Ounces	9x12 envelope, 9x12 SASE number of pages	9x12 SASE (for return trips) number of pages	First Class Postage	Third Class Postage	Postage from U.S. to Canada
under 2	...	1 to 2	$ .35*	$ .45	$ .40*
2	1 to 4	3 to 8	.45	.45	.52
3	5 to 10	9 to 12	.65	.65	.74
4	11 to 16	13 to 19	.85	.85	.96
5	17 to 21	20 to 25	1.05	1.00	1.18
6	22 to 27	26 to 30	1.25	1.00	1.40
7	28 to 32	31 to 35	1.45	1.10	1.62
8	33 to 38	36 to 41	1.65	1.10	1.84
9	39 to 44	42 to 46	1.85	1.20	2.06
10	45 to 49	47 to 52	2.05	1.20	2.28
11	50 to 55	53 to 57	2.25	1.30	2.50

*This cost includes an assessment for oversized mail that is light in weight.

1990 Writer's Market

Distributed in Canada by Prentice-Hall of
Canada Ltd., 1870 Birchmount Road,
Scarborough, Ontario M1P 2J7.
Also distributed in Australia by Kirby Books, Private Bag No. 19, P.O. Alexandria NSW2015.

Managing Editor, Market Books Department:
Constance J. Achabal

Library of Congress Catalog Number
31-20772
International Standard Serial Number
0084-2729
International Standard Book Number
0-89879-374-2

Information in U.S. Postage by the Page chart
supplied by Carolyn Hardesty;
Canadian Postage by the Page by Barbara Murrin

Cover illustration © 1989 PhotoDesign Tim
Grondin

1990

Writer's Market

Where & How
To Sell What You Write

Editor: **Glenda Tennant Neff**

Assistant Editor: **Deborah Cinnamon**

Cincinnati, Ohio

The Writing Profession

1 **From the Editors**

3 **How to Use Writer's Market**

5 **Key to Symbols and Abbreviations**

6 **Since You Asked . . . Questions about Writing and Publishing,** *by Glenda Tennant Neff*
Answers to 20 of the most frequently-asked questions about writing, publishing and use of Writer's Market.

13 **The Business of Writing**

13 *Marketing your manuscripts*

13 *Writing tools*

16 *Approaching markets*

18 *Sample magazine query*

19 *Sample book query*

21 *Manuscript mechanics*

22 *Mailing submissions*

24 *Recording submissions*

24 *Bookkeeping*

25 *Tax information*

25 *Rights and the writer*

28 *Copyrighting your writing*

31 *How much should I charge?*

Special Business Feature:

40 **Writers' Roundtable**
Three fulltime writers discuss common business problems and share techniques freelancers can use to solve them.

The Markets

47 **Book Publishers**

112 Close-up:
Dennis Hensley and Holly Miller
Two Indiana authors, successful on their own, discuss their collaboration and offer tips on choosing a partner and maintaining a good working relationship.

132 Close-up:
Margery Facklam, Author
Children's writing requires a different, but not easier, set of skills than writing for adults, says this author.

Contents

206 Close-up:
Susan Williamson,
Williamson Publishing
Writers should propose books that fill needs, not follow trends, says this self-help publisher.

212 Subsidy Publishers

Special Feature:

213 **First Novelists**
Six authors discuss their first novels — from writing to promotion — and give you tips for avoiding publishing pitfalls.

221 **Small Presses**

224 **Book Packagers and Producers**

229 Other Book Publishers and Packagers

231 **Consumer Publications**

231 *Animal*

241 *Art and Architecture*

245 *Associations*

252 *Astrology, Metaphysical and New Age*

255 *Automotive and Motorcycle*

263 *Aviation*

265 *Business and Finance*

277 *Career, College and Alumni*

287 *Child Care and Parental Guidance*

288 *Close-up:*
Sacramento Non-fiction Network
A unique writers' group supplies the advice, support and expertise its members need to keep them selling.

295 *Comic Books*

297 *Consumer Service and Business Opportunity*

300 *Contemporary Culture*

304 *Detective and Crime*

304 *Disabilities*

308 *Entertainment*

316 *Ethnic/Minority*

324 *Food and Drink*

327 *Games and Puzzles*

328 *General Interest*

338 *Close-up:*
Keith Bellows, Special Reports
This series of general interest magazines is looking for top writers who can write timely, well-researched articles.

339 *Health and Fitness*

350 *History*

356 *Hobby and Craft*

377 *Home and Garden*

385 *Close-up:*
Joe Provey,
Practical Homeowner
This editor explains why writers must think visually when submitting to his home improvement magazine.

388 *Humor*

391 *In-Flight*

394 *Juvenile*

403 *Close-up:*
Sylvia Funston, Owl Magazine
One key to break in at this magazine is to write for children on an international level.

409 *Literary and "Little"*

427 *Men's*

433 **Military**

439 **Music**

446 **Mystery**

447 **Nature, Conservation and Ecology**

449 **Close-up:
Kristin Merriman,
Outdoor America**
*Writers who can let readers know how
conservation issues affect their lives are
in demand at this publication.*

455 **Personal Computers**

465 **Photography**

467 **Politics and World Affairs**

469 **Close-up:
Doug Foster, Mother Jones**
*Why a freelancer must adapt his
approach to keep up with a magazine's
changing editorial coverage and design
is explained by the editor of* Mother
Jones.

472 **Psychology and
Self-Improvement**

473 **Regional**

491 **Close-up:
Marilyn Moore, South Florida**
*Writers for regional magazines should
look for local angles and fresh ideas
that haven't been covered by other area
media, says this editor.*

527 **Relationships**

533 **Religious**

563 **Retirement**

568 **Romance and Confession**

571 **Rural**

573 **Science**

576 **Science Fiction, Fantasy
and Horror**

583 **Sports**
*Archery and Bowhunting, Baseball,
Basketball, Bicycling, Boating,
Bowling, Football, Gambling, General
Interest, Golf, Guns, Horse Racing,
Hunting and Fishing, Martial Arts,
Miscellaneous, Skiing and Snow
Sports, Soccer, Tennis, Water Sports*

631 **Teen and Young Adult**

638 **Travel, Camping and Trailer**

652 **Women's**

667 **Close-up:
Mary McLaughlin,
Working Mother**
*This editor talks about the difference
between proposing an article on a
"topic" and proposing an idea with a
solution.*

668 **Other Consumer Publications**

671 **Trade, Technical and
Professional Journals**

673 **Advertising, Marketing
and PR**

676 **Art, Design and Collectibles**

680 **Auto and Truck**

685 **Aviation and Space**

687 **Beverages and Bottling**

689 **Close-up:
William Moffett, Vineyard &
Winery Management**
*Trade magazines are looking for writers
knowledgeable about industry and
willing to do the necessary research,
says this editor.*

Contents

690 **Book and Bookstore**

691 **Brick, Glass and Ceramics**

691 **Building Interiors**

693 **Business Management**

697 **Close-up:**
Ruth Benedict,
Magna Publications
Trade newsletters offer a special
opportunity for writers who have
expertise and write succinctly, says this
editor.

701 **Church Administration**
and Ministry

704 **Clothing**

705 **Coin-Operated Machines**

706 **Confectionery and**
Snack Foods

707 **Construction and Contracting**

712 **Dental**

714 **Drugs, Health Care**
and Medical Products

715 **Education and Counseling**

721 **Electronics and**
Communication

726 **Energy and Utilities**

728 **Engineering and Technology**

731 **Entertainment and the Arts**

734 **Farm**
Agricultural Equipment, Crops and
Soil Management, Dairy Farming,
Livestock, Management,
Miscellaneous, Regional

745 **Finance**

749 **Fishing**

750 **Florists, Nurseries**
and Landscaping

753 **Government and**
Public Service

758 **Groceries and Food Products**

764 **Hardware**

764 **Home Furnishings and**
Household Goods

767 **Hospitals, Nursing and**
Nursing Homes

769 **Hotels, Motels, Clubs, Resorts**
and Restaurants

774 **Industrial Operations**

776 **Information Systems**

780 **Insurance**

782 **International Affairs**

783 **Jewelry**

784 **Journalism and Writing**

795 **Law**

799 **Leather Goods**

800 **Library Science**

802 **Lumber**

803 **Machinery and Metal**

803 **Maintenance and Safety**

805 **Management and**
Supervision

811 **Marine and Maritime**
Industries

811 **Medical**

820 **Music**

822 **Office Environment**
and Equipment

822 **Paint**

823 **Paper**

823 **Pets**

825 *Photography Trade*

827 *Plumbing, Heating, Air Conditioning and Refrigeration*

829 *Printing*

831 *Real Estate*

833 *Resources and Waste Reduction*

834 *Selling and Merchandising*

838 *Sport Trade*

843 *Stone and Quarry Products*

844 *Toy, Novelty and Hobby*

845 *Transportation*

847 *Travel*

850 *Veterinary*

850 *Other Trade Journals*

852 **Scriptwriting**

852 *Business and Educational Writing*

863 *Playwriting*

890 *Screenwriting*

895 *Other Scriptwriting Markets*

896 **Syndicates**

906 *Other Syndicates*

907 **Greeting Card Publishers**

911 *Close-up:*
Ann Asel-Wagner, Hallmark
Greeting cards cover a variety of relationships today, but the key is still writing a "me-to-you" sentiment readers want to send.

917 *Other Greeting Card Publishers*

Services & Opportunities

918 **Author's Agents**

966 *Other Author's Agents*

967 **Contests and Awards**

988 *Close-up:*
Deborah Purcell, Redbook *Fiction Contest*
Good storytelling with entertainment value is the key to competing in this prestigious short story contest.

995 *Other Contests and Awards*

996 **Glossary**

1000 **Book Publishers Subject Index**

1000 *Nonfiction*

1017 *Fiction*

1021 **Author's Agents Subject Index**

1021 *Nonfiction*

1024 *Fiction*

1027 **General Index**

The Writing Profession

_____ From the Editors

This is the 61st edition of *Writer's Market* and it's amazing how the publishing industry continues to change and move into new areas.

During the past year, companies have gone on-line with publications, allowing you to read books and magazines from a personal computer; Whittle Communications is planning books with advertising; and publications have started up that are distributed exclusively by facsimile (fax) machines. You can now polish your writing with computer software programs, listen to horror stories on Embassy Cassette tapes and read short stories published on puzzles. And, of course, mergers and buyouts have continued this year, creating larger and larger conglomerates.

At *Writer's Market* we give you the information you need to keep up with the evolving publishing world. This year we've included a number of new features and have updated the ones you've told us you found helpful.

Writers just entering the field, as well as those who've been around for a while, constantly have questions about the publishing industry and about *Writer's Market*. We've answered the most frequently-asked questions this year in a feature, Since You Asked...The Basics of Writing and Publishing.

We want *Writer's Market* to be a forum where writers can share ideas as well as obtain them, so we've included two new features. First Novelists contains interviews with six authors about their experiences, ranging from writing to promoting their first novels. Three fulltime freelancers discuss common business problems and some of their solutions in Writers' Roundtable at the end of the Business of Writing section.

You'll also find information about how your unsolicited material is handled in each of the major section introductions. We surveyed more than 1,000 editors and agents about ways in which they handle unsolicited queries and manuscripts, so we could let you know what the industry standards and practices are in dealing with submissions.

The new nonfiction and fiction indexes for the Author's Agents section will give writers a quicker method for finding agents interested in topics about which they write.

We've updated three features that writers told us they found useful and interesting. How Much Should I Charge?, a guide in the Business of Writing section to setting freelance fees, has been updated after our annual survey of professional groups and individuals. New samples of a magazine query letter and book manuscript query will provide writers with examples of successful selling tools. Again this year you'll find section-by-section lists (see the end of each section) to give you additional information about markets that have changed or no longer accept freelance submissions.

As always, you'll find Close-up interviews with writers and editors who share their experience, advice and insights on the writing profession. In addition, we have more than 800 new markets for your writing plus changes in existing markets, including 560 editor changes, 198 address changes and 15 publication name changes since the 1989 edition.

Writer's Market no longer has a Gag Writing section. Those listings of comedians and cartoonists will be contained in a new, specialized book covering humor writing and illustrating. *1990 Humor and Cartoon Markets* will be available from Writer's Digest Books in March, 1990.

All the changes and updated information will make the process of marketing your work easier and more efficient. In order to keep up with the increased emphasis on speed and timeliness in the industry, we've included facsimile or fax machine numbers for book publishers, magazine editors and agents who wanted the information listed. In addition, we're launching a computer disk version with 1990 *Writer's Market* listings. Instead of reading through numerous listings to find the best market for your work, this software allows you to search quickly through the entire database of listings for the information you want. If you have an IBM or IBM-compatible personal computer and want more information about this version, see the bind-in card included in this book.

We hope you understand that between the time this edition goes to press and the time you read it, some details in the market listings may change. We make additions, corrections and changes in the listings until the book is sent to the printer, but often publishers go out of business; editors find other jobs; and publications change their needs, payment or submission policies. Listings for new markets and changes in others can be found throughout the year in many publishing industry and writers' magazines, including *Writer's Digest*, the monthly magazine for freelance writers.

As editors, we appreciate it when you send us information about new market opportunities you discover. And we want to know if you have complaints about nonpayment or lack of response from any market we've listed. In addition, we're always interested in hearing how you use *Writer's Market* and how we can make it more useful for you. Always enclose a self-addressed, stamped envelope with your letter if you expect a reply.

Best wishes for success in 1990 — and beyond.

Glenda Tennant Neff

Deborah Cinnamon

How to Use Writer's Market

Before beginning your search for markets to send your writing to, take a moment to read this section. It will help you make full use of the individual listings and will explain the symbols and abbreviations used throughout the book. (Check the glossary for unfamiliar words.) Specific symbols and abbreviations are explained in the table on page 5. The most important abbreviation is SASE—self-addressed, stamped envelope. *Always* enclose one when you send unsolicited queries or manuscripts to editors, publishers or agents. This requirement is not included in the individual market listings because it's a "given" that you must follow if you expect to receive a reply.

For an explanation of the information given in the listings, match the numbered phrases in this sample listing with the corresponding numbers in the copy that follows.

(1)‡COOKING LIGHT, The Magazine of Food and Fitness, Southern Living, Inc., Box 1748, Birmingham AL 35201. **(2)** (205)877-6000. FAX: (205)877-6600. **(3)** Editor: Katherine M. Eakin. Managing Editor: B. Ellen Templeton. **(4)** 75% freelance written. **(5)(6)** Bimonthly magazine on healthy recipes and fitness information. "*Cooking Light* is a positive approach to a healthier lifestyle. It's written for healthy people on regular diets who are counting calories or trying to make calories count toward better nutrition. Moderation, balance and variety are emphasized. The writing style is fresh, upbeat and encouraging, emphasizing that eating a balanced, varied, lower-calorie diet and exercising regularly do not have to be boring." Circ. 650,000. **(7)** Pays on acceptance. Publishes ms an average of 6-12 months after acceptance. Byline sometimes given. Offers 25% of original contract fee as kill fee. Buys all rights. **(8)** Submit seasonal/holiday material 12 months in advance. Computer printout submissions OK; prefers letter-quality. **(9)(10)** Free sample copy and writer's guidelines.

(11) Nonfiction: (12) Personal experience, nutrition, healthy recipes, fitness/exercise. **(13)** Buys 150 mss/year. **(14)** Query with published clips. **(15)** Length: 400-2,000 words. **(16)** Pays $250-2,000 for assigned articles. **(17)** Pays expenses of writers on assignment.

Columns/Departments: (18) Profile (an incident or event that occurred in one's life that resulted in a total lifestyle change) 2,000-2500 words; Children's Fitness (emphasis on prevention and intervention in regard to fitness, exercise, nutrition) 1,000-1,500 words; Taking Aim (a personal account of progression from desire to obstacle to achievement for incorporating exercise into one's routine schedule) 1,000-1,500 words and Downfall (a humorous personal account of desire to obstacle to the continuing struggle to overcome a particular food habit or addiction) 1,000-1,500 words. Buys 30 mss/year. Query. Length: 1,000-2,000 words. Pays $250-2,000.

(19) Tips: "Emphasis should be on achieving a healthier lifestyle through food, nutrition, fitness, exercise information. In submitting queries, include information on professional background. Food writers should include examples of healthy recipes which meet the guidelines of *Cooking Light*."

(1) Symbols, names and addresses. One or more symbols (*, ‡,□) may precede the name and address of the publication or market; check the key on page 5 for their meanings. (This double dagger signifies a new listing.)

(2) Phone and FAX numbers. A phone number or FAX number in a listing does not mean the market accepts phone queries. Make a phone query only when your story's timeliness would be lost by following the usual procedures. As a rule, don't call or FAX information unless you have been invited to do so.

(3) Contact names. In most listings, names of contact persons are given in the first paragraph or under the bold subheadings. Address your query or submission to a specific name when possible. If the name is not easily recognizable by gender, use the full name (e.g., Dear Dale Smith:). If no contact name is given, consult a sample copy. As a last resort, you can address your query to "Articles editor" or what is appropriate. For more information, read Approaching Markets in the Business of Writing.

(4) Size of market. A market's general openness to writers is indicated by the percentage of freelance material used or by the percentage of published manuscripts from new, unagented writers.

(5) Copyright information. Since most publications are copyrighted, the information is only given in this spot when the publication is not copyrighted. For information on copyrighting your own work, see Rights and the Writer in the Business of Writing.

(6) Emphasis and readership. A description of the market provides the focus and audience. Established dates are listed for most sections only if 1988 or later. (All agents have established dates.) The date a market was established can help you evaluate its stability. New markets may be open to freelancers, but they can also be riskier. Circulation figures listed are the total of subscriptions plus off-the-shelf sales.

(7) Rights purchased. General business policies give information about rights purchased and time of payment. Book publishers list average royalty and agents list commission rates. For more information on types of rights for sale, see Rights and the Writer in the Business of Writing.

(8) Submission requirements. Submission requirements include how far in advance to submit seasonal material and whether or not previously published and photocopied material will be considered. Send manuscripts or queries to one market at a time unless it indicates simultaneous submissions are OK. If you send your manuscript to more than one market at a time, always mention in your cover letter that it is a simultaneous submission. Computer printouts and electronic submissions are mentioned only if the market accepts them. See Writing Tools in the Business of Writing for more information.

(9) Reporting time. Reporting times indicate how soon a market will respond to your query or manuscript, but times listed are approximate. Quarterly publications, book publishers, literary magazines and all new listings may be slower to respond. Wait three weeks beyond the stated reporting time before you send a polite inquiry. If no reporting time is listed, wait 2 months for a reply.

(10) Writer's guidelines and sample copies. If you're interested in writing for a particular market, request the writer's guidelines and/or a sample copy if the market indicates availability. "Writer's guidelines for SASE" means that a business-size envelope (#10) with one First Class stamp will be adequate. You should request a sample copy if you are unable to find the publication at a newsstand or library. A sample copy or book catalog is often available for a 9x12 self-addressed envelope with a specified number of stamps or International Reply Coupons. Most publishers will send, at no extra charge, writer's guidelines with sample copies if you request them.

(11) Subheads. Subheads in bold (Nonfiction, Photos, etc.) guide you to requirements for those types of materials.

(12) Types of nonfiction needed. The specific material desired (and often material *not* desired) is listed. Follow the guidelines. Do not send fiction to a publication that only uses nonfiction; do not send a children's book manuscript to a publisher of men's adventure novels.

(13) Manuscripts purchased. The number of manuscripts purchased per issue or per year will give you an idea of how easy or difficult it may be to sell your work to a particular market. With new listings, these figures may change dramatically depending on the submissions they receive or changes in policy.

(14) Submission information. If the market wants to see queries, that's what you should send. The same goes for outlines and sample chapters, etc. Don't send a complete manuscript unless the listing indicates it's acceptable.

(15) Word length. Editors know the length of most material they buy; follow their range of words or pages. If your manuscript is longer or shorter (by a wide margin) than the stated requirements, find another market.

(16) Payment rates. Payment ranges tell you what the market usually paid at the time *Writer's Market* was published.

(17) Expenses. Whether a market sometimes or usually pays expenses of writers on assignment is listed. No mention is made when a market does *not* pay expenses.

(18) Photos, columns, fiction, poetry and fillers. Needs, rates and policies for specified material.

(19) Tips. Helpful suggestions are listed under the subhead Tips in many listings. They describe the best way to submit manuscripts or give special insight into needs and preferences of the market.

Key to Symbols and Abbreviations

‡ New listing in all sections
* Subsidy publisher in Book Publishers section
☐ Cable TV market in Scriptwriting section
ms-manuscript; **mss**-manuscripts
b&w-black and white (photo)
SASE-self-addressed, stamped envelope
SAE-self-addressed envelope
IRC-International Reply Coupon, for use on reply mail in Canada and foreign markets.
FAX-a communications system used to transmit documents over the telephone lines.

(See Glossary for definitions of words and expressions used in writing/publishing.)

Important Listing Information

● Listings are based on editorial questionnaires and interviews. They are *not* advertisements; publishers do not pay for their listings. The markets are *not* endorsed by *Writer's Market* editors.

● All listings have been verified before publication of this book. If a listing has not changed from last year, then the editor told us the market's needs have not changed and the previous listing continues to accurately reflect its policies. We require documentation in our files for each listing and never run a listing without its editorial office's approval.

● *Writer's Market* reserves the right to exclude any listing.

● When looking for a specific market, check the index. A market may not be listed for one of these reasons.

1. It doesn't solicit freelance material.
2. It doesn't pay for material.
3. It has gone out of business.
4. It has failed to verify or update its listing for the 1990 edition.
5. It was in the middle of being sold at press time, and rather than disclose premature details, we chose not to list it.
6. It hasn't answered *Writer's Market* inquiries satisfactorily. (To the best of our ability, and with our readers' help, we try to screen out fraudulent listings.)
7. It buys few manuscripts, thereby constituting a very small market for freelancers.

● See the index of additional markets at the end of each major section for specific information on individual markets not listed.

Since You Asked . . . The Basics of Writing and Publishing

by Glenda Tennant Neff

At *Writer's Market* we receive letters and phone calls every day from writers who have questions and comments about the publishing industry, about freelancing and even about *Writer's Market* itself. Over the years we have observed a pattern of common problems and concerns writers have and we present here, in a question-and-answer format, 20 of the most-asked questions along with the answers we provide.

We hope this compilation will answer the important questions for those of you new to the business of freelancing or new to using *Writer's Market* as a source of markets for your work. Other frequent questions we receive about copyright, manuscript mechanics and query letters are answered in The Business of Writing section beginning on page 13. Terms are defined in the Glossary and the Key to Symbols and Abbreviations appears on page 5. If you have a topic that isn't discussed here, write to us at the address on the copyright page. Please include a self-addressed, stamped envelope (SASE) for reply.

About the listings...

1. How do the editors obtain listings for Writer's Market?

Throughout the year, we send letters and questionnaires to about 15,000 book publishers, magazine editors, script producers, greeting card publishers, syndicate editors, agents and contest directors. In addition, some of the information is gathered by phone interviews. Sources for these mailings include industry reference guides, publishing journals, magazines and the industry grapevine. We also follow up on any leads submitted to us by writers. There is never a charge for a listing in *Writer's Market*; the listings are not advertisements but compilations of information from our questionnaires.

2. How is listing information verified and updated in succeeding years?

Between editions of *Writer's Market*, we send out copies of the information we have listed for each entry in the book—we call them verifications. We ask editors, publishers and agents to review the information, update or make changes as needed, and return the signed verification form to us. In some cases, this process is completed with a phone call to the editor, publisher or agent. Before we run a listing in *Writer's Market*, we *must* have documentation on file; we will not run information that has not been approved. Between editions, we make changes in information on our database and pass along the updates to *Writer's Digest* magazine, so writers can get the latest information on our listings throughout the year.

3. Some publishers and magazines I know of are not listed. Why?

There are several reasons a book publisher or magazine may not be listed in *Writer's Market*. Certain publishers and editors do not accept unsolicited or unagented material and do not want to encourage submission of it with a listing. Other magazines are entirely staff-written, while some use only authors they know well and therefore don't accept outside submissions. In addition, many specialized, small and regional publishing houses and magazines do not want to be listed in *Writer's Market* because they do not want the number of submissions a listing in a national publication attracts. Finally, some publications do not pay writers or pay only in copies and we do not list these publications. To give writers as much information as possible, we have a list at the end of each major section of the book. In it, we let writers know why a publisher, magazine or agent may not be listed in that particular edition. If you find a potential market which isn't listed in *Writer's Market*, write to the magazine and ask for its writer's guidelines. Then study back issues as you would before submitting to any magazine. If you find a good market for freelancers, we'd love to hear about it and will be happy to send a questionnaire so they can be included in the next edition of the book.

4. Are there any shortcuts in searching through listings in the book?

Browsing through *Writer's Market* listings is interesting. Reading through listings sometimes can help you generate ideas and probably will let you know about markets you didn't even know existed. We don't want you to spend more time searching than writing, though, so we have a variety of features to speed your search. The Table of Contents provides you with a breakdown of categories, with page numbers, for all the major sections of the book. We also let you know in each section introduction if other sections in the book contain related information and markets. Each listing in the book appears in the Index, and we have an additional index according to subject for the Book Publishers and Author's Agents sections. Both are designed to give you ready access to the names of publishers and agents who have indicated an interest in specific subjects. In addition, we have developed with the Folio Corp. a software package with *Writer's Market* on computer disk. If you own an IBM or IBM-compatible PC, you may be interested in the fast searching and linking capabilities this software offers. For more information, see the bind-in card in this book.

Charges and submissions

5. How do I know if charges relating to my writing are legitimate?

Writers often are concerned, and rightly so, about fees they are asked to pay. The key to knowing if and how much to pay is knowing about standard industry practices. Two years ago, we encountered the first listing for a book publisher who charged a fee to read a manuscript. Publishers instituting this type of fee say they do it because they receive a large number of unsolicited manuscripts. Other publishers control this problem by accepting only queries or agented submissions. It is not standard practice in the industry for book publishers to charge fees or to make purchase of books a condition of acceptance, and we have instituted a policy in which we will not run listings for publishers who do either. Subsidy publishers—those who ask you to pay part or all of the cost of producing your book—appear in *Writer's Market*. Those that publish more than 50% of their books with author subsidies are listed in a section for subsidy publishers. Those 50% or under are marked with an asterisk (*) in the Book Publishers section. For more specific information about subsidy publishing, see the section introduction to Book Publishers.

Magazine editors, script producers, greeting card publishers and syndicates do not normally charge fees to consider queries and manuscripts, but agents and contests are two areas in which fees often are charged. About 85% of agents charge some kind of fee, ranging from long-distance phone calls to evaluation and criticism fees. The types of fees and typical charges are covered more fully in the section introduction to Author's Agents.

Contests may or may not charge an entrance fee. Normally the fee is charged to pay the judges involved. A small fee is typical in the industry, but writers should be wary of any contest which charges a fee and doesn't offer a prize or offers a prize that is not much more than an individual entry fee. In no event should a contest entrant be obligated to purchase anything as a condition of winning.

6. Is it better to send a query letter or a complete manuscript?

The best submission is the one that the listing specifies. This is the way the publisher, editor or agent prefers to receive material; some will not even consider material submitted another way. A few have even asked us to delete their listings in *Writer's Market* when they received too many inappropriate submissions.

In general, most book publishers want to see a proposal for a nonfiction book. A proposal is some combination of a query letter, outline and/or synopsis and sample chapters. For fiction, it's usually best to send a cover letter with up to three sample chapters. Many writers submit complete manuscripts, but this method usually costs the author large postage bills and long waits for evaluation. Sample chapters give the editor enough material to decide whether or not he is interested in seeing the complete manuscript. This same method also works for most material sent to agents.

Most magazine editors prefer a query for nonfiction and a full manuscript for short fiction. Writers of fillers, humor and opinion pieces generally send complete manuscripts. Fillers are short and can be evaluated quickly. Humor and opinion simply can't be evaluated in a query; editors must see them to know if they'll work in their magazines.

Remember that these are only guidelines to submission methods. Always follow the submission method specified in the *Writer's Market* listing.

7. Can I submit queries and manuscripts simultaneously?

It depends. Some book publishers and magazine editors don't object to simultaneous submissions. Their listings indicate that with the statement "Simultaneous submissions OK."

In general, simultaneous queries to book publishers and agents are acceptable and save an author valuable marketing time. Simultaneous queries to magazine editors are not usually necessary since they generally report back on queries sooner than book publishers and agents will. If you do send simultaneous queries to magazines, you need to decide what you'll do if more than one editor accepts the article. Will you go with the first one to call or the highest paying and risk the other editor's anger? Will you try to write two different articles from the same material?

We do not recommend sending complete manuscripts as simultaneous submissions to magazines. The exception to this may be literary magazines, which often have long reporting times. Some editors do not object to simultaneous submissions; others refuse to consider further material from an author who withdraws an accepted piece because it also was accepted by a more prestigious or better-paying magazine. Most book publishers and agents do not like to spend time reading and evaluating a complete manuscript they're not sure they will have a chance to acquire. To avoid any confusion, you should let the publisher or agent know that it's a simultaneous submission, or you may offer it exclusively for a short amount of time, say three weeks, before you submit it elsewhere.

8. How do publishers, editors and agents handle unsolicited manuscripts?

Unsolicited manuscripts are handled in a variety of ways. Some review unsolicited material just as they would solicited manuscripts; some give it a cursory review; while others will not review it at all and only return the material if a self-addressed, stamped envelope (SASE) is enclosed. To provide you with more complete information, this year we've surveyed hundreds of book publishers, magazine editors and agents on this question. The results are included in the section introductions for Book Publishers; Consumer Publications; Trade, Technical and Professional Journals; and Author's Agents.

Two important points were repeated often by those participating in the survey. Although they'd like to, publishers, editors and agents receive too many manuscripts to offer personal letters or constructive criticism. Most will send a form rejection, and some simply return the material without comment. Additionally, inclusion of a self-addressed, stamped envelope or International Reply Coupons for Canadian submissions, is mandatory when you submit any unsolicited material and want it returned. Never submit unsolicited your only copy of a manuscript or original artwork or photos.

Finding the right market

9. Can Writer's Market editors recommend a publisher, magazine or agent for my work?

We want to provide you with the best information about markets for your work, but we can't recommend a publisher, editor or agent for you. We don't know your work like you do. With the market information we provide, *you* are the best person to select places to send your work.

10. How do I find the best book publisher to publish my writing?

To speed up your search, first look in the Book Publishers Subject Index under the nonfiction or fiction heading that matches your manuscript subject. The book publishers listed there have indicated an interest in manuscripts on that subject. Then read the complete listings for each of those book publishers. See how many books they publish, how many new and unagented authors they deal with, and what submission method they prefer. The listing also will give you some basics about the payment terms they offer and will tell you if the publisher does subsidy publishing. Check *Books in Print* (available at most public libraries) to see what other titles they publish and find out what the competition is for your book. Take a look at some of the publisher's other titles too. Do you like their editing and production (the jacket, the back copy, the paper, etc.)? This will let you know whether or not you have a compatible approach to publishing. Be sure to order a copy of the publisher's most recent catalog. It helps you determine where your book fits in with the publisher's complete list of titles. Many writers blanket the market without researching it, just hoping to get an acceptance from someone, but the skillful writer will eliminate much of the wasted time and money by doing this research before submitting.

11. What are some keys to finding the right magazine markets for my articles?

Before submitting, study magazine listings for those using the type of articles you write. Then look at several issues of the magazine to get a feel for its approach and style. Your local library or newsstand are the best places to find magazines, but you may need to send for sample copies for magazines not circulated in your area. Magazines offering sample copies indicate this in their listings. This will help you determine whether or not your article and style of writing fit in with the current editorial content. Magazine editors, like the rest of us, have pet peeves, and one of them is submission of material that's totally inappropriate.

Before you send a query or manuscript, you should send for a copy of the magazine's writer's guidelines if they supply them. A magazine's guidelines will give you specific requirements and will give you the latest information if editors have changed policies since *Writer's Market* went to press. It can also give you more detail about requirements for specific columns, departments or sections of the magazine.

When you're considering a magazine, also look for payment rates, payment on acceptance, kill fee, rights purchased, payment of expenses and additional payment for photos. Most writers simply look at total payment, but these other factors should influence your choice too. If you are paid $100 for all rights, but another magazine offers $80 for first North American serial rights, you may want to accept the lower offer if you think the article has reprint value. Although you won't make as much with the first sale, you still have an opportunity to market other rights by choosing the second magazine. Payment on acceptance is preferred over payment on publication since publication may be several months after an article is accepted. You should also look for magazines that offer the extras: kill fees if an acceptable article is not used, additional payment for photos, and payment of expenses incurred in producing the article. These extras add up.

12. How do I know if I need an agent to represent my work?

You will need an agent to represent your work if you want to approach book publishers that only consider agented submissions. You may want an agent if you write book manuscripts fulltime. (Most agents will not consider selling articles and short stories, or they'll only do it for clients they represent on book contracts.) You also may want an agent if you don't feel knowledgeable enough to negotiate your own contract or if your volume of writing doesn't leave you with enough time to handle marketing and other business details. A complete discussion of the author-agent relationship is in the Author's Agents section introduction.

13. How can I choose the best agent for my material?

Agents aren't required to have any particular qualifications to set up shop, so writers often find it difficult to know who to approach. First, look for an agent who is interested in handling the type of material you write. We've included an Author's Agents Subject Index in this edition. Check it for the names of agents who specialize in your subject area, then look up their individual listings. Agents list these specialities because they have contacts in those publishing areas. Also note the type of writer (new or experienced) the agent deals with and any publishing requirements for writers who submit work. Agents usually charge 10-15% commission, but their fees vary widely. Be sure you know what you'll receive if you pay a fee, and remember that paying a fee does *not* mean that the agent has to accept your manuscript for representation. Finally, look at books the agent has sold. It will give you a good idea of the agent's client list, contacts in the industry and negotiating ability. Some agents consider this information confidential, while others simply did not answer the question on our questionnaire. We attempt to distinguish between the two in our listings.

Look for an agent's professional affiliations. Many professional groups like Independent Literary Agents Association and Writers Guild have a set of ethical standards for their members. And don't overlook your own contacts with other writers. Many times, agents acquire clients as referrals from their other clients.

14. How do Writer's Market editors respond to complaints about listings?

When we receive a complaint, we always respond to the writer and keep the correspondence on file. If the complaint involves lack of payment or response, we will contact the editor or agent about it, so the matter can be resolved. If the problem involves actions that conflict with information in our listing, we ask the editor or agent to correct the information. After correction, if the publisher, magazine or agent no longer meets our standards for inclusion, we will delete the listing. If we have three or more unresolved complaints on file for a particular listing when we go to press, we will not run the listing in that edition. The listing may appear in future editions of *Writer's Market* if the complaints are resolved.

Business and etiquette

15. What should I do when I don't get a reply to my query or manuscript in the listing's stated reporting time?

Wait three or four weeks beyond the stated reporting time and send a polite letter inquiring about the status of your manuscript. Sometimes writers are quick to send accusatory letters when a delay can mean that the manuscript is making its way up the ladder and being considered seriously for publication. Delays do happen, however, and occasionally material is lost or misplaced. To cut down on these problems, always submit your work in the way the publisher or magazine prefers; never send your only copy; and remember that most editors will not return manuscripts without a self-addressed, stamped envelope. Some writers also send self-addressed, stamped postcards with the manuscript, so editors can drop the postcard back in the mail, notifying the writer that the material was received. If you do not receive a reply to your inquiry in four weeks, send a certified letter withdrawing the manuscript from consideration and begin submitting it elsewhere.

16. Is it OK to call an editor?

Rarely. The few editors who are willing to accept phone queries say so in their listings. Editors you work with regularly may not object to phone calls; some actually *prefer* a phone call on timely pieces that can't be delayed. You probably will be encouraged to call if you're sending your article by modem because you'll need to discuss compatibility and requirements of the systems. If you run into a major problem when working on an article, you may need to call an editor, but be prepared to offer a solution.

17. What do I do if the publication doesn't pay on time?

If you don't receive your payment within two weeks of the time you expected it, follow up with a note to your editor. Sometimes it's an honest mistake, a backup in paperwork, a cut-off date that wasn't met, etc. Most problems can be corrected with a simple inquiry note. If you still don't receive payment, some writers find that sending an invoice to the accounting department works well. If you still do not receive payment, consider sending a certified letter, having your attorney contact the magazine or going to small claims court. If you do not receive payment from a market listed in this edition, we also want you to notify us at *Writer's Market*.

18. What rights do editors buy for articles?

The most common purchase of rights for articles is first North American serial rights. That means the publication has the right to publish your article for the first time in any periodical in North America. North America is generally used instead of U.S. or Canadian rights because many U.S. magazines are circulated in both countries. Some magazines will buy both first serial rights and second serial or reprint rights, allowing them to print the article for the first time and also reprint it another time. If you do not sell reprint rights with the first sale, you can market the article's reprint rights to another publication. Some magazines buy all rights. Editors say they do this because they want exclusive material and pay well for it, while other specialized magazines don't want to give competitors the chance to reprint material they've had. If you sell all rights to an article, you cannot sell it again, but occasionally an editor who has bought all rights will reassign rights to the writer. It's worth a written request if you have another potential sale. Finally, some publications ask writers to sign work-for-hire agreements. This is the worst deal for writers since they sign over the copyright to the article and do not retain any rights to the work. For a complete discussion of rights, see Rights and the Writer and Copyrighting your Writing in The Business of Writing section.

19. Can I sell an article for publication more than once?

Yes, if you haven't sold the rights already. If you have sold first North American serial rights, first rights or one-time rights to an article, you can sell the exact article for reprint to other publications. When you submit the article, send a fresh copy marked with the rights you are selling (usually second serial rights or one-time rights). If the article already has been published, send a photocopy of it too. If it hasn't been published, let the editor know in your cover letter where and when it's scheduled to be published.

20. How much should I charge for my work when the fee is negotiable?

Rates can be developed several ways. You can charge by the total project, by the number of words written, or by the hour. In general, writing assignments receive a flat fee or by-the-word rate, and editing assignments usually involve a flat fee, a per-hour or per-page rate. Rates for freelance work vary widely, depending on your experience, the competition, and your geographic location. At a recent *Folio* seminar, magazine editors said they paid freelance rates ranging from $7.50-25 per hour, and technical writers often commanded $40 or more per hour. In How Much Should I Charge? in The Business of Writing section, we supply ranges for many writing and editing services, along with a formula for figuring out a per-hour rate to charge.

The Business of Writing

During the past year, tax laws for freelancers have been changed, work-for-hire has been challenged in the Supreme Court and the National Writers Union has negotiated work rule changes or labor contracts with publications ranging from *Village Voice* to *Ploughshares*. Many freelancers concentrate on the artistic side of their writing and overlook new business developments. Whether you freelance fulltime or just want to make a little extra money and see your work in print, you must also plan to invest some time in managing the business side of your writing and keeping up with changes in the industry. The following information will help you do both.

Marketing your manuscripts

Often writers find a subject that interests them, write about it, and then begin to look for a publisher. While this approach is common, it reduces your chances of success. Instead, try choosing writing categories that interest you and study those sections in *Writer's Market*. Select several listings that you consider good prospects for your kind of writing.

Next, develop several ideas, and make a list of the potential markets for each idea. Make the initial contact with markets using the method stated in the market listings.

If you exhaust your list of possibilities, don't give up. Re-evaluate the idea, revise it, or try another angle. Continue developing ideas and approaching markets with them. Identify and rank potential markets for an idea and continue the process, but don't approach a market a second time until you've received a response to your first submission.

Prepare for rejection and the sometimes lengthy process that publishing takes. When a submission is returned, check the file folder of potential markets for that idea. Cross off the current market and immediately mail an appropriate submission to the next market on your list. If the editor has given you suggestions or reasons the manuscript was not accepted, you might want to incorporate these when revising your manuscript. In any event, remember the first editor didn't reject *you*, but simply chose not to buy your product. A rejection only means that your particular piece did not fit the needs of the publisher at that time. Veteran writers also find it helps to have several projects going at once, so you don't dwell on the one that's out for consideration.

Writing tools

Like anyone involved in a trade or business, you need certain tools and supplies to produce your product or provide your service. While writers often compose their work in a variety of ways, there are some basics you'll need for your writing business. We've also included information about some you may want in the future.

Typewriter. Many writers use electric or electronic typewriters that produce either pica or elite type. Pica type has 10 characters to a horizontal inch and elite has 12; both have six single-spaced, or three double-spaced, lines to a vertical inch. The slightly larger pica type is easier to read and many editors prefer it, although they don't object to elite.

Editors do dislike, and often refuse to read, manuscripts that are single-spaced, typed in all caps or in an unusual type style like script, italic or Old English. Reading these manuscripts is hard on the eyes. You should strive for clean, easy-to-read manuscripts and correspondence that reflect a professional approach to your work and consideration for your reader.

Use a good black (never colored) typewriter ribbon and clean the keys frequently. If the enclosures of the letters a, b, d, e, g, o, etc., become inked in, a cleaning is overdue.

Even the best typists make errors. *Occasional* retyping over erasures is acceptable, but strikeovers give your manuscript a sloppy, careless appearance. Hiding typos with large splotches of correction fluid makes your work look amateurish; use it sparingly. Some writers prefer to use typing correction film for final drafts and correction fluid for rough drafts. Better yet, a self-correcting electric typewriter with a correction tape makes typos nearly invisible. Whatever method you use, it's best to retype a page that has several noticeable corrections. Sloppy typing is taken by many editors as a sign of sloppy work habits—and the possibility of careless research and writing.

Personal computers. More and more writers are working on personal computers. A personal computer can make a writer's work much more efficient. Writing, revising and editing are usually faster and easier on a computer than on a typewriter, eliminating tedious retyping. Writers also can rely on their computers to give them fresh, readable copy as they revise rough drafts into finished manuscripts.

When a manuscript is written on a computer, it can come out of the computer in three ways: as hard copy from the computer's printer; stored on a removable 5¼" floppy disk or 3½" diskette that can be read by other computers; or as an electronic transfer over telephone lines using a modem (a device that allows one computer to transmit to another).

● Hard copy—Most editors are receptive to computer printout submissions if they look like neatly-typed manuscripts. Some older and cheaper printers produce only a low-quality dot-matrix printout with hard-to-read, poorly shaped letters and numbers. Many editors are not willing to read these manuscripts and have indicated that in their listings. (In addition, most editors dislike copy with even, or justified, right margins.) New dot-matrix printers, however, produce near letter-quality (NLQ) printouts that are almost indistinguishable from a typewritten manuscript. These are acceptable to editors who indicate they prefer letter-quality submissions. Remember that readability is the key. Whether you use a $100 24-pin dot-matrix printer or a $1,000 laser printer doesn't matter to the editor. He just wants to be able to read it easily.

When you submit hard copy to an editor, be sure you use quality paper. Some computer printers use standard bond paper that you'd use in a typewriter. Others are equipped with a tractor-feed that pulls continuous form paper with holes along the edges through the machine. If you use continuous form paper, be sure to remove the perforated tabs on each side and separate the pages.

● Disk—You'll find that more publishers are accepting or even requesting submissions on disk. A few publishers pay more for electronic submissions, nearly all publishers appreciate it, and some won't accept anything but submissions on disk. Eventually, industry observers say electronic submissions will be the norm, just as typewritten submissions became the norm over handwritten manuscripts earlier in the century.

● Modem—Some publishers who accept submissions on disk also will accept electronic submissions by modem. This is the fastest method of getting your manuscript to the publisher.

When you receive an assignment to send by modem, ask the editor about his computer requirements. You'll need to know the name of your computer; its manufacturer and model; the operating system (MS-DOS or OS/2); and word processing software before you compare information. Because most editors want hard copy along with an electronic submission, you may wonder why you should even consider using a disk or modem. Editors like it because they can revise manuscripts more quickly on a computer screen as well as save typesetting expenses. If you have a particularly timely topic or a manuscript that needs to be submitted quickly, a disk or modem submission is an asset that also can save you and the editor time on deadline.

Publishers that accept submissions by disk or modem have this phrase in their listings: Query for electronic submissions. We give the information this way because you'll need to speak with someone before you send anything by these methods. Also, many magazines and publishers change system requirements each year as equipment and software is updated. Instead of listing information which you may find is outdated when you begin to send the submission, we have put just general information in the listing.

Facsimile machines and boards. This year we have added information to the listings concerning publishers' and agents' facsimile machine numbers. These machines, known commonly as fax machines, transmit copy across phone lines. Those publishers who wanted to list their facsimile machine numbers have done so.

Between businesses, the fax has come into standard daily usage for materials which have to be sent quickly. In addition, some public fax machines are being installed in airports, hotels and libraries. Unfortunately, the convenience of the machines has also given rise to "junk" fax transmissions, including unwanted correspondence and advertisements.

The information we have included is not to be used to transmit queries or entire manscripts to editors, unless they specifically request it. Although some machines transmit on regular bond paper, most still use a cheaper grade that is difficult to write on, making it unsuitable for editing. In most cases, this paper also fades with time, an undesirable characteristic for a manuscript. Writers should continue to use traditional means for sending manuscripts and queries and use the fax number we list only when an editor asks to receive correspondence by this method.

Some computer owners also have fax boards installed to allow transmissions to the screen or computer printer. Unless the fax board can operate independently from the computer's main processor, an incoming fax forces the user to halt whatever work is in process until the transmission ends. You should never send anything by this method without calling or arranging with the editor for this type of transmission.

Types of paper. The paper you use must measure 8½x11 inches. That's a standard size and editors are adamant—they don't want unusual colors or sizes. There's a wide range of white 8½x11 papers. The cheaper ones are made from wood pulp. They will suffice, but are not recommended. Editors also discourage the use of erasable bond for manuscripts; typewriter ribbon ink on erasable bond tends to smear when handled and is difficult to write on. Don't use less than a 16 lb. bond paper; 20 lb. is preferred. Your best bet is paper with a 25% cotton fiber content. Its texture shows type neatly and it holds up under erasing and corrections.

You don't need fancy letterhead for your correspondence with editors. Plain bond paper is fine; just type your name, address, phone number and the date at the top of the page—centered or in the right-hand corner. If you decide to use letterhead, make it as simple and businesslike as possible. Many quick print shops have standard typefaces and can supply letterhead stationery at a relatively low cost. Never use letterhead for typing your manuscripts; only the first page of queries, cover letters and other correspondence should be typed on letterhead.

Photocopies. Always make copies of your manuscripts and correspondence before putting them in the mail. Don't learn the hard way, as many writers have, that manuscripts get lost in the mail and publishers sometimes go out of business without returning submissions.

You might want to make several copies of your manuscript while it is still clean and crisp. Some writers keep their original manuscript as a file copy and submit good quality photocopies. Submitting copies can save you the expense and effort of retyping a manuscript if it becomes lost in the mail. If you submit a copy, it's a good idea to explain to the editor whether or not you are making a simultaneous (or multiple) submission to several markets. Some editors will not consider material submitted simultaneously, and they assume a photocopied submission is simultaneous. Follow the requirements in the individual listings, and see Approaching Markets later in this article for more detailed information about simultaneous submissions.

Some writers include a self-addressed post card with a photocopied submission and suggest in their cover letter that if the editor is not interested in the manuscript, it may be tossed out and a reply returned on the post card. This practice is recommended when dealing with foreign markets. If you find that your personal computer generates copies more cheaply than you can pay to have them returned, you might choose to send disposable manuscripts. Submitting a.disposable manuscript costs the writer some photocopy or computer printer expense, but it can save on large postage bills.

The cost of personal photocopiers is coming down, but they remain too expensive for many writers to consider purchasing. If you need to make a large number of photocopies, you should ask your print shop about quantity discounts. One advantage of owning a personal computer and printer is that you can quickly print copies of any text you have composed on it.

Assorted supplies. Where will you put all your manuscripts and correspondence? A two- or four-drawer filing cabinet with file folders is a good choice, but some writers find they can make do with manila envelopes and cardboard boxes. It's important to organize and label your correspondence, manuscripts, ideas, submission records, clippings, etc., so you can find them when you need them. See sections on Recording Submissions and Bookkeeping for other helpful hints on keeping records.

You will also need stamps and envelopes; see Mailing Submissions in this article and the U.S. and Canadian Postage by the Page tables on the inside covers of the book. If you decide to invest in a camera to increase your sales, you'll find details on submitting and mailing photos in the sections on Approaching Markets and Mailing Submissions.

Approaching markets

Before submitting a manuscript to a market, be sure you've done the following:
● Familiarize yourself with the publication or other type of market that interests you. Your first sales probably will be to markets you already know through your reading. If you find a listing in *Writer's Market* that seems a likely home for an idea you've been working on, study a sample copy or book catalog to see if your idea fits in with their current topics. If you have a magazine article idea, you may also want to check the *Reader's Guide to Periodical Literature* to be sure the idea hasn't been covered with an article in the magazine during the past year or two. For a book idea, check the Subject Guide to *Books in Print* to see what other books have been published on the subject.
● Always request writer's guidelines if they're available. Guidelines give a publication's exact requirements for submissions and will help you focus your query letter or manuscript. If a publication has undergone editorial changes since this edition of *Writer's Market* went to press, those changes will usually be reflected in its writer's guidelines. Some publications also have theme or other special issues, or an editorial calendar planned in advance that will be included in its guidelines. The response to your request for guidelines can also let you know if a publication has folded or if it has an unreasonably long response time.
● Check submission requirements. A publication that accepts only queries may not respond at all to a writer who submits an unsolicited complete manuscript. Don't send an unpublished manuscript to a publication that publishes only reprints, and if you're submitting photos, be sure the publication reviews prints or slides, and find out if they require model releases and captions. An editor is impressed when a writer carefully studies a publication and its requirements before making a submission.
● With unsolicited submissions or correspondence, enclose a self-addressed, stamped envelope (SASE). Editors appreciate the convenience and the savings in postage. Some editorial offices deal with such a large volume of mail that their policies do not allow them to

respond to mail that does not include a SASE. If you submit to a foreign market, enclose a self-addressed envelope (SAE) with International Reply Coupons (IRCs) purchased from the post office. (You don't need to send an SASE if you send a disposable manuscript or your manuscript is an assignment, but be sure you mention that in your cover letter.)

Those are the basics; now you're ready to learn the details of what you should send when you contact an editor.

Query letters. A query letter is a brief, but detailed letter written to interest an editor in your manuscript. Some beginners are hesitant to query, thinking an editor can more fairly judge an idea by seeing the entire manuscript. Actually, most editors of nonfiction prefer to be queried.

Do your best writing when you sit down to compose your query. There is no query formula that guarantees success, but there are some points to consider when you begin:

● Queries are single-spaced business letters, usually limited to one page. Address the current editor by name, if possible. (If you cannot tell whether an editor is male or female from the name in the listing, address the editor by a full name: Dear Chris Dodd:). Don't show unwarranted familiarity by immediately addressing an editor by a first name; follow the editor's lead when responding to your correspondence.

● Your major goal is to convince the editor that your idea would be interesting to the publication's readership and that you are the best writer for the job. Mention any special training or experience that qualifies you to write the article. If you have prior writing experience, you should mention it; if not there's no need to call attention to the fact. Some editors will also ask to look at clips or tearsheets — actual pages or photocopies of your published work. If possible, submit something related to your idea, either in topic or style.

● Be sure you use a strong opening to pique the editor's interest. Some queries begin with a paragraph that approximates the lead of the intended article.

● Briefly detail the structure of the article. Give some facts and perhaps an anecdote and mention people you intend to interview. Give editors enough information to make them want to know more, but don't feel the need to give them details of the whole story. You want to sell the sizzle now and save the steak for later.

● If photos are available to accompany the manuscript, let the editor know, but never send original photos, transparencies or artwork on your initial contact with a publisher. You should always have duplicates, so if your material is lost, you haven't lost your only copy.

● Your closing paragraph should include a direct request to do the article; it may specify the date the manuscript can be completed and an approximate length. Don't discuss fees or request advice from the editor at this time. Editors are put off by presumption that they are beyond the point of consideration and to the point of negotiation. Treat the query like a short introductory job interview. You wouldn't presume to discuss money at this early a stage in a job interview; treat the query the same way.

● Fiction is rarely queried since most fiction editors want to see the complete manuscript before making a judgment. If a fiction editor does request a query, briefly describe the main theme and story line, including the conflict and resolution of your story.

● Some writers state politely in their query letters that after a specified date (slightly beyond the listed reporting time), they will assume the editor is not currently interested in their topic and will submit their query elsewhere. It's a good idea to do this only if your topic is a timely one that will suffer if not considered quickly.

For more information about writing query letters and biographical notes, read *How to Write Irresistible Query Letters*, by Lisa Collier Cool (Writer's Digest Books).

Cover letters. A brief cover letter enclosed with your manuscript is helpful in personalizing a submission. If you have previously queried the editor on the article or book, the note should be a brief reminder: "Here is the piece on changes in the Fair Housing Act, which we discussed previously. I look forward to hearing from you at your earliest convenience."

Christine Dodd
(address)

Hope M. Daniels
Editor
Military Lifestyle
Downey Communications Inc.
1732 Wisconsin Avenue NW
Washington, D.C. 20007

Dear Ms. Daniels:

With the link between cholesterol and heart disease so much in the news, Americans are becoming increasingly aware of the need to lower their blood cholesterol in a variety of ways.

In the last year, new drugs have been developed to treat patients with familial hypercholesteremia (an inherited predisposition to high blood cholesterol), and two members of our family have benefited from that technology.

But there was a catch for our youngest brother Tim, who was also found to have elevated cholesterol levels. Tim is an Air Force pilot and feared he would have been taken off active flying status had he been put on medication as well. He decided to see if diet alone could make a difference in his cholesterol, and six months ago went on the regimen prescribed in the book *How to Lower Your Blood Cholesterol in Eight Weeks*. At last report, he had lowered his level from the mid-300s to 265 on the diet. And he's still on flying status, presently stationed in Washington after a year's tour of duty in Egypt and the Middle East.

I'd like to propose a story on Tim for readers of *Military Lifestyle* (even if their military status isn't affected, their health might well be!) I'd describe the modifications he's made in his diet and lifestyle (he's taken up running), and would include some of the low-fat recipes he and I both use (maybe even one for a Middle East dish!)

I wrote a story about the rest of the family's experiences for the February issue of *Health* magazine (Tim, incidentally, took the picture for that story), a copy of which I've enclosed. Other clips are available on request.

Regarding my credentials, I've been a freelance writer and newspaper reporter for the past eighteen years. Besides the *Health* piece, I've written for such publications as *Bride's* magazine, *Writer's Digest*, *Ladies' Circle* and others.

Thank you for your consideration of this story idea, Ms. Daniels. I look forward to hearing from you.

Sincerely,

Chris Dodd

Magazine query. This sample query for a magazine article presents a timely idea, ties it in well with the targeted magazine and presents the author's qualifications. Note that the same information—with a different slant—can result in sales to more than one magazine. Reprinted with permission of the author, ©Chris Dodd.

(Address)

Ms. Irma Genary
Author's Representative
(Address)

Dear Ms. Genary:

I am a mystery writer who has sold five stories to *Hitchcock's Mystery Magazine* in the past eighteen months. The first of these stories appeared in (date); the last is not yet in print.

Two of the stories involve the hero of a murder mystery I have written entitled *Murder at the War*. The novel is traditional in structure and set in an "exotic locale" — a simulated medieval war. Every year 3000-plus members of the Society for the Advancement of Medievalism gather at a campground in western Pennsylvania to hold a mock war. Everyone dresses in medieval garb (including steel armor for the fighters), and the campground joyously drops out of the twentieth century for a three-day weekend. During the course of a mock battle in the woods, however, a man is found dead — really dead, not mock dead. The woman who finds him becomes the chief suspect. She also happens to be the wife of Peter Brichter, a police detective from out of state.

The local law enforcement officers are startled at the sight of all these oddly-dressed people and half-convinced they are some kind of cult. Brichter, trying to clear his wife, begins his own unofficial investigation, but the local police angrily call a halt to his activities and confine him to his encampment.

Meanwhile, the clues lead to a certain Lord Christopher, who, dressed in armor, participated in a mock skirmish beside the victim shortly before the murder. Lord Christopher's armor is found abandoned in the woods near the body, and it seems that no one had seen or heard of him before he appeared in the woods, dressed for battle.

All of this suggests that there is, in fact, no Lord Christopher — that he was a SAM member who assumed that persona (and armor) as a disguise only for a few minutes, for the specific purpose of killing his victim and then escaping detection. There were two hundred participants in the woods battle; any one of them might have slipped away for a brief time.

While the local police struggle with the esoterica of the Society, Brichter welcomes visitors to his tent, fitting the pieces together in classic detective style.

There really is a medievalist society which holds an annual mock war in Pennsylvania. I am a member, and drew on my experiences at several of these wars in writing this book.

The novel is in finished form, about 90,000 words long. Please let me know if you would be interested in reading it with an eye toward representing it.

Sincerely,

Mary Kuhfeld

Book query. This query for a novel could be sent either to a publisher or an agent. It details the author's experience and provides an overview of the book. A nonfiction book query often will contain information about the author's expertise to write and promote the book and will be accompanied by a chapter outline. Reprinted with permission, ©Mary Kuhfeld.

Don't use the letter to make a sales pitch. Your manuscript must stand on its own at this point.

If you are submitting to a market that considers unsolicited complete manuscripts, your cover letter should tell the editor something about your manuscript and about you—your publishing history and any particular qualifications you have for writing the enclosed manuscript.

If the manuscript you are submitting is a photocopy, indicate in the letter if that means it is a simultaneous submission. An editor may assume it is, unless you tell him otherwise. Markets that are open to simultaneous submissions indicate that in their listings.

Once your manuscript has been accepted, offer to get involved in the editing process. This process varies from magazine to magazine. According to a poll in *Publishing News*, 55% of magazine editors don't send galleys to authors before publication. If the magazine regularly sends authors copies of the edited versions of their manuscripts, you should return the galleys as promptly as possible after you've reviewed them. If the editors don't regularly send galleys, you should ask to be involved in the editing process. Don't hesitate to rewrite your article to the magazine's specifications. Writers almost always prefer to rework their own prose rather than have someone else do it.

Book proposals. Book proposals are some combination of a cover letter, a synopsis, an outline and/or two or three sample chapters. The exact combination of these will depend on the publisher.

Some editors use the terms synopsis and outline interchangeably. If the publisher requests only a synopsis or an outline, not both, be sure you know which format the publisher prefers. Either a synopsis or outline is appropriate for a novel, but you may find an outline is more effective for a nonfiction book.

● A synopsis is a very brief summary of your book. Cover the basic plot or theme of your book and reveal the ending. Make sure your synopsis flows well, is interesting and easy to read.

● An outline covers the highlights of your book chapter-by-chapter. If your outline is for a novel, include all major characters, the main plot, subplots and any pertinent details. An outline may run three to 30 pages, depending on the complexity and length of the book. Be sure your outline is clear; you will lose the reader with a tangle of ideas and events.

● Sample chapters are also requested by many editors. Most are interested in the first two or three chapters to see how well you develop your book. A few want a beginning chapter, a chapter from the middle of your book, and the final chapter, so they can see how well you follow through. *How to Write a Book Proposal*, by Michael Larsen (Writer's Digest Books), also provides helpful details about submitting a book proposal.

Some writers are finding a distinct advantage in providing marketing information with their nonfiction book proposals. The marketing information tells the editor what competition there is for the potential book, who the potential audience is—including statistics—and any special ways the book could be marketed. An author who does this kind of homework will impress an editor with his knowledge of business considerations.

Reprints. You can get more mileage—and money—out of your research and writing time by marketing your previously published material for reprint sales. You may use a photocopy of your original manuscript and/or tearsheets from the publication in which it originally appeared. With your reprint submission, be sure to inform the editor that you are marketing the article as a reprint, especially if you send a photocopy without tearsheets. The editor will also need to know when and in what publication it appeared.

If you market for reprint an article that has not yet been published by the original purchaser, inform editors that it cannot be used before it has made its initial appearance. Give them the intended publication date and be sure to inform them if any changes take place.

Photographs and slides. The availability of good quality photos can be a deciding factor when an editor is considering a manuscript. Most publications also offer additional pay for photos accepted with a manuscript. When submitting black and white prints, editors usually want to see 8x10 glossy photos, unless they indicate another preference in the listing. The universally accepted format for color transparencies is 35mm; few buyers will look at color prints.

On all your photos and slides, you should stamp or print your copyright notice and "Return to:" followed by your name, address and phone number. Rubber stamps are preferred for labeling photos since they are less likely to cause damage. You can order them from many stationery or office supply stores. If you use a pen to write this information on the back of your photos, be careful not to damage the print by pressing too hard or allowing ink to bleed through the paper. A felt tip pen is best, but you should take care not to put photos or copy together before the ink dries or it will smear.

● Captions can be typed on a sheet of paper and taped to the back of the prints. Some writers, when submitting several transparencies or photos, number the photos and type captions (numbered accordingly) on an 8½x11 sheet of paper.

● Submit prints rather than negatives or consider having duplicates made of your slides or transparencies. Don't risk having your original negative or slide lost or damaged. Look for a photography lab that does custom work in prints and transparencies.

Manuscript mechanics

Your good writing may be hurt by your presentation if it's not done in correct form. Follow these rules of manuscript mechanics to present your work in its best form.

Manuscript format. Do not use a cover sheet or title page. Use a binder only if you are submitting a play or a television or movie script. You can use a paper clip to hold pages together, but never use staples.

The upper corners of the first page contain important information about you and your manuscript. This information is always single-spaced. In the upper left corner list your name, address, phone number and Social Security number (publishers must have this now to file accurate payment records with the government). If you are using a pseudonym for your byline, your legal name still must appear in this space. In the upper right corner, indicate the approximate word count of the manuscript, the rights you are offering for sale and your copyright notice (© 1990 Chris Jones). A handwritten copyright symbol is acceptable. For a book manuscript, do not specify the rights you are offering; that will be covered in your contract. Do not number the first page of your manuscript.

There is much discussion about the necessity of this information. Many writers of short fiction and poetry do not feel it necessary to put the rights or word count on manuscripts they submit to literary magazines. Some writers also consider the copyright notice unnecessary or think editors will consider it amateurish. Others use it only for unsolicited complete manuscripts and not for assigned or solicited manuscripts. A copyright notice is not required to obtain copyright protection or to avoid losing it, but persons who use protected works without authorization can claim "innocent infringement" if the notice is not on the manuscript. U.S. copyright owners also must register their works with the U.S. Copyright Office before they file a copyright infringement lawsuit; otherwise, registration is not necessary.

Center the title in capital letters one-third of the way down the page. To center, set the tabulator to stop halfway between the right and left edges of the page. Count the letters in the title, including spaces and punctuation, and backspace half that number. Type the title. Set your typewriter to double-space. Type "by" centered one double-space under your title, and type your name or pseudonym centered one double-space beneath that.

After the title and byline, drop down two double-spaces, paragraph indent, and begin the body of your manuscript. Always double-space your manuscript and use standard paragraph indentations of five spaces. Margins should be about 1¼ inches on all sides of each full page of typewritten manuscript. You may lightly pencil in a line to remind you when you reach the bottom margin of your page, but be sure to erase it before submitting your manuscript.

On every page after the first, type your last name, a dash and the page number in the upper left corner. (This is sometimes called the slug line.) The title of your manuscript may, but need not, be typed on this line or beneath it. Page number two would read: Jones—2. If you are using a pseudonym, type your real name, followed by your pen name in parentheses, then a dash and the page number: Jones (Smith)—2. Then drop down two double-spaces and continue typing. Follow this format throughout your manuscript.

If you are submitting novel chapters, leave the top one-third of the first page of each chapter blank before typing the chapter title. Subsequent pages should include the author's last name, the page number, and a shortened form of the book's title: Jones—2—Skating. (In a variation on this, some authors place the title before the name on the left side and put the page number on the right-hand margin.)

When submitting poetry, the poems should be typed single-spaced (double-space between stanzas), one poem per page. For a long poem requiring more than one page, paper clip the pages together.

On the final page of your manuscript, after you've typed your last word and period, skip three double-spaces and center the words "The End." Some nonfiction writers use ### or the old newspaper symbol -30- to indicate the same thing. Further information on formats for books, articles, scripts, proposals and cover letters, with illustrated examples, is available in *The Writer's Digest Guide to Manuscript Formats*, by Dian Dincin Buchman and Seli Groves (Writer's Digest Books).

Estimating word count. To estimate word count in manuscripts, count the number of characters and spaces in an average line and divide by six for the average words per line. Then count the number of lines of type on a representative page. Multiply the words per line by the lines per page to find out the average number of words per page. Then count the number of manuscript pages (fractions should be counted as fractions, except in book manuscript chapter headings, which are counted as a full page.) Multiply the number of pages by the number of words per page you already determined. This will give you the approximate number of words in the manuscript. For short manuscripts, it's often quicker to count each word on a representative page and multiply by the total number of pages.

Mailing submissions

No matter what size manuscript you're mailing, always include sufficient return postage and a self-addressed envelope large enough to contain your manuscript if it is returned.

A manuscript of fewer than six pages may be folded in thirds and mailed as if it were a letter using a #10 (business-size) envelope. The enclosed SASE should be a #10 folded in thirds or a #9 envelope which will slip into the mailing envelope without being folded. Some editors also appreciate the convenience of having a manuscript folded into halves in a 6x9 envelope.

For larger manuscripts, use 9x12 envelopes for both mailing and return. The return SASE may be folded in half.

A book manuscript should be mailed in a sturdy, well-wrapped box. Your typing paper, computer paper or envelope box is a suitable mailer. Enclose a self-addressed mailing label and paper clip your return postage stamps or International Reply Coupons to the label.

Always mail photos and slides First Class. The rougher handling received by Fourth Class mail could damage them. If you are concerned about losing prints or slides, send them certified or registered mail. For any photo submission that is mailed separately from a manuscript, enclose a short cover letter of explanation, separate self-addressed label, adequate return postage, and an envelope. Never submit photos or slides mounted in glass.

To mail up to 20 prints, you can buy photo mailers that are stamped "Photos—Do Not

Bend" and contain two cardboard inserts to sandwich your prints. Or use a 9x12 manila envelope, write "Photos—Do Not Bend" and devise your own cardboard inserts. Some photography supply shops also carry heavy cardboard envelopes that are reusable.

When mailing a number of prints, say 25 to 50 for a book with illustrations, pack them in a sturdy cardboard box. A box for typing paper or photo paper is an adequate mailer. If, after packing both manuscript and photos, there's empty space in the box, slip in enough cardboard inserts to fill the box. Wrap the box securely.

To mail transparencies, first slip them into protective vinyl sleeves, then mail as you would prints. If you're mailing a number of sheets, use a cardboard box as for photos above.

Types of mail service

- First Class is the most expensive way of mailing a manuscript, but many writers prefer it. First Class mail generally receives better handling and is delivered more quickly. Mail sent First Class is forwarded for one year if the addressee has moved, and is returned automatically if it is undeliverable.
- Fourth Class rates are available for packages but you must pack materials carefully when mailing Fourth Class since they will be handled the same as Parcel Post—roughly. If a letter is enclosed with your Fourth Class package, write "First Class Letter Enclosed" on the package and add adequate First Class postage for your letter. To make sure your package will be returned to you if it is undeliverable, print "Return Postage Guaranteed" under your address.
- Certified Mail must be signed for when it reaches its destination. If requested, a signed receipt is returned to the sender. There is an 85¢ charge for this service, in addition to the required postage, and a 90¢ charge for a return receipt.
- Registered Mail is a high security method of mailing. The package is signed in and out of every office it passes through, and a receipt is returned to the sender when the package reaches its destination. This service begins at $4.40 in addition to the postage required for the item. If you obtain insurance for the package, the cost begins at $4.50.
- United Parcel Service may be slightly cheaper than First Class postage if you drop the package off at UPS yourself. UPS cannot legally carry First Class mail, so your cover letter needs to be mailed separately. Check with UPS in your area for current rates. The cost depends on the weight of your package and the distance to its destination.
- Overnight mail services are provided by both the U.S. Postal Service and several private firms. These services can be useful if your manuscript or revisions *must* be at an editor's office quickly. More information on next day service is available from the U.S. Post Office in your area, or check your Yellow Pages under "Delivery Services."

Other important details

- Money orders should be used if you are ordering sample copies or supplies and do not have checking services. You'll have a receipt and money orders are traceable. Money orders for up to $35 can be purchased from the U.S. Postal Service for a 75¢ service charge. Banks, savings and loans, and some commercial businesses also carry money orders; their fees vary. *Never* send cash through the mail for sample copies.
- Insurance is available for items handled by the U.S. Postal Service but is payable only on typing fees or the tangible value of the item in the package—such as typing paper—so your best insurance when mailing manuscripts is to keep a copy of what you send.
- When corresponding with foreign publications and publishers, International Reply Coupons (IRCs) must be used for return postage. Surface rates in foreign countries differ from those in the U.S., and U.S. postage stamps are of no use there. Currently, one IRC costs 95¢ and is sufficient for one ounce traveling at surface rate; two must be used for airmail return. Since some post offices don't carry IRCs many writers dealing with foreign publishers mail photocopies and tell the publisher to dispose of them if they're not appropriate.

When you use this method, it's best to set a deadline for withdrawing your manuscript from consideration, so you can market it elsewhere.

● International money orders are also available from the post office for a $3 charge.

● See U.S. and Canadian Postage by the Page on the inside covers for specific mailing costs.

Recording submissions

A number of writers think once they've mailed a manuscript, the situation is out of their hands; all they can do is sit and wait. But submitting a manuscript doesn't mean you've lost control of it. Manage your writing business by keeping copies of all manuscripts and correspondence, and by recording the dates of submissions.

One way to keep track of your manuscripts is to use a record of submissions that includes the date sent, title, market, editor and enclosures (such as photos). You should also note the date of the editor's response, any rewrites that were done, and, if the manuscript was accepted, the publication date and payment information. You might want to keep a similar record just for queries.

Also remember to keep a separate file for each manuscript or idea along with its list of potential markets. You may want to keep track of expected reporting times on a calendar, too. Then you'll know if a market has been slow to respond and you can follow up on your query or submission.

Bookkeeping

Whether or not you are profitable in your writing, you'll need to keep accurate financial records. These records are necessary to let you know how you're doing, and, of course, the government is also interested in your financial activities.

If you have another source of income, you should plan to keep separate records for your writing expenses and income. Some writers open separate checking accounts for their writing-related expenses.

The best financial records are the ones that get used, and usually the simpler the form, the more likely it will be used regularly. Get in the habit of recording every transaction related to your writing. You can start at any time; it doesn't need to be on Jan. 1. Because you're likely to have expenses before you have income, start keeping your records whenever you make your first purchase related to writing—such as this copy of *Writer's Market*.

A simple bookkeeping system. For most freelance writers, a simple type of single-entry bookkeeping is adequate. The heart of the single-entry system is the journal, an accounting book available at any stationery or office supply store. You record all of the expenses and income of your writing business in the journal.

The single-entry journal's form is similar to a standard check register. Instead of withdrawals and deposits, you record expenses and income. You'll need to describe each transaction clearly—including the date; the source of the income (or the vendor of your purchase); a description of what was sold or bought; whether the payment was by cash, check or credit card; and the amount of the transaction.

Your receipt file. Keep all documentation pertaining to your writing expenses or income. This is true whether you have started a bookkeeping journal or not. For every payment you receive, you should have a check stub from the publisher's check, a cover letter or contract stating the amount of payment, or your own bank records of the deposit. For every check you write to pay business expenses, you should have a record in your check register as well as a cancelled check. Keep credit card receipts, too. And for every cash purchase, you should have a receipt from the vendor—especially if the amount is over $25. For small expenses, you can usually keep a list if you don't record them in a journal.

Tax information

The application of federal income tax laws was modified last year after lobbying by freelance writers, artists and photographers. A subsection has been added to the Internal Revenue Code that exempts freelance authors, photographers and artists from having to capitalize "qualified creative expenses" incurred while in the business as a freelancer. The expenses can be allowed as deductions. (Changes in the 1986 Tax Reform Act originally required writers to deduct expenses for a project over the entire income-producing lifetime of the work. If no income was produced, no deductions could be taken.) Individuals who are involved in related but separate business and freelance activities, such as self-publishers who are writers and publishers, probably will have to keep the expenses separate and capitalize expenses related to publishing, while they deduct expenses from freelancing.

There also is an office-in-home deduction that can be used if an area in your home is used strictly for business. Contact the IRS for information on requirements for this deduction. The deduction is limited to net income after all other deductions have been made; you cannot declare a loss on your deductions from your business. The law also requires a business to be profitable three out of five years to avoid being treated as a hobby.

If your freelance income exceeds your expenses, regardless of the amount, you must declare that profit. If the profit is $400 or more, you also must pay quarterly Self-Employment Social Security Tax and fill out that self-employment form on your 1040 tax form. While we cannot offer you tax advice or interpretations, we can suggest several sources for the most current information.

● Call your local IRS office. Look in the white pages of the telephone directory under U.S. Government—Internal Revenue Service. Someone will be able to respond to your request for IRS publications and tax forms or other information. Ask about the IRS Tele-tax service, a series of recorded messages you can hear by dialing on a touch-tone phone. If you need answers to complicated questions, ask to speak with a Taxpayer Service Specialist.

● Obtain the basic IRS publications. You can order them by phone or mail from any IRS office; most are available at libraries and some post offices. Start with *Your Federal Income Tax* (Publication 17) and *Tax Guide for Small Business* (Publication 334). These are both comprehensive, detailed guides—you'll need to find the regulations that apply to you and ignore the rest. You may also want to get a copy of *Business Use of Your Home* (Publication 587) and *Self-Employment Tax* (Publication 533).

● Consider other information sources. Many public libraries have detailed tax instructions available on tape. Some colleges and universities offer free assistance in preparing tax returns. And if you decide to consult a professional tax preparer, the fee is a deductible business expense on your tax return.

Rights and the writer

We find that writers and editors sometimes define rights in different ways. To eliminate any misinterpretations, read the following definitions of each right—and you'll see the definitions upon which editors updated the information in their listings.

Occasionally, we hear from a writer who is confused because an editor claims never to acquire or buy rights. The truth is, any time an editor buys a story or asks you for permission to publish a story, even without payment, the editor is asking you for rights. In some cases, however, editors will reassign those rights to the author after publishing the story.

Sometimes people start magazines in their areas of expertise but don't have extensive knowledge of publishing terms and practices. And sometimes editors simply don't take the time to specify the rights. In a *Publishing News* survey, 15% of the editors say they don't attempt to purchase any specific rights to manuscripts. If you sense that an editor is interested in getting stories but doesn't seem to know what his and the writer's responsibilities are regarding rights, be wary. In such a case, you'll want to explain what rights you're offering (preferably one-time rights only) and that you expect additional payment for subsequent use of your work. Writers may also agree to sell first rights, for example to a magazine, but then never receive a check for the manuscript and subsequent inquiries bring no response. In a case like this, we recommend that the writer send a certified letter, return receipt requested, notifying the magazine that the manuscript is being withdrawn from that publication for submission elsewhere. There is no industry standard for how long a writer should wait before using this procedure. The best bet is to check the *Writer's Market* listing for what the magazine lists as its usual reporting time and then, after a reasonable wait beyond that, institute the withdrawal.

For a complete discussion about book and magazine agreements and information on rights and negotiations, see *A Writer's Guide to Contract Negotiations*, by Richard Balkin (Writer's Digest Books).

Selling rights to your writing. The Copyright Law that went into effect Jan. 1, 1978, said writers were primarily selling one-time rights to their work (plus any revision of that collective work and any later collective work in the same series) unless they—and the publisher—agreed otherwise in writing. In some cases, however, a writer may have little say in the rights sold to an editor. The beginning writer, in fact, can jeopardize a sale by arguing with an editor who is likely to have other writers available who are eager to please. As long as there are more writers than there are markets, this situation will remain.

As a writer acquires skill, reliability, and professionalism on the job, he becomes more valued by editors—and rights become a more important consideration. Though a beginning writer will accept modest payment just to get in print, an experienced writer cannot afford to give away good writing just to see a byline. At this point the writer must become concerned with selling reprints of articles already sold to one market, using previously published articles as chapters in a book on the same topic, seeking markets for the same material overseas, or offering rights to TV or the movies.

You should strive to keep as many rights to your work as you can from the outset, because before you can resell any piece of writing, you must own the rights to negotiate. If you have sold "all rights" to an article, for instance, it can be reprinted without your permission and without additional payment to you. Some writers will not deal with editors who buy all rights. What an editor buys will determine whether you can resell your own work. Here is a list of the rights most editors and publishers seek. (Book rights will be covered by the contract submitted to the writer by a book publisher. The writer does not indicate any such rights offered.)

● First Serial Rights—First serial rights means the writer offers the newspaper or magazine the right to publish the article, story or poem for the first time in any periodical. All other rights to the material belong to the writer. Variations on this right are, for example, first North American serial rights. Some magazines use this purchasing technique to obtain the right to publish first in both the U.S. and Canada since many U.S. magazines are circulated in Canada. If an editor had purchased only first U.S. serial rights, a Canadian magazine could come out with prior or simultaneous publication of the same material. When material is excerpted from a book scheduled to be published and it appears in a magazine or newspaper prior to book publication, this is also called first serial rights.

● First North American Serial Rights—Magazine publishers that distribute in both the United States and Canada frequently buy these first rights covering publication in both countries.

● One-Time Rights—This differs from first serial rights in that the buyer has no guarantee he will be the first to publish the work. One-time rights often apply to photos, but also apply to writing sold to more than one market over a period of time. See also Simultaneous Rights.

● Second Serial (Reprint) Rights—This gives a newspaper or magazine the opportunity to print an article, poem or story after it has already appeared in another newspaper or magazine. The term is also used to refer to the sale of part of a book to a newspaper or magazine after a book has been published, whether or not there has been any first serial publication. Income derived from second serial rights to book material is often shared 50/50 by author and book publisher.

● All Rights — Some magazines buy all rights because of the top prices they pay for material or the exclusive nature of the publication; others have book publishing interests or foreign magazine connections.

About 40% of the trade magazines and 31% of the consumer magazines in a *Publishing News* survey bought all rights or asked for work-for-hire agreements. A writer who sells an article, story or poem to a magazine under these terms forfeits the rights to use his material in its present form elsewhere. If he signs a work-for-hire agreement, he signs away all rights and the copyright to the company making the assignment. (Work-for-hire rules may undergo change with the recent review of a U.S. Supreme Court case in which a sculptor claimed copyright ownership of work he created under such an agreement.)

If the writer thinks he may want to use his material later (perhaps in book form), he must avoid submitting to such markets or refuse payment and withdraw his material if he discovers it later. Ask the editor whether he is willing to buy only first rights instead of all rights before you agree to an assignment or sale. Some editors will reassign rights to a writer after a given period, such as one year. It's worth an inquiry in writing.

● Simultaneous Rights — This term covers articles and stories sold to publications (primarily religious magazines) that do not have overlapping circulations. A Catholic publication, for example, might be willing to buy simultaneous rights to a Christmas story they like very much, even though they know a Presbyterian magazine may be publishing the same story in its Christmas issue. Publications that buy simultaneous rights indicate this fact in their listings in *Writer's Market*.

Always advise an editor when the material you are sending is a simultaneous submission to another market. Some writers put the information in their cover letters while others also add it to the upper right-hand corner of the first page of the manuscript under the approximate word count.

● Foreign Serial Rights — Can you resell a story you had published in the U.S. or North America to a foreign magazine? If you sold only first U.S. serial rights or first North American rights, yes, you are free to market your story abroad. Of course, you must contact a foreign magazine that buys material that has previously appeared in the U.S. or North American periodicals.

● Syndication Rights — This is a division of serial rights. For example, a book publisher may sell the rights to a newspaper syndicate to print a portion of a book in 12 installments in each of 20 U.S. newspapers. If they did this after book publication, they would be syndicating second serial rights to the book. In either case, the syndicate would be taking a commission on the sales it made to newspapers, so the remaining percentage would split between author and publisher.

● Subsidiary Rights — The rights, other than book publication rights, that should be specified in a book contract. These may include various serial rights, dramatic rights, translation rights, etc. The contract lists what percentage of these sales goes to the author and what percentage to the publisher. Be careful when signing away these rights. If the publisher is unlikely to market them, you may be able to retain them and market them yourself or through an agent.

● Dramatic, Television and Motion Picture Rights — This means the writer is selling his material for use on the stage, in television or in the movies. Often a one-year option to buy such rights is offered (generally for 10% of the total price). The interested party then tries to sell the idea to other people — actors, directors, studios or television networks, etc. — who become part of the project, which then becomes a script. Some properties are optioned over and over again, but most fail to become dramatic productions. In such cases, the writer can sell his rights again and again—as long as there is interest in the material. Though dramatic, TV and motion picture rights are more important to the fiction writer than the nonfiction writer, producers today are increasingly interested in nonfiction material; many biographies and topical books, and "true-life stories" are being dramatized.

Communicate and clarify. Before submitting material to a market, check its listing in this book to see what rights are purchased. Most editors will discuss rights they wish to purchase before any exchange of money occurs. Some buyers are adamant about what rights they will accept; others will negotiate. In any case, the rights purchased should be stated specifically in writing sometime during the course of the sale, usually in a contract, memo or letter of agreement. If the editor doesn't put this information in writing, you should. Summarize what you talked about and send it a copy to the editor.Give as much attention to the rights you haven't sold as you do to the rights you have sold. Be aware of the rights you retain, with an eye for additional sales.

Regardless of the rights you sell or keep, make sure all parties involved in any sale understand the terms of the sale. Keep in mind, too, that if there is a change in editors or publishers from the edition of *Writer's Market* you're using, the rights purchased may also change. Communication, coupled with these guidelines and some common sense, will preclude misunderstandings with editors over rights.

Copyrighting your writing

The copyright law, effective since Jan. 1, 1978, protects your writing, unequivocally recognizes the creator of the work as its owner, and grants the creator all the rights, benefits and privileges that ownership entails.

In other words, the moment you finish a piece of writing—whether it is a short story, article, novel or poem—the law recognizes that only you can decide how it is to be used.

This law gives writers power in dealing with editors and publishers, but they should understand how to use that power. They should also understand that certain circumstances can complicate and confuse the concept of ownership. Writers must be wary of these circumstances or risk losing ownership of their work. Here are answers to frequently asked questions about copyright law:

To what rights am I entitled under copyright law? The law gives you, as creator of your work, the right to print, reprint and copy the work; to sell or distribute copies of the work; to prepare "derivative works"—dramatizations, translations, musical arrangement, novelizations, etc.; to record the work; and to perform or display literary, dramatic or musical works publicly. These rights give you control over how your work is used, and assure you (in theory) that you receive payment for any use of your work.

If, however, you create the work as a "work-for-hire," you do not own any of these rights. The person or company that commissioned the work-for-hire owns the copyright.

When does copyright law take effect, and how long does it last? A piece of writing is copyrighted the moment it is put to paper and you indicate your authorship with the word Copyright or the ©, the year and your name. Protection lasts for the life of the author plus 50 years, thus allowing your heirs to benefit from your work. For material written by two or more people, protection lasts for the life of the last survivor plus 50 years. The life-plus-50 provision applies if the work was created or registered with the Copyright Office after January 1, 1978, when the updated copyright law took effect. The old law protected works for a 28-year term, and gave the copyright owner the option to renew the copyright for an additional 28 years at the end of that term. Works copyrighted under the old law that are in their second 28-year term automatically receive an additional 19 years of protection (for a total of 75 years). Works in their first term also receive the 19-year extension beyond the 28-year second term, but must still be renewed when the first term ends.

If you create a work anonymously or pseudonymously, protection lasts for 100 years after the work's creation, or 75 years after its publication, whichever is shorter. The life-plus-50 coverage takes effect, however, if you reveal your identity to the Copyright Office any time before the original term of protection runs out.

Works created on a for-hire basis are also protected for 100 years after the work's creation or 75 years after its publication, whichever is shorter. But the copyright is held by the publisher, not the writer.

Must I register my work with the Copyright Office to receive protection? No. Your work is copyrighted whether or not you register it, although registration offers certain advantages. For example, you must register the work before you can bring an infringement suit to court. You can register the work *after* an infringement has taken place, and *then* take the suit to court, but registering after the fact removes certain rights from you. You can sue for actual damages (the income or other benefits lost as a result of the infringement), but you can't sue for statutory damages and you can't recover attorney's fees unless the work has been registered with the Copyright Office *before* the infringement took place. Registering before the infringement also allows you to make a stronger case when bringing the infringement to court.

If you suspect that someone might infringe on your work, register it. If you doubt that an infringement is likely (and infringements are relatively rare), you might save yourself the time and money involved in registering the material.

I have an article that I want to protect fully. How do I register it? Request the proper form from the Copyright Office. Send the completed form, a $10 registration fee, and one copy (if the work is unpublished; two if it's published) of the work to the Register of Copyrights, Library of Congress, Washington, DC 20559. You needn't register each work individually. A group of articles can be registered simultaneously (for a single $10 fee) if they meet these requirements: They must be assembled in orderly form (simply placing them in a notebook binder is sufficient); they must bear a single title ("Works by Chris Jones," for example); they must represent the work of one person (or one set of collaborators); and they must be the subject of a single claim to copyright. No limit is placed on the number of works that can be copyrighted in a group.

If my writing is published in a "collective work" — such as a magazine — does the publication handle registration of the work? Only if the publication owns the piece of writing. Although the copyright notice carried by the magazine covers its contents, you must register any writing to which *you* own the rights if you want the additional protection registration provides.

Collective works are publications with a variety of contributors. Magazines, newspapers, encyclopedias, anthologies, etc., are considered collective works. If you sell something to a collective work, state in writing what rights you're selling. If you don't specify rights, the law allows one-time rights plus publication in any revision of the collective work and any later collective work in the same series. For example, a publishing company could reprint a contribution from one issue in a later issue of its magazine without paying you. The same is true for other collective works, so always detail in writing what rights you are selling before actually making the sale.

When contributing to a collective work, ask that your copyright notice be placed on or near your published manuscript (if you still own the manuscript's rights). Prominent display of your copyright notice on published work has two advantages: It signals to readers and potential reusers of the piece that it belongs to you, and not to the collective work in which it appears; and it allows you to register all published work bearing such notice with the Copyright Office as a group for a single $10 fee. A published work *not* bearing notice indicating you as copyright owner can't be included in a group registration.

Display of copyright notice is especially important when contributing to an uncopyrighted publication — that is, a publication that doesn't display a copyright symbol and doesn't register with the Copyright Office. When the United States joined the Berne Copyright Convention on March 1, 1989, mandatory notice of copyright was no longer required and failure to place a notice of copyright on copies no longer results in loss of copyright. It can still be important to display a copyright notice so no one will innocently infringe on your copyright, however.

Official notice of copyright consists of the symbol ©, the word "Copyright," or the abbreviation "Copr."; the name of the copyright owner or owners; and the year date of first publication (for example, "© 1990 by Chris Jones"). A hand-drawn copyright symbol is acceptable.

Under what circumstances should I place my copyright notice on unpublished works that haven't been registered? Place official copyright notice on the first page of any manuscript. This procedure is not intended to stop a buyer from stealing your material (editorial piracy is very rare, actually), but to demonstrate to the editor that you understand your rights under copyright law, that you own that particular manuscript, and that you want to retain your ownership after the manuscript is published.

How do I transfer copyright? A transfer of copyright, like the sale of any property, is simply an exchange of the property for payment. The law stipulates, however, that the transfer of any exclusive rights (and the copyright is the most exclusive of rights) must be made in writing to be valid. Various types of exclusive rights exist, as outlined above. Usually it is best not to sell your copyright. If you do, you lose control over the use of the manuscript, and forfeit future income from its use.

What is a "work-for-hire assignment"? This is a work that another party commissions you to do. Two types of work-for-hire works exist: Work done as a regular employee of a company, and commissioned work that is specifically called "work-for-hire" in writing at the time of assignment. The phrase "work-for-hire" or something close must be used in the written agreement, though you should watch for similar phrasings. The work-for-hire provision was included in the new copyright law so that no writer could unwittingly sign away his copyright. The phrase "work-for-hire" is a bright red flag warning the writer that the agreement he is about to enter into will result in loss of rights to any material created under the agreement.

Some editors offer work-for-hire agreements when making assignments, and expect writers to sign them routinely. By signing them, you forfeit the potential for additional income from a manuscript through reprint sales, or sale of other rights. Be careful, therefore, in signing away your rights in a "work-for-hire" agreement. Many articles written as works-for-hire or to which all rights have been sold are never resold, but if you retain the copyright, you might try to resell the article—something you couldn't do if you forfeited your rights to the piece.

Can I get my rights back if I sell all rights to a manuscript, or if I sell the copyright itself? Yes. You or your heirs can terminate the transfer of rights 40 years after the grant was made or, in the case of publication, 35 years after publication—whichever comes first. You can do this by serving written notice, within specified time limits, to the person to whom you transferred rights. Consult the Copyright Office for the procedural details.

Must all transfers be in writing? Only work-for-hire agreements and transfers of exclusive rights *must* be in writing. However, getting any agreement in writing before the sale is wise. Beware of other statements about what rights the buyer purchases that may appear on checks, writer's guidelines or magazine mastheads. If the publisher makes such a statement elsewhere, you might insert a phrase like "No statement pertaining to purchase of rights other than the one detailed in this letter—including masthead statements or writer's guidelines—applies to this agreement" into the letter that outlines your rights agreement. Some publishers put their terms in writing on the back of a check that, when endorsed by the writer, becomes in their view a "contract." If the terms on the back of the check do not agree with the rights you are selling, then change the endorsement to match the rights you have sold before signing the check for deposit. Contact the editor to discuss this difference in rights.

Are ideas and titles copyrightable? No. Nor can facts be copyrighted. Only the actual expression of ideas or information can be copyrighted. You can't copyright the idea to do a solar energy story, and you can't copyright lists of materials for building solar energy converters. But you can copyright the article that results from that idea and that information.

Where can I get more information about copyright law? Write the Copyright Office (Library of Congress, Washington, DC 20559) for a free Copyright Information Kit. Call (not collect) the Copyright Public Information Office at (202)479-0700 weekdays between 8:30 a.m. and 5 p.m. if you need forms for registration of a claim to copyright. The Copyright Office will answer specific questions but won't provide legal advice. For more information about copyright and other laws, consult the latest edition of *The Writer's Friendly Legal Guide*, edited by Kirk Polking (Writer's Digest Books).

How much should I charge?

You have just learned from a friend that the company he works for will be marking its 100th anniversary in about a year. The president would like to have a history of the firm prepared as part of the celebration, but no one has the time to research and write the project. Aha! you think — just the job for you while your first novel is making the rounds and your latest magazine article check only paid for part of your new printer. You think you can convince the president you have the skills he needs, but how do you decide what to bid on the job?

First, of course, you should see if your friend has any information on whether a budget has been established for the project. The company may have budgeted money for the printing but is asking writers to supply their fees when the present their credentials. Have they hired outside writers for other projects your friend may know about?

Without revealing who *your* potential client is, contact friends in related businesses or advertising agencies to find out what has been paid locally for comparable writing jobs. If you belong to the local chapter of a professional writers organization such as the Society of Professional Journalists or Women in Communications, seek out those members who may have information from their own experience or contacts that could help you set the parameters for your project fee or hourly rate. The size of the business can make a difference too. One freelancer comments, "Some big corporations think you're not very good if you don't charge enough."

A company history is just one kind of freelance job available in your own backyard. Business anniversaries usually incorporate a variety of public relations "events" that need skilled media professionals. New businesses, competition among existing firms, cities vying with each other for economic development or tourist dollars are all fair game for the freelance writer. Don't wait for the lucky conversation with a friend, though. Create your own opportunities. Maureen Healy, a former advertising copywriter, got tired of reading the same old thing in her fortune cookies. She started Make a Fortune Ltd. in San Francisco turning out "misfortune" cookies, such as "If you can read this, the poison hasn't worked yet," or "Look forward to love and marriage, but not with the same person."

Another woman in Ohio established "An Apology Service." While she gives you a clean conscience by making a telephone call to your mother-in-law or the friend you offended, some freelancers might want to consider putting the soothing words in writing for a fee.

These creative communications can be fun and rewarding, but there also are plenty of potential clients who need freelancers to produce the newsletters, brochures or speeches they use to lure and keep customers.

When setting your freelance fees, keep these factors in mind: pay rates in your area; amount of competition; how much you think the client is willing or able to pay for the job; and how much you want to earn for your time. For example, if something you write helps a businessman get a $50,000 order or a school board to get a $100,000 grant, that may influence your fees. How much you want to earn for your time should take into consideration not only an hourly rate for the time you spend writing, but also the time involved in travel, meeting with the client, doing research, rewriting and, where necessary, handling details with a printer or producer. One way to figure your hourly rate is to determine what an annual salary might be for a staff person to do the same job you are bidding on, and figure an hourly wage on that. If, for example, you think the buyer would have to pay a staff person $20,000 a year, divide that by 2,000 (approximately 40 hours per week for 50 weeks) and you will arrive at $10 an hour. Then add another 20% to cover the amount of fringe benefits that an employer normally pays (but you must now absorb) in Social Security, unemployment insurance, paid vacations, hospitalization, retirement funds, etc. Then add another dollars-per-hour figure to cover your actual overhead expense for office space, equipment, supplies; plus time spent on professional meetings, readings, and making unsuccessful proposals. (To get this figure, add up one year's expenses and divide by the number of hours per year you work on freelancing. In the beginning you may have to adjust this to avoid pricing yourself out of the market.)

Example:

$20,000 (salary) ÷ 2,000 (hours) = $10 per hour
+ 2 (20% to cover fringe benefits, taxes, etc.)
+ 2 (overhead based on annual expenses of $4,000)
_____
$14 per hour charge

Regardless of the method by which you arrive at your fee for the job, be sure to get a letter of agreement signed by both parties covering the work to be done and the fee to be paid.

If there is any question about how long the project will take you, be sure the agreement indicates that you are estimating the time and your project fee is based on X hours. If more time is required, you should be able to renegotiate with the client. This is a good reason to require partial payment as parts of the job are completed, so both you and the client have a better idea of the time involved.

You will, of course, from time to time handle certain jobs at less than desirable rates because they are for a cause you believe in, allow you to get your foot in the door, or because the job offers additional experience or exposure to some profitable client for the future. Some clients pay hourly rates; others pay flat fees for the job. Both kinds of rates are listed when the data were available so you have as many pricing options as possible.

A

Advertising copywriting: Advertising agencies and the advertising departments of large companies need part-time help in rush seasons. Newspapers, radio and TV stations also need copywriters for their small business customers who do not have agencies. Depending on the client and the job, the following rates could apply: $50-100 per hour, $250 and up per day, $500 and up per week, $1,000-2,000 as a monthly retainer. Flat-fee-per-ad rates could range from $100 and up per page depending upon size and kind of client.

Annual reports: A brief report with some economic information and an explanation of figures, $20-35 per hour; 12-page report, $600-1,500; a report that must meet Securities and Exchange Commission (SEC) standards and reports that use legal language could bill at $40-65 per hour. Some writers who provide copywriting and editing services charge flat fees ranging from $5,000-10,000.

Anthology editing: Variable advance plus 3-15% of royalties. Flat-fee-per-manuscript rates could range from $500-5,000 or more if it consists of complex, technical material.

Article manuscript critique: 3,000 words, $40.

Arts reviewing: For weekly newspapers, $15-35; for dailies, $45 and up; for Sunday supplements, $100-400; regional arts events summaries for national trade magazines, $35-100.

Associations: Miscellaneous writing projects, small associations, $15-25 per hour; larger groups, up to $85 per hour; or a flat fee per project, such as $550-900 for 10-12 page magazine articles, or $1,200-1,800 for a 10-page booklet.

Audio cassette scripts: $10-50 per scripted minute, assuming written from existing client materials, with no additional research or meetings; otherwise $75-100 per minute, $750 minimum.

Audiovisuals: For writing, $250-350 per requested scripted minute; includes rough draft, editing conference with client, and final shooting script. For consulting, research, producing, directing, soundtrack oversight, etc., $400-600 per day plus travel and expenses. Writing fee is sometimes 10% of gross production price as billed to client.

B

Book, as-told-to (ghostwriting): Author gets full advance and 50% of author's royalties; subject gets 50%. Hourly rate for subjects who are self-publishing ($25-50 per hour).

Book, ghostwritten, without as-told-to credit: For clients who are either self-publishing or have no royalty publisher lined up, $5,000 to $35,000 (plus expenses) with one-fourth down payment, one-fourth when book half finished, one-fourth at three quarters mark and last fourth of payment when manuscript completed; or chapter by chapter.

Book content editing: $12-50 per hour and up; $600-5,000 per manuscript, based on size and complexity of the project.

Book copyediting: $9-22 per hour and up.

Book indexing: $10-22.50 per hour; $25 per hour using computer indexing software programs that take fewer hours; $1.50-6 per printed book page; 40-70¢ per line of index; or flat fee of $250-500, depending on length.

Book jacket blurb writing: Up to $600 for front cover copy plus inside and back cover copy summarizing content and tone of the book.

Book manuscript criticism: $160 for outline and first 20,000 words; $300-500 for up to 100,000 words.

Book manuscript reading, nonspecialized subjects: $20-50 for a half page summary and recommendation. **Specialized subject:** $100-500 and up, depending on complexity of project.

Book proofreading: $8.50-25 per hour and up; sometimes $1.50-3 per page.

Book proposal consultation: $25-35 per hour.

Book proposal writing: $300-1,000 or more depending on length and whether client provides full information or writer must do some research.

Book query critique: $50 for letter to publisher and outline.

Book research: $5-20 per hour and up, depending on complexity.

Book reviews: For byline and the book only, on small newspapers; to $35-300 on larger publications.

Book rewriting: $18-50 per hour; sometimes $5 per page. Some writers have combination ghostwriting and rewriting short-term jobs for which the pay could be $350 per day and up. Some participate in royalties on book rewrites.

Book summaries for business people: $400 for 4-8 printed pages.

Book summaries for book clubs, film producers: $50-100/ book. Note: You must live in the area where the business is located to get this kind of work.

Brochures: $200-7,500 and up depending on client (small nonprofit organization to large corporation), length, and complexity of job.

Business booklets, announcement folders: Writing and editing, $100-1,000 depending on size, research, etc.

Business facilities brochure: 12-16 pages, $1,000-4,000.

Business letters: Such as those designed to be used as form letters to improve customer relations, $100 per letter for small businesses; $500 and up per form letter for corporations.

Business meeting guide and brochure: 4 pages, $200; 8-12 pages, $400.

Business writing: On the local or national level, this may be advertising copy, collateral materials, speechwriting, films, public relations or other jobs—see individual entries on these subjects for details. General business writing rates could range from $25-60 per hour; $100-200 per day, plus expenses.

Business writing seminars: $250 for a half-day seminar, plus travel expenses.

C

Catalogs for business: $25-40 per hour or $60-75 per printed page; more if many tables or charts must be reworked for readability and consistency.

Church history: $200-1,000 for writing 15 to 50 pages.

Collateral materials for business: See Business Booklets, Catalogs for business, etc.

Comedy writing for night club entertainers: Gags only, $2-25 each. Routines, $100-1,000 per minute. Some new comics may try to get a five-minute routine for $150; others will pay $2,500 for a five-minute bit from a top writer.

Commercial reports for businesses, insurance companies, credit agencies: $6-10 per page; $5-20 per report on short reports.

Company newsletters and inhouse publications: Writing and editing 2-4 pages, $200-500; 4-8 pages, $500-1,000; 12-48 pages, $1,000-2,500. Writing, $20-50 per hour; editing, $15-40 per hour.

College/university history: $35 per hour for research through final ms.

Consultation on communications: $250 per day plus expenses for nonprofit, social service and religious organizations; $400 per day to others.

Consultation on magazine editorial: $1,000-1,500 per day plus expenses.

Consultation to business: On writing, PR, $25-50 per hour.

Consultant to publishers: $25-50 per hour.

Consumer complaint letters: $25 each.

Contest judging: Short manuscripts, $5 per entry; with one-page critique, $15-25. Overall contest judging: $100-500.

Copyediting and content editing for other writers: $10-50/hour or $2 per page. (See also Manuscript consultation and Manuscript criticism.)

Copyediting for advertising: $25 per hour.

Copyediting for book publishers: see Book copyediting.

Copyediting for nonprofit organizations: $15 per hour.

Copywriting for book club catalogs: $85-200.

Corporate history: $1,000-20,000, depending on length, complexity and client resources.

Corporate profile: Up to 3,000 words, $1,250-2,500.

D

Dance criticism: $25-400 per article. (See also Arts reviewing.)

Direct-mail catalog copy: $10-50 per page for 3-20 blocks of copy per page of a 24-48 page catalog.

Direct-mail packages: Copywriting direct mail letter, response card, etc., $1,500-5,000 depending on writer's skill, reputation.

Direct response card on a product: $250.

E

Editing: See Book copyediting, Company newsletters, Magazine editing, etc.

Educational consulting and educational grant and proposal writing: $250-750 per day and or $25-75 per hour.

Encyclopedia articles: Entries in some reference books, such as biographical encyclopedias, 500-2,000 words; pay ranges from $60-80 per 1,000 words. Specialists' fees vary.

Executive biography: (based on a resume, but in narrative form): $100.
English teachers — lay reading for: $6 per hour.

F

Fact checking: $17-25 per hour.
Family histories: See Histories, family.
Filmstrip script: See Audiovisuals.
Financial presentation for a corporation: 20-30 minutes, $1,500-4,500.
Flyers for tourist attractions, small museums, art shows: $50 and up for writing a brief bio, history, etc.
Fund-raising campaign brochure: $5,000 for 20 hours' research and 30 hours to write a major capital campaign brochure, get it approved, lay out and produce with a printer. For a standard fund-raising brochure, many fund-raising executives hire copywriters for $50-75 an hour to do research which takes 10-15 hours and 20-30 hours to write/produce.

G

Gags: see Comedy writing for nightclub entertainers.
Genealogical research: $25 per hour.
Ghostwriting: $25-100 per hour; $200 per day plus expenses. Ghostwritten professional and trade journal articles under someone else's byline, $400-4,000. Ghostwritten books: see Book, as-told-to (ghostwriting) and Book, ghostwritten, without as-told-to credit.
Ghostwriting a corporate book: 6 months' work, $13,000-25,000.
Ghostwriting article for a physician: $2,500-3,000.
Ghostwriting speeches: See Speechwriting.
Government public information officer: Part-time, with local governments, $25 per hour; or a retainer for so many hours per period.
Grant appeals for local non-profit organizations: $50 an hour or flat fee.
Grant proposals: $40 per hour.

H

Histories, family: Fees depend on whether the writer need only edit already prepared notes or do extensive research and writing; and the length of the work, $500-15,000.
Histories, local: Centennial history of a local church, $25 per hour for research through final manuscript for printer.
House organ editing: See Company newsletters and inhouse publications.

I

Industrial product film: $1,000 for 10-minute script.
Industrial promotions: $15-40 per hour. See also Business writing.

J

Job application letters: $10-25.

L

Lectures to local librarians or teachers: $50-100.
Lectures to school classes: $25-75; $150 per day; $250 per day if farther than 100 miles.
Lectures at national conventions by well-known authors: $2,500-20,000 and up, plus expenses; less for panel discussions.
Lectures at regional writers' conferences: $300 and up, plus expenses.

M

Magazine, city, calendar of events column: $150.

Magazine column: 200 words, $25. Larger circulation publications pay fees related to their regular word rate.

Magazine editing: Religious publications, $200-500 per month; $15-30 per hour.

Magazine stringing: 20¢-$1 per word based on circulation. Daily rate: $100-200 plus expenses; weekly rate: $750 plus expenses. Also $7.50-35 per hour plus expenses.

Manuscript consultation: $25-50 per hour.

Manuscript criticism: $25 per 16-line poem; $40 per article or short story of up to 3,000 words; book outlines and sample chapters of up to 20,000 words, $160.

Manuscript typing: Depending on ms length and delivery schedule, $1.50-2 per page with one copy; $15 per hour.

Market research survey reports: $10 per report; $15-30 per hour; writing results of studies or reports, $500-1,200 per day.

Medical editing: $25-65 per hour.

Medical proofreading: $12-30 per hour.

Medical writing: $25-80 per hour; manuscript for pharmeceutical company submitted to research journal, $4,500-5,000.

N

New product release: $300-500 plus expenses.

News release: See Press release.

Newsletters: See Company newsletters and Retail business newsletters.

Newspaper column, local: 80¢ per column inch to $5-10 for a weekly; $7.50-15 for dailies of 4,000-6,000 circulation; $10-20 for 7,000-10,000 dailies; $15-20 for 11,000-25,000 dailies; and $25 and up for larger dailies.

Newspaper feature: 35¢ to $1.50 per column inch or $15-30 per article for a weekly; $70-80 for a daily.

Newspaper feature writing, part-time: $1,000 a month for an 18-hour week.

Newspaper reviews of art, music, drama: See Arts reviewing.

Newspaper stringing: 50¢-2.50 per column inch up to $7.50 per column inch for some national publications. Also publications like *National Enquirer* pay lead fees up to $250 for tips on page one story ideas.

Newspaper ads for small business: $25 for a small, one-column ad, or $10 per hour and up.

Novel synopsis for film producer: $150 for 5-10 pages typed single-spaced.

Novel synopsis for literary agent: $150 for 5-10 pages typed single-spaced.

O

Obituary copy: Where local newspapers permit lengthier than normal notices paid for by the funeral home (and charged to the family), $15. Writers are engaged by funeral homes.

Opinion research interviewing: $4-6 per hour or $15-25 per completed interview.

P

Party toasts, limericks, place card verses: $1.50 per line.

Permission fees to publishers to reprint article or story: $75-500; 10-15¢ per word; less for charitable organizations.

Photo brochures: $700-15,000 flat fee for photos and writing.

Photo research: $12-25 per hour.

Poetry criticism: $25 per 16-line poem.

Political writing: See Public relations and Speechwriting.

Press background on a company: $500-1,200 for 4-8 pages.

Press kits: $500-3,000.

Press release: 1-3 pages, $85-300.

Printers' camera-ready typewritten copy: Negotiated with individual printers, but see also Manuscript typing.

Product literature: Per page, $100-150.

Programmed instruction consultant fees: $300-700 per day; $50 per hour.

Programmed instruction materials for business: $50 per hour for inhouse writing and editing; $500-700 a day plus expenses for outside research and writing. Alternate method: $2,000-5,000 per hour of programmed training provided, depending on technicality of subject.

Public relations for business: $200-500 per day plus expenses.

Public relations for conventions: $500-1,500 flat fee.

Public relations for libraries: Small libraries, $5-10 per hour; larger cities, $35 an hour and up.

Public relations for nonprofit or proprietary organizations: Small towns, $100-500 monthly retainers.

Public relations for politicians: Small town, state campaigns, $10-50 per hour; incumbents, congressional, gubernatorial, and other national campaigns, $25-100 per hour.

Public relations for schools: $15-20 per hour and up in small districts; larger districts have full-time staff personnel.

R

Radio advertising copy: Small towns, up to $5 per spot; $20-65 per hour; $100-250 per week for a four- to six-hour day; larger cities, $250-400 per week.

Radio continuity writing: $5 per page to $150 per week, part-time.

Radio documentaries: $200 for 60 minutes, local station.

Radio editorials: $10-30 for 90-second to two-minute spots.

Radio interviews: For National Public Radio, up to 3 minutes, $25; 3-10 minutes, $40-75; 10-60 minutes, $125 to negotiable fees. Small radio stations would pay approximately 50% of the NPR rate; large stations, double the NPR rate.

Readings by poets, fiction writers: $25-600 depending on the author.

Record album cover copy: $100-250 flat fee.

Recruiting brochure: 8-12 pages, $500-1,500.

Research for writers or book publishers: $15-30 an hour and up; $15-200 per day and all expenses. Some quote a flat fee of $300-500 for a complete and complicated job.

Restaurant guide features: Short article on restaurant, owner, special attractions, $15; interior, exterior photos, $15.

Résumé writing: $25-150 per résumé.

Retail business newsletters for customers: $175-300 for writing four-page publications. Some writers work with a local printer and handle production details as well, billing the client for the total package. Some writers also do their own photography.

Rewriting: Copy for a local client, $27.50 per hour.

S

Sales brochure: 12-16 pages, $750-3,000.

Sales letter for business or industry: $150-500 for one or two pages.

Science writing: For newspapers $150-600; magazines $2,000-5,000; encyclopedias $1 per line; textbook editing $40 per hour; professional publications $500-1,500 for 1,500-3,000 words.

Script synopsis for agent or film producer: $75 for 2-3 typed pages, single-spaced.

Scripts for nontheatrical films for education, business, industry: Prices vary among producers, clients, and sponsors and there is no standardization of rates in the field. Fees include $75-120 per minute for one reel (10 minutes) and corresponding increases with each successive reel; approximately 10% of the production cost of films that cost the producer more than $1,500 per release minute.

Services brochure: 12-18 pages, $1,250-2,000.

Shopping mall promotion: $500 monthly retainer up to 15% of promotion budget for the mall.

Short story manuscript critique: 3,000 words, $40.

Slide film script: See Audiovisuals.

Slide presentation: Including visual formats plus audio, $1,000-1,500 for 10-15 minutes.

Slide/single image photos: $75 flat fee.

Slide/tape script: $75-100 per minute, $750 minimum.

Software manual writing: $35-50 per hour for research and writing.

Special news article: For a business's submission to trade publication, $250-400 for 1,000 words.

Special occasion booklet: Family keepsake of a wedding, anniversary, Bar Mitzvah, etc., $115 and up.

Speech for government official: $4,000 for 20 minutes plus up to $1,000 travel and miscellaneous expenses.

Speech for local political candidate: $150-250 for 15 minutes.

Speech for national congressional candidate: $1,000 and up.

Speech for owners of a small business: $100 for six minutes.

Speech for owners of larger businesses: $500-3,000 for 10-30 minutes.

Speech for statewide candidate: $500-800.

Speechwriting: $20-75 per hour.

Syndicated newspaper column, self-promoted: $2-8 each for weeklies; $5-25 per week for dailies, based on circulation.

T

Teaching adult education course: $10-60 per class hour.

Teaching adult seminar: $350 plus mileage and per diem for a 6- or 7-hour day; plus 40% of the tuition fee beyond the sponsor's breakeven point.

Teaching business writing to company employees: $60 per hour.

Teaching college course or seminar: $15-70 per class hour.

Teaching creative writing in school: $15-60 per hour of instruction, or $1,500-2,000 per 12-15 week semester; less in recessionary times.

Teaching elementary and middle school teachers how to teach writing to students: $75-120 for a 1-1½ hour session.

Teaching home-bound students: $5-10 per hour.

Teaching journalism in high school: Proportionate to salary scale for full-time teacher in the same school district.

Technical editing: $15-60 per hour.

Technical typing: $1-4 per double-spaced page.

Technical writing: $35 per ms page or $35-75 per hour, depending on degree of complexity and type of audience.

Textbook copyediting: $14-20 per hour, depending on el-hi, college, technical, non-technical.

Textbook editing: $15-30 per hour.

Textbook proofreading: $9-18.50 per hour.

Textbook writing: $14-50 per hour.

Trade journal ad copywriting: $250-500.

Trade journal article: For business client, $500-1,500.

Translation, commercial: Final draft from one of the common European languages, $115-120 per thousand words.

Translation for government agencies: Up to $125 per 1,000 foreign words into English.
Translation, literary: $50-100 per thousand English words.
Translation through translation agencies: Less 33⅓% (average) for agency commission.
Translation, technical: $125 per thousand words.
Tutoring: $25 per 1-1½ hour private session.
TV documentary: 30-minute 5-6 page proposal outline, $250 and up; 15-17 page treatment, $1,000 and up; less in smaller cities.
TV editorials: $35 and up for 1-minute, 45 seconds (250-300 words).
TV home shopping: Local ad copy: $6 an hour. Writing, misc. freelance: $15-85 per hour; $.50-1 per word.
TV information scripts: Short 5- to 10-minute scripts for local cable TV stations, $10-15 per hour.
TV instruction taping: $150 per 30-minute tape; $25 residual each time tape is sold.
TV news film still photo: $3-6 flat fee.
TV news story: $16-25 flat fee.
TV filmed news and features: From $10-20 per clip for 30-second spot; $15-25 for 60-second clip; more for special events.
TV, national and local public stations: $35-100 per minute down to a flat fee of $100-500 for a 30- to 60-minute script.
TV scripts: (Teleplay only), 60 minutes, prime time, Writers Guild rates: $11,780; 30 minutes, $8,733.

V

Video script: See Audiovisuals.

W

Writer-in-schools: Arts council program, $130 per day; $650 per week. Personal charges vary from $25 per day to $100 per hour depending on school's ability to pay.
Writer's workshop: Lecturing and seminar conducting, $50-150 per hour to $750 per day plus expenses; local classes, $35-50 per student for 10 sessions.

_____ *Writers' Roundtable*

Writers face a number of unique challenges in freelancing—from securing interviews to working on that final rewrite—but they often find the business side most frustrating. If you don't know other freelancers, you may feel unsure about how to solve business problems and keep them from cropping up again.

This year, we asked three fulltime writers about the most common business problems freelancers face. In addition to identifying pitfalls, they've also offered a variety of solutions from their own experiences and provided some perspective on the publishing industry from the writer's viewpoint. Analyze which solutions best fit your own personality and writing career and try them the next time you're faced with similar problems.

We're happy to share responses from the following writers:

Katy Williams, a writer from Boulder, Colorado, worked for two Knight-Ridder newspapers after college. In 1983 she quit her job to write a book with one of the winners of the Boston Marathon. When the book project fell through, she began freelancing fulltime. She's a specialist in running, health and fitness and has been published in *The Runner*, *Runner's World*, *The Walking Magazine* and *Campus USA*.

James McKimmey, a writer from South Lake Tahoe, California, sold his first short story in 1949 to a small literary magazine. After selling 25 more short stories and his first novel, he began writing fulltime in 1956. He has published 17 books to such houses as Morrow and Random House and sold 400 articles and short stories to a wide variety of periodicals. He also takes photos for use with his own articles as well as sales for magazine covers, brochures, advertising and other writers' works.

Lisa Napell is a former New York City writer who recently relocated to Scottsdale, Arizona. She began freelancing in college and has been a fulltime freelancer since June, 1987. She founded LMN Editorial to incorporate the wide range of her writing. Napell's work has appeared in the *New York Times*, *Newsday*, *Publishing News* and *Bride's*.

How do you handle late payment problems?

Katy Williams: I have had only one bad debt of $400 over the years, and that was for a public relations job. I have called and written the individual numerous times; I have also sworn never to do business with him again. I look back on the experience as a big lesson in the life of a freelance writer. Since, I have not pursued any jobs that may produce similar headaches. My luck with magazines has been excellent—maybe because I take assignments from magazines which are not likely to fold (and leave writers unpaid), and which have a record of paying decent amounts to begin with.

James McKimmey: I try a polite query. But when a payment gets well overdue, I send the publishing company a billing on a printed statement form. Accounting departments understand formal billings. The most extreme step I've taken was when *Argosy*—which published a novel and short story of mine without paying—appeared to be and was heading for bankruptcy. I put an attorney on it. I got most of my money, less a very reasonable attorney's fee. Other writers who were reluctant to take that action got 5¢ on the dollar owed them. But unreasonably late payments have been fairly rare in my experience.

Lisa Napell: Late payment is one of the most persistent and aggravating problems facing freelance writers. It is especially hard on those of us who depend on our writing for our livelihood. The landlord and the telephone company won't wait until some publisher feels like paying me. They demand payment on schedule. If a contracted payment is 30 days past due, I generally call and ask if it's been mailed. I am polite and friendly at this point (and always). "Just checking," I say, placing assumed blame on the U.S. mail. After another 10 days or so, I call again. The second call is followed immediately by a letter from myself or my "comptroller." (My husband signs these; anyone with a different last name will do.) The letter states that payment is X number of days past due and requests immediate remittance. I always use formal collection letter terminology and include a copy of the original invoice (which I gave them with the manuscript when it was first delivered).

Should this fail, I call the bookkeeping department directly—sometimes they never received the original invoice. This combination of friendly reminder calls and letters is usually effective. If they really want to screw you out of the money, they'll do it. Small claims court is an option, if the sum in dispute is worth the trouble and small expense. Mentioning that you are a member of the National Writers Union and will refer the case to them is generally quite effective. There's power in numbers. (Be sure to join the Union first, though—it's inexpensive and invaluable). If all else fails, you can always write it off your taxes as a bad debt.

How do you cope with the writer's nightmare of erratic funds—big checks followed by droughts? Do you have any techniques for bringing in money more steadily?

Katy Williams: I never "spend" a check until it's in the bank. I accept as one of the realities of freelancing that I may write an article in January but not receive payment until after publication, in April or May. For my bookkeeping—and for a sense of steady accomplishment—I keep tabs of my monthly earnings by what I write each month.

I think my mother worries more about my "life as a freelance writer" than I do! Money indeed arrives in spurts...but I know a big check will come in a month if I've already written the piece. If I am without an assignment or a big check headed my way, I suppose I could get some work—say one or two big Sunday features—from the local newspaper. Although the pay isn't great, it's money I can count on almost immediately (within two weeks).

James McKimmey: I haven't coped very damned well with it in my long and checkered career. The solution to the problem might very well be diversification of your work. The certain solution is definitely found by becoming a household name. My problem has been that if I find a highly receptive and lucrative market, I am tempted to place all of my eggs there. But if something happens, such as the basket's editor changing, drought follows the big checks. Count on it.

Lisa Napell: Techniques for bringing in money more steadily:

A) Get a regularly appearing column.

B) Create relationships with editors so they'll give you work more regularly, think of you when they have a story or a hole to fill at the last minute.

C) Send out more queries (better the odds).

D) Get a part-time job in the field. Some possibilities include a few days a week as an assistant editor, paste-up artist, editor, proofreader, copy or line editor.

E) Take a part-time job as a word processor. Legal firms pay quite well and need evening, night and weekend workers. It's best to start out with a reputable temporary agency.

F) Marry money, or inherit it, or win the lottery.

As for coping, keep a smile on your face, a song in your heart and your American Express card where you can't get at it.

How do you determine what to charge when a fee is negotiable?

Katy Williams: This is really tricky, especially if I am unfamiliar with the magazine's editorial budget and what has been paid in the past. I will shoot high but settle for less. And if my high figure is accepted, I will live up to it by delivering the piece on time and with no holes, etc.

James McKimmey: It's the time and expense that's involved. If it's an article on a subject I'm already knowledgeable about and if I already have photos in my stock file to illustrate it, it's naturally a lower fee. If I have to do extensive research and use up 20 rolls of film to illustrate it, the fee has got to be greater.

Lisa Napell: As much as I can get them to pay me. It's almost always too little overall, anyway. Time and research required, complexity and length of article are considerations. So is whether I've worked with them before. Sometimes, if I feel a relationship will develop, I'll go a little lower to start, making sure to tell the editor what I'm doing and why and that my price will go up in the future. Remember, they'll never pay you more than they can afford, no matter what they say. So take what you can get; you deserve it.

If you write articles, do you have any strategies to share about ways to resell articles or write several pieces from the same interview(s)? Do you look for reprint or reslant value in potential articles?

Katy Williams: I think this is a technique you develop the longer you're in the business. At first, I was so pleased just to have an assignment from X magazine and focused entirely on doing the piece well. Now, as I do research for an article, a number of things strike me — people, quotes, resources, statistics — that would be useful (and marketable) in other articles on the same subject. I think this comes from having studied the magazine market and realizing the dozens of magazines I could see myself writing for.

James McKimmey: The criteria is simply to do it for markets that do not compete with one another, such as religious markets of different faiths. For reprint potential, I pore over *Writer's Market* for markets that are open to buying reprint rights. As an example, I resold a slightly edited version of a short-short that had originally appeared in *Good Housekeeping* to *Virtue*, *The Lookout* and *St. Joseph's Messenger & Advocate of the Blind* . . . absolute no-effort bonuses.

Lisa Napell: Resale is the best way to make money in this business. Trade magazines are great markets. I did a piece on window display for an optical magazine and, by writing a form letter to one magazine in every retail-oriented trade listed in *Writer's Market*, sold the identical story over a dozen times. I just pulled up a copy of the story on my word processor, called my experts and made the necessary changes in examples to suit the new market. The original piece was commissioned at $400. Follow-up sales required a maximum of half an hour of research and writing and brought in between $50 and $250 per piece.

Asking unrelated questions during the interview and allowing your subject to get off on interesting tangents are ways of creating material for second and third articles. For example, if you're interviewing a celebrity (large or small) about her success, ask about her hobbies, childhood, pets as well. You can then do other pieces focusing on these angles.

Do you have any tips to offer writers on additional outlets for writing that they might not have considered – or you didn't consider when you started writing?

Katy Williams: I didn't read enough when I started freelancing. Today, when I see a publication in the library or wherever for the first time, I peruse to see what kinds of articles they use and whether I spot any familiar bylines. Then I make a copy of the masthead for my files and send for writer's guidelines. And when I travel, I *always* read the in-flight magazines with particular interest to see what they are publishing. The potential for new work is *everywhere*, not only in *Writer's Market* (although it's a wonderful starting point).

James McKimmey: There are books that offer better advice on this than I could. The best I've read is *Turning Words Into Cash*, published by Writer's Digest Books. (Ed. note: This book is no longer in print, but writers may find helpful *How to Make $25,000 a Year as a Writer*, available in spring 1990).

Lisa Napell: Trade journals. They're smaller and more accessible than large consumer publications. You can develop a portfolio and a relationship with an editor more easily. They need good writers. They generally pay OK and closer to on time than small consumer books. And they will not hurt your consumer career.

What about lack of response to a submission? Do you wait it out, follow up, or withdraw your submission? How long are you willing to wait for a response?

Katy Williams: If I don't hear from an editor within six weeks or so, I check my source (the magazine's writer's guidelines or else *Writer's Market*) for the stated length of response. If it does say "wait two months," then I continue to wait. But often extended wait kills the lead time necessary to prepare, say a seasonal piece. That's a real frustration. If I have submitted an idea I am very excited about, I do send a follow-up reminder – a letter, not a post card. I am not in the practice of withdrawing submissions, although I suppose I should. I have a lot of patience instead. And if one magazine doesn't respond to a great – but seasonal – idea, then I look to submit it elsewhere the next year.

James McKimmey: I follow up with polite queries when no response goes a month or so beyond the market's stated response time. If two or more queries, spread about a month apart, don't draw a response, I feel free to market the material elsewhere. That polite query on an overdue response has brought more than a few sales, by the way. It's simply that if there is serious editorial consideration about buying your submission, that decision usually takes longer than one to reject.

Lisa Napell: If I've had no response to a query two weeks after the stated response time (as listed in *Writer's Market*), I call. I ask if they've received my query. If not – I send another immediately. If they've received it, I ask if they have any idea as to when they'll reach a decision – stressing that I am not pushing for a reply, just interested in a time frame. This friendly, pressure-less approach usually speeds things up. Sometimes I even get an answer right then. As far as I know, this tactic has never influenced the decision of the editor either way.

What do you do when an editor gives you information about payment, etc., that differs from information you've found in a market source (like Writer's Market)? What do you do if the terms seem to change from what you felt was the original agreement?

Katy Williams: Unless I'm absolutely desperate for work (and cash), I won't solicit work from a magazine with low pay rates. I have a minimum amount that I will write for, and it's not worth my time to accept less. This honestly hasn't been a problem for me—the agreements changing in mid-stream. I've managed to avoid it by conversing regularly and often with the editor—they always like progress reports, even when the due date is still two or three weeks out. If I discover I need to make a $20 international telephone call, I will tell the editor (in expectation of his or her approval in advance for repayment). I learned in five years as a reporter for daily newspapers that "no surprises" is a rule that works everywhere.

James McKimmey: Sometimes the practice isn't really an actual reversal of the market-source promise. But it can be just as annoying as though it were. As an example, the market source lists a magazine as reporting in two weeks and paying on acceptance, exactly as the magazine gave the information to the market source. But after a submission is made, the writer receives a post card (yes, within two weeks) indicating that the material has been received by the magazine. Then actual acceptance may not follow for another six months, about when the story is published, and the writer is indeed paid. Well, the magazine did report in two weeks and it did pay on acceptance as promised. But it wasn't done exactly as you'd expected when you chose that magazine over another promising a six-week response and payment upon publication.

Lisa Napell: If the price is higher, I take it. If it's lower, I ask why. I've never had terms changed, so I can't address that except in theory. I always get everything in writing. Sometimes that means sending a letter re-capping a phone conversation before I begin work. Save copies of everything. Take notes of all your conversations with editors and keep them in your file on that magazine or that project. It's not paranoid. It's useful for disputes, but more often serves to remind you of what you promised to do and when. I keep a looseleaf notebook with a page for every client. All addresses and names are there, and every time I call, send a letter, whatever, I make a note of the date and the basics of the transaction.

Do you supply photos with your articles? Do you take the photos yourself, use a professional photographer, or find other sources like stock photo agencies for photos? Do you find that many editors want writers to supply photos?

Katy Williams: Since I don't do photos or even own a camera, I don't query editors who indicate they want photos as part of the submission. However, if I know photos have been taken by professionals at the local newspaper, I indicate this because I know I can follow up and secure appropriate photos. Because I used to work at my local newspaper, I know the individuals and their talents...and whether they're agreeable to shooting something on speculation.

I'm happy to find an editor who says, "Oh, we'll handle the photos." My feeling is, there are hundreds of magazines out there, and you can work with ones that have photo and graphic departments or ones that depend on photos coming from their writers. Since I admit a limitation for photos, I guess that limits me as a freelance writer. But I haven't felt limited yet.

James McKimmey: I take the photos myself because it's not financially feasible to bring in a photographer. But I think most any editor would appreciate a writer being able to photograph as well as he or she writes. In the nature field, for instance, you'll almost always have to supply good photography with your article in order to sell to, say *American Forests*; economics demand it. *National Wildlife* or *Audubon*, on the other hand, *can*, if they have to, afford to buy top-quality stock photos. But if you can supply photography of that same quality, they would prefer to buy your combined talents in a package, which is both easier and more economical for them.

Lisa Napell: When I can, or when I must. I own and can operate a 35mm camera and often offer photos as a bonus. My experience has included everything from editors who won't assign without guaranteed photos to those who won't let me shoot.

Travel photos are free from most tourist agencies. Just call and ask. They'll send them to you or your editor. They're OK; nothing you'd sell to *Travel & Leisure*, but serviceable.

Most writers have had their work edited in ways they didn't like. How do you handle this problem?

Katy Williams: I never like these kinds of conversations, because, obviously, the editor feels that what ended up in print was best. Usually I am not insulted or embarrassed with what ends up under my byline, but I'm livid when an editor's rewriting results in factual errors. I do appreciate when editors send galleys of how my article will appear, so I can correct beforehand the very serious mistakes.

James McKimmey: I've come to believe that complaining, which I've done, is fairly useless. Good editors don't edit in that fashion. It's done by foolish, misguided novices who, when they have finished, believe the result to be so brilliant that they become more sensitive about the piece than you were in the first place. On the other hand, after I've decided that something's been hopelessly mangled, I try to reestimate as objectively as I can, remembering how I, novice that I was, thought sincerely that the first story I sold to a major market had been horribly edited when it was published. That same story has been reprinted more than any other I've written and is in print right now. So I have, of course, taken full credit for exactly the way it reads, which is to say exactly the way the editor revised it.

Lisa Napell: Always request to be involved with the editing process. Volunteer to do your own cuts and rewrites. This sometimes works. When I've been manhandled, I call and complain — immediately. Generally there's no excuse for it. Next, I write to the National Writers Union so the magazine will be mentioned as a manhandler in their newsletter and other writers will be forewarned. We must stick together and let editors know that mistreating one writer is mistreating us all.

Do you send out simultaneous submissions to editors, agents and publishers? Do you feel differently about queries vs. complete manuscripts? Have you ever faced a situation in which two competitors wanted the manuscript? If so, how did you handle it?

Katy Williams: For book proposals to publishers, yes; for magazine queries to editors, *never*.

I've had just one instance when one article was wanted by two magazines. That happened because I had mailed the query to a big-time city magazine whose editor I didn't know, but I ran into the editor of another magazine, who was a long-time friend. Verbally, he showed interest in the piece, but a few days later I got a favorable response from the first editor. Very embarrassed, I settled the situation by printing the article in 2,000-word form in the April issue of the city magazine, and in 3,500-word form in the May issue of the other (in a specialty, noncompeting market). I felt lucky it worked out..but I knew the city editor wasn't happy. I haven't worked with her since.

James McKimmey: Sensibly or not, I don't send out either submissions or queries simultaneously.

Lisa Napell: I send out simultaneous submissions only to noncompeting magazines, so I've never had that happen. I try to avoid working on spec (obvious exceptions are humor and opinion pieces). Why do all that work with no guarantee of at least a kill fee? I think spec should be illegal. Do you have the opportunity to go home and cook the roast and taste it before you pay the butcher? Of course not! Only writers allow that sort of nonsense. And only because each writer feels that if he or she doesn't do it exactly as the editor asks, another writer will take the job (and the resulting paycheck). We must band together so that no writer has to work for insulting wages or write on speculation. Without us, the magazine, newspaper and book industries cannot survive. They tend to forget that. We need to remind them.

I urge every writer in America to join the National Writers Union. Membership dues are small and on a sliding scale according to how much money you earn "as a writer." Raise your voice with your fellow writers and improve our lot in this crazy industry we love so much.

The Markets

Book Publishers

The book publishing field continued to evolve last year with mergers creating $10 billion communications giants, companies planning to use corporate advertising in books and authors writing about products in their books so they could be used for promotional tie-ins. Meanwhile, about 50,000 books were published, so many that *New York Times Book Review* author Arthur Krystal wrote: "If you were to read 135 books a day, every day for a year, you wouldn't finish all the books published annually in the United States."

Here are more changes and figures about the industry:

● Sales of adult trade paperbacks are expected to be up about 10% this year, with children's hardcovers and paperbacks up 2.5% and 11.9%. Mass market paperbacks declined 4.5% the past year.

● The comic book format is now being used for comedy, adventure, drama, horror, science fiction or even contemporary work. These graphic novels use illustrations to advance and develop the story as much as the prose.

● Men's adventure novels with continuing characters are becoming more popular. The novels often have strong technological or social overtones.

● Gardening books continue to be strong, especially large-format books with lavish use of color. Specialty books on landscaping, weekend gardening, wildflowers, regional and herb gardening have all done well.

● Historical romances continue to be strong and plots are becoming increasingly more inventive as readers become more selective. Non-category contemporary romances, more like mainstream novels, are being published.

● In science fiction, the total books published rose 12% from the year before, and a record 177 publishers produced science fiction and fantasy books.

● One of the fastest-growing book categories in the past few years has been New Age, a catch-all for everything from spirituality to extraterrestrial travel and spirit possession. A glut of these titles appears inevitable as publishers squeeze books into the category.

● Some areas of publishing, in general, are more receptive to unsolicited material. These include religious, children's, romance and science fiction fields. You should always follow the individual publisher's stated preference for submitting material, however.

● Self-help books have shown strength in accounting, law and medical areas. One-third of Americans have bought a self-help book with the majority sold to women age 35-49.

● Travel books have been so popular in the past few years that three firms have brought out guides to the guide books. A slowdown in this category appears inevitable.

● Mergers continue to affect the industry and writers. Currently, 2% of U.S. publishers are putting out 75% of the titles. This means fewer houses are bidding competitively for books. Literary agents have varied views about this development. "I have never had a worthy book that I couldn't sell," agent Morton Janklow told *Publishers Weekly*. Agent Richard Curtis told the magazine the proposed merger of Time Inc. and Warner Communications, one of many during the year, ". . . is one more step in the alarming movement toward consolidation, which means that rich authors and agents will get richer and poor ones will get poorer."

If you've finished a manuscript or have an idea for a book, you may be wondering about your next step. You probably have put a lot of work into writing already, but if you plan to get your work in print, you'll also need to pay attention to the business side of publishing. Submitting appropriate manuscripts means knowing the differences between publishers, knowing the way they want to receive material and knowing how to work effectively with editors.

What to consider

When choosing a publisher, try to match the publisher's area of specialization to yours. Our Book Publishers Subject Index for nonfiction and fiction will help you quickly identify the publishers who are interested in the subjects on which you write. Find out about the imprints or subsidiaries of publishing houses and the special focus of those imprints. "Each imprint has its own editorial staff, editorial identity and reputation," an editor wrote in *Writer's Digest* magazine. "These distinctions can be important to you in deciding where to submit your work. Be aware of which imprints publish the kinds of books you write (you can do so by looking in bookstores) and then submit to them." As a special feature at the end of the Book Publishers section, we have included interviews with six first novelists who share their experiences in writing and selling their first novels.

Don't overlook small presses, university presses and regional publishers in your search for a publisher. Many different types of independent presses have been started by consultants, teachers and former trade-house editors. They are often more approachable and offer more personal attention than the larger houses, especially for first-time authors. They also tend to keep books in print longer and have become increasingly sophisticated in marketing and production.

Study the general business statements of the publisher as they are detailed in the *Writer's Market* listings. What is their average advance, royalty payment and number of books published? This information will give you general guidelines for contracts, although most publishers are willing to negotiate these terms.

Industry trends

Predicting book sales and trends is tricky. Some novelists are always popular; a new book by Stephen King is *expected* to be a bestseller before it ever comes off the press. Sometimes publishing houses overestimate the popularity of a title, while other times they are pleasantly surprised by strong sales of a title they had expected to sell moderately well. Writers should keep up with trends in the industry to make their manuscripts as timely and salable as possible, but they should also be aware that a book written today may not be published for a year or more. The manuscript must rely on its own strengths, not its adherence to trends.

Develop a marketing plan

After finding several possible publishers, order a copy of their book catalogs to see their new titles and backlist and how your manuscript will fit in. Check *Books in Print* to see what other titles have been published on the subject. "Read the magazines important to publishing, bookselling and libraries, as well as the particular field for which you're writing," counsels Linda Peterson of Hazeldon Educational Materials. "It helps when making the pitch in the query."

Show a knowledge of the audience for your book, the competition and market savvy. "Research markets and target your audience. Research other books on the same subject.

Make yours different," advises John Rimel of Mountain Press Publishing Co. "Don't present your manuscript to a publisher—sell it to him. Give him the information he needs to make a decision on a title."

Submit your proposal according to the publisher's preference. Most nonfiction is sold by proposal and most fiction is sold by sample chapters. And always send your manuscript to the correct person. If no editor is specified, call to see who would be appropriate. Never send unsolicited material to a publisher who only accepts submissions through agents.

The editorial process

Manuscripts, queries and proposals are considered by methods that vary from one publishing house to the next and even from one imprint to the next. Three hundred-three publishers responded to a survey we conducted on the handling of unsolicited submissions. The number of unsolicited manuscripts received by publishers ranged from four per year to 7,500, with an average of 395 per publisher. About 33% say they review all proposals, but they may be sent out-of-house for initial review or may wait a long time for inhouse review. Sixteen percent of the respondents "strongly" preferred a query, outline or sample chapters and wouldn't guarantee review of materials submitted another way. Of the responses to the review question, 8% said they *never* review material which is not submitted according to their specifications.

Although we did not mention it in the survey, 24% of the respondents specifically mentioned they require a self-addressed stamped envelope (SASE) for return of unsolicited material, and 35% of those said they would discard material without it. Only 2 respondents said they never returned manuscripts, while 4% said they did not accept unsolicited material and would return it without review if a SASE was enclosed. Only 2% of the publishers who responded read agented material only.

Response time on unsolicited material varies from one week to eight months or more. The average among respondents to our survey was two to three months.

Working with editors

Manuscripts must go through several steps before they become books and you will likely encounter a number of editors in the process. The initial reading probably will be done by a freelancer or an editor who usually has only authority to reject, not to accept. If you do receive a rejection, you rarely will get more than a form letter. Editors simply don't have the time to offer instruction and personal advice.

Editors acquire books in a variety of ways: some are submitted by agents, some are sent by authors, and some are generated by the editor. The percentage is different from house to house. In large trade houses, the majority come from agents; in smaller houses they are more likely to be sent by the author or generated by an editor.

If an editor shows interest in your manuscript, it has only cleared one of many hurdles. Your book will go to an editorial meeting for book proposals. Editorial meetings are held with marketing and editorial staff once a week to once a quarter, depending on the size of the publishing house. In this meeting, the editor will try to sell your idea to others who will want to know who will buy the book, including the size of the audience; what the competition is and how your book is different or better; how it fits in with their line of titles; and whether or not the publishing house can make money on the title.

If your book is accepted at this meeting, an editor will notify you. If you sent a proposal or an outline, you will begin to write the complete manuscript. If you have submitted a complete manuscript, you may begin contract negotiations.

Contract negotiations

Writers often feel uneasy about negotiating contracts. This work will be done by an agent if you have one. If you don't, you should be aware that contracts vary widely—some publishers offer six-figure advances on royalties, while others never offer an advance. In general, an advance is determined by multiplying the number of books in the first printing by the price of the book and the royalty rate. This is generally the amount the publisher expects the book to earn in a year.

We encourage you to work with publishers who pay writers through a royalty arrangement. Most publishers pay the author 3-25% of the wholesale, retail or net price. Whenever a copy is sold, both the writer and the publisher make money. Some publishers buy manuscripts outright. This is an option for writers, but it often means the author does not retain the copyright to the work and receives a flat amount of money whether the book sells five copies or 500,000. For more information about contracts, see *A Writer's Guide to Contract Negotiations*, by Richard Balkin (Writer's Digest Books).

Other options

Self-publishing has become an option chosen by writers as desktop publishing becomes more popular. Some authors choose to self-publish because they are unable to place their books with publishing houses; others want to be in control of everything from production to distribution of their titles. A few have found enormous success with this option. Bernard Kamaroff self-published *Small-time Operator* for small business owners and has sold more than 300,000 copies. Ken Keyes Jr. has nearly 3 million copies of his nine personal-growth titles in print. His *Handbook to Higher Consciousness*, originally published in 1972, has sold 900,000 copies.

The successful self-published book has a potential audience and fills a need not filled by current books on the topic. If a large publishing house determined that it couldn't generate enough sales, remember that books do not have to sell in the same quantities for a self-published book to make money as for a large publisher to profit.

Your consideration of self-publishing should include answering these questions. Are you willing to pay for a few hundred to several thousand copies of your book? Can you supervise all stages of its production? Do you have the time and energy to promote and distribute the book yourself? "Done properly, self-publishing is an exciting and viable way to get your book into print," say Marilyn and Tom Ross, authors of *The Complete Guide to Self-Publishing* (Writer's Digest Books).

Subsidy publishers expect writers to pay part or all of the cost of producing a book and they rarely market books as effectively as major publishing companies. They make money by selling their services to writers, not by selling their products to bookstores and libraries. Subsidy publishers are sometimes called "vanity" presses because of the appeal to a writer's ego in wanting to have his book published. Any publisher that asks the writer to pay all or part of the cost of his book is identified in *Writer's Market* with an asterisk (*). Companies which subsidy publish more than 50% of their titles are listed at the end of the Book Publishers section.

This doesn't mean that subsidy publishing is always a bad choice. In Canada, for example, books are often subsidized by government grants. In the U.S., a special interest book may be subsidized by the writer's friends, a foundation or church. We attempt to distinguish in the listings between subsidies provided by the author and nonauthor subsidies.

For a list of publishers according to their subjects of interest, see the nonfiction and fiction sections of the Book Publishers Subject Index. Information on some book publishers and packagers not included in this edition of *Writer's Market* can be found in Other Book Publishers and Packagers at the end of the Book Packagers and Producers section.

AASLH PRESS, American Association for State and Local History, 172 2nd Ave. N., Nashville TN 37201. (615)255-2971. AASLH Press Director: Bob Summer. Publishes hardcover and softcover originals and reprints. Averages 6 titles/year; receives 20-30 submissions annually. 50% of books from first-time authors; 100% of books from unagented writers. Pays 5-10% royalty on retail price. Publishes book an average of 1 year after acceptance. Photocopied submissions OK. Computer printout submissions acceptable; prefers letter-quality. Reports in 3 months on submissions. Free book catalog.

Nonfiction: How-to, reference, self-help and textbook. "We publish books, mostly technical, that help people do effective work in historical societies, sites and museums, or do research in, or teach, history. No manuscripts on history itself—that is, on the history of specific places, events, people." Submit outline/synopsis and sample chapters. Reviews artwork/photos.

Recent Nonfiction Title: *A Graveyard Preservation Primer*, by Lynette Strangstad.

Tips: "Explain why our market will buy your book, use it, need it. The emphasis is on materials that can be practically utilized by historic preservationists."

ABBOTT, LANGER & ASSOCIATES, 548 1st St., Crete IL 60417. (312)672-4200. President: Dr. Steven Langer. Publishes trade paperback originals and loose-leaf books. Averages 14 titles/year; receives 25 submissions annually. 15% of books from first-time authors; 100% of books from unagented writers. Pays 10-15% royalty; no advance. Publishes book an average of 1 year after acceptance. Photocopied submissions OK. Query for electronic submissions. Computer printout submissions OK. Book catalog for 6x9 SAE with 2 first class stamps. Reports in 2 weeks on queries; 2 months on mss.

Nonfiction: How-to, reference, technical on some phase of personnel administration, industrial relations, sales management, etc. Especially needs "a very limited number (3-5) of books dealing with very specialized topics in the field of personnel management, wage and salary administration, sales compensation, training, recruitment, selection, labor relations, etc." Publishes for personnel directors, wage and salary administrators, training directors, sales/marketing managers, security directors, etc. Query with outline. Reviews artwork/photos.

Recent Nonfiction Title: *How to Build a Motivated Work Force Using Non-Monetary Incentives*, by Lynn Grensing.

Tips: "A how-to book in personnel management, sales/marketing management or security management has the best chance of selling to our firm."

ABC-CLIO, INC., 130 Cremona, Santa Barbara CA 93117 (head office). All submissions to Suite 300, 180 Cook St., Denver CO 80206. (303)333-3003. Subsidiaries include ISIS, Clio Press, Ltd. Vice President: Heather Cameron. Publishes hardcover originals. Firm averages 35 titles/year. Receives 250 submissions/year. 50% of books from first-time authors; 95% from unagented writers. Pays royalty on net price. Publishes ms an average of 8 months after acceptance. Query for electronic submissions. Computer printout submissions OK; prefers letter-quality. Reports in 3 weeks on queries; 1 month on mss. Free book catalog and manuscript guidelines.

Nonfiction: How-to, reference. Subjects include art/architecture, education, government/politics, history, military/war, women's issues/studies. "Looking for reference books on/for older adults, current world issues, teen issues, women's issues, and for high school social studies curriculum. No monographs or textbooks." Query or submit outline/synopsis and sample chapters.

Recent Nonfiction Title: *Place Names in Classical Mythology: Greece*, by Robert Bell (general reference).

ABINGDON PRESS, 201 8th Ave. S., Box 801, Nashville TN 37202. (615)749-6301. Editor Trade Books: Mary Catherine Dean. Senior Editor Reference/Academic Books: Davis Perkins. Senior Editor Church Resources: Ronald P. Patterson. Editor Professional Books: Greg Michael. Publishes paperback originals and reprints; church supplies. Receives approximately 2,500 submissions annually. Published 100 titles last year. Few books from first-time authors; 90-95% of books from unagented writers. Average print order for a writer's first book is 4,000-5,000. Pays royalty. Publishes book an average of 18 months after acceptance. Query for electronic submissions. Computer printout submissions acceptable; prefers letter-quality. Ms guidelines for SASE. Reports in 2 months.

Nonfiction: Religious-lay and professional, children's religious books and academic texts. Length: 32-300 pages. Query with outline and samples only. Reviews artwork/photos.

Recent Nonfiction Title: *Mixed Blessings*, by William and Barbara Christopher.

Fiction: Juveniles/religious (12 and up).

Recent Fiction Title: *God's Love Is for Sharings*, by Helen Caswell.

ACCELERATED DEVELOPMENT INC., 3400 Kilgore Ave., Muncie IN 47304. (317)284-7511. President: Dr. Joseph W. Hollis. Executive Vice President: Marcella Hollis. Publishes textbooks/paperback originals and software. Averages 10-15 titles/year; receives 170 submissions annually. 50% of books from first-time authors; 100% of books from unagented writers. Query for electronic submissions. Computer printout submissions acceptable; prefers letter-quality. Pays 6-15% royalty on net price. Publishes book an average of 1 year after acceptance. Reports in 3 months. Book catalog for 9x12 SAE with 3 first class stamps.

Nonfiction: Reference books and textbooks on psychology, counseling, guidance and counseling, teacher education and death education. Especially needs "psychologically-based textbook or reference materials, death education material, theories of counseling psychology, techniques of counseling, and gerontological counseling." Publishes for professors, counselors, teachers, college and secondary students, psychologists,

death educators, psychological therapists, and other health-service providers. "Write for the graduate level student." Submit outline/synopsis, 2 sample chapters, prospectus, and author's resume. Reviews artwork/photos.
Recent Nonfiction Title: *Adlerian Counseling: A Practical Approach for a New Decade*, by Tom Sweeney, Ph.D.
Tips: "Freelance writers should be aware of American Psychological Association style of preparing manuscripts."

ACCENT BOOKS, A division of Accent Publications, 12100 W. 6th Ave., Box 15337, Denver CO 80215. (303)988-5300. Executive Editor: Mary B. Nelson. Publishes evangelical Christian paperbacks, the majority of which are nonfiction. Averages 18-24 titles/year. 30% of books from first-time authors; 100% of books from unagented writers. Pays royalty on cover price. Publishes book an average of 1 year after acceptance. Computer printout submissions acceptable; no dot-matrix. Query or submit 3 sample chapters with a brief synopsis and chapter outline. Do not submit full ms unless requested. Reports in 1 year. Book catalog for 9x12 SAE with 2 first class stamps.
Recent Nonfiction Title: *Children and Stress*, by Arnold Burron.
Fiction: "Fiction titles have strong evangelical message woven throughout plot and characters, and are either contemporary mystery/romance or frontier romance."
Recent Fiction Title: *Vow of Silence*, by B.J. Hoff.
Tips: "How-to books designed for personal application of Biblical truth and/or dealing with problems/solutions of philosophical, societal, and personal issues from a Biblical perspective have the best chance of selling to our firm. We also consider books for the professional and volunteer in church ministries."

ACROPOLIS BOOKS, LTD., Subsidiary of Colortone Press, 2400 17th St. NW, Washington DC 20009. (202)387-6805. Publisher: Kathleen P. Hughes. President: John R. Hackl. Publishes hardcover and trade paperback originals. Averages 25 titles/year. Pays individually negotiated royalty. Publishes book an average of 7 months after acceptance. Query for electronic submissions. Computer printout submissions acceptable; prefers letter-quality. Reports in 2 months. Book catalog $2.
Nonfiction: How-to, reference and self-help. Subjects include health, beauty/fashion, cooking, parenting, business and money management. "We will be looking for manuscripts dealing with fashion and beauty, and self development. Our audience includes general adult consumers, professionals from all walks of life, but to also include elementary school teachers and children." Submit outline/synopsis and sample chapters. Reviews artwork/photos as part of ms package.
Recent Nonfiction Title: *Earn College Credit for What You Know*, by Susan Simosko.

ACS PUBLICATIONS, INC., Box 34487, San Diego CA 92103-0802. (619)297-9203. Editorial Director: Maritha Pottenger. Publishes trade paperback originals and reprints. Averages 8 titles/year; receives 400 submissions annually. 50% of books from first-time authors; 95% of books from unagented writers. Average print order for a writer's first book is 3,000. Pays 15% royalty "on monies received through wholesale and retail sales." No advance. Publishes book an average of 2 years after acceptance. Photocopied submissions OK "if neat." Query for electronic submissions. Computer printout submissions acceptable; prefers letter-quality. Reports in 1 month on queries; 2 months on mss. Book catalog and guidelines for 9x12 SAE with 3 first class stamps.
Nonfiction: Astrology and New Age. Subjects include astrology, holistic health alternatives, channeled books, numerology, and psychic understanding. "Our most important market is astrology. We are seeking pragmatic, useful, immediately applicable contributions to field; prefer psychological approach. Specific ideas and topics should enhance people's lives. Research also valued. No determinism ('Saturn made me do it.') No autobiographies. No airy-fairy 'space cadet' philosophizing. Keep it grounded, useful, opening options (not closing doors) for readers." Query or submit outline and 3 sample chapters.
Recent Nonfiction Title: *Houses of the Horoscope*, by Bill Herbst.
Tips: "The most common mistake writers make when trying to get their work published is to send works to inappropriate publishers. We get too many submissions outside our field or contrary to our world view."

BOB ADAMS, INC., 260 Center St., Holbrook MA 02343. (617)767-8100. Managing Editor: Brandon Toropov. Publishes hardcover and trade paperback originals. Averages 7 titles/year. Receives 25 submissions/year. 25% of books from first-time authors; 25% of books from unagented writers. Variable royalty "determined on case-by-case basis." Publishes book an average of 12-18 months after acceptance. Computer printout submissions OK; prefers letter-quality. Reports in 6 months "if interested. We accept no responsibility for unsolicited manuscripts." Book catalog for 9x12 SAE and $2.40 postage.
Nonfiction: Reference books on careers and business. Query.
Recent Nonfiction Title: *Why Love is Not Enough*, by Sol Gordon.

‡ADVOCACY PRESS, Division of The Girls Club of Santa Barbara, Box 236, Santa Barbara CA 93102. (805)962-2728. Director of Operations: Kathy Araujo. Firm publishes hardcover and trade paperback originals. Publishes average 4 titles/year. Receives 100-150 submissions/year. 25% from first-time authors; 100%

from unagented writers. Publishes ms an average of 6 months after acceptance. Simultaneous and photocopied submissions OK. Computer printout submissions OK; prefers letter-quality. Reports in 6 weeks. Free book catalog and ms guidelines.

Nonfiction: Biography, juvenile, self-help. Subjects include education, psychology and women's issues/studies. "Children's picture books needed. Non-sexist, issue-oriented adult and young adult materials." Submit outline/synopsis and sample chapters.

Recent Nonfiction Title: *More Choices*, by Bingham/Stryker (young adult self-help).

Fiction: Adventure, feminist, historical, juvenile, picture books, young adult. Submit outline/synopsis and sample chapters.

Recent Fiction Title: *My Way Sally*, by Bingham (children's picture book).

*AEGINA PRESS, INC., 59 Oak Lane, Spring Valley, Huntington WV 25704. (304)429-7204. Subsidiaries include University Editions. Managing Editor: Ira Herman. Publishes trade paperback originals and reprints. Publishes approximately 20 titles per year; receives 300 submissions per year. Buys 50% of books from first-time authors; 95% from unagented writers. Subsidy publishes 40% of books. "If the manuscript meets our quality standards but is financially high risk, self-publishing through the University Editions imprint is offered. All sales proceeds go to the author until the subsidy is repaid. The author receives a 40% royalty thereafter. Remaining unsold copies belong to the author." Pays 15% royalty on net sales. Publishes book an average of 6 months after acceptance. Simultaneous and photocopied submissions OK. Query for electronic submissions. Computer printout submissions OK; prefers letter-quality. Reports in 2 weeks on queries; 1 month on ms. Book catalog for $1 and 9x12 SAE with 4 first class stamps; ms guidelines for #10 SASE.

Nonfiction: Biography, how-to, humor, general nonfiction. Subjects include ethnic, health/medicine, regional (local histories), travel guides. "No racist, sexist or hate materials." Query or submit outline/synopsis and sample chapters, or complete ms. Reviews artwork/photos as part of ms package.

Recent Nonfiction Title: *Down Home Gynecology*, by Marvin and Mary Sue Jaffee.

Fiction: Adventure, experimental, fantasy, historical, horror, humor, juvenile (all ages), literary, mainstream/contemporary, mystery, science fiction, short story collections, young adult. Query or submit outline/synopsis and sample chapters or complete ms.

Recent Fiction Title: *The Child Abuse Man*, by James McGovern.

Poetry: Submit 4-6 samples or complete ms.

Recent Poetry Title: *Swim in the Void*, by Gary Horn.

Tips: "If I were a writer trying to market a book today, I would vigorously try the small presses. Too many new writers give up after being rejected by the large publishers."

‡AFRICAN AMERICAN IMAGES, Suite 308, 9204 Commercial, Chicago IL 60617. (312)375-9682. Editor: Jawanza Kunjufu. Publishes trade paperback originals. Averages 6 titles/year. Receives 25 submissions/year. 90% of books from first-time authors. 100% from unagented writers. Pays royalty on wholesale price. Offers $500 average advance. Publishes book an average of 6-9 months after acceptance. Simultaneous submissions OK. Computer printout submissions OK; prefers letter-quality. Reports in 1 week on queries; 3 weeks on mss. Free book catalog and manuscript guidelines.

Nonfiction: Juvenile and self-help. Subjects include child guidance/parenting, education, ethnic (Black), history, psychology and sociology. Submit complete ms. Reviews artwork/photos as part of ms package.

Recent Nonfiction Title: *Color Me Light of the World*, by Sharon Carter (juvenile).

Fiction: Juvenile and young adult. "Only children's books on Black culture." Submit complete ms.

AGLOW PUBLICATIONS, A ministry of Women's Aglow Fellowship International, Box 1548, Lynnwood WA 98046-1557. (206)775-7282. Editor: Gwen Weising. Publishes trade paperback originals. Averages 10 titles/year; receives 1,000 submissions annually. 50% of books from first-time authors; 95% of books from unagented writers. Average print order of a writer's first book is 10,000. Pays up to 10% maximum royalty on retail price "depending on amount of editorial work needed"; buys some mss outright. Publishes book 18 months after acceptance. Photocopied submissions OK. Computer printout submissions acceptable; prefers letter-quality. Reports in 1 month on queries; 2 months on mss. Book catalog and guidelines for 9x12 SAE with 3 first class stamps.

Nonfiction: Biblically-oriented support group books, self-help and inspirational. Subjects include religion (Christian only). "Familiarize yourself with our materials before submitting. Our needs and formats are very specific." Query or submit outline/synopsis and first 3 sample chapters.

Recent Nonfiction Title: *Healing the Angry Heart*, by Kathy Collard Miller.

Tips: "The writer has the best chance of selling our firm a book that shows some aspect of the Christian life."

 The double dagger before a listing indicates that the listing is new in this edition. New markets are often the most receptive to freelance submissions.

ALA BOOKS, 50 East Huron St., Chicago IL 60611. (312)944-6780. Subsidiary of American Library Association. Senior Editor: Herbert Bloom. Publishes hardcover and paperback originals. Firm averages 35-40 titles/year. Receives approximately 200 submissions/year. 60% of books from first-time authors; 100% from unagented writers. Pays royalty of "not more than 20% of our receipts from sales." Publishes ms an average of 7 months after acceptance. High resolution computer printout submissions OK; no dot-matrix. Reports in 2 weeks on queries; 2 months on mss. Free ms guidelines.

Nonfiction: Reference and technical. Subjects include library science, child and adult guidance, education, library service. Professional books for librarians. "We are looking for management of information centers generally; and application of electronic technologies to such management particularly." Query.

Recent Nonfiction Title: *Movie Characters of Leading Performers*, by Nowlan (general reference).

Tips: "If I were a writer trying to market a book today, I would choose a topic people beyond myself are interested in, say something new about the topic, and say it well."

THE ALBAN INSTITUTE, INC., 4125 Nebraska Ave. NW, Washington DC 20016. (202)244-7320. Director of Publications: Celia A. Hahn. Publishes trade paperback originals. Averages 7 titles/year; receives 100 submissions annually. 100% of books from unagented writers. Pays 7% royalty on books; $50 on publication for 2- to 8-page articles relevant to congregational life—practical—ecumenical. Publishes book an average of 1 year after acceptance. Computer printout submissions acceptable. Reports in 2 months. Prefers queries. Book catalog and ms guidelines for 9x12 SAE and 3 first class stamps.

Nonfiction: Religious—focus on local congregation—ecumenical. Must be accessible to general reader. Research preferred. Needs mss on the task of the ordained leader in the congregation, the career path of the ordained leader in the congregation, problems and opportunities in congregational life, and ministry of the laity in the world and in the church. No sermons, devotional, children's titles, inspirational type or prayers. Query or submit outline/synopsis and sample chapters.

Recent Nonfiction Title: *The Inviting Church: A Study of New Member Assimilation*, by Roy M. Oswald and Speed B. Leas.

Tips: "Our audience is intelligent, probably liberal mainline Protestant and Catholic clergy and lay leaders, executives and seminary administration/faculty—people who are concerned with the local church at a practical level and new approaches to its ministry. We are looking for titles on the ministry of the laity and how the church can empower it."

ALLEN PUBLISHING CO., 7324 Reseda Blvd., Reseda CA 91335. (818)344-6788. Owner/Publisher: Michael Wiener. Publishes mass market paperback originals. Firm averages 4 titles/year. Receives 50-100 submissions/year. 50% of books from first-time authors. 100% from unagented writers. Buys mss outright for negotiable sum. Publishes book an average of 6 months after acceptance. Simultaneous and photocopied submissions OK. Computer printout submissions OK; no dot-matrix. Reports in 2 weeks. Book catalog for #10 SAE; with 1 first class stamp.

Nonfiction: How-to and self-help. Subjects include business and economics and money/finance. "We want self-help material, 25,000 words approximately, aimed at wealth-builders, opportunity seekers, aspiring entrepreneurs. Material must be original and authoritative, not rehashed from other sources. All our books are marketed exclusively by mail, in soft-cover, 8½x11 format. We are a specialty publisher and will not consider anything that does not exactly meet our needs. Query. Reviews artwork/photos as part of ms package.

Recent Nonfiction Title: *Start a Money-Making Business for $15*, by Jack Erbe (how-to, self-help).

Tips: "There are more and more people who call themselves writers but who do not have the expertise to write nonfiction books on the subjects they choose. We prefer books by people who really know their subject. Choose a very specialized subject, learn all you about it, and write."

*ALPINE PUBLICATIONS, INC., 2456 E. 9th St., Loveland CO 80537. (303)667-2017. Publisher: B.J. McKinney. Publishes hardcover and trade paperback originals. Averages 6-10 titles/year. Subsidy publishes 2% of books when "book fits into our line but has a market so limited (e.g., rare dog breed) that we would not accept it on royalty terms." Occasional small advance. Pays 7-15% royalty. Publishes book an average of 1½ years after acceptance. Computer printout submissions OK; prefers letter-quality. Reports in 3 weeks on queries; 2 months on mss. Writer's guidelines for #9 SAE with 2 first class stamps.

Nonfiction: How-to books about animals. "We need comprehensive breed books on the more popular AKC breeds, books for breeders on showing, breeding, genetics, gait, new training methods, and cat and horse books. No fiction or fictionalized stories of real animals; no books on reptiles; no personal experience stories except in case of well-known professional in field." Submit outline/synopsis and sample chapters or complete ms. Reviews artwork/photos as part of manuscript package.

Recent Nonfiction Title: *Retriever Puppy Training*, by Rutherford.

*ALYSON PUBLICATIONS, INC., 40 Plympton St., Boston MA 02118. (617)542-5679. Publisher: Sasha Alyson. Publishes trade paperback originals and reprints. Averages 20 titles/year; receives 500 submissions annually. 50% of books from first-time authors; 80% of books from unagented writers. Average print order for a writer's first book is 6,000. Subsidy publishes 5% of books. Pays 8-15% royalty on net price; buys some mss outright for $200-1,000; offers $500-1,000 advance. Publishes book an average of 15 months after acceptance. Computer printout submissions acceptable; no dot-matrix. Reports in 2 weeks on queries; 5 weeks on mss. Looks for "writing ability and content suitable for our house." Book catalog and ms guidelines for #10 SAE and 3 first class stamps.

Nonfiction: Gay/lesbian subjects. "We are especially interested in nonfiction providing a positive approach to gay/lesbian issues." Accepts nonfiction translations. Submit one-page synopsis. Reviews artwork/photos as part of ms package.

Recent Nonfiction Title: *Unbroken Ties: Lesbian Ex-Lovers*, by Carol Becker, Ph.D.

Fiction: Gay novels. Accepts fiction translations. Submit one-page synopsis.

Recent Fiction Title: *Shadows of Love: American Gay Fiction*, by Charles Jurrist.

Tips: "We publish many books by new authors. The writer has the best chance of selling to our firm well-researched, popularly-written nonfiction on a subject (e.g., some aspect of gay history) that has not yet been written about much. With fiction, create a strong storyline that makes the reader want to find out what happens. With nonfiction, write in a popular style for a non-academic audience."

‡AMERICA WEST PUBLISHERS, Box K, Boulder CO 80306. (303)494-8134. Review Editor: George Green. Publishes hardcover and trade paperback originals and hardcover and trade paperback reprints. Averages 5 titles/year. Receives 50 submissions/year. 30% of books from first-time authors. 90% from unagented writers. Pays 10-15% on wholesale price. Offers $300 average advance. Publishes book an average of 6 months after acceptance. Simultaneous and photocopied submissions OK. Reports in 2 weeks on queries; 3 months on mss. Free book catalog and manuscript guidelines.

Nonfiction: UFO—metaphysical. Subject includes health/medicine (holistic self-help). Submit outline/synopsis and sample chapters. Reviews artwork/photos as part of ms package.

Recent Nonfiction Title: *The Bridge to Infinity—Harmonic 371244*, by Bruce Cathie.

Tips: "We currently have materials in all bookstores that have areas of UFO's and also metaphysical information and New Age."

AMERICAN ASTRONAUTICAL SOCIETY, Univelt, Inc., Publisher, Box 28130, San Diego CA 92128. (619)746-4005. Editorial Director: H. Jacobs. Publishes hardcover originals. Averages 8 titles/year; receives 12-15 submissions annually. 5% of books from first-time authors; 5% of books from unagented writers. Average print order for a writer's first book is 600-2,000. Pays 10% royalty on actual sales; no advance. Publishes book an average of 4 months after acceptance. Simultaneous and photocopied submissions OK. Computer printout submissions acceptable; prefers letter-quality. Reports in 1 month. Book catalog and ms guidelines for 9x12 SAE and 3 first class stamps.

Nonfiction: Proceedings or monographs in the field of astronautics, including applications of aerospace technology to Earth's problems. "Our books must be space-oriented or space-related. They are meant for technical libraries, research establishments and the aerospace industry worldwide." Submit outline/synopsis and 1-2 sample chapters. Reviews artwork/photos as part of ms package.

Recent Nonfiction Title: *Soviet Space Programs 1980-1985*, by N.L. Johnson.

*AMERICAN ATHEIST PRESS, American Atheists, Box 2117, Austin TX 78768-2117. (512)458-1244. Editor: R. Murray-O'Hair. Small press. Imprints include Gusttav Broukal Press. Publishes trade paperback originals and trade paperback reprints. Averages 12 titles/year; receives 200 submissions annually. 40-50% of books from first-time authors; 100% of books from unagented writers. Pays 5-10% royalty on retail price. Publishes book an average of 1 year after acceptance. Simultaneous and photocopied submissions OK. Computer printout submissions acceptable; prefers letter-quality. Reports in 6 weeks on queries; 3 months on submissions. Book catalog for 6½x9½ SAE; writer's guidelines for 9x12 SAE.

Nonfiction: Biography, humor, reference and general. Subjects include history (of religion and Atheism, of the effects of religion historically); philosophy and religion (from an Atheist perspective, particularly criticism of religion); politics (separation of state and church, religion and politics); Atheism (particularly the lifestyle of Atheism; the history of Atheism; applications of Atheism). "We are interested in hard-hitting and original books expounding the lifestyle of Atheism and criticizing religion. We would like to see more submissions dealing with the histories of specific religious sects, such as the L.D.S., the Worldwide Church of God, etc.

An asterisk preceding a listing indicates that subsidy publishing or co-publishing (where author pays part or all of publishing costs) is available. Firms whose subsidy programs comprise more than 50% of their total publishing activities are listed at the end of the Book Publishers section.

We are generally not interested in biblical criticism." Submit outline/synopsis and sample chapters or complete ms. Reviews artwork/photos.

Recent Nonfiction Title: *Robertson: The Pulpit and the Power*, by Arthur F. Ide.

Fiction: Humor (satire of religion or of current religious leaders); anything of particular interest to Atheists. "We rarely publish any fiction. But we have occasionally released a humorous book." No mainstream. "For our press to consider fiction, it would have to tie in with the general focus of our press, which is the promotion of Atheism and free thought." Submit outline/synopsis and sample chapters.

Tips: "We plan two new periodicals (start dates: 1990). This will enable us to publish a greater variety of material in regard to both length and content. We will need more how-to types of material—how to argue with creationists, how to fight for state/church separation, etc. We have an urgent need for literature for young Atheists."

AMERICAN CATHOLIC PRESS, 16160 South Seton Dr., South Holland IL 60473. (312)331-5845. Editorial Director: Father Michael Gilligan, Ph.D. Publishes hardcover originals and hardcover and paperback reprints. "Most of our sales are by direct mail, although we do work through retail outlets." Averages 4 titles/year. Pays by outright purchase of $25-100; no advance. Publishes book an average of 8 months after acceptance. Simultaneous and photocopied submissions OK. Computer printout submissions acceptable. Reports in 2 months.

Nonfiction: "We publish books on the Roman Catholic liturgy—for the most part, books on religious music and educational books and pamphlets. We also publish religious songs for church use, including Psalms, as well as choral and instrumental arrangements. We are interested in new music, meant for use in church services. Books, or even pamphlets, on the Roman Catholic Mass are especially welcome. We have no interest in secular topics and are not interested in religious poetry of any kind." Query.

Recent Nonfiction Title: *The Role of Music in the New Roman Liturgy*, by W. Herring (educational).

AMERICAN HOSPITAL PUBLISHING, INC., American Hospital Association, 211 East Chicago Ave., Chicago IL 60611. (312)440-6800. Vice President, Books: Brian Schenk. Publishes trade paperback originals. Firm averages 20-30 titles/year. Receives 75-100 submissions/year. 20% of books from first-time writers; 100% from unagented writers. Pays 10-12% royalty on retail price. Offers $1,000 average advance. Publishes book an average of 1 year after acceptance. Computer printout submissions OK; prefers letter-quality. Reports in 1 month on queries; 6 weeks on mss. Book catalog and manuscript guidelines for #10 SASE.

Nonfiction: Reference, technical, textbook. Subjects include business and economics (specific to health care institutions); health/medicine (never consumer oriented). Need field-based, reality-tested responses to changes in the health care field directed to hospital CEO's, planners, boards of directors, or other senior management. No personal histories, untested health care programs or clinical texts. Query.

Recent Nonfiction Title: *Integrated Quality Assessment*, by Dan Longo.

Tips: "The successful proposal demonstrates a clear understanding of the needs of the market and the writer's ability to succinctly present practical knowledge of demonstrable benefit that comes from genuine experience that readers will recognize, trust and accept. The audience is senior and middle management of health care institutions."

‡AMERICAN INSTITUTE OF PHYSICS, 335 East 45th Street, New York NY 10017-3483. FAX: (212)661-2036. Manager, Books Divison: Dr. R. G. Lerner. Publishes hardcover originals and reprints. Averages 30 titles/year. Receives 90 submissions/year. Pays 6% minimum royalty on wholesale price. Publishes book an average of 6-8 months after acceptance. Simultaneous and photocopied submissions OK. Computer printout submissions OK; prefers letter-quality. Reports in 2 weeks on queries; 2 months on mss. Free book catalog.

Nonfiction: Technical. Subjects include science. "We need physics and physics-related books." Submit outline/synopsis and sample chapters or complete ms.

Recent Nonfiction Title: *The Cosmic Onion*, by Frank Close (monograph).

THE AMERICAN PSYCHIATRIC PRESS, INC. (associated with the American Psychiatric Association), 1400 K St. NW, Washington DC 20005. (202)682-6268. Editor-in-Chief: Carol C. Nadelson, M.D. Publishes hardcover and trade paperback originals. Averages 40 titles/year, 2-4 trade books/year; receives about 300 submissions annually. About 10% of books from first-time authors; 95% of books from unagented writers. Pays 10% minimum royalty based on all money actually received, maximum varies; offers average $3,000-5,000 advance. Publishes book an average of 9 months after acceptance. Simultaneous and photocopied submissions OK (if made clear in cover letter). Query for electronic submissions. Computer printout submissions acceptable; no dot-matrix. Reports in 6 weeks "in regard to an *initial* decision regarding our interest. A *final* decision requires more time." Author questionnaire and proposal guidelines available for SASE.

Nonfiction: Reference, technical, textbook and general nonfiction. Subjects include psychiatry and related subjects. Authors must be well qualified in their subject area. No first-person accounts of mental illness or anything not clearly related to psychiatry. Query with outline/synopsis and sample chapters.

Recent Nonfiction Title: *Cocaine*, by Roger D. Weiss, M.D., and Steven M. Mirin, M.D.
Tips: "Because we are a specialty publishing company, books written by or in collaboration with a psychiatrist have the best chance of acceptance. Make it authoritative and professional."

AMERICAN REFERENCES INC., 919 N. Michigan, Chicago IL 60611. (312)951-6200. President: Les Krantz. Publishes hardcover and trade paperback originals. Averages 4-10 titles/year. Payment negotiable. Simultaneous and photocopied submissions OK. Reports in 6 weeks on queries.
Nonfiction: Illustrations and reference. Subjects include art and photography.
Nonfiction Title: *The California Art Review*, second edition.

AMERICAN STUDIES PRESS, INC., 13511 Palmwood Lane, Tampa FL 33624. (813)961-7200 or 974-2857. Imprints include ASP Books, Rattlesnake Books, Harvest Books and Marilu Books (Marilu imprint includes Herland—poems by women about women—and Woman). Editor-in-Chief: Donald R. Harkness. Publishes trade paperback originals. Receives 250-300 submissions/year. 80% of books from first-time authors. 100% of books from unagented writers. Averages 6 titles/year. Pays 10 copies plus 10% royalty on retail price after printing cost is met. Publishes book an average of 6 months after acceptance. Computer printout submissions OK; prefers letter-quality. Reports in 2 weeks on queries; 2 months on mss. Book list for #10 SASE.
Nonfiction: Biography, humor and illustrated book. Subjects include Americana, history, psychology. "I might consider a book of generalized family history, of interest to an audience wider than the immediate circle of relatives." Query or submit outline/synopsis and sample chapters or complete ms. Reviews artwork/photos as part of ms package.
Recent Nonfiction Title: *A Boy Grows in Brooklyn*, by William M. Firshing (autobiography).
Poetry: Submit 6 poems from a unified book or submit complete ms.
Recent Poetry Title: *Poetica Erotica*, by Normajean MacLeod.
Tips: "Our audience is intelligent and appreciative college graduates, not taken in by the slick and fancy package but more concerned with content. Good poetry, or satire—that's what I like best. Please don't send a bulky ms without advance query (with SASE, of course)."

ANCESTRY INCORPORATED, Box 476, Salt Lake City UT 84110. (801)531-1790. Managing Editor: Robert J. Welsh. Publishes hardcover and mass market paperback originals. Averages 10 titles/year; receives 10-20 submissions annually. 70% of books from first-time authors; 100% of books from unagented writers. Pays 8-12% royalty or purchases mss outright. Advances are discouraged but considered if necessary. Publishes book an average of 1 year after acceptance. Simultaneous and photocopied submissions OK. Query for electronic submissions. Computer printout submissions acceptable. Reports in 1 month on queries; 2 months on mss. Free book catalog and ms guidelines.
Nonfiction: How-to, reference and genealogy. Subjects include Americana; history (family and local); and hobbies (genealogy). "Our publications are aimed exclusively at the genealogist. We consider everything from short monographs to book length works on immigration, migration, record collections, etc. Good local histories and heraldic topics are considered." No mss that are not genealogical or historical. Query, or submit outline/synopsis and sample chapters, or complete ms. Reviews artwork/photos.
Recent Nonfiction Title: *Applied Genealogy*, by Eugene A. Stratton.
Tips: "Genealogical reference, how-to, and descriptions of source collections have the best chance of selling to our firm. Be precise in your description."

*ANDERSON PUBLISHING CO., Box 1576, Cincinnati OH 45201-1576. (513)421-4142. Editorial Director: Dale Hartig. Publishes hardcover, paperback originals, journals and software and reprints. Publishes 13-15 titles/year. Subsidy publishes 10% of books. Pays 15-18% royalty; "advance in selected cases." Publishes book an average of 7 months after acceptance. Simultaneous and photocopied submissions OK. Computer printout submissions acceptable; prefers letter-quality. Reports in 2 months. Book catalog for 8½x11 SASE; guidelines for SASE.
Nonfiction: Law and law-related books, and criminal justice criminology texts (justice administration legal series). Query or submit outline/chapters with vitae.
Recent Nonfiction Title: *Economic Damages*, by Michael L. Brookshire, Ph.D. (law/economics).

ANDREWS AND McMEEL, 4900 Main St., Kansas City MO 64112. Editorial Director: Donna Martin. Publishes hardcover and paperback originals. Averages 30 titles/year. Pays royalty on retail price. "Query only. No unsolicited manuscripts. Areas of specialization include humor, how-to, and consumer reference books, such as *The Writer's Art* by James J. Kilpatrick, and *Roger Ebert's Movie Home Companion*."

‡APOLLO BOOKS, 5 Schoolhouse Lane, Poughkeepsie NY 12003. (914)462-0040. Owner: Glenn Opitz. Averages 4-6 titles/year. Receives 12 submissions/year. Pays royalty or outright purchase. Publishes book an average of 6 months after acceptance. Simultaneous or photocopied submissions OK. Query for electronic submissions. Computer printout submissions OK. Reports in 1 week on queries; 1 month on mss. Book catalog for SAE and 90¢ postage.

Nonfiction: Biography, coffee table book and reference. Subjects include art/architecture and gardening. Reviews artwork as part of ms package.
Recent Nonfiction Title: *Chinese and Other Far Eastern Art.*

APPALACHIAN MOUNTAIN CLUB BOOKS, 5 Joy St., Boston MA 02108. (617)523-0636. FAX: (617)523-0722. Publisher: Susan Cummings. Publishes hardcover and trade paperback originals. Averages 8 titles/year; receives 100 submissions annually. 50% of books from first-time authors; 90% of books from unagented writers. Pays 10% royalty on retail price; offers $1,000 advance. Publishes book an average of 6 months after receipt of acceptable manuscript. Simultaneous and photocopied submissions OK. Query for electronic submissions. High quality computer printout submissions acceptable. Reports in 1 month on queries; 4 months on mss. Book brochure for #10 SAE.
Nonfiction: How-to, reference, field guides and guidebooks. Subjects include history (Northeast, mountains), nature, outdoor recreation, and travel. "We want manuscripts about the environment, mountains and their history and culture and outdoor recreation (such as hiking, climbing, skiing, canoeing, kayaking, bicycling)." No physical fitness manuals. Query or submit outline/synopsis and sample chapters.
Recent Nonfiction Title: *Classic Backcountry Skiing: A Guide to the Best Ski Tours in New England,* by David Goodman.
Tips: "We are expanding into travel outside the U.S. that offers opportunities for outdoor recreation. We have also begun to publish children's books on outdoor recreation and nature."

‡APPLEZABA PRESS, Box 4134, Long Beach CA 90804. (213)591-0015. Publisher: D.H. Lloyd. Publishes hardcover and trade paperback originals. Firm averages 4 titles/year. Receives 1,000 submissions/year. 5% of books from first-time authors; 95% from unagented writers. Pays 8-15% royalty on retail price. Publishes book average of 3 years after acceptance. Simultaneous and photocopied submissions OK. Computer printout submission OK; letter-quality preferred. Reports in 2 weeks on queries; 3 months on mss. Free book catalog; mss guidelines for #10 SASE.
Nonfiction: Cookbook. Subjects include cooking, foods and nutrition. Query or submit complete ms. Reviews artwork/photos as part of ms package.
Recent Nonfiction Title: *College Quickies Survival Cookbook,* by Sandy Sieg.
Fiction: Literary and short story collections. Query or submit outline/synopsis and sample chapters.
Recent Fiction Title: *Flight to Freedom,* by F.N. Wright.
Recent Poetry Title: *Blood & Bones,* by Clifton Snider.

THE AQUARIAN PRESS LTD., Denington Estate, Wellingborough, Northamptonshire NN8 2RQ England. Editor-in-Chief: Eileen Campbell. Hardcover and paperback originals. Averages 70-80 titles/year. Pays 7½-10% royalty. Photocopied submissions OK. Computer printout and disk submissions acceptable; prefers letter-quality. Reports in 1 month. Free book catalog.
Nonfiction: Publishes books on all forms of divination, magic, the paranormal, personal development and general New Age topics. "Crucible is a sub-imprint of The Aquarian Press and publishes in the field of transformation—religion and spirituality, psychology and psychotherapy and philosophy and esoteric thought." Length: 30,000-100,000 words.
Tips: "We look for a clear indication that the author has thought about his market; a fundamental ability to *communicate* ideas—authority in combination with readability."

ARBOR HOUSE, Imprint of William Morrow, 105 Madison Ave., New York NY 10016. President and Publisher: Eden Collinsworth. Publishes hardcover and trade paperback originals and selected reprints. Averages 50-60 titles/year. Pays standard royalty; offers negotiable advance. Publishes book an average of 9 months after acceptance. Computer printout submissions acceptable; prefers letter-quality. Free book catalog.
Nonfiction: Autobiography, cookbook, how-to and self-help. Subjects include Americana (possibly), art (possibly), business and economics, cooking and foods, health, history, politics, psychology, recreation, inspiration and sports. Query first to "The Editors." Reviews artwork/photos as part of ms package.
Recent Nonfiction Title: *The Equilibrium Plan: Balancing Diet and Exercise,* by Sally Edwards.
Fiction: "Quality fiction—everything from romance to science fiction, fantasy, adventure and suspense." Query or submit outline/synopsis and sample chapters to "The Editors."
Recent Fiction Title: *Killshot,* by Elmore Leonard.
Tips: "Freelance writers should be aware of a greater emphasis on agented properties and market resistance to untried fiction."

ARCsoft PUBLISHERS, Box 132, Woodsboro MD 21798. (301)845-8856. Publisher: Anthony R. Curtis. Publishes trade paperback originals. Averages 20 titles/year. "We now offer only 'buyout' contracts in which all rights are purchased. Typically, an advance of 20 percent is paid at contract signing and 80 percent at acceptable completion of work. Royalties are no longer offered since writers suffer under royalty contracts for small-volume technical books." Offers variable advance. Publishes book an average of 6 months after acceptance. Computer printout submissions acceptable; no dot-matrix. Reports in 1 month on queries; 10 weeks on mss. Free book catalog.

Nonfiction: Technical. "We publish technical books including space science, desktop publishing, personal computers and hobby electronics, especially for beginners." Accepts nonfiction translations. Query or submit outline/synopsis and 1 sample chapter. Reviews artwork/photos as part of ms package.

Recent Nonfiction Title: *Space Almanac*, by A.R. Curtis.

Tips: "We look for the writer's ability to cover our desired subject thoroughly, writing quality and interest."

*M. ARMAN PUBLISHING, INC., 740 S. Ridgewood Ave., Ormond Beach FL 32074. (904)673-5576. Mailing address: Box 785, Ormond Beach FL 32074. Contact: Mike Arman. Publishes trade paperback originals, reprints and software. Averages 6-8 titles/year; receives 20 submissions annually. 20% of books from first-time authors; 100% of books from unagented writers. Average print order for a writer's first book is 2,500. Subsidy publishes 20% of books. Pays 10% royalty on wholesale price. No advance. Publishes book (on royalty basis) an average of 8 months after acceptance; 6 weeks on subsidy basis. Photocopied submissions OK. "We now set type directly from author's disks. Our equipment can read most computer disks, most operating systems, most word processing programs." Computer printout submissions acceptable. Reports in 1 week on queries; 3 weeks on mss. Book catalog for #10 SASE.

Nonfiction: How-to, reference, technical, and textbook. "Motorcycle and aircraft technical books only." Accepts nonfiction translations. Publishes for enthusiasts. Submit complete ms. Reviews artwork/photos as part of ms package.

Recent Nonfiction Title: *V-Twin Thunder*, by Carl McClanahan (motorcycle performance manual).

Fiction: "Motorcycle or aircraft-related only." Accepts fiction translations. Immediate needs are "slim," but not non-existent. Submit cover letter and complete ms.

Tips: "The type of book a writer has the best chance of selling to our firm is how-to fix motorcycles — specifically Harley-Davidsons. We have a strong, established market for these books."

ASHER-GALLANT PRESS, Division of Caddylak Systems, Inc., 131 Heartland Blvd., Box W, Brentwood NY 11717-0698. Publishes softcover and loose-leaf format originals (sold mostly through direct marketing). Averages 20 titles/year; receives 150 submissions annually. 50% of books from first-time authors; 95% of books from unagented writers. "Many of our authors are first-time authors when they begin working with us, but write several subsequent books for us. Payment for each project is treated individually, but generally, the rights to smaller works (up to about 25,000 words) are purchased on a flat fee basis, and rights to larger works are purchased on a royalty basis." Advance varies by project. Publishes books an average of 6 months after acceptance. Simultaneous and photocopied submissions OK. Computer printout submissions acceptable; prefers letter-quality. Ms returned only if requested. "We prefer to keep a writer's sample on file for possible future assignments." Reports negative results in 2 weeks on queries; 1 month on mss. Free book catalog.

Nonfiction: How-to, reference, audio cassette programs and business directories. Subjects include business (general) and management topics. "We plan to do 35 to 40 new titles during the next two years. The list will consist of individual business titles, more technical management reports, and longer, more comprehensive books that will be published in binder format. All subject matter must be appropriate to our broad audience of middle-level corporate managers. No sensational, jazzy nonfiction without solid research behind it." Submit outline/synopsis and sample chapters.

Recent Nonfiction Title: *Words for Telemarketing*, by Steven R. Isaac.

Tips: "The deciding factors in whether or not we publish a certain book are: (1) we believe there will be a very sizeable demand for the book, (2) the outline we review is logically structured and very comprehensive, and (3) the sample chapters are concisely and clearly written and well-researched."

ASIAN HUMANITIES PRESS, Box 4177, Santa Clara CA 95054-0177. (408)727-3151. Editor: Lew Lancaster. Publishes hardcover originals, trade paperback originals and reprints. Firm averages 8 titles/year. Receives 25 submissions/year. 100% of books from unagented authors. Pays up to 7.5% royalty on retail price. Publishes book an average of 9 months after acceptance. Photocopied submissions OK. Query for electronic submissions. Computer printout submission OK; no dot-matrix. Reports on queries in 1 month; 2 months on mss. Free book catalog.

Nonfiction: Reference, textbook. Subjects include language/literature (Asian), philosophy (Asian and comparative), religion (Asian and comparative), translation (Asian religions, cultures and philosophy), women's issues/studies (Asian), humanities, spiritual. "We publish books pertaining to Asian religions, cultures and thought directed toward scholars, libraries and specialty bookstores." Submit complete ms. Reviews artwork/photos as part of ms package.

Recent Nonfiction Title: *Zibo: The Last Great Zen Master of China*, by J.C. Cleary.

Tips: "Scholars and general readers interested in Asian and comparative religions, cultures and philosophy are our audience."

ATHENEUM CHILDREN'S BOOKS, Macmillan, Inc., 866 3rd Ave., New York NY 10022. (212)702-7894. Editorial Director: Jonathan J. Lanman or editors Marcia Marshall and Gail Paris. Publishes hardcover originals. Averages 60 titles/year; receives 7,000-8,000 submissions annually. 8-12% of books from first-time authors; 50% of books from unagented writers. Pays 10% royalty on retail price; offers average $2,000-3,000 advance. Publishes book an average of 18 months after acceptance. Photocopied submissions (outline and first 3 chapters only, please) OK. Computer printout submissions acceptable; prefers letter-quality. Reports in 2 weeks on queries; 3 months on outline and sample chapters. Book catalog and ms guidelines for 7x10 SAE and 2 first class stamps.

Nonfiction: Biography, how-to, humor, illustrated book, juvenile (pre-school through young adult) and self-help, all for juveniles. Subjects include: Americana, animals, art, business and economics, cooking and foods, health, history, hobbies, music, nature, philosophy, photography, politics, psychology, recreation, religion, sociology, sports, and travel, all for young readers. "Do remember, most publishers plan their lists as much as two years in advance. So if a topic is 'hot' right now, it may be 'old hat' by the time we could bring it out. It's better to steer clear of fads. Some writers assume juvenile books are for 'practice' until you get good enough to write adult books. Not so. Books for young readers demand just as much 'professionalism' in writing as adult books. So save those 'practice' manuscripts for class, or polish them before sending them." Query, submit outline/synopsis and sample chapters. Reviews artwork/photos as part of ms package; prefers photocopies of artwork.

Recent Nonfiction Title: *Dead Serious*, by Jane Mersky Leder (teenage suicide).

Fiction: Adventure, ethnic, experimental, fantasy, gothic, historical, horror, humor, mainstream, mystery, romance, science fiction, suspense, and western, all in juvenile versions. "We have few specific needs except for books that are fresh, interesting and well written. Again, fad topics are dangerous, as are works you haven't polished to the best of your ability. (The competition is fierce.) We've been inundated with dragon stories (misunderstood dragon befriends understanding child), unicorn stories (misunderstood child befriends understanding unicorn), and variations of 'Ignatz the Egg' (Everyone laughs at Ignatz the egg [giraffe/airplane/accountant] because he's square [short/purple/stupid] until he saves them from the eggbeater [lion/storm/I.R.S. man] and becomes a hero). Other things we don't need at this time are safety pamphlets, ABC books, and rhymed narratives. In writing picture book texts, avoid the coy and 'cutesy.' " Query, submit outline/synopsis and sample chapters for novels; complete ms for picture books.

Recent Fiction Title: *The Return*, by Sonia Levitin (young adult novel).

Poetry: "At this time there is a growing market for children's poetry. However, we don't anticipate needing any for the next year or two, especially rhymed narratives."

Tips: "Our books are aimed at children from pre-school age, up through high school. Our young adult novels and much of our science fiction and fantasy also cross over into adult markets."

‡ATLANTIC MONTHLY PRESS, 19 Union Sq. W., New York NY 10107. (212)645-4462. FAX: (212)727-0180. Publisher: Carl Navarre. Editorial Director: Gary Fisketjon. Executive Editor: Ann Godoff. Associate and Assistant Editors: Anne Rumsey and Nancy Lewin. Averages 75 titles/year. "Advance and royalties depend on the nature of the book, the stature of the author, and the subject matter." Publishes book an average of 1 year after acceptance.

Nonfiction: Publishes general nonfiction, biography, autobiography, science, philosophy, the arts, belles lettres, history and world affairs. Length: 70,000-200,000 words. Query.

Recent Nonfiction Title: *Changes in Latitude*, by Joanna McIntyre Varawa.

Fiction: Publishes general fiction and poetry. Prefers complete fiction and poetry mss.

Recent Fiction Title: *Nebraska*, by Ron Hansen.

AUGSBURG BOOKS, 426 S. 5th St., Box 1209, Minneapolis MN 55440. (612)330-3563. Senior Editor: Robert Moluf. Publishes mostly paperback originals. Publishes 40 titles/year; receives 5,000 queries annually. 20% of books from first-time authors; 95% of books from unagented writers. Average print order for a writer's first book is 5,000. Pays 10% royalty on retail price; offers variable advance. Publishes book an average of 1 year after acceptance. Simultaneous and photocopied queries OK. Manuscript submissions only upon request. Computer printout submissions acceptable; must be near-letter quality. Book catalog and ms guidelines for 8½x11 SAE and 4 first class stamps. Reports in 1 month.

Nonfiction: Publishes for a wide Christian market. Books for children, youth or intergenerational family use; books of practical help, guidance, and encouragement; resources for Christian leadership and ministry; nontechnical books dealing with scripture, church history, ethics, theology, and related fields.

Recent Nonfiction Title: *Trust*, by Ira Tanner.

If you have an IBM or IBM-compatible personal computer and would like to know more about Writer's Market on disk, see the bind-in card between pages 904 and 905.

AVALON BOOKS, Imprint of Thomas Bouregy & Co., Inc., 401 Lafayette St., New York NY 10003. Editor and Publisher: Barbara J. Brett. Publishes 60 titles/year. Pays $500 for first book and $600 thereafter, which is applied against sales of the first 3,500 copies of the book (initial run is 2,100 copies). Computer printout submissions acceptable; no dot-matrix. Reports in 3 months. Writer's guidelines for #10 SASE.
Fiction: "We publish wholesome romances, westerns and adventure novels that are sold to libraries throughout the country. Our books are read by adults as well as teenagers, and their characters are all adults. All the romances and adventures are contemporary; all the westerns are historical." Length: 35,000 to 50,000 words. Submit first chapter and a brief, but complete summary of the book, or, if you are sure the book fits our requirements, submit the complete manuscript. Enclose manuscript size SASE.
Recent Fiction Title: *Reach for a Star*, by Charlene Bowen.
Tips: "We do not want old-fashioned, predictable, formula-type books. We are looking for contemporary characters and fresh, contemporary plots and storylines. Every heroine should have an interesting career or profession."

AVIATION BOOK CO., 1640 Victory Blvd., Glendale CA 91201-2999. (818)240-1771. Editor: Walter P. Winner. Publishes hardcover and paperback originals and reprints. Averages 5 titles/year; receives 25 submissions annually. 90% of books from first-time authors; 10% of books from unagented writers. Pays royalty on retail price. No advance. Query with outline. Publishes book an average of 9 months after acceptance. Computer printout submissions acceptable; prefers letter-quality. Reports in 2 months. Book catalog for 9x12 SAE with $1 postage.
Nonfiction: Aviation books, primarily of a technical nature and pertaining to pilot training. Young adult level and up. Also aeronautical history. Asks of ms, "Does it fill a void in available books on subject?" or "Is it better than available material?" Reviews artwork/photos as part of ms package.
Recent Nonfiction Title: *Instrument Flight Training Manual*, by Peter Dogan.

AVON BOOKS, 105 Madison, New York NY 10016. Publisher: Carolyn Reidy. Editor-in-Chief: Susanne Jaffe. Publishes paperback originals and paperback reprints. Averages 300 titles/year. Pay and advance are negotiable. Publishes ms an average of 2 years after acceptance. Simultaneous and photocopied submissions OK. Computer printout submissions acceptable; prefers letter-quality. Reports in 2 months. Book catalog for SASE.
Nonfiction: How-to, popular psychology, self-help, health, history,war, sports, business/economics, biography and politics. No textbooks.
Recent Nonfiction Title: *Communion*, by Whitley Strieber.
Fiction: Romance (contemporary), historical romance, science fiction, fantasy, men's adventure, suspense/thriller, mystery, and western. Submit query letter only.
Recent Fiction Title: *Bound by Desire*, by Rosemary Rogers.

AVON FLARE BOOKS, Young Adult Imprint of Avon Books, a division of the Hearst Corp., 105 Madison Ave., New York NY 10016. (212)481-5609. FAX: (212)532-2693. Editorial Director: Ellen Krieger. Publishes mass market paperback originals and reprints. Imprint publishes 24 new titles annually. 25% of books from first-time authors; 15% of books from unagented writers. Pays 6-8% royalty; offers average $2,000 advance. Publishes book an average of 15 months after acceptance. Simultaneous and photocopied submissions OK. Computer printout submissions acceptable; prefers letter-quality. Reports in 10 weeks. Book catalog and manuscript guidelines for 8x10 SAE and 5 first class stamps.
Nonfiction: General. Submit outline/synopsis and 6 sample chapters. "*Very* selective with young adult nonfiction."
Fiction: Adventure, ethnic, experimental, humor, mainstream, mystery, romance, suspense and contemporary. "Very selective with mystery." Mss appropriate to ages 12-18. Query with sample chapters or synopsis.
Recent Fiction Title: *What's In a Name?*, by Peter Filichia.

AZTEX CORP., 1126 N. 6th Ave., Box 50046, Tucson AZ 85703. (608)882-4656. Publishes hardcover and paperback originals. Averages 15 titles/year; receives 250 submissions annually. 100% of books from unagented writers. Average print order for a writer's first book is 3,500. Pays 10% royalty. Publishes book an average of 18 months after acceptance. Query for electronic submissions. Computer printout submissions acceptable; prefers letter-quality. Reports in 3 months. Free catalog.
Nonfiction: "We specialize in transportation subjects (how-to and history)." Accepts nonfiction translations. Submit outline/synopsis and 2 sample chapters or complete ms. Reviews artwork/photos as part of ms package.
Recent Nonfiction Title: *The Amateur Astronomer's Catalog of 500 Deep-Sky Objects*, by Ronald J. Morales.
Tips: "We look for accuracy, thoroughness and interesting presentation."

BACKCOUNTRY PUBLICATIONS, Imprint of The Countryman Press, Inc., Box 175, Woodstock VT 05091. (802)457-1049. Publishes trade paperback originals. Averages 8 titles/year. 50% of books from first-time authors; 95% from unagented writers. Pays 5-10% royalty on retail price. Offers $500 average advance.

Publishes book average of 9 months after acceptance. Simultaneous and photocopied submissions OK. Computer printout submissions OK; prefers letter-quality. Reports on queries in 2 weeks; on mss in 6 weeks. Free book catalog.

Nonfiction: Reference. Subjects include recreation. "We're looking for regional guides to hiking, bicycling, cross-country skiing, canoeing, and fishing for all parts of the country." Submit outline/synopsis and sample chapters. Reviews artwork/photos as part of ms package.

Recent Nonfiction Title: *Fifty Hikes in New Jersey*, by Scofield, Green and Zimmerman (hiking guide).

BAEN PUBLISHING ENTERPRISES, Distributed by Simon & Schuster, 260 Fifth Ave., New York NY 10001. (212)532-4111. Publisher and Editor-in-Chief: Jim Baen. Publishes hardcover, trade paperback and mass market paperback originals and mass market paperback reprints. Averages 80-100 titles/year; receives 1,000 submissions annually. 5% of books from first-time authors; 10% of books from unagented writers. Pays 6-8% royalty on cover price. Photocopied submissions OK. Computer printout submissions acceptable if letter-quality. Reports in 2 weeks on queries; 2 months on mss. Ms guidelines for #10 SASE.

Nonfiction: High-tech science or futuristic topics such as space technology, artificial intelligence, etc. Submit outline/synopsis and sample chapters.

Recent Nonfiction Title: *Artificial Intelligence*, by F. David Peat.

Fiction: Fantasy and science fiction. Submit outline/synopsis and sample chapters or (preferred) synopsis and complete ms.

Recent Fiction Title: *After the Fact*, by Fred Saberhagen.

Tips: "Our audience includes those who are interested in *hard* science fiction and quality fantasy pieces that engage the mind as well as entertain."

*BAKER BOOK HOUSE COMPANY, Box 6287, Grand Rapids MI 49516-6287. (616)676-9185. FAX: (616)676-9573. Editor, trade books: Dan Van't Kerkhoff. Editor, academic books: Allan Fisher. Publishes hardcover and trade paperback originals and reprints. Averages 120 titles/year. 25% of books from first-time authors; 85% of books from unagented writers. Subsidy publishes 1% of books. Pays 10% royalty. Publishes book within 1 year after acceptance. Simultaneous and photocopied submissions OK. Computer printout submissions OK; prefers letter-quality. Reports in 3 weeks on queries; 6 weeks on ms. Book catalog for 9x12 SAE and $1.20 postage. Manuscript guidelines for #10 SASE.

Nonfiction: Biography, juvenile, humor, reference, self-help (gift books, Bible study), Bible commentaries and textbook. Subjects include child guidance/parenting, language/literature, philosophy, psychology, religion, sociology, women's-issues/studies. "We're looking for books from a religious perspective — devotional, Bible study, self-help, textbooks for Christian colleges and seminaries, counseling and humorous books." Query or submit outline/synopsis and sample chapters.

Recent Nonfiction Title: *Your Hidden Half*, by Mark R. McMinn.

Tips: "Our books are sold through Christian bookstores to customers with religious background."

BALE BOOKS, Division of Bale Publications, Box 2727, New Orleans LA 70176. Editor-in-Chief: Don Bale Jr. Publishes hardcover and paperback originals and reprints. Averages 10 titles/year; receives 25 submissions annually. 50% of books from first-time authors; 90% of books from unagented writers. Average print order for a writer's first book is 1,000. Offers standard 10-12½-15% royalty contract on wholesale or retail price; sometimes purchases mss outright for $500. Offers no advance. Publishes book an average of 3 years after acceptance. Will consider photocopied submissions. Computer printout submissions acceptable; no dot-matrix. "Send manuscript by registered or certified mail. Be sure copy of manuscript is retained." Book catalog for SAE and 2 first class stamps.

Nonfiction: Numismatics. "Our specialty is coin and stock market investment books; especially coin investment books and coin price guides. Most of our books are sold through publicity and ads in the coin newspapers. We are open to any new ideas in the area of numismatics. The writer should write for a teenage through adult level. Lead the reader by the hand like a teacher, building chapter by chapter. Our books sometimes have a light, humorous treatment, but not necessarily." Looks for "good English, construction and content, and sales potential." Submit outline and 3 sample chapters.

Recent Nonfiction Title: *A Gold Mine in Gold*, by Bale (discusses gold coins as an investment).

BALLANTINE/EPIPHANY BOOKS, Imprint of Ballantine Books, 201 E. 50th St., New York NY 10022. (212)572-1699. Editor: Toni Simmons. Publishes inspirational hardcover and trade paperback originals, mass market paperback originals and reprints. Averages 20 titles/year. Receives 2,500 submissions/year. 30% of books from first-time authors. Pays 8-10% royalty on retail price. Publishes book an average of 1 year after acceptance. Simultaneous and photocopied submissions OK. Reports in 6 weeks. Book catalog for 9x12 SAE with 2 first class stamps.

Nonfiction: Inspirational, biography, how-to, humor and self-help. Subjects include health, psychology, religion and sociology. "Nonfiction proposals should enrich the Christian's life in some way and be written in a style that will also appeal to and be accessible to nonChristians." No poetry, sermons, eschatology, devotionals, books for children or books on controversial issues. Query or submit outline/synopsis and sample chapters. Reviews artwork/photos as part of ms package.

Recent Nonfiction Title: *And God Created Wrinkles*, by E. Jane Mall (aging).

Fiction: Inspirational. "We publish very little fiction; while it need not be overly religious, our fiction must contain some inspirational qualities." No "fiction for children, fiction about the end of time, prairie romances, inspirational romances, biblical/historical fiction, science fiction, or New Age fiction." Query or submit outline/synopsis and sample chapters.

Recent Fiction Title: *The Last Exile*, by Charles Durham.

Tips: "Examine possible similar books already on the market, then compare your own manuscript to others. Be sure to write for a general audience; Epiphany does not publish books of limited interest to a small segmented audience. A common mistake writers make is that they state how much of an advance they want in their query letters."

BANKS-BALDWIN LAW PUBLISHING CO., 1904 Ansel Rd., Cleveland OH 44106. (216)721-7373. FAX: (216)721-8055. Editor-in-Chief: P.J. Lucier. Publishes law books and services in a variety of formats. Averages approximately 5 new titles/year; receives 5-10 submissions annually. 5% of books from first-time authors; 90% of books from unagented writers. "Most titles include material submitted by outside authors." Pays 8-16% on net revenue, or fee. Offers advance not to exceed 25% of anticipated royalty or fee. Publishes book an average of 18 months after acceptance, 3 months after receipt of ms. Photocopied submissions OK. Query for electronic submissions. Computer printout submissions acceptable; prefers letter-quality. Reports in 3 weeks on queries; 6 weeks on submissions. Free book catalog; ms guidelines for SASE.

Nonfiction: Reference, law/legal. Query.

Recent Nonfiction Title: *Ohio Driving Under the Influence Law*, by Mark P. Painter and James M. Looker (handbook).

Tips: "We publish books for attorneys, government officials and professionals in allied fields. Trends in our field include more interest in handbooks, less in costly multi-volume sets; electronic publishing. Writer has the best chance of selling us a book on a hot new topic of law. Check citations and quotations carefully."

BANTAM BOOKS, Subsidiary of Bantam/Doubleday/Dell, 666 Fifth Ave., New York NY 10010. (212)765-6500. Imprints include Spectra, Windstone, New Age, Bantam Classics, Bantam New Fiction, Loveswept. Publishes hardcover, trade paperback and mass market paperback originals, trade paperback and mass market paperback reprints. Publishes 650 titles/year. Buys no books from unagented writers. Pays 4-15% royalty. Publishes book an average of 1 year after ms is accepted. Simultaneous and photocopied submissions OK. Computer printout submissions OK; prefers letter-quality. Reports in 3 weeks on queries; 1 month on ms.

Nonfiction: Biography, coffee table book, how-to, cookbook, humor, illustrated book, juvenile and self-help. Subjects include Americana, anthropology/archaelogy, business/economics, child guidance/parenting, computers and electronics, cooking, foods and nutrition, gay/lesbian, government/politics, health/medicine, history, language/literature, military/war, money/finance, music/dance, philosophy, psychology, religion, science, sociology, sports and travel. Query or submit outline/synopsis or complete ms through agent only. All unsolicited mss are returned unopened.

Recent Nonfiction Title: *A Brief History of Time*, by Stephen Hawking.

Fiction: Adventure, fantasy, feminist, gay/lesbian, historical, horror, juvenile, literary, mainstream/contemporary, mystery, romance, science fiction, suspense, western, young adult. Query or submit outline/synopsis or complete ms through agent only. All unsolicited mss are returned unopened.

Recent Fiction Title: *The Negotiator*, by Frederick Forsythe.

BARRON'S EDUCATIONAL SERIES, INC., 250 Wireless Blvd., Hauppauge NY 11788. FAX: (516)434-3723. Publishes hardcover and paperback originals and software. Publishes 170 titles/year. 10% of books from first-time authors; 90% of books from unagented writers. Pays royalty, based on both wholesale and retail price. Publishes book an average of 9 months after acceptance. Simultaneous and photocopied submissions OK. Computer printout OK; prefers letter-quality. Reports in 3 months. Book catalog $5.

Nonfiction: Adult education, art, business, cookbooks, crafts, foreign language, review books, guidance, pet books, travel, literary guides, juvenile, young adult sports, test preparation materials and textbooks. Reviews artwork/photos as part of package. Query or submit outline/synopsis and 2-3 sample chapters. Accepts nonfiction translations.

Recent Nonfiction Title: *Wild About Munchies*, by Dotty Griffith.

Tips: "The writer has the best chance of selling us a book that will fit into one of our series."

‡BART BOOKS, Imprint of Interpub Communications, Inc., 155 East 34th St., New York NY 10016. (212)696-9141. Publisher: Norman Goldfind. Publishes trade and mass market paperback originals and mass market paperback reprints. Averages 60 titles/year. Receives 200 submissions/year. 10% of books from first-time authors; 20% from unagented writers. Pays 6-10% minimum on retail price. Offers $1,500 average advance.

Publishes book an average of 1 year after acceptance. Simultaneous and photocopied submissions OK. Reports in 3 weeks on queries; 2 months on mss. Free book catalog.

Nonfiction: Biography, cookbook, how-to, humor, reference and self-help. Subjects include child guidance/parenting, cooking, foods and nutrition, health/medicine, psychology, sports and true crime. Query. Submit outline/synopsis and sample chapters. All unsolicited mss are returned unopened. Reviews artwork/photos as part of ms package.

Recent Nonfiction Title: *The Nut Cookbook*, by William I. Kaufman (cookbook).

Fiction: Adventure, historical, horror, humor, mainstream/contemporary, occult and suspense. Query. Submit outline/synopsis and sample chapters. All unsolicited mss are returned unopened.

Recent Fiction Title: *The Hucksters of Holiness*, by Ron Gorton.

‡**BEACON HILL PRESS OF KANSAS CITY**, Box 419527, Kansas City MO 64141. Book division of Nazarene Publishing House. Coordinator: Betty Fuhrman. Publishes hardcover and paperback originals. Averages 65-70 titles/year. Offers "standard contract (sometimes flat rate purchase). Advance on royalty is paid on first 1,000 copies at publication date. On standard contract, pays 10% on first 10,000 copies and 12% on subsequent copies at the end of each calendar year." Publishes book an average of 2 years after acceptance. Computer printout submissions acceptable; prefers letter-quality. Reports in 4-8 months unless immediately returned. "Book Committee meets quarterly to select from the manuscripts which will be published."

Nonfiction: Inspirational, Bible-based. Doctrinally must conform to the evangelical, Wesleyan tradition. Conservative view of Bible. No autobiography, poetry, devotional collections, or children's picture books. Accent on holy living; encouragement in daily Christian life. Popular style books usually under 128 pages. Query. Textbooks "almost exclusively done on assignment." Full ms or outline/sample chapters. Length: 20,000-40,000 words.

Recent Nonfiction Title: *No! The Positive Response to Alcohol*, by Jerry D. Hull.

BEAR AND CO., INC., Drawer 2860, Santa Fe NM 87504-2860. (505)983-9868. Vice President Editorial: Barbara Clow. Publishes trade paperback originals. Averages 12 titles/year. Receives 6,000 submissions/year. 20% of books from first-time authors; 80% of books from unagented writers. Pays 8-10% royalty. Publishes book an average of 18 months after acceptance. Query for electronic submissions. Computer printout submissions OK; prefers letter-quality. Reports in 1 month on queries; 3 months on mss. "No response without SASE." Free book catalog.

Nonfiction: Illustrated books, science, theology, mysticism, religion and ecology. "We publish books to 'heal and celebrate the earth.' Our interest is in New Age, western mystics, new science, ecology. We are not interested in how-to, self-help, etc. Our readers are people who are open to new ways of looking at the world. They are spiritually oriented but not necessarily religious; interested in healing of the earth, peace issues, and receptive to New Age ideas." Query or submit outline/synopsis and sample chapters. Reviews artwork/photos as part of ms package.

Recent Nonfiction Title: *Medicine Cards*, by David Carson and Jamie Sams.

‡**BEAR FLAG BOOKS**, Subsidiary of Padre Productions, Box 840, Arroyo Grande CA 93420-0840. (805)473-1947. Publisher: Lachlan P. MacDonald. Publishes hardcover and trade paperback originals and reprints. Publishes 6-8 titles/year. Receives 500 submissions/year. 80% of books from first-time authors; 90% from unagented writers. Pays 6-10% royalty on retail price; offers varying advance. Publishes book an average of 2 years after acceptance. Simultaneous and photocopied submissions OK. Computer printout submissions OK. Reports in 2 weeks on queries; 2 months on ms. Book catalog for 9 × 12 SAE and 2 first class stamps. Manuscript guidelines for #10 SAE.

Nonfiction: Biography, illustrated book and reference. Subjects include Americana, animals, anthropology/archaeology, history (California and West), nature/environment, photography, recreation, regional and travel. "Best bet is photo-illustrated to a specific county or park or region of California. No children's picture books. We prefer adult-level material." Submit outline/synopsis and sample chapters or complete ms.

Recent Nonfiction Title: *Sierra Mountaineering*, by Leonard Daughenbauth (history).

Fiction: "We would only consider historical fiction with a strong basis in California history and biography."

Tips: "Travelers of all ages, teachers, local residents and libraries are our audience. If I were a writer trying to market a book today, I would complete a guidebook or biography or history, then offer as many unique illustrations as possible, especially unpublished material. Try to fill a market niche."

BEAU LAC PUBLISHERS, Box 248, Chuluota FL 32766. Publishes hardcover and paperback originals.

Nonfiction: "Military subjects. Specialist in social side of service life." Query.

Recent Nonfiction Title: *The Officer's Family Social Guide*, by Mary Preston Gross.

‡**BEHRMAN HOUSE INC.**, 235 Watchung Ave., W. Orange NJ 07052. (202)669-0447. Subsidiary includes Rossel Books. Managing Editor: Adam Bengal. Publishes trade paperback originals and reprints. Averages 20 titles/year. Receives 200 submissions/year. 20% of books from first-time authors; 95% from unagented writers. Pays 2-10% on wholesale price or retail price. Buys mss outright for $500-10,000. Offers $1,000

average advance. Publishes book an average of 18 months after acceptance. Simultaneous and photocopied submissions OK. Computer printout submissions OK; prefers letter-quality. Reports in 2 weeks on queries; 1 month on mss. Free book catalog and manuscript guidelines.
Nonfiction: Juvenile (1-18), reference and textbook. Subjects include religion. "We want Jewish textbooks for the El-Hi market." Query. Submit outline/synopsis and sample chapters.

THE BENJAMIN COMPANY, INC., One Westchester Plaza, Elmsford NY 10523. (914)592-8088. FAX (914)997-7214. President: Ted Benjamin. Publishes hardcover and paperback originals. Averages 20-25 titles/year. 90-100% of books from unagented writers. "Usually commissions author to write specific book; seldom accepts proffered manuscripts." Publishes book an average of 6 months after acceptance. Buys mss by outright purchase. Offers advance. Simultaneous and photocopied submissions OK. Query for electronic submissions. Computer printout submissions acceptable; prefers letter-quality. Reports in 2 months.
Nonfiction: Business/economics, cookbooks, cooking and foods, health, hobbies, how-to, self-help, sports and consumerism. "Ours is a very specialized kind of publishing—for clients (industrial and association) to use in promotional, PR, or educational programs. If an author has an idea for a book and close connections with a company that might be interested in using that book, we will be very interested in working together with the author to 'sell' the program and the idea of a special book for that company. Once published, our books do get trade distribution through a distributing publisher, so the author generally sees the book in regular book outlets as well as in the special programs undertaken by the sponsoring company. We do not encourage submission of manuscripts. We usually commission an author to write for us. The most helpful thing an author can do is to let us know what he or she has written, or what subjects he or she feels competent to write about. We will contact the author when our needs indicate that the author might be the right person to produce a needed manuscript." Query. Submit outline/synopsis and 1 sample chapter. Looks for "possibility of tie-in with sponsoring company or association."
Recent Nonfiction Title: *A Century of Caring*, for Upjohn.

ROBERT BENTLEY, INC., Automotive Publishers, 1000 Massachusetts Ave., Cambridge MA 02138. (617)547-4170. Publisher: Michael Bentley. Publishes hardcover and trade paperback originals and reprints. Publishes 15-20 titles/year. 20% of books are from first-time authors; 90% from unagented writers. Pays 5-15% royalty on wholesale price; or makes outright purchase. Offers $2,000-6,000 average advance. Publishes book an average of 5 months after acceptance. Query for electronic submissions. Computer printout submissions OK; prefers letter-quality. Reports in 1 month. Book catalog and ms guidelines for SAE and 45¢ postage.
Nonfiction: Coffee-table book, how-to, technical, automotive only. Subjects include automotive specialties. Query or submit outline/synopsis and sample chapters or complete ms. Reviews artwork/photos as part of manuscript package.
Recent Nonfiction Title: *The Design and Tuning of Competitive Engines*, by Philip H. Smith (automotive).
Tips: "We are excited about the possibilities and growth in the automobile enthusiast book market. Our audience is primarily composed of serious and intelligent, automobile, sports car, or racing enthusiasts, automotive technicians and high performance tuners."

‡*BERGH PUBLISHING, INC., Subsidiary of Bergh & Bergh Verlagsanstalt GmbH, Switzerland, Suite 715, 276 Fifth Ave., New York NY 10001. (212)686-8551. Contact: Sven-Erik Bergh. Publishes hardcover originals and reprints. Firm averages 10-15 titles/year. Receives 74 submissions/year. 40% of books from first-time authors; 60% from unagented writers. Subsidy publishes 2% of books. Pays 10-15% on wholesale price. Offers $3000 average advance. Publishes book an average of 6 months after acceptance. Simultaneous submissions OK. Computer printout submissions OK; no dot-matrix. Reports in 2 weeks on queries. Free book catalog.
Nonfiction: Biography, cookbook, illustrated book and juvenile. Subjects include animals, cooking, foods and nutrition, government/politics, music/dance, psychology, sports and travel. Query. Reviews artwork/photos as part of ms package.
Recent Nonfiction Title: *My Name is Regine*, by Regine.
Fiction: Adventure, erotica, fantasy, feminist, literary, mainstream/contemporary, mystery, occult, picture books, suspense and young adult. Query.

BETHANY HOUSE PUBLISHERS, Subsidiary of Bethany Fellowship, Inc., 6820 Auto Club Rd., Minneapolis MN 55438. (612)944-2121. Editorial Director: Carol Johnson. Publishes hardcover and paperback originals and reprints. "Contracts negotiable." Averages 60 titles/year; receives 1,200 submissions annually. 15% of books from first-time authors; 95% of books from unagented writers. Publishes book an average of 9-18

For information on book publishers' areas of interest, see the nonfiction and fiction sections in the Book Publishers Subject Index.

months after acceptance. Simultaneous and photocopied submissions OK. Query for electronic submissions. Computer printout submissions acceptable. Reports in 2 months. Book catalog and ms guidelines for 9x12 SAE and 5 first class stamps.

Nonfiction: Publishes reference (lay-oriented); devotional (evangelical, charismatic); and personal growth books. Submit outline and 2-3 sample chapters. Looks for "provocative subject, quality writing style, authoritative presentation, unique approach, sound Christian truth." Reviews artwork/photos as part of ms package.

Recent Nonfiction Title: *Kingdom of the Cults*, by Dr. Walter Martin.

Fiction: Well written stories with a Christian message. No poetry. Submit synopsis and 2-3 sample chapters to Acquisitions Editor. Guidelines available.

Recent Fiction Title: *Vienna Prelude*, by Bodie Thoene.

Tips: "The writer has the best chance of selling our firm a book that will market well in the Christian bookstore. In your query, list other books in this category (price, length, main thrust), and tell how yours is better or unique."

BETTER HOMES AND GARDENS BOOKS, Division of the Meredith Corporation, 1716 Locust St., Des Moines IA 50336. FAX: (515)284-2700. Managing Editor: David A. Kirchner. Publishes hardcover and trade paperback originals. Averages 40 titles/year. "The majority of our books are produced by on-staff editors, but we often use freelance writers on assignment for sections or chapters of books already in progress." Will consider photocopied submissions. Reports in 6 weeks.

Nonfiction: "We publish nonfiction in many family and home-service categories, including gardening, decorating and remodeling, crafts, money management, handyman's topics, cooking and nutrition, Christmas activities, and other subjects of home-service value. Emphasis is on how-to and on stimulating people to action. We require concise, factual writing. Audience is primarily husbands and wives with home and family as their main center of interest. Style should be informative and lively with a straightforward approach. Stress the positive. Emphasis is entirely on reader service. Because most of our books are produced by on-staff editors, we're less interested in book-length manuscripts than in hearing from freelance writers with solid expertise in gardening, do-it-yourself, health/fitness, and home decorating. We have no need at present for cookbooks or cookbook authors. Publisher recommends careful study of specific Better Homes and Gardens Books titles before submitting material." Prefers outline and sample chapters. "Please include SASE with appropriate return postage."

Recent Nonfiction Title: *Come Home to Country*.

Tips: "Writers often fail to familiarize themselves with the catalog/backlist of the publishers to whom they are submitting. We expect heavier emphasis on health/fitness, gardening and do-it-yourself titles. But, again, we're most interested in hearing from freelance writers with subject expertise in these areas than in receiving queries for book-length manuscripts. Queries/mss may be routed to other editors in the publishing group."

BETTERWAY PUBLICATIONS, INC., White Hall VA 22987. (804)823-5661. Senior Editor: Hilary Swinson. Publishes hardcover and trade paperback originals. Averages 24-25 titles/year; receives 1,200 submissions annually. 50-60% of books from first-time authors; 90% of books from unagented writers. Pays 12-16% royalty on wholesale price; offers $500-1,500 advance. Publishes book an average of 8 months after acceptance. Simultaneous and (quality copies please) photocopied submissions OK. Query for electronic submissions. Computer printout submissions acceptable; no dot-matrix. Reports in 6 weeks on queries; 2 months on mss. Book catalog for 9x12 SAE and 3 first class stamps; ms guidelines for #10 SAE and 2 first class stamps.

Nonfiction: How-to, illustrated book, juvenile (10-14), reference, and self-help on business and economics, cooking and foods, health, hobbies, psychology, sociology, genealogy, small businesses, all aspects of homebuilding and ownership ("e.g., contracting your own home, remodeling, decorating, painting, buying/selling real estate, etc."). "We are seeking to expand our list in small and home-based business guides or handbooks, parenting books, genealogy books (advanced how-to), theater crafts books, popular music/jazz reference books, 'collectibles' source books." No cookbooks. Submit outline/synopsis and sample chapters. Reviews artwork/photos.

Recent Nonfiction Title: *Collecting Stamps for Pleasure & Profit*, by Barry Krause.

Tips: "We are continuing our emphasis on small and home business books and all aspects of housing/home ownership. We're also looking for distinctive (if not unique) how-to books, like *Gameplan—The Game Inventor's Handbook*, *The Theater Props Handbook*, and *Garage Sale Mania!*"

BETWEEN THE LINES INC., 394 Euclid Ave., Toronto, Ontario M6G 259 Canada. (416)925-8260. FAX: (416)324-8268. Editor: Robert Clarke. Publishes trade paperback originals. Averages 9-10 titles/year. Receives 150 submissions/year. 75% of books are from first-time authors; 100% from unagented writers. Pays 8-15% royalty. Offers average advance of $500. Publishes ms an average of 10 months after acceptance. Simultaneous and photocopied submissions OK. Query for electronic submissions. Computer printout submissions OK; prefers letter-quality. Reports in 2 months on queries; 3 months on mss. Free book catalog. Ms guidelines for #10 SASE.

Nonfiction: Subjects include agriculture/horticulture, business and economics, education, ethnic, gay/lesbian, government/politics, health/medicine, women's issues/studies. Query or submit outline/synopsis and sample chapters. Reviews artwork/photos as part of ms package.

Recent Nonfiction Title: *The Colonized Eye: Rethinking the Grierson Legend*, by Joyce Nelson (culture/politics).

*BINFORD & MORT PUBLISHING, 1202 N.W. 17th Ave., Portland OR 97209. (503)221-0866. Publisher: James Gardenier. Publishes hardcover and paperback originals and reprints. Receives 500 submissions annually. 60% of books from first-time authors; 90% of books from unagented writers. Average print order for a writer's first book is 5,000. Pays 10% royalty on retail price; offers variable advance (to established authors). Publishes about 10-12 titles annually. Occasionally does some subsidy publishing (10%), at author's request. Publishes book an average of 1 year after acceptance. Reports in 4 months. Computer printout submissions acceptable; prefers letter-quality.

Nonfiction: Books about the Pacific Coast and the Northwest. Subjects include Western Americana, biography, history, nature, maritime, recreation, reference, and travel. Query with sample chapters and SASE. Reviews artwork/photos as part of ms package.

Recent Nonfiction Title: *Kid on the River*, by Dean Nichols.

‡JOHN F. BLAIR, PUBLISHER, 1406 Plaza Dr., Winston-Salem NC 27103. (919)768-1374. Editor: Stephen Kirk. Publishes hardcover originals, trade paperbacks and occasional reprints; receives 1,000 submissions annually. 20-30% of books from first-time authors; 90% of books from unagented writers. Average print order for a writer's first book is 3,500. Royalty to be negotiated. Publishes book an average of 1-1½ years after acceptance. Query for electronic submissions. Computer printout submissions acceptable; no dot-matrix. Reports in 2 months. Book catalog and ms guidelines for 9x12 SAE and 85¢ postage.

Nonfiction: Especially interested in well-researched adult biography and history. Preference given to books dealing with Southeastern United States. Also interested in environment and Americana; query on other nonfiction topics. Looks for utility and significance. Submit synopsis/outline and first 3 chapters or complete ms. Reviews artwork/photos as part of ms package.

Recent Nonfiction Title: *Being a Boy*, by Paxton Davis (memoirs/autobiography).

Fiction: "We are most interested in serious novels of substance and imagination. Preference given to material related to Southeastern United States." No category fiction, juvenile fiction, picture books or poetry.

Recent Fiction Title: *The Hatterask Incident*, by John D. Randall.

‡BLUE BIRD PUBLISHING, #306, 1713 E. Broadway, Tempe AZ 85282. (602)968-4088. Publisher: Cheryl Gorder. Publishes trade paperback originals. Firm averages 6 titles/year. 50% of books from first-time authors. 100% from unagented writers. Pays 10% royalty on wholesale price; 15% on retail price. Publishes book an average of 9 months after acceptance. Simultaneous and photocopied submissions OK. Computer printout submissions OK. Reports in 6 weeks. Free book catalog and manuscript guidelines.

Nonfiction: How-to, juvenile and reference. Subjects include child guidance/parenting, education (especially home education) and sociology (current social issues). "The home schooling population in the U.S. is exploding. We have a strong market for anything that can be targeted to this group: i.e., home education manuscripts; parenting guides, home business ideas. We would also like to see complete nonfiction manuscripts in current issues, how-to, and juvenile topics." Submit complete ms. Reviews artwork/photos as part of ms package.

Recent Nonfiction Title: *Homeless: Without Addresses in America*, by Gorder.

Fiction: Historical and juvenile. "We have just published our first fiction title (a juvenile fiction)." Submit complete ms.

Recent Fiction Title: *Spacedog's Best Friend*, by Sweeney (juvenile).

Tips: "We are interested if we see a complete manuscript that is aimed toward a general adult nonfiction audience. We are impressed if the writer has really done his homework and the manuscript includes photos, artwork, graphs, charts, and other graphics."

‡BLUE DOLPHIN PUBLISHING, INC., Box 1908, 13386 N. Bloomfield Rd., Nevada City CA 95959. (916)265-6923. President: Paul M. Clemens. Publishes hardcover and trade paperback originals. Firm averages 8 titles/year. Receives 75-100 submissions/year. 75% of books from first-time authors. 90% from unagented writers. Pays 7.5-12.5% on wholesale price. Offers average $1,000 advance. Publishes book an average of 6-9 months after acceptance. Simultaneous and photocopied submissions OK. Query for electronic submissions. Computer printout submissions OK. Reports in 1 month on queries; 2-3 months on mss. Free book catalog and manuscript guidelines.

Nonfiction: Biography, cookbook, how-to, humor, juvenile and self-help. Subjects include anthropology/archaeology, cooking, foods and nutrition, health/medicine, psychology and religion. "We are interested primarily in new age self-help psychology, and comparative spiritual traditions, especially translations from Tibetan or Zen traditions." Submit outline/synopsis and sample chapters. Reviews artwork as part of package.

Recent Nonfiction Title: *Daughter of Fire*, by Irina Tweedie (spiritual/psychological).
Fiction: Feminist, humor, literary, occult and religious. Submit outline/synopsis and sample chapters.
Recent Fiction Title: *A Practical Guide to Creative Senility*, by Donovan Bess (humor/old age).
Poetry: "We will only consider previously published authors of some merit; translations from Japanese, Chinese, Tibetan, Sanskrit." Submit complete ms.
Recent Poetry Title: *Lightly the Harper*, by Jack Tootell (Americana).
Tips: "The new age spiritual seeker interested in self-growth and awareness for oneself and the planet is our audience."

‡BNA BOOKS, Division of The Bureau of National Affairs, Inc., 1231 25th St. NW, Washington DC 20037. (202)452-4276. FAX: (202)452-9186. Harriet G. Berlin, Product Development Manager. Publishes hardcover and softcover originals. Averages 35 titles/year. Receives 200 submissions/year. 20% of books from first-time authors; 95% of books from unagented writers. Pays 5-15% royalty on retail price; offers $1,000 average advance. Simultaneous submissions OK. Publishes book an average of 1 year after acceptance. Reports in 2 months on queries; 3 months on mss. Free book catalog and ms guidelines.
Nonfiction: Reference and professional/scholarly. Subjects include business law and regulation, environment and safety, legal practice, labor relations and human resource management. No biographies, bibliographies, cookbooks, religion books, humor or trade books. Submit detailed table of contents or outline.
Recent Nonfiction Title: *Supreme Court Practice*, sixth edition, by Stern, Gressman and Shapiro (law).
Tips: "Our audience is practicing lawyers and business executives; managers, federal, state, and local government administrators; unions; and libraries. We look for authoritative and comprehensive works on subjects of interest to executives, professionals, and managers, that relate to the interaction of government and business."

BOOKCRAFT, INC., 1848 W. 2300 S., Salt Lake City UT 84119. (801)972-6180. Editorial Manager: Cory H. Maxwell. Publishes (mainly hardcover) originals and reprints. Pays standard 7½-10-12½-15% royalty on retail price; "we rarely give a royalty advance." Averages 40-45 titles/year; receives 500-600 submissions annually. 20% of books from first-time authors; virtually 100% of books from unagented writers. Publishes book an average of 6 months after acceptance. Will consider photocopied submissions. Computer printout submissions acceptable; prefers letter-quality. Reports in about 2 months. Will send general information to prospective authors on request; ms guidelines for #10 SASE.
Nonfiction: "We publish for members of The Church of Jesus Christ of Latter-Day Saints (Mormons) and do not distribute to the national market. All our books are closely oriented to the faith and practices of the LDS church, and we will be glad to review such mss. Mss which have merely a general religious appeal are not acceptable. Ideal book lengths range from about 80 to 240 pages or so, depending on subject, presentation, and age level. We look for a fresh approach—rehashes of well-known concepts or doctrines not acceptable. Mss should be anecdotal unless truly scholarly or on a specialized subject. Outlook must be positive. We do not publish anti-Mormon works. We also publish short and moderate length books for Mormon youth, about ages 14 to 19, mostly nonfiction. These reflect LDS principles without being 'preachy'; must be motivational. 30,000-45,000 words is about the right length, though good, longer mss are not entirely ruled out. This is a tough area to write in, and the mortality rate for such mss is high. We publish only 2 or 3 new juvenile titles annually." No "poetry, plays, personal philosophizings, or family histories." Query. "Include contents page with manuscript."
Recent Nonfiction Title: *Pure in Heart*, by Dallin H. Oaks.
Fiction: Must be closely oriented to LDS faith and practices.
Recent Fiction Title: *On the Side of the Angels*, by Kristen D. Randle.

BOOKMAKERS GUILD, INC., Subsidiary of Dakota Graphics, Inc., 9655 W. Colfax Ave., Lakewood CO 80215. (303)772-7322 or (303)442-5774. Managine Editor: Leah Ann Crussell. Publisher: Barbara J. Ciletti. Publishes hardcover and trade paperback originals. Averages 6-8 titles/year; receives 700 submissions annually. 30% of books from first-time authors; 90% of books from unagented writers. Pays 10% royalty on net receipts. Publishes books an average of 12-18 months after acceptance. Photocopied submissions OK. Letter-quality computer printout submissions acceptable. Mss will not be returned without SASE. Reports in 2 weeks on queries; 2 months on mss after query, 4 months on ms without query. Book catalog and guidelines available.
Nonfiction: Adult reference; contemporary social issues; health; natural history; and psychology (focus on children and family). "We see a continuing focus on families, children and youth, especially books on child advocacy, behavior and education. Also seeking juvenile nonfiction. No how-to, cookbooks, local history, novels, poetry, sci-fi, computers, fashion, sports or works ill-written and ill-conceived." Query or submit outline/synopsis and sample chapters. Sometimes reviews artwork/photos.
Recent Nonfiction Title: *The Future as if it Really Mattered*, by James Garbarino.
Fiction: Juvenile, age 8 and up. "We seek folklore, folktale and saga along classical themes with educational merit. Primarily focus on language and literature." 100 page minimum required. No picture books, but will look at collections of stories that could make a good volume. Query first.

Recent Fiction Title: *The Stolen Appaloosa*, by Levitt and Guralnick.

Tips: "Current concerns regarding the family unit and adolescent growth and development have influenced the type of material that we look for. We focus on those works which seek to educate and inform. We are specifically seeking educational nonfiction in the natural sciences for young adults, as well as adult nonfiction that addresses the issues concerning the well-being of the adolescent, the aged, and the family. Books that are sensitively written, well-researched, and on topics that are not already flooding the market have the best chances of being considered for publication by our firm."

BOREALIS PRESS, LTD., 9 Ashburn Dr., Nepean, Ontario K2E 6N4 Canada. Editorial Director: Frank Tierney. Senior Editor: Glenn Clever. Publishes hardcover and paperback originals. Averages 4 titles/year; receives 400-500 submissions annually. 80% of books from first-time authors; 95% of books from unagented writers. Pays 10% royalty on retail price; no advance. Publishes book an average of 18 months after acceptance. "No multiple submissions or electronic printouts on paper more than 8½ inches wide." Computer printout submissions acceptable; prefers letter-quality. Reports in 8 months. Book catalog $1 with SAE and IRCs.

Nonfiction: "Only material Canadian in content." Query. Reviews artwork/photos as part of ms package. Looks for "style in tone and language, reader interest, and maturity of outlook."

Recent Nonfiction Title: *Canadian Parliamentary Handbook*, by Bejermi.

Fiction: "Only material Canadian in content and dealing with significant aspects of the human situation." Query.

Recent Fiction Title: *Annie*, by Hortie (novel).

Tips: "Ensure that creative writing deals with consequential human affairs, not just action, sensation, or cutesy stuff."

THE BORGO PRESS, Box 2845, San Bernardino CA 92406. (714)884-5813. Publisher: Robert Reginald. Editor: Mary A. Burgess. Publishes hardcover and paperback originals. Averages 30 titles/year; receives 200 submissions annually. 5% of books from first-time authors; 80% of books from unagented writers. Pays royalty on retail price: "10% of gross." No advance. Publishes book an average of 1-2 years after acceptance. "Virtually all of our sales are to the academic library market." Query for electronic submissions. Computer printout submissions acceptable. Reports in 3 months minimum. Book catalog and writer's guidelines for #10 SAE and 3 first class stamps.

Nonfiction: Publishes literary critiques, bibliographies, historical research, film critiques, theatrical research, interview volumes, biographies, social studies, political science, and reference works for the academic library market. Query with letter or outline/synopsis and 1 sample chapter. "All of our books, without exception, are published in open-ended, numbered, monographic series. Do not submit proposals until you have looked at actual copies of Borgo Press publications. We are *not* a market for fiction, poetry, popular nonfiction, artwork, or anything else except scholarly monographs in the humanities and social sciences. We discard unsolicited manuscripts from outside of our subject fields which are not accompanied by SASEs."

Recent Nonfiction Title: *The Work of Colin Wilson: An Annotated Bibliography and Guide*, by Stanley.

Tips: "We are currently buying comprehensible, annotated bibliographies of twentieth-century writers; these must be produced to a strict series format (available on request)."

‡*DON BOSCO PUBLICATIONS, 475 N. Ave., Box T, New Rochelle NY 10802. (914)576-0122. Subsidiaries include Salesiana Publishers. Editorial Director: James Hurley. Publishes hardcover and trade paperback originals. Averages 6-10 titles/year; receives 50 submissions annually. 15% of books from first-time authors; 100% of books from unagented writers. Average print order for a writer's first book is 3,000. Subsidy publishes 10% of books. Subsidy publishes (nonauthor) 30% of books. "We judge the content of the manuscript and quality to be sure it fits the description of our house. We subsidy publish for nonprofit and religious societies." Pays 5-10% royalty on retail price; offers average $100 advance. Publishes book an average of 10 months after acceptance. Computer printout submissions acceptable; no dot-matrix. Reports in 2 weeks on queries; 2 months on mss. Free book catalog.

Nonfiction: Biography, juvenile and textbook on Roman Catholic religion. "Biographies of outstanding Christian men and women of today. We are a new publisher with wide experience in school marketing, especially in religious education field." Accepts nonfiction translations from Italian and Spanish. Query or submit outline/synopsis and 2 sample chapters. Occasionally reviews artwork/photos as part of ms package.

Recent Nonfiction Title: *First Lady of the World*, by Peter Lappin.

Tips: Queries/mss may be routed to other editors in the publishing group.

THE BOSTON MILLS PRESS, 132 Main St., Erin, Ontario N0B 1T0 Canada. (519)833-2407. President: John Denison. Publishes hardcover and trade paperback originals. Averages 16 titles/year; receives 100 submissions annually. 75% of books from first-time authors; 90% of books from unagented writers. Pays 6-10% royalty on retail price; no advance. Publishes book an average of 8 months after acceptance. Simultaneous and photocopied submissions OK. Query for electronic submissions. Computer printout submissions acceptable. Reports in 2 weeks on queries; 1 month on mss. Free book catalog.

Nonfiction: Illustrated book. Subjects include history. "We're interested in anything to do with Canadian or American history—especially transportation. We like books with a small, strong market." No autobiographies. Query. Reviews artwork/photos as part of ms package.

Recent Nonfiction Title: *Next Stop Grand Central*, by Stan Fischler (railway history).

Tips: "We can't compete with the big boys so we stay with short-run specific market books that bigger firms can't handle. We've done well this way so we'll continue in the same vein. We tend to accept books from completed manuscripts."

BRADBURY PRESS, Affiliate of Macmillan, Inc., 866 3rd Ave., New York NY 10022. (212)702-9809. Editorial Director: Barbara Lalicki. Publishes hardcover originals for children and young adults. Averages 30 titles/year. Pays royalty and offers advance. Reports in 3 months. Book catalog and ms guidelines for 9x12 SAE with 4 first class stamps.

Fiction: Picture books, concept books, photo essays and novels for elementary school children. Also "stories about real kids; special interest in realistic dialogue." No adult ms. No religious material. Submit complete ms.

Recent Fiction Title: *Hatchet*, by Gary Paulsen (novel).

Tips: "We're looking for historically accurate material that will interest kids in the past. We also look for science writers who can explain concepts of physics and biology on an elementary school level."

ALLEN D. BRAGDON PUBLISHERS, INC., Tupelo Rd., South Yarmouth MA 02664. (508)398-4440. Subsidiaries include Brownstone Library and Munchie Books. Publisher: Allen Bragdon. Publishes hardcover originals and reprints and trade paperback originals. Averages 8 titles/year.

Nonfiction: Cookbook, how-to and illustrated book. Subjects include Americana, cooking and foods and hobbies.

Recent Nonfiction Title: *Joy Through the World*, by UNICEF.

Tips: "We are looking for old time Americana at 500 words; home skills with color photos or illustrations." Our mss are bought outright for a multi-volume continuity encyclopedia.

BRANDEN PUBLISHING CO., INC., 17 Station St., Box 843, Brookline Village MA 02147. (617)734-2045. President: Adolph Caso. Subsidiaries include International Pocket Library and Popular Technology, Four Seas and Brashear. Publishes hardcover and trade paperback originals, hardcover and trade paperback reprints and software. Averages 10 titles/year; receives 400 submissions annually. 80% of books from first-time authors; 90% of books from unagented writers. Average print order for a writer's first book is 3,000. Pays 5-10% royalty on wholesale price; offers $1,000 maximum advance. Publishes book an average of 10 months after acceptance. Query for electronic submissions. Computer printout submissions acceptable; prefers letter-quality. Reports in 1 week on queries; 2 months on mss. Book catalog for #10 SASE.

Nonfiction: Biography, illustrated book, juvenile, reference, technical and textbook. Subjects include Americana, art, computers, health, history, music, photography, politics, sociology, software and classics. Especially looking for "about 10 manuscripts on national and international subjects, including biographies of well-known individuals." No religion or philosophy. Prefers paragraph query with author's vita and SASE; no unsolicited mss. Reviews artwork/photos as part of ms package.

Recent Nonfiction Title: *Pay Dirt—Divorces of Rich & Famous*.

Fiction: Adventure (well-written, realistic); ethnic (histories, integration); historical (especially biographies); mainstream (emphasis on youth and immigrants); religious (historical-reconstructive); romance (novels with well-drawn characters). No science, mystery or pornography. Paragraph query with author's vita and SASE; no unsolicited mss.

Recent Fiction Title: *The Saving Rain*, by Elsie Webber.

Poetry: No religious, humorous or autobiographical poetry books. Submit 5 poems.

Recent Poetry Title: *Dante's Inferno*, by D. Alighieri.

Tips: "Branden publishes only manuscripts determined to have a significant impact on modern society. Our audience is a well-read general public, professionals, college students, and some high school students. If I were a writer trying to market a book today, I would thoroughly investigate the number of potential readers interested in the content of my book. We like books by or about women."

‡BREAKWATER BOOKS, Box 2188, St. John's Newfoundland A1C 6E6 Canada. (709)722-6680. Firm publishes hardcover and trade paperback originals. Publishes 25-30 titles/year. Pays 10% royalty on retail price. Publishes book an average of 2 years after acceptance. Simultaneous and photocopied submissions OK. Computer printout submissions OK. Reports in 3 months. Free book catalog.

For explanation of symbols, see the Key to Symbols and Abbreviations on Page 5. For unfamiliar words, see the Glossary.

Nonfiction: Biography, coffee table book, cookbook, humor, illustrated book, juvenile, reference, software, textbook. Subjects include computers and electronics, cooking, foods and nutrition, education, history, language/literature, nature/environment, photography, recreation, regional, religion, sociology and folklore. Submit outline/synopsis and sample chapters or send complete ms. Reviews artwork/photos as part of ms package.

Recent Nonfiction Title: *The Vexed Question: Denominational Education in a Secular Age*, by William McKim, et. al.

Fiction: Adventure, ethnic, experimental, fantasy, feminist, historical, humor, juvenile, literary, mainstream/contemporary, mystery, picture books, plays, romance, science fiction, short story collections, suspense, young adult. Submit outline/synopsis and sample chapters or send complete ms.

Recent Fiction Title: *January, February, June or July*, by Helen Porter.

Poetry: Submit complete ms.

Recent Poetry Title: *The Edge of Beulah*, by David Elliott.

*BRETHREN PRESS, 1451 Dundee Ave., Elgin IL 60120. (312)742-5100. Owned and managed by The Church of the Brethren General Board. Book Editor: Jeanne Donovan. Publishes hardcover and trade paperback originals, and trade paperback reprints. Averages 10-12 titles/year; receives 150 queries/submissions annually. 30% of books from first-time authors; 90% of books from unagented writers. Subsidy publishes (nonauthor) 30% of books. Payment depends on target market, "some manuscripts are purchased outright." Typical contract: up to $1,000 advance against 10% net royalties for first 5,000 copies; 12% net on 5,001 copies and up. Publishes book an average of 1 year after acceptance. Simultaneous and photocopied submissions OK. Query for electronic submissions. Computer printout submissions acceptable; prefers letter-quality. Reports in 2 months on queries; 6 months ("hopefully") on mss. Book catalog and mss guidelines for #10 SAE with 2 first class stamps.

Nonfiction: Subjects include business and economics, health, history, philosophy, politics, psychology, religion and sociology. All titles should be from a faith perspective. Needs theology, Bible study, devotional, peace-related, practical discipleship, social issues, simple living, family life, "Plain People" heritage, and current and international events. Query or submit outline/synopsis and sample chapters. Reviews artwork/photos as part of ms package.

Recent Nonfiction Title: *Glimpses of China*, by Ingrid Rogers.

Fiction: Religious. "The only fiction published in recent years has been inspirational, with historical settings in 'Pennsylvania Dutch'/Plain People context." No romances. Query.

Tips: "We prefer timely issues with solid theological content, well-written for the average reader or religious professionals. Adhere to Chicago *Manual of Style* and *Church of the Brethren Handbook of Style*."

*BRIARCLIFF PRESS PUBLISHERS, 11 Wimbledon Ct., Jericho NY 11753. Editorial Director: Trudy Settel. Senior Editor: J. Frieman. Publishes hardcover and paperback originals. Averages 5-7 titles/year; receives 250 submissions annually. 10% of books from first-time authors; 60% of books from unagented writers. Average print order for a writer's first book is 5,000. Subsidy publishes 20% of books. Pays $4,000-5,000 for outright purchase; offers average of $1,000 advance. Publishes book an average of 6 months after acceptance. Computer printout submissions acceptable; no dot-matrix. "We do not use unsolicited manuscripts. Ours are custom books prepared for businesses, and assignments are initiated by us."

Nonfiction: How-to, cookbooks, sports, travel, fitness/health, business and finance, diet, gardening and crafts. "We want our books to be designed to meet the needs of specific businesses." Accepts nonfiction translations from French, German and Italian. Query. Submit outline and 2 sample chapters. Reviews artwork/photos as part of ms package.

Recent Nonfiction Title: *Eat to Your Heart's Content*, by Alisone Corete.

BRICK HOUSE PUBLISHING CO., Box 134, 11 Thoreau Rd, Acton MA 01720. (508)635-9800. Publisher: Robert Runck. Publishes hardcover and trade paperback originals. Averages 12 titles/year; receives 500 submissions annually. 20% of books from first-time authors; 100% of books from unagented writers. Pays 10-15% royalty on wholesale price. Offers average $1,000 advance. Publishes book an average of 6 months after acceptance. Simultaneous and photocopied submissions OK. Query for electronic submissions. Computer printout submissions acceptable; prefers letter-quality. Reports in 2 weeks on queries; 3 months on mss. Book catalog and ms guidelines for 9x12 SAE with 3 first class stamps.

Nonfiction: How-to, reference, technical and textbook. Subjects include business and consumer advice. "We are looking for writers to do books in the following areas: practical guidance and information for people running small businesses, consumer trade books on money and job topics, and college business textbooks." Query with synopses.

Recent Nonfiction Title: *Planning and Financing the New Venture*, by Jeffry Timmons.

Tips: "A common mistake writers make is not addressing the following questions in their query/proposals: What are my qualifications for writing this book? Why would anyone want the book enough to pay for it in a bookstore? What can I do to help promote the book?"

BRISTOL PUBLISHING ENTERPRISES, INC., Box 1737, 14692 Wicks Blvd., San Leandro CA 94577. (415)895-4461. Imprints include Nitty Gritty Cookbooks. Chairman: Patricia J. Hall. Publishes 6-8 titles/year. Receives approximately 200 proposals/year. 75% of books from first/time authors; 100% from unagented writers. Pays 3-6% royalty on wholesale price. Average advance is $100. Publishes ms an average of 1 year after acceptance. Computer printout submissions OK; prefers letter-quality. Reports in 2 months. Book catalog for 6x9 SAE with 2 first class stamps.
Nonfiction: Cookbooks. Submit outline/synopsis and sample chapters.
Recent Nonfiction Title: *Creative Lunch Box*, by Simmons.

BROADMAN PRESS, 127 9th Ave. N, Nashville TN 37234. Editorial Director: Harold S. Smith. Publishes hardcover and paperback originals (85%) and reprints (15%). Averages 75 titles/year. Pays 10% royalty on retail price; no advance. Photocopied submissions OK "only if they're sharp and clear." Computer printouts acceptable; prefers letter-quality. Reports in 2 months.
Nonfiction: Religion. "We are open to freelance submissions in the children's and inspirational areas. Materials in both areas must be suited for a conservative Protestant readership. No poetry, biography, sermons, or anything outside the area of the Protestant tradition." Query, submit outline/synopsis and sample chapters, or submit complete ms. Reviews artwork/photos as part of ms package. Writer's guidelines for #10 SAE with 2 first class stamps.
Fiction: Religious. "We publish almost no fiction—less than five titles per year. For our occasional publication we want not only a very good story, but also one that sets forth Christian values. Nothing that lacks a positive Christian emphasis; nothing that fails to sustain reader interest." Submit complete ms with synopsis.
Tips: "Textbook and family material are becoming an important forum for us—Bible study is very good for us, but our publishing is largely restricted in this area to works that we enlist on the basis of specific author qualifications. Preparation for the future and living with life's stresses and complexities are trends in the subject area."

BROADWAY PRESS, Suite 407, 120 Duane St., New York NY 10007. (212)693-0570. Publisher: David Rodger. Publishes trade paperback originals. Averages 5-10 titles/year; receives 20-30 submissions annually. 50% of books from first-time authors; 75% of books from unagented writers. Pays negotiable royalty. Publishes book an average of 18 months after acceptance. Simultaneous and photocopied submissions OK. Computer printout submissions acceptable. Reports in 1 month on queries.
Nonfiction: Reference and technical. Subjects include theatre, film, television and the performing arts. "We're looking for professionally-oriented and authored books. Most of our books are in-house publications, but we will accept author's queries for titles fitting the above criteria." Submit outline/synopsis and sample chapters.
Recent Nonfiction Title: *Backstage Handbook*, by Paul Carter.
Tips: "A common mistake writers make is not following up on submissions and queries."

C Q PRESS, Imprint of Congressional Quarterly, Inc., 1414 22nd St. NW, Washington DC 20037. (202)887-8642. Director: Joanne Daniels. Publishes hardcover and paperback originals. Receives 20-30 submissions annually. 90% of books from unagented writers. Pays standard college royalty on wholesale price; offers college text advance. Publishes book an average of 5 months after acceptance of final ms. Simultaneous and photocopied submissions OK. Computer printout submissions acceptable; no dot-matrix. Reports in 3 months. Free book catalog.
Nonfiction: College text. All levels of political science texts. "We are one of the most distinguished publishers in the area of political science textbooks." Submit outline and sample chapter.
Recent Nonfiction Title: *Mass Media and American Politics 3/E*, 6/e, by Doris Graber.

*C.S.S. PUBLISHING COMPANY, 628 South Main St., Lima OH 45804. (419)227-1818. Imprints include Fairway Press. Editorial Director: Dawn Lausa. Publishes trade paperback originals. Publishes 50 titles/year. Receives 300 mss/year. 40% of books from first-time authors; 100% from unagented writers. Subsidy publishes 20%. "If books have limited market appeal and/or deal with basically same subject matter as title already on list, we will consider subsidy option." Pays 4-12% royalty on wholesale price or outright purchase of $25-250. Publishes book 2 years after acceptance. Simultaneous submissions OK. Query for electronic submissions. Computer printout submissions OK; no dot-matrix. Reports on mss in 6 months. Book catalog free on request; ms guidelines for #10 SASE.
Nonfiction: Humor (religious) and self-help (religious). Subjects include religion: "Christian resources for mainline Protestant denominations; some Catholic resources. We are interested in sermon and worship resources, preaching illustrations, sermon seasonings, some Bible study, inspirationals, pastoral care, plays, practical theology, newsletter and bulletin board blurbs, church growth, success stories, teacher helps/training helps, church program material. Also sermon and worship resources based on the three-year lectionary; marriage helps and wedding services. We are not interested in the 'born again' movement or hellfire and brimstone stuff. No heavy theology, philosophy or scholarly themes." Reviews photos/artwork as part of ms package.

Recent Nonfiction Title: *The Penguin Principles*, by David Belasic and Paul Schmidt (practical theology).
Tips: "Books that sell well for us are seasonal sermon and worship resources; books aimed at clergy on professional growth and survival; also books of children's object lessons; seasonal plays (i.e. Christmas/Lent/Easter etc.). With church attendance declining, books on creative church growth will be popular. Our primary market is the clergy in all mainline denominations; others include church leaders, movers and shakers, education directors, Sunday school teachers, women's groups, youth leaders; to a certain extent we publish for the Christian layperson. Write something that makes Christianity applicable to the contemporary world, something useful to the struggling, searching Christian. The treatment might be humorous, certainly unique. We have published a few titles that other houses would not touch—with some degree of success. We are open to new ideas and would be pleased to see anything new, different, creative, and well-written that fits our traditional markets."

‡CAMBRIDGE CAREER PRODUCTS, Box 2153, Charleston WV 25328-2153. (800)468-4227. Subsidiaries include: Cambridge Home Economics, Cambridge Physical Education & Health. President: Edward T. Gardner, Ph.D. Publishes hardcover and trade paperback originals. Firm averages 12 titles/year. Receives 20 submissions/year. 20% of books from first-time authors. 90% from unagented writers. Pays 6-15% on wholesale price, $1,500-18,500 outright purchase. Offers $1,200 average advance. Publishes book an average of 8 months after acceptance. Simultaneous and photocopied submissions OK. Computer printout submissions OK. Reports in 2 weeks on queries; 1 month on mss. Free book catalog and manuscript guidelines.
Nonfiction: How-to, juvenile and self-help. Subjects include child guidance/parenting, cooking, foods and nutrition, education, health/medicine, money/finance, recreation and sports. "We need high quality books written for young adults (13 to 24 years old) on job search, career guidance, educational guidance, personal guidance, home economics, physical education, coaching, recreation, health, personal development, substance abuse, and sports. We only publish books written for young adults and primarily sold to libraries, schools, etc. We do not seek books targeted to adults or written at high readability levels." Query or submit outline/synopsis and sample chapters or send complete ms. Reviews artwork/photos as part of ms package.
Recent Nonfiction Title: *Cambridge Financial Aid Planner*, by J. Lupia.
Tips: "We encourage the submission of high-quality books on timely topics written for young adult audiences at moderate to low readibility levels. Call and request a copy of all our current catalogs, talk to the management about what is timely in the areas you wish to write on, thoroughly research the topic, and write a manuscript that will be read by young adults without being overly technical. Low to moderate readibility yet entertaining, informative and accurate."

‡*CAMDEN HOUSE, INC., Box 2025, Columbia SC 29202. (803)788-8689. President: Jim Hardin. Publishes hardcover and trade paperback originals. Averages 12 titles/year. Receives 50-80 submissions/year. 40% of books from first-time authors; 90% from unagented writers. Subsidy publishes 10% of books. Pays 8-15% maximum on wholesale price. Publishes book an average of 8 months after acceptance. Photocopied submissions OK. Computer printout submissions OK. Reports in 2 weeks. Book catalog for #10 SAE with 45¢ postage.
Nonfiction: Reference and technical. Subjects include Americana, health/medicine, language/literature and translation. We want "nonfiction works by experts in fields where good reference works are needed." Submit outline/synopsis and sample chapters.
Recent Nonfiction Title: *Getting into a Residency*, by Kenneth Iserson (medical reference).
Fiction: Mystery. Submit outline/synopsis and sample chapters.
Recent Poetry Title: *Sonnets to Orpheus*, by R.M. Rilke.

CAMELOT BOOKS, Children's Book Imprint of Avon Books, a division of the Hearst Corp., 8th Floor, 105 Madison Ave., New York NY 10016. (212)481-5609. FAX: (212)532-2172. Editorial Director: Ellen Krieger. Publishes paperback originals and reprints. Averages 48 titles/year; receives 1,000-1,500 submissions annually. 10-15% of books from first-time authors; 75% of books from unagented writers. Pays 6-8% royalty on retail price; offers minimum advance of $2,000. Publishes book an average of 15 months after acceptance. Simultaneous and photocopied submissions OK. Computer printout submissions acceptable; prefers letter-quality. Reports in 10 weeks. Free book catalog and ms guidelines for 8x10 SAE and 5 first class stamps.
Fiction: Subjects include adventure, fantasy, humor, juvenile (Camelot, 8-12 and Young Camelot, 7-10, Flare, 12 and up) mainstream, mystery, ("very selective with mystery and fantasy") and suspense. Submit entire ms or 3 sample chapters and a brief "general summary of the story, chapter by chapter."
Recent Fiction Title: *Racing the Sun*, by Paul Pitts.
Tips: "The YA market is not as strong as it was 5 years ago; we are more selective with young adult fiction."

*CANADIAN PLAINS RESEARCH CENTER, University of Regina, Regina, Saskatchewan S4S 0A2 Canada. (306)585-4795. Manager: Gillian Wadsworth Minifie. Publishes scholarly and trade paperback originals and some casebound originals. Averages 6-8 titles/year; receives 45-50 submissions annually. 35% of books from first-time authors; 90% of books from unagented writers. Subsidy publishes 80% (nonauthor) of books. Determines whether an author should be subsidy published through a scholarly peer review. Pays 5-10%

royalty on retail price. "Occasionally academics will waive royalties in order to maintain lower prices." Publishes book an average of 18 months after acceptance. Query for electronic submissions. Reports in 2 months. Free book catalog and ms guidelines. Also publishes *Prairie Forum*, a scholarly journal.

Nonfiction: Biography, coffee table book, illustrated book, technical, textbook and scholarly. Subjects include animals, business and economics, history, nature, politics and sociology. "The Canadian Plains Research Center publishes the results of research on topics relating to the Canadian Plains region, although manuscripts relating to the Great Plains region will be considered. Material *must* be scholarly. Do not submit health, self-help, hobbies, music, sports, psychology, recreation or cookbooks unless they have a scholarly approach. For example, we would be interested in acquiring a pioneer manuscript cookbook, with modern ingredient equivalents, if the material relates to the Canadian Plains/Great Plains region." Submit complete ms. Reviews artwork/photos as part of ms package.

Recent Nonfiction Title: *Emporium of the North: Fort Chipewyan and the Fur Trade to 1835*, by James Parker (fur-trade history co-published with Alberta Culture and Multiculturalism).

Tips: "Pay great attention to manuscript preparation and accurate footnoting."

*ARISTIDE D. CARATZAS, PUBLISHER, Box 210/30 Church St., New Rochelle NY 10801. (914)632-8487. FAX: (914)636-3650. Managing Editor: John Emerich. Publishes hardcover originals and reprints. Averages 12 titles/year; receives 100 submissions annually. 35% of books from first-time authors; 80% of books from unagented writers. Subsidy publishes 25% of books. "We seek grants/subsidies for limited run scholarly books; granting organizations are generally institutions or foundations." Pays royalty; offers $1,500 average advance. Publishes book an average of 18 months after acceptance. Simultaneous and photocopied submissions OK. Query for electronic submissions. Computer printout submissions OK. Reports in 1 month on queries; 3 months on mss. Free book catalog.

Nonfiction: Reference, technical and textbook. Subjects include art, history (ancient, European, Russian), politics, religion, travel, classical languages (Greek and Latin), archaeology and mythology. Nonfiction book ms needs for the next year include "scholarly books in archaeology; mythology; ancient and medieval history; and art history." Query or submit outline/synopsis and sample chapters. Reviews artwork/photos as part of ms package.

Recent Nonfiction Title: *Spartan Twilight*, by L. Piper (history).

CAREER PUBLISHING, INC., Box 5486, Orange CA 92613-5486. (714)771-5155. FAX: (714)532-0180. Editor-in-Chief: Sherry Robson. Publishes paperback originals and software. Averages 6-20 titles/year; receives 300 submissions annually. 80% of books from first-time authors; 90% of books from unagented writers. Average print order for a writer's first book is 5,000-10,000. Pays 10% royalty on actual amount received; no advance. Publishes book an average of 6 months after acceptance. Simultaneous (if so informed with names of others to whom submissions have been sent) and photocopied submissions OK. Query for electronic submissions. Computer printout submissions acceptable; prefers letter-quality. Reports in 2 months. Book catalog for 8½x11 SAE with 2 first class stamps; ms guidelines for #10 SASE.

Nonfiction: Microcomputer material, educational software, word processing, guidance material, allied health, dictionaries, etc. "Textbooks should provide core upon which class curriculum can be based: textbook, workbook or kit with 'hands-on' activities and exercises, and teacher's guide. Should incorporate modern and effective teaching techniques. Should lead to a job objective. We also publish support materials for existing courses and are open to unique, marketable ideas with schools in mind. Reading level should be controlled appropriately—usually 8th-9th grade equivalent for vocational school and community college level courses. Any sign of sexism or racism will disqualify the work. No career awareness masquerading as career training." Submit outline/synopsis, 2 sample chapters and table of contents or complete ms. Reviews artwork/photos as part of ms package. If material is to be returned, enclose SAE and return postage.

Recent Nonfiction Title: *WordStar 2000 Plus, Release 3*, by Richard C. Bonen, Ed. D., and Darla S. Babcock.

Tips: "Authors should be aware of vocational/career areas with inadequate or no training textbooks and submit ideas and samples to fill the gap. Trends in book publishing that freelance writers should be aware of include education—especially for microcomputers."

‡*CAROL PUBLISHING, 600 Madison Ave., New York NY 10022. (212)486-2200. Imprints include: Lyle Stuart, Birch Lane Press, Citadel Press, University Books. Publisher: Steven Schragis. Firm publishes hardcover originals, and trade paperback originals and reprints. Firm averages 100 titles/year. Receives 1,000 submissions/year. 15% of books from first-time authors; 50% from unagented writers. Subsidy publishes 5% of books. Pays 10-15% royalty on retail price. As little as $1,000, as much as $250,000 advance. Publishes book an average of 1 year after acceptance. Simultaneous and photocopied submissions OK. Computer printout submissions OK. Reports in 2 months. Free book catalog.

Nonfiction: Biography, how-to, humor, illustrated book and self-help. Subjects include Americana, animals, art/architecture, business and economics, child guidance/parenting, computers and electronics, cooking, foods and nutrition, ethnic, gay/lesbian, health/medicine, history, hobbies, money/finance, music/dance, nature/environment, philosophy, psychology, recreation, regional, science, sports, travel and women's issues/studies. Submit outline/synopsis and sample chapters.

Recent Nonfiction Title: *A Woman Named Jackie*, by C. David Heymann.
Fiction: Adventure, confession, fantasy, gay/lesbian, horror, humor, literary, mystery, science fiction and short story collections. Submit outline/synopsis and sample chapters.
Recent Fiction Title: *Earthly Remains*, by Peter Hernon.

‡**CAROLINA BIOLOGICAL SUPPLY CO.,** 2700 York Rd., Burlington NC 27215. (919)584-0381. Head, Scientific Publications: Dr. Phillip L. Owens. Publishes paperback originals. Averages 15 titles/year; receives 30 submissions annually. 25% of books from first-time authors; 100% of books from unagented writers. Pays 10% royalty on sales. Publishes book an average of 1½ years after acceptance. Simultaneous and photocopied submissions OK. Query for electronic submissions. Computer printout submissions acceptable; no dot-matrix. Reports in 2 weeks on queries.
Nonfiction: Self-help, technical, field and study guides on animals, health, nature, biology and science. "We will consider short (10,000 words) manuscripts of general interest to high school and college students on health, computers, biology, physics, astronomy, microscopes, etc. Longer manuscripts less favored but will be considered." Query. Reviews photos/artwork as part of ms package.
Recent Nonfiction Title: *AIDS*, by Donald Armstrong.

CAROLRHODA BOOKS, INC., 241 1st Ave. N., Minneapolis MN 55401. (612)332-3344. Submissions Editor: Rebecca Poole. Publishes hardcover originals. Averages 25-30 titles/year. Receives 1,300-1,500 submissions/year. 25% of books from first-time authors; 95% of books from unagented writers. Pays 4-7% royalty on wholesale price, makes outright purchase, or negotiates cents per printed copy. Publishes book an average of 18 months after acceptance. Simultaneous and photocopied submissions OK. Computer printout submissions OK; no dot-matrix. Reports in 3 months. Book catalog and ms guidelines for 9x12 SASE.
Nonfiction: Publishes only children's books. Subjects include biography, animals, art, history, music and nature. Needs "biographies in story form on truly creative individuals—25 manuscript pages in length." Query or send full ms. Reviews artwork/photos as part of ms package.
Recent Nonfiction Title: *Arctic Explorer: The Story of Matthew Henson*, by Jeri Ferris.
Fiction: Children's historical. No anthropomorphized animal stories. Submit complete ms.
Recent Fiction Title: *The Gift of the Willows*, by Helena Clare Pittman.
Tips: "Our audience is children ages four to eleven. We publish very few picture books. Nonfiction science topics, particularly nature, do well for us, as do biographies, photo essays, and easy readers. We prefer manuscripts that can fit into one of our series. Spend time developing your idea in a unique way or from a unique angle; avoid trite, hackneyed plots and ideas."

CARROLL & GRAF PUBLISHERS, INC., 260 5th Ave., New York NY 10001. (212)889-8772. Contact: Kent Carroll. Publishes hardcover, trade and mass market paperback originals, and trade and mass market paperback reprints. Averages 85 titles/year; receives 1,000 submissions annually. 10% of books from first-time authors; 10% of books from unagented writers. Pays 6-10% royalty on retail price. Publishes book an average of 9 months after acceptance. Photocopied submissions OK. Reports in 3 weeks on queries; 1 month on mss. Book catalog for 6x9 SASE.
Nonfiction: Biography, history, psychology, current affairs. Query. Reviews artwork/photos as part of ms package.
Recent Nonfiction Title: *The Peter Lawford Story: Life with the Kennedys, Monroe and the Rat Pack*, by Patricia Seaton Lawford with Ted Schwarz.
Fiction: Erotica, mainstream, mystery and suspense. Query with SASE.

CARSTENS PUBLICATIONS, INC., Hobby Book Division, Box 700, Newton NJ 07860. (201)383-3355. Publisher: Harold H. Carstens. Publishes paperback originals. Averages 8 titles/year. 100% of books from unagented writers. Pays 10% royalty on retail price; offers average advance. Publishes book an average of 2 years after acceptance. Query for electronic submissions. Computer printout submissions acceptable; prefers letter-quality. Book catalog for SASE.
Nonfiction: Model railroading, toy trains, model aviation, railroads and model hobbies. "We have scheduled or planned titles on several railroads as well as model railroad and model airplane books. Authors must know their field intimately since our readers are active modelers. Our railroad books presently are primarily photographic essays on specific railroads. Writers cannot write about somebody else's hobby with authority. If they do, we can't use them." Query. Reviews artwork/photos as part of ms package.
Tips: "No fiction. We need lots of good b&w photos. Material must be in model, hobby, railroad field only."

‡**CASSANDRA PRESS,** Box 868, San Rafael CA 94915. (415)382-8507. President: Gurudas. Publishes trade paperback originals. Averages 6 titles/year. Receives 30 submissions/year. 50% of books from first-time authors. 50% from unagented writers. Pays 6-8% maximum royalty on retail price. Advance rarely offered, but to $4,000. Publishes book an average of 1 year after acceptance. Simultaneous and photocopied submissions OK. Computer printout submissions OK; prefers letter-quality. Reports in 3 weeks on queries; 1-2 months on mss. Free book catalog and manuscript guidelines.

Nonfiction: Cookbook, how-to, self-help and New Age. Subjects include cooking, foods and nutrition, health/medicine (holistic health), philosophy, psychology, religion (New Age) and metaphysical. "We like to do around six titles a year in the general New Age, metaphysical and holistic health fields so we continue to look for good material." Submit outline/synopsis and sample chapters or complete ms. Reviews artwork/photos as part of ms package.

Recent Nonfiction Title: *Spiritual Nutrition and the Rainbow Diet*, by Gabriel Cousens, MD (health care, cookbook).

Fiction: Occult and religious. Submit outline/synopsis and sample chapters or complete ms.

‡**CASSELL PUBLICATIONS**, Cassell Communications Inc., Box 9844, Ft. Lauderdale FL 33310. (305)485-0795. Executive Editor: Dana K. Cassell. Firm publishes trade paperback originals. Publishes 8 titles/year; receives 300 submissions/year. 50% from first-time authors; 100% from unagented writers. Pays 10% royalty on retail price. Pays $500 average advance. Publishes book an average of 6 months after acceptance. Simultaneous and photocopied submissions OK. Query for electronic submissions. Computer printout submissions OK. Reports in 1 month on queries; 2 months on mss. Book catalog for #10 SAE with 2 first class stamps. Ms guidelines for #10 SASE.

Nonfiction: How-to, reference. Subjects include business and economics, language/literature. Wants books covering writing, advertising, promotion, marketing and how-to treatments for freelance writers, professionals and independent retailers and services businesses. Query or submit outline/synopsis and sample chapters. Reviews artwork/photos as part of ms package.

THE CATHOLIC HEALTH ASSOCIATION OF THE UNITED STATES, 4455 Woodson Rd., St. Louis MO 63134-0889. (314)427-2500. FAX: (314)427-0029. Books Editor: Robert J. Stephens. Publishes hardcover originals and reprints, trade paperback originals and reprints. Averages 20 titles/year. Receives 50 submissions/year. 5% of books from first-time authors; 100% of books from unagented writers. Pays 10-15% royalty on net proceeds. Offers variable advance. Publishes book an average of 9 months after acceptance. Query for electronic submissions. Reports in 1 month on queries; 3 months on mss. Book catalog for 9x12 SASE; ms guidelines for 8½x11 SASE.

Nonfiction: Textbook, ethics and management. Subjects include health and ethics. Needs manuscripts for pamphlets on ethical health care topics for lay people and religious practices in health care, health care management and financing. No books for nonprofessionals. Submit outline/synopsis and sample chapters. Reviews artwork/photos as part of ms package.

Recent Nonfiction Title: *Caring for Persons with AIDS and Cancer*, by John Tuohey.

CATHOLIC UNIVERSITY OF AMERICA PRESS, 620 Michigan Ave. NE, Washington DC 20064. (202)635-5052. Director: Dr. David J. McGonagle. Marketing Manager: Miryam B. Hirsch. Averages 15-20 titles/year; receives 100 submissions annually. 50% of books from first-time authors; 100% of books from unagented writers. Average print order for a writer's first book is 1,000. Pays variable royalty on net receipts. Publishes book an average of 1 year after acceptance. Query for electronic submissions. Computer printout submissions acceptable; no dot-matrix. Reports in 2 months. Book catalog for #10 SASE.

Nonfiction: Publishes history, biography, languages and literature, philosophy, religion, church-state relations, political theory and social sciences. No unrevised doctoral dissertations. Length: 200,000-500,000 words. Query with sample chapter plus outline of entire work, along with curriculum vitae and list of previous publications. Reviews artwork/photos.

Recent Nonfiction Title: *The Inner Experience of Law: A Jurisprudence of Subjectivity*.

Tips: Freelancer has best chance of selling "scholarly monographs and works suitable for adoption as supplementary reading material in courses."

THE CAXTON PRINTERS, LTD., 312 Main St., Caldwell ID 83605. (208)459-7421. Vice President: Gordon Gipson. Publishes hardcover and trade paperback originals. Averages 6-10 titles/year; receives 250 submissions annually. 50% of books from first-time authors; 60% of books from unagented writers. Audience includes Westerners, students, historians and researchers. Pays royalty; advance is $500-2,000. Publishes book an average of 18 months after acceptance. Simultaneous and photocopied submissions OK. Computer printout submissions acceptable; no dot-matrix. Reports in 2 weeks on queries; 2 months on mss. Book catalog for 9x12 SASE.

Market conditions are constantly changing! If this is 1991 or later, buy the newest edition of Writer's Market at your favorite bookstore or order directly from Writer's Digest Books.

Nonfiction: Coffee table, Americana and Western Americana. "We need good Western Americana, especially the Northwest, preferably copiously illustrated with unpublished photos." Query. Reviews artwork/photos as part of ms package.
Recent Nonfiction Title: *Two-Story Outhouse*, by Weis.

CCC PUBLICATIONS, 20306 Tau Place, Chatsworth CA 91311. (818)407-1661. Attn: Editorial Dept. Publishes trade paperback originals and mass market paperback originals. Averages 5-10 titles/year; receives 400-600 mss/year. 50% of books from first-time authors; 50% of books from unagented writers. Pays 5-10% royalty on wholesale price. Publishes book an average of 1 year after acceptance. Simultaneous and photocopied submissions OK. Computer printout submissions OK; prefers letter-quality. Reports in 1 month on queries; reports in 3 months on mss.
Nonfiction: Humorous how-to/self-help. "We are looking for *original, clever* and *current* humor that is not too limited in audience appeal or that will have a limited shelf life. All of our titles are as marketable 5 years from now as they are today. No rip-offs of previously published books, or too special interest mss." For best results: Query first with SASE; will review complete ms only. Reviews artwork/photos as part of ms package.
Recent Nonfiction Title: *No Hang-Ups*, by John Carfi and Cliff Carle (humor).
Tips: "Humor—we specialize in the subject and have a good reputation with retailers and wholesalers for publishing super-impulse titles. SASE is a must!"

‡**CENTER FOR APPLIED LINGUISTICS**, 1118 22nd St. NW, Washington DC 20007. (202)429-9292. Publications Coordinator: Whitney Stewart. Publishes trade paperback originals. Firm averages 4 titles/year. 100% of books from unagented writers. Pays $500 maximum for outright purchase. Publishes book an average of 6 months after acceptance. Query for electronic submissions. Computer printout submissions OK (prefers hard copy and computer disk). Reports in 1 month.
Nonfiction: Textbook on language in education. Subjects include child language, computers and language, education and linguistics. "We want texts on teaching foreign language and reading; texts on special education; on bilingual education; texts on child language acquisition. No foreign language textbooks. We want only theory and practical methodology on language instruction." Query.
Recent Nonfiction Title: *More Than Meets the Eye: Foreign Language Reading*, by Marva Barnett.
Tips: "We need manuscripts of 100-200 pages—texts on classroom theory and practice—written for the teacher, the parent or the linguistics student. We want theory but with an emphasis on practical application."

*****CHATHAM PRESS**, Box A, Old Greenwich CT 06870. FAX: (203)622-6688. Publishes hardcover and paperback originals, reprints and anthologies relating to New England and the Atlantic coastline. Averages 15 titles/year; receives 50 submissions annually. 30% of books from first-time authors; 75% of books from unagented writers. Subsidy publishes mainly poetry or ecological topics (nonauthor) 10% of books. "Standard book contract does not always apply if the book is heavily illustrated. Average advance is low." Publishes book an average of 6 months after acceptance. Query for electronic submissions. Computer printout submissions acceptable; prefers letter-quality. Reports in 2 weeks. Book catalog and ms guidelines for 6x9 SAE with 10 first class stamps.
Nonfiction: Publishes mostly "regional history and natural history, involving mainly Northeast seaboard to the Carolinas, mostly illustrated, with emphasis on conservation and outdoor recreation." Accepts nonfiction translations from French and German. Query with outline and 3 sample chapters. Reviews artwork/photos as part of ms package.
Recent Nonfiction Title: *Beachcomber's Companion*, by Wesemann.
Recent Poetry Title: *Weapons Against Chaos*, by M. Ewald.
Tips: "Illustrated New England-relevant titles have the best chance of selling to our firm. We have a slightly greater (15%) skew towards cooking and travel titles."

CHELSEA GREEN, Box 283, Chelsea VT 05038. (802)685-3108. Editor: Ian Baldwin Jr. Fiction Editor: Michael Moore. Publishes hardcover and paperback trade originals. Averages 10 titles/year.
Nonfiction: Biography, nature, politics, travel, art history. Query only and include SASE.
Recent Nonfiction Title: *On Watching Birds*, by Laurence Kilham.
Fiction: Serious contemporary fiction (no genre fiction). Please submit query with SASE.
Recent Fiction Title: *The Eight Corners of the World*, by Gordon Weaver.

‡**CHERIBE PUBLISHING COMPANY**, Box 100, Wolverton MN 56594. (218)557-8710. Editor-in-Chief: Michael Lee. Publishes hardcover and trade paperback originals. Imprint averages 6-8 titles/year. Receives 50 submissions/year. 75% of books from first-time authors; 100% from unagented writers. Pays 10-15% maximum royalty on wholesale price or buys mss outright for $1,000 minimum. Offers $500 average advance. Publishes book an average of 9 months after acceptance. Simultaneous and photocopied submissions OK (with notification). Query for electronic submissions. Computer printout submissions OK. Reports in 2 weeks on queries; 6 weeks on mss. Free book catalog and manuscript guidelines.

Nonfiction: How-to (entrepreneurism only), reference, self-help, software, technical and textbook. Subjects include art/architecture (computer applications), business and economics (facility magagement), computers and electronics, architecture design (management), health/medicine (stress management), money/finance (entrepreneurism), psychology (stress management) and women's issues/studies (entrepreneurism). "We want reference books in the area of facility management, stress management, productivity issues in the white collar environment and ethics in the workplace; also social applications of entrepreneurism." Query. Submit outline/synopsis and sample chapters or complete ms.
Recent Nonfiction Title: *101 Ways to Ease Out of the Rat Race*, by Michael Lee (stress management).
Tips: "We believe that our society is becoming more sensitive to the pressures of the workplace and can contribute to maximum worker productivity by increasing job satisfaction. We want material that supports this premise."

‡CHEROKEE PUBLISHING COMPANY, subsidiary of Larlin Corporation, Box 1730, Marietta GA 30061. (404)424-6210. Imprints include: University Press of Washington, DC. Editor: Alexa Selph. Publishes hardcover and trade paperback originals and reprints. Firm averages 10-15 titles/year. Receives 100 submissions/year. 50% of books from first-time authors; 90% from unagented writers. Pays 12½-15% royalty on wholesale. Publishes book an average of 18 months after acceptance. Simultaneous submissions OK. Computer printout submissions OK; no dot-matrix. Reports in 3 months on queries; 4 months on manuscripts. Free book catalog.
Nonfiction: Biography. Subjects include Americana, health/medicine, history and regional. Query or submit outline/synopsis and sample chapters.
Recent Nonfiction Title: *Chief William McIntosh*, by George Chapman (biography).

*CHILD WELFARE LEAGUE OF AMERICA, Suite 310, 440 First St. NW, Washington DC 20001. (202)638-2952. Director, Publications: Susan Brite. Publishes hardcover and trade paperback originals. Publishes 10-12 titles/year. Receives 60-100 submissions/year. 95% of writers are unagented. 50% of books are nonauthor subsidy published. Pays 0-10% royalty on net domestic sales. Publishes book an average of 1 year after acceptance. Query for electronic submissions. Computer printout submissions OK; prefers letter-quality. Reports on queries in 2 months; on mss in 3 months. Free book catalog and manuscript guidelines.
Nonfiction: Child Welfare. Subjects include child guidance/parenting, sociology. Submit outline/synopsis and sample chapters or complete ms.
Recent Nonfiction Title: *Adoption Agency Directory*, by Julia Posner.
Recent Fiction Title: *Floating*, by Mark Krueger.
Tips: "Our audience is child welfare workers, administrators, agency execs, parents, etc."

CHILTON BOOK CO., Chilton Way, Radnor PA 19089. Editorial Director: Alan F. Turner. Publishes hardcover and trade paperback originals. Publishes 90 titles/year. Pays royalty; average advance. Simultaneous and photocopied submissions OK. Query for electronic submissions. Computer printout submissions acceptable. Reports in 3 weeks.
Nonfiction: Business/economics, crafts, how-to and technical. "We only want to see any manuscripts with informational value." Query or submit outline/synopsis and 2-3 sample chapters.
Recent Nonfiction Title: *Opportunity Knocks-Using PR*, by Laurie J. Mercer and Jennifer Singer.

‡CHOCKSTONE PRESS, INC., Box 3505, Evergreen CO 80439. (303)377-1970. President: George Meyers. Publishes hardcover and trade paperback originals. Averages 8 titles/year. Receives 15 submissions/year. 90% of books from first-time authors; 100% from unagented writers. Pays 12-15% maximum on retail price. Offers varied advance. Publishes book an average of 5 months after acceptance. Simultaneous and photocopied submissions OK. Query for electronic submissions. Computer printout submissions OK; prefers letter-quality. Reports in 1 month. Free book catalog.
Nonfiction: Biography, coffee table book, how-to, illustrated book, reference and guides. Subjects include recreation and sports. Query.
Recent Nonfiction Title: *Grand Canyon Loop Hikes I*, by George Steele.
Fiction: Adventure. Query.

CHOSEN BOOKS PUBLISHING CO., LTD., Imprint of Fleming H. Revell Co., 184 Central Ave., Old Tappan NJ 07675. (201)768-8060. FAX: (201)768-2749. Editor: Jane Campbell. Publishes hardcover and trade paperback originals. Averages 16 titles/year; receives 600 submissions annually. 15% of books from first-time authors; 99% of books from unagented writers. Pays royalty on retail price. Publishes book an average of 1 year after acceptance. Simultaneous and photocopied submissions OK. Computer printout submissions acceptable; prefers letter-quality. Reports in 2 months. Occasionally makes work-for-hire assignments. Book catalog not available; ms guidelines for #10 SASE.
Nonfiction: How-to, self-help, and a very limited number of first-person narratives. "We publish books reflecting the current acts of the Holy Spirit in the world, books with a charismatic Christian orientation." No New Age, poetry, fiction, or children's books. Submit synopsis, chapter outline and SASE. No complete mss.

Recent Nonfiction Title: *Love On Its Knees*, by Dick Eastman.

Tips: "In expositional books we look for solid, practical advice for the growing and maturing Christian from authors with professional or personal experience platforms. Narratives must have a strong theme and reader benefits. No conversion accounts or chronicling of life events, please. State the topic or theme of your book clearly in your cover letter."

for life." Query or submit outline/synopsis and sample chapters. Reviews artwork/photos as part of ms package.

*THE CHRISTOPHER PUBLISHING HOUSE, 24 Rockland St., Commerce Green, Hanover MA 02339. (617)826-7474. Managing Editor: Susan Lukas. Publishes hardcover and trade paperback originals. Averages 20-30 titles/year; receives 300-400 submissions annually. 30% of books from first-time authors; 100% of books from unagented writers. Subsidy publishes 50% of books. Pays 5-30% royalty on wholesale price; offers no advance. Publishes book an average of 2 years after acceptance. Simultaneous and photocopied submissions OK. Query for electronic submissions. Computer printout submissions acceptable; prefers letter-quality. Reports in 1 month. Book catalog for #10 SAE with 2 first class stamps; ms guidelines for SASE.

Nonfiction: Biography, how-to, reference, self-help, textbook and religious. Subjects include Americana, animals, art, business and economics, cooking and foods (nutrition), health, history, philosophy, politics, psychology, religion, sociology and travel. "We will be glad to review all nonfiction manuscripts, particularly college textbook and religious-oriented." Submit complete ms. Reviews artwork/photos as part of ms package.

Recent Nonfiction Title: *Man: Computer, Ape, or Angel*, by Larry Azar, Ph.D.

Poetry: "We will review all forms of poetry." Submit complete ms.

Recent Poetry Title: *So Many Crossroads*, by Alannah Van Boven.

Tips: "Our books are for a general audience, slanted toward college-educated readers. There are specific books targeted toward specific audiences when appropriate."

CITADEL PRESS, Subsidiary of Lyle Stuart Inc., 120 Enterprise Ave., Secaucus NJ 07094. (212)736-0007. FAX: (201)866-8159. Editorial Director: Allan J. Wilson. Publishes hardcover originals and paperback reprints. Averages 60-80 titles/year. Receives 800-1,000 submissions annually. 7% of books from first-time authors; 50% of books from unagented writers. Average print order for a writer's first book is 5,000. Pays 10% royalty on hardcover, 5-7% on paperback; offers average $5,000 advance. Publishes book an average of 1 year after acceptance. Simultaneous and photocopied submissions OK. Computer printout submissions acceptable; no dot-matrix. Reports in 2 months. Book catalog for $1.

Nonfiction: Biography, film, psychology, humor and history. Also seeks "off-beat material," but no "poetry, religion, politics." Accepts nonfiction and fiction translations. Query. Submit outline/synopsis and 3 sample chapters. Reviews artwork/photos as part of ms package.

Recent Nonfiction Title: *Lost Films of the Fifties*.

Recent Fiction Title: *The Rain Maiden*, by Jill M. Phillips.

Tips: "We concentrate on biography, popular interest, and film, with limited fiction (no romance, religion, poetry, music)."

CLARION BOOKS, Ticknor & Fields: a Houghton Mifflin Company, 52 Vanderbilt Ave., New York NY 10017. Editor and Publisher: James C. Giblin. Executive Editor for Nonfiction: Ann Troy. Publishes hardcover originals. Averages 30-35 titles/year. Pays 5-10% royalty on retail price; $1,000-3,000 advance, depending on whether project is a picture book or a longer work for older children. Photocopied submissions OK. No multiple submissions. Computer printout submissions acceptable; no dot-matrix. Reports in 2 months. Publishes book an average of 18 months after acceptance. Ms guidelines for #10 SASE.

Nonfiction: Americana, biography, holiday, humor, nature, photo essays and word play. Prefers books for younger children. Reviews artwork/photos as part of ms package. Query.

Recent Nonfiction Title: *Lincoln: A Photobiography*.

Fiction: Adventure, humor, mystery, strong character studies, and suspense. "We would like to see more humorous contemporary stories that young people of 8-12 or 10-14 can identify with readily." Accepts fiction translations. Query on ms of more than 50 pages. Looks for "freshness, enthusiasm—in short, life" (fiction and nonfiction).

Recent Fiction Title: *Following the Mystery Man*, by Mary Downing Hahn.

*ARTHUR H. CLARK CO. , Box 14907, Spokane WA 99214. (509)928-9540. Editorial Director: Robert A. Clark. Publishes hardcover originals. Averages 8 titles/year; receives 40 submissions annually. 40% of books from first-time authors; 100% of books from unagented writers. Subsidy publishes 15% of books based on whether they are "high-risk sales." Subsidy publishes (nonauthor) 5% of books. Pays 10% minimum royalty on wholesale price. Publishes book an average of 9 months after acceptance. Photocopied submissions OK. Computer printout submissions acceptable; prefers letter-quality. Reports in 1 week on queries; 6 months on mss. Book catalog for 6x9 SASE.

Nonfiction: Biography, reference and historical nonfiction. Subjects include Americana and history. "We're looking for documentary source material in Western American history." Query or submit outline/synopsis with SASE. Looks for "content, form, style." Reviews artwork/photos as part of ms package.

Recent Nonfiction Title: *Encyclopedia of Frontier Biography*, by Dan L. Thrapp.

Tips: "Western Americana (nonfiction) has the best chance of selling to our firm."

*CLEANING CONSULTANT SERVICES, INC., 1512 Western Ave., Seattle WA 98101. (206)682-9748. President: William R. Griffin. Publishes trade paperback originals and reprints. Averages 4-6 titles/year; receives 15 submissions annually. 75% of books from first-time authors; 100% of books from unagented writers. Subsidy publishes 5% of books. "If they (authors) won't sell it and won't accept royalty contract, we offer our publishing services and often sell the book along with our books." Pays 5-15% royalty on retail price or outright purchase, $100-2,500, depending on negotiated agreement. Publishes book an average of 6-12 months after acceptance. Photocopied submissions OK. Computer printout submissions acceptable; prefers letter-quality. Reports in 6 weeks on queries; 3 months on mss. Free book catalog; ms guidelines for SASE.

Nonfiction: How-to, illustrated book, reference, self-help, technical, textbook and directories. Subjects include business, health, and cleaning and maintenance. Needs books on anything related to cleaning, maintenance, self-employment or entrepreneurship. Query or submit outline/synopsis and sample chapters or complete ms. Reviews artwork/photos as part of ms package.

Recent Nonfiction Title: *How to Sell and Price Contract Cleaning*, by William Griffin and John Davis.

Tips: "Our audience includes those involved in cleaning and maintenance service trades, opportunity seekers, schools, property managers, libraries—anyone who needs information on cleaning and maintenance. How-to and self-employment guides are doing well for us in today's market. We are now seeking books on fire damage restoration and also articles for a service business quarterly magazine."

CLEIS PRESS, Box 14684, San Francisco CA 94114. Co-editor, Acquisitions Coordinator: Frederique Delacoste. Publishes trade paperback originals and reprints. Publishes 4 titles/year. 75% of books are from first-time authors; 90% from unagented writers. Royalties vary on retail price. Publishes book an average of 1 year after acceptance. Simultaneous and photocopied submissions OK "only if accompanied by an original letter stating where and when ms was sent." Query for electronic submissions. Computer printout submissions OK; prefers letter-quality. Reports in 1 month. Books catalog for #10 SAE and 2 first class stamps.

Nonfiction: Human rights, feminist. Subjects include gay/lesbian, government/politics, sociology (of women), women's issues/studies. "We are interested in books that: a) will sell in feminist and progressive bookstores and b) will sell in Europe (translation rights). We are interested in books by and about women in Latin America; on lesbian and gay rights; and other feminist topics which have not already been widely documented. We do not want religious/spiritual tracts; we are not interested in books on topics which have been documented over and over, unless the author is approaching the topic from a new viewpoint." Query or submit outline/synopsis and sample chapters or submit complete ms.

Recent Nonfiction Title: *AIDS: The Women*, edited by Ines Rieder and Patricia Ruppelt.

Fiction: Feminist, gay/lesbian, literary. "We are looking for high quality novels by women. We are especially interested in translations of Latin American women's fiction. No romances!" Submit complete ms.

Recent Fiction Title: *Unholy Alliances: New Fiction by Women*, edited by Rafkin (anthology).

Tips: "An anthology project representing the work of a very diverse group of women . . . an anthology on a very hot, very unique, risk-taking theme. These books sell well for us; they're our trademark. If I were trying to market a book today, I would become very familiar with the presses serving my market. More than reading publishers' catalogs, I think author should spend time in a bookstore whose clientele closely resembles her intended audience; be absolutely aware of her audience; have researched potential market; present fresh new ways of looking at her topic; avoid 'PR' language in query letter."

*CLEVELAND STATE UNIVERSITY POETRY CENTER, R.T. 1815, Cleveland State University, Cleveland OH 44115. (216)687-3986. Editor: Leonard M. Trawick. Publishes trade paperback and hardcover originals. Averages 5 titles/year; receives 400 queries, 500 mss annually. 60% of books from first-time authors; 100% of books from unagented writers. 30% of titles subsidized by CSU, 30% by government subsidy. CSU poetry series pays one-time, lump-sum royalty of $200-400 plus 50 copies; Cleveland Poetry Series (Ohio poets only) pays 100 copies. $1,000 prize for best manuscript each year. No advance. Publishes book an average of 1 year after acceptance. Simultaneous and photocopied submissions OK. Computer printout submissions acceptable; prefers letter-quality. Reports in 2 weeks on queries; 6 months on mss. Book catalog for 6x9 SAE with 2 first class stamps; ms guidelines for SASE.

Poetry: No light verse, "inspirational," or greeting card verse. ("This does not mean that we do not consider poetry with humor or philosophical/religious import.") Query—ask for guidelines. Submit only December-February. Reviews artwork/photos if applicable (i.e., concrete poetry).

Recent Poetry Title: *Returning the Question*, by Trish Reeves.

Tips: "Our books are for serious readers of poetry, i.e. poets, critics, academics, students, people who read *Poetry, Field, American Poetry Review, Antaeus*, etc." Trends include "movement from 'confessional' poetry; greater attention to form and craftsmanship. Try to project an interesting, coherent personality; link poems so as to make coherent unity, not just a miscellaneous collection." Especially needs "poems with *mystery*, i.e., poems that reflect profound thought, but do not tell all—suggestive, tantalizing, enticing."

CLIFFHANGER PRESS, Box 29527, Oakland CA 94604-9527. (415)763-3510. Editor: Nancy Chirich. Publishes hardcover originals for libraries. Averages 5 titles/year. Pays 10% royalty on retail price. Publishes book an average of 1 year after acceptance. Simultaneous and photocopied submissions OK. Reports in 2 weeks on 2-3 sample chapters and one-page synopsis. Do not send full ms unless requested. Book·catalog for #10 SASE. Computer printout submissions OK; prefers letter-quality.
Fiction: Mystery and suspense. "Manuscripts should be about 75,000 words, heavy on American regional or foreign atmosphere. No cynical, hardboiled detectives or spies." Submit synopsis/outline and 2-3 sample chapters. "No returns without SASE."
Recent Fiction Title: *The Druze Document*, by Gregory Fitz Gerald and John Dillon.
Tips: "Mystery/suspense is our only specialty. Have believable characters, a strong, uncomplicated story and heavy regional or foreign atmosphere. No justified right margins on manuscripts submitted. They're very hard to read at length. Please send SASE (#10) for writer's guidelines before submitting *anything*."

CLIFFS NOTES, INC., Box 80728, Lincoln NE 68501. (402)423-5050. General Editor: Michele Spence. Notes Editor: Gary Carey. Publishes trade paperback originals. Averages 20 titles/year. 100% of books from un-agented writers. Pays royalty on wholesale price. Buys some mss outright; "full payment on acceptance of ms." Publishes book an average of 1 year after acceptance. Computer printout submissions acceptable. Reports in 1 month. "We provide specific guidelines when a project is assigned."
Nonfiction: Self-help and textbook. "We publish self-help study aids directed to junior high through graduate school audience. Publications include *Cliffs Notes*, *Cliffs Test Preparation Guides*, *Cliffs Teaching Portfolios*, and other study guides. Most authors are experienced teachers, usually with advanced degrees. *Teaching Portfolio* authors are experienced high school English teachers who can provide practical, proven classroom material designed for junior high and high school English teachers. Some books also appeal to a general lay audience. Among these are those in a new series, *Bluffer's Guides*, published under our Centennial Press imprint. The books are both informative and humorous and cover a wide range of subject areas." Query.
Recent Nonfiction Title: *Bluff Your Way in Public Speaking*.

COLES PUBLISHING CO., LTD., 90 Ronson Dr., Rexdale Ontario, M9W 1C1 Canada. (416)243-3132. FAX: (416)243-8964. Publishing Assistant: Janina Lucci. Publishes paperback originals and reprints. Averages 10 titles/year; receives 350 submissions annually. 80% of books from first-time authors; 100% of books from unagented writers. Average print order for a writer's first book is 3,000. "We are a subsidiary company of 'Coles, the Book People,' a chain of 200 bookstores throughout Canada." Pays by outright purchase of $500-$2,500; advance averages $1,000. Publishes book an average of 8 months after acceptance. Simultaneous and photocopied submissions OK. Reports in 1 month. Send SAE and International Reply Coupons.
Nonfiction: "We publish in the following areas: education, language, technical and do-it-yourself, crafts and hobbies. We also publish a complete line of literary study aids sold worldwide." No philosophy, religion, history or biography. Submit outline/synopsis and sample chapters.
Recent Nonfiction Title: *Teach Yourself Keyboarding*.
Tips: "The writer has the best chance of selling us wide appeal, practical self-help books."

THE COLLEGE BOARD, Imprint of College Entrance Examination Board, 45 Columbus Ave., New York NY 10023-6917. (212)713-8000. Senior Editor: Carolyn Trager. Publishes trade paperback originals. Firm publishes 30 titles/year; imprint publishes 8 titles/year. Receives 20-30 submissions/year. 25% of books from first-time authors; 50% from unagented writers. Pays royalty on retail price of books sold through bookstores. Offers advance based on anticipated first year's earnings. Publishes book an average of 9 months after acceptance. Photocopied submissions OK. Computer printout submissions OK; prefers letter-quality. Reports in 2 weeks on queries; 1 month on ms. Book catalog free on request.
Nonfiction: How-to, reference, self-help. Subjects include child guidance/parenting, education, language/literature, science. "We want books to help students make a successful transition from high school to college." Query or send outline/synopsis and sample chapters. Reviews artwork/photos as part of ms package.
Recent Nonfiction Title: *College Bound: The Students' Handbook for Getting Ready, Moving In, and Succeeding on Campus*, by Evelyn Kaye and Janet Gardner.
Tips: "Our audience is college-bound high school students, beginning college students and/or their parents."

***COLLEGE PRESS PUBLISHING CO., INC.**, 205 N. Main, Box 1132, Joplin MO 64802. (417)623-6280. Contact: Steven F. Jennings. Publishes hardcover and trade paperback originals and reprints. Publishes 25 titles/year. Receives 150 submissions/year. 25% of books are from first-time authors; 100% from unagented writers. Subsidy publishes 5% of books. Subsidy considered "if we really want to publish a book, but don't have room in schedule at this time or funds available." Pays 10% royalty on net receipts. Publishes book an average of 1 year after acceptance. Simultaneous and photocopied submissions OK. Computer printout submissions OK. Reports on queries in 1 month; on ms in 3 months. Free book catalog.

Nonfiction: Textbooks. Subjects include religious (Christian church, Church of Christ). Query.
Recent Nonfiction Title: *What the Bible Says About the Holy Spirit*, by Russell Boatman.
Fiction: Historical, religious. Query.
Tips: "Topical Bible study books have the best chance of selling to our firm. Our audience is Christians interested in reading and studying Bible-based material."

COLORADO ASSOCIATED UNIVERSITY PRESS, 1344 Grandview Ave., Boulder CO 80302. (303)492-7191. Editor: Luther Wilson. Publishes hardcover and paperback originals. Averages 10 titles/year; receives 350 submissions annually. 50% of books from first-time authors; 99% of books from unagented writers. Average print order for a writer's first book is 1,500-2,000. Pays 10-12½-15% royalty contract on net price; "no advances." Publishes book an average of 18 months after acceptance. Will consider photocopied submissions "if not sent simultaneously to another publisher." Electronic submissions encouraged. Computer printout submissions acceptable; prefers letter-quality. Reports in 3 months. Free book catalog.
Nonfiction: Scholarly, regional and environmental subjects. Length: 250-500 pages. Query first with table of contents, preface or opening chapter. Reviews artwork/photos as part of ms package.
Recent Nonfiction Title: *Colorado Flora: Western Slope*, by William A. Weber.
Tips: "Books should be solidly researched and from a reputable scholar, because we are a university press. We have a new series on world resources and environmental issues."

‡COMMERCE CLEARING HOUSE, INC., 4025 W. Peterson Ave, Chicago IL 60646. (312)940-4600. Book Acquisitions Editor: Richard J. Vittenson. Publishes hardcover and trade paperback originals. Firm averages 300 titles/year; imprint averages 50 titles/year. Receives 100 submissions/year. 50% from first-time authors; 100% from unagented writers. Pays 10-15% royalty on retail price. Publishes book an average of 2 years after acceptance. Simultaneous and photocopied submissions OK. Query for electronic submissions. Computer printout submissions OK; prefers letter-quality. Reports in 2 weeks on queries; 3 weeks on mss. Free book catalog.
Nonfiction: Technical and textbook. Subjects include tax law and business law. "We publish practical books in the areas of tax law and business law, written for lawyers, CPAs, and other tax and business law professionals." Query or submit outline/synopsis and sample chapters. Reviews artwork/photos as part of ms package.
Recent Nonfiction Title: *Franchising: A Planning and Sales Compliance Guide*, by Norman D. Axelrod and Lewis G. Rudnick.
Tips: "We prefer practical books written by tax law and business law professionals."

COMMUNICATIONS PRESS, Imprint of Broadcasting Publications, Inc., 1705 DeSales St. NW, Washington DC 20036. (202)659-2340. Manager: David Dietz. Publishes hardcover, trade paperback, and professional/text paperback originals. 95% of books from unagented writers. Pays royalty or honorarium; offers "nominal, if any" advance. Publishes book an average of 9 months after acceptance. Computer printout submissions acceptable; no dot-matrix. Reports in 1 month.
Nonfiction: Reference, technical and textbook. Subjects include broadcast and cable television, radio and satellite communications. Emphasis on business, management and government regulation. Submit outline/synopsis and 2 sample chapters. Reviews artwork/photos.
Recent Nonfiction Title: *Cable Programming Resource Directory*.

COMPACT BOOKS, 2131 Hollywood Blvd., Hollywood FL 33020. (305)925-5242. FAX: (305)925-5244. Imprint of Frederick Fell. Publisher: Donald L. Lessne. Publishes hardcover and trade paperback originals. Averages 10 titles/year; receives 1,000 submissions annually. 25% of books from first-time authors; 25% of books from unagented writers. Pays royalty. Publishes book an average of 1 year after acceptance. Simultaneous and photocopied submissions OK. Query for electronic submissions. Computer printout submissions OK. Reports in 6 months on mss. Free book catalog.
Nonfiction: Cookbook, how-to, humor, reference and self-help. Subjects include business and economics, cooking and foods, health, hobbies, psychology, recreation, religion and sociology. "We're looking for easy-to-read, general interest books on current issues and health." Submit outline/synopsis and sample chapters. Reviews artwork/photos as part of ms package.
Recent Nonfiction Title: *Teenage Alcoholism and Substance Abuse*, by Carmella and John Bartimole (family/child care).
Tips: "Our list is fairly well consistent year-to-year. We look to fill in our list in the various categories of trade publishing when there is something new in the media or complements our current list. We also look strongly at those authors who are promotional-minded and are able to work hard to get their titles sold."

‡COMPCARE PUBLISHERS, 18551 Von Karman, Irvine CA 92715. (714)851-2273. Managing Editor: Bonnie Hesse. Publishes trade paperback originals and reprints. Averages 15 titles/year. Receives 5,000 submissions/year. 40% of books from first-time authors; 90% from unagented writers. Pays 10-15% royalty on wholesale price. Offers $5,000 average advance. Publishes book an average of 1 year after acceptance. Simultaneous and photocopied submissions OK. Computer printout submissions OK. Reports in 1 month on queries; 3 months on mss. Free book catalog and manuscript guidelines.

Nonfiction: Self-help. Subjects include child guidance/parenting, health/medicine, psychology and addiction recovery. "Wants mss covering emotional, psychological aspects of coping with life's problems; personal growth and inspiration." Submit query, outline/synopsis and sample chapters or complete ms. Reviews artwork/photos as part of m's package.

Recent Nonfiction Title: *Raise Your Right Hand Against Fear*, by Sheldon Kopp (fear management).

‡COMPUTE! BOOKS, A Division of Chilton Book Company, Box 5406, Greensboro NC 27403. (919)275-9809. Editor-in-Chief: Stephen Levy. Publishes trade paperback originals and software. Averages 36-48 titles/year. Pays royalties based on gross wholesale receipts. Photocopied submissions OK. Publishes ms an average of 6 months after acceptance. Query for electronic submissions. Computer printout submissions acceptable (dot-matrix OK if clear). Reports in 3 months.

Nonfiction: Books on computers. "We publish books for the home and business computer user and are always looking for reference books, teaching books, and programming books. Books must be aimed at the users of a *specific* computer with a specific and limited purpose in mind. For instance, our *Writing Excel Macros* teaches how to write macros using Microsoft's *Excel* spreadsheet on the PC and Macintosh. Writers should think of their audience as intelligent people who want their computers to improve their lives and the lives of their loved ones. We are also interested in entertainment programs and programming; home applications; educational programs; and books that teach programming at different levels—if a family or individual would find them useful and interesting." Submit outline and synopsis with sample chapters. "Writers who are known to us through articles in *COMPUTE! Magazine* and *COMPUTE!'s Gazette* already have our trust—we know they can come through with the right material—but we have often bought from writers we did not know, and from writers who had never published anything before."

Recent Nonfiction Title: *Mastering PC Works*, by Brian Flynn.

Tips: "If I were trying to create a marketable computer book today, I would become intimately familiar with one computer, then define a specific area to explain to less-familiar computer users, and write a clear, concise outline of the book I meant to write, along with a sample chapter from the working section of the book (not the introduction). Then send that proposal to a publisher whose books you believe are excellent and who targets the same audience you are aiming at. Once the proposal was in the mail, I'd forget about it. Keep learning more about the computer and develop another book proposal. *Don't write a book without a go-ahead from a publisher*. The chances are too great that you will spend 6 months writing a book, only to discover that there are nine on the market with the same concept by the time your manuscript is ready to send out."

COMPUTER SCIENCE PRESS, INC., 1803 Research Blvd., Rockville MD 20850. (301)251-9050. Imprint of W.H. Freeman and Company. Editor: Barbara B. Friedman. Editor-in-Chief: Dr. Arthur D. Friedman. Publishes hardcover and paperback originals and software. Averages 20 titles/year. 25% of books from first-time authors; 98% of books from unagented writers. All authors are recognized subject area experts. Pays royalty on net price. Publishes book an average of 6-9 months after acceptance. Computer printout submissions acceptable. Reports ASAP.

Nonfiction: "Technical books in all aspects of computer science, computer engineering, computer chess, electrical engineering, computers and math, and telecommunications. Both text and reference books. Will also consider public appeal 'trade' books in computer science, manuscripts and diskettes. Query or submit complete ms. Requires "3 copies of manuscripts." Looks for "technical accuracy of the material and the reason this approach is being taken. We would also like a covering letter stating what the author sees as the competition for this work and why this work is superior."

Recent Nonfiction Title: *Principles of Database and Knowledge Base Systems Vol. I & II*, by Ullman.

‡THE CONSULTANT PRESS, Subsidiary of The Photographic Arts Center, Ltd., 163 Amsterdam Ave., #201, New York NY 10023. FAX: (212)873-7065. Publisher: Bob Persky. Publishes hardcover and trade paperback originals. Firm averages 7 titles/year; Receives 10 submissions/year. 50% of books from first-time authors. 100% from unagented writers. Buys mss outright for $1,000-2,500. Publishes book an average of 6 months after acceptance. Simultaneous and photocopied submissions OK. Computer printout submissions OK. Reports in 2 weeks on queries; 1 month on mss. Free book catalog.

Nonfiction: Subjects include art/architecture, business and economics, photography. "We want books filling needs of artists, photographers and galleries—business oriented. No books of pictures or books on how to take pictures or paint pictures."

Recent Nonfiction Title: *Art Of Selling Art*, by Zella Jackson.

Tips: "Artists, photographers, galleries, museums, curators and art consultants are our audience."

CONTEMPORARY BOOKS, INC., 180 N. Michigan Ave., Chicago IL 60601. (312)782-9182. Subsidiaries include Congdon & Weed. Editorial Director: Nancy J. Crossman. Publishes hardcover originals and trade paperback originals and reprints. Averages 100 titles/year; receives 2,500 submissions annually. 25% of books from first-time authors; 25% of books from unagented writers. Pays 6-15% royalty on retail price. Publishes book an average of 10 months after acceptance. Query for electronic submissions. Computer printout submissions OK. Simultaneous and photocopied submissions OK. Reports in 3 weeks. Book catalog and ms guidelines for 9x12 SAE and 6 first class stamps.

Nonfiction: Biography, cookbook, how-to, humor, reference and self-help. Subjects include business, finance, cooking, health, fitness, psychology, sports, real estate, nutrition, popular culture and women's studies. Submit outline/synopsis and sample chapters. Reviews artwork/photos as part of ms package.

Tips: "The New Age market has become saturated. Also, competition in cookbooks mean we need professional, accomplished cooks instead of amateurs to write them."

‡**COPYRIGHT INFORMATION SERVICES**, Box 1460-A, Friday Harbor WA 98250-1460. (206)378-5128. Subsidiary of Harbor View Publications. President: Jerome K. Miller. Publishes hardcover originals. Averages 6-8 titles/year. 50% of books from first-time authors; 100% from unagented writers. Publishes book an average of 6 months after acceptance. Simultaneous and photocopied submissions OK. Computer printout submissions OK. Reports in 6 weeks on queries. Book catalog for #10 SAE with 45¢ postage.

Nonfiction: "Almost any topic relating to the copyright law." Query. All unsolicited mss are returned unopened.

Recent Nonfiction Title: *A Copyright Primer For Educational and Industrial Media Producers*, by E.R. Sinofsky.

CORKSCREW PRESS, 2915 Fenimore Rd., Silver Spring MD 20902. (301)933-0407. President: Richard Lippman. Publishes trade paperback originals. Publishes 4 books/year. 50% of books from first-time authors. Pays 5-10% royalty on retail price. Publishes book an average of 12-15 months after acceptance. Simultaneous and photocopied submissions OK. Computer printout submissions OK; no dot-matrix. Reports in 2 weeks on queries; 5 weeks on mss.

Nonfiction: Humor only. Submit outline/synopsis and sample chapters.

Fiction: Humor. (No novels or satire please.) Submit outline/synopsis and sample chapters.

CORNELL MARITIME PRESS, INC., Box 456, Centreville MD 21617. Editor: Willard A. Lockwood. Imprint is Tidewater Publishers. Publishes hardcover originals and quality paperbacks. Averages 15-18 titles/year; receives 150 submissions annually. 41% of books from first-time authors; 99% of books from unagented writers. Payment is negotiable but royalties do not exceed 10% for first 5,000 copies, 12½% for second 5,000 copies, 15% on all additional. Royalties for original paperbacks and regional titles are invariably lower. Revised editions revert to original royalty schedule. Publishes book an average of 10 months after acceptance. Query for electronic submissions. Computer printout submissions acceptable; prefers letter-quality. Send queries first, accompanied by writing samples and outlines of book ideas. Reports in 1 month. Free book catalog and ms guidelines.

Nonfiction: Marine subjects (highly technical); manuals; and how-to books on maritime subjects. Tidewater Publishers imprint publishes books on regional history, folklore and wildlife of the Chesapeake Bay and the Delmarva Peninsula.

Recent Nonfiction Title: *Modern Towing*, by Capt. John S. Blank, 3rd (professional text/reference).

COTEAU BOOKS, Imprint of Thunder Creek Publishing Cooperative, Suite 209, 1945 Scarth St., Regina Saskatchewan S4P 2H2 Canada. (306)352-5346. Subsidiaries include Coteau Books and Caragana Records. Managing Editor: Shelley Sopher. Publishes hardcover, trade paperback and mass market paperback originals. Publishes 8-9 titles/year; receives approximately 500 queries and mss/year. 60% of books from first-time authors; 100% from unagented writers. Pays 10% royalty on retail price or outright purchase of $50-200 for anthology contributors. Publishes book an average of 12-18 months after acceptance. Photocopied submissions OK. Computer printout submissions OK; prefers letter-quality. Reports in 1 month on queries; 6 months on ms. Free book catalog.

Nonfiction: Humor, illustrated book, juvenile, reference, desk calendars. Subjects include art/architecture, ethnic, history, language/literature, photography, regional and women's issues/studies. "We do not want to see manuscripts from the U.S.; we are a Canadian publisher. We are interested in history for our region and books on multicultural themes pertaining to our region." Reviews artwork/photos as part of ms package.

Recent Nonfiction Title: *Plainspeaking*, by Doris Hillis.

Fiction: Ethnic, experimental, fantasy, feminist, humor, juvenile, literary, mainstream/contemporary, picture books, plays, short story collections. "No popular, mass market sort of stuff. We are a literary press." Submit complete ms.

Recent Fiction Title: *Women of Influence*, by Bonnie Burnard.

THE COUNTRYMAN PRESS, INC., Box 175, Woodstock VT 05091. (802)457-1049. Fiction: Louis Kannenstine, president. Nonfiction: Carl Taylor, vice president. Publishes hardcover and trade paperback originals and paperback reprints. Publishes 24 titles/year. Receives 150 submissions/year. 50% of books from first-time authors; 75% from unagented writers. Pays 5-10% royalty on retail price. Offers $500 average advance. Publishes book an average of 1 year after acceptance. Simultaneous and photocopied submissions OK.

Computer printout submissions OK; prefers letter-quality. Reports in 2 weeks on queries; in 6 weeks on mss. Free book catalog.

Nonfiction: Cookbook, how-to, humor, travel guides. Subjects include cooking, foods and nutrition, history, nature/environment, recreation, regional (New England, especially Vermont), travel. "We want good 'how-to' books, especially those related to rural life." Submit outline/synopsis and sample chapters. Review artwork/photos as part of ms package.

Recent Nonfiction Title: *Maine, An Explorer's Guide*, by Tree/Steadman (travel guide).

Fiction: Mystery. "We're looking for good mysteries of any type—new, reprint, or U.S. publication of mysteries already published abroad." Submit outline, sample chapter, and SASE.

Recent Fiction Title: *The Long Kill*, by Reginald Hill writing as Patrick Ruell (mystery).

‡**THE COUNTRYWOMAN'S PRESS**, Subsidiary of Padre Productions, Box 840, Arroyo Grande CA 93420-0840. (805)473-1947. Editor and Publisher: Karen L. Reinecke. Publishes hardcover and trade paperback originals. Firm averages 4 titles/year. Receives 100 submissions/year. 100% from first-time authors; 100% from unagented writers. Pays 6-10% royalty on retail price.

Nonfiction: Cookbook, how-to. Subjects include agriculture/horticulture, animals (domestic), cooking, foods and nutrition, gardening, nature/environment and recreation. Submit outline/synopsis and sample chapters. Reviews artwork/photos as part of ms package.

CRAFTSMAN BOOK COMPANY, 6058 Corte Del Cedro, Box 6500, Carlsbad CA 92008. (619)438-7828. FAX (619)438-0398. Editor-in-Chief: Laurence D. Jacobs. Publishes paperback originals. Averages 8-12 titles/year; receives 20 submissions/year. 50% of books from first-time authors; 98% of books from unagented writers. Pays 12.5% royalty on wholesale price; pays 12.5% royalty on retail price "when we retail by mail." Publishes book an average of 18 months after acceptance. Simultaneous and photocopied submissions OK. Query for electronic submissions. Computer printout submissions OK; prefers letter-quality. Reports in 1 month on queries; 10 weeks on mss. Free book catalog and ms guidelines.

Nonfiction: How-to and technical. All titles are related to construction for professional builders. Submit outline/synopsis and sample chapters. Reviews artwork/photos as part of ms package.

Recent Nonfiction Title: *Residential Electrician's Handbook*, by Traister.

Tips: "The book should be loaded with step-by-step instructions, illustrations, charts, reference data, forms, samples, cost estimates, rules of thumb, and examples that solve actual problems in the builder's office and in the field. The book must cover the subject completely, become the owner's primary reference on the subject, have a high utility-to-cost ratio, and help the owner make a better living in his chosen field."

CREATIVE ARTS BOOK COMPANY, Donald S. Ellis, San Francisco; Black Lizard Books; Creative Arts Communications Books; 833 Bancroft Way, Berkeley CA 94710. (415)848-4777. Publisher: Donald S. Ellis. Senior Editor: Peg O'Donnell. Publishes hardcover and paperback originals and paperback reprints. Averages 38 titles/year; receives 800-1,000 submissions annually. 10% of books from first-time authors; 20% of books from unagented writers. Pays 5-15% royalty on retail price. Offers minimum $500 advance. Publishes book an average of 12-18 months after acceptance. Simultaneous and photocopied submissions OK. Computer printout submissions acceptable. Reports in 6 weeks. Free book catalog.

Nonfiction: Biographies and essays. Especially interested in music and works on California.

Recent Nonfiction Title: *Russia*, by Nikos Kazantzakis.

Fiction: "Looking for serious literary fiction of broad appeal," especially books by and/or about women and crime fiction (Black Lizard Books).

Recent Fiction Title: *California Childhood: Recollections and Stories of the Golden State*, edited by Gary Soto.

CREATIVE PUBLISHING CO., The Early West, Box 9292, College Station TX 77840. (409)775-6047. Contact: Theresa Earle. Publishes hardcover originals. Receives 20-40 submissions/year. 50% of books from first-time authors; 100% from unagented writers. Royalty varies on wholesale price. Publishes book an average of 8 months after acceptance. Photocopied submissions OK. Computer printout submissions OK; prefers letter-quality. Reports in "several" week on queries; "several" months on mss. Free book catalog.

Nonfiction: Biography. Subjects include Americana (western), history. No mss other than 19th century western America. Query. Reviews artwork/photos as part of ms package.

Recent Nonfiction Title: *Garrett & Roosevelt*, by Jack DeMattos.

THE CROSSING PRESS, 22-D Roache Rd., Box 1048, Freedom CA 95019. (408)722-0711. Co-Publishers: Elaine Goldman Gill, John Gill. Publishes hardcover and trade paperback originals. Averages 30 titles/year; receives 1,600 submissions annually. 30% of books from first-time authors; 90% of books from unagented writers. Pays royalty. Publishes book an average of 18 months after acceptance. Simultaneous and photocopied submissions OK. Query for electronic submissions. Computer printout submissions acceptable. Reports in 2 weeks on queries; 2 months on mss. Free book catalog.

Nonfiction: Cookbook, how-to, men's studies, literary and feminist. Subjects include cooking, health, gays and feminism. Submissions to be considered for the feminist series must be written by women. Submit outline and sample chapter. Reviews artwork/photos as part of ms package.
Recent Nonfiction Title: *Salad Dressings*, by Jane M. Dieckmann (cookbook).
Fiction: Good literary material. Submit outline and sample chapter.
Recent Fiction Title: *Class Porn*, by Molly Hite (novel).
Tips: "Simple intelligent query letters do best. No come-ons, no cutes. It helps if there are credentials. Authors should research the press first to see what sort of books it publishes."

CROSSWAY BOOKS, Subsidiary of Good News Publishers, 9825 W. Roosevelt Rd., Westchester IL 60154. Managing Editor: Ted Griffin. Publishes hardcover and trade paperback originals. Averages 35 titles/year; receives 2,000 submissions annually. 10% of books from first-time authors; 50% of books from unagented writers. Average print order for a writer's first book is 3,000. Pays negotiable royalty; offers negotiable advance. Publishes book an average of 1 year after acceptance. Send query and synopsis, not whole manuscript. No phone queries! Reports in 3 months. Book catalog and ms guidelines for 6x9 SAE and $1 postage.
Nonfiction: Subjects include issues on Christianity in contemporary culture, Christian doctrine, and church history. "All books must be written out of Christian perspective or world view." No unsolicited mss. Query with synopsis.
Recent Nonfiction Title: *Sanctified Through the Truth*, by Martyn Lloyd-Jones.
Fiction: Mainstream; science fiction; fantasy (genuinely creative in the tradition of C.S. Lewis, J.R.R. Tolkien and Madeleine L'Engle); and juvenile (10-14; 13-16). No formula romance. Query with synopsis. "All fiction must be written from a genuine Christian perspective."
Recent Fiction Title: *Piercing the Darkness*, by Frank E. Peretti.
Tips: "The writer has the best chance of selling our firm a book which, through fiction or nonfiction, shows the practical relevance of biblical doctrine to contemporary issues and life."

CROWN PUBLISHERS, INC., 225 Park Ave. S., New York NY 10003. (212)254-1600. Imprints include Clarkson N. Potter, Orion Books, Harmony and Julian Press. Publishes hardcover and paperback originals. Publishes 250 titles/year. Simultaneous submissions OK. Reports in 2 months.
Nonfiction: Americana, animals, art, biography, cookbooks/cooking, health, history, hobbies, how-to, humor, juveniles, military history, nature, photography, politics, psychology, recreation, reference, science, self-help and sports. Query with letter only.

HARRY CUFF PUBLICATIONS LIMITED, 1 Dorset St., St. John's, Newfoundland A1B 1W8 Canada. (709)726-6590. Editor: Harry Cuff. Publishes hardcover and trade paperback originals. Averages 12 titles/year; receives 50 submissions annually. 50% of books from first-time authors; 100% of books from unagented writers. Pays 10% royalty on retail price. No advance. Publishes book an average of 8 months after acceptance. Photocopied submissions OK. Computer printout submissions acceptable; no dot-matrix. Reports in 6 months on mss. Book catalog for 5x9 SAE.
Nonfiction: Biography, humor, reference, technical, and textbook, all dealing with Newfoundland. Subjects include history, photography, politics and sociology. Query.
Recent Nonfiction Title: *A History of the Newfoundland Railway, Volume I*, by A.R. Penney.
Fiction: Ethnic, historical, humor and mainstream. Needs fiction about Newfoundlanders or Newfoundland. Submit complete ms.
Recent Fiction Title: *A Fresh Breeze From Pigeon Inlet*, by Ted Russell.
Tips: "We are currently dedicated to publishing book about Newfoundland. We will return 'mainstream' manuscripts from the U.S. unread."

***DANCE HORIZONS,** Imprint of Princeton Book Co., Publishers, Box 57, Pennington NJ 08534. (609)737-8177. Editorial Director: Richard Carlin. Publishes hardcover and paperback originals and paperback reprints. Averages 10 titles/year; receives 50-75 submissions annually. 50% of books from first-time authors; 100% of books from unagented writers. Subsidy publishes 20% of books. Pays 10% royalty on net receipts; offers no advance. Publishes book an average of 10 months after acceptance. Simultaneous and photocopied submissions OK. Computer printout submissions acceptable; no dot-matrix. Reports in 3 months. Free book catalog.
Nonfiction: "Anything dealing with dance." Query first. Reviews artwork/photos.
Recent Nonfiction Title: *People Who Dance*, by John Gruen.

JOHN DANIEL AND COMPANY, PUBLISHERS, Box 21922, Santa Barbara CA 93121. (805)962-1780. Publisher: John Daniel. Publishes trade paperback originals. Averages 10 titles/year; receives 600 submissions annually. 50% of books from first-time authors; 100% of books from unagented writers. Pays 10% royalty on wholesale price. Publishes book an average of 8 months after acceptance. Simultaneous and photocopied submissions OK. Query for electronic submissions. Computer printout submissions acceptable. Reports in 3 weeks on queries; 2 months on mss. Book catalog and ms guidelines for #10 SASE.

Nonfiction: Autobiography, biography, humor, self-help, travel, nature, philosophy and essays. "We'll look at anything, but are particularly interested in books in which literary merit is foremost — as opposed to books that simply supply information. No libelous, obscene, poorly written or unintelligent manuscripts." Query or submit outline and sample chapters.
Recent Nonfiction Title: *A Year in Baghdad*, by Albert V. Baez and Joan Baez Sr. (travel memoir).
Fiction: Adventure, ethnic, experimental, fantasy, historical, humor, mainstream and mystery. "We do best with books by authors who have demonstrated a clear, honest, elegant style. No libelous, obscene, poorly written, or boring submissions." Query or submit synopsis and sample chapters.
Recent Fiction Title: *Big Chocolate Cookies*, by E.S. Goldman (novel).
Poetry: "We're open to anything, but we're very cautious. Poetry's hard to sell." Submit complete ms.
Recent Poetry Title: *A Soldier's Time*, by R.L. Barth.
Tips: "If I were a writer trying to market a book today, I would envision my specific audience and approach publishers who demonstrate that they can reach that audience. Writing is not always a lucrative profession; almost nobody makes a living off of royalties from small press publishing houses. That's why the authors we deal with are dedicated to their art and proud of their books — but don't expect to appear on the Carson show. Small press publishers have a hard time breaking into the bookstore market. We try, but we wouldn't be able to survive without a healthy direct-mail sale."

DANTE UNIVERSITY OF AMERICA PRESS, INC., Box 843, Brookline VA 02147. Contact: Manuscripts Editor. Publishes hardcover originals and reprints, and trade paperback originals and reprints. Averages 5 titles/ year; receives 50 submissions annually. 50% of books from first-time authors; 50% of books from unagented writers. Average print order for a writer's first book is 3,000. Pays royalty; offers negotiable advance. Publishes book an average of 10 months after acceptance. Simultaneous and photocopied submissions OK. Query for electronic submissions. Computer printout submissions acceptable. Reports in 2 weeks on queries only; 2 months on mss.
Nonfiction: Biography, reference, reprints, and nonfiction and fiction translations from Italian and Latin. Subjects include general scholarly nonfiction, Renaissance thought and letter, Italian language and linguistics, Italian-American history and culture, and bilingual education. Query first with SASE. Reviews artwork/ photos as part of ms package.
Poetry: "There is a chance that we would use Renaissance poetry translations."
Recent Poetry Title: *Tales of Suicide*, by Pirandello.

*MAY DAVENPORT, PUBLISHERS, 26313 Purissima Rd., Los Altos Hills CA 94022. (415)948-6499. Editor/ Publisher: May Davenport. Imprint is md Books (nonfiction and fiction). Publishes hardcover and trade paperback originals. Averages 4 titles/year; receives 1,000-2,000 submissions annually. 95% of books from first-time authors; 95% of books from unagented writers. May consider subsidy publishing on jr.-sr. high school textbooks and games only. Pays 15% royalty on retail price; no advance. Publishes book an average of 1-3 years after acceptance. Reports in 3 weeks. Ms guidelines for #10 SASE.
Nonfiction: Juvenile (13-17). Subjects include art, music, economics, money and banking. "Our readers are students in elementary and secondary public school districts, as well as correctional institutes of learning, etc." No "hack writing." Query.
Recent Nonfiction Title: *Willy, Zilly and The Little Bantams*, by Grace Collins (a pair of bantams use chicken sense to survive.).
Fiction: Adventure, ethnic, fantasy. "We're overstocked with picture books and first readers; prefer stage and teleplays for TV-oriented teenagers (30 min. one act). "Be entertaining while informing." No sex or violence. Query with SASE.
Recent Fiction Title: *Comic Tales Anthology #2*, edited by May Davenport.
Tips: "Make people laugh. Humor has a place, too."

DAVIS PUBLICATIONS, INC., 50 Portland St., Worcester MA 01608. (617)754-7201. Managing Editor: Wyatt Wade. Averages 5-10 titles/year. Pays 10-15% royalty. Publishes book an average of 1 year after acceptance. Computer printout submissions acceptable; prefers letter-quality. Write for copy of guidelines for authors.
Nonfiction: Publishes art, design and craft books. Accepts nonfiction translations. "Keep in mind the intended audience. Our readers are visually oriented. All illustrations should be collated separately from the text, but keyed to the text. Photos should be good quality transparencies and black and white photographs. Well selected illustrations should explain, amplify, and enhance the text. We average 2-4 photos/page. We like to see technique photos as well as illustrations of finished artwork, by a variety of artists. Recent books have been on papermaking, airbrush painting, jewelry, design, puppets, quilting, and watercolor painting." Submit outline, sample chapters and illustrations. Reviews artwork/photos as part of ms package.

STEVE DAVIS PUBLISHING, Box 190831, Dallas TX 75219. (214)954-4469. Publisher: Steve Davis. Publishes hardcover and trade paperback originals. Averages 4 titles/year. Query for electronic submissions. Computer printout submissions acceptable. "Manuscripts should be professionally proofed for style, grammar and spelling before submission." Reports in 3 weeks on queries *if interested*. Not responsible for unsolicited material. Book catalog for SASE.

Nonfiction: Books on current issues and some reference books. "We are very selective about our list. We look for material that is professionally prepared, takes a fresh approach to a timely topic, and offers the reader helpful information." No religious or occult topics, no sports, and no mass market material such as diet books, joke books, exercise books, etc. Query with outline/summary, sample chapter and SASE. "We can only respond to projects that interest us."

Recent Nonfiction Title: *The Writer's Yellow Pages*, edited by Steve Davis (reference).

DAW BOOKS, INC., 1633 Broadway, New York NY 10019. Submissions Editor: Peter Stampfel. Publishes science fiction and fantasy hardcover and paperback originals and reprints. Publishes 60-80 titles/year. Pays in royalties with an advance that is negotiable on a book-by-book basis. Sends galleys to author. Simultaneous submissions "returned at once, unread unless prior arrangements are made by agent." Computer printout submissions acceptable; prefers letter-quality. Reports in 6 weeks "or longer, if a second reading is required." Free book catalog.

Fiction: "We are interested in science fiction and fantasy novels only. We do not publish any other category of fiction. We accept both agented and unagented ms. We are not seeking collections of short stories or ideas for anthologies. We do not want any nonfiction manuscripts." Submit complete ms.

DEL REY BOOKS, Imprint of Ballantine Books, 201 E. 50th St., New York NY 10022. (212)572-2677. Editor-in-Chief: Owen Lock. Vice President and Fantasy Editor: Lester del Rey. Publishes hardcover, trade paperback and mass market originals and mass market paperback reprints. Averages 80 titles/year; receives 1,600 submissions annually. 10% of books from first-time authors; 40% of books from unagented writers. Pays royalty on retail price. Offers competitive advance. Publishes book an average of 1 year after acceptance. Photocopied submissions OK. Computer printout submissions acceptable; legible dot-matrix acceptable. Reporting time slow. Writer's guidelines for #10 SASE.

Fiction: Fantasy ("should have the practice of magic as an essential element of the plot") and science fiction ("well-plotted novels with good characterization, exotic locales, and detailed alien cultures. Novels should have a 'sense of wonder' and be designed to please readers"). Will need "144 original fiction manuscripts of science fiction and fantasy suitable for publishing over the next two years. No flying-saucers, Atlantis, or occult novels." Submit complete ms or detailed outline and first three chapters.

Recent Fiction Title: *Dragonsdawn*, by Anne McCaffrey.

Tips: "Del Rey is a reader's house. Our audience is anyone who wants to be pleased by a good entertaining novel. We do very well with original fantasy novels, in which magic is a central element, and with hard-science science fiction novels. Pay particular attention to plotting and a satisfactory conclusion. It must be/feel believable. That's what the readers like."

DELACORTE PRESS, Imprint of Dell Publishing and division of Bantam Doubleday Dell, 666 5th Ave., New York NY 10103. (212)765-6500. Editor-in-Chief: Jackie Farber. Publishes hardcover originals. Publishes 36 titles/year. Royalty varies. Average advance. Publishes book an average of 2 years after acceptance, but varies. Simultaneous and photocopied submissions OK. Computer printout submissions acceptable; prefers letter-quality. Reports in 2 months. Book catalog and guidelines for SASE.

Fiction and Nonfiction: *Query, outline or brief proposal, or complete ms accepted*. No mss for children's or young adult books accepted in this division.

Recent Nonfiction Title: *MD*, by John Pekkanen.

Recent Fiction Title: *The Telling of Lies*, by Timothy Findley.

‡DELTA BOOKS, Division of Bantam Doubleday Dell Publishing Co., 666 Fifth Ave., New York NY 10103. (212)765-6500. Editorial Director: Bob Miller. Publishes trade paperback reprints and originals. Averages 20 titles/year. Pays 6-7½% royalty; offers advance. Simultaneous and photocopied submissions OK. Computer printout submissions acceptable; prefers letter-quality. Reports in 2 months. Book catalog for 8½x11 SASE.

Nonfiction: Biography, childcare, film, music, New Age, science. "We are expanding our base of strong childcare and New Age titles, while also looking for good books on popular culture (film, music, television) and developing a line of literary biographies." Query or submit outline/synopsis and sample chapters. *Prefers submissions through agents*.

Fiction: "We are looking for original, innovative and contemporary novels." Submit through an agent.

The double dagger before a listing indicates that the listing is new in this edition. New markets are often the most receptive to freelance submissions.

DEMBNER BOOKS, Division of Red Dembner Enterprises, Corp., 80 8th Ave., New York NY 10011. (212)924-2525. Editor: S. Arthur Dembner. Publishes hardcover and trade paperback originals, and hardcover and trade paperback reprints. Averages 10-15 titles/year; receives 500-750 submissions annually. 20% of books from first-time authors; 75% of books from unagented writers. Pays 10-15% royalty on hardcover; 6-7½% royalty on paperback, both on retail price. Offers average $1,000-5,000 advance. Publishes book an average of 1 year after acceptance. Simultaneous and photocopied submissions OK. Readable computer printout submissions acceptable; no dot-matrix. Reports in 2 weeks on queries; 10 weeks on mss. Book catalog available from W.W. Norton, 500 5th Ave., New York NY 10110. Writer's guidelines available for #10 SASE.
Nonfiction: How-to, reference. Subjects include health, film, history (popular), music, sports and social causes. "We want books written by knowledgeable authors who focus on a problem area (health/home) and offer an insightful guidance toward solutions." No surveys or collections—books that do not focus on one specific, promotable topic. No first-person accounts of tragic personal events. Also, no books on heavily published topics, such as weight loss and exercise programs. Query.
Recent Nonfiction Title: *Alfred Hitchcock and the Making of a Psycho*, by Stephen Rebello.
Fiction: Mystery, suspense and literary. "We look for genre fiction (mystery, suspense, etc.), that keeps pace with the times, deals with contemporary issues, and has three-dimensional characters. Occasionally we publish literary novels, but the writing must be of excellent quality." No indulgent, self-conscious fiction. Query and two sample chapters.
Recent Fiction Title: *Haunt of the Nightingale*, by John R. Riggs.
Tips: "We take a great deal of pride in the books we publish. No humor books or fad books. We're developing a strong backlist and want to continue to do so. Small hardcover houses such as ourselves are being very careful about the books they choose for publication primarily because secondary rights sales have dropped, and the money is less. Quality is of utmost importance."

T.S. DENISON & CO., INC., 9601 Newton Ave. S., Minneapolis MN 55431. Editor-in-Chief: Sherrill B. Flora. Publishes teacher aid materials; receives 500 submissions annually. 90% of books from first-time authors; 100% of books from unagented writers. Average print order for a writer's first book is 3,000. Royalty varies; no advance. Publishes book an average of 1-2 years after acceptance. Photocopied submissions OK. Computer printout submissions acceptable; no dot-matrix. Reports in 1 month. Book catalog and ms guidelines for SASE.
Nonfiction: Specializes in early childhood and elementary school teaching aids. Send prints if photos are to accompany ms. Submit complete ms. Reviews artwork/photos as part of ms package.

DENLINGERS PUBLISHERS, LTD., Box 76, Fairfax VA 22030. (703)830-4646. Publisher: William W. Denlinger. Publishes hardcover and trade paperback originals, hardcover and trade paperback reprints. Averages 12 titles/year; receives 250 submissions annually. 5% of books from first-time authors; 95% of books from unagented writers. Average print order for a writer's first book is 3,000. Pays variable royalty. No advance. Publishes book an average of 18 months after acceptance. Simultaneous and photocopied submissions OK. Query for electronic submissions. Computer printout submissions acceptable; prefers letter-quality. Reports in 1 week on queries; 6 weeks on mss. Book catalog for SASE.
Nonfiction: How-to and technical books; dog-breed books only. Query. Reviews artwork/photos as part of ms package.
Recent Nonfiction Title: *Dogs in Sports*, by Steven Rufe.

*DEVIN-ADAIR PUBLISHERS, INC., 6 N. Water St., Greenwich CT 06830. (203)531-7755. Editor: Jane Andrassi. Publishes hardcover and paperback originals, reprints and software. Averages 20 titles/year; receives up to 500 submissions annually. 30% of books from first-time authors; 70% of books from unagented writers. Average print order for a writer's first book is 7,500. Subsidy publishes 5% of books. Royalty on sliding scale, 5-25%; "average advance is low." Publishes book an average of 9 months after acceptance. No simultaneous submissions. Query for electronic submissions. Computer printout submissions acceptable; prefers letter-quality. Book catalog and guidelines for 6x9 SAE and 5 first class stamps.
Nonfiction: Publishes Americana, business, how-to, conservative politics, history, medicine, nature, economics, sports and travel books. New line: homeopathic books. Accepts translations. Query or submit outline/synopsis and sample chapters. Looks for "early interest, uniqueness, economy of expression, good style, and new information." Reviews artwork/photos as part of ms package.
Recent Nonfiction Title: *Exploring Old Block Island*, by H. Whitman and R. Fox.
Tips: "We seek to publish books of high quality manufacture. We spend 8% more on production and design than necessary to ensure a better quality book. Trends include increased specialization and a more narrow view of a subject. General overviews in computer publishing are now a thing of the past. Better a narrow subject in depth than a wide superficial one."

‡*DEVONSHIRE PUBLISHING CO., Box 85, Elgin IL 60121-0085. (312)242-3846. Vice President: Don Reynolds. Publishes hardcover and trade paperback originals. Averages 4 titles/year; receives 1,000 submissions annually. 85% of books from first-time authors; 75% of books from unagented writers. Subsidy publishes

20% of books. "Although we do not generally subsidy publish we will enter into 'cooperative publishing agreements' with an author if the subject matter is of such limited appeal that we doubt its profitability, or if the author desires a more extravagant finished product than we planned to produce." Pays 10-15% royalty on retail price. "Royalty would be higher if author engaged in cooperative venture." Offers negotiable advance. Publishes book an average of 1 year after acceptance. Simultaneous and photocopied submissions OK. Computer printout submissions acceptable; prefers letter-quality. Reports in 1 month on queries; 2 months on submissions. Book catalog and guidelines for #10 SASE.

Nonfiction: Reference, technical and textbook. Subjects include business and economics, history, hobbies, nature, psychology, religion and sociology. "We will be looking for books that have an impact on the reader. A history or religious book will have to be more than just a recitation of past events. Our books must have some relation to today's problems or situations." No works of personal philosophy or unverifiable speculation. Query and/or submit outline/synopsis.

Recent Nonfiction Title: *The Way We Were*, by Mace Crandall Erandall (history).

Fiction: Erotica, experimental, historical, horror, religious and science fiction. "All works must have some relevance to today's reader and be well written. We hope to produce one or two titles, but our main thrust will be in the nonfiction area. However, if a work is thought-provoking and/or controversial, we may give it priority. Query and/or submit outline/synopsis.

Recent Fiction Title: *The Making of Bernie Trumble*, by Robert Wetherall (adult humor).

Tips: "Since we are a small publishing company, we can aim for the smaller, more specialized market. We envision that the audience for our books will be well educated with a specific area of interest. We can afford to look at work that other publishers have passed over. Although we are not looking for works that are controversial just for the sake of controversy, we are looking for topics that go beyond the norm. If it is documented and has a strong basis or foundation, we will endeavor to publish it."

DIAL BOOKS FOR YOUNG READERS, Division of NAL Penguin Inc., 2 Park Ave., New York NY 10016. (212)725-1818. Submissions Editor: Phyllis J. Sogelman. Imprints include Dial Easy-to-Read Books and Dial Very First Books. Publishes hardcover originals. Averages 60 titles/year; receives 6,000-7,000 submissions annually. 15% of books from first-time authors. Pays variable royalty and advance. Simultaneous and photocopied submissions OK, but not preferred. Computer printout submissions acceptable. Reports in 2 weeks on queries; 3 months on mss. Book catalog and ms guidelines for 9x12 SASE.

Nonfiction: Juvenile picture books and young adult books. Especially looking for "quality picture books and well-researched young adult and middle-reader mss." Not interested in alphabet books, riddle and game books, and early concept books. Query with outline/synopsis and sample chapters. Reviews artwork/photos.

Recent Nonfiction Title: *Getting Your Period: A Book About Menstruation*, by Jean Marzollo.

Fiction: Adventure, fantasy, historical, humor, mystery, romance (appropriate for young adults), and suspense. Especially looking for "lively and well written novels for middle grade and young adult children involving a convincing plot and believable characters. The subject matter or theme should not already be overworked in previously published books. The approach must not be demeaning to any minority group, nor should the roles of female characters (or others) be stereotyped, though we don't think books should be didactic, or in any way message-y." No "topics inappropriate for the juvenile, young adult, and middle grade audiences. No plays or poetry." Submit complete ms.

Recent Fiction Title: *Where It Stops, Nobody Knows*, by Amy Ehrlich.

Tips: "Our readers are anywhere from preschool age to teenage. Picture books must have strong plots, lots of action, unusual premises, or universal themes treated with freshness and originality. Humor works well in these books. A very well thought out and intelligently presented book has the best chance of being taken on. Genre isn't as much of a factor as presentation."

‡*DIGITAL PRESS, Subsidiary of Digital Equipment Corp., 12 Crosby Dr., Bedford MA 01730. (617)276-4809. Executive Editor: Michael Meehan. Publishes hardcover and trade paperback originals. Firm averages 15 titles/year. Receives 75-100 submissions/year. 75% of books from first-time authors; 100% from unagented writers. Subsidy publishes 50% of books. Pays 10-15% royalty on wholesale price. Publishes book an average of 7 months after acceptance. Simultaneous and photocopied submissions OK. Query for electronic submissions. Computer printout submissions OK. Reports in 6 weeks. Free book catalog.

Nonfiction: Software and technical. Subjects include computers and electronics. "We will consider all proposed manuscripts on Digital's computer systems. VAX hardware, VMS operating system—also in the area of networking. No manuscripts based on other systems, IBM, etc." Submit outline/synopsis and sample chapters. Reviews artwork/photos as part of package.

DILLON PRESS, INC., 242 Portland Ave. S., Minneapolis MN 55415. (612)333-2691. Editorial Director: Uva Dillon. Senior Editor: Tom Schneider. Nonfiction Editor: Lora Polack. Publishes hardcover originals. Averages 30-40 titles/year; receives 3,000 submissions annually. 30% of books from first-time authors; 90% of books from unagented writers. Average print order for a writer's first book is 3,000-5,000. Pays royalty or by outright purchase. Publishes book an average of 18 months after acceptance. Computer printout submissions acceptable; no dot-matrix. Reports in 2 months. Book catalog for 10x12 SAE with 4 first class stamps.

Nonfiction: "We are actively seeking mss for the juvenile educational market." Subjects include world and U.S. geography, international festivals and holidays, U.S. states and cities, contemporary and historical biographies for elementary and middle grade levels, unusual approaches to science topics for primary grade readers, unusual or remarkable animals, and contemporary issues of interest and value to young people. Submit complete ms or outline and 2 sample chapters; query letters if accompanied by book proposal. Reviews artwork/photos as part of ms package.
Recent Nonfiction Title: *San Francisco*, by Patricia Haddock.
Tips: "Before writing, authors should check out the existing competition for their book idea to determine if it is really needed and stands a reasonable chance for success, especially for a nonfiction proposal."

‡**DIMENSION BOOKS, INC.**, Box 811, Denville NJ 07834-0811. (201)627-4334. Contact: Thomas P. Coffey. Publishes 25 titles/year; receives 450-500 submissions annually. 10% of books from first-time authors; 60% of books from unagented writers. Pays "regular royalty schedule" based on retail price; advance is negotiable. Publishes book an average of 3-5 months after acceptance. Computer printout submissions acceptable. Book catalog and guidelines for SAE and 2 first class stamps. Reports in 2 weeks.
Nonfiction: Publishes general nonfiction including religion, principally Roman Catholic. Also psychology. Accepts nonfiction translations. Query. Submit outline/synopsis and 3 sample chapters. Length: 40,000 words minimum. Reviews artwork/photos as part of ms package.
Recent Nonfiction Title: *The Enneagram: A Journey of Self-Discovery*, by Beesing, Nogosek, and O'Leary.

DOLL READER, Subsidiary of Hobby House Press, Inc., 900 Frederick St., Cumberland MD 21502. (301)759-3770. FAX: (301)759-4940. Subsidiaries include *Doll Reader* and *The Teddy Bear and Friends Magazine*. Publisher: Gary R. Ruddell. Publishes hardcover and paperbound originals. Averages 24 titles/year. 20% of books from first-time authors; 90% of books from unagented writers. Pays royalty. Publishes book an average of 24 months after acceptance. Simultaneous and photocopied submissions OK. Computer printout submissions acceptable; prefers letter-quality. Reports in 1 month. Ms guidelines for 9x12 SAE.
Nonfiction: Doll-related books. "We publish books pertaining to dolls, teddy bears and crafts as a collector's hobby; we also publish pattern books. The *Doll Reader* is published 8 times a year dealing with the hobby of doll collecting. We appeal to those people who are doll collectors, miniature collectors, as well as people who sew for dolls. Our magazine has a worldwide circulation of close to 72,000." Query or submit outline/ synopsis. Reviews artwork/photos as part of ms package. *The Teddy Bear and Friends Magazine* is published bimonthly.
Recent Nonfiction Title: *9th Blue Book of Dolls and Values*, by Jan Foulke (price guide for dolls).

DOUBLEDAY & CO., INC., 666 5th Ave., New York NY 10103. (212)765-6500. Publishes hardcover and paperback originals. Offers royalty on retail price; offers variable advance. Reports in 2½ months. "At present, Doubleday is *only* able to consider fiction for mystery/suspense, science fiction, and romance imprints." Send proposal/synopsis to Crime Club Editor, Science Fiction Editor, or Loveswept Editor as appropriate. Sufficient postage for return via fourth class mail must accompany manuscript.

DOWN EAST BOOKS, Division of Down East Enterprise, Inc., Box 679, Camden ME 04843. (207)594-9544. Editor: Karin Womer. Publishes hardcover and trade paperback originals and trade paperback reprints. Averages 10-14 titles/year; receives 300 submissions annually. 50% of books from first-time authors; 90% of books from unagented writers. Average print order for a writer's first book is 2,500. Pays 10-15% on receipts. Offers average $200 advance. Publishes book an average of 1 year after acceptance. Simultaneous and photocopied submissions OK. Computer printout submissions acceptable; prefers letter-quality. Reports in 2 weeks on queries; 2 months on mss. Book catalog and ms guidelines for 9x12 SAE with 2 first class stamps.
Nonfiction: Books about the New England region, Maine in particular. Subjects include Americana, cooking and foods, history, nature, traditional crafts and recreation. "All of our books must have a Maine or New England emphasis." Query. Reviews artwork/photos as part of ms package.
Recent Nonfiction Title: *Maine's Natural Heritage: Rare Species and Unique Natural Features*, by Dean Bennett.
Fiction: "We publish no fiction except for an occasional juvenile title (average 1/year)."
Recent Fiction Title: *The Amazing Marsh: Alex Discovers a Hidden World*, by Eve Knowles.

DRAMA BOOK PUBLISHERS, 260 Fifth Ave., New York NY 10001. (212)725-5377. Contact: Ralph Pine or Judith Holmes. Publishes hardcover and paperback originals and reprints. Averages 4-15 titles/year; receives 500 submissions annually. 70% of books from first-time authors; 90% of books from unagented writers. Royalty varies; advance varies; negotiable. Publishes book an average of 18 months after acceptance. Computer printout submissions acceptable; prefers letter-quality. Reports in 2 months.
Nonfiction: Books—texts, guides, manuals, directories, reference—for and about performing arts theory and practice: acting, directing; voice, speech, movement, music, dance, mime; makeup, masks, wigs; costumes, sets, lighting, sound; design and execution; technical theatre, stagecraft, equipment; stage management; producing; arts management, all varieties; business and legal aspects; film, radio, television, cable, video;

theory, criticism, reference; playwriting; theatre and performance history. Accepts nonfiction, drama and technical works in translations also. Query; accepts 1-3 sample chapters; no complete mss. Reviews artwork/photos as part of ms package.

Fiction: Professionally produced plays and musicals.

‡**DUNDURN PRESS LTD.**, 2181 Queen St. E., Toronto, Ontario M4E 1E5 Canada. (416)698-0454. Publisher: Kirk Howard. Publishes hardcover, trade paperback and hardcover reprints. Averages 15 titles/year; receives 500 submissions annually. 45% of books from first-time authors; 90% of books from unagented writers. Average print order for a writer's first book is 2,000. Pays 10% royalty on retail price; 8% royalty on some paperback children's books. Publishes book an average of 1 year after acceptance. "Easy-to-read" photocopied submissions OK. Computer printout submissions acceptable; prefers letter-quality. Query for electronic submissions.

Nonfiction: Biography, coffee table books, juvenile (12 and up), literary and reference. Subjects include Canadiana, art, history, hobbies, Canadian history and literary criticism. Especially looking for Canadian biographies. No religious or soft science topics. Query with outline/synopsis and sample chapters. Reviews artwork/photos as part of ms package.

Tips: "Publishers want more books written in better prose styles. If I were a writer trying to market a book today, I would visit bookstores and watch what readers buy and what company publishes that type of book 'close' to my manuscript."

*DUQUESNE UNIVERSITY PRESS, 600 Forbes Ave., Pittsburgh PA 15282. (412)434-6610. Averages 9 titles/year; receives 400 submissions annually. 25% of books from first-time authors; 100% of books from unagented writers. Average print order for a writer's first book is 1,500. Subsidy publishes 20% of books. Pays 10% royalty on net sales; no advance. Publishes book an average of 1 year after acceptance. Query for electronic submissions. Computer printout submissions acceptable; no dot-matrix. Query. Reports in 3 months.

Nonfiction: Scholarly books in the humanities, social sciences for academics, libraries, college bookstores and educated laypersons. Length: open. Looks for scholarship.

Recent Nonfiction Title: *Imaginative Thinking*, by Edward L. Murray.

DUSTBOOKS, Box 100, Paradise CA 95967. (916)877-6110. Publisher: Len Fulton. Publishes hardcover and paperback originals. Averages 7 titles/year. Offers 15% royalty. Offers average $500 advance. Simultaneous and photocopied submissions OK if so informed. Computer printout submissions acceptable. Reports in 2 months. Free book catalog; writer's guidelines for #10 SASE.

Nonfiction: Technical. "DustBooks would like to see manuscripts dealing with microcomputers (software, hardware) and water (any aspect). Must be technically sound and well-written. We have at present no titles in these areas. These represent an expansion of our interests. Our specialty is directories of small presses, poetry publishers, and a monthly newsletter on small publishers (*Small Press Review*)." Submit outline/synopsis and sample chapters.

DUTTON CHILDREN'S BOOKS, Penguin Books USA Inc., 2 Park Ave., New York NY 10016. (212)725-1818. Editor-in-Chief: Lucia Monfried. Firm publishes hardcover originals. Publishes 70 titles/year. 15% from first-time authors. Pays royalty on retail price. Simultaneous and photocopied submissions OK. Computer printout submissions OK. Reports in 1 month on queries; 3 months on mss. Book catalog for 9½x11 SAE with $1.65 postage; ms guidelines for #10 SASE.

Nonfiction: Juvenile. Subjects include animals, nature/environment and science. Submit outline/synopsis and sample chapters.

Fiction: Adventure, fantasy, juvenile, picture books, science fiction, and young adult.

EES* PUBLICATIONS, Subsidiary of Education for Emergency Services, Inc. (EES*), 6801 Lake Worth Rd. Lake Worth FL 33467. (407)642-3340. Director: Candace Brown-Nixon. Publishes trade paperback originals. Firm averages 3-6 titles/year. 10% of books from first-time authors. Pays 10-15% royalty on retail price. Negotiable re: outright purchase. Publishes book an average of 2 months after acceptance. Computer printout submissions OK. Reports in 2 weeks on queries; 1 month on mss. Free book catalog and ms guidelines, "just send legible address."

Nonfiction: How-to, reference, technical and textbook. Subjects include education (EMS field only) and health/medicine (EMS related only). "We're interested in specialized EMS, law enforcement, fire-related topics. Authors must be properly credentialed for the topic." No pictorial history, how to read an EKG, general topic initial education textbooks, or nursing topics. Query or submit outline/synopsis and sample chapters.

Recent Nonfiction Title: *Documentation: The Big CYA*, by C. Brown-Nixon.

Tips: "Writers have the best chance of selling us a specialized topic about which the author is acutely knowledgeable and properly credentialed-i.e., an EMT should not attempt to write on an ALS level. EMTs, paramedics, rescue personnel, students and educators in EMS/rescue are our audience."

‡**E.P. DUTTON**, Division of Penguin USA, 2 Park Ave., New York NY 10016. (212)725-1818. Publishes hardcover and trade paperback originals and reprints. Firm averages 160 titles/year. Receives 4,000 submissions/year. 10% of books from first-time authors. 2% from unagented writers. Pays royalty. Simultaneous and photocopied submissions OK. Computer printout submissions OK. Reports in 2 months on queries; 4 months on mss. Manuscript guidelines for #10 SAE and 1 first-class stamp.

Nonfiction: Biography, coffee table book, cookbook, how-to, humor, illustrated book and self-help. Query with outline/synopsis and sample chapters.

Fiction: Mainstream/contemporary. "We don't publish genre romances or westerns." Query with outline/synopsis and sample chapters and complete ms.

EAKIN PUBLICATIONS, INC., Box 23069, Austin TX 78735. (512)288-1771. Imprints include Eakin Press and Nortex Press. Editorial Director: Edwin M. Eakin. Publishes hardcover and paperback originals and reprints. Averages 40 titles/year; receives 500 submissions annually. 80% of books from first-time authors; 90% of books from unagented writers. Average print order for a writer's first book is 2,000-5,000. Pays 10-12-15% in royalty. Publishes book an average of 1 year after acceptance. Simultaneous and photocopied submissions OK. Query for electronic submissions. Computer printout submissions acceptable; prefers letter-quality. Reports in 3 months. Book catalog and ms guidelines for #10 SAE with 4 first class stamps.

Nonfiction: Adult nonfiction categories include Western Americana, World War II, business, sports, biographies, Early Americana, contemporary topics, women's studies, Civil War, cookbooks, regional Texas history. Juvenile nonfiction includes biographies of historic personalities, prefer with Texas or regional interest, or nature studies. Easy read illustrated books for grades one through three.

Recent Nonfiction Title: *Centaur of the North*, by Dr. Manuel A. Machado.

Fiction: "Adult fiction mostly by published writers." Juvenile fiction for grades four through seven, preferably relating to Texas and the southwest or contemporary. Query or submit outline/synopsis and sample chapters.

***ECW PRESS**, Subsidiaries include Emerson House, Essays on Canadian Writing. 307 Coxwell Ave., Toronto, Ontario M4L 3B5 Canada. (416)694-3348. President: Jack David. Publishes hardcover and trade paperback originals. Publishes 12-15 titles/year; receives 120 submissions annually. 50% of books from first-time authors; 80% of books from unagented writers. Subsidy publishes (nonauthor) up to 5% of books. Pays 10% royalty on retail price. Simultaneous and photocopied submissions OK. Query for electronic submissions. Computer printout submissions acceptable; prefers letter-quality. Reports in 2 weeks. Free book catalog.

Nonfiction: Reference and Canadian literary criticism. "ECW is interested in all literary criticism aimed at the undergraduate and graduate university market." Query. Reviews artwork/photos as part of ms package.

Recent Nonfiction Title: *John Glassco's Richer World*, by Philip Kokotailo (literary criticism).

Tips: "The writer has the best chance of selling literary criticism to our firm because that's our specialty and the only thing that makes us money."

‡***EDICIONES UNIVERSAL**, 3090 S.W. 8th St., Miami FL 33135. (305)642-3355. FAX: (305)642-7978. Director: Juan M. Salvat. Publishes trade paperback originals in Spanish. Publishes 50 titles/year; receives 150 submissions/year. 40% of books from first-time authors. 90% of books from unagented writers. Subsidy publishes 10% of books. Pays 5-10% royalty on retail price. Publishes book an average of 9 months after acceptance. Simultaneous and photocopied submissions OK. Computer printout submissions OK; prefers letter-quality. Reports in 1 month on queries; 2 months on mss. Book catalog free.

Nonfiction: Biography, cookbook, humor and reference. Subjects include cooking and foods, philosophy, politics, psychology and sociology. "We specialize in Cuban topics." All manuscripts must be in Spanish. Submit outline/synopsis and sample chapters. Reviews artwork/photos as part of ms package.

Recent Nonfiction Title: *Cuba: Destiny as Choice*, by Wilfredo del Prado.

Fiction: "We will consider everything as long as it is written in Spanish." Submit outline/synopsis and sample chapters.

Recent Fiction Title: *El Rumbo*, by Joaquin Delgado-Sanchez.

Poetry: "We will consider any Spanish-language poetry." Submit 3 or more poems.

Recent Poetry Title: *Antologia De Poesia Infantil*, by Ana Rosa Nunez.

Tips: "Our audience is composed entirely of Spanish-language readers. This is a very limited market. Books on Cuban or Latin American topics have the best chance of selling to our firm."

***EDUCATION ASSOCIATES**, Division of The Daye Press, Inc., Box 8021, Athens GA 30603. (404)542-4244. Editor, Text Division: D. Keith Osborn. Publishes hardcover and trade paperback originals. Averages 2-6 titles/year; receives 300 submissions annually. 1% of books from first-time authors; 100% of books from unagented writers. Subsidy publishes 5% of books. "We may publish a textbook which has a very limited audience and is of unusual merit ... but we still believe that the book will make a contribution to the educational field." Buys mss "on individual basis." Publishes book an average of 9 months after acceptance. Do not send ms; query first. No reponse without SASE. Reports in 1 month on queries.

Nonfiction: How-to and textbook. Subjects include psychology and education. "Books in the fields of early childhood and middle school education. Do not wish basic textbooks. Rather, are interested in more specific areas of interest in above fields. We are more interested in small runs on topics of more limited nature than general texts." Query only with one-page letter. If interested will request synopsis and sample chapters. Absolutely no reply unless SASE is enclosed. No phone queries.

Recent Nonfiction Title: *Discipline and Classroom Management*, by Janie D. Osborn (college textbook).

Tips: College textbooks—usually dealing with early childhood, middle school, or child development—have the best chance of selling to Education Associates.

*WILLIAM B. EERDMANS PUBLISHING CO., Christian University Press, 255 Jefferson Ave. SE, Grand Rapids MI 49503. (616)459-4591. FAX: (616)459-6540. Editor-in-Chief: Jon Pott. Managing Editor: Charles Van Hof. Publishes hardcover and paperback originals and reprints. Averages 65-70 titles/year; receives 3,000-4,000 submissions annually. 25% of books from first-time authors; 95% of books from unagented writers. Average print order for a writer's first book is 4,000. Subsidy publishes 1% of books. Pays 7½-10% royalty on retail price; usually no advance. Publishes book an average of 1 year after acceptance. Simultaneous and photocopied submissions OK if noted. Computer printout submissions acceptable; no dot-matrix. Reports in 3 weeks for queries; 4 months for mss. Looks for "quality and relevance." Free book catalog.

Nonfiction: Reference, textbooks and tourists guidebooks. Subjects include history, philosophy, psychology, religion, sociology, regional history and geography. "Approximately 80% of our publications are religious—specifically Protestant—and largely of the more academic or theological variety (as opposed to the devotional, inspirational or celebrity-conversion books). Our history and social studies titles aim, similarly, at an academic audience; some of them are documentary histories. We prefer that writers take the time to notice if we have published anything at all in the same category as their manuscript before sending it to us." Accepts nonfiction translations. Query. Accepts outline/synopsis and 2-3 sample chapters. Reviews artwork/photos.

Recent Nonfiction Title: *The Illuminating Icon*, by Anthony Ugolnik.

ELYSIUM GROWTH PRESS, 5436 Fernwood Ave., Los Angeles CA 90027. (213)455-1000. FAX (213)455-2007. Publishes hardcover and paperback originals, and hardcover and trade paperback reprints. Averages 4 titles/year; receives 20 submissions/year. 20% of books from first-time authors; 100% of books from unagented writers. Pays $5,000 average advance. Publishes book an average of 18 months after acceptance. Photocopied submissions OK. Query for electronic submissions. Computer printout submissions OK; no dot-matrix. Reports in 2 weeks on queries; 6 weeks on submissions. Book catalog free on request.

Nonfiction: Illustrated book, self-help and textbook. Subjects include health, nature, philosophy, photography, psychology, recreation, sociology and travel. A nudist, naturist, special niche publisher. Needs books on "body self-image, body self-appreciation, world travel and subjects depicting the clothing-optional lifestyle." Query. All unsolicited mss are returned unopened. Reviews artwork/photos as part of ms package.

Recent Nonfiction Title: *Therapy—Nudity and Joy!*, by Aileen Goodson.

ENSLOW PUBLISHERS, Bloy St. and Ramsey Ave., Box 777, Hillside NJ 07205. (201)964-4116. Editor: Ridley Enslow. Publishes hardcover and paperback originals. Averages 30 titles/year. 30% require freelance illustration. Pays 10-15% royalty on retail price or net price; offers $500-5,000 advance. Publishes book an average of 8 months after acceptance. Photocopied submissions OK. Computer printout submissions acceptable. Reports in 2 weeks. Free book catalog for SASE with 25¢ postage.

Nonfiction: Interested in manuscripts for young adults and children. Some areas of special interest are science, social issues, biography, reference topics and recreation. Also, business/economics, health, hobbies, how-to, juveniles, philosophy, psychology, self-help, sports and technical. Accepts nonfiction translations. Submit outline/synopsis and 2 sample chapters. Reviews artwork/photos as part of ms package.

Recent Nonfiction Title: *Prisons, A System in Trouble*, by Anne E. Weiss.

ENTELEK, Ward-Whidden House/The Hill, Box 1303, Portsmouth NH 03801. Editor-in-Chief: Albert E. Hickey. Publishes paperback originals. Offers royalty on retail price of 5% trade; 10% textbook. No advance. Averages 5 titles/year. Photocopied and simultaneous submissions OK. Submit outline and sample chapters or submit complete ms. Reports in 1 week. Book catalog for SASE.

An asterisk preceding a listing indicates that subsidy publishing or co-publishing (where author pays part or all of publishing costs) is available. Firms whose subsidy programs comprise more than 50% of their total publishing activities are listed at the end of the Book Publishers section.

Nonfiction: Publishes computer books and software of special interest to educators. Length: 3,000 words minimum.
Recent Nonfiction Title: *Sail Training for Young Offenders*, edited by A. Hickey (education).

ENTERPRISE PUBLISHING CO., INC., 725 N. Market St., Wilmington DE 19801. (302)654-0110. FAX: (302)654-0277. Publisher: T.N. Peterson. Publishes hardcover and paperback originals, "with an increasing interest in newsletters and periodicals." Averages 8 titles/year; receives 150 submissions annually. 50% of books from first-time authors; 90% of books from unagented writers. Pays royalty on wholesale or retail price. Offers $1,000 average advance. Publishes book an average of 6 months after acceptance. Simultaneous and photocopied submissions OK, but "let us know." Query for electronic submissions. Computer printout submissions acceptable; prefers letter-quality. Catalog and ms guidelines for SASE.
Nonfiction: "Subjects of interest to small business executives/entrepreneurs. They are highly independent and self-sufficient, and of an apolitical to conservative political leaning. They need practical information, as opposed to theoretical: self-help topics on business, including starting and managing a small enterprise, advertising, marketing, raising capital, public relations, tax avoidance and personal finance. Business/economics, legal self-help and business how-to." Queries only. All unsolicited mss are returned unopened. Reviews artwork/photos.
Recent Nonfiction Title: *Golden Mailbox*, by Ted Nicholas.

*PAUL S. ERIKSSON, PUBLISHER, 208 Battell Bldg., Middlebury VT 05753. (802)388-7303; Summer: Forest Dale VT 05745. (802)247-8415. Publisher/Editor: Paul S. Eriksson. Associate Publisher/Co-Editor: Peggy Eriksson. Publishes hardcover and paperback trade originals and paperback trade reprints. Averages 5-10 titles/year; receives 1,500 submissions annually. 25% of books from first-time authors; 95% of books from unagented writers. Average print order for a writer's first book is 3,000-5,000. Subsidy publishes 1% of books. Pays 10-15% royalty on retail price; advance offered if necessary. Publishes book an average of 6 months after acceptance. Catalog for #10 SASE.
Nonfiction: Americana, birds (ornithology), art, biography, business/economics, cookbooks/cooking/foods, health, history, hobbies, how-to, humor, music, nature, philosophy, photography, politics, psychology, recreation, self-help, sociology, sports and travel. Query.
Recent Nonfiction Title: *Make That Scene: A Writer's Guide to Setting, Mood and Atmosphere*, by William Noble.
Fiction: Mainstream. Query.
Recent Fiction Title: *Norman Rockwell's Greatest Painting*, by Hollis Hodges.
Tips: "We look for intelligence, excitement and salability. We prefer manuscripts written out of deep, personal knowledge or experience."

*ETC PUBLICATIONS, Drawer ETC, Palm Springs CA 92263. (619)325-5352. Editorial Director: LeeOna S. Hostrop. Senior Editor: Dr. Richard W. Hostrop. Publishes hardcover and paperback originals. Averages 6-12 titles/year; receives 100 submissions annually. 75% of books from first-time authors; 90% of books from unagented writers. Average print order for a writer's first book is 2,500. Subsidy publishes 5-10% of books. Offers 5-15% royalty, based on wholesale and retail price. No advance. Publishes book an average of 9 months after acceptance. Simultaneous and photocopied submissions OK. Computer printout submissions acceptable; prefers letter-quality. Reports in 3 weeks.
Nonfiction: Educational management, gifted education, futuristics and textbooks. Accepts nonfiction translations in above areas. Submit complete ms with SASE. Reviews artwork/photos as part of ms package.
Recent Nonfiction Title: *The Effective School Administrator*, by Richard W. Hostrop.
Tips: "ETC will seriously consider textbook manuscripts in any knowledge area in which the author can guarantee a first-year adoption of not less than 500 copies. Special consideration is given to those authors who are capable and willing to submit their completed work in camera-ready, typeset form."

M. EVANS AND CO., INC., 216 E. 49 St., New York NY 10017. FAX: (212)486-4544. Editor-in-Chief: George C. deKay. Publishes hardcover originals. Royalty schedule to be negotiated. Averages 30-40 titles/year. 5% of books from unagented writers. Publishes book an average of 8 months after acceptance. Will consider photocopied submissions. Computer printout submissions OK; no dot-matrix. "No mss should be sent unsolicited. A letter of inquiry is essential." Reports in 8 weeks. SASE essential.
Nonfiction and Fiction: "We publish a general trade list of adult fiction and nonfiction, cookbooks and semireference works. The emphasis is on selectivity since we publish only 30 titles a year. Our general fiction list, which is very small, represents an attempt to combine quality with commercial potential. We also publish westerns and romance novels. Our most successful nonfiction titles have been related to health and the behavioral sciences. No limitation on subject. A writer should clearly indicate what his book is all about, frequently the task the writer performs least well. His credentials, although important, mean less than his ability to convince this company that he understands his subject and that he has the ability to communicate a message worth hearing." Reviews artwork/photos.

Tips: "Writers should review our catalog (available for 9x12 envelope with 3 first class stamps) or the *Publishers Trade List Annual* before making submissions."

FABER & FABER, INC., Division of Faber & Faber, Ltd., London, England; 50 Cross St., Winchester MA 01890. (617)721-1427. Editor: Betsy Uhrig. Publishes hardcover and trade paperback originals, and trade paperback reprints. Averages 12 titles/year; receives 600 submissions annually. 10% of books from first-time authors; 25% of books from unagented writers. Pays 7½-10% royalty on wholesale or retail price; advance varies. Publishes book an average of 1 year after acceptance. Simultaneous and photocopied submissions OK. Computer printout submissions acceptable; prefers letter-quality. Reports in 6 weeks on queries; 2-3 months on mss. Book catalog for 8½x11 SAE and 4 first class stamps; writer's guidelines for #10 SASE.
Nonfiction: Anthologies, biography, humor, contemporary culture, film and screenplays. Subjects include Americana, animals, pop/rock music, New England, and sociology. Query with synopsis and outline with SAE. Reviews artwork/photos as part of ms package.
Recent Nonfiction Title: *Back in the USSR: The True Story of Rock in Russia*, by Troitsky.
Fiction: Collections, ethnic, experimental, juvenile (8-12), mainstream and regional. No historical/family sagas or mysteries. Query with synopsis and outline with SAE.
Recent Fiction Title: *Adele at the End of the Day*, by Marshall.
Tips: "We are concentrating on subjects that have consistently done well for us. These include popular culture; serious, intelligent rock and roll books; anthologies; and literary, somewhat quirky fiction. Please do not send entire ms; please include SASE for reply."

FACTS ON FILE, INC., 460 Park Ave. S., New York NY 10016. (212)683-2244. Editor in Chief: Gerard Helferich. Publishes hardcover originals and hardcover reprints. Averages 125 titles/year; receives approximately 1,000 submissions annually. 25% of books from unagented writers. Pays 10-15% royalty on retail price. Offers average $10,000 advance. Simultaneous and photocopied submissions OK. Query for electronic submissions. Computer printout submissions acceptable; prefers letter-quality. Reports in 2 weeks on queries; 1 month on mss. Free book catalog.
Nonfiction: Reference and other informational books on business and economics, cooking and foods (no cookbooks), health, history, hobbies (but no how-to), music, natural history, philosophy, psychology, recreation, religion, language and sports. "We need serious, informational books for a targeted audience. All our books must have strong library interest, but we also distribute books effectively to the book trade." No cookbooks, biographies, pop psychology, humor, do-it-yourself crafts or poetry. Query or submit outline/synopsis and sample chapters. Reviews artwork/photos.
Recent Nonfiction Title: *Bears of the World*, by Terry Domico.
Tips: "Our audience is school and public libraries for our more reference-oriented books and libraries, schools and bookstores for our less reference-oriented informational titles."

*FAIRCHILD BOOKS & VISUALS, Book Division, Subsidiary of Capital Cities, Inc., 7 E. 12th St., New York NY 10003. FAX: (212) 887-1865. Manager: E.B. Gold. Publishes hardcover and paperback originals. Offers standard minimum book contract; no advance. Pays 10% of net sales distributed twice annually. Averages 12 titles/year; receives 100 submissions annually. 50% of books from first-time authors; 99% of books from unagented writers. Subsidy publishes 2% of books—1% subsidized by authors, 1% by organizations. Publishes book an average of 1 year after acceptance. Photocopied submissions OK. Computer printout submissions acceptable; prefers letter-quality. Book catalog and ms guidelines for 9x12 SASE.
Nonfiction: Publishes business books and textbooks relating to fashion, marketing, retailing, career education, advertising, home economics and management. Length: open. Query, giving subject matter, brief outline and at least 1 sample chapter. Reviews artwork/photos as part of ms package.
Recent Nonfiction Title: *A Survey of Historic Costume*, by Phyllis Tortora and Keith Eubank.
Tips: "The writer has the best chance of selling our firm fashion, retailing or textile related books that can be used by both the trade and schools. If possible, the writer should let us know what courses would use the book."

*FAIRLEIGH DICKINSON UNIVERSITY PRESS, 285 Madison Ave., Madison NJ 07940. (201)593-8564. Director: Harry Keyishian. Publishes hardcover originals. Averages 30 titles/year; receives 300 submissions annually. 33% of books from first-time authors; 100% of books from unagented writers. Average print order for a writer's first book is 1,000. "Contract is arranged through Associated University Presses of Cranbury, New Jersey. We are a *selection* committee only." Subsidy publishes (nonauthor) 2% of books. Publishes book an average of 18 months after acceptance. Computer printout submissions acceptable; prefers letter-quality. Reports in 2 weeks on queries; 4 months average on mss.
Nonfiction: Reference and scholarly books. Subjects include art, business and economics, Civil War, film, history, Jewish studies, literary criticism, music, philosophy, politics, psychology, sociology and women's studies. Looking for scholarly books in all fields. No nonscholarly books. Query with outline/synopsis and sample chapters. Reviews artwork/photos as part of ms package.

Recent Nonfiction Title: *The Presence of the Past in Modern American Drama*, by Patricia R. Schroeder.
Tips: "Research must be up to date. Poor reviews result when authors' bibliographies and notes don't reflect current research. We follow University of Chicago style in scholarly citations. We continue to accept submissions in all fields, but stress books on film, the Civil War, Jewish studies, American history."

*FALCON PRESS PUBLISHING CO., INC., Box 1718, Helena MT 59624. (406)442-6597. Publisher: Bill Schneider. Publishes hardcover and trade paperback originals. Averages 20-30 titles/year. Subsidy publishes 20% of books. Pays 8-15% royalty on net price or pays flat fee. Publishes book an average of 6 months after ms is in final form. Reports in 3 weeks on queries. Free book catalog.
Nonfiction: "We're primarily interested in ideas for recreational guidebooks and books on regional outdoor subjects for either adults or children.We can only respond to submissions that fit these categories." No fiction or poetry. Query only; do not send ms.
Recent Nonfiction Title: *Montana on My Mind*, by Michael S. Sample and Larry Mayer.

*THE FAMILY ALBUM, Rt. 1, Box 42, Glen Rock PA 17327. (717)235-2134. Contact: Ron Lieberman. Publishes hardcover originals and reprints and software. Averages 4 titles/year; receives 150 submissions annually. 30% of books from first-time authors; 100% of books from unagented writers. Average print order for a writer's first book is 1,000. Subsidy publishes 20% of books. Pays royalty on wholesale price. Publishes book an average of 10 months after acceptance. Simultaneous and photocopied submissions OK. Query for electronic submissions. Computer printout submissions acceptable; prefers letter-quality. Reports in 2 months.
Nonfiction: "Significant works in the field of (nonfiction) bibliography. Worthy submissions in the field of Pennsylvania history, biography, folk art and lore. We are also seeking materials relating to books, literacy, and national development. Special emphasis on Third World countries, and the role of printing in international development." No religious material. Submit outline/synopsis and sample chapters.

FARRAR, STRAUS AND GIROUX, INC., 19 Union Sq. W., New York NY 10003. Publisher, Books for Young Readers: Stephen Roxburgh. Editor-in-Chief: Margaret Ferguson. Publishes hardcover originals. Receives 3,600 submissions annually. Pays royalty; advance. Publishes book an average of 18 months after acceptance. Photocopied submissions OK. Computer printout submissions acceptable; prefers letter-quality. Reports in 3 months. Catalog for #10 SAE and 3 first class stamps.
Nonfiction and Fiction: "We are primarily interested in fiction picture books and novels for children and middle readers." Submit outline/synopsis and sample chapters. Reviews artwork/photos as part of ms package.
Recent Nonfiction Title: *Grace in the Wilderness*, by Aranka Siegal.
Recent Fiction Title: *Sweet Creek Holler*, by Ruth White.
Recent Picture Book Title: *The Incredible Painting of Felix Clousseau*, by Jon Agee.
Tips: Fiction of all types has the best chance of selling to this firm. Farrar, Straus and Giroux publishes a limited number of nonfiction titles.

‡FAWCETT JUNIPER, Imprint of Ballantine/Del Rey/Fawcett/Ivy, 201 E. 50th St., New York NY 10022. (212)751-2600. Editor-in-Chief, Vice President: Leona Nevler. Publishes 24 titles/year. Pays royalty. Publishes book an average of 1 year after acceptance. Simultaneous and photocopied submissions OK. Computer printout submissions OK; no dot-matrix. Reports in 2 months on queries; in 4 months on mss. Free book catalog.
Nonfiction: Juvenile.
Fiction: Juvenile, mainstream/contemporary, young adult. Query.

‡FEARON EDUCATION, Subsidiary of Simon & Schuster, 500 Harbor Blvd., Belmont CA 94002. (415)592-7810. Publisher: Carol Hegarty. Publisher, Fearon Teacher Aids: Ina Tabibian. Averages 100-120 titles/year. Pays royalty or fee outright. Photocopied submissions OK. Computer printout submissions acceptable; prefers letter-quality. Reports in 1 month. Book catalog and ms guidelines for 9x12 SASE.
Nonfiction: Educational. Query or submit synopsis.
Recent Nonfiction Title: *Our Century Magazine*, (social studies).
Fiction: "Fearon Education is looking for easy-to-read fiction suitable for middle school and up. We prefer the major characters to be young adults or adults. Solid plotting is essential." Length: varies with series; write for specific guidelines.
Recent Fiction Title: *An American Family*, by Bledsoe/Jones.

‡FEDERAL BUYERS GUIDE, INC., 600 Ward Dr., Santa Barbara CA 93111. (805)683-6181. FAX: (805) 683-8593. President: Stuart Miller. Publishes hardcover and trade originals. Averages 25 titles/year. Receives 50 submissions/year. 80% of books from first-time authors; 50% from unagented writers. Buys mss outright for $500-$5,000. Publishes book an average of 6 months after acceptance. Reports in 2 weeks on queries; 1 month on mss. Free book catalog for #10 SASE.

Nonfiction: How-to and technical. Subjects include business, government. Query or submit outline/synopsis and sample chapters. All unsolicited mss are returned unopened.

‡**FEDERAL PERSONNEL MANAGEMENT INSTITUTE, INC.**, Box 16021, Huntsville AL 35802-6021. (205)882-3042. President: Ralph Smith. Publishes trade paperback originals. Averages 4-6 titles/year. Receives 4-5 submissions/year. 60% of books from first-time authors; 100% from unagented writers. Pays 15% on retail price. Publishes book an average of 1 year after acceptance. Simultaneous and photocopied submissions OK. Query for electronic submissions. Computer printout submissions OK; prefers letter-quality. Reports in 3 weeks on queries; 2 months on mss. Free book catalog.
Nonfiction: Technical. Subjects include government/politics, labor relations and personnel issues. "We will be publishing books for government and business on topics such as sexual harassment, drug testing, and how to deal with leave abuse by employees. Our books are practical, how-to books for a supervisor or manager. Scholarly theoretical works do not interest our audience." Submit outline/synopsis and sample chapters or send complete ms.
Recent Nonfiction Title: *Federal Manager's Guide to EEO*, by Robert J. Gilson.
Tips: "We are interested in books that are practical, easy-to-read and less than 150 pages. Primary audience is for managers and supervisors—particularly first and second level. If I were a writer trying to market a book today, I would emphasize practical topics with plenty of examples in succinct, concrete language."

FREDERICK FELL PUBLISHERS, INC., 2131 Hollywood Blvd., Hollywood FL 33020. (305)925-5242. FAX (305)925-5244. Imprints include Compact Books. Publisher: Donald L. Lessne. Publishes hardcover and trade paperback originals and reprints. Averages 20 titles/year; receives 1,000 submissions annually. 20% of books from first-time authors; 20% of books from unagented writers. Pays royalty. Publishes book an average of 1 year after acceptance. Simultaneous and photocopied submissions OK. Query for electronic submissions. Computer printout submissions OK. Reports in 6 months on mss. Free book catalog.
Nonfiction: Biography, coffee table book, cookbook, how-to, humor, self-help, technical and textbook. Subjects include business and economics, cooking and foods, health, hobbies, philosophy, psychology, recreation, religion and sociology. Especially looking for manuscripts on current issues of interest; how-to, health and business. Submit outline/synopsis and sample chapters. Reviews artwork/photos as part of ms package.
Recent Nonfiction Title: *Cholesterol Cure Made Easy*, by Sylvan Lewis, M.D.

*****FICTION COLLECTIVE**, Manuscript Central, English Department, Univ. of Colorado, CB 226, Boulder CO 80309. Managing Editor: Erin Van Rheenen. Publishes hardcover and trade paperback originals. Averages 6 titles/year; receives 100-150 submissions/year. 30% of books from first-time authors; 50% of books from unagented writers. Subsidy publishes (nonauthor) 50% of books. Pays 10% royalty on wholesale price after production costs are covered. Publishes book an average of 15 months after acceptance. Simultaneous and photocopied submissions OK. Computer printout submissions OK; no dot-matrix. Reports in 2 months on queries. Free book catalog.
Fiction: Ethnic and experimental. "We publish high-quality, innovative fiction (novels and story collections) completely on the basis of literary merit. We are always looking for quality fiction, but can publish only a very small percentage of what we receive. No genre fiction." Query.
Recent Fiction Title: *Uncle Ovid's Exercise Book*, by Don Webb.

‡**FIDDLEHEAD POETRY BOOKS & GOOSE LANE EDITIONS**, 248 Brunswick, Fredericton, New Brunswick E3B 1G9 Canada. (506)454-8319. General Editor: Peter Thomas. Publishes hardcover and trade paperback originals. Averages 12 titles/year; receives 350 submissions annually. 33⅓% of books from first-time authors; 75-100% of books from unagented writers. Pays royalty on retail price. Small advances. Computer printout submissions preferred. Reports in 3 weeks on queries; 2 months on mss. Book catalog free on request.
Imprints: Goose Lane Editions (nonfiction and fiction), Peter Thomas, general editor.
Nonfiction: Coffee table books and reference on Canadian and maritime provinces, history, photography, regional literature and linguistics.
Recent Nonfiction Title: *No Faster Than a Walk: The Covered Bridges of New Brunswick*, by J. Gillis and S. Gillis.
Fiction: Experimental, mainstream, "first" novel authors and others. "Erotica, confession, or dull or immature fiction is not required. SASE absolutely necessary for return of manuscript." Submit complete ms.
Recent Fiction Title: *Married Love*, by Kent Thompson (novella).
Poetry: Open to collections of poetry; modern/experimental preferable. Submit complete ms with SASE.
Recent Poetry Title: *Landscape Turned Sideways*, by Yvonne Trainer.

Tips: "No one will ever grow rich by publishing poetry. Although we have a much easier time marketing fiction and nonfiction we feel a cultural obligation to publish poetry as a small literary press."

FINANCIAL SOURCEBOOKS, Division of Sourcebooks, Inc., Box 313, Naperville IL 60566. (312)961-2161. Publisher: Dominique Raccah. Publishes hardcover and trade paperback originals. Firm averages 7 titles/year. 50% of books from first-time authors; 100% from unagented writers. Pays 5-15% royalty on wholesale price, or buys mss outright. Publishes book an average of 6 months after acceptance. Simultaneous and photocopied submissions OK. Query for electronic submissions. Computer printout submissions OK. Reports in 1 month on queries. "We do not want to see complete manuscripts." Book catalog free for SASE.

Nonfiction: Reference, technical and textbook. Subjects include business and economics, computers and electronics, government/politics, and money/finance. "We publish books, directories and newsletters for financial executives. Our books are largely developed in-house or assigned to a freelancer specializing in the area. We are now looking for additional projects. The books of interest to us will establish a standard in their domain. We look for books with a well-defined, strong market such as reference works or books with a technical, informative bent." Query or submit outline/synopsis and sample chapters (2-3 chapters, not the 1st). Reviews artwork/photos as part of ms package.

Recent Nonfiction Title: *Competitive Intelligence in Financial Services*, (handbook).

Tips: "Financial executives today are bombarded with information in most every form through much of their working day. Writers can easily sell us books that will help a busy professional deal with the workload more productively. That means books that 1.) compile otherwise difficult to obtain (but useful) information; or 2.) develop new concepts or ideas that will help executives "work smarter"; or 3.) reformat concepts or information executives need into some more useful or digestible form (e.g. graphics, tutorials, etc.)."

‡DONALD I. FINE, INC., 128 E. 36th St., New York NY 10016. (212)696-1838. Imprints include Primus Library of Contemporary Americana. Publishes hardcover originals and trade paperback originals and reprints. Firm averages 60-75 titles/year. Receives 1,000 submissions/year. 30% of books from first-time authors. Pays royalty on retail price. Advance varies. Publishes book an average of 1 year after acceptance. Computer printout submissions OK; no dot-matrix. Book catalog for SAE.

Nonfiction: Biography, cookbook, humor, self-help. Subjects include history, military/war and sports. All unsolicited mss are returned unopened. Reviews artwork/photos as part of ms package.

Recent Nonfiction Title: *Miss Peggy Lee*, by Peggy Lee (biography).

Fiction: Adventure, ethnic, fantasy, historical, horror, humor, literary, mainstream/contemporary, mystery, science fiction, suspense and western. All unsolicited mss are returned unopened.

Recent Fiction Title: *Redeye*, by Richard Allen (suspense).

FIREBRAND BOOKS, 141 The Commons, Ithaca NY 14850. (607)272-0000. Publisher: Nancy K. Bereano. Publishes hardcover and trade paperback originals and hardcover and trade paperback reprints. Averages 6-8 titles/year; receives 200-300 submissions annually. 50% of books from first-time authors; 75% of books from unagented writers. Pays 7-9% royalty on retail price, or makes outright purchase. Publishes book an average of 18 months after acceptance. Simultaneous and photocopied submissions OK "with notification." Computer printout submissions acceptable; prefers letter-quality. Reports in 2 weeks on queries; 2 months on mss. Free book catalog.

Nonfiction: Criticism and essays. Subjects include feminism and lesbianism. Submit complete ms.

Recent Nonfiction Title: *A Burst of Light*, by Audre Lorde.

Fiction: Will consider all types of feminist and lesbian fiction.

Recent Fiction Title: *Trash*, by Dorothy Allison.

Recent Poetry Title: *Living as a Lesbian*, by Cheryl Clarke.

Tips: "Our audience includes feminists, lesbians, ethnic audiences, and other progressive people."

FISHER BOOKS, Box 38040, Tucson AZ 85740-8040. (602)292-9080. Publishes trade paperback originals and trade paperback reprints. Firm averages 20 titles/year. 25% of books from first-time authors; 50% from unagented writers. Pays 10-15% royalty on wholesale price. Pays advances sometimes. Simultaneous and photocopied submissions OK. Computer printout submissions OK; prefers letter-quality. Reports in 1 month. Free book catalog.

ALWAYS submit unsolicited manuscripts or queries with a self-addressed, stamped envelope (SASE) within your country or International Reply Coupons (IRC) purchased from the post office for other countries.

Nonfiction: Cookbook, how-to and self-help. Subjects include child guidance/parenting, cooking, foods and nutrition, gardening, health/medicine, psychology and sports. Submit outline/synopsis and sample chapters.
Recent Nonfiction Title: *Good Fat, Bad Fat, How to Lower Your Cholesterol & Beat the Odds of a Heart Attack*, by Griffin & Castelli.

‡**FITZHENRY & WHITESIDE, LTD.**, 195 Allstate Parkway, Markham, Ontario L3R 4T8 Canada. (416)477-0030. Vice President: Robert Read. Publishes hardcover and paperback originals and reprints. Royalty contract varies; advance negotiable. Publishes 50 titles/year, text and trade. Photocopied submissions OK. Reports in 3 months. Enclose return postage.
Nonfiction: "Especially interested in topics of interest to Canadians, and by Canadians." Textbooks for elementary and secondary schools, also biography, business, history, health, fine arts. Submit outline and sample chapters. Length: open.
Recent Title: *Northrop Frye on Shakespeare*.

‡**FIVE STAR PUBLICATIONS**, Box 3142, Scottsdale AZ 85271-3142. (602)941-0770. Publisher: Linda F. Radke. Publishes hardcover and trade paperback originals. Firm averages 4 titles/year. Pays 6-15% on wholesale price, sometimes buys by outright purchase. Offers $500 average advance. Publishes book an average of 9 months after acceptance. Simultaneous submissions OK. Reports in 2 months on queries; 3 months on mss. Book catalog for #10 SAE and 2 first class stamps.
Nonfiction: Cookbook, how-to, illustrated book, juvenile and directories. Subjects include child guidance/parenting, cooking, foods and nutrition, education and women's issues/studies. Submit outline/synopsis and sample chapters. Reviews artwork/photos as part of package.
Recent Nonfiction Title: *Options: A Directory of Child & Senior Services*, by Linda F. Radke (directory).
Fiction: Humor, picture books. Submit outline/synopsis and sample chapters.
Recent Fiction Title: *Shakespeare for Children: The Story of Romeo & Juliet*, by Cass Foster (children's literature).
Tips: "Research your topic thoroughly and see what else has already been done. Join professional publishing associations."

FLEET PRESS CORP., 160 5th Ave., New York NY 10010. (212)243-6100. Editor: Phoebe Scott. Publishes hardcover and paperback originals and reprints; receives 200 submissions annually. 10% of books from first-time authors; 25% of books from unagented writers. Royalty schedule and advance "varies." Publishes book an average of 15 months after acceptance. Computer printout submissions acceptable; no dot-matrix. Reports in 2 months. Free book catalog.
Nonfiction: History, biography, arts, religion and general nonfiction. Length: 45,000 words. Publishes juveniles. Stresses social studies; for ages 8-15. Length: 25,000 words. Query with outline; no unsolicited mss.

FLORA AND FAUNA PUBLICATIONS, 2406 N.W. 47th Terrace, Gainesville FL 32606. (904)371-9858. Publisher: Ross H. Arnett, Jr. Book publisher/packager. Publishes hardcover and trade paperback originals. Entire firm publishes 350 annually; imprint averages 10-12 titles/year; receives 70 submissions annually. 50% of books from first-time authors; 100% of books from unagented writers. Average print order for a writer's first book is 500. Pays 10% royalty on list price; negotiable advance. Publishes book an average of 1 year after acceptance. Photocopied submissions OK. Query for electronic submissions. Computer printout submissions acceptable; prefers letter-quality. Reports in 2 weeks on queries; 3 months on mss.
Nonfiction: Reference, technical, textbook and directories. Subjects include plants and animals (for amateur and professional biologists), and natural history. Looking for "books dealing with kinds of plants and animals, new nature guide series underway. No nature stories or 'Oh My' nature books." Query with outline and 2 sample chapters. Reviews artwork/photos as part of ms package.
Recent Nonfiction Title: *Butterflies of Florida*, by E.G. Gerberg.
Tips: "Well-documented books, especially those that fit into one of our series, have the best chance of selling to our firm — biology, natural history, no garden books."

J. FLORES PUBLICATIONS, Box 163001, Miami FL 33116. Editor: Eliezer Flores. Publishes trade paperback originals and reprints. Averages 10 titles/year. 99% of books from unagented writers. Pays 10-15% royalty on net sales; no advance. Publishes book an average of 10 months after acceptance. Simultaneous and photocopied submissions OK. Computer printout submissions acceptable; prefers letter-quality. Reports in 1 month on queries; 6 weeks on mss. Book catalog and ms guidelines for 6x9 SAE with 2 first class stamps.
Nonfiction: How-to, illustrated book and self-help. "We need original nonfiction manuscripts on military science, weaponry, current events, self-defense, survival, police science, the martial arts, guerrilla warfare and military history. How-to manuscripts are given priority." No pre-World War II material. Query with outline and 2-3 sample chapters. Reviews artwork/photos. "Photos are accepted as part of the manuscript package and are strongly encouraged."

Recent Nonfiction Title: *Nuclear War Survival*, by Duncan Long.
Tips: "Trends include illustrated how-to books on a specific subject. Be thoroughly informed on your subject and technically accurate."

FOCAL PRESS, Subsidiary of Butterworth Publishers, 80 Montvale Ave., Stoneham MA 02180. (617)438-8464. Senior Editor: Karen M. Speerstra. Imprint publishes hardcover and paperback originals and reprints. Averages 20-25 UK-US titles/year; entire firm averages 40-50 titles/year; receives 500-700 submissions annually. 25% of books from first-time authors; 90% of books from unagented writers. Pays 10-15% royalty on wholesale price; offers $1,500 average advance. Publishes book an average of 1 year after acceptance. Simultaneous and photocopied submissions OK. Computer printout submissions OK. Reports in 3 months. Free book catalog and ms guidelines.
Nonfiction: How-to, reference, technical and textbooks in media arts: photography, film and cinematography, and broadcasting. High-level scientific/technical monographs are also considered. We generally do not publish collections of photographs or books composed primarily of photographs. Our books are text-oriented, with artwork serving to illustrate and expand on points in the text." Query preferred, or submit outline/synopsis and sample chapters or complete ms. Reviews artwork/photos as part of ms package.
Recent Nonfiction Title: *Photography: Art & Technique*, by Al Blaker.

FORMAN PUBLISHING, Suite 201, 2932 Wilshire Blvd., Santa Monica CA 90403. FAX: (213)453-8553. President: Len Forman. Executive Vice President: Claudia Forman. Publishes hardcover and trade paperback. Averages 6 titles/year; receives 1,000 submissions/year. 100% of books from first-time authors. 90% of books from unagented writers. Pays 6-15% royalty. Simultaneous and photocopied submissions OK. Publishes book an average of 18 months after acceptance. Reports in 1 month on queries; 3 months on mss. Book catalog for 8½×11 SASE.
Nonfiction: Cookbooks, how-to and self-help. Subjects include art, business and economics, cooking and foods, health, nature and psychology. Submit outline/synopsis and sample chapters. Reviews artwork/photos as part of ms package.
Recent Nonfiction Title: *Stepmothering, Another Kind of Love*.

FOUR WINDS PRESS, Macmillan Children's Books Group, 866 Third Ave., New York NY 10022. (212)702-2000. Editor-in-Chief: Cindy Kane. Publishes hardcover originals. Publishes 24 titles/year; receives 500 queries/year and 3,570 manuscripts per year. 10% of books from first-time authors; 20% from unagented writers. Pays 5-10% royalty on retail price. Average advance is $4,000. Publishes book an average of 18 months after acceptance. Simultaneous and photocopied submissions OK. Computer printout submissions OK; prefers letter-quality. Reports in 2 weeks on queries; 6 weeks on mss. Free book catalog and ms guidelines for SASE.
Nonfiction: Juvenile. Subjects—all juvenile—include: Americana, animals, ethnic, nature/environment. Query. Reviews artwork/photos with ms package.
Recent Nonfiction Title: *Dinosaurs, Dragonflies and Diamonds*, Gail Gibbons (picture book/nonfiction).
Fiction: Juvenile, young adult. Wants picture books, early readers middle grade (ages 8-12) and young adult (ages 12 and up). No overworked themes such as sibling rivalry, alphabet and counting books, retellings of fairy tales—all at picture book level. Submit complete ms.
Recent Fiction Title: *The Delphic Choice*, by Norma Johnston (YA novel).
Tips: "We're looking for fresh older fiction that is both funny and moving and that only the author could have written. Our audience is children—either being read to (ages 3-7) or reading on their own. Study the books curently being published in your chosen field."

*FRANCISCAN HERALD PRESS, Sacred Heart Province of the Order of Friars Minor, 1434 W. 51st St., Chicago IL 60609. (312)254-4462. Managing Director: Gabriel Brinkman, OFMP. Publishes hardcover originals and trade paperback originals. Firm averages 9-12 titles/year. 20% of books from first-time authors; 99% from unagented writers. Subsidy publishes 10% of books. Pays 7-10% royalty on retail price. Publishing of book varies after acceptance. Query for electronic submissions. Reports in 2 weeks on queries; 1 month on mss.
Nonfiction: Religion. Submit complete ms.
Recent Nonfiction Title: *St. Francis of Assisi*, by R. Manselli.

THE FRASER INSTITUTE, 626 Bute St., Vancouver, British Columbia V6E 3M1 Canada. (604)688-0221. FAX: (604) 688-8539. Assistant Director: Sally Pipes. Publishes trade paperback originals. Averages 4-6 titles/year; receives 30 submissions annually. Pays honorarium. Publishes book an average of 6 months after acceptance. Simultaneous and photocopied submissions OK. Query for electronic submissions. Computer printout submissions acceptable; prefers letter-quality. Reports in 6 weeks. Free book catalog; ms guidelines for SAE and IRC.
Nonfiction: Analysis, opinion, on economics, social issues and public policy. Subjects include business and economics, politics, religion and sociology. "We will consider submissions of high-quality work on economics, social issues, economics and religion, public policy, and government intervention in the economy." Submit complete ms.

Recent Nonfiction Title: *Privatization: Tactics and Techniques*, edited by Michael Walker.

Tips: "Our books are read by well-educated consumers, concerned about their society and the way in which it is run and are adopted as required or recommended reading at colleges and universities in Canada, the U.S. and abroad. Our readers feel they have some power to improve society and view our books as a source of the information needed to take steps to change unproductive and inefficient ways of behavior into behavior which will benefit society. Recent trends to note in book publishing include affirmative action, banking, broadcasting, insurance, health care and religion. A writer has the best chance of selling us books on government, economics, finance, or social issues."

THE FREE PRESS, Division of the Macmillan Publishing Co., Inc., 866 3rd Ave., New York NY 10022. President/Publisher: Erwin A. Glikes. Averages 65 titles/year; receives 3,000 submissions annually. 15% of books from first-time authors; 50% of books from unagented writers. Royalty schedule varies. Publishes book an average of 11 months after acceptance. "Prefers camera-ready copy to machine-readable media." Computer printout submissions acceptable; prefers letter-quality. Reports in 6 weeks.

Nonfiction: Professional books and textbooks. Publishes college texts, adult nonfiction, and professional books in the social sciences, humanities and business. Reviews artwork/photos as part of ms package "but we can accept no responsibility for photos or art." Looks for "identifiable target audience, evidence of writing ability." Accepts nonfiction translations. Send 1-3 sample chapters, outline, and query letter before submitting mss.

SAMUEL FRENCH, INC., 45 W. 25th St., New York NY 10010. (212)206-8990. Subsidiaries include Samuel French Ltd. (London); Samuel French (Canada) Ltd. (Toronto); Samuel French, Inc. (Hollywood); and Baker's Plays (Boston). Editor: Lawrence Harbison. Publishes paperback acting editions of plays. Averages 80-90 titles/year; receives 1,200 submissions annually, mostly from unagented playwrights. About 10% of publications are from first-time authors; 20% from unagented writers. Pays 10% book royalty on retail price. Pays 90% stock production royalty; 80% amateur production royalty. Offers variable advance. Publishes book an average of 6 months after acceptance. Simultaneous and photocopied submissions OK. Computer-generated mss acceptable; no dot-matrix. Reports immediately on queries; from 6 weeks to 8 months on mss. Book catalog $1.25; ms guidelines $3.

Nonfiction: Acting editions of plays.

Tips: "Broadway and Off-Broadway hit plays, light comedies and mysteries have the best chance of selling to our firm. Our market is theater producers—both professional and amateur—and actors. Read as many plays as possible of recent vintage to keep apprised of today's market; write small-cast plays with good female roles; and be one hundred percent professional in approaching publishers and producers (see guidelines)."

FULCRUM, INC., 350 Indiana St., Golden CO 80401. (303)277-1623. Contact: Submissions Editor. Publishes hardcover and trade paperback originals, and reprints. Averages 12-20 titles/year; receives up to 1,500 submissions/year. 75% of books from first-time authors; 85% of books from unagented writers. Pays royalty on retail price; offers $1,500-5,000 average advance. Average first print run is 5,000-10,000. Publishes book an average of 1 year after acceptance. Query for electronic submissions. Computer printout submissions OK; no dot-matrix. Reports in 1 month on queries; 6 weeks on mss. Book catalog for 8x10 SAE with 3 first class stamps; ms guidelines for SASE.

Nonfiction: Nature, history, biography, self-development and other subjects of general interest. No how-to, sports, cookbooks, reference. Submit outline/synopsis and sample chapters. Reviews artwork/photos as part of ms package.

Recent Nonfiction Title: *Keepers of the Earth: Native American Stories and Environmental Activities for Children*, by Michael Caduto and Joseph Bruchac.

‡GALLAUDET UNIVERSITY PRESS, 800 Florida Ave. NE, Washington DC 20002. (202)651-5488. Imprints include Kendall Green Publications, Clerc Books, Gallaudet University Press. Editorial Assistant: Julie Humpert. Publishes hardcover originals, and trade paperback and mass market paperback originals and reprints. Firm averages 12 titles/year. Receives 65 submissions/year. 50% of books from first-time authors; 95% from unagented writers. Pays 10-15% royalty on wholesale price (net). Publishes book an average of 12-18 months after acceptance. Simultaneous and photocopied submissions OK. Query for electronic submissions. Computer printout submissions OK. Reports in 3 months. Free book catalog and manuscript guidelines.

Nonfiction: Biography, coffee table book, illustrated book, juvenile, reference, self-help, technical, textbook and sign language. Subjects include child guidance/parenting, education, health/medicine, history, language/literature, psychology, regional, science, sociology, sports, translation and travel. All topics must relate to hearing impairment/deafness in some way (though topic doesn't have to focus on hearing impairment/deafness). "Because of the press's mission to publish books for and about deafness/hearing impairment, we'll accept books on any topic as long as they're somehow related." Submit outline/synopsis and sample chapters or complete ms. Reviews artwork/photos as part of ms package.

Recent Nonfiction Title: *The Week the World Heard Gallaudet*, by Jack R. Gannon (photo essay).
Fiction: Adventure, ethnic, fantasy, historical, humor, juvenile, literary, mainstream/contemporary, mystery, picture books, plays, science fiction, short story collections, suspense, young adult (most categories are considered as long as they relate to hearing impairment in some way.) "We need fiction for 8-12-year-olds and young adults with hearing-impaired character(s), although the hearing-impairment does not need to be the focus of the story." Submit outline/synopsis and sample chapters or complete ms.
Recent Fiction Title: *Buffy's Orange Leash*, by Golder & Memling (children's story).
Tips: "The market is wide open and growing for books relating to hearing impairment due especially to an increased awareness of deafness and sign language among the public. Individuals in our audience come from many walks of life and include every age group. The common denominator among them is an interest and / or openness to learn more about hearing impairment/deafness."

GARBER COMMUNICATIONS, INC., (affiliates: Steinerbooks, Spiritual Fiction Publications, Spiritual Science Library, Rudolf Steiner Publications, Freedeeds Library, Biograf Publications), 5 Garber Hill Rd., Blauvelt NY 10913. (914)359-9292. Editor: Bernard J. Garber. Publishes hardcover and paperback originals and reprints. Does not accept unsolicited submissions. "We will refuse and return unsolicited submissions at the author's expense." Averages 15 titles/year; receives 250 submissions annually. 10% of books from first-time authors; 10% of books from unagented writers. Average print order for a writer's first book is 500-1,000 copies. Pays 5-7% royalty on retail price; offers average $500 advance. Publishes book an average of 1 year after acceptance. Will consider photocopied submissions.
Nonfiction: Spiritual sciences, occult, philosophical, metaphysical and ESP. These are for our Steiner Books division only. Serious nonfiction. Philosophy and Spiritual Sciences: Bernard J. Garber. Query only (with SASE or no response).
Fiction: Patricia Abrams, editor; the new genre called Spiritual Fiction Publications. "We are now looking for original manuscripts or rewrites of classics in modern terms." Query only with SASE.

‡*GARDNER PRESS, INC., 19 Union Square West, New York NY 10003. (212)924-8293. Publisher: Gardner Spungin. Publishes hardcover originals and reprints. Firm averages 22 titles/year. Receives 150 submissions/year. 10% of books from first-time authors; 90% from unagented writers. Subsidy publishes 10% of books. Pays 6-15% royalty on wholesale price. Publishes book an average of 8-10 months after acceptance. Simultaneous and photocopied submissions OK. Computer printout submissions OK; no dot-matrix. Reports in 3 weeks. Free book catalog.
Nonfiction: Biography, reference, self-help and textbook. Subjects include child guidance/parenting, education, ethnic, gay/lesbian, health/medicine, psychology, recreation, religion, sociology, sports, translation and women's issues/studies. Query.
Recent Nonfiction Title: *Relationships: Adult Children of Alcoholics*, by Joe Perez (self-help).

GARLAND PUBLISHING, INC., 136 Madison Ave., New York NY 10016. (212)686-7492. Vice President: Gary Kuris. Publishes hardcover originals. Averages 150 titles/year. 99% of books from unagented writers. Pays 10-15% royalty on wholesale price. "Depending on marketability, authors may prepare camera-ready copy." Publishes book an average of 9 months after acceptance. Simultaneous and photocopied submissions OK. Computer printout submissions acceptable; prefers letter-quality. Reports in 2 weeks on queries; 1 month on mss. Free book catalog; ms guidelines for SASE.
Nonfiction: Reference books for libraries. Subjects include humanities and social sciences. Accepts nonfiction translations. "We're interested in reference books—encyclopedias, bibliographies, sourcebooks, indexes, etc.—in all fields." Submit outline/synopsis and 1-2 sample chapters. Reviews artwork/photos as part of ms package.
Recent Nonfiction Title: *Ulysses*, by James Joyce (a synoptic edition).

‡GASLIGHT PUBLICATIONS, 626 North College Ave., Bloomington IN 47404. (812)332-5169. Imprints include McGuffin Books. Publisher: Jack Tracy. Publishes hardcover originals. Averages 6 titles/year. Receives 15-20 submissions/year. 75% of books from first-time authors; 90% from unagented writers. Pays 10% royalty on retail price. Publishes book an average of 1 year after acceptance. Simultaneous and photocopied submissions OK. Computer printout submissions OK. Reports in 1 month. Free book catalog.
Nonfiction: "We publish specialized studies of the mystery genre and related fields: biography, criticism, analysis, reference, film. Submissions should be serious, well-researched, not necessarily for the scholar, but for readers who are already experts in their own right. 12,000 words minimum." Query, submit outline/synopsis and sample chapters or send complete ms. Reviews artwork/photos as part of ms package.
Recent Nonfiction Title: *A Study in Surmise: The Making of Sherlock Holmes*, by Michael Harrison (literary analysis).
Tips: "Our purchasers tend to be public libraries and knowledgeable, affluent mystery aficionados."

‡*GENEALOGICAL PUBLISHING CO., INC., 1001 N. Calvert St., Baltimore MD 21202. (301)837-8271. Editor-in-Chief: Michael H. Tepper, Ph.D. Publishes hardcover originals and reprints. Subsidy publishes 10% of books. Averages 80 titles/year; receives 400 submissions annually. 50% of books from first-time authors;

100% of books from unagented writers. Average print order for a writer's first book is 2,000-3,000. Offers straight 10% royalty on retail price. Publishes book an average of 6 months after acceptance. Photocopied submissions OK. Computer printout submissions acceptable; no dot-matrix. Reports "immediately." Enclose SAE and return postage.

Nonfiction: Reference, genealogy, and immigration records. "Our requirements are unusual, so we usually treat each author and his subject in a way particularly appropriate to his special skills and subject matter. Guidelines are flexible, but it is expected that an author will consult with us in depth. Most, though not all, of our original publications are offset from camera-ready typescript. Since most genealogical reference works are compilations of vital records and similar data, tabular formats are common. We hope to receive more ms material covering vital records and ships' passenger lists. We want family history compendia, basic methodology in genealogy, heraldry, and immigration records." Prefers query first, but will look at outline and sample chapter or complete ms. Reviews artwork/photos as part of ms package.

GIFTED EDUCATION PRESS, The Reading Tutorium, 10201 Yuma Ct., Box 1586, Manassas VA 22110. (703)369-5017. Publisher: Maurice D. Fisher. Publishes paperback originals for school districts and libraries. Averages 5 titles/year; receives 50 submissions annually. 100% of books from first-time authors; 100% of books from unagented writers. Pays royalty of $1 per book. Publishes book an average of 6 months after acceptance. Simultaneous and photocopied submissions OK. Computer printout submissions acceptable; prefers letter-quality. Reports in 4 months. Book catalog and ms guidelines for #10 SAE with 2 first class stamps. Send letter of inquiry first.

Nonfiction: How-to. Subjects include philosophy, psychology, education of the gifted; and how to teach adults to read. "Need books on how to educate gifted children—both theory and practice, and adult literacy. Also, we are searching for books on using computers with the gifted, and teaching the sciences to the gifted. Need rigorous books on procedures, methods, and specific curriculum for the gifted. Send letter of inquiry only. Do not send manuscripts or parts of manuscripts."

Recent Nonfiction Title: *Adventures in Prehistoric Archaeology*, by Robert Bleiweiss.

Tips: "If I were a writer trying to market a book today, I would develop a detailed outline based upon intensive study of my field of interest. Present creative ideas in a rigorous fashion. Be knowledgeable about and comfortable with ideas. We are looking for books on using computers with gifted students; books on science and humanities education for the gifted; and books on how to teach adults to read."

GLENBRIDGE PUBLISHING LTD., 4 Woodland Lane, Macomb IL 61455. (309)833-5104. Editor: James A. Keene. Publishes hardcover originals and reprints, and trade paperback originals. Publishes 6 titles/year. Pays 10% royalty. Publishes book an average of 1 year after acceptance. Simultaneous and photocopied submissions OK. Computer printout submissions OK; prefers letter-quality. Reports in 1 week on queries; 1 month on mss. Ms guidelines for #10 SASE.

Nonfiction: Reference and textbook. Subjects include Americana, business and economics, history, music, philosophy, politics, psychology and sociology. "Academic and scholarly" books desired. Query or submit outline/synopsis and sample chapters. Include SASE.

Recent Nonfiction Title: *Maximum Performance Management*, by Joseph H. Boyett and Henry P. Conn.

‡*GLOBAL BUSINESS AND TRADE COMMUNICATIONS, Suites 209-255, 386 East "H" St., Chula Vista CA 92010. (619)421-5923. Managing Editor: Monica A. Nelson. Publishes hardcover, trade paperback and mass market paperback originals and video cassettes. Averages 4 titles/year. Receives 25 submissions/year. 25% of books from first-time authors; 25% from unagented writers. Subsidy publishes 25% of books. Pays 7-15% royalty on net receipts. Offers $1,000 average advance. Publishes book an average of 9 months after acceptance. Simultaneous and photocopied submissions OK. Query for electronic submissions. Computer printout submissions OK. Reports in 3 weeks on queries; 2 months on mss.

Nonfiction: Biography, how-to, self-help and textbook. Subjects include business and economics, education, military/war, money/finance and international business. Submit outline/synopsis and sample chapters.

Recent Nonfiction Title: *Your Own Import-Export Business: Winning the Trade Game* (how-to/educational).

DAVID R. GODINE, PUBLISHER, 300 Masachusetts Ave., Boston MA 02115. (617)536-0761. Subsidiary: Nonpareil Books. Contact: Julia Hanna, Assistant Editor. Publishes hardcover and trade paperback originals and reprints. Publishes 50-70 titles/year. 30% of books from first-time authors; 5-10% from unagented writers. Pays royalty on retail price. Publishes ms an average of 18 months after acceptance. Simultaneous and photocopied submissions OK. Computer printout submissions OK; prefers letter-quality. Reports in 6 weeks. Book catalog free on request.

Nonfiction: Biography, cookbooks, illustrated books, juvenile. Subjects include Americana, art/architecture, cooking, foods and nutrition, gardening, history, language/literature, music/dance, nature/environment, photography, regional, translation, travel. Needs more history and biography, less photography. No genealogies, sports books, college theses, celebrity address books, or adventure/suspense. Query or submit ms. Reviews artwork/photos as part of complete ms package.

Recent Nonfiction Title: *The High Spirits*, by David Huddle.
Fiction: Literary, mainstream/contemporary and mystery. No science fiction, fantasy, adventure, or religious books. Query or submit complete ms.
Recent Fiction Title: *Masters of the Italic Letter*, by Kay Atkins.
Tips: "In fiction, literary works appeal to us the most; that is, books that are thoughtful and well written as well as original in plot and intent. We also like beautifully illustrated books."

‡GOLDEN WEST BOOKS, Box 80250, San Marino CA 91118. (213)283-3446. Editor-in-Chief: Donald Duke. Managing Editor: Vernice Dagosta. Publishes hardcover and paperback originals. Averages 4 titles/year. Receives 50 submissions annually. 50% of books from first-time authors; 100% of books from unagented writers. Pays 10% royalty contract; no advance. Publishes book an average of 3 months after acceptance. Simultaneous and photocopied submissions OK. Computer printout submissions acceptable; prefers letter-quality. Reports in 1 month. Free book catalog.
Nonfiction: Publishes selected Western Americana and transportation Americana. Query or submit complete ms. "Illustrations and photographs will be examined if we like manuscript."

GOLDEN WEST PUBLISHERS, 4113 N. Longview, Phoenix AZ 85014. (602)265-4392. Editor: Hal Mitchell. Publishes trade paperback originals. Averages 5-6 titles/year; receives 200 submissions annually. 50% of books from first-time authors; 100% of books from unagented writers. Average print order for a writer's first book is 5,000. Pays 6-10% royalty on retail price or makes outright purchase of $500-2,500. No advance. Publishes book an average of 6 months after acceptance. Simultaneous and photocopied submissions OK. Query for electronic submissions. Computer printout submissions acceptable; no dot-matrix. Reports in 2 weeks on queries; 1 month on mss. Book catalog for #10 SASE.
Nonfiction: Cookbooks, books on the Southwest and West. Subjects include cooking and foods, southwest history and outdoors, and travel. Query or submit outline/synopsis and sample chapters. Prefers query letter first. Reviews artwork/photos as part of ms package.
Recent Title: *The Other Mexico*, by E.J. Guarino.
Tips: "We are primarily interested in Arizona and Southwest material and welcome material in this area."

‡GOLLEHON PRESS INC., Box 88324, 3105 Madison S.E., Grand Rapids MI 49518-0324. (616)247-8231. President: John Gollehon. Publishes trade paperback and mass market paperback originals. Averages 6-8 titles/year. Receives 50 submissions/year. 100% of books from first-time authors; 75% from unagented writers. Pays 7% royalty on retail price. Offers $1,000-2,000 average advance. Publishes book an average of 4 months after acceptance. Photocopied submissions OK. Computer printout submissions OK; prefers letter-quality. Reports in 3 weeks on queries; 2 months on mss. Free book catalog and manuscript guidelines.
Nonfiction: How-to, humor and self-help. Subjects include business and economics, hobbies, money/finance, recreation, travel and casino gambling. "Titles relating to gambling, Las Vegas, casinos, etc., are one of our primary interests. We want first-time authors writing work for wide audience in fields of how-to, self-help, travel, games, hobbies, humor, etc." Query or submit outline/synopsis and sample chapters. Reviews artwork/photos as part of ms package.
Recent Nonfiction Title: *Slot Machine Mania*, by Dwight and Louise Crevelt.

GORDON AND BREACH, 50 West 23rd St., New York NY 10010. (212)206-8900. Subsidiaries include Gordon and Breach; Hardwood Academic Publishers. Editorial Director: Dr. Philip C. Manor. Publishes hardcover and trade paperback originals and reprints. Firm publishes 120 titles/year. Receives 50 submissions/year. 80% of books from first-time authors; 100% from unagented writers. Pays 10% royalty on wholesale price or outright purchase of $1,000. Publishes book an average of 9 months after acceptance. Photocopied submissions OK. Query for electronic submissions. Computer printout submissions OK; no dot-matrix. Reports in 2 months. Free book catalog.
Nonfiction: Biography, reference, technical and textbook. Subjects include agriculture/horticulture, anthropology/archaeology, art/architecture, business and economics, computers and electronics, education, ethnic, health/medicine, music/dance, nature/environment, philosophy, photography, psychology, science and sociology. "We publish *scholarly works*, usually from academic authors, in the sciences, mathematics, medicine, the social sciences, and the arts." Submit outline/synopsis and sample chapters or complete ms. Reviews artwork/photos as part of ms package.
Recent Nonfiction Title: *DNA in Clinical Medicine*, by Wilkin (medical).
Tips: "We publish scholarly monographs and graduate level texts; increasing program in medicine and in humanities/social sciences. Research scientists, scholars, graduate level and above are our audience."

GOSPEL PUBLISHING HOUSE, Imprint of Assemblies of God General Council, 1445 Boonville Ave., Springfield MO 65802-1894. (417)862-2781. Book Editor: Glen Ellard. Firm publishes hardcover, trade and mass market paperback originals. Publishes 18 titles/year. Receives 380 submissions/year. 90% of books from first-time authors; 90% from unagented writers. Pays 10% royalty on retail price. Publishes book an average of 18 months after acceptance. Simultaneous submissions OK. Computer printout submissions OK; no dot-matrix. Reports in 2 weeks on queries; 2 months on mss. Free book catalog and ms guidelines.

Nonfiction: Biography and self-help. Subjects include education (Christian or deaf), history (Assemblies of God), religion (Bible study, Christian living, devotional, doctrinal, evangelism, healing, Holy Spirit, missionary, pastoral, prophecy). "Gospel Publishing House is owned and operated by the Assemblies of God. Therefore, the doctrinal viewpoint of all books published is required to be compatible with our denominational positions." Query or submit outline/synopsis and sample chapters.

Recent Nonfiction Title: *Choosing to Cope*, by Mary J. Beggs (autobiography).

Fiction: Adventure, fantasy, historical, humor, juvenile (ages 9-18), mystery, religious, young adult. Query or submit outline/synopsis and sample chapters.

Recent Fiction Title: *Mystery at Pier Fourteen*, by Betty Swinford (juvenile Christian).

GOVERNMENT INSTITUTES, INC., Suite 24, 966 Hungerford Dr., Rockville MD 20850. (301)251-9250. Vice President, Publishing: G. David Williams. Publishes hardcover and softcover originals. Averages 30 titles/year; receives 20 submissions annually. 50% of books from first-time authors; 100% of books from unagented writers. Pays variable royalty or fee. No advance. Publishes book an average of 2 months after acceptance. Simultaneous and photocopied submissions OK. Computer printout submissions acceptable; prefers letter-quality. Reports in 1 month on queries; 2 months on mss. Book catalog and ms guidelines available on request.

Nonfiction: Reference and technical. Subjects include environmental law, health, safety, real estate and energy. Needs professional-level titles in environmental law, health, safety, real estate and energy. Submit synopsis in narrative style and sample chapters. Reviews artwork/photos as part of ms package.

Recent Nonfiction Title: *Environmental Law Handbook, 10th Edition*, by J. Gordon Arbuckle, et al. (professional).

‡*GOWER PUBLISHING COMPANY, Old Post Rd., Brookfield VT 05036. (802)276-3162. FAX (802)276-3837. Subsidiaries include Avebury, Scolar Press, Edward Elgar and Wildwood House. President: James W. Gerard. Publishes hardcover originals and reprints and trade paperback originals. Averages 250 titles/year. Receives 100 submissions/year. 25% of books from first-time authors; 100% from unagented writers. Subsidy publishes 10% of books. Pays royalty on retail price or buys mss outright. Publishes book an average of 3 months after acceptance. Simultaneous and photocopied submissions OK. Query for electronic submissions. Computer printout submissions OK; prefers letter-quality. Reports in 1 week on queries; 1 month on mss. Free book catalog and manuscript guidelines.

Nonfiction: Reference, technical and textbook. Subjects include agriculture/horticulture, art/architecture, business and economics, government/politics, military/war, money/finance, philosophy, religion and sociology. Submit outline/synopsis and sample chapters.

GRAPEVINE PUBLICATIONS, INC., Box 118, Corvallis OR 97339. (503)754-0583. Editor: Christopher M. Coffin. Publishes trade paperback originals. Averages 6-10 titles/year; receives 100-200 submissions/year. 20% of books from first-time authors; 100% of books from unagented writers. Pays 9% royalty on retail price. Publishes book an average of 6 months after acceptance. Simultaneous and photocopied submissions OK. Query for electronic submissions. Computer printout submissions OK; prefers letter-quality. Reports in 2 weeks on queries; 1 month on mss.

Nonfiction: How-to, self-help, technical and textbook. Subjects include math, science, computers, calculators, software and other technical tools. Submit complete ms.

Recent Nonfiction Title: *An Easy Course In Creating Easy Courses with HyperCard*, by Williams.

Tips: "We place heavy emphasis on readability, visual presentation, clarity, and reader participation. We will insist on numerous diagrams and illustrations, loosely-spaced text, large, easy-to-read formats, friendly, conversational writing, but tight, well-designed instruction. We disguise top-flight teaching as merely refreshing reading. The writer must be first and foremost a teacher who holds an engaging one-on-one conversation with the reader through the printed medium."

GRAPHIC ARTS CENTER PUBLISHING CO., 3019 NW Yeon Ave., Box 10306, Portland OR 97210. (503)226-2402. General Manager and Editor: Douglas Pfeiffer. Publishes hardcover originals. Averages 10 titles/year. Makes outright purchase, averaging $3,000.

Nonfiction: "All titles are pictorials with text. Text usually runs separately from the pictorial treatment. Authors must be previously published and are selected to complement the pictorial essay." Query.

‡GRAPHIC ARTS TECHNICAL FOUNDATION, 4615 Forbes Ave., Pittsburgh PA 15213-3796. (412)621-6941. Editor: Thomas M. Destree. Publishes trade paperback originals. Firm averages 15 titles/year; imprint averages 10 titles/year. Receives 10 submissions/year. 50% of books from first-time authors; 100% from unagented writers. Pays 5-15% royalty on member price. Publishes book an average of 1 year after acceptance. Photocopied submissions OK. Query for electronic submissions. Computer printout submissions OK; no dot-matrix. Reports in 1 month on queries; 2 months on mss. Free book catalog and manuscript guidelines.

Nonfiction: How-to, reference, technical and textbook. Subjects include printing/graphic arts. "We want textbook/reference relating to printing and related technologies, providing that the content does not overlap appreciably with any other GATF books in print or in production. Although original photography is related to printing, we do not anticipate publishing any books on that topic." Query or submit outline/synopsis and sample chapters. Reviews artwork/photos as part of ms package.

Recent Nonfiction Title: *Lithographers Manual*, by Ray Blair and Thomas M. Destree (textbook on lithographic printing).

Tips: "Our typical audience would be students in high schools and colleges as well as trainees in the printing industry."

‡GRAYWOLF PRESS, Box 75006, St. Paul MN 55175. (612)222-8342. Assistant Editor: Rosie O'Brien. Publishes hardcover and trade paperback originals and hardcover and trade paperback reprints. Averages 12-16 titles/year. Receives 2,000 submissions/year. 20% of books from first-time authors. Pays 6-12½% royalty on retail price. Offers $2,000 average advance. Publishes book an average of 9 months after acceptance. Simultaneous and photocopied submissions OK. Computer printout submissions OK; prefers letter-quality. Reports in 1 month on queries. Free book catalog.

Nonfiction: Literary essays and memoirs. Query.

Fiction: Ethnic, feminist, literary, mainstream/contemporary and short story collections. Query.

GREAT NORTHWEST PUBLISHING AND DISTRIBUTING COMPANY, INC., Box 10-3902, Anchorage AK 99510-3902. (907)373-0122. President: Marvin H. Clark Jr. Publishes hardcover and trade paperback originals. Averages 5 titles/year; receives 22-25 submissions annually. 30% of books from first-time authors; 100% of books from unagented writers. Pays 10% royalty. Publishes book an average of 1 year after acceptance. Simultaneous and photocopied submissions OK. Query for electronic submissions. Computer printout submissions OK; no dot-matrix. Reports in 2 weeks on queries; 2 months on mss. Free book catalog.

Nonfiction: Biography and how-to. Subjects include Alaska and hunting. "Alaskana and hunting books by very knowledgeable hunters and residents of the Far North interest our firm." Query.

Recent Nonfiction Title: *Glacier Wings and Tales*, by Jack Wilson.

Tips: "Pick a target audience first, subject second. Provide crisp, clear journalistic prose."

GREEN TIGER PRESS INC., 1061 India St., San Diego CA 92101. (619)238-1001. FAX: (619)234-4501. Submit to Editorial Committee. Publishes picture books, greeting cards, calendars, posters and stationery. Averages 12-15 titles/year; receives 2,500 submissions annually. 5% of books from first-time authors; 80% of books from unagented writers. Pays royalty on retail price; rights purchased vary according to each project.

Tips: "We look for manuscripts containing a romantic, visionary or imaginative quality, often with a mythic feeling where fantasy and reality co-exist. We also welcome nostalgia and the world of the child themes. We do not publish science fiction. Since we are a visually-oriented house, we look for manuscripts whose texts readily conjure up visual imagery. Never send originals. Samples will be returned only if accompanied by SASE. Please allow three months before inquiring about your submission."

THE STEPHEN GREENE PRESS/PELHAM BOOKS, 15 Muzzey St., Lexington MA 02173. (617)861-0170. Editorial Director: Thomas Begner. Publishes hardcover and paperback originals, and hardcover and paperback reprints. Averages 30 titles/year. Royalty "variable; advances are small." Send query letter and SASE. Reports in 3 months.

Nonfiction: How-to (self-reliance); nature and environment; recreation; self-help; sports (outdoor and horse); popular psychology and social science; and regional (New England). "We see our audience as mainly college-educated men and women, 30 and over. They are regular book buyers and readers. They probably have pronounced interests, hobby or professional, in subjects that our books treat. Authors can assess their needs by looking critically at what we have published."

GREENHAVEN PRESS, INC., Box 289009, San Diego CA 92128-9009. Senior Editor: Bonnie Szumski. Publishes hard and softcover educational supplementary materials and (nontrade) juvenile nonfiction. Averages 20-30 juvenile manuscripts published/year; all are works for hire; receives 100 submissions/year. 50% of juvenile books from first-time authors; 100% of juvenile books from unagented writers. Makes outright purchase for $1,500-3,500. Publishes book an average of 1 year after acceptance. Simultaneous (if specified) and clear photocopied submissions OK. Computer printout submissions OK; prefers letter-quality. Book catalog for 9x12 SAE with 2 first class stamps.

Nonfiction: Biography, illustrated book, juvenile, reference and textbook. Subjects include animals, business and economics, history, nature, philosophy, politics, psychology, religion and sociology. "We produce tightly formatted books for young people grades 4-6 and 7-9. Each series has specific requirements: Great Mysteries (5th-8th grade); Overviews (5th-8th grade); Opposing Viewpoints Juniors (5th-6th grade). Potential writers should familiarize themselves with our catalog and senior high material. No unsolicited manuscripts." Query or submit outline/synopsis and sample chapters. Reviews artwork/photos as part of manuscript package.

Recent Nonfiction Title: *AIDS: Opposing Viewpoints*, edited by Tom Modl and Lynn Hall.
Nonfiction Juvenile: *Great Mysteries: The Solar System*, by Peter and Connie Roop.

GREENLEAF CLASSICS, INC., Box 20194, San Diego CA 92120. Editor: Paul J. Estok. Publishes paperback originals. Publishes 450 titles/year; receives 1,000-2,000 submissions annually. 15% of books from first-time authors; 90% of books from unagented writers. Pays by outright purchase about 6 months after acceptance. Computer printout submissions acceptable; no dot-matrix. Reports in 1-2 months. "No manuscripts will be returned unless accompanied by return postage." Ms guidelines for SASE.
Fiction: Specializes in adult erotic novels. "All stories must have a sexual theme. They must be contemporary novels dealing with the serious problems of everyday people. All plots are structured so that characters must get involved in erotic situations. Write from the female viewpoint (third person). Request our guidelines before beginning any project for us." Preferred length: 35,000 words. Send complete ms (preferred); or at least 3 sample chapters.

*GUERNICA EDITIONS, Box 633, Station N.D.G., Montreal, Quebec H4A 3R1 Canada. (514)481-5569. President/Editor: Antonio D'Alfonso. Publishes hardcover and trade paperback originals, hardcover and trade paperback reprints and software. Averages 10 titles/year; receives 1,000 submissions annually. 5% of books from first-time authors. Average print order for a writer's first book is 750-1,000. Subsidy publishes (nonauthor) 50% of titles. "Subsidy in Canada is received only when the author is established, Canadian-born and active in the country's cultural world. The others we subsidize ourselves." Pays 3-10% royalty on retail price. Makes outright purchase of $200-5,000. Offers 10¢/word advance for translators. Photocopied submissions OK. IRCs required. "American stamps are of no use to us in Canada." Reports in 1 month on queries; 6 weeks on mss. Book catalog for SASE.
Nonfiction: Biography, humor, juvenile, reference and textbook. Subjects include art, history, music, philosophy, politics, psychology, recreation, religion and Canadiana.
Recent Nonfiction Title: *The Courage of Poetry*, by Paul Chamberland (essays).
Fiction: Ethnic, historical, mystery. "We wish to open up into the fiction world. No country is a country without its fiction writers. Canada is growing some fine fiction writers. We'd like to read you. No first novels." Query.
Poetry: "We wish to have writers in translation. Any writer who has translated Italian poetry is welcomed. Full books only. Not single poems by different authors, unless modern, and used as an anthology. First books will have no place in the next couple of years." Submit samples.
Recent Poetry Title: *Formentera*, by Bert Schierbeek (Holland).
Tips: "We are seeking less poetry, more modern novels, and translations into the English or French."

ALEXANDER HAMILTON INSTITUTE, 197 W. Spring Valley Ave., Maywood NJ 07607. (201)587-7050. Editor-in-Chief: Brian L.P. Zevnik. Publishes 3-ring binder and paperback originals. Averages 18 titles/year; receives 150 submissions annually. 40% of books from first-time authors; 90% of books from unagented writers. "We pay advance against negotiated royalty or straight fee (no royalty)." Offers average $3,000 advance. Publishes book an average of 10 months after acceptance. Simultaneous submissions OK. Computer printout submissions acceptable; no dot-matrix. Reports in 1 month on queries; 2 months on mss.
Nonfiction: Executive/management books for two audiences. One is overseas, upper-level manager. "We need how-to and skills building books. *No* traditional management texts or academic treatises." The second audience is U.S. personnel executives and high-level management. Subject is legal personnel matters. "These books combine court case research and practical application of defensible programs." Query or submit outline or synopsis. Preferred form is outline, three paragraphs on each chapter, examples of lists, graphics, cases.
Recent Nonfiction Title: *Team-Building*.
Tips: "We sell exclusively by direct mail to managers and executives around the world. A writer must know his/her field and be able to communicate practical systems and programs."

HANCOCK HOUSE PUBLISHERS LTD., 1431 Harrison Ave., Blaine WA 98230. (604)538-1114. Publisher: David Hancock. Publishes hardcover and trade paperback originals, and hardcover and trade paperback reprints. Averages 12 titles/year; receives 400 submissions annually. 50% of books from first-time authors; 100% of books from unagented writers. Pays 10% maximum royalty on wholesale price. Simultaneous submissions OK. Publishes book an average of 6 months after acceptance. Computer printout submissions acceptable; prefers letter-quality. Reports in 6 months. Book catalog free on request. Ms guidelines for SASE.

For information on book publishers' areas of interest, see the nonfiction and fiction sections in the Book Publishers Subject Index.

Nonfiction: Biography, cookbook, how-to and self-help. Subject include Americana; cooking and foods; history (Northwest coast Indians); nature; recreation (sports handbooks for teachers); sports; and investment guides. Query with outline/synopsis and sample chapters. Reviews artwork/photos.
Recent Nonfiction Title: *The Ships of British Columbia*, by Bannerman (history).

‡**HARBINGER HOUSE, INC.**, Suite 106, 3131 N. Country Club, Tucson AZ 85741. (602)326-9595. Editor: Zdenek Gerych. Publishes hardcover originals and trade paperback originals and reprints. Averages 20 titles/year. Receives 250 submissions/year. 50% of books from first-time authors. 80% from unagented writers. Pays 8-15% royalty on retail price. Offers $1,500 average advance. Publishes book an average of 7 months after acceptance. Simultaneous and photocopied submissions OK. Computer printout submissions OK. Reports in 1 month on queries; 3 months on mss. Book catalog for 7½ × 10½ SAE and 4 first class stamps. Manuscript guidelines for #10 SAE and 1 first-class stamp.
Nonfiction: Personal growth, social issues, biography, juvenile and self-help. Subjects include child guidance/parenting, health/medicine, history, nature/environment, psychology, sociology, translation and women's issues/studies. Submit outline/synopsis and sample chapters for adult titles; complete ms for children's books. Reviews artwork as part of ms package.
Recent Nonfiction Title: *The Joyful Child*, by Peggy Jenkins, Ph.D. (sourcebook of activities and ideas for parents and teachers).
Fiction: Literary, mainstream/contemporary, picture books and short story collections. No mystery, adventure, horror, occult or plays. Submit outline/synopsis and sample chapters.

HARBOR HOUSE PUBLISHERS INC., 221 Water St., Boyne City MI 49712. (616)582-2814. Chairman: Jacques LesStrang. Publishes hardcover and trade paperback originals and hardcover and trade paperback reprints. Averages 10 titles/year. Pays 10-15% royalty on wholesale price. Advance varies. Photocopied submissions OK. Reports in 1 month. Book catalog free on request.
Nonfiction: Coffee table book, illustrated book, and maritime. Subjects include business and economics, cooking and foods, and Great Lakes subjects. "Our manuscript needs include pictorials of all kinds, books conceived within the Great Lakes region and maritime subjects." Submit outline/synopsis and sample chapters or complete ms.

HARCOURT BRACE JOVANOVICH, Children's Books Division, 1250 Sixth Ave., San Diego CA 92101. (619)699-6810. Imprints include HBJ Children's Books, Gulliver Books, Voyager and Odyssey Paperbacks, and Jane Yolen Books. Attn: Manuscript Submissions. Publishes hardcover originals and trade paperback reprints. Division publishes 40-60 hardcover originals/year and 20-30 paperback reprints/year. Royalty varies. Advance varies. Publishes ms an average of 1-2 years after acceptance. Photocopied submissions OK. Computer printout submissions OK; prefers letter-quality. Reports in 6 weeks on queries; 2 months on mss. Book catalog for 9x12 SAE with 3 first class stamps. Manuscript guidelines for #10 SAE wth 1 first class stamp.
Nonfiction: Juvenile. Query. Reviews artwork/photos as part of ms package "but requests that no originals are sent."
Fiction: Query or submit outline/synopsis and sample chapters for middle-grade and young-adult novels; or complete ms for picture books.
Tips: "The trade division of Harcourt Brace Jovanovich does not accept any unsolicited manuscripts. The children's division is the only one open to unsolicited submissions."

MAX HARDY—PUBLISHER, Box 28219, Las Vegas NV 89126-2219. (702)368-0379. Owner: Max Hardy. Publishes trade paperback originals. Averages 5 titles/year; receives few submissions/year. Small percentage of books from first-time authors. 100% of books from unagented writers. Pays 10% royalty on retail price. Publishes book an average of 8 months after acceptance. Query for electronic submissions. Computer printout submissions OK; prefers letter-quality. Reports in 2 weeks. Book catalog free on request.
Nonfiction: Textbooks on bridge. Especially needs "quality educational material preferably from known bridge authorities. No other topics." Query.
Recent Nonfiction Title: *Better Bidding With Bergen*, by Marty Bergen.
Fiction: Bridge fiction only. Query.
Recent Fiction Title: *The Jake of Diamonds*, by Don Von Elsner (bridge novel).

HARLEQUIN BOOKS, Subsidiary of Torstar, 225 Duncan Mill Rd., Don Mills, Ontario M3B 3K9 Canada. (416)445-5860. Divisions include Worldwide Library and Silhouette Books, editorial offices, 300 E. 42nd St., New York NY 10017. Vice President and Editor-in-Chief: Horst Bausch. Vice President and Executive Editor

If you have an IBM or IBM-compatible personal computer and would like to know more about Writer's Market on disk, see the bind-in card between pages 904 and 905.

(Harlequin and Silhouette): Karen Solem. Editorial Director: Randall Toye (Worldwide Library/Gold Eagle Books). Publishes mass market paperback originals. Averages 675 titles/year; receives 10,000 submissions annually. 10% of books from first-time authors; 20% of books from unagented writers. Pays 6-10% "escalating" royalty on retail price. Offers advance. Publishes book an average of 1 year after acceptance. Photocopied submissions OK. Computer printout submissions acceptable; prefers letter-quality. Reports in 2 weeks on queries; 2 months on mss. Free ms guidelines.

Imprints: Harlequin Books of North America, 8 fiction series. Harlequin Romance. Presents. American Romance. Superromance. Intrigue. Temptation. Silhouette Books, 4 fiction series. Romance. Desire. Special Edition. Intimate Moments.

Fiction: Historicals and Regency, intrigue, traditional, short contemporary sensuals, long contemporary romances, historicals. "We're always looking for new authors." Query.

Tips: "Harlequin readership comprises a wide variety of ages, backgrounds, income and education levels. The audience is predominantly female. Because of the high competition in women's fiction, readers are becoming very discriminating. They look for a quality read. Read as many recent romance books as possible in all series to get a feel for the scope, new trends, acceptable levels of sensuality, etc."

HARPER & ROW PUBLISHERS, INC., 10 E. 53rd St., New York NY 10022. (212)207-7000. Imprints include Barnes & Noble; Harper & Row-San Francisco (religious books only); Perennial Library; and Torchbooks. Managing Editor: Helen Moore. Publishes hardcover and paperback originals, and paperback reprints. Trade publishes over 400 titles/year. Pays standard royalties; advances negotiable. No unsolicited queries or mss. Reports on solicited queries in 6 weeks.

Nonfiction: Americana, animals, art, biography, business/economics, cookbooks, health, history, how-to, humor, music, nature, philosophy, politics, psychology, reference, religion, science, self-help, sociology, sports and travel.

Recent Nonfiction Title: *The Eight-Week Cholesterol Cure* (revised edition).

Fiction: Adventure, fantasy, gothic, historical, mystery, science fiction, suspense, western and literary. "We look for a strong story line and exceptional literary talent."

Recent Fiction Title: *Talking God*, by Tony Hillerman.

Tips: "Strongly suggest that you go through a literary agent before submitting any ms. Any unsolicited query or ms will be returned unread."

‡HARPER & ROW, SAN FRANCISCO, Division of Harper & Row, Publishers, Icehouse One #401; 151 Union St., San Francisco CA 94111-1299. (415)477-4400. Editor-in-Chief: Thomas Grady. Firm publishes hardcover and trade paperback originals and trade paperback reprints. Publishes 150 titles/year. Receives about 10,000 submissions/year. 5% of books from first-time authors; 50% from unagented writers. Pays royalty. Publishes book an average of 18 months after acceptance. Simultaneous (if notified) and photocopied submissions OK. Computer printout submissions OK. Reports in 2 months on queries; 6 months on mss. Free book catalog and ms guidelines.

Nonfiction: Biography, how-to, reference, self-help. Subjects include addiction/recovery, philosophy, psychology, religion, women's issues/studies, theology, New Age. Query or submit outline/synopsis and sample chapters.

HARPER JUNIOR BOOKS GROUP, WEST COAST, Division of Harper & Row Publishers, Box 6549, San Pedro CA 90734. (213)547-4262. Executive Editor, West Coast: Linda Zuckerman. Publishes hardcover originals. Averages 15 titles/year; receives 1500 submissions annually. 10% of books from first-time authors. 40% of books from unagented writers. Pays royalty on invoice price. Advance negotiable. Publishes book an average of 18 months after acceptance. Simultaneous and photocopied submissions OK. Computer printout submissions OK; no dot-matrix. Reports in 4 months. Book catalog and guidelines for 10x13 SAE with 4 first class stamps.

Nonfiction: Juvenile. Query or submit complete ms. Reviews artwork/photos as part of ms package.

Recent Nonfiction Title: *Whales*, by Seymour Simon.

Fiction: Juvenile. Submit complete ms only. No queries.

Recent Fiction Title: *The Best of Friends*, by Margaret Rostkowsbi.

Poetry: No Dr. Seuss-type verse. Submit complete ms.

Recent Poetry Title: *Under the Sunday Tree*, by Eloise Greenfield.

Tips: "Our audience is categorized into children, ages 3-6; 4-8; 8-12; 10-14; 12-16. Read contemporary children's books at all age levels; try to take some writing or children's literature courses; talk to children's librarians and booksellers in independent bookstores; read *Horn Book, Booklist, School Library Journal* and *Publishers Weekly*; take courses in book illustration and design."

HARROW AND HESTON, Stuyvesant Plaza, Box 3934, Albany NY 12203. (518)456-4894. Editor-in-Chief: Graeme Newman. Small press. Publishes hardcover and trade paperback originals and paperback reprints. Averages 4 titles/year; receives 10-20 submissions annually. 80% of books from first-time authors; 100% of books from unagented writers. Pays 10% royalty on wholesale price. Publishes book an average of 3 months after acceptance. Simultaneous and photocopied submissions OK. Query for electronic submissions. Computer printout submissions acceptable. Reports in 2 months on queries; 6 months on mss.

Nonfiction: Textbooks on sociology and criminal justices. Query.

Recent Nonfiction Title: *A Primer in the Sociology of Law*, by Dragan Milovanovic.

Tips: "Submissions must be clearly written with no jargon, and directed to upper undergraduate or graduate criminal justice students, on central criminal justice topics."

THE HARVARD COMMON PRESS, 535 Albany St., Boston MA 02118. (617)423-5803. President: Bruce P. Shaw. Publishes hardcover and trade paperback originals and reprints. Averages 6 titles/year; receives "thousands" of submissions annually. 75% of books from first-time authors; 75% of books from unagented writers. Average print order for a writer's first book is 7,500. Pays royalty; offers average $1,000 advance. Publishes book an average of 9 months after acceptance. Simultaneous and photocopied submissions OK. Computer printout submissions acceptable; no dot-matrix. Reports in 1 month. Book catalog for 9x11½ SAE and 3 first class stamps; ms guidelines for SASE.

Nonfiction: Travel, cookbook, how-to, reference and self-help. Emphasis on travel, family matters and cooking. "We want strong, practical books that help people gain control over a particular area of their lives, whether it's family matters, business or financial matters, health, careers, food or travel. An increasing percentage of our list is made up of books about travel and travel guides; in this area we are looking for authors who are well traveled, and who can offer a different approach to the series guidebooks. We are open to good nonfiction proposals that show evidence of strong organization and writing, and clearly demonstrate a need in the marketplace. First-time authors are welcome." Accepts nonfiction translations. Submit outline/synopsis and 1-3 sample chapters. Reviews artwork/photos.

Recent Nonfiction Title: *Going Places: The Guide to Travel Guides*, by Greg Hayes and Joan Wright (travel, reference).

HARVEST HOUSE PUBLISHERS, 1075 Arrowsmith, Eugene OR 97402. (503)343-0123. Editor-in-Chief: Eileen L. Mason. Manuscript Coordinator: LaRae Weikert. Publishes hardcover, trade paperback and mass market originals and reprints. Averages 55-60 titles/year; receives 1,200 submissions annually. 10% of books from first-time authors; 90% of books from unagented writers. Pays 14-18% royalty on wholesale price. Publishes book an average of 1 year after acceptance. Simultaneous and photocopied submissions OK. Computer printout submissions acceptable; prefers letter-quality. Reports in 10 weeks. Book catalog for 8½x11 SAE with 2 first class stamps; manuscript guidelines for SASE.

Nonfiction: Biography, how-to, illustrated book, juvenile (picture books ages 2-8; ages 9-12), reference, self-help, textbook and gift books on Evangelical Christian religion. No cookbooks, theses, dissertations or music.

Recent Nonfiction Title: *When the World Will Be As One*, by Tai Brooke.

Fiction: Historical, mystery and religious. No romances or short stories. Query or submit outline/synopsis and sample chapters.

Recent Fiction Title: *When Morning Comes Again*, by June Bacher.

Tips: Audience is women ages 25-40 and high school youth—evangelical Christians of all denominations.

‡*HAWKES PUBLISHING, INC., 1055 South 700 W., Salt Lake City UT 84104. (801)262-5555. President: John Hawkes. Publishes hardcover and trade paperback originals. Averages 24 titles/year; receives 200 submissions annually. 70% of books from first-time authors; 90% of books from unagented writers. Subsidy publishes 25-50% of books/year based on "how promising they are." Pays varying royalty of 10% on retail price to 10% on wholesale; no advance. Publishes book an average of 6 months after acceptance. Letters preferred describing book. Computer printout submissions acceptable; prefers letter-quality. Reports in 1 month on queries; 3 months on mss. Free book catalog.

Nonfiction: Cookbook, how-to and self-help. Subjects include cooking and foods, health, history, hobbies and psychology. Query or submit outline/synopsis and sample chapters. Reviews artwork/photos.

‡HAZELDEN EDUCATIONAL MATERIALS, 15251 Pleasant Valley Rd., Center City MN 55012. (612)257-4010. Imprints include Harper-Hazeldon. Publishes trade paperback originals. Averages 100 titles/year. 50% of books from first-time authors. 50% from unagented writers. Pays 7-9% royalty on retail price. Publishes ms an average of 6 months after acceptance. Simultaneous and photocopied submissions OK. Computer printout submissions acceptable. Reports in 6 weeks. Free book catalog and mss guidelines.

Nonfiction: Juvenile, self-help, psychology, textbook, health/medicine, eating disorders, AIDS and addictions. No autobiographies. Submit outline/synopsis sample chapters. Reviews artwork/photos as part of ms package.

Recent Nonfiction Title: *Beyond Codependency*, by Melodie Beattie.

Tips: "Common mistakes writers make include not doing their homework; i.e., they do not thoroughly investigate existing works on their topic and are unaware that they have reinvented the wheel. They do not investigate the publisher's niche and submit totally inappropriate proposals."

Close-up

Dennis Hensley
Holly Miller
Collaborators

"Find someone to collaborate with who is on your own level," advises Dr. Dennis E. Hensley. "You don't want to be a teacher, nor do you want to be so intimidated by the other person's credentials that you're afraid to make a suggestion. The irony is that while you need to find someone with similar talent, you also should look for someone who is different from you."

The advice on choosing a collaborator comes from someone who should know; Hensley has successfully collaborated on five books with colleague Holly G. Miller. Miller is a contributing editor to *The Saturday Evening Post*, instructor at Anderson University and frequent speaker at writers' workshops. Her most recent solo book is *How to Earn More than Pennies for Your Thoughts*, a Christian writers' handbook, for Warner Press. Hensley holds a doctorate in English and is the author of 20 books and more than 2,000 freelance articles. His 1983 bestseller, *Positive Workaholism* (Bobbs-Merrill), is considered a classic among motivation books. Hensley also is a frequent speaker at writers' workshops.

The two are co-authors of a three-book series written under the pen name Leslie Holden. They devised the name by saying it's "Les" of a "lie" to admit they're "Hol" and "Den." They decided to use a pen name because individually they write nonfiction books and they didn't want their following of readers to be confused and think the novels were self-help or motivation books.

The first novel of the series, *The Legacy of Lillian Parker* (Harvest House), is a mystery/romance novel written from a Christian viewpoint—no four-letter words or vivid sex scenes—but fast-paced action and an interesting subplot. Harvest House started a whole new line with the book since it didn't fit into the typical romance genre.

Miller describes how she and Hensley divide up the writing: "We used to split it every other chapter, but that became too predictable because people would guess who wrote what." They found it works better to write the outline and then assign each chapter, always aiming for 50/50. "It winds up where we share parts of chapters, too," Hensley says. "The subplot will come in and one of us will carry a certain character along. The other thing about it is once Holly has edited my chapter by adding more dialogue or a transition line, it becomes a 'Leslie Holden' chapter."

Hensley thinks his strength is developing strong plots, which combines well with Miller's strength in developing characters. Some things are simply more interesting to one than the other, so they choose to write certain scenes. In their second book, *The Compton Connection*, Miller plans a wedding for one of the characters. While writing the scene, a friend called and Miller answered the phone with a whispered "hello." Her friend asked why she was whispering. "Because I'm at a wedding," she quietly replied.

The differences in their perspectives and abilities give their characters greater depth and dimension, they believe, which enhance the plot and enable it to move in directions only "Leslie Holden" could choose. They've had different jobs and experiences and feel the male and female characters they write about are more believable than if only a man or only a woman was writing about them.

The two often are asked how they collaborate when they live more than 100 miles apart. Hensley says they send chapters to each other through the mail and also include a cassette tape. Then they edit each other's work meticulously. "There are times when we don't agree with what the other has done, so we'll take a stand, and that's why one of us serves as 'head writer' for each book," explains Hensley. "Somebody has to have the ultimate authority."

For their most recent novel, *The Gift*, they used their real names. The book combines a science fiction thriller with a strong Christian message. "Dennis wrote a couple of key scenes early and they're the heart of the whole book," Miller says. "That was good because it kept us on track so we remembered that everything had to lead to that." Hensley says, "The problem with *The Gift* was that we had to make what was impossible, not only sound possible, but probable, so we put in a lot of scientific research. It is all genuine, and putting that in lends an authenticity—not only *could* this happen, but this *might* happen. I think readers can read our books and be entertained, but think at the same time."

When collaborating, Miller says writers should "be aware that the odds are against you. Most collaborations don't work—at least not for long. Famous collaborations have gone on the skids. I think we have been aware of this and that kind of conflict could have grown, but we backed off and thought, 'No what we're doing is bigger than this little spat. We have a nice relationship and some good things are happening because of it, so let's not blow it.' "

"It's always more work than you think it is. The work is not cut in half," Hensley says, "and collaborators must have a similar approach to work." He suggests looking for these traits in a collaborator: quality of talent; diversity of background; and ability to see things through to the end.

"Our partnership is downright fun," declares Miller. "We enjoy surprising each other with twists and turns of the plot, and we like producing good exchanges of dialogue that we know will please the other. Getting instant feedback is one of the benefits of working with a partner.

"Also, I think we constantly are learning from each other. When Dennis sends me a chapter to edit, I not only look for flaws (and I don't find many!), but I like to pay attention to the way his transitions flow, how he successfully inserts flashbacks, and how he maintains tension in order to keep the reader turning pages. I can honestly say that 'Leslie' is a far better writer today than she/he was a couple of years ago."

— Cynthia Kephart

HEALTH ADMINISTRATION PRESS, Foundation of the American College of Healthcare Executives, 1021 East Huron St., Ann Arbor MI 48104. (313)764-1380. FAX: (313)763-1105. Imprints include Health Administration Press, Health Administration Press Perspectives and ACHE Management Series. Director: Daphne M. Grew. Publishes hardcover and trade paperback originals. Publishes 12 titles/year. Pays 10-15% royalty on net revenue from sale of book. Occasionally offers small advance. Publishes book an average of 10 months after acceptance. Photocopied submissions OK. Computer printout submissions OK; prefers letter-quality. Query for electronic submissions. Reports in 6 weeks on queries; 19 weeks on mss. Book catalog free on request.
Nonfiction: Reference or textbook. Subjects include business and economics, government/politics, health/medicine, sociology, health administration. "We are always interested in good, solid texts and references, and we are adding to our management series; books in this series offer health services CEOs and top managers immediately useful information in an accessible format." Submit outline/synopsis and sample chapters.
Recent Nonfiction Title: *Hospital Mergers in the Making,* by David B. Starkweather.
Tips: "We publish books primarily for an audience of managers of health care institutions and researchers and scholars in health services administration. The books we like to see have something to say and say it to our audience."

*HEART OF THE LAKES PUBLISHING, 2989 Lodi Rd., Interlaken NY 14847-0299. (607)532-4997. Imprints include Empire State Books and Windswept Press. Contact: Walter Steesy. Publishes hardcover and trade paperback originals and hardcover and trade paperback reprints. Averages 20-25 titles/year; receives 15-20 submissions annually. 100% of books from unagented writers. Average print order for a writer's first book is 500-1,000. Subsidy publishes 50% of books, "depending on type of material and potential sales." 15% author subsidized; 35% nonauthor subsidized. Payment is "worked out individually." Publishes book an average of 1-2 years after acceptance. Simultaneous and photocopied submissions OK. Query for electronic submissions. Computer printouts acceptable. Reports in 1 week on queries; 2 weeks on mss. Current books flyer for #10 SAE and 1 first class stamp.
Nonfiction: New York state and regional, history and genealogy source materials. Query. Reviews artwork/photos.
Recent Nonfiction Title: *Cheese Making in New York State,* by Eunice Stamm.
Fiction: Will review only fiction that deals with New York state historical subjects.

HENDRICKSON PUBLISHERS, INC., 137 Summit St., Box 3473, Peabody MA 01961-3473. (617)532-6546. Executive Editor: Dr. Ben Aker. Publishes hardcover and trade paperback originals, and hardcover and trade paperback reprints. Averages 6-12 titles/year; receives 85 submissions annually. 5% of books from first-time authors; 100% of books from unagented writers. Pays 5-15% royalty on wholesale and retail price. Average advance depends on project. Publishes book an average of 6 months after acceptance. Simultaneous (if so notified) and photocopied submissions OK. Computer printout submissions acceptable; prefers letter-quality. Free book catalog. Ms guidelines for SASE.
Nonfiction: Religious. "We will consider any quality manuscripts within the area of religion, specifically related to Biblical studies and related fields. Popularly written manuscripts are not acceptable." Submit outline/synopsis and sample chapters or complete ms.
Recent Nonfiction Title: *1 and 2 Timothy, Titus,* by Gordon D. Fee.

VIRGIL W. HENSLEY, INC., 6116 E. 32nd St., Tulsa OK 74135. (918)644-8520. Editor: Terri Kalfas. Publishes hardcover originals. Publishes 5 titles/year (will increase that number). Receives 100 submissions/year. 50% of books from first-time authors; 50% from unagented writers. Pays 5% minimum royalty on retail price or outright purchase of $250 minimum for study aids. Publishes ms an average of 18 months after acceptance. Computer printout submissions OK; prefers letter-quality. Reports in 6 weeks on queries; 2 months on mss. Book catalog for 9x12 SAE and $1 postage. Manuscript guidelines for #10 SAE and 1 first class stamp.
Nonfiction: Bible study curriculum. Subjects include child guidance/parenting, money/finance, religion, women's issues/studies. "We look for subjects that lend themselves to long-term Bible studies—prayer, prophecy, family, faith, etc. We do not want to see anything non-Christian." Query with brief synopsis then submit outline/sample chapters or complete ms.
Recent Nonfiction Title: *Understanding the Bible,* by Chip Ricks.
Tips: "Submit something that crosses denominational lines; Bible studies which are directed toward the large Christian market, not small specialized groups; heavy emphasis on student activities and student involvement. We serve an interdenominational market—churches of all sizes and Christian persuasions. Our books are used by both pastors and Christian education leaders in Bible studies, Sunday Schools, home Bible studies, and school classrooms."

HERALD PRESS, Subsidiary of Mennonite Publishing House, 616 Walnut Ave., Scottdale PA 15683. (412)887-8500. General Book Editor: David Garber. Publishes hardcover, trade and mass market paperback originals, trade paperback and mass market paperback reprints. Averages 30 titles/year; receives 700 submissions annually. 15% of books from first-time authors. 95% of books from unagented writers. Pays minimum royalty

of 10% wholesale, maximum of 12% retail. Advance seldom given. Publishes book an average of 14 months after acceptance. Photocopied submissions OK. Query for electronic submissions. Computer printout submissions OK; no dot-matrix. Reports in 3 weeks on queries; 2 months on submissions. Book catalog 50¢.
Nonfiction: Christian inspiration, Bible study, current issues, missions and evangelism, peace and justice, family life, Christian ethics and theology, self-help and juveniles (mostly ages 9-14). No drama or poetry. Query or submit outline/synopsis and sample chapters. Reviews artwork/photos as part of ms package.
Recent Nonfiction Title: *When Good People Quarrel*, by Robert S. Kreider and Rachel Waltner Goossen.
Fiction: Religious. Needs some fiction for youth and adults reflecting themes similar to those listed in nonfiction, also "compelling stories that treat social and Christian issues in a believable manner." No fantasy. Query or submit outline/synopsis and sample chapters.
Recent Fiction Title: *Yesterday, Today, and Forever*, by Kathi Mills.

HERE'S LIFE PUBLISHERS, INC., Subsidiary of Campus Crusade for Christ, Box 1576, San Bernardino CA 92404. (714)886-7981. FAX: (714)886-7985. President: Les Stobbe. Editorial Director: Dan Benson. Publishes hardcover and trade paperback originals. Averages 25 titles/year; receives 400 submissions annually. 40% of books from first-time authors; 100% of books from unagented writers. Average print order for a writer's first book is 5,000. Pays 15% royalty on wholesale price. Publishes book an average of 1 year after acceptance. Simultaneous and photocopied proposal submissions OK. Query for electronic submissions. Computer printout submissions acceptable; no dot-matrix. Reports in 1 month on queries; 3 months on mss. Ms guidelines for 8½x11 SAE with 2 first class stamps.
Nonfiction: Biography, how-to, reference and self-help. Needs "books in the areas of evangelism, Christian growth and family life; must reflect basic understanding of ministry and mission of Campus Crusade for Christ. No metaphysical or missionary biography." Query or submit outline/synopsis and sample chapters. Reviews artwork/photos.
Recent Nonfiction Title: *Memories that Bind*, by Fred and Florence Littauer.
Tips: "The writer has the best chance of selling our firm a sharply focused how-to book that provides a Biblical approach to a felt need."

*HERITAGE BOOKS, INC., 3602 Maureen, Bowie MD 20715. (301)464-1159. Editorial Director: Laird C. Towle. Publishes hardcover and paperback originals and reprints. Averages 100 titles/year; receives 100 submissions annually. 25% of books from first-time authors; 100% of books from unagented writers. Subsidy publishes 5% or less of books. Pays 10% royalty on retail price; no advance. Publishes book an average of 6 months after acceptance. Simultaneous and photocopied submissions OK. Computer printout submissions acceptable; prefers letter-quality. Reports in 1 month. Book catalog for SAE.
Nonfiction: "We particularly desire nonfiction titles dealing with history and genealogy including how-to and reference works, as well as conventional histories and genealogies. Ancestries of contemporary people are not of interest. The titles should be either of general interest or restricted to Eastern U.S. Material dealing with the present century is usually not of interest. We prefer writers to query or submit an outline/synopsis." Reviews artwork/photos.
Recent Nonfiction Title: *Historic Districts of America: New England*, by Richardson.
Tips: "The quality of the book is of prime importance; next is its relevance to our fields of interest."

‡HERMES HOUSE PRESS, 39 Adare Place, Northampton MA 01060. (413)584-8402. General Editor: Richard Mandell. Small press. Publishes trade paperback originals. Averages 8 titles/year; receives 45 submissions annually. 50% of books from first-time authors. "Pays in copies; after cost of publication is covered by income, pays small royalty." Publishes book an average of 8 months after acceptance. Photocopied submissions OK. Query for electronic submissions. Computer printout submissions OK; prefers letter-quality. Reports in 2 weeks on queries; 2 months on mss. Book catalog for #10 SAE.
Fiction: Ethnic, experimental, feminist, historical, mainstream and science fiction. "We are presently backed up with submissions and therefore not accepting new submissions. Literary fiction, with some attention made to language, has the best chance of selling to our firm."
Recent Fiction Title: *Crossings*, by Marie Diamond.
Poetry: "We are not currently accepting poetry submissions."
Recent Poetry Title: *Going West*, by Stanley Diamond (narrative).

HEYDAY BOOKS, Box 9145, Berkeley CA 94709. (415)549-3564. Publisher: Malcolm Margolin. Publishes hardcover and trade paperback originals, trade paperback reprints. Averages 4-9 titles/year; receives 200 submissions annually. 50% of books from first-time authors; 75% of books from unagented writers. Pays 8-10% royalty on retail price; offers average $1,000 advance. Publishes book an average of 8 months after acceptance. Computer printout submissions acceptable; no dot-matrix. Reports in 1 week on queries; up to 5 weeks on mss. Book catalog for 7x9 SAE and 2 first class stamps.
Nonfiction: Books about California only; how-to and reference. Subjects include Americana, history, nature and travel. "We publish books about native Americans, natural history, history, and recreation, with a strong California focus." Query with outline and synopsis. Reviews artwork/photos.

Recent Nonfiction Title: *Disorderly House*, by James Mills.
Tips: "Give good value, and avoid gimmicks. We are accepting *only* nonfiction books with a California focus."

HIPPOCRENE BOOKS INC.,171 Madison Ave., New York NY 10016. (212)685-4371. President: George Blagowidow. Publishes hardcover originals and trade paperback originals and reprints. Averages 100 titles/year. Receives 250 submissions annually. 25% of books from first-time authors; 50% of books from unagented writers. Pays 6-15% royalty on retail price. Offers "few thousand" dollar advance. Publishes book an average of 11 months after acceptance. Simultaneous submissions OK. Ms guidelines for SASE.
Nonfiction: Biography, how-to, reference, self-help, travel guides. Subjects include history, recreation and travel. Submit outline/synopsis and 2 sample chapters. Reviews artwork/photos as part of ms package.
Recent Nonfiction Titles: *The Paycheck Disruption*, by Dan Lacey.
Tips: "Our recent successes in publishing general books considered midlist by larger publishers is making us more of a general trade publisher. We continue to do well with travel books and reference books like dictionaries, atlases, quiz books etc."

HOLLOWAY HOUSE PUBLISHING CO., 8060 Melrose Ave., Los Angeles CA 90046. (213)653-8060. Publishes paperback originals (75%) and reprints (25%). Averages 30 titles/year; receives 300-500 submissions annually. 50% of books from first-time authors; 60% of books from unagented writers. Average print order for a writer's first book is 15,000-20,000. Pays royalty based on retail price. Publishes book an average of 6 months after acceptance. Photocopied submissions OK. Query for electronic submissions. Submit outline and 3 sample chapters. Reports in 6-9 weeks. Free book catalog and ms guidelines for SASE. Unsolicited manuscripts without SASE will not be returned nor acknowledged.
Nonfiction: Gambling and game books—from time to time publishes gambling books along the line of *How to Win*, *World's Greatest Winning Systems*, *Backgammon*, *How to Play and Win at Gin Rummy*, etc. Send query letter and/or outline with one sample chapter. Length: 60,000 words. Reviews artwork/photos as part of ms package.
Recent Nonfiction Title: *The King Conspiracy*, by Michael Newton.
Fiction: "Holloway House is the largest publisher of Black Experience literature. We are in the market for easily identifiable characters and locations. Dialogue must be realistic. Some sex is acceptable but not essential (refer to writer's guidelines). Action, people and places must be thoroughly depicted and graphically presented."
Recent Fiction Title: *Reunion*, by Mark Boone.

*HOLMES & MEIER PUBLISHERS, INC., 30 Irving Place, New York NY 10003. (212)254-4100. Publisher: Max J. Holmes. Associate Publisher: Barbara Lyons. Editors: Kevin Davis, Sheila Friedling. Managing Editor: Katharine Turok. Subsidy publishes books with organizations, not with individual authors. Publishes hardcover and paperback originals. Publishes 60 titles/year. Pays variable royalty. Publishes book an average of 9 months after acceptance. Computer printout submissions acceptable; prefers letter-quality. Reports in 3 months. Free book catalog.
Nonfiction: Americana, Africana, art, biography, business/economics, education, history, Judaica, Latin American studies, literary criticism, music, nature, politics, reference, sociology, textbooks and women's studies. Accepts translations. "We are noted as an academic publishing house and are pleased with our reputation of excellence in the field. However, we are also expanding our list to include books of more general interest." Reviews artwork/photos as part of ms package. Query first and submit outline/synopsis, sample chapters, curriculum vitae and idea of intended market/audience.
Recent Nonfiction Title: *Centerstage: American Diplomacy Since World War II*, edited by L. Carl Brown.

HOMESTEAD PUBLISHING, Box 193, Moose WY 83102. Editor: Carl Schreier. Publishes hardcover and trade paperback originals and trade paperback reprints. Averages 5 titles/year; receives 100 submissions annually. 60% of books from first-time authors. 90% of books from unagented writers. Pays 8-12% royalty on net receipts; offers $1,000 average advance. Publishes book an average of 1 year after acceptance. Simultaneous and photocopied submissions OK. Query for electronic submissions. Computer printout submissions OK. Reports in 2 weeks on queries; 2 months on submissions. Book catalog for #10 SAE with 2 first class stamps.
Nonfiction: Biography, coffee table book, illustrated book, juvenile and reference. Subjects include animals, art, history, nature, photography and travel. Especially needs natural history and nature books for children. No textbooks. Query; or submit outline, synopsis and sample chapters or complete ms. Reviews artwork/photos as part of ms package.
Recent Nonfiction Title: *Yellowstone: Selected Photographs 1870-1960*.
Tips: "Illustrated books on natural history are our specialty. Our audiences include professional, educated people with an interest in natural history, conservation, national parks, and western art. Underneath the visual aspects, a book should be well written, with a good grasp of the English language. We are looking for professional work and top quality publications."

‡**HORIZON PUBLISHERS & DISTRIBUTORS,** 50 South 500 West, Box 490, Bountiful UT 84010. (801)295-9451. President/Sr. Editor: Duane S. Crowther. Publishes hardcover and trade paperback originals and reprints. Averages 30 titles/year. Receives 800-1,500 submissions/year. Pays 8-14% on wholesale price or $500 maximum outright purchase. Photocopied submissions OK. Computer printout submissions OK. Reports in 1 week on queries; 5 months on mss. Free manuscript guidelines.
Nonfiction: Biography, cookbook, how-to, humor, illustrated book, juvenile, self-help and textbook. Subjects include anthropology/archaeology, child guidance/parenting, cooking, foods and nutrition, education, gardening, health/medicine, history, hobbies, money/finance, music/dance, nature/environment, psychology, recreation, religion and women's issues/studies. Query or submit complete ms.
Recent Nonfiction Title: *. . . And Justice For All?*, by John C. Sullivan (law).
Fiction: Adventure, experimental, fantasy, historical, humor, juvenile, mystery, picture books, religious, science fiction, short story collections, suspense, western and young adult. Query or submit complete ms.
Recent Fiction Title: *The Coachman and the Bells*, by Ted C. Hindmarsh (Christmas story).

HOUGHTON MIFFLIN CO., Adult Trade Division, 2 Park St., Boston MA 02108. (617)725-5000. Submissions Editor: Janice Harvey. Hardcover and paperback originals and paperback reprints. Royalty of 6-7½% on retail price for paperbacks; 10-15% on sliding scale for standard fiction and nonfiction; advance varies widely. Publishes book an average of 18 months after acceptance. Publishes 100 titles/year. Simultaneous submissions OK. Computer printout submissions acceptable; no dot-matrix. SASE required with all submissions. Reports in 2 months. Book catalog for 8½x11 SAE.
Nonfiction: Natural history, biography, health, history, current affairs, psychology and science. Query.
Recent Nonfiction Title: *Landslide: The Unmaking of the President, 1984-1988*, by Jane Mayer and Doyle McManus.
Fiction: Historical, mainstream and literary. Query.
Recent Fiction Title: *Emperor of the Air*, by Ethan Canin.
Tips: "No unsolicited manuscripts will be read. Submit query letter and outline or synopsis to Submissions Editor. (Include one sample chapter for fiction.) The query letter should be short and to the point—that is, it should *not* incorporate the book's synopsis. The letter should say who the writer is (including information on previous publications in magazines or wherever) and the subject of the book."

HOUGHTON MIFFLIN CO., Children's Trade Books, 2 Park St., Boston MA 02108. Contact: Editor. Publishes hardcover originals and trade paperback reprints (some simultaneous hard/soft). Averages 45-50 titles/year. Pays standard royalty; offers advance. Computer printout submissions acceptable; no dot-matrix; and no justified right margins. Reports in 1 month on queries; 2 months on mss. Free book catalog.
Nonfiction: Submit outline/synopsis and sample chapters. Reviews artwork/photos as part of ms package.
Fiction: Submit complete ms.

‡**HOWELL PRESS, INC.,** Suite B, 700 Harris St., Charlottesville, VA 22901. (804)977-4006. FAX: (804)979-5588. Dir. of Communications: Kathleen D. Valenzi. Publishes hardcover originals. Firm averages 8 titles/year. Receives 20-30 submissions/year. 30% of books from first-time authors. 80% from unagented writers. Pays 5-10% on whosesale price. "We generally offer an advance, but amount differs with each project and is generally negotiated with authors on a case-by-case basis." Publishes book an average of 2 years after acceptance. Simultaneous and photocopied submissions OK. Computer printout submissions OK; prefers letter-quality. Reports in 2 months. Book catalog for 7x10 SAE with 4 first class stamps.
Nonfiction: Coffee table book, illustrated book. Subjects include anthropology/archaeology, art/architecture, history, military/war, photography, religion, sports, regional travel, motorsports, aviation. "Generally open to most ideas, as long as writing is not scholarly (easily accessible to average adult reader) and can be illustrated in some fashion with photography. While our line is esoteric, it would be advisable to look over our catalog before querying to better understand what Howell Press does." Query. Submit outline/synopsis and sample chapters. Reviews artwork/photos as part of ms package.
Recent Nonfiction Title: *People of the High Plateau*, by Carl Berman (art).
Tips: "We're looking for books with built-in buyers (aviation enthusiasts, motorsports fans, etc.); books that can be beautifully illustrated with four-color art/photography."

HUDSON HILLS PRESS, INC., Suite 1308, 230 5th Ave., New York NY 10001-7704. (212)889-3090. President/Editorial Director: Paul Anbinder. Publishes hardcover and paperback originals. Averages 10 titles/year; receives 50-100 submissions annually. 15% of books from first-time authors; 90% of books from unagented writers. Average print order for a writer's first book is 3,000. Offers royalties of 5-8% on retail price. Average

For explanation of symbols, see the Key to Symbols and Abbreviations on Page 5. For unfamiliar words, see the Glossary.

advance: $5,000. Publishes book an average of 1 year after acceptance. Simultaneous and photocopied submissions OK. Computer printout submissions acceptable; prefers letter-quality. Reports in 1 month. Book catalog for SAE with 2 first class stamps.

Nonfiction: Art and photography. "We are only interested in publishing books about art and photography, including monographs." Query first, then submit outline/synopsis and sample chapters. Reviews artwork/photos as part of ms package.

Recent Nonfiction Title: _Berthe Morisot — Impressionist._

HUMAN KINETICS PUBLISHERS, INC., Box 5076, Champaign IL 61825-5076. (217)351-5076. FAX: (217)351-2674. Publisher: Rainer Martens. Imprints include Leisure Press and Human Kinetics Books. Publishes hardcover and paperback text and reference books and trade paperback originals. Averages 80 titles/year; receives 300 submissions annually. 50% of books from first-time authors; 97% of books from unagented writers. Pays 10-15% royalty on net income. Publishes book an average of 18 months after acceptance. Simultaneous and photocopied submissions OK. Query for electronic submissions. Computer printout submissions acceptable; prefers letter-quality. Reports in 2 months. Free book catalog.

Nonfiction: How-to, reference, self-help, technical and textbook. Subjects include health, recreation, sports, sport sciences and sports medicine, and physical education. Especially interested in books on wellness, including stress management, weight management, leisure management, and fitness; books on all aspects of sports technique or how-to books and coaching books; books which interpret the sport sciences and sports medicine, including sport physiology, sport psychology, sport pedagogy and sport biomechanics. No sport biographies, sport record or statistics books or regional books. Submit outline/synopsis and sample chapters. Reviews artwork/photos as part of ms package.

Recent Nonfiction Title: _Osteoporosis: A Guide to Prevention and Treatment_, by John F. Aloia, M.D.

Tips: "Books which accurately interpret the sport sciences and health research to coaches, athletes and fitness enthusiasts have the best chance of selling to us."

HUMANICS PUBLISHING GROUP, Suite 370, 1389 Peachtree St. NE, Atlanta GA 30309. (404)874-2176. President: Gary B. Wilson. Contact: Robert Grayson Hall, Executive Editor. Publishes softcover, educational and trade paperback originals. Averages 12 titles/year; receives 500 submissions annually. 20% of books from first-time authors; 100% of books from unagented writers. Average print order for a writer's first book is 5,000. Pays average 10% royalty on net sales; buys some mss outright. Publishes book an average of 1 year after acceptance. Computer printout submissions acceptable; prefers letter-quality. Reports in 4 months. Book catalog and ms guidelines for SASE.

Nonfiction: Self-help teacher resource books and psychological assessment instruments for early education. Subjects include health, psychology, sociology, education, business and New Age. Submit outline/synopsis and at least 3 sample chapters. Reviews artwork/photos as part of ms package.

Recent Nonfiction Title: _The Tao of Management_, by Bob Messing (New Age).

Tips: "Be resourceful, bold and creative. But be sure to have the facts and expertise in hand to back up your work."

‡*HUMANITIES PRESS INTERNATIONAL, INC., 171 First Ave., Atlantic Highlands NJ 07716. (201)872-1441. President: Keith M. Ashfield. Publishes hardcover originals and trade paperback originals and trade paperback reprints. Averages 80-100 titles/year. Receives 500 submissions/year. 5% of books from first-time authors. 80% from unagented writers. Subsidy publishes 2% of books. Pays 5-12½% royalty on retail price. Offers $500 average advance. Publishes book an average of 1 year after acceptance. Computer printout submissions OK. Reports in 3 weeks on queries; 10 weeks on mss. Free book catalog.

Nonfiction: Subjects include politics (international/theory), history (European Early Modern to Modern), language/literature, philosophy and sociology. "We want books for senior level undergraduates and upward."

Recent Nonfiction Title: _Lenin & the Revolutionary Party_, by LeBlanc (Marxist theory/politics).

Tips: "We want well-written contributions to scholarly investigation or synthesis of recent thought. Serious students and scholars are our audience."

CARL HUNGNESS PUBLISHING, Box 24308, Speedway IN 46224. (317)244-4792. Editorial Director: Carl Hungness. Publishes hardcover and paperback originals. Pays "negotiable" outright purchase. Reports in 3 weeks. Free book catalog.

Nonfiction: Stories relating to professional automobile racing. No sports car racing or drag racing material. Query.

*HUNTER HOUSE, INC., PUBLISHERS, Box 1302, Claremont CA 91711. FAX: (714)626-1636. General Manager: K.S. Rana. Publishes hardcover and trade paperback originals. Averages 8 titles/year; receives 200 submissions annually. 50% of books from first-time authors; 50% of books from unagented writers. Subsidy publishes 10% of books. "We determine whether an author should be subsidy published based upon subject matter, quality of the work, and if a subsidy is available." Pays 7½-12½% royalty on retail price. Offers $101 advance. Publishes book an average of 12-18 months after acceptance and receipt of final manuscript.

Simultaneous and photocopied submissions OK. Query for electronic submissions. Computer printout submissions acceptable. Reports in 1 month on queries; 5 months on mss. Book catalog and ms guidelines for 9x12 SAE with 3 first class stamps.

Nonfiction: How-to, young adult, and self-help. Subjects include family, health, psychology. Needs mss on "family and health, especially emerging areas in women's health, men's opening up and single parenting, older people, young adult, especially on health and intergenerational concerns." No evangelical, political, Americana, esoteric or erotica. Query or submit outline/synopsis and sample chapters. Reviews artwork/photos. "Please enclose return postage for material."

Recent Nonfiction Title: *Writing from Within: A Step-by-Step Guide to Writing Your Life's Stories*, by Bernard Selling.

Tips: "Manuscripts on family and health, or psychology for an aware public do well for us. Write simply, with established credentials and imagination. We respect writers and do not mistreat them. We ask for the same consideration."

HUNTER PUBLISHING, INC., 300 Raritan Center Pkwy., Edison NJ 08818. President: Michael Hunter. Averages 100 titles/year; receives 300 submissions annually. 10% of books from first-time authors. 75% of books from unagented writers. Pays royalty; offers $0-2,000 average advance. Publishes book on average 9 months after acceptance. Simultaneous submissions OK. Query for electronic submissions. Computer printout submissions OK. Reports in 3 weeks on queries; 1 month on submissions. Book catalog for #10 SAE with 4 first class stamps.

Nonfiction: Reference. Subjects include travel. "We need travel guides to areas covered by few competitors: Caribbean Islands, Pacific Islands, Canada, Mexico, regional U.S. from an active 'adventure' perspective. Walking and climbing guides to all areas—from Australia to India." No personal travel stories or books not directed to travelers. Query or submit outline/synopsis and sample chapters. Reviews artwork/photos as part of ms package.

Recent Nonfiction Title: *Charming Small Hotels of Italy.*

Tips: "Study what's out there, pick some successful models, and identify ways they can be made more appealing. We need active adventure-oriented guides and more specialized guides for travelers in search of the unusual."

HUNTINGTON HOUSE, INC., Box 53788, Lafayette LA 70505.(318)237-7049. President: Bill Keith. Publishes hardcover, trade paperback, and mass market paperback originals, trade paperback reprints. Averages 10-20 titles/year; receives 600 submissions annually. 50% of books from first-time authors; 20% of books from unagented writers. Average print order for a writer's first book is 10,000. Pays 10-15% royalty on wholesale and retail price. Publishes book an average of 18 months after acceptance. Simultaneous and photocopied submissions OK. Query for electronic submissions. Computer printout submissions acceptable. Free book catalog and ms guidelines.

Nonfiction: Current social and political issues, biographies, self-help, inspirational and childrens books. Query with descriptive outline or ms.

Recent Nonfiction Title: *Gold in the Furnace: South Africa on Trial*, by Jed Smock.

Tips: "Write clear, crisp and exciting mss that grab the reader. The company's goal is to educated and keep readers abreast of critical current events and to expose the effects of secular humanism specifically in regards to its impact on public, private and political institutions."

ILR PRESS, Division of The New York State School of Industrial and Labor Relations, Cornell University, Ithaca NY 14851-0952. (607)255-3061. Managing Editor: E. Fox. Publishes hardcover and trade paperback originals and reprints. Averages 5-10 titles/year. Pays royalty. Photocopied submissions OK. Computer printout submissions acceptable; no dot-matrix. Reports in 2-3 weeks on queries; 8-12 weeks on mss. Free book catalog.

Nonfiction: All titles relate to industrial and labor relations. Biography, reference, technical, and academic books. Subjects include history, sociology of work and the workplace, and business and economics. Book manuscript needs for the next year include "manuscripts on workplace problems, employment policy, women and work, personnel issues, and dispute resolution that will interest academics and practitioners." Query or submit outline/synopsis and sample chapters or complete ms.

Recent Nonfiction Title: *Teachers on Trial: Values, Standards, and Equity in Judging Conduct and Competence*, by James A. Gross.

Tips: "We are interested in manuscripts that address topical issues in industrial and labor relations that concern both academics and the general public. These must be well documented to pass our editorial evaluation, which includes review by academics in the industrial and labor relations field."

IMAGINE, INC., Box 9674, Pittsburgh PA 15226. (412)571-1430. President: R.V. Michelucci. Publishes trade paperback originals. Averages 3-5 titles/year; receives 50 submissions annually. 50% of books from first-time authors; 75% of books from unagented writers. Pays 6-10% royalty on retail price. Offers average $500 advance. Publishes book an average of 1 year after acceptance. Photocopied submissions OK. Reports in 2 weeks on queries; 2 months on mss. Book catalog for #10 SAE with 1 first class stamp.

Nonfiction: Coffee table book, how-to, illustrated book and reference. Subjects include films, science fiction, fantasy and horror films. Submit outline/synopsis and sample chapters or complete ms with illustrations and/or photos.

Recent Nonfiction Title: *Drive-In Madness*, by Bill George.

Tips: "If I were a writer trying to market a book today, I would research my subject matter completely before sending a manuscript. Our audience is between ages 18-45 and interested in film, science fiction, fantasy and the horror genre."

INCENTIVE PUBLICATIONS, INC., 3835 Cleghorn Ave., Nashville TN 37215. (615)385-2934. Editor: Sally Sharpe. Publishes paperback originals. Averages 15-25 titles/year; receives 350 submissions annually. 25% of books from first-time authors; 95% of books from unagented writers. Pays royalty or makes outright purchase. Publishes book an average of 1 year after acceptance. Photocopied submissions OK. Computer printout submissions acceptable; prefers letter-quality. Reports in 2 weeks on queries; 3 weeks on mss. Book catalog and ms guidelines for 8½x12 SAE.

Nonfiction: Teacher resources and books on educational areas relating to children. Submit outline/synopsis and sample chapters. Query with synopsis and detailed outline. Reviews artwork/photos as part of ms package.

Recent Nonfiction Title: *The Early Childhood Teacher's Every-Day-All-Year-Long Book* (early childhood units, activities, patterns and more).

Tips: "A common mistake writers make is demanding too much, such as the inclusion of their own artwork. Often they overwhelm the editor with too much copy—a short synopsis often receives much more attention."

*INDIANA UNIVERSITY PRESS, 10th & Morton Sts., Bloomington IN 47405. (812)337-4203. FAX: (812)855-7931. Director: John Gallman. Publishes hardcover and paperback originals and paperback reprints. Averages 134 titles/year. 30% of books from first-time authors. 98% from unagented writers. Average print order for a writer's first book is 1,000. Subsidy publishes (nonauthor) 9% of books. Pays maximum 10% royalty on retail price; offers occasional advance. Publishes book an average of 1 year after acceptance. Photocopied submissions OK. Computer printout submissions acceptable; no dot-matrix. Reports in 2 months. Free book catalog and ms guidelines.

Nonfiction: Scholarly books on humanities, history, philosophy, religion, Jewish studies, Black studies, translations, semiotics, public policy, film, music, linguistics, social sciences, regional materials, African studies, women's studies, and serious nonfiction for the general reader. Query or submit outline/synopsis and sample chapters. "Queries should include as much descriptive material as is necessary to convey scope and market appeal to us." Reviews artwork/photos.

Recent Nonfiction Title: *Harps and Harpists*, by Roslyn Rensch.

INDUSTRIAL PRESS INC., 200 Madison Ave., New York NY 10016. (212)889-6330. FAX: (212)545-8327. Editorial Director: Woodrow Chapman. Small press. Publishes hardcover originals. Averages 12 titles/year; receives 25 submissions annually. 2% of books from first-time authors; 100% of books from unagented writers. Publishes book an average of 1 year after acceptance of finished ms. Query for electronic submissions. Computer printout submissions acceptable; no dot-matrix. Reports in 1 month. Free book catalog.

Nonfiction: Reference and technical. Subjects include business and economics, science and engineering. "We envision professional engineers, plant managers, on-line industrial professionals responsible for equipment operation, professors teaching manufacturing, engineering, technology related courses as our audience." Especially looking for material on manufacturing technologies and titles on specific areas in manufacturing and industry. Computers in manufacturing are a priority. No energy-related books or how-to books. Query.

Recent Nonfiction Title: *Computer Graphics, An Introduction to the Mathematics & Geometry*, by Michael Mortenson.

INFORMATION RESOURCES PRESS, A Division of Herner and Company, Suite 700, 1700 N. Moore St., Arlington VA 22209. (703)558-8270. FAX: (703)558-4979. Vice President/Publisher: Ms. Gene P. Allen. Publishes hardcover originals. Averages 6 titles/year; receives 25 submissions annually. 80% of books from first-time authors; 100% of books from unagented writers. Pays 10-15% royalty on net cash receipts after returns and discounts. Publishes book an average of 1 year after acceptance. Simultaneous and photocopied submissions OK. Query for electronic submissions. Reports in 2 weeks on queries; 2 months on mss. Free book catalog and ms guidelines.

Nonfiction: Reference, technical and textbook. Subjects include health and library and information science. Needs basic or introductory books on information science, library science, and health planning that lend themselves for use as textbooks. Preferably, the mss will have been developed from course notes. No works on narrow research topics (nonbasic or introductory works). Submit outline/synopsis and sample chapters or complete ms.

Recent Nonfiction Title: *A Basic Guide to Online Information; on Systems for Health Care Professionals*, by Ronald G. Albright, Jr.
Tips: "Our audience includes libraries (public, special, college and university); librarians, information scientists, college-level faculty; schools of library and information science; health planners, graduate-level students of health planning, and administrators; economists. Our marketing program is slanted toward library and information science and health planning, and we can do a better job of marketing in these areas."

INSTRUCTOR BOOKS, 7500 Old Oak Blvd., Cleveland OH 44130. Editor: Christine Van Huysse, Ph.D. "U.S. and Canadian school supervisors, principals and teachers purchase items in our line for instructional purposes or professional development." 90% freelance written. Buys 6-10 scripts/year from published or unpublished writers. Most scripts produced are unagented submissions. Buys all rights. Writer should have "experience in preparing materials for elementary students, including suitable teaching guides to accompany them, and demonstrate knowledge of the appropriate subject areas, or demonstrate ability for accurate and efficient research and documentation." Computer printout submissions acceptable. Catalog for 8½x11 SAE.
Needs: Elementary curriculum enrichment—all subject areas. Display material, copy and illustration should match interest and reading skills of children in grades for which material is intended. Production is limited to printed matter: resource handbooks, teaching guides and idea books. Length: 6,000-12,000 words. Query. Standard contract, but fees vary considerably, depending on type of project.
Tips: "Writers who reflect current educational practices can expect to sell to us."

INTERCULTURAL PRESS, INC., Box 768, Yarmouth ME 04096. (207)846-5168. Contact: David S. Hoopes, Editor-in-Chief, 130 North Rd., Vershire VT 05079. (802)685-4448. Publishes hardcover and trade paperback originals. Averages 5-7 titles/year; receives 50-80 submissions annually. 50% of books from first-time authors; 95% of books from unagented writers. Pays royalty; occasionally offers small advance. Publishes book an average of 2 years after acceptance. Simultaneous and photocopied submissions OK. Query for electronic submissions. Computer printout submissions acceptable; prefers letter-quality. Reports in "several weeks" on queries; 2 months on mss. Free book catalog and ms guidelines.
Nonfiction: How-to, reference, self-help, textbook and theory. Subjects include business and economics, philosophy, politics, psychology, sociology, travel, or "any book with an international or domestic intercultural, multicultural or cross-cultural focus, i.e., a focus on the cultural factors in personal, social, political or economic relations. We want books with an international or domestic intercultural or multicultural focus, especially those on business operations (how to be effective in intercultural business activities) and education (textbooks for teaching intercultural subjects, for instance). Our books are published for educators in the intercultural field, business people who are engaged in international business, and anyone else who works in an international occupation or has had intercultural experience. No manuscripts that don't have an intercultural focus." Accepts nonfiction translations. Query "if there is any question of suitability (we can tell quickly from a good query)," or submit outline/synopsis. Do not submit mss unless invited.
Recent Nonfiction Title: *Toward Multiculturalism: A Reader in Multicultural Education*, by Jaime Wurzel.

‡*INTERGALACTIC PUBLISHING CO., 321 New Albany Rd., Moorestown NJ 08057. (609)778-8700. Contact: Samuel W. Valenza, Jr. Intergalactic is a division of Regal Communications Corporation, publishers of *Lottery Player's Magazine*. Averages 3-10 titles/year; receives 10-20 submissions annually. 80% of books from first-time authors; 100% of books from unagented writers. Average print order for a writer's first book is 1,000-5,000. Subsidy publishes 30-40% of books. Publishes book an average of 1 year after acceptance. Query for electronic submissions. Computer printout submissions acceptable; no dot-matrix.
Nonfiction: The publisher invites mss dealing with lottery in general and *systems of play* in particular. The company also produces and sells lottery and gaming related products and games, and invites submissions of ideas for same. Reviews artwork/photos.
Recent Nonfiction Title: *Lotto and Daily Numbers Playing Techniques*, by Steve Player.

INTERNATIONAL FOUNDATION OF EMPLOYEE BENEFIT PLANS, Box 69, Brookfield WI 53008-0069. (414)786-6700. FAX: (414)786-6647. Director of Publications: Dee Birschel. Publishes hardcover and trade paperback originals. Averages 30 titles/year; receives 10 submissions annually. 15% of books from first-time authors. 80% of books from unagented writers. Pays 5-15% royalty on wholesale and retail price. Publishes book an average of 1 year after acceptance. Photocopied submissions OK. Computer printout submissions OK; no dot-matrix. Reports in 3 months on queries. Book catalog free on request; ms guidelines for SASE.
Nonfiction: Reference, technical, consumer information and textbook. Subjects include health care, pensions, retirement planning, business and employee benefits. "We publish general and technical monographs on all aspects of employee benefits—pension plans, health insurance, etc." Query with outline.
Recent Nonfiction Title: *Self-Funding of Health Care Benefits*, by Carlton Harker.
Tips: Be aware of "interests of employers and the marketplace in benefits topics, i.e., how AIDS affects employers, health care cost containment."

INTERNATIONAL MARINE PUBLISHING CO., Division of TAB Books, Inc., Route 1, Box 220, Camden ME 04843. Imprints include Seven Seas Press. Editor-in-Chief: Jonathan Eaton. Publishes hardcover and paperback originals. Averages 22 titles/year; receives 500-700 submissions annually. 30% of books from first-time authors; 80% of books from unagented writers. Pays standard royalties, based on net price, with advances. Publishes book an average of 8 months after acceptance. Computer printout submissions acceptable; prefers letter-quality. Reports in 6 weeks. Book catalog and ms guidelines for SASE.

Nonfiction: "Mostly marine nonfiction but a wide range of subjects within that category: boatbuilding, boat design, yachting, seamanship, boat maintenance, maritime history, etc." All books are illustrated. "Material in all stages welcome. We prefer queries first with outline and 2-3 sample chapters." Reviews artwork/photos as part of ms package.

Recent Nonfiction Title: *The Fiberglass Boat Repair Manual*, by Allan Vaitses.

Fiction: "Marine fiction of excellence will be considered."

Tips: "Freelance writers should be aware of the need for clarity, accuracy and interest. Many progress too far in the actual writing, with an unsalable topic."

INTERNATIONAL PUBLISHERS CO., INC., #1301, 381 Park Ave. S., New York NY 10016. (212)685-2864. President: Betty Smith. Publishes hardcover and trade paperback originals and trade paperback reprints. Averages 15-20 titles/year; receives 200 submissions annually. 15% of books from first-time authors. Pays 5% royalty on paperbacks; 10% royalty on cloth. No advance. Publishes book an average of 6 months after acceptance. Simultaneous and photocopied submissions OK. Computer printout submissions acceptable; prefers letter-quality. Reports in 1 month on queries; 6 months on mss. Book catalog and ms guidelines for SASE with 45¢ postage.

Nonfiction: Biography, reference and textbook. Subjects include Americana, economics, history, philosophy, politics, social sciences, and Marxist-Leninist classics. "Books on labor, black studies and women's studies based on Marxist science have high priority." Query or submit outline and sample chapters. Reviews artwork/ photos as part of ms package.

Recent Nonfiction Title: *Superprofits and Crises*, by Victor Perlo.

Fiction: "We publish very little fiction." Query or submit outline and sample chapters.

Recent Fiction Title: *A Bird in Her Hair*, by Phillip Bonosky (short stories).

Poetry: "We rarely publish individual poets, usually anthologies."

Recent Poetry Title: *New and Old Voices of Wah'Kon-Tah*, editors Dodge and McCullough (contemporary native American Indian poetry).

‡INTERNATIONAL RESOURCES, Box 840, Arroyo Grande CA 93420-0840. (805)473-1947. Subsidiary of Padre Productions. Publisher: Lachlan P. MacDonald. Publishes hardcover and trade paperback originals. Averages 6-10 titles/year. Receives 500 submissions/year. 90% of books from first-time authors. 95% from unagented writers. Pays 6-10% on retail price. Advance varies. Publishes book an average of 3 years after acceptance. Simultaneous and photocopied submissions OK. Computer submissions OK; prefers letter-quality. Reports in 2 weeks on queries; 2 months on mss. Book catalog for 9x12 SAE and 2 first class stamps. Manuscript guidelines for #10 SAE and 1 first class stamp.

Nonfiction: Biography, how-to, illustrated book, reference, self-help and textbook. Subjects include Americana, animals, anthropology, archaeology, history, hobbies, nature/environment, photography, travel and women's issues/studies. "We want hot business leadership and finance topics, top-level advice for corporate CEOs, management techniques. No 'how to make millions in stocks, bonds or whatever'—usually submitted by writers with modest accomplishments. We only consider such books from self-made millionaires. Financial statement will be required." No fiction or poetry. Query or submit outline/synopsis and sample chapters. Reviews artwork/photos as part of ms package.

Recent Nonfiction Title: *An Uncommon Guide to Easter Island*, by Georgia Lee, Ph.D. (travel guide).

Tips: "We prefer authorites who offer useful information to high achievers: people active in business and industry who need guidelines. Chief executives, public relations and personnel vice presidents, active traveling retirees are our audience."

INTERNATIONAL SELF-COUNSEL PRESS, LTD., 1481 Charlotte Rd., North Vancouver, British Columbia V7J 1H1 Canada. (604)986-3366. President: Diana R. Douglas. Senior Editor: Ruth Wilson. Publishes trade paperback originals. Averages 10-15 titles/year; receives 500 submissions annually. 50% of books from first-time authors; 100% of books from unagented writers. Average print order for a writer's first book is 4,000. Pays 10% royalty on wholesale price; no advance. Publishes book an average of 9 months after submission of contracted ms. Simultaneous and photocopied submissions OK. Computer printout submissions acceptable; prefers letter-quality. Reports in 6 weeks. Book catalog for 9x6 SAE with IRCs.

Nonfiction: Specializes in self-help and how-to books in law, business, reference, and psychology for lay person. Submit outline and sample chapters. Follow Chicago *Manual of Style*.

Recent Nonfiction Title: *Marketing Your Service*, by Withers and Vipperman (business—how-to).

INTERNATIONAL WEALTH SUCCESS, Box 186, Merrick NY 11566. (516)766-5850. Editor: Tyler G. Hicks. Averages 10 titles/year; receives 100 submissions annually. 100% of books from first-time authors; 100% of books from unagented writers. Average print order for a writer's first book "varies from 500 and up, depending on the book." Pays 10% royalty on wholesale or retail price. Buys all rights. Usual advance is $1,000, but this varies, depending on author's reputation and nature of book. Publishes book 4 months after acceptance. Photocopied and dot-matrix submissions OK. Query for electronic submissions. Computer printout submissions acceptable. Reports in 1 month. Book catalog and ms guidelines for 9x12 SAE with 3 first class stamps.

Nonfiction: Self-help and how-to. "Techniques, methods, sources for building wealth. Highly personal, how-to-do-it with plenty of case histories. Books are aimed at the wealth builder and are highly sympathetic to his and her problems." Financing, business success, venture capital, etc. Length: 60,000-70,000 words. Query. Reviews artwork/photos as part of ms package.

Recent Nonfiction Title: *Money Agency Planning Guide*, by Brisky.

Tips: "With the mass layoffs in large and medium-size companies there is an increasing interest in owning your own business. So we will focus on more how-to hands-on material on owning—and becoming successful in—one's own business of any kind. Our market is the BWB—Beginning Wealth Builder. This person has so little money that financial planning is something they never think of. Instead, they want to know what kind of a business they can get into to make some money without a large investment. Write for this market and you have millions of potential readers. Remember—there are a lot more people *without* money than *with* money."

*INTERSTATE PUBLISHERS, INC., 19 N. Jackson St., Box 50, Danville IL 61834-0050. (217)446-0500. Acquisitions/Vice President-Editorial: Ronald L. McDaniel. Hardcover and paperback originals and software. Publishes about 50 titles/year. 50% of books from first-time authors; 100% of books from unagented writers. Subsidy publishes 5% of books; 3% nonauthor subsidy. Usual royalty is 10%; no advance. Markets books by mail and exhibits. Publishes book an average of 9-12 months after acceptance. Computer printout submissions acceptable; prefers letter-quality. Reports in 3-4 months. Book catalog for 9x12 SAE. "Our guidelines booklet is provided only to persons who have submitted proposals for works in which we believe we might be interested. If the booklet is sent, no self-addressed envelope or postage from the author is necessary."

Nonfiction: Publishes high school and undergraduate college-level texts and related materials in agricultural education (production agriculture, agriscience and technology, agribusiness, agrimarketing, horticulture). Also publishes items in correctional education (books for professional training and development and works for use by and with incarcerated individuals in correctional facilities). "We favor, but do not limit ourselves to, works that are designed for class—quantity rather than single-copy sale." Query or submit synopsis and 2-3 sample chapters. Reviews artwork/photos as part of ms package.

Recent Nonfiction Title: *Our Soils and Their Management*, 6th ed.

Tips: "Freelance writers should be aware of strict adherence to the use of nonsexist language; fair and balanced representation of the sexes and of minorities in both text and illustrations; and discussion of computer applications wherever applicable. Writers commonly fail to identify publishers who specialize in the subject areas in which they are writing. For example, a publisher of textbooks isn't interested in novels, or one that specializes in elementary education materials isn't going to want a book on auto mechanics."

INTERURBAN PRESS/TRANS ANGLO BOOKS, Box 6444, Glendale CA 91205. (213)240-9130. Subsidiaries include PRN/PTJ Magazines and Interurban Films. President: Mac Sebree. Publishes hardcover and trade paperback originals. Averages 10-12 titles/year; receives 50-75 submissions yearly. 35% of books from first-time authors; 99% of books from unagented writers. Average print order for a writer's first book is 2,000. Pays 5-10% royalty on gross receipts; offers no advance. Computer printout submissions acceptable. Reports in 2 weeks on queries; 2 months on mss. Free book catalog.

Nonfiction: Western Americana and transportation. Subjects include Americana, history, hobbies and travel. "We are interested mainly in manuscripts about railroads, local transit, local history, and Western Americana (gold mining, logging, early transportation, etc.). Also anything pertaining to preservation movement, nostalgia." Query. Reviews artwork/photos.

Recent Nonfiction Title: *The Surfliners—50 Years of the San Diegan*, by Dick Stephenson.

Tips: "Our audience is comprised of hobbyists in the rail transportation field ('railfans'); those interested in Western Americana (logging, mining, etc.); and students of transportation history, especially railroads and local rail transit (streetcars)."

*INTERVARSITY PRESS, Division of Intervarsity Christian Fellowship, Box 1400, Downers Grove IL 60515. (312)964-5700. Managing Editor: Andrew T. LePeau. Publishes hardcover and paperback originals and reprints. Averages 50 titles/year; receives 800 submissions annually. 25% of books from first-time authors; 95% of books from unagented writers. Subsidy publishes (nonauthor) 6% of books. Pays average 10% royalty on retail price; offers average $1,000 advance. Sometimes makes outright purchase for $600-2,500. Publishes book an average of 15 months after acceptance of final draft. "Indicate simultaneous submissions." Computer printout submissions acceptable; no dot-matrix. Reports in 3 months. Writer's guidelines for SASE.

Nonfiction: "InterVarsity Press publishes books geared to the presentation of Biblical Christianity in its various relations to personal life, art, literature, sociology, psychology, philosophy, history and so forth. Though we are primarily publishers of trade books, we are cognizant of the textbook market at the college, university and seminary level within the general religious field. The audience for which the books are published is composed primarily of adult Christians. Stylistic treatment varies from topic to topic and from fairly simple popularizations to scholarly works primarily designed to be read by scholars." Accepts nonfiction translations. Query or submit outline/synopsis and 2 sample chapters.

Recent Nonfiction Title: *When Christians Clash*, by Horace L. Fenton, Jr. (Christian living).

Fiction: Fantasy, humor, mainstream, religious, science fiction. "While fiction need not be explicity Christian or religious, it should rise out of a Christian perspective." Submit outline/synopsis and sample chapters.

Recent Fiction Title: *The Toy Campaign*, by John Bibee (juvenile fantasy).

Tips: "Religious publishing has become overpublished. Books that fill niches or give a look at a specific aspect of a broad topic (such as marriage or finances or Christian growth) are doing well for us. Also, even thoughtful books need lower reading levels, more stories and illustrative materials. If I were a writer trying to market a book today, I would read William Zinsser's *On Writing Well* and do as he says. Writers commonly send us types of mss that we don't publish, and act as if we should publish their work—being too confident of their ideas and ability."

‡INTERWEAVE PRESS, 306 N. Washington Ave., Loveland CO 80537. (303)669-7672. Book Coordinator: Barbara Liebler. Firm publishes hardcover and trade paperback originals. Publishes 8 titles/year; receives 50 submissions/year. 60% from first-time authors; 98% from unagented writers. Pays 10% royalty on net receipts. Offers $500 average advance. Publishes book an average of 1 year after acceptance. Simultaneous (if clearly identified) and photocopied submissions OK. Query for electronic submissions. Computer printout submissions OK. Reports in 2 months. Free book catalog and ms guidelines.

Nonfiction: How-to, technical. Subjects include fiber arts—basketry, spinning, knitting, dyeing and weaving. Submit outline/synopsis and sample chapters, or send complete ms. Reviews artwork/photos as part of ms package.

Recent Nonfiction Title: *Splint Woven Basketry*, by Robin Daughtery (basketry how-to).

Tips: "We are looking for very clear, informally written, technically correct manuscripts, generally of a how-to nature, in our specific fiber fields. Our audience includes a variety of creative self-starters who like fibers and appreciate inspiration and clear instruction. They are often well educated and skillful in many areas."

*IOWA STATE UNIVERSITY PRESS, 2121 S. State Ave., Ames IA 50010. (515)292-0140. Director: Richard Kinney. Managing Editor: Bill Silag. Hardcover and paperback originals. Averages 70 titles/year; receives 350 submissions annually. 98% of books from unagented writers. Average print order for a writer's first book is 2,000. Subsidy publishes (nonauthor) 25% of titles, based on sales potential of book and contribution to scholarship. Pays 10-12½-15% royalty on wholesale price; no advance. Publishes book an average of 1 year after acceptance. Simultaneous submissions OK, if advised; photocopied submissions OK. Query for electronic submissions. Computer printout submissions acceptable; prefers letter-quality. Reports in 4 months. Free book catalog; ms guidelines for SASE.

Nonfiction: Publishes biography, history, scientific/technical textbooks, the arts and sciences, statistics and mathematics, economics, aviation, and medical and veterinary sciences. Accepts nonfiction translations. Submit outline/synopsis and several sample chapters, preferably not in sequence; must be double-spaced throughout. Looks for "unique approach to subject; clear, concise narrative; and effective integration of scholarly apparatus." Send contrasting b&w glossy prints to illustrate ms. Reviews artwork/photos.

Recent Nonfiction Title: *Portrait of an Explorer: Hiram Bingham, Discoverer of Machu Picchu*, by Alfred M. Bingham.

IRON CROWN ENTERPRISES, Box 1605, Charlottesville VA 22902. (804)295-3918. Managing Editor: John Ruemmler. Imprint includes Fantasy & Sci-Fi Novels (fiction)—John Ruemmler, editor. Publishes 8½x11 paperback and mass market paperback originals. Averages 50-60 titles/year; receives 200 submissions annually. 25% of books from first-time authors; 75% of books from unagented writers. Pays 2-6% royalty on wholesale price, or makes outright purchase for $1,000-2,500. Offers average $1,000 advance. Publishes book an average of 1 year after acceptance. Photocopied submissions OK. Computer printout submissions acceptable; prefers letter-quality. Reports in 1 month on queries; 3 months on mss. Book catalog and ms guidelines for #10 SASE.

Fiction: Fantasy and science fiction and fantasy role-playing supplements. Query. "We do not accept unsolicited manuscripts."

Recent Fiction Title: *War in a Distant Moon*, by Tod Foley (game).

Tips: "Our basic audience for gaming books is role-players, who are mostly ages 12-25. Iron Crown Enterprises publishes only a very specific sub-genre of fiction, namely fantasy role-playing supplements. We own the exclusive worldwide rights for such material based on J.R.R. Tolkien's *Hobbit* and *Lord of the Rings*. We also have a line of science fiction supplements and are planning a line of fantasy books of our own. We are currently concentrating on a very specific market, and potential submissions must fall within stringent guidelines. Due to the complexity of our needs, please query."

*ISHIYAKU EUROAMERICA, INC., Subsidiary of Ishiyaku Publishers, Inc., Tokyo, Japan: 716 Hanley Industrial Court, St. Louis MO 63144. (314)644-4322. FAX: (314)644-9532. President: Manuel L. Ponte. Inquiries should be directed to Dr. Gregory Hacke, Editor-in-Chief. Publishes hardcover originals. Averages 15 titles/year; receives 50 submissions annually. Subsidy publishes (nonauthor) 100% of books. 75% of books from first-time authors; 100% of books from unagented writers. Average print order for a writer's first book is 3,000. Pays 10% minimum royalty on retail price or pays 35% of all foreign translation rights sales. Offers average $1,000 advance. Simultaneous submissions OK. Query for electronic submissions. Computer printout submissions acceptable; no dot-matrix. Reports in 2 weeks on queries; 1 week on mss. Free book catalog; ms guidelines for SASE.
Nonfiction: Reference and medical/nursing textbooks. Subjects include health (medical and dental); psychology (nursing); and psychiatry. Especially looking for "all phases of nursing education, administration and clinical procedures." Query, or submit outline/synopsis and sample chapters or complete ms. Reviews artwork/photos as part of ms package.
Recent Nonfiction Title: *When You Face the Chemically Dependent Patient: A Practical Guide for Nurses*, by Judy Bluhm, R.N., M.A., (nursing).
Tips: "Medical authors often feel that their incomplete works deserve to be published; dental authors have a tendency to overstress facts, thereby requiring considerable editing. We prefer the latter to the former."

*JALMAR PRESS, INC., Subsidiary of B.L. Winch & Associates, 45 Hitching Post Dr., Bldg. 2, Rolling Hills Estates CA 90274-4297. (213)547-1240. FAX (213)547-1644. Editorial Director: B.L. Winch. Senior Editor: Suzanne Mikesell. Publishes hardcover and trade paperback originals. Averages 4-8 titles/year. Pays 5-15% royalty on net sales. Subsidy publishes 10% of books; subsidy publishes (nonauthor) 20% of books. Publishes book an average of 18 months after acceptance. Simultaneous and photocopied submissions OK. Query for electronic submissions. Computer printout submissions acceptable. Reports in 3 months. Book catalog for 8½x11 SAE with 4 first class stamps.
Nonfiction: Positive self-esteem materials for parenting and teaching; right-brain/whole-brain learning materials; peacemaking skills activities for parenting and teaching; and inspirational titles on self-concept and values. Reviews artwork/photos as part of ms package. "Prefer completed ms."
Recent Nonfiction Title: *Good Morning Class, I Love You*, by Esther Wright.
Tips: "A continuing strong effort by Jalmar in the areas of self-esteem, right brain/whole brain learning, peacemaking skills and creative thinking/problem solving will be made."

‡*JAVA PUBLISHING COMPANY, Box 25203, Colorado Springs CO 80936. (719)548-1844. Publisher: Bruce Fife. Firm publishes hardcover and trade paperback originals and trade paperback reprints. Publishes 3-8 titles/year; receives 40 submissions/year. 70% of books from first-time authors; 100% from unagented writers. Subsidy publishes 10% of books. Pays 5-10% royalty on retail price, or buys ms for $250-5,000 outright. Offers $250 average advance. Publishes book an average of 9 months after acceptance. Simultaneous and photocopied submissions OK. Computer printout submissions OK. Reports in 1 month on queries; 2 months on mss. Book catalog of 6x9 SAE and 2 first class stamps; ms guidelines for #10 SASE.
Nonfiction: Biography, how-to, humor, self-help. Subjects include hobbies, recreation, sports, entertainment and performing arts. Submit complete ms. Reviews artwork/photos as part of ms package.
Recent Nonfiction Title: *Creative Clowning*, by Tony Blanco, et. al. (how-to).
Fiction: Humor. Submit complete ms.

JONATHAN DAVID PUBLISHERS, 68-22 Eliot Ave., Middle Village NY 11379. (718)456-8611. Editor-in-Chief: Alfred J. Kolatch. Publishes hardcover and paperback originals. Averages 15 titles/year; receives 750-1,000 submissions annually. 50% of books from first-time authors; 90% of books from unagented writers. Pays standard royalty. Publishes book an average of 18 months after acceptance. Computer printout submissions acceptable; no dot-matrix. Photocopied submissions OK. Reports in 2 weeks on queries; 2 months on ms.
Nonfiction: Adult nonfiction books for a general audience. Cookbooks, cooking and foods, how-to, baseball and football, reference, self-help, Judaica. Query.
Recent Nonfiction Title: *Great Jews on Stage and Screen*, by Darryl Lyman (biographical reference).

KALMBACH PUBLISHING CO., 21027 Crossroads Circle, Waukesha WI 53186. Books Editor: Bob Hayden. Publishes hardcover and paperback originals and paperback reprints. Averages 6-8 titles/year; receives 25 submissions annually. 85% of books from first-time authors; 100% of books from unagented writers. Offers 5-8% royalty on retail price. Average advance is $1,000. Publishes book an average of 18 months after acceptance. Computer printout submissions acceptable; prefers letter-quality. Reports in 2 months.
Nonfiction: Hobbies, how-to, and recreation. "Our book publishing effort is in railroading and hobby how-to-do-it titles *only*." Query first. "I welcome telephone inquiries. They save me a lot of time, and they can save an author a lot of misconceptions and wasted work." In written query, wants to see "a detailed outline

of two or three pages and a complete sample chapter with photos, drawings, and how-to text." Reviews artwork/photos as part of ms package.

Recent Nonfiction Title: *Basic Electricity and Electronics for Model Railroaders*, by Don Fiehmann.

Tips: "Our books are about half text and half illustrations. Any author who wants to publish with us must be able to furnish good photographs and rough drawings before we'll consider contracting for his book."

KAR-BEN COPIES INC., 6800 Tildenwood Ln., Rockville MD 20852. (301)984-8733. President: Judye Groner. Publishes hardcover and trade paperback originals. Averages 8-10 titles/year; receives 150 submissions annually. 25% of books from first-time authors; 100% from unagented writers. Average print order for a writer's first book is 5,000. Pays 6-8% royalty on net receipts; makes negotiable outright purchase; offers average $1,000 advance. Publishes book an average of 1 year after acceptance. Computer printout submissions acceptable. Reports in 1 week on queries; 1 month on mss. Free book catalog; ms guidelines for 9x12 SAE with 2 first class stamps.

Nonfiction: Jewish juvenile (ages 1-12). Especially looking for books on Jewish life-cycle, holidays, and customs for children—"early childhood and elementary." Send only mss with Jewish content. Query with outline/synopsis and sample chapters or submit complete ms. Reviews artwork/photos as part of ms package.

Recent Nonfiction Title: *Kids Love Israel. Israel Loves Kids—A Travel Guide for Families*, by Barbara Sofer.

Fiction: Adventure, fantasy, historical and religious (all Jewish juvenile). Especially looking for Jewish holiday and history-related fiction for young children. Submit outline/synopsis and sample chapters or complete ms.

Recent Fiction Title: *Not Yet, Elijah!*, by Harriet Feder.

Tips: "We envision Jewish children and their families, and juveniles interested in learning about Jewish subjects, as our audience."

*KENT STATE UNIVERSITY PRESS, Kent State University, Kent OH 44242. (216)672-7913. Director: John T. Hubbell. Editor: Julia Morton. Publishes hardcover and paperback originals and some reprints. Averages 15-20 titles/year. Subsidy publishes (nonauthor) 20% of books. Standard minimum book contract on net sales; rarely offers advance. "Always write a letter of inquiry before submitting manuscripts. We can publish only a limited number of titles each year and can frequently tell in advance whether or not we would be interested in a particular manuscript. This practice saves both our time and that of the author, not to mention postage costs. If interested we will ask for complete manuscript. Decisions based on in-house readings and two by outside scholars in the field of study." Computer printout submissions acceptable; prefers letter-quality. Reports in 6-10 weeks. Enclose return postage. Free book catalog.

Nonfiction: Especially interested in "scholarly works in history and literary studies of high quality, any titles of regional interest for Ohio, scholarly biographies, archaeological research, the arts, and general nonfiction."

Recent Nonfiction Title: *A Photo Album of Ohio's Canal Era, 1825-1913*, by Jack Gieck (history, Ohio studies).

Reports in 2 weeks. Book catalog and ms guidelines for 8½x11 SASE.

Nonfiction: How-to, technical, textbook and computer software in book form. Subjects include recreation, business, finance, science and engineering. We are interested in books that include computer program listings. Of special interest are how-to books in this area. We are also interested in nontechnical books and programs, such as business applications, as long as they relate to microcomputers. Of special interest are computer-aided design and manufacturing, robotics, computer graphics, and computer-aided instruction. Also, our publications must be of immediate interest to the computer and educational communities and must be highly professional in technical content. No mss of merely academic interest." Query or submit outline/synopsis and sample chapters. Reviews artwork/photos.

Recent Nonfiction Title: *Stock Market Charting*, by A. Hogue (investment).

MICHAEL KESEND PUBLISHING, LTD., 1025 5th Ave., New York NY 10028. (212)249-5150. Director: Michael Kesend. Publishes hardcover and trade paperback originals, and hardcover and trade paperback reprints. Averages 4-6 titles/year; receives 150 submissions annually. 50% of books from first-time authors; 50% of books from unagented writers. Pays 3-12½% royalty on wholesale price or retail price, or makes outright purchase for $500 minimum. Advance varies. Publishes book an average of 18 months after acceptance. Computer printout submissions acceptable; prefers letter-quality. Reports in 2 months on queries; 3 months on mss. Guidelines for #10 SASE.

Nonfiction: Biography, how-to, illustrated book, self-help and sports. Subjects include animals, health, history, hobbies, nature, sports, travel, the environment, and guides to several subjects. Needs sports, health self-help and environmental awareness guides. No photography mss. Submit outline/synopsis and sample chapters. Reviews artwork/photos as part of ms package.

Recent Nonfiction Title: *Clearing the Bases, Baseball Then & Now*, by Bill Starr.

Fiction: Literary fiction only. No science fiction or romance. No simultaneous submissions. Submit outline/synopsis and 2-3 sample chapters.

Recent Fiction Title: *Dan Yack*, by Blaise Cendrars.

Tips: "We are now more interested in nature-related topics and also regional guides."

‡**KINSEEKER PUBLICATIONS**, Box 184, Grawn MI 49637. (616)276-6745. Editor: Victoria Wilson. Publishes trade paperback originals. Averages 6 titles/year. 100% of books from unagented writers. Pays 10-25% royalty on retail price. Publishes book an average of 8 months after acceptance. Simultaneous and photocopied submissions OK. Computer printout submissions OK; prefers letter-quality. Reports in 2 weeks. Book catalog and manuscript guidelines for #10 SASE.
Nonfiction: Reference books. Subjects include history and genealogy. Query or submit outline/synopsis and sample chapters. Reviews artwork/photos as part of ms package.

‡**B. KLEIN PUBLICATIONS**, Box 8503, Coral Springs FL 33065. (305)752-1708. Editor-in-Chief: Bernard Klein. Hardcover and paperback originals. Specializes in directories, annuals, who's who type of books, bibliography, business opportunity, reference books. Averages 5 titles/year. Pays 10% royalty on wholesale price, "but we're negotiable." Advance "depends on many factors." Markets books by direct mail and mail order. Simultaneous and photocopied submissions OK. Reports in 2 weeks. Book catalog for #10 SASE.
Nonfiction: Business, hobbies, how-to, reference, self-help, directories and bibliographies. Query or submit outline/synopsis and sample chapters or complete ms.
Recent Nonfiction Title: *Guide to American Directories*, by Bernard Klein.

KNIGHTS PRESS, Box 454, Pound Ridge NY 10576. Publisher: Elizabeth G. Gershman. Publishes trade paperback originals. Averages 16 titles/year; receives 500 submissions annually. 50% of books from first-time authors; 50% of books from unagented writers. Pays 10% plus escalating royalty on retail price; offers average $500 advance. Publishes book an average of 1 year after acceptance. Photocopied submissions OK. Computer printout submissions acceptable; prefers letter-quality. Reports in 1 month on queries; 3 months on mss. Book catalog and ms guidelines for #10 SASE.
Fiction: Adventure, erotica (very soft-core considered), ethnic, experimental, fantasy, gothic, historical, humor, mystery, romance, science fiction, suspense and western. "We publish *only* gay men's fiction; must show a positive gay lifestyle or positive gay relationship." No young adult or children's; no pornography; no formula plots, especially no formula romances; or no hardcore S&M. No lesbian fiction. Query a must. Submit outline/synopsis and sample chapters. Do not submit complete manuscript unless requested.
Recent Fiction Title: *The Boys in the Bars*, by Christopher Davis (short stories).
Tips: "We are interested in well-written, well-plotted gay fiction. We are looking only for the highest quality gay literature."

ALFRED A. KNOPF, INC., 201 E. 50th St., New York NY 10022. (212)751-2600. Senior Editor: Ashbel Green. Children's Book Editor: Ms. Frances Foster. Publishes hardcover and paperback originals. Averages 200 titles annually. 15% of books from first-time authors; 40% of books from unagented writers. Royalties and advance "vary." Publishes book an average of 10 months after acceptance. Simultaneous (if so informed) and photocopied submissions OK. Reports in 1 month. Book catalog for 7x10 SAE (7 oz.).
Nonfiction: Book-length nonfiction, including books of scholarly merit. Preferred length: 40,000-150,000 words. "A good nonfiction writer should be able to follow the latest scholarship in any field of human knowledge, and fill in the abstractions of scholarship for the benefit of the general reader by means of good, concrete, sensory reporting." Query. Reviews artwork/photos as part of ms package.
Recent Nonfiction Title: *The First Salute*, by Barbara Tuchman (history).
Fiction: Publishes book-length fiction of literary merit by known or unknown writers. Length: 30,000-150,000 words. Submit complete ms.
Recent Fiction Title: *Breathing Lessons*, by Anne Tyler.

KNOWLEDGE INDUSTRY PUBLICATIONS, INC., 701 Westchester Ave., White Plains NY 10604. (914)328-9157. Senior Vice President: Janet Moore. Publishes hardcover and paperback originals. Averages 10 titles/year; receives 30 submissions annually. 50% of books from first-time authors; 100% of books from unagented writers. Average print order for a writer's first book is 2,500. Offers negotiable advance. Publishes book an average of 6 months after acceptance. Photocopied submissions OK. Query for electronic submissions. Computer printout submissions acceptable; no dot-matrix. Reports in 2 weeks. Free book catalog; ms guidelines for SASE.
Nonfiction: Business and economics, also corporate, industrial video, interactive video. Especially needs TV and video. Query first, then submit outline/synopsis and sample chapters. Reviews artwork/photos as part of ms package.
Recent Nonfiction Title: *Video Editing and Post-Production, A Professional Guide*, by Gary Anderson.

ROBERT E. KRIEGER PUBLISHING CO. INC., Box 9542, Melbourne FL 32902-9542. (305)724-9542. FAX (407)951-3671. Subsidiary, Orbit Book Company (space technology). Executive Assistant: Marie Bowles. Publishes hardcover and paperback originals and reprints. Averages 120 titles/year; receives 50-60 submissions annually. 30% of books from first-time authors; 100% of books from unagented writers. Pays royalty on net realized price. Publishes book an average of 8 months after acceptance. Computer printout submissions acceptable; prefers letter-quality. Reports in 1 month. Free book catalog.

Nonfiction: College reference, technical, and textbook. Subjects include business, history, music, philosophy, psychology, recreation, religion, sociology, sports, chemistry, physics, engineering and medical. Reviews artwork/photos as part of ms package.

Recent Nonfiction Title: *Introduction to Space: The Science of Spaceflight*, by Thomas D. Damon.

*PETER LANG PUBLISHING, 62 W. 45th St., New York NY 10036. (212)302-6740. Subsidiary of Verlag Peter Lang AG, Bern, Switzerland. Executive Director: Brigitte D. McDonald. Acquisitions Editor: Michael Flamini. West Coast Acquisitions Editor: Robert West. Publishes mostly hardcover originals. Averages 120 titles/year. 75% of books from first-time authors; 98% of books from unagented writers. Subsidy publishes 50% of books. All subsidies are guaranteed repayment plus profit (if edition sells out) in contract. Subsidy published if ms is highly specialized and author relatively unknown. Pays 10-20% royalty on net price. Translators get flat fee plus percentage of royalties. No advance. Publishes book an average of 1 year after acceptance. Photocopied submissions OK. Computer printout submissions acceptable; prefers letter-quality. Reports in 1 month on queries; 2 months on mss. Free book catalog and ms guidelines.

Nonfiction: General nonfiction, reference works, and scholarly monographs. Subjects include literary criticism, Germanic and Romance languages, art history, business and economics, American and European political science, history, music, philosophy, psychology, religion, sociology and biography. All books are scholarly monographs, textbooks, reference books, reprints of historic texts, critical editions or translations. "We are expanding and are receptive to any scholarly project in the humanities and social sciences." No mss shorter than 200 pages. Submit complete ms.

Fiction and Poetry: "We do not publish original fiction or poetry. We seek scholarly and critical editions only. Submit complete ms."

Tips: "Besides our commitment to specialist academic monographs, we are one of the few U.S. publishers who publish books in most of the modern languages."

‡LAURA BOOKS, INC., Box 918, Davenport FL 33837. (813)422-9135. President: J. Jones. Publishes mass market paperback originals. Receives 70 submissions/year. 50% of books from first-time authors. 100% from unagented writers. Buys mss outright for $500 minumum. Publishes book an average of 6 months after acceptance. Computer printout submissions OK; prefers letter-quality. Reports in 3 months on queries.

Fiction: Adventure, fantasy, gothic, mystery, occult, science fiction, western and war. Submit outline/synopsis and sample chapters.

LEISURE BOOKS, Division of Dorchester Publishing Co., Inc., Suite 1008, 276 Fifth Ave., New York NY 10001. (212)725-8811. Editor: Audrey LaFehr. Publishes mass market paperback originals and reprints. Averages 144 titles/year; receives thousands of submissions annually. 20% of books from first-time authors; 40% of books from unagented writers. Pays royalty on retail price. Advance negotiable. Publishes book an average of 18 months after acceptance. Computer printout submissions acceptable; no dot-matrix. Reports in 1 month on queries; up to 2 months on mss. Book catalog and ms guidelines for #10 SASE.

Nonfiction: "Our needs are minimal as we publish perhaps four nonfiction titles a year." Query.

Fiction: Historical (90,000 words); horror (80,000 words); futuristic romance (80,000 words). "We are strongly backing horror and historical romance." No sweet romance, science fiction, western, erotica, contemporary women's fiction, mainstream or male adventure. Query or submit outline/synopsis and sample chapters. "No material will be returned without SASE."

Recent Fiction Title: *Fallen Angel*, by Catherine Hart (historical romance).

Tips: "Horror and historical romance are our best sellers."

‡LEISURE PRESS, Box 5076, Champaign IL 61820. (217)351-5076. Director: Brian Holding. Publishes hardcover, trade paperback and mass market paperback originals. Averages 30 titles/year; receives 100-150 submissions annually. 70% of books from first-time authors; 90% from unagented writers. Pays 10-15% royalty on wholesale price. Offers average $1,000 advance. Publishes ms an average of 9 months after acceptance. Simultaneous submissions OK. Query for electronic submissions. Computer printout submissions OK; prefers letter-quality. Reports in 2 weeks on queries; 6 weeks on ms. Free book catalog; writer's guidelines for SASE.

Nonfiction: How-to, reference, technical. Subjects include sports, fitness and wellness. "We want coaching-related books, technique books on sports and fitness. No fitness or coaching books that are not based on sound physical education principles and research." Reviews artwork/photos as part of ms package. Query or submit outline/synopsis and sample chapters.

Recent Nonfiction Title: *Serious Training for Serious Athletes*, by Sleamaker (fitness).

Tips: "Our audience is coaches, athletes and physical education students. Target my audience and cater to their needs."

‡HAL LEONARD PUBLISHING CORP., 7777 W. Bluemound Rd., Box 13819, Milwaukee WI 53213. (414)774-3630. FAX: (414)774-3259. Managing Editor: Glenda Herro. Publishes hardcover and trade paperback originals. Averages 20 titles/year; receives 25 submissions annually. 95% of books from unagented writers. Pays 5-10% royalty on wholesale or retail price. Publishes book an average of 1 year after acceptance. Simultaneous

and photocopied submissions OK. Reports in 2 months on queries; 3 months on mss. Free book catalog.
Nonfiction: Especially interested in "subject matter related to pop and rock music, Broadway theatre, film and television personalities, and general interest material in the music and entertainment industry." Query. Reviews artwork/photos.
Recent Nonfiction Title: *How to Have Your Hit Song Published*, by Jay Warner.
Tips: "Our books are for all age groups interested in music and entertainment."

LEXIKOS, Box 296, Lagunitas CA 94938. (415)488-0401. Imprints include Don't Call It Frisco Press. Editor: Mike Witter. Publishes hardcover and trade paperback originals and trade paperback reprints. Averages 8 titles/year; receives 200 submissions annually. 50% of books from first-time authors; 90% of books from unagented writers. Average print order for a writer's first book is 5,000. Royalties vary from 8-12½% according to books sold. "Authors asked to accept lower royalty on high discount (50% plus) sales." Offers average $1,000 advance. Publishes book an average of 10 months after acceptance. Simultaneous and photocopied submissions OK. Computer printout submissions acceptable. Reports in 1 month. Book catalog and ms guidelines for 6x9 SAE and 2 first class stamps.
Nonfiction: Coffee table book, illustrated book. Subjects include regional, outdoors, oral histories, Americana, history and nature. Especially looking for 50,000-word "city and regional histories, anecdotal in style for a general audience; books of regional interest about *places*; adventure and wilderness books; annotated reprints of books of Americana; Americana in general." No health, sex, European travel, diet, broad humor, fiction, quickie books (we stress backlist vitality), religion, children's or nutrition. Submit outline/synopsis and sample chapters. Reviews artwork/photos as part of ms package.
Recent Nonfiction Title: *A Short History of Santa Fe*, by Hazen-Hammond.
Tips: "A regional interest or history book has the best chance of selling to Lexikos. Submit a short, cogent proposal; follow up with letter queries. Give the publisher reason to believe you will help him *sell* the book (identify the market, point out the availability of mailing lists, distinguish your book from the competition). Avoid grandiose claims."

LIBERTY HOUSE, Imprint of Tab Books, Inc., #1101, 10 E. 21st St., New York NY 10010. (212)475-1446. Vice President/Editorial Director: David J. Conti. Publishes hardcover originals and trade paperback originals and reprints. Publishes 25 titles/year. Receives 200 submissions/year. 50% of books from first-time authors; 80% from unagented writers. Pays 5-15% royalty on wholesale price. Offers $3,000 average advance. Publishes book an average of 5 months after acceptance. Simultaneous and photocopied submissions OK. Computer printout submissions OK. Reports on queries in 2 weeks; on ms in 1 month. Book catalog free on request; writer's guidelines for #10 SASE.
Nonfiction: Subjects include small business, investing, money/finance, real estate. "We're engaged in a wide-ranging business publishing program. We're looking for books written for sophisticated investors, business people and for professionals as well as the general public." Submit outline/synopsis and sample chapter.
Recent Nonfiction Title: *No-Loads: Mutual Fund Profits Using Technical Analysis*, by James E. Kearis.
Tips: "We publish very practical, how-to, results-oriented books. Study the competition, study the market, then submit a proposal."

*LIBRA PUBLISHERS, INC., Suite 383, 3089C Clairemont Dr., San Diego CA 92117. (619)581-9449. Contact: William Kroll. Publishes hardcover and paperback originals. Specializes in the behavioral sciences. Averages 15 titles/year; receives 300 submissions annually. 60% of books from first-time authors; 85% of books from unagented writers. 10-15% royalty on retail price; no advance. "We will also offer our services to authors who wish to publish their own works. The services include editing, proofreading, production, artwork, copyrighting, and assistance in promotion and distribution." Publishes book an average of 8 months after acceptance. Computer printout submissions acceptable; prefers letter-quality. Reports in 2 weeks. Free book catalog; writer's guidelines for #10 SASE.
Nonfiction: Mss in all subject areas will be given consideration, but main interest is in the behavioral sciences. Prefers complete manuscript but will consider outline/synopsis and 3 sample chapters. Reviews artwork/photos as part of ms package.
Recent Nonfiction Title: *Emotional Abuse of the Child*, by Dory Renn, Ph.D.
Recent Fiction Title: *Tarnished Hero*, by Steve Berman.

LIBRARIES UNLIMITED, Box 3988, Englewood CO 80155-3988. Imprints include Ukranian Academic Press. Editor-in-Chief: Bohdan S. Wynar. Publishes hardcover and paperback originals. Averages 50 titles/year; receives 100-200 submissions annually. 10-20% of books from first-time authors. Average print order for a writer's first book is 2,000. 10% royalty on net sales; advance averages $500. Publishes book an average of 1 year after acceptance. Reports in 2 months. Free book catalog and ms guidelines.
Nonfiction: Publishes reference and library science textbooks. Looks for professional experience. Query or submit outline and sample chapters; state availability of photos/illustrations with submission. All prospective authors are required to fill out an author questionnaire.
Recent Nonfiction Title: *Theory and Practice*, by Charles W. Ulcek and Raymond V. Wiman.

LIBRARY RESEARCH ASSOCIATES, INC., Subsidiaries include Empire State Fiction, RD #5, Box 41, Dunderberg Rd., Monroe NY 10950. (914)783-1144. President: Matilda A. Gocek. Publishes hardcover and trade paperback originals. Averages 4 titles/year; receives about 30 submissions annually. 100% of books from first-time authors; 100% of books from unagented writers. Pays 10% maximum royalty on retail price. Offers 20 copies of the book as advance. Publishes book an average of 14 months after acceptance. Photocopied submissions OK. Computer printout submissions acceptable; no dot-matrix. Reports in 3 weeks on queries; 3 months on mss. Book catalog free on request.
Nonfiction: Biography, coffee table book, how-to, reference, technical and American history. Subjects include Americana, art, business and economics, history, philosophy, politics and travel. "Our nonfiction book manuscript needs for the next year or two will include books about American artists, graphics and photography, historical research of some facet of American history, and definitive works about current or past economics or politics." No astrology, occult, sex, adult humor or gay rights. Submit outline/synopsis and sample chapters.
Recent Nonfiction Title: *By the Dim and Flaring Lamp: A Civil War Diary.*
Fiction: Send fiction to Empire State Fiction, Patricia E. Clyne, senior editor. Adventure (based in an authentic NY location); historical (particularly in or about New York state); mystery; and suspense. "I try to publish at least three novels per year. Characterization is so important! The development of people and plot must read well. The realism of world events (war, terrorism, catastrophes) is turning readers to a more innocent world of reading for entertainment with less shock value. Free speech (free *everything*!) is reviving old values. Explicit sex, extreme violence, vile language in any form will not be considered." Submit outline/synopsis and sample chapters.
Recent Fiction Title: *Beyond the Thunder of the Waters*, by Janice Doyle Collins.
Tips: "Our audience is adult, over age 30, literate and knowledgeable in business or professions. The writer has the best chance of selling our firm historical fiction or nonfiction and scientific texts. If I were a writer trying to market a book today, I would try to write about people in a warm human situation—the foibles, the loss of self, the unsung heroism—angels with feet of clay."

LIFE CYCLE BOOKS, Subsidiary of Life Cycle Books, Ltd., Toronto, Canada. Box 420, Lewiston NY 14092-0420. (416)690-5860. President: Paul Broughton. Publishes trade paperback originals and reprints, brochures and pamphlets. Receives 150 submissions annually. 30% of books from first-time authors. 100% of books from unagented authors. Averages 5-10 titles/year. Pays 8% royalty on net price for books; makes outright purchase of $200-1,000 for pamphlets and books. Offers average $150 advance. Publishes book an average of 18 months after acceptance. Photocopied submissions OK if good quality reproduction. Computer printout submissions acceptable; no dot-matrix. Reports in 1 month on queries; 3 months on mss. Free book catalog.
Nonfiction: Health, history, politics, religion, sociology. Specifically "we publish materials on human life issues (i.e. abortion, infanticide, euthanasia, child abuse, sex education, etc.) written from a pro-life perspective." Query for books; submit complete ms for pamphlets or brochures. Reviews artwork/photos as part of ms package.
Recent Nonfiction Titles: *Abortion, the Bible and the Church*, by T. J. Bosgra.

LIGUORI PUBLICATIONS, Book and Pamphlet Dept., 1 Liguori Dr., Liguori MO 63057-9999. (314)464-2500. FAX: (314)464-8449. Managing Editor: Thomas Artz, C.SS.R. Associate Editor: Julie Kelemen. Editorial Assistant: Theresa Lewis. Publishes paperback originals. Specializes in Catholic-Christian religious materials. Averages 35 titles/year; receives about 200 submissions annually. About 40% of books from first-time authors; 95% of books from unagented writers. Average print order for a writer's first book is 10,000-16,000. Pays royalty on books; flat fee on pamphlets and teacher's guides. Publishes book an average of 1 year after acceptance. Query for electronic submissions. Computer printout submissions OK. Reports in 5 weeks. Book catalog and ms guidelines for 9x12 SAE with 4 first class stamps.
Nonfiction: Publishes doctrinal, inspirational, biblical, self-help and educational materials. Looks for "thought and language that speak to basic practical religious concerns of contemporary Catholic Christians." Query or submit synopsis and 1 sample chapter; "never submit total book."
Recent Nonfiction Title: *Pathways to Serenity*, by Philip St. Romain.
Tips: "We seek manuscripts that deal with topics of current interest to Catholics: biblical study, prayer, RCIA programs, women and the Church, Catholic health care, etc."

LINCH PUBLISHING, INC., Box 75, Orlando FL 32802. (305)647-3025. Vice President: Valeria Lynch. Editor: Peggy H. Maddox. Publishes hardcover and trade paperback originals. Averages 10 titles/year. Pays 6-8% royalty on retail price. Rarely pays advances. Publishes book an average of 9 months after acceptance. Simultaneous and photocopied submissions OK. Computer printout submissions acceptable; prefers letter-quality. Reports in 6 weeks. Book catalog for $1 and #10 SAE with 2 first class stamps.
Nonfiction: Publishes books only on estate planning and legal how-to books which must be applicable in all 50 states. "We are interested in a book on getting through probate, settling an estate, and minimizing federal estate and/or state inheritance taxes." Query editor by phone before submitting mss—"we could have already accepted a manuscript and be in the process of publishing one of the above."

Recent Nonfiction Title: *Ask an Attorney*, by J. Pippen.
Tips: Currently interest is mainly estate planning and legal "how-to."

‡**LION PUBLISHING CORPORATION**, 1705 Hubbard Ave., Batavia IL 60510. (312)879-0707. Editor: La-Vonne Neff. Publishes hardcover and trade paperback originals. Firm averages 15 titles/year. Pays royalty. Publishes book an average of 18 months after acceptance. Photocopied submissions OK. Computer printout submissions OK; prefers letter-quality. Reports in 1 month on queries; 2 months on mss. Book catalog for 9x12 SAE and $1.05 postage. Manuscript guidelines for #10 SAE and 2 first class stamps.
Nonfiction: Subjects include child guidance/parenting, health/medicine and religion. "We are especially interested in manuscripts on relationships and on spirituality. We do not want Bible studies or sermons." Query or submit outline/synopsis and sample chapters.
Recent Nonfiction Title: *A Transforming Friendship*, by Jim Houston.
Fiction: Fantasy, historical, juvenile (ages 8-12). "Stories that create meaty, believable characters, not puppets or simplistic representations of certain values or beliefs. Give us a story that anyone would be intrigued with – and write it from a Christian perspective." Submit complete ms.
Recent Fiction Title: *Pangur Ban*, by Fay Sampson (fantasy).
Tips: "All Lion books are written from a Christian perspective. However, they must speak to a general audience that includes people of all faiths or no faith at all."

LITTLE, BROWN AND CO., INC., 34 Beacon St., Boston MA 02108. Contact: Editorial Department, Trade Division. Publishes hardcover and paperback originals and paperback reprints. Averages 100 titles/year. "Royalty and advance agreements vary from book to book and are discussed with the author at the time an offer is made. Submissions only from authors who have had a book published or have been published in professional or literary journals, newspapers or magazines." Computer printout submissions acceptable; prefers letter-quality. Reports in 3 months for queries/proposals.
Nonfiction: "Some how-to books, distinctive cookbooks, biographies, history, science and sports." Query or submit outline/synopsis and sample chapters. Reviews artwork/photos as part of ms package.
Recent Nonfiction Title: *The Last Lion: Winston Spenser Churchill Alone*, by William Manchester.
Fiction: Contemporary popular fiction as well as fiction of literary distinction. Query or submit outline/synopsis and sample chapters.
Recent Fiction Title: *Rivals*, by Janet Dailey.

‡**LITURGICAL PUBLICATIONS, INC.**, 1025 S. Moorland Rd., Brookfield WI 55005. (414)785-1188. Publisher: Keith B. Lawson. Publishes hardcover and trade paperback originals. Averages 8 titles/year. Receives 15-20 submissions/year. 12% of books from first-time authors. 100% from unagented writers. Pays 10% royalty on wholesale price. Publishes book an average of 3 months after acceptance. Photocopied submissions OK. Query for electronic submissions. Computer printout submissions OK. Reports in 1 week on queries; 1 month on mss. Free book catalog.
Nonfiction: Biography, how-to, reference, self-help and textbook. Subject includes religion. "We want ministerial aid, preaching, homily, and prayer." Query. All unsolicited mss are returned unopened. Reviews artwork/photos as part of ms package.
Recent Nonfiction Title: *Merton & Walsh on the Person*, by Dr. Rosert Imperato (theological controversy).

‡**LIVING FLAME PRESS**, 325 Rabro Dr., Hauppauge NY 11788. (516)348-5251. Editor: Nancy Benvenga. Publishes mass market paperback originals. Averages 8-10 titles/year. Receives 75-100 submissions/year. 25% of books from first-time authors. 100% from unagented writers. Pays 5% minimum on retail price. Publishes book an average of 18 months after acceptance. Photocopied submissions OK. Computer printout submissions OK; no dot-matrix. Reports in 2 weeks on queries; 6 weeks on mss. Free book catalog. Manuscript guidelines for #10 SAE and 1 first class stamp.
Nonfiction: Self-help. Subject includes religion. "We want books on prayer, spirituality, Christian living, theology, liturgy." Submit outline/synopsis and sample chapters. Reviews artwork/photos as part of ms package.
Recent Nonfiction Title: *Communion of Saints*, by George Maloney (spirituality).
Tips: "We seek books in which deeply-felt personal experience combines with coherent, professional writing to produce an edifying or educational book for the reader."

LODESTAR BOOKS, Imprint of E. P. Dutton, 2 Park Ave., New York NY 10016. (212)725-1818. FAX: (212)532-6568. Editorial Director: Virginia Buckley. Senior Editor: Rosemary Brosnan. Publishes hardcover originals. Publishes juveniles, young adults, fiction and nonfiction; and picture books. Averages 20 titles/year; receives 800 submissions annually. 10-20% of books from first-time authors; 25-30% of books from unagented writers. Average print order for a writer's first book is 5,000-6,000. Pays royalty on invoice list price; advance offered. Publishes book an average of 18 months after acceptance. Photocopied submissions OK. Computer printout submissions acceptable; prefers letter-quality. Reports in 4 months. Ms guidelines for SASE.

Close-up

Margery Facklam
Author

Like many writers of children's books, Margery Facklam says she began writing when she read a children's book and thought, "I can do better than that!" Now the writer of 12 books in the past 10 years says writing for children is not nearly as simple as she originally thought. "It's not easier, just different," she says. "It requires different skills to write a tight, short first chapter novel for young readers, for example, than to write a 300-page romance for adults. I've done four picture books; they were *not* easy."

Facklam was home with five children when she began writing. "It was as though I'd found what mythologist Joseph Campbell calls 'my bliss,' " she says. Facklam sold her first book on her fifth submission to a publisher "after I'd revised it completely for the first publisher, who then rejected it," she says. The first sale was just the beginning of the learning process, she found out. "After that it took a while to find out what I'd done right in that first book before I could do it again. I hadn't paid my dues yet, but I had written what I knew. More people would see their first stories published if they did that."

As an instructor at conferences, Facklam counsels writers to draw on their own childhood experiences for ideas. "You draw on your childhood fears and interests when you're writing just as you draw upon adult fears and interests. Sometimes it's just the memory of a moment...the monster in the closet, the embarrassment of being the new kid that is still real," she says. "Sometimes it's an event from childhood that triggers an idea for a book or story. Sometimes it's a game, a chant, a celebration that is suddenly there again, as real as the day it happened."

Like many writers, Facklam says ideas come to her at various times. "I get ideas in the bathtub, driving the car or ironing—yes, I still iron now and then. I jot down ideas whenever they pop into mind...sometimes it's a title, or a bit of dialogue or just a few words I know will work to open a scene."

Facklam has written nonfiction, fiction and numerous magazine articles. She often draws on her knowledge of biology but doesn't limit her topics. "I do draw heavily on my biology background because it interests me," she says. "But I write about lots of different subjects, not just biology. I think it's more accurate to say that it's important for me to write what I know or what I'm curious about. That's meant articles about being a grandmother to books about censorship as well as science." Her latest book, *The Trouble with Mothers*, is about censorship and how it affects a student whose mother wrote a controversial novel and also uses it in teaching her history class.

Now a published veteran, Facklam advises writers to "avoid trends in book publishing like the plague. By the time you write a book and it's published, two or three years may pass, and in the meantime, so has the trend. Publishers are buying lots of nonfiction for young kids right now, but next year, who knows? The best trend is one toward good writing and a good story."

—Glenda Tennant Neff

Nonfiction: Query or submit outline/synopsis and 2-3 sample chapters including "theme, chapter-by-chapter outline, and 1 or 2 completed chapters." State availability of photos and/or illustrations. Queries/mss may be routed to other editors in the publishing group. Reviews artwork/photos as part of ms package.
Recent Nonfiction Title: *Spanish Pioneers of the Southwest*, by Joan Anderson.
Fiction: Publishes for young adults (middle grade) and juveniles (ages 5-17): adventure, fantasy, historical, humorous, contemporary, mystery, science fiction, suspense and western books, also picture books. Submit complete ms.
Recent Fiction Title: *The Honorable Prison*, by Lyll Becerra de Jenkins.
Tips: "A young adult or middle-grade novel that is literary, fast-paced, well-constructed (as opposed to a commercial novel); well-written nonfiction on contemporary issues, photographic essays, and nonfiction pictures have been our staples. We are now expanding into the picture book market as well."

LOMOND PUBLICATIONS, INC., Box 88, Mt. Airy MD 21771. (301)829-1496. Publisher: Lowell H. Hattery. Publishes hardcover originals. Averages 3-10 titles/year; receives 30 submissions annually. 50% of books from first-time authors; 100% of books from unagented writers. Pays 10% royalty on net price or makes outright purchase. No advance. Publishes book an average of 18 months after acceptance. Simultaneous submissions OK. Computer printout submissions acceptable. Reports in 1 month. Free book catalog.
Nonfiction: Technical, professional and scholarly. Subjects include business and economics, politics, sociology, public policy, technological change and management. Query or submit complete ms.
Recent Nonfiction Title: *How to Successfully Keep R&D Projects on Track!*, by Robert Szakonyi.
Tips: "We publish for the scholarly, professional, and well-informed lay readers of all countries. We publish only English titles, but some are subsequently reprinted and translated in other languages. A writer's best bet with us is an interdisciplinary approach to management, technology or public policy."

‡LONGMAN FINANCIAL SERVICES PUBLISHING, 520 N. Dearborn St., Chicago IL 60610. (312)836-4400. FAX: (312)836-1021. Subsidiary includes Longman, Real Estate Education Co. Senior Vice President: Anita Constant. Publishes hardcover originals. Averages 200 titles/year. Receives 200 submissions/year. 50% of books from first-time authors. 50% from unagented writers. Pays 1-15% on wholesale price. Publishes book an average of 8 months after acceptance. Simultaneous and photocopied submissions OK. Query for electronic submissions. Reports in 2 weeks; 1 month on mss. Free book catalog and manuscript guidelines.
Nonfiction: How-to, reference and textbook. Subjects include business and economics and money/finance. Query.
Recent Nonfiction Title: *Modern Real Estate Practice, 11th Edition*, by Allaway, Galaty, Kyle (real estate text).
Tips: "People seeking real estate, insurance, broker's licenses are our audience; also business professionals interested in information on managing their finances, improving their business skills, broadening their knowledge of the financial services industry."

‡LONGWOOD ACADEMIC, Box 2069, Wolfeboro NH 03894. (603)569-4576. FAX: (207)324-0349. A division of Longwood Publishing Group, Inc. Other imprints include Tanager Books and Longwood Press. Editor-in-Chief: Wyatt Benner. Publishes hardcover and mass market paperback originals and hardcover and trade paperback reprints. Firm averages 35 titles/year; imprint averages 24 titles/year. Receives 100 submissions/year. 25% of books from first-time authors. 90% from unagented writers. Pays 5-10% on retail price. Publishes book an average of 6 months after acceptance. Simultaneous and photocopied submissions OK. Computer printout submissions OK. Reports in 1 month on queries; 2 months on mss. Free book catalog and manuscript guidelines.
Nonfiction: Biography, reference and textbook. Subjects include education, health/medicine, history, language/literature, music/dance, philosophy, religion, science, translation, women's issues/studies, literary criticism and Asian studies. "We publish primarily scholarly books of high quality aimed at academics and college libraries. We'll consider all topics for which there is an academic audience. That eliminates coffee-table books, juvenile books, cookbooks, how-to books, etc." Submit complete ms. Reviews artwork/photos as part of ms package.
Recent Nonfiction Title: *Pattern Biology*, by Michael J. Katz (scholarly—science).
Fiction: Literary (translations of classics). "We'll consider new translations or first translations of neglected foreign writers, usually non-contemporaries—writers like Nicholas Chamfort, Leon Bloy, Valle-Inclan. No original contemporary fiction or poetry." Query.
Recent Fiction Title: *Imaginary Lives*, by Marcel Schwob (imaginary portraits based on historical characters).
Poetry: "We don't accept original poetry."

LOOMPANICS UNLIMITED, Box 1197, Port Townsend WA 98368. Book Editor: Michael Hoy. Publishes trade paperback originals. Publishes 12 titles/year; receives 50 submissions annually. 40% of books from first-time authors; 100% of books from unagented writers. Average print order for a writer's first book is 1,000. Pays 7½-15% royalty on wholesale or retail price; or makes outright purchase of $100-1,200. Offers average $500 advance. Publishes book an average of 10 months after acceptance. Simultaneous and photocopied submissions OK. Computer printout submissions acceptable; prefers letter-quality. Reports in 6 weeks. Free book catalog.

Nonfiction: How-to, reference and self-help. Subjects include business and economics, philosophy, politics, travel, and "beat the system" books. "We are looking for how-to books in the fields of espionage, investigation, the underground economy, police methods, how to beat the system, crime and criminal techniques. No cookbooks, inspirational, travel, or cutesy-wutesy stuff." Query, or submit outline/synopsis and sample chapters. Reviews artwork/photos.

Recent Nonfiction Title: *Methods of Disguise*, by John Sample (how-to).

Tips: "Our audience is young males looking for hard-to-find information on alternatives to 'The System.' "

*LOYOLA UNIVERSITY PRESS, 3441 N. Ashland Ave., Chicago IL 60657. (312)281-1818. Editorial Director: George A. Lane. Imprints include Campion Books. Publishes hardcover and trade paperback originals, and hardcover and trade paperback reprints. Averages 12 titles/year; receives 100 submissions annually. 40% of books from first-time authors; 95% of books from unagented writers. Subsidy publishes 2% of books. Pays 10% royalty on wholesale price; offers no advance. Publishes book an average of 1 year after acceptance. Simultaneous and photocopied submissions acceptable. Query for electronic submissions. Computer printout submissions acceptable; prefers letter-quality. Reports in 1 month. Book catalog for 6x9 SAE.

Nonfiction: Biography and textbook. Subjects include art (religious); history (church); and religion. The four subject areas of Campion Books include Jesuitica (Jesuit history, biography and spirituality); Literature-Theology interface (books dealing with theological or religious aspects of literary works or authors); contemporary Catholic concerns (books on morality, spirituality, family life, pastoral ministry, prayer, worship, etc.); and Chicago/art (books dealing with the city of Chicago from historical, artistic, architectural, or ethnic perspectives, but with religious emphases). Query before submitting ms. Reviews artwork/photos.

Recent Nonfiction Titles: *Married to a Catholic Priest*, by Mary Dolly.

Tips: "Our audience is principally the college-educated reader with religious, theological interest."

LURAMEDIA, Box 261668, 10227 Autumnview Lane, San Diego CA 92126. (619)578-1948. Editorial Director: Lura Jane Geiger. Publishes trade paperback originals and reprints. Averages 8 titles/year; receives 250 submissions annually. 75% of books from first-time authors. 90% of books from unagented writers. Pays 10-15% royalty on wholesale price. Publishes book an average of 9 months after acceptance. Photocopied submissions OK. Query for electronic submissions. Computer printout submissions OK; prefers letter-quality. Reports in 3 weeks on queries; 1 month on mss. Book catalog and ms guidelines for #10 SAE with 1 first class stamp.

Nonfiction: Self-help. Subjects include health, spirituality, psychology, and creativity. "Books on renewal . . . body, mind spirit . . . using the right brain and relational material. Books on creativity, journaling, women's issues, black Christian, relationships. I want well digested, thoughtful books. No 'Jesus Saves' literature; books that give all the answers; poetry; or strident politics." Submit outline/synopsis, biography and sample chapters. Reviews artwork/photos as part of ms package.

Recent Nonfiction Title: *No Time for NonSense: Self-Help for the Seriously Ill*, by Ronna Fay Jeune and Alexander Levitan.

Tips: "Our audience are people who want to grow and change; who want to get in touch with their spiritual side; who want to relax; who are creative and want creative ways to live. We have recently published a book, *Just a Sister Away*, for black Christian women. This is a new market for us."

‡LYONS & BURFORD, PUBLISHERS, INC., 31 W. 21 St., New York NY 10010. (212)620-9580. Publisher: Peter Burford. Publishes hardcover and trade paperback originals and hardcover and trade paperback reprints. Averages 30-40 titles/year. Averages 200 titles/year. 50% of books from first-time authors. 75% from unagented writers. Pays varied royalty on retail price. Publishes book an average of 1 year after acceptance. Simultaneous and photocopied submissions OK. Computer printout submissions OK; prefers letter-quality. Reports in 2 weeks on queries and mss. Free book catalog.

Nonfiction: Cookbook and how-to. Subjects include agriculture/horticulture, Americana, animals, art/architecture, cooking, foods & nutrition, gardening, hobbies, nature/environment, science, sports and travel. Query.

Recent Nonfiction Title: *Mississippi Solo*, by Harris (travel).

Tips: "We want practical, well written books on any aspect of the outdoors."

MARGARET K. McELDERRY BOOKS, Macmillan Publishing Co., Inc., 866 3rd Ave., New York NY 10022. Editor: Margaret K. McElderry. Publishes hardcover originals. Publishes 20-25 titles/year; receives 1,300-1,500 submissions annually. 8% of books from first-time authors; 45% of books from unagented writers. The average print order is 6,000-7,500 for a writer's first teen book; 7,500-10,000 for a writer's first picture book. Pays royalty on retail price. Publishes book an average of 1½ years after acceptance. Reports in 6 weeks. Computer printout submissions acceptable; no dot-matrix. Ms guidelines for #10 SASE.

Nonfiction and Fiction: Quality material for preschoolers to 16-year-olds. Looks for "originality of ideas, clarity and felicity of expression, well-organized plot (fiction) or exposition (nonfiction); quality." Reviews artwork/photos as part of ms package.

Recent Title: *Who Said Red?*, by Mary Serfozo, illustrated by Keiko Narahashi.

Tips: "There is not a particular 'type' of book that we are interested in above others though we always look for humor; rather, we look for superior quality in both writing and illustration." Freelance writers should be aware of the swing away from teen-age problem novels to books for younger readers.

McFARLAND & COMPANY, INC., PUBLISHERS, Box 611, Jefferson NC 28640. (919)246-4460. President and Editor-in-Chief: Robert Franklin. Business Manager: Rhonda Herman. Editor: Virginia Hege. Publishes hardcover and "quality" paperback originals; a non-"trade" publisher. Averages 75 titles/year; receives 700 submissions annually. 70% of books from first-time authors; 95% of books from unagented writers. Average print order for a writer's first book is 1,000. Pays 10-12½% royalty on net receipts; no advance. Publishes book an average of 11 months after acceptance. Computer printout submissions acceptable; prefers letter-quality. Reports in 1 week.

Nonfiction: Reference books and scholarly, technical and professional monographs. Subjects include Americana, art, business, chess, drama/theatre, health, cinema/radio/TV (very strong here), history, literature, librarianship (very strong here), music, parapsychology, religion, sociology, sports/recreation (very strong here), women's studies, and world affairs (very strong here). "We will consider *any* scholarly book—with authorial maturity and competent grasp of subject." Reference books are particularly wanted—fresh material (i.e., not in head-to-head competition with an established title). "We don't like manuscripts of fewer than 200 double-spaced typed pages. Our market consists mainly of libraries." No memoirs, poetry, children's books, devotional/inspirational works or personal essays. Query or submit outline/synopsis and sample chapters. Reviews artwork/photos as part of ms package.

Recent Nonfiction Title: *Commonsense Copyright: A Guide to the New Technologies*, by R.S. Talab (comprehensive handbook for teachers and librarians).

Tips: "We do *not* accept novels or fiction of any kind or personal Bible studies. Don't worry about writing skills—we have editors. What we want is well-organized *knowledge* of an area in which there is not good information coverage at present, plus reliability so we don't feel we have to check absolutely everything."

McGRAW HILL RYERSON, Subsidiary of McGraw-Hill, 330 Progress Ave., Scarborough, Ontario M1P 2Z5 Canada. (416)293-1911. Editorial Director: Denise Schon. Publishes hardcover originals, trade paperback originals and reprints. Firm publishes 200 titles/year; division publishes 25 titles/year. Receives 400 submissions/year. 10% of books from first-time authors; 40% from unagented writers. Pays 8-15% royalty on retail price. Publishes book an average of 8 months after acceptance. Simultaneous submissions OK. Query for electronic submissions. Computer printout submissions OK; no dot-matrix. Reports in 1 month on queries; 3 months on ms.

Nonfiction: Canadian biography, cookbook, how-to, reference, self-help. Subjects include art/architecture, business and economics, cooking, foods and nutrition, gardening, Canadian government/politics, health/medicine, Canadian history, money/finance, recreation, sports. No exercise books. Submit outline/synopsis and sample chapters.

Recent Nonfiction Title: *Lanny*, by Lanny McDonald (sports autobiography).

MACMILLAN PUBLISHING COMPANY, Children's Book Department, 866 3rd Ave., New York NY 10022. Publishes hardcover originals. Averages 65 titles/year. Will consider juvenile submissions only. Fiction and nonfiction. Enclose return postage. See Margaret McElderry Books, Charles Scribner's Sons, Four Winds Press, Atheneum and Bradbury Press. New name: Maxwell Macmillan.

MADISON BOOKS, University Press of America, Inc., 4720 Boston Way, Lanham MD 20706. (301)459-5308. FAX: (301)459-2118. Imprints include Hamilton Press. Associate Publisher: Charles Lean. Publishes hardcover originals and trade paperback originals and reprints. Averages 20 titles/year. Receives 350 submissions/year. 20% of books from first-time authors; 50% from unagented writers. Pays 10-15% royalty on wholesale price. Offers average advance of $2,000. Publishes ms an average of 1 year after acceptance. Simultaneous and photocopied submissions OK. Computer printout submissions OK; no dot-matrix. Book catalog and manuscript guidelines for 9 × 12 SASE and $1 postage.

Nonfiction: Biography, reference. Subjects include Americana, business, government/politics, popular culture, history, sociology. "We are specifically looking for film and culture studies; history; biography; current affairs; and social sciences. Nothing on hobbies, gardening, cooking or translation." Query or submit outline/synopsis and sample chapters. No complete mss.

Recent Nonfiction Title: *The Book of Video Lists*, by Tom Wiener (popular culture).

THE MAIN STREET PRESS, William Case House, Pittstown NJ 08867. (201)735-9424. Editorial Director: Martin Greif. Publishes hardcover and trade paperback originals. Averages 30 titles/year; receives 1,000 submissions annually. 10% of books from first-time authors; 15% of books from agented writers; 75% of books from unagented writers. Pays 5-7½% royalty on paperbacks, 10-15% on a sliding scale for hardcover books; advance varies widely. Sometimes makes outright purchase. Publishes book an average of 1 year after acceptance. Simultaneous and photocopied submissions OK. Computer printout submissions OK. Reports in 2 months on queries; 3 months on mss. Reviews artwork/photos (photocopies OK) as part of ms package. Book catalog $1.25.

Nonfiction: Subjects include Americana, art, hobbies, gardening, film, architecture, popular culture and design. "We publish *heavily illustrated* books on the subjects above; we publish *only* illustrated books." Especially needs how-to quilting books. "We do not want to consider any nonfiction book with fewer than 75 illustrations." Query or submit outline/synopsis and sample chapters. "We will *not* return queries without SASE, and we will *not* return unsolicited manuscripts without return postage."

Recent Nonfiction Title: *Childhood Dreams: A Book of Crib Quilt Projects*, by Susan Bennett Gallagher.

Tips: "Our books are largely for the 'carriage trade' "

MARATHON INTERNATIONAL PUBLISHING COMPANY, INC., Dept. WM, Box 33008, Louisville KY 40232. President: Jim Wortham. Publishes hardcover originals, and trade paperback originals and reprints. Averages 4-10 titles/year. Pays 10% royalty on wholesale. Publishes book an average of 10 months after acceptance. Simultaneous and photocopied submissions OK. Computer printout submissions acceptable. Reports in 3 weeks.

Nonfiction: "We are looking for manuscripts in the area of alcohol and drug addictions; and codependency. We are urgently in need of any reports or manuscripts dealing with 'sex addiction.' Other manuscripts in the area of mental health are being considered. No biography, textbooks or poetry. Query.

MAZDA PUBLISHERS, Box 2603, 2991 Grace Ln., Costa Mesa CA 92626. (714)751-5252. Editor-in-Chief/ Publisher: Ahmad Jabbari. Publishes hardcover and trade paperback originals and trade paperback reprints. Averages 6 titles/year; receives approximately 25 submissions annually. 90% of books from first-time authors; 100% of books from unagented writers. Pays royalty on wholesale price; no advance. Publishes book an average of 4 months after acceptance. Photocopied submissions OK. Query for electronic submissions. Computer printout submissions acceptable; prefers letter-quality. Reports in 2 weeks on queries; 6 weeks on mss. Free book catalog; ms guidelines for SASE.

Nonfiction: Cookbook, juvenile, reference, textbook, scholarly books. Subjects include art, business and economics, cooking and foods, history, politics, sociology, and social sciences in general. "Our primary objective is to publish scholarly books and other informational books about the Middle East and North Africa. All subject areas will be considered with priority given to the scholarly books." Query with outline/synopsis and sample chapters. Reviews artwork/photos as part of ms package.

Recent Nonfiction Title: *The Wade Cup in the Cleveland Museum of Art*, by D.S. Rice (art).

Recent Fiction Title: *Cry for My Revolution: IRAN*, Manoucher Parvin (novel).

Poetry: Translations and scholarly presentation of poetry from the poets of the Middle Eastern countries only. Submit 5 poems.

Recent Poetry Title: *The Homely Touch: Folk Poetry of Old India* (translated from Sanscrit).

Tips: "We publish books for an academic audience and laymen."

MEADOWBROOK PRESS, 18318 Minnetonka Blvd., Deephaven MN 55391. (612)473-5400. Contact submissions editor. Publishes trade paperback originals and reprints. Averages 20 titles/year. Receives 250 queries annually. 25% of books from first-time authors. 75% of books from unagented writers. Pays 5-7.5% royalty; offers $2,000 average advance. Publishes book an average of 1 year after acceptance. Simultaneous and photocopied submissions OK. Computer printout submissions OK. Reports in 3 weeks on queries; 4-6 weeks on mss. Book catalog and ms guidelines for #10 SASE.

Nonfiction: How-to, humor, juvenile, illustrated book and reference. Subjects include baby and childcare; senior citizen's; children's activities; travel; relationships; business; cooking. No academic, autobiography, semi-autobiography or fiction. Query with outline and sample chapters. "We prefer a query first; then we will request an outline and/or sample material."

Recent Nonfiction Title: *The Parent's Guide to Dirty Tricks*, by Bill Dodds.

Tips: "We like how-to books in a simple, accessible format and any new advice on parenting. We look for a fresh approach to overcoming traditional problems (e.g. potty training)."

‡MEDIA FORUM INTERNATIONAL, LTD., RFD 1, Box 107, W. Danville VT 05873. (802)592-3444, or Box 65, Peacham VT 05862. (802)592-3310. Imprint includes Media Forum Books; Division: Há Penny Gourmet. Managing Director: D.K. Bognár. Publishes hardcover and trade paperback originals. Averages 4 titles/year. Pays 10% minimum royalty.

Nonfiction: Biography, cookbook, humor and reference. Subjects include cooking, ethnic, broadcast/film and drama. "All mss are assigned."

Recent Nonfiction Title: *An Evening with Chechov*, by A. Achinn (theater/plays).

MEDIA PRODUCTIONS AND MARKETING, INC., Division include Media Publishing and Midgard Press, Suite 202, 2440 O Street, Lincoln NE 68510. (402)474-2676. President: Jerry Kromberg. Publishes hardcover originals and trade paperback originals and reprints. Averages 9-12 titles annually. Receives 200 submissions/year. 60% of books from first-time writers; 95% from unagented writers. Pays 2-15% royalty based on net sales. Makes some work-for-hire assignments. "Midgard Press is contract publishing; Media Publishing is trade publishing." Publishes book an average of 6 months after acceptance. Simultaneous submissions OK; photocopied submissions OK. Query for electronic submissions. Computer printout submissions acceptable. Reports in 1 month. Book catalog for #10 SASE.

Nonfiction: Biography, how-to, reference, self-help, textbook. Subjects include Americana, history, politics and general interest. "We will consider manuscripts of general interest with good commercial appeal to regional or special interest markets." Query or submit outline/synopsis and sample chapters or submit complete ms. Reviews artwork/photos as part of ms package.

Recent Nonfiction Title: *Women and Medicine*, by Beatrice Levin.

‡MEDMASTER, INC., 17500 NE 9th Ave., N. Miami Beach FL 33162. (305)653-3480. Vice President: Harriet Sabinson. Publishes hardcover and trade paperback orignals. Publishes 10 titles/year. Receives 3-4 submissions/year. 50% of books from first-time authors. 100% from unagented writers. Pays 10-15% royalty. Publishes book an average of 7 months after acceptance. Simultaneous and photocopied submissions OK. Query for electronic submissions. Computer printous submissions OK; prefers letter-quality. Reports in 2 weeks on queries; 6 weeks on mss. Free book catalog and manuscript guidelines.

Nonfiction: Technical. Subject includes health/medicine. Submit outline/synopsis and sample chapters. Reviews artwork/photos as part of ms package.

Recent Nonfiction Title: *Clinical Anatomy Made Ridiculously Simple*, by S. Goldberg (medical)

Tips: "We want brief clear, clinically relevant books at the level of need of the family physician."

MELIOR PUBLICATIONS, Suite 550, N. 10 Post, Box 1905, Spokane WA 99210-1905. (509)455-9617. Vice President: Barbara Greene Chamberlain or President: John C. Shideler. Publishes hardcover and trade paperback originals. Publishes 4-5 titles/year; receives 20-30 proposals/year. 50% of books from first-time authors; 100% from unagented writers (but will accept agented submissions). Pays 8-12% royalty on retail price. Publishes ms an average of 18 months after acceptance. Simultaneous and photocopied submissions OK. Query for electronic submissions. Computer printout submissions OK; prefers letter-quality. Reports in 1 month on queries; 9 months on mss. Ms guidelines for #10 SASE.

Nonfiction: Biography, coffee table book, illustrated book, "Contemporary American Voices" series. CAV is an essay series seeking works on matters of current interest in such fields as politics, the environment, economics, and religion. First book in the series: *Infinity in Your Hand: A Guide for the Spiritually Curious*, by William H. Houff (New Age/metaphysical work by Unitarian Universalist minister and founder of the Hanford Education Action League). Subjects include history, folklore, regional interest, current interest. Query with outline. Reviews artwork/photos as part of ms package.

Recent Nonfiction Title: *Washington: Images of a State's Heritage*, Carlos Schwantes, general editor; contributing editors: Katherine Morrissey, David Nicandri and Susan Strasser.

Fiction: Historical (with Pacific Northwest setting). Query.

Recent Fiction Title: *Fireweed: An American Saga*, by Nellie Buxton Picken (historical fiction).

*MERCER UNIVERSITY PRESS, Macon GA 31207. (912)744-2880. Director: Edd Rowell. Publishes hardcover originals. Averages 25 titles/year. Receives 250 submissions annually. 30% of books from first-time authors. 100% of books from unagented writers. Subsidy publishes 90% of books. "We usually ask for a subsidy from the author's institution (university). We do not accept personal subsidies from the authors themselves." Publishes book an average of 1 year after acceptance. Computer printout submissions acceptable; no dot-matrix. Reports in 1 month on queries; 3 months on mss. Free book catalog; writer's guidelines for SASE.

Nonfiction: Biography, reference, textbook and scholarly monographs. Subjects include history (of the American South); philosophy; religion and sociology. "We are very interested in Southern history, biblical studies and theology. We also favor books that may be adapted as textbooks in college courses. Our audience includes professors, students, researchers and libraries." Query or submit outline/synopsis and sample chapters or submit complete ms. Reviews artwork/photos as part of ms package.

Recent Nonfiction Title: *To See the Promised Land: The Faith Pilgrimage of Martin Luther King, Jr.*, by Frederick L. Downing.

Tips: "In scholarly publishing, there has been a substantial increase in the cost of books and decrease in print runs. We see more university presses publishing coffee table books that appeal to a general audience rather than to a scholarly one. Writers have the best chance of selling us scholarly monographs or original research in theology, religion, or history. Extensive documentation and a manuscript addressed to a specific (usually academic) market usually impress us."

*MERCURY HOUSE INC., Suite 700, 300 Montgomery St., San Francisco CA 94104. (415)433-7042. President: William M. Brinton. Executive Editor: Alev Lytle. Publishes hardcover originals. Averages 10-15 titles/year; receives 500 submissions annually. 20% of books come from first-time authors; 10% of books from unagented writers. Average print order for a writer's first book is 5,000. Subsidy publishes "only if there is a good market and author has something unique to say, and can say it well." Pays standard royalties and advances. Publishes books an average of 9 months after acceptance. Simultaneous and photocopied submissions OK only if publisher is informed prior to arrangement. Computer printout submissions acceptable in letter-quality type only. Reports in 1 month on queries; 6 weeks on mss.

Nonfiction: Original and unusual adult nonfiction, on a limited basis. Query with outline/synopsis and sample chapters.

Recent Nonfiction Title: *The Psychic Detectives.*

Fiction: Original adult fiction, translations, reprints. Query with outline/synopsis and sample chapters. All unsolicited mss are returned unopened.

Recent Fiction Title: *Irish Wine.*

Tips: "Our audience is adult. The editorial process is highly rigorous. Mercury House uses electronic marketing of its titles through computer users, as well as traditional distribution channels."

MERIWETHER PUBLISHING LTD., 885 Elkton Dr., Colorado Springs CO 80907. (303)594-4422. Editors: Arthur or Theodore Zapel. Publishes hardcover and trade paperback originals and reprints. Firm publishes 5-10 books/year; 35-50 plays/year. Receives 1,200 submissions/year. 50% of books from first-time authors; 90% from unagented writers. Pays 10% royalty on retail price or outright purchase of $250-2,500. Publishes book an average of 6 months after acceptance. Simultaneous and photocopied submissions OK. Computer printout submissions OK; no dot-matrix. Reports in 2 weeks on queries; 1 month on ms. Book catalog and ms guidelines available for $1 and SASE.

Nonfiction: How-to, reference, self-help, humor and inspirational. Also textbooks. Subjects include art/theatre/drama, hobbies, music/dance, recreation, religion. "We're looking for unusual textbooks or trade books related to the communication or performing arts. We are not interested in religious titles with fundamentalist themes or approaches—we prefer mainstream religion titles." Query or submit outline/synopsis and sample chapters.

Recent Nonfiction Title: *The Mime Book*, by Claude Kipnis.

Fiction: Plays. "Plays only—humorous, mainstream, mystery, religious, suspense."

Tips: "Our educational books are sold to teachers and students at college and high school levels. Our religious books are sold to youth activity directors, pastors and choir directors. Our trade books are directed at the public with a sense of humor. Another group of buyers is the professional theatre, radio and TV category. We expect to publish several new trade book titles dealing with how-to information in a humorous style. We will focus more on books of plays and acting texts."

METAMORPHOUS PRESS, 3249 NW 29th Ave., Box 10616, Portland OR 92710. (503)228-4972. Publisher: David Balding. Acquisitions Editor: Anita Sullivan. Publishes hardcover and trade paperback originals and hardcover and trade paperback reprints. Averages 8-12 titles/year; receives 600 submissions annually. 90% of books from first-time authors; 90% of books from unagented writers. Average print order for a writer's first book is 2,000-5,000. Pays minimum 10% profit split on wholesale prices. No advance. Publishes book an average of 8 months after acceptance. Simultaneous and photocopied submissions OK. Query for electronic submissions. Computer printout submissions acceptable; prefers letter-quality. Free book catalog; ms guidelines for #10 SASE.

Nonfiction: Biography, how-to, illustrated book, reference, self-help, technical and textbook—all related to behavioral science and personal growth. Subjects include business and sales, health, psychology, sociology, education, children's books, science and new ideas in behavioral science. "We are interested in any well-proven new idea or philosophy in the behavioral science areas. Our primary editorial screen is 'will this book further define, explain or support the concept that we are responsible for our reality or assist people in gaining control of their lives.'" Submit idea, outline, and table of contents only. Reviews artwork/photos as part of ms package.

Recent Nonfiction Title: *Recreating Your Self*, by Christopher Stone.

THE MGI MANAGEMENT INSTITUTE, INC., 378 Halstead Ave., Harrison NY 10528. (914)835-5790. President: Dr. Henry Oppenheimer. Averages 5-10 new titles/year; receives 10-15 submissions annually. 50% of books from first-time authors; 100% of those books from unagented writers. Pays 4% royalty on retail price of correspondence course or training manual (price is usually in $100 range). Does not publish conventional books. Publishes course or manual an average of 6 months after acceptance. Query for electronic submissions. Computer printout submissions acceptable. Reports in 2 weeks. Free course catalog.

Nonfiction: How-to, technical and correspondence courses. Subjects include business and economics, engineering, computer, and manufacturing-related topics. Needs correspondence courses in management, purchasing, manufacturing management, production and inventory control, quality control, computers and marketing professional services. Reviews artwork/photos.

Recent Nonfiction Title: *Computers in Purchasing Management*, by Bruce Wright (correspondence course).

Tips: "Our audience includes quality and inventory control managers, purchasing managers, graduate engineers and architects, manufacturing supervisors and managers, and real estate investors."

*MICHIGAN STATE UNIVERSITY PRESS, Room 25, 1405 S. Harrison Rd., East Lansing MI 48824. (517)355-9543. Director: Richard Chapin. Publishes hardcover and softcover originals. Averages 12 titles annually. Receives 100 submissions/year. 95% of books from first-time writers; 100% from unagented writers. Pays 10% royalty on net sales. Publishes ms an average of 9 months after acceptance. Photocopied submissions OK. Query for electronic submissions. Computer printout submissions OK; prefers letter-quality. Book catalog and manuscript guidelines for #10 SASE.

Nonfiction: Reference, software, technical, textbook and scholarly. Subjects include agriculture, business and economics, history, literature, philosophy, politics and religion. Looking for "scholarly publishing representing strengths of the university." Query with outline/synopsis and sample chapters. Reviews artwork/photos.

Recent Nonfiction Title: *Global Bioethics*, by Potter.

‡MIDDLE ATLANTIC PRESS, Box 945, Wilmington DE 19899. (302)654-9922. Publisher: Norman Goldfind. Publishes hardcover and mass market paperback originals and hardcover and tradepaperback reprints. Averages 10 titles/year. 10% of books from first-time authors; 10% from unagented writers. Pays 5-12% royalty on retail price. Offers $1,000 average advance. Publishes book an average of 1 year after acceptance. Simultaneous and photocopied submissions OK. Computer printout submissions OK; no dot-matrix. Reports in 1 month on queries. Free book catalog.

Nonfiction: Coffee table book, cookbook, how-to, humor, illustrated book, juvenile, self-help. Subjects include Americana, child guidance/parenting, cooking, foods and nutrition, health/medicine, history, regional, travel. Submit outline/synopsis and sample chapters. All unsolicited mss are returned unopened. Reviews artwork/photos as part of ms package.

Recent Nonfiction Title: *The Cook's Handbook*, by Prue Leith (cooking).

Fiction: Adventure, historical, horror, humor, juvenile, mainstream/contemporary, occult, science fiction, suspence, western, young adult. Submit outline/synopsis and sample chapters. All unsolicited mss are returned unopened.

Recent Fiction Title: *Passengers*, by Thomas G. Foxworth, Michael Guren (techno-thriller).

MILADY PUBLISHING COMPANY, Division of Delmar Publishers, Inc., 3839 White Plains Rd., Bronx NY 10467. (212)881-3000. FAX: (212)881-5624. President: Thomas R. Severance. Publishes technical books, particularly for occupational education. Averages 25 titles/year; receives 75 submissions annually. 25% of books from first-time authors; 100% of books from unagented writers. Pays 8-12% royalty on wholesale price. Offers average $750 advance. Publishes book an average of 1 year after acceptance. Photocopied submissions OK. Query for electronic submissions. Computer printout submissions acceptable; prefers letter-quality. Reports in 6 weeks. Book catalog for $1.

Nonfiction: How-to, reference, textbook, software workbooks and exam reviews on occupational education. No academic. Query or submit outline/synopsis and sample chapters. Reviews artwork/photos as part of ms package.

Tips: "Our audience is vocational students."

MILKWEED EDITIONS, Box 3226, Minneapolis MN 55403. (612)332-3192. Managing Editor: Deborah Keenan. Publishes hardcover originals and paperback originals and reprints. Averages 8-10 titles/year. Receives 1,560 submissions/year. 30% of books from first-time authors; 70% from unagented writers. Pays 8-12% royalty on wholesale price. Offers average advance of $400. Publishes work an average of 1 year after acceptance. Simultaneous and photocopies submissions OK. Computer printout submissions OK; no dot-matrix. Reports in 2 weeks on queries; 6 months on mss. Book catalog and ms guidelines for SASE.

Nonfiction: Illustrated book. Subjects include anthropology/archaeology, art/architecture, government/politics, history, language/literature, nature/environment, photography, regional, sports, women's issues/studies. Query. Reviews artwork/photos as part of ms package.

Recent Nonfiction Title: *The Mythic Family*, by Judith Guest (essay).

Recent Fiction Title: *Ganado Red*, by Susan Lowell.

Tips: "We are looking for three different collaborative works between writers and visual artists for our 1989 list. We want to emphasize visual art in 1990. Also, write for our fiction contest guidelines. Two fiction collections will be chosen still for our 1990 list."

MILLER BOOKS, 2908 W. Valley Blvd., Alhambra CA 91803. (818)284-7607. Subsidiaries include *San Gabriel Valley Magazine*, Miller Press and Miller Electric. Publisher: Joseph Miller. Publishes hardcover and trade paperback originals, hardcover reprints and software. Averages 4 titles/year. Pays 10-15% royalty on retail price; buys some mss outright. Simultaneous and photocopied submissions OK. Computer printout submissions acceptable. Reports in 2 weeks on queries; 2 months on mss. Free book catalog.

Nonfiction: Cookbook, how-to, self-help, textbook and remedial textbooks. Subjects include Americana, animals, cooking and foods, history, philosophy and politics. "Remedial manuscripts are needed in most fields." No erotica. Submit complete ms. Reviews artwork/photos as part of ms package. "Please don't send letters. Let us see your work."

Recent Nonfiction Title: *Every Feeling is Desire*, by James Smith, M.D.
Fiction: Adventure, historical, humor, mystery and western. No erotica; "no returns on erotic material." Submit complete ms.
Recent Fiction Title: *The Magic Story*, by F.V.R. Dey (positive thinking).
Tips: "Write something good about people, places and our country. Avoid the negative—it doesn't sell."

MILLS & SANDERSON, PUBLISHERS, Suite 6, 442 Marrett Rd., Lexington MA 02173. (617)861-0992. Publisher: Georgia Mills. Publishes trade paperback originals. Publishes 8 titles/year; receives 400 submissions annually. 50% of books from first-time authors; 75% of books from unagented writers. Pays 12½-13% royalty on wholesale price; offers average $1,000 advance. Publishes book 1 year after acceptance. Simultaneous and photocopied submissions OK. Query for electronic submissions. Computer printout submissions OK; prefers letter-quality. Reports in 6 weeks on queries; 2 months on mss. Ms guidelines for #10 SASE.
Nonfiction: Self-help. Subjects include health, travel and contemporary issues. "All our books are aimed at improving the individual's life in some way. No religion, music, art or photography." Query.
Recent Nonfiction Title: *Your Food-Allergic Child*, by Janet Meizel.
Tips: "We only publish nonfiction with broad general consumer appeal because it normally is less chancy than fiction. It must be an interesting subject with broad appeal by an author whose credentials indicate he/she knows a lot about the subject, be well researched and most importantly, must have a certain uniqueness about it."

‡*MODERN BOOKS AND CRAFTS, INC., 147 McKinley Ave., Bridgeport CT 06606. (203)366-5494. President: Alex M. Yupkin. Publishes hardcover originals and reprints. Averages 6 titles/year. Receives 25 submissions/year. 10% of books from first-time authors. 70% from unagented writers. Subsidy publishes 50% of books. Buys by outright purchase. Publishes book an average of 4 months after acceptance. Simultaneous and photocopied submissions OK. Reports in 1 month on queries.
Nonfiction: How-to and self-help. Subjects include military/war and books on antiques, gambling. Query. Reviews artwork as part of package.

MODERN LANGUAGE ASSOCIATION OF AMERICA, 10 Astor Pl., New York NY 10003. (212)475-9500. FAX: (212)477-9863. Director of Book Publications: Walter S. Achtert. Publishes hardcover and paperback originals. Averages 15 titles/year; receives 100 submissions annually. 100% of books from unagented writers. Pays 5-10% royalty on net proceeds. Publishes book an average of 11 months after acceptance. Photocopied submissions OK. Query for electronic submissions. Computer printout submissions acceptable; prefers letter-quality. Reports in 3 weeks on queries; 3 months on mss. Book catalog free on request.
Nonfiction: Reference and professional. Subjects include language and literature. Needs mss on current issues in research and teaching of language and literature. No critical monographs. Query or submit outline/synopsis and sample chapters.
Recent Nonfiction Title: *Language, Gender and Professional Writing*, by Francine Wattman Frank and Paula A. Treichler.

MONITOR BOOK CO., INC., Box 9078, Palm Springs CA 92263. Editor-in-Chief: Alan F. Pater. Hardcover originals. Pays 10% minimum royalty or by outright purchase, depending on circumstances; no advance. Reports in 4 months. Book catalog for SASE.
Nonfiction: Americana, biographies (only of well-known personalities), law and reference books. Send prints if photos and/or illustrations are to accompany ms.

‡MOONFALL PUBLISHING, INC., Box 2397, Springfield VA 22152. (703)866-9207. Director: George Simon. Publishes hardcover and paperback originals. Averages 5 titles/year. Pays 20-50% on retail price. Publishes book an average of 8 months after acceptance. Simultaneous and photocopied submissions OK. Computer printout submissions OK. Reports in 2 weeks on queries; 2 months on mss. Free book catalog and manuscript guidelines.
Nonfiction: Biography, coffee table book, how-to, self-help. subjects include government/politics, philosophy, psychology, religion, sociology. "Need New Age and religion books." Query or submit through agent. All unsolicited mss are returned unopened.
Recent Nonfiction Title: *Homo Spiritus*, by Silvia Cinca (self-improvement).
Fiction: Adventure, confession, fantasy, literary, mystery, occult, religious, romance, science fiction, suspense. Query or submit through agent. All unsolicited mss are returned unopened.
Recent Fiction Title: *Comrade Dracula*, by Silvia Cinca (suspense).

*MOREHOUSE PUBLISHING CO., 78 Danbury Rd., Wilton CT 06897. FAX: (203)762-0727. Publisher: E. Allen Kelley. Senior Editor: Deborah Graham-Smith. Juvenile and Special Projects Editor: Stephanie Oda. Academic Editor: Theodore A. McConnell. Publishes hardcover and paperback originals. Averages 45 titles/year; receives 500 submissions annually. 40% of books from first-time authors; 75% of books from unagented writers. Pays 10% royalty on retail price. Publishes book an average of 8 months after acceptance. Computer

printout submissions acceptable; no dot-matrix. Book catalog for 9x12 SAE with 2 first class stamps.
Nonfiction: Specializes in Christian publishing (with an Anglican emphasis). Theology, ethics, church history, pastoral counseling, liturgy, religious education and children's books (preschool-teen); beginning tapes and videos. No poetry or drama. Accepts outline/synopsis and 2-4 sample chapters. Reviews artwork/photos as part of ms package.
Recent Nonfiction Title: *Banners for Beginners,* by Cory Atwood (craft book—religious subjects).

MORGAN-RAND PUBLICATIONS INC., 2200 Sansom St., Philadelphia PA 19103. (215)557-8200. FAX: (215)259-4810. Contact: M. Weakley. Publishes trade paperback originals. Publishes 7 titles/year. Receives 20 submissions/year. 50% of books from first-time authors; 100% from unagented writers. Pays 20-45% royalty, or outright purchase of $500-1,000. Publishes book an average of 3 months after acceptance. Simultaneous submissions OK. Query for electronic submissions. Computer printout submissions OK; prefers letter-quality. Reports in 2 weeks on queries; 5 weeks on mss. Book catalog free on request.
Nonfiction: Reference, technical. Subjects include business and economics. Query.
Recent Nonfiction Title: *Directory Industry Buyer's Guide,* by Perkins.
Tips: "Books offering specific business and technical information to publishing and information industry professionals are wanted."

WILLIAM MORROW AND CO., 105 Madison Ave., New York NY 10016. (212)889-3050. Publisher: James D. Landis. Imprints include Arbor House, Greenwillow Books (juveniles), Susan Hirschman, editor. Lothrop, Lee and Shepard (juveniles), Dorothy Briley, editor. Morrow Junior Books (juveniles), David Reuther, editor. Quill (trade paperback), Douglas Stumpf and Andrew Ambraziejus, editors. Affiliates include Hearst Books (trade). Editorial Director: Ann Bramson. Hearst Marine Books (nautical). Connie Roosevelt, editor, Beech Tree Books, James D. Landis, Publisher. Silver Arrow Books, Sherry W. Arden, Publisher. Receives 10,000 submissions annually. 30% of books from first-time authors; 5% of books from unagented writers. Payment is on standard royalty basis. Publishes book an average of 1-2 years after acceptance. Computer printout submissions acceptable; prefers letter-quality to dot-matrix. Query letter on all books. *No* unsolicited mss or proposals. Mss and proposals should be submitted through a literary agent.
Nonfiction and Fiction: Publishes adult fiction, nonfiction, history, biography, arts, religion, poetry, how-to books and cookbooks. Length: 50,000-100,000 words. Query only; mss and proposals should be submitted only through an agent.

MORROW JUNIOR BOOKS, Division of William Morrow & Company, Inc., 105 Madison Ave., New York NY 10016. (212)889-3050. Editor-in-Chief: David L. Reuther. Executive Editor: Meredith Charpentier. Senior Editor: Andrea Curley. Publishes hardcover originals. Publishes 50 titles/year. All contracts negotiated separately; offers variable advance. Book catalog and guidelines for 8½x11 SAE with 2 first class stamps.
Nonfiction: Juveniles (trade books). No textbooks. Query. Reviews artwork/photos as part of ms package.
Recent Nonfiction Title: *A Girl from Yamhill,* by Beverly Cleary (autobiography).
Fiction: Juveniles (trade books).
Recent Fiction Title: *Teacher's Pet,* by Johanna Hurwitz (middle grade novel).
Tips: "Please query us after Jan. 1, 1990."

MOSAIC PRESS MINIATURE BOOKS, 358 Oliver Rd., Cincinnati OH 45215. (513)761-5977. Publisher: Miriam Irwin. Publishes hardcover originals. Averages 4 titles/year; receives 150-200 submissions annually. 49% of books from first-time authors. Average print order for a writer's first book is 2,000. Buys mss outright for $50. Publishes book an average of 30 months after acceptance. Computer printout submissions acceptable; no dot-matrix. Reports in 2 weeks; "but our production, if manuscript is accepted, often takes 2 or 3 years." Book catalog $3. Writer's guidelines for #10 SAE and 2 first-class stamps.
Nonfiction: Biography, cookbook, humor, illustrated book and satire. Subjects include Americana, animals, art, business and economics, cooking and foods, health, history, hobbies, music, nature, sports and travel. Interested in "beautifully written, delightful text. If factual, it must be extremely correct and authoritative. Our books are intended to delight, both in their miniature size, beautiful bindings and excellent writing." No occult, pornography, science fiction, fantasy, haiku, or how-to. Query or submit outline/synopsis and sample chapters or complete ms. Reviews artwork/photos as part of ms package.
Recent Nonfiction Title: *Victorian Christmas,* by Maria von Stauffer.
Tips: "I want a book to tell me something I don't know."

MOTHER COURAGE PRESS, 1533 Illinois St., Racine WI 53405. (414)634-1047. Managing Editor: Barbara Lindquist. Publishes trade paperback originals. Averages 4 titles/year; receives 300-400 submissions annually. 100% of books from first-time authors; 100% of books from unagented writers. Pays 10-15% royalty on wholesale and retail price; offers $250 average advance. Publishes book an average of 1 year after acceptance. No unsolicited manuscripts. Simultaneous and photocopied submissions OK. Query for electronic submissions. Computer printout submissions OK. Reports in 2 weeks on queries; 6 weeks on mss. Free book catalog; writer's guidelines for #10 SASE.

Nonfiction: Biography, how-to and self-help. Subjects include health, psychology and sociology. "We are looking for books on difficult subjects—explaining death to children (no talking animals); teen pregnancy; sexual abuse (no personal stories); and rape." Submit outline/synopsis and sample chapters. Reviews artwork/photos as part of ms package.

Recent Nonfiction Title: *Warning, Dating May Be Hazardous to Your Health*, by Claudette McShane.

Fiction: Adventure, fantasy, historical, humor, mystery, romance, science fiction and lesbian. "We are looking for lesbian/feminist or strictly feminist themes. Don't send male-oriented fiction of any kind." Submit outline/synopsis and sample chapters or complete ms.

Recent Fiction Title: *Night Lights*, by Bonnie Arthur (lesbian romance).

Tips: "We like to do books that have 'Women of Courage' as the theme."

MOTORBOOKS INTERNATIONAL PUBLISHERS & WHOLESALERS, INC., Box 2, Osceola WI 54020. FAX: (715)294-4448. Director of Publications: Tim Parker. Managing Editor: Barbara K. Harold. Hardcover and paperback originals. Averages 50 titles/year. 100% of books from unagented writers. Offers 7-15% royalty on net receipts. Offers average $4,000 advance. Publishes book an average of 1 year after acceptance. Simultaneous and photocopied submissions OK. Query for electronic submissions. Computer printout submissions acceptable; prefers letter-quality. Reports in 3 months. Free book catalog; ms guidelines for #10 SASE.

Nonfiction: Biography, history, how-to, photography, and motor sports (as they relate to cars, trucks, motorcycles, R/C modeling, motor sports and aviation—domestic and foreign). Accepts nonfiction translations. Submit outline/synopsis, 1-2 sample chapters and sample of illustrations. "State qualifications for doing book." Reviews artwork/photos as part of ms package.

Recent Nonfiction Title: *Stealth Bomber*, by Bill Sweetman.

‡MOTT MEDIA, INC., PUBLISHERS, 1000 E. Huron, Milford MI 48042. (313)685-8773. Senior Editor: George Mott. Hardcover and paperback originals and reprints. Averages 15 titles/year; receives 900 submissions annually. 20% of books from first-time authors; 100% of books from unagented writers. Average print order for a writer's first book is 3,500-5,000. Pays variable 7-10% royalty on retail, depending on type of book, and makes outright purchases. Publishes book an average of 20 months after acceptance. Simultaneous and photocopied submissions OK. Computer printout submissions acceptable; no dot-matrix. Reports in 2 months. Book catalog for 8½x11 SAE with 39¢ postage; ms guidelines for SASE.

Nonfiction: Specializes in religious books, including trade and Christian school textbooks. Publishes Americana (religious slant); biography (for juveniles on famous Christians, adventure-filled; for adults on Christian people, scholarly, new slant for marketing); how-to (for pastors, Christian laymen); juvenile (biographies, 30,000-40,000 words); politics (conservative, Christian approach); religious (conservative Christian); self-help (religious); and textbooks (all levels from a Christian perspective, all subject fields). No preschool materials. Main emphasis of all mss must be religious. Wants to know "vocation, present position and education of author; brief description of the contents of the book; basic readership for which the manuscript was written; brief explanation of why the manuscript differs from other books on the same subject; the author's interpretation of the significance of this manuscript." Submit outline/synopsis and sample chapters or complete ms.

Recent Nonfiction Title: *Process Theology*, by Ron Nash.

‡MOUNTAIN PRESS PUBLISHING COMPANY, Box 2399, Missoula MT 59806. (406)728-1900. Imprints include Roadside Geology Series, Roadside History Series, Classics of the Fur Trade. Publisher: David Flaccus. Publishes hardcover and trade paperback originals. Averages 15 titles/year. Receives 100 submissions/year. 70% of books from first-time authors. 95% of books from unagented writers. Pays 6-15% on wholesale price. Publishes book an average of 6 months after acceptance. Simultanous and photocopied submissions OK. Query for electronic submissions. Computer printout submissions OK; prefers letter-quality. Reports in 1 month on queries. Free book catalog.

Nonfiction: Technical. Subjects include Americana, nature/environment, recreation, regional, science, travel. "We are expanding our Roadside Geology and Roadside History series (done on a state by state basis.) We would also be interested in how-to books (related to horses, fishing). Also well written regional outdoor guides—plant, flower and bird. No personal histories or journals." Query or submit outline/synopsis and sample chapters or complete ms. Reviews artwork/photos as part of ms package.

Tips: "It is obvious that small- to medium-size publishers are becoming more important, while the giants are becoming harder and less accessible. If I were a writer trying to market a book today, I would find out what kind of books a publisher was interested in and tailor my writing to them. Research markets and target my audience. Research other books, on the same subjects. Make yours different. Don't present your manuscript to a publisher—*sell* it to him. Give him the information he needs to make a decision on a title."

THE MOUNTAINEERS BOOKS, The Mountaineers, 306-2nd Ave W., Seattle WA 98119. (206)285-2665. FAX: (206)285-8992. Director: Donna DeShazo. Publishes hardcover and trade paperback originals (85%) and reprints (15%). Averages 10-15 titles/year; receives 150-250 submissions annually. 25% of books from first-time authors; 98% of books from unagented writers. Average print order for a writer's first book is 2,000-5,000. Offers royalty based on net sales. Offers advance on occasion. Publishes book an average of 1 year after acceptance. Dot-matrix submissions are acceptable with new ribbon and double-spaced. Reports in 2 months. Book catalog and ms guidelines for 9x12 SAE with 2 first class stamps.

Nonfiction: Adventure travel, recreation, non-competitive sports, and outdoor how-to books. "We specialize only in books dealing with mountaineering, hiking, backpacking, skiing, snowshoeing, canoeing, bicycling, etc. These can be either how-to-do-it, where-to-do-it (guidebooks), or accounts of similar outdoor or mountain-related experiences." Does *not* want to see "anything dealing with hunting, fishing or motorized travel." Submit outline/synopsis and minimum of 2 sample chapters. Accepts nonfiction translations. Looks for "expert knowledge, good organization."

Recent Nonfiction Title: *Walking Austria's Alps, Hut-to-Hut*, by Jon Hurdle (guidebook).

Fiction: "We might consider an exceptionally well-done book-length manuscript on mountaineering." Does *not* want poetry or mystery. Query first.

Tips: "The type of book the writer has the best chance of selling our firm is an authoritative guidebook (*in our field*) to a specific area not otherwise covered; or a first-person narrative of outdoor adventure otherwise unduplicated in print."

‡**JOHN MUIR PUBLICATIONS**, Box 613, Santa Fe NM 87504. (505)982-4078. FAX: (505)988-1680. President: Ken Luboff. Publishes trade paperback originals and reprints. Averages 30 titles/year. Receives 300 submissions/year. 30% of books from first-time authors. 90% of books from unagented writers. Pays 8-12% on wholesale price. Offers $750-1,000 average advance. Publishes book an average of 1 year after acceptance. Simultaneous and photocopied submissions OK. Computer printout submissions OK; prefers letter-quality. Reports in 2 weeks on queries; 1 month on mss. Free book catalog.

Nonfiction: How-to, reference. Subjects include business and economics, ethnic, health/medicine, nature/environment, recreation, science, sports, travel, auto repair. We want "unique and/or original treatments of ideas which inform, enlighten and stimulate our readers." Query or submit outline/synopsis and sample chapters. Reviews artwork/photos as part of ms package.

Recent Nonfiction Title: *Mona Winks: Self-Guided Tours of Europe's Top Museums*, by Rick Steves and Gene Openshaw.

MULTNOMAH PRESS, A division of Multnomah School of The Bible, 10209 SE Division St., Portland OR 97266. (503)257-0526. Senior Editors: Liz Heaney and Al Janssen. Publishes hardcover and trade paperback originals, and a limited number trade paperback reprints. Averages 30 titles/year; receives 500 submissions annually. 20% of books from first-time authors; 100% of books from unagented writers. Pays royalty on wholesale price. Publishes books an average of 9 months after acceptance. Photocopied submissions OK. Query for electronic submissions. Computer printout submissions acceptable; no dot-matrix. Reports in 6 weeks on queries; 10 weeks on mss. Book catalog and ms guidelines for SASE.

Nonfiction: Coffee table book and self-help. Subjects include religion. "We publish issue-related books linking social/ethical concerns and Christianity; books addressing the needs of women from a Christian point of view; books addressing the needs of the traditional family in today's society; illustrated books for children; and books explaining Christian theology in a very popular way to a lay audience." No daily devotional, personal experience, scripture/photo combinations or poetry. Submit outline/synopsis and sample chapters.

Recent Nonfiction Title: *Living, Loving, Leading*, by David and Karen Mains.

Fiction: Realistic fiction with a Christian world view for the middle reader (8-11-year-olds).

Tips: "We have a reputation for tackling tough issues from a Biblical view; we need to continue to deserve that reputation. Avoid being too scholarly or detached. Although we like well-researched books, we do direct our books to a popular market, not just to professors of theology."

*****MUSEUM OF NORTHERN ARIZONA PRESS**, Subsidiary of Museum of Northern Arizona, Box 720, Rt. 4, Flagstaff AZ 86001. (602)774-5211. Publisher: Diana Clark Lubick. Publishes hardcover and trade paperback originals, and also quarterly magazine. Averages 10-12 titles/year; receives 35 submissions annually. 10% of books from first-time authors; 100% of books from unagented writers. Subsidy publishes (nonauthor) 15% of books. Pays one-time fee on acceptance of ms. No advance. Publishes book an average of 1 year after acceptance. Queries only. Query for electronic submissions. Computer printout submissions acceptable; prefers letter-quality. Reports in 1 month. Book catalog for 8½x11 SAE and ms guidelines for #10 SASE.

Nonfiction: Coffee table book, reference and technical. Subjects include Southwest, art, nature, science. "Especially needs manuscripts on the Colorado Plateau that are written for a well-educated general audience." Query or submit outline/synopsis and 3-4 sample chapters. Reviews artwork/photos as part of ms package.

Recent Nonfiction Title: *A Separate Vision*, by Linda Eaton (ethnology and art).

MUSTANG PUBLISHING CO., Box 9327, New Haven CT 06533. (203)624-5485. President: Rollin Riggs. Publishes hardcover and trade paperback originals. Averages 6 titles/year; receives 1,000 submissions annually. 50% of books from first-time authors; 100% of books from unagented writers. Pays 6-9% royalty on retail price. Publishes book an average of 1 year after acceptance. Simultaneous and photocopied submissions OK. No electronic submissions. No phone calls, please. Computer printout submissions acceptable; prefers letter-quality. Reports in 1 month. SASE a must. Book catalog available from address above—include #10 SASE for catalog.

Nonfiction: How-to, humor and self-help. Subjects include Americana, hobbies, recreation, sports and travel. "Our needs are very general—humor, travel, how-to, nonfiction, etc.—for the 18-to 35-year-old market." Query or submit synopsis and sample chapters.

Recent Nonfiction Title: *Let's Blow thru Europe*, by Neenan and Hancock.

Tips: "From the proposals we receive, it seems that many writers never go to bookstores and have no idea what sells. Before you waste a lot of time on a nonfiction book idea, ask yourself, 'How often have my friends and I actually *bought* a book like this?' Know the market!"

‡THE MYSTERIOUS PRESS, 129 W. 56th St., New York NY 10019. (212)765-0901. Editor-in-Chief: William Malloy. Subsidiaries include Penzler Books (non-mystery fiction by mystery authors) and *The Armchair Detective* (magazine). Publishes hardcover originals, trade paperback reprints and mass market paperback reprints. Averages 40-50 titles/year; receives 750 submissions annually. 10% of books from first-time authors. 5% of books from unagented writers. Pays standard, but negotiable, royalty on retail price; amount of advance varies widely. Publishes book an average of 1 year after acceptance. Photocopied submissions OK. Computer printout submissions OK; prefers letter-quality. Reports in 2 months. Book catalog and guidelines for 8½x11 SAE with $1 postage.

Nonfiction: Reference books on criticism and history of crime fiction. Submit complete ms. Reviews artwork/ photos as part of ms package.

Recent Nonfiction Title: *Cornell Woolrich: First You Dream, Then You Die*, by Francis M. Nevins, Jr. (biography).

Fiction: Mystery, suspense and espionage. "We will consider publishing any outstanding crime/espionage/ suspense/detective novel that comes our way. No short stories." Submit complete mss.

Recent Fiction Title: *The Fourth Durango*, by Ross Thomas (suspense).

Tips: "We no longer read unagented material. Agents only, please."

THE NAIAD PRESS, INC., Box 10543, Tallahassee FL 32302. (904)539-9322. FAX: (904)539-9731. Editorial Director: Barbara Grier. Publishes paperback originals. Averages 24 titles/year; receives 255 submissions annually. 20% of books from first-time authors; 99% of books from unagented writers. Average print order for a writer's first book is 12,000. Pays 15% royalty on wholesale or retail price; no advance. Publishes book an average of 1 year after acceptance. Reports in 2 months. Book catalog and ms guidelines for #10 SAE and 45¢ postage.

Fiction: "We publish lesbian fiction, preferably lesbian/feminist fiction. We are not impressed with the 'oh woe' school and prefer realistic (i.e., happy) novels. We emphasize fiction and are now heavily reading manuscripts in that area. We are working in a lot of genre fiction—mysteries, science fiction, short stories, fantasy—all with lesbian themes, of course." Query.

Recent Fiction Title: *The Beverly Malibu*, by Katherine V. Forrest.

Tips: "There is tremendous world-wide demand for lesbian mysteries from lesbian authors published by lesbian presses, and we are doing several such series."

NATIONAL ASSOCIATION OF SOCIAL WORKERS, 7981 Eastern Ave., Silver Springs MD 20910. FAX: (301)587-1321. Contact: Director of Publications. Averages 8 titles/year; receives 100 submissions annually. 20% of books from first-time authors. 100% of books from unagented writers. Pays 10-15% royalty on net prices. Publishes book an average of 1 year after acceptance. Computer printout submissions OK; prefers letter-quality. Reports in 3 months on submissions. Free book catalog and ms guidelines.

Nonfiction: Textbooks of interest to professional social workers. "We're looking for books on social work in health care, mental health and occupational social work. Books must be directed to the professional social worker and build on the current literature." Submit outline/synopsis and sample chapters. Rarely reviews artwork/photos as part of ms package.

Recent Nonfiction Title: *Ethnicity and Race: Critical Concepts in Social Work*, by Carolyn Jacobs and Dorcas Bowles, editors.

Tips: "Our audience includes social work practitioners, educators, students and policy makers. They are looking for practice-related books that are well grounded in theory. The books that do well are those that have direct application to the work our audience does. New technology, AIDS, welfare reform and health policy will be of increasing interest to our readers."

NATIONAL BOOK COMPANY, Division of Educational Research Associates, Box 8795, Portland OR 97207-8795. (503)228-6345. Imprints include Halcyon House. Editorial Director: Carl W. Salser. Senior Editor: John R. Kimmel. Manager of Copyrights: Lucille Fry. Publishes hardcover and paperback originals, paperback reprints, and software. Averages 23 titles/year. Pays 5-15% royalty on wholesale or retail price; no advance. Publishes book an average of 1 year after acceptance. Computer printout submissions acceptable. Reports in 2 months. Free catalog for 9x12 SAE with 2 first class stamps.

Nonfiction: Only materials suitable for educational uses in all categories. Art, business/economics, health, history, music, politics, psychology, reference, science, technical and textbooks. "The vast majority of titles are multimedia Individualized Instruction/Mastery Learning programs for educational consumers. Prospective authors should be aware of this and be prepared for this type of format, although content, style and appropriateness of subject matter are the major criteria by which submissions are judged. We are most interested in materials in the areas of the language arts, social studies and the sciences." Query, submit outline/synopsis and 2-5 sample chapters or complete ms. Reviews artwork/photos as part of ms package.
Recent Nonfiction Title: *The Last Angry Principal*, by Howard L. Hurwitz.

*NATIONAL GALLERY OF CANADA, Publications Division, 380 Sussex Dr., Ottawa, Ontario K1N 9N4 Canada. (613)990-0540. Acting Head: Serge Theriault. Editorial Coordinator: Irene Lillico. Publishes hardcover and paperback originals. Averages 15 titles/year. Subsidy publishes (nonauthor) 100% of books. Pays in outright purchase of $1,500-2,500; offers average $700 advance. Photocopied submissions OK. Reports in 3 months. Free sales catalog.
Nonfiction: "In general, we publish only *solicited* manuscripts on art, particularly Canadian art, and must publish them in English and French. Exhibition catalogs are commissioned, but we are open (upon approval by Curatorial general editors) to manuscripts for the various series, monographic and otherwise, that we publish. All manuscripts should be directed to our Editorial Coordinator, who doubles as manuscript editor. Since we publish translations into French, authors have access to French Canada and the rest of Francophonia. Because our titles are distributed by the University of Chicago Press, authors have the attention of European as well as American markets."
Recent Nonfiction Title: *Catalogue of the National Gallery of Canada, Canadian Art, Volume 1, (A-F)*, general editors: Charles C. Hill and Pierre B. Landry.

NATIONAL TEXTBOOK CO., 4255 W. Touhy Ave., Lincolnwood IL 60646. (312)679-5500. FAX: (312)679-2494. Editorial Director: Leonard I. Fiddle. Publishes originals for education and trade market, and software. Averages 100-150 titles/year; receives 200 submissions annually. 10% of books from first-time authors; 80% of books from unagented writers. Mss purchased on either royalty or buy-out basis. Publishes book an average of 1 year after acceptance. Computer printout submissions acceptable; no dot-matrix. Reports in 4 months. Book catalog and ms guidelines for SAE and 2 first class stamps.
Nonfiction: Textbook. Major emphasis being given to foreign language and language arts texts, especially secondary level material, and business and career subjects (marketing, advertising, sales, etc.). Raymond B. Walters, Language Arts Editor. Michael Ross, Foreign Language and ESL. Michael Urban, Career Guidance. Casimir Psujek, Business Books. Send sample chapter and outline or table of contents.
Recent Nonfiction Title: *Building Your Advertising Business*, by David M. Lockett.

NATUREGRAPH PUBLISHERS, INC., Box 1075, Happy Camp CA 96039. (916)493-5353. Imprint, Prism Editions. Editor: Barbara Brown. Averages 5 titles/year; receives 300 submissions annually. 75% of books from first-time authors; 100% of books from unagented writers. Average print order for a writer's first book is 2,500. "We offer 10% of wholesale; 12½% after 10,000 copies are sold." Publishes book an average of 18 months after acceptance. Photocopied submissions OK. Computer printout submissions acceptable; prefers letter-quality. Reports in 2 months. Book catalog and ms guidelines for #10 SAE with 3 first class stamps.
Nonfiction: Primarily publishes nonfiction for the layman in 7 general areas: natural history (biology, geology, ecology, astronomy); American Indian (historical and contemporary); outdoor living (backpacking, wild edibles, etc.); land and gardening (modern homesteading); crafts and how-to; holistic health (natural foods and healing arts); and PRISM Editions (Baha'i and other New Age approaches to harmonious living). All material must be well-grounded; author must be professional, and in command of effective style. Our natural history and American Indian lines can be geared for educational markets. "To speed things up, queries should include summary, detailed outline, comparison to related books, 2 sample chapters, availability and samples of any photos or illustrations, and author background. Send manuscript only on request." Reviews artwork/photos as part of ms package.
Recent Nonfiction Title: *The Mushroom Manual*, by Lorentz C. Pearson.

‡NAVAL INSTITUTE PRESS, Annapolis MD 21402. Manager, Acquisitions and Subsidiary Rights: Deborah Guberti Estes. Press Director: Thomas F. Epley. Averages 60 titles/year; receives 400-500 submissions annually. 80% of books from first-time authors; 70% of books from unagented writers. Average print order for a writer's first book is 4,000. Pays 14-18-21% royalty based on net sales; advance. Publishes book an average of 1 year after acceptance. Computer printout submissions acceptable; no dot-matrix. Reports in 2 weeks on queries; 6-8 weeks on other submissions. Free book catalog; ms guidelines for SASE.

For information on setting your freelance fees, see How Much Should I Charge? in the Business of Writing section.

Nonfiction: "We are interested only in naval and maritime subjects: tactics, strategy, navigation, naval history, biographies of naval leaders and naval aviation." Reviews artwork/photos as part of ms package.
Recent Nonfiction Title: *Flights of Passage: Reflections of a World War II Aviator*, by Samuel Hynes.
Fiction: Limited, very high quality fiction on naval and maritime themes.
Recent Fiction Title: *Flight of the Intruder*, by Stephen Coonts.

‡NAVPRESS, Division of The Navigators, Box 6000, Colorado Springs CO 80934. (719)598-1212. Editorial Director: Bruce Nygren. Publishes hardcover, trade paperback and mass market paperback originals. Averages 40 titles/year. Receives 300-350 submissions/year. 25% of books from first-time authors; 90% from unagented writers. Pays royalty on wholesale price. Publishes book an average of 18 months after acceptance. Simultaneous and photocopied submissions OK. Computer printout submissions OK. Reports in 1 month on queries; 10 weeks on mss. Free book catalog and manuscript guidelines.
Nonfiction: Juvenile and Christian instruction. Subjects include business and economics, child guidance/ parenting, money/finance, psychology, religion and women's issues/studies. Query or submit outline/synopsis and sample chapters.
Recent Nonfiction Title: *Stuck Like Glue*, by Paula Rinehart (children's).
Fiction: Adventure, juvenile, religious, young adult. "NavPress now publishes only Christian fiction for youth (ages 8 to 18) but will consider adult proposals. We do not want to receive fiction that is non-Christian in tone, content, or style." Query or submit outline/synopsis and sample chapters.
Tips: "We want fresh insights on the relevancy of the Christian faith in contemporary society; books that creatively respond to felt needs. Aggressively study existing books and seek to find niches in the market where specific needs of significant groups of readers are not being met."

NELSON-HALL PUBLISHERS, 111 N. Canal St., Chicago IL 60606. (312)930-9446. Editorial Director: Harold Wise, Ph.D. Publishes hardcover and paperback originals. Averages 90 titles/year. Pays 15% maximum royalty on retail price; offers average advance. Photocopied submissions OK. Reports in 1 month. Free book catalog.
Nonfiction: Textbooks and general scholarly books in the social sciences. Query.
Recent Nonfiction Title: *Men and Society*, by Clyde W. Franklin, II.

NEW AMERICAN LIBRARY, 1633 Broadway, New York NY 10019. (212)397-8000. Imprints include Signet, Mentor, Signet Classics, Plume, Meridian, D.A.W. Books, Onyx and NAL Books. Publisher: Elaine Koster. Executive Editor Mass Market: Kevin Mulroy. Editor-in-Chief/Trade Books: Arnold Dolin. Executive Editor/ Hardcover: Michaela Hamilton. Publishes hardcover and paperback originals and hardcover reprints. Publishes 350 titles/year. Royalty is "variable"; offers "substantial" advance. Query letters *only*. Replies in 1 month. Free book catalog.
Tips: Queries may be routed to other editors in the publishing group.

THE NEW ENGLAND PRESS, INC., Box 575, Shelburne VT 05482. (802)863-2520. President: Alfred Rosa. Publishes hardcover and trade paperback originals and trade paperback reprints. Averages 6-12 titles/year; receives 200 submissions annually. 25% of books from first-time authors; 75% of books from unagented writers. Pays 10-15% royalty on wholesale price. Publishes ms an average of 1 year after acceptance. Photocopied submissions OK. Computer printout submissions acceptable; no dot-matrix. Reports in 2 weeks on queries; 1 month on mss.
Nonfiction: Biography, how-to, nature and illustrated book. Subjects include Americana (Vermontiana and New England); history (New England orientation); and essays (New England orientation). No juvenile or psychology. Query or submit outline/synopsis and sample chapters. Reviews artwork/photos.
Recent Nonfiction Title: *Love: Proverbs of the Heart*, by Wolfgang Mieder.
Fiction: Historical (New England orientation). No novels. Query.

‡*NEW IDEA PRESS, INC., Box 13683, Boulder CO 80308-3683. (303)666-5242. Editor: Martha Gorman. Publishes trade paperback originals. Firm averages 4 titles/year. Receives 30 submissions/year. 10% of books from first-time authors; 80% from unagented writers. Subsidy publishes 20% of books. Determines subsidy "based on marketing considerations." Pays 5-10% royalty on retail price. Publishes book an average of 6 months after acceptance. Simultaneous and photocopied submissions OK. Query for electronic submissions. Computer printout submissions OK; prefers letter-quality. Reports in 3 weeks on queries; 6 weeks on mss.
Nonfiction: Subjects include health/medicine, psychology, sociology. "Innovative, unorthodox and controversial approaches welcome. We are looking for mss on the physiological bases of addiction and for well-written children's books on mental illness and on grieving. Also, soliciting short pieces written in Spanish and/or English by Central American refugees. No religious, no poetry, no cookbooks." Query or submit outline/synopsis and sample chapters. Reviews artwork/photos as part of ms package.

Recent Nonfiction Title: *Ill, Not Insane*, by Bonnie S. Busick (self-help medical).
Fiction: Juvenile and picture books. "Juvenile on mental illness or grieving. Will also consider mainstream adult and young adult books with these themes." Query.
Tips: "If I were a writer trying to market a book today, I would do my research carefully, write up the results in a lively, anecdotal manner, using case histories and metaphors, and be open to editing and editorial suggestions."

NEW LEAF PRESS, INC., Box 311, Green Forest AR 72638. Editor-in-Chief: Harriett Dudley. Publishes hardcover and paperback originals. Specializes in charismatic books. Publishes 15 titles/year; receives 236 submissions annually. 15% of books from first-time authors; 90% of books from unagented writers. Average print order for a writer's first book is 10,000. Pays 10% royalty on first 10,000 copies, paid once a year; no advance. Send photos and illustrations to accompany ms. Publishes book an average of 10 months after acceptance. Simultaneous and photocopied submissions OK. Reports in 3 months. Reviews artwork/photos as part of ms package. Book catalog and guidelines for 8½x11 SAE with 5 first class stamps.
Nonfiction: Biography and self-help. Charismatic books; life stories, and how to live the Christian life. Length: 100-400 pages. Submit complete ms.
Recent Nonfiction Title: *Pentecostals In Crisis*, by Ron Aoch.
Tips: "Biographies, relevant nonfiction, and Bible-based fiction have the best chance of selling to our firm. Honest and real-life experience help make a book or query one we can't put down."

NEW READERS PRESS, Publishing division of Laubach Literacy International, Box 131, Syracuse NY 13210. Acquisitions Editor: Kay Koschnick. Publishes paperback originals. Averages 30 titles/year; receives 200 submissions/year. 40% of books by first-time authors; 100% of books by unagented writers. Average print order for a writer's first book is 5,000. "Most of our sales are to high school classes for slower learners, special education, and adult basic education programs, with some sales to volunteer literacy programs, private human services agencies, prisons, and libraries with outreach programs for poor readers." Pays royalty on retail price, or by outright purchase. Rate varies according to type of publication and length of manuscript. Advance is "different in each case, but does not exceed projected royalty for first year." Publishes book an average of 1 year after acceptance. Photocopied submissions OK. Query for electronic submissions. Computer printout submissions acceptable; prefers letter-quality. Reports in 2 months. Free book catalog and authors' brochure.
Nonfiction: "Our audience is adults and older teenagers with limited reading skills (6th grade level and below). We publish basic education materials in reading and writing, math, social studies, health, science, and English-as-a-second-language for double illiterates. We are particularly interested in materials that fulfill curriculum requirements in these areas. Manuscripts must be not only easy to read (3rd-6th grade level) but mature in tone and concepts. We are not interested in poetry or anything at all written for children." Submit outline and 1-3 sample chapters.
Recent Nonfiction Title: *Easing into Essays: Getting Ready to Write the GED Test Essay*, by Nan Phifer.
Fiction: Short novels (12,000-15,000 words) at third grade reading level on themes of interest to adults and older teenagers. Submit synopsis.
Recent Fiction Title: *Barrio Ghosts*, by Esther and Alex Cervantes.

NEW VICTORIA PUBLISHERS, Box 27, Norwich VT 05055. (802)649-5297. Editor: Claudia Lamperti. Publishes trade paperback originals. Averages 4 titles/year; receives 100 submissions/year. 100% of books from first-time authors; 100% of books from unagented writers. Pays 10% royalty on wholesale price. Publishes book an average of 6 months after acceptance. Photocopied submissions OK. Query for electronic submissions. Computer printout submissions OK. Reports on queries in 2 weeks; on mss in 1 month. Free book catalog.
Nonfiction: History. "We are interested in feminist history or biography and interviews with or topics relating to lesbians. No poetry." Submit outline/synopis and sample chapters.
Recent Nonfiction Title: *Radical Feminists of Hetereodoxy*, by Judith Schwarz (feminist history).
Fiction: Adventure, erotica, fantasy, historical, humor, mystery, romance, science fiction and western. "We will consider most anything if it is well written and appeals to lesbian/feminist audience." Submit outline/synopsis and sample chapters.
Recent Fiction Title: *As The Road Curves*, by Elizabeth Dean.
Tips: "Try to appeal to a specific audience and not write for the general market."

*****NEW YORK ZOETROPE, INC.**, 838 Broadway, New York NY 10003. (212)420-0590. FAX: (212)529-3330. Contact: Susan Schenker. Publishes hardcover and trade paperback originals, hardcover and trade paperback reprints and software. Averages 10 titles/year; receives 100 submissions annually. 25% of books from first-time authors; 75% of books from unagented writers. Subsidy publishes (nonauthor) 3% of books. Pays 10-20% royalty on wholesale prices or makes outright purchase of $500-1,000. Offers average $1,000 advance. Publishes book an average of 9 months after acceptance. Simultaneous and photocopied submissions OK. Query for electronic submissions. Computer printout submissions acceptable; prefers letter-quality. Reports in 2 weeks on queries; 2 months on mss. Book catalog and guidelines for 6x9 SAE.

Nonfiction: Reference, technical and textbook. Subjects include film, T.V., entertainment industry and media. Interested especially in film and computer subjects. No fiction. Query with synopsis and outline.

Recent Nonfiction Title: *The Laser Video Disc Companion: A Guide to the Best (and Worst) Laser Video Discs*, by Douglas Pratt.

Tips: "Film- or media-oriented (academic and popular) subjects have the best chance of selling to our firm. Media books (reference) are our strongest line."

NEWCASTLE PUBLISHING CO., INC., 13419 Saticoy, North Hollywood CA 91605. (213)873-3191. Editor-in-Chief: Alfred Saunders. Publishes trade paperback originals and reprints. Averages 10 titles/year; receives 300 submissions annually. 70% of books from first-time authors; 95% of books from unagented writers. Average print order for a writer's first book is 3,000-5,000. Pays 5-10% royalty on retail price; no advance. Publishes book an average of 8 months after acceptance. Simultaneous and photocopied submissions OK. Computer printout submissions acceptable; prefers letter-quality. Reports in 3 weeks on queries; 6 weeks on mss. Free book catalog; ms guidelines for SASE.

Nonfiction: How-to, self-help, metaphysical and New Age. Subjects include health (physical fitness, diet and nutrition), psychology and religion. "Our audience is made up of college students and college-age nonstudents; also, adults ages 25 and up. They are of above average intelligence and are fully aware of what is available in the bookstores." No biography, travel, children's books, poetry, cookbooks or fiction. Query or submit outline/synopsis and sample chapters. Looks for "something to grab the reader so that he/she will readily remember that passage."

Recent Nonfiction Title: *Authentic I Ching*, by Henry Wei, Ph.D (translation of I Ching by a Chinese national).

Tips: "Check the shelves in the larger bookstores on the subject of the manuscript being submitted. A book on life extension, holistic health, or stress management has the best chance of selling to our firm."

NICHOLS PUBLISHING, Subsidiary of GP Publishing Inc., Box 96, New York NY 10024. (212)580-8079. Subsidiaries include GP Courseware. Vice President and Publisher: Linda Kahn. Publishes hardcover and paperback originals. Firm publishes 50 titles/year; division publishes 40 titles/year. 15% of books from first-time authors; 98% from unagented writers. Pays 5-15% royalty on wholesale price. Offers $300-500 average advance. Publishes book an average of 9 months after acceptance. Simultaneous and photocopied submissions OK. Query for electronic submissions. Computer printout submissions OK; prefers letter-quality. Reports on queries in 1 week; 6 weeks on mss. Book catalog and ms guidelines free on request.

Nonfiction: Reference, technical. Subjects include architecture, business and economics, computers and electronics, education, money/finance, training, energy, engineering. Submit outline/synopsis and sample chapters or complete ms.

Recent Nonfiction Title: *Design for Hospitality*, by Davies and Beaseley.

‡NIMBUS PUBLISHING LIMITED, Subsidiary of H.H. Marshall Ltd., Box 9301, Station A, Halifax, Nova Scotia B3K 5N5 Canada. (902)454-8381. Contact: Dorothy Blythe. Imprints include Petheric Press (nonfiction and fiction). Publishes hardcover and trade paperback originals and trade paperback reprints. Averages 12 titles/year; receives 60 submissions annually. 50% of books from first-time authors; 100% of books from unagented writers. Average print order for a writer's first book is 3,000. Pays 10% royalty on retail price. Publishes book an average of 2 years after acceptance. Photocopied submissions OK. Query for electronic submissions. Computer printout submissions acceptable. Reports in 2 months on queries; 4 months on mss. Free book catalog.

Nonfiction: Biography, coffee table books, cookbooks, how-to, humor, illustrated books, juvenile and books of regional interest. Subjects include art, cooking and foods, history, nature, travel and regional. "We do some specialized publishing, otherwise our audience is the tourist and trade market in Atlantic Canada." Query or submit outline/synopsis and a minimum of 1 sample chapter. Reviews artwork/photos as part of ms package.

Tips: "Titles of regional interest, with potential for national or international sales, have the best chance of selling to our firm."

‡THE NOBLE PRESS, INCOPORATED, Suite #48A, 111 E. Chestnut, Chicago IL 60611. (312)951-8891. President: David Driver. Firm publishes hardcover and trade paperback originals. Publishes 8 titles/year; receives 200 submissions/year. 50% of books from first-time authors; 80% from unagented writers. Pays 5-15% royalty on retail price. Advance varies. Publishes book an average of 6 months after acceptance. Simultaneous and photocopied submissions OK. Computer printout submissions OK; no dot-matrix. Reports in 6 weeks. Free ms guidelines.

Nonfiction: Biography, how-to, illustrated book, juvenile, reference, self-help. Subjects include education, ethnic, government/politics, history, nature/environment, philosophy, religion, sociology, women's issues/ studies. No cookbooks, technical manuals, texts in full. Submit outline/synopsis and sample chapters.

Recent Nonfiction Title: *The Good Heart Book*, by David Driver (guide to human care volunteering).
Tips: "The writer has the best chance of selling us a nonfiction book that addresses contemporary issues of importance to our society."

NORTH LIGHT, Imprint of F&W Publications, 1507 Dana Ave., Cincinnati OH 45207. Editorial Director: David Lewis. Publishes hardcover and trade paperback originals. Averages 30-35 titles/year. Pays 10% royalty on net receipts. Offers $3,000 advance. Simultaneous submissions OK. Reports in 3 weeks on queries; 2 months on mss. Book catalog for 9x12 SAE with 6 first class stamps.
Nonfiction: Art and graphic design instruction books. Interested in books on watercolor painting, oil painting, basic drawing, pen and ink, airbrush, markers, basic design, computer graphics, desktop publishing, desktop design, color, illustration techniques, layout and typography. Do not submit coffee table art books with no how-to art instruction. Query or submit outline/synopsis and examples of artwork (transparencies and photographs of artwork are OK).
Recent Nonfiction Title: *Light: How to See It, How to Paint It*.

NORTHERN ILLINOIS UNIVERSITY PRESS, DeKalb IL 60115. (815)753-1826/753-1075. Director: Mary L. Lincoln. Pays 10-15% royalty on wholesale price. Free book catalog.
Nonfiction: "The NIU Press publishes mainly history, political science, literary criticism and regional studies. It does not consider collections of previously published articles, essays, etc., nor do we consider unsolicited poetry." Accepts nonfiction translations. Query with outline/synopsis and 1-3 sample chapters.
Recent Nonfiction Title: *Chicago Divided: The Making of a Black Mayor*, by Paul Kleppner.

‡NORTHLAND PUBLISHING CO., INC., Box N, Flagstaff AZ 86002. (602)774-5251. FAX: (602)774-0592. Editorial Director: Susan McDonald. Publishes hardcover and trade paperback originals. Firm averages 20 titles/year. Receives 250 submissions/year. 30% of books from first-time authors. 75% from unagented writers. Pays 8-15% on net receipts; amount varies depending upon terms book is sold under. Offers $1,000 average advance. Publishes book an average of 10 months after acceptance. Simultaneous and photocopied submissions OK. Computer printout submissions OK. Reports in 1 month on queries; 2 months on mss. Free book catalog and manuscript guidelines.
Nonfiction: Biography, coffee table, cookbook, how-to and illustrated books. Subjects include animals, anthropology/archaeology, art/architecture, history, nature/environment, photography and regional (American west/Southwest). "We are seeking authoritative, well-written manuscripts on natural history subjects. We do not want to see poetry, general fiction, children's stories, or new age/science fiction material." Query or submit outline/synopsis and sample chapters. Reviews artwork/photos as part of ms package.
Recent Nonfiction Title: *Beyond Tradition*, by Jacka.
Tips: "In general, our audience is composed of general interest readers and those interested in specialty subjects such as Native American culture and crafts. It is not necessarily a scholarly market, but is sophisticated."

W.W. NORTON CO., INC., 500 5th Ave., New York NY 10110. (212)354-5500. Editor: Liz Malcolm. Imprints include Shoreline Books. Publishes 300 titles/year; receives 5,000 submissions annually. Often publishes new and unagented authors. Royalty varies on retail price; advance varies. Publishes book an average of 1 year after acceptance. Photocopied and simultaneous submissions OK. Computer printout submissions acceptable. Submit outline and/or 2-3 sample chapters for fiction and nonfiction. Return of material not guaranteed without return packaging and postage. Reports in 2 months. Book catalog and guidelines for 8½x11 SAE with 2 first class stamps.
Nonfiction and Fiction: "General, adult fiction and nonfiction of the highest quality possible." No occult, paranormal, religion, genre fiction, formula romances, science fiction or westerns, cookbooks, arts and crafts, young adult or children's books. Last year there were 100 book club rights sales; 36 mass paperback reprint sales; and "innumerable serializations, second serial, syndication, translations, etc." Looks for "clear, intelligent, creative writing on original subjects or with original characters."
Recent Nonfiction Title: *Freud: A Life for Our Time*, by Peter Gay.
Recent Fiction Title: *The Watch*, by Rick Bass.
Tips: "Long novels are too expensive—keep them under 350 (manuscript) pages."

NOYES DATA CORP., Imprints include Noyes Press and Noyes Publications, Noyes Bldg., Park Ridge NJ 07656. Publishes hardcover originals. Averages 60 titles/year. Pays 10%-12% royalty on retail price; advance varies, depending on author's reputation and nature of book. Reports in 2 weeks. Free book catalog.
Nonfiction: Noyes Press publishes art, classical studies, archaeology, and history. "Material directed to the intelligent adult and the academic market." Noyes Publications publishes technical books on practical industrial processing, science, economic books pertaining to chemistry, chemical engineering, food, textiles, energy, electronics, pollution control—primarily of interest to the business executive. Length: 50,000-250,000 words. Query Editorial Department.

OCTAMERON ASSOCIATES, 820 Fontaine St., Alexandria VA 22302. (703)823-1882. Editorial Director: Karen Stokstad. Publishes trade paperback originals. Averages 15 titles/year; receives 150 submissions annually. 10% of books from first-time authors; 100% of books from unagented writers. Average print order for a writer's first book is 8,000-10,000. Pays 7½% royalty on retail price. Publishes book an average of 6 months after acceptance. Simultaneous submissions OK. Query for electronic submissions. Computer printout submissions acceptable; prefers letter-quality. Reports in 2 weeks. Book catalog and guidelines for #10 SAE and 2 first class stamps.
Nonfiction: Reference, career and post-secondary education subjects. Especially interested in "paying-for-college and college admission guides." Query. Submit outline/synopsis and 2 sample chapters. Reviews artwork/photos as part of ms package.
Recent Nonfiction Title: *Campus Daze: Easing the Transition from High School to College*, by George Gibbs.

ODDO PUBLISHING, INC., Box 68, Redwine Rd., Fayetteville GA 30214. (404)461-7627. Managing Editor: Genevieve Oddo. Publishes hardcover and paperback originals. Averages 4 titles/year; receives 300 submissions annually. 25% of books from first-time authors; 100% of books from unagented writers. Average print order for a writer's first book is 3,500. Makes outright purchase. "We judge all scripts independently." Royalty considered for special scripts only. Publishes book an average of 2-3 years after acceptance. Computer printout submissions acceptable; no dot-matrix. Reports in 4 months. Book catalog for 9x12 SAE with $1.25 postage.
Nonfiction and Fiction: Publishes juvenile books (ages 4-10) in language arts, workbooks in math, writing (English), photophonics, science (space and oceanography), and social studies for schools, libraries, and trade. Interested in children's supplementary readers in the areas of language arts, math, science, social studies, etc. "Texts run from 1,500 to 3,500 words. Ecology, space, patriotism, oceanography and pollution are subjects of interest. Manuscripts must be easy to read, general, and not set to outdated themes. They must lend themselves to full color illustration. No stories of grandmother long ago. No love angle, permissive language, or immoral words or statements." Submit complete ms. Reviews artwork/photos as part of ms package.
Recent Fiction Title: *Bobby Bear's Treasure Hunt*, by Marilue.
Tips: "We are currently expanding our line to include materials more acceptable in the trade market. To do so, we are concentrating on adding titles to our top selling series in lieu of developing new series; however, we will consider other scripts."

OHARA PUBLICATIONS, INC., 1813 Victory Place, Box 7728, Burbank CA 91510-7728. Contact: Editor. Publishes trade paperback originals. Averages 12 titles/year. Pays royalty. Photocopied submissions OK. Write for guidelines. Reports in 3 weeks on queries; 8 weeks on mss.
Nonfiction: Martial arts. "We decide to do a book on a specific martial art, then seek out the most qualified martial artist to author that book. 'How to' books are our mainstay, and we will accept no manuscript that does not pertain to martial arts systems (their history, techniques, philosophy, etc.)." Query first, then submit outline/synopsis and sample chapter. Include author biography and copies of credentials.
Recent Nonfiction Title: *The Bruce Lee Story*, by Linda Lee (biography).

OHIO STATE UNIVERSITY PRESS, 1070 Carmack Rd., Columbus OH 43210. (614)292-6930. Director: Peter J. Givler. Pays royalty on wholesale or retail price. Averages 30 titles/year. Reports in 3 months; ms held longer with author's permission.
Nonfiction: Publishes history, biography, philosophy, the arts, political science, law, literature, criminology, education, sociology and general scholarly nonfiction. Query with outline and sample chapters.
Recent Nonfiction Title: *David Lloyd George: A Political Life, The Architect of Change*, by Bentley B. Gilbert.
Tips: Publishes some poetry and fiction.

‡OHIO UNIVERSITY PRESS, Scott Quad, Ohio University, Athens OH 45701. (614)593-1155. Imprints include Ohio University Press and Swallow Press. Director: Duane Schneider. Publishes hardcover and paperback originals and reprints. Averages 25-30 titles/year. No advance. Photocopied submissions OK. Reports in 5 months. Free book catalog.
Nonfiction: "General scholarly nonfiction with particular emphasis on 19th century literature and culture. Also history, social sciences, philosophy, western regional works and miscellaneous categories." Query.
Recent Nonfiction Title: *In the Shadow of the Giant: Thomas Wolfe: Correspondence of Edward C. Aswell and Elizabeth Nowell, 1949-1958*, edited by Mary Aswell Doll and Clara Stites.
Tips: Does not accept unsolicited mss.

*OISE PRESS, Subsidiary of Ontario Institute for Studies in Education, 252 Floor, W., Toronto, Ontario M5S 1V6 Canada. (416)923-6641, ext. 2531. FAX: (416)926-4725. Editor-in-Chief: Hugh Oliver. Publishes trade paperback originals. Averages 25 titles/year; receives 100 submissions annually. 20% of books from first-time authors; 90% of books from unagented writers. Subsidy publishes (nonauthor) 5% of books. Pays 10-15% royalty; rarely offers an advance. Simultaneous and photocopied submissions OK. Query for electronic sub-

missions. Computer printout submissions OK; prefers letter-quality. Reports in 1 week on queries; 2 months on submissions. Free book catalog and guidelines.
Nonfiction: Textbooks and educational books. "Our audience includes educational scholars; educational administrators, principals and teachers and students. In the future, we will be publishing fewer scholarly books and more books for teachers and students." Submit complete ms. Reviews artwork/photos as part of ms package.
Recent Nonfiction Title: *Care and Moral Motivation*, by Debra Shogan.

THE OLD ARMY PRESS, Box 2243, Ft. Collins CO 80522. (303)484-5535. General Manager: Dee Koury. Publishes hardcover and trade paperback originals; hardcover and trade paperback reprints. Averages 6 titles/year; receives 30 submissions annually. 50% of books from first-time authors. 100% of books from unagented writers. Pays 5-10% royalty on wholesale price. Publishes book an average of 18 months after acceptance. Photocopied submissions OK. Query for electronic submissions. Computer printout submissions OK; prefers letter-quality. Reports in 3 weeks on queries; 3 months on submissions.
Nonfiction: Biography and reference—all related to western military history. Especially needs mss on Indian wars and Texas history. Query. Reviews artwork/photos as part of ms package.
Recent Nonfiction Title: *Custer For President*, by Craig Repass.

ONCE UPON A PLANET, INC., 65-42 Fresh Meadow Lane, Fresh Meadows NY 11365. (718)961-9240. Susidiaries include Planet Books and Greeting Books. President: Charles Faraone. Publishes humorous, novelty 32-page books for the international gift and stationery market. Publishes 12-20 titles/year. Pays authors 5-15% royalty on wholesale price, outright $500-3,000 purchase or flat amount per book printed or per book sold. Offers average advance of $500-1,500. Publishes ms an average of 4 months after acceptance. Simultaneous and photocopied submissions OK. Computer printout submissions OK. Reports in 2 weeks on queries and 3 weeks on mss. Book catalog and ms guidelines for #10 SAE.
Nonfiction: Humor, illustrated books. Query or submit outline/synopsis and sample chapters.
Fiction: Humor. "We'd like to find 10-15 funny books each year to fit our format." Query or submit outline/synopsis and sample chapters.

*OREGON HISTORICAL SOCIETY PRESS, Oregon Historical Society, 1230 SW Park, Portland OR 97205. (503)222-1741. Director—Publications: Bruce Taylor Hamilton. Publishes hardcover originals and trade paperback originals and reprints. Publishes 12-14 titles/year. Receives 300 submissions/year. 75% of books from first-time authors; 100% from unagented writers. Subsidy publishes 70% (nonauthor) of books. Pays royalty on wholesale price or makes outright purchase. Publishes book an average of 18 months after acceptance. Simultaneous and photocopied submissions OK. Query for electronic submissions. Reports in 1 week on queries; 3 months on mss. Free book catalog. Ms guidelines for #10 SASE.
Nonfiction: Subjects include Americana, art/architecture, biography, ethnic, government/politics, history, military/war, nature/environment, North Pacific Studies, photography, reference, regional. Query or submit outline/synopsis and sample chapters or submit complete ms. Reviews artwork/photos as part of ms package.
Recent Nonfiction Title: *That Balance So Rare: The Story of Oregon*, by Terence O'Donell (history).

*OREGON STATE UNIVERSITY PRESS, 101 Waldo Hall, Corvallis OR 97331. (503)754-3166. Publishers hardcover and paperback originals. Averages 6 titles/year; receives 100 submissions annually. 75% of books from first-time authors; 100% of books from unagented writers. Average print order for a writer's first book is 1,500. Subsidy publishes (nonauthor) 40% of books. Pays royalty on wholesale price. No advance. Publishes book an average of 1 year after acceptance. Query for electronic submissions. Computer printout submissions acceptable; no dot-matrix. Reports in 1 month. Book catalog for 6x9 SAE with 2 first class stamps.
Nonfiction: Publishes scholarly books in history, biography, geography, literature, life sciences and natural resource management, with strong emphasis on Pacific or Northwestern topics. Submit outline/synopsis and sample chapters.
Recent Nonfiction Title: *William L. Finley: Pioneer Wildlife Photographer*, by Worth Mathewson (biography/photos).

ORYX PRESS, 2214 N. Central Ave., Phoenix AZ 85004. (602)254-6156. President/Editorial Director: Phyllis B. Steckler. Publishes hardcover and paperback originals. Averages 55 titles/year; receives 300 submissions annually. 40% of books from first-time authors; 100% of books from unagented writers. Average print order for a writer's first book is 1,500. Pays 10% royalty on net receipts; no advance. Publishes book an average of 9 months after acceptance. Query for electronic submissions. Computer printout submissions acceptable; prefers letter-quality. Reports in 2 months. Free book catalog and ms guidelines.
Nonfiction: Bibliographies, directories, general reference, library and information science, business reference, health care, gerontology, automation, and agriculture monographs. Publishes nonfiction for public, college and university, junior college, school and special libraries; agriculture specialists, health care deliverers; and managers. Query or submit outline/synopsis and 1 sample chapter, or complete ms. Queries/mss may be routed to other editors in the publishing group.

Recent Nonfiction Title: *The Nonsexist Word Finder: A Dictionary of Gender-Free Usage*, by Rosalie Maggio.

OUR SUNDAY VISITOR, INC., 200 Noll Plaza, Huntington IN 46750. (219)356-8400. Director: Robert Lockwood. Publishes paperback originals and reprints. Averages 20-30 titles a year; receives 75 submissions annually. 10% of books from first-time authors; 90% of books from unagented writers. Pays variable royalty on net receipts; offers average $500 advance. Publishes book an average of 1 year after acceptance. Query for electronic submissions. Computer printout submissions acceptable; prefers letter-quality. Reports in 1 month on most queries and submissions. Author's guide and catalog for SASE.
Nonfiction: Catholic viewpoints on current issues, reference and guidance, Bibles and devotional books, and Catholic heritage books. Prefers to see well-developed proposals as first submission with "annotated outline, three sample chapters, and definition of intended market." Reviews artwork/photos as part of ms package.
Recent Nonfiction Title: *Cults, Sects and the New Age*, by Fr. James J. LeBar.
Tips: "Solid devotional books that are not first person, well-researched church histories or lives of the saints and self-help for those over 55 have the best chance of selling to our firm. Make it solidly Catholic, unique, without pious platitudes."

OUTBOOKS INC., 2487 Industrial Blvd., Unit #2, Grand Junction CO 81505. (303)243-0205. President: William R. Jones. Publishes trade paperback originals and reprints. Firm averages 5 titles/year. Receives 50 submissions/year. 100% from unagented writers. Pays 5% royalty on retail price. Publishes book an average of 4 months after acceptance. Simultaneous and photocopied submissions OK. Query for electronic submissions. Computer printout submissions OK. Reports in 1 week on queries; 2 weeks on mss. Free book catalog.
Nonfiction: Biography, cookbook and reference. Subjects include Americana, animals, anthropology/archaeology, cooking, foods and nutrition, history, military/war, nature/environment, recreation, regional, science and travel. Query.
Recent Nonfiction Title: *What's Cooking in our National Parks* (cookbook).

THE OVERLOOK PRESS, Distributed by Viking/Penguin, 12 W. 21st St., New York NY 10010. (212)337-5200. Contact: Editorial Department. Imprints include Tusk Books. Publishes hardcover and trade paperback originals and hardcover reprints. Averages 40 titles/year; receives 300 submissions annually. Pays 3-15% royalty on wholesale or retail price. Submissions accepted only through literary agents. Reports in 2 months. Free book catalog.
Nonfiction: How-to and reference. Subjects include Americana, business and economics, history, nature, recreation, sports, and travel. No pornography.
Fiction: Adventure, ethnic, fantasy/science fiction, historical, mainstream, mystery/suspense. "We tend not to publish commercial fiction."
Recent Fiction Title: *The Universe and Other Fictions*, by Paul West.
Poetry: "We like to publish poets who have a strong following—those who read in New York City regularly or publish in periodicals regularly." No poetry from unpublished authors. Submit complete ms.
Recent Poetry Title: *Disappearances*, by Paul Auster.
Tips: "We are a very small company. If authors want a very quick decision, they should go to another company first and come back to us. We try to be as prompt as possible, but it sometimes takes over 3 months for us to get to a final decision."

P.P.I. PUBLISHING, 603 Congress Park, Box 335, Dayton OH 45459. (513)433-2709. Publishes booklets. Averages 30-40 titles/year; receives 200 submissions annually. 40% of books from first-time authors; 100% of books from unagented writers. Average print order for a writer's first book is 1,000. Pays 10% royalty on retail selling price to customer (some customer discounts). Publishes book an average of 3 months after acceptance. Simultaneous and photocopied submissions OK. Computer printout submissions acceptable; no dot-matrix. Reports in 6 weeks on queries; 3 months on mss. Book catalog and guidelines for SAE and 2 first class stamps.
Nonfiction: Juvenile and teens (ages 12 and up). Subjects include controversial issues and current events. "We publish nonfiction booklets of 20,000 words or larger for junior and senior high schools, libraries, colleges, universities and other specialized markets such as social service organizations. Our main subjects include controversial issues and items in the news. Topics that students are preparing for research papers or debates are of particular interest. We keep our markets informed on what's happening today in the world, in the home, in schools, and for the future. Some recent topics that were published include nuclear energy, AIDS, drug and alcohol abuse, teen suicide, violence in society, national healthcare, industrial/chemical leaks and accidents, and nuclear war. We are especially looking for 20,000-word manuscripts or larger on current events. We're not interested in how-to, technical material, travel or cookbooks." Submit outline/synopsis, sample chapters or complete ms. "For new authors we prefer outlines or queries to save them time and effort." Reviews artwork/photos as part of ms package "on a limited basis."

Recent Nonfiction Title: *Sex Education for Teenagers and Young Adults*, by Dr. Anne E. Jordheim.
Tips: "Abortion, capital punishment, gun control, nuclear energy, AIDS are but a few areas that have been of interest to us and society for quite a while and should remain current throughout the near future. Our largest market is high schools."

PACIFIC BOOKS, PUBLISHERS, Box 558, Palo Alto CA 94302. (415)965-1980. Editor: Henry Ponleithner. Averages 6-12 titles/year. Royalty schedule varies with book. No advance. Send complete ms. Computer printout submissions OK "if clean, typewriter-quality." Reports "promptly." Book catalog and guidelines for 9x12 SAE.
Nonfiction: General interest, professional, technical and scholarly nonfiction trade books. Specialties include western Americana and Hawaiiana. Looks for "well-written, documented material of interest to a significant audience." Also considers text and reference books; high school and college. Accepts artwork/photos and translations.
Recent Nonfiction Title: *Really Now, Why Can't Our Johnnies Read?*, by Jon Eisenson.

PACIFIC PRESS PUBLISHING ASSOCIATION, Book Division, Seventh-day Adventist Church, Box 7000, Boise ID 83707. (208)465-2595. Vice President for Editorial Development: Ken McFarland. Publishes hardcover and trade paperback originals and hardcover and trade paperback reprints. Averages 50 titles/year; receives 600 submissions annually. Up to 50% of books from first-time authors; 100% of books from unagented writers. Pays 8-14% royalty on wholesale price. Offers average $300 advance. Publishes books an average of 6 months after acceptance. Photocopied submissions OK. Query for electronic submissions. Computer printout submissions acceptable; prefers letter-quality. Reports in 1 month on queries; 2 months on mss. Ms guidelines for #10 SASE.
Nonfiction: Biography, cookbook (vegetarian), how-to, juvenile, self-help and textbook. Subjects include cooking and foods (vegetarian only), health, nature, religion, and family living. "We are an exclusively religious publisher. We are looking for practical, how-to oriented manuscripts on religion, health, and family life that speak to human needs, interests and problems from a Biblical perspective. We can't use anything totally secular or written from other than a Christian perspective." Query or submit outline/synopsis and sample chapters. Reviews artwork/photos as part of ms package.
Recent Nonfiction Title: *The Answer is Prayer*, by Morris L. Venden.
Tips: "Our primary audiences are members of our own denomination (Seventh-day Adventist), the general Christian reading market, and the secular or nonreligious reader. Books that are doing well for us are those that relate the Biblical message to practical human concerns and those that focus more on the experiential rather than theoretical aspects of Christianity."

‡PALADIN PRESS, Box 1307, Boulder CO 80306. (303)443-7250. FAX: (303)442-8741. President/Publisher: Peder C. Lund. General Manager: Kim R. Hood. Editorial Director: Jon Ford. Publishes hardcover and paperback originals and paperback reprints. Averages 36 titles/year. 50% of books from first-time authors; 100% of books from unagented writers. Pays 10-12-15% royalty on net sales. Publishes book an average of 1 year after acceptance. Simultaneous and photocopied submissions OK. Computer printout submissions acceptable. Reports in 2 months. Free book catalog.
Nonfiction: "Paladin Press primarily publishes original manuscripts on martial arts, military science, weaponry, self-defense, police science, action careers, guerrilla warfare, fieldcraft and 'creative revenge' humor. How-to manuscripts are given priority. Manuals on building weapons, when technically accurate and clearly presented, are encouraged. If applicable, send sample photographs and line drawings with complete outline and sample chapters." Query or submit outline/synopsis and sample chapters.
Recent Nonfiction Title: *Combat Revolvers*, by Duncan Long.
Tips: "We need lucid, instructive material aimed at our market and accompanied by sharp, relevant illustrations and photos. As we are primarily a publisher of 'how-to' books, a manuscript which has step-by-step instructions, written in a clear and concise manner (but not strictly outline form) is desirable. No fiction, first-person accounts, children's, religious or joke books."

‡*PARAGON HOUSE PUBLISHERS, 2 Hammarskjold Plaza, New York NY 10017. (212)223-6433. Editor-in-Chief: Ken Stuart. Publishes hardcover and trade paperback originals and reprints. Averages 100 titles/year; receives 1,000 submissions annually. 10-20% of nonfiction from first-time authors; 50% of books from unagented writers. Subsidy publishes 2% of books/year (mostly translations). Whether an author is subsidy published is determined by "how much subsidy there is, as well as how much market." Royalty and advance negotiable. Simultaneous and photocopied submissions OK. Query for electronic submissions. Computer printout submissions acceptable; no dot-matrix. Reports in 2 weeks on queries; 6 weeks on mss. Book catalog free on request.
Nonfiction: Biography, reference and college textbook. Subjects include Americana, history, philosophy, politics, religion. Especially needs history, biography and serious nonfiction. No self help, diet, gardening, crafts, occult or humor. Query or submit outline/synopsis and sample chapters. Reviews artwork/photos as part of ms package.

Recent Nonfiction Title: *Roosevelt and Hitler: Robert Henzstein*.
Poetry: Journals and letters only. No new or unestablished writers.
Recent Poetry Title: *Collected Poems*, by Lonis Simpson.
Tips: "We are looking for books that fall between the cracks, such as books which are too mid-list for trade houses and not scholarly enough for university presses."

‡**PARENTING PRESS, INC.**, 7744 31st Ave. NE, Seattle WA 98115. (206)527-2900. Editor: Shari Steelsmith. Publishes hardcover and trade paperback originals. Averages 10 titles/year; receives 200 submissions annually. 80% of books from first-time authors; 100% of books from unagented writers. Pays 8-10% royalty on retail price. Offers average $150 advance. Publishes book an average of 9 months after acceptance. Simultaneous and photocopied submissions OK. Computer printout submissions acceptable; no dot-matrix. Reports in 1 month on queries; 6 weeks on mss. Book catalog and ms guidelines for #10 SASE.
Nonfiction: Illustrated book, juvenile, self-help and parenting. "We need books that build competence in parents and children and improve the quality of family life. No fiction or 'should' books—we instead like to see manuscripts that provide a variety of ways to do things—not just one 'right' way." Submit query or book proposal *first*. Send manuscript only upon request. Unsolicited manuscripts will be returned.
Recent Nonfiction Title: *Bully on the Bus*, by Carl Bosch.
Tips: "Our audience is thinking adults who are looking for ways to improve the quality of family life. The writer has the best chance of selling our firm a book that provides alternatives in child guidance and child-rearing issues. We are 'alternative' oriented. Books on child guidance are doing well for us. Make certain there is a wide enough need for the book before writing, and field test it yourself. I would say field testing the manuscript with parents and children improves it immensely."

PASSPORT PRESS, Box 1346, Champlain NY 12919. (514)937-8155. Publisher: B. Houghton. Publishes trade paperback originals. Averages 4 titles/year. 25% of books from first-time authors; 100% from unagented writers. Pays 8-12% royalty on retail price. Publishes book an average of 9 months after acceptance. Send query only. Unsolicited manuscripts or samples will not be returned.
Nonfiction: Travel books only. Especially looking for manuscripts on practical travel subjects and travel guides on specific countries. Query. Reviews artwork/photos as part of ms package.
Recent Nonfiction Title: *Latin America on Bicycle*, by J.P. Panet.

*****PAULIST PRESS**, 997 Macarthur Blvd., Mahwah NJ 07430. (201)825-7300. Publisher: Rev. Kevin A. Lynch. Managing Editor: Donald Brophy. Publishes hardcover and paperback originals and paperback reprints. Averages 90-100 titles/year; receives 500 submissions annually. 5-8% of books from first-time authors; 95% of books from unagented writers. Subsidy publishes (nonauthor) 1-2% of books. Pays royalty on retail price. Usually offers advance. Publishes book an average of 10 months after acceptance. Photocopied submissions OK. Query for electronic submissions. Computer printout submissions acceptable; prefers letter-quality.
Nonfiction: Philosophy, religion, self-help and textbooks (religious). Accepts nonfiction translations from German, French and Spanish. "We would like to see theology (Catholic and ecumenical Christian), popular spirituality, liturgy, and religious education texts." Submit outline/synopsis and 2 sample chapters. Reviews artwork/photos as part of ms package.
Recent Nonfiction Title: *What is Religion?*, by John Haught.

PBC INTERNATIONAL INC., Subsidiary is The Photographic Book Company, 1 School St., Glen Cove NY 11542. (516)676-2727. FAX: (516)676-2738. Managing Director: Penny Sibal-Samonte. Imprints include Library of Applied Design (nonfiction), Great Graphics Series (nonfiction) and Design In Motion Series (nonfiction). Publishes hardcover and trade paperback originals. Averages 15 titles/year; receives 100-200 submissions annually. Most of books from first-time authors and unagented writers done on assignment. Pays royalty and/or flat fees. Simultaneous and photocopied submissions OK. Computer printout submissions acceptable; prefers letter-quality. Book catalog for 8½x11 SASE.
Nonfiction: Subjects include design, graphic art, and photography. The Library of Applied Design needs books that show the best in current design trends in all fields. No submissions not covered in the above listed topics. Query with outline/synopsis and sample chapters. Reviews artwork/photos as part of ms package.
Recent Nonfiction Title: *International Hotel and Resort Design*, by Anne M. Schmid and Mary Scoviak-Lerner.

PEACHTREE PUBLISHERS, LTD., 494 Armour Circle NE, Atlanta GA 30324. (404)876-8761. Publishes hardcover and trade paperback originals. Averages 20-25 titles/year; receives up to 2,000 submissions annually. 50% of books from first-time authors; 75% of books from unagented writers. Average print order for a writer's first book is 5,000-10,000. Publishes book an average of 1 year after acceptance. Computer printout submissions acceptable; prefers letter-quality. Reports in 3 weeks on queries; 5 months on mss. Book catalog for SAE with 3 first class stamps.

Nonfiction: General and humor. Subjects include cooking and foods, history, recreation and travel. No technical, reference, art, juvenile or animals. Submit outline/synopsis and sample chapters. Reviews artwork/photos as part of ms package.

Recent Nonfiction Title: *Traveler's Guide to Major U.S. Airports*, by Richard Barbara and Linda Hafendorfer.

Fiction: Literary, humor and mainstream. "We are particularly interested in fiction with a Southern feel." No fantasy, juvenile, science fiction or romance. Submit complete manuscript.

Recent Fiction Title: *The Song of Daniel*, by Philip Lee Williams.

Tips: "We're looking for mainstream fiction and nonfiction of general interest; although our books are sold throughout North America. We consider ourselves the national publisher with a Southern accent."

PELICAN PUBLISHING COMPANY, 1101 Monroe St., Box 189, Gretna LA 70053. (504)368-1175. FAX: (504)368-1195. Associate Editor: Dean Shapiro. Publishes hardcover, trade paperback and mass market paperback originals and reprints. Averages 30-40 titles/year; receives 2,000 submissions annually. 30% of books from first-time authors; 97% of books from unagented writers. Pays royalty on publisher's actual receipts. Publishes book an average of 18 months after acceptance. Photocopied submissions OK. Computer printout submissions acceptable; no dot-matrix. Reports in 3 weeks on queries; 4 months on mss. Writer's guidelines for SASE.

Nonfiction: Biography, coffee table book (limited), cookbook, how-to, humor, illustrated book, juvenile (ages 8-12), self-help, motivational, inspirational, and Scottish. Subjects include Americana (especially Southern regional, Ozarks, Texas and Florida); business and economics (popular how-to and motivational); cooking and food; health; history; music (American artforms: jazz, blues, Cajun, R&B); politics (special interest in conservative viewpoint); recreation; religion (for popular audience mostly, but will consider others); and travel. *Travel*: Regional and international (especially areas in Pacific). *Motivational*: with business slant. *Inspirational*: author must be someone with potential for large audience. *Cookbooks*: "We look for authors with strong connection to restaurant industry or cooking circles, i.e. someone who can promote successfully." *How-to*: will consider broad range. Query. "Although our company does accept and review unsolicited manuscripts, we prefer that a query be made first. This greatly expedites the review process and can save the writer additional postage expenses." Does not consider multiple queries or submissions. Reviews artwork/photos as part of ms package.

Recent Nonfiction Title: *Adventuring on the Eurail Express*, by Jay Brunhouse (travel).

Fiction: Historical, humor, mainstream, Southern, juvenile and young adult. "Fiction needs are *very* limited. We are most interested in Southern novels. We are also looking for good mainstream juvenile/young adult works." No romance, science fiction, fantasy, gothic, mystery, erotica, confession, horror; no sex or violence. Submit outline/synopsis and sample chapters.

Recent Fiction Title: *Once Upon a Time on a Plantation*, by Nancy Rhyne (juvenile).

Tips: "We do extremely well with travel, motivational, cookbooks, and children's titles. We will continue to build in these areas. The writer must have a clear sense of the market and this includes knowledge of the competition. Pelican Publishing Company will accept unsolicited manuscripts. We accept no responsibility for returning them. However, if each is accompanied by a self-addressed stamped envelope (SASE) sufficient to cover the cost of return mail, we will make every effort to return it if we are unable to use it. Due to the large number of submissions we receive, we strongly advise all writers to send us a query letter and SASE first, describing their project briefly and concisely."

THE PENKEVILL PUBLISHING COMPANY, Box 212, Greenwood FL 32443. (904)569-2811. Director: Stephen H. Goode. Publishes hardcover originals. Averages 6-8 titles/year; receives approximately 50 submissions annually. 40% of books from first-time authors; 100% of books from unagented writers. Pays 10-15% royalty on wholesale price. Publishes book an average of 18 months after acceptance. Simultaneous and photocopied submissions OK. Computer printout submissions acceptable; prefers letter-quality. Reports in 1 month on queries; 2 months on submissions. Free book catalog.

Nonfiction: Reference, textbook and scholarly/critical. Subjects include history (19th, 20th Century American and European; Civil War and current interest); psychology; sociology (of current interest, divorce, terrorism); and literature and the arts and humanities. "Substantively, there are three areas of current interest: 1. Scholarly and critical works in the arts and humanities from about the Renaissance forward (e.g., a new edition [Translation] of Chaucer); 2. 19th and 20th century American and Continental history, such as the American Civil War (e.g. Wheeler's Last Raid or a collection of essays on the literature, film, and art arising from the Vietnam war); 3. modern social currents, such as divorce, terrorism, the [Jewish] Holocaust, etc. (e.g., an annual bibliography and survey of divorce in America; an annual bibliography of terrorism, etc.). On another level, we are interested in the following genres: diaries, correspondence, histories of movements, biographies, critical and scholarly editions, sources (e.g. Faulkner's library); and in the following kinds of reference works; bibliographies, preferably annotated, checklists; dictionaries (of authors' works, such as a Proust dictionary), etc." Query.

Recent Nonfiction Title: *The Letters of William Hazlitt, Leigh Hunt, and Their Circle.*
Tips: "The type of book a writer has the best chance of selling to us is something unique in modern letters; that is, that hasn't been done before—such as the *Art and Artists of Protest: The Vietnam War*, (a forthcoming title); the sources of Melville [either externally (his personal library) or internally (an examination of references in his works) arrived at]; or an index to the magazines that are members of the CCLM (Coordinating Council of Literary Magazines)."

PENNSYLVANIA HISTORICAL AND MUSEUM COMMISSION, The official history agency for the Commonwealth of Pennsylvania, Box 1026, Harrisburg PA 17108-1026. (717)787-8312. Chief, Marketing, Sales and Publications Division: Douglas H. West. Publishes hardcover originals and reprints, trade paperback originals and reprints, mass market paperback originals and reprints. Averages 6 titles/year; receives 50 submissions annually. 50% of books from first-time authors; 95% of books from unagented writers. Pays 5-10% royalty on wholesale or retail price. May make outright purchase of $500-1,000; sometimes makes special assignments; offers $350 average advance. Publishes book an average of 15 months after acceptance. Simultaneous and photocopied submissions OK. Query for electronic submissions. Computer printout submissions OK. Reports in 6 weeks on queries; 3 months on mss. Manuscripts prepared according to the Chicago *Manual of Style.*
Nonfiction: All books must be related to Pennsylvania, its history and its culture, biography, coffee table book, cookbook, how-to, illustrated book, reference, technical, visitor attractions and historic travel guidebooks. "The Commission is seeking manuscripts on Pennsylvania in general, but most specifically on archaeology, history, art (decorative and fine), politics, religion, travel, photography, nature, sports history, and cooking and food." Query or submit outline/synopsis and sample chapters.
Recent Nonfiction Title: *The Covered Bridges of Pennsylvania: A Guide*, by Susan M. Zecher (revised).
Tips: "Our audience is diverse—professional and avocational historians, students and scholars, specialists and generalists—all of whom are interested in one or more aspects of Pennsylvania's history and culture. Manuscripts must be well researched and documented (footnotes not necessarily required depending on the nature of the manuscript) and interestingly written. Because of the expertise of our reviewers, manuscripts must be factually accurate, but in being so, writers must not sacrifice style. We have always had a tradition of publishing scholarly and reference works, and although we intend to continue doing so, we want to branch out with more popularly styled books which will reach an even broader audience."

PERSPECTIVES PRESS, Box 90318, Indianapolis IN 46290-0318. (317)872-3055. Publisher: Pat Johnston. Publishes hardcover and trade paperback originals. Averages 4 titles/year; receives 200 queries annually. 95% of books from first-time authors. 95% of books from unagented writers. Pays 5-15% royalty on net sales. Publishes book an average of 6 months after acceptance. Simultaneous and photocopied submissions OK. Computer printout submission OK; no dot-matrix. Reports in 2 weeks on queries. Book catalog and writer's guidelines for #10 SAE and 2 first class stamps.
Nonfiction: How-to, juvenile and self-help books on health, psychology and sociology—all related to adoption or infertility. Query.
Recent Nonfiction Title: *Sweet Grapes: How to Stop Being Infertile and Start Living Again*, by Mike and Jean Carter.
Fiction: Adoption/infertility for adults or children. Query.
Recent Fiction Title: *Real for Sure Sister*, by Ann Angel (children).
Tips: "For adults we are seeking decision-making materials, books dealing with parenting issues, books to use with children, books to share with others to help explain infertility or adoption or foster care, special programming or training manuals, etc. For children we will consider manuscripts that are appropriate for preschoolers, for early elementary, for later elementary or middle school children, for high schoolers. While we would consider a manuscript from a writer who was not personally or professionally involved in these issues, we would be more inclined to accept a manuscript submitted by an infertile person, an adoptee, a birthparent, an adoptive parent, a professional working with any of these."

PETER PAUPER PRESS, INC., 202 Mamaroneck Ave., White Plains NY 10601. (914)681-0144. Co-Publisher: Nick Beilenson. Publishes hardcover originals. Averages 8 titles/year; receives 50 submissions annually. Buys some mss outright for $1,000. Offers no advance. Publishes ms an average of 9 months after acceptance. Simultaneous and photocopied submissions OK. Computer printout submissions OK. Reports in 2 weeks. Book catalog for #10 SAE.
Nonfiction: Cookbook and humor. Subjects include Americana, cooking and foods, inspirational, and religion. Submit complete ms. Reviews artwork/photos as part of ms package.
Recent Nonfiction Title: *Reigning Cats and Dogs*, by L.L. Kaufman.
Tips: Books on women's subjects have done well for Peter Pauper Press.

PETERSON'S, Box 2123, Princeton NJ 08543. (609)243-9111. Publisher/President: Peter W. Hegener. Executive Vice President: Karen C. Hegener. Vice President, Trade & Reference Division: Wayne Anderson. Publishes paperback originals and software (for the educational/career market). Averages 55-75 titles/year.

Receives 200-250 submissions annually. 30% of books from first-time authors; 90% from unagented writers. Average print order for a writer's first book is 10,000-15,000. Pays 8-10% royalty on net sales; offers advance. Publishes book an average of 1 year after acceptance. Photocopied submissions OK. Computer printout submissions acceptable; prefers letter-quality. Responds in 3 weeks. Free catalog.

Nonfiction: Educational and career reference and guidance works for professionals, libraries, and trade. Submit complete ms or detailed outline and sample chapters. Looks for "appropriateness of contents to our market, accuracy of information, author's credentials, and writing style suitable for audience." Reviews artwork/photos as part of ms package.

Recent Nonfiction Title: *Full Disclosure: Do You Really Want to be a Lawyer?*, by Susan Bell.

Tips: "We're expanding into educational travel."

PHAROS BOOKS, Publisher of *The World Almanac*, 200 Park Ave., New York NY 10166. (212)692-3824. Editor-in-Chief: Hana Umlauf Lane. Editor: Eileen Schlesinger. Assistant Editor: Sharilyn K. Jee. Publishes hardcover and trade paperback originals. Averages 30 titles/year. Pays 6-15% on retail price. Publishes book an average of 1 year after acceptance. Computer printout submissions acceptable; prefers letter-quality. Reports in 3 weeks. Free book catalog.

Nonfiction: "We look for books under three imprints: Pharos Books for nonfiction with strong consumer interest; World Almanac for innovative reference books; Topper for humor books. We expect at least a synopsis/outline and sample chapters, and would like to see the completed manuscript." Reviews artwork/photos as part of ms package.

PHILOMEL BOOKS, Division of The Putnam Publishing Group, 200 Madison Ave., New York NY 10016. (212)951-8700. Editor-in-Chief: Patricia Lee Gauch. Senior Editor: Paula Wiseman. Publishes hardcover originals. Publishes 25-30 titles/year; receives 2,600 submissions annually. 15% of books from first-time authors; 30% of books from unagented writers. Pays standard royalty. Advance negotiable. Publishes book an average of 1-2 years after acceptance. Computer printout submissions acceptable; no dot-matrix. Reports in 1 month on queries. Book catalog for 8½x11 SAE with 4 first class stamps. Request book catalog from marketing department of Putnam Publishing Group.

Nonfiction: Young adult and children's picture books (ages 2-17). No alphabet books or workbooks. Query first. Looks for quality writing, unique ideas, suitability to our market.

Recent Nonfiction Title: *Anno's Math Games*, by Mitsumassa Anno.

Fiction: Young adult and children's books (ages 2-17) on any topic. Particularly interested in fine regional fiction and quality picture books. Query to department.

Recent Fiction Title: *A White Romance*, by Virginia Hamilton.

Tips: "We prefer a very brief synopsis that states the basic premise of the story. This will help us determine whether or not the manuscript is suited to our list. If applicable, we'd be interested in knowing the author's writing experience or background knowledge. We are always looking for beautifully written manuscripts with stories that engage. We try to be less influenced by the swings of the market than in the power, value, essence of the manuscript itself."

‡THE PICKERING PRESS, Suite 601, 2665 S. Bayshore Dr., Miami FL 33133. (305)858-1321. FAX: (305)856-0873. Managing Editor: Charity H. Johnson. Publishes hardcover and trade paperback originals and trade paperback reprints. Firm averages 4-5 titles/year. Receives 25 submissions/year. 45% of books from first-time authors; 100% from unagented writers. Pays 6-15% on wholesale price. Buys mss outright for $2,500. Publishes book an average of 9 months after acceptance. Photocopied submissions OK. Query for electronic submissions. Computer printout submissions OK. Reports in 1 month on queries; 1 month on mss. Free book catalog.

Nonfiction: How-to, illustrated book and self-help. Subjects include art/architecture, health/medicine, history, psychology and regional. Looking for regional/Florida history; psychology/self-help; medical/self-help ms. No regional books outside of Florida. Submit query or outline/synopsis and sample chapters. Reviews artwork/photos as part of ms package.

Recent Nonficiton Title: *The Heart Surgery Handbook, a Patient's Guide*, by Carol Cohan, June B. Pimm, Ph.D. and James R. Jude, M.D., (medical self-help).

Tips: "Nonfiction, regional history, and medical self/help have the best chance of selling to our firm. If I were a writer trying to market a book today, I would clearly define the market for my book prior to approaching publishers, and be prepared to offer non-book trade suggestions in addition to traditional techniques."

‡*PICKWICK PUBLICATIONS, 4137 Timberlane Dr., Allison Park PA 15101. Editorial Director: Dikran Y. Hadidian. Publishes paperback originals and reprints. Averages 6-8 titles/year; receives 10 submissions annually. 50% of books from first-time authors; 90% of books from unagented writers. Subsidy publishes 10% of books. Publishes book an average of 18-24 months after acceptance. Photocopied submissions OK. Computer printout submissions acceptable. Reports in 4 months. Free book catalog.

Nonfiction: Religious and scholarly mss in Biblical archeology, Biblical studies, church history and theology. Also reprints of outstanding out-of-print titles and original texts and translations. Accepts nonfiction translations from French or German. No popular religious material. Query or submit outline/synopsis and 2 sample chapters. Consult *MLA Style Sheet* or Turabian's *A Manual for Writers*.
Recent Nonfiction Title: *Luke the Theologian*, edited by Francois Bovon.

PILOT BOOKS, 103 Cooper St., Babylon NY 11702. (516)422-2225. President: Sam Small. Publishes paperback originals. Averages 20-30 titles/year; receives 300-400 submissions annually. 20% of books from first-time authors; 90% of books from unagented writers. Average print order for a writer's first book is 3,000. Offers standard royalty contract based on wholesale or retail price. Usual advance is $250, but this varies, depending on author's reputation and nature of book. Publishes book an average of 8 months after acceptance. Computer printout submissions acceptable; prefers letter-quality. Reports in 1 month. Book catalog and guidelines for SASE.
Nonfiction: Financial, business, travel, career, personal guides and training manuals. "Our training manuals are utilized by America's major corporations as well as the government." Directories and books on travel and moneymaking opportunities. Wants "clear, concise treatment of subject matter." Length: 8,000-30,000 words. Send outline. Reviews artwork/photos as part of ms package.
Recent Nonfiction Title: *Developing and Enforcing a Code of Business Ethics*, by Gary Ward.

PINEAPPLE PRESS, INC., Drawer 16008, Sarasota FL 34239. (813)952-1085. Editor: June Cussen. Publishes hardcover and trade paperback originals. Averages 12 titles/year; receives 600 submissions annually. 20% of books from first-time authors; 80% of books from unagented writers. Pays 6½-15% royalty on retail price. Seldom offers advance. Publishes book an average of 1 year after acceptance. Simultaneous and photocopied submissions OK. Query for electronic submissions. Computer printout submissions acceptable; no dot-matrix unless high quality. Reports in 1 month on queries; 6 weeks on mss. Book catalog for 8½x11 SAE and 2 first class stamps.
Nonfiction: Biography, how-to, reference, nature and young adult. Subjects include animals, history and nature. "We will consider most nonfiction topics. We are seeking quality nonfiction on diverse topics for the library and book trade markets." No heavily illustrated submissions, pop psychology, or autobiographies. Query or submit outline/brief synopsis and sample chapters.
Recent Nonfiction Title: *Organizing Special Events*, by Darcy Devney.
Fiction: Literary, historical and mainstream. No romance, science fiction, or children's (below the young adult level). Submit outline/brief synopsis and sample chapters.
Recent Fiction Title: *A Court for Owls*, by Richard Adicks.
Tips: "If I were a writer trying to market a book today, I would learn everything I could about book publishing and book publicity and agree to actively participate in promoting my book. A query on a novel without a brief sample seems useless."

‡PIPPIN PRESS, 229 E. 85th St., Gracie Station, Box 92, New York NY 10028. (212)288-4920. Publisher/President: Barbara Francis. Publishes hardcover originals. Publishes 6-8 titles/year; receives 3,000 submissions/year. 80% of books from unagented writers. Pays royalty. Publishes book an average of 9-18 months after acceptance. Simultaneous and photocopied submissions OK. Reports in 3 weeks on queries; 2 months on mss. Book catalog for 6x9 SASE; ms guidelines for #10 SASE.
Nonfiction: Biography, humor, juvenile, picture books. Animals, history, language/literature, nature, science. General nonfiction for children ages 4-12. Query. Reviews copies of artwork/photos as part of ms package.
Recent Nonfiction Title: *I Did it with My Hatchet: A Story of George Washington*, by Robert Quackenbush (humorous).
Fiction: Adventure, fantasy, historical, humor, juvenile, mystery, picture books, suspense. Wants humorous fiction for agents 7-11. Query.
Recent Fiction Title: *An Autumn Tale*, by David Updike, illustrated by Robert Andrew Parker (juvenile fantasy).
Tips: "Read as many of the best children's books published in the last five years as you can. I would pay particular attention to children's books favorably reviewed in *School Library Journal*, *The Booklist*, *The New York Times*, and *Publishers Weekly*."

‡PLATT & MUNK PUBLISHERS, Division of Grosset & Dunlap, 200 Madison Ave., New York NY 10016. Editor-in-Chief: Bernette G. Ford. Publishes hardcover and paperback originals. Averages 100 titles/year; receives more than 10,000 submissions annually. Pays $500-2,000 in outright purchase; advance negotiable. Publishes book an average of 18 months after acceptance. Simultaneous and photocopied submissions OK. Reports in 10 weeks.

Nonfiction: Juveniles. Submit proposal or query first. "Nature, science, and light technology are of interest." Looks for "new ways of looking at the world of a child."

Fiction: Juveniles, picture books for 3-7 age group and some higher. Also interested in anthologies and collections with a fresh approach.

Tips: "Nonfiction that is particularly topical or of wide interest in the mass market; a new concept for novelty format for preschoolers; and very well-written fiction on topics that appeal to parents of preschoolers have the best chance of selling to our firm. We want something new—a proposal for a new series for the ordinary picture book. You have a better chance if you have new ideas."

*PLAYERS PRESS, INC., Box 1132, Studio City CA 91604. (818)789-4980. Vice President, Editorial: Robert W. Gordon. Publishes hardcover and trade paperback originals, and trade paperback reprints. Averages 15-25 titles/year; receives 75-300 submissions annually. 10% of books from first-time authors; 90% of books from unagented writers. Subsidy publishes 1% of books; subsidy publishes (nonauthor) 2% of books. Pays royalty on retail price. Publishes book an average of 20 months after acceptance. Photocopied submissions OK. Reports in 4 months. Book catalog and guidelines for 6x9 SAE and 3 first class stamps.

Nonfiction: Juvenile and theatrical drama/entertainment industry. Subjects include the performing arts. Needs quality plays and musicals, adult or juvenile. Submit complete ms. Reviews artwork/photos as part of ms package.

Recent Nonfiction Title: *Techniques of the Actor, by William-Alan Landes.*

Fiction: Adventure, confession, ethnic, experimental, fantasy, historical, horror, humor, mainstream, mystery, religious, romance, science fiction, suspense and western. Submit complete ms for theatrical plays only. "No novels are accepted. We publish plays only."

Recent Fiction Title: *A Frog King's Daughter*, by Cheryl Thurstin.

Tips: "Plays, entertainment industry texts and children's story books have the best chance of selling to our firm."

PLAYWRIGHTS CANADA, Imprint of Playwrights Union of Canada, 54 Wolseley St., 2nd floor, Toronto, Ontario M5J 1A5 Canada. (416)947-0201. Publishes paperback originals and reprints of plays by Canadian citizens or landed immigrants which have been professionally produced on stage. Receives 100 member submissions/year. 50% of plays from first-time authors; 50% from unagented authors. Pays 10% royalty on list price. Publishes about 1 year after acceptance. Simultaneous, photocopied and computer printout submissions OK; perfers letter-quality. Free play catalog and ms guidelines. Non-members should query. Accepts children's plays.

Recent Fiction Title: *Lucky Strike*, by Hrant Alianak (play).

PLENUM PUBLISHING, 233 Spring St., New York NY 10013. (212)620-8000. Senior Editor, Trade Books: Linda Greenspan Regan. Publishes hardcover originals. Averages 350 titles/year; trade division publishes 12. Receives 250 submissions annually. 50% of books from first-time authors. 90% of books from unagented writers. Publishes book an average of 8 months after acceptance. Simultaneous and photocopied submissions OK. Query for electronic submissions. Reports in several months on queries; several months on mss.

Nonfiction: Subjects include politics, current events, sociology, psychology, and science. "We need popular books in the social sciences, sciences and the humanities." Query only.

Recent Nonfiction Title: *The Supernova Story*, by Laurence Marschall.

Tips: "Our audience is intelligent laymen and professionals. Authors should be experts on subject matter of book. They must compare their books with competitive works, explain how theirs differs, and define the market for their books."

PLEXUS PUBLISHING, INC., 143 Old Marlton Pike, Medford NJ 08055. (609)654-6500. FAX: (609)654-4309. Editorial Director: Thomas Hogan. Publishes hardcover and paperback originals. Averages 4-5 titles/year; receives 10-20 submissons annually. 70% of books from first-time authors; 90% of books from unagented writers. Pays 10-20% royalty on wholesale price; buys some booklets outright for $250-1,000. Offers $500-1,000 advance. Simultaneous and photocopied submissions OK. Computer printout submissions acceptable; prefers letter-quality. Reports in 2 months. Book catalog and guidelines for SASE.

Nonfiction: Biography (of naturalists) and reference. Subjects include plants, animals, nature and life sciences. "We will consider any book on a nature/biology subject, particularly those of a reference (permanent) nature that would be of lasting value to high school and college audiences, and/or the general reading public (ages 14 and up). Authors should have authentic qualifications in their subject area, but qualifications may be by experience as well as academic training." No gardening; no philosophy or psychology; generally not interested in travel but will consider travel that gives sound ecological information. Also interested in mss of about 20-40 pages in length for feature articles in *Biology Digest* (guidelines available with SASE). Query. Reviews artwork/photos as part of ms package.

Recent Nonfiction Title: *Dinosaurs in the Garden: An Evolutionary Guide to Backyard Biology*, by Gary Raham.

Tips: "We will give serious consideration to well-written manuscripts that deal even indirectly with biology/nature subjects. For example, *Exploring Underwater Photography* (a how-to for divers) and *The Literature of Nature* (an anthology of nature writings for college curriculum) were accepted for publication."

POCKET BOOKS, 1230 Avenue of the Americas, New York NY 10020. Imprints include Washington Square Press (high-quality mass market), Poseidon Press (hardcover fiction and nonfiction), Archway and Minstrel (juvenile/YA imprints). Publishes paperback originals and reprints, mass market and trade paperbacks. Averages 300 titles/year; receives 750 submissions annually. 15% of books from first-time authors. Pays royalty on retail price. Publishes book an average of 1 year after acceptance. *No unsolicited mss or queries.* "All submissions must go through a literary agent."
Nonfiction: History, biography, reference and general nonfiction, cookbooks, humor, calendars.
Fiction: Adult (mysteries, thriller, psychological suspense, Star Trek ® novels, romance, westerns).

‡POMEGRANATE PRESS, LTD., 3236 Bennett Dr., Los Angeles CA 90068-1702. (213)850-6719. Publisher: Kathryn Leigh Scott. Firm publishes hardcover and trade paperback originals. Publishes 4 titles/year. Receives 15-25 submissions/year. 50% of books from first time authors. 50% from unagented writers. Pays 10% royalty on retail price. Offers $1,000-2,000 average advance. Publishes book an average of 6 months after acceptance. Simultaneous and photocopied submissions OK. Computer printout submissions OK; no dot-matrix. Reports in 2 weeks on queries; 6 weeks on mss. Free book catalog.
Nonfiction: Biography, coffee table book, how-to, humor, self-help, textbook and guide books. Subjects include Americana, art/architecture, hobbies, music/dance, photography, travel. "Entertainment industry oriented." Query or submit outline/synopsis and sample chapters or complete ms. Reviews artwork/photos a part of ms package.
Recent Nonfiction Title: *Lobby Cards: The Classic Films* (coffee table book).

*PORCÉPIC BOOKS, 4252 Commerce Circle, Victoria British Columbia V8Z 4M2 Canada. (604)381-5502. Imprints include Softwords and Tesseract Books. Imprint publishes hardcover and trade paperback originals. Averages 5 titles/year; receives 300 submissions annually. 20% of books from first-time authors. 90% of books from unagented writers. Subsidy publishes (nonauthor) 100% of books. Pays 10% royalty on retail price; offers $300-500 advance. Publishes ms an average of 10 months after acceptance. Simultaneous (if so advised) and photocopied submissions OK. Computer printout submissions OK; prefers letter-quality. Reports in 2 weeks on queries; 3 months on mss.
Nonfiction: "Not actively soliciting nonfiction books."
Fiction: Experimental, science fiction and speculative fiction. "We are interested in hearing from new Canadian writers of mainstream or experimental fiction." Press publishes Canadian authors only. Prefer query first, then sample chapters.
Recent Fiction Title: *The Silent City*, edited by Elizabeth Vonarburg.
Tips: "Make sure the manuscript is well written. We see so many mss that only the unique and excellent can't be put down."

PORTER SARGENT PUBLISHERS, INC., 11 Beacon St., Boston MA 02108. (617)523-1670. Publishes hardcover and paperback originals, reprints, translations and anthologies. Averages 4 titles/year. Pays royalty on retail price. "Each contract is dealt with on an individual basis with the author." Computer printout submissions acceptable. Book catalog for SASE.
Nonfiction: Reference, special education and academic nonfiction. "Handbook Series and Special Education Series offer standard, definitive reference works in private education and writings and texts in special education. The Extending Horizons Series is an outspoken, unconventional series which presents topics of importance in contemporary affairs and the social sciences." This series is particularly directed to the college adoption market. Accepts nonfiction translations from French and Spanish. Contact: Donna Vierra. Send query with brief description, table of contents, sample chapter and information regarding author's background.
Recent Nonfiction Title: *Workplace Democracy and Social Change.*

‡POSEIDON PRESS, Division of Simon and Schuster, 1230 Avenue of the Americas, New York NY 10020. (212)698-7290. Vice President/Publisher: Ann E. Patty. Publishes hardcover and trade paperback originals. Averages 20 titles/year; receives 1,000 submissions annually. 20% of books from first-time authors; none from

The double dagger before a listing indicates that the listing is new in this edition. New markets are often the most receptive to freelance submissions.

unagented writers. Pays 10-15% royalty on hardcover retail price. Publishes book an average of 1 year after acceptance. Computer printout submissions acceptable; no dot-matrix. Does not accept unsolicited material.
Nonfiction: Autobiography, biography and self-help. Subjects include business and economics, culture, history, politics, psychology and biography, autobiography and self-help. No religious/inspirational, cookbooks, diet or exercise.
Recent Nonfiction Title: *Behind the Mountain*, by Peter Conrad.
Fiction: Literary, historical, contemporary and mainstream.
Recent Fiction Title: *The Grotesque*, by Patrick McGrath.

POTENTIALS DEVELOPMENT FOR HEALTH & AGING SERVICES, 775 Main St., Buffalo NY 14203. (716)842-2658. Publishes paperback originals. Averages 6 titles/year; receives 30-40 submissions annually. 90% of books from first-time authors; 100% of books from unagented writers. Average print order for a writer's first book is 1,000. Pays 5% royalty on sales of first 3,000 copies; 8% thereafter. Publishes book an average of 1 year after acceptance. Computer printout submissions acceptable; no dot-matrix. Reports in 6 weeks. Book catalog and ms guidelines for #10 SASE.
Nonfiction: "We seek material of interest to those working with elderly people in the community and in institutional settings. We need tested, innovative and practical ideas." Query or submit outline/synopsis and 3 sample chapters to J.A. Elkins. Looks for "suitable subject matter, writing style and organization."
Recent Nonfiction Title: *Realistic Alzheimer's Activities*, by Madelyn Lewis-Long.
Tips: "The writer has the best chance of selling us materials of interest to those working with elderly people in nursing homes, senior and retirement centers. Our major market is activity directors. Give us good reasons why activity directors would want or need the material submitted."

‡POTOMAC-PACIFIC PRESS, 5120 Kenwood Drive, Annandale VA 22003. Editor: George Mair. Publishes hardcover originals, trade paperback originals. Firm averages 10-15 titles/year. 20% of books from first-time authors. 100% from unagented writers. Pays royalty on retail price. Simultaneous and photocopied submissions OK. Computer printout submissions OK; prefers letter-quality. Reports in 2 weeks on queries. Book catalog and manuscript guidelines free on request.
Nonfiction: Biography, how-to, humor and self-help. Subjects include Americana, business and economics, child guidance/parenting, government/politics, health/medicine, history, psychology, sociology, self-help, and New Age. Query with outline/synopsis and sample chapters.
Recent Nonfiction Title: *Personal Power Writing*, by George Briechle (self-improvement/business).

CLARKSON N. POTTER, INC., 225 Park Ave., New York NY 10003. (212)254-1600. Imprint of Crown Publishers. Editorial Director, Potter: Carol Southern, associate publisher, Crown. Publishes hardcover and trade paperback originals. Averages 55 titles/year; receives 1,500 submissions annually. 18% of books from first-time authors, but many of these first-time authors are well-known and have had media coverage. Pays 10% royalty on hardcover; 5-7½% on paperback; 5-7% on illustrated hardcover, varying escalations; advance depends on type of book and reputation or experience of author. No unagented mss can be considered. Photocopied submissions OK. Computer printout submissions acceptable. Reports in 1 month. Book catalog for 7x10 SASE.
Nonfiction: Publishes art, autobiography, biography, cooking and foods, design, how-to, humor, juvenile, nature, photography, self-help, style and annotated literature. Accepts nonfiction translations. "Manuscripts must be cleanly typed on 8½x11 nonerasable bond; double-spaced. Chicago *Manual of Style* is preferred." Query or submit outline/synopsis and sample chapters. Reviews artwork/photos as part of ms package.
Recent Nonfiction Title: *Weddings*, by Martha Stewart.
Fiction: Will consider "quality fiction."
Recent Fiction Title: *Doctors and Women*, by Susan Cheever.

THE PRAIRIE PUBLISHING COMPANY, Box 2997, Winnipeg, Manitoba R3C 4B5 Canada. (204)885-6496. Publisher: Ralph Watkins. Publishes trade paperback originals. Averages 4 titles/year; receives 25 submissions annually. 4% of books from first-time authors; 85% of books from unagented writers. Average print order for a writer's first book is 2,000. Pays 10% royalty on retail price. Photocopied submissions OK. Computer printout submissions acceptable; no dot-matrix. Reports in several weeks. Book catalog and guidelines for 8x10½ SAE with IRCs.
Nonfiction: Biography and cookbook. Subjects include cooking and foods. "We would look at any submissions." Reviews artwork/photos as part of ms package.
Recent Nonfiction Title: *The Homeplace*, by Jean James.
Tips: "The Prairie Publishing Company will be looking for marketable material from American authors as it pushes aggressively into that market."

PRAKKEN PUBLICATIONS, INC., Box 8623, Ann Arbor MI 48107. (313)769-1211. Publisher/Executive Editor: Alan H. Jones. Publishes hardcover and trade paperback originals. Averages 5 titles/year; receives 50 submissions annually. 50% of books from first-time authors; 100% of books from unagented writers. Pays 10%

royalty on net price. Publishes book an average of 6 months after acceptance. Simultaneous and photocopied submissions OK. Computer printout submissions acceptable; prefers letter-quality. Reports in 2 weeks on queries; 1 month on mss. Book catalog for #10 SASE.

Nonfiction: General education, vocational and technical education. "We are interested in manuscripts with broad appeal in any of the specific subject areas of the industrial arts, vocational-technical education, and in the general education field." Submit outline/synopsis and sample chapters. Reviews artwork/photos as part of ms package.

Recent Nonfiction Title: *Judicious Discipline*, by Forrest Gathercoal.

Tips: "We have a continuing interest in magazine and book manuscripts which reflect emerging policy issues in the field of education."

PRENTICE-HALL CANADA, INC., College Division, Subsidiary of Simon & Schuster, 1870 Birchmount Road, Scarborough, Ontario M1P 2J7 Canada. (416)293-3621. Editorial Director: Cliff Newman. Publishes hardcover and paperback originals and software. Averages 30 titles/year. Receives 200-300 submissions annually. 30-40% of books from first-time authors; 100% of books from unagented writers. Pays 10-15% royalty on net price. Publishes book an average of 14 months after acceptance. Query for electronic submissions. Computer printout submissions acceptable; prefers letter-quality.

Nonfiction: The College Division publishes textbooks suitable for the community college and large university market. Most submissions should be designed for existing courses in all disciplines of study. Will consider software in most disciplines, especially business and sciences. Canadian content is important. The division also publishes books in computer science, technology and mathematics.

Recent Nonfiction Title: *Investment Management in Canada*, by Hatch.

Tips: "Manuscripts of interest to Canadians and/or by authors resident in Canada should be forwarded to above address. All other manuscripts should be sent to Prentice-Hall, Inc., Englewood Office, N.J. 07632."

PRENTICE-HALL CANADA, INC., Secondary School Division, A subsidiary of Simon & Schuster, 1870 Birchmount Road, Scarborough, Ontario M1P 2J7 Canada. (416)293-3621. FAX: (416)299-2529. President: Rob Greenaway. Averages 30 titles annually.

Nonfiction: Publishes texts, workbooks, and instructional media including computer courseware for junior and senior high schools. Subjects include business, computer studies, geography, history, language arts, mathematics, science, social studies, technology, and French as a second language. Query.

Recent Nonfiction Title: *Physics Today*, by T.J. Elgin Wolfe.

PRENTICE-HALL CANADA, INC., Trade Division, 1870 Birchmount Road, Scarborough, Ontario M1P 2J7 Canada. (416)293-3621. Acquisitions Editor: Tanya Long. Publishes hardcover and trade paperback originals. Averages 25-30 titles/year; receives 750-900 submissions annually. 30% of books from first-time authors; 40% of books from unagented writers. Negotiates royalty and advance. Publishes book an average of 9 months after acceptance. Query for electronic submissions. Computer printout submissions acceptable; prefers letter-quality. Reports in 10 weeks. Ms guidelines for #10 SAE and 1 IRC.

Nonfiction: Subjects of Canadian and international interest; art, politics and current affairs, sports, business, travel, health and food. Send outline and sample chapters. Reviews artwork/photos as part of ms package.

Recent Nonfiction Title: *Champions: The Making of the Edmonton Oilers*, by Kevin Lowe with Stan and Shirley Fischler (sports).

Tips: Needs general interest nonfiction books on topical subjects. "Present a clear, concise thesis, well-argued with a thorough knowledge of existing works. We are looking for more books on social and political issues."

PRENTICE HALL PRESS, Trade Division, Gulf & Western Building, 1 Gulf & Western Plaza, New York NY 10023. Publisher: Elizabeth Perle. Publishes nonfiction hardcover and trade paperback originals. Publishes book an average of 10 months after acceptance. Will not consider unsolicited submissions.

Nonfiction: Categories include: self-help, New Age, psychology, business, health, diet, fitness, cookbooks, gardening, arts, and crafts, design, art architecture, photography, performing arts, travel, sports, nature, equestrian, military and illustrated gift books. Does not publish fiction, poetry, romances, westerns and other fiction genres.

THE PRESERVATION PRESS, National Trust for Historic Preservation, 1785 Massachusetts Ave. NW, Washington DC 20036. FAX: (202)673-4038. Director: Diane Maddex. Publishes nonfiction books on historic preservation (saving and reusing the "built environment"). Averages 6 titles/year; receives 30 submissions annually. 40% of books from first-time authors; 50% of books from unagented writers. Books are often commissioned by the publisher. Publishes book an average of 2 years after acceptance. Query for electronic submissions. Computer printout submissions acceptable; no dot-matrix. Book catalog for 9x12 SASE.

Nonfiction: Subject matter encompasses architecture and architectural history, building restoration and historic preservation. No local history. Looks for "relevance to national preservation-oriented audience; educational or instructional value; depth; uniqueness; need in field." Query. Reviews artwork/photos as part of ms package.

Recent Nonfiction Title: *Lighting for Historic Buildings*, by Roger W. Moss.

Tips: "The writer has the best chance of selling our press a book clearly related to our mission—historic preservation—that covers new ideas and is unique and practical. If it fills a clear need, we will know immediately."

PRICE STERN SLOAN INC., PUBLISHERS, 360 N. La Cienega Blvd., Los Angeles CA 90048. Imprints include Serendipity Books, Bugg Books, Wee Sing Books, Troubador Press and Laughter Library. Publishes trade paperback originals. Averages 200 titles/year; receives 6,000 submissions annually. 20% of books from first-time authors; 60% of books from unagented writers. Pays royalty on wholesale price, or by outright purchase. Offers small or no advance. Publishes book an average of 1 year after acceptance. Computer printout submissions acceptable; no dot-matrix. Reports in 3 months. Ms guidelines for SASE.

Nonfiction: Subjects include humor, self-help (limited), and satire (limited). Juveniles (all ages). Query *only*. "Most titles are unique in concept as well as execution and are geared for the so-called gift market." Reviews artwork/photos as part of ms package. "Do not send original artwork."

Tips: "Humor and satire were the basis of the company's early product and are still the mainstream of the company."

PRIMA PUBLISHING AND COMMUNICATIONS, Cal Co Am., Inc., Box 1260, Rocklin CA 95677. (916)624-5718. Publisher: Ben Dominitz. Publishes hardcover and trade paperback originals and trade paperback reprints. Publishes 30 titles/year. Receives 500 queries/year. Buys 10% of books from first-time authors; 50% from unagented writers. Pays 15-20% royalty on wholesale price. Advance varies. Publishes books an average of 6-9 months after acceptance. Simultaneous and photocopied submissions OK. Query for electronic submissions. Computer printout submissions OK; no dot-matrix. Reports in 2 months. Catalog for 9x12 SAE with $1.25 postage; writer's guidelines for #10 SASE.

Nonfiction: Biography, cookbook, how-to, self-help. Subjects include business and economics, cooking and foods, health, music, politics and psychology. "We want books with originality, written by highly qualified individuals. No fiction at this time." Query.

Recent Nonfiction Title: *Good Cholesterol, Bad Cholesterol*, by Eli Roth, M.D. and Sandra Streicher, R.N.

Tips: "Prima strives to reach the primary and secondary markets for each of its books. We are known for promoting our books aggressively. Books that genuinely solve problems for people will always do well if properly promoted. Try to picture the intended audience while writing the book. Too many books are written to an audience that doesn't exist."

*PRINCETON ARCHITECTURAL PRESS, 37 East 7th St., New York NY 10003. (212)995-9620. Publishes hardcover and trade paperback originals and hardcover reprints. Averages 20 titles/year; receives 20 submissions annually. 50% of books from first-time authors; 100% of books from unagented writers. Subsidy publishes 10% of books; subsidy publishes (nonauthor) 20% of books. Pays 6-10% royalty on wholesale price. Simultaneous and photocopied submissions OK. Query for electronic submissions. Computer printout submissions acceptable; no dot-matrix. Reports in 1 month. Book catalog and guidelines for 8½x11 SAE with 3 first class stamps. "Manuscripts will not be returned unless SASE is enclosed."

Nonfiction: Illustrated book and textbook. Subjects include architecture, landscape architecture and design. Needs texts on architecture, landscape architecture, architectural monographs, and texts to accompany a possible reprint, architectural history and urban design. Submit outline/synopsis and sample chapters or complete ms. Reviews artwork/photos as part of ms package.

Recent Nonfiction Title: *Building Modern Italy, 1914-1936*, by Dennis Doordan.

Tips: "Our audience is architects, designers, urban planners, architectural theorists, and architectural-urban design historians, and many academicians and practitioners. We are still focusing on architecture and architectural history but would like to increase our list of books on design."

*PRINCETON BOOK COMPANY, PUBLISHERS, Box 57, Pennington NJ 08534. (609)737-8177. Imprints include Dance Horizons. President: Charles H. Woodford. Vice President: Richard Carlin. Publishes hardcover originals, trade paperback originals and trade paperback reprints. Firm averages 15 titles/year. Receives 100 submissions/year. 25% of books from first-time authors. 100% from unagented writers. Subsidy publishes 25% of books. Subsidy determined by cost involved in the project. Pays 5-10% on wholesale price. Publishes book an average of 10 months after acceptance. Simultaneous and photocopied submissions OK. Computer printout submissions OK; prefers letter-quality. Reports in 2 weeks on queries; 1 month on mss. Free book catalog.

Nonfiction: Biography, coffee table book, how-to, reference, self-help and textbook. Subjects include education, health/medicine, dance, recreation, sociology, sports and women's issues/studies. "We're looking for textbooks in the fields of dance, physical education, and general education. No autobiographies or special-interest books in dance that have no possibility for use as college texts." Query or submit outline/synopsis and sample chapters. Reviews artwork/photos as part of manuscript package.

Recent Nonfiction Title: *People Who Dance*, by John Gruen (dance trade book).

Tips: "Books that have appeal to both trade and text markets are of most interest to us. Our audience is dance professors, students and professionals. If I were a writer trying to market a book today, I would write with a clear notion of the market in mind. Don't produce a manuscript without first considering what is needed in your field."

‡*PRINCETON UNIVERSITY PRESS, 41 William St., Princeton NJ 08540. (609)452-4900. Imprints include Bollingen Series. Editor-in-Chief: Sanford G. Thatcher. Publishes hardcover and trade paperback originals, hardcover and trade paperback reprints. Averages 265 titles/year. Receives 10,800 submissions/year. Receives 50% of books from first-time authors. 99% from unagented writers. Subsidy publishes 30% of books. "A subsidy is applied in order to make possible selling the book at a reasonable price for its market." Pays 15% on net receipts. Offers advance between $500 and $10,000. Publishes book an average of 1 year after acceptance. Simultaneous and photocopied submissions OK. Query for electronic submission. Computer printout submissions OK; no dot-matrix. Reports in 2 weeks on queries; 1 month on mss. Book catalog and manuscript guidelines free on request.

Nonfiction: Biography, reference, technical, and scholarly works. Subjects include anthropology/archaeology, art/architecture, business and economics, computer science, government/politics, history, language/literature, military/war, music/dance, nature/environment, philosophy, religion, science, sociology, translation, and women's issues/studies. "The books we publish all undergo a process of review by scholarly experts; we welcome submission of books that make significant contributions to scholarship as judged by these experts." Query. Reviews artwork/photos as part of ms package.

Recent Nonfiction Title: *The Complete Works of W.H. Auden, Vol. I: Plays and Other Dramatic Writings, 1928-1938*, edited by Edward Mendelson.

Poetry: "We have two poetry series, but submission is by invitation only."

‡PROBUS PUBLISHING CO., 118 N. Clinton, Chicago IL 60606. (312)346-7985. FAX: (312)346-1184. Executive Vice President: J. Michael Jeffers. Publishes hardcover and paperback originals and trade paperback reprints. Averages 40 titles/year; receives 250 submissions annually. 50% of books from first-time authors; 100% of books from unagented writers. Pays 10-15% royalty on wholesale price; offers average $2,500 advance. Publishes book an average of 5 months after acceptance. Simultaneous and photocopied submissions OK. Query for electronic submissions. Computer printout submissions acceptable; prefers letter-quality. Reports in 1 week on queries; 1 month on mss. Free book catalog; ms guidelines for SASE.

Nonfiction: How-to and technical. Subjects include business, economics and investments. Query or submit outline/synopsis and sample chapters.

Recent Nonfiction Title: *The Intelligent Investor's Guide to Profiting from Stock Market Inefficiencies*, by D. Robert Coulson.

PROFESSIONAL PUBLICATIONS, INC., 1250 Fifth Ave., Belmont CA 94002. (415)593-9119. FAX: (415)592-4519. Acquisitions Editor: Wendy Nelson. Publishes hardcover and paperback originals. Averages 6 titles/year; receives 20-50 submissions annually. Pays 8-12% royalty on wholesale price; offers $2,000 average advance. Sometimes makes outright purchase for $1,000-$2,000. Publishes book an average of 6-18 months after acceptance. Simultaneous and photocopied submissions OK. Query for electronic submissions. Computer printout submissions OK; prefers letter-quality. Reports in 2 weeks on queries; 1 month on mss. Free book catalog.

Nonfiction: Reference, technical and textbook. Subjects include business and economics, mathematics, engineering, accounting, architecture, contracting and building. Especially needs "licensing examination review books for general contractors and lawyers." Query or submit outline/synopsis and sample chapters or complete ms. Reviews artwork/photos as part of ms package.

Recent Nonfiction Title: *Architecture Exam Review*, by David Ballast.

Tips: "We specialize in books for working professionals: engineers, architects, contractors, accountants, etc. The more complex technically the manuscript is the happier we are. We love equations, tables of data, complex illustrations, mathematics, etc. In technical/professional book publishing, it isn't always obvious to us if a market exists. We can judge the quality of a ms, but the author should make some effort to convince us that a market exists. Facts, figures, and estimates about the market—and marketing ideas from the author—will help sell us on the work. Besides our interest in highly technical materials, we will be trying to broaden our range of titles in each discipline. Specifically, we will be looking for career guides for accountants and architects, as well as for engineers."

‡PROLINGUA ASSOCIATES, 15 Elm St., Brattleboro VT 05301. (802)207-7779. Publisher: Arthur A. Burrows. Publishes text paperback originals. Averages 6 titles/year; receives 10 submissions annually. 25% of books from first-time authors. 100% of books from unagented writers. Pays 5-10% royalty on wholesale price; offers $200 average advance. Publishes book an average of 12 months after acceptance. Simultaneous and photocopied submissions OK. Computer printout submissions OK; prefers letter-quality. Reports in 2 weeks on queries; 3 months on mss. Free book catalog.

Nonfiction: Reference and textbook. Subjects include English as a second language, French and Spanish. "We are always willing to consider innovative language texts and language teacher resources which fit with our approach to language teaching. Also interested in intercultural training." Query or submit outline/ synopsis and sample chapters.
Recent Nonfiction Title: *Language Teaching Techniques*, by R.C. Clark (reference).
Tips: "Get a catalog of our books, take a couple of books by ProLingua out of the library or from a nearby language department, ask about ProLingua, and in general try to determine whether your book would fit into ProLingua's list."

‡**PURDUE UNIVERSITY PRESS**, South Campus Courts, Bldg. D, West Lafayette IN 47907. (317)494-2035. Managing Editor: Verna Emery. Publishes hardcover and trade paperback originals and trade paperback reprints. Averages 6 titles/year; receives 100 submissions annually. Pays 10% royalty on retail price. No advance. Publishes book an average of 15 months after acceptance. Photocopied submissions OK. Computer printout submissions acceptable. Reports in 8 weeks on mss. Book catalog and ms guidelines for SASE.
Nonfiction: Biography, textbook, scholarly and regional. Subjects include Americana (especially Indiana), business and economics, history, philosophy, politics, religion, sociology, theories of biology and literary criticism. "The writer must present good credentials, demonstrate good writing skills, and above all explain how his/her work will make a significant contribution to scholarship/regional studies. Our purpose is to publish scholarly and regional books. We are looking for manuscripts on these subjects: theory of biography, Balkan and Danubian history, interdisciplinary, regional interest, horticulture, history, literature, criticism, and effects of science and technology on society. No cookbooks, nonbooks, textbooks, theses/dissertations, manuals/pamphlets, or books on how-to, fitness/exercise or fads." Submit complete ms. Reviews artwork/ photos as part of ms package.
Recent Nonfiction Title: *The Moral Picturesque: Studies in Hawthorne's Fiction*, by Darrel Abel.
Tips: "Scholarly publishers are gearing books in the humanities especially toward the educated layperson so as to widen their audiences, make academic knowledge more accessible, and increase sales. If I were a writer trying to market a book today, I would show a press why publishing my book would help them meet their own long-term goals."

Q.E.D. INFORMATION SCIENCES, INC., 170 Linden St., Box 181, Wellesley MA 02181. (617)237-5656. FAX: (617)235-0826. Executive Vice President: Edwin F. Kerr. Publishes computer books, reports and journals for MIS professionals. Averages 30 titles/year. Pays 10-15% royalty on net sales. Publishes book an average of 4-6 months after acceptance. Query for electronic submissions. Preliminary reports in 1 week on queries; 3 weeks on mss. Free book catalog.
Nonfiction: Technical. Subjects include computers, systems development, personal computing, and database technology. "Our books are read by data processing managers and technicians." Submit outline/synopsis and 2 sample chapters. Reviews artwork/photos as part of ms package.
Recent Nonfiction Title: *SQL Spoken Here*, by Sayles.

***Q.E.D. PRESS OF ANN ARBOR, INC.**, Suite 112, 1008 Island Drive Ct., Ann Arbor MI 48105-2025. (313)994-0371. Managing Editor: Dan Fox. Publishes hardcover and trade paperback originals. Publishes 7 titles/year. Receives 100 submissions/year. 60% of books from first-time authors; 75% from unagented writers. Pays 6-10% royalty on retail price. Publishes book an average of 4 months after acceptance. Simultaneous submissions OK. Query for electronic submissions. Computer printout submissions OK; prefers letter-quality. Subsidy publishes "if the book might not be easily marketable to begin with and we would like to publish it at this point in time but budgetary constraints make it difficult; the option would be we will pick up the tab for reprints." Reports in 3 months on queries; 5 months on mss.
Nonfiction: How-to. Subjects include art/architecture, music/dance (classical, how to set up a studio, piano-related topics), literary criticism, philosophy (existentialism, theory of tragedy). "Music criticism and teaching are high on the list with literary criticism following a close second. How-to and informational books are welcome as well as books about computer technology and in particular, desk-top publishing." Query or submit outline/synopsis and sample chapters.
Recent Nonfiction Title: *Beyond Mystery: A New Look at the Old Testament and Vice Versa.*
Fiction: Literary. Query or submit outline/synopsis and sample chapters.
Recent Fiction Title: *Half Dozen Dutch: Six Writers-in-Residence at American Universities*, edited by Jon Broos.
Tips: "How-to books, informational books and books about computers (desk-top publishing) technology have the best chance of selling to us. Our audience is university professors, local university bookstores, college students, artists and intellectuals. We're looking for books for targeted audience where a small press can better compete with bigger, established publishers."

‡**QUALITY PUBLICATIONS**, Box 770604, Lakewood OH 44107-0030. Publishes mass market paperback originals and reprints. Averages 4 titles/year; receives 96 submissions annually. 75% of books from first-time authors; 100% from unagented writers. Pays 15-25% royalty on retail price. Publishes book average of 1 year after acceptance. Simultaneous and photocopied submissions OK. Computer printout submissions accept-

able. Reports on queries in 1 week; 2-4 months on submissions. Book catalog for #10 SAE with first class stamp; ms guidelines for SASE.

Fiction: Adventure, erotica, historical, mainstream and western. "I'm looking for westerns, and more Vietnam—related stories. Never any pornography." Query or submit outline/synopsis and sample chapters. Reviews artwork/photos.

Recent Fiction Title: *From the Carriage Step*, by Leith Mahren.

Tips: "Our books reach a wide spectrum of the public from blue-collar working people to academics; a pretty fair split of men and women; and through all age ranges from early 20's on up. A writer should simply treat his/her writing as a business, and a tough one at that—that I say from personal experience as a writer."

‡**QUE CORPORATION**, 11711 N. College Ave., Carmel IN 46032. (317)573-2500. Executive Editor/Acquisitions: Terrie Lynn Solomon. Publishes tutorials and application books on popular business software, and trade paperback originals, programming languages and systems and technical books. Receives 500 submissions. 80% of books from first-time authors; 90% of books from unagented writers. Pays 2-15% escalating royalty on net price. Many work-for-hire titles pay a flat fee. Publishes book an average of 4 months after acceptance. Simultaneous (if so advised) and photocopied submissions OK. Computer printout submissions acceptable; prefers letter-quality to dot-matrix. Reports in 1 month. Free book catalog.

Nonfiction: How-to, technical, and reference books relating to microcomputers; textbooks on business use of microcomputers; software user's guides and tutorials; operating systems user's guides; computer programming language reference works; books on microcomputer systems, spreadsheet software business applications, word processing, data base management, time management, popular computer programs for the home, computer graphics, networking, communications, languages, educational uses of microcomputers, computer-assisted instruction in education and business and course-authoring applications. "We will consider books on specific subjects relating to microcomputers." Query or submit outline/synopsis and sample chapters. Reviews artwork/photos as part of ms package.

Recent Nonfiction Title: *Using WordPerfect 5.0*, by Charles Stewart, et al.

‡**QUILL**, Imprint of William Morrow and Co., Inc., subsidiary of The Hearst Corporation, 105 Madison Ave., New York NY 10016. (212)889-3050. Managing Editor: Andrew Ambraziejus. Publishes trade paperback originals and reprints. Averages 40 titles/year; receives over 2,000 submissions annually. 40% of books from first-time authors; 5% of books from unagented writers. Pays royalty on retail price. Offers variable advance. Publishes ms an average of 1 year after acceptance. Simultaneous and photocopied submissions OK. Computer printout submissions acceptable; prefers letter-quality to dot-matrix. No unsolicited mss or proposals; mss and proposals should be submitted through a literary agent. Reports in 3 months.

Nonfiction: Biography and trade books. Subjects include cooking and foods, history, music, psychology, science, and puzzles and games. Needs nonfiction trade paperbacks with enduring importance; books that have backlist potential and appeal to educated people with broad intellectual curiosities. No fiction, poetry, fitness, diet, how-to, self-help or humor. Query.

Recent Nonfiction Title: *The Supreme Court*, by William Rehnquist.

‡*R&E PUBLISHERS**, Box 2008, Saratoga CA 95070. (408)866-6303. Publisher: R. Reed. Hardcover and trade paperback originals. Averages 30 titles/year. Receives 300 submissions/year. 80% of books from first-time authors. 80% from unagented writers. Subsidy publishes 5% of books. Pays 10-20% on wholesale price. Publishes book an average of 6 months after acceptance. Simultaneous and photocopied submissions OK. Query for electronic submissions. Computer printout submissions OK. Reports in 2 months. Free book catalog and manuscript guidelines.

Nonfiction: How-to, humor, illustrated book, reference, self-help, software, technical and textbook. Subjects include business and economics, child guidance/parenting, computers and electronics, cooking, foods and nutrition, education, ethnic, government/politics, health/medicine, history, money/finance, music/dance, nature/environment, philosophy, psychology, regional, science, sociology, travel and women's issues/studies. Query or submit outline/synopsis and sample chapters. Reviews artwork as part of package.

Recent Nonfiction Title: *Rewards Offered by the United States*, by Larry Dreyfus (how-to).

RAINBOW BOOKS, Box 1069, Moore Haven FL 33471. (813)946-0293. Associate Editor: B. A. Lampe. Publishes hardcover, trade paperback originals, video (VHS) and audio tapes. Averages 10-20 titles/year; receives 600 submissions annually. 70% of books from first-time authors; 50% of books from unagented writers. Publishes book an average of 8 months after acceptance. Reports in 2 weeks on queries. Book catalog for 9x6 SAE and 3 first class stamps; ms guidelines for #10 SAE and 2 first class stamps.

Nonfiction: Reference, self-help, how-to and resource books. "Writers without agents query only please."

Recent Nonfiction Title: *Time Out for War*, by E.C. Cury.

Tips: "We may be interested in seeing good fiction. However, by query letter and synopsis only please. We are always interested in seeing good reference and resource books. Please query with what you have before sending it along. No materials returned without proper postage and mailer."

RANDOM HOUSE, INC., Subsidary of Advance Publications, 201 E. 50th St., New York NY 10022. Random House Trade Division publishes 120 titles/year; receives 3,000 submissions annually. Imprints include Vintage, Villard and Random House Juvenile. Pays royalty on retail price. Simultaneous and photocopied submissions OK. Reports in 3 weeks on queries; 6 weeks on mss. Free book catalog; ms guidelines for #10 SASE.

Nonfiction: Biography, cookbook, humor, illustrated book, self-help. Subjects include Americana, art, business and economics, cooking and foods, health, history, music, nature, politics, psychology, religion, sociology and sports. No juveniles or textbooks (separate division). Query with outline/synopsis and sample chapters.

Fiction: Adventure, confession, experimental, fantasy, historical, horror, humor, mainstream, mystery, and suspense. Submit outline/synopsis and sample chapters. "SASE is helpful."

Tips: "If I were a writer trying to market a book today, I would get an agent."

RANDOM HOUSE, INC./ALFRED A. KNOPF, INC. JUVENILE BOOKS, 201 E. 50th St., New York NY 10022. (212)572-2653. Subsidiaries include Knopf Children's Books, Knopf Children's Paperbacks (Bullseye Books, Dragonfly Books and Borzoi Sprinters), Random House Children's Books, Crown Children's Books. Juvenile Division: J. Schulman, Publisher. Managing Editor: R. Abend. Alfred A. Knopf: S. Spinner, Executive Editor. Random House Juvenile: S. Spinner. Associate Publisher: J. O'Connor, Editor-in-Chief. Firm publishes hardcover, trade paperback and mass market paperback originals, and mass market paperback reprints. Publishes 250 titles/year. Simultaneous submissions OK.

Nonfiction: Biography, humor, illustrated book, juvenile. Subjects include animals, nature/environment, recreation, science, sports. Query or submit outline/synopsis and sample chapters. Submit ms through agent only.

Fiction: Adventure, confession (young adult), fantasy, historical, horror, humor, juvenile, mystery, picture books, science fiction (juvenile/young adult), suspense, young adult. Submit through agent only.

Tips: Books for children 6 months to 15 years old.

THE REAL COMET PRESS, Subsidiary of Such a Deal Corporation, #410, 3131 Western Ave., Seattle WA 98121. (206)283-7827. Publisher: Catherine Hillenbrand. Publishes hardcover and trade paperback originals and trade paperback reprints. Averages 6 titles/year; receives 500 submissions annually. 30% of books from first-time authors; 80% from unagented writers. Pays royalty on list or wholesale price. Publishes book an average of 15-24 months after acceptance. Simultaneous and photocopied submissions OK. Computer printout submissions OK. Free book catalog; writer's guidelines for 6×9 SASE.

Nonfiction: Visual books, exhibition catalogs. Subjects include art, contemporary culture, music, photography, politics and social commentary. "Art books, political commentary, social criticism, and books on popular culture have the best chance of selling to our firm." Submit outline/synopsis and sample chapters. Reviews artwork/photos.

Recent Nonfiction Title: *Putting Myself in the Picture*, by Jo Spence.

Tips: "We are increasing the titles on our flipbook list, and are looking for new visual artists/storytellers, who don't necessarily need to be experienced animators. Also looking for unusual autobiographies, especially from people who have been involved in contemporary culture, politics, social issues and activism."

REGNERY/GATEWAY, INC., Imprints/divisions include The American Citizen Reader's Catalogue, Cahill and Co., Gateway Distribution and Fullfillment Services and Gateway Editions, Suite 600, 1130 17th St. N.W., Washington DC 20036. Editor: Harry Crocker. Vice President: Thomas A. Palmer. Publishes hardcover and paperback originals and paperback reprints. Averages 25 titles/year. Pays royalty. "Responds only to submissions in which there is interest." Book catalog for 8½x11 SAE.

Nonfiction: Politics, classics. Queries preferred. Looks for "expertise of the author and salability of the proposed work."

Recent Nonfiction Title: *Senatorial Privilege*, by Leo Damore.

RELIGIOUS EDUCATION PRESS, 5316 Meadow Brook Rd., Birmingham AL 35242. (205)991-1000. Editor: James Michael Lee. Publishes trade paperback originals. Averages 5 titles/year; receives 120 submissions annually. 40% of books from first-time authors; 100% of books from unagented writers. Pays 10% royalty on actual selling price. "Many of our books are work for hire. We do not have a subsidy option." Offers no advance. Photocopied submissions OK. Query for electronic submissions. Computer printout submissions OK; no dot-matrix. Reports in 1 month on queries; 2 months on mss. Free book catalog.

Nonfiction: Technical and textbook. Scholarly subjects on religion and religious education. "We publish serious, significant and scholarly books on religious education and pastoral ministry." No mss under 200 pages, no poetry, books on Biblical interpretation, or "popular" books. Query. Reviews artwork/photos as part of ms package.

Recent Nonfiction Title: *Intergenerational Religious Education*, by James W. White.
Tips: "Write clearly, reason exactly and connectively, and meet deadlines."

‡**RENAISSANCE HOUSE PUBLISHERS**, Subsidiary of Jende-Hagan, Inc., Box 177, 541 Oak St., Frederick CO 80530. (303)833-2030. Editor: Eleanor Ayer. Publishes hardcover and trade paperback originals and trade paperback reprints. Averages 8 titles/year; receives 125 submissions annually. 60% of books from first-time authors; 75% of books from unagented writers. Pays 8-12% royalty on net receipts. Offers average advance of 10% of anticipated first printing royalties. May consider work for hire by experts in specific fields of interest. Publishes book an average of 18 months after acceptance. Simultaneous and photocopied submissions OK. Query for electronic submissions. Computer printout submissions acceptable. Reports in 1 month on queries; 2 months on mss. Book catalog free on request.
Nonfiction: General interest nonfiction. Subjects include Americana, history, regional guidebooks and naturalist philosophy. No fiction, personal reminiscences, general traditional philosophy, children's books, general cookbooks, books on topics totally unrelated to subject areas specified above. Submit outline/synopsis and sample chapters. Reviews artwork/photos as part of ms package.
Recent Nonfiction Title: *Witness to the Execution: The Odyssey of Amelia Earhart*, by T.C. Buddy Brennan.
Tips: "We are going more and more toward in-house generation of book concepts and then finding authors who will write for hire to our specifications. Therefore our acceptance of outside ms will be much less frequent in the future."

*****RESOURCE PUBLICATIONS, INC.**, Suite 290, 160 E. Virginia St., San Jose CA 95112. Editorial Director: Kenneth E. Guentert. Publishes paperback originals. Publishes 14 titles/year; receives 100-200 submissions annually. 30% of books from first-time authors; 99% of books from unagented writers. Average print order for a writer's first book is 2,000. Subsidy publishes 10% of books. "If the author can present and defend a personal publicity effort or otherwise demonstrate demand and the work is in our field, we will consider it." Pays 8% royalty; occasionally offers advance in the form of books. Publishes book an average of 18 months after acceptance. Photocopied submissions (with written assurance that work is not being submitted simultaneously) OK. Query for electronic submissions. Computer printout submissions acceptable; prefers letter-quality. Reports in 2 months.
Nonfiction: "We look for imaginative but practical books relating to celebration, professional growth, and spirituality. How-to books, especially for contemporary religious art forms, are of particular interest (dance, mime, drama, choral reading, singing, music, musicianship, bannermaking, statuary, or any visual art form). No heavy theoretical, philosophical, or theological tomes. Query or submit outline/synopsis and sample chapters. "Prepare a clear outline of the work and an ambitious schedule of public appearances to help make it known and present both as a proposal to the publisher. With our company a work that can be serialized or systematically excerpted in our periodicals is always given special attention." Accepts translations. Reviews artwork/photos as part of ms package.
Recent Nonfiction Title: *Symbols For All Seasons*, by Katherine Krier.
Fiction: "We are not interested in novels or collections of short stories in the usual literary sense. But we look for storytelling resources and collections of short works in the area of drama, dance, song, and visual art, especially if related to worship celebrations, festivals, or mythology." Query or submit outline/synopsis and sample chapters.
Tips: "Books that provide readers with practical, usable suggestions and ideas pertaining to worship, celebration, education, and the arts have the best chance of selling to our firm. We've moved more clearly into the celebration resources field and are looking for resources on popular—as well as little known—celebrations, feasts, and rituals to complement our strong backlist of worship resources."

‡**FLEMING H. REVELL CO.**, Subsidiary of Guideposts, Inc., Central Ave., Old Tappan NJ 07675. Imprints include Power Books and Spire. Vice President/Editor-in-Chief: William J. Petersen. Managing Editor: Jean Pease. Publishes hardcover and paperback originals and reprints. Averages 90 titles/year. 10% of books from first-time authors; 95% of books from unagented writers. Pays royalty on retail price; sometimes offers advance. Publishes book an average of 1 year after acceptance. Computer printout submissions acceptable if letter-quality. No unsolicited mss. Must query.

ALWAYS submit unsolicited manuscripts or queries with a self-addressed, stamped envelope (SASE) within your country or International Reply Coupons (IRC) purchased from the post office for other countries.

Nonfiction: Religion and inspirational. "All books must appeal to Protestant-evangelical readers." Query. Reviews artwork/photos as part of ms package.
Recent Nonfiction Title: *When Caring Parents Have Problem Kids*, by Finley Sizemore.
Fiction: Protestant-evangelical religion and inspiration. Query.
Recent Fiction Title: *Call of the Isles*, by Molly Glass.
Tips: "The writer has the best chance of selling our firm Christian books if she or he has credentials, degree and area of professional expertise."

REVIEW AND HERALD PUBLISHING ASSOCIATION, 55 West Oak Ridge Dr., Hagerstown MD 21740. Acquisitions Editor: Penny Estes Wheeler. Publishes hardcover and paperback originals. Specializes in religious-oriented books. Averages 30-40 titles/year; receives 300 submissions annually. 15% of books from first-time authors; 100% of books from unagented writers. Average print order for a writer's first book is 5,000-7,500. Pays 14% of retail price, hardcover; 12% of retail price, softcover; offers average $500 advance. Publishes book an average of 1 year after acceptance. Computer printout submissions acceptable; prefers letter-quality. Encourages computer diskette submissions. Reports in 3 months. Free brochure; ms guidelines for SASE.
Nonfiction: Juveniles (religious-oriented only), nature, and religious, all 20,000-60,000 words; 128 pages average. Query or submit outline/synopsis and 2-3 sample chapters. Prefers to do own illustrating. Looks for "literary style, constructive tone, factual accuracy, compatibility with Adventist theology and lifestyle, and length of manuscript." Reviews artwork/photos as part of ms package.
Tips: "Familiarize yourself with Adventist theology because Review and Herald Publishing Association is owned and operated by the Seventh-day Adventist Church. We are accepting fewer but better-written manuscripts."

‡**REYMONT ASSOCIATES**, Box 2013, Boca Raton FL 33427. Editor-in-Chief: D.J. Scherer. Managing Editor: Felicia Scherer. Publishes softcover originals. Averages 4 titles annually. Receives 30 submissions annually. 20% from first-time authors; 100% from unagented writers. Average print order for a writer's first book is 1,000. Pays 10-15% royalty on wholesale price; no advance. Publishes book an average of 3 months after acceptance. Computer printout submissions acceptable. Reports in 2 weeks. Book catalog for #10 SASE.
Nonfiction: Publishes business reports, how-to, unique directories, and bibliographies. " 'Net' writing; no rhetoric. Aim for 7,500-10,000 words." Submit outline/synopsis and sample chapter.
Recent Nonfiction Title: *Radon in the Home*, (guide to dealing with risks from radon).
Tips: Trends in book publishing that freelance writers should be aware of include "the need for sharply focused single-subject reports of 7,000-8,000 words in length."

THE RIVERDALE COMPANY, INC., PUBLISHERS, Suite 102, 5506 Kenilworth Ave., Riverdale MD 20737. (301)864-2029. President: John Adams. Vice President: Adele Adams. Editor: Mary Power. Publishes hardcover originals. Averages 16-18 titles/year; receives 100 submissions annually. 20% of books from first-time authors; 100% of books from unagented writers. Pays 0-15% royalty on wholesale price. Publishes book an average of 8 months after acceptance. Computer printout submissions acceptable; prefers letter-quality. Reports in 1 week on queries; 2 months on mss. Book catalog for SASE.
Nonfiction: "We publish technical and social science books for scholars, students, policymakers; and tour, restaurant and recreational guides for the mass market." Subjects include economics, history, humanities, politics, psychology, sociology and travel. Especially needs social science and travel mss on South Asia or Africa. Will consider college text proposals in economics and Third World studies; travel guides of any sort. Query. Accepts outline/synopsis and 2-3 sample chapters.
Recent Nonfiction Title: *Industrial Change in India, 1970-2000*, by George Rosen.

ROCKY TOP PUBLICATIONS, Subsidiary of Rocky Top Industries, Box 33, Stamford NY 12167. President/Publisher: Joseph D. Jennings. Publishes hardcover and paperback originals. Averages 4-6 titles/year. 70% of books from first-time authors; 95% of books from unagented writers. Pays 4-10% royalty (may vary) on wholesale price. Publishes book an average of 6 months after acceptance. Photocopied submissions OK. Computer printout submissions acceptable; prefers letter-quality. No unsolicited mss.
Nonfiction: How-to, reference, self-help and technical. Subjects include animal health; health; hobbies (crafts); medical; nature; philosophy (Thoreau or environmental only); and science. "We are actively looking for exposé-type material on science, medicine and health—well written and researched only." No autobiographies, biographies, business "get rich quick" or fad books.
Recent Nonfiction Title: *The Hydroponic Workbook*, by J. Gooze (technical).
Tips: "Our readers range from self-sufficiency people, to medical and health professionals, environmentalists, and gardeners. Scientific, medical, health, pharmaceutical, and environmental (conservation, naturalist) books have the best chance of selling to us."

RODALE PRESS, Health Books Division, 33 E. Minor St., Emmaus PA 18049. (215)967-5171. Senior Editor: Sharon Faelten. Publishes hardcover and trade paperback originals and reprints. Averages 8-10 titles/year; receives 100 submissions annually. 20% of books from first-time authors; 25% of books from unagented writers. Pays royalty on retail price: 10-15% trade hardcover; 6-7% trade paperback; 2% major mail order or 5% book club. Offers average $10,000 advance. Publishes book an average of 1 year after acceptance. Simultaneous and photocopied submissions OK. Query for electronic submissions. Computer printout submissions acceptable; prefers letter-quality. Reports in 1 month.

Nonfiction: Cookbook, how-to, reference, self-help—all health books. Subjects include health, health psychology and fitness. Especially interested in "how-to books on health care with practical, self-help information by doctors and other health professionals, or by collaborations between experienced medical writers and health care professionals. Also looking for books on walking, bicycling, backpacking, cross-country skiing and other lifetime sports." No technical, textbook, non-health related books. Query with outline/synopsis and sample chapters. Reviews artwork/photos.

Recent Nonfiction Title: *The Healing Foods*, by Patricia Housman and Judith Benn Hurley.

Tips: "Our audience is over 50 years of age, health conscious, mostly women. Writers have the best chance of selling us health books that focus on practical, self-help health care information, with emphasis on mind-body interaction and alternative therapies, especially by pioneers in their field. No childcare/parenting books."

*RONIN PUBLISHING INC., Box 1035, Berkeley CA 94701. (415)540-6278. Publisher: Sebastian Orfal. Publishes originals and trade paperback reprints. Averages 6-8 titles/year; mostly repackaged previously published books.

Nonfiction: How-to (business), humor. Subjects include business and psychology (psychoactive). Query.

Recent Nonfiction Title: *Ecstacy: The MDMA Story*, by Eisner.

THE ROSEN PUBLISHING GROUP, 29 E. 21st St., New York NY 10010. (212)777-3017. President: Roger Rosen. Imprints include Pelion Press (music titles). Publishes hardcover originals. Entire firm averages 46 titles/year; young adult division averages 35 titles/year. 45% of books from first-time authors; 80% of books from unagented writers. Pays royalty or makes outright purchase. Publishes book an average of 9 months after acceptance. Simultaneous and photocopied submissions OK. Computer printout submissions acceptable; prefers letter-quality. Reports in 1 month. Book catalog and guidelines for 8½x11 SAE with 3 first class stamps.

Nonfiction: Young adult, reference, self-help and textbook. Subjects include art, health (coping), and music. "Our books are geared to the young adult audience whom we reach via school and public libraries. Most of the books we publish are related to career guidance and personal adjustment. We also publish material on the theatre, music and art, as well as journalism for schools. Interested in supplementary material for enrichment of school curriculum. We have begun a high/low division and are interested in material that is supplementary to the curriculum written at a 4 reading level for teenagers who are reluctant readers." Mss in the young adult nonfiction areas include vocational guidance, personal and social adjustment, journalism and theatre. For Pelion Press, mss on classical music, emphasis on opera and singing. Query or submit outline/synopsis and sample chapters. Reviews artwork/photos as part of ms package.

Recent Nonfiction Title: *Coping with Sexual Abuse*, by Judith Cooney.

Tips: "The writer has the best chance of selling our firm a book on vocational guidance or personal social adjustment, or high-interest, low reading level material for teens."

ROSS BOOKS, Box 4340, Berkeley CA 94704. FAX: (415)841-2695. President: Franz Ross. Small press. Publishes hardcover and paperback originals, paperback reprints, and software. Averages 7-10 titles/year; receives 200 submissions annually. 90% of books from first-time authors; 99% of books from unagented writers. Average print order for a writer's first book is 5,000-10,000. Offers 8-12% royalty on net price. Offers average advance of 2% of the first print run. Publishes book an average of 1 year after acceptance. Simultaneous and photocopied submissions OK. Query for electronic submissions. Computer printout submissions acceptable; prefers letter-quality. Reports in 1 month. Book catalog for 6x9 SAE with 2 first class stamps.

Nonfiction: Popular how-to on science, business, general how-to. No political, religious or children's books. Accepts nonfiction translations. Submit outline or synopsis of no more than 3 pages and 1 sample chapter with SASE. Reviews artwork/photos as part of ms package.

Recent Nonfiction Title: *Holography Marketplace 1989*, edited by F. Ross, E. Yerkes.

Tips: "We are looking for books on holography and desktop publishing."

ROUNDTABLE PUBLISHING, INC., 933 Pico Blvd., Santa Monica CA 90405. (213)450-9777. Senior Editor: Darrell Houghton. Publishes hardcover and trade paperback originals. Averages 10 titles/year. 25% of books from first-time authors; 10% of books from unagented writers. Pays royalty on retail price. Publishes book an average of 9 months after acceptance. Photocopied submissions OK. Computer printout submissions acceptable; prefers letter-quality. Reports in 2 months.

Nonfiction: Biography, how-to and self-help. Subjects include motion pictures and TV, business and economics, health, politics and psychology. Especially interested in celebrity biographies, how-to or self-help. No cookbooks, history or textbooks. Submit outline/synopsis and sample chapters. Reviews artwork/photos as part of ms package.

Recent Nonfiction Titles: *The Senator Must Die*, by Robert D. Morrow.
Tips: "Our books are for a mainstream audience—children and adult. Writers have the best chance of selling us biographies."

ROUTLEDGE, CHAPMAN & HALL, INC., 29 W. 35th St., New York NY 10001. (212)244-3336. 30 subject editors in the U.K. Editorial Director (New York): William P. Germano. Editor for philosophy, psychoanalysis, education: Maureen MacGrogan. Editor for politics and psychology: Jay Wilson. Editor for women's history: Cecelia Cancellaro. Editor for life sciences: Gregory Payne. Science books published under Chapman and Hall. Humanities and social sciences published under Routledge. New corporate name comprises former imprints Methuen; Routledge & Kegan Paul; Croom Helm; Tavistock. Also publishers of Theatre Arts Books. Chapman & Hall list includes scientific and technical books in life and physical sciences, statistics, allied health, science reference. Routledge list includes humanities, social sciences, business and economics, reference. Monographs, reference works, hardback and paperback upper-level texts, academic general interest. Averages 800 titles/year; receives 5,000 submissions annually. 10% of books from first-time authors; 95% of books from unagented authors. Average royalty 10% net receipts; offers average $1,000 advance. High-quality computer printout submissions acceptable. No simultaneous submissions. Reports in 6 weeks on queries. Do not send manuscripts at initial stage. No replies to unsolicited inquiries without SASE.
Nonfiction: Monograph, textbook, reference work. Academic subjects include reference, biography, philosophy, literary criticism, psychoanalysis, social sciences, business and economics, history, psychology, women's studies, political science, anthropology, geography, education. Scientific subjects include biology, ecology, statistics, materials science, chemistry.

ROXBURY PUBLISHING CO., Box 491044, Los Angeles CA 90049. (213)653-1068. Executive Editor: Claude Teweles. Publishes hardcover and paperback originals and reprints. Averages 10 titles/year. Pays royalty. Simultaneous, photocopied and computer printout submissions OK. Reports in 2 months.
Nonfiction: College-level textbooks only. Subjects include business and economics, humanities, philosophy, psychology, social sciences and sociology. Query, submit outline/synopsis and sample chapters, or submit complete ms.
Recent Nonfiction Title: *The Writing Cycle*, by Clela Allphin-Hoggatt.

‡RUSSELL SAGE, INC., 112 East 64 St., New York NY 10021. (212)750-6037. Director of Publications: Priscilla Lewis. Publishes hardcover and trade paperback originals. Averages 20 titles/year. Receives 50 submissions/year. "Usually, payment is through grant support; book is end result." Publishes book an average of 9 months after acceptance.
Nonfiction: Social science research. Subjects include business and economics, education, ethnic, government, history, psychology, sociology, women's issues/studies, public policy. Query or submit outline/synopsis and sample chapters.
Recent Nonfiction Title: *The Two New Yorks: State-City Relations in the Changing of Federal System*, by Gerald Benjamin and Charles Brecher, editors (politics and public policy).

RUTGERS UNIVERSITY PRESS, 109 Church St., New Brunswick NJ 08901. FAX: (201)932-7039. Averages 50 titles/year; receives 600 submissions annually. 30% of books from first-time authors; 80% of books from unagented writers. Average print order for a writer's first book is 2,000. Pays royalty on retail price. Publishes book an average of 1 year after acceptance. Query for electronic submissions. Computer printout submissions acceptable; no dot-matrix. Final decision depends on time required to secure competent professional reading reports. Book catalog and ms guidelines for 9x12 SAE with 4 first class stamps.
Nonfiction: Scholarly books in history, literary criticism, film studies, art history, anthropology, sociology, science, technology, women's studies and criminal justice. Regional nonfiction must deal with mid-Atlantic region. Length: 60,000 words minimum. Query. Reviews artwork/photos as part of ms package.
Recent Nonfiction Title: *Black Pearls: Blues Queens of the 1920s*, by Daphne Duval Harrison.

‡RUTLEDGE HILL PRESS, 513 Third Ave. S, Nashville TN 37210. (615)244-2700. President: Lawrence Stone. Vice President: Ron Pitkin. Publishes hardcover and trade paperback originals and hardcover and trade paperback reprints. Averages 20 titles/year; receives 250 submissions annually. 40% of books from first-time authors; 90% of books from unagented writers. Pays 10-20% royalty on wholesale price. Publishes book an average of 10 months after acceptance. Photocopied submissions OK. Computer printout submissions OK; prefers letter-quality. Reports in 5 weeks on queries; 3 months on mss. Book catalog for 9x12 SAE and 65¢ postage.
Nonfiction: Biography, "coffee table", cookbook, humor, reference and self-help. "The book must have a market that is primarily in the Southeast." Submit outline/synopsis and sample chapters. Reviews artwork/photos as part of ms package.
Recent Nonfiction Title: *The Moon is Always Full*, by David Hunter.

S.C.E.-EDITIONS L'ETINCELLE, Suite 206, 4920 Blvd. de Maisonneuve W. Westmount, Montreal, Quebec H3Z 1N1 Canada. (514)488-9531. FAX: (514)488-9532. President: Robert Davies. Publishes trade paperback originals in French translation. Averages 12 titles/year; receives 200 submissions annually. 10% of books from first-time authors; 80% of books from unagented writers. Average print order for a writer's first book is 4,000. Pays 8-12% royalty on retail price; offers average $1,000 advance. Publishes book an average of 1 year after acceptance. Simultaneous and photocopied submissions OK. Query for electronic submissions. Computer printout submissions acceptable. Reports in 2 months on queries; 4 months on mss. Book catalog and ms guidelines for 9x12 SAE with 2 IRCs. Imprints include: L'Etincelle (nonfiction and fiction). Memoire Vive (microcomputer books).

Nonfiction: Biography, cookbook, how-to, humor, reference and self-help. Subjects include animals, business and economics, cooking and foods, health, history, hobbies, microcomputers, nature, philosophy, politics, psychology, recreation, sociology, sports and travel. Accepts nonfiction translations. "We are looking for about five translatable works of nonfiction, in any popular field. Our audience includes French-speaking readers in all major markets in the world." No topics of interest only to Americans. Query or submit outline/synopsis and 3 sample chapters. Reviews artwork/photos as part of ms package.

Recent Nonfiction Title: *Starsailing*, by Louis Friedman.

S.O.C.O. PUBLICATIONS, Rd #1, Box 71, Mohawk NY 13407. Publisher: Carol Ann Vercz. Publishes trade paperback originals. Firm averages 15-20 titles/year. Receives 500 submissions/year. 85% of books from first-time authors. 75% from unagented writers. Pays royalty. Simultaneous submissions OK. Query for electronic submissions. Computer printout submissions OK; prefers letter-quality. Reports in 4-6 weeks on queries; 2-4 weeks on mss. Book catalog, manuscript guidelines for 9x12 SAE and $1 postage.

Nonfiction: Biography, coffee table book, cookbook, how-to, humor, self-help, technical and textbook. Subjects include Americana, animals, business and economics, cooking, foods and nutrition, history, hobbies, nature/environment, photography, sports and travel. "Americana, natural history, animals, cookbooks, history and how-to books are our needs. We are not interested in politics or automotive books." Query. Reviews artwork/photos as part of manuscript package.

Recent Nonfiction Title: *Such Agreeable Friends*, by Gay L. Balliet (animals).

Fiction: Subjects include adventure, historical, mainstream/contemporary, mystery, romance, suspense and western. "Suspense, historical and mainstream novels are our needs. We are not interested in erotica or gothic novels." Query.

Poetry: Submit 6-12 samples.

Recent Poetry Title: *To Peter With Love*.

ST. ANTHONY MESSENGER PRESS, 1615 Republic St., Cincinnati OH 45210. Editor-in-Chief: The Rev. Norman Perry, O.F.M. Publishes paperback originals. Averages 14 titles/year; receives 250 submissions annually. 10% of books from first-time authors; 100% of books from unagented writers. Pays 10-12% royalty on net receipts of sales. Offers $600 average advance. Publishes book an average of 1 year after acceptance. Books are sold in bulk to groups (study clubs, high school or college classes, and parishes) and in bookstores. Photocopied submissions OK if they are not simultaneous submissions to other publishers. Query for electronic submissions. Computer printout submissions acceptable; no dot-matrix. Book catalog and ms guidelines for 9x12 SAE with 2 first-class stamps.

Nonfiction: Religion. "We try to reach the Catholic market with topics near the heart of the ordinary Catholic's belief. We want to offer insight and inspiration and thus give people support in living a Christian life in a pluralistic society. We are not interested in an academic or abstract approach. Our emphasis is on popular writing with examples, specifics, color and anecdotes." Length: 25,000-40,000 words. Query or submit outline and 2 sample chapters. Reviews artwork/photos as part of ms package.

Recent Nonfiction Title: *A Story of Jesus: For Those Who Have Only Heard Rumors*, by Leonard Foley, O.F.M. (inspirational).

Tips: "We are looking for aids to parish ministry, prayer, spirituality and liturgy and the sacraments. Also, we are seeking manuscripts that deal with the Catholic identity—explaining it, identifying it, understanding it. The book cannot be the place for the author to think through a subject. The author has to think through the subject first and then tell the reader what is important to know. Style uses anecdotes, examples, illustrations, human interest, 'colorful' quotes, fiction techniques of suspense, dialogue, characterization, etc. Address practical problems, deal in concrete situations, free of technical terms and professional jargon."

‡*ST. BEDE'S PUBLICATIONS, Subsidiary of St. Scholastica Priory, Box 545, Petersham MA 01366. (508)724-3407. Editorial Director: Sr. Mary Joseph, OSB. Publishes hardcover originals, trade paperback originals and reprints. Averages 8-12 titles/year; receives 100 submissions annually. 30-40% of books from first-time authors; 90% of books from unagented writers. Subsidy publishes (nonauthor) 10% of books. Pays 5-10% royalty on wholesale price or retail price. No advance. Publishes book an average of 2 years after acceptance. Simultaneous and photocopied submissions OK. Query for electronic submissions. Computer printout submissions acceptable; no dot-matrix. Reports in 2 weeks on queries; 3 months on mss. Book catalog and ms guidelines for #10 SAE and 45¢ postage.

Nonfiction: Textbook (theology), religion, prayer, spirituality, hagiography, theology, philosophy, church history and related lives of saints fields. "We are always looking for excellent books on prayer, spirituality, liturgy, church or monastic history. Theology and philosophy are important also. We publish English translations of foreign works in these fields if we think they are excellent and worth translating." No submissions unrelated to religion, theology, spirituality, etc. Query or submit outline/synopsis and sample chapters.
Recent Nonfiction Title: *Hammer and Fire*, by Raphael Simon.
Fiction: Historical (only if religious) and religious. "Generally we don't do fiction – but we are willing to look over a manuscript if it fits into our categories." No fiction submissions unrelated to religion. Query or submit outline/synopsis and sample chapters.
Tips: "There seems to be a growing interest in monasticism among lay people and we will be publishing more books in this area during the next couple of years. For our theology/philosophy titles our audience is scholars, colleges and universities, seminaries, etc. For our other titles (i.e. prayer, spirituality, lives of saints, etc.) the audience is above-average readers interested in furthering their knowledge in these areas. Theology seems to be swinging back to studying more conservative lines. We're finding a lot of excellent books being published in France and are getting the rights to translate these. Also, there's a great, general interest in prayer and spirituality so we try to publish really excellent titles in these areas, too. New material, or newly translated material, gets priority."

‡*ST. LUKE'S PRESS, Division of Peachtree Publishers, Ltd., 494 Armour Circle NE, Atlanta GA 30324; Memphis office, Mid-Memphis Tower, 1407 Union, Memphis TN 38104. (901)357-5441. Managing Editor: Roger Easson, Ph.D. Averages 8-10 titles/year; receives 3,000 submissions annually. 90% of books from unagented writers. Average print order for a writer's first book is 5,000. Subsidy publishes (nonauthor) 10% of books. Pays 10% minimum royalty on monies received; offers average $1,000-5,000 advance. Publishes book an average of 2 years after acceptance. Query for electronic submissions. Computer printout submissions acceptable. Reports in 3 months. Book catalog $1.
Fiction: Submit story line and 3 sample chapters.
Recent Fiction Title: *Edge*, by John Osier.

ST. MARTIN'S PRESS, 175 5th Ave., New York NY 10010. Averages 1,100 titles/year; receives 3,000 submissions annually. 15-20% of books from first-time authors; 30% of books from unagented writers. Query for electronic submissions. Computer printout submission acceptable; prefers letter-quality. Reports "promptly."
Nonfiction and Fiction: General and textbook. Publishes general fiction and nonfiction; major interest in adult fiction and nonfiction, history, self-help, political science, popular science, biography, scholarly, popular reference, etc. Query. Reviews artwork/photos as part of ms package. "It takes very persuasive credentials to prompt us to commission a book or outline."
Recent Title: *Hot Flashes*, by Barbara Raskin.
Tips: "We do almost every kind of book there is – trade, textbooks, reference and mass market. Crime fiction has the best chance of selling to our firm – over fifteen percent of all the trade books we published are this category."

ST. PAUL BOOKS AND MEDIA, Daughters of St. Paul, 50 St. Paul's Ave., Boston MA 02130. (617)522-8911. FAX: (617)522-4081. Director, Editorial Department: Sister Mary Mark, FSP. Firm publishes hardcover, trade paperback originals, and hardcover and trade paperback reprints. Average 20 titles/year; receives approximately 200 proposals/year. Pays authors 10-15% royalty on wholesale price. Advance is negotiable. Publishes ms an average of 12-18 months after acceptance. Photocopied submissions OK. Computer printout submissions OK; no dot-matrix. Reports in 2 weeks on queries; in 6 weeks on mss. Book catalog free; ms guidelines for #10 SASE.
Nonfiction: Biography, juvenile, self-help. Subjects include child guidance/parenting, psychology and religion. "No strictly secular manuscripts." Query or submit outline/synopsis and sample chapters.
Recent Nonfiction Title: *Living in Love*, by Rhonda Chervin (Christian ethics).
Fiction: Juvenile, religious, young adult. "We want books promoting moral values for children, adolescents and young adults." Query or submit outline/synopsis and sample chapters.
Tips: "We are looking for books with a religious and/or moral orientation."

***ST. VLADIMIR'S SEMINARY PRESS**, 575 Scarsdale Rd., Crestwood NY 10707. (914)961-8313. Managing Director: Theodore Bazil. Publishes hardcover and trade paperback originals and reprints. Averages 15 titles/ year. Subsidy publishes 20% of books. Market considerations determine whether an author should be subsidy published. Pays 7% royalty on retail price. Simultaneous and photocopied submissions OK. Computer printout submissions acceptable; prefers letter-quality. Reports in 3 months on queries; 9 months on mss. Free book catalog and ms guidelines.
Nonfiction: Religion dealing with Eastern Orthodox theology. Query. Reviews artwork/photos as part of ms package.
Tips: "We have an interest in books that stand on firm theological ground; careful writing and scholarship are basic."

‡**SAN FRANCISCO PRESS, INC.**, Box 6800, San Francisco CA 94101-6800. (415)524-1000. President: Terry Gabriel. Publishes hardcover originals and trade paperback originals and reprints. Averaes 5-10 titles/year. Receives 25-50 submissions/year. 50% of books from first-time authors. 100% from unagented writers. Pays 10-15% on wholesale price. Publishes book an average of 6 months after acceptance. Simultaneous and photocopied submissions OK. Computer printout submissions OK. Reports in 1 month on queries; 2 weeks on mss. Book catalog for #10 SAE and 1 first-class stamp.

Nonfiction: Biography, technical and textbook. Subjects include computers and electronics, education, government/politics, history, music and science. Submit outline/synopsis and sample chapters.

Recent Nonfiction Title: *Sound Judgment: Basic Ideas About Music*, by J.P. Swain (textbook).

Tips: "Our books are aimed at specialized audiences (e.g., engineers, public health specialists, scholars, students)."

SANDLAPPER PUBLISHING, INC., Box 1932, Orangeburg SC 29116. (803)531-1658. Acquisitions: Nancy M. Drake. Publishes hardcover and trade paperback originals and reprints. Averages 6 titles/year; receives 200 submissions annually. 80% of books from first-time authors; 95% of books from unagented writers. Pays 15% maximum royalty on net receipts. Publishes book on average of 20 months after acceptance. Photocopied submissions OK; simultaneous submissions OK if informed. Computer printout submissions acceptable. Reports in 1 month on queries; 6 months on mss. Book catalog and ms guidelines for 9x12 SAE with 4 first class stamps.

Nonfiction: History, biography, illustrated books, humor, cookbook, juvenile (ages 9-14), reference and textbook. Subjects are limited to history, culture and cuisine of the Southeast and especially South Carolina. "We are looking for manuscripts that reveal underappreciated or undiscovered facets of the rich heritage of our region. If a manuscript doesn't deal with South Carolina or the Southeast, the work is probably not appropriate for us. We don't do self-help books, children's books about divorce, kidnapping, etc., and absolutely no religious manuscripts." Query or submit outline synopsis and sample chapters "if you're not sure it's what we're looking for, otherwise complete ms." Reviews artwork/photos as part of ms package.

Recent Nonfiction Title: *The South Carolina Story*, by Anne R. Osborne.

Fiction: We do not need fiction submissions at present, "but I will look at good strong fiction by South Carolinians and other regional writers. We will not consider any horror, romance or religious fiction." Query or submit outline/synopsis and sample chapters. "Do check with us on books dealing with regional nature, science and outdoor subjects."

Tips: "Our readers are South Carolinians, visitors to the region's tourist spots, and friends and family that live out-of-state. We are striving to be a leading regional publisher for South Carolina. We will be looking for more history and biography."

SASQUATCH BOOKS, 1931 Second Ave., Seattle WA 98101. (206)441-5555. FAX: (206)441-6213. Managing Editor: Anne DePue. Firm publishes hardcover and trade paperback originals. Averages 6-8 titles/year. 25% of books from first-time authors; 95% from unagented writers. Pays authors 5-12% royalty on net price. Offers wide range of advances. Publishes ms an average of 6 months after acceptance. Simultaneous and photocopied submissions OK. Query for electronic submissions. Computer printout submissions OK. Reports in 1 month. Free book catalog.

Nonfiction: Subjects include art/architecture, business and economics, cooking, foods and nutrition, gardening, government/politics, history, language/literature, nature/environment, photography, recreation, regional, sports and travel. "We are only seeking quality nonfiction works by, about or for people of the Pacific Northwest region. In this sense we are a regional publisher, but we do distribute our books nationally, depending on the title." Submit outline/synopsis and sample chapters.

Recent Nonfiction Title: *Seattle Best Places*, by Brewster and Robinson.

Tips: "We sell books through a range of channels in addition to the book trade. Our audience consists of active, literate residents of the Pacific Northwest."

SCARECROW PRESS, INC., 52 Liberty St., Metuchen NJ 08840. Vice President of Editorial: Norman Horrocks. Senior Editor: Barbara Lee. Publishes hardcover originals. Averages 110 titles/year; receives 600-700 submissions annually. 70% of books from first-time authors; 100% of books from unagented writers. Average print order for a writer's first book is 1,000. Pays 10% royalty on net of first 1,000 copies; 15% of net price thereafter. 15% initial royalty on camera-ready copy. Offers no advance. Publishes book 1 year after receipt of ms. Photocopied submissions OK. Query for electronic submissions. Computer printout submissions acceptable. Reports in 2 weeks. Free book catalog.

Nonfiction: Books about music. Needs reference books and meticulously prepared annotated bibliographies, indexes, women's studies, movies and stage. Query. Occasionally reviews artwork/photos as part of ms package.

Tips: "Essentially we consider any scholarly title likely to appeal to libraries. Emphasis is on reference material, but this can be interpreted broadly, provided author is knowledgeable in the subject field."

‡**SCHIFFER PUBLISHING LTD.**, 1469 Morstein Rd., West Chester PA 19380. (215)696-1001. President: Peter Schiffer. Publishes originals and reprints, trade paperback originals and reprints. Firm averages 50 titles/year; imprint averages 40 titles/year. Receives 500 submissions/year. 90% of books from first-time authors. 95% from unagented writers. Royalty on wholesale price. Publishes book an average of 6 months after acceptance. Simultaneous and photocopied submissions OK. Computer printout submissions OK; prefers letter-quality. Reports in 1 week on queries. Free book catalog.
Nonfiction: Coffeetable book, how-to, illustrated book, reference and textbook. Subjects include Americana, art/architecture, history, hobbies, military/war and regional. "We want books on collecting, hobby carving, military, architecture, aeronautic history and natural history." Query. Submit outline/synopsis and sample chapters. Reviews artwork/photos as part of ms package.
Recent Nonfiction Title: *American Wristwatches*, by Faber & Unger, (history of American wristwatch).

SCHIRMER BOOKS, Macmillan Publishing Co., Inc., 866 3rd Ave., New York NY 10022. FAX: (212)319-1216. Editor-in-Chief: Maribeth Anderson Payne. Publishes hardcover and paperback originals, related audio recordings, paperback reprints and some software. Averages 20 books/year; receives 250 submissions annually. 40% of books from first-time authors; 95% of books from unagented writers. Average print order for a writer's first book is 3,000-5,000. Pays royalty on wholesale or retail price; offers small advance. Submit photos and/or illustrations "if central to the book, not if decorative or tangential." Publishes book an average of 1 year after acceptance. Query for electronic submissions. Computer printout submissions acceptable; prefers letter-quality. Reports in 2 months. Book catalog and ms guidelines for SASE.
Nonfiction: Publishes college texts, biographies, scholarly, reference and how-to on the performing arts specializing in music, also dance and theatre. Needs texts or scholarly mss for college or scholarly audience. Submit outline/synopsis and sample chapters and current vita. Reviews artwork/photos as part of ms package.
Recent Nonfiction Title: *Listen to the Music*, by Jonathan Kramer.
Tips: "The writer has the best chance of selling our firm a music book with a clearly defined, reachable audience, either scholarly or trade. Must be an exceptionally well-written work of original scholarship prepared by an expert in that particular field who has a thorough understanding of correct manuscript style and attention to detail (see the Chicago *Manual of Style*)."

SCHOLASTIC, INC., 730 Broadway, New York NY 10003. (212)505-3000. Executive Editor: Ann Reit. Publishes trade paperback originals. Averages 36 titles/year. Pays 6% royalty on retail price. Computer printout submissions acceptable; no dot-matrix. Reports in 3 months. Ms guidelines for #10 SASE.
Fiction: Romance and historical romance scholastic, family mysteries, school and friendships for ages 8-12. YA fiction, romance, family and mystery for ages 12-16. Also nonfiction. Books should be 40,000-45,000 words for girls ages 12-15 who are average to good readers. Query.
Tips: Queries/mss may be routed to other editors in the publishing group.

‡*SCIENCE TECH PUBLISHERS, INC.**, 701 Ridge St., Madison WI 53705. (608)238-8664. Book publisher and independent book producer/packager. Managing Editor: Katherine Brock. Publishes hardcover originals and reprints and paperback originals. Firm averages 8-10 titles/year. Receives 20 submissions/year. 90% of books from first-time authors. 95% from unagented authors. Subsidy publishes 5-10% of books. "Subsidy used only if his book is outside our normal area, so that we can't market it well." Pays 10% on wholesale price. Offers $500-1,000 average advance. Publishes book an average of 1 year after acceptance. Simultaneous and photocopied submissions OK. Query for electronic submissions. Computer printout submissions OK; prefers letter-quality. Reports in 3 weeks on queries; 3 weeks on mss. Book catalog free. Manuscript quidelines "available on individual basis."
Nonfiction: Biography, reference, technical and textbook. Subjects include agriculture, health/medicine, history of science and science. "We will examine high-level references or monographs in various areas of science, history of science, biographies of scientists." Query. Submit outline/synopsis and sample chapters or complete mss. Reviews artwork/photos as part of ms package.
Recent Nonfiction Title: *Robert Koch, a Life in Medicine and Bacteriology*, by T.D. Brock, (biography).
Fiction: "Possibly YA fiction with solid *science* orientation." Query. Submit outline/synopsis and sample chapters or complete ms.
Tips: "Writers have the best chance of selling us high quality monographs in field of research specialty. Authors generally are scientists. Biographies also welcome, at high academic level in general. Research and professional scientists; university and public libraries are our audience."

‡*SCOJTIA PUBLISHING CO., INC.**, Imprint of The Lion, 6457 Wilcox Station, Box 38002, Los Angeles CA 90038. (213)734-7384. Managing Editor: Patrique Quintahlen. Publishes hardcover originals and trade paperback originals and reprints. Firm averages 5 titles/year. Receives 150 submissions/year. 80% of books from first-time authors. 20% from unagented writers. Subsidy publishes 1% of books. "If a book project has a sentimental, family, romantic interest to the author, we will consider it for subsidy publishing." Pays 8-15% on retail price. Offers $1,000-$5,000 average advance. Publishes book an average of 1-1½ years after acceptance. Simultaneous and photocopied submissions OK. Query for electronic submissions. Computer

printout submissions OK; prefers letter-quality. Reports in 4 months on queries; 6 months on mss.

Nonfiction: Biography, cookbook, how-to, humor, illustrated book, juvenile, reference, self-help, technical and textbook. Subjects include agriculture/horticulture, anthropology/archaeology, art/architecture, business (job search and career planning; international and national marketing and sales, investing) and economics, child guidance/parenting, computers and electronics, cooking, foods and nutrition, education, ethnic, gardening, government/politics, health/medicine, history, language/literature, military/war, money/finance, music/dance, nature/environment, philosophy, photography, psychology, recreation, religion (books on spiritual progress), science, translation, travel and women's issues/studies. "We are looking for works of nonfiction on the subjects of new trends in college living; books on starting, managing and selling a business today (entrepreneuring); books on writing fiction and nonfiction books, self publishing, editing and publishing; nutrition and vitamin therapy (enzymes); relationship problems, overcoming them; finding love, breaking the cycle of divorce in today's generations." Query first; submit outline/synopsis with 3 sample chapters. Reviews artwork/photos as part of ms package.

Recent Nonfiction Title: *Roommates, College Sublets, and Living in the Dorm*, by Prentiss Van Daves, (how to/self-help).

Fiction: Adventure, experimental, fantasy, historical, humor, juvenile, literary, mainstream/contemporary, mystery, plays, romance, science fiction, short story collections, suspense, western and young adult. "We are looking for literary works of science fiction, romance or those that are historical in subject matter."

Poetry: "Submissions must be written from a self-help perspective. The subjects must be inspiring, uplifting and enlightening from insights in psychology, philosophy, and the American traditional way of life anew in today's world. We are particularly interested in poetry about love, and the new male female relationships today." Submit 3 samples.

CHARLES SCRIBNER'S SONS, Children's Books Department, 866 Third Ave., New York NY 10022. (212)702-7885. FAX: (212)319-1216. Editorial Director, Children's Books: Clare Costello. Publishes hardcover originals and paperback reprints of own titles. Averages 20-25 titles/year. Pays royalty on retail price; offers advance. Publishes book an average of 1 year after acceptance. Photocopied submissions OK. Computer printout submissions acceptable. Reports in 2 weeks on queries; in 10 weeks on mss. Free book catalog and ms guidelines.

Nonfiction: Subjects include animals, biography, health, hobbies, humor, nature, photography, recreation, science, sports and juvenile, for ages 3-14. Query. Reviews artwork/photos as part of ms package.

Recent Nonfiction Title: *The Birth of a Nation*, by Harold and Doris Faber.

Fiction: Adventure, fantasy, historical, humor, mystery, picture books, science fiction and suspense. Submit outline/synopsis and sample chapters.

Recent Fiction Title: *Lisa's War*, by Carol Matas.

SECOND CHANCE PRESS/PERMANENT PRESS, #2, Noyac Rd., Sag Harbor NY 11963. (516)725-1101. Editor: Judith Shepard. Publishes hardcover originals and reprints. Second Chance Press devotes itself exclusively to re-publishing fine books that are out of print and deserve continued recognition. Permanent Press publishes original fiction and some books of social and/or political significance. Averages 12 titles/year; receives 1,000 submissions annually. 25% of books from first-time authors; 75% of books from unagented writers. Average print order for a writer's first book is 2,000. Pays 10% maximum royalty on wholesale price; offers average $1,000 advance for Permanent Press books only. Publishes book an average of 18 months after acceptance. Simultaneous and photocopied submissions OK. Computer printout submissions acceptable; prefers letter-quality. Reports in 2 weeks on queries; 3 months on mss. Book catalog for $2 postage.

Nonfiction: Biography, autobiography and current events. Subjects include Americana, history, philosophy and politics. No scientific and technical material or academic studies. Query.

Recent Nonfiction Title: *1933*, by Philip Metcalfe.

Fiction: Adventure, confession, ethnic, experimental, fantasy, historical, humor, mainstream, mystery, and suspense. Especially looking for fiction with a unique point of view—"original and arresting" suitable for college literature classes. No mass market romance. Query.

Recent Fiction Title: *Who Dwelt by a Churchyard*, by Berry Fleming.

SERVANT PUBLICATIONS, 840 Airport Blvd., Box 8617, Ann Arbor MI 48107. (313)761-8505. Editor: Ann Spangler. Publishes hardcover, trade and mass market paperback originals and trade paperback reprints. Averages 30 titles/year. 5% of books from first-time authors; 95% of books from unagented writers. Pays 8-10% royalty on retail price. Publishes book an average of 1 year after acceptance. Computer printout submissions acceptable. Reports in 2 months. Free book catalog; writer's guidelines for #10 SASE.

Nonfiction: Subjects include religion. "We're looking for practical Christian teaching, scripture, current problems facing the Christian church, and inspiration." No heterodox or non-Christian approaches. Query or submit brief outline/synopsis and 1 sample chapter. All unsolicited mss are returned unopened. Reviews artwork/photos as part of ms package.

Recent Nonfiction Title: *Against the Night*, by Chuck Colson.

SEVEN LOCKS PRESS, INC., Box 27, Cabin John MD 20818. (301)320-2130. Imprint is Isidore Stephanus Sons Publishing. President/Publisher: James McGrath Morris. Editor: Anne Stanfield. Publishes hardcover and trade paperback originals, and hardcover and trade paperback reprints. Averages 6-9 titles/year; receives 100 submissions annually. 50% of books from first-time authors; 50% of books from unagented writers. Pays 8-15% royalty of retail price. Simultaneous and photocopied submissions OK. Computer printout submissions acceptable; no dot-matrix. Reports in 1 month on queries; 3 months on mss. Free book catalog.

Nonfiction: Biography, reference and textbook. Subjects include Americana, business and economics, history, international relations, nature, politics, religion and sociology. Especially needs "books that promise to enlighten public policy; also, books of regional interest that are entertaining." Query or submit outline/synopsis and sample chapters. Reviews artwork/photos as part of ms package.

Recent Nonfiction Title: *The Secret Government: The Constitution In Crisis*, by Bill Moyers (public affairs).

Tips: "Literate, intelligent, socially conscious men and women are our readers."

*SHAPOLSKY PUBLISHERS, 136 W. 22nd St., New York NY 10011. (212)633-2022. FAX: (212)633-2123. Editorial Director: Isaac Mozeson. Publishes hardcover and paperback originals, hardcover and trade paperback reprints. 75% originals and 25% reprints. Averages 35 titles/year; receives 300 submissions annually. 60% of books from first-time authors; 40% of books from unagented writers. Subsidy publishes 2% of books. Pays 5-10% royalty on retail price. Offers average $1,000 advance. Publishes ms an average of 15 months after acceptance. Simultaneous and photocopied submissions OK. Query for electronic submissions. Computer printout submissions OK; prefers letter-quality. Reports on queries in 3 weeks; 5 weeks on ms. Free book catalog.

Nonfiction: Subjects include art, cooking and foods, history, juvenile (for ages 4 and up.) Philosophy, photography, politics, religion, sports and travel. "The major thrust of our list is light and lively Judaica. No memoirs." Query or submit outline/synopsis and sample chapters. Reviews artwork/photos as part of package.

Recent Nonfiction Title: *Contract On America: The Mafia Murder of President John F. Kennedy*, by David E. Scheim.

Fiction: "Must be by a well established author." Query.

Recent Fiction Title: *Uncle Misha's Partisans: The Story of Young Freedom Fighters in Nazi-Occupied Europe*.

Tips: "Religious and ethnic books enjoy a growing demand. 60% of our books are general interest; 40% are Jewish interest."

HAROLD SHAW PUBLISHERS, 388 Gundersen Dr., Box 567, Wheaton IL 60189. (312)665-6700. Director of Editorial Services: Ramona Cramer Tucker. Publishes hardcover and trade paperback originals and reprints. Averages 26 titles/year; receives 2,000 submissions annually. 10% of books from first-time authors; 90% of books from unagented writers. Offers 5-10% royalty on retail price. Sometimes makes outright purchase for $1,000-2,500. Publishes book an average of 15 months after acceptance. Photocopied submissions OK. Reports in 1 month on queries; 6 weeks on mss. Book catalog and ms guidelines for 9x12 SAE with $1 postage.

Nonfiction: Juvenile (Bible studies only), reference and self-help. Subjects include history (of religious movements/evangelical/charismatic), psychology (self-help) and religion (Bible study guides and general religion). "We are looking for general nonfiction, with different twists—self-help manuscripts on issues and topics with fresh insight and colorful, vibrant writing style. We already have how to forgive yourself, or defend yourself, and how to deal with cancer, death and handicaps. No autobiographies or biographies accepted. Must have an evangelical Christian perspective for us even to review the ms." Query. Reviews artwork/photos as part of ms package.

Recent Nonfiction Title: *When You Feel Like Screaming*, by Pat Holt and Grace Ketterman.

Tips: "Get an editor who is not a friend or a spouse who will tell you honestly whether your book is marketable. It will save a lot of your time and money and effort. Then do an honest evaluation of yourself and the book. Most writers who send in mss say this is for everyone. Most books that are written are for no one but the writer. Evaluate who would actually read the book other than yourself—will it do others enough good to sell 5,000 copies?"

‡THE SHEEP MEADOW PRESS, Box 1345, Riverdale-on-Hudson NY 10471. (212)549-3321. Publisher: Stanley Moss. Editor-in-Chief: George Wen. Publishes trade paperback originals. Firm averages 8-9 titles/year. receives 20 submissions/year. 75% of books from first-time authors. 100% from unagented writers. Pays royalty. Computer printout submissions OK; no dot-matrix. Reports in 3 weeks on queries; 3 months on mss. Book catalog for 6x9 SAE with 1 first class stamp.

Poetry: "We are always in the market for original manuscripts." Submit complete ms.

Recent Poetry Title: *The Lime Orchard Woman*, by Alberto Rios.

SHOE TREE PRESS, (formerly McDonald Press), Imprint of Betterway Publications, RD2, Box 1162, Hemlock Rd., Columbia NJ 07832. (201)496-4441. Editor: Joyce McDonald. Publishes juvenile/hardcover and trade paperback originals and reprints. Averages 4 titles/year. 25% of books from first-time authors; 25% of books from unagented writers. Pays 10% royalty on hardcover; 5-7% on trade paperbacks; "sometimes on wholesale price, usually on retail price. Maximum royalty on hardcover only." Advance negotiable. Publishes book an average of 18 months after acceptance. Simultaneous and photocopied submissions OK. Computer printout submissions OK; prefers letter-quality. Reports in 1 month on queries; 3 months on mss. Guidelines for #10 SASE.

Nonfiction: Juvenile books on Americana, animals, art, cooking and foods, health, history, hobbies, music, nature, recreation, sports and travel. "Books focusing on the problems of growing up have the best chance of being considered. We are also looking for nature and environmental books. No textbook manuscripts." Query with proposal. Reviews artwork/photos as part of ms package. No unsolicited mss.

Recent Nonfiction Title: *Four Feet*, by Gretchen Alday.

Fiction: Juvenile adventure, historical, humor, mainstream. "Humorous novels and adventure stories are preferred. We do not publish picture books. No 'formula' books." Query.

Tips: "Authors have the best chance of selling us timely nonfiction for 8-11-year-olds."

MICHAEL SHORE ASSOCIATES, 24 Westfield Rd., Milford CT 06460. (203)877-9218. Owner/Director: Michael Shore. Publishes trade paperback originals. Firm averages up to 5 titles/year. Receives 10 submissions/year. 75% of books from unagented writers. Pays 10% maximum royalty on retail price. Publishes book an average of 1 year in advance. Simultaneous and photocopied submissions OK. Computer printout submissions OK; prefers letter-quality. Reports on queries in 6 weeks; on mss in 3 months.

Nonfiction: How-to and self-help. "We prefer to see self-help manuscripts for the average reader which aid him in dealing with everyday problems and situations, i.e., 'What to do When You've Been Fired,' 'Relating to Your Family and Friends More Positively,' etc. We do not want first-person anecdotes (How I Lost 75 Pounds on the Grapefruit Diet, Dealing with My Two-Year-Old) or pop psychology manuscripts not thoroughly researched." Query or submit complete ms. Reviews artwork/photos as part of ms package.

Recent Nonfiction Title: *Acting Techniques for Salespeople*.

Tips: "We've noticed a taste for simple, usable techniques for self-improvement. Self-instruction and practical exercises are popular for us. We expect this trend to continue. Our audience is comprised of anyone who envisions an improved life-style for himself, whether materially (better job, better pay) or psychologically (fewer fears, more ability to cope, better relationships)."

SIERRA CLUB BOOKS, 730 Polk St., San Francisco CA 94109. (415)776-2211. Editor-in-Chief: Daniel Moses. Publishes hardcover and paperback originals and reprints. Averages 20 titles/year; receives 500 submissions annually. 50% of books from unagented writers. Pays 7-12½% royalty on retail price. Offers average $3,000-5,000 advance. Publishes book an average of 12-18 months after acceptance. Computer printout submissions acceptable. Reports in 2 months. Free book catalog.

Nonfiction: Animals; health; history (natural); how-to (outdoors); juveniles; nature; philosophy; photography; recreation (outdoors, nonmechanical); science; sports (outdoors); and travel (by foot or bicycle). "The Sierra Club was founded to help people to explore, enjoy and preserve the nation's forests, waters, wildlife and wilderness. The books program looks to publish quality trade books about the outdoors and the protection of natural resources. Specifically, we are interested in nature, environmental issues such as nuclear power, self-sufficiency, natural history, politics and the environment, and juvenile books with an ecological theme." Does *not* want "personal, lyrical, philosophical books on the great outdoors; proposals for large color photographic books without substantial text; how-to books on building things outdoors; books on motorized travel; or any but the most professional studies of animals." Query first, submit outline/synopsis and sample chapters. Reviews artwork/photos ("duplicates, not originals") as part of ms package.

Recent Nonfiction Title: *History of the Sierra Club 1892-1970*, by Michael Cohen.

Fiction: Adventure, historical, mainstream and ecological fiction. "We do very little fiction, but will consider a fiction manuscript if its theme fits our philosophical aims: the enjoyment and protection of the environment." Does *not* want "any manuscript with animals or plants that talk; apocalyptic plots." Query first, submit outline/synopsis and sample chapters, or submit complete ms.

SILHOUETTE BOOKS, Division of Harlequin Enterprises, 300 E. 42nd St., New York NY 10017. (212)682-6080. Vice President and Executive Editor, Harlequin and Silhouette: Karen Solem. Publishes mass market paperback originals. Averages 336 titles/year; receives 4,000 submissions annually. 10% of books from first-time authors; 25% of books from unagented writers. Pays royalty. Publishes book an average of 1 year after acceptance. Computer printout submissions acceptable; no dot-matrix. No unsolicited mss. Send query letter; 2 page synopsis and SASE to head of imprint. Ms guidelines for #10 SASE.

Imprints: Silhouette Romances (contemporary adult romances), Tara Hughes, Senior Editor; 53,000-58,000 words. Silhouette Special Editions (contemporary adult romances), Leslie Kazanjian, Senior Editor; 75,000-80,000 words. Silhouette Desires (contemporary adult romances), Isabel Swift, Senior Editor and Editorial Coordinator; Lucie Macro, Senior Editor; 55,000-60,000 words. Silhouette Intimate Moments (contemporary adult romances), Leslie Wainger, Senior Editor; 80,000-85,000 words. Harlequin Historicals (adult historical romances), Tracy Farrell and Eliza Schallcross, Editors; 95-105,000 words.

Fiction: Romance (contemporary and historical romance for adults). "We are interested in seeing submissions for all our lines. No manuscripts other than the types outlined above." Ms should "follow our general format, yet have an individuality and life of its own that will make it stand out in the readers' minds."

Recent Fiction Title: *Meckeneir's Mountain*, by Linda Howard.
Tips: "The romance market is constantly changing, so when you read for research, read the latest books and those that have been recommended to you by people knowledgeable in the genre. We are actively seeking new authors for all our lines, contemporary and historical."

‡**SILVER BURDETT PRESS**, Imprint of Simon & Schuster, 190 Sylvan Ave., Englewood Cliffs NJ 07632. FAX: (201)592-8005. President: Carole Cushmore, Editor-in-Chief: Bonnie Brook. Publishes hardcover and paperback originals. Averages 65-80 titles/year; does not accept unsolicited manuscripts. Publishes book an average of one year after acceptance. Offers variable advance. Simultaneous submissions OK. Free book catalog.
Nonfiction: Juvenile and young adult reference. Subjects include Americana, science, history, nature, and geography. "We're primarily intersted in nonfiction for students on subjects which supplement the classroom curricula, but are graphically apealing and, in some instances, have commercial as well as institutional appeal."
Recent Nonfiction Title: *The Tet Offensive* (Turning Point Series).
Tips: "Our books are primarily bought by school and public librarians for use by students and young readers. Virtually all are nonfiction and done as part of a series."

SIMON & SCHUSTER, Trade Books Division, 1230 Avenue of the Americas, New York NY 10020. "We do not accept unsolicited manuscripts. Only manuscripts submitted by agents or recommended to us by friends or actively solicited by us will be considered. In such cases, our requirements are as follows: Manuscripts must be typewritten, double-spaced, on one side of the sheet only. We suggest margins of about one and one half inches all around and the standard 8x11 typewriter paper." Computer printout submissions acceptable; prefers letter-quality.
Nonfiction and Fiction: "Simon and Schuster publishes books of general adult fiction, history, biography, science, philosophy, the arts and popular culture, running 50,000 words or more. Our program does not, however, include school textbooks, extremely technical or highly specialized works, or, as a general rule, poetry or plays. Exceptions have been made, of course, for extraordinary manuscripts of great distinction or significance."

GIBBS SMITH, PUBLISHER, Peregrine Smith Books, Box 667, Layton UT 84041. (801)544-9800. Editorial Director: Madge Baird. Publishes hardcover and paperback originals and reprints. Averages 25-30 titles/ year; receives 1,000 submissions annually. 25% of books from first-time authors; 40% of books from un-agented writers. Average print order for a writer's first book is 3,000-5,000. Starts at 10% royalty on wholesale price. Offers average $1,000 advance. Publishes book an average of 1½ years after acceptance. Photocopied submissions OK. Reports in 2 months. Book catalog for 6x9 SAE and 3 first class stamps; ms guidelines for #10 SASE.
Nonfiction: "Subjects include western American history, natural history, architecture, art history, and fine arts. "We consider biographical, historical, descriptive and analytical studies in all of the above. Emphasis is also placed on pictorial content." Query. Reviews artwork/photos as part of ms package.
Recent Nonfiction Title: *Bernard Shaw on Photography*, ed. Bill Jay and Margaret Moore.
Fiction: "We publish contemporary literary fiction." Looks for "style, readable, intelligent, careful writing, contribution to the social consciousness of our time." Query.
Recent Fiction Title: *Mr. Wahlquist in Yellowstone*, by Douglas Thayer.
Tips: "We're looking for art books (visual arts and music and architecture on the leading edge of our culture. In fiction we are interested in work with literary merit, work that demonstrates a control of subject with a distinctive and original voice will be seriously considered. We are not interested in potboilers, bodice-rippers, science fiction, techno-thrillers or anything that deals with a subject that claims to be 'as current as today's headlines.' "

‡**SOHO PRESS, INC.**, One Union Square, New York NY 10003. (212)243-1527. Editor-in-Chief: Juris Jurjevics. Publishes hardcover and trade paperback originals. Firm averages 12 titles/year. Receives 1,000 submisisons/year. 75% of books from first-time authors. 50% of books from unagented writers. Pays 10-15% on retail price. Publishes book an average of 1 year after acceptance. Simultaneous and photocopied submissions OK. Computer printout submissions OK; prefers letter-quality. Reports in 2 weeks on queries; 2 months on mss. Free book catalog.
Nonfiction: Biography. "We want literary non-fiction: travel, autobiography, biography, etc. no self-help." Submit outline/synopsis and sample chapters or complete ms.
Recent Nonfiction Title *O Come Ye Back to Ireland*, by Nialll Williams and Christine Breen, (travel and biography).
Fiction: Adventure, ethnic, feminist, historical, literary, mainstream/contemporary, mystery and suspense. Submit complete ms with SASE.
Recent Fiction Title: *High Crimes*, by John Westermann.

SOUTHERN ILLINOIS UNIVERSITY PRESS, Box 3697, Carbondale IL 62901. (618)453-2281. Director: Kenney Withers. Averages 60 titles/year; receives 500 submissions annually. 50% of books from first-time authors; 99% of books from unagented writers. Publishes book an average of 1 year after acceptance. Computer printout submissions acceptable; no dot-matrix. Reports in 6 weeks. Free book catalog.
Nonfiction: "We are interested in scholarly nonfiction on the humanities, social sciences and contemporary affairs. No dissertations or collections of previously published articles." Accepts nonfiction translations from French, German, Scandinavian and Hebrew. Query.
Recent Nonfiction Title: *Plato, Derrida, and Writing*, by Jasper Neel (literary/criticism).

‡SOUTHFARM PRESS, Haan Graphic Publishing Services, Ltd., Box 1296, Middletown CT 06457. (203)344-9137. Publisher: Walter J. Haan. Publishes trade paperback originals. Firm averages 5 titles/year. 100% from first-time authors; 100% from unagented writers. Pays 5-10% royalty on retail price. Offers $500 average advance. Publishes book an average of 1 year after acceptance. Simultaneous and photocopied submissions OK. Computer printout submissions OK; letter-quality preferred. Reports in 1 month. Free book catalog.
Nonfiction: Subjects include animals, history, military/war and "B"movies. Submit outline/synopsis and sample chapters.
Recent Nonfiction Title: *Reel Wars*, by Monica Jacoby and Frederick Fulfer (fact/quiz book).

‡SPARROW PRESS, Subsidiaries include Sparrow Poverty Pamphlets and Vagrom Chap Books, 103 Waldron St., West Lafayette IN 47906. (317)743-1991. Editor/Publisher: Felix Stefanile. Publishes trade paperback originals. Averages 3 pamphlets and 1-3 chapbooks/year; receives 1,200 submissions annually. 25% of books from first-time authors; 100% of books from unagented writers. Pays $30 advance on royalties, 20% of profits after cost is recovered. No simultaneous submissions. Publishes book an average of 10 months after acceptance. Reports in 1 month on queries; 6 weeks on mss. Ms guidelines for SASE. Sample pamphlet $2; book catalog for 50¢.
Imprints: Sparrow Poverty Pamphlets (poetry), Felix Stefanile, editor/publisher. Vagrom Chap Books (poetry, by invitation), Felix Stefanile, editor/publisher.
Poetry: "We need the best poetry we can find. We plan at least three volumes a year. We are not interested in seeing any humor, or religious verse. We don't want prose poems. We do not want cut-up prose confessional poems." 28 page typescript only, one poem/page. "If we want to see more, we'll ask." *No* queries answered without SASE.
Recent Poetry Title: *Prisms*, by Gray Burr (formal verse).
Tips: "Our readers are contemporary-minded fellow poets, creative writing students, serious readers and teachers. Poetry is becoming more formal again, more literate. The better poets write out of their hearts, and find their own genuine, if not too large, following. One of our poets has gone through three printings, another two. Recent Sparrow poets have won the Guggenheim, the Carl Sandburg Memorial Award, etc. Under no circumstances do we return submitted manuscripts not accompanied by SASE."

‡THE SPEECH BIN, INC., 231 Clarksville Road, Box 218, Princeton Junction NJ 08550-0218. (609)799-3935. Senior Editor: Jan Binney. Publishes trade paperback originals. Publishes 5-10 titles/year. Receives 50-75 manuscripts per year. 50% of books from first-time authors; 90% from unagented writers. Pays negotiable royalty on wholesale price. Publishes ms average of 6 months after acceptance. Photocopied submissions OK. Query for electronic submissions. Computer printout submissions acceptable. Reports in one month on queries, six weeks on manuscripts. Book catalog for 9 × 12 SASE.
Nonfiction: How-to, illustrated book, juvenile (preschool-teen), reference, textbook, educational material and games. Subjects include health, communication disorders and education for handicapped persons. Query or submit outline synopsis and sample chapters. Reviews artwork/photos as part of ms package.
Recent Nonfiction Title: *RULES: Reading Unintelligible Linguistic Expressions of Speech*, by Jane Webb and Barbara Duckett.
Fiction: Booklets or books "for children and adults about handicapped persons, especially with communication disorders." Query or submit outline/synopsis and sample chapters. "This is a potentially new market for The Speech Bin."
Tips: "Our audience is special educators, speech-language pathologists and audiologists, parents, caregivers, and teachers of children and adults with developmental and post-trauma disabilities. Books and materials must be research-based, clearly presented, well written, competently illustrated, and unique. We'll be adding books and materials for use by occupational and physical therapists and other allied health professionals."

‡SPENCE PUBLISHING, Division of Spence Research Inc., 11 East 22 St., Tulsa OK 74114-1119. (918)592-4415. Subsidiaries include Health Edco, Health Fair. President: Tom Spence. Publishes trade paperback originals and reprints. Firm publishes 40 titles/year. Receives 400 submissions/year. 20% from first-time authors; 95% from unagented writers. Pays 8-12% royalty on retail price or buys ms outright for $2,000-5,000. Offers $1,000 average advance. Publishes book an average of 9 months after acceptance. Simultaneous and photocopied submission OK. Computer printout submissions OK. Reports in 3 weeks on queries; 6 weeks on mss. Free book catalog; mss guidelines for #10 SAE and 2 first class stamps.

Nonfiction: How-to, illustrated book, self-help. Subjects include child guidance/parenting, cooking, foods and nutrition, health/medicine. "We need 40-50 titles, 100-140 pages, general reader books covering all common health subjects, from arthritis to potty training. We sell heavily to libraries and doctors' offices, and must have reliable but interesting manuscripts." Query. Reviews artwork/photos as part of the ms package.
Recent Nonfiction Title: *Courting Disaster: STD's*, by B. Seaman.

SPINSTERS/AUNT LUTE BOOKS, Box 410687, San Francisco CA 94141. (415)558-9655. Editors: Sherry Thomas and Joan Pinkvoss. Publishes trade paperback originals and reprints. Averages 6-8 titles/year; receives 200 submissions annually. 50% of books from first-time authors; 95% of books from unagented writers. Pays 7-11% royalty on retail price. Publishes book an average of 1 year after acceptance. Photocopied submissions OK. Computer printout submissions acceptable; prefers letter-quality to dot-matrix. Reports in 3 weeks on queries; 6 months on mss. Free book catalog; ms guidelines for SASE.
Nonfiction: Self-help and feminist analysis for positive change. Subjects include women's issues. "We are interested in books that not only name the crucial issues in women's lives, but show and encourage change and growth. We do not want to see work by men, or anything that is not specific to women's lives (ie. humor, childrens' books, etc.). We do not want genre fiction (romances, etc.)." Query. Reviews artwork/photos as part of ms package.
Recent Nonfiction Title: *Borderlands/LaFrontera*, by Gloria Anzuidua (ethnic/women's history).
Fiction: Ethnic, women's, lesbian. Submit outline/synopsis and sample chapters.
Recent Fiction Title: *Child of Her People*, by Anne Cameron.
Poetry: Minimal. Submit complete ms.
Recent Poetry Title: *We Say We Love Each Other*, by Minnie Bruce Pratt (Southern lesbian).

ST PUBLICATIONS, INC., Signs of the Times Pubishing Co., Book Division, 407 Gilbert Ave., Cincinnati OH 45202. (513)421-4050. FAX: (513)421-5144. Book Division Coordinator: Carole Singleton Emery. Publishes hardcover and trade paperback originals and hardcover reprints. Averages 6 titles/year; receives 15-20 submissions annually. 50% of books from first-time authors; 100% of books from unagented writers. Pays royalty on wholesale price: 10% until recovery of production costs; 12½% thereafter; and 15% on straight reprints. Publishes book an average of 9 months after acceptance. Photocopied submissions OK. Computer printout submissions acceptable. Reports in 6 weeks on queries; 2 months on mss. Free book catalog and ms guidelines.
Nonfiction: How-to, reference, technical and textbook. Subjects include art (collections of copyright-free artwork suitable for sign, display or screen printing industries). "We need technical how-to books for professionals in three specific industries: the sign industry, including outdoor advertising, electric and commercial signs; the screen printing industry, including the printing of paper products, fabrics, ceramics, glass and electronic circuits; and the visual merchandising and store design industry. We are not interested in submissions that do not relate specifically to those three fields." Submit outline/synopsis and sample chapters. Reviews artwork/photos as part of ms package.
Recent Nonfiction Title: *Silent Selling: The Complete Guide to Fashion Merchandise Presentation*, by Judith A. Bell.
Tips: "The writer has the best chance of selling our firm how-to books related to our industries: signs, screen printing, and visual merchandising. These are the fields our marketing and distribution channels are geared to. Request copies of, and thoroughly absorb the information presented in, our trade magazines (*Signs of the Times*, *Visual Merchandising*, and *Screen Printing*). Our books are permanent packages of this type of information. We are taking a closer look at submissions which we can sell outside our primary range of customers, yet still confining our subject interests to sign painting and design, visual merchandising, display and store design, and screen printing (both technical and art aspects)."

STACKPOLE BOOKS, Company of Commonwealth Communications Services, Box 1831, Harrisburg PA 17105. FAX: (717)233-7411. Editorial Director: Judith Schnell. Publishes hardcover and paperback originals. Publishes 40-50 titles/year. "Proposals should begin as a one-page letter, leading to chapter outline on request only. If author is unknown to Stackpole, supply credentials." Publishes book an average of 9 months after acceptance. Computer printout submissions acceptable; prefers letter-quality.
Nonfiction: Outdoor-related subject areas—fishing, hunting, firearms, wildlife, adventure, outdoor skills, gardening, military guides, military history, decoy carving/woodcarving, space exploration and contemporary issues. Reviews artwork/photos as part of ms package.
Recent Nonfiction Title: *The Edge of Everest*, by Sue Cobb.

STANDARD PUBLISHING, A division of Standex International Corp., 8121 Hamilton Ave., Cincinnati OH 45231. (513)931-4050. Publisher/Vice President: Eugene H. Wigginton. Publishes hardcover and paperback originals and reprints. Specializes in religious books. Averages 125 titles/year; receives 1,500 submissions annually. 25% of books from first-time authors; 90% of books from unagented writers. Average print order for a writer's first book is 5,000. Pays 8-10% royalty on wholesale price "for substantial books. Lump sum for smaller books." Offers $200-1,500 advance. Publishes book an average of 1 year after acceptance. Query for electronic submissions. Computer printout submissions acceptable; no dot-matrix. Reports in 2-3 months. Ms guidelines for #10 SASE.

Nonfiction: Publishes how-to; crafts (to be used in Christian education); juveniles; reference; Christian education; quiz; puzzle and religious books; and college textbooks (religious). All mss must pertain to religion. Query or submit outline/synopsis and 2-3 sample chapters. Reviews artwork/photos as part of ms package.

Recent Nonfiction Title: *Living Stones*, by Earl Comfort.

Fiction: Religious, devotional books.

Recent Fiction Title: *Runaway*, by Janet Willig.

Tips: "Children's books (picture books, ages 4-7), juvenile fiction (8-11 and 12-15), Christian education, activity books, and helps for Christian parents and church leaders are the types of books writers have the best chance of selling to our firm."

*STANFORD UNIVERSITY PRESS, Imprint of Stanford University, Stanford CA 94305. (415)723-9434. Editor: William W. Carver. Averages 65 titles/year; receives 900 submissions annually. 40% of books from first-time authors, 95% of books from unagented writers. Subsidy (nonauthor) publishes 65% of books. Pays up to 15% royalty ("typically 10%, often none"); sometimes offers advance. Publishes book an average of 13 months ("typically a year") after acceptance. Photocopied submissions OK. Query for electronic submissions. Computer printout submissions acceptable; no dot-matrix. Reports in 3 weeks on queries; 5 weeks on mss. Free book catalog.

Nonfiction: Scholarly books in the humanities, social sciences, and natural sciences: history and culture of China, Japan, and Latin America; European history; biology, natural history, and taxonomy; anthropology, linguistics, and psychology; literature, criticism, and literary theory; political science and sociology; archaeology and geology; and medieval and classical studies. Also high-level textbooks and books for a more general audience. Query. "We like to see a prospectus and an outline." Reviews artwork/photos as part of ms package.

Recent Nonfiction Title: *The Butterflies of North America*, by James A. Scott.

Tips: "The writer's best chance is a work of original scholarship with an argument of some importance and an appeal to a broad audience."

STARRHILL PRESS, Box 32342, Washington DC 20007. (202)686-6703. Co-presidents: Liz Hill and Marty Starr. Publishes trade paperback originals. Firm averages 4 titles/year. Receives 10 submissions/year. 90% of books from first-time authors. 100% from unagented writers. Pays 5-10% royalty on retail price. Publishes book an average of 1 year after acceptance. Simultaneous and photocopied submissions OK. Computer printout submissions OK; prefers letter-quality. Reports in 2 weeks on queries. Book catalog for #10 SASE.

Nonfiction: Reference. Subjects include art/architecture, music/dance, nature/environment and travel. "American arts, decoration, literary guide books, performing arts, short nonfiction (with line drawings only) are our needs. No popular junk, coffee table books or expensive artwork." Query or submit outline/synopsis and sample chapters. Reviews artwork/photos as part of manuscript package.

Recent Nonfiction Title: *Clues to American Furniture*, by Jean Taylor Federico.

STEMMER HOUSE PUBLISHERS, INC., 2627 Caves Rd., Owings Mills MD 21117. (301)363-3690. President: Barbara Holdridge. Publishes hardcover originals. Averages 12 titles/year; receives 500 submissions annually. 10% of books from first-time authors; 90% of books from unagented writers. Average print order for a writer's first book is 4,000-10,000. Pays royalty on wholesale price. Publishes book an average of 1 year after acceptance. Computer printout submissions acceptable; no dot-matrix. Reports in 2 weeks on queries; 3 months on mss. Book catalog for 9x12 SAE and 4 first class stamps.

Nonfiction: Biography, cookbook, illustrated book, juvenile (ages 4-14) and design books. Subjects include Americana, animals, art, cooking and foods, history and nature. Especially looking for "quality biography, history, and art and design." No humor. Query or submit outline/synopsis and sample chapters.

An asterisk preceding a listing indicates that subsidy publishing or co-publishing (where author pays part or all of publishing costs) is available. Firms whose subsidy programs comprise more than 50% of their total publishing activities are listed at the end of the Book Publishers section.

Recent Nonfiction Title: *A Heritage of Roses*, by Hazel Le Rougetel.
Fiction: Adventure, ethnic, historical, mainstream and philosophical. "We want only manuscripts of sustained literary merit. No popular-type manuscripts written to be instant bestsellers." Query.
Recent Fiction Title: *The Fringe of Heaven*, by Margaret Sutherland (contemporary novel).
Tips: "We are interested in finding original manuscripts on gardens and gardening. If I were a writer trying to market a book today, I would not imitate current genres on the bestseller lists, but strike out with a subject of intense interest to me." Freelancer has best chance of selling a book with a universal theme, either for adults or children, exceptionally well written, and marketable internationally. "Our goal is a list of perennial sellers of which we can be proud."

STERLING PUBLISHING, 387 Park Ave. South, New York NY 10016. (212)532-7160. Acquisitions Manager: Sheila Anne Barry. Publishes hardcover and paperback originals and reprints. Averages 80 titles/year. Pays royalty; offers advance. Publishes book an average of 8 months after acceptance. Computer printout submissions acceptable; prefers letter-quality. Reports in 6 weeks. Guidelines for SASE.
Nonfiction: Alternative lifestyle, fiber arts, games and puzzles, health how-to, business, foods, hobbies, how-to, children's humor, militaria, occult, pets, photography, recreation, reference, self-help, sports, technical, wine and woodworking. Query or submit complete chapter list, detailed outline/synopsis and 2 sample chapters with photos if necessary. Reviews artwork/photos as part of ms package.
Recent Nonfiction Title: *The Great Rift: Africa's Changing Valley*, by Anthony Smith.

‡GARETH STEVENS, INC., 7317 W. Green Tree Rd., Milwaukee WI 53223. (414)466-7550. Acquisitions Editor: Kathy Keller. Publishes hardcover originals. Averages 150 titles/year. Receives 1,000 submissions/year. 50% of books from first-time authors. 100% from unagented writers. Pays 5% on wholesale price or buys mss outright for $1,500. Offers $500-1,000 average advance. Publishes book average of 1 year after acceptance. Simultaneous (but limited to 2) and photocopied submissions OK. Computer printout submissions OK, prefers letter-quality. Reports in 1 month on queries. Book catalog for 9½×12½ SAE and 2 oz. postage.
Nonfiction: Biography, cookbook, juvenile, reference (all children's books). Subjects include animals, anthropology/archaeology, art/architecture, history, nature/environment and sociology. "No religious." Submit outline/synopsis and sample chapters or complete ms. Reviews artwork/photos as part of ms package.
Recent Nonfiction Title: *Isaac Asimov's Library of Universe*, by Isaac Asimov (astronomy).
Fiction: Adventure, feminist, historical, humor, juvenile, mystery, picture books (all children's books, ages 5-8). "No religious."
Recent Fiction Title: *Enoch the Emu*, by Gordon Wind (picture book).

STIPES PUBLISHING CO., 10-12 Chester St., Champaign IL 61820. (217)356-8391. FAX: (217)356-5753. Contact: Robert Watts. Publishes hardcover and paperback originals. Averages 15-30 titles/year; receives 150 submissions annually. 50% of books from first-time authors; 100% of books from unagented writers. Pays 15% maximum royalty on retail price. Publishes book an average of 4 months after acceptance. Computer printout submissions acceptable; prefers letter-quality. Reports in 2 weeks on queries; 2 months on mss.
Nonfiction: Technical (some areas), textbooks on business and economics, music, chemistry, agriculture/horticulture, and recreation and physical education. "All of our books in the trade area are books that also have a college text market." No "books unrelated to educational fields taught at the college level." Submit outline/synopsis and 1 sample chapter.
Recent Nonfiction Title: *Discerning Art: Concepts and Issues*, by George Hardiman and Ted Zernich.

‡STOEGER PUBLISHING COMPANY, 55 Ruta Court, S. Hackensack NJ 07606. (201)440-2700. Subsidiary includes Stoeger Industries. Publisher: Paul G. Emberley. Publishes trade paperback originals. Averages 12-15 titles/year. Royalty varies, depending on ms. Simultaneous and photocopied submissions OK. Reports in 1 month on queries; 3 months on mss. Book catalog for SASE.
Nonfiction: Subjects include sports, outdoor sports, cooking and foods, and hobbies. Especially looking for how-to books relating to hunting, fishing, or other outdoor sports. Submit outline/synopsis and sample chapters.
Recent Nonfiction Title: *Antique Guns*, by John E. Traister.

STORIE/MCOWEN PUBLISHERS, INC., Box 308, Manteo NC 27954. (919)473-1225. Editorial Assistant: Melissa Powell. Publishes trade paperback originals. Firm averages 7 titles/year. 20% of books from first-time authors; 100% of books from unagented writers. Pays 5% royalty on retail price. Offers $2,000 average advance. Publishes book an average of 1 year in advance. Query for electronic submissions. Computer printout submissions OK; no dot-matrix. Reports in 1 week on queries. Free book catalog.
Nonfiction: Reference. Subjects include travel/newcomer guides. Query. All unsolicited mss are returned unopened. Reviews artwork/photos as part of ms package.
Recent Nonfiction Title: *Insider's Guide to the Outer Banks of NC*, by Dave Poyer and Chris Kidder (travel).
Tips: "Travelers/vacationers, business people, and newcomers to an area are our audience."

‡STORMLINE PRESS, Box 539, Urbana IL 61801. (217)328-2665. Imprints include: Blue Heron Books. Publisher: Raymond Bial. Publishes hardcover and trade paperback originals. Averages 4-5 titles/year. Receives 500 submissions/year. Pays 15% on retail price (after production costs are met). Publishes book an average of 1 year after acceptance. Book catalog for #10 SAE and 1 first-class stamp.

Nonfiction: Biography, cookbook, humor, illustrated book and juvenile. Subjects include agriculture/horticulture, Americana, animals, art/architecture, cooking, foods and nutrition, ethnic, gardening, history, photography and regional. "We publish by invitation only. We do not like to receive unsolicited manuscripts or query letters. We announce those times in which we are prepared to consider manuscripts." Reviews artwork as part of ms package.

Recent Nonfiction Title: *Living With Lincoln: Life and Art in the Heartland*, by Dan Guillory (essays on life in the Midwest).

Fiction: "We are presently overcommitted and will not be considering manuscripts until 1991."

Tips: "Do not submit unsolicited manuscripts or query our press. When we are able to consider manuscripts we will place an announcement in a number of literary journals. If I were a writer trying to market a book today, I would be more interested in creating a work of enduring nature rather than simply trying to publish a book."

STUDIO PRESS, Box 1268, Twain Harte CA 95383. (209)533-4222. Publisher: Paul Castle. Publishes hardcover and paperback originals. Averages 4 titles/year; receives 10-15 submissions annually. 100% of books from first-time authors; 100% of books from unagented writers. Average print order for a writer's first book is 2,000-3,000. Pays 15% royalty on wholesale or retail price; no advance. Publishes book an average of 3-6 months after acceptance. Simultaneous and photocopied submissions OK. Computer printout submissions acceptable; prefers letter-quality. Reports in 1 month. Ms guidelines for #10 SASE.

Nonfiction: Photography. "We are always interested in good manuscripts on technique and the business of photography. We especially want manuscripts on *marketing* one's photography. We don't want manuscripts on art criticism of photography, collections of art photos, basic photo teaching books, or anything other than books on the technique and/or business of photography. Query; if the idea is good, we'll ask for outline and sample chapters." Reviews artwork/photos as part of ms package. "Artwork/photos are essential to acceptance."

Recent Nonfiction Title: *Family Portraiture*, by John Hartman.

Tips: "We need more anecdotes and word illustrations to amplify the writer's points. We particularly look for skilled photographers who are doing something very well and can communicate their expertise to others. We are willing to work with such individuals on extensive rewrite and editing, if what they have to say is valuable."

SUNSTONE PRESS, Box 2321, Santa Fe NM 87504-2321. (505)988-4418. Editor-in-Chief: James C. Smith Jr. Publishes paperback originals; few hardcover originals. Averages 20 titles/year; receives 400 submissions annually. 70% of books from first-time authors; 100% of books from unagented writers. Average print order for writer's first book is 2,000-5,000. Pays royalty on wholesale price. Publishes book an average of 1 year after acceptance. Computer printout submissions acceptable; prefers letter-quality. Reports in 2 months.

Nonfiction: How-to series craft books. Books on the history and architecture of the Southwest. Looks for "strong regional appeal (Southwestern)." Reviews artwork/photos as part of ms package.

Recent Nonfiction Title: *Rural Architecture*, by Myrtle Stedman.

Fiction: Publishes "material with Southwestern theme."

Recent Fiction Title: *Love Lies Bleeding*, by Robert Swisher.

Poetry: Traditional or free verse. Poetry book not exceeding 64 pages. Prefers Southwestern theme.

Recent Poetry Title: *Signature of the Spiral*, by Daniel Schreck.

SYBEX, INC., 2021 Challenger Dr., Alameda CA 94501. (415)848-8233. Editor-in-Chief: Dr. Rudolph S. Langer. Acquisitions Editor: Dianne King. Publishes paperback originals. Averages 75 titles/year. Royalty rates vary. Offers average $2,500 advance. Publishes book an average of 3 months after acceptance. Simultaneous and photocopied submissions OK. Query for electronic submissions. Computer printout submissions acceptable. Reports in 2 months. Free book catalog.

Nonfiction: Computers and computer software. "Manuscripts most publishable in the field of personal computers, desktop computer business applications, hardware, programming, languages, and telecommunications." Submit outline/synopsis and 2-3 sample chapters. Accepts nonfiction translations from French or German. Looks for "clear writing; technical accuracy; logical presentation of material; and good selection of material, such that the most important aspects of the subject matter are thoroughly covered; well-focused subject matter; and well-thought-out organization that helps the reader understand the material." Reviews artwork/photos as part of ms package.

Recent Nonfiction Title: *Mastering Word Perfect 5*.

Tips: Queries/mss may be routed to other editors in the publishing group.

‡*SYMMES SYSTEMS, Box 8101, Atlanta GA 30306. Editor-in-Chief: E. C. Symmes. Publishes hardcover and paperback originals. 50% of books from first-time authors; 100% of books from unagented writers. Pays 10% royalty on wholesale price. "Contracts are usually written for the individual title and may have different terms." No advance. Subsidy publishes 40% of books. Publishes book an average of 14 months after acceptance. Will consider photocopied and simultaneous submissions. Computer printout submissions acceptable; no dot-matrix. Acknowledges receipt of submission in 10 days; evaluates within 1 month.

Nonfiction: Nature. "Our books have mostly been in the art of bonsai (miniature trees). We are publishing quality information for laypersons (hobbyists). Most of the titles introduce information that is totally new for the hobbyist." Text must be topical, showing state-of-the-art. All books so far have been illustrated with photos and/or drawings. Would like to see more material on self-help business subjects; also photography and collecting photographica. Length: open. Query. Reviews artwork/photos as part of ms package.

Recent Nonfiction Title: *The Physician's Guide to Nutritional Therapy*, by Anderson.

*SYRACUSE UNIVERSITY PRESS, 1600 Jamesville Ave., Syracuse NY 13244-5160. (315)443-5534. Director: Charles Backus. Averages 40 titles/year; receives 350 submissions annually. 40% of books from first-time authors; 95% of books from unagented writers. Subsidy publishes (nonauthor) 20% of books. Pays royalty on net sales. Publishes book an average of 10 months after acceptance. Simultaneous and photocopied submissions OK "if we are informed." Computer printout submissions acceptable. Reports in 2 weeks on queries; "longer on submissions." Book catalog and ms guidelines for SASE.

Nonfiction: "Special opportunity in our nonfiction program for freelance writers of books on New York state. We have published regional books by people with limited formal education, but authors were thoroughly acquainted with their subjects, and they wrote simply and directly about them. Provide precise descriptions about subjects, along with background description of project. The author must make a case for the importance of his or her subject." Query. Accepts outline/synopsis and at least 2 sample chapters. Reviews artwork/photos as part of ms package.

Recent Nonfiction Title: *The Man Who Tried to Burn New York*, by Nat Brandt (history/Civil War).

TAB BOOKS, INC., Blue Ridge, Summit PA 17214. (717)794-2191. Director of Acquisitions: Ron Powers. Imprint is Windcrest (microcomputer books). Publishes hardcover and paperback originals and reprints. Publishes 275 titles/year; receives 600 submissions annually. 50% of books from first-time authors; 85% of books from unagented writers. Average print order for writer's first book is 10,000. Pays variable royalty; buys some mss outright for a negotiable fee. Offers advance. Photocopied submissions OK (except for art). Query for electronic submissions. Computer printout submissions acceptable; prefers letter-quality or laser quality. Reports in 6 weeks. Free book catalog and ms guidelines.

Nonfiction: TAB publishes titles in such fields as computer hardware, computer software, business, solar and alternate energy, marine line, aviation, automotive, music technology, consumer medicine, electronics, electrical and electronics repair, amateur radio, shortwave listening, model railroading, toys, hobbies, drawing, animals and animal power, woodworking, practical skills with projects, building furniture, basic how-to for the house, building large structures, calculators, robotics, telephones, model radio control, TV servicing, audio, recording, hi-fi and stereo, electronic music, electric motors, electrical wiring, electronic test equipment, video programming, CATV, MATV and CCTV, broadcasting, photography and film, appliance servicing and repair, advertising, antiques and restoration, bicycles, crafts, farmsteading, hobby electronics, home construction, license study guides, mathematics, metalworking, reference books, schematics and manuals, small gasoline engines, two-way radio and CB, military fiction, and woodworking. Accepts nonfiction translations. Query with outline/synopsis. Reviews artwork/photos as part of ms package.

Tips: "Many writers believe that a cover letter alone will describe their proposed book sufficiently; it rarely does. The more details we receive, the better the chances are that the writer will get published by us. We expect a writer to tell us what the book is about, but many writers actually fail to do just that."

TABOR PUBLISHING, a division of DLM, Inc. #130, 25115 Avenue Stanford, Valencia CA 91355. (805)257-0911. President: Cullen W. Schippe. Publishes hardcover originals and trade paperback originals. Firm averages 12-20 titles/year. Receives 150 submissions/year. 75% of books from first-time authors. 80% from unagented writers. Pays 4-12% royalty on wholesale price. Buys mss outright for $500-2,000. "Specific arrangements are made for specialized work." Offers $1,000 average advance. Publishes book an average of 18 months after acceptance. Photocopied submissions OK. Computer printout submissions OK; prefers letter-quality. Reports in 6 weeks on queries; 4 months on mss.

Nonfiction: Textbook. Subjects include child guidance/parenting (religious slant), education (religious), philosophy (religious), psychology, religion (Roman Catholic) and adult education. "No private revelations, poetry, get-rich schemes, health and fitness with religious twist or Bible interpretation." Query or submit outline/synopsis and sample chapter. All unsolicited mss are returned.

Recent Nonfiction Title: *Touchstone*, by Miller & Weber (adult activities for religious education).

Tips: "Best shot is a program type book that fits a specific institutional or personal need in the Roman Catholic or mainline Christian market."

‡**LANCE TAPLEY, PUBLISHER, INC.**, 86 Winthrop St., Box 2439, Augusta ME 04330. (207)622-1179. Imprints include Kennebec Press; Blue Heron Books. President: Lance Tapley. Publishes hardcover, trade paperback and mass market paperback originals and hardcover and trade paperback reprints. Firm averages 8-10 titles/year. Receives 250 submissions/year. 50% of books from first-time authors. 90% from unagented writers. Pays 5-15% royalty on wholesale price or retail price. Offers negotiable advance. Publishes book an average of 6 months after acceptance. Simultaneous and photocopied submissions OK. Computer printout submissions OK. Reports in 2 weeks on queries and 2-4 months on mss. Free book catalog.

Nonfiction: Biography, coffee table book, cookbook, how-to, humor, illustrated book, juvenile, reference, self-help. Subjects include Americana, animals, anthropology/archaeology, art/architecture, child guidance/parenting, cooking, foods and nutrition, government/politics, history, language/literature, nature/environment, photography, recreation, regional, religion and sports. Query before sending ms. Reviews artwork/photos as part of ms package.

Recent Nonfiction Title: *Bette, Rita & the Rest of My Life*, by Gary Merrill (autobiography).

Fiction: Adventure, erotica, historical, humor and picture books. Query.

Recent Fiction Title: *Best Stories of Sarah Orne Sewett* (collection of stories).

‡**TAYLOR PUBLISHING COMPANY**, Subsidiary of Insilco, 1550 W. Mockingbird Ln., Dallas TX 75235. (214)637-2800. FAX: (214)637-2800, ext. 220. Editorial Assistant—Trade Books Division. Publishes hardcover and softcover originals. Averages 24 titles/year; receives 1,000 submissions annually. 25% of books from first-time authors; 10% of books from unagented writers. Buys some mss outright. Publishes book 1 year after acceptance. Simultaneous and photocopied submissions OK. Computer printout submissions acceptable. Reports in 6 weeks on queries and unsolicited mss. Book catalog and ms guidelines for 7x9 SASE.

Nonfiction: True crime, cookbook, humor, sports, travel, self-help and trivia. Submit outline/synopsis and sample chapters. Reviews artwork/photos as part of ms package.

Recent Nonfiction Title: *Men of Autumn*, by Dom Forker.

TEACHERS COLLEGE PRESS, 1234 Amsterdam Ave., New York NY 10027. (212)678-3929. Director: Carole P. Saltz. Publishes hardcover and paperback originals and reprints. Averages 40 titles/year. Pays royalty. Publishes book an average of 1 year after acceptance. Reports in 1 year. Free book catalog.

Nonfiction: "This university press concentrates on books in the field of education in the broadest sense, from early childhood to higher education: good classroom practices, teacher training, special education, innovative trends and issues, administration and supervision, film, continuing and adult education, all areas of the curriculum, computers, guidance and counseling and the politics, economics, philosophy, sociology and history of education. The press also issues classroom materials for students at all levels, with a strong emphasis on reading and writing and social studies." Submit outline/synopsis and sample chapters.

Recent Nonfiction Title: *The Empowerment of Teachers*, by Gene Maeroff.

*****TEXAS A&M UNIVERSITY PRESS**, Drawer C, College Station TX 77843. (409)845-1436. Director: John F. Stetter. Publishes 30 titles/year. Subsidy publishes 3% of books; subsidy publishes (nonauthor) 15% of books. Pays in royalties. Publishes book an average of 1 year after acceptance. Query for electronic submissions. Computer printout submissions acceptable; prefers letter-quality. Reports in 1 week on queries: 1 month on submissions. Free book catalog.

Nonfiction: History, natural history (juvenile, ages 5-15), environmental history, military history, economics, agriculture and regional studies (juvenile, ages 5-15). Receives artwork/photos as part of ms package. "We do not want poetry." Query. Accepts outline/synopsis and 2-3 sample chapters. "We prefer an introductory statement, table of contents, and sample chapter, which may be a combination of a synopsis and an outline." Reviews artwork/photos as part of ms package.

Recent Nonfiction Title: *Enduring Women*, by Diane Koos Gentry.

*****TEXAS CHRISTIAN UNIVERSITY PRESS**, Box 30783, TCU, Fort Worth TX 76129. (817)921-7822. Director: Judy Alter. Publishes hardcover originals, some reprints. Averages 8 titles/year; receives 100 submissions annually. 10% of books from first-time authors; 75% of books from unagented writers. Subsidy publishes (nonauthor) 10% of books. Pays royalty. Publishes book an average of 16 months after acceptance. Computer printout submissions acceptable; no dot-matrix. Reports "as soon as possible."

Nonfiction: American studies, juvenile (Chaparral Books, 10 and up), Texana, literature and criticism. "We are looking for good scholarly monographs, other serious scholarly work and regional titles of significance." Query. Reviews artwork/photos as part of ms package.

Recent Nonfiction Title: *Eats, a Folk History of Texas Foods*, by Ernestine Sewell Linck & Joyce Gibson Roach.

Fiction: Adult and young adult regional fiction. Query.

Recent Fiction Title: *Wanderer Springs*, by Robert Flynn (regional novel).

Tips: "Regional and/or Texana nonfiction or fiction have best chance of breaking into our firm."

TEXAS MONTHLY PRESS, INC., Subsidiary of Mediatex Communications Corp., Box 1569, Austin TX 78767. (512)476-7085. Director: Cathy Casey Hale. Publishes hardcover and trade paperback originals, and trade paperback reprints. Averages 30 titles/year; receives 400 submissions annually. 60% of books from first-time authors; 85% of books from unagented writers. Pays royalty; offers advance. Publishes book an average of 1 year after acceptance. Simultaneous and photocopied submissions OK. Query for electronic submissions. Computer printout submissions acceptable. Reports in 1 month on queries; 2 months on mss. Free book catalog.

Nonfiction: Politics and history with comtemporary subject matter, biography, coffee table book, cookbook, humor, guidebook, illustrated book and reference. Subjects include Southwest, art, business and economics, cooking and foods, nature, photography, recreation, sports and travel. Query or submit outline/synopsis and 3 sample chapters. Reviews artwork/photos as part of ms package.

Recent Nonfiction Title: *And Deliver Us From Evil*, by Mike Cochran.

Fiction: Ethnic, mainstream. "All stories must be set in the South or Southwest." No experimental, erotica, confession, gothic, romance or poetry. Query or submit outline/synopsis and 3 sample chapters. No unsolicited mss.

Recent Fiction Title: *Baby Houston*, by June Arnold.

TEXAS WESTERN PRESS, Imprint of The University of Texas at El Paso, El Paso TX 79968-0633. (915)747-5688. Director: Dale L. Walker. Editor: Nancy Hamilton. Publishes hardcover and paperback originals. Publishes 7-8 titles/year. "This is a university press, 35 years old; we do offer a standard 10% royalty contract on our hardcover books and on some of our paperbacks as well. We try to treat our authors professionally, produce handsome, long-lived books and aim for quality, rather than quantity of titles carrying our imprint." Photocopied submissions OK. Free book catalog and ms guidelines. Reports in 1-3 months.

Nonfiction: Scholarly books. Historic and cultural accounts of the Southwest (West Texas, New Mexico, northern Mexico and Arizona). Occasional technical titles. "Our *Southwestern Studies* use manuscripts of up to 30,000 words. Our hardback books range from 30,000 words up. The writer should use good exposition in his work. Most of our work requires documentation. We favor a scholarly, but not overly pedantic, style. We specialize in superior book design." Query with outlines. Follow Chicago *Manual of Style*.

Recent Nonfiction Title: *Literature and Landscape: Writers of the Southwest*, by Cynthia Farah.

Tips: "Texas Western Press is interested in books relating to the history of Hispanics in the U.S., will experiment with photo-documentary books, and is interested in seeing more 'popular' history and books on Southwestern culture/life."

THE THEOSOPHICAL PUBLISHING HOUSE, Subsidiary of The Theosophical Society in America, 306 W. Geneva Rd., Wheaton IL 60189. (312)665-0123. Imprint, Quest (nonfiction). Senior Editor: Shirley Nicholson. Publishes trade paperback originals. Averages 12 titles/year; receives 750-1,000 submissions annually. 50-60% of books from first-time authors; 95% of books from unagented writers. Average print order for a writer's first book is 5,000. Pays 12.5% royalty on net price; offers average $1,500 advance. Publishes book an average of 9 months after acceptance. Simultaneous and photocopied submissions OK. Computer printout submissions acceptable; prefers letter-quality. Reports in 2 weeks on queries, 2 months on mss. Free book catalog; ms guidelines for SASE.

Nonfiction: Subjects include self-development, self-help, philosophy (holistic), psychology (transpersonal), Eastern and Western religions, comparative religion, holistic implications in science, health and healing, yoga, meditation and astrology. "TPH seeks works which are compatible with the theosophical philosophy. Our audience includes the 'new age' community, seekers in all religions, general public, professors, and health professionals. No submissions which do not fit the needs outlined above." Accepts nonfiction translations. Query or submit outline/synopsis and sample chapters. Reviews artwork/photos as part of ms package.

Recent Nonfiction Title: *The Goddess Reawakening: The Feminine Principle Today*, compiled by Shirley Nicholson.

Tips: "The writer has the best chance of selling our firm a book which illustrates a connection between spiritually-oriented philosophy or viewpoint and some field of current interest."

*THISTLEDOWN PRESS, 668 East Place, Saskatoon, Saskatchewan S7J 2Z5 Canada. (306)244-1722. Editor-in-Chief: Paddy O' Rourke. Publishes hardcover and trade paperback originals by resident Canadian authors *only*. Averages 10-12 titles/year; receives 150 submissions annually. 50% of books from first-time authors; 100% of books from unagented writers. Average print order for a writer's first (poetry) book is 750 or (fiction) 1,500. Subsidy publishes (nonauthor) 100% of books. Pays standard royalty on retail price. Publishes book an average of 18-24 months after acceptance. Computer printout submissions acceptable; no .dot-matrix. Reports in 2 weeks on queries; 2 months on poetry mss; 3 months on fiction mss. Book catalog and guidelines for #10 SASE.

Fiction: Juvenile (ages 12 and up), literary. Interested in fiction mss from resident Canadian authors only. Minimum of 30,000 words. Accepts no unsolicited work. Query first.

Recent Fiction Title: *Paradise Cafe and Other Stories*, by Martha Brooks (young adult).

Poetry: "The author should make him/herself familiar with our publishing program before deciding whether or not his/her work is appropriate." No poetry by people *not* citizens and residents of Canada. Submit complete ms. Minimum of 60 pages. Prefers poetry mss that have had some previous exposure in literary magazines. Accepts no unsolicited work. Query first.

Recent Poetry Title: *Sticks & Strings: Selected and New Poems*, by John V. Hicks.

Tips: "We prefer to receive a query letter first before a submission. We're looking for quality, well-written literary fiction—for young adults and for our adult fiction list as well."

THOMAS PUBLICATIONS, Subsidiary of Thomas Graphics, Inc., Box 33244, Austin TX 78764. (512)832-0355. Contact: Ralph D. Thomas. Publishes trade paperback originals and trade paperback reprints. Averages 8-10 titles/year; receives 20-30 submissions annually. 90% of books from first-time authors; 90% of books from unagented writers. Pays 10-15% royalty on wholesale or retail price, or makes outright purchase of $500-2,000. Publishes book an average of 1 year after acceptance. Simultaneous and photocopied submissions OK. Computer printout submissions acceptable; no dot-matrix. Reports in 2 weeks on queries; 1 month on mss. Book catalog $1.

Nonfiction: How-to, reference and textbook. Subjects include sociology and investigation and investigative techniques. "We are looking for hardcore investigative methods books, manuals on how to make more dollars in private investigation, private investigative marketing techniques, and specialties in the investigative professions." Query or submit outline/synopsis and sample chapters. Reviews artwork/photos as part of ms package.

Recent Nonfiction Title: *How to Find Anyone Anywhere*, by Ralph Thomas (investigation).

Tips: "Our audience includes private investigators, those wanting to break into investigation, related trades such as auto repossessors, private process servers, news reporters, and related security trades."

CHARLES C. THOMAS, PUBLISHER, 2600 South First St., Springfield IL 62794. (217)789-8980. Editor: Payne E.L. Thomas. Publishes hardcover originals and paperback originals. Firm averages 150 titles/year. Receives 1,000 submissions/year. 95% of books from first-time authors. 94% from unagented writers. Pays 10% royalty on retail price. Publishes book an average of 6 months after acceptance. Simultaneous submissions OK. Computer printout submissions OK; prefers letter-quality. Reports in 1 week on queries; 1 week on mss. Free book catalog and ms guidelines.

Nonfiction: Self-help, technical and textbook. Subjects include anthropology, archaeology, child guidance/ parenting, education, health/medicine, language/literature, nature/environment, philosophy, psychology, recreation, religion, science, sociology and sports. "Biomedical sciences, rehabilitation, behavioral and social sciences, education and special education, criminal justice are our manuscript needs." Submit outline/synopsis and sample chapters or submit complete ms. Reviews artwork/photos as part of manuscript package.

*THREE CONTINENTS PRESS, 1636 Connecticut Ave. NW, Washington DC 20009. Publisher/Editor-in-Chief: Donald E. Herdeck. General Editor: Norman Ware. Publishes hardcover and paperback originals and reprints. Averages 12-14 titles/year. Receives 200 submissions annually. 15% of books from first-time authors; 100% of books from unagented writers. Average print order for a writer's first book is 1,000. Subsidy publishes (nonauthor) 10% of books. Pays 10% royalty; advance "only on delivery of complete manuscript which is found acceptable; usually $300." Photocopied (preferred) and simultaneous submissions OK. State availability of photos/illustrations. Computer printout submissions acceptable; prefers letter-quality. Reports in 2 months. Book catalog and guidelines for 8x11 SAE.

Nonfiction and Fiction: Specializes in African, Caribbean and Middle Eastern (Arabic and Persian) literature and criticism and translation, Third World literature and history. Scholarly, well-prepared mss; creative writing. Fiction, poetry, criticism, history and translations of creative writing. "We search for books which will make clear the complexity and value of non-western literature and culture, including bilingual texts (Arabic language/English translations). We are always interested in genuine contributions to understanding non-western culture." Length: 50,000-125,000 words. Query. "Please do not submit manuscript unless we ask for it. We prefer an outline, and an annotated table of contents, for works of nonfiction; and a synopsis, a plot summary (one to three pages), for fiction. For poetry, send two or three sample poems." Reviews artwork/photos as part of ms package.

Recent Nonfiction Title: *The Emperishable Empire: A Study of British Fiction on India*, by Rashna B. Singh.

Recent Fiction Title: *The Fantasy Eaters, Stories from Fiji*, by Subramani.

Tips: "We need a *polished* translation, or original prose or poetry by non-Western authors *only*."

TIMBER PRESS, INC., 9999 S.W. Wilshire, Portland OR 97225. (503)292-0745. Imprints include Dioscorides Press (botany), Amadeus Press (music) and Areopagitica Press, (history). Editor: Richard Abel. Small press. Publishes hardcover and paperback originals. Publishes 40 titles/year; receives 300-400 submissions annually. 90% of books from first-time authors; 100% of books from unagented writers. Pays 10-20% royalty; sometimes offers advance to cover costs of artwork and final ms completion. Publishes book an average of 1 year after acceptance. Query for electronic submissions. Computer printout submissions acceptable; prefers letter-quality. Reports in 2 months. Book catalog for 9x12 SAE with 3 first class stamps.

Nonfiction: Horticulture (ornamental and economic), botany, plant sciences, natural history, Northwest regional material, forestry, serious music and history. Accepts nonfiction translations from all languages. Query or submit outline/synopsis and 3-4 sample chapters. Reviews artwork/photos as part of ms package.

Recent Nonfiction Title: *Foliage Plants for Decorating Indoors*, by Elbert.

Tips: "The writer has the best chance of selling our firm good books on botany, plant science, horticulture, forestry, agriculture and serious music and history."

TIME-LIFE BOOKS INC., 777 Duke St., Alexandria VA 22314. (703)838-7000. Editor: George Constable. Publishes hardcover originals. Averages 40 titles/year. Books are almost entirely staff-generated and staff-produced, and distribution is primarily through mail order sale. Query to the Director of Corporate Development.

Nonfiction: "General interest books. Most books tend to be heavily illustrated (by staff), with text written by assigned authors. We very rarely accept mss or book ideas submitted from outside our staff." Length: open.

Recent Nonfiction Title: *The Computerized Society*.

TIMES BOOKS, Division of Random House, Inc., 201 East 50 St., New York NY 10022. (212)872-8110. Vice President and Editorial Director: Jonathan B. Segal. Executive Editor: Hugh O'Neill. Publishes hardcover and paperback originals and reprints. Publishes 45 titles/year. Pays royalty; average advance. Publishes book an average of 1 year after acceptance. Computer printout submissions acceptable.

Nonfiction: Business/economics, science and medicine, history, biography, women's issues, the family, cookbooks, current affairs and sports. Accepts only solicited manuscripts. Reviews artwork/photos as part of ms package.

Recent Nonfiction Title: *Buying Into America*, by Martin and Susan Tolchin.

TOR BOOKS, Subsidiary of St. Martin's Press, 9th Floor, 49 W. 24th St., New York NY 10010. (212)741-3100. Editor-in-Chief: Beth Meacham. Publishes mass market, hardcover and trade paperback originals and reprints. Averages 300 books/year. Pays 6-8% royalty; offers negotiable advance. Book catalog for 9x12 SASE.

Fiction: Horror, science fiction, occult, chillers, suspense, espionage, historical and fantasy. "We prefer an extensive chapter-by-chapter synopsis and the first 3 chapters complete." Prefers agented mss or proposals.

Recent Fiction Title: *Seventh Son*, by Orson Scott Card (fantasy).

Tips: "We're pretty broad in the occult, horror and fantasy but more straightforward in science fiction and thrillers, tending to stay with certain authors and certain types of work."

‡*TRANSACTION BOOKS, Rutgers University, New Brunswick NJ 08903. (201)932-2280. FAX: (201)932-3138. President: I.L. Horowitz. Publisher: Scott Bramson. Book Division Director: Mary E. Curtis. Publishes hardcover and paperback originals and reprints. Specializes in scholarly social science books. Averages 135 titles/year; receives 700-800 submissions annually. 15% of books from first-time authors; 85% of books from unagented writers. Average print order for a writer's first book is 1,000. Subsidy publishes 10% of books. Royalty "depends almost entirely on individual contract; we've gone anywhere from 2-15%." No advance. Publishes book an average of 8 months after acceptance. Electronic submissions OK, but requires hard copy also. Computer printout submissions acceptable; prefers letter-quality to dot-matrix. Reports in 4 months. Book catalog and ms guidelines for SASE.

Nonfiction: Americana, biography, economics, history, law, medicine and psychiatry, music, philosophy, politics, psychology, reference, scientific, sociology, technical and textbooks. "All must be scholarly social science or related." Strong emphasis on applied social research. Query or submit outline/synopsis. "Do not submit sample chapters. We evaluate complete manuscripts only." Accepts nonfiction translations. Use Chicago *Manual of Style*. Looks for "scholarly content, presentation, methodology, and target audience." State availability of photos/illustrations and send one photocopied example. Reviews artwork/photos as part of ms package.

Recent Nonfiction Title: *The Gun in Politics*, by J. Bowyer Bell (military history).

TRANSNATIONAL PUBLISHERS, INC., Box 7282, Ardsley-on-Hudson NY 10503. (914)693-0089. Publisher: Ms. Heike Fenton. Publishes hardcover originals. Averages 10-15 titles/year; receives 50 submissions annually. 10% of books from first-time authors; 100% of books from unagented writers. Pays 5-10% royalty. Publishes book an average of 6 months after acceptance. Simultaneous and photocopied submissions OK. Computer printout submissions acceptable. Reports in 2 weeks on queries; 1 month on mss. Book and ms guidelines free on request.

Nonfiction: Reference, textbook and books for professionals. Subjects include politics, international law, criminal law, human rights, women's studies and political theory. Needs scholarly works in the area of international law and politics. No submissions on topics other than those listed above. Submit outline/synopsis and sample chapters.

Recent Nonfiction Title: *Acid Rain and Ozone Layer Depletion*, by Jutta Brunnee.
Tips: "The audience for our books includes law libraries, public libraries, universities, government personnel, military personnel, college students and women's rights groups."

‡**TRANSPORTATION TRAILS**, Subsidiary of National Bus Trader, Inc., 9698 W. Judson Road, Polo IL 61064. (815)946-2341. Editor: Larry Plachino. Publishes hardcover and trade paperback originals and mass market paperback originals. Firm averages 8 titles/year. Receives 10 submissions/year. 50% of books from first-time authors. 100% from unagented writers. Pays 10-15% on retail price. Publishes book an average of 1 year after acceptance. Simultaneous and photocopied submissions OK. Reports in 2 weeks on queries; 2 months on mss. Free book catalog and manuscript guidelines.
Nonfiction: Subject includes travel. "We are only interested in transportation history—prefer electric interurban railroads or trolley lines but will consider steam locomotives, horsecars, buses, aviation and maritime." Query. Reviews artwork/photos as part of ms package.
Recent Nonfiction Title: *The Lake Shore & Michigan Southern*, by Dave McLellan and Bill Warrack.

TRAVEL KEYS, Box 160691, Sacramento CA 95816. (916)452-5200. Publisher: Peter B. Manston. Publishes hardcover and trade paperback originals. Averages 4 titles/year; receives 35 submissions annually. 20% of books from first-time authors; 90% of books from unagented writers. Pays 6-15% royalty ("rarely, we mostly use work for hire"); or makes outright purchase for $500 minimum. Offers minimum $500 advance. Publishes book an average of 10 months after acceptance. Simultaneous and photocopied submissions OK. Query for electronic submissions. Reports in 1 month. Book catalog for #10 SAE with 1 first class stamp.
Nonfiction: How-to on travel (mainly Europe), antiques and flea market guides and home security. "We need carefully researched, practical travel manuscripts. No science or technical submissions." Submit outline/synopsis and sample chapters. Reviews artwork/photos as part of ms package.
Recent Nonfiction Title: *Manston's Travel Key '89*.
Tips: "We will continue in the travel field, but we are broadening out from destination guides to more general travel topics."

TREND BOOK DIVISION, Box 611, St. Petersburg FL 33731. (813)821-5800. Chairman: Eugene C. Patterson. President: Andrew Barnes. Publisher: Richard Edmonds. Publishes paperback originals and reprints. Specializes in books on Florida—all categories. Pays royalty; no advance. Books are marketed through *Florida Trend* magazine. Publishes book an average of 8 months after acceptance. Computer printout submissions acceptable; no dot-matrix. Reports in 1 month.
Nonfiction: Business, economics, history, law, politics, reference, textbooks and travel. "All books pertain to Florida." Query. Reviews artwork/photos as part of ms package.
Tips: "We are shifting to more emphasis on books of a Florida business/economics nature."

TRILLIUM PRESS, Subsidiaries include Cloud 10, Box 209, Monroe NY 10950. (914)783-2999. Editor: William Neumann. Publishes hardcover and paperback originals, software, video tapes and audio tapes. Averages 150 titles/year; receives 800 submissions annually. 33% of books from first-time authors; 95% of books from unagented writers. Publishes book an average of 1 year after acceptance. Photocopied submissions OK. Computer printout submissions OK; prefers letter-quality. Reports in 1 month on queries. Book catalog and guidelines for 8½x11 SAE and 4 first class stamps.
Nonfiction: Self-help and textbook. Subjects include inspirational and education. Submit complete ms. Review artwork/photos as part of ms.
Recent Nonfiction Title: *Educating Children for Life*, by Annemarie Roeper.
Fiction: Children's (ages 4-17). Submit complete ms.
Recent Fiction Title: *Anna's Blanket*, by Sue Hood.

TROUBADOR PRESS, Subsidiary of Price Stern Sloan, Inc., 360 N. La Cienega Blvd., Los Angeles CA 90048. (213)657-6100. Publishes paperback originals. Averages 4 titles/year; receives 300 submissions annually. 95% of books from unagented writers. Average print order for a writer's first book is 10,000. Pays royalty. Offers average $500 advance. Publishes book an average of 6 months after acceptance. Computer printout submissions acceptable; prefers letter-quality. Reports in 3 months. Book catalog and ms guidelines for SASE.
Nonfiction: "Troubador Press publishes mainly, but is not limited to, children's activity books: coloring, cut-out, mazes, games, paper dolls, etc. All titles feature original art and exceptional graphics. Age range varies. We like books which have the potential to develop into series." Query or submit outline/synopsis and 2-3 sample chapters with conciseness and clarity of a good idea. Reviews artwork as part of ms package. "Do not send original artwork."
Recent Nonfiction Title: *The Second Dinosaur Action Set*, by M. Whyte and artist Dan Smith (dinosaurs punch-out and play book with dinosaur dictionary text incorporated).
Tips: "We continue to publish new authors along with established writers/artists. We feel the mix is good and healthy." Queries/mss may be routed to other editors in the publishing group.

‡TSR, INC., Box 756, Lake Geneva WI 53147. (414)248-3625. Imprints include Dragonlance, Forgotten Realms, Greyhawk, TSR Books and Buck Rogers. Managing Editor: Mary Kirchoff. Publishes trade paperback originals. Firm averages 70-80 titles/year; imprint averages 20-25 titles/year. Receives 250 submissions/year. 30-40% of books from first-time authors. 5% from unagented authors. Pays 4% on retail price. Offers $4,000 average advance. Publishes book an average of 6 months after acceptance. Simultaneous and photocopied submissions OK. Computer printout submissions OK; no dot-matrix. Reports in 1 month on queries; 6 weeks on mss.
Nonfiction: "All of our nonfiction books are generated in-house."
Fiction: Fantasy, horror, mainstream/contemporary, mystery and science fiction. "We won't be contracting for any new books until April 1990. We have a very small market for good science fiction and fantasy for the TSR Book line, but also need samples from writers willing to do work-for-hire for our other lines. We do not need occult, new age, or adult theme fiction. Nor will we consider excessively violent or gory fantasy, science fiction or horror." Query. Submit outline/synopsis and sample chapters or ms through agent only.
Recent Fiction Title: *Darkness and Light*, by Paul Thompson and Tonya Carter.
Tips: Our audience is highly imaginative 12-40 year-old males.

‡*CHARLES E. TUTTLE PUBLISHING COMPANY, INC., 2-6 Suido 1-Chome, Tokyo 112, Japan. Managing Editor: Ray Furse. Publishes hardcover and trade paperback originals and reprints. Averages 36 titles/year. Receives 750 submissions/year. 10% of books from first-time authors; 80% from unagented writers. Subsidy publishes 5% of books. Pays 6-10% on wholesale price. Offers $1,000 average advance. Publishes book an average of 8-12 months after acceptance. Simultaneous and photocopied submissions OK. Query for electronic submissions. Computer printout submissions OK. Reports in 2 weeks on queries; 2 months on manuscripts. Free book catalog and manuscript guidelines.
Nonfiction: Cookbook, how-to, humor, illustrated book and reference. Subjects include art/architecture, business and economics, cooking, foods and nutrition, government/politics, history, language/literature, money/finance, philosophy, regional, religion, sports and travel. "We want Asia-related, but specifically Japan-related manuscripts on various topics, particularly business, martial arts, language, etc." Query with outline/synopsis and sample chapters. Reviews artwork as part of ms package.
Recent Nonfiction Title: *Sho: Japanese Calligraphy*, by C.J. Earnshaw (language art).
Fiction: Literature of Japan or Asia in English translation. Query with outline/synopsis and sample chapters.
Recent Fiction Title: *More Max Danger*, by R.J. Collins (humor).
Poetry: Submit samples.
Recent Poetry Title: *Kyoto Dwelling*, by Edith Shiffert (haiku).
Tips: "Readers with an interest in Japan and Asia—culture, language, business, foods, travel, etc.—are our audience."

‡TWIN PEAKS PRESS, Box 129, Vancouver WA 98666. (206)694-2462. President: Helen Hecker. Publishes hardcover originals and reprints and trade paperback originals and reprints. Averages 7-10 titles/year. Receives 24 submissions/year. 25% of books from first-time authors. 100% from unagented writers. Payment varies—individual agreement. Publishes book an average of 6 months after acceptance. Simultaneous and photocopied submissions OK. Computer printout submissions OK; prefers letter-quality. Reports in 2 weeks on queries; 2 weeks on mss. Book catalog for $1.
Nonfiction: Cookbook, how-to, reference and self-help. Subjects include business and economics, cooking, foods & nutrition, health/medicine, hobbies, recreation, sociology, sports and travel. Query.
Recent Nonfiction Title: *Travel for the Disabled*, by Hecker, (travel/health).

*TYNDALE HOUSE PUBLISHERS, INC., 336 Gundersen Dr., Wheaton IL 60187. (312)668-8300. Editor-in-Chief/Acquisitions: Wendell Hawley. Publishes hardcover and trade paperback originals and hardcover and mass paperback reprints. Averages 100 titles/year; receives 3,000 submissions annually. 15% of books from first-time authors; 99% of books from unagented writers. Average print order for a writer's first book is 7,000-10,000. Subsidy publishes 2% of books. Pays 10% royalty; offers negotiable advance. Publishes book an average of 18 months after acceptance. Computer printout submissions acceptable; no dot-matrix. Reports in 6 weeks. Free book catalog; ms guidelines for #10 SAE with 1 first class stamp.
Nonfiction: Religious books only: personal experience, family living, marriage, Bible reference works and commentaries, Christian living, devotional, inspirational, church and social issues, Bible prophecy, theology and doctrine, counseling and Christian psychology, Christian apologetics and church history. Submit table of contents, chapter summary, preface, first 2 chapters and 1 later chapter.
Fiction: Biblical novels. Submit outline/synopsis and sample chapters.

*UAHC PRESS, Union of American Hebrew Congregations, 838 5th Ave., New York NY 10021. (212)249-0100. Managing Director: Stuart L. Benick. Publishes hardcover and trade paperback originals. Averages 15 titles/year. 50% of books from first-time authors; 90% of books from unagented writers. Subsidy publishes 40% of books. Pays 5-15% royalty on wholesale price. Publishes book an average of 9 months after acceptance.

Simultaneous and photocopied submissions OK. Computer printout submissions OK. Book catalog and ms guidelines for SASE.

Nonfiction: Illustrated, juvenile and Jewish textbooks. Subjects include Jewish religion. "We need Jewish textbooks which fit into our curriculum." Reviews artwork/photos as part of ms package.

Fiction: Jewish religion. "We publish books that teach values."

ULI, THE URBAN LAND INSTITUTE, 1090 Vermont Ave. N.W., Washington DC 20005. (202)289-8500. Staff Vice President of Publications: Frank H. Spink, Jr. Publishes hardcover and trade paperback originals. Averages 15-20 titles/year. Receives 20 submissions annually. No books from first-time authors; 100% of books from unagented writers. Pays 10% royalty on gross sales. Offers advance of $1,500-2,000. Publishes book an average of 6 months after acceptance. Query for electronic submissions. Computer printout submissions acceptable; prefers letter-quality. Book catalog and writer's guidelines for 9x12 SAE.

Nonfiction: Technical books on real estate development and land planning. "The majority of mss are created in-house by research staff. We acquire two or three outside authors to fill schedule and subject areas where our list has gaps. We are not interested in real estate sales, brokerages, appraisal, making money in real estate, opinion, personal point of view, or mss negative toward growth and development." Query. Reviews artwork/photos as part of ms package.

Recent Nonfiction Title: *Density by Design*, by A/A Housing Committee.

ULTRALIGHT PUBLICATIONS, INC., Box 234, Hammelstown PA 17036. (717)566-0468. Editor: Michael A. Markowski. Imprints includes Aviation Publishers and Medical Information Systems Division. Publishes hardcover and trade paperback originals. Averages 6 titles/year; receives 30 submissions annually. 50% of books from first-time authors; 100% of books from unagented writers. Average print order for a writer's first book is 5,000. Pays 10-15% royalty on wholesale price; buys some mss outright. Offers average $1,000-1,500 advance. Publishes book an average of 9 months after acceptance. Simultaneous and photocopied submissions OK. Computer printout submissions acceptable; no dot-matrix. Reports in 3 weeks on queries; 2 months on mss. Book catalog and ms guidelines for #10 SAE with 2 first class stamps.

Nonfiction: How-to, technical on hobbies (model airplanes, model cars, and model boats) and aviation. Publishes for "aviation buffs, dreamers and enthusiasts. We are looking for titles in the homebuilt, ultralight, sport and general aviation fields. We are interested in how-to, technical and reference books of short to medium length that will serve recognized and emerging aviation needs." Also interested in automotive historical, reference and how-to; popular health, medical, and fitness for the general public. Self-help, motivation and success are also areas of interest. Query or submit outline/synopsis and 3 sample chapters. Reviews artwork/photos as part of ms package.

Recent Nonfiction Title: *Canard: A Revolution in Flight*, by Lennon (aviation history).

‡UMBRELLA BOOKS, Harbor View Publications Group, Box 1460-A, Friday Harbor WA 98250. (206)378-5128. Publishes 4-6 titles/year. Pays on wholesale price. Advance varies. Publishes book an average of 6 months after acceptance. Simultaneous and photocopied submissions OK. Query for electronic submissions. Computer printout submissions OK; prefers letter-quality. Reports in 1 month on queries. Manuscript guidelines for #10 SAE with 1 first class stamp.

Nonfiction: Travel (Pacific Northwest). Query. Reviews artwork/photos as part of ms package.

Recent Nonfiction Title: *Umbrella Guide to Friday Harbor and San Juan Island*.

UMI RESEARCH PRESS, University Microfilms, Inc., Bell & Howell, 300 N. Zeeb Rd., Ann Arbor MI 48106. Editorial Development Manager: Christine B. Hammes. Publishes hardcover originals and some revised dissertations. Averages 60-70 titles/year; receives 400 or more submissions annually. 70% of books from first-time authors. Average print order for a writer's first book is 700. Pays 5% royalty on net sales. Offers average $100 advance. Publishes book an average of 6 months after acceptance. Photocopied submissions OK. Query for electronic submissions. Computer printout submissions acceptable "if good quality."

Nonfiction: Scholarly and professional research and critical studies in arts and humanities. Subjects include film and TV (theory, criticism, and aesthetics); art (theory, criticism, and history); theatre (history and theory); musicology; folk art; American material culture; literary criticism and women's studies. Especially looking for "scholarly works, original conclusions resulting from careful academic research. Primarily aimed at undergraduate, graduate, and professional level. Academics, research librarians, art, music, and literary communities, are our audience." No mass market books. Query.

Recent Nonfiction Title: *Warhol: Conversations about the Artist*, by Patrick S. Smith.

Tips: "Send detailed proposal to publisher *before* devoting hours to complete a manuscript. Get feedback at the outline/prospectus stage. Sell us on your manuscript: Why is the work an important and original contribution to its field? Who are its prospective readers and what are your ideas for helping us get word out to them (should we agree to publish the ms)?"

‡UNION SQUARE PRESS, Imprint of NJ Sambul & Co., Inc. 5 E. 16th St., New York NY 10003. (212)924-2800. FAX: (212)675-5479. Managing Editor: Karen Raugust. Publishes hardcover originals and trade paperback originals and reprints. Firm averages 7 titles/year. 50% of books from first-time authors. 90% from

unagented writers. Pays 10% on wholesale price. Offers $500-1,000 average advance. Publishes book an average of 9 months after acceptance. Simultaneous submissions OK. Query for electronic submissions. Computer printout submissions OK; prefers letter-quality. Reports in 3 months on queries; 3 months on mss.
Nonfiction: Coffee table books, how-to, illustrated books, reference and technical. Subjects include business and economics, computers and electronics, hobbies/crafts, science (broadcast engineering) and media. Submit outline/synopsis and sample chapters. Reviews artwork/photos as part of ms package.
Recent Nonfiction Title: *The Embroidery of Madeira*, by Holman/Walker (crafts, coffee-table).

‡**UNITED RESOURCE PRESS**, 4521 Campus Dr. #388, Irvine CA 92715. General Manager: Sally Black. Publishes hardcover, trade paperback and mass market paperback originals. Publishes 6 titles/year. 50% of books from first-time authors. 50% from unagented writers. Pays 5-7% on retail price. Publishes book an average of 1 year after acceptance. Simultaneous and photocopied submissions. Query for electronic submissions. Computer printout submissions OK. Reports in 2 months. Book catalog for $1. Manuscript guidelines for #10 SAE and 1 first-class stamp.
Nonfiction: Personal finance. Subjects include money/finance. "For next two years we will focus on personal finance (primary)." Submit outline/synopsis and sample chapters and complete ms.
Recent Nonfiction Title: *Financial Literacy*.
Tips: "Write for or buy samples of the publishers' best selling or favorite titles to see what they want."

***UNIVELT, INC.**, Box 28130, San Diego CA 92128. (619)746-4005. Publisher: H. Jacobs. Publishes hardcover originals. Averages 8 titles/year; receives 20 submissions annually. 5% of books from first-time authors; 5% of books from unagented writers. Subsidy publishes (nonauthor) 10% of books. Average print order for a writer's first book is 1,000-2,000. Pays 10% royalty on actual sales; no advance. Publishes book an average of 4 months after acceptance. Computer printout submissions acceptable; prefers letter-quality. Reports in 1 month. Book catalog and ms guidelines for SASE.
Nonfiction: Publishes in the field of aerospace, especially astronautics and technical communications, but including application of aerospace technology to Earth's problems, also astronomy. Submit outline/synopsis and 1-2 sample chapters. Reviews artwork/photos as part of ms package.
Recent Nonfiction Title: *Soviet Space Programs 1980-1985*.
Tips: "Writers have the best chance of selling manuscripts on the history of astronautics (we have a history series) and astronautics/spaceflight subjects. We publish for the American Astronautical Society." Queries/mss may be routed to other editors in the publishing group.

‡**UNIVERSITY ASSOCIATES, INC.**, 8517 Production Ave., San Diego CA 92121. (619)578-5900. FAX: (619)578-2042. President: J. William Pfeiffer. Publishes paperback and hardback originals and reprints. Averages 12-15 titles/year. Specializes in practical materials for human resource development, consultants, etc. Pays average 10% royalty; no advance. Publishes book an average of 6 months after acceptance. Markets books by direct mail. Simultaneous submissions OK. Computer printout submissions acceptable; no dot-matrix. Reports in 4 months. Book catalog and guidelines for SASE.
Nonfiction: Richard Roe, Vice President, Publications. Publishes (in order of preference) human resource development and group-oriented material, management education and community relations and personal growth, and business. No materials for grammar school or high school classroom teachers. Use *American Psychological Association Style Manual*. Query. Send prints or completed art or rough sketches to accompany ms.
Recent Nonfiction Title: *The 1989 Annual: Developing Human Resources*, J.W. Pfeiffer, editor.

UNIVERSITY OF ALABAMA PRESS, Box 2877, Tuscaloosa AL 35487. Director: Malcolm MacDonald. Publishes hardcover originals. Averages 40 titles/year; receives 200 submissions annually. 80% of books from first-time authors; 100% of books from unagented writers. "Pays maximum 10% royalty on wholesale price; no advance." Publishes book an average of 16 months after acceptance. Computer printout submissions acceptable. Free book catalog; ms guidelines for SASE.
Nonfiction: Biography, history, philosophy, politics, religion, sociology and anthropology. Considers upon merit almost any subject of scholarly interest, but specializes in linguistics and philology, political science and public administration, literary criticism and biography, philosophy and history. Accepts nonfiction translations. Reviews artwork/photos as part of ms package.
Recent Nonfiction Title: *Black Eagle: General Daniel "Chappie" James* (biography).

THE UNIVERSITY OF ALBERTA PRESS, 141 Athabasca Hall, Edmonton, Alberta T6G 2E8 Canada. (403)432-3662. FAX: (403)492-7219. Imprint, Pica Pica Press. Director: Norma Gutteridge. Publishes hardcover and trade paperback originals, and trade paperback reprints. Averages 10 titles/year; receives 200-300 submissions annually. 60% of books from first-time authors; majority of books from unagented writers. Average print order for a writer's first book is 1,000. Pays 10% royalty on retail price. Publishes book an average of 1 year after acceptance. Query for electronic submissions. Computer printout submissions acceptable; no dot-matrix. Reports in 1 week on queries; 3 months on mss. Free book catalog and ms guidelines.

Nonfiction: Biography, how-to, reference, technical, textbook, and scholarly. Subjects include art, history, nature, philosophy, politics, and sociology. Especially looking for "biographies of Canadians in public life, and works analyzing Canada's political history and public policy, particularly in international affairs. No pioneer reminiscences, literary criticism (unless in Canadian literature), reports of narrowly focused studies, unrevised theses." Submit complete ms. Reviews artwork/photos as part of ms package.

Recent Nonfiction Title: *The Windmill Turning: Nursery Rhymes, Maxims and Other Expressions of Western Canadian Mennonites*, by Victor Carl Friesen.

Tips: "We are interested in original research making a significant contribution to knowledge in the subject."

‡**UNIVERSITY OF ARIZONA PRESS**, 1230 N. Park Ave., No. 102, Tucson AZ 85719. (602)621-1441. Director: Stephen Cox. Publishes hardcover and paperback originals and reprints. Averages 40 titles/year; receives 300-400 submissions annually. 30% of books from first-time authors; 90% of books from unagented writers. Average print order is 1,500. Royalty terms vary; usual starting point for scholarly monograph is after sale of first 1,000 copies. Publishes book an average of 1 year after acceptance. Photocopied submissions OK. Query for electronic submissions. Computer printout submissions acceptable; no dot-matrix. Reports in three months. Book catalog for 9x12 SAE; ms guidelines for #10 SAE.

Nonfiction: Scholarly books about the American West, Mexico and natural history, and about subjects strongly identified with the universities in Arizona—anthropology, philosophy, arid lands studies, space sciences, Asian studies, Southwest Indians, Mexico and creative nonfiction. Query and submit outline, list of illustrations and sample chapters. Reviews artwork/photos as part of ms package.

Recent Nonfiction Title: *Blue Desert*, by Charles Bowden.

Tips: "Perhaps the most common mistake a writer might make is to offer a book manuscript or proposal to a house whose list he or she has not studied carefully. Editors rejoice in receiving material that is clearly targeted to the house's list, 'I have approached your firm because my books complement your past publications in. . .', presented in a straightforward, businesslike manner."

***THE UNIVERSITY OF CALGARY PRESS**, 2500 University Drive NW, Calgary, Alberta T2N 1N4 Canada. (403)220-7578. Assistant Director: L. D. Cameron. Publishes scholarly paperback originals. Averages 12-16 titles/year; receives 100 submissions annually. 50% of books from first-time authors; 100% of books from unagented authors. Subsidy publishes (nonauthor) 100% of books. "As with all Canadian University presses, UCP does not have publication funds of its own. Money must be found to subsidize each project. We do not consider publications for which there is no possibility of subvention." Publishes book average of 1 year after acceptance. Pays negotiable royalties. "Ms must pass a two tier review system before acceptance." Photocopied submissions OK. Query for electronic submissions. Computer printout submissions OK; prefers letter-quality. Reports on 2 weeks on queries; 2 months on mss. Free book catalog and guidelines.

Nonfiction: The University of Calgary Press (UCP) has developed an active publishing program that includes up to 12 new scholarly titles each year and 10 scholarly journals. UCP publishes in a wide variety of subject areas and is willing to consider any innovative scholarly publication. The intention is not to restrict the publication list to specific areas.

Recent Nonfiction Title: *Roland Gissing: The Peoples' Painter*, by Max Foran with Nonie Houlton.

Tips: "If I were trying to interest a scholarly publisher, I would prepare my manuscript on a word processor and submit a completed prospectus, including projected market, to the publisher."

UNIVERSITY OF CALIFORNIA PRESS, 2120 Berkeley Way, Berkeley CA 94720. Director: James H. Clark. Assistant Director: Lynne E. Withey. Los Angeles office: Suite 613, 10995 Le Conte Ave., UCLA, Los Angeles CA 90024. New York office: Room 513, 50 E. 42 St., New York NY 10017. London office: University Presses of California, Columbia, and Princeton, Avonlea, 10 Watlington Rd., Cowley, Oxford OX4 5NF England. Publishes hardcover and paperback originals and reprints. "On books likely to do more than return their costs, a standard royalty contract beginning at 7% is paid; on paperbacks it is less." Published 230 titles last year. Queries are always advisable, accompanied by outlines or sample material. Accepts nonfiction translations. Send to Berkeley address. Reports vary, depending on the subject. Enclose return postage.

Nonfiction: "Most of our publications are hardcover nonfiction written by scholars." Publishes scholarly books including art, literary studies, social sciences, natural sciences and some high-level popularizations. No length preferences.

Fiction and Poetry: Publishes fiction and poetry only in translation, usually in bilingual editions.

***UNIVERSITY OF ILLINOIS PRESS**, 54 E. Gregory, Champaign IL 61820. (217)333-0950. FAX: (217)244-8082. Director/Editor: Richard L. Wentworth. Publishes hardcover and trade paperback originals, and hardcover and trade paperback reprints. Averages 90-100 titles/year. 50% of books from first-time authors; 95% of books from unagented writers. Subsidy publishes (nonauthor) 30% of books. Pays 0-10% royalty on net sales; offers average $1,000-1,500 advance (rarely). Publishes book an average of 1 year after acceptance. Query for electronic submissions. Computer printout submissions acceptable; no dot-matrix. Reports in 1 week on queries; 3 months on mss. Free book catalog.

Nonfiction: Biography, reference and scholarly books. Subjects include Americana, business and economics, history (especially American history), music (especially American music), politics, sociology, sports and literature. Always looking for "solid scholarly books in American history, especially social history; books on American popular music, and books in the broad area of American studies." Query with outline/synopsis.

Recent Nonfiction Title: *Waiting for Prime Time: The Women of Television News*, by Marlene Sanders and Marcia Rock.

Fiction: Ethnic, experimental and mainstream. "We publish four collections of stories by individual writers each year. We do not publish novels." Query.

Recent Fiction Title: *The Christmas Wife*, by Helen Norris (stories).

Tips: "Serious scholarly books that are broad enough and well-written enough to appeal to non-specialists are doing well for us in today's market. Writers of nonfiction whose primary goal is to earn money (rather than get promoted in an academic position) are advised to try at least a dozen commercial publishers before thinking about offering the work to a university press."

UNIVERSITY OF IOWA PRESS, Westlawn, Iowa City IA 52242. (319)353-3181. Director: Paul Zimmer. Publishes hardcover and paperback originals. Averages 30 titles/year; receives 300-400 submissions annually. 30% of books from first-time authors; 95% of books from unagented writers. Average print order for a writer's first book is 1,200-1,500. Pays 7-10% royalty on net price. "We market mostly by direct mailing of flyers to groups with special interests in our titles and by advertising in trade and scholarly publications." Publishes book an average of 1 year after acceptance. Query for electronic submissions. Readable computer printout submissions acceptable. Reports within 4 months. Free book catalog and ms guidelines.

Nonfiction: Publishes anthropology, archaeology, British and American literary studies, history (Victorian, U.S., German, medieval, Latin American), and natural history. Currently publishes the Iowa School of Letters Award for Short Fiction, and Iowa Poetry Prize selections. "Please query regarding poetry or fiction before sending manuscript." Looks for "evidence of original research; reliable sources; clarity of organization, complete development of theme with documentation and supportive footnotes and/or bibliography; and a substantive contribution to knowledge in the field treated." Query or submit outline/synopsis. Use Chicago *Manual of Style*. Reviews artwork/photos as part of ms package.

UNIVERSITY OF MASSACHUSETTS PRESS, Box 429, Amherst MA 01004. (413)545-2217. Director: Bruce Wilcox. Publishes hardcover and paperback originals, reprints and imports. Averages 30 titles/year; receives 600 submissions annually. 20% of books from first-time authors; 90% of books from unagented writers. Average print order for a writer's first book is 1,500. Royalties generally 10% of net income. Advance rarely offered. No author subsidies accepted. Publishes book an average of 1 year after acceptance. Query for electronic submissions. Computer printout submissions acceptable; prefers letter-quality. Preliminary report in 1 month. Free book catalog.

Nonfiction: Publishes Afro-American studies, art and architecture, biography, criticism, history, natural history, philosophy, poetry, public policy, sociology and women's studies in original and reprint editions. Accepts nonfiction translations. Submit outline/synopsis and 1-2 sample chapters. Reviews artwork/photos as part of ms package.

Recent Nonfiction Title: *Black Yankees: The Development of an Afro-American Subculture in Eighteenth-Century New England*, by William D. Piersen.

UNIVERSITY OF MICHIGAN PRESS, 839 Greene St., Ann Arbor MI 48106. (313)764-4388. Director: Colin Day. Editors: Mary C. Erwin, LeAnn Fields. Publishes hardcover and paperback originals and reprints. Averages 40-50 titles/year. Pays royalty on net price; offers advance. Query for electronic submissions. Computer printout submissions acceptable. Reports in 2 months. Free book catalog.

Nonfiction: Archaeology, advanced textbooks, anthropology, biology, classics, economics, English as a second language, Great Lakes regional, history, law, literary criticism, music, political science, reference, theater, women's studies. Query first.

‡*UNIVERSITY OF MINNESOTA PRESS, 2037 University Ave. S.E., Minneapolis MN 55414. (612)624-2516. Senior Editor: Terry Cochran. Publishes hardcover and trade paperback originals and reprints. Averages 50 titles/year. Receives 350 submissions/year. 20% of books from first-time authors. 95% from unagented writers. Subsidy publishes 20% of books. Subsidies are traditionally sought for translations. Pays 4-12.5% royalty on retail price. Offers $1,000 average advance. Publishes book an average of 18 months after acceptance. Simultaneous and photocopied submissions. Query for electronic submissions. Computer printout submissions OK. Reports in 1 month. Free book catalog and ms guidelines.

Nonfiction: Illustrated books, reference, technical and textbook. Subjects include agriculture/horticulture, Americana (popular culture), art/architecture (criticism), business and economics, child guidance/parenting (health-related), gay/lesbian, health/medicine, language/literature (literature theory), music/dance (music/criticism), nature/environment (regional geology and biology), philosophy, photography (media studies), psychology: MMPI (multi-phasic inventory), regional, and women's issues/studies. Query or submit outline/synopsis and sample chapters. Reviews artwork as part of package.

Recent Nonfiction Title: *Schooling and the Struggle for Public Life*, by Henry Giroux (education/American studies).
Fiction: Ethnic, experimental, feminist, gay/lesbian, historical, literary and plays. Query or submit outline/synopsis and sample chapters.
Recent Fiction Title: *The Trickster of Liberty*, by Gerald Vizenor (American Indian fiction).

UNIVERSITY OF MISSOURI PRESS, 200 Lewis Hall, Columbia MO 65211. (314)882-7641. Director: Beverly Jarrett. Associate Director: Susan McGregor Denny. Publishes hardcover and paperback originals and paperback reprints. Averages 40 titles/year; receives 300 submissions annually. 40% of books from first-time authors; 100% of books from unagented writers. Average print order for a writer's first book is 1,000. Pays up to 10% royalty on net receipts; no advance. Publishes book an average of 1 year after acceptance. Photocopied submissions OK. Query for electronic submissions. Computer printout submissions acceptable; prefers letter-quality. Reports in 6 months. Free book catalog; ms guidelines for SASE.
Nonfiction: Scholarly publisher interested in history, literary criticism, political science, social science, art and art history. Also regional books about Missouri and the Midwest. No mathematics or hard sciences. Query or submit outline/synopsis and sample chapters. Consult Chicago *Manual of Style*.
Fiction: "Fiction, poetry and drama manuscripts are taken by submission only in February and March of odd-numbered years. We publish original short fiction in the Breakthrough Series, not to exceed 35,000 words. May be short story collection or novella. We also publish poetry and drama in the same series. No limitations on subject matter." Query with SASE.
Recent Fiction Title: *The Wrong-Handed Man*, by Lawrence Millman (stories).

UNIVERSITY OF NEVADA PRESS, Reno NV 89557. (702)784-6573. Acting Director: Nicholas M. Cady. Publishes hardcover and paperback originals and reprints. Averages 12 titles/year; receives 50 submissions annually. 20% of books from first-time authors; 100% of books from unagented writers. Average print order for a writer's first book is 2,000. Pays 5-10% royalty on net price. Publishes book an average of 2 years after acceptance. Computer printout submissions acceptable; high quality dot-matrix is OK. Preliminary report in 2 months. Free book catalog and ms guidelines.
Nonfiction: Specifically needs regional history and natural history, anthropology, biographies and Basque studies. "We are the first university press to sustain a sound series on Basque studies—New World and Old World." No juvenile books. Submit complete ms. Reviews photocopies of artwork/photos as part of ms package.
Recent Nonfiction Title: *Casino Accounting and Financial Management*, by E. Malcolm Greenlees.
Recent Fiction Title: *Chester's Last Stand*, by Richard Brown.

UNIVERSITY OF OKLAHOMA PRESS, 1005 Asp Ave., Norman OK 73019. (405)325-5111. Editor-in-Chief: John Drayton. Publishes hardcover and paperback originals; and reprints. Averages 50 titles/year. Pays royalty comparable to those paid by other publishers for comparable books. Publishes book an average of 12-18 months after acceptance. Query for electronic submissions. Computer printout submissions acceptable; prefers letter-quality. Reports in 4 months. Book catalog $1.
Nonfiction: Publishes American Indian studies, Western U.S. history, literacy theory, and classical studies. No poetry and fiction. Query, including outline, 1-2 sample chapters and author resume. Chicago *Manual of Style* for ms guidelines. Reviews artwork/photos as part of ms package.
Recent Nonfiction Title: *Hoover Dam: An American Adventure*, by Joseph E. Stevens.

***UNIVERSITY OF PENNSYLVANIA PRESS**, University of Pennsylvania, 418 Service Dr., Philadelphia PA 19104. (215)898-6261. Director: Thomas M. Rotell. Publishes hardcover and paperback originals and reprints. Averages 65 titles/year; receives 600 submissions annually. 10-20% of books from first-time authors; 99% of books from unagented writers. Subsidy publishes (nonauthor) 4% of books. Subsidy publishing is determined by evaluation obtained by the press from outside specialists; work approved by Faculty Editorial Committee; subsidy approved by funding organization. Royalty determined on book-by-book basis. Publishes book an average of 9 months after delivery of completed ms. Photocopied submissions OK. Query for electronic submissions. Computer printout submissions acceptable; prefers letter-quality. Reports in 3 months. Book catalog and ms guidelines for 8½x11 SAE and 5 first class stamps.
Nonfiction: Publishes Americana, biography, business, economics, history, medicine, biological sciences, computer science, physical sciences, law, anthropology, folklore and literary criticism. "Serious books that serve the scholar and the professional." Follow the Chicago *Manual of Style*. Query with outline and letter

For information on book publishers' areas of interest, see the nonfiction and fiction sections in the Book Publishers Subject Index.

describing project, state availability of photos and/or illustrations to accompany ms, with copies of illustrations.
Recent Nonfiction Title: *Clara Barton: Professional Angel*, edited by Elizabeth Pryor.
Tips: Queries/mss may be routed to other editors in the publishing group.

*THE UNIVERSITY OF TENNESSEE PRESS, 293 Communications Bldg., Knoxville TN 37996-0325. Contact: Acquisitions Editor. Averages 30 titles/year; receives 300 submissions annually. 50% of books from first-time authors; 99% of books from unagented writers. Average print order for a writer's first book is 1,250. Subsidy publishes (nonauthor) 10% of books. Pays negotiable royalty on retail price. Publishes book an average of 1 year after acceptance. Photocopied submissions OK. Computer printout submissions acceptable; no dot-matrix. Reports in 1 month. Book catalog for $1 and 12x16 SAE; ms guidelines for SASE.
Nonfiction: American history, political science, religious studies, vernacular architecture and material culture, literary criticism, Black studies, women's studies, Caribbean, anthropology, folklore and regional studies. Prefers "scholarly treatment and a readable style. Authors usually have Ph.D.s." Submit outline/synopsis, author vita, and 2 sample chapters. No fiction, poetry or plays. Reviews artwork/photos as part of ms package.
Recent Nonfiction Title: *Seeking Many Inventions: The Idea of Community in America*, by Philip Abbott.
Tips: "Our market is in several groups: scholars; educated readers with special interests in given scholarly subjects; and the general educated public interested in Tennessee, Appalachia and the South. Not all our books appeal to all these groups, of course, but any given book must appeal to at least one of them."

UNIVERSITY OF TEXAS PRESS, Box 7819, Austin TX 78713. Executive Editor: Theresa May. Averages 60 titles/year; receives 1,000 submissions annually. 50% of books from first-time authors; 99% of books from unagented writers. Average print order for a writer's first book is 1,000. Pays royalty usually based on net income; occasionally offers advance. Publishes book an average of 18 months after acceptance. Query for electronic submissions. Computer printout submissions acceptable; no dot-matrix. Reports in 2 months. Free book catalog and writer's guidelines.
Nonfiction: General scholarly subjects: astronomy, natural history, economics, American, Latin American and Middle Eastern studies, native Americans, classics, films, medicine, biology, contemporary architecture, archeology, anthropology, geography, ornithology, ecology, Chicano studies, physics, health, sciences, international relations, linguistics, photography, 20th-century and women's literature. Also uses specialty titles related to Texas and the Southwest, national trade titles, and regional trade titles. Accepts nonfiction and fiction translations (generally Latin American fiction). Query or submit outline/synopsis and 2 sample chapters. Reviews artwork/photos as part of ms package.
Recent Nonfiction Title: *The Mockingbird*, by Robin Doughty.
Recent Fiction Translation: *Sanitary Centennial and Selected Stories*, by Fernando Sorrentino (translated from Spanish).
Tips: "It's difficult to make a manuscript over 400 double-spaced pages into a feasible book. Authors should take special care to edit out extraneous material." Looks for sharply focused, in-depth treatments of important topics.

‡UNIVERSITY OF UTAH PRESS, University of Utah, 101 University Services Bldg., Salt Lake City UT 84112. (801)581-6771. Director: David Catron. Publishes hardcover and paperback originals and reprints. Averages 18 titles/year; receives 500 submissions annually. 30% of books from first-time authors. Average print order for writer's first book is 1,000. Subsidy publishes (nonauthor) 10% of books. Pays 10% royalty on net sales on first 2,000 copies sold; 12% on 2,001 to 4,000 copies sold; 15% thereafter. Publishes book an average of 18 months after acceptance. Computer printout submissions acceptable. Reports in 10 weeks. Free book catalog; ms guidelines for SASE.
Nonfiction: Scholarly books on Western history, philosophy, anthropology, Mesoamerican studies, folklore, and Middle Eastern studies. Accepts nonfiction translations. Popular, well-written, carefully researched regional studies for Bonneville Books Series. Query with synopsis and 3 sample chapters. Author should specify ms length in query. Reviews artwork/photos as part of ms package.
Recent Nonfiction Title: *Indians of Yellowstone*, by Joel Janetski.
Fiction: Regional (western) authors or subjects.
Recent Fiction Title: *The Wake of the General Bliss*, by Edward Lueders.
Poetry: One volume per year selected in an annual competition (submissions in March).
Recent Poetry Title: *A Day at the Races*, by Sidney Burris.

UNIVERSITY OF WISCONSIN PRESS, 114 N. Murray St., Madison WI 53715. (608)262-4928. Director: Allen N. Fitchen. Acquisitions Editor: Barbara J. Hanrahan. Publishes hardcover and paperback originals and reprints. Averages 50 titles/year. Pays standard royalties on retail price. Reports in 3 months.
Nonfiction: Publishes general nonfiction based on scholarly research. Looks for "originality, significance, quality of the research represented, literary quality, and breadth of interest to the educated community at large." Follow Chicago *Manual of Style*. Send letter of inquiry and prospectus.
Recent Nonfiction Title: *The Rights of Nature*, by Roderick-Frazier Nash.

UNIVERSITY PRESS OF AMERICA, INC., 4720 Boston Way, Lanham MD 20706. (301)459-3366. Publisher: James E. Lyons. Publishes hardcover and paperback originals and reprints. Averages 450 titles/year. Pays 5-15% royalty on retail price; occasional advance. No computer printout submissions. Reports in 6 weeks. Book catalog and guidelines for SASE.
Nonfiction: Scholarly monographs, college, and graduate level textbooks in history, economics, business, psychology, political science, African studies, Black studies, philosophy, religion, sociology, music, art, literature, drama and education. No juvenile, elementary or high school material. Submit outline.
Recent Nonfiction Title: *Thomas Jefferson: A Strange Case of Mistaken Identity*, by Alf J. Mapp Jr. (biography).

UNIVERSITY PRESS OF KANSAS, 329 Carruth, Lawrence KS 66045. (913)864-4154. Editor: Fred Woodward. Hardcover and paperback originals. Averages 30 titles/year; receives 500-600 submissions annually. 25% of books from first-time authors; 95% of books from unagented writers. Royalties negotiable; occasional advances. Markets books by advertising, direct mail, publicity, and sales representation to the trade; 55% of sales to bookstores. "State availability of illustrations if they add significantly to the manuscript." Publishes book an average of 10 months after acceptance. Computer printout submissions acceptable; no dot-matrix. Reports in 4 months. Free book catalog; ms guidelines for #10 SASE.
Nonfiction: Publishes biography, history, sociology, philosophy, politics, military studies, regional subjects (Kansas, Great Plains, Midwest), and scholarly. Reviews artwork/photos as part of ms package. Query.
Recent Nonfiction Title: *The Middle West: Its Meaning in American Culture* (geography).

UNIVERSITY PRESS OF KENTUCKY, 663 South Limestone, Lexington KY 40506-0336. (606)257-2951. Associate Director: Jerome Crouch. Publishes hardcover originals and hardcover and trade paperback reprints. Averages 35 titles/year; receives 200 submissions annually. 25-50% of books from first-time authors; 98% of books from unagented writers. Pays 10-15% royalty on wholesale price. "As a nonprofit press, we generally exclude the first 1,000 copies from royalty payment." No advance. Publishes ms an average of 1 year after acceptance. Photocopied submissions OK if clearly legible. Computer printout submissions acceptable; prefers letter-quality. Reports in 1 month on queries; 3 months on mss. Free book catalog.
Nonfiction: Biography, reference and monographs. Subjects include Americana, history, politics and sociology. "We are a scholarly publisher, publishing chiefly for an academic and professional audience. Strong areas are history, literature, political science, folklore, anthropology, and sociology. Our books are expected to advance knowledge in their fields in some measure. We would be interested in the treatment of timely topics in the fields indicated, treatments that would be solid and substantial but that would be readable and capable of appealing to a general public." No "textbooks; genealogical material; lightweight popular treatments; how-to books; and generally books not related to our major areas of interest." Query. Reviews artwork/photos, but generally does not publish books with extensive number of photos.
Recent Nonfiction Title: *National Security Planning: Roosevelt Through Reagan*, by Michael M. Boll.
Tips: "Most of our authors are drawn from our primary academic and professional audience. We are probably not a good market for the usual freelance writer, unless his work fits into our special requirements. Moreover, we do not pay advances and income from our books is minimal; so we cannot offer much financial reward to a freelance writer."

UNIVERSITY PRESS OF MISSISSIPPI, 3825 Ridgewood Rd., Jackson MS 39211. (601)982-6205. FAX: (601)982-6610. Director: Richard Abel. Acquisitions Editor: Seetha Srinivasan. Publishes hardcover and paperback originals and reprints. Averages 30 titles/year; receives 250 submissions annually. 25% of books from first-time authors; 95% of books from unagented writers. "Competitive royalties and terms." Publishes book an average of 1 year after acceptance. Computer printout submissions acceptable. Reports in 2 months. Free book catalog.
Nonfiction: Americana, biography, history, politics, folklife, literary criticism, ethnic/minority studies, natural sciences and popular culture with scholarly emphasis. Interested in southern regional studies and literary studies. Submit outline/synopsis and sample chapters and curriculum vita to Acquisitions Editor. "We prefer a proposal that describes the significance of the work and a chapter outline." Reviews artwork/photos as part of ms package.
Recent Nonfiction Title: *Come Retribution: The Confederate Secret Service and the Assassination of Lincoln*, by William A. Tidwell.
Fiction: Commissioned trade editions by prominent writers.
Recent Fiction Title: *Morgana*, by Eurdora Welty.

‡*UNIVERSITY PRESS OF VIRGINIA**, Box 3608, University Station, Charlottesville VA 22903. (804)924-3468. Publishes hardcover and paperback originals and reprints. Averages 50 titles/year; receives 250 submissions annually. 70% of books from first-time authors; 100% of books from unagented writers. Average print order for a writer's first book is 1,000. "We subsidy publish 35% of our books, based on cost versus probable market." Royalty on retail depends on the market for the book; sometimes none is made. Publishes book an average of 1 year after acceptance. Computer printout submissions acceptable; no dot-matrix. Returns re-

jected material within a week; reports on acceptances in 2 months. Free catalog; ms guidelines for SASE.
Nonfiction: Publishes Americana, history, medicine and psychiatry, literary criticism, women's studies, Afro-American, bibliography, and decorative arts books. "Write a letter to the acquisitions editor, describing content of the manuscript, plus length. Also specify if maps, tables, illustrations, etc., are included." No educational, sociological or psychological mss. Reviews artwork/photos as part of ms package.
Recent Nonfiction Title: *Poetries of America: Essays on the Relation of Character to Style*, by Irvin Ehrenpreis.

‡*UNLIMITED PUBLISHING CO., Rt. 17K, Box 240, Bullville NY 10915. (914)361-1299. Publisher: John J. Prizzia Jr. Imprints includes UPC Publications, Inc. Publishes trade paperback originals. Averages 12 titles/year; receives 25 submissions annually. 90% of books from first-time; 95% of books from unagented writers. Subsidy publishes 20% of books. Pays 10-40% royalty on retail price or makes outright purchase for $500-4,000; offers $1,000 average advance. Publishes book an average of 6 months after acceptance. Photocopied submissions OK. Computer printout submissions OK; prefers letter-quality. Reports in 1 month on queries; 6 months on submissions. Book catalog for SASE.
Nonfiction: Biography, cookbook, how-to, humor, illustrated book, reference, self-help and technical. Subjects include business and economics, cooking and foods, hobbies, nature and sociology. "Prefers self-help and how-to books pertaining to cooking, traveling, hobbies, small business, advertising for small business, start your own business, etc." Submit outline/synopsis and sample chapters or complete ms.
Recent Nonfiction Title: *The Little People of Guadalcanal*, by Joseph T. Webber, MD.
Fiction: Adventure, experimental, historical, humor and mystery. "War stories, adventures of successful business people, the beginnings of millionaires, etc." Submit outline/synopsis and sample chapters or complete ms.
Recent Fiction Title: *Nicaragua Incident*, by Joseph Musso.

*UTAH STATE UNIVERSITY PRESS, Utah State University, Logan UT 84322-7800. (801)750-1362. Director: Linda Speth. Publishes hardcover and trade paperback originals and hardcover and trade paperback reprints. Averages 6 titles/year; receives 170 submissions annually. 8% of books from first-time authors. Average print order for a writer's first book is 1,000. Subsidy publishes 10% of books; subsidy publishes (nonauthor) 45% of books. Pays royalty on net price; no advance. Publishes book an average of 18 months after acceptance. Electronic submissions OK on Televideo 803, but requires hard copy also. Computer printout submissions acceptable; prefers letter-quality. Reports in 2 weeks on queries; 2 months on mss. Free book catalog; ms guidelines for SASE.
Nonfiction: Biography, reference and textbook on folklore, Americana (history and politics). "Particularly interested in book-length scholarly manuscripts dealing with folklore, Western history, Western literature. All manuscript submissions must have a scholarly focus." Submit complete ms. Reviews artwork/photos as part of ms package.
Recent Nonfiction Title: *Folk Groups*, by Elliot Oring (folklore).
Poetry: "At the present time, we have accepted several poetry manuscripts and will not be reading poetry submissions for one year."
Recent Poetry Title: *War On War*, by Lowell Jaeger.

VEHICULE PRESS, Box 125, Place du Parc Station, Montreal, Quebec H2W 2M9 Canada. (514)844-6073. Imprints include Signal Editions (poetry) and Dossier Quebec (history, memoirs). President/Publisher: Simon Dardick. Publishes trade paperback originals by Canadian authors *only*. Averages 8 titles/year; receives 250 submissions annually. 20% of books from first-time authors; 95% of books from unagented writers. Pays 10-15% royalty on retail price; offers $200-500 advance. Publishes book an average of 1 year after acceptance. Photocopied submissions OK. Query for electronic submissions. Computer printout submissions acceptable; prefers letter-quality. "We would appreciate receiving an IRC with SAE rather than U.S. postage stamps which we cannot use." Reports in 1 month on queries; 2 months on mss. Book catalog for 9x12 SAE with IRCs.
Nonfiction: Biography and memoir. Subjects include Canadiana, history, politics, social history and literature. Especially looking for Canadian social history. Query. Reviews artwork/photos as part of ms package.
Recent Nonfiction Title: *Swinging in Paradise: The Story of Jazz in Montreal*, by John Gilmore.
Poetry: Contact Michael Harris, editor. Looking for Canadian authors only. Submit complete ms.
Recent Poetry Title: *Infinite Worlds: The Poetry of Louis Dudek*.
Tips: "We are only interested in Canadian authors."

*VESTA PUBLICATIONS, LTD., Box 1641, Cornwall, Ontario K6H 5V6 Canada. (613)932-2135. Editor-in-Chief: Stephen Gill. Paperback and hardcover originals. 10% minimum royalty on wholesale price. Subsidy publishes 5% of books. "We ask a writer to subsidize a part of the cost of printing; normally, it is 50%. We do so when we find that the book does not have a wide market, as in the case of university theses and the author's first collection of poems. The writer gets 25 free copies and 10% royalty on paperback editions." No advance. Publishes 16 titles/year; receives 350 submissions annually. 80% of books from first-time authors; 100% of books from unagented writers. Simultaneous submissions OK if so informed. Photocopied submissions OK. Query for electronic submissions. Computer printout submissions acceptable; prefers letter-quality. Reports in 1 week on queries; 1 month on mss. Send SAE with IRCs. Free book catalog.

Nonfiction: Publishes Americana, art, biography, cookbooks, cooking and foods, history, philosophy, poetry, politics, reference, and religious books. Accepts nonfiction translations. Query or submit complete ms. Reviews artwork/photos. Looks for knowledge of the language and subject. "Query letters and mss should be accompanied by synopsis of the book and biographical notes." State availability of photos and/or illustrations to accompany ms.

Recent Nonfiction Title: *Famine*, by Edward Pike.

THE VESTAL PRESS, LTD., 320 N. Jensen Rd., Box 97, Vestal NY 13851-0097. (607)797-4872. President: Grace L. Houghton. Publishes hardcover and trade paperback originals and reprints. Averages 6-8 titles/year; receives 50-75 submissions annually. 20% of books from first-time writers; 95% of books from unagented authors. Pays 10% maximum royalty on net sales. Publishes books an average of 1 year after acceptance. Simultaneous and photocopied submissions OK. Computer printout submissions OK; prefers letter-quality. Reports in 2 weeks. Book catalog for $2.

Nonfiction: Technical antiquarian hobby topics in antique radio, mechanical music (player pianos, music boxes, etc.), reed organs, carousels, antique phonographs, early cinema history, regional history based on postcard collections. Query or submit outline/synopsis and sample chapters or submit complete ms.

Recent Nonfiction Title: *Speaking of Silence*, by William M. Drew.

VGM CAREER HORIZONS, Division of National Textbook Co., 4255 W. Touhy Ave., Lincolnwood IL 60646-1975. (312)679-5500. FAX: (312)679-2494. Editorial Director: Leonard Fiddle. Senior Editor: Michael Urban. Publishes hardcover and paperback originals and software. Averages 20-30 titles/year; receives 150-200 submissions annually. 10% of books from first-time authors; 95% of books from unagented writers. Pays royalty or makes outright purchase. Advance varies. Publishes book an average of 1 year after acceptance. Simultaneous and photocopied submissions OK. Query for electronic submissions. Computer printout submissions OK, prefers letter-quality. Reports in 3 weeks. Book catalog and ms guidelines for 9x12 SAE with 5 first class stamps.

Nonfiction: Textbook and general trade on careers and jobs. Nonfiction book manuscript needs are for careers in eye care, performing arts, information systems, welding, etc. Query or submit outline/synopsis and sample chapters. Reviews artwork/photos as part of ms package.

Recent Nonfiction Title: *How to Write a Winning Resume*, by Deborah Perlmutter Bloch.

Tips: "Our audience is job seekers, career planners, job changers, and students and adults in education and trade markets. Study our existing line of books before sending proposals."

VICTOR BOOKS, Division of Scripture Press Publications, Inc. 1825 College Ave., Wheaton IL 60187. (312)668-6000. Address mss to Acquisitions Editor. Imprints include SonFlower, Winner, SonPower. Publishes hardcover and trade paperback originals. Firm averages 75 titles/year. Receives 1,400 submissions/year. 5% of books from first-time authors; 98% from unagented writers. Royalty negotiable on retail price. Publishes book an average of 18 months after acceptance. Simultaneous and photocopied submissions OK. Computer printout submissions OK; prefers letter-quality. Reports in 1 month on queries; 2 months on mss. Ms guidelines for #10 SAE with 1 first class stamp; 4 first class stamps for a catalog and guidelines.

Nonfiction: Juvenile, reference and self-help. Subjects include child guidance/parenting, psychology, life-related Bible study and women's issues/studies. "We are interested in manuscripts with a fresh approach to Bible study and Christian living/leadership topics, written from an evangelical perspective. Issues-type books are also welcome." Query or submit outline/synopsis and sample chapters.

Recent Nonfiction Title: *Help! I'm a Baby-Boomer*, by Hans Finzel (issues).

Fiction: For ages 2-12. "We are looking for simple Bible-related stories that could be developed into shape or picture books for the preschooler or young reader. For the 8-12-year-old, we are interested in action stories with a Christian take-away message. Fiction should also be series oriented. No romance or science fiction." Query or submit outline/synopsis and sample chapters or submit complete ms.

Recent Fiction Title: *The Mystery of the Black Hole Mine*, by Lee Roddy (adventure, 8-12).

Tips: "Too many books rehash the same topic and there are many shallow books that require no thinking. A writer has the best chance of selling Victor a well-conceived and imaginative manuscript that helps the reader apply Christianity to his/her life in practical ways. Christians active in the local church and their children are our audience."

‡WADSWORTH PUBLISHING COMPANY, Division of Wadsworth, Inc., 10 Davis Dr., Belmont CA 94002. (415)595-2350. Other divisions include Brooks/Cole Pub. Co., Kent Pub. Co., Prindle, Weber and Schmidt Pub. Co. Editor-in-Chief for Wadsworth Publishing Company: Stephen D. Rutter. Publishes hardcover and paperback originals and software. Publishes 350 titles/year. 35% of books from first-time authors; 99% of books from unagented writers. Pays 5-15% royalty on net price. Advances not automatic policy. Publishes ms an average of 1 year after acceptance. Simultaneous and photocopied submissions OK. Query for electronic submissions. Computer printout submissions acceptable; prefers letter-quality. Reports in 1 week. Book catalog (by subject area) and ms guidelines available.

Nonfiction: Textbook: higher education only. Subjects include mathematics, music, social sciences, economics, philosophy, religious studies, speech and mass communications, English, and other subjects in higher education. "We need books that use fresh teaching approaches to all courses taught at schools of higher education throughout the U.S. and Canada. We specifically do not publish textbooks in art and history." Query or submit outline/synopsis and sample chapters.

Recent Nonfiction Title: *Biology: The Unity and Diversity of Life,* by Cecie Starr and Ralph Taggart.

‡**WAKE FOREST UNIVERSITY PRESS,** Box 7333, Winston-Salem NC 27109. (919)724-3750. Director: Dillon Johnston. Manager: Guinn Batten. Publishes hardcover and trade paperback originals. Firm averages 5 titles/year. Receives 80 submissions/year. Pays 10% on retail price. Offers $500 average advance. Publishes book an average of 6 months after acceptance. Photocopied OK. Computer printout submissions OK. Reports in 1 month on queries; 2-3 months on mss. Free book catalog.

Nonfiction: Subjects include language/literature and photography. "We publish exclusively poetry, photography, and criticism of the poetry of Ireland and bilingual editions of contemporary French poetry." Query.

Recent Nonfiction Title: *Selected Poems of Philippe Jaccottet,* by Jaccottet translated by Derek Mahon, (bilingual edition of the poetry).

Tips: "Readers of contemporary poetry and of books of Irish interest or French interest are our audience."

J. WESTON WALCH, PUBLISHER, Box 658, Portland ME 04104. (207)772-2846. Managing Editor: Richard S. Kimball. Editor: Jane Carter. Math/Science Editor: Eric Olson. Computer Editor: Robert Crepeau. Publishes paperback originals and software. Averages 110 titles/year; receives 300 submissions annually. 10% of books from first-time authors; 95% of books from unagented writers. Average print order for a writer's first book is 700. Offers 10-15% royalty on gross receipts; buys some titles by outright purchase for $100-2,500. No advance. Publishes book an average of 18 months after acceptance. Query for electronic submissions. Computer printout submissions acceptable; prefers letter-quality. Reports in 3-6 weeks. Book catalog for 9x12 SAE with $1.05 postage; ms guidelines for #10 SASE.

Nonfiction: Subjects include art, business, computer education, economics, English, foreign language, government, health, history, mathematics, music, physical education, psychology, science, social science, sociology and special education. "We publish only supplementary educational material for sale to secondary schools throughout the U.S. and Canada. Formats include books, posters, master sets, card sets, cassettes, filmstrips, microcomputer courseware, video and mixed packages. Most titles are assigned by us, though we occasionally accept an author's unsolicited submission. We have a great need for author/artist teams and for authors who can write at third- to tenth-grade levels. We do *not* want basic texts, anthologies or industrial arts titles. Most of our authors—but not all—have secondary teaching experience. I cannot stress too much the advantages that an author/artist team would have in approaching us and probably other publishers." Query first. Looks for "sense of organization, writing ability, knowledge of subject, skill of communicating with intended audience." Reviews artwork/photos as part of ms package.

Recent Nonfiction Title: *Developing Creativity: A Classroom Resource,* by William Reid.

WALKER AND CO., Division of Walker Publishing Co., 720 5th Ave., New York NY 10019. FAX: (212)307-1764. Contact: Submissions Editor. Hardcover and trade paperback originals and reprints of British books. Averages 100 titles/year; receives 3,500 submissions annually. 50% of books from first-time authors; 50% of books from unagented writers. Pays 10-12-15% royalty on retail price or makes outright purchase. Advance averages $1,000-3,000 "but could be higher or lower." Photocopied submissions OK. Do not telephone submissions editors. Material without SASE will not be returned. Book catalog and guidelines for 8½x11 SAE with 56¢ postage.

Nonfiction: Publishes biography, business, histories, science and natural history, health, music, nature, parenting, psychology, reference, popular science, and self-help books. Query or submit outline/synopsis and sample chapter. Reviews artwork/photos as part of ms package (photographs). Do not send originals.

Recent Nonfiction Title: *Fathers' Rights,* by Jon Contre.

Fiction: Mystery, juvenile (ages 5 and up), suspense, regency romance, western, action adventure/suspense and espionage.

Recent Fiction Title: *The Murder of Frau Schütz,* by J. Madison Davis.

Tips: "We also need preschool to young adult nonfiction, science fiction, historical novels, biographies and middle-grade novels. Query."

***WASHINGTON STATE UNIVERSITY PRESS,** Washington State University, Pullman WA 99164-5910. (509)335-3518. Editor-in-chief: Fred C. Bohm. Publishes hardcover originals, trade paperback originals and reprints. Averages 10-15 titles/year; receives 50-75 submissions annually. 50% of books from first-time writers; 100% of books from unagented authors. Subsidy publishes 20% of books. "The nature of the manuscript and the potential market for the manuscript determine whether it should be subsidy published." Pays 10% royalty. Publishes book an average of 1 year after acceptance. Simultaneous and photocopied submissions OK. Query for electronic submissions. Computer printout submissions are acceptable. Reports on queries in 1 month; on submissions in 1-4 months.

Nonfiction: Biography, academic and scholarly. Subjects include Americana, art, business and economics, history (especially of the American West and the Pacific Northwest), nature, philosophy, politics, psychology, and sociology. Needs for the next year are "quality manuscripts that focus on the development of the Pacific Northwest as a region, and on the social and economic changes that have taken place and continue to take place as the region enters the 21st century. No romance novels, historical fiction, how-to books, gardening books, or books specifically written as classroom texts." Submit outline/synopsis and sample chapters. Reviews artwork/photos as part of ms package.

Recent Nonfiction Title: *Looking at the Land of Promise*, by William H. Goetzmann (Pacific Northwest history).

Tips: "Our audience consists of scholars, specialists and informed general readers who are interested in well-documented research presented in an attractive format." Writers have the best chance of selling to our firm "completed manuscripts on regional history. We have developed our marketing in the direction of regional and local history and have attempted to use this as the base around which we hope to expand our publishing program. In regional history, the secret is to write a good narrative—a good story—that is substantiated factually. It should be told in an imaginative, clever way. Have visuals (photos, maps, etc) available to help the reader envision what has happened. Tell the local or regional history story in a way that ties it to larger, national, and even international events. Weave it into the large pattern of history."

SAMUEL WEISER, INC., Box 612, York Beach ME 03910. (207)363-4393. Editor: Susan Smithe. Publishes hardcover originals and trade paperback originals and reprints. Publishes 18-20 titles/year; receives 100-200 submissions annually. 50% of books from first-time authors; 98% of books from unagented writers. Pays 10% royalty on wholesale or retail price; offers average $500 advance. Publishes book an average of 1-1½ years after acceptance. Query for electronic submissions. Computer printout submissions OK; prefers letter-quality. Reports in 3 months. Free book catalog.

Nonfiction: How-to and self-help. Subjects include health, music, philosophy, psychology and religion. "We look for strong books in our specialty field—written by teachers and people who know the subject. Don't want a writer's rehash of all the astrology books in the library, only texts written by people with strong background in field. No poetry or novels." Submit complete ms. Reviews artwork/photos as part of ms package.

Recent Nonfiction Title: *Games of the Gods*, by Nigel Pennick.

Tips: "Most new authors do not check permissions, nor do they provide proper footnotes. If they did, it would help. We specialize in new age material, oriental philosophy, metaphysics, esoterica of all kinds (tarot, astrology, qabalah, magic, crystals, etc.) and our emphasis is still the same. We still look at all manuscripts submitted to us. We are interested in seeing freelance art for book covers."

WESTERN MARINE ENTERPRISES, INC., Division of ProStar Publications, Suite 14, 4051 Glencoe Ave., Marina Del Ray CA 90292. (213)306-2094. Editor: Sue Artof. Publishes hardcover and trade paperback originals. Averages 7 titles/year. Pays 15% royalty on net sales price. Computer printout submissions acceptable; prefers floppy disks. Reports in 3 weeks.

Nonfiction: Boating. "We specialize in boating books—mainly how-to and when-to." No "simple narrative accounts of how someone sailed a boat from here to there." First-time book authors should submit complete ms.

Recent Nonfiction Title: *How to Name Your Boat*, by Michael Deer.

WESTERNLORE PRESS, Box 35305, Tucson AZ 85740. Editor: Lynn R. Bailey. Publishes 6-12 titles/year. Pays standard royalties on retail price "except in special cases." Query. Reports in 2 months. Enclose return postage with query.

Nonfiction: Publishes Western Americana of a scholarly and semischolarly nature: anthropology, history, biography, historic sites, restoration, and ethnohistory pertaining to the greater American West. Re-publication of rare and out-of-print books. Length: 25,000-100,000 words.

*WESTGATE PRESS, Westgate Co. 8 Bernstein Blvd., Center Moriches NY 11934. (516)878-2901. Editor, Books: Lorraine Chandler. Publishes trade paperback originals and trade paperback reprints. Firm averages 5-7 titles/year. Receives 100 submissions/year. 50% of books from first-time authors. 100% from unagented writers. Subsidy publishes 10% of books. Subsidy titles are determined by book content and author enthusiasm. Pays 10% minimum royalty on wholesale price. Outright purchase negotiable. Offers $0-1,000 average advance. Publishes book an average of 18 months after acceptance. Simultaneous and photocopied submissions OK. Computer printout submissions OK; prefers letter-quality. Reports in 2 weeks on queries; 2 months on mss. Free book catalog. Ms guidelines for #10 SASE.

Nonfiction: Illustrated book. Subjects include art, metaphysics, occult/new age and related topics. "Westgate deals exclusively in the lesser known, esoteric areas of metaphysics. We'll look at mss that are not covered already by other authors and presses. Nothing already so overplayed that it's simply a rehash. No channeling, crystals, or other generic new age material. Check what we're currently doing before submitting." Reviews artwork/photos as part of manuscript package.

Recent Nonfiction Title: *The Book of Azrael: An Intimate Encounter With the Angel of Death*, by Leilah Wendell (metaphysics).

Tips: "As many times as we ask for the *truly unusual*, we still receive repetitive topics and angles. Give us the uncommon rarity of the blockbuster status as *The Book of Azrael* is fast becoming. If I were a writer trying to market a book today, I would choose an area in which I'm comfortable, learned and sincere, find an angle not presently being used and procure a blockbuster that is timeless in its message and awesome in its impact."

‡**WESTPORT PUBLISHERS, INC.**, 4050 Pennsylvania, Kansas City MO 64111. (816)756-1490. Subsidiaries include Test Corporation of America. Managing Editor: Barbara Cochrane. Publishes hardcover originals and trade paperback originals. Averages 5-6 titles/year. Receives 100 submissions/year. 50% of books from first-time authors. 100% from unagented writers. Pays royalty. Advance varies. Publishes book an average of 6-9 months after acceptance. Photocopied submissions OK. Computer printout submissions OK. Reports in 3 weeks on queries; 6 weeks on mss. Ms guidelines for #10 SAE and 2 first class stamps.

Nonfiction: Coffee table book, cookbook, and reference works. Subjects include child guidance/parenting, cooking, foods & nutrition, psychology, recreation, and regional studies. "Topics to consider are child guidance/parenting; psychology related; regional topics; family issues. However, we will consider all topics except books with sensational topics (mass murderers, etc.)" Submit complete ms. Reviews artwork/photos as part of ms package.

Recent Nonfiction Title: *Little People: Guidelines for Commonsense Childrearing*, by Edward R. Christophersen (parenting).

Tips: "Books with a well-defined audience have the best chance of succeeding. An author must have demonstrated expertise in the topic on which he or she is writing."

‡*****WHITAKER HOUSE**, 580 Pittsburgh St., Springdale PA 15144. (412)274-4440. Publishes trade and mass market paperback originals and reprints. Averages 10-12 titles/year. Subsidy publishes (author and nonauthor) 25% of books. "We publish only Christian books for the adult reader." Unsolicited mss returned. Book catalog for 9x12 SAE with 39 postage. Ms guidelines for SASE.

Nonfiction: How-to and personal growth books centered on biblical teaching and related to everyday life — especially topics of interest to women and related to diet, health, and exercise. Looking for teaching books supported by author's research and personal experience. Wants typewritten copy or computer printout, double-spaced, 50,000-90,000 words. Prefers synopsis of chapters with query letter. Interested in receiving queries from Christian leaders with a recognized ministry. No booklets, poetry, or children's books considered.

Recent Nonfiction Title: *Creating a Lifestyle You Can Live Wtih*, by Ron Frank, Ph.D.

WHITFORD PRESS, Schiffer Publishing, 1469 Morstein Rd., West Chester PA 19380. (215)696-1001. Managing Editor: Ellen Taylor. Publishes trade paperback originals. Averages 10-12 titles/year; receives 400-500 submissions annually. 50% of books from first-time authors; 90% of books from unagented writers. Pays royalty on wholesale price; advances vary. Publishes on an average of 9-12 months after acceptance and receipt of complete ms. Simultaneous and photocopied submissions OK. Computer printout submissions OK; prefers letter-quality. Reports in about 1 month. Free book catalog; ms guidelines for SASE.

Nonfiction: How-to, self-help, reference. Subjects include astrology, metaphysics, new age topics. "We are looking for well written, well-organized, originals books on all metaphysical subjects (except channeling and past lives). Books that empower the reader or show him/her ways to develop personal skills are preferred. New aproaches, techniques, or concepts are best. No personal accounts unless they directly relate to a general audience. No moralistic, fatalistic, sexist or strictly philosophical books. Query first or send outline. Enclose SASE large enough to hold your submission if you want it returned.

Recent Nonfiction Title: *Planets in Signs*.

Tips: "Our audience is knowledgeable in metaphysical fields, well-read and progressive in thinking. Please check bookstores to see if your subject has already been covered thoroughly. Expertise in the field is not enough; your book must be clean, well written and well organized. A specific and unique marketing angle is a plus. No Sun-sign material; we prefer more advanced work. Please don't send entire ms unless we request it, and be sure to include SASE. Let us know if the book is available on computer diskette and what type of hardware/software. Mss should be between 60,000 and 110,000 words."

‡**WHITNEY LIBRARY OF DESIGN**, Imprint of Watson-Guptill Publishers, 1515 Broadway, New York NY 10036. Senior Editor: Cornelia Guest. Publishes hardcover and trade paperback originals and reprints. Averages 10 titles/year. Receives 250 submissions/year. 30% of books from first-time authors. 100% from unagented writers. Pays 7½-15% royalty on wholesale price. Offers $3,000 average advance. Publishes book an average of 9 months after acceptance. Simultaneous and photocopied submissions OK. Computer submissions OK. Reports in 3 weeks on queries. Free book catalog.

Nonfiction: Subjects include architecture/interior design. "I am looking for professionally oriented titles in the fields of architecture, landscape architecture, and interior design by practitioners and teachers of these specialties." Query or submit outline/synopsis and sample chapter.

Recent Nonfiction Title: *Architectural Illustration Inside and Out*, by Albert Lovenz and Leonard Lizak (art instruction).

Tips: "Writers who are well-known architects or designers or teach in these fields have the best chance of selling to us. Professionals and students in architecture, landscape architecture, and interior design are our audience."

THE WHITSTON PUBLISHING CO., Box 958, Troy NY 12181. (518)283-4363. Editorial Director: Jean Goode. Publishes hardcover originals. Averages 20 titles/year; receives 100 submissions annually. 50% of books from first-time authors; 100% of books from unagented writers. Pays 10% royalty on wholesale price; no advance. Publishes book an average of 30 months after acceptance. Computer printout submissions acceptable; no dot-matrix. Reports in 1 year. Book catalog for $1.

Nonfiction: "We publish scholarly and critical books in the arts, humanities and some of the social sciences. We also publish reference books, bibliographies, indexes, checklists and monographs. We do not want author bibliographies in general unless they are unusual and unusually scholarly. We are, however, much interested in catalogs and inventories of library collections of individuals, such as the catalog of the Evelyn Waugh Collection at the Humanities Research Center, the University of Texas at Austin; and collections of interest to the specific scholarly community, such as surveys of early Black newspapers in libraries in the U.S., etc." Query or submit complete ms. Reviews artwork/photos as part of ms package.

Recent Nonfiction Title: *Following Percy: Essays on Walker Percy's Work*, by Lewis A. Lawson.

‡*WILDERNESS ADVENTURE BOOKS, Box 968, Fowlerville MI 48836. Editor: Clayton Klein. Publishes hardcover and trade paperback originals and reprints. Firm averages 4 titles/year. Receives 20 submissions/year. 90% of books from first-time authors. 100% from unagented writers. Subsidy publishes 25% of books. Pays 5-10% royalty on retail price. Offers $200 average advance. Publishes book an average of 10 months after acceptance. Simultaneous and photocopied submissions OK. Query for electronic submission. Computer printout submissions OK; prefers letter-quality. Reports in 2 weeks on queries; 6 weeks on mss. Free book catalog.

Nonfiction: Biography, how-to and illustrated book. Subjects include Americana, animals, anthropology/archaeology, history, nature/environment, regional, sports and travel. Query. Submit outline/synopsis and sample chapters or complete ms. Reviews artwork/photos as part of ms package.

Recent Nonfiction Title: *Cruise of the Blue Flujin*, by Ken C. Wise.

Fiction: Adventure, historical and young adult. Query. Submit outline/synopsis and sample chapters or complete ms.

Recent Fiction Title: *Challenge the Wilderness*, by Clayton Klein.

Poetry: Submit samples.

Recent Poetry Title: *For Better or Verse*, by Ben Howard.

WILDERNESS PRESS, 2440 Bancroft Way, Berkeley CA 94704. (415)843-8080. Editorial Director: Thomas Winnett. Publishes paperback originals. Averages 5 titles/year; receives 150 submissions annually. 20% of books from first-time authors; 95% of books from unagented writers. Average print order for a writer's first book is 5,000. Pays 8-10% royalty on retail price; offers average $1,000 advance. Publishes book an average of 6 months after acceptance. Computer printout submissions acceptable; prefers letter-quality. Reports in 2 weeks. Book catalog for 9x12 SAE with $2.50 postage.

Nonfiction: "We publish books about the outdoors. Most of our books are trail guides for hikers and backpackers, but we also publish how-to books about the outdoors and perhaps will publish personal adventures. The manuscript must be accurate. The author must thoroughly research an area in person. If he is writing a trail guide, he must walk all the trails in the area his book is about. The outlook must be strongly conservationist. The style must be appropriate for a highly literate audience." Query, submit outline/synopsis and sample chapters, or submit complete ms demonstrating "accuracy, literacy, and popularity of subject area." Reviews artwork/photos as part of ms package.

Recent Nonfiction Title: *Hiking the Big Sur Country*, by Jeffrey Schaffer (outdoor guide).

JOHN WILEY & SONS, INC., 605 3rd Ave., New York NY 10158. (212)850-6000. Editor: Katherine R. Schowalter. Publishes hardcover and trade paperback nonfiction originals. Receives 150 submissions annually. 40% of books from first-time authors; 65% of books from unagented writers. Pays royalty. Publishes book an average of 18 months after acceptance. Photocopied submissions OK. Query for electronic submissions. Computer printout submissions OK; prefers letter-quality. Reports in 2 weeks on queries; 6 weeks on mss. Manuscript guidelines for SASE.

Nonfiction: General interest, how-to, reference and self-help. Subjects include business, mathematics, travel, language and careers. Needs travel, hospitality, small business, mathematics, business skills, and careers. "In all areas information needs to be new and it is important to do a thorough competitive search to determine how your manuscript is different from other books on the subject. No sales skills, low-level business books or crafts." Submit outline/synopsis and sample chapters. Reviews artwork/photos as part of ms package.

Recent Nonfiction Title: *Building Your Own Home*, by Waspi Youssef.

Tips: "It is important to have as complete a proposal as possible—information on the audience, competition, how the book will be used, and how the reader will benefit from reading the book."

WILLIAMSON PUBLISHING CO., Box 185, Church Hill Rd., Charlotte VT 05445. (802)425-2102. Editorial Director: Susan Williamson. Publishes trade paperback originals. Averages 12 titles/year; receives 450 submissions annually. 50% of books from first-time authors; 80% of books from unagented writers. Average print order for a writer's first book is 5,000-10,000. Pays 10-12% royalty on sales dollars received or makes outright purchase if favored by author. Advance negotiable. Publishes book an average of 1 year after acceptance. Simultaneous and photocopied submissions OK. Computer printout submissions acceptable; prefers letter-quality. Reports in 1 month on queries; 3 months on mss. Book catalog for 6x9 SAE and 3 first class stamps.

Nonfiction: How-to, cookbook, illustrated book and self-help. Subjects include business, education, gardening, careers, home crafts, parenting, building, animals, cooking and foods, travel, hobbies, nature, landscaping, and children. "Our areas of concentration are people-oriented business and psychology books, cookbooks, travel books, gardening, small-scale livestock raising, family housing (all aspects), health and education." No children's fiction books, photography, politics, religion, history, art or biography. Query with outline/synopsis and sample chapters. Reviews photos as part of ms package.

Recent Nonfiction Title: *Doing Children's Museums: A Guide to 225 Hands-On Museums*, by Joanne Cheaver.

Tips: "We're most interested in authors who are experts in their fields—doers, not researchers. Give us a good, solid manuscript with original ideas and we'll work with you to refine the writing. We also have a highly skilled staff to develop the high quality graphics and design of our books."

WILLOW CREEK PRESS, Box 300, Wautoma WI 54982. (414)787-3005. Editor-in-chief: Chuck Petrie. Publishes hardcover original and reprints. Averages 5-7 titles/year. 10% of books from first time authors; 80% of books from unagented writers. Pays 10-15% royalties on wholesale or retail price depending on individual contract. Offers average advance of $2,000-5,000. Publishes book an average of 1 year after acceptance. Simultaneous and photocopied submissions OK. Computer printout submissions OK. Reports on queries in 5 weeks; on submissions in 6 weeks. Book catalog for 8½x11 SAE with 3 first class stamps; writer's guidelines for SASE.

Nonfiction: Coffee-table book, how-to, humor, illustrated and technical books. Subjects include wildlife, nature, hunting and fishing. "We do not want to see submissions on dog training, taxidermy or fly tying, any compilations of stories previously published in outdoor magazines or any submissions not suitable for publishing in trade hardcover format." Submit outline/synopsis and sample chapters. Reviews artwork/photos as part of ms package.

Recent Nonfiction Title: *Sporting Clays*, by A.J. Smith.

Fiction: Historical and humorous fiction, all related to hunting and fishing. "No mss concerning hunting and/or fishing in 'exotic' countries." Submit outline/synopsis and sample chapters.

Recent Fiction Title: *Those of the Forest*, by Wallace B. Grange.

Tips: "We will consider over-the-transom submissions in the fields where we specialize. Writers wishing to be published by Willow Creek Press should familiarize themselves with the types of books we have published and not submit proposals or mss outside those categories."

WILSHIRE BOOK CO., 12015 Sherman Rd., North Hollywood CA 91605. (213)875-1711. Editorial Director: Melvin Powers. Publishes paperback originals and reprints. Publishes 50 titles/year; receives 6,000 submissions annually. 25% of books from first-time authors; 75% of books from unagented writers. Average print order for a writer's first book is 5,000. Pays standard royalty; offers variable advance. Computer printout submissions acceptable; no dot-matrix. Reports in 2 weeks. Book catalog for SASE.

Nonfiction: Health, hobbies, how-to, psychology, recreation, self-help, entrepreneurship, how to make money, and mail order. "We are always looking for self-help and psychological books such as *Psycho-Cybernetics, The Magic of Thinking Big* and *Guide to Rational Living*. We need manuscripts teaching mail order, entrepreneur techniques, how to make money and advertising. We publish 70 horse books. "All that I need is the concept of the book to determine if the project is viable. I welcome phone calls to discuss manuscripts with authors." Reviews artwork/photos as part of ms package.

Recent Nonfiction Title: *The Knight in the Rusty Amor*, by Robert Fisher (adult fable).

Tips: "We are looking for such books as *Jonathan Livingston Seagull, The Little Prince*, and *The Greatest Salesman in the World*."

WINDRIVER PUBLISHING COMPANY, Two Dallas Communications Complex, Suite 100, 6309 North O'Connor Rd., Irving TX 75039-3510. (214)869-7625. President/Publisher: Brim Crow. Publishes hardcover originals. Firm averages 20 titles/year. Pays royalty on wholesale price. Outright purchase varies. Advance varies.

Simultaneous and photocopied submissions OK. Reports in 2 weeks on queries; 2 months on mss. Free book catalog; ms guidelines for #10 SASE.

Nonfiction: Biography. Subjects include Americana, history, film history and nostalgia. "We specifically need film books. Nothing sensational (unauthorized bios, etc.)." Query or submit outline/synopsis and sample chapters.

Recent Nonfiction Title: *Time of Your Life*, by Jack H. Smith.

Fiction: Mystery. "We need mysteries of all types. *We no longer accept romance.* No occult or science fiction or overt sex." Query or submit outline/synopsis and sample chapters.

Recent Fiction Title: *The Conquerors*, by Rose M. Poole.

Editor's Note: We learned at press time that Windriver Publishing Co. has gone out of business.

WINDSOR BOOKS, Subsidiary of Windsor Marketing Corp., Box 280, Brightwaters NY 11718. (516)321-7830. Managing Editor: Stephen Schmidt. Publishes hardcover and trade paperback originals, reprints, and very specific software. Averages 8 titles/year; receives approximately 40 submissions annually. 60% of books from first-time authors; 90% of books from unagented writers. Pays 10% royalty on retail price; 5% on wholesale price (50% of total cost); offers variable advance. Publishes book an average of 6 months after acceptance. Simultaneous and photocopied submissions OK. Computer printout submissions acceptable; prefers letter-quality. Reports in 2 weeks on queries; 3 weeks on mss. Free book catalog and ms guidelines.

Nonfiction: How-to and technical. Subjects include business and economics (investing in stocks and commodities). Interested in books on strategies, methods for investing in the stock market, options market, and commodity markets. Query or submit outline/synopsis and sample chapters. Reviews artwork/photos as part of ms package.

Recent Nonfiction Title: *The Price Spiral Method*, by B.J. Howard (investing).

Tips: "Our books are for serious investors; we sell through direct mail to our mailing list and other financial lists. Writers must keep their work original; this market tends to have a great deal of information overlap among publications."

WINE APPRECIATION GUILD LTD., Vintage Image, Wine Advisory Board, 155 Connecticut St., San Francisco CA 94107. (514)864-1202. Director: Maurice Sullivan. Imprints include Vintage Image and Wine Advisory Board (nonfiction). Publishes hardcover and trade paperback originals, trade paperback reprints, and software. Averages 12 titles/year; receives 30-40 submissions annually. 30% of books from first-time authors; 100% of books from unagented writers. Pays 5-15% royalty on wholesale price or makes outright purchase. Publishes book an average of 18 months after acceptance. Simultaneous and photocopied submissions OK. Query for electronic submisstions. Reports in 2 months. Book catalog for $2.

Nonfiction: Cookbook and how-to—wine related. Subjects include wine, cooking and foods and travel. Must be wine-related. Submit outline/synopsis and sample chapters. Reviews artwork/photos as part of ms package.

Tips: "Our books are read by wine enthusiasts—from neophytes to professionals, and wine industry and food industry people. We are interested in anything of a topical and timely nature connected with wine, by a knowledgeable author. We do not deal with agents of any type. We prefer to get to know the author as a person and to work closely with him/her."

WINGBOW PRESS, Subsidiary of Bookpeople, 2929 Fifth St., Berkeley CA 94710. (415)549-3030. Editor: Randy Fingland. Small press. Publishes trade paperback originals. Averages 4 titles/year; receives 450 submissions annually, "mostly fiction and poetry, which we aren't even considering." 50% of books from first-time authors; 100% of books from unagented writers. Pays 7-10% royalty on retail price; offers average $250 advance. Publishes book an average of 15 months after acceptance. Photocopied submissions OK. Query for electronic submissions. Computer printout submissions OK; prefers letter-quality. Reports in 2 weeks on queries; 2 months on mss. Book catalog for #10 SAE and 1 first class stamp.

Nonfiction: Reference and self-help. Subjects include philosophy/metaphysics, psychology and women's issues. "We are currently looking most seriously at women's studies; religion/metaphysics/philosophy; psychology and personal development. Our readers are receptive to alternative/New Age ideas. No business/finance how-to." Query or submit outline/synopsis and sample chapters.

Recent Nonfiction Title: *Illuminations: The Healing Image*, by Madeline McMurray.

*WINSTON-DEREK PUBLISHERS, INC., Pennywell Dr., Box 90883, Nashville TN 37209. (615)329-1319/321-0535. FAX: (615)329-4811. Publisher: James W. Peebles. Pubishes hardcover, trade, and mass market paperback originals. Averages 60-65 titles/year; receives 3,500 submissions annually. 60% of books from first-time authors; 75% of books from unagented authors. Average print order for writer's first book is 3,000-5,000. "We will co-publish exceptional works of quality and style only when we reach our quota in our trade book

For information on setting your freelance fees, see How Much Should I Charge? in the Business of Writing section.

Close-up

Susan Williamson
Editorial Director
Williamson Publishing Company

Walk into almost any bookstore these days and you're sure to find several books on how to get the most out of your desktop publishing system. A few years ago shelves were packed with books on fitness and before that management books were the craze. It seems a small publisher could do well building on the success of a trendy subject, yet many find it hard to keep up with what's in—once a trend dies, book sales can plummet.

Success in the how-to and self-help publishing field, says Susan Williamson, cannot rely on trends. Publishers must avoid publishing "just one more book on a popular subject." Instead publishers should look for how-to titles that fill a need—one that has not previously been addressed. Williamson is the editorial director of Williamson Publishing, a company she and her husband started six years ago.

With 30 years combined experience in the publishing business, the Williamsons saw many small publishers fail because they could not compete with the larger houses. The solution, they found, was in choosing books on subjects not being treated by other houses. "Our goal was to be different, to create our own niche in the how-to and self-help field," Williamson explains.

Williamson publishes books dealing with a broad range of subjects—from sheep raising to a guide to children's museums. "Many of our books are on topics of concern to people dealing with transitions in their lives—raising children, planning retirement, going to college. We especially want books on improving the quality of family life."

Of the 500 manuscripts she receives each year, Williamson usually publishes six or seven books, although she may hold over a few for the following year. "We're looking for books with a long life of sales, so we do a concentrated marketing effort over a long time. That's why we do only six or seven books—we're better able to market this amount." In addition to distribution and marketing to bookstores and libraries, Williamson's books are often distributed to speciality stores, museum gift shops and special interest organizations.

Although she does relatively few books, Williamson is always looking for new ideas. Writers interested in Williamson Publishing should submit a query letter, writing samples and a well-thought-out proposal.

The writer must display both a knowledge of the subject and a very clear awareness of the market, she says. "We want a well-rounded idea, not a researcher's viewpoint." This does not necessarily mean the writer must be a professional in the field, but must exhibit a working knowledge. For example, Williamson recently published a book for children on nature. The author was not a professional naturalist, but she was an experienced outdoor hobbyist with an intense interest in nature education.

Above all, Williamson says, it's the idea that's important. "We're most interested in an author who has an original idea, as well as a thorough knowledge of a subject. Writing is almost secondary to content for us, but it's a real pleasure to find a gifted writer."

—Robin Gee

division." Subsidy publishes 20% of books. Pays 10-15% of the net amount received on sales. Advance varies. Simultaneous and photocopied submissions OK. Computer printout submissions acceptable; prefers letter-quality. Queries and mss without SASE will be discarded. Reports in 1 month on queries; 6 weeks on mss. Book catalog and guidelines for 9x12 SASE.

Nonfiction: Biography (current or historically famous) and behavioral science and health (especially interested in mss of this category for teenagers and young adults). Subjects include Americana; theology; philosophy (nontechnical with contemporary format); religion (noncultist); and inspirational. Length: 65,000-85,000 words or less. Submit outline and first 2 or 4 chapters. Reviews artwork/photos as part of ms package.

Recent Nonfiction Title: *Go Ahead—Make Your Day: The One-Shot Self Development Book*, by Jim Davidson and Gordon Shea.

Fiction: Ethnic (non-defamatory); religious (theologically sound); suspense (highly plotted); and Americana (minorities and whites in positive relationships). Length: 85,000 words or less. "We can use fiction with a semi-historical plot; it must be based or centered around actual facts and events—Americana, religion, and gothic. We are looking for juvenile books (ages 9-15) on relevant aspects of growing up and understanding life's situations. No funny animals talking." Children's/juvenile books must be of high quality. Submit complete ms for children and juvenile books with illustrations, which are optional.

Recent Fiction Title: *Sisters of A Different Dawn*, by Darcy Williamson.

Poetry: Should be inspirational and with meaning. Poetry dealing with secular life should be of excellent quality. "We will accept unusual poetry books of exceptional quality and taste. We do not publish avant-garde type poetry." Submit complete ms. No single poems.

Recent Poetry Title: *Champagne Mist*, by Marla Spevak Hess.

Tips: "We do not publish material that advocates violence or is derogative of other cultures or beliefs. There is now a growing concern for books about seniors, aging, and geriatic care. Outstanding biographies are quite successful, as are books dealing with the simplicity of man and his relationship with his environs. Our imprint Scythe Books for children needs material for adolescents within the 9-13 age group. These manuscripts should help young people with motivation for learning and succeeding at an early age, goal setting and character building. Biographies of famous women and men as role models are always welcomed. Always there is a need for books about current minority, scholars, issues and concerns. Stories must have a new twist and be provocative."

‡WIZARDS BOOKSHELF, Box 6600, San Diego CA 92106. (619)297-9879. Contact: R.I. Robb. Publishes hardcover and trade paperback originals and reprints. Firm averages 5 titles per year. Pays royalty or buys mss outright. Publishes book an average of 1 year after acceptance. Photocopied submissions OK. Reports in 1 month on queries; 1 month on mss. Free book catalog and manuscript guidelines.

Nonfiction: Hermetic philosophy. Subjects include translation and antiquities. Submit outline/synopsis and sample chapters.

Recent Nonfiction Title: *Qabbalah*, by Isaac Myers, comparative religion and philosophy.

Tips: "Theosophists, Masons, Rosecrusians and neoplatonists are our audience."

‡WOLGEMUTH & HYATT, PUBLISHERS, Box 1941, Nashville TN 37214. (615)371-1210. Publisher: Michael Hyatt. Publishes hardcover and trade paperback originals. Averages 24 titles/year. 20% of books from first-time authors. 90% from unagented writers. Pays royalty on wholesale price. Publishes book an average of 9 months after acceptance. Simultaneous and photocopied submissions OK. Query for electronic submissions. Computer printout submissions OK. Reports in 6 weeks on queries; 2 months on mss.

Nonfiction: Coffee table book, how-to, self-help. Subjects include religion. Query or submit outline/synopsis and sample chapters.

Recent Nonfiction Title: *Out of the Blue*, by Orel Hershiser with Jerry B. Jenkins (autobiography).

Fiction: Religious—(evangelical). Query.

WOODBINE HOUSE, 10400 Connecticut Ave., #512, Kensington MD 20895. (301)949-3590. Editor: Susan Stokes. Publishes hardcover and trade paperback originals. Averages 8-10 titles/year; receives 400-500 submissions annually. 60% of books from first-time authors; 60% of books from unagented writers. Pays royalty; buys some mss outright. Publishes book an average of 18 months after acceptance. Simultaneous and photocopied submissions OK. Query for electronic submissions. Computer printout submissions OK; prefers letter-quality. Reports in 1 month on queries; 3 months on mss. Free book catalog; ms guidelines for #10 SAE and 45¢ postage.

For explanation of symbols, see the Key to Symbols and Abbreviations on Page 5. For unfamiliar words, see the Glossary.

Nonfiction: Biography, reference, travel and self-help. Subjects include Americana, health, history, hobbies, natural history, science, (juvenile, ages 5-18), sociology, parents' guides for special needs children. Especially needs parents' guides for special needs children and history. No exercise or diet books. Submit outline/synopsis and sample chapters. Review artwork/photos as part of ms.
Recent Nonfiction Title: *The Retirement Sourcebook*, by Edward Palder.
Tips: "We are always impressed by authors who can write with clarity, authority, and style and can demonstrate that their book has a clearly defined market that they know how to reach."

‡WOODBRIDGE PRESS, Box 6189, Santa Barbara CA 93160. (805)965-7039. Imprint includes Banquo Books. Contact: Howard Weeks. Publishes hardcover and trade paperback originals. Firm averages 4-5 titles/year. Receives 250 submissions/year. 60% of books from first-time authors. 80% from unagented writers. Pays 10-15% on wholesale price. Publishes book an average of 8 months after acceptance. Simultaneous and photocopied submissions OK. Computer printout submissions OK; prefers letter-quality. Reports in 3 weeks on queries; 1 month on mss. Free book catalog.
Nonfiction: Cookbook (vegetarian) and self-help. Subjects include agriculture/horticulture, cooking, foods, & nutrition, gardening, health/medicine, nature/environment and psychology (popular). Query. Submit outline/synopsis and sample chapters or complete ms. Reviews artwork/photos as part of ms package.
Recent Nonfiction Title: *The Great Car Craze*, by Ashleigh Brilliant, (social history /Americana).

*WOODSONG GRAPHICS, INC., P.O. Box 238, New Hope PA 18938. (215)794-8321. Editor: Ellen P. Bordner. Publishes hardcover and trade paperback originals. Averages 6-8 titles/year; receives 2,500-3,000 submissions annually. 40-60% of books from first-time authors; 100% of books from unagented writers. Average print order for writer's first book is 2,500-5,000. Will occasionally consider subsidy publishing based on "quality of material, motivation of author in distributing his work, and cost factors (which depend on the type of material involved), plus our own feelings on its marketability." Subsidy publishes 20% of books. Pays royalty on net price; offers average $100 advance. Publishes book an average of 1 year after acceptance. Simultaneous submissions OK. Computer printout submissions acceptable; prefers letter-quality. Reports in 1 month on queries; reports on full mss *can* take several months, depending on the amount of material already in house. "We do everything possible to facilitate replies, but we have a small staff and want to give every manuscript a thoughtful reading." Book catalog for #10 SAE and 1 first class stamp. "Manuscripts not returned unless SASE enclosed."
Nonfiction: Biography, cookbook, how-to, humor, illustrated book, juvenile, reference, and self-help. Subjects include cooking and foods, hobbies, philosophy and psychology. "We're happy to look at anything of good quality, but we're not equipped to handle lavish color spreads at this time. Our needs are very open, and we're interested in seeing any subject, provided it's handled with competence and style. Good writing from unknowns is also welcome." No pornography; only minimal interest in technical manuals of any kind. Query or submit outline/synopsis and at least 2 sample chapters. Reviews artwork/photos as part of ms package.
Recent Nonfiction Title: *The Herb Gardener's Mail Order Source Book*, by Elayne Moos.
Fiction: Adventure, experimental, fantasy, gothic, historical, humor, mainstream, mystery, romance, science fiction, suspense and western. "In fiction, we are simply looking for books that provide enjoyment. We want well-developed characters, creative plots, and good writing style." No pornography or "sick" material. Submit outline/synopsis and sample chapters.
Tips: "Good nonfiction with an identified target audience and a definite slant has the best chance of selling to our firm. We rarely contract in advance of seeing the completed manuscript. We prefer a synopsis, explaining what the thrust of the book is without a chapter-by-chapter profile. If the query is interesting enough, we'll look at the full manuscript for further details."

*WORD BEAT PRESS, Box 22310, Flagstaff AZ 86002. Publishes trade paperback originals and reprints. Averages 4 titles/year; receives 500 submissions annually. 50% of books from first-time authors. Average print order for a writer's first book is 1,000. Pays 10% royalty on wholesale price. Currently, only accepting queries from agents for new books.
Fiction: Short story collections and novellas; "open to fine writing in any category." Query first.
Recent Fiction Title: *Four-Minute Fictions: Best Short-Short Stories from The North American Review*, edited by Robley Wilson, Jr.

*WORDWARE PUBLISHING, INC., Suite 101, 1506 Capital Ave., Plano TX 75074. (214)423-0090. FAX: (214)881-9147. Book packager producing 5 titles/year. Publisher: Russell A. Stultz. Publishes hardcover and trade paperback originals. Averages 30-40 titles/year; receives 200 submissions annually. 40% of books from first-time authors; 95% of books from unagented writers. Subsidy publishes 5% of books. "We review manuscripts on a case-by-case basis. We are primarily a trade publisher dealing with authors on a royalty basis." Pays royalty on wholesale price; advance varies. Publishes book an average of 1 year after acceptance. Simultaneous and photocopied submissions OK. "We prefer electronic submissions." Reports in 2 weeks. Free book catalog; ms guidelines for 9x12 and 5 first class stamps.

Nonfiction: Regional (Texas) which will include 8-10 titles in 1989; technical. Subjects include business and economics and computer. "I am always interested in books that improve upon specific software documentation. Additionally, I am willing to consider manuscripts on any new software products or 'hot' topics in the field of computers. I do not want to see anything that is not computer or business related." Query or submit outline/synopsis and sample chapters. Reviews artwork/photos as part of ms package.
Recent Nonfiction Title: *The Illustrated Autocad*, by Dr. Tom Berghauser and Dr. Paul Schlieve (reference).
Tips: "Our audience covers the spectrum from computer novice to the professional who needs advanced reference manuals. We have very stringent deadlines that our authors must meet to access the window of opportunity for our products. So many computer books are time-sensitive and any author interested in signing with me should expect to give an all-out effort to his manuscript."

WORKMAN PUBLISHING COMPANY, INC., 708 Broadway, New York NY 10003. (212)254-5900. Publishes hardcover and trade paperback originals and hardcover and trade paperback reprints and calendars. Averages 25 titles/year (and 33 calendars). Pays royalty. Simultaneous and photocopied submissions OK. Reports in 6 months. Book catalog free on request.
Nonfiction: Coffee table book, cookbook, how-to, humor, illustrated book, juvenile, and self-help. Subjects include Americana, art, cooking and foods, health, history, hobbies, nature, photography, recreation, religion, sports, travel. Query or submit outline/synopsis and sample chapters.
Recent Nonfiction Titles: *What to Expect in the First Year*, by Eisenburg, Murkoff and Hathaway.

WORLDWIDE LIBRARY, a Division of Harlequin Books, 225 Duncan Mill Rd., Don Mills, Ontario M3B 3K9 Canada. (416)445-5860. Imprints: Gold Eagle Books, Worldwide Mysteries. Editorial Director: Randall Toye. Publishes mass market paperback originals and reprints. Averages 72 titles/year; receives 1,100 submissions annually. 20% of books from first-time authors; 25% of books from unagented writers. Offers negotiable royalty on retail price; offers average $3,000-7,000 advance. Publishes book an average of 1 year after acceptance. Photocopied submissions OK. Reports in 1 month on queries; 2 months on mss. Book catalog for 8½x11 SAE and IRC.
Fiction: Action-adventure and mystery. Prefers complete ms; will accept synopsis and first 3 chapters. Query Senior Editor: Feroze Mohammed for action-adventure and Dianne Moggy for mystery.
Recent Fiction Title: *Murder on Safari*, by Hillary Waugh.
Tips: "We are an excellent market for action-adventure and near-future fiction."

WRITER'S DIGEST BOOKS, Imprint of F & W Publications, 1507 Dana Ave., Cincinnati OH 45207. Editorial Director: B. Leslie Koch. Publishes hardcover and paperback originals (nonfiction only). Averages 45 titles/year. Pays advance and 10% royalty on net receipts. Simultaneous (if so advised) and photocopied submissions OK. Computer printout submissions OK; prefers letter-quality. Publishes book an average of 1 year after acceptance. Enclose return postage. Book catalog for 9x12 SAE with 6 first class stamps.
Nonfiction: Writing, photography, music, and other creative pursuits, as well as general-interest subjects. "We're seeking up-to-date, how-to treatments by authors who can write from successful experience. Should be well-researched, yet lively and readable. Query or submit outline/synopsis and sample chapters. Be prepared to explain how the proposed book differs from existing books on the subject. We are also very interested in republishing self-published nonfiction books and good instructional or reference books that have gone out of print before their time. No fiction or poetry. Send sample copy, sales record, and reviews if available. If you have a good idea for a book that would be updated annually, try us. We're willing to consider freelance compilers of such works." Reviews artwork/photos as part of ms package.
Recent Nonfiction Title: *Successful Lyric Writing: A Step-By-Step Course and Workbook*.

YANKEE BOOKS, Division of Yankee Publishing Inc., Main St., Dublin NH 03444. (603)563-8111. Editorial Director: Sharon Smith. Publishes trade paperback and hardcover originals. Averages 6 titles/year, mainly based on material related to *Yankee Magazine* or topics found in the magazine. Average print order for a writer's first book is 5,000-10,000. Pays royalty with $1,000-5,000 advance. Publishes book an average of 18 months after acceptance. Query for electronic submissions. Computer printout submissions acceptable; no dot-matrix. Reports in 1 month on queries; 6 weeks on mss. Book catalog for 9x12 SAE with 5 first class stamps.
Nonfiction: Query or submit proposal, outline/synopsis and sample chapters or complete ms. Reviews artwork/photos as part of ms package.
Recent Nonfiction Title: *Yankee Folk Crafts*, by Carole Yeager.
Tips: "We are now focusing on large, coffee table type books about New England to be sold primarily via direct mail marketing."

YORK PRESS LTD., Box 1172, Fredericton, New Brunswick E3B 5C8 Canada. (506)458-8748. General Manager/Editor: Dr. S. Elkhadem. Publishes trade paperback originals. Averages 10 titles/year; receives 50 submissions annually. 10% of books from first-time authors; 100% of books from unagented writers. Pays 5-20% royalty on wholesale price. Publishes book an average of 6 months after acceptance. Photocopied submissions

OK. Computer printout submissions acceptable; prefers letter-quality. Reports in 1 week on queries; 1 month on ms. Free book catalog; ms guidelines for $2.50.

Nonfiction and Fiction: Reference, textbook and scholarly. Especially needs literary criticism, comparative literature and linguistics and fiction of an experimental nature by well-established writers. Query.

Recent Nonfiction Title: *Authoritative Studies in World Literature*, ASWL.

Tips: "If I were a writer trying to market a book today, I would spend a considerable amount of time examining the needs of a publisher *before* sending my manuscript to him. Scholarly books and creative writing of an experimental nature are the only kinds we publish. The writer must adhere to our style manual and follow our guidelines exactly."

ZEBRA BOOKS, Subsidiary of Kensington Publishing Corp., 475 Park Ave. S., New York NY 10016. (212)889-2299. Editorial Director: Leslie Gelbman. Publishes mass market paperback originals and reprints. Averages 600 titles/year; receives thousands of submissions annually. 50% of books from first-time authors. Pays royalty on retail price or makes outright purchase. Publishes book an average of 12-18 months after acceptance. Simultaneous and photocopied submissions OK. Computer printout submissions acceptable; no dot-matrix. Reports in 3 months on queries; 4 months on mss. Book catalog for business size SAE and 39 postage.

Nonfiction: Biography, how-to, humor and self-help. Subjects include health, history and psychology. "We are open to many areas, especially self-help, stress, money management, child-rearing, health, war (WWII, Vietnam), and celebrity biographies." No nature, art, music, photography, religion or philosophy. Query or submit outline/synopsis and sample chapters.

Fiction: Adventure, men's action, confession, erotica, gothic, historical, horror, humor, mainstream, medical novels, romance and suspense. Tip sheet on historical romances, gothics, family sagas, adult romances and women's contemporary fiction is available. No poetry or short story collections. Query with synopsis and several sample chapters. SASE is a must.

‡ZOLAND BOOKS, INC., Box 2766 Cambridge MA 02238. (617)864-6252. Publisher: Roland Pease, Jr.. General Manager: Peter Siegenthaler. Publishes hardcover and trade paperback originals. Averages 5-10 titles/year. Receives 50 submissions/year. 50% of books from first-time authors. 50% from unagented writers. Pays 10% royalty on wholesale price. Publishes book an average of 1 year after acceptance. Photocopied submissions OK. Computer printout submissions OK; no dot-matrix. Reports in 2 months on mss. Book catalog for 6½"x9½" SAE with 2 first class stamps.

Nonfiction: Biography, coffee table book. Subjects include art/architecture, language/literature, nature/environment, photography, regional, translation, travel, women's issues/studies. Query or submit complete ms.. Reviews artwork/photos as part of ms package.

Recent Nonfiction Title: *Recognitions: Images of a Woman Artist*, by Nancy Roberts (photography).

Fiction: Literary, plays and short story collections. "We are seeking to publish 7-15 books in the next year or two." Submit complete ms.

Recent Poetry Title: *No Free Will in Tomatoes*, by Peter Payack.

Tips: "We are most likely to publish books which provide original, thought-provoking ideas, books which will captivate the reader, and are evocative."

THE ZONDERVAN CORP., 1415 Lake Drive, SE, Grand Rapids MI 49506. (616)698-6900. Publishes hardcover and trade paperback originals and reprints. Averages 100 titles/year; receives 3,000 submissions annually. 20% of books from first-time authors; 80% of books from unagented writers. Average print order for a writer's first book is 5,000. Pays royalty of 14% of the net amount received on sales of cloth and softcover trade editions and 12% of net amount received on sales of mass market paperbacks. Offers variable advance. Computer printout submissions are acceptable; prefers letter-quality. The author should separate the perforated pages. Reports in 6 weeks on queries; 3 months on proposals. Book catalog for 9x12 SASE. Ms guidelines for #10 SASE. Send queries, requests and proposals to Manuscript Review.

Nonfiction: Biography, autobiography, self-help, devotional, Bible study resources, references for lay audience; some adult fiction; youth and children's ministry, teens and children. Academic and Professional Books: college and seminary textbooks (biblical studies, theology, church history, the humanities); preaching, counseling, discipleship, worship, and church renewal for pastors, professionals, and lay leaders in ministry; theological and biblical reference books; variety of books written from the Wesleyan perspective. All from religious perspective (evangelical). Immediate needs listed in guidelines. Query or submit outline/synopsis, and 1 sample chapter.

Recent Nonfiction Title: *Disappointment With God*, by Phillip Yancey.

Recent Fiction Title: *Men of Kent*, by Elizabeth Gibson.

Subsidy publishers

The following publishers produce more than 50% of their books on a subsidy or cooperative basis, or they supply publishing services to writers for a fee. What they charge and what they offer to each writer varies, so you'll want to judge each publisher on its own merit. Because subsidy publishing can cost you several thousand dollars, make sure the number of books, the deadlines and services offered by the publisher are detailed in your contract. If you are willing to pay to have your book published, you should also be willing to hire an attorney to review the contract. This step prevents misunderstandings between you and your prospective publisher. Never agree to terms you don't understand in a contract. Consult the Book Publishers introduction for more information on subsidy publishing and publishing services.

Authors' Unlimited
#201, 3330 Barham Blvd., Los Angeles CA 90068

Brunswick Publishing Company
Box 555, Lawrenceville VA 23868

Carlton Press, Inc.
11 W. 32nd St., New York NY 10001

De Young Press
Box 7252, Spencer IA 51301-7252

Eastview Editions
Box 783, Westfield NJ 07091

Fairway Press
C.S.S. Publishing Company, Inc.,
628 South Main St., Lima OH 45804

Fithian Press
Box 1525, Santa Barbara CA 93102

The Golden Quill Press
Avery Rd., Francestown NH 03043

Laser Publishing Systems, Inc.
1803 Huge Oaks, Houston TX 77055

Peter Randall Publisher
500 Market St., Box 4726, Portsmouth NH 03801

Rivercross Publishing, Inc.
127 East 59th St., New York NY 10022

Howard W. Sams and Co., Inc.
4300 W 62nd St., Indianapolis IN 46268

Vantage Press
516 W. 34th St., New York NY 10001

First Novelists
by Deborah Cinnamon

The odds are stacked against a writer becoming a "first novelist." Few of the major publishers will wade through voluminous piles of unsolicited manuscripts to find a "first novel." But it does happen—the six first novelists interviewed here are proof.

To succeed in getting a first book published, a writer must arm himself with knowledge of the publishing industry and research the market as thoroughly as he researched his book.

We talked to six writers who have the distinction of being "first novelists." They want to share their experiences with those about to embark on a similar journey.

The six novelists had varying experiences in getting their books published. Three of the books were hardcover; three were paperback originals. Four of the authors had agents, two did not. All are working on new titles; two have planned sequels to their first books. They all worked hard on promoting their books since first novels generally have little or no budget for promotion.

As first novelist Bill Kent says, "A first novelist should not care about *how* he is going to write his novel. There is no *right* way to do it the first time around. You have to find your own way. Forget about the *how*, just start doing it."

Bill Kent
Under the Boardwalk (Arbor House/William Morrow)

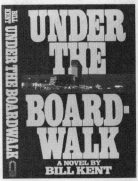

"I had several reasons for writing *Under the Boardwalk*," says Bill Kent. "First, I wanted to write a novel. It's something I've wanted to do since I was about 11 years old, primarily because books just always pleased me the most. The second reason was that I wanted to get some things off my chest about Atlantic City. The mob is not in control. The people are not creeps or scumbags and I wanted to tell the story of the city as I see it. Third, as a reader, a good book is something that I enjoy so much. When I come across a good book, it's better than a play and it's better than going to Europe. A book can take you places where nothing else can. I wanted to provide that feeling to other people. I feel that for a first effort, I came very close to doing so."

Under the Boardwalk took three years and 10 rewrites to complete. It was published as a hardcover original by Arbor House/William Morrow in November, 1988. The print run was 4,500 with a reprint of 1,500.

Bill Kent knows a great deal about the setting of his novel, Atlantic City. He has reported and written about the city, including a weekly column, for 10 years. He has written articles for more than 35 different publications. Currently, he has several books in various stages of completion and a planned sequel to *Under the Boardwalk*.

"One of the bitter truths of writing a first novel is the discovery of how much your vanity has to do with it. When the book does come out, there are a lot of things that happen that are totally unforeseen," says Kent. He says he probably lost money by writing this novel; he says he could have made triple the amount by writing articles for other publications. "But that's not the point of writing a book. That's not why you write a 'first novel.' You don't do it for the money. It's more important right now to get things accomplished.

"Media doesn't do first novels," he says he was told when he asked about getting his book reviewed. As a member of the media himself he was offended by this, not believing it to be quite true. He says he was told there would be no promotion of his book. So, he hired a publicist and set about promoting the book himself. He sent out 500 press kits to the media. They were designed with the help of his wife, a former art director, and printed at his own expense. He also bought about 100 copies of the book to send out as review copies. "To be fair, the publisher did come through. They offered to compensate me for the cost involved in the printing and mailing of the media kits. We are working together for the benefit of both of us."

Kent has an agent and advises a first novelist to get an agent as early as possible. "An agent has his ear to the ground and knows what publishers want or don't want. This information is invaluable to a writer. But more important, the negotiation process for a book is very complex and should be handled by someone knowledgeable about the process. As a first novelist, the publisher owns you. This happens to many artists who are entering into the commercial mainstream because they don't have much to negotiate with. There is also a degree of anxiety and tension with every submission from a two-page article to a 400-page manuscript. Sometimes it's good not to know who has passed on it. It's very difficult, if not impossible, not to take writing personally. Your agent doesn't have to tell you about the rejections.

"Ultimately, though, you are working for people out there who like to read, who are crazy enough, or rich enough, to spend real good money on what you have written. They're going to want a lot of things from you and you're not going to be able to please all of them. But, you owe something to your reader. You owe them the best possible job you can do. I have faith that if you are good for your reader, if you give your reader a good book, they'll take care of you by reading what you do, enjoying what you do.

"Basically," he says, "a first novelist can expect to gain only two moments of satisfaction. The first moment comes from finishing the book, and even then there's this incredible postpartum depression. The second satisfaction happens when you hold that book in your hand. I will never forget that moment. If it should happen to you, and when it does happen to you, then you will know *how* it happened. But until it does, forget about the *how*, just do."

Ann Tonsor Zeddies
Deathgift (Del Rey)

"I always intended to be a writer, but never took any creative writing courses. I also never attended any workshops. I didn't have an agent, and I hadn't published any short stories. Yet, to my extreme astonishment, the first publisher I sent my first novel to bought it a month after I sent it. Surprised? I was," says Ann

Tonsor Zeddies, author of *Deathgift*, a science fiction paperback novel.

Zeddies grew up in Ann Arbor, Michigan. She was an English major at the University of Michigan. She now lives in Lawrence, Kansas, with her husband and four children and is currently working on a sequel to her book.

"Some people think that genre writing is in some way easier than 'real' writing—easier to write, easier to get published. That's not why I write SF. I was working on a mainstream novel when I started this one, but *Deathgift* won out, because I became more interested and more involved in it than I was in my 'realistic' fiction. Writing good SF is just as demanding as any other kind of good writing. However, it may be true that it's easier to publish a first novel in SF than in mainstream literature.

"The nature of the field and the market may be more welcoming to new writers. If you've never written science fiction, though, you have a great deal of research ahead of you. You can't just have a neat idea and decide to write a novel. Chances are your great new idea was already written in 1953, and your editor will point this out to you!"

It took only one month for an editor to call and offer her a contract, on the condition that she would agree to rewrite a couple of problem areas. "I accepted eagerly, but rewriting turned out to be harder than I thought." She says it took two years for her manuscript to become an actual book. She sent it to Del Rey in December of 1986 and saw her first copy in December of 1988.

"Although I didn't have an agent, I did what I could to get my book to the top of the slush pile. I never was the kind of person who had connections. Racking my brain before submitting the manuscript, I thought of two friends who knew editors at Del Rey. One worked in the same building so I asked him to hand-deliver the manuscript for me. The other, a fellow writer, put in a good word for me," says Zeddies.

Zeddies says although she didn't have an agent to sell the book, she did get someone knowledgeable to look at her contract. He confirmed that she was getting a good, standard first-book contract. She says that eventually, though, she will probably want an agent to keep track of rights and royalties, as well as to negotiate contracts.

Her advice to writers: "Don't get defensive about your writing. I'm grateful to have had the chance to rewrite. In many ways I think it improved the book. Rewriting takes even more concentration than writing, since cutting any thread disturbs the whole closely planned fabric of the story. I pulled all-nighters to get the uninterrupted time I needed.

"If your editor is the kind of person you should be dealing with, she wants the book to succeed as much as you do. If she sees a problem, chances are it's really there. Apply your mind to creative alternatives, rather than explaining how wrong she is."

To promote the book, she sent numerous review copies to people she had contacts with at the Ann Arbor newspapers. She also printed and distributed flyers. She attended the science fiction conventions in the spring. But, she warns that "self-promotion is not easy with a family to work around.

"What would I have done differently? I would have tried even harder to write faster! Productivity is important in this business, as my editor keeps pointing out to me. That's true of unpublished writing as well. Although *Deathgift* is my first sale, it wasn't my first piece of writing. As well as a stack of unpublished but finished stories, I have written book reviews, newspaper articles and precis. The more I wrote, the better I wrote.

"I've been lucky—but a little over two years ago I was down in the basement, typing. If you write enough, and well enough, they *will* read your books. That's the bottom line."

Penny Colvin
Blood and Wine (Pocket Books)

Penny Colvin, a fulltime writer, says she began taking a writing class about five years ago. Now she is working on her third novel. Her first novel, *Blood and Wine*, is a paperback original. Although marketed as a romance, she says it is packed with action and suspense.

Her writing instructor, a man who has published more than 200 books, encouraged his students to write about World War II, a subject which was selling very well at the time. She says the original premise of her book was a generational novel. But instead she narrowed the scope of her book to cover WWII. Her instructor gave her the name of his agent in New York and she sent it to his office. "Ironically, they liked the story; they liked the characters; but they were tired of WWII!"

She says she learned a great deal from her class. "Just learning the craft, the techniques of writing fiction, was very important to me. Writing teachers who have never published or never written don't have the same kind of practical experience in writing as someone who's already been doing it for many years. The kind of advice I got from my instructor was very practical. Not just in terms of the writing technique but also in terms of how to market your book."

She sent her proposal to the agency recommended by her instructor. They wanted some changes, which she made; they accepted it and a few weeks later, they sold it.

"I've had an extraordinary experience. The agency worked with me to make sure that the manuscript was acceptable and they seemed to know the tastes of the editors they were submitting to. That really cuts down on the time that might have been wasted otherwise. I would definitely recommend going this route for anybody. What it meant for me was that I did not write my book first. I wrote a 35-page proposal and the first 75 pages of the book and I sent that to the agency. We worked on the proposal for three or four months, polishing it. Of course that necessitated some changes in the chapters before they sold it. It wasn't wasted time. I didn't put in two years of my life writing a book and then another year waiting to see if it would be accepted."

She says the only frustrations were those experienced in the amount of time that everything takes during the publishing process. She received the copyedited manuscript only three days before the galleys arrived. Although she says she wasn't pleased with the copy editing, she admits that is probably because she is a former English teacher and a perfectionist. She says she was disappointed that all her corrections weren't transferred to the finished manuscript. Also, she says her contract specified her book would be published 18 months from the time of acceptance, but it was actually two years later. "But, that was a trade off for a lead slot, number two behind *Rock Star*, by Jackie Collins," she adds.

Colvin says there was little promotion by Pocket Books but her print run was 130,000 in mass market paperback. She has received favorable comments in *Publishers Weekly*. Her contract with Pocket Books was for two books and she says she has finished the second book.

Dan Bentley-Baker
The Paper Boat (Pineapple Press)

"The first draft of *The Paper Boat* was written longhand on legal pads. Never again. Discovery of word processing has lifted me out of the Dark Ages. I can't imagine writing without my computer. I sold my boat to buy the tools of my trade and I have no regrets," says Dan Bentley-Baker.

He began writing at age 12. "I wrote end-of-the-world stories with my friends as main characters. I gave them all one sex scene, one action scene, and one death scene. Then I sold it to them for fifty cents apiece."

Bentley-Baker says, "It is a great feeling to accomplish a coherent, complete and fully embellished extension of myself like this first novel." He says he hadn't known before that writing the novel was just the beginning of his odyssey. "I sent mailings out to 10 publishers—five big houses and five little ones." Pineapple Press, a smaller house, accepted his manuscript.

Bentley-Baker says, "There was a cycle to my relationship with *The Paper Boat*. I loved it, got lost in it and lived in it. I molded it and caressed it and drifted off to sleep with it for almost two years. Then in the rewrites I saw the blemishes, saw the awkward phrases, the crippled paragraphs, the pointless pages. And I hated it. I hit the 18-mile wall of disillusionment. The marathon could have been lost at that point without the one quality you'll hear every author mention: persistence."

He didn't have an agent. "I don't think agents are an important advantage for beginning writers. Their efforts will only match your experience and their estimate of your selling power. What the new writer provides is sweat equity—a do-it-yourself term for hard work. There's no substitute for it.

"Why do I work harder than an agent? Because I believe in my book and I believe in myself. Those are nearly spiritual realizations without which no creative process within the complexity of book publishing can succeed."

Five thousand copies of *The Paper Boat* were printed in hardcover edition. "I took full responsibility for the promotion of my book and cooperated with my publisher eagerly. Because the press is small, the capital investment couldn't be too speculative. But, we worked together," he adds. "I made personal contact with all the bookstores in my area and renewed the contacts regularly. I think it paid off." He says sales have been so-so but, "I'm in print."

Bentley-Baker says he has finished a second draft of a new novel, *The Egyptian Heresy*. He says he will probably look for an agent for his second book.

"The result of all this is growth. I know now just how tough the business of writing is, but I know better how to play the game. It is always a blow to read an unfair review or get the cold shoulder from a national chain store. But it is worth it just to turn off the computer at the end of a long night of pecking the keys and know you're playing hardball in the national arena."

Denise Ohio
The Finer Grain (Naiad Press)

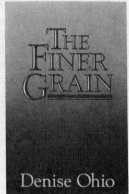

Denise Ohio, a fulltime writer who also works three jobs, says writing her first novel, *Finer Grain*, "was a gas." She says that while she had done well in college creative writing classes, she hadn't found a character who could hold her interest long enough to complete a novel. Instead, she worked on short stories and poetry. That changed one summer night. "I was sitting outside, sighing over a passionate love affair that ended that afternoon, when into the moonlight and melodrama, Amory Walker rushed into my imagination, laughing at my misery as she lit a cigarette."

Amory Walker, 19, is the protagonist of Ohio's novel. "I listened as closely as I could over the next several months and scratched down everything she (Amory) said or thought. I typed up the first 30 pages for writing class. After reading the first 10 pages at a roundtable, I waited for response. Everyone was kind and nice. I knew I'd flopped in a big way." She says her professor urged her to return to writing short stories and poetry again, but she says she knew she had a book to write.

Ohio says after several years of stopping and starting the manuscript, and making "every mistake a writer can—poor characterization, nonexistent plot, overwriting, underwriting, and slipping in a few cliches," she spent the next 15-20 drafts making repairs. "The work was exciting, much like walking on the floor of a new treehouse for the first time. And frustrating, like realizing there was more than one nail sticking business-end up through the boards. But, I hammered away at my errors and loved it."

When she had done all she could to the manuscript, going over it carefully to get rid of typographical and grammatical mistakes, she researched the fields of publishing and agenting before sending her manuscript out. She says she taped every rejection notice she received onto her kitchen wall. "That one-half wall covered with nice stationery tempted me to write crude things on those letters, which I did in red marker to exorcise any retaliatory thoughts."

After she was accepted by a literary agent, her book was sold in three months to Naiad Press as a trade paperback original. Ohio says the actual publishing process took about 16 months. She says she did a great deal of self-promotion, sending out a mass mailing of promotional flyers for her book. She says writers should be prepared to humble themselves to the fact of self-promotion.

Ohio says she got along very well with her editor. She didn't especially like the jacket cover or the jacket blurbs, but she says she can live with them. She advises writers to be prepared for long delays, but also short deadlines, including a small amount of time to turn around galley proofs, and the disappointment of not getting all the corrections in that you asked for.

"I got to sign my first autograph and I'm in the Library of Congress. Most important, people all over the world have read *The Finer Grain*. My book."

Patricia Weaver Francisco
Cold Feet (Simon & Schuster)

"Yoder, the character in my novel, *Cold Feet*, was born in a short story written in a creative writing class at the University of Michigan," says Patricia Weaver Francisco. Despite her instructor's encouragement to do more with the story, it wasn't until six years later that she began working again with the character Yoder, a process which led to her novel, *Cold Feet*.

Francisco has lived in Minneapolis, Minnesota for about 15 years. She teaches writing at Hamline University, and at The Loft, Minnesota's literary center. "I am fortunate to be part of a remarkable community of writers who have supported me in my work," she says.

"When I began to write *Cold Feet*, I wanted to write about the sensation I had of living in a country where I felt like a stranger. I had lived through the closing years of the Vietnam War as if in an eternal present—everything in question, no perspective available nor even desired. I wanted to write about the wounds the war left in those who did not face death in a nameless jungle," says Francisco. The story is an exploration of a difficult complicated man whose life and character were shaped by the historical forces of his time.

Francisco says her book was sold to Simon & Schuster in February, 1986, only one month after she had delivered the completed manuscript to her agent. She had sent him seven sample chapters the previous summer, at which time he agreed to represent her. He suggested selling the novel based on those chapters, but she decided to finish the story first. "At the time I felt it important to complete the novel first, though, looking back, it may have been a very good idea to sell the book at that early stage."

Francisco says that because of the speed with which her agent sold the book, and the terms he negotiated, that part of the publishing process was "surprisingly painless. I frankly can't imagine taking on the business of the publishing without an agent, and without an agent with whom I feel comfortable."

Francisco suggests that writers investigate how an agent feels about various issues first, such as multiple submissions, and also about the agent's view of his role after the sale. Her agent was involved in post-publication publicity and promotion. She warns that not all agents define their role as broadly as this. "Since my experience of every phase of the publication of *Cold Feet* was colored by *my expectations*, it's wise to clarify such issues before signing with an agent."

In addition, she hired a lawyer to review the contract. Her agent then negotiated a long list of revisions to the contract, resulting, she says, in a contract which has proven to be both fair and reasonable.

The process, she advises writers, while not painful, is complicated. In the middle of the publishing process her editor left Simon & Schuster and she became, in publishing lingo— "an orphan." The term, she says, is appropriate. "There is no denying the loss of the champion which a good and enthusiastic purchasing editor can be." She says her book was eventually reassigned to a new editor who moved the book into production. The book was published November, 1988, two and a half years after it was sold.

She was assigned a publicist from Simon & Schuster who sent copies of *Cold Feet* out for review. S&S also purchased space in a Christmas catalog that had wide distribution in magazines, newspapers and bookstores in the Midwest.

She participated in the Upper Midwest Booksellers Convention where she had a chance to speak with independent booksellers in the region and she hired a publicist to coordinate publicity and appearances. She also made promotional trips in the region at her own expense.

"A first novel needs the kind of doting attention only its author can give. Promoting one's novel is easily a fulltime job for two to three months. Show me the publishing house that does justice to *all* its first novelists, and I'll pipe down, but until then, my advice is unequivocally: Become involved. Take time to put your book into the hands of the press, the independent bookseller, and as many writers and readers as you can reach," she says.

"My primary advice to first novelists: Ask many, many questions. More than that, find someone who can tell you what questions you need to ask. In general, I was not given much warning about the occurrence of various steps in the publishing process. Deadlines for permissions (watch out for song lyrics and beloved quotes from obscure sources), jacket blurbs, flap copy and cover art, for example, sometimes came up too quickly for there to be as much accomplished as I wanted.

"As in all brushes with reality, publishing for the first time with a major publisher was a balanced experience, full of the sound of dreams coming true—and the illusions shattering. Were I to do it all over again I'd ask more questions about the publishing process itself, spend more time in New York, magically arrange to have the necessary two to three months to correctly promote my book, and make a fool of myself in bookstores.

"There's an electric thrill set off by the sight of one's own book in a store or library; there's a temptation to shout a bit. There's room for a bit more shouting whenever a novelist is born."

Small Presses

Following are additional listings of small presses which publish three or fewer titles per year or new presses which had not published four books by the time they completed a questionnaire to be listed in this edition of *Writer's Market*. This means the publishing opportunity is more limited, but these companies are still legitimate markets and have expressed an interest in being listed in *Writer's Market*. Write for more information and query before sending manuscripts.

AHSAHTA PRESS, Boise State University, Dept. of English, 1910 University Dr., Boise ID 83725. (208)385-1246. Co-Editor: Tom Trusky. Publishes poetry in trade paperback.

‡AMADEUS PUBLISHING COMPANY, Box 6141, San Jose CA 95150-6141. (408)295-6427. Proprietor: George D. Snell. Books relative to late 18th century musicians and composers.

‡AMERICAN SHOWCASE, INC., 724 5th Ave., New York NY 10019. (212)245-0981. Marketing Director: Ann Middlebrook. Publishes graphic design books—both trade and consumer and sourcebooks on all topics.

‡ANDERSON MCLEAN, INC., #508, 5 Town & Country Village, San Jose CA 95128. (408)972-0401. Sr. Editor: Jan Scott. How-to market, install, and select microcomputer accounting software.

AUTO BOOK PRESS, P.O. Bin 711, San Marcos CA 92069. (619)744-3582. Editorial Director: William Carroll. Publishes hardcover and paperback originals. Automotive material only: technical or definitive how-to.

‡BERKSHIRE TRAVELLER PRESS, Pine Street, Stockbridge MA 01262. (413)298-3636. Editor: Virginia Rowe. Publishes books on country inn-related subjects and Americana; history folk art, cookbooks, crafts, and how-to.

‡CLARITY PRESS, 3277 Roswell Rd. NE, #469, Atlanta GA 30305. (519)945-6092. Editorial Committee contact: Annette Gordon. Publishes manuscripts on minorities, human rights in US, Middle East and Africa.

‡CORBIN HOUSE, 227 Corbin Place, Brooklyn NY 11235. (718)648-2161. Editorial Director: Jus Kimmel. Publishes trade paperback originals on health, food, diet, finances, economics, how-to, self-help and education.

‡CRADDOCK PUBLISHING, Box 252, Laramie WY 82070. (307)322-5448. Managing Editor: Ellen Moss. Publishes hardcover and trade paperback originals. Publishes nonfiction education books for parents of school children. Fiction: erotica, experimental, historical and humor.

DIAMOND PRESS, Box 2458, Doycestown PA 18901. (215)345-6094. Marketing Director: Paul Johnson. Publishes trade paperback originals on sports, antiques.

‡DIMI PRESS, 3820 Oak Hollow Lane, SE, Salem OR 97302. (503)364-7698. FAX: (503)769-6207. President: Dick Lutz. Trade paperback originals of health and psychology.

‡DRY CANYON PRESS, 914 River Hts. Blvd., Logan UT 84321. Editor: Thad Box. Publishes trade paperback originals of mainstream/contemporary fiction and poetry.

‡EARTH STAR PUBLICATIONS, Box 174, Delta CO 81416-0174. Publisher: Ann Ulrich. Publishes trade paperback originals on UFOs; New Age concepts, including spirituality, health, metaphysics.

‡FREE SPIRIT PUBLISHING INC., Suite 716, 123 N. Third St., Minneapolis MN 55401. (612)338-2068. President: Judy Galbraith. Publishes psychology and self-help materials for kids, educational/parenting books for adults.

FRONT ROW EXPERIENCE, 540 Discovery Bay Blvd., Byron CA 94514. (415)634-5710. Editor: Frank Alexander. Publishes teacher/educator edition paperback originals.

GREAT OCEAN PUBLISHERS, 1823 N. Lincoln St., Arlington VA 22207. Vice President: Mark Esterman. Publishes hardcover and trade paperback originals and hardcover reprints. In nonfiction, biography, how-to, illustrated book, reference, self-help and technical.

GREEN TIMBER PUBLICATIONS, Box 3884, Portland ME 04104. (207)797-4180. President: Tirrell H. Kimball. Publishes trade paperback originals in juvenile nonfiction, fiction and poetry.

GRYPHON HOUSE, INC., 3706 Otis St., Box 275, Mt. Rainier MD 20712. (301)779-6200. President/Editor: Larry Rood. Publishes trade paperback originals of how-to and creative educational activities for teachers to do with preschool children ages 1-5.

HELIX PRESS, 4410 Hickey, Corpus Christi TX 78413. (512)852-8834. Editor: Aubrey R. McKinney. Publishes hardcover originals on science for adults.

‡HELM PUBLISHING, Subsidiary of Padre Productions, Box 840, Arroyo Grande CA 93420-0840. (805)473-1947. Editor: Louise Fox. Publishes marine or naval history dealing with California coast and including unpublished historical photos and drawings.

‡INSTITUTE FOR POLICY STUDIES, 1601 Connecticut Ave., NW, Washington DC 20009. (202)234-9382. Director of Publishing: M.S. Smalhout. Publishes interpretive essays.

‡JAMENAIR LTD., Box 241957, Los Angeles CA 90024-9757. (213)470-6688. Publisher: P.K. Studner. Publishes hardcover, trade paperback and mass market paperback originals and trade paperback reprints. Subjects are: business and economics, computers and electronics, education and career—advancement/job search.

‡JONES 21ST CENTURY, INC., 9697 E. Mineral Ave., Englewood CO 80112. (303)792-3111. Editorial Director: Kim Dority. Publishes hardcover originals on reference books for cable television industry.

‡LINTEL, Box 8609, Roanoke VA 24014. (703)345-2886. Editorial Director: Walter James Miller. Publishes nonfiction, fiction and poetry.

‡MAVERICK PUBLICATIONS, 10245 W. 14th Ave., Denver CO 80215. (303)238-5782. Publisher: Harry E. Chrisman. Publishes hardcover and trade paperback originals and reprints of western biography, western Americana and history.

*MEYERBOOKS, PUBLISHER, Box 427, Glenwood IL 60425. (312)757-4950. Publisher: David Meyer. Publishes hardcover and trade paperback originals and hardcover and trade paperback reprints. History, reference and self-help works published on subjects of Americana, cooking and foods, health, hobbies and nature.

MISTY HILL PRESS, 5024 Turner Rd., Sebastopol CA 95472. (415)892-0789. Managing Editor: Sally C. Karste. Publishes trade paperback originals. In nonfiction, publishes biography; in fiction, historical.

‡NATIONAL PUBLISHING COMPANY, Box 8386, Philadelphia PA 19101-8386. (215)732-1863. Editor: Peter F. Hewitt. Publishes Bibles, New Testament and foreign language New Testaments.

OAK TREE PUBLICATIONS, 3870 Murphy Canyon Rd., San Diego CA 92123. (619)560-5163. Editor: Linda Alioto. Publishes hardcover originals for juveniles.

OHIO PSYCHOLOGY PUBLISHING CO., Suite 020, 400 E. Town St., Columbus OH 43215. (614)224-3228. Vice President: Henry Saeman. Acquisitions Editor: Patricia Kleine. Publishes hardcover and trade paperback original textbooks on parenting, personal growth, gifted children, psychology and health.

PARTNERS IN PUBLISHING, Box 50374, Tulsa OK 74150. (918)584-5906. Editor: P.M. Fielding. Publishes biography, how-to, reference, self-help, technical and textbooks on learning disabilities.

‡PATHFINDER PUBLICATIONS, Suite 401, 150 Hamakua, Kailua HI 96734. (808)263-4278. Chief Editing Officer: Donna Allison. Publishes trade paperback originals on history (military, modern) and hobbies.

‡*PEACOCK BOOKS, College Square, Cuttack Orissa 753003, India. 0671-22733. Editor: Bibhu Padhi. "We are looking for 3-4 good, 56-80 page (typed, double-spaced) poetry collections from new writers, who have had at least *some* magazine publication."

‡**PEN DRAGON PUBLISHING CO.**, 8623 Pen Dragon, San Antonio TX 78250. (512)681-0499. Contact: Sherman Morgan.

THE PERFECTION FORM CO., 10520 New York Ave., Des Moines IA 50322. (515)278-0133. Publishes supplement on educational material grades K-12.

‡**V. POLLARD PRESS**, Box 19864, Jacksonville FL 32245. (904)724-8441. Owner: M.L. Lum. Publishes trade paperback and mass market paperback originals on cooking, foods and nutrition, education, hobbies, and recreation.

‡**THE PRESS OF MACDONALD & REINECKE**, Subsidiary of Padre Productions, Box 840, Arroyo Grande CA 93420-0840. (805)473-1947. Publisher: Lachlan P. MacDonald. Publishes literary criticism, usually by invitation. Critics should submit examples of published articles devoted to a particular theme. Also publishes fiction, poetry and drama.

PUCKERBRUSH PRESS, 76 Main St., Orono ME 04473. (207)581-3832/866-4808. Publisher/Editor: Constance Hunting. Publishes trade paperback originals of literary fiction and poetry.

‡**RESOLUTION BUSINESS PRESS**, Suite 208, 713-110th Ave., NE, Bellevue WA 98004. (206)455-4611. Contact: John Spilker. "Our focus is on books dealing with management issues related to the computer industry (hardware and software manufacturers and developers) and compiling computer industry directories emphasizing career and product development opportunities."

SANDPIPER PRESS, Box 286, Brookings OR 97415. (503)469-5588. Editor: Marilyn Riddle. Publishes first-person material on handicaps.

‡**SIGNPOST BOOKS**, 8912 192nd SW, Edmonds WA 98020. Owner/Publisher: Cliff Cameron. Hiking guides and outdoor recreation (*except* hunting and fishing) for the Pacific Northwest.

SOUND VIEW PRESS, 206 Boston Post Rd., Madison CT 06443. President: Peter Falk. Publishes hardcover and trade paperback originals on 19th-mid 20th century American art (reference).

SQUARE ONE PUBLISHERS, Box 4385, Madison WI 53711. (608)255-8425. Editorial Director: Lyn Miller-Lachman. Publishes trade paperback originals of young adult fiction.

STILL POINT PRESS, 4222 Willow Grove Rd., Dallas TX 75220. (214)352-8282. Editor/Publisher: Charlotte T. Whaley. Publishes hardcover originals of biographies and fine limited editions in the humanities. No unsolicited ms accepted.

STONE WALL PRESS, INC., 1241 30th St. NW, Washington DC 20007. President/Publisher: Henry Wheelwright. Publishes hardcover and trade paperback originals of how-to and environmental/outdoor instruction.

TGNW PRESS, 2429 E. Aloha, Seattle WA 98112. (206)328-9656. Proprietor: Roger Herz. Publishes mass market paperback originals on baseball, and children's books with a humorous subject matter.

‡**VICTORY PRESS**, 543 Lighthouse Ave., Monterey CA 93940. (408)372-8438. Editor: Eileen Hu. Interested in topics on Chinese philosophy and medicine; martial arts books that fit in with the philosophy of Buddhism and Taoism.

‡**VORTEX COMMUNICATIONS**, Box 1008, Topanga CA 90290. (213)455-0097. President: Cynthia Riddle. Articles on health care, exercise, fitness, nutrition, spiritual well being from a holistic perspective, 1,000 to 2,500 words.

‡**WATERFRONT BOOKS**, 98 Brookes Ave., Burlington VT 05401. (802)658-7477. Publisher: Sherrill N. Musty. Publishes books on children's issues, books that empower children, books on prevention, mental health, whatever addresses increasing opportunities for children. Fiction or non-fiction.

WESTERN TANAGER PRESS, 1111 Pacific Ave., Santa Cruz CA 95060. (408)425-1111. Publisher: Hal Morris. Publishes biography, hiking and biking guides and regional history hardcover and trade paperback originals and reprints.

Although book packagers develop books most frequently in the areas of art, history, cooking, self-help and reference, they're moving into a variety of other subject areas. You'll also find that some book packagers have developed specialties which are included in their listings in this section.

Book packaging is an opportunity for writers who can supply innovative ideas or who specialize in particular topics. While it originated in England in the 1940s, book packaging didn't pick up in the U.S. on a large scale until the 1970s. While they originally were known as book packagers, today many firms prefer to be called book producers or book developers. They provide a book publisher with services ranging from hiring writers, photographers or artists, to editing and delivering the finished book.

In most instances, a book packager or producer develops a book proposal, assembles the people to prepare it and submits it to a publisher. When a proposal is accepted by a publisher, the producer serves several functions. When the manuscript is in preparation, the producer is an editor. As the manuscript and illustrations or photo package are put together, the function changes to managing editor. Then the producer takes over coordination of production and may also serve as a sales consultant for the project. In other cases, a book publisher who already has a book idea will contract with a packager or producer to perform one or more of these functions on the title instead of using inhouse staff to do it.

The term book developer may be used to refer to a book packager or producer, or it may apply to a literary agent who joins with writers to provide writing and editorial services. An agent who functions as a book packager or developer often provides additional writing support for the author as they work together to produce a proposal. Then the agent uses his contacts within the industry to sell the work. Agents who work in book packaging have that information included in their listings in the Author's Agents section.

What makes book packagers' and producers' services so attractive to publishers? Primarily, it's speed and specialties. Many publishers with small editorial staffs use packagers and producers as extensions of their companies. An inhouse staff member can provide 20% of the work on the book and rely on the packager to produce the remaining 80%. This frees the staff member to move on to other projects. In some cases, publishers work with packagers to provide resources or knowledge they don't need fulltime but do need for a specific book. Many book packagers and producers also are experts at producing high-quality illustrated books, an area where small publishers may lack inhouse expertise. Book packagers are doing an increasing amount of business with major and medium-size publishers too.

Writers who want to work in the field should be aware of differences between book publishers and book packagers. Publishers accept book proposals and ideas for books submitted to them by writers. Book packagers and agents who act as book packagers most often assign topics to writers. Occasionally, a packager will develop an idea brought in by a writer, but this is rare. When you submit material, packagers most often want to see a query with your writing credentials and list of areas of expertise. Some indicate they want a resume and a history of the writer's published credits. Book packagers which accept material for fiction most often want to see a proposal and a sample of your writing.

Writers who are trying to establish themselves in the industry may consider this an attractive option but should be aware that it doesn't always provide you with credit for your writing since many books require several writers. Book producers and packagers often make outright purchases of writing, contract on work-for-hire agreements or offer a large advance and low royalty percentage. Don't expect to receive a book catalog from a book producer or book packager; they produce books for other publishers' catalogs. If you ask for a sample of titles they've produced, however, you may be surprised to find some bestsellers on the list.

More than 200 book packagers, producers and agents work in the field but most prefer to make their own contacts with writers and do not accept unsolicited queries. In this section, we've only included those who say they are interested in being contacted by writers. For a list of other book packagers and producers, see the latest edition of *Literary Market Place* in your local library.

‡**BASCOM COMMUNICATIONS**, 399 East 72nd St., New York NY 10021. (212)988-4212. Contact: Elizabeth Ryan. Publishes hardcover, trade and mass market paperback originals. Averages 15 titles/year. 50% of books from first-time authors; 90% unagented writers. Makes outright purchase. Offers $4,000 average advance. Computer printout submissions OK. Does not return submissions accompanied with SASE. Reports in 2 months.
Nonfiction: Cookbook, humor, juvenile, reference and self-help. Subjects include child guidance/parenting, cooking, foods and nutrition, education and health. Query with publishing history. Reviews artwork/photos as part of freelance ms package.
Recent Nonfiction Title: *Getting into the College of Your Choice* for G.P. Putnam's Sons, (education).
Fiction: Adventure, confession, historical, horror, humor, juvenile, mainstream, mystery, picture books, romance, suspense and young adult. Query with publishing history.
Recent Fiction Title: *Tightcase*, for Macmillan (crime).

‡**BOOK CREATIONS, INC.**, Schillings Crossing Rd., Canaan NY 12029. (518)781-4171. Editorial Director: Laurie Rosin. Produces trade paperback and mass market paperback orginals. Averages 30-40 titles/year. 10% of books from first-time authors; 75% unagented writers. Pays royalty on net receipts or outright purchase. Advance varies with project. Query for electronic submissions. Computer printout submissions OK. Reports in 2 months.
Nonfiction: Self-help. Subjects include cooking, foods and nutrition, health and recreation. Submit resume, publishing history and clips.
Recent Nonfiction Titles: *Pearl Buck's Book of Christmas* for Simon & Schuster (Christmas stories).
Fiction: Adventure, historical, literary, mystery and western. Submit proposal and 50 pages of the work in progress.
Recent Fiction Titles: *Celebration!* (WAGONS WEST Series) for Bantam (historical).

BOOKWORKS, INC., 119 South Miami St., West Milton OH 45383. (513)698-3619. FAX: (513)698-3654. President: Nick Engler. Firm averages 6 titles/year. Receives 1-10 submissions/year. 20-40% of books from first-time authors. 100% from unagented writers. Pays 2½-5% royalty on retail price. Buys mss outright for $3,000-10,000. Offers $7,500 average advance. Publishes book an average of 8 months after acceptance. Simultaneous and photocopied submissions OK. Computer printout submissions OK; prefers letter-quality. Reports in 6 weeks on queries; 2 months on mss.
Nonfiction: How-to. Subjects include hobbies, woodworking and home improvement. Nothing other than crafts/woodworking/home improvement. Query or submit outline/synopsis and sample chapters. Reviews artwork/photos as part of manuscript package.
Recent Nonfiction Title: *Country Furniture*, by Engler.
Tips: "In the how-to field, there is more emphasis on projects, less emphasis on techniques and methods. We publish how-to books for do-it-yourselfers, hobbyists and craftsmen."

CARPENTER PUBLISHING HOUSE, Suite 4602, 175 E. Delaware Place, Chicago IL 60611. (312)787-3569. President: Allan Carpenter. Develops hardcover originals. "We develop on contract for major publishers. We assign work to authors and artists." Negotiates fee. Reports promptly on queries.
Nonfiction: Biography, juvenile, reference and supplementary texts. Subjects include Americana, history and directory/resource annuals. "We do not solicit mss. We specialize in books in large series. We would consider proposals for American biographies for school use." Query. All unsolicited mss are returned unopened.
Recent Nonfiction Title: *Encyclopedia of the Medieval*, by Allan Carpenter.

MICHAEL FRIEDMAN PUBLISHING GROUP, 15 W. 26th St., New York NY 10010. (212)685-6610. FAX (212)685-1300. Subsidiaries include Friedman Group; Tern Enterprises; The Wainscott Group. Editorial Director: Karla Olson. Packages hardcover originals and trade paperback originals working with all major publishers. Firm averages 60 packages/year. "We work with many first-time authors and almost exclusively with unagented authors." Buys mss outright "under certain circumstances (when an author approaches us with an idea) we will pay a small royalty on reprints based on our price to publisher." Produces book an average of 1 year after acceptance; Friedman group responsible for all illustrative material included in book. Query for electronic submissions. Computer printout submissions OK. Free book catalog.

Nonfiction: Coffee table book, cookbook, how-to and illustrated book. Subjects include Americana, animals, anthropology/archaeology, art/architecture, cooking, foods and nutrition, gardening, health and fitness, hobbies, nature/environment, recreation and sports. Query.

Recent Nonfiction Title: *Regatta*, by Benjamin Ivvy.

HELENA FROST ASSOCIATES, 117 East 24th St., New York NY 10010. (212)475-6642. FAX: (212)353-2984. President: Helena Frost. Editorial Director: Lauren Fedorko. Packages approximately 50 titles/year. Receives approximately 100 queries/year. Authors paid by flat or hourly fees or on freelance assignments. Query for electronic submissions. Computer printout submissions OK; prefers letter-quality. Reports in 3 weeks. Completed projects list available; ms guidelines available per project.

Nonfiction: Textbook ancillaries, some general trade titles. Subjects include business and economics, education, government/politics, health/medicine, history, language/literature, psychology. Query.

Tips: "Although we are not interested in over-the-transom mss, we do request writers' and editors' resumes and will review school-related proposals and outlines for submission to major publishers."

THE K S GINIGER COMPANY INC., 1133 Broadway, New York NY 10010. (212)645-5150. President: Kenneth S. Giniger. Publishes hardcover, trade paperback and mass paperback originals. Averages 8 titles/year; receives 250 submissions annually. 25% of books from first-time authors; 75% of books from unagented writers. Pays 5-15% royalty on retail price; offers $3,500 average advance. Publishes book an average of 18 months after acceptance. Computer printout submissions OK; prefers letter-quality. Reports in 2 weeks on queries.

Nonfiction: Biography, coffee table book, illustrated book, reference and self-help. Subjects include business and economics, health, history, religion and travel. "No religious books, cookbooks, personal histories or personal adventure." Query with SAE. All unsolicited mss are returned unread (if postage is enclosed for return of ms).

Recent Nonfiction Title: *The Bed and Breakfast Guide to Britain*, by Elsie Dillard and Susan Causin.

Tips: "We look for a book whose subject interests us and which we think can achieve success in the marketplace; most of our books are based on ideas originating with us by authors we commission, but we have commissioned books from queries submitted to us."

LUCAS-EVANS BOOKS, 1123 Broadway, New York NY 10010. (212)929-2583. Contact: Barbara Lucas. Packages hardcover, trade paperback originals and mass market paperback originals for major publishers. Averages 10 titles/year. 20% of books from first-time authors. Pays 1-8% royalty, "depends on our contract agreement with publisher." Makes work-for-hire assignments. Offers $3,000 average advance. Reports in 1 month on queries; 2 months on mss.

Nonfiction: Reference. "We are looking for series proposals and selected single juvenile books: preschool through high school, prefer picture book and middle grade novels." Submit complete ms.

Recent Nonfiction Title: *Partners for Life*, by Margery Facklam (animal symbiosis).

Fiction: Preschool through high school. No rhyming verse.

Recent Fiction Title: *Nathan's Fishing Trip*, by Lulu Delacre (picture book).

*MAVERICK PUBLICATIONS, Drawer 5007, Bend OR 97708. (503)382-6978. FAX: (503)382-4831. Publisher: Ken Asher. Publishes hardcover and trade paperback originals. Averages 150 titles/year; receives 200 submissions annually. "Like every other publisher, the number of books we can publish is limited. We would like to suggest to any writer who has a timely manuscript and is having trouble getting it published to consider publishing it themselves. We will be glad to discuss this alternative with anyone who might be interested." 50% of books from first-time authors; 99% of books from unagented writers. Pays 15% royalty on wholesale price. Publishes book an average of 6 months after acceptance. Simultaneous and photocopied submissions OK. Computer printout submissions acceptable; prefers letter-quality. Reports in 2 weeks on queries; 3 weeks on mss. Book catalog for $1.

Nonfiction: Biography, cookbook, illustrated book, self-help and textbook. Subjects include Americana, cooking and foods, health, history, hobbies, music and travel. Submit proposal.

Recent Nonfiction Title: *Sally Rand—From Film to Fans* (biography).

Fiction: Historical, literary, mainstream, plays, short stories and science fantasy. Submit outline/synopsis and sample chapters.

Recent Fiction Title: *Boxer Rebellion* (sports).

Tips: "We love a good query. One that would be material suitable for back cover copy. We like an author who believes so strongly in his manuscript he might consider self-publishing or would be willing to suggest ideas for promoting the book. Tell us how you can sell 1,000 copies of your book in your own area."

‡MOUNT IDA PRESS, 4 Central Ave., Albany NY 12210. (518)426-5935. President: Diana S. Waite. Firm publishes hardcover and trade paperback originals. Averages 5 titles/year. Works with 50% first-time authors; 100% unagented writers. Pays royalty. Query for electronic submissions, "if hard copy also is available". Computer printout submissions OK. Reports in 1 month. Catalog for #10 SASE.
Nonfiction: Coffee table book, illustrated book and reference. Subjects include art/architecture, history, regional and commemorative histories. Query. Reviews artwork/photos as part of freelance ms package.
Recent Nonfiction Title: *Pavilion I, University of Virginia, an Historic Structure Report*, for Mendel, Mesick, Cohen, Waite Hall Architects (architectural report).

‡OTTENHEIMER PUBLISHERS, INC., 300 Reisterstown Rd., Baltimore MD 21208. (301)484-2100. Chairman of the Board: Allan T. Hirsh Jr. President: Allan T. Hirsh III. Vice President: Steven Bloom. Publishes hardcover and paperback originals and reprints. Publishes 250 titles/year; receives 500 submissions annually. 20% of books from first-time authors; 100% of books from unagented writers. Average print order for a writer's first book is 15,000. Negotiates royalty and advance, sometimes makes outright purchase for $25-3,000. Publishes book an average of 6 months after acceptance. Photocopied submissions OK. Computer printout submissions acceptable; prefers letter-quality to dot-matrix. Reports in 3 months.
Nonfiction: Cookbooks, reference, gardening, home repair and decorating, children's nonfiction activities, automotive and medical for the layperson. Submit outline/synopsis and sample chapters or complete ms. Reviews artwork/photos as part of ms package.
Tips: "We're looking for nonfiction adult books in the how-to information area, for mass market—we're a packager."

BYRON PREISS VISUAL PUBLICATIONS, INC., Subsidiaries include General Licensing Co., 12th Floor, 24 West 25th St., New York NY 10010. (212)645-9870. FAX: (212)645-9874. Executive Editor: David M. Harris. Publishes hardcover, trade paperback and mass market paperback originals. Averages 60 titles/year; receives 50-100 submissions annually. 2% of books from first-time authors; 30% of books from unagented writers. Pays 2-6% royalty on retail price; offers $4,000 average advance. Publishes book an average of 1 year after acceptance. Photocopied submissions OK. Computer printout submissions OK; prefers letter-quality. Reports in 1 month on queries; 2 months on mss.
Nonfiction: Biography and juvenile (all ages). Subjects include history and science. "All of our books are commissioned. We need authors who are familiar with a specialized field and capable of writing for younger readers. Series under development at present include dinosaurs, business and biographies for young adults. Since all our books are commissioned, no completed manuscripts should be submitted." Query. Reviews artwork/photos as part of ms package.
Recent Nonfiction Title: *My Life With The Chimpanzees*, by Jane Goodall (autobiography).
Fiction: Adventure, fantasy, historical, horror, mystery and science fiction. "We need people who can work to our specifications and who are familiar with the conventions of genre fiction." Query.
Recent Fiction Title: *Joe Gosh*, by Tom de Haven (science fiction).
Tips: "Science fiction is doing particularly well for us lately, as part of the resurgence of category fiction in the market. Interactive fiction seems to be consolidating as a part of the publishing scene, and may be moving from young adult into the mainstream. We will be looking more at mysteries in the future, and our interest in the natural sciences is growing. Contact Ruth Ashby for these topics."

QUINLAN PRESS, 131 Beverly St., Boston MA 02114. (617)227-4870/1-800-551-2500. FAX: (617)227-4689. Executive Editor: Kevin Stevens. Publishes hardcover and trade paperback originals. Averages 25-40 titles/year; receives 1,500 submissions annually. 75% of books from first-time authors; 90% of books from unagented writers. Pays 7-12% royalty on retail price; buys one ms outright for $1,000-5,000. Offers average $500 advance. Publishes book 1 year after acceptance. Simultaneous submissions OK. Electronic submissions preferred. Computer printout submissions acceptable. Reports in 5 weeks on queries; 2 months on mss. Guidelines for 8½ SAE and 4 first class stamps.
Nonfiction: Biography, illustrated book and self-help. Subjects include Americana, animals, history, hobbies, music, photography, politics, recreation, religion, sociology and sports. "We are interested in publishing any nonfiction book we feel is consumable by the population in general. Nothing too esoteric." Submit outline/synopsis and sample chapters. Reviews artwork/photos as part of ms package.
Recent Nonfiction Title: *Schirra's Space*, by Walter M. Schirra, Jr., with Richard N. Billings.

‡SCHUETTGE & CARLETON, 458 Gravatt, Berkeley CA 94705. (415)841-6962. Editor: Dick Carleton. Firm produces hardcover and trade paperback originals. Produces 10-20 titles/year. 75% from first-time authors; 100% from unagented writers. Pays 6-12% royalty on retail price. Offers average $4,000 advance. Computer printout submissions OK. Reports in 3 weeks. Free ms guidelines.
Nonfiction: Biography, coffee table book, cookbook, how-to, illustrated book, juvenile. Subjects include Americana, animals, art/architecture, cooking, foods and nutrition, education, ethnic, gardening, health, history, language/literature, music, nature/environment, photography, travel. Submit proposal. Reviews artwork/photos as part of ms package.

Recent Nonfiction Title: *Shrimp* for Chronicle Books (cookbook).
Fiction: Fantasy, juvenile, picture books. Query or submit proposal.
Recent Fiction Title: *Alma the Scow Schooner*.
Tips: "We are working toward a single specialty of children's books, with clever, special and well-prepared art. We will develop the manuscript and art if the idea is unusual and fits the surprise we put on the market."

T.F.H. PUBLICATIONS, INC., 1 T.F.H. Plaza; Third and Union Avenues; Neptune City NJ 07753. Imprint: Paganiniana Publications. (201)988-8400. Managing Editor: Neal Pronek. Publishes hardcover originals. Averages 100 titles/year; receives 200 submissions annually. 80% of books from first-time authors; 95% of books from unagented writers. Royalty varies, depending on type of book, etc. Usually makes outright purchase of up to $20 per page. Offers advance of ½ of total based upon estimation of total pages in final printed work. Publishes book an average of 1 year after acceptance. Simultaneous and photocopied submissions OK. Query for electronic submissions. Computer printout submissions acceptable; prefers letter-quality. Reports in 3 weeks.
Nonfiction: Coffee table book, how-to, illustrated book, reference, technical and textbook. Subjects include animals. "Our nonfiction book manuscript needs are for books that deal with specific guidelines for people who own or are interested in purchasing a particular type of pet. No books exclusively devoted to personal experiences with a particular pet, for example, *My Pet Sam*." Submit outline/synopsis and sample chapters. Reviews artwork/photos as part of ms package.
Recent Nonfiction Title: *The Boston Terrier*, by Anna Katherine Nicholas.
Tips: "Our audience is any and everyone who owns a pet. We do well with books that have a lot of photographs, and those that offer good sound advice for caring for a particular type of pet."

WELCOME ENTERPRISES, INC., 164 E. 95th St., New York NY 10128. (212)722-7533. President: Lena Tabori. Agent: Richard Barber. Managing Editor: Timothy Gray. Firm packages 12 books per year; agents 25. Receives approximately 100-200 submissions/year. "A publisher always contractually commits to us before we package a book for them." Keeps 25% of the royalties negotiated on packaged books, 15% for agented books. Simultaneous and photocopied submissions OK. Computer printout submissions OK; prefers letter-quality. Reports in 1 month on queries; 3 months on mss. Ms guidelines for #10 SAE.
Nonfiction: Coffee table book, cookbook, how-to, humor, illustrated book, reference and self-help. Subjects include animals, anthropology/archaeology, child guidance/parenting, cooking, foods and nutrition, gardening, government/politics, health/medicine, history, hobbies, literature, music/dance, nature/environment, photography, psychology, recreation, science, sociology and New Age/occult. Submit outline/synopsis, sample chapters and SASE. Reviews artwork/photos as part of ms package.
Recent Nonfiction Title: *The Joys of Entertaining*, by Beverly Reese Church and Bethany Ewald Bultman (home entertaining for Abbeville Press).
Fiction: Occassionally handles fiction.

‡WIESER & WIESER, INC., 118 East 25th St. New York NY 10010. (212)260-0860. FAX (212)505-7186. Producer: George J Wieser. Firm produces hardcover, trade paperback and mass market paperback originals. Averages 25 titles/year. Works with 10% first-time authors; 90% unagented writers. Makes outright purchase for $5,000 or other arrangement. Offers $5,000 average advance. Computer printout submissions OK. Reports in 2 weeks.
Nonfiction: Coffee table book, cookbook, how-to, juvenile and reference. Subjects include Americana, business and economics, cooking, foods and nutrition, gardening, health, history, hobbies, military/war, money/finance, nature/environment, photography, recreation, sports and travel. Query. Reviews artwork/photos as part of freelance ms package.
Recent Nonfiction Title: *Associated Press History of World War II*, for Henry Holt & Co.
Tips: "Have an original idea and pursue it completely and competently before contacting us."

WINGRA WOODS PRESS, Box 9601, Madison WI 53715. Acquisitions Editor: M.G. Mahoney. Publishes trade paperback originals. Averages 6-10 titles/year; receives 200 submissions annually. 70% of books from first-time authors; 100% of books from unagented writers. Pays 10-12% royalty on retail price, sometimes makes outright purchase of $500-10,000. Publishes book an average of 18 months after acceptance. Simultaneous and photocopied submissions OK. Computer printout submissions acceptable. Reports in 6 weeks.
Nonfiction: Coffee table, cookbook, how-to, juvenile, self-help. Subjects include Americana, popular history and science, animals, art, and nature, psychology and spiritual. Especially looking for popularized book-length treatments of specialized knowledge; interested in proposals from academics and professionals. Query with outline/synopsis. Do not send complete ms. Reviews artwork/photos as part of ms package.

Recent Nonfiction Title: *The Christmas Cat.*
Tips: "Put your 'good stuff' in the very first paragraph . . . tell us why we should care. Consider page 1 of the query as distilled flap copy. Then follow up with facts and credentials."

Other Book Publishers and Packagers

The following listings are inactive for the 1990 edition because the firms are backlogged with submissions or indicated a need for few freelance submissions in 1990.

Celestial Arts
Community Intervention
Critic's Choice Paperbacks
Globe Press Books
Pallas Communications
Publishing Horizons
Taplinger Publishing Co. Inc.

The following firms did not return a verification to update an existing listing or a questionnaire to begin a new listing by press time.

Abbey Press
Harry N. Abrams, Inc.
Academy Chicago
Ace Science Fiction
Addison-Wesley Publishing
    Co., Inc.
Alaska Nature Press
Alaska Northwest Publishing
Alba House
Almar Press
Alpha Publishing Co.
Amphoto
And Books
APA Productions
Architectural Book Publishing
    Co., Inc.
Art Direction Book Co.
Associated Faculty Press, Inc.
Avant Books
Ballinger Publishing Co.
Beacon Press
Beaufort Books Publishers
Bennett & McKnight Publish-
    ing Co.
Berkley Publishing Group
R.R. Bowker
Brevet Press
Bridge Publishing
Brunner/Mazel
Bucknell University Press
Bull Publishing Co.
Caedmon
Cambridge University Press
Canterbury Press
Carson-Dellosa Publishing Co.,
    Inc.
Cay-Bel Publishing Co.
Center for Migration Studies of
    New York, Inc.
Center for Thanatology Re-
    search
Chariot Books
Chicago Review Press
Childrens Press
China Books & Periodicals, Inc.
Chronicle Books
Coach House Press, Inc.
Collector Books
Communication Skill Builders,
    Inc.

Consumer Reports Books
David C. Cook
Cynthia Publishing Co.
Dartnell Corp.
Decalogue Books
Donning Co./Publishers, Inc.
Dragon's Teeth Press
Durst Publications
Eden Press
Educational Technology Publi-
    cations
Feminist Press
Fisher's World, Inc.
Fodor's Travel Publications,
    Inc.
Garden Way Publishing
Gay Sunshine Press & Leyland
    Publications
General Licensing Co.
J. Paul Getty Museum
Globe Pequot Press, Inc.
Golden Books
Green Hill Publishers, Inc.
Warren H. Green, Inc.
Gulf Publishing Co.
H.P. Books
Hanley & Belfus, Inc.
Harper & Row Junior Books
    Group
Hartley & Marks Publishers
Health Profession Division
Heinle + Heinle Publications,
    Inc.
Herald Publishing House
Holt, Rinehart & Winston
Jamestown Publishers, Inc.
Jist Works, Inc.
Johnson Books
Judson Press
John Knox Press
Loizeaux Brothers, Inc.
Lone Eagle Publishing Co.
Lone Star Publishers, Inc.
Longman
Lothrop, Lee and Shepherd
    Books
McClelland & Stewart
McCutchan Publishing Corp.
McGraw-Hill Book Co.
Markus Wiener Publishing Inc.

Marlor Press
MCN Press
Medical Economics Books
Melius & Peterson Publishing,
    Inc.
Menasha Ridge Press, Inc.
Moon Publications
Mountain Lion, Inc.
Multipath Gamebooks, West
    End Games, Inc.
Museum of New Mexico Press
Music Sales Corp.
National Health Publishing
National Publishers of the
    Black Hills, Inc.
New Society Publications
Newmarket Press
Open Court Publishing Co.
Orbis Books
Ortho Information Services
Owl Creek Press
Panjandrum Books
Pantheon Books
Parker & Son Publishers, Inc.
Petrocelli Books, Inc.
Police Bookshelf
Presidio Press
Pruett Publishing Co.
PSG Publishing Co. Inc.
Publications International, Ltd.
Publishers Associates
Putnam's
Reading Rainbow Gazette, Inc.
Regal Books
Richboro Press
Routledge
Rowman & Littlefield Pub-
    lishers
Royal Publishing Co.
RPM Press, Inc.
Santa Barbara Press
Saybrook Publishing Co.
Schenkman Books Inc.
Scott, Foresman
Shameless Hussy Press
Shoe String Press
South End Press
Springer-Verlag New York,
    Inc.
Jeremy Tarcher, Inc.

Temple University Press
Theatre Arts Books
Thunder's Mouth Press
Twayne Publishers
Unique Publications
Universe Books
University of Arkansas Press
University of Chicago Press
University of Idaho Press
University of Nebraska Press
University of North Carolina

Press
University Press of New
    England
Alfred Van Der Marck
    Editions
Vance Bibliographies
Viking Penguin
Wallace-Homestead Book Co.
Warner
Watson-Guptill
Franklin Watts

Weidenfeld & Nicolson (merg-
    ing with Grove)
West End Games, Inc.
Western Producer Prarie
    Books
Westview Press
Alan Wofsy Fine Arts
Word Books Publishers
Yee Wen Publishing Co.

The following listings were deleted following the 1989 edition of *Writer's Market* because the company asked to have the listing removed, went out of business, or is no longer accepting unsolicited submissions.

Andrion Books (no longer accepting submissions)
Bancroft-Sage Publishing (doesn't accept unsolicited submissions)
Barnes & Noble (see Harper & Row listing for information)
Byls Press (unable to contact)
Council Oak Books (doesn't accept unsolicited submissions)
Credo Publishing Corp. (unable to contact)
Dodd, Mead & Co. (being sold)
Dell (see Delacorte listing for information)
Fantagraphics Books, Inc. (asked to be deleted)
Fjord Press (asked to be deleted)
Gemstone Books (line discontinued)
Guidance Centre (consolidated with Oise Press)
Harbour Publishing Co. Ltd. (asked to be deleted)
Harpswell Press, Inc. (received too many unsolicited manuscripts)
JH Press (asked to be deleted)
Logical Extension Ltd. (no longer accepts outside submissions)
M.H. Macy & Co. (out of business)
New City Press (asked to be deleted)
Oasis Press (asked to be deleted)
Prentice-Hall Business and Professional Division (asked to be deleted)
Ragweed Press (asked to be deleted)
Randall House (asked to be deleted)
Irving Rockwood & Associates Inc. (only operating part-time)
Shepherd Books (doesn't accept unsolicited material)
SOS Publications (out of business)
Stein & Day (out of business)
Success Publishing (unable to contact)
Lyle Stuart (sold to Carol Publications)
Ten Speed Press (asked to be deleted)
Tompson & Rutter (out of business)
Unicorn Publishing House, Inc. (asked to be deleted)
Vanguard (asked to be deleted)
Westport Publishing Group (not accepting manuscript submissions)

Consumer Publications

Change continues to be the name of the game in consumer publications. Since the last edition of _Writer's Market_, about 500 new magazines appeared—although some not for long—others were redesigned and still others adapted to the marketplace by changing focus or name. Although the magazine racks are overflowing with choices, not all these magazines have staying power. The business is a competitive one and growth in the industry is running at a sluggish 6.3% rate.

In addition to new titles, many old favorites adopted a new look. _Esquire, Ms., Mother Jones, HG_ and _Mademoiselle_ were among the magazines getting a new look to update their images, reflect their readers' wishes and respond to increasing competition in the marketplace. Many other magazines also started using heavier, glossy paper, oversize formats and many reorganized features to make them easier to read.

Magazine titles also changed with the times. Some, like _House and Garden_'s change to _HG_, were part of an overall change. Others, including some computer magazines, changed to become more specific about their editorial focus. For example: _Home Office Computing_, a new listing in this edition, used to be called _Family Computing_.

The past year has also been a year of sales, with such venerable titles as _TV Guide_ changing hands and many other sales are pending. Editors have kept on the move too. Grace Mirabella was replaced at _Vogue_ by Anna Wintour and almost immediately began planning her own fashion magazine, _Mirabella_, which began publication in spring 1989.

Popular growth areas in the market include "maturity" magazines, hobby and craft, home and garden, travel, and child guidance and parenting titles. Many business magazines, especially those for small business, have found a strong following. On the down side, a number of astrology and New Age titles, as well as airline magazines, have gone out of business.

In addition, we've found that fewer magazines are accepting poetry and fillers this year. Many magazines also are backlogged with fiction—especially those that pay well for short stories.

To keep up with new magazines, make regular trips to your local bookstore, newsstand or library. Read magazines like _Folio, Writer's Digest, Magazine Week_ and _Publishing News_ to learn about changes that have happened since _Writer's Market_ went to press. Then read the magazine or write for a sample copy if you can't locate a recent issue. Before you submit a manuscript, also write for the publication's writer's guidelines.

Consumer magazines have a variety of response times and methods. In a survey we conducted, 338 magazine editors said they receive 409,203 unsolicited queries and manuscripts per year, an average of 1,233 each. Response times vary from one week to eight months. A full 76% said they respond within two months. Although we didn't mention it, one-third of the editors said a self-addressed, stamped envelope (SASE) was necessary; 74% of those said they discard material without SASEs.

The typical consumer magazine editor in a _Publishing News_ survey used an average of nine to 10 freelancers per issue, so you must remember the editor is probably juggling a number of inhouse and freelance projects at once. For information on the best way to handle your submissions and dealings with editors, see The Business of Writing section and the accompanying Writers' Roundtable.

Most editors will have an established fee schedule, but if you are asked for an estimate or you must negotiate the fee, refer to How Much Should I Charge? in The Business of Writing section for information on establishing your fees.

The type of article you write, rather than length, tends to govern what most magazine editors will pay for an article, according to the *Publishing News* survey. About 44.8% of the editors will pay for manuscripts at a regular rate and pay for photos separately; 37.9% pay for it as one package. Thirty-six percent say they always pay a kill fee when an article is assigned but later cannot be used, while another 23% say they never pay a kill fee. The majority, 54%, don't send an edited manuscript or galley proof to the author before publication.

Information on publications not included in *Writer's Market* can be found in Other Consumer Publications at the end of this section.

Animal

The publications in this section deal with pets, racing and show horses, and other pleasure animals and wildlife. Magazines about animals bred and raised for the market are classified in the Farm category. Publications about horse racing can be found in the Sports section.

‡AMERICAN FARRIERS JOURNAL, The Laux Company Publishers, Inc., 63 Great Rd., Maynard MA 01754. (508)897-5552. FAX: (508)897-6824. Contact: Editor. Published 7 times/year. Magazine covering horseshoeing, horse health related to legs and feet of horses and metalworking for a professional audience of full-time and part-time horseshoers, veterinarians, horseowners and horse trainers. Circ. 10,000. Pays on publication. Byline given. Buys all rights. Submit material 3 months in advance. Computer printout submissions acceptable; dot-matrix submissions accepted only when double-spaced. Writer's guidelines for SAE and 1 first class stamp.
Nonfiction: Book excerpts, general interest, historical/nostalgic, how-to, interview/profile, new product, personal experience, photo feature and technical. Buys 50 mss/year. Send complete ms. Length: 800-3,000 words. Pays 30¢ per published line.
Photos: Send photos with ms. Reviews b&w contact sheets, b&w negatives, 35mm color transparencies, and 8x10 b&w or color prints. Pays $10 per published photo. Captions and identification of subjects required. Buys one-time rights.

ANIMAL KINGDOM, New York Zoological Society, 185 St. and Southern Blvd., Bronx NY 10460. (212)220-5121. Editor: Eugene J. Walter, Jr. Executive Editor: Penelope J. O'Prey. 89% freelance written. A bimonthly magazine on zoology, animal behavior and conservation. Circ. 130,000. Pays on acceptance. Byline given. Offers $100 kill fee. Buys all rights. Submit seasonal/holiday material 9 months in advance. Simultaneous submissions OK. Computer printout submissions OK; prefers letter-quality, double spaced. Reports in 1 month. Sample copy $2 with 9x12 SAE and 6 first class stamps. Free writer's guidelines.
Nonfiction: Nancy Simmons Christie, articles editor. Book excerpts, essays, historical, how-to, humor, personal experience, photo feature and travel. No pet stories. Buys 24 mss/year. Query with published clips. Length: 1,500-2,500 words. Pays $550-800. Pays in copies "at request of author."
Photos: Miriam Helbok, Copy Editor/Photo Researcher. State availability of photos with submission. Reviews transparencies. Offers $35-200 per photo. Identification of subjects required. Buys one-time rights.
Columns/Departments: Bookshelf (reviews of wildlife books for adults/children), 300-600 words. Buys 18 mss/year. Query with published clips. Pays $75-150.

ANIMAL WORLD, RSPCA, Causeway, Horsham, West Sussex England RH12 1HG. 0403-64181. Editor: Elizabeth Winson. 20% freelance written. Bimonthly magazine on animal welfare for students ages 5-17. Circ. 65,000. Pays on publication. Publishes ms an average of 2 months after acceptance. Byline given. Not copyrighted. Buys first North American serial rights. Simultaneous and photocopied submissions OK. Computer printout submissions OK. Reports in 2 weeks on queries; 6 months on mss.
Nonfiction: Animals. "No anthropomorphism, please." Buys 20 mss/year. Send complete ms. Length: 600-1,000 words. Pays 8-18 pounds for assigned articles. Sometimes pays expenses of writers on assignment.
Photos: Send photos with submission. Reviews transparencies and prints. Pays 6 pounds for b&w; 12 pounds for color photos.
Fiction: Animal. Buys 20 mss/year. Send complete ms. Length: 600-1,000 words. Pays 18 pounds maximum.

ANIMALS, Massachusetts Society for the Prevention of Cruelty to Animals, 350 S. Huntington Ave., Boston MA 02130. (617)522-7400. Editor: Joni Praded. Managing Editor: Paula Abend. 90% freelance written. Bimonthly magazine covering animals. "*Animals* publishes articles on wildlife (American and international), domestic animals, balanced treatments of controversies involving animals, conservation, animal welfare issues, pet health and pet care." Circ. 70,000. Pays on publication. Publishes ms an average of 5 months after acceptance. Byline given. Offers negotiable kill fee. Buys one-time rights or makes work-for-hire assignments. Submit seasonal/holiday material 6 months in advance. Photocopied submissions OK. Computer printout submissions OK; prefers letter-quality. Reports in 6 weeks. Sample copy $2.50 with 9x12 SAE and 4 first class stamps. Writer's guidelines for #10 SASE.

Nonfiction: Essays, expose, general interest, how-to, opinion and photo feature on animal and environmental issues and controversies, plus practical pet-care topics. "*Animals* does not publish breed-specific domestic pet articles or 'favorite pet' stories. Poetry and fiction are also not used." Buys 6 mss/year. Query with published clips. Length: 3,000 words maximum. Pays $300 maximum. Sometimes pays the expenses of writers on assignment.

Photos: State availability of photos with submission. Reviews contact sheets, 35mm transparencies and 5x7 or 8x10 prints. Payment depends on usage size and quality. Captions, model releases and identification of subjects required. Buys one-time rights.

Columns/Departments: Books (book reviews of books on animals and animal-related subjects), 300 words. Buys 18 mss/year. Query with published clips. Length: 300 words maximum. Pays $75 maximum.

Tips: "Present a well-researched proposal. Be sure to include clips that demonstrate the quality of your writing. Stick to categories mentioned in *Animals'* editorial description. Combine well-researched facts with a lively, informative writing style. Feature stories are written almost exclusively by freelancers. We continue to seek proposals and articles that take a humane approach. Articles should concentrate on how issues affect animals, rather than humans."

‡AQUARIUM FISH MAGAZINE, Fancy Publications, Box 6050, Mission Viejo CA 92690. (714)855-8822. FAX: (714)855-3045. Editor: Edward Bauman. 100% freelance written. Bimonthly magazine on aquariums, tropical fish, ponds and pond fish. "We need well-written feature articles, preferably with color transparencies, dealing with all aspects of the hobby and directed toward novices and experienced hobbyists." Estab. 1988. Circ. 48,000. Pays on publication. Buys first North American serial rights. Query for electronic submissions. Computer printout submissions OK; prefers near letter-quality. Reports in 2 weeks on queries; 1 month on mss. Sample copy $3.50 Free writer's guidelines.

Nonfiction: "Articles on biology, care and breeding of aquarium and pond fish; pond and aquarium set-up and maintenance. No pet fish stories." Buys 45-60 mss/year. Query. Length: 1,500-3,500 words. Pays $100-300 for assigned articles.

Photos: Send slides with submission. Reviews contact sheets and transparencies. Offers $50-150 for color; up to $25 for b&w. Buys one-time rights.

Tips: "Know the subject; write tight, well-organized copy. Avoid 'my first aquarium' type of articles. Too many writers avoid adequate research. Many readers are knowledgeable about hobby and want solid information."

ARABIAN HORSE TIMES, Adams Corp., Rt. 3, Waseca MN 56093. (507)835-3204. FAX: (507)835-5138. Editor: Ronda Morehead. Managing Editor: Joyce Denn. 20% freelance written. Works with a small number of new/unpublished writers each year. Monthly magazine about Arabian horses. Editorial format includes hard news (veterinary, new products, book reports, etc.), lifestyle and personality pieces, and bloodline studies. Circ. 22,000. Pays on publication. Publishes ms an average of 6 months after acceptance. Byline given. Buys first serial rights. Submit seasonal/holiday material 3 months in advance. Simultaneous queries OK. Computer printout submissions acceptable; prefers letter-quality. Sample copy and writer's guidelines for 9x12 SAE and $6.

Nonfiction: General interest, how-to, interview/profile, new product and photo feature. Buys at least 12 mss/year. Query with published clips. Length: 1,000-5,000 words. Pays $50-350. Sometimes pays expenses of writers on assignment.

Photos: Prefers 5x7 color prints. Payment depends on circumstances. Captions and identification of subjects required. Buys one-time rights.

Fiction: Will look at anything about Arabians except erotica. Buys 1-2 mss/year. Send complete ms. Length: 1,500-5,000 words. Pays $75-250.

Poetry: Horse-related poetry only. Buys 1-2 poems/year. Submit maximum of 1 poem. Pays $25.

Tips: "As our periodical is specific to Arabian horses, we are interested in anyone who can write well and tightly about them. Send us something timely. Also, narrow your topic to a specific horse, incident, person or problem. 'Why I Love Arabians' will not work."

 The double dagger before a listing indicates that the listing is new in this edition. New markets are often the most receptive to freelance submissions.

BIRD TALK, Dedicated to Better Care for Pet Birds, Fancy Publications, Box 6050, Mission Viejo CA 92690. (714)855-8822. FAX: (714)855-3045. Editor: Karyn New. 85% freelance written. Works with a small number of new/unpublished writers each year. Monthly magazine covering the care and training of cage birds for men and women who own any number of pet or exotic birds. Circ. 170,000. Pays latter part of month in which article appears. Publishes ms an average of 6 months after acceptance. Byline given. Buys first North American serial rights. Submit seasonal/holiday material 7 months in advance. Photocopied and previously published submissions OK. Computer printout submissions acceptable; prefers letter-quality. Reports in 3 weeks on queries; 2 months on mss. Sample copy $3.50; writer's guidelines for #10 SASE.

Nonfiction: General interest (anything to do with pet birds); historical/nostalgic (of bird breeds, owners, cages); how-to (build cages, aviaries, playpens and groom, feed, breed, tame); humor; interview/profile (of bird and bird owners); new product; how-to (live with birds—compatible pets, lifestyle, apartment adaptability, etc.); personal experience (with your own bird); photo feature (humorous or informative); travel (with pet birds or to see exotic birds); and articles giving medical information, legal information, and description of breeds. No juvenile or material on wild birds not pertinent to pet care; everything should relate to *pet* birds. Buys 150 mss/year. Query or send complete ms. Length: 500-3,000 words. Pays 10-15¢/word.

Photos: State availability of photos. Reviews b&w contact sheets; prefers prints. Pays $50-150 for color transparencies; $15 minimum for 5x7 b&w prints. Model release and identification of subjects required. Buys one-time rights.

Columns/Departments: Editorial (opinion on a phase of owning pet birds) and Small Talk (short news item of general interest to bird owners). Buys 20 mss/year. Send complete ms. Length: 300-1,200 words. Pays 10-15¢/word and up.

Fiction: "Only fiction with pet birds as primary focus of interest." Adventure, fantasy, historical, humorous, mystery, suspense. No juvenile, and no birds talking unless it's their trained vocabulary. Buys 1 ms/year. Send complete ms. Length: 2,000-3,000 words. Pays 7¢/word and up.

Tips: "Send grammatical, clean copy on a human-interest story about a pet bird or about a medical or health-related topic. We also need how-tos on feather crafts; cage cover making; aviary, perch and cage building; and planting plants in aviaries safe and good for birds. Keep health, nutrition, lack of stress in mind regarding pet birds. Study back issues to learn our style."

‡BIRDER'S WORLD, The Magazine Exploring Wild Birds and Birding, 720 E. 8th St., Holland MI 49423. (616)396-5618. Editor: Eldon D. Greij. Managing Editor: Julie G. Ridl. 80% freelance written. Bimonthly magazine on wild birds, birding and bird watching. "*Birder's World* is designed for people with a broad interest in wild birds and birding. Readers have varying degrees of experience in the world of birds, ranging from the absolute novice to the studied ornithologist. They are well educated, curious readers." Circ. 40,000. Publishes ms an average of 6 months after acceptance. Byline given. Negotiable kill fee. Buys first North American serial rights and makes work-for-hire assignments. Submit seasonal/holiday material 8 months in advance. Photocopied submissions OK. Query for electronic submissions. Computer printout submissions OK; prefers letter-quality. Sample copy for $3.50. Writer's guidelines for #10 SASE.

Nonfiction: Book excerpts, essays, general interest, historical/nostalgic, how-to, humor, interview/profile, opinion, personal experience, photo feature, technical and travel. Buys 40-70 mss/year. Query with or without published clips, or send complete ms. Length: 1,000-2,500 words. Pays $100-400 for assigned articles. Sometimes pays expenses of writers on assignment.

Photos: State availability of photos with submission. Reviews transparencies and prints. Offers $75-100 per inside photo; $150 for a two-page spread; and $200 for covers. Model releases and identification of subjects required. Buys one-time rights.

Columns/Departments: Buys 20 mss/year. Query with published clips. Length: 1,000-2,500 words. Pays $100-400.

Tips: "We strongly encourage interested writers to send for our writer's guidelines before submitting work."

CAT FANCY, Fancy Publications, Inc., Box 6050, Mission Viejo CA 92690. (714)855-8822. Managing Editor: K. E. Segnar. 80-90% freelance written. Monthly magazine for men and women of all ages interested in all phases of cat ownership. 80 pages. Circ. 200,000. Pays after publication. Publishes ms an average of 6 months after acceptance. Buys first North American serial rights. Byline given. Submit seasonal/holiday material 4 months in advance. Computer printout submissions acceptable. Reports in 6 weeks. Sample copy $3; writer's guidelines for SASE.

Nonfiction: Historical, medical, how-to, humor, informational, personal experience, photo feature and technical. Buys 5 mss/issue. Query or send complete ms. Length: 500-3,000 words. Pays 5¢/word; special rates for photo/story packages.

Photos: Photos purchased with or without accompanying ms. Pays $15 minimum for 8x10 b&w glossy prints; $50-150 for 35mm or 2¼x2¼ color transparencies. Send prints and transparencies. Model release required.
Fiction: Adventure, fantasy, historical and humorous. Nothing written with cats speaking. Buys 1 ms/issue. Send complete ms. Length: 500-3,000 words. Pays 5¢/word.
Fillers: Newsworthy or unusual; items with photo and cartoons. Buys 10 fillers/year. Length: 100-500 words. Pays $20-35.
Tips: "We receive more filler-type articles than we can use. It's the well-researched, hard information article we need."

CATS MAGAZINE, Cats Magazine Inc., Box 290037, Port Orange FL 32029. (904)788-2770. Editor: Linda J. Walton. 50% freelance written. A monthly magazine for cat lovers, veterinarians, breeders and show enthusiasts. Circ. 148,000. Pays on publication. Byline given. Buys one-time rights. Submit seasonal/holiday material 7 months in advance. Reports in 1 month on queries; 3 months on manuscripts (sometimes longer depending on the backlog.) Sample copy and writer's guidelines with 9x12 SAE and $1.05 postage.
Nonfiction: Book excerpts; general interest (concerning cats); how-to (care for cats); humor; interview/profile (on cat owning personalities); new product; personal experience; photo feature; and technical (veterinarian writers). No talking cats. Buys 36 mss/year. Send complete ms. Length 800-2,500 words. Pays $25-300.
Photos: Send photos with submission. Reviews transparencies. Offers $5-25/photo. Identification of subjects required. Buys one-time rights.
Fiction: Fantasy, historical, mystery, science fiction, slice-of-life vignettes and suspense. "We rarely use fiction, but are not averse to using it if the cat theme is handled in smooth, believable manner. All fiction must involve a cat or relationship of cat and humans, etc." No talking cats. Buys 4-6 mss/year. Send complete ms. Length: 800-2,500 words. Pays $25-300.
Poetry: Avant-garde, free verse, haiku, light verse and traditional. Length: 4-64 lines. Pays 50¢/line.
Tips: "Well researched articles are the freelancer's best bet. Writers must at least like cats. Writers who obviously don't, miss the mark."

THE CHRONICLE OF THE HORSE, Box 46, Middleburg VA 22117. (703)687-6341. Editor: John Strassburger. Managing Editor: Nancy Comer. 80% freelance written. Weekly magazine about horses. "We cover English riding sports, including horse showing, grand prix jumping competitions, steeplechase racing, foxhunting, dressage, endurance riding, handicapped riding and combined training. We are the official publication for the national governing bodies of many of the above sports. We feature news of the above sports, and we also publish how-to articles on equitation and horse care, and interviews with leaders in the various fields." Circ. 22,000. Pays for features on acceptance; news and other items on publication. Publishes ms an average of 3 months after acceptance. Byline given. Buys first North American rights and makes work-for-hire assignments. Submit seasonal/holiday material 3 months in advance. Computer printout submissions acceptable only if double-spaced, 8½x11 format; prefers letter-quality. Simultaneous queries and photocopied submissions OK. Reports in 2-3 weeks. Sample copy for 9x12 SAE and $2; writer's guidelines for #10 SAE.
Nonfiction: General interest; historical/nostalgic (history of breeds, use of horses in other countries and times, art, etc.); how-to (trailer, train, design a course, save money, etc.); humor (centered on living with horses or horse people); interview/profile (of nationally known horsemen or the very unusual); technical (horse care, articles on feeding, injuries, care of foals, shoeing, etc.); and news (of major competitions, clear assignment with us first). Special issues include Steeplechasing; Grand Prix Jumping; Combined Training; Dressage; Hunt Roster; Junior and Pony; and Christmas. No Q&A interviews, clinic reports, Western riding articles, personal experience, or wild horses. Buys 300 mss/year. Query or send complete ms. Length: 300-1,225 words. Pays $25-200.
Photos: State availability of photos. Reviews 5x7 b&w prints. Color may be considered for b&w reproduction. Pays $10-25. Identification of subjects required. Buys one-time rights.
Columns/Departments: Dressage, Combined Training, Horse Show, Horse Care, Polo, Racing, Racing over Fences, Young Entry (about young riders, geared for youth), Horses and Humanities, and Hunting. Query or send complete ms. Length: 300-1,225 words. Pays $25-200.
Poetry: Light verse and traditional. No free verse. Buys 75 mss/year. Length: 5-30 lines. Pays $15.
Fillers: Anecdotes, short humor, newsbreaks and cartoons. Buys 300 mss/year. Length: 50-175 lines. Pays $10-25.
Tips: "Get our guidelines. Our readers are sophisticated, competitive horsemen. Articles need to go beyond common knowledge. Freelancers often attempt too broad or too basic a subject. We welcome well-written news stories on major events, but clear the assignment with us."

DOG FANCY, Fancy Publications, Inc., Box 6050, Mission Viejo CA 92690. (714)855-8822. Editor: Kim Thornton . 75% freelance written. Eager to work with unpublished writers. "We'd like to see a balance of both new and established writers." Monthly magazine for men and women of all ages interested in all phases of dog ownership. Circ. 150,000. Pays after publication. Publishes ms an average of 6 months after acceptance. Buys first American serial rights. Byline given. Submit seasonal/holiday material 4 months in advance. Computer printout submissions acceptable; prefers letter-quality. Sample copy $3.50; writer's guidelines for #10 SASE.

Nonfiction: Historical, medical, how-to, humor, informational, interview, personal experience, photo feature, profile and technical. "We're planning one or two *major* features covering significant events in the dog world. We'll be looking for (and paying more for) high quality writing/photo packages on topics outside of our normal range of features. Interested writers should query with topics." Buys 5 mss/issue. Query or send complete ms. Length: 500-3,000 words. Pays 5/word.

Photos: Photos purchased with or without accompanying ms. Pays $15 minimum for 8x10 b&w glossy prints; $50-150 for 35mm or 2¼x2¼ color transparencies. Send prints and transparencies. Model release required.

Fillers: "Need short, punchy photo fillers and cartoons." Buys 10 fillers/year. Pays $20-35.

Tips: "We're looking for the unique experience that communicates something about the dog/owner relationship—with the dog as the focus of the story, not the owner. Articles that provide hard information (medical, etc.) through a personal experience are appreciated. Note that we write for a lay audience (non-technical), but we do assume a certain level of intelligence: no talking down to people. If you've never seen the type of article you're writing in *Dog Fancy*, don't expect to."

‡**EQUINEWS, All Breeds - All Disciplines**, Whitehouse Publishing, Box 1778, Vernon B.C. V1T 8C3 Canada. (604)545-9896. Editor Dr. B.J. White. 50% freelance written. Monthly tabloid on horses. Serves the horse industry with current news and information. Circ. 17,492. Pays on publication. Publishes ms an average of 2 months after acceptance. Byline given. Buys first rights or second serial (reprint) rights. Submit seasonal/holiday material 2 months in advance. Simultaneous, photocopied and previously published submissions OK (if advised). Query for electronic submissions. Computer printout submissions OK; prefers letter-quality. Reports in 2 months on queries. Sample copy for 9x12 SAE and $1.50 Canadian postage; writer's guidelines for #10 SAE with 44¢ USA, 38¢ for Canada postage.

Nonfiction: General interest, humor, interview/profile (English trainers and internationally known riders) and travel. Also sponsors Christmas horse story contest for prizes. Nov. 1 deadline. "No veterinary or how-to." Buys 15 mss/year. Send complete ms. Length: 500-1,500 words. Pays $75. Pays exchange for advertising if desired at double value.

Photos: State availability of photos with submission. Reviews prints. Offers $5 per photo. Captions, model releases and identification of subjects required. Buys one-time rights.

Columns/Departments: Profiles on Trainers (background, facilities, fees, charges, successes, students philosophy), 500-1,500 words. Buys 10 mss/year. Send complete ms. Pays $25-75.

Fiction: Adventure, historical, humorous, and slice-of-life vignettes, all with equine slant. Buys 4 mms/year. Send complete mss. Length: 500-1,500 words. Pays $25-75.

Poetry: Buys 3 or 4 poems/year. Submit maximum 5 poems. Pays $10-25.

Fillers: Anecdotes, facts, gags to be illustrated by cartoonist, newsbreaks and short humor. Buys 12/year. Pays $5-25.

Tips: "Submit sample mss with introductory letter giving brief background of writer, 'horse' knowledge and any published works."

‡**THE HORSE DIGEST**, Equine Excellence Management Group, Box 3039, Berea KY 40403. (606)986-4644. FAX: (606)986-1770. Editor: James Bloomquist. 75% freelance written. Monthly magazine on the US horse industry. Circ. 15,000. Pays on publication. Byline given. Offers negotiable kill fee. Buys first North American serial rights. Previously published submissions OK. Reports in 1 month on queries. Free sample copy and writer's guidelines.

Nonfiction: Exposé (business oriented), how-to (should be serious, useable, business information), interview/profile (with industry people). No girl-and-her-horse, how-to clean your tack, or historical pieces. Also, we do not want "great horse" profiles. We are not a "backyard", casual interest horse magazine. No fiction. Buys 60 mss/year. Query with published clips. Length: 1,000-2,500 words. Pays $100-200 for assigned articles; $75-125 for unsolicited articles. Rarely pays expenses of writers on assignment.

Photos: State availability of photos with submission or send photos with submission. Reviews 3½x5 prints. Offers $5-15 per photo (negotiable). Captions or model releases required. Buy one-time rights.

Columns/Departments: International (international, overseas business-interest pieces), 1,000 words; The Entrepreneurs (stories about business success in the equine industry), 1,000 words. Buys 10 mms/year. Query with published clips. Pays $50-100.

Tips: "Read *THD* and *other* horse publications. Understand that we serve the professional or semi-pro equine business community and not the casual horse owner. Understand the U.S. horse industry. If you write informative articles for business, gear your articles that way. If you go to a horse show or race or event, we aren't necessarily interested in who won, but how much money the event generated, how it was organized. People in the horse business are like other business-people; they have employees, need insurance, they travel, own computers, advertise, need basic and not so basic information like other business-people."

HORSE ILLUSTRATED, The Magazine for Responsible Horse Owners, Fancy Publications, Inc., Box 6050, Mission Viejo CA 92690. (714)855-8822. Editor: Jill-Marie Jones. 90% freelance written. Prefers to work with published/established writers but eager to work with new/unpublished writers. Monthly magazine covering all aspects of horse ownership. "Our readers are adult women between the ages of 18 and 40; stories should be geared to that age group and reflect responsible horse care." Circ. 110,000. Pays on publication. Publishes ms an average of 8 months after acceptance. Byline given. Buys one-time rights. Submit seasonal/holiday material 6 months in advance. Computer printout submissions acceptable; prefers letter-quality. Reports in 6 weeks on queries; 2 months on mss. Sample copy $3.25. Writer's guidelines for #10 SASE.

Nonfiction: How-to (horse care, training, veterinary care), humor, personal experience and photo feature. No "little girl" horse stories; "cowboy and Indian" stories; anything not *directly* relating to horses. "We are beginning to look for longer, more in-depth features on trends and issues in the horse industry. Such articles must be queried first with a detailed outline of the article and clips." Buys 100 mss/year. Query or send complete ms. Length: 1,000-2,500 words. Pays $100-250 for assigned articles. Pays $50-200 for unsolicited articles. Sometimes pays telephone bills for writers on assignment.

Photos: Send photos with submission. Reviews contact sheet, 35mm transparencies and 5x7 prints. Occasionally offers additional payment for photos accepted with ms.

Tips: "Freelancers can break in at this publication with feature articles on Western and English training methods and trainer profiles (including training tips); veterinary and general care how-to articles; and horse sports articles. While we use personal experience articles (six to eight times a year), they must be extremely well-written and have wide appeal; humor in such stories is a bonus. Submit photos with training and how-to articles whenever possible. We have a very good record of developing new freelancers into regular contributors/columnists. We are always looking for fresh talent, but certainly enjoy working with established writers who 'know the ropes' as well."

HORSE WORLD USA, Garri Publications, Inc., 114 West Hills Rd., Box 249, Huntington Station NY 11746. (516)549-3557. FAX: (516)423-0567. Editor: Diana DeRosa. 25% freelance written. A magazine published 13 times per year about horses. Circ. 16,500. Pays on publication. Byline given. Buys first North American serial rights. Submit seasonal/holiday material 6 months in advance. Query for electronic submissions. Computer printout submissions OK; no dot-matrix. Reports in 3 months on queries. Sample copy for 9x12 SAE, and 6 first class stamps. Writer's guidelines for #10 SASE.

Nonfiction: "Anything horse-related (see topics listed in columns/departments section below)." Buys 25 mss/year. Query with published clips. Length: 100-2,000 words. Pays $5-125 or offers complimentary ad in directory on in classifieds as payment.

Photos: State availability of photos with submission or send photos with submission. Reviews 5x7 prints. Offers $5-10 per photo. Captions, model releases and identification of subjects required. Buys one-time rights. "No name on front of photo; give creditline."

Columns/Departments: Stable management/Horse care, Puzzles, Equine spotlight, Equestrian Spotlight, Celebrity Corner, Diet/Health/Fitness, Horoscopes, The Judge's Coral, From The Horse's Mouth, The Foal's Paddock (does not pay). "Remember these must all be related to horses or horse people." Features: Horse Show, Driving, Dressage, Polo, Racing, Side-Saddle, Eventing, Breeding, Gift Mart, Grand Prix, Western, Youth, Saratoga in August. Query with published clips. Length: 500-1,000 words. Pays $75 maximum.

Fillers: Anecdotes, facts, gags to be illustrated by cartoonist, and short humor. Buys 18/year. Length: 25 words minimum. Pays $5.

Tips: "We are an information center for horse people. Write for guidelines. We like to work with writers and artists who are new and are not necessarily looking for money but rather a chance to be published. When writing please specify whether payment is required."

HORSEMAN MAGAZINE, Horseman Publishing Corporation, Suite 390, 25025 I45 N., Spring TX 77380. (713)367-5151. Editor: Kathy Kadash. 60% freelance written. Monthly magazine covering the western performance horse industry. "Articles should convey quality information on western horses and horsemanship within the warmth of journalistic prose." Circ. 140,000. Publishes ms an average of 9 months after acceptance. Byline given. Pays $50 kill fee. Buys first North American serial rights. Photocopied submissions OK. Computer printout submissions OK; prefers letter quality. Reports in 2 weeks. Sample copy for 10x13 SAE and $1 postage; writer's guidelines for #10 SASE.

Nonfiction: How-to, general interest, historical/nostalgic, humor, interview/profile, personal experience, photo feature, technical. No horse health articles. Buys 100 articles/year. Query or send complete ms. Length: 1,000-2,000 words. Pays $100-250.

Photos: Send photos with manuscript submission. Reviews transparencies (35mm) and prints (5x7). Captions required. Buys one-time rights. Rarely buys freelance photography.

Columns/Departments: "Columns are done by freelance contributors but they are assigned over a long period and are not open to other freelance writers."

HORSEMEN'S YANKEE PEDLAR NEWSPAPER, 785 Southbridge St., Auburn MA 01501. (508)832-9638. Publisher: Nancy L. Khoury. Editor: Tracy Thomson. 40% freelance written. "All-breed monthly newspaper for horse enthusiasts of all ages and incomes, from one-horse owners to large commercial stables. Covers region from New Jersey to Maine." Circ. 12,000. Pays on publication. Buys all rights for one year. Submit seasonal/holiday material 3 months in advance of issue date. Query for electronic submissions. Computer printout submissions acceptable; prefers letter-quality. Publishes ms an average of 5 months after acceptance. Reports in 1 month. Sample copy $3.75.

Nonfiction: Humor, educational and interview about horses and the people involved with them. Pays $2/published inch. Buys 100 mss/year. Query or submit complete ms or outline. Length: 1,500 words maximum.

Photos: Purchased with ms. Captions and photo credit required. Submit b&w prints. Pays $5.

Columns/Departments: Area news column. Buys 85-95/year. Length: 1,200-1,400 words. Query.

Tips: "Query with outline of angle of story, approximate length and date when story will be submitted. Stories should be people oriented and horse focused. Send newsworthy, timely pieces, such as stories that are applicable to the season, for example: foaling in the spring or how to keep a horse healthy through the winter. We like to see how-tos, features about special horse people and anything that has to do with the preservation of horses and their rights as creatures deserving a chance to survive."

HORSEPLAY, Box 130, Gaithersburg MD 20877. (301)840-1866. FAX: (301)840-5722. Editor: Cordelia Doucet. 50% freelance written. Works with published/established writers and a small number of new/unpublished writers each year. Monthly magazine covering horses and English horse sports for a readership interested in horses, show jumping, dressage, combined training, hunting, and driving. 60-80 pages. Circ. 48,000. Pays end of publication month. Buys all rights, first North American serial rights, and second serial (reprint) rights. Offers kill fee. Byline given. Query first. Deadline is 2 months prior to issue date. Nothing returned without SASE. Computer printout submissions acceptable; no dot-matrix. Reports within 3 weeks. Sample copy $3 with 9x12 SAE; writer's and photographer's guidelines for #10 SASE.

Nonfiction: Instruction (various aspects of horsemanship, course designing, stable management, putting on horse shows, etc.); competitions; interview; photo feature; profile and technical. Length: 1,000-3,000 words. Pays 10¢/word, all rights; 9¢/word, first North American serial rights; 7/word, second rights. Sometimes pays extra to writers on assignment.

Photos: Cathy Kuehner, art director. Purchased on assignment. Write captions on separate paper attached to photo. Query or send contact sheet, prints or transparencies. Pays $22.50 for 8x10 b&w glossy prints; $200 for color transparencies for cover; $45 for inside color.

Tips: Don't send fiction, Western riding, or racing articles.

HORSES ALL, Box 9, Hill Spring Alberta T0K 1E0 Canada. (403)626-3344. Editor: Jacki French. 30% freelance written. Eager to work with new/unpublished writers. Monthly tabloid for horse owners, 75% rural, 25% urban. Circ. 11,200. Pays on publication. Publishes ms an average of 6 months after acceptance. Buys one-time rights. Phone queries OK. Submit seasonal material 3 months in advance. Simultaneous, photocopied (if clear), and previously published submissions OK. Computer printout submissions acceptable; no dot-matrix. Reports on queries in 5 weeks; on mss in 6 weeks. Sample copy for 9x12 SAE and $2.

Nonfiction: Interview, humor and personal experience. Query. Pays $20-100. Sometimes pays the expenses of writers on assignment.

Photos: State availability of photos. Captions required.

Columns/Departments: Open to suggestions for new columns/departments. Send query to Doug French. Length: 1-2 columns.

Fiction: Historical and western. Query. Pays $20-100.

Tips: "We use more short articles. The most frequent mistakes made by writers in completing an article assignment for us are poor research, wrong terminology, and poor (terrible) writing style."

‡HORSES WEST, The Rocky Mountain Region's Largest News Magazine Dedicated to Horses for Sport and Performance, Box 129, Castle Rock CO 80104. (303)688-1117. Editor: Phyllis Squiccimara. Tabloid published 10 times/year on the horse industry. "*Horses West* is a regional magazine serving the Rocky Mountain states. Our audience includes those horsemen of English riding disciplines." Pays on publication. Publishes ms an average of 3 months after acceptance. Byline given. Offers 25% kill fee. Buys first North American serial rights or second serial (reprint) rights. Submit seasonal/holiday material 3 months in advance. Photocopied and previously published submissions OK. Computer printout submissions OK; prefers letter-quality. Reports in 2 weeks on queries; 1 month on mss. Sample copy for 9x12 SAE with 5 first class stamps. Writer's guidelines for #10 SASE.

Nonfiction: Submissions sent to Articles Editor. Book excerpts, how-to (training, riding, care of the horse), humor, interview/profile, new product and photo feature. Buys 50 mss/year. Query with or without published clips, or send complete ms. Length: 250-5,000 words. Pays $10-150 for assigned articles. Sometimes pays expenses of writers on assignment.

Photos: State availability of photos with submission. Reviews contact sheets and 5x7 prints. Offers $5-25 per photo. Buys one-time rights.

Columns/Departments: Send to Column Editor. Book Review (reviews of recent high quality books on English disciplines); Trainers/Judges (training and showing hints from professionals in the field), 250-1,000 words; Sports Psychologist (monthly advise on various problems in horse/rider), 250-1,000 words. Buys 20 mss/year. Query with published clips. Length: 250-1,000 words. Pays $10-75.

Poetry: Send to Poetry Editor. Free verse, haiku, light verse and traditional. "No *bad* poetry—sentimental, syrupy, abstract tributes to a favorite pony or old gray mare." Buys 6 poems/year. Submit maximum 15 poems. Length: 3-150 lines. Pays $5-35.

Fillers: Send to Fillers Editor. Facts, gags to be illustrated by cartoonist, newsbreak and short humor. Buys up to 20/year. Length: 25-250 words. "*Must be horse related*" Pays $5-25.

Tips: "Please query the editor first. Write a paragraph or two outlining your story idea. Indicate photo or graphic availability in your query. Querying us first saves your time and our time. *Horses West* is looking for skillfully written articles in a feature style photojournalism format. Be clear, concise and precise in your wording. We're expanding our focus to include Western riding disciplines. We will accept profiles on trainers and how-to articles on training and showing methods for the Western discipline."

‡**THE INTERNATIONAL HORSE'S MOUTH**, Extenda Productions, Inc., #207 4020-17 Ave. SE, Calgary Alberta T2A 0S7 Canada. (403)248-5412. U.S. Office: (206)766-6400. FAX: (403)248-1190. Editor: Leo T. Maxwell. 55% freelance written. Monthly magazine on the equine industry in Canada, US and Europe. "Our publication reaches new equine enthusiasts in addition to long time breeders. Our articles reflect our readers interests in training, breeding and product knowledge." Circ. 10,000 Europe; 28,000 Canada and US. Pays on publication. Byline given. Offers 25% kill fee. Buys first North American serial rights, first rights or second serial (reprint) rights. Submit seasonal/holiday material 4 months in advance. Previously published submissions OK. Query for electronic submissions. Computer printout submissions OK; prefers letter-quality. Free sample copy and writer's guidelines.

Nonfiction: Historical/nostalgic, equine only; how-to, equine only; interview/profile, equine only; new product, equine only; personal experience, equine only; photo feature, equine only; and technical, equine only. "No poetry." Buys 50-60 mss/year. Query. Length: 1,000-5,000 words. Pays $35-150 for assigned articles.

Photos: State availability of photos with submission. Reviews contact sheets. Offers $5 per photo. Buys one-time rights.

Columns/Departments: Cowhorse Corner (reining, roping, cutting, cattle penning), 1,000-2500 words; Competitive Edge (endurance, ride & tie), 1,000-2,500; Track Talk (Quarter horse, Arab, Appaloosa and Paint racing), 1,000-2,500. Buys 30-40 mss/year. Query. Pays $35-150.

Tips: "We like to publish quality writing from new writers. Writers may contact us regarding their ideas, or for suggestions from us."

PAINT HORSE JOURNAL, American Paint Horse Association, Box 18519, Fort Worth TX 76118. (817)439-3412. Editor: Bill Shepard. 10% freelance written. Works with a small number of new/unpublished writers each year. For people who raise, breed and show Paint horses. Monthly magazine. Circ. 12,000. Pays on acceptance. Publishes ms an average of 3 months after acceptance. Buys first North American serial rights plus reprint rights occasionally. Pays negotiable kill fee. Byline given. Phone queries OK, but prefers written query. Submit seasonal/holiday material 3 months in advance. Photocopied and previously published submissions OK. Computer printout submissions acceptable; prefers letter-quality. Reports in 1 month. Sample copy for 9x12 SAE and 5 first class stamps; writer's guidelines for #10 SASE.

Nonfiction: General interest (personality pieces on well-known owners of Paints); historical (Paint horses in the past—particular horses and the breed in general); how-to (train and show horses); photo feature (Paint horses); and articles on horse health. Now seeking informative well-written articles on recreational riding. Buys 4-5 mss/issue. Send complete ms. Pays $50-250.

Photos: Send photos with ms. Offers no additional payment for photos accepted with accompanying ms. Uses 3x5 or larger b&w glossy prints; 35mm or larger color transparencies. Captions required.

Tips: "*PHJ* needs breeder-trainer articles, Paint horse marketing and timely articles from areas throughout the U.S. and Canada. We are looking for more horse health articles, recreational and how-to articles. We are beginning to cover more equine activity outside the show ring. This can include such things as trail riding, orienteering, and other outdoor events. Photos with copy are almost always essential. Well-written first person articles are welcomed. Submit well-written items that show a definite understanding of the horse business. Be sure you understand precisely what a Paint Horse is as defined by the American Paint Horse Association. Use proper equine terminology and proper grounding in ability to communicate thoughts."

‡**PETS MAGAZINE**, Moorshead Publications, 1300 Don Mills Rd., Toronto Ontario M3B 3M8 Canada. (416)445-5600. FAX: (416)445-8149. Editor: Marie Hubbs. Editorial Director/Veterinarian: Dr. Tom Frisby. 40% freelance written. Bimonthly magazine on pets. Circ. 67,000 distributed by vet clinics; 5,500 personal subscriptions. Pays on publication. Publishes ms an average of 6-12 months after acceptance. Buys all rights. Submit seasonal/holiday material 4 months in advance. Photocopied submissions OK. Previously published

submissions (sometimes). Query for electronic submissions. Computer submissions OK; prefers letter-quality. Sample copy for #10 SAE with 91¢ IRC. Free writer's guidelines.

Nonfiction: General interest, historical, how-to (train, bathe/groom, build dog houses, make cat toys and photograph pets), profile, personal experience and photo feature. No "I remember Fluffy." Buys 12-18 mss/year. Query with outline. Length: 600-1,500 words. Pays 12-18¢ (Canadian)/ word; 1-3 copies included with payment check. Pays expenses of writers on assignment only by prior agreement.

Photos: Send photos with submission. Reviews prints 3x5 and larger, b&w preferred. Offers $25 per photo. Model releases and identification of subjects required. Buys all rights.

Fillers: Facts, gags to be illustrated by cartoonist; query with samples. Buys 1-2/year. Length: 100-400 words. Pays 12-15¢(Canadian)/word. "Always call or send topic outline first; we always have backlog of freelance articles waiting to be run. Prefers factual, information pieces, not anecdotal or merely humorous, but can be written with humor; we do not cover controversial areas such as product testing, vivisection, puppy mills, pound seizure."

PURE-BRED DOGS AMERICAN KENNEL GAZETTE, American Kennel Club, 51 Madison Ave., New York NY 10010. (212)696-8331. Executive Editor: Marion Lane. 80% freelance written. Monthly association publication on pure-bred dogs. "Material is slanted to interests of fanciers of pure-bred dogs as opposed to commercial interests." Circ. 58,000. Pays on acceptance. Publishes ms an average of 6 months after acceptance. Byline given. Offers 30% kill fee. Buys first North American serial rights. Submit seasonal/holiday material 6 months in advance. Photocopied submissions OK. Computer submissions OK; no dot-matrix. Reports in 3 weeks. Sample copy and writer's guidelines for 9x12 SAE and 11 first class stamps.

Nonfiction: General interest, historical, how-to, humor, photo feature, travel. No profiles, poetry, tributes to individual dogs, or fiction. Buys about 85 mss/year. Query with or without published clips, or send complete ms. Length: 1,000-2,500 words. Pays $100-300. Sometimes pays expenses of writers on assignment.

Fiction: Annual short fiction contest only. Guidelines for #10 SASE.

Photos: Send photos with submission. Reviews tranparencies and prints. Offers $25-$100/photo. Captions required. Buys one-time rights. (Photo contest guidelines for #10 SASE).

Tips: "Contributors should be involved in dog fancy or be expert in the area they write about (veterinary, showing,field trialing, obedience, training, dogs in legislation, dog art or history or literature). All submissions are welcome and are read but the author must be credible. Veterinary articles must be written by or with veterinarians. Humorous features are personal experiences relative to pure-bred dogs. For features generally, know the subject thoroughly and be conversant with jargon peculiar to dog sport."

PURRRR! THE NEWSLETTER FOR CAT LOVERS, The Meow Company, HCR 227 Rd., Islesboro ME 04848. (207)734-6745. Publisher/Editor Agatha Cabaniss. 85% freelance written. Works with a small number of new/unpublished writers each year. A bimonthly newsletter for the average cat owner. "The publication is designed to amuse while providing cat lovers with information about the care, feeding and enjoyment of house cats." Circ. 1,000. Pays on acceptance. Publishes ms an average of 4-5 months after acceptance. Byline given. Buys first serial rights and second serial (reprint) rights. Submit seasonal/holiday material 6 months in advance. Photocopied and previously published submissions OK unless it's been published in a competing publication, such as *Cats* and *Cat Fancy*. Query for electronic submissions. Computer printout submissions acceptable; prefers letter-quality. Reports in 2 weeks. Sample copy $2; writer's guidelines for #10 SASE.

Nonfiction: General interest; historical; how-to; literary cat lovers (have featured Colette, Mark Twain and May Sarton); humor; interview/profile; new product; travel, off-beat unusual. "We want a humorous slant wherever possible; writing should be tight and professional. Avoid the first person." Special Christmas issue. No shaggy cat stories, sentimental stories, "I taught Fluffy to roll over" or no "reformed cat hater" stories. "We would like to receive articles on humane societies and animal rescue leagues." Absolutely no fiction. Buys 50/mss year. Query with published clips, or send complete ms. Length: 250-1,500 words. Pays: $15-100.

Photos: Avoid "cute" photos. State availability of photos. Pays $5-10 for 5x8 b&w prints. Buys one-time rights.

Poetry: Accepts some poetry.

Fillers: Clippings, anecdotes, short humor/cartoons and newsbreaks. Buys 20/year. Length: 25-75 words. Pays $5.

Tips: "You should know pet cats, their foibles and personalities. We are interested in good writing but also in a good story about a cat. We are interested in people who work with and for animal welfare and how-to articles on making things for cats or for people who live with cats, i.e. how to 'cat proof' a crib. We will work with a writer who has an interesting cat story. We are not interested in show cats or breeding. Query or send article and a SASE for reply."

THE QUARTER HORSE JOURNAL, Box 32470, Amarillo TX 79120. (806)376-4811. FAX: (806)372-6806. Editor-in-Chief: Audie Rackley. 10% freelance written. Prefers to work with published/established writers. Official publication of the American Quarter Horse Association. Monthly magazine. Circ. 70,000. Pays on acceptance. Publishes ms an average of 3 months after acceptance. Buys first North American serial rights.

Submit seasonal/holiday material 2 months in advance. Computer printout submissions acceptable; no dot-matrix. Reports in 2 weeks. Free sample copy and writer's guidelines.

Nonfiction: Historical ("those that retain our western heritage"); how-to (fitting, grooming, showing, or anything that relates to owning, showing, or breeding); informational (educational clinics, current news); interview (feature-type stories—must be about established horses or people who have made a contribution to the business); personal opinion; and technical (equine updates, new surgery procedures, etc.). Buys 20 mss/year. Length: 800-2,500 words. Pays $50-250.

Photos: Purchased with accompanying ms. Captions required. Send prints or transparencies. Uses 5x7 or 8x10 b&w glossy prints; 2¼x2¼ or 4x5 color transparencies. Offers no additional payment for photos accepted with accompanying ms.

Tips: "Writers must have a knowledge of the horse business. We will be purchasing more material on quarter horse racing."

TROPICAL FISH HOBBYIST, "The World's Most Widely Read Aquarium Monthly," TFH Publications, Inc., 211 W. Sylvania Ave., Neptune City NJ 07753. (201)988-8400. Editor: Ray Hunziker. Managing Editor: Neal Pronek. 75% freelance written. Monthly magazine covering the tropical fish hobby. "We favor articles well illustrated with good color slides and aimed at both the neophyte and veteran tropical fish hobbyist." Circ. 60,000. Pays on acceptance. Publishes ms an average of 4 months after acceptance. Byline given. Buys all rights. Submit seasonal/holiday material 4 months in advance. Photocopied submissions OK. Computer printout submissions acceptable; no dot-matrix. Reports in 2 weeks. Sample copy $3; writer's guidelines for #10 SASE.

Nonfiction: General interest, how-to, photo feature, technical, and articles dealing with beginning and advanced aspects of the aquarium hobby. No "how I got started in the hobby" articles that impart little solid information. Buys 20-30 mss/year. Length: 500-2,500 words. Pays $25-100.

Photos: State availability of photos or send photos with ms. Pays $10 for 35mm color transparencies. Identification of subjects required. "Originals of photos returned to owner, who may market them elsewhere."

Fiction: "On occasion, we will review a fiction piece relevant to the aquarium hobby."

Tips: "We cater to a specialized readership—people knowledgeable in fish culture. Prospective authors should be familiar with subject; photography skills are a plus. It's a help if an author we've never dealt with queries first or submits a short item."

THE WESTERN HORSEMAN, World's Leading Horse Magazine Since 1936, Western Horseman, Inc., 3850 N. Nevada Ave., Box 7980, Colorado Springs CO 80933. (719)633-5524. Editor: Randy Witte. 50% freelance written. Works with a small number of new/unpublished writers each year. Monthly magazine covering western horsemanship. Circ. 168,086. Pays on acceptance. Publishes ms an average of 5 months after acceptance. Buys North American serial rights or second serial (reprint) rights. Byline given. Computer printout submissions acceptable; prefers letter-quality. Submit seasonal/holiday material 9 months in advance. Reports in 2 weeks. Sample copy $2.25; free writer's guidelines.

Nonfiction: How-to (horse training, care of horses, tips, etc.); and informational (on rodeos, ranch life, historical articles of the West emphasizing horses). Buys 100 mss/year. Length: 500-2,000 words. Payment begins at $35-300; "sometimes higher by special arrangement."

Photos: Send photos with ms. Offers no additional payment for photos. Uses 5x7 or 8x10 b&w glossy prints and 35mm transparencies. Captions required.

Fiction: Humorous, western. Buys 2-3 mss/year. Send complete ms. Length: 1,000-1,500 words. Pays $300 maximum.

Tips: "Submit clean copy with professional quality photos. Stay away from generalities. Writing style should show a deep interest in horses coupled with a wide knowledge of the subject."

_____ *Art and Architecture*

Listed here are publications about art, art history, specific art forms and architecture written for art patrons, architects and artists. Publications addressing the business and management side of the art industry are listed in the Art, Design and Collectibles category of the Trade section. Trade publications for architecture can be found in Building Interiors and Construction and Contracting sections.

‡**THE AMERICAN ART JOURNAL,** Kennedy Galleries, Inc. 400 W. 57th St., 5th Floor, New York NY 10019. (212)541-9600. Editor-in-Chief: Jane Van N. Truman. Prefers to work with published/established writers; works with a small number of new/unpublished writers each year. Scholarly magazine of American art history

of the 17th, 18th, 19th and 20th centuries, including painting, sculpture, architecture, decorative arts, etc., for people with a serious interest in American art, and who are already knowledgeable about the subject. Readers are scholars, curators, collectors, students of American art, or persons who have a strong interest in Americana. Quarterly magazine; 96 pages. Circ. 2,000. pays on acceptance. Publishes ms an average of 6 months after acceptance. Buys all rights, but will reassign rights to a writer. Byline given. Photocopied submissions OK. Computer printout submissions acceptable but with reluctance. Reports in 2 months. Sample copy $11.

Nonfiction: "All articles are about some phase or aspect of American art history." No how-to articles or reviews of exhibitions. No book reviews or opinion pieces. No human interest approaches to artists' lives. No articles written in a casual or "folksy" style. *Writing style must be formal and serious*. Buys 25-30 mss/year. Submit complete ms "with good cover letter. No queries. Length: 2,500-8,000 words. Pays $300-400.

Photos: Purchased with accompanying ms. Captions required. Uses b&w only. Offers no additional payment for photos accepted with accompanying ms.

Tips: "Articles *must be* scholarly, thoroughly documented, well-researched, well-written, and illustrated. Whenever possible, all manuscripts must be accompanied by b&w photographs which have been integrated into the text by the use of numbers."

AMERICAN INDIAN ART MAGAZINE, American Indian Art, Inc., 7314 E. Osborn Dr., Scottsdale AZ 85251. (602)994-5445. Managing Editor: Roanne P. Goldfein. 97% freelance written. Works with a small number of new/unpublished writers each year. Quarterly magazine covering Native American art, historic and contemporary, including new research on any aspect of Native American art. Circ. 15,000. Pays on publication. Publishes ms an average of 3 months after acceptance. Byline given. Buys one-time and first rights. Simultaneous queries OK. Computer printout submissions OK; prefers letter-quality. Reports in 2 weeks on queries; 2 months on mss. Writer's guidelines for #10 SASE.

Nonfiction: New research on any aspect of Native American art. No previously published work or personal interviews with artists. Buys 12-18 mss/year. Query. Length: 1,000-2,500 words. Pays $75-300.

Tips: "The magazine is devoted to all aspects of Native American art. Some of our readers are knowledgeable about the field and some know very little. We seek articles that offer something to both groups. Articles reflecting original research are preferred to those summarizing previously published information."

ART TIMES, A Cultural and Creative Journal, Box 730, Mount Marion NY 12456. (914)246-5170. Editor: Raymond J. Steiner. 10% (just fiction and poetry) freelance written. Prefers to work with published/established writers; works with a small number of new/unpublished writers each year; and eager to work with new/unpublished writers. Monthly tabloid covering the arts (visual, theatre, dance, etc.). "*Art Times* covers the art fields and is distributed in locations most frequented by those enjoying the arts. Our 15,000 copies are distributed throughout three upstate New York counties rich in the arts as well as in most of the galleries in Soho, 57th Street and Madison Avenue in the metropolitan area; locations include theatres, galleries, museums, cultural centers and the like. Subscriptions come from across U.S. and abroad. Our readers are mostly over 40, affluent, art-conscious and sophisticated." Circ. 15,000. Pays on publication. Publishes ms an average of 1 year after acceptance. Byline given. Buys first serial rights. Submit seasonal/holiday material 8 months in advance. Simultaneous queries, and simultaneous and photocopied submissions OK. Computer printout submissions OK; prefers letter-quality. Reports in 3 months on queries; 6 months on mss. Sample copy for 9x12 SAE and 6 first class stamps; writer's guidelines for #10 SASE.

Fiction: "We're looking for short fiction that aspires to be *literary*. No excessive violence, sexist, off-beat, erotic, sports, or juvenile fiction." Buys 8-10 mss/year. Send complete ms. Length: 1,500 words maximum. Pays $15 maximum (honorarium) and 1 year's free subscription.

Poetry: Poet's Niche. Avant-garde, free verse, haiku, light verse and traditional. "We prefer well-crafted 'literary' poems. No excessively sentimental poetry." Buys 30-35 poems/year. Submit maximum 6 poems. Length: 20 lines maximum. Offers contributor copies and 1 year's free subscription.

Tips: "We are now receiving 300 to 400 poems and 40-50 short stories per month. We only publish 2 to 3 poems and one story each issue. Competition is getting very great. We only pick the best. Be familiar with *Art Times* and its special audience. *Art Times* has literary leanings with articles written by a staff of scholars knowledgeable in their respective fields. Our readers expect quality. Although an 'arts' publication, we observe no restrictions (other than noted) in accepting fiction/poetry other than a concern for quality writing—subjects can cover anything and not specifically arts."

THE ARTIST'S MAGAZINE, F&W Publications, Inc., 1507 Dana Ave., Cincinnati OH 45207. Editor: Michael Ward. 80% freelance written. Works with a small number of new/unpublished writers each year. Monthly magazine covering primarily two-dimensional art instruction for working artists. "Ours is a highly visual approach to teaching the serious amateur artist techniques that will help him improve his skills and market his work. The style should be crisp and immediately engaging." Circ. 212,000. Pays on acceptance. Publishes ms an average of 4 months after acceptance. Byline given; bionote given for feature material. Offers 20% kill fee. Buys first North American serial rights and second serial (reprint) rights. Simultaneous queries, and photocopied and previously published submissions OK "as long as noted as such." Computer printout submissions acceptable; prefers letter-quality. Reports in 1 month. Sample copy $2.25 with 9x12 SAE and 3 first class stamps; writer's guidelines for #10 SASE.

Nonfiction: Instructional only — how an artist uses a particular technique, how he handles a particular subject or medium, or how he markets his work. "The emphasis must be on how the reader can learn some method of improving his artwork, or the marketing of it." No unillustrated articles; no seasonal/holiday material; no travel articles; no profiles of artists (except for "Artist's Life," below). Buys 60 mss/year. Query first; all queries must be accompanied by slides, transparencies, prints or tearsheets of the artist's work as well as the artist's bio, and the writer's bio and clips. Length: 1,000-2,500 words. Pays $100-350 and up. Sometimes pays the expenses of writers on assignment.

Photos: "Color transparencies are required with every accepted article since these are essential for our instructional format. Full captions must accompany these." Buys one-time rights.

Departments: Two departments are open to freelance writers: The Artist's Life and P.S. The Artist's Life (profiles and brief items about artists and their work. Also, art-related games and puzzles and art-related poetry). Query first with samples of artist's work for profiles; send complete ms for other items. Length: 600 words maximum. Pays $50 and up for profiles; up to $25 for brief items and poetry. P.S. (a humorous look at art from the artist's point of view, or at least sympathetic to the artist). Send complete ms. Pays $50 and up.

Tips: "Look at several current issues and read the author's guidelines carefully. Remember that our readers are fine and graphic artists."

EQUINE IMAGES, The National Magazine of Equine Art, Heartland Communications Group, Inc., 1003 Central Ave., Fort Dodge IA 50501. (800)247-2000, ext. 1208. Co-Editors: Sandy Geier and Deborah Schneider. Publisher: Susan Badger, Heartland Communications Group, Inc. 20% freelance written. A quarterly magazine of equine art. "*Equine Images* serves artists, collectors, and equine art enthusiasts. We write for a sophisticated, culturally-oriented audience." Circ. 5,000. Pays on publication. Byline given. Offers $25 kill fee. Publication not copyrighted. Buys first rights and makes work for hire assignments. Previously published submissions OK. Reports in 2 weeks on queries; 3 weeks on mss. Sample copy for 9x12 SAE and $7.50; writer's guidelines for #10 SASE.

Nonfiction: Historical/nostalgic (history of the horse in art), how-to (art and art collections), interview/profile (equine artists, galleries, collectors), personal experience (of equine artists and collectors), photo feature (artworks or collections). "No articles about horses in general — just horse art. No casual writing style." Buys 4-8 mss/year. Query with published clips. Length: 500-3,000 words. Pays $150-500 for assigned articles; $100-350 for unsolicited articles.

Photos: State availability of photos with submission. Reviews contact sheets, transparencies, prints. Offers no additional payment for photos accepted with ms. Identification of subjects required. Buys one-time rights.

Tips: "We are interested only in art-related subjects. Writers should have an art background or be knowledgeable of the field. Experience with horses is also a plus. The most promising categories for writers are profiles of prominent artists and equine galleries or museums. If you know of a talented artist in your area, or a gallery or museum that specializes in equine art, send a good query letter with accompanying visuals, along with published clips or writing samples."

‡EXHIBIT, Magazine of Art, Allied Publications, 1776 Lake Worth Rd., Lake Worth FL 33460. (407)582-2099. FAX: (407)582-4667. Editor: Richard Champlin. 10% freelance written. Bimonthly magazine on fine art museum exhibits. Pays on publication. Publishes ms an average of 3 months after acceptance. Byline given. Buys first North American serial rights or one-time rights, or second serial (reprint) rights, or simultaneous rights. Submit seasonal/holiday material 6-8 months in advance. Simultaneous, photocopied and previously published submissions OK. Query for electronic submissions. Computer printout submissions OK. Reports in 2 weeks on queries; 6 months on mss. Sample copy for $1. Free writer's guidelines.

Nonfiction: Essays (art) and technical (fine art framing). Buys 6-12 mss/year. Query with or without published clips, or send complete ms. Length: 600-1,500 words. Pays $5-25 for unsolicited articles.

Photos: State availability of photos with submission. Reviews contact sheets and transparencies. Offers $5 per photo. Captions, model releases and identification of subjects required. Buys one-time rights.

HANDMADE ACCENTS, The Buyer's Guide to American Artisans, Creative Publications, Inc., 488-A River Mountain Rd., Lebanon VA 24266. (703)873-7402. Editor: Steve McCay. 15% freelance written. A quarterly magazine covering art, craft and photography. Audience is art patrons — collectors, investors, art directors, buyers for stores. "Most stories are profiles of contemporary artistic talents who market their wares

ALWAYS submit unsolicited manuscripts or queries with a self-addressed, stamped envelope (SASE) within your country or International Reply Coupons (IRC) purchased from the post office for other countries.

directly to the public—our readers." Circ. 50,000. Pays on publication. Publishes ms an average of 6 months after acceptance. Byline given. Buys first rights. Submit seasonal/holiday material 6 months in advance. Computer printout submissions acceptable; prefers letter-quality. Reports in 6 weeks. Sample copy $5.

Nonfiction: Humor, inspirational, interview/profile, personal experience and photo feature. No how-to-make specific craft, pattern, etc. Buys 16 mss/year. Query with or without published clips. Length: 1,000-2,500 words. Pays 5¢/word for articles. "Whenever article is autobiographical we pay 20 copies of issue and one year subscription."

Photos: Send photos with submission. Reviews 35mm slides and 4x5 transparencies. Offers $5 payment for each photo accepted with ms. Captions required. Buys one-time rights.

Columns/Departments: Book Reviews (art books of interest to art patrons); Art Beat (news releases and shorts of interest to our audience). Buys 32 mss/year. Query with published clips. Length: 500-2,000 words. Pays $10-25.

Poetry: Light verse and traditional. Must have slant on the art world/community. Buys 4 poems/year. Submit maximum 3 poems. Length: 50 lines maximum. Pays $10.

Fillers: Anecdotes, facts, gags to be illustrated by cartoonist, newsbreaks and short humor. Must have appeal to art patrons. Length: 100-500 words. Pays $5-25.

Tips: "Superior quality photos are a must. We feature creative talents of the arts community—primarily those willing to sell their wares direct to a retail market via mail order. We like to see slides of art and craft work first. Mostly we use autobiographical or first-person self portrait/profiles. We'd like to have a feature collector each issue with photos of the collection—be it art, pottery, metal, fiber, wood, etc.—with details on the pieces collected, philosophy of collectors, tips on displaying a collection. We provide a media for fine artists, photographers and craftspeople to reach their market also, direct mail offerings of fine crafts by their makers."

‡**MUSEUM & ARTS/WASHINGTON,** Museum & Arts/Washington, Inc., Suite 222, 1707 L St. NW, Washington D.C. 20036. (202)659-5973. Editor: Jeff Stein. 90% freelance written. Bimonthly magazine on the arts. "*Museum & Arts/Washington* is a lively guide to the arts in the Washington area. It seeks to interest and enliven its readers appreciation of art and artists in the capitol city." Circ. 50,000. Pays on publication. Publishes ms an average of 2 months after acceptance. Byline given. Offers 33⅓% kill fee. Buys first North American serial rights and makes work-for-hire assignments. Submit seasonal/holiday material 4 months in advance. Photocopied submissions OK. Query for electronic submissions. Computer printout submissions OK; prefers letter-quality. Reports in 2 weeks. Sample copy for 11x13 SAE with $2 first class postage.

Nonfiction: Submit to Jeff Stein, Editor. Book excerpts, essays, exposé, historical, interview/profile, opinion, personal experience and technical. Do *not* want anything that does not clearly relate to the Washington arts scene. Length: 750-6,000 words. Pays $75-2,500 for assigned articles. Sometimes pays expenses of writers on assignment.

Photos: State availability of photos with submission or send photos with submission. Reviews transparencies. Payment negotiable. Identification of subjects required. Buys one-time rights.

THE ORIGINAL ART REPORT, Box 1641, Chicago IL 60690. Editor and Publisher: Frank Salantrie. 1% freelance written. Eager to work with new/unpublished writers. Emphasizes "visual art conditions from the visual artists' and general public's perspectives." Newsletter; 6-8 pages. Pays on publication. Reports in 4 weeks. Sample copy $1.25 and 1 first class stamp.

Nonfiction: Expose (art galleries, government agencies ripping off artists, or ignoring them); historical (perspective pieces relating to now); humor (whenever possible); informational (material that is unavailable in other art publications); inspirational (acts and ideas of courage); interview (with artists, other experts; serious material); personal opinion; technical (brief items to recall traditional methods of producing art); travel (places in the world where artists are welcomed and honored); philosophical, economic, aesthetic, and artistic. "We would like to receive investigative articles on government and private arts agencies, and non-profits, too, perhaps hiding behind status to carry on for business entities. No vanity profiles of artists, arts organizations, and arts promoters' operations." Buys 4-5 mss/year. Query or submit complete ms. Length: 1,000 words maximum. Pays 1¢/word.

Columns/Departments: In Back of the Individual Artist. Artists express their views about non-art topics. After all, artists are in this world, too. WOW (Worth One Wow), Worth Repeating, and Worth Repeating Again. Basically, these are reprint items with introduction to give context and source, including complete name and address of publication. Looking for insightful, succinct commentary. Submit complete ms. Length: 500 words maximum and copy of item. Pays ½¢/word.

Tips: We have a stronger than ever emphasis on editorial opinion or commentary, based on fact, of the visual art condition: economics, finances, politics, and manufacture of art and the social and individual implications of and to fine art."

‡**THEDAMU, The Black Arts Magazine,** Detroit Black Arts Alliance, 13217 Livernois, Detroit MI 48238. (313)931-3427. Editor: David Rambeau. Managing Editor: Titilaya Akanke. 50% freelance written. Monthly literary magazine on the arts. "We publish Afro-American feature articles on local artists." Circ. 2,000. Pays

on publication. Publishes 4 months after acceptance. Byline given. Buys one-time rights. Submit seasonal/holiday material 4 months in advance. Simultaneous, photocopied and previously published submissions OK. Query for electronic submissions. Computer printout submissions OK; prefers letter-quality. Reports in 1 month on queries; 2 months on mss. Sample copy $2 with 1 SAE and 4 first class stamps. Writer's guidelines for SAE with 1 first class stamp.

Nonfiction: Essays and interview/profile. Buys 120 mss/year. Send complete ms. Length: 500-1,500 words. Pays $10-25 for unsolicited articles. Pays with contributor copies or other premiums if writer agrees.

Photos: State availability of photos with submission. Reviews 5x7 prints. Offers no additional payment for photos accepted with ms. Captions, model releases and identification of subjects required. Buys one-time rights.

Tips: "Send a résumé and sample ms. Query for fiction and poetry."

‡**U.S. ART, The Magazine of Realism in America,** Adams Publishing, Suite 400, 12 South 6th St., Minneapolis MN 55402. (612)339-7571. FAX: (612)339-5806. Editor: Paul Froiland. Associate Editor: Laura Silver. 90% freelance written. Magazine published 9 issues/year. "We are a mainstream publication covering American realist art of all genres—wildlife, landscape, still life, Western, Americana, etc. We are directed at the consumer, and feature artist profiles and articles on historical and contemporary issues in representational art." Circ. 32,000. Pays on publication. Publishes ms an average of 3 months after acceptance. Byline given. Offers 25% kill fee. Buys first North American serial rights. Submit seasonal/holiday material 6 months in advance. Simultaneous submissions OK, if they are identified as such. Computer printout submissions OK; prefers letter-quality. Reports in 6 weeks on queries; 2 months on mss. Sample for $2.50 with 9x12 SAE and 3 first class stamps. Writer's guidelines for #10 SASE.

Nonfiction: Essays, general interest, historical, interview/profile and opinion (does not mean letters to the editor). October: Western Art theme and March: Wildlife Art theme issue. Buys 45 mss/year. Query with published clips. Length: 2,000-2,500 words. Pays $400-500 for assigned articles. Pays only telephone and mileage expenses.

Columns/Departments: Collector's Window (news from the art world—accounts of gallery openings, auction news, museum news, changes or events in art law), 250 words; Museums (reviews of museum exhibitions, preferably travelling), 750 words; and Remarques (back-page opinion piece—humorous or serious), 500 words. Buys 23 mss/year. Query with published clips. Pays $50-200.

Tips: Queries should be very focused, and topics should be geared toward a mainstream audience—nothing too obscure, and nothing academically written. If they are querying on a particular artist, slides or 4x5 transparencies must be submitted.

WESTART, Box 6868, Auburn CA 95604. (916)885-0969. Editor-in-Chief: Martha Garcia. Emphasizes art for practicing artists and artists/craftsmen; students of art and art patrons. Semimonthly tabloid; 20 pages. Circ. 6,500. Pays on publication. Buys all rights. Byline given. Phone queries OK. Photocopied submissions OK. Sample copy $1; free writer's guidelines.

Nonfiction: Informational, photo feature and profile. No hobbies. Buys 6-8 mss/year. Query or submit complete ms. Length: 700-800 words. Pays 50¢/column inch.

Photos: Purchased with or without accompanying ms. Send b&w prints. Pays 50¢/column inch.

Tips: "We publish information which is current—that is, we will use a review of an exhibition only if exhibition is still open on the date of publication. Therefore, reviewer must be familiar with our printing deadlines and news deadlines."

‡**WOMEN ARTISTS NEWS,** Midmarch Associates, Box 3304, Grand Central Station, New York NY 10163. Editor: Judy Seigel. 70-90% freelance written. Works with small number of new/unpublished writers each year; eager to work with new/unpublished writers. Bimonthly magazine for "artists and art historians, museum and gallery personnel, students, teachers, crafts personnel, art critics and writers." Circ. 5,000. Buys first serial rights only when funds are available. "Token payment as funding permits." Publishes ms an average of 2 months after acceptance. Byline given. Submit seasonal material 2 months in advance. Computer printout submissions acceptable; no dot-matrix. Reports in 1 month. Sample copy $3.

Nonfiction: Features, informational, historical, interview, opinion, personal experience, photo feature and technical. Query or submit complete ms. Length: 500-2,500 words.

Photos: Used with or without accompanying ms. Query or submit contact sheet or prints. Pays $5 for 5x7 b&w prints when money is available. Captions required.

Associations

Association publications allow writers to write for national audiences while covering local stories. If your town has a Kiwanis, Lions or Rotary Club chapter, one of its projects might merit a story in the club's magazine. If you are a member of the organization, find out before you write an article if the publication pays members of the organization for stories; some associations do not. Association publications link members who live continents from one another or just across town and keep members abreast of ideas, objectives, projects and activities of the organization. Club-financed magazines that carry material not directly related to the group's activities are classified by their subject matter in the Consumer and Trade sections.

‡ASSOCIATION EXECUTIVE, An Independent News Magazine Serving Association, Hospitality and Meeting Executives, Special Editions Publishing, Inc. 450 Wymore Rd., Winter Park FL 32789. (407)644-0031. Editor: Kevin Fritz. 1% freelance written. Monthly tabloid on association and hospitality news. "We are primarily a news magazine, with special sections for features and news features. Our magazine is read by people who run associations. They are interested in things that affect their members and their associations." Circ. 4,300. Pays on publication on an individual basis. Byline given. Buys all rights. Submit seasonal/holiday material 2 months in advance. Simultaneous, photocopied and previously published submissions OK. Query for electronic submissions. Computer printout submissions OK; prefers letter-quality. Reports in 1 month on queries; 1 month (usually much faster) on mss. Sample copy and writer's guidelines for 8½x11 SAE with 4 first class stamps.

Nonfiction: Opinion (the effect of current affairs on the association industry), travel (especially cities with convention facilities) and legislative. Feature sections on convention facilities in: May: Carolinas, August: Georgia, October: Central Florida, November: Tennessee and December: South Florida. Buys 1 ms/year. Query with or without published clips, or send complete ms. Length: 500-2,500 words. Pays $1-250 for assigned articles; $1-50 for unsolicited articles. Sometimes pays expenses of writers on assignment.

Photos: Send photos with submission. Reviews transparencies (1x1¼) and 4x5 prints. Offers no additional payment for photos accepted with.ms. Buys all rights.

Columns/Departments: Executive to Executive (ways and ideas for effective managament). Buys 1 ms/year. Send complete ms. Length: 500-1,500 words. Pays $1-50.

Tips: "Our magazine is easy to break into. Either a phone call or a query letter will be answered right away, with explanations on our readers interests. Make sure that it relates to the interests of the association or convention planning industries. It can also effect business. Example: legislation, taxes, union movement."

CALIFORNIA HIGHWAY PATROLMAN, California Association of Highway Patrolmen, 2030 V St., Sacramento CA 95818. (916)452-6751. Editor: Carol Perri. 80% freelance written. Will work with established or new/unpublished writers. Monthly magazine. Circ. 20,000. Pays on publication. Publishes ms an average of 1 year after acceptance. Buys one-time rights. Submit seasonal/holiday material 6 months in advance. Computer printout submissions acceptable. Reports in 3 months. Sample copy and writer's guidelines for 9x12 SAE and 4 first class stamps.

Nonfiction: Publishes articles on transportation safety, driver education, consumer interest, California history, humor and general interest. "Topics can include autos, boats, bicycles, motorcycles, snowmobiles, recreational vehicles and pedestrian safety. We are also in the market for California travel pieces and articles on early California. We are *not* a technical journal for teachers and traffic safety experts, but rather a general interest publication geared toward the layman." Pays 2½¢/word.

Photos: "Illustrated articles always receive preference." Pays $5/b&w photo; no transparencies please. Captions required.

Tips: "If a writer feels the article idea, length and style are consistent with our magazine, submit the manuscript for me to determine if I agree. We are especially looking for articles for specific holidays."

CATHOLIC FORESTER, Catholic Order of Foresters, 425 W. Shuman Blvd., Naperville IL 60566. (312)983-4920. Editor: Barbara Cunningham. 35% freelance written. Prefers to work with published/established writers; works with a small number of new/unpublished writers each year. A bimonthly magazine of short, general interest articles and fiction for members of the Order, which is a fraternal insurance company. Family type audience, middle class. Circ. 150,000. Pays on acceptance. Publishes ms an average of 6 months after acceptance. Byline given. Buys one-time rights, second serial (reprint) rights, and simultaneous rights. Submit seasonal/holiday material 6 months in advance. Simultaneous, photocopied, and previously published submissions OK. Computer printout submissions acceptable; prefers letter-quality. Reports in 6 weeks on ms. Sample copy for 9x12 SAE with 73¢ postage; writer's guidelines #10 SASE.

Nonfiction: General interest; historical/nostalgic; humor; inspirational; interview/profile; new product; opinion; personal experience; photo feature; technical (depends on subject); and travel. "Short feature articles are most open to freelancers." No blatant sex nor anything too violent. Send complete ms. Length: 1,000-3,000 words. Pays 5¢/word; more for excellent ms.

Photos: Prefers something of unusual interest or story-telling. State availability of photos, or send photos with ms. Reviews any size b&w and color prints. Payment to be determined. Captions, model releases, and identification of subjects required. Buys one-time rights.

Columns/Departments: Needs unusual items on what is going on in the world; new, interesting products, discoveries or happenings. Would like about 800 word opinion for our View Point column. Send complete ms. Length: 1,000 words. Payment to be determined.

Fiction: Adventure, historical, humorous, mainstream, mystery, religious (Catholic), suspense and western. No sex or extreme violence. Length: up to 3,000 words (prefers shorter fiction). Pays 5¢/word; more for excellent ms.

Poetry: Free verse, haiku, light verse, traditional and humorous. Submit maximum 5 poems. Payment to be determined.

Fillers: Cartoons, jokes, anecdotes and short humor. Length: 300-500 words. Payment to be determined.

CLUB COSTA MAGAZINE, Club Costa Corp., Suite 200, 7701 College Blvd., Overland Park KS 66210. (913)451-3462. Editor: Joseph D. Brenneman. 50-65% freelance written. Prefers to work with published/established writers; works with a small number of new/unpublished writers each year. A quarterly magazine available only to club members covering discounted accommodations, travel and other savings available through Club Costa. "We offer 'discount' prices to our members on a variety of worldwide hotel and resort accommodations, cruises, flights, car rentals and activities. Our format features money-saving tips for vacations and destination features for the areas in which we have properties available. Readers are reasonably sophisticated travelers with above average incomes." Circ. 20,000. Pays on publication. Publishes ms an average of 3 months after acceptance. Byline given. Buys one-time rights, simultaneous rights and second serial (reprint) rights. Submit seasonal/holiday material 6 months in advance. Simultaneous, photocopied, and previously published submissions OK. Computer printout submissions acceptable. Reports in 6 weeks. Sample copy $3; writer's guidelines for #10 SASE. "If requesting both sample copy and writer's guidelines, include 25¢ stamp, no envelope necessary."

Nonfiction: Travel-related historical/nostalgic, how-to, personal experience and humor. "Articles may relate to saving money while on vacation. We need features about destinations, activities, background/history of area(s), bargain purchases, how to plan a vacation, and tips for the business or leisure traveler." No camping, hunting, fishing, or "my favorite vacation" articles. Buys 15-20 mss/year. Query with SASE. No mss sent back unless accompanied with envelope and proper postage. Length: 1,200 words, features; up to 500 words, shorts. Pays $25-125.

Photos: Photos are required with most articles. State availability.

Tips: "We need short travel-related humor and shorts that give an insight to an area or its people. We are putting more emphasis on international travel."

COMEDY WRITERS ASSOCIATION NEWSLETTER, Box 023304, Brooklyn NY 11202-0066. (718)855-5057. Editor: Robert Makinson. 10% freelance written. Quarterly newsletter on comedy writing for association members. Circ. 125. Pays on acceptance. Publishes ms an average of 3 months after acceptance. Byline given. Buys all rights. Submit seasonal/holiday material 6 months in advance. Computer printout submissions OK. Reports in 2 weeks on queries; 3 weeks on mss. Sample copy $4; writer's guidelines for #10 SASE.

Nonfiction: How-to, humor, opinion, personal experience. "No exaggerations about the sales that you make and what you are paid. Be accurate." Query. Length: 250-500 words. Pays 3¢/word.

Photos: State availability of photos with submission. Offers no additional payment for photos accepted with ms.

Fillers: Facts. Length: 100 words maximum. Pays 3¢/word.

Tips: "The easiest way to be mentioned in the publication is to submit short jokes. (Payment is $1-3 per joke.)

THE ELKS MAGAZINE, 425 W. Diversey, Chicago IL 60614. Editor: Fred D. Oakes. 50% freelance written. Prefers to work with published/established writers. Emphasizes general interest with family appeal. Magazine published 10 times/year. Circ. 1 million. Pays on acceptance. Publishes ms an average of 4 months after acceptance. Buys first North American serial rights. Computer printout submissions acceptable; no dot-matrix. Reports in 6 weeks. Sample copy and writer's guidelines for 9x12 SAE with 85¢ postage.

Nonfiction: Articles of information, business, contemporary life problems and situations, nostalgia, or just interesting topics, ranging from medicine, science, and history, to sports. "The articles should not just be a rehash of existing material. They must be fresh, thought-provoking, well-researched and documented." No fiction, political articles, fillers or verse. Buys 2-3 mss/issue. Query; no phone queries. Length: 1,500-3,000 words. Pays from $100.

For explanation of symbols, see the Key to Symbols and Abbreviations on Page 5. For unfamiliar words, see the Glossary.

Tips: "Requirements are clearly stated in our guidelines. Loose, wordy pieces are not accepted. A submission, following a query letter go-ahead, should include several b&w prints if the piece lends itself to illustration. We offer no additional payment for photos accepted with manuscripts. We expect to continue targeting our content to an older (50+) demographic."

FEDCO REPORTER, A Publication Exclusively for FEDCO Members, Box 2605, Terminal Annex, Los Angeles CA 90051. (213)946-2511. Editor: Michele A. Brunmier. 90% freelance written. Works with a small number of new/unpublished writers each year. A monthly catalog/magazine for FEDCO department store members. Circ. 2 million. Pays on acceptance. Publishes ms an average of 4 months after acceptance. Byline given. Offers $50 kill fee. Buys first rights. Query for electronic submissions. Computer printout submissions acceptable; prefers letter-quality. Reports in 6 weeks. Sample copy for 9x12 SAE with 4 first class stamps; writer's guidelines for SASE.
Nonfiction: General interest, historical. The magazine publishes material on historical events, personalities, and little-known happenings (especially relating to California); general interst stories on common, everyday items with an unusual background or interesting use. Seasonal stories (especially relating to California); and stories about South California wildlife. No first person narrative. Buys 75 mss/year. Query with or without published clips, or send complete manuscript. Length: 450 words. Pays $100.
Photos: State availability of photos. Reviews b&w and color slides. Pays $25.
Tips: "We will publish excellent writing that is well-researched regardless of prior writings. Articles should be tightly written and not stray from subject."

KIWANIS, 3636 Woodview Trace, Indianapolis IN 46268. FAX: (317)879-0204. Executive Editor: Chuck Jonak. 90% of feature articles freelance written. Magazine published 10 times/year for business and professional persons and their families. Circ. 300,000. Pays on acceptance. Buys first North American serial rights. Pays 20-40% kill fee. Publishes ms an average of 6 months after acceptance. Byline given. Computer printout submissions acceptable. Reports within 2 months. Sample copy and writer's guidelines for 9x12 SAE and 5 first class stamps.
Nonfiction: Articles about social and civic betterment, small-business concerns, science, education, religion, family, sports, health, recreation, etc. Emphasis on objectivity, intelligent analysis and thorough research of contemporary problems. Positive tone preferred. Concise, lively writing, absence of cliches, and impartial presentation of controversy required. When applicable, information and quotation from international sources are required. Avoid writing strictly to a U.S. audience. Especially needs articles on business and professional topics that will directly assist the readers in their own businesses (generally independent retailers and companies of less than 25 employees) or careers. "We have a continuing need for articles of international interest. In addition, we are very interested in proposals that concern helping youth, particularly in regard to their character development, self-images, future goals, and social and emotional needs." Length: 2,500-3,000 words. Pays $400-1,000. "No fiction, personal essays, fillers, or verse of any kind. A light or humorous approach is welcomed where the subject is appropriate and all other requirements are observed." Usually pays the expenses of writers on assignment. Query first. Must include SASE for response.
Photos: "We accept photos submitted with manuscripts. Our rate for a manuscript with good photos is higher than for one without." Model release and identification of subjects required. Buys one-time rights.
Tips: "We will work with any writer who presents a strong feature article idea applicable to our magazine's audience and who will prove he or she knows the craft of writing. First, obtain writer's guidelines and a sample copy. Study for general style and content. When querying, present detailed outline of proposed manuscript's focus, direction, and editorial intent. Indicate expert sources to be used for attribution, as well as article's tone and length. Present well-researched, smoothly written manuscript that contains a 'human quality' with the use of anecdotes, practical examples, quotation, etc."

THE LION, 300 22nd St., Oak Brook IL 60570. (312)571-5466. Editor-in-Chief: Mark C. Lukas. Senior Editor: Robert Kleinfelder. 35% freelance written. Works with a small number of new/unpublished writers each year. Covers service club organization for Lions Club members and their families. Monthly magazine. Circ. 670,000. Pays on acceptance. Publishes ms an average of 5 months after acceptance. Buys all rights. Byline given. Phone queries OK. Photocopied submissions OK. Computer printout submissions acceptable; no dot-matrix. Reports in 2 weeks. Free sample copy and writer's guidelines.
Nonfiction: Informational (stories of interest to civic-minded individuals) and photo feature (must be of a Lions Club service project). No travel, biography, or personal experiences. No sensationalism. Prefers anecdotes in articles. Buys 4 mss/issue. Query. Length: 500-2,200. Pays $50-750. Sometimes pays the expenses of writers on assignment.
Photos: Purchased with or without accompanying ms or on assignment. Captions required. Query for photos. B&w and color glossies at least 5x7 or 35mm color slides. Total purchase price for ms includes payment for photos, accepted with ms. "Be sure photos are clear and as candid as possible."
Tips: "Incomplete details on how the Lions involved actually carried out a project and poor quality photos are the most frequent mistakes made by writers in completing an article assignment for us. We are geared increasingly to an international audience."

THE MODERN WOODMEN, Public Relations Department, Mississippi River at 17th St., Rock Island IL 61201. (309)786-6481. Editor: Gloria Bergh. Address manuscripts to Sandy Howell, staff writer. 5-10% freelance written. Works with both published and new writers. "Our publication is for families who are members of Modern Woodmen of America. Modern Woodmen is a fraternal life insurance society, and most of our members live in smaller communities or rural areas throughout the United States. Various age groups read the magazine." Quarterly magazine, 24 pages. Circ. 350,000. Not copyrighted. Pays on acceptance. Keeps a file of good manuscripts to meet specific future needs and to balance content. Buys one-time rights or second serial (reprint) rights to material. Photocopied and simultaneous submissions OK. Reports in 1 month if SASE included. Sample copy and guidelines for 9x12 SAE and 2 first class stamps; writer's guidelines for #10 SASE.
Nonfiction: For children and adults. "We seek lucid style and rich content. We need manuscripts that center on family-oriented subjects, human development, and educational topics."
Fiction: "Publish an occasional fiction story for children and teens. We stress plot and characterization. A moral is a pleasant addition, but not required." Length: about 1,200 words. Pays $50 minimum.
Tips: "We want articles that appeal to young families, emphasize family interaction, community involvement, and family life. We also consider educational, historical, patriotic, and humorous articles. We don't want religious articles, teen romances, or seasonal material. Focus on people, whether the article is about families or is educational, historical or patriotic or humorous."

MOOSE MAGAZINE, Loyal Order of Moose, Supreme Lodge Building, Mooseheart IL 60539. (312)859-2000. Managing Editor: Raymond Dickow. A monthly (10 issues/year) fraternal magazine. "Distributed to men, ages 21 and older, who are members of 2,300 Moose lodges located throughout the U.S. and Canada." Circ. 1.3 million. Pays on acceptance. Byline given. Buys first North American serial rights. Submit seasonal/holiday material 4 months in advance. Photocopied submissions OK. No computer printout submissions. Reports in 5 weeks on mss. Free sample copy and writer's guidelines.
Nonfiction: General interest, historical/nostalgic and sports. No politics or religion. Send complete ms. Length: 1,000-2,000 words. Pays $300-1,000 for unsolicited articles.
Photos: Send photos with submission. Offers no additional payment for photos accepted with ms.
Tips: Freelancers can best break in at this publication with "feature articles involving outdoor sports (fishing, hunting, camping) as well as golf, bowling, baseball, football, etc., and with articles of general interest reflective of community and family living in addition to those of nostalgic interest. Features should include anecdotes and provide the kind of information that is interesting, educational, and entertaining to our readers. Style of writing should show rather than tell. Submit appropriate photo(s) with manuscript whenever possible."

THE NEIGHBORHOOD WORKS, Resources for Urban Communities, Center for Neighborhood Technology, 2125 West North Ave., Chicago IL 60647. (312)278-4800. Editor: Mary O'Connell. 15-25% freelance written. A bimonthly magazine on community organizing, housing, energy, environmental and economic issues affecting city neighborhoods. "Writers must understand the importance of empowering people in low- and moderate-income city neighborhoods to solve local problems in housing, environment and local economy." Circ. 2,000. Pays on publication. Publishes ms an average of 2 months after acceptance. Byline given. Buys all rights. Submit seasonal/holiday material 2 months in advance. Photocopied and previously published submissions OK. Reports in 1 month on queries; 2 months on mss. Sample copy and writer's guidelines for 9x12 SAE and 2 first class stamps.
Nonfiction: Exposes, historical (neighborhood history), how-to (each issue has "reproducible feature" on such topics as organizing a neighborhood block watch, a community garden, recycling, etc.), interview/profile (of someone active on one of our issues), personal experience (in our issue areas, e.g, community organizing), technical (on energy conservation and alternative energy). Buys 6-10 mss/year. Query with or without published clips or send complete ms. Length: 750-2,000 words. Pays $100-500. "We pay professional writers (people who make living at it). We don't pay nonprofessionals and students but offer them a free subscription." Sometimes pays expenses of writers on assignment by previous agreement.
Photos: State availability of photos with submission. Reviews contact sheets and prints. Offers $10-25/photo. Captions and identification of subjects required. Buys one-time rights.
Columns/Departments: Reproducible features (how-to articles on issues of interest to neighborhood organizations), 1,000-2,000 words. Query with published clips. Pays $100-250.
Tips: We are increasingly interested in stories from cities other than Chicago (our home base).

PERSPECTIVE, Pioneer Clubs, Division of Pioneer Ministries, Inc., Box 788, Wheaton IL 60189-0788. (312)293-1600. Editor: Rebecca Powell Parat. 15% freelance written. Works with a small number of new/unpublished writers each year. "All subscribers are volunteer leaders of clubs for girls and boys in grades K-12. Clubs are sponsored by local churches throughout North America." Quarterly magazine. Circ. 24,000. Pays on acceptance. Publishes ms an average of 8 months after acceptance. Buys first North American serial rights and second serial (reprint) rights to material originally published elsewhere. Submit seasonal/holiday material 9 months in advance. Simultaneous submissions OK. Computer printout submissions acceptable if double-spaced; prefers letter-quality. Reports in 6 weeks. Writer's packet for 9x12 SAE and $1.50; includes writer's guidelines and sample magazine.

Nonfiction: Informational (relationship skills, leadership skills); inspirational (stories of leaders and children in Pioneer Clubs); interview (Christian education leaders, club leaders); personal experience (of club leaders). Buys 8-12 mss/year. Byline given. Query. Length: 500-1,500 words. Pays $20-60. Sometimes pays expenses of writers on assignment.

Columns/Departments: Storehouse (game, activity, outdoor activity, service project suggestions—all related to club projects for any age between grades K-12). Buys 4-6 mss/year. Submit complete ms. Length: 150-250 words. Pays $8-15.

Tips: "We only assign major features to writers who have proven previously that they know us and our constituency. Submit articles directly related to club work, practical in nature, i.e., ideas for leader training in communication, discipline, teaching skills. They must have practical application. We want substance—not ephemeral ideas. In addition to a summary of the article idea and evidence that the writer has knowledge of the subject, we want evidence that the author understands our purpose and philosophy."

‡**RECREATION NEWS, Official Publication of the League of Federal Recreation Associations, Inc.,** Icarus Publishers, Inc., Box 32335, Washington DC 20007. (202)965-6960. Editor: Annette Licitra. 50% freelance written. A monthly guide to leisure activities for federal workers covering outdoor recreation, federal issues, travel, fitness and indoor pastimes. Circ. 108,000. Pays on publication. Publishes ms an average of 6 months after acceptance. Byline given. Offers 20% kill fee on 4th assignment (first 3 on speculation). Buys one-time rights, first rights and second serial (reprint) rights. Submit seasonal/holiday material 8 months in advance. Simultaneous queries, simultaneous, photocopied and previously published submissions OK. Computer printout submissions acceptable. Reports in 1 month. Sample copy and writer's guidelines for 9x12 SAE with 85¢ postage.

Nonfiction: Karen Hannigan, articles editor. Book excerpts (on recreation, travel), general interest (on recreation, outdoors); historical/nostalgic (Washington-related); humor (on working, home life); interview/profile (sports or entertainment angle); and personal experience (with recreation, life in Washington). Special issues feature skiing (December); Chesapeake Bay (June); education (August). Buys 45 mss/year. Query with clips of published work. Length: 500-3,000 words. Pays $35-300. Sometimes pays the expenses of writers on assignment.

Photos: Kathy Velis, photo editor. State availability of photos with query letter or ms. Reviews contact sheets, transparencies, and 5x7 b&w prints. Pays $25-40/b&w photo ordered from contact sheet, $50-125 for color. Captions and identification of subjects required.

Columns/Departments: Julie Barnett, columns, departments editor. Books (recreation, outdoors, hobbies, travel); Good sport (first person sports/recreation column); Reflections (humor); Buys 15-20 mss/year. Query with clips of published work or send complete ms (on speculation only). Length: 500-1,200 words. Pays $25-75.

Tips: "Our writers generally have a few years of professional writing experience and their work runs to the lively and conversational. We'll need more manuscripts in a wider range of recreational topics, including the off-beat. The areas of our publication most open to freelancers are general articles, and the Reflections column."

REVIEW, A Publication of North American Benefit Association, 1338 Military St., Box 5020, Port Huron MI 48061-5020. (313)985-5191, ext. 77. Editor: Virginia E. Farmer. Associate Editor: Patricia Pfeifer. 10-15% freelance written. Prefers to work with published/established writers, and works with a small number of new/unpublished writers each year. Quarterly trade journal on insurance/fraternal deeds. Family magazine. Circ. 44,000. Pays on acceptance. Publishes ms an average of 2 years after acceptance. Byline given. Not copyrighted. Buys one-time rights, simultaneous rights, and second serial (reprint) rights. Submit seasonal/holiday material 6 months in advance. Simultaneous, photocopied and previously published submissions OK. Computer printout submissions acceptable; no dot-matrix. Reports in 2 months. Sample copy for 9x12 SAE with 4 first class stamps; writer's guidelines for #10 SASE.

Nonfiction: General interest, historical/nostalgic, how-to (improve; self-help); humor; inspirational; personal experience; and photo feature. No political/controversial. Buys 4-10 mss/year. Send complete ms. Length: 600-1,500 words. Pays 3-5/word.

Photos: Prefers ms with photos if available. Send photos with ms. Reviews 5x7 or 8x10 b&w prints and color slides or prints. Pays $10-15. Model release and identification of subjects required. Buys one-time rights.

Fiction: Adventure, humorous and mainstream. Buys 2-4 mss/year. Send complete ms. Length: 600-1,500 words. Pays 3-5/word.

Tips: "We like articles with accompanying photos; articles that warm the heart; stories with gentle, happy humor. Give background of writer as to education and credits. Manuscripts and art material will be carefully considered, but received only with the understanding that North American Benefit Association shall not be responsible for loss or injury."

THE ROTARIAN, Official Magazine of Rotary International, 1560 Sherman Ave., Evanston IL 60201. (312)866-3000. Editor: Willmon L. White. 50% freelance written. Works with published and unpublished writers. For Rotarian business and professional men and women and their families; for schools, libraries, hospitals, etc. Monthly. Circ. 540,000. Usually buys all rights. Pays on acceptance. Query preferred. Computer printout submissions acceptable; prefers letter-quality. Reports in 1 month. Sample copy for SAE and 7 first class stamps; writer's guidelines for SAE and 1 first class stamp.

Nonfiction: "The field for freelance articles is in the general interest category. These run the gamut from guidelines for daily living to such concerns as AIDS, famine and conservation. Recent articles have dealt with modern office communications tools, retail theft, architecture and design and waste management worldwide. Articles should appeal to an international audience and should in some way help Rotarians help other people. An article may increase a reader's understanding of world affairs, thereby making him or her a better world citizen. It may educate him in civic matters, thus helping him improve his town. It may help him to become a better employer, or a better human being. We are interested in articles on unusual Rotary club projects or really unusual Rotarians. We carry debates and symposiums, but are careful to show more than one point of view. We present arguments for effective politics and business ethics, but avoid expose and muckraking. Controversy is welcomed if it gets our readers to think but does not offend minority, ethnic or religious groups. In short, the rationale of the organization is one of hope and encouragement and belief in the power of individuals talking and working together." Query preferred. Length: 1,000-2,000 words. Payment varies. Seldom pays the expenses of writers on assignment. Does not pay for information about club projects.

Photos: Purchased with mss or with captions only. Prefers 2¼x2¼ or larger color transparencies, but also uses 35mm. B&w prints and photo essays. Vertical shots preferred for covers. Scenes of international interest. Color cover.

SCOUTING, Boy Scouts of America, 1325 Walnut Hill Ln., Irving TX 75038-3096. (214)580-2355. Editor: Walter Babson. Executive Editor: Ernest Doclar. 90% freelance written. A bimonthly magazine on scouting activities for adult leaders of the Boy Scouts. Circ. 1 million. Pays on acceptance. Publishes ms an average of 4 months after acceptance. Byline given. Buys first North American serial rights. Submit seasonal/holiday material 4 months in advance. Computer printout submissions OK; no dot-matrix. Reports in 2 weeks. Sample copy for #10 SAE with $1 postage; writer's guidelines for #10 SAE with 1 first class stamp.

Nonfiction: Buys 60 mss/year. Query with published clips. Length: 1,500-2,000 words. Pays $300-600 for assigned articles; pays $200-500 for unsolicited articles. Pays expenses of writers on assignment.

Photos: State availability of photos with submission. Reviews contact sheets and transparencies. Identification of subjects required. Buys one-time rights.

Columns/Departments: Family Quiz (quiz on topics of family interest), 1,000 words; and Way it Was (Scouting history), 1,200 words. Buys 6 mss/year. Query. Pays $200-300.

‡**THE SONS OF NORWAY VIKING**, Sons of Norway, 1455 W. Lake St., Minneapolis MN 55408. (612)827-3611. FAX: (612)827-0658. Editor: Gaelyn Beal. 50% freelance written. Prefers to work with published/established writers. A monthly magazine for the Sons of Norway, a fraternal and cultural organization, covering Norwegian culture, heritage, history, Norwegian-American topics, modern Norwegian society, genealogy and travel. "Our audience is Norwegian-Americans (middle-aged or older) with strong interest in their heritage and anything Norwegian. Many have traveled to Norway." Circ. 70,000. Pays on publication. Publishes ms an average of 8 months after acceptance. Byline given. Offers $25 kill fee. Buys first North American serial rights and second serial (reprint) rights. Submit seasonal/holiday material 6 months in advance. Photocopied and previously published submissions OK. Computer printout submissions acceptable; prefers letter-quality to dot-matrix. Reports in 6 weeks on queries; 8 weeks on mss. Free sample copy and writer's guidelines on request.

Nonfiction: General interest, historical/nostalgic, humor, interview/profile, and travel—all having a Norwegian angle. "Articles should not be personal impressions nor a colorless spewing of facts, but well-researched and conveyed in a warm and audience-involving manner. Does it entertain *and* inform?" Buys 30 mss/year. Query. Length: 1,500-3,000 words. Pays $75-250.

Photos: Reviews transparencies and prints. Pays $10-20/photo; pays $100 for cover color photo. Identification of subjects required. Buys one-time rights.

Tips: "Show familiarity with Norwegian culture and subject matter. Our readers are somewhat knowledgeable about Norway and quick to note misstatements. Articles about modern Norway are most open to freelancers—the society, industries—but historical periods also okay. Call before a scheduled trip to Norway to discuss subjects to research or interview while there."

THE TOASTMASTER, Toastmasters International, 2200 N. Grand Ave., Box 10400, Santa Ana CA 92711. (714)542-6793. Editor: Suzanne Frey. Associate Editor: Susan Messner. 50% freelance written. A monthly magazine on public speaking, leadership and club concerns. "This magazine is sent to members of Toastmasters International, a nonprofit educational association of men and women throughout the world who are interested in developing their communication and leadership skills. Members range from novice speakers to professional orators and come from a wide variety of backgrounds." Circ. 145,000. Pays on acceptance.

Publishes ms an average of 8 months after acceptance. Byline given. Buys second serial (reprint) rights or all rights. Submit seasonal/holiday material 3 months in advance. Simultaneous, photocopied and previously published submissions OK. Query for electronic submissions. Computer printout submissions OK; no dot-matrix. Reports in 2 weeks on queries; 3 weeks on mss. Sample copy for 9x12 SAE and 2 first class stamps; writer's guidelines for #10 SASE.

Nonfiction: Book excerpts, how-to (communications related), humor (only if informative; humor cannot be off-color or derogatory), interview/profile (only if of a very prominent member or former member of Toast-masters International or someone who has a valuable perspective on communication and leadership). Buys 50 mss/year. Query. Length: 1,500-3,000 words. Pays $75-250. Sometimes pays expenses of writers on assignment. "Toastmaster members are requested to view their submissions as contributions to the organization. Some-times asks for book excerpts and reprints without payment, but original contribution from individuals outside Toastmasters will be paid for at stated rates."

Photos: Reviews b&w prints. Offers no additional payment for photos accepted with ms. Captions are required. Buys all rights.

Tips: "We are looking primarily for 'how-to' articles on subjects from the broad fields of communications and leadership which can be directly applied by our readers in their self-improvement and club programming efforts. Concrete examples are useful. Avoid sexist or nationalist language."

‡**VFW MAGAZINE,** Veterans of ForeignWar of the United States, Suite 523, 34th & Broadway, Kansas City MO 64111. (816)968-1171. FAX: (816)968-1157. Editorial Director: Warren Maus. 75% freelance written. Monthly magazine on veterans' affairs. *"VFW Magazine* goes to its members worldwide, all having served honorably in the armed forces overseas during periods of conflict or war and earning a campaign medal." Circ. 2.1 million. Pays on acceptance. Publishes 3-6 months after acceptance. Offers 100% kill fee. Buys first rights. Submit seasonal/holiday material 6 months in advance. Photocopied submissions OK. Query for electronic submissions. Computer printout submissions OK; prefers letter-quality. Reports in 1-4 weeks on queries; 4-6 weeks on mss. Free sample copy.

Nonfiction: Interview/profile and veterans' affairs. Buys 10-15 mss/year. Query. Length: 500-3,000 words. Pays $200-750.

Photos: Send photos with submission. Reviews contact sheets, negatives, transparencies and prints. Captions, model releases and identification of subjects required. Buys all rights.

WOODMEN OF THE WORLD MAGAZINE, 1700 Farnam St., Omaha NE 68102. (402)342-1890, ext. 302. Editor: Leland A. Larson. 20% freelance written. Works with a small number of new/unpublished writers each year. Published by Woodmen of the World Life Insurance Society for "people of all ages in all walks of life. We have both adult and child readers from all types of American families." Monthly. Circ. 467,000. Not copyrighted. Buys 20 mss/year. Pays on acceptance. Byline given. Buys one-time rights. Publishes ms an average of 2 months after acceptance. Will consider photocopied and simultaneous submissions. Computer printout submissions acceptable; prefers letter-quality. Submit seasonal material 3 months in advance. Re-ports in 5 weeks. Free sample copy.Writer's guidelines for #10 SASE.

Nonfiction: "General interest articles which appeal to the American family—travel, history, art, new prod-ucts, how-to, sports, hobbies, food, home decorating, family expenses, etc. Because we are a fraternal benefit society operating under a lodge system, we often carry stories on how a number of people can enjoy social or recreational activities as a group. No special approach required. We want more 'consumer type' articles, humor, historical articles, think pieces, nostalgia, photo articles." Buys 15-24 unsolicited mss/year. Submit complete ms. Length: 2,000 words or less. Pays $10 minimum, 5¢/word depending on count.

Photos: Purchased with or without mss; captions optional "but suggested." Uses 8x10 glossy prints, 4x5 transparencies ("and possibly down to 35mm"). Payment "depends on use." For b&w photos, pays $25 for cover, $10 for inside. Color prices vary according to use and quality. Minimum of $25 for inside use; up to $150 for covers.

Fiction: Humorous and historical short stories. Length: 1,500 words or less. Pays "$10 minimum or 5¢/word, depending on count."

——— *Astrology, Metaphysical and New Age*

A number of new magazines have started publication in this category during the past few years, but many also have gone out of business. Magazines in this section carry articles ranging from the occult to holistic healing. The following publications regard astrology, psychic phenomena, metaphysical experiences and related subjects as sciences or as objects of serious study. Each has an individual personality and approach to these phenomena. If you want to write for these publications, be sure to read them carefully.

ASTRO SIGNS, T-Square Publications, 566 Westchester Ave., Rye Brook NY 10573. (914)939-2111. Editor: Nancy Frederick Sussan. 20% freelance written. Monthly miniature magazine (2½x3") covering astrology. Circ. 1,000,000. Pays on publication. Byline given (listing on masthead). Buys all rights. Submit seasonal/holiday material 6 months in advance. Computer printout submissions OK. Reports in 2 weeks. Sample copy and writer's guidelines for #10 SASE (send to publisher, 566 Westchester Ave., Rye Brook, NY 10573).
Nonfiction: Sun sign articles on general interest, humor, technical, travel. "We use upbeat, positive articles focusing on sun signs as a way to make the reader's life better." Buys 60 mss/year. Do not send unsolicited manuscripts. Query first. No reply without SASE. Pays $100 minimum.
Tips: "A writer must have some astrological sophistication as well as a positive, helpful approach. Usually a query letter is best and then a phone call. We need at least two small features a month on love, travel, health, etc."

BODY, MIND & SPIRIT, Island Publishing Co. Inc., Box 701, Providence RI 02901. (401)351-4320. Editor: Paul Zuromski. Managing Editor: Carol Kramer. 75% freelance written. Prefers to work with published/established writers; works with many new/unpublished writers each year. Bimonthly magazine covering New Age, natural living, and metaphysical topics. "Our editorial is slanted toward assisting people in their self-transformation process to improve body, mind and spirit. We take a holistic approach to the subjects we present. They include spirituality, health, healing, nutrition, new ideas, interviews with new age people, travel, books and music. We avoid sensationalizing and try to present material objectively to allow the individual to decide what to accept or believe." Circ. 150,000. Pays on publication. Publishes ms an average of 3-6 months after acceptance. Byline given. Offers negotiable kill fee. Buys first North American serial rights. Submit seasonal/holiday material 8 months in advance. Simultaneous queries OK. Computer printout submissions acceptable. Reports in 2 months on queries; 4 months on mss. Sample copy for 9x12 SAE and $1.45 postage; writer's guidelines for #10 SASE stamp.
Nonfiction: Book excerpts, historical/nostalgic (research on the roots of the New Age movement and related topics); how-to (develop psychic abilities, health, healing, proper nutrition, etc., based on holistic approach); inspirational; interview/profile (of New Age people); new product (or services offered in this field—must be unique and interesting); opinion (on any New Age, natural living or metaphysical topic); and travel (example: to Egypt based on past life research). Don't send "My life as a psychic" or "How I became psychic" articles. Buys 30-40 mss/year. Query with published clips. Length: 2,000-5,000 words. Pays $100-300. Sometimes pays the expenses of writers on assignment.
Photos: State availability of photos with query. Pays $10-20 for b&w contact sheets. Captions, model releases and identification of subjects required. Buys one-time rights.
Fillers: Clippings, anecdotes or newsbreaks on any interesting or unusual New Age, natural living, or metaphysical topic. Buys 10-20 fillers/year. Length: 500 words maximum. Pays $10-40.
Tips: "Examine our unique approach to the subject matter. We avoid sensationalism and overly strange or unbelievable stories. Reading an issue should give you a good idea of our approach to the subject."

FATE, Llewellyn Publications, Box 64383, St. Paul MN 55164-0383. FAX: (612)291-1908. Editor: Donald Michael Kraig. 70% freelance written. Buys all rights; occasionally North American serial rights only. Byline given. Pays on publication. Sample copy $3. Query. Reports in 2 months.
Nonfiction and Fillers: Personal psychic and magical experiences, 300-500 words. Pays $10. Articles on parapsychology, occultism, witchcraft, magic, spiritual healing, flying saucers, new frontiers of science, and mystical aspects of ancient civilizations, 2,000-3,000 words. *Must* include complete authenticating details. Prefers interesting accounts of single events rather than roundups. "We very frequently accept manuscripts from new writers; the majority are individual's first-person accounts of their own psychic/magical/spiritual experiences. We do need to have all details, where, when, why, who and what, included for complete documentation. We ask for notarized statement attesting to truth of article." Pays minimum of 5¢/word. Fillers must be be fully authenticated also, and on similar topics. Length: 100-300 words.

Photos: Buys good glossy prints with mss. Pays $5-10.

Tips: "For the past several years *Fate* has moved toward archeological and debunking types of articles. We will be moving back to the original concept of *Fate*—looking at the unusual in the world—the things that science doesn't like to talk about. Our focus will be more New Age-oriented, including more parapsychology, spirituality, divination, magic, UFO's, etc."

NEW AGE JOURNAL, Rising Star Associates, 342 Western Ave., Brighton MA 02135. (617)787-2005. Editor: Florence Graves. Editorial Manager: Gail Whitney. 35% freelance written. Works with a small number of new/unpublished writers each year. A bimonthly magazine emphasizing "personal fulfillment and social change. The audience we reach is college-educated, social-service/hi-tech oriented, 25-45 years of age, concerned about social values, humanitarianism and balance in personal life." Payment negotiated. Publishes ms an average of 5 months after acceptance. Byline given. Offers 25% kill fee. Buys first North American serial rights and reprint rights. Submit seasonal/holiday material 6 months in advance. Simultaneous and photocopied submissions OK. Computer printout submissions are acceptable provided they are double-spaced "and dark enough. Reports in 2 months on queries. Sample copy for 9 × 12 SAE and $3.50. Writers' guidelines for letter-size SAE with 1 first class stamp.

Nonfiction: Book excerpts, exposé, general interest, how-to (travel on business, select a computer, reclaim land, plant a garden, behavior, trend pieces), humor, inspirational, interview/profile, new product, food, sci-tech, nutrition, holistic health, education and personal experience. Buys 60-80 mss/year. Query with published clips. "Written queries only—no phone calls. The process of decision making takes time and involves more than one editor. An answer cannot be given over the phone." Length: 500-4,000 words. Pays $50-2,500. Pays the expenses of writers on assignment.

Photos: State availability of photos with submission. Model releases and identification of subjects required. Buys one-time rights.

Columns/Departments: Body/Mind; Reflections; First Person. Buys 60-80 mss/year. Query with published clips. Length: 750-1,500 words. Pays $100-400.

Tips: "Submit short, specific news items to the Upfront department. Query first with clips. A query is one to two paragraphs—if you need more space than that to *present* the idea, then you don't have a clear grip on it. The next open area is columns: First Person and Reflections often take first-time contributors. Read the magazine and get a sense of type of writing run in these two columns. In particular we are interested in seeing inspirational, first-person pieces that highlight an engaging idea, experience or issue. We are also looking for new cutting edge thinking."

NEW REALITIES, Oneness of Self, Mind, and Body, Heldref Publications, 4000 Albemarle St. NW, Washington DC 20016. (202)362-6445. Editor: Neal Vahle. Managing Editor: Joy O'Rourke. 50% freelance written. A bimonthly magazine of new age interests. "Our emphasis is on the positive elements of life, those things that add, rather than detract, from people's lives." Circ. 18,000. Pays on publication. Byline given. Buys first North American serial rights, first rights or one-time rights. Submit seasonal/holiday material 4 months in advance. Simultaneous, photocopied and previously published submissions OK. Reports in 1 month. Sample copy for $2; writer's guidelines for #10 SASE.

Nonfiction: Book excerpts, general interest, how-to, inspirational, interview/profile. No fiction, poetry, or purely reflective personal experience pieces. Buys 40 mss/year. Query with or without published clips, or send complete ms. Length: 1,000-5,000 words. Pays up to $350 for unsolicited articles. Rarely assigns articles. Sometimes pays expenses of writers on assignment.

Photos: State availability of photos with submission. Reviews contact sheets and any size prints. Offers $10-100 per photo (cover shots more). Identification of subjects required. Buys one-time rights.

Columns/Departments: Column/Department Editor: Anne Mattison. Sights and Sounds (reviews of books, audio and video cassettes) 250 words; Tools for Transformation (experiential exercises, concrete tips on holistic living) 2,500 words. Buys 30 mss/year. Send complete ms. Length: 250-2,500 words. Pays $10-100.

Tips: "We appreciate seeing the entire manuscript, along with clips of other work. We look for a journalistic, third-party, concrete approach to what usually are rather subjective topics."

RAINBOW CITY EXPRESS, Adventures on the Spiritual Path, Box 8447, Berkeley CA 94707. Editor: Helen B. Harvey. 50-75% freelance written. Quarterly magazine on "spiritual awakening and evolving consciousness, especially feminist spirituality and women's issues. We take an eclectic, mature and innovative approach to the topics of spiritual awakening and evolution of consciousness. A positive, constructive, healing tone is required, not divisive, separatist slant." Estab. 1988. Circ. 1,000. Pays on publication. Byline given. Buys first North American serial rights or second serial (reprint) rights. Submit seasonal/holiday material 4-6 months in advance. Photocopied and previously published (only when full publishing information accompanies ms showing where previously published) submissions OK. Computer printout submissions OK; no dot-matrix. Reports in 1 month on queries; 3 months on mss. Sample copy for $5.50; writer's guidelines for #10 SASE.

Nonfiction: Book excerpts, essays, general interest, historical/nostalgic, how-to, humor, inspirational, interview/profile, opinion, personal experience, religious, travel. "No get-rich-quick or how-to channel spirits, how-to manipulate the cosmos/others, occult/voodoo/spellcasting diatribes and no glorification of victimization/

scapegoating or addictions." Buys 50-100 mss/year. Query with or without published clips, or send complete ms. Length: 250-2,000 words. Pays $5-50 per piece, negotiated individually.

Photos: State availability of photos with submissions or send photos with submission. Reviews contact sheets and prints. Offers no additional payment for photos accepted with ms. Captions, model releases and identification of subjects required. Buys one-time rights.

Columns/Departments: Book Reviews (spirituality, goddess consciousness, New Age topics), 250-500 words; Readers' Forum. Acquires 30 mss/year. Send complete ms. Pays in contributor copies.

Fiction: Adventure, fantasy, historical, religious. "Fiction should relate directly to our slant which is about spiritual/consciousness evolution. No science fiction, thriller, sex, drugs or violence mss." Acquires about 12 mss/year. Query. Length: 500-1,000 words. Pays in contributor copies.

Poetry: Avant-garde, free verse, haiku, light verse, traditional. Acquires about 30 poems/year. Submit 3 poems maximum. Length: 8-30 lines.

Fillers: Anecdotes, short humor. "Fillers must relate to our spirituality slant."

Tips: "We feature true life experiences and accounts of spiritual awakenings/attendant phenomena, and consciousness evolution. Readers/writers who have experienced some of these phenomena and know what they're talking about are likely to be well received. We are particularly interested in actual experiences with Kundalini activation and archetypal stirring. We aim to demonstrate the often unsuspected connections between spiritual awakening and everyday realities. Note: *Please* obtain sample copy prior to submitting mss! No mss returned without SASE. Also sponsors writing contests. Send SASE for details. All material submitted on speculation."

TRANSFORMATION TIMES, Life Resources Unlimited, Box 425, Beavercreek OR 97004. (503)632-7141. Editor: Connie L. Faubel. Managing Editor: E. James Faubel. 100% freelance written. A tabloid covering new age, metaphysics, and natural health, published 10 times/year. Circ. 8,000. Pays on publication. Publishes ms an average of 2 months after acceptance. Byline given. Buys one-time rights. Submit seasonal/holiday material 2 months in advance. Simultaneous, photocopied and previously published submissions OK. Query for electronic submissions. Computer printout submissions OK. Sample copy and writer's guidelines for 9x12 SAE and 5 first class stamps.

Nonfiction: Book excerpts, inspirational, interview/profile, women's issues, metaphysical. "No articles with emphasis on negative opinions and ideas." Buys 60 mss/year. Send complete ms. Length: 500-1,000 words. Pays 1-3¢/word.

Photos: Send photos with submission. Reviews 3x5 prints. Offers $3-5/photo. Captions and identification of subjects required. Buys one-time rights.

Columns/Departments: Woman's Way (women's issues) 500-1,000 words. Buys 20 mss/year. Send complete ms. Pays 1-3/word.

Tips: "In addition, to present interests we plan on adding articles on environmental quality issues and socially responsible investing."

Automotive and Motorcycle

Publications in this section detail the maintenance, operation, performance, racing and judging of automobiles and recreational vehicles. Publications that treat vehicles as means of shelter instead of as a hobby or sport are classified in the Travel, Camping and Trailer category. Journals for service station operators and auto and motorcycle dealers are located in the Trade Auto and Truck section.

AMERICAN MOTORCYCLIST, American Motorcyclist Association, Box 6114, Westerville OH 43081-6114. (614)891-2425. Executive Editor: Greg Harrison. For "enthusiastic motorcyclists, investing considerable time and money in the sport. We emphasize the motorcyclist, not the vehicle." Monthly magazine. Circ. 140,000. Pays on publication. Rights purchased vary with author and material. Pays 25-50% kill fee. Byline given. Query with SASE. Submit seasonal/holiday material 4 months in advance. Reports in 1 month. Free sample copy and writer's guidelines.

Nonfiction: How-to (different and/or unusual ways to use a motorcycle or have fun on one); historical (the heritage of motorcycling, particularly as it relates to the AMA); interviews (with interesting personalities in the world of motorcycling); photo feature (quality work on any aspect of motorcycling); and technical or how-to articles. No product evaluations or stories on motorcycling events not sanctioned by the AMA. Buys 20-

25 mss/year. Query. Length: 500 words minimum. Pays minimum $4.50/published column inch.

Photos: Purchased with or without accompanying ms, or on assignment. Captions required. Query. Pays $20 minimum per published photo.

Tips: "Accuracy and reliability are prime factors in our work with freelancers. We emphasize the rider, not the motorcycle itself. It's always best to query us first and the further in advance the better to allow for scheduling."

‡AMERICAN WOMAN ROAD RIDER, Ladylike Enterprises, Inc. #5, 1038 7th St., Santa Monica CA 90403. (213)395-1171. Editor: Courtney Caldwell. Managing Editor: Marcy Meyer. 40% freelance written. Bimonthly magazine on women in motorcycling. "We are geared towards career, professional, and/or goal-oriented women who enjoy the sport of motorcycling. The magazine is upscale and is dedicated to image enhancement." Estab. 1988. Circ. 20,000. Pays on publication an average of 2 months after acceptance. Byline sometimes given. Buys first rights, second serial (reprint) rights or makes work-for-hire assignments. Submit seasonal/holiday material 4 months in advance. Photocopied and previously published submissions OK. Query for electronic submissions. Computer printout submissions OK; prefers letter-quality. Reports in 2 months. Free sample copy.

Nonfiction: Humor, inspirational, interview/profile, new product, photo feature, technical, travel and biker friendly restaurants around us, all motorcycle related. We have a section called "Man of the Month" our special issue will be "Man of the Year!" No articles depicting women in motorcycling or professions that are degrading, negative or not upscale. Buys 30 mss/year. Send complete ms. Length 250-1,000 words. Pays $30-50 for assigned articles; $20-35 for unsolicited articles. Sometimes pays expenses of writers on assignment.

Photos: Send photos with submission. Reviews contact sheets. Offers $10-50 per photo. Captions, model releases and identification of subjects required. Buys all rights.

Columns/Departments: Product Evaluations (M/C's and related products), 200-250 words; Man of the Month (Highlight and profile select gentlemen who ride motorcycles and are making positive contributions to industry and community), 500-1,000 words; Phantom Diner (Biker friendly restaurants), 250-400 words; Hot Sports (Motorcycle people gathering places), 250-400 words and Tech Talk (Technical), 200-300 words. Buys 20-30 mss/year. Send complete ms. Pays $25-40.

Fillers: Anecdotes, facts, gags to illustrated by cartoonist, newsbreaks and short humor. Buys 12/year. Length: 25-100 words. Pays $10-25.

Tips: "It helps if the writer is into motorcycles. It is a special sport. If he/she doesn't ride, should have a positive point of view of motorcycling and be willing to learn more about the subject. We are a 'people' type of publication more than a technical magazine. Positive attitudes wanted."

BMX PLUS MAGAZINE, Daisy/Hi-Torque Publishing Co., Inc., 10600 Sepulveda Blvd., Mission Hills CA 91345. (818)545-6012. FAX: (818)361-4512. Editor: John Ker. Monthly magazine covering the sport of bicycle motocross for a youthful readership (95% male, aged 8-25). 3% freelance written. Prefers to work with published/established writers. Circ. 87,000. Pays on publication. Byline given. Buys one-time rights. Submit seasonal/holiday material 4 months in advance. Simultaneous queries and manuscripts OK. Computer print-out submissions acceptable; prefers letter-quality. Reports in 2 months. Publishes ms an average of 3 months after acceptance. Sample copy $2; writer's guidelines for #10 SASE.

Nonfiction: Historical/nostalgic, how-to, humor, interview/profile, new product, photo feature, technical, travel. "No articles for a general audience; our readers are BMX fanatics." Buys 20 mss/year. Send complete ms. Length: 500-1,500 words. Pays $30-250.

Photos: "Photography is the key to our magazine. Send us some exciting and/or unusual photos of hot riders in action." Send photos with ms. Pays $40-50 for color photo published; $25 for b&w photos. Reviews 35mm color transparencies and b&w negatives and 8x10 prints. Captions and identification of subjects required.

Tips: "We would like to receive more material on hot freestylers from areas other than California. Photo/story submissions would be welcomed. We also need more material about racing and freestyle from foreign countries. The sport of BMX is very young. The opportunities for talented writers and photographers in this field are open. Send us a good interview or race story with photos. Race coverage is the area that's easiest to break in to. It must be a *big* race, preferably national or international in scope. Submit story within one week of completion of race."

BRITISH CAR, Box 9099, Canoga Park CA 91309. (818)710-1234. Editor: Dave Destler. 50% freelance written. A bimonthly magazine covering British cars. "We focus upon the cars built in Britain, the people who buy them, drive them, collect them, love them. Writers must be among the aforementioned. Written by enthusiasts for enthusiasts." Circ. 30,000. Pays on publication. Publishes ms an average of 3 months after acceptance. Byline given. Buys all rights, unless other arrangements made. Submit seasonal/holiday material 4 months in advance. Photocopied submissions OK. Electronic submissions (Apple IIe). Computer printout submissions acceptable. Reports in 1 month. Sample copy $2.95; writer's guidelines for #10 SASE.

Nonfiction: Historical/nostalgic; how-to (on repair or restoration of a specific model or range of models, new technique or process); humor (based upon a realistic nonfiction situation); interview/profile (famous racer, designer, engineer, etc.); photo feature and technical. "No submissions so specific as to appeal or relate to a very narrow range of readers; no submissions so general as to be out-of-place in a specialty publication. Buys 30 mss/year. Send complete ms. "Include SASE if submission is to be returned." Length: 750-4,500 words. Pays $2-5/column inch for assigned articles; pays $2-3/column inch for unsolicited articles. Sometimes pays writers with contributor copies or other premiums rather than cash on prior arrangement.

Photos: Send photos with submission. Reviews transparencies and prints. Offers $15-75/photo. Captions and identification of subjects required. Buys all rights, unless otherwise arranged.

Columns/Departments: Update (newsworthy briefs of interest, not too timely for bimonthly publication), approximately 50-175 words; Lifestyle: A column about the people and various situations and lifestyles of British car enthusiasts. Buys 20 mss/year. Send complete ms.

Tips: "Our magazine has changed from *British Car & Bike* to *British Car*. The bikes are deleted, and the magazine will focus on the more upmarket British car scene. Thorough familiarity of subject is essential. *British Car* is read by experts and enthusiasts who can see right through superficial research. Facts are important, and must be accurate. Writers should ask themselves 'I know I'm interested in this story, but will most of *British Car's* readers appreciate it?' "

CAR AND DRIVER, 2002 Hogback Rd., Ann Arbor MI 48105. (313)971-3600. Editor: William Jeanes. For auto enthusiasts; college-educated, professional, median 24-35 years of age. Monthly magazine; 160 pages. Circ. 900,000. Pays on acceptance. Rights purchased vary with author and material. Buys all rights or first North American serial rights. Buys 3-4 unsolicited mss/year. Submit seasonal material 4 months in advance. Reports in 2 months.

Nonfiction: Non-anecdotal articles about the more sophisticated treatment of autos and motor racing. Exciting, interesting cars. Automotive road tests, informational articles on cars and equipment; some satire and humor. Personalities, past and present, in the automotive industry and automotive sports. "Treat readers as intellectual equals. Emphasis on people as well as hardware." Informational, how-to, humor, historical, think articles, and nostalgia. Query with clips of previously published work. Length: 750-2,000 words. Pays $200-1,500. Also buys mini-features for FYI department. Length: about 500 words. Pays $100-500.

Photos: B&w photos purchased with accompanying mss with no additional payment.

Tips: "It is best to start off with an interesting query and to stay away from nuts-and-bolts stuff since that will be handled in-house or by an acknowledged expert. Our goal is to be absolutely without flaw in our presentation of automotive facts, but we strive to be every bit as entertaining as we are informative."

‡CAR AUDIO AND ELECTRONICS, CurtCo Publishing, 4827 Sepulveda Blvd., Sherman Oaks CA 91403. (818)784-0700. FAX: (818)784-8504. Editor: William A. Burton. Managing Editor: Bill Neill. 89-90% freelance written. Monthly magazine on electronic products designed for cars. "We help people buy the best electronic products for their cars. The magazine is about electronics, how to buy, how to use, and so on: *CA&E* explains complicated things in simple ways. The articles are accurate, easy, and fun." Estab. 1988. Circ. 225,000. Pays on acceptance. Publishes ms an average of 3-5 months after acceptance. Byline given. Offers 50% kill fee. Buys all rights. Submit seasonal/holiday material 3-4 months in advance. Simultaneous and photocopied submissions OK. Query for electronic submissions. Computer printout submissions OK; prefers letter-quality. Reports in 1 week on queries; 1 week on mss. Sample copy $3.95 with 9x12 SAE and 4 first class stamps; writer's guidelines for #10 SASE.

Nonfiction: How-to (buy electronics for your car), interview/profile, new product, opinion, photo feature and technical. Buys 60-70 mss/year. Query with or without published clips, or send complete ms. Length: 500-1,700 words. Pays $300-1,000. Sometimes pays expenses of writers on assignment.

Photos: Send photos with submission. Review transparencies, any size.

Fillers: Gags to be illustrated by cartoonist and cartoons. Pays $20-50.

Tips: "Write clearly and knowledgeably about car electronics."

CAR COLLECTOR/CAR CLASSICS, Classic Publishing, Inc., Suite 144, 8601 Dunwoody Pl., Atlanta GA 30350. Editor: Donald R. Peterson. 90% freelance written. Works with a small number of new/unpublished writers each year. For people interested in all facets of collecting classic, milestone, antique, special interest and sports cars; also mascots, models, restoration, garaging, license plates and memorabilia. Monthly magazine; 68 pages. Circ. 35,000. Pays on cover date. Publishes ms an average of 4 months after acceptance. Buys first rights. Submit seasonal/holiday material 4 months in advance. Photocopied submissions OK. Computer printout submissions acceptable; no dot-matrix. Reports in 2 months. Sample copy for $2; writer's guidelines for #10 SASE.

Nonfiction: General interest, historical, how-to, humor, inspirational, interview, nostalgia, personal opinion, profile, photo feature, technical and travel—but must be automobile-related. Buys 50-75 mss/year; buys 24-36 unsolicited mss/year. Query with clips of published work. Length: 300-2,500 words. Pays 5¢/word minimum. Sometimes pays the expenses of writers on assignment.

Photos: "We have a continuing need for high-quality color positives (e.g., 2¼ or 35mm) *with* copy." State availability of photos with ms. Offers additional payment for photos with accompanying mss. Uses b&w glossy prints; color transparencies. Pays a minimum of $75 for cover and centerfold color; $10 for inside color; $5 for inside b&w. Captions and model releases required.

Columns/Departments: "Rarely add a new columnist but we are open to suggestions." Buys 36 mss/year. Query with clips of published work. Length: 2,000 maximum; prefers 1,000-2,000 words. Pays 5¢/word minimum.

Tips: "The most frequent mistakes are made by writers who are writing to a 'Sunday supplement' audience rather than to a sophisticated audience of car collectors and who are submitting stories that are often too basic and assume no car knowledge at all on the part of the reader."

‡**CARROZZERIA**, Restorative Publications, Box 533, Oyster Bay NY 11771. (718)743-1002. Editor: Richard A. Lentinello. 50% freelance written. Quarterly magazine on classic car restoration for automobile restorers and collectors—semi-technical. Circ. 5,000. Pays on publication. Publishes ms an average of 3-6 months after acceptance. Byline sometimes given. Buys first rights. Free sample copy and writer's guidelines.

Nonfiction: General interest, how-to (technical, about restoration), interview/profile and technical. "No fiction." Buys 10 mss/year. Query with published clips. Length: 1,500-4,000 words. Pays $150-500 for assigned articles; $100-200 for unsolicited articles. If writer has associated business, will offer free ad. Sometimes pays expenses of writers on assignment.

Photos: Send photos with submission. Reviews contact sheets and 5x7 prints. Offers $50 maximum per photo. Identification of subjects required. Buys one-time rights.

Columns/Departments: In Restoration (technical explanation) and Metalcrafting (side of each craft). Buys 8 mss/year. Send complete ms. Length: 500-1,000 words. Pays $150 maximum.

Tips: "Writer should be an avid enthusiast of classic cars and have an appreciation of craftsman's skills." Interviews with professional restorers and features about restoration facilities are areas most open to freelance writers.

‡**CLASSIC AUTO RESTORER**, Fancy Publishing, Inc., Box 6050, Mission Viejo CA 92690. (714)855-8822. FAX: (714)855-3045. Editor: Steve Kimball. 85% freelance written. Bimonthly magazine on auto restoration. "Our readers own old cars and they work on them. We help our readers by providing as much practical, how-to information as we can about restoration and old cars." Estab. 1989. Pays on publication. Publishes an average of 3 months after acceptance. Offers $50 kill fee. Buys first North American serial rights or one-time rights. Submit seasonal/holiday material 4 months in advance. Query for electronic submissions. Computer printout submissions OK; prefers letter-quality. Reports in 2 weeks on queries. Sample copy $3.95; free writer's guidelines.

Nonfiction: How-to (auto restoration), new product, photo feature, technical and travel. Buys 60 mss/year. Query with or without published clips, or send complete ms. Length: 200-5,000 words. Pays $100-500 for assigned articles; $75-500 for unsolicited articles.

Photos: Send photos with submission. Reviews contact sheets, transparencies and 5x7 prints. Offers no additional payment for photos accepted with ms.

Columns/Departments: Buys 12 mss/year. Send complete ms. Length: 400-1,000 words. Pays $75-200.

Tips: "Send a story. Include photos. Make it something that the magazine regularly uses. Do automotive how-tos. We need lots of them. We'll help you with them."

CORVETTE FEVER, Dobbs Publications, Inc., 3816 Industry Blvd., Lakeland FL 33811. (813)644-0449. FAX: (813)644-8373. Publisher: Larry Dobbs. Editorial Director: Paul Zazarine. 30-40% freelance written. Will work with new/unpublished writers. Monthly magazine. Circ. 55,000. Pays on publication. Publishes ms an average of 2-4 months after acceptance. Buys first rights and second serial (reprint) rights. Byline given. Phone queries OK. Submit seasonal/holiday material 5 months in advance. Computer printout submissions OK; prefers letter-quality. Reports in 1 month. Free writer's/photographers guidelines.

Nonfiction: General interest (event coverage, personal experience); historical (special or unusual Corvette historical topics); how-to (technical and mechanical articles, photos are a must); humor (Corvette-related humor); interviews and profiles (with important Corvette personalities, race drivers, club officials, prominent Chevrolet personnel); travel and leisure (relating to Corvette use and adventure); photo feature (color spreads on restored and vintage race Corvettes). Buys 3-6 mss/issue. Query with outline recommended prior to ms submission. Length: 500-2,500 words. Pays $100-1,000. Sometimes pays the expenses of writers on assignment.

Photos: Send photos with ms. Payment is incorporated with ms on per-printed-page basis. Captions preferred; model release required.

Columns/Departments: Restoration, Tech Line, Inside Track, Performance Portfolio, What's New, and Motorsports.

Fiction: Will publish fiction on occasion based on quality of story. Send complete ms. Length: 500-2,000 words.

Fillers: Clippings, anecdotes, short humor and newsbreaks associated with new or vintage Corvettes. Length: 25-100 words. Pays $10-25.

‡**CYCLE WORLD**, DCI Communications, Inc., 853 W. 17th St., Costa Mesa CA 92627. (714)720-5300. Editor: David Edwards. 20% freelance written. For active motorcyclists, "young, affluent, educated, very perceptive." Subject matter includes "road tests (staff-written), features on special bikes, customs, racers, racing events;

technical and how-to features involving mechanical modifications." Monthly. Circ. 275,000. Pays on acceptance. Publishes ms an average of 3 months after acceptance. Buys all rights. Query for electronic submissions. Computer printout submissions acceptable. Reports in 1 week on queries; 1 month on mss. Sample copy $2; free writer's guidelines.

Nonfiction: Buys informative, well-researched, technical, theory and how-to articles; interviews; profiles; humor; and historical pieces. Buys 20 mss/year. Query. Length: 1,000-2,000 words. Pays variable rates. Sometimes pays the expenses of writers on assignment.

Photos: Purchased with or without ms, or on assignment. "We need funny photos with a motorcycle theme." Reviews contact sheets and transparencies. Pays $75 minimum. Buys one-time rights and reprint rights.

Tips: "Area most open to freelancers is short nonfiction features. They must contain positive and fun experience regarding motorcycle travel, sport and lifestyle."

‡**DIRT BIKE,** Hi-Torque Publication, 10600 Sepulveda, Mission Hills CA 91345. (818)365-6831. FAX: (818)361-4512. Editor: Eddie Arnet. Managing Editor: Tim Tolleson. 30% freelance written. Monthly magazine. "Targeted at the motorcycle enthusiast. Follow the format of the magazine. No written guidelines." Circ. 150,000. Pays on publication. Publishes ms an average of 2-3 months after acceptance (immediately, if special late breaking news). Buys one-time rights. Simultaneous and photocopied submissions OK. Query for electronic submissions. Computer printout submissions OK. Free sample copy and writer's guidelines (call or write for info.).

Nonfiction: Exposé, general interest, how-to (riding & mechanical), interview/profile, photo feature and technical. Query. Length: 500 words. Pays $50 for assigned and unsolicited articles (depends on length). Sometimes pays expenses of writers on assignment.

Photos: Send photos with submission. Reviews negatives and transparencies. Offers $10-50 per photo. Identification of subjects required. Buys one-time rights.

Columns/Departments: Bits and Pieces (gossip/new news); New Products (new products). Buys 100 mss/year. Query. Query with published clips. Length: 1,500-3,000 words. Pays $50.

Fiction: Historical. Query with published clips. Length: 1,500 words. Pays $50 (depends on length).

Fillers: Newsbreaks. Buys 100/year. Length: 250 words. Pays: $50.

Tips: "Need background or insight on dirt bike riding."

4-WHEEL & OFF-ROAD, Petersen Publishing Co., 8490 Sunset Blvd., Los Angeles CA 90069. (213)854-2360. Editor: Steve Campbell. Managing Editor: Cecily Chittick. A monthly magazine covering four-wheel-drive vehicles, "devoted to new-truck tests, buildups of custom 4x4s, coverage of 4WD racing, trail rides and other competitions." Circ. 300,000. Pays on acceptance. Publishes ms an average of 4 months after acceptance. Byline given. Pays 20% kill fee. Buys first North American serial rights or all rights. Submit seasonal/holiday material 4 months in advance. Computer printout submissions OK. Reports in 3 weeks. Free sample copy; writer's guidelines for #10 SASE.

Nonfiction: How-to (on four-wheel-drive vehicles—engines, suspension, drive systems, etc.), new product, photo feature, technical and travel. Buys 12-16 mss/year. Send complete ms. Length: 1,000-2,500 words. Pays $200-500 for assigned and unsolicited articles. Sometimes pays the expenses of writers on assignment.

Photos: Send photos with submission. Reviews transparencies and 7x9 prints. Offers no additional payment for photos accepted with ms. Captions, model releases and identification of subjects required. Buys all rights.

Fillers: Anecdotes, facts, gags, newsbreaks and short humor. Buys 12-16/year. Length: 50-150 words. Pays $15-50.

Tips: "Attend 4x4 events, get to know the audience. Present material only after full research. Manuscripts should contain *all* of the facts pertinent to the story. Technical/how-to articles are most open to freelancers."

‡**FOUR WHEELER MAGAZINE,** 6728 Eton Ave., Canoga Park CA 91303. (818)992-4777. FAX: (818)992-4979. Editor: John Stewart. 20% freelance written. Works with a small number of new/unpublished writers each year. Emphasizes four-wheel-drive vehicles, competition and travel/adventure. Monthly magazine; 164 pages. Circ. 316,941. Pays on publication. Publishes ms an average of 4 months after acceptance. Buys all rights. Submit seasonal/holiday material at least 4 months in advance. Query for electronic submissions. Computer printout submissions acceptable; prefers letter-quality. Free sample copy; writer's guidelines for #10 SAE.

Nonfiction: 4WD competition and travel/adventure articles, technical, how-tos, and vehicle features about unique four-wheel drives. "We like the adventure stories that bring four wheeling to life in word and photo: mud-running deserted logging roads, exploring remote, isolated trails, or hunting/fishing where the 4x4 is a necessity for success." See features by Bruce Smith, Gary Wescott, Matt Conrad and Dick Stansfield for examples. Query with photos before sending complete ms. Length: 1,200-2,000 words; average 4-5 pages when published. Pays $100/page minimum for complete package. Sometimes pays the expenses of writers on assignment.

Photos: Requires professional quality color slides and b&w prints for every article. Captions required. Prefers Kodachrome 64 or Fujichrome 50 in 35mm or 2¼ formats. "Action shots a must for all vehicle features and travel articles."

Tips: "Show us you know how to use a camera as well as the written word. The easiest way for a new writer/photographer to break in to our magazine is to read several issues of the magazine, then query with a short vehicle feature that will show his or her potential as a creative writer/photographer."

KEEPIN' TRACK OF VETTES, Box 48, Spring Valley NY 10977. (914)425-2649. Editor: Shelli Finkel. 70% freelance written. Works with a small number of new/unpublished writers each year. Monthly magazine; 60-68 pages. For Corvette owners and enthusiasts. Circ. 38,000. Pays on publication. Publishes ms an average of 3 months after acceptance. Buys all rights. Byline given. Submit seasonal/holiday material 3 months in advance. Computer printout submissions acceptable; prefers letter-quality. Reports in 1 month. Free sample copy and writer's guidelines.

Nonfiction: Expose (telling of Corvette problems with parts, etc.); historical (any and all aspects of Corvette developments); how-to (restorations, engine work, suspension, race, swapmeets); humor; informational; interview (query); nostalgia; personal experience; personal opinion; photo feature; profile (query); technical; and travel. Buys 1-2 mss/issue. Query or submit complete ms. Pays $50-200. Sometimes pays the expenses of writers on assignment.

Photos: Send photo with ms. Pays $10-35 for b&w contact sheets or negatives; $10-50 for 35mm color transparencies; offers no additional payment for photos with accompanying ms.

Tips: The writer "must have more than a passing knowledge of Corvettes specifically and automobiles in general. We're looking for more material covering '63-67' Corvettes—as they appreciate in value, interest in those years is rising."

MOTOR TREND, Petersen Publishing Co., 8490 Sunset Blvd., Los Angeles CA 90069. (213)854-2222. Editor: Jack Nerad. 15-20% freelance written. Prefers to work with published/established writers. For automotive enthusiasts and general interest consumers. Monthly. Circ. 750,000. Publishes ms an average of 3 months after acceptance. Buys all rights. "Fact-filled query suggested for all freelancers." Computer printout submissions acceptable; prefers letter-quality. Reports in 1 month.

Nonfiction: Automotive and related subjects that have national appeal. Emphasis on domestic and imported cars, roadtests, driving impressions, auto classics, auto, travel, racing, and high-performance features for the enthusiast. Packed with facts. Freelancers should confine queries to feature material; road tests and related activity handled inhouse.

Photos: Buys photos, particularly of prototype cars and assorted automotive matter. Pays $25-250 for b&w glossy prints or color transparencies.

NISSAN DISCOVERY, The Magazine for Nissan Owners, Donnelley Marketing, Box 4617, N. Hollywood CA 91607. (818)506-4081 Editor: Wayne Thoms. 50% freelance written. Prefers to work with published/established writers and photographers. Bimonthly magazine for Nissan owners and their families. Circ. 500,000. Pays on acceptance. Publishes ms an average of 3-6 months after acceptance. Byline given. Buys first North American serial rights. Submit seasonal/holiday material 5 months in advance. Photocopied and previously published submissions OK. Computer printout submissions acceptable; no dot-matrix. Reports in 1 month. Sample copy 9x12 SAE and 4 first class stamps; writer's guidelines for #10 SASE.

Nonfiction: Historical/nostalgic, humor, photo feature, travel. "We need general family interest material with heavy emphasis on outstanding color photos: travel, humor, food, lifestyle, sports, entertainment." Buys 25 mss/year. Query. Length: 1,300-1,800 words. Pays $300-1,000. Sometimes pays the expenses of writers on assignment.

Photos: State availability of photos. Reviews 2¼" and 35mm color transparencies. No b&w photos. "Payment usually is part of story package—all negotiated." Captions and identification of subjects required. Buys one-time rights.

Tips: "A freelancer can best break in to our publication by submitting a brief idea query with specific information on color slides available. Offer a package of copy and art."

‡ON TRACK, The Auto Racing News Magazine, OT Publishing, Inc., Box 8509, Fountain Valley CA 92728. (714)966-1131. Editor: Craig Fischer, Andrew Crask. 90% freelance written. Biweekly magazine on auto racing (no drag racing, sprint cars, etc.). Circ. 40,000. Pays on publication. Publishes 2 months after acceptance. Byline given. Buys first North American serial rights. Query for electronic submissions. Computer printout submissions OK; prefers letter-quality. Reports on queries. Sample copy $2. Free writer's guidelines.

Nonfiction: Interview/profile and technical. Opinions, stories about race drivers without quotes from driver. Buys 3-4 mss/year. Query with or without published clips, or send complete ms. Length: 800-2,000 words. Pays $5/column inch. Sometimes pays expenses of writers on assignment.

Photos: State availability of photos with submission. Review 5x7 prints. Offers $10 per photo when used. Captions and identification of subjects required. Buys one-time rights.

Columns/Departments: Inside Line (look at subjects affecting trends, safety rules, etc.), 850; Broadcast Booth (TV, radio), 850. Buys 40 mss/year. Send complete ms. Pays $5.25 per column inch.

Tips: "Show some knowledge on the subject. Our readers are very knowledgeable and are quick to spot mistakes that get by us. Most of the magazine is done by a select few, but there are openings."

OPEN WHEEL MAGAZINE, Lopez Publications, Box 715, Ipswich MA 01938. (617)356-7030. FAX: (508)356-2492. Editor: Dick Berggren. 80% freelance written. Monthly magazine. "*OW* covers sprint cars, midgets, supermodifieds and Indy cars. *OW* is an enthusiast's publication which speaks to those deeply involved in oval track automobile racing in the United States and Canada. *OW*'s primary audience is a group of men and women actively engaged in competition at the present time, those who have recently been in competition and those who plan competition soon. That audience includes drivers, car owners, sponsors and crew members who represent perhaps 50-70 percent of our readership. The rest who read the magazine are those in the racing trade (part manufacturers, track operators and officials) and serious fans who see 30 or more races per year." Circ. 150,000. Pays on publication. Publishes ms an average of 3-6 months after acceptance. Byline given. Buys first rights. Submit seasonal/holiday material 2 months in advance. Computer printout submissions OK; prefers letter-quality. Reports in 3 weeks on queries. Sample copy for 9x12 SAE and $2 postage; writer's guidelines for #10 SASE.

Nonfiction: General interest, historical/nostalgic, how-to, humor, interview/profile, new product, photo feature and technical. "We don't care for features that are a blow-by-blow chronology of events. The key word is interest. We want features which allow the reader to get to know the main figure very well. Our view of racing is positive. We don't think all is lost, that the sport is about to shut down and don't want stories that claim such to be the case, but we shoot straight and avoid whitewash." Buys 125+ mss/year. Query with or without published clips, or send complete ms.

Photos: State availability of photos with submission. Reviews contact sheets, negatives, transparencies and prints. Buys one-time rights.

Fillers: Anecdotes, facts and short humor. Buys 100/year. Length: 1-3 pages, double-spaced. Pays $35.

Tips: "Virtually all our features are submitted without assignment. An author knows much better what's going on in his backyard than we do. We ask that you write to us before beginning a story theme. Judging of material is always a combination of a review of the story and its support illustrations. Therefore, we ask for photography to accompany the manuscript on first submission. We've gone from bi-monthly to monthly - so we are looking to use more quality material."

ROAD KING MAGAZINE, Box 250, Park Forest IL 60466. Editor-in-Chief: George Friend. 10% freelance written. Eager to work with new/unpublished writers. Truck driver leisure reading publication. Quarterly magazine; 72 pages. Circ. 231,000. Pays on acceptance. Publishes ms an average of 2 months after acceptance. Usually buys all rights; sometimes buys first rights. Byline given "always on fiction—if requested on nonfiction." Submit seasonal/holiday material 3 months in advance. Sample copy for 7x10 SAE and 85¢ postage or get free sample copy at any Unocal 76 truck stop; writer's guidelines for #10 SASE.

Nonfiction: Trucker slant or general interest, humor, and photo feature. No articles on violence or sex. Name and quote release required. No queries. Submit complete ms. Length: 500-1,200 words. Pays $50-400.

Photos: Submit photos with accompanying ms. No additional payment for b&w contact sheets or 2¼x2¼ color transparencies. Captions preferred. Buys first rights. Model release required.

Fiction: Adventure, historical, humorous, mystery, rescue-type suspense and western. Especially about truckers. No stories on sex and violence. "We're looking for quality writing." Buys 4 mss/year. Submit complete ms. Length: approximately 1,200 words. Pays up to $400. Writer should quote selling price with submission.

Fillers: Jokes, gags, anecdotes and short humor about truckers. Buys 20-25/year. Length: 50-500 words. Pays $5-100.

Tips: "No collect phone calls or postcard requests. Never phone for free copy as we will not handle such phone calls. We don't appreciate letters we have to answer. Do not submit manuscripts, art or photos using registered mail, certified mail or insured mail. Publisher will not accept such materials from the post office. Publisher will not discuss refusal with writer. Nothing personal, just legal. Do not write and ask if we would like such and such article or outline. We buy only from original and complete manuscripts submitted on speculation. Do not ask for writer's guidelines. See above and/or get a copy of the magazine and be familiar with our format before submitting anything. We are a trucker publication whose readers are often family members and sometimes Bible Belt. We refrain from violence, sex, nudity, etc."

ROD & CUSTOM, Peterson Publishing Co., 8490 Sunset Blvd., Los Angeles CA 90069. (213)854-2250. Editor: Patrick Ganahl. Managing Editor: Kristin Kelly. 30% freelance written. Bimonthly magazine on street rods and custom cards. "*R&C* is a special interest automotive magazine covering street rods, custom cards, '50s cars and vintage race cars. All articles are photo illustrated and the slant is toward hands-on enthusiasts and how-to subjects." Circ. 85,000. Pays on acceptance. Byline given. Buys all rights. Computer printout submissions OK. Reports in 2 weeks. Sample copy $3.

Nonfiction: Historical/nostalgic, how-to, interview/profile, new product, photo feature, technical: Buys 25 mss/year. Query with or without published clips, or send complete ms. Length: 250-2,000 words. Pays $150-1,000. Seldom pays the expenses of writers on assignment.

Photos: Send photos with submission. Reviews contact sheets, transparencies and 5x7 or larger prints. Offers no additional payment for photos accepted with ms; pays $50-100 for photos alone. Captions and model releases required. Buys all rights.

Columns/Departments: Roddin' Around (newsy, unusual, interesting, historical short subjects on rod/custom topics), 250-500 words. Buys 20 mss/year. Query or send complete ms. Pays $50-250.

Fillers: Anecdotes, facts, newsbreaks and illustrations. Buys 25/year. Length 50-250 words. Pays $50-200.

Tips: "You must know the subject matter intimately and be able to speak the language. Professional quality photos are a must with any submission. We need technical, how-to and event articles more than we need photo features of individual cars. Other than car features, most of our photography is black and white; color features should also include b&w."

SCHNEIDER PERFORMANCE SERIES, Vette, Pontiac, Mopar & Muscle Cars, CSK Publishing Co., Inc., 175 Hudson St., Hackensack NJ 07601. (201)488-7171. Editor: Steve Collison. Managing Editor: Sue Elliott. 35% freelance written. Automotive enthusiast magazines dedicated to all makes and models within the individual marque. Circ. 50,000. Pays on acceptance. Publishes ms an average of 3 months after acceptance. Byline given. Buys all rights. Query for electronic submission. Computer printout submissions OK; no dot-matrix. Reports in 2 weeks on queries; 1 month on mss. Sample copy for 8½x11 SAE.

Nonfiction: Jeff Bauer, articles editor. Historical/nostalgic, how-to, interview/profile, photo feature, technical. Buys 150 mss/year. Query with or without published clips, or send complete ms. Length: 1,000-5,000 words. Pays $150-350. Sometimes pays expenses of writers on assignment.

Photos: Send photos with submission. Reviews contact sheets, transparencies and prints. Offers no additional payment for photos accepted with mss. Identification of subjects required.

STOCK CAR RACING MAGAZINE, Box 715, Ipswich MA 01938. Editor: Dick Berggren. 80% freelance written. Eager to work with new/unpublished writers. For stock car racing fans and competitors. Monthly magazine; 120 pages. Circ. 400,000. Pays on publication. Publishes ms an average of 3 months after acceptance. Buys all rights. Byline given. Query for electronic submissions. Computer printout submissions acceptable; prefers letter-quality. Reports in 6 weeks. Free writer's guidelines.

Nonfiction: General interest, historical/nostalgic, how-to, humor, interviews, new product, photo features and technical. "Uses nonfiction on stock car drivers, cars, and races. We are interested in the story behind the story in stock car racing. We want interesting profiles and colorful, nationally interesting features. We are looking for more technical articles, particularly in the area of street stocks and limited sportsman." Query with or without published clips, or submit complete ms. Buys 50-200 mss/year. Length: 100-6,000 words. Pays up to $450.

Photos: State availability of photos. Pays $20 for 8x10 b&w photos; up to $250 for 35mm or larger color transparencies. Captions required.

Fillers: Anecdotes and short humor. Buys 100 each year. Pays $35.

Tips: "We get more queries than stories. We just don't get as much material as we want to buy. We have more room for stories than ever before. We are an excellent market with 12 issues per year. Virtually all our features are submitted without assignment. An author knows much better what's going on in his backyard than we do. We ask that you write to us before beginning a story theme. If nobody is working on the theme you wish to pursue, we'd be glad to assign it to you if it fits our needs and you are the best person for the job. Judging of material is always a combination of a review of the story and its support illustration. Therefore, we ask for photography to accompany the manuscript on first submission."

‡3 & 4 WHEEL ACTION, Hi-Torque Publications, 10600 Sepulveda, Mission Hills CA 91345. (818)365-6831. Editor: Steve Casper. Managing Editor: Jeff Maas. 20% freelance written. Monthly magazine on off-road all-terrain vehicles (3 & 4 wheelers). "Nearly 100% male readers, mostly in the 18-24 age group—the magazine is designed to inform ATV enthusiasts on new products, machines, races and riding areas." Circ. 50,000. Pays on publication. Byline given. Buys one-time rights. Submit seasonal/holiday material 3 months in advance. Computer printout submissions OK; prefers letter-quality. Free sample copy.

Nonfiction: How-to (technical stories on ATVs), personal experience, photo features, technical, travel (to great riding areas); all about ATV's. Query. Length: 500-1,250 words. Pays $40-120.

Photos: Send photos with submission. Reviews negatives, 35mm transparencies and 5x7 prints. Offers $15-40 per photo. Buys one-time rights.

Tips: "What we need from other areas of the country are photo features on scenic riding spots and hunting and fishing on your ATV stories. These stories can also have a personal slant to them. A writer's best bet is to contact a local ATV club or enthusiast (the local dealers should know these people) and go on a scenic *legal* ride with them and take good photographs of the trip—same goes for hunting and fishing."

‡VETTE MAGAZINE, CSK Publishing, Inc., 299 Market St., Saddle Brook NJ 07622. (201)488-7171. FAX: (201)488-8259. Editor: D. Randy Riggs. Managing Editor: Sue Elliott. 60% freelance written. Monthly magazine. All subjects related to the Corvette automobile. "Our readership is extremely knowledgeable about the subject of Corvettes. Therefore, writers had better know the subject thoroughly and be good at fact checking." Circ. 60,000. Offers 50% kill fee. Buys first North American serial rights. Submit seasonal/holiday material 3 months in advance. Query for electronic submissions. Computer printout submissions OK; letter-quality

only. Reports in 3 weeks on queries; 2 weeks on mss. Sample copy for 9x12 SAE with $1.45 postage; writer's guidelines for #10 SASE.
Nonfiction: General interest, historical/nostalgic, how-to, interview/profile, new product, personal experience, photo feature, technical and travel. Buys 120 mss/year. Query with published clips. Length: 4pp-2,700 words. Pays $150-750 for assigned articles; $100-350 for unsolicited articles. Sometimes pays expenses of writers on assignment.
Photos: State availability of photos with submission. Reviews contact sheets. Offers no additional payment for photos accepted with ms. Captions and model releases are required. Buys one-time rights.
Columns/Departments: Reviews (books/videos), 400-500 words. Buys 12 mss/year. Query. Pays $50-150.
Fiction: Adventure, fantasy and slice-of-life vignettes. Buys 4 mss/year. Query with published clips. Length: 400-2,500 words. Pays $100-500.

VOLKSWAGEN'S WORLD, Volkswagen of America, 888 W. Big Beaver Rd., Box 3951, Troy MI 48007. Editor: Marlene Goldsmith. 75% freelance written. Magazine published 4 times/year for Volkswagen owners in the United States. Circ. 300,000. Pays on acceptance. Buys first North American serial rights. Byline given. Query for electronic submissions. Computer printout submissions acceptable; no dot-matrix. Reports in 6 weeks. Sample copy for 9x12 SAE and $1.05 postage. Free writer's guidelines.
Nonfiction: "Interesting stories on people using Volkswagens; travel pieces with the emphasis on people, not places; Volkswagenmania stories; personality pieces, including celebrity interviews; and inspirational and true adventure articles. The style should be light. Our approach is subtle, however, and we try to avoid obvious product puffery, since *Volkswagen's World* is not an advertising medium. We prefer a first-person, people-oriented handling. No basic travelogues; stay away from Beetle stories. With all story ideas, query first. All unsolicited manuscripts will be returned unopened. We strongly advise writers to read at least 2 past issues before working on a story." Buys 10-12 mss/year. Length: 750 words maximum; "shorter pieces, some as short as 450 words, often receive closer attention." Pays minimum $150 per printed page for photographs and text; otherwise, a portion of that amount, depending on the space allotted. Most stories are 2 pages; some run 3 or 4 pages.
Photos: Submit photo samples with query. Photos purchased with ms; captions required. "We prefer color transparencies, 35mm or larger. All photos should carry the photographer's name and address. If the photographer is not the author, both names should appear on the first page of the text. Where possible, we would like a selection of at least 40 transparencies. Quality photography can often sell a story that might be otherwise rejected. Every picture should be identified or explained." Model releases required. Pays $500 maximum for front cover photo.
Fillers: "Short, humorous anecdotes about current model Volkswagens." Pays $15.
Tips: "Style of the publication and its content are being structured toward more upscale, affluent buyers. VW drivers are not the same as those who used to drive the Beetle."

Aviation

Professional and private pilots and aviation enthusiasts read the publications in this section. Editors at aviation magazines want material for audiences who know commercial aviation. Magazines for passengers of commercial airlines are grouped in the In-flight category. Technical aviation and space journals and publications for airport operators, aircraft dealers and others in aviation businesses are listed under Aviation and Space in the Trade section.

‡AERO ART, Hermes Publications, Inc., 15 W. 44th St., 9th Fl., New York NY 10036. (212)921-2473. Editor: Bernard Kent. Quarterly professional journal devoted to all facets of aviation art. "Official publication of the American Society of Aviation Artists, non-profit, educational/professional society. Reaches broad spectrum of aviation enthusiasts, art collectors, dealers, pilots, military, media, airport executives, museums, gallery-owners, etc." Pays on publication. Publishes ms an average of 5 months after acceptance. Byline sometimes given. Offers 50% kill fee. Buys all rights and makes work-for-hire assignments. Submit seasonal/holiday material 6 months in advance. Simultaneous and photocopied submissions OK. Computer printout submissions OK; prefers letter-quality. Sample copy $5 with 8½x11 SAE and $1 postage. Free writer's guidelines.
Nonfiction: Essays, historical/nostalgic, interview/profile and photo feature. Coverage of Annual Aviation Art Forum. Buys 6 mss/year. Query with or without published clips "Submit brief treatment of proposed article along with professional resume and samples. Do not submit complete ms. OK to phone." Length: 1,000-3,000 words. Pays $100 per page in print. Sometimes pays expenses of writers on assignment.

Photos: Reviews transparencies. Offers no additional payment for photos accepted with ms. Captions, model releases and identification of subjects required. Buys one-time rights. Protection of artists' copyrights is a must.

Fiction: Might consider fiction, but primarily non-fiction used in our genre publication. Historical and science fiction (involving aviation, space illustrated by established artists). "No fiction unrelated to aviation/space art."

‡**AIR ALASKA,** Pacific Rim Publishing Company, Suite 410, 900 W 5th, Box 99007, Anchorage AK 99509. (907)272-7500. FAX: (907)279-1037. Managing Editor: Steve Grissom. 75% freelance written. Monthly tabloid on aviation, piloting in the far north region. "*Air Alaska* targets readers who actively use their small aircraft in recreation and business in far north regions. Writing must appeal to that audience and be good, clear and concise." Circ. 10,000. Pays within 30 days of publication. Byline given. Offers 40% kill fee. Buys first North American serial rights and second serial (reprint) rights. Submit seasonal/holiday material 6 months in advance. Simultaneous, photocopied and previously published submissions OK. Query for electronic submissions. Computer printout submissions OK; no dot-matrix. Reports in 1 month. Sample copy for 9x12 SAE with 5 first class stamps; free writer's guidelines.

Nonfiction: General interest, historical/nostalgic, how-to (secure floats, fly skis, winter maintenance, etc.), humor, inspirational, interview/profile, new product, personal experience, photo feature, technical, travel (to and from far north areas, far north generally means above 45°N latitude). Fly-in fishing articles - April; Fly-in hunting articles - August; Pilot's Gift guide (product description/gift ideas) - November. "If it does not relate to general aviation, it will not be considered. Exception: hang gliding, parachuting, ultralights. *No* remote control/model stuff." Buys 200 mss/year. Query. Length: 600-800 words. Pays 5-10¢/word for assigned articles; 3-8¢/word for unsolicited articles. Sometimes pays expenses of writers on assignment.

Photos: State availability of photos with submission and briefly describe. Reviews contact sheets. Offers $15-30 per photo. Captions, model releases and identification of subjects required. Buys first rights and rights to reprint. Not exclusive rights or rights to resale.

Fiction: Adventure and novel excerpts (aviation related *only*).

Fillers: Anecdotes, facts, gags, newsbreaks, and short humor. Buys 24/year. Length: 200 words. Pays 5-10¢/word.

Tips: "Limit query with one page or less. Action stopping b&w photos are paramount. People in photos necessary. We rarely use poses. We also pay more for electronic submission."

AIR & SPACE/SMITHSONIAN MAGAZINE, Joe Bonsignore-Smithsonian, 900 Jefferson Dr., Washington DC 20560. (202)357-4414. Editor: Tom Huntington. Managing Editor: Philip Hayward. 80% freelance written. Prefers to work with published/established writers. A bimonthly magazine covering aviation and aerospace for a non-technical audience. "Features are slanted to a technically curious, but not necessarily technically knowledgeable audience. We are looking for unique angles to aviation/aerospace stories, history, events, personalities, current and future technologies, that emphasize the human-interest aspect." Circ. 310,000. Pays on acceptance. Byline given. Offers kill fee. Buys first North American serial rights. Photocopied submissions OK. Reports in 5 weeks. Sample copy for $3.50 plus 9½x13 SASE; free writer's guidelines.

Nonfiction: Book excerpts, essays, general interest (on aviation/aerospace), historical/nostalgic, how-to, humor, interview/profile, photo feature and technical. Buys 50 mss/year. Query with published clips. Length: 1,500-3,000 words. Pays $2,000 maximum. Pays the expenses of writers on assignment.

Columns/Departments: Above and Beyond (first person), 2,000-2,500 words; Flights and Fancy (whimsy, insight), approximately 1,200 words; Oldies & Oddities (weird, wonderful and old), 1,200 words; Groundling's Notebook (looking upward), length varies. Buys 25 mss/year. Query with published clips. Pays $1,000 maximum. Soundings (brief items, timely but not breaking news), 500-800 words. Pays $300.

Tips: "Soundings is the section most open to freelancers. State availability of illustrations with submission. Reviews 35mm transparencies. We will be buying more stories about space flight than aviaiton now that space program is heating up again."

‡**AIR LINE PILOT,** Air Line Pilots Association, 535 Herndon Parkway, Box 1169, Herndon VA 22070. (703)689-4176. Editor: Esperison Martinez, Jr. 10% freelance written. Prefers to work with published/established writers; works with a small number of new/unpublished writers each year. A monthly magazine for airline pilots covering "commercial aviation industry information—economics, avionics, equipment, systems, safety—that affects a pilot's life in professional sense." Also includes information about management/labor relations trends, contract negotiations, etc. Circ. 40,000. Pays on acceptance. Publishes ms an average of 6 months after acceptance. Offers 50% kill fee. Buys all rights. Submit seasonal/holiday material 6 months in advance. Query for electronic submissions. Computer printout submissions acceptable. Reports in 2 months. Sample copy $1; writer's guidelines for #10 SASE.

Nonfiction: Humor, inspirational, photo feature and technical. "We are backlogged with historical submissions and prefer not to receive unsolicited submissions at this time." Buys 20 mss/year. Query with or without published clips, or send complete ms. Length: 700-3,000 words. Pays $200-600 for assigned articles; pays $50-600 for unsolicited articles.

Photos: Send photos with submission. Reviews contact sheets, 35mm transparencies and 8x10 prints. Offers $10-25/photo. Identification of subjects required. Buys one-time rights.

Tips: "For our feature section, we seek aviation industry information that affects the life of a professional airline pilot from a career standpoint. We also seek material that affects his life from a job security and work environment standpoint. Any airline pilot featured in an article must be an Air Line Pilot Association member in good standing."

FREQUENT FLYER, 888 7th Ave., New York NY 10106. Managing Editor: Jane L. Levere. 50% freelance written. Monthly magazine covering business travel (airlines/airports/aviation) for mostly male high-level business executive readership. Circ. 350,000. Pays on acceptance. Publishes ms an average of 6 months after acceptance. Byline given. Offers kill fee. Buys all rights. Submit seasonal/holiday material 8 months in advance. Computer printout submissions acceptable. Reports in 2 months. Free sample copy and writer's guidelines.

Nonfiction: Expose, new product, technical, travel, and news reporting, in particular on airports/aircraft/airlines/hotels/credit cards/car rentals. Not interested in anything written in the first person. "*FF* reports on travel as part of an executive's job. We do not assume that he enjoys travel, and neither should the freelancer." Buys 100 mss/year. Query with published clips. Length: 800-3,000 words. Pays $100-750.

Photos: "We accept both b&w and color contact sheets, transparencies and prints; rates negotiable." Buys one-time rights.

Tips: "As always, we will seek articles that in some way address the reader as a mobile executive. These can cover such topics as airports, airlines hotels, car rentals and cities frequently visited by business travelers; they also can deal with subjects such as international banking, credit cards, import/export developments, cross-cultural communications, health and safety while traveling, telecommunications and management problems associated with frequent travel. The majority of our stories are third-person news features. We also buy a *very limited* number of destination articles, which represent many of the queries we receive and less than 5% of our assignments and purchase."

WESTERN FLYER, N.W. Flyer, Inc., Box 98786, Tacoma WA 98498-0786. (206)588-1743. FAX: (206)588-4005. Editor: Dave Sclair. 30% freelance written. Prefers to work with published/established writers; works with a small number of new/unpublished writers each year; and will work with new/unpublished writers. Biweekly tabloid covering general aviation. Provides "coverage of aviation news, activities, regulations and politics of general and sport aviation with emphasis on timely features of interest to pilots and aircraft owners." Circ. 35,000. Pays 1 month after publication. Publishes ms an average of 3 months after acceptance. Byline given. Buys one-time rights and first North American seral rights, on occasion second serial (reprint) rights. Submit seasonal/holiday material 2 months in advance. Simultaneous queries, photocopied and previously published submissions from noncompetitive publications OK but must be identified. Query for electronic submissions. Computer printout submissions acceptable. Reports in 2 weeks on queries; 1 month on mss. Sample copy $2; writer's guidelines, style guidelines for #10 SASE.

Nonfiction: Features of current interest about aviation businesses, developments at airports, new products and services, safety, flying technique and maintenance. "Good medium-length reports on current events—controversies at airports, problems with air traffic control, FAA, etc. We want solid news coverage of breaking stories." Query first on historical, nostalgic features and profiles/interviews. Many special sections throughout the year, send SASE for list. Buys 100 mss/year. Query or send complete ms. Length: 500-2,000 words. Pays up to $3/printed column inch maximum. Rarely pays the expenses of writers on assignment.

Photos: "Good pics a must." Send photos (b&w or color prints preferred, no slides) with ms. All photos must have complete captions and carry photographer's ID. Pays $10/b&w photo used.

Tips: "We always are looking for features on places to fly and interviews or features about people and businesses using airplanes in unusual ways. Travel features must include information on what to do once you've arrived, with addresses from which readers can get more information. Get direct quotations from the principals involved in the story. We want current, first-hand information."

Business and Finance

Business publications give executives and consumers a range of information from local business news and trends to national overviews and laws which affect them. National and regional publications are listed below in separate categories. Magazines that have a technical slant are in the Trade section under Business Management, Finance or Management and Supervision categories.

National

BARRON'S, Business and Financial Weekly, Dow Jones and Co. Inc., 200 Liberty St., New York NY 10028. (212)416-2759. Editor: Alan Abelson. Managing Editor: Kathryn M. Welling. 10% freelance written. Weekly tabloid covering the investment scene. *"Barron's* is written for active participants in and avid spectators of the investment scene. We require top-notch reporting *and* graceful, intelligent and irreverent writing." Circ. 296,000. Pays on publication. Byline given. Offers 25% kill fee. Buys all rights. Computer printout submissions OK. Reports in 1 month. Writer's guidelines for SASE.
Nonfiction: Book excerpts, general interest and interview/profile. Publishes quarterly mutual fund sections. Buys 100 mss/year. Query with published clips. Length: 1,500-2,000 words. Pays $500-2,000 for assigned articles. Pays expenses of writers on assignment.
Photos: State availability of photos with submission. Reviews contact sheets, negatives and 8x10 prints. Offers $150-300/photo (day rate). Model releases and identification of subjects required. Buys one-time rights.
Columns/Departments: Richard Donnelly, column/department editor. Barron's on Books (business/investment books). Buys 100 mss/year. Query with published clips. Length: 250-500 words. Pays $150.

BETTER BUSINESS, National Minority Business Council, Inc., 235 E. 42nd St., New York NY 10017. (212)573-2385. Editor: John F. Robinson. 50% freelance written. Semiannual magazine covering small/minority business issues. Circ. 10,000. Pays on publication. Publishes ms an average of 2 months after acceptance. Byline given. Buys first North American serial rights and all rights. Submit seasonal material 1 month in advance. Computer printout submissions acceptable; prefers letter-quality. Sample copy $5 and 9x12 SAE and 6 first class stamps; free writer's guidelines.
Nonfiction: Interview/profile and technical. Buys 5 mss/year. Query with clips. Length: 3,000-5,000 words. Pays $200-250.
Photos: State availability of photos. Reviews b&w prints. Captions required. Buys all rights.
Tips: "Materials are not returned if not used."

BUSINESS AGE, The Magazine for Small Business, Business Trends Communication Corp., 135 W. Wells St., 7th Floor, Milwaukee WI 53203. (414)276-7612. Editor: Claire A. Bremer. 10% freelance written. Monthly magazine for owners/managers of businesses with 1-250 employees. Articles should emphasize useful information for effective business operation. Circ. 190,000. Pays on publication. Publishes ms an average of 5 months after acceptance. Byline given. Buys all rights. Computer printout submissions acceptable; prefers letter-quality. Reports in 3 months. Sample copy for $3.75. Writer's guidelines for #10 SASE.
Nonfiction: How-to information in the areas of: finance, accounting, marketing, management, business law, personnel management, customer relations, planning, taxes, international businesses; interview/profile (successful businesses and small business advocates). All articles should have clear application to small business. Query or send complete ms. State availability of photos. Length: 1,500-2,000 words. Pays $50-250.
Tips: "Small business people want information that can help them increase the productivity and profitability of their operations. Articles must provide practical, hands-on information."

‡BUSINESS MONTH, 488 Madison Ave., New York NY 10022. (212)605-9400. Editor: Niles Howard. 20% freelance written. Prefers to work with published/established writers. Emphasizes business, management and financial trends for a readership "concentrated among senior executives of those companies that have a net worth of $1 million or more." Monthly magazine. Circ. 301,000. Pays on acceptance. Buys first world rights. Submit seasonal/holiday material 3 months in advance. Photocopied submissions OK. Computer printout submissions OK; prefers letter-quality to dot-matrix. Reports in 1 month. Sample copy and writer's guidelines are available.
Nonfiction: Business and government, historical (business; i.e., law or case history), management (new trends, composition), finance and accounting, informational, interview, personal opinion and company profile. Buys 12 mss/year. Query first. Length: 3,500-5,000 words. Pays $200 maximum. Pays expenses of writers on assignment if approved in advance.
Photos: Contact art director. Photos purchased with accompanying ms. Query first. Pays $75 for b&w photos; $150 for color.
Tips: "Make your query short and clearly to the point. Also important—what distinguishes proposed story from others of its type?"

CZESCHIN'S MUTUAL FUND OUTLOOK & RECOMMENDATIONS, Agora, Inc., Box 1423, Baltimore MD 21203. (301)558-1699. Editor: Bob Czeschin. A monthly on mutual fund investing. Circ. 1,000. Pays on publication. Publishes ms an average of 3 months after acceptance. Byline given. Buys first North American serial rights. Submit seasonal/holiday material 3 months in advance. Simultaneous, photocopied and previously published submissions OK. Query for electronic submissions. Computer printout submissions acceptable. Reports in 1 month. Sample copy for $5 and SAE with 2 first class stamps.

Nonfiction: Expose, how-to, interview/profile. Send complete ms. Length: 500-2,000 words. Pays $50-250 for assigned articles; $50-100 for unsolicited articles. Sometimes pays expenses of writers on assignment.
Columns/Departments: Recent issues, new funds coming on the market, minimum investment, investment objectives, fees and expenses, investment restrictions, etc. Length: 200-600 words. Send complete ms. Pays $50-150.

D&B REPORTS, The Dun & Bradstreet Magazine for Small Business Management, Dun & Bradstreet, 299 Park Ave., 24th Floor, New York NY 10171. (212)593-6723. Editor: Patricia W. Hamilton. 10% freelance written. Works with a small number of new/unpublished writers each year. A bimonthly magazine for small business. "Articles should contain useful information that managers of small businesses can apply to their own companies. *D&B Reports* focuses on companies with $15 million in annual sales and under." Circ. 76,000. Pays on acceptance. Publishes ms an average of 2 months after acceptance. Byline given. Buys all rights. Query for electronic submissions. Computer printout submissions acceptable. Reports in 3 weeks on manuscripts. Free sample copy and writer's guidelines.
Nonfiction: How-to (on management); and interview/profile (of successful entrepreneurs). Buys 5 mss/year. Query. Length: 1,500-2,500 words. Pays $500 minimum. Sometimes pays expenses of writers on assignment.
Photos: State availability of photos with submission. Identification of subjects required. Buys one-time rights.
Tips: "The area of our publication most open to freelancers is profiles of innovative companies and managers."

EXECUTIVE FEMALE, NAFE, 127 W. 24th St., 4th Fl., New York NY 10011. (212)645-0770. Editor: Mary E. Terzella. Managing Editor: Jane Mintzer. Emphasizes "upbeat and useful career and financial information for the upwardly mobile female." 60% freelance written. Prefers to work with published/established writers; works with a small number of new/unpublished writers each year. Bimonthly magazine. Circ. 190,000. Byline given. Pays on publication. Publishes an average of 2 months after acceptance. Submit seasonal/holiday material 6 months in advance. Buys first rights, all rights and second serial (reprint) rights to material originally published elsewhere. Previously published submissions OK. Query for electronic submissions. Computer printout submissions acceptable; no dot-matrix. Reports in 2 months. Sample copy $2.50; writer's guidelines for #10 SASE.
Nonfiction: "Articles on any aspect of career advancement and financial planning are welcomed." Needs how-tos for managers and articles about coping on the job, trends in the workplace, financial planning, trouble shooting, business communication, time and stress management, career goal-setting and get-ahead strategies. "We would also like to receive humorous essays dealing with aspects of the job/workplace." Written queries only. Length: 1,500-2,500 words. Pays $50-400. Pays for local travel and telephone calls.
Columns/Departments: More Money (saving, financial advice, interesting tips); Small Business Briefs (how to run your own business better); Working Smart (tips on managing people, getting ahead). Buys 20 mss/year. Query with published clips or send complete ms. Department length: 500-2,000 words. Pays $50-100.

FORBES, 60 5th Ave., New York NY 10011. (212)620-2200. Managing Editor: Sheldon Zalaznick. "We occasionally buy freelance material. When a writer of some standing (or whose work is at least known to us) is going abroad or into an area where we don't have regular staff or bureau coverage, we have given assignments or sometimes helped on travel expenses." Pays negotiable kill fee. Byline usually given.

HOME BUSINESS NEWS, The Newsletter for Home-based Entrepreneurs, 12221 Beaver Pike, Jackson OH 45640. (614)988-2331. Editor: Ed Simpson. 60% freelance written. Works with a small number of new/unpublished writers each year. A bimonthly magazine covering home-based businesses and marketing. Pays on publication. Publishes ms an average of 2 months after acceptance. Byline sometimes given. Buys first North American serial rights and second serial (reprint) rights. Submit seasonal/holiday material 4 months in advance. Simultaneous, photocopied and previously published submissions OK. Query for electronic submissions. Computer printout submissions acceptable; prefers letter-quality. Reports in 1 week on queries; 5 weeks on mss. Sample copy $2; writer's guidelines for #10 SAE with 1 first class stamp.
Nonfiction: Book excerpts, inspirational, interview/profile (of home business owners), new products, personal experience, computer-based home businesses and mail order success stories. Buys 15-20 mss/year. Query with published clips. Length: 800-3,000 words. Pays $20-100; will pay with ad space if agreed upon.
Photos: State availability of photos with submission. Offers no additional payment for photos accepted with ms. Captions and identification of subjects required. Buys one-time rights.
Columns/Departments: Home Business Profiles (profiles of home business owners), 2,000 words. Buys 15-20 mss/year. Query with published clips. Pays $20-100.
Fillers: Facts and newsbreaks. Buys 10/year. Length: 50-300 words. Pays $5-10.

‡MODERN SECRETARY, Allied Publications, 1776 Lake Worth Rd., Lake Worth FL 33460. (407)582-2099. FAX: (407)582-4667. Editor: Richard Champlin. 95% freelance written. Monthly magazine on business/ personal topics for secretaries. Pays on publication. Publishes ms an average of 2-3 months after acceptance. Buys first North American serial rights or one-time rights or second serial (reprint) rights or simultaneous rights. Submit seasonal/holiday material 8 months in advance. Simultaneous, photocopied submissions and previously published submissions OK. Query for electronic submissions. Computer printout submissions OK; prefers letter-quality. Samply copy $1. Free writer's guidelines with SASE.

Nonfiction: How-to (business activities), humor, interview/profile (successful secretaries), personal experience (as a secretary) and photo feature. Buys 50 mss/year. Query with or without published clips, or send complete ms. Length: 600-1,500 words. Pays $5-25 for unsolicited articles. Pays in contributor copies or other premiums only at writer's request.

Photos: Reviews contacts sheets and transparencies. Offers $5 per photo. Captions, model releases (when necessary) and identification of subjects required. Buys one-time rights.

Columns/Departments: Wordwise (origins of words), 500-600 words; Writestyle (grammar, office procedure), 600 words. Buys 24 mss/year. Query with published clips.

Fiction: Humorous (business related). Buys 8-12 mss/year. Send complete ms. Length: 600-1,200 words. Pays $5-25.

Fillers: Anecdotes, gags to be illustrated by cartoonist and short humor. Buys 40-50/year. Pays $5.

MONEY MAKER, Your Guide to Financial Security and Wealth, Consumers Digest Inc., 5705 N. Lincoln Ave., Chicago IL 60659. (312)275-3590. Editor: Dennis Fertig. 90% freelance written. A bimonthly magazine on personal investing. "We cover the broad range of topics associated with personal finance — the strongest emphasis is on traditional investment opportunities." Circulation: 165,000. Pays on acceptance. Publishes ms an average of 2 months after acceptance. Byline given. Offers 50% kill fee. Buys first rights and second serial (reprint) rights. Photocopied submissions OK. Computer printout submissions OK; prefers letter-quality. Reports in 3 months on queries. Sample copy for 8½x11 SAE with $1 postage; writer's guidelines for #10 SASE.

Nonfiction: How-to. "No personal success stories or profiles of one company." Buys 25 mss/year. Send complete ms or query and clips. Include stamped, self-addressed postcard for more prompt response. Length: 1,500-3,000 words. Pays 20¢/word for assigned articles. Pays expenses of writers on assignment. State availability of photos with submission. Offers no additional payment for photos accepted with ms.

Tips: "Know the subject matter. Develop real sources in the investment community. Demonstrate a reader-friendly style that will help make the sometimes complicated subject of investing more accessible to the average person."

‡MONEY WORLD, World Perspective Communications, Inc. 3443 Parkway Center Ct., Orlando FL 32808. (407)290-9600. Editor: Eric Jones. Managing Editor: Elaine Wilson. 90% freelance written. Monthly newspaper on financial/economic/investment news. "*Money World* reaches astute business leaders and serious investors. Writers must be knowledgeable about world economic affairs and write in an interesting fashion." Circ. 200,000. Pays 1 month after publication. Byline given. Buys all rights. Submit seasonal/holiday material 3 months in advance. Simultaneous and photocopied submissions OK. Reports in 2 weeks on queries; 3 weeks on mss. Free sample copy and writer's guidelines.

Nonfiction: Essays, exposé how-to ("consumer reports" investments strategies), interview/profile (with successful people) and other investing news. No "advertorials" for products or companies. Buys 200 mss/year. Query with published clips. Length: 1,500-3,000 words. Pays $20 for assigned articles. Pays in contributor copies in addition to cash payment. Sometimes pays expenses of writers on assignment.

Photos: Send photos with submission. Reviews negatives, transparencies and prints. Prefers negatives. Offers $10-25 per photo. Captions required. Buys one-time rights.

Tips: "We need only in-depth reports and analyses. We encourage new writers, with the understanding that there are plenty of unpublished writers who will become tomorrow's 'stars', but we do scrutinize vehemently."

‡NEW BUSINESS OPPORTUNITIES, Entrepreneur Group, Inc., 2392 Morse Ave., Irvine CA 92714. (714)261-2083. Editor: Rieva Lesonsky. 20-25% freelance written. Monthly magazine on small business. "Provides how-to information for starting a small business and profiles of entrepreneurs who have started small businesses." Estab. 1989. Circ. 200,000. Pays on acceptance. Byline given. Offers 20% kill fee. Buys all rights. Submit seasonal/holiday material 6 months in advance. Previously published submissions OK (if in non-competing publication). Computer printout submissions OK; prefers letter-quality. Reports in 6-8 weeks on queries. Sample copy $3. Writer's guidelines for SAE with 1 first class stamp.

Nonfiction: How-to-start a small business and interview/profile on entrepreneurs. Query. Length: 500-2,000 words. Pays $150-350.

Photos: State availability of photos with submission. Identification of subjects required.

‡OFFSHORE FINANCIAL REPORT, Wealth Publications, Inc., Suite 3552, 144 Fairport Village Landing, Fairport NY 14450. (716)425-3493. FAX: (716)425-3493. Editor: Henri Pallas. 65% freelance written. Monthly newsletter on global financial and investment news. Pays on acceptance. Publishes ms an average of 2 months after acceptance. Byline given. Offers 25% kill fee. Buys first rights world-wide. Simultaneous, photocopied and previously published submissions OK. Query for electronic submissions. Computer printout submission OK; prefers letter-quality. Reports in 2 weeks on queries; 1 month on mss. Sample copy $5. Free writer's guidelines.

Nonfiction: General interest, inspirational and technical. Publishes 40-page world report twice a year—in May and October. No how-to. Buys 200 mss/year. Send complete ms w/ published clips. New writers OK. Length: 250-2,000 words. Pays 25¢/word. Pays expenses of writers on assignment.

Photos: State availability of photos with submission. Reviews contact sheets. Offers $10 per photo. Buys one-time rights.

Columns/Departments: Buys 20 mss/year.

Tips: "Keep global focus of readers in mind. 55% of our readers are outside of the US."

‡REPORT ON BUSINESS MAGAZINE, Globe and Mail, 444 Front St. W., Toronto Ontario M5V 2S9 Canada. (416)585-5499. Editor: Margaret Wente. Managing Editor: James Fleming. 50% freelance written. Monthly magazine. "A business magazine like *Forbes* or *Manhattan, Inc.* which tries to capture major trends and personalities." Circ. 300,000. Pays on acceptance. Publishes ms an average of 4 months after acceptance. Byline given. Offers 50% kill fee. Buys first North American serial rights. Query for electronic submissions. Computer printout submissions OK. Reports in 3 weeks. Free sample copy.

Nonfiction: Book excerpts, exposé, interview/profile, new product and photo feature. Buys 30 mss/year. Query with published clips. Length: 2,000-4,000 words. Pays $200-3,000. Pays expenses of writers on assignment.

Tips: "For features send a 1 page story proposal. We prefer to write about personalities involved in corporate events."

TECHNICAL ANALYSIS OF STOCKS & COMMODITIES, The Trader's Magazine, 9131 California Ave. SW, Box 46518, Seattle WA 98146-0518. (206)938-0570. Publisher: Jack K. Hutson. 75% freelance written. Eager to work with new/unpublished writers. Magazine covers methods of investing and trading stocks, bonds and commodities (futures), options, mutual funds, and precious metals. Circ. 18,000. Pays on publication. Publishes ms an average of 3 months after acceptance. Byline given. Offers 50% kill fee. Buys all rights; however, second serial (reprint) rights revert to the author, provided copyright credit is given. Photocopied and previously published submissions OK. Query for electronic submissions. Computer printout submissions acceptable; prefers letter-quality. Reports in 3 weeks on queries; 1 month on mss. Sample copy $5; detailed writer's guidelines for #10 SAE and 1 first class stamp.

Nonfiction: Melanie Bowman, managing editor. Reviews (new software or hardware that can make a trader's life easier; comparative reviews of software books, services, etc.); how-to (trade); technical (trading and software aids to trading); utilities (charting or computer programs, surveys, statistics, or information to help the trader study or interpret market movements); humor (unusual incidents of market occurrences, cartoons). No newsletter-type, buy-sell recommendations. The article subject must relate to trading psychology, technical analysis, charting or a numerical technique used to trade securities or futures. Virtually requires graphics with every article. Buys 120 mss/year. Query with published clips if available, or send complete ms. Length: 1,000-4,000 words. Pays $100-500. (Applies per inch base rate and premium rate—write for information). Sometimes pays expenses of writers on assignment.

Photos: Christine M. Morrison, photo editor. State availability of photos. Pays $20-150 for 5x7 b&w glossy prints or color slides. Captions, model releases and identification of subjects required. Buys one-time rights.

Columns/Departments: Buys 10 mss/year. Query. Length: 800-1,600 words. Pays $50-200.

Fillers: Karen Webb, fillers editor. Jokes and cartoons, on investment humor. Must relate to trading stocks, bonds, options, mutual funds or commodities. Buys 20/year. Length: 500 words. Pays $20-50.

Tips: "Describe how to use technical analysis, charting, or computer work in day-to-day trading of stocks, bonds, mutual funds, options or commodities. A blow-by-blow account of how a trade was made, including the trader's thought processes, is, to our subscribers, the very best received story. One of our prime considerations is to instruct in a manner that the lay person can comprehend. We are not hyper-critical of writing style. The completeness and accuracy of submitted material are of the utmost consideration. Write for detailed writer's guidelines."

WOMAN'S ENTERPRISE for entrepreneurs, Paisano Publications Inc., Box 3100, 28210 Dorothy Dr., Aqoura CA 91301. (818)889-8740. FAX: (818)889-4726. Editor: Caryne Brown. 40% freelance written. A bimonthly small business magazine on entrepreneurship by women. "The magazine is devoted to why and how women have created, in whole or significant part, a small business of their own. Readership comprises corporate-executive women seeking to strike out on their own, entrepreneurial homemakers, and women who are already in business." Pays on acceptance. Publishes ms an average of 4 months after acceptance. Byline given. Offers 15% kill fee. Buys all rights and makes work-for-hire assignments. Photocopied submissions OK. Query for electronic submissions. Reports in 1 month on queries; 1 month on mss. Sample copy for 10x13 SAE with $1.50 postage. Writer's guidelines for #10 SAE with 1 first class stamp.

Nonfiction: Business features, management features and new business ideas. "Our editorial calendar is still being developed. Theme issues may appear from time to time. No personality profiles of entrepreneurs. We want to know how, why, and how much." Buys 80 mss/year. Query. Length: 1,000-2,000 words. Pays 20¢/word minimum. Sometimes pays expenses of writers on assignments.

Photos: State availability of photos with submission. Reviews transparencies and prints. Offers no additional payment for photos accepted with ms. Captions, model releases and subjects required. Buys all rights.

Tips: "Our readers are either in business or want to be. The more practical, how-to, specific information about what it takes for any business to succeed, the better suited it is to the magazine. A definite plus is a short, quick-hit sidebar that details key how-to information. *Woman's Enterprise* is a publication readers should be able to use to make money for themselves. When specific businesses are being profiled, specific cost, returns, and profit figures are *essential*. Otherwise we can't use the piece."

‡**WORLD TRADE, The Magazine for Companies with International Sales**, World Trade, Building 137, 3100 Airway Ave. Costa Mesa CA 92626. (714)641-1404. FAX: (714)957-0922. Editor: Drew Lawler. Managing Editor: William Lobdell. 75% freelance written. Quarterly magazine on world trade. Estab. 1988. Circ. 40,000. Pays on publication. Publishes ms an average of 2 months after acceptance. Byline given. Buys first North American serial rights. Query for electronic submissions. Computer printout submissions OK; prefers letter-quality. Reports in 2 weeks. Sample copy for 10x13 SAE with $2.05 postage.

Nonfiction: Exposé, interview/profile (country profiles and company profiles), new product, finance and joint ventures. Buys 75 mss/year. Query with published clips. Length: 2,000-3,000 words. Pays $150-500 for assigned articles.

Photos: State availability of photos with submission.

Regional

ARIZONA BUSINESS GAZETTE, Phoenix Newspapers Inc. Box 1950, Phoenix AZ 85001. (602)271-8491. FAX: (602)271-7363. Editor: Bill Chronister. 30-40% freelance written. Weekly business newspaper on Arizona business issues. "Articles must have a strong business angle and be of local interest to Arizona, primarily the Phoenix area." Circ. 9,500. Pays on publication 2-3 weeks after acceptance. Byline given. Offers 10-25% kill fee. Buys first rights. Computer printout submissions OK; prefers letter-quality. Reports in 1 month on queries; 1 month on mss. Sample copy for $4. Writer's guidelines SAE with 1 first class stamp.

Nonfiction: Arizona business news and features. No fiction, no advice columns, no how-tos. Buys 50+ mss/year. Query with published clips. Length: 500-1,000 words. Pays $50-100 for assigned articles. Sometimes pays expenses of writers on assignment. State availability of photos with submission. Offers $10-20 per photo. Captions and identification of subjects required. Buys one-time rights.

Tips: "We can afford to use only those freelancers with background and training as news reporters and news writers. Solid journalism skills and some general expertise in business, economics, etc. are necessary. Most open to freelancers would be business features on Arizona companies, industries or business people. They should be legitimate news, not public relations promotions. Must be written in a lively style but accurately and thoroughly reported."

ARIZONA TREND, Magazine of Business and Finance, Trend Magazines, Inc., Suite 2004, 3003 N. Central Ave., Phoenix AZ 85012. (602)230-1117. Editor and Publisher: Thomas Kunkel. Managing Editor: Kevin Helliker. A monthly regional business magazine. Estab. 1986. Circ. 28,000. Pays on acceptance. Byline given. Offers variable kill fee. Buys first North American serial rights. Computer printout submissions acceptable; no dot-matrix. Reports in 2 weeks on queries; 1 week on mss. Sample copy $2.95 with 9x12 SAE and 7 first class stamps.

Nonfiction: Essays, interview/profile, and new product. Query. Length: 2,000-3,000 words. Pays $300-1,200. Pays some expenses of writers on assignment.

Photos: State availability of photos with submission. Reviews transparencies. Offers $50 minimum/photo. Captions and identification of subjects required. Buys one-time rights.

‡**ARKANSAS BUSINESS**, Journal Publishing, Inc., Suite 200, 201 E. Markham, Little Rock AR 72203. (501)372-1443. FAX: (501)375-3623. Editor: Tom Honeycutt. 40% freelance written. Biweekly tabloid on the Arkansas business community. "While most business publications cover the who, what, when, where and why of business, *Arkansas Business* answers the 'so what'. What does a trend or idea or strategy mean to the local business community?" Circ. 11,000. Pays on acceptance. Publishes ms an average of 2 weeks after acceptance. Byline given. 10% kill fee. Buys first rights. Submit seasonal/holiday material 6 weeks in advance. Query for electronic submissions. Computer printout submissions OK; prefers letter-quality. Reports in 2 weeks. Free sample copy and writer's guidelines.

Nonfiction: Exposé (business methods) how-to (business concepts, products) and interview/profile (local business executives). "We do not print articles that do not have a local (i.e. Arkansas) angle on a business topic." Buys 100 mss/year. Query with published clips. Length: 800-1,200 words. Pays $60-300 for assigned articles. Pays expenses of writers on assignment.

Photos: State availability of photos with submission. Reviews contact sheets. Offers $15-200 per photo. Captions and identification of subjects required. Buys one-time rights.

Columns/Departments: Buys 1-10 mss/year. Query with published clips. Length: 400-1,000 words. Pays $45-300.

‡**BNH MAGAZINE,The Business of New Hampshire,** The Joliecoeur Companies, 177 E Industrial Dr., Manchester NH 03103. Editor: Dan Wise. Managing Editor: Eric Pope. 15% freelance written. Monthly magazine with focus on business, politics, life and people of New Hampshire. "Our audience consists of the owners and top managers of New Hampshire businesses and others interested in business and state affairs. Circ. 20,000. Pays on acceptance. Publishes an average of 1-2 months after acceptance. Byline given. Buys first North American serial rights. Reports in 1 month on queries. Free sample and writer's guidelines to likely contributors.

Nonfiction: Essays, how-to, interview/profile and opinion. Buys 14 mss/year. Query with published clips. "No unsolicited ms; interested in local writers only." Length: 500-1,800 words. $50-600 for assigned articles. Sometimes pays expenses of writers on assignment.

Photos: State availability of photos with submission. Reviews contact sheets. Model releases and identification of subjects required. Buys one-time rights.

Columns/Departments: Personal Business (how-to lifestyle, health, personal finance, travel by local writers), 1,000 words. Buys 6 mss/year.

Tips: "I *always* want clips with queries. Writers must be from the area and be experienced writers. Follow up of phone call at least 3 weeks. People and how-to pieces best for new writers."

BOULDER COUNTY BUSINESS REPORT, 1830 N. 55th St., Boulder CO 80301. (303)440-4950. FAX: (303)440-8954. Editor: Jerry W. Lewis. 75% freelance written. Prefers to work with published/established writers; works with a small number of new/unpublished writers each year. Monthly newspaper covering Boulder County business issues. Offers "news tailored to a monthly theme and read primarily by Colorado businesspeople and by some investors nationwide. Philosophy: Descriptive, well-written articles that reach behind the scene to examine area's business activity." Circ. 14,000. Pays on publication. Publishes ms an average of 1 month after acceptance. Byline given. Buys one-time rights and second serial (reprint) rights. Simultaneous queries and photocopied submissions OK. Computer printout submissions acceptable; prefers letter-quality. Query for electronic submissions. Reports in 1 month on queries; 2 weeks on mss. Sample copy free on request.

Nonfiction: Book excerpts, interview/profile, new product, photo feature of company, examination of competition in a particular line of business. "All our issues are written around a monthly theme. No articles are accepted in which the subject has not been pursued in depth and both sides of an issue presented in a writing style with flair." Buys 120 mss/year. Query with published clips. Length: 250-2,000 words. Pays $50-300.

Photos: State availability of photos with query letter. Reviews b&w contact sheets. Pays $10 maximum for b&w contact sheet. Identification of subjects required. Buys one-time rights and reprint rights.

Tips: "It would be difficult to write for this publication if a freelancer were unable to localize a subject. In-depth articles are written by assignment. The freelancer located in the Colorado area has an excellent chance here."

BUSINESS VIEW, Florida Business Publications Inc., Box 9859, Naples FL 33941. (813)263-7525. Editor: Ken Gooderham. 100% freelance written. Prefers to work with published/established writers; works with a small number of new/unpublished writers each year. A monthly magazine covering business trends and issues in southwest Florida. Circ. 14,200. Pays on publication. Publishes ms an average of 3-6 months after acceptance. Byline given. Buys all rights or makes work-for-hire assignments. Simultaneous, photocopied and previously published submissions OK. Computer printout submissions acceptable; prefers letter-quality. Reports in 2 months. Sample copy $2.50 with 8½x11 SAE and 8 first class stamps; writer's guidelines for #10 SASE.

Nonfiction: Book excerpts (business); how-to (management); humor (business); interview/profile (regional); and technical. Buys 24-36 mss/year. Query with published clips. Length: 100-3,000 words. Pays $15-300 for assigned articles; pays $15-200 for unsolicited articles. Sometimes pays the expenses of writers on assignment.

Photos: State availability of photos with submission. Reviews contact sheets and 5x7 prints. Offers $15-25/photo. Buys one-time rights.

Columns/Departments: Finance (general investment opportunities); Management; Marketing; Profiles; Viewpoint; Regional View. Buys 12-20 mss/year. Send complete ms. Length: 750-1,200 words. Pays $25-100.

Tips: "Our readers like specific answers to specific problems. Do not send generalized how-to articles that do not offer concrete solutions to management problems. Be concise, informed, and upbeat in style. Profiles of southwest Florida business leaders are most open to freelance writers. These are short (1,000 words) articles that present local, interesting personalities. How-to articles in the areas of management, personal finance, retailing, accounting, investing, personnel, and stress management are also open."

CRAIN'S DETROIT BUSINESS, Crain Communications, Inc., 1400 Woodbridge, Detroit MI 48207. (313)446-0460. FAX: (313)446-0383. Editor: Mary Kramer. Managing Editor: Matt Gryczan. 20% freelance written. Weekly tabloid covering Detroit area businesses. *"Crain's Detroit Business* reports the activities of local businesses. Our readers are mostly executives; many of them own their own companies. They read us to keep track of companies not often reported about in the daily press—privately held companies and small public companies. Our slant is hard news and news features. We do not report on the auto companies, but other businesses in Wayne, Oakland, Macomb, and Washtenaw counties are part of our turf." Circ. 33,500. Pays on publication. Byline given. Offers negotiable kill fee. Buys first rights and "the right to make the story available to the other 25 Crain publications, and the right to circulate the story through the Crain News Service." Photocopied submissions OK. Query for electronic submissions. Computer printout submissions OK; prefers letter-quality. Sample copy 50¢; writer's guidelines for SASE.

Nonfiction: Cindy Goodaker, articles editor. Book excerpts and interview/profile. No "how-tos, new product articles, or fiction." Looking for local and statewide news. Buys 200 mss/year. Query. Length: 800 words average. Pays $6/inch and expenses for assigned articles. Pays $6/inch without expenses for unsolicited articles. Pays expenses of writers on assignment.

Tips: "What we are most interested in are specific news stories about local businesses. The fact that Widget Inc. is a great company is of no interest to us. However, if Widget Inc. introduced a new product six months ago and sales have gone up from $20 million to $30 million, then that's a story. The same is true if sales went down from $20 million to $10 million. I would strongly encourage interested writers to contact me directly. Although we don't have a blanket rule against unsolicited manuscripts, they are rarely usable. We are a general circulation publication, but we are narrowly focused. A writer not familiar with us would have trouble focusing the story properly, In addition writers may not have a business relationship with the company they are writing about."

FLORIDA TREND, Magazine of Florida Business and Finance, Box 611, St. Petersburg FL 33731. (813)821-5800. Editor and Publisher: Rick Edmonds. Managing Editor: Thomas J. Billitteri. A monthly magazine covering business economics and public policy for Florida business people and investors. Circ. 50,000. Pays on final acceptance. Byline given. Buys first North American serial rights. Computer printout submissions acceptable. Reports in 1 month. Sample copy $2.95.

Nonfiction: Business and finance. Buys 10-12 mss/year. Query with or without published clips. Length: 1,200-2,500 words.

‡GREATER WINNIPEG BUSINESS, Harvard Publishing Co. Ltd., #2, 1835 Sargent, Winnipeg Manitoba R3H 0E2 Canada. (204)783-2681. Editor: Guy R. Rochom. 75% freelance written. Monthly magazine on business trends, strategies and profiles of interest to business owners. Circ. 15,000. Pays on publication. Byline sometimes given. Offers 10% kill fee. Buys first rights. Submit seasonal/holiday material 4 months in advance. Simultaneous, photocopied and previously published submissions OK. Computer printout submissions OK; prefers letter-quality. Reports in 1 month. Sample copy for 9x12 SAE with 1 first class stamp. Free writer's guidelines.

Nonfiction: General interest, how-to maintain cash flow, interview/profile, new product, technical, and travel; strictly Canadian articles. Buys 24 mss/year. Query with published clips. Length: 300-800 words. Pays 5¢/word.

Photos: Send photos with submission. Review contact sheets. Offers $10 per photo. Captions, model releases and identification of subjects required. Buys one-time rights.

Fillers: Facts and newsbreaks. Buys 24/year. Length: 100-300 words. Pays 5¢/word.

‡HAWAII HIGH TECH JOURNAL, East West Magazine Co., Ltd., 832 Halekauwila St., Honolulu HI 96813. (808)538-0934. Editor: Barry Hampe. Publisher: Chris Pearce. 90% freelance written. Quarterly magazine on the high-tech industry in Hawaii; business use of computer technology. "We are covering high-tech projects in Hawaii for a non-technical audience. The writer must *understand* the subject well enough to explain it to a lay person. We want interesting, exciting writing, not dry, technical journal articles." Circ. 5,500. Pays on acceptance. Byline given. Negotiable kill fee. Not copyrighted. Buys first North American serial rights. Submit seasonal/holiday material 6 months in advance. Query for electronic submission. Computer printout submissions OK; prefers letter-quality. Reports in 4 weeks on queries. Sample copy for 9x12 SAE with $1.75 postage. Free writer's guidelines.

Nonfiction: General interest, how-to (optimize computer use in the high-tech workplace), interview profile (of major players in Hawaii's high-tech industry). Buys 20 mss/year. Query with published clips. Length: 1,000-3,000 words. Pays $100-600 for assigned articles. Pays expenses of writers on assignment.

Photos: State availability of photos with submission. Reviews 35mm and up transparencies. Offers $50-200 per photo. Captions, model releases and identification of subjects required.

Columns/Departments: The High Tech Workplace (Development in computer use in business.), 1,000 words; Wrapping It Up (Light [even humorous] essay with a high-tech focus.), 300-400 words and High Tech Notes (Brief industry reports about Hawaii's high-tech industry.), 200 words. Query with published clips. Pays 12¢/word.

Tips: "Be a sponge for facts that you can translate into an exciting query and easy, readable, interesting prose. Be involved in some aspect of the high-tech industry in Hawaii (even if you are on the mainland.) Get out in the field and see what's going on—then tell us about it."

INDIANA BUSINESS, 1000 Waterway Blvd., Indianapolis IN 46202. (317)633-2026. FAX: (317)634-9751. Editor: David Dawson. 50% freelance written. Statewide publication focusing on business in Indiana. "We are a general business publication that reaches 30,000 top executives in Indiana, covering all business categories." Circ. 30,000. Pays 30-60 days after acceptance. Publishes ms an average of 2 months after acceptance. Rights negotiable. Submit seasonal/holiday material 4 months in advance. Photocopied submissions OK. Computer printout double-spaced submissions acceptable. Byline given. Reports in 1 month. Sample copy $2.

Nonfiction: Expose; interview/profile; and opinion. No first person experience stories. "All articles must relate to Indiana business and must be of interest to a broad range of business and professional people." Especially interested in articles on agribusiness, international affairs as they affect Indiana business, executive health issues, new science and technology projects happening in Indiana. "We would like to hear about business success stories but only as they pertain to current issues, trends (i.e., a real estate company that has made it big because they got in on the Economic Development Bonds and invested in renovation property)." Buys 40-50 mss/year. Query. Length: 500-2,500 words. Pay negotiable. Pays expenses of writers on assignment.

Photos: State availability of photos. Reviews contact sheets, negatives, transparencies and 5x7 prints. Pay negotiable for b&w or color photos. Captions, model releases and subject identification required.

Columns/Departments: "Writers need to check with us. We may publish a column once a year or six times a year, and we will consider any business-related subject." Buys 30 mss/year. Query. Length: 1,000-1,500 words. Pays $50-200.

Fillers: Anecdotes and newsbreaks. Length: 125-250 words.

Tips: "Give us a concise query telling us not only why we should run the article but why you should write it. Be sure to indicate available photography or subjects for photography or art. We look first for good ideas. Our readers are sophisticated businessmen who are interested in their peers as well as how they can run their businesses better. We will look at non-business issues if they can be related to business in some way."

MANHATTAN, INC., The Business of New York, Metrocorp. 18th Floor, 420 Lexington Ave., New York NY 10170. (212)697-2100. Editor: Clay S. Felker. A monthly magazine about the business of New York and the people who do business in New York. "*Manhattan, inc.* stories are best told through the narrative of a personality rather than an overview essay. We are most interested in Manhattan-based businesses." Pays on acceptance. Publishes ms an average of 1 month after acceptance. Byline given. Offers 15% kill fee. Buys first North American serial rights. Submit seasonal/holiday material 2 months after acceptance. Query for electronic submissions. Computer printout submissions OK. Reports in 2 months on queries. Sample copy for $3.00.

Nonfiction: Book excerpts, exposé, general interest, historical/nostalgic, how-to, humor, interview/profile, personal experience, photo feature. No general overviews or articles on businesses not related to New York. Buys 100 mss/year. Query with published clips. Length: 500-5,000 words. Pays $250-5,000 for assigned articles. Sometimes pays expenses of writers on assignment.

Photos: State availability of photos with submission. Reviews contact sheets, negatives, transparencies and prints. Offers no additional payment for photos accepted with ms. Captions, model releases and identification of subjects required. Buys one-time rights.

Columns/Departments: Executive Editor: Ken Emerson. On The Books (book reviews—business books), 1,000-2,000 words; Dossier (short glimpses of unusual trends in the business world) 250-1,000 words; Corporate Culture (business of art), 800-3,000 words; Hot Properties (real estate in NY), 1,000-3,000 words; Infrastructure (infrastructure of NY), 1,000-3,000. Buys 50 mss/year. Query with published clips. Length: 1,000-3,000 words. Pays $1,000 minimum.

Fiction: Contact: Judy Daniels. Adventure, condensed novels, experimental, fantasy, historical, horror, humorous, mainstream, mystery, novel excerpts, romance, slice-of-life vignettes, suspense and other. Buys 12 mss/year. Send complete ms. Length: 1,000-5,000 words. Pays $1,000 minimum.

Tips: "Submit writing that has solid reporting behind it. Dossier is the best place to start."

MEMPHIS BUSINESS JOURNAL, Mid-South Communications, Inc., Suite 102, 88 Union, Memphis TN 38103. (901)523-0437. Editor: Barney DuBois. Weekly tabloid covering industry, trade, agribusiness and finance in west Tennessee, north Mississippi, east Arkansas, and the Missouri Bootheel. "Articles should be timely and relevant to business in our region." Circ. 12,500. Pays on acceptance. Byline given. Pays $50 kill fee. Buys one-time rights, and makes work-for-hire assignments. Computer printout submissions acceptable; prefers letter-quality. Free sample copy.
Nonfiction: Exposé, historical/nostalgic, interview/profile, business features and trends. "All must relate to business in our area." Query with or without clips of published work, or send complete ms. Length: 750-2,000 words. Pays $100-250. Sometimes pays the expenses of writers on assignment.
Photos: State availability of photos or send photos with ms. Pays $25-50 for 5x7 b&w prints. Identification of subjects required. Buys one-time rights.
Tips: "We are interested in news—and this means we can accept short, hard-hitting work more quickly. We also welcome freelancers who can do features and articles on business in the smaller cities of our region. We are a weekly, so our stories need to be timely."

‡METRO TORONTO BUSINESS JOURNAL, Business Journal, Metro Toronto Board of Trade, 3 1st Canadian Place 60, Toronto Ontario M5X 1C1 Canada. (416)366-6811. FAX: (416)366-5620. Editor: Peter Carter. Managing Editor: Douglas Bell. 90% freelance written. Monthly magazine on Toronto business. Circ. 46,000. Pays on acceptance. Offers 50% kill fee. Buys first North American serial rights. Computer printout submissions OK; prefers letter-qualtiy. Reports in 2 weeks on queries; 1 week on mss. Free sample copy.
Nonfiction: Book excerpts, essays, exposé, general interest, historical/nostalgic, humor, interview/profile, opinion, personal experience and photo feature. Buys 300 mss/year. Query. Length: 150-3,000 words. Pays $150-2,500 for assigned articles. Sometimes pays expenses of writers on assignment.
Photos: State availability of photos with submission. Reviews contact sheets. Captions required. Buys all rights.
Columns/Departments: City Business (Toronto related, innovative business ideas, personalities), 50-300 words; Landmarks (Toronto business landmarks, historic sites), 900 words; In Progress (changing Toronto landscapes), 900 words. Buys 300 mss/year. Query. Pays $150-500. .

‡MISSISSIPPI BUSINESS JOURNAL, Venture Publications, Box 4566, Jackson MS 39216. (601)352-9035. Editor: Kevin Jones. Managing Editor: Laura Treischmann. 90% freelance written. Monthly magazine. "Our readers are in business in Mississippi or interested in the economy of Mississippi." Circ. 13,500. Pays on publication. Publishes ms an average of 2 months after acceptance. Byline given. Buys one-time rights and makes work-for-hire assignments. Submit seasonal/holiday material 3 months in advance. Simultaneous and previously published submissions OK. Query for electronic submissions. Computer printout submissions OK. Reports in 2 weeks on queries. Sample copy for 9x12 SAE. Writer's guidelines for #10 SAE.
Nonfiction: General interest, how-to and interview/profile. Features on who's getting power, who's losing power, in Mississippi. Buys 100 mss/year. Query with or without published clips, or send complete ms. Length: 1,000-2,000 words. Pays $100-300 for assigned articles. Sometimes pays expenses of writers on assignment.
Photos: State availability of photos with submission. Review contact sheets and transparencies.

‡NOVA SCOTIA BUSINESS JOURNAL, N S Business Publishing Limited, 5426 Portland Pl., Halifax B3K 1A1 Nova Scotia. (902)420-0437. Editor: Bette Tetreault. 25% freelance written. Monthly tabloid. "We are a business to business newspaper, publishing stories to keep provincial businesses aware of what is happening in the province." Circ. 31,000. Pays on publication. Publishes ms an average of 1 month after acceptance. Byline given. Buys first rights. Photocopied submissions OK. Query for electronic submissions. Computer printout submissions OK. Sample copy for 8½x11 SAE with $1 postage. Writer's guidelines for #10 SAE with 1 first class stamp.
Nonfiction: Interview/profile, new product and technical. "Editorial calendar available with writer's guidelines if requested." Buys 120 mss/year. Query with published clips. Length: 150-1,000 words. Pays 10¢/word. Sometimes pays expenses of writers on assignment.
Photos: State availability of photos with submission. Offers no additional payment for photos accepted with ms.

OHIO BUSINESS, Business Journal Publishing Co., 3rd floor, 1720 Euclid Ave., Cleveland OH 44115. (216)621-1644. Editor: Robert W. Gardner. Managing Editor: Michael E. Moore. 10% freelance written. Prefers to work with published/established writers. A monthly magazine covering general business topics. "*Ohio Business* serves the state of Ohio. Readers are business executives in the state engaged in manufacturing, agriculture, mining, construction, transportation, communications, utilities, retail and wholesale trade, services, and government." Circ. 43,000. Pays for features on acceptance; news on publication. Publishes ms an average of 4 months after acceptance. Byline sometimes given. Kill fee can be negotiated. Buys first serial rights; depends on projects. Submit seasonal/holiday material 3-4 months in advance. Simultaneous queries, and simultaneous, photocopied, and previously published submissions OK. Computer printout submissions acceptable; prefers letter-quality. Reports in 2 weeks on queries; 1 month on mss. Sample copy $2; writer's guidelines for SAE and 1 first class stamp.

Nonfiction: Book excerpts, general interest, how-to, interview/profile, opinion and personal experience. "In all cases, write with an Ohio executive in mind. Stories should give readers useful information on business within the state, trends in management, ways to manage better, or other developments which would affect them in their professional careers." Buys 14-20 mss/year. Query with published clips. Length: 800-2,500 words. Pays $100 minimum. Sometimes pays expenses of writers on assignment.

Photos: State availability of photos. Reviews b&w and color transparencies and prints. Captions and identification of subjects required. Buys variable rights.

Columns/Departments: News; People (profiles of Ohio business execs); High-Tech (leading edge Ohio products and companies); Made in Ohio (unusual Ohio product/services). Query with published clips. Length: 100-600 words. Pay varies.

Tips: "Features are most open to freelancers. Come up with new ideas or information for our readers: Ohio executives in manufacturing and service industries. Writers should be aware of the trend toward specialization in magazine publishing with strong emphasis on people in coverage."

OREGON BUSINESS, Media America Publications, Suite 500, 208 SW Stark, Portland OR 97204. (503)223-0304. Editor: Robert Hill. 60% freelance written. Works with a small number of new/unpublished writers each year. Monthly magazine covering business in Oregon. Circ. 20,000. Pays on publication. Publishes ms an average of 4 months after acceptance. Byline given. Buys first rights. Submit seasonal/holiday material 3 months in advance. Photocopied and previously published submissions OK. Computer printout submissions acceptable; prefers letter-quality. Reports in 1 month. Sample copy for 9x12 SAE and 5 first class stamps.

Nonfiction: General interest (real estate, business, investing, small business); interview/profile (business leaders); and new products. Special issues include tourism, world trade, finance. "We need articles on real estate or small business in Oregon, outside the Portland area." Buys 50 mss/year. Query with published clips. Length: 900-2,000 words. Pays 10¢/word minimum; $200 maximum. Sometimes pays expenses of writers on assignment.

ORLANDO MAGAZINE, Orlando Media Affiliates, Box 2207, Suite 290, 341 N. Maitland Ave., Orlando FL 32802. (407)539-3939. 50% freelance written. Monthly magazine covering city growth, development, trends, entertainment. "We use first-person experiential pieces on subjects of interest to people in central Florida. Our business, personality and trends stories are staff written." Circ. 35,000. Pays on acceptance. Publishes ms an average of 2 months after acceptance. Byline given. Offers negotiable kill fee. Submit seasonal/holiday material 3 months in advance. Simultaneous and photocopied submissions OK. Computer printout submissions OK. Reports in 3 weeks. Free sample copy and writer's guidelines.

Nonfiction: Exposé, how-to (business, and interview. Buys 60 mss/year. Send complete ms. Length: 1,000-2,500 words. Pays $50-350 for assigned articles.

Photos: State availability of photos with submission. Reviews transparencies. Offers $5 per photo. Captions and identification of subjects required. Buys one-time rights.

Columns/Departments: Media, Medicine, Sports and Arts. Length: 1,200-1,500. Buys 24 mss/year. Pays $100-150.

Fillers: Newsbreaks. "Have a well-researched query. Give me a call; I'll answer the phone, but be prepared." Buys 36/year. Length: 100-500 words. Pays $25-50.

‡REGARDIES: THE MAGAZINE OF WASHINGTON BUSINESS, 1010 Wisconsin Ave., NW, Washington DC 20007. (202)342-0410. Editor: Brian Kelly. 80% freelance written. Works with a small number of new/unpublished writers each year. Monthly magazine covering business and general features in the Washington DC metropolitan area for Washington business executives. Circ. 60,000. Pays within 30 days after publication. Publishes ms an average of 2 months after acceptance. Byline given. Offers variable kill fee. Buys first serial rights and second serial (reprint) rights. Computer printout submissions acceptable; prefers letter-quality. Submit seasonal/holiday material 3 months in advance. Reports in 3 weeks. Sample copy for $8 and 9x12 SAE.

Nonfiction: Profiles (of business leaders), investigative reporting, real estate, advertising, politics, lifestyle, media, retailing, communications, labor issues, and financial issues — all on the Washington business scene. "If it is the kind of story that could just as easily run in a city magazine or a national magazine like *Harper's*, *Atlantic*, *Esquire*, etc., I don't want to see it." Also buys book mss for excerpt. No how-to. Narrative nonfiction only. Buys 90 mss/year. Length: 4,000 words average. Buys 5-6/issue. Pays negotiable rate. Pays the expenses of writers on assignment.

Columns/Departments: Length: 1,500 words average. Buys 8-12/issue. Pays negotiable rates.

Tips: "The most frequent mistake writers make is not including enough information and data about business which, with public companies, is easy enough to find. This results in flawed analysis and a willingness to accept the 'official line.' "

‡SACRAMENTO BUSINESS JOURNAL, MCP, Inc., 2030 J St., Sacramento CA 95814. (916)447-7661. Editor: Lee Wessman. Managing Editor: Beth Davis 20% freelance written. Weekly tabloid. "Insightful and timely coverage of events that affect business and economics in the Sacramento region, and of how business and economics help shape the region itself."Circ. 48,000. Pays on publication. Byline given. Offers 25% kill fee. Buys first rights and second serial (reprint) rights. Submit seasonal/holiday material 2 months in advance. Computer printout submissions OK. Reports in 2 weeks on queries. Sample copy $1.

Nonfiction: Exposé, interview/profile (business or political figures), and opinion (on current events.) Special report stories on business trends are done on assignment. Yearly special report calendars are available upon request. Buys 100 mss/year. Query with published clips. Length: 750-2,000 words. Pays $75-300 for assigned articles; $50-125 for unsolicited articles. Sometimes pays expenses of writers on assignment.

Photos: State availability of photos with submission. Reviews contact sheets, 35mm transparencies, and 5x7 prints. Offers $25-50 per photo. Captions and identification of subjects required.

Columns/Departments: Another Voice (opinion on current events), 750-1,000 words; Personal Finance (investment or tax advice), 750-1,000 words ; Management (tips on managing people or companies), 750-1,000 words. Buys 25 mss/year. Query with published clips. Pays $50-75.

Tips: "Most freelance work is on assignment and we like our freelancers to work closely with assignment editors as they go about reporting and structuring a story. We seek a small, stable pool of quality freelancers from the region who can tackle two or three stories a month. Send résumés clips, follow up with phone call, interview. Our weekly special reports use 4-7 freelance stories each. We want them in a journalistic style modeled after *The Wall Street Journal*. There's a two week turnaround on each assignment. Writers must be good at research and interviewing. We also assign 100-page projects to top freelancers, that pay in neighborhood of $1,500-3,000."

SEATTLE BUSINESS, Vernon Publications, Suite 200, 3000 Northup Way, Bellevue WA 98004. (206)827-9900. Editorial Director: Roberta S. Lang. Editor: Michele Andrus Dill. 20% freelance written. Monthly magazine covering business news in Greater Seattle area. "Articles must pertain to concerns of Seattle businesses, emphasis on local, not national." Circ. 9,000. Publishes ms an average of 3 months after acceptance. Byline given. Buys all rights. Simultaneous and photocopied submissions OK. Computer printout submissions OK; prefers letter quality. Reports only on submissions used. Sample copy for 9x12 SAE with 54¢ postage; writer's guidelines for #10 SASE.

Nonfiction: Expose, general interest, how-to (succeed in business, be more efficient, increase profitability, etc.), humor, interview/profile, opinion, technical. Buys 5 mss/year. Query. Length: 500-2,000 words. Pays $100-250. Sometimes pays expenses of writers on assignment.

Photos: State availability of photos with submission. Reviews contact sheets, prints. Offers no additional payment for photos accepted with ms. Identification of subjects required. Buys one-time rights.

Tips: "We are interested in any feature-length (1,200-2,000 words) submission on some aspect of business in Seattle area. It is best to query first; freelancer would do well to obtain a copy of our editorial calendar and use that as a guide."

VERMONT BUSINESS MAGAZINE, Manning Publications, Inc., Brattleboro Professional Center, Box 6120, Brattleboro VT 05301. (802)257-4100. FAX: (802)257-5266. Editor: Robert W. Lawson. 80% freelance written. A monthly tabloid covering business in Vermont. Circ. 15,000. Pays on publication. Publishes ms an average of 1 month after acceptance. Byline given. Offers $50-full payment kill fee. Not copyrighted. Buys one-time rights. Simultaneous submissions OK. Query for electronic submissions. Computer printout submissions acceptable. Free sample copy.

Nonfiction: Business trends and issues. Buys 200 mss/year. Query with published clips. Length: 800-1,800 words. Pays $50-150. Pays the expenses of writers on assignment.

Photos: Send photos with submission. Reviews contact sheets. Offers $5-15 per photo. Identification of subjects required.

Tips: "Read daily papers and look for business angles for a follow-up article. We look for issue and trend articles rather than company or businessman profiles. Note: Magazine accepts Vermont-specific material *only*. The articles *must* be about Vermont."

‡VICTORIA'S BUSINESS REPORT, Monday Publications Ltd., 1609 Blanshard St., Victoria BC V8W 2J5 Canada. (604)382-7777. FAX: (604)381-2662. Editor: Norman Gidney. 20% freelance written. Monthly magazine that covers Vancouver Island business. "*Victoria's Business Report* is small business-oriented and focuses on Victoria and southern Vancouver Island." Pays on publication. Publishes ms an average of 1-2 months after acceptance. Byline given. Buys first North American serial rights. Simultaneous, photocopied submissions and previously published submissions OK. Query for electronic submisions. Computer printout submissions OK. Reports in 3 weeks on queries. Sample copy $2.75.

Nonfiction: Length: 500-3,000 words. Pays $75-400 for assigned articles. Sometimes pays expenses of writers on assignment.

Photos: State availability of photos with submission. Offers $10-35 per photo. Captions and identification of subjects required. Buys one-time rights.

WESTERN INVESTOR, Western States Investment Information, Willamette Publishing, Inc., Suite 1115, 400 SW 6th Ave., Portland OR 97204. (503)222-0577. FAX: (503)222-7392. Editor-In-Chief and Publisher: S.P. Pratt. Managing Editor: Kate Alley. 50% freelance written. Quarterly magazine for the investment community of the 13 western states. For stock brokers, corporate officers, financial analysts, trust officers, CPAs, investors, etc. Circ. 13,000. Pays on publication. Publishes ms an average of 6 months after acceptance. Byline given. Buys one-time and second serial (reprint) rights and makes work-for-hire assignments. Simultaneous queries and simultaneous, photocopied and previously published submissions OK. Computer submissions acceptable; prefers letter-quality. Sample copy for 8½x11 SAE and $2.40 postage; free writer's guidelines.

Nonfiction: General business interest ("trends, people, public, listed in our Investment Data Section"). "Each issue carries a particular industry theme." Query. Length: 200-2,000 words. Pays $50 minimum.

Photos: State availability of photos. Pays $10 minimum for 5x7 (or larger) b&w prints. Buys one-time rights.

Tips: "All editorial copy must pertain or directly relate to companies and/or industry groups included in our listed companies. Send us a one-page introduction including your financial writing background, story ideas, availability for assignment work, credits, etc. What we want at this point is a good working file of authors to draw from; let us know your special areas of interest and expertise. Newspaper business-page writers would be good candidates. If you live and work in the West, so much the better."

WESTERN NEW YORK MAGAZINE, Greater Buffalo Chamber Services Corporation, 107 Delaware Ave., Buffalo NY 14202. (716)852-7100. Editor: J. Patrick Donlon. 10% freelance written. Monthly magazine of the Buffalo-Niagara Falls-Southern Ontario area. "Tells the story of Buffalo and Western New York, balancing business with quality-of-life topics" Circ. 8,000. Pays on acceptance. Publishes ms an average of 3 months after acceptance. Byline given. Offers $150 kill fee. Not copyrighted. Buys all rights. Submit seasonal/holiday material 3 months in advance. Simultaneous queries OK. Computer printout submissions acceptable; no dot-matrix. Reports in 1 month. Sample copy for $2, 9x12 SAE and 3 first class stamps; writer's guidelines for #10 SASE.

Nonfiction: General interest (business, finance, commerce); historical/nostalgic (Buffalo, Niagara Falls); how-to (business management); interview/profile (community leader); and Western New York industry, quality of life. "Broad-based items preferred over single firm or organization. Submit articles that provide insight into business operations, marketing, finance, promotion, and nuts-and-bolts approach to small business management. No nationwide or even New York statewide articles or pieces on specific companies, products, services." Buys 30 mss/year. Query with published clips. Length: 1,000-2,500 words. Pays $150-300. Sometimes pays the expenses of writers on assignment.

Photos: Pamela Mills, art director. State availability of photos. Reviews contact sheets. Pays $10-25 for 5x7 b&w prints.

Career, College and Alumni

Three types of magazines are listed in this section: university publications written for students, alumni and friends of a specific institution; publications about college life for students; and publications on career and job opportunities. A number of national campus magazines have gone out of business during the past year, including *Newsweek on Campus*, *Business Week Careers* and Whittle Communications' *Campus Voice*. Several others have stepped in to try to fill the gap, including an annual magazine on spring breaks called *Breaker's Guide '90*, and others have turned to wall media (oversize posters with articles, graphics and advertising) to attract student interest.

AIM, A Resource Guide for Vocational/Technical Graduates, Communications Publishing Group, 3100 Broadway, 225 PennTower, Kansas City MO 64111. (816)756-3039. Editor: Georgia Clark. 40% freelance written. A quarterly educational and career source guide "designed to assist experienced voc/tech students in their search for career opportunities and aid in improving their life survival skills. For Black and Hispanic young adults — ages 21-35." Circ. 350,000. Pays on acceptance. Byline sometimes given. Buys second serial (reprint) rights or makes work-for-hire assignments. Submit seasonal/holiday material 6 months in advance. Simultaneous, photocopied and previously published submissions OK. Computer printout submissions OK; prefers letter-quality. Reports in 2 months. Sample copy for 9x10 SAE with 4 first class stamps. Writer's guidelines for #10 SASE.

Nonfiction: Book excerpts or reviews, general interest, how-to (dealing with careers or education), humor, inspirational, interview/profile (celebrity or "up and coming" young adult), new product (as it relates to young adult market), personal experience, photo feature, technical, travel. Query or send complete ms.

278 Writer's Market '90

Length: 750-3,000 words. Pays $150-400 for assigned articles; 10¢/word for unsolicited articles. Sometimes pays expenses of writers on assignment.

Photos: State availability of photos with submission. Prefers transparencies. Offers $10-50/photo. Captions, model releases and identification of subjects required. Buys all rights.

Columns/Departments: Profiles of Achievement (striving and successful minority young adult ages 21-35 in various technical careers). Buys 15 mss/year. Send complete ms. Length: 500-1,000 words. Pays $50-250.

Fiction: Adventure, ethnic, historical, humorous, mainstream, slice-of-life vignettes. Buys 3 mss/year. Send complete ms. Length: 1,000-5,000 words. Pays $100-400.

Poetry: Free verse. Buys 5 poems/year. Submit up to 5 poems at one time. Length: 10-25 lines. Pays $10-50.

Fillers: Anecdotes, facts, gags to be illustrated by cartoonist, newsbreaks, short humor. Buys 10/year. Length: 25-250 words. Pays $25-100.

Tips: "For new writers, submit full manuscript that is double spaced; clean copy only. Include on first page of manuscript your name, address, phone, Social Security Number and number of words in article. Need to have clippings of previous published works and resume. Resume should tell when available to write. Most open are profiles of successful and striving Black or Hispanic young adult (age 21-35). Include photo."

ALCALDE, Box 7278, Austin TX 78713. (512)471-3799. FAX: (512)471-8832. Editor: Ernestine Wheelock. 20% freelance written. Works with a small number of new/unpublished writers each year. Bimonthly magazine. Circ. 48,000. Pays on publication. Publishes an average of 6 months after acceptance. Buys all rights. Submit seasonal/holiday material 5 months in advance. Query for electronic submissions. Computer printout submission OK; prefers letter-quality. Reports in 1 month. Sample copy 8½×11 and 90¢ postage. Writer's guidelines for #10 SASE.

Nonfiction: General interest; historical (University of Texas, research and faculty profile); humor (humorous Texas subjects); nostalgia (University of Texas traditions); profile (students, faculty, alumni); and technical (University of Texas research on a subject or product). No subjects lacking taste or quality, or not connected with the University of Texas. Buys 12 mss/year. Query. Length: 1,000-2,400 words. Pays according to importance of article.

THE BLACK COLLEGIAN, The National Magazine of Black College Students, Black Collegiate Services, Inc., 1240 S. Broad St., New Orleans LA 70125. (504)821-5694. FAX: (504)821-5113. Editor: K. Kazi-Ferrouillet. 25% freelance written. Magazine for black college students and recent graduates with an interest in career and job information, black cultural awareness, sports, news, personalities, history, trends and current events. Published bimonthly during school year; (4 times/year). Circ. 121,000. Buys one-time rights. Byline given. Pays on publication. Computer printout submissions OK; prefers letter quality. Submit seasonal and special interest material 2 months in advance of issue date (Careers, September; Computers/Grad School and Travel/summer programs, November; Engineering and Black History programs, January; finance and jobs, March). Reports in 3 weeks on queries; 1 month on mss. Sample copy for 9x12 SAE and $4. Writer's guidelines for #10 SASE.

Nonfiction: Material on careers, sports, black history, news analysis. Articles on problems and opportunities confronting black college students and recent graduates. Book excerpts, exposé, general interest, historical/nostalgic, how-to (develop employability), opinion, personal experience, profile, inspirational, humor. Buys 40 mss/year (6 unsolicited). Query with published clips or send complete ms. Length: 500-1,500 words. Pays $25-350.

Photos: State availability of photos with query or ms, or send photos with query or ms. B&w photos or color transparencies purchased with or without ms. 8x10 prints preferred. Captions, model releases and identification of subjects required. Pasy $35/b&w; $50/color.

Tips: "Career features area is most open to freelancers."

‡BREAKER'S GUIDE '90, OP Publishing, Inc., 1143 S. Semoran Blvd., Winter Park FL 32792. (407)679-1906. Editor: Andrew Owens. Managing Editor: Brad Partridge. 33% freelance written. Annual magazine on spring breaks. Circ. 105,000. Pays on acceptance. Publishes ms an average of 1 month after acceptance. Byline given. Offers 25% kill fee. Buys simultaneous rights. Simultaneous and previously published submissions OK. Query for electronic submissions. Computer printout submissions OK; prefers letter-quality. Free sample copy and writer's guidelines.

Nonfiction: General interest, historical/nostalgic, how-to, humor, inspirational, interview/profile, new product, opinion, personal experience, photo feature and travel. Buys 2 mss/year. Query with or without published clips, or send complete ms. Length: 500-2,500. Pays $300 for assigned articles; $250 for unsolicited articles. Sometimes pays expenses of writers on assignment.

Photos: State availibity of photos with submission. Captions, model releases and identification of subjects required. Buys all rights.

Columns/Departments: Inside Cities (native look at what to do, where to go); Interview (with interesting, contemporary personality) and Features (humorous, interesting, relevant). Buys 4 mss/year. Query. Length: 500-2,500 words. Pays $300 maximum.

Fiction: Adventure, experimental, fantasy, historical, humorous, mystery, romance, science fiction and suspense. Buys 2-3 mss/year. Query. Length: 500-2,500 words. Pays $300 maximum.

Poetry: Free verse, light verse and traditional. Length: 1,000 lines maximum.

Fillers: Anecdotes, facts, gags to be illustrated by cartoonist, newsbreaks and short humor. Length: 1,000 words. Pays $150 maximum.

Tips: "Submit articles that today's college market would find interesting and entertaining; as well as travel information for the young at heart."

CAREER FOCUS, For Today's Professional, Communications Publishing Group, Inc., Suite 225, 3100 Broadway, Kansas City MO 64111. (816)756-3039. Editor: Georgia Clark. 40% freelance written. Bimonthly magazine "devoted to providing positive insight, information, guidance and motivation to assist Black and Hispanics (ages 21-35) in their career development and attainment of goals." Estab. 1988. Circ. 750,000. Pays on acceptance. Byline given often. Buys second serial (reprint) rights and makes work-for-hire assignments. Submit seasonal/holiday material 6 months in advance. Simultaneous, photocopied and previously published submissions OK. Computer printout submissions OK. Reports in 2 months. Sample copy for 9x12 SAE and 4 first class stamps; writer's guidelines for #10 SASE.

Nonfiction: Book excerpts, general interest, historical, how-to, humor, inspirational, interview/profile, personal experience, photo feature, technical, travel. Length: 750-3,000 words. Pays $150-400 for assigned articles; pays 10¢/word for unsolicited articles. Sometimes pays expenses of writers on assignment.

Photos: State availability of photos with submission. Reviews transparencies. Pays $10-50. Captions, model releases and identification of subjects required. Buys all rights.

Columns/Departments: Profiles (striving and successful Black and Hispanic young adult, ages 21-35). Buys 15 mss/year. Send complete ms. Length: 500-1,000 words. Pays $50-250.

Fiction: Adventure, ethnic, historical, humorous, mainstream, slice-of-life vignettes. Buys 3 mss/year. Send complete ms. Length: 1,500-5,000 words. Pays $100-400.

Poetry: Free verse. Buys 4 poems/year. Length: 10-25 lines. Pays $10-50.

Fillers: Anecdotes, facts, gags to be illustrated by cartoonist, newsbreaks, short humor. Buys 10/year. Length: 25-250 words. Pays $25-100.

Tips: "For new writers: Submit full manuscript that is double-spaced; clean copy only. Need to have clippings and previously published works and resume. Should also tell when available to write. Most open to freelancers are profiles of successful and striving person including photo. Profile must be of a Black or Hispanic adult living in the U.S. Include on first page of manuscript your name, address phone, Social Security number, and number of words in article."

‡CAREER VISION, The College Magazine, Career Vision, 600 Madison Ave., 14th Floor, New York NY 10020. (212)755-4800. Editor: Marion L. Salzman. Managing Editor: Madeline Hutcheson. 80% freelance written. Quarterly magazine covering careers and lifestyle for college students. "We are a cross between *Folio, Rolling Stone* and *Sassy*—upbeat editorial about the real world for college students." Estab. 1988. Circ. 1.2 million. Pays on acceptance. Publishes ms an average of 6 months after acceptance. Byline given. Offers 25% kill fee. Buys second serial or all rights. Submit seasonal/holiday material 6 months in advance. Simultaneous and previously published submissions OK. Computer printout submissions OK; prefers letter-quality. Reports in 2 weeks on queries; 3 weeks on ms. Free sample copy and writer's guidelines.

Nonfiction: Book excerpts, essays, expose, general interest, how-to, humor, interview/profile, new product, personal experience, photo feature and travel. Buys 40 mss/year. Query with published clips. Length: 1,000-3,000 words. Pays $1,000-2,500 for assigned articles; $500-2,500 for unsolicited articles. Pays expenses of writers on assignment.

Photos: State availability of photos with submission. Reviews contact sheets. Offers $50-500 per photo. Model releases and identification of subjects required. Buys one-time or all rights.

Tips: "We are anxious to find young freelancers in out-of-the-way locations, as well as in cities outside the Northeast. Further, we look for writers with new angles on old subjects such as the job hunt, breaking away from your parents, college living, life after graduation, etc."

CARNEGIE MELLON MAGAZINE, Carnegie Mellon University, Pittsburgh PA 15213. (412)268-6967. Editor: Ann Curran. Alumni publication issued fall, winter, spring, summer covering university activities, alumni profiles, etc. Circ. 52,000. Pays on acceptance. Byline given. Not copyrighted. Reports in 1 month.

Nonfiction: Book reviews (faculty alumni), general interest, humor, interview/profile, photo feature, "We use general interest stories linked to CMU activities and research." No unsolicited mss. Buys 5 features and 5-10 alumni profiles/year. Query with published clips. Length: 800-2,000 words. Pays $100-400 or negotiable rate. Sample copy for 9x12 SAE and $2 postage.

Poetry: Avant-garde or traditional. No previously published poetry. No payment.

Tips: "Concentration is given to professional writers among alumni."

CIRCLE K MAGAZINE, 3636 Woodview Trace, Indianapolis IN 46268. FAX: (317)879-0204. Executive Editor: Nicholas K. Drake. 60% freelance written. "Our readership consists almost entirely of above-average college students interested in voluntary community service and leadership development. They are politically and socially aware and have a wide range of interests." Publishes 5 times/year. Circ. 10,000. Pays on acceptance. Normally buys first North American serial rights. Byline given. Submit seasonal/holiday material 6 months in advance. Computer printout submissions OK; no dot-matrix. Reports in 1 month. Sample copy and writer's guidelines for large SAE with 3 first class stamps.

Nonfiction: Articles published in *Circle K* are of two types—serious and light nonfiction. "We are interested in general interest articles on topics concerning college students and their lifestyles, as well as articles dealing with community concerns and leadership development." No "first person confessions, family histories, or travel pieces." Query. Length: 2,000-2,500 words. Pays $200-300.

Photos: Purchased with accompanying ms. Captions required. Total purchase price for ms includes payment for photos.

Tips: "Query should indicate author's familiarity with the field and sources. Subject treatment must be objective and in-depth, and articles should include illustrative examples and quotes from persons involved in the subject or qualified to speak on it. We are open to working with new writers who present a good article idea and demonstrate that they've done their homework concerning the article subject itself, as well as concerning our magazine's style. We're interested in college-oriented trends i.e., Entrepreneur schooling now a major shift; more awareness of college crime; health issues."

COLLEGE MONTHLY, New England, Lapierre & Associates, Suite 805, 332 Main St., Worcester MA 01608. (508)253-2550. Editor: Maureen Castillo. Managing Editor: Randy Cohen. 25% freelance written. College lifestyle and entertainment magazine published 8 times/year. Circ. 73,000. Pays on publication. Byline given. Offers $5 kill fee. Buys one-time rights. Query for electronic submissions. Computer printout submissions OK. Free sample copy and writer's guidelines.

Nonfiction: Humor, interview/profile, opinion, personal experience and travel. Query with published clips. Length: 500-2,000 words. Pays $25-100 for assigned articles; $5-25 for unsolicited articles. Sometimes pays the expenses of writers on assignment.

Photos: State availability of photos with submission. Offers no additional payment for photos accepted with ms. Caption required. Buys one-time rights.

Columns/Departments: Fashion (trends in the college market for clothes); Lifestyle (off-the-wall things students do); Sports (national sports and college); Politics (national level/hot social issues), all 500-750 words.

Fillers: Newsbreaks, short humor. Length: 100 words. Pays $5-25.

COLLEGE PREVIEW, A Guide for College-Bound Students, Communications Publishing Group, 3100 Broadway, 225 PennTower, Kansas City MO 64111. (816)756-3039. Editor: Georgia Clark. 40% freelance written. A quarterly educational and career source guide. "Contemporary guide is designed to inform and motivate Black and Hispanic young adults, ages 16-21 years old about college preparation, career planning and life survival skills." Circ. 600,000. Pays on acceptance. Byline often given. Buys second serial (reprint) rights or makes work-for-hire assignments. Submit seasonal/holiday material 6 months in advance. Simultaneous, photocopied and previously published submissions OK. Computer printout submissions OK; prefers letter-quality. Reports in 2 months. Sample copy for 9x10 SAE with 4 first class stamps. Writer's guidelines for #10 SASE.

Nonfiction: Book excerpts or reviews, general interest, how-to (dealing with careers or education), humor, inspirational, interview/profile (celebrity or "up and coming" young adult), new product (as it relates to young adult market), personal experience, photo feature, technical, travel. Send complete ms. Length: 750-3,000 words. Pays $150-400 for assigned articles; 10¢/word for unsolicited articles. Sometimes pays expenses of writers on assignment.

Photos: State availability of photos with submission. Reviews transparencies. Offers $10-$50/photo. Captions, model releases and identification of subjects required. Buys all rights.

Columns/Departments: Profiles of Achievement (striving and successful minority young adult ages 16-35 in various careers). Buys 15 mss/year. Send complete ms. Length: 500-1,500. Pays $50-250.

Fiction: Adventure, ethnic, historical, humorous, mainstream, slice-of-life vignettes. Buys 3 mss/year. Send complete ms. Length: 1,000-5,000 words. Pays $100-400.

Poetry: Free verse. Buys 5 poems/year. Submit up to 5 poems at one time. Length: 10-25 lines. Pays $10-50.

Fillers: Anecdotes, facts, gags to be illustrated by cartoonist, newsbreaks, short humor. Buys 10/year. Length: 25-250 words. Pasy $25-100.

Tips: For new writers—Send complete manuscript that is double spaced; clean copy only. If available, send clippings of previous published works and resume. Should state when available to write. Include on first page of manuscript your name, address, phone, Social Security number and word count.

COLLEGIATE CAREER WOMAN, For Career-Minded Women, Equal Opportunity Publications, Inc., 44 Broadway, Greenlawn NY 11740. (516)261-8917. FAX: (516)261-8935. Editor: Anne Kelly. 80% freelance written. Works with small number of new/unpublished writers each year. Magazine published 3 times/year (fall, winter, spring) covering career-guidance for college women. Strives to "aid women in developing career abilities to the fullest potential; improve job hunting skills; present career opportunities; provide personal resources; help cope with discrimination." Audience is 92% college juniors and seniors; 8% working graduates. Circ. 10,500. Controlled circulation, distributed through college guidance and placement offices. Pays on publication. Publishes ms an average of 3-12 months after acceptance. Byline given. Buys all rights. Simultaneous queries and submissions OK. Computer printout submissions OK; no dot-matrix. Sample copy and writer's guidelines for 9x12 SAE with 5 first class stamps.
Nonfiction: "We want career-related articles describing for a college-educated woman the how-tos of obtaining a professional position and advancing her career." Looks for practical features detailing self-evaluation techniques, the job-search process, and advice for succeeding on the job. Emphasizes role-model profiles of successful career women. Needs manuscripts presenting information on professions offering opportunities to young women—especially the growth professions of the future. Special issues emphasize career opportunities for women in fields such as health care, communications, sales, marketing, banking, insurance, finance, science, engineering, and computers as well as opportunities in government, military and defense. Query first.
Photos: Send with ms. Prefers 35mm color slides, but will accept b&w prints. Captions and identification of subjects required. Buys all rights.
Tips: "Articles should focus on career-guidance, role model, and industry prospects for women and should have a snappy, down-to-earth writing style."

DIRECTIONS, A Guide to Career Alternatives, Communications Publishing Group, 3100 Broadway, 225 PennTower, Kansas City MO 64111. (816)756-3039. Editor: Georgia Clark. 40% freelance written. A quarterly magazine that focuses on evaluating career possibilities and enhancement of life survival skills for Black and Hispanic young adults, ages 18-25. Circ. 500,000. Pays on acceptance. Byline often given. Buys second serial (reprint) rights or makes work-for-hire assignments. Submit seasonal/holiday material 6 months in advance. Simultaneous, photocopied and previously published submissions OK. Computer printout submissions OK; prefers letter-quality. Reports in 2 months. Sample copy for 9x12 SAE with 4 first class stamps. Writer's guidelines for #10 SASE.
Nonfiction: Book excerpts or reviews, general interest, how-to (dealing with careers or education), humor, inspirational, interview/profile (celebrity or "up and coming" young adult), new product (as it relates to young adult market), personal experience, photo feature, technical, travel. Send complete ms. Length: 750-3,000 words. Pays $150-400 for assigned articles; 10¢/word for unsolicited articles. Sometimes pays expenses of writers on assignment.
Photos: State availability of photos with submission. Reviews transparencies. Offers $10-50/photo. Captions, model releases and identification of subjects required. Buys all rights.
Columns/Departments: Profiles of Achievement (striving and successful minority young adult age 16-35 in various careers). Buys 15 mss/year. Send complete ms. Length: 500-1,500. Pays $50-250.
Fiction: Adventure, ethnic, historical, humorous, mainstream, slice-of-life vignettes. Buys 3 mss/year. Send complete ms. Length: 1,000-5,000 words. Pays $100-400.
Poetry: Free verse. Buys 5 poems/year. Submit up to 5 poems at one time. Length: 10-25 lines. Pays $10-50.
Fillers: Anecdotes, facts, gags to be illustrated by cartoonist, newsbreaks, short humor. Buys 10/year. Length: 25-250 words. Pays $25-100.
Tips: "For new writers—Send complete manuscript that is double spaced; clean copy only. If available, send clippings of previous published works and resume. Should state when available to write. Must include on first page of ms—name, address, phone, Social Security and number of words in article."

EQUAL OPPORTUNITY, The Nation's Only Multi-Ethnic Recruitment Magazine for Black, Hispanic, Native American & Asian American College Grads, Equal Opportunity Publications, Inc., 44 Broadway, Greenlawn NY 11740. (516)261-8917. FAX: (516)261-8935. Editor: James Schneider. 50% freelance written. Prefers to work with published/established writers. Magazine published 3 times/year (fall, winter, spring) covering career guidance for minorities. "Our audience is 90% college juniors and seniors; 10% working graduates. An understanding of educational and career problems of minorities is essential." Circ. 15,000. Controlled circulation, distributed through college guidance and placement offices. Pays on publication. Publishes ms an average of 2 months after acceptance. Byline given. Buys all rights. Deadline dates: fall, June 15; winter, August 15: spring, November 1. Simultaneous queries and simultaneous, photocopied and previously published submissions OK. Computer printout submissions OK; prefers letter-quality. Sample copy and writer's guidelines for 9x12 SAE and 5 first class stamps.
Nonfiction: Book excerpts and articles (on job search techniques, role models), general interest (on specific minority concerns), how-to (on job-hunting skills, personal finance, better living, coping with discrimination); humor (student or career related), interview/profile (minority role models), opinion (problems of minorities),

personal experience (professional and student study and career experiences), technical (on career fields offering opportunities for minorities), travel (on overseas job opportunities), and coverage of Black, Hispanic, Native American and Asian American interests. Special issues include career opportunities for minorities in industry and government in fields such as banking, insurance, finance, communications, sales, marketing, engineering, computers, military and defense. Query or send complete ms. Length: 1,000-2,000 words. Sometimes pays expenses of writers on assignment. Pays 10¢/word.

Photos: Prefers 35mm color slides and b&w. Captions and identification of subjects required. Buys all rights at $15 per photo use.

Tips: "Articles must be geared toward questions and answers faced by minority and women students."

ETC MAGAZINE, Student Media—University of North Carolina at Charlotte, Cone University Center UNCC, Charlotte NC 28223. (704)547-2146. Editor: Bill Hartley. Managing Editor: Linda Culbertson. 90% freelance written. A sëmiannual magazine on collegiate lifestyle. "*Etc. Magazine* is a student publication serving the University of North Carolina at Charlotte that features general interest articles dealing with collegiate lifestyles." Circ. 5,000. Pays on publication. Byline given. Buys one-time rights. Submit seasonal/holiday material 6 months in advance. Photocopied submissions and previously published material OK. Computer printout submissions OK. Reports in 6 months. Free sample copy and writer's guidelines.

Nonfiction: General interest, historical/nostalgic, how-to, humor, interview/profile, personal experience, photo feature, travel. Special issues: freshman orientation issue and graduate section. Send complete ms. Length: 500-2,500 words. Pays $10 minimum. Sometimes pays expenses of writers on assignment.

Photos: State availability of photos with submission or send photos with submission.

FIRST OPPORTUNITY, A Guide for Vocational/Technical Students, Communications Publishing Group, 3100 Broadway, 225 PennTower, Kansas City MO 64111. (816)756-3039. Editor: Georgia Clark. 40% freelance written. A quarterly resource publication focuses on advanced voc/tech educational opportunities and career preparation for Black and Hispanic young adults, ages 16-21. Circ. 500,000. Pays on acceptance. Byline sometimes given. Buys second serial (reprint) rights or makes work-for-hire assignments. Submit seasonal/holiday material 6 months in advance. Simultaneous, photocopied and previously published submissions OK. Computer printout submissions OK; prefers letter-quality. Reports in 2 months. Sample copy for 9x12 SAE with 4 first class stamps. Writer's guidelines for #10 SASE.

Nonfiction: Book excerpts or reviews, general interest, how-to (dealing with careers or education), humor, inspirational, interview/profile (celebrity or "up and coming" young adult), new product (as it relates to young adult market), personal experience, photo feature, technical, travel. Length: 750-3,000 words. Pays $150-400 for assigned articles; 10¢/word for unsolicited articles. Sometimes pays expenses of writers on assignment.

Photos: State availability of photos with submission. Prefers transparencies. Offers $10-50/photo. Captions, model releases and identification of subjects required. Buys all rights.

Columns/Departments: Profiles of Achievement (striving and successful minority young adult, age 16-35 in various vocational or technical careers). Buys 15 mss/year. Send complete ms. Length: 500-1,500. Pays $50-250.

Fiction: Adventure, ethnic, historical, humorous, mainstream, slice-of-life vignettes. Buys 3 mss/year. Send complete ms. Length: 1,000-5,000 words. Pays $100-400.

Poetry: Free verse. Buys 5 poems/year. Submit up to 5 poems at one time. Length: 10-25 lines. Pays $10-50.

Fillers: Anecdotes, facts, gags to be illustrated by cartoonist, newsbreaks, short humor. Buys 10/year. Length: 25-250 words. Pays $25-100.

Tips: For new writers—Send complete manuscript that is double spaced; clean copy only. If available, send clippings of previous published works and resume. Should state when available to write. Include on first page your name, address, phone, Social Security number and number of words in article.

FLORIDA LEADER, Box 14081, Gainesville FL 32604. (904)373-6907. Publisher: W.H. "Butch" Oxendine, Jr. Editor: Christine Lenyo. Nearly 40% freelance written. "Florida's college magazine, feature oriented, with hard hitting, issue conscious stories. We specialize in interviews with leaders from all walks of life." Published 4 times/year. Circ. 28,000. Publishes ms an average of 6 months after acceptance. Byline given. Submit seasonal/holiday material 6 months in advance. Query for electronic submissions. Reports in 1 month on queries. Sample copy and writer's guidelines for 9x12 SAE with 5 first class stamps.

Nonfiction: How-to, humor, interview/profile, and feature—all Florida college related. Special issues include spring break (February); back to school (August). Query. Length: 500 words or less. Payment varies; may pay writer contributor's copies or other premiums rather than cash. Sometimes pays expenses of writers on assignment.

Photos: State availability of photos with submission. Reviews negatives and transparencies. Captions, model releases and identification of subjects requested.

FORDHAM MAGAZINE, Fordham University, Suite 313, 113 West 60th St., New York NY 10023. (212)841-5360. Editor: Tricia Gallagher-Hempel. 75% freelance written. A quarterly magazine on Fordham University alumni and student life. "We are heavy on feature and personality profiles on our alumni: e.g. actor Denzel

Washington, author Mary Higgins Clark, and how education influenced their careers." Pays on acceptance. Publishes ms an average of 8 months after acceptance. Byline given. Offers $50-100 kill fee. Makes work-for-hire assignments. Submit seasonal/holiday material 10 months in advance. Previously published submissions OK. Computer printout submissions OK; prefers letter-quality. Reports in 1 month on queries; 2 months on mss. Free sample copy; writer's guidelines for #10 SAE and 2 first class stamps.

Nonfiction: Book excerpts, essays, general interest, historical/nostalgic, humor, inspirational, interview/profile (alumni, faculty, students); photo feature. Buys 12 mss/year. Query with published clips. Length: 1,500-3,500. Pays $150-700 for assigned articles; $50-500 for unsolicited articles. Sometimes pays expenses of writers on assignment.

Photos: State availability of photos with submission. Reviews contact sheets, transparencies, prints. Offers additional payment for photos accepted with ms. Model releases and identification of subjects required.

Fillers: Anecdotes, facts, newsbreaks, short humor. "All must be specific to Fordham University." Buys 1-2/year. Length: 150-350 words. Pays $25-50.

Tips: "Have a good familiarity with alumni publications in general: research some of the schools and see what they use, what they look for. Research alumni of the school and see if there is a noted personality you might interview—someone who might live in your area. Be prepared to narrow the proposed idea down to the publication's very specific needs. Feature articles and personality profiles are most open to freelancers. These include interviews with famous or interesting alumni and faculty or students, as well as in-depth analytical articles on trends in university life today (pertinent to Fordham) and features on student life in New York. This includes articles on ways that our school interacts with the community around it. Redesign of magazine is planned."

JOURNEY, A Success Guide for College and Career Bound Students, Communications Publishing Group, 3100 Broadway, 225 PennTower, Kansas City MO 64111. (816)756-3039. Editor: Georgia Clark. 40% freelance written. A quarterly educational and career source guide for Asian-American high school and college students who have indicated a desire to pursue higher education through college, vocational and technical or proprietary schools. For students ages 16-25. Circ. 200,000. Pays on acceptance. Byline sometimes given. Buys second serial (reprint) rights or makes work-for-hire assignments. Submit seasonal/holiday material 6 months in advance. Simultaneous, photocopied and previously published submissions OK. Computer printout submissions OK; prefers letter-quality. Reports in 2 months. Sample copy for 9x12 SAE with 4 first class stamps. Writer's guidelines for #10 SASE.

Nonfiction: Book excerpts or reviews, general interest, how-to (dealing with careers or education), humor, inspirational, interview/profile (celebrity or "up and coming" young adult), new product (as it relates to young adult market), personal experience, photo feature, technical, travel and sports. First time writers with *Journey* must submit complete manuscript for consideration. Length: 750-3,000 words. Pays $150-400 for assigned articles; 10¢/word for unsolicited articles. Sometimes pays expenses of writers on assignment.

Photos: State availability of photos with submission. Prefers transparencies. Offers $10-50/photo. Captions, model releases and identification of subjects required. Buys all rights or one-time rights.

Columns/Departments: Profiles of Achievement (striving and successful minority young adult, age 16-35 in various careers). Buys 15 mss/year. Send complete ms. Length: 500-1,500. Pays $50-200.

Fiction: Adventure, ethnic, historical, humorous, mainstream, slice-of-life vignettes. Buys 3 mss/year. Send complete ms. Length: 1,000-3,000 words. Pays $100-400.

Poetry: Free verse. Buys 5 poems/year. Submit up to 5 poems at one time. Length: 10-25 lines. Pays $10-50.

Fillers: Anecdotes, facts, gags to be illustrated by cartoonist, newsbreaks, short humor. Buys 10/year. Length: 25-250 words. Pays $25-100.

Tips: For new writers—Must submit complete manuscript that is double spaced; clean copy only. If available, send clippings of previous published works and resume. Should state when available to write. Include on first page your name, address, phone, Social Security number and number of words in article.

MISSISSIPPI STATE UNIVERSITY ALUMNUS, Mississippi State University, Alumni Association, Editorial Office, Box 5328, Mississippi State MS 39762. (601)325-3442. Editor: Mr. Linsey H. Wright. Up to 10% freelance written. Works with small number of new/unpublished writers each year. Emphasizes articles about Mississippi State graduates and former students. For well-educated and affluent audience. Quarterly magazine. Circ. 16,000. Pays on publication. Publishes ms 3-6 months after acceptance. Buys one-time rights. Pays 25% kill fee. Byline given. Submit seasonal/holiday material 3 months in advance. Simultaneous, photocopied and previously published submissions OK. Computer printout submissions acceptable; prefers letter-quality. Reports in 1 month. Sample copy for 9x12 SAE and 5 first class stamps.

Nonfiction: Historical, humor (with strong MSU flavor; nothing risque), informational, inspirational, interview (with MSU grads), nostalgia (early days at MSU), personal experience, profile and travel (by MSU grads, but must be of wide interest to other grads). Buys 5-6 mss/years. Send complete ms. Length: 500-2,000 words. Pays $50-150 (including photos, if used).

Photos: Offers no additional payment for photos purchased with accompanying ms. Captions required. Uses 5x7 and 8x10 b&w photos and color transparencies of any size.

Columns/Departments: Statements, "a section of the *Mississippi State Alumnus* that features briefs about alumni achievements and professional or business advancement. We do not use engagements, marriages or births. There is no payment for Statements briefs."

Tips: "All stories *must* be about Mississippi State University or its alumni. We're putting more emphasis on people and events on the campus—teaching, research, and public service projects. But we're still eager to receive good stories about alumni in all parts of the world. We welcome articles about MSU grads in interesting occupations and have used stories on off-shore drillers, miners, horse trainers, etc. We also want profiles on prominent MSU alumni and have carried pieces on Senator John C. Stennis, comedian Jerry Clower, professional football players and coaches, and Eugene Butler, former editor-in-chief of *Progressive Farmer* magazine. We feature 2-4 alumni in each issue, alumni who have risen to prominence in their fields or who are engaged in unusual occupations or who are involved in unusual hobbies. We're using more short features (500-700 words) to vary the length of our articles in each issue. We pay $50-75 for these, including 1 b&w photo."

‡THE NEW HAMPSHIRE ALUMNUS, University Publications, Schofield House, UNH, Durham NH 03824. (603)862-1463. Editor: Drew Sanborn. 25% freelance written. "*The Alumnus* provides the alumni audience of the University of New Hampshire with features, news, and notes on alumni achievements nationwide and on university people and programs two times/year." Circ. 40,000. Pays on acceptance. Publishes ms an average of 6 months after acceptance. Byline given. Kill fee to be negotiated. Not copyrighted. Makes work-for-hire assignments. Simultaneous and previously published submissions OK. Query for electronic submissions. Computer printout submissions OK; prefers letter-quality. Free sample copy and writer's guidelines.

Nonfiction: General interest, interview/profile, photo feature. Buys variable mss/year. Query with published clips. Length: 350-1,500 words. Pays $100-400 for assigned articles; pays $50-150 for unsolicited articles. Sometimes pays the expenses of writers on assignment.

Photos: State availability of photos with submission. Reviews negatives and 5x8 prints. Identification of subjects required. Buys one-time rights.

Columns/Departments: Alumni Profile (UNH alumni achievements). Query with published clips. Length: 350-750 words. Pays $200 maximum.

Tips: "We give preference to University of New Hampshire (alumni and campus) features, articles, and news briefs. We like writers to submit samples of work first with story ideas and fee requirements."

NOTRE DAME MAGAZINE, University of Notre Dame, Room 415, Administration Bldg., Notre Dame IN 46556. (219)239-5335. FAX: (219)239-6947. Editor: Walton R. Collins. Managing Editor: Kerry Temple. 75% freelance written. Quarterly magazine covering news of Notre Dame and education and issues affecting the Roman Catholic Church. "We are interested in the moral, ethical and spiritual issues of the day and how Christians live in today's world. We are universal in scope and Catholic in viewpoint and serve Notre Dame alumni, friends and other constituencies." Circ. 110,000. Pays on acceptance. Publishes ms an average of 6-12 months after acceptance. Byline given. Kill fee negotiable. Buys first rights. Simultaneous queries OK. Query for electronic submissions. Computer printout submissions acceptable; prefers letter-quality. Reports in 1 month. Free sample copy.

Nonfiction: Opinion, personal experience, religion. "All articles must be of interest to Christian/Catholic readers who are well educated and active in their communities." Buys 35 mss/year. Query with clips of published work. Length: 600-3,000 words. Pays $500-1,500. Sometimes pays the expenses of writers on assignment.

Photos: State availability of photos. Reviews b&w contact sheets, color transparencies, and 8x10 prints. Model releases and identification of subjects required. Buys one-time rights.

OLD OREGON, The Magazine of the University of Oregon, University of Oregon, 101 Chapman Hall, Eugene OR 97403. (503)686-5047. Editor: Tom Hager. 50% freelance written. A quarterly university magazine of people and ideas at the University of Oregon. Circ. 87,000. Pays on acceptance. Publishes ms an average of 3 months after acceptance. Byline given. Offers 20% kill fee. Buys first North American serial rights. Query for electronic submissions. Computer printout submissions OK; no dot-matrix. Reports in 3 weeks. Sample copy for 9x12 SAE with 2 first class stamps.

Nonfiction: Historical/nostalgic, interview/profile, personal experience relating to U.O. issues and alumni. Buys 30 mss/year. Query with published clips. Length: 750-3,000 words. Pays $75-300. Sometimes pays expenses of writers on assignment.

Photos: State availability of photos with submission. Reviews 8x10 prints. Offers $10-25/photo. Identification of subjects required. Buys one-time rights.

Tips: "Query with strong, colorful lead; clips."

PRINCETON ALUMNI WEEKLY, Princeton University Press, 41 William St., Princeton NJ 08540. (609)452-4885. Editor: Michelle Preston. Associate Editor: Andrew Mytelka. 50% freelance written. Eager to work with new/unpublished writers. Biweekly (during the academic year) magazine covering Princeton University and higher education for Princeton alumni, students, faculty, staff and friends. "We assume familiarity with and interest in the university." Circ. 52,000. Pays on publication. Publishes ms an average of 3 months after acceptance. Byline given. Offers $100 kill fee. Buys first serial rights and one-time rights. Submit seasonal/holiday material 2 months in advance. Simultaneous queries or photocopied submissions OK. Query for electronic submissions. Computer printout submissions acceptable; prefers letter-quality. Sample copy for 9x12 SAE and 5 first class stamps.

Nonfiction: Book excerpts, general interest, historical/nostalgic, interview/profile, opinion, personal experience, photo feature. "Connection to Princeton essential. Remember, it's for an upscale educated audience." Special issue on education and economics (February). Buys 20 mss/year. Query with clips of published work. Length: 1,000-6,000 words. Pays $100-600. Pays expenses of writers on assignment.

Photos: State availability of photos. Pays $25-50 for 8x10 b&w prints; $50-100 for color transparencies. Reviews (for ordering purposes) b&w contact sheet. Captions and identification of subjects required.

Columns/Departments: "Columnists must have a Princeton connection (alumnus, student, etc.)." Buys 50 mss/year. Query with clips of published work. Length: 750-1,500 words. Pays $75-150.

THE PURDUE ALUMNUS, Purdue Alumni Association, Purdue Memorial Union 160, West Lafayette IN 47907. (317)494-5184. Editor: Gay L. Totten. 30% freelance written. Prefers to work with published/established writers; works with small number of new/unpublished writers each year. Magazine published 9 times/year (except February, June, August) covering subjects of interest to Purdue University alumni. Circ. 72,000. Pays on publication. Publishes ms an average of 2 months after acceptance. Byline given. Buys first rights and makes work-for-hire assignments. Submit seasonal/holiday material 3 months in advance. Simultaneous queries, and simultaneous, photocopied, and previously published submissions OK. Computer printout submissions acceptable; prefers letter-quality. Reports in 1 week on queries; 2 weeks on mss. Sample copy for 8½x11 SAE and 2 first class stamps.

Nonfiction: Book excerpts, general interest, historical/nostalgic, humor, interview/profile, personal experience. Focus is on campus news, issues, opinions of interest to 72,000 members of the Alumni Association. Feature style, primarily university-oriented. Issues relevant to education. Buys 12-20 mss/year. Length: 1,500-2,500 words. Pays $25-250. Sometimes pays expenses of writers on assignment.

Photos: State availability of photos. Reviews b&w contact sheet or 5x7 prints.

Tips: "We are still aiming to be more broadly issue-focused, moving away from the rah-rah type of traditional alumni magazine article. We are interested in issues of concern to educated people, with a university perspective. We want carefully researched, in-depth material, and would prefer, if at all possible, that it somehow include a Purdue authority, alumnus, or citation. For instance, in a recent article on Nicaragua, we cited some 25 sources for information, two were Purdue-related."

SCORECARD, Falsoft, Inc., 9509 US Highway 42, Box 385, Prospect KY 40059. (502)228-4492. FAX: (502)228-5121. Editor: John Crawley. 50% freelance written. Prefers to work with published/established writers. A weekly sports fan tabloid covering University of Louisville sports only. Circ. 3,000. Pays on publication. Publishes ms an average of 1 month after acceptance. Byline given. Buys first rights. Submit seasonal/holiday material 1 month in advance. Previously published submissions OK "rarely." Computer printout submissions acceptable; prefers letter-quality. Reports in 2 weeks. Free sample copy and writer's guidelines.

Nonfiction: Assigned to contributing editors. Buys 100 mss/year. Query with published clips. Length: 750-1,500 words. Pays $20-50. Sometimes pays expenses of writers on assignment.

Photos: State availability of photos.

Columns/Departments: Notes Page (tidbits relevant to University of Louisville sports program or former players or teams). Buys 25 mss/year. Length: Approximately 100 words. Pay undetermined.

Tips: "Be very familiar with history and tradition of University of Louisville sports program. Contact us with story ideas. Know the subject."

SHIPMATE, U.S. Naval Academy Alumni Association Magazine, Alumni House, Annapolis MD 21402. (301)263-4469. Editor: Col. J.W. Hammond, Jr., USMC (retired). 100% freelance written. A magazine published 10 times a year by and for alumni of the U.S. Naval Academy. Circ. 31,000. Pays on publication. Byline given. Buys first North American serial rights. Submit seasonal/holiday material 10 months in advance. Computer printout submissions OK; prefers letter-quality. Reports in 1 week. Sample copy for 8½x11 SAE and 6 first class stamps.

Nonfiction: Buys 50 mss/year. Send complete ms. Length: 2,000-7,500 words. Pays $100 for unsolicited articles.

Photos: Send photos with submission. Offers no additional payment for photos accepted with ms. Identification of subjects required. Buys one-time rights.

Tips: "The writer should be a Naval Academy alumnus (not necessarily a graduate) with first-hand experience of events in the Naval Service."

THE STUDENT, 127 9th Ave. N., Nashville TN 37234. Editor: Milt Hughes. 10% freelance written. Works with a small number of new/unpublished writers each year. Publication of Student Ministry Department of the Southern Baptist Convention. For college students; focusing on freshman and sophomore levels. Published 12 times during the school year. Circ. 45,000. Buys all rights. Payment on acceptance. Publishes ms an average of 10 months after acceptance. Mss should be double-spaced on white paper with 50-space line, 25 lines/page. Reports usually in 6 weeks. Computer printout submissions acceptable; no dot-matrix. Sample copy and guidelines for 8x10 SAE.

Nonfiction: Contemporary questions, problems, and issues facing college students viewed from a Christian perspective to develop high moral and ethical values. Cultivating interpersonal relationships, developing self-esteem, dealing with the academic struggle, coping with rejection, learning how to love, developing a personal relationship with Jesus Christ. Prefers complete ms rather than query. Length: 1,000 words maximum. Pays 5¢/word after editing with reserved right to edit accepted material. Extra payment for use of computer diskette.

Fiction: Satire and parody on college life, humorous episodes; emphasize clean fun and the ability to grow and be uplifted through humor. Contemporary fiction involving student life, on campus as well as off. Length: 900 words. Pays 5¢/word.

VISIONS, A Success Guide for Native American Students, Communications Publishing Group, 3100 Broadway, 225 Penntower, Kansas City MO 64111. (816)756-3039. Editor: Georgia Clark. 40% freelance written. A quarterly education and career source guide designed for Native American students who want to pursue a higher education through colleges, vocational and technical schools, or proprietary schools, to focus on insight, motivational and career planning informations. For young adults, ages 16-25. Circ. 100,000. Pays on acceptance. Byline sometimes given. Buys second serial (reprint) rights or makes work-for-hire assignments. Submit seasonal/holiday material 6 months in advance. Simultaneous, photocopied and previously published submissions OK. Computer printout submissions OK; prefers letter-quality. Reports in 2 months. Sample copy for 9x10 SAE with 4 first class stamps; writer's guidelines for #10 SASE.

Nonfiction: Book excerpts or reviews, general interest, how-to, humor, inspirational, interview/profile, new product, personal experience, photo feature, technical, travel and sports. Query or send complete ms. Length: 750-3,000 words. Pays $150-400 for assigned articles; 10¢/word for unsolicited articles. Sometimes pays expenses of writers on assignment.

Photos: State availability of photos with submission. Reviews transparencies. Offers $10-50/photo. Captions, model releases, and identification of subjects required. Buys all rights.

Columns/Departments: Profiles of Achievement (striving and successful Native American young adults, age 16-35, in various careers). Length: 500-1,500 words. Buys 15 mss/year. Send complete ms. Pays $50-250.

Fiction: Adventure, ethnic, historical, humorous, mainstream, slice-of-life vignettes. Buys 3 mss/year. Send complete ms. Length: 1,000-5,000 words. Pays $100-400.

Poetry: Free verse. Buys 5 poems/year. Submit up to 5 poems at one time. Length: 10-25 lines. Pays $10-50.

Fillers: Anecdotes, facts, gags to be illustrated by cartoonist, newsbreaks, short humor. Buys 10 fillers/year. Length: 25-250 words. Pays $25-100.

Tips: For new writers—Submit complete manuscript that is double spaced; clean copy only. If available, send clippings of previous published works and resume. Should state when available to write. Include on first page of manuscript your name, address, phone, Social Security number and number of words in article.

WPI JOURNAL, Worcester Polytechnic Institute, 100 Institute Rd., Worcester MA 01609. FAX: (508)831-5604. Editor: Michael Dorsey. 75% freelance written. A quarterly alumni magazine covering science and engineering/education/business personalities for 17,000 alumni, primarily engineers, scientists, managers; parents of students, national media. Circ. 22,500. Pays on publication. Publishes ms an average of 3 months after acceptance. Byline given. Buys one-time rights. Submit seasonal/holiday material 6 months in advance. Simultaneous queries, and simultaneous, photocopied and previously published submissions OK. Query for electronic submissions. Requires hard copy also. Computer printout submissions acceptable; prefers letter-quality to dot-matrix. Reports in 2 weeks on queries; 1 month on mss.

Nonfiction: Book excerpts; exposé (education, engineering, science); general interest; historical/nostalgic; humor; interview/profile (people in engineering, science); personal experience; photo feature; and technical (with personal orientation). Query with published clips. Length: 1,000-4,000 words. Pays negotiable rate. Sometimes pays the expenses of writers on assignment.

Photos: State availability of photos with query or ms. Reviews b&w contact sheets. Pays negotiable rate. Captions required.

Tips: "Submit outline of story and/or ms of story idea or published work. Features are most open to freelancers. Keep in mind that this is an alumni magazine, so most articles focus on the college and its community."

If you have an IBM or IBM-compatible personal computer and would like to know more about Writer's Market on disk, see the bind-in card between pages 904 and 905.

Child Care and Parental Guidance

Readers of today's parenting magazines are starting families later and having fewer children but they want more information on pregnancy, infancy, child development and parenting research. Child care magazines address these and other issues from many different perspectives: Some are general interest parenting magazines while others for child care providers combine care information with business tips. Other markets that buy articles about child care and the family are included in the Education, Religious and Women's sections.

AMERICAN BABY MAGAZINE, For Expectant and New Parents, 475 Park Ave. South, New York NY 10016. (212)689-3600. Editor: Judith Nolte. 70% freelance written. Prefers to work with published/established writers; works with a small number of new/unpublished writers each year. A monthly magazine covering pregnancy, child care, and parenting. "Our readership is composed of women in late pregnancy and early new motherhood. Most readers are first-time parents; some have older children. A simple, straightforward, clear approach is mandatory." Circ. 1,150,000. Pays on acceptance. Publishes ms an average of 3 months after acceptance. Byline given. Buys first North American serial rights. Submit seasonal holiday material 5-6 months in advance. Simultaneous, photocopied and previously published submissions OK. Computer printout submissions acceptable; prefers letter-quality. Reports in 3 weeks on queries; 2 months on mss. Sample copy for 9x12 SAE with 6 first class stamps. Writer's guidelines for SASE.
Nonfiction: Book excerpts, essays, how-to (on some aspect of pregnancy or child care), humor, opinion and personal experience. "No 'hearts and flowers' or fantasy pieces." Buys 60 mss/year. Query with published clips, or send complete ms. Length: 1,000-2,500 words. Pays $200-1,000 for assigned articles; pays $100-500 for unsolicited articles. Pays the expenses of writers on assignment.
Photos: State availability of photos with submission. Reviews transparencies and prints. Model release and identification of subjects required. Buys one-time rights.
Columns/Departments: One View (an opinion or personal experience essay on some aspect of pregnancy, birth, or parenting), 1,000 words. Buys 12 mss/year. Send complete ms.
Tips: "Articles should either give 'how to' information on some aspect of pregnancy or child care, cover some common problem of child raising, along with solutions, or give advice to the mother on some psychological or practical subject."

BABY TALK MAGAZINE, Parenting/Excellence, 686 Avenue of the Americas, New York NY 10011. (212)989-8181. Editor: Susan Linned Strecker. 50% freelance written. Monthly magazine covering "topics of interest to expectant and new parents—baby care—child development." Circ. 975,000. Pays on acceptance. Publishes ms an average of 3-6 months after acceptance. Byline given. Buys one-time rights. Submit seasonal/holiday material 3-6 months in advance. Previously published submissions sometimes OK. Computer printout submissions OK; no dot-matrix. Reports in 2 months. Sample copy and writer's guidelines for 9x12 SAE and 85¢ postage.
Nonfiction: Essays (on parental topics); how-to (on baby care); opinions; personal experience; photo feature; and travel. No articles under 1,000 words, hand-written articles, humor or fiction. Buys 40 mss/year. Query or send complete ms. Length: 1,500-3,000 words. Pays $50-200.
Photos: Send photos with submission. Reviews color transparencies. Captions and model releases required. Buys one-time rights.
Columns/Departments: One Mother's View (personal experience). Length: 1,500-3,000 words. Buys 6-8 mss/year. Query or send complete ms. Pays $50.
Tips: "Writing for *Baby Talk* is highly competitive. Due to a lack of available editorial space, less than one in 100 submitted manuscripts can be accepted."

BAY AREA PARENT, The Santa Clara News Magazine, for Parents, Kids Kids Kids Publications, Inc., 455, Los Gatos Blvd. #103, Los Gatos CA 95023. Editor: Lynn Berardo. 80% freelance written. Works with locally-based published/established writers. Monthly tabloid of resource information for parents and teachers. Circ 60,000. Pays on publication. Publishes ms an average of 3 months after acceptance. Byline given. Buys one-time rights. Submit seasonal/holiday material 3 months in advance. Simultaneous, photocopied, and previously published submissions OK. Query for electronic submissions. Computer printout submissions acceptable. Sample copy for 9x12 SAE and $1.75 postage; writer's guidelines for #10 SASE.

Close-up

Sacramento Non-fiction Network

"Since freelance writing is a lonely profession, we needed a way to exchange information." With this idea, freelancer Grace Ertel initiated Sacramento's Non-fiction Network.

The Network is unique among writers' groups because it exists primarily to offer marketing strategies. Instead of manuscripts, members tote sample copies, clips, editorial calendars, conference flyers—anything pertinent to the freelance business. Materials circulate while members make brief reports of current projects and sales. Writers are able to take home "updates on editors' needs and quirks—which editors respond, which pay promptly, and especially, who is buying what," Ertel says.

The roster now contains about two dozen regulars, most belonging to the California Writers' Club, of which the Network is an unofficial sub-group. Represented are published writers in many areas of expertise. "As it doesn't operate like critique groups, the Network accommodates a larger and sometimes changing core group," Ertel says. Beginners or long-time pros all find the Network essential to keep them on top of the freelance business. They steer each other away from problems *before* they become horror stories. Newcomers are welcome—the group appears able to self-limit its membership to active writers—and members remain loyal.

Michele McCormick, columnist and book author, enjoys being with working writers. "It's tremendously energizing. I get so many ideas for new angles and markets that I usually spend the day or two following our meeting working up a new batch of queries."

"It's easier to be productive with suggestions from other writers," agrees freelancer Susan Cort Johnson. From query to publication, tips apply to every stage. "I took advantage of suggestions for publicizing my self-published history book," says Bill Holden.

Marilyn Pribus, who publishes regularly on family issues, has discovered new topics to explore. "A 'comp' that a member received in Las Vegas inspired me. Now I'm doing travel assignments for periodicals around the country," she says. Editor Kathleen Reimer stayed with her freelance interests but expanded them when she was invited to the group shortly after relocating. "I realized what a dedicated and prolific group of writers lived here, and I determined to concentrate on larger markets."

"So many writers forget they are running a business; the key here is that everybody is professional," Laura St. George says of the group's membership. "When I wanted to syndicate articles on home-based business, the group saved me headaches by sharing what works and what doesn't in a column." In a highly competitive field, this group demonstrates remarkable cooperation. Reviewer Lilyan Mastrolia sums up the Network's support and knowledge in a single benefit: "The encouragement to keep writing." And selling.

Fortunately for those unable to make the commute, this concept travels well, and Ertel exhorts other freelancers to start their own networks. "Get together with people who are doing what you're doing. As word spreads, the group—and your resources—will get larger. Inviting like-minded working writers together is a good professional move in any community."

—Lynn Narlesky

Nonfiction: Book excerpts (related to our interest group); expose (health, psychology); historical/nostalgic ("History of Diapers"); how-to (related to kids/parenting); humor; interview/profile; photo feature; and travel (with kids, family). Special issues include Music (February); Art (March); Kid's Birthdays (April); Summer Camps (May); Family Fun (June); Pregnancy and Childbirth (July); Fashion (August); Health (September); and Mental Health (October). No opinion or religious articles. Buys 36-50 mss/year. Query or send complete ms. Length: 150-1,500 words. Pays $10-50. Sometimes pays expenses of writers on assignment.

Photos: State availability of photos. Prefers b&w contact sheets and/or 3x5 b&w prints. Pays $5-25. Model release required. Buys one-time rights.

Columns/Departments: Child Care, Family Travel, Birthday Party Ideas, Baby Page, Toddler Page, Adolescent Kids. Buys 36 mss/year. Send complete ms. Length: 400-1,200 words. Pays $20-60.

Fiction: Humorous.

Tips: "Submit new, fresh information concisely written and accurately researched. Publisher also producer *Bay Area Baby Magazine* a semi-annual publication."

CENTRAL COAST PARENT, Box 12407, San Luis Obispo CA 93406. (805)544-8609. Editor: Rhonda Jones. 90% freelance written. Monthly tabloid on child-rearing, health, behavior, parenting. Readers are pregnant women and parents of children 18 and under. Estab. 1989. Circ. 20,000. Pays on publication. Publishes ms an average of 4 months after acceptance. Byline given. Buys first rights or second serial (reprint) rights. Submit seasonal/holiday material 4 months in advance. Simultaneous, photocopied and previously published submissions OK. Computer printout submissions OK; no dot-matrix. Reports in 1 month. Sample copy for 9x12 SAE with $1.25 postage; writer's guidelines and editorial calendar for #10 SASE.

Nonfiction: Book excerpts, general interest, how-to, inspirational, in-depth features, critical assessment of issues, personal experience and travel—all related to parenting and child development. Buys 20-40 mss/year. Query with or without published clips or send complete ms. Length: 500-1,500 words. Pays 1-3¢/word.

Photos: Send photos with submission. Reviews 5x7 or 3x5 prints. Pays $1. Captions required. Buys one-time rights.

Columns/Departments: Kids Korner (craft, art, educational activities for children 12 and under), 50-500 words; Family Travel (getaways, things to do with kids), 300-500 words; Babies; Expectant Parents; Teens; Growing Child; 500-750 words. Buys 20 mss/year. Send complete ms. Length: 300-750 words. Pays 1-3¢/word.

Fillers: Anecdotes, consumer tips, facts, newsbreaks, short humor. Buys 20/year. Length: 50-500 words. Pays $2.50.

‡CHILD, The New York Times Magazine Group, 110 Fifth Ave., New York NY 10011. (212)463-1000. Editor-in-Chief: Kate White. Executive Editor: Laura Manske. 75% freelance written. Bimonthly magazine covering parents and children. "*Child* is written for sophisticated parents who want the best for their children—the best information, health care, products, etc." Circ. 300,000. Pays on acceptance. Publishes ms an average of 3 months after acceptance. Byline given. Offers 25% kill fee. Buys first North American serial rights, one-time rights or second serial (reprint) rights. Submit seasonal/holiday material 6 months in advance. Simultaneous and photocopied submissions OK. Computer printout submissions OK; prefers letter-quality. Prefers query letters rather than complete ms. Reports in 6-8 weeks. Sample copy for 9x12 SAE with $2.40 postage and $1.50; writer's guidelines for #10 SASE.

Nonfiction: Book excerpts, humor, and travel. No poetry, children's stories, fiction. Buys 75 mss/year. Query with *published clips*. Length: 1,000-2,500 words. Pays $500 and up for assigned articles. Sometimes pays expenses of writers on assignment if approved in advance.

Columns/Departments: Child's Play (toys, child-related businesses, activities); Best Behavior (psychological issues); and Health (medical concerns for parents). Parent Principle; Stages; Learning. Buys 30 mss/year. Query with published clips. Length: 1,500-2,000 words. Pays $500-1,000.

‡CHILD & FAMILY, Canada's Family Magazine, Ontario Child and Parent Publications Ltd., #966, 50 Charles Street East, Toronto, Ontario M4Y 2N9 Canada. (416)963-5988. Editor: Joseph Holmes. Associate Editor: Wolfgang Dios. 80% freelance written. Quarterly magazine on parenting, children (5-15) and families. "We are a young, progressive magazine aimed at educated Canadian families with children ages 5-15. Past articles have included such topics as midwifery and ethics (the teaching of). Also publish children's stories." Circ. 45,000. Pays approximately 6 weeks after acceptance. Byline given. Offers 20% kill fee. Buys all rights. Submit seasonal/holiday material 6 months in advance. Photocopied submissions OK. Query for electronic submissions. Computer printout submissions OK; prefers letter-quality. Reports in 3 weeks. Free sample copy.

Nonfiction: Essays, exposé, general interest, humor, interview/profile, personal experience and photo feature. Buys 15 mss/year. Send complete ms. Length: 1,000-3,500 words. Pays $100-400.
Photos: Send photos with submission. Reviews contact sheet, negatives, transparencies and prints. Offers $15-30 per photo. Captions, model releases and identification of subjects required. Buys all rights.
Columns/Departments: Veni, Vidi, Video (video reviews on parenting, or for children), 500-1,000 words; More than Mother Goose (reviews of books for children), 500-1,000 words; Adults Only (reviews of books for adults on parenting), 500-1,000 words. Buys 40 mss/year. Query. Pays $35-200.
Fiction: Slice-of-life vignettes; and stories for children. Buys 4 mss/year. Send complete ms. Length: 500-3,000 words. Pays $150-425.
Poetry: Avant-garde, free verse and traditional. Must be about childhood. We only use poetry in conjunction with photo features, so must be highly visual, lending themselves to this purpose. We do not publish poems separately. Excerpts from plays for or about children also welcome. Buys 2 poems/year. Submit maximum 3 poems. Length: 15-35 lines. Pays $25-50.
Fillers: Anecdotes and short humor. Buys 5/year. Length: 500-2,000 words. Pays $35-250.
Tips: "Generally, we prefer finished manuscripts to queries. Information articles are our biggest need, and these should have a Canadian slant. We do not like hype, or 'trendy' thoughtless pieces, ditto sentimentality. Since we prefer to work closely with our freelancers, most are from the Toronto area. However, we also have writers in Calgary and Vancouver, and are branching out. Generally, pieces should be intelligent and imaginative. We place a high priority on imagination."

‡**FATHERS,** Fathers, Inc., 643 E. Capitol St., SE, Washington D.C. 20003. (202)544-4220. Editor: D.C. Spencer. Managing Editor: Kathy Davis. 50% freelance written. Bimonthly magazine. "Fathers who have graduated from *Esquire* and *Playboy*, etc., and are involved with their families and children." Circ. 500,000. Pays on publication. Publishes ms an average of 1 month after acceptance. Byline given. Buys first North American serial rights. Simultaneous submissions OK. Computer printout submissions OK. Free sample copy.
Nonfiction: Book excerpts, how-to, humor, interview/profile, opinion, personal experience and travel. Buys 60-100 mss/year. Query with published clips. Length: 500-3,000 words. Pays $200-700. Sometimes pays expenses of writers on assignment.
Photos: State availability of photos with submission.

GIFTED CHILDREN MONTHLY, For the Parents of Children with Great Promise, Box 115, Sewell NJ 08080. (609)582-0277. Editor: Dr. James Alvino. Managing Editor: Robert Baum. 50% freelance written. Prefers to work with published/established writers. Monthly newsletter covering parenting and education of gifted children for parents. Circ. 50,000. Pays on acceptance. Publishes ms an average of 3-6 months after acceptance. Buys all rights and first rights. Submit seasonal/holiday material 4 months in advance. Simultaneous queries, and simultaneous, photocopied, and previously published submissions OK. Computer printout submissions acceptable; prefers letter-quality. Reports in 1 month on queries; 2 months on mss. Sample copy and writer's guidelines for 9x12 SAE and 3 first class stamps.
Nonfiction: Book excerpts; personal accounts; how-to (on parenting of gifted kids); research into practice; outstanding programs; interview/profile; and opinion. Also puzzles, brainteasers and ideas for children's Spin-Off section. "Our Special Reports and Idea Place sections are most accessible to freelancers." Query with clips of published work or send complete ms. Buys 36 unsolicited mss/year. Length: Idea Place 500-750 words; Special Reports 1,000-2,500 words. Pays $10-200. Sometimes pays expenses of writers on assignment.
Tips: "We look forward to working with both new and veteran writers who have something new to say to the parents of gifted and talented children. It is helpful if freelancers provide copies of research papers to back up the article."

GROWING PARENT, Dunn & Hargitt, Inc., 22 N. 2nd St., Box 1100, Lafayette IN 47902. (317)423-2624. Editor: Nancy Kleckner. 40-50% freelance written. Works with a small number of new/unpublished writers each year. "We do receive a lot of unsolicited submissions but have had excellent results in working with some unpublished writers. So, we're always happy to look at material and hope to find one or two jewels each year." A monthly newsletter which focuses on parents—the issues, problems, and choices they face as their children grow. "We want to look at the parent as an adult and help encourage his or her growth not only as a parent but as an individual." Pays on acceptance. Publishes ms an average of 6 months after acceptance. Byline given. Buys first North American serial rights; maintains exclusive rights for three months. Submit seasonal/holiday material 6 months in advance. Photocopied submissions and previously published submissions OK. Computer printout submissions acceptable; prefers letter-quality. Reports in 2 weeks. Sample copy and writer's guidelines for 5x8 SAE with 2 first class stamps.
Nonfiction: "We are looking for informational articles written in an easy-to-read, concise style. We would like to see articles that help parents deal with the stresses they face in everyday life—positive, upbeat, how-to-cope suggestions. We rarely use humorous pieces, fiction or personal experience articles. Writers should keep in mind that most of our readers have children under three years of age." Buys 15-20 mss/year. Query. Length: 1,500-2,000 words; will look at shorter pieces. Pays 8-10¢/word (depends on article).
Tips: "Submit a very specific query letter with samples."

HOME EDUCATION MAGAZINE, Box 1083, Tonasket WA 98855. Editors: Mark J. Hegener and Helen E. Hegener. 80% freelance written. Eager to work with new/unpublished writers each year. A bimonthly magazine covering home-based education. "We feature articles which address the concerns of parents who want to take a direct involvement in the education of their children—concerns such as socialization, how to find curriculums and materials, testing and evaluation, how to tell when your child is ready to begin reading, what to do when home schooling is difficult, teaching advanced subjects, etc." Circ. 5,500. Pays on publication. Publishes ms an average of 4-6 months after acceptance. Byline given ("Please include a 30-50 word credit with your article"). Buys first North American serial rights, first rights, one-time rights, second serial (reprint) rights, simultaneous rights, all rights, and makes work-for-hire assignments. Submit seasonal/holiday material 6 months in advance. Simultaneous, photocopied and previously published submissions OK. Query for electronic submission requirements. Computer printout submissions acceptable; prefers letter-quality. Reports in 6-8 weeks. Sample copy $4.50; writer's guidelines for #10 SASE.

Nonfiction: Book excerpts, essays, how-to (related to home schooling), humor, inspirational, interview/profile, personal experience, photo feature and technical. Buys 40-50 mss/year. Query with or without published clips, or send complete ms. Length: 750-3,500 words. Pays $10 per our typeset page, (about 750 words). Sometimes pays expenses of writers on assignment.

Photos: Send photos with submission. Reviews 5x7, 35mm prints and b&w snapshots. Write for photo rates. Identification of subjects required. Buys one-time rights.

Poetry: "Accepts previously published as well as original poetry." Pays $5-10/poem.

Tips: "We would like to see how-to articles (that don't preach, just present options); articles on testing, accountability, working with the public schools, socialization, learning disabilities, resources, support groups, legislation and humor. We need answers to the questions that home schoolers ask."

HOME LIFE, Sunday School Board, 127 9th Ave. N., Nashville TN 37234. (615)251-2271. Editor-in-Chief: Charlie Warren. 40-50% freelance written. Prefers to work with published/established writers; eager to work with new/unpublished writers. Emphasizes Christian marriage and Christian family life. For married adults of all ages, but especially newlyweds and middle-aged marrieds. Monthly magazine. Circ. 725,000. Pays on acceptance. Publishes ms an average of 15 months after acceptance. Buys first rights, first North American serial rights and all rights. Byline given. Phone queries OK, but written queries preferred. Submit seasonal/holiday material 1 year in advance. Computer printout submissions acceptable; prefers letter-quality. Reports in 6 weeks. Sample copy $1; writer's guidelines for #10 SASE.

Nonfiction: How-to (good articles on marriage and family life); informational (about some current family-related issue of national significance such as "Television and the Christian Family" or "Whatever Happened to Family Worship?"); personal experience (informed articles by people who have solved marriage and family problems in healthy, constructive ways); marriage and family life with a masculine slant. "No column material. We are not interested in material that will not in some way enrich Christian marriage or family life." Buys 150-200 mss/year. Query or submit complete ms. Length: 600-1,800 words. Pays up to 5¢/word.

Fiction: "Fiction should be family-related and should show a strong moral about how families face and solve problems constructively." Buys 12-20 mss/year. Submit complete ms. Length: 600-1,800 words. Pays up to 5¢/word.

Tips: "Study the magazine to see our unique slant on Christian family life. We prefer a life-centered case study approach, rather than theoretical essays on family life. Our top priority is marriage enrichment material."

L.A. PARENT, The Magazine for Parents in Southern California, Box 3204, Burbank CA 91504. (818)846-0400. Editor: Jack Bierman. 80% freelance written. Prefers to work with published/established writers, and works with a small number of new/unpublished writers each year. Monthly tabloid covering parenting. Circ. 100,000. Pays on publication. Publishes ms an average of 4 months after acceptance. Byline given. Buys first rights. Submit seasonal/holiday material 3 months in advance. Simultaneous queries and previously published submissions OK. Query for electronic submission requirements. Computer printout submissions acceptable. Reports in 1 month. Sample copy and writer's guidelines for $2.

Nonfiction: David Jameison, articles editor. General interest, how-to. "We focus on southern California activities for families, and do round-up pieces, i.e., a guide to private schools, fishing spots." Buys 60-75 mss/year. Query with clips of published work. Length: 700-1,200 words. Pays $150 plus expenses.

Tips: "We will be using more contemporary articles on parenting's challenges. If you can write for a 'city magazine' in tone and accuracy, you may write for us. The 'Baby Boom' has created a need for more generic parenting material."

‡LIVING WITH CHILDREN, Baptist Sunday School Board, 127 9th Ave. N., Nashville TN 37234. (615)251-2229. Editor: Phillip H. Waugh. 50% freelance written. Works with a small number of new/unpublished writers each year. Quarterly magazine covering parenting issues for parents of elementary-age children (ages 6 through 11). "Written and designed from a Christian perspective." Circ. 50,000. Pays on acceptance. Publishes ms an average of 2 years after acceptance. Byline given. "We generally buy all rights to mss; first serial rights on a limited basis. First and reprint rights may be negotiated at a lower rate of pay." Submit seasonal/holiday material 1 year in advance. Previously published submissions (on limited basis) OK. Computer printout submissions acceptable; no dot-matrix. Reports in 1 month on queries; 2 months on mss. Sample copy for 9x12 SASE; free writer's guidelines.

Nonfiction: How-to (parent), humor, inspirational, personal experience, and articles on child development. No highly technical material or articles containing more than 15-20 lines quoted material. Buys 60 mss/year. Query or send complete ms (queries preferred). Length: 800-1,800 words (1,450 words preferred). Pays 5¢/word.

Photos: "Submission of photos with mss is strongly discouraged."

Fiction: Humorous (parent/child relationships); and religious. "We have very limited need for fiction." Buys maximum of 4 mss/year. Length: 800-1,450 words. Pays 5¢/word.

Poetry: Light verse and inspirational. "We have limited need for poetry and buy only all rights." Buys 15 poems/year. Submit maximum 3 poems. Length: 4-30 lines. Pays $1.75 (for 1-7 lines) plus $1 for each additional line; pays $4.50 for 8 lines and more plus 65¢ each additional line.

Fillers: Jokes, anecdotes and short humor. Buys 15/year. Length: 100-400 words. Pays $5 minimum, 5¢/word.

Tips: "Articles must deal with an issue of interest to parents. A mistake some writers make in articles for us is failing to write from a uniquely Christian perspective; that is very necessary for our periodicals. Material should be 850, 1,450 or 1,800 words in length. All sections, particularly articles, are open to freelance writers. Only regular features are assigned."

‡**LIVING WITH PRESCHOOLERS**, Baptist Sunday School Board, 127 9th Ave. N., Nashville TN 37234. (615)251-2229. Editor: Phillip H. Waugh. 50% freelance written. Works with a small number of new/unpublished writers each year. Quarterly magazine covering parenting issues for parents of preschoolers (infants through 5-year-olds). The magazine is "written and designed from a Christian perspective." Circ. 152,000. Pays on acceptance. Publishes manuscript an average of 2 years after acceptance. Byline given. "We generally buy all rights to manuscripts. First and reprint rights may be negotiated at a lower rate of pay." Submit seasonal/holiday material 2 years in advance. Previously published submissions (on limited basis) OK. Computer printout submissions acceptable; no dot-matrix. Reports in 1 month on queries; 2 months on mss. Sample copy for 9x12 SASE; free writer's guidelines.

Nonfiction: How-to (parent), humor, inspirational, personal experience, and articles on child development. No highly technical material or articles containing more than 15-20 lines quoted material. Buys 60 mss/year. Query or send complete ms (queries preferred). Length: 800-1,800 words (1,450 words preferred). Pays 5¢/word for manuscripts offered on all-rights basis.

Photos: "Submission of photos with mss is strongly discouraged."

Fiction: Humorous (parent/child relationships); and religious. "We have very limited need for fiction." Buys maximum of 4 mss/year. Length: 800-1,450 words. Pays 5¢/word.

Poetry: Light verse and inspirational. "We have limited need for poetry and buy only all rights." Buys 15 poems/year. Submit maximum 3 poems. Length: 4-30 lines. Pays $1.75 (for 1-7 lines) plus $1 for each additional line; pays $4.50 for 8 lines and more plus 65¢ each additional line.

Fillers: Jokes, anecdotes and short humor. Buys 15/year. Length: 100-400 words. Pays $5 minimum, 5¢/word maximum.

Tips: "Articles must deal with an issue of interest to parents. A mistake some writers make in writing an article for us is failing to write from a uniquely Christian perspective; that is very necessary for our periodicals. Material should be 850, 1,450, or 1,800 words in length. All sections, particularly articles, are open to freelance writers. Only regular features are assigned."

‡**NANNY TIMES**, Jack & Jill Enterprises, Inc., Box 31, Rutherford NJ 07070. (201)935-5575. 90% freelance written. Biweekly magazine on child care. "Our magazine goes to nannies (usually untrained) and parents in need of a nanny. We cover safety, nutrition, child psychology, health and articles on how-to fit in with family, communication, etc." Estab. 1988. Circ. 25,000. Pays on publication. Publishes ms an average of 3 months after acceptance. Byline given. Buys one-time rights. Submit seasonal/holiday material 3 months in advance. Simultaneous, photocopied and previously published submissions OK. Query for electronic submissions. Computer printout submissions OK. Reports in 6 weeks. Sample copy $1.50; free writer's guidelines.

Nonfiction: General interest, how-to and personal experience. All relating to child care or the business of being a nanny. Send complete ms. Length: 1,000-2,000. Pays 10¢/word. Sometimes pays with advertisements.

Photos: Send photos with submissions. Reviews contact sheets, negatives, transparencies and prints. Offers no additional payment for photos accepted with ms. Model releases are required.

NETWORK, For Public Schools, National Committee for Citizens in Education, Suite 301, 10840 Little Patuxent Pkwy., Columbia MD 21044. (301)997-9300. Editor: Chrissie Bamber. 10% freelance written. Works with a small number of new/unpublished writers each year. Published 6 times during the school year covering parent/citizen involvement in public schools. Circ. 8,000. Pays on publication. Publishes ms an average of 6 months after acceptance. Byline given. Buys first serial rights, first North American serial rights, one-time rights, second serial (reprint) rights, simultaneous rights, all rights and makes work-for-hire assignments. Submit seasonal/holiday material 3 months in advance. Simultaneous queries and photocopied submissions

OK. Computer printout submissions OK; prefers letter-quality. Reports in 6 weeks. Free sample copy; writer's guidelines for #10 SAE and 2 first class stamps.

Nonfiction: Book excerpts (elementary and secondary public education); exposé (of school systems which attempt to reduce public access); how-to (improve schools through parent/citizen participation); humor (related to public school issues); opinion (school-related issues); personal experience (school-related issues). "We want to provide balanced coverage of current developments and continuing issues and to place the facts about schools in a perspective useful to parents. No highly technical or scholarly articles about education; no child rearing articles or personal opinion not backed by research or concrete examples." Buys 4-6 mss/year. Query with clips of published work or send complete ms. Length: 1,000-1,500 words. Pays $25-100. Sometimes pays the expenses of writers on assignment.

Tips: "We are seeking more local examples of parent/community and school partnerships that have succeeded in raising student achievement. Readers want articles of substance with information they can use and act on, not headlines which promise much but deliver only the most shallow analysis of the subject. Information is first, style second. A high personal commitment to public schools and preferably first-hand experience are the greatest assets. A clear and simple writing style, easily understood by a wide range of lay readers, is a must."

‡PARENTING MAGAZINE, 501 Second St., #110, San Francisco CA 94107. Editor: David Markus. Magazine published 10 times/year. "Edited for parents of children from birth to ten years old, with the most emphasis put on the under-sixes." Pays on acceptance. Byline given. Offers 25% kill fee. Buys first rights. Query for electronic submissions. Computer printout submissions OK; prefers letter-quality. Reports in 1 month on queries; 6 weeks on mss. Sample copy $1.20 with 9x12 SAE and $1.20 postage. Writer's guidelines for SASE.

Nonfiction: Rebecca Poole. Book excerpts, humor, new product (to Elizabeth Moore), personal experience and photo feature. Buys 20-30 mss/year. Query with or without published clips, or send complete ms. Length: 1,000-3,500 words. Pays $750-2,000. Sometimes pays expenses of writers on assignment.

Columns/Departments: Extra (news items relating to children/family), 100-400 words; Care and Feeding (health, nutrition), 100-300 words. Buys 50-60 mss/year. Pays $50-100.

Fillers: Length: 150-500. Pays $50-100.

‡PARENTS & TEENAGERS, Thom Schultz Publications, Inc., 2890 N. Monroe, Box 481, Loveland CO 80539. (303)669-3836. Editorial Director: Joani Schultz. Managing Editor: Cindy Parolini. 90% freelance written. Bimontly newsletter, practical helps for Christian parents of teenagers. Estab. 1988. Circ. 7,000. Pays on acceptance. Publishes ms an average of 4 months after acceptance. Byline given. Offers $25 kill fee for longer articles. Buys all rights. Submit seasonal/holiday material 6 months in advance. Computer printout submissions OK. Reports in 2 weeks on queries; 1 month on mss. Sample copy for 9x12 SAE with $1; free writer's guidelines.

Nonfiction: Barbara Beach. How-to (ideas to build closer family; personal help ideas for marriage, single parents; understanding teenagers, self), personal experience (family success stories, parenting, family life). Query with published clips. Length: 200-1,400 words. Pays $25-100 for assigned articles; $15-100 for unsolicited articles. Sometimes pays expenses of writers on assignment.

Photos: State availability of photos with submission. Reviews contact sheets, 35mm transparencies and 8 × 10 prints. Offers $25-50/b&w photo and $50-150 for color.

Columns/Departments: Barbara Beach. Personal Help for Parenting (practical ideas to help parents deal with their frustrations with teenagers and parenting), 200-300 words; Building a Closer Family (practical helps for parents to build closer families—communication), 200 words; and Family Success Stories (personal stories of surviving family tough times with teenagers—with how-to's for others to cope), 600-700 words. Query. Pays $25-75.

PARENTS MAGAZINE, 685 3rd Ave., New York NY 10017. Editor: Ann Pleshette Murphy. 25% freelance written. Monthly. Circ. 1,740,000. Pays on acceptance. Publishes ms an average of 8 months after acceptance. Usually buys first serial rights or first North American serial rights; sometimes buys all rights. Byline given "except for Almanac." Pays $100-350 kill fee. Computer printout submissions acceptable; prefers letter-quality. Reports in approximately 6 weeks. Writer's guidelines for #10 SASE.

Nonfiction: "We are interested in well-documented articles on the development and behavior of preschool, school-age, and adolescent children and their parents; good, practical guides to the routines of baby care; articles that offer professional insights into family and marriage relationships; reports of new trends and significant research findings in education and in mental and physical health; and articles encouraging informed citizen action on matters of social concern. Especially need articles on women's issues, pregnancy, birth, baby care and early childhood. We prefer a warm, colloquial style of writing, one which avoids the extremes of either slang or technical jargon. Anecdotes and examples should be used to illustrate points which can then be summed up by straight exposition." Query. Length: 2,500 words maximum. Payment varies; pays $400 minimum; $50 minimum for Almanac items. Sometimes pays the expenses of writers on assignment.

PEDIATRICS FOR PARENTS, The Newsletter for Caring Parents, Pediatrics for Parents, Inc., 176 Mt. Hope Ave., Bangor ME 04401. (207)942-6212. Editor: Richard J. Sagall, M.D. 20% freelance written. Eager to work with new/unpublished writers. Monthly newsletter covering medical aspects of rearing children and educating parents about children's health. Circ. 2,000. Pays on publication. Publishes ms an average of 3-4 months after acceptance. Byline given. Buys first North American serial rights, first and second rights to the same material, and second (reprint) rights to material originally published elsewhere. Rights always include right to publish article in our books on "Best of . . ." series. Submit seasonal/holiday material 6 months in advance. Simultaneous queries, and simultaneous, photocopied and previously published submissions OK. Query for electronic submissions. Computer printout submissions acceptable. Reports in 1 month on queries; 6 weeks on mss. Sample copy for $2; writer's guidelines for #10 SAE and 2 first class stamps.
Nonfiction: Book reviews; how-to (feed healthy kids, exercise, practice wellness, etc.); new product; technical (explaining medical concepts in shirtsleeve language). No general parenting articles. Query with published clips or submit complete ms. Length: 25-1,000 words. Pays 2-5¢/edited word.
Columns/Departments: Book reviews; Please Send Me (material available to parents for free or at nominal cost); Pedia-Tricks (medically-oriented parenting tips that work). Send complete ms. Pays $15-250. Pays 2/edited word.
Tips: "We are dedicated to taking the mystery out of medicine for young parents. Therefore, we write in clear and understandable language (but not simplistic language) to help people understand and deal intelligently with complex disease processes, treatments, prevention, wellness, etc. Our articles must be well researched and documented. Detailed references must always be attached to any article for documentation, but not for publication. We strongly urge freelancers to read one or two issues before writing."

SESAME STREET MAGAZINE, Parent's Guide, Children's Television Workshop, One Lincoln Plaza, New York NY 10023. (212)595-3456. FAX: (212)580-3845. Editor-in-Chief: Marge Kennedy. Articles Editor: Rebecca Herman. 60% freelance written. A monthly magazine for parents of preschoolers. Circ. 1.3 million. Pays ½ on acceptance, ½ on publication. Byline given. Offers 50% kill fee. Buys all rights. Submit seasonal/holiday material 7 months in advance. Reports in 1 month on queries. Sample copy for 9x12 SAE with 6 first class stamps. Writer's guidelines for #10 SAE.
Nonfiction: Book excerpts, essays, general interest (child development/parenting), how-to (practical tips for parents of preschoolers), interview/profile, personal experience, photo feature and travel (with children). Buys 20 mss/year. Query with or without published clips, or send complete ms. Length: 800-4,000 words. Pays $200-900 for assigned articles. Pays $200-500 for unsolicited articles.
Photos: State availability of photos with submission. Model releases and identification of subjects required. Buys one-time rights or all rights.

‡**THE SINGLE PARENT**, Parents Without Partners, Inc., 8807 Colesville Rd., Silver Spring MD 20910. (301)588-9354. Editor: Allan N. Glennon. 60% freelance written. Works with small number of new/unpublished writers each year. Magazine, published 6 times/year; 48 pages. Emphasizes single parenting, family, divorce, widowhood and children. Distributed to members of Parents Without Partners, plus libraries, universities, psychologists, psychiatrists, subscribers, etc. Circ. 120,000. Pays on publication. Publishes ms an average of 6-9 months after acceptance. Buys one-time rights. Simultaneous, photocopied, and previously published submissions OK. No electronic submissions. Computer printout submissions acceptable. Reports in 2 months. Sample copy $1, writer's guidelines for #10 SASE.
Nonfiction: Informational (parenting, legal issues, single parents in society, programs that work for single parents, children's problems); how-to (raise children alone, travel, take up a new career, cope with life as a new or veteran single parent; short lists of how-to tips). No first-hand accounts of bitter legal battles with former spouses. No "poor me" articles. Buys 30 unsolicited mss/year. Query not required. Mss not returned unless SASE is enclosed. Length: 1,000-3,000 words. Payment $50-150, based on content, not length.
Columns/Departments: F.Y.I., for short news items, reports on research, tips on how to do things better, and new products, Letters to Editor column.
Photos: Purchased with accompanying ms. Also, use freelance stock shots. Query. Pays negotiable rates. Model release required.
Tips: "Be familiar with our magazine and its readership before trying to write for us. We publish constructive, upbeat articles that present new ideas for coping with and solving the problems that confront single parents. Articles on origins of Halloween customs, tribal behavior in Ghana, or how to predict the weather have little likelihood of acceptance unless there is a clear tie-in to single parent issues."

TWINS, The Magazine for Parents of Multiples, Box 12045, Overland Park KS 66212. (913)722-1090. FAX: (913)722-1767. Editor: Barbara C. Unell. 100% freelance written. Eager to work with new/unpublished writers. A bimonthly national magazine designed to give professional guidance to help multiples, their parents and those professionals who care for them learn about twin facts and research. Circ. 40,000. Pays on publication. Publishes ms an average of 6 months after acceptance. Byline given. Buys all rights. Submit seasonal/holiday material 10 months in advance. Simultaneous, photocopied and previously published submissions OK. Computer printout submissions acceptable; prefers letter-quality. Reports in 6 weeks on queries; 2

months on mss. Sample copy $3.50 plus $1.50 postage and handling; writer's guidelines for #10 SASE.

Nonfiction: Book excerpts, general interest, how-to, humor, interview/profile, personal experience and photo feature. "No articles which substitute the word 'twin' for 'child'—those that simply apply the same research to twins that applies to singletons without any facts backing up the reason to do so." Buys 150 mss/ year. Query with or without published clips, or send complete ms. Length: 1,250-3,000 words. Payment varies; sometimes pays in contributor copies or premiums instead of cash. Sometimes pays the expenses of writers on assignment.

Photos: Send photos with submission. Reviews contact sheets, 4x5 transparencies, and all size prints. Captions, model releases, and identification of subjects required. Buys all rights.

Columns/Departments: Resources, Supertwins, Prematurity, Family Health, Twice as Funny, Double Focus (series from pregnancy through adolescence), Personal Perspective (first-person accounts of beliefs about a certain aspect of parenting multiples), Home-Grown Advice (specific tips that have worked for the writer in raising multiples), Consumer Matters, Feelings on Fatherhood, Research, On Being Twins (first-person accounts of growing up as a twin), On Being Parents of Twins (first-person accounts of the experience of parenting twins), Double Takes (fun photographs of twins), and Education Matters. Buys 70 mss/year. Query with published clips. Length: 1,250-2,000 words. Payment varies.

Fillers: Anecdotes and short humor. Length: 75-750 words. Payment varies.

Tips: "Features and columns are both open to freelancers. Columnists write for *Twins* on a continuous basis, so the column becomes their column. We are looking for a wide variety of the latest, well-researched practical information. There is no other magazine of this type directed to this market." We are interested in "personal interviews with celebrity twins or celebrity parents of twins, and tips on rearing twins from experienced parents and/or twins themselves, as well as reports on national and international research studies involving twins."

Comic Books

Comic books aren't just for kids. Today, this medium also attracts a reader who is older and wants stories presented visually on a wide variety of topics. This doesn't mean you have to be an artist to write for comic books. Most of these publishers want to see a synopsis of one to two double-spaced pages. Highlight the story's beginning, middle and end, and tell how events will affect your main character emotionally. Be concise. Comics use few words and rely on graphics as well as words to forward the plot.

Once your synopsis is accepted, either an artist will draw the story from your plot, returning these pages to you for dialogue and captions, or you will be expected to write a script. Scripts run approximately 23 typewritten pages and include suggestions for artwork as well as dialogue. Try to imagine your story on actual comic book pages and divide your script accordingly. The average comic has six panels per page, with a maximum of 35 words per panel.

If you're submitting a proposal to Marvel or DC, your story should center on an already established character. If you're dealing with an independent publisher, characters are often the property of their creators. Your proposal should be for a new series. Include a background sheet for main characters who will appear regularly, listing origins, weaknesses, powers or other information that will make your character unique. Indicate an overall theme or direction for your series. Submit story ideas for the first three issues. If you're really ambitious, you may also include a script for your first issue. As with all markets, read a sample copy before making a submission.

AMAZING HEROES, Fantagraphics Books, 7563 Lake City Way, Seattle WA 98115. Editor: Chris McCubbin. 80% freelance written. Eager to work with new/unpublished writers. A biweekly magazine for comic book fans of all ages and backgrounds. "*Amazing Heroes* focuses on both historical aspects of comics and current doings in the industry." Circ. 15,000. Pays on publication. Publishes ms an average of 2 months after acceptance. Byline given. Offers $25 kill fee on solicited ms. Buys first North American serial rights and second serial (reprint) rights. Submit seasonal/holiday material 3 months in advance. Photocopied and previously published submissions OK. Computer printout submissions OK; prefers letter-quality. Reports in 2 weeks on queries; 1 month on mss. Sample copy for 7½x10½ SAE and $2.50.

Nonfiction: Essays, historical/nostalgic, interview/profile, new product. Query with published clips and interests. Length: 300-7,500 words. Pays $5-125 for assigned articles; pays $5-75 for unsolicited articles. Pays writers with double payment in Fantagraphics book merchandise if requested. Sometimes pays the expenses of writers on assignment.

Photos: State availability of photos on profile pieces and interviews.

Tips: "Recently, there has been a renaissance, though some refer to it as a glut, of new material and new publishers in the comic book industry. This has called for a greater need for more writers who are not just interested in super-heroes or just books produced by DC and Marvel. There is now, more than ever, a need to be open-minded as well as critical. Writers for *Amazing Heroes* must have a much broader knowledge of the entire, ever-widening spectrum of the comic book industry."

CARTOON WORLD, Box 30367, Dept. WM, Lincoln NE 68503. Editor: George Hartman. 100% freelance written. Works with published/established writers and a small number of new/unpublished writers each year. "Monthly newsletter for professional and amateur cartoonists who are serious and want to utilize new cartoon markets in each issue." Buys only from paid subscribers. Circ. 150-300. Pays on acceptance. Publishes ms an average of 2 months after acceptance. Byline given. Buys second (reprint) rights to material originally published elsewhere. Not copyrighted. Submit seasonal/holiday material 3 months in advance. Simultaneous submissions OK. Computer printout submissions acceptable; no dot-matrix. Reports in 1 month. Sample copy $5.

Nonfiction: "We want only positive articles about the business of cartooning and gag writing." Buys 10 mss/year. Query. Length: 1,000 words. Pays $5/page.

COMICO THE COMIC COMPANY, 1547 DeKalb St., Norristown PA 19401. (215)277-4305. FAX: (215)277-5651. Publisher: Phil LaSorda. 100% freelance written. "Due to market conditions, Comico will not consider *any* new material until early in 1990. We work only with writers, published or unpublished, who can tell a strong, solid, and visual story." One-shot, limited and continuing series comic books. Circ. approximately 70,000 per title. Pays 1 month after acceptance. Publishes ms an average of 9-12 months after acceptance. Byline given. Buys first rights, makes work-for-hire assignments or offers creator ownership contracts. Simultaneous, photocopied and previously published submissions OK. Computer printout submissions OK; no dot-matrix. Reports in 1 month on queries; 2 months on mss. Sample copy for $2.50 and 7½x10½ SAE and 3 first class stamps; writer's guidelines for #10 SASE.

Fiction: Various genres. "We are always interested in seeing submissions of new and innovative material. Due to the words-and-pictures format of comic books, it is usually preferable, though not essential, that the writer submit material in conjunction with an artist of his or her choice." No pornography or dogma. Buys 100 mss/year. Query. Length: 24 story pages. Payment varies.

Tips: "Our industry in general and our company in particular are beginning to look more and more at the limited series format as a means of properly conveying solid stories, beautifully illustrated for the adult marketplace, as opposed to the standard continuing serials. Be familiar with comics medium and industry. Show that writer can write in script format and express intentions to artist who will create images based on writer's descriptions. The area of licensed properties is most open to freelancers. Writer must be faithful to licensed characters, to licensor's wishes, and be willing to make any requested changes."

COMICS SCENE, O'Quinn Studios, 475 Park Avenue S, 8th Floor, New York NY 10016. (212)689-2830. FAX: (212)889-7933. Editor: David McDonnell. Bi-monthly magazine on comic books, comic strips, and animated cartoons; those who create them and TV/movie adaptations of both. Pays on publication. Byline given. Offers 25% kill fee. Buys first North American serial rights or second serial (reprint) rights. Submit seasonal/holiday material 5-6 months in advance. Simultaneous (*if* informed), photocopied and previously published submissions (in certain cases) OK. Computer printout submissions OK. Reports in 6 weeks on queries; 2 months on mss. Sample copy $3.50; writer's guidelines for #10 SASE.

Nonfiction: Book excerpts, historical/nostalgic, interview/profile, new product, personal experience. Buys 60 mss/year. Query with published clips. Length: 750-3,500 words. Pays $75-200. Sometimes pays expenses of writers on assignment. Does *not* publish ficiton.

Photos: State availability of photos and comic strip/book/animation artwork with submission. Reviews contact sheets, transparencies, 8x10 prints. Offers $5-25 for original photos. Captions, model releases, identification of subjects required. Buys all rights.

Columns/Departments: The Comics Scene (interviews with comic book artists, writers and editors on upcoming projects and new developments), 100-500 words; The Comics Reporter ("newsy" interviews with writer, director, producer of TV series, and movie adaptations of comic books and strips). Buys 50 mss/year. Query with published clips. Length: 100-750 words. Pays $15-50.

Tips: "We really need small department items, re: independent comics companies' products and creators. We're also especially in need of interviews with specific comic strip creators. Comics are hot and comics—based movies (thanks to Batman) should be even hotter in '90. We anticipate no changes in focus. And most any writer can break in with interviews with hot comic book writers and artists—and with comic book creators who don't work for the big five companies. We do *not* want nostalgic items or interviews. Do not burden us with your own personal comic book stories or artwork. Want to sell us something? Get us interviews we can't get or haven't thought to pursue. Out-thinking overworked editors is a great way to sell a story."

ECLIPSE COMICS, Box 1099, Forestville CA 95436. (707)887-1521. Publisher: Dean Mullaney. Editor-in-Chief: Catherine Yronwode. 100% freelance written. Works with a small number of new/unpublished writers each year. Publishers of various four-color comic books. *Eclipse* publishes comic books with high-quality paper and color reproduction, geared toward the discriminating comic book fan; and sold through the "direct sales" specialty store market. Circ. varies (35,000-85,000). Pays on acceptance (net 1 month). Publishes ms an average of 3 months after acceptance. Byline given. Buys first North American serial rights, second serial (reprint) rights with additional payment, and first option on collection and non-exclusive rights to sell material to South American and European markets (with additional payments). Simultaneous queries, and simultaneous and photocopied submissions OK. Computer printout submissions acceptable; no dot-matrix. Reports in 2 months. Sample copy $1.75; writer's guidelines for #10 SASE.
Fiction: "Most of our comics are fictional." Adventure, fantasy, mystery, science fiction, horror. "No sexually explicit material, please." Buys approximately 200 mss/year (mostly from established comics writers). Send sample script or plot synopsis for a back-up story staring one of our lesser-known characters (The Heap, Black Angel, Iron Ace, etc.). Length: 8-11 pages. Pays $30 minimum/page.
Tips: "At the present time we are publishing both adventure and super-heroic series but we are currently scheduling fewer 32-page periodical adventure comics and more 48-96 page graphic albums, some of which are nonfiction current events journalism in graphic format. We are moving into the arena of political and social commentary and current events in graphic form. We have also expanded our line of classic newspaper strip reprints. Because all of our comics are creator-owned, we do not buy fill-in plots or scripts for our periodicals. Plot synopsis less than a page can be submitted; we will select promising concepts for development into full script submissions. All full script submissions should be written in comic book or 'screenplay' form for artists to illustrate. Writers who are already teamed with artists stand a better chance of selling material to us, but if necessary we'll find an artist. Our special needs at the moment are for heroic, character-oriented series with overtones of humanism, morality, political opinion, philosophical speculation, and/or social commentary. Comic book adaptations (by the original authors) of previously published science fiction and horror short stories are definitely encouraged. Queries about current events/nonfiction albums should be discussed with us prior to a full-blown submission."

MARVEL COMICS, 387 Park Ave. S., New York NY 10016. (212)576-9200. Editor-in-Chief: Tom DeFalco. 99% freelance written. Publishes 60 comics and magazines per month, 6-12 graphic novels per year, and specials, storybooks, industrials, and paperbacks for all ages. Over 9 million copies sold/month. Pays a flat fee for most projects, plus a royalty type incentive based upon sales. Also works on advance/royalty basis on many projects. Pays on acceptance. Publishes manuscript an average of 6 months after acceptance. Byline given. Offers variable kill fee. Rights purchased depend upon format and material. Submit seasonal/holiday material 1 year in advance. Simultaneous and photocopied submissions OK. Computer printout submissions OK; no dot-matrix. Reports in 6 months. Writer's guidelines for #10 SASE. Additional guidelines on request.
Fiction: Super hero, action-adventure, science fiction, fantasy, and other material. No noncomics. Buys 600-800 mss/year. Query with brief plot synopses only. Do not send scripts, short stories or long outlines. A plot synopsis should be less than two typed pages; send two synopses at most. Pays expenses of writers on assignment.

_____ *Consumer Service and Business Opportunity*

Some of these magazines are geared to investing earnings or starting a new business; others show how to make economical purchases. Publications for business executives and consumers interested in business topics are listed under Business and Finance. Those on how to run specific businesses are classified by category in the Trade section.

BUSINESS TODAY, Meridian Publishing, Box 10010, Ogden UT 84409. (801)394-9446. Editor: Libby Hyland. 40% freelance written. Monthly magazine covering all aspects of business. Particularly interested in tips to small/medium business managers. Pays on acceptance. Publishes ms an average of 8 months after acceptance. Byline given. Buys first rights, second serial (reprint) rights and nonexclusive reprint rights. Computer printout submissions acceptable; prefers letter-quality. Reports in 2 months. Sample copy for $1 and 9x12 SAE;

writer's guidelines for #10 SASE. All requests for samples and guidelines should be addressed Attn: Editorial Assistant.

Nonfiction: General interest articles about employee relations, management principles, advertising methods and financial planning. Articles covering up-to-date practical business information are welcome. Cover stories are often profiles of people who have expertise and success in a specific aspect of business. Buys 40 mss/year. Query. Length: 1,000-1,200 words. Pays 15¢/word for first rights plus non-exclusive reprint rights. Payment for second rights is negotiable.

Photos: State availability of photos or send photos with query. Reviews 35mm or larger transparencies. Pays $35 for inside photo; pays $50 for cover photo. Captions, model releases and identification of subjects required.

Tips: "We're looking for meaty, hard-core business articles with practical applications. Profiles should be prominent business-people, preferably Fortune-500 league. The key is a well-written query letter that: 1) demonstrates that the subject of the article is tried-and-true and has national appeal 2) shows that the article will have a clear, focused theme 3) outlines the availability (from writer or a photographer or a PR source) of top-quality color photos 4) gives evidence that the writer/photographer is a professional, even if a beginner."

CHANGING TIMES, The Kiplinger Magazine, 1729 H St. NW, Washington DC 20006. Editor: Ted Miller. Less than 10% freelance written. Prefers to work with published/established writers. For general, adult audience interested in personal finance and consumer information. Monthly. Circ. 1,350,000. Pays on acceptance. Publishes ms an average of 2 months after acceptance. Buys all rights. Reports in 1 month. Query for electronic submissions. Computer printout submissions acceptable; prefers letter-quality. Thorough documentation required for fact-checking.

Nonfiction: "Most material is staff-written, but we accept some freelance." Query with clips of published work. Pays expenses of writers on assignment.

Tips: "We are looking for a heavy emphasis on personal finance topics."

COMMERCE MAGAZINE, 200 N. LaSalle St., Chicago IL 60601. (312)580-6900. Editor: Carol Johnson. For top businessmen and industrial leaders in greater Chicago area. Monthly magazine; varies from 100 to 300 pages, (8½x11½). Circ. 15,000. Buys all rights. Buys 30-40 mss/year. Pays on acceptance. Query.

Nonfiction: Business articles and pieces of general interest to top business executives. "We select our freelancers and assign topics. Many of our writers are from local newspapers. Considerable freelance material is used but almost exclusively on assignment from Chicago-area specialists within a particular business sector."

CONSUMER ACTION NEWS, Suite 216, 1106 E. High St., Springfield OH 45505. (513)325-2001. Editor: Victor Pence. 10% freelance written. Eager to work with new/unpublished writers. A monthly newsletter circulated in the state of Ohio for readers who are interested in knowing how to handle any type of consumer complaint. "We handle consumer complaints and publish results in newsletter." Pays on acceptance. Byline given. Buys one-time rights. Simultaneous queries, and simultaneous, photocopied, and previously published submissions OK. Computer printout submissions acceptable; prefers letter-quality. Reports in 6 weeks. Sample copy for 9x12 SAE and $1.25 postage; writer's guidelines for #10 SASE.

Nonfiction: Send complete ms. Length: 1,000 words or less. Pays $10-25.

Tips: "We want only experiences with complaints that were solved when the usual protection sources couldn't solve them. Creative ways of finding solutions without legal actions. If the problem has not been solved, we will offer possible solutions to the problem anywhere in the U.S., Canada or Mexico at no charge."

‡CONSUMERS DIGEST MAGAZINE, for People who Demand Value, Consumers Digest, Inc., 5705 N. Lincoln Ave., Chicago IL 60201. (312)275-3590. Editor: John Manos. Executive Editor: Elliott H. McCleary. 75% freelance written. Prefers to work with published/established writers. Emphasizes anything of consumer interest. Recommends products and services for a middle-American audience, specifying brands and models as Best Buys. Bi-monthly magazine. Circ. 900,000. Pays on acceptance. Publishes ms an average of 3 months after acceptance. Offers 50% kill fee. Buys all rights. Computer printout submissions acceptable; prefers letter-quality to dot-matrix. Reports in 1 month. Free guidelines for SAE and 1 first class stamp to published writers only.

Nonfiction: Product-testing, evaluating; general interest (on advice to consumers, service, health, home, business, investments, insurance and money management); new products and travel. Query. Length: 500-3,500 words. Pays $150-1,200 for assigned articles, $150-500 for unsolicited articles. Pays expenses of writers on assignment.

Photos: State availability of photos with submission. Model releases and identification of subjects required. Buys one-time rights.

Columns/Departments: Buys 3 mss/year. Length: 100-400 words. Pays $50-200.

Tips: "Study writer's guidelines and sample copy, try for a fresh subject."

ECONOMIC FACTS, The National Research Bureau, Inc., 424 N. 3rd St., Burlington IA 52601. FAX: (319)752-3421. Editor: Rhonda Wilson. Editorial Supervisor: Doris J. Ruschill. 25% freelance written. Eager to work with new/unpublished writers; works with a small number of new/unpublished writers each year. Magazine for industrial workers of all ages. Published 4 times/year. Pays on publication. Publishes ms an average of 1 year after acceptance. Buys all rights. Byline given. Submit seasonal/holiday material 7 months in advance of issue date. Previously published submissions OK. Computer printout submissions acceptable; prefers letter-quality. Reports in 1 week. Free sample copy, writer's guidelines for #10 SASE.
Nonfiction: General interest (private enterprise, government data, graphs, taxes and health care). Buys 3-5 mss/year. Query with outline of article. Length: 400-600 words. Pays 4¢/word.

ENTREPRENEUR MAGAZINE, 2392 Morse Ave., Box 19787, Irvine CA 92714-6234. Editor: Rieva Lesonsky. 40% freelance written. "We are eager to work with any writer who takes the time to see *Entrepreneur*'s special 'angle' and who turns in copy on time." For a readership looking for opportunities in small business, as owners, franchisees or seeking "tips and tactics to help them better run their existing small business." Circ. 300,000. Pays on acceptance. Publishes ms an average of 3-5 months after acceptance. Buys all rights. Byline given. Submit seasonal/holiday material 6 months in advance of issue date. Computer printout submissions acceptable. Reports in 2 months. Sample copy $3; writer's guidelines for #10 SASE.
Nonfiction: How-to (information on running a business, profiles on unique entrepreneurs). Buys 60-70 mss/year. Query with clips of published work and SASE. Length: 750-2,000 words. Payment varies.
Photos: "We need color transparencies to illustrate articles." Offers additional payment for photos accepted with ms. Uses standard color transparencies. Captions preferred. Buys all rights. Model release required.
Tips: "It's rewarding to find a freelancer who reads the magazine *before* he/she submits a query. We get so many queries with the wrong angle. I can't stress enough the importance of reading and understanding our magazine and our audience before you write. We're looking for writers who can perceive the difference between *Entrepreneur* and 'other' business magazines."

‡FDA CONSUMER, 5600 Fishers Lane, Rockville MD 20857. (301)443-3220. Editor: William M. Rados. 20% freelance written. Prefers to work with experienced health and medical writers. Monthly magazine. December/January and July/August issues combined. For "all consumers of products regulated by the Food and Drug Administration." A federal government publication. Circ. 25,000. Pays after acceptance. Publishes ms an average of 3 months after acceptance. Byline given. Not copyrighted. Pays 50% kill fee. "All purchases automatically become part of public domain." Buys 10-20 freelance mss a year. "We cannot be responsible for any work by writer not agreed upon by prior contract." Query for electronic submissions. Computer printout submissions acceptable; prefers letter-quality. Free sample copy.
Nonfiction: "Articles of an educational nature concerning purchase and use of *FDA regulated* products and specific FDA programs and actions to protect the consumer's health and pocketbook. Authoritative and official agency viewpoints emanating from agency policy and actions in administrating the Food, Drug and Cosmetic Act and a number of other statutes. All articles subject to clearance by the appropriate FDA experts as well as acceptance by the editor. Articles based on health topics with the proviso that the subjects be connected to food, drugs, medicine, medical devices, and other products regulated by FDA. All articles based on prior arrangement by contract." Query. Length: 2,000-2,500 words. Pays $1,000 average. Sometimes pays the expenses of writers on assignment.
Photos: B&w photos are purchased on assignment only.
Tips: "Besides reading the feature articles in *FDA Consumer*, a writer can best determine whether his/her style and expertise suit our needs by submitting a query letter, resume and sample clips for our review."

INCOME OPPORTUNITIES, 380 Lexington Ave., New York NY 10017. FAX: (212)986-7313. Editor: Stephen Wagner. Managing Editor: Dara Wertheimer. 90% freelance written. Works with a small number of new/unpublished writers each year. Monthly magazine. For all who are seeking business opportunities, full- or part-time. Publishes ms an average of 5 months after acceptance. Buys all rights. Two special directory issues contain articles on selling techniques, mail order, import/export, franchising and home business ideas. Query for details on electronic submissions. Computer printout submissions acceptable. Reports in 2 weeks. Writer's guidelines for #10 SASE.
Nonfiction and Photos: Regularly covered are such subjects as mail order, home business, direct selling, franchising, party plans, selling techniques and the marketing of handcrafted or homecrafted products. Wanted are ideas for the aspiring entrepreneur; examples of successful business methods that might be duplicated. No material that is purely inspirational. Buys 50-60 mss/year. Query with outline of article development. Length: 800 words for a short; 2,000-3,000 words for a major article. "Payment rates vary according to length and quality of the submission." Sometimes pays expenses of writers on assignment.
Tips: "Study recent issues of the magazine. Best bets for newcomers: Interview-based report on a successful small business venture. Our emphasis is on home-based business."

TOWERS CLUB, USA NEWSLETTER, The Original Information-By-Mail, Direct-Marketing Newsletter, Towers Club Press, Box 2038, Vancouver WA 98668. (206)574-3084. Editor: Jerry Buchanan. 5-10% freelance written. Works with a small number of new/unpublished writers each year. Newsletter published 10 times/

year (not published in May or December) covering entrepreneurism (especially selling useful information by mail). Circ. 8,000. Pays on publication. Publishes ms an average of 2 months after acceptance. Byline given. Buys one-time rights. Submit seasonal/holiday material 10 weeks in advance. Simultaneous, photocopied, and previously published submissions OK. Query for electronic submissions. Reports in 2 weeks. Sample copy for $5 and 6x9 SAE; writer's guidelines for $1 and #10 SAE.

Nonfiction: Exposé (of mail order fraud); how-to (personal experience in self-publishing and marketing); book reviews of new self-published nonfiction how-to-do-it books (must include name and address of author). "Welcomes well-written articles of successful self-publishing/marketing ventures. Must be current, and preferably written by the person who actually did the work and reaped the rewards. There's very little we will not consider, *if* it pertains to unique money-making enterprises that can be operated from the home." Buys 10 mss/year. Send complete ms. Length: 500-1,500 words. Pays $10-35. Pays extra for b&w photo and bonus for excellence in longer manuscript.

Tips: "The most frequent mistake made by writers in completing an article for us is that they think they can simply rewrite a newspaper article and be accepted. That is only the start. We want them to find the article about a successful self-publishing enterprise, and then go out and interview the principal for a more detailed how-to article, including names and addresses. We prefer that writer actually interview a successful self-publisher. Articles should include how idea first came to subject; how they implemented and financed and promoted the project; how long it took to show a profit and some of the stumbling blocks they overcame; how many persons participated in the production and promotion; and how much money was invested (approximately) and other pertinent how-to elements of the story. Glossy photos (b&w) of principals at work in their offices will help sell article."

———— Contemporary Culture

These magazines combine politics, gossip, fashion and entertainment in a single package. Their approach to institutions is typically irreverent and the target is primarily a young adult audience. Although most of the magazines are centered in large metropolitan areas, some like *Spy* have a following throughout the country.

BOMB, New Art Productions, Suite 177, Franklin St., New York NY 10013. Editor: Betsy Sussler. 100% freelance written. Quarterly magazine on new art, writing, theater and film for artists and writers. Circ. 10,000. Publishes ms an average of 3 months after acceptance. Byline given. Buys one-time rights. Photocopied submissions OK. Computer printout submissions OK; prefers letter-quality. Reports in 3-6 months. Sample copy for 12x15 SAE and $1.50 postage; writer's guidelines for #10 SASE.

Nonfiction: Buys 4 mss/year. Length: 2,500-3,000 words. Pays $50-100.

Photos: State availability of photos with submission. Offers $25-100 per photo. Captions required. Buys one-time rights.

Fiction: Experimental, novel excerpts. Buys 20 mss/year. Send complete ms. Length: 1,200-4,000 words. Pays $50-100.

BOSTON REVIEW, 33 Harrison Ave., Boston MA 02111. (617)350-5353. Editor: Margaret Ann Roth. 100% freelance written. Works with a small number of new/unpublished writers each year. Bimonthly magazine of the arts, politics and culture. Circ. 10,000. Pays on acceptance. Publishes ms an average of 2 months after acceptance. Buys first American serial rights. Byline given. Photocopied and simultaneous submissions OK. Computer printout submissions acceptable; prefers letter-quality. Reports in 2 months. Sample copy $3; writer's guidelines for #10 SASE.

Nonfiction: Critical essays and reviews, natural and social sciences, literature, music, painting, film, photography, dance and theatre. Buys 20 unsolicited mss/year. Length: 1,000-3,000 words. Sometimes pays expenses of writers on assignment.

Fiction: Length: 2,000-4,000 words. Pays according to length and author, ranging from $50-200.

Poetry: Pays according to length and author.

Tips: "Short (500 words) color pieces are particularly difficult to find, and so we are always on the look-out for them. We look for in-depth knowledge of an area, an original view of the material, and a presentation which makes these accessible to a sophisticated reader who will be looking for more and better articles which anticipate ideas and trends on the intellectual and cultural frontier."

CANADIAN DIMENSION, Dimension Publications Inc., #801-44 Princess St., Winnipeg, Manitoba, R3B 1K2 Canada. 80% freelance written. A magazine on economics, politics and popular cultures, published 8 times/year. Circ. 5,000. Pays on publication. Publishes ms an average of 6 months after acceptance. Not copyrighted. Simultaneous and photocopied submissions OK. Query for electronic submissions. Computer printout submissions OK; prefers letter-quality. Reports in 6 weeks on queries. Sample copy $1; writer's guidelines for #10 SAE.

Nonfiction: General interest, humor, interview/profile, opinion, personal experience and reviews. Buys 8 mss/year. Length: 500-2,000 words. Pays $25-300 for assigned articles. Send photos and/or graphics with submission.

‡DETAILS, Details Publishing Corp., Suite 711, 611 Broadway, New York NY 10012. (212)420-1113. Editor: Annie Flanders. Managing Editor: Alan Weitz. Appears 10 times per year, a magazine on fashion, style, nightlife, lifestyle. "We call *Details* the fashion statement of the Avant-Garb. We cover fashion, nightlife, arts and entertainment, interior design, all with an alternative slant." Circ. 100,000. Pays on publication. Publishes ms an average of 3 months after acceptance. Byline given. Offers 50% kill fee (of agreed price – usually). Buys all rights. Submit seasonal/holiday material 3 months in advance. Simultaneous sumbissions OK. Computer printout submissions OK; prefers letter-quality. Reports in 1 month. Free sample copy.

Nonfiction: Essays, humor, interview/profile, personal experience, photo feature and travel. Buys 100 mss/year. Query with published clips. Length: 500-3,000 words. Pays $75-750 for assigned articles. Sometime pays expenses of writers on assignment.

Photos: State availability of photos with submission. Offers $50-100 per photo. Captions, model releases and identification of subjects required. Buys all rights.

Columns/Departments: Film (reviews of unique or important films), 1,000 words; Music (reviews of unique or important groups or artists), 1,000 words; Art (reviews of unique or important artists), 1,000 words; Knifestyles (personal cosmetic surgery reports), 1,000 words and Fashion (reviews of unique & important designers), 1,000 words. Query with published clips. Buys 50 mss/year. Pays $50-500.

Fiction: Experimental, humorous and slice-of-life vignettes. Buys 20 mss/year. Query with published clips. Length: 1,000-3,000 words. Pays $100-500.

Poetry: Avant-garde and free verse. Buys 5 poems/year. Pays $50-250.

Tips: "All articles, whether on film, music, fashion, nightlife, lifestyle, design, art, entertainment, should be treated with passion. We want our writers to feel strongly about what they're covering, to be involved with their subject. There should be a point of view."

‡FOLLOW ME, Brugi Design Pty. Ltd., 2nd Floor, 2-4 Bellevue St., Surry Hills, Sydney NSW Australia 2010. (2)212-5344. FAX: 61-2-2126037. Editor: Robin Powell. 50% freelance written. Bimonthly magazine "for ages 25-40 professionals, interested in fashion, art, photography, writing film etc.;; Circ. 60,000. Pays on acceptance. Publishes ms an average of 5-6 months after acceptance (long lead-time as we print overseas). Offers $100 kill fee commissioned stories only. Buys first Australian serial rights. Submit seasonal/holiday material 6 months in advance. Computer printout submissions OK; prefers letter-quality. Sample copy US $10 covers sea postage.

Nonfiction: Book excerpts, essays, historical, humor, interview/profile, photo feature and travel. Buys 30 mss/year. Query with published clips. "We will discuss individual assignments by phone, fax or mail." Length: 700-4,000 words. Pays $150-200/1,000 words.

Photos: State availability of photos with submission. Reviews 35 mm transparencies and 8x10 prints. Offers $50-200 per photo. Captions, model releases and identificaiton of subjects required. Buys one-time rights.

Columns/Departments: All columns currently on permanent freelance basis. Will take suggstions for new permanent columns. Buys 26 mss/year. Query with published clips. Length: 700-1,500 words. Pays $150-250.

Fiction: Erotica, historical, humorous, novel excerpts and slice-of-life vignettes. Buys 10 mss/year. Query with published clips. Length: 2,000-4,500 words. Pays $350 – set fee.

‡FOLLOW ME GENTLEMAN, Brugi Design Pty. Ltd., 2nd Fl., 2-4 Bellevue St., Surry Hills, Sydney NSW Australia 2010. (2)212-5344. Editor: Robin Powell. 50% freelance written. Quarterly magazine. See *Follow Me.*

HIGH TIMES, Trans High Corp., Floor 20, 211 E. 43rd St., New York NY 10017. (212)972-8484. Editor: Steve Hager. Executive Editor: John Holmstrom. 75% freelance written. Monthly magazine covering marijuana. Circ. 250,000. Pays on publication. Byline given. Offers 20% kill fee. Buys one-time rights, all rights, or makes work-for-hire assignments. Submit seasonal/holiday material 6 months in advance. Simultaneous and photocopied submissions OK. Computer printout submissions OK. Reports in 1 month on queries; 2 months on mss. Sample for $5 and SASE; writer's guidelines for SASE.

Nonfiction: Book excerpts, expose, humor, interview/profile, new product, personal experience, photo feature and travel. Special issues include indoor Growers issue in September. No stories on "my drug bust." Buys 30 mss/year. Send complete ms. Length: 1,000-10,000 words. Pays $150-400. Sometimes pays in trade for advertisements. Sometimes pays expenses of writers on assignment.

Photos: Send photos with submission. Pays $50-300. Captions, model releases and identification of subjects required. Buys all rights or one-time use.

Columns/Departments: Steve Bloom, news editor. Drug related books; drug related news. Buys 10 mss/year. Query with published clips. Length: 100-2,000 words. Pays $25-300.

Fiction: Adventure, fantasy, humorous and stories on smuggling. Buys 5 mss/year. Send complete ms. Length: 2,000-5,000 words. Pays $250-400.

Poetry: Edie Barrett, poetry editor. Avant-garde, free verse. Buys 1 poem/year. Pays $5-50.

Fillers: Gags to be illustrated by cartoonist, newsbreaks and short humor. Buys 10/year. Length: 100-500 words. Pays $10-50. Cartoon Editor: John Holmstrom.

Tips: "All sections are open to good, professional writers."

‡**MTL MAGAZINE, ENGLISH,** Canam Publications, 8270 Mountain Sights #201, Montreal, Quebec H4P 2B7 Canada. (514)731-9517. Publisher: James Dawe. Assistant to Publisher: Ava Chisling. 80% freelance written. Monthly magazine that deals with social issues mostly concerned with Montrealers. "We do not strive for mediocrity and demand that our writers write about what they know best. We ask that submissions be original in thought and can be learned from in at least one of the many ways possible." Estab. 1988. Circ. 55,000. Pays on publication. Publishes ms an average of 1 month after acceptance. Byline given. Buys first rights, second serial (reprint) rights. Submit seasonal/holiday material 3 months in advance. Query for electronic submissions. Computer printout submissions OK; prefers letter-quality. Free writer's guidelines with SAE.

Nonfiction: Humor, inspirational, interview/profile, personal experience, photo feature and image pieces, i.e. health, fitness, grooming etc. Buys 50 mss/year. Query with published clips. Length: 250-2,000 words. Pays $75-1,000. Sometimes pays expenses of writers on assignment.

Photos: State availability of photos with submission. Reviews negatives, transparencies and prints. Captions and identification of subjects required. Buys one-time rights.

Columns/Departments: Figures (a look at people not usually highlighted. i.e. a choreographer), 350 words; Interview (famous person profile), 750 words and Urban Epicure (cooking for real people – a new way to look at what you eat), 750 words. Buys 50 mss/year. Query with published clips. Pays $75-500.

Tips: "The best way to get into *MTL* is to take a stance on something you know and send it to us! We like all kinds of opinions on topics and definitely encourage original and 'off-beat' submissions. We are not very departmental here at *MTL*. We examine all queries and then decide, as an editorial group, where the idea can best be directed. A writer should concentrate more on excellent skills and originality than our sections!"

‡**PLENTY,** Brugi Design Pty. Ltd., 2nd Fl., 2-4 Bellevue St., Surry Hills, Sydney NSW Australia 2010. (2)212-5344. Editor: Robin Powell. 50% freelance written. Quarterly magazine. See *Follow Me*.

‡**QUALITY LIVING, A Magazine for the Study of Values,** Quality Living Publications, Inc. 3218 E. Pima, Tucson AZ 85716. (602)323-6480. Quarterly magazine. "Reflections on what deepens the best qualities in our living." Circ. 600. Pays on publication. Publishes ms an average of 6 months after acceptance. Byline given. Offers $25 kill fee. Buys first North American serial rights. Submit seasonal/holiday material 6 months in advance. Computer printout submissions OK; prefers letter-quality. Reports in 3 weeks on queries; 2 months on mss. Writer's guidelines for #10 SASE.

Nonfiction: Essays, inspirational, interview/profile, opinion, personal experience, book reviews and movie reviews. "No pure problem-presentation, no cynicism, no highly technical, no exposé." Buys 30 mss/year. Query with or without published clips, or send complete ms. Length: 1,000-1,700 words. Pays $50 maximum.

Columns/Departments: Quality Reviews (of book or movies, from standpoint of their positive contribution to quality in life, or their exploration of this question). Buys 12 mss/year. Send complete ms. Length: 500-1,000 words. Pays $25 maximum.

Tips: "*Quality Living* has a subject focus for each issue. The bulk of our work is done 6 months ahead of publication date. Last minute submissions will not be read. Please note that we also accept two articles per issue that are not focus-topic articles. Write for a list of focus topics. Essays are most open to freelancers. Our audience is well educated, yet not academic. Style and vocabulary should be comfortable, not complex, highly readable. Ideas can be challenging if clearly handled. We like some sparkle!"

SPLASH, International Magazine, Art, Fashion and Contemporary Culture, #4B, 561 Broadway, New York NY 10012. (212)966-3218. Publisher/Editor: Jordan Crandall. 75% freelance written. A bimonthly magazine covering the arts, "but we are eclectic. *Splash* is devoted to art, fashion and comtemporary culture. Our audience is generally well-educated and interested in culture. There is no special slant, per se, but we are decidedly progressive in thought and style." Circ. 50,000. Pays on publication. Publishes ms an average of 2 months after acceptance. Byline given. Buys first rights. Submit seasonal/holiday material 4 months in advance. Simultaneous and photocopied submissions OK. Computer printout submissions OK; prefers letter-quality. Reports in 1 month. Sample copy $4; writer's guidelines for SASE.

Nonfiction: Educated art essays, general interest, humor, interview/profile, personal experience. "We like to receive social satire (subtle, dry, educated wit); absurdist and/or surreal literature or humor." Does not want anything in a subjective or journalistic mode—no newspaper-type mss will be considered. Buys 50-60 mss/year. Query with published clips, or send complete ms. Length: 250-3,000 words. Pays $50-500.

Columns/Departments: Expo (essays on the arts and science—national as well as international *not* reviews), 500-1,100 words; Opine (non-polemical educated opinions on culture, art, religion, current issues, etc.), 750-1,250 words; Arena (short, sophisticated humor), 150-500 words. Buys 25 mss/year. Query with published clips. Length: 250-1,250 words. Pays $50-250.

Fiction: "We use short, experimental fiction at present." Surreal, experimental, fantasy, novel excerpts and objective slice-of-life vignettes. "No lengthy stories (no book-size texts)—the shorter the fiction, and the more avant garde, the better the chances are that we will use it." Buys 15 mss/year. Query with published clips. Length: 250-1,000 words. Pays $50-350.

Fillers: Short educated humor. Buys 20/year. Length: 150-500 words. Pays $15-75. "Our style is progressive, objective, avant garde. In a word, our magazine is *style-oriented* and decidedly *not* journalistic. If a manuscript is approached aesthetically and literarily as opposed to journalistically it has a much better chance of being published. All areas are open to freelancers. Essays must be topical, interesting, insightful and succinct. The interviews we do are generally with accomplished, well-known people in all fields—art, literature, politics, entertainment. Writings of an academic nature will be considered, so long as the work is not too specialized."

SPY, Spy Publishing Partners, 295 Lafayette, New York NY 10012. (212)925-5509. Editor: K. Andersen and G. Carter. 50% freelance written. "*Spy* is a non-fiction satirical magazine published monthly." Circ. 130,000. Pays on acceptance. Publishes ms an average of 3 months after acceptance. Byline given. Offers 25% kill fee. Buys first and second North American serial rights, non-exclusive anthology rights. Submit seasonal/holiday material 6 months in advance. Simultaneous and photocopied submissions OK. Query for electronic submissions. Computer printout submissions OK; prefers letter-quality. Reports in 2 weeks on queries; 1 month on mss. Sample copy $4.

Nonfiction: Jamie Malanowski and JoAnne Gruber, senior editors. Book excerpts, essays, exposé, humor, interview/profile, opinion. Buys 100 mss/year. Query with published clips. Length: 200-4,000 words. Pays $50-1,500. Sometimes pays expenses of writers on assignment.

Photos: State availability of photos with submission. Reviews contact sheets. Offers $40-200/photo. Model release and identification of subjects required. Buys one-time rights.

‡SUPERCUTS STYLE, Allied Publications, 1776 Lake Worth Rd., Lake Worth FL 33460. (407)582-2099. FAX: (407)582-4667. Editor: Richard Champlin. 95% freelance written. Bimonthly magazine. "This is a unisex lifestyle magazine with emphasis on 'style.' " Estab. 1989. Pays on publication. Byline given. Buys first North American serial rights, one-time rights or second serial (reprint) rights. Submit seasonal/holiday material 8 months in advance. Simultaneous, photocopied and previously published submissions OK. Query for electronic submissions. Computer printout submissions OK; prefers letter-quality. Reports in 2 weeks on queries; 6 months on mss. Sample copy $1. Free writer's guidelines.

Nonfiction: Book excerpts, general interest, how-to, humor, interview/profile, personal experience and photo feature. Buys 12-20 mss/year. Query with or without published clips, or send complete ms. Length: 600-1,500 words. Pays $5-25 for unsolicited articles. Pays with contributor copies or other premiums only at their request.

Photos: State availability of photos with submission. Reviews contact sheets, transparencies and b&w photos. Pays $5 maximum. Captions, model releases and identification of subjects required. Buys one-time rights.

Fiction: Humorous, mainstream and slice-of-life vignettes. Buys 2-6 mss/year. Query with published clips. Length: 600-800 words. Pays $5-250.

Fillers: Anecdotes, facts, gags illustrated by cartoonist, newsbreaks and short humor. Buys 20/year. Pays $5.

‡TATTOO ADVOCATE JOURNAL, Tattoo Advocacy Inc., Box 8390, Haledon NJ 07538-0429. (201)790-0429. Editor: Cathy Weber. 80% freelance written. Semiannual magazine on tattoo art. Circ. 5,000. Pays on acceptance. By line given. Offers $50 kill fee. Buys first North American serial rights, second serial (reprint) rights, all rights and makes work-for- hire assignments. Query for electronic submissions. Computer printout submissions OK. Reports in 6 weeks on queries; 2 months on mss. Sample copy $5; free writer's guidelines.

Nonfiction: Shotsie Gorman, articles editor. Book excerpts, essays, general interest historical/nostalgic, humor, inspirational, interview/profile, opinion (does not mean letters to the editor), personal experience, photo feature, religious, technical and travel. "No motorcycle lifestyle, sexist, racist, or sexually oriented (unless in context)." Query with published clips or send complete ms. Length: 500-7,000. Pays $50-800 for assigned articles; $25-500 for unsolicited articles. Sometimes pays expenses of writers on assignment.

Photos: State availability of photos with submission. Reviews contact sheets, transparencies, and prints. Offers $20-300 per photo. Buys one-time rights and all rights.

Fiction: Adventure, ethnic, experimental, fantasy, historical, horror, humorous, mainstream, mystery, novel excerpts, religious, romance, science fiction, serialized novels, slice-of-life vignettes and suspense. No biker lifestyle fiction. Buys 3 mss/year. Send complete ms. Length: 1,000-7,000 words. Pays $100-700.

Poetry: Avant-garde, haiku, light verse and traditional. Buys 3 poems/year. Submit maximum 6 poems. Length: No minimum, no epics. Pays $25-400.

Detective and Crime

Fans of detective stories want to read accounts of actual criminal cases and espionage. The following magazines specialize in nonfiction, but a few buy some fiction. Markets specializing in crime fiction are listed under Mystery publications.

DETECTIVE CASES, Detective Files Group, 1350 Sherbrooke St. W., Montreal, Quebec H3G 2T4 Canada. Editor-in-Chief: Dominick A. Merle. Bimonthly magazine. See *Detective Files.*

DETECTIVE DRAGNET, Detective Files Group, 1350 Sherbrooke St. W., Montreal, Quebec H3G 2T4 Canada. Editor-in-Chief: Dominick A. Merle. Bimonthly magazine; 72 pages. See *Detective Files.*

DETECTIVE FILES, Detective Files Group, 1350 Sherbrooke St. W., Montreal, Quebec H3G 2T4 Canada. Editor-in-Chief: Dominick A. Merle. 100% freelance written. Bimonthly magazine; 72 pages. Pays on acceptance. Publishes ms an average of 3 months after acceptance. Buys all rights. Photocopied submissions OK. Include international reply coupons. Reports in 1 month. Free sample copy and writer's guidelines.
Nonfiction: True crime stories. "Do a thorough job; don't double-sell (sell the same article to more than one market); and deliver, and you can have a steady market. Neatness, clarity and pace will help you make the sale." Query. Length: 3,500-6,000 words. Pays $250-350.
Photos: Purchased with accompanying ms; no additional payment.

HEADQUARTERS DETECTIVE, Detective Files Group, 1350 Sherbrooke St. W., Montreal, Quebec H3G 2T4 Canada. Editor-in-Chief: Dominick A. Merle. Bimonthly magazine; 72 pages. See *Detective Files.*

‡P. I. MAGAZINE, Fact and Fiction about the World of Private Investigators, 755 Bronx, Toledo OH 43609. (419)382-0967. Editor: Bob Mackowiak. 60% freelance written. "Not a trade journal. Audience includes professional investigators and mystery/private eye fans." Estab. 1988. Circ. 500. Pays on publication. Publishes ms an average of 3 months after acceptance. Buys one-time rights. Submit seasonal/holiday material 3 months in advance. Simultaneous, photocopied and previously published submissions OK. Reports in 1 month on queries; 3 months on mss. Sample copy $3.75.
Nonfiction: Interview/profile, new product and personal experience (investigators only). Buys 4-10 mss/year. Send complete ms. Length: 500 words. Pays $10-25 for unsolicited articles.
Photos: Send photos with submission. Offers no additional payment for photos accepted with ms. Model releases and identification of subjects required. Buys one-time rights.
Columns/Departments: Profile (personality stories—what makes this person different from other investigators), 1,000-2,000 words. Buys 4 mss/year. Send complete ms. Pays $25.
Fiction: Adventure, humorous and mystery (Main character *must* be a private detective—not police detective, spy, or little old lady who happens to solve murders on the side. "No explicit sex.") Buys 16-20 mss/year. Length: 2,000-5,000 words. Send complete ms. Pays $25.

STARTLING DETECTIVE, Detective Files Group, 1350 Sherbrooke St. W., Montreal, Quebec H3G 2T4 Canada. Editor-in-Chief: Dominick A. Merle. Bimonthly magazine; 72 pages. See *Detective Files.*

TRUE POLICE CASES, Detective Files Group, 1350 Sherbrooke St. W., Montreal, Quebec H3G 2T4 Canada. Editor-in-Chief: Dominick A. Merle. Bimonthly magazine; 72 pages. Buys all rights. See *Detective Files.*

Disabilities

These magazines are geared toward disabled persons and those who care for or teach them. A knowledge of disabilities and lifestyles is important for writers trying to break in to this field; editors regularly discard material without a realistic focus. Some of these magazines will accept manuscripts only from disabled persons or those with a background in caring for disabled persons.

ARTHRITIS TODAY, Arthritis Foundation. 1314 Spring St., N.W., Atlanta GA 30309. (404)872-7100. FAX: (404)872-0457. Editor: Cindy T. McDaniel. 50% freelance written. A bimonthly magazine about living with arthritis; latest in research/treatment. *"Arthritis Today* is written for the 37 million Americans who have arthritis and for the millions of others whose lives are touched by an arthritis-related disease. The editorial content is designed to help the person with arthritis live a more productive, independent and painfree life. The articles are upbeat and provide practical advice, information and inspiration." Estab. 1987. Circ. 700,000. Requires unlimited reprint rights in Arthritis Foundation publications. Submit seasonal/holiday material 6 months in advance. Simultaneous, photocopied and previously published submissions OK. Computer printout submissions OK; prefers letter-quality. Reports in 1 month on queries; 6 weeks on mss. Sample copy for 9x11 SAE with 4 first class stamps. Writer's guidelines for #10 SAE with 1 first class stamp.
Nonfiction: General interest, arts and entertainment, how-to (tips on any aspect of living with arthritis), humor, inspirational, interview/profile, new product, opinion, personal experience, photo feature, technical and travel. Buys 30 mss/year. Query with published clips. Length: 1,000-2,500. Pays $250-750. Sometimes pays expenses of writers on assignment.
Photos: State availability of photos with submission. Reviews 3x5 transparencies and 5x7 prints. Offers $25-100 per photo. Captions, model releases and identification of subjects required. Buys one-time rights or all rights.
Columns/Departments: Of Interest (general news and information); Personality Profiles (upbeat profiles of people living positively in spite of arthritis); Scientific Frontier (research news about arthritis) 100-250 words. Buys 4-6 mss/year. Query with published clips. Pays $50-200.
Fiction: Dianne Witter, fiction editor. Experimental, fantasy, humorous and slice-of-life vignettes. Must not necessarily relate to living with arthritis. Buys 4-6 mss/year. Query with published clips. Length: 750-2,500 words. Pays $300-750.
Fillers: Anecdotes, facts, gags to be illustrated by cartoonist, newsbreaks and short humor. Buys 2-4/year. Length: 75-150 words. Pays $25-150.
Tips: "In addition to articles specifically about living with arthritis, we look for fiction and nonfiction articles to appeal to an older audience on subjects such as travel, history, arts and entertainment, hobbies, general health, etc."

CAREERS & THE HANDICAPPED, Equal Opportunity Publications, 44 Broadway, Greenlawn, NY 11740. (516)261-8917. Editor: James Schneider. 60% freelance written. A semi-annual career guidance magazine distributed through college campuses for disabled college students and professionals. "The magazine offers role-model profiles and career guidance articles geared toward disabled college students and professionals." Pays on publication. Publishes ms an average of 6 months after acceptance. Circ. 10,000. Byline given. Buys all rights. Simultaneous, photocopied and previously published submissions OK. Reports in 2 weeks. Sample copy and writer's guidelines for 7x10 SAE and $1.25 postage.
Nonfiction: General interest, interview/profile, opinion and personal experience. Buys 15 mss/year. Query. Length: 1,000-2,500 words. Pays $100-300 for assigned articles. Sometimes pays the expenses of writers on assignment.
Photos: State availability of photos with submission. Reviews prints. Offers $15 per photo. Captions. Buys one-time rights.
Tips: "Be as targeted as possible. Role model profiles which offer advice to disabled college students are most needed."

DIALOGUE, The Magazine for the Visually Impaired, Dialogue Publications, Inc., 3100 Oak Park Ave., Berwyn IL 60402. (312)749-1908. Editor: Bonnie Miller. 50% freelance written. Works with published/established writers and a small number of new/unpublished writers each year. Quarterly magazine of issues, topics and opportunities related to the visually impaired. Pays on acceptance. Publishes ms an average of 6 months after acceptance. Byline given. Buys all rights "with generous reprint rights." Submit seasonal/holiday material 6 months in advance. Photocopied submissions OK. Computer printout submissions acceptable; no dot-matrix. Reports in 2 weeks on queries; 1 month on mss. Free sample copy to visually impaired writers. Writer's guidelines in print for #10 SASE; send a 60-minute cassette for guidelines on tape.
Nonfiction: "Writers should indicate nature and severity of visual handicap." How-to (cope with various aspects of blindness); humor; interview/profile; new product (of interest to visually impaired); opinion; personal experience; technical (adaptations for use without sight); travel (personal experiences of visually impaired travelers); and first person articles about careers in which individual blind persons have succeeded. No "aren't blind people wonderful" articles; articles that are slanted towards sighted general audience. Buys 60 mss/year. Query with published clips or submit complete ms. Length: 3,000 words maximum. Prefers shorter lengths but will use longer articles if subject warrants. Pays $10-50. Sometimes pays the expenses of writers on assignment.

Columns/Departments: ABAPITA ("Ain't Blindness a Pain in the Anatomy") — short anecdotes relating to blindness; Recipe Round-Up; Around the House (household hints); Vox Pop (see magazine); Puzzle Box (see magazine and guidelines); book reviews of books written by visually impaired authors; Beyond the Armchair (travel personal experience); and Backscratcher (a column of questions, answers, hints). Buys 80 mss/year. Send complete ms. Payment varies.

Fiction: "Writers should state nature and severity of visual handicap." Adventure, fantasy, historical, humorous, mainstream, mystery, science fiction, and suspense. No plotless fiction or stories with unbelievable characters; no horror; no explicit sex and no vulgar language. Buys 12 mss/year. Send complete ms. Length: 3,000 words maximum; shorter lengths preferred. Pays $10-50.

Poetry: "Writers should indicate nature and severity of visual impairment." Free verse, haiku, and traditional. No religious poetry or any poetry with more than 20 lines. Buys 30 poems/year. Submit maximum 3 poems. Length: 20 lines maximum. Pays in contributor's copies.

Fillers: Jokes, anecdotes, and short humor. Buys few mss/year. Length: 100 words maximum. Payment varies.

Tips: "*Dialogue* cannot consider manuscripts from authors with 20/20 vision or those who can read regular print with ordinary glasses. Any person unable to read ordinary print who has helpful information to share with others in this category will find a ready market. We believe that blind people are capable, competent, responsible citizens, and the material we publish reflects this view. We are *not* interested in scholarly journal-type articles; 'amazing blind people I have known,' articles written by sighted writers; articles and fiction that exceed our 3,000-word maximum length; and material that is too regional to appeal to an international audience. No manuscript can be considered without a statement of visual impairment, nor can it be returned without a SASE."

‡INDEPENDENT LIVING, The Magazine Serving Dealers and Their Clients, Equal Opportunity Publications, Inc. 44 Broadway, Greenlawn NY 11740. (516)-261-8917. Editor: Anne Kelly. 75% freelance written. Quarterly magazine on home health care and disability issues. "*Independent Living* magazine is written for persons with disabilities and the home care dealers, manufacturers, and health care professionals who serve their special needs." Circ. 35,000. Pays on publication. Byline given. Buys all rights. Simultaneous and photocopied submissions OK. Query for electronic submissions. Computer printout submissions OK; prefers letter-quality. Reports in 1 month. Free sample copy and writer's guidelines.

Nonfiction: Essays, how-to, humor, inspirational, interview/profile, new product, opinion, personal experience and travel. Buys 40 mss/year. Query. Length: 500-2,500 words. Pays 10¢/word.

Photos: Send photos with submission. Reviews prints. Offers $15 per photo. Captions and identification of subjects required. Buys all rights.

Tips: "The best way to have a manuscript published is to first send a detailed query on a subject related to the health care and independent lifestyles of persons who have disabilities. We need articles on innovative ways that home health care dealers are meeting their clients needs."

KALEIDOSCOPE: International Magazine of Literature, Fine Arts, and Disability, Kaleidoscope Press, 326 Locust St., Akron OH 44302. (216)762-9755. Editor: Darshan C. Perusek, Ph.D. 75% freelance written. Works with a small number of new/unpublished writers each year; eager to work with new/unpublished writers. Semiannual magazine with international collection of disability-related literature and art by disabled/nondisabled people. Circ. 1,500. Pays on publication. Publishes ms an average of 6 months after acceptance. Byline given. Buys first North American serial rights. Simultaneous queries OK. Previously published submissions "at editor's discretion." Computer printout submissions acceptable; no dot-matrix. Reports in 6 months. Sample copy $2. Writer's guidelines for #10 SASE.

Nonfiction: Disability-related literary criticism, book reviews, personal experience essays, interview/profiles/photo features on literary and/or art personalities. Publishes 8-10 mss/year. Payment $25-50 for up to 2,500 words. Maximim 3,500 words. Feature length ms (15-20 pp) up to $100. All contributors receive 2 complimentary copies.

Photos: Pays up to $25/photo. Reviews 3x5, 5x7, 8x10 b&w and color prints. Captions and identification of subjects required.

Fiction: Short stories, excerpts. Traditional and experimental. Theme generally disability-related, occasional exceptions. Humor encouraged. Publishes 8-10 mss/year. Length: 5,000 words maximum. Pays $25; editor's discretion for higher payment. 2 complimentary copies.

Poetry: Traditional and experimental. Theme experience of disability. Submit up to 12 poems. Publishes 16-20 poems a year. Payment up to $25 for multiple publication.

Tips: "Avoid the trite and sentimental. Treatment of subject should be fresh, original and imaginative. Always send photocopies. Make sure black and white photos, color slides are clean, or reproductions will suffer."

MAINSTREAM, Magazine of the Able-Disabled, Exploding Myths, Inc., 2973 Beech St., San Diego CA 92102. (619)234-3138. Editor: Cyndi Jones. 100% freelance written. Eager to develop writers who have a disability. A magazine published 10 times/year (monthly except January and June) covering disability-related topics, geared to disabled consumers. Circ. 15,500. Pays on publication. Publishes ms an average of 3 months after acceptance. Byline given. Buys all rights. Submit seasonal/holiday material 4 months in advance. Computer printout submissions OK; prefers letter-quality. Reports in 2 months. Sample copy $4.25 or 9x12 SAE with $3 and 5 first class stamps. Writer's guidelines for #10 SASE.

Nonfiction: Book excerpts, exposé, how-to (daily independent living tips), humor, interview/profile, personal experience (dealing with problems/solutions), photo feature, technical, travel and legislation. "All must be disability-related, directed to disabled consumers." No articles on " 'my favorite disabled character', 'my most inspirational disabled person', poster child stories." Buys 50 mss/year. Query with or without published clips, or send complete ms. Length: 6-12 pages. Pays $50-100. May pay subscription if writer requests.

Photos: State availability of photos with submission. Reviews contact sheets, 1½x¾ transparencies and 5x7 or larger prints. Offers $5-25 per b&w photo. Captions and identification of subjects required. Buys all rights.

Columns/Departments: Creative Solutions (unusual solutions to common aggravating problems); Personal Page (deals with personal relations: dating, meeting people). Buys 10 mss/year. Send complete ms. Length: 500-800 words. Pays $25-50.

Fiction: Humorous. Must be disability-related. Buys 4 mss/year. Send complete ms. Length: 800-1,200 words. Pays $50-100.

Tips: "It seems that politics and disability are becoming more important."

‡**NEW WAYS to Bring a Better Life to People With Mental Retardation**, First Publications, Inc., Box 5072, Evanston IL 60204. (312)869-7210. Editor-in-Chief/Co-Publisher: Mark Russell. 75% freelance written. A quarterly national magazine searching for excellence and innovations in areas like housing, work, education, leisure, day programs, quality assurance, money matters, health, fitness, nutrition, psychology, guardianship and support services. Pays on acceptance. Publishes ms 6 months after acceptance. Byline given. Computer printout submissions OK "if easy to read." Reports in 2 months. Sample copy for 9x11 SAE with 90¢ postage. Writer's guidelines for #10 SASE.

Nonfiction: Short, interesting articles slanted for readers concerned with assuring quality of life for people with mental retardation, teaching them, coping, planning for their future or increasing their integration with nondisabled people. Buys 20-30 mss/year. Query with published clips or send complete ms. Query should include the subject, proposed angle, authorities to be quoted, an example involving a person with mental retardation (if applicable) and your qualifications to write the article. Length: 700-2,000 (including sidebars). Pays $35-100. Pays some expenses of writers if approved in advance.

Photos: Pays $7.50-10 on acceptance for 5x7 or 8x10 b&w glossy print. (If possible, send contact sheets.) Buys one-time rights. Needs releases for people identifiable in photo.

Columns/Departments: Sharing (memorable moments, ironic happenings or turning points involving people with mental retardation, their relatives, caregivers, teachers or friends), 200-700 words. Buys one-time rights for 4-8 mss/year. Send complete ms. Pays $10-35 on acceptance.

Tips: If you know at least one person with mental retardation, you have a better chance of finding a topic and approach suitable for our readers. The focus may be on autism, cerebral palsy, Down syndrome or epilepsy, as long as mental retardation is involved. For most articles, *New Ways* looks for the cutting edge combined with common sense, compassion and commitment.

A POSITIVE APPROACH, A National Magazine for the Physically Challenged, 1600 Malone St., Municipal Airport, Millville NJ 08332. (609)327-4040. FAX: (609)825-4804. Publisher: Patricia M. Johnson. 80% freelance written. A bimonthly magazine for the physically disabled/handicapped. "We're a positive profile on living and for the creation of a barrier-free lifestyle. Each profile is aimed at encouraging others with that same handicap to better their situations and environments. Covers all disabilities." Circ. 200,000. Pays on publication. Publishes ms an average of 4 months after acceptance. Byline given. Buys one-time rights and second serial (reprint) rights. Submit seasonal/holiday material 4-6 months in advance. Simultaneous, photocopied and previously published submissions OK. Computer printout submissions acceptable; no dot-matrix. Reports in 2 weeks on queries; 3 weeks on mss. Sample copy $2.50; writer's guidelines for #9 SASE.

Nonfiction: Ann Miller, articles editor. Book excerpts, general interest, how-to (make life more accessible), humor, inspirational, interview/profile, personal experience, photo feature and travel (for the disabled). No depressing, poorly researched, death and dying articles. Buys 60-70 mss/year. Query with or without published clips, or send complete ms. Length: 500 words. Pays 10/word for unsolicited articles. Sometimes pays the expenses of writers on assignment.

Photos: State availability of photos with submission. Reviews 3x5 or larger prints. Offers $5/photo. Identification of subjects required. Buys one-time rights.

Columns/Departments: Ann Miller, column/department editor. Hair Styling (easy hairdo for the disabled), 500 words; Wardrobe (fashionable clothing/easy dressing), 500 words; Travel (accessible travel throughout U.S. and Europe), 500-700 words; Workshops (employment, self-improvement), 500 words; and Profiles

The double dagger before a listing indicates that the listing is new in this edition. New markets are often the most receptive to freelance submissions.

(positive approach on life with goals), 500 words. Buys 30 mss/year. Query with published clips or send complete ms. Pays 10/word.

Tips: "Research newspapers. Learn what problems exist for the physically challenged. Know that they want to better their lifestyles and get on with their lives to the best of their abilities. Learn their assets and write on what they can do and not on what can't be done! The area of our publication most open to freelancers is profiles."

Entertainment

This category's publications cover live, filmed or videotaped entertainment, including home video, TV, dance, theater and adult entertainment. Besides celebrity interviews, most publications want solid reporting on trends and upcoming productions. Magazines in the Contemporary Culture section also use articles on entertainment. For those publications with an emphasis on music and musicians, see the Music section.

AMERICAN SQUAREDANCE, Burdick Enterprises, Box 488, Huron OH 44839. (419)433-2188. Editors: Stan and Cathie Burdick. 10% freelance written. Works with a small number of new/unpublished writers each year. Monthly magazine of interviews, reviews, topics of interest to the modern square dancer. Circ. 23,000. Pays on publication. Publishes ms an average of 3-6 months after acceptance. Byline given. Buys all rights. Submit seasonal/holiday material 3 months in advance. Computer printout submissions acceptable; prefers letter-quality. Reports in 2 weeks on queries. Sample copy for 6x9 SAE with $1.05 postage; writer's guidelines for #10 SASE.

Nonfiction: General interest, historical/nostalgic, humor, inspirational, interview/profile, new product, opinion, personal experience, photo feature, travel. Must deal with square dance. Buys 6 mss/year. Send complete ms. Length: 1,000-1,500 words. Pays $2/column inch.

Photos: Send photos with ms. Reviews b&w prints. Captions and identification of subjects required.

Fiction: Subject related to square dancing only. Buys 1-2 mss/year. Send complete ms. Length: 2,000-2,500 words. Pays $2/column inch.

Poetry: Avant-garde, free verse, haiku, light verse, traditional. Square dancing subjects only. Buys 6 poems/year. Submit maximum 3 poems. Pays $2 for 1st 4 lines; $2/verse thereafter.

‡ANGLOFILE, British Entertainment & Pop Culture, The Goody Press, Box 33515, Decatur GA 30033. (404)633-5587. Editor: William P. King. Managing Editor: Leslie T. King. 15% freelance written. A bimonthly newsletter. "News and interviews on British entertainment, past and present, from an American point of view." Circ. 3,000. Pays on publication. Publishes ms an average of 6 months after acceptance. Byline given. Buys all rights. Computer printout submissions OK; prefers letter-quality. Reports in 2 months. Free sample copy.

Nonfiction: Articles Editor: Justin Stonehouse. Book excerpts, essays, historical/nostalgic, interview/profile, opinion, personal experience, photo feature, and travel. "No articles written for general audience." Buys 5/mss/year. Send complete ms. Length: 1,500 words. Pays $25-250.

Photos: Send photos with submission. Reviews prints. Offers $10-25 per photo. Identification of subjects required. Buys all rights.

CINEASTE, America's Leading Magazine on the Art and Politics of the Cinema, Cineaste Publishers, Inc., #1320, 200 Park Ave. South, New York NY 10003. (212)982-1241. Managing Editor: Gary Crowdus. 50% freelance written. A quarterly magazine on motion pictures, offering "social and political perspective on the cinema." Circ. 7,000. Pays on publication. Publishes ms an average of 3 months after acceptance. Byline given. Offers 50% kill fee. Buys first North American serial rights. Photocopied submissions OK. Computer printout submissions OK; prefers letter-quality. Reports in 3 weeks on queries; 1 month on mss. Sample copy $6. Writer's guidelines for #10 SASE.

Nonfiction: Essays, interview/profile, criticism. Buys 40-50 mss/year. Query with or without published clips, or send complete ms. Length: 3,000-6,000 words. Pays $20.

Photos: State availability of photos with submissions. Reviews prints. Offers no additional payment for photos accepted with ms. Identification of subjects required.

CINEFANTASTIQUE MAGAZINE, The review of horror, fantasy and science fiction films, Box 270, Oak Park IL 60303. (312)366-5566. Editor: Frederick S. Clarke. 100% freelance written. Eager to work with new/unpublished writers. A bimonthly magazine covering horror, fantasy and science fiction films. Circ. 25,000. Pays on publication. Publishes ms an average of 6 months after acceptance. Byline given. Buys all magazine rights. Simultaneous queries and photocopied submissions OK. Computer printout submissions acceptable. Sample copy for $6 and 9x12 SAE. Reports in 2 months or longer.

Nonfiction: Historical/nostalgic (retrospects of film classics); interview/profile (film personalities); new product (new film projects); opinion (film reviews, critical essays); technical (how films are made). Buys 100-125 mss/year. Query with published clips. Length: 1,000-10,000 words. Sometimes pays the expenses of writers on assignment.

Photos: State availability of photos with query letter or ms.

Tips: "Study the magazine to see the kinds of stories we publish. Develop original story suggestions; develop access to film industry personnel; submit reviews that show a perceptive point-of-view."

DANCE CONNECTION, Alberta Dance Alliance, 603, 815 1st St. S.W., Calgary AB T2P IN3, Canada. (403)263-3232 or 237-7327. Editor: Heather Elton. 75% freelance written. A bimonthly magazine devoted to dance with a broad editorial scope reflecting a deep commitment to a view of dance that embaces its diversity of style and fuction. Articles have ranged in subject matter from the changing role of dance in Native Indian culture from the buffalo days to the modern powwow, to the history of belly dancing, to modern dance. Circ. 5,000. Pays on publication. Byline given. Buys first rights or second serial (reprint) rights. Submit material 3 months in advance. Simultaneous, photocopied, and previously submissions OK. Computer printout submissions OK. Query for electronic submissions. Sample copy for 8½x11 SAE with IRCs.

Nonfiction: A variety of writing styles including criticism, essay, exposé, general interest, historical/nostalgic, humor, opinion, interview, performance review, forum debate, literature and photo feature. Query with published clips, or send complete ms. Length 800-2,500 words. Pays $5-150.

Fiction: Literature and poetry relating to dance.

Columns/Departments: Education, Children in Dance, Multiculturalism, and Movement.

DANCE MAGAZINE, 33 W. 60th St., New York NY 10023. (212)245-9050. FAX: (212)956-6487. Editor-in-Chief: Richard Philp. 25% freelance written. Monthly magazine covering dance. Circ. 51,000. Pays on publication. Byline given. Offers up to $150 kill fee (varies). Makes work-for-hire assignments. Submit seasonal/holiday material 4 months in advance. Computer printout submission OK; no dot-matrix. Reports in "weeks." Sample copy and writer's guidelines for 8x10 SAE.

Nonfiction: Interview/profile. Buys 50 mss/year. Query with or without published clips, or send complete ms. Length: 300-1,500 words. Pays $15-350. Sometimes pays expenses of writers on assignment.

Photos: State availability of photos with submission. Reviews transparencies and prints. Offers $15-285/photo. Captions and identification of subjects required. Buys one-times rights.

Columns/Departments: Presstime News (topical, short articles on current dance world events) 150-400 words. Buys 40 mss/year. Query with published clips. Pays $20-75.

Tips: Writers must have "thorough knowledge of dance and take a sophisticated approach."

‡DANCSCENE—THE MAGAZINE OF BALLROOM DANCE, Koine Publishing Company, Box 801371, Dallas TX 75380. (214)750-0275. Editor: Suzanna Penn. 20% freelance published. Bimonthly magazine on ballroom dancing, especially competitive. "Carries feature articles and news covering the ballroom dance field including articles of general and technical interest." Circ. 2,100. Pays on acceptance. Publishes ms an average of 6 months after acceptance. Byline given. Buys all rights. Query for electronic submissions. Computer printout submissions OK; prefers letter-quality. Free sample copy and writer's guidelines.

Nonfiction: Historical/nostalgic, how-to, interview/profile, photo feature, technical and travel. "No gossip; exposé; no articles that emphasize immoral conduct or lack of ethics." Buys 3 mss/year. Query with published clips. Length: 150-1,500 words. Pays $150-400. Sometimes pays expenses of writers on assignment.

Photos: Send photos with submission. Reviews 3x5 prints. Offers $5-100 per photo. Captions, model releases and identificaton of subjects required. Buys one-time rights or all rights, depends on subject.

Columns/Departments: Right and Wrong (One or two steps of dance illustrated verbally and with right and wrong pictures), 50-150 words; Stitch in Time (How to design, construct, ballroom dance costumes), 100-250 words; DancScope (Anything instructive about ballroom dance, except right and wrong), 100-200 words. Buys 18 mss/year. Query. Length: 50-250 words. Pays $30-150.

Poetry Free verse, light verse and traditional. "Must pertain to ballroom dance." Buys 2-3 poems/year. No limit. Length: 42 lines. Pays $10-25.

Fillers: Gags to be illustrated by cartoonist and short humor. Pays $10-25.

Tips: "Writers should have some knowledge of ballroom dance either as an amateur or professional. All instructive articles, must be submitted by qualified ballroom dancers—recognized teachers, adjudicators, etc."

DRAMATICS MAGAZINE, International Thespian Society, 3368 Central Pkwy., Cincinnati OH 45225. (513)559-1996. Editor-in-Chief: Donald Corathers. 70% freelance written. Works with small number of new/unpublished writers. For theater arts students, teachers and others interested in theater arts education. Magazine published monthly, September through May. Circ. 35,000. Pays on acceptance. Publishes ms an average of 3 months after acceptance. Buys first North American serial rights. Byline given. Submit seasonal/

holiday material 3 months in advance. Simultaneous, photocopied and previously published submissions OK. Query for electronic submissions. Computer printout submissions acceptable; prefers letter-quality. Reports in 1 month. Sample copy for $2 and a 9x12 SAE with 5 first class stamps; free writer's guidelines.

Nonfiction: How-to (technical theater), informational, interview, photo feature, humorous, profile and technical. Buys 30 mss/year. Submit complete ms. Length: 750-3,000 words. Pays $30-200. Rarely pays expenses of writers on assignment.

Photos: Purchased with accompanying ms. Uses b&w photos and color transparencies. Query. Total purchase price for ms includes payment for photos.

Fiction: Drama (one-act plays). No "plays for children, Christmas plays, or plays written with no attention paid to the conventions of theatre."Buys 5-9 mss/year. Send complete ms. Pays $50-200.

Tips: "The best way to break in is to know our audience – drama students, teachers and others interested in theater – and to write for them. Writers who have some practical experience in theater, especially in technical areas, have a leg-up here, but we'll work with anybody who has a good idea. Some freelancers have become regular contributors. Others ignore style suggestions included in our writer's guidelines."

EMMY MAGAZINE, Academy of Television Arts & Sciences, Suite 700, 3500 W. Olive, Burbank CA 91505-4628. (818)953-7575. Editor and Publisher: Hank Rieger. Managing Editor: Gail Polevoi. 100% freelance written. Works with a small number of new/unpublished writers each year. Bimonthly magazine on television – a "provocative, critical – though not necessarily fault-finding – treatment of television and its effects on society." Circ. 12,000. Pays on publication. Publishes ms an average of 3 months after acceptance. Byline given. Offers 20% kill fee. Buys first North American serial rights. Computer printout submissions acceptable; no dot-matrix. Reports in 1 month. Sample copy for 9x12 SAE with 5 first class stamps.

Nonfiction: Provocative and topical articles, nostalgic, humor, interview/profile, opinion – all dealing with television. Buys 40 mss/year. Query with published clips. Length: 1,500-2,000 words. Pays $500-900. Sometimes pays expenses of writers on assignment.

Columns/Departments: Opinion or point-of-view columns dealing with TV. Buys 18-20 mss/year. Query with published clips. Length: 800-1,200 words. Pays $250-550.

Tips: "Query in writing with a thoughtful description of what you wish to write about. Please do not call. The most frequent mistake made by writers in completing an article for us is that they misread the magazine and send fan-magazine items."

FANGORIA: Horror in Entertainment, Starlog Group, 475 Park Ave. South, 8th Floor, New York NY 10016. (212)689-2830. Editor: Anthony Timpone. 90% freelance written. Works with a small number of new/unpublished writers each year. Published 10 times/year. Magazine covering horror films, TV projects and literature and those who create them. Pays on publication. Publishes ms an average of 3 months after acceptance. Byline given. Buys first North American serial rights with option for second serial (reprint) rights to same material. Submit seasonal/holiday material 6 months in advance. Simultaneous queries OK. Query for electronic submissions. Computer printout submissions acceptable; no dot-matrix. Reports in 6 weeks. "We provide an assignment sheet (deadlines, info) to writers, thus authorizing queried stories that we're buying." Sample copy $4.50; writers' guidelines for #10 SASE.

Nonfiction: Book excerpts, interview/profile of movie directors, makeup FX artists, screenwriters, producers, actors, noted horror novelists and others – with genre credits. No "think" pieces, opinion pieces, reviews, or sub-theme overviews (i.e., vampire in the cinema). Buys 100 mss/year. Query with published clips. Length: 1,000-3,000 words. Pays $100-225. Rarely pays the expenses of writers on assignment. Avoids articles on science fiction films – see listing for sister magazine *Starlog* in *Writer's Market* science fiction magazine section.

Photos: State availability of photos. Reviews b&w and color transparencies and prints. "No separate payment for photos provided by film studios." Captions or identification of subjects required. Photo credit given. Buys all rights.

Columns/Departments: Monster Invasion (news about new film productions; must be exclusive, early information; also mini-interviews with filmmakers and novelists). Query with published clips. Length: 300-500 words. Pays $25-35.

Fiction: "We do *not* publish any fiction. *Don't* send any."

Tips: "Other than recommending that you study one or several copies of *Fangoria*, we can only describe it as a horror film magazine consisting primarily of interviews with technicians and filmmakers in the field. Be sure to stress the interview subjects' words – not your own opinions. We're very interested in small, independent filmmakers working outside of Hollywood. These people are usually more accessible to writers, and more cooperative. *Fangoria* is also sort of a *de facto* bible for youngsters interested in movie makeup careers and for young filmmakers. We are devoted only to *reel* horrors – the fakery of films, the imagery of the horror fiction of a Stephen King or a Peter Straub – we *do not* want nor would we *ever* publish articles on real-life horrors, murders, etc. A writer must *like* and *enjoy* horror films and horror fiction to work for us. If the photos in *Fangoria* disgust you, if the sight of (*stage*) blood repels you, if you feel 'superior' to horror (and its fans), you aren't a writer for us and we certainly aren't the market for you. *Fangoria's* frequency has increased over the last years and, with an editorial change reducing staff written articles, this has essentially doubled the number of stories we're buying. In 1990, we expect such opportunities only to increase for freelancers. *Fangoria* will try for a lighter, more 'Gonzo' tone in the year ahead."

FILM QUARTERLY, University of California Press, Berkeley CA 94720. (415)642-6333. FAX: (415)643-7127. Editor: Ernest Callenbach. 100% freelance written. Eager to work with new/unpublished writers. Quarterly. Buys all rights. Byline given. Pays on publication. Publishes ms an average of 3 months after acceptance. Query; "sample pages are very helpful from unknown writers. We must have hard-copy printout and don't care how it is produced, but we cannot use dot-matrix printouts unless done on one of the new printers that gives type-quality letters." Sample copy and writer's guidelines for SASE.

Nonfiction: Articles on style and structure in films, articles analyzing the work of important directors, historical articles on development of the film as art, reviews of current films and detailed analyses of classics, book reviews of film books. Must be familiar with the past and present of the art; must be competently, although not necessarily breezily, written; must deal with important problems of the art. "We write for people who like to think and talk seriously about films, as well as simply view them and enjoy them. We use no personality pieces or reportage pieces. Interviews usually work for us only when conducted by someone familiar with most of a filmmaker's work. (We don't use performer interviews.)" Length: 6,000 words maximum. Pay is about 2¢/word.

Tips: "*Film Quarterly* is a specialized academic journal of film criticism, though it is also a magazine (with pictures) sold in bookstores. It is read by film teachers, students, and die-hard movie buffs, so unless you fall into one of those categories, it is very hard to write for us. Currently, we are especially looking for material on independent, documentary, etc. films not written about in the national film reviewing columns."

‡FILMCLIPS, Box 1335, New York NY 10013. (718)899-3947. Editor: Dan Karpf. 100% freelance written. Quarterly newsletter on movie memorabilia. Estab. 1988. Circ. 1,000. Pays on acceptance. Publishes ms an average of 2 months after acceptance. Byline given. Not copyrighted. Buys one-time rights. Submit seasonal/holiday material 3 months in advance. Simultaneous, photocopied and previously published submissions OK. Computer printout submissions OK; prefers letter-quality. Reports in 1 month. Sample copy for $2.

Nonfiction: General interest, humor, interview/profile and personal experience. Buys 15 mss/year. Send complete ms. Length: 500-2,500 words. Pays $5-50 for unsolicited articles.

Photos: State availability of photos with submission. Reviews contact sheets. Offers no additional payment for photos accepted with ms. Model releases and identification of subjects required. Buys one-time rights.

‡THE MAYBERRY GAZETTE, The World Authority on Mayberry, NC, The Andy Griffith Show Appreciation Society, Box 330, Clemmons NC 27012. (919)998-2860. Editor: John Meroney. 5% freelance written. Bimonthly newsletter. "We deal with material relating to 'The Andy Griffith Show' TV series (CBS, 1960-1968). Virtually any material relating to the old series, and the individuals involved, is of interest to us. The audience is broad-based." Circ. 5,000. Pays on acceptance. Publishes ms an average of 4 months after acceptance. Byline sometimes given. Buys all rights. Submit seasonal/holiday material 4 months in advance. Simultanous and previously published submissions OK. Computer printout submissions OK; prefers letter-quality. Reports in 1 month. Sample copy $1. Writer's guidelines for 3 first class stamps and 9x12 envelope.

Nonfiction: Essays, historical/nostalgic, humor, interview/profile, new product, personal experience and photo feature. "Each year the Society publishes a special convention program which may require freelance material. We suggest that the individual writers, if interested, contact us about writing for the convention program and we will provide them with specifics. Time may vary in terms of publication." Buys 6 mss/year. Query with published clips. Length: 25-1,080 words. Pays $4-150. Pays in contributor copies or other premiums depending on individual situation; please inquire. Sometimes pays expenses of writers on assignment.

Photos: Send photos with submission. Reviews 8x10 prints. Offers no additional payment for photos accepted with ms. Identification of subjects required. Will make determination about rights upon seeing photographs.

Columns/Departments: Mayberry Alumni (Deals with individuals, on-screen and off, who were involved in some facet with the show), 250-300 words; Mayberry After Midnite (Discusses activities of the membership of the AGSAS. Sometimes includes brief updates on the cast and crew of the series), 900-1,080 words. Buys 6 mss/year. Query with published clips. Pays $5-150 (depends on size—we could pay for small tidbits).

Fiction: Humorous and slice-of-life vignettes. "We publish fiction very rarely—if ever. We suggest that the individual writer be very clear and specific in their initial query as to what they plan to do." Buys 1 ms/year. Query with published clips. Length: 250-1,080 words. Pays $5-150.

Poetry: Light verse and traditional. Buys 3 poems/year. Submit maximum 10 poems. Pays $5-50.

Fillers: Anecdotes, facts, gags to be illustrated by cartoonist and short humor. Buys 6/year. Length: 50-250 words. Pays $5-15.

Tips: "We suggest that they be very familiar with the subjects they are writing about. Perhaps the best suggestion we could give them is to watch "Andy Griffith Show" reruns—endlessly. The best suggestion is that the material be somewhat timely, entertaining, and above all, interesting to admirers of 'The Andy Griffith Show.' "

‡MOVIE COLLECTOR'S WORLD, The Marketplace For Film & Video Collectors, Box 58, Annandale MN 55302. (612)274-5230. Editor: Jon E. Johnson. 90% freelance written. Eager to work with new/unpublished writers. Biweekly tabloid covering film-collecting movie and video reviews, profiles, features and technical subjects. "We strive to serve the varied interests of our readers, ranging from film and video enthusiasts to still and poster collectors." Circ. 10,000. Pays on publication. Publishes ms an averge of 3 months after acceptance. Byline given. Buys first serial rights and second serial (reprint) rights. Submit seasonal/dated material 3 months in advance. Photocopied submissions OK. Computer printout submissions OK "if close to double-spaced;" prefers letter quality to dot matrix. Reports in 6 weeks. Sample copy and writer's guidelines for 9x12 SAE and $2 postage.

Nonfiction: Book excerpts; expose (investigative or extensive profile-type submissions); how-to; opinion (in the form of reviews); technical subjects ("one very popular feature we ran was on Cinemascope"). "We'd like to see more historical retrospective-type pieces on films. For instance our stories on *The Thin Man* series and *Ma and Pa Kettle* were two recent favorites." No personal experience/first person articles other than interview, profile or general interest. "We do not need very elementary pieces on 'buying your first VCR' or humorous commentary." Send complete ms or query. Pays 3¢/word or $100 maximum.

Photos: State availability of photos with query or ms. Pays $3-5 for 8x10 b&w prints. Model release required. Buys one-time rights.

Columns/Departments: Book (film/video-related topics) and tape/disc reviews. Send ms or query. Pays $5 minimum for short reviews, word rates for longer pieces.

Tips: "We're looking for more historical-type retrospectives and interviews, rather than currently available video reviews that can be found anywhere. *MCW* uses freelance material for nearly its entire content, and as a result it is very easy for a freelancer to break in to the publication, provided his/her material suits our needs and they know what they're writing about. Once writers get a feel for what *MCW* is, and we get an idea of their work, they tend to become one of our 'family' of regular contributors. Writers who know and care about their subject should have no problem when it comes to writing for *MCW* (providing it suits our needs). We actually encourage unsolicited submissions. A look at your wares just might land you a quicker sale than if there has to be a lot of counseling, advising or hand-holding involved. With a biweekly schedule we work quick. If there is a tie-in date, please make a note of it on the upper left-hand corner of the manuscript."

MOVIELINE MAGAZINE, 1141 S. Beverly Dr., Los Angeles CA 90035. (213)282-0711. Editor: Laurie Halpern Smith. Senior Editor: Virginia Campbell. 60% freelance written. Biweekly magazine covering motion pictures. Circ. 100,000. Pays on publication. Publishes ms an average of 1 month after acceptance. Byline given. Offers variable kill fee. Buys first North American serial rights or simultaneous rights ("if not in our market"). Submit seasonal/holiday material 2 months in advance. Simultaneous submissions OK. Computer printout submissions OK. Reports in 2 months. Free sample copy.

Nonfiction: Book excerpts, film business-oriented pieces, essays, humor and interview/profile. No historical pieces, *please*. Buys 75-100 mss/year. Query with published clips. Length: 150-2,500 words. Pays $35-500. Sometimes pays expenses of writers on assignment.

Photos: State availability of photos with submission. Reviews contact sheets, 2¼ transparencies and 5x7 photos. Offers $10-100/photo. Identification of subjects required. Buys one-time rights.

Columns/Departments: Buzz (short, funny pieces on movie-related personalities and incidents) 150-300 words. Buys 75 mss/year. Pays $50-75.

Tips: "*Movieline* is a consumer-oriented publication devoted to film. We publish interviews with actors and actresses, directors, cinematographers, producers, writers, costume designers, and others with a creative involvement in motion pictures. We also seek behind-the-scenes stories relating to the movie business; fresh, insightful overviews of trends and genres; on-location pieces; and short, anecdotal items relating to any of the above. We are not, repeat not, seeking pieces on dead movie stars, like 'When Errol Flynn Came Through Town.' We consider our audience to be seasoned moviegoers, and consequently look for a knowledgeable, sophisticated approach to the subject; avoid a breathless, "fan"-like attitude, especially in star interviews. Pieces should be exciting, stylish and, because of our space limitations, tightly written."

‡ON VIDEO, The Home Movie Guide, LFP, Inc., Suite 300, 9171 Wilshire Blvd., Beverly Hills CA 90210. (213)858-7866. Editor: Scott Mallory. 100% freelance written. Bimonthly magazine on movies/home videos. "Devoted to movies, with 80% of content being movie reviews. Audience is people 12-65 who watch movies." Estab. 1988. Circ. 200,000. Pays on acceptance. Publishes ms an average of 3 months after acceptance. Byline given. Offers 50% kill fee. Buys all rights. Submit seasonal/holiday material 8 months in advance. Computer printout submissions OK; prefers letter-quality. Reports in 2 weeks on queries; 1 month on ms. Sample copy $2.95. Free writer's guidelines.

Nonfiction: Essays, humor, interview/profile and opinion. Buys 500 mss/year. Query with published clips. Length: 750-2,500 words. Reviews: 250 words. Pays $100-350 for assigned articles. Reviews pay $30. Pays expenses of writers on assignment.

Photos: State availability of photos with submission. Reviews 2x5 transparencies and 8x10 prints. Offers $10-50 per photo. Identification of subjects required. Buys all rights.

Columns/Departments: Quiet, Please (a day on the movie set) 1,500 words; Look (profiles of costume designers and F/X artists) 1,500 words. Buys 12 mss/year. Query with published clips. Pays $200-350.

Tips: "Keep a light touch. We have fun with movies."

THE OPERA COMPANION, 40 Museum Way, San Francisco CA 94114. (415)626-2741. Editor: James Keolker, Ph.D. 25% freelance written. Eager to work with new/unpublished writers. A magazine published 14 times yearly covering "opera in particular, music in general. We provide readers with an in depth analysis of 14 operas per year—the personal, philosophical, and political content of each composer and his works." Circ. 8,000. Pays on acceptance. Publishes ms an average of 2 months after acceptance. Byline given. Buys first rights. Photocopied submissions OK. Computer printout submissions acceptable; prefers letter-quality. Reports in 1 week on queries; 1 month on mss. Sample copy and writer's guidelines for 9x12 SAE and 3 first class stamps.

Nonfiction: Essay, historical/nostalgic, humor and interview/profile (opera composers, singers, producers and designers). No Master's or Doctoral theses. Buys 10 mss/year. Query with published clips. Length: 500-5,000 words. Pays $50-250.

Fillers: Anecdotes and short humor. Buys 25/year. Length: 150-500 words. Pays $50-250.

Tips: "Be pointed, pithy in statement, accurate in research. Avoid florid, excessive language. Writers must be musically sensitive, interested in opera as a continuing vocal art. Enthusiasm for the subject is important. Contact us for which operas/composers we will be featuring each year. It is those areas of research, anecdote, analysis and humor, we will be filling first."

PERFORMING ARTS IN CANADA, 5th Fl., 263 Adelaide St. W., Toronto, Ontario M5H 1Y2 Canada. (416)971-9516. Editor: Alex Newman. Assistant Editor: Patricia Michael. 80% freelance written. Prefers to work with published/established writers; works with a small number of new/unpublished writers each year. Quarterly magazine for professional performers and general readers with an interest in Canadian theatre, dance, music, opera and film. Covers "modern and classical theatre arts, plus articles on related subjects (government arts policy, etc.)." Pays 1 month following publication. Publishes ms an average of 3 months after acceptance. Byline given. Buys first serial rights. Query for electronic submissions. Computer printout submissions acceptable. Reports in 6 weeks. Sample copy for $1 and 9x12 SAE with IRCs; writer's guidelines for #10 SASE.

Nonfiction: "Lively, stimulating, well-researched articles on Canadian performing artists or groups. Most often in need of good classical music and dance articles." No nonCanadian, nonperforming arts material. Buys 30-35 mss/year. Query preferably with an outline plus tearsheets. Writers new to this publication should include clippings. Length: 1,000-2,000 words. Pays $150-200. Sometimes pays the expenses of writers on assignment.

Tips: "We have a continuing need for articles that hale from the smaller centers in Canada. Ontario and particularly Toronto events are well covered."

PLAYBILL, Playbill Inc., Suite 320, 71 Vanderbilt Ave., New York NY 10169. (212)557-5757. Editor: Joan Alleman. 50% freelance written. Monthly magazine covering NYC, Broadway and Off-Broadway theatre. Circ. 1,040,000. Pays on acceptance. Publishes ms an average of 2 months after acceptance. Byline given. Buys all rights. Computer printout submissions OK; no dot-matrix. Reports in 2 months.

Nonfiction: Book excerpts, humor, interview/profile, personal experience—must all be theatre related. Buys approximately 10 mss/year. Query with published clips. Length: 1,500-1,800 words. Pays $250-500.

Photos: State availability of photos with submission. Offers no additional payment for photos accepted with ms. Identification of subjects required.

Fillers: Anecdotes, facts and short humor. Buys 10 mss/year. Length: 350-700 words. Pays $50-100. Must all be theatre related.

‡PREMIERE, Murdoch Publications, Inc., 2 Park Ave., 4th Fl, New York NY 10016. (212)725-7927. Editor: Susan Lyne. Monthly magazine. "Monthly magazine for young adults (18-34 years old) that takes readers behind the scenes of movies in release and in production." Pays on acceptance. Byline given. Offers 25% kill fee. Buys first North American serial rights and world rights for 3 months. Submit seasonal/holiday material 4 months in advance. Computer printout submissions OK; prefers letter-quality. Reports in 2-3 weeks on queries. Writer's guidelines for #10 SASE.

ALWAYS submit unsolicited manuscripts or queries with a self-addressed, stamped envelope (SASE) within your country or International Reply Coupons (IRC) purchased from the post office for other countries.

Nonfiction: Film. Video issue (January), Year-End Issue (February), Academy Award Issue (April), Summer Preview Issue (June), Fall Preview Issue (October). Buys 60 mss/year. Query with published clips. Maximum length 2,500 words. Pays $1/word maximum. Pays expenses of writers on assignment.

Columns/Departments: Buys 40 mss/year. Maximum length 1,000 word. Pays $1/word maximum.

Fillers: Features, columns etc. Buys 60/year. Maximum length 500 words. Pays 50¢/word maximum.

Tips: "*Premiere* looks for articles that go behind the scenes of movies in release and in production; that answer questions about creative strategy, development, financing and distribution as well as focusing on the producers, directors and stars who create the films. Feature articles include interviews, profiles and film commentary and analysis. Monthly departments look for coverage of the movie business, video technology and hardware, home video, movie music/scoring and books."

SOAP OPERA UPDATE, The Magazine of Stars and Stories, 158 Linwood Plaza, Ft. Lee NJ 07024. (201)592-7002. Editor: Allison Waldman. 50% freelance written. Tri-weekly magazine on daytime serials. "We cover the world of soap operas, daytime and nighttime. Feature interviews, history, character sketches, events where soap stars are seen and participate." Estab. 1988. Pays on publication. Byline given. Buys first North American serial rights. Submit seasonal/holiday material 3 months in advance. Simultaneous submissions OK. Computer printout submissions OK. Reports in 3 weeks. Sample copy $1.95 with 3 first class stamps.

Nonfiction: Humor, interview/profile. "Only articles directly about actors, shows or history of a soap opera." Buys 100 mss/year. Query with published clips. Length: 750-2,200 words. Pays $100-150. Sometimes pays expenses of writers on assignment.

Photos: State availability of photos with submission. Reviews transparencies. Offers $25. Captions and identification of subjects required. Buys all rights.

Tips: "Come up with fresh, new approaches to stories about soap operas and their people. Submit ideas and writing samples, previously published. Take a serious approach; don't talk down to the reader. All articles must be well written and the writer knowledgeable about his subject matter."

STV GUIDE, Triple D Publishing, Inc., Box 2384, Shelby NC 28151. (704)482-9673. FAX: (704)484-8558. Editor: David B. Melton. 70% freelance written. Monthly magazine covering home satellite TV. "We look for articles on satellite television entertainment, new equipment, how-to for the consumer, communications legislation, and programming for the home satellite television enthusiast." Circ. 60,000. Byline given. Pays on publication. Offers 30% kill fee. Buys all rights. Submit seasonal/holiday material 3 months in advance. Simultaneous and photocopied submissions OK. Query for electronic submissions. Reports in 2 weeks. Free sample copy and writer's guidelines.

Nonfiction: How-to, interview/profile, new product, opinion, personal experience, photo feature, technical. Buys 45 mss/year. Query with or without published clips, or send complete ms. Length: 1,800-3,600 words. Pays $150-300. Sometimes pays expenses of writers on assignment.

Photos: State availability of photos with submission or send photos with submission. Reviews contact sheets, transparencies and prints. Offers $5-50 per photo. Captions, model release and identification of subjects required.

Columns/Departments: At Home (personal experiences of readers) 1,000 words. Query. Length: 1,000-1,800 words. Pays $50-100.

Tips: "A writer who is a satellite TV user or has knowledge of it would be of great help. Familiarity with television transmission and some programming knowledge would also be helpful."

‡TV ENTERTAINMENT, The Crosby Vandenburgh Group, 420 Boylston St., Boston MA 02116. Editor: Cable Neuhaus. 60% freelance written. Monthly magazine on TV and motion-picture entertainment. "We are read by U.S. cable-TV subscribers who are interested in behind-the-scenes and exclusive info about TV and motion-picture personalities as well as information about Americans whose lives are portrayed, in one way or another, on TV." Estab. 1989. Circ. 4,000,000. Pays on publication. Publishes ms an average of 2 months after acceptance. Byline given. Negotiated kill fee. Buys first North American serial rights. Submit seasonal/holiday material 4 months in advance. Computer printout submissions OK; prefers letter-quality. Reports in 3 weeks. Sample copy for 8x10 SAE with 7 first class stamps. Writer's guidelines for #10 SAE with 1 first class stamp.

Nonfiction: Book excerpts, exposé, general interest, historical/nostalgic, humor, interview/profile, new product, personal experience, photo feature. "No stock celebrity interviews/profiles." Buys 37 mss/year. Query with published clips. Length: 100-2,000 words. Pays $50-1,300.

Photos: State availability of photos with submission. Reviews contact sheets, negatives, transparencies, prints. Payment negotiated. Captions, model releases, and identifications of subjects required. Rights negotiated.

Fillers: Editor: Michael Rosenstein. Facts. Buys 20/year. Length: 25-300 words. Payment negotiated.

Tips: "Land exclusive interviews with difficult U.S. celebrities or have access to *verifiable* information concerning our subject matter. We are a *general-interest* consumer magazine that is pegged to cable-TV programming. All feature areas and our Talk/Show department are open to freelancers."

TV GUIDE, Radnor PA 19088. Editor (National Section): David Sendler. Editor (Local Sections): Roger Youman. Managing Editor: Dick Friedman. 70% freelance written. Prefers to work with published/established writers; works with a small number of new/unpublished writers each year; eager to work with new/unpublished writers. Weekly. Circ. 16.3 million. Publishes ms an average of 2 months after acceptance. Computer printout submissions acceptable; prefers letter-quality.
Nonfiction: Wants offbeat articles about TV people and shows. This magazine is not interested in fan material. Also wants stories on the newest trends of television, but they must be written in clear, lively English. Study publication. Query to Andrew Mills, assistant managing editor. Length: 1,000-2,000 words.
Photos: Uses professional high-quality photos, normally shot on assignment by photographers chosen by *TV Guide*. Prefers color. Pays $350 day rate against page rates—$450 for 2 pages or less.

TV WEEK MAGAZINE, Canada Wide Magazines, 401-4180 Lougheed Highway, Burnaby BC V5C 6A7 Canada. (604)299-7311. Managing Editor: Louise Leger. 60% freelance written. Weekly magazine on television and entertainment. "Our readers are interested in television and the entertainment industry. We focus on different areas-on local Canadian and American celebrities. We are interested in upbeat articles with fresh angles which inform and entertain." Circ. 85,000. Pays on publication. Byline given. Offers 75% kill fee. Not copyrighted. Buys first North American serial rights. Submit seasonal/holiday material 2 months in advance. Simultaneous, photocopied and previously published submissions OK. Computer printout submissions OK; no dot-matrix. Reports in 1 month. Free sample copy and writer's guidelines.
Nonfiction: Nostalgic, interview/profile, photo feature; as they relate to TV. "We want a current hook on a story to justify printing it." Buys 30 mss/year. Query with or without published clips, or send complete ms. Length: 500-2,000 words. Pays $50-450. Sometimes pays expenses of writers on assignment.
Photos: State availability of photos with submission. Reviews contact sheets, transparencies and prints. Pays $25-300. Identification of subjects required. Buys one-time rights.

‡VIDEO, 460 W. 34th St., New York, NY 10001. (212)947-6500. FAX: (212)947-6727. Editor: Judith Sawyer. Managing Editor: Stan Pinkwas. 75% freelance written. Prefers to work with published/established writers; works with a small number of new/unpublished writers each year. A monthly magazine covering home video equipment, technology and prerecorded tapes. Circ. 450,000. Pays on acceptance. Publishes ms an average of 2 months after acceptance. Byline given. Buys one-time rights. Query for electronic submissions. Requires hard copy also. Computer printout submissions acceptable; prefers letter-quality. Reports in 2 weeks on queries; 1 month on manuscripts. Free writer's guidelines.
Nonfiction: Buys 80 mss/year. Query with published clips. Pays $300-1,000. Sometimes pays the expenses of writers on assignment.
Tips: The entire feature area is open to freelancers. Write a brilliant query and send samples of published articles.

VIDEO CHOICE MAGAZINE, The Leading Review Magazine for the Video Enthusiast, Connell Communications, 331 Jaffrey Rd., Peterborough, New Hampshire 03458. Editor: Deborah Navas. Senior Editor: Ann E. Graves. 80% freelance written. Monthly magazine on special interest (non-theatrical) and feature-film videos, and video-related hardware topics. "Our audience is middle-class consumers who own a VCR and are interested in using it for personal enrichment as well as entertainment. The magazine serves varied interests: sports, children, exercise, business, education, arts, etc." Estab. 1988. Circ. 70,000. Pays on acceptance. Publishes ms an average of 3 months after acceptance. Byline sometimes given. Offers 25% kill fee for assigned article. Buys all rights. Submit seasonal/holiday material 3 months in advance. Simultaneous and photocopied submissions OK. Query for electronic submissions. Reports in 2 weeks on queries; 1 month on mss. Sample copy $3; writer's guidelines for #10 SASE.
Nonfiction: Interview/profile, new product, opinion, technical, reviews of videotapes. Buys 240 mss/year. Query or query with published clips. Length: 250-2,000 words. Pays $30-500. Sometimes pays expenses of writers on assignment.
Photos: State availability of photos with submission. Reviews transparencies, prints. Offers no additional payment for photos accepted with ms, or sometimes offers $50-100 per photo. Identification of subjects required. Buys one-time rights.
Columns/Departments: Industry Insight; Video Soundtrack, Collector's Choice; Fast Forward. Query with published clips. Length: 1,200 words. Pays $250.

‡VIDEO MAGAZINE, Reese Communications, 460 West 34 St., New York NY 10001. (212)947-6500. Monthly magazine on home video in all its aspects. Circ. 450,000. Pays on acceptance. Publishes ms an average of 2-4 months after acceptance. Byline given. Buys first North American serial rights. Submit seasonal/holiday material 5 months in advance. Query for electronic submissions. Computer printout submissions OK; prefers letter-quality. Reports in 2-4 weeks on queries; 1-2 weeks on mss. Sample copy for 8x11 SAE.
Nonfiction: Stan Pinkwas. Book excerpts (pre-publication galleys), how-to (editing and camera shooting), interview/profile, personal experience and technical. Buys 50-60 mss/year. Query with published clilps. Length: 1,000-2,500 words. Pays $400-750 for assigned articles. Pays expenses of writers on assignment.

Photos: State availability of photos with submission. Captions, model releases and identification of subjects required. Buys one-time rights.
Columns/Departments: Camcorner (How-to shoot/edit home videos), 1,200 words; Technically Speaking (Technical aspects of home video gear), 1,200; Gazette (Celebrity interviews/offbeat video applications), 200-500 words. Query with published clips. Length: 700-1,800 words. Pays $100-500.
Fillers: Lou Kesten. Facts. Length: 100-200 words. Pays $25.

VIDEO MARKETPLACE MAGAZINE, World Publishing Co., 4th Floor, 990 Grove St., Evanston IL 60201. (312)491-6440. Editor: Robert Meyers. 90% freelance written. A monthly magazine on video software. "The magazine is broken down into 15-20 categories: music, travel, health, sports, how-to, etc. plus feature film movies. Each category starts off with a related feature article of 700-900 or 1,200-1,400 words." Circ. 150,000. Pays on acceptance. Publishes ms an average of 4 months after acceptance. Byline given. Offers $75-125 kill fee. Buys one-time rights. Submit seasonal/holiday material 6 months in advance. Previously published submissions OK. Reports in 2 weeks on queries; 3 weeks on mss. Sample copy $2.50; writer's guidelines for #10 SASE.
Nonfiction: General interest, historical/nostalgic (documentary), how-to (instructional, educational), humor (in general areas), interview/profile (celebrity, all fields), photo feature (all categories), technical (general). Query with published clips or send complete ms. Length: 700-1,500 words. Pays $125-350; $75-125 for reprints.
Photos: State availability of photos with submission. Reviews transparencies. Offers no additional payment for photos accepted with ms. Offers $20-50/photo; $100 for cover. Captions required. Buys one-time rights.
Columns/Departments: Video Views (just released or upcoming video cassettes—what's new on video, etc.) 1,400-1,500 words. Buys 8-10 mss/year. Query. Length: 1,400-1,800 words. Pays $250-350.
Tips: "Any topic is acceptable so long as it is related to a subject currently available on video. Example titles: Changing Trends in Conntry Music (music), History of the American Auto (documentary), The Blue Angels (aviation/space)."

VIDEOMANIA, "The Video Collector's Newspaper", Legs Of Stone Publishing Co., Box 47, Princeton WI 54968. Editor: Bob Katerzynske. 70% freelance written. Eager to work with new/unpublished writers. A monthly tabloid for the home video hobbyist. "Our readers are very much 'into' home video: they like reading about it—including both video hardware and software—98% also collect video (movies, vintage TV, etc.)." Circ. 5,000. Pays on publication. Publishes ms an average of 3 months after acceptance. Byline given. Buys all rights; may reassign. Submit seasonal/holiday material 6 months in advance. Computer printout submissions acceptable; prefers letter-quality. Reports in 3 weeks on mss. Sample copy for 9x12 SAE and $2.50 postage; writer's guidelines for #10 SASE .
Nonfiction: Book excerpts, videotape and book reviews, expose, general interest, historical/nostalgic, how-to, humor, interview/profile, new product, opinion, personal experience, photo feature, technical and travel. "All articles should deal with video and/or film. We always have special holiday issues in November and December." No "*complicated* technical pieces." Buys 24 mss/year. Send complete ms. Length: 500-1,000 words. Pays $2.50 maximum. "Contributor copies also used for payment."
Photos: Send photos with submissions. Reviews contact sheets and 3x5 prints. Offers no additional payment for photos accepted with ms. Model releases and identification of subjects required. Buys all rights; may reassign.
Fiction: Adventure, horror and humorous. "We want short, video-related fiction only on an occasional basis. Since we aim for a general readership, we do not want any pornographic material." Buys 5 mss/year. Send complete ms. Length: 500 words. Pays $2.50 maximum plus copies.
Tips: "We want to offer more reviews and articles on offbeat, obscure and rare movies, videos and stars. Write in a plain, easy-to-understand style. We're not looking for a highhanded, knock-'em-dead writing style . . . just something good! We want more short video, film and book reviews by freelancers."

Ethnic/Minority

Ethnic magazines, especially for Hispanics, have started up and done well during the past year. Writers also are looking forward to the publication of *Emerge*, a general-interest magazine targeted at middle-class black professionals partially owned by Time, Inc., which will appear this year. Traditions are kept alive, new ones become established and people are united by ethnic publications. Some ethnic magazines seek material that unites people of all races. Ideas, interests and concerns of nationalities and religions are covered by publications in this category. General interest lifestyle magazines for these groups are also included. Additional markets for writing with an ethnic orientation are located in the following sections: Career, College and Alumni; Juvenile; Men's; Women's; and Teen and Young Adult.

‡**AFRICAN-AMERICAN HERITAGE**, Dellco Publishing Company, Suite 103, 8443 S. Crenshaw Blvd., Inglewood CA 90305. (213)752-3706. Editor: Dennis W. DeLoach. 30% freelance written. Bimonthly magazine looking for "positive, informative, educational articles that build self-esteem, pride and an appreciation for the richness of culture and history." Circ. 25,000. Pays on publication. Publishes ms an average of 3-6 months after acceptance. Byline given. Offers 25% kill fee. Buys First North American serial rights, one-time rights or simultaneous rights. Submit seasonal/holiday material 6 months in advance. Simultaneous, photocopied and previously published submissions OK. Computer printout submissions OK; prefers letter-quality. Reports in 1 month on queries; two months on mss. Free sample copy. Writer's guidelines for 1 SAE with 4 first class stamps.

Nonfiction: Book excerpts, essays, general interest, historical/nostalgic, how-to, humor, inspirational, interview/profile, new product, opinion, personal experience, photo feature, religious and travel. Black History Month (February). Buys 6 mss/year. Query. Length: 200-2,500 words. Pays $25-300 for assigned articles. Sometimes pays expenses of writers on assignment.

Photos: State availability of photos with submission. Reviews 5x7 prints. Offers no additional payment for photos accepted with ms. Identification of subject required. Buys one-time rights.

Columns/Departments: History (historical profiles); Commentary (letters to the editor) 2,500 max.; Interviews (personalities, unusual careers, positive experiences) 2,500 max.; Short Stories (well written, entertaining) 2,500 max. Buys 12 mss/year. Query. Pays $25-300.

Fiction: Adventure, ethnic, historical, humorous, mystery, religious, romance and slice-of-life vignettes. "No erotica, horror, fantasy." Buys 6 mss/year. Query. Length: 200-2,500 words. Pays $25-300.

Poetry: Avant-garde, free verse, haiku, light verse and traditional. Buys 60 poems/year. Submit maximum 5 poems. Length: 4-36 lines. Pays $10-25.

Fillers: Anecdotes and facts. Buys 12/year. Length: 10-200 words. Pays $25-100.

AIM MAGAZINE, AIM Publishing Company, 7308 S. Eberhart Ave., Chicago IL 60619. (312)874-6184. Editor: Ruth Apilado. Managing Editor: Dr. Myron Apilado. 75% freelance written. Works with a small number of new/unpublished writers each year. Quarterly magazine on social betterment that promotes racial harmony and peace for high school, college and general audience. Circ. 10,000. Pays on publication. Publishes ms an average of 3 months after acceptance. Offers 60% of contract as kill fee. Not copyrighted. Buys one-time rights. Submit seasonal/holiday material 6 months in advance. Simultaneous queries, and simultaneous and photocopied submissions OK. Computer printout submissions acceptable; prefers letter-quality. Reports in 6 weeks on queries. Sample copy and writer's guidelines for $3.50, 8½x11 SAE and 4 first class stamps.

Nonfiction: Exposé (education); general interest (social significance); historical/nostalgic (Black or Indian); how-to (create a more equitable society); and profile (one who is making social contributions to community); and book reviews and reviews of plays "that reflect our ethnic/minority orientation." No religious material. Buys 16 mss/year. Send complete ms. Length: 500-800 words. Pays $25-35.

Photos: Reviews b&w prints. Captions and identification of subjects required.

Fiction: Ethnic, historical, mainstream, and suspense. Fiction that teaches the brotherhood of man. Buys 20 mss/year. Send complete ms. Length: 1,000-1,500 words. Pays $25-35.

Poetry: Avant-garde, free verse, light verse. No "preachy" poetry. Buys 20 poems/year. Submit maximum 5 poems. Length: 15-30 lines. Pays $3-5.

Fillers: Jokes, anecdotes and newsbreaks. Buys 30/year. Length: 50-100 words. Pays $5.

Tips: "Interview anyone of any age who unselfishly is making an unusual contribution to the lives of less fortunate individuals. Include photo and background of person. We look at the nations of the world as part of one family. Short stories and historical pieces about blacks and Indians are the areas most open to freelancers. Subject matter of submission is of paramount concern for us rather than writing style. Articles and stories showing the similarity in the lives of people with different racial backgrounds are desired."

THE AMERICAN CITIZEN ITALIAN PRESS, 13681 V St., Omaha NE 68137. (402)896-0403. Publisher/Editor: Diana C. Failla. 40% freelance written. Quarterly newspaper of Italian-American news/stories. Circ. 8,000. Pays on publication. Publishes ms an average of 3 months after acceptance. Byline given. Not copyrighted. Buys first North American serial rights. Submit seasonal/holiday material 2 months in advance. Previously published submissions OK. Computer printout submissions acceptable; prefers letter-quality. Reports in 1 month. Sample copy for 10x13 SAE and $1.50 postage; writer's guidelines for #10 SAE with 2 first class stamps.

Nonfiction: Book excerpts, general interest, historical/nostalgic, opinion, photo feature, celebrity pieces, travel, fashions, profiles and sports (Italian players). Query with published clips. Length: 400-600 words. Pays $15-20.

Photos: State availability of photos. Reviews b&w prints. Pays $5. Captions and identification of subjects required. Buys all rights.
Columns/Departments: Query.
Fiction: Query. Pays $15-20.
Poetry: Submit maximum 5 poems. Pays $5-10.
Tips: "Human interest stories are the most open to freelancers. We would also like some work dealing with current controversial issues involving those of Italian/American descent."

AMERICAN DANE, The Danish Brotherhood in America, 3717 Harney St., Box 31748, Omaha NE 68131. (402)341-5049. Editor: Jerome L. Christensen. Managing Editor: Pamela K. Dorau. 50% freelance written. Prefers to work with published/ established writers; works with a small number of new/unpublished writers each year. The monthly magazine of the Danish Brotherhood in America. All articles must have Danish ethnic flavor. Circ. 10,000. Pays on publication. Publishes ms an average of 1 year after acceptance. Byline given. Not copyrighted. Buys first rights. Submit seasonal/holiday material 1 year in advance. Photocopied submissions OK. Computer printout submissions acceptable; prefers letter-quality. Reports in 2 weeks on queries. Sample copy for 9½x4 SAE and 3 first class stamps; writer's guidelines for #10 SASE.
Nonfiction: Historical, humor, inspirational, personal experience, photo feature and travel, all with a Danish flavor. Buys 12 mss/year. Query. Length: 1,500 words maximum. Pays $50 maximum for unsolicited articles.
Photos: Send photos with submission. Reviews prints. Offers no additional payment for photos accepted with ms. Captions and identification of subjects required. Buys one-time rights.
Fiction: Adventure, historical, humorous, mystery, romance and suspense, all with a Danish flavor. Buys 6-12 mss/year. Query with published clips. Length: 1,500 words maximum. Pays $50 maximum.
Poetry: Traditional. Buys 1-6 poems/year. Submit maximum 6 poems. Pays $35 maximum.
Fillers: Anecdotes and short humor. Buys up to 12/year. Length: 300 words maximum. Pays $15 maximum.
Tips: "Feature articles are most open to freelancers. Reviews unsolicited manuscripts in August only."

AMERICAN JEWISH WORLD, AJW Publishing Inc., 4509 Minnetonka Blvd., Minneapolis MN 55416. (612)920-7000. Managing Editor: Marshall Hoffman. 10% freelance written. Weekly Jewish newspaper covering local, national and international stories. Circ.: 6,500. Pays on publication. Publishes ms an average of 1-4 months after acceptance. Byline given. Offers 50% kill fee. Publication copyrighted. Makes work-for-hire assignments. Submit seasonal/holiday material 6 months in advance. Simultaneous and photocopied submissions OK. Computer printout submissions OK. Free sample copy and writer's guidelines.
Nonfiction: Essays, expose, general interest, historical/nostalgic, humor, inspirational, interview/profile, opinion, personal experience, photo feature, religious, travel. Buys 30-50 mss/year. Query with or without published clips, or send complete ms. Length: 1,500-2,000 maximum. Pays $10-75. Sometimes pays expenses of writers on assignment.
Photos: State availability of photos with submission. Reviews prints. Pays $5 per photo. Identification of subjects required. Buys one-time rights.

ARARAT, 585 Saddle River Rd., Saddle Brook NJ 07662. Editor-in-Chief: Leo Hamalian. 80% freelance written. Emphasizes Armenian life and culture for Americans of Armenian descent and Armenian immigrants. "Most are well-educated; some are Old World." Quarterly magazine. Circ. 2,400. Pays on publication. Publishes ms an average of 1 year after acceptance. Buys first North American serial rights and second (reprint) rights to material originally published elsewhere. Submit seasonal/holiday material at least 3 months in advance. Photocopied and previously published submissions OK. Computer printout submissions acceptable. Reports in 6 weeks. Sample copy $3 plus 4 first class stamps.
Nonfiction: Historical (history of Armenian people, of leaders, etc.); interviews (with prominent or interesting Armenians in any field, but articles are preferred); profile (on subjects relating to Armenian life and culture); personal experience (revealing aspects of typical Armenian life); and travel (in Armenia and Armenian communities throughout the world and the US). Buys 3 mss/issue. Query. Length: 1,000-6,000 words. Pays $25-100.
Columns/Departments: Reviews of books by Armenians or relating to Armenians. Buys 6/issue. Query. Pays $25. Open to suggestions for new columns/departments.
Fiction: Any stories dealing with Armenian life in America or in the old country. Buys 4 mss/year. Query. Length: 2,000-5,000 words. Pays $35-75.
Poetry: Any verse that is Armenian in theme. Buys 6/issue. Pays $10.
Tips: "Read the magazine, and write about the kind of subjects we are obviously interested in, e.g., Kirlian photography, Aram Avakian's films, etc. Remember that we have become almost totally ethnic in subject matter, but we want articles that present (to the rest of the world) the Armenian in an interesting way. The most frequent mistake made by writers in completing an article for us is that they are not sufficiently versed in Armenian history/culture. The articles are too superficial for our audience."

EBONY MAGAZINE, 820 S. Michigan Ave., Chicago IL 60605. Editor: John H. Johnson. Managing Editor: Charles L. Sanders. 10% freelance written. For Black readers of the U.S., Africa, and the Caribbean. Monthly. Circ. 1,800,000. Buys first North American serial rights and all rights. Buys about 10 mss/year. "We are now fully staffed, buying few manuscripts." Pays on publication. Publishes ms an average of 3 months after acceptance. Submit seasonal material 2 months in advance. Query. Reports in 1 month.

Nonfiction: Achievement and human interest stories about, or of concern to, Black readers. Interviews, profiles and humor pieces are bought. Length: 1,500 words maximum. "Study magazine and needs carefully. Perhaps one out of 50 submissions interests us. Most are totally irrelevant to our needs and are simply returned." Pays $200 minimum. Sometimes pays the expenses of writers on assignment.

Photos: Purchased with mss, and with captions only. Buys 8x10 glossy prints, color transparencies, 35mm color. Submit negatives and contact sheets when possible. Offers no additional payment for photos accepted with mss.

GREATER PHOENIX JEWISH NEWS, Phoenix Jewish News, Inc., Box 26590, Phoenix AZ 85068. (602)870-9470. Executive Editor: Flo Eckstein. Managing Editor: Leni Reiss. 10% freelance written. Prefers to work with published/established writers. Weekly tabloid covering subjects of interest to Jewish readers. Circ. 7,000. Pays on publication. Publishes ms an average of 3 months after acceptance. Byline given. Submit seasonal/holiday material 3 months in advance. Simultaneous queries, and simultaneous, photocopied, and previously published submissions OK. Computer printout submissions acceptable; prefers letter-quality. (Must be easy to read, with upper and lower case.) Reports in 1 month. Sample copy $1.

Nonfiction: General interest, issue analysis, interview/profile, opinion, personal experience, photo feature and travel. Special sections include Fashion and Health; House and Home; Back to School; Summer Camps; Party Planning; Bridal; Travel; Business and Finance; and Jewish Holidays. Buys 25 mss/year. Send complete ms. Length: 1,000-2,500 words. Pays $15-75 for simultaneous rights; $1.50/column inch for first serial rights. Sometimes pays the expenses of writers on assignment.

Photos: Send photos with query or ms. Pays $10 for 8x10 b&w prints. Captions required.

Tips: "We are looking for lifestyle and issue-oriented pieces of particular interest to Jewish readers. Our newspaper reaches across the religious, political, social and economic spectrum of Jewish residents in this burgeoning southwestern metropolitan area. We stay away from cute stories as well as ponderous submissions."

HADASSAH MAGAZINE, 50 W. 58th St., New York NY 10019. Executive Editor: Alan M. Tigay. 90% freelance written. Works with small number of new/unpublished writers each year. Monthly, except combined issues (June-July and August-September). Circ. 334,000. Publishes ms 1-18 months after acceptance. Buys first rights (with travel articles, we buy all rights). Computer printout submissions acceptable. Reports in 6 weeks. Free sample copy and writer's guidelines.

Nonfiction: Primarily concerned with Israel, Jewish communities around the world, and American civic affairs. Buys 10 unsolicited mss/year. Length: 1,500-2,000 words. Pays $200-400, less for reviews. Sometimes pays the expenses of writers on assignment.

Photos: "We buy photos only to illustrate articles, with the exception of outstanding color from Israel which we use on our covers. We pay $175 and up for a suitable cover photo." Offers $50 for first photo; $35 for each additional. "Always interested in striking cover (color) photos, especially of Israel and Jerusalem."

Columns/Departments: "We have a Parenting column and a Travel column, but a query for topic or destination should be submitted first to make sure the area is of interest and the story follows our format."

Fiction: Contact Zelda Shluker. Short stories with strong plots and positive Jewish values. No personal memoirs, "schmaltzy" fiction, or women's magazine fiction. "We continue to buy very little fiction because of a backlog. We are also open to art stories that explore trends in Jewish art, literature, theatre, etc." Length: 3,000 words maximum. Pays $300 minimum.

Tips: "We are interested in reading articles that offer an American perspective on Jewish affairs (1,500 words). Send query of topic first. (For example, a look at the presidential candidates from a Jewish perspective."

‡HERITAGE FLORIDA JEWISH NEWS, 207 O'Brien Rd. Box 742, Fern Park FL 32730. (407)834-8787. Associate Editor: Edith Schulman. Publisher/Editor: Jeffrey Gaeser. 30% freelance written. Weekly tabloid on Jewish subjects of local, national and international scope, except for special issues. "Covers news of local, national and international scope of interest to Jewish readers and not likely to be found in other publications." Circ. 10,000. Pays on publication. Publishes ms an average of 2 months after acceptance. Byline given. Buys first North American serial rights or first rights or one-time rights or second serial (reprint) rights or simultaneous rights. Submit seasonal/holiday material 2 months in advance. Photocopied and previously published submissions OK. Computer printout submissions OK; prefers letter-quality. Sample copy 50¢.

Nonfiction: General interest, interview/profile, opinion (does not mean letters to the editor), photo feature, religious and travel. "Especially need articles for these annual issues: Rosh Hashanah, Financial, Chanukah, Celebration (wedding & bar mitzvah), Passover, Health and Fitness, Education. No fiction, poems, 1st person experiences." Buys 50 mss/year. Send complete ms. Length: 500-1,000 words. Pays $15-30. Sometimes pays expenses of writers on assignment.

Photos: State availability of photos with submission. Reviews 5x7 prints. Offers $5 per photo. Captions and identification of subjects required. Buys one-time rights.

THE HIGHLANDER, Angus J. Ray Associates, Inc., Box 397, Barrington IL 60011. (312)382-1035. FAX: (312)382-0322. Editor: Angus J. Ray. Managing Editor: Ethyl Kennedy Ray. 50% freelance written. Works with a small number of new/unpublished writers each year. Bimonthly magazine covering Scottish history, clans, genealogy, travel/history, and Scottish/American activities. Circ. 40,000. Pays on acceptance. Publishes ms an average of 6 months after acceptance. Byline given. Buys first North American serial rights and second serial (reprint) rights to material originally published elsewhere. Submit seasonal/holiday material 6 months in advance. Photocopied and previously published submissions OK. Computer printout submissions acceptable. Reports in 1 month. Sample copy for $1 and 9x12 SAE. Free writer's guidelines.

Nonfiction: Historical/nostalgic. "No fiction; no articles unrelated to Scotland." Buys 50 mss/year. Query. Length: 750-2,000 words. Pays $75-150. Sometimes pays the expenses of writers on assignment.

Photos: State availability of photos. Pays $5-10 for 8x10 b&w prints or transparencies. Reviews b&w contact sheets. Identification of subjects required. Buys one-time rights.

Tips: "Submit something that has appeared elsewhere."

INSIDE, The Jewish Exponent Magazine, Federation of Jewish Agencies of Greater Philadelphia, 226 S. 16th St., Philadelphia PA 19102. (215)893-5700. Editor: Jane Biberman. Managing Editor: Jodie Green. 95% freelance written (by assignment). Works with published/established writers and a small number of new/unpublished writers each year. Quarterly Jewish community magazine—for a 25 years and older general interest Jewish readership. Circ. 100,000. Pays on acceptance. Publishes ms an average of 2 months after acceptance. Byline given. Offers 20% kill fee. Buys one-time rights. Submit seasonal/holiday material 3 months in advance. Simultaneous queries OK. Computer printout submissions acceptable; no dot-matrix. Reports in 2 weeks on queries; 3 weeks on mss. Sample copy for 9x12 SAE and $2; writer's guidelines for #10 SASE.

Nonfiction: Book excerpts, general interest, historical/nostalgic, humor, interview/profile. Philadelphia angle desirable. No personal religious experiences or trips to Israel. Buys 80 mss/year. Query. Length: 600-3,000 words. Pays $100-700. Pays the expenses of writers on assignment.

Fiction: Short stories. Query.

Photos: State availability of photos. Reviews color and b&w transparencies. Identification of subjects required.

Tips: "Personalities—very well known—and serious issues of concern to Jewish community needed. We can use 600-word 'back page' pieces—humorous, first person articles."

IRISH & AMERICAN REVIEW, The Newspaper of the International Irish Community, Interstate News Services, Inc., Suite 250, 500 Airport Rd., St. Louis MO 63135. (314)522-1300. Editor: Michael J. Olds. 80% freelance written. Quarterly tabloid of Irish and Irish-American features and photographs. "Our newspaper is strictly a feature-lifestyle publication. The only hard news is business information. No politics." Circ. 20,000. Pays on publication. Publishes ms an average of 2 months after acceptance. Byline given. Buys all rights. Submit seasonal/holiday material 4 months in advance. Query for electronic submissions. Computer printout submissions OK. Reports in 1 month. Free writer's guidelines.

Nonfiction: Historical/nostalgic, humor, inspirational, interview/profile, new product, personal experience, photo feature, religious, travel. Special issues: St. Patrick's Day (March edition); Irish travel season. Buys 20 mss/year. Query. Length: 300-2,000 words. Pays $20-250 for assigned articles; $20-100 for unsolicited articles. Sometimes pays expenses of writers on assignment.

Photos: State availability of photos with submission. Reviews contact sheets, transparencies and 5x7 prints. Offers $5 minimum for photos. Captions, model releases and identification of subjects required. Usually buys one-time rights.

Columns/Departments: Books (of interest to Irish, Irish-Americans), 250-400 words; Food (cooking and review or Irish food and restaurants), Travel Dept., 250-400 words. Buys 4-8 mss/year. Query or send complete ms. Pays $15 minimum.

Fiction: Historical, humorous, novel excerpts. Nothing political. Buys 1-4 mss/year. Query. Length: 250-1,000 words. Pays $15 minimum.

Poetry: Traditional. Buys up to 4 poems/year. Pays $10 minimum.

Tips: "We are interested in features and photo features about Irish-Americans; Irish; American cities and events with an Irish flavor; Irish travel stories; stories about Irish commerce. Look for the Irish interest."

‡THE ITALIAN TIMES, Italian-American Publications, Inc., Box 20241, Baltimore MD 21284-2024. (301)254-1300. Publisher and Managing Editor: Stephen J. Ferrandi. 55% freelance written. Eager to work with new/unpublished writers. Quarterly magazine covering anything of interest to Italian-Americans. Circ. 32,500. Pays on publication. Publishes ms an average of 3 months after acceptance. Byline given. Buys first rights, one-time rights, or second serial (reprint) rights. Submit seasonal/holiday material 5 months in advance. Simultaneous and previously published submissions OK. Computer printout submissions acceptable; no dot-matrix. Reports in 6 weeks on queries; 1 month on mss. Sample copy $2.

Nonfiction: Essays, exposé, general interest, historical/nostalgic, humor, interview/profile, opinion, personal experience, travel and young Italian-American success stories. Articles on Italy very much wanted. Special issues include Italian Easter; all Italy issue with personal experiences, travel hints, food and wine featured (August); and Italian Christmas. Buys 30 mss/year. Send complete ms. Length: 100-10,000 words. Pays $2-100; mainly pays in copies "if new author with only average writing skills but good idea." Sometimes pays the expenses of writers on assignment.

Photos: Send photos or slides with submission. Reviews 8x10 prints. Captions and identification of subjects required.

Poetry: F. Joseph Sebastian, poetry editor. Free verse, haiku, light verse and traditional. Buys 6 poems/year. Length: 50 lines maximum. Pays $2-25.

Fillers: Anecdotes, facts, newsbreaks and short humor. Buys 100/year. Length: 750 words maximum. Pays $2-25.

Tips: "We encourage good writers who haven't been published to send a manuscript for consideration. Stories and articles should be fast paced, easily digested and worth reading a second time. We welcome phone calls to answer any questions (9-5). We publish mostly freelance general interest and cover stories."

THE JEWISH MONTHLY, B'nai B'rith International, 1640 Rhode Island Ave. NW, Washington DC 20036. (202)857-6645. Editor: Jeff Rubin. 75% freelance written. Prefers to work with published/established writers. A monthly magazine covering Jewish politics, lifestyles, religion and culture for a family audience. Circ. 180,000. Pays on publication. Publishes ms an average of 4 months after acceptance. Byline given. Offers 25% kill fee. Buys first North American serial rights. Submit seasonal/holiday material 6 months in advance. Photocopied submissions OK. Query for electronic submissions. Computer printout submissions acceptable; prefers letter-quality. Reports in 2 weeks on queries; 1 month on mss. Sample copy $1; free writer's guidelines.

Nonfiction: Book excerpts, general interest, historical/nostalgic, humor, interview/profile, opinion, personal experience, photo feature, religious and travel. "I am looking for articles that offer fresh perspectives on familiar issues in the Jewish community (such as assimilation, Middle East conflict, religious tensions) and articles that focus on new trends and problems." No immigrant reminiscences. Buys 25 mss/year. Query with published clips. Length: 500-5,000 words. Pays 10-25¢/word. Sometimes pays the expenses of writers on assignment.

Photos: State availability of photos with submission. Reviews contact sheets, transparencies and prints. Offers $25-75/photo. Captions, model releases, and identification of subjects required. Buys one-time rights.

JEWISH NEWS, Suite 240, 20300 Civic Center Dr., Southfield MI 48076. (313)354-6060. Editor: Gary Rosenblatt. Associate Editor: Alan Hitsky. 10% freelance written. Works with a small number of new/unpublished writers each year. A weekly tabloid covering news and features of Jewish interest. Circ. 20,000. Pays on publication. Publishes ms an average of 3 months after acceptance. Byline given. No kill fee "unless stipulated beforehand." Buys first North American serial rights. Simultaneous queries and photocopied submissions OK. Computer printout submissions acceptable; prefers letter-quality. Reports in 2 weeks on queries; 1 month on mss. Sample copy $1; writer's guidelines for #10 SASE.

Nonfiction: Book excerpts, humor, and interview/profile. Buys 10-20 mss/year. Query with or without published clips, or send complete ms. Length: 500-2,500 words. Pays $40-125.

Fiction: Ethnic. Buys 1-2 mss/year. Send complete ms. Length: 500-2,500 words. Pays $40-125.

‡LA RED/THE NET, The Hispanic Journal of Education, Floricanto Press, Suite 830, 16161 Ventura Blvd., Encino CA 91436. (818)990-1885. Editor: Giselle K. Cabello. 80% freelance written. Quarterly magazine on Hispanic issues, particularly education. Circ. 5,000. Pays 90 days after publication. Byline sometimes given. Buys all rights. Query for electronic submissions. Computer printout submissions OK; prefers letter-quality. Sample copy $5 with 9x12 SAE and $1.20 postage. Writer's guidelines for SAE with 50¢ postage.

Nonfiction: Hispanic issues. "No mainstream general articles." Buys 10 mss/year. Query or send complete manuscript. Length: 2,000-6,000 words. Pays $50-150 for assigned articles; $50 maximum for unsolicited articles. Sometimes pays writers with contributor copies or other premiums rather than cash on articles that are not very high interest.

Photos: Send photos with submission. Reviews 3½x1½ transparencies, 3x3 prints. Offers no additional payment for photos accepted with ms. Captions and identification of subjects required. Buys one-time rights.

Columns/Departments: Feature Review (a lengthy review of a high interest book) 3,000 words; Feature Article (a lengthy review on a high interest topic) 6,000 words. Buys 4 mss/year. Send complete ms. Pays $50-150.

Tips: "Take a high interest issue affecting Hispanics and write a well researched article; it must be informative, no jargon, please."

LECTOR, The Hispanic Book Review Journal, Floricanto Press, Suite 830, 16161 Ventura Blvd., Encino CA 91436. (818)990-1885. Editor: Roberto Cabello-Argandona. Managing Editor: Giselle K. Cabello. 95% freelance written. Works with a small number of new/unpublished writers each year and is eager to work with new/unpublished writers. A semiannual journal of U.S. Hispanic cultural articles Latin American literature, and English reviews of books in Spanish (published in Spain, Central America, and Latin America). "We desire cultural articles, particularly of Hispanic arts and literature, written for a popular level (as opposed to an academic level). Articles are to be nonsexist, nonracist." Circ. 3,000. Pays on publication. Publishes ms an average of 6-12 months after acceptance. Byline given. Buys first rights or makes work-for-hire assignments. Photocopied submissions OK; previously published submissions sometimes accepted. Computer printout submissions acceptable ("desirable"); prefers letter-quality. Reports in 3 months. Sample copy $5; writer's guidelines for #10 SASE.

Nonfiction: Interview/profile, photo feature and articles on art, literature and Latino small presses. No personal experience, religious or how-to. Buys 25 mss/year. "No unsolicited manuscripts; query us first." Length: 2,000-3,500 words. Pays $50-150. "Writers, along with payment, always get five copies of magazine."

Photos: Send photos with submission. Reviews contact sheets. Captions required. Buys one-time rights.

Columns/Departments: Publisher's Corner (covers publishing houses in Latin America or U.S. [Latin]), 2,000-2,500 words; Perspective (cultural articles dealing with aspect of Hispanic art/lit), 2,500-3,500 words; Events in Profile (occasional column covering particular event in Chicano Studies), 1,500-2,000 words; Feature Review (in-depth review of particularly important published work), 2,500-3,000 words, Author's Corner (interview with recently published author), 1,500-2,000 words, and Inquiry (literary criticism) 2,000-2,500 words. Buys 15 mss/year. Query with published clips. Pays $50-150.

‡**MIDSTREAM, A Monthly Jewish Review**, 515 Park Ave., New York NY 10022. Editor: Murray Zuckoff. 90% freelance written. Works with a small number of new/unpublished writers each year. Monthly. Circ. 10,000. Buys first North American serial rights. Byline given. Pays after publication. Publishes ms an average of 6 months after acceptance. Computer printout submissions acceptable; no dot-matrix. Reports in 2 months. Fiction guidelines for SAE with 1 first class stamp.

Nonfiction: "Articles offering a critical interpretation of the past, searching examination of the present, and affording a medium for independent opinion and creative cultural expression. Articles on the political and social scene in Israel, on Jews in Russia, the U.S. and elsewhere; generally it helps to have a Zionist orientation." Buys historical and think pieces, primarily of Jewish and related content. Pays 5¢/word.

Fiction: Primarily of Jewish and related content. Pays 5¢/word.

Tips: "A book review is a good way to start. Send us a sample review or a clip, let us know your area of interest, suggest books you would like to review. For longer articles, give a brief account of your background or credentials in this field. Send query describing article or ms with cover letter. Since we are a monthly, we look for critical analysis rather than a 'journalistic' approach."

NATIVE PEOPLES MAGAZINE, The Arts and Lifeways, 1833 North 3rd St., Phoenix AZ 85004. (602)252-2236. Editor: Gary Avey. Quarterly magazine on Native Americans. "The primary purpose of this magazine is to offer a sensitive portrayal of the arts and lifeways of native peoples around the world." Estab. 1987. Circ. 18,000. Pays on publication. Byline given. Buys one-time rights. Query for electronic submissions. Computer printout submissions OK. Reports in 1 month on queries; 2 weeks on mss. Sample copy for 8½x11 SAE with 5 first class stamps. Free writer's guidelines.

Nonfiction: Book excerpts, historical/nostalgic, interview/profile, personal experience, photo feature. Buys 35 mss/year. Query with published clips. Length: 1,400-2,000 words. Pays 25-50¢/word. Sometimes pays expenses of writer's on assignment.

Photos: State availability of photos with submission. Reviews transparencies (all formats). Offers $75-150 per-page rates. Identification of subjects required. Buys one-time rights.

‡**POLISH AMERICAN JOURNAL, Polonia's Voice**, Panagraphics, Inc., 774 Fillmore Ave., Buffalo NY 14212. (716)852-8211. Editor: Mark A. Kohan. Managing Editor: William Falkowski. 20% freelance written. Monthly tabloid for Polonia (Polish and Polish-American events, people, etc.). "Stories/reports should be about Polish-Americans active in their community on either a local or national level. Prefer biographies/ histories of these people or essays on their accomplishments." Circ. 20,000. Pays on publication. Publishes ms an average of 2 months after acceptance. Byline given. Offers $2 kill fee. Not copyrighted. Buys one-time rights. Submit seasonal/holiday material 3 months in advance. Photocopied and previously published submissions OK. Query for electronic submissions. Computer printout submissions OK; prefer letter-quality. Sample copy for 9x12 SAE with 3 first class stamps.

Nonfiction: Exposé (story on Polish-Americans), general interest (community news), historical/nostalgic (retrospectives on events), how-to (organize groups, etc.), interview/profile (background on local Pol-Ams), opinion (historical observations, anti-defamation, etc.), personal experience (growing up Polish). Special issues on Easter and Christmas celebrations—how practiced in other areas; travel to Poland/airfare and comparisons, etc.; salute to prominent Polish-American, business leaders, clergy, media personalities, etc. Buys 6-8 mss/year. Query. Length: 200-1,000 words. Pays $10-50 ($2 per 1,000 characters or $1/100 words). Sometimes pays expenses of writers on assignment.

Photos: State availability of photos with submission. Reviews 8½x11 prints. Offers $2-10 per photo. Identification of subjects required. Buys one-time rights.

Columns/Departments: Forum Viewpoints (observations on recent decisions/events), 1,000-2,000 words; culture (music/art developments), 1,000-2,000 words; scholarships/studies (grants and programs available), 1,000-2,000 words. Buys 6 mss/year. Query. Length: 100-500 words. Pays $10-50.

Fillers: Anecdotes, facts, gags to be illustrated by cartoonist, newsbreaks, and short humor. Buys 25/year. Length: 50-200 words. Pays $2-10.

Tips: "Get a sample issue to get feel of paper. Best bet is to call editor to find out what stories need writers (there are, on average, 1-2 doz. articles/ideas 'on deck' that need writers.) Human interest stories are good but should not be run-of-the-mill. Freelancers can best break in by writing for: Cover and feature—need fresh blood, new perspectives on ethnicity, art and music reviews—need someone to cover work of Pol-Am artist, etal, and Polka music columnists are needed, also."

PRESENT TENSE, 165 E. 56th St., New York NY 10022. (212)751-4000. FAX: (212)319-0975. Editor: Murray Polner. 95% freelance written. Prefers to work with published/established writers. For college-educated, Jewish-oriented audience interested in Jewish life throughout the world. Bimonthly magazine. Circ. 45,000. Buys all rights. Queries only, accompanied by SASE. Byline given. Buys 60 mss/year. Pays on publication. Publishes ms an average of 6 months after acceptance. Computer printout submissions acceptable. Reports in 2 months. Sample copy $4.50.

Nonfiction: Quality reportage of contemporary events (a la *Harper's, New Yorker*, etc.). Personal journalism, reportage, profiles and photo essays. Query. Length: 3,000 words maximum. Pays $150-250.

Tips: "Read our magazine."

‡QUE PASA, D. S. Magazines, 1086 Teaneck Rd., Teaneck NJ 07032. (201)833-1800. FAX: (201)833-1428. Editor: Celeste Gomes. 25% freelance written. Bimonthly magazine on Hispanic artists/lifestyles. "QP is a magazine for the Hispanic community—mostly ages 13-25. It is a magazine with a positive outlook." Circ. 100,000. Pays on publication. Publishes ms an average of 3-4 months after acceptance. Byline given. Offers $25 kill fee. Buys first North American serial rights. Submit seasonal/holiday material 4 months in advance. Computer printout submissions OK; no dot-matrix. NLQ only. Reports in 2 weeks on queries. Free sample copy and writer's guidelines.

Nonfiction: General interest, interview/profile, new product and travel; all dealing with either entertainment or Hispanic community. Buys 50 mss/year. Query with published clips. Pays $50.

Photos: State availability of photos with submission. Reviews transparencies and 5x7 prints. Offers $25 b&w-$75 per color photo. Identification of subjects required. Buys one-time rights.

‡THE SOUTHERN JEWISH WEEKLY, Southern Independent Operators, Inc. Box 3297, Jacksonville FL 32206. (904)634-1469. Editor: Isadore Moscovitz. 10% freelance written. Weekly tabloid looking for "items and articles of Jewish interest throughout the South, the nation, Israel and throughout the world." Circ. 28,500. Pays on publication. Publishes ms an average of 1 month after acceptance. Byline given. Not copyrighted. Buys one-time rights. Submit seasonal/holiday material 1 month in advance. Computer submissions OK; no dot-matrix. Sample copy for #10 SAE with 2 first class stamps.

Nonfiction: Humor, inspirational, photo feature and travel, all pertaining to Jewish interset. August for Jewish New Year; February for Passover and November for Chanukah. Buys 15 mss/year. Send complete ms. Length: 250-1,500 words. Pays $10-200 for assigned articles; $10-100 for unsolicited articles. Pays expenses of writers on assignment.

Photos: Send photos with submission. Offers $5-50 per photo. Captions required. Buys one-time rights.

Fiction: Ethnic, humorous and religious. "We use only material specifically directed toward a Jewish audience." Buys 5 mss/year. Send complete ms. Length: 500-1,500 words. Pays $10-250.

THE UKRAINIAN WEEKLY, Ukrainian National Association, 30 Montgomery St., Jersey City NJ 07302. (201)434-0237. Editor: Roma Hadzewycz. 30% freelance written (mostly by a corps of regular contributors). "We are backlogged with submissions and prefer not to receive unsolicited submissions at this time." A weekly tabloid covering news and issues of concern to Ukrainian community. Circ. 8,000. Pays on publication. Publishes ms an average of 1-2 months after acceptance. Byline given. Buys first North American serial rights, second serial (reprint) rights or makes work-for-hire assignments. Submit seasonal/holiday material 1 month in advance. Reports in 1 month. Free sample copy.

Nonfiction: Book excerpts, essays, exposé, general interest, historical/nostalgic, interview/profile, opinion, personal experience, photo feature and news events. Special issues include Easter, Christmas, anniversary of Helsinki Accords, anniversary of Ukrainian Helsinki monitoring group. Buys 80 mss/year. Query with published clips. Length: 500-2,000 words. Pays $45-100 for assigned articles. Pays $25-100 for unsolicited articles. Sometimes pays the expenses of writers on assignment.

Photos: Send photos with submission. Reviews contact sheets, negatives and 3x5, 5x7 or 8x10 prints. Offers no additional payment for photos accepted with ms.
Columns/Departments: News & Views (commentary on news events), 500-1,000 words. Buys 10 mss/year. Query. Pays $25-50.
Tips: "Become acquainted with the Ukrainian community in the U.S. and Canada. The area of our publication most open to freelancers is community news—coverage of local events. We'll put more emphasis on events in Ukraine during this period of perestroika in the USSR."

Food and Drink

Magazines appealing to gourmets are classified here. Journals aimed at food processing, manufacturing and retailing are in the Trade section. Many magazines in General Interest and Women's categories also buy articles on food topics.

BON APPETIT, America's Food and Entertaining Magazine, Knapp Communications Corporation, 5900 Wilshire Blvd., Los Angeles CA 90036. (213)965-3600. Editor-in-Chief: William J. Garry. 50% freelance written. Works with small number of new/unpublished writers each year. Monthly magazine. "Our articles are written in the first person voice and are directed toward the active cook. Emphasis on recipes intended for use by the dedicated amateur cook." Circ. 1,300,000. Pays on acceptance. Publishes ms an average of 6 months after acceptance. Byline given. Buys first North American serial rights and all rights. Submit seasonal/holiday material 6 months in advance. Computer printout submissions acceptable; no dot-matrix. Reports in 1 month. Writer's guidelines for #10 SASE.
Nonfiction: Barbara Fairchild, executive editor. How-to (cooking) and travel. No articles which are not food related. Buys 120 mss/year. Query with published clips. Length: 1,000-3,000 words. Pays $600-2,000.
Photos: State availability of photos with submission. Reviews 35mm transparencies. Offers $175-550/photo. Captions, model releases and identification of subjects required. Buys one-time rights.
Columns/Departments: Tricia Cauas, column/department editor. Bon Voyage (travel articles featuring a specific city which cover, in a lively manner, interesting sights and landmarks and, especially, local restaurants and foods of note). Will need recipes from these restaurants. Buys 12 mss/year. Query. Length: 1,000-1,800 words. Pays $600-1,200.
Tips: We will probably be buying more "fast and easy" and "healthy/low calorie" stories in the next year.

CHOCOLATIER, The Haymarket Group/Ion International, #500, 45 W. 34th St., New York NY 10001. (212)239-0855. Editor-in-Chief: Barbara Albright. 33% freelance written. A bimonthly magazine "devoted to people who exemplify their passion for the good life by their love of fine quality desserts. While *Chocolatier* focuses on a national indulgence, feature articles cover desserts, spirits, and entertaining." Circ. 350,000. Pays on acceptance. Publishes ms an average of 6 months after acceptance. Byline given. Offers 25% kill fee. Buys first worldwide serial rights (publication elsewhere not earlier than 4 months after publication in *Chocolatier*). Submit seasonal/holiday material 8 months in advance. Simultaneous and photocopied submissions OK. Computer printout submissions acceptable; prefers letter-quality. Reports in 2 months. Writer's guidelines for #10 SASE.
Nonfiction: New products, food/recipe and technical. Buys 10 mss/year. Query with published clips. Length: 500-2,500 words. Pays $100-800.
Photos: State availability of photos with submission. Identification of subjects required. Buys one-time rights.
Columns/Departments: Submit ideas for departments. Query with published clips. Length: 500-1,000 words. Pays variable rates.

‡COOKING LIGHT, The Magazine of Food and Fitness, Southern Living, Inc. Box 1748, Birmingham AL 35201. (205)877-6000. FAX: (205)877-6600. Editor: Katherine M. Eakin. Managing Editor: B. Ellen Templeton. 75% freelance written. Bimonthly magazine on healthy recipes and fitness information. "*Cooking Light* is a positive approach to a healthier lifestyle. It's written for healthy people on regular diets who are counting calories or trying to make calories count toward better nutrition. Moderation, balance and variety are emphasized. The writing style is fresh, upbeat and encouraging, emphasizing that eating a balanced, varied, lower-calorie diet and excercising regularly do not have to be boring." Circ. 650,000. Pays on acceptance. Publishes ms an average of 6-12 months after acceptance. Byline sometimes given. Offers 25% of original contract fee as kill fee. Buys all rights. Submit seasonal/holiday material 12 months in advance. Computer printout submissions OK; prefers letter-quality. Free sample copy and writer's guidelines.
Nonfiction: Personal experience nutrition, healthy recipes, fitness/exercise. Buys 150 mss/year. Query with published clips. Length: 400-2,000 words. Pays $250-2,000 for assigned articles. Pays expenses of writers on assignment.

Columns/Departments: Profile (an incident or event that occurred in one's life that resulted in a total lifestyle change) 2,000-2500 words; Children's Fitness (emphasis on prevention and intervention in regard to fitness, exercise, nutrition) 1,000-1,500 words; Taking Aim (a personal account of progression from desire to obstacle to achievement for incorporating exercise into one's routine schedule) 1,000-1,500 words and Downfall (a humorous personal account of desire to obstacle to the continuing struggle to overcome a particular food habit or addiction) 1,000-1,500 words. Buys 30 mss/year. Query. Length: 1,000-2,000 words. Pays $250-2,000.

Tips: "Emphasis should be on achieving a healthier lifestyle through food, nutrition, fitness, exercise information. In submitting queries, include information on professional background. Food writers should include examples of healthy recipes which meet the guidelines of *Cooking Light*."

COOK'S, The Magazine of Cooking in America, Pennington Publishing, 2710 North Ave., Bridgeport CT 06604. (203)366-4155. Senior Editor: Deborah Hartz. 50% freelance written. A magazine published 10 times/year covering food and cooking in America. "*Cook's* publishes lively informative articles that describe food and restaurant trends in the U.S. or that describe hands-on cooking techniques. Almost all of our articles include recipes." Circ. 235,000. Pays on acceptance. Publishes ms an average of 4-5 months after acceptance. Byline given. Offers 50% kill fee. Makes work for hire arrangements. Submit seasonal/holiday material 1 year in advance. Photocopied submissions OK. Computer printout submissions acceptable; prefers letter-quality. Reports in 2 months. Sample copy for 10x13 SAE with 6 first class stamps

Nonfiction: Food and cooking. No travel, personal experience or nostalgia pieces, history of food and cuisine, or recipes using prepared ingredients (e.g., canned soups, "instant" foods, mixes, etc.). Buys 60 mss/year. Query with clips and sample first page. Length: 1,000-2,000 words plus recipes. Pays $300-750. Paying of expenses, etc. determined on a contract basis.

‡FOOD & WINE, American Express Publishing Corp., 1120 Avenue of the Americas, New York NY 10036. (212)382-5618. Editor: Ila Stanger. Managing Editor: Warren Picower. Monthly magazine for "active people for whom eating, drinking, entertaining, dining out, travel and all the related equipment and trappings are central to their lifestyle." Circ. 800,000. Pays on acceptance. Byline given. Offers 25% kill fee. Buys first world rights. Submit seasonal/holiday material 9 months in advance. Query for electronic submissions. Computer printout submissions OK; prefers letter-quality. Reports in 2-3 weeks on queries; 2 weeks on mss. Sample copy $3. Free writer's guidelines.

Nonfiction: Essays, how-to, humor, new product and travel. Query. Query with published clips. Buys 150 mss/year. Query with published clips. Length: 1,000-3,000 words. Pays $800-2,000. Pays expenses of writers on assignment.

Photos: State availability of photos with submission. No unsolicited photos or art. Offers $100-450 page rate per photo. Model releases and identification of subjects required. Buys one-time rights.

Columns/Departments: What's New, Eating Out, The Traveler, Setting the Scene (see magazine). Buys 140 mss/year. Query with published clips. Length: 800-3,000 words. Pays $800-2,000.

Tips: "Good service, good writing, up-to-date information, interesting article approach and appropriate point of view for F&W's audience."

KASHRUS MAGAZINE, The Bimonthly for the Kosher Consumer, Yeshiva Birkas Reuven, Box 96, Parkville Station, Brooklyn NY 11204. (718)998-3201. Editor: Rabbi Yosef Wikler. 25% freelance written. Prefers to work with published/established writers, and is eager to work with new/unpublished writers. Bimonthly magazine covering kosher food industry. Circ. 10,000. Pays on acceptance. Publishes ms an average of 2 months after acceptance. Byline given. Offers 50% kill fee. Buys first or second serial (reprint) rights. Submit seasonal/holiday material 2 months in advance. Simultaneous, photocopied and previously published submissions OK. Query for electronic submissions. Computer printout submissions OK; prefers letter-quality. Reports in 1 week on queries; 2 weeks on mss. Sample copy and writer's guidelines for $1.

Nonfiction: General interest, interview/profile, new product, personal experience, photo feature, religious, technical and travel. Special issues feature International Kosher Travel (October) and Passover (March). Buys 8-12 mss/year. Query with published clips. Length: 1,000-2,000 words. Pays $100-250 for assigned articles; pays up to $100 for unsolicited articles. Sometimes pays the expenses of writers on assignment.

Photos: State availability of photos with submission. Offers no additional payment for photos accepted with ms. Buys one-time rights.

Columns/Departments: Book Review (cooking books, food technology, kosher food), 250-500 words; People in the News (interviews with kosher personalities), 1,000-2,000 words; Regional Kosher Supervision (report on kosher supervision in a city or community), 1,000-3,000 words; Food Technology (new technology or current technology with accompanying pictures), 1,000-2,000 words. Buys 5 mss/year. Query with published clips. Pays $50-250.

Tips: "*Kashrus Magazine* will do more writing on general food technology, production, and merchandising as well as human interest travelogs and regional writing in 1990 than we have done in the past. Areas most open to freelancers are interviews, food technology, regional reporting and travel. We welcome stories on the availability and quality of Kosher foods and services in communities across the U.S. and throughout the world."

NATURAL FOOD & FARMING, Natural Food Associates, Highway 59, Box 210, Atlanta TX 75551. (214)796-3612. 80% freelance written. Eager to work with new/unpublished writers. Executive Director: Bill Francis. A monthly magazine covering organic gardening and natural foods, preventive medicine, and vitamins and supplements. Circ. 50,000. Pays on acceptance. Publishes ms an average of 3 months after acceptance. Byline given sometimes. Not copyrighted. Buys first rights or second serial (reprint) rights. Submit seasonal/holiday material 2-3 months in advance. Simultaneous, photocopied and previously published submissions OK. Computer printout submissions acceptable. Free sample copy and writer's guidelines.
Nonfiction: Book excerpts; exposé; how-to (gardening, recipes and canning), new product; opinion; personal experience (organic gardening) and photo feature. Buys approximately 150 mss/year. Query with or without published clips, or send complete ms. Length: 1,000-3,000 words. Pays $50-100; sometimes pays in free advertising for company, books or products. Sometimes pays the expenses of writers on assignment.
Photos: State availability or send photos with submission.
Columns/Departments: Bugs, Weeds & Free Advice (organic gardening), 800 words; Food Talk (tips on cooking and recipes), 300-1,500 words; Of Consuming Interest (shorts on new developments in field), 800-1,500 words; and The Doctor Prescribes (questions and answers on preventive medicine), 800-1,500 words. Buys 96 mss/year. Send complete ms. Pays $50-100 (negotiable).
Fillers: Facts and short humor.
Tips: "Articles on subjects concerning gardening organically or cooking with natural foods are most open to freelancers."

‡PROST!, A Toast to Good Health, Brandon-Chase Publications, Ltd., 11 S. Second Ave., St. Charles IL 60174. (312)584-8978. Editor: Catherine Wanner. 50% free lance written. Quarterly magazine about drinking. *"Prost!* is the first national consumer magazine that toasts healthy drinking. Each issue will present timely information on the positive aspects of alcohol beverages; provocative insight into contemporary alcohol-related issues; and entertaining features about celebrities and party planning." Estab. 1988. Pays on acceptance. Byline given. Offers 35% kill fee. Buys first rights or second serial (reprint) rights. Submit seasonal/holiday material 6 months in advance. Computer printout submissions OK; prefers letter-quality. Sample copy $2.50. Free writer's guidelines.
Nonfiction: Historical/nostalgic, humor, interview/profile, new product and entertaining w/alcohol beverages. Query with published clips. Length: 750-1,500 words. Pays $250-1,000 for assigned articles; $250-500 for unsolicited articles. Sometimes pays expenses of writers on assignment.
Photos: State availability of photos with submission. Reviews transparencies. Offers no additional payment for photos accepted with ms. Captions and model releases required. Buys one-time rights.
Fillers: Anecdotes, newsbreaks and new products and services. Length: 50-250 words. Pays $25-50.

THE WINE SPECTATOR, M. Shanken Communications, Inc., Opera Plaza, Suite 2040, 601 Van Ness Ave., San Francisco CA 94102. (415)673-2040. Managing Editor: Jim Gordon. 20% freelance written. Prefers to work with published/established writers. Twice monthly consumer news magazine covering wine. Circ. 70,000. Pays on publication. Publishes ms an average of 2 months after acceptance. Byline given. Buys first rights and makes work-for-hire assignments. Submit seasonal/holiday material 3 months in advance. Query for electronic submissions. Computer printout submissions acceptable "as long as they are legible." Reports in 3 weeks. Sample copy $1.75; free writer's guidelines.
Nonfiction: General interest (news about wine or wine events); humor; interview/profile (of wine, vintners, wineries); opinion; and photo feature. No "winery promotional pieces or articles by writers who lack sufficient knowledge to write below just surface data." Query. Length: 100-2,000 words average. Pays $50-300.
Photos: Send photos with ms. Pays $75 minimum for color transparencies. Captions, model releases and identification of subjects required. Buys all rights.
Tips: "A solid knowledge of wine is a must. Query letters essential, detailing the story idea. New, refreshing ideas which have not been covered before stand a good chance of acceptance. *The Wine Spectator* is a consumer-oriented *news magazine* but we are interested in some trade stories; brevity is essential."

WINE TIDINGS, Kylix Media Inc., 5165 Sherbrooke St. W., 414, Montreal, Quebec H4A 1T6 Canada. (514)481-5892. Publisher: Judy Rochester. Editor: Barbara Leslie. 90% freelance written. Works with small number of new/unpublished writers each year. Magazine published 8 times/year primarily for men with incomes of more than $50,000. "Covers anything happening on the wine scene in Canada." Circ. 28,000. Pays

For explanation of symbols, see the Key to Symbols and Abbreviations on Page 5. For unfamiliar words, see the Glossary.

on publication. Publishes ms an average of 3-4 months after acceptance. Byline given. Buys all rights. Submit seasonal/holiday material 3 months in advance. Computer printout submissions acceptable; prefers letter-quality. Reports in 1 month.

Nonfiction: General interest; historical; humor; interview/profile; new product (and developments in the Canadian and U.S. wine industries); opinion; personal experience; photo feature; and travel (to wine-producing countries). "All must pertain to wine or wine-related topics and should reflect author's basic knowledge of and interest in wine." Buys 20-30 mss/year. Send complete ms. Length: 500-2,000 words. Pays $35-300.

Photos: State availability of photos. Pays $20-100 for color prints; $10-25 for b&w prints. Identification of subjects required. Buys one-time rights.

Games and Puzzles

These publications are written by and for game enthusiasts interested in both traditional games and word puzzles and newer role-playing adventure, computer and video games. Crossword fans also will find markets here. Additional home video game publications are listed in the Entertainment section. Other puzzle markets may be found in the Juvenile section.

CHESS LIFE, United States Chess Federation, 186 Route 9W, New Windsor NY 12550. (914)562-8350. Editor: Boris Baczynsky. 15% freelance written. Works with a small number of new/unpublished writers each year. Monthly magazine covering the chess world. Circ. 60,000. Pays variable fee. Publishes ms an average of 5 months after acceptance. Byline given. Offers kill fee. Buys first or negotiable rights. Submit seasonal/holiday material 8 months in advance. Simultaneous queries, and simultaneous, photocopied and previously published submissions OK. Computer printout submissions acceptable. Reports in 1 month. Sample copy and writer's guidelines for 9x11 SAE.

Nonfiction: General interest, historical, interview/profile, and technical—all must have some relation to chess. No "stories about personal experiences with chess." Buys 30-40 mss/year. Query with samples "if new to publication." Length: 3,000 words maximum. Sometimes pays the expenses of writers on assignment.

Photos: Reviews b&w contact sheets and prints, and color prints and slides. Captions, model releases and identification of subjects required. Buys all or negotiable rights.

Fiction: "Chess-related, high quality." Buys 1-2 mss/year. Pays variable fee.

Tips: "Articles must be written from an informed point of view—not from view of the curious amateur. Most of our writers are specialized in that they have sound credentials as chessplayers. Freelancers in major population areas (except New York and Los Angeles, which we already have covered) who are interested in short personality profiles and perhaps news reporting have the best opportunities. We're looking for more personality pieces on chessplayers around the country; not just the stars, but local masters, talented youths, and dedicated volunteers. Freelancers interested in such pieces might let us know of their interest and their range. Could be we know of an interesting story in their territory that needs covering."

COMPUTER GAMING WORLD, The Journal of Computer Gaming, Golden Empire Publications, Inc., Suite B, 515 S. Harbor Blvd., Anaheim CA 92805. (714)535-4435. Editor: Russell Sipe. 75% freelance written. Works with a small number of new/unpublished writers each year. Monthly magazine covering computer games. "*CGW* is read by an adult audience looking for detailed reviews and information on strategy, adventure and action games." Circ. 30,000. Pays on publication. Publishes ms an average of 3 months after acceptance. Byline given. Buys first rights. Submit seasonal/holiday material 4 months in advance. Query for electronic submissions; electronic submissions preferred, but not required. Computer printout submissions OK. Reports in 1 month. Sample copy $3.50. Free writer's guidelines.

Nonfiction: Reviews, strategy tips, industry insights. Buys 60 mss/year. Query. Length: 500-3,500 words. Pays $25-200. Sometimes pays the expenses of writers on assignment.

Photos: State availability of photos with submission. Reviews contact sheets. Offers $10-50 per photo. Buys one-time rights.

DRAGON® Magazine, TSR, Inc., Box 111, 201 Sheridan Springs Rd., Lake Geneva WI 53147. (414)248-3625. Editor: Roger E. Moore. Monthly magazine of fantasy and science-fiction role-playing games. 90% freelance written. Eager to work with published/established writers as well as new/unpublished writers. "Most of our readers are intelligent, imaginative teenage males." Circ. about 100,000, primarily across the United States, Canada, and Great Britain. Byline given. Offers kill fee. Submit seasonal/holiday material 8 months in advance. Photocopied or computer printout submissions acceptable only if clearly legible; prefers letter-

quality print. Pays on publication for articles to which all rights are purchased; pays on acceptance for articles to which first/worldwide rights in English are purchased. Publishing dates vary from 1-24 months after acceptance. Writer's guidelines for #10 SAE and 1 first-class stamp or International Reply Coupon.
Nonfiction: Articles on the hobby of science fiction and fantasy role-playing. No general articles on gaming hobby; "our article needs are *very* specialized. Writers should be experienced in gaming hobby and role-playing. No strong sexual overtones or graphic depictions of violence." Buys 120 mss/year. Query. Length: 1,000-8,000 words. Pays $50-500 for assigned articles; pays $5-400 for unsolicited articles.
Fiction: Barbara G. Young, fiction editor. Adventure, fantasy and suspense. "No strong sexual overtones or graphic depictions of violence." Buys 8-12 mss/year. Send complete ms. Length: 2,000-8,000 words. Pays $150-650.
Tips: "*Dragon® Magazine* and the related publications of Dragon Publishing are *not* periodicals that the 'average reader' appreciates or understands. A writer must *be* a reader and must share the serious interest in gaming our readers possess."

‡**GAMES JUNIOR** and **GAMES**, PSC Publications Limited Partnership, 810 7th Ave., New York NY 10019. (212)246-4640. Editor: Wayne Schmittberger. 70-75% freelance written. Bimonthly magazine on puzzles and games (for children and adults). "Our goal is to entertain children ages 6-12 and their parents with a variety of puzzles and games involving wordplay, picture and logic. *Games* has an educated, adult audience of casual and serious puzzlesolvers and game players." Estab. 1988. Circ. 250,000; *Games*, 700,000. Pays on acceptance. Publishes ms an average of 4 months after acceptance. Byline given. Offers 25% kill fee. Buys first North American serial rights, first rights, one-time rights or all rights. Submit seasonal/holiday material 6 months in advance. Simultaneous and photocopied submissions OK. Computer printout submissions OK, prefers letter-quality. Reports in 3 months. Writer's guidelines for #10 SASE. "No material other than puzzles and games." Query. *Games Junior* pays $50-125 per page, depending on novelty, complexity and originality of the puzzle. *Games* pays $1,000-1,750. Sometimes pays expenses of writers on assignment.
Columns/Departments: Pencilwise and Pencilwise Plus. Query for *Games Special Edition*; Gamebits (offbeat events, ingenious or imaginative feats), 100-450/words. Query. Wild Cards and Your Move (short, original puzzles of all kinds), 25-150 words. Buys 100 mss/year. Pays $25-200.
Fiction: Mystery. Buys 1-2 mss/year. Query. Length: 400-1,000 words. "Most often, photomysteries with little copy."
Tips: "We are looking for novel kinds of puzzles, especially ones with a visual element, whether requiring illustration or photography. A description of the visual element is all that we require in a submission—we can assign the final art or photograpy. Try testing the puzzle on children you know to see if it is inviting, solvable and entertaining. Educational value in a puzzle is a plus, but entertainment value is our primary concern. For the most standard kinds of puzzles (crosswords, mazes, hidden pictures, word searches, acrostics), most of our needs are met by staff and regular contributors. Puzzles of the types that have not previously appeared in the magazine are the most likely to be accepted. Puzzles based on a pop culture subject (provided it is familiar to most children) are also highly desirable. *Games* is most often in need of 1-2 page puzzles or quizzes that have strong visual appeal. Photocrimes, our picture mysteries that readers must solve, are always needed by us."

GIANT CROSSWORDS, Scrambl-Gram, Inc., Puzzle Buffs International, 1772 State Road, Cuyahoga Falls OH 44223. (216)923-2397. Editors: C.J. Elum and C.R. Elum. 40% freelance written. Eager to work with new/unpublished writers. Crossword puzzle and word game magazines issued quarterly. Pays on acceptance. Publishes ms an average of 10 days after acceptance. No byline given. Buys all rights. Simultaneous queries OK. Reports in several weeks. "We furnish constructors' kits, master grids and clue sheets and offer a 'how-to-make-crosswords' book for $17.50 postpaid."
Nonfiction: Crosswords only. Query. Pays according to size of puzzle and/or clues.
Tips: "We are expanding our syndication of original crosswords and our publishing schedule to include new titles and extra issues of current puzzle books."

SCHOOL MATES, U.S. Chess Federation, 186 Route 9W, New Windsor NY 12550. (914)562-8350. Editor: Jennie L. Simon. 15% freelance written. Quarterly magazine on youth chess. Circ. 5,000. Pays on publication. Publishes ms an average of 6 months after acceptance. Byline given. Buys all rights. Free sample copy and writer's guidelines.
Nonfiction: Historical/nostalgic, humor, interview/profile. Buys 4 mss/year. Query. Length: 250-800 words. Pays $40/1,000 words.
Photos: State availability of photos with submission. Reviews contact sheets. Pays $25 for first time rights; $12.50 for each subsequent use. Identification of subjects required.

General Interest

General interest magazines need writers who can appeal to a varied audience—teens and senior citizens, wealthy readers and the unemployed. Each magazine still has a personality that suits its audience—one that a writer should study before sending material to an editor. Other markets for general interest material are in these Consumer categories: Contemporary Culture, Ethnic/Minority, In-flight, Men's, Regional and Women's.

THE AMERICAN LEGION MAGAZINE, Box 1055, Indianapolis IN 46206. (317)635-8411. Editor: Michael D. La Bonne. Monthly. 95% freelance written. Prefers to work with published/established writers, eager to work with new/unpublished writers, and works with a small number of new/unpublished writers each year. Circ. 2,700,000. Buys first North American serial rights. Computer printout submissions acceptable; prefers letter-quality. Reports on submissions "promptly." Pays on acceptance. Publishes ms an average of 6 months after acceptance. Byline given. Sample copy for 9x12 SAE and 6 first class stamps. Writer's guidelines for #10 SASE.
Nonfiction: Query first, but will consider unsolicited mss. "Prefer an outline query. Relate your article's thesis or purpose, tell why you are qualified to write it, the approach you will take and any authorities you intend to interview. War-remembrance pieces of a personal nature (vs. historic in perspective) should be in ms form." Uses current world affairs, topics of contemporary interest, little-known happenings in American history, 20th century war-remembrance pieces, and 750-word commentaries on contemporary problems and points of view. No personality profiles, or regional topics. Buys 75 mss/year. Length: 1,500 words maximum. Pays $300-2,000. Pays phone expenses of writers on assignment.
Photos: On assignment.
Fillers: Short, tasteful jokes and humorous anecdotes. Pays $15.
Tips: Query should include author's qualifications for writing a technical or complex article. Also include thesis, length, outline and conclusion. "Send a thorough query. Submit material that is suitable for us, showing that you have read several issues. Attach a few clips of previously published material. *The American Legion Magazine* considers itself '*the* magazine for a strong America.' Any query that reflects this theme (which includes strong economy, educational system, moral fiber, infrastructure and armed forces) will be given priority. Humor is welcomed—must touch on universal themes applicable to most people. No longer accepting unsolicited cartoons or jokes."

‡ANGLO-AMERICAN SPOTLIGHT, Spotlight Verlag, Freihamer Strasse 4b (Box 1629), 8032 Gräfelfing/Munich, Federal Republic of Germany D-8032, (049)89 85 48 221. FAX: (049)898548223. Editor: Kevin Perryman. 30% freelance written. Monthly magazine on current events, travel, personalities and history in English-speaking countries. "*Spotlight* is a general interest magazine for German-speakers who are trying to brush up and improve their English. In general we prefer an informal newsy style with relatively simple sentence structure and vocabulary." Circ. 75,000. Pays on publication. Byline given. Offers DM 150, kill fee (maximum). Buys one-time rights for West-Germany, Austria, Switzerland. Submit seasonal/holiday material 6 months in advance. Simultaneous, photocopied, and previously published submissions OK. Computer printout submissions OK; prefers letter-quality. Reports in 1 month. Free sample copy.
Nonfiction: General interest, historical/nostalgic, interview/profile, photo feature and travel. No pieces that have nothing to do with the English-speaking world. Buys at least 20 mss/year. Query with published clips. Length: 1,000-2,000 words. Pays DM 150 per printed column line, (about seven words). Sometimes pays expenses of writers on assignment.
Photos: State availability of photos with submission. Reviews color transparencies and b&w prints. Offers $25-100 per photo. Buys one-time rights.
Tips: "Try a travel story (a national park, a state, an event), a city portrait (history, current problems, travel info), an article about a current issue or trend, interview or article about a well-known person. Please type flush left, 40 characters per line, triple space. It's best from an 'insider's point of view. Tell our German readers something beyond what they can already find in travel brochures. Fill the story with anecdotes, honest information and advice about what to do and what not to do."

THE ATLANTIC MONTHLY, 745 Boylston St., Boston MA 02116. (617)536-9500. Editor: William Whitworth. Managing Editor: Cullen Murphy. Monthly magazine of arts and public affairs. Circ. 470,000. Pays on acceptance. Byline given. Buys first North American serial rights. Simultaneous submissions OK but not encouraged. Reporting time varies.
Nonfiction: Book excerpts, essays, general interest, humor, personal experience, religious, travel. Query with or without published clips or send complete ms. Length: 1,000-6,000 words. Payment varies. Sometimes pays expenses of writers on assignment.
Fiction: C. Michael Curtis, fiction editor. Buys 15-18 mss/year. Send complete ms. Length: 2,000-6,000 words preferred. Pays $2,500.
Poetry: Peter Davison, poetry editor. Buys 40-60 poems/year.

A BETTER LIFE FOR YOU, The National Research Bureau, Inc., 424 N. 3rd St., Burlington IA 52601. (319)752-5415. Editor: FAX: (319)752-3421. Rhonda Wilson. Editorial Supervisor: Doris J. Ruschill. 75% freelance written. Works with a small number of new/unpublished writers each year, eager to work with new/unpublished writers. Quarterly magazine. Pays on publication. Publishes ms an average of 1 year after acceptance. Buys all rights. Submit seasonal/holiday material 7 months in advance of issue date. Previously published submissions OK. Computer printout submissions acceptable; no dot-matrix. Reports in 3 weeks. Writer's guidelines for #10 SASE.

Nonfiction: General interest (steps to better health, on-the-job attitudes); and how-to (perform better on the job, do home repair jobs, and keep up maintenance on a car). Buys 10-12 mss/year. Query or send outline. Length: 400-600 words. Pays 4¢/word.

Tips: "Writers have a better chance of breaking in at our publication with short articles."

CAPPER'S, Stauffer Communications, Inc., 616 Jefferson St., Topeka KS 66607. (913)295-1108. Editor: Nancy Peavler. 25% freelance written. Works with a small number of new/unpublished writers each year. Emphasizes home and family for readers who live in small towns and on farms. Biweekly tabloid. Circ. 385,000. Pays for poetry on acceptance; articles on publication. Publishes ms an average of 3 months after acceptance. Buys first serial rights only. Submit seasonal/holiday material at least 2 months in advance. Computer printout submissions OK; prefers letter-quality. Reports in 1 month; 8 months for serialized novels. Sample copy 80¢; writer's guidlelines for #10 SASE.

Nonfiction: Historical (local museums, etc.), inspirational, nostalgia, travel (local slants) and people stories (accomplishments, collections, etc.). Buys 50 mss/year. Submit complete ms. Length: 700 words maximum. Pays $1/inch.

Photos: Purchased with accompanying ms. Submit prints. Pays $5-10 for 8x10 or 5x7 b&w glossy prints. Total purchase price for ms includes payment for photos. Limited market for color photos (35mm color slides); pays $20-25 each.

Columns/Departments: Heart of the Home (homemakers' letters, recipes, hints), and Hometown Heartbeat (descriptive). Submit complete ms. Length: 300 words maximum. Pays $1-10.

Fiction: "We have begun to buy some fiction pieces—longer than short stories, shorter than novels." Adventure and romance mss. No explicit sex, violence or profanity. Buys 4-5 mss/year. Query. Pays $75-250.

Poetry: Free verse, haiku, light verse, traditional, nature and inspiration. "The poems that appear in *Capper's* are not too difficult to read. They're easy to grasp. We're looking for everyday events, and down-to-earth themes." Buys 4-5/issue. Limit submissions to batches of 5-6. Length: 4-16 lines. Pays $3-6.

Tips: "Study a few issues of our publication. Most rejections are for material that is too long, unsuitable or out of character for our paper (too sexy, too much profanity, etc.). On occasion, we must cut material to fit column space."

THE CHRISTIAN SCIENCE MONITOR, 1 Norway St., Boston MA 02115. (617)450-2303. Contact: Submissions. International newspaper issued daily except Saturdays, Sundays and holidays in North America; weekly international edition. March and September: fashion. Circ. 150,000. Buys all newspaper rights for 3 months following publication. Buys limited number of mss, "top quality only." Publishes original (exclusive) material only. Pays on acceptance or publication, "depending on department." Reports in 1 month. Submit complete original ms or letter of inquiry. Writer's guidelines available.

Nonfiction: David Holmstrom, feature editor. In-depth features and essays. Please query by mail before sending mss. "Style should be bright but not cute, concise but thoroughly researched. Try to humanize news or feature writing so reader identifies with it. Avoid sensationalism, crime and disaster. Accent constructive, solution-oriented treatment of subjects. Home Forum page buys essays of 400-900 words. Pays $70-140. Education, people, books, food and science pages will consider articles not usually more than 800 words appropriate to respective subjects." Pays $100-150.

Poetry: Traditional, blank and free verse. Seeks non-religious poetry of high quality and of all lengths up to 75 lines. Pays $25 average.

Tips: "We prefer neatly typed originals. No handwritten copy. Enclosing an SAE and postage with ms is a must."

CHRYSALIS, See Religious section.

EQUINOX: THE MAGAZINE OF CANADIAN DISCOVERY, Equinox Publishing, 7 Queen Victoria Dr., Camden East, Ontario K0K 1J0 Canada. (613)378-6661. Editorial Director: Barry Estabrook. Editor: Bart Robinson. Bimonthly magazine. "We publish in-depth profiles of people, places and wildlife to show readers the real stories behind subjects of general interest in the fields of science and geography." Circ. 166,000. Pays on acceptance. Byline given. Offers 50% kill fee. Buys first North American serial rights only. Submit seasonal queries 1 year in advance. Computer printout submissions acceptable; prefers letter-quality. Reports in 6 weeks. Sample copy $5; free writer's guidelines.

Nonfiction: Book excerpts (occasionally), geography, science and art. No travel articles. Buys 40 mss/year. Query. "Our biggest need is for science stories. We do not touch unsolicited feature manuscripts." Length: 5,000-10,000 words. Pays $1,500-negotiated.

Photos: Send photos with ms. Reviews color transparencies—must be of professional quality; no prints or negatives. Captions and identification of subjects required.

Columns/Departments: Nexus (current science that isn't covered by daily media) and Habitat (Canadian environmental stories not covered by daily media). Buys 80 mss/year. Query with clips of published work. Length: 200-300 words. Pays $200.

Tips: "Submit Habitat and Nexus ideas to us—the 'only' route to a feature is through these departments if writers are untried."

FORD TIMES, 1 Illinois Center, Suite 1700, 111 E. Wacker Dr., Chicago IL 60601. Editor: John Fink. 85% freelance written. Works with a small number of new/unpublished writers each year. "General-interest magazine designed to attract all ages." Monthly. Circ. 1,200,000. Pays on acceptance. Publishes ms an average of 8-9 months after acceptance. Buys first rights only. Offers kill fee. Byline given. Submit seasonal material 6 months in advance. Computer printout submissions acceptable; prefers letter-quality. Reports in 1 month. Sample copy and writer's guidelines for 8½x11 SAE with 5 first class stamps.

Nonfiction: "Almost anything relating to contemporary American life that is upbeat and positive. Topics include lifestyle trends, outdoor activities and sports, profiles, food, narrow-scope destination stories, and the arts. We are especially interested in subjects that appeal to readers in the 18-35 age group. We strive to be colorful, lively and, above all, interesting. We try to avoid subjects that have appeared in other publications or in our own." Buys 100 mss/year. Length: 1,500 words maximum. Query required unless previous contributor. Pays $550-800 for full-length articles. Pays up to $200 in expenses for writers on assignment.

Photos: "Speculative submission of high-quality color transparencies and b&w photos with mss is welcomed. We need bright, graphically strong photos showing people. We need releases for people whose identity is readily apparent in photos."

FRIENDLY EXCHANGE, Meredith Publishing Services, Locust at 17th, Des Moines IA 50336. Publication Office: (515)284-2008. Editor (702)786-7419. Editor: Adele Malott. 80% freelance written. Works with a small number of new/unpublished writers each year. Quarterly magazine exploring travel and leisure topics of interest to active western families. For policyholders of Farmers Insurance Group of Companies. "These are traditional families (median adult age 39) who live in the area bounded by Ohio on the east and the Pacific Ocean on the west." Circ. 4.2 million. Pays on acceptance. Publishes ms an average of 5 months after acceptance. Offers 25% kill fee. Buys all rights. Submit seasonal/holiday material 1 year in advance. Simultaneous queries and photocopied queries OK. Query for electronic submissions. Computer printout submissions acceptable; prefers letter-quality. Reports in 2 months. Sample copy for 9x12 SAE and 5 first class stamps; writer's guidelines for #10 SAE and 1 first class stamp.

Nonfiction: Travel and leisure activities such as gardening, crafts, pets, photography, etc.—topics of interest to the western family. "Travel and leisure topics can be addressed from many different perspectives, including health and safety, consumerism, heritage and education. Articles offer a service to readers and encourage them to take some positive action such as taking a trip. Style is colorful, warm, and inviting, making liberal use of anecdotes and quotes. The only first-person articles used are those assigned; all others in third person. Domestic locations in the western half of the continent are emphasized." Buys 8 mss/issue. Query. Length: 600-1,800 words. Pays $300-800/article, plus agreed-upon expenses.

Photos: Peggy Fisher, art director. Pays $150-250 for 35mm color transparencies; and $50 for b&w prints. Cover photo payment negotiable. Pays on publication.

Columns/Departments: All columns and departments rely on reader-generated materials; none used from professional writers.

Tips: "We are now concentrating exclusively on the travel and leisure hours of our readers. Do not use destination approach in travel pieces—instead, for example, tell us about the people, activities, or events that make the location special. Concentrate on what families can do together."

FUTURIFIC MAGAZINE, 280 Madison Ave., New York NY 10016. (212)684-4913. Editor-in-Chief: Balint Szent-Miklosy. 50-75% freelance written. Monthly. "Futurific, Inc. "The Foundation for Optimism," is an independent, nonprofit organization set up in 1976 to study the future, and *Futurific Magazine* is its monthly report on findings. We report on what is coming in all areas of life from international affairs to the arts and sciences. Readership cuts across all income levels and includes leadership, government, corporate and religious circles." Circ. 10,000. Pays on publication. Publishes ms an average of 1 month after acceptance. Byline given in most cases. Buys one-time rights and will negotiate reprints. Computer printout submissions OK. Reports within 1 month. Sample copy for $3 and 9x12 SAE. Writer's guidelines for #10 SASE.

Nonfiction: All subjects must deal with the future: book, movie, theatre and software reviews, general interest, how to forecast the future—seriously, humor, interview/profile, new product, photo feature and technical. No historical, opinion or gloom and doom. Send complete ms. Length: 5,000 words maximum. Payment negotiable.

Photos: Send photos with ms. Reviews b&w prints. Pay negotiable. Identification of subjects required.
Columns/Departments: Medical breakthroughs, new products, inventions, book, movie and theatre reviews, etc. "Anything that is new or about to be new." Send complete ms. Length: 5,000 words maximum.
Poetry: Avant-garde, free verse, haiku, light verse and traditional. "Must deal with the future. No gloom and doom or sad poetry." Buys 6/year. Submit unlimited number of poems. Length: open. Pays in copies.
Fillers: Clippings, jokes, gags, anecdotes, short humor, and newsbreaks. "Must deal with the future." Length: open. Pays in copies.
Tips: "It's not who you are; it's what you have to say that counts with us. We seek to maintain a light-hearted, professional look at forecasting. Be upbeat and show a loving expectation for the marvels of human achievement. Take any subject or concern you find in regular news magazines and extrapolate as to what the future will be. Use imagination. Get involved in the excitement of the international developments, social interaction. Write the solution—not the problem."

GOOD READING, for Everyone, Henrichs Publications, Inc., Box 40, Sunshine Park, Litchfield IL 62056. (217)324-3425. Editor: Peggy Kuethe. Managing Editor: Garth Henrichs. 80% freelance written. Works with a small number of new/unpublished writers, and is eager to work with new/unpublished writers each year. A monthly general interest magazine with articles and stories based on a wide range of current or factual subjects. Circ. 7,500. Pays on acceptance. Publishes ms an average of 6 months after acceptance. Byline given. Buys first North American serial rights. Submit seasonal/holiday material 5 months in advance. Photocopied submissions OK. Computer printout submissions acceptable; prefers letter-quality. Reports in 2 months. Sample copy for 50¢, 6x10 SAE and 2 first class stamps; writer's guidelines for #10 SAE with 1 first class stamp.
Nonfiction: General interest, historical/nostalgic, humor, photo feature and travel. Also stories about annual festivals, new products, people who make a difference. "No material that deals with the sordid side of life, nothing about alcohol, smoking, drugs, gambling. Nothing that deals with the cost of travel, or that is too technical." Send complete ms. Length: 100-1,000 words. Pays $20-100 for unsolicited articles.
Photos: Send photos with submission. Reviews contact sheets and 3x5, 5x7, or 8x10 prints. Offers no additional payment for photos accepted with ms. Identification of subjects required. Buys one-time rights.
Columns/Departments: Youth Today (directed at young readers), 100 words maximum. Buys 6-9 mss/year. Send complete ms. Pays $10-50.
Poetry: Light verse. No limit to number of poems submitted at one time. Length: 4-16 lines. Pays in copies.
Fillers: Anecdotes, facts and short humor. Length: 50-150 words. Pays $10-30.
Tips: "The tone of *Good Reading* is wholesome; the articles are short. Keep writing informal but grammatically correct. *Good Reading* is general interest and directed at the entire family—so we accept only material that would be of interest to nearly every age group."

HARPER'S MAGAZINE, 666 Broadway, 11th Floor, New York NY 10012. (212)614-6500. Editor: Lewis H. Lapham. 40% freelance written. For well-educated, socially concerned, widely read men and women who value ideas and good writing. Monthly. Circ. 186,000. Rights purchased vary with author and material. Pays negotiable kill fee. Pays on acceptance. Computer printout submissions acceptable if double-spaced. Reports in 2 weeks. Publishes ms an average of 3 months after acceptance. Sample copy $2.50.
Nonfiction: "For writers working with agents or who will query first only, our requirements are: public affairs, literary, international and local reporting, and humor." No interviews; no profiles. Complete mss and queries must include SASEs. No unsolicited poems will be accepted. Publishes one major report per issue. Length: 4,000-6,000 words. Publishes one major essay per issue. Length: 4,000-6,000 words. "These should be construed as topical essays on all manner of subjects (politics, the arts, crime, business, etc.) to which the author can bring the force of passionately informed statement." Publishes one short story per month. Generally pays 50¢-$1/word.
Photos: Deborah Rust, art director. Occasionally purchased with mss; others by assignment. Pays $50-500.

KNOWLEDGE, Official Publication of the World Olympiads of Knowledge, Knowledge, Inc., 3863 Southwest Loop 820, S 100, Ft. Worth TX 76133-2076. (817)292-4272. Editor: Dr. O.A. Battista. Managing Editor: N.L. Matous. 90% freelance written. For lay and professional audiences of all occupations. Quarterly magazine; 60 pages. Circ. 3,000. Pays on publication. Publishes ms an average of 6 months after acceptance. Buys all rights. "We will reassign rights to a writer after a given period." Byline given. Submit seasonal/holiday material 6 months in advance. Computer printout submissions acceptable; prefers letter-quality. Reports in 1 month. Sample copy $5; writer's guidelines for #10 SASE.
Nonfiction: Informational—original new knowledge that will prove mentally or physically beneficial to all readers. Buys 30 unsolicited mss/year. Query. Length: 1,500-2,000 words maximum. Pays $100 minimum. Sometimes pays the expenses of writers on assignment.

For information on setting your freelance fees, see How Much Should I Charge? in the Business of Writing section.

Columns/Departments: Journal section uses maverick and speculative ideas that other magazines will not publish and reference. Payment is made, on publication, at the following minimum rates: Why Don't They, $50; Salutes, $25; New Vignettes, $25; Quotes To Ponder, $10; and Facts, $5.

Tips: "The editors of *Knowledge* welcome submissions from contributors. Manuscripts and art material will be carefully considered but received *only* with the unequivocal understanding that the magazine will not be responsible for loss or injury. Material from a published source should have the publication's name, date, and page number. Submissions cannot be acknowledged and will be returned only when accompanied by a SAE having adequate postage."

LEFTHANDER MAGAZINE, Lefthander International, Box 8249, Topeka KS 66608. (913)234-2177. Managing Editor: Suzan Ireland. 80% freelance written. Eager to work with new/unpublished writers. Bimonthly. "Our readers are lefthanded people of all ages and interests in 50 U.S. states and 12 foreign countries. The one thing they have in common is an interest in lefthandedness." Circ. 26,000. Pays on publication. Publishes ms an average of 4 months after acceptance. Byline usually given. Offers 25% kill fee. Rights negotiable. Simultaneous queries OK. Computer printout submissions acceptable; prefers letter-quality. Reports on queries in 4-6 weeks. Sample copy for 8½x11 SAE and $2. Writer's guidelines for #10 SAE and 1 first class stamp.

Nonfiction: Interviews with famous lefthanders; features about lefthanders with interesting talents and occupations; how-to features (sports, crafts, hobbies for lefties); research on handedness and brain dominance; exposé on discrimination against lefthanders in the work world; features on occupations and careers attracting lefties; education features relating to ambidextrous right brain teaching methods. Length: Buys 50-60 mss/year. 750-1,000 words for features. Buys 6 personal experience shorts/year. Query with SASE. Length 750 words. Pays $25. Pays expenses of writer on assignment.

Photos: State availability of photos for features. Pays $10-15 for b&w, good contrast b&w glossies. Rights negotiable.

Tips: "All material must have a lefthanded hook. We prefer quick, practical, self-help and self-awareness types of editorial content; keep it brief, light, and of general interest. More of our space is devoted to shorter pieces. A good short piece gives us enough evidence of writer's style, which we like to have before assigning full-length features. In addition we are looking for short fiction pieces for 10-16 year olds for a children's supplement."

‡**LEISURE ONTARIO**, Ontario Motorist Publishing Company, 1215 Ovellette Ave., Box 580, Windsor, Ontario N9A 6N3 Canada. (519)255-1212. FAX: (519)255-7379. Editor: Douglas O'Neil. 30% freelance written. Bimonthly magazine. "*Leisure Ontario* is distributed to members of the Canadian Automobile Association in Southwestern Ontario. Editorial content is focused on travel, entertainment and leisure time pursuits of interst to CAA members." Circ. 200,000. Pays on publication. Publishes ms an average of 2 months after acceptance. Buys first rights and second serial (reprint) rights. Submit seasonal/holiday material 4 months in advance. Computer printout submissions OK. Sample copy $2. Free writer's guidelines.

Nonfiction: General interest, historical/nostalgic, humor, new product and travel. Buys 20 mss/year. Send complete ms. Length: 800-2,000 words. Pays $50-150.

Photos: Reviews negatives. Offers $15-40 per photo. Captions and model releases required. Buys one-time rights.

Columns/Departments: Query with published clips. Length: 400-800 words. Pays $40-60.

Fiction: Mainstream and slice-of-life vignettes. Buys 3-4 mss/year. Query with published clips. Length: 1,200-2,400 words. Pays $150-250.

Fillers: Marlene Lancaster. Anecdotes, facts and short humor. Buys 20/year. Length: 50-150 words. Pays $10-25.

Tips: "We are most interested in travel destination articles that offer a personal, subjective and positive point of view on international (including U.S.A.) destinations. Good quality color slides are a must."

‡**MACLEAN'S, Canada's Weekly News Magazine**, Maclean Hunter Ltd., 777 Bay St., Toronto, Ontario M5W 1A7 Canada. (416)596-5386. Editor: Kevin Doyle. 15% freelance written. Works with a small number of new/unpublished writers each year. For news-oriented audience. Weekly news magazine. Circ. 615,000. Byline given. Frequently buys all rights. Pays on acceptance. Publishes ms "immediately" after acceptance. "Query with 200- or 300-word outline before sending material." Reports in 2 weeks. Query for electronic submissions. Computer printout submissions acceptable. SAE and IRCs. Sample copy for 9x12 SAE.

Nonfiction: Book excerpts (nonfiction), exposé and interview/profile. "We have the conventional news magazine departments (Canada, world, business, people; also science, medicine, law, art, music, etc.) with roughly the same treatment as other news magazines. We specialize in subjects that are primarily of Canadian interest, and there is now more emphasis on international — particularly US — news. Most material is now written by staffers or retainer freelancers, but we are open to suggestions from abroad, especially in world, business and departments (medicine, lifestyles, etc.). Freelancers should write for a copy of the magazine and study the approach." Length: 350-10,000 words. Pays 40-75¢/word.

NATIONAL EXAMINER, Globe Communications, Inc., 5401 N.W. Broken Sound Blvd., Boca Raton FL 33487. (407)997-7733. FAX: (407)997-7733, ext. 239. Editor: Bill Burt. Executive Editor: Cliff Linedecker. 15% freelance written. Works with a small number of new/unpublished writers each year. "We are a weekly supermarket tabloid that covers celebrity news, human interest features, true crime, medical breakthroughs, astrology, UFOs and the supernatural. Nonfiction stories should be well researched and documented, concise and fun to read." Circ. 1,000,000. Pays on publication. Publishes ms an average of 1 month after acceptance. Byline given. Buys first North American serial rights. Submit seasonal/holiday material 2 months in advance. Photocopied submissions OK. Computer printout submissions acceptable; prefers letter-quality. Writer's guidelines for #10 SASE.
Nonfiction: Historical/nostalgic; interview/profile (of celebrities); photo feature (color preferred); and the supernatural. No fillers or political material. Buys 200 mss/year. Query with published clips. Length: 250-750 words. Pays $25-300.
Photos: Send photos with submission. Reviews contact sheets, 35mm transparencies, and 8x10 prints. Offers $35-100/photo. Captions and identification of subjects required. Buys one-time rights.
Tips: "Send us a well crafted, carefully documented story. The areas of our publication most open to freelancers are celebrity interviews and color photo spreads featuring celebrities or general subjects."

NATIONAL GEOGRAPHIC MAGAZINE, 17th and M Sts. NW, Washington DC 20036. Editor: Wilbur E. Garrett. Approximately 50% freelance written. Prefers to work with published/established writers, and works with a small number of new/unpublished writers each year. For members of the National Geographic Society. Monthly. Circ. more than 10,000,000. Query for electronic submissions. Computer printout submissions OK; prefers letter-quality.
Nonfiction: *National Geographic* publishes first-person, general interest, heavy illustrated articles on science, natural history, exploration and geographical regions. Almost half of the articles are staff-written. Of the freelance writers assigned, most are experts in their fields; the remainder are established professionals. Fewer than one percent of unsolicited queries result in assignments. Query (500 words) by letter, not by phone, to Senior Assistant Editor (Contract Writers). Do not send manuscripts. Before querying, study recent issues and check a *Geographic Index* at a library since the magazine seldom returns to regions or subjects covered within the past ten years. Pays expenses of writers on assignment.
Photos: Photographers should query in care of the Illustration Division.

THE NEW YORKER, 25 W. 43rd St., New York NY 10036. Editor: Robert Gottlieb. Weekly. Circ. over 500,000. Reports in 2 months. Pays on acceptance. Computer printout submissions acceptable; prefers letter-quality.
Nonfiction, Fiction, Poetry, and Fillers: Long fact pieces are usually staff-written. So is "Talk of the Town," although freelance submissions are considered. Pays good rates. Uses fiction, both serious and light. About 90% of the fillers come from contributors with or without taglines (extra pay if the tagline is used).

OUT WEST, America's On the Road Newspaper, Box 19894, Sacramento CA 95819. (916)457-4006. Editor: Chuck Woodbury. 10% freelance written. Quarterly tabloid for general audience. Estab. 1988. Circ. 10,000. Pays on acceptance and publication (negotiated). Byline given. Buys one-time or reprint rights. Submit seasonal/holiday material 6 months in advance. Simultaneous, photocopied and previously published submissions OK. Computer printout submissions OK; prefers letter-quality. Reports in 6 weeks. Sample copy $1.50 and 9x12 SAE; writer's guidelines for #10 SASE.
Nonfiction: Essays, general interest, historical, humor, interview/profile, photo feature, travel. No travel destinations reached primarily by air, nothing over 1,000 words, travel to expensive hotels, locations in large urban areas, and no foreign travel except perhaps western Canada. Buys 50 mss/year. Query with or without published clips, or send complete ms. Length: 150-1,000 words. Pays $20-100.
Photos: State availability of photos with submission. Reviews 5x7 or 8x10 b&w prints only. Pays $6-15. Captions required. Buys one-time rights.
Columns/Departments: Ghost Towns, Small Town Media, Wildlife, Road of the Month, Eating on the Road, all 300-700 words. Query or send complete ms. Length: 500-700 words. Pays. $20-50. "I'm looking for a few good columnists who can become regular in the paper."
Fillers: Anecdotes, facts, newsbreaks, short humor. Buys 50/year. Length: 25-150 words. Pays $2-12.
Tips: "It's critically important to read the publication before submitting work."

PARADE, Parade Publications, Inc., 750 3rd Ave., New York NY 10017. (212)573-7000. Editor: Walter Anderson. Weekly magazine for a general interest audience. 90% freelance written. Circ. 33 million. Pays on acceptance. Publishes ms an average of 3 months after acceptance. Kill fee varies in amount. Buys first North American serial rights. Computer printout submissions acceptable. Reports in 5 weeks on queries. Writer's guidelines for 4x9 SAE and 1 first class stamp.
Nonfiction: General interest (on health, trends, social issues, business or anything of interest to a broad general audience); interview/profile (of news figures, celebrities and people of national significance); and "provocative topical pieces of news value." Spot news events are not accepted, as *Parade* has a 6-week lead time. No fiction, fashion, travel, poetry, quizzes, or fillers. Address three-paragraph queries to Articles Editor.

Length: 800-1,500 words. Pays $1,000 minimum. Pays expenses of writers on assignment.
Tips: "Send a well-researched, well-written query targeted to our market. Please, no phone queries. We're interested in well-written exclusive manuscripts on topics of news interest. The most frequent mistake made by writers in completing an article for us is not adhering to the suggestions made by the editor when the article was assigned."

PEOPLE IN ACTION, Meridian Publishing Company, Box 10010, Ogden UT 84409. (801)394-9446. Editor: Libby Hyland. 40% freelance written. A monthly inhouse magazine featuring personality profiles. Pays on acceptance. Publishes ms an average of 8 months after acceptance. Byline given. Buys first rights, second serial (reprint) rights and non-exclusive reprint rights. Simultaneous, photocopied and previously published submissions OK. Computer printout submissions acceptable. Query first. Reports in 2 months. Publishes ms an average of 6 months after acceptance. Sample copy for $1 and 9x12 SAE; writer's guidelines for SAE and 1 first class stamp. All requests for sample copies and guidelines and queries should be addressed Attn: Editorial Assistant.
Nonfiction: General interest personality profiles. Cover stories focus on nationally noted individuals in the fine arts, literature, entertainment, communications, business, sports, education, health, science and technology. The lives of those featured exemplify positive values; overcoming obstacles, helping others, advancing culture, creating solutions. Buys 40 mss/year. Query. Length: 1,000-1,400 words. Pays 15¢/word for first rights plus non-exclusive reprint rights. Payment for second rights is negotiable.
Photos: State availability of photos or send photos with query. Pays $35/inside photo, $50/cover photo; uses glossy professional-quality color prints and transparencies (slides to 8x10). Prefers transparencies. Captions, model releases and identification of subjects required.
Columns/Departments: Regular column features: a 700-word profile of a gourmet chef, first-class restaurant manager, food or nutrition expert, or a celebrity who is also a top-notch cook; a recipe and 1-2 good color transparencies are essential. Buys 10 mss/year. Query. Pays 15¢/word.
Tips: "The key is a well-written query letter that: 1) demonstrates that the subject of the article has national appeal; 2) shows that a profile of the person interviewed will have a clear, focused theme; 3) outlines the availability (from the writer, photographer or PR source) of top-quality color photos; and 4) gives evidence that the writer/photographer is a professional, even if a beginner."

READ ME, 1118 Hoyt Ave., Everett WA 98201. Editor: Ron Fleshman. 95% freelance written. Quarterly general interest tabloid. Estab. 1988. Circ. 2,000. Pays on publication. Publishes ms an average of 10 months after acceptance. Byline given. Buys first North American serial rights, one-time rights or second serial (reprint) rights. Submit seasonal/holiday material 6 months in advance. Photocopied and previously published submissions (if identified) OK. Computer printout submissions OK; prefers letter-quality. Reports in 3 months. Sample copy $1.50; writer's guidelines for #10 SASE.
Nonfiction: Book excerpts, essays, expose, general interest, historical/nostalgic, humor, opinion, personal experience, travel. Buys 30 mss/year. Query with or without published clips, or send complete ms. Length: 500-2,000. Pays $20 maximum.
Columns/Departments: Outreach (first-person statements from forgotten members of society or those who work with or serve them), 1,000 words maximum; Contention (strongly expressed personal opinion on controversial issues), 1,000 words maximum; Travel (single interesting aspect of a distant place), 750 words maximum. Humor (mild to brutally sardonic, essays, short-short stories), 1,000 words maximum. Buys 80 mss/year. Send complete ms. Pays $1-20.
Fiction: Linda McMichael and Kay Nelson, editors. Adventure, confession, ethnic, fantasy, historical, horror, humorous, mainstream, mystery, novel excerpts, romance, science fiction, suspense, western. Buys 60 mss/year. Send complete ms. Length: 100-2,500 words. Pays $1-20.
Poetry: Elizabeth Strong, editor. Free verse, traditional. No obscenity, no academic poetry. Buys 30 poems/year. Submit maximum of 6 poems at one time. Length: 50 lines maximum. Pays $1-5.
Fillers: Ellie Brauer, fillers editor. Anecdotes, facts, short humor. Buys 40/year. Length: 5-50 words. Pays $1-5.
Tips: "Reward our readers with new insight, unusual slant, fresh perspective. Material may reassure or outrage, teach or tickle. Perimeter testing is encouraged – but must be accessible to a non-academic readership. Avoid subjects quickly dated. Regarding style: less is more."

READER'S DIGEST, Pleasantville NY 10570. Monthly. Circ. 16.5 million. Publishes general interest articles "as varied as all human experience." The *Digest* does not read or return unsolicited mss. Address proposals and tearsheets of published articles to the editors. Considers only previously published articles; pays $1,200/ *Digest* page for World Digest rights. (Usually split 50/50 between original publisher and writer.) Tearsheets of submitted article must include name of original publisher and date of publication.
Columns/Departments: "Original contributions become the property of *Reader's Digest* upon acceptance and payment. Life-in-these-United States contributions must be true, unpublished stories from one's own experience, revealing adult human nature, and providing appealing or humorous sidelights on the American scene. Length: 300 words maximum. Pays $400 on publication. True and unpublished stories are also solicited

for Humor in Uniform, Campus Comedy and All in a Day's Work. Length: 300 words maximum. Pays $400 on publication. Towards More Picturesque Speech—the first contributor of each item used in this department is paid $50 for original material, $35 for reprints. Contributions should be dated, and the source must be given. For items used in Laughter, the Best Medicine, Personal Glimpses, Quotable Quotes, and elsewhere in the magazine payment is as follows; to the *first* contributor of each from a published source, $35. For original material, $30 per *Digest* two-column line, with a minimum payment of $50. Send complete anecdotes to excerpt editor."

READERS REVIEW, The National Research Bureau, Inc., 424 N. 3rd St., Burlington IA 52601. Editor: Rhonda Wilson. Editorial Supervisor: Doris J. Ruschill. 75% freelance written. Works with a small number of new/unpublished writers each year, and is eager to work with new/unpublished writers. Quarterly magazine. Pays on publication. Publishes ms an average of 1 year after acceptance. Buys all rights. Previously published submissions OK. Computer printout submissions acceptable; prefers letter-quality. Submit seasonal/holiday material 7 months in advance of issue date. Reports in 3 weeks. Writer's guidelines for #10 SASE.
Nonfiction: General interest (steps to better health, attitudes on the job); how-to (perform better on the job, do home repairs, car maintenance); and travel. Buys 10-12 mss/year. Query with outline or submit complete ms. Length: 400-600 words. Pays 4¢/word.
Tips: "Writers have a better chance of breaking in at our publication with short articles."

REAL PEOPLE, The Magazine of Celebrities and Interesting People, Main Street Publishing Co., Inc., 950 Third Ave. 16th Fl., New York NY 10022-2705. (212)371-4932. FAX: (212)838-8420. Editor: Alex Polner. 75% freelance written. Bimonthly magazine of profiles, human interest and self-help articles for audience, ages 28-45. Circ. 125,000. Pays on publication. Byline given. Pays 33% kill fee. Buys first North American serial rights, first rights, or one-time rights. Submit seasonal/holiday material 6 months in advance. Photocopied submissions OK. Computer printout submissions OK; prefers letter-quality. Reports in 1 month. Sample copy for $3 with 6x9 SAE and 65¢ postage. Writer's guidelines for #10 SASE.
Nonfiction: Book excerpts, how-to, interview/profile, photos essays. Buys 100 mss/year. Query with published clips. Length: 500-1,200 words. Pays $150-200 for assigned articles; $75-150 for unsolicited articles.
Photos: State availability of photos with submissions. Reviews 5x7 prints. Offers no additional payment for photos accepted with ms. Captions, model releases and identification of subjects required. Buys one-time rights.

RIGHT HERE, The Hometown Magazine, Right Here Publications, Box 1014, Huntington IN 46750. Editor: Emily Jean Carroll. 90% freelance written. Works with a small number of new/unpublished writers each year. Bimonthly magazine of general family interest. Circ. 2,000. Pays 2 weeks after date of issue. Publishes ms an average of 4 months after acceptance. Byline given. Buys first serial rights, one-time rights, simultaneous rights, and second serial (reprint) rights. Submit seasonal/holiday material 5 months in advance. Simultaneous, photocopied, and previously published submissions OK. Computer printout submissions acceptable; prefers letter-quality. Reports in 4 months on mss. No queries please. Sample copy $1.25; writer's guidelines for SASE.
Nonfiction: General interest, historical/nostalgic, how-to, humor, inspirational, interview/profile, opinion and travel. "We are looking for short pieces on all aspects of family life—40-plus age range." Profiles, nostalgia, history, recreation, travel and music. Buys 18 mss/year. Send complete ms. Length: 900-2,000 words. Pays $5-25.
Photos: Send photos with ms. Reviews b&w prints. Pays $2-5. Model releases and identification of subjects required. Buys one-time rights.
Columns/Departments: Listen To This (opinion pieces of about 1,000 words); Remember? (nostalgia, up to 2,000 words); Keeping Up (mental, spiritual, self-help, uplifting, etc., to 2,000 words); and My Space (writers 19 years old and under, to 1,000 words). Buys 30-40 mss/year. Send complete ms. Length: 800-2,000 words. Pays $5-25.
Fiction: Humorous, mainstream, mystery and romance. Needs short stories of about 2,000 words. Buys 6-8 mss/year. Send complete ms. Length: 900-2,500 words. Pays $5-25.
Poetry: Free verse, light verse and traditional. Uses 30-40/year. Submit maximum 6 poems. Length: 4-48 lines. Pays $1-4 for poetry featured separately; pays one copy for poetry used as filler or on poetry page.
Fillers: Anecdotes and short humor. Buys 6-8/year. Length: 300 words maximum. Pays $3 maximum. Pays one copy for material under 300 words.
Tips: "We sometimes fall behind in answering mail. It is best not to send second and third manuscript before hearing back on the first."

SELECTED READING, The National Research Bureau, Inc., 424 N. 3rd St., Burlington IA 52601. FAX (319)752-3421. Editor: Rhonda Wilson. Editorial Supervisor: Doris J. Ruschill. 75% freelance written. Eager to work with new/unpublished writers, works with a small number of new/unpublished writers each year. Quarterly magazine. Pays on publication. Publishes ms an average of 1 year after acceptance. Buys all rights.

Previously published submissions OK. Computer printout submissions acceptable; prefers letter-quality. Submit seasonal/holiday material 6-7 months in advance of issue date. Reports in 3 weeks. Writer's guidelines for #10 SASE.

Nonfiction: General interest (economics, health, safety, working relationships); how-to; and travel (out-of-the way places). No material on car repair. Buys 10-12 mss/year. Query. A short outline or synopsis is best. Lists of titles are no help. Length: 400-600 words. Pays 4¢/word.

Tips: "Writers have a better chance of breaking in at our publication with short articles."

‡SPECIAL REPORTS, America's General-Interest Magazine, 505 Market St., Knoxville TN 37902. (615)595-5000. Editor: Keith Bellows. 95% freelance written. Quarterly magazine. "*Special Reports* consists of 6 special interest editions—Fiction, Personalities, Living, Family, Health and Sports. Distributed to doctor's offices. Core readers are mothers ages 25-40, with one or more children. These women are active and balance child-rearing with the demands of work, exercise and travel." Estab. 1988. Circ. 1 million. Pays on acceptance. Publishes ms an average of 3 months after acceptance. Byline given. Offers 30% kill fee. Buys first North American serial rights, second serial (reprint) rights or makes work-for-hire assignments. Query for electronic submission. Computer printout submissions OK; prefers letter-quality. Reports in 1 months on queries. Sample copy $3.50 (each) with 11½x16 SAE and $2 postage. Free writer's guidelines for SASE.

Nonfiction: Book excerpts, essays, exposé, general interest, historical/nostalgic, how-to, humor, interview/profile, opinion, personal experience, photo feature, travel and other. "No unsolicited ms." Buys 300 mss/year. Send published clips before querying. Length: 100-4,500 words. Pays 50¢-$5/word for assigned articles. Pays expenses of writers on assignment.

Fiction: Ethnic, fantasy, horror, humorous, mainstream, mystery, novel excerpts, romance, science fiction, slice-of-life vignettes and suspense. Buys 65 mss/year. Query with published clips. Length: 100-4,500 words. Pays 50¢-$2/word.

Poetry: Free verse and light verse. Buys 20 poems/year. Submit maximum 5 poems. Length: 5-200 lines. Pays $5/word.

Tips: "While we don't accept unsolicited ms or ideas, we encourage you to send a cover letter outlining your professional experience and strengths and 5-8 examples of your best *published* work. If it's strong enough, an editor may follow up with a specific assignment. You'll hear words of encouragement or rejection from us within a month of receiving your material (enclose SASE). Each of the six editors of *Special Reports* has a distinct identity and approach." Individual guidelines for each should be read before querying.

THE STAR, 660 White Plains Rd., Tarrytown NY 10591. (914)332-5000. Editor: Richard Kaplan. Executive Editors: Bill Ridley and Phil Bunton. 40% freelance written. Prefers to work with published/established writers. "For every family; all the family—kids, teenagers, young parents and grandparents." Weekly magazine; 48 pages. Circ. 3.5 million. Publishes ms an average of 1 month after acceptance. Buys first North American serial rights, occasional second serial book rights. Query for electronic submissions. Computer printout submissions acceptable; prefers letter-quality. Pays expenses of writers on assignment.

Nonfiction: Exposé (government waste, consumer, education, anything affecting family); general interest (human interest, consumerism, informational, family and women's interest); how-to (psychological, practical on all subjects affecting readers); interview (celebrity or human interest); new product; photo feature; profile (celebrity or national figure); health; medical; and diet. No first-person articles. Query or submit complete ms. Length: 500-1,000 words. Pays $50-1,500.

Photos: Alistair Duncan, photo editor. State availability of photos with query or ms. Pays $25-100 for 8x10 b&w glossy prints, contact sheets or negatives; $150-1,000 for 35mm color transparencies. Captions required. Buys one-time or all rights.

SUNSHINE MAGAZINE, Henry F. Henrichs Publications, Box 40, Sunshine Park, Litchfield IL 62056. (217)324-3425. Editor: Peggy Kuethe. Managing Editor: Garth Henrichs. 95% freelance written. Eager to work with new/unpublished writers. A monthly magazine. "Primarily human interest and inspirational in its appeal, *Sunshine Magazine* provides worthwhile reading for all the family." Circ. 70,000. Pays on acceptance. Publishes ms an average of 6 months after acceptance. Byline given. Buys first North American serial rights or one-time rights. Submit seasonal/holiday material 6 months in advance. Photocopied submissions OK. Computer printout submissions acceptable; prefers letter-quality. Reports in 2 months. Sample copy for 50¢, 6x9 SAE and 2 first class stamps; writer's guidelines for #10 SAE with 1 first class stamp.

Nonfiction: Essays, historical/nostalgic, inspirational and personal experience. "No material dealing with specifically religious matters or that is depressing in nature (divorce, drug abuse, alcohol abuse, death, violence, child abuse)." Send complete ms. Length: 200-1,250. Pays $10-100.

Columns/Departments: Extraordinary Experience (personal experience), 500 words; Let's Reminisce (reminiscent, nostalgia), 500 words; Guidelines (inspirational), 200 words; and Favorite Meditation (inspirational essay), 200 words. Buys 85-90 mss/year. Send complete ms. Pays $15-50.

Close-up

Keith Bellows
Group Editor
Special Reports

Special Reports, a general interest magazine consisting of six single theme editions—Family, Fiction, Health, Living, Personalities and Sports, is published quarterly. The magazines, 24 issues per year, are distributed exclusively to doctors' offices and are also available by subscription. "The closed circulation enables *Special Reports* editors to target their readers very precisely," says Keith Bellows, editor of the magazines and vice president of Whittle Communications.

Before joining Whittle Communications, Bellows freelanced for various publications and was assistant editor at *Reader's Digest* in Canada. He has headed the development of over 20 publishing properties, produced a daily national college radio show and was also host of a weekly cable TV segment. In addition, he has written two books.

Bellows says *Special Reports* is a browser's magazine that employs high graphic impact, dramatic photography and stories that play on the emotions. The stories are meant to seduce a reader into reading the magazine. Because each issue is devoted to a single theme, the articles are fairly short pieces, 500 to 4,000 words.

"While the issues deal with important bedrock themes in family life, the stories are very narrowly focused," he says. Writers are urged to try to take a different approach to a story, to have fun with it. For example, in the Sports issue, they look for the offbeat, not information that can be found in newspapers. He says their Sports Edition is something of a *People Magazine* of sports.

Competition for freelance assignments at *Special Reports* is keen. Approximately 1,000 bylines are offered a year. To write for *Special Reports* a writer must first submit clips of his published work. These are evaluated and if they show promise, kept on file. Only those writers will receive advance article schedules and be considered for future assignments.

"I demand articles that are timely, well-reported, well-researched and well-written. We are very specific about what we want. When we do stories, we like to peg them to that one person whose story is universal. A writer must furnish research notes and phone numbers of contact people. Good writing is details," says Bellows. "We demand you do intense research, that you bring your stories to life by loading them with observation and specific detail. I hate generalities like 'big' and 'beautiful.' " As one of the top paying freelance markets, they can afford to choose only the best writers. "Take the articles and analyze them. Look at the leads, the transitions, the tone and the vocabulary that is used, the use of anecdotes, the depth of detail," Bellows advises writers. "Finally, we take care to respect our readers. We avoid editing by guilt ('Your kids are on drugs, you're too fat') or overpromising ('We have a quick and easy solution for your problems')."

—Deborah Cinnamon

Fiction: Inspirational and human interest. Buys 75-80 mss/year. Send complete ms.
Poetry: Light verse and traditional. No avant-garde, free verse or haiku. Buys 12-15 poems/year. No limit to the number of poems submitted at one time. Length: 4-16 lines. Pays $15-80, or may pay in copies.
Fillers: Anecdotes and short humor. Buys 1-5/year. Length: 50-150 words. Pays $10-20.
Tips: "Make a note that *Sunshine* is not religious—but it is inspirational. After reading a sample copy, you should know that we do not accept material that is very different from what we've been doing for over 60 years. Don't send a manuscript that is longer than specified or that is 'different' from anything else we've published—that's not what we're looking for. The whole magazine is written primarily by freelancers. We are just as eager to publish new writers as they are to get published."

‡USA WEEKEND, Gannett Co., Inc., Box 500-W, Washington DC 20044. (703)276-6445. Managing Editor: Marcia Bullard. 70% freelance written. Weekly Sunday newspaper magazine. Circ. 15.3 million. Pays on acceptance. Publishes ms an average of 3 months after acceptance. Byline given. Offers 25% kill fee. Buys first North American serial rights. Submit seasonal/holiday material 5 months in advance. Photocopied submissions OK. Query for electronic submissions. Reports in 5 weeks.
Nonfiction: Food and Family Issues, Connie Kurz; Trends, Entertainment, Mei-Mei Chan; Recreation, Tim McQuay; Current Events, Brenda Turner. Book excerpts, general interest, how-to, interview/profile, travel, food and recreation. No first-person essays, historic pieces, retrospectives. Buys 200 mss/year. Query with published clips. No unsolicited mss accepted. Length: 50-2,000 words. Pays $75-2,000. Sometimes pays expenses of writers on assignment.
Photos: State availability of photos with submission.
Columns/Departments: Food, Travel, Entertainment, Books, Recreation. "All stories must be pegged to an upcoming event, must report new and refreshing trends in the field and must include high profile people." Length: 50-1,000 words. Query with published clips. Pays $250-500.
Tips: "We are looking for authoritative, lively articles that blend the author's expertise with our style. All articles must have a broad, timely appeal. One-page query should include peg or timeliness of the subject matter. We generally look for sidebar material to accompany each article."

WHAT MAKES PEOPLE SUCCESSFUL, The National Research Bureau, Inc., 424 N. 3rd St., Burlington IA 52601. Editor: Rhonda Wilson. Editorial Supervisor: Doris J. Ruschill. 75% freelance written. Eager to work with new/unpublished writers, and works with a small number of new/unpublished writers each year. For industrial workers of all ages. Published quarterly. Pays on publication. Publishes ms an average of 1 year after acceptance. Buys all rights. Previously published submissions OK. Computer printout submissions acceptable; prefers letter-quality. Submit seasonal/holiday material 8 months in advance of issue date. Reports in 3 weeks. Writer's guidelines for #10 SASE.
Nonfiction: How-to (be successful); general interest (personality, employee morale, guides to successful living, biographies of successful persons, etc.); experience; and opinion. No material on health. Buys 3-4 mss/issue. Query with outline. Length: 400-600 words. Pays 4¢/word.
Tips: Short articles and fillers (rather than major features) have a better chance of acceptance because all articles are short.

WORLD'S FAIR, World's Fair, Inc., Box 339, Corte Madera CA 94925. (415)924-6035. Editor: Alfred Heller. 75% freelance written. Quarterly magazine covering fairs and expositions, (past, present and future). "The people, politics and pageantry of fairs and expositions, in historical perspective; lively, good-humored articles of fact and analysis." Circ. 5,000. Pays on acceptance. Publishes ms an average of 3 months after acceptance. Byline given. Offers 50% kill fee. Buys all rights. Photocopied submissions OK. Computer printout submissions OK; prefers letter-quality. Reports in 3 weeks. Free sample copy and writer's guidelines.
Nonfiction: Essays, historical/nostalgic, humor, interview/profile, personal experience and photo feature. Buys 10-12 mss/year. Query with published clips. Length: 750-3,000 words. Pays $50-400. Sometimes pays expenses of writers on assignment.
Photos: State availability of photos or line drawings with submission. Reviews contact sheets and 8x10 b&w prints. Identification of subjects required. Buys one-time rights.
Tips: Looking for "correspondents in cities planning major expositions, in the U.S. and abroad."

_____ Health and Fitness

The magazines listed here specialize in covering health and fitness topics for a general audience. Magazines covering health topics from a medical perspective are listed in the Medical category of Trade. Also see the Sports/Miscellaneous section where publications dealing with health and particular sports may be listed. Many general interest publications are also potential markets for health or fitness articles. A new consumer health magazine, *Good Health Magazine*, also is slated to appear in April 1990 in five major metropolitan newspapers.

ACCENT ON LIVING, Box 700, Bloomington IL 61702. (309)378-2961. Editor: Betty Garee. 75% freelance written. Eager to work with new/unpublished writers. For physically disabled persons and rehabilitation professionals. Quarterly magazine. Circ. 20,000. Buys first rights and second (reprint) rights to material originally published elsewhere. Byline usually given. Buys 50-60 unsolicited mss/year. Pays on publication. Publishes ms an average of 6 months after acceptance. Photocopied submissions OK. Computer printout submissions acceptable; prefers letter-quality. Reports in 2 weeks. Sample copy with writer's guidelines for $2.50, 6x8 SAE and four first class stamps; writer's guidelines alone for #10 SAE and 1 first class stamp.
Nonfiction: Articles about new devices that would make a disabled person with limited physical mobility more independent; should include description, availability, and photos. Medical breakthroughs for disabled people. Intelligent discussion articles on acceptance of physically disabled persons in normal living situations; topics may be architectural barriers, housing, transportation, educational or job opportunities, organizations, or other areas. How-to articles concerning everyday living, giving specific, helpful information so the reader can carry out the idea himself/herself. News articles about active disabled persons or groups. Good strong interviews. Vacations, accessible places to go, sports, organizations, humorous incidents, self improvement, and sexual or personal adjustment – all related to physically handicapped persons. No religious-type articles. "We are looking for upbeat material." Query. Length: 250-1,000 words. Pays 10¢/word for article as it appears in magazine (after editing and/or condensing by staff).
Photos: Pays $10 minimum for b&w photos purchased with accompanying captions. Amount will depend on quality of photos and subject matter. Pays $50 and up for four-color slides used on cover. "We need good-quality transparencies or slides with submissions – or b&w photos."
Tips: "Ask a friend who is disabled to read your article before sending it to *Accent*. Make sure that he/she understands your major points and the sequence or procedure."

AMERICAN HEALTH MAGAZINE, Fitness of Body and Mind, American Health Partners, 80 Fifth Ave., New York NY 10011. (212)242-2460. Editor-in-Chief: T. George Harris. Editor: Joel Gurin. 70% freelance written. Prefers to work with published/established writers. 10 issues/year. General interest magazine that covers both scientific and "lifestyle" aspects of health, including laboratory research, clinical advances, fitness, holistic healing and nutrition. Circ. 1,000,000. Pays on acceptance. Publishes ms an average of 4-6 months after acceptance. Byline given. Offers 25% kill fee. Buys first North American serial rights, "and certain other rights that are negotiable, in some cases." Computer printout submissions acceptable. Reports in 1-2 months. Sample copy for $3; writer's guidelines for #10 SAE and 1 first class stamp.
Nonfiction: Mail to Editorial/Features. Book excerpts; how-to; humor; interview/profile (health or fitness related); photo feature (any solid feature or news item relating to health); and technical. No mechanical research reports, quick weight-loss plans or unproven treatments. "Stories should be written clearly, without jargon. Information should be new, authoritative and helpful to the readers." Buys 60-70 mss/year (plus many more news items). Query with 2 clips of published work. "Absolutely *no* complete mss." Length: 1,000-3,000 words. Pays $600-2,000 upon acceptance. Pays the expenses of writers on assignment.
Photos: Mail to Editorial/Photo. Send photos with query. Pays $100-600 for 35mm transparencies and 8x10 prints "depending on use." Captions and identification of subjects required. Buys one-time rights.
Columns/Departments: Mail to Editorial/News. Medical News, Fitness Report, Nutrition Report, Mind/Body News, Family Report, Family Pet, Tooth Report, and Skin, Scent and Hair. Other news sections included from time to time. Buys about 300 mss/year. Query with clips of published work. Prefers 2 pages-500 words. Pays $125-375 upon acceptance.
Tips: "*American Health* has no full-time staff writers; we have chosen to rely on outside contributors for most of our articles. The magazine needs good ideas, and good articles, from professional journalists, health educators, researchers and clinicians. Queries should be short (no longer than a page), snappy and to the point. Think short; think news. Give us a good angle and a paragraph of background. Queries only. We do not take responsibility for materials not accompanied by SASE."

BACK TO HEALTH MAGAZINE, (formerly *Back Pain Magazine*) Suite 203, 1761 W. Hillsboro Blvd., Deerfield Beach FL 33442. (305)360-0700. FAX: (305)429-9896. Executive Editor: Herbert Siegel. 50% freelance written. Monthly magazine on overall health with emphasis on pain relief for men and women over 40. Estab. 1987. Circ. 200,000. Pays on publication. Byline given. Simultaneous and previously published submissions OK. Computer printout submissions OK; prefers letter quality (double-spaced). "We reply within 15 days." Sample copy for $1.95, includes writer's guidelines. Writer's guidelines alone for SAE and first class stamp.
Nonfiction: Innovative therapies, techniques for "open-minded" readers, personal experience, expose, interview, general interest (health), new product, research reports. Query only. No unsolicited manuscripts. Length: 500-5,000. Pay negotiable.

Photos: Send photos with submission, 4-color transparencies preferred.
Fillers: Cartoons: Send 6 non-returnable samples. Pay negotiable.
Tips: "We are not a literary magazine but we expect some degree of respect for the rules of grammar and correct spelling. Health care professionals must submit curriculum vitae with query letter. Writers should send brief bio. Assignments possible."

‡**BEAUTY DIGEST**, Regent Media, Suite 802, 126 5th Ave., New York NY 10011. (212)627-1440. Editor: Trisa McMahon Drain. 50% freelance written. Bimonthly magazine on beauty, health and fitness. Circ. 375,000. Pays on publication. Byline given. Buys first North American serial rights. Submit seasonal/holiday material 4-6 months in advance. Computer printout submissions OK; prefers letter-quality. Reports in 2 months. Sample copy $2.50 and 9x12 SAE. Writer's guidelines for SAE with 1 first class stamp.
Nonfiction: Book excerpts, how-to (how to get more out of your fitness plan; find a good doctor, etc.), interview/profile, new product and travel. Query with published clips. Length: 1,000-2,000 words. Pays $150-500. Sometimes pays expenses of writers on assignment.
Photos: State availability of photos with submission. Captions, model releases and identification of subjects required. Buys all rights.
Columns/Departments: Your Body (Makeup, hair, skin stories); Your Body (Step by step exercises for a particular body part. Any fitness related angle.); Your Health (Health problems OB/Gyn plus other relating to wormen); and Your Life (Emotional self help).
Tips: "We are looking for 'knockout' tight text, a one page query letter with an outline of proposed article idea with strong title, and fresh ideas—not rehashed versions of old topics."

BETTER HEALTH, Better Health Press, 1384 Chapel St., New Haven CT 06511. (203)789-3972. Managing Editor: Susan Blum. 50% freelance written. Prefers to work with published/established writers; works with small number of new/unpublished writers each year. A bimonthly magazine covering health related topics. Circ. 120,000. Pays on publication. Byline given. Buys first and second serial rights. Submit seasonal/holiday material 2 months in advance. Simultaneous, photocopied and previously published submissions OK. Query for electronic submissions. Computer printout submissions OK. Free sample copy for 9x12 SAE.
Nonfiction: Medical general interest. Query with published clips. Length: 800-3,000 words. Pays $100-300.
Photos: State availability of photos with submission. Reviews contact sheets. Offers no additional payment for photos accepted with ms.

‡**CONCEIVE MAGAZINE, The Magazine of Infertility Issues**, Larson Publishing, Inc., Box 2047, Danville CA 94526. (415)685-9489. Editor: Catherine C. Knipper. 10% freelance written. Bimonthly magazine on infertility and alternatives. "*Conceive* is edited to support and inform infertile couples about current medical technologies and advances in layman's terms, the emotional side of infertility and how to cope, as well as alternatives to family building such as adoption and child-free living. No special slant or philosophy." Pays on publication. Publishes ms an average of 4 months after acceptance. Byline given. Offers $25 kill fee. Buys first North American serial rights. Simultaneous, photocopied and previously published submissions OK. Computer printout submissions OK; prefers letter-quality. Reports in 2 weeks on queries; 1 month on mss. Sample copy for $3.95 and 9x12 SAE. Writer's guidelines for SASE.
Nonfiction: Book excerpts, general interest, historical/nostalgic, humor, inspirational, interview/profile, new product, opinion (does not mean letters to the editor), personal experience, photo feature, religious and technical. Query with or without published clips. Length: 400-4,000 words. Pays $50-175.
Photos: Send photos with submission. Reviews contact sheets, negatives. and 8x10 prints. Offers $25 per photo. Buys one-time rights.
Poetry: Avant-garde, free verse, haiku, light verse and traditional. Buys 6 poems/year. No maximum number of poems. Length: 4-30 lines. Pays $1/line.
Fillers: Anecdotes, facts, gags to be illustrated by cartoonist, newsbreaks and short humor. Buys 15/year. Length: 10-250 words. Pays $10 up to 100 words.

‡**COPING, Living with Cancer**, Pulse Publications, Box 1677, Franklin TN 37065-1677. (615)791-5900. Associate Editor: Jacki Moss. Managing Editor: Susan Prudowsky. 25% freelance written. Quarterly magazine. "All material must be cancer-specific, detailing information relevant to patients and families living with cancer—features on lifestyle, survivors, physicians, cancer issues and treatments—positive, helpful in nature." Circ. 50,000. Pays within 30 days of publication. Byline given. Offers $25 kill fee. Buys first North American serial rights. Submit seasonal/holiday material six months in advance. Computer printout submissions OK; prefers letter-quality. Reports in 1 month. Sample copy $2.50. Free writer's guidelines.
Nonfiction: How-to overcome difficulties in living w/cancer; humor, inspirational, interview/profile, personal experience, technical, travel, and research; all related to oncology. Does not want to see "articles too health-generic. Must have oncology applications clearly drawn." Buys 20 mss/year. Query with or without published clips, or send complete ms. Length: 500-1,500 words. Pays $50-250 for assigned articles; $25-200 for unsolicited articles. Sometimes pays expenses of writers on assignment.

Photos: State availability of photos with submission. Reviews contact sheets, transparencies and prints. Offers $10-25 per photo. Captions, model releases and identification of subjects required. Buys one-time rights.

Columns/Departments: Upfront (upbeat look at cancer lifestyles or progress), 750 words; First Person (first-person account of cancer experience), 750 words; Second Opinion (editorial-type comment on cancer issues), 1,000 words; Survivors (profile/personality of cancer survivors), 1,000 words and Treatment (innovations, improvements in treatment), 1,000 words. Buys 12 mss/year. Query with published clips. Pays $50-200.

Tips: "Freelancers must understand the needs of *Coping*'s readership and be sensitive to the issues readers face. If not touched themselves by cancer (self or family), freelancers benefit by increasing their understanding of the disease's challenges and triumphs by observing survivors, speaking w/physicians or patients. 'How-to' is a good area for freelancers, though ideas must be practical and suggestions medically correct. All material used as background for technical articles must be timely—six months aged maximum, since oncology research is always ongoing w/new results."

‡EAST WEST, The Journal of Natural Health & Living, Kushi Foundation, Inc., 17 Station St., Box 1200, Brookline Village MA 02147. (617)232-1000. FAX: (617)232-1572. Editor: Mark Mayell. 40% freelance written. Works with a small number of new/unpublished writers each year. Monthly magazine emphasizing natural health for "people of all ages seeking balance in a world of change." Circ. 100,000. Pays on publication. Publishes ms an average of 6 months after acceptance. Buys first serial rights or second (reprint) rights. Byline given. Submit seasonal/holiday material 6 months in advance. Simultaneous and photocopied submissions OK. Computer printout submissions acceptable; prefers letter-quality to dot-matrix. Reports in 1 month. Sample copy $1 and 8½x11 SAE; writer's guidelines for SAE and 1 first class stamp.

Nonfiction: Major focus is on issues of natural health and diet; interviews and features (on the natural foods industry, sustainable farming and gardening, natural healing, human-potential movement, diet and fitness). No negative, politically-oriented, or New Age material. "We're looking for original, first-person articles without jargon or opinions of any particular teachings. Articles should be well documented." Buys 15-20 mss/year. Query. Length: 2,000-3,000 words. Pays 10-15¢/word. Sometimes pays expenses of writers on assignment.

Photos: Send photos with ms. Pays $15-40 for b&w prints; $15-175 for 35mm color transparencies. Captions preferred; model releases required.

Columns/Departments: Body, Whole Foods, Natural Healing, Gardening, and Cooking. Buys 15 mss/year. Submit complete ms. Length: 1,500-2,000 words. Pays 10-15¢/word.

Tips: "Read another issue. Too many freelancers don't take the time to truly understand their market and thus waste their time and ours with inappropriate submissions."

HEALTH EXPRESS, Shaping Up Body and Mind, Good Health, Inc., 13521 Cedar Rd., Cleveland OH 44118. (216)662-6969. Editor: Suzanne Pelisson. Managing Editor: Walitha Griffey. 75% freelance written. Bimonthly magazine on health and fitness of mind and body. "*Health Express* is a health and fitness magazine for busy men and women who aren't too busy to take an active role in maintaining good health—for themselves and their families." Circ. 100,000. Pays on publication. Byline given. Buys one-time rights or second serial (reprint) rights. Submit seasonal/holiday material 4 months in advance. Simultaneous, photocopied and previously published submissions OK. Computer printout submissions OK; prefers letter-quality. Reports in 3 weeks. Sample copy $2.50; writer's guidelines for #10 SAE with 1 first class stamp.

Nonfiction: Book excerpts, how-to (health related fitness), inspirational, interview/profile, new product, photo feature. Buys 60-70 mss/year. Query with or without published clips, or send complete ms. Length: 1,000 words. Pays $25-150. Sometimes pays expenses of writers on assignment.

Photos: State availability of photos with submission or send photos with submission. Reviews contacts and 8x10 prints. Model release and identification of subjects required. Buys one-time rights.

Columns/Departments: The Whole Tooth (dental health); Psychology (mindbody—behavior); Food (nutrition, disease control). Buys 15 mss/year. Query or send complete ms. Length: 500-700 words. Pays $50-75.

Fillers: Contact: Michael Cohen. Newsbreaks. Buys 150 mss/yar. Length: 10-60 words. Pays $5-20.

HEALTH MAGAZINE, Getting the Best From Yourself, Family Media, Inc., 3 Park Ave., New York NY 10016. (212)340-9261. Editor: Dianne Partie Lange. Executive Editor: Bonnie Gordon. Managing Editor: Jennifer Cook. 75% freelance written. A monthly magazine covering women's health issues. "*Health* is a service magazine for women twenty to fifty. We run pieces on medicine and health, behavior and psychology, fitness, food, beauty and fashion." Circ. 1,000,000. Pays on acceptance. Publishes ms an average of 4 months after acceptance. Byline given. Offers 20% kill fee. Buys first North American serial rights. Submit seasonal/holiday material 6 months in advance. Computer printout submissions acceptable; prefers letter-quality. Reports in 2 months. Sample copy for 9 × 12 SAE and $1.45 postage; free writer's guidelines.

Nonfiction: Investigative, general interest, humor, interview/profile, new product and personal experience. Buys 325 mss/year. Query with published clips. Length: 175-2,500 words. Pays $150-2,000. Pays the expenses of writers on assignment.

Photos: State availability of photos with submission. Reviews transparencies.

Tips: "A freelancer's best first query to *Health* should be well researched and backed up by clips."

HIPPOCRATES, The Magazine of Health & Medicine, Suite 100, 475 Gate 5 Rd., Sausalito CA 94965. (415)332-5866. Editor: Eric Schrier. Managing Editor: Michael Gold. 75% freelance written. A bimonthly magazine on health and medicine. "Articles should be written with wit, reflection and authority." Circ. 500,000. Pays on acceptance. Publishes ms an average of 6 months after acceptance. Offers 20% kill fee. Buys first North American serial rights. Submit seasonal/holiday material 6 months in advance. Comptuer printout submissions OK.

Nonfiction: Essays, general interest, how-to, interview/profile, photo feature. Query with published clips. Length: 1,000-5,000 words. Pays $850-4,000. Sometimes pays expenses of writers on assignment.

Columns/Departments: Editorial Coordinator: John Kiefer. Food, Family, Sports, Drugs, Mind, all 800-1,300 words. Buys 12 mss/year. Query with published clips. Pays $600-850.

Fillers: Clippings: verbatim from other publications or book, $50 each *used*; nothing if unused.

Tips: "Send sharply focused queries with the proposed style and sources clearly defined. Departments are the best place to start. Queries can run to 250 words per topic and should demonstrate the finished story's structure and character. Departments are Food, Family, Sports, Drugs and Mind. Tightly focused stories, with real voices and touches of humor used. *Always* query first."

‡INTERNATIONAL MEDICAL ADVANCES NOW!, International Medical Advances Now, Ltd., US address: 4416 N. Scottsdale Rd. #700, Scottsdale AZ 85251. (602)829-8888. Editor: Susan Orlando. Monthly newsletter on medical & health advances *currently available* and where in North America and Europe. "Readers are individuals in North America and Europe who are interested in discovering medical and health advances which can help them solve medical problems, reduce pain, and prolong their lives." Estab. 1988. Circ. 10,000. Pays on publication. Publishes ms an average of 1 month after acceptance. Byline given. Buys all rights. Photocopied and previously submitted submissions OK. Computer printout submissions OK; prefers letter-quality. Reports in 1 mongh. Sample copy $3.

Nonfiction: Book excerpts, how-to (medical & health advances), interview/profile and new product. No articles not related to medical & health advances. Buys 50 mss/year. Query with or without published clips, or send complete ms. Length: 500-5,000 words. Pays $50-500.

Photos: Send photos with submission. Reviews prints. Offers $10-50 per photo. Captions, model releases and identification of subjects required. Buys all rights.

Columns/Departments: You Are What You Eat (health/medical benefits and problems associated with specific foods & beverages), 500-1,000 words. Buys 5 mss/year. Query with published clips or send complete ms. Pays $50-200.

LET'S LIVE MAGAZINE, Oxford Industries, Inc., 444 N. Larchmont Blvd., Box 74908, Los Angeles CA 90004. (213)469-8379. FAX: (213)469-9597. Editor: Debra A. Jenkins. Emphasizes nutrition. 40% freelance written. Works with a small number of new/unpublished writers each year. Monthly magazine. Circ. 140,000. Pays on publication. Publishes ms an average of 4 months after acceptance. Buys first North American serial rights. Byline given. Submit seasonal/holiday material 6 months in advance. Computer printout submissions acceptable; prefers letter quality. Reports in 1 month on queries; 6 weeks on mss. Sample copy for $2.50 and 10x13 SAE with 5 first class stamps; writer's guidelines for SAE and 1 first class stamp.

Nonfiction: General interest (effects of vitamins, minerals and nutrients in improvement of health or afflictions); historical (documentation of experiments or treatment establishing value of nutrients as boon to health); how-to (acquire strength and vitality, improve health of adults and/or children and prepare tasty health-food meals); interview (benefits of research in establishing prevention as key to good health); personal opinion (views of orthomolecular doctors or their patients on value of health foods toward maintaining good health); and profile (background and/or medical history of preventive medicine, M.D.s or Ph.D.s, in advancement of nutrition). Manuscripts must be well-researched, reliably documented, and written in a clear, readable style. Buys 2-4 mss/issue. Query with published clips. Length: 1,000-1,200 words. Pays $150. Sometimes pays expenses of writers on assignment.

Photos: State availability of photos with ms. Pays $17.50 for 8x10 b&w glossy prints; $35 for 8x10 color prints and 35mm color transparencies; and $150 for good cover shot. Captions and model releases required.

Tips: "We want writers with experience in researching nonsurgical medical subjects and interviewing experts with the ability to simplify technical and clinical information for the layman. A captivating lead and structural flow are essential. The most frequent mistakes made by writers are in writing articles that are too technical; in poor style; written for the wrong audience (publication not thoroughly studied), or have unreliable documentation or overzealous faith in the topic reflected by flimsy research and inappropriate tone."

LISTEN MAGAZINE, 6830 Laurel St. NW, Washington DC 20012. (202)722-6726. Editor: Gary B. Swanson. 75% freelance written. Works with a small number of new/unpublished writers each year. Specializes in drug prevention, presenting positive alternatives to various drug dependencies. "*Listen* is used in many high school classes, in addition to use by professionals: medical personnel, counselors, law enforcement officers, educators, youth workers, etc." Monthly magazine, 32 pages. Circ. 100,000. Buys first rights. Byline given. Pays on acceptance. Publishes ms an average of 6 months after acceptance. Computer printout submissions acceptable; prefers letter-quality. Reports in 1 month. Sample copy $1 and 8½x11 SASE; free writer's guidelines.

Nonfiction: Seeks articles that deal with causes of drug use such as poor self-concept, family relations, social skills or peer pressure. Especially interested in youth-slanted articles or personality interviews encouraging nonalcoholic and nondrug ways of life. Teenage point of view is essential. Popularized medical, legal and educational articles. Also seeks narratives which portray teens dealing with youth conflicts, especially those related to the use of or temptation to use harmful substances. Growth of the main character should be shown. "We don't want typical alcoholic story/skid-row bum, AA stories. We are also being inundated with drunk-driving accident stories. Unless yours is unique, consider another topic." Buys 15-20 unsolicited mss/year. Query. Length: 1,200-1,500 words. Pays 5-7¢/word. Sometimes pays the expenses of writers on assignment.
Photos: Purchased with accompanying ms. Captions required. Color photos preferred, but b&w acceptable.
Fillers: Word square/general puzzles are also considered. Pays $15.
Tips: "True stories are good, especially if they have a unique angle. Other authoritative articles need a fresh approach. In query, briefly summarize article idea and logic of why you feel it's good."

LONGEVITY, Omni Publications, 1965 Broadway, New York NY 10023. (212)496-6100. FAX: (212)580-3693. Editor-in-Chief: Rona Cherry. A monthly magazine on medicine, health, fitness and aging research. "*Longevity* is written for an audience with a median age of 40 who want to prolong their ability to lead a productive, vibrant, healthy life, and to look as good as they feel at their best." Circ. 225,000. Pays on acceptance. Publishes ms an average of 2 months after acceptance. Byline given. Offers 25% kill fee. Makes work-for-hire assignments. Query for electronic submissions.
Nonfiction: Interview/profile, new product, health. Query. Length: 150-950 words. Pays $100-2,500. Pays expenses of writers on assignment.
Columns/Departments: Antiaging News, Outer Limits, Nutrition.

‡MASSAGE MAGAZINE, Keeping Those Who Touch—In Touch, Noah Publishing Co., Suite 14A, 74-5543 Kaiwi St., Box 1389, Kailua-Kona HI 96740. (808)329-2433. Editor: Robert Calvert. 80% freelance written. Prefers to work with published/established writers, and works with a small number of new/unpublished writers each year. A bimonthly magazine on massage-bodywork and related healing arts. Circ. 35,000. Pays on publication. Publishes ms an average of 6 months after acceptance. Byline given. Buys first North American rights. Previously published submissions OK. Query for electronic submissions. Computer printout submissions OK; no dot-matrix. Reports in 1 month on queries; 2 months on mss. Sample copy $4. Free writer's guidelines.
Nonfiction: Book excerpts, essays, general interest, historical/nostalgic, how-to, humor, inspirational, interview/profile, new product, photo feature, technical and travel. Buys 2-3/year. Query. Length: 600-2,000 words. Pays $50-100 for assigned articles; $25-50 for unassigned. Sometimes pays the expenses of writers on assignment.
Photos: Send photos with submission. Offers $10-25 per photo. Identification of subjects required. Buys one-time rights.
Columns/Departments: In Sports (massage/bodywork and sports); In Class (how-to technical pieces on aspects of the profession); Interactions (between practitioner and client). Query. Length: 800-1,200 words. Pays $25-50.
Fillers: Anecdotes, facts, newsbreaks and short humor. Buys 5/year. Length: 100 words. Pays $25 maximum.
Tips: "For first articles accepted, we don't pay much, but as a writer establishes with us, we pay more. Wholesome stories with facts, interviews and industry insight are welcomed. We're leaning away from a strong emphasis on the touch professions to more consumer (general) touch-related materials."

MATURE HEALTH, (formerly *AIM* plus), The Haymarket Group, Inc., Suite 500, 45 West 34th St., New York NY 10001. (212)239-0855. Editor: Tim Moriarty. Managing Editor: Gayle Turim. 75% freelance written. Prefers to work with published/established writers, and works with a small number of new/unpublished writers each year. Magazine published 10 times/year covering health for mature (50-65) market. Circ. 200,000. Pays 2 months after publication. Byline given. Offers 25% kill fee. Buys first North American serial rights. Submit seasonal/holiday material 5 months in advance. Computer printout submissions OK; no dot-matrix. Reports in 6 weeks on queries. Sample copy $2.50 with 9x12 SAE and 3 first class stamps; writer's guidelines for #10 SAE and 1 first class stamp.
Nonfiction: Health, nutrition, medical news, book excerpts, how-to, humor, interview/profile, new product and personal experience. No travel, no clippings, no articles slanted to those 50 and under. Query with published clips. Length: 300-1,500 words. Pays 30-40¢/word. Usually pays expenses of writers on assignment.
Photos: State availability of photos with submission. Identification of subjects required. Buys one-time rights.
Fillers: Anecdotes, facts and short humor. Length: 50-300 words. Pays $25-60.
Tips: "Send a well-written query that outlines, in detail, what your article will cover. Avoid the obvious. Queries that convey a sense of humor stand out; we need upbeat material."

‡MEN'S HEALTH, Rodale Press, 33 E. Minor St., Emmaus PA 18098. (215)967-5171. Editor: Michael Lafavore. Managing Editor: Jan Bresnick. 90% freelance written. Quarterly magazine. "We publish health articles with a male slant. We take a broad view of health to encompass the physical and emotional." Circ. 250,000.

Pays on acceptance. Publishes ms an average of 2 months after acceptance. Byline given. Offers 15% kill fee. Buys first North American serial rights or second serial (reprint) rights. Submit seasonal/holiday material 6-8 months in advance. Previously published submissions OK. Query for electronic submissions. Computer printout submissions OK; prefers letter-quality. Reports in 2 weeks. Sample copy $2.95 with SAE and postage.

Nonfiction: Book excerpts, essays, exposé, interview/profile, personal experience and travel. Buys 50 mss/year. Query with published clips. Length: 100-2,000 words. Pays 25-50¢/word. Sometimes pays expenses of writers on assignment.

Photos: State availability of photos with submission. Offers no additional payment for photos accepted with ms. Model releases required. Buys one-time rights.

Columns/Departments: Eating Right (nutrition); Couples (relationships); Clinic (deals with a specific health problem) and Malegrams (short news items). Buys 10 mss/year. Query. Length: 800-1,000 words. Pays 25-50¢/word.

MUSCLE MAG INTERNATIONAL, 52 Bramsteele Rd., Unit 2, Brampton, Ontario L6W 3M5 Canada. Editor: Robert Kennedy. 80% freelance written. "We do not care if a writer is known or unknown; published or unpublished. We simply want good instructional articles on bodybuilding." For 16 to 50-year-old men and women interested in physical fitness and overall body improvement. Monthly magazine. Circ. 225,000. Buys all rights. Pays on acceptance. Publishes ms an average of 4 months after acceptance. Byline given. Buys 80 mss/year. Sample copy $4 and 9x12 SAE. Computer printout submissions acceptable; no dot-matrix. Reports in 1 month. Submit complete ms with IRCs.

Nonfiction: Articles on ideal physical proportions and importance of supplements in the diet, training for muscle size. Should be helpful and instructional and appeal to young men and women who want to live life in a vigorous and healthy style. "We would like to see articles for the physical culturist on new muscle building techniques or an article on fitness testing." Informational, how-to, personal experience, interview, profile, inspirational, humor, historical, exposé, nostalgia, personal opinion, photo, spot news, new product, and merchandising technique articles. Length: 1,200-1,600 words. Pays 10¢/word. Sometimes pays the expenses of writers on assignment.

Columns/Departments: Nutrition Talk (eating for top results) and Shaping Up (improving fitness and stamina). Length: 1,300 words. Pays 10¢/word.

Photos: B&w and color photos are purchased with or without ms. Pays $15 for 8x10 glossy exercise photos; $15 for 8x10 b&w posing shots. Pays $100-200 for color cover and $20 for color used inside magazine (transparencies). More for "special" or "outstanding" work.

Fillers: Newsbreaks, puzzles, quotes of the champs. Length: open. Pays $5 minimum.

Tips: "The best way to break in is to seek out the muscle-building 'stars' and do in-depth interviews with biography in mind. Color training picture support essential. Writers have to make their articles informative in that readers can apply them to help gain bodybuilding success."

NEW BODY, The Magazine of Health & Fitness, GCR Publishing Group, Inc., 888 7th Ave., New York NY 10106. (212)541-7100. Editor: Kate Samples. Managing Editor: Sandra Kosherick. 75% freelance written. Works with a small number of new/unpublished writers each year. A bimonthly magazine covering fitness and health for young, middle-class women. Circ. 125,000. Pays on publication. Publishes ms an average of 6 months after acceptance. Byline given. Offers negotiable kill fee. Buys all rights. Submit seasonal/holiday material 6 months in advance. Simultaneous and photocopied submissions OK. Computer printout submissions acceptable; prefers letter-quality. Reports in 2 months.

Nonfiction: Health, exercise, psychology, relationships, diet, celebrities, and nutrition. "We do not cover bodybuilding—please no queries." No articles on "How I do exercises." Buys 75 mss/year. Query with published clips. Length: 800-1,500 words. Pays $100-300 for assigned articles; $50-150 for unsolicited articles.

Photos: Reviews contact sheets, transparencies and prints. Model releases and identification of subjects required. Buys all rights.

Tips: "We are moving toward more general interest women's material on relationships, emotional health, nutrition, etc. We look for a fresh angle—a new way to present the material. Celebrity profiles, fitness tips, and health news are good topics to consider. Make a clean statement of what your article is about, what it would cover—not why the article is important. We're interested in new ideas, new trends or new ways of looking at old topics."

OSTOMY QUARTERLY, United Ostomy Association, Inc., Suite 120, 36 Executive Park, Irvine CA 92714. Editor: TennieBee M. Hall. 10% freelance written. Works with a small number of new/unpublished writers each year and is eager to work with new/unpublished writers. Quarterly magazine on ostomy surgery and living with ostomies. "The *OQ* is the official publication of UOA and should cover topics of interest to patients who underwent abdominal ostomy surgery (ileostomy, colostomy, urostomy). Most articles should be 'upbeat' in feeling; also, we cover new surgical techniques in ostomy surgery." Circ. 50,000. Pays on publication. Publishes ms an average of 6 months after acceptance. Byline given. Buys first North American serial rights; makes work-for-hire assignments. Submit seasonal/holiday material 3 months in advance. Simultaneous queries and photocopied submissions OK. Query for electronic submissions. Computer printout submissions acceptable; prefers letter-quality. Print must be dark and readable. Reports in 3 months. Sample copy for $2.50 and 8½x11 SAE with 8 first class stamps; writer's guidelines for SASE.

Nonfiction: General interest (parenting, psychology); humor (coping humorously with problems with ostomies); interview/profile (important MDs in gastroenterology, urology); personal experience (living with abdominal ostomies); technical (new surgical techniques in ostomy); and travel (with ostomies). No testimonials from members, "How I overcame . . . with ostomy and life is great now." Buys 6 mss/year. Query. Length: 800-2,400 words. Usually asks for pages of copy. Pays $50-150 maximum. Sometimes pays the expenses of writers on assignment but no more than $150 total (expenses plus fee) per article will be paid. No kill fee offered.

Photos: Reviews b&w and color transparencies. "We like to use photographs with articles, but price for article includes use of photos. We return photos on request." Captions and model releases required.

Columns/Departments: Book reviews (on ostomy care, living with ostomies); Ostomy World (any news items relating to ostomy, enterostomal therapy, medical); Q&A (answers medical questions from members); nutrition; financial; psychology. Primarily staff-written.

Tips: "We will be looking mainly for articles from freelancers about ostomy management, ostomy advances, people important to ostomates. Send different topics and ideas than we have published for 25 years. Be willing to attend free meeting of UOA chapter to get a 'flavor' of the group. UOA is a nonprofit association which accounts for the fees offered."

‡**SHAPE, Merging Mind and Body Fitness**, Weider Enterprises, 21100 Erwin St., Woodland Hills CA 91367. (818)595-0593. Editor: Barbara Harris. 10% freelance written. Prefers to work with published/established writers, works with a small number of new/unpublished writers each year, and is eager to work with new/unpublished writers. Monthly magazine covering women's health and fitness. Circ. 785,000. Pays on publication. Publishes ms an average of 6 months after acceptance. Offers 1/3 kill fee. Buys all rights and reprint rights. Submit seasonal/holiday material 8 months in advance. Computer printout submissions acceptable; prefers letter-quality to dot-matrix. Reports in 2 months.

Nonfiction: Book excerpts; expose (health, fitness related); how-to (get fit); interview/profile (of fit women); travel (spas). "We use health and fitness articles written by professionals in their specific fields. No articles which haven't been queried first." Query with clips of published work. Length: 500-2,000 words. Pays negotiable fee. Pays expenses of writers on assignment.

TOTAL HEALTH, Body, Mind and Spirit, Trio Publications, Suite 300, 6001 Topanga Cyn Blvd., Woodland Hills CA 91367. (818)887-6484. Editor: Robert L. Smith. Managing Editor: Rosemary Hofer. Prefers to work with published/established writers. 80% freelance written. A bimonthly magazine covering fitness, diet (weight loss), nutrition and mental health—"a family magazine about wholeness." Circ. 70,000. Pays on publication. Publishes ms an average of 2 months after acceptance. Byline given. Buys first rights. Submit seasonal/holiday material 4 months in advance. Photocopied submissions OK. Reports in 1 month. Sample copy $1 with 9x12 SAE and 5 first class stamps; writer's guidelines for SAE.

Nonfiction: Exposé; how-to (pertaining to health and fitness); and religious (Judeo-Christian). Especially needs articles on skin and body care and power of positive thinking articles. No personal experience articles. Buys 48 mss/year. Send complete ms. Length: 2,000 words. Pays $50-75. Sometimes pays the expenses of writers on assignment.

Photos: State availability of photos with submission. Offers no additional payment for photos accepted with ms. Captions, model releases and identification of subjects required.

Columns/Departments: Query with or without published clips. Length: 1,000 words maximum. Pays $50 maximum.

Tips: "Feature-length articles are most open to freelancers. We are looking for more family fitness-exercise articles."

VEGETARIAN JOURNAL, Box 1463, Baltimore MD 21203. (301)752-VEGV. Editors: Charles Stahler/Debra Wasserman. A monthly newsletter on vegetarianism and animal rights. "*Vegetarian* issues include health, nutrition, animal rights and world hunger. Articles related to nutrition should be documented by established (mainstream) nutrition studies." Circ. 3,000. Pays on publication. Publishes ms an average of 3-5 months after acceptance. Byline given. Makes work-for-hire assignments. Submit seasonal/holiday material 6 months in advance. Computer printout submissions OK. Reports in 1 month. Sample copy and writer's guidelines for #10 SAE with 2 first class stamps.

Nonfiction: Book excerpts, expose, how-to, interview/profile, new products, travel. "At present we are only looking for in-depth articles on selected nutrition subjects from registered dieticians or M.D.'s. Please query with your background. Possibly some in-depth practical and researched articles from others. No miracle cures or use of supplements." Buys 1-5 mss/year. Query with or without published clips or send complete ms. Length: 2,500-8,250 words. Pays $10-25. Sometimes pays writers with contributor copies or other premiums "if not a specific agreed upon in-depth article." Sometimes pays the expenses of writers on assignment.

Photos: State availability of photos with submission. Reviews prints. Offers no additional payment for photos accepted with ms. Identification of subjects required. Buys one-time rights.

Poetry: Avant-garde, free verse, haiku, light verse, traditional "Poetry should be related to vegetarianism, world hunger, or animal rights. No graphic animal abuse. We do not want to see the word, blood, in any form." Pays in copies.

Tips: "We are most open to vegan-oriented medical professionals or vegetarian/animal rights activists who are new to freelancing."

VEGETARIAN TIMES, Box 570, Oak Park IL 60303. (312)848-8100. FAX: (312)848-8175. Executive Editor: Sally Hayhow. Managing Editor: Lucy Moll. 30% freelance written. Prefers to work with published/established writers; works with small number of new/unpublished writers each year. Monthly magazine. Circ. 170,000. Rights purchased vary with author and material. Buys first serial rights or all rights. Byline given unless extensive revisions are required or material is incorporated into a larger article. Pays on acceptance. Publishes ms an average of 6 months after acceptance. Computer printout submissions acceptable; prefers letter-quality. Submit seasonal material 6 months in advance. Reports in 1 month. Query. Sample copy $3; writer's guidelines for #10 SASE.

Nonfiction: Features articles inform readers about how vetetarianism relates to diet, cooking, lifestyle, health, consumer choices, natural foods, environmental concerns and animal welfare. "All material should be well documented and researched, and written in a sophisticated yet lively style." Informational, how-to, personal experience, interview, profile. Length: average 2,000 words. Pays 20¢/word and up, though a flat rate may be negotiated. Will also use 500-word items for new digest. Sometimes pays expenses of writers on assignment.

Photos: Pays $40 for b&w; $40 for color photos used.

Tips: "You don't have to be a vegetarian to write for *Vegetarian Times*, but it is VITAL that your article has a vegetarian slant. The best way to pick up that slant is to read several issues of the magazine (no doubt a tip you've heard over and over). We are very particular about the articles we run and thus tend to ask for rewrites. The best way to break in is by querying us on a well-defined topic that is appropriate for our news digest section. Make sure your idea is well thought out before querying."

VIBRANT LIFE, A Christian Guide for Total Health, Review and Herald Publishing Assn., 55 W. Oak Ridge Dr., Hagerstown MD 21740. (301)791-7000. 95% freelance written. Enjoys working with published/established writers; works with a small number of new/unpublished writers each year. Bimonthly magazine covering health articles (especially from a prevention angle and with a Christian slant). Circ. 50,000. Pays on acceptance. "The average length of time between acceptance of a freelance-written manuscript and publication of the material depends upon the topics; some immediately used; others up to 2 years." Byline always given. Offers 25% kill fee. Buys first serial rights, first North American serial rights, or sometimes second serial (reprint) rights. Computer printout submissions acceptable; no dot-matrix. Submit seasonal/holiday material 6 months in advance. Photocopied (if clear) submissions OK. Reports in 2 months. Sample copy $1; free writer's guidelines for #10 SASE.

Nonfiction: Interview/profile (with personalities on health). "We seek practical articles promoting better health, and a more fulfilled life. We especially like features on breakthroughs in medicine, and most aspects of health. Buys 90-100 mss/year. Send complete ms. Length: 750-2,800 words. Pays $125-450. Pays the expenses of writers on assignment.

Photos: Send photos with ms. Needs 35mm transparencies. Not interested in b&w photos.

Tips: *"Vibrant Life* is published for the typical man/woman on the street, age 20-50. Therefore articles must be written in an interesting, easy-to-read style. Information must be reliable; no faddism. We are more conservative than other magazines in our field. Request a sample copy, and study the magazine and writer's guidelines."

WALKWAYS, Update on Walkers and Walking, The WalkWays Center, 1400 16th St., NW, Washington DC 20036. (202)234-5299. Editor: Marsha L. Wallen. 50% freelance written. Works with a small number of new/unpublished writers each year, and is eager to work with new/unpublished writers. A bimonthly newsletter on walking. Circ. 5,000. Pays on publication. Publishes ms an average of 1 month after acceptance. Byline given. Buys first North American serial rights. Submit seasonal/holiday material 6 months in advance. Simultaneous and photocopied submissions OK. Computer printout submissions OK. Reports in 2 weeks. Sample copy $1.50 with #10 SASE.

Nonfiction: Essays, how-to, humor, interview/profile, opinion, personal experience and travel. "No general travelogues, how walking is a religious experience, or narrow-scope articles about a type of walking with no examples of where it can be done in other places." Buys 6 mss/year. Send complete ms. Length: 200-750 words. Pays $20-75.

Photos: State availability of photos with submissions. Photos should include people walking or some other activity; should not be just scenery. Reviews contact sheets, 35mm transparencies, and 5x7 and 8x10 prints. Offers $10/photo. Captions required. Buys one-time rights.

Columns/Departments: Health Notes, 350 words maximum, with art or photo; Networking (an information sharing department on specific subjects to familiarize readers, such as Volksmarching, race walking, how to form walking club), 350 words maximum, with art or photo; and Footloose (a walk or series of walks in special places with how-to and sidebar information on how to get there, best time, best places to see, who was leader, etc.), 750 words maximum, with art or photo. Buys 32 mss/year. Send complete ms. Offers $10/photo.

Fillers: Medical facts and short humor. Length: 30-50 words. Pays $5.

Tips: "We need writers who can concentrate more on the walk and less about the scenery and extraneous details, although they are appreciated. If writing about a walking trip or experience, give details on how to get there, costs, etc., plus *other* places you can do similar walks. We like to approach themes versus single event or experiences, if possible and applicable."

WEIGHT WATCHERS MAGAZINE, 360 Lexington Ave., New York NY 10017. Editor-in-Chief: Lee Haiken. Senior Editor: Nelly Edmondson. 50% freelance written. Works with a small number of new/unpublished writers each year. Monthly publication for those interested in weight loss and weight maintenance through sensible eating and health/nutrition guidance. Circ. 1,000,000. Buys first North American serial rights only. Pays on acceptance. Publishes ms an average of 6 months after acceptance. Offers 25% kill fee. Computer printout submissions acceptable; prefers letter-quality. Reports in 1-2 months. Sample copy and writer's guidelines for 8½x11 SAE and $1.75.

Nonfiction: "We are interested in general health and medical articles; nutrition pieces based on documented research results; fitness stories that feature types of exercises that don't require special skills or excessive financial costs; and weight loss stories that focus on interesting people and situations. While our articles are authoritative, they are written in a light, upbeat style; a humorous tone is acceptable as long as it is in good taste. To expedite the fact-checking process, we require a second copy of your manuscript that is annotated in the margins with the telephone numbers of all interview subjects, and with citations from such written sources as books, journal articles, magazines, newsletters, newspapers, or press releases. You must attach photocopies of these sources to the annotated manuscript with relevant passages highlighted and referenced to your margin notes. We will be happy to reimburse you for copying costs." Send detailed queries with published clips and SASE. No full-length mss; send feature ideas, as well as before-and-after weight loss story ideas dealing either with celebrities or "real people" Length: 1,000-1,200 words. Pays $250-500.

Tips: "Though we prefer working with established writers, *Weight Watchers Magazine* welcomes new writers as well. As long as your query is tightly written, shows style and attention to detail, and gives evidence that you are knowledgeable about your subject matter, we won't reject you out-of-hand just because you don't have three clips attached. When developing a story for us, keep in mind that we prefer interview subjects to be medical professionals with university appointments who have published in their field of expertise."

WHOLE LIFE, The Journal for Holistic Health and Natural Living, Whole Life Enterprises Inc., Box 2058, Madison Square Station, New York NY 10159. (212)353-3395. Editor and Publisher: Marc Medoff. 25% freelance written. Prefers to work with published/established writers and works with a small number of new/unpublished writers each year. Tabloid covering holistic health, natural living, nutrition and related topics. Circ. 60,000. Pays 90 days after publication. Publishes ms 3-18 months after acceptance. Byline given. Buys first North American serial rights, all rights, and second serial (reprint) rights, and makes work-for-hire assignments; depends on topic and author. Submit seasonal/holiday material 6 months in advance. Simultaneous queries, and simultaneous, photocopied, and previously published submissions OK. Reports in 4 months. Sample copy $7.50; writer's guidelines $3 and #10 SASE.

Nonfiction: Book excerpts (health, nutrition, natural living); general interest (health sciences, holistic health, environment, alternative medicine);how-to (exercise, relaxation, fitness, appropriate technology, outdoors); interview/profile (on assignment); and new product (health, music, spiritual, psychological, natural diet). No undocumented opinion or narrative. Buys 20-40 mss/year. Query with published clips and resume. Length: 1,150-3,000 words. Pays $25-150. Sometimes pays expenses of writers on assignment.

Photos: Reviews b&w contact sheets, any size b&w and color transparencies and any size prints. Model releases and identification of subjects required. Buys all rights.

Columns/Departments: Films, Recipes, Herbs & Health, Resources, Whole Health Network, Living Lightly (appropriate technology), News Views, Whole Life Person, Music, In the Market, Animal Rights—Human Wrongs, Whole Life Experience, Healthy Travel, Restaurant Review, Alternative Fitness, Whole Foods in the News, Whole Frauds in the News, People and Food. Buys 20-40 mss/year. Query with published clips and resume. Length: 150-1,000 words. Pays $25-80.

THE YOGA JOURNAL, California Yoga Teachers Association, 2054 University Ave., Berkeley CA 94704. (415)841-9200. FAX: (415)644-2877. Editor: Stephan Bodian. 75% freelance written. Bimonthly magazine covering yoga, holistic health, conscious living, spiritual practices, and nutrition. "We reach a middle-class, educated audience interested in self-improvement and higher consciousness." Circ. 60,000. Pays on publication. Publishes ms an average of 6 months after acceptance. Byline given. Offers $50 kill fee. Buys first North American serial rights only. Submit seasonal/holiday material 4 months in advance. Simultaneous queries and photocopied submissions OK. Reports in 6 weeks on queries; 2 months on mss. Sample copy $3; free writer's guidelines.

Nonfiction: Book excerpts; how-to (exercise, yoga, massage, etc.); inspirational (yoga or related); interview/profile; opinion; photo feature; and travel (if about yoga). "Yoga is our main concern, but our principal features in each issue highlight other new age personalities and endeavors. Nothing too far-out and mystical. Prefer stories about Americans incorporating yoga, meditation, etc., into their normal lives." Buys 40 mss/year. Query. Length: 750-3,500 words. Pays $150-400.

Photos: Lawrence Watson, art director. Send photos with ms. Pays $200-300 for color cover transparencies; $15-25 for 8x10 b&w prints. Model release (for cover only) and identification of subjects required. Buys one-time rights.

Columns/Departments: Forum; Cooking; Well-Being; Psychology; Profiles; Music (reviews of new age music); and Book Reviews. Buys 12-15 mss/year. Pays $50-150 for columns; $35-60 for book reviews.

Tips: "We always read submissions. We are very open to freelance material and want to encourage writers to submit to our magazine. We're looking for out-of-state contributors, particularly in the Midwest and east coast."

‡YOUR HEALTH, (Florida), Globe Communications Corp. 5401 NW Broken Sound Blvd., Boca Raton FL 33487. (407)997-7733. Editor: Susan Gregg. Associate Editor: Lisa Rappa. 50% freelance written. Semi-monthly magazine on health and fitness. "*Your Health* is a lay-person magazine covering the entire gamut of health, fitness and medicine." Circ. 50,000. Pays on publication. Byline given. Offers $10 kill fee. Buys first North American serial rights and second serial (reprint) rights. Submit seasonal/holiday material 3 months in advance. Photocopied and previously published submissions OK. Computer printout submissions OK; prefers letter-quality. Reports in 1 month on queries; 6 weeks on mss. Free sample copy and writer's guidelines.

Nonfiction: Book excerpts, exposé, general interest, how-to (on general health and fitness topics), inspirational, interview/profile, new product and personal experience. "No general articles, such as 'Why vitamins are good for you.' Give us something new and different." Buys 75-100 mss/year. Query with published clips or send complete ms. Length: 300-1,000 words. Pays $15-75. Sometimes pays expenses of writers on assignment.

Photos: Send photos with submission. Reviews contact sheet, negatives, transparencies and prints. Offers $50-100 per photo. Captions, model releases and identification of subjects required. Buys one-time rights.

Tips: "We are especially interested in profiles and features on common people and celebrities who have conquered illness or who participate in a unique physical fitness regimen. Freelancers can best break in by offering us stories of national interest that we won't find through other channels, such as wire services."

YOUR HEALTH, Meridian Publishing Inc., Box 10010, Ogden UT 84409. (801)394-9446. 65% freelance written. A monthly in-house magazine covering personal health, customized with special imprint titles for various businesses, organizations and associations. "Articles should be timeless, noncontroversial, upscale and positive, and the subject matter should have national appeal." Circ. 40,000. Pays on acceptance. Publishes ms an average of 8 months after acceptance. Byline given. Buys first rights and non-exclusive reprint rights. Simultaneous, photocopied, and previously published submissions OK. Computer printout submissions acceptable; prefers letter-quality. Reports in 6 weeks. Sample copy $1 with 9x12 SAE; writer's guidelines for #10 SAE with 1 first class stamp. (All requests for sample copies and guidelines should be addressed to—Attention: Editorial Assistant.)

Nonfiction: General interest stories about individual's health care needs, including preventative approaches to good health. Topics include advances in medical technology, common maladies and treatments, fitness and nutrition, hospital and home medical care, and personality profiles of both health care professionals and exceptional people coping with disability or illness. Also articles slanted to geriatric readership. "We almost never use a first person narrative. No articles about chiropractic, podiatry or lay midwifery articles." Medical pieces must be accompanied by a list of checkable resources. Buys 40 mss/year. Query. Length: 1,000-1,200 words. Pays 15¢/word for first rights plus non-exclusive reprint rights. Payment for second rights is negotiable. Authors retain the right to resell material after it is printed by *Your Health*.

Photos: Send photos or state availability with submission. Reviews 35mm and 2¼x2¼ transparencies and 5x7 or 8x10 prints. Offers $35/inside photo and $50/cover photo. Captions, model releases and identification of subjects required.

Tips: "The key for the freelancer is a well-written query letter that demonstrates that the subject of the article has national appeal; establishes that any medical claims are based on interviews with experts and/or reliable documented sources; shows that the article will have a clear, focused theme; outlines the availability (from the writer, photographer, or a PR source) of top-quality color photos; and gives evidence that the writer/photographer is a professional, even if a beginner. The best way to get started as a contributor to *Your Health* is to prove that you can submit a well-focused article, based on facts, written cleanly per AP style, along with a variety of beautiful color transparencies to illustrate the story. Material is reviewed by a medical board and must be approved by them."

‡**YOUR HEALTH & FITNESS**, General Learning Corp., 60 Revere Dr., Northbrook IL 60062-1563. (312)564-4070. Executive Editor: Laura Rueckberg. Managing Editor: Carol Lezak. 90-95% freelance written. Prefers to work with published/established writers. A bimonthly magazine covering health and fitness. Needs "general, educational material on health, fitness and safety that can be read and understood easily by the layman." Circ. 1,000,000. Pays within 30 days after acceptance. Publishes ms an average of 6 months after acceptance. No byline given. Offers 50% kill fee. Buys all rights. Submit seasonal/holiday material 6 months in advance. Computer printout submissions OK; no dot-matrix. Sample copy for 9x12 SAE with 2 first class stamps. Free writer's guidelines.

Nonfiction: General interest. "All article topics assigned; send resumes and writing samples. All topics are determined a year in advance of publication by editors; no unsolicited manuscripts." Buys approximately 65 mss/year. Length: 350-1,400 words. Pays $100-700 for assigned articles. Sometimes pays the expenses of writers on assignment.

Photos: Offers no additional payment for photos accepted with ms.

Tips: "Write to a general audience which has only a surface knowledge of health and fitness topics. Possible subjects include exercise and fitness, psychology, nutrition, safety, disease, drug data, and health concerns."

History

Listed here are magazines and other periodicals written for historical collectors, genealogy enthusiasts, historic preservationists and researchers. Editors of history magazines look for fresh accounts of past events in a readable style. Some publications cover an era, like the Civil War, or a region while others specialize in historic preservation.

AMERICAN HERITAGE, 60 Fifth Ave., New York NY 10011. Editor: Byron Dobell. 70% freelance written. 8 times/year. Circ. 275,000. Usually buys first North American rights or all rights. Byline given. Pays on acceptance. Publishes ms an average of 6-12 months after acceptance. Before submitting material, "check our index to see whether we have already treated the subject." Submit seasonal material 1 year in advance. Computer printout submissions acceptable; prefers letter-quality. Reports in 1 month. Writer's guidelines for SAE and 1 first class stamp.

Nonfiction: Wants "historical articles by scholars or journalists intended for intelligent lay readers rather than for professional historians." Emphasis is on authenticity, accuracy and verve. "Interesting documents, photographs and drawings are always welcome. Query." Style should stress "readability and accuracy." Buys 30 unsolicited mss/year. Length: 1,500-5,000 words. Sometimes pays the expenses of writers on assignment.

Tips: "We have over the years published quite a few 'firsts' from young writers whose historical knowledge, research methods and writing skills met our standards. The scope and ambition of a new writer tell us a lot about his or her future usefulness to us. A major article gives us a better idea of the writer's value. Everything depends on the quality of the material. We don't really care whether the author is 20 and unknown, or 80 and famous, or vice versa."

AMERICAN HISTORY ILLUSTRATED, Box 8200, Harrisburg PA 17105. (717)657-9555. Editor: Ed Holm. 60% freelance written. "We are backlogged with submissions and prefer not to receive unsolicited submissions at this time." A bimonthly magazine of cultural, social, military and political history published for a general audience. Circ. 150,000. Pays on acceptance. Byline given. Buys all rights. Query for electronic submissions. Computer printout submissions acceptable; no dot-matrix. Reports in 10 weeks on queries; 4 months on mss. Writer's guidelines for #10 SAE and 1 first class stamp; sample copy and guidelines for $3 (amount includes 3rd class postage) or $2.50 and 9x12 SAE with 4 first class stamps.

Nonfiction: Regular features include American Profiles (biographies of noteworthy historical figures); Artifacts (stories behind historical objects); Portfolio (pictorial features on artists, photographers and graphic subjects); Digging Up History (coverage of recent major archaeological and historical discoveries); and Testaments to the Past (living history articles on major restored historical sites). "Material is presented on a popular rather than a scholarly level." Writers are required to query before submitting ms. "Query letters should be limited to a concise 1-2 page proposal defining your article with an emphasis on its unique qualities." Buys 30-40 mss/year. Length: 1,000-5,000 words depending on type of article. Pays $125-650. Sometimes pays the expenses of writers on assignment.

Photos: Occasionally buys 8x10 glossy prints or color transparencies with mss; welcomes suggestions for illustrations. Pays for the reproduced color illustrations that the author provides.

Tips: "Key prerequisites for publication are thorough research and accurate presentation, precise English usage and sound organization, a lively style, and a high level of human interest. We are especially interested in publishing 'Testaments to the Past' articles (on significant ongoing living history sites), as well as top-quality articles on significant American women, on the Vietnam era, and on social/cultural history. Submissions received without return postage will not be considered or returned. Inappropriate materials include: fiction, book reviews, travelogues, personal/family narratives not of national significance, articles about collectibles/antiques, living artists, local/individual historic buildings/landmarks and articles of a current editorial nature."

AMERICA'S CIVIL WAR, Empire Press, A Cowles Media Co. Affiliate, 105 Loudoun St. SW, Leesburg VA 22075. (703)771-9400. Editor: Roy Morris, Jr. 95% freelance written. Bimonthly magazine of "popular history and straight historical narrative for both the general reader and the Civil War buff." Estab. 1988. Circ. 75,000. Pays on publication. Publishes ms up to 2 years after acceptance. Byline given. Buys first North American serial rights. Query for electronic submissions. Computer printout submissions OK; no dot-matrix. Reports in 2 months on queries; 3 months on mss. Sample copy $3.95; writer's guidelines for #10 SAE with 1 first class stamp.
Nonfiction: Book excerpts, historical, travel. No fiction or poetry. Buys 48 mss/year. Query. Length: 4,000 words maximum. Pays $300 maximum.
Photos: State availability of photos with submission. Pays up to $100/photo. Captions and identification of subjects required. Buys one-time rights.
Columns/Departments: Personality (probes); Ordnance (about weapons used); Commands (about units); Travel (about appropriate historical sites). Buys 24 mss/year. Query. Length: 2,000 words. Pays up to $150.

ANCESTRY NEWSLETTER, Ancestry, Inc., Box 476, Salt Lake City UT 84110. (801)531-1790. Editor-in-Chief: Robb Barr. 95% freelance written. Eager to work with new/unpublished writers. A bimonthly newsletter covering genealogy and family history. "We publish practical, instructional, and informative pieces specifically applicable to the field of genealogy. Our audience is the active genealogist, both hobbyist and professional." Circ. 8,200. Pays on publication. Publishes ms an average of 9 months after acceptance. Byline given. Buys first North American serial rights or all rights. Submit seasonal/holiday material 4 months in advance. Simultaneous and photocopied submissions OK. Computer printout submissions acceptable; prefers letter-quality. Reports in 2 weeks. Sample copy and writer's guidelines for 3 first class stamps.
Nonfiction: General interest (genealogical); historical; how-to (genealogical research techniques); instructional; and photo feature (genealogically related). No unpublished or published family histories, genealogies; the "story of my great-grandmother," nor personal experiences. Buys 25-30 mss/year. Send complete ms. Length: 1,000-3,000 words. Pays $50.
Photos: Send photos with submission. Reviews contact sheets and 5x7 prints. Offers no additional payment for photos accepted with ms. Identification of subjects required. Buys one-time rights.
Tips: "You don't have to be famous, but you must know something about genealogy. Our readers crave any information which might assist them in their ancestral quest."

THE ARTILLERYMAN, Cutter & Locke, Inc., Publishers, 4 Water St., Box C, Arlington MA 02174. (617)646-2010. FAX: (617)643-1864. Editor: C. Peter Jorgensen. 60% freelance written. Quarterly magazine covering antique artillery, fortifications, and crew-served weapons 1750 to 1900 for competition shooters, collectors and living history reenactors using artillery; "emphasis on Revolutionary War and Civil War but includes everyone interested in pre-1900 artillery and fortifications, preservation, construction of replicas, etc." Circ. 2,600. Pays on publication. Publishes ms an average of 3-6 months after acceptance. Byline given. Not copyrighted. Buys one-time rights. Simultaneous queries, and simultaneous, photocopied and previously published submissions OK. Computer printout submissions acceptable; prefers letter-quality. Reports in 3 weeks. Sample copy and writer's guidelines for 8½x11 SAE and 4 first class stamps.
Nonfiction: Historical/nostalgic; how-to (reproduce ordinance equipment/sights/implements/tools/accessories, etc.); interview/profile; new product; opinion (must be accompanied by detailed background of writer and include references); personal experience; photo feature; technical (must have footnotes); and travel (where to find interesting antique cannon). Interested in "artillery *only*, for sophisticated readers. Not interested in other weapons, battles in general." Buys 24-30 mss/year. Send complete ms. Length: 300 words minimum. Pays $20-60. Sometimes pays the expenses of writers on assignment.
Photos: Send photos with ms. Pays $5 for 5x7 and larger b&w prints. Captions and identification of subjects required.
Tips: "We regularly use freelance contributions for Places-to-Visit, Cannon Safety, The Workshop and Unit Profiles departments. Also need pieces on unusual cannon or cannon with a known and unique history. To judge whether writing style and/or expertise will suit our needs, writers should ask themselves if they could knowledgeably talk *artillery* with an expert. Subject matter is of more concern than writer's background."

‡CANADIAN WEST, Box 3399, Langley, British Columbia V3A 4R7 Canada. (604)534-9378. Editor-in-Chief: Garnet Basque. 80-100% freelance written. Works with a small number of new/unpublished writers each year. Emphasizes pioneer history, primarily of British Columbia, Alberta and the Yukon. Quarterly magazine; 48 pages. Circ. 8,000. Pays on publication. Publishes ms an average of 3 months after acceptance. Buys first North American serial rights. Phone queries OK. Electronic submissions acceptable via IBM compatible disks, but requires hard copy also. Computer printout submissions acceptable; prefers letter-quality to dot-matrix. Previously published submissions OK. Reports in 2 months. Sample copy and writer's guidelines for $1.50 and 9x12 SAE.

Nonfiction: How-to (related to gold panning and dredging); historical (pioneers, shipwrecks, massacres, battles, exploration, logging, Indians, ghost towns, mining camps, gold rushes and railroads). Interested in an occasional U.S. based article from states bordering B.C. when the story also involves some aspect of Canadian history. No American locale articles. Buys 28 mss/year. Submit complete ms. Length: 2,000-3,500 words. Pays $100-300.

Photos: All mss must include photos or other artwork. Submit photos with ms. Pays $10 per b&w photo and $20 per color photo. Captions preferred. "Photographs are kept for future reference with the right to re-use. However, we do not forbid other uses, generally, as these are historical prints from archives."

Columns/Departments: Open to suggestions for new columns/departments.

CHICAGO HISTORY, The Magazine of the Chicago Historical Society, Chicago Historical Society, Clark St. at North Ave., Chicago IL 60614. (312)642-4600. FAX: (312)266-2077. Editor: Russell Lewis. Associate Editor: Meg Moss. Assistant Editor: Aleta Zak. Editorial Assistant: Margaret Welsh. 100% freelance written. Works with a small number of new/unpublished writers each year. A quarterly magazine covering Chicago history: cultural, political, economic, social, architectural. Circ. 8,000. Pays on publication. Publishes ms an average of 6-12 months after acceptance. Byline given. Buys all rights. Submit seasonal/holiday material 9 months in advance. Photocopied submissions OK. Query for electronic submissions. Computer printout submissions acceptable; no dot-matrix. Reports in 6 weeks. Sample copy $3.25; free writer's guidelines.

Nonfiction: Book excerpts, essays, historical/nostalgic, interview/profile and photo feature. Articles to be "analytical, informative, and directed at a popular audience with a special interest in history." No "cute" articles. Buys 16-20 mss/year. Query; send complete ms. Length: approximately 4,500 words. Pays $250.

Photos: State availability of photos with submission and submit photocopies. Would prefer no originals. Offers no additional payment for photos accepted with ms. Identification of subjects required.

Columns/Departments: Book Reviews (Chicago and/or urban history), 500-750 words; and Review Essays (author reviews, comparatively, a compilation of several books on same topic—Chicago and/or urban history), 2,500 words. Buys 20 mss/year. Query; send complete ms. Pays $75-100 "but book review authors receive only one copy of book, no cash."

Tips: "A freelancer can best break in by 1) calling to discuss an article idea with editor; and 2) submitting a detailed outline of proposed article. All sections of *Chicago History* are open to freelancers, but we suggest that authors do not undertake to write articles for the magazine unless they have considerable knowledge of the subject and are willing to research it in some detail. We require a footnoted manuscript, although we do not publish the notes."

EL PALACIO, The Magazine of the Museum of New Mexico, Box 2087, Santa Fe NM 87504. (505)982-8594. Editor-in-Chief: Karen Meadows. 15% freelance written. Prefers to work with published/established writers. Emphasizes the collections of the Museum of New Mexico and anthropology, ethnology, history, folk and fine arts, Southwestern culture, and natural history as these topics pertain to the Museum of New Mexico and the Southwest. Triannual magazine; 64 pages. Circ. 4,500. Pays on publication. We hope "to attract professional writers who can translate scholarly and complex information into material that will interest and inform a general educated readership." Acquires first North American serial rights. Byline given. Submit seasonal/holiday queries 1 year in advance. Photocopied submissions OK. Query for electronic submissions. Computer printout submissions acceptable; no dot-matrix. Reports in 6 weeks. Sample copy $6 and 9x12 SAE with $1.85 postage. Writer's guidelines for #10 SASE.

Nonfiction: Historical (on Southwest; substantive but readable—not too technical); folk art; archaeology; fine art (Southwest); photo essay; anthropology; material culture of the Southwest. Buys 3-4 unsolicited mss/year. Recent articles documented the history of Las Vegas, New Mexico; women in New Mexico; collections of the Museum of New Mexico; and contemporary photography. "Other articles that have been very successful are a photo-essay on Chaco Canyon and other archaeological spots of interest in the state and an article on Indian baskets and their function in Indian life." Query with credentials. Length: 1,750-4,000 words. Pays $50 honorarium.

Photos: Photos often purchased with accompanying ms, some on assignment. Prefers b&w prints. Informative captions required. Pays "on contract" for 5x7 (or larger) b&w photos and 5x7 or 8½x11 prints or 35mm color transparencies. Send prints and transparencies. Total purchase price for ms includes payment for photos.

Columns/Departments: Curator's Choice and Books (reviews of interest to *El Palacio* readers).

Tips: "*El Palacio* magazine offers a unique opportunity for writers with technical ability to have their work published and seen by influential professionals as well as avidly interested lay readers. The magazine is highly regarded in its field. The writer should have strong writing skills, an understanding of the Southwest and of the field written about. Be able to communicate technical concepts to the educated reader. We like to have a bibliography, list of sources, or suggested reading list with nearly every submission."

‡**GHOST TOWN QUARTERLY**, William and Donna McLean, McLean Enterprises, Box 714, Philipsburg MT 59858. (406)859-3365. Editor: Donna B. McLean. 90% freelance written. Quarterly magazine on ghost towns & ghosted areas - U.S., Canada and Mexico. "Materials should be factual yet interesting to the general public. We want to present history in such a manner that we are a human-interest magazine yet valuable to historians." Estab. 1988. Circ. 6,000. Byline given. Offers $20 kill fee. Buys first North American serial rights, first rights, one-time rights, second serial (reprint) rights or simultaneous rights. Submit seasonal/holiday material 6 months in advance. Simultaneous, photocopied and (only occasionally) previously published submissions. Computer printout submissions OK. Reports in 3 weeks on queries; 3 months on mss. Sample copy for $3.50. Writer's guidelines for SAE with 1 first class stamp.

Nonfiction: General interest, historical/nostalgic, interview/profile, interesting, unusual up-coming events of a historical nature. Buys 80 mss/year. Send complete ms. Length: 300-6,500 words. Pays 5¢/word. Pays in contributor copies only if requested by the writer.

Photos: Send photos with submission. Reviews 5x7 prints, smaller or larger also OK. Also review picture postcards (old). Offers $5-50 per photo (cover photo). Captions required. Buys one-time rights.

Columns/Departments: Student's Corner (materials submitted by students from kindergarten thru 12th grade. 2 pages reserved in each issue for this feature. Follow same guidelines as for adult contributors. Photos, artwork, poetry, and articles acceptable.), 1,500 words maximum. Buys 30 mss/year. Send complete ms. Pays 5¢/word.

Poetry: Avant-garde, free verse, haiku, light verse and traditional. No foul language or lewdness. No extreme negativism unless it has in important purpose relevant to our themes. Buys 20 poems/year. Submit maximum 3 poems. Pays 5¢/word.

Fillers: Anecdotes, facts, gags to be illustrated by cartoonist, short humor and cartoons (pays $10). Buys 20/year. Length: 30-300 words. Pays $1.50-15.

Tips: "If submitting an article, research facts and include bibliographical information. Interview people who may have first-hand knowledge, and include interesting facts you uncover, quotes from diaries, photocopies of old documents and historical photographs when available. We like to feature the unusual, things people may not have realized before—such as silver being found in trees."

GOOD OLD DAYS, America's Premier Nostalgia Magazine, House of White Birches, 306 E. Parr Rd., Berne Indiana 46711. (219)589-8741. Editor: Edgar Harrison. Managing Editor: Rebekah Montgomery. 100% freelance written. A monthly magazine of first person nostalgia, 1900-1949. "We look for strong narratives showing life as it was in the first part of this century. Our readership is nostalgia buffs and history enthusiasts." Pays on publication. Publishes ms an average of 8 months after acceptance. Byline given. Buys all rights, first North American serial rights or one-time rights. Submit seasonal/holiday material 8 months in advance. Computer printout submissions OK; prefers letter-quality. Reports in 2 weeks. Sample copy $1.50; writer's guidelines for #10 SASE.

Nonfiction: Historical/nostalgic, humor, interview/profile, personal experience, photo feature. Buys 300 mss/year. Query or send complete ms. Length: 5,000 words maximum. Pays 2-4¢/word.

Photos: Send photos with submission. Offers $5/photo. Indentification of subjects required. Buys one-time or all rights.

MEDIA HISTORY DIGEST, Media History Digest Corp., % Editor and Publisher, 11 W. 19th St., New York NY 10011. Editor: Hiley H. Ward. 100% freelance written. Semiannual (will probably return to being quarterly) magazine. Circ. 2,000. Pays on publication. Publishes ms an average of 4 months after acceptance. Byline given. Buys first or second serial (reprint) rights. Submit seasonal/holiday material 8 months in advance. Previously published submissions OK. Reports in 2 months. Sample copy $2.50.

Nonfiction: Historical/nostalgic (media); humor (media history); and puzzles (media history). Buys 15 mss/year. Query. Length: 1,500-3,000 words. Pays $125 for assigned articles; pays $100 for unsolicited articles. Pays in contributor copies for articles prepared by university graduate students. Sometimes pays the expenses of writers on assignment.

Photos: Send photos with submission. Buys first or reprint rights.

Columns/Departments: Quiz Page (media history) and "Media Hysteria" (media history humor). Query. Pays $50-125 for humor; $25 for puzzles.

Fillers: Anecdotes and short humor on topics of media history.

Tips: "Present in-depth enterprising material targeted for our specialty—media history, pre-1970."

MILITARY HISTORY, Empire Press, 105 Loudoun St. SW, Leesburg VA 22075. (703)771-9400. Editor: C. Brian Kelly. 95% freelance written. Circ. 200,000. "We'll work with anyone, established or not, who can provide the goods and convince us as to its accuracy." Bimonthly magazine covering all military history of the world. "We strive to give the general reader accurate, highly readable, often narrative popular history, richly accompanied by period art." Pays on publication. Publishes ms 1-2 years after acceptance. Byline given. Buys first North American serial rights. Submit anniversary material 1 year in advance. Computer printout submissions acceptable; no dot-matrix. Reports in 2 months on queries; 6 months on mss. Sample copy $3.95; writer's guidelines for SAE with 1 first class stamp.

Nonfiction: Historical; interview (military figures of commanding interest); personal experience (only occasionally). Buys 18 mss, plus 6 interviews/year. Query with published clips. "To propose an article, submit a short, self-explanatory query summarizing the story proposed, its highlights and/or significance. State also your own expertise, access to sources or proposed means of developing the pertinent information." Length: 4,000 words. Pays $400.

Columns/Departments: Espionage, weaponry, personality, travel (with military history of the place) and books—all relating to military history. Buys 24 mss/year. Query with published clips. Length: 2,000 words. Pays $200.

Tips: "We would like journalistically 'pure' submissions that adhere to basics, such as full name at first reference, same with rank, and definition of prior or related events, issues cited as context or obscure military 'hardware.' Read the magazine, discover our style, and avoid subjects already covered. Pick stories with strong art possibilities (*real* art and photos), send photocopies, tell us where to order the art. Avoid historical overview, focus upon an event with appropriate and accurate context. Provide bibliography. Tell the story in popular but elegant style."

MILITARY IMAGES, RD2, Box 2542, East Stroudsburg PA 18301. (717)476-1388. Editor: Harry Roach. 100% freelance written. A bimonthly journal reaching a broad spectrum of military historians, antiquarians, collectors and dealers. *MI* covers American military history from 1839 to 1900, with heavy concentration on the Civil War. Circ. 3,000. Pays on publication. Byline given. Buys first North American serial rights. Submit seasonal/holiday material 2 months in advance. Photocopied submissions OK. Query for electronic submissions. Computer printout submissions OK; prefers letter-quality. Reports in 2 weeks on queries; 1 month on mss. Sample copy for $3; free writer's guidelines.

Nonfiction: Book excerpts, historical, humor, interview/profile, photo feature and technical. No articles not tied to, or illustrated by, period photos. Buys 36 mss/year. Query. Length: 1,000-12,000 words. Pays $40-200.

Photos: State availability of photos with submission, or send photocopy with query. Reviews 5x7 or larger b&w prints. Offers no additional payment for photos accepted with ms. Captions required.

Columns/Departments: The Darkroom (technical, 19th-century photo processes, preservation), 1,000 words. Buys 6 mss/year. Query. Length: 1,000-3,000 words. Pays $20-75.

Tips: "Concentrate on details of the common soldier, his uniform, his equipment, his organizations. We do not publish broad-brush histories of generals and campaigns. Articles must be supported by period photos."

OLD MILL NEWS, Society for the Preservation of Old Mills, 604 Ensley Dr., Rt. 29, Knoxville TN 37920. (615)577-7757. Editor: Michael LaForest. 70% freelance written. Quarterly magazine covering "water, wind, animal, steam power mills (usually grist mills)." Circ. 2,500. Pays on acceptance. Byline given. Buys first North American serial rights or first rights. Simultaneous and photocopied submissions OK. Computer printout submissions OK; prefers letter-quality. Reports in 2 weeks. Sample copy $3.

Nonfiction: Historical and technical. "No poetry, recipes, mills converted to houses, commercial, or alternative uses, nostalgia." Buys 8 mss/year. Query with or without published clips, or send complete ms. Length: 400-1,000 words. Pays $15-50.

Photos: Send photos with submission. "At least one recent photograph of subject is highly recommended." Uses b&w or color prints only; no transparencies. Offers $5-10 per photo. Identification of subjects required. Buys one-time rights.

Fillers: Short humor. Buys 3-4/year. Length: 50-200 words. Pays $10 maximum.

Tips: "An interview with the mill owner/operator is usually necessary. Accurate presentation of the facts and good English are required."

OLD WEST, Western Periodicals, Inc., Box 2107, Stillwater OK 74076. (405)743-3370. Quarterly magazine. Byline given. See *True West*.

PERSIMMON HILL, 1700 NE 63rd St., Oklahoma City OK 73111. Editor: Marcia Preston. 70% freelance written. Prefers to work with published/established writers and works with a small number of new/unpublished writers each year. For an audience interested in Western art, Western history, ranching and rodeo, including historians, artists, ranchers, art galleries, schools, and libraries. Publication of the National Cowboy Hall of Fame and Western Heritage Center. Quarterly. Circ. 15,000. Buys first rights. Byline given. Buys 12-14 mss/year. Pays on scheduling of article. Publishes ms an average of 6 months after acceptance. Reporting time on mss varies. Computer printout submissions acceptable; no dot-matrix. Sample copy $5 plus 5 first class stamps; writer's guidelines for #10 SASE.

Nonfiction: Historical and contemporary articles on famous Western figures connected with pioneering the American West, Western art, rodeo, cowboys, etc. (or biographies of such people), stories of Western flora and animal life, and environmental subjects. "We want thoroughly researched and historically authentic material written in a popular style. May have a humorous approach to subject. No broad, sweeping, superficial pieces; i.e., the California Gold Rush or rehashed pieces on Billy the Kid, etc." Length: 2,000-3,000 words. Query with clips. Pays $100-250; special work negotiated.

Photos: B&w glossy prints or color transparencies purchased with ms, or on assignment. Pays according to quality and importance for b&w and color photos. Suggested captions appreciated.
Tips: "Excellent illustrations for articles essential!"

PRESERVATION NEWS, National Trust for Historic Preservation, 1785 Massachusetts Ave. NW, Washington DC 20016. (202)673-4075. FAX: (202)673-4038. Editor: Arnold M. Berke. 30% freelance written. Prefers to work with published/established writers. A monthly tabloid covering preservation of historic buildings in the U.S. "We cover proposed or completed preservation projects and controversies involving historic buildings and districts. Most entries are news stories, features or opinion pieces." Circ. 200,000. Pays on publication. Publishes ms an average of 1 month after acceptance. Byline given. Offers variable kill fee. Buys one-time rights. Simultaneous queries, and photocopied and previously published submissions OK. Computer printout submissions acceptable. Reports in 2 months on queries. Sample copy for $1 and 10x14 SAE with 56¢ postage; writer's guidelines for SAE and 1 first class stamp.
Nonfiction: News, interview/profile, opinion, humor, personal experience, photo feature and travel. Buys 12 mss/year. Query with published clips. Length: 500-1,200 words. Pays $150-300. Sometimes pays the expenses of writers on assignment.
Photos: State availability of photos with query or ms. Reviews b&w contact sheet. Pays $25-100. Identification of subjects required.
Columns/Departments: "We seek an urban affairs reporter who can give a new slant on development conflict throughout the United States. We also are looking for foreign coverage, and profiles of preservation craftspersons." Buys 6 mss/year. Query with published clips. Length: 600-1,200 words. Pays $150-250.
Tips: "Do not send or propose histories of buildings, descriptive accounts of cities or towns or long-winded treatises on any subjects. This is a *newspaper*. Proposals for coverage of fast-breaking events are especially welcome."

TIMELINE, Ohio Historical Society, 1985 Velma Ave., Columbus OH 43211. (614)297-2360. Editor: Christopher S. Duckworth. 90% freelance written. Works with a small number of new/unpublished writers each year. A bimonthly magazine covering history, natural history, archaeology, and fine and decorative arts. Circ. 11,000. Pays on acceptance. Publishes ms an average of 1 year after acceptance. Byline given. Offers $75 minimum kill fee. Buys first North American serial rights or all rights. Submit seasonal/holiday material 6 months in advance. Photocopied submissions OK. Query for electronic submissions. Computer printout submissions acceptable; no dot-matrix. Reports in 3 weeks on queries; 6 weeks on manuscripts. Sample copy $5 and 8½x11 SAE. Writer's guidelines for #10 SASE.
Nonfiction: Book excerpts, essays, historical, profile (of individuals) and photo feature. Buys 22 mss/year. Query. Length: 500-6,000 words. Pays $100-900.
Photos: State availability of photos with submission. Will not consider submissions without ideas for illustration. Reviews contact sheets, transparencies, and 8x10 prints. Captions, model releases, and identification of subjects required. Buys one-time rights.
Tips: "We want crisply written, authoritative narratives for the intelligent lay reader. An Ohio slant may strengthen a submission, but it is not indispensable. Contributors must know enough about their subject to explain it clearly and in an interesting fashion. We use high-quality illustration with all features. If appropriate illustration is unavailable, we can't use the feature. The writer who sends illustration ideas with a manuscript has an advantage, but an often-published illustration won't attract us."

‡TRACES OF INDIANA AND MIDWESTERN HISTORY, Indiana Historical Society, 315 W Ohio St., Indianapolis IN 46202. (317)232-1884. Editor: Thomas Mason. Managing Editor: Kent Calder. 100% freelance written. Quarterly magazine on Indiana and Midwestern history. Estab. 1989. Circ. 7,000. Pays on acceptance. Publishes ms an average of 6 months after acceptance. Byline given. Buys one-time rights. Submit seasonal/holiday material 1 year in advance. Previously published submissions OK. Computer printout submissions OK; prefers letter-quality. Reports in 3 months on mss. Sample copy $5; free writer's guidelines.
Nonfiction: Book excerpts, essays, historical/nostalgic and photo feature. Buys 20 mss/year. Send complete ms. Length: 2,000-5,000 words. Pays $100-500.
Photos: State availability of photos with submission. Reviews contact sheets, transparencies and prints. Offers $10-30 per photo. Captions, model releases and identification of subjects required. Buys one-time rights.
Columns/Departments: Profile; Midwestern Made and Now and Then (Editors seek short articles on significant people, places, and artifacts in Indiana and Midwestern history.), 750-1,500 words. Query. Pays $50-100.
Tips: "Freelancers should be aware of prerequisites for writing history in general and popular history in particular. Should have some awareness of other magazines of this type published by midwestern and western historical societies. Preference is sometimes given to subjects with an Indiana connection. Quality of potential illustration is also important. Departments are not yet fully developed. Editors will consider queries in regard to departments on any aspect of midwestern history, including art, politics, sports, industry, transportation, etc. Freelancers should submit at least 3 fully developed mss. for each department."

TRUE WEST, Western Periodicals, Inc., Box 2107, Stillwater OK 74076. (405)743-3370. Editor: John Joerschke. 100% freelance written. Works with a small number of new/unpublished writers each year. Magazine on Western American history before 1940. "We want reliable research on significant historical topics written in lively prose for an informed general audience." Circ. 30,000. Pays on acceptance. Publishes ms an average of 4 months after acceptance. Byline given. Buys first North American serial rights. Submit seasonal/holiday material 6 months in advance. Simultaneous queries OK. Computer printout submissions acceptable; prefers letter-quality. Reports in 1 month on queries; 6 weeks on mss. Sample copy for 8½x11 SAE and $2; writer's guidelines for #10 SAE and 1 first class stamp.
Nonfiction: Historical/nostalgic, how-to, photo feature and travel. "We do not want rehashes of worn-out stories, historical fiction, or history written in a fictional style." Buys 150 mss/year. Query. Length: 500-4,500 words. Pays 3-5¢/word.
Photos: Send photos with accompanying query or manuscript. Pays $10 for b&w prints. Identification of subjects required. Buys one-time rights.
Columns/Departments: Western Roundup—200-300 word short articles on historically oriented places to go and things to do in the West with one b&w print. Buys 12-16 mss/year. Send complete ms. Pays $35.
Tips: "Do original research on fresh topics. Stay away from controversial subjects unless you are truly knowledgeable in the field. Read our magazines and follow our writer's guidelines. A freelancer is most likely to break in with us by submitting thoroughly researched, lively prose on relatively obscure topics. First person accounts rarely fill our needs."

VIRGINIA CAVALCADE, Virginia State Library and Archives, Richmond VA 23219-3491. (804)786-2312. Primarily for readers with an interest in Virginia history. 90% freelance written. "Both established and new writers are invited to submit articles." Quarterly magazine. Circ. 12,000. Buys all rights. Byline given. Pays on acceptance. Publishes ms an average of 6-12 months after acceptance. Rarely considers simultaneous submissions. Submit seasonal material 15-18 months in advance. Reports in 1-3 months. Computer printout submissions acceptable; prefers letter-quality. Sample copy $2; free writer's guidelines.
Nonfiction: "We welcome readable and factually accurate articles that are relevant to some phase of Virginia history. Art, architecture, literature, education, business, technology and transportation are all acceptable subjects, as well as political and military affairs. Articles must be based on thorough, scholarly research. We require footnotes but do not publish them. Any period from the age of exploration to the mid-20th century, and any geographical section or area of the state may be represented. Must deal with subjects that will appeal to a broad readership, rather than to a very restricted group or locality. Articles must be suitable for illustration, although it is not necessary that the author provide the pictures. If the author does have pertinent illustrations or knows their location, the editor appreciates information concerning them." Buys 12-15 mss/year. Query. Length: 3,500-4,500 words. Pays $100.
Photos: Uses 8x10 b&w glossy prints; color transparencies should be at least 4x5.
Tips: "*Cavalcade* employs a narrative, anecdotal style. Too many submissions are written for an academic audience or are simply not sufficiently gripping."

WILD WEST, Empire Press, 105 Loudoun St. SW, Leesburg VA 22075. (703)771-9400. Editor: William M. Vogt. 95% freelance written. Bimonthly magazine on history of the American West. "*Wild West* covers the popular (narrative) history of the American West—events, trends, personalities, anything of general interest." Estab. 1988. Circ. 75,000. Pays on publication. Byline given. Buys first North American serial rights. Submit seasonal/holiday material 1 year in advance. Query for electronic submissions. Computer printout submissions OK; no dot-matrix. Sample copy $3.95; writer's guidelines for #10 SASE.
Nonfiction: Historical/nostalgic, humor, travel. No fiction or poetry—nothing current. Buys 24 mss/year. Query. Length: 4,000 words. Pays $300.
Photos: State availability of photos with submission. Captions and identification of subjects required. Buys one-time rights or all rights.
Columns/Departments: Travel; Gun Fighters & Lawmen; Personalities; Warriors & Chiefs; Books Reviews. Buys 16 mss/year. Length: 2,000. Pays $150 for departments, by the word for book reviews.

Hobby and Craft

Magazines in this category range from gem collecting to home video. Craftspeople and hobbyists who read these magazines want new ideas while collectors need to know what is most valuable and why. Collectors, do-it-yourselfers and craftspeople look to these magazines for inspiration, research and information. Publications covering antiques and miniatures are also listed here, while additional publications for electronics and radio hobbyists are included in the Science classification.

THE ANTIQUE TRADER WEEKLY, Box 1050, Dubuque IA 52001. (319)588-2073. Editor: Kyle D. Husfloen. 50% freelance written. Works with a small number of new/unpublished writers each year. For collectors and dealers in antiques and collectibles. Weekly newspaper; 90-120 pages. Circ. 90,000. Publishes ms an average of 1 year after acceptance. Buys all rights. Payment at beginning of month following publication. Photocopied and simultaneous submissions OK. Computer printout submissions acceptable; no dot-matrix. Submit seasonal/holiday material 4 months in advance. Sample copy 50¢; free writer's guidelines.
Nonfiction: "We invite authoritative and well-researched articles on all types of antiques and collectors' items and in-depth stories on specific types of antiques and collectibles. No human interest stories. We do not pay for brief information on new shops opening or other material printed as a service to the antiques hobby." Buys about 60 mss/year. Query or submit complete ms. Pays $5-75 for feature articles; $75-150 for feature cover stories.
Photos: Submit a liberal number of good b&w photos to accompany article. Uses 35mm or larger color transparencies for cover. Offers no additional payment for photos accompanying mss.
Tips: "Send concise, polite letter stating the topic to be covered in the story and the writer's qualifications. No 'cute' letters rambling on about some 'imaginative' story idea. Writers who have a concise yet readable style and know their topic are always appreciated. I am most interested in those who have personal collecting experience or can put together a knowledgeable and informative feature after interviewing a serious collector/authority."

ANTIQUES & AUCTION NEWS, Route 230 West, Box 500, Mount Joy PA 17552. (717)653-9797, ext. 254. Editor: Doris Ann Johnson. Works with a small number of new/unpublished writers each year. A weekly tabloid for dealers and buyers of antiques, nostalgics and collectibles, and those who follow antique shows, shops and auctions. Circ. 40,000. Pays on publication. Submit seasonal/holiday material 3 months in advance. Computer printout submissions OK; no dot-matrix. Free sample copy available if you mention *Writer's Market*. Writer's guidelines for #10 SASE.
Nonfiction: "Our readers are interested in collectibles and antiques dating approximately from the Civil War to the present, originating in the U.S. or western Europe. We normally will consider any story on a collectible or antique if it is well-written, slanted toward helping collectors, buyers and dealers learn more about the field, and is focused on the aspect of collecting. This could be an historical perspective, a specific area of collecting, an especially interesting antique or unusual collection. Issues have included material on old Christmas ornaments, antique love tokens, collections of fans, pencils and pottery, and 'The Man from U.N.C.L.E.' books and magazines. Articles may be how-to, informational research, news and reporting and even an occasional photo feature." Call or write before submitting any manuscript. Length: 1,000 words or less preferred, but will consider up to 2,000 words. Pays $12.50 for articles without photos; $15 for articles with usable photos. "We also accept an occasional short article—about one typed page, with a good photo—for which we will pay $7.50, $5 without photo."
Photos: Purchased as part of ms package. "We prefer b&w photos, usually of a single item against a simple background. Color photos can be used if there is good contrast between darks and lights." Captions required.

BASEBALL CARDS, Krause Publications, 700 E. State St., Iola WI 54990. (715)445-2214. FAX: (715)445-4087. Editor: Kit Kiefer. 50% freelance written. A monthly magazine covering sports memorabilia collecting. "Geared for the novice collector or general public who might become interested in the hobby." Circ. 230,000. Pays on publication. Publishes ms an average of 6 months after acceptance. Byline given. Buys first North American serial rights and second serial (reprint) rights. Submit seasonal/holiday material 6 months in advance. Photocopied submissions OK. Computer printout submissions acceptable; no dot-matrix. Reports in 2 weeks. Sample copy for 8½x11 SAE with 3 first class stamps. Writer's guidelines for #10 SASE.
Nonfiction: General interest, historical/nostalgic, how-to (enjoy or enhance your collection) and photo feature. No personal reminiscences of collecting baseball cards as a kid or articles that relate to baseball, rather than cards. Buys 36-50 mss/year. Query. Length: 2,000-4,000 words. Pays up to $400.
Photos: Send photos with submission. Reviews contact sheets and transparencies. Payment negotiated. Identification of subjects required.
Tips: "We would like to receive knowledgeable features on specific collectibles: card sets, team items, etc. We want to identify the collecting trends of the 90s and be the first to report on them."

BECKETT BASEBALL CARD MONTHLY, Statabase, Inc., Suite 110, 3410 MidCourt, Carrollton TX 75006. (214)991-6657. Editor: Dr. James Beckett. Managing Editor: Fred Reed. 85% freelance written. Monthly magazine on baseball card and sports memorabilia collecting. "Our readers expect our publication to be entertaining and informative. Our slant is that hobbies are for fun and rewarding. Especially wanted are how-to collect articles." Circ. 300,000. Pays on acceptance. Publishes ms an average of 4 months after acceptance. Byline given. Pays $50 kill fee. Buys first North American serial rights. Submit seasonal/holiday material

6 months in advance. "No simultaneous submissions, please!" Query for electronic submissions. Computer printout submissions OK; prefers letter-quality. Reports in 1 month. Sample copy $2.50; free writer's guidelines.

Nonfiction: Book excerpts, historical/nostalgic, how-to, humor, interview/profile, new product, opinion, personal experience, photo feature, technical. Special issues include: March (spring training/new card sets issued); July (Hall of Fame/All Star Game issue); October (World Series issue); November (autograph special issue). No articles that emphasize speculative prices and investments. Buys 145 mss/year. Send complete ms. Length: 300-2,000 words. Pays $100-400 for assigned articles; $50-200 for unsolicited articles. Sometimes pays expenses of writers on assignment.

Photos: Send photos with submission. Reviews 35mm transparencies, 5x7 or larger prints. Offers $10-200 per photo. Captions, model releases and identification of subjects required. Buys one-time rights.

Columns/Departments: Pepper Hastings, editor. Autograph Experiences (memorable experience with baseball star), 50-400 words; Prospects (players on the verge of major league stardom), 300-500 words; Collecting Tips (basic but overlooked helpful hints), 300-500 words; Trivia (major league baseball odd or humorous facts), 20-50 words; Player Vignettes (general baseball articles featuring emerging or proven superstars). Buys 60 mss/years. Send complete ms. Length: 50-400 words. Pays $25-100.

Fiction: Humorous only.

Tips: "A writer for *Becket Baseball Card Monthly* should be an avid sports fan and/or a collector with an enthusiasm for sharing his/her interests with others. First person (not research) articles presenting the writer's personal experiences told with wit and humor, and emphasizing the stars of the game, are *always* wanted. Acceptable articles must be of interest to our two basic reader segments: teenaged boys and their middle-aged fathers who are reexperiencing a nostalgic renaissance of their own childhoods. Prospective writers should write down to neither group!"

THE COIN ENTHUSIAST'S JOURNAL, Masongate Publishing, Box 1383, Torrance CA 90505. Editor: William J. Cook. 50% freelance written. Prefers to work with published/established writers, and works with a small number of new/unpublished writers each year. Monthly newsletter covering numismatics (coin collecting) and bullion trading. "Our purpose is to give readers information to help them make sound investment decisions in the areas we cover and to help them get more enjoyment out of their hobby." Circ. 2,000. Pays on publication. Publishes ms an average of 2 months after acceptance. Byline given. Offers $25 kill fee. Buys all rights. Submit seasonal/holiday material 3 months in advance. Simultaneous queries and simultaneous and photocopied submissions OK. Computer printout submissions acceptable; prefers letter-quality. Reports in 3 weeks. Sample copy for $1 and #10 SAE with 2 first class stamps (must mention *Writer's Market*). Guidelines sent free with sample when requested.

Nonfiction: How-to (make money from your hobby and be a better trader); opinion (what is the coin market going to do?); personal experience (insiders' "tricks of the trade"); and technical (why are coin prices going up [or down]?). No "crystal ball" predictions, i.e., "I see silver going up to $200 per ounce by mid-1989." Query with published clips. Length: 500-2,500 words. Buys 36-40 mss/year. Pays mostly $75-100. Also looking for "staff writers" who will submit material each month or bimonthly.

Photos: State availability of photos with query. Pays $5-25 for b&w prints. Buys one-time rights.

Tips: "Occasionally we buy cartoons. We are buying a few more short articles but the majority are longer articles (i.e.1,500 words and up). We are also buying more 'human interest' and humorous articles. More entertainment as opposed to just technical information. Try to make articles interesting—we get *too* much dry, boring stuff."

COINS, Krause Publications, 700 E. State St., Iola WI 54990. (715)445-2214. Editor: Arlyn G. Sieber. 75% freelance written. Eager to work with new/unpublished writers. Monthly magazine about U.S. and foreign coins for all levels of collectors, investors and dealers. Circ. 65,000. Computer printout submissions acceptable; prefers letter-quality. Sample copy and writer's guidelines free upon request.

Nonfiction: "We'd like to see articles on any phase of the coin hobby; collection, investing, displaying, history, art, the story behind the coin, unusual collections, profiles on dealers and the business of coins." No news items. "Our staff covers the hard news." Buys 8 mss/issue. Send complete ms. Length: 500-5,000 words. Pays 3¢/word to first-time contributors; fee negotiated for later articles. Sometimes pays the expenses of writers on assignment.

Photos: Pays $5 minimum for b&w prints. Pays $25 minimum for 35mm color transparencies used. Captions and model releases required. Buys first rights.

‡COLLECTOR EDITIONS QUARTERLY, Collector Communications Corp., 170 5th Ave., New York NY 10010. (212)989-8700. Editor: R. C. Rowe. Managing Editor: Joan Muyskens Pursley. 40% freelance written. Works with a small number of new/unpublished writers each year. Bimonthly magazine on porcelain and glass collectibles. "We specialize in contemporary (post-war ceramic and glass) collectibles, including reproductions, but also publish articles about antiques, if they are being reproduced today and are generally available."Circ. 80,000. Rights purchased vary with author and material. Buys first North American serial rights and sometimes second serial (reprint) rights. "First assignments are always done on a speculative basis."

Pays within 30 days of acceptance. Publishes ms an average of 6 months after acceptance. Photocopied submissions OK. Computer printout submissions acceptable; no dot-matrix. Reports in 2 months. Sample copy $2; writer's guidelines for #10 SASE.

Nonfiction: "Short features about collecting, written in tight, newsy style. We specialize in contemporary (postwar) collectibles. Values for pieces being written about should be included." Informational, how-to, interview, profile, exposé and nostalgia. Buys 8-10 mss/year. Query with sample photos. Length: 500-2,500 words. Pays $100-300. Sometimes pays expenses of writers on assignments.

Columns/Departments: Columns cover porcelain, glass, auction reports and artist profiles. Query. Length: 750 words. Pays $75.

Photos: B&w and color photos purchased with accompanying ms with no additional payment. Captions are required. "We want clear, distinct, full-frame images that say something."

Tips: "Unfamiliarity with the field is the most frequent mistake made by writers in completing an article for us."

COLLECTORS NEWS & THE ANTIQUE REPORTER, 506 2nd St., Box 156, Grundy Center IA 50638. (319)824-5456. Editor: Linda Kruger. 20% freelance written. Works with a small number of new/unpublished writers each year. A monthly tabloid covering antiques, collectibles and nostalgic memorabilia. Circ. 15,000. Byline given. Pays on publication. Publishes ms an average of 1 year after acceptance. Buys first rights and makes work-for-hire assignments. Submit seasonal material (holidays) 3 months in advance. Computer printout submissions acceptable. Reports in 2 weeks on queries; 6 weeks on mss. Sample copy for $2 and 9x12 SAE; free writer's guidelines.

Nonfiction: General interest (any subject re: collectibles, antique to modern); historical/nostalgic (relating to collections or collectors); how-to (display your collection, care for, restore, appraise, locate, add to, etc.); interview/profile (covering individual collectors and their hobbies, unique or extensive; celebrity collectors, and limited edition artists); technical (in-depth analysis of a particular antique, collectible or collecting field); and travel (coverage of special interest or regional shows, seminars, conventions – or major antique shows, flea markets; places collectors can visit, tours they can take, museums, etc.). Special issues include January and June show/flea market issues; and usual seasonal emphasis. Buys 100 mss/year. Query with sample of writing. Length: 1,200-1,600 words. Pays 75¢/column inch; $1/column inch for color features.

Photos: Reviews b&w prints and 35mm color slides. Payment for photos included in payment for ms. Captions required. Buys first rights.

Tips: Articles most open to freelancers are on celebrity collectors; collectors with unique and/or extensive collections; music collectibles; transportation collectibles; advertising collectibles; bottles; glass, china and silver; primitives; furniture; toys; political collectibles; and movie memorabilia.

CRAFTS 'N THINGS, 14 Main St., Park Ridge IL 60068. (312)825-2161. Editor: Nancy Tosh. Associate Editor: Jackie Thielen. Published 8 times a year, covering quality crafts for today's creative woman. Circ. 320,000. Pays on publication. Byline, photo and brief bio given. Buys first North American serial rights. Submit seasonal/holiday material 6 months in advance. Reports in 1 month. Free sample copy.

Nonfiction: How-to (do a craft project). Buys 7-14 mss/issue. "Send in a photo of the item and complete directions. We will consider it and return if not accepted." Length: 1-4 magazine pages. Pays $50-200, "depending on how much staff work is required."

Photos: "Generally, we will ask that you send the item so we can photograph it ourselves."

Tips: "We're looking more for people who can craft than people who can write."

DECORATIVE ARTIST'S WORKBOOK, F&W Publishing, 1507 Dana Ave., Cincinnati OH 45207. Editorial Director: Michael Ward. 50% freelance written. Bimonthly magazine covering tole and decorative painting and related art forms. Offers "straightforward, personal instruction in the techniques of tole and decorative painting." Circ. 100,000. Pays on acceptance. Byline given. Offers 20% kill fee. Buys first North American serial rights. Submit seasonal/holiday material 6 months in advance. Photocopied submissions OK. Computer printout submissions OK; no dot-matrix. Reports in 1 month. Sample copy for $2.95 with 9x12 SAE and 7 first class stamps.

Nonfiction: How-to (related to tole and decorative painting), new product and technical. No profiles and/or general interest topics. Buys 30 mss/year. Query with slides or photos. Length: 1,200-1,800 words. Pays 10-12¢/word.

Photos: State availability of photos and slides with submission or send photos with submission. Reviews 35mm, 4x5 transparencies or good quality photos. Offers no additional payment for photos accepted with ms. Captions required. Buys one-time rights.

Fillers: Anecdotes, facts and short humor. Buys 10/year. Length: 50-200 words. Pays $10-20.

Tips: "The more you know – and can prove you know – about decorative painting the better your chances. I'm looking for experts in the field who, through their own experience, can artfully describe the techniques involved. How-to articles are most open to freelancers. Be sure to query with slides or transparencies, and show that you understand the extensive graphic requirements for these pieces and are able to provide progressives – slides that show works in progress."

DOLLS, The Collector's Magazine, Collector Communications Corp., 170 5th Ave., New York NY 10010. (212)989-8700. Editor: Krystyna Poray Goddu. 75% freelance written. Works with a small number of new/unpublished writers each year. Bimonthly magazine covering doll collecting "for collectors of antique, contemporary and reproduction dolls. We publish well-researched, professionally written articles that are illustrated with photographs of high quality, color or black-and-white." Circ. 70,000. Pays within 1 month of acceptance. Publishes ms an average of 6 months after acceptance. Byline given. "Almost all first manuscripts are on speculation. We rarely kill assigned stories, but fee would be about 33% of article fee." Buys first serial rights, first North American serial rights ("almost always"), second serial rights if piece has appeared in a non-competing publication. Submit seasonal/holiday material 6 months in advance. Photocopied submissions considered (not preferred); previously published submissions OK. Computer printout submissions acceptable; no dot-matrix. Reports in 2 months. Sample copy $2; writer's guidelines for #10 SASE.

Nonfiction: Book excerpts; historical (with collecting angle); interview/profile (on collectors with outstanding collections); new product (just photos and captions; "we do not pay for these, but regard them as publicity"); opinion ("A Personal Definition of Dolls"); technical (doll restoration advice by experts only); and travel (museums and collections around the world). "No sentimental, uninformed 'my doll collection' or 'my grandma's doll collection' stories or trade magazine-type stories on shops, etc. Our readers are knowledgeable collectors." Query with clips. Length: 500-2,500 words. Pays $100-350. Sometimes pays expenses of writers on assignment.

Photos: Send photos with accompanying query or ms. Reviews 4x5 color transparencies; 4x5 or 8x10 b&w prints and also 35mm slides. "We do not buy photographs submitted without manuscripts unless we have assigned them; we pay for the manuscript/photos package in one fee." Captions required. Buys one-time rights.

Columns/Departments: Doll Views—a miscellany of news and views of the doll world includes reports on upcoming or recently held events. "*Not* the place for new dolls, auction prices or dates; we have regular contributors or staff assigned to those columns." Query with clips if available or send complete ms. Length: 200-500 words. Pays $25-75. Doll Views items are rarely bylined.

Fillers: "We don't really use fillers but would consider them if we got something very good. Hints on restoring, for example, or a nice illustration." Length: 500 words maximum. Pays $25-75.

Tips: "We need experts in the field who are also good writers. The most frequent mistake made by writers in completing an article assignment for us is being unfamiliar with the field; our readers are very knowledgeable. Freelancers who are not experts should know their particular story thoroughly and do background research to get the facts correct. Well-written queries from writers outside the NYC area are especially welcomed. Non-experts should stay away from technical or specific subjects (restoration, price trends). Short profiles of unusual collectors or a story of a local museum collection, with good photos, might catch our interest. Editors want to know they are getting something from a writer they cannot get from anyone else. Good writing should be a given, a starting point. After that, it's what you know."

EARLY AMERICAN LIFE, Cowles Magazines, Inc. Box 8200, Harrisburg PA 17105. Editor: Frances Carnahan. 60-70% freelance written. Bimonthly magazine for "people who are interested in capturing the warmth and beauty of the 1600 to 1840 period and using it in their homes and lives today. They are interested in arts, crafts, travel, restoration and collecting." Circ. 300,000. Buys all rights. Buys 50 mss/year. Pays on acceptance. Publishes ms an average of 1 year after acceptance. Photocopied submissions OK. Computer printout submissions OK; no dot-matrix. Sample copy and writer's guidelines for 9x12 SAE and 4 first class stamps. Reports in 1 month. Query or submit complete ms with SASE.

Nonfiction: "Social history (the story of the people, not epic heroes and battles), travel to historic sites, country inns, antiques and reproductions, refinishing and restoration, architecture and decorating. We try to entertain as we inform. While we're always on the lookout for good pieces on any of our subjects, the 'travel to historic sites' theme is most frequently submitted. Would like to see more on how real people did something great to their homes." Buys 40 mss/year. Query or submit complete ms. Length: 750-3,000 words. Pays $50-600. Pays expenses of writers on assignment.

Photos: Pays $10 for 5x7 (and up) b&w photos used with mss, minimum of $25 for color. Prefers 2¼x2¼ and up, but can work from 35mm.

Tips: "Our readers are eager for ideas on how to bring early America into their lives. Conceive a new approach to satisfy their related interests in arts, crafts, travel to historic sites, and especially in houses decorated in the early American style. Write to entertain and inform at the same time, and be prepared to help us with illustrations, or sources for them."

‡ELECTRONICS EXPERIMENTERS HANDBOOK, Gernsback Publications, Inc., 500 B Bi-County Blvd., Farmingdale NY 11735. (516)293-3000. Editor: Brian C. Fenton. 100% freelance written. Annual magazine on hobby electronics. "Radio *Electronics Experimenters Handbook* is directed toward projects. It combines the best articles published in radio-electronics with new features and updates." Circ. 150,000. Buys all rights. Submit seasonal/holiday material 6 months in advance. Simultaneous submission OK. Query for electronic submissions. Computer printout submissions OK; prefers letter-quality. Free sample copy and writer's guidelines.

Nonfiction: How-to (project construction), humor (cartoons) and new product. Buys 150-200 mss/year. Send complete ms. Length: 1,000-10,000 words. Pays $200-800 for assigned articles; $100-800 for unsolicited articles.

Photos: Send photos with submission. Offers no additional payment for photos accepted with ms. Captions, model releases and identification of subjects required. Buys all rights.

FIBERARTS, The Magazine of Textiles, Nine Press, 50 College St., Asheville NC 28801. (704)253-0467. Editor: Ann Batchelder. 100% freelance written. Eager to work with new/unpublished writers; works with a small number of new/unpublished writers each year. Magazine appears 5 times/year, covering textiles as art and craft (weaving, quilting, surface design, stitchery, knitting, fashion, crochet, etc.) for textile artists, craftspeople, hobbyists, teachers, museum and gallery staffs, collectors and enthusiasts. Circ. 23,000. Pays 60 days after publication. Publishes ms an average of 4 months after acceptance. Byline given. Offers 50% kill fee. Buys first rights. Submit seasonal/holiday material 8 months in advance. Editorial guidelines and style sheet available. Computer printout submissions acceptable; prefers letter-quality. Reports within 2 weeks. Sample copy $4 and 10x12 SAE with 2 first class stamps; writer's guidelines for #10 SAE with 2 first class stamps.

Nonfiction: Book excerpts; historical/nostalgic; how-to; humor; interview/profile; opinion; personal experience; photo feature; technical; travel (for the textile enthusiast, e.g., collecting rugs in Turkey); and education, trends, exhibition reviews and textile news. Buys 25-50 mss/year. Query. "Please be very specific about your proposal. Also an important consideration in accepting an article is the kind of photos—35mm slides and/or b&w glossies—that you can provide as illustration. We like to see photos in advance." Length: 250-1,200 words. Pays $40-300, depending on article. Sometimes (rarely) pays the expenses of writers on assignment.

Tips: "Our writers are very familiar with the textile field, and this is what we look for in a new writer. Familiarity with textile techniques, history or events determines clarity of an article more than a particular style of writing. The writer should also be familiar with *Fiberarts*, the magazine. We outline our upcoming issues in regular Editorial Agendas far enough in advance for a prospective writer to be aware of our future needs."

‡FINE WOODWORKING, The Taunton Press, 63 S. Main St., Box 355, Newtown CT 06470. (203)426-8171. Editor: Dick Burrows. Bimonthly magazine on woodworking in the small shop. "All writers are also skilled woodworkers. It's more important that a contributor be a woodworker than a writer. Our editors (also woodworkers) will fix the words." Circ. 280,000. Pays on publication. Byline given. Kill fee varies; "editorial discretion." Buys first rights and rights to republish in anthologies and use in promo pieces. Submit seasonal/ holiday material 6 months in advance. Simultaneous and photocopied submissions OK. Query for electronic submissions. Computer printout submissions OK; prefers letter-quality. Reports in 2 months. Sample copy $4.50.

Nonfiction: How-to (woodworking). Buys 120 mss/year. "No specs—our editors would rather see more than less." Pays $150 per magazine page. Sometimes pays expenses of writers on assignment.

Photos: Send photos with submission. Reviews contact sheets, negatives, transparencies and prints. Captions, model releases and identification of subjects required. Buys one-time rights.

Columns/Departments: Notes & Comment (topics of interest to woodworkers); Question & Answer (woodworking Q & A); Follow-Up (information on past articles/readers' comments); and Methods of Work (shop tips). Buys 400 items/year. Length varies. Pays $10 minumum-150/published page.

Tips: "Send for authors guidelines and follow them. Stories about woodworking reported by non-woodworkers *not* used. Our magazine is essentially reader-written by woodworkers."

FINESCALE MODELER, Kalmbach Publishing Co., 21027 Crossroads Circle, Box 1612, Waukesha WI 53187. (414)272-2060. Editor: Bob Hayden. 80% freelance written. Eager to work with new/unpublished writers. Magazine published 8 times/year "devoted to how-to-do-it modeling information for scale model builders who build non-operating aircraft, tanks, boats, automobiles, figures, dioramas, and science fiction and fantasy models." Circ. 80,000. Pays on acceptance. Publishes ms an average of 14 months after acceptance. Byline given. Buys all rights. Computer printout submissions acceptable; prefers letter-quality. Reports in 6 weeks on queries; 3 months on mss. Sample copy for 9x12 SAE and 3 first class stamps; free writer's guidelines.

Nonfiction: How-to (build scale models); and technical (research information for building models). Query or send complete ms. Length: 750-3,000 words. Pays $30/published page minimum.

Photos: Send photos with ms. Pays $7.50 minimum for color transparencies and $5 minimum for 5x7 b&w prints. Captions and identification of subjects required. Buys one-time rights.

Columns/Departments: *FSM* Showcase (photos plus description of model); and *FSM* Tips and Techniques (modelbuilding hints and tips). Buys 25-50 Tips and Techniques/year. Query or send complete ms. Length: 100-1,000 words. Pays $5-75.

Tips: "A freelancer can best break in first through hints and tips, then through feature articles. Most people who write for *FSM* are modelers first, writers second. This is a specialty magazine for a special, quite expert audience. Essentially, 99% of our writers will come from that audience."

GEM SHOW NEWS, Shows of Integrity, Rt. #2, Box 78, Blue Ridge TX 75004. (214)752-5192. Editor: Judi Tripp. Managing Editor: Stacy Hobbs. 50% freelance written. A bimonthly newspaper on precious stones, mineral collecting and jewelry. "Slant should be gem/collectible investments including gold, gold coins, silver, silver jewelry and original silver designs." Circ. 12,000-30,000. Pays on acceptance. Publishes ms an average of 2 months after acceptance. Byline given. Publication not copyrighted. Buys first rights and makes work-for-hire assignments. Submit seasonal/holiday material 4 months in advance. Simultaneous, photocopied and previously published submissions OK. Computer printout submissions OK; prefers letter-quality. Reports in 6 weeks. Sample copy for 9x12 SAE and 5 first class stamps. Writer's guidelines for #10 SASE.
Nonfiction: How-to (gem collecting; gem cutting/collecting), humor, interview/profile, new product, personal experience, photo feature, technical, travel. Buys 30 mss/year. Send complete ms. Length: 1,000-3,000 words. Pays $50-150.
Photos: Send photos with submission. Reviews prints (3x5). Offers $5-10/photo. Captions, model releases and identification of subjects required. Buys one-time rights.
Fillers: Anecdotes, facts, gags to be illustrated by cartoonist, newsbreaks, short humor. Buys 30 mss/year. Length: 500 words maximum. Pays $10-25.
Tips: "Attend gem and jewelry shows to see the interest in this field. The gem and mineral collecting field is the second most popular hobby (second only to coin and stamp collecting) in the U.S. All areas are open, including current fads and trends such as articles on the current quartz crystals and crystal healing craze and related subjects."

HANDWOVEN, Interweave Press, 306 N. Washington, Loveland CO 80537. (303)669-7672. Editor: Jane Patrick. 75% freelance written. Bimonthly magazine (except July) covering handweaving, spinning and dyeing. Audience includes "practicing textile craftsmen. Article should show considerable depth of knowledge of subject, although tone should be informal and accessible." Circ. 35,000. Pays on publication. Publishes ms an average of 10 months after acceptance. Byline given. Pays 50% kill fee. Buys first North American serial rights. Simultaneous queries and photocopied submissions OK. Computer printout submissions acceptable; prefers letter-quality. Sample copy $4.50; writer's guidelines for #10 SASE.
Nonfiction: Historical and how-to (on weaving and other craft techniques; specific items with instructions); and technical (on handweaving, spinning and dyeing technology). "All articles must contain a high level of in-depth information. Our readers are very knowledgeable about these subjects." Query. Length: 500-2,000 words. Pays $35-150.
Photos: State availability of photos. Identification of subjects required.
Tips: "We prefer work written by writers with an in-depth knowledge of weaving. We're particularly interested in articles about new weaving and spinning techniques as well as applying these techniques to finished products."

‡HEDDLE MAGAZINE, Muskoka Publications Group, Box 1600, Bracebridge, Ontario P0B 1C0 Canada. (705)645-4463. FAX (705)645-3928. Editor: Verna Wilson. Managing Editor: Doug Brenner. 90% freelance written. Bimonthly magazine on weaving and spinning. "Magazine caters to skilled spinners and weavers designs, patterns etc." Circ. 3,000. Pays on publication. Publishes ms an average of 2 months after acceptance. Byline given. Buys second serial (reprint) rights. Submit seasonal/holiday material 2 months in advance. Simultaneous submissions OK. Computer printout submissions OK; prefers letter-quality. Reports in 2 weeks. Free sample copy and writer's guidelines.
Nonfiction: Book excerpts, general interest, how-to, humor, inspirational, interview/profile, new product, opinion, personal experience, technical and book reviews. Buys 50 mss/year. Query with or without published clips, or send complete ms. Length: 1,500-3,000 words. Pays $35-50.
Photos: Send photos with submission. Reviews 5x7 prints. Offers $10 per photo. Identification of subjects required. Buys one-time rights.

HOME MECHANIX, 2 Park Ave., New York NY 10016. (212)779-5000. Editor: Michael Morris. Managing Editor: Jim Wigdahl. 50% freelance written. Prefers to work with published/established writers. "If it's good, and it fits the type of material we're currently publishing, we're interested whether writer is new or experienced." Monthly magazine for the active home and car owner. "Articles emphasizing an active, home-oriented lifestyle. Includes information useful for maintenance, repair and renovation to the home and family car. Information on how to buy, how to select products useful to homeowners/car owners. Emphasis in home-oriented articles is on good design, inventive solutions to styling and space problems, useful home-workshop projects." Circ. 1.2 million. Pays on acceptance. Publishes ms an average of 6 months after acceptance. Byline given. Buys first North American serial rights. Computer printout submissions acceptable; prefers letter-quality. Query.
Nonfiction: Feature articles relating to homeowner/car owner, 1,500-2,500 words. "This may include personal home-renovation projects, professional advice on interior design, reports on different or unusual construction methods, energy-related subjects, outdoor/backyard projects, etc. We are no longer interested in high-tech subjects such as aerospace, electronics, photography or military hardware. Most of our automotive features are written by experts in the field, but fillers, tips, how-to repair, or modification articles on the

family car are welcome. Workshop articles on furniture, construction, tool use, refinishing techniques, etc., are also sought. Pays $300 minimum for features; fees based on number of printed pages, photos accompanying mss., etc." Pays expenses of writers on assignment.

Photos: Photos should accompany mss. Pays $600 and up for transparencies for cover. Inside color: $300/1 page; $500/2, $700/3, etc. Captions and model releases required.

Fillers: Tips and fillers useful to tool users or for general home maintenance. Pays $25 and up for illustrated and captioned fillers.

Tips: "The most frequent mistake made by writers in completing an article assignment for *Home Mechanix* is not taking the time to understand its editorial focus and special needs."

THE HOME SHOP MACHINIST, 2779 Aero Park Dr., Box 1810, Traverse City MI 49685. (616)946-3712. FAX: (616)946-3289. Editor: Joe D. Rice. 95% freelance written. Bimonthly magazine covering machining and metalworking for the hobbyist. Circ. 24,000. Pays on publication. Publishes ms an average of 18 months after acceptance. Byline given. Buys first North American serial rights only. Simultaneous submissions OK. Computer printout submissions acceptable; prefers letter-quality. Reports in 3 weeks. Free sample copy and writer's guidelines for 9x12 SASE.

Nonfiction: How-to (projects designed to upgrade present shop equipment or hobby model projects that require machining); and technical (should pertain to metalworking, machining, drafting, layout, welding or foundry work for the hobbyist). No fiction. Buys 50 mss/year. Query or send complete ms. Length: open—"whatever it takes to do a thorough job." Pays $40/published page, plus $9/published photo; $70/page for camera-ready art; and $40 for b&w cover photo.

Photos: Send photos with ms. Pays $9-40 for 5x7 b&w prints. Captions and identification of subjects required.

Columns/Departments: Sheetmetal; Book Reviews; New Product Reviews; Micro-Machining; and Foundry. "Writer should become familiar with our magazine before submitting. Query first." Buys 25-30 mss/year. Length: 600-1,500 words. Pays $40-70/page.

Fillers: Machining tips/shortcuts. No news clippings. Buys 12-15/year. Length: 100-300 words. Pays $30-48.

Tips: "The writer should be experienced in the area of metalworking and machining; should be extremely thorough in explanations of methods, processes—always with an eye to safety; and should provide good quality b&w photos and/or clear drawings to aid in description. Visuals are of increasing importance to our readers. Carefully planned photos, drawings and charts will carry a submission to our magazine much farther along the path to publication."

INTERNATIONAL WOODWORKING, Box 706, Rt. 3 and Cummings Hill Rd., Plymouth NH 03264. (603)536-3876. Editor: Doug Werbeck. 90% freelance written. Quarterly magazine on woodworking for hobbyists and professionals. Articles with drawn plans and diagrams are encouraged. Circ. 8,000. Pays on acceptance. Byline given. 50% kill fee offered. Buys one-time rights. Submit seasonal/holiday material 6 months in advance. Simultaneous, photocopied and previously published submissions OK. Query for electronic submissions. Computer printout submissions OK. Reports in 1 month. Free sample copy and writer's guidelines for 9x12 SAE and postage for 5 ounces.

Nonfiction: "Articles and project plans on all aspects of woodworking, including machinery, tool maintenance and repair, furniture making, woodturning, antique repair, restoration and refinishing, musical instrument making, miniatures, wooden crafts, jigs and accessories. Our woodworking readership are interested in completing these projects in their individual shops." Buys 25 mss/year. Query with or without clips, or send complete ms. Length: 500-2,000 words. Pays $25-250. Pays expenses of writers on assignment.

Photos: Send photos with submission. Reviews contact sheets, transparencies and 3x5 or larger prints. Offers $5-15 per photo. Caption, model releases and identification of subjects required. Buys one-time rights.

Fillers: Anecdotes, facts, cartoons, newsbreaks and short humor. Buys 50/year. Length: 100-1,000 words. Pays $10-100.

Tips: "We are an easy-to-work-with publication whose purpose is to disseminate information, how-to's and helpful tips and techniques to woodworking professionals and serious hobbyists."

‡JEWEL, Collector Communications Corp., Suite 1200, 170 5th Ave., New York NY 10010. (212)989-8700. Editor: Neil Letson. 90% freelance written. Quarterly magazine about jewels, gems, precious objects. Estab. 1988. Circ. 50,000 (expected). Pays on acceptance. Byline given. Buys first rights. Offers kill fee. Computer printout submissions OK; prefers letter-quality. Reports in 4 weeks on queries. Free sample copy.

Nonfiction: General interest, historical/nostalgic, how-to, interview/profile, new product, personal experience, photo feature and travel. "Only jewelry or gem related material." Buys 12-20 mss/year. Query. Length: 1,200-1,500 words. Pays $550-1,200. Pays expenses of writers on assignment.

Photos: State availability of photos with submission. Reviews contact sheets, negatives, transparencies and prints. Offers no additional payment for photos accepted with ms. Captions, model releases and identification of subjects required. Buys one-time rights.

Tips: "Types of articles most open to freelancers are pieces on historical jewels or new designs."

JUGGLER'S WORLD, International Jugglers Association, Box 443, Davidson NC 28036. (704)892-1296. FAX: (704)892-2526. Editor: Bill Giduz. 25% freelance written. A quarterly magazine on juggling. "*Juggler's World* publishes news, feature articles, fiction and poetry that relates to juggling. We also encourage 'how to' articles describing how to learn various juggling tricks." Circ. 3,500. Pays on acceptance. Publishes ms an average of 6 months after acceptance. Byline given. Buys all rights. Submit seasonal/holiday material 6 months in advance. Simultaneous, photocopied and previously published submissions OK. Query for electronic submissions. Computer printout submissions OK. Reports in 1 week. Sample copy for 8½x11 SAE with 5 first class stamps. Writer's guidelines for #10 SASE.

Nonfiction: Essays, general interest, historical/nostalgic, how-to, humor, interview/profile, opinion, personal experience, photo feature and travel. Buys 10 mss/year. Query. Length: 500-2,000 words. Pays $50-100 for assigned articles. Pays expenses of writers on assignment.

Photos: State availability of photos with submission. Reviews contact sheets, negatives and prints. Offers no additional payment for photos accepted with ms. Captions required. Buys one-time rights.

Fiction: Ken Letko, fiction editor. Adventure, fantasy, historical, humorous, science fiction and slice-of-life vignettes. Buys 2 mss/year. Query. Length: 250-1,000 words. Pays $25-50.

Tips: "The best approach is a feature article on or an interview with a leading juggler. Article should include both human interest material to describe the performer as a individual and technical juggling information to make it clear to a knowledgeable audience the exact tricks and skits performed."

KITPLANES, For designers, builders and pilots of experimental aircraft, Fancy Publications, Box 6050, Mission Viejo CA 92690. (714)240-6001. Editor: Dave Martin. 70% freelance written. Eager to work with new/unpublished writers. Monthly magazine covering self-construction of private aircraft for pilots and builders. Circ. 52,000. Pays on publication. Publishes ms an average of 3 months after acceptance. Byline given. Offers negotiable kill fee. Buys first North American serial rights. Submit seasonal/holiday material 6 months in advance. Query for electronic submissions. Computer printout submissions acceptable; dot-matrix must be caps and lower case printing. Reports in 2 weeks on queries; 6 weeks on mss. Sample copy $3; free writer's guidelines.

Nonfiction: How-to, interview/profile, new product, personal experience, photo feature, technical and general interest. "We are looking for articles on specific construction techniques, the use of tools, both hand and power, in aircraft building, the relative merits of various materials, conversions of engines from automobiles for aviation use, installation of instruments and electronics." No general-interest aviation articles, or "My First Solo" type of articles. Buys 80 mss/year. Query. Length: 500-5,000 words. Pays $100-400 including story photos.

Photos: Send photos with query or ms, or state availability of photos. Pays $250 for cover photos. Captions and identification of subjects required. Buys one-time rights.

Tips: "*Kitplanes* contains very specific information — a writer must be extremely knowledgeable in the field. Major features are entrusted only to known writers. I cannot emphasize enough that articles must be directed at the individual aircraft builder. We need more 'how-to' photo features in all areas of homebuilt aircraft."

THE LEATHER CRAFTSMAN, Craftsman Publishing, Box 1386, Fort Worth TX 76101. (817)923-6787. Editor: Nancy Sawyer. 95% freelance written. Eager to work with new/unpublished writers. A bimonthly magazine covering leathercrafting or leather art. "We are dedicated to the preservation of leather craft and leather art. Each issue contains articles on leather crafters, helpful hints and projects that our readers try at home or in their businesses." Circ. 10,000. Pays on publication. Publishes ms an average of 6-12 months after acceptance. Byline given. Buys first rights. Submit seasonal/holiday material 6 months in advance. Computer printout submissions acceptable; prefers letter-quality. Reports in 6 weeks on queries; 1 month on mss. Sample copy $3.50, 10x13 SAE and $1.25 postage; free writer's guidelines for SASE.

Nonfiction: How-to on leathercrafting projects. No articles not related to leather in some way. Send complete ms. Pays $25-200.

Photos: Send photos or completed project with submission. Reviews transparencies and prints. Offers no additional payment for photos accepted with ms. Captions required.

Tips: "*The Leather Craftsman* is dedicated to the preservation of leather craft and leather art. All aspects of the craft including carving, stamping, dyeing, sewing, decorating, etc., are presented to our readers through the use of step by step instructions. We are interested in more articles concerning leather apparel."

‡LEGACY MAGAZINE, For the Contemporary Numismatist, Ivy Press/Heritage Capital Corp., 311 Market St., Dallas TX 75202. (800-527-9250. Editor: Michael W. Sherman. Managing Editor: Mark Van Winkle. Quarterly magazine with general articles on U.S. coinage, collecting, investing, analysis of coin market. Readers are upper middle class and have about 5 years collecting experience. Circ. 12,000. Pays on publication. Byline given. Buys one-time rights. Simultaneous, photocopied and previously published submissions OK. Query for electronic submissions. Computer printout submissions OK. Reports in 2 weeks. Free sample copy and writer's guidelines.

Nonfiction: Essays, expose, historical/nostalgic, interview/profile, opinion, personal experience. Buys 15 mss/year. Query. Length: 1,500-3,000 words. Pays $50-500.

Photos: Send photos with submission. Offers no additional payment for photos accepted with ms. Identification of subjects required. Buys one-time rights.

Tips: "The magazine is aimed at intermediate to advanced coin collectors. We have features on historical, investing, collecting and analytical aspects of U.S. numismatics."

‡**LINN'S STAMP NEWS**, Amos Press, 911 Vandemark Rd. Box 29, Sidney OH 45365. (513)498-0801. FAX: (513)498-0806. Editor: Michael Laurence. Managing Editor: Elaine Boughner. 50% freelance written. Weekly tabloid on the stamp collecting hobby. "All articles must be about philatelic collectibles." Circ. 75,000. Pays on publication. Publishes ms an average of 1 month after acceptance. Byline given. Buys first North American serial rights. Submit seasonal/holiday material 2 months in advance. Reports on queries; 2 weeks on mss. Free sample copy. Writer's guidelines for #10 SAE with 2 first class stamps.

Nonfiction: General interest, historical/nostalgic, how-to, interview/profile and technical. "No articles merely giving information on background of stamp subject. Must have philatelic information included." Buys 300 mss/year. Send complete ms. Length: 500 words maximum. Pays $10-50. Rarely pays expenses of writers on assignment.

Photos: State availability of photos with submission. Prefers glossy b&w prints. Offers no additional payment for photos accepted with ms. Captions required. Buys all rights.

LIVE STEAM, Live Steam, Inc., 2779 Aero Park Dr., Box 629, Traverse City MI 49685. (616)941-7160. Editor: Joe D. Rice. 90% freelance written. Eager to work with new/unpublished writers. Monthly magazine covering steam-powered models and full-size engines (i.e., locomotives, traction, cars, boats, stationary, etc.) "Our readers are hobbyists, many of whom are building their engines from scratch. We are interested in anything that has to do with the world of live steam-powered machinery." Circ. 12,800. Pays on publication. Publishes ms an average of 18 months after acceptance. Byline given. Buys first North American serial rights only. Computer printout submissions acceptable; prefers letter-quality. Reports in 3 weeks. Free sample copy and writer's guidelines.

Nonfiction: Historical/nostalgic; how-to (build projects powered by steam); new product; personal experience; photo feature; and technical (must be within the context of steam-powered machinery or on machining techniques). No fiction. Buys 50 mss/year. Query or send complete ms. Length: 500-3,000 words. Pays $30/published page – $500 maximum. Sometimes pays the expenses of writers on assignment.

Photos: Send photos with ms. Pays $50/page of finished art. Pays $8 for 5x7 b&w prints; $40 for cover (color). Captions and identification of subjects required.

Columns/Departments: Steam traction engines, steamboats, stationary steam, and steam autos. Buys 6-8 mss/year. Query. Length: 1,000-3,000 words. Pays $20-50.

Tips: "At least half of all our material is from the freelancer. Requesting a sample copy and author's guide will be a good place to start. The writer must be well-versed in the nature of live steam equipment and the hobby of scale modeling such equipment. Technical and historical accuracy is an absolute must. Often, good articles are weakened or spoiled by mediocre to poor quality photos. Freelancers must learn to take a *good* photograph."

LOST TREASURE, Box 1589, Grove OK 74344. Managing Editor: Kathy Dyer. 95% freelance written. For treasure hunting hobbyists, relic collectors, amateur prospectors and miners. Monthly magazine; 72 pages. Circ. 55,000. Buys first rights only. Byline given. Buys 100 mss/year. Pays on publication. Will consider photocopied submissions. No simultaneous submissions. Computer printout submissions acceptable. Reports in 2 months. Submit complete ms. Publishes ms an average of 2 months after acceptance. Sample copy and writer's guidelines for 9x12 SASE.

Nonfiction: How-to articles about treasure hunting, coinshooting, personal profiles, and stories about actual hunts, stories that give an unusual twist to treasure hunting – using detectors in an unorthodox way, odd sidelights on history, unusual finds. *Avoid* writing about the more famous treasures and lost mines. No bottle hunting stories. Length: 1,000-3,000 words. "If an article is well-written and covers its subject well, we'll buy it – regardless of length." Pays 3¢/word.

Photos: B&w glossy prints with mss help sell your story. Captions required.

Tips: "Read *Lost Treasure* before submitting your stories. We are especially interested in stories that deal with the more unusual aspects of treasure hunting and metal detecting. Try to avoid the obvious – give something different. Also – good photos and graphics are a *must*."

‡**LOTTERY!, The Magazine for the Winning Lifestyle**, International Media Corp. 951 Broken Sound Pkwy. N.W., Box 5008, Boca Raton FL 33431-0808. (407)241-1800. Editor: Judy Strauss. 75% freelance written. Bimonthly magazine on lotteries. "Designed to entertain as well as to inform, the magazine includes articles for the novice as well as the experienced player. Featured are lifestyle stories on big winners and basic 'how-to advice'." Pays on acceptance. Publishes ms an average of 2 months after acceptance. Byline given. Offers 5¢/word kill fee. Buys all rights. Submit seasonal/holiday material 4 months in advance. Photocopied submis-

sions OK. Query for electronic submissions. Computer printout submissions OK; prefers letter-quality. Reports in 2 weeks. Free sample copy.

Nonfiction: General interest, how-to (how to play to improve chances of winning), humor, interview/profile (limited to winner of at least $10 million jackpot), personal experience and photo feature. "No negative articles about the lottery." Buys 30-40 mss/year. Query with or without published clips, or send complete ms. Length: 750-3,000 words. Pays 20¢/word. Sometimes pays in contributor copies or other premiums. Sometimes pays expenses of writers on assignment.

Photos: State availability of photos with submission. Offers no additional payment for photos accepted with ms. Captions, model releases and identification of subjects required. Buys one-time rights.

‡**MAINLINE MODELER**, Hundman Publishing, 5115 Monticello Dr., Edmonds WA 98020. (206)743-2607. FAX: (206)743-2607 (call first). Editor: Robert L. Hundman. 50% freelance written. Monthly magazine on railroad history and modeling. "Must have accurate information on the history of railroads or details on modeling techniques." Circ. 14,000. Pays 3-6 months after publication. Byline given. Buys all rights. Submit seasonal/holiday material 3-6 months in advance. Simultaneous submissions OK.

Nonfiction: Historical/nostalgic, how-to, interview/profile, personal experience, photo feature and technical. Buys 120 mss/year. Send complete ms. Length: 500-6,000 words. Pays $100-600.

Photos: Send photos or photocopies with submission. Captions, model releases and identification of subjects required.

‡**MINIATURE COLLECTOR**, Collector Communications Corp., 170 5th Ave., New York NY 10010. (212)989-8700. FAX: (212)645-8976 Managing Editor: A. Christian Revi. 50% freelance written. Works with a small number of new/unpublished writers each year. Quarterly magazine; 56 pages. Circ. 24,000. Byline given. Buys first North American serial rights. Pays within 30 days of acceptance. Publishes ms an average of 4 months after acceptance. Submit seasonal/holiday material 6 months in advance. Photocopied submissions OK. Computer printout submissions acceptable; no dot-matrix. Reports in 2 months. Sample copy $2; writer's guidelines for #10 SASE.

Nonfiction: General interest, how-to (detailed furniture and accessories projects in l/12th scale with accurate patterns and illustrations); new product (very short-caption type pieces—no payment); photo feature (show reports, heavily photographic, with captions stressing pieces and availability of new and unusual pieces); and profile (of collectors, artists and other personalities in the field with photos). Buys 24 mss/year. Query. Length: 800-1,800 words. Pays $100-250. "Most short pieces, such as news stories, are staff written. We welcome both short and long stories from freelancers." First manuscripts usually on speculation.

Photos: Send photos with ms; usually buys photo/manuscript package. Buys one-time rights. Captions required.

Columns/Departments: News & Views (news about established miniatures club contests and special projects—with b&w photos, if available. Length: 200 words maximum. Buys 6 mss/year. Send complete ms. Pays $10-25.

Tips: "We need feature material on museum collections and top-quality artisans (as opposed to hobbyists)."

MINIATURES SHOWCASE, Kalmbach Publishing Co., 21027 Crossroads Circle, Waukesha WI 53186. Editor: Geraldine Willems. 65% freelance written. A quarterly magazine about dollhouse miniatures. "We feature a different decorating theme each issue—our articles support the miniature room scene we focus on." Circ. 40,000. Pays on publication. Publishes ms an average of 3 months after acceptance. Byline given. Buys all rights. Submit seasonal/holiday material 4 months in advance. Photocopied submissions OK. Query for electronic submissions. Computer printout submissions OK; prefers letter-quality. Reports in 1 month. Sample copy $3; writer's guidelines for SASE.

Nonfiction: Historical/social. Buys 12 mss/year. Query. Length: 100-1,500 words. Pays 10¢/word.

Photos: State availability of photos with submission. Reviews contact sheets, negatives, transparencies and 4 color prints only. Offers no additional payment for photos accepted with ms. Captions and identificaiton of subjects required.

Tips: "Our articles are all assigned—a freelancer should query before sending in anything. Our features are open to freelancers—each issue deals with a different topic, often historical."

MODEL RAILROADER, 1027 N. 7th St., Milwaukee WI 53233. Editor: Russell G. Larson. For hobbyists interested in scale model railroading. Monthly. Buys exclusive rights. Study publication before submitting material. Reports on submissions within 1 month.

Nonfiction: Wants construction articles on specific model railroad projects (structures, cars, locomotives, scenery, benchwork, etc.). Also photo stories showing model railroads. Query. First-hand knowledge of subject almost always necessary for acceptable slant. Pays base rate of $75/page.

Photos: Buys photos with detailed descriptive captions only. Pays $7.50 and up, depending on size and use. Pays double b&w rate for color; full color cover earns $210.

MONITORING TIMES, Grove Enterprises Inc., Box 98, Brasstown NC 28902. (704)837-9200. Managing Editor: Larry Miller. Publisher: Robert Grove. 80% freelance written. A monthly magazine for shortwave and scanner hobbyists. Circ. 25,000. Pays on acceptance. Publishes ms an average of 2 months after acceptance. Byline given. Buys first North American serial rights. Submit seasonal/holiday material 4 months in advance. Simultaneous and photocopied submissions OK. Query for electronic submissions. Computer printout submissions OK; prefers letter-quality. Reports in 1 month. Free sample copy for 8½x11 SAE and $1 postage; free writer's guidelines.

Nonfiction: General interest, how-to, humor, interview/profile, opinion, personal experience, photo feature, technical. Buys 275 mss/year. Query. Length: 1,000-2,500 words. Pays $75-100.

Photos: State availability of photos with submission. Offers $10-25/photo. Captions required. Buys one-time rights.

Columns/Departments: "Requires extensive, specialized expertise. Query managing editor with résumé."

MOUNTAIN STATES COLLECTOR, Spree Publishing, Box 2525, Evergreen CO 80439. Editor: Carol Rudolph. Managing Editor: Peg DeStefano. 85% freelance written. A monthly tabloid covering antiques and collectibles. Circ. 8,000. Pays on publication. Publishes ms an average of 3-6 months after acceptance. Byline given. Not copyrighted. Buys first rights, one-time rights or second serial (reprint) rights to material published elsewhere. Submit seasonal/holiday material at least 3 months in advance. Simultaneous and previously published submissions OK. Computer printout submissions acceptable; prefers letter-quality. Reports in 6 weeks. Sample copy for 9x12 SAE with 4 first class stamps; writer's guidelines for SASE.

Nonfiction: About antiques and/or collectibles — book excerpts, historical/nostalgic, how-to (collect), interview/profile (of collectors) and photo feature. Buys 75 mss/year. Query with or without published clips, or send complete ms. Length: 500-1,500 words. Pays $15. Sometimes pays the expenses of writers on assignment (mileage, phone — not long distance travel).

Photos: Send photos with submission. Reviews contact sheets, and 5x7 b&w prints. Offers $5/photo used. Captions required. Buys one-time rights.

Tips: "Writers should know their topics well or be prepared to do in-depth interviews with collectors. We prefer a down-home approach. We need articles on antiques and on collectors and collections; how-to articles on collecting; how a collector can get started; or clubs for collectors. We would like to see more articles in 1990 with high-quality b&w photos."

‡NATIONAL DOLL WORLD, House of White Birches, 306 E. Parr Rd., Berne IN 46711. (219)589-8741. Editor: Rebekah Montgomery. Bimonthly magazine on collecting or making dolls. "Our people collect and restore dolls as well as make them." Circ. 55,000. Pays on publication. Publishes ms an average of 6-8 months after acceptance. Byline given. Buys first rights. Submit seasonal/holiday material 6-12 months in advance. Reports in 1 week on queries; 1 month on mss. Sample copy $2.50. Writer's guidelines for #8 SAE with 1 first class stamp.

Nonfiction: Historical/nostalgic and how-to repair, restore, dress or make. Christmas issue: dolls and teddy bear patterns. "No 'why I collect dolls' stories." Buys 65 mss/year. Send complete ms. Length: 2,500 words maximum. Pays $200.

Photos: Send photos with submission. Reviews transparencies and prints. Offers $5-25 per photo. Identification of subjects required. Buys one-time rights or all rights.

THE NUMISMATIST, American Numismatic Association, 818 N. Cascade Ave., Colorado Springs CO 80903. (719)632-2646. Editor: Barbara Gregory. Monthly magazine "for collectors of coins, medals, tokens and paper money." Circ. 35,000. Pays on publication. Publishes ms an average of 1 year after acceptance. Byline given. Buys first North American serial rights or second serial (reprint) rights. Submit seasonal/holiday material 1 year in advance. Previously published submissions OK. Computer printout submissions OK. Reports in 2 months. Free sample copy and writer's guidelines for #10 SASE.

Nonfiction: Essays, exposé, general interest, historical/nostalgic, humor, interview/profile, new product, opinion, personal experience, photo feature and technical. No articles that are lengthy or non-numismatic. Buys 48-60 mss/year. Send complete ms. Length: 1,000-3,500 words. Pays "on rate-per-published-page basis." Sometimes pays the expenses of writers on assignment.

Photos: Send photos with submission. Reviews contact sheets and 4x5 or 5x7 prints. Offers $2.50-5/photo. Captions and identification of subjects required. Buys one-time rights.

Columns/Departments: Buys 6 mss/year. Length: 775-2,000 words. "Pays negotiable flat fee per column."

OLD CARS WEEKLY, Krause Publications, 700 E. State St., Iola WI 54990. (715)445-2214. FAX: (715)445-4087. Editor: John Gunnell. 50% freelance written. Weekly tabloid; 44-48 pages. Circ. 80,000. Pays on publication. Publishes ms an average of 2 months after acceptance. Buys all rights. Phone queries OK. Byline given. Computer printout submissions OK; prefers letter-quality. Reports in 2 weeks. Free sample copy and writer's guidelines.

Nonfiction: Short (2-3 pages) timely news reports on old car hobby with 1 photo. Buys 20 mss/issue. Query. Pays 3¢/word. Sometimes pays the expenses of writers on auction assignments.
Photos: Pays $5 for 5x7 b&w glossy prints. Captions required. Buys all rights.
Fillers: Newsbreaks. Buys 50/year. Pays 3¢/word. Pays $10 bonus for usable news tips.
Tips: "We have converted basically to a news package and buy only news. This would include post-event coverage of antique auto shows, summary reports on auctions with list of prices realized and 'hard' news concerning old cars or people in the hobby. For example, the stock market crash has enhanced values of collectible cars, and collectible autos are growing newer and newer each year."

PAPER COLLECTORS MARKETPLACE, Watson Graphic Designs, Inc., Box 127, Scandinavia WI 54977. (715)467-2379. Editor: Doug Watson. 100% freelance written. A monthly magazine on paper collectibles. "All articles must relate to the hobby in some form. Whenever possible values should be given for the collectibles mentioned in the article." Circ. 4,000. Pays on publication. Byline given. Offers 25% kill fee on commissioned articles. Buys first North American serial rights. Submit seasonal/holiday material 2 months in advance. Reports in 2 weeks. Free sample copy; writer's guidelines for #10 SASE.
Nonfiction: Historical/nostalgic, how-to, photo feature, technical. Buys 60 mss/year. Query with published clips. Length: 1,000-2,000 words. Pays 3-5¢/words.
Photos: Send photos with submissions. Offers no additional payment for photos accepted with ms. Captions, model releases and identification of subjects required. Buys one-time rights.
Tips: "We presently plan on publishing four special issues a year: February (December 1 deadline) Mystery/Detective; June (April 1 deadline) Sports Special; August (June 1 deadline) Science-Fiction Special."

‡PIPE SMOKER & TOBACCIANA TRADER, Journal of Kapnismology, Pipe Collectors International Inc., 6172 Airways Blvd., Chattanooga TN 37422. (615)892-7277. Editor: C. Bruce Spencer. 30% freelance written. Works with a small number of new/unpublished writers each year who are already involved with collectibles. A bimonthly magazine about collecting smoking pipes and tobacciana. Features articles relative to the past, present and future of smoking pipes, tobacciana and the people and companies involved. Circ. 5,000. Pays on publication. Publishes ms an average of 2-6 months after acceptance. Byline given. Buys one-time rights. Submit seasonal/holiday material 3 months in advance. Query for electronic submissions. Computer printout submissions OK. Sample copy $1.
Nonfiction: Book excerpts, essays, historical/nostalgic, how-to, interview/profile, personal experience, new product, personal experience and photo feature. No anti-smoking articles. Buys 8-10 mss/year. Send complete ms. Length: 1,500 words maximum. Pays 7¢/word.
Photos: Send photos with submission. Reviews contact sheets; contract on color. Offers $5 maximum/b&w photo. Captions, model releases and identification of subjects required. Buys one-time rights.
Fillers: Facts. Buys 2-3/year. Length: 1,200 words maximum. Pays 7¢/word. "It helps to be a pipe-smoker—visit smokeshops—go to some pipe shows, etc.; learn about the hobby."
Tips: "Features on related subjects are most open to freelancers, especially if writer is a pipe smoker."

‡PLATE WORLD, The Magazine of Collector's Plates, 9200 N. Maryland Ave. Niles IL 60648. (312)763-7773. Editor-in-Chief: Tina Panoplos. 5% freelance written. Bimonthly magazine. "We write exclusively about limited-edition collector's plates—artists, makers, dealers and collectors. Our audience is involved in plates mostly as collectors; also dealers, makers or producers." Circ. 55,000. Pays on acceptance. Publishes ms an average of 2 months after acceptance. Byline given. Offers 50% kill fee. Buys various rights. Submit seasonal/holiday material 5 months in advance. Computer printout submissions OK; prefers letter-quality. Reports in 1 month on queries; 2 weeks on mss. Sample copy $3.50; free writer's guidelines. Pays some expenses of writers on assignment—"travel plus phone."
Nonfiction: Interview/profile (how artists create, biography or artist profile of exceptional plate collector); photo feature (about artist or plate manufacturer). "Writers can submit short profiles of interesting and exceptional plate collectors. Also, we have departments where we publish short items of interest." No critical attacks on industry. No articles on antique plates. Buys 10 mss/year. Query and send samples of work. Pays $100-500.
Photos: Albert Scharpou, art director. Human interest, technical. State availability of photos. Reviews transparencies. Pays negotiable rate. Identification of subjects required. Usually buys all rights; occasionally buys one-time rights.
Tips: Profiles of artists or collectors are the areas most open to freelancers. "The most frequent mistakes made by writers in completing an article for us are: not enough research, profiles not objective, articles too promotional. Also, writers must understand our editorial content—only limited-edition collector's plates (no antiques, etc.)."

POPULAR ELECTRONICS, (formerly *Hands-On-Electronics*), Gernsback Publications, Inc., 500B Bi-County Blvd., Farmingdale NY 11735. (516)293-3000. Editor: Julian Martin. 100% freelance written. Monthly magazine covering hobby electronics—"features, projects, ideas related to audio, CB, radio, experimenting, test equipment, antique radio, communications, state-of-the-art, etc." Circ. 80,000. Pays on acceptance. Byline given. Buys all rights. Submit seasonal/holiday material 6 months in advance. Photocopied and previously published submissions OK. Query for electronic submissions. Computer printout submissions OK; prefers letter-quality. Reports in 2 weeks. Free sample copy, "include label." Writer's guidelines for SASE.

Nonfiction: General interest, how-to, photo feature and technical. Buys 200 mss/year. Query or send complete ms. Length: 1,000-3,500 words. Pays $100-350.

Photos: Send photos with submission. "Wants b&w glossy photos." Offers no additional payment for photos accepted with ms. Captions required. Buys all rights.

Tips: "All areas are open to freelancers. Project-type articles and other 'how-to' articles have best success."

‡POPULAR ELECTRONICS HOBBYIST'S HANDBOOK, Gernsback Publications, Inc., 500 B Bi-County Blvd., Farmingdale NY 11735. (516)293-3000. Editor: Julian S. Martin. Managing Editor: Carl Laron. 100% freelance written. Monthly magazine on hobby electronics. Estab. 1989. Circ. 126,000. Pays on acceptance. Byline given. Buys all rights. Submit seasonal/holiday material 5-6 months in advance. Photocopied submissions OK. Query for electronic submissions. Computer printout submissions OK; prefers letter-quality. Reports in 2 weeks. Free sample copy and writer's guidelines.

Nonfiction: General interest, historical/nostalgic, how-to (build projects, fix consumer products, etc., all of which must "have a wire in it!"), photo feature and technical. "No product reviews!" Buys 5-6 mss/year. Send complete ms. Length: 1,000-5,000 words. Pays $100-500 for assigned articles; $100-400 for unsolicited articles. Sometimes pays expenses of writers on assignment.

Photos: Send photos with submission. "We want b&w glossy photos." Reviews 5x7 or 8x10 b&w prints. Offers no additional payment for photos accepted with ms. Captions and model releases are required. Buys all rights.

Tips: "Read the magazine. Know and understand the subject matter. Write it. Submit it."

POSTCARD COLLECTOR, Joe Jones Publishing, Box 337, Iola WI 54945. (715)445-5000. Editor: Deb Lengkeck. 70% freelance written. Monthly magazine. "Publication is for postcard collectors; all editorial content relates to postcards in some way." Circ. 6,000. Pays on publication. Publishes ms an average of 6 months after acceptance. Byline given. Buys one-time rights, first rights or second serial rights. Submit seasonal/holiday material 3 months in advance. Previously published submissions OK. Reports in 2 weeks on queries; 1 month on mss. Free sample copy and writer's guidelines.

Nonfiction: General interest, historical/nostalgic, how-to (e.g. preservatives), new product, opinion, personal experience, photo feature and travel. Buys 40 mss/year. Send complete ms. Length: 200-1,800 words. Pays 3-8¢/word for assigned articles; 3-5¢/word for unsolicited articles.

Photos: State availability of postcards with submission. Offers $1-3/photo. Captions and identification of subjects required. Buys perpetual, but nonexclusive rights.

Columns/Departments: 50-150 words. Buys 20-30 mss/year. Query. Pays $2.

Tips: "We publish information about postcards written by expert topical specialists. The writer must be knowledgeable about postcards and have acquired 'expert' information. We plan more complete listings of postcard sets and series—old and new." Areas most open to freelancers are feature-length articles on specialized areas (600-1,800 words) with 1 to 10 illustrations."

THE PROFESSIONAL QUILTER, Oliver Press, Box 75277, St. Paul MN 55175-0277. (612)426-9681. Editor: Jeannie M. Spears. 80% freelance written. Works with a small number of new/unpublished writers each year. Quarterly magazine on the quilting business. Emphasis on small business, preferably quilt related. Circ. 2,000. Payment negotiated. Publishes ms an average of 6 months after acceptance. Byline given. Buys first North American serial rights, first serial rights and second serial (reprint) rights. Simultaneous queries, and photocopied and previously published submissions OK. Computer printout submissions acceptable; prefers letter-quality. Reports in 2 weeks on queries; 1 month on mss. Sample copy for 9x12 SAE with 4 first class stamps and $4; writer's guidelines for #10 SASE.

Nonfiction: How-to (quilting business); humor; interview/profile; new product; opinion; and personal experience (of problems and problem-solving ideas in a quilting business). No quilting or sewing *techniques* or quilt photo spreads. Buys 20 mss/year. Query or send complete ms. Length: 500-1,500 words. Pays $25-75.

Tips: "Each issue will focus in depth on an issue of concern to the professional quilting community, such as ethics, art vs. craft, professionalism, etc. We would also like to receive articles on time and space (studio) organization, stress and family relationships. Remember that our readers already know that quilting is a time-honored tradition passed down from generation to generation, that quilts reflect the life of the maker, that quilt patterns have revealing names, etc. Ask yourself: If my grandmother had been running a quilting business for the last 5 years, would she have found this article interesting? Send a letter describing your quilt, craft or business experience with a query or manuscript."

QUILT WORLD, House of White Birches, 306 E. Parr Rd., Berne IN 46711. (219)589-8741. Editor: Sandra L. Hatch. 100% freelance written. Works with a small number of new/unpublished writers each year. Bimonthly magazine covering quilting. "We publish articles on quilting techniques, profile of quilters and coverage of quilt shows. Reader is 50-70 years old, midwestern." Circ. 130,000. Pays on publication. Publishes ms an

average of 6 months after acceptance. Byline given. Buys all rights, first rights, one-time rights and second serial (reprint) rights. Submit seasonal/holiday material 6 months in advance. Previously published submissions OK. Query for electronic submissions. Computer printout submissions are acceptable. Reports in 3 weeks. Sample copy $2.50; writer's guidelines for SASE.
Nonfiction: How-to, interview/profile (quilters), technical, new product (quilt products) and photo feature. Buys 18-24 mss/year. Query. Length: open. Pays $35-100.
Photo: Send photos with submission. Reviews transparencies and prints. Offers $15/photo (except covers). Identification of subjects required. Buys all rights or one-time rights.
Tips: "Send list of previous articles published with resume and a SASE. List ideas which you plan to base your articles around."

‡**QUILTING TODAY MAGAZINE, The International Quilt Magazine**, Chitra Publications, 300 Church St., Box 437, New Milford PA 18834. (717)465-3306. Editor: Patti Bachelder. 80% freelance written. Bimonthly magazine on quilting, traditional and contemporary. "We seek articles that will cover one or two full pages (800 words each); informative to the general quilting public, present new ideas, interviews, instructional, etc." Circ. 90,000. Pays on publication. Publishes ms an average of 3 months after acceptance. Byline given. Buys second serial (reprint) rights and makes work-for-hire assignments. Submit seasonal/holiday material 3-4 months in advance. Query for electronic submissions. Computer printout submissions OK; prefers letter-quality. Reports in 1 month on queries; 2 months on mss. Free sample copy and writer's guidelines.
Nonfiction: Books excerpts, essays, how-to (for various quilting techniques), humor, interview/profile, new product, opinion, personal experience and photo feature. "Special section, 64-pages with advertising devoted entirely to miniature quilts. Deadline late October. No articles about family history related to a quilt or quilts unless the quilt is a masterpiece of color and design, impeccable workmanship." Buys 20-30 mss/year. Query with or without published clips, or send complete mss. Length: 800-1,600 words. Pays $50-75/page. Sometimes pays expenses of writers on assignment.
Photos: Send photos with submission. Reviews 2x3 transparencies and 5x7 prints. Offers $20 per photo. Captions, identification of subjects required. Buys all rights unless rented from a museum.
Columns/Departments: Bits & Pieces (philosophical and emotional with positive ideas and suggestions, currently written by one writer), 300 words maximum; Quilting B'tween the Lines (instructional from personal view; also written by same writer), 300 words maximum. Buys 10-12 ms/year. Send complete ms. Pays $40-50 per column.
Fiction: Fantasy, historical and humorous. Buys 1 mss/year. Send complete ms. Length: 300-1,600 words. Pays $50-75/page.
Tips: "Query with ideas; send samples of prior work so that we can assess and suggest assignment. Our publications appeal to traditional quilters (generally middle-aged) who use the patterns in each issue."

‡**RADIO-ELECTRONICS**, Gernsback Publicaitons, Inc., 500 B Bi-County Blvd., Farmingdale NY 11735. (516)293-3000. Editor: Brian C. Fenton. 75% freelance written. Monthly magazine on electronics technology. "*Radio-Electronics* presents features on electronics technology and electronics construction." Circ. 250,000. Pays on acceptance. Publishes ms an average of 4 months after acceptance. Byline given. Buys all rights. Submit seasonal/holiday material 5-6 months in advance. Simultaneous submissions OK. Query for electronic submissions. Computer printout submissions OK; prefers letter-quality. Reports in 2 months on queries; 4 months on mss. Free sample copy and writer's guidelines.
Nonfiction: How-to (electronic project construction), humor (cartoons) and new product. Buys 150-200 mss/year. Send complete ms. Length: 1,000-10,000 words. Pays $200-800 for assigned articles; $100-800 for unsolicited articles.
Photos: Send photos with submission. Offers no additional payment for photos accepted with ms. Captions, model releases and identification of subjects required. Buys all rights.

RAILROAD MODEL CRAFTSMAN, Box 700, Newton NJ 07860. (201)383-3355. Editor: William C. Schaumburg. 75% freelance written. Works with a small number of new/unpublished writers each year. For model railroad hobbyists, in all scales and gauges. Monthly. Circ. 97,000. Buys all rights. Buys 50-100 mss/year. Pays on publication. Publishes ms an average of 9 months after acceptance. Submit seasonal material 6 months in advance. Computer printout submissions acceptable; prefers letter-quality. Sample copy $2; writer's and photographer's guidelines for SASE.
Nonfiction: "How-to and descriptive model railroad features written by persons who did the work are preferred. Almost all our features and articles are written by active model railroaders. It is difficult for non-modelers to know how to approach writing for this field." Pays minimum of $1.75/column inch of copy ($50/page).
Photos: Purchased with or without mss. Buys sharp 8x10 glossy prints and 35mm or larger color transparencies. Pays minimum of $10 for photos or $2/diagonal inch of published b&w photos, $3 for color transparencies and $100 for covers, which must tie in with article in that issue. Caption information required.
Tips: "We would like to emphasize freight car modeling based on actual prototypes, as well as major prototype studies of them."

SAGEBRUSH JOURNAL, The Best Danged Western Newspaper Going!, Allied Publishing, 430 Haywood Rd., Asheville NC 28806. Editor: Linda Hagan. Publisher: Bill Hagan. 90% freelance written. A monthly tabloid covering Western genre films and print (books and magazines). "We are oriented toward people who love the thrill of the Western genre – from the glorious B westerns of yesteryear, pulp stories and novels, to the Western revival of today." Circ. 5,000. Pays on publication. Byline given. Buys first North American serial, one-time and second serial (reprint) rights. Submit seasonal/holiday material 6 months in advance. Photocopied and previously published submissions OK. Query for electronic submissions. Computer printout submissions OK; prefers letter-quality to dot-matrix. Reports in 2 weeks on queries; 2 months on mss. Sample copy for $2.50 and SAE with $2 postage. Writer's guidelines for #10 SASE.

Nonfiction: General interest, historical/nostalgic, humor, interview/profile, personal experience, photo feature, Western convention reports, reviews of Western films and books. Buys 40-50 mss/year. Query with or without published clips, or send complete ms. Length: 200-5,000 words. Pays 25¢/column inch.

Photos: Send photos with submission. Reviews prints. Offers 25¢/column inch for photo (included with article payment); "no separate photos." Captions and identification of subjects required. Buys one-time rights.

Fillers: Judy Hagan, fillers editor. Western-related anecdotes, facts, newsbreaks and short humor. Buys 15-20/year. Length: 50-200 words. Pays 25¢/column inch.

SCOTT STAMP MONTHLY, Box 828, Sidney OH 45365. (513)498-0802. Editor: Richard L. Sine. 40% freelance written. Works with a small number of new/unpublished writers each year. For stamp collectors, from the beginner to the sophisticated philatelist. Monthly magazine; 84 pages. Circ. 24,000. Rights purchased vary with author and material; usually buys first North American serial rights. Byline given. Buys 60 unsolicited mss/year. Pays on publication. Publishes ms an average of 7 months after acceptance. Submit seasonal or holiday material at least 6 months in advance. Computer printout submissions acceptable; prefers letter-quality. Query for electronic submissions. Reports in 1 month. Sample copy for $1.50.

Nonfiction: "We are in the market for articles, written in an engaging fashion, concerning the remote byways and often-overlooked aspects of stamp collecting. Writing should be clear and concise, and subjects must be well-researched and documented. Illustrative material should also accompany articles whenever possible." Query. Pays about $100.

Photos: State availability of photos. Offers no additional payment for b&w photos used with mss.

Tips: "It's rewarding to find a good new writer with good new material. Because our emphasis is on lively, interesting articles about stamps, including historical perspectives and human interest slants, we are open to writers who can produce the same. Of course, if you are an experienced philatelist, so much the better. We do not want stories about the picture on a stamp taken from a history book or an encyclopedia and dressed up to look like research. If an idea is good and not a basic rehash, we are interested."

SEW NEWS, The Fashion Magazine for People Who Sew, PJS Publications, Inc., News Plaza, Box 1790, Peoria IL 61656. (309)682-6626. Editor: Linda Turner Griepentrog. 90% freelance written. Works with a small number of new/unpublished writers each year. Monthly newspaper covering fashion-sewing. "Our magazine is for the beginning home sewer to the professional dressmaker. It expresses the fun, creativity and excitement of sewing." Circ. 200,000. Pays on acceptance. Publishes ms an average of 6 months after acceptance. Byline given. Buys all rights. Submit seasonal/holiday material 6 months in advance. Photocopied submissions OK. Computer printout submissions acceptable. Reports in 2 months. Sample copy $3; writer's guidelines for #10 SAE and 2 first class stamps.

Nonfiction: How-to (sewing techniques) and interview/profile (interesting personalities in home-sewing field). Buys 200-240 ms/year. Query with published clips. Length: 500-2,000 words. Pays $25-400. Rarely pays expenses of writers on assignment.

Photos: State availability of photos. Prefers b&w contact sheets and negatives. Payment included in ms price. Identification of subjects required. Buys all rights.

Tips: "Query first with writing sample. Areas most open to freelancers are how-to and sewing techniques; give explicit, step-by-step instructions plus rough art."

SHUTTLE SPINDLE & DYEPOT, Handweavers Guild of America, 120 Mountain Road, Bloomfield CT 06002. Editor: Judy Robbins. 60% freelance written. A quarterly magazine covering handweaving, spinning and dyeing. "We take the practical and aesthetic approach to handweaving, handspinning, and related textile arts." Pays on publication. Publishes ms 4-15 months after acceptance. Byline given. Buys first North American serial rights. Submit seasonal/holiday material 1 year in advance. Photocopied submissions OK. Rarely accepts previously published submissions. Computer printout submissions acceptable; prefers letter-quality. Reports in 1 month on queries; 2 months on mss. Sample copy $6.50; free writer's guidelines.

Nonfiction: How-to, interview/profile, personal experience, photo feature and technical. "We want interesting, practical, technical information in our field." Buys 30 mss/year. Query with or without published clips, or send complete ms. Length: 500-1,500 words. Pays $25-100.

Photos: Send photos or state availability of photos with submission. Reviews contact sheets and transparencies. Payment varies. Captions, model releases and identification of subjects required. Buys one-time rights.
Tips: "We read all submissions, especially from weavers and weaving teachers."

SPIN-OFF, Interweave Press, 306 N. Washington, Loveland CO 80537. (303)669-7672. Editor: Deborah Robson. 10-20% freelance written. Quarterly magazine covering handspinning, dyeing, techniques and projects for using handspun fibers. Audience includes "practicing textile/fiber craftsmen. Article should show considerable depth of knowledge of subject, although the tone should be informal and accessible." Circ. 10,000. Pays on publication. Publishes ms an average of 6-12 months after acceptance. Byline given. Pays 50% kill fee. Buys first North American serial rights. Simultaneous queries and photocopied submissions OK. Computer printout submissions acceptable; prefers letter-quality. Sample copy $3.50 and 8½x11 SAE; free writer's guidelines for #10 SAE and 37¢ postage.
Nonfiction: Historical and how-to (on spinning; knitted, crocheted, woven projects from handspun fibers with instructions); interview/profile (of successful and/or interesting fiber craftsmen); and technical (on spinning, dyeing or fiber technology, use, properties). "All articles must contain a high level of in-depth information. Our readers are very knowledgeable about these subjects." Query. Length: 2,000 words. Pays $15-100.
Photos: State availability of photos. Identification of subjects required.
Tips: "You should display an in-depth knowledge of your subject, but you can tailor your article to reach beginning, intermediate or advanced spinners. Try for thoughtful organization, a personal informal style and an article or series segment that is self-contained. New approaches to familiar topics are welcomed."

SPORTS COLLECTORS DIGEST, Krause Publications, 700 E. State St., Iola WI 54990. (715)445-2214. FAX: (715)445-4087. Editor: Tom Mortenson. 60% freelance written. Eager to work with new/unpublished writers; works with a small number of new/unpublished writers each year. Sports memorabilia magazine published weekly. "We serve collectors of sports memorabilia—baseball cards, yearbooks, programs, autographs, jerseys, bats, balls, books, magazines, ticket stubs, etc." Circ. 46,000. Pays after publication. Publishes ms an average of 3 months after acceptance. Byline given. Buys first North American serial rights only. Submit seasonal/holiday material 3 months in advance. Simultaneous queries and photocopied submissions OK. Computer printout submissions acceptable; prefers letter-quality. Reports in 5 weeks on queries; 2 months on mss. Free sample copy; writer's guidelines for #10 SASE.
Nonfiction: General interest (new card issues, research on older sets); historical/nostalgic (old stadiums, old collectibles, etc.); how-to (buy cards, sell cards and other collectibles, display collectibles, ways to get autographs, jerseys and other memorabilia); interview/profile (well-known collectors, ball players—but must focus on collectibles); new product (new card sets) and personal experience ("what I collect and why"-type stories). No sports stories. "We are not competing with *The Sporting News*, *Sports Illustrated* or your daily paper. Sports collectibles only." Buys 200-300 mss/year. Query. Length: 300-3,000 words; prefers 1,000 words. Pays $20-75.
Photos: Unusual collectibles. State availability of photos. Pays $5-15 for b&w prints. Identification of subjects required. Buys all rights.
Columns/Departments: "We have all the columnists we need but welcome ideas for new columns." Buys 100-150 mss/year. Query. Length: 600-3,000 words. Pays $15-60.
Tips: "If you are a collector, you know what collectors are interested in. Write about it. No shallow, puff pieces; our readers are too smart for that. Only well-researched articles about sports memorabilia and collecting. Some sports nostalgia pieces are OK. Write only about the areas you know about."

‡STORYBOARD, Your Disneyana Magazine, Bobit Publishing, 2512 Artesia Blvd., Redondo Beach CA 90278. (213)376-8788. FAX: (213)376-9043. Editor: Glenn Shaffer. 50% freelance written. Bimonthly magazine on Disneyana-Collectors, enthusiasts and fans. "Magazine covers the world of Disneyana—collectible merchandise, studio history, theme park history, animation art, movie and book reviews, collector profiles and artist interviews." Pays on publication. Publishes ms an average of 2-3 months after acceptance. Byline given. Offers 100% kill fee. Buys first North American serial rights. Submit seasonal/holiday material 2-3 months in advance. Query for electronic submissions. Computer printout submissions OK; prefers letter quality. Reports in 2 weeks on queries; 3 weeks on mss. Free sample copy and writer's guidelines.
Nonfiction: Essays, exposé, general interest, historical/nostalgic, humor, interview/profile, new product, opinion, personal experience, photo feature and travel. Buys 25-30 mss/year. Query. Length: 500-3,000 words. Pays $250-500 for assigned articles; $100-250 for unsolicited articles. Pays in contributor copies or other premiums at writer's request only. Sometimes pays expenses of writers on assignment.
Photos: Reviews contact sheets, negatives, 35mm and up transparencies and 3x5 and up prints. Offers no additional payment for photos accepted with ms (ms payment based on photos or no photos).
Columns/Departments: Collector's Profile (brief look at collector and their collection), 500 words; New Products (information on new merchandise available), 500 words; Book/Movie Review (about author, director, star; plus review) 500 words. Buys 10 mss/year. Query. Pays $50-150.

Fillers: Anecdotes, newsbreaks and short humor. Buys 50-75/year. Length: 100-250 words. Pays $10-50.
Tips: "Please call for additional information and sample copy of magazine. Refer to other collectibles magazines for style and content."

SUNSHINE ARTISTS USA, The Voice Of The Nation's Artists and Craftsmen, Sun Country Enterprises, 1700 Sunset Dr., Longwood FL 32750. (407)323-5937. Editor: Joan L. Wahl. Managing Editor: 'Crusty' Sy. A monthly magazine covering art and craft shows in the United States. "We are a top marketing magazine for professional artists, craftspeople and photographers working street and mall shows. We list 10,000+ shows a year, critique many of them and publish articles on marketing, selling and improving arts and crafts. Circ. 16,000. Pays on publication. Publishes ms an average of 3 months after acceptance. Byline given. Buys first North American serial rights. Reports in 2 weeks on queries; 6 weeks on manuscripts. Sample copy $2.50.
Nonfiction: "We are interested in articles that relate to artists and craftsmen traveling the circuit. Although we have a permanent staff of 40 writers, we will consider well-written, thoroughly researched articles on successful artists making a living with their work, new ways to market arts and crafts, and rags to riches profiles. Attend some art shows. Talk to the exhibitors. Get ideas from them." No how-tos. Buys 20 mss/year. Query. Length: 550-2,000 words. Pays $15-50 for assigned articles.
Photos: State availability of photos with submission. Offers no additional payment for photos accepted with ms. Captions, model releases and identification of subjects required.

TEDDY BEAR REVIEW, Collector Communications Corp., 170 5th Ave., New York NY 10010. FAX: (212)645-8976. Editor: A. Christian Revi. 25% freelance written. Works with a small number of new/unpublished writers each year. A quarterly magazine on teddy bears. Pays 30 days after acceptance. Byline given. Buys first North American serial rights. Submit seasonal/holiday material 6 months in advance. Computer printout submissions OK; no dot-matrix. Reports in 2 months. Sample copy and writer's guidelines for $2 and 9x12 SAE.
Nonfiction: Book excerpts, historical, how-to and interview/profile. No nostalgia on childhood teddy bears. Buys 10 mss/year. Query with published clips. Length: 500-1,500 words. Pays $75-200. Sometimes pays the expenses of writers on assignment "if approved ahead of time."
Photos: Send photos with submission. Reviews transparencies and b&w prints. Offers no additional payment for photos accepted with ms. Captions required. Buys one-time rights.
Tips: "We are interested in good, professional writers around the country with a strong knowledge of teddy bears. Historical profile of bear companies, profiles of contemporary artists and knowledgeable reports on museum collections are of interest."

‡TRADITIONAL QUILTWORKS, The Pattern Magazine for Innovative Quilters, Chitra Publications, 300 Church St., Box 437, New Milford PA 18834. (717)465-3306. Editor: Linda Halpin. Managing Editor: Patti Bachelder. 60% freelance written. Quarterly magazine on quilting. "We seek articles of an instructional nature, profiles of talented teachers, articles on the history of specific areas of quiltmaking (patterns, fiber, regional, etc.)." Estab. 1988. Circ. 90,000. Pays on publication. Publishes ms an average of 4 months after acceptance. Byline given. Buys second serial (reprint) rights. Submit seasonal/holiday material 4 months in advance. Query for electronic submissions. Computer printout submissions OK; prefers letter-quality. Reports in 2-4 weeks on queries; 6-8 weeks on mss. Free sample copy and writer's guidelines.
Nonfiction: Historical, instructional and quilting education. "No light-hearted entertainment." Buys 5-10 mss/year. Query with or without published clips, or send complete ms. Length: 600 words maximum. Pays $75/page.
Photos: Send photos with submission. Reviews transparencies (color) and prints (b&w). Offers $20 per photo. Captions, model releases and identification of subjects required. Buys all rights.
Tips: "Query with ideas; send samples of prior work so that we can assess and suggest assignment. Our publications appeal to traditional quilters, generally middle-aged and mostly who use the patterns in the magazine."

TREASURE, Jess Publishing, 6745 Adobe Rd., 29 Palms CA 92277. (619)367-3531. Editor: Jim Williams. Emphasizes treasure hunting and metal detecting. 90% freelance written. Eager to work with new/unpublished writers. Monthly magazine. Circ. 40,000. Pays on publication. Publishes ms an average of 6 months after acceptance. Buys all rights. Byline given. Phone queries OK. Submit seasonal/holiday material 4 months in advance. Previously published submissions OK. Computer printout submissions acceptable; prefers letter-quality. Reports in 2 months. Sample copy for 8½x11 SAE and $1.05 postage; writer's guidelines for SAE and $1.
Nonfiction: Lee Chandler, articles editor. How-to (coinshooting and treasure hunting tips); informational and historical (location of lost treasures with emphasis on the lesser-known); interviews (with treasure hunters); profiles (successful treasure hunters and metal detector hobbyists); personal experience (treasure hunting); technical (advice on use of metal detectors and metal detector designs). "We would like more coverage of archaeological finds, both professional and amateur, and more reports on recently found caches, whether

located purposefully or accidentally—both types should be accompanied by photos of the finds." Buys 6-8 mss/issue. Send complete ms. Length: 300-3,000 words. Pays $30-200. "Our rate of payment varies considerably depending upon the proficiency of the author, the quality of the photographs, the importance of the subject matter, and the amount of useful information given."

Photos: Offers no additional payment for 5x7 or 8x10 b&w glossy prints used with mss. Pays $75 minimum for color transparencies (35mm or 2¼x2¼. Color for cover only. "Clear photos and other illustrations are a must." Model release required.

Tips: "We hope to increase our news coverage of archaeological digs and cache finds, opening the doors to writers who would like simply to use their journalistic skills to report a specific event. No great knowledge of treasure hunting will be necessary. The most frequent mistakes made by writers in completing an article for *Treasure* are failure to list sources of information and to supply illustrations or photos with a story."

‡**TREASURE CHEST, The Information Source & Marketplace for Collectors and Dealers,** Venture Publishing Co., 211A 253 West 72nd St., New York NY 10023. (212)496-2234. Editor: Howard E. Fischer. 60% freelance written. Monthly newspaper on antiques and collectibles. Estab. 1988. Circ. 50,000. Pays on publication. Publishes an average of 2 months after acceptance. Byline given. Buys first rights and second serial (reprint) rights. Photocopied and previously published submissions OK. Reports in 1 month on queries; 2 months on mss. Sample copy for 9x12 SAE with 3 first class stamps; writer's guidelines for #10 SASE.

Nonfiction: Exposé, general interest, historical/nostalgic, how-to (detect reproductions, find new sources of items, etc.), humor, interview/profile, personal experience and photo feature. Buys 20-35 mss/year. Query with published clips. Length: 700-1,000 words. Pays $20-50. Payment in contributor copies or other premiums negotiable.

Photos: State availability of photos with submission. Reviews contact sheets, 5x7 and 8x10 prints. Offers no additional payment for photos accepted with ms. Captions and identification of subjects required. Buys one-time rights.

Columns/Departments: Investing in Antiques & Collectibles (what's hot; investing tips, etc.) and Show Reviews (unusual items displayed; sales figures, etc.). Query with published clips.

Fillers: Anecdotes, facts, gags to be illustrated by cartoonist and short humor. Buys 12-30/year. Length: 30-200 words. Pays $10-25.

‡**TREASURE SEARCH,** Jess Publishing Co., 6745 Adobe Rd., 29 Palms CA 92277. (619)367-3531. Editor: Jim Williams. 80% freelance written. Bimonthly magazine on treasure hunts. "We publish true stories about treasures, great and small, yet to be discovered as well as about potential coin and relic hunting sites; also product reviews, how-to articles and descriptions of both successful and unsuccessful searches. The magazine is intended to be a practical handbook for the active searcher." Pays on publication. Publishes ms an average ot 2 months after acceptance. Byline given. Buys all rights. Submit seasonal/holiday material 3 months in advance. Photocopied submissions OK. Query for electronic submissions. Computer printout submissions OK. Reports in 2 weeks. Sample copy for 9x12 SAE with $1.05 in postage. Free writer's guidelines.

Nonfiction: Exposé (of treasures not worth searching), historical/nostalgic (treasures backed by history), how-to (how-to research, and search), humor (humorous experiences in the field), inspirational (accounts of treasures found), interview/profile (a treasure hunter's biography), new product (any kind of detection or recovery equipment), personal experience (accounts of searches), photo feature (showing the search for or recovery of a treasure) and technical (explaining how related equipment works). "No fiction—fabricated treasures or experiences." Buys 50 mss/year. Query. Length: 500-15,000 words. Pays $30 per magazine page. Sometimes pays expenses of writers on assignment.

Photos: Send photos with submissions. Reviews contact sheets and 2¼ or 35mm color transparencies. Offers $2-75 per photo. Identification of subjects required. Buys one-time rights.

Columns/Departments: "Then And Now" (clues to treasures or sites worth exploring), 1,000 words and "The Printing Press" (reviews of books of interest to the treasure hunter), 250-400 words. Buys 12 mss/year. Query. Pays $35-45.

Tips: "Freelancers should be aware they are writing for an experienced, skeptical audience and can help themselves by being accurate in all details, getting to know treasure hunters and even practicing some of the techniques themselves. We immediately publish truthful stories of recovered treasures backed by pertinent photos and clues to previously unreported treasures yet to be found if backed by historical documentation."

THE TRUMPETER, Croatian Philatelic Society, 1512 Lancelot, Borger TX 79007. (806)273-7225. Editor: Eck Spahich. 80% freelance written. Eager to work with new/unpublished writers. A quarterly magazine covering stamps, coins, currency, military decorations and collectibles of the Balkans, and of central Europe. Circ. 800. Pays on publication. Publishes ms an average of 9 months after acceptance. Byline given. Buys first and one-time rights. Submit seasonal/holiday material 6 months in advance. Simultaneous and photocopied submissions OK. Computer printout submissions acceptable; no dot-matrix. Reports in 2 months on queries; 1 month on mss. Sample copy $3; free writer's guidelines with #10 SASE.

Nonfiction: Book excerpts, general interest, historical/nostalgic, how-to (on detecting forged stamps, currency etc.) interview/profile, photo features and travel. Buys 15-20 mss/year. Send complete ms. Length: 500-1,500 words. Pays for $25-50 for assigned articles; pays $5-25 for unsolicited articles. Sometimes pays the expenses of writers on assignment.

Photos: State availability of photos with submission. Reviews 3x5 prints. Offers $5-10/photo. Captions and identification of subjects required. Buys one-time rights.

Columns/Departments: Book Reviews (stamps, coins, currency of Balkans), 200-400 words; Forgeries (emphasis on pre-1945 period), 500-1,000 words. Buys 10 mss/year. Send complete ms. Length: 100-300 words. Pays $5-25.

Fillers: Facts. Buys 15-20/year. Length: 20-50 words. Pays $1-5.

Tips: "We desperately need features on Zara, Montenegro, Serbia, Bulgaria, Bosnia, Croatia, Romania and Laibach."

VIDEOMAKER™, The Video Camera User's Magazine, Videomaker Inc., Box 4591, Chico CA 95927. (916)891-8410. FAX: (916)891-9443. Editor: Bradley Kent. 75% freelance written. A bimonthly magazine on video production. "Our audience is a range of hobbyist and low-end professional video camera users." Editorial emphasis is on video*making* (production and exposure), *not* reviews of commercial videos. Personal video phenomenon is a young 'movement'—readership encouraged to participate—get in on the act, join the fun." Circ. 50,000. Pays on publication. Publishes ms an average of 4-6 months after acceptance. Byline given. Buys all rights. Submit seasonal/holiday material 6 months in advance. Simultaneous, photocopied and previously published submissions OK. Query for electronic submissions. Computer printout submissions OK. Reports in 2 months on queries; 1 month on mss. Sample copy for 9x12 SAE with 5 first-class stamps. Free writer's guidelines.

Nonfiction: How-to (tools, tips, techniques for better videomaking), interview/profile (notable videomakers), product probe (review of latest and greatest or innovative), personal experience (lessons to benefit other videomakers), technical (state-of-the-art audio/video). Articles with comprehensive coverage of product line or aspect of videomaking preferred. Buys 35 mss/year. Query with or without published clips or send complete ms. Length: open. Pays $150-300.

Photos: Send photos with submissions. Reviews contact sheets, transparencies and prints. Captions required. Payment for photos accepted with ms included as package compensation. Buys one-time rights.

Columns/Departments: Computer Video (state-of-the art products, applications, potentials for computer-video interface); Profile (highlights videomakers using medium in unique/worthwhile ways); Book/Tape Mode (brief reviews of current works pertaining to video production); Videocrafts (projects, gadgets, inventions for videomaking). Buys 40 mss/year. Pays $35-175.

Fillers: Anecdotes, facts, cartoons, newsbreaks, short humor. Negotiable pay.

Tips: "Comprehensiveness a must. Article on shooting tips covers *all* angles. Buyer's guide to special-effect generators cites *all* models available. Magazine strives for an 'all-or-none' approach, given bimonthly status. Most topics covered once (twice tops) per year, so we must be thorough. Manuscript/photo package submissions helpful. *Videomaker* wants videomaking to be fulfilling for all."

WESTERN & EASTERN TREASURES, People's Publishing Co., Inc., Box 1095, Arcata CA 95521. Editor: Rosemary Anderson. Emphasizes treasure hunting and metal detecting for all ages, entire range in education, coast-to-coast readership. 90% freelance written. Monthly magazine. Circ. 70,000. Pays on publication. Publishes ms an average of 1 year after acceptance. Buys all rights. Computer printout submissions acceptable; no dot-matrix. Sample copy and writer's guidelines for $2 and 8½x11 SAE.

Nonfiction: How-to "hands on" use of metal detecting equipment, how to locate coins, jewelry and relics, prospect for gold, where to look for treasures, rocks and gems, etc., "first-person" experiences. "No purely historical manuscripts or manuscripts that require two-part segments or more." Buys 200 unsolicited mss/year. Submit complete ms. Length: maximum 1,500 words. Pays 2¢/word—negotiable.

Photos: Purchased with accompanying ms. Captions required. Submit b&w prints or 35mm Kodachrome color transparencies. Pays $5 maximum for 3x5 and up b&w glossy prints; $35 and up for 35mm Kodachrome cover slides. Model releases required.

Tips: "The writer has a better chance of breaking in at our publication with short articles and fillers as these give the readers a chance to respond to the writer. The publisher relies heavily on reader reaction. Not adhering to word limit is the main mistake made by writers in completing an article for us. Writers must clearly cover the subjects described above in 1,500 words or less."

WOMEN'S CIRCLE COUNTED CROSS-STITCH, House of White Birches, Inc., 306 E. Parr Rd., Berne IN 46711. Editor: Denise Lohr. 100% freelance written. Eager to work with new/unpublished writers. Bimonthly magazine featuring counted cross-stitch. Circ. 165,000. Pays on publication. Publishes ms an average of at least 6 months after acceptance. Byline given. Buys all rights. Submit seasonal/holiday material 6 months in advance. Computer printout submissions OK. Reports in 1 month. Sample copy $3. Make checks payable to House of White Birches. Contributor tips, guidelines and deadline schedule for large SAE and 2 first class stamps.

Nonfiction: How-to, interview/profile, new product and charted designs. Buys 12-15 mss/year. Query with published clips. "Submit cross-stitch designs with cover letter, complete ms and snapshot or 35mm slide of project *or* send complete ms and finished project. Include sufficient postage for project return." Length: open. Pays $25 and up. Also publishes cross-stitch leaflets.
Tips: "We'd like larger, more complicated designs using the latest techniques and products."

WOMEN'S HOUSEHOLD CROCHET, House of White Birches, Inc., 306 E. Parr Rd., Berne IN 46711. Editor: Susan Hankins Andrews. 99% freelance written. A quarterly magazine. "We appeal to crochet lovers—young and old, city and country, thread and yarn lovers alike. Our readers crochet for necessity as well as pleasure. Articles are 99% pattern-oriented. We need patterns for all expertise levels—beginner to expert. No knit patterns please." Circ. 75,000. Pays on publication. Publishes ms an average of 1 year after acceptance. Byline given. Buys all rights. Submit seasonal/holiday material 6 months in advance. Computer printout submissions OK. Reports in 1 month on queries; 6 weeks on mss. Sample copy for $2; free writer's guidelines.
Nonfiction: General interest, historical/nostalgic, how-to, humor, personal experience and technical. Needs seasonal patterns by March 1. Christmas Annual (December). Must be Christmas oriented. "Nothing of explicit sexual nature—our readers are true Bible-belt types. Even articles of a suggestive nature are apt to offend. Stay away from themes having to do with alcohol." Buys 10 mss/year. Send complete ms. Length: 500-2,000 words. Pays $50 and up for unsolicited articles.
Photos: Buys no photos. Must send crocheted item for staff photography.
Columns/Departments: Designer's Debut Contest (1st and 2nd prizes chosen each issue for crochet design). Buys 8 mss/year. Send complete ms. Length: 500-2,000 words. Pays competitive designer rates.
Poetry: Light verse and traditional. "No long poems over 20 lines. None of a sexual nature." Buys 6 poems/year. Submit maximum 2 poems. Length: 5-20 lines. Pays $5-20.
Fillers: Anecdotes, crochet cartoons, facts and short humor. Buys 24/year. Length: 35-70 words. Pays $5-20.
Tips: "Freelancers have the best chance of selling articles incorporating new trends in crochet. Look around you at the latest fashions, home decor, etc., for ideas—how to make money at crocheting (success stories from those who have marketed their needlework successfully) and patterns (keep materials inexpensive or moderately priced). Make sure crochet directions are complete and exact (no errors). Use standard crochet abbreviations. Send crocheted items with manuscripts; we will return them if return postage is included."

THE WORKBASKET, 4251 Pennsylvania Ave., Kansas City MO 64111. Editor: Roma Jean Rice. Issued monthly except bimonthly June-July and November-December. Buys first rights. Pays on acceptance. Reports in 6 weeks.
Nonfiction: Step-by-step directions for craft projects (400-500 words) and gardening articles (200-500 words). Query. Pays 7¢/word.
Photos: Pays $7-10 for 8x10 glossies with ms.

WORKBENCH, 4251 Pennsylvania Ave., Kansas City MO 64111. (816)531-5730. Editor: Robert N. Hoffman. 75% freelance written. Prefers to work with published/established writers; works with a small number of new/unpublished writers each year. For woodworkers. Circ. 830,000. Pays on acceptance. Publishes ms an average of 1 year after acceptance. Byline given if requested. Buys all rights then returns all but first rights upon request, after publication. Computer printout submissions acceptable; prefers letter-quality. Reports in 2 months. Sample copy for 8½x11 SAE and 6 first class stamps; free writer's guidelines.
Nonfiction: "We have continued emphasis on do-it-yourself woodworking, home improvement and home maintenance projects. We provide in-progress photos, technical drawings and how-to text for all projects. We are very strong in woodworking, cabinetmaking and classic furniture construction. Projects range from simple toys to complicated reproductions of furniture now in museums. We would like to receive contemporary and furniture items that can be duplicated by both beginning do-it-yourselfers and advanced woodworkers." Query. Pays $175/published page, up or down depending on quality of submission. Additional payment for good color photos. "If you can consistently provide good material, including photos, your rates will go up and you will get assignments."
Columns/Departments: Shop Tips bring $20-50 with a line drawing and/or b&w photo. Workbench Solver pays $50 to experts providing answers to readers problems related to do-it-yourself projects and home repair.
Tips: "Our magazine will focus on wood working, covering all levels of ability. We will continue to present home improvment projects from the do-it-yourselfer's viewpoint, emphasizing the most up-to-date materials and procedures. We would like to receive articles on indoor home improvements and remodeling, home improvement on manufactured and mobile homes, and/or simple contemporary furniture. We place a heavy emphasis on well-designed projects, that is projects that are both functional and classic in design. We can photograph projects worthy for publication, so feel free to send snapshots."

WORLD COIN NEWS, Krause Publications, 700 E. State, Iola WI 54990. (715)445-2214. FAX: (715)445-4087. Editor: John Kolbeck. 30% freelance written. Works with a small number of new/unpublished writers each year. Weekly newsmagazine about non-U.S. coin collecting for novices and advanced collectors of foreign coins, medals, and other numismatic items. Circ. 15,000. Pays on publication. Publishes ms an average of 1 month after acceptance. Byline given. Buys first North American serial rights and reprint rights. Submit seasonal material 1 month in advance. Simultaneous and photocopied submissions OK. Computer printout submissions acceptable. Reports in 2 weeks. Free sample copy.

Nonfiction: "Send us timely news stories related to collecting foreign coins and current information on coin values and markets." Send complete ms. Buys 30 mss/year. Length: 500-2,000 words. Pays 3¢/word to first-time contributors; fees negotiated for later articles. Sometimes pays the expenses of writers on assignment.

Photos: Send photos with ms. Pays $5 minimum for b&w prints. Captions and model release required. Buys first rights and first reprint rights.

YESTERYEAR, Yesteryear Publications, Box 2, Princeton WI 54968. (414)787-4808. Editor: Michael Jacobi. 25% freelance written. Prefers to work with published/established writers. For antique dealers and collectors, people interested in collecting just about anything, and nostalgia buffs. Monthly tabloid. Circ. 7,000. Pays on publication. Publishes ms an average of 2-3 months after acceptance. Buys one-time rights. Byline given. Submit seasonal/holiday material 3 months in advance. Simultaneous, photocopied and previously published submissions OK. Computer printout submissions acceptable; prefers letter-quality. Reports in 1 month. Sample copy $1.

Nonfiction: General interest (basically, anything pertaining to antiques, collectible items or nostalgia in general); historical (again, pertaining to the above categories); and how-to (refinishing antiques, how to collect). The more specific and detailed, the better. "We do not want personal experience or opinion articles." Buys 24 mss/year. Send complete ms. Pays $5-25. Pays expenses of writers on assignment.

Photos: Send photos with ms. Pays $5 for 5x7 b&w glossy or matte prints; $5 for 5x7 color prints. Captions preferred.

Columns/Departments: "We will consider new column concepts as long as they fit into the general areas of antiques and collectibles." Buys 1 ms/issue. Send complete ms. Pays $5-25.

Home and Garden

Some magazines here concentrate on gardens; others on the how-to of interior design. Still others focus on homes and gardens in specific regions of the country.

BETTER HOMES AND GARDENS, 1716 Locust St., Des Moines IA 50336. (515)284-3000. Editor (Building): Joan McCloskey. Editor (Furnishings): Denise Caringer. Editor (Foods): Nancy Byal. Editor (Travel): Mark Ingelbrentson. Editor (Garden Outdoor Living): Doug Jimerson. Editor (Health & Education): Paul Krantz. Editor (Money Management, Automotive, Features): Margaret Daly. 10-15% freelance written. Pays on acceptance. Buys all rights. "We read all freelance articles, but much prefer to see a letter of query rather than a finished manuscript."

Nonfiction: Travel, education, health, cars, money management, and home entertainment. "We do not deal with political subjects or with areas not connected with the home, community, and family." Pays rates "based on estimate of length, quality and importance."

Tips: Direct queries to the department that best suits your story line.

CANADIAN WORKSHOP, The Do-It-Yourself Magazine, Camar Publications (1984) Inc., 130 Spy Ct., Markham, Ontario L3R 5H6 Canada. (416)475-8440. Editor: Cindy Lister. 90% freelance written; half of these are assigned. Monthly magazine covering the "do-it-yourself market including woodworking projects, renovation and restoration, maintenance and decoration. Canadian writers only." Circ. 110,000. Pays on publication. Publishes ms an average of 5 months after acceptance. Byline given. Offers 75% kill fee. Rights are negotiated with the author. Submit seasonal/holiday material 6 months in advance. Simultaneous queries OK. Computer printout submissions acceptable; no dot-matrix. Reports in 3 weeks. Sample copy for 8 × 11 SASE; free writer's guidelines with #10 SASE.

Nonfiction: How-to (home maintenance, renovation projects, woodworking projects and features). Buys 20-40 mss/year. Query with clips of published work. Length: 1,500-4,000 words. Pays $225-600. Pays expenses of writers on assignment.

Photos: Send photos with ms. Payment for photos, transparencies negotiated with the author. Captions, model releases, and identification of subjects required.

Tips: "Freelancers must be aware of our magazine format. Products used in how-to articles must be readily available across Canada. Deadlines for articles are 5 months in advance of cover date. How-tos should be detailed enough for the amateur but appealing to the experienced. A frequent mistake made by writers is not directing the copy towards our reader. Stories sometimes have a tendency to be too basic."

COLORADO HOMES & LIFESTYLES, Suite 154, 2550 31st St., Denver CO 80216. (303)455-1944. FAX: (303)455-7490. Editor: Darla Worden. 60% freelance written. Bimonthly magazine covering Colorado homes and lifestyles for upper-middle-class and high income households as well as designers, decorators and architects. Circ. 30,000. Pays on acceptance. Publishes ms an average of 4 months after acceptance. Byline given. Buys all rights. Submit seasonal/holiday material 6 months in advance. Simultaneous queries and photocopied submissions OK. Query for electronic submissions. Computer printout submissions acceptable: prefers letter-quality. Reports in 1 month. Free writer's guidelines.
Nonfiction: Fine home furnishings, interesting personalities and lifestyles, gardening and plants, decorating and design, fine food and entertaining—all with a Colorado slant. Buys 40 mss/year. Send complete ms. Length: 1,000-2,000 words. "For celebrity features (Colorado celebrity and home) pay is $300-800. For unique, well-researched pieces on Colorado people, places, etc., pay is 15-25¢/word. For regular articles, 10¢/word. The more specialized and Colorado-oriented your article is, the more generous we are." Sometimes pays the expenses of writers on assignment.
Photos: Send photos with ms. Reviews 35mm, 4x5 and 2¼ color transparencies and b&w glossy prints. Identification of subjects required.
Tips: "The more interesting and unique the subject the better. A frequent mistake made by writers is failure to provide material with a style and slant appropriate for the magazine, due to poor understanding of the focus of the magazine."

FINE GARDENING, Taunton Press, 63 S. Main St., Box 355, Newtown CT 06470. 1-800-243-7252. FAX: (203)426-3434. Editor: Roger Holmes. Bimonthly magazine on gardening. "Focus is broad subject of landscape and ornamental gardening, with selective interest in food gardening. Reader written by avid gardeners—first person, hands-on gardening experiences." Estab. 1988. Circ. 85,000. Pays on publication. Byline given. Buys first North American serial rights. Simultaneous, photocopied and previously published submissions OK. Query for electronic submissions. Computer printout submissions OK. Reports in 1 month. Free writer's guidelines.
Nonfiction: Book review, essays, how-to, new product, opinion, personal experience, photo feature. Buys 50-60 mss/year. Query. Length: 1,000-3,000 words. Pays $150/page.
Photos: Send photos with submission. Reviews 35mm transparencies. Offers no additional payment for photos accepted with ms. Buys one-time rights.
Columns/Department: Book reviews (on gardening); Gleanings (essays, stories, opinions, research); Last Word (essays/serious, humorous, fact or fiction). Query. Length: 100-1,000 words. Pays $10-150.
Tips: "It's most important to have solid first-hand experience as a gardener. Tell us what you've done with your own landscape and plants."

FLORIDA HOME & GARDEN, #207, 600 Brickell Ave., Miami FL 33131. (305)374-5011. Editor: Kathryn Howard. Managing Editor: Sylvia Wood. 20% freelance written. Works with a small number of new/unpublished writers each year. Monthly magazine of Florida homes, interior design, architecture, landscape architecture, gardens, cuisine, lifestyles and home entertainment. "We want beautiful, practical coverage of the subjects listed as they relate to Florida." Circ. 65,000. Pays on publication. Publishes ms an average of 3 months after acceptance. Byline given. Offers $25 kill fee by pre-agreement only. Buys first North American serial rights for one year, plus unlimited reuse in our magazine (no resale). Submit seasonal/holiday material 6 months in advance. Query for electronic submissions. Computer printout submissions OK. Sample copy $2.50; writer's guidelines for #10 SASE.
Nonfiction: General interest (in our subjects); how-to (interior design, cuisine, recipes, but with a Florida twist, and gardening for Florida climate); and travel Caribbean/Florida (home architecture or garden destinations only). Buys 36 mss/year. Query with published clips. length: 1,000-2,000 words. Pays $200-400. Pays expenses of writers on assignment by prior agreement only.
Photos: Fathia Lyn, art director. State availability of photos or send photos with query. Reviews 35mm, 4x5 or 2″ color transparencies. Captions and identification of subjects required. Buys one-time rights plus unlimited editorial re-use of magazine's separations.
Columns/Departments: How-to (specific home how-to); Garden Care; What's Hot (Florida products); Developments; Who's Hot (Florida); Antiques & Collectibles; Art; Cuisine; Florida Gardener; Travel (Florida, Caribbean); Books (reviews); New Products (b&w photos). Buys 36 mss/year. Query with published clips. Length: 500-1,500 words. Pays $200-400.
Tips: "We're looking for stories that visually show the beauty of Florida and impart practical information to our readers. Must relate to Florida's tropicality in all subjects."

FLOWER AND GARDEN MAGAZINE, 4251 Pennsylvania, Kansas City MO 64111. Editor: A. Cort Sinnes. 50% freelance written. Works with a small number of new/unpublished writers each year. For home gardeners. Bimonthly. Picture magazine. Circ. 600,000. Buys first rights only. Byline given. Pays on acceptance. Publishes ms an average of 6-12 months after acceptance. Computer printout submissions acceptable; no dot-matrix. Reports in 6 weeks. Sample copy $2.50 and 9½ × 12½ SAE; writer's guidelines for SASE.

Nonfiction: Interested in illustrated articles on how to do certain types of gardening and descriptive articles about individual plants. Flower arranging, landscape design, house plants, patio gardening are other aspects covered. "The approach we stress is practical (how-to-do-it, what-to-do-it-with). We try to stress plain talk, clarity and economy of words. An article should be tailored for a national audience." Buys 20-30 mss/year. Query. Length: 500-1,500 words. Rates vary depending on quality and kind of material.

Photos: Pays up to $12.50/5x7 or 8x10 b&w prints, depending on quality, suitability. Also buys color transparencies, 35mm and larger. "We are using more four-color illustrations." Pays $30-125 for these, depending on size and use.

Tips: "The prospective author needs good grounding in gardening practice and literature. Offer well-researched and well-written material appropriate to the experience level of our audience. Use botanical names as well as common. Illustrations help sell the story. Describe special qualifications for writing the particular proposed subject."

GARDEN DESIGN, The Fine Art of Residential Landscape Architecture, American Society of Landscape Architects, Suite 500, 4401 Connecticut Ave. NW, Washington DC 20008. (202)686-2752. Editor: Karen D. Fishler. 80% freelance written. Works with a small number of new/unpublished writers each year. A quarterly magazine focusing on the design of public and private gardens. "Our attitude is that garden design is a fine art and craft, and that gardening is a way of life." Circ. 41,500. May pay part on acceptance if long interval between acceptance and publication. Publishes ms an average of 9 months after acceptance. Byline given. Offers $100 kill fee. Buys first North American rights. Submit seasonal/holiday material 6 months in advance. Computer printout submissions OK; no dot-matrix. Reports in 2 months. Sample copy $5; writer's guidelines for 10 SASE.

Nonfiction: "We look for literate, imaginative writing that conveys how a specific garden's design works, both how it was achieved and the experience it provides." No how-to, such as gardening techniques. Buys 15-20 mss/year. Query with published clips. Length: 1,000-2,500 words. Pays $350 maximum. Sometimes pays the expenses of writers on assignment.

Photos: Send scouting photos with submission (preferably transparencies, not prints). Reviews transparencies and prints. Offers $75-200/photo. Captions and identification of subjects required. Buys one-time rights.

Columns/Departments: Subjects include: personality; plants; design details; design (as a problem solver); the garden as a social setting. Buys 35-40 mss/year. Query with published clips. Pays $75-250.

Tips: "Our greatest need is for small to mid-size private gardens, designed by professionals in collaboration with owners. Scouting locations is a valuable service freelancers can perform, by contacting designers and garden clubs in the area, visiting gardens and taking snapshots for our review. It helps to submit a plan drawing of the garden's layout (the designer usually can supply this). All feature articles and departments are open to freelancers. Writing should be intelligent and well-informed, a pleasure to read. Avoid pretension and flowery devices. Check proper plant names in Hortus III."

GARDEN MAGAZINE, The Garden Society, A Division of the New York Botanical Garden, Bronx Park, Bronx NY 10458. FAX: (212)220-6504. Editor: Ann Botshon. 50% freelance written. Works with a small number of new/unpublished writers each year. Bimonthly magazine, emphasizing horticulture, environment and botany for a diverse readership, largely college graduates and professionals united by a common interest in plants and the environment. Most are members of botanical gardens and arboreta. Circ. 32,000. Publishes ms an average of 1 year after acceptance. Buys first North American serial rights. Submit seasonal/holiday material 6 months in advance. Photocopied submissions OK. Query for electronic submissions. Computer printout submissions acceptable; prefers letter-quality. Reports in 2 months. Sample copy $3.50 and 9×11 SAE; guidelines for SASE.

Nonfiction: "All articles must be of high quality, meticulously researched and botanically accurate." Exposé (environmental subjects); how-to (horticultural techniques, must be unusual and verifiable); general interest (plants in art and history, botanical news, ecology); humor (pertaining to botany and horticulture); and travel (great gardens of the world). Buys 15-20 unsolicited mss/year. Query with clips of published work. Length: 1,000-2,500 words. Pays $100-300. Sometimes pays the expenses of writers on assignment.

Photos: Karen Polyak, managing editor. Pays $35-50/5x7 b&w glossy print; $40-150/4x5 or 35mm color transparency. Captions preferred. Buys one-time rights.

Tips: "We appreciate some evidence that the freelancer has studied our magazine and understands our special requirements. A writer should write from a position of authority that comes from either personal experience (horticulture); extensive research (environment, ecology, history, art); adequate scientific background; or all three. Style should be appropriate to this approach."

THE HERB COMPANION, Interweave Press, 306 N. Washington, Loveland CO 80537. (303)669-7672. Editor: Linda Ligon. 80% freelance written. Bimonthly magazine about herbs: culture, history, culinary use, crafts, medicinal.. Audience includes a wide range of herb enthusiasts. Circ. 30,000. Pays on publication. Byline given. Buys first North American serial rights. Sample copy $4; writer's guidelines for #10 SASE. Query. Length: 10-16 pages. Typical payment is $100 per published page. State availability of photos.

Tips: "Articles must show depth and working knowledge of the subject, though tone should be informal and accessible."

HERB QUARTERLY, Box 548, Boiling Springs PA 17007. FAX: (717)245-2764. Publisher: Linda Sparrowe. 80% freelance written. Quarterly magazine for herb enthusiasts. Circ. 25,000. Pays on publication. Publishes ms an average of 1 year after acceptance. Buys first North American serial rights and second (reprint) rights to manuscripts originally published elsewhere. Query for electronic submissions. Computer printout submissions acceptable. Query letters recommended. Reports in 1 month. Sample copy $5 and 9 × 12 SAE; writer's guidelines for #10 SASE.
Nonfiction: Gardening (landscaping, herb garden design, propagation, harvesting); herb businesses; medicinal and cosmetic use of herbs; crafts; cooking; historical (folklore, focused piece on particular period—*not* general survey); interview of a famous person involved with herbs or folksy herbalist; personal experience; and photo essay ("cover quality" 8x10 b&w prints). "We are particularly interested in herb garden design, contemporary or historical." No fiction. Send double-spaced ms. Length: 2,000-10,000 words. Pays $50. Reports in 1 month.
Tips: "Our best submissions are narrowly focused on herbs with much practical information on cultivation and use for the gardener."

‡HOME MAGAZINE, Allied Publications, 1776 Lake Worth Rd., Lake Worth FL 33460. (407)582-2099. FAX: (407)582-4667. Editor: Richard Champlin. 95% freelance written. Bimonthly magazine. Pays on publication. Publishes ms an average of 2-3 months after acceptance. Byline given. Buys first North American serial rights, one-time rights, second serial (reprint) rights or simultaneous rights. Submit seasonal/holiday material 6-8 months in advance. Simultaneous, photocopied and previously published submissions OK. Query for electronic submissions. Computer printout submissions OK; prefers letter-quality. Reports in 2 weeks on queries; 6 months on mss. Sample copy $1. Free writer's guidelines with SASE.
Nonfiction: Book excerpts, general interest, how-to, humor, interview/profile, personal experience, photo feature and travel (domestic). Query with or without published clips. Length: 600-1,500 words. Pays $5-25 for unsolicited articles. Pays in contributor copies or other premiums only at writer's request.
Photos: State availability of photos with submission. Reviews contact sheets, transparencies and b&w prints. Offers $5 per photo. Captions, model releases (when necessary) and identification of subjects required. Buys one-time rights.
Columns/Departments: Homework (first person stories/newsbreak), 600 words. Buys 6 mss/year. Query. Send complete ms. Pays $5-25.
Fiction: Humorous, mainstream and slice-of-life vignettes. Buys 6 mss/year. Send complete ms. Length: 600-1,200 words. Pays $5-25.
Fillers: Anecdotes, facts, gags to be illustrated by cartoonist, newsbreaks and short humor. Pays $5.

HOMEOWNER, Family Media Inc., 3 Park Ave., New York NY 10016. Editor-in-chief: Joe Carter. Managing Editor: Michael Hartnett. 75% freelance written. Monthly (combined Jan/Feb; July/Aug) magazine on home improvement, including remodeling, maintenance and repair. Aimed at men and women with helpful information of planning, design options, new products and do-it-yourself techniques. Circ. 700,000. Pays on acceptance. Publishes ms an average of 4 months after acceptance. Byline given. Offers kill fee. Buys first North American serial rights. Computer printout submissions acceptable. Reports in 1 month. Sample copy on request; writer's guidelines for #10 SASE.
Nonfiction: Remodeling, home repair and maintenance, how-to; personal experience (hands-on experience with building a home, remodeling or carpentry project); and some technical information on products, materials, how things work. Length: 1,500 maximum. Rates start at $400 for short articles plus some expenses of writers on assignment.

‡HORTICULTURE, The Magazine of American Gardening, Suite 1220, 20 Park Plaza, Boston MA 02116. Published by Horticulture Limited Partnership. Editor: Thomas C. Cooper. 90% freelance written. Works with a small number of new/unpublished writers each year. Monthly. Buys first North American serial rights. Byline given. Publishes ms an average of 9 months after acceptance. Computer submissions OK; query for electronic submissions. Sample copy and writer's guidelines for 8½ × 11 SASE and 85¢ postage. Reports in 10 weeks.
Nonfiction: All aspects of gardening. "We cover indoors and outdoors, edibles and ornamentals, garden design, noteworthy gardens and gardeners." Length: 1,500-3,000 words. Query. Study publication. Pays expenses of writers on assignment.
Photos: Color transparencies and top quality b&w prints, 8x10 only; "accurately identified." Buys one-time rights.
Tips: "We'd like to see some writing by accomplished vegetable gardeners. We continue to seek good pieces on garden design as well as visits to interesting small gardens."

HOUSE BEAUTIFUL, The Hearst Corp., 1700 Broadway, New York NY 10019. (212)903-5000. Editor: JoAnn Barwick. Executive Editor: Margaret Kennedy. Editorial Director: Mervyn Kaufman. Features Director: Joanna Krotz. (212)903-5224. 15% freelance written. Prefers to work with published/established writers. Emphasizes design, architecture and building. Monthly magazine. Circ. 850,000. Pays on acceptance. Publishes ms an average of 4 months after acceptance. Byline given. Submit seasonal/holiday material 4 months in advance of issue date. Computer printout submissions acceptable; prefers letter-quality. Reports in 5 weeks.

Nonfiction: Historical (landmark buildings and restorations); how-to (kitchen, bath remodeling); interviews; new product; and profile. Submit query with detailed outline or complete ms. Length: 300-1,000 words. Pays varying rates.

Photos: State availability of photos or submit with ms.

‡THE ISLAND GROWER, The Magazine of Coastal Gardening and Living, Greenheart Publications, 7007 Richview Dr., RR4, Sooke, B.C. V0S 1N0 Canada. (604)642-4129. Editor: Phyllis Kusch. 90% freelance written. Monthly magazine (excluding January) on gardening and outdoor coastal living. "As we have a targeted, paid readership, we address editorial to those interested in gardening with most of slant towards natural methods." Pays within three months after publication. Byline given. Buys one-time rights. Submit seasonal/holiday material 3 months in advance. Simultaneous, photocopied and previously published submissions OK. Query for electronic submissions. Computer printout submissions OK. Reports in 1 month on queries; 6 weeks on mss. Free sample copy and writer's guidelines.

Nonfiction: How-to (steps to complete gardening project—comprehensive), humor, interview/profile, new product, opinion (concerning environment), photo feature and travel (horticulture shows, events, tours, places of interest). "No general, philosophical articles that are not practical use to readers, and articles that require sources but are not included." Query with published clips. Length: 1,000-2,000 words. Pays $20-75 for assigned articles; $20-110 for unsolicited articles. Pays in contributor copies or other premiums "if known personally and can arrange agreeable payment."

Photos: Send photos with submission. Reviews 5x7 or 8x10 prints. Offers no additional payment for photos accepted with ms. Model releases and identification of subjects required.

Columns/Departments: Bulbs and Vegetables (how to plant, varieties available, pertinent geographical area), 1,000-2,000 words and New Products (of interest to environment; specifically pest control methods without chemical reliance), 500-1,000 words. Query with published clips. Pays $20-110.

Tips: "Study and observe publication to appreciate quality of publication; reflect this in query letters and submissions. We do not appreciate sloppy or poorly researched submissions."

‡LOG HOME LIVING, Home Buyer Publications Inc., Suite 500, 610 Herndon Pkwy., Box 370, Herndon VA 22070. (703)478-0435. Editor: John R. Kupferer. Managing Editor: Roland Sweet. Less than 10% freelance written. Quarterly magazine that covers contemporary log homes. "*Log Home Living* is a quarterly magazine for people who own or are planning to build contemporary manufactured and handcrafted kit log homes. Our audience comprises married couples 30-45 years old. Estab. 1989. Pays on acceptance. Publishes ms an average of 6 months after acceptance. Byline given. Offers $100 kill fee. Buys one-time rights. Submit seasonal/holiday material 9-12 months in advance. Reports in 6-8 weeks. Sample copy $3.25. Writer's guidelines for SAE with 1 first class stamp.

Nonfiction: How-to (buy or build log home), interview/profile (log home owners and companies), photo feature (log homes) and technical (design/decor topics). "We do not want historical/nostalgic material." Buys 2-3 mss/year. Query with published clips. Length: 750-1,500 words. Pays $100-600. Sometimes pays expenses of writers on assignment.

Photos: Send photos with submission. Reviews contact sheets, 2½x2½ transparencies and 5x7 prints. Offers $50-200 per photo. Captions, model releases and identification of subjects required. Buys one-time rights.

Tips: "Owner profiles are most open to freelancers. Reveal how they planned for, designed and bought/built their dream home; how they decorated it; how they like it; advice for others thinking of buying."

‡METROPOLITAN HOME, Meredith Corporation, 750 Third Ave., New York NY 10017. (212)557-6600. Editor: Dorothy Kalins. Articles Editor: Barbara Graustark. 50% freelance written. Monthly magazine on home furnishings, interior design and architects. Circ. 720,000. Pays on acceptance. Byline given. Offers 25% kill fee. Buys all rights. Submit seasonal/holiday material 5 months in advance. Computer printout submissions OK. Reports in 1 month on queries. Free writer's guidelines. "Encourages writers to pick up magazine on newsstand."

Nonfiction: Book excerpts, essays, interview/profile, personal experience, real estate and travel. Buys 60-100 mss/year. Query with published clips. Length: 350-2,000 words. Pays $350-2,000 for assigned articles. Pays expenses of writers on assignment if agreed in advance.

Photos: State availability of photos with submission.

Tips: "The Metro section is most open for freelancers. It provides a variety of subjects to which writers can contribute."

NATIONAL GARDENING, National Gardening Association, 180 Flynn Ave., Burlington VT 05401. (802)863-1308. Editor: Katharine Anderson. 85% freelance written. Willing to work with new/unpublished writers. Monthly magazine covering all aspects of food gardening and ornamentals. "We publish not only how-to garden techniques, but also news that affects gardeners, like science advances. Detailed, experienced-based articles with carefully worked-out techniques for planting, growing, harvesting and using garden fruits and vegetables sought. Our material is for both experienced and beginning gardeners." Circ. 200,000. Pays on acceptance. Publishes ms an average of 9 months after acceptance. Byline given. Buys first serial rights and occasionally second (reprint) rights to material originally published elsewhere. Submit seasonal/holiday material 8 months in advance. Photocopied and previously published submissions OK, but original material preferred. Computer printout submissions acceptable; prefers letter-quality. Reports in 1 month. Sample copy for 8½x11 SAE and $1; writer's guidelines for #10 SASE.
Nonfiction: How-to, humor, inspirational, interview/profile, new product, personal experience, photo feature and technical. Buys 80-100 mss/year. Query first. Length: 500-3,000 words. Pays $30-450/article. Sometimes pays the expenses of writers on assignment; must have prior approval.
Photos: Vicky Congdon, photo manager. Send photos with ms. Pays $20-40 for b&w photos; $50 for color photos. Captions, model releases and identification of subjects required.
Tips: "Wordiness is a frequent mistake made by writers. Few writers understand how to write 'tight'. We have increased coverage of ornamentals, although primary focus will remain food gardening."

NEW HOME, The Magazine for Imaginative Homeowners, Gilford Publishing, Box 2008, Village West, Laconia NH 03247. Managing Editor: Steven Maviglio. 90% freelance written. Bimonthly magazine. "*New Home* is mailed to homebuyers (new and existing within one month of filing the deed). The magazine goes to those who have purchased homes costing $85,000 or more. The first few months of living in a new house means decorating, remodeling and buying products. We show them how to make quality decisions." Circ. 300,000. Pays on acceptance. Publishes ms an average of 2 months after acceptance. Byline given. Kill fee varies $100-500. Buys all rights. Submit seasonal/holiday material 6 months in advance. Simultaneous submissions OK; no dot-matrix. Computer printout submissions OK. Reports in 2 weeks. Sample copy for $5 and 8½x11 SAE with 6 first class stamps. Free writer's guidelines.
Nonfiction: Essays, how-to, interview/profile, new product, technical. No articles on "How I dealt with My New Kitchen," "Why Moving Is So Terrible." Buys 50 mss/year. Query with published clips. Pays $200-3,000 words. Pays $200-1,500 for assigned articles; $200-500 for unsolicited articles. Sometimes pays expenses of writers on assignment.
Photos: State availability of photos with submission. Reviews transparencies (5x7) and prints. Offers $50-250/photo. Captions, model release and identification of subjects required. Buys all rights.
Columns/Departments: Out-of-Doors (lawn and garden, landscaping) 1,000-1,500 words; The Kitchen (kitchen cabinets, countertops, small appliances); The Bath (new tubs, working with color, Victorian baths); Details (do-it-yourself, fun projects); Back Porch (essay of a new home experience). Buys 50 mss/year. Query with published clips. Length: 250-2,000 words. Pays $200-1,500.
Fillers: "Homefront" (news and trends). Facts. Buys 20 mss/year. Length: 50-250 words. Pays up to $250.
Tips: "We assign nearly all of our stories. But it doesn't hurt for a writer to query with samples and present their idea in a one-page letter. No unsolicited manuscripts except for our Back Porch section."

N.Y. HABITAT MAGAZINE, For Co-op, Condominium and Loft Living, The Carol Group, Ltd., 928 Broadway, New York NY 10010. (212)505-2030. Editor: Carol J. Ott. Managing Editor: Lloyd Chrein. 75% freelance written. Prefers to work with published/established writers. Published 8 times/year, covering co-op, condo and loft living in metropolitan New York. "Our primary readership is boards of directors of co-ops and condos, and we are looking for material that will help them fulfill their responsibilities." Circ. 10,000. Pays on publication. Publishes ms an average of 3 months after acceptance. Byline given. Offers negotiable kill fee. Buys first North American serial rights. Submit seasonal/holiday material 3 months in advance. Computer printout submissions acceptable. Reports in 3 weeks. Sample copy for $5, 9x12 SAE and 5 first class stamps; writer's guidelines for #10 SASE.
Nonfiction: Only material relating to co-op and condominium living in New York metropolitan area. Buys 20 mss/year. Query with published clips. Length: 750-1,500 words. Pays $25-1,000. Sometimes pays the expenses of writers on assignment.
Tips: "We would like to receive manuscripts dealing with co-op or condo management."

‡**1,001 HOME IDEAS**, Family Media, Inc., 3 Park Ave., New York NY 10016. (212)340-9250. Editor: Errol Croft. Executive Editor: Kathryn Larson. 40% freelance written. Prefers to work with published/established writers. A monthly magazine covering home furnishings, building, remodeling and home equipment. "We are a family shelter magazine edited for young, mainstream homeowners, providing ideas for decorating, remodeling, outdoor living, and at-home entertaining. Emphasis on ideas that are do-able and affordable." Circ. 1,500,000. Pays on acceptance. Publishes ms an average of 6 months after acceptance. Byline given. Offers 25% kill fee. Buys first North American serial rights, second serial (reprint) rights, or makes work-for-hire assignments. Submit seasonal/holiday material 12 months in advance. Computer printout submissions

acceptable. Reports in 1 month. Sample copy $2.50; writer's guidelines for business size SASE.

Nonfiction: Book excerpts (on interior design and crafts only); how-to (on decorating, remodeling and home maintenance); interview/profile (of designers only); new product; photo feature (on homes only); crafts; home equipment; and home furnishings and decor. No travel, religious, technical or exposés. Buys 25 mss/year. Query with or without published clips, or send complete ms. Length: 300-2,000 words. Pays $100-750 for assigned articles; pays $100-500 for unsolicited articles. Sometimes pays the expenses of writers on assignment.

Photos: State availability of photos with submission. Reviews transparencies and prints. Offers $10-100/photo. Captions, model releases, and identification of subjects required. Buys one-time rights.

Columns/Departments: Kathie Robitz, column/department editor. 1,001 Ways to Save $$$ (consumer buymanship, housing, finance, home furnishings, products, etc.) 1,500 words. Buys 12 mss/year. Query. Pays $300-400.

Tips: "The idea is what sells an article to us ... good ideas for decorating, remodeling and improving the home, and well-researched information on how-to, with any necessary directions and patterns, to help the reader carry out the idea. The department, 1,001 Ways to Save, is the area most open to freelance writers. We also look for features which we can turn into photo features on decorating, remodeling and improving the home."

PHOENIX HOME & GARDEN, PHG, Inc., 3136 N. 3rd Ave., Phoenix AZ 85013. (602)234-0840. Editor: Manya Winsted. Managing Editor: Nora Burba Trulsson. 50% freelance written. Works with a small number of new/unpublished writers each year. Monthly magazine covering homes, furnishings, entertainment, lifestyle and gardening for Phoenix area residents interested in better living. Circ. 35,000. Pays on publication. Publishes ms an average of 2 months after acceptance. Byline given. Buys all rights. Submit seasonal/holiday material 6 months in advance. Computer printout submissions acceptable. Reports in 2 weeks on queries. Sample copy $2, plus 9 first class stamps.

Nonfiction: General interest (on interior decorating, architecture, gardening, entertainment, food); historical (Arizona history); and travel (of interest to Phoenix residents). Buys 100 or more mss/year. Query with published clips. Length: 1,200 words maximum. Pays $75-300/article. Pays expenses of writers on assignment.

Tips: "It's not a closed shop. I want the brightest, freshest, most accurate material available. Study the magazine to see our format and style. Major features are assigned to contributing editors."

PRACTICAL HOMEOWNER, Practical Homeowner Publishing Co., 27 Unquowa, Fairfield CT 06430. (203)259-9877. Editor: Joe Provey. 75% freelance written. Works with a small number of new/unpublished writers each year. Magazine published 9 times/year about well-designed remodelings, home improvements and new home construction. Circ. 750,000. Pays on acceptance. Publishes ms an average of 3 months after acceptance. Submit seasonal material at least 1 year in advance. Query for electronic submissions. Computer printout submissions acceptable; no dot-matrix. Reports in 6 weeks.

Nonfiction: "*Practical Homeowner* is a do-it-yourself magazine for people who want to create a safe, efficient and healthy home environment. Its aim is to put the reader in control of all decisions affecting his home, which may mean simplifying day-to-day maintenance and improving an existing structure or the more involved overseeing of new home construction." Feature articles relating to the home, including—but not limited to—remodeling, home repair, home management, improving energy efficiency, landscaping, home design, construction techniques, building materials and technology, home ownership trends, and home health issues. Length: 1,000-1,500 words. Buys all rights. Payment $400-2,500.

Photos: Horst Weber, art director. State availability of photos. Pays $35-100 for b&w; $75-400 for color transparencies or 35mm slides, depending on size and use. Captions and model releases required. Buys one-time rights.

Columns/Departments: Healthy Home (maintaining a safe, healthy home environment), Financial Advisor (managing home and home improvement finances), Well-Crafted Home (projects for the intermediate to advanced do -it-yourselfer), Trade Secrets (professional tradesmen explain techniques), Practical Products (building supplies, home furnishings, tools) and Life at My House (anecdotal essays on life at home). Length: 600-1,000 words. All columns are on assignment basis. Pays: $150-600.

SAN DIEGO HOME/GARDEN, Westward Press, Box 1471, San Diego CA 92112. (714)233-4567. Editor: Peter Jensen. Managing Editor: Gretchen Pelletier. 50% freelance written. Works with a small number of new/unpublished writers each year. Monthly magazine covering homes, gardens, food and local travel for residents of San Diego city and county. Circ. 31,000. Pays on acceptance. Publishes ms an average of 3 months after acceptance. Byline given. Buys first North American serial rights only. Submit seasonal material 3 months in advance. Photocopied submissions OK. Computer printout submissions acceptable. Reports in 1 month. Sample copy $4.

Nonfiction: Residential architecture and interior design (San Diego-area homes only); remodeling (must be well-designed—little do-it-yourself), residential landscape design; furniture; other features oriented towards upscale readers interested in living the cultured good life in San Diego. Articles must have local angle. Buys 0-5 unsolicited mss/year. Query with published clips. Length: 700-2,000 words. Pays $50-200.

Tips: "No out-of-town, out-of-state subject material. Most freelance work is accepted from local writers. Gear stories to the unique quality of San Diego. We try to offer only information unique to San Diego— people, places, shops, resources, etc. We plan more food and entertaining-at-home articles and more articles on garden products. We also need more in-depth reports on major architecture, environmental, and social aspects of life in San Diego and the border area (LaFrontera)."

SOUTHERN HOMES, Atlanta's Magazine for Better Living, Haas Publishing Co., Inc., Georgia regional office: 3119 Campus Dr., Norcross GA 30071. (404)446-6585. Editor: Jane F. Schneider. Managing Editor: Lynn B. McGill. 80% freelance written. Bimonthly magazine on shelter design, lifestyle in the home. "*Southern Homes* is designed for the achievement-oriented, well-educated reader who is concerned about the quality of his/her shelter, its design and construction, its environment, and how to best enjoy living and entertaining in it." Circ. 25,000. Pays on acceptance. Byline given. Publishes ms an average of 6 months after acceptance. Pays 25% kill fee. Buys all rights. Photocopied submissions OK. Computer printout submissions OK; prefers letter-quality. Reports in 3 months. Sample copy #10 SAE with 1 first class stamp.

Nonfiction: Lynn B. McGill, managing editor. Historical/nostalgic, interview/profile, new product, well-designed homes, antiques, photo feature, gardens, local art. "We do not want articles outside respective market area, not written for magazine format, or that are excessively controversial, investigative or that cannot be appropriately illustrated with attractive photography." Buys 35 mss/year. Query with published clips. Length: 1,000-1,500 words. Pays $375-450. Sometimes pays expenses of writers on assignment "if agreed upon in advance of assignment."

Photos: State availability of photos with submission "but, most photography is assigned." Reviews transparencies. Offers $50-75/photo. Captions, model releases, and identification of subjects required. Buys one-time rights.

Columns/Departments: Decorative Arts (profile of Atlanta-area artist's work), Design, South Looks Back, Outer View (gardening) and Destinations. Query with published clips. Buys 25-30 mss/year. Length: 750-900 words. Pays $250-350.

‡SOUTHERN PRESTIGIOUS HOMES & INTERIORS, D&B Publishing, Box 306, Mt. Pleasant SC 29465. (803)723-2496. Editor: David Cornwell. 80% freelance written. Bimonthly magazine on Southeastern real estate/lifestyle. "Writing for higher income residents, particularly in Northern states, interested in Southern real estate and lifestyle. Our focus is presently on the coast of NC, SC and Georgia, but we are expanding." Estab. 1988. Circ. 30,000. Pays on publication. Publishes ms an average of 3 months after acceptance. Byline given. Buys one-time rights. Photocopied submissions OK. Computer printout submissions OK. Reports in 1 month on queries. Sample copy $1.50.

Nonfiction: Interview, photo feature, travel and real estate development, resorts, prestigious homes and interiors. Buys 30 mss/year. Query. Length: 1,000 words maximum. Pays $50 maximum for assigned articles. Sometimes pays expenses of writers on assignment.

Photos: Send photos with submission. Reviews 3x5 prints. Offers $5 per photo. Captions and identification of subjects required. Buys one-time rights.

Tips: "We are not looking for articles on home repair, do-it-yourself decorating or profiles of realtors who had a million dollar year. Our readers are primarily affluent and in the market for a second home or a more expensive primary residence. We are interested in profiles of developers with a national reputation, prestigious homes of the rich, famous or infamous and interiors of the same, and articles targeting resorts and resort living. Unless it's about the Southeast, however, we're not interested."

THE SPROUTLETTER, Sprouting Publications, Box 62, Ashland OR 97520. (503)488-2326. Editor: Michael Linden. 50% freelance written. Quarterly newsletter covering sprouting, live foods and indoor food gardening. "We emphasize growing foods (especially sprouts) indoors for health, economy, nutrition and food self-sufficiency. We also cover topics related to sprouting, live foods and holistic health." Circ. 2,500. Pays on publication. Publishes ms an average of 3 months after acceptance. Byline given. Buys North American serial rights and second (reprint) rights to material originally published elsewhere. Submit seasonal/holiday material 4 months in advance. Previously published submissions OK. Computer printout submissions acceptable; prefers letter-quality. Reports in 2 weeks on queries; 3 weeks on mss. Sample copy $2.50.

Nonfiction: General interest (raw foods, sprouting, holistic health); how-to (grow sprouts, all kinds of foods indoors; build devices for sprouting or indoor gardening); personal experience (in sprouting or related areas); and technical (experiments with growing sprouts). No common health food/vitamin articles or growing ornamental plants indoors (as opposed to food producing plants). Buys 4-6 mss/year. Query. Length: 500-2,400 words. Pays $15-50. Trades for merchandise are also considered.

Columns/Departments: Book Reviews (books oriented toward sprouts, nutrition or holistic health). Reviews are short and informative. News Items (interesting news items relating to sprouts or live foods); Recipes (mostly raw foods). Buys 5-10 mss/year. Query. Length: 100-450 words. Pays $3-10.

Close-up

Joseph Provey
Editor
Practical Homeowner

In 1980 a new magazine, *New Shelter*, offered an alternative to traditional home improvement magazines by presenting a broader range of subjects than were typically covered by such publications. In addition to remodeling projects and building plans, the magazine featured articles aimed at helping readers improve their home environments, such as articles on health, gardening and alternative home energy use. The name was changed to *Practical Homeowner* in 1986 and two years later the magazine was sold.

The new owners, under the name Practical Homeowner Publishing, have begun to update the magazine. Editor Joseph Provey came on board last winter—he brought with him 15 years of experience in the magazine and home improvement fields. He'd been editor of *Home Mechanics*, *Family Handyman*, building editor at *House Beautiful* and home and shop editor at *Popular Mechanics*. Add to this his experience as a handyman and carpenter and Provey's career seems tailor-made for this position.

In his first editorial Provey said he had been attracted to the magazine years ago by its "spunky" attitude and willingness to "break the mold." His plans for *Practical Homeowner*, therefore, include keeping the magazine fresh in its approach to and treatment of home improvement information.

"There's going to be a smaller market for the traditional do-it-yourself-type stories," he says. Two-career families, longer commuting times and other lifestyle changes have left people with less time to do their own repairs or improvements, he explains. "People now need information that will help them make wise buying decisions about both products and services." Readers, he says, are looking for information needed before hiring a contractor, decorator or architect to do the job.

In this field writers must have a practical knowledge of the subject matter, says Provey. The magazine buys 80 percent of its material from freelancers. Yet it is not easy to break in. "We are always looking for new talent, but for 85 percent of the work we buy we turn to known quantities—people who have worked with us before."

"Work for a home improvement magazine is always very visual," says Provey. "*Practical Homeowner* has a network of scouts—designers and architects—who look for interesting remodeling and building projects. They send in study shots for review." The editors will choose from the shots and then assign a writer and a photographer to do the story. Although many features are assigned in this way, writers querying the magazine with an idea must also think of visuals. Provey rarely buys photos from writers, but it helps to send in study shots to be later reshot by a professional photographer. Writers can also check supply or equipment manufacturers or industry organizations for photos.

"Be sure to investigate and mention these sources in your query or cover letter. Queries are good," says Provey, but "you can take a short cut by sending a cover letter and the manuscript."

—Robin Gee

Fillers: Short humor and newsbreaks. Buys 3-6/year. Length: 50-150 words. Pays $2-6.

Tips: "Writers should have a sincere interest in holistic health and in natural whole foods. We like tight writing which is optimistic, interesting and informative. Consumers are demanding more thorough and accurate information. Articles should cover any given subject in depth in an enjoyable and inspiring manner. A frequent mistake is that the subject matter is not appropriate. Also buys cartoon strips and singles. Will consider series."

‡**TEXAS GARDENER, The Magazine for Texas Gardeners, by Texas Gardeners**, Suntex Communications, Inc., Box 9005, Waco TX 76714. (817)772-1270. Editor: Chris S. Corby. 80% freelance written. Works with a small number of new/unpublished writers each year. Bimonthly magazine covering vegetable and fruit production, ornamentals and home landscape information for home gardeners in Texas. Circ. 37,000. Pays on publication. Publishes ms an average of 4 months after acceptance. Byline given. Buys first North American serial rights and all rights. Submit seasonal/holiday material 6 months in advance. Query for electronic submissions. Computer printout submissions acceptable; prefers letter-quality to dot-matrix. Reports in 6 weeks. Sample copy $2.75; writer's guidelines for business size SASE.

Nonfiction: How-to, humor, interview/profile and photo feature. "We use feature articles that relate to Texas gardeners. We also like personality profiles on hobby gardeners and professional horticulturists who are doing something unique." Buys 50-100 mss/year. Query with clips of published work. Length: 800-2,400 words. Pays $50-200.

Photos: "We prefer superb color and b&w photos; 90% of photos used are color." State availability of photos. Pays negotiable rates for 2¼, 35mm color transparencies and 8x10 b&w prints and contact sheets. Model release and identification of subjects required.

Tips: "First, be a Texan. Then come up with a good idea of interest to home gardeners in this state. Be specific. Stick to feature topics like 'How Alley Gardening Became a Texas Tradition.' Leave topics like 'How to Control Fire Blight' to the experts. High quality photos could make the difference. We would like to add several writers to our group of regular contributors and would make assignments on a regular basis. Fillers are easy to come up with in-house. We want good writers who can produce accurate and interesting copy. Frequent mistakes made by writers in completing an article assignment for us are that articles are not slanted toward Texas gardening, show inaccurate or too little gardening information or lack good writing style. We will be doing more 'people' features and articles on ornamentals."

‡**TWENTYONE® MAGAZINE, The Magazine of the Century 21® Preferred Client Club**, The Quarton Group, Suite 430, 2701 Troy Center Dr., Troy MI 48084. (313)362-0044. Editor: Tom Morrisey. Associate Editor: Dee Ann Maki. 90% freelance written. Bimonthly magazine on home ownership. "Our readers have all either recently purchased or are about to purchase a new home. We're here to make that experience more productive and enjoyable." Circ. 500,000. Pays on acceptance. Publishes ms an average of 4 months after acceptance. Byline given. Offers 25% kill fee. Buys first North American serial and second serial (reprint) rights. Submit seasonal/holiday material 6 months in advance. Photocopied submissions OK. Query for electronic submissions. Computer printout submissions OK; prefers letter-quality. Reports in 3 weeks on queries; 2 months on ms. Sample copy for 9 × 12 SAE with 8 first class stamps. Writer's guidelines for #10 SAE with 2 first class stamps.

Nonfiction: Book excerpts, how-to, interview/profile, new product, personal experience, photo feature and technical. "No food stories. We are strictly a home-owning and real estate investment publication." Buys 42 mss/year. Query with published clips. Length: 600-3,000 words. Pays $250-500 for assigned articles; $100-400 for unsolicited articles. Sometimes pays expenses of writers on assignment.

Photos: Send photos with submission. Reviews transparencies (any size). Offers $25-100 per photo. Model releases and photo captions required. Buys one-time rights.

Columns/Departments: The Welcome Mat (potpourri of home-related items), length open; Dollars & Sense (home-buying/investment/tax tips), 1200-1500 words; Home Library (book and video reviews), length open. Buys 20 mss/year. Query with published clips. Pays $100-500.

Fiction: Humorous. "Nothing that does not relate to home ownership in a light manner." Buys 6 mss/year. Send complete ms. Length: 400-1,200 words. Pays $100.

Fillers: Newsbreaks and short humor. Buys 24/year. Length: 25-150 words.

Tips: "Bring something you know well to our attention. If you just built a greenhouse—or better still, just wrote a book on them—write us about greenhouses!"

‡**THE WEEKEND GARDENER**, Tel-A-Cast Inc., Box 1607, Aiken SC 29802. (803)648-9537. Editor: Paula Daniel. Assistant Editor: Debbie Burns. 95% freelance written. Magazine appearing 8 times/year on gardening. "The magazine is aimed at the weekend gardener and carries articles on all aspects of food and ornamental gardening, garden related crafts and projects. Articles should be accurate, well-researched, in-depth (but not *too* technical) and to the point." Pays on publication. Publishes an average of 2 months after acceptance. Buys first North American rights and will consider second serial (reprint) rights. Submit seasonal/holiday material 3 months in advance. Photocopied submissions OK. Computer printout submissions OK; prefers

letter-quality. Reports in 1 month. Sample copy $1 and 10 × 12½ SAE with 75¢ postage. Free writer's guidelines for #10 SASE.

Nonfiction: General garden interest, how-to (gardening and building gardening aids) and personal gardening experience. Buys 170 mss/year. Send complete ms. Length: 800-1,100 words. Pays $60-135 (occasionally higher).

Photos: Send photos with submission. Reviews transparencies. Offers $15-50 per photo. Model releases and identification of subjects required. Buys one-time rights.

Poetry: "No poetry that does not relate to gardening." Pays $30-60.

Fillers: Anecdotes, facts and short humor. Pays $10-30.

Tips: "Submit only clear concise, readable manuscripts with color photos. We work with new writers eagerly. We like to emphasize appropriate seasonal material and encourage such submissions. Where possible, make stories applicable to all parts of the U.S. Most of our features are freelance written. We prefer that these features not be too technical and that they relate to the weekend gardener. Our readers enjoy gardening as a hobby, not a career."

‡**YANKEE HOMES**, Yankee Publishing Incorporated, Main St., Dublin NH 03444. (603)563-8111. Editor: Jim Collins. 75% freelance written. Prefers to work with published/established writers. "*Yankee Homes* is a monthly publication geared toward people interested in buying, owning and restoring New England homes. Feature articles tend to be factual and service-oriented, with an emphasis on information." Circ. 35,000. Pays on acceptance. Publishes ms an average of 2 months after acceptance. Byline given. Kill fee varies. Buys first and second serial (reprint) rights. Query for electronic submissions. Computer printout submissions OK. Reports in 2 weeks. Free sample copy.

Nonfiction: Essays, historical/nostalgic, how-to, interview/profile and new product. "No meditations on 'How I built my dream house,' or anything we've already seen in *Better Homes and Gardens* and *Country Living*." Buys 35 mss/year. Query with or without published clips, or send complete ms. Length: 400-2,000 words. Pays $150-600 for assigned articles; pays $50-400 for unsolicited articles. Sometimes pays the expenses of writers on assignment.

Photos: State availability of photos with submission. Reviews 5x7 prints. Offers no additional payment for photos accepted with ms. Identification of subjects required. Buys one-time rights.

Columns/Departments: Dave Nelson, mail order products. A View From Our House (first-person thoughts and reminiscences on some concept of "home" in New England. Generally assigned), 400-800 words; The Advisor (concise, informational articles on trends, new products), 200-600 words. Buys 15 mss/year. Send complete ms. Pays $50-250.

Tips: "Feature articles that focus on unusual or new or atypical topics relating to homes in New England are most open to freelancers. Articles should be both entertaining and informative. In some cases, timeliness can be very important. *Yankee Homes* only publishes black and white photographs."

YOUR HOME, Meridian Publishing, Inc., Box 10010, Ogden UT 84409. (801)394-9446. 65% freelance written. A monthly in-house magazine covering home/garden subjects. Pays on acceptance. Publishes ms an average of 8 months after acceptance. Byline given. Buys first rights and second serial (reprint) rights. Eight-month lead time. Submit seasonal material 10 months in advance. Simultaneous, photocopied and previously published submissions OK. Computer printout submissions acceptable; prefers letter-quality. Reports in 6 weeks. Sample copy for $1 and 9x12 SAE; writer's guidelines for #10 SASE. All requests for samples and guidelines and queries should be addressed Attn: Editor.

Nonfiction: General interest articles about fresh ideas in home decor, ranging from floor and wall coverings to home furnishings. Subject matter includes the latest in home construction (exteriors, interiors, building materials, design), the outdoors at home (landscaping, pools, patios, gardening), remodeling projects, home management and home buying and selling. "No do-it-yourself pieces." Buys 40 mss/year. Length: 1,000-1,400 words. Pays 15¢/word for first rights plus nonexclusive reprint rights. Payment for second serial rights is negotiable.

Photos: State availability of photos with query. Reviews 35mm or larger transparencies and 5x7 or 8x10 "sharp, professional-looking" color prints. Pays $35 for inside photo; pays $50 for cover photo. Captions, model releases and identification of subjects required.

Tips: "Always looking for upscale, universal pieces. No do-it-yourself articles. The key is a well-written query letter that: (1) demonstrates that the subject of the article is practical and useful and has national appeal; (2) shows that the article will have a clear, focused theme and will be based on interviews with experts; (3) outlines the availability (from the writer, a photographer or a PR source) of top-quality color photos; (4) gives evidence that the writer/photographer is a professional."

Humor

Publications listed here specialize in gaglines or prose humor. Other publications that use humor can be found in nearly every category in this book. Some have special needs for major humor pieces; some use humor as fillers; many others are interested in material that meets their ordinary fiction or nonfiction requirements but has a humorous slant. The majority of humor articles must be submitted as complete manuscripts on speculation. Editors can't know from a query whether or not the piece will be right for them. For more information and markets for humor, see *Humor and Cartoon Markets* (Writer's Digest Books) appearing in April 1990.

CURRENT COMEDY FOR SPEAKERS, Suite 4D, 165 West 47th St., New York NY 10036. Editor: Gary Apple. For "speakers, toastmasters, business executives, public officials, educators, public relations specialists and communication professionals." Pays on publication (at end of month material published). Buys all rights. Computer printout submissions acceptable, prefers letter quality. "Unused material will be returned only if #10 SASE is enclosed."
Fillers: "We are looking for funny, performable one-liners and short jokes that deal with happenings in the news, fads, trends, and other topical subjects. The accent is on laugh-out-loud comedy. We are particularly interested in material that can be used by speakers and toastmasters: lines for beginning a speech, ending a speech, acknowledging an introduction, specific speaking occasions – any clever, original comments that would be of use to a person making a speech. We are also in the market for jokes used to respond to specific speaking situations (microphone feedback, broken air conditioning, hecklers). Short, sharp comment on business trends and events is also desirable. No puns, poems, sexist or stereotype jokes." Pays $12/joke.
Tips: "The material *must be original*. Do not send jokes you have heard, only those from your own creativity. Send only your strongest material. We'd rather receive 5 truly funny jokes than 50 so-so ones. If you're not sure that your jokes are funny, try them out on some friends before trying them out on us."

‡EXPRESSIONS, Humor Ink., Suite 200, 3121 Greenfield Rd., Glenshaw PA 15116. (412)487-6657. Editor: Sal Greco. Managing Editor: John Clark. 75% freelance written. Bimonthly magazine on humor. Estab. 1988. Circ. 5,000. Pays on publication. Publishes ms 2 months after acceptance. Byline given. Offers 50% kill fee. Buys first North American rights. Submit seasonal/holiday material 4 months in advance. Simultaneous, photocopied and previously published submissions OK. Computer printout submissions OK; prefers letter-quality. Reports in 2 weeks on queries; 1 month on mss. Sample copy $2 with SAE and 5 first class stamps. Writer's guidelines for SAE with 1 first class stamp.
Nonfiction: Essays, exposé general interest, humor, interview/profile and personal experience. "No sentimental, heavy, serious material." Send complete ms. Length 500-1,000 words. Pays $10-30. Sometimes pays expenses of writers on assignment.
Photos: State availability of photos with submission. Reviews contact sheets. Offers no additional payment for photos accepted with ms. Identification of subjects required. Buys one-time rights.
Columns/Departments: Review (humorous review of anything), 500 words and Neighborhood (local humor). Buys 12 mss/year. Send complete ms. Length: 250-500 words. Pays $10-30.
Poetry: Light verse. No "SERIOUS" poetry. Buys 12 poems/year. Submit maximum 3 poems. Length: 6-24 lines. Pays $10-20.
Fillers Anecdotes, gags to be illustrated by cartoonist and short humor. Buys 12/year Length: 25-100 words. Pays $5-100. "Looking for creative ideas and concepts that can become a series."

‡FUNNY BUSINESS, Funny Biz, Funny Business Enterprises, 210 Hollywood St. Fitchburg MA 01420-6134. (508)342-1074. Editor: Jack Raymond. Managing Editor: Charlene Raymond. 50% freelance written. Monthly newsletter on humor. Writers should have the "ability to write topical, humorous and original one-liner jokes." Pays on acceptance. Not copyrighted. Buys all rights. Submit seasonal/holiday material 2 months in advance. Simultaneous and photocopied submissions OK. Computer printout submissions OK; prefers letter-quality. Free sample copy and writer's guidelines.
Nonfiction: Humor and one-liner jokes. No "old jokes and comedy skits or bits." Buys 600 mss/year. Query with or without published clips or send complete ms. Length 5-20 words. Pays $1-2.
Tips: Send us 10-20 one liners and if we like'em the check is issued immediately and all material including purchased is returned within 10 days."

KNUCKLEHEAD PRESS, Box 305, Burbank CA 91503. Editors: Chris Miksanek and Jim Riley. A quarterly humor newsletter. "We print anything that's funny, but not morally or sexually offensive." Circ. 600. Pays on publication. Publishes ms an average of 6 months after acceptance. "We include writer in editorial bar as

Contributing Editor." Buys all rights. Submit seasonal/holiday material 6 months in advance. Simultaneous, photocopied and previously published submissions OK. Query for electronic submissions. Computer printout submissions OK. Reports in 3 weeks on mss. Sample copy for 9x12 SAE with 2 first class stamps; or $1. Free writer's guidelines with sample copy request. "Please request a sample issue before trying to write for us."

Nonfiction: Everything in Knucklehead Press is fiction in that it's not true, but we would welcome parodies of: exposé, general interest, historical/nostalgic, how-to, interview/profile, new product and technical. "We're always doing special 1 or 2 page sections. They're not planned, but based on material submitted. For example, if we have 3 or 4 food pieces, we might do a special restaurant/dining out section. Nothing unfunny or (and we're not prudes) something religiously or sexually offensive." Buys 10-15 mss/year. Send complete ms. Length: 50-500 words. Pays $5-20 for unsolicited articles. Send photos with submission. Reviews prints (b&w only). Offers no additional payment for photos accepted with ms. Captions, model releases and identification of subjects required. Buys all rights.

Columns/Departments: Newsbriefs (short news-type bits), 25-50 words. Buys 10 mss/year. Send complete ms. Length: 10-100 words. Pays $3-5.

Fiction: Adventure, historical, horror, humorous, novel excerpts and slice-of-life vignettes. Buys 4 mss/year. Send complete ms. Length: 250-500 words. Pays $5-20.

Fillers: Newsbreaks, short humor and gag classifieds. Buys 15/year. Length: 20-50 words. Pays $1-3.

Tips: "A comedy writer has to ask himself, 'Does my material entertain me? Can I read my own material and laugh as I would reading someone else's?' If the answer is 'yes' then we want to see your stuff. Every part of our newsletter is open to freelancers. If they can do something funnier than us, we're more than happy to step aside. Our goal is to publish a gut-busting newsletter, and any way that we accomplish that goal is OK by us. Make every word count. There's nothing more agonizing than a long not-so-funny piece; make your point and exit. Short and sweet."

LATEST JOKES, Box 3304, Brooklyn NY 11202-0066. (718)855-5057. Editor: Robert Makinson. 20% freelance written. Monthly newsletter of humor for TV and radio personalities, comedians and professional speakers. Circ. 250. Pays on acceptance. Byline given. Buys all rights. Submit seasonal/holiday material 3 months in advance. Reports in 3 weeks. Sample copy $3 and 1 first class stamp.

Nonfiction: Humor (short jokes). No "stupid, obvious, non-funny vulgar humor. Jokes about human tragedy also unwelcome." Send complete ms. Pays $1-3 for each joke.

Fiction: Humorous jokes. Pays $1-3.

Poetry: Light verse (humorous). Submit maximum 3 poems at one time. Line length: 2-8 lines. Pays 25¢/line.

Tips: "No famous personality jokes. Clever statements are not enough. Be original and surprising."

LONE STAR HUMOR, Lone Star Publications of Humor, Suite 103, Box 29000, San Antonio TX 78229. Editor: Lauren I. Barnett. Less than 25% freelance written. Eager to work with new/unpublished writers. A humor book-by-subscription for "the general public and 'comedy connoisseur' as well as the professional humorist." Pays on publication, "but we try to pay before that." Publishes ms an average of 8 months after acceptance. Buys variable rights. Submit seasonal/holiday material 6 months in advance. Photocopied submissions and sometimes previously published work OK. Query for electronic submissions. Computer printout submission acceptable; no dot-matrix. Reports in 2-4 months on queries; 3-4 months on mss. Inquire with SASE for prices and availability of sample copy. Writer's guidelines for #10 SASE.

Nonfiction: Humor (on anything topical/timeless); interview/profile (of anyone professionally involved in humor); and opinion (reviews of stand-up comedians, comedy plays, cartoonists, humorous books, *anything* concerned with comedy). "Inquire about possible theme issues." Buys 15 mss/year. Query with clips of published work if available. Length: 500-1,000 words; average is 700-800 words. Pays $5-30 and contributor's copy.

Fiction: Humorous. Buys variable mss/year. Send complete ms. Length: 500-1,000 words. Pays $5-30 and contributor's copy.

Poetry: Free verse, light verse, traditional, clerihews and limericks. "Nothing too 'artsy' to be funny." Buys 10-20/year. Submit maximum 5 poems. Length: 4-16 lines. Inquire for current rates.

Fillers: Clippings, jokes, gags, anecdotes, short humor and newsbreaks—"must be humorous or humor-related." Buys 20-30 mss/year. Length: 450 words maximum. Inquire for current rates.

Tips: "Our needs for freelance material will be somewhat diminished; writers should inquire (with SASE) before submitting material. We will be generating more and more of our humor inhouse, but will most likely require freelance material for books and other special projects. If the words 'wacky, zany or crazy' describe the writer's finished product, it is *not* likely that his/her piece will suit our needs. The best humor is just slightly removed from reality."

MAD MAGAZINE, 485 Madison Ave., New York NY 10022. (212)752-7685. Editors: Nick Meglin and John Ficarra. 100% freelance written. Magazine published 8 times/year. Circ. 1 million. Pays on acceptance. Publishes ms an average of 6 months after acceptance. Byline given. Buys all rights. Submit seasonal/holiday material 6 months in advance. Photocopied submissions OK. Computer printout submissions acceptable; prefers letter-quality. Reports in 6 weeks. Writer's guidelines for #10 SASE.

Nonfiction: Satire, parody. "We're always on the lookout for new ways to spoof and to poke fun at hot trends — music, computers, fashions etc. We're *not* interested in formats we're already doing or have done to death like... 'you know you're a when....'" Buys 400 ms yearly. Submit a premise with 3 or 4 examples of how you intend to carry it through, describing the action and visual content. Rough sketches are not necessary. Pays minimum $350/*MAD* page. One-page gags: 2-8 panel cartoon continuities in the style and tradition of *MAD*. Buys 30 yearly. Pays minimum of $350/*MAD* page. Don't send riddles, advice columns, TV or movie satires, book manuscripts, articles about Alfred E. Neuman or text pieces.

Tips: "Have fun! We're interested in anything and everything that you think is funny. Remember to think visually! Freelancers can best break in with nontopical material. If we see even a germ of talent, we will work with that person. We like outrageous, silly and/or satirical humor. Recent first-time sale — *The FBI's 10 Most Wanted Renegade Clowns*. So don't be afraid to be dumb."

‡NATIONAL LAMPOON, National Lampoon Inc., 155 Ave. of the Americas, New York NY 10013. (212)645-5040. FAX: (212)645-9219. Executive Editor: Larry Sloman. 50% freelance written. Works with small number of new unpublished writers each year. But "We are backlogged with submissions and prefer not to receive unsolicited submissions at this time." A bimonthly magazine of "offbeat, irreverent satire." Circ. 200,000. Pays on acceptance. Publishes ms an average of 4 months after acceptance. Byline given. Offers 20% kill fee. Buys first North American serial rights. Simultaneous submissions OK. Computer printout submissions acceptable; prefers letter-quality to dot-matrix. Reports in 2-3 months. Sample copy $3.95 with SAE.

Nonfiction: Humor. Buys 60 mss/year. Query with published clips. Length: approximately 2,000 words. Pays 20-40¢/word. Pays the expenses of writers on assignment.

Columns/Departments: John Bendel, column/department editor. True Facts (weird true-life stories). Special True Facts issue during first quarter of each year. Buys 240/year. Send complete ms. Length: 200 words maximum. Pays $10/item; $20/photo. Offers t-shirt for ideas, $10 and t-shirt for photos.

Tips: "We use very few new freelancers for major articles." True Facts section is most open to freelancers.

THE ONION, Suite 270, 33 University Square, Madison WI 53715. (608)256-1372. Editor Scott Dikkers. 80% freelance written. Weekly humor-entertainment newspaper. "*The Onion* is an irreverent humor publication with witty and outrageous stories, articles and cartoons satirizing college life, or any subject of interest to a college audience." Estab. 1988. Circ. 25,000. Pays on publication. Publishes manuscript an average of 1 month after acceptance. Byline given. Buys one-time rights. Submit seasonal/holiday material 3 months in advance. Simultaneous, photocopied and previously published submissions OK. Computer printout submissions OK. Reports in 1 month. Sample copy and writer's guidelines for #10 SASE.

Nonfiction: Humor, personal experience and imaginative parodies. Buys 20 mss/year. Send complete ms. Length: 100-1,000. Pays $10-60. Sometimes pays with copies if writer prefers.

Photos: Send photos with submission. Offers $5-10. Identification of subjects required. Buys one-time rights.

Columns/Departments: "We do not publish columns for which freelancers may write; we publish columns by freelancers willing to create their own column of engaging, original and humorous thoughts. Buys 2 mss/year. Send complete ms. Length: 50-300. Pays $10-60.

Fiction: Humorous, slice-of-life vignettes and humorous, inventive and offbeat stories. Buys 180 mss/year. Send complete ms. Length: 50-1,000. Pays $10-60.

Fillers: Anecdotes, gags to be illustrated by cartoonist and short humor. Buys 100/year. Length: 1-300 words. Pays $5-30.

Tips: "Hip, funny and unconventional submissions are always taken seriously. First-time writers are welcome. We plan to expand to other cities around the country, and we'd like creative, witty and reliable writers to expand with us. We are most interested in short short stories and satirical articles of interest to a college audience. Our tone is sharp, intelligent and irreverent, but deviations for comic effect are encouraged. Be original."

THE P.U.N., Play on Words, The Silly Club and Michael C. Raynes, Box 536-583, Orlando FL 32853. (407)648-2028. Editor: Danno Sullivan. 15% freelance written. Eager to work with new/unpublished writers. A bimonthly newsletter for a nonexistent organization, The Silly Club. "The P.U.N. readers enjoy humor bordering on intellectual, all the way down or up to just plain silliness. Politeness, though, above all. Despite the title, we very rarely use puns as such. *P.U.N.* is an acronym, not an indication of content." Circ. 400. Pays on acceptance. Publishes ms an average of 2 months after acceptance. Byline given, "listed in credits." Buys one-time rights. Submit seasonal/holiday material 1-2 months in advance. Simultnaeous, photocopied and previously published submissions OK. Computer printout submissions OK; prefers letter-quality. Reports in 3 weeks on mss. Sample copy for #10 SASE and $1.

Nonfiction: Humor. "Nothing rude, no foul language and no naughty things." Buys 10-25 mss/year. Send complete ms. Length: 10-1,000 words. Pays $1-25 for unsolicited articles.
Columns/Departments: Buys 10-15 mss/year. Send complete ms. Length: 10-100 words. Pays $1-25.
Fiction: Humorous. Buys 3-5 mss/year. Send complete ms. Length: 10-2,000 words. Pays $1-25. Also single panel cartoons. "Our fiction is mostly 'fictional nonfiction.'"
Poetry: Humorous poetry. Buys 5 poems/year. Submit maximum 10 poems. Pays $1-10.
Fillers: Gags and short humor. Buys 15/year. Pays $1-25.

In-flight

Most major in-flight magazines cater to business travelers and vacationers who will be reading, during the flight, about the airline's destinations and other items of general interest. Airline mergers and acquisitions continue to decrease the number of magazines published in this area. The writer should watch for airline announcements in the news and in ads and read the latest sample copies and writer's guidelines for current information.

ABOARD, North-South Net, Inc., Suite 6100, N.W. 153 St., Miami Lakes FL 33014. (305)827-3649. Editor: Cristina Juri Arencibia. 50% freelance written. Eager to work with new/unpublished writers. Bimonthly magazine covering destinations for the Equatorian, Dominican, Paraguayan, Bolivian, Chilean, Salvadoran, Hondruan, Guatemalan and Venezuelan national airlines. Entertaining, upbeat stories for the passengers. Circ. 100,000. Pays on publication. Publishes ms an average of 2 months after acceptance. Byline given. Buys first rights. Photocopied submissions OK. Query for electronic submissions. Computer printout submissions acceptable; prefers letter-quality. Reports in 1 week. Free sample copy and writer's guidelines.
Nonfiction: General interest, historical, humor, interview/profile, new product, travel, tourist attractions in Central and Latin America. Nothing "controversial, political, downbeat or in any way offensive to Latin American sensibilities." Buys 60 mss/year. Query. Length: 1,000-2,000 words. Pays $150 (with photos).
Photos: State availability of photos with query. Reviews b&w photos and color transparencies. Offers no additional payment for photos accepted with ms. Captions, model release and identification of subjects required.
Tips: "Study *Aboard* and other inflights, write exciting, succinct stories with an upbeat slant and enclose photos with captions. Break in with destination pieces for the individual airline or those shared by all nine. Writers must be accurate. Photos are always indispensable. Manuscripts are accepted either in English or Spanish. Translation rights must be granted. All manuscripts are subject to editing and condensation."

‡AIR DESTINATIONS, Stout Publishing Corp. Suite 225, 3980 Quebec, Denver CO 80207. (303)399-3000. FAX: (303)399-3021. Editor-in-Chief: Jeff Miller. Managing Editor: Rod Manuel. Monthly and bimonthly magazine. Circ. 40,000. Pays on publication. Publishes ms an average of 2 months after acceptance. Byline given. Offers 50% kill fee. Buys first North American serial rights and second serial (reprint) rights. Submit seasonal/holiday material 4-6 months in advance. Simultaneous, photocopied and previously published submissions OK. Query for electronic submissions. Computer printout submissions OK; prefers letter-qualtiy. Reports in 1 month on queries; 6 weeks on mss. Sample copy for 9x13 SAE with 8 first class stamps. Free writer's guidelines for #10 SAE and 2 first-class stamps.
Nonfiction: Historical/nostalgic (on our airline destinations), humor (short essay type), interview/profile (with famous people) and photo feature. Buys more than 100 mss/year. Query with or without published clips, or send complete ms. Length: 800-1,200 words. Pays $150 maximum in trade—hotels, restaurants and sometimes airline tickets. Pays in contributor copies or other premiums. Sometimes pays expenses of writers on assignment.
Photos: Send photos with submission. Reviews contact sheets and transparencies. Offers 50-300 per photo in trade—hotels, restaurants and sometimes airline tickets. Identification of subjects required. Buys one-time rights.
Columns/Departments: Final Approach (humor—any kind), 800-1,200 words. Buys 15-20 mss/year. Query with published clips or send complete ms.
Tips: "Because we have no set audience—ours is the diverse airline passenger audience—we are wide open to suggestions for articles. Although most of our pieces are oriented to our airline's destinations, we also carry 'cross-over' articles for all our magazines."

AMERICA WEST AIRLINES MAGAZINE, Skyword Marketing, Inc., Suite 236, 7500 N. Dreamy Draw Dr., Phoenix AZ 85020. (602)997-7200. FAX: (602)997-9875. Editor: Michael Derr. Managing Editor: Carrie Sears Bell. 80% freelance written. Works with small number of new/unpublished writers each year. A monthly "general interest magazine emphasizing the western and southwestern U.S. Some midwestern, northwestern and eastern subjects also appropriate. We look for ideas and people that celebrate opportunity, and those who put it to positive use." Query with published clips and SASE. Pays on publication. Publishes ms an average of 4 months after acceptance. Byline given. Offers 15% kill fee. Buys first North American rights. Submit seasonal/holiday material 6-8 months in advance. Simultaneous submissions OK, "if indicated as such." Query for electronic submissions. Computer printout submissions OK; prefers letter quality. Reports in 1 month on queries; 5 weeks on mss. Sample copy for $2; writer's guidelines for 9x12 SAE with 3 first class stamps.

Nonfiction: General interest, creative leisure, events, profile, photo feature, science, sports, business issues, entrepreneurs, nature, health, history, arts, book excerpts, travel and trends. Also considers essays and humor. No puzzles, reviews or highly controversial features. Buys 130-140 mss/year. Query with published clips. Length: 500-2,200. Pays $200-750. Pays some expenses.

Photos: State availability of original photography. Offers $50-250/photo. Captions, model releases and identification of subjects required. Buys one-time rights.

Fiction: Will consider exceptional pieces with a regional slant. No horror, inspirational or political. Send complete ms. Length: 800-1,800. Pays $200-500.

‡AMERICAN WAY, Mail Drop 2G23, Box 619616, Dallas/Fort Worth Airport TX 75261-9616. (817)355-1804. FAX: (817)355-1571. Editor: Doug Crichton. 98% freelance written. Prefers to work with published/ established writers. Fortnightly inflight magazine for passengers flying with American Airlines. Pays on acceptance. Publishes ms an average of 6 months after acceptance. Buys first serial rights. Computer printout submissions acceptable; prefers letter-quality to dot-matrix.

Nonfiction: Business and CEO profiles, the arts and entertainment, sports, personalities, technology, food, science and medicine and travel. "We are amenable to almost any subject that would be interesting, entertaining or useful to a passenger of American Airlines." Also humor, trivia, trends, and will consider a variety of ideas. Buys 450 mss/year. Query with published clips. Length: 1,500-4,000 words. Pays $500 and up. Usually pays the expenses of writers on assignment.

‡BRANIFF MAGAZINE, Pace Communications, Inc., 1301 Carolina St., Greensboro NC 27401. (919)378-6065. Editor Melinda L. Stovall. 100% freelance written. Monthly inflight magazine about business and travel. "We are a general interest magazine edited for passengers of Braniff Airlines. We look for informed, energetic, nontechnical writing on subjects that speak particularly to the professional business executive." Pays on acceptance. Publishes manuscript an average of 6 months after acceptance. Byline given. Offers 25% kill fee. Buys first North American serial rights. Submit seasonal/holiday material 6 months in advance. Query for electronic submissions. Computer printout submissions OK, prefers letter-quality. Reports in 2 months. Sample copy for $3; writer's guidelines for #10 SASE.

Nonfiction: General interest, business, interview/profile and travel. Query with or without published clips, or send complete ms. Length: 1,500-2,000. Pays $50-600.

Photos: State availability of photos with submission. Offers no additional payment for photos accepted with ms. Identification of subjects required. Buys one-time rights.

Columns/Departments: Business Beat (sales strategies, marketing techniques, climbing the corporate ladder); Sports (popular sports topic with business or travel angle); Sidelines (historical parks, roller coasters or other leisure-time activities); Personality Profile (newsworthy person in business, arts, entertainment, sports, science, etc.). Length: 1,500-2,000. Query.

MIDWAY MAGAZINE, Skies America Publishing Co., Suite 310, 9600 S.W. Oak St., Portland OR 97223. (503)244-2299. Editor: Terri J. Wallo. 50% freelance written. Monthly magazine. Circ. approximately 40,000. Pays on publication. Publishes ms an average of 2 months after acceptance. Byline given. Submit seasonal/ holiday material 6 months in advance. Simultaneous submissions OK. Computer printout submissions acceptable; prefers letter-quality. Reports in 1 month. Sample copy for 8½x11 SAE $3; writer's guidelines only, include #10 SASE.

Nonfiction: Interview/profile, photo feature and travel. "Business features should be timely, well-researched and well-focused. Corporate profiles and personality profiles are encouraged. Travel destination pieces should be original, detailed and lively. No stale pieces that sound like canned promotions." Buys 24 mss/ year. Query with published clips. Length: 1,000-2,500 words. Pays $150-400 for assigned articles; pays $150-250 for unsolicited articles. Sometimes pays the expenses of writers on assignment.

The double dagger before a listing indicates that the listing is new in this edition. New markets are often the most receptive to freelance submissions.

Photos: Send photos with submission. Reviews color transparencies and 8x10 b&w prints. Offers no additional payment for photos accepted with ms. Identification of subjects required. Buys one-time rights.

Tips: "The cities we focus on are: New York; Boston; Chicago; Indianapolis; Miami; Pittsburgh; Columbus; New Orleans; all Florida cities; New York; Minneapolis; Dallas; Cleveland; Detroit; New Orleans; Washington, D.C.; Virgin Islands; Cincinnati; Kansas City; Philadelphia; Las Vegas; Denver and Atlanta. Write to us with specific ideas relating to these cities. A fresh, original idea with excellent photo possibilities will receive our close attention. Areas most open to freelancers are corporate profiles; destination travel pieces with an unusual slant; personality profiles on businessmen and women, entrepreneurs."

SKY, Inflight Magazine of Delta Air Lines, Halsey Publishing Co., 12955 Biscayne Blvd., N. Miami FL 33181. (305)893-1520. Editor: Lidia De Leon. 90% freelance written. Monthly magazine. "Delta *SKY* is a general interest, nationally oriented magazine with a primary editorial focus on business and management, with the main purpose to entertain and inform business travelers aboard Delta Air Lines." Circ. 410,000. Pays on acceptance. Publishes ms an average of 2 months after acceptance. Byline given. Offers 100% kill fee when cancellation is through no fault of the writer. Buys first North American serial rights. Submit seasonal/holiday material 9 months in advance. Simultaneous and photocopied submissions OK. Computer printout submissions OK; prefers letter-quality. Reports in 1 month. Sample copy for 9x12 SAE; free writer's guidelines for SASE.

Nonfiction: General interest and photo feature. "No excerpts, essays, personal experience, opinion, religious, reviews, poetry, fiction or fillers." Buys 200 mss/year. Query with published clips. Length: 1700-2500 words. Pays $500-700 for assigned articles; pays $300-450 for unsolicited articles. Pays expenses of writers on assignment.

Photos: State availability of photos with submission. Reviews transparencies (4x5) and prints (5x7). Offers $25-50/photo. Captions, model releases and identification of subject required. Buys one-time rights.

Columns/Departments: On Management (managerial techniques, methods of topical nature). Buys 40 mss/year. Query with published clips. Length: 1500-1800 words. Pays $400-450.

Tips: "Send a comprehensive, well detailed query tied in to one of the feature categories of the magazine along with clips of previously published work. Since our lead times call for planning of editorial content 6-9 months in advance, that should also be kept in mind when proposing story ideas. We are always open to good feature story ideas that have to do with business and technology. Next in order of priority would be leisure, sports, entertainment and consumer topics. All feature story categories (Business, Lifestyle, Sports, Arts/Entertainment, Consumer, Technology and Collectibles) are open to freelancers, with the exceptions of Travel (areas are predetermined by the airline) and the executive Profile Series (which is also predetermined)."

‡SPIRIT, (formerly *Southwest Spirit*), East/West Network, Inc., 34 East 51st St., New York NY 10022. Editor: John Cade. 95% freelance written. Monthly magazine. "In-flight magazine for Southwest Airlines, is written with the business traveler in mind." Circ. 125,000. Pays on acceptance. Byline given. Offers 25% kill fee. Buys first rights. Submit seasonal/holiday material 6 months in advance. Computer printout submissions OK; prefers letter-quality. Reports in 3 weeks on queries. Sample copy $3. Free writer's guidelines for SASE.

Nonfiction: General interest, interview/profile, new product and travel. Buys 72 mss/year. Query with published clips. Length: 2,300 words maximum. Pays $800-1,200 for assigned articles. Pays 10% of writer's expenses on assignment.

Columns/Departments: Buys 60 mss/year. Length: 1,500-2,000 words. Pays $200 maximum.

Tips: "Definitely be familiar with *Spirit*. We are heavily formatted and although we are sent many good ideas, very few fit our format. Sending a SASE for writer's guidelines and $3 for sample copy really a must." Queries only.

USAIR MAGAZINE, Pace Communications, 1301 Carolina St., Greensboro NC 27401. (919)378-6065. Editor: Maggie Oman. Assistant Editor: Terry Barnes. 95% freelance written. Prefers to work with published/established writers. A monthly general interest magazine published for airline passengers, many of whom are business travelers, male, with high incomes and college educations. Circ. 475,000. Pays before publication. Publishes ms an average of 4 months after acceptance. Buys first rights only. Submit seasonal material 4 months in advance. Photocopied submissions OK. Computer printout submissions acceptable; prefers letter-quality. Reports in 6 weeks. Sample copy $4; free writer's guidelines with SASE.

Nonfiction: Travel, business, sports, health, food, personal finance, nature, the arts, science/technology and photography. Buys 100 mss/year. Query with clips of previously published work. Length: 1,500-2,800 words. Pays $400-800. Pays expenses of writers on assignment, if requested.

Photos: Send photos with ms. Pays $75-150/b&w print, depending on size; color from $100-250/print or slide. Captions preferred; model release required. Buys one-time rights.

Columns/Departments: Sports, food, money, health, business, living and science. Buys 8-10 mss/issue. Query. Length: 1,200-1,800 words. Pays $300-500.

Tips: "Send irresistible ideas and proof that you can write. It's great to get a clean manuscript from a good writer who has given me exactly what I asked for. Frequent mistakes are not following instructions, not delivering on time, etc."

Juvenile

Just as children change and grow, so do juvenile magazines. Children's magazine editors stress that writers must read recent issues. This section lists publications for children ages 2-12. Magazines for young people 13-19 appear in the Teen and Young Adult category. Many of the following publications are produced by religious groups and, where possible, the specific denomination is given. For the writer with a story or article slanted to a specific age group, the following children's index is a quick reference to markets for each age group. A book of juvenile markets, *Children's Writer's and Illustrator's Market*, is available from Writer's Digest Books.

Juvenile publications classified by age

Two- to Five-Year-Olds: *Chickadee, Playmate, The Friend, Humpty Dumpty, Nature Friend Magazine, R-A-D-A-R, Stone Soup, Story Friends, Turtle, Wee Wisdom.*

Six- to Eight-Year-Olds: *Boys' Life, Chickadee, Children's Digest, Cobblestone, Cricket, The Dolphin Log, The Friend, Humpty Dumpty, Kid City, Nature Friend Magazine, Noah's Ark, Odyssey, Pennywhistle Press, Pockets, R-A-D-A-R, Ranger Rick, Shofar, Sports Illustrated for Kids, Stone Soup, Story Friends, 3-2-1 Contact, Touch, Wee Wisdom, Wonder Time, Young American.*

Nine- to Twelve-Year-Olds: *Action, Boys' Life, Children's Digest, Chickadee, Clubhouse, Cobblestone, Cricket, Crusader, Discoveries, The Dolphin Log, The Friend, High Adventure, Junior Scholastic, Junior Trails, Kid City, Nature Friend Magazine, Noah's Ark, Odyssey, On the Line, Pennywhistle Press, Pockets, Ranger Rick, Shofar, Sports Illustrated for Kids, Stone Soup, Story Friends, 3-2-1 Contact, Touch, Venture, Wee Wisdom, The World of Business Kids, Young American.*

BOYS' LIFE, Boy Scouts of America, 1325 Walnut Hill Lane, Irving TX 75038-3096. Editor-in-chief: William B. McMorris. 75% freelance written. Prefers to work with published/established writers; works with small number of new/unpublished writers each year. Monthly magazine covering activities of interest to all boys ages 8-18. Most readers are Scouts or Cub Scouts. Circ 1.4 million. Pays on acceptance. Publishes ms an average of 6-12 months after acceptance. Buys one-time rights. Computer printout submissions OK; prefers letter-quality. Reports in 2 weeks. Sample copy for 9x12 SAE and $2.50. Writer's guidelines for 4x6½ or #10 SASE.

Nonfiction: Major articles run 1,200-2,000 words. Preferred length is about 1,500 words. Pays minimum $500 for major article text. Uses strong photo features with about 750 words of text. Separate payment or assignment for photos. "Much better rates if you really know how to write for our market." Buys 60 major articles/year. Also needs how-to features and hobby and crafts ideas. "We pay top rates for ideas accompanied by sharp photos, clean diagrams, and short, clear instructions." Query first in writing. Buys 30-40 how-tos/year. Query all nonfiction ideas in writing. Pays expenses of writers on assignment. Also buys freelance comics pages and scripts. Query first.

Columns: "Food, Health, Pets, Bicycling and Magic Tricks are some of the columns for which we use 400-600 words of text. This is a good place to show us what you can do. Query first in writing." Pays $150 minimum. Buys 75-80 columns/year.

Fiction: Short stories 1,000-1,500 words; occasionally longer. Send complete ms. Pays $500 minimum. Buys 15 short stories/year.

Tips: "We strongly recommend reading at least 12 issues of the magazine and learning something about the programs of the Boy Scouts of America before you submit queries. We are a good market for any writer willing to do the necessary homework."

CHICKADEE MAGAZINE, For Young Children from *OWL*, The Young Naturalist Foundation, 56 The Esplanade, Suite 306, Toronto, Ontario M5E 1A7 Canada. (416)868-6001. Editor-in-Chief: Sylvia Funston. 25% freelance written. Magazine published 10 times/year (except July and August) for 4-9 year-olds. "We aim to interest young children in the world around them in an entertaining and lively way." Circ. 100,000 Canada; 50,000 U.S. Pays on publication. Byline given. Buys all rights. Submit seasonal/holiday material up to 1 year in advance. Computer printout submissions acceptable. Reports in 2½ months. Sample copy for $2.50 and SAE; writer's guidelines for 50¢ and SAE.

Nonfiction: How-to (arts and crafts, easy experiments for children); personal experience (real children in real situations); and photo feature (wildlife features). No articles for older children; no religious or moralistic features. Sometimes pays the expenses of writers on assignment.

Photos: Send photos with ms. Reviews 35mm transparencies. Identification of subjects required.

Fiction: Adventure (relating to the 4-9 year old), humor. No science fiction, fantasy, talking animal stories or religious articles. Send complete ms with $1 money order for handling and return postage. No IRCs. Pays $100-300.

Tips: "A frequent mistake made by writers is trying to teach too much—not enough entertainment and fun."

CHILDREN'S DIGEST, Children's Better Health Institute, Box 567, Indianapolis IN 46206. (317)636-8881. Editor: Elizabeth Rinck. 85% freelance written. Works with a small number of new/unpublished writers each year. Magazine published 8 times/year covering children's health for children ages 8-10. Pays on publication. Publishes ms an average of 1 year after acceptance. Byline given. Buys all rights. Submit seasonal/holiday material 8 months in advance. Submit *only* complete manuscripts. "No queries, please." Photocopied submissions acceptable (if clear). Computer printout submissions acceptable; prefers letter-quality. Reports in 2 months. Sample copy for 75¢; writer's guidelines for #10 SASE.

Nonfiction: Historical, interview/profile (biographical), craft ideas, health, nutrition, hygiene, exercise and safety. "We're especially interested in factual features that teach readers about the human body or encourage them to develop better health habits. We are *not* interested in material that is simply rewritten from encyclopedias. We try to present our health material in a way that instructs *and* entertains the reader." Buys 15-20 mss/year. Send complete ms. Length: 500-1,200 words. Pays 8¢/word. Sometimes pays the expenses of writers on assignment.

Photos: State availability of full color or b&w photos. Payment varies. Model releases and identification of subjects required. Buys one-time rights.

Fiction: Adventure, humorous, mainstream and mystery. Stories should appeal to both boys and girls. "We need some stories that incorporate a health theme. However, we don't want stories that preach, preferring instead stories with implied morals. We like a light or humorous approach." Buys 15-20 mss/year. Length: 500-1,500 words. Pays 8¢/word.

Poetry: Pays $10 minimum.

Tips: "Many of our readers have working mothers and/or come from single-parent homes. We need more stories that reflect these changing times while communicating good values."

CHILDREN'S PLAYMATE, 1100 Waterway Blvd., Box 567, Indianapolis IN 46206. (317)636-8881. Editor: Elizabeth Rinck. 75% freelance written. Eager to work with new/unpublished writers. "We are looking for articles, stories, and activities with a health, safety, exercise or nutritionally oriented theme. Primarily we are concerned with preventative medicine. We try to present our material in a positive—not a negative—light, and we try to incorporate humor and a light approach wherever possible without minimizing the seriousness of what we are saying." For children ages 5-7. Magazine published 8 times/year. Buys all rights. Byline given. Pays on publication. Publishes ms an average of 1 year after acceptance. Submit seasonal material 8 months in advance. Computer printout submissions acceptable; prefers letter-quality. Reports in 2 months. Sometimes may hold mss for up to 1 year, with author's permission. Write for guidelines. "Material will not be returned unless accompanied by a self-addressed envelope and sufficient postage." Sample copy 75¢; free writer's guidelines with SASE.

Nonfiction: Beginning science, 600 words maximum. A feature may be an interesting presentation on animals, people, events, objects or places, especially about good health, exercise, proper nutrition and safety. Include number of words in articles. Buys 30 mss/year. "We do not consider outlines. Reading the whole manuscript is the only way to give fair consideration. The editors cannot criticize, offer suggestions, or review unsolicited material that is not accepted." No queries. Pays about 8¢/word.

Fiction: Short stories for beginning readers, not over 700 words. Seasonal stories with holiday themes. Humorous stories, unusual plots. "We are interested in stories about children in different cultures and stories about lesser-known holidays (not just Christmas, Thanksgiving, Halloween, Hanukkah)." Vocabulary suitable for ages 5-7. Submit complete ms. Pays about 8¢/word. Include number of words in stories.

Fillers: Puzzles, dot-to-dots, color-ins, hidden pictures and mazes. Buys 30 fillers/year. Payment varies.

Tips: Especially interested in stories, poems and articles about special holidays, customs and events.

CLUBHOUSE, Your Story Hour, Box 15, Berrien Springs MI 49103. (616)471-3701. Editor: Elaine Trumbo. 75% freelance written. Works with a small number of new/unpublished writers each year. Magazine published 6 times/year covering many subjects with Christian approach, though not associated with a church. "Stories and features for fun for 9-14 year-olds. Main objective: To provide a psychologically 'up' magazine that lets kids know that they are acceptable, 'neat' people." Circ. 15,000. Pays on acceptance. Publishes ms an average of 1 year after acceptance. Byline given. Buys first serial rights or first North American serial rights, one-time rights, simultaneous rights, and second serial (reprint) rights. Simultaneous queries, and simultaneous, photocopied and previously published submissions OK. Computer printout submissions acceptable; prefers letter-quality. Reports in 4-5 weeks. Sample copy for 6x9 SAE and 3 first class stamps; writer's guidelines for #10 SASE.

Nonfiction: How-to (crafts), personal experience and recipes (without sugar or artificial flavors and colors). "No stories in which kids start out 'bad' and by peer or adult pressure or circumstances are changed into 'good' people." Send complete ms. Length: 750-800 words ($25); 1,000-1,200 words ($30); feature story, 1,200 words ($35).

Photos: Send photos with ms. Pays on publication according to published size. Buys one-time rights.

Columns/Departments: Body Shop (short stories or "ad" type material that is anti-smoking, drugs and alcohol and pro-good nutrition, etc.); and Jr. Detective (secret codes, word search, deduction problems, hidden pictures, etc.). Buys 20/year. Send complete ms. Length: 400 words maximum for Jr. Detective; 1,000 maximum for Body Shop. Pays $10-30.

Fiction: Adventure, historical, humorous and mainstream. "Stories should depict bravery, kindness, etc., without a preachy attitude." No science fiction, romance, confession or mystery. Cannot use Santa-elves, Halloween or Easter Bunny material. Buys 40 mss/year. Send query or complete ms (prefers ms). Length: 750-800 words ($20); 1,000-1,200 words ($30); lead story ($35).

Poetry: Free verse, light verse and traditional. Buys 6-10/year. Submit maximum 5 poems. Length: 4-24 lines. Pays $5-20.

Fillers: Cartoons. Buys 18/year. Pay $12 maximum.

Tips: "Send all material during March or April. (Not accepting material until April 1990.) By the middle of June acceptance or rejection notices will be sent. Material chosen will appear the following year. Basically, kids are more and more informed and aware of the world around them. This means that characters in stories for *Clubhouse* should not seem too simple, yet maintain the wonder and joy of youth."

COBBLESTONE: The History Magazine for Young People, Cobblestone Publishing, Inc., 20 Grove St., Peterborough NH 03458. (603)924-7209. Editor-in-Chief: Carolyn P. Yoder. 80% freelance written (approximately 2 issues/year are by assignment only). Prefers to work with published/established writers; works with small number of new/unpublished writers each year. Monthly magazine covering American history for children ages 8-14. "Each issue presents a particular theme, approaching it from different angles, making it exciting as well as informative. Half of all subscriptions are for schools." Circ. 45,000. Pays on publication. Publishes ms an average of 4 months after acceptance. Byline given. Buys all rights; makes work-for-hire assignments. All material must relate to monthly theme. Simultaneous and previously published submissions OK. Computer printout submissions acceptable; prefers letter-quality. Sample copy for 7½x10½ SAE with 5 first class stamps and $4.95; writer's guidelines for SASE.

Nonfiction: Historical/nostalgic, how-to, interview, plays, biography, recipes, activities and personal experience. "Request a copy of the writer's guidelines to find out specific issue themes in upcoming months." No material that editorializes rather than reports. Buys 5-8 mss/issue. Length: 800-1,200 words. Supplemental nonfiction 200-800 words. Query with published clips, outline and bibliography. Pays up to 15¢/word. Rarely pays expenses of writers on assignment.

Fiction: Adventure, historical, humorous and biographical fiction. "Has to be very strong and accurate." Buys 1-2 mss/issue. Length: 800-1,200 words. Request free editorial guidelines that explain upcoming issue themes and give query deadlines. "Message" must be smoothly integrated with the story. Query with written samples. Pays up to 15¢/word.

Poetry: Free verse, light verse and traditional. Submit maximum 2 poems. Length: 5-100 lines. Pays on an individual basis.

Tips: "All material is considered on the basis of merit and appropriateness to theme. Query should state idea for material simply, with rationale for why material is applicable to theme. Request writer's guidelines (includes themes and query deadlines) before submitting a query. Include SASE."

CRICKET, The Magazine for Children, Open Court Publishing Co., 315 5th St., Peru IL 61354. (815)224-6643. Editor: Marianne Carus. Monthly magazine. Circ. 120,000. Pays on publication. Byline given. Buys first North American serial rights. Submit seasonal/holiday material 1 year in advance. Photocopied and previously published submissions OK. Computer printout submissions acceptable; prefers letter-quality. Reports in 2 months. Sample copy $2; writer's guidelines for SASE.

Nonfiction: Historical/nostalgic, lively science, personal experience and travel. Send complete ms. Length: 200-1,200 words. Pays $50-300.

Fiction: Adventure, ethnic, fantasy, historical, humorous, mystery, novel excerpts, science fiction, suspense and western. No didactic, sex, religious or horror stories. Buys 24-36 mss/year. Send complete ms. Length: 200-1,500 words. Pays $50-375.

Poetry: Buys 8-10 poems/year. Length: 50 lines maximum. Pays $3/line on publication.

CRUSADER MAGAZINE, Box 7259, Grand Rapids MI 49510. FAX: (616)241-5558. Editor: G. Richard Broene. 40% freelance written. Works with a small number of new/unpublished writers each year. Magazine published 7 times/year. "*Crusader Magazine* shows boys (9-14) how God is at work in their lives and in the world around them." Circ. 12,000. Buys 20-25 mss/year. Pays on acceptance. Byline given. Publishes ms an average of 8 months after acceptance. Rights purchased vary with author and material; buys first serial rights, one-time rights, second serial (reprint) rights, and simultaneous rights. Submit seasonal material (Christmas, Easter) at least 5 months in advance. Photocopied and simultaneous submissions OK. Computer printout submissions acceptable; prefers letter-quality. Reports in 1 month. Free sample copy and writer's guidelines for 9x12 SAE and 3 first class stamps.

Nonfiction: Articles about young boys' interests: sports, outdoor activities, bike riding, science, crafts, etc., and problems. Emphasis is on a Christian multi-racial perspective, but no simplistic moralisms. Informational, how-to, personal experience, interview, profile, inspirational and humor. Submit complete ms. Length: 500-1,500 words. Pays 2-5¢/word.

Photos: Pays $4-25 for b&w photos purchased with mss.

Fiction: "Considerable fiction is used. Fast-moving stories that appeal to a boy's sense of adventure or sense of humor are welcome. Avoid preachiness. Avoid simplistic answers to complicated problems. Avoid long dialogue and little action." Length: 900-1,500 words. Pays 2¢/word minimum.

Fillers: Uses short humor and any type of puzzles as fillers.

DISCOVERIES, 6401 The Paseo, Kansas City MO 64131. Editor: Middler Editor. 75% freelance written. For boys and girls ages 9-12 in the Church of the Nazarene. Weekly. Publishes ms an average of 1 year after acceptance. Buys first serial rights and second (reprint) rights. "We process only letter-quality manuscripts; word processing with letter-quality printers acceptable. Minimal comments on pre-printed form are made on rejected material." Reports in 1 month. Sample copy and guidelines for #10 SASE.

Fiction: Stories with Christian emphasis on high ideals, wholesome social relationships and activities, right choices, Sabbath observance, church loyalty and missions. Informal style. Submit complete ms. Length: 500-700 words. Pays 3½¢/word for first serial rights and 2¢/word for second (reprint) rights.

Photos: Color photos only.

Tips: "The freelancer needs an understanding of the doctrine of the Church of the Nazarene and the Sunday school material for third to sixth graders."

THE DOLPHIN LOG, The Cousteau Society, 8440 Santa Monica Blvd., Los Angeles CA 90069. (213)656-4422. Editor: Pamela Stacey. 60% freelance written. Prefers to work with published/established writers; works with a small number of new/unpublished writers each year. Bimonthly magazine covering marine biology, ecology, environment, natural history, and water-related stories. "The *Dolphin Log* is an educational publication for children ages 7-15 offered by The Cousteau Society. Subject matter encompasses all areas of science, history and the arts which can be related to our global water system. The philosophy of the magazine is to delight, instruct and instill an environmental ethic and understanding of the interconnectedness of living organisms, including people." Circ. 82,000. Pays on publication. Publishes ms an average of 1 year after acceptance. Byline given. Buys one-time and translation rights. Submit seasonal/holiday material 4 months in advance. "Encourages disk submissions which are IBM-PC compatible (ASCII character file)." Computer printout submissions acceptable; prefers letter-quality. Reports in 2 months. Sample copy for $2 with 9x12 SAE and 3 first class stamps; writer's guidelines for SASE.

Nonfiction: General interest (per guidelines); how-to (water-related crafts or science); personal experience (ocean related); and photo feature (marine subject). "Of special interest are articles on specific marine creatures, and games involving an ocean/water-related theme which develop math, reading and comprehension skills. Humorous articles and short jokes based on scientific fact are also welcome. Experiments that can be conducted at home and demonstrate a phenomenon or principle of science are wanted as are clever crafts or art projects which also can be tied to an ocean theme. Try to incorporate such activities into any articles submitted." No fiction or "talking" animals. Buys 8-12 mss/year. Query or send complete ms. Length: 500-1,000 words. Pays $50-150.

Photos: Send photos with query or ms (duplicates only). Prefers underwater animals, water photos with children, photos that explain text. Pays $25-100/photo. Identification of subjects required. Buys one-time and translation rights.

Columns/Departments: Discovery (science experiments or crafts a young person can easily do at home), 50-500 words; Creature Feature (lively article on one specific marine animal), 500-700 words. Buys 1 mss/year. Send complete ms. Pays $25-150.

Poetry: No "talking" animals. Buys 1-2 poems/year. Pays $10-100.

Tips: "Find a lively way to relate scientific facts to children without anthropomorphizing. We need to know material is accurate and current. Articles should feature an interesting marine creature and yet contain factual material that's fun to read. We will be increasingly interested in material which draws information from current scientific research."

THE FRIEND, 50 East North Temple, Salt Lake City UT 84150. Managing Editor: Vivian Paulsen. 60% freelance written. Eager to work with new/unpublished writers as well as established writers. Appeals to children ages 3-11. Monthly publication of The Church of Jesus Christ of Latter-Day Saints. Circ. 205,000. Pays on acceptance. Buys all rights. Submit seasonal material 8 months in advance. Computer printout submissions acceptable. Publishes ms an average of 1 year after acceptance. Sample copy and writer's guidelines for 8½x11 with SAE with 4 first class stamps.

Nonfiction: Subjects of current interest, science, nature, pets, sports, foreign countries, and things to make and do. Special issues for Christmas and Easter. "Submit only complete ms—no queries, please." Length: 1,000 words maximum. Pays 8¢/word minimum.

Fiction: Seasonal and holiday stories and stories about other countries and their children. Wholesome and optimistic; high motive, plot, and action. Character-building stories preferred. Length: 1,200 words maximum. Stories for younger children should not exceed 250 words. Pays 8¢/word minimum.

Poetry: Serious, humorous and holiday. Any form with child appeal. Pays $15.

Tips: "Do you remember how it feels to be a child? Can you write stories that appeal to children ages 3-11 in today's world? We're interested in stories with an international flavor and those that focus on present-day problems. Send material of high literary quality slanted to our editorial requirements. Let the child solve the problem—not some helpful, all-wise adult. No overt moralizing. Nonfiction should be creatively presented—not an array of facts strung together. Beware of being cutesy."

HIGH ADVENTURE, Assemblies of God, 1445 Boonville, Springfield MO 65802. (417)862-2781, ext. 1497. Editor: Johnnie Barnes. Eager to work with new/unpublished writers. Quarterly magazine "designed to provide boys with worthwhile, enjoyable, leisure reading; to challenge them in narrative form to higher ideals and greater spiritual dedication; and to perpetuate the spirit of the Royal Rangers program through stories, ideas and illustrations." Circ. 87,000. Pays on acceptance. Byline given. Buys one-time rights. Submit seasonal/holiday material 9 months in advance. Simultaneous queries, and simultaneous, photocopied and previously published submissions OK. Computer printout submission OK; prefers letter-quality. Reports in 1 month. Sample copy for 9x12 SAE with 3 first class stamps; free writer's guidelines.

Nonfiction: Historical/nostalgic, how-to, humor and inspirational. Buys 25-50 mss/year. Query or send complete ms. Length: 800-1,800 words. Pays 3¢/word.

Photos: Reviews b&w negatives, color transparencies and prints. Identification of subjects required. Buys one-time rights.

Fiction: Adventure, historical, humorous, religious and western. Buys 25-50 mss/year. Query or send complete ms. Length: 800-1,800 words maximum. Pays 3¢/word.

Fillers: Jokes, gags and short humor. Pays $7.50 for jokes; others vary.

HIGHLIGHTS FOR CHILDREN, 803 Church St., Honesdale PA 18431. Editor: Kent L. Brown Jr. 80% freelance written. Magazine published 11 times/year for children ages 2-12. Circ. 2,300,000. Pays on acceptance. Buys all rights. Computer printout submissions acceptable; prefers letter-quality. Reports in about 2 months. Sample copy $2.25; writer's guidelines for #10 SASE.

Nonfiction: "We prefer factual features, including history and natural, technical and social science, written by persons with rich background and mastery in their respective fields. Contributions always welcomed from new writers, especially engineers, scientists, historians, teachers, etc., who can make useful, interesting and authentic facts accessible to children. Also writers who have lived abroad and can interpret the ways of life, especially of children, in other countries. Sports material, biographies and general articles of interest to children. Direct, original approach, simple style, interesting content, without word embellishment; not rewritten from encyclopedias. State background and qualifications for writing factual articles submitted. Include references or sources of information. Length: 900 words maximum. Pays $75 minimum. Also buys original party plans for children ages 7-12, clearly described in 300-800 words, including drawings or sample of items to be illustrated. Also, novel but tested ideas in crafts, with clear directions and made-up models. Projects must require only free or inexpensive, easy-to-obtain materials. Especially desirable if easy enough for early primary grades. Also, fingerplays with lots of action, easy for very young children to grasp and parents to

ALWAYS submit unsolicited manuscripts or queries with a self-addressed, stamped envelope (SASE) within your country or International Reply Coupons (IRC) purchased from the post office for other countries.

dramatize. Avoid wordiness. Pays minimum $50 for party plans; $15 for crafts ideas; $25 for fingerplays.

Fiction: Unusual, meaningful stories appealing to both girls and boys, ages 2-12. Vivid, full of action. "Engaging plot, strong characterization, lively language." Prefers stories in which a child protagonist solves a dilemma through his or her own resources. Seeks stories that the child ages 8-12 will eagerly read, and the child ages 2-7 will begin to read and/or will like to hear when read aloud (600 words maximum). "We publish stories in the suspense/adventure/mystery, fantasy and humor category, all requiring interesting plot and a number of illustration possiblities. Also need rebuses (picture stories 150 words or under), stories with urban settings, stories for beginning readers (500 words), humorous and horse stories. We also would like to see more material of 1-page length (300-500 words), both fiction and factual. We need creative-thinking puzzles that can be illustrated, optical illusions, brain teasers, games of physical agility, and other 'fun' activities. War, crime and violence are taboo. Some folk-tale retelling stories published." Length: 400-900 words. Pays $65 minimum.

Tips: "We are pleased that many authors of children's literature report that their first published work was in the pages of *Highlights*. It is not our policy to consider fiction on the strength of the reputation of the author. We judge each submission on its own merits. With factual material, however, we do prefer either authorities in their field or people with first-hand experience. In this manner we can avoid the encyclopedic article that merely restates information readily available elsewhere. We don't make assignments. Query with simple letter to establish whether the nonfiction *subject* is likely to be of interest. A beginning writer should first become familiar with the type of material which *Highlights* publishes. Include special qualifications, if any, of author. Write for the child, not the editor."

HUMPTY DUMPTY'S MAGAZINE, Children's Better Health Institute, 1100 Waterway Blvd., Box 567, Indianapolis IN 46206. Editor: Christine French Clark. 90% freelance written. "We try not to be overly influenced by an author's credits, preferring instead to judge each submission on its own merit." Magazine published 8 times/year stressing health, nutrition, hygiene, exercise and safety for children ages 4-6. Combined issues: February/March, April/May, June/July and August/September. Pays on publication. Publishes ms at least 8 months after acceptance. Buys all rights. Submit seasonal material 8 months in advance. Computer printout submissions OK; prefers letter-quality. Reports in 10 weeks. Sample copy 75¢; writer's guidelines for SASE.

Nonfiction: "We are open to nonfiction on almost any age-appropriate subject, but we especially need material with a health theme—nutrition, safety, exercise, hygiene. We're looking for articles that encourage readers to develop better health habits without preaching. Very simple factual articles that creatively teach readers about their bodies. We use simple crafts, some with holiday themes. We also use several puzzles and activities in each issue—dot-to-dot, hidden pictures and other activities that promote following instructions, developing finger dexterity and working with numbers and letters. Submit complete ms. "Include number of words in manuscript and Social Security number." Length: 600 words maximum. Pays approximately 8¢/word.

Fiction: "We use some stories in rhyme and a few easy-to-read stories for the beginning reader. All stories should work well as read alouds. Currently we need seasonal stories with holiday themes. We use contemporary stories and fantasy, some employing a health theme. We try to present our health material in a positive light, incorporating humor and a light approach wherever possible. Avoid sexual stereotyping. Characters in contemporary stories should be realistic and up-to-date. Remember, many of our readers have working mothers and/or come from single-parent homes. We need more stories that reflect these changing times but at the same time communicate good, wholesome values." Submit complete ms. "Include number of words in manuscript and Social Security number." Length: 600 words maximum. Pays about 8¢/word.

Poetry: Short, simple poems. Pays $10 minimum.

Tips: "Writing for *Humpty Dumpty* is similar to writing picture book manuscripts. There must be a great economy of words. We strive for 50% art per page (in stories and articles), so space for text is limited. Because the illustrations are so important, stories should lend themselves well to visual imagery."

JUNIOR SCHOLASTIC, Scholastic Inc.. 730 Broadway, New York NY 10003. (212)505-3071. Editor: Lee Baier. 25% freelance written. Educational classroom magazine publishing 18 issues during school year on social studies for grades 6-8. "We strive to present all sides of important issues, written so as to appeal to young people ages 11-14." Circ. 700,000. Pays on acceptance. Byline given. Buys first rights. Submit seasonal/holiday material 2 months in advance. Simultaneous and photocopied submissions OK. Computer printout submissions OK; prefers letter-quality. Reports in 6 months on queries. Sample copy $1.75 with 9x12 SAE. Free writer's guidelines.

Nonfiction: Geography adventure and articles about young people, ages 11-14, in the U.S. and foreign countries, accompanied by 35mm color transparencies. Buys 25 mss/year. Query. Length: 500-1,000 words. Pays $175-300 for assigned articles. Sometimes pays the expenses of writers on assignment. Send photos with submission. Reviews contact sheets and transparencies (35mm). Offers $75-125 per photo. Model releases. Buys one-time rights.

Columns/Departments: Health self-improvement (slanted toward teens 11-14), 500 words. Pays $150-175.

Tips: "Keep writing simple, easy to understand, filled with quotes and anecdotes. Articles should convey important information about the subject in a lively, interesting manner. Bring young people ages 11-14 into the story—lead with them if at all possible. We are mainly looking for articles about foreign countries, using interviews with people from that country—especially young people 11-14—to illustrate the current situation in that country, problems that country is facing and what it is like to live there. Also interested in stories about outstanding young people in the U.S. Need color transparencies to accompany all such stories."

JUNIOR TRAILS, Gospel Publishing House, 1445 Boonville Ave., Springfield MO 65802. (417)862-2781. Editor: Cathy Ketcher. 100% freelance written. Eager to work with new/unpublished writers. Weekly tabloid covering religious fiction; and biographical, historical and scientific articles with a spiritual emphasis for boys and girls ages 10-11. Circ. 75,000. Pays on acceptance. Publishes ms an average of 9-12 months after acceptance. Byline given. Not copyrighted. Buys simultaneous rights, first rights, or second (reprint) rights to material originally published elsewhere. Submit seasonal/holiday material 1 year in advance. List Social Security number and number of words in ms. Simultaneous and previously published submissions OK. Computer printout submissions acceptable; prefers letter-quality. Reports in 6 weeks on queries; 2 months on mss. Sample copy and writer's guidelines for 9x12 SAE and 2 first class stamps.
Nonfiction: Biographical, historical and scientific (with spiritual lesson or emphasis). "Junior-age children need to be alerted to the dangers of drugs, alcohol, smoking, etc. They need positive guidelines and believable examples relating to living a Christian life in an ever-changing world. Buys 20-30 mss/year. Send complete ms. Length: 500-1,000 words. Pays 2-3¢/word.
Fiction: Adventure (with spiritual lesson or application); and religious. "We're looking for fiction that presents believable characters working out their problems according to Biblical principles. No fictionalized accounts of Bible stories or events." Buys 60-80 mss/year. Send complete ms. Length: 1,000-1,800 words. Pays 2-3¢/word.
Poetry: Free verse and light verse. Buys 6-8 mss/year. Pays 20¢/line.
Fillers: Anecdotes (with spiritual emphasis). Buys 15-20/year. Length: 200 words maximum. Pays 2-3¢/word.
Tips: "We like to receive stories showing contemporary children positively facing today's world. These stories show children who are aware of their world and who find a moral solution to their problems through the guidance of God's Word. They are not 'super children' in themselves. They are average children learning how to face life through God's help. We tend to get settings in stories that are out of step with today's society. We will tend to turn more and more to purely contemporary settings unless we are using a historical or biographical story. We will have the setting, characters and plot agree with each other in order to make it more believable to our audience."

KID CITY™, (formerly *The Electric Company Magazine*), Children's Television Workshop, 1 Lincoln Plaza, New York NY 10023. (212)595-3456. Editor: Maureen Hunter-Bone. Associate Editor: Christina Meyer. 10% freelance written. Works with small number of new/unpublished writers each year. Magazine published 10 times/year. "We are a humor/reading/activity magazine for children 6-10 years old." Circ. 250,000. Pays on acceptance. Publishes ms an average of 8 months after acceptance. Byline given. Offers 50% kill fee. Buys all rights. Submit seasonal/holiday material at least 6 months in advance. Simultaneous and photocopied submissions OK. Computer printout submissions acceptable. Reports in 2 weeks. Sample copy for 9x12 SAE with 6 first class stamps.
Nonfiction: General interest, humor and photo feature. Buys 5-6 mss/year. Query with or without published clips, or send complete ms. Length: 700 words maximum. Pays $25-400.
Photos: State availability of photos with submission. Reviews transparencies. Offers $75 maximum/photo. Model releases and identification of subjects required.
Fiction: Adventure, fantasy, historical, humorous, mystery and western. "No stories with heavy moral messages; or those about child abuse, saying 'no,' divorce, single parent households, handicapped children, etc." Buys 3 mss/year. Query or send complete ms. Length: 250-700 words. Pays $400 maximum.
Tips: "Just think about what you liked to read about when you were a kid and write it down. No stories about doggies, bunnies or kitties. No stories with heavy moral message. We're looking for more interesting items about *real* kids who have done something newsworthy or exceptional."

‡NATURE FRIEND MAGAZINE, Pilgrim Publishers, 22777 State Rd. 119, Goshen IN 46526. (219)534-2245. Editor: Stanley K. Brubaker. 50% freelance written. Prefers to work with published/established writers. Monthly magazine appreciating God's marvelous creation. Audience includes children ages 4-14 and older of Christian families who hold a literal view of Creation. Circ. 12,000. Pays on publication. Publishes ms an average of 1 year after acceptance. Byline given. Buys one-time rights. Submit seasonal material 3 or more months in advance. Simultaneous queries, and simultaneous, photocopied, and previously published submissions OK if notified of other submissions or past use. Computer printout submissions acceptable; prefers letter-quality. Reports in 1 month. Sample copy for 8x10 SAE and 3 first class stamps; writer's guidelines $1, 6x9 SAE and 3 first class stamps.
Nonfiction: General interest (various length articles on popular and odd creatures); how-to (for children in learning or building, working with nature); inspirational (praise; humbled by God's handiwork); new product (each issue has Nature's Workshop product page); personal experience (especially from child's point of view); and puzzles, projects, etc. "We buy no manuscripts which feature talking or (humanly) thinking creatures." Buys 30-40 mss/year. Send complete ms. Length: 300-1,200 words. Pays $15-55.

Fiction: Uses some true-to-life nature study stories with animals or other creatures as main character (from animal's perspective). Also families enjoying nature discovery. Buys 30-50 mss/year. Length: 300-1,200 words. Pays $15-55.

Tips: "Subscribe to *Nature Friend Magazine* or study back issues—it has a definite targeted market of fundamental Christians. We want all materials to have a cheerful factual reverential mood. Writers will notice in studying *Nature Friend* that we prefer stories with our particular usage of conversation, questions and concise, fast-flowing description to give accurate and interesting stories for instant reader rapport. We welcome fascinating animal and wildlife biographies, whether stories from human point of view or animal's, but we will *not* use stories where animals think or talk like humans."

NOAH'S ARK, A Newspaper for Jewish Children, 7726 Portal, Houston TX 77071. (713)771-7143. Editors: Debbie Israel Dubin and Linda Freedman Block. A monthly tabloid that "captures readers' interest and reinforces learning about Jewish history, holidays, laws and culture through articles, stories, recipes, games, crafts, projects, Hebrew column and more." For Jewish children, ages 6-12. Circ. 450,000. Pays on acceptance. Byline given. Buys first North American serial rights. Submit seasonal/holiday material 4 months in advance. Simultaneous and photocopied submissions OK. Computer printout submissions OK; prefers letter-quality. Reports in 6 weeks on queries; 2 months on mss. Sample copy and writer's guidelines for #10 SASE.

Nonfiction: Historical/nostalgic, craft projects, recipes, humor, interview/profile. Send complete ms. Length: 350 words maximum. Pays usually 5¢/word.

Photos: State availability of photos with submission or send photos with submission. Offers no additional payment for photos accepted with ms. Identification of subjects required. Buys one-time rights.

Fiction: All must be of Jewish interest: Historical, humorous, religious (Jewish), slice-of-life vignettes. Any and all suitable for Jewish children. Buys 2-3 mss/year. Send complete ms. Length: 600 words maximum. Pays 5¢/word.

Poetry: Light verse and traditional. Buys 1 poem/year. Submit maximum 1 poem. Payment varies.

Fillers: All must be of Jewish interest: Anecdotes, facts, gags, short humor and games. Buys 3-5/year. Payment varies.

Tips: "We're just looking for high quality material suitable for entertainment as well as supplemental religious school use." Encourages freelancers to take an "unusual approach to writing about holidays. All submissions must have Jewish content and positive Jewish values. Content should not be exclusively for an American audience."

ODYSSEY, Kalmbach Publishing Co., 21027 Crossroads Circle, Box 1612, Waukesha WI 53187. (414)796-8776. FAX: (414)796-0126. Editor: Nancy Mack. 50% freelance written. Works with a small number of new/unpublished writers each year. Monthly magazine emphasizing astronomy and outer space for children ages 8-12. Circ. 100,000. Pays on publication. Publishes ms an average of 8 months after acceptance. Buys one-time rights. Submit seasonal/holiday material 4 months in advance. Photocopied and previously published submissions OK. Computer printout submissions acceptable; prefers letter-quality. Reports in 2 months. "Material with little news connection may be held up to one year." Sample copy and writer's guidelines for 8½x12½ SAE and 5 first class stamps.

Nonfiction: General interest (astronomy, outer space, spacecraft, planets, stars, etc.); how-to (astronomy projects, experiments, etc.); and photo feature (spacecraft, planets, stars, etc.). "We like short, off-beat articles with some astronomy or space-science tie-in. A recent example: an article about a baseball game that ended with the explosion of a meteorite over the field. Study the styles of the monthly columnists. No general overview articles; for example, a general article on the Space Shuttle, or a general article on stars. We do not want science fiction articles." Buys 12 mss/year. Query with published clips. Length: 750-2,000 words. Pays $100-350 depending on length and type of article. Sometimes pays expenses of writers on assignment.

Photos: State availability of photos. Buys one-time rights. Captions preferred; model releases required. Payment depends upon size and placement.

Tips: "Since I am overstocked and have a stable of regular writers, a query is very important. I often get several manuscripts on the same subject and must reject them. Write a very specific proposal and indicate why it will interest kids. If the subject is very technical, indicate your qualifications to write about it. I will be buying short articles almost exclusively in 1990 because most major features are being handled by staff or contributing editors. Frequent mistakes writers make are trying to fudge on material they don't understand, using outdated references, and telling me their articles are assignments for the Institute of Children's Literature."

ON THE LINE, Mennonite Publishing House, 616 Walnut Ave., Scottdale PA 15683-1999. (412)887-8500. Editor: Virginia A. Hostetler. 100% freelance written. Works with a small number of new/unpublished writers each year. Weekly magazine for children ages 10-14. Circ. 10,000. Pays on acceptance. Publishes ms an average of 1 year after acceptance. Byline given. Buys one-time rights. Submit seasonal/holiday material 6 months in advance. Simultaneous, photocopied and previously published submissions OK. Computer printout submissions acceptable; prefers letter-quality. Reports in 1 month. Sample copy for 8½x11 SAE and 2 first class stamps.

Nonfiction: How-to (things to make with easy-to-get materials); and informational (500-word articles on wonders of nature, people who have made outstanding contributions). Buys 95 unsolicited mss/year. Send complete ms. Length: 500-900 words. Pays $10-24.

Photos: Photos purchased with or without ms. Pays $10-25 for 8x10 b&w photos. Total purchase price for ms includes payment for photos.

Columns/Departments: Fiction, adventure, humorous and religious. Buys 52 mss/year. Send complete ms. Length: 800-1,200 words. Pays $15-30.

Poetry: Light verse and religious. Length: 3-12 lines. Pays $5-15.

Tips: "Study the publication first. We need short well-written how-to and craft articles. Don't send query; we prefer to see the complete manuscript."

OWL MAGAZINE, The Discovery Magazine for Children, The Young Naturalist Foundation, 56 The Esplanade, Suite 306, Toronto, Ontario M5E 1A7 Canada. (416)868-6001. FAX: (416)868-6009. Editor-in-Chief: Sylvia Funston. 25% freelance written. Works with small number of new/unpublished writers each year. Magazine published 10 times/year (no July or August issues) covering science and nature. Aims to interest children in their environment through accurate, factual information about the world around them presented in an easy, lively style. Circ. 160,000. Pays on publication. Publishes ms an average of 3 months after acceptance. Byline given. Buys all rights; makes work-for-hire assignments. Submit seasonal/holiday material 1 year in advance. Computer printout submissions acceptable; no dot-matrix. Reports in 10 weeks. Sample copy $2.50; free writer's guidelines. Send SAE (large envelope if requesting sample copy) and a money order for $1 to cover postage (no stamps please).

Nonfiction: How-to (activities, crafts); personal experience (real life children in real situations); photo feature (natural science, international wildlife, and outdoor features); and science and environmental features. No problem stories with drugs, sex or moralistic views, or talking animal stories. "We accept short, well-written articles about up-to-the-minute science discoveries or developments for our HOOT CLUB News section." Query with clips of published work.

Photos: State availability of photos. Reviews 35mm transparencies. Identification of subjects required. Send for photo package before submitting material.

Tips: "Write for editorial guidelines first. Review back issues of the magazine for content and style. Know your topic and approach it from an unusual perspective. Our magazine never talks down to children."

‡PENNYWHISTLE PRESS, Gannett Co., Inc., Box 500-P, Washington DC 20044. (703)276-3796. Editor: Anita Sama. 15% freelance written. Works with a very small number of new/unpublished writers each year. A weekly tabloid newspaper supplement with stories and features for children ages 6-12. Circ. 2,900,000. Pays on acceptance. Publishes ms an average of 1 year after acceptance. Byline given. Buys all rights. Submit seasonal/holiday material 3-6 months in advance. Reports in 3 months. Sample copy for 75¢ and SASE. Writer's guidelines for SASE.

Nonfiction: How-to (sports, crafts). Buys 15 mss/year. Length: 500 words maximum. Pays variable rate.

Fiction: For children. Buys 25 mss/year. Send complete ms. Length: 250-850 words. Pays variable rate.

Poetry: Traditional poetry for children. Buys 5-10 poems/year. Submit maximum 1 poem. Pays variable rate.

Tips: Fiction is most open to freelancers.

POCKETS, The Upper Room, 1908 Grand Ave., Box 189, Nashville TN 37202. (615)340-3300. Editor: Janet M. Bugg. 40% freelance written. Eager to work with new/unpublished writers. A monthly themed magazine (except combined January and February issues) covering children's and families spiritual formation. "We are a Christian, non-denominational publication for children 6 to 12 years of age." Circ. 70,000. Pays on acceptance. Byline given. Offers 4¢/word kill fee. Buys first North American serial rights. Submit seasonal/holiday material 1 year in advance. Photocopied and previously published submissions OK. Computer printout submissons acceptable; prefers letter-quality. Reports in 10 weeks on manuscripts. Sample copy for 5x7 SAE with 4 first class stamps; writer's guidelines and themes for #10 SASE.

Nonfiction: Learmond Chapman, articles editor. Interview/profile, religious (retold scripture stories) and personal experience. List of themes for special issues available with SASE. No violence or romance. Buys 3 mss/year. Send complete ms. Length: 600-1,500 words. Pays 7¢-10¢/word.

Photos: Send photos with submission. Reviews contact sheets, transparencies and prints. Offers $25-50/photo. Buys one-time rights.

Columns Departments: Refrigerator Door (poetry and prayer related to themes), 25 lines; Pocketsful of Love (family communications activities), and Loaves and Fishes (simplified lifestyle and nutrition), both 300 words. Buys 20 mss/year. Send complete ms. Pays 7¢-10¢/word; recipes $25.

Fiction: Adventure, ethnic and slice-of-life. "Stories should reflect the child's everyday experiences through a Christian approach. This is often more acceptable when stories are not preachy or overtly Christian." Buys 15 mss/year. Send complete ms. Length: 750-1,600 words. Pays 7-10¢/word.

Close-up

Sylvia Funston
Editor-in-Chief
Owl Magazine

"Television has had a tremendous impact on print material for children. Magazines have been forced to compete with the small screen by being less wordy, more instantly accessible, more visually exciting. These have not always been bad developments," says Sylvia Funston, editor of *Owl Magazine*. "I believe *Owl* has adapted to the print medium of TV-based communication ideas, resulting in a successful integration of words and pictures that children can't help but want to read."

Owl Magazine, the flagship publication of the nonprofit Young Naturalist Foundation, is a nature and science discovery magazine published 10 times a year for children ages 9-12. The magazine began publication in 1976 and has since launched a sister publication, *Chickadee Magazine*, for young children. They are unique among North American children's publications because of their international focus. They are published in Canada, the U.S., Italy, France, Sweden, Finland and the U.K.

"Getting children to want to read should be part of a children's magazine's mandate. Another is to have a point of view, a philosophy that's worth examining and defending. It's okay to produce an up-to-the-minute magazine with slick production values, providing the magazine also has integrity and something worth saying," says Funston.

Funston was raised and educated in England, later emigrating to Canada. She joined the staff of the newly formed *Owl Magazine* in 1976. She became managing editor of *Owl* the following year, editor in 1979 and editor-in-chief of *Owl* and *Chickadee* magazines in 1989. "*Owl* has provided me with the wonderful opportunity to bring together several lifelong interests—nature, photography, writing, design, science and children—and get paid for doing it! The three things I like most about editing *Owl*: First, the job allows me to slip back into that natural state of curiosity we all experience as children. No question is too dumb to ask if it unlocks traditional barriers to problem solving and creative thinking. Second, *Owl*'s international focus grew out of the fact that the environment doesn't recognize boundaries. Looking at ideas from a global rather than a national perspective is both challenging and liberating. And finally, I love the contact my job provides with children. Their letters are a source of great joy and inspiration."

Owl receives approximately 500 unsolicited manuscripts a year, and of these, only about 10 are considered for publication. "This tells us two things. First, we probably aren't explaining our needs carefully enough in our editorial guidelines—so we're working on these right now. Second, writers aren't doing enough homework on our publication before submitting material for consideration," says Funston.

Funston's advice to writers is: "Acquire several back issues of the magazine to get a feel for the scope and content of the editorial material. Send for the editorial guidelines. Also, decide on a topic that interests you. Try it out on children and see if it holds their interest. Ask yourself, what do they really want to know about your topic?"

—Deborah Cinnamon

Poetry: Buys 8 poems/year. Length: 4-25 lines. Pays $25-50.

Tips: "Theme stories, role models and retold scripture stories are most open to freelancers. Poetry is also open, but we rarely receive an acceptable poem. It's very helpful if writers send for our themes. These are *not* the same as writer's guidelines."

R-A-D-A-R, 8121 Hamilton Ave., Cincinnati OH 45231. (513)931-4050. Editor: Margaret Williams. 75% freelance written. Prefers to work with published/established writers; works with a small number of new/unpublished writers each year. Weekly for children in grades 3-6 in Christian Sunday schools. Rights purchased vary with author and material; prefers buying first serial rights, but will buy second (reprint) rights. Occasionally overstocked. Pays on acceptance. Publishes ms an average of 1 year after acceptance. Submit seasonal material 1 year in advance. Computer printout submissions acceptable; prefers letter-quality. Reports in 1-2 months. Free sample copy; writer's guidelines for #10 SASE.

Nonfiction: Articles on hobbies and handicrafts, nature, famous people, seasonal subjects, etc., written from a Christian viewpoint. No articles about historical figures with an absence of religious implication. Length: 500-1,000 words. Pays 3¢/word maximum.

Fiction: Short stories of heroism, adventure, travel, mystery, animals and biography. True or possible plots stressing clean, wholesome, Christian character-building ideas, but not preachy. Make prayer, church attendance and Christian living a natural part of the story. "We correlate our fiction and other features with a definite Bible lesson. Writers who want to meet our needs should send for a theme list." No talking animal stories, science fiction, Halloween stories or first-person stories from an adult's viewpoint. Length: up to 1,000 words. Pays 3¢/word maximum.

RANGER RICK, National Wildlife Federation, 1412 16th St. NW, Washington DC 20036. (703)790-4274. Editor: Gerald Bishop. 30% freelance written. Works with a small number new/unpublished writers each year. Monthly magazine for children from ages 6-12, with the greatest concentration in the 7-10 age bracket. Buys all world rights unless other arrangements made. Byline given "but occasionally, for very brief pieces, we will identify author by name at the end. Contributions to regular columns usually are not bylined." Pays on acceptance. Publishes ms an average of 18 months after acceptance. Computer printout submissions acceptable. Reports in 6 weeks. "Anything written with a specific month in mind should be in our hands at least 10 months before that issue date." Writer's guidelines for #10 SASE.

Nonfiction: "Articles may be written on anything related to nature, conservation, the outdoors, environmental problems or natural science." Buys 20-25 unsolicited mss/year. Query. Pays from $50-550, depending on length, quality and content (maximum length, 900 words).

Fiction: "Same categories as nonfiction plus fantasy and science fiction. The attributing of human qualities to animals is limited to our regular feature, 'The Adventures of Ranger Rick,' so please do not humanize wildlife. The publisher, The National Wildlife Federation, discourages keeping wildlife as pets."

Photos: "Photographs, when used, are paid for separately. It is not necessary that illustrations accompany material."

Tips: "Include in query details of what manuscript will cover; sample lead; evidence that you can write playfully and with great enthusiasm, conviction and excitement (formal, serious, dull queries indicate otherwise). Think of an exciting subject we haven't done recently, sell it effectively with query, and produce a manuscript of highest quality. Read past issues to learn successful styles and unique approaches to subjects. If your submission is commonplace, we won't want it."

SHOFAR Magazine, Senior Publications Ltd. 43 Northcote Dr., Melville NY 11747. (516)643-4598. Managing Editor: Gerald H. Grayson. 80-90% freelance written. A monthly children's magazine on Jewish subjects. Circ. 10,000. Pays on publication. Byline given. Buys one-time rights. Submit seasonal/holiday material 6 months in advance. Simultaneous, photocopied and previously published submissions OK. Computer printout submissions OK; prefers letter-quality. Sample copy and writer's guidelines for 9x12 SAE and 4 first class stamps.

Nonfiction: Dr. Gerald H. Grayson, publisher. Historical/nostalgic, humor, inspirational, interview/profile, personal experience, photo feature, religious and travel. Buys 15 mss/year. Send complete ms. Length: 750-1,000 words. Pays 7¢-10¢/word. Sometimes pays the expenses of writers on assignment.

Photos: State availability of photos with submission or send photos with submission. Offers $10-50 per photo. Identification of subjects required. Buys one-time rights.

Fiction: Adventure, historical, humorous and religious. Buys 15 mss/year. Send complete ms. Length: 750-1,000 words. Pays 7-10¢/word.

Poetry: Free verse, light verse and traditional. Buys 4-5 poems/year. Length: 8-50 words. Pays 7-10¢/word.

Tips: "Submissions should be geared to readers who are 8 to 12 years old."

‡SPORTS ILLUSTRATED FOR KIDS, Time Incorporated, Time & Life Building, New York NY 10020. (212)522-5437. FAX: (212)522-0120. Managing Editor: John Papanek. 50% freelance written. Monthly magazine on sports for children eight years old and up. Content is divided 50/50 between sports as played by kids, and sports as played by professionals. Pays on acceptance. Publishes ms an average of 3 months after acceptance. Byline given. Offers 25% kill fee. Buys all rights. Computer printout submissions OK. Sample copy $1.75. Writer's guidelines for SAE.

Nonfiction: Patricia Berry, articles editor. Games, general interest, how-to, humor, inspirational, interview/profile, photo feature and puzzles. Buys 60 mss/year. Query with published clips. Length: 100-1,500 words. Pays $75-1,000 for assigned articles; $75-800 for unsolicited articles. Pays expenses of writers on assignment.

Photos: State availability of photos with submission. Buys one-time rights.

Columns/Departments: The Worst Day I Ever Had (tells about day in pro athlete's life when all seemed hopeless), 500-600 words; Hotshots (young [8-15] athlete getting good things out of sports), 100-250 words; and Home Team (son, daughter, brother, sister of famous athlete), 500-600 words. Buys 30-40 mss/year. Query with published clips. Pays $75-600.

STONE SOUP, The Magazine by Children, Children's Art Foundation. Box 83, Santa Cruz CA 95063. (408)426-5557. Editor: Ms. Gerry Mandel. 100% freelance written. A bimonthly magazine of writing and art by children, including fiction, poetry, book reviews, and art by children through age 13. Audience is children, teachers, parents, writers, artists. "We have a preference for writing and art based on real-life experiences; no formula stories or poems." Pays on acceptance. Publishes ms an average of 3 months after acceptance. Buys all rights. Submit seasonal/holiday material 6 months in advance. Photocopied submissions OK. Computer printout submissions OK; prefers letter-quality. Reports in 2 weeks on queries; 6 weeks on mss. Sample copy $4. Free writer's guidelines.

Nonfiction: Book reviews. Buys 10 mss/year. Query. Pays $15 for assigned articles. "We pay book reviewers (solicited writers) and illustrators (solicited artists) in cash. We pay for unsolicited fiction, poetry and art in copies."

Fiction: Adventure, ethnic, experimental, fantasy, historical, humorous, mystery, science fiction, slice-of-life vignettes and suspense. "We do not like assignments or formula stories of any kind." Accepts 35 mss/year. Send complete ms. Pays in copies only.

Poetry: Avant-garde and free verse. Accepts 10 poems/year. Pays in copies only.

Tips: "We can't emphasize enough how important it is to read a couple of issues of the magazine. We have a strong preference for writing on subjects that mean a lot to the author. If you feel strongly about something that happened to you or something you observed, use that feeling as the basis for your story or poem. Stories should have good descriptions, realistic dialogue and a point to make. In a poem, each word must be chosen carefully. Your poem should present a view of your subject and a way of using words that are special and all your own."

STORY FRIENDS, Mennonite Publishing House, 616 Walnut Ave., Scottdale PA 15683. (412)887-8500. Editor: Marjorie Waybill. 80% freelance written. Monthly story paper for children ages 4-9. "*Story Friends* is planned to provide wholesome Christian reading for the 4- to 9-year-old. Practical life stories are included to teach moral values and remind the children that God is at work today. Activities introduce children to the Bible and its message for them." Circ.: 11,500. Pays on acceptance. Publishes ms an average of 1 year after acceptance. Byline given. Publication not copyrighted. Buys one-time rights and second serial (reprint) rights. Submit seasonal/holiday material 6 months in advance. Simlutaneous, photocopied and previously published material OK. Computer printout submissions OK; prefers letter quality. Sample copy for 8½x11 SAE with 2 first class stamps. Writer's guidelines for #10 SASE.

Nonfiction: How-to (craft ideas for young children), photo feature. Buys 20 mss/year. Send complete ms. Length: 400-800 words. Pays 3-5/word.

Photos: Send photos with submission. Reviews 8½x11 b&w prints. Offers $10-20/photo. Model releases required. Buys one-time rights.

Fiction: See writer's guidelines for *Story Friends*. Buys 50 mss/year. Send complete ms. Length: 300-800 words. Pays 3-5¢/word.

Poetry: Traditional. Buys 20 poems/year. Length: 4-16 lines. Pays $5-10/poem.

Tips: "Send stories that children from a variety of ethnic backgrounds can relate to; stories that deal with experiences similar to all children. For example, all children have fears but their fears may vary depending on where they live."

‡3-2-1 CONTACT, Children's Television Workshop, One Lincoln Plaza, New York NY 10023. (212)595-3456. FAX: (212)580-3845. Editor-in-Chief: Jonathan Rosenbloom. Senior Editor: Eric Weiner. 40% freelance written. Magazine published 10 times/year covering science and technology for children ages 8-14. Circ. 400,000. Pays on acceptance. Publishes ms 6 months after acceptance. Buys all rights "with some exceptions." Submit seasonal material 8 months in advance. Simultaneous, photocopied and previously published submissions OK if so indicated. Computer printout submissions acceptable; prefers letter-quality to dot-matrix. Reports in 1 month. Sample copy $1.50 with 8½x11 SAE; free writer's guidelines with SASE.

Nonfiction: General interest (space exploration, the human body, animals, computers and the new technology, current science issues); profile (of interesting scientists or children involved in science or with computers); photo feature (centered around a science theme); and role models of women and minority scientists. No articles on travel not related to science. Buys 5 unsolicited mss/year. Query with published clips. Length:

700-1,000 words. Pays $150-400. Sometimes pays expenses of writers on assignment.

Photos: Do *not* send photos on spec.

Tips: "I prefer a short query, without manuscript, that makes it clear that an article is interesting. When sending an article, include your telephone number. Don't call us, we'll call you. Many submissions we receive are more like college research papers than feature stories. We like articles in which writers have interviewed kids or scientists, or discovered exciting events with a scientific angle. Library research is necessary; but if that's all you're doing, you aren't giving us anything we can't get ourselves. If your story needs a bibliography, chances are, it's not right for us."

‡TOUCH, Box 7259, Grand Rapids MI 49510. Editor: Joanne Ilbrink. 80% freelance written. Prefers to work with published/established writers. Monthly magazine. Purpose of publication is to show girls ages 7-14 how God is at work in their lives and in the world around them. "The May/June issue annually features the material written by our readers." Circ. 14,000. Pays on acceptance. Publishes ms an average of 1 year after acceptance. Byline given. Buys second serial (reprint) rights and first North American serial rights. Submit seasonal/holiday material 9 months in advance. Simultaneous, photocopied and previously published submissions OK. Computer printout submissions acceptable; no dot-matrix. Reports in 6 weeks. Free sample copy and writer's guidelines for 9x12 SASE and 3 first class stamps.

Nonfiction: How-to (crafts girls can make easily and inexpensively); informational (write for issue themes); humor (need much more); inspirational (seasonal and holiday); interview; multicultural materials; travel; personal experience (avoid the testimony approach); and photo feature (query first). "Because our magazine is published around a monthly theme, requesting the letter we send out twice a year to our established freelancers would be most helpful. We do not want easy solutions or quick character changes from bad to good. No pietistic characters. Constant mention of God is not necessary if the moral tone of the story is positive. We do not always want stories that have a good ending." Buys 36-45 unsolicited mss/year. Submit complete ms. Length: 100-1,000 words. Pays 2.5¢/word, depending on the amount of editing.

Photos: Purchased with or without ms. Reviews 5x7 clear b&w (only) glossy prints. Appreciate multicultural subjects. Pays $5-25 on publication.

Fiction: Adventure (that girls could experience in their hometowns or places they might realistically visit); humorous; mystery (believable only); romance (stories that deal with awakening awareness of boys are appreciated); suspense (can be serialized); and religious (nothing preachy). Buys 20 mss/year. Submit complete ms. Length: 300-1,500 words. Pays 2¢/word.

Poetry: Free verse, haiku, light verse and traditional. Buys 10/year. Length: 30 lines maximum. Pays $5 minimum.

Fillers: Puzzles, short humor and cartoons. Buys 3/issue. Pays $2.50-7.

Tips: "Prefers not to see anything on the adult level, secular material or violence. Writers frequently oversimplify the articles and often write with a Pollyanna attitude. An author should be able to see his/her writing style as exciting and appealing to girls ages 7-14. The style can be fun, but also teach a truth. The subject should be current and important to *Touch* readers. We would like to receive material that features a multicultural slant."

TURTLE MAGAZINE FOR PRESCHOOL KIDS, Children's Better Health Institute, Benjamin Franklin Literary & Medical Society, Inc., 1100 Waterway Blvd., Box 567, Indianapolis IN 46206. (317)636-8881. Editor: Beth Wood Thomas. 95% freelance written. Monthly magazine (bimonthly February/March, April/May, June/July, August/September) for preschoolers emphasizing health, safety, exercise and good nutrition. Pays on publication. Publishes ms an average of 1 year after acceptance. Byline given. Buys all rights. Submit seasonal/holiday material 8 months in advance. Reports in 10 weeks. Sample copy 75¢; writer's guidelines for #10 SASE.

Fiction: Fantasy, humorous and health-related stories. "Stories that deal with a health theme need not have health as the primary subject but should include it in some way in the course of events." No controversial material. Buys 40 mss/year. Submit complete ms. Length: 700 words maximum. Pays approximately 8¢/word.

Poetry: "We use many stories in rhyme—vocabulary should be geared to a 3- to 5-year-old. Anthropomorphic animal stories and rhymes are especially effective for this age group to emphasize a moral or lesson without 'lecturing'." Pays variable rates.

Tips: "We are primarily concerned with preventive medicine. We try to present our material in a positive—not a negative—light and to incorporate humor and a light approach wherever possible without minimizing the seriousness of what we are saying. We would like to see more stories, articles, craft ideas and activities with the following holiday themes: New Year's Day, Valentine's Day, President's Day, St. Patrick's Day, Easter, Independence Day, Thanksgiving, Christmas and Hannukah. We like new ideas that will entertain as well as teach preschoolers. Publishing a writer's first work is very gratifying to us. It is a great pleasure to receive new, fresh material."

VENTURE, Christian Service Brigade, Box 150, Wheaton IL 60189. (312)665-0630. Editor: Steven P. Neideck. 15% freelance written. Works with a small number of new/unpublished writers each year. "Venture is a bimonthly company publication published to support and compliment *CSB's* Stockade and Battalion programs. We aim to provide wholesome, entertaining reading for boys ages 10-15." Circ. 25,000. Pays on publication. Publishes ms an average of 4-6 months after acceptance. Byline given. Offers $35 kill fee. Buys first North American serial, one-time and second serial (reprint) rights. Submit seasonal/holiday material 6 months in advance. Photocopied submissions and previously published submissions OK. Computer printout submissions OK; prefers letter-quality. Reports in 2 weeks. Sample copy $1.50 with 9x12 SAE and 4 first class stamps; writer's guidelines for #10 SASE.

Nonfiction: Exposé, general interest, historical/nostalgic, humor, inspirational, interview/profile, personal experience, photo feature and religious. Buys 10-12 mss/year. Query. Length: 1,000-1,500 words. Pays $75-125 for assigned articles; pays $40-100 for unsolicited articles. Sometimes pays expenses of writers on assignment.

Photos: Send photos with submission. Reviews contact sheets and 5x7 prints. Offers $35-125/photo. Buys one-time rights.

Fiction: Adventure, humorous, mystery and religious. Buys 10-12 mss/year. Query. Length: 1,000-1,500 words. Pays $40-125.

Tips: "Talk to young boys. Find out the things that interest them and write about those things. We are looking for material relating to our theme: Building Men to Serve Christ."

WEE WISDOM, Unity Village MO 64065. Editor: Ms. Judy Gehrlein. 90% freelance written. "We are happy to work with any freelance writers whose submissions and policies match our needs." Magazine published 10 times/year "for children aged 13 and under, dedicated to the truth that each person has an inner source of wisdom, power, love and health that can be applied in a practical manner to everyday life." Circ. 175,000. Publishes ms an average of 8 months after acceptance. Submit seasonal/holiday material 10-12 months in advance. Pays on acceptance. Byline given. Buys first serial rights only. Computer printout submissions acceptable; must be clearly legible. Sample copy and editorial policy for 5¾x8¾ SAE and 4 first class stamps.

Fiction: Character-building stories that encourage a positive self-image. Although entertaining enough to hold the interest of the older child, they should be readable by the third grader. "Characters should be appealing; plots should be imaginative but plausible, and all stories should be told without preaching. Life combines fun and humor with its more serious lessons, and our most interesting and helpful stories do the same thing. Language should be universal, avoiding the Sunday school image." Length: 500-800 words. Rates vary, depending on excellence.

Poetry: Limited. Prefers short, seasonal and general poems for children. Pays $15 minimum, 50¢ per line after 15 lines. Rhymed prose (read aloud) stories are paid at about the same rate as prose stories, depending on excellence.

Fillers: Pays $8-10 for puzzles and games.

WONDER TIME, 6401 The Paseo, Kansas City MO 64131. (816)333-7000. Editor: Evelyn Beals. 75% freelance written. "Willing to read and consider appropriate freelance submissions." Published weekly by Church of the Nazarene for children ages 6-8. Pays on acceptance. Publishes ms an average of 1 year after acceptance. Byline given. Buys first serial rights, second serial (reprint) rights, simultaneous rights and all rights for curriculum assignments. Computer printout submissions acceptable; prefers letter-quality. Sample copy and writer's guidelines for 9x12 SAE with 3 first class stamps.

Fiction: Buys stories portraying Christian attitudes without being preachy. Uses stories for special days—stories teaching honesty, truthfulness, kindness, helpfulness or other important spiritual truths, and avoiding symbolism. Also, stories about real life problems children face today. "God should be spoken of as our Father who loves and cares for us; Jesus, as our Lord and Savior." Buys 52/mss year. Length: 350-550 words. Pays 3½¢/word on acceptance.

Poetry: Uses verse which has seasonal or Christian emphasis. Length: 4-8 lines. Pays 25¢/line, minimum $2.50.

Tips: "Any stories that allude to church doctrine must be in keeping with Nazarene beliefs. Any type of fantasy must be in good taste and easily recognizable. We are overstocked now with poetry and stories with general themes. We plan to reprint more than before to save art costs, therefore we will be more selective and purchase fewer manuscripts."

‡**THE WORLD OF BUSINES$ KIDS, Busine$$ Kids/America's Future,** Lemonade Kids, Inc., Suite 330, 301 Almeria Ave., Coral Gables FL 33134. (305)445-8869. Editor: Jacky Robinson. Quarterly newsletter on business, specifically young entrepreneurs. "We cover stories about young entrepreneurs, how teens and preteens can become entrepreneurs, and useful information for effective business operation and management." Estab. 1988. Circ. 25,000. Pays on publication. Publishes ms an average of 6 months after acceptance. Teens get byline. Buys first rights. Submit seasonal/holiday material 6 months in advance. Computer printout submissions OK; prefers letter-quality. Reports in 10 weeks on mss. Free sample copy and writer's guidelines.

Nonfiction: Any nonfiction pertaining to teens in the business world. How-to choose, build, improve, market or advertise a business. When, and how, to hire (or fire) employees. Profiles of successful young entrepreneurs. The latest in any field, entertainment, sports, medicine, etc., where teens are making megabucks or just movie money. New products, book reviews on children and money; motivational articles; how-to invest/ save money, news releases, tax information, stock market tips, bonds, banking, precious metals, cartoons, puzzles, poetry, games. "No articles with inappropriate language; any mention of alcohol, drugs or tobacco, religious articles; product advertising; inappropriate themes for teens; cheesecake; inappropriate photo backgrounds." Buys 50 mss/year. Send complete ms. Length: 200-600 words. Pays 15¢/word.

Photos: Send photos with submission. Reviews 5x7 or 8x10 b&w prints. Offers $5-10 per photo. Captions, model releases and identification of subjects required. Buys all rights.

Columns/Departments Parentally Speaking (book review for parents, what teens should know about money), 15¢/word; Movie Review (critique of recent films written by teens only, payment free admission). Buys 8 mss/year. Send complete ms. Length: 200-400 words.

Poetry: Avant-garde, free verse, haiku, light verse and traditional. Nothing unrelated to business. Buys 2-4 poems/year. No limit on number of poem submissions. Length: open. Pays $15-20.

Fillers: Cartoons, puzzles and games. Buys 2-4/year. Length: 25-100 words. Pays cartoons $15-20; puzzles and games $25-50.

Tips: "Write thoroughly researched, entertaining, factual and *positive* how-tos. No sermonettes or abstract concepts. Understanding teens is a prerequisite. Study our guidelines. Use words economically, and submit clean copy with SASE.

YOUNG AMERICAN, America's Newspaper for Kids, Young American Publishing Co., Inc., Box 12409, Portland OR 97212. (503)230-1895. FAX: (503)236-0440. Editor: Kristina T. Linden. 3% freelance written. Eager to work with new/unpublished writers. A tabloid-size newspaper supplement to suburban newspapers for children and their families. Circ. 4.6 million. Pays on publication. Publishes ms an average of 6 months after acceptance. Buys first North American serial rights. Submit seasonal/holiday material 6 months in advance. Photocopied submissions OK. Computer printout submissions acceptable; prefers letter-quality. Reports in 4 months on mss. Sample copy $1.50; writer's guidelines for SASE.

Nonfiction: General interest; historical/nostalgic; how-to (crafts, fitness); humor; interview/profile (of kids, or people particularly of interest to them); and newsworthy kids. No condescending articles or articles relating to religion, sex, violence, drugs or substance abuse. Buys 30 mss/year. *No queries*; send complete ms. Length: 350 words maximum. Pays $5-75. Sometimes pays the expenses of writers on assignment.

Photos: Send photos with submission. Offers negotiable maximum/photo. Identification of subjects required. Buys one-time rights.

Columns/Departments: You and the News (stories about newsworthy kids), science (new developments, things not covered in textbooks). Length 350 words maximum. Buys 20 mss/year. Send complete ms. Pays $5-75.

Fiction: Adventure, ethnic, fantasy, humorous, mystery, science fiction, suspense, western and lore. No condescending stories or stories relating to religion, sex, drugs or substance abuse. Buys 24 mss/year. Send complete ms. Length: 500-1,000 words. Pays $35-75.

Poetry: Light verse. No "heavy" or depressing poetry. Buys 30 poems/year. Length: 4 lines, 500 words maximum. Pays $5-35.

Fillers: Facts and short humor. Buys 20/year. Length: 30-300 words. Pays $2.10-21.

Tips: "*Young American* is particularly interested in publishing articles about newsworthy kids. These articles should be under 350 words and accompanied by photos—we prefer color transparencies to black and white. The *Young American* focus is on children—and they are taken seriously. Articles are intended to inform, entertain, stimulate and enlighten. They give children a sense of being a part of today's important events and a recognition which is often denied them because of age. If applicable, photos, diagrams or information for illustration helps tremendously as our publication is highly visual. The fiction we have been receiving is excellent. We are now distributed nationwide and now have a more national perspective. Kids want to read about what other kids in different places are doing."

THE YOUNG SOLDIER, The Salvation Army, 799 Bloomfield Ave., Verona NJ 07044. Editor: Robert R. Hostetler. 75% freelance written. Monthly Christian/religious magazine for children, ages 8-12. "Only material with clear Christian or Biblical emphasis is accepted." Circ. 48,000. Pays on acceptance. Publishes ms an average of 6 months after acceptance. Byline given. Buys first North American serial rights, first rights, one-time rights or second serial (reprint) rights. Submit seasonal/holiday material 6 months in advance. Photocopied and previously published submissions OK. Computer printout submissions OK; prefers letter-quality. Reports in 1 month. Sample copy for 8½x11 SAE with 3 first class stamps. Writer's guidelines for #10 SASE.

Nonfiction: How-to (craft, Bible study, etc.), religious, games, puzzles, activities. Buys 12 mss/year. Send complete ms. Length: 300-1,000 words. Pays 3-5¢/word.

Photos: State availability or send photos with submission. Reviews contact sheets, negatives, transparencies and prints. Payment varies for photos accepted with ms. Buy one-time rights.

Fiction: Adventure, religious. "Must have Christian emphasis." Buys 10-12 mss/year. Send complete ms. Length: 500-1,000 words. Pays 3-5¢/word.

Poetry: Free verse, light verse, traditional. Buys 6 poems/year. Length: 4-20 lines. Pays 5¢/word ($5 minimum).

_____ *Literary and "Little"*

Literary and "little" magazines contain fiction, poetry, book reviews, essays and literary criticism. Many are published by universities and have a regional or scholarly focus.

Literary magazines launch many writers into print. Serious writers will find great opportunities here; some agents read the magazines to find promising potential clients, and many magazines also sponsor annual contests. Writers who want to get a story printed may have to be patient. Literary magazines, especially semiannuals, will buy good material and save it for future editions. Submitting work to a literary, the writer may encounter frequent address changes or long response times. On the other hand, many editors carefully read submissions several times and send personal notes to writers.

Many literary magazines do not pay writers or pay in contributor's copies. Only literary magazines which pay are included in *Writer's Market* listings. However, *Novel and Short Story Writer's Market*, published by Writer's Digest Books, includes nonpaying fiction markets and has indepth information about fiction techniques and markets. Literary and "little" magazine writers will notice that *Writer's Market* does not have a Poetry section, although Poetry subheads can be found in this section and in many consumer magazine listings. Writer's Digest Books also publishes *Poet's Market*, edited by Judson Jerome, with detailed information for poets.

ALASKA QUARTERLY REVIEW, College of Arts & Sciences, University of Alaska Anchorage, Dept. of English, 3221 Providence Dr., Anchorage AK 99508. (907)786-1731. Executive Editors: Ronald Spatz and James Liszka. 100% freelance written. Prefers to work with published/established writers; eager to work with new/unpublished writers. A semiannual magazine publishing fiction and poetry, both traditional and experimental styles, and literary criticism and reviews, with an emphasis on contemporary literature. Circ. 1,000. Pays honorariums on publication when funding permits. Publishes ms an average of 6 months after acceptance. Byline given. Buys first North American serial rights. Upon request, rights will be transferred back to author after publication. Photocopied submissions OK. Computer printout submissions acceptable; prefers letter-quality. Reports in 4 months. Sample copy $3 and 8x10 SAE; writer's guidelines for #10 SAE.
Nonfiction: Essays, literary criticism, reviews and philosophy of literature. Buys 1-5 mss/year. Query. Length: 1,000-20,000 words. Pays $50-100 subject to funding; pays in copies when funding is limited.
Fiction: Ronald Spatz, fiction editor. Experimental and traditional literary forms. No romance, children's or inspirational/religious. Buys 10-20 mss/year. Send complete ms. Length: 500-20,000 words. Pays $50-150 subject to funding; sometimes pays in contributor's copies only.
Poetry: Thomas Sexton, poetry editor. Avant-garde, free verse, haiku and traditional. No light verse. Buys 10-30 poems/year. Submit maximum 10 poems. Pays $10-50 subject to availability of funds.
Tips: "All sections are open to freelancers. We rely exclusively on unsolicited manuscripts. *AQR* is a nonprofit literary magazine and does not always have funds to pay authors."

AMELIA MAGAZINE, Amelia Press, 329 E St., Bakersfield CA 93304. (805)323-4064. Editor: Frederick A. Raborg Jr. 100% freelance written. Eager to work with new/unpublished writers. "*Amelia* is a quarterly international magazine publishing the finest poetry and fiction available, along with expert criticism and reviews intended for all interested in contemporary literature. *Amelia* also publishes three supplements each year: *Cicada*, which publishes only high quality traditional or experimental haiku and senryu plus fiction, essays and cartoons pertaining to Japan; *SPSM&H*, which publishes the highest quality traditional and experimental sonnets available plus romantic fiction and essays pertaining to the sonnet; and the annual winner of the Charles William Duke long poem contest." Circ. 1,250. Pays on acceptance. Publishes ms an average of 6 months after acceptance. Byline given. Offers 50% kill fee. Buys first North American serial rights. Submit seasonal/holiday material 2 months in advance. Computer printout submissions acceptable; prefers letter-quality. Reports in 2 months on mss. Sample copy $6.50 (includes postage); writer's guidelines for #10 SASE. Sample copy of any supplement $4.
Nonfiction: Historical/nostalgic (in the form of belles lettres); humor (in fiction or belles lettres); interview/profile (poets and fiction writers); opinion (on poetry and fiction only); personal experience (as it pertains to poetry or fiction in the form of belles lettres); travel (in the form of belles lettres only); and criticism and book reviews of poetry and small press fiction titles. "Nothing overtly slick in approach. Criticism pieces must have depth; belles lettres must offer important insights into the human scene." Buys 8 mss/year. Send complete ms. Length: 1,000-2,000 words. Pays $25 or by arrangement. "Ordinarily payment for all prose is a flat rate of $25/piece, more for exceptional work." Sometimes pays the expenses of writers on assignment.

Fiction: Adventure; book excerpts (original novel excerpts only); erotica (of a quality seen in Anaïs Nin or Henry Miller only); ethnic; experimental; fantasy; historical; horror; humorous; mainstream; mystery; novel excerpts; science fiction; suspense; and western. "We would consider slick fiction of the quality seen in *Redbook* and more excellent submissions in the genres—science fiction, wit, Gothic horror, traditional romance, stories with complex *raisons d'être*; avant-garde ought to be truly avant-garde and not merely exercises in vulgarity (read a few old issues of *Evergreen Review* or *Avant-Garde*)." No pornography ("good erotica is not the same thing"). Buys 24-36 mss/year. Send complete ms. Length: 1,000-5,000 words. Pays $35 or by arrangement for exceptional work.

Poetry: Avant-garde, free verse, haiku, light verse and traditional. "No patently religious or stereotypical newspaper poetry." Buys 100-160 poems/year depending on lengths. Prefers submission of at least 3 poems. Length: 3-100 lines. Pays $2-25; additional payment for exceptional work, usually by established professionals. *Cicada* pays $10 each to three "best of issue" poets; *SPSM&H* pays $14 to two "best of issue" sonnets; winner of the long poem contest receives $100 plus copies and publication.

Tips: *"Have something to say* and say it well. If you insist on waving flags or pushing your religion, then do it with subtlety and class. We enjoy a good cry from time to time, too, but sentimentality does not mean we want to see mush. Read our fiction carefully for depth of plot and characterization, then try very hard to improve on it. With the growth of quality in short fiction, we expect to find stories of lasting merit. I also hope to begin seeing more critical essays which, without sacrificing research, demonstrate a more entertaining obliqueness to the style sheets, more 'new journalism' than MLA. In poetry, we also often look for a good 'storyline' so to speak. Above all we want to feel a sense of honesty and value in every piece. As in the first issue of *Amelia*, 'name' writers are used, but newcomers who have done their homework suffer no disadvantage here. So often the problem seems to be that writers feel small press publications allow such a sloughing of responsibility. It is not so."

THE AMERICAN VOICE, 332 W. Broadway, Louisville KY 40202. (502)562-0045. Editors: Sallie Bingham and Frederick Smock. Works with small number of new/unpublished writers each year. A quarterly literary magazine "for readers of varying backgrounds and educational levels, though usually college-educated. Radical, feminist, unpredictable, we publish new writers' work along with the more radical work of established writers. Avant-garde, open-minded." Circ. 1,500. Pays on publication. Publishes ms an average of 4 months after acceptance. Byline given. Offers 50% kill fee. Buys first North American rights. Photocopied submissions OK. Computer printout submissions acceptable; prefers letter-quality. Reports in 1 month on queries; 2 months on mss. Sample copy $5.

Nonfiction: Essays, opinion, photo feature and criticism. Buys 15 mss/year. Send complete ms. Length: 10,000 words maximum. Pays $400/essay; $150 to translator.

Fiction: Buys 10 mss/year. Send complete ms. Pays $400/story; $150 to translator.

Poetry: Avant-garde and free verse. Buys 35 poems/year. Submit maximum 10 poems. Pays $150/poem; $75 to translator.

Tips: "We are looking only for vigorously original fiction, poetry and essays, from new and established writers, and will consider nothing that is in any way sexist, racist or homophobic."

ANTIOCH REVIEW, Box 148, Yellow Springs OH 45387. Editor: Robert S. Fogarty. 80% freelance written. Quarterly magazine for general, literary and academic audience. Buys all rights. Byline given. Pays on publication. Publishes ms an average of 10 months after acceptance. Computer printout submissions acceptable; prefers letter-quality. Reports in 6 weeks. Sample copy for $5; writer's guidelines for #10 SASE.

Nonfiction: "Contemporary articles in the humanities and social sciences, politics, economics, literature and all areas of broad intellectual concern. Somewhat scholarly, but never pedantic in style, eschewing all professional jargon. Lively, distinctive prose insisted upon." Length: 2,000-8,000 words. Pays $10/published page.

Fiction: Quality fiction only, distinctive in style with fresh insights into the human condition. No science fiction, fantasy or confessions. Pays $10/published page.

Poetry: Concrete visual imagery. No light or inspirational verse. Contributors should be familiar with the magazine before submitting.

BAD HAIRCUT, Box 6631, Kent WA 98064. Editors: Ray Goforth and Kim Goforth. 99% freelance written. Quarterly literary magazine. Circ. 400. Pays on publication. Byline given. Buys first North American serial rights. Submit seasonal/holiday material 4 months in advance. Simultaneous, photocopied and previously published submissions OK. Computer printout submissions OK; no dot-matrix. Reports in 1 week on queries; 1 month on mss. Sample copy $4; writer's guidelines for #10 SASE.

Nonfiction: Essays, expose (government), general interest, interview/profile (political leaders, activists), opinion, photo feature. No pornography or hate-oriented articles. Buys 6 mss/year. Query with or without published clips, or send complete ms. Length: 500-5,000. Pays $50 maximum. Sometimes pays writers with contributor copies or other premiums rather than a cash payment.

Photos: Send photos with submission. Reviews 5x7 prints. Offers $5-100/photo. Model release and identification of subjects required. Buys one-time rights.

Fiction: Adventure, experimental, historical, science fiction. Buys 6 mss/year. Send complete ms. Length: 500-5,000 words. Pays $50 maximum, (usually copies).

Poetry: Avant-garde, free verse. Buys 300 poems/year. Submit up to 10 poems at one time. Length: 1-100 lines. Pays with tear sheets or copy.

Fillers: Anecdotes, facts, newsbreaks. Buys 20 mss/year. Length: 7-100 words. Pays $2.

Tips: "There is a rising tide of activism—a caring for others and the common future we all share. Tap into this—let your heart guide you along the path to peace."

‡BLACK WARRIOR REVIEW, University of Alabama, Box 2936, Tuscaloosa AL 35487. (205)348-4518. Editor: Mark Dawson. Managing Editor: Dale Prince 95% freelance written. A semiannual magazine of fiction and poetry. Circ. 2,000. Pays on publication. Publishes ms an average of 6 months after acceptance. Byline given. Buys first rights. Photocopied submissions OK. Computer printout submissions OK; prefers letter-quality to dot-matrix. Reports in 2 weeks on queries; 3 months on mss. Sample copy $4; writer's guidelines for #10 SASE.

Nonfiction: Interview/profile and book reviews. Buys 5 mss/year. Query or send complete ms. No limit on length. Payment varies.

Photos: State availability of photos with submission. Offers no additional payment for photos accepted with ms. Identification of subjects required. Buys one-time rights.

Fiction: Alicia Griswold, fiction editor. Good fiction only. Buys 10 mss/year.

Poetry: Glenn Mott, poetry editor. Good poetry. Submit 3-6 poems. Long poems encouraged. Buys 50 poems/year.

Tips: "Read the *BWR* before submitting."

BOOK FORUM, Crescent Publishing Co, Inc., Box 585, Niantic CT 06357. Editor: Clarence Driskill. 95% freelance written. Works with small number of new/unpublished writers each year. "Serious writers not yet recognized are welcome to query." Quarterly magazine emphasizing contemporary literature, the arts and foreign affairs for "intellectually sophisticated and knowledgeable professionals: university-level academics, writers, and the professions." Circ. 5,200. Pays on publication. Publishes ms an average of 6 months after acceptance. Pays 33⅓% kill fee. Byline given. Buys first serial rights. Photocopied submissions OK. Letter-quality submissions only. Reports in 1 month. Sample copy for 8½x11 SAE, 5 first class stamps and $3.

Nonfiction: "We seek highly literate essays that would appeal to the same readership as, say, the *London Times Literary Supplement* or *Encounter*. Our readers are interested in professionally written, highly literate and informative essays, profiles and reviews in literature, the arts, behavior, and foreign and public affairs. We cannot use material designed for a mass readership." General interest, interview (with select contemporary writers, scientists, educators, artists, film makers); profiles and essays about contemporary innovators. Buys 20-40 unsolicited mss/year. Query. Length: 800-2,000 words. Pays $25-100.

Tips: "To break in, send with the query letter a sample of writing in an area relevant to our interests. If the writer wants to contribute book reviews, send a book review sample, published or not, of the kind of title we are likely to review—literary, social, biographical, art. We will be looking for more short book reviews in the future and are interested in additional interviews in philosophy, foreign affairs, art."

CALYX, A Journal of Art & Literature by Women, Calyx, Inc., P.O. Box B, Corvallis OR 97339. (503)753-9384. Editors: Margarita Donnelly et al. A literary triannual magazine publishing "Work by women: literature, art, interviews and reviews." Circ. 5,000. Pays on publication. Publishes ms an average of 6 months to 1 year after acceptance. Byline given. Buys first rights and second serial reprint rights. Photocopied submissions OK. Computer printout submissions OK. Reports in 3 weeks on queries; 2-3 months on mss. Sample copy for $6.50 plus $1 postage; writer's guidelines for #10 SASE.

Nonfiction: "We are interested in well-crafted writing by women." Essays, interview/profile and book reviews. "We use 10-30 book reviews per issue and 3-6 interviews and essays per year." Send complete ms. Query the editors for book review list. Length for book reviews: 1,000 words; interviews/essays: 3,000 words. Pays in copies or $5/page depending on grant support.

Fiction: Contact: Editorial Board. Serious literary fiction. Buys 10-15 mss/year. Send complete ms. Length: 5,000 words maximum. Pays $5/published page or in copies of journal.

Poetry: Publishes 150-250 poems/year. Submit maximum 6 poems. Pays $5/poem per page or in copies of the journal.

Tips: "Send well-crafted writing with SASE and brief biographical statement. Be familiar with our publication."

CANADIAN FICTION MAGAZINE, Box 946, Station F, Toronto, Ontario M4Y 2N9 Canada. Editor: Geoffrey Hancock. Quarterly magazine; 148 pages. Publishes only Canadian fiction, short stories and novel excerpts. Circ. 1,800. Pays on publication. Buys first North American serial rights. Byline given. Reports in 6 weeks. Back issue $6 (in Canadian funds); current issue $7.50 (in Canadian funds).

Nonfiction: Interview (must have a definite purpose, both as biography and as a critical tool focusing on problems and techniques) and book reviews (Canadian fiction only). Buys 35 mss/year. Query. Length: 1,000-3,000 words. Pays $10/printed page plus 1-year subscription.

Photos: Purchased on assignment. Send prints. Pays $10 for 5x7 b&w glossy prints; $50 for cover. Model releases required.

Fiction: "No restrictions on subject matter or theme. We are open to experimental and speculative fiction as well as traditional forms. Style, content and form are the author's prerogative. We also publish self-contained sections of novel-in-progress and French-Canadian fiction in translation, as well as an annual special issue on a single author such as Mavis Gallant, Leon Rooke, Robert Harlow or Jane Rule. Please note that *CFM* is an anthology devoted *exclusively* to Canadian fiction. We publish only the works of writers and artists residing in Canada and Canadians living abroad." Pays $10/printed page.

Tips: "Prospective contributors must study several recent issues carefully. *CFM* is a serious professional literary magazine whose contributors include the finest writers in Canada."

CANADIAN LITERATURE, #223-2029 West Mall, University of British Columbia, Vancouver, British Columbia V6T 1W5 Canada. Editor: W.H. New. 70% freelance written. Works with "both new and established writers depending on quality. Quarterly. Circ. 2,000. Not copyrighted. Buys first Canadian rights only. Pays on publication. Publishes ms an average of 2 years after acceptance. Computer printout submissions acceptable; prefers letter-quality. Query "with a clear description of the project." Sample copy and writer's guidelines for $7.50 (Canadian) and 7x10 SAE with $2.50 Canadian postage.

Nonfiction: Articles of high quality only on Canadian books and writers written in French or English. Articles should be scholarly and readable. Length: 2,000-5,500 words. Pays $5/printed page.

CAROLINA QUARTERLY, University of North Carolina, Greenlaw Hall 066A, Chapel Hill NC 27514. (919)962-0244. Editor: Rebecca Barnhouse. Managing Editor: Michael Evans. 100% freelance written. Eager to work with new/unpublished writers. Literary journal published 3 times/year. Circ. 1,000. Pays on publication. Publishes ms an average of 4 months after acceptance. Byline given. Buys first North American serial rights. Photocopied submissions OK. Computer printout submissions acceptable; prefers letter-quality. Reports in 4 months. Sample copy $4 (includes postage); writer's guidelines for SASE.

Nonfiction: Book reviews and photo feature. Publishes 6 reviews/year, 12 photographs/year.

Fiction: "We are interested in maturity: control over language; command of structure and technique; understanding of the possibilities and demands of prose narrative, with respect to stylistics, characterization, and point of view. We publish a good many unsolicited stories; *CQ* is a market for newcomer and professional alike." No pornography. Buys 12-18 mss/year. Send complete ms. Length: 7,000 words maximum. Pays $3/printed page.

Poetry: "*CQ* places no specific restrictions on the length, form or substance of poems considered for publication." Submit 2-6 poems. Buys 60 mss/year. Pays $5/printed poem.

Tips: "Send *one* fiction manuscript at a time; no cover letter is necessary. Address to appropriate editor, not to general editor. Look at the magazine, a recent number if possible."

THE CHARITON REVIEW, Northeast Missouri State University, Kirksville MO 63501. (816)785-4499. Editor: Jim Barnes. 100% freelance written. Semiannual (fall and spring) magazine covering contemporary fiction, poetry, translation and book reviews. Circ. 600. Pays on publication. Publishes ms an average of 6 months after acceptance. Byline given. Buys first North American serial rights. Computer printout submissions acceptable; no dot-matrix. Reports in 1 week on queries; 2 weeks on mss. Sample copy for $2, 7x10 SAE and 3 first class stamps.

Nonfiction: Essays and essay reviews of books. Buys 2-5 mss/year. Query or send complete ms. Length: 1,000-5,000. Pays $15.

Fiction: Ethnic, experimental, mainstream, novel excerpts and traditional. "We are not interested in slick material." Buys 6-8 mss/year. Send complete ms. Length: 1,000-6,000 words. Pays $5/page.

Poetry: Avant-garde, free verse and traditional. Buys 50-55 poems/year. Submit maximum 10 poems. Length: open. Pays $5/page.

Tips: "Read *Chariton* and similar magazines. Know the difference between good literature and bad. Know what magazine might be interested in your work. We are not a trendy magazine. We publish only the best. All sections are open to freelancers. Know your market or you are wasting your time—and mine. Do *not* write for guidelines; the only guideline is excellence in all matters."

CONFRONTATION, C.W. Post College of Long Island University, Brookville NY 11548. (516)299-2391. Editor: Martin Tucker. 90% freelance written. Works with a small number of new/unpublished writers each year. Semiannual magazine emphasizing creative writing for a "literate, educated, college-graduate audience." Circ. 2,000. Pays on publication. Pays 50% kill fee. Publishes ms an average of 9 months after acceptance. Byline given. Buys first serial rights. Phone queries, simultaneous and photocopied submissions OK. Query for electronic submissions. Computer printout submissions acceptable; no dot-matrix. Reports in 2 months. Sample copy $3.

Nonfiction: "Articles are, basically, commissioned essays on a specific subject." Memoirs wanted. Buys 6 mss/year. Query. Length: 1,000-3,000 words. Pays $10-100.

Fiction: William Fahey, fiction editor. Experimental, humorous and mainstream. Buys 25-50 mss/year. Submit complete ms. Length: open. Pays $15-100.

Poetry: Katherine Hill-Miller, poetry editor. Avant-garde, free verse, haiku, light verse and traditional. Buys 60 poems/year. Submit maximum 8 poems. No length requirement. Pays $5-50.

Tips: "We discourage proselytizing literature. We do, however, read all manuscripts. It's rewarding discovering a good manuscript that comes in unsolicited."

‡**THE DENVER QUARTERLY,** University of Denver, Denver CO 80208. (303)871-2892. Editor: Donald Revell. 100% freelance written. Works with a small number of new/unpublished writers. Quarterly magazine for generally sophisticated readership. Circ.1,000. Pays on publication. Publishes ms an average of 6-12 months after acceptance. Buys first North American serial rights. Photocopied submissions OK. Computer printout submissions acceptable; no dot-matrix. Reports in 3 months. Sample copy $5.

Nonfiction: "Most reviews are solicited; we do publish a few literary essays in each number. Use non-sexist language, please." Send complete ms. Pays $5/printed page.

Fiction: Buys 10 mss/year. Send complete ms. Pays $5/printed page.

Poetry: Buys 50 poems/year. Send poems. Pays $5/printed page.

Tips: "We decide on the basis of quality only. Prior publication is irrelevant. Promising material, even though rejected, may receive some personal comment from the editor; some material can be revised to meet our standards through such criticism. I receive more good stuff than *DQ* can accept, so there is some subjectivity and a good deal of luck involved in any final acceptance. *DQ* is becoming interested in issues of aesthetics and *lucid* perspectives and performances of the avant-garde. We are also interested in topics and translations in the literature of Eastern Europe. Please look at a *recent* issue before submitting. Reading unsolicited mss during academic year only; we do *not* read between May 15 and Sept. 15."

ELDRITCH TALES, Magazine in the Weird Tales Tradition, Yith Press, 1051 Wellington Rd., Lawrence KS 66044. (913)843-4341. Editor: Crispin Burnham. 90% freelance written. A quarterly magazine of supernatural horror. Circ. 500. Pays on publication. Byline given. Buys first North American rights. Photocopied and previously published submissions OK. Computer printout submissions acceptable; prefers letter-quality. Reports in 1 week on queries; 5 months on mss. Sample copy $6; free writer's guidelines.

Nonfiction: Essays and interview/profile. Buys 1-2 mss/year. Send complete ms. Length: 10-500 words. Pays ¼-1¢/word; pays in copies if author prefers.

Photos: State availability of photos with submission.

Columns/Departments: Eldritch Eye (film review columns) and Book Reviews. Buys 1-2 mss/year. Query. Length: 200 words. Pays ¼-1¢/word.

Fiction: Horror, novel excerpts, serialized novels and suspense. No "mad slashers, sword and sorcery, or hard science fiction." Buys 10-12 mss/year. Send complete ms. Length: 50-10,000 words. Pays ¼-1¢/word.

Poetry: Free verse. Buys 5-10 poems/year. Submit maximum 3 poems. Length: 5-20 lines. Pays 10-25¢/line.

Fillers: Facts and newsbreaks. Buys 10/year. Length: 5-25 words. Pays 10-25¢/line.

EPOCH, Cornell University, 251 Goldwin Smith, Ithaca NY 14853. (607)256-3385. Editor: C.S. Giscombe. 50-98% freelance written. Works with a small number of new/unpublished writers each year. Literary magazine of original fiction and poetry published 3 times/year. Circ. 1,000. Pays on publication. Publishes ms 2-12 months after acceptance. Byline given. Buys first North American serial rights. Computer printout submissions OK; prefers letter-quality. Sample copy $3.50.

Fiction: "Potential contributors should *read* a copy or two. There is *no other way* for them to ascertain what we need or like." Buys 15-20 mss/year. Send complete ms. Pays $10/page.

Poetry: "Potential contributors should read magazine to see what type of poetry is used." Buys 20-30 poems/year. Pays $1/line.

Tips: Mss received over the summer (15 May- 1 Sept) will be returned unread."

‡**EVENT,** c/o Douglas College, Box 2503, New Westminster, British Columbia V3L 5B2 Canada. Managing Editor: Bonnie Bauder. 100% freelance written. Works with a small number of new/unpublished writers each year; eager to work with new/unpublished writers. Triannual magazine (March, July and November) for "those interested in literature and writing." Circ. 1,000. Uses 80-100 mss/year. Small payment and contributor's copy only. Publishes ms an average of 3 months after acceptance. Buys first serial rights. Byline given. Photocopied submissions OK. Computer printout submissions acceptable; prefers letter-quality to dot-matrix. Reports in 4 months. Submit complete ms with IRCs.

Nonfiction: "High quality work." Reviews of Canadian books and essays.

Fiction: Short stories and drama.

Poetry: Submit complete ms. "We are looking for high quality modern poetry."

‡**FAMILY FICTION DIGEST**, Blue Ribbon Publishing Company, 1273 Birkes Rd., Eufaula OK 74432. (918)689-5551. Managing Editor: Bill Sunday. 92% freelance written. Monthly magazine; covers all subjects of fiction."Our publication is designed to reach every member of the American family. We will cover 10 subjects monthly of interest to men, women, children and teens." Estab. 1988. Pays on publication. Publishes ms an average of 1-3 months after acceptance. Byline given. Buys one-time rights. Submit seasonal/holiday material 3 months in advance. Simultaneous and photocopied submissions OK. Query for electronic submissions. Computer printout submissions OK; prefers letter-quality. Reports in 2 weeks on queries; 1 month on mss.

Fiction: Adventure, experimental, fantasy, crime fiction, mainstream, mystery, romance, science fiction, suspense, western, teen life, war. "No erotica, occult, perversions or unnecessarily graphic violence." Buys 133 mss/year. Send complete ms. Length: 3,000-6,500 words. Pays $125-250.

Tips: "We appreciate each writer for his/her own unique ability to reach our readers. We want them to be themselves and not try to be a Hemingway or Clancy. The only requirement we have is that they know their audience and be in touch with the attitudes of today. If freelancers select an area such as war; they should be familiar with tactics and with the equipment in use at the time of their battle. In the crime fiction area they should use good investigative techniques to solve their crime."

FICTION NETWORK MAGAZINE, Fiction Network, Box 5651, San Francisco CA 94101. (415)391-6610. Editor: Jay Schaefer. 100% freelance written. Eager to work with new/unpublished writers. Semiannual magazine of short stories. Circ. 7,000. Pays on publication. Publishes ms an average of 10 months after acceptance. Byline given. Buys first serial rights. Holds annual $1,500 fiction competition; rules in magazine. Photocopied submissions OK. Computer printout submissions acceptable; prefers letter-quality. Reports within 4 months. Does not return foreign submissions—notification only with SASE. Sample copy $5 U.S. and Canada; $7 elsewhere. Writer's guidelines for #10 SASE.

Fiction: All types of stories and subjects are acceptable; novel excerpts will be considered only if they stand alone as stories. Considers unpublished fiction only. No poetry, essays, reviews or interviews. No children's or young adult material. Buys 25 mss/year. Send complete ms. "Do not submit a second manuscript until you receive a response to the first." Pays $25 minimum.

Tips: "We are looking for high-quality fiction and offer both known and unknown writers excellent exposure. Contributors include Alice Adams, Ann Beattie, Andre Dubus, Lynne Sharon Schwartz, Marian Thurm, Ken Chowder and Bobbie Ann Mason and Joyce Carol Oates."

THE FIDDLEHEAD, University of New Brunswick, Old Arts Bldg., Box 4400, Fredericton, New Brunswick E3B 5A3 Canada. (506)454-3591. Editor: Michael Taylor. 90% freelance written. Eager to work with new/unpublished writers. Quarterly magazine covering poetry, short fiction, drawings and photographs and book reviews. Circ. 1,100. Pays on publication. Publishes ms an average of 6-12 months after acceptance. Not copyrighted. Buys first North American serial rights. Submit seasonal/holiday material 6 months in advance. Simultaneous queries and photocopied submissions (if legible) OK. Computer printout submissions acceptable. Reports in 3 weeks on queries; 2 months on mss. Sample copy $5.50.

Fiction: Michael Taylor, Anthony Boxill, William Cragg, fiction editors. "Stories may be on any subject— acceptance is based on quality alone. Because the journal is heavily subsidized by the Canadian government, some preference is given to Canadian writers." Buys 20 mss/year. Pays $12/page.

Poetry: Robert Gibbs, Robert Hawkes, poetry editors. "Poetry may be on any subject—acceptance is based on quality alone. Because the journal is heavily subsidized by the Canadian government, some preference is given to Canadian writers." Buys average of 60 poems/year. Submit maximum 10 poems. Pays $12/page; $100 maximum.

Tips: "Quality alone is the criterion for publication. Return postage (Canadian, or IRCs) should accompany all manuscripts."

THE GAMUT, A Journal of Ideas and Information, Cleveland State University, RT 1216, Cleveland OH 44115. (216)687-4679. Editor: Louis T. Milic. Managing Editor: Mary Grimm. 50-60% freelance written. Triannual magazine. Circ. 1,000. Pays on publication. Publishes ms an average of 6 months after acceptance. Byline given. Buys one-time rights. Submit seasonal/holiday material 6 months in advance. Simultaneous and photocopied submissions OK. Computer printout submissions acceptable. Reports in 1 month on queries; 3 months on mss. Sample copy $2.50; writer's guidelines for #10 SASE.

Nonfiction: Essays, general interest, historic/nostalgic, humor, opinion, personal experience, photo feature and technical.Buys 15-20 mss/year. Query with or without published clips, or send complete ms. Length: 1,000-6,000 words. Pays $25-250. Pays authors associated with the university with contributor copies.

Photos: State availability of photos with submission. Offers no additional payment for photos accepted with ms. Captions, model releases and identification of subjects required. Buys one-time rights.
Columns/Departments: Languages of the World (linguistic). Length: 2,000-4,000. Buys 1-2 mss/year. Query with published clips or send complete ms. Pays $75-125.
Fiction: Ethnic, experimental, historical, humorous, mainstream, novel excerpts and science fiction. No condensed novels or genre fiction. Buys 1-2 mss/year. Send complete ms. Length: 1,000-6,000 words. Pays $25-150.
Poetry: Leonard Trawick, poetry editor. Buys 6-15 poems/year. Submit up to 10 at one time. Pays $25-75.
Tips: "Get a fresh approach to an interesting idea or subject; back it up with solid facts, analysis, and/or research. Make sure you are writing for an educated, but general and not expert reader."

HIBISCUS MAGAZINE, Short Stories, Poetry, Art, Hibiscus Press, Box 22248, Sacramento CA 95822. Editor: Margaret Wensrich. 100% freelance written. Works with a small number of new/unpublished writers each year. Magazine "for people who like to read." Circ. 2,000. Pays on publication. Publishes ms 6-18 months after acceptance. Byline given. Buys first North American serial rights. Photocopied submissions OK. Computer printout submissions OK; no dot-matrix. Reports in 4 months on queries. Sample copy $4; writer's guidelines for #10 SASE.
Fiction: Adventure, fantasy, humorous, mainstream, mystery, romance, science fiction, slice-of-life vignettes, suspense and western. Buys 9-12 mss/year. Send complete ms. Length: 1,500-3,000 words. Pays $15-25.
Poetry: Joyce Odam, poetry editor. Free verse, haiku, light verse and traditional. No subject or line limit. Buys 20-25 poems/year. Submit maximum 4 poems. Pays $5-25.
Fillers: Short humor. Buys 4-6/year. Length: 25-100 words. Pays $2-5.
Tips: "We receive hundreds of submissions each month. All queries must have an SASE. International mail must come with sufficient IRC to pay return postage. Canadian and other international mail needs a minimum of 2 IRCs. Heavier mail needs 3 or more IRCs. Writers and poets need to have mail weighed at post office and enclose sufficient IRCs. We do not return mail with insufficient postage. We regret this, but volume of mss with insufficient postage too high. All queries must have an SASE for reply. We are slow to read and return manuscripts, but we do serve each writer and poet as fast as we can. We are a limited market. We regret we must return work that ought to be published because we do not have enough space."

THE HUDSON REVIEW, 684 Park Ave., New York NY 10021. Managing Editor: Ronald Koury. Quarterly. Pays on publication. Buys first world serial rights in English. Reports in 6-8 weeks.
Nonfiction: Articles, translations and reviews. Length: 8,000 words maximum.
Fiction: Uses "quality fiction." Length: 10,000 words maximum. Pays 2½¢/word.
Poetry: 50¢/line for poetry.
Tips: Unsolicited mss will be read according to the following schedule: *Nonfiction:* Jan. 1-March 31, and Oct. 1-Dec. 31; *Poetry:* April 1-Sept. 30; *Fiction:* June 1-Nov. 30.

THE IOWA REVIEW, 369 EPB, The University of Iowa, Iowa City IA 52242. (319)335-0462. Editor: David Hamilton, with the help of colleagues, graduate assistants, and occasional guest editors. Magazine published 3 times/year. Buys first serial rights. Photocopied submissions OK. Reports in 3 months.
Nonfiction, Fiction and Poetry: "We publish essays, stories and poems and would like for our essays not always to be works of academic criticism." Buys 65-85 unsolicited mss/year. Submit complete ms. Pays $1/line for verse; $10/page for prose.

JAM TO-DAY, 372 Dunstable Rd., Tyngsboro MA 01879. Editors: Judith Stanford and Don Stanford. 90% freelance written. Eager to work with new/unpublished writers. Annual literary magazine featuring high quality poetry, fiction and reviews. Especially interested in unknown or little-known authors. Circ. 300. Pays on publication. Publishes ms an average of 6 months after acceptance. Byline given. Buys first rights and nonexclusive anthology rights. Photocopied submissions OK. Computer printout submissions acceptable; prefers letter-quality. Reports in 6 weeks. Sample copy $4 (includes postage).
Fiction: "We will consider quality fiction of almost any style or genre. However, we prefer not to receive material written to mass-market formulas, or that is highly allegorical, abstruse, or heavily dependent on word play for its effect." Buys 2-4 mss/year. Send complete ms. Length: 1,500-7,500 words. Pays $5/page.
Poetry: Avant-garde, free verse, shaped-concrete, found, haiku and traditional. No light verse. Buys 30-50/year. Submit 5 poems maximum. Length: open. Pays $5/poem; higher payment for poems more than 3 pages in length.

JAPANOPHILE, Box 223, Okemos MI 48864. Editor: Earl Snodgrass. 80% freelance written. Works with a small number of new/unpublished writers each year. Quarterly magazine for literate people who are interested in Japanese culture anywhere in the world. Pays on publication. Publishes ms an average of 5 months after acceptance. Buys first North American serial rights. Previously published submissions OK. Computer printout submissions acceptable; no dot-matrix. Reports in 1 month. Sample copy $4, postpaid. Writer's guidelines with #10 SASE.

Nonfiction: "We want material on Japanese culture in *North America or anywhere in the world*, even Japan. We want articles, preferably with pictures, about persons engaged in arts of Japanese origin: a Michigan naturalist who is a haiku poet, a potter who learned raku in Japan, a vivid 'I was there' account of a Go tournament in California. We use some travel articles if exceptionally well-written, but we are *not* a regional magazine about Japan. We are a little magazine, a literary magazine. Our particular slant is a certain kind of culture wherever it is in the world: Canada, the U.S., Europe, Japan. The culture includes flower arranging, haiku, religion, art, photography and fiction. It is important to study the magazine." Buys 8 mss/issue. Query preferred but not required. Length: 1,600 words maximum. Pays $8-20.

Photos: State availability of photos. Pays $10-20 for 8x10 b&w glossy prints.

Fiction: Experimental, mainstream, mystery, adventure, science fiction, humorous, romance and historical. Themes should relate to Japan or Japanese culture. Length: 1,000-6,000 words. Pays $20. Contest each year pays $100 to best short story. Should include one or more Japanese and non-Japanese characters.

Columns/Departments: Regular columns and features are Tokyo Scene and Profile of Artists. "We also need columns about Japanese culture in other cities." Query. Length: 1,000 words. Pays $20 maximum.

Poetry: Traditional, avant-garde and light verse related to Japanese culture or in a Japanese form such as haiku. Length: 3-50 lines. Pays $1-100.

Fillers: Newsbreaks, puzzles, clippings and short humor of up to 200 words. Pays $1-5.

Tips: "We prefer to see more articles about Japanese culture in the U.S., Canada and Europe." Lack of convincing fact and detail is a frequent mistake.

‡LETTERS MAGAZINE, Maine Writers' Workshop, Box 905, Rd. 1, Stonington ME 04681. (May-October), Sapphire Bay West, Apt. A-19, St. Thomas USVI 00802, (November-April). (207)367-2484. Editor: Helen Nash. 90% freelance written. A quarterly literary magazine. Circ. 6,500. Pays on acceptance. Publishes ms an average of 1 month after acceptance. No byline given. Buys all rights. Submit seasonal/holiday material 6 months in advance. Simultaneous submissions OK. Computer printout submissions OK; no dot-matrix. Reports in 1 month. Sample copy for #10 SAE with 1 U.S. first class stamp with free writer's guidelines.

Nonfiction: Essays, general interest, historical/nostalgic, humor and travel. Buys 5 mss/year. Query. Length: 2,000 maximum words. Pays $10-50. Pays expenses of writers on assignment.

Photos: State availability of photos with submission.

Fiction: Historical, humorous, mainstream, novel excerpts and science fiction. Buys 2 mss/year. Query. Length: 2,000-7,000 words. Pay varies.

Poetry: Free verse, light verse and traditional. Buys 10 poems/year. Submit maximum 3 poems. Length: 10-40 lines. Pays $5-50.

Tips: "Write and edit three times before submitting."

LIGHTHOUSE, Box 1377, Auburn WA 98071-1377. Editor: Tim Clinton. 100% freelance written. A bimonthly literary magazine. Circ. 500. Pays on publication. Byline given. Buys first North American serial rights and first rights. Photocopied submissions OK. Computer printout submissions OK; prefers letter quality. Reports in 2 months. Sample copy for $2; writer's guidelines for #10 SASE.

Fiction: Lynne Trindl, fiction editor. Adventure, humorous, mainstream, mystery, romance, science fiction, suspense, western. "No murder mysteries or anything not G-rated." Buys 66 mss/year. Send complete ms. Length: 5,000 words maximum. Pays up to $50.

Poetry: Lorraine Clinton, poetry editor. Free verse, light verse, traditional. Buys 24 poems/year. Submit up to 5 poems at one time. Pays up to $5.

Tips: "Both fiction and poetry are open to freelancers; just follow the guidelines."

LITERARY MAGAZINE REVIEW, KSU Writers Society, English Dept., Denison Hall, Kansas State University, Manhattan KS 66506. (913)532-6106. Editor: G.W. Clift. 98% freelance written. "Most of our reviewers are recommended to us by third parties." A quarterly literary magazine devoted almost exclusively to reviews of the current contents of small circulation serials publishing some fiction or poetry. Circ. 500. Pays on publication. Publishes ms an average of 1 month after acceptance. Byline given. Buys first rights. Photocopied submissions OK. Query for electronic submissions. Computer printout submissions OK; prefers letter-quality. Reports in 2 weeks. Sample copy $4.

Nonfiction: Buys 60 mss/year. Query. Length: 1,500+ words. Pays $25 maximum for assigned articles and two contributor's copies. Sometimes pays expenses of writers on assignment.

Photos: State availability of photos with submission. Identification of subjects required.

Tips: Interested in "omnibus reviews of magazines sharing some quality, editorial philosophy, or place of origin and in articles about literary magazine editing and the literary magazine scene."

LITERARY SKETCHES, Box 810571, Dallas TX 75381-0571. (214)243-8776. Editor: Olivia Murray Nichols. 33% freelance written. Works with small number of new/unpublished writers each year and is willing to work with new/unpublished writers. Monthly newsletter for readers with literary interests; all ages. Circ 500.

Byline given. Pays on publication. Publishes ms an average of 1 year after acceptance. Computer printout submissions acceptable; prefers letter-quality; no photocopies. Reports in 1 month. Sample copy for #10 SASE.

Nonfiction: Interviews of well-known writers and biographical material of more than common knowledge on past writers. Concise, informal style. Centennial pieces relating to a writer's birth, death or famous works. Buys 4-6 mss/year. Submit complete ms. Length: up to 750 words. Pays ½¢/word, plus copies.

Tips: "Articles need not be footnoted, but a list of sources should be submitted with the manuscript. We appreciate fillers of 100 words or less if they concern some little known information on an author or book."

LOS ANGELES TIMES BOOK REVIEW, Times Mirror, Times Mirror Sq., Los Angeles CA 90053. (213)237-7777. Editor: Jack Miles. 70% freelance written. Weekly tabloid reviewing current books. Circ. 1.4 million. Pays on publication. Publishes ms an average of 3 weeks after acceptance. Byline given. Offers variable kill fee. Buys first North American serial rights. Computer printout submissions acceptable; prefers letter-quality. Accepts no unsolicited book reviews or requests for specific titles to review. "Query with published samples — book reviews or literary features." Buys 500 mss/year. Length: 200-1,500 words. Pays $75-500.

THE MALAHAT REVIEW, The University of Victoria, Box 1700, Victoria, British Columbia V8W 2Y2 Canada. Contact: Editor. 100% freelance written. Eager to work with new/unpublished writers. Magazine published 4 times/year covering poetry, fiction, drama and criticism. Circ. 1,700. Pays on acceptance. Publishes ms up to 1 year after acceptance. Byline given. Offers 100% kill fee. Buys first serial rights. Photocopied submissions OK. Computer printout submissions acceptable; prefers letter-quality. Reports in 2 weeks on queries; 3 months on mss. Sample copy $6.

Nonfiction: Interview/profile (literary/artistic). Buys 2 mss/year. Query first. Length: 1,000-8,000. Pays $35-175.

Photos: Pays $25-50 for b&w prints. Captions required.

Fiction: Buys 20 mss/year. Send complete ms. Length: no restriction. Pays $40/1,000 words.

Poetry: Avant-garde, free verse and traditional. Buys 100/year. Pays $20/page.

THE MASSACHUSETTS REVIEW, Memorial Hall, University of Massachusetts, Amherst MA 01003. (413)545-2689. Editors: Mary Heath and Fred Robinson. "As pleased to consider new writers as established ones." Quarterly. Pays on publication. Publishes ms 6-18 months after acceptance. Buys first North American serial rights. Computer printout submissions acceptable; no dot-matrix. Reports in 3 months. Mss will not be returned unless accompanied by SASE. Sample copy for $4 plus 3 first class stamps.

Nonfiction: Articles on literary criticism, women, public affairs, art, philosophy, music and dance. Length: 6,500 words average. Pays $50.

Fiction: Short stories or chapters from novels when suitable for independent publication. Length: max. 25 typed pages (approx.). Pays $50.

Poetry: 35/line or $10 minimum.

Tips: No fiction manuscripts are considered from June to October.

MICHIGAN QUARTERLY REVIEW, 3032 Rackham Bldg., University of Michigan, Ann Arbor MI 48109. Editor: Laurence Goldstein. 75% freelance written. Prefers to work with published/established writers; works with a small number of new/unpublished writers each year. Quarterly. Circ. 2,000. Publishes ms an average of 1 year after acceptance. Pays on publication. Buys first serial rights. Computer printout submissions acceptable; no dot-matrix. Reports in 1 month for mss submitted in September-May; in summer, 2 months. Sample copy $2 with 2 first class stamps.

Nonfiction: "*MQR* is open to general articles directed at an intellectual audience. Essays ought to have a personal voice and engage a significant subject. Scholarship must be present as a foundation, but we are not interested in specialized essays directed only at professionals in the field. We prefer ruminative essays, written in a fresh style and which reach interesting conclusions. We also like memoirs and interviews with significant historical or cultural resonance. " Length: 2,000-5,000 words. Pays $100-150, sometimes more.

Fiction and Poetry: No restrictions on subject matter or language. "We publish about 10 stories a year and are very selective. We like stories which are unusual in tone and structure, and innovative in language." Send complete ms. Pays $10/published page.

Tips: "Read the journal and assess the range of contents and the level of writing. We have no guidelines to offer or set expectations; every manuscript is judged on its unique qualities. On essays — query with a very thorough description of the argument and a copy of the first page. Watch for announcements of special issues, which are usually expanded issues and draw upon a lot of freelance writing. Be aware that this is a university quarterly that publishes a limited amount of fiction and poetry; that it is directed at an educated audience, one that has done a great deal of reading in all types of literature."

MID-AMERICAN REVIEW, Dept. of English, Bowling Green State University, Bowling Green OH 43403. (419)372-2725. Editor: Ken Letko. 100% freelance written. Eager to work with new/unpublished writers. Semiannual literary magazine of "the highest quality fiction, poetry and translations of contemporary poetry and fiction." Also publishes critical articles and book reviews of contemporary literature. Pays on publication. Publishes ms an average of 3-6 months after acceptance. Byline given. Buys one-time rights. Photocopied submissions OK. Computer printout submissions OK; prefers letter-quality. Reports in 2 months or less. Sample copy $4.50, back issues for $3.

Fiction: Character-oriented, literary. Buys 12 mss/year. Send complete ms; do not query. Pays $5/page up to $75.

Poetry: Strong imagery, strong sense of vision. Buys 60 poems/year. Pays $5/page.

Tips: "We are seeking translations of contemporary authors from all languages into English; submissions must include the original; essays in feminist criticism."

‡**MIDWEST POETRY REVIEW**, Box 776, Rock Island IL 61201. Editor: Hugh Ferguson. Managing Editor: Tom Tilford. 100% freelance written. Eager to work with new/unpublished writers. A quarterly magazine of poetry. Pays on acceptance. Publishes ms an average of 3 months after acceptance. Byline given. Buys first North American serial rights. Submit seasonal/holiday material 6 months in advance. Computer printout submissions acceptable; no dot-matrix. Reports in 2 weeks. Sample copy $3; writer's guidelines for #10 SASE.

Nonfiction: Poetry reviews and technical (on poetry). Buys 4 mss/year. Query. Length: 800-1,500 words. Pays $10 minimum. Sometimes pays expenses of writers on assignment.

Columns/Departments: Comment (poetry enhancement, improvement) 800-1,500 words. Buys 4 mss/year. Query. Pays $10 minimum.

Poetry: Avant-garde, free verse haiku, light verse and traditional. No jingles. Buys 400 poems/year. Submit maximum 5 poems; must be subscriber to submit. Pays $5 minimum.

Tips: "We would like authenticated live interviews with known poets."

MINNESOTA INK, INC., Box 9148, N. St. Paul MN 55109. (612)433-3626. Publisher/Managing Editor: Valerie Hockert. Contributing Editors: Marilyn Bailey, Betty Ulrich, Denis Hensley, Herman Holtz, Jeffrey Lant. Associate Editor: John Hall. Poetry Editor: Esther Leiper. 75% freelance written. A bimonthly literary magazine. Pays on publication. Byline given. Buys first rights. Photocopied submissions OK. Computer printout submissions OK; prefers letter-quality. Reports in 1 month on queries; 2 months on mss. Sample copy for $2. Writer's guidelines for #10 SASE.

Nonfiction: How-to, interview/profile. Query with or without published clips, or send complete ms. Length: 500-1,500 words. Pays $5-50.

Photos: May send photos with submission. Reviews contact sheets, negatives, transparencies. Sometimes offers additional payment for photos accepted with ms. Identification of subjects required. Buys one-time rights.

Fiction: Adventure, ethnic, experimental, fantasy, historical, humorous, mainstream, mystery, romance, science fiction, suspense, western. Send complete ms. Length: 500-1,500 words. Pays $5-50.

‡**MODERN SHORT STORIES**, Claggk Inc., 500B Bicounty Blvd., Farmingdale NY 11735. (516)293-3751. Editor: Glenn Steckler. 100% freelance written. Bimonthly magazine on short fiction. Estab. 1988. Circ. 90,000. Pays on acceptance. Publishes ms an average of 3-6 months after acceptance. Byline given. Buys first North American serial rights, first rights and second serial (reprint) rights. Submit seasonal/holiday material 6-9 months in advance. Query for electronic submissions. Computer printout submissions OK; prefers letter-quality. Reports in 1 month. Sample copy for $2. Free writer's guidelines.

Fiction: Adventure, confession, erotica, ethnic, experimental, fantasy, historical, horror, humorous, mainstream, mystery, religious, romance, science fiction, suspense and western. Buys 72 mss/year. Send complete ms. Length: 1,000-5,000 words. Pays $25-75.

‡**THE MOUNTAIN**, Thomas Shaw Publications, Inc., 110 Center St., Box 1010, Galax VA 24333. (703)236-7112. Editor: Lynn Webb. 99% freelance written. Bimonthly magazine on the mountain regions of U.S.; 40% Appalachia. Circ. 10,000. Pays on publication. Byline given. Kill fee subject to negotiation and rewrite status. Buys first North American serial rights or all rights (rare). Submit seasonal/holiday material 6 months in advance. Simultaneous, photocopied and previously submissions OK with cover letter and SASE. Computer printout submissions OK; prefers letter-quality. Reports 2 months. Sample copy $3.50. Writer's guidelines for SAE.

Nonfiction: Essays, exposé, general interest, historical/nostalgic, humor, interview/profile, new product, opinion, photo feature, technical (environmental essays), travel, book reviews (major and out of print books), art reviews and articles on Mountain education. "No personal experience, religious or inspirational." Buys 30 mss/year. Query with or without published clips, or send complete ms. Length: 800-6,000 words. Pays $100-1,000 for assigned articles; $50-500 for unsolicited articles. Sometimes pays expenses of writers on assignment.

Photos: Send photos with submission. Reviews 4x5 prints. Offers no additional payment for photos accepted with ms. Captions, model releases and identification of subjects required.

Columns/Departments: Fire on The Mountain, A Day in the Life, Tour the Mountain, Intellectual Hillbilly, Folk Tales. Query with published clips or send complete ms. Length: 500-2,000 words. Pays $50-1,000.

Fiction: Adventure, ethnic, experimental, fantasy, historical, humorous, mainstream, mystery, science fiction, serialized novels, suspense. "No confession, religious, horror or erotica." Buys 25-30 mss/year. Send complete ms. Length: 2,000-10,000. Pays $75-1,200.

Poetry: Avant-garde, free verse, light verse and traditional. Buys 20-30 poems/year. Submit maximum 12 poems. Length: 5-100 lines. Pays $5 minimum. "When budget allows. Otherwise we pay in contributor's copies."

Fillers: Editor: C.E. Thomas. Anecdotes, facts, gags to be illustrated by cartoonist, newsbreaks, short humor. Buys 100/year. Length: 10-50 words. Pays $10-25.

Tips: "Absolutely all submissions, including poetry, should come with a well-written cover letter and self-addressed-stamped envelope. Articles should be well researched and documented in journalistic style. All submissions should be well typed, neat and clean. No handwritten submissions will be accepted. We like to see a cover letter telling a little about the writer's personal self. Our magazine is 99% freelance. We are looking for the best American writers. We are open to new writers with professional styles. We pay close attention to previously unpublished writers of fiction and poetry in hopes of discovering new talent. We also do serialization of new unpublished novels."

MUSES MILL, Box 2117, Ashland KY 41105-2117. Publisher: Robert L. Vinson. 90% freelance written. Quarterly magazine of short fiction. "We are publishing well written original fiction (short stories) to 5,000 words. Pays on publication. Publishes ms an average of 6 months after acceptance. Byline given. Offers 25% kill fee. Buys first North American serial rights or first rights. Submit seasonal/holiday material 6 months in advance. Simultaneous submissions OK. Query for electronic submissions. Computer printout submissions OK; prefers letter-quality. Reports in 2 weeks on queries; 1 month on mss. Writer's guidelines for #10 SASE.

Photos: State availability of photos with submission. Offers no additional payment for photos accepted with ms. Model release and identification of subjects required.

Fiction: Adventure, experimental, fantasy, horror, humorous, mainstream, mystery, science fiction, suspense. Buys 40-48 mss/year. Send complete ms. Length: 1,000-5,000 words. Pays $10-100.

Poetry: Free verse, light verse, traditional. No haiku, epic, or stream of consciousness poetry. Buys 12 poems/year. Submit up to 6 poems at one time. Pays in copies.

Tips: "We are interested in any kind of fiction (short stories) that are original and preferably unpublished, although we will not rule out something that has been published before. Good stories, with an opening that gets your attention and strong characterizations will be appreciated and given serious consideration."

THE NEBRASKA REVIEW, Writer's Workshop/University of Nebraska-Omaha, 60th & Dodge, Omaha NE 68182-0324. (402)554-4801. Editors: Richard Duggin/Art Homer. 100% freelance written. A semiannual literary magazine. "We publish the best available contemporary fiction and poetry." Circ. 600. Pays on publication. Byline given. Buys first North American serial rights. Photocopied submissions OK. Computer printout submissions OK; prefers letter-quality. Reports in 4 months on mss. Sample copy for $2.

Fiction: Richard Duggin, fiction editor. Mainstream. "No straight genre fiction." Buys 8-10 mss/year. Send complete ms. Length: 6,000 words. Pays $5/page maximum.

Poetry: Art Homer, poetry editor. Free verse and traditional. Buys 40-50 poems/year. Submit maximum 5 poems or 6 pages. Pays $5 maximum.

NEW ENGLAND REVIEW/BREAD LOAF QUARTERLY, NER/BLQ Middlebury College, Middlebury VT 05753. (802)388-3711, Ext 5075. Editors: Sydney Lea and Maura High. Managing Editor: Toni Best. 99% freelance written. Quarterly magazine covering contemporary literature. "We print a wide range of contemporary poetry, fiction, essays and reviews. Our readers tend to be literary and intellectual, but we're not academic, over-refined or doctrinaire." Circ. 3,100. Pays on publication. Publishes ms an average of 6 months after acceptance. Byline given. Buys first-time rights. Photocopied submissions OK. Computer printout submissions OK; prefers letter quality. Reports in 1 week on queries; 2 months on ms. Sample copy $4; writer's guidelines for #10 SASE.

Nonfiction: Book excerpts, essays, general interest, humor and personal experience. Buys 10 mss/year. Send complete ms. Length: 500-6,000 words. Pays $5/page, $10 minimum.

Photos: Also accepts drawings, woodcuts and etchings. Send with submission. Reviews transparencies and prints. Offers $60 minimum for cover art. Captions and identification of subjects required. Buys one-time rights.

Fiction: Ethnic, experimental, mainstream, novel excerpts, slice-of-life vignettes. Buys 18 mss/year. Send complete ms. Pays $5/page, $10 minimum.

Poetry: Avant-garde, free verse and traditional. Buys 50 poems/year. Submit up to 6 at one time. Pays $5/page, $10 minimum.

Tips: "Read at least one issue to get an idea of our range, standards and style. Don't submit simultaneously to other publications. All sections are open. We look for writing that's intelligent, well informed and well crafted."

THE NORTH AMERICAN REVIEW, University of Northern Iowa, Cedar Falls IA 50614. (319)273-2681. Editor: Robley Wilson Jr. 50% freelance written. Quarterly. Circ. 4,000. Buys all rights for nonfiction and North American serial rights for fiction and poetry. Pays on acceptance. Publishes ms an average of 1 year after acceptance. Computer printout submissions acceptable; no dot-matrix. Familiarity with magazine helpful. Reports in 10 weeks. Sample copy $2.50.

Nonfiction: No restrictions, but most nonfiction is commissioned by magazine. Query. Rate of payment arranged.

Fiction: No restrictions; highest quality only. Length: open. Pays minimum $10/page. Fiction department closed (no mss read) from April 1 to December 31.

Poetry: Peter Cooley, department editor. No restrictions; highest quality only. Length: open. Pays 50¢/line minimum.

THE OHIO REVIEW, Ellis Hall, Ohio University, Athens OH 45701-2979. (614)593-1900. Editor: Wayne Dodd. 40% freelance written. Published 3 times/year. "A balanced, informed engagement of contemporary American letters, with special emphasis on poetics." Circ. 2,000. Publishes ms an average of 8 months after acceptance. Rights acquired vary with author and material; usually buys first serial rights or first North American serial rights. Submit complete ms. Unsolicited material will be read only September-May. Computer printout submissions acceptable; prefers letter-quality. Reports in 10 weeks.

Nonfiction, Fiction and Poetry: Buys essays of general intellectual and special literary appeal. Not interested in narrowly focused scholarly articles. Seeks writing that is marked by clarity, liveliness, and perspective. Interested in the best fiction and poetry. Buys 75 unsolicited mss/year. Pays minimum $5/page, plus copies.

Tips: "Make your query very brief, not gabby—one that describes some publishing history, but no extensive bibliographies. We publish mostly poetry—short fiction, some book reviews."

THE PARIS REVIEW, 45-39 171st Place, Flushing NY 11358. Submit to 541 E. 72nd St., New York NY 10021. Editor: George A. Plimpton. Quarterly. Buys all rights. Pays on publication. Address submissions to proper department and address. Computer printout submissions acceptable; no dot-matrix. Sample copy $6.90. Writer's guidelines for #10 SASE.

Fiction: Study publication. No length limit. Pays up to $250. Makes award of $1,000 in annual fiction contest. Awards $1,500 in John Train Humor Prize contest, and $1,000 in Bernard F. Conners, Poetry Prize contest.

Poetry: Patricia Storace, poetry editor. Study publication. Pays $35/1-24 lines; $50/25-59 lines; $75/60-99 lines; and $150-175/100 lines and over.

PARTISAN REVIEW, 236 Bay State Rd., Boston MA 02215. (617)353-4260. Editor: William Phillips. 90% freelance written. Works with a small number of new/unpublished writers each year. Quarterly literary journal covering world literature, politics and contemporary culture for an intelligent public with emphasis on the arts and political/social commentary. Circ. 8,200. Pays on publication. Publishes ms an average of 6-12 months after acceptance. Buys first serial rights. Byline given. Photocopied submissions OK. Computer printout submissions acceptable; prefers letter-quality. Reports in 3-4 months. Sample copy $5 and 4 first class stamps; writer's guidelines for #10 SASE. "All manuscripts and requests must be accompanied by a SASE."

Nonfiction: Essays; interviews and book reviews. Buys 30-40 mss/year. Send complete ms. Pays $50-250.

Fiction: High quality, serious and contemporary fiction. No science fiction, mystery, confession, romantic or religious material. Buys 8-10 mss/year. Send complete ms. Pays $100-250.

Poetry: Buys 60 poems/year. Submit maximum 6 poems. Pays $50.

Tips: "If, after reading *PR* a writer or poet feels that he or she writes with comparable originality and quality, then of course he or she may well be accepted. Standards of self-watchfulness, originality and hard work apply and reap benefits."

PASSAGES NORTH, William Bonifas Fine Arts Center, Escanaba MI 49829. (906)786-3833. Editor: Elinor Benedict. Managing Editor: Carol R. Hackenbruch. 100% freelance written. Eager to work with emerging writers. A semiannual tabloid of poetry, fiction and graphic arts. Circ. 2,000. Pays on publication. Publishes ms an average of 2-4 months after acceptance. Byline given. Buys first rights. Computer printout submissions acceptable. Reports in 1 month on queries; 3 months on manuscripts. Sample copy $1.50; writer's guidelines for #10 SASE.

Fiction: "High quality" fiction. Buys 6-8 mss/year. Send complete ms. Length: 4,000 words maximum. Pays 3 copies minimum, $50 maximum.

Poetry: No "greeting card" or sentimental poetry and no song lyrics. Buys 80 poems/year. Submit maximum 4 poems. Length: prefers 40 lines maximum. Pays 3 copies minimum, $20 maximum.

Tips: "We want poems and stories of high quality that make the reader see, imagine and experience."

THE PENNSYLVANIA REVIEW, University of Pittsburgh, English Dept./526 CL, Pittsburgh PA 15260. (412)624-0026. Managing Editor: Deborah Pursifull. A semiannual magazine publishing contemporary fiction, poetry, book reviews and interviews with authors. Circ. approximately 1,200. Manuscripts accepted from September 1 to March 1. Pays on publication. Publishes ms an average of 6-8 months after acceptance. Byline given. An SASE must accompany all submissions or manuscript will not be returned. Photocopied submissions OK. Reports in 13 weeks. Sample copy $5; writer's guidelines for #10 SAE.

Columns/Departments: Book reviews. Phil Orr, editor. Buys 5-10 reviews of contemporary work a year. Maximum 5 pages. Pays $5/page. Interviews. Deborah Pursifull, managing editor. Buys 1-2 interviews with recognizable authors a year. Send complete interview. Pays $5/page.

Fiction: Jill Weaver, fiction editor. Interested in publishing strong, mainstream fiction. Attention paid to character voice, movement and resolution. Genre discouraged. Buys 6-8 mss/year. Send complete ms. Maximum 20 pages. Pays $5/page.

Poetry: Jan Beatty, poetry editor. Buys 50-75 poems/year. Submit maximum 6 poems. Length: open. Pays $5/page.

PIG IRON MAGAZINE, Pig Iron Press, Box 237, Youngstown OH 44501. (216)783-1269. Editors-in-Chief: Jim Villani, Naton Leslie and Rose Sayre. 90% freelance written. Annual magazine emphasizing literature/art for writers, artists and intelligent lay audience interested in popular culture. Circ. 1,500. Buys one-time rights. Pays on publication. Publishes ms an average of 6-18 months after acceptance. Byline given. Photocopied and previously published submissions OK. Computer printout submissions acceptable. Reports in 4 months. Sample copy $3; writer's guidelines and list of current themes with #10 SASE.

Nonfiction: General interest, personal opinion, criticism, new journalism and lifestyle. Buys 3 mss/year. Query. Length: 8,000 words maximum. Pays $3/page minimum.

Photos: Submit photo material with query. Pays $3 minimum for 5x7 or 8x10 b&w glossy prints. Buys one-time rights.

Fiction: Narrative fiction, psychological fiction, epistolary fiction, avant-garde, experimental, metafiction, satire and parody. Buys 4-12 mss/issue. Submit complete ms. Length: 8,000 words maximum. Pays $3 minimum.

Poetry: Avant-garde and free verse. Buys 25-50/issue. Submit in batches of 5 or less. Length: open. Pays $3 minimum.

Tips: "Looking for epistolary fiction for 1990 project. Looking for any work that explores the significance of the 'letter' as a discourse form and its impact upon culture and the individual."

PLOUGHSHARES, Box 529, Dept. M, Cambridge MA 02139. Director: DeWitt Henry. Quarterly magazine for "readers of serious contemporary literature: students, educators, adult public." Circ. 3,500. Pays on publication. Publishes ms an average of 6 months after acceptance. Buys first North American serial rights. Photocopied submissions OK. Computer printout submissions OK; prefers letter quality. Reports in 6 months. Sample/back issue $5; writer's guidelines for SASE.

Nonfiction: Interview and literary essays. Length: 5,000 words maximum. Pays $50. Reviews (assigned). Length: 500 words maximum. Pays $15.

Fiction: Literary and mainstream. Buys 25-35 unsolicited mss/year. Length: 300-6,000 words. Pays $10-50.

Poetry: Traditional forms, blank verse, free verse and avant-garde. Length: open. Pays $10/poem.

Tips: "Because of our policy of rotating editors, we suggest writers check the current issue for news of reading periods and upcoming editors and/or themes."

POETRY, The Modern Poetry Association, 60 West Walton St., Chicago IL 60610. (312)280-4870. Editor: Joseph Parisi. Managing Editor: Helen Lothrop Klaviter. 100% freelance written. A monthly poetry magazine. Circ. 7,000. Pays on publication. Byline given. Buys all rights. "Copyright assigned to author on request." Submit seasonal/holiday material 6 months in advance. Photocopied submissions OK. Reports in 2 months. Sample copy $3.50. Writer's guidelines for #10 SASE.

Poetry: All styles and subject matter. Buys 180-250 poems/year. Submit maximum 6 poems. All lengths considered. Pays $2/line.

THE PRAIRIE JOURNAL of Canadian Literature, Box 997, Station G., Calgary, Alberta T3A 3G2 Canada. Editor: A. Burke. 100% freelance written. A semiannual magazine of Canadian literature. Circ. 400. Pays on publication; "honorarium depends on grant." Byline given. Buys first North American serial rights. Photocopied submissions OK. Computer printout submissions OK; no dot-matrix. Reports 1 month on queries. Sample copy $3 and IRCs.

Nonfiction: Interview/profile and scholarly. Buys 5 mss/year. Query with published clips. "Include IRC." Pays $25 maximum. Pays contributor copies or honoraria for literary work.
Photos: Send photos with submission. Offers no additional payment for photos accepted with ms. Identification of subjets required. Buys one-time rights.
Fiction: Literary. Buys 10 mss/year. Send complete ms. No payment for fiction.
Poetry: Avant-garde and free verse. Buys 10 poems/year. Submit maximum 6-10 poems. No payment for poetry.
Tips: "Commercial writers are advised to submit elsewhere. Art needed, b&w originals or good-quality photocopy. We are strictly small press editors interested in highly talented, serious artists. We are oversupplied with fiction but seek more high-quality poetry, especially the contemporary long poem or sequences from longer works."

PRISM INTERNATIONAL, Department of Creative Writing, University of British Columbia, Vancouver, British Columbia V6T 1W5 Canada. Editor-in-Chief: Debbie Howlett. Executive Editor: Neal Anderson. 100% freelance written. Eager to work with new/unpublished writers. Quarterly magazine emphasizing contemporary literature, including translations. For university and public libraries, and private subscribers. Circ. 1,000. Pays on publication. Publishes ms an average of 3 months after acceptance. Buys first North American serial rights. Photocopied submissions OK. Computer printout submissions acceptable; prefers letter-quality. Reports in 6-12 weeks. Sample copy $4. Writer's guidelines for #10 SAE with 1 first class Canadian stamp (Canadian entries) or 1 IRC (U.S. entries).
Nonfiction: Memoirs, belles-lettres, etc. "*Creative* nonfiction that possibly reads like fiction." No reviews, tracts or scholarly essays.
Fiction: Fiction Editor: Barb Parkin. Experimental and traditional. Buys 3-5 mss/issue. Send complete ms. Length: 5,000 words maximum. Pays $25/printed page and 1-year subscription.
Poetry: Poetry Editor: Mary Cameron. Avant-garde and traditional. Buys 30 poems/issue. Submit maximum 6 poems. Pays $25/printed page and 1-year subscription.
Drama: One-acts preferred. Pays $25/printed page and 1-year subscription.
Tips: "We are looking for new and exciting fiction. Excellence is still our number one criterion. As well as poetry, imaginative nonfiction and fiction, we are especially open to translations of all kinds, very short fiction pieces and drama which works well on the page. This year we also plan to feature writing from the Pacific Rim as well as stories from the oral tradition and sound poetry."

QUEEN'S QUARTERLY, A Canadian Review, Queen's University, Kingston, Ontario K7L 3N6 Canada. (613)545-2667. Editors: Dr. Clive Thomson and Ms. Martha J. Bailey. Quarterly magazine covering a wide variety of subjects, including science, humanities, arts and letters, politics and history for the educated reader. 15% freelance written. Circ. 1,900. Pays on publication. Publishes ms an average of 1 year after acceptance. Byline given. Buys first North American serial rights. Photocopied submissions OK. Computer printout submissions acceptable; prefers letter-quality. Reports in 3 months on mss. Sample copy $5.
Fiction: Fantasy, historical, humorous, mainstream and science fiction. Buys 8-12 mss/year. Send complete ms. Length: 5,000 words maximum. Pays $80-150.
Poetry: Avant-garde, free verse, haiku, light verse and traditional. No "sentimental, religious, or first efforts by unpublished writers." Buys 25/year. Submit maximum 6 poems. Length: open. Pays $20-35.
Tips: "Poetry and fiction are most open to freelancers. Don't send less than the best. No multiple submissions. No more than 6 poems or one story per submission. We buy very a few freelance submissions."

ROOM OF ONE'S OWN, A Feminist Journal of Literature & Criticism, Growing Room Collective, Box 46160, Station G, Vancouver, British Columbia V6R 4G5 Canada. Editors: Sylvia Arnold, Susan Cooper, Laura Leach, Janet Pollock, Robin Van Heck, Yvonne Van Ruskenveld. 100% freelance written. Eager to work with new/unpublished writers. Quarterly magazine of original fiction, poetry, literary criticism, and reviews of feminist (literary) concern. Circ 1,200. Pays on publication. Publishes ms an average of 3 months after acceptance. Byline given. Buys first serial rights. Photocopied submissions OK. Computer printout submissions acceptable "if readable and not in all caps"; no dot-matrix. Reports in 4 months. Sample copy $4.
Nonfiction: Interview/profile (of authors) and literary criticism. Buys 4 mss/year. Send complete ms. Length: 1,500-6,000 words. Pays $50.
Fiction: Quality short stories by women with a feminist outlook. Not interested in fiction written by men. Buys 12 mss/year. Send complete ms. Length: 1,500-6,000 words. Pays $50.
Poetry: Avant-garde, eclectic free verse and haiku. Not interested in poetry from men. Buys 32 poems/year. Submit maximum 8 poems. Length: open. Pays $10-25.

‡SEWANEE REVIEW, University of the South, Sewanee TN 37375. (615)598-1246. Editor: George Core. Works with a small number of new/unpublished writers each year. Quarterly magazine for audience of "variable ages and locations, mostly college-educated and with interest in literature." Circ. 3,400. Pays on publication. Publishes ms an average of 9 months after acceptance. Computer printout submissions acceptable; prefers letter-quality to dot-matrix. Reports in 1 month. Sample copy $5.75, writer's guidelines for #10 SASE.

Nonfiction and Fiction: Short fiction (but not drama); essays of critical nature on literary subjects (especially modern British and American literature); and essay-reviews and reviews (books and reviewers selected by the editor). Unsolicited reviews rarely accepted. Length: 5,000-7,500 words. Payment varies: averages $12/printed page.

Poetry: Selections of 4 to 6 poems preferred. In general, light verse and translations not acceptable. Maximum payment is 70¢ per line.

SHOOTING STAR REVIEW, Black Literary Magazine, Timbuctu Express, 7123 Race St., Pittsburgh PA 15208. (412)731-7039. Publisher: Sandra Gould Ford. 85% freelance written. Quarterly African-American literary magazine. "*Shooting Star Review* is an educational magazine that uses the literary and visual arts to increase understanding and appreciation of the African-American experience." Circ. 1,500. Pays on publication. Publishes ms an average of 3-9 months after acceptance. Byline given. Buys first North American serial rights. Submit seasonal/holiday material 6 months in advance. Simultaneous and photocopied submissions OK. Query for electronic submissions. Computer printout submissions OK. Reports in 2 weeks on queries; 2 months on mss. Sample copy for $3 and a 9x12 SAE with $1 postage; writer's guidelines for SASE.

Nonfiction: Book excerpts, essays, historical/nostalgic, interview/profile, opinion, personal experience, photo feature and book reviews. Each issue has a special theme: Spring, 1990, Rhythm and Blues; Summer, 1990, Behind Bars; Autumn, 1990, Marching to a Different Beat; Winter, 1990, Salute to Black Male Writers. Buys 25 mss/year. Query. Length: 750-3,500 words. Pays $10-25 plus 2 contributor copies. Sometimes pays expenses of writers on assignment.

Photos: Send photos with submission. Reviews contact sheets, 35mm and 4x5 transparencies and 8x10 prints. Payment negotiated. Captions, model releases and identification of subjects required. Buys one-time rights.

Fiction: Sharon Flake, fiction coordinator. Adventure, experimental, fantasy, historical, mainstream, novel excerpts, romance, science fiction, and slice-of-life vignettes. Buys 8 mss/year. Send complete ms. Length: 3,500 words maximum. Pays $30 maximum plus 2 contributor copies.

Poetry: Leslie Clark, poetry coordinator. Avant-garde, free verse and traditional. Buys 60-80 poems/year. Submit maximum 6 poems at one time. Length: 50 lines maximum. Pays $8 maximum plus 2 contributor copies.

Tips: "Writers should keep in mind that *Shooting Star Review* regularly reprints classic fiction about the black experience. From modern writers, we look for innovative, well structured, challenging, even controversial, creative writing. Short fiction is most open to freelancers. We get very excited about innovative subject treatment by writers who understand the elements of fine writing and demonstrate familiarity with the specific needs of short fiction."

‡THE SOUTH FLORIDA POETRY REVIEW, South Florida Poetry Institute, 7190 NW 21st St., Ft. Lauderdale FL 33313. (305)742-5624. Editor: S.A. Stirnemann. Assistant Editor: Virginia Wells. Managing Editor: Shirley Blum. 100% freelance written. Quarterly magazine on poetry. "*SFPR* invites submissions of contemporary poetry of the highest literary quality. We are also interested in essay-reviews of books of poetry published in previous year, Q&A interviews with established poets, and essays on current American poetry." Circ. 750. Pays on publication. Publishes ms an average of 3-12 months after acceptance. Byline given. Buys first rights. Photocopied submissions OK. Reports in 3 months on ms. Sample copy $3.50. Writer's guidelines for #10 SASE.

Nonfiction: Essays (reviews and American poetry), interview/profile (Q&A). Do not want to see "anything that is *not* related to poetry." Buys 12 mss/year. Query. Length: 300-2,000 words. Pays $5-25 for unsolicited articles.

Poetry: Avant-garde, free verse and traditional. Buys 125 poems/year. Submit 8 maximum poems.

Tips: "All sections are open to freelancers. They should be familiar with contemporary American poetry as it is defined in most national literary journals."

THE SOUTHERN REVIEW, 43 Allen Hall, Louisiana State University, Baton Rouge LA 70803. (504)388-5108. Editor: James Olney. 75% freelance written. Works with a moderate number of new/unpublished writers each year. Quarterly magazine for academic, professional, literary, intellectual audience. Circ. 3,100. Buys first serial rights only. Byline given. Pays on publication. Publishes ms an average of 18 months after acceptance. No queries. Computer printout submissions acceptable; prefers letter-quality. Reports in 2 to 3 months. Sample copy $5. Writer's guidelines for #10 SASE.

ALWAYS submit unsolicited manuscripts or queries with a self-addressed, stamped envelope (SASE) within your country or International Reply Coupons (IRC) purchased from the post office for other countries.

Nonfiction: Essays with careful attention to craftsmanship, technique and to seriousness of subject matter. "Willing to publish experimental writing if it has a valid artistic purpose. Avoid extremism and sensationalism. Essays exhibit thoughtful and sometimes severe awareness of the necessity of literary standards in our time." Emphasis on contemporary literature, especially Southern culture and history. Minimum number of footnotes. Buys 45 mss/year. Length: 4,000-10,000 words. Pays $12/page for prose.

Fiction and Poetry: Short stories of lasting literary merit, with emphasis on style and technique. Length: 4,000-8,000 words. Pays $12/page for prose; $20/page for poetry.

SOUTHWEST REVIEW, 6410 Airline Rd., Southern Methodist University, Dallas TX 75275. (214)373-7440. Editor: Willard Spiegelman. 100% freelance written. Works with a small number of new/unpublished writers each year. Quarterly magazine for "adults and college graduates with literary interests and some interest in the Southwest, but subscribers are from all over America and some foreign countries." Circ. 1,500. Pays on publication. Publishes ms an average of 1 year after acceptance. Buys first North American serial rights. Computer printout submissions acceptable; prefers letter-quality. Byline given. Buys 65 mss/year. Reports immediately or within 3 months. Sample copy $5.

Nonfiction: "Literary essays, social and political problems, history (especially Southwestern), folklore (especially Southwestern), the arts, etc. Articles should be appropriate for literary quarterly; no feature stories. Critical articles should consider writer's whole body of work, not just one book. History should use new primary sources or new perspective, not syntheses of old material." Interviews with writers, historical articles. Query. Length: 3,500-7,000 words.

Fiction: No limitations on subject matter for fiction; high literary quality is only criterion. Prefers stories of experimental and mainstream. Submit complete ms. Length: 1,500-7,000 words. The John H. McGinnis Memorial Award of $1,000 made in alternate years for fiction and nonfiction pieces that appeared in *SWR* during preceding two years.

Poetry: No limitations on subject matter. Not particularly interested in broadly humorous, religious or sentimental poetry. Free verse, some avant-garde forms; open to all serious forms of poetry. "There are no arbitrary limits on length, but we find shorter poems are easier to fit into our format." The Elizabeth Matchett Stover Memorial Award of $100 made annually for a poem published in *SWR*.

Tips: "The most frequent mistakes we find in work that is submitted for consideration are lack of attention to grammar and syntax and little knowledge of the kind of thing we're looking for. Writers should look at a couple of issues before submitting."

SPECTRUM, Spectrum/Anna Maria College. Box 72-F, Sunset Lane, Paxton MA 01612. (508)757-4586. Editor: Robert H. Goepfert. Managing Editor: Robert Lemieux. A literary magazine, "*Spectrum* is a multidisciplinary national publication aimed particularly at scholarly generalists affiliated with small liberal arts colleges." Circ. 1,000. Pays on publication. Publishes ms an average of 6 months after acceptance. Byline given. Publication copyrighted. Buys first North American serial rights. Photocopied submissions OK. Computer printout submissions OK; prefers letter-quality. Reports in 3 weeks on queries; 6 weeks on ms. Sample copy $3. Writer's guidelines for #10 SASE.

Nonfiction: Louise N. Soldani, articles editor. Essays, general interest, historical/nostalgic, inspirational, opinion and interdisciplinary. Buys 8 mss/year. Send complete ms. Length: 3,000-15,000 words. Pays $20 for unsolicited articles. State availability of photos with submission. Prints (8x10) b&w only. Offers no additional payment for photos accepted with ms. Model releases and identification of subjects required. Buys one-time rights.

Columns/Departments: Sandra Rasmussen, reviews and correspondence editor. Reviews (books/recordings/audio-visual aids), 300-500 words; (educational computer software), up to 2,000 words. Buys 2 mss/year. Send complete ms. Length: 300-2,000 words. Pays $20.

Fiction: Joseph Wilson, fiction editor. Ethnic, experimental, fantasy, historical, humorous, mainstream, romance and slice-of-life vignettes. "No erotica, mystery, western or science fiction." Buys 2 ms/year. Send complete ms. Length: 3,000 words. Pays $20.

Poetry: Joseph Wilson, poetry editor. Avant-garde, free verse, light verse and traditional. No long poems (over 100 lines). Buys 8 poems/year. Submit maximum 6 poems.

Tips: "We welcome short fiction and poetry, as well as short to medium-length articles that are interdisciplinary or that deal with one discipline in a manner accessible to the scholarly-generalist reader. Articles referring to or quoting work of other authors should be footnoted appropriately. All areas are equally open to freelancers. In general, originality and relative brevity are paramount, although we will occasionally publish longer works (e.g., articles) that explore ideas not subject to a briefer treatment."

‡STORY, F&W Publications, Inc., 1507 Dana Ave., Cincinnati OH 45207. (513)531-2222. Editor: Lois Rosenthal. Associate Editor: Jack Heffron. 100% freelance written. Quarterly literary magazine of short fiction. "We want short stories of general interest that are extremely well-written. Our audience is well-educated, sophisticated and accustomed to the finest imaginative writing available." Circ. 20,000. Byline given. Buys first North American serial rights. Photocopied submissions OK. Computer printout submissions acceptable. Reports in 1 month. Sample copy $5 with 9x12 SAE and $2.40 in postage. Writer's guidelines for #10 SASE.

Fiction: Novel excerpts, experimental and mainstream. No genre fiction. Buys 40-50 mss/year. Send complete ms. Length: 1,000-10,000 words. Pays $100.
Tips: "We treat submissions by unknown writers with the same courtesy and respect we give to those by well-known writers. We publish the best work we can find."

THE SUN, A Magazine Of Ideas, The Sun Publishing Company, Inc., 107 N. Roberson St., Chapel Hill NC 27516. (919)942-5282. Editor: Sy Safransky. 75% freelance written. Monthly magazine. Circ. 10,000. Pays on publication. Publishes ms an average of 2 months after acceptance. Byline given. Buys first-rights. Photocopied and previously published submissions OK. Reports in 1 month. Sample copy $3, 9x12 SAE and 3 first class stamps; writer's guidelines for #10 SASE.
Nonfiction: General interest. Buys 40 mss/year. Send complete ms. Length: 10,000 words maximum. Pays $100 and up plus copies and a subscription.
Photos: Send photos with submissions. Offers $25 for photos accepted with ms. Model releases required. Buys one-time rights.
Fiction: General. Buys 15 mss/year. Send complete ms. Length: 10,000 words maximum. Pays $100 and up.
Poetry: General. Buys 25 poems/year. Submit maximum 6 poems. Length: open. Pays $25.
Tips: "We're interested in any writing that makes sense and enriches our common space."

TAMPA REVIEW, Humanities Division, University of Tampa, Tampa FL 33606. (813)253-3333. Editor of Fiction: Andy Solomon, Box 135F. Editors of Poetry: Don Morrill, Box 115F; Kathy Van Spanckeren, Box 16F. 100% freelance written. Annual magazine of literary fiction and poetry. Estab. 1988. Circ. 5,000. Pays on publication. Publishes ms an average of 4 months after acceptance. Byline given. Buys first North American serial rights. Photocopied submissions OK. Computer printout submissions OK; prefers letter-quality. .Reports in 6 weeks on mss. Sample copy $7; writer's guidelines for 9x12 SAE with 2 first class stamps.
Fiction: Experimental, mainstream. "We are far more concerned with quality than genre." Buys 4-6 mss/year. Send complete ms. Length: 1,000-6,000 words; slight preference for mss less than 20 pp. Pays $10/printed page.
Poetry: Buys 30 poems/year. Submit up to 5 poems at one time. Pays $10/printed page.

THE THREEPENNY REVIEW, Box 9131, Berkeley CA 94709. (415)849-4545. Editor: Wendy Lesser. 100% freelance written. Works with small number of new/unpublished writers each year. A quarterly literary tabloid. "We are a general interest, national literary magazine with coverage of politics, the visual arts and the performing arts as well." Circ. 8,000. Pays on acceptance. Publishes ms an average of 12 months after acceptance. Byline given. Buys first North American serial rights. Photocopied submissions OK. Computer printout submissions OK; prefers letter-quality. Reports in 1 month on queries; 2 months on mss. Sample copy for 10x13 SAE, 5 first class stamps and $4; writer's guidelines for SASE.
Nonfiction: Essays, exposé, historical, interview/profile, personal experience, book, film, theater, dance, music and art reviews. Buys 40 mss/year. Query with or without published clips, or send complete ms. Length: 1,500-4,000 words. Pays $100.
Fiction: No fragmentary, sentimental fiction. Buys 10 mss/year. Send complete ms. Length: 800-4,000 words. Pays $100.
Poetry: Free verse and traditional. No poems "without capital letters or poems without a discernible subject." Buys 30 poems/year. Submit maximum 10 poems. Pays $50.
Tips: Nonfiction (political articles, reviews) is most open to freelancers.

TRIQUARTERLY, 2020 Ridge Ave., Northwestern University, Evanston IL 60208. (312)491-3490. Editor: Reginald Gibbons. 70% freelance written. Eager to work with new/unpublished writers. Published 3 times/year. Publishes fiction, poetry, and essays, as well as artwork. Pays on publication. Publishes ms an average of 1 year after acceptance. Buys first serial rights and nonexclusive reprint rights. Computer printout submissions acceptable; no dot-matrix. Reports in 3 months. Study magazine before submitting. Sample copy $4. Writer's guidelines for #10 SASE.
Nonfiction: Query before sending essays (no scholarly or critical essays except in special issues).
Fiction and Poetry: No prejudice against style or length of work; only seriousness and excellence are required. Buys 20-50 unsolicited mss/year. Pays $40/page.

UNIVERSITY OF TORONTO QUARTERLY, University of Toronto Press, 10 St. Mary St., Suite 700, Toronto, Ontario M4Y 2W8 Canada. Editor-in-Chief: T.H. Adamowski. 66% freelance written. Eager to work with new/unpublished writers. Quarterly magazine restricted to criticism on literature and the humanities for the university community. Pays on publication. Publishes ms an average of 1 year after acceptance. Acquires all rights. Byline given. Photocopied submissions OK. Computer printout submissions acceptable; prefers letter-quality; double spaced, non-justified right margin. Sample copy $8.95, SAE and IRCs.
Nonfiction: Scholarly articles on the humanities; literary criticism and intellectual discussion. Buys 12 unsolicited mss/year. Pays $50 maximum.

‡**THE UNSPEAKABLE VISIONS OF THE INDIVIDUAL INC.**, Box 439, California PA 15419. Editors-in-Chief: Arthur Winfield Knight, Kit Knight. 50% freelance written. Annual magazine/book for an adult audience, generally college-educated (or substantial self-education) with an interest in Beat (generation) writing. Circ. 2,000. Payment (if made) on acceptance. Publishes ms an average of 2 months after acceptance. Buys first North American serial rights. Computer printout submissions acceptable; no dot-matrix. Reports in 2 months. Sample copy $3.50.
Nonfiction: Interviews (with Beat writers), personal experience and photo feature. "Know who the Beat writers are—Jack Kerouac, Allen Ginsberg, William S. Burroughs, etc." Uses 20 mss/year. Query or submit complete ms. Length: 300-15,000 words. Pays 2 copies, "sometimes a small cash payment, i.e., $10."
Photos: Used with or without ms or on assignment. Send prints. Pays 2 copies to $10 for 8x10 b&w glossies. Uses 40-50/year. Captions required.
Fiction: Uses 10 mss/year. Submit complete ms. Pays 2 copies to $10.
Poetry: Avant-garde, free verse and traditional. Uses 10 poems/year. Submit maximum 10 poems. Length: 100 lines maximum. Pays 2 copies to $10.

THE VIRGINIA QUARTERLY REVIEW, 1 W. Range, Charlottesville VA 22903. (804)924-3124. Editor: Staige Blackford. 50% freelance written. Quarterly. Pays on publication. Publishes ms an average of 2 years after acceptance. Byline given. Buys first serial rights. Reports in 1 month. Sample copy $5.
Nonfiction: Articles on current problems, economic, historical; and literary essays. Length: 3,000-6,000 words. Pays $10/345-word page.
Fiction: Good short stories, conventional or experimental. Length: 2,000-7,000 words. Pays $10/350-word page. Prizes offered for best short stories and poems published in a calendar year.
Poetry: Generally publishes 15 pages of poetry in each issue. No length or subject restrictions. Pays $1/line.
Tips: Prefers not to see pornography, science fiction or fantasy.

WEBSTER REVIEW, Webster University, 470 E. Lockwood, Webster Groves MO 63119. (314)432-2657. Editor: Nancy Schapiro. 100% freelance written. A semiannual magazine. "*Webster Review* is an international literary magazine publishing fiction, poetry, essays and translations of writing in those categories. Our subscribers are primarily university and public libraries, and writers and readers of quality fiction and poetry." Circ. 1,000. Pays on publication. Publishes ms an average of 1 year after acceptance. Byline given. Buys first North American serial rights. Simultaneous and photocopied submissions OK. Reports in 6 weeks on manuscripts. Sample copy for 9½x6½ SAE with 4 first class stamps.
Nonfiction: Essays. Send complete ms.
Fiction: Will consider all types of literature. Buys 6 mss/year. Send complete ms. Pays $25-50, (if funds are available).
Poetry: Pamela White Hadas, poetry editor. Buys 100 poems/year. Pays $10-50 (if funds are available).

WEST COAST REVIEW, A Literary Quarterly, West Coast Review Publishing Society, Department of English, Simon Fraser University, Burnaby British Columbia V5A 156 Canada. (604)291-4287. Quarterly magazine covering poetry, fiction, book reviews. "We publish original creative writing regardless of style, subject, etc.; the only criterion is the quality of the writing." Circ. 800. Pays on publication. Publishes ms an average of 6 months after acceptance. Byline given. Buys first North American serial rights. Submit seasonal/holiday material 6 months in advance. Photocopied submissions OK. Computer printout submissions OK; prefers letter-quality. Reports in 2 months. Sample copy $4; writer's guidelines for SAE with 1 Canadian first class stamp or IRC.
Nonfiction: Essays, mainly dealing with literary matters. Buys 10-12 ms/year. Send complete ms. Length: 1,000-5,000 words. Pays $10/page for assigned articles; pays $10/page for unsolicited articles.
Photos: State availability of photos with submission. Offers no additional payment for photos accepted with mss. Buys one-time rights.
Fiction: Experimental, mainstream and novel excerpts. Buys 10-12 mss/year. Send complete ms. Length: 2,000-10,000 words. Pays $10/page.
Poetry: Avant-garde and traditional. Buys 50-60 poems/year. Submit maximum 10 poems. Length: 4-500 lines. Pays $10-50.

WESTERN HUMANITIES REVIEW, University of Utah, Salt Lake City UT 84112. (801)581-7438. Managing Editor: Elizabeth Tornes. Quarterly magazine for educated readers. Circ. 1,200. Pays on acceptance. Publishes ms an average of 3 months after acceptance. Buys all rights. Phone queries OK. Simultaneous and photocopied submissions OK. Computer printout submissions acceptable; prefers letter-quality. Reports in 3 months.
Nonfiction: Barry Weller, editor-in-chief. Authoritative, readable articles on literature, art, philosophy, current events, history, religion and anything in the humanities. Interdisciplinary articles encouraged. Departments on film and books. "We commission book reviews." Buys 40 unsolicited mss/year. Pays $50-150.

Fiction: Larry Levis, fiction editor. Any type or theme. Buys 2 mss/issue. Send complete ms.

Poetry: Richard Howard, poetry editor. "See magazine. Recent contributors include Joseph Brodsky, Charles Simic, Charles Wright, Carol Muske, David St. John, Thomas Lux and Sandra McPherson."

Tips: "The change in editorial staff will probably mean a slight shift in emphasis. We will probably be soliciting more submissions and relying less on uninvited materials. More poetry and scholarly articles (and perhaps less fiction) may be included in the future."

THE YALE REVIEW, 1902A Yale Station, New Haven CT 06520. Editor: Kai Erikson. Associate Editor: Penelope Laurans. Managing Editor: Wendy Wipprecht. 20% freelance written. Buys first North American serial rights. Pays on publication. Publishes ms an average of 1 year after acceptance. Computer printout submissions acceptable; no dot-matrix. Writer's guidelines for #10 SASE.

Nonfiction and Fiction: Authoritative discussions of politics, literature and the arts. Buys quality fiction. Pays $100. Length: 3,000-5,000 words.

YELLOW SILK, Journal of Erotic Arts, verygraphics, Box 6374, Albany CA 94706. (415)841-6500. Editor: Lily Pond. 90% freelance written. Prefers to work with published/established writers; works with a small number of new/unpublished writers each year. A quarterly magazine of erotic literature and visual arts. "Editorial policy: All persuasions; no brutality." Our publication is artistic and literary, not pornographic or pandering. Humans are involved: heads, hearts and bodies—not just bodies alone; and the quality of the literature is as important as the erotic content." Circ. 15,000. Pays on publication. Publishes ms an average of 6 months after acceptance. Byline given. Buys all publication rights for one year, at which time they revert to author; and reprint and anthology rights for duration of copyright. Photocopied submissions OK. Computer printout submissions acceptable; prefers letter-quality. Reports in 2 months on mss. Sample copy $6.

Nonfiction: Book excerpts, essays, humor and reviews. "We often have theme issues, but non-regularly and usually not announced in advance. No pornography, romance-novel type writing, sex fantasies. No first-person accounts or blow-by-blow descriptions. No articles. No novels." Buys 5-10 mss/year. Send complete ms. All submissions should be typed, double-spaced, with name, address and phone number on each page; always enclose SASE. No specified length requirements. Pays minimum $10 and 3 contributor copies.

Photos: Photos may be submitted independently, not as illustration for submission. Reviews photocopies, contact sheets, transparencies and prints. We accept 4-color and b&w artwork. Offers varying payment for series of 9-12 used, plus copies. Buys one-time rights and reprint rights.

Columns/Departments: Reviews (book, movie, art, dance, food, anything). "Erotic content and how it's handled is focus of importance. Old or new does not matter. Want to bring readers information of what's out there." Buys 8-10 mss/year. Send complete ms or query. Pays minimum of $10 plus copies.

Fiction: Erotica, including ethnic, experimental, fantasy, humorous, mainstream, novel excerpts and science fiction. See "Nonfiction." Buys 12-16 mss/year. Send complete ms. Pays $1/printed column inch, plus copies.

Poetry: Avant-garde, free verse, haiku, light verse and traditional. "No greeting-card poetry." Buys 80-100 poems/year. No limit on number of poems submitted, "but don't send book-length manuscripts." Pays .375¢/ line, plus copies.

Tips: "The best way to get into *Yellow Silk* is produce excellent, well-crafted work that approaches erotica with freshness, strength of voice, beauty of language, and insight into character. I'll tell you what I'm sick of and have, unfortunately, been seeing more of lately: the products of 'How to Write Erotica' classes. This is not brilliant fiction; it is poorly written fantasy and not what I'm looking for."

ZYZZYVA, The Last Word: West Coast Writers and Artists, Suite 1400, 41 Sutter St., San Francisco CA 94104. (415)255-1282. Editor: Howard Junker. 100% freelance written. Works with a small number of new/ unpublished writers each year. Quarterly magazine. "We feature work by West Coast writers only. We are essentially a literary magazine, but of wide-ranging interests and a strong commitment to nonfiction." Circ. 3,500. Pays on acceptance. Publishes ms an average of 3 months after acceptance. Byline given. Buys first North American serial rights and one-time anthology rights. Photocopied submissions OK. Computer print-out submissions acceptable; prefers letter-quality. Reports in 1 week on queries; 2 weeks on mss. Sample copy $8.

Nonfiction: Book excerpts, general interest, historical/nostalgic, humor and personal experience. Buys 15 mss/year. Query. Length: open. Pays $25-100.

Fiction: Ethnic, experimental, humorous, mainstream and mystery. Buys 20 mss/year. Send complete ms. Length: open. Pays $25-100.

Poetry: Buys 20 poems/year. Submit maximum 5 poems. Length: 3-200 lines. Pays $25-50.

Men's

Men's magazines, for the most part, have been able to stabilize the downward spiral that has affected them during the past few years. Very few new magazines in this category are succeeding, but they are becoming more specialized and many are showing an increased emphasis on fashion. Magazines that also use material slanted toward men can be found in Business and Finance, Relationships, Military and Sports sections.

CAVALIER, Suite 204, 2355 Salzedo St., Coral Gables FL 33134. (305)443-2378. Editor: Douglas Allen. 80% freelance written. Works with published/established and new/unpublished writers each year. Monthly magazine for "young males, ages 18-29, 80% college graduates, affluent, intelligent, interested in current events, sex, sports, adventure, travel and good fiction." Circ. 250,000. Pays on publication. Publishes ms an average of 3 months after acceptance. Byline given. Buys first serial and second serial (reprint) rights. Buys 44 or more mss/year. See past issues for general approach to take. Submit seasonal material at least 3 months in advance. Computer printout submissions acceptable; prefers letter-quality. Reports in 5 weeks. Writer's guidelines for #10 SAE.

Nonfiction: Personal experience, interview, humor, think pieces, exposé and new product. "Be frank—we are open to dealing with controversial issues. No timely material (have 4 month lead time). Prefers 'unusual' subject matter as well as sex-oriented (but serious) articles." Query. Length: 2,800-3,500 words. Pays maximum $500 with photos. Sometimes pays the expenses of writers on assignment.

Photos: Photos purchased with or without captions. No cheesecake.

Fiction: Nye Willden, department editor. Mystery, science fiction, humorous, adventure and contemporary problems "with at least one explicit sex scene per story." Send complete ms. Length: 2,500-3,500 words. Pays $250 maximum, higher for special.

Tips: "Our greatest interest is in originality—new ideas, new approaches; no tired, overdone stories—both feature and fiction. We do not deal in 'hack' sensationalism but in high quality pieces. Keep in mind the intelligent 18- to 29-year-old male reader. We will be putting more emphasis in articles and fiction on sexual themes. We prefer serious articles. Pornography—fiction can be very imaginative and sensational."

CHIC MAGAZINE, Larry Flynt Publications, Suite 300, 9171 Wilshire Blvd., Beverly Hills CA 90210. FAX: (213)275-3857. Executive Editor: Allan MacDonell. 40% freelance written. Prefers to work with published/ established writers. Monthly magazine for men, ages 20-35 years, college-educated and interested in current affairs, entertainment and sports. Circ. 100,000. Pays 1 month after acceptance. Publishes ms an average of 3 months after acceptance. Buys all rights. Pays 20% kill fee. Computer printout submissions acceptable; prefers letter-quality. Byline given unless writer requests otherwise. Reports in 2 months. Writer's guidelines for #10 SASE.

Nonfiction: Sex-related topics of current national interest; interview (personalities in news and entertainment); and celebrity profiles. Buys 12-18 mss/year. Query. Length: 3,000 words. Pays $750. Sometimes pays the expenses of writers on assignment.

Columns/Departments: Odds and Ends (front of the book shorts; study the publication first), 100-300 words. Pays $50. Third Degree (short Q&As) columns, 2,000 words. Pays $350.

Fiction: "At present we are buying stories with emphasis on erotic themes. These may be adventure, action, mystery, horror or humorous stories, but the tone and theme must involve sex and eroticism. The erotic nature of the story should not be subordinate to the characterizations and plot; the sex must grow logically from the people and the plot, not be contrived or forced."

Tips: "We do not buy poetry or non-erotic science fiction. Refrain from stories with drug themes, sex with minors, incest and bestiality."

ESQUIRE, 1790 Broadway, New York NY 10019. (212)459-7500. Editor-in-Chief: Lee Eisenberg. 99% freelance written. Monthly. Pays on acceptance. Publishes ms an average of 6 months after acceptance. Usually buys first serial rights. Computer printout submissions acceptable; prefers letter-quality. Reports in 3 weeks. "We depend chiefly on solicited contributions and material from literary agencies. We are unable to accept responsibility for unsolicited material." Query.

Nonfiction: Articles vary in length, but features usually average 3,000-7,000 words. Articles should be slanted for sophisticated, intelligent readers; however, not highbrow in the restrictive sense. Wide range of subject matter. Rates run roughly between $300 and $3,000, depending on length, quality, etc. Sometimes pays expenses of writers on assignment.

Photos: Temple Smith, photo editor. Payment depends on how photo is used, but rates are roughly $300 for b&w; $500-750 for color. Guarantee on acceptance. Buys first periodical publication rights.

Fiction: L. Rust Hills, fiction editor. "Literary excellence is our only criterion." Discourages genre fiction (horror, science fiction, murder mystery, etc.). Length: about 1,000-6,000 words. Payment: $1,000-5,000.

Tips: The writer sometimes has a better chance of breaking in at *Esquire* with short, lesser-paying articles and fillers (rather than with major features) "because we need more short pieces."

FLING, Relim Publishing Co., Inc., 550 Miller Ave., Mill Valley CA 94941. (415)383-5464. Editor: Arv Miller. Managing Editor: Ted Albert. 30% freelance written. Prefers to work with published/established writers; works with a small number of new/unpublished writers each year. Bimonthly magazine in the men's sophisticate field. Young male audience of adults ages 18-34. Sexual-oriented field. Circ. 100,000. Pays on acceptance.

Publishes ms an average of 3 months after acceptance. Buys first North American serial rights and second serial (reprint) rights; makes work-for-hire assignments. Submit seasonal/holiday material 8 months in advance. Computer printout submissions acceptable; prefers letter-quality. Does not consider multiple submissions. Reports in 1 week on queries; 2 weeks on mss. Sample copy $4; writer's guidelines for SASE.

Nonfiction: Exposé; how-to (better relationships with women, better lovers); interview/profile; personal experience; photo feature; and taboo sex articles. Buys 15 mss/year. Query. Length: 1,500-3,000 words. Pays $150-250. Sometimes pays expenses of writers on assignment.

Photos: Send photos with query. Reviews b&w contact sheets and 8x10 prints; 35mm color transparencies. Pays $10-25 for b&w; $20-35 for color. Model releases required. Buys one-time rights.

Columns/Departments: Buys 12 mss/year. Query or send complete ms. Length: 100-200 words. Pays $15-125.

Fiction: Confession, erotica and sexual. No science fiction, western, plotless, private-eye, "dated" or adventure. Buys 20 mss/year. Send complete ms. Length: 2,000-3,000 words. Pays $135-200.

Fillers: Clippings. Buys 50/year. Length: 100-500 words. Pays $5-15.

Tips: "Nonfiction and fiction are wide open areas to freelancers. Always query with one-page letter to the editor before proceeding with any writing. Also send a sample photocopy of published material, similar to suggestion."

‡FORUM, The International Journal of Human Relations, Penthouse International, 1965 Broadway, New York NY. (212)496-6100. Editor: Don Myrus. 100% freelance written. Works with small number of new/unpublished writers each year. A monthly magazine. "*Forum* is the only serious publication in the U.S. to cover human sexuality in all its aspects for the layman—not only the erotic, but the medical, political, legal, etc." Circ. 300,000. Pays on acceptance. Publishes ms an average of 4-6 months after acceptance. Byline given. "Pseudonym mandatory for first-person sex stories." Offers 25% kill fee. Buys all rights. Submit seasonal/holiday material 6 months in advance. Photocopied submissions OK. Query for electronic submissions. Computer printout submissions OK; no dot matrix. Reports in 1 month on queries.

Nonfiction: Book excepts and personal experience "Most of our freelance submissions are true first-person sexual tales." No submissions of a specialized nature, medical, fiction or poetry. Buys 100 mss/year. Query or send complete ms. Length: 2,000-3,000 words. Pays $1,250. Sometimes pays expenses of writers on assignment.

Photos: State availability of photos with submission. Reviews transparencies and 8x11 prints. Offers $50 minimum/photo. Captions, model releases and identification of subjects required.

GALLERY MAGAZINE, Montcalm Publishing Corp., 401 Park Ave. S., New York NY 10016-8802. (212)779-8900. FAX: (212)725-7215. Editorial Director: Marc Lichter. Managing Editor: Barry Janoff. 50% freelance written. Prefers to work with published/established writers. Monthly magazine "focusing on features of interest to the young American man." Circ. 500,000. Pays 50% on acceptance, 50% on publication. Byline given. Pays 25% kill fee. Buys first North American serial rights; makes work-for-hire assignments. Submit seasonal/holiday material 6 months in advance. Photocopied submissions OK. Computer printout submissions OK; prefers letter-quality. Reports in 1 month on queries; 2 months on mss. Sample copy $3.50 plus $1.75 postage and handling. Free writer's guidelines.

Nonfiction: Investigative pieces, general interest, how-to, humor, interview, new products and profile. "We *do not* want to see pornographic articles." Buys 7-9 mss/issue. Query or send complete mss. Length: 1,000-3,000 words. Pays $300-2,000. "Special prices negotiated." Sometimes pays expenses of writers on assignment.

Photos: Send photos with accompanying mss. Pay varies for b&w or color contact sheets and negatives. Buys one-time rights. Captions preferred; model release required.

Fiction: Adventure, erotica, experimental, humorous, mainstream, mystery and suspense. Buys 1 ms/issue. Send complete ms. Length: 1,000-3,000 words. Pays $350-1,000.

GEM, G&S Publications, 1472 Broadway, New York NY 10036. (212)840-7224. Editor: Will Martin. Managing Editor: R.B. Kendennis. 70% freelance written. Bimonthly magazine. Pays when ms is assigned to a specific issue.

Nonfiction: Sex-related but nonpornographic articles. Pays $50-100. Length: 700-2,000 words.

Fiction: Sex-related but nonpornographic. Same length as above. Pays $50-100.

Tips: "We do not use explicit, graphic descriptions of sex acts or manuscripts with violence. Humor, satire and spoofs of sexual subjects that other magazines treat seriously are welcome."

GENT, Suite 204, 2355 Salzedo St., Coral Gables FL 33134. (305)443-2378. Editor: Bruce Arthur. 75% freelance written. Prefers to work with published/established writers. Monthly magazine for men from every strata of society who enjoy big breasted, full-figured females. Circ. 200,000. Buys first North American serial rights. Byline given. Pays on publication. Publishes ms an average of 2 months after acceptance. Computer printout submissions acceptable; prefers letter-quality. Reports in 6 weeks. Sample copy $5; writer's guidelines for #10 SASE.

Nonfiction: Looking for traditional men's subjects (cars, racing, outdoor adventure, science, gambling, etc.) as well as sex-related topics. Query first. Length: 2,000-3,500 words. Buys 70 mss/year. Pays $100-250.

Photos: B&w photos and color transparencies purchased with mss. Captions (preferred).

Fiction: Erotic. "Stories should contain a huge-breasted female character, as this type of model is *Gent's* main focus. And this character's endowments should be described in detail in the course of the story." Submit complete ms. No fiction queries. Length: 2,000-4,000 words. Pays $100-200.

Tips: "Our efforts to make *Gent* acceptable to Canadian censors as a condition for exportation to that country have forced some shifting of editorial focus. Toward this end, we have de-emphasized our editorial coverage of pregnancy, lactation, anal intercourse and all forms of sadism and masochism. Study sample copies of the magazine before trying to write for it. We like custom-tailored stories and articles."

GENTLEMEN'S QUARTERLY, Condé Nast, 350 Madison Ave., New York NY 10017. (212)880-8800. Editor-in-Chief: Arthur Cooper. Managing Editor: Eliot Kaplan. 60% freelance written. Circ. 675,000. Monthly magazine emphasizing fashion, general interest and service features for men ages 25-45 with a large discretionary income. Pays on acceptance. Byline given. Pays 25% kill fee. Submit seasonal/holiday material 6 months in advance. Computer printout submissions acceptable; prefers letter-quality. Reports in 1 month.

Nonfiction: Politics, personality profiles, lifestyles, trends, grooming, nutrition, health and fitness, sports, travel, money, investment and business matters. Buys 4-6 mss/issue. Query with published clips. Length: 1,500-4,000 words. Pay varies.

Columns/Departments: Eliot Kaplan, managing editor. Body & Soul (fitness, nutrition and grooming); Private Lives; Health; Games (sports); All About Adam (nonfiction by women about men). Query with published clips. Length: 1,000-2,500 words. Pay varies.

Tips: "Major features are usually assigned to well-established, known writers. Pieces are almost always solicited. The best way to break in is through the columns, especially Male Animal, All About Adam, Games, Health or Humor."

HIGH SOCIETY, 801 2nd Ave., New York NY 10017. (212)661-7878. Editor: Stephen Loshiauo. Managing Editor: Paul Proch. Articles Editor: Stephen Loshiavo. 80% freelance written. Monthly magazine of erotic adult entertainment. Circ. 300,000. Pays on acceptance. Publishes ms an average of 4 months after acceptance. Byline given. Makes work-for-hire assignments. Submit seasonal/holiday material 6 months in advance. Computer printout submissions acceptable; no dot-matrix. Reports in 2 weeks. Sample copy $4.50; free writer's guidelines.

Nonfiction: Exposé (political/entertainment); how-to (sexual, self-help); humor (bawdy); interview/profile (sports, music, politics); opinion (sexual subjects); and personal experience (sexual). Query with published clips. Length: 1,000-1,500 words. Pays $200 minimum. Sometimes pays expenses of writers on assignment.

Photos: State availability of photos or send photo with query. Reviews 1" color transparencies. Model release and identification of subjects required.

Columns/Departments: Silver Spoonfuls: Newsbits, health, reviews. Buys 50 mss/year. Query with published clips. Length: 250-1,000 words. Pays $200-400.

Fiction: Confession (sex oriented), erotica and humorous (sex oriented). Buys 12 mss/year. Query with published clips. Length: 1,000-1,500 words. Pays $150-250.

MAGNA, Fashion & Lifestyle Magazine for Big & Tall Men, The Magna Corp., Box 286, Cabin John MD 20818. (301)320-2745. Editor: Jack Shulman. Publisher: Marlene Solomon. A quarterly magazine for big and tall men. "We deal with problems particular to large men and to universal interests and problems." Circ. 120,000. Pays on publication. Publishes ms an average of 7 months after acceptance. Byline given. Buys first rights. Submit seasonal/holiday material 9 months in advance. Simultaneous and photocopied submissions OK. Computer printout submissions OK; prefers letter-quality. Reports in 2 months on queries; 2 weeks on mss. Sample copy $3.50 with 7 first class stamps.

Nonfiction: General interest, how-to, humor, interview/profile, personal experience and travel. No fiction or any article that does not treat big or tall men sympathetically. Buys 16 mss/year. Send complete ms. Length: 250-2,500 words. Pays $150-275.

Photos: State availability of photos with submission. Reviews 35mm transparencies. Offers no additional payment for photos accepted with ms. Model releases and identification of subjects required. Buys one-time rights.

Columns/Departments: Gerry Green, column/department editor. Buys 24 mss/year. Send complete ms. Length: 50-150 words. Pays $25-100.

Fillers: Facts about big and tall men. Buys 12/year. Length: 75-300 words. Pays $25-60.

NUGGET, Suite 204, 2355 Salzedo St., Coral Gables FL 33134. (305)443-2378. Editor: Jerome Slaughter. 75% freelance written. Magazine "primarily devoted to fetishism." Pays on publication. Publishes ms an average of 2 months after acceptance. Byline given. Buys first North American serial rights. Computer printout submissions acceptable; prefers letter-quality. Reports in 6 weeks. Sample copy $5; writer's guidelines for SASE.

Nonfiction: Articles on fetishism — every aspect. Buys 20-30 mss/year. Submit complete ms. Length: 2,000-4,000 words. Pays $100-200.

Photos: Erotic pictorials of women and couples — essay types on fetish clothing (leather, rubber, underwear, etc.) or women wrestling or boxing other women or men, preferably semi-nude or nude. Captions or short accompanying ms desirable. Reviews color transparencies or b&w photos.

Fiction: Erotic and fetishistic. Should be oriented to *Nugget's* subject matter. Length: 2,000-4,000 words. Pays $100-200.

Tips: "We require queries on articles only, and the letter should be a brief synopsis of what the article is about. Originality in handling of subject is very helpful. It is almost a necessity for a freelancer to study our magazine first, be knowledgeable about the subject matter we deal with and able to write explicit and erotic fetish material."

OPTIONS, The Bi-Monthly, AJA Publishing, Box 470, Port Chester NY 10573. (914)939-2111. Editor: Don Stone. Assistant Editor: Diana Sheridan. Mostly freelance written. Sexually explicit magazine for and about bisexuals and homosexuals, published 10 times/year. "Articles, stories and letters about bisexuality. Positive approach. Safe-sex encounters unless the story clearly pre-dates the AIDS situation." Circ. 100,000. Pays on publication. Publishes ms an average of 4-8 months after acceptance. Byline given. Buys all rights. Submit seasonal/holiday material 6-8 months in advance; buys very little seasonal material. Photocopied submissions OK. Computer printout submissions OK. Reports in 3 weeks. Sample copy $2.95 with 6x9 SAE and 5 first class stamps. Writer's guidelines for SASE.

Nonfiction: Essays (occasional), how-to, humor, interview/profile, opinion and (especially) personal experience. All must be bisexually related. Does not want "anything not bisexually related, anything negative, anything opposed to safe sex, anything dry/boring/ponderous/pedantic; write even serious topics informally if not lightly." Buys 70 mss/year. Send complete ms. Length: 2,000-3,000. Pays $100.

Photos: Reviews transparencies and prints. Pays $10 for b&w photos; $200 for full color. Previously published photos acceptable.

Fiction: "We don't usually get enough true first-person stories and need to buy some from writers. They must be bisexual, usually man/man, hot and believable. They must not read like fiction." Buys 60 ms/year. Send complete ms. Length: 2,000-3,000. Pays $100.

Tips: "We use many more male/male pieces than female/female. Use only 1 serious article per issue. A serious/humorous approach is good here, but only if it's natural to you; don't make an effort for it."

PLAYBOY, 919 N. Michigan, Chicago IL 60611. 50% freelance written. Prefers to work with published/established writers; works with a small number of new/unpublished writers each year. Monthly. Pays on acceptance. Publishes ms an average of 6 months after acceptance. Offers 20% kill fee. Buys first serial rights and others. Computer printout submissions acceptable; prefers letter-quality. Reports in 1 month. Writer's guidelines for #10 SASE.

Nonfiction: John Rezek, articles editor. "We're looking for timely, topical pieces. Articles should be carefully researched and written with wit and insight. Little true adventure or how-to material. Check magazine for subject matter. Pieces on outstanding contemporary men, sports, politics, sociology, business and finance, music, science and technology, games, all areas of interest to the contemporary urban male." Query. Length: 3,000-5,000 words. Pays $3,000 minimum. *Playboy* interviews run between 10,000 and 15,000 words. After getting an assignment, the freelancer outlines the questions, conducts and edits the interview, and writes the introduction. Pays $5,000 minimum. For interviews contact G. Barry Golson, Executive Editor, 747 3rd Ave., New York NY 10017. Pays expenses of writers on assignment.

Photos: Gary Cole, photography director, suggests that all photographers interested in contributing make a thorough study of the photography currently appearing in the magazine. Generally all photography is done on assignment. While much of this is assigned to *Playboy's* staff photographers, approximately 50% of the photography is done by freelancers, and *Playboy* is in constant search of creative new talent. Qualified freelancers are encouraged to submit samples of their work and ideas. All assignments made on an all rights basis with payments scaled from $600/color page for miscellaneous features such as fashion, food and drink, etc.; $300/b&w page; $1,000/color page for girl features; cover, $1,500. Playmate photography for entire project: $10,000-13,000. Assignments and submissions handled by senior editor: Jeff Cohen and associate editors: James Larson and Michael Ann Sullivan, Chicago; Marilyn Grabowski and Linda Kenney, Los Angeles. Assignments made on a minimum guarantee basis. Film, processing, and other expenses necessitated by assignment honored.

Fiction: Alice Turner, fiction editor. Both light and serious fiction. "Entertainment pieces are clever, smoothly written stories. Serious fiction must come up to the best contemporary standards in substance, idea and style. Both, however, should be designed to appeal to the educated, well-informed male reader." General types include comedy, mystery, fantasy, horror, science fiction, adventure, social-realism, "problem" and psychological stories. Fiction lengths are 3,000-6,000 words; short-shorts of 1,000 to 1,500 words are used. Pays $2,000; $1,000 short-short. Rates rise for additional acceptances.

Fillers: Party Jokes are always welcome. Pays $100 each. Also interesting items for Playboy After Hours section (check it carefully before submitting). The After Hours front section pays $75 for humorous or unusual news items (submissions not returned). Send to After Hours editor. Has regular movie, book and record reviewers. Ideas for Playboy Potpourri pay $75. Query to David Stevens, Chicago. Games, puzzles and travel articles should be addressed to New York office.

SCREW, Box 432, Old Chelsea Station, New York NY 10113. Managing Editor: Manny Neuhaus. 95% freelance written. Eager to work with new/unpublished writers. Weekly tabloid newspaper for a predominantly male, college-educated audience; ages 21 through mid-40s. Circ. 125,000. Pays on publication. Publishes ms an average of 3 months after acceptance. Byline given. Buys all rights. Computer printout submissions acceptable; prefers letter-quality. Reports in 3 months. Free sample copy and writer's guidelines.
Nonfiction: "Sexually-related news, humor, how-to articles, first-person and true confessions. Frank and explicit treatment of all areas of sex; outrageous and irreverent attitudes combined with hard information, news and consumer reports. Our style is unique. Writers should check several recent issues." Buys 150-200 mss/year. Will also consider material for Letter From . . ., a consumer-oriented wrap-up of commercial sex scene in cities around the country; Submit complete ms or query. Length: 1,000-3,000 words. Pays $100-250. Also, My Scene, a sexual true confession. Length: 1,000-2,500 words. Pays $40.
Photos: Reviews b&w glossy prints (8x10 or 11x14) purchased with or without manuscripts or on assignment. Pays $10-50.
Tips: "All mss get careful attention. Those written in *Screw* style on sexual topics have the best chance. I anticipate a need for more aggressive, insightful political humor."

‡SWANK, GCR Publishing Corp., 888 7th Ave., New York NY 10106. (212)541-7100. Editor: W.B. Gerard. 75% freelance written. Eager to work with new/unpublished writers. Monthly magazine on "sex and sensationalism, lurid. High quality adult erotic entertainment." Audience of men ages 18-38, high school and some college education, medium income, skilled blue-collar professionals, union men. Circ. 350,000. Pays on publication. Publishes ms an average of 4 months after acceptance. Byline given; pseudonym, if wanted. Pays 20% kill fee. Buys first North American serial rights. Submit seasonal/holiday material 4 months in advance. Reports in 2 weeks on queries; 6 weeks on mss. Sample copy $3.50; writer's guidelines for SASE.
Nonfiction: Exposé (researched) and adventure must be accompanied by photographs. "We buy non-sex articles and articles on sex-related topics, which don't need to be accompanied by photos." Interested in lifestyle (unusual) pieces. Buys photo pieces on autos. Buys 34 mss/year. Query with or without published clips. Pays $350-500. Sometimes pays the expenses of writers on assignment.
Photos: Bruce Perez, photo editor. State availability of photos. "If you have good photographs of an interesting adventure/lifestyle subject, the writing that accompanies is bought almost automatically." Model releases required.
Tips: "Don't even bother to send girl photos unless you are a published professional." Looks for "lifestyle and adventure pieces that are accompanied by color 35mm chromes and articles about sex-related topics. We carry one photo/journalism piece about automobiles or related subjects per issue."

TURN-ON LETTERS, AJA Publishing, Box 470, Port Chester NY 10573. Editor: Julie Silver. Magazine published 9 times/year covering sex. "Adult material, must be positive, no pain or degradations. No incest, no underage." Circ. 100,000. Pays on publication. Publishes ms an average of 4-8 months after acceptance. Buys all rights. No byline. No kill fee; "assigned mss are not killed unless they do not fulfill the assignment and/or violate censorship laws." Submit seasonal/holiday material 6 months in advance. Computer printout submissions OK. Reports in 3 weeks. Sample copy $2.50 with 6x9 SAE and 4 first class stamps. Writer's guidelines for #10 SASE.
Fiction: Sexually explicit material in the format of a letter. Buys 441 "letters"/year. Send complete ms. Length: 500-750 words (2-3 typed pages). Pays $15.
Photos: Reviews transparencies and prints. Buys b&w for $10 and full color for $200. Previously published pictures OK. Buys all rights.
Tips: "When you write, be different, be believable."

UNCENSORED LETTERS, Sportomatic Publishers, Box 470, Port Chester NY 10573. Editor: Tammy Simmons. 100% freelance written. Magazine covering sex published nine times/year. "Adult material, must be positive in approach, no pain or degradation. No incest; no underage." Circ. 100,000. Pays on publication. Publishes ms an average of 4-6 months after acceptance. No byline given. No kill fee; "assigned mss are not killed unless they do not fulfill assignment and/or they violate censorship laws." Buys all rights. Computer printout submissions OK. Reports in 3 weeks. Sample copy $2.95 with 9x12 envelope and 5 first class stamps; writer's guidelines for SASE.

Fiction: Sexually explicit material written as true-to-life in the format of a letter. Buys 594 mss/year. Send complete ms. Length: 300-750 (2-3 typed, double-spaced pages). Pays $15.

Photos: Buys b&w's, $10 each; full color, $200. Previously published photos OK. Buys all rights.

Tips: "Read spec sheet, available for SASE. When you write, be different, yet believable. Manuscripts accepted by *UL* may now be used in our sister magazine, *Turn-On Letters*, and vice-versa. We look to buy a few manuscripts detailing hot 'safe-sex' for each issue."

Military

These publications emphasize military or paramilitary subjects or other aspects of military life. Technical and semitechnical publications for military commanders, personnel and planners, as well as those for military families and civilians interested in Armed Forces activities are listed here.

AMERICAN SURVIVAL GUIDE, McMullen Publishing, Inc., 2145 W. La Palma Ave., Anaheim CA 92801. (714)635-9040. FAX: (714)533-9979. Editor: Jim Benson. 50% freelance written. Monthly magazine covering "self-reliance, defense, meeting day-to-day and possible future threats—survivalism for survivalists." Circ. 72,000. Pays on publication. Publishes ms up to 1 year after acceptance. Byline given. Submit seasonal/holiday material 5 months in advance. Computer printout submissions acceptable; prefers letter-quality. Sample copy $3.50; writer's guidelines for SASE.

Nonfiction: Expose (political); how-to; interview/profile; personal experience (how I survived); photo feature (equipment and techniques related to survival in all possible situations); emergency medical; health and fitness; communications; transportation; food preservation; water purification; self-defense; terrorism; nuclear dangers; nutrition; tools; shelter; etc. "No general articles about how to survive. We want specifics and single subjects." Buys 60-100 mss/year. Query or send complete ms. Length: 1,500-2,000 words. Pays $140-350. Sometimes pays the expenses of writers on assignment.

Photos: Send photos with ms. "One of the most frequent mistakes made by writers in completing an article assignment for us is sending photo submissions that are inadequate." Captions, model releases and identification of subjects mandatory. Buys all rights.

Tips: "Prepare material of value to individuals who wish to sustain human life no matter what the circumstance. This magazine is a text and reference."

ARMED FORCES JOURNAL INTERNATIONAL, Suite 520, 2000 L St. NW, Washington DC 20036. FAX: (202)296-5727 or (202)296-4872. Editor: Benjamin F. Schemmer. 30% freelance written. Monthly magazine for "senior career officers of the U.S. military, defense industry, Congressmen and government officials interested in defense matters, international military and defense industry." Circ. 45,000. Pays on publication. Publishes ms an average of 2 months after acceptance. Buys all rights. Photocopied submissions OK. Computer printout submissions acceptable; no dot-matrix. Reports in 1 month. Sample copy $2.75.

Nonfiction: Publishes "national and international defense issues: weapons programs, research, personnel programs and international relations (with emphasis on defense issues). We do not want broad overviews of a general subject; we are more interested in detailed analysis which lays out *both* sides of a specific program or international defense issue. Our readers are decision-makers in defense matters—hence, subject should not be treated too simplistically. Be provocative. We are not afraid to take issue with our own constituency when an independent voice needs to be heard." Buys informational, profile and think pieces. No poetry, biographies, or non-defense topics. Buys 80-100 mss/year. Send complete ms with photos. Length: 1,000-3,000 words. Pays $250/page.

Tips: "The most frequent mistakes made by writers are: 1) one-dimensional and one-sided articles; 2) broadbrush generalities versus specificity; and 3) poorly written gobbledygook."

FAMILY MAGAZINE, The Magazine for Military Wives, Box 4993, Walnut Creek CA 94596. (415)284-9093. Editor: Janet A. Venturino. 100% freelance written. Works with a small number of new/unpublished writers each year. A monthly magazine for military wives who are young, high school educated and move often. Circ. 545,000. Pays on publication. Publishes ms an average of 6-12 months after acceptance. Byline given. Buys first North American serial rights. Submit seasonal/holiday material 6 months in advance. Simultaneous and photocopied submissions OK. Computer printout submissions acceptable; prefers letter-quality. Reports in 1 month. Sample copy $1.25; writer's guidelines for SASE.

Nonfiction: Humor, personal experience, photo feature and travel, of interest to military wives. No romance, anything to do with getting a man or aging. Buys 30 mss/year. Send complete ms. Length: 2,000 words maximum. Pays $75-200.

Photos: Send photos with submissions. Reviews contact sheets, transparencies and prints. Offers $25-100/photo. Identification of subjects required. Buys one-time rights.
Fiction: Humorous, mainstream and slice-of-life vignettes. No romance or novel excerpts. Buys 5 mss/year. Length: 2,000 words maximum. Pays $75-150.

INFANTRY, Box 2005, Fort Benning GA 31905-0605. (404)545-2350. Editor: Albert N. Garland. 90% freelance written. Eager to work with new/unpublished writers. Bimonthly magazine published primarily for combat arms officers and noncommissioned officers. Circ. 15,000. Not copyrighted. Buys first serial rights. Pays on publication. Payment cannot be made to U.S. government employees. Publishes ms an average of 1 year after acceptance. Computer printout submissions acceptable; prefers letter-quality. Reports in 1 month. Free sample copy and writer's guidelines.
Nonfiction: Interested in current information on U.S. military organizations, weapons, equipment, tactics and techniques; foreign armies and their equipment; lessons learned from combat experience, both past and present; and solutions to problems encountered in the Active Army and the Reserve Components. Departments include Letters, Professional Forum, Training Notes and Book Reviews. Uses 70 unsolicited mss/year. Length of articles: 1,500-3,500 words. Length for Book Reviews: 500-1,000 words. Query with writing sample. Accepts 75 mss/year.
Photos: Used with mss.
Tips: "Start with letters to editor and book reviews to break in."

LIFE IN THE TIMES, Times Journal Co., Springfield VA 22159-0200. (703)750-8666. FAX: (703)750-8622. Editor: Barry Robinson. Managing Editor: Roger Hyneman. 30% freelance written. Eager to work with new/unpublished writers. Weekly lifestyle section of Army, Navy and Air Force Times covering current lifestyles and problems of career military families around the world. Circ. 300,000. Pays on acceptance. Publishes ms an average of 2 months after acceptance. Byline given. Offers negotiable kill fee. Buys first rights. Submit seasonal/holiday material 6 months in advance. Query for electronic submissions. Double- or triple-spaced computer printout submissions acceptable; no dot-matrix. Reports in about 2 months. Writer's guidelines for #10 SASE.
Nonfiction: Exposé (current military); how-to (military wives); interview/profile (military); opinion (military topic); personal experience (military only); and travel (of military interest). "We accept food articles and short items about unusual things military people and their families are doing." No poetry, cartoons or historical articles. Buys 110 mss/year. Query with published clips. Length: 750-2,000 words. Pays $75-350. Sometimes pays the expenses of writers on assignment.
Photos: State availability of photos or send photos with ms. Reviews 35mm color contact sheets and prints. Captions, model releases and identification of subjects required.
Tips: "In your query write a detailed description of story and how it will be told. A tentative lead is nice. Just one good story 'breaks in' a freelancer. Follow the outline you propose in your query letter and humanize articles with quotes and examples."

MARINE CORPS GAZETTE, Professional Magazine for United States Marines, Marine Corps Association, Box 1775, Quantico VA 22134. (703)640-6161. FAX: (703)640-2628. Editor: Col. John E. Greenwood, USMC (Ret.). Managing Editor: Joseph D. Dodd. Less than 5% freelance written. "Will continue to welcome and respond to queries, but will be selective due to large backlog from Marine authors." Monthly magazine. "*Gazette* serves as a forum in which serving Marine officers exchange ideas and viewpoints on professional military matters." Circ. 37,000. Pays on publication. Publishes ms an average of 6 months after acceptance. Byline given. Buys all rights. Computer printout submissions acceptable. Reports in 3 weeks on queries; 2 months on mss. Free sample copy and writer's guidelines.
Nonfiction: Historical/nostalgic (Marine Corps operations only); and technical (Marine Corps related equipment). "The magazine is a professional journal oriented toward hard skills, factual treatment, technical detail—no market for lightweight puff pieces—analysis of doctrine, lessons learned goes well. A very strong Marine Corps background and influence are normally prerequisites for publication." Buys 4-5 mss/year from non-Marine Corps sources. Query or send complete ms. Length: 2,500-5,000 words. Pays $200-400; short features, $50-100.
Photos: "We welcome photos and charts." Payment for illustrative material included in payment forms. "Photos need not be original, nor have been taken by the author, but they must support the article."
Columns/Departments: Book Reviews (of interest and importance to Marines); and Ideas and Issues (an assortment of topical articles, e.g., opinion or argument, ideas of better ways to accomplish tasks, reports on weapons and equipment, strategies and tactics, etc., also short vignettes on history of Corps). Buys 60 book reviews and 120 Ideas and Issues mss/year, most from Marines. Query. Length: 500-1,500 words. Pays $25-50 plus book for 750-word book review; $50-100 for Ideas and Issues.
Tips: "Book reviews or short articles (500-1,500 words) on Marine Corps related hardware or technological development are the best way to break in. Sections/departments most open to freelancers are Book Reviews and Ideas & Issues sections—query first. We are not much of a market for those outside U.S. Marine Corps or who are not closely associated with current Marine activities."

THE MILITARY ENGINEER, 607 Prince St., Box 21289, Alexandria VA 22320-2289. (703)549-3800. Editor: John J. Kern. 90% freelance written. Prefers to work with published/established writers, but willing to work with new authors. Bimonthly magazine. Circ. 30,000. Pays on publication. Publishes ms an average of 9 months after acceptance. Byline given. Buys all rights. Phone queries OK. Computer printout submissions acceptable (double-spaced). Query for electronic submissions. Reports in 1 month. Sample copy and writer's guidelines $4.

Nonfiction: Well-written and illustrated semitechnical articles by experts and practitioners of civil and military engineering, constructors, equipment manufacturers, defense contract suppliers and architect/engineers on these subjects and on subjects of military biography and history. "Subject matter should represent a contribution to the fund of knowledge, concern a new project or method, be on R&D in these fields; investigate planning and management techniques or problems in these fields, or be of militarily strategic nature." Buys 50-70 unsolicited mss/year. Length: 1,000-2,000 words. Query.

Photos: Mss must be accompanied by 6-10 well-captioned photos, maps or illustrations; b&w glossy, generally. Pays approximately $50/page.

MILITARY LIFESTYLE, Downey Communications, Inc., 1732 Wisconsin Ave. NW, Washington DC 20007. FAX: (202)333-0499. Editor: Hope M. Daniels. 80-90% freelance written. Works with equal balance of published and unpublished writers. For military families in the U.S. and overseas. Published 10 times a year. Magazine. Circ. 520,000. Pays on publication. Publishes ms an average of 4-6 months after acceptance. Buys first North American serial rights. Submit seasonal/holiday material at least 6 months in advance. Computer printout submissions acceptable. Reports in approximately 2 months. Sample copy $1.50 and 9x12 SAE. Writer's guidelines for #10 SASE.

Nonfiction: "All articles must have special interest for military families. General interest articles are OK if they reflect situations our readers can relate to." Food, humor, profiles, childrearing, health, home decor and travel. "Query letter should name sources, describe focus of article, use a few sample quotes from sources, indicate length, and should describe writer's own qualifications for doing the piece." Length: 1,000-2,000 words. Pays $300-700/article. Negotiates expenses on a case-by-case basis.

Photos: Purchased with accompanying ms and on assignment. Uses 35mm or larger color transparencies. Captions and model releases are required. Query art director Judi Connelly.

Columns/Departments: Your Point of View—personal experience pieces by military family members. Also, Your Pet, Your Money and Your Baby. Query. Length: 800-1,200 words. Rates vary.

Fiction: Slice-of-life, family situation, contemporary tableaux. "Military family life or relationship themes only." Buys 6-8 mss/year. Query. Length: 1,500-2,000 words. Pays $250-350.

Tips: "We are a magazine for military families, not just women. Our editorial attempts enthusiastically to reflect that. Our ideal contributor is a military family member who can write. However, I'm always impressed by a writer who has analyzed the market and can suggest some possible new angles for us. Sensitivity to military issues is a must for our contributors, as is the ability to write good personality profiles and/or do thorough research about military family life. We don't purchase household hints, historical articles, WW II-era material or parenting advice that is too personal and limited only to the writer's own experience."

MILITARY LIVING R&R REPORT, Box 2347, Falls Church VA 22042. (703)237-0203. Publisher: Ann Crawford. Bimonthly newsletter for "military travelers worldwide. Please state when sending submission that it is for the *R&R Report Newsletter* so as not to confuse it with our monthly magazine which has different requirements." Pays on publication. Buys first serial rights but will consider other rights. Sample copy $1.

Nonfiction: "We use information on little-known military facilities and privileges, discounts around the world and travel information. Items must be short and concise. Most reports are done by *R&R*'s subscribers on a 'sharing with others' basis with no fee paid. Used only a few freelance pieces in last year. Payment is on an honorarium basis, 1-1½¢/word."

MILITARY REVIEW, U.S. Army Command and General Staff College, Fort Leavenworth KS 66027-6910. (913)684-5642. Editor-in-Chief: Col. Phillip W. Childress. Managing Editor: Maj. Chris LeBlanc. Associate Editor: Lt. Col. Lynn Havach. 75% freelance written. Eager to work with new/unpublished writers. Monthly journal (printed in three languages; English, Spanish and Brazilian Portuguese), emphasizing the military for military officers, students and scholars. Circ. 27,000. Pays on publication. Publishes ms an average of 8 months after acceptance. Byline given. Buys first serial rights and reserves right to reprint for training purpose. Phone queries and photocopied submissions OK. Query for electronic submissions. Computer printout submissions acceptable; prefers letter-quality. Reports in 1 month. Writer's guidelines for #10 SASE.

Nonfiction: Operational level of war, military history, international affairs, tactics, new military equipment, strategy and book reviews. Prefers not to get poetry or cartoons. Buys 100-120 mss/year. Query. Length: 2,000-3,000 words. Pays $50-200.

Tips: "We need more articles from military personnel experienced in particular specialties. Examples: Tactics from a tactician, military engineering from an engineer, etc. By reading our publication, writers will quickly recognize our magazine as a forum for any topic of general interest to the U.S. Army. They will also discover the style we prefer: concise and direct, in the active voice, with precision and clarity, and moving from the specific to the general."

OVERSEAS!, Military Consumer Today, Inc., Kolpingstr 1, 6906 Leimen, West Germany 011-49-6224-7060. Editorial Director: Charles L. Kaufman. Managing Editor: Greg Ballinger. 95% freelance written. Eager to work with new/unpublished writers; "we don't get enough submissions." Monthly magazine. *"Overseas!* is aimed at the U.S. military in Europe. It is the leading men's military lifestyle magazine slanted toward life in Europe, specifically directed to males ages 18-35." Circ. 83,000. Pays on publication. Publishes ms an average of 3 months after acceptance. Byline given. Publishes photos, bio of new writers in editor's column. Offers kill fee depending on circumstances and writer. Buys one-time rights. Submit seasonal/holiday material at least 4 months in advance. Simultaneous queries, and simultaneous, photocopied and previously published submissions OK. Computer printout submissions acceptable; prefers letter-quality. Reports in 2 weeks on queries; 1 month on mss. Sample copy for SAE and 4 IRCs; writer's guidelines for SAE and 1 IRC.
Nonfiction: General interest (lifestyle for men and other topics); how-to (use camera, buy various types of video, audio, photo and computer equipment); humor ("We want travel/tourist in Europe humor like old *National Lampoon* style. Must be funny."); interview/profile (music, personality interviews; current music stars for young audience); technical (video, audio, photo, computer; how to purchase and use equipment); travel (European, first person adventure; write toward male audience); men's cooking; and men's fashion/ lifestyle. Special issues include Video, Audio, Photo, and Military Shopper's Guide. Needs 250-750-word articles on video, audio, photo and computer products. Published in September every year. No articles that are drug- or sex-related. No cathedrals or museums of Europe stories. Buys 30-50 mss/year "but would buy more if we got better quality and subjects." Query with or without pulished clips or send complete ms. Length: 750-2,000 words. Pays 10/word. Usually pays expenses of writers on assignment; negotiable.
Photos: Send photos with accompanying query or ms. Pays $20 minimum, b&w; $35 color transparencies, 35mm or larger. Photos must accompany travel articles—"color slides. Also, we are always looking for photographs of pretty women for our covers." Pays $250 minimum. Identification of subjects required. Buys one-time rights. Buys 12 covers/year.
Columns/Departments: Back Talk—potpourri page of humor, cartoons and other materials relating to tourist life in Europe and the military. Buys 20-50 mss/year. Length: 150 words maximum. Pays $25-150/piece used. "Would buy more if received more."
Tips: "We would like more submissions on travel in Europe and humor for the 'Back Talk' page. Writing should be lively, interesting, with lots of good information. We anticipate a change in the length of articles. Articles will be shorter and livelier with more sidebars, because readers don't have time to read longer articles. *Overseas!* magazine is the *Travel and Leisure/GQ/Esquire* of this market; any articles that would be suitable for these magazines would probably work in *Overseas!*"

PARAMETERS: U.S. ARMY WAR COLLEGE QUARTERLY, U.S. Army War College, Carlisle Barracks PA 17013. (717)245-4943. Editor: Col. Lloyd J. Matthews, U.S. Army Retired. Quarterly. 100% freelance written. Prefers to work with published/established writers or experts in the field. Readership consists of senior leadership of U.S. defense establishment, both uniformed and civilian, plus members of the media, government, industry and academia interested in national and international security affairs, military strategy, military leadership and management, art and science of warfare, and military history (provided it has contemporary relevance). Most readers possess a graduate degree. Circ. 10,000. Not copyrighted; unless copyrighted by author, articles may be reprinted with appropriate credits. Buys first serial rights. Byline given. Pays on publication. Publishes ms an average of 6 months after acceptance. Computer printout submissions acceptable. Reports in 1 month. Free writer's guidelines.
Nonfiction: Articles preferred that deal with current security issues, employ critical analysis and provide solutions or recommendations. Liveliness and verve, consistent with scholarly integrity, appreciated. Theses, studies and academic course papers should be adapted to article form prior to submission. Documentation in complete endnotes. Submit complete ms. Length: 4,500 words average, preferably less. Pays $150 average (including visuals).
Tips: "Make it short; keep it interesting; get criticism and revise accordingly. Tackle a subject only if you are an authority."

PERIODICAL, Council on America's Military Past, 4970 N. Camino Antonio, Tucson AZ 85718. Editor-in-Chief: Dan L. Thrapp. 90% freelance written. Works with a small number of new/unpublished writers each year. Quarterly magazine emphasizing old and abandoned forts, posts and military installations; military subjects for a professional, knowledgeable readership interested in one-time defense sites or other military installations. Circ. 1,500. Pays on publication. Publishes ms an average of 6 months after acceptance. Buys one-time rights. Simultaneous, photocopied, and previously published (if published a long time ago) submissions OK. Computer printout submissions OK; prefers letter-quality. Reports in 3 weeks. Writer's guidelines for #10 SASE.

Nonfiction: Historical, personal experience, photo feature and technical (relating to posts, their construction/operation and military matters). Buys 4-6 mss/issue. Query or send complete ms. Length: 300-4,000 words. Pays $2/page minimum.

Photos: Purchased with or without ms. Query. Reviews glossy, single-weight 8x10 b&w prints. Offers no additional payment for photos accepted with accompanying ms. Captions required.

Tips: "We plan more emphasis on appeal to professional military audience and military historians."

R&R ENTERTAINMENT DIGEST, R&R Communications GmbH, 1 Kolpingstrasse, 6906 Leimen, W. Germany 06224-7060. FAX: 06224-70676. Editor: Marji Hess. 50% freelance written. Monthly entertainment guide for military and government employees and their families stationed in Europe "specializing in travel in Europe, audio/video/photo information, music and the homemaker scene. Aimed exclusively at military/DoD based in Europe – Germany, Britain and the Mediterranean." Circ. 170,000. Pays on publication. Publishes ms an average of 2-6 months after acceptance. Byline given. "We offer 50% of payment as a kill fee, but this rarely happens – if story can't run in one issue, we try to use it in a future edition." Buys first serial rights for military market in Europe only. "We will reprint stories that have run in stateside publications if applicable to us." Submit seasonal/holiday material 3 months in advance. Computer printout submissions acceptable; prefers letter-quality. Simultaneous queries, and simultaneous, photocopied, and previously published submissions OK. Reports in 2 months. Sample copy and writer's guidelines available for #10 SAE and 5 IRCs.

Nonfiction: Humor (limited amount used – dealing with travel experiences in Europe), and travel (always looking for good travel in Europe features). "We buy only articles by writers who have been to or lived in the destination on which they write. Not interested in tourist articles. Our readers live in Europe, average age 26.5, married with 2 children. Over 50% travel by car. Annual vacation is 1 week or more. Weekend trips are also popular. Should always include restaurant/clubs/hotel recommendations. Looking for bargains." No interviews of singers, historical pieces, album/movie/book reviews, or technical stories. Buys 15 mss/year. Query with published clips or send complete ms. Length: 600-1,000 words. Pays in Deutsche Marks – DM 90 (an estimated $45) /page; partial payment for partial page.

Photos: State availability of photos or send photos with query or mss. Pays DM 80 for 35mm color transparencies. Captions required. "We pay once for use with story but can reuse at no additional cost."

Columns/Departments: Monthly audio, video and photo stories. "We need freelancers with solid background in these areas who can write for general public on a variety of topics." Buys 10 mss/year. Query with published clips or send complete ms. Length: 1,300-1,400 words. Pays DM 90/magazine page.

Fiction: Very little fiction accepted. Query. "It has to be exceptional to be accepted." Length: 600-1,200 words. Pays DM 90/page.

Fillers: Cartoons pertaining to television. Buys 5/year. Pays DM 80/cartoon.

Tips: "Best chance would be a tie-in travel or first-person story with an American holiday: Mother's Day in Paris, Labor Day, Thanksgiving, St. Pat's Day in Europe, etc. Stories must be written with an American military member and family in mind – young married, 2 children with car, 2 weeks annual leave, several 3-day weekends. Sports/adventure travel stories are popular with our readers."

THE RETIRED OFFICER MAGAZINE, 201 N. Washington St., Alexandria VA 22314. (703)549-2311. Editor: Col. Charles D. Cooper, USAF-Ret. 60% freelance written. Prefers to work with published/established writers. Monthly for officers of the 7 uniformed services and their families. Circ. 363,000. Pays on acceptance. Publishes ms an average of 9-12 months after acceptance. Byline given. Buys first serial rights. Submit seasonal material (holiday stories with a military theme) at least 9-12 months in advance. Reports on material accepted for publication within 2 months. Sample copy and writer's guidelines for 9x12 SAE with 5 first class stamps.

Nonfiction: Current military/political affairs, health and wellness, recent military history, humor, hobbies, travel, second-career job opportunities and military family lifestyle. Also, upbeat articles on aging, human interest and features pertinent to a retired military officer's milieu. True military experiences are also useful. "We rarely accept unsolicited mss. We look for detailed query letters with resumé and sample clips attached. We do not publish poetry or fillers." Buys 48 mss/year. Length: 750-2,000 words. Pays up to $500.

Photos: Query with list of stock photo subjects. Reviews 8x10 b&w photos (normal halftone). Pays $20. Original slides or transparencies must be suitable for color separation. Pays up to $125 for inside color; up to $200 for cover.

Tips: "Our readers are 55-65. We never write about them as senior citizens, yet we look for upbeat stories that take into consideration the demographic characteristics of their age group."

SEA POWER, 2300 Wilson Blvd., Arlington VA 22201-3308. Editor: James D. Hessman. Issued monthly by the Navy League of the U.S. for sea service personnel and civilians interested in naval maritime and defense matters. 10% freelance written. "We prefer queries from experts/specialists in maritime industry." Computer printout submissions acceptable; prefers letter-quality. Pays on publication. Buys all rights. Free sample copy.

Nonfiction: Factual articles on sea power and national defense in general, U.S. industrial base, mineral resources, and the U.S. Navy, U.S. Marine Corps, U.S. Coast Guard, U.S. Merchant Marine, oceanographic industries and other navies of the world. Should illustrate and expound the importance of the seas and sea power to the U.S. and its allies. Wants timely, clear, nonpedantic writing for audience that is intelligent and well-educated but not necessarily fluent in military/hi-tech terminology. No personal analysis. Material should be presented in the third person, well documented with complete attribution. No historical articles, commentaries, critiques, abstract theories, poetry or editorials. Query first. Length: 500-2,500 words. Pays $100-500 depending upon length and research involved.
Photos: Purchased with ms.
Tips: "The writer should be invisible. Copy should be understandable without reference to charts, graphs or footnotes."

SOLDIER OF FORTUNE, The Journal of Professional Adventurers, Omega Group, Ltd., Box 693, Boulder CO 80306. (303)449-3750. FAX: (303)444-5617. Editor: Robert K. Brown. 50% freelance written. A monthly magazine covering military, paramilitary, police and combat subjects. "We are an action-oriented magazine; we cover combat hot spots around the world such as Afghanistan, Central America, Angola, etc. We also provide timely features on state-of-the-art weapons and equipment; elite military and police units; and historical military operations. Readership is primarily active-duty military, veterans and law enforcement." Circ. 175,000. Pays on acceptance. Publishes ms an average of 5 months after acceptance. Byline given. Offers 25% kill fee. Buys first North American serial rights. Submit seasonal/holiday material 5 months in advance. Photocopied submissions OK. Computer printout submissions OK; prefers letter-quality. Reports in 3 weeks on queries; 1 month on mss. Sample copy $3.50; writer's guidelines for #10 SASE. Send ms to articles editor; queries to managing editor.
Nonfiction: Exposé; general interest; historical/nostalgic; how-to (on weapons and their skilled use); humor; profile; new product; personal experience; photo feature ("number one on our list"); technical; travel; combat reports; military unit reporters and solid Vietnam history. "No 'How I won the war' pieces; no op-ed pieces *unless* they are fully and factually backgrounded; no knife articles (staff assignments only). *All* submitted articles should have good art; art will sell us on an article. Buys 75 mss/year. Query with or without published clips, or send complete ms. Length: 2,500-5,000 words. Pays $300-1,200 for assigned articles; pays $200-1,000 for unsolicited articles. Sometimes pays the expenses of writers on assignment.
Photos: Send photos with submission (copies only, no originals). Reviews contact sheets and transparencies. Offers no additional payment for photos accepted with ms. Pays $46 for cover photo. Captions and identification of subjects required. Buys one-time rights.
Columns/Departments: Address to appropriate column editor (i.e., I Was There Editor). Combat weaponcraft (how-to military and police survival skills) and I Was There (first-person accounts of the arcane or unusual based in a combat or law enforcement environment), all 600-800 words. Buys 16 mss/year. Send complete ms. Length: 600-800 words. Combat weaponcraft pays $200; I was There pays $50.
Fillers: Bulletin Board editor. Newsbreaks; military/paramilitary related, "*has* to be documented." Length: 100-250 words. Pays $25.
Tips: "Submit a professionally prepared, complete package. All artwork with cutlines, double-spaced typed manuscript, cover letter including synopsis of article, supporting documentation where applicable, etc. Manuscript must be factual; writers have to do their homework and get all their facts straight. One error means rejection. We will work with authors over the phone or by letter, tell them if their ideas have merit for an acceptable article, and help them fine-tune their work. I Was There is a good place for freelancers to start. Vietnam features, if carefully researched and art heavy, will always get a careful look. Combat reports, again, with good art, are number one in our book and stand the best chance of being accepted. Military unit reports from around the world are well received as are law enforcement articles (units, police in action). If you write for us, be complete and factual; pros read *Soldier of Fortune*, and are *very* quick to let us know if we (and the author) err. We plan more articles on terrorism."

WORLD WAR II, Empire Press, 105 Loudoun Street SW, Leesburg VA 22075. (703)771-9400. Editor: C. Brian Kelly. 95% freelance written. Prefers to work with published/established writers. A bimonthly magazine covering "military operations in World War II—events, personalities, strategy, national policy, etc." Circ. 200,000. Pays on publication. Publishes ms an average of 1-2 years after acceptance. Byline given. Buys first North American serial rights. Submit anniversary-related material 1 year in advance. Reports in 2 months on queries; 3 months or more on mss. Sample copy $4; writer's guidelines for #10 SASE.
Nonfiction: World War II military history. No fiction. Buys 24 mss/year. Query. Length: 4,000 words. Pays $200.
Photos: State availability of art and photos with submission. (For photos and other art, send photocopies and cite sources. "We'll order.") Sometimes offers additional payment for photos accepted with ms. Captions and identification of subjects required. Buys one-time rights.
Columns/Department: Undercover (espionage, resistance, sabotage, intelligence gathering, behind the lines, etc.); Personalities (WW II personalities of interest); and Armaments (weapons, their use and development), all 2,000 words. Book reviews, 300-750 words. Buys 18 mss/year (plus book reviews). Query. Pays $100.

Tips: "List your sources and suggest further readings in standard format at the end of your piece — as a bibliography for our files in case of factual challenge or dispute. All submissions are on speculation. When the story's right, but the writing isn't, we'll pay a small research fee for use of the information in our own style and language."

Music

Music fans follow the latest music industry news in these publications. Types of music and musicians or specific instruments are the sole focus of some magazines. Publications geared to music industry and professionals can be found in the Trade Music section. Additional music and dance markets are included in the Entertainment section.

‡**AMERICAN SONGWRITER**, 27 Music Square E, Nashville TN 37203. (615)244-6065. Editor: Vernell Hackett. Managing Editor: Deborah Price. 50% freelance written. Bimonthly magazine, educating amateur songwriters while informing professionals. Circ. 4,000. Pays on publication. Publishes ms an average of 2 months after acceptance. Offers $10 kill fee. Buys first North American serial rights. Submit seasonal/holiday material 2 months in advance. Simultaneous submissions OK. Query for electronic submissions. Computer printout submissions OK. Reports in 2 months. Sample copy $3. Writer's guidelines for SAE.
Nonfiction: General interest, interview/profile, new product, photo feature and technical. March/April - Gospel Songwriting; July/August - Country Songwriting. "No fiction." Buys 30 mss/year. Query with published clips. Length: 300-2,000 words. Pays $25-100 for assigned articles.
Photos: State availability of photos with submission. Reviews 3x5 prints. Offers no additional payment for photos accepted with ms. Identification of subjects required. Buys one-time rights.
Columns/Departments: Artists Viewpoint (what artist looks for in a song); Producers Viewpoint (record producers' views of songwriting), 900 words; and Publisher's Viewpoint (music publisher's views of songwriting), 900 words. Buys 20 mss/year. Query with published clips. Length: 600-1,000 words. Pays $30-50.

BANJO NEWSLETTER, Box 364, Greensboro MD 21639. (301)482-6278. Editor: Hub Nitchie. 10% freelance written. Monthly magazine covering the "instructional and historical treatment of the 5-string banjo. Covers all aspects of the instrument. Tablature is used for musical examples." Circ. 7,000. Pays on publication. Byline given. Buys one-time rights. Query for electronic submissions. Computer printout submissions OK; prefers letter-quality. Reports in 1 month on queries. Free sample copy.
Nonfiction: Interviews with 5-string banjo players, banjo builders, shop owners, etc. No humorous fiction from anyone unfamiliar with the popular music field. Buys 6 mss/year. Query. Length: 500-4,000 words. Pays $20-100. Sometimes pays writers with contributor copies or other premiums "if that is what writer wants." Very seldom pays expenses of writers on assignment. "We can arrange for press tickets to musical events."
Photos: State availability of photos with submission. Reviews b&w prints. Offers $10-40/photo. Captions and identification of subjects required whenever possible. Buys one-time rights.
Columns/Departments: Buys 60 mss/year. Query. Length: 500-750 words. Payment varies.
Poetry: Poetry Editor: Don Nitchie, General Delivery, West Tisbury, MA 02575. Buys 2 poems/year. Submit maximum 1 poem at one time.
Tips: "The writer should be motivated by being a student of the 5-string banjo or interested in the folk or bluegrass music fields where 5-string banjo is featured. Writers should be able to read and write banjo tablature and know various musicians or others in the field."

BLUEGRASS UNLIMITED, Bluegrass Unlimited, Inc., Box 111, Broad Run VA 22014. (703)349-8181. Editor: Peter V. Kuykendall. 80% freelance written. Prefers to work with published/established writers. Monthly magazine on bluegrass and old-time country music. Circ. 21,500. Pays on publication. Publishes ms an average of 4 months after acceptance. Byline given. Kill fee negotiated. Buys first North American serial rights, one-time rights, all rights and second serial (reprint) rights. Submit seasonal/holiday material 4 months in advance. Photocopied submissions OK. Computer printout submissions are OK; prefers letter-quality. Reports in 2 weeks on queries; 2 months on mss. Free sample copy and writer's guidelines for #10 SASE.
Nonfiction: General interest, historical/nostalgic, how-to, interview/profile, personal experience, photo feature and travel. No "fan" style articles. Buys 75-80 mss/year. Query with or without published clips. No set word length. Pays 6-8¢/word.
Photos: State availability of photos or send photos with query. Reviews 35mm color transparencies and 3x5, 5x7 and 8x10 b&w and color prints. Pays $25-50 for b&w transparencies; $50-150 for color transparencies; $25-50 for b&w prints; and $50-150 for color prints. Identification of subjects required. Buys one-time rights and all rights.

Fiction: Ethnic and humorous. Buys 3-5 mss/year. Query. No set word length. Pays 6-8¢/word.
Tips: "We would prefer that articles be informational, based on personal experience or an interview with lots of quotes from subject, profile, humor, etc."

B-SIDE, B-Side Publishing, Box 1387, Fort Washington PA 19034. (215)542-9754 or (215)561-9027. Editor: Carol Schutzbank. Managing Editor: Sandra Garcia. 75% freelance written. A bimonthly tabloid on entertainment. *"B-Side* offers an alternative look at alternative music. It delivers in-depth interviews and intelligent reviews. It bridges the gap between larger more 'commercial' publications and grass roots, 'gonzo-styled' home grown fanzines." Circ. 5,000. Byline given. Buys first rights. Simultaneous and photocopied submissions OK. Computer printout submissions OK; prefers letter-quality. Reports in 1 month on queries; 3 months on ms. Sample copy $3. Writer's guidelines for #10 SASE.
Nonfiction: Essays, exposé, humor, interview/profile, new product, opinion, personal experience, photo feature and technical. Query with published clips. Length: 300-2,000 words. Pays up to $25 for assigned articles but sometimes pays in copies for unsolicited mss. Sometimes pays expenses of writers on assignment. State availability of photos with submission. Reviews contact sheets. Offers no additional payment for photos accepted with ms. Identification of subjects required. Buys one-time rights.
Fiction: Humorous and slice-of-life vignettes. Fiction must be oriented to music. Send complete ms. Pays in contributor's copies.
Poetry: Avant-garde, free verse and haiku. Submit maximum 3 poems. "Read the writer's guidelines."

‡FRETS MAGAZINE, GPI Publications, 20085 Stevens Creek Blvd., Cupertino CA 95014. (408)446-1105. FAX: (408)257-1088. Editor: Phil Hood. 40% freelance written. Prefers to work with published/established writers. Monthly magazine for amateur and professional acoustic string music enthusiasts; for players, makers, listeners and fans. Country, jazz, classical, blues, pop and bluegrass. For instrumentalists interested in banjo, mandolin, guitar, violin, upright bass, dobro, and others. Circ. open. Pays on acceptance. Publishes ms an average of 6 months after acceptance. Buys first serial rights. Submit seasonal/holiday material 6 months in advance. Computer printout submissions on 8½x11 sheets with legible type acceptable if not a photocopy or multiple submission. "All-caps printout unacceptable." Reports in 6 weeks. Free sample copy and writer's guidelines.
Nonfiction: General interest (artist-oriented); historical (instrument making or manufacture); how-to (instrument craft and repair); interview (with artists or historically important individuals); profile (music performer); and technical (instrument making, acoustics, instrument repair). Prefers not to see humor; poetry; general-interest articles that really belong in a less-specialized publication; articles (about performers) that only touch on biographical or human interest angles, without getting into the "how-to" nuts and bolts of musicianship. Buys 24 mss/year. Query with published clips or sample lead paragraph. Length: 1,000-2,500 words. Pays $150-350. Experimental (instrument design, acoustics), pays $100-175. Sometimes pays expenses of writers on assignment.
Photos: State availability of photos. Pays $25 minimum for b&w prints (reviews contact sheets); $200 and up for cover shot color transparencies. Captions and credits required. Buys one-time rights.
Columns/Departments: Repair Shop (instrument craft and repair); and *Frets* Visits (on-location visit to manufacturer or major music festival). Buys 10 mss/year. Query. Length: 1,200-1,700 words. Pays $75-175, including photos.
Fillers: Newsbreaks, upcoming events and music-related news.
Tips: "Our focus also includes ancillary areas of string music—such as sound reinforcement for acoustic musicians, using personal computers in booking and management, recording techniques for acoustic music, and so on. We enjoy giving exposure (and encouragement) to talented new writers. We do not like to receive submissions or queries from writers who have only a vague notion of our scope and interest. We do not cover electric guitarists. We want to see more in-depth instructional features and stories on younger artists."

‡GIG MAGAZINE, for Working Musicians, Premier Publishing, Suite 209, 17042 Devonshire, Northridge CA 91325. (818)360-6673. Editor: Greg Hofmann. 75% freelance written. Monthly magazine for musicians. "We emphasize practical information for musicians." Circ. 50,000. Pays on publication. Publishes ms an average of 2 months after acceptance. Byline given. Offers 50% kill fee. Buys first North American serial rights. Simultaneous, photocopied and previously published submissions OK. Query for electronic submissions. Computer printout submissions OK; prefers letter-quality. Reports in 2 weeks on queries. Sample copy for 9x12 SAE with 4 first class stamps. Free writer's guidelines.
Nonfiction: How-to, interview/profile, new product and technical. Buys 100 mss/year. Query with published clips. Length: 1,200-3,000 words. Pays $60-150. Sometimes pays expenses of writers on assignment.
Photos: State availability of photos with submission. Offers no additional payment for photos accepted with ms. Identification of subjects required. Buys one-time rights.
Columns/Departments: Buys 80 mss/year. Query with published clips. Length: 600-1,000 words. Pays $30-50.
Tips: "Articles must be informative and expand a musician's knowledge of the craft or business."

GUITAR PLAYER MAGAZINE, GPI Publications, 20085 Stevens Creek, Cupertino CA 95014. (408)446-1105. Editor: Tom Wheeler. 70% freelance written. Monthly magazine for persons "interested in guitars, guitarists, manufacturers, guitar builders, bass players, equipment, careers, etc." Circ. 180,000. Buys first serial and limited reprint rights. Pays on acceptance. Publishes ms an average of 3 months after acceptance. Byline given. Computer printout submissions acceptable; prefers letter-quality. Reports in 6 weeks. Free sample copy; writer's guidelines for #10 SASE.

Nonfiction: Publishes "wide variety of articles pertaining to guitars and guitarists: interviews, guitar crafts-men profiles, how-to features — anything amateur and professional guitarists would find fascinating and/or helpful. On interviews with 'name' performers, be as technical as possible regarding strings, guitars, tech-niques, etc. We're not a pop culture magazine, but a magazine for musicians." Also buys features on such subjects as a guitar museum, role of the guitar in elementary education, personal reminiscences of past greats, technical gadgets and how to work them, analysis of flamenco, etc. Buys 30-40 mss/year. Query. Length: open. Pays $100-300. Sometimes pays expenses of writers on assignment.

Photos: Reviews b&w glossy prints. Pays $50-100. Buys 35mm color transparencies. Pays $250 (for cover only). Buys one time rights.

‡HOME & STUDIO RECORDING, the Magazine for the Recording Musician, Music Maker Publications, Suite 118, 22024 Lassen St., Chatsworth CA 91311, (818)407-0744. FAX: (818)407-0882. Editor: Amy V. Ziffer. 50% freelance written. Monthly magazine on home recording, small format recording. "We rely heavily on application/technique articles in which practical information is made available to readers. Our primary purpose is to help people improve their recordings and otherwise keep them informed as to ways of making a living in music/recording." Circ. 50,000. Pays 30 days after publication. Byline given. Buys all rights. Submit seasonal/holiday material 3 months in advance. Simultaneous, photocopied and previously published submissions OK. Query for electronic submissions. Computer printout submissions OK; prefers letter-quality. Reports in 1 month. Free sample copy and writer's guidelines.

Nonfiction: Historical/nostalgic, how-to (recording techniques, studio construction, anything concerning studios), humor, interview/profile, new product, personal experience and technical. "No articles about people and studios who have gotten lots of press in the past; about high end audio and audio products; articles that do not contain practical info." Buys 50 mss/year. Query with published clips. Length: 500-4,000 words. Pays 10-11¢/word. Sometimes pays expenses of writers on assignment, must be cleared in advance.

Photos: State availability of photos with submission or send photos with submission. Reviews contact sheets, negatives, 4x5 and 2¼ transparencies, slides and prints. Offers $25 per photo. Identification of subjects required. Buys one-time rights.

Columns/Departments Scott Wilkinson, Technical Editor. Studio Focus (close-up look at a studio with something of interest for our readership. MUST contain practical info re: studio construction, equipment selection and purchase, etc.); Making It Pay (focuses on a person or group of persons who have developed a novel way of making a living in the music/recording industry) and Crosstalk (interview with an employee or principal of a manufacturer of recording products who has something to share with readers regarding technical aspects of their products). Buys 10 mss/year. Query with published clips. Length: 1,500-2,500 words. Pays 10-11¢/word.

Fillers: Anecdotes, facts, gags to illustrated by cartoonist and short humor. Buys 2/year. Length: 500-1,000 words. Pays 10-11¢/word.

Tips: "Call our offices, ask for editor or editorial assistant John Schroeder and talk over ideas before proceed-ing. We will generally request an outline of the article first to make sure it's going in the right direction. Interviews are area most open to freelancers. Again, make sure interview contains practical information and the interviewee is willing to share insights into their success and methods."

ILLINOIS ENTERTAINER, Suite 192, 2200 E. Devon, Des Plaines IL 60018. (312)298-9333. FAX: (312)298-7973. Editor: Bill Dalton. 95% freelance written. Prefers to work with published/established writers but open to new writers with "style." Monthly tabloid covering music and entertainment for consumers within 100-mile radius of Chicago interested in music. Circ. 80,000. Pays on publication. Publishes ms an average of 2 months after acceptance. Byline given. Offers 10% kill fee. Buys one-time rights. Simultaneous queries OK. Computer printout submissions acceptable "if letters are clear"; no dot-matrix. Reports in 1 month on queries; 2 months on mss. Sample copy $5.

Nonfiction: Interview/profile (of entertainment figures). No Q&A interviews. Buys 75 mss/year. Query with published clips. Length: 500-2,000 words. Pays $15-100. Sometimes pays expenses of writers on assignment.

Photos: State availability of photos. Pays $20-30 for 5x7 or 8x10 b&w prints; $125 for color cover photo, both on publication only. Captions and identification of subjects required.

Columns/Departments: Software (record reviews stress record over band or genre). Buys 50 mss/year. Query with published clips. Length: 150-250 words. Pays $6-20.

Tips: "Send clips (published or unpublished) with phone number, and be patient. Full staff has seniority, but if you know the ins and outs of the entertainment biz, and can balance that knowledge with a broad sense of humor, then you'll have a chance."

INTERNATIONAL MUSICIAN, American Federation of Musicians, Suite 600, Paramount Building, 1501 Broadway, New York NY 10036. (212)869-1330. Editor: Kelly L. Castleberry II. 10% freelance written. Prefers to work with published/established writers. Monthly for professional musicians. Pays on acceptance. Publishes ms an average of 3 months after acceptance. Byline given. Computer printout submissions OK; no dot-matrix. Reports in 2 months.
Nonfiction: Articles on prominent instrumental musicians (classical, jazz, rock or country). Send complete ms. Length: 1,500 words.

KEYBOARD MAGAZINE, GPI Publications, 20085 Stevens Creek Blvd., Cupertino CA 95014. (408)446-1105. FAX: (408)446-1088. Editor: Dominic Milano. 20% freelance written. Prefers to work with published/established writers; works with a small number of new/unpublished writers each year. Monthly magazine for those who play synthesizer, piano, organ, harpsichord, or any other keyboard instrument. All styles of music; all levels of ability. Circ. 82,000. Pays on acceptance. Publishes ms 6 months after acceptance. Byline given. Buys first serial rights and second serial (reprint) rights. Phone queries OK. Query for electronic submissions. Computer printout submissions acceptable; prefers letter-quality. Reports in 1 month. Free sample copy and writer's guidelines.
Nonfiction: "We publish articles on a wide variety of music-related topics. We're most interested in how-to oriented pieces relating to keyboard playing and/or the application of electronic music technology written in a conversational, non-academic tone. The instruments covered regularly include synthesizers, samplers, piano (electronic and acoustic), sequencers, drum machines, computers w/music software, and alternate MIDI controllers, as well as harpsichord, organ, and accordion. We cover all styles of music and our readers range from top professionals to absolute beginners. Note: All product and record reviews are done in-house." Buys 10 unsolicited mss/year. Query: "Letter should mention topic and length of article and describe basic approach." Length: 800-2,500 words. Pays $200-500 +. Sometimes pays expenses of wrtiers on assignment.
Tips: "Query first (just a few ideas at a time, rather than twenty). A musical background helps, and a knowledge of keyboard instruments is essential."

‡THE LISTEN AGAIN MUSIC NEWSLETTER, Listen Again Music, 165 Beaver St., New Brighton PA 15066. Editor: William E. Watson. 50% freelance written. Monthly newsletter on songwriting. "The newsletter seeks to improve songwriter's and musician's understanding of how to break into the music business, how to increase their income, with specific tips." Circ. 1,100. Pays on acceptance. Byline sometimes given. Offers $25 kill fee. Buys one-time rights. Submit seasonal/holiday material 3 months in advance. Photocopied submissions OK. Computer printout submissions OK; prefers letter-quality. Reports in 2 weeks on queries; 1 month on manuscripts. Sample copy $5 (note: 2 samples are sent). Free writer's guidelines.
Nonfiction: How-to (improve demos and improve songwriting), personal experience (related to music, either writing or playing) and technical (article should show how new equipment can improve a songwriter's product). "No articles about rock stars or articles that are too general." Buys 24 mss/year. Send complete ms. Length: 500-800 words. Pays $25-75.
Columns/Departments Demo Tips (specific ways to improve the sound quality of a demo tape); Writing Tips (specific ways to improve songwriting abilities). Buys 24 mss/year. Send complete ms. Length: 500-800 words. Pays $25-75.
Tips: "Writing about music can be boring. All articles submitted should have some humor to lighten things up but *must* teach our readers something about music. For the past two years all articles have been staff-written. We want to open up to outside writers but don't want to change the slant we started with. Study samples and guidelines *thoroughly*. Be open to rewriting."

THE MISSISSIPPI RAG, "The Voice of Traditional Jazz and Ragtime," 5644 Morgan Ave. S, Minneapolis MN 55419. (612)861-2446 or (612)920-0312. Editor: Leslie Johnson. 70% freelance written. Works with small number of new/unpublished writers each year. A monthly tabloid covering traditional jazz and ragtime. Circ. 3,000. Pays on publication. Publishes ms an average of 4 months after acceptance. Byline given. Buys all rights, "but writer may negotiate if he wishes to use material later." Submit seasonal/holiday material 3 months in advance. Computer printout submissions OK; prefers letter-quality. Sample copy and writer's guidelines for 9x12 SAE with 85¢ postage.
Nonfiction: Historical, interview/profile, personal experience, photo features, current jazz and ragtime, festival coverage, book reviews and record reviews. Reviews are always assigned. No "long-winded essays on jazz or superficial pieces on local ice cream social Dixieland bands." Buys 24-30 mss/year. Query with or without published clips, or send complete ms. Length: 1,500-4,000 words. Pays 1½¢/word.

For explanation of symbols, see the Key to Symbols and Abbreviations on Page 5. For unfamiliar words, see the Glossary.

Photos: Send photos with submission. Prefers b&w 5x7 or 8x10 prints. Offers $4 minimum per photo. Identification of subjects required. Buys one-time rights.

Columns/Departments: Book and Record reviews. Buys 60 assigned mss/year. Query with published clips. Pays 1½¢/word.

Tips: "Become familiar with the jazz world. The *Rag* is read by musicians, jazz/ragtime writers, historians and jazz/ragtime buffs. We want articles that have depth—solid facts and a good basic grasp of jazz and/or ragtime history. Not for the novice jazz writer. Interviews with jazz and ragtime performers are most open to freelancers. It's wise to query first because we have already covered so many performers."

MODERN DRUMMER, 870 Pompton Ave., Cedar Grove NJ 07009. (201)239-4140. Editor-in-Chief: Ronald Spagnardi. Senior Editor: Rick Mattingly. Managing Editor: Rick Van Horn. Monthly for "student, semi-pro and professional drummers at all ages and levels of playing ability, with varied specialized interests within the field." 60% freelance written. Circ. 85,000. Pays on publication. Publishes ms an average of 3 months after acceptance. Buys all rights. Photocopied and previously published submissions OK. Computer printout submissions acceptable; prefers letter-quality. Reports in 1 month. Sample copy $2.95; free writer's guidelines.

Nonfiction: How-to, informational, interview, new product, personal experience and technical. "All submissions must appeal to the specialized interests of drummers." Buys 20-30 mss/year. Query or submit complete ms. Length: 5,000-8,000 words. Pays $200-500. Pays expenses of writers on assignment.

Photos: Purchased with accompanying ms. Reviews 8x10 b&w prints and color transparencies.

Columns/Departments: Jazz Drummers Workshop, Rock Perspectives, In The Studio, Show Drummers Seminar, Teachers Forum, Drum Soloist, The Jobbing Drummer, Strictly Technique, Book Reviews and Shop Talk. "Technical knowledge of area required for most columns." Buys 40-50 mss/year. Query or submit complete ms. Length: 500-2,500 words. Pays $25-150.

‡MUSIC EXPRESS, Rock Express Communications., 47 Jefferson Ave., Toronto, Ontario M6K 1Y3 Canada. (416)538-7500. Editor: Dean Haynes. Managing Editor: Keith Sharp. 50% freelance written. Monthly magazine on contemporary music. "A contemporary consumer music covering all forms of popular music slanted at a demographic between 18-25 with equal appeal for male and female readers." Circ. 678,000. Pays 30 days after publication. Byline given. Offers 20% kill fee. Buys first North American serial rights. Submit seasonal/holiday material 2 months in advance. Simultaneous and photocopied submissions OK. Computer printout submissions OK; prefers letter-quality. Reports in 6 weeks on queries; 1 month on mss. Free sample copy and writer's guidelines.

Nonfiction: Humor, interview/profile and photo feature. Spring Audio Special; Summer Special Activities; Special College Issue; and Fall Audio Special. Buys 18 mss/year. Query. Length: 500-3,000 words. Pays $75-1,000. Sometimes pays expenses of writers on assignment.

Photos: State availability of photos with submission. Reviews transparencies and 5x7 and 8x10 prints. Offers $35-500 per photo. Captions, model releases and identification of subjects required. Buys one-time rights.

Columns/Departments: Kerry Poole. Regional (local news); Video (latest releases); Specific Music Columns (jazz, country, blues, hard rock); and Film (latest movie releases). Buys 80 mss/year. Query. Length: 200-500 words. Pays $60-250.

MUSIC MAGAZINE, Future Perfect Publishing, Box 96 Station R, Toronto Ontario M4G 323 Canada. Publisher: Valerie Fletcher. 90% freelance written. Prefers to work with published/established writers; works with a small number of new/unpublished writers each year. Quarterly magazine emphasizing classical music. Circ. 10,000. Pays on publication. Publishes ms an average of 4 months after acceptance. Byline given. Buys first North American rights, one-time rights and second serial (reprint) rights. Submit seasonal/holiday material 4 months in advance. Photocopied and previously published submissions (book excerpts) OK. Query for electronic submissions. Computer printout submissions acceptable; prefers letter-quality. Reports in 2 months. Sample copy and writer's guidelines for 9x12 SAE and $3.

Nonfiction: Interview, historical articles, photo feature and profile. "All articles should pertain to classical music and people in that world. We do not want any academic analysis or short pieces of family experiences in classical music." Query with published clips; phone queries OK. Unsolicited articles will not be returned. Length: 1,500-3,500 words. Pays $100-500. Sometimes pays expenses of writers on assignment.

Photos: State availability of photos. Pays $15-25 for 8x10 b&w glossy prints or contact sheets; $100 for color transparencies. No posed promotion photos. "Candid, lively material only." Captions required. Buys one-time rights.

Tips: "Send a sample of your writing with suggested subjects. Off-beat subjects are welcome but must be thoroughly interesting to be considered. A famous person or major subject in music are your best bets."

MUSICAL AMERICA/OPUS, 825 7th Ave., New York NY 10019. FAX: (212)586-1364. Editor: Shirley Fleming. 50% freelance written. Bimonthly. Circ. 20,000. Pays on publication. Publishes ms an average of 3-4 months after acceptance. Buys all rights. Computer printout submissions acceptable; no dot-matrix. Free sample copy and writer's guidelines.

Nonfiction: Articles on classical music and classical record reviews are generally prepared by acknowledged writers and authorities in the field, but uses freelance material. Query with published clips. Length: 1,200 words maximum. Pays $200 minimum.

Photos: New b&w photos of musical personalities, events, etc.

ONE SHOT, Attentive Writing for Neglected Rock 'N' Roll, One Shot Enterprises, Box 1284, Cincinnati OH 45201. (415)527-7121. Editor: Steve Rosen. 80% freelance written. Eager to work with new/unpublished writers. "*One Shot* is a quarterly magazine dedicated to remembering now-obscure or under-appreciated performers of rock and related musics; expecially the one-hit wonders. Uses interviews, essays and journalism." Circ. 200. Pays on publication. Publishes ms up to 1 year after acceptance. Byline given. Buys one-time, second serial (reprint) or simultaneous rights and makes work-for-hire assignments. Simultaneous, photocopied and previously published submissions OK. Computer printout submissions OK; prefers letter-quality. Reports in 1 month. Sample copy $3. Writer's guidelines for #10 SASE.

Nonfiction: Book excerpts, essays, exposé, general interest, historical/nostalgic, interview/profile, opinion, personal experience and travel. No religious/inspirational articles. Buys 16 mss/year. Query. Length: 2,500 maximum words. Pays up to $100 maximum for assigned articles. Pays with copies for nonjournalism work. Sometimes pays expenses of writers on assignment.

Photos: State availability of photos with submission. Reviews contact sheets and 8½x11 prints. Offers additional payment for photos accepted with ms. Buys one-time rights.

Columns/Departments: Speak, Memory! (personal experiences with now-obscure rock, etc., performers); and Travel (update on a place that once figured in a rock song, or performer's career, such as "Hitsville USA" studios in Detroit). Buys 10 mss/year. Query with or without published clips or send complete ms. Length: 1,000 maximum words. Pays about $50.

Tips: "*One Shot* needs 'Where are They Now' articles on obscure and neglected rock performers who once were popular. Those pieces should include interviews with the performer and others; and provide a sense of 'being there'. *One Shot* will pay for such stories. Just send me a note explaining your interests, and I'll respond with detailed suggestions. I won't disqualify anyone for not following procedures; I want to encourage a body of work on this topic. Also looking for remembrances, travel pieces, etc., concerning neglected rock."

‡OPERA CANADA, Suite 433, 366 Adelaide St. E., Toronto, Ontario M5A 3X9 Canada. (416)363-0395. Editor: Ruby Mercer. 80% freelance written. Prefers to work with published/established writers. Quarterly magazine for readers who are interested in serious music; specifically, opera. Circ. 7,000. Pays on publication. Publishes ms an average of 1 year after acceptance. Byline given. Not copyrighted. Buys first serial rights. Photocopied and simultaneous submissions OK. Computer printout submissions acceptable; no dot-matrix. Reports on material accepted for publication within 1 year. Sample copy $3.95.

Nonfiction: "Because we are Canada's only opera magazine, we like to keep 75% of our content Canadian, i.e., by Canadians or about Canadian personalities and events. We prefer informative and/or humorous articles about any aspect of music theater, with an emphasis on opera. The relationship of the actual subject matter to opera can be direct or indirect. We accept interviews with major operatic personalities. Please, no reviews of performances; we have staff reviewers." Buys 10 mss/year. Query or submit complete ms. Length (for all articles except reviews of books and records): 1,000-3,000 words. Pays $50-200.

Photos: Photos with cutlines (i.e. captions) to accompany mss are welcome. No additional payment for photos used with mss. Captions required.

Tips: "We are interested in articles with an emphasis on current or controversial issues in opera."

‡OVATION, 33 W. 60th St., New York NY 10023. Managing Editor: Charles Passy. 75% freelance written. Prefers to work with published/established writers; works with small number of new/unpublished writers each year. Monthly magazine of the classical music lifestyle, with articles detailing the personalities, trends, issues, events, recordings and audio and video products. Also articles on travel, food and wine, fashion, art and antiques. Average issue includes 4 music features, 3 lifestyle features plus audio and video product, book and record reviews and other departments. Pays on publication. Publishes ms an average of 4 months after acceptance. Byline given. Buys all rights. Submit seasonal material 8 months in advance. Computer printout submissions acceptable. Sample copy for SASE with $2.40 postage.

Nonfiction: Buys 5 unsolicited mss/year. Query with published clips. Length: 250-1,000 words (record reviews), 500-1,200 (other departments), 1,200-3,000 (features). Pays $50-750. Sometimes pays expenses of writers on assignment.

Photos: State availability of photos. May offer additional payment for photos accepted with ms. Captions required. Buys one-time rights.

RELIX MAGAZINE, Music for the Mind, Box 94, Brooklyn NY 11229. Editor: Toni A. Brown. 60% freelance written. Eager to work with new/unpublished writers. Bimonthly magazine covering rock 'n' roll music and specializing in Grateful Dead and other San Francisco and '60's related groups for readers ages 15-45. Circ. 26,000. Pays on publication. Publishes ms an average of 6 months after acceptance. Byline given. Buys all rights. Photocopied submissions OK. Computer printout submissions acceptable; prefers letter-quality. Sample copy $3.

Nonfiction: Historical/nostalgic, interview/profile, new product, personal experience, photo feature and technical. Special issues include year-end special. Query with published clips if available or send complete ms. Length open. Pays $1.50/column inch.

Columns/Departments: Query with published clips, if available, or send complete ms. Length: open. Pays variable rates.

Fiction: "We are seeking science fiction, rock and roll stories for a potential book." Query with published clips, if available, or send complete ms. Length: open. Pays variable rates.

Tips: "The most rewarding aspects of working with freelance writers are fresh writing and new outlooks."

‡**ROCK**, D.S. Magazines, 1086 Teaneck Rd., Teaneck NJ 07666. (201)833-1800. FAX: (201)833-1428. Editor: Celeste Gomes. 15% freelance written. Monthly magazine on rock'n'roll. Audience: male and female; ages 14-25. Entertainment magazine about the world of rock 'n' roll. Circ. 175,000. Pays on publication. Publishes ms an average of 2 months after acceptance. Byline given. Offers $25 kill fee. Buys first North American serial rights. Computer printout submissions OK; letter quality only. Reports in 3 weeks on queries. Free sample copy and writer's guidelines.

Nonfiction: General interest, interview/profile, new product, photo feature and technical, all dealing with music, concerts, rockers, etc. Buys approx. 50 mss/year. Query with published clips. Pays $50-100 for assigned articles.

Photos: State availability of photos with submission. Reviews any transparencies and 5x7 prints. Offers $25 b&w and $75 color per photo. Identification of subjects required. Buys one-time rights.

‡**THE ROCK HALL REPORTER**, Big "O" Publications, Box 24124, Cleveland OH 44124. Editor: Professor Witt. Managing Editor: Martha L. Rutty. 50% freelance written. Bimonthly newsletter on the Rock and Roll Hall of Fame. Circ. 10,000. Pays on publication. Publishes ms an average of 1 month after acceptance. Sometimes offers byline. Offers 25% kill fee. Makes work-for-hire assignments. Submit seasonal/holiday material 3 months in advance. Photocopied submissions OK. Computer printout submissions OK; prefers letter-quality. Reports in 6 weeks on queries; 2 months on mss. Sample copy $2 with 9x12 SAE and 2 first class stamps.

Nonfiction: Essays, exposé, general interest, historical/nostalgic, humor, interview/profile, new product, opinion, personal experience, photo feature, technical, travel and other—inside stories on Rock Hall of Fame. "No fiction." Buys 10 mss/year. Send complete ms. Length: 150-500 words. Pays $25-500 for assigned articles; $25-200 for unsolicited articles. Sometimes pays expenses of writers on assignments.

Photos: Send photos with submission. Offers no additional payment for photos accepted with ms. Identification of subjects required. Buys all rights.

THE $ENSIBLE SOUND, 403 Darwin Dr., Snyder NY 14226. Editor/Publisher: John A. Horan. 80% freelance written. Eager to work with new/unpublished writers. Quarterly magazine. "All readers are high fidelity enthusiasts, and many have a high fidelity industry-related job." Circ. 6,900. Pays on acceptance. Publishes ms an average of 3-6 months after acceptance. Byline given. Buys all rights. Simultaneous, photocopied and previously published submissions OK. Computer printout submissions OK. Reports in 2 weeks. Sample copy $2, or free with writing sample, outline, ideas.

Nonfiction: Exposé; how-to; general interest; humor; historical; interview (people in hi-fi business, manufacturers or retail); new product (all types of new audio equipment); nostalgia (articles and opinion on older equipment); personal experience (with various types of audio equipment); photo feature (on installation, or how-to tips); profile (of hi-fi equipment); and technical (pertaining to audio). "Subjective evaluations of hi-fi equipment make up 70% of our publication. We will accept 10 per issue." Buys 8 mss/year. Submit outline. Pays $25 maximum. Pays expenses of writers on assignment.

Columns/Departments: Bits & Pieces (short items of interest to hi-fi hobbyists); Ramblings (do-it-yourself tips on bettering existing systems); and Record Reviews (of records which would be of interest to audiophiles and recordings of an unusual nature). Query. Length: 25-400 words. Pays $10/page.

SONG HITS, Charlton Publications, Charlton Bldg., Division St., Derby CT 06418. (203)735-3381. Editor: Mary Jane Canetti. 60% freelance written. Works with a small number of new/unpublished writers each year. A bimonthly magazine covering recording artists—rock, heavy metal. "*Song Hits* readers are between the ages of 10 and 21. Our philosophy in writing is to gear our material toward what is currently popular with our audience." Circ. 100,000. Pays on publication. Publishes ms an average of 3 months after acceptance. Byline given. Buys all rights. Simultaneous and photocopied submissions OK. Computer printout submissions acceptable; prefers letter-quality. Reports in 2 weeks. Free sample copy.

Nonfiction: Interview/profile. Query with published clips. Length: 1,250-3,000 words.
Photos: State availability of photos with submission. Reviews contact sheets, 2x2 transparencies and 8x10 prints. Identification of subjects required. Buys one-time rights.
Columns/Departments: Concert Review (current reviews of popular touring groups), and Pick of the Litter (album reviews of current and/or up and coming talent; 8-10 per issue). Query with published clips. Length: 500-1,000 words.

SOUNDTRACK, Metropolitan Music Magazine, SoundTrack Publishing, Box 609, Ringwood NJ 07456. (201)831-1317. Editor: Don Kulak. 60% freelance written. Bimonthly music and acoustics magazine. Estab. 1988. Circ. 20,000. Pays on acceptance. Publishes ms an average of 3-4 months after acceptance. Byline sometimes given. Buys first and second serial (reprint) rights. Submit seasonal/holiday material 4 months in advance. Simultaneous, photocopied and previously published submissions OK. Computer printout submissions OK; no dot-matrix. Reports in 1 week on queries; 3 weeks on mss. Free sample copy and writer's guidelines for 9x12 SAE and $1.85 postage.
Nonfiction: Book excerpts, expose, how-to, interview/profile, new product, opinion, technical. Buys 36 mss/year. Query with published clips. Length: 1,500-5,000 words.. Pays $50-200 for assigned articles; $20-75 for unsolicited articles. Sometimes pays writers with contributor copies or other premiums rather than cash by "mutually beneficial agreement." Sometimes pays expenses of writers on assignment.
Photos: State availability of photos with submissions. Offers $10-20 per photo. Buys all rights.
Columns/Departments: The Business of Music (promotion, distribution, forming a record label; alternative markets—film scores, jingles, etc.; how-to's on generating more income from own music); Sound Input (in-depth and objective reporting on audio equipment and technology, emphasizing acoustical ramifications); Acousticraft (in-depth articles on acoustics in general, including acoustic instruments, concert halls, hearing). Buys 24 mss/year. Query with published clips. Length: 1,500-3,500 words.
Tips: "Write a letter explaining background, interests, and areas of special study and what you hope to get out of writing for our publication. All sections are open to freelancers. Writing should be fluid and direct. When describing music, the writing should paint an aural picture with good use of metaphors, and not be overly critical or pretentious. Technical writing should be well documented."

STEREO REVIEW, Diamandis Communications, Inc., 1515 Broadway, New York NY 10036. (212)719-6000. Editor-in-Chief: Louise Boundas. Music Editor: Christie Barter. Executive Editor: Michael Smolen. 75% freelance written, almost entirely by established contributing editors, and on assignment. A monthly magazine. Circ. 530,000. Pays on acceptance. Publishes ms an average of 5 months after acceptance. Byline given. Buys first North American rights or all rights. Computer printout submissions acceptable; prefers letter-quality. Sample copy for 9x12 SAE with $1.24 postage.
Nonfiction: Equipment and music reviews, how-to-buy, how-to-use, stereo and interview/profile. Buys approximately 25 mss/year. Query with published clips. Length: 1,500-3,000 words. Pays $500-800.

TRADITION, Prairie Press, Box 438, Walnut IA 51577. (712)366-1136. Editor: Robert Everhart. 20% freelance written. Bimonthly magazine emphasizing traditional country music and other aspects of pioneer living. Circ. 2,500. Pays on publication. Not copyrighted. Byline given. Buys one-time rights. Submit seasonal/holiday material 6 months in advance. Simultaneous queries, and simultaneous, photocopied, and previously published submissions OK. Computer printout submissions acceptable. Reports in 1 month. Sample copy for $1 to cover postage and handling.
Nonfiction: Historical (relating to country music); how-to (play, write, or perform country music); inspirational (on country gospel); interview (with country performers, both traditional and contemporary); nostalgia (pioneer living); personal experience (country music); and travel (in connection with country music contests or festivals). Query. Length: 800-1,200 words. Pays $25-50.
Photos: State availability of photos with query. Payment included in ms price. Reviews 5x7 b&w prints. Captions and model releases required. Buys one-time rights.
Poetry: Free verse and traditional. Buys 4 poems/year. Length: 5-20 lines. Submit maximum 2 poems with SASE. Pays $2-5.
Fillers: Clippings, jokes and anecdotes. Buys 5/year. Length: 15-50 words. Pays $5-10.
Tips: "Material must be concerned with what we term 'real' country music as opposed to today's 'pop' country music. Freelancer must be knowledgable of the subject; many writers don't even know who the father of country music is, let alone write about him."

Mystery

These magazines buy fictional accounts of crime, detective work and mystery. Additional mystery markets can be found in the Literary and "Little" section. Several magazines in the Detective and Crime category also buy mystery fiction. Skim through other sections to identify markets for fiction; many of these will buy mysteries.

ALFRED HITCHCOCK'S MYSTERY MAGAZINE, Davis Publications, Inc., 380 Lexington Ave., New York NY 10017. Editor: Cathleen Jordan. Magazine published 13 times a year emphasizing mystery fiction. Circ. 225,000. Pays on acceptance. Byline given. Buys first serial rights, second serial (reprint) rights and foreign rights. Submit seasonal/holiday material 7 months in advance. Photocopied submissions OK. Reports in 2 months. Writer's guidelines for SASE.
Fiction: Original and well-written mystery and crime fiction. Length: up to 14,000 words.

ELLERY QUEEN'S MYSTERY MAGAZINE, Davis Publications, Inc., 380 Lexington Ave., New York NY 10017. Editor: Eleanor Sullivan. 100% freelance written. Magazine published 13 times/year. Circ. 375,000. Pays on acceptance. Publishes ms an average of 6 months after acceptance. Byline given. Buys first serial rights or second serial (reprint) rights. Submit seasonal/holiday material 7 months in advance. Simultaneous, photocopied and previously published submissions OK. Computer printout submissions acceptable; prefers letter-quality. Reports in 1 month. Writer's guidelines for #10 SASE.
Fiction: Special consideration will be given to "anything timely and original. We publish every type of mystery: the suspense story, the psychological study, the deductive puzzle—the gamut of crime and detection from the realistic (including stories of police procedure) to the more imaginative (including 'locked rooms' and impossible crimes). We always need detective stories, and do not want sex, sadism or sensationalism-for-the-sake-of-sensationalism." No gore or horror; seldom publishes parodies or pastiches. Buys up to 13 mss/issue. Length: 6,000 words maximum; occasionally higher but not often. Pays 3-8¢/word.
Tips: "We have a department of First Stories to encourage writers whose fiction has never before been in print. We publish an average of 13 first stories a year."

——— *Nature, Conservation and Ecology*

These publications promote reader awareness of the natural environment, wildlife, nature preserves and ecosystems. They do not publish recreation or travel articles except as they relate to conservation or nature. Other markets for this kind of material can be found in the Regional, Sports, and Travel, Camping and Trailer categories, although magazines listed there require that nature or conservation articles be slanted to their specialized subject matter and audience. Some juvenile and teen publications also buy nature-related material for young audiences.

‡ALL OF NATURE, 382 E. Westfield Ave., Roselle Park NJ 07204. (201)245-3622. Editor: Richard Marranca. 60% freelance written. Biannual magazine on nature, ecology, vegetarianism and New Age. "Our journal is a forum for those concerned about nature in all its facets. We want to reach people who wish to preserve nature and respect animals." Estab. 1989. Circ. 2,000-3,000. Pays on publication. Publishes ms an average of 3-6 months after acceptance. Byline given. Buys one-time rights. Submit seasonal/holiday material 6 months in advance. Simultaneous and photocopied submissions OK. Computer printout submissions OK; prefers letter-quality. Reports in 1 month on queries; 2 months on mss.
Nonfiction: Book excerpts, essays, exposé, general interest, historical/nostalgic, humor, inspirational, interview/profile, new product, opinion, personal experience, photo feature, religious, technical, travel, New Age and vegetarianism. Buys 10 mss/year. Send complete ms. Length: 3,000 words maximum. Pays $10-30.
Photos: Send photos with submission. Offers $5-10 per photo. Buys one-time rights.
Columns/Departments: Book Reviews (on ecology, health, vegetarianism, spirituality, New Age), 500-2,000 words; and The New Age (essays on the New Age movement). Buys 5-10 mss/year. Send complete ms. Pays $10-30.
Fiction: Literary, adventure, experimental, fantasy, historical, mainstream and religious/spiritual. Buys 6-8 mss/year. Send complete ms. Pays $10-30.
Poetry: Avant-garde, free verse, haiku, light verse and traditional. Buys 10-15 poems/year. Submit maximum 3 poems. Pays $5-20.
Fillers: Anecdotes, facts, gags to be illustrated by cartoonist, newsbreaks and short humor. Pays $5-10.
Tips: "We are looking for finely crafted, substantial works that deal with the authenticity and wonderment of nature. Submissions can be about saving and upholding nature, or they can show the beauty of nature—as Wordsworth did so well."

AMERICAN FORESTS, American Forestry Association, 1516 P St. NW, Washington DC 20005. (202)667-3300. Editor: Bill Rooney. 70% freelance written. Bimonthly magazine. "The magazine of trees and forests, published by a citizens' organization for the advancement of intelligent management and use of our forests, soil, water, wildlife and all other natural resources necessary for an environment of high quality." Circ. 30,000. Pays on acceptance. Publishes ms an average of 8 months after acceptance. Byline given. Buys one-time rights. Phone queries OK but written queries preferred. Submit seasonal/holiday material 5 months in advance. Computer printout submissions acceptable; no dot-matrix. Reports in 2 months. Sample copy $1.20; writer's guidelines for SASE.
Nonfiction: General interest, historical, how-to, humor and inspirational. All articles should emphasize trees, forests, forestry and related issues. Buys 7-10 mss/issue. Query. Length: 2,000 words. Pays $300-700.
Photos: State availability of photos. Offers no additional payment for photos accompanying ms. Uses 8x10 b&w glossy prints; 35mm or larger color transparencies, originals only. Captions required. Buys one-time rights.
Tips: "Query should have honesty and information on photo support."

THE AMICUS JOURNAL, Natural Resources Defense Council, 40 N. 20th St., Rm. 4500, New York NY 10011. (212)727-2700. Editor: Peter Borrelli. 80% freelance written. Quarterly magazine covering national and international environmental policy. "*The Amicus Journal* is intended to provide the general public with a journal of thought and opinion on environmental affairs, particularly those relating to policies of national and international significance." Circ. 110,000. Pays on acceptance. Publishes ms an average of 6 months after acceptance. Byline given. Offers 50% kill fee. Buys first North American serial rights. Submit seasonal/ holiday material 6 months in advance. Query for electronic submissions. Computer printout submissions OK; prefers letter-quality. Reports in 6 weeks. Sample copy for 9x12 SAE with 4 first class stamps. Writer's guidelines for #10 SASE.
Nonfiction: Exposé and interview/profile. No articles not concerned with environmental issues of national or international policy significance. Buys 25 mss/year. Query with published clips. Length: 200-1,500 words. Payment negotiable. Sometimes pays expenses of writers on assignment.
Photos: State availability of photos with submssion. Reviews contact sheets, negatives, transparencies and 8x10 prints. Offers negotiable payment for photos. Captions, model releases and identification of subjects required. Buys one-time rights.
Columns/Departments: News and Comment (summary reporting of environmental issues, usually tied to topical items), 200-500 words; Articles (in-depth reporting on issues and personalities), 750-1,500 words; Book Reviews (well-informed essays on books of general interest to environmentalists interested in policy and history), 500-1,000 words. Buys 25 mss/year. Query with published clips. Payment negotiable.
Poetry: Poetry Editor: Brian Swann. Avant-garde and free verse. All poetry should be rooted in nature. Buys 20 poems/year. Pays $25.
Tips: "Except for editorials, all departments are open to freelance writers. Queries should precede manuscripts, and manuscripts should conform to the *Chicago Manual of Style*. Writers are asked to be sensitive to tone. As a policy magazine, we do not publish articles of a personal or satirical nature."

APPALACHIAN TRAILWAY NEWS, Appalachian Trail Conference, Box 807, Harpers Ferry WV 25425. (304)535-6331. 50% freelance written. Bimonthly magazine "subject matter must relate to Appalachian Trail." Circ. 22,000. Pays on acceptance. Byline given. Buys first North American serial rights or second serial (reprint) rights. Submit seasonal/holiday material 4 months in advance. Photocopied and previously published submissions OK. Reports in 1 month. Sample copy and guidelines $2.50; guidelines only for #10 SASE.
Nonfiction: Essays, general interest, historical/nostalgic, how-to, humor, inspirational, interview/profile, photo feature, technical and travel. No poetry or religious materials. Buys 15-20 mss/year. Query with or without published clips, or send complete ms. Length: 250-3,000 words. Pays $25-300. Pays expenses of writers on assignment. Publishes, but does not pay for "hiking reflections."
Photos: State availability of b&w photos with submission. Reviews contact sheets, negatives and 5x7 prints. Offers $25-125 per photo. Identification of subjects required. Negotiates future use by ATC.
Tips: "Contributors should display an obvious knowledge of or interest in the Appalachian Trail. Those who live in the vicinity of the Trail may opt for an assigned story and should present credentials and subject in which interested to the editor."

THE ATLANTIC SALMON JOURNAL, The Atlantic Salmon Federation, Suite 1030, 1435 St. Alexandre, Montreal, Quebec H3A 2G4 Canada. (514)842-8059. Editor: Terry Davis. 50-68% freelance written. Works with a small number of new/unpublished writers each year. A quarterly magazine covering conservation efforts for the Atlantic salmon. Caters to "affluent and responsive audience – the dedicated angler and conservationist of the Atlantic salmon." Circ. 20,000. Pays on publication. Publishes ms an average of 3-6 months after acceptance. Byline given. Buys first serial rights to articles and one-time rights to photos. Submit seasonal/holiday material 3 months in advance. Simultaneous queries, and simultaneous and photocopied submissions OK. Query for electronic submissions. Computer printout submissions acceptable; no dot-matrix. Reports in 2 months. Sample copy for 9x12 SAE and $1 (Canadian), or SAE with IRC; free writer's guidelines.

Close-up

Kristin Merriman
Editor
Outdoor America

Outdoor America is the quarterly magazine of the Izaak Walton League of America, a 50,000-member national conservation organization. First published in 1922, the magazine is one of the nation's most established voices for conservation. Because it serves primarily as a membership magazine for the League, its content strongly reflects the goals and the interests of the organization.

Outdoor America receives 24-36 submissions a month. Since the magazine is about 50 percent staff-written, editors generally only buy two to three articles per issue. Current editor Kristin Merriman and former editor Kevin Kasowski say the two strongest selling points for submissions are originality and authoritativeness. Original ideas or fresh angles on old ideas that jump right out when you see them are rare, they say. "Freelancers should strive to come up with ideas that editors haven't already thought of," says Kasowski.

Merriman, the new editor of the magazine, wants to see one or two well-outlined queries at a time from writers, something that proves that the idea has been well researched and well written. She encourages writers to define and explain the issue, cite specific examples but place them in a national context, then offer solutions.

Merriman has a B.S. in journalism and political science. Before she came to *Outdoor America*, she edited a book on acid rain for the Friends of the Earth, U.K. She also worked as a news and features reporter at newspapers and magazines for eight years before becoming involved in environmental issues.

Merriman advises writers to send for writer's guidelines and to read the magazine to see what kind of material is used. She says writers should not only proof and double-proof their work, but have someone else check it as well. Almost half the submissions they receive have misspellings and grammatical errors, not to mention typos, scribbles and handwritten queries. "Why should an editor think a sloppy writer would handle manuscripts — or facts — any differently? We also get a lot of good ideas for articles, but they're simply not the kind of stories our members would read or want."

Merriman says in the coming months the League will be looking for articles on ethics and the outdoors (poaching problems, vandalism in parks, angling ethics, landowner-hunter relationships, etc.); trap-shooting; groundwater pollution; state efforts to tackle pollution issues; and natural/manmade threats to national parks and wildlife refuges. Also, the magazine has used articles on general wildlife and nonfiction photo essays.

Kasowski says: "It has become increasingly clear that many conservation concerns are really all of our concerns. Conservationists need to broaden their appeal to include people who haven't really thought of themselves as environmentalists. You can't do this with one-sided propaganda and half-truths, as if the conservation world existed in a vacuum. People are smart, and you need to hit them where they live — in other words, write about conservation, but also write about how it affects their lives — not just their health, but the economy, their lifestyles, and so on. In other words, it's time to 'get real.' "

—Deborah Cinnamon

Nonfiction: Exposé, historical/nostalgic, how-to, humor, interview/profile, new product, opinion, personal experience, photo feature, technical, travel, conservation, cuisine, science, research and management. "We are seeking articles that are pertinent to the focus and purpose of our magazine, which is to inform and entertain our membership on all aspects of the Atlantic salmon and its environment, preservation and conservation." Buys 15-20 mss/year. Query with published clips and state availability of photos. Length: 1,500-3,000 words. Pays $150-300. Sometimes pays the expenses of writers on assignment.

Photos: State availability of photos with query. Pays $50 for 3x5 or 5x7 b&w prints; $50-100 for 2¼x3¼ or 35mm color slides. Captions and identification of subjects required.

Columns/Departments: Adventure Eating (cuisine) and First Person (nonfiction, anecdotal, from first person viewpoint, can be humorous). Buys about 6 mss/year. Length: 1,000-1,500 words. Pays $100.

Fiction: Adventure, fantasy, historical, humorous and mainstream. "We don't want to see anything that does not deal with Atlantic salmon directly or indirectly. Wilderness adventures are acceptable as long as they deal with Atlantic salmon." Buys 3 ms/year. Query with published clips. Length: 3,000 words maximum. Pays $150-300.

Fillers: Clippings, jokes, anecdotes and short humor. Length: 100-300 words average. Does not pay. Cartoons, single panel, $25-50.

Tips: "We will be buying more consumer oriented articles—travel, equipment. Articles must reflect informed and up-to-date knowledge of Atlantic salmon. Writers need not be authorities, but research must be impeccable. Clear, concise writing is a plus, and submissions must be typed. Anecdote, River Log and photo essays are most open to freelancers. The odds are that a writer without a background in outdoors writing and wildlife reporting will not have the 'informed' angle I'm looking for. Our readership is well-read and critical of simplification and generalization."

‡AUDUBON, The Magazine of the National Aubudon Society, National Audubon Society, 950 Third Ave., New York NY 10022. Editor: Les Line. 85% freelance written. Bimonthly magazine on conservation, environment and natural history. "We are edited for people who delight in, care about and are willing to fight for the protection of wildlife and natural resources." Circ. 430,000. Pays on acceptance. Byline given. Offers negotiable kill fee, but prefers not to use. Buys first North American serial rights, first rights and second serial (reprint) rights (rarely). Query for electronic submissions. Computer printout submissions OK; prefers letter-quality. Reports in 6-12 weeks. Sample copy $4 with 8½x11 SAE and $2.40 in postage. Free writer's guidelines.

Nonfiction: Book excerpts (well in advance of publication), essays, exposé, historical, humor, interview/profile, opinion and photo feature. "No poorly written, ill-researched or duplicative articles; things that sound as if they were written for a small-town newspaper or encyclopedia." Length: 250-5,000 words. Pays $250-2,500. Pays expenses of writers on assignment.

Photos: Reviews 35mm transparencies. Offers page rates per photo on publication. Caption info and identification of subjects required. Write for photo guidelines.

Fiction: Appropriate to our audience. Send complete ms. Length: 500-3,000 words. Pays $250-2,000.

Tips: "Because we are presently overstocked, we are not actively soliciting freelance submissions. However, a *good* story, *well* written, always seems to find room. But, please, study the magazine carefully before querying."

BIRD WATCHER'S DIGEST, Pardson Corp., Box 110, Marietta OH 45750. Editor: Mary Beacom Bowers. 60% freelance written. Works with a small number of new/unpublished writers each year. Bimonthly magazine covering natural history—birds and bird watching. "*BWD* is a nontechnical magazine interpreting ornithological material for amateur observers, including the knowledgeable birder, the serious novice and the backyard bird watcher; we strive to provide good reading and good ornithology." Circ. 80,000. Pays on publication. Publishes ms an average of 1 year after acceptance. Byline given. Buys one-time rights, first serial rights and second serial (reprint) rights. Submit seasonal/holiday material 6 months in advance. Previously published submissions OK. Computer printout submissions acceptable; no dot-matrix. Reports in 6 weeks. Sample copy $3; writer's guidelines for #10 SASE.

Nonfiction: Book excerpts, how-to (relating to birds, feeding and attracting, etc.), humor, personal experience and travel (limited—we get many). "We are especially interested in fresh, lively accounts of closely observed bird behavior and displays and of bird watching experiences and expeditions. We often need material on less common species or on unusual or previously unreported behavior of common species." No articles on pet or caged birds; none on raising a baby bird. Buys 75-90 mss/year. Send complete ms. Length: 600-3,500 words. Pays $25-50 minimum.

Photos: Send photos with ms. Pays $10 minimum for b&w prints; $25 minimum for color transparencies. Buys one-time rights.

Poetry: Avant-garde, free verse, light verse and traditional. No haiku. Buys 12-18 poems/year. Submit maximum 3 poems. Length 8-20 lines. Pays $10.

Tips: "We are aimed at an audience ranging from the backyard bird watcher to the very knowledgeable birder; we include in each issue material that will appeal at various levels. We always strive for a good geographical spread, with material from every section of the country. We leave very technical matters to others, but we want facts and accuracy, depth and quality, directed at the veteran bird watcher and at the enthusiastic novice. We stress the joys and pleasures of bird watching, its environmental contribution, and its value for the individual and society."

ENVIRONMENT, 4000 Albemarle St. NW, Washington DC 20016. Managing Editor: Barbara T. Richman. 2% freelance written. For citizens, scientists, business and government executives, teachers, high school and college students interested in environment or effects of technology and science in public affairs. Magazine published 10 times/year. Circ. 17,000. Buys all rights. Byline given. Pays on publication to professional writers. Publishes ms an average of 5 months after acceptance. Photocopied submissions OK. Computer printout submissions acceptable; no dot-matrix. Reports in 6-8 weeks. Query or submit 3 double-spaced copies of complete ms. Sample copy $4.50.
Nonfiction: Scientific and environmental material, and effects of technology on society. Preferred length: 2,500-4,500 words for full-length article. Pays $100-300, depending on material. Also accepts shorter articles (1,100-1,700 words) for "Overview" section. Pays $75. "All full-length articles must be annotated (referenced), and all conclusions must follow logically from the facts and arguments presented." Prefers articles centering around policy-oriented, public decision-making, scientific and technological issues.

ENVIRONMENTAL ACTION, 1525 New Hampshire Ave. NW, Washington DC 20036. (202)745-4870. FAX: (202)745-4880. Editors: Rose Marie Audette and Hawley Truax. 30% freelance written. Bimonthly magazine on environmental news and policy. *"Environmental Action* provides balanced reporting on key environmental issues facing the U.S. — particularly at a national level. Articles are written for a general audience — we don't assume any knowledge of environmental conditions or problems." Circ. 16,000. Pays on publication. Publishes ms an average of 2 months after acceptance. Kill fee negotiated. Byline given. Buys first North American serial rights or second serial (reprint) rights. Simultaneous and photocopied submissions OK (author must specify that material is being submitted elsewhere). Computer printout submissions OK; prefers letter-quality. Reports in 4 months. Sample copy for 9x12 SAE with 4 first class stamps; free writer's guidelines.
Nonfiction: Exposé, profile, news feature, political analysis, book reviews. No nature appreciation, personal history, adventure in nature, academic/journal articles, or opinion articles. Buys 20 mss/year. Query with published clips and résumé, or send complete ms. Length: 250-3,000 words. Pays $40-300. Sometimes pays expenses of writers on assignment.
Photos: State availability of photos (b&w prints preferred) with submission. Reviews contact sheets, negatives and prints. Offers $25/photo, $50/cover. Captions required. Buys one-time rights.

‡FORESTS & PEOPLE, Official Publication of the Louisiana Forestry Association, Louisiana Forestry Association, Drawer 5067, Alexandria LA 71301. (318)443-2558. Editor: John R. Gormley. 50% freelance written. Works with a small number of new/unpublished writers each year. Quarterly magazine covering forests, forest industry, wood-related stories, wildlife for general readers, both in and out of the forest industry. Circ. 8,500, readership 39,000. Pays on acceptance. Publishes ms an average of 6 months after acceptance. Byline given. Not copyrighted. Submit seasonal/holiday material 2 months in advance. Simultaneous queries, and simultaneous, photocopied, and previously published submissions OK. Computer printout submissions OK; no dot-matrix. Reports in 2 weeks on queries; 3 weeks on mss. Sample copy $1.75; writer's guidelines for #10 SASE.
Nonfiction: General interest (recreation, wildlife, crafts with wood, festivals); historical/nostalgic (logging towns, historical wooden buildings, forestry legends); interview/profile (of forest industry execs, foresters, loggers, wildlife managers, tree farmers); photo feature (of scenic forest, wetlands, logging operations); and technical (innovative equipment, chemicals, operations, forestland studies, or industry profiles). No research papers. Articles may cover a technical subject but must be understandable to the general public." Buys 12 mss/year. Query with published clips. Length: open. Pays $100.
Photos: State availability of photos. Reviews b&w and color slides. Identification of subjects required.

HIGH COUNTRY NEWS, High Country Foundation, Box 1090, Paonia CO 81428. (303)527-4898. Editor: Betsy Marston. 80% freelance written. Works with a small number of new/unpublished writers each year. Biweekly tabloid covering environment and natural resource issues in the Rocky Mountain states for environmentalists, politicians, companies, college classes, government agencies, etc. Circ. 7,500. Pays on publication. Publishes ms an average of 2 months after acceptance. Byline given. Buys one-time rights. Computer printout submissions acceptable if "double-spaced (at least) and legible"; prefers letter-quality. Reports in 1 month. Free sample copy and writer's guidelines.
Nonfiction: Reporting (local issues with regional importance); exposé (government, corporate); interview/profile; opinion; personal experience; and centerspread photo feature. Special issues include those on states in the region. Buys 100 mss/year. Query. Length: 3,000 words maximum. Pays 5-10¢/word. Sometimes pays the expenses of writers on assignment.

Photos: Send photos with ms. Reviews b&w prints. Captions and identification of subjects required.
Poetry: Chip Rawlins, poetry editor, 67½ S. 500 W., Logan UT 84321. Avant-garde, free verse, haiku, light verse and traditional. Pays in contributor copies.
Tips: "We use a lot of freelance material, though very little from outside the Rockies. Start by writing short, 500-word news items of timely, regional interest."

INTERNATIONAL WILDLIFE, National Wildlife Federation, 1400 16th St. NW, Washington DC 20036-2266. FAX: (703)442-7332. Editor: Jonathan Fisher. 85% freelance written. Prefers to work with published/established writers. Bimonthly for persons interested in natural history, outdoor adventure and the environment. Circ. 400,000. Pays on acceptance. Publishes ms an average of 4 months after acceptance. Usually buys all rights to text. "We are now assigning most articles but will consider detailed proposals for quality feature material of interest to a broad audience." Computer printout submissions acceptable; prefers letter quality. Reports in 6 weeks. Writer's guidelines for #10 SASE.
Nonfiction: Focuses on world wildlife, environmental problems and man's relationship to the natural world as reflected in such issues as population control, pollution, resource utilization, food production, etc. Stories deal with non-U.S. subjects. Especially interested in articles on animal behavior and other natural history, first-person experiences by scientists in the field, well-reported coverage of wildlife-status case studies which also raise broader themes about international conservation, and timely issues. Query. Length: 2,000-2,500 words. Also in the market for short, 750-word "one pagers." Examine past issue for style and subject matter. Pays $1,200 minimum. Sometimes pays expenses of writers on assignment.
Photos: Purchases top-quality color photos; prefers packages of related photos and text, but single shots of exceptional interest and sequences also considered. Prefers Kodachrome or Fujichrome transparencies. Buys one-time rights.

MICHIGAN NATURAL RESOURCES MAGAZINE, State of Michigan Department of Natural Resources, Box 30034, Lansing MI 48909. (517)373-9267. Editor: N.R. McDowell. Managing Editor: Richard Morscheck. 60% freelance written. Works with a small number of new/unpublished writers each year. Bimonthly magazine covering natural resources in the Great Lakes area. Circ. 125,000. Pays on acceptance. Publishes ms an average of 6 months after acceptance. Byline given. Offers 100% kill fee. Buys first rights. Submit seasonal/holiday material 1 year in advance. Computer printout submissions acceptable; no dot-matrix. Reports in 1 month. Sample copy for $2.50 and 9x12 SAE; writer's guidelines for #10 SASE.
Nonfiction: "All material must pertain to this region's natural resources: lakes, rivers, wildlife, flora and special features. No personal experience, domestic animal stories or animal rehabilitation." Buys 24 mss/year. Query with clips of published work. Length: 1,000-4,000 words. Pays $150-400. Sometimes pays the expenses of writers on assignment.
Photos: Gijsbert (Nick) vanFrankenhuyzen, photo editor. "Photos submitted with an article can help sell it, but they must be razor sharp in focus." Send photos with ms. Pays $50-200 for 35mm color transparencies; Fuji or Kodachrome preferred. Model releases and identification of subjects required. Buys one-time rights.
Tips: "We hope to exemplify why Michigan's natural resources are valuable to people and vice versa."

NATIONAL WILDLIFE, National Wildlife Federation, 8925 Leesburg Pike, Vienna VA 22184. (703)790-4510. Editor-in-Chief: Bob Strohm. Editor: Mark Wexler. 90% freelance written. Works with a small number of new/unpublished writers each year. Bimonthly magazine on wildlife, natural history and environment. "Our purpose is to promote wise use of the nation's natural resources and to conserve and protect wildlife and its habitat. We reach a broad audience that is largely interested in wildlife conservation and nature photography. We avoid too much scientific detail and prefer anecdotal, natural history material." Circ. 900,000. Pays on acceptance. Publishes ms an average of 1 year after acceptance. Offers 25% kill fee. Buys all rights. Submit seasonal/holiday material 8 months in advance. Computer printout submissions acceptable; prefers letter-quality. Reports in 6 weeks. Sample copy for 9x12 SAE and 4 first class stamps; writer's guidelines for #10 SASE.
Nonfiction: General interest (2,500-word features on wildlife, new discoveries, behavior, or the environment); how-to (an outdoor or nature related activity); personal experience (outdoor adventure); photo feature (wildlife); and short 700-word features on an unusual individual or new scientific discovery relating to nature. Buys 50 mss/year. Query with or without published clips. Length: 750-2,500 words. Pays $500-1,750. Sometimes pays expenses of writers on assignment.
Photos: John Nuhn, photo editor. State availability of photos or send photos with query. Reviews 35mm color transparencies. Pays $250-750. Buys one-time rights.
Tips: "Writers can break in with us more readily by proposing subjects (initially) that will take only one or two pages in the magazine (short features)."

‡OCEAN REALM, Magazine of the Sea, 342 W. Sunset Rd., San Antonio TX 78209. (512)824-8099. Editors: Charlene deJori and Cheryl Schorp. 90% freelance written. Quarterly magazine covering all subjects relating to the sea—scuba diving, natural history, travel, adventure, science, ecology, oceanography, geography, people and cultures, seafood—all with emphasis on expanding some awareness of the ocean. Circ. 40,000. Pays on publication. Computer printout submissions OK; prefer letter-quality. Reports in 1 month on queries. Sample copy $5.95 with 9x12 SASE; writer's guidelines for #10 SASE.

Nonfiction: Historical/nostalgic, personal experience, travel, science and anything relating to the sea. Query with or without published clips, or send complete ms. Length: 3,000-4,000 words. Pays $50 per page for articles and photographs.

Photos: Send photos with submission, registered—return postage for photos a must. Offers $25 per photo, purchased with or without ms.

Columns/Departments: Marine Life (sea animals), 1,000 words; Ocean Art (artists of marine subjects), 500 words; Ocean Profile (unsung heroes working in the sea), 1,000 words; Marine Cuisine (seafood and seafood industry), 1,000-1,500 words.

Tips: "This is an excellent market for new, untried writers who have something to say about places they've gone and things they've seen. We're as much interested in personal experience and unusual approaches to a foreign land and culture as we are in the scenery underwater; the influence of the ocean on the land, however, should be a central point of a story."

OCEANS, Ocean Magazine Associates, Inc., 2001 W. Main St., Stamford CT 06902. Editor: Richard Covington. 100% freelance written. Prefers to work with published/established writers and works with small number of new/unpublished writers each year. Bimonthly magazine; 72 pages. For people who love the sea. Circ. 50,000. Pays on acceptance. Publishes ms an average of 3 months after acceptance. Byline given. Buys first serial rights; some second serial (reprint) rights. Submit seasonal/holiday material 4 months in advance. Simultaneous and photocopied submissions OK, if identified as such. Query for electronic submissions. Computer printout submissions acceptable if legible. Reports in 2 months. Sample copy $3.50; writer's guidelines for SASE.

Nonfiction: "We want articles on the worldwide realm of salt water: marine life (biology and ecology), oceanography, maritime history, marine painting and other arts, geography, undersea exploration, voyages, ships, coastal areas including environmental problems, seaports and shipping, islands, aquaculture, peoples of the sea, including anthropological materials. Writing should be direct, factual, very readable; not cute, flippant or tongue-in-cheek. Buys 60 mss/year. Query with SASE. Length: 1,000-6,000 words. Pays $750-1,000. Sometimes pays expenses of writers on assignment.

Tips: "*Oceans*' purpose is how to use, enjoy and learn from the world's seas without damaging them. The magazine takes as its province travel, personalities, sporting, cultural and recreational pursuits, scientific explorations and historical discoveries—anything under the sun having to do with the sea. We could use more profiles of important people in the marine world, and more articles of interest to cruise ship passengers."

OCEANUS, The International Magazine of Marine Science and Policy, Woods Hole Oceanographic Institution, Woods Hole MA 02543. (508)548-1400, ext. 2386. FAX: (508)548-1400, ext. 2600. Editor: T.M. Hawley. Assistant Editor: James Hain. 10% freelance written. "*Oceanus* is an international quarterly magazine that monitors significant trends in ocean research, technology and marine policy. Its basic purpose is to encourage wise, environmentally responsible use of the oceans. In addition, two of the magazine's main tasks are to explain the significance of present marine research to readers and to expose them to the substance of vital public policy questions." Circ. 15,000. Pays on publication. Publishes ms an average of 3 months after acceptance. Byline given. Buys all rights. Simultaneous queries OK. Computer printout submissions acceptable; no dot-matrix. Reports in 2 months. Sample copy $4; free writer's guidelines.

Nonfiction: Interview/profile and technical. *Oceanus* publishes 4 thematic issues/year. Most articles are commissioned. Length: 2,700-3,500 words. Pays $300 minimum. Sometimes pays expenses of writers on assignment.

Photos: State availability of photos. Reviews b&w and color contact sheets and 8x10 prints. Pays variable rates depending on size; $125/full-page b&w print. Captions required. Buys one-time rights.

Tips: The writer has a better chance of breaking in at this publication with short articles and fillers. "Most of our writers are top scientists in their fields."

OUTDOOR AMERICA, 1401 Wilson Blvd., Level B, Arlington VA 22209. (703)528-1818. Editor: Kristin Merriman. 50-75% freelance written. Prefers to work with published/established writers. Quarterly magazine about natural resource conservation and outdoor recreation for sports enthusiasts and local conservationists who are members of the Izaak Walton League. Circ. 50,000. Pays on publication. Publishes ms an average of 4 months after acceptance. Byline given. Buys all rights or first serial rights, depending on arrangements with author. "Considers previously published material if there's not a lot of audience overlap." Query first. Submit seasonal material 6 months in advance. Simultaneous and photocopied submissions OK, if so indicated. Computer printout submissions acceptable; no dot-matrix. Reports in 2 months. Sample copy $1.50 with 9x12 SAE; writer's guidelines for SASE.

Nonfiction: "We are interested in thoroughly researched, well-written pieces on current natural resource and recreation issues of national importance (threats to water, fisheries, wildlife habitat, air, public lands, soil, etc.); articles on wildlife management controversies, and first-person essays and humor pieces on outdoor recreation themes (fishing, hunting, camping, ethical outdoor behavior, etc.)." Length: 1,500-2,500 words. Payment: minimum 20¢/word.

Columns/Departments: Interested in shorter articles for the following departments: "Closer to Home" (short articles on enviromental/consumer problems—e.g. radon, lawn chemicals, etc.); "From the Naturalist's Notebook" (pieces that give insight into the habits and behavior of animals, fish, birds). Length: 500-600 words. Payment: minimum 10¢/word.

Photos: Reviews 5x7 b&w glossy prints and 35mm and larger color transparencies. Additional payment for photos with ms negotiated. Pays $225 for covers. Captions and model releases required. Buys one-time rights.

Tips: "Writers should obtain guidelines and sample issue *before* querying us. They will understand our needs and editorial focus much better if they've done this. Queries submitted without the writer having read the guidelines are *almost always* off base and almost always rejected."

‡**PACIFIC DISCOVERY**, California Academy of Sciences, Golden Gate Park, San Francisco CA 94118. (415)750-7117. Editor: Janet Cox. 100% freelance written. Prefers to work with published/established writers. "A journal of nature and culture around the world read by scientists, naturalists, teachers, students, and others having a keen interest in knowing the natural world more thoroughly." Published quarterly by the California Academy of Sciences. Circ. 25,000. Buys first North American serial rights on articles; one-time rights on photos. Pays on publication. Publishes ms an average of 1 year after acceptance. Query for electronic submissions. Computer printout submissions acceptable; Usually reports within 3 months. Sample copy for 9×12 SAE and $1.10 postage; writer's guidelines for #10 SASE.

Nonfiction: "Subjects of articles include behavior and natural history of animals and plants, ecology, evolution, anthropology, geology, paleontology, biogeography, taxonomy and related topics in the natural sciences. Occasional articles are published on the history of natural science, exploration, astronomy and archaeology. Emphasis is on current research findings. Authors need not be scientists; however, all articles must be based, at least in part, on firsthand fieldwork." Query with 100-word summary of projected article for review before preparing finished ms. Length: 1,000-3,000 words. Pays 24¢/word.

Photos: Send photos with submission "even if an author judges that his own photos should not be reproduced. Referrals to professional photographers with coverage of the subject will be greatly appreciated." Reviews 35mm, 4x5 or other color transparencies or 8x10 b&w glossy prints. Offers $75-175 and $200 for the cover. Buys one-time rights.

SEA FRONTIERS, 3979 Rickenbacker Causeway, Virginia Key, Miami FL 33149. (305)361-5786. Executive Editor: Jean Bradfisch. 95% freelance written. Works with a small number of new/unpublished writers each year. Bimonthly. "For anyone interested in the sea, its conservation, and the life it contains. Our audience is professional people for the most part; people in executive positions and students." Circ. 25,000. Pays on acceptance. Publishes ms an average of 4-10 months after acceptance. Byline given. Buys first serial rights. Will consider photocopied submissions "if very clear." Computer printout submissions acceptable; no dot-matrix. Reports on submissions in 2 months. Sample copy $3; writer's guidelines for SASE.

Nonfiction: "Articles (with illustrations) covering interesting and little known facts about the sea, marine life, chemistry, geology, physics, fisheries, mining, engineering, navigation, influences on weather and climate, ecology, conservation, explorations, discoveries or advances in our knowledge of the marine sciences, or describing the activities of oceanographic laboratories or expeditions to any part of the world. Emphasis should be on research and discoveries rather than personalities involved." Buys 40-50 mss/year. Query. Length: 1,000-3,000 words. Pays $150-450.

Photos: Reviews 8x10 b&w glossy prints and 35mm (or larger) color transparencies. Pays $100 for color used on front and $60 for the back cover.

Tips: "Query should include a paragraph or two that tells the subject, the angle or approach to be taken, and the writer's qualifications for covering this subject or the authorities with whom the facts will be checked."

SIERRA, 730 Polk St., San Francisco CA 94109. (415)923-5656. Editor-in-Chief: Jonathan F. King. Managing Editor: Annie Stine. Senior Editor: Joan Hamilton. Associate Editors: Reed McManus, Barbara Fuller. 80% freelance written. Works with a small number of new/unpublished writers each year. Bimonthly magazine emphasizing conservation and environmental politics for people who are well educated, activist, outdoor-oriented and politically well informed with a dedication to conservation. Circ. 375,000. Pays on acceptance. Publishes ms an average of 6 months after acceptance. Byline given. Buys first North American serial rights. Photocopied submissions OK. Query for electronic submissions. Computer printout submissions acceptable; prefers letter-quality. Reports in 6 weeks. Writer's guidelines for SAE and 2 first class stamps.

Nonfiction: Exposé (well-documented on environmental issues of national importance such as energy, wilderness, forests, etc.); general interest (well-researched pieces on areas of particular environmental concern); historical (relevant to environmental concerns); how-to and equipment pieces (on camping, climbing, outdoor photography, etc.); profiles (of environmental activists); interview (with very prominent figures in the field); photo feature (photo essays on threatened or scenic areas); and journalistic treatments of semi-technical topics (energy sources, wildlife management, land use, waste management, etc.). No "My trip to . . ." or "why we must save wildlife/nature" articles; no poetry or general superficial essays on environmentalism and local environmental issues. Buys 10-15 mss/issue. Query with published clips. Length: 300-3,000 words. Pays $75-1,500. Sometimes pays limited expenses of writers on assignment.

Photos: Silvana Nova, art and production manager. State availability of photos. Pays $300 maximum for color transparencies; more for cover photos. Buys one-time rights.

Columns/Departments: Book reviews. Buys 20-25 mss/year. Length: 750-1,000 words. Pays $100; submit queries to Mark Mardon, assistant editor. For Younger Readers, natural history and conservation topics presented for children ages 8 to 13. Pays $200-500; submit queries to Reed McManus, associate editor.

Tips: "Queries should include an outline of how the topic would be covered and a mention of the political appropriateness and timeliness of the article. Familiarity with Sierra Club positions and policies is recommended. Statements of the writer's qualifications should be included. We don't have fillers in our format. Our redesign introduced new departments (Afield and Hot Spots) that use shorter pieces than we've been able to previously use."

‡SNOWY EGRET, The Fair Press, RR #1, Box 354, Poland IN 47868. (812)829-4339. Editor: Karl Barnebey. 95% freelance written. Semiannual magazine about natural history from literary, artistic, philosophical and historical perspectives. "We are interested in works that celebrate the abundance and beauty of nature, encourage a love and respect for the natural world, and examine the variety of way, both positive and negative, through which human beings interact with the environment." Circ. 400. Pays on publication. Publishes ms an average of 6 months after acceptance. Buys first North American serial rights and one-time rights. Submit seasonal/holiday material 6 months in advance. Simultaneous and photocopied submissions OK. Computer printout submissions OK; prefers letter-quality. Reports in 2 weeks on queries; 1 month on mss. Sample copy $5 with 9x12 SAE and 6 first class stamps. Writer's guidelines for #10 SASE.

Nonfiction: Essays, general interest, historical, how-to, humor, inspirational, interview/profile, opinion, personal experience and travel. "No topical, dated articles, highly scientific or technical pieces." Buys 20 mss/year. Send complete ms. Length: 500-10,000. Pays $2/page.

Fiction: Literary with natural history orientation. "No popular and genre fiction." Buys up to 10 mss/year. Send complete ms. Length: 500-10,000. Pays $2/page.

Poetry: Alan Seabury, 67 Century St., West Medford, MA 02155. Nature-oriented: avant-garde, free verse, haiku, light verse and traditional. Buys 20 poems/year. Pays $2/poem to $4/page.

Tips: "Make sure that all general points, ideas, messages, etc. are thoroughly rooted in detailed observations, shared wtih the reader through description, dialogue, and narrative. The reader needs to see what you've seen, live what you've lived. Whenever possible the subject shown should be allowed to carry its own message, to speak for itself. We look for book reviews, essays, poetry, fiction, conservation and environmental studies based on first-hand observations of plants and animals that show an awareness of detail and a thoroughgoing familiarity with the organism in question."

Personal Computers

Personal computer magazines continue to change and evolve. The most successful have a strong focus on a particular family of computers or widely-used applications and carefully target a specific type of computer use. Magazines serving MS-DOS and Macintosh families of computers are expected to grow, while new technology also will offer opportunities for new titles. Some of the magazines offer an on-line service for readers in which they can get the magazine alone or with a supplement on computer disk. Be sure you see the most recent issue of a magazine before submitting material to it.

‡A.N.A.L.O.G. COMPUTING, The Magazine for ATARI Computer Owners, LFP, Inc., 9171 Wilshire Blvd., Suite 300, Beverly Hills CA 90210. (213)858-7100. 80% freelance written. Monthly magazine covering the Atari home computer. Pays on publication. Publishes ms an average of 2-6 months after acceptance. Byline given. Buys all rights. Submit seasonal/holiday material 4 months in advance. Photocopied submissions OK. Computer printout submissions acceptable; prefers letter-quality to dot-matrix. Query for electronic submissions. Reports in 2 weeks. Sample copy $3; writer's guidelines for #10 SASE.

Nonfiction: How-to and technical. "We publish beginner's articles, educational programs, utilities, multifunction tutorials, do-it-yourself hardware articles and games (preferably arcade-style in Basic and/or Assembly language). We also publish reviews of Atari software and hardware." Buys 150 mss/year. Send complete ms. Length: open. Pays $75-400. Sometimes pays expenses of writers on assignment.

Photos: Send photos with ms. Captions required, "clipped to the photo or taped to the back." Buys all rights.

Columns/Departments: Atari software and hardware reviews. Buys 30 mss/year. Send complete ms. Length: open.

Tips: "Almost all submissions are from people who read the magazine regularly and use the Atari home computers. We have published many first-time authors. We have published programs written in BASIC, ASSEMBLY, PILOT, FORTH, LISP, and some information on PASCAL. When submitting any program over 30 lines, authors must send a copy of the program on magnetic media, either cassette or disk. We strive to publish personable, down-to-earth articles as long as the style does not impair the technical aspects of the article. Authors should avoid sterile, lifeless prose. Occasional humor (detailing how the author uses his or her computer or tackles a programming problem) is welcome."

AMAZING COMPUTING, PiM Publications, Inc., 1 Currant Place, Box 869, Fall River MA 02720. (617)678-4200. Submissions Editor: Elizabeth G. Fedorzyn. Managing Editor: Donald D. Hicks. 90% freelance written. Monthly magazine for the Commodore Amiga computer system user. Circ. 35,000. Pays on publication. Publishes ms an average of 1-2 months after acceptance. Byline given. Buys all rights. Query for electronic submissions. Computer printout submissions OK. Sample copy for $5; free writer's guidelines.

Nonfiction: How-to, new product, technical, reviews and tutorials. Buys 100 mss/year. Query. Length: 1,000 words minimum. Pays $65/page. Sometimes pays the expenses of writers on assignment.

Photos: Send photos with submission. Reviews 4x5 prints. Offers $25 per photo. Captions required. Buys all rights.

Columns/Departments: Reviews, Programs. Buys 200 mss/year. Query. Length: 1,000-5,000 words.

AMIGAWORLD, Exploring the Amiga, IDGC/P, 80 Elm St., Peterborough NH 03458. (603)924-9471. FAX: (603)924-9384. Editor: Guy Wright. Managing Editor: Shawn Laflamme. 90% freelance written. Eager to work with new/unpublished writers. Monthly magazine for users of the Amiga computer from Commodore. "We help people understand the inner workings of the machine so that they can better use and enjoy their computer." Circ. 75,000. Pays on publication. Publishes ms an average of 3 months after acceptance. Byline given. Buys all rights. Submit seasonal/holiday material 4 months in advance. Photocopied submissions OK. Query for electronic submissions. Computer printout submissions OK; prefers letter-quality. Reports in 1 month on queries; 2 months on mss. Writer's guidelines for #10 SASE.

Nonfiction: Bob Ryan, articles editor. General interest, how-to, humor (rarely), personal experience and technical—all related to programming or using Amiga computer. "The magazine features informative, interesting, high quality articles, tutorials, hints and tips, news and reviews about the Amiga. We don't want to see any program listings over 20 lines or articles on 'how I got started' or 'why the Amiga computer is so great.' " Buys 50 mss/year. Query with or without published clips, or send complete ms. Length: 2,000-4,000 words. Pays $100-1,500 for assigned articles; pays $100-800 for unsolicited articles. Sometimes pays the expenses of writers on assignment.

Photos: Send photos with submission. Reviews negatives, transparencies and prints. Offers no additional payment for photos accepted with ms. Captions required. Buys all rights.

Columns/Departments: Barbara Gefvert, reviews editor. Reviews (hardware and software reviews). "All reviews are assigned by us. Send one page and biography and areas of expertise and we will contact you." Buys 40 mss/year. Length: 500-1,500 words. Pays $50-300. Reviewer's guidelines for #10 SASE.

Tips: "The author should have a good knowledge of the Amiga computer or have access to one. Most of our articles are about the computer itself, but we do publish features about famous people using Amigas or unique applications. If you have an idea for an article give us a call first. We are more than happy to discuss on the phone and even suggest topics. The expected sales of the new Commodore Amiga 500 and Amiga 2000 will mean we plan more beginner level articles dealing with the Amiga computer."

ANTIC MAGAZINE, The Atari Resource, Antic Publishing Co., 544 2nd St., San Francisco CA 94107. (415)957-0886. Editor: Nat Friedland. 75% freelance written. Eager to work with new/unpublished writers. Monthly magazine for Atari 400/800, XL/XE, users. Circ. 60,000. Pays on publication. Publishes ms an average of 3 months after acceptance. Byline given. Offers $60 kill fee. Buys all rights. Submit seasonal/holiday material 3 months in advance. Simultaneous queries and photocopied submissions OK. Query for electronic submissions. Computer printout submissions acceptable. Reports in 2 weeks on queries; 1 month on mss. Sample copy $3; free writer's guidelines. Request text files on disks and printout.

Nonfiction: How-to, interview/profile, new product, photo feature and technical. Especially wants article plus programs—games, utilities, productivity, etc. Special issues include Education (October) and Buyer's Guide (December). No generalized, nontechnical articles. Buys 250 mss/year. Send complete ms. Length: 500-2,500 words. Pays $50-600. Pays expenses of writers on assignment.

Photos: State availability of photos or send photos with ms. Reviews color transparencies and b&w prints; b&w should accompany article. Identification of subjects required.

Columns/Departments: Game of the Month (computer games); Starting Line (beginner's column); Assembly Language (for advanced programmers); Profiles (personalities in the business); and Product Reviews (software/hardware products). Buys 36 mss/year. Send complete ms. Length: 1,500-2,500 words. Pays $120-180.

Tips: "Write for the Product Reviews section. We need 400- to 600-word articles on a new software or hardware product for the Atari computers. Give a clear description; personal experience with product; comparison with other available product; or product survey with charts. The most frequent mistakes made by writers in completing an article are failure to be clear and specific, and writing overly long submissions."

THE APPLE IIGS BUYER'S GUIDE, 24 New England Executive Park, Burlington MA 01803. Editor: Paul Pinella. 90% freelance written. A quarterly magazine on Apple IIGS hardware and software markets. "*The Apple IIGS Buyer's Guide* examines what's available for Apple IIGS owners by providing in-depth product reviews, how-to feature articles, answers technical questions from readers, and provides an in-depth product directory in each issue." Circ. 70,000. Pays on acceptance. Byline given. Offers 70% kill fee. Buys all rights. Submit seasonal/holiday material 2 months in advance. Query for electronic submissions. Computer printout submissions OK, but must be accompanied with diskette. Reports in 3 weeks. Sample copy for $2; writer's guidelines for #10 SASE.

Nonfiction: How-to, interview/profile, new product, technical and reviews. Buys 40 mss/year. Query with or without published clips, or send complete ms. Length: 400-5,000 words. Pays $100-700. Pays expenses of writers on assignment. State availability of photos with submission. Reviews transparencies. Offers $30-100 per photo. Buys one-time rights.

Columns/Departments: Reviews (hardware/software), 350-800 words; IIGS Address (technical reader questions), 800-2,000 words; 'IIGS Press,' (desktop publishing column); 'R&R,' (games column); 'Shareware Solutions,' (public domain software column); 'Class Action,' (education column); and 'Inside Appleworks GS,' (Appleworks column). Buys 10 mss/year. Query. Length: 350-800 words. Pays $200-550.

Tips: "All copy must now be submitted in electronic form."

ATARI EXPLORER, The Official Atari Journal, Atari Explorer Publications Corp., 7 Hilltop Rd., Mendham NJ 07945. Editor: Elizabeth B. Staples. 70% freelance written. A bimonthly magazine about Atari computers. "Our audience consists of users of Atari 8-bit and ST computers, and our objective is to help them make good use of those computers." Circ. 70,000. Pays on acceptance. Publishes ms an average of 4 months after acceptance. Byline given. Offers $100 kill fee. Buys first North American serial rights or all rights. Photocopied submissions OK. Query for electronic submissions. Reports in 6 weeks. Sample copy $3 with 9x13 SAE and $1.24 postage.

Nonfiction: How-to (programming), interview/profile (of people who use Atari computers in interesting ways), technical and product reviews. No non-technical or "How I learned to love my computer." Buys 50 mss/year. Send complete ms. Length: 750-4,000 words. Pays $35-600. Sometimes pays the expenses of writers on assignment. Send photos with submission. Offers no additional payment for photos accepted with ms. Captions required. Buys one-time rights.

Tips: "Writers must have access to and use Atari computers. All submissions must be relevant to Atari computer users."

BYTE MAGAZINE, 1 Phoenix Mill Lane, Peterborough NH 03458. (603)924-9281. Editor: Fred Langa. Monthly magazine covering personal computers for college-educated, professional users of computers. 50% freelance written. Circ. 455,000. Pays on acceptance. Byline given. Buys all rights. Computer printout submissions acceptable; prefers letter-quality. Reports on rejections in 6 weeks; 3 months if accepted. Electronic submissions accepted, IBM or Macintosh compatible. Sample copy $3.50; writer's guidelines for #10 SASE.

Nonfiction: In-depth discussions of technical topics related to microcomputers or technology that will be available to micros within five years. Buys 160 mss/year. Query. Length: 1,500-5,000 words. Pay is $50-1,000 for assigned articles; $500-750 for unassigned.

Tips: "Read technical journals to stay on the cutting edge of new technology and trends. Send us a proposal with a short outline of an article explaining some new technology, programming technique, software trend, and the relevance to advanced users of personal computers. Our readers want accurate, useful, technical information; not fluff and not meaningless data presented without insight or analysis."

CLOSING THE GAP, INC., Box 68, Henderson MN 56044. (612)248-3294. Managing Editor: Paul M. Malchow. 40% freelance written. Eager to work with new/unpublished writers. Bimonthly tabloid covering microcomputers for handicapped readers, special education and rehabilitation professionals. "We focus on currently available products and procedures written for the layperson that incorporate microcomputers to enhance the educational opportunities and quality of life for persons with disabilities." Circ. 10,000. Pays on publication. Publishes ms an average of 2 months after acceptance. Byline given. Buys first serial rights. Simultaneous queries, and simultaneous, photocopied and previously published submissions OK. Query for electronic submissions. Computer printout submissions acceptable (dot-matrix with descenders). Reports in 2 weeks. Free sample copy and writer's guidelines.

Nonfiction: How-to (simple modifications to computers or programs to aid handicapped persons); interview/profile (users or developers of computers to aid handicapped persons); new product (computer products to aid handicapped persons); personal experience (by a handicapped person or on use of microcomputer to aid a handicapped person); articles of current research on projects on microcomputers to aid persons with disabilities; and articles that examine current legislation, social trends and new projects that deal with computer technology for persons with disabilities. No highly technical "computer hobbyist" pieces. Buys 25 mss/year. Query. Length: 500-2,000 words. Pays $25 and up (negotiable). "Many authors' material runs without financial compensation." Sometimes pays expenses of writers on assignment.

Tips: "Knowledge of the subject is vital, but freelancers do not need to be computer geniuses. Clarity is essential; articles must be able to be understood by a layperson. All departments are open to freelancers. We are looking for new ideas. If you saw it in some other computer publication, don't bother submitting. *CTG*'s emphasis is on increasing computer user skills in our area of interest, not developing hobbyist or technical skills. The most frequent mistakes made by writers in completing an article for us is that their submissions are too technical – they associate 'computer' with hobbyist, often their own perspective – and don't realize our readers are not hobbyists or hackers."

COMMODORE MAGAZINE, Commodore Business Machines, 1200 Wilson Dr., West Chester PA 19380. (215)431-9100. FAX: (215)431-9156. Editor: Susan West. 90% freelance written. Monthly magazine for owners of Commodore and Amiga computers, who use them for business, programming, education, communications, art, recreation, etc. Circ. 200,000. Pays on publication. Publishes ms an average of 3 months after acceptance. Byline given. Buys all rights; makes occasional work-for-hire assignments. Submit seasonal/holiday material 5 months in advance. Simultaneous queries and previously published submissions OK. Query for electronic submissions. Reports in 1 month on queries; 2 months on mss. Free sample copy; writer's guidelines for #10 SASE.

Nonfiction: Book reviews; how-to (write programs, use software); new product (reviews); personal experience; photo feature; and technical. "Write for guidelines." Buys 360 mss/year. Query or send complete ms. Length: 750-2,500 words. Pays $60-100/published page.

Photos: Send photos with ms. Reviews 5x7 b&w and color prints. Captions required. Buys all rights.

Tips: "Write to the editor with several specific ideas. Use Commodore computers. We're open to programming techniques and product reviews."

COMPUTER LANGUAGE, Miller Freeman Publications, 500 Howard Street, San Francisco CA 94105. (415)397-1881. FAX: (415)543-0256. Editor: J.D. Hildebrand. Managing Editor: Brett Warren. 100% freelance written. Monthly magazine covering programming languages and software design. Circ. 65,000. Pays on publication. Byline given. Buys first rights. Photocopied submissions OK. Query for electronic submissions. Computer printout submissions OK; prefers letter-quality. Reports in months. Free sample copy and writer's guidelines. Query author's BBS: (415)882-9915 (300/1,200 baud).

Nonfiction: Interview/profile, new product, technical and product reviews. Buys 150 mss/year. Query. Length: 1,500-4,000. Pays $100-650.

Columns/Departments: Product Wrap-Up (in-depth software review); Software Review; and Computer Visions (interviews with experts in the field). Buys 24 mss/year. Query or send complete ms. Length: 1,500-4,000.

Tips: "Introduce idea for article and/or send manuscripts to editor; propose to become software reviewer. Current hot topics: object-oriented programming, OS/2, multitasking, 80386, TSRs, C, Pascal, Ada, BASIC."

COMPUTER SHOPPER, Coastal Associates Publishing L.P., 5211 S. Washington Ave., Box F, Titusville FL 32780. (407)269-3211. FAX: (407)267-2950. Editor: Stanley Veit. 50% freelance written. Prefers to work with published/established writers; works with a small number of new/unpublished writers each year. A monthly tabloid covering personal computing. "Our readers are experienced computer users. They are interested in using and comparing machines and software, and in saving money." Circ. 283,000. Pays on publication. Publishes ms an average of 2 months after acceptance. Byline given. Offers $25 kill fee. Buys all rights. Submit seasonal/holiday material 4 months in advance. Query for electronic submissions. Computer printout submissions acceptable; prefers letter-quality. Reports in 1 week on queries; 2 weeks on mss. Sample copy $2.95.

Nonfiction: How-to (computer boards), new product reviews, and technical. "No rank beginner articles." Buys 250 mss/year. Query. Length: 1,500-2,500 words. Pays 10-20¢/word. Sometimes pays expenses of writers on assignment.

Photos: State availability of photos with submission. Reviews b&w prints or line drawings. Offers no additional payment for photos or drawings accepted with ms.

Tips: "Current interests include new equipment for PS/2, Amiga 2000, Macintosh II, OS/2, CD-ROM, WORMS."

COMPUTE!'S PC MAGAZINE, For IBM, Tandy, & PC and Compatibles, COMPUTE! Publications, Inc., 324 West Wendover Ave., Greensboro NC 27408. (919)275-9809. Editor: Clifton Karnes. 90% freelance written. An MS-DOS-specific publication that appears six times a year. Each issue includes articles, departments, software and hardware reviews, programs and a software disk. Free writer's guidelines.

Nonfiction: "*COMPUTE!'s PC Magazine* is looking for interesting and entertaining how-to articles, features and tutorials. Articles should be aimed at beginning to intermediate home or small-business users with MS-DOS machines. Length varies from 1500 to 4000 words. Pay is competitive. If you're an experienced writer with an idea that you think would interest our readers, send a query letter with writing samples to Clifton Karnes, editor."

Columns/Departments: "*COMPUTE!'s PC Magazine* publishes as many as 20 reviews per issue. We're always looking for qualified reviewers, but we don't accept unsolicited reviews. Please send a query letter with writing samples, software interests, and system specifics to Tom Netsel, Assistant Features Editor." Each issue also includes a disk containing "several MS-DOS programs written by freelancers. We're looking for professional-quality, original applications with easy-to-use interfaces. High-quality games are always welcome submissions. Send program and article on disk to David Hensley, PC Disk Submissions."

‡COMPUTING NOW!, Canada's Personal Computing Magazine, Moorshead Publications, 1300 Don Mill Rd., Toronto, Ontario, M3B 3M8 Canada. (416)445-5600. FAX: (416)445-8149. Editor: Frank Lenk. 15-20% freelance written. A monthly magazine covering micro computing, the use of micro computers in business, software/reviews, programming. Circ. 17,000. Pays on publication. Publishes ms an average of 6 months after acceptance. Byline given. Buys first rights. Electronic submissions acceptable; whether hard copy is required depends on the article. Computer printout submissions acceptable; prefers letter-quality.

Nonfiction: How-to (hardware/software); new product (occasional hardware or software review); and technical. No humor, inspirational or general/historical articles. Query. Length: 2,000-3,000 words. Pays 12¢(Canadian)/word. Sometimes pays the expenses of writers on assignment.

Photos: State availability of photos with submission. Reviews prints. Captions, model releases and identification of subjects required.

Tips: "Will work with authors knowledgeable in specific subject areas—operating systems, software applications, connectivity, hardware."

COMPUTOREDGE, San Diego's-Computer Magazine, The Byte Buyer, Inc., Box 83086, San Diego CA 92138. (619)573-0315. Editors: Dan Gookin, Tina Berke and Wally Wang. 90% freelance written. A biweekly magazine on computers. "We cater to the novice/beginner/first-time computer buyer. Humor is welcome. Nothing too technical." Circ. 65,000. Pays on publication. Byline given. Offers $15 kill fee. Buys first North American serial rights. Submit seasonal/holiday material 2 months in advance. Query for electronic submissions. Photocopied submissions OK. Reports in 2 weeks. Writer's guidelines for #10 SASE.

Nonfiction: General interest (computer), how-to, humor and personal experience. Buys 80 mss/year. Send complete ms. Length: 300-1,500 words. Pays 10-15¢/word for assigned articles. Pays 5-10¢/word for unsolicited articles. State availability of photos with submission. Reviews prints (8x10). Offers $15-50 per photo. Captions and identification of subjects required. Buys one-time rights.

Columns/Departments: Beyond Personal Computing (a reader's personal experience). Buys 80 mss/year. Send complete ms. Length: 500-1,000 words. Pays $50-100.

Fiction: Confession, fantasy and slice-of-life vignettes. Buys 5 mss/year. Send complete ms. Length: 500-1,500 words. Pays $50-150.

Poetry: Light verse and traditional. "We're not big on poems, but we might find some interesting." Buys 25 poems/year. Submit maximum 20 poems. Length: 6-30 words. Pays $15.

Tips: "Be relentless. Don't be technical. We like light material, but not fluff. Write as if you're speaking with a friend."

‡ELECTRONIC COMPOSITION AND IMAGING, Youngblood Publishing, 200 Yorkland Blvd, Toronto, Ontario M2J 1R5 Canada. (416)492-5777. FAX: (416)422-0212. Editor: Chris Dickman. 70% freelance written. Bimonthly magazine on desktop publishing, computer graphics, video and animation. Circ. 25,000. Pays on acceptance. Publishes ms an average of 2 months after acceptance. Byline given. Offers $100 kill fee. Buys first North American serial rights. Query for electronic submissions. Computer printout submissions OK; prefers letter-quality. Reports in 1 week on queries; 2 weeks on mss. Free sample copy and writer's guidelines.

Nonfiction: How-to (computers and graphics or publishing), interview/profile, new product, technical. "No humor." Buys 60 mss/year. Query with published clips. Length: 1,000-3,000 words. Pays $200-600 for assigned articles; $100-300 for unsolicited articles.

Photos: Sometimes pays the expenses of writers on assignment. State availability of photos with submission. Reviews negatives, 4x5 transparencies and 4x5 prints. Offers $10-50 per photo. Captions required. Buys one-time rights.

Tips: "Call to discuss article ideas, or fax query, or mail. Writers must know their areas of electronic composition and imaging in depth."

GENEALOGICAL COMPUTING, Ancestry Inc., Box 476, Salt Lake City UT 84110. (801)531-1790. Editor: Robert Passaro. 50% freelance written. Quarterly magazine on genealogy, using computers. "Each issue contains up-to-date articles, new software announcements, reviews of software and shareware. Designed for genealogists who use computers for records management. We publish articles on all types of computers: PC, Macintosh, Apple II, etc." Circ. 2,500. Pays on publication. Publishes ms an average of 4 months after acceptance. Byline given. Buys all rights. Query for electronic submissions. Computer printout submissions OK. Reports in 2 months.

Nonfiction: New product, personal experience (with software), technical (telecommunications, data exchange, data base development) how-to, reviews. "Articles on pure genealogy cannot be accepted; this also applies to straight computer technology." Query with outline/summary. Length: 1,300-4,000 words. Pays $100.

Tips: "We need articles expressing a personal experience with software, or a comparison of one program with another. We can also use light technical articles on telecommunications, data exchange and data base developments."

‡**HOME OFFICE COMPUTING**, Scholastic Inc., 730 Broadway, New York NY 10003. Editor: Claudia Cohl. Executive Editor: Bernadette Grey. 75% freelance written. Monthly magazine on home/small business and computing. Circ. 400,000. Pays on acceptance. Publishes ms an average of 3 months after acceptance. Byline given. Offers 25% kill fee. Buys all rights or makes work-for-hire assignments. Submit seasonal/holiday material 6 months in advance. Simultaneous and photocopied submissions OK. Query for electronic submissions. Free sample copy and writer's guidelines for 8½ × 11 SAE.

Nonfiction: How-to, interview/profile, new product, technical, reviews. "No fiction, humor, opinion." Buys 12 mss/year. Query with published clips. Length: 200-4,000 words. Pays $100-2,000.

Photos: Sometimes pays the expenses of writers on assignment. State availability of photos with submission.

Columns/Departments: Word Processing, Desktop Publishing, Business Basics, Spreadsheets, Family Computing, Hardware/Software Reviews. Length: 500-1,000 words. Pays $100-2,000.

Tips: "Submission must be on disk or telecommunicated."

‡**INCIDER, The Apple II Magazine**, IDG Communications/Peterborough, 80 Elm St., Peterborough NH 03458. (603)924-9471. Editor: Dan Muse. Managing Editor: Eileen Terrill. 50% freelance written. Monthly magazine on Apple II computers, hardware and software. "*InCider* is a magazine for Apple II computer users, dedicated to helping them get the most out of their hardware and software." Circ. 130,000. Pays on acceptance. Publishes ms an average of 5 months after acceptance. Byline given. Offers ½ kill fee. Buys all rights. Submit seasonal/holiday material 9 months in advance. Query for electronic submissions. Computer printout submissions OK; prefers letter-quality. Reports in 1 month.

Nonfiction: Paul Statt, articles editor. How-to (repair or use hardware, and how to build software), interview/profile (with software or hardware developer), technical (strictly limited to Apple II computers) and reviews of Apple II hardware and software. No fiction or poetry. Buys 18 mss/year. Query with published clips. Length: 200-2,500 words. Pays $100-500 for assigned articles; $25-200 for unsolicited articles.

Photos: Sometimes pays the expenses of writers on assignment. State availability of photos with submission. Offers no additional payment for photos accepted with ms.

Tips: "Reviews are most open to freelancers at *InCider*. In addition to 'read the magazine.' I would advice freelance reviewers to 'have an opinion.' A review should not explain how to use a product, or tell how the reviewer used it. The question is: 'What's it like to use it?' "

‡**LINK-UP, The Newsmagazine for Users of Online Services**, Learned Information, Inc., 143 Old Marlton Pike, Medford NJ 08055. (609)654-4888. Editor: Joseph A. Webb. 33% freelance written. Bimonthly tabloid. "*Link-Up* covers the dynamic new world of online services for business, personal and educational use. Our readers are executives, hobbyists, students, office workers and researchers who share a common goal: they own a computer and modem and are eager to go online." Circ. 10,000. Pays on publication. Publishes ms an average of 2 months after acceptance. Byline given. Buys first rights. Submit seasonal/holiday material 2 months in advance. Photocopied submissions OK. Query for electronic submissions. Computer printout submissions OK; no dot-matrix. Reports in 3 weeks on queries; 1 month on mss. Free sample copy and writer's guidelines.

Nonfiction: General interest, how-to get the most from going online, interview/profile, new product, opinion (does not mean letters to the editor), personal experience, technical, book reviews (we pay $50 for these; length: 500-800 words). "No overly technical pieces or strictly hobbyist articles." Buys 30 mss/year. Send complete ms. Length: 500-2,000 words. Pays $80-200.

Photos: Sometimes pays the expenses of writers on assignment. Send photos with submission. Reviews negatives and prints. Offers no additional payment for photos accepted with ms. Identification of subjects required. Buys one-time rights.

Columns/Departments: Hardware Review (must write about and evaluate a specific hardware product that has something to do with telecommunications.) Length: 1,000-2,000. Buys 6 mss/year. Query. Pays $80-200.
Fillers: Cartoons. Buys 12/year. Pays $25.
Tips: "Become familiar with the online industry. Writers must know what they are talking about in order to inform our readers. We appreciate articles on new developments. Our features section is most open to freelancers. Articles should be well-structured and lively."

MacBUSINESS JOURNAL, PiM Publications Inc., 1 Currant Place, Fall River MA 02720. (617)678-4200. Submissions Editor: Michael K. Creeden. Managing Editor: Donald D. Hicks. 80% freelance written. Bi-monthly magazine of tutorials, reviews and vertical programs designed for both the small business owner and the corporate executive. Estab. 1988. Circ. 15,000. Pays on publication. Publishes ms an average of 2-4 months after acceptance. Byline given. Negotiable kill fee. Buys all rights. Submit seasonal/holiday material 4 months in advance. Query for electronic submissions. Computer printout submissions OK. Free writer's guidelines.
Nonfiction: Book excerpts, how-to, interview/profile, new product, opinion, personal experience, technical. "Almost any article dealing with the Macintosh and its use in business will be considered." Buys 130 mss/year. Query. Length: 1,000 words minimum. Pays $65/page minimum. Sometimes pays expenses of writers on assignment.
Photos: Send photos with submission. Reviews contact sheets, negatives and 4x6 prints. Captions and identification of subjects required. Buys all rights.
Columns/Departments: Reviews, Programs. Buys 120 mss/year. Query. Length: 1,000 words.

THE MACINTOSH BUYER'S GUIDE, Redgate Communications Corp., 660 Beachland Blvd., Vero Beach FL 32963. (407)231-6904. FAX: (407)231-6847. Editor-in-Chief: Jordan Gold. 80% freelance written. Quarterly magazine covering Macintosh software, hardware and peripherals. Circ. 125,000. Pays 45 days after acceptance. Publishes ms an average of 3 months after acceptance. Byline given. Buys all rights. Submit seasonal/holiday material 3 months in advance. Electronic submissions preferred. Reports in 3 weeks on queries. Sample copy $2.50 with 10×13 SAE; free writer's guidelines.
Nonfiction: General interest, how-to, new product, personal experience and technical. No humor—"we're business related." Buys 35 mss/year. Query with published clips. Length: 600-5,000 words. Pays $100-1,000. Pays expenses of writers on assignment.
Photos: State availability of photos with submission. Reviews transparencies. Offers $25-300 per photo. Buys one-time rights.
Columns/Departments: Quarterly Report (news of interest to the Macintosh computer community), 1500 words; and Reviews (software, hardware and peripherals), 1,000 words and up. Buys 40 mss/year. Query with published clips. Pays $100-800.
Tips: "Please call the editor to ascertain current business topics of interest. By far, most freelancers are users of Macintosh computers." Looking for "feature article writing and new product reviews."

MICROAGE QUARTERLY, MicroAge Computer Stores, Inc., Box 1920, Tempe AZ 85281. (602)968-3168. Managing Editor: Dirk Weisheit. 90% freelance written. Prefers to work with published/established writers. A quarterly magazine for business users of microcomputers. Circ. 350,000. Pays on acceptance. Publishes ms an average of 3 months after acceptance. Byline given. Offers kill fee. Buys first North American serial rights, one-time rights and second serial (reprint) rights. Computer printout submissions acceptable; prefer accompanying diskette. Sample copy and writer's guidelines for 9x12 SAE with $1.50 postage.
Nonfiction: Query with published clips. Length: 800-3,000 words. Pays $200-1,200. Pays the phone expenses of writers on assignment.
Columns/Departments: Changing Market (changes in uses of business-oriented microcomputer equipment—what affects the market, and how it changes); Changing Technology (changes/improvements in microcomputer technology that affect the business user); and Changing Industry (adaptations in the microcomputer industry); all 1,000-3,000 words; User Focus (specific vertical markets—construction, accounting, etc.—and how microcomputers are used in these markets), 2,000-2,500 words.
Tips: "We're looking for problem-solving articles on office automation and microcomputer applications oriented toward small- and medium-sized businesses. We're willing to discuss ideas with experienced business or computer-literate writers. Please, no queries on home-computer subjects."

MICROpendium, Covering the TI99/4A, Myarc 9640 compatibles, Burns-Koloen Communications Inc., Box 1343, Round Rock TX 78664. (512)255-1512. Editor: Laura Burns. 40% freelance written. Eager to work with new/unpublished writers. A monthly magazine for users of the "orphaned" TI99/4A. "We are interested in helping users get the most out of their home computers." Circ. 6,000. Pays on publication. Publishes ms an average of 2-3 months after acceptance. Byline given. Buys second serial rights. Photocopied and previously published submissions OK. Query for electronic submission. Computer printout submissions acceptable. Reports in 2 weeks on queries; 2 months on manuscripts. Free sample copy and writer's guidelines.

Nonfiction: Book excerpts; how-to (computer applications); interview/profile (of computer "personalities," e.g. a software developer concentrating more on "how-to" than personality); and opinion (product reviews, hardware and software). Buys 30-50 mss/year. Query with or without published clips, or send complete ms. "We can do some articles as a series if they are lengthy, yet worthwhile." Pays $10-150, depending on length. No pay for product announcements. Sometimes pays the expenses of writers on assignment.

Photos: Send photos with submission. Reviews contact sheets, negatives, transparencies, and prints (b&w preferred). Buys negotiable rights.

Columns/Departments: User Notes (tips and brief routines for the computer) 100 words and up. Buys 35-40 mss/year. Send complete ms. Pays $10.

Tips: "We have more regularly scheduled columnists, which may reduce the amount we accept from others. The area most open to freelancers is product reviews on hardware and software. The writer should be a sophisticated TI99/4A computer user. We are more interested in advising our readers of the availability of good products than in 'panning' poor ones. We are interested in coverage of the Geneva 9640 by Myarc."

NIBBLE, The Reference for Apple Computing, Micro-SPARC Inc., 52 Domino Dr., Concord MA 01742. (617)371-1660. Managing Editor: Paul MacMillan. 90% freelance written. Eager to work with new/unpublished writers. A monthly magazine for Apple II computer reference. Authors should submit programs that run on Apple computers. Pays on acceptance. Publishes ms an average of 4 months after acceptance. Byline given. Buys all rights. Submit seasonal/holiday material 4 months in advance. Photocopied submissions OK. Query for electronic submissions. Computer printout submissions acceptable. Reports in 1 week on queries; 1 month on manuscripts. Free sample copy and writer's guidelines.

Nonfiction: New product and technical. No product reviews or fiction. Buys 175 mss/year. Query. Length: 500-3,000 words. Pays $50-500. Sometimes pays expenses of writers on assignment.

Photos: State availability of photos with submission. Offers no additional payment for photos accepted with ms. Buys all rights.

Tips: "Authors should submit original Apple programs along with descriptive articles."

PC COMPUTING, America's Computing Magazine, Ziff-Davis Publishing Co., 4 Cambridge Ctr., Cambridge MA 02142. (617)492-7500. Editor: Steve Smith. Monthly magazine on personal computing. Estab. 1988. Circ. 150,000. Pays on publication. Byline given. Offers negotiable kill fee. Makes work-for-hire assignments. Query for electronic submissions. Computer printout submissions OK; no dot-matrix. Reports in 1 month. Sample copy for $2.95; writer's guidelines for #10 SASE.

Nonfiction: Book excerpts, how-to, interview/profile, new product, technical. Query with published clips. Payment negotiable. Sometimes pays expenses of writers on assignment.

Photos: State availability of photos with submission. Reviews 35mm transparencies. Payment negotiable. Captions, model releases and identification of subjects required. Buys all rights.

PCM, The Personal Computing Magazine for Tandy Computer Users, Falsoft, Inc., Falsoft Bldg., 9509 U.S. Highway 42, Box 385, Prospect KY 40059. (502)228-4492. FAX: (302)228-5121. Editor: Lawrence C. Falk. Managing Editor: Judy Hutchinson. 75% freelance written. A monthly (brand specific) magazine for owners of the Tandy Model 100, 200 and 600 portable computer and the Tandy 1000, 1200, 2000 and 3000, 4000 and 5000. Circ. 51,096. Pays on publication. Publishes ms an average of 3 months after acceptance. Byline given. Buys full rights, and rights for disk service reprint. Submit seasonal/holiday material 4 months in advance. Photocopied submissions OK. Query for electronic submissions. Computer printout submissions acceptable. Reports in 2 months. Sample copy for SASE; free writer's guidelines.

Nonfiction: Tony Olive, submissions editor. How-to. "We prefer articles with programs." No general interest material. Buys 80 mss/year. Send complete ms. "Do not query." Length: 300 words minimum. Pays $40-50/page.

Photos: State availability of photos. Rarely uses photos.

Tips: "At this time we are only interested in submissions for the Tandy MS-DOS and portable computers. Strong preference is given to submissions accompanied by brief program listings. All listings must be submitted on tape or disk as well as in hard copy form."

PERSONAL COMPUTING MAGAZINE, VNU Business Publications, Inc., Ten Holland Dr., Hasbrouck Heights NJ 07604. (201)393-6187. Editor: Fred Abatemarco. Executive Editor: Peter McKie. 15% freelance written. Monthly magazine written, edited, and illustrated for professionals and managers who use personal computers as a tool in day-to-day business tasks. *Personal Computing* is a service-oriented consumer magazine that details hands-on computing tips and techniques, personal computing management strategies, product trends, and manufacturer profiles and product analyses. Circ. 525,000. Pays on acceptance. Publishes ms an average of 4 months after acceptance. Byline given. Offers 30% kill fee. Buys all rights. Submit seasonal/holiday material 5 months in advance. Simultaneous submissions OK. Computer printout submissions acceptable; prefers letter-quality. Reports in 2 weeks. Sample copy and writer's guidelines for 9x12 SAE and 11 first class stamps.

Nonfiction: Peter McKie. Essays, how-to and interview/profile. "All of our articles are written from the user's perspective. We focus on ways business executives can improve the quality of their work or increase their productivity. In addition, we cover stories on the personal computing industry that we deem of merit in helping our readers develop an effective personal computing strategy. No product-based stories, computer neophyte stories or reviews." Query with published clips. Length: 2,500-3,000 words. Pays expenses of writers on assignment.

Fillers: Jack Bell, editor. Any shortcuts readers discover in using applications.

Tips: "Hands-on, applications-oriented features and relevant industry stories are most open to freelancers. We will be looking for occasional articles that target a sophisticated, corporate user involved in micro-to-mainframe communications."

PORTABLE 100, Tandy Laptop Computing, Portable Computing International Corp., 145 Grove St. Ext., Box 428, Peterborough NH 03458. (603)924-7949. Editor: Terry Kepner. 80% freelance written. Eager to work with new/unpublished writers. Monthly magazine covering laptop computers, their software and peripherals. Pays on publication. Publishes ms an average of 4 months after acceptance. Byline given. Offers 30% kill fee. Buys first North American serial rights and the right to use the article again in a yearbook, compendium or "best of . . ." magazine or book. Submit seasonal/holiday material 6 months in advance. Previously published submissions OK. Query for electronic submissions. Computer printout submissions OK; prefers letter-quality. Reports in 2 weeks. Sample copy $3.95 with 9x12 SAE and 5 first class stamps; writer's guidelines for #10 SASE.

Nonfiction: General interest, humor (April), interview/profile, new product reviews and technical. No articles on how to write programs in BASIC, "my first computer," etc. Buys 120 mss/year. Query with published clips, or send complete ms. Length: 1,000-4,000 words. Pays $22-330 for assigned articles; pays $22-264 for unsolicited articles. Sometimes pays the expenses of writers on assignment.

Photos: Send photos with submission. Especially reviews 8x10 prints; 3x5 prints acceptable. Offers $10-16.50 per photo. Identification of subjects required. Buys one-time and reprint rights.

Columns/Departments: "Columns are arranged case by case; some are written in-house, some are written by freelance authors." Send complete ms. Length: 700-1,000 words. Pays $52-82.50.

Fiction: Humorous (April). Buys 2-3 mss/year. Query. Length: 500-1,000 words. Pays $33-66.

Tips: "We want *application* stories: how lap top computers are being integrated into business and society. In general, the easiest way to break in is via a review of some software or hardware. You must write in first person."

PUBLISH!, The How-To Magazine of Desktop Publishing, PCW Communications, Inc., 501 Second St., San Francisco CA 94107. (415)546-7722. Editor-in-Chief: Susan Gubernat. Managing Editor: Leslie Steere. 80% freelance written. Monthly magazine on desktop publishing. "*Publish!* helps communications professionals learn to effectively use desktop publishing. The emphasis is on practical hands-on advice for computer novice and publishing professional alike." Circ. 80,000. Pays on acceptance. Publishes ms an average of 3 months after acceptance. Byline given. Buys first international rights. Query for electronic submissions. Computer printout submissions OK; prefers letter-quality. Reports in 3 weeks. Free writer's guidelines.

Nonfiction: Book excerpts, product reviews, how-to (publishing topics), interview/profile, news, new products, technical tips. Buys 120 mss/year. Query with published clips. Length: 300-2,500 words. Pays $300-2,000. Sometimes pays expenses of writers on assignment.

Photos: State availability of photos with submission. Reviews contact sheets. Captions and identification of subjects required.

‡SHAREWARE MAGAZINE, Software for the IBM & Compatible, PC-SIG, Inc., 1030-D East Duane Ave., Sunnyvale CA 94086. (408)730-9291. FAX: (408)730-2107. Editor: Michelle Ramage. 80% freelance written. Bimonthly magazine on shareware software. Circ. 75,000. Pays on publication. Publishes ms an average of 3-4 months after acceptance. Byline given. Buys first North American serial rights. Submit seasonal/holiday material 4 months in advance. Simultaneous, photocopied and previously published submissions OK. Query for electronic submissions. Computer printout submissions OK; prefers letter-quality. Reports in 2 weeks. Sample copy and writer's guidelines for 9×12 SAE and 3 first class stamps.

Nonfiction: How-to (computers), humor, interview/profile, new product, personal experience, photo feature, technical. "No articles reviewing software not related to shareware." Buys 40 mss/year. Query with or without published clips, or send complete ms. Length: 1,200-6,000 words. Pays $50-400.

Photos: Send photos with submission. Reviews contact sheets. Payment for photos included in total payment for article. Captions, model releases and identification of subjects required. Buys one-time rights.

‡ST-LOG, The Magazine for ATARI ST Computer Owners, LFP, Inc., Suite 300, 9171 Wilshire Blvd., Beverly Hills CA 90210. (213)858-7100. Publisher: Lee H. Pappas. Editor: Clayton Walnum. 80% freelance written. Monthly magazine covering the Atari ST home computer. Pays on acceptance. Publishes ms an average of 2-6 months after acceptance. Byline given. Buys all rights. Submit seasonal/holiday material 4 months in advance. Photocopied submissions OK. Computer printout submissions acceptable; prefers letter-quality to dot-matrix. Reports in 2 weeks. Sample copy $3; writer's guidelines for #10 SASE.

Nonfiction: How-to and technical. "We publish beginner's articles, educational programs, utilities, multi-function tutorials, do-it-yourself hardware articles and games. We also publish reviews of Atari software and hardware." Buys 150 mss/year. Send complete ms. Length: open. Payment ranges from $75-1,000. Sometimes pays expenses of writers on assignment.

Photos: Send photos with ms. Captions required, "clipped to the photo or taped to the back." Buys all rights.

Columns/Departments: Atari ST software and hardware reviews. Buys 50 mss/year. Send complete ms. Length: open.

Tips: "Almost all submissions are from people who read the magazine regularly and use the Atari ST home computers. We have published many first-time authors. We have published programs written in BASIC, Assembly, C, Pascal and Modula-2. When submitting any program over 30 lines, authors must send a copy of the program on magnetic media, either cassette or disk. We strive to publish personable, down-to-earth articles as long as the style does not impair the technical aspects of the article. Authors should avoid sterile, lifeless prose. Occasional humor (detailing how the author uses his or her computer or tackles a programming problem) is welcome."

TEXAS HI-TECH REVIEW, The Magazine for Texas Computer Users, Publications and Communications, Inc., 251 Live Oak, Marlin TX 76661. (817)883-2533. FAX (817)883-2536. Editor: Larry Storer. 40% freelance written. Works with small number of new/unpublished writers each year. A monthly newspaper with articles of interest to owners/managers of small to mid-size businesses in Texas. Includes high technology from copiers to computers as well as management and other issues. Also book, hardware, software and service reviews. Circ. 25,000. Pays on publication. Publishes ms an average of 3 months after acceptance. Byline given. Buys first North American serial rights and reprints from other PCI magazines. Submit seasonal/holiday material 5 months in advance. Simultaneous submissions and photocopied submissions OK. Query for electronic submissions. Computer printout submissions acceptable; prefers letter-quality. Free sample copy and writer's guidelines.

Nonfiction: How-to, interview/profile, new product, opinion and technical on high technology related articles. Also book, hardware, software and services reviews. Query with or without published clips, or send complete ms. Length: 500-1,000. Fees negotiable upon assignment, acceptance. Occasionally pays with subscription or other premiums; will negotiate. Sometimes pays the expenses of writers on assignment.

Photos: State availability of photos with submission. Reviews contact sheets, transparencies, and prints. Offers $10 maximum/photo. Captions, model releases and identification of subjects required. Buys one-time rights.

TI COMPUTING, An Independent Newspaper for Texas Instruments Computer Users, Publications and Communications, Inc., 251 Live Oak, Marlin TX 76661. (817)883-2533. FAX: (817)883-2536. Editor: Larry Storer. 50-60% freelance written. Works with small number of new/unpublished writers each year. A monthly newspaper of technical articles relating to all Texas Instruments computer applications. Circ. 15,000. Pays on publication. Publishes ms an average of 2-3 months after acceptance. Byline given. Buys first North American serial rights and reprints from other PCI magazines. Submit seasonal/holiday material 5 months in advance. Simultaneous submissions and photocopied submissions OK. Query for electronic submissions. Computer printout submissions acceptable; prefers letter-quality. Free sample copy for 9×12 SAE and writer's guidelines.

Nonfiction: How-to, interview/profile, new product, opinion and technical on TI-related articles only. Query with or without published clips, or send complete ms. Length 500-1,500 words. Fees negotiable upon assignment, acceptance. Occasionally pays with subscription or other premiums; will negotiate. Sometimes pays the expenses of writers on assignment.

Photos: State availability of photos with submissions. Reviews contact sheets, transparencies and prints. Offers $10 maximum/photo. Captions, model releases and identification of subjects required. Buys one-time rights.

Tips: "We now accept submissions from Value Added Resellers of TI, and solicit material on all TI computers, applications and related artificial intelligence. We no longer limit coverage to a specific machine—all TI computers are covered."

‡**WANG IN THE NEWS, an independent newspaper for Wang Computer Users**, Publications and Communications, Inc., 251 Live Oak, Marlin TX 76661. (817)883-2533. FAX: (817)883-2536. Editor: Larry Storer. 30-40% freelance written. Works with small number of new/unpublished writers each year. A monthly newspaper of technical articles relating to all Wang computer applications. Circ. 25,000. Pays on publication. Publishes ms an average of 2-3 months after acceptance. Byline given. Buys first North American serial rights and reprints from other PCI magazines. Submit seasonal/holiday material 5 months in advance. Simultaneous submissions and photocopied submissions OK. Query for electronic submissions. Computer printout submissions acceptable; prefers letter-quality. Sample copy and writer's guidelines for 9×12 SASE.

Nonfiction: How-to, interview/profile, new product, opinion and technical on Wang-related articles only. Query with or without published clips, or send complete ms. Length 500-1,500 words. Fees negotiable upon assignment, acceptance. Occasionally pays with subscription or other premiums; will negotiate. Sometimes pays the expenses of writers on assignment.

Photos: State availability of photos with submissions. Reviews contact sheets, transparencies, and prints. Offers $10 maximum/photo. Captions, model releases and identification of subjects required. Buys one-time rights.

Tips: "We accept submissions from Value Added Resellers of Wang and solicit material on all Wang computers and applications."

‡**WORDPERFECT, THE MAGAZINE,** WordPerfect Publishing Co., 270 W. Center St., Orem UT 84057. (801)226-5555. Editor: Clair F. Rees. 85% freelance written. Monthly magazine of "how-to" articles for users of various WordPerfect computer software. "Easy-to-understand articles written with *minimum* of jargon. Articles should provide readers good useful information about word processing and other computer functions." Estab. 1988. Circ. 100,000. Publishes ms 6-8 months after acceptance. Byline given. Negotiable kill fee. Buys all rights (but negotiable). Submit seasonal/holiday material 8 months in advance. Query for electronic submissions only (WordPerfect 4.2 or 5.0). Reports in 2 months. Sample copy for 9x12 SAE with $1.25 postage. Free writer's guidelines.

Nonfiction: How-to, humor, interview/company profile, new product and technical. Buys 120-160 mss/year. Query with or without published clips. Length: 800-2,000 words. Pays $400-1,000.

Photos: State availability of photos with submission. Reviews transparencies (35mm or larger). Offers no additional payment for photos accepted with ms. Captions and identification of subjects required. Buys one-time rights.

Columns/Departments: Macro Magic (WordPerfect macros), 1,000-1,400 words; Booting Up (tips for beginners), 1,000-1,400 words; Final Keystrokes (professional writers who are WordPerfect users, views about writing), 800 words. Buys 90-120 mss/year. Query with published clips. Pays $400-700 for column-length materials.

Tips: "Studying publication provides best information. We're looking for writers who can both inform *and* entertain our specialized group of readers."

Photography

Readers of these magazines use their cameras as a hobby and for weekend assignments. Magazines geared to the professional photographer can be found in the Photography Trade section.

‡**AMERICAN PHOTOGRAPHER,** 1515 Broadway, New York NY 10036. Editor: David Schonauer. Managing Editor: Sudie Redmond. Monthly magazine for advanced amateur, sophisticated general interest and pro-photographer. Pays on acceptance. Byline given. Offers 25% kill fee. Buys first North American serial rights. Sample copy $2.50.

Nonfiction: Length: 2,000-2,500 words. Sometimes pays writers expenses on assignment (reasonble).

Columns/Departments: Buys 10-30 mss/year. Length: 700 words maximum.

‡**DARKROOM & CREATIVE CAMERA TECHNIQUES,** Preston Publications, Inc., Box 48312, 7800 Merrimac Ave., Niles IL 60648. (312)965-0566. FAX: (312)965-7639. Publisher: Seaton Preston. Editor: David Alan Jay. 85% freelance written. Prefers to work with experienced photographer-writers; happy to work with excellent photographers whose writing skills are lacking. "Article conclusions often require experimental support." Bimonthly publication covering the most technical aspects of photography: photochemistry, lighting, optics, processing and printing, Zone System, special effects, sensitometry, etc. Aimed at advanced workers. Circ. 45,000. Pays within about 2 weeks of publication. Publishes ms an average of 6 months after acceptance. Byline given. Buys one-time rights. Photocopied submissions OK. Query for electronic submissions. Computer printout submissions OK. Sample copy $4.50; writer's guidelines with #10 SASE.

Nonfiction: Special interest articles within above listed topics; how-to, technical product reviews and photo features. Query or send complete ms. Length open, but most features run approximately 2,500 words or 3-4 magazine pages. Pays $100/published page for well-researched technical articles.

Photos: "Don't send photos with ms. Will request them at a later date." Ms payment includes photo payment. Prefers color transparencies and 8x10 b&w prints. Captions, model releases (where appropriate) and technical information required. Buys one-time rights.

Tips: "We like serious photographic articles with a creative or technical bent. Successful writers for our magazine are doing what they write about. Also, any ms that addresses a serious problem facing many photographers will get our immediate attention."

‡DARKROOM PHOTOGRAPHY MAGAZINE, Suite 300, 9171 Wilshire Blvd., Beverly Hills CA 90210. (213)858-7100. FAX: (213)275-3857. Editorial Director: Thomas Harrop. Senior Editor: Anna Ercegovac. Editorial Assistant: Patricia Koury. A photography magazine with darkroom emphasis, published 12 times/year for both professional and amateur photographers "interested in what goes on after the picture's been taken: processing, printing, manipulating, etc." Circ. 80,000. Pays on publication; pays regular writers on acceptance. Byline given. Buys one-time rights. Photocopied submissions OK. Computer printouts acceptable. Query for electronic submissions. Reports in 6 weeks. Sample copy and writer's guidelines for 8½x11 SASE.
Nonfiction: Historical/nostalgic (some photo-history pieces); how-to (darkroom equipment build-its); interview/profile (famous photographers); and technical (articles on darkroom techniques, tools, and tricks). No stories on shooting techniques, strobes, lighting, or in-camera image manipulation. Query or send complete ms. Length: varies. Pays $50-500, depending on project.
Photos: State availability or send photos with query or ms. Reviews transparencies and prints. "Supporting photographs are considered part of the manuscript package."
Columns/Departments: Darkroom Basics, Tools & Tricks, Special Effects, Making Money and Larger Formats. Query or send complete ms. Length: 800-1,200 words. "Published darkroom-related 'tips' receive free one-year subscriptions." Length: 100-150 words.

‡OUTDOOR PHOTOGRAPHER, Werner & Werner Corp., 16200 Ventura Blvd., Encino CA 91436. (818)986-8400. Editor: Steve Werner. Managing Editor: Jim Lawrence. 80% freelance written. A magazine published 10 times a year covering sports, nature and travel photography. Circ. 150,000. Pays on publication. Byline given. Submit seasonal/holiday material 6 months in advance. Simultaneous, photocopied and previously published submissions OK. Reports in 1 month. Sample copy for 9x12 SAE with $4.35 postage.
Nonfiction: How-to, interview/profile, new product, personal experience, photo feature, technical and travel. Buys 50 mss/year. Query with or without published clips, or send complete ms. Length: 1,000-3,000 words. Pays $200-600. Sometimes pays expenses of writers on assignment.
Photos: Send photos with submission. Reviews transparencies and prints. Offers $75-350/photo. Captions and identification of subjects required. Buys one-time rights.
Tips: "*Outdoor Photographer* takes a fresh look at our modern photographic world by encouraging photography as part of a lifestyle associated with outdoor recreation. Editorial is intended to de-mystify the use of modern equipment by emphasizing the practical use of the camera in the field, highlighting the technique rather than the technical."

PETERSEN'S PHOTOGRAPHIC MAGAZINE, Petersen Publishing Co., 8490 Sunset Blvd., Los Angeles CA 90069. (213)854-2000. Publisher: Jackie Augustine. Editor: Bill Hurter. 50% freelance written. Prefers to work with published/established writers; eager to work with new/unpublished writers. Monthly magazine; 100 pages. Emphasizes how-to photography. Circ. 275,000. Pays on publication. Byline given. Publishes ms an average of 9 months after acceptance. Buys all rights. Submit seasonal/holiday material 6 months in advance. Photocopied submissions OK. Computer printout submissions acceptable (IBM compatible disk sent with submission). Reports in 2 months. Sample copy $3; writer's guidelines for #10 SASE.
Nonfiction: Book excerpts, how-to (equipment reports, darkroom, lighting, special effects and studio photography). Buys 75 unsolicited mss/year. Length: 2,000-5,000 words. Send story, photos and captions. Pays $65 minimum, negotiated.
Photos: Photos purchased only with accompanying ms. Articles only not accepted. Reviews 2x2 transparencies and 8x10 prints. Cover photos purchased independently. Pays $25-35 for b&w and color photos; offers negotiable rates for covers. Model releases and technical details required.
Tips: "Freelancers should study the easy conversational style of our articles. We are a how-to-do-it magazine which requires clearly detailed text and step-by-step illustration. Write for our free writer's and photographer's guide for details of our requirements."

‡POPULAR PHOTOGRAPHY, 1515 Broadway, New York NY 10036. Editorial Director: Jason Schneider. 25% freelance written. Monthly. "The magazine is designed for advanced amateur and professional photographers." Circ. 725,000. Pays on acceptance. Publishes ms an average of 4 months after acceptance. Byline given. "Rights purchased vary occasionally but are usually one-time." Submit material 4 months in advance. Computer printout submissions acceptable; prefers letter-quality to dot-matrix. Reports in 1 month. SASE.
Nonfiction: "This magazine is mainly interested in instructional articles on photography that will help photographers improve their work. This includes all aspects of photography, from theory to camera use and darkroom procedures. Utter familiarity with the subject is a prerequisite to acceptance. It is best to submit article ideas in outline form since features are set up to fit the magazine's visual policies. Style should be easily readable but with plenty of factual data when a technique story is involved." Buys how-to, interviews,

profiles, historical articles. Query. Length: 500-2,000 words. Pays $250/page.
Photos: Jeanne Stallman, picture editor. Interested in seeing portfolios in b&w and color of highest quality in terms of creativity, imagination and technique.

‡WESTERN PHOTO TRAVELER, Photo Traveler Publications, Box 39912, Los Angeles CA 90039. (213)660-0473. Editor: Nadine Orabona. 40% freelance written. Bimonthly newsletter on photo travel. "Travel articles on places or events in California and the West written from a photographer's point of view. Audience is amateur photographers." Circ. 2,000. Pays on publication. Publishes ms an average of 3 months after acceptance. Byline given. Buys first, one-time or second serial (reprint) rights. Submit seasonal/holiday material 6 months in advance. Simultaneous, photocopied and previously published submissions OK. Query for electronic submissions. Computer printout submissions OK. Reports in 1 month on queries; 6 weeks on mss. Sample copy $3.95; writer's guidelines for SASE.
Nonfiction: Travel. "No regular travel articles." Buys 24 mss/year. Query with or without published clips, or send complete ms. Length: 500-2,500 words. Pays $25 for feature articles of more than 1,500 words and $10 for short articles of under 1,500 words.'
Photos: State availability of photos with submission. Reviews 35mm transparencies and 5x7 prints. Offers no additional payment for photos accepted with ms. Identification of subjects required. Buys one-time rights.
Tips: "Writer should know photography and should visit the site or event. We want specifics such as best photo spots, best time of day or year, photo tips, recommended equipment, etc., but not a lot of technical advice. We like maps, showing best photo spots."

‡WILDLIFE PHOTOGRAPHY, The Wildlife Photography Association, Box 691, Greenville PA 16125. (412)588-3492. Editor: Rich Faler. 90% freelance written. Eager to work with new/unpublished writers. Bimonthly newsletter. "We are dedicated to the pursuit and capture of wildlife on film. Emphasis on how-to." Circ. 3,000. Pays on acceptance. Publishes ms an average of 1 year after acceptance. Byline given. Buys first rights, one-time rights or second serial (reprint) rights. Submit seasonal/holiday material 4 months in advance. Simultaneous, photocopied and previously published submissions OK. Computer printout submissions acceptable; prefers letter-quality to dot-matrix. Reports in 2 weeks on queries; 6 weeks on mss. Sample copy for $2 and 9x12 SAE; free writer's guidelines.
Nonfiction: Book excerpts; how-to (work with animals to take a good photo); interview/profile (of professionals); new product (of particular interest to wildlife photography); personal experience (with cameras in the field); and travel (where to find superb photo opportunities of plants and animals). No fiction or photography of pets, sports and scenery. Buys 30 mss/year. Query or send complete ms. Length: 500-2,000 words. Pays $30-100.
Photos: Send sharp photos with submission. Reviews contact sheets, negatives, transparencies and 5x7 prints as part of ms package. Photos not accepted separate from ms. Offers no additional payment for photos accepted with ms. Captions and identification of subjects required. Buys one-time rights.
Fillers: Anecdotes and facts. Buys 12/year. Length: 50-200 words. Pays $5-15.
Tips: "Give solid how-to info on how to photograph a specific species of wild animal. Send photos, not only of the subject, but of the photographer and his gear in action. The area of our publication most open to freelancers is feature articles."

Politics and World Affairs

These publications cover politics for the reader interested in current events. Other publications that will consider articles about politics and world affairs are listed under Business and Finance, Contemporary Culture, Regional and General Interest. For listings of publications geared toward the professional, see Government and Public Service and International Affairs in the Trade section.

AFRICA REPORT, 833 United Nations Plaza, New York NY 10017. (212)949-5731. FAX: (212)286-9493. Editor: Margaret A. Novicki. 60% freelance written. Prefers to work with published/established writers. A bimonthly magazine for U.S. citizens and residents with a special interest in African affairs for professional, business, academic or personal reasons. Not tourist-related. Circ. 10,500. Pays on publication. Publishes ms an average of 2 months after acceptance. Rights purchased vary with author and material; usually buys all rights, very occasionally first serial rights. Offers negotiable kill fee. Byline given unless otherwise requested. Computer printout submissions OK. Sample copy for $4.50; free writer's guidelines.

Nonfiction: Interested in "African political, economic and cultural affairs, especially in relation to U.S. foreign policy and business objectives. Style should be journalistic but not academic or light. Articles should not be polemical or long on rhetoric but may be committed to a strong viewpoint. I do not want tourism articles." Would like to see in-depth topical analyses of lesser known African countries, based on residence or several months' stay in the country. Buys 15 unsolicited mss/year. Pays $150-250.

Photos: Photos purchased with or without accompanying mss with extra payment. Reviews b&w only. Pays $25. Submit 12x8 "half-plate."

Tips: "Read *Africa Report* and other international journals regularly. Become an expert on an African or Africa-related topic. Make sure your submissions fit the style, length and level of *Africa Report*."

ARETE, Forum for Thought, (formerly *A Critique of America*), Suite 418, 405 W. Washington, San Diego CA 92103. (619)237-0074. FAX: (619)237-9366. Publisher/Editor: Alden Mills. Managing Editor: Dana Plank. 75% freelance written. A bimonthly political/social/arts and literary magazine. "We are dedicated to presenting high-quality work of any viewpoint, providing an unbiased forum of thought-provoking ideas." Circ. 25,000. Pays on acceptance. Publishes ms an average of 2 months after acceptance. Byline given. Offers 15% kill fee. Not copyrighted. Buys one-time rights. Photocopied and previously published submissions OK. Query for electronic submissions. Computer printout submissions OK; prefers letter-quality. Reports in 1 month. Sample copy $3.50. Free writer's/photographer's guidelines.

Nonfiction: Harlan Lewin-political/social commentary editor; Doug Balding-arts editor. Book excerpts, essays, exposé, general interest, historical/nostalgic, humor, interview/profile, opinion, personal experience, photo feature and travel (features on the arts). Send complete ms. Length: 1,000-9,000 words (negotiable). Pays $100-2,000 (negotiable). Sometimes pays expenses of writers on assignment.

Photos: Send photos with submission to Tina Cravat. Reviews contact sheets and negatives. Pays $225 a page (negotiable). Buys one-time rights.

Fiction: Erica Lowe, fiction editor. Adventure, condensed novels, ethnic, experimental, fantasy, historical, horror, humorous, mainstream, mystery, novel excerpts, science fiction, slice-of-life vignettes and suspense. No dry academic pieces. Buys 25-30 mss/year. Send complete ms. Length: 500-9,000 words. Pays $100-2,000 (negotiable).

Poetry: Erica Lowe, poetry editor. Free verse, light verse and traditional. Buys 60-100 poems/year. Submit maximum 6 poems. "Prefer shorter poetry." Pays $20-200 (negotiable).

C.L.A.S.S. MAGAZINE, C.L.A.S.S. Promotions, Inc., 27 Union Square West, New York NY 10003. Editor: René John-Sandy. 70% freelance written. Prefers to work with published/established writers; eager to to work with new/unpublished writers. Monthly magazine covering Caribbean/American Third World news and views. Circ. 200,000. Pays on acceptance. Publishes ms an average of 1-2 months after acceptance. Byline given. Buys first rights and second (reprint) rights to material originally published elsewhere. Submit seasonal/holiday material 4 months in advance. Simultaneous queries and previously published submissions OK. Computer printout submissions acceptable; prefers letter-quality. Reports in 1 month on queries; 6 weeks on mss. Sample copy and writer's guidelines for 6x9 SAE and 10 first class stamps.

Nonfiction: Features, book excerpts, general interest, historical/nostalgic, inspirational, interview/profile, travel and international news, views and lifestyles in Third World countries. Query or send complete ms. Length: 150-2,500 words. Articles over 700 words must be of international flavor in content. Sometimes pays expenses of writers on assignment.

Poetry: Avant-garde, free verse, haiku, light verse and traditional. Buys 10-20 poems/year. Submit maximum 10 poems. Length: 22-30 lines. Pays $10 minimum.

Tips: "Submit written queries; stick to Afro American/Third World interests and relate to an international audience."

CALIFORNIA JOURNAL, 1714 Capitol Ave., Sacramento CA 95814. (916)444-2840. Editor: Richard Zeiger. Managing Editor: A.G. Block. 50% freelance written. Prefers to work with published/established writers. Monthly magazine that emphasizes analysis of California politics and government. Circ. 20,000. Pays on publication. Publishes ms an average of 2 months after acceptance. Byline given. Buys all rights. Query for electronic submissions. Computer printout submissions acceptable; prefers letter-quality. Writer's guidelines for #10 SASE.

Nonfiction: Profiles of state and local government and political analysis. No outright advocacy pieces. Buys 25 unsolicited mss/year. Query. Length: 900-3,000 words. Pays $150-500. Sometimes pays the expenses of writers on assignment.

‡COMMONWEAL, A Review of Public Affairs, Religion, Literature and the Arts, Commonweal Foundation, 15 Dutch St., New York NY 10038. (212)732-0800. Editor: Margaret O'Brien Steinfels. Biweekly magazine. Circ. 18,000. Pays on acceptance. Byline given. Buys all rights. Submit seasonal/holiday material 2

Close-up

Doug Foster
Editor
Mother Jones Magazine

A "retooling"...a "repositioning"...a redesign.

No matter what editors call it, even the grandest of grand old magazines may get a periodic facelift—anything from a new logo and the addition of a few new features to a fine-tuning of the magazine's total focus to keep up with a changing audience.

If you're relying on five-year-old sample copies of magazines stashed in your storeroom, better think again. It's imperative that writers keep abreast of what's going on at their favorite magazines.

Consider the changes at *Mother Jones*, the journal of political commentary, which left its "love beads" image in mothballs this spring in favor of a more contemporary—though no less socially committed—magazine. Readers and writers were generally pleased, reports Editor Doug Foster.

The changes in *Mother Jones* were due to "a combination of things," Foster says. A new cover strategy (featuring celebrities such as Susan Sarandon) "was our response to increased competition on the newsstand. There's been a 100 percent increase in the number of titles on the stands over the last six or seven years. That means you have to do some things to be noticeable, to be viable there."

A magazine, if it is to stay in business, must also keep in touch with the changing needs of its readers, Foster adds.

A survey by Mediamark Research Inc., for example, showed that *Mother Jones*'s readers had changed since the publication started in 1976. "We found our readers had more disposable income, had grown older, now had children, were spending more time with the magazine and were looking for a broader, more diverse publication."

The magazine added two new sections—Outfront, which carries "short, interesting zippy items" of interest to readers, and an expanded review section at the back of an issue for books, music and the arts. Columns on travel and personal finance were also added.

Doing a little homework in advance can help freelancers deal more smoothly with a magazine going through a redesign, Foster advises. If you're a regular contributor, "and you hear through the grapevine or read that a redesign is in the works, a new editor's coming in or there's going to be an editorial shift, talk with your editor" about what features might be dropped or added, squeezed or expanded. You'll have a better chance of continuing to sell. Most editors would prefer a brief conversation with a contributor to "re-educate" him in the new format than continue to receive material that may no longer be suitable.

If a personal conversation isn't feasible, Foster has another suggestion: Study the promotional materials the magazine's circulation department has prepared to announce the magazine's new look to readers and advertisers. That material contains a wealth of information about where the magazine intends to go. "If you see the clarity with which editorial direction is expressed in that material, I think it helps," he says.

—*Chris Dodd*

months in advance. Computer printout submissions OK; prefers letter-quality. Reports in 3-4 weeks on mss. Free sample copy.

Nonfiction: Essays, general interest, interview/profile, personal experience, religious. Buys 20 mss/year. Query with published clips. Length: 1,200-3,000 words. Pays $50-100.

Poetry: Rosemary Dunn, editor. Free verse, traditional. Buys 25-30 poems/year. Pays 50¢/line.

EUROPE, 2100 M St. NW, 707, Washington DC 20037. Managing Editor: Anker Middelmann. 20% freelance written. Magazine published 10 times a year for anyone with a professional or personal interest in Western Europe and European/U.S. relations. Circ. 25,000. Pays on acceptance. Publishes ms an average of 2 months after acceptance. Buys first serial rights and all rights. Submit seasonal material 3 months in advance. Computer printout submissions acceptable; prefers letter-quality. Reports in 1 month.

Nonfiction: Interested in current affairs (with emphasis on economics and politics), the Common Market and Europe's relations with the rest of the world. Publishes occasional cultural pieces, with European angle. "High quality writing a must. We publish anything that might be useful to people with a professional interest in Europe." Query or submit complete ms or article outline. Include résumé of author's background and qualifications. Length: 500-2,000 words. Pays $75-150.

Photos: Photos purchased with or without accompanying mss. Buys b&w and color. Pays $25-35 for b&w print, any size; $100 for inside use of color transparencies; $450 for color used on cover; per job negotiable.

THE FREEMAN, 30 S. Broadway, Irvington-on-Hudson NY 10533. (914)591-7230. FAX: (914)591-8910. Senior Editor: Brian Summers. 75% freelance written. Eager to work with new/unpublished writers. Monthly for "the layman and fairly advanced students of liberty." Buys all rights, including reprint rights. Byline given. Pays on publication. Publishes ms an average of 5 months after acceptance. Computer printout submissions acceptable; prefers letter-quality. Sample copy for 7½x10½ SASE with 4 first class stamps.

Nonfiction: "We want nonfiction clearly analyzing and explaining various aspects of the free market, private enterprise, limited government philosophy. Though a necessary part of the literature of freedom is the exposure of collectivistic clichés and fallacies, our aim is to emphasize and explain the positive case for individual responsibility and choice in a free economy. Especially important, we believe, is the methodology of freedom—self-improvement, offered to others who are interested. We try to avoid name-calling and personality clashes and find satire of little use as an educational device. Ours is a scholarly analysis of the principles underlying a free market economy. No political strategy or tactics." Buys 60 mss/year. Length: 3,500 words maximum. Pays 10¢/word. Sometimes pays expenses of writers on assignment.

Tips: "It's most rewarding to find freelancers with new insights, fresh points of view. Facts, figures and quotations cited should be fully documented, to their original source, if possible."

‡MOTHER JONES MAGAZINE, The Foundation for National Progress, 1663 Mission St., Second Floor, San Francisco CA 94103. (415)558-8881. Editor: Doug Foster. Managing Editor: Bruce Dancis. 90% freelance written. Monthly magazine of investigative reporting (corporate, governmental). "*Mother Jones* is the largest magazine of political opinion in the United States. Our emphasis is on social change, progressive politics and investigative reporting." Circ. 185,000. Pays on acceptance. Byline given. Offers 25% kill fee. Buys first North American serial rights. Submit seasonal/holiday material 4 months in advance. Computer printout submissions OK; no dot-matrix. Sample copy $5; free writer's guidelines for #10 SASE.

Nonfiction: Book excerpts, essays, exposé, interview/profile, personal experience and photo feature. Buys 35 mss/year. Query with published clips. Length: 3,000-5,000 words. Pays $1,500-2,000. Pays expenses of writers on assignment.

Photos: State availablility of photos with submission. Reviews contact sheets, negatives, transparencies and prints. Offers $75 minimum/photo. Captions, model releases and identification of subjects required. Buys one-time rights.

Columns/Departments: Global Notebook (international coverage) and The Arts (various topics in popular culture). Buys 20 mss/year. Length: 1,000-2,500 words. Query with published clips. Pays $500-900.

Fiction: "Please read our magazine to get a feel for our fiction." No western, romance or confession. Buys 3 mss/year. Send complete ms. Length: 1,500-5,000 words. Pays $400-2,000.

Fillers: Frontlines Editor: Bernard Ohanian. Newsbreaks and short humor. Buys 75 mss/year. Length: 100-600 words. Pays $75-200.

Tips: "Frontlines are the best way to break in. Write and ask for Frontlines guidelines. Do not telephone."

THE NATION, 72 5th Ave., New York NY 10011. FAX: (212)463-9712. Editor: Victor Navasky. 75% freelance written. Works with a small number of new/unpublished writers each year. Weekly. Buys first serial rights. Query for electronic submissions. Computer printout submissions acceptable; prefers letter-quality. Free sample copy and writer's guidelines for #10 SASE.

Nonfiction: "We welcome all articles dealing with the social scene, from an independent perspective." Queries encouraged. Buys 100 mss/year. Length: 2,500 words maximum. Modest rates. Sometimes pays expenses of writers on assignment.

Tips: "We are firmly committed to reporting on the issues of labor, national politics, business, consumer affairs, environmental politics, civil liberties and foreign affairs."

NEWSWEEK, 444 Madison Ave., New York NY 10022. (212)350-4000. My Turn Editor: Olwen Clark. Although staff written, accepts unsolicited mss for My Turn, a column of opinion. The 1,000- to 1,100-word essays for the column must be original and contain verifiable facts. Payment is $1,000, on publication, for all rights. Computer printout submissions acceptable; no dot-matrix. Reports in 1 month.

THE PRAGMATIST, A Utilitarian Approach, Box 392, Forest Grove PA 18922. Editor: Jorge Amador. Publisher: Hans G. Schroeder. 67% freelance written. Bimonthly magazine on politics and current affairs. "*The Pragmatist* is a free-market magazine with a social conscience. We explore the practical benefits of tolerance, civil liberties and the market order, with emphasis on helping the poor and the underprivileged." Circ. 1,550. Pays on publication. Publishes ms an average of 4 months after acceptance. Byline given. Publication not copyrighted "but will run copyright notice for individual author on request." Buys first rights and/or second serial (reprint) rights. Submit seasonal/holiday material 6 months in advance. Photocopied and previously published submissions OK. Query for electronic submissions. Computer printout submissions OK; prefers letter-quality. Reports in 1 month. Sample copy $2; writer's guidelines for #10 SASE.
Nonfiction: Essays, humor, opinion. "*The Pragmatist* is solution-oriented. We seek facts and figures, no moralizing or abstract philosophy, and focus on the issues, not personalities. Recent articles have surveyed alternatives to government schools and examined how subsidies hurt farmers." Buys 35 mss/year. Query with published clips or send complete ms. Length: 500-3,000 words. Pays 1¢/published word plus copies.
Columns/Departments: Book Review (history/current affairs, dealing with the dangers of power or the benefits of civil liberties and market relations). Buys 10-15 mss/year. Query with published clips or send complete ms. Length: 1,000-1,500 words. Pays 1¢/published word plus copies.
Fiction: "We use very little fiction, and then only if it makes a political point."
Tips: "We welcome new writers. Most of our authors are established, but the most important article criteria are clear writing and sound reasoning backed up by facts. Write for an educated lay audience, not first-graders or academics. Polite correspondence gets answered first. No phone calls, please. Don't get discouraged by initial rejections; keep working on your writing and your targeting."

THE PROGRESSIVE, 409 E. Main St., Madison WI 53703. (608)257-4626. Editor: Erwin Knoll. 75% freelance written. Monthly. Pays on publication. Publishes ms an average of 6 weeks after acceptance. Byline given. Buys all rights. Computer printout submissions acceptable "if legible and double-spaced"; prefers letter-quality. Reports in 2 weeks. Sample copy for 8½x11 SAE and $1.05 postage. Writer's guidelines for #10 SASE.
Nonfiction: Primarily interested in articles which interpret, from a progressive point of view, domestic and world affairs. Occasional lighter features. "*The Progressive* is a *political* publication. General-interest material is inappropriate." Query. Length: 3,000 words maximum. Pays $75-250.
Tips: "Display some familiarity with our magazine, its interests and concerns, its format and style. We want query letters that fully describe the proposed article without attempting to sell it—and that give an indication of the writer's competence to deal with the subject."

REASON MAGAZINE, Suite 1062, 2716 Ocean Park Blvd., Santa Monica CA 90405. (213)392-0443. Editor: Mary Zupan. 50% freelance written. Eager to work with new/unpublished writers. A monthly magazine for a readership interested in individual liberty, economic freedom, private enterprise alternatives to government services and individualist cultural and social perspectives. Circ. 32,000. Pays on acceptance. Publishes ms an average of 2 months after acceptance. Rights purchased vary with author and material. Byline given. Offers kill fee by pre-arrangement. Photocopied submissions OK. Computer printout submission OK; double- or triple-spaced mss only. Query for electronic submissions. Reports in 2 months. Sample copy for $2 and 9x12 SAE with $1.24 postage.
Nonfiction: "*Reason* deals with social, economic and political issues, supporting both individual liberty and economic freedom. The following kinds of articles are desired: investigative articles exposing government wrongdoing and bungling; investigative articles revealing examples of private (individual, business, or group) ways of meeting needs; individualist analysis of policy issues (e.g., education, victimless crimes, regulation); think pieces exploring implications of individual freedom in economic, political, cultural and social areas." Query. Buys 50-70 mss/year. Length: 1,000-5,000 words. Sometimes pays expenses of writers on assignment.

REPORT ON THE AMERICAS, North American Congress on Latin America, 475 Riverside Dr., Room 454, New York NY 10115. (212)870-3146. Editor: Mark Fried. Managing Editor: Sandra Necchi. 75% freelance written. A bimonthly magazine on Latin America and Caribbean U.S. foreign policy. Circ. 11,000. Pays on publication. Byline given. Offers ¼ kill fee. Buys one-time rights. Simultaneous and photocopied submissions OK. Query for electronic submissions. Computer printout submissions OK; prefers letter-quality. Sample copy $4.40.

Nonfiction: Exposé, opinion, and photo feature. Buys 25 mss/year. Query with published clips or send complete ms. Length: 1,000-2,500 words. Pays $75-150.
Photos: State availability of photos with submission. Reviews contact sheets and prints (5x7). Pays $25 minimum. Identification of subjects required. Buys one-time rights.

RIPON FORUM, Ripon Society, 6 Library Ct. SE, Washington DC 20003. (202)546-1292. Editor: William P. McKenzie. 20% freelance written. Eager to work with new/unpublished writers. A bimonthly magazine on progressive Republicanism/GOP politics. Circ. 3,000. Pays on publication. Publishes ms an average of 2-4 months after acceptance. Byline given. Simultaneous and photocopied submissions OK. Computer printout submissions OK. Reports in 2 months. Sample copy for 9x12 SAE and 4 first class stamps. Writer's guidelines for #10 SASE.
Nonfiction: Essays and opinion. Query with published clips. Length: 800-1,500 words. Pays $80-150.

WASHINGTON MONTHLY, 1611 Connecticut Ave., Washington DC 20009. (202)462-0128. Editor-in-Chief: Charles Peters. 35% freelance written. Works with a small number of new/unpublished writers each year. For "well-educated, well-read people interested in politics, the press and government." Monthly. Circ. 30,000. Rights purchased depend on author and material; buys all rights, first rights, or second serial (reprint) rights. Buys 20-30 mss/year. Pays on publication. Sometimes does special topical issues. Query or submit complete ms. Computer printout submissions acceptable. Tries to report in 2 months. Publishes ms an average of 2-6 weeks after acceptance. Sample copy $4.
Nonfiction: Responsible investigative or evaluative reporting about the U.S. government, business, society, the press and politics. "No editorial comment/essays." Also no poetry, fiction or humor. Length: "average 2,000-6,000 words." Pays 4-10¢/word.
Photos: Buys b&w glossy prints.
Tips: "Best route is to send 1-2 page proposal describing article and angle. The most rewarding aspect of working with freelance writers is getting a solid piece of reporting with fresh ideas that challenge the conventional wisdom."

WORLD POLICY JOURNAL, World Policy Institute, 777 UN Plaza, New York NY 10017. (212)490-0010. Editor: Sherle Schwenninger. 80% freelance written. "We are eager to work with new or unpublished writers as well as more established writers." A quarterly magazine covering international politics, economics and security issues. "We hope to bring a new sense of imagination, principle and proportion, as well as a restored sense of reality and direction to America's discussion of its role in the world." Circ. 10,000. Pays on acceptance. Publishes ms an average of 3 months after acceptance. Byline given. Offers variable kill fee. Buys all rights. Photocopied submissions OK. Computer printout submissions acceptable; prefers letter-quality. Reports in 2 months. Sample copy for 7½x10½ SAE, 10 first class stamps and $5.25.
Nonfiction: Articles that "define policies that reflect the shared needs and interests of all nations of the world." Query. Length: 30-40 pages (8,500 words maximum). Pays variable commission rate. Sometimes pays the expenses of writers on assignment.
Tips: "By providing a forum for many younger or previously unheard voices, including those from Europe, Asia, Africa and Latin America, we hope to replace lingering illusions and fears with new priorities and aspirations. Articles submitted on speculation very rarely suit our particular needs—the writers clearly haven't taken time to study the kind of article we publish."

Psychology and Self-Improvement

These publications focus on psychological topics, how and why readers can improve their own outlooks, and how to understand people in general. Many General Interest, Men's and Women's publications also publish articles in these areas.

JOURNAL OF GRAPHOANALYSIS, 111 N. Canal St. Chicago IL 60606. Publisher: V. Peter Ferrara. For an audience interested in self-improvement. Monthly magazine. Buys all rights. Pays negotiable kill fee. Byline given. Pays on acceptance. Reports on submissions in 1 month.
Nonfiction: Self-improvement material helpful for ambitious, alert, mature people. Applied psychology and personality studies, techniques of effective living, etc.; all written from intellectual approach by qualified writers in psychology, counseling and teaching, preferably with advanced degrees. Length: 2,000 words. Pays 5¢/word, minimum.

‡NEWSERVICE, D.I.N. Publications, Box 21126, Phoenix AZ 85036. (602)257-0764. Editor: James D. Parker. Managing Editor: Christina Dye. 20% freelance written. "Award winning bimonthly newsletter on health and behavior, published by Do It Now Foundation." Circ. 2,500. Pays on publication. Byline given. Buys first North American serial rights and one-time rights. Simultaneous, photocopied and previously published submissions OK. Query for electronic submissions. Computer printout submissions acceptable. Reports in 1-3 months. Sample copy $2.50; writer's guidelines for SASE.
Nonfiction: Short features, profiles and opinion. Focus on personal health, personal growth and fitness. Buys 10 mss/year. Query. Length 100-2,000 words. Pays $25-250.
Photos: State availability of photos with query; send photos with submission. Reviews contact sheets. Offers $5-50/photo. Buys one-time rights.
Columns/Departments: Backwords (off-beat, humor, unusual mini-features), 50-250 words; Newsfronts (new developments in behavior and health), 50-400 words; Guestcolumn (opinion); and Postscripts (personal commentary). Length: 500 words. Pays $20-100.
Tips: "Be concise. Since adopting a newsletter format, we've come to see the virtue in brevity. Use frequent quotes in news. We're interested in new developments in health and behavior—from AIDS to zoophobia. Focus especially on actions that individuals can take to better manage their lives. Mostly staff-written, but always open to change."

‡PRACTICAL KNOWLEDGE, 111 N. Canal St., Chicago IL 60606. Editor: Lee Arnold. A monthly self-advancement magazine for active and involved men and women. Buys all rights, "but we are happy to cooperate with our authors." Pays on acceptance. Reports in 3 weeks.
Nonfiction and Photos: Uses success stories of famous people, past or present, applied psychology, articles on mental hygiene and personality by qualified writers with proper degrees to make subject matter authoritative. Also human interest stories with an optimistic tone. Length: 5,000 words maximum. Photographs and drawings are used when helpful. Pays 5¢/word minimum; $40 each for illustrations.

PSYCHOLOGY TODAY, P.T. Partners, L.P., 80 5th Ave., New York NY 10011. (212)886-2840. Editor: Julia Kagan. 85% freelance written. Published 10 times/year, magazine covering psychology and the social and behavioral sciences. Circ. 875,000. Pays on acceptance. Publishes ms an average of 5 months after acceptance. Byline given. Offers 20% kill fee. Buys first North American serial rights, one-time rights, second serial (reprint) rights or all rights. Submit seasonal/holiday material 6 months in advance. Photocopied submissions OK. Computer printout submissions acceptable; prefers letter-quality. Reports in 6 weeks. Sample copy for 8½x11 SAE with $3 postage. Writer's guidelines for #10 SASE.
Nonfiction: Book excerpts, essays, exposé, general interest, interview/profile, opinion, and technical. No inspirational/personal experience. Buys 60 mss/year. Query with published clips. Length: 1,000-3,500 words. Pays $500-2,500. Pays expenses of writers on assignment.
Photos: State availability of photos with submission.
Columns/Departments: Covering Health (work, family matters, men and women, media, sports, brain, therapy, and some first-person articles, book reviews. Contact: Wray Herbert.) Query: Jack Horn, news editor. Length: 300-1,000 words. Pays $150-750.

Regional

Many regional publications rely on staff-written material, but others accept work from freelance writers who live in or know the region. Many of these magazines are among the bestselling magazines in a particular area and are read carefully, so writers must be able to supply accurate, up-to-date material. The best regional publication is usually the one in your hometown, whether it's a city or state magazine or a Sunday supplement in a newspaper. (Since you are familiar with the region, it is easier to propose suitable story ideas.)

Listed first are general interest magazines slanted toward residents of and visitors to a particular region. Next, regional publications are categorized alphabetically by state, followed by Canada. Publications that report on the business climate of a region are grouped in the regional division of the Business and Finance category. Recreation and travel publications specific to a geographical area are listed in the Travel, Camping and Trailer section. Regional publications are not listed if they only accept material from a select group of freelancers in their area or if they did not want to receive the number of queries and manuscripts a national listing would attract. If you know of a regional magazine that is not listed, approach it by asking for writer's guidelines before you send unsolicited material.

General

AMERICAS, Organization of American States, Editorial Offices, General Secretariat Bldg., 1889 F Street NW, Washington DC 20006. FAX: (202)458-6421. Managing Editor: Catherine Healy. 20% freelance written. Official magazine of Organization of American States. Editions published in English and Spanish. Bimonthly. Circ. 75,000. Buys first publication and reprint rights. Byline given. Pays on publication. Publishes ms an average of 6 months after acceptance. Queries preferred. Articles received on speculation only. Include cover letter with writer's background.

Nonfiction: Articles of general New World interest on history, art, literature, theatre, development, archaeology, etc. Emphasis on modern, up-to-date Latin America. Taboos are religious and political themes or articles with noninternational slant. "Photos are not required, but are a big plus." Buys 6-10 unsolicited mss/year. Length: 2,500 words maximum. Pays $200 for features.

Tips: "Send excellent photographs in both color and b&w. Address an international readership, not a local or national one. We want something insightful culturally."

‡BLUERIDGE COUNTRY, Leisure Publishing, 3424 Brambleton Ave. SW, Box 21535, Roanoke VA 24018-1535. (703)989-6138. Editor: Kurt Rheinheimer. 75% freelance written. Bimonthly magazine on the Blue Ridge region from Virginia to Georgia. "The magazine is designed to celebrate the history, heritage and beauty of the Blue Ridge region. It is aimed at the adult, upscale readers who enjoy living or traveling in the mountain regions of Virginia, North Carolina, West Virginia, Kentucky, Tennessee and Georgia." Circ. 30,000. Pays on publication. Publishes ms an average of 6-8 months after acceptance. Byline given. Offers $50 kill fee. Buys first and second serial (reprint) rights. Submit seasonal/holiday material 6 months in advance. Photocopied submissions OK. Query for electronic submissions. Computer printout submissions OK; prefers letter-quality. Reports in 3-5 weeks. Sample copy for 9x12 SAE with $1.65 postage. Writer's guidelines for #10 SASE.

Nonfiction: General interest interest, historical/nostalgic, interview/profile, personal expeerience, photo feature, travel, history. Buys 25-30 mss/year. Query with or without published clips or send complete ms. Length: 500-4,000 words. Pays $50-350 for assigned articles; $25-300 for unsolicited articles.

Photos: State availability of photos with submission. Reviews transparencies. Offers $10-25 per photo. Identification of subjects required. Buys all rights.

Columns/Departments: Country Roads (stories on people, events, ecology, history, antiques, books); Mountain Living (profiles of cooks and their recipes, garden tips, weather info); 50-300 words. Buys 6-12 mss/year. Query. Pays $10-25.

Tips: Freelancers needed for departmental shorts and "macro" issues affecting whole region. Also need field reporters from all areas of Blue Ridge region. Also, we need updates on the Blue Ridge, Appalachian trail, national forests, ecological issues, preservation movements."

COUNTRY ROADS QUARTERLY, Appalachian Life for Today, Box 479, Oakland MD 21550. Editor/Publisher: Carol L. Fox. Associate Editor: Lori Cooley. 75% freelance written. Quarterly regional magazine of Appalachia. "*CRQ* is designed to inform, interest and entertain readers about Maryland, Pennsylvania, and West Virginia people, places and things that make this area appealing." Pays on acceptance, or before publication. Byline given. Offers 20% kill fee. Buys first North American serial rights. Submit seasonal/holiday material 2 months in advance. Simultaneous and previously published submissions OK. Computer printout submissions OK; prefers letter-quality. Reports in 1 month on queries; 2 months on mss. Sample copy for $2 and 9x12 SAE with 4 first class stamps; free writer's guidelines.

Nonfiction: General interest, historical/nostalgic, humor, interview/profile, opinion, personal experience, photo features, religious, travel. "No first-person material, no fiction." Buys 40 mss/year. Query with or without published clips, or send complete ms. Length: 500-3,000 words. Pays $5-150. Sometimes pays expenses of writers on assignment.

Photos: Send photos with submission. Reviews 5x7 prints. Offers $2.50-10. Captions and identification of subjects required. Buys one-time rights.

Columns/Departments: Country Food/Cooking (homestyle cuisine/outdoor cooking), 500-2,000 words; Nostalgia (bygone days in Pennsylvania, Maryland, West Virginia portion of Appalachia), 500-3,000 words. Buys 20-30/year. Send complete ms. Length: 500-2,000 words. Pays $5-75.

Poetry: Free verse, haiku, light verse, traditional. Buys 10 poems/year. Length: 6-20 lines. Pays $5-10.

Fillers: Anecdotes, short humor. Buys 10/year. Length: 500 words maximum. Pays $5-15.

Tips: "I'm anxious to work with new writers but only if they follow my guidelines. Anyone who's lived in Appalachia would understand the uniqueness of mountains and rural living. All areas are open to freelancers—particularly profile, nostalgia, culture and history of the land. Material must have relevance to coverage area."

INLAND, The Magazine of the Middle West, Inland Steel Co., 18 S. Home Ave., Park Ridge IL 60068. Managing Editor: Sheldon A. Mix. 35-50% freelance written. Prefers to work with published/established writers, and eager to work with new/unpublished writers. Quarterly magazine that emphasizes steel products, services and company personnel. Circ. 8,000. Pays on acceptance. "Articles assigned are published within 4 months usually, but pieces in the inventory may remain years without being published." Buys first serial rights and first North American serial rights. "We have always paid the full fee on articles that have been killed." Byline given. Submit seasonal/holiday material at least 1 year in advance. Query for electronic submissions. Computer printout submissions acceptable; prefers letter-quality. Tries to report in 4 months. Free sample copy.

Nonfiction: Essays, humorous commentaries, profile, historical, think articles, personal opinion and photo essays. "We encourage individuality. At least half of each issue deals with staff-written steel subjects; half with widely ranging nonsteel matter. Articles and essays related somehow to the Midwest (Illinois, Wisconsin, Minnesota, Michigan, Missouri, Iowa, Nebraska, Kansas, North Dakota, South Dakota, Indiana and Ohio) in such subject areas as business, entertainment, history, folklore, sports, humor, current scene generally. But subject is less important than treatment. We like perceptive, thoughtful writing, and fresh ideas and approaches. Please don't send slight, rehashed historical pieces or any articles of purely local interest." Buys 5-10 unsolicited mss/year. Length: 1,200-5,000 words. Payment depends on individual assignment or unsolicited submission (usual range: $300-750). Sometimes pays expenses of writers on assignment.

Photos: Purchased with or without mss. Captions required. "Payment for pictorial essay same as for text feature."

Tips: "We are overstocked with nostalgia and are not looking for folksy treatments of family life and personal experiences. Our publication particularly needs humor that is neither threadbare nor in questionable taste, and shorter pieces (800-1,500 words) in which word choice and wit are especially important. The most frequent mistake made by writers in completing an article for us is untidiness in the manuscript (inattentiveness to good form, resulting in errors in spelling and facts, and in gaping holes in information). A writer who knows our needs and believes in himself or herself should keep trying. 'The Education of a Steel Hauler's Daughter'; 'How the Midwest was Won' (bicentennial of Northwest Ordinance); 'Adventures of a Young Balzac' (Vincent Starrett's early newspaper days in Chicago); articles on the gold rush to Pikes Peak in 1859; first steamboat in the Middle West; Illinois-Michigan Canal National Heritage Corridor; kayaking on Wisconsin's Wolf River; origins of unusual place names in the Middle West; the Battle of Lake Erie (1812) are recent article examples."

INTERNATIONAL LIVING, Agora Publishing, 824 E. Baltimore St., Baltimore MD 21202. (301)234-0515. Editor: Kathleen Peddicord. 60% freelance written. "We prefer established writers and unpublished writers with original, first-hand experience." Monthly newsletter covering international lifestyles, travel and investment for Americans. Aimed at affluent and not-so-affluent dreamers to whom the romance of living overseas has a strong appeal, especially when it involves money-saving angles. Circ. 65,000. Pays within 1 month of publication. Publishes ms an average of 6 months after acceptance. Byline given. Buys all rights. Submit seasonal/holiday material 2 months in advance. Query for electronic submissions. Computer printout submissions acceptable; prefers letter-quality. Reports in 1 month on queries; 6 weeks on mss. Sample copy $2.50; writer's guidelines for #10 SASE.

Nonfiction: Book excerpts (overseas, travel, retirement, investment, save money overseas, invest overseas); how-to (save money, find a job overseas); interview/profile (famous people and other Americans living abroad); personal experience; travel (unusual, imaginative destinations—give how-to's and costs); and other (humor, cuisine). "We want pithy, fact-packed articles. No vague, long-winded travel articles on well-trodden destinations. No articles on destinations in the United States." Buys 100 mss/year. Query with published clips or send complete ms. Length: 200-1,500 words. Pays $15-200.

Tips: "We are looking for writers who can combine original valuable information with a style that suggests the romance of life abroad. Break in with highly specific, well-researched material combining subjective impressions of living in a foreign country or city with information on taxes, cost of living, residency requirements, real estate, employment and entertainment possibilities. We do heavy rewrites and usually reorganize because of tight space requirements. We are moving toward more how-to and source lists."

ISLANDS, An International Magazine, Islands Publishing Company, 3886 State St., Santa Barbara CA 93105. Editor: Joan Tapper. 95% freelance written. Works with established writers. Bimonthly magazine covering islands throughout the world. "We cover accessible and once-in-a-lifetime islands from many different perspectives: travel, culture, lifestyle. We ask our authors to give in the essence of the island and do it with literary flair." Circ. 130,000. Pays 50% on acceptance and 50% within 30 days after publication. Publishes ms an average of 8 months after acceptance. Byline given. Buys all rights. Query for electronic submissions. Computer printout submissions acceptable; prefers letter-quality. Reports in 1 month on queries; 6 weeks on ms. Sample copy for $5.25; writer's guidelines with #10 SASE.

Nonfiction: General interest, historical/nostalgic, interview/profile, personal experience, photo feature, technical, and any island-related material. "Each issue contains a major centerpiece of up to 3,500 words, 3 or 4 feature articles of roughly 2,000-3,000 words, and 4 or 5 topical articles for departments, each of which runs approximately 500-1,500 words. Any authors who wish to be commissioned should send a detailed proposal for an article, an estimate of costs (if applicable) and samples of previously published work." Buys 25 mss/year. "The majority of our manuscripts are commissioned." Query with published clips or send complete ms. Length: 500-4,000 words. Pays $100-3,000. Pays expenses of writers on assignment.

Photos: State availability or send photos with query or ms. Pays $50-300 for 35mm color transparencies. "Fine color photography is a special attraction of *Islands*, and we look for superb composition, image quality and editorial applicability." Label slides with name and address, include captions, and submit in protective plastic sleeves. Identification of subjects required. Buys one-time rights.

Columns/Departments: "Columns and departments are generally assigned, but we have accepted short features for our Island Hopping department or very short items for our Logbook section. These should be highly focused on some specific aspect of islands." Buys 50 mss/year. Query with published clips. Length: 500-1,000 words. Pays $100-500.

Tips: "A freelancer can best break in to our publication with short (500-1,000 word) features that are highly focused on some aspect of island life, history, people, etc. Stay away from general, sweeping articles. We are always looking for topics for our Islanders and Logbook pieces. These are a good place to break in. We will be using big name writers for major features; will continue to use newcomers and regulars for columns and departments."

NORTHWEST LIVING!, Northwest Living Company, 130 2nd Ave. S., Edmonds WA 98020. (206)774-4111. Editor: Terry W. Sheely. 85% freelance written. A bimonthly magazine publishing information on "people, places of the Northwest from Montana west to Washington, north to Alaska south to Northern California. Country-style information." Circ. 30,000. Pays on publication. Publishes ms an average of 1 year after acceptance. Byline given. Buys one-time rights. Submit queries 1 year in advance. Previously published submissions OK. Computer printout submissions OK; double-space; no dot-matrix. Reports in 1 month on queries. Sample copy for 10x13 SAE and $1. Writer's guidelines for SASE (required!).

Nonfiction: How-to, interview/profile, living style, photo feature and travel, garden and kitchen. No poetry or fiction. Buys 120 mss/year. Length: 500-1,200 words.

Photos: Send photos with query. Reviews 35mm transparencies and 5x7 prints. Offers no additional payment for photos accepted with ms. Buys one-time rights.

Columns/Departments: Query.

Fillers: Regional shorts. See brief section. Buys 25/year. Length: 25-300 words.

Tips: "Query in detail with specific Northwest-oriented material. Include photo support if available. No telephone queries."

NORTHWEST MAGAZINE, the Sunday magazine of *The Oregonian*, 1320 SW Broadway, Portland OR 97201. FAX: (503)227-5306. Editor: Ellen Heltzel. 90% freelance written. Prefers to work with published/established writers. Weekly newspaper Sunday supplement magazine. For an upscale, 25-49-year-old audience distributed throughout the Pacific Northwest. Circ. 420,000. Buys first serial rights for Oregon and Washington state. Pays mid-month in the month following acceptance. Publishes ms an average of 4 months after acceptance. Simultaneous submissions considered. Computer printout submissions acceptable; prefers letter-quality. Query for electronic submissions. Reports in 2 weeks. Sample copy for 10x12 SAE and 65¢ postage. Free writer's guidelines.

Nonfiction: "Contemporary, regional articles with a strong hook to concerns of the Pacific Northwest. Cover stories usually deal with regional issues and feature 'professional-level' reporting and writing. Personality profiles focus on young, Pacific Northwest movers and shakers. Short humor, personal essays, regional destination travel, entertainment, the arts and lifestyle stories also are appropriate. No history without a contemporary angle, boilerplate features of the type that are mailed out en masse with no specific hook to our local audience, poorly documented and highly opinionated issue stories that lack solid journalistic underpinnings, routine holiday features, or gushy essays that rhapsodize about daisies and rainbows. We expect top-quality writing and thorough, careful reporting. A contemporary writing style that features involving literary techniques like scenic construction stands the best chance." Buys 400 mss/year. Query much preferred, but complete ms considered. All mss on speculation. Length: 800-3,000 words. Pays $75-1,000.

Photos: Photographs should be professional quality Kodachrome slides. Pays $75-150.

Fiction: Address submissions to fiction editor. Short-short stories that reflect the culture and social structure of the Pacific Northwest in a way that relates to contemporary life in the region as well as to the magazine's target audience. New writers welcomed; Northwest writers preferred. Buys 20-24 mss/year. Length: 1,500-2,500 words. Pays $200-225.

Poetry: Paul Pintarich, book review editor. "*Northwest Magazine* seeks poetry with solid imagery, skilled use of language and having appeal to a broad and intelligent audience. We do not accept cutesy rhymes, jingles, doggeral or verse written for a specific season, i.e., Christmas, Valentine's Day, etc. We currently are accepting poems only from poets in the Pacific Northwest region (Oregon, Washington, Idaho, Montana, Northern California, British Columbia and Alaska). Poems from Nevada and Hawaii receive consideration. We are looking for a few fine and distinctive poems each week. Poems on dot-matrix printers accepted if near letter-quality only. No handwritten submissions or threats." Send at least 3 poems for consideration. Length: 23 lines maximum. Pays $10 on acceptance.

Tips: "Pay rates and editing standards are up, and this market will become far more competitive. However, new writers with talent and good basic language skills still are encouraged to try us. Printing quality and flexibility should improve, increasing the magazine's potential for good color photographers and illustrators."

NOW AND THEN, Center for Appalachian Studies and Services, East Tennessee State University, Box 19180A, Johnson City TN 37614. (615)929-5348. 80% freelance written. A tri-annual regional magazine. Circ. 1,500. Pays on publication. Publishes ms an averge of 6 months after acceptance. Byline given. Buys one-time rights. Simultaneous, photocopied and previously published submissions OK. Computer printout submissions OK; prefers letter-quality. Reports in 1 month on queries; 3 months on mss. Sample copy $2.50; free writer's guidelines for #10 SASE.

Nonfiction: Book excerpts, essays, historical, humor, interview/profile, personal experience, photo feature. "We do have a special focus in each issue—we've featured Appalachian Blacks, Cherokees, women, music and veterans. Write for future themes. Stereotypes (especially granny rocking on the front porch), generalizations, sentimental writing are rejected. It must have to do with Appalachia." Buys 8 mss/year. Query with or without published clips, or send complete ms. Length: 2,500 words. Pays $15-60 for assigned articles; $10-60 for unsolicited articles. Sometimes pays expenses of writers on assignment.

Photos: Send photos with submission. Reviews contact sheets and prints. Offers no additional payment for photos accepted with ms. Captions, model releases and identification of subjects required. Buys one-time rights.

Fiction: Ethnic, experimental, historical, humorous, novel excerpts, slice-of-life vignettes. "Everything we publish has to be by or about Appalachians. No stereotypes, generalizations, or sentimentality." Buys 2 mss/ year. Send complete ms. Length: 2,500 words maximum. Pays $10-50.

Poetry: Avant-garde, free verse. "Must have something to do with the Appalachian region. Avoid stereotypes, generalizations and sentimentality." Buys 30-35 poems/year. Pays 2 contributor's copies and a year subscription.

Tips: "Everything we publish has something to do with life in Appalachia present and past. Profiles of people living and working in the region, short stores that convey the reality of life in Appalachia (which can include malls, children who wear shoes and watch MTV) are the kinds of things we're looking for."

RURALITE, Box 558, Forest Grove OR 97116. (503)357-2105. Editor: Ken Dollinger. 50-70% freelance written. Works with new/unpublished writers each year. Monthly magazine primarily slanted toward small town and rural families, served by consumer-owned electric utilities in Washington, Oregon, Idaho, Nevada, Alaska and northern California. "Ours is an old-fashioned down-home publication, with something for all members of the family." Circ. 223,000. Pays on acceptance. Buys first serial rights and occasionally second serial (reprint) rights. Byline given. Submit seasonal material at least 3 months in advance. Computer printout submissions acceptable; prefers letter-quality. Sample copy and writer's guidelines for $1 and 10x13 SAE.

Nonfiction: Walter J. Wentz, nonfiction editor. Primarily human-interest stories about rural or small-town folk, preferably living in areas (Northwest states and Alaska) served by Rural Electric Cooperatives. Articles emphasize self-reliance, overcoming of obstacles, cooperative effort, hard or interesting work, unusual or interesting avocations, odd or unusual hobbies or histories, public spirit or service and humor. Also considers how-to, advice for rural folk, little-known and interesting Northwest history, people or events. Stories on economic recovery or development, or unusual small businesses in our service areas, inventors, entrepreneurs innovators in small towns or rural areas will be carefully considered. As always, energy-related stories pertaining to publicly-owned utilities will be of interest. No "sentimental nostalgia or subjects outside the Pacific Northwest; nothing racy." Buys 15-20 mss/year. Query. Length: 500-900 words. Pays $30-140, depending upon length, quality, appropriateness and interest, number and quality of photos.

Photos: Reviews b&w negatives with contact sheets. Illustrated stories have better chance for acceptance.

Tips: "Freelance submissions are evaluated and decided upon immediately upon arrival. We need good, solid, well-illustrated 'first-feature' articles to lead off the magazine each month. These receive our best pay rate. We are overloaded with second- and third-feature stories already. We will be placing more emphasis on illustrations and layout; good, professional-quality b&w negatives will add to the appeal of any mss. Due to a loss of feature pages, we will be judging freelance submissions much more critically."

‡SOUTHERN SENSATIONS, Good Fairey Publications, 330 E. Richards St., Box 322, Denmark SC 29042. (803)793-3856. Editor: J. Kelley Fairey. Managing Editor: Evelyn W. Fairey. 70% freelance written. Bimonthly magazine on small Southern towns and people. Estab. 1988. Circ. 25,000. Pays on acceptance.

Byline given. Buys one-time rights or second serial (reprint) rights. Submit seasonal/holiday material 1 year in advance. Simultaneous and photocopied submissions OK. Computer printout submissions OK; prefers letter-quality. Reports in 1 month on queries; 2 months on mss. Sample copy for $3, 9 × 12 SAE and $1.85.
Nonfiction: General interest, historical/nostalgic, humor, inspirational, interview/profile, new product and personal experience, photo feature and travel. Buys 24 mss/year. Query with or without published clips or send complete ms. Length: 300-3,500 words. Pays $50-200 for assigned articles; $25-100 for unsolicited articles. Sometimes pays students with contributor copies or other premiums rather than a cash payment. Sometimes pays expenses of writers on assignment.
Photos: State availability of photos with submission. Reviews negatives, transparencies and b&w prints only. Offers no additional payment for photos accepted with ms. Identification of subjects required.
Columns/Departments: Publisher's Award (Students only, life in the South, any subject), 300-2,000 words and Down the Dirt Road (Southern Nostalgic), 500-2,500 words. Buys 50 mss/year. Query. Length: 300-2,500 words. Pays $25-75.
Fiction: Adventure, historical, humorous, mainstream, slice-of-life vignettes and Southern. "No erotica, science fiction." Buys 10 mss/year. Query. Length: 300-2,500 words. Pays $25-100.
Poetry: Traditional. We want nothing but traditional Southern. Buys 6 poems/year. Pays $5-15.
Fillers: Anecdotes, facts and short humor. Pays $5.
Tips: "If you don't *love* the South—*Forget it*! Small towns and unusual Southern people are what we want. We are looking for small out-of-the-way places that actually represent the true South where all neighbors are friends (we *know* them). We wish to cover 16½ states from *Southern* California to West Virginia."

‡**SUNDAY JOURNAL MAGAZINE**, Providence Journal Co., 75 Fountain St., Providence RI 02902. (401)277-7349. Editor: Elliot Krieger. 50% freelance written. Weekly Sunday supplement magazine about news of Rhode Island and New England. Circ. 250,000. Pays on publication. Byline given. Buys first North American serial rights. Submit seasonal/holiday 3 months in advance. Simultaneous and photocopied submissions OK. Query for electronic submissions. Computer printout submissions OK. Reports in 2 weeks on queries.
Nonfiction: Book excerpts, exposé, general interest, historical/nostalgic, interview/profile and photo feature. No fiction, poetry or personal opinion. Buys 100 mss/year. Query. Length: 750-5,000. Pays $100-1,000.
Photos: State availability of photos with submission. Offers $25-100/photo. Captions and identification of subjects required.
Fiction: Mainstream, historical. Must relate to Rhode Island. Buys 5-10 mss/year. Send complete ms. Length: 10,000 words maximum. Pays $100-750.

YANKEE, Dublin NH 03444. (603)563-8111. FAX: (603)563-8252. Editor-in-Chief: Judson D. Hale. Managing Editor: John Pierce. 25% freelance written. Works with a small number of new/unpublished writers each year. Monthly magazine emphasizing the New England region. Circ. 1 million. Pays on acceptance. Publishes ms an average of 10 months after acceptance. Byline given. Buys all rights, first North American serial rights or one-time rights. Submit seasonal/holiday material at least 4 months in advance. Query for electronic submissions. Computer printout submissions acceptable; no dot-matrix. Reports in 6 weeks. Sample copy for 7 × 10 SAE; writer's guidelines for #10 SASE.
Nonfiction: Historical (New England history, especially with present-day tie-in); how-to (especially for Forgotten Arts series of New England arts, crafts, etc.); humor; interview (especially with New Englanders who have not received a great deal of coverage); nostalgia (personal reminiscence of New England life); photo feature (prefers color, captions essential); profile; travel (to the Northeast only, with specifics on places, prices, etc.); current issues; antiques; and food. Buys 50 mss/year. Query with brief description of how article will be structured (its focus, etc.); articles must include a New England "hook." Length: 1,500-3,000 words. Pays $150-1,000. Pays expenses of writers on assignment.
Photos: Purchased with ms or on assignment; purchased without accompanying ms for This New England feature only; color only. Captions required. Reviews prints or transparencies. Pays $25 minimum for 8x10 b&w glossy prints; $150/page for 2¼x2¼ or 35mm transparencies; 4x5 for cover or centerspread.
Columns/Departments: Traveler's Journal (with specifics on places, prices, etc.); Antiques to Look For (how to find, prices, other specifics); and At Home in New England (recipes, gardening, crafts). Buys 10-12 mss/year. Query. Length: 1,000-2,500 words. Pays $150-400.
Fiction: Edie Clark, fiction editor. Emphasis is on character development. Buys 8-10 mss/year. Send complete ms. Length: 1,500-3,500 words. Pays $1,000.
Poetry: Jean Burden, poetry editor. Free verse or traditional. Buys 3-4 poems/issue. Send poems. Length: 32 lines maximum. Pays $50 for all rights, $35 for first magazine rights. Annual poetry contest with awards of $150, $100 and $50 for three best poems during the year.

Alabama

‡**ALABAMA HERITAGE**, University of Alabama, Box 870342, Tuscaloosa AL 35487-0342. (205)348-7467. Editor: Suzanne Wolfe. Managing Editor: G. Ward Hubbs. 50% freelance written. Quarterly magazine on

Alabama history and culture." *Alabama Heritage* is a nonprofit historical quarterly published by the University of Alabama for the intelligent lay reader. We are interested in lively, well written and thoroughly researched articles on Alabama/Southern history and culture. Readability and accuracy are essential." Pays on publication. Byline given. Buys first rights and second serial (reprint) rights. Photocopied submissions OK. Query for electronic submissions. Computer printout submissions OK; prefers letter-quality. Reports in 1 month. Sample copy $3.50. Writer's guidelines for #10 SASE.

Nonfiction: Historical. "We do not want fiction, poetry, book reviews, articles on current events or living artists and personal/family reminiscences." Buys 10 mss/year. Query. Length: 1,500-5,000 words. Pays $100 minimum. Pays 10 copies to each author.

Photos: Reviews contact sheets. Identification of subjects required. Buys one-time rights.

Tips: "Authors need to remember that we regard history as a fascinating subject, not as a dry recounting of dates and facts. Articles that are lively and engaging, in addition to being well researched, will find interested readers among our editors. No term papers, please. All areas of our magazine are open to freelance writers. Best approach is a written query."

Alaska

ALASKA, The Magazine of Life on the Last Frontier, Suite 200, 808 E. St., Anchorage AK 99501. (907)272-6070. Editor: Ron Dalby. Managing Editor: Shannon Lowry. 60% freelance written. Eager to work with new/unpublished writers. A monthly magazine covering topics "uniquely Alaskan." Circ. 235,000. Pays on acceptance. Publishes ms an average of 6 months after acceptance. Byline given. Buys first rights or one-time rights. Submit seasonal/holiday material 1 year in advance. Query for electronic submissions. Computer printout submissions acceptable; prefers letter-quality. Reports in 1 month on queries; 2 months on manuscripts. Sample copy $3; writer's guidelines for #10 SASE.

Nonfiction: Historical/nostalgic, how-to (on anything Alaskan), humor, interview/profile, personal experience and photo feature. Also travel articles and Alaska destination stories. Does not accept fiction or poetry. Buys 60 mss/year. Query. Length: 100-2,500 words. Pays $100-1,250. Pays expenses of writers on assignment.

Photos: Send photos with submission. Reviews 35mm transparencies. Captions and identification of subjects required. Offers no additional payment for photos accepted with ms.

‡ALASKA OUTDOORS MAGAZINE, Swensen's Alaska Outdoors Corporation, Suite 200, 400 "D" St., Box 190324, Anchorage AK 99519. (907)276-2672. Editor: Evan Swensen. Managing Editor: Diane Clawson. 90% freelance written. Monthly magazine on outdoor recreation in Alaska. Circ. 55,000. Pays 30 days after publication. Publishes ms an average of 4 months after acceptance. Byline given. Offers 50% kill fee. Buys first North American serial rights. Submit seasonal/holiday material 4 months in advance. Photocopied submissions OK. Query for electronic submissions. Computer printout submissions OK; prefers letter-quality. Reports in 3 weeks on queries; 4 weeks on mss. Sample copy $1 with 8½x11 SAE and 3 first class stamps. Free writer's guidelines.

Nonfiction: Essays, how-to (outdoor recreation), humor, personal experience, photo feature and travel. Buys 150-175 mss/year. Query with or without published clips or send complete ms. Length: 800-2,400 words. Pays $75-200. Pays in advertising.

Photos: Send photos with submission. Reviews transparencies and prints. Offers no additional payment for photos accepted with ms (except cover). Captions, model releases and identification of subjects required. Buys one-time rights.

Arizona

‡ARIZONA HIGHWAYS, 2039 W. Lewis Ave., Phoenix AZ 85009. (602)258-6641. FAX: (602)254-4505. Managing Editor: Richard G. Stahl. 90% freelance written. Prefers to work with published/established writers. State-owned magazine designed to help attract tourists into and through the state. Pays on acceptance. Publishes ms an average of 6 months after acceptance. Computer printout submissions acceptable; no dot-matrix. Writer's guidelines for SASE.

Nonfiction: Contact managing editor. Subjects include narratives and exposition dealing with contemporary events, popular geography, history, anthropology, nature, special things to see and do, outstanding arts and crafts, travel, etc.; all must be oriented toward Arizona and the Southwest. Buys 6 mss/issue. Buys first serial rights. Query with "a lead paragraph and brief outline of story. We deal with professionals only, so include list of current credits." Length: 1,500-2,500 words. Pays 35-50¢/word. Sometimes pays expenses of writers on assignment.

Photos: "We will use transparencies of 2¼, 4x5 or larger, and 35 mm when it displays exceptional quality or content. We prefer Kodachrome in 35mm. Each transparency *must* be accompanied by information attached to each photograph: where, when, what. No photography will be reviewed by the editors unless the photographer's name appears on *each* and *every* transparency." Pays $80-350 for "selected" color transparencies. Buys one-time rights.

Tips: "Writing must be of professional quality, warm, sincere, in-depth, well-peopled and accurate. Avoid themes that describe first trips to Arizona, the Grand Canyon, the desert, Colorado River running, etc. Emphasis is to be on Arizona adventure and romance as well as flora and fauna, when appropriate, and themes that can be photographed. Double check your manuscript for accuracy."

ARIZONA LIVING MAGAZINE, AZ Com Publishing, Inc., 4518 N. 12th St., Suite 200, Phoenix AZ 85014. (602)264-4295. Managing Editor: Kiana Dicker. 30% freelance written. Works with new/unpublished writers. Monthly magazine covering general interest subjects relating to Arizona. "*Arizona Living* magazine is the highest circulation, statewide, general interest feature magazine in Arizona. Our subscriber base consists of upscale, affluent, on-the-move Arizonans. We don't want to cramp your style, but we demand a solid journalistic approach." Circ. 16,500. Pays on publication. Byline given. Buys first North American serial rights. Submit seasonal/holiday material 4 months in advance. Simultaneous submissions OK. Computer printout submissions OK; prefers letter-quality. Sample copy $2.50 and 8½×11 SAE; writer's guidelines for #10 SASE.

Nonfiction: No "advetorial" submissions. Buys 48 mss/year. Query only. Ideal article length: 1,000-2,000 words. Pays 5-10¢/word. Pays the expenses of writers on assignment, when pre-approved.

Photos: State availability of photos or send photos with submission. Reviews contact sheets, transparencies and prints. Offers cost of film for photos. Captions, model releases and identification of subjects required.

Fiction: Slice-of-life vignettes (if anything). "We only very rarely print fiction."

Tips: "We don't care as much whether or not you have been published; we mainly care that you are a good writer. Query first. Be concise, be complete, be interesting. Be prepared to change the angle of your article to fit our exact requirements. Be organized. Write for us what you promise. Good writers will be used again and again. Most freelance articles are written by assignment, but we are always looking for interesting ideas by good writers. Also, don't confine your thoughts to Arizona topics; we write about art, fashion, travel from outside the state. If it's well written and interesting, we'll probably use it."

Arkansas

ARKANSAS TIMES, Arkansas Writers' Project, Inc., Box 34010, Little Rock AR 72203. (501)375-2985. Editor: Mel White. 25% freelance written. Monthly magazine. "We are an Arkansas magazine. We seek to appreciate, enliven and, where necessary, improve the quality of life in the state." Circ. 32,000. Pays on acceptance. Publishes ms an average of 3 months after acceptance. Byline given. Buys first serial rights. Submit seasonal/holiday material 5 months in advance. Simultaneous, photocopied and previously published submissions OK. Computer printout submissions acceptable. Reports in 2 weeks on queries; 1 month on mss. Sample copy $3.50; writer's guidelines for SASE.

Nonfiction: Book excerpts; exposé (in investigative reporting vein); general interest; historical/nostalgic; humor; interview/profile; opinion; recreation; and entertainment, all relating to Arkansas. "The Arkansas angle is all-important." Buys 24 mss/year. Query. Length: 250-6,000 words. Pays $100-500. Sometimes pays the expenses of writers on assignment.

Photos: Chris Kiesler, art director. State availability of photos. Pays $25-75. Identification of subjects required. Buys one-time rights.

Columns/Departments: Mike Trimble, column editor. In Our Times (articles on people, places and things in Arkansas or with special interest to Arkansans). "This is the department that is most open to freelancers." Buys 15 mss/year. Query. Length: 250-1,000 words. Pays $100-150.

Tips: "The most annoying aspect of freelance submissions is that so many of the writers have obviously never seen our magazine. Only writers who know something about Arkansas should send us mss."

California

CALIFORNIA MAGAZINE, 11601 Wilshire Blvd., Los Angeles CA 90025. (213)479-6511. FAX: (213)477-1710. Editor: Bob Roe. Managing Editor: Rebecca Levy. 90% freelance written. Prefers to work with published/established writers. Monthly magazine about California—lifestyle, the arts, politics, business, crime, education, technology, etc. Circ. 363,000. Pays on acceptance. Publishes ms an average of 3 months after acceptance. Byline given. Offers variable kill fee. Buys first North American serial rights. Photocopied submissions OK. Computer printout submissions acceptable; prefers letter-quality to dot-matrix. Reports in 6 weeks on queries. Sample copy $2 and 9x12 SAE.

Nonfiction: Greg Critzer and Sean Elder, features editors. Exposé (environment, government, education, business), general interest, historical/nostalgic, humor, interview/profile, new product, photo feature and travel; *all* must pertain to California. Length: 800-4,000 words. Pays expenses of writers on assignment.

Photos: Assigns most photos; reviews portfolios. Captions, model releases and identification of subjects required. Buys one-time rights.

Columns/Departments: Open to freelance: Home, New West. Query with published clips. Length: 750-2,000 words. Pays $450-1,500.

Tips: "Query first with clips. *Don't* send complete manuscript. *Read* the magazine."

‡CENTURY CITY MAGAZINE, Affinity Publishing, 23919 Ventura Blvd., Calabasas CA 91302. (818)347-5953. Managing Editor: A. Henry Shaw. 50% freelance written. Bimonthly magazine about local business in Century City and surrounding area. Estab. 1989. Circ. 30,000. Pays on publication. Byline given. Buys all rights. Simultaneous and photocopied submissions OK. Query for electronic submissions. Computer printout submissions OK. Sample copy and writer's guidelines for 9x12 SASE with $2.50 in postage.

Nonfiction: Book excerpts, essays, expose, general interest and humor. Query. Length: 500-3,000. Pays $500-1,000 for assigned articles; $250-500 for unsolicited articles. Sometimes pays expenses of writers on assignment.

Photos: State availability of photos with submission. Reviews contact sheets. Offers no additional payment for photos accepted with ms. Captions, model releases and identification of subjects required. Buys one-time or all rights.

Columns/Departments: Get Outa Town (local travel). Length: 500-1,000 words. Pays $250-500.

Fillers: Anecdotes, facts and newsbreaks. Pays $50-100.

L.A. STYLE, 6834 Hollywood Blvd., Los Angeles CA 90028. (213)467-4244. Editor: Ms. Joie Davidow. Managing Editor: Michael Lassell. 80% freelance written. Monthly magazine on Los Angeles lifestyle. "Our readers are highly educated and affluent; they are involved in the artistic, social and political whirlwind of Los Angeles and they are always interested in what is new—*L.A. Style* attempts to discover and re-discover Los Angeles." Circ. 65,000. Pays within 30 days of acceptance. Byline given. Offers 25% kill fee—"one rewrite may be required before kill fee is paid." Buys first rights. Submit seasonal/holiday material 4 months in advance. Simultaneous and photocopied submissions OK. Computer printout submissions OK; prefers letter-quality. Reports in "one week to two months depending on editorial load." Sample copy $3; writer's guidelines for #10 SASE.

Nonfiction: Book excerpts, essays, exposé, general interest, historical/nostalgic, how-to, humor, interview/profile, opinion, personal experience, photo feature, technical, travel. No "health and beauty stereotyped women's magazine stories; any story that does not have a strong L.A. angle." Buys 100 mss/year. Query with published clips or send complete ms. Length: 1,000-5,000 words. Pays $300-1,500. Sometimes pays expenses of writers on assignment.

Photos: "We prefer to assign our own art." Buys one-time rights.

Fiction: Bob LaBrasca, senior editor. Erotica, ethnic, experimental, humorous, novel excerpts, slice-of-life vignettes. "No teen, genre, romance, devotional—what we do want is sophisticated, highly literate, innovative fiction." Buys 4-8 mss/year. Send complete ms. Length: 1,000-5,000 words. Pays $300-1,000.

Tips: "It is not impossible to write for *L.A. Style* without living in Los Angeles—it is just very unlikely that writers who do not know the evolving city intimately will be able to find the contemporary slant we require. Service pieces, how-to pieces, humor pieces and overview pieces are the hardest to come by and the most eagerly considered."

L.A. WEST, Santa Monica Bay Printing & Publishing Co., #245, 919 Santa Monica Blvd., Santa Monica CA 90401. (213)458-3376. Editor-in-Chief: Jan Loomis. Editor: Mary Daily. 75% freelance written. Works with a small number of new/unpublished writers each year. Monthly magazine of the community of West Los Angeles. "We are a sophisticated magazine with local events and people as our focus, sent free to the entire community." Circ. 60,000. Pays on acceptance. Publishes ms an average of 6-12 months after acceptance. Byline and author bionote given. Buys first North American serial rights and all rights; makes work-for-hire assignments. Submit seasonal/holiday material 6 months in advance. Photocopied submissions OK. Query for electronic submissions. Computer printout submissions acceptable; prefers letter-quality. Reports in 3 months on queries. Sample copy and writer's guidelines for 9x12 SAE with 7 first class stamps.

Nonfiction: Historical/nostalgic, interview/profile, opinion, lifestyle articles, photo features and travel. No extreme positions, titillation, pornography, etc. Buys 20 mss/year. Query with published clips. Length: 200-1,500 words. Pays $25-500.

Photos: State availability of photos. Reviews color and b&w contact sheets, 4x4 transparencies and 8x10 glossy prints. Pays $35 for b&w; $40 for color.
Tips: "We're looking for well-written articles on subjects that will interest our upscale readers (average income $125,900; average age 39)."

LOS ANGELES MAGAZINE, ABC/Capital Cities, 1888 Century Park East, Los Angeles CA 90067. (213)557-7569. Editor: Geoff Miller. 98% freelance written. Monthly magazine about southern California. "The primary editorial role of the magazine is to aid a literate, upscale audience in getting the most out of life in the Los Angeles area." Circ. 174,000. Pays on acceptance. Publishes ms an average of 4 months after acceptance. Byline given. Offers 30% kill fee. Buys first North American serial rights. Submit seasonal/holiday material 3-6 months in advance. Computer printout submissions acceptable; prefers letter-quality. Reports in 6 weeks. Sample copy $4; writer's guidelines for #10 SASE.
Nonfiction: Rodger Claire, articles editor. Book excerpts (about L.A. or by famous L.A. author); exposé (any local issue); general interest; historical/nostalgic (about L.A. or Hollywood); and interview/profile (about L.A. person). Buys 400 mss/year. Query with published clips. Length: 250-3,500 words. Pays $50-1,200. Sometimes pays expenses of writers on assignment.
Photos: Rodger Claire, photo editor. State availability of photos.
Columns/Departments: Rodger Claire, column/department editor. Buys 170 mss/year. Query with published clips. Length: 250-1,200 words. Pays $50-500.

LOS ANGELES TIMES MAGAZINE, Los Angeles Times, Times Mirror Sq., Los Angeles CA 90053. Editorial Director: Wallace Guenther. Editor: Linda Mathews. 50% freelance written. Weekly magazine of regional general interest. Circ. 1 million. Payment schedule varies. Publishes ms an average of 2 months after acceptance. Byline given. Buys first North American serial rights. Submit seasonal/holiday material 3 months in advance. Simultaneous queries and submissions OK. Computer printout submissions acceptable; no dot-matrix. Reports in 1 month. Sample copy for 9x12 SAE and 6 first class stamps. Writer's guidelines for SAE and 2 first class stamps.
Nonfiction: General interest, historical/nostalgic, interview/profile, personal experience and photo feature. Must have California tie-in, but no need to be set in California. Query with published clips. "We welcome all queries." Length: 400-1,800 words. Pays $400-2,000. Sometimes pays the expenses of writers on assignment.
Photos: Query first. Reviews color transparencies and b&w prints. Payment varies. Captions, model releases and identification of subjects required. Buys one-time rights.
Tips: "The writer should know the subject well or have researched it adequately. As for style, the best style is when the writer goes to the trouble of employing proper English and self-edits an article prior to submission."

‡**METRO, Santa Clara Valley's Weekly**, Metro Publishing Ltd., 410 S. First St., San Jose CA 95113. (408)298-8000. Editor: Dan Pulcrano. Asst. Editor: Leslie Ariel. 50% freelance written. Weekly tabloid; news, features, arts and entertainment. "Fresh, original and lively writing targeted towards young adults in Silicon Valley (San Jose metropolitan area)." Circ. 50,000. Pays on publication. Publishes ms an average of 1 month after acceptance. Byline given. Offers 35% minimum kill fee on assigned pieces; request assignment memorandum. Buys first North American serial rights and nonexclusive anthology rights. Submit seasonal/holiday material 2 months in advance. Simultaneous, photocopied and previously published submissions OK only if it hasn't been published in Northern California or national publication. Query for electronic submissions. Computer printout submissions OK; prefers letter-quality. Reports in 1 month. Sample copy for 9x12 SAE with 3 first class stamps. Writer's guidelines for #10 SASE.
Nonfiction: Book excerpts, essays, exposé, general interest, humor, interview/profile, opinion (does not mean letters to the editor) and photo feature (fashion). Buys 100 mss/year. Query with published clips, or send complete ms. Length: 800-5,000 words. Pays 75-250 for assigned articles. Pays $40-150 for unsolicited articles. Sometimes pays expenses of writers on assignment, by prior arrangement only.
Photos: State availability of photos with submission. Send photos with submission. Reviews contact sheets, color 35mm or 2¼ transparencies and b&w prints. Offers $15-25 per photo (more for color covers). Model releases (for non-news photos) and identification of subjects required. Buys one-time rights.
Columns/Departments: Buys 150 mss/year. Send complete ms. Length: 1,000-1,200 words. Pays $15-75.

‡**MONTEREY LIFE MAGAZINE, The Magazine of California's Spectacular Central Coast**, Box 2107, Monterey CA 93942. (408)372-9200. FAX: (408)372-6259. Editor: Ann Sage. 50% freelance written. Prefers to work with published/established writers. Monthly magazine covering art, regional affairs, music, sports, environment and lifestyles for "a sophisticated readership in the central California coast area." Circ. 25,000. Pays on publication. Publishes ms an average of 3 months after acceptance. Byline given. Submit seasonal/holiday material 4 months in advance. Simultaneous queries, and simultaneous and photocopied submissions OK. Electronic submissions acceptable via IBM format but requires hard copy also. Computer printout submissions acceptable. Reports in 3 weeks on queries; 6 weeks on mss. Sample copy for $1.85 postage and SAE.

Nonfiction: Historical/nostalgic, humor, interview/profile, photo feature and travel. No poetry. "All articles must pertain to issues and lifestyles within the counties of Monterey, Santa Cruz and San Benito." Buys 75 mss/year. Query with published clips if available. Length: 175-3,000 words. Pays 5-10¢/word. Sometimes pays expenses of writers on assignment.

Photos: State availability of photos. Pays $20-100 for color transparencies; $15-25 for 5x7 and 8x10 b&w prints. Captions, model releases and identification of subjects required.

Columns/Departments: Community Focus. Query with published clips. Length: 250-1,000 words. Pays $25-40.

Tips: "Since we have a core of very capable freelance writers for longer articles, it is easier to break in with short articles and fillers. Ask probing questions."

NORTHCOAST VIEW, Blarney Publishing, Box 1374, Eureka CA 95502. (707)443-4887. Publishers/Editors: Scott K. Ryan and Damon Maguire. 95% freelance written. Works with a small number of new/unpublished writers each year. A monthly magazine covering entertainment, recreation, the arts, consumer news, in-depth news, fiction and poetry for Humboldt and Del Norte counties audience, mostly 18-50-year-olds. Circ. 22,500. Pays on publication. Publishes ms an average of 1-6 months after acceptance. Byline given. Generally buys all rights, but will reassign. Submit seasonal/holiday material 6 months in advance. Simultaneous queries, and simultaneous (so long as not in our area), photocopied and previously published (so long as rights available) submissions OK. Query for electronic submissions. Computer printout submissions acceptable; no dot-matrix. Reports in 2 months on queries; 6 months on mss. Sample copy $2; writer's guidelines for SASE.

Nonfiction: Book excerpts (locally written); expose (consumer, government); historical/nostalgic (local); humor; interview/profile (entertainment, recreation, arts or political people planning to visit county); new product (for arts); photo feature (local for art section); and travel (weekend and short retreats accessible from Humboldt County). "Most features need a Humboldt County slant." Special issues include Christmas (December). Buys 30-40 mss/year. Query with published clips or send complete ms. Length: 1,250-2,500 words. Pays $25-75.

Photos: State availability of photos with query letter or ms and send proof sheet, if available. Pays $5-15 for 5x7 b&w prints; $25-100 for 35mm Ecktachrome slides. Captions, model releases and identification of subjects required. Buys all rights but will reassign.

Columns/Departments: A La Carte (restaurant reviews of county restaurants); Ex Libris (books); Reel Views (film); Vinyl Views (albums); Cornucopia (calendar); Poetry; Rearview (art). Buys 80-100 mss/year. Send complete ms. Length: 500-750 words. Pays $25-75.

Fiction: Adventure, condensed novels, erotica (light), experimental, fantasy, horror, humorous, mystery, novel excerpts (local), science fiction and suspense. "We are open to most ideas and like to publish new writers. Topic and length are all very flexible—quality reading is the only criteria." No clichéd, contrived or predictable fiction." Buys 10-15 mss/year. Send complete ms. Length: 600-4,500 words; "a longer good piece may run 2-3 months consecutively, if it breaks well."

Poetry: Stephen Miller, poetry editor. Avant-garde, free verse, haiku, light verse and traditional. Open to all types. No "sappy, overdone or symbolic poetry." Buys work of 12-20 poets (3-4 poems each)/year. Submit maximum 5 poems. Length: 12-48 lines. Pays $25.

Tips: "Our greatest need always seems to be for reviews—book, album and film. Films need to be fairly current, but remember that some films take a while to get up to Humboldt County. Book and album—we're always looking for somewhat current but lesser known works that are exceptional. The most frequent mistakes made by writers are using too few quotes and too much paraphrasing."

PENINSULA MAGAZINE, 656 Bair Island Rd., 2nd Fl., Redwood City CA 94063. (415)368-8800. FAX: (415)368-6251. Editor: David Gorn. Managing Editor: Dale Conour. 50% freelance written. A monthly magazine on San Mateo and Santa Clara counties. "We have an educated and affluent readership, so we need stories with a little bite." Circ. 40,000. Pays on acceptance. Publishes ms an average of 2 months after acceptance. Byline given. 30% kill fee. Buys first rights. Submit seasonal/holiday material 4 months in advance. Simultaneous, photocopied and previously published submissions OK. Query for electronic submissions. Computer printout submissions OK. Reports in 2 months. Sample copy for 9x12 SAE with $4 postage. Writer's guidelines for #10 SAE with 42¢ postage.

Nonfiction: Exposé, general interest, interview/profile, photo feature, environment, innovations, power and money, the arts, history, fashion, finance, food, health, fitness and medicine. Buys 30 mss/year. Send complete ms. Length: 2,000-4,000 words. Pays $125-600 for assigned articles. Pays $75-350 for unsolicited articles. Sometimes pays the expenses of writers on assignment. State availability of photos with submission or send photos with submission. Reviews transparencies and prints. Offers $10-100 per photo. Model releases and identification of subjects required. Buys one-time rights.

SACRAMENTO MAGAZINE, Box 2424, Sacramento CA 95812-2424. Editor: Nancy Martini Curley. 60-70% freelance written. Works with a small number of new/unpublished writers each year. Monthly magazine emphasizing a strong local angle on politics, local issues, human interest and consumer items for readers in the middle to high income brackets. Pays on publication. Publishes ms an average of 3 months after acceptance. Rights vary; generally buys first North American serial rights, rarely second serial (reprint) rights. Original mss only (no previously published submissions). Computer printout submissions acceptable; prefers letter-quality. Reports in 8 weeks. Sample copy $3.50; writer's guidelines for #10 SASE.

Nonfiction: Local issues vital to Sacramento quality of life. Buys 15 unsolicited feature mss/year. Query first; no phone queries. Length: 2,000-3,000 words, depending on author, subject matter and treatment. Sometimes pays expenses of writers on assignment.

Photos: State availability of photos. Payment varies depending on photographer, subject matter and treatment. Captions (including IDs, location and date) required. Buys one-time rights.

Columns/Departments: Business, home and garden, media, parenting, first person essays, local travel, gourmet, profile, sports and city arts (850-1,250 words); City Lights (250 words).

‡SAN DIEGO MAGAZINE, Box 85409, San Diego CA 92138. (619)225-8953. Managing Editor: Winke Self. Editor-in-Chief: Edwin F. Self. 30% freelance written. Prefers to work with published/established writers; works with a small number of new/unpublished writers each year. A monthly magazine emphasizing San Diego; 310 pages. Circ. 69,000. Pays on publication. Publishes ms an average of 3 months after acceptance. Buys all rights, but will negotiate. Byline given. Submit seasonal/holiday material 6 months in advance of issue date. Simultaneous and photocopied submissions OK. Computer printout submissions acceptable; prefers letter-quality. Query for electronic submissions (prefers stories by disk or modem). Reports in 2 months. Sample copy $3.

Nonfiction: Exposé (serious, documented); general interest (to San Diego region); historical (San Diego region); interview (with notable San Diegans); nostalgia; photo essays; profile; service guides; and travel. Buys variable number of mss/issue. Prefers query with clips of published work. Send photocopies. Length: 2,000-5,000 words. Pays $600 maximum. Pays the expenses of writers on assignment.

Photos: State availability of photos with query. Fee negotiable. Captions required. Model release required. Buys one-time rights.

Columns/Departments: Topics include Up and Coming (fine and popular arts); Books; Music and Dance; Films; and Urban Eye (San Diego related short items). Length: 500-100 words. Pays $50-75.

Tips: "Write better lead paragraphs; write shorter, with greater clarity; wit and style appreciated; stick to basic magazine journalism principles."

‡SAN FRANCISCO BAY GUARDIAN, 2700 19th St., San Francisco CA 94110. (415)824-7660. Editor/Publisher: Bruce Brugmann. 60% freelance written. Works with a small number of new/unpublished writers each year. An urban newsweekly specializing in investigative, consumer and lifestyle reporting for a sophisticated, urban audience. Circ. 65,000, Pays 1 month after publication. Publishes ms an average of 2 months after acceptance. Byline given. Buys 200 mss/year. Buys first rights. Photocopied submissions OK; no simultaneous or multiple submissions. Query for electronic submissions. Computer printout submissions acceptable.

Nonfiction: Tim Redmond, city editor; Jean Fields, arts and entertainment editor; Eileen Ecklund features and book editor. Publishes "incisive local news stories, investigative reports, features, analysis and interpretation, how-to, consumer and entertainment reviews. Most stories have a Bay Area angle." Freelance material should have a "public interest advocacy journalism approach." Sometimes pays the expenses of writers on assignment.

Photos: John Schmitz, photo editor. Purchased with or without mss.

Tips: "Work with our volunteer and intern projects in investigative, political and consumer reporting. We teach the techniques and send interns out to do investigative research. We like to talk to writers in our office before they begin doing a story."

SAN FRANCISCO FOCUS, The City Magazine for the San Francisco Bay Area, 680 8th St., San Francisco CA 94103. (415)553-2800. Editor: Mark K. Powelson. Managing Editor: Rick Clogher. 80% freelance written. Prefers to work with published/established writers. A monthly city/regional magazine. Circ. 200,000. Pays on acceptance. Publishes ms an average of 2 months after acceptance. Byline given. Offers 33% kill fee. Buys one-time rights. Submit seasonal/holiday material 5 months in advance. Simultaneous queries and previously published submissions OK. Query for electronic submissions. Computer printout submissions acceptable; prefers letter-quality. Reports in 6 weeks. Sample copy $2.50; free writer's guidelines.

Nonfiction: Expose, humor, interview/profile, the arts, politics, public issues and travel. All stories should relate in some way to the San Francisco Bay Area (travel excepted). Query with published clips or send complete ms. Length: 750-4,000 words. Pays $75-750. Sometimes pays the expenses of writers on assignment.

THE SAN GABRIEL VALLEY MAGAZINE, Miller Books, 2908 W. Valley Blvd., Alhambra CA 91803. (213)284-7607. Editor-in-Chief: Joseph Miller. 75% freelance written. Bimonthly magazine. For middle- to upper-income people who dine out often at better restaurants in Los Angeles County. Circ. 3,400. Pays on publication. Publishes ms an average of 45 days after acceptance. Buys simultaneous rights, second serial (reprint) rights and one-time rights. Phone queries OK. Submit seasonal/holiday material 1 month in advance.

Simultaneous, photocopied, and previously published submissions OK. Computer printout submissions acceptable. Reports in 2 weeks. Sample copy $1.

Nonfiction: Exposé (political); informational (restaurants in the Valley); inspirational (success stories and positive thinking); interview (successful people and how they made it); profile (political leaders in the San Gabriel Valley); and travel (places in the Valley). Interested in 500-word humor articles. Buys 18 unsolicited mss/year. Length: 500-10,000 words. Pays 5¢/word.

Columns/Departments: Restaurants, Education, Valley News and Valley Personality. Buys 2 mss/issue. Send complete ms. Length: 500-1,500 words. Pays 5¢/word.

Fiction: Historical (successful people) and western (articles about Los Angeles County). Buys 2 mss/issue. Send complete ms. Length: 500-10,000 words. Pays 5¢/word.

Tips: "Send us a good personal success story about a Valley or a California personality. We are also interested in articles on positive thinking."

‡VALLEY MAGAZINE, World of Communications, Inc., Suite 275, 16800 Devonshire St., Granada Hills CA 91344. (818)368-3353. Editor: Barbara Wernik. 90% freelance written. Monthly magazine covering topics and people of interest to the San Francisco Valley. Circ. 40,000. Pays within 2 months of acceptance. Publishes ms an average of 3 months after acceptance. Byline given. Offers 20% kill fee. Buys first North American serial rights. Submit seasonal/holiday material 6 months in advance. Simultaneous, photocopied and previously published submissions OK. Computer printout submissions acceptable; no dot-matrix. Reports in 2 weeks. Sample copy for $3 and 10×13 SAE; writer's guidelines for #10 SASE.

Nonfiction: Book excerpts, education, business, essays, general interest, how-to, humor, interview/profile, personal experience and travel. "General interest articles range from health to business to personality profiles. There must be a Valley slant. Audience is upscale, mature professionals." Special issues include, Dining, Travel, Health and Local Business. Buys 130 mss/year. Query with published clips. Length: 750-2,000 words. Pays $50-350 for assigned articles; pays $25-250 for unsolicited articles. Sometimes pays the expenses of writers on assignment.

Photos: State availability of photos with submission. Reviews transparencies. Captions, model releases and identification of subjects required.

VENTURA COUNTY & COAST REPORTER, VCR Inc., Suite 213, 1583 Spinnaker Dr., Ventura CA 93001. (805)658-2244; (805)656-0707. Editor: Nancy Cloutier. 12% freelance written. Works with a small number of new/unpublished writers each year. Weekly tabloid covering local news. Circ. 35,000. Pays on publication. Publishes ms an average of 2 weeks after acceptance. Byline given. Buys first North American serial rights. Computer printout submissions acceptable; no dot-matrix. Reports in 3 weeks.

Nonfiction: General interest (local slant), humor, interview/profile and travel (local—within 500 miles). Local (Ventura County) slant predominates. Length: 2-5 double-spaced typewritten pages. Pays $10-25.

Photos: State availability of photos with ms. Reviews b&w contact sheet.

Columns/Departments: Entertainment, Sports, Dining News, Real Estate and Boating Experience (Southern California). Send complete ms. Pays $10-25.

Tips: "As long as topics are up-beat with local slant, we'll consider it."

WEST, 750 Ridder Park Dr., San Jose CA 95190. (408)920-5796. Editor: Jeffrey Klein. 50% freelance written. Prefers to work with published/established writers. Weekly newspaper/magazine, published with the *San Jose Mercury News*. Circ. 320,000. Pays on acceptance. Publishes ms an average of 3 months after acceptance. Byline given. Buys first serial rights and occasionally second serial (reprint) rights. Submit seasonal material (skiing, wine, outdoor living) 3 months in advance. Will consider photocopied and simultaneous submissions (if the simultaneous submission is out of the area). Computer printout submissions acceptable; prefers letter-quality. Reports in 1 month.

Nonfiction: A general newspaper-magazine requiring that subjects be related to California (especially the Bay Area) and the interests of California. Length: 1,000-4,000 words. Query with published clips. Pays $250-600. Sometimes (but infrequently) pays expenses of writers on assignment.

Photos: Sandra Eisert, art director. Payment varies for b&w and color photos purchased with or without mss. Captions required.

Colorado

SUNDAY MAGAZINE, *Rocky Mountain News*, 400 W. Colfax Ave., Denver CO 80204. (303)892-5000. FAX: (303)892-5499. Magazine Editor: Joe Rassenfoss. Sunday supplement of daily newspaper covering general interest topics; newspaper circulates throughout Colorado and southern part of Wyoming. Circ. 380,000. Pays on publication. Byline given. Buys one-time rights. Submit seasonal/holiday material 2 months in advance. Simultaneous and previously published submissions OK ("if outside circulation area—Colorado and Southern Wyoming"). Reports in 1 month.

Nonfiction: Investigative; general interest; historical; photo feature; articles with Western angle on an out-of-the-way place; travel articles. Also looking for commentary pieces for Sunday newspapers; query Jean Otto. Buys 20 mss/year. Send complete ms. Length: 1,500-2,000 words. Pays $30-100.

Photos: State availability of photos or send photos with ms ("if article covers an event we can't cover ourselves"). Reviews color transparencies and 8x10 b&w glossy prints. Pay varies. Captions required. Buys one-time rights.

Tips: "The magazine is increasingly interested in people, events and trends that face Coloradans. We are less and less interested in personal columns."

‡VAIL MAGAZINE, Vail Magazine, Inc., Suite 109, 2077 N. Frontage Rd., W., Box 368, Vail CO 81658. (303) 476-6600. Editor: Connie Knight. 60% freelance written. Magazine published 3 times/year on skiing and anything relating to Vail, Colorado. *"Vail Magazine* is geared toward residents, tourists and second-homeowners ages 18-86. Articles must pertain to the Vail Valley (Eagle County), sports, lifestyles, etc." Circ. 20,000. Pays on publication. Publishes ms an average of 4 months after acceptance. Byline given. Offers $50 kill fee. Buys first rights. Submit seasonal/holiday material 6 months in advance. Query for electronic submissions. Computer printout submissions OK, prefers letter-quality. Reports in 1 month on queries, 2 months on ms. Sample copy $3. Writer's guidelines for SASE.

Nonfiction: General interest, how-to (ski, visit Vail, etc.), humor, interview/profile, opinion, personal experience, photo feature, technical (ski) and cooking at high altitudes. Buys 30-40 mss/year. Query with published clips. Length: 500-2,500. Pays $50-250. Sometimes pays with premiums in addition to cash payment. Sometimes pays expenses of writers on assignment.

Photos: State availability of photos with submission. Reviews 1x1 transparencies and 5 × 7 prints. Offers $25-150/photo. Captions, model releases and identification of subjects required. Buys one-time rights.

Columns/Departments: Profiles (second homeowners and/or locals with color) 1,200-2,200 words; Fashion (ski-oriented or summer sports) 750-1,200 words; Fishing (in the Rocky Mountains, prefer Eagle County) 500-750 words; Cooking (only as it pertains to high-altitude cooking) 500-750 words; Skiing ("ski scoops" tips for beginners through experts) 500-750 words. Buys 4-6 mss/year. Query with published clips. Pays 50-220.

Poetry: Free verse and light verse. Buys 1 poem/year. Submit 2-3 maximum at one time. Pays $25-100.

Tips: "Lively, accurate, well-researched articles will find a spot with us, providing they pertain to Vail, Beaver Creek and the outdoors lifestyle of the area. Our readers are well-traveled, educated and sophisticated."

Connecticut

‡HARTFORD MONTHLY, Hartford Monthly, Inc. 486 New Park Ave., West Hartford CT 06110. (203)236-7272. Editor: Debra A. Martorelli. 95% freelance written. Monthly magazine on Greater Hartford area. Estab. 1988. Circ. 31,000. Pays on publication. Publishes ms ms an average of 2 months after acceptance. Byline given. Offers 20% kill fee. Buys first North American serial rights. Submit holiday/seasonal material 6 months in advance. Photocopied submissions OK. Computer printout submissions OK; prefers letter-quality. Reports in 3 weeks on queries; 2 months on mss. Sample copy for 8½x11 SAE with $1.45 postage. Free writer's guidelines.

Nonfiction: Essays, exposé, historical/nostalgic, how-to (gardening, home repair, cooking, decorating, etc.), humor, interview/profile, opinion, personal experience, photo feature and travel. Buys 38-42 mss/year. Query with published clips or send complete ms. Length: 1,000-4,000 words. Pays $185-500. Sometimes pays expenses of writers on assignment.

Photos: State availability of photos with submission or send photos with submission. Reviews 4x5 transparencies and 5x7 prints. Model releases and identification of subjects required. Buys one-time rights.

Fiction: Adventure, ethnic, experimental, fantasy, historical, horror, humorous, mainstream, mystery, science fiction, slice-of-life vignette and suspense. "No erotica, religious." Buys 6 mss/year. Query with published clips or send complete ms. Length: 1,500-4,000 words. Pays $250-500.

Poetry: Avant-garde, free verse, haiku, light verse and traditional. "No erotica, religious." Buys 6 poems/year. Submit maximum 6 poems. Length: 15-45 lines. Pays $100-175.

Fillers: Anecdotes, facts, newsbreaks and short humor. Buys 36/year. Length: 50-150 words. Pays $25-75.

HARTFORD WOMAN, a women's newspaper, Gamer Publishing, 595 Franklin Ave., Hartford CT 06114. (203)278-3800. Editor: Susan Phillips Plese. 100% freelance written. Monthly tabloid covering women's issues. "Publication is for and about working women in the Hartford area. Any valid women's issue will be given serious editorial consideration." Circ. 40,000. Pays on publication. Publishes ms an average of 3 months after acceptance. Byline given. Offers 50% kill fee. Buys first rights and reprint rights. Submit seasonal/holiday material 3 months in advance. Simultaneous (unless within our geographic area), photocopied and previously published submissions OK. Reports in 2 weeks on queries; 1 month on mss. Sample copy for 9x12 SASE and $1.25 postage; writer's guidelines for #10 SASE.

Nonfiction: Exposé, general interest (women's), historical/nostalgic, how-to, humor, opinion, jobs and education. All submissions must meet gender and geographic criteria. Special issues include Health and Bridal (January); Fashion (April and September); Education (August); and Gift Guide (November). Buys 150 mss/year. Query with published clips or send complete ms. Length: 500-1,500 words. Pays $25-60.

Photos: Send photos with submission. Offers $7.50/photo. Identification of subjects required. Buys one-time rights.

Columns/Departments: Arts, Auto, Finance, Health, Government, Fashion. Buys 50 mss/year. Query with published clips or send complete ms. Length: 800-1,000 words. Pays $35. Most open to new freelance writers is "Last Word," monthly opinion piece, which may be humorous, reflective or serious. Send complete ms. Length: 750-1,000 words. Buys 12/year. Pays $35.

Tips: "Telephone the editor. Women writers are given preference over men writers; please don't try the same old angles; we're looking for fresh ideas. We have limited editorial space, and must plan issues three months in advance. In addition, each month has an editorial focus; most of the features assigned must relate to that focus."

District of Columbia

THE WASHINGTON POST, 1150 15th St. NW, Washington DC 20071. (202)334-7591. Travel Editor: Linda L. Halsey. 60% freelance written. Works with small number of new/unpublished writers each year. Prefers to work with published/established writers. Weekly newspaper travel section (Sunday). Pays on publication. Publishes ms an average of 3-6 months after acceptance. Byline given. "We are now emphasizing staff-written articles as well as quality writing from other sources. Stories are rarely assigned; all material comes in on speculation; there is no fixed kill fee." Buys first North American serial rights. Query for electronic submissions. Computer printout submissions acceptable if legible; no dot-matrix. Usually reports in 3 weeks.

Nonfiction: Emphasis is on travel writing with a strong sense of place, color, anecdote and history. Query with published clips. Length: 1,500-2,500 words, plus sidebar for practical information.

Photos: State availability of photos with ms.

THE WASHINGTON POST MAGAZINE, *The Washington Post*, 1150 15th St. NW, Washington DC 20071. Managing Editor: Stephen Petranek. 40% freelance written. Prefers to work with published/established writers. Weekly magazine featuring articles of interest to Washington readers. Circ. 1.2 million (Sunday). Average issue includes 3-5 feature articles and 4-6 columns. Pays on acceptance. Publishes ms an average of 2 months after acceptance. Byline given. Buys all rights or first North American serial rights, depending on fee. Submit seasonal material 4 months in advance. Photocopied submissions OK. Computer printout submissions acceptable; no dot-matrix unless near letter-quality. Reports in 6 weeks on queries; 3 weeks on mss. Sample copy for 9x12 SAE and 2 first class stamps.

Nonfiction: Controversial and consequential articles. Subject areas include children, science, politics, law and crime, media, money, arts, behavior, sports, society and photo feature. Buys 2 mss/issue. Query with published clips. Length: 1,500-6,500 words. Pays $200-up; competitive with major national magazine rates. Pays expenses of writers on assignment.

Photos: Reviews 4x5 or larger b&w glossy prints and 35mm or larger color transparencies. Model releases required.

THE WASHINGTONIAN MAGAZINE, 1828 L St. NW, Washington DC 20036. Editor: John A. Limpert. 20% freelance written. Prefers to work with published/established writers who live in the Washington area. For active, affluent and well-educated audience. Monthly magazine; 310 pages. Circ. 156,000. Buys first rights only. Pays on publication. Publishes ms an average of 2 months after acceptance. Simultaneous and photocopied submissions OK. Computer printout submissions acceptable; prefers letter-quality. Reports in 4-6 weeks. Sample copy for $3 and 9x12 SAE; writer's guidelines for #10 SASE.

Nonfiction: *"The Washingtonian* is written for Washingtonians. The subject matter is anything we feel might interest people interested in the mind and manners of the city. The style, as Wolcott Gibbs said, should be the author's—if he is an author, and if he has a style. The only thing we ask is thoughtfulness and that no subject be treated too reverently. Audience is literate. We assume considerable sophistication about the city, and a sense of humor." Buys how-to, personal experience, interview/profile, humor, coverage of successful business operations, think pieces and exposes. Buys 75 mss/year. Length: 1,000-7,000 words; average feature 4,000 words. Pays 30¢/word. Sometimes pays the expenses of writers on assignment. Query or submit complete ms.

Photos: Photos rarely purchased with mss.

Fiction and Poetry: Margaret Cheney, department editor. Must be Washington-oriented. No limitations on length for fiction; poetry not to exceed 30 lines. Pays 20¢/word for fiction. Payment is negotiable for poetry.

Florida

CORAL SPRINGS MONTHLY/PLANTATION MONTHLY, Box 8783, 7452 Wiles Rd., Coral Springs FL 33067. (305)344-8090. Editor: Karen King. Monthly magazine covering people who work and/or live in Coral Springs. "This family-oriented community in South Florida is also one of the fastest-growing and most affluent communities in the Southeastern United States. Our residents are well-educated and care a great deal about raising their children in today's world. We focus on the entire family, offering a variety of topics each month, from psychology and health to fashion, classic cars and interior design." Distributed to residents and businesses as well as people who plan to move here. 99% positive material." Circ. 8,000 each. Pays on publication. Publishes ms an average of 2-3 months after acceptance. Byline given. Offers $20 kill fee. Buys first rights and second serial (reprint) rights; all rights for assigned story. Submit seasonal/holiday material 5-6 months in advance. Photocopied submissions OK. Computer printout submissions OK; prefers letter-quality. Reports in 1 month. Sample copy $1.95.

Nonfiction: General interest (must interest yuppies or high class), how-to (on home decorating, gardening, fashion and beauty), humor (relating to family and children), interview/profile (Coral Springs people or celebrities who might frequent here), new products (pertaining to yuppies or high class) and travel. Buys 60 mss/year. Send complete ms; will return if not used. Length: 500-1,000 words. Pays $55-75.

Photos: Send photos with submission. Reviews transparencies (2½x2½ or 4x5); 5x7 prints. Captions, model releases and identification of subjects required. Fees negotiable.

Columns/Departments: On the Light Side (humorous slants on family life, raising children, etc.).Query with published clips. Length: 800-1,000 words. Pays $55.

Tips: "Send complete manuscript! We are too small and busy to respond back and forth with query letters. Anything which might appeal to families would be a good start. Our residents love to travel, care about world and community issues and like to learn about new things."

‡FOLIO WEEKLY, Landmark Communications, Suite 14, 8101 Phillips Highway, Jacksonville FL 32256. (904)733-3103. Editor: Judy Wells. 60% freelance written. Weekly tabloid on arts, entertainment, lifestyle. "An arts and entertainment direct distribution newsprint magazine aimed at young, active affluent residents of greater Jacksonville, Florida." Circ. 30,000. Pays on publication. Publishes ms an average of 1-2 months after acceptance. Byline given. Negotiable kill fee. Buys first North American serial rights, second serial (reprint) rights or makes work-for-hire assignments. Submit seasonal/holiday material 4 months in advance. Simultaneous and photocopied submissions OK. Computer printout submissions OK; prefers letter-quality. Reports in 2-3 weeks on queries; 2-4 weeks on mss. Sample copy for 9x12 SAE.

Nonfiction: Humor and opinion. Buys 80-100 mss/year. Query with published clips. Length: 100-3,000 words. Pays $10-200 for assigned articles. Sometimes pays expenses of writers on assignment.

Photos: State availability of photos with submission. Offers $10 minimum per photo. Captions, model releases and identification of subjects required.

Columns/Departments: Folio Finish (locally oriented editorials), 1,000 words; Vanities (trendy items in local market), 250 words; Habitat (new developments, resales, condos, renovation), 300 words; Preview/Reviews (theatre, movies, dance, art, music, records, sports, restaurants), 600 words; and Briefcases (news nuggets, inside stories), 100-150 words. Buys 200-250 mss/year. Query with published clips. Pays $10-70.

Tips: "Currently seeking editorialists to write on issues of interest in N. Florida area every other week. Easiest way to catch my attention: write bright, hip, brief about something going on hereabouts we don't already know about, always keeping in mind that our readers are young (20-45) and affluent ($30,000 up salaries/incomes)."

‡GULF COAST, The Magazine of Southwest Florida, Gulfcoast Media Affiliates, 205 S. Airport Rd., Naples FL 33942. (813)643-4232. Editor: Warren Miller. 65% freelance written. Monthly magazine. "We reach an affluent, literate readership with information on Florida's Gulf Coast." Circ. 25,000. Pays within 30 days of acceptance. Byline given. Offers $50 kill fee. Buys first North American serial rights, one-time rights or makes work-for-hire assignments. Submit seasonal/holiday material 4 months in advance. Query for electronic submission. Computer printout submissions OK; no dot-matrix. Reports in 3 weeks on queries; 2 months on mss. Sample copy for 9x12 SAE with 6 first class stamps. Writer's guidelines for #10 SASE.

Nonfiction: General interest and interview/profile. "We are heavily regional and use very little material that is not written by area writers." Buys 100 mss/year. Query. Length: 800-3,000 words. Pays $120-500 for assigned articles. Pays expenses of writers on assignment.

Photos: State availability of photos with submission. Reviews contact sheets, 35mm to 4x5 transparencies and prints. Pays $25 minimum per photo. Captions, model releases and identification of subjects required. Buys one-time rights.

Columns/Departments: Outdoors, Business, Travel, Media, The Arts and People, 800-1,200 words. Buys 50 mss/year. Query. Pays $80-300.

ISLAND LIFE, The Enchanting Barrier Islands of Florida's Southwest Gulf Coast, Island Life Publications, Box X, Sanibel FL 33957. (813)472-4344. Editor: Joan Hooper. Editorial Associate: Susan Shores. 40% freelance written. Prefers to work with published/established writers, but works with a small number of new/unpublished writers each year. Quarterly magazine of the Barrier Islands from Anna Maria Island to Key West, for upper-income residents and vacationers of Florida's Gulf Coast area. Circ. 20,000. Pays on publication. Publishes ms an average of 1 year after acceptance. Byline given. Buys first serial rights and second serial (reprint) rights. Simultaneous queries, and simultaneous and photocopied submissions OK. Computer printout submissions acceptable; no dot-matrix. Reports in 1 month on queries; 3 months on mss. Sample copy and writer's guidelines for $3; writer's guidelines only for #10 SASE.
Nonfiction: General interest, historical. "Travel and interview/profile done by staff. Our past use of freelance work has been heavily on Florida wildlife (plant and animal), Florida cuisine, and Florida parks and conservancies. We are a regional magazine. No fiction or first-person experiences. No poetry. Our editorial emphasis is on the history, culture, wildlife, art, scenic, sports, social and leisure activities of the area." Buys 10-20 mss/year. Query with ms and photos. Length: 500-1,500 words. Pays 3-8¢/word.
Photos: Send photos with query. No additional payment. Captions, model releases, and identification of subjects required.
Tips: "Submissions are rejected, most often, when writer does not show adequate knowledge of subject. Send something new and fresh, not same old rehashed subjects. Please, no first person."

‡JACKSONVILLE MAGAZINE, Box 329, Jacksonville FL 32201. (904)353-0300. 75% freelance written. Works with a small number of new/unpublished writers each year. Published 8 times/year. Circ. 15,000. Pays on acceptance. Publishes ms an average of 6 months after acceptance. Buys all rights. Query. Submit seasonal material 3-6 months in advance. Query for electronic submissions. Computer printout submissions acceptable; prefers letter-quality. Reports in 3 weeks.
Nonfiction: Historical, business and other feature articles mostly pertaining specifically to Jacksonville or Northeast Florida. No fiction or poetry. Buys 30-40 mss/year. Length: usually 1,000-2,000 words. Pays $100-300. Sometimes pays expenses of writers on assignment.
Photos: Reviews b&w glossy prints with good contrast, and color transparencies. Pays $30 minimum for b&w; color terms to be arranged.
Tips: "Stories with a business/economic and/or northeastern Florida angle are strongly preferred."

‡PALM BEACH COUNTY MAGAZINE, Skyline Publishing, Inc., Suite 300-P, 515 N. Flagler Dr., West Palm Beach FL 33401. (407)659-6468. Editor: Anita Kirchen. Managing Editor: Kathy Stark. 80% freelance written. Monthly magazine about Palm Beach County. Circ. 8,200. Pays on publication. Publishes ms an average of 1 month after acceptance. Offers 25% kill fee. Buys all rights. Submit seasonal/holiday material 3-4 months in advance (prefers to assign). Computer printout submissions OK; prefers letter-quality. Reports in 1 week on queries; 2-3 weeks on mss. Free sample copy and writer's guidelines.
Nonfiction: General interest, historical/nostalgic, humor, interview/profile and photo feature. "No articles not pertaining to Palm Beach County; theater or movie reviews." Buys 30-40 mss/year. Query with published clips. Length: 1,000-3,000 words. Pays $150 minimum for assigned articles. Sometimes pays expenses for writers on assignment (pre-approved).
Photos: Send photos with submission. Offers $25-50 per photo. Model releases and identification of subjects required. Buys all rights.
Columns/Departments: Environment, Personal Finance and Real Estate (all pertaining to Palm Beach County residents), 1,000 words. Buys 25 mss/year. Query with published clips. Length: 500-1,000 words. Pays $100-150.
Poetry Morris Tobias, poetry editor. Free verse and light verse. Buys 3 poems/year. Submit maximum 3 poems. Length: 20-40 lines. Pays $50-100.

‡PALM BEACH LIFE, Palm Beach Newspapers Irrc./Cox Enterprises, 265 Royal Poinciana Way, Palm Beach FL 33486. (407)837-4750. Editor: Joyce Harr. 100% freelance written. Monthly magazine, a regional publication for Palm Beach County and South Florida. Circ. 19,971. Pays on acceptance. Publishes ms an average of 3 months after acceptance. Byline given. Buys first North American serial rights. Submit seasonal/holiday material 6 months in advance. Photocopied submissions OK. Query for electronic submission. Computer printout submissions OK; prefers letter-quality. Reports in 1 month.
Nonfiction: Essays, exposé, general interest, historical/nostalgic, humor, interview/profile, photo feature and travel. Buys 100 mss/year. Query with published clips. Length: 900-5,000 words. Pays $150-700 for assigned articles; $75-400 for unsolicited articles. Sometimes pays expenses of writers on assignment (depending on agreed-upon fee).
Photos: Send photos with submission. Reviews transparencies. Offers $35-200 per photo. Captions, model releases and identification of subjects required. Buys one-time rights.
Columns/Departments: Traveler's Journal (specifically focused topical travel pieces), 1,500 words; High Profile (profiles of people of interest to readers in our region), 2,500 words. Buys 36 mss/year. Query with published clips. Pays Pays $75-300.

‡SOUTH FLORIDA, Florida Media Affiliates, Suite 207, 600 Brickell Ave., Miami FL 33131. (305)374-5011. FAX: (305)374-7691. Editor: Marilyn A. Moore. Managing Editor: Joseph McQuay. 90% freelance written. Monthly magazine; general interest, must relate to Miami, Fort Lauderdale or Palm Beach County. Circ. 43,000. Pays on acceptance. Publishes ms an average of 3 months after acceptance. Byline given. Offers 50% kill fee. Buys first North American serial rights, one-time rights or second serial (reprint) rights. Submit seasonal/holiday material 4 months in advance. Simultaneous and previously published submissions OK. Query for electronic submissions. Computer printout submissions OK. Reports in 6 weeks on queries. Sample copy $2.65 plus $1.50 postage. Writer's guidelines for #10 SASE.

Nonfiction: Exposé, general interest, humor, interview/profile, photo feature, South Florida Lifestyles and travel. Buys 120 mss/year. Query with or without published clips, or send complete ms. Length: 3,500 words maximum. Pays $300-1,000 for assigned articles. Sometimes pays expenses of writers on assignment.

Photos: State availability of photos with submission. Identification of subjects required. Buys one-time rights.

Columns/Departments: Business, Media, Arts, Home and "Lunch With" (profile of a locally connected celebrity). Buys 12 mss/year. Query with published clips. Length: 1,200-1,500 words. Pays $300-400.

SUNSHINE: THE MAGAZINE OF SOUTH FLORIDA, The News & Sun-Sentinel Co., 101 N. New River Dr., Fort Lauderdale FL 33301-2293. (305)761-4017. Editor: John Parkyn. 50% freelance written. Prefers to work with published/established writers, and works with a small number of new/unpublished writers each year. A general interest Sunday magazine for the *News/Sun-Sentinel's* 750,000 readers in South Florida. Circ. 300,000. Pays within 1 month of acceptance. Publishes ms an average of 2 months after acceptance. Byline given. Offers 25% kill fee for assigned material. Buys first serial rights or one-time rights in the state of Florida. Submit seasonal/holiday material 2 months in advance. Simultaneous queries, and simultaneous, photocopied and previously published submissions OK. Computer printout submissions OK; prefers letter-quality. Reports in 2 weeks on queries; 1 month on mss. Free sample copy and writer's guidelines.

Nonfiction: General interest, how-to, interview/profile and travel. "Articles must be relevant to the interests of adults living in South Florida." Buys about 100 mss/year. Query with published clips. Length: 1,000-3,000 words; preferred length 1,500-2,500 words. Pays 20-25¢/word to $1,000 maximum.

Photos: State availability of photos. Pays negotiable rate for 35mm and 2¼ color slides and 8x10 b&w prints. Captions and identification of subjects required; model releases required for sensitive material. Buys one-time rights for the state of Florida.

Tips: "Do not phone—we don't have the staff to handle calls of this type—but do include your phone number on query letter. Keep your writing tight and concise—readers don't have the time to wade through masses of 'pretty' prose. We are always in the market for first-rate profiles, human-interest stories and travel stories (which must spotligt destinations within easy access of South Florida (e.g. S.E. U.S., Caribbean Central America.) Be as sophisticated and stylish as you can—Sunday magazines have come a long way from the Sunday supplements of yesteryear."

TAMPA BAY MAGAZINE, Tampa Bay Publications, Suite 101, 2531 Landmark Dr., Clearwater FL 34621. (813)791-4800. Editor: Aaron Fodiman. Associate Editor: DeAnn G. Semler. 60% freelance written. Bimonthly magazine, with quarterly spinoff publication, *Dining and Entertainment.* Editorial needs mostly local or statewide, with national/international fashion, travel and design interests. Circ. 20,000. Pays 1 week following publication. Publishes ms an average of 2 months after acceptance. Byline given. Offers 50% kill fee. Buys all North American rights. Submit seasonal/holiday material 4 months in advance. Simultaneous submissions OK. Computer printout submissions, double-spaced OK. Reports in 2 months on queries.

Nonfiction: General interest, humor, local interview/profile, photo feature, travel, food/dining, the arts and entertainment. Buys 6-8 mss/year. Query with 2 published clips. Length: 500-2,000 words. Pays $75-300. Sometimes pays expenses of writers on assignment.

Photos: State availability of photos with submission. Reviews 35mm or 4x5 transparencies and 4x5 prints. Offers no additional payment for photos with ms. Identification of subjects required. Buys one-time rights.

Tips: "Clean, double-spaced mss written in decent prose preferred. Since most of our needs are relative to the Tampa Bay area, it follows that most of our writers are local. For those who are residents, we are looking for upbeat, fresh approaches and idea or new, interesting stories. Delight us with something extraordinary."

TROPIC MAGAZINE, Sunday Magazine of the Miami Herald, Knight Ridder, 1 Herald Plaza, Miami FL 33132. (305)376-3432. Executive Editor: Gene Weingarten. Editor: Tom Shroder. 20% freelance written. Works with small number of new/unpublished writers each year. Weekly magazine covering general interest, locally oriented topics for local readers. Circ. 500,000. Pays on publication. Publishes ms an average of 2 months after acceptance. Byline given. Buys first serial rights. Submit seasonal/holiday material 2 months in advance. Computer printout submission OK; prefers letter-quality. Reports in 6 weeks. Sample copy for 11x14 SAE; writer's guidelines for #10 SAE.

Nonfiction: General interest; interview/profile (first person); and personal experience. No fiction or poetry. Buys 20 mss/year. Query with published clips or send complete ms. Length: 1,500-3,000 words. Pays $200-1,000/article.

Photos: Philip Brooker, art director. State availability of photos.

Close-up

Marilyn A. Moore
Editor
South Florida

The key to selling articles to *South Florida* magazine "is to write about something that will be of interest to everyone in the region," says Editor Marilyn A. Moore. "We strive to give our readers a mix of hard news, service journalism and fun features—always trying to beat the dailies in a journalistically competitive marketplace of ideas."

Moore says *South Florida* covers three counties "that are just beginning to think of themselves as a region. In a sense, we are helping to create the region by covering the things that everyone from Palm Beach to Key West has to cope with: traffic, dangers to the environment, crime, social problems, trends." The magazine also must target its content to an average reader who "is about 40 years old, is a college-educated professional or manager, has a household income of more than $100,000, and is intensely interested in eating out, getting the best buy and following culture," Moore says.

Moore brings experience as a reporter, college journalism instructor and freelancer to her job at *South Florida*. She received her bachelor's degree in journalism from Ohio State University and started her career working on small dailies in Ohio.

"Because I had lived overseas as a child, I am fluent in Spanish and gravitated naturally to Miami and its international flavor," Moore says. She worked for seven years as a city desk reporter and copy editor at the now-defunct *Miami News* and left that paper to freelance in 1985. As a freelancer, she covered regional news for *U.S. News and World Report* and wrote for a variety of magazines and newspapers. Moore also wrote an award-winning business column for *South Florida* magazine. When the previous editor left in 1988, she says the publisher invited her to apply for the job.

About 90 percent of *South Florida*'s stories are freelance written, "so we're always looking for good writers," Moore says. "What we buy is mostly based on queries, but I have also bought complete manuscripts if they fit into something we had planned and can be localized with a sidebar. The important thing is how it fits into our format, whether or not the idea is really intriguing and interesting, and how well it can be localized." Like most editors, Moore dislikes phone queries. "There's never enough time or enough tranquility to consider an unknown writer's idea over the phone. I'd much rather look over a letter in a quiet moment of the day," she says.

Moore advises writers to read *South Florida* carefully before they query. "A query should be well written with a clear 'peg' that fits our regional or local approach. The writer should tell me how he or she is going to quote local sources, possibly listing one or two. I also like to see a new writer's resume and published clips." The most common mistake freelancers make is proposing stories already done in regional newspapers. "We are in a very competitive marketplace and we don't run stories that everyone has seen in the newspapers unless there's a new twist," she says. "Once you've gotten the assignment, put in lots of color detail. Be thoughtful, analytical. Keep it regional."

— Glenda Tennant Neff

WATERFRONT NEWS, Ziegler Publishing Co., Inc., 1224 S.W. 1st Ave., Ft. Lauderdale FL 33315. (305)524-9450. Editor: John Ziegler. 75% freelance written. A monthly tabloid covering marine and boating topics for the Greater Ft. Lauderdale waterfront community. Circ. 35,000. Pays on publication. Publishes ms an average of 2 months after acceptance. Byline given. Buys first serial rights; second serial (reprint) rights or simultaneous rights. Submit seasonal/holiday material 3 months in advance. Computer printout submissions acceptable; prefers letter-quality. Reports in 1 month on queries. Sample copy for 9x12 SAE and 4 first class stamps; free writer's guidelines.

Nonfiction: Historical/nostalgic (nautical or Southern Florida); new marine products; opinion (on marine topics); technical (on marine topics); and marine travel. Buys 50 mss/year. Query with or without published clips, or send complete ms. Length: 500-1,000 words. Pays $50-200 for assigned articles; pays $25-200 for unsolicited articles. Sometimes pays the expenses of writers on assignment.

Photos: State availability of photos or send photos with submission. Reviews contact sheets and 3x5 or larger prints. Offers $5/photo. Buys one-time rights.

Columns/Departments: Query with published clips. Length 500-1,000 words. Pays $25-100.

Fillers: Anecdotes, facts, nautical one-liners to be illustrated by cartoonist, newsbriefs and short humor. Buys 12/year. Length 100-500 words. Pays $10-200.

Tips: "Nonfiction marine, nautical or South Florida stories are more likely to be published. Keep it under 1,000 words. Photos or illustrations help."

Georgia

GEORGIA JOURNAL, Grimes Publications, Inc., Box 27, Athens GA 30603-0027. Editor: Millard Grimes. 75% freelance written. Works with a small number of new/unpublished writers each year. Quarterly magazine covering the state of Georgia. Circ. 13,000. Pays on acceptance. Publishes ms an average of 3-6 months after acceptance. Byline given. Buys first serial rights. Submit seasonal/holiday material 4-6 months in advance. Photocopied submissions OK. Computer printout submissions acceptable; no dot-matrix. Reports in 1 month. Sample copy $3; writer's guidelines for #10 SASE.

Nonfiction: "We are interested in almost everything going on within the state. Although we specialize in an area, we maintain a general interest format. We do prefer to get pieces that are current and that have a human interest slant. We are also very interested in natural science pieces. We do our special focus issues and suggest that writers send for special focus schedule. We are not interested in sentimental reminiscences, anything risqué, specifically political or religious pieces." Buys 30-40 mss/year. Query. Length: 1,200-2,000 words. Pays $50-100. Pays expenses of writers on assignment.

Photos: State availability of photos or send photos with query or ms. Reviews sharp 8x10 b&w glossies. Captions, model releases and identification of subjects required.

Columns/Departments: "We have a section called Your Guide to Adventure, originated by Alfred W. Brown, former editor, *Brown's Guide*, *Brown's Newsletter*. Features what to do and where to go in and around Georgia."

Poetry: Janice Moore, poetry editor. Free verse, haiku, light verse and traditional. No poetry specifically dealing with another part of the country (out of the South) or anything not suitable for a general audience. "Most of our school-age readers are middle school and older." Uses 20 poems/year. Submit maximum 4 poems. Length: 25 lines. Pays in copies.

Tips: "We are now a quarterly publication, which will limit the number of freelance articles we accept. We have a section of short pieces (3-8 paragraphs) called Under the Chinaberry Tree where we always need good general interest submissions. These pieces are usually on topics not meriting feature article length. See a sample copy for Chinaberry Tree pieces that have been used."

NORTH GEORGIA JOURNAL, Legacy Communications, Inc., 110 Hunters Mill, Woodstock GA 30188. (404)928-7739. Editor: Olin Jackson. 75% freelance written. A quarterly magazine feature-length history articles and of travel opportunities to historic sites in the Southeast. "The *North Georgia Journal* is bought and subscribed to by persons interested in traveling to and reading about scenic attractions and historic sites and information indigenous to the north Georgia region and areas contiguous to the north Georgia area." Pays on publication. Publishes ms an average of 6 months after acceptance. Byline given. Buys first publication rights or all rights. Simultaneous submissions OK. Computer printout submissions OK; prefers letter-quality. Reports in 6 weeks. Sample copy $3.95 with 9x12 SAE and 8 first class stamps; free writer's guidelines.

Nonfiction: Historical/nostalgic, personal experiences, photo feature, travel. "I'm interested primarily in a first-person account of experiences involving the exploration of unique historic sites and travel opportunities indigenous to north Georgia and areas contiguous to north Georgia in other states." Buys 20-30 mss/year. Query. Length: 2,500-3,500 words. Pays $75-250.

Photos: Send photos with submission. "Photos are crucial to the acceptance of submissions." Reviews contact sheets and 8x10 and 5x7 prints. Offers no additional payment for photos accepted with ms. Captions and identification of subjects required. Buys first publication rights or all rights.

Tips: "We're interested in first person accounts of experiences involving travel to and exploration of unique and interesting historic sites and travel opportunities indigenous to the Appalachian Mountains of north Georgia and areas contiguous to north Georgia in Tennessee, North Carolina, South Carolina and Alabama. An approach similar to that taken by submissions in National Geographic magazine is most desired. Subject matter of particular interest includes gold mining; pioneers in the area; Indian/early settlements/communities; catastrophic events and occurrences; and travel subject matter related to present-day travel opportunities to scenic and historic sites such as historic bed and breakfast/mountain inns, etc."

Hawaii

ALOHA, THE MAGAZINE OF HAWAII AND THE PACIFIC, Davick Publishing Co., 49 S. Hotel St., #309, Honolulu HI 96813. FAX: (808)523-9875. Editor: Cheryl Tsutsumi. 50% freelance written. *Aloha* is a bimonthly regional magazine of international interest. "Most of our readers do not live in Hawaii, although most readers have been to the Islands at least once. Even given this fact, the magazine is directed primarily to residents of Hawaii in the belief that presenting material to an immediate critical audience will result in a true and accurate presentation that can be appreciated by everyone. *Aloha* is not a tourist publication and is not geared to such a readership, although travelers will find it to be of great value." Circ. 65,000. Pays on publication. Publishes ms an average of 6 months after acceptance; unsolicited ms can take a year or more. Byline given. Offers variable kill fee. Buys first-time rights. Submit seasonal/holiday material 1 year in advance. Photocopied submissions OK. Computer printout submissions acceptable; no dot-matrix. Reports in 2 months. Sample copy $2.95 with $2.75 postage; writer's guidelines for SASE.
Nonfiction: Book excerpts; historical/nostalgic (historical articles must be researched with bibliography); interview/profile; and photo features. Subjects include the arts, business, flora and fauna, people, sports, destinations, food, interiors and history of Hawaii. "We don't want stories of a tourist's experiences in Waikiki or odes to beautiful scenery. We don't want an outsider's impressions of Hawaii, written for outsiders." Buys 24 mss/year. Query with published clips. Length: 1,000-4,000 words. Pay ranges from $250-400. Sometimes pays expenses of writers on assignment.
Photos: State availability of photos with query. Pays $25 for b&w prints; prefers negatives and contact sheets. Pays $60 for 35mm (minimum size) color transparencies used inside; $125 for double-page bleeds; $175 for color transparencies used as cover art. "*Aloha* features Beautiful Hawaii, a collection of photographs illustrating that theme, in every issue. A second photo essay by a sole photographer on a theme of his/her own choosing is also run occcasionally. Queries are essential for the sole photographer essay." Model releases and identification of subjects required. Buys one-time rights.
Fiction: Ethnic and historical. "Fiction depicting a tourist's adventures in Waikiki is not what we're looking for. As a general statement, we welcome material reflecting the true Hawaiian experience." Buys 2 mss/year. Send complete ms. Length: 1,000-2,500 words. Pays $300.
Poetry: Haiku, light verse and traditional. No seasonal poetry or poetry related to other areas of the world. Buys 6 poems/year. Submit maximum 6 poems. Prefers "shorter poetry." Pays $25.
Tips: "Read *Aloha*. Be meticulous in research and have good illustrative material available."

HONOLULU, Honolulu Publishing Co., Ltd., 36 Merchant St., Honolulu HI 96813. (808)524-7400. FAX: (808)531-2306 Editor: Brian Nicol. 20% freelance written. Prefers to work with published/established writers. Monthly magazine covering general interest topics relating to Hawaii. Circ. 35,000. Pays on acceptance. Publishes ms an average of 4 months after acceptance. Byline given. Offers $50 kill fee. Buys first serial rights. Submit seasonal/holiday material 5 months in advance. Simultaneous queries, and simultaneous and photocopied submissions OK. Computer printout submissions acceptable; prefers letter-quality. Sample copy $2 with 9x12 SAE and $2.40 postage; free writer's guidelines..
Nonfiction: Exposé, general interest, historical/nostalgic, and photo feature—all Hawaii-related. "We run regular features on fashion, interior design, travel, etc., plus other timely, provocative articles. No personal experience articles." Buys 10 mss/year. Query with published clips if available. Length: 2,000-4,000 words. Pays $250-500. Sometimes pays expenses of writers on assignment.
Photos: Teresa Black, photo editor. State availability of photos. Pays $15 maximum for b&w contact sheet; $25 maximum for 35mm color transparencies. Captions and identification of subjects required. Buys one-time rights.
Columns/Departments: Calabash (light, "newsy," timely, humorous column on any Hawaii-related subject). Buys 15 mss/year. Query with published clips or send complete ms. Length: 250-1,000 words. Pays $25-35.

Idaho

‡**OH! IDAHO, The Idaho State Magazine,** Peak Media, Inc., 118 River St. N., Hailey ID 83333. (208)788-4500. FAX: (208)788-5098. Editor: Colleen Daly. 80% freelance written. Quarterly magazine on Idaho related topics. Estab. 1988. Circ. 20,000. Pays on publication. Publishes ms an averge of 2 months after

acceptance. Byline given. Buys first North American serial rights. Submit seasonal/holiday material 6 months in advance. Simultaneous submissions and previously published submissions (if not in an Idaho publication within same year) OK. Query for electronic submissions. Computer printout submissions OK; prefers letter-quality. Reports in 6 weeks. Sample copy $3 with 8½x11 SAE. Writer's guidelines for letter SAE with 1 first class stamp.

Nonfiction: Buys 15-20 mss/year. Query. Length: 1,500-2,500 words. Pays $100-250 (more for *top quality*).

Photos: Send photos in response to want list (generated 4 times/year). Reviews transparencies. Offers $25-200 per photo, more for cover shot. Captions, model releases and identification of subjects required. Buys one-time rights.

Columns/Departments: Education (exciting topics from Idaho universities or schools), food; general interest; interview/profile; new product; opinion; and travel, all Idaho related. "No descriptions of small business unless it has an Idaho base and a national impact." Buys 30-40 mss/year. Query or send complete ms. Length: 900-1,500 words. Pays $90-150, more for top quality.

Tips: "All articles must specifically be related to Idaho. Most willing to consider all queries and submissions. Writing should *sparkle* and avoid journalistic approach."

Illinois

CHICAGO MAGAZINE, 414 N. Orleans, Chicago IL 60610. Editor: Hillel Levin. Managing Editor: Joanne Trestrail. 40% freelance written. Prefers to work with published/established writers; works with a small number of new/unpublished writers each year. Monthly magazine for an audience which is "95% from Chicago area; 90% college-trained; upper income; overriding interests in the arts, politics, dining, good life in the city and suburbs. Most are in 25-50 age bracket, well-read and articulate." Circ. 210,000. Buys first serial rights. Pays on acceptance. Publishes ms an average of 6 months after acceptance. Submit seasonal material 4 months in advance. Computer printout submissions acceptable "if legible." Reports in 2 weeks. Query; indicate "specifics, knowledge of city and market, and demonstrable access to sources." For sample copy, send $3 to Circulation Dept.; writer's guidelines for #10 SASE.

Nonfiction: "On themes relating to the quality of life in Chicago: past, present, and future." Writers should have "a general awareness that the readers will be concerned, influential longtime Chicagoans reading what the writer has to say about their city. We generally publish material too comprehensive for daily newspapers." Personal experience and think pieces, profiles, humor, spot news, historical articles and exposés. Buys about 50 mss/year. Length: 500-6,000 words. Pays $100-$2,500. Pays expenses of writers on assignment.

Photos: Reviews b&w glossy prints, 35mm color transparencies or color prints. Usually assigned separately, not acquired from writers.

Tips: "Submit detailed queries, be business-like and avoid clichéd ideas."

ILLINOIS MAGAZINE, The Magazine of the Prairie State, Sunshine Park, Box 40, Litchfield IL 62056. (217)324-3425. Editor: Peggy Kuethe. 85% freelance written. Works with a small number of new/unpublished writers each year, and is eager to work with new/unpublished writers. A bimonthly magazine devoted to the heritage of the state. Emphasizes history, current interest and travel in Illinois for historians, genealogists, students and others who are interested in the state. Circ. 16,000. Pays on publication. Publishes ms an average of 6 months after acceptance. Byline given. Buys first North American serial rights or one-time rights. Submit seasonal/holiday material 6 months in advance. Photocopied submissions OK. Computer printout submissions acceptable; prefers letter-quality. Reports in 2 months on queries; 4 months on mss. Sample copy for 10x12 SAE and 5 first class stamps; writer's guidelines for #10 SASE.

Nonfiction: Essays, general interest, historical/nostalgic, interview/profile, photo feature and travel. Also, festivals (annual events, county fairs), biography, points of interest, botany, animals, scenic areas that would be of interest to travelers. "We do not want to see family history/family tree/genealogy articles." Buys 75-85 mss/year. Send complete ms. Length: 100-2,000 words. Pays $10-200.

Photos: Send photos with submission. Reviews contact sheets, 35mm or 4x5 transparencies and 3x5, 5x7 and 8x10 prints. Offers $5-50 photo. Captions, model releases, and identification of subjects required. Buys one-time rights.

Fillers: Anecdotes, facts and short humor. Buys 3-5/year. Length: 50-200 words. Pays $10-$25.

Tips: "Be sure to include a phone number where you can be reached during the day. Also, try if at all possible to obtain photographs for the article if it requires them. And don't forget to include sources or references for factual material used in the article."

INSIDE CHICAGO, Signature Publishing, 2501 W. Peterson Ave., Chicago IL 60659. (312)784-0800. Editor: Barbara J. Young. 90% freelance written. Bimonthly magazine. Estab. 1987. Circ. 70,000. Pays within 30 days of publication. Byline given. Offers 20% kill fee. Buys first rights. Submit seasonal/holiday material 3 months in advance. Query for electronic submissions. Computer printout submissions OK; prefers letter-quality. Reports in 1 month. Sample copy $4.40; writer's guidelines for SASE.

Nonfiction: Business, general and special interest, humor, interview/profile, photo feature, travel, music, art, theatre, design and political. "Send only material with an offbeat, local angle." Buys 60 mss/year. Query with published clips.

Columns/Departments: Architecture, Snapshots, Album, Music, Art, Nightlife, Travel, Dining, Accent/Lifestyle, Zip Code, Books and Film. Length: approximately 600 words. Pays $100 and up.

Fillers: Needs short pieces for The Front and Power Play. Buys 30/year. Length: 100-300 words.

‡NORTH SHORE, The Magazine of Chicago's Northern Suburbs, PB Communications, 874 Green Bay Rd., Winnetka IL 60093. (312)441-7892. Editor: Asher Birnbaum. Features Editor: Mark Mandernach. 75% freelance written. Monthly magazine. "Our readers are a diverse lot, from middle-class communities to some of the country's wealthiest ZIP codes. But they all have one thing in common—our proximity to Chicago." Pays on publication. Publishes ms an average of 3 months after acceptance. Byline given. 50% kill fee. Buys first North American serial rights. Submit seasonal/holiday material 5 months in advance. Photocopied and previously published submissions OK. Computer printout submissions OK; prefers letter quality. Reports in 2 weeks on queries; 1 month on mss. Free sample copy and writer's guidelines.

Nonfiction: Book excerpts, exposé, general interest, historical/nostalgic, how-to, interview/profile, photo feature and travel. Fitness—February; Weddings—January, July; Homes/Gardens—March, September; Weekend Travel—May; Dining and Nightlife—October. Buys 50 mss/year. Query with published clips. Length: 500-4,000 words. Pays $100-800. Sometimes pays expenses of writers on assignment.

Photos: State availability of photos with submission. Reviews contact sheets, negatives, transparencies and prints. Offers $25-100 per photo. Identification of subjects required. Buys one-time rights.

Columns/Departments: "Prelude" (shorter items of local interest), 400-900 words. Buys 12 mss/year. Query with published clips. Pays $50-100.

Tips: "We're always looking for something of local interest that's fresh and hasn't been reported elsewhere. Look for local angle and read the magazine. Study the product. Offer us a story that's exclusive in the crowded Chicago-area media marketplace. Well-written feature stories have the best chance of being published. Also, we cover the all of Chicago's north and northwest suburbs together with some Chicago material, not just the North Shore."

‡STYLE, Chicago Tribune, Room 400, 435 N. Michigan Ave., Chicago IL 60011. (312)222-4176. Associate Style Editor: Marcia Lythcott. 55% freelance written. Prefers to work with published/established writers. A weekly (Wednesday) lifestyle/fashion tabloid section of the *Chicago Tribune*. Circ. 760,000. Pays on publication. Publishes an average of 1 month after acceptance. Buys first North American serial rights or second serial (reprint) rights. Submit seasonal/holiday material 6 months in advance. Simultaneous, photocopied and previously published submissions OK. Computer printout submissions acceptable. Reports in 6 weeks on mss.

Nonfiction: Essays about some kind of relationship for alternating "He" and "She" column. Buys 50 mss/year. Send complete ms. Length: 800 words. Pays $100.

SUNDAY, The Chicago Tribune Magazine, Chicago Tribune Co.. 435 N. Michigan Ave., Chicago IL 60611. (312)222-3573. Editor: Denis Gosselin. Managing Editor: Ruby Scott. 35% freelance written. A weekly Sunday magazine. "*SUNDAY* looks for unique, compelling, all researched, eloquently written articles on subjects of general interest." Circ. 1 million. Pays on publication. Publishes ms an average of 2 months after acceptance. Offers 35-50% kill fee. Buys one-time rights. Submit seasonal/holiday material 6 months in advance. Query for electronic submissions. Computer printout submissions OK; prefers letter-quality. Reports in 1 month on queries; 6 weeks on manuscripts.

Nonfiction: Book excerpts, exposé, general interest, interview/profile, photo feature, technical and travel. No humor, first person or casual essays. Buys 35 mss/year. Query or send complete ms. Length: 3,000-8,000 words. Pays $1,000. Sometimes pays the expenses of writers on assignment. State availability of photos with submission. Offer varies for photos. Captions and identification of subjects required. Buys one-time rights.

Columns/Departments: First Person (Chicago area subjects only, talking about their occupations), 1,000 words. Buys 52 mss/year. Query. Pays $250.

Indiana

‡ARTS INDIANA, Arts Indiana, Inc. Suite 701, 47 S. Pennsylvania, Indianapolis IN 46204. (317)632-7894. Editor: N.J. Stanley. 95% freelance written. Monthly, Sept.-June tabloid on artists and arts organizations working in Indiana—literary, visual and performing. Circ. 12,000. Pays on publication. Publishes ms an average of 3-6 months after acceptance. Byline given. Offers 50% kill fee. Buys first North American serial rights. Submit seasonal/holiday material 4 months in advance. Computer printout submissions OK; prefers letter-quality. Reports in 3 months. Free sample copy and writer's guidelines.

Nonfiction: Essays, historical/nostalgic, interview/profile, opinion, photo feature and interviews with reviews; Q & A format. "No straight news reportage." Query with published clips. Length: 1,000-3,000 words. Pays $50-250 for assigned articles; $50-150 for unsolicited articles. Complimentary one-year subscription is given in addition to cash payment. Sometimes pays expenses of writer on assignment.

Photos: Send photos with submission. Reviews 5x7 or larger prints. Offers no additional payment for photos accepted with ms. Captions and identification of subjects required. Buys one-time rights.

Tips: "We are looking for people-oriented and issue-oriented articles. Articles about people should reveal the artist's personality as well as describe his artwork. Contributing writers must reside in Indiana."

INDIANAPOLIS MONTHLY, Emmis Publishing Corp., Suite 225, 8425 Keystone Crossing, Indianapolis IN 46260. (317)259-8222. Editor: Deborah Paul. Managing Editor: Sam Stall. 20% freelance written. Prefers to work with published/established writers. A monthly magazine of "upbeat material reflecting current trends. Heavy on lifestyle, homes and fashion. Material must be regional in appeal." Circ. 45,000. Pays on publication. Publishes ms an average of 2 months after acceptance. Byline given. Offers 50% kill fee in some cases. Buys first North American serial rights and makes work-for-hire assignments. Submit seasonal/holiday material 3 months in advance. Computer printout submissions acceptable; prefers letter-quality. Reports in 1 month. Sample copy for 9x12 SAE and $3.05; writer's guidelines for #10 SASE.

Nonfiction: General interest, historical/nostalgic, interview/profile and photo feature. Special issue is the 500 Mile Race issue (May). No poetry, domestic humor or stories without a regional angle. "We prefer stories with a timely or topical angle or 'hook' as opposed to topics plucked out of thin air." Buys 25 mss/year. Query with published clips or send complete ms. Length: 200-5,000 words. Pays $35-400. Sometimes pays the expenses of writers on assignment.

Photos: Send photos with submission. Reviews 35mm or 2¼ transparencies. Offers $25 minimum/photo. Identification of subjects required. Buys one-time rights.

Columns/Departments: Business (local made-goods), Sport (heroes, trendy sports), Health (new specialties, technology) and Retrospect (regional history), all 1,000 words. Buys 6-9 mss/year. Query with published clips or send complete mss. Pays $100-300.

Tips: "Monthly departments are open to freelancers. We also run monthly special sections—write for editorial special section lineups."

Kentucky

KENTUCKY HAPPY HUNTING GROUND, Kentucky Dept. of Fish and Wildlife Resources, 1 Game Farm Rd., Frankfort KY 40601. (502)564-4336. FAX: (502)564-6508. Editor: John Wilson. Works with a small number of new/unpublished writers each year. A bimonthly state conservation magazine covering hunting, fishing, general outdoor recreation, conservation of wildlife and other natural resources. Circ. 35,000. Pays on publication. Publishes ms an average of 6 months-1 year after acceptance. Byline given. Buys one-time rights. Submit seasonal/holiday material 6 months in advance. Previously published submissions OK. Computer printout submissions acceptable. Reports in 3 weeks on queries; 2 months on mss. Sample copy for 8½x11 SAE. Free sample copy and writer's guidelines.

Nonfiction: General interest, historical/nostalgic, how-to, humor, interview/profile, personal experience and photo feature. All articles should deal with some aspect of the natural world, with outdoor recreation or with natural resources conservation or management, and should relate to Kentucky. "No 'Me and Joe' stories (i.e., accounts of specific trips); nothing off-color or otherwise unsuitable for a state publication." Buys 3-6 mss/year. Query or send complete ms. Length: 500-2,000 words. Pays $75-250 (with photos).

Photos: State availability of photos with query; send photos with accompanying ms. Reviews color transparencies (2¼ preferred, 35mm acceptable) and b&w prints (5x7 minimum). No separate payment for photos, but amount paid for article will be determined by number of photos used.

Tips: "We would be much more kindly disposed toward articles accompanied by several good photographs (or other graphic material) than to those without."

KENTUCKY LIVING, (formerly *Rural Kentuckian*)Box 32170, 4515 Bishop Lane, Louisville KY 40232. (502)451-2430. Editor: Gary W. Luhr. Mostly freelance written. Prefers to work with published/established writers. Monthly feature magazine primarily for Kentucky residents. Circ. 300,000. Pays on acceptance. Publishes ms on average 2-8 months after acceptance. Byline given. Buys first serial rights for Kentucky. Submit seasonal/holiday material at least 6 months in advance. Will consider photocopied, previously published and simultaneous submissions (if previously published and/or simultaneous submissions outside Kentucky). Computer printout submissions acceptable; prefers letter-quality. Reports in 2 weeks. Sample copy for 8½x11 SAE and 4 first class stamps.; writer's guidelines for #10 SASE.

Nonfiction: Prefers Kentucky-related profiles (people, places or events), history, biography, recreation, travel, leisure or lifestyle articles or book excerpts; articles on contemporary subjects of general public interest and general consumer-related features including service pieces. Publishes some humorous and first-person articles of exceptional quality and opinion pieces from qualified authorities. No general nostalgia. Buys 24-36 mss/year. Query or send complete ms. Length: 800-2000 words. Pays $50-$250. Sometimes pays the expenses of writers on assignment.

Photos: Send photos with submission. Reviews color slide transparencies and b&w prints. Identification of subjects required. Payment for photos included in payment for ms. Pays extra if photo used on cover.

Tips: The quality of writing and reporting (factual, objective, thorough) is considered in setting payment price. We prefer well-documented pieces filled with quotes and anecdotes. Avoid boosterism. Well-researched, well-written feature articles, particularly on subjects of a serious nature, are given preference over light-weight material.

Louisiana

SUNDAY ADVOCATE MAGAZINE, Box 588, Baton Rouge LA 70821. (504)383-1111, ext. 319. Editor: Larry Catalanello. 5% freelance written. We are backlogged, but still welcome submissions. Byline given. Pays on publication. Publishes ms up to 1 year after acceptance. Query for electronic submissions. Computer printout submissions acceptable.

Nonfiction and Photos: Well-illustrated, short articles; must have local, area or Louisiana angle, in that order of preference. Also interested in travel pieces. Photos purchased with mss. Rates vary.

Tips: Styles may vary. Subject matter may vary. Local interest is most important. No more than 4-5 typed, double-spaced pages.

Maine

GREATER PORTLAND MAGAZINE, Chamber of Commerce of the Greater Portland Region, 142 Free St., Portland ME 04101. (207)772-2811. Editor: Shirley Jacks. 75% freelance written. Works with a small number of new/unpublished writers each year. "We enjoy offering talented and enthusiastic new writers the kind of editorial guidance they need to become professional freelancers." A quarterly magazine covering metropolitan and island lifestyles of Greater Portland. "We cover the arts, night life, islands, people and progressive business in and around Greater Portland." Circ. 10,000. Pays on publication. Publishes ms an average of 2 months after acceptance. Byline given. Buys first serial rights or second serial reprint rights. Submit seasonal/holiday material 6 months in advance. Query for electronic submissions. Computer printout submissions acceptable; prefers letter-quality. Reports in 1 week on queries; 2 weeks on mss. Sample copy $2; writer's guidelines for #10 SASE.

Nonfiction: Articles about people, places, events, institutions and the arts in greater Portland. "*Greater Portland* is largely freelance written. We are looking for well-researched, well-focused essayistic features. First-person essays are welcome." Buys 20 mss/year. Query with published clips or send complete ms. Length: 1,500-3,500 words. Pays 10¢/word maximum. Sometimes pays expenses of writers on assignment.

Photos: Buys b&w and color slides with or without ms. Captions required.

Tips: "Send some clips with several story ideas. We're looking for informal, essayistic features structured around a well-defined point or theme. A lively, carefully crafted presentation is as important as a good subject. We enjoy working closely with talented writers of varying experience to produce a literate (as opposed to slick or newsy) magazine."

ISLESBORO ISLAND NEWS,, (formerly Linking the Dots), Islesboro Publishing, HCR 222, Islesboro ME 04848. (207)734-6745. Publisher/Editor: Agatha Cabaniss. 20% freelance written. Bimonthly magazine on Penobscot Bay islands and people. Pays on acceptance. Byline given. Buys first rights and second serial (reprint) rights. Computer printout submissions OK. Sample copy $2; writer's guidelines for #10 SAE with 3 first class stamps.

Nonfiction: Articles about contemporary issues on the islands, historical pieces, personality profiles, arts, lifestyles and businesses on the islands. Any story must have a definite Maine island connection. No travel pieces. Query or send complete ms. Pays $20-50.

Photos: State availability of photos with submission.

Tips: "Writers must know the Penobscot Bay Islands. We are not interested in pieces of generic island nature unless it relates to development problems, or the viability of the islands as year round communities. We do not want 'vacation on a romantic island,' but we are interested in island historical pieces."

Maryland

CHESAPEAKE BAY MAGAZINE, Suite 200, 1819 Bay Ridge Ave., Annapolis MD 21403. (301)263-2662. Editor: Betty D. Rigoli. 40% freelance written. Works with a small number of new/unpublished writers each year. "*Chesapeake Bay Magazine* is a monthly regional publication for those who enjoy reading about the Chesapeake and its tributaries. Our readers are yachtsmen, boating families, fishermen, ecologists—anyone who is part of Chesapeake Bay life." Circ. 30,000. Pays either on acceptance or publication, depending on "type of article, timeliness and need." Publishes ms an average of 14 months after acceptance. Buys first North American serial rights and all rights. Submit seasonal/holiday material 4 months in advance. Simultaneous (if not to magazines with overlapping circulations) and photocopied submissions OK. Computer printout submissions acceptable; no dot-matrix. Reports in 1 month. Sample copy $2; writer's guidelines for SASE.
Nonfiction: "All material must be about the Chesapeake Bay area—land or water." How-to (fishing and sports pertinent to Chesapeake Bay); general interest; humor (welcomed, but don't send any "dumb boater" stories where common safety is ignored); historical; interviews (with interesting people who have contributed in some way to Chesapeake Bay life: authors, historians, sailors, oystermen, etc.); and nostalgia (accurate, informative and well-paced—no maudlin ramblings about "the good old days"); personal experience (drawn from experiences in boating situations, adventures, events in our geographical area); photo feature (with accompanying ms); profile (on natives of Chesapeake Bay); technical (relating to boating, fishing); and Chesapeake Bay folklore. "We do not want material written by those unfamiliar with the Bay area, or general sea stories. No personal opinions on environmental issues or new column (monthly) material and no rehashing of familiar ports-of-call (e.g., Oxford, St. Michaels)." Buys 25-40 unsolicited mss/year. Query or submit complete ms. Length: 1,000-2,500 words. Pays $85-100. Sometimes pays the expenses of writers on assignment.
Photos: Virginia Leonard, art director. Submit photo material with ms. Reviews 8x10 b&w glossy prints and color transparencies. Pays $100 for 35mm, 2¼x2¼ or 4x5 color transparencies used for cover photos; $50, $30 or $15 for color photo used inside. Captions and model releases required. Buys one-time rights with reprint permission.
Fiction: "All fiction must deal with the Chesapeake Bay and be written by persons familiar with some facet of bay life." Adventure, fantasy, historical, humorous, mystery and suspense. "No general stories with Chesapeake Bay superimposed in an attempt to make a sale." Buys 3-4 mss/year. Query or submit complete ms. Length: 1,000-2,500 words. Pays $85-100.
Tips: "We are a regional publication entirely about the Chesapeake Bay and its tributaries. Our readers are true 'Bay' lovers, and·look for stories written by others who obviously share this love. We are particularly interested in material from the Lower Bay (Virginia) area and the Upper Bay (Maryland/Delaware) area. We are looking for personal experience Chesapeake boating articles/stories, especially from power boaters."

Massachusetts

‡BOSTON GLOBE MAGAZINE, *Boston Globe,* Boston MA 02107. Editor-in-Chief: Ms. Ande Zellman. 25% freelance written. Weekly magazine; 64 pages. Circ. 805,099. Pays on publication. Publishes ms an average of 2 months after acceptance. No reprints of any kind. Buys first serial rights. Submit seasonal/holiday material 3 months in advance. Computer printout submissions acceptable; no dot-matrix. SASE must be included with ms or queries for return. Reports in 1 month.
Nonfiction: Expose (variety of issues including political, economic, scientific, medical and the arts); interview (not Q&A); profile; and book excerpts (first serial rights only). No travelogs or personal experience pieces. Buys 65 mss/year. Query. Length: 3,000-5,000 words. Payment negotiable from $750.
Photos: Purchased with accompanying ms or on assignment. Reviews contact sheets. Pays standard rates according to size used. Captions required.

BOSTON MAGAZINE, 300 Massachusetts Ave., Boston MA 02115. (617)262-9700. Editor: David Rosenbaum. Managing Editor: Betsy Buffington. 30% freelance written. Monthly magazine. "Looks for strong reporting of locally based stories with national interest." Circ. 129,248. Pays on publication. Publishes ms an average of 2 months after acceptance. Byline given. Offers 20% kill fee. Buys first North American serial rights. Submit seasonal/holiday material 3 months in advance. Query for electronic submissions. Reports in 1 month. Sample copy for 9x12 SAE with $2.40 postage; writer's guidelines for #10 SASE.
Nonfiction: General interest, humor, personal experience and photo feature. No fiction or poetry. Buys 36 mss/year. Query with published clips or send complete ms. Length: 1,500-5,000 words. Pays $500-2,000. Sometimes pays the expenses of writers on assignment.
Photos: State availability of photos with submission. Reviews transparencies and prints. Offers payment for photos accepted with ms. Captions, model releases and identification of subjects required. Buys one-time rights.

Columns/Departments: Profile (portraits of Bostonians), Local Color (odd facts about Boston); Good Spirits (stories about alcohol—wines, beers, drinks, etc.); First Person (experiences of general interest); Sports (Boston short stories). Buys 50 mss/year. Send complete ms. Length: 1,500-2,500 words. Pays $300-800.

Tips: "Query should contain an outline of proposed story structure, including sources and source material. Stories should seek to be controversial. Area most open to freelancers is investigative journalism. Stories concerning newsworthy scandals that are unreported. Look for something everyone believes to be true—then question it."

‡BOSTONIA, The Magazine of Culture & Ideas, Boston University, 10 Lenox St., Brookline MA 02146. (617)353-3081. Editor: Laura Fried. Managing Editor: Lori Calabro. 90% freelance written. Bimonthly magazine on culture and ideas in New England. Circ. 140,000. Pays on acceptance. Publishes ms an average of 2 months after acceptance. Byline given. Offers 20% kill fee. Buys first rights. Submit seasonal/holiday material 4 months in advance. Simultaneous submissions OK. Query for electronic submissions. Computer printout submissions OK; prefers letter-quality. Reports in 2 months. Free sample copy and writer's guidelines.
Nonfiction: Exposé, general interest, historical/nostalgic, humor, interview/profile and new product. Buys 30-40 mss/year. Query with published clips. Length: 2,000-4,500 words. Pays $400-800. Sometimes pays expenses of writers on assignment.
Photos: State availability of photos with submission. Reviews transparencies and prints. Offers $50 minimum per photo. Model releases and identification of subjects required.
Columns/Departments: In Our Backyard (humor), 750 words; Ideas (open; politics, history, etc.), 1,500 words; and Art View (film, theatre, dance, art opinions), 1,500 words. (All must have New England angle.) Buys 30 mss/year. Query with published clips. Pays $300-500.
Fiction: Buys 6 mss/year. Send complete ms. Length: 1,500-4,000 words. Pays $300-800.
Fillers: Newsbreaks and short humor. Buys 30/year. Length: 150-500 words. Pays $50-200.
Tips: Send queries for commonwealth section of magazine (short pieces and fillers).

CAPE COD COMPASS, Quarterdeck Communications, Inc., 935 Main St., Box 375, Chatham MA 02633. (508)945-3542. Editor: Andrew Scherding. Managing Editor: Donald Davidson. 80% freelance written. A quarterly magazine about Cape Cod, Martha's Vineyard and Nantucket (Mass.) region. Circ. 21,000. Pays on acceptance. Publishes ms an average of 6 months after acceptance. Byline given. Offers variable kill fee. Buys first North American serial rights or one-time rights. Photocopied submissions OK. Computer printout submissions acceptable. Reports in 1 month. Sample copy $4; writer's guidelines for 9x12 SAE.
Nonfiction: Essays, general interest, historical/nostalgic, interview/profile and photo feature. "Articles must have a theme connected with this region of New England. We rarely publish first-person articles." Buys 40 mss/year. Query with published clips, or send complete ms. Length: 1,500-7,000 words. Pays $400-800 for assigned articles; pays $250-500 for unsolicited articles. Sometimes pays the expenses of writers on assignment.
Photos: Send photos with submission, if any. Reviews transparencies. Offers $75-90/photo. Model releases and identification of subjects required. Buys one-time rights.
Tips: "We are now accepting more topical submissions about the Cape and islands (current events, trends, upcoming issues). Telephone calls initiated by the contributor are discouraged. We would suggest that the writer become thoroughly knowledgeable about a subject before he or she writes about it with the intention of submitting it to our magazine."

‡CAPE COD LIFE, Including Martha's Vineyard and Nantucket, Cape Cod Life, Inc., Box 222, Osterville MA 02655. (508)428-5706. Editor: Brian F. Shortsleeve. Managing Editor: Laurel Kornhiser. 80% freelance written. Magazine published 6 times/year, focusing on "area lifestyle, history and culture, people and places, business and industry, and issues and answers." Readers are "year-round and summer residents of Cape Cod as well as non-residents who spend their leisure time on the Cape." Circ. 32,000. Pays within 30 days of publication. Byline given. Offers 20% kill fee. Buys first North American serial rights; makes work-for-hire assignments. Submit seasonal/holiday material 6 months in advance. Simultaneous queries and photocopied submissions OK. Computer printout submissions acceptable; no dot-matrix. Reports in 6 weeks on queries; 2 months on mss. Sample copy $3; writer's guidelines for #10 SASE.
Nonfiction: General interest, historical, gardening, interview/profile, photo feature, travel, marine, nautical, nature, arts and antiques. Buys 20 mss/year. Query with or without published clips. Length: 1,000-4,000 words. Pays $100-400.
Photos: State availability of photos with query. Pays $7.50-20 for photos. Captions and identification of subjects required. Buys first rights with right to reprint.
Tips: "Those freelancers who submit *quality* spec articles generally have a good chance at publication. We do like to see a wide selection of writer's clips before giving assignments. We accept more spec work written about Cape and Islands history than any other area."

WHAT'S NEW MAGAZINE, The Good Times Magazine, Multicom 7 Inc., 11 Allen Rd., Boston MA 02135. (617)787-3636. Editor: Bob Leja. 80% freelance written. A monthly magazine covering music, entertainment, sports and lifestyles for the "baby-boom" generation. Circ. 125,000. Pays on publication. Publishes ms an average of 2 months after acceptance. Byline given. Offers 25% kill fee. Buys one-time rights. Submit seasonal/holiday material 4 months in advance. Photocopied submissions OK. Electronic submissions OK; call system operator. Computer printout submissions acceptable; prefers letter-quality. Reports in 2 months. Sample copy $3 with 9x12 SAE and $1.40 postage.
Nonfiction: Book excerpts, general interest, humor, new product, photo feature and travel. Special issues include motorcycle buyer's guide, consumer elect buyer's guide, and automotive buyer's guide. Buys 120 mss/year. Query with published clips. Length: 150-3,000 words. Pays $25-250 for assigned articles. Sometimes pays the expenses of writers on assignment.
Photos: State availability of photos with submission. Reviews contact sheets. Offers $15 for first photo, $5 for each additional photo published in 1 issue. Captions, model releases and identification of subjects required. Buys one-time rights.
Columns/Departments: Great Escapes (undiscovered or under-explored vacation possibilities); Food Department (new and unusual developments in food and drink); and Fads, Follies and Trends (weird things that everyone is doing—from buying breakdancing accessories to brushing with pump toothpaste). Buys 150 mss/year. Query with published clips. Length: 150-3,000 words. Pays $25-250.
Tips: *"What's New* will remain a unique magazine by continuing to combine informative coverage of established, mainstream artists with reports on the newest bands, movies, fads or trends and by writing about them in the same snappy, witty and irreverent style that has singled it out in the past. The magazine will remain creative enough to find the angle that others fail to see. This calls for some extraordinary talent, and the magazine is fortunate to have such a resource in its national network of freelance writers."

Michigan

ABOVE THE BRIDGE MAGAZINE, Star Rt. 550, Box 189-C, Marquette MI 49855. Editor: Jacqueline J. Miller. Managing Editor: Judith A. Hendrickson. 100% freelance written. A quarterly magazine on the upper peninsula of Michigan. "Most material, including fiction, has an upper peninsula of Michigan slant. Our readership is past and present upper peninsula residents." Circ. 1,500. Pays on publication. Publishes ms an average of 6 months after acceptance. Byline given. Offers 50% kill fee. Buys one-time rights. Submit seasonal/holiday material 6 months in advance. Previously published submissions. Query for electronic submissions. Computer printout submissions OK; prefers letter-quality. Reports in 2 months. Sample copy for $3.50. Writer's guidelines for #10 SASE.
Nonfiction: Book excerpts (books on upper peninsula or UP writer), essays, historical/nostalgic (UP), interview/profile (UP personality or business) personal experience, photo feature (UP). Note: Travel by assignment only. "This is a family magazine; therefore, no material in poor taste." Buys 60 mss/year. Send complete ms. Length: 1,000-2,500 words. Pays 2¢/word. Send photos with submission. Reviews prints (5x7 or larger). Offers $5 ($15-20 if used for cover). Captions, model releases and identification of subjects required. Buys one-time rights.
Fiction: Ethnic (UP heritage), humorous, mainstream and mystery. No horror or erotica. "Material set in UP has preference for publication. Accepts children's fiction." Buys 20 mss/year. Send complete ms. Length: 2,500 words (1,000 maximum for children's). Pays 2¢/word.
Poetry: Free verse, haiku, light verse and traditional. No erotica. Buys 30 poems/year. Shorter poetry preferred. Pays $5.
Fillers: Anecdotes and short humor. Buys 25/year. Length: 100-500 words. Pays $5 or 2¢/word maximum.
Tips: "Material on the shorter end of our requirements has a better chance for publication. We're very well-stocked at the moment, so if we receive a submission that might not be published for a year of more, we'll pay on acceptance. As the budget allows we're attempting to eventually pay for all material on acceptance. Much material is by out-of-state writers with content not tied to upper peninsula of Michigan. Know the area and people, read the magazine. Most material received is too long. Stick to our guidelines. We love to publish well written material by previously unpublished writers."

ANN ARBOR OBSERVER, Ann Arbor Observer Company, 206 S. Main, Ann Arbor MI 48104. Editor: John Hilton. 25% freelance written. Works with a small number of new/unpublished writers each year. Monthly magazine featuring stories about people and events in Ann Arbor. Circ. 50,000. Pays on publication. Publishes ms an average of 2 months after acceptance. Byline given. Buys one-time rights. Query for electronic submissions. Computer printout submissions acceptable. Reports in 3 weeks on queries; 1 month on mss. Sample copy for 12½x15 SAE and $2.40 postage; free writer's guidelines.
Nonfiction: Historical, investigative features, profiles and brief vignettes. Must pertain to Ann Arbor. Buys 75 mss/year. Length: 100-7,000 words. Pays up to $1,000/article. Sometimes pays expenses of writers on assignment.

Tips: "If you have an idea for a story, write up a 100-200-word description telling us why the story is interesting. We are most open to intelligent, insightful features of up to 5,000 words about interesting aspects of life in Ann Arbor."

THE DETROIT FREE PRESS MAGAZINE, *The Detroit Free Press*, 321 W. Lafayette Blvd., Detroit MI 48231. (313)222-6559. 20% freelance written. Prefers to work with published/established writers; works with a small number of new/unpublished writers each year. For a general newspaper readership; urban and suburban. Weekly magazine. Circ. 800,000. Pays within 6 weeks of publication. Publishes ms an average of 2-3 months after acceptance. Buys first or second serial rights. Offers kill fee of ⅓ the agreed-upon price. Byline given. Query for electronic submissions. Computer printout submissions acceptable. Reports in 6 weeks. Sample copy for #10 SAE and 2 first class stamps. Writer's guidelines for #10 SASE.
Nonfiction: "Seeking quality magazine journalism on subjects of interest to Detroit and Michigan readers: lifestyles and better living, trends, behavior, health and body, business and political intrigue, crime and cops, money, success and failure, sports, fascinating people, arts and entertainment. *Detroit Magazine* is bright and cosmopolitan in tone. Most desired writing style is literate but casual—the kind you'd like to read—and reporting must be unimpeachable." Buys 75-100 mss/year. Query or submit complete ms. "If possible, the letter should be held to one page. It should present topic, organizational technique and writing angle. It should demonstrate writing style and give some indication as to why the story would be of interest to us. It should not, however, be an extended sales pitch." Length: 1,000-1,500 words maximum. Pays $125-$1,000. Sometimes pays the expenses of writers on assignment.
Photos: Purchased with or without accompanying ms. Pays $25 for b&w glossy prints or color transparencies used inside; $100 for color used as cover.
Tips: "We will be accepting fewer nostalgia, history and first-person stories than in the past. We are aiming to be more polished, sophisticated and 'slicker' and have recently redesigned our magazine to reflect this. Try to generate fresh ideas, or fresh approaches to older ideas. Always begin with a query letter and not a telephone call. If sending a complete ms, be very brief in your cover letter; we really are not interested in previous publication credits. If the story is good for us, we'll know, and if the most widely published writer sends us something lousy, we aren't going to take it."

‡**DETROIT MONTHLY,** Crain Communications, 1400 Woodbridge, Detroit MI 48207. (313)446-0600. Editor: Diane Brozek. 50% freelance written. Monthly magazine. "We are a city magazine for educated, reasonably well-to-do, intellectually curious Detroiters." Circ. 100,000. Pays on acceptance. Byline given. Offers negotiable kill fee. Buys first North American serial rights. Submit seasonal/holiday material 4 months in advance. Query for electronic submissions. Computer printout submissions OK. Reports in 6 weeks.
Nonfiction: Book excerpts, exposé and travel. Buys 25 mss/year. Query with published clips. Length: 1,000-5,000 words. Pays $100-1,200. Sometimes pays the expenses of writers on assignment.
Photos: State availability of photos with submission.

GRAND RAPIDS MAGAZINE, Suite 1040, Trust Bldg., 40 Pearl St., NW, Grand Rapids MI 49503. (616)459-4545. FAX: (616)459-4800. Publisher: John H. Zwarensteyn. Editor: Carol Valade Smith. 45% freelance written. Eager to work with new/unpublished writers. Monthly general feature magazine serving western Michigan. Circ. 12,000. Pays on 15th of month of publication. Publishes ms an average of 4 months after acceptance. Buys first serial rights. Phone queries OK. Submit seasonal material 3 months in advance. Photocopied and previously published submissions OK. Query for electronic submissions. Computer printout submissions acceptable; prefers letter-quality. Reports in 2 months. Sample copy $2 and $1.50 postage.
Nonfiction: Western Michigan writers preferred. Western Michigan subjects only: government, labor, investigative, criminal justice, environment, health/medical, education, general interest, historical, interview/profile and nostalgia. Inspirational and personal experience pieces discouraged. No breezy, self-centered "human" pieces or "pieces not only light on style but light on hard information." Humor appreciated but must be specific to region. Buys 5-8 unsolicited mss/year. "If you live here, see the managing editor before you write. If you don't, send a query letter with published clips, or phone." Length: 500-4,000 words. Pays $25-200. Sometimes pays the expenses of writers on assignment.
Photos: State availability of photos. Pays $25 + /5x7 glossy print and $35 + /35 or 120mm color transparency. Captions and model releases required.
Tips: "Television has forced city/regional magazines to be less provincial and more broad-based in their approach. People's interests seem to be evening out from region to region. The subject matters should remain largely local, but national trends must be recognized in style and content. And we must *entertain* as well as inform."

‡**JACKSON TOWN & COUNTRY MAGAZINE,** Bridges Publishing Co., Suite 657, One Jackson Square, Jackson MI 49201. (517)782-5118. Editor: Tauné M. Beiser. 90% freelance written. Bimonthly magazine on news/events in Jackson County and South Central Michigan. "Avoid presenting 'negatives' without presenting solutions to problems. Controversial topics should be handled without deliberate writer bias except in 'The Back Fence'." Estab. 1988. Circ. 10,000. Pays within 1 month of publication. Publishes ms an average of 2

months after acceptance. Byline given. Buys first rights, one-time rights, second serial (reprint) rights or makes work-for-hire assignments. Submit seasonal/holiday material 2 months in advance. Simultaneous, photocopied and previously published submissions OK. Query for electronic submissions. Computer printout submissions OK; prefers letter-quality. Reports in 1 week. Sample copy for 9x12 SAE with 3 first class stamps.

Nonfiction: Essays (on issues of moral/political), exposé, general interest, how-to (outdoor subjects/health subjects/general interest, humor, interview/profile), opinion, photo feature (fashion, outdoors) and travel, all pertaining to local issues. "No articles pertaining to the use of controlled substances, alcohol, cigarettes unless cleared first with editor. No foul language." Buys 36-50 mss/year. Query. Length: 300-1,200 words. Pays $5-75 for assigned articles; $5-50 for unsolicited articles. Pay cash plus dinner for restaurant reviews. Sometimes pays expenses of writers on assignment.

Photos: Send photos with submission. Reviews b&w prints *only*. Offers $5 maximum per photo. Captions, model releases and identification of subjects required. Buys one-time rights.

Columns/Departments: Health & Fitness (covers varying health related topics); On Time (covers local arts events, profiles); The Back Fence (examines moral issues), all 600 words. Buys 16 mss/year. Query. Length: 500-600 words. Pays $10-25.

Fiction: "At this time, we accept *no* fiction. Would consider very short works from local writers, however."

Poetry: Avant-garde, free verse and traditional. "Poetry purchased for 1 magazine per year only. No foul language." Pays $5 maximum.

Tips: "Call me. I'll listen, and we'll talk about your ideas. If they fit, are solid and well researched, we'll use them, provided we have room. Visiting or queries wil produce the same results. All areas except Master Mechanic and Fashion are open to freelancers. I like new ideas, fresh slants and creative people. Write about what you care about. It shows in people's work."

THE MICHIGAN WOMAN, 30400 Telegraph, Suite 374, Birmingham, MI 48010. (517)563-2500. FAX: (313)540-6683. Editor: Susan Hipsley 90%. 40% freelance written. Bimonthly magazine covering "lifestyles of working/active Michigan women." Circ. 25,000. Pays on publication. Byline given. *Michigan writers only.* Writer's guidelines for 9x12 SASE.

Nonfiction: Book reviews, essays, exposé, general interest, historical/nostalgic, how-to, humor, inspirational, interview/profile, new product, opinion, personal experience, photo feature, technical and travel. Query with published clips. Length: 200-2,000 words. Pays 10¢/word.

Photos: Send photos with submission. Identification of subjects required.

Columns/Departments: Finance, Health, Legal (issues in Michigan affecting women), Cuisine, Book Reviews, Kids, Arts, Male Viewpoint, Decorating. Query with clips. Length: 700 words. Pays 10¢/word.

‡MONROE, The Magazine for and about Monroe County, Miotke Media & Marketing, 477 N. Dixie, Monroe MI 48161. (313)242-8788. FAX: (313)242-5973.Editor: Dave Meagher. 10% freelance written. Monthly magazine. "Articles should center on Monroe County Michigan or be written by Monroe County writers." Estab. 1988. Circ. 18,000. Pays on publication. Publishes ms an average of 2 months after acceptance. Byline given. Buys one-time rights. Submit seasonal/holiday material 3 months in advance. Simultaneous, photocopied and previously published submissions OK. Query for electronic submissions. Computer printout submissions OK; prefers letter-quality. Sample copy for 10x14 SAE with 4 first class stamps. Writer's guidelines for #10 SASE.

Nonfiction: General interest, historical/nostalgic, humor, interview/profile, personal experience, photo feature and travel. Large Christmas issue every year. Buys 4-6 mss/year. Send complete ms. Length: 1,000-4,000 words. Pays $50-100 for assigned articles; $25-50 for unsolicited articles. Sometimes pays expenses of writers on assignment.

Photos: State availability of photos with submission. Reviews contact sheets, negatives and 2¼x1¼ transparencies. Offers $5-10 per photo. Captions, model releases and identification of subjects required. Buys one-time rights.

Columns/Departments: I Remember (a time before 1968 in Monroe County), 1,000-4,000 words and First Person (a story written in first person about Monroe County or by a writer from Monroe County), 1,000-4,000 words. Buys 2-4 mss/year. Send Complete ms. Pays $25-50.

Fiction: Adventure, historical, humorous, mainstream, novel excerpts and slice-of-life vignettes. Buys 2-3 mss/year. Send complete ms. Length: 1,000-4,000 words. Pays $25-50.

Tips: "We are looking for stories of 'Country' interest, and stories about Monroe County, MI. Articles written by Monroe County writers are more likely to be published than others."

Minnesota

LAKE SUPERIOR MAGAZINE, Lake Superior Port Cities, Inc., P.O. Box 16417, Duluth MN 55816-6417. (218)722-5002. Editor: Paul L. Hayden. 60% freelance written. Works with a small number of new/

unpublished writers each year. A bimonthly regional magazine covering contemporary and historic people, places and current events around Lake Superior. Circ. 16,000 (subscribers in all states and 56 foreign countries). Pays on publication. Publishes ms an average of 8-10 months after acceptance. Byline given. Offers $25 kill fee. Buys first North American serial rights and some second rights. Submit seasonal/holiday material 8-12 months in advance. Photocopied submissions OK. Query for electronic submissions. Computer printout submissions acceptable; prefers letter-quality to dot-matrix. Reports in 3 months on manuscripts. Sample copy $3.95 and 6 first class stamps; writer's guidelines for #10 SASE.

Nonfiction: Book excerpts, general interest, historic/nostalgic, humor, interview/profile (local), personal experience, photo feature (local), travel (local), city profiles, regional business, some investigative. Buys 45 mss/year. Query with published clips. Length 300-3,500 words. Pays $80-400 maximum. Sometimes pays the expenses of writers if on assignment.

Photos: Quality photography is our hallmark. State availability of photos with submission. Reviews contact sheets, 2x2 transparencies and 4x5 prints. Offers $20 for b&w and $30 for color transparencies. Captions, model releases and identification of subjects required.

Columns/Departments: Current events and things to do (for Events Calendar section) short, under 300 words; Shore Lines (letters and short pieces on events and highlights of the Lake Superior Region), up to 150 words; Life Lines (single personality profile with b&w), up to 350 words; and Book Reviews (regional targeted or published books), up to 450 words. Direct book reviews to book review editor. Buys 20 mss/year. Query with published clips. Pays $10-45.

Fiction: Ethnic, historic, humorous, mainstream, slice-of-life vignettes and ghost stories. Must be regionally targeted in nature. Buys 2-3 mss/year. Query with published clips. Length: 300-2,500 words. Pays $1-300.

Tips: "Well-researched queries are attended to. We actively seek queries from writers in Lake Superior communities. We prefer manuscripts to queries. Provide enough information on why the subject is important to the region and our readers, or why and how something is unique. We want details. The writer must have a thorough knowledge of the subject and how it relates to our region. We prefer a fresh, unused approach to the subject which provides the reader with an emotional involvement. Almost all of our articles feature quality photography, color or black and white. It is a prerequisite of all nonfiction. All submissions should include a *short* biography of author/photographer."

MPLS. ST. PAUL MAGAZINE, Suite 400, 12 S. 6th St., Minneapolis MN 55402. (612)339-7571 FAX: (612)339-5806. Editor: Brian Anderson. Executive Editor: Sylvia Paine. Managing Editor: Claude Peck. 90% freelance written. Monthly general interest magazine covering the metropolitan area of Minneapolis/St. Paul and aimed at college-educated professionals who enjoy living in the area and taking advantage of the cultural, entertainment and dining out opportunities. Reports on people and issues of importance to the community. Circ. 60,000. Pays on acceptance. Publishes ms an average of 3 months after acceptance. Byline given. Offers 25% kill fee. Buys first North American serial rights. Submit seasonal/holiday material 5 months in advance. Query for electronic submissions. Computer printout submissions acceptable; prefers letter-quality. Reports in 1 month. Sample copy $3.50; free writer's guidelines.

Nonfiction: Book excerpts; general interest; historical/nostalgic; interview/profile (local); new product; photo feature (local); and travel (regional). Buys 250 mss/year. Query with published clips. Length: 1,000-4,000 words. Pays $100-1,200. Sometimes pays expenses of writers on assignment.

Photos: Chris Greco, photo editor.

Columns/Departments: Nostalgia—Minnesota historical; Home—interior design, local. Query with published clips. Length: 750-2,000 words. Pays $100-400.

Tips: People profiles (400 words) and·Nostalgia are areas most open to freelancers.

Missouri

‡ST. LOUIS MAGAZINE, Box 88908, St. Louis MO 63118. (314)231-7200. Editor: Barry Murov. Managing Editor: Steve Friedman. 80% freelance written. A monthly magazine about St. Louisans and St. Louis events. Pays on acceptance. Publishes ms an average of 2 months after acceptance. Byline given. Buys first rights; makes work-for-hire assignments. Submit seasonal/holiday material 4 months in advance. Computer printout submissions OK; prefers letter-quality. Reports in 2 months on queries; 3 months on mss.

Nonfiction: Historical, interview/profile, photo feature and travel. Query with published clips. Length: 250-2,000 words. Pays $25-300. Sometimes pays the expenses of writers on assignment.

Photos: State availability of photos with submission.

Columns/Departments: Travel, Arts, Health, Money, Sports, Entertaining. Buys 36 mss/year. Query with published clips. Length: 500-1,250 words. Pays $125 maximum.

Tips: "Columns are the best ways to break in."

Montana

MONTANA MAGAZINE, American Geographic Publishing, Box 5630, 3020 Bozeman Ave., Helena MT 59604. (406)443-2842. FAX: (406)443-5480. Managing Editor: Barbara Fifer. Editor: Carolyn Zieg Cunningham. 35% freelance written. Bimonthly magazine; "*Montana Magazine* is a strictly Montana-oriented magazine that features community profiles, personality profiles, contemporary issues, travel pieces." Circ. 72,000. Publishes ms an average of 6-8 months after acceptance. Byline given. Offers $50 kill fee on assigned stories only. Buys one-time rights. Submit seasonal material at least 6 months in advance. Simultaneous submissions OK. Reports in 6 weeks. Sample copy $2; writer's guidelines for #10 SASE.
Nonfiction: Essays, general interest, interview/profile, new product, opinion, photo feature and travel. Special features on "summer and winter destination points. Query by January for summer material; July for winter material. No 'me and Joe' hiking and hunting tales; no blood-and-guts hunting stories; no poetry; no fiction; no sentimental essays." Buys 30 mss/year. Query. Length: 300-2,500 words. Pays $75-500 for assigned articles; pays $50-350 for unsolicited articles. Sometimes pays the expenses of writers on assignment.
Photos: Send photos with submission. Reviews contact sheets, 35mm or larger format transparencies; and 5x7 prints. Offers no additional payment for photos accepted with ms. Captions, model releases and identification of subjects required. Buys one-time rights.
Columns/Departments: Over the Weekend (destination points of interest to travelers, family weekends and exploring trips to take), 300 words plus b&w photo; Food and Lodging (great places to eat; interesting hotels, resorts, etc.), 700-1,000 words plus b&w photo; Made in MT (successful cottage industries), 700-1,200 words plus b&w photo. Query. Pays $75-125.

Nevada

NEVADA MAGAZINE, Capitol Complex, Carson City NV 89710. (702)885-5416. Managing Editor: David Moore. 50% freelance written. Works with a small number of new/unpublished writers each year. Bimonthly magazine published by the state of Nevada to promote tourism in the state. Circ. 80,000. Pays on publication. Publishes ms an average of 6 months after acceptance. Byline given. Buys first North American serial rights. Phone queries OK. Submit seasonal/holiday material at least 6 months in advance. Query for electronic submissions. Computer printout submissions acceptable; no dot-matrix. Reports in 2 months. Sample copy $1; free writer's guidelines.
Nonfiction: Nevada topics only. Historical, nostalgia, photo feature, people profile, recreational, travel and think pieces. "We welcome stories and photos on speculation." Buys 40 unsolicited mss/year. Submit complete ms or queries to Associate Editor Jim Crandall. Length: 500-2,000 words. Pays $75-300.
Photos: Send photo material with accompanying ms. Pays $10-50 for 8x10 glossy prints; $15-75 for color transparencies. Name, address and caption should appear on each photo or slide. Buys one-time rights.
Tips: "Keep in mind that the magazine's purpose is to promote tourism in Nevada. Keys to higher payments are quality and editing effort (more than length). Send cover letter, no photocopies. We look for a light, enthusiastic tone of voice without being too cute; articles bolstered by amazing facts and thorough research; and unique angles on Nevada subjects."

THE NEVADAN, *The Las Vegas Review Journal*, Box 70, Las Vegas NV 89125-0070. (702)383-0270. Editor-in-Chief: A.D. Hopkins. 75% freelance written. Works with a small number of new/unpublished writers each year. Weekly magazine supplement. For Las Vegas and surrounding small town residents of all ages "who take our Sunday paper—affluent, thinking people." Circ. 160,000. Pays on publication. Publishes ms an average of 2 months after acceptance. Byline given. Buys one-time rights and simultaneous rights. Submit seasonal/holiday material 3 months in advance. Photocopied and previously published submissions OK. Computer printout submissions acceptable; prefers letter-quality. Reports in 3 weeks. Sample copy and writer's guidelines for 9x12 SAE with 65¢ postage; mention *Writer's Market* in request. Writer's guidelines for #10 SASE.
Nonfiction: Historical, travel, always linked to Nevada, southern Utah, northern Arizona and Death Valley); personalities; personal experience (any with strong Nevada angle, current or pioneer; pioneer can be 1948 in some parts of Nevada). "We also buy contemporary pieces of about 2,400-5,000 words. An advance query is absolutely essential for these. No articles on history that are based on doubtful sources; no current show business material; and no commercial plugs." Buys 110 mss/year. Query. Phone queries OK. Length: average 1,200 words (contemporary pieces are longer). Usually pays $200-650.
Photos: State availability of photos. Pays $20 for 5x7 or 8x10 b&w glossy prints, or 35 or 120mm color transparencies. Captions required. Buys one-time rights on both photos and text. Also buys photo essays on case-by-case basis and arrangement for payment.

Tips: "We are shifting emphasis of our main pieces from people to issues. We still need strong, several-source pieces about important and interesting people with strong Las Vegas connections—investors or sport figures for example. But we need more stories relating to issues which can be national in scope, but addressed from a Nevada standpoint: for instance, what happens to couples who work different hours, particularly in Nevada where a lot of people do it. In queries, come to the point. Tell me what sort of photos are available, whether historic or contemporary, black-and-white or color transparency. Be specific in talking about what you want to write."

New Hampshire

FOREST NOTES, Society for the Protection of New Hampshire Forests, 54 Portsmouth St., Concord NH 03301. (603)224-9945. Editor: Richard Ober. 25% freelance written. Works with a small number of new/unpublished writers each year. A quarterly non-profit journal covering forestry, conservation, wildlife and land protection. "Our readers are concerned with in-depth examinations of natural resource issues in New Hampshire." Circ. 10,000. Pays on acceptance. Publishes ms an average of 3 months after acceptance. Byline given. Buys first or second serial (reprint) rights; makes work-for-hire assignments. Previously published submissions OK. Query for electronic submissions. Computer printout submissions OK; prefers letter-quality. Reports in 2 weeks on queries; 1 month on mss. Free sample copy.
Nonfiction: Interview/profile (on assignment only); photo feature (b&w photos of New Hampshire) and technical (on forestry). Query. Length: 500-2,000 words. Pay varies; or pays membership in organization. Sometimes pays the expenses of writers on assignment.
Photos: State availability of photos with submission. Reviews 5x7 prints. Offers no additional payment for photos accepted with ms. Captions required. Buys one-time rights.
Columns/Departments: Book review. Buys 1 mss/year. Query. Length: 150-500 words. Pays $25-75.
Tips: "Live in New Hampshire or New England; know your subject."

‡NEW HAMPSHIRE PROFILES, Goals Communications, Inc., Box 4638, Portsmouth NH 03801. (603)433-1551. Editor: Jack Savage. 90% freelance written. Prefers to work with published/established writers; works with small number of new/unpublished writers each year. Monthly magazine; articles concentrate on audience ages 25 and up, consumer-oriented readers who want to know more about the quality of life in New Hampshire. Pays on acceptance. Publishes ms an average of 4 months after acceptance. Offers 25% kill fee. Buys first North American serial rights. Submit seasonal/holiday material 9 months in advance. Query for electronic submissions. Computer printout submissions acceptable; prefers letter-quality. Reports in 2 months. Sample copy $2.50 with 9½x12 SAE. Writer's guidelines for #10 SASE.
Nonfiction: Interview, profile, photo feature and interesting activities for and about the state of New Hampshire and people who live in it. Buys 100 mss/year. Query with published clips or send complete ms. Length varies from 1,000-3,000 words, depending on subject matter. Pays $75-350. Sometimes pays expenses of writers on assignment.
Photos: State availability of photos. Reviews transparencies. Pays $35-50 per photo.
Columns/Departments: Buys 50 mss/year. Query with published clips. Length: 1,000-1,500 words. Pays $100-200.
Tips: "Query before submitting manuscript, and don't send us your only copy of the manuscript—photocopy it. Familiarity with magazine is essential."

New Jersey

ATLANTIC CITY MAGAZINE, 1637 Atlantic Ave., Atlantic City NJ 08401. (609)348-6886. FAX: (609)344-8996. Editor: Tom McGrath. Managing Editor: Ken Weatherford. 60% freelance written. Works with small number of new/unpublished writers each year. Monthly city magazine covering issues pertinent to the South Jersey area. Circ. 50,000. Pays on acceptance. Publishes ms an average of 4 months after acceptance. Byline given. Buys one-time rights. Offers variable kill fee. Submit seasonal/holiday material 4 months in advance. Computer printout submissions OK; no dot-matrix. Reports in 1 month. Sample copy $3; free writer's guidelines.
Nonfiction: Entertainment, exposé, general interest, how-to, interview/profile, photo feature and trends. "No travel pieces or any article without a South Jersey shore area/Atlantic City slant." Query. Length: 100-5,000 words. Pays $50-800 for assigned articles; pays $50-500 for unsolicited articles. Sometimes pays the expenses of writers on assignment.

Photos: State availability of photos. Reviews contact sheets, negatives, 2¼x2¼ transparencies and 8x10 prints. Pay varies. Captions, model releases and identification of subjects required. Buys one-time rights.
Columns/Departments: Art, Business, Entertainment, Environment, Sports, Style and Real Estate. Query with published clips. Length: 500-2,500 words. Pays $150-400.
Tips: "We're looking for interesting personalities and good stories with a strong local angle. Don't approach us with story ideas though, until you have studied two or three issues of the magazine. Try to propose articles that the magazine just can't live without."

NEW JERSEY LIVING, 830 Raymond Road, R.D. 4, Princeton NJ 08540. (201)329-2100. FAX: (201)329-2342. Editor: Marion Burdick. 75% freelance written. A monthly magazine. Circ. 30,000. Pays on publication. Publishes ms an average of 4 months after acceptance. Byline given. Buys first rights and second serial (reprint) rights. Submit seasonal/holiday material 4 months in advance. Simultaneous, photocopied and previously published submissions OK. Computer printout submissions acceptable; prefers letter-quality. Reports in 3 weeks on queries. Sample copy $2.50 with 9x12 SASE; writer's guidelines for #10 SASE.
Nonfiction: Books excerpts, general interest, historical/nostalgic, humor, inspirational, lifestyle interview/profile, personal experience, photo feature and travel. Query with published clips. Length: 1,500-3,000 words. Pays $50 and up.
Photos: Reviews contact sheets, negatives, 4x5 transparencies and 4x5 prints. Offers no additional payment for photos accepted with ms. Captions, model releases, and identification of subjects required.
Poetry: Light verse and traditional. Submit maximum 5 poems. Length: 5-50 lines. No cash payment.
Fillers: Anecdotes, facts, gags to be illustrated by cartoonist and short humor. Length: 5-100 words. No cash payment.
Tips: Features are most open to freelancers.

NEW JERSEY MONTHLY, Box 920, Morristown NJ 07963-0920. (201)539-8230. Executive Editor: Patrick Sarver. 85% freelance written. Monthly magazine covering New Jersey. "Almost anything that's New Jersey related." Circ. 106,000. Pays on acceptance. Byline given. Offers 33% kill fee. Buys first rights. Submit seasonal/holiday material 6 months in advance. Query for electronic submissions. Computer printout submissions OK; prefers letter-quality. Reports in 6 weeks. Sample copy $3.75; writer's guidelines for #10 SASE.
Nonfiction: Book excerpts, essays, exposé, general interest, historical, humor, interview/profile, opinion, personal experience and travel. Special issue features Dining Out and Bridal (Jan.); Real Estate (March); Home & Garden (April); Great Weekends (May); Shore Guide (June); Summer Pleasures (July); Dining Out (Aug.); Fall Getaways (Oct.); Entertaining (Nov.); Holiday Gala (Dec.). No experience pieces from people who used to live in New Jersey or general pieces that have no New Jersey angle. Buys 180 mss/year. Query with published magazine clips. Length: 2,000-3,000 words. Pays 35¢/word and up. Pays expenses of writers on assignment.
Photos: State availability of photos with submission. Payment negotiated. Identification of subjects required. Buys one-time rights.
Columns/Departments: New Jersey & Co. (company profile, trends, individual profiles); Health (trends, how-to, personal experience, service); Politics (perspective pieces from writers working the political beat in Trenton); Home & Garden (homes, gardens, how-tos, trends, profiles, etc.); Health; Media; Travel (in and out-of-state); Education. Buys 60 mss/year. Query with published clips. Length: 1,500-1,800 words. Pays 35¢ and up per word.
Fiction: Adventure, humorous, mystery and novel excerpts. All must relate to New Jersey. Writer must provide condensation, excerpt. Buys 1-2 mss/year. Length: 1,500-3,000 words. Pays 35¢ and up per word.
Tips: "Almost everything here is open to freelancers, since most of the magazine is freelance written. However, to break in, we suggest contributing short items to our front-of-the-book section, 'Upfront' (light, off-beat items, trends, people, things; short service items, such as the 10 best NJ-made ice creams; short issue-oriented items; gossip; media notes. We pay 35¢ per published word. This is the only section we pay for on publication."

NEW JERSEY REPORTER, A Journal of Public Issues, The Center for Analysis of Public Issues, 16 Vandeventer Ave., Princeton NJ 08542. (609)924-9750. Editor: Rick Sinding. 30% freelance written. Prefers to work with published/established writers. Magazine published 10 times/year covering New Jersey politics, public affairs and public issues. "*New Jersey Reporter* is a hard-hitting and highly respected magazine published for people who take an active interest in New Jersey politics and public affairs, and who want to know more about what's going on than what newspapers and television newscasts are able to tell them. We publish a great variety of stories ranging from analysis to exposé." Circ. 3,000. Pays on publication. Publishes ms an average of 2 months after acceptance. Byline given. Buys all rights. Simultaneous queries and submissions, and photocopied and previously published submissions OK. Computer printout submissions acceptable; no dot-matrix. Reports in 1 month. Sample copy $3.50.

Nonfiction: Book excerpts, exposé, interview/profile and opinion. "We like articles from specialists (in planning, politics, economics, corruption, etc.), but we reject stories that do not read well because of jargon or too little attention to the actual writing of the piece. Our magazine is interesting as well as informative." Buys 10 mss/year. Query with published clips or send complete ms. Length: 2,000-6,000 words. Pays $100-250. Pays expenses of writers on assignments.

Tips: "Queries should be specific about how the prospective story represents an issue that affects or will affect the people of New Jersey. The writer's résumé should be included. Stories—unless they are specifically meant to be opinion—should come to a conclusion but avoid a 'holier than thou' or preachy tone. Allegations should be scrupulously substantiated. Our magazine represents a good opportunity for freelancers to acquire great clips. Our publication specializes in longer, more detailed, analytical features. The most frequent mistake made by writers in completing an article for us is too much personal opinion versus reasoned advocacy. We are less interested in opinion than in analysis based on sound reasoning and fact. *New Jersey Reporter* is a well-respected publication, and many of our writers go on to nationally respected newspapers and magazines."

THE SANDPAPER, Newsmagazine of the Jersey Shore, The SandPaper, Inc., 1816 Long Beach Blvd., Surf City NJ 08008. (609)494-2034. FAX: (609)494-1437. Editor: Curt Travers. Managing Editor: Jack Germain. 20% freelance written. Weekly tabloid covering subjects of interest to Jersey shore residents and visitors. "*The Sandpaper* publishes three editions covering many of the Jersey Shore's finest resort communities. Each issue includes a mix of hard news, human interest features, opinion columns and entertainment/calendar listings." Circ. 85,000. Pays on publication. Publishes ms an average of 1 month after acceptance. Byline given. Offers 100% kill fee. Buys first rights or all rights. Submit seasonal/holiday material 3 months in advance. Simultaneous, photocopied and previously published submissions OK. Computer printout submissions acceptable; prefers letter-quality. Reports in 1 month. Free sample copy.

Nonfiction: Essays, general interest, historical/nostalgic, humor, opinion and environmental submissions relating to the ocean, wetlands and pinelands. Must pertain to New Jersey shore locale. Also, arts and entertainment news and reviews if they have a Jersey shore angle. Buys 25 mss/year. Send complete ms. Length: 200-2,000 words. Pays $15-100. Sometimes pays the expenses of writers on assignment.

Photos: State availability of photos with submission. Offers $6-25/photo. Buys one-time rights or all rights.

Columns/Departments: Speak Easy (opinion and slice-of-life; often humorous); Food for Thought (cooking); and Commentary (forum for social science perspectives); all 500-1,500 words. Buys 50 mss/year. Send complete ms. Pays $15-35.

Fiction: Humorous and slice-of-life vignettes. Buys 25 mss/year. Send complete ms. Length: 500-1,500 words. Pays $15-35.

Tips: "Anything of interest to sun worshippers, beach walkers, nature watchers, water sports lovers is of potential interest to us. There is an increasing coverage of environmental issues. The opinion page and columns are most open to freelancers. We are steadily increasing the amount of entertainment-related material in our publication."

New Mexico

NEW MEXICO MAGAZINE, Joseph Montoya State Bldg., 1100 St. Francis Drive, Santa Fe NM 87503. Editor: Emily Drabanski. Managing Editor: Jon Bowman. Associate Editor: Arnold Vigil. 85% freelance written. Monthly magazine; 64-96 pages. Emphasizes New Mexico for a college-educated readership, above average income, interested in the Southwest. Circ. 100,000. Pays on acceptance. Publishes ms an average of 6 months after acceptance. Buys first North American serial rights. Submit seasonal/holiday material 8 months in advance. Computer printout submissions acceptable; no dot-matrix. Reports in 8 weeks. Sample copy for $2.25; free writer's guidelines.

Nonfiction: New Mexico subjects of interest to travelers. Historical, cultural, humorous, nostalgic and informational articles. "We are looking for more short, light and bright stories for the 'Asi Es Nuevo Mexico' section." No columns, cartoons, poetry or non-New Mexico subjects. Buys 5-7 mss/issue. Query with 3 published writing samples. Length: 250-2,000 words. Pays $75-350.

Photos: Purchased with accompanying ms or on assignment. Query or send contact sheet or transparencies. Pays $30-50 for 8x10 b&w glossy prints; $30-75 for 35mm—prefers Kodachrome; (photos in plastic-pocketed viewing sheets). Captions and model releases required. Buys one-time rights.

Tips: "We're publishing more personality profiles. Send a superb short (300 words) manuscript on a little-known person, event, aspect of history or place to see in New Mexico. Faulty research will ruin a writer's chances for the future. Good style, good grammar. No generalized odes to the state or the Southwest. No sentimentalized, paternalistic views of Indians or Hispanics. No glib, gimmicky 'travel brochure' writing."

SOUTHWEST PROFILE, Whitney Publishing Co., Suite #102, 941 Calle Mejia, Box 1236, Santa Fe NM 87504-1236. (505)984-1773. Editor: Stephen Parks. 50% freelance written. Magazine on the southwest, published 10 times per year. "*Southwest Profile* is a guide to travel and adventure, art and culture, and living and leisure in the Southwest, with special emphasis on Arizona and New Mexico." Circ. 20,000. Pays on publication. Publishes ms an average of 2 months after acceptance. Byline given. Offers 50% kill fee. Buys first North American serial rights. Submit seasonal/holiday material 6 months in advance. Photocopied submissions OK. Query for electronic submissions. Computer printout submissions OK. Reports in 1 month. Sample copy for 9x12 SAE with $1.25 postage; writer's guidelines for #10 SASE..

Nonfiction: General interest, interview/profile, photo feature, travel and art. Buys 30 mss/year. Query with published clips. Length: 1,000-2,500 words. Pays $150-300. Sometimes pays expenses of writers on assignment.

Photos: Send photos with submission. Reviews 35mm or larger transparencies and 5x7 prints. Offers $25-50 per photo. Captions required. Buys one-time rights.

New York

ADIRONDACK LIFE, Route 86, Box 97, Jay NY 12941. FAX (518)946-7461. Editor: Christopher Shaw. 50% freelance written. Prefers to work with published/established writers; works with a small number of new/unpublished writers each year. Emphasizes the Adirondack region and the North Country of New York State in articles concerning outdoor activities, history, and natural history directly related to the Adirondacks. Bimonthly magazine. Circ. 40,000. Pays on acceptance. Publishes ms an average of 6 months after acceptance. Buys one-time rights. Byline given. Submit seasonal/holiday material 1 year in advance. Computer printout submissions acceptable; prefers letter-quality. Reports in 1 month. Sample copy for 9x12 SAE and $1.65 postage; writer's guidelines for #10 SASE.

Nonfiction: *Adirondack Life* attempts to capture the unique flavor and ethos of the Adirondack mountains and North Country region through feature articles directly pertaining to the qualities of the area and through department articles examining specific aspects. Example Barkeater: personal essay; Special Places: unique spots in the Adirondacks; Working: careers in the Adirondacks; Wilderness: environmental issues, personal experiences. Buys 10-16 unsolicited mss/year. Query. Lenght: for features, 3,000 words maximum; for departments, 1,000 words. Pays up to 25¢/word. Sometimes pays expenses of writers on assignment.

Photos: All photos must have been taken in the Adirondacks. Each issue contains a photo feature. Purchased with or without ms or on assignment. All photos must be identified as to subject or locale and must bear photographer's name. Submit color slides or b&w prints. Pays $25 for b&w transparencies; $50 for color transparencies; $300 for cover (color only, vertical in format). Credit line given.

Tips: "We are looking for clear, concise, well-organized manuscripts, written with flair. We are continually trying to upgrade the editorial quality of our publication."

CAPITAL MAGAZINE, Capital Region Magazine, Inc., 4 Central Ave., Albany NY 12210. (518)465-3500. Editor-in-Chief: Dardis McNamee. 40% freelance written. Prefers to work with published/established writers. A monthly city/regional magazine for New York's capital region. Circ. 35,000. Pays 30 days from acceptance. Publishes ms an average of 3 months after acceptance. Byline given. Offers 25% kill fee. Buys one-time and second serial (reprint) rights. Submit seasonal/holiday material 3 months in advance. Photocopied submissions OK. Query for electronic submissions. Computer printout submissions OK; prefers letter-quality. Reports in 2 months. Sample copy for 9x12 SAE with $1.95; writer's guidelines for #10 SASE.

Nonfiction: Book excerpts, essays, exposé, general interest, historical/nostalgic, humor, interview/profile, arts and culture, photo feature, travel, business and politics. Buys 75 mss/year. Query with published clips (preferred) or send complete ms. Length: 1,500-3,000. Pays $120-400. Fees set at approximately 10¢/word. Pays the expenses of writers on assignment "if agreed upon in advance."

Photos: State availability of photos with submission. Pays $300 plus expenses for covers; $350 plus expenses for features. Identification of subjects required. Buys one-time rights.

Columns/Departments: Politics, Business, Culture, Food & Wine, Design, Destinations and Media, all 1,000-1,400 words. Buys 30 mss/year. Query with published clips or send complete ms. Length: 1,000-1,400 words. Pays $150 maximum.

Fiction: "One fiction issue per year, July; short stories, novel excerpts, poetry. Deadline Feburary 15. For writers with a link to the region. Professional quality only; one slot for writers previously unpublished in a general circulation magazine."

Fillers: Vignettes, short essays, newsbreaks and short humor. Buys 30/year. Length: 150-750 words. Pays $25-75.

Tips: "Exclusively local focus, although we welcome pieces seen in larger context. Investigative reporting, profiles, business stories, trend pieces, behind-the-scenes, humor, service features, arts and culture, nitty-gritty. Looking for The Great Read in every story."

‡**CITY GUIDE**, Bill of Fare, Inc., Suite 1A, 853 Seventh Ave., New York NY 10019. (212)315-0800. Editor: Peter Insalaco. Managing Editor: Joyce Snadecky. 90% freelance written. Weekly magazine. Circ. 40,125. Pays on acceptance. Byline given. Submit seasonal/holiday material 3 months in advance. Query for electronic submissions. Computer printout submissions OK; prefers letter quality. Free sample copy.

Nonfiction: General interest. All articles should pertain to New York City. Query. Length: 750 words maximum. Pays with restaurant certificates and theatre tickets.
Photos: Send photos with submission. Reviews contact sheets. Offers no additional payment for photos accepted with ms. Captions required.

CITY LIMITS, City Limits Community Information Service, Inc., 40 Prince St., New York NY 10012. (212)925-9820. FAX: (212)996-3407. Editor: Doug Turetsky. Associate Editor: Lisa Glazer. 50% freelance written. Works with a small number of new/unpublished writers each year. A monthly magazine covering housing and related urban issues. "We cover news and issues in New York City as they relate to the city's poor, moderate and middle-income residents. We are advocacy journalists with a progressive or 'left' slant." Circ. 5,000. Pays on publication. Publishes ms an average of 1-2 months after acceptance. Byline given. Buys first North American serial rights, one-time rights, or second serial (reprint) rights. Query for electronic submissions. Computer printout submissions acceptable; prefers letter-quality. Reports in 3 weeks. Sample copy $2.
Nonfiction: Expose, interview/profile, opinion, hard news and community profile. "No fluff, no propaganda." Length: 600-2,500 words. Pays $50-150. Sometimes pays expenses of writers on assignment.
Photos: Reviews contact sheets and 5x7 prints. Offers $10-40/photo, cover only. Identification of subjects required. Buys one-time rights.
Columns/Departments: Short Term Notes (brief descriptions of programs, policies, events, etc.), 250-400 words; Book Reviews (housing, urban development, planning, etc.), 250-600 words; Pipeline (covers community organizations, new programs, government policies, etc.), 600-800 words. People (who are active in organizations, community groups, etc.), 600-800 words; and Organize (groups involved in housing, job programs, health care, etc.), 600-800 words. Buys 50-75 mss/year. Query with published clips or send complete ms. Pays $25-35.
Tips: "We are open to a wide range of story ideas in the community development field. If you don't have particular expertise in housing, urban planning etc., start with a community profile or pertinent book or film review. Short Term Notes is also good for anyone with reporting skills. We're looking for writing that is serious and informed but not academic or heavy handed."

‡LONG ISLAND MONTHLY, CMP Publications, 600 Community Dr., Manhasset NY 11030. (516)562-5000. Editor: John Atwood. 90% freelance written. Monthly magazine, general-interest, usually with Long Island connection. Estab. 1988. Circ. 70,000. Byline given. Offers 25% kill fee. Buys first North American serial rights. Submit seasonal/holiday material 4 months in advance. Simultaneous and photocopied submissions OK. Query for electronic submissions. Computer printout submissions OK; prefers letter-quality. Reports in 6 weeks. Sample copy $3.50. Writer's guidelines for #10 SASE.
Nonfiction: Book excerpts, essays, exposé, general interest, historical/nostalgic, humor, interview/profile, personal experience, photo feature and travel. Buys 250 mss/year. Query with published clips. Pays 10¢-$1/word for assigned articles. Pays expenses of writers on assignment.
Photos: State availability of photos with submission. Captions, model releases and identification of subjects required. Buys one-time rights.

NEW YORK ALIVE, The Magazine of Life and Work in the Empire State, The Business Council of New York State, Inc., 152 Washington Ave., Albany NY 12210. (518)465-7511. Editor: Mary Grates Stoll. 85% freelance written. Works with a small number of new/unpublished writers each year. Bimonthly magazine about New York state—people, places, events, history. "Devoted to promoting the culture, heritage and lifestyle of New York state. Aimed at people who enjoy living and reading about the New York state experience. All stories must be positive in tone and slanted toward promoting the state." Circ. 35,000. Pays within 45 days of acceptance. Publishes ms an average of 8 months after acceptance. Byline given. Offers 25% of agreed-upon purchase price as kill fee. Buys one-time rights. Submit seasonal/holiday material 4 months in advance. Simultaneous queries and previously published submissions OK. Query for electronic submissions. Computer printout submissions acceptable. Reports in 3 months on queries; 1 month on mss. Sample copy $2.50; writer's guidelines for #10 SASE.
Nonfiction: Historical/nostalgic, humor, interview/profile, personal experience, photo feature and travel. In all cases subject must be a New York state person, place, event or experience. No stories of general nature (e.g. nationwide trends); political; religious; nonNew York state subjects. Query with published clips. Buys 30-40 mss/year. Length: 1,500-3,000 words. Pays $200-350. Pays expenses of writers on assignment.
Photos: State availability of photos. Reviews b&w contact sheets, 35mm color transparencies, and b&w prints. Pays $15-30 for b&w and $30-250 for color. Model releases and identification of subjects required.
Columns/Departments: Buys 80-100 mss/year. Query with published clips. Length: 500-1,000 words. Pays $50-150.
Tips: "We buy more short articles. The writer should enjoy and feel comfortable with writing straightforward, promotional type of material."

NEW YORK DAILY NEWS, Travel Section, 220 E. 42 St., New York NY 10017. (212)210-1699. FAX: (212)661-4675. Travel Editor: Harry Ryan. 30% freelance written. Prefers to work with published/established writers. Weekly tabloid. Circ. 1.8 million. "We are the largest circulating newspaper travel section in the country and take all types of articles ranging from experiences to service oriented pieces that tell readers how to make a certain trip." Pays on publication. Publishes ms an average of 3 months after acceptance. Byline given. Submit seasonal/holiday material 4 months in advance. Contact first before submitting electronic submissions; requires hard copy also. Computer printout submissions acceptable "if crisp"; prefers letter-quality. Reports "as soon as possible." Writer's guidelines for #10 SASE.

Nonfiction: General interest, historical/nostalgic, humor, inspirational, personal experience and travel. "Most of our articles involve practical trips that the average family can afford—even if it's one you can't afford every year. We put heavy emphasis on budget saving tips for all trips. We also run stories now and then for the Armchair Traveler, an exotic and usually expensive trip. We are looking for professional quality work from professional writers who know what they are doing. The pieces have to give information and be entertaining at the same time. No 'How I Spent My Summer Vacation' type articles. No PR hype." Buys 60 mss/year. Query with SASE. Length: 1,500 words maximum. Pays $75-150.

Photos: "Good pictures always help sell good stories." State availability of photos with ms. Reviews contact sheets and negatives. Captions and identification of subjects required. Buys all rights.

Columns/Departments: Short Hops is based on trips to places within a 300-mile radius of New York City. Length: 800-1,000 words. Travel Watch gives practical travel advice.

Tips: "A writer might have some luck gearing a specific destination to a news event or date: In Search of Irish Crafts in March, for example, but do it well in advance."

‡**NEW YORK HABITAT, For Co-Op, Condominium and Loft Living,** Carol Group Ltd., Suite 1105, 928 Broadway, New York NY 10010. (212)505-2030. FAX: (212)254-6795. Editor: Carol Ott. Managing Editor: Lloyd Chrein. 75% freelance written. Publishes 8 issues/year. "*N.Y. Habitat* is a magazine directed to owners, board members, and potential owners of co-ops and condos. All articles should be instructive to these readers, offering them information in an easy-to-read and entertaining manner." Circ. 10,000. Pays on publication. Byline given. Offers 50% kill fee. Buys one-time rights. Submit seasonal/holiday material 6 months in advance. Photocopied submissions OK. Computer printout submissions OK; no dot-matrix. Reports in 2 weeks on queries; 1 month on mss. Sample copy $5; writer's guidelines for #10 SASE.

Nonfiction: How-to (run a co-op); interview/profile (of co-op/condo managers, board members, etc.); personal experience; news stories on trends in co-ops and condos. Special issues include Annual Management Issue (July/August). No articles on lifestyles or apartment furnishings. Buys 30 mss/year. Query with published clips. Length: 2,000-4,500 words. Pays $75-700 for assigned articles. Pays expenses of writers on assignment.

Photos: State availability of photos with submission. Reviews contact sheets. Offers $50-75 per photo. Captions, model releases and identification of subjects required. Buys one-time rights.

Columns/Departments: Hotline (short, timely news items about co-op and condo living), 500 words; Finances (financial information for buyers and owners), 1000-1,500 words. Westchester Report (news, profiles, management. stories pertaining to Westchester County), 1,000-1,500 words. Buys 15 mss/year. Query with published clips. Pays $75-500.

Tips: "The Hotline section is the most accessible to freelancers. This calls for light (but informative) news and personality pieces pertaining to co-op/condo concerns. If you have ideas for our other columns, however, query, as most of them are completely freelance written."

NEW YORK MAGAZINE, News America Publishing, Inc., 755 2nd Ave., New York NY 10017. (212)880-0700. Editor: Edward Kosner. Managing Editor: Laurie Jones. 25% freelance written. Weekly magazine focusing on current events in the New York metropolitan area. Circ. 433,813. Pays on acceptance. Offers $150-250 kill fee. Buys first North American serial rights. Submit seasonal/holiday material 2 months in advance. Photocopied submissions OK. Computer printout submissions acceptable; prefers letter-quality. Reports in 1 month. Sample copy for $3.50 if the individual has the copy mailed. Otherwise, the charge is $2. Free writer's guidelines.

Nonfiction: Exposé, general interest, profile, new product, personal experience, travel. Query. Pays 75¢-$1/word. Pays expenses of writers on assignment.

Tips: "Submit a detailed query to Laurie Jones, *New York's* managing editor. If there is sufficient interest in the proposed piece, the article will be assigned."

‡**NEW YORK'S NIGHTLIFE AND LONG ISLAND'S NIGHTLIFE,** MJC Publications Inc., 1770 Deer Park Ave., Deer Park NY 11729. (516)242-7722. Publisher: Michael Cutino. Managing Editor: Fred Goodman. 35% freelance written. Eager to work with new/unpublished writers. A monthly entertainment magazine. Circ. 50,000. Pays on publication. Publishes ms an average of 3 months after acceptance. Byline given. Offers $15 kill fee. Buys first North American serial rights and all rights. Submit seasonal/holiday material 10 weeks in advance. Simultaneous queries and photocopied submissions OK. Query for electronic submissions. Computer printout submissions OK; prefers letter-quality. Reports in 10 weeks. Free sample copy and writer's guidelines for 8½x11 SAE and $1.25 postage.

Nonfiction: General interest, humor, inspirational, interview/profile, new product, photo feature, travel and entertainment. Length: 500-1,500 words. Pays $25-75.
Photos: Send photos with ms. Reviews b&w and color contact sheets. Pays $10 for color transparencies and b&w prints. Captions and model releases required. Buys all rights.
Columns/Departments: Films, Movies, Albums, Sports, Fashion, Entertainment and Groups. Buys 150 mss/year. Send complete ms. Length: 400-600 words. Pays $25.
Fillers: Clippings, jokes, gags, anecdotes, short humor and newsbreaks. Buys 10/year. Length: 25-100 words. Pays $10.

NEWSDAY, Long Island NY 11747. Viewpoints Editor: James Lynn. Opinion section of daily newspaper. Byline given. Computer printout submissions acceptable.
Nonfiction: Seeks "opinion on current events, trends, issues – whether national or local government or lifestyle. Must be timely, pertinent, articulate and opinionated. Strong preference for authors within the circulation area. It's best to consult before you start writing." Length: 600-2,000 words. Pays $150-400.
Tips: "The writer has a better chance of breaking in at our publication with short articles since the longer essays are commissioned from experts and well-known writers."

OUR TOWN, East Side/West Side Communications Corp., 451 E. 83rd St., New York NY 10028. (212)439-7800. FAX: (212)439-7808. Editor: Ed Kayatt. 80% freelance written. Eager to work with new/unpublished writers. Weekly tabloid covering neighborhood news of Manhattan (96th St.-14th St.). Circ. 119,000. Pays on publication. Publishes ms an average of 1 month after acceptance. Byline given. Buys first serial rights. Submit seasonal/holiday material 1 month in advance. Computer printout submissions OK; prefers letter-quality.
Nonfiction: Expose (especially consumer ripoffs); historical/nostalgic (Manhattan, 14th St.-96th St.); interview/profile (of local personalities); photo feature (of local event); and animal rights. "We're looking for local news (Manhattan only, mainly 14th St.-96th St.). We need timely, lively coverage of local issues and events, focusing on people or exposing injustice and good deeds of local residents and business people. (Get *full names, spelled right*.)" Special issues include Education (January, March and August); and Summer Camps (March). Query with published clips. Length: 1,000 words maximum. Pays "70¢/20-pica column-inch as published." Sometimes pays expenses of writers on assignment.
Photos: Pays $2-5 for 8x10 b&w prints. Buys all rights.
Tips: "Come by the office and talk to the editor. (Call first.) Bring samples of writing."

‡**ROCHESTER BUSINESS MAGAZINE,** Rochester Business, Inc., 1600 Lyell Ave. Rochester NY 14606. (716)458-8280. Editor: Douglas Sprei. 25% freelance written. Monthly magazine. "*RBM* is a colorful tutorial business publication targeted specifically toward business owners and upper level managers in the Rochester metropolitan area. Our audience is comprised of upscale decision-makers with keen interest in the 'how-to' of business. Some features deal with lifestyle, travel, cultural focus, etc." Circ. 17,000. Pays on publication. Publishes ms an average of 2-6 months after acceptance. Byline given. Buys all rights. Previously published submissions OK. Computer printout submissions OK; prefers letter-quality. Reports in 1 month. Sample $2.
Nonfiction: Essays, historical/nostalgic, how-to, humor, interview/profile and personal experience, all with business slant. Buys 12-24 mss/year. Query with published clips. Length: 1,500 words maximum. Pays $50-100. Pays barter (trade dollars) to interested writers.
Photos: State availability of photos with submission. Offers no additional payment for photos accepted with ms. Captions required.

‡**SOUTHERN TIER IMAGES,** Broome County Chamber of Commerce, Binghamton, NY 13902. Editor: Karen Hammond. Box 205A, Rd. 1, Endicott NY 13760. 85% freelance written. Quarterly magazine; strictly regional, covering Broome, Tioga, Schuyler, Chemung, Tompkins, Cortland, Madison, Chenango and Delaware counties. "We cannot consider material not directly related to these areas." Estab. 1988. Circ. 5,000. Pays on publication. Publishes an average of 3-6 months after acceptance. Byline given. Buys first North American serial rights or one-time (reprint) rights. Submit seasonal/holiday material 6 months in advance. Photocopied and previously published submissions OK. Computer printout submissions OK; prefers letter-quality. Reports in 4-6 weeks. Sample copy $2.50. Free writer's guidelines. All queries, requests for guidelines, etc. should be sent to the editor at the Endicott address listed above.
Nonfiction: Essays, general interest, historical/nostalgic, how-to, humor, interview/profile, opinion, personal experience, photo feature and travel. "All submissions must be *strictly regional*, pertaining to the Southern Tier of New York and surrounding areas only, or of particular interest to residents of these areas." Query with or without published clips, or send complete ms. Length: 1,500 words maximum. Pays $50-100 for assigned feature articles; $25-100 for unsolicited feature articles. Sometimes pays expenses of writers on assignment.
Photos: State availability of photos with submission. Reviews contact sheets, negatives, transparencies and prints. Model releases and identification of subjects required.
Columns/Departments: Day Tripper (regional travel articles), 350-1,000 words; Centerfold (photo spread – usually 2 pages), captions required; Parting Shots (humor), about 500 words; Reflections (nostalgia), 500-750 words. Buys 20 mss/year. Query or query with published clips or send complete ms.

Poetry Free verse, haiku, light verse, humorous and traditional. "Regional poetry preferred—nothing off the wall." Buys at least 4 poems/year. Pays $15-30.

Fillers: Anecdotes, gags to be illustrated by cartoonist, short humor and cartoons.

Tips: "Send for sample copy and guidelines. Do *not* call. Submit queries or complete ms to editor-in-chief Karen Hammond at Endicott address listed above. We are happy to work with beginners who produce professional quality work, but all work must be strictly regional in focus. For the most part our writers 1.) Live here; 2.) Travel here on business; 3.) Vacation here."

UPSTATE MAGAZINE, *Democrat and Chronicle*, 55 Exchange Blvd., Rochester NY 14614. (716)232-7100. Editor: James Leunk. 90-100% freelance written. Works with a small number of new/unpublished writers each year. A Sunday magazine appearing weekly in the *Democrat and Chronicle*. A regional magazine covering topics of local interest written for the most part by area writers. Circ. 280,000. Pays on publication. Publishes ms an average of 4 months after acceptance. Byline given. Buys first North American serial rights and occasionally buy second (reprint) rights to material originally published elsewhere. Submit seasonal/holiday material 3 months in advance. Computer printout submissions acceptable. Reports in 2 months. Sample copy and writer's guidelines for 12x16 and postage for 2 oz. SAE.

Nonfiction: General interest (places and events of local interest); historical/nostalgic; humor; interview/ profile (of outstanding people in local area); personal experience; photo feature (with local angle). Buys 100 mss/year. Query. Length: 750-1,500 words; shorter is better. Pays $60-250. Do not send fiction or fillers.

North Carolina

‡CHARLOTTE MAGAZINE, New South Press, Inc., 119 E. 8th St., Charlotte NC 28202. (704)332-0148. Editor: Jack Bacot. 90% freelance written. Bimonthly magazine. "The editorial content is slanted to upscale and affluent readers within the Charlotte Metrolina region of North Carolina." Estab. 1988. Circ. 15,000. Pays on publication. Publishes ms an average of 2 months after acceptance. Byline given. Buys one-time rights. Submit seasonal/holiday material 2 months in advance. Simultaneous, photocopied and previously published submissions OK. Query for electronic submission. Computer printout submissions OK. Reports in 1 month on queries; 2 months on ms. Sample copy $2.95; free writer's guidelines.

Nonfiction: Book excerpts, essays, general interest, historical/nostalgic, humor, interview/profile, photo feature, religious, travel and other consumer articles. Special Travel section-May/June issue. Buys 40 mss/ year. Query with published clips. "No phone calls, please." Length: 500-2,500. Pays 15¢/word. Sometimes pays expenses of writers on assignment.

Photos: State availability of photos with submission. Reviews contact sheets, negatives, up to 4x5 transparencies and 5x7 prints. Offers negotiable pay for photos. Captions, model releases and identification of subjects required. Buys one-time rights.

Columns/Departments: Reviews (books, New Age music, jazz music) 250-500 words; Random Thoughts (general interest, unique tidbits of information) 250 words; Business (trends, ideas) 250-1,000 words. Buys 12 mss/year. Query with published clips or send complete ms. Pays 15¢/word.

Fiction: Adventure, historical, humorous, mainstream, mystery, novel excerpts, religious, romance, slice of life vignettes and suspense. No science fiction, horror, ethnic or erotica. Buys 6 mss/year. Send complete ms. Length 1,500-2,500. Pays $150.

Poetry: Avant-garde, free verse, haiku, light verse and traditonal. Buys 6 poems/year. Submit maximum 3 poems. Length: 4-50 lines. Pays $25/poem selected.

Fillers: Anecdotes, facts and short humor. Buys 12/year. Length: 25-100 words. Pays 15¢/word.

SOUTHERN EXPOSURE, Box 531, Durham NC 27702. (919)688-8167. Contact: Editor. Quarterly Journal for Southerners interested in "left-liberal" political perspective and the South; all ages; well-educated. Circ. 7,500. Pays on publication. Buys all rights. Offers kill fee. Byline given. Will consider photocopied and simultaneous submissions. Submit seasonal material 6 months in advance. Reports in 3 months. "Query is appreciated, but not required." Sample copy $4. Writer's guidelines for #10 SASE.

Nonfiction: "Ours is one of the few publications about the South *not* aimed at business or upper-class people; it appeals to all segments of the population. *And*, it is used as a resource—sold as a magazine and then as a book—so it rarely becomes dated." Needs investigative articles about the following subjects as related to the South: politics, energy, institutional power from prisons to universities, women, labor, black people and the economy. Informational interview, profile, historical, think articles, exposé, opinion and book reviews. Length: 6,000 words maximum. Pays $50-200. Smaller fee for short items.

Photos: "Very rarely purchase photos, as we have a large number of photographers working for us." 8x10 b&w preferred; no color. Payment negotiable.

Tips: "Because we will be publishing shorter issues on a quarterly basis, we will be looking for clear and thoughtful writing, articles that relate specific experiences of individual southerners or grass roots groups to larger issues."

THE STATE, *Down Home in North Carolina*, Suite 550, 1900 Rexford Rd., Charlotte NC 28211. Editor: Jim Duff. 70% freelance written. Publishes material from published and unpublished writers from time to time. Monthly. Buys first serial rights. Pays on acceptance. Deadlines 1 month in advance. Computer printout submissions acceptable; prefers letter-quality to dot-matrix. Sample copy $1.
Nonfiction: General articles about places, people, events, history, nostalgia and general interest in North Carolina. Emphasis on travel in North Carolina. Will use humor if related to region. Length: 1,000-1,200 words average. Pays $15-100, including illustrations.
Photos: B&w photos. Pays $3-20, "depending on use."

North Dakota

‡**NORTH DAKOTA REC,** North Dakota Association of Rural Electric Cooperatives, Box 727, Mandan ND 58554. (701)663-6501. Editor: Karl Karlgaard. Managing Editor: Jo Ann Winistorfer. Monthly magazine. "We cover the rural electric program, primarily funded through the Rural Electrification Administration, and the changes the REA program brought to rural North Dakota. Our focus is on the member/owners of North Dakota's 21 rural electric cooperatives, and we try to report each subject through the eyes of our members." Circ. 75,000. Pays on publication. Byline given. Buys first rights or second serial (reprint) rights. Submit seasonal/holiday material 3-5 months in advance. Simultaneous queries, photocopied submissions and previously published submissions OK. Computer printout submissions acceptable. Query for electronic submissions. Reports 3 months. Sample copy for 9x12 SAE and $2.05 postage; writer's guidelines with #10 SASE.
Nonfiction: General interest (changes in ND agriculture); historical/nostalgic (on changes REA brought to country); how-to (on efficient use of electricity). No articles that do not show impact/benefit/applicability to rural North Dakotans. Buys 20 mss/year. Length: 750-2,500 words. Pays $50-250.
Photos: State availability of photos with query letter or ms. Offers $25-200 per photo. Captions, model releases and identification of subjects required. Buys one-time rights.
Tips: "Write about a North Dakotan—one of our members who has done something notable in the ag/energy/rural electric/rural lifestyle areas. Also needs energy efficiency articles on North Dakotans who make wise use of rural electric power."

Ohio

‡**BEACON MAGAZINE, Akron Beacon Journal,** 44 E. Exchange St., Akron OH 44328. (216)375-8269. Editor: Ann Sheldon Mezger. 25% freelance written. Eager to work with new/unpublished writers and works with a small number of new/unpublished writers each year. Sunday newspaper magazine of general interest articles with a focus on Northeast Ohio. Circ. 225,000. Pays on publication. Publishes ms an average of 2 months after acceptance. Byline given. Offers 50% kill fee. Buys one-time rights, simultaneous rights and second serial (reprint) rights. Submit seasonal/holiday material 3 months in advance. Simultaneous queries, and simultaneous and previously published submissions OK. Computer printout submissions acceptable; no dot-matrix. Reports in 1 month. Free sample copy and writer's guidelines.
Nonfiction: General interest, historical/nostalgic, short humor and interview/profile. Buys 50 mss/year. Query with or without published clips. Include Social Security number with story submission. Length: 500-3,000 words. Pays $75-450. Sometimes pays expenses of writers on assignment.
Photos: State availability of photos. Pays $25-50 for 35mm color transparencies and 8x10 b&w prints. Captions and identification of subjects required. Buys one-time rights.

BEND OF THE RIVER® MAGAZINE, 143 W. Third St., Box 239, Perrysburg OH 43551. (419)874-7534. Publishers: Christine Raizk Alexander and R. Lee Raizk. 90% freelance written. Works with a small number of new/unpublished writers each year, and eager to work with new/unpublished writers. "We buy material that we like whether by an experienced writer or not." Monthly magazine for readers interested in Ohio history, antiques, etc. Circ. 3,400. Pays on publication. Publishes ms an average of 6 months after acceptance. Byline given. Buys one-time rights. Submit seasonal material 2 months in advance; deadline for holiday issue is October 15. Reports in 6 weeks. Sample copy $1.
Nonfiction: "We deal heavily in Ohio history. We are looking for well-researched articles about local history and modern day pioneers doing the unusual. We'd like to see interviews with historical (Ohio) authorities; travel sketches of little-known but interesting places in Ohio; articles about grass roots farmers, famous people from Ohio like Doris Day, Gloria Steinem, etc. and preservation. Our main interest is to give our readers happy thoughts and good reading. We strive for material that says 'yes' to life, past and present." No personal reflection or nostalgia unless you are over 65. Buys 75 unsolicited mss/year. Submit complete ms.

Length: 1,500 words. Pays $10-25. Sometimes pays the expenses of writers on assignment.
Photos: Purchases b&w or color photos with accompanying mss. Pays $1 minimum. Captions required.
Tips: "Any Toledo area, well-researched history will be put on top of the heap. Send us any unusual piece that is either cleverly humorous, divinely inspired or thought provoking. We like articles about historical topics treated in down-to-earth conversational tones. We pay a small amount (however, we're now paying more) but usually use our writers often and through the years. We're loyal."

‡COLUMBUS MONTHLY, 171 E. Livingston Ave., Columbus OH 43215. (614)464-4567. Editor: Lenore E. Brown. 20-40% freelance written. Prefers to work with published/established writers; works with a small number of new/unpublished writers each year. Monthly magazine emphasizing subjects specifically related to Columbus and central Ohio. Pays on publication. Publishes ms an average of 2 months after acceptance. Byline given. Buys all rights. Query for electronic submissions. Computer printout submissions acceptable; prefers letter-quality to dot-matrix. Reports in 1 month. Sample copy $3.35.
Nonfiction: No humor, essays or first person material. "I like query letters which are well-written, indicate the author has some familiarity with *Columbus Monthly*, give me enough detail to make a decision and include at least a basic biography of the writer." Buys 4-5 unsolicited mss/year. Query. Length: 400-4,500 words. Pays $50-400. Sometimes pays the expenses of writers on assignment.
Photos: State availability of photos. Pay varies for b&w or color prints. Model release required.
Columns/Departments: Art, business, food and drink, movies, politics, sports and theatre. Buys 2-3 columns/issue. Query. Length: 1,000-2,000 words. Pays $100-175.
Tips: "It makes sense to start small—something for our Around Columbus section, perhaps. Stories for that section run between 400-1,000 words."

OHIO MAGAZINE, Ohio Magazine, Inc., Subsidiary of Dispatch Printing Co., 40 S. 3rd St., Columbus OH 43215. Editor-in-Chief: Robert B. Smith. 65% freelance written. Works with a small number of new/unpublished writers each year. Monthly magazine. Emphasizes news and feature material of Ohio for an educated, urban and urbane readership. Circ. 103,327. Pays on publication. Publishes ms an average of 5 months after acceptance. Buys all rights, second serial (reprint) rights, one-time rights, first North American serial rights or first serial rights. Byline given except on short articles appearing in sections. Submit seasonal/holiday material 5 months in advance. Simultaneous, photocopied and previously published submissions OK. Computer printout submissions acceptable; no dot-matrix. Reports in 2 months. Sample copy $2.50 and 9x12 SAE; writer's guidelines for #10 SASE.
Nonfiction: Features: 2,000-8,000 words. Pays $250-700. Cover pieces $600-850; Ohioana and Ohioans (should be offbeat with solid news interest; 50-250 words, pays $15-50); Ohioguide (pieces on upcoming Ohio events, must be offbeat and worth traveling for; 100-300 words, pays $10-15); Diner's Digest ("We are still looking for writers with extensive restaurant reviewing experience to do 5-10 short reviews each month in specific sections of the state on a specific topic. Fee is on a retainer basis and negotiable"); Money (covering business related news items, profiles of prominent people in business community, personal finance—all Ohio angle; 300-1,000 words, pays $50-250); and Living (embodies dining in, home furnishings, gardening and architecture; 300-1,000 words, pays $50-250). Send submissions for features to Robert B. Smith, editor-in-chief, or Ellen Stein Burbach, managing editor; Ohioguide and Diner's Digest to services editor; and Money to Ellen Stein Burbach, managing editor. No political columns or articles of limited geographical interest (must be of interest to all of Ohio). Buys 40 unsolicited mss/year. Sometimes pays expenses of writers on assignment.
Columns/Departments: Ellen Stein Burbach, managing editor. Sports, Last Word, travel, fashion and wine. Open to suggestions for new columns/departments.
Photos: Ellen Stein Burbach, managing editor. Rate negotiable.
Tips: "Freelancers should send a brief prospectus prior to submission of the complete article. All articles should have a definite Ohio application."

‡PLAIN DEALER MAGAZINE, Plain Dealer Publishing Co., 1801 Superior Ave., Cleveland OH 44114. (216)344-4546. FAX: (216)344-4122. Managing Editor: Janet Fillmore. 50% freelance written. A Sunday newspaper magazine covering people and issues relating to Cleveland. Circ. 550,000. Pays on publication. Publishes ms an average of 1 year after acceptance. Byline given. Buys first or one-time rights. Submit seasonal/holiday material 3 months in advance. Simultaneous, photocopied and previously published submissions OK. Computer printout submissions OK. Reports in 6 weeks on queries; 3 months on mss. Sample copy $1.
Nonfiction: Book excerpts, essays, exposé, general interest, historical/nostalgic, humor, interview/profile, personal experience and travel. Buys 20 mss/year. Query with published clips, or send complete ms. Length: 800-5,000 words. Pays $75-500.
Photos: State availability of photos with submission. Buys one-time rights.
Fiction: Adventure, confession, fantasy, humorous, mainstream and slice-of-life vignettes. Buys 5 mss/year. Send complete ms. Length: 1,000-5,000 words. Pays $100-500.

TOLEDO MAGAZINE, The Blade, 541 Superior St., Toledo OH 43660. (419)245-6121. Editor: Sue Stankey. 60% freelance written. Prefers to work with published/established writers and works with a small number of new/unpublished writers each year. Weekly general interest magazine that appears in the Sunday newspaper. Circ. 225,000. Pays on publication. Publishes ms an average of 3 months after acceptance. Byline given. Buys one-time rights. Submit seasonal/holiday material 4-6 months in advance. Simultaneous queries and submissions OK. Computer printout submissions acceptable; no dot-matrix. Reports in 2 weeks on queries; 1 month on mss. Sample copy for 9x12 SASE.
Nonfiction: General interest, historical/nostalgic, humor, interview/profile and personal experience. Buys 100-200 mss/year. Query with or without published clips. Length: 500-6,000 words. Pays $75-500.
Photos: State availability of photos. Reviews b&w and color contact sheets. Payment negotiable. Captions, model release and identification of subjects required. Buys one-time rights.
Tips: "Submit a well-organized story proposal and include copies of previously published stories."

TRISTATE MAGAZINE, The Cincinnati Enquirer (Gannett), 617 Vine St., Cincinnati OH 45201. (513)369-1954. Editor: Alice Hornbaker. 20% freelance written. Eager to work with new/unpublished writers. Sunday newspaper magazine covering a wide range of all local topics. Circ. 330,000. Pays on publication. Publishes ms an average of 4 months after acceptance. Byline given. Buys first serial rights. Submit seasonal/holiday material 6 months in advance. Simultaneous queries, and simultaneous, photocopied and previously published submissions OK. Query for electronic submissions. Computer printout submissions acceptable; prefers letter-quality. Reports in 2 weeks on queries. Writer's guidelines for #10 SASE.
Nonfiction: General interest, historical/nostalgic, humor (tristate writers only) and interview/profile pertaining to the Cincinnati, Northern Kentucky, Indiana, tristate area only. No editorials, how-to, new products, inspirational or technical material. Buys 25-50 mss/year. Query first except for humor and short fiction. Length: 4 pages maximum. Pays $100 (inside), $200 (cover).
Fiction: Short-short fiction to 4 pages, all locally based. Pays $100.
Photos: State availability of photos. Pays $25 per photo. Identification of subjects required. Buys one-time rights.

Oklahoma

‡OKLAHOMA HOME & LIFESTYLE, ColorGraphics Corporation, 4129 S. 72nd E. Ave. Tulsa OK 74145. (918)622-3730. Editor: M.J. Van Deventer. 50% freelance written. Bimonthly magazine on Oklahoma lifestyles, interior design, fine arts, fashion and travel. Circ. 15,000. Pays on publication. Publishes an average of 4 months after acceptance. Byline given. Buys first North American serial rights. Submit seasonal/holiday material 9 months in advance. Query for electronic submissions. Computer printout submissions OK; only letter-quality. Reports in 2 months on queries; 1 month on mss. Sample copy $3 with 8½x11 SASE. Writer's guidelines for SAE and $1.
Nonfiction: General interest, interview/profile, photo feature and travel. "No personal experience or religious." Buys 35-50 mss/year. Query with published clips. Length: 1,000-1,500 words. Pays $150 maximum for assigned articles.
Photos: Send photos with submission. Reviews 2½ transparencies and 8x10 prints. Offers $50 minimum per photo. Captions, model releases and identification of subjects required.
Columns/Departments: Remodeling (from attics to bathroom renovation); Travel (exotic locales as well as weekend getaways) and Food and Entertaining (topics that relate to seasonal trends), all 1,000 words. Buys 18 mss/year. Query with published clips. Pays $100-150.
Tips: "Features on interior design and travel are most open to freelancers. We are a statewide publication that caters to an affluent readership. Interior design stories should reflect current market trends more than how to decorate on a shoestring. Travel should focus on the interesting, the unusual, but not offbeat trips."

OKLAHOMA TODAY, Oklahoma Department of Tourism and Recreation, Box 53384, Oklahoma City OK 73152. Editor-in-Chief: Sue Carter. Managing Editor: Jeanne Devlin. 99% freelance written. Works with a small number of new/unpublished writers each year. Bimonthly magazine covering travel and recreation in the state of Oklahoma. "We are interested in showing off the best Oklahoma has to offer; we're pretty serious about our travel slant but will also consider history, nature and personality profiles." Circ. 45,000. Pays on acceptance. Publishes ms an average of 3 months after acceptance. Byline given. Buys first serial rights. Submit seasonal/holiday material 1 year in advance "depending on photographic requirements." Simultaneous queries and photocopied submissions OK. Reports in 2 months. Sample copy $2.50 with 8½x11 SASE; writer's guidelines for #10 SASE.
Nonfiction: Book excerpts (pre-publication only, on Oklahoma topics); photo feature and travel (in Oklahoma). "We are a specialized market; no first-person reminiscences or fashion, memoirs, though just about any topic can be used if given a travel slant." Buys 35-40 mss/year. Query with published clips; no phone queries. Length: 1,000-1,500 words. Pays $150-250.

Photos: High-quality color transparencies, b&w prints. "We are especially interested in developing contacts with photographers who either live in Oklahoma or have shot here. Send samples and price range." Free photo guidelines with SASE. Send photos with ms. Pays $50-100 for b&w and $50-250 for color; reviews 2¼ and 35mm color transparencies. Model releases, identification of subjects and other information for captions required. Buys one-time rights plus right to use photos for promotional purposes.

Tips: "The best way to become a regular contributor to *Oklahoma Today* is to query us with one or more story ideas, each developed to give us an idea of your proposed slant. We're looking for *lively* writing, writing that doesn't need to be heavily edited and is not newspaper style. We have a two-person editorial staff, and freelancers who can write and have done their homework get called again and again."

Oregon

CASCADES EAST, 716 NE 4th St., Box 5784, Bend OR 97708. (503)382-0127. Editor: Geoff Hill. 100% freelance written. Prefers to work with published/established writers. Quarterly magazine. For "all ages as long as they are interested in outdoor recreation in central Oregon: fishing, hunting, sight-seeing, golf, tennis, hiking, bicycling, mountain climbing, backpacking, rockhounding, skiing, snowmobiling, etc." Circ. 10,000 (distributed throughout area resorts and motels and to subscribers). Pays on publication. Publishes ms an average of 6 months after acceptance. Buys all rights. Byline given. Submit seasonal/holiday material 6 months in advance. Computer printout submissions acceptable; no dot-matrix. Reports in 6 weeks. Sample copy and writer's guidelines for $4 and 9x12 SAE.

Nonfiction: General interest (first person experiences in outdoor central Oregon—with photos, can be dramatic, humorous or factual); historical (for feature, "Little Known Tales from Oregon History," with b&w photos); and personal experience (needed on outdoor subjects: dramatic, humorous or factual). "No articles that are too general, sight-seeing articles that come from a travel folder, or outdoor articles without the first-person approach." Buys 20-30 unsolicited mss/year. Query. Length: 1,000-3,000 words. Pays 3-10¢/word.

Photos: "Old photos will greatly enhance chances of selling a historical feature. First-person articles need black and white photos, also." Pays $8-20 for b&w; $15-75 for color transparencies. Captions preferred. Buys one-time rights.

Tips: "Submit stories a year or so in advance of publication. We are seasonal and must plan editorials for summer '91 in the spring of '90, etc., in case seasonal photos are needed."

Pennsylvania

PENNSYLVANIA, Pennsylvania Magazine Co., Box 576, Camp Hill PA 17011. (717)761-6620. Editor: Albert E. Holliday. Managing Editor: Joan Holliday. 90% freelance written. Bimonthly magazine. Circ. 40,000. Pays on acceptance for assigned articles. Publishes ms an average of 6 months after acceptance. Byline given. Offers 33% kill fee. Buys first North American serial rights or one-time rights. Computer printout submissions acceptable; prefers letter-quality. Reports in 2 weeks on queries; 3 weeks on mss. Sample copy $2.95 and 9x12 SAE; writer's guidelines for #10 SASE.

Nonfiction: General interest, historical/nostalgic, photo feature and travel—all dealing with or related to Pennsylvania. Nothing on Amish topics, hunting or skiing. Buys 50-75 mss/year. Query. Length: 250-2,500 words. Pays $25-250. Sometimes pays the expenses of writers on assignment. All articles must be illustrated; send photocopies of possible illustrations with query.

Photos: Reviews 35mm and 2¼ color transparencies and 5x7 to 8x10 color and b&w prints. Pays $10-50 for b&w; $10-100 for color. Captions required. Buys one-time rights.

Columns/Departments: Panorama—short items about people, unusual events; Made in Pennsylvania-short items about family and individually owned consumer-related businesses. Scrapbook (short historical items).

PENNSYLVANIA HERITAGE, Pennsylvania Historical and Museum Commission, Box 1026, Harrisburg PA 17108-1026. (717)787-7522. Editor: Michael J. O'Malley III. 90% freelance written. Prefers to work with published/established writers. Quarterly magazine covering Pennsylvania history and culture. "*Pennsylvania Heritage* introduces readers to Pennsylvania's rich culture and historic legacy, educates and sensitizes them to the value of preserving that heritage and entertains and involves them in such as way as to ensure that Pennsylvania's past has a future. The magazine is intended for intelligent lay readers." Circ. 9,000. Pays on acceptance. Publishes ms an average of 8-12 months after acceptance. Byline given. Buys all rights. Simultaneous queries, and simultaneous and photocopied submissions OK. Computer printout submissions acceptable; prefers letter-quality. Reports in 3 weeks on queries; 6 weeks on mss. Sample copy for 9x12 SAE and $2.50; free writer's guidelines for #10 SASE.

Nonfiction: Art, science, biographies, industry, business, politics, transportation, military, historic preservation, archaeology, photography, etc. No articles which in no way relate to Pennsylvania history or culture. "Our format requires feature-length articles. Manuscripts with illustrations are especially sought for publication." Buys 20-24 mss/year. Query. Length: 2,000-3,500 words. Pays $0-500.

Photos: State availability or send photos with query or ms. Pays $25-100 for color transparencies; $5-10 for b&w photos. Captions and identification of subjects required. Buys one-time rights.

Tips: "We are looking for well-written, interesting material that pertains to any aspect of Pennsylvania history or culture. Potential contributors should realize that, although our articles are popularly styled, they are not light, puffy or breezy; in fact they demand strident documentation and substantiation (sans footnotes). The most frequent mistake made by writers in completing articles for us is making them either too scholarly or too nostalgic. We want material which educates, but also entertains. Authors should make history readable and entertaining."

PHILADELPHIA MAGAZINE, 1500 Walnut St., Philadelphia PA 19102. Editor: Ron Javers. 40% freelance written. Prefers to work with published/established writers; works with a small number of new/unpublished writers each year. Monthly magazine for sophisticated middle- and upper-income people in the Greater Philadelphia/South Jersey area. Circ. 152,272. Pays on acceptance. Publishes ms an average of 2 months after acceptance. Buys first serial rights. Pays 20% kill fee. Byline given. Computer printout submissions acceptable; prefers letter-quality. Reports in 1 month. Writer's guidelines for SASE.

Nonfiction: Bill Tonelli, articles editor. "Articles should have a strong Philadelphia (city and suburbs) focus but should avoid Philadelphia stereotypes—we've seen them all. Submit lifestyles, city survival, profiles of interesting people, business stories, music, the arts, sports and local politics, stressing the topical or unusual. Intelligent, entertaining essays on subjects of specific local interest. No puff pieces. We offer lots of latitude for style." Buys 50 mss/year. Length: 1,000-7,000 words. Pays $100-1,000. Sometimes pays expenses of writers on assignment.

Rhode Island

RHODE ISLAND MONTHLY, 60 Branch Ave., Providence RI 02904. (401)421-2552. FAX: (401)831-5624. Editor: Dan Kaplan. Managing Editor: Vicki Sanders. 50% freelance written. Monthly magazine on Rhode Island living. Estab. 1988. Circ. 15,000. Pays on publication. Publishes ms an average of 2 months after acceptance. Byline given. Kill fee varies. Buys first rights. Submit seasonal/holiday material 4 months in advance. Query for electronic submissions. Computer printout submissions OK; prefers letter-quality. Reports in 1 month. Sample copy $1.95 with 8x½x11 SAE with $1.20 postage.

Nonfiction: Book excerpts, exposé, photo feature. "We do not want material unrelated to Rhode Island." Buys 48 mss/year. Query with published clips. Length: 200-6,000 words. Pays $100-1,000. Sometimes pays expenses of writers on assignment.

Photos: State availability of photos with submission. Reviews contact sheets and 5x7 prints. Offers $50-200. Captions, model releases and identification of subjects required. Buys one-time rights.

South Dakota

‡DAKOTA OUTDOORS, South Dakota, Hipple Publishing Co., Box 669, Pierre SD 57501. (605)224-7301. FAX: (605)224-9210. Editor: Kevin Hipple. 50% freelance written. Monthly magazine on Dakota outdoor life. Circ. 3,250. Pays on publication. Publishes ms an average of 2 months after acceptance. Byline given. Submit seasonal/holiday material 3 months in advance. Simultaneous, photocopied and previously published submissions (if notified) OK. Query for electronic submissions. Computer printout submissions OK; prefers letter-quality. Sample copy for 9x12 SAE with 2 first class stamps.

Nonfiction: General interest, how-to, humor, interview/profile, new product, opinion, personal experience, photo feature and technical (all on outdoor topics—prefer in Dakotas). Buys 50 mss/year. Query with or without published clips, or send complete ms. Length: 200-1,000 words. Pays $5-40 for assigned articles; $40 maximum for unsolicited articles. Pays in contributor copies or other premiums (inquire).

Photos: Send photos with submission. Reviews 5x7 prints. Offers no additional payment for photos accepted with ms. Identification of subjects preferred. Buys one-time rights.

Fillers: Anecdotes, facts, gags to be illustrated by cartoonist, newsbreaks and short humor. Buys 4/year. Also publishes line drawings of fish and game. Prefers 5x7.

Tips: "Submit samples of manuscript or previous works for consideration, photos or illustrations with manuscript are helpful."

Tennessee

CHATTANOOGA LIFE & LEISURE, Metro Publishing, 1085 Bailey Ave., Chattanooga TN 37404. (615)629-5375. Editor: Mark Northern. 90% freelance written. Monthly magazine on the Chattanooga region. Circ. 10,000. Pays on publication. Byline given. Offers 50% kill fee. Buys first North American serial rights or second serial (reprint) rights. Submit seasonal/holiday material 1 year in advance. Query for electronic submissions. Computer printout submissions OK. Sample copy $1.95; writer's guidelines for SASE.
Nonfiction: Book excerpts, expose, general interest, historical, interview/profile and photo feature. Buys 120 mss/year. Query with or without published clips. Length: 150-3,000 words. Pays $20-200.
Photos: Send photos with submission. Reviews b&w contact sheets, 35mm or larger transparencies, and any size color prints. Offers $20 per photo. Captions, model releases and identification of subjects required. Buys one-time rights.
Tips: "Contributors must know their subjects. We expect all material to be in-depth and about a local subject. We present complex subjects in a clear manner so our readers can see the entire picture in perspective. I am most satisfied when my readers stop me in the street and say 'I read such-and-such article. I have lived here all my life and I didn't know that.' "

MEMPHIS, MM Corporation, Box 256, Memphis TN 38101. (901)521-9000. Editor: Larry Conley. 60% freelance written. Works with a small number of new/unpublished writers. Circ. 26,500. Pays on publication. Publishes ms an average of 3 months after acceptance. Byline given. Buys first North American serial rights. Pays $35-100 kill fee. Simultaneous, photocopied and previously published submissions OK. Computer printout submissions acceptable; prefers letter-quality. Reports in 6 weeks. Sample copy for 9x12 SAE and $2.50 postage; writer's guidelines for SASE.
Nonfiction: Exposé, general interest, historical, how-to, humor, interview and profile. "Virtually all our material has strong mid-South connections." Buys 25 freelance mss/year. Query or submit complete ms or published clips. Length: 1,500-5,000 words. Pays $100-1,000. Sometimes pays expenses of writers on assignment.
Tips: "The kinds of manuscripts we most need have a sense of story (i.e., plot, suspense, character), an abundance of evocative images to bring that story alive, and a sensitivity to issues at work in Memphis. The most frequent mistakes made by writers in completing an article for us are lack of focus, lack of organization, factual gaps and failure to capture the magazine's style. Tough investigative pieces would be especially welcomed."

Texas

"D" MAGAZINE, Southwest Media Corporation, Suite 1200, 3988 N. Central Expressway, Dallas TX 75204. (214)827-5000. Editor: Ruth Miller Fitzgibbons. 25% freelance written. Monthly magazine. "We are a general interest magazine with emphasis on events occuring in Dallas." Circ. 100,000. Pays on acceptance. Publishes ms an average of 2 months after acceptance. Byline given. Offers 25% kill fee. Buys first North American serial rights. Submit seasonal/holiday material 2 months in advance. Query for electronic submissions. Computer printout submissions OK; prefers letter-quality. Reports in 1 month. Sample copy $2.50 with SAE and 5 first class stamps; free writer's guidelines.
Nonfiction: Essays, exposé, general interest, historical/nostalgic, how-to, interview/profile and travel. Buys 20-30 mss/year. Query with published clips. Length: 1,000-5,000 words. Pays $75-750 for assigned articles; pays $50-500 for unsolicited articles. Pays expenses of writers on assignment.
Photos: State availability of photos with submission. Reviews transparencies and 35mm prints. Offers $50-75 per photo. Captions required. Buys one-time rights.
Columns/Departments: Business, Politics, Travel and Relationships. Query with published clips or send complete ms. Length: 1,500-2,000 words. Pays $250-350.
Tips: "Tell us something about our city that we have not written about. We realize that is very difficult for someone outside of Dallas to do—that's why 90% of our magazine is written by people who live in the North Texas area."

DALLAS LIFE MAGAZINE, Sunday Magazine of *The Dallas Morning News,* Belo Corporation, Communications Center, Dallas TX 75265. (214)745-8432. Editor: Melissa Houtte. Weekly magazine. "We are a lively, topical, sometimes controversial city magazine devoted to informing, enlightening and entertaining our urban Sunbelt readers with material which is specifically relevant to Dallas lifestyles and interests." Pays on acceptance. Byline given. Buys first North American serial rights or simultaneous rights. Simultaneous queries and submissions OK ("if not competitive in our area"). Computer printout submissions acceptable; prefers letter-quality. Reports in 1 month on queries; 6 weeks on mss.

Nonfiction: General interest; humor (short); interview/profile. "All material must, repeat *must*, have a Dallas metropolitan area frame of reference." Special issues include: spring and fall home furnishings theme and travel. Buys 5-10 unsolicited mss/year. Query with published clips or send complete ms. Length: 1,200-3,000 words. Pays $200-650.

DENTON TODAY MAGAZINE, Community Life Publications, Inc., Suite #304, 207 W. Hickory, Denton TX 76201. (817)566-3464. Editor: Jonathan B. Cott. 100% freelance written. Quarterly magazine of news/entertainment in North Texas. Circ. 5,000. Pays on publication. Publishes ms an average of 1 month after acceptance. Byline given. Buys first North American serial rights, second serial (reprint) rights or makes work-for-hire assignments. Submit seasonal/holiday material 2 months in advance. Previously published submissions OK. Computer printout submissions OK; no dot-matrix. Reports in 2 weeks. Sample copy $1.95 with 9x12 SAE and $1.50 postage; writer's guidelines for #10 SASE.
Nonfiction: Essays, general interest, historical/nostalgic, how-to, humor, inspirational, interview/profile, new product, personal experience, photo feature. No religious or controversial articles. Buys 40 mss/year. Send ocmplete ms. Length: 500-3,000. Pays $25-210 for assigned articles; $25-150 for unsolicited articles. Sometimes pays expenses of writers on assignment.
Photos: Send photos with submission. Offers $5-50 per photo. Captions, model releases and identification of subjects required. Buys one-time rights.
Columns/Departments: Business/economy, Government/services, Education, Health, Arts/entertainment. All with north Texas, positive slant. Buys 40 mss/year. Send complete ms. Length: 500-750 words. Pays $25-50.
Fiction: Historical, humorous, mainstream, slice-of-life vignettes. Buys 5 mss/year. Send complete ms. Length: 1,000-3,000 words. Pays $50-210.

EL PASO MAGAZINE, El Paso Chamber of Commerce, 10 Civic Center Plaza, El Paso TX 79901. (915)534-0500. Executive Editor: David Stewart. 75% freelance written. Prefers to work with published/established writers; works with a small number of new/unpublished writers each year. Monthly magazine that "takes a positive look at El Paso, its people and its businesses. Readers are owners and managers of El Paso businesses." Circ. 4,000. Pays on publication. Publishes ms an average of 3 months after acceptance. Byline given. Buys first North American serial rights. Submit seasonal/holiday material 3 months in advance. Simultaneous queries, and simultaneous and photocopied submissions OK. Computer printout submissions acceptable; prefers letter-quality. Reports in 2 months. Free sample copy and writer's guidelines.
Nonfiction: General interest, business, historical/nostalgic, interview/profile and photo feature. Query with published clips. Length: 1,000-2,500 words. Pay varies.
Photos: Send photos with ms. Captions, model releases and identification of subjects required. Buys one-time rights with ms.
Tips: "An article for *El Paso Magazine* must talk about El Paso area business and its successes or community leaders. *El Paso Magazine* will rely more on experienced writers in 1990. Writers must know El Paso."

HOUSTON MAGAZINE, The Chamber of Commerce Magazine, Texas Cities Publishing, 2323 S. Voss, Suite 400, Houston TX 77057. (713)784-0555. Editor-in-Chief: Larry Storer. 65-85% freelance written. Magazine is oriented exclusively toward Houston businesses. Circ. 25,000. Pays on publication. Publishes ms an average of 3-4 months after acceptance. Byline given. Buys first North American serial rights and reprints from other PCI magazines. Submit seasonal/holiday material 5 months in advance. Simultaneous submissions and photocopied submissions OK. Query for electronic submissions. Computer printout submissions acceptable; prefers letter-quality. Free sample copy and writer's guidelines.
Nonfiction: Articles of use to small to mid-size Houston firms only. Length: 250-750 words. Query with or without published clips, or send complete ms. Fees negotiable upon assignment, acceptance. Occasionally pays with subscription or other premiums; will negotiate. Sometimes pays the expenses of writers on assignment.
Photos: State availability of photos with submissions. Review contact sheets, transparencies, and prints. Offers $25 maximum/b&w photo. Cover shots are negotiated. Captions, model releases and identification of subjects required. Buys one-time rights.
Tips: No lifestyles or arts-related stories.

HOUSTON METROPOLITAN MAGAZINE, City Home Publishing, Box 25386, Houston TX 77265. (713)524-3000. Editorial Director: Gabrielle Cosgriff. Managing Editor: Barbara Burgower. 85% freelance written. A monthly city magazine. Circ. 87,500. Pays on acceptance. Publishes ms an average of 3 months after acceptance. Byline given. Offers 25% kill fee. Buys first North American serial rights. Submit holiday/seasonal material 6 months in advance. Query for electronic submissions. Simultaneous and photocopied submissions OK. Computer printout submissions OK; no dot-matrix. Reports in 2 weeks on queries; 1 month on mss. Sample copy for 9½x12 SAE and 8 first class stamps.

Nonfiction: Issue-oriented features, profiles, lifestyle/entertainment, food features, visual stories, and humorous features. Query with published clips or send complete ms. Length: 300-2,500 words. Pays $50-1,000.

Photos: Carla Poindexter, art director. State availability of photos with submission. Buys one-time rights. "Also assigns photographers at day or job rates."

Columns/Departments: City Insight and Artbeat. All must have strong Houston-area slant. Length: 300-2,500 words. Pays $50-1,000.

Tips: "Submit clips demonstrating strong writing and reporting skills with detailed queries, bearing in mind that this is a city magazine. Our intent is to be a lively, informative city book, addressing the issues and people who affect our lives objectively and fairly. But also with affection and, where suitable, a sense of humor. Only those familiar with the Houston metropolitan area should approach us."

‡**THE WEST TEXAS SUN**, NJN Inc., Box 61541, San Angelo TX 76906. (915)944-8918. Editor: Soren W. Nielsen. 95% freelance written. Semi-monthly magazine on West Texas. "This is a chronicle of the West Texas experience. All freelance submissions should have a relevant hook or have impact on the West Texas reader." Estab. 1989. Circ. 5,000. Pays on publication. Publishes ms an average of 2 months after acceptance. Byline given. Offers $100 kill fee. Buys one-time rights. Submit seasonal/holiday material 3 months in advance. Simultaneous, photocopied and previously published submissions OK. Computer printout submissions OK; prefers letter-quality. Reports 2 weeks. Writer's guidelines for #10 SASE.

Nonfiction: Book excerpts, essays, exposé, general interest, historical/nostalgic, how-to, humor, inspirational, interview/profile, personal experience, photo feature, and vignettes of life in West Texas — fillers. Special issues: Rodeo—March 1; Football season opener—August 15. Buys 65 mss/year. Query. Length: 40-4,000 words. Pays $50-400. Sometimes pays expenses of writers on assignment.

Photos: State availability of photos with submission. Reviews contact sheets. Offers $10-25 maximum per photo. Captions and identification of subjects required. Buys one-time rights.

Columns/Departments: The Way It Was (historical pieces, personal recollections of West Texas), 2,000 words. Query. Pays $50-200.

Fiction: Adventure, historical, humorous, mainstream, mystery, novel excerpts, science fiction, slice-of-life vignettes, Western. "No erotica." Buys 20 mss/year. Query. Length: 1,000-4,000. Pays $50-400.

Fillers: Anecdotes, facts, short humor. Buys 100/year. Length: 20-200 words. Pays $5-25.

Tips: "Submissions of quality ideas and writing about West Texas will always get full consideration. Well-researched historical pieces and well-written fiction stand the best chance of being published. Vignettes of the West Texas experience, even if short, are also likely candidates."

Utah

‡**UTAH HOLIDAY MAGAZINE, Utah**, Tuesday Publishing Co. 419 E. 100 S. Box 985, Salt Lake City UT 84111. (801)532-3737. Editor: Bruce Lee. Managing Editor: Mildren Evans. 100% freelance written. Monthly magazine on Utah oriented—subjects newspapers do not print, provocative opinion. Theatre, art, movie reviews. Circ. 10,000. Pays on 15th of month of publication. Byline given. Offers $50 kill fee. Buys first North American serial rights. Submit seasonal/holiday material 3 months in advance. Photocopied submissions OK. Query for electronic submissions. Computer printout submissions OK; prefers letter-quality. Reports in 3 weeks on queries. Sample copy for 10x12 SAE and 5 first class stamps; writer's guidelines for #10 SASE.

Nonfiction: Essays, exposé, interview/profile, opinion and personal experience. "No travel outside Utah, humor or personal essays." Buys 1 ms/year. Query with or without published clips, or send complete ms. Length: 2,500-8,000 words. Pays $90-350 for assigned articles. Pays in contributor copies or other premiums. Sometimes pays expenses of writers on assignment.

Photos: State availability of photos with submission. Send photos with submission. Reviews contact sheets and transparencies. Offers $15-70 per photo. Identification of subjects required. Buys one-time rights.

Columns/Departments: Movie Reviews, Opera, Theatre, Ballet and Art (all slanted to current Utah productions), 1,500 words. Buys 10 mss/year. Query with published clips. Pays $90-120.

Vermont

VERMONT LIFE MAGAZINE, 61 Elm St., Montpelier VT 05602. (802)828-3241. Editor-in-Chief: Thomas K. Slayton. 90% freelance written. Prefers to work with published/established writers. Quarterly magazine. Circ. 120,000. Publishes ms an average of 9 months after acceptance. Byline given. Offers kill fee. Buys first serial rights. Submit seasonal/holiday material 1 year in advance. Simultaneous queries, and simultaneous, photocopied, and previously published submissions OK. Computer printout submissions acceptable; prefers letter-quality. Reports in 1 month. Writer's guidelines for #10 SASE.

Nonfiction: Wants articles on today's Vermont, those which portray a typical or, if possible, unique aspect of the state or its people. Style should be literate, clear and concise. Subtle humor favored. No Vermont dialect attempts as in "Ayup," outsider's view on visiting Vermont, or "Vermont clichés" — maple syrup, town meetings or stereotyped natives. Buys 60 mss/year. Query by letter essential. Length: 1,500 words average. Pays 20¢/word. Seldom pays expenses of writers on assignment.

Photos: Buys photographs with mss; buys seasonal photographs alone. Prefers b&w contact sheets to look at first on assigned material. Color submissions must be 4x5 or 35mm transparencies. Rates on acceptance: $75-150 inside, color; $200 for cover. Gives assignments but only with experienced photographers. Query in writing. Captions, model releases, and identification of subjects required. Buys one-time rights, but often negotiates for re-use rights.

Tips: "Writers who read our magazine are given more consideration because they understand that we want authentic articles about Vermont. If a writer has a genuine working knowledge of Vermont, his or her work usually shows it. Vermont is changing and there is much concern here about what this state will be like in years ahead. It is a beautiful, environmentally sound place now and the vast majority of residents want to keep it so. Articles reflecting such concerns in an intelligent, authoritative, non-hysterical way will be given very careful consideration. The growth of tourism makes *Vermont Life* interested in intelligent articles about specific places in Vermont, their history and attractions to the traveling public."

VERMONT MAGAZINE, 14 School St., Box 288, Bristol VT 05443. (802)453-3200. Managing Editor: Wanda Shipman. Bimonthly magazine about Vermont. Buys first North American serial rights. Submit seasonal/holiday material 5-6 months in advance. Simultaneous and photocopied submissions OK. Query for electronic submissions. Computer printout submissions OK. Reports in 6 weeks. Writer's guidelines for #10 SASE.

Nonfiction: Book excerpts, essays, expose, general interest, historical, how-to, humor, interview/profile, new product, personal experience, photo feature, calendar. Buys 50 mss/year. Query with published clips, or send complete ms. Length: 900-3,500 words. Pays $400-1,000. Sometimes pays expenses of writers on assignment.

Photos: Send photos with submission. Reviews contact sheets, 35mm transparencies and 8x10 b&w prints. Captions, model releases (if possible) and identification of subjects required. Buys one-time rights.

Columns/Departments: Vermont Kitchen (food); Real Estate Report (buying and selling Vermont property). Buys 12 mss/year. Query with published clips. Length: 200-1,000 words. Pays $150-750.

Fiction: Adventure, historical, humorous, mainstream, mystery, slice of life vignettes and suspense. Buys 3 stories/year.

Tips: "Our readers *know* their state well, and they know the 'real' Vermont can't be slipped inside a glib and glossy brochure. If you keep this in mind you stand a good chance of placing your work in *Vermont Magazine*."

VERMONT VANGUARD PRESS, Statewide Weekly, Vanguard Publishing, 87 College St., Burlington VT 05401. (802)864-0506. Editor: Joshua Mamis. Managing Editor: Pamela Polston. 70% freelance written. Works with a small number of new/unpublished writers each year. A weekly alternative newspaper, locally oriented, covering Vermont politics, environment, arts, etc. Circ. 25,000. Pays on publication. Byline given. Offers 50% kill fee only after written acceptance. Buys first serial rights. Submit seasonal/holiday material 1 month in advance. Simultaneous queries, and simultaneous, photocopied and previously published submissions OK. Query for electronic submissions. Computer printout submissions acceptable; no dot-matrix. Reports in 1 month.

Nonfiction: Exposé and humor. Articles must have a Vermont angle. Buys about 12 mss/year. Query with published clips. Length: 500-2,500 words. Pays $20-100.

Photos: Rob Swanson, photo editor. State availability of photos. Pays $10-20 for b&w contact sheets and negatives. Captions, model releases and identification of subjects required. Buys one-time rights.

Tips: "Short news stories are most open to freelancers. Knowledge of Vermont politics is essential."

Virginia

NORTHERN VIRGINIAN MAGAZINE, 135 Park St., Box 1177, Vienna VA 22180. (703)938-0666. Editor: Goodie Holden. 80% freelance written. Bimonthly magazine concerning the five counties of northern Virginia. Pays first of month following publication. Publishes ms an average of 3 months after acceptance. Byline given. Buys first serial rights and second serial (reprint) rights. Submit seasonal/holiday material 3 months in advance. Simultaneous queries, and simultaneous, photocopied and previously published submissions OK. Computer printout submissions acceptable. "Send photocopy of manuscript as we can't guarantee its return." Reports in 2 weeks on queries; 1 month on mss. Sample copy $1; free writer's guidelines.

Nonfiction: "Freelance manuscripts welcomed on speculation. We are particularly interested in articles about or related to northern Virginia. Articles on 'the Lighter Side of Northern Virginia' preferred." Buys 75 mss/year. Query or send complete ms. Length: 2,500 words minimum. Pays 1½¢/word.

Photos: Prefers good, clear b&w glossy photos. Pays $5/photo or photo credit line. Captions, model releases and identification of subjects required.

Tips: Longer articles preferred, minimum 2,500 words. History articles accepted only if unique.

‡**NOVASCOPE**, Novascope, Inc., Box 1590, Middleburg VA 22117. (703)687-3314. Editor: Mark Smith and Joy Smith. 75% freelance written. Monthly magazine on human interest, environmental issues, history and events pertinent to northern Virginia. Circ. 50,000. Pays on publication. Byline given. Buys first North American serial rights. Submit seasonal/holiday 3 months in advance. Simultaneous and photocopied submissions OK. Computer printout submissions OK. Reports in 2 weeks. Free sample copy and writer's guidelines.

Nonfiction: General interest, historical and interview/profile, all pertinent to Northern Virginia. Buys 50 mss/year. Query with published clips. Length: 1,000 words maximum. Pays $50 maximum for unsolicited articles. Sometimes pays expensee of writers on assignment.

Photos: State availability of photos with submission. Reviews 35mm transparencies. Offers $10 maximum per photo. Identification of subjects required. Buys one-time rights.

THE ROANOKER, Leisure Publishing Co., 3424 Brambleton Ave., Box 21535, Roanoke VA 24018. (703)989-6138. Editor: Kurt Rheinheimer. 75% freelance written. Works with a small number of new/unpublished writers each year. Monthly magazine covering people and events of Western Virginia. "*The Roanoker* is a general interest city magazine edited for the people of Roanoke, Virginia, and the surrounding area. Our readers are primarily upper-income, well-educated professionals between the ages of 35 and 60. Coverage ranges from hard news and consumer information to restaurant reviews and local history." Circ. 14,000. Pays on publication. Publishes ms an average of 4 months after acceptance. Byline given. Buys all rights; makes work-for-hire assignments. Submit seasonal/holiday material 4 months in advance. Simultaneous submissions OK. Computer printout submissions acceptable. Reports in 2 months. Sample copy for $2 and 9x12 SAE with $1.45 postage; writer's guidelines for #10 SASE.

Nonfiction: Exposé; historical/nostalgic; how-to (live better in western Virginia); interview/profile (of well-known area personalities); photo feature; and travel (Virginia and surrounding states). "We are attempting to broaden our base and provide more and more coverage of western Virginia, i.e., that part of the state west of Roanoke. We place special emphasis on consumer-related issues and how-to articles." Periodic special sections on fashion, real estate, media, banking, investing. Buys 100 mss/year. Query with published clips or send complete ms. Length: 3,000 words maximum. Pays $35-200. Sometimes pays expenses of writers on assignment.

Photos: Send photos with ms. Reviews color transparencies. Pays $5-10 for 5x7 or 8x10 b&w prints; $10 maximum for 5x7 or 8x10 color prints. Captions and model releases required. Rights purchased vary.

Tips: "It helps if freelancer lives in the area. The most frequent mistake made by writers in completing an article for us is not having enough Roanoke area focus: use of area experts, sources, slants, etc."

THE VIRGINIAN, Shenandoah Valley Magazine Corp., Box 8, New Hope VA 24469. (703)885-0388. Manuscript Editor: Hunter S. Pierce IV. Bimonthly magazine. 10% freelance written. Circ. 20,000. Pays on publication. Byline given. Buys first-time and other rights. Submit seasonal/holiday material 4 months in advance. Simultaneous queries, and simultaneous and photocopied submissions OK. Reports in 1 month. Sample copy $4.

Nonfiction: Book excerpts, general interest, historical/nostalgic, food, how-to, humor, inspirational, interview/profile, personal experience, photo feature and travel. Buys 20 mss/year. "Don't send unless there is a direct relation to Virginians and Virginia." Query with or without published clips, or send complete ms. Length: 1,000-1,500 words. Pays negotiable rate.

Photos: State availability of photos. Buys one-time rights.

Tips: "Be familiar enough with the magazine to know the tone and character of the feature articles."

Washington

THE SEATTLE WEEKLY, Sasquatch Publishing, 1931 2nd Ave., Seattle WA 98101. (206)441-5555. Editor: David Brewster. 30% freelance written. Eager to work with new/unpublished writers, especially those in the region. Weekly tabloid covering arts, politics, food, business, sports and books with local and regional emphasis. Circ. 32,000. Pays 2 weeks after publication. Publishes ms an average of 1 month after acceptance. Byline given. Offers variable kill fee. Buys first North American serial rights. Submit seasonal/holiday material 2 months in advance. Simultaneous queries OK. Computer printout submissions acceptable; prefers letter-quality. Reports in 1 month. Sample copy $2; writer's guidelines for #10 SASE.

Nonfiction: Book excerpts; expose; general interest; historical/nostalgic (Northwest); how-to (related to food and health); humor; interview/profile; opinion; travel; and arts-related essays. Buys 25 cover stories/year. Query with resume and published clips. Length: 700-4,000 words. Pays $75-800. Sometimes pays the expenses of writers on assignment.

Fiction: Annual Holiday Short Story Contest. Writers must be residents of the state of Washington. "We prefer that the stories have Northwest locales."

Tips: "The *Weekly* publishes stories on Northwest politics and art, usually written by regional and local writers, for a mostly upscale, urban audience; writing is high quality magazine style. We may decide to publish a new regional magazine, either quarterly or bimonthly, for a slightly different audience."

WASHINGTON, The Evergreen State Magazine, Evergreen Publishing Co., 200 W. Thomas, Seattle WA 98119. FAX: (206)285-3248. Editor: J. Kingston Pierce. Associate Editor: Heather M. Doran. 80% freelance written. A seven-times-per-year magazine covering all facets of life in Washington for an in-state audience. Circ. 72,000. Pays 30 days after acceptance for assigned pieces; on publication for spec material. Publishes mss an average of 6 months after acceptance. Byline given. Offers 20% kill fee on accepted stories. Submit seasonal/holiday material 6 months in advance. Query before submitting any material. Reports in 1 month on queries; 6 weeks on mss. Sample copy for $3.50; free writer's guidelines.

Nonfiction: Interview/profile; travel; historical; humor; book excerpts (unpublished Washington-related); newsfeatures; personal experience; business; food; home and garden; style. "No subjects not related specifically to Washingtonians." Query with published clips. Length: features, 1,500-3,000 words; sidebars, 200-600 words. Pays $350-800.

Photos: Carrie Seglin, picture editor. Original transparencies only. State availability of photos with query or send photos with query. Pays $50-250 for b&w; $125-325 for 35mm color transparencies. Captions, model releases and identification of subjects required. Buys one-time rights.

Columns/Departments: State Fare (a compendium of short news and insight pieces); High Stakes (business); The Wild Life (nature); State of Mine (thoughts and perspectives on the Evergreen State); Good Sports (professional and participatory sports); The Lively Arts (arts and entertainment profiles); Reading Matters (books); Ground Rules (gardening); Appearance's Sake (fashion/health and fitness); Time Capsule (state history). Buys about 70 mss/year. Length: 500-1,500 words. Pays $100-350.

Fiction: Must be written by a Washington author and offer perspective on how Washington residents think and live. Interested only in material from previously published writers. Length: 1,500-3,000 words. Pays $500.

Tips: "All areas are open, but the writer has a better chance of breaking in at our publication with short features and news stories. Our articles emphasize people—sometimes writers get sidetracked. We're also looking for original thinking, not tired approaches."

Wisconsin

‡INDIANHEAD STAR, Indianhead Publication Ltd., 104 S. Main St., Box 50, Deer Park WI 54007. (715)263-2445. Editor: Carole Inez Santoro. 75% freelance written. Weekly newspaper on small town life in Wisconsin. "Focus on people who reflect rural lifestyle. Where to visit in Wisconsin, profiles of 'ordinary' people, history, entrepreneurs, farming." Circ. 4,000. Pays on publication. Publishes ms an average of 1 month after acceptance. Buys first North American serial rights, first rights, one-time rights, second serial (reprint) rights and makes work-for-hire assignments. Submit seasonal/holiday material 2 months in advance. Simultaneous, photocopied and previously published submissions OK. Computer printout submissions OK; prefer letter-quality. Reports in 1 month on mss. Sample copy for SAE with $1.50 postage. Writer's guidelines for SAE with 2 first class stamps.

Nonfiction: Book excerpts, essays (historical link to Wisconsin), general interest, historical/nostalgic, how-to (fix old houses, cooking, raising children), humor, inspirational, interview/profile, new product, opinion, personal experience, photo feature (rural life), religious, travel (what's happening in Wisconsin), nostalgia, 30's depression, growing up, grandparents. All pertaining to Wisconsin. Special issues: Spring farming issue; Auto (old car stories welcome); Christmas—growing up; Veteran rememberances, (war stories women waiting at home, child's viewpoint). Buys 200 mss/year. Send complete ms and published clips. Length: 300-2,000. Pays $20-100 for assigned articles; $10-50 for unsolicited articles. Pays with contributor's copies to new columnists (plus $5). Sometimes pays expenses of writers on assignment.

Photos: Send photos with submission. Reviews negatives and prints. Offers no additional payment for photos accepted with ms, but ms has greater chance of acceptance. Captions and identification of subjects required. Buys one-time rights.

Columns/Departments: Lest We Forget (war stories); Farming Page (farm issues); Cooking Page (recipe, hints column); Out & About (What's happening in Wisconsin). Buys 100 mss/year. Send complete ms. Length: 300 words. Pays $5-15.

Fiction: Ethnic, historical (Wisconsin or war remembrances), humorous, slice-of-life vignettes (historical, growing-up). Buys 100 mss/year. Send complete ms. Length: 300-1,500 words. Pays $10-25.

Fillers: Anecdotes, facts, gags to be illustrated by cartoonist, newsbreaks and short humor. Buys 50/year. Pays $5.

Tips: "Accept small pay now—grow with us. We need reporters to cover hard news and political news."

MADISON MAGAZINE, Box 1604, Madison WI 53701. Editor: James Selk. 50% freelance written. Prefers to work with published/established writers. Monthly magazine; 100-150 pages. General city magazine aimed at upscale audience. Circ. 24,000. Pays on publication. Publishes ms an average of 2 months after acceptance. Buys all rights. Reports on material accepted for publication 10 days after acceptance. Returns rejected material immediately. Query. Computer printout submissions acceptable; prefers letter-quality. Sample copy $3 and 9x12 SAE.

Nonfiction: General human interest articles with strong local angles. Buys 100 mss/year. Length: 1,000-5,000 words. Pays $25-500. Pays the expenses of writers on assignment.

Photos: Offers no additional payment for b&w photos used with mss. Captions required.

WISCONSIN, *The Milwaukee Journal Magazine,* Box 661, Milwaukee WI 53201. (414)224-2341. Editor: Alan Borsuk. 20% freelance written. Prefers to work with published/established writers. Weekly general interest magazine appealing to readers living in Wisconsin. Circ. 520,000. Pays on publication. Publishes ms an average of 4 months after acceptance. Byline given. Buys first serial rights. Submit seasonal/holiday material 4 months in advance. Simultaneous queries OK. Computer printout submissions acceptable; prefers letter-quality. Reports in 1 month on queries; 6 months on mss. Free sample copy; writer's guidelines for #10 SASE.

Nonfiction: Expose, general interest, humor, interview/profile, opinion, personal experience and photo feature. No nostalgic reminiscences. Buys 50 mss/year. Query. Length: 150-2,500 words. Pays $75-500. Sometimes pays expenses of writers on assignment.

Photos: State availability of photos.

Columns/Departments: Opinion, Humor and Essays. Buys 50 mss/year. Query. Length: 300-1,000 words. Pays $100-200.

Tips: "We are primarily Wisconsin-oriented and are becoming more news-oriented."

WISCONSIN TRAILS, Box 5650, Madison WI 53705. (608)231-2444. Managing Editor: Geri Nixon. 70% freelance written. Prefers to work with published/established writers; works with a small number of new/unpublished writers each year. Bimonthly magazine for readers interested in Wisconsin; its contemporary issues, personalities, recreation, history, natural beauty; and the arts. Circ. 40,000. Buys first serial rights, and one-time rights sometimes. Pays on publication. Submit seasonal material at least 1 year in advance. Publishes ms an average of 6 months after acceptance. Byline given. Photocopied submissions OK. Computer printout submissions acceptable; prefers letter-quality. Reports in 1 month. Writer's guidelines for #10 SASE.

Nonfiction: "Our articles focus on some aspect of Wisconsin life; an interesting town or event, a person or industry, history or the arts and especially outdoor recreation. We do not use first-person essays or biographies about people who were born in Wisconsin but made their fortunes elsewhere. No poetry. No articles that are too local for our regional audience, or articles about obvious places to visit in Wisconsin. We need more articles about the new and little-known." Buys 3 unsolicited mss/year. Query or send outline. Length: 1,000-3,000 words. Pays $100-400 (negotiable), depending on assignment length and quality. Sometimes pays expenses of writers on assignment.

Photos: Purchased with or without mss or on assignment. Uses 35mm transparencies; larger format OK. Color photos usually illustrate an activity, event, region or striking scenery. Prefer photos with people in scenery. B&w photos usually illustrate a given article. Pays $50 each for b&w on publication. Pays $50-75 for inside color; $100-200 for covers. Captions preferred.

Tips: "We're looking for active articles about people, places, events and outdoor adventures in Wisconsin. We want to publish one in-depth article of state-wide interest or concern per issue, and several short (1,000-word) articles about short trips, recreational opportunities, restaurants, inns and cultural activities. We will be looking for more articles about out-of-the-way places in Wisconsin that are exceptional in some way."

Canada

CANADIAN GEOGRAPHIC, 39 McArthur Ave., Ottawa, Ontario K1L 8L7 Canada. FAX: (613)744-0947. Publisher: Susan Hudson. Editor: Ross W. Smith. Managing Editor: Ian Darragh. 90% freelance written. Works with a small number of new/unpublished writers each year. Circ. 215,000. Bimonthly magazine. Pays on acceptance. Publishes ms an average of 3 months after acceptance. Buys first Canadian rights; interested only in first-time publication. Computer printout submissions acceptable; prefers letter-quality. Sample copy for 9x12 SAE and $5; free writer's guidelines.

Nonfiction: Buys authoritative geographical articles, in the broad geographical sense, written for the average person, not for a scientific audience. Predominantly Canadian subjects by Canadian authors. Buys 30-45 mss/year. Always query first. Length: 1,500-3,000 words. Pays 30¢/word minimum. Usual payment for articles ranges between $500-2,500. Higher fees reserved for commissioned articles on which copyright remains with publisher unless otherwise agreed. Sometimes pays the expenses of writers on assignment.
Photos: Reviews 35mm slides, 2¼ transparencies or 8x10 glossies. Pays $60-300 for color photos, depending on published size.

‡**GEORGIA STRAIGHT**, Vancouver Free Press Publishing Corp., 2nd Floor, 1235 W. Pender St., Vancouver, B.C. V6E 2V6 Canada. (604)681-2000. FAX: (604)681-0272. Managing Editor: Charles Campbell. 90% freelance written. Weekly tabloid on arts/entertainment/lifestyle/civic issues. Circ. 70,000. Pays on publication. Byline given. Offers 75-100% kill fee. Buys first North American serial rights or second serial (reprint) rights. Simultaneous, photocopied and previously published submissions OK. Computer printout submissions OK; prefers letter-quality. Reports in 1 month. Sample copy for 8½x11 SAE and $1.
Nonfiction: General interest, humor, interview/profile, travel, and arts and entertainment. Buys 600 mss/year. Query with published clips. Length: 250-4,000 words. Pays $20-300. Sometimes pays expenses of writers on assignment.
Photos: Send photo with submission. Reviews, contact sheets, transparencies and 8x10 prints. Offers $30-70 per photo. Captions, model releases and identification of subjects required. Buys one-time rights.
Tips: "Be aware of entertainment events in the Vancouver area and expansion of our news coverage. Most stories relate to those events."

‡**HIGHLIGHTS**, The Fairway Group (Canada), 215 Fairway Rd., Kitchener, Ontario N2G 4E5 Canada. (519)894-1630. FAX: (519)894-2173 . Editor: Tawny Sinasac. Editorial Assistant: Katherine Brenner. General Manager: Scott Murray. 90% freelance written. Bimonthly magazine on human interest, fashion and homes. Circ. 37,000. Pays on publication. Publishes ms an average of 2 months after acceptance. Byline given. Offers 25% kill fee. Buys first North American serial rights. Submit seasonal/holiday material 4 months in advance. Previously published submissions OK for 2nd rights only; therefore, reduced fee. Computer printout submissions OK; prefers letter-quality. Reports in 6 weeks. Free sample copy and writer's guidelines with IRC (44¢/letter, $1.50/magazine).
Nonfiction: General interest, how-to (home improvements etc.), humor, interview/profile (local people) and travel. Query with published clips. Length: 500-2,500 words. Pays $70-400 for assigned articles. Sometimes pays expenses of writers on assignment.
Photos: State availability of photos with submission. Reviews contact sheets, transparencies and 8x10 prints. Offers payment sliding scale depending on professional quality.

‡**KEY TO VICTORIA/ESSENTIAL VICTORIA**, Key Pacific Publishers Co. Ltd. 3rd Fl. 1001 Wharf St., Victoria, B.C. V8W 1T6 Canada. (604)388-4324. FAX: (604)388-6166. Editor: Janice Strong. 40% freelance written. Monthly magazine on Victoria and Vancouver Island. Circ. 30,000. Pays on publication. Publishes ms an average of 1-2 months after acceptance. Byline given. Buys first North American serial rights and all rights. Query for electronic submissions. Computer printout submissions OK. Reports in 3 months. Free sample copy.
Nonfiction: General interest and travel. Essential Victoria. Buys 30 mss/year. Query with published clips. Length: 500-2,500 words. Pays 20-40¢/word.
Photos: State availability of photos with submission. Reviews contact sheets, transparencies and prints. Offers $50-150 per photo. Model releases and identification of subjects required. Buys one-time rights.

THE MIRROR, The Mirror-Northern Report, Box 269, High Prairie, Alberta T0G 0X0 Canada. (403)523-3706. 25% freelance written. Weekly magazine of northern Alberta news and features. Circ. 2,000. Pays on publication. Publishes ms an average of 2 months after acceptance. Byline given. Publication not copyrighted. Buys one-time rights. Simultaneous, photocopied and previously published submissions OK. Computer printout submissions OK; prefers letter-quality. Reports in 2 weeks on queries; 1 month on mss. Sample copy for 9x12 SAE and $2.
Nonfiction: Buys 20 mss/year. Send complete ms. Length: 2,000 words maximum. Pays 1¢/word.
Photos: Send photos with submission. Reviews prints. Offers no additional payment for photos accepted with ms. Captions and identification of subjects required. Buys one-time rights.
Fiction: Buys 20 mss/year. Send complete ms. Length: 1,500 words.
Poetry: Traditional. Buys 10 poems/year.

‡**ONTARIO OUT OF DOORS**, 227 Front St. E., Toronto, Ont. M5A 1E8 Canada. (416)368-0815. Editor-in-Chief: Burton J. Myers. 80% freelance written. "We prefer a blend of both experienced and new writers." Emphasizes hunting, fishing, camping, and conservation. Monthly magazine; 80 pages. Circ. 55,000. Pays on acceptance. Publishes ms an average of 6 months after acceptance. Buys first North American serial rights. Phone queries OK. Computer printout submissions acceptable; no dot-matrix. Submit seasonal/holiday

material 5 months in advance of issue date. Reports in 6 weeks. Free sample copy and writer's guidelines; mention *Writer's Market* in request.

Nonfiction: Exposé of conservation practices; how-to (improve your fishing and hunting skills); humor; photo feature (on wildlife); travel (where to find good fishing and hunting); and any news on Ontario. "Avoid 'Me and Joe' articles or funny family camping anecdotes." Buys 20-30 unsolicited mss/year. Query. Length: 150-3,500 words. Pays $35-350. Sometimes pays the expenses of writers on assignment.

Photos: Submit photo material with accompanying query. No additonal payment for b&w contact sheets and 35mm color transparencies. "Should a photo be used on the cover, an additional payment of $350-500 is made."

Fillers: Outdoor tips. Buys 100 mss/year. Length 20-50 words. Pays $15-35.

Tips: "It's rewarding for us to find a freelancer who reads and understands a set of writer's guidelines, but it is annoying when writers fail to submit supporting photography."

OTTAWA MAGAZINE, Ottawa Magazine Inc., 192 Bank St., Ottawa, Ontario K2P 1W8 Canada. (613)234-7751. Editor: Louis Valenzuela. 80% freelance written. Prefers to work with published/established writers. Magazine, published 11 times/year, covering life in Ottawa and environs. "*Ottawa Magazine* reflects the interest and lifestyles of its readers who tend to be married, ages 35-55, upwardly mobile and urban." Circ. 50,000. Pays on acceptance. Publishes ms an average of 6 months after acceptance. Byline given. "Kill fee depends on agreed-upon fee; very seldom used." Buys first North American serial rights and second serial (reprint) rights. Simultaneous queries, and photocopied and previously published submissions OK. Computer printout submissions acceptable. Reports in 2 months. Sample copy $1.

Nonfiction: Book excerpts (by local authors or about regional issues); exposé (federal or regional government, education); general interest; interview/profile (on Ottawans who have established national or international reputations); photo feature (for recurring section called Freezeframe); and travel (recent examples are Brazil, Trinidad & Tobago, Copenhagen). "No articles better suited to a national or special interest publication." Buys 100 mss/year. Query with published clips. Length: 2,000-3,500 words. Pays $500/1,000 (Canadian).

Tips: "A phone call to our associate editor is the best way to assure that queries receive prompt attention. Once a query interests me the writer is assigned a detailed 'treatment' of the proposed piece which is used to determine viability of story. We will be concentrating on more issue-type stories with good, solid fact-researched base, also doing more fluffy pieces—best and worst of Ottawa—that sort of stuff. Harder for out-of-town writers to furnish. The writer should strive to inject a personal style and avoid newspaper-style reportage. *Ottawa Magazine* also doesn't stoop to boosterism and points out the bad along with the good. Good prospects for U.S. writers are interiors (house and garden type), gardening (for Northern climate), leisure/lifestyles. Second rights OK."

TORONTO LIFE, 59 Front St. E., Toronto, Ontario M5E 1B3 Canada. (416)364-3333. Editor: Marq de Villiers. 95% freelance written. Prefers to work with published/established writers. Monthly magazine emphasizing local issues and social trends, short humor/satire, and service features for upper income, well educated and, for the most part, young Torontonians. Uses some fiction. Pays on acceptance. Publishes ms an average of 3-4 months after acceptance. Byline given. Buys first North American serial rights. Pays 50% kill fee "for commissioned articles only." Phone queries OK. Reports in 3 weeks. Sample copy $2.50 with SAE and IRCs.

Nonfiction: Uses most types of articles. Buys 17 mss/issue. Query with published clips. Buys about 40 unsolicited mss/year. Length: 1,000-5,000 words. Pays $800-3,000.

Photos: State availability of photos. Uses good color transparencies and clear, crisp b&w prints. Seldom uses submitted photos. Captions and model release required.

Columns/Departments: "We run about five columns an issue. They are all freelanced, though most are from regular contributors. They are mostly local in concern and cover politics, money, fine art, performing arts, movies and sports." Length: 1,800 words. Pays $1,500.

WESTERN CANADA OUTDOORS, McIntosh Publishing Company, Ltd., 1132-98th St., Box 430, North Battleford, Saskatchewan S9A 2Y5 Canada. (306)445-4401. Contact: Stanley Nowakowski. 15% freelance written. Bimonthly tabloid covering fish and wildlife. Circ. 36,700. Pays on publication. Publishes ms an average of 2 months after acceptance. Byline given. Buys one-time rights. Submit seasonal/holiday material 1 month in advance. Simultaneous submissions OK. Computer printout submissions OK; prefers letter-quality. Reports in 3 weeks.

Nonfiction: Exposé, general interest, humor, personal experience and photo feature. Buys 4 mss/year. Query with or without published clips, or send complete ms. Length: 200-800 words. Pays $25-50 for assigned articles. Sometimes pays the expenses of writers on assignment.

Photos: State availability of photos with submission. Reviews contact sheets. Offers $10-25 per photo. Captions and identification of subjects required. Buys one-time rights.

Columns/Departments: Buys 18 mss/year. Query. Length: 700-800 words. Pays $25-50.

Fillers: Anecdotes. Buys 6/year.

WESTERN PEOPLE, Supplement to the Western Producer, Western Producer Publications, Box 2500, Saskatoon, Saskatchewan S7K 2C4 Canada. (306)665-3500. Managing Editor: Liz Delahey. Weekly farm newspaper supplement covering rural Western Canada. "Our magazine reflects the life and people of rural Western Canada both in the present and historically." Circ. 135,000. Pays on acceptance. Publishes ms an average of 6 months after acceptance. Byline given. Buys first rights. Submit seasonal/holiday material 3 months in advance. Reports in 2 weeks on queries; 1 month on mss. Sample copy for 9x12 SAE and 74¢ postage; writer's guidelines for #10 SAE and 38¢ postage.

Nonfiction: General interest, historical/nostalgic, humor, interview/profile, personal experience and photo feature. Buys 450 mss/year. Send complete ms. Length: 500-2,500 words. Pays $50-250.

Photos: Send photos with submission. Reviews transparencies and prints. Offers $5-25 per photo. Captions and identification of subjects required. Buys one-time rights.

Fiction: Adventure, historical, humorous, mainstream, mystery, novel excerpts, romance, serialized novels, suspense and western stories reflecting life in rural Western Canada. Buys 50 mss/year. Send complete ms. Length: 1,000-2,000 words. Pays $50-200.

Poetry: Free verse, traditional, haiku and light verse. Buys 75 poems/year. Submit maximum 3 poems. Length: 4-50 lines. Pays $10-35.

Tips: "Western Canada is geographically very large. The approach for writing about an interesting individual is to introduce that person *neighbor-to-neighbor* to our readers."

‡THE WESTERN PRODUCER, Western Producer Publications, Box 2500, Saskatoon, Saskatchewan S7K 2C4 Canada. (306)665-3500. FAX: (306)653-1255. Editor: Keith Dryden. Managing Editor: Garry Fairbairn. 30% freelance written. Weekly newspaper covering agriculture and rural life. Publishes "informative material for 135,000 western Canadian farm families." Pays on acceptance. Byline given. Kill fee varies. Not copyrighted. Buys one-time rights. Submit seasonal/holiday material 2 months in advance. Simultaneous, photocopied and previously published submissions OK. Query for electronic submissions. Computer printout submissions OK; prefers letter-quality to dot-matrix. Reports in 1 week on queries; 3 weeks on mss. Sample copy for 11x14 SAE with IRC; writer's guidelines for #10 SAE.

Nonfiction: General interest, historical/nostalgic, how-to (on farm machinery or construction), humor, new product, technical and rural cartoons. Special issue includes Weeds and Chemical issue (March). Nothing "non-Canadian, over 1,500 words." Buys 600 mss/year. Query. Length: 2,000 words. Pays $100-400 for assigned articles; pays $150 maximum for unsolicited articles. Sometimes pays the expenses of writers on assignment.

Photos: Send photos with submission. Reviews contact sheets, negatives, transparencies and prints. Offers $15-50 per photo. Captions required. Buys one-time rights.

Columns/Departments: Liz Delahey, editor. Western People (magazine insert focusing on Western Canadian personalities, hobbies, history, fiction), 500-2,000 words. Buys 350 mss/year. Query. Length: 500-2,000 words. Pays $50-500.

Fiction: Ethnic, historical, humorous, slice-of-life vignettes, western and rural settings. No non-western Canadian subjects. Buys 40 mss/year. Query. Length: 500-2,000. Pays $50-500.

Poetry: Free verse, light verse and traditional. Buys 20 poems/year. Length: 10-100 lines. Pays $10-100.

Tips: "Use CP/AP/UPI style and a fresh ribbon." Areas most open to freelancers are "cartoons, on-farm profiles, rural Canadian personalities."

‡YORK MAGAZINE, Suite 800, 1881 Yonge St., Toronto, Ontario M4S 3C4 Canada. (416)489-7553. FAX: (416)486-1704. Editor: Lorie Sculthorp. 100% freelance written. Magazine appears 10 times a year, on York region (north of Toronto). Circ. 50,000. Pays on acceptance. Publishes ms an average of 3 months after acceptance. Offers kill fee. Buys one-time rights or second serial (reprint) rights. Submit seasonal/holiday material 3 months in advance. Photocopied and previously published submissions OK. Query for electronic submissions. Computer printout submissions OK. Free sample copy.

Nonfiction: Exposé (investigative), how-to and interview/profile (people in York region). "No fiction." Buys 50 mss/year. Length: 2,000-3,000 words. Pays up to $1,500 for assigned articles; $500-700 for unsolicited articles. Pays expenses of writers on assignments.

Photos: State availability of photos with submissions. Reviews negatives. Offers $50-200 per photo. Captions, model releases and identification of subjects required. Buys one-time rights.

Tips: "We are a small but friendly publication—give us a call with your ideas. If we like what you say we'll ask for a query. We pay promptly!"

Relationships

These publications focus on lifestyles and relationships. These magazines are read and often written by single people, gays and lesbians and those interested in these lifestyles or in alternative outlooks. They may offer writers a forum for unconventional views or serve as a voice for particular audiences or causes.

ATLANTA SINGLES MAGAZINE, Sigma Publications, Inc., Suite 320, 3423 Piedmont Rd. NE., Atlanta GA 30305 and Box 52700, Atlanta GA 30355. (404)239-0642. FAX: (404)261-2214. Editor: Margaret Anthony. Associate Editor: Diana Porter. 10% freelance written. Works with a small number of new/unpublished writers each year. A bi-monthly magazine for single, widowed or divorced adults, medium to high income level, many business and professionally oriented; single parents, ages 25 to 55. Circ. 15,000. Pays on publication. Publishes ms an average of 6 months after acceptance. Byline given. Buys one-time rights, second serial (reprint) rights and simultaneous rights. Submit seasonal/holiday material 6 months in advance. Simultaneous, photocopied and previously published submissions OK. Computer printout submissions acceptable; prefers letter-quality. Sample copy $2; writer's guidelines for #10 SASE.
Nonfiction: General interest, humor, personal experience, photo feature and travel. No pornography. Buys 5 mss/year. Send complete ms. Length: 600-1,200 words. Pays $100-200 for unsolicited articles; sometimes trades for personal ad.
Photos: Send photos with submission. Cover photos also considered. Reviews prints. Offers no additional payment for photos accepted with ms. Model releases and identification of subjects required. Buys one-time rights.
Columns/Departments: Will consider ideas. Query. Length: 600-800 words. Pays $100-200 per column/department.
Fiction: "We rarely print fiction, unless it is outstanding and relates to single readers exceptionally well." Length: 600-1,200 words. Pays $100-200.
Tips: "We are open to articles on *any* subject that would be of interest to singles, i.e., travel, autos, movies, love stories, fashion, investments, real estate, etc. Although singles are interested in topics like self-awareness, being single again, and dating, they are also interested in many of the same subjects that married people are, such as those listed."

BAY WINDOWS, New England's Largest Gay and Lesbian Newspaper, Bay Windows, Inc.. 1523 Washington St., Boston MA 02118. (617)266-6670. Editor: Jeff Epperly; Arts Editor: Ruby Kikel. 30-40% freelance written. A weekly newspaper of gay news and concerns. "*Bay Windows* covers predominantly news of New England, but will print non-local news and features depending on the newsworthiness of the story. We feature hard news, opinion, news analysis, arts reviews and interviews." Publishes ms within 2 months of acceptance, pays within 2 weeks of publication. Byline given. Offers 50% kill fee. Rights obtained varies, usually first serial rights. Simultaneous submissions accepted if other submissions are outside of New England. Submit seasonal-holiday material 3 months in advance. Sample copies $1; writer's guidelines for #10 SASE.
Nonfiction: Hard news, general interest with a gay slant, interview/profile, opinion and photo features. Publishes 100 mss/year. Query with published clips, or send complete ms. Length: 500-1,500 words. Pay varies: $25-100 news; $10-60 arts.
Photos: $25 per published photo, b&w photos only. Model releases and identification of subjects required.
Columns/Departments: Film, music, dance, books, art. Length: 500-1,500 words. Buys 200 mss/year. Pays $10-100.
Poetry: All varieties. Publishes 50 poems per year. Length: 10-30 lines. No payment.
Tips: "Too much gay-oriented writing is laden with the clichés and catch phrases of the movement. Writers must have intimate knowledge of gay community; however, this should not mean that standard English usage is not required. We look for writers with new—even controversial perspectives on the lives of gay men and lesbians. While we assume gay is good, we will print stories which examine problems within the community and movement. No pornography."

CHANGING MEN, Issues in Gender, Sex and Politics, Feminist Men's Publications, 306 N. Brooks St., Madison WI 53715. Editor: Rick Cote. Managing Editor: Michael Birnbaum. 80% freelance written. Works with a small number of new/unpublished writers each year. A feminist men's journal published two times a year. "We are a forum for anti-sexist men and women to explore the politics of gender, the complexities of sexual relations, and the expressions of love in a changing world." Circ. 4,000. Publishes ms an average of 1 year after acceptance. Byline given. Buys one-time rights. Simultaneous queries, simultaneous, photocopied and previously published submissions OK. Computer printout submissions acceptable; prefers letter-quality. Reports in 2 months. Sample copy $4.50; writer's guidelines for #10 SASE.
Nonfiction: Book excerpts, humor, interview/profile, opinion, personal experience and photo feature. Plans special issues on male/female intimacy. Future issues expected to focus on fathering, feminism, divorce, prisons. No theoretical articles. Query with published clips. Length: 3,500 words maximum. Pays $25 maximum.
Columns/Departments: Men and War (focus on masculinity and how culture shapes male values), Sports (with a feminist slant), and Book Reviews (focus on sexuality and masculinity). Query with published clips. Length: 500-1,500 words. Pays $15 maximum.

Fiction: Jeff Kirsch, fiction editor. Erotica, ethnic, experimental, humorous and novel excerpts. Buys 1 ms/year. Query with published clips. Length: 3,500 words maximum. Pays $20 maximum.
Poetry: Free verse, haiku and light verse. Submit maximum 3 poems. Length: 50 lines maximum. No payment for poetry.
Fillers: Clippings, jokes and newsbreaks. Length: 300 words. No payment for fillers.

‡COLUMBUS BRIDE & GROOM MAGAZINE, National Bridal Publications, Inc., 303 East Livingston Ave., Columbus OH 43215. (614)224-1992. Editor: Marvin Brown. Managing Editor: Lori Meeker. 5% freelance written. Semiannual magazine on weddings. Circ. 13,000. Pays on publication. Publishes ms an average of 4 months after acceptance. Byline given. Offers 50% kill fee. Buys all rights. Submit seasonal/holiday material 6 months in advance. Reports in 3-4 weeks. Sample copy $1.50.
Nonfiction: General interest (within our specialized field), how-to (plan and execute a wedding and take up married life), humor and inspirational. "No articles promoting a specifically named product and/or service." Buys 4-5 mss/year. Query. Length: 250-1,500 words. Pays $40-250 for assigned articles; $25-150 for unsolicited articles. Sometimes pays expenses of writers on assignment.
Photos: State availability of photos with submission. Reviews contact sheets 35mm and up transparencies and 5x7 and up prints. Captions and model releases required. Buys one-time rights.
Fillers: Anecdotes, facts, newsbreaks and short humor. Length: 40-200 words.

DRUMMER, Desmodus, Inc., Box 11314, San Francisco CA 94101. (415)864-3456. Editor: Tony DeBlase. 80% freelance written. Gay male leather and related fetish erotica/news. Monthly magazine publishes "erotic aspects of leather and other masculine fetishes for gay men." Circ. 60,000. Pays on publication. Publishes ms an average of 3 months after acceptance. Byline given. Buys first North American serial rights or makes work-for-hire assignments. Submit seasonal/holiday material 9 months in advance. Photocopied and previously published submissions OK. Computer printout submissions OK; prefers letter-quality. Reports in 1 month on queries; in 2-3 months on mss. Sample copy $5; writer's guidelines for #10 SASE.
Nonfiction: Book excerpts, essays, historical/nostalgic, how-to, humor, interview/profile, new product, opinion, personal experience, photo feature, technical and travel. No feminine slanted pieces. Buys 25 mss/year. Query with or without published clips, or send complete ms. Length: 1,000-15,000 words. Pays $50-200 for assigned articles; $50-100 for unsolicited articles. Sometimes pays writers with contributor copies "if author is willing." Rarely pays expenses of writers on assignment.
Photos: Send photos with submission (photocopies OK). Reviews contact sheets and transparencies. Offers $10-100 per photo. Model releases and identification of subjects required. Buys one-time rights or all rights.
Fiction: Adventure, condensed novels, erotica, ethnic, fantasy, historical, horror, humorous, mystery, novel excerpts, science fiction, slice-of-life vignettes, suspense and western. Must have gay "macho" erotic elements. Buys 60-75 mss/year. Send complete ms. Length: 1,000-20,000 words. Occasionally serializes stories. Pays $100.
Fillers: Anecdotes, facts, gags and newsbreaks. Buys 50/year. Length: 10-100 words. pay $10-50.
Tips: "All they have to do is write—but they must be knowledgeable about some aspect of the scene. While the magazine is aimed at gay men, we welcome contributions from straight men and from straight, bisexual and gay women who understand leather and s/m and kinky erotic fetishes. Fiction is most open to freelancers."

DUNGEON MASTER, Desmodus Inc., Box 11314, San Francisco CA 94101. (415)978-5377. Editor: Tony DeBlase. 50% freelance written. Quarterly magazine covering gay male erotic s/m. "Safety is emphasized. This is not a fantasy magazine but is for real how-to articles on equipment, techniques, etc." Circ. 5,000. Most articles are unpaid—except by complimentary subscriptions, ads, etc. Byline given. Buys first North American serial rights, one-time rights, simultaneous rights or makes work-for-hire assignments. Photocopied submissions and previously published submissions OK. Computer printout submissions OK; prefers letter-quality. Sample copy $5; writer's guidelines for #10 SASE.
Nonfiction: Book excerpts, essays, historical/nostalgic, how-to (mainly), humor, interview/profile, new product, opinion, personal experience, photo feature (may be paid), technical, travel and safety. No fiction or unsafe practices. Buys 40 mss/year. Query with or without published clips, or send complete ms. Length: no limit. Pays $25-200 for assigned articles. Usually pays writers with contributor copies or other premiums rather than a cash payment. Rarely pays expenses of writers on assignment.
Photos: Send photos with submission. (photocopies OK). Reviews contact sheets and transparencies. Offers $10-100/photo. Model releases and identification of subjects required. Buys one-time rights or all rights.
Fillers: Anecdotes, facts, gags to be illustrated and newbreaks. Buys 10/year. Pays $5-25.
Tips: "Must be knowledgeable in specialized field. While publication is aimed at gay men, submission by straight men and straight and gay women are welcome."

FIRST HAND, Experiences For Loving Men, Firsthand, Ltd., 310 Cedar Lane, Teaneck NJ 07666. (201)836-9177. Editor: Lou Thomas. Publisher: Jackie Lewis. 75% freelance written. Eager to work with new/unpublished writers. Monthly magazine of homosexual erotica. Circ. 70,000. Pays 8 months after acceptance or on publication, whichever comes first. Publishes ms an average of 8 months after acceptance. Byline given. Buys all rights (exceptions made) and second serial (reprint) rights. Submit seasonal/holiday material 10 months in advance. Photocopied submissions OK. Computer printout submissions acceptable; no dot-matrix. Reports in 2 months. Sample copy $3; writer's guidelines for #10 SASE.

Nonfiction: "We seldom use nonfiction except for our 'Survival Kit' section, but will consider full-length profiles, investigative reports, and so on if they are of information/inspirational interest to gay people. Erotic safe sex stories are acceptable." Length: 3,000 words maximum. Pays $100-150. "We will consider original submissions only." Query.

Columns/Departments: Survival Kit (short nonfiction articles, up to 1,000 words, featuring practical information on safe sex practices, health, travel, books, video, psychology, law, fashion, and other advice/consumer/ lifestyle topics of interest to gay or single men). "These should be written in the second or third person." Query. "For this section, we sometimes also buy reprint rights to appropriate articles previously published in local gay newspapers around the country." Pays $35 to $70, depending on length, if original; if reprint, pays half that rate.

Fiction: Erotic fiction up to 5,000 words in length, average 2,000-3,000 words. "We prefer fiction in the first person which is believable—stories based on the writer's actual experience have the best chance. We're not interested in stories which involve underage characters in sexual situations. Other taboos include bestiality, rape—except in prison stories, as rape is an unavoidable reality in prison—and heavy drug use. Writers with questions about what we can and cannot depict should write for our guidelines, which go into this in more detail. We print mostly self-contained stories; we will look at novel excerpts, but only if they stand on their own."

Poetry: Free verse and light verse. Buys 12/year. Submit maximum 5 poems. Length: 10-30 lines. Pays $25.

Tips: "*First Hand* is a very reader-oriented publication for gay men. Half of each issue is comprised by letters from our readers describing their personal experiences, fantasies and feelings. Our readers are from all walks of life, all races and ethnic backgrounds, all classes, all religious and political affiliations, and so on. They are very diverse, and many live in far-flung rural areas or small towns; for some of them, our magazines are the primary source of contact with gay life, in some cases the only support for their gay identity. Our readers are very loyal and save every issue. We return that loyalty by trying to reflect their interests—for instance, by striving to avoid the exclusively big-city bias so common to national gay publications. So bear in mind the diversity of the audience when you write."

‡FQ, Foreskin Quarterly, Desmodus Inc., Box 11314, San Francisco CA 94101. (415)864-3456. Editor: Tony DeBlase. 90% freelance written. Quarterly magazine covering circumcision. "Most writers are anti-circumcision but both sides are solicited and pro-circumcision writers are also invited to submit." Circ. 15,000. Pays on publication. Publishes ms an average of 4-8 months after acceptance. Byline given. Buys first North American serial rights. Photocopied and previously published submissions OK. Computer printout submissions OK; prefers letter-quality to dot-matrix. Reports in 4-6 weeks on queries; 2-4 months on mss. Sample copy $4; writer's guidelines for #10 SASE.

Nonfiction: Book excerpts, essays, expose, historical/nostalgic, how-to, humor, interview/profile, new product, opinion, personal experience, photo feature, technical and travel. Buys 40 mss/year. Query with or without published clips or send complete ms. Length varies. Pays $0-150 for assigned articles; $0-100 for unsolicited material. Pays writers with contributor copies or other premiums "depending on author's willingness."

Photos: Send photos with submission (photocopies OK). Reviews contact sheets and transparencies. Offers $10-100/photo. Model releases and identification of subjects required. Buys one-time rights or all rights.

Fiction: Adventure, confession, erotica, ethnic, fantasy, historical, humorous, religious, science fiction and suspense. Must have foreskin/circumcision slant. Buys 4-8 mss/year. Send complete ms. Length varies. Pays $25-100.

Fillers: Anecdotes, facts, gags to be illustrated. Buys 10-20/year. Pays $10-50.

Tips: "Writers must have genuine interest in subject."

THE GUIDE, To The Gay Northeast, Fidelity Publishing. Box 593, Boston MA 02199. (617)266-8557. Editor: French Wall. 50% freelance written. A monthly magazine on the gay and lesbian community. Circ. 22,000. Pays on acceptance. Publishes ms an average of 2 months after acceptance. Kill fee negotiable. Buys all rights. Submit seasonal/holiday material 2 months in advance. Simultaneous and photocopied submissions OK. Computer printout submissions OK; prefers letter-quality. Sample copy for 9x12 SAE with 8 first class stamps; writer's guidelines for #10 SASE.

Nonfiction: Book excerpts (if yet unpublished), essays, exposé, general interest, historical/nostalgic, humor, interview/profile, opinion, personal experience, photo feature and religious. "We prefer upbeat articles with focus on Northeast United States or Eastern Canada." Buys 48 mss/year. Query with or without published clips, or send complete ms. Length: 500-5,000 words. Pays $30-120. Send photos with submission. Reviews contact sheets. Offers no additional payment for photos accepted with ms/negotiable. Captions, model releases, identification of subjects prefered; releases required sometimes. Buys one-time rights.

Fiction: Adventure, erotica, ethnic, experimental, fantasy, historical, humorous, novel excerpts, religious, romance, science fiction, slice-of-life vignettes and suspense. "We are seeking to add fiction to our magazine; format allows for only short (500-4,000 word) pieces, though serialization could be a possibility." Query with published clips. Length: 500-4,000 words. Pays $30-120.

Tips: "Brevity, humor and militancy appreciated."

IN TOUCH FOR MEN, In Touch Publications International, Inc., 7216 Varna, North Hollywood CA 91605. (818)764-2288. Editor-in-Chief: Tom Quinn. 80% freelance written. Works with a small number of new/unpublished writers each year. A monthly magazine covering the gay male lifestyle, gay male humor and erotica. Circ. 70,000. Pays on acceptance. Byline given. Buys one-time rights. Submit seasonal/holiday material 4 months in advance. Simultaneous and photocopied submissions OK. Computer printout submissions acceptable. Reports in 2 weeks on queries; 6 weeks on mss. Sample copy $4.95; writer's guidelines for #10 SAE.

Nonfiction: Buys 36 mss/year. Send complete ms. Length: 1,000-3,500 words. Pays $25-75.

Photos: State availability of photos with submission. Reviews contact sheets, transparencies, and prints. Offers $35/photo. Captions, model releases and identification of subjects required. Buys one-time rights.

Columns/Departments: Touch and Go (brief comments on various items or pictures that have appeared in the media), 50-500 words. Buys 12 mss/year. Send complete ms. Pays $25.

Fiction: Adventure, confession, erotica, historical, horror, humorous, mainstream, mystery, romance, science fiction, slice-of-life vignettes, suspense, and western; all must be gay male erotica. No "heterosexual, heavy stuff." Buys 36 mss/year. Send complete ms. Length: 2,500-3,500 words. Pays $75 maximum.

Fillers: Short humor. Buys 12/year. Length: 1,500-3,500 words. Pays $50-75.

Tips: "Our publication features male nude photos plus three fiction pieces, several articles, cartoons, humorous comments on items from the media, photo features, and gay travel. We try to present the positive aspects of the gay lifestyle, with an emphasis on humor. Humorous pieces may be erotic in nature. We are open to all submissions that fit our gay male format; the emphasis, however, is on humor and the upbeat. We receive many fiction manuscripts but not nearly enough articles and humor."

MANSCAPE 2, First Hand Ltd., Box 1314, Teaneck NJ 07666. (201)836-9177. Editor: Lou Thomas. 75% freelance written. A bimonthly magazine focusing on "gay male sexual fetishes, kink and leather sex." Circ. 70,000. Pays on publication or 240 days, whichever comes first. Publishes ms an average of 9 months after acceptance. Byline given. Buys first North American serial rights or all rights. Submit seasonal/holiday material 9 months in advance. Photocopied submissions OK. "No simultaneous submisions." Computer printout submissions OK; no dot-matrix. Reports in 1-2 months. Sample copy $5; writer's guidelines for #10 SASE.

Nonfiction: Interview/profile and health. "All nonfiction articles must have gay angle." Buys 6 mss/year. Query with or without published clips, or send complete ms. Length: 2,000-3,750. Pays $100-150 for unsolicited articles (no assigned articles).

Fiction: Erotica and novel excerpts. "All fiction must be gay erotica. We don't want to see downbeat attitudes in stories." Buys 30 mss/year. Send complete ms. Length: 2,000-3,750 words. Pays $100-150.

Poetry: Free verse, haiku, light verse, traditional. Must be erotic. Buys 6 poems/year. Submit 3 poems maximum at one time. Length: 5-20 lines. Pays $25.

Tips: "The fiction section is the best area for freelancers to break in with. Fiction we publish must be written in the first person. Stories should be strongly erotic, with at least an edge of kinkiness. And stories should be a celebration of masculinity, of maleness."

METRO SINGLES LIFESTYLES, Metro Publications, Box 28203, Kansas City MO 64118. (816)436-8424. Editor: R.L. Huffstutter. 40% freelance written. Eager to work with new/unpublished writers. A tabloid appearing 9 times/year covering singles lifestyles. Pays on acceptance. Publishes ms an average of 2 months after acceptance. Byline given. Buys one-time rights and second serial (reprint) rights. Submit seasonal/holiday material 3 months in advance. Photocopied submissions OK. Computer printout submissions acceptable; prefers letter-quality. Reports in 1 month. Sample copy $2 and 9x12 SAE with 5 first class stamps.

Nonfiction: Essay, general interest, how-to (on meeting the ideal mate, recovering from divorce, etc.), inspirational, interview/profile, personal experience and photo feature. No sexually-oriented material. Buys 2-6 mss/year. Send complete ms. Length: 700-1,200 words. Pays $100 maximum for assigned articles; pays $20-50 for unsolicited articles. Will pay in copies or other if writer prefers.

Photos: Send photos with submission. Reviews 3x5 prints. Offers no additional payment for photos accepted with ms. Captions, model releases and identification of subjects required. Buys one-time rights.

Columns/Departments: Movie Reviews, Lifestyles, Singles Events, and Book Reviews (about singles), all 400-1,000 words. Buys 3 mss/year. Send complete ms. Pays $20-50.

Fiction: Confession, humorous, romance and slice-of-life vignettes. No political, religion, ethnic or sexually-oriented material. Buys 6 mss/year. Send complete ms. Length: 700-1,200 words. Pays $20-50.

Poetry: Free verse and light verse. Buys 6 poems/year. Submit maximum 3 poems. Length: 21 lines. Pays $5-10.

Tips: "A freelancer can best approach and break in to our publication with positive articles, photo features about singles and positive fiction about singles. Photos and short bios of singles (blue collar, white collar, and professional) at work needed. Photos and a few lines about singles enjoying recreation (swimming, sports, chess, etc.) always welcome. Color photos, close-up, are suitable."

MOM GUESS WHAT NEWSPAPER, New Helvetia Communications, Inc., 1725 L. St., Sacramento CA 95814. (916)441-6397. Editor: Linda Birner. 80% freelance written. Works with small number of new/unpublished writers each year. A monthly tabloid covering gay rights and gay lifestyles. Circ. 21,000. Publishes ms an average of 3 months after acceptance. Byline given. Buys all rights. Submit seasonal/holiday material 3 months in advance. Photocopied submissions OK. Computer printout submissions acceptable; no dot-matrix. Reports in 2 months. Sample copy $1; writer's guidelines for 8½x11 SAE with 3 first class stamps.
Nonfiction: Interview/profile and photo feature of international, national or local scope. Buys 8 mss/year. Query. Length: 200-1,500 words. Payment depends on article. Pays expenses of writers on special assignment.
Photos: State availability of photos with submission. Reviews 5x7 prints. Offers no additional payment for photos accepted with ms. Captions and identification of subjects required. Buys one-time rights.
Columns/Departments: Restaurants, Political, Health, and Film, Video and Book Reviews. Buys 12 mss/year. Query. Payment depends on article.

ON THE SCENE MAGAZINE, 3507 Wyoming NE, Albuquerque NM 87111. (505)299-4401. Editor: Gail Skinner. 60% freelance written. Eager to work with new/unpublished writers. Monthly tabloid covering lifestyles for all ages. Pays on publication. Publishes ms an average of 6 months after acceptance. Byline given. Submit seasonal/holiday material 3 months in advance. Query for electronic submissions. Computer printout submissions acceptable; prefers letter-quality. Reports in 3 months. Sample copy $3. Writer's guidelines and sample copy for 9x12 SAE and 5 first class stamps; writer's guidelines for #10 SASE.
Nonfiction: General interest; how-to; humor; inspirational; opinion; personal experience; relationships; consumer guide; travel; finance; real estate; parenting; and astrology. No suggestive or pornographic material. Buys 100 mss/year. Send complete ms. "Ms returned only if adequate SASE is included." Also publishes some fiction. Length: 300-1,500 words. Pays $20-60. Sometimes pays expenses of writers on assignment.
Photos: State availability of photos with ms. Captions, model releases, and identification of subjects required.
Tips: "We are looking for articles that deal with every aspect of living—whether on a local or national level. Our readers are of above-average intelligence, income and education. The majority of our articles are chosen from 'relationships' and 'humor' submissions. Expanded format from 'singles only' to general readership."

‡TORSO, Varsity Communications, 462 Broadway, New York NY 10013. (212)966-8400. Editor: Stan Leventhal. 75% freelance written. Works with a small number of new/unpublished writers each year. A monthly magazine for gay men. "Divergent viewpoints are expressed in both feature articles and fiction, which examine values and behavior patterns characteristic of a gay lifestyle. *Torso* has a continuing commitment to well-documented investigative journalism in areas pertaining to the lives and well-being of homosexuals." Circ. 60,000. Pays on publication. Publishes ms an average of 5 months after acceptance. Byline given. Buys first North American serial rights. Submit seasonal/holiday material 3 months in advance. Simultaneous queries, and simultaneous and photocopied submissions OK. Reports in 2 weeks on queries; 1 month on mss. Sample copy $5; writer's quidelines for #10 SASE.
Nonfiction: Exposé, general interest, humor, interview/profile, opinion, personal experience, photo feature and travel. "*Torso* also regularly reports on cultural and political trends, as well as the arts and entertainment, often profiling the people and personalities who affect them. The tone must be positive regarding the gay experience." Buys 12 mss/year. Query with or without published clips or send complete ms (typewritten and double-spaced). Length: 2,000-4,000 words. Pays $100.
Fiction: Erotica, adventure, fantasy, humorous, novel excerpts and romance. "No long, drawn-out fiction with no form, etc." Buys 35 mss/year. Query with or without published clips or send complete ms. Length: 2,000-4,000 words. Pays $100.
Tips: "Write about what is happening—what you as a gay male (if you are) would care to read."

THE WASHINGTON BLADE, Washington Blade, Inc., 8th Floor, 724 9th St. NW, Washington DC 20001. (202)347-2038. FAX: (202)393-6510. Senior Editor: Lisa M. Keen. 20% freelance written. Works with a small number of new/unpublished writers each year. Weekly news tabloid covering the gay/lesbian community. "Articles (subjects) should be written from or directed to a gay perspective." Circ. 22,500. Pays in 1 month. Publishes ms an average of 1 month after acceptance. Byline given. Offers $15 kill fee. Buys first North American serial rights. Submit seasonal/holiday material 1 month in advance. Photocopied submissions OK. Computer printout submissions acceptable; prefers letter-quality. Sample copy and writer's guidelines for 8½x11 SASE and $1.
Nonfiction: Exposé (of government, private agency, church, etc., handling of gay-related issues); historical/nostalgic; interview/profile (of gay community/political leaders; persons, gay or nongay, in positions to affect gay issues; outstanding achievers who happen to be gay; those who incorporate the gay lifestyle into their professions); photo feature (on a nationally or internationally historic gay event); and travel (on locales that welcome or cater to the gay traveler). *The Washington Blade* basically covers two areas: news and lifestyle. News coverage of D.C. metropolitan area gay community, local and federal government actions relating to gays, as well as national news of interest to gays. Section also includes features on current events. Special issues include: Annual gay pride issue (early June). No sexually explicit material. Articles of interest to the community must include and be written for both gay men and lesbians. Buys 30 mss/year, average. Query

with published clips and resume. Length: 500-1,500 words. Pays 5-10¢/word. Sometimes pays the expenses of writers on assignment.

Photos: "A photo or graphic with feature/lifestyle articles is particularly important. Photos with news stories are appreciated." State availability of photos. Reviews b&w contact sheets and 5x7 glossy prints. Pays $25 minimum. Captions preferred; model releases required. On assignment, photographer paid mutually agreed upon fee, with expenses reimbursed. Publication retains all rights.

Tips: "Send good examples of your writing and know the paper before you submit a manuscript for publication. We get a lot of submissions which are entirely inappropriate. We're looking for more features, but fewer AIDS-related features." Greatest opportunity for freelancers resides in current events, features, interviews and book reviews.

‡WASHINGTON JEWISH SINGLES NEWSLETTER, WJSN, Suite L, 444 N. Frederick Av., Box 239, Gaithersburg MD 20877. (301)990-0210, Editor: Ben Levitan. Managing Editor: Ellen Caswell. 100% freelance written. Monthly newsletter for singles (unmarried professionals). "All articles should have a singles slant. Must relate to life/career/humor, etc. for singles." Pays on publication. Byline given. Buys first North American serial rights or second serial (reprint) rights. Submit seasonal/holiday material 2 months in advance. Simultaneous, photocopied and previously published submissions OK. Query for electronic submissions. Computer printout submissions OK. Query for electronic submissions. Reports in 3 weeks on queries; 1 week on mss. Sample copy $1 with 9x12 SAE and 2 first class stamps.

Nonfiction Book excerpts, exposé, general interest, how-to (travel alone, manage finance/career, write "personal" ads), humor (especially dating romance), inspirational, interview/profile (new/unusual single activities in other cities), opinion personal experience, religious (Jewish only), technical and travel. Every May—"State of Jewish American singles" report and survey results. "We try to maintain an upbeat/light mood. We discourage negative/depressing articles." Send complete ms. "Queries are discouraged." Length: 300-800 words. Pays $10-35.

Photos: State availability of photos with submissions. Reviews contact sheets and negatives. Offers no additional payment for photos accepted with ms. Identification of subjects required. Buys one-time rights.

Columns/Departments: Where Shall We Go? (fun/different dates in DC area), 300 words; For What It's Worth (offbeat items/fun current facts), 100 words; Dynamic People (DC area singles of special note), 400 words; The Bright Side (humor/comedy), 100-400 words and Your Money (finance for singles), 50-300 words. Buys 12 mss/year. Send complete ms. Pays $10-35.

Fiction: Confession, historical (singles related), humorous, mystery, romance, serialized novels and slice-of-life vignettes. Buys 3 mss/year. Send complete ms.

Fillers: Anecdotes, facts, gags to be illustrated by cartoonist, newsbreaks and short humor. Length: 20-150 words. Pays 2 copies to $10.

Tips: "Short, to-the-point articles and fillers are always appreciated—especially humor. All *must* have a slant to unmarried singles."

THE WEEKLY NEWS, The Weekly News Inc., 901 NE 79th St., Miami FL 33138. (305)757-6333. Editor: Chip Halvorsen. Managing Editor: Bill Watson. 40% freelance written. Weekly gay tabloid. Circ. 32,000. Pays on publication. Byline given. Buys one-time rights. Submit seasonal/holiday material 2 months in advance. Simultaneous, photocopied and previously published submissions OK. Sample copy for 9½x12½ SAE with $1.50 postage.

Nonfiction: Exposé, humor and interview/profile. Buys 8 mss/year. Send complete ms. Length: 1,000-5,000 words. Pays $25-125. Sometimes pays the expenses of writers on assignment.

Photos: State availability of photos with submission. Reviews 3x5 prints. Offers $5-20/photo. Buys first and future use.

Columns/Departments: Send complete ms. Length: 900 words maximum. Pays $15-30.

Fillers: Anecdotes, gags to be illustrated by cartoonist and short humor. Pays $15-30.

Religious

Religious magazines focus on a variety of subjects, styles and beliefs. Many are publishing articles relating to current affairs like AIDS, cults, or substance abuse. Fewer religious publications are considering poems and personal experience articles, but many emphasize special ministries to singles, seniors and deaf people. Such diversity makes reading each magazine essential for the writer hoping to break in. Educational and inspirational material of interest to church members, workers and leaders within a denomination or religion is needed by the publications in this category. Publications intended to assist professional religious workers in teaching and managing church affairs are classified in Church Administration and Ministry in the Trade section. Religious magazines for children and teenagers can be found in the Juvenile and Teen and Young Adult classifications.

AGLOW, For the Spirit-Renewed Christian Woman, Aglow Publications, Box 1548, Lynnwood WA 98046-1557. (206)775-7282. Editor: Gwen Weising. 66% freelance written. Works with a small number of new/unpublished writers each year. Bimonthly nondenominational Christian charismatic magazine for women. Pays on acceptance. Publishes ms an average of 6 months to 1 year after acceptance. Byline given. Buys first North American serial rights, and reprint rights for use in *Aglow* magazine in other countries. Submit seasonal/holiday material 8 months in advance. Simultaneous queries and photocopied submissions acceptable. Computer printout submissions OK; prefers letter-quality. Reports in 2 months. Sample copy for 9x12 SAE and 2 first class stamps; writer's guidelines for #10 SASE.
Nonfiction: Contact Gloria Chisholm, Acquisitions Editor. Christian women's spiritual experience articles (first person) and some humor. "Each article should be either a personal experience of or teaching about Jesus as Savior, as Baptizer in the Holy Spirit, or as Guide and Strength in everyday circumstances." Queries only. "We would like to see material about 'Women of Vision' who have made and are making an impact on their world for God." Length: 1,000-2,000 words. Pays up to 10¢/word. Sometimes pays expenses of writers on assignment.

THE ANNALS OF SAINT ANNE DE BEAUPRE, Redemptorist Fathers, 9597 St. Anne Blvd., St. Anne De Beaupre, Quebec G0A 3C0 Canada. (418)827-4538. Editor: Bernard Mercier. Managing Editor: Roch Achard. 80% freelance written. Works with a small number of new/unpublished writers each year. "Anyone can submit manuscripts. We judge." Monthly magazine on religion. "Our aim is to promote devotion to St. Anne and Christian family values." Circ. 50,000. Pays on acceptance. Publishes ms an average of 1 year after acceptance. Byline given. Buys first North American serial rights. Submit seasonal/holiday material 2½months in advance. Simultaneous queries and photocopied submissions OK. Computer printout submissions OK; prefers letter-quality. Reports in 2 weeks. Free sample copy and writer's guidelines.
Nonfiction: Exposé, general interest, inspirational and personal experience. No articles without spiritual thrust. Buys 30 mss/year. Send complete ms. Length: 500-1,200 words. Pays 3-4¢/word.
Fiction: Religious. Buys 15 mss/year. Send complete ms. Length: 500-1,200 words. Pays 3-4¢/word.
Poetry: Traditional. Buys 12/year. Submit maximum 2-3 poems. Length: 12-20 lines. Pays $5-8.
Tips: "Write something educational, inspirational, objective and uplifting. Reporting rather than analysis is simply not remarkable."

THE ASSOCIATE REFORMED PRESBYTERIAN, Associate Reformed Presbyterian General Synod, 1 Cleveland St., Greenville SC 29601. (803)232-8297. Editor: Ben Johnston. 10% freelance written. Works with a small number of new/unpublished writers each year. A Christian publication serving a conservative, evangelical and Reformed denomination, most of whose members are in the Southeast U.S. Circ. 7,000. Pays on acceptance. Publishes ms an average of 3 months after acceptance. Byline given. Not copyrighted. Buys first rights, one-time rights, or second serial (reprint) rights. Submit seasonal/holiday material 4 months in advance. Simultaneous submissions and previously published submissions OK. Computer printout submissions acceptable; prefers letter-quality. Reports in 1 month. Sample copy $1.50; writer's guidelines for #10 SASE.
Nonfiction: Book excerpts, essays, inspirational, opinion, personal experience and religious. Buys 10-15 mss/year. Query. Length: 400-2,000 words. Pays $50 maximum.
Photos: State availability of photos with submission. Reviews 5x7 reprints. Offers $25 maximum per photo. Captions and identification of subjects required. Buys one-time rights. Sometimes pays expenses of writers on assignment.
Fiction: Religious and children's. Pays $50 maximum.
Tips: "Feature articles are the area of our publication most open to freelancers. Focus on a contemporary problem and offer Bible-based solutions to it. Provide information that would help a Christian struggling in his daily walk. Writers should understand that we are denominational, conservative, evangelical, Reformed and Presbyterian. A writer who appreciates these nuances would stand a much better chance of being published here than one who does not."

AXIOS, 800 S. Euclid St., Fullerton CA 92632. (714)526-4952. Computer number for Axios BBS (714)526-2387. Editor: David Gorham. 10% freelance written. Eager to work with new/unpublished writers. Monthly journal seeking spiritual articles mostly on Orthodox Christian background, either Russian, Greek, Serbian, Syrian or American. Circ. 8,789. Pays on publication. Publishes ms an average of 6 months after acceptance. Byline given. Offers 50% kill fee. Buys all rights. Submit seasonal/holiday material 4 months in advance. Simultaneous queries, and simultaneous, photocopied and previously published submissions OK. Query for electronic submissions. Computer printout submissions acceptable; prefers letter-quality. Reports in 1 month. Sample copy for $2 and 9x12 SAE with 50¢ postage.

Nonfiction: Book excerpts; exposé (of religious figures); general interest; historical/nostalgic; interview/profile; opinion; personal experience; photo feature; and travel (shrines, pilgrimages). Special issues include the persecution of Christians in Iran, Russia, behind Iron Curtain or in Arab lands; Roman Catholic interest in the Orthodox Church. Nothing about the Pope or general "all-is-well-with-Christ" items. Buys 14 mss/year. Send complete ms. Length: 1,000-3,000 words. Pays 4¢/word minimum.
Columns/Departments: Reviews religious books and films. Buys 80 mss/year. Query.
Tips: "We need some hard hitting articles on the 'political' church – the why, how and where of it and why it lacks the timelessness of the spiritual. Here in *Axios* you can discuss your feelings, your findings, your needs, your growth; give us your outpouring. Don't mistake us for either Protestant or Roman Catholic; we are the voice of Catholics united with the Eastern Orthodox Church, also referred to as the Greek Orthodox Church. We are most interested in the western rite within eastern Orthodoxy; and the return of the Roman Catholic to the ancient universal church. Very interested in the old calendar."

BAPTIST LEADER, Valley Forge PA 19482-0851. (215)768-2153. Editor: Linda Isham. For pastors, teachers and leaders in Sunday church schools. 5% freelance written. Works with a small number of new/unpublished writers each year. Bimonthly. Buys first serial rights. Pays on acceptance. Publishes ms an average of 8 months after acceptance. Deadlines are 8 months prior to date of issue. Computer printout submissions acceptable; prefers letter-quality. Sample copy for $1.25; writer's guidelines for #10 SASE.
Nonfiction: Educational topics. How-to articles for local church school teachers and leaders. Length: 1,500-2,000 words. Pays $25-75.
Tips: "We're planning more emphasis on church school and Christian education administration and planning."

‡BELIEVERS BY THE BAY, Believers By the Bay Inc., Box 109, Traverse City MI 49685. Editor: Pat Murphy. Managing Editor: David Bivins. 80% freelance written. Quarterly magazine on subjects of interest to Christians. Circ. 5,000. Pays on publication. Publishes ms an average of 6 months after acceptance. Byline given. Buys first rights. Submit holiday/seasonal material 6 months in advance. Previously published submissions OK. Query for electronic submissions. Computer printout submissions OK; prefers letter quality. Sample copy for $2 SAE with 5 first class stamps; writer's guidelines for #10 SASE.
Nonfiction: Essays, historical/nostalgic, humor, inspirational, interview/profile, personal experience and photo feature. Nothing preachy or the same old ingrained doctrine Christians already know. Buys 10 mss/year. Query. Length: 250-1,500 words. Pays $2-20.
Photos: State availability of photos with submission. Reviews prints. Buys one-time rights.
Columns/Departments: Today's Youth, 500-1,000 words; Silver Moments, 500-2,000 words; Articles/Features, 1,500-2,000 words; and Personal Profile, 1,500-2,000 words all Christian related. Query. Length: 500-2,000. Pays $2-20.
Fiction: Adventure, ethnic, historical, humorous, religious, romance and slice-of-life vignettes. Query. Length: 1,500-2,000. Pays $2-20.
Poetry: Free verse, light verse and traditional. Buys 6 poems/year. Submit maximum 3 poems. Pays $2-5.
Fillers: Gags to be illustrated by cartoonist and short humor. Length: 10-250 words. Pays $2-5.

‡THE CATHOLIC ANSWER, Our Sunday Visitor, Inc., 200 Noll Plaza, Huntington IN 46750. (219)356-8400. Editor: Father Peter M.J. Stravinskas. Managing Editor: Kelley L. Renz. 50% freelance written. Bimonthly magazine on the Catholic faith. "*The Catholic Answer* seeks to inform, interpret and apply solid, fundamental Catholic belief for orthodox Catholics, converts and those wishing to learn more about the traditional Catholic faith." Circ. 100,000. Pays on publication. Publishes ms an average of 6 months after acceptance. Byline given. Buys all rights. Submit seasonal/holiday material 6 months in advance. Simultaneous and photocopied submissions OK. Query for electronic submissions. Computer printout submissions OK; prefers letter-quality. Free sample copy and writer's guidelines.
Nonfiction: Essays, general interest (Catholic), historical/nostalgic, inspirational. "No superficial treatments of the Faith." Buys 80 mss/year. Query with published clips. Length: 1,200-2,200 words. Pays $100 flat payment.
Tips: "Write for guidelines and begin sending material according to those specifications. *TCA* has 3 sections that are most open to freelance writers. Two regular columnists and the remainder is freelance – average of 5-8 articles per issue."

CATHOLIC DIGEST, Box 64090, St. Paul MN 55164. Editor: Henry Lexau. Managing Editor: Richard Reece. 50% freelance written. Works with small number of new/unpublished writers each year. Monthly magazine covering the daily living of Roman Catholics for an audience that is 60% female, 40% male; 37% is college educated. Circ. 600,000. Publishes ms an average of 6 months after acceptance. Byline given. Buys first North American serial rights or one-time reprint rights. Submit seasonal material 6 months in advance. Previously published submissions OK, if so indicated. Computer printout submissions acceptable; prefers letter-quality. Reports in 1 month. Free sample copy and writer's guidelines.

Nonfiction: General interest (daily living and family relationships); interview (of outstanding Catholics, celebrities and locals); nostalgia (the good old days of family living); profile; religion; travel (shrines); humor; inspirational (overcoming illness, role model people); and personal experience (adventures and daily living). Buys 30 articles/issue. No queries. Send complete ms. Length: 500-3,000 words, 2,000 average. Pays on acceptance—$200-400 for originals, $100 for reprints.

Columns/Departments: "Check a copy of the magazine in the library for a description of column needs. Payment varies and is made on publication. We buy about 5/issue."

Fillers: Jokes, anecdotes and short humor. Buys 10-15 mss/issue. Length: 10-300 words. Pays $3-50 on publication.

CATHOLIC LIFE, 35750 Moravian Dr., Fraser MI 48026. Editor-in-Chief: Robert C. Bayer. 20% freelance written. Monthly (except July or August) magazine. Emphasizes foreign missionary activities of the Catholic Church in Burma, India, Bangladesh, the Philippines, Hong Kong, Africa, etc., for middle-aged and older audience with either middle incomes or pensions. High school educated (on the average), conservative in both religion and politics. Circ. 17,600. Pays on publication. Publishes ms an average of 3 months after acceptance. Buys all rights. Byline given. Submit seasonal/holiday material 4 months in advance. Simultaneous submissions OK. Computer printout submissions acceptable. Reports in 2 weeks.

Nonfiction: Informational and inspirational foreign missionary activities of the Catholic Church. Buys 10-15 unsolicited mss/year. Query or send complete ms. Length: 1,000-1,500 words. Pays 4¢/word.

Tips: "Query with short, graphic details of what the material will cover or the personality involved in the biographical sketch. Also, we appreciate being advised on the availability of good black-and-white photos to illustrate the material."

CATHOLIC NEAR EAST MAGAZINE, Catholic Near East Welfare Association, 1011 1st Ave., New York NY 10022. (212)826-1480. Editor: Michael Healy. 90% freelance written. Quarterly magazine. For a Roman Catholic audience with interest in the Near East, particularly its religious and cultural aspects. Circ. 150,000. Pays on publication. Publishes ms an average of 4 months after acceptance. Byline given. Buys all rights. Submit seasonal material (Christmas and Easter in different Near Eastern lands or rites) 6 months in advance. Photocopied submissions OK if legible. Computer printout submissions acceptable; no dot-matrix. Reports in 1 month. Sample copy and writer's guidelines for 9½x6½ SAE with 2 first class stamps.

Nonfiction: "Cultural, territorial, devotional material on the Near East, its history, peoples and religions (especially the Eastern Rites of the Catholic Church). Style should be simple, factual, concise. Articles must stem from personal acquaintance with subject matter, or thorough up-to-date research. No preaching or speculations." Length: 1,200-1,800 words. Pays 10¢/word.

Photos: "Photographs to accompany manuscript are always welcome; they should illustrate the people, places, ceremonies, etc. which are described in the article. We prefer color transparencies but occasionally use black and white. Pay varies depending on the quality of the photos."

Tips: "Writers please heed: Stick to the people of the Near East, the Balkans through the Middle East to India. Send factual articles; concise, descriptive style preferred, not flowery. Pictures are a big plus; if you have photos to accompany your article, please send them—with captions—at the same time."

CHICAGO STUDIES, Box 665, Mundelein IL 60060. (312)566-1462. Editor: Rev. George J. Dyer. 50% freelance written. Magazine published 3 times/year; 112 pages. For Roman Catholic priests and religious educators. Circ. 10,000. Pays on acceptance. Buys all rights. Photocopied submissions OK. Computer printout submissions acceptable. Reports in 2 months. Sample copy $5; free writer's guidelines.

Nonfiction: Nontechnical discussion of theological, Biblical and ethical topics. Articles aimed at a nontechnical presentation of the contemporary scholarship in those fields. Submit complete ms. Buys 30 mss/year. Length: 3,000-5,000 words. Pays $35-100.

CHRISTIAN HOME & SCHOOL, Christian Schools International, 3350 East Paris Ave. SE, Box 8709, Grand Rapids MI 49508. (616)957-1070. Editor: Gordon L. Bordewyk. Associate Editor: Judy Zylstra. 30% freelance written. Works with a small number of new/unpublished writers each year. Magazine published 8 times/year covering family life and Christian education. "The magazine is designed for parents who support Christian education. We feature material on a wide range of topics of interest to parents." Pays on publication. Publishes ms an average of 4 months after acceptance. Byline given. Buys first North American serial rights. Submit seasonal/holiday material 4 months in advance. Simultaneous queries and photocopied submissions OK. Computer printout submissions acceptable; prefers letter-quality. Reports in 3 weeks on queries; 1 month on mss. Sample copy for 9x12 SAE and 4 first class stamps; writer's guidelines for #10 SASE.

Nonfiction: Book excerpts, interview/profile, opinion, personal experience and articles on parenting and school life. "We publish features on issues which affect the home and school and profiles on interesting individuals, providing that the profile appeals to our readers and is not a tribute or eulogy of that person." Buys 40 mss/year. Send complete ms. Length: 500-2,000 words. Pays $25-85. Sometimes pays the expenses of writers on assignment.

Photos: "If you have any black-and-white photos appropriate for your article, send them along."

Tips: "Features are the area most open to freelancers. We are publishing articles that deal with contemporary issues which affect parents; keep that in mind. Use an informal easy-to-read style rather than a philosophical, academic tone. Try to incorporate vivid imagery and concrete, practical examples from real life."

CHRISTIAN OUTLOOK, Hutton Publications, Box 1870, Hayden ID 83835. (208)772-6184. Editor: Linda Hutton. 50% freelance written. Quarterly newsletter of inspirational material. "Send us uplifting poetry and fiction, with a subtle moral, but nothing overly religious or preachy." Estab. 1988. Circ. 200. Pays on acceptance. Publishes ms an average of 9 months after acceptance. Byline given. Buys one-time rights or second serial (reprint) rights. Submit seasonal/holiday material 9 months in advance. Simultaneous, photocopied and previously published submissions OK. Computer printout submissions OK; prefers letter-quality. Reports in 1 month on mss. Sample copy and writer's guidelines for #10 SAE with 2 first class stamps.

Fiction: Relgious. Buys 4 mss/year. Send complete ms. Length: 300-1,500 words. Pays ¼-1¢/word.

Poetry: Free verse, light verse, traditional, "Nothing overly religious, merely uplifting and inspirational." Buys 8 poems/year. Submit up to 3 poems at one time. Length: 4-8 lines. Pays 10-25¢/line.

CHRISTIAN SINGLE, Family Ministry Dept., Baptist Sunday School Board, 127 9th Ave. N., Nashville TN 37234. (615)251-2228. Editor: Cliff Allbritton. 50-70% freelance written. Prefers to work with published/ established writers; works with a small number of new/unpublished writers each year. Monthly magazine covering items of special interest to Christian single adults. "*Christian Single* is a contemporary Christian magazine that seeks to give substantive information to singles for living the abundant life. It seeks to be constructive and creative in approach." Circ. 105,000. Pays on acceptance "for immediate needs"; on publication "for unsolicited manuscripts." Publishes ms 1-2 years after acceptance. Byline given. Buys all rights; makes work-for-hire assignments. Submit seasonal/holiday material 1½ years in advance. Computer printout submissions acceptable; no dot-matrix. Reports in 6 weeks. Sample copy and writer's guidelines for 9x12 SASE with 85¢ postage.

Nonfiction: Humor (good, clean humor that applies to Christian singles); how-to (specific subjects which apply to singles; query needed); inspirational (of the personal experience type); high adventure personal experience (of single adults); photo feature (on outstanding Christian singles; query needed); well researched financial articles targeted to single adults (query needed). No "shallow, uninformative mouthing off. This magazine says something, and people read it cover to cover." Buys 120-150 unsolicited mss/year. Query with published clips. Length: 300-1,200 words. Pays 5¢/word.

Tips: "We look for freshness and creativity, not duplication of what we have already done. Don't write on loneliness! Need more upbeat personal experience articles written by Christian *single men*! We are backlogged with submissions by women and with poetry at this time. We give preference to Christian single adult writers but publish articles by *sensitive* and *informed* married writers also. Remember that you are talking to educated people who attend church. Study the magazine before submitting materials."

CHRISTIAN SOCIAL ACTION, 100 Maryland Ave. NE, Washington DC 20002. (202)488-5632. Editor: Lee Ranck. 2% freelance written. Works with a small number of new/unpublished writers each year. Monthly for "United Methodist clergy and lay people interested in in-depth analysis of social issues, with emphasis on the church's role or involvement in these issues." Circ. 4,500. May buy all rights. Pays on publication. Publishes ms an average of 2 months after acceptance. Rights purchased vary with author and material. Photocopied submissions OK, but prefers original. Computer printout submissions acceptable; prefers letter-quality. Returns rejected material in 4-5 weeks. Reports on material accepted for publication in several weeks. Free sample copy and writer's guidelines for #10 SASE.

Nonfiction: "This is the social action publication of the United Methodist Church published by the denomination's General Board of Church and Society. Our publication tries to relate social issues to the church— what the church can do, is doing; why the church should be involved. We only accept articles relating to social issues, e.g., war, draft, peace, race relations, welfare, police/community relations, labor, population problems, drug and alcohol problems." No devotional, 'religious,' superficial material, highly technical articles, personal experiences or poetry. Buys 25-30 mss/year. "Query to show that writer has expertise on a particular social issue, give credentials, and reflect a readable writing style." Query or submit complete ms. Length: 2,000 words maximum. Pays $75-100. Sometimes pays the expenses of writers on assignment.

Tips: "Write on social issues, but not superficially; we're more interested in finding an expert who can write (e.g., on human rights, alcohol problems, peace issues) than a writer who attempts to research a complex issue."

CHRISTIANITY & CRISIS, 537 W. 121st St., New York NY 10027. (212)662-5907. Editor: Leon Howell. Managing Editor: Gail Hovey. 10% freelance written. Works with a small number of new/unpublished writers each year. Biweekly Protestant journal of opinion. "We are interested in foreign affairs, domestic, economic and social policy, and theological developments with social or ethical implications, e.g., feminist, black and liberation theologies. As an independent religious journal it is part of *C&C*'s function to discuss church policies from a detached and sometimes critical perspective. We carry no 'devotional' material but welcome solid contemplative reflections. Most subscribers are highly educated, well-informed." Circ. 14,000. Pays on publication. Publishes ms an average of 2 months after acceptance. Byline given. Offers variable kill fee. Submit seasonal/holiday material 2 months in advance. Simultaneous queries and photocopied submissions OK. Computer printout submissions acceptable if double-spaced. Reports in 1 month. Sample copy $1.75 with 9x12 SAE and 2 first class stamps; writer's guidelines for #10 SASE.

Nonfiction: Buys 150 mss/year. Query with or without published clips. Length: 1,000-4,000 words. Pays 3¢/word. Rarely pays expenses of writers on assignment.

Tips: "We have been publishing more international stories and need to build up reporting on U.S. issues."

CHRISTIANITY TODAY, 465 Gundersen Dr., Carol Stream IL 60188. 80% freelance written. Works with a small number of new/unpublished writers each year. Emphasizes orthodox, evangelical religion. Semimonthly magazine. Circ. 180,000. Publishes ms an average of 6 months after acceptance. Usually buys first serial rights. Submit seasonal/holiday material at least 8 months in advance. Computer printout submissions acceptable; prefers letter-quality. Reports in 2 months. Sample copy and writer's guidelines for 9x12 SAE and 3 first class stamps.

Nonfiction: Theological, ethical, historical and informational (not merely inspirational). Buys 4 mss/issue. *Query only.* Unsolicited mss not accepted and not returned. Length: 1,000-4,000 words. Pays negotiable rates. Sometimes pays the expenses of writers on assignment.

Columns/Departments: The Arts (Christian review of the arts). Buys 12 mss/year. Send complete ms. Length: 800-900 words. Pays negotiable rates.

Tips: "We are developing more of our own manuscripts and requiring a much more professional quality of others."

CHRISTMAS, The Annual of Christmas Literature and Art, Augsburg Fortress, Publishers, 426 S. 5th St., Box 1209, Minneapolis MN 55440. (612)330-3437. Editor: Gloria E. Bengtson. 100% freelance written. "An annual literary magazine that celebrates Christmas focusing on the effect of the Christmas love of God on the lives of people, and how it colors and shapes traditions and celebrations." Pays on acceptance. Byline given. Buys first rights, one-time rights and all rights; makes work-for-hire assignments. Submit seasonal/holiday material 18 months in advance. Reports in 2 weeks on queries; 3 weeks on mss. Sample copy $8.95 plus 5 first class stamps.

Nonfiction: Historical/nostalgic (on Christmas customs); inspirational, interview/profile, personal experience and travel. Focusing on more family-oriented articles with stories for children and young adults. Articles on art and music with Christmas relationships. Buys 6-8 mss/year. Query with published clips, or send complete ms. Length: 2,500-7,500 words. Pays $200-450 for assigned articles; pays $150-300 for unsolicited articles.

Photos: State availability of photos with submission. Reviews transparencies. Offers $15-100 per photo. Captions and identification of subjects required. Buys one-time rights.

Fiction: Jennifer Huber, editor. Ethnic, historical and slice-of-life vignettes. "No stories of fictionalized characters at the Bethlehem stable. Fiction should show the effect of God's love on the lives of people." Buys 2 mss/year. Send complete ms. Length: 5,000 words maximum. Pays $150-300.

Poetry: Jennifer Huber, editor. Free verse, light verse and traditional. No poetry dealing with Santa Claus. Buys 3 poems/year. Submit maximum 30 poems. Pays $35-40.

CHRYSALIS, Journal of the Swedenborg Foundation, 139 East 23rd St., New York NY 10010. Send inquiries and manuscripts directly to the editorial office: Route 1, Box 184, Dillwyn VA 23936. Editor: Carol S. Lawson. Managing Editor: Susanna van Rensselaer. 50% freelance written. A literary magazine published 3 times per year on spiritually related topics. (*It is very important to send for writer's guidelines and sample copies before submitting.*) "Content of fiction, articles, reviews, poetry, etc., should be directly focused on that issue's theme and directed to the educated, intellectually curious reader." Circ. 1,000. Pays at page-proof stage. Publishes ms an average of 9 months after acceptance. Byline given. Buys first rights and makes work-for-hire assignments. Computer printout submissions OK; prefers letter-quality (with word count). Reports in 2 weeks on queries; 2 months on mss. Sample copy and writer's guidelines for 9x12 SAE and $5. For writer's guidelines and copy deadlines for SASE. Upcoming Themes: Spring 1990: "Journeys"; Summer 1990: "Eastern European Mysticism"; Autumn 1990: "Home"; Spring 1991: "Eastern Religions in America."

Nonfiction: Essays and interview/profile. Buys 15 mss/year. Query. Length: 750-2,500 words. Pays $75-250 for assigned articles. Pays $75-150 for unsolicited articles.

Photos: Send suggestions for illustrations with submission. Offers no additional payment for photos accepted with ms. Captions and identification of subjects required. Buys original artwork for cover and inside copy, $25-150. Buys one-time rights.

Columns/Departments: Vital Issues (articles and material related to practical psychology, health, healing), 750-2,000 words; Patterns (philosophical inquiry into the underlying patterns found within reality), 750-2,000 words; Currents (articles and material on the fine and visionary arts); 750-2,000 words; and Fringe Benefits (book, film, art, video reviews relevant to *Chrysalis* subject matter), 350-500 words. Buys 12 mss/year. Length: 350-2,000. Pays $75-250.

Fiction: Phoebe Loughrey, fiction editor. Adventure, experimental, historical, mainstream, mystery and science fiction, realted to theme of issue. Buys 6 mss/year. Query. Length: short more likely to be published, 500-2,000 words. Pays $75-150.
Poetry: Avante-garde and traditional. Buys 10 poems/year. Pays $25. Submit maximum 6.

CHURCH & STATE, Americans United for Separation of Church and State, 8120 Fenton St., Silver Spring MD 20910. (301)589-3707. Managing Editor: Joseph Conn. 10% freelance written. Prefers to work with published/established writers. Monthly magazine. Emphasizes religious liberty and church/state relations matters. Readership "includes the whole spectrum, but is predominantly Protestant and well-educated." Circ. 50,000. Pays on acceptance. Publishes ms an average of 2 months after acceptance. Buys all rights. Simultaneous, photocopied and previously published submissions OK. Computer printout submissions OK; prefers letter-quality. Reports in 1 month. Sample copy and writer's guidelines for 9x12 SAE and 3 first class stamps.
Nonfiction: Expose, general interest, historical and interview. Buys 11 mss/year. Query. Length: 3,000 words maximum. Pays negotiable fee.
Photos: State availability of photos with query. Pays negotiable fee for b&w prints. Captions preferred. Buys one-time rights.

THE CHURCH HERALD, 6157 28th St., SE, Grand Rapids MI 49546. Editor: Rev. Dr. John Stapert. Managing Editor: Jeff Japinga. 20% freelance written. Prefers to work with published/established writers; works with small number of new/unpublished writers each year. Monthly magazine covering contemporary Christian life. "The *Church Herald* is the denominational publication of the Reformed Church in America, a Protestant denomination in the Presbyterian-Reformed family of churches. We solicit carefully researched and well-written articles on almost any subject, but they all must have a distinctively Christian perspective." Circ. 50,000. Pays on acceptance. Publishes ms an average of 3 months after acceptance. Byline given. Offers 50% kill fee. Buys first rights, one-time rights, second serial (reprint) rights, simultaneous rights and all rights. Submit seasonal/holiday material 3 months in advance. Simultaneous and previously published submissions OK. Query for electronic submissions. Computer printout submissions OK; no dot-matrix. Reports in 1 month on queries; 2 months on mss. Sample copy and writer's guidelines for $2 and 9x12 SAE.
Nonfiction: Essays, general interest, humor, inspirational, personal experience, religious. Buys 30 mss/year. Send complete ms. Length: 400-1,500 words. Pays $45-150 for assigned articles. Pays $45-120 for unsolicited articles. Sometimes pays expenses of writers on assignment.
Photos: State availability of photos with submission. Reviews color transparencies and 8x10 b&w prints. Offers $25-50 per photo. Model releases required. Buys one-time rights.
Fiction: Religious. "We consider good fiction written from a Christian perspective. Avoid pious sentimentality and obvious plots." Buys 15 mss/year. Send complete ms. Length: 400-1,500. Pays $45-120.
Poetry: Free verse and traditional. Buys 6 poems/year. Submit maximum of 10 poems at one time. Length: up to 30 lines. Pays $25-45.
Tips: "Research articles carefully. Superficial articles are immediately recognizable; they cannot be disguised by big words or professional jargon. Writers need not have personally experienced everything they write about, but they must have done careful research. Also, what our readers want are new solutions to recognized problems. If a writer doesn't have any, he or she should try another subject. Section most open to freelancers is feature articles."

COLUMBIA, Drawer 1670, New Haven CT 06507. Editor: Richard McMunn. Monthly magazine for Catholic families; caters particularly to members of the Knights of Columbus. Circ. 1 million. Pays on acceptance. Buys first time serial rights. Submit seasonal material 6 months in advance. Reports in 1 month. Free sample copy and writer's guidelines.
Nonfiction: Fact articles directed to the Catholic layman and his family dealing with current events, social problems, Catholic apostolic activities, education, ecumenism, rearing a family, literature, science, humor, satire, arts, sports and leisure. Color glossy prints, transparencies or contact prints with negatives are required for illustration. Articles without ample illustrative material are not given consideration. Pays up to $500, including photos. Photo stories are also wanted. Buys 30 mss/year. Query. Length: 1,000-1,500 words. Pays $200.
Photos: Pays $50 per photo used. Pays 10¢/word.

COMMENTS, From the Friends, Box 840, Stoughton MA 02072. Editor: David A. Reed. 20% freelance written. A quarterly Christian newsletter written especially for "Jehovah's Witnesses, ex-Jehovah's Witnesses and persons concerned about Jehovah's Witness, relatives, friends, and neighbors." Circ. 1,500. Pays on publication. Publishes ms an average of 3 months after acceptance. Byline sometimes given. Buys second serial (reprint) and simultaneous rights. Submit seasonal/holiday material 4 months in advance. Simultaneous, photocopied and previously published submissions OK. Query for electronic submissions. Computer printout submissions acceptable; prefers letter-quality. Reports in 1 month on mss. Sample copy $1; writer's guidelines for #10 SAE with 2 first class stamps.

Nonfiction: Book excerpts, essays, exposé, how-to (witnessing tips), humor, inspirational, interview/profile, personal experience, religious and book reviews of books on cults only. Special issue topic will be The Next Watchtower President (replacing Fred Franz). "No general religious material not written specifically for our unique readership." Buys 8 mss/year. Send complete ms. Length: 200-1,000 words. Pays $2-20. May pay with contributor copies rather than a cash payment "when a writer contributes an article as a gift to this ministry."
Columns/Departments: Witnessing Tips (brief, powerful and effective approaches), 250-300 words; and News Briefs (current events involving Jehovah's Witnesses and ex-Jehovah's Witnesses), 60-240 words. Buys 4 mss/year. Send complete ms. Length: 60-300 words. Pays $2-10.
Fillers: Facts, newsbreaks and quotes. Buys 4/year. Length: 10-50 words. Pays $1-5.
Tips: "Acquaint us with your background that qualifies you to write in this field. Write well-documented, germane articles in layman's language."

CONFIDENT LIVING, Box 82808, Lincoln NE 68501. (402)474-4567. Editor: Warren Wiersbe. 40% freelance written. Monthly interdenominational magazine for adults, mostly age 50 and up. Circ. 95,000. Pays on acceptance. Buys first serial rights or first North American serial rights, or second serial (reprint) rights. Submit seasonal material at least 1 year in advance. Computer printout submissions acceptable if double spaced; no dot-matrix. Reports in 5 weeks. Sample copy $1.75; writer's guidelines with SASE.
Nonfiction: Managing Editor, Jan E. Reeser. Articles which will help the reader learn and apply Christian Biblical principles to his life from the writer's or the subject's own experience. Writers are required "to affirm agreement with our doctrinal statement. We are especially looking for true, personal experience 'salvation,' church, 'how to live the Christian life' articles, reports and interviews regarding major and interesting happenings and people in fundamental, evangelical Christian circles." Nothing rambling or sugary sweet, or without Biblical basis. Details or statistics should be authentic and verifiable. Style should be conservative but concise. Prefers that Scripture references be from the *New American Standard Bible* or the *Authorized Version* or the *New Scofield Reference Bible*. Buys approximately 100 mss/year. Length: 1,500 words maximum. Pays 4-10¢/word. "When you can get us to assign an article to you, we pay nearer the maximum.
Photos: Pays $25 maximum for b&w glossies; $50 maximum for color transparencies inside, $85 cover. Photos paid on publication.
Tips: "The basic purpose of the magazine is to explain the Bible and how it is relevant to life because we believe this will accomplish one of two things—to present Christ as Savior to the lost or to promote the spiritual growth of believers, so don't ignore our primary purposes when writing for us. Nonfiction should be Biblical and timely; at the least Biblical in principle. Use illustrations of your own experiences or of someone else's when God solved a problem similar to the reader's. Be so specific that the meanings and significance will be crystal clear to all readers."

CONSCIENCE, A Newsjournal of Prochoice Catholic Opinion, Catholics for a Free Choice, Suite 301, 1436 U St., NW, Washington DC 20009-3916. (202)638-1706. Editor: Nancy H. Evans. 80% freelance written. Eager to work with new/unpublished writers. Bimonthly newsjournal covering reproductive rights, specifically abortion rights in area of church and church and government in U.S. and worldwide. "A feminist, prochoice perspective is a must, and knowledge of Christianity and specifically Catholicism is helpful." Circ. 10,000. Pays on publication. Publishes ms an average of 4 months after acceptance. Byline given. Buys first North American serial rights; makes work-for-hire assignments. Submit seasonal/holiday material 4 months in advance. Simultaneous queries, and simultaneous, photocopied and previously published submissions OK. Query for electronic submissions. Computer printout submissions acceptable. Reports in 2 months; free sample copy for #10 SAE with 2 first class stamps; free writer's guidelines for #10 SASE.
Nonfiction: Book excerpts, interview/profile, opinion and personal experience. Especially needs "expose/refutation of antichoice misinformation and specific research into the implications of new reproductive technology and fetal personhood bills/court decisions." Buys 8-12 mss/year. Query with published clips or send complete ms. Length: 1,000-3,500 words. Pays $25-100. "Writers should be aware that we are a nonprofit organization." A substantial number of articles are contributed without payment by writers. Sometimes pays the expenses of writers on assignment.
Photos: State availability of photos with query or ms. Prefers 5x7 b&w prints. Identification of subjects required. Buys all rights.
Columns/Departments: Book reviews. Buys 6-10 mss/year. Send complete ms. Length: 1,000-2,000 words. Pays $25.
Fillers: Clippings and newsbreaks. Uses 6/year. Length: 25-100 words. No payment.
Tips: "Say something new on the abortion issue. Thoughtful, well-researched and well-argued articles needed. The most frequent mistakes made by writers in completing an article for us are untimeliness and wordiness. When you have shown you can write thoughtfully, we may hire you for other types of articles."

CORNERSTONE, Jesus People USA, 4707 N. Malden, Chicago IL 60640. Editor: Dawn Herrin. 10% freelance written. Works with a small number of new/unpublished writers each year; eager to work with new/unpublished writers. A bimonthly magazine covering contemporary issues in the light of Evangelical Christianity. Circ. 90,000. Pays after publication. Publishes ms an average of 4-6 months after acceptance. Byline given.

Buys first serial rights. Submit seasonal/holiday material 6 months in advance. Simultaneous, photocopied and previously published submissions OK. Computer printout submissions acceptable. Reports in 1 month. Sample copy and writer's guidelines for 9x12 SAE with 4 first class stamps.

Nonfiction: Essays, personal experience, religious. Buys 3-4 mss/year. Query. Length: 2,700 words maximum. Pays negotiable rate. Sometimes pays the expenses of writers on assignment.

Photos: Send photos with accompanying ms. Reviews 8x10 b&w and color prints and 35mm slides. Identification of subjects required. Buys negotiable rights.

Columns/Departments: Music (interview with artists, mainly rock, focusing on artist's world view and value system as expressed in his/her music); Current Events; Personalities; Film and Book Reviews (focuses on meaning as compared and contrasted to Biblical values). Buys 2-6 mss/year. Query. Length: 100-2,500 words (negotiable). Pays negotiable rate.

Fiction: "Articles may express Christian world view but should not be unrealistic or 'syrupy.' Other than porn, the sky's the limit. We want fiction as creative as the Creator." Buys 1-4 mss/year. Send complete ms. Length: 250-2,500 words (negotiable). Pays negotiable rate.

Poetry: Avant-garde, free verse, haiku, light verse and traditional. No limits *except* for epic poetry ("We've not the room!"). Buys 10-50 poems/year. Submit maximum 10 poems. Payment negotiated.

Fillers: Anecdotes, facts, short humor and newsbreaks. Buys 5-15 year. Length: 20-200 words (negotiable). Payment negotiable.

Tips: "A display of creativity which expresses a biblical world view without clichés or cheap shots at non-Christians is the ideal. We are known as the most avant-garde magazine in the Christian market, yet attempt to express orthodox beliefs in language of the '80s. *Any* writer who does this may well be published by *Cornerstone*. Creative fiction is begging for more Christian participation. We anticipate such contributions gladly. Interviews where well-known personalities respond to the gospel are also strong publication possibilities. Please address all submissions to: Sarah Sullivan, assistant editor."

THE COVENANT COMPANION, Covenant Publications of the Evangelical Covenant Church, 5101 N. Francisco Ave., Chicago IL 60625. (312)784-3000. Editor: James R. Hawkinson. 10-15% freelance written. "As the official monthly organ of The Evangelical Covenant Church, we seek to inform, stimulate and gather the denomination we serve by putting Covenants in touch with each other and assisting them in interpreting contemporary issues. We also seek to inform them on events in the church. Our background is evangelical and our emphasis is on Christian commitment and life." Circ. 25,000. Publishes ms an average of 2 months after acceptance. Byline given. Buys first or all rights. Submit seasonal/holiday material 4 months in advance. Simultaneous and previously published submissions OK. Query for electronic submissions. Computer printout submissions acceptable; prefers letter-quality. Sample copy $2; writer's guidelines for #10 SASE. Unused mss only returned if accompanied by SASE.

Nonfiction: Humor, inspirational and religious. Buys 10-15 mss/year. Send complete ms. Length: 500-2,000 words. Pays $15-50 for assigned articles; pays $15-35 for unsolicited articles.

Photos: Send photos with submissions. Reviews prints. Offers no additonal payment for photos accepted with ms. Identification of subjects required. Buys one-time rights.

Poetry: Traditional. Buys 10-15 poems/year. Submit maximum 10 poems. Pays $10-15.

Tips: "Seasonal articles related to church year and on national holidays are welcome."

DAILY MEDITATION, Box 2710, San Antonio TX 78299. Editor: Ruth S. Paterson. Quarterly. Byline given. Rights purchased vary. Payment on acceptance. Submit seasonal material 6 months in advance. Sample copy 50¢.

Nonfiction: "Inspirational, self-improvement and nonsectarian religious articles, 750-1,600 words, showing the path to greater spiritual growth." Pays 1½-2¢/word.

Fillers: Length: 400 words maximum.

Poetry: Inspirational. Length: 16 lines maximum. Pays 14¢/line.

Tips: "All our material is freelance submission for consideration except our meditations, which are staff written. We buy approximately 250 manuscripts a year. We must see finished manuscripts; no queries, please. Checking copy is sent upon publication."

DAILY WORD, Unity School of Christianity, Unity Village MO 64065. (816)524-3550. Editor: Colleen Zuck. A monthly magazine of articles, poems, lessons and meditation. Circ. 2.5 million. Pays on acceptance. Publishes ms an average of 6 months after acceptance. Byline given on articles and poetry only. Buys first rights. Submit seasonal/holiday material 8 months in advance. Computer printout submissions OK; prefers letter-quality. Reports in 6 weeks on mss. Free sample copy and writer's guidelines.

Nonfiction: Inspirational and religious. Buys 250 mss/year. Send complete ms. Length: 1,500 words. Pays $20/page.

Poetry: Free verse and traditional. Buys 12-15 poems/year. Pays $1/line.

DECISION, Billy Graham Evangelistic Association, 1300 Harmon Place, Minneapolis MN 55403-1988. (612)338-0500. Editor: Roger C. Palms. 25% freelance written. Works each year with small number of new/unpublished writers, as well as a solid stable of experienced writers. A magazine, published 11 times per year, "to set forth to every reader the Good News of salvation in Jesus Christ with such vividness and clarity that he or she will be drawn to make a commitment to Christ; to encourage, teach and strengthen Christians." Circ. 2 million. Pays on publication. Byline given. Buys first rights and assigns work-made-for-hire manuscripts, articles, projects. Include telephone number with submission. Submit seasonal/holiday material 8 months in advance; other mss published up to 1 year after acceptance. No simultaneous submissions. Photocopied submissions OK. Computer printout submissions OK; no dot-matrix. Reports in 2 months on mss. Sample copy for 8½x11 SAE and 4 first class stamps; writer's guidelines for #10 SASE.

Nonfiction: How-to, motivational, personal experience and religious. "No personality-centered articles or articles which are issue oriented or critical of denominations." Buys approximately 50 mss/year. Send complete ms. Length: 400-1.800 words. Pays $35-200. Pays expenses of writers on assignment.

Photos: State availability of photos with submission. Reviews prints. Captions, model releases and identification of subjects required. Buys one-time rights.

Poetry: Free verse and traditional. No long or secular poems. Buys 15-20 poems/year. Submit maximum 7 poems. Length: 4-20 lines. Pays approximately 50¢/word.

Tips: "We are seeking personal conversion testimonies, personal experience articles which show how God intervened in a person's daily life and the way in which Scripture was applied to the experience in helping to solve the problem. We also are looking for vignettes on various aspects of personal evangelism. SASE required with submissions."

THE DISCIPLE, Box 179, St. Louis MO 63166. Editor: James L. Merrell. 10% freelance written. Monthly published by Christian Board of Publication of the Christian Church (Disciples of Christ). For ministers and church members, both young and older adults. Circ. 50,000. Pays month after publication. Publishes ms an average of 9 months after acceptance. Buys first serial rights. Photocopied and simultaneous submissions OK. Computer printout submissions acceptable; no dot-matrix. Submit seasonal material at least 6 months in advance. Reports in 1 month. Sample copy $1.50; free writer's guidelines for SASE.

Nonfiction: Articles and meditations on religious themes, short pieces and some humorous. No fiction. Buys 100 unsolicited mss/year. Length: 500-800 words. Pays $10-50.

Photos: Reviews 8x10 b&w glossy prints. Occasional b&w glossy prints, any size, used to illustrate articles. Occasional color. "We are looking for b&w photos of church activities – adult baptism, worship, prayer, dinners, etc." Pays $10-25; $35-100/cover. Pays for photos at end of month after acceptance.

Poetry: Uses 3-5 poems/issue. Traditional forms, blank verse, free verse and light verse. Length: 16 lines maximum. Themes may be seasonal, historical, religious and occasionally humorous. Pays $3-20.

Tips: "We're looking for personality features about lay disciples, churches. Give a good summary of story idea in query. Queries on Christian values in television, radio, film and music desired. We use articles primarily from disciples ministers and lay persons since our magazine is written to attract our members. We are barraged with features that mainly deal with subjects that don't interest our readers; fillers are more general, thus more easily placed. We work with more secular poets than writers and the poets write religious themes for us."

DISCIPLESHIP JOURNAL, NavPress, a division of The Navigators, Box 6000, Colorado Springs CO 80934. (719)528-5363 ext. 291. FAX: (719)598-7128. Editor: Susan Maycinik. 90% freelance written. Works with a small number of new/unpublished writers each year. Bimonthly magazine on Christian discipleship. "The mission of *Discipleship Journal* is to help people examine, understand and practice the truths of the Bible, so that they may know Jesus Christ, become like Him and labor for His Kingdom." Circ. 90,000. Pays on acceptance. Publishes ms an average of 4 months after acceptance. Byline given. Buys first North American serial rights and second serial (reprint) rights. Submit seasonal/holiday material 6 months in advance. Simultaneous queries, and simultaneous and previously published submissions OK. Query for electronic submissions. Computer printout submissions acceptable; prefers letter-quality. Reports in 1 month on queries; 2 months on mss. Sample copy and writer's guidelines for 9x12 SAE and 7 first class stamps.

Nonfiction: Book excerpts (rarely); how-to (grow in Christian faith and disciplines; help others grow as Christians; serve people in need; understand and apply the Bible); inspirational; interview/profile (focusing on one aspect of discipleship); and interpretation/application of the Bible. No personal testimony; humor; anything not directly related to Christian life and faith; politically partisan articles. Buys 80 mss/year. Query with published clips or send complete ms. Length: 500-3,000 words. Pays 3¢/word reprint; 10-12¢/word first rights. Pays the expenses of writers on assignment.

Tips: "Our articles are meaty, not fluffy. Study writers guidelines and back issues and try to use similar approaches. Don't preach. Polish before submitting. About half of the articles in each issue are related to one theme. Freelancers should write to request theme list. We are looking for more practical articles on ministering to others and more articles dealing with world missions."

THE EPISCOPALIAN, 1201 Chestnut St., Philadelphia PA 19107. (215)564-2010. Publisher: Richard Crawford. Managing Editor: Richard H. Schmidt. 60% freelance written. Accepts submissions from a small number of new/unpublished writers each year. Monthly tabloid about the Episcopal Church for Episcopalians. Circ. 250,000. Pays on publication. Publishes ms an average of 2 months after acceptance. Byline given. Submit seasonal/holiday material 2 months in advance. Previously published submissions OK. Computer printout submissions acceptable; prefers letter-quality. Reports in 1 month. Sample copy for 3 first class stamps.

Nonfiction: Inspirational and interview/profile (of Episcopalians participating in church or community activities). "I like action stories about people doing things and solving problems. I like quotes, photos and active voice." No personal experience articles. Buys 24 mss/year. Send complete ms. Length: 750-1,000 words. Pays up to $50. Rarely pays expenses of writers on assignment.

Photos: Pays $10 for b&w glossy prints. Identification of subjects required. Buys one-time rights.

Tips: "Stories must have an Episcopal Church connection."

EVANGEL, Free Methodist Publishing House, 999 College Ave., Winona Lake IN 46590. (219)267-7161. Editor: Vera Bethel. 100% freelance written. Weekly magazine. Audience is 65% female, 35% male; married, 25-31 years old, mostly city dwellers, high school graduates, mostly nonprofessional. Circ. 35,000. Pays on publication. Publishes ms an average of 1 year after acceptance. Buys simultaneous rights, second serial (reprint) rights or one-time rights. Submit seasonal/holiday material 3 months in advance. Computer printout submissions acceptable; no dot-matrix. Reports in 1 month. Sample copy and writer's guidelines for 6x9 SAE with 2 first class stamps.

Nonfiction: Interview (with ordinary person who is doing something extraordinary in his community, in service to others); profile (of missionary or one from similar service profession who is contributing significantly to society); and personal experience (finding a solution to a problem common to young adults; coping with handicapped child, for instance, or with a neighborhood problem. Story of how God-given strength or insight saved a situation). Buys 100 mss/year. Submit complete ms. Length: 300-1,000 words. Pays $10-25.

Photos: Purchased with accompanying ms. Captions required. Send prints. Pays $5-10 for 8x10 b&w glossy prints; $2 for snapshots.

Fiction: Religious themes dealing with contemporary issues dealt with from a Christian frame of reference. Story must "go somewhere." Buys 50 mss/year. Submit complete ms. Length: 1,200 words. Pays $45.

Poetry: Free verse, haiku, light verse, traditional and religious. Buys 50 poems/year. Submit maximum 6 poems. Length: 4-24 lines. Pays $10.

Tips: "Seasonal material will get a second look (won't be rejected so easily) because we get so little. Write an attention grabbing lead followed by a body of article that says something worthwhile. Relate the lead to some of the universal needs of the reader—promise in that lead to help the reader in some way. Remember that everybody is interested most in himself. Lack of SASE brands author as a nonprofessional; I seldom even bother to read the script. If the writer doesn't want the script back, it probably has no value for me, either."

THE EVANGELICAL BEACON, 1515 E. 66th St., Minneapolis MN 55423. (612)866-3343. Editor: George Keck. 30% freelance written. Works with a small number of new/unpublished writers each year. Denominational magazine of the Evangelical Free Church of America—evangelical Protestant readership; published 17 times/year (every third Monday, except for a 4 week interval, June-August). Pays on publication. Publishes ms an average of 6 months after acceptance. Rights purchased vary with author and material. Buys first rights or all rights, and some reprints. Computer printout submissions acceptable; prefers letter-quality. Reports in 8-10 weeks. Sample copy and writer's guidelines for 75¢.

Nonfiction: Articles on the church, Christ-centered human interest and personal testimony articles, well researched on current issues of religious interest. Desires crisp, imaginative, original writing—not sermons on paper. Length: 250-2,000 words. Pays 3¢/word with extra payment on some articles, at discretion of editor.

Photos: Prefers 8x10 b&w photos. Pays $10 minimum.

Fiction: Not much fiction used, but will consider. Length: 100-1,500 words.

Poetry: Very little poetry used. Pays variable rate, $3.50 minimum.

Tips: "Articles need to be helpful to the average Christian—encouraging, challenging, instructive. Also needs material presenting reality of the Christian faith to nonChristians. Some tie-in with the Evangelical Free Church of America is helpful but not required."

EVANGELIZING TODAY'S CHILD, Child Evangelism Fellowship Inc., Warrenton MO 63383. (314)456-4321. Editor: Elsie Lippy. 75% freelance written. Prefers to work with published/established writers. Bimonthly magazine; 72 pages. "Our purpose is to equip Christians to win the world's children to Christ and disciple them. Our readership is Sunday school teachers, Christian education leaders and children's workers in every phase of Christian ministry to children up to 12 years old." Circ. 26,000. Pays within 90 days of acceptance. Publishes ms an average of 6 months after acceptance. Byline given. Pays a kill fee if assigned. Buys first serial rights. Submit seasonal/holiday material 6 months in advance. Simultaneous queries and photocopied submissions OK. Computer printout submissions acceptable; no dot-matrix. Reports in 3 weeks on queries; 2 months on mss. Free sample copy; writer's guidelines with SASE.

Nonfiction: Unsolicited articles welcomed from writers with Christian education training or current experience in working with children. Buys 25 mss/year. Query. Length: 1,200-1,500. Pays 6-8¢/word.

Photos: Submissions of photos on speculation accepted. Needs photos of children or related subjects. Pays $25 for 8x10 b&w glossy prints; $100 for color transparencies.

‡**THE FAMILY,** Daughters of St. Paul, 50 St. Paul's Ave., Boston MA 02130. (617)522-8911. Editor: Sr. Mary Lea Hill. Managing Editor: Sr. Janet Peter Figurant. Monthly magazine on Christian family life. *"The Family* magazine stresses the special place of the family within society as an irreplaceable center of life, love and faith. Articles on timely, pertinent issues help families approach today's challenges with a faith perspective and a spirit of commitment to the Gospel of Jesus Christ." Pays on publication. Publishes ms an average of 5 months after acceptance. Byline given. Buys first and second serial (reprint) rights. Submit seasonal/holiday material 5 months in advance. Previously published submissions OK. Computer printout submissions OK; no dot-matrix. Sample copy $1.25 with 8½x11 SAE with 5 first class stamps. Writer's guidelines for #10 SASE.

Nonfiction: Humor, inspirational, interview/profile, religious. Buys 70 mss/year. Send complete ms. Length: 500-1,500 words. Pays $50-150. Pays in contributor's copies.

Photos: Send photos with submission. Reviews 4x5 transparencies. Offers $50-200 per photo. Captions, model releases and identification of subjects required. Buys one-time rights.

Fiction: Humorous, religious, slice-of-life vignettes, family. Buys 12 mss/year. Send complete ms. Length: 1,000-2,000 words. Pays $50-150.

Fillers: Anecdotes, short humor. Buys 30/year. Length: 100-300 words. Pays $20.

FUNDAMENTALIST JOURNAL, Old-Time Gospel Hour, 2220 Langhorne Rd., Lynchburg VA 24514. (804)528-4112. Publisher: Jerry Falwell. Editor: Deborah Wade Huff. 40% freelance written. Works with a small number of new/unpublished writers. A Christian magazine (nonprofit organization) published monthly (July/August combined) covering "matters of interest to all Fundamentalists, providing inspirational articles, features on current issues, human interest stories, profiles, reviews and news reports." Audience is 65% Baptist; 35% other denominations; 30% pastors, 70% other. Circ. 85,000. Pays on publication. Publishes ms an average of 4-12 months after acceptance. Byline given. Offers kill fee on assigned articles. Buys all rights, first North American serial rights, makes work-for-hire assignments. Submit seasonal/holiday material 6 months in advance. Previously published submissions OK. Computer printout submissions acceptable; prefers letter-quality. Reports in 3 months. Sample copy for 9x12 SAE with 4 first class stamps; writer's guidelines for #10 SASE.

Nonfiction: Earlene R. Goodwin, articles editor. Book excerpts; expose (government, communism, education); general interest; historical/nostalgic (regarding the Bible, Christianity, great Christians of old); inspirational, interview/profile; opinion, and personal experience. "Writing must be consistent with Fundamentalist doctrine. We do not want articles that are critical in naming leaders of churches or Christian organizations." Buys 77 mss/year. Query. Length: 500-2,000 words. Pays 10¢/printed word for major articles; 20¢/printed word for shorter articles in special sections. Sometimes pays the expenses of writers on assignment.

Columns/Departments: Length: 300-2,000 words. Pays 10¢/printed word.

Tips: "We are looking for more articles to encourage and support the Christian family. We ask writers to submit query first. News is usually by assignment; various articles of general interest to Fundamentalist Christian readers, perspective, profiles, missions articles, family living articles and brief articles dealing with pastoring are most open to freelancers."

‡**THE GEM,** Churches of God, General Conference, Box 926, Findlay OH 45839. (419)424-1961. Editor: Marilyn Rayle Kern. 98% freelance written. Works with a small number of new/unpublished writers each year. "We are backlogged with submissions but still hope to find new submissions of high quality." Weekly magazine; adult and youth church school take-home paper. "Our readers expect to find true-to-life help for daily living as growing Christians." Circ. 8,000. Pays on publication. Publishes ms an average of 9 months after acceptance. Byline given. Not copyrighted. Buys simultaneous rights, first serial rights or second serial (reprint) rights. Submit seasonal/holiday material 3 months in advance. Simultaneous, photocopied and previously published submissions OK. Query for electronic submission. Computer printout submissions acceptable; prefers letter-quality to dot-matrix. Reports in 6 months. Sample copy and writer's guidelines for #10 SASE (unless more than 1 copy).

Nonfiction: General interest, historical/nostalgic, humor, inspirational and personal experience. No preachy, judgmental articles, or use of quotes from other sources. Buys 50 mss/year. Send complete ms. Length: 600-1,600 words. Pays $10-15.

Fiction: Adventure, historical, humorous and religious. No mss which are preachy or inauthentic. Buys 50 mss/year. Send complete ms. Length: 1,000-1,600 words. Pays $10-15.

Fillers: Anecdotes and short humor. Buys 40/year. Length: 100-500 words. Pays $5-7.50.

Tips: "Humor, which does not put down people and leads the reader to understand a valuable lesson, is always in short supply."

GOOD NEWS, The Bimonthly Magazine For United Methodists, Box 150, Wilmore KY 40390. (606)858-4661. Editor: James V. Heidinger II. Executive Editor: James S. Robb. 20% freelance written. Prefers to work with published/established writers; works with a small number of new/unpublished writers each year. Bimonthly magazine for United Methodist lay people and pastors, primarily middle income; conservative and Biblical religious beliefs; broad range of political, social and cultural values. "We are the only evangelical magazine with the purpose of working within the United Methodist Church for Biblical reform and evangelical renewal." Circ. 20,000. Pays on acceptance. Publishes ms an average of 8 months after acceptance. Byline given. Buys first serial rights, simultaneous rights, and second serial (reprint) rights. Submit seasonal/holiday material 6 months in advance. Simultaneous submissions with noncompeting publications OK. Prefers original mss and not photocopies of reprinted material. Computer printout submissions acceptable. Reports in 3 months. Sample copy $2.75; free writer's guidelines.

Nonfiction: Historical (prominent people or churches from the Methodist/Evangelical United Brethren tradition); how-to (build faith, work in local church); humor (good taste); inspirational (related to Christian faith); personal experience (case histories of God at work in individual lives); and any contemporary issues as they relate to the Christian faith and/or the United Methodist Church. No sermons or secular material. Buys 25 mss/year. Must query first with a "brief description of the article, perhaps a skeleton outline. Show some enthusiasm about the article and writing (and research). Tell us something about yourself including whether you or the article has United Methodist tie-in. Send manuscripts % editor." Length: 1,500-1,800 words. Pays 5-7¢/word, more on occasion for special assignments. Sometimes pays the expenses of writers on assignment.

Photos: Extra payment for photos with accompanying ms. Uses fine screen b&w prints. Total purchase price for ms includes payment for photos. Payment negotiable. Captions required.

Tips: "Writers must be either United Methodists themselves or intimately familiar with the mindset of our church members. Evangelical slant is a must for all articles, yet we are not fundamentalist or sentimental. We are now moving away from predictable testimony pieces (though there is still room for the fresh testimony which ties in with burning issues, especially when written by Methodists). What we are looking for now are 1,200-word, newspaper style sketches of vibrant, evangelically oriented United Methodist churches. Photos are a must. We'll hire a pro if we need to. We also need personality profiles of dynamic, unusual United Methodists with accompanying professional quality photo (evidence of vital faith in subject is required)."

THE GOSPEL TRUTH, Gospel Truth Ministries, Inc., Box 4148, Brockton MA 02403. Editor: David A. Reed. 25% freelance written. Quarterly newsletter covering religious cults and evangelism. "Our articles are written from an evangelical Christian perspective to an evangelical Christian audience." Circ. 1,000. Pays on publication. Publishes ms an average of 3 months after acceptance. Byline given. Buys one-time rights or second serial (reprint) rights. Simultaneous and previously published submissions OK. Query for electronic submissions. Computer printout submissions OK. Reports in 1 month. Sample copy for #10 SAE with 2 first class stamps; writer's guidelines for #10 SASE.

Nonfiction: Book excerpts on cults, exposé on cults, how-to evangelize particular segments of society, personal experience (brief testimonies), religious (on evangelism), technical (apologetics), other news on cults and religious freedom issues. No general religious or inspirational material. Buys 8 mss/year. Send complete ms. Length: 100-1,000 words. Pays $5-50.

Photos: Offers $5-50.

Columns/Departments: Book Reviews (books on cults, issues confront the Church, religious freedom issues), 300-600 words; Witnessing Tips (how to share the Gospel with members of a particular cult or population segment), 300-800 words. Buys 4 mss/year. Send complete ms. Pays $15-40.

Tips: "When writing on a cult group, please furnish your credentials that make you an authority on the subject. When submitting on religious freedom issues or news items, please include thorough documentation. Book reviews are most readily accepted from first-time writers. The book should be one relevant to this publication's field of interest."

GROUP'S JUNIOR HIGH MINISTRY MAGAZINE, Thom Schultz Publications, Inc., 2890 N. Monroe Ave., Box 481, Loveland CO 80539. (303)669-3836. Editorial Director: Joani Schultz. 90% freelance written (assigned). Magazine published 5 times/year for leaders of junior-high Christian youth groups. "How-to articles for junior high membership building, worship planning, handling specific group problems and improving as a leader; hints for parents of junior highers; special style-formatted junior high group meetings on topics like competition, faith in action, seasonal themes, friendship, dealing with life situations and service projects." Circ. 27,000. Pays on acceptance. Publishes ms an average of 3 months after acceptance. Byline given. Offer $25 kill fee. Buys all rights and makes work-for-hire assignments. Submit seasonal/holiday material 6 months in advance. Query for electronic submissions. Computer printout submissions OK; no dot-matrix. Sample copy for 9x12 SAE with $1 postage; writer's guidelines for SASE.

Nonfiction: How-to, humor, inspirational/motivational, personal experience, religious/Bible studies, and curriculum. No fiction. Buys 65 assigned mss/year. Query. Length: 500-1,700. Pays $75-100 for assigned articles. Sometimes pays expenses of writers on assignment.

Photos: Send photos with submission. Reviews contact sheets, transparencies and prints. Offers $20-50/b&w photo; $50-150/color photo. Model releases required. Buys one-time rights (occasionally buys additional rights).

Columns/Departments: Parent's Page (brief helps for parents of junior highers; for example, tips on discipline, faith communication, building close family, parent-self understanding, practical help, understanding junior highers and values). One Group's Success, (a one-page article on a successful junior high group).

Length: 500 words. Pays $75. New Jr. High Resources, (reviews on books, curriculum and videos for junor high leaders.) 200 words. The actual resource serves as payment. Buys 30 mss/year. Send complete ms. Length: 150 words. Pays $25.

Tips: "Writers who are also successful junior high workers or teachers have the best chance of being published in *Jr. High Ministry* simply because they know the kids. We need authors who can give our readers practical tips for ministry with junior highers. We need step-by-step experiential, Bible-oriented, fun meetings for leaders to do with junior high youth groups. The meetings must help the kids apply their Christian faith to life and must follow the standard format in the magazine."

GUIDEPOSTS MAGAZINE, 747 3rd Ave., New York NY 10017. Editor: Van Varner. 30% freelance written. "Works with a small number of new/unpublished writers each year, and reads all unsolicited manuscripts. *Guideposts* is an inspirational monthly magazine for people of all faiths, in which men and women from all walks of life tell in first-person narrative how they overcame obstacles, rose above failures, handled sorrow, learned to master themselves and became more effective people through faith in God." Publishes ms an "indefinite" number of months after acceptance. Pays 25% kill fee for assigned articles. Byline given. "Most of our stories are ghosted articles, so the writer would not get a byline unless it was his/her own story." Buys all rights and second serial (reprint) rights. Computer printout submissions acceptable; prefers letter-quality.

Nonfiction and Fillers: Articles and features should be written in simple, anecdotal style with an emphasis on human interest. Short mss of approximately 250-750 words (pays $50-200) would be considered for such features as Quiet People and general one-page stories. Full-length mss, 750-1,500 words, pays $200-400. All mss should be typed, double-spaced and accompanied by a stamped, self-addressed envelope. Annually awards scholarships to high school juniors and seniors in writing contest. Buys 40-60 unsolicited mss/year. Pays expenses of writers on assignment.

Tips: "Study the magazine before you try to write for it. Each story must make a single spiritual point. The freelancer would have the best chance of breaking in by aiming for a one-page or maybe two-page article. That would be very short, say two and a half pages of typescript, but in a small magazine such things are very welcome. Sensitively written anecdotes are extremely useful. And they are much easier to just sit down and write than to have to go through the process of preparing a query. They should be warm, well written, intelligent and upbeat. We like personal narratives that are true and have some universal relevance, but the religious element does not have to be driven home with a sledge hammer. A writer succeeds with us if he or she can write a true article in short-story form with scenes, drama, tension and a resolution of the problem presented." Address short items to Rick Hamlin.

HICALL, Gospel Publishing House, 1445 Boonville Ave., Springfield MO 65802. (417)862-2781, ext. 4349. Editor: Sinda Zinn. Mostly freelance written. Eager to work with new/unpublished writers. Assemblies of God (denominational) weekly magazine of Christian fiction and articles for church-oriented teenagers, 12-17. Circ. 95,000. Pays on acceptance. Publishes ms an average of 6 months after acceptance. Byline given. Buys first North American serial rights, one-time rights, simultaneous rights and second serial (reprint) rights. Submit seasonal/holiday material 1 year in advance. Simultaneous, photocopied and previously published submissions OK—if typed, double-spaced, on 8½x11 paper. Computer printout submissions acceptable; prefers letter-quality. Reports in 6 weeks. Sample copy for 8x11 SAE and 2 first class stamps; writer's guidelines for SAE.

Nonfiction: Book excerpts; historical; general interest; how-to (deal with various life problems); humor; inspirational; and personal experience. Buys 80-100 mss/year. Send complete ms. Length: 500-1,500 words. Pays 2-3¢/word.

Photos: Photos purchased with or without accompanying ms. Pays $25/8x10 b&w glossy print; $30/35mm.

Fiction: Adventure, humorous, mystery, romance, suspense, western and religious. Buys 80-100 mss/year. Send complete ms. Length: 500-1,500 words. Pays 2-3¢/word.

Poetry: Free verse, light verse and traditional. Buys 30 poems/year. Length: 10-30 lines. Pays 25¢/line, minimum of $5 (first rights).

Fillers: Clippings, anecdotes, short humor and newsbreaks. Buys 30/year. Pays 2-3¢/word.

INTERLIT, David C. Cook Foundation, Cook Square, Elgin IL 60120. (312)741-2400, ext. 316. Editor: Tim Bascom. 90% freelance written on assignment. Works with a small number of new/unpublished writers each year. Quarterly journal. Emphasizes sharpening skills in Christian journalism and publishing. Especially for editors, publishers and writers in the third world (developing countries). Also goes to missionaries, broadcasters and educational personnel in the U.S. Circ. 6,000. Pays on acceptance. Publishes ms an average of 6 months after acceptance. Buys all rights. Photocopied submissions OK. Computer printout submissions acceptable. Reports in 4-6 weeks. Free sample copy.

Nonfiction: Technical and how-to articles about all aspects of publishing, writing and literacy. "Please study publication and query before submitting manuscripts." Also photo features. Buys 7 mss/issue, mostly on assignment. Length: 500-1,500 words. Pays 6¢/word.

Photos: Purchased with accompanying ms only. Uses b&w. Query or send prints. Captions required.

THE JEWISH WEEKLY NEWS, Bennett-Scott Publications Corp., 99 Mill St., Box 1569, Springfield MA 01101. (413)739-4771. 25% freelance written. Jewish news and features, secular and non-secular; World Judaism; arts (New England based). Circ. 2,500. Pays on publication. Publishes ms an average of 2 months after acceptance. Byline given. Not copyrighted. Buys first North American serial rights and second serial (reprint) rights. Submit seasonal/holiday material 2 months in advance. Simultaneous, photocopied and previously published submissions OK. Query for electronic submissions. Computer printout submissions OK. Sample copy for 9x12 SAE with 5 first class stamps.

Nonfiction: Interview/profile, religious and travel. Special issues include Jewish New Year (September); Chanukah (December); Home Issues (March); Bar/Bat Mitzvahs (May). Buys 61 mss/year. Query with published clips. Length: 300-1,000 words. Pays $5.

Photos: Send photos with submission. Reviews 5x7 prints. Offers no additional payment for photos accepted with ms. Identification of subjects required.

Columns/Departments: Jewish Kitchen (Kosher recipes), 300-500 words. Buys 10 mss/year. Query with published clips. Length: 300-5,000 words. Pays 50¢/inch.

Fiction: Sheila Thompson, editor. Slice-of-life vignettes. Buys 5 mss/year. Query with published clips. Length: 750-1,000 words. Pays 50¢/inch.

LIGHT AND LIFE, Free Methodist Church of North America, 901 College Ave., Winona Lake IN 46590. FAX: (219)269-7431. Editor: Bob Haslam. 35% freelance written. Works with a small number of new/unpublished writers each year. Monthly magazine. Emphasizes evangelical Christianity with Wesleyan slant for a cross section of adults. Circ. 40,000. Pays on publication. Publishes ms an average of 6 months after acceptance. Byline given. Prefers first serial rights; rarely buys second serial (reprint) rights. Submit seasonal/holiday material 6 months in advance. Computer printout submissions acceptable; no dot-matrix. Reports in 6 weeks. Sample copy and guidelines $1.50; writer's guidelines for SASE.

Nonfiction: "Each issue includes a mini-theme (3 or 4 articles addressing contemporary topics such as entertainment media, personal relationships, Christians as citizens), so freelancers should request our schedule of mini-theme topics. We also need fresh, upbeat articles showing the average layperson how to be Christ-like at home, work and play." Submit complete ms. Buys 70-80 unsolicited ms/year. Pays 4¢/word. Sometimes pays expenses of writers on assignment.

Photos: Purchased without accompanying ms. Send prints. Pays $5-35 for b&w photos. Offers additional payment for photos accepted with accompanying ms.

LIGUORIAN, Liguori MO 63057. Editor: Rev. Norman Muckerman. Managing Editor: Francine M. O'Connor. 50% freelance written. Prefers to work with published/established writers; works with a small number of new/unpublished writers each year. Monthly. For families with Catholic religious convictions. Circ. 525,000. Pays on acceptance. Publishes ms an average of 3-4 months after acceptance. Byline given "except on short fillers and jokes." Buys all rights but will reassign rights to author *after* publication upon written request. Submit seasonal material 6 months in advance. Query for electronic submissions. Computer printout submissions acceptable; no dot-matrix. Reports in 6 weeks. Sample copy and writer's guidelines for 6x9 SAE with 3 first class stamps.

Nonfiction: "Pastoral, practical and personal approach to the problems and challenges of people today. No travelogue approach or unresearched ventures into controversial areas. Also, no material found in secular publications—fad subjects that already get enough press, pop psychology, negative or put-down articles." Buys 60 unsolicited mss/year. Length: 400-2,000 words. Pays 10¢/word. Sometimes pays expenses of writers on assignment.

Photos: Photographs on assignment only unless submitted with and specific to article.

LIVE, 1445 Boonville Ave., Springfield MO 65802. (417)862-2781. Editor: John T. Maempa. 100% freelance written. Works with several new/unpublished writers each year. Weekly. For adults in Assemblies of God Sunday schools. Circ. 200,000. Pays on acceptance. Publishes ms an average of 1 year after acceptance. Not copyrighted. Submit seasonal material 1 year in advance; do not mention Santa Claus, Halloween or Easter bunnies. Computer printout submissions acceptable. Reports on material within 3-6 weeks. Submissions held for further consideration may require more time. Free sample copy and writer's guidelines for 7½x10½ SASE and 35¢ postage. Letters without SASE will not be answered.

Nonfiction: Articles with reader appeal emphasizing some phase of Christian living presented in a down-to-earth manner. Biography or missionary material using fiction techniques. Historical, scientific or nature material with spiritual lesson. "Be accurate in detail and factual material. Writing for Christian publications is a ministry. The spiritual emphasis must be an integral part of your material." Prefers not to see material on highly controversial subjects but would appreciate articles on contemporary issues and concerns (e.g. substance abuse, AIDS, euthanasia, cults, integrity, etc.). Buys about 120 mss/year. Length: 1,000-1,600 words. Pays 3¢/word for first serial rights; 2¢/word for second serial (reprint) rights, according to the value of the material and the amount of editorial work necessary. "Please do not send large numbers of articles at one time."

Photos: Color photos or transparencies purchased with mss, or on assignment. Pay open.

Fiction: "Present believable characters working out their problems according to Bible principles; in other words, present Christianity in action without being preachy. We use very few serials, but we will consider three- to four-part stories if each part conforms to average word length for short stories. Each part must contain a spiritual emphasis and have enough suspense to carry the reader's interest from one week to the next. Stories should be true to life but not what we would feel is bad to set before the reader as a pattern for living. Stories should not put parents, teachers, ministers or other Christian workers in a bad light. Setting, plot and action should be realistic, with strong motivation. Characterize so that the people will live in your story. Construct your plot carefully so that each incident moves naturally and sensibly toward crisis and conclusion. An element of conflict is necessary in fiction. Short stories should be written from one viewpoint only. We do not accept fiction based on incidents in the Bible." Length: 1,200-1,600 words. Pays 3¢/word for first serial rights; 2¢/word for second serial (reprint) rights. "Please do not send large numbers of articles at one time."

Poetry: Traditional, free and blank verse. Length: 12-20 lines. "Please do not send large numbers of poems at one time." Pays 20¢/line.

Fillers: Brief and purposeful, usually containing an anecdote, and always with a strong evangelical emphasis. Length: 200-600 words.

LIVING WITH TEENAGERS, Baptist Sunday School Board, 127 9th Ave. N., Nashville TN 37234. (615)251-2273. Editor: Jimmy Hester. 50-75% freelance written. Works with a small number of new/unpublished writers each year. Quarterly magazine about teenagers for Baptist parents of teenagers. Circ. 50,000. Pays within 2 months of acceptance. Publishes ms an average of 18 months after acceptance. Buys all rights. Submit seasonal material 1 year in advance. Computer printout submissions OK; prefers letter-quality. Reports in 2 months. Sample copy for 9x12 SAE with 4 first class stamps, writer's guidelines for #10 SASE.

Nonfiction: "We are looking for a unique Christian element. We want a genuine insight into the teen/parent relationship." General interest (on communication, emotional problems, growing up, drugs and alcohol, leisure, sex education, spiritual growth, working teens and parents, money, family relationships and church relationships); inspirational; and personal experience. Buys 60 unsolicited mss/year. Query with clips of previously published work. Length: 600-2,000 words. Pays 5¢/published word.

Fiction: Humorous and religious, but must relate to parent/teen relationship. "No stories from the teen's point of view." Buys 2 mss/issue. Query with clips of previously published work. Length: 600-2,000 words. Pays 5¢/published word.

Poetry: Free verse, light verse, traditional and devotional inspirational; all must relate to parent/teen relationship. Buys 3 mss/issue. Submit 5 poems maximum. Length: 33 characters maximum. Pays $2.10 plus $1.25/line for 1-7 lines; $5.40 plus 75¢/line for 8 lines minimum.

Tips: "A writer can meet our needs if they have something to say to parents of teenagers concerning an issue the parents are confronting with the teenager."

THE LOOKOUT, 8121 Hamilton Ave., Cincinnati OH 45231. (513)931-4050. Editor: Mark A. Taylor. 50-60% freelance written. Eager to work with new/unpublished writers. Weekly for adults and young adults attending Sunday schools and Christian churches. Pays on acceptance. Publishes ms an average of 4 months after acceptance. Byline given. Buys first serial rights, one-time rights, second serial (reprint) rights, or simultaneous rights. Simultaneous submissions OK. Computer printout submissions acceptable; prefers letter-quality. Reports in 2 months, sometimes longer. Sample copy and writer's guidelines 50¢. Guidelines only for #10 SASE.

Nonfiction: "Seeks stories about real people or Sunday school classes; items that shed Biblical light on matters of contemporary controversy; and items that motivate, that lead the reader to ask, 'Why shouldn't I try that?' or 'Why couldn't our Sunday school class accomplish this?' Articles should tell how real people are involved for Christ. In choosing topics, *The Lookout* considers timeliness, the church and national calendar, and the ability of the material to fit the above guidelines. Tell us about ideas that are working in your Sunday school and in the lives of its members. Remember to aim at laymen." Submit complete ms. Length: 1,200-1,800 words. Pays 4-7¢/word. We also use inspirational short pieces. "About 600-800 words is a good length for these. Relate an incident that illustrates a point without preaching." Pays 4-6¢/word.

Fiction: "A short story is printed in many issues; it is usually between 1,200-1,800 words long and should be as true to life as possible while remaining inspirational and helpful. Use familiar settings and situations. Most often we use stories with a Christian slant." Pays 5-6¢/word.

Photos: Reviews b&w prints, 4x6 or larger. Pays $5-35. Pays $50-150 for color transparencies for covers and inside use. Needs photos of people, especially adults in a variety of settings. Send to Photo Editor, Standard Publishing, at the above address.

LUTHERAN FORUM, at the Wartburg, Bradley Ave., Mt. Vernon NY 10552. (914)699-1226. Editor: Dr. Paul R. Hunlicky, Executive Director: Dr. Thomas R. Sluberski. 25% freelance written. Works with a small number of new/unpublished writers each year. Quarterly magazine. For church leadership, clerical and lay. Circ. 4,500. Pays on publication. Publishes ms an average of 3 months after acceptance. Byline given. Rights purchased vary with author and material; buys all rights, first North American serial rights, second serial (reprint) rights and simultaneous rights. Will consider photocopied and simultaneous submissions. Computer printout submissions acceptable; prefers letter-quality to dot-matrix. Reports in 9 weeks. Sample copy $1.50, SAE and $1 postage; writer's guidelines for #10 SASE.

Nonfiction: Articles about important issues and developments in the church's institutional life and in its cultural/social setting. Special interest in articles on the Christian's life in secular vocations. No purely devotional/inspirational material. Buys 8-10 mss/year. Query or submit complete ms. Length: 1,000-3,000 words. Payment varies; $30 minimum. Informational, how-to, interview, profile, think articles and exposé. Length: 500-3,000 words. Pays $25-75.

Photos: Purchased with ms and only with captions. Prefers 4x5 prints. Pays $15 minimum.

THE LUTHERAN JOURNAL, 7317 Cahill Rd., Edina MN 55435. Editor: Rev. Armin U. Deye. Quarterly magazine. Family magazine for Lutheran Church members, middle age and older. Circ. 136,000. Pays on publication. Byline given. Will consider photocopied and simultaneous submissions. Reports in 2 months. Free sample copy.

Nonfiction: Inspirational, religious, human interest and historical articles. Interesting or unusual church projects. Informational, how-to, personal experience, interview, humor and think articles. Buys 25-30 mss/year. Submit complete ms. Length: 1,500 words maximum; occasionally 2,000 words. Pays 1-3¢/word.

Photos: B&w and color photos purchased with accompanying ms. Captions required. Payment varies.

Fiction: Mainstream, religious and historical fiction. Must be suitable for church distribution. Length: 2,000 words maximum. Pays 1-1½¢/word.

Poetry: Traditional poetry, blank verse and free verse, related to subject matter.

MARIAN HELPERS BULLETIN, Eden Hill, Stockbridge MA 01263. (413)298-3691. FAX: (413)298-3583. Editor: Rev. Gerald Ornowski, M.I.C. 60% freelance written. Bimonthly magazine for average Catholics of varying ages with moderate religious views and general education. Circ. 1 million. Pays on acceptance. Byline given. Submit seasonal material 6 months in advance. Computer printout submissions OK; prefers letter-quality. Reports in 2 months. Sample copy $1.

Nonfiction: "Articles on spiritual, devotional and moral topics for a Catholic audience. Use a positive, practical approach, well done without being sophisticated. Unsolicited mss will not be returned." Buys 18-24 mss/year. Length: 300-900 words. Pays 3-10¢/word.

Photos: Photos should be sent to complement articles.

Tips: "Human interest stories are very valuable, from which personal reflection is stimulated."

MARRIAGE & FAMILY, St. Meinrad IN 47577. (812)357-8011. Managing Editor: Kass Dotterweich. 75% freelance written. Monthly magazine. Circ. 28,000. Pays on acceptance. Byline given. Buys first international serial rights, first book reprint option, and control of other reprint rights. Query. Computer printout submissions acceptable; prefers letter-quality. Reports in 6 weeks. Sample copy $1 with 9x12 SAE; writer's guidelines for #10 SASE.

Nonfiction: Articles which affirm marriage and parenting as an awesome vocation created by God; and personal essays relating amusing, heartwarming or insightful incidents which reflect the rich human side of marriage and family life. Length: 1,500-2,000 words maximum. Pays 7¢/word. Pays expenses of writers on assignment.

Photos: Attention, art director. Reviews 8x10 b&w glossy prints and color transparencies or 35mm slides. Pays $150/4-color cover or center spread photo. Uses approximately 6-8 b&w photos and an occasional illustration inside. Pays variable rate on publication. Photos of couples, families and individuals especially desirable. Model releases required.

Poetry: Short, free verse. Pays $15 on publication; please include phone number.

MENNONITE BRETHREN HERALD, 3-169 Riverton Ave., Winnipeg, Manitoba R2L 2E5 Canada. Contact: Editor. 25% freelance written. Family publication "read mainly by people of the Mennonite faith, reaching a wide cross section of professional and occupational groups, but also including many homemakers. Readership includes people from both urban and rural communities." Biweekly. Circ. 13,500. Pays on publication. Publishes ms an average of 4-6 months after acceptance. Not copyrighted. Byline given. Computer printout submissions OK. Sample copy for $1 with 9x12 SAE and IRCs. Reports in 6 months.

Nonfiction: Articles with a Christian family orientation; youth directed, Christian faith and life, and current issues. Wants articles critiquing the values of a secular society, attempting to relate Christian living to the practical situations of daily living; showing how people have related their faith to their vocations. Length: 1,500 words. Pays $30-40. Pays the expenses of writers on assignment.

Photos: Photos purchased with mss; pays $5.

THE MESSENGER OF THE SACRED HEART, Apostleship of Prayer, 661 Greenwood Ave., Toronto, Ontario M4J 4B3 Canada. (416)466-1195. Editor: Rev. F.J. Power, S.J. For "Canadian and U.S. Catholics interested in developing a life of prayer and spirituality; stresses the great value of our ordinary actions and lives." 20%

freelance written. Monthly. Circ. 16,500. Buys first rights only. Byline given. Pays on acceptance. Submit seasonal material 5 months in advance. Computer printout submissions acceptable; prefers letter-quality. Reports in 1 month. Sample copy $1 and 7½x10½ SAE; writer's guidelines for #10 SASE.

Fiction: Religious/inspirational. Stories about people, adventure, heroism, humor, drama. Buys 12 mss/year. Send complete ms with SAE and IRCs. Unsolicited manuscripts, unaccompanied by return postage, will not be returned. Length: 750-1,500 words. Pays 4¢ word.

Tips: "Develop a story that sustains interest to the end. Do not preach, but use plot and characters to convey the message or theme. Aim to move the heart as well as the mind. Before sending, cut out unnecessary or unrelated words or sentences. If you can, add a light touch or a sense of humor to the story. Your ending should have impact, leaving a moral or faith message for the reader."

THE MIRACULOUS MEDAL, 475 E. Chelten Ave., Philadelphia PA 19144. Editorial Director: Rev. Robert P. Cawley, C.M. 40% freelance written. Quarterly. Pays on acceptance. Publishes ms an average of 2 years after acceptance. Buys first North American serial rights. Buys articles only on special assignment. Computer printout submissions acceptable; no dot-matrix. Sample copy for 6x9 SAE with 2 first class stamps.

Fiction: Should not be pious or sermon-like. Wants good general fiction—not necessarily religious, but if religion is basic to the story, the writer should be sure of his facts. Only restriction is that subject matter and treatment must not conflict with Catholic teaching and practice. Can use seasonal material; Christmas stories. Length: 2,000 words maximum. Occasionally uses short-shorts from 750-1,250 words. Pays 2¢/word minimum.

Poetry: Maximum of 20 lines, preferably about the Virgin Mary or at least with religious slant. Pays 50¢/line minimum.

MODERN LITURGY, Suite 290, 160 E. Virginia St., San Jose CA 95112. Editor: Kenneth Guentert. 80% freelance written. Magazine; 40-48 pages published 10 times/year for artists, musicians and creative individuals who plan group worship, services; teachers of religion. Circ. 15,000. Buys first serial rights. Pays on publication. Publishes ms an average of 6 months after acceptance. Byline given. Query for electronic submissions. Computer printout submissions acceptable; prefers letter-quality. Reports in 6 weeks. Sample copy $4; free writer's guidelines for SASE.

Nonfiction and Fiction: Articles (historical, theological and practical) which address special interest topics in the field of liturgy; example services; and liturgical art forms (music, poetry, stories, dances, dramatizations, etc.). Practical, creative ideas; and art forms for use in worship and/or religious education classrooms. "No material out of our field." Buys 10 mss/year. Query. Length: 750-2,000 words. Pays with subscriptions, copies, and negotiated cost stipend for regular contributors.

MOODY MONTHLY, Moody Bible Institute, 820 N. LaSalle Dr., Chicago IL 60610. (312)329-2163. Senior Editors: Mike Umlandt and Andrew Scheer. 20% freelance written. A monthly magazine for evangelical Christianity. "Our readers are conservative, evangelical Christians highly active in their churches and concerned about family living." Circ. 200,000. Pays on acceptance. Publishes ms an average of 6 months after acceptance. Byline given. Offers $50 kill fee. Buys first North American serial rights. Submit seasonal/holiday material 8 months in advance. Photocopied submissions OK. Query for electronic submissions. Computer printout submissions OK. Reports in 1 month on queries; 2 months on mss. Sample copy for 10x13 SASE; writer's guidelines for #10 SASE.

Nonfiction: How-to (on living the Christian life), humor and personal experience. Buys 50 mss/year. Query. Length: 750-2,000 words. Pays 10-15¢/word for assigned articles. Sometimes pays the expenses of writers on assignment.

Photos: State availability of photos with submission. Offers $35-50 per photo. Buys one-time rights.

Columns/Departments: First Person (The only article written for non-Christians; a personal testimony written by the author [we will accept 'as told to's']; the objective is to tell a person's testimony in such a way that the reader will understand the gospel and want to receive Christ as Savior); Parenting (provides practical guidance for parents solidly based on biblical principles). Buys 30 mss/year. Query. Length: 750-1,200 words. Pays 10-15¢/word.

MY DAILY VISITOR, Our Sunday Visitor, Inc., 200 Noll Plaza, Huntington IN 46750. (219)356-8400. Editor: Jacquelyn M. Eckert. 99% freelance written. Bimonthly magazine on spirituality and scripture meditations. Circ. 40,000. Pays on acceptance. Publishes ms an average of 1 year after acceptance. Byline given. Not copyrighted. Buys one-time rights. Reports in 2 months. Sample copy for #10 SAE with 2 first class stamps. Writer's guidelines for #10 SASE. "Guest editors write on assignment basis."

Nonfiction: Inspirational, personal experience, religious. Buys 12 mss/year. Query with published clips. Length: 175 words. Pays $100-200. Sometimes pays writers 25 gratis copies.

NATIONAL CHRISTIAN REPORTER, Box 222198, Dallas TX 75222. (214)630-6495. Editor/General Manager: Spurgeon M. Dunnam III. Managing Editor: John A. Lovelace. 5% freelance written. Prefers to work with published/established writers. Weekly newspaper for an interdenominational national readership. Circ.

25,000. Pays on publication. Publishes ms an average of 1 month after acceptance. Byline given. Not copyrighted. Free sample copy and writer's guidelines.

Nonfiction: "We welcome short features, approximately 500 words. Articles need to have an explicit 'mainstream' Protestant angle. Write about a distinctly Christian response to human need or how a person's faith relates to a given situation. Preferably including evidence of participation in a local Protestant congregation." Send complete ms. Pays 4¢/word. Sometimes pays the expenses of writers on assignment.

Photos: Purchased with accompanying ms. "We encourage the submission of good action photos (5x7 or 8x10 b&w glossy prints) of the persons or situations in the article." Pays $10.

Poetry: "Good poetry welcomed on a religious theme." Length: 4-20 lines. Pays $2.

THE NEW ERA, 50 E. North Temple, Salt Lake City UT 84150. (801)240-2951. Managing Editor: Richard M. Romney. 60% freelance written. "We work with both established writers and newcomers." Monthly magazine. For young people of the Church of Jesus Christ of Latter-day Saints (Mormon); their church leaders and teachers. Circ. 180,000. Pays on acceptance. Publishes ms an average of 1 year after acceptance. Byline given. Buys all rights. Submit seasonal material 1 year in advance. Query for electronic submissions. Computer printout submissions acceptable; prefers letter-quality. Reports in 1 month. Query preferred. Sample copy $1 and 9x12 SAE; writer's guidelines for SASE.

Nonfiction: Material that shows how the Church of Jesus Christ of Latter-day Saints is relevant in the lives of young people today. Must capture the excitement of being a young Latter-day Saint. Special interest in the experiences of young Mormons in other countries. No general library research or formula pieces without the *New Era* slant and feel. Uses informational, how-to, personal experience, interview, profile, inspirational, humor, historical, think pieces, travel and spot news. Length: 150-3,000 words. Pays 3-12¢/word. *For Your Information* (news of young Mormons around the world). Pays expenses of writers on assignment.

Photos: Uses b&w photos and color transparencies with mss. Payment depends on use in magazine, but begins at $10.

Fiction: Adventure, science fiction and humorous. Must relate to young Mormon audience. Pays minimum 3¢/word.

Poetry: Traditional forms, blank verse, free verse, light verse and all other forms. Must relate to editorial viewpoint. Pays minimum 25¢/line.

Tips: "The writer must be able to write from a Mormon point of view. We anticipate using more staff-produced material. We're especially looking for stories about successful family relationships. This means freelance quality will have to improve."

NEW WORLD OUTLOOK, Room 1351, 475 Riverside Dr., New York NY 10115. (212)870-3758. Executive Editor: George M. Daniels. 60% freelance written. Eager to work with new/unpublished writers. Bimonthly magazine for United Methodist lay people; not clergy generally. Circ. 40,000. Pays on publication. Publishes ms an average of 4 months after acceptance. Buys first serial rights. Query for electronic submissions. Computer printout submissions acceptable; no dot-matrix. Sample copy for $2 and 9x12 SASE; writer's guidelines for 9x12 SASE.

Nonfiction: Articles about the involvement of the church around the world, including the U.S. in outreach and social concerns and Christian witness. "Write with good magazine style. Facts and actualities are important. Use quotes. Relate what Christians are doing to meet problems. Use specifics. Though we want material on large urban areas as New York, Chicago, Los Angeles and Detroit, we need more good journalistic efforts from smaller places in U.S. and articles by freelancers in out-of-the-way places in the U.S." Buys 40-50 mss/year. Query or submit complete ms. Length: 1,000-2,000 words. Usually pays $150-250 but considerably more on occasion. "Writers are encouraged to illustrate their articles photographically if possible." Pays expenses of writers on assignment "if it originates with us or if article is one in which we have a special interest."

Photos: "Generally use b&w but covers (4-color) and 4-color photo features will be considered. Photos are purchased separately at standard rates."

Tips: "A freelancer should have some understanding of the United Methodist Church, or else know very well a local situation of human need or social problem which the churches and Christians have tried to face. Too much freelance material we get tries to paint with broad strokes about world or national issues. The local story of meaning to people elsewhere is still the best material. Avoid pontificating on the big issues. Write cleanly and interestingly on the 'small' ones. We're interested in major articles and photos (including photo features from freelancers)."

NORTH AMERICAN VOICE OF FATIMA, Fatima Shrine, Youngstown NY 14174. Editor: Rev. Paul M. Keeling, C.R.S.P. 40% freelance written. Works with a small number of new/unpublished writers each year. For Roman Catholic readership. Circ. 3,000. Pays on publication. Publishes ms an average of 2 months after acceptance. Not copyrighted. Buys first North American serial rights. Reports in 6 weeks. Computer printout submissions acceptable; no dot-matrix. Free sample copy.

Nonfiction and Fiction: Inspirational, personal experience, historical and think articles. Religious and historical fiction. Length: 700 words. All material must have a religious slant. Pays 2¢/word.

Photos: B&w photos purchased with ms.

OBLATES MAGAZINE, Missionary Association of Mary Immaculate, 15 S. 59th St., Belleville IL 62222. (618)233-2238. Editor of Contributions: Jacqueline Lowery Corn. 30-50% freelance written. Prefers to work with professional writers; but will work with new/unpublished writers. Bimonthly religious magazine for Christian families; audience mainly older adults. Circ. 430,000. Pays on acceptance. Publishes ms within 1 year after acceptance. Byline given. Buys first North American serial rights. Submit seasonal/holiday material 8 months in advance. Computer printout submissions acceptable. Reports in 2 months. Sample copy and writer's guidelines for 9x6 or larger SAE with 2 first class stamps.

Nonfiction: Inspirational and personal experience with positive spiritual insights. No preachy, theological or research articles. Avoid current events and controversial topics. Send complete ms. Length: 500 words. Pays $75.

Poetry: Light verse—reverent, well written, perceptive, with traditional rhythym and rhyme. "Emphasis should be on inspiration, insight and relationship with God." Submit maximum 2 poems. Length: 8-16 lines. Pays $25.

Tips: "Our readership is made up mostly of mature Americans who are looking for comfort, encouragement, and a positive sense of applicable Christian direction to their lives. Focus on sharing of personal insight to problem (i.e. death or change), but must be positive, uplifting, only subtly spiritual. We are very selective for a very narrow market, but always on the lookout for exceptional work."

ORT REPORTER, Woman's American ORT, Inc., 315 Park Ave. So., New York NY 10010. (212)505-7700. Editor: Eve Jacobson. Assistant to the Editor: Freyda Reiss Weiss. 85% freelance written. Nonprofit journal published by Jewish women's organization. Quarterly tabloid covering "Jewish topics, education, Mideast and women." Circ. 155,000. Payment time varies. Publishes ms ASAP after acceptance. Byline given. Buys first North American serial rights or second serial (reprint) rights. Submit seasonal/holiday material 6 months in advance. Reports "as soon as possible." Free sample copy.

Nonfiction: Book excerpts, essays, general interest, humor, opinion and religious. Buys approximately 40 mss/year. Send complete ms. Length: 500-3,000. Pays 8-15¢/word.

Photos: Send photos with submission. Reviews 5x7 prints. Offers $50-85 per photo. Identification of subjects required. Purchases "whatever rights photographer desires."

Columns/Departments: Books, Film, Stage. Buys 4-10 mss/year. Send complete ms. Length: 200-2,000 words. Pays 15¢/word.

Fiction: Ethnic, novel excerpts. Buys 2 ms/year. Send complete ms. Pays 15¢/word, less for reprints.

Tips: "Simply send ms; do not call. First submission must be 'on spec.' Open Forum (opinion section) is most open to freelancers, although all are open. Looking for well-written essay on relevant topic that makes its point strongly—evokes response from reader."

THE OTHER SIDE, 1225 Dandridge St., Fredericksburg VA 22401. Editor: Mark Olson. Associate Editor: John Linscheid. 50% freelance written. Prefers to work with published/established writers; works with a small number of new/unpublished writers each year. Magazine published bimonthly, focusing on "peace, justice and economic liberation from a radical Christian perspective." Circ. 15,000. Pays on acceptance. Publishes ms an average of 4 months after acceptance. Byline given. Buys first serial rights. Query for electronic submissions. Computer printout submissions acceptable. Reports in 6 weeks. Sample copy $4; free writer's guidelines with #10 SASE.

Nonfiction: Nidi Amarantides, articles editor. Current social, political and economic issues in the U.S. and around the world: personality profiles, interpretative essays, interviews, how-to's, personal experiences and investigative reporting. "Articles must be lively, vivid and down-to-earth, with a radical Christian perspective." Length: 500-6,000 words. Pays $25-300. Sometimes pays expenses of writers on assignment.

Photos: Cathleen Boint, art director. Photos or photo essays illustrating current social, political, or economic reality in the U.S. and Third World. Pays $15-75 for b&w and $50-300 for color.

Fiction: Barbara Moorman, fiction editor. "Short stories, humor and satire conveying insights and situations that will be helpful to Christians with a radical commitment to peace and justice." Length: 300-4,000 words. Pays $25-250.

Poetry: Rod Jellema, poetry editor. "Short, creative poetry that will be thought-provoking and appealing to radical Christians who have a strong commitment to spirituality, peace and justice." Length: 3-50 lines. Pays $15-20.

Tips: "We're looking for tightly written pieces (500-1,000 words) on interesting and unusual Christians (or Christian groups) who are putting their commitment to peace and social justice into action in creative and useful ways. We're also looking for practical, down-to-earth articles (500-6,000 words) for Christian parents who seek to instill in their children their values of personal faith, peace, justice, and a concern for the poor."

OUR FAMILY, Oblate Fathers of St. Mary's Province, Box 249, Battleford, Saskatchewan S0M 0E0 Canada. (306)937-7772. FAX: (306)937-7644.Editor: Nestor Gregoire. 60% freelance written. Prefers to work with published/established writers; works with a small number of new/unpublished writers each year. Monthly magazine for average family men and women with high school and early college education. Circ. 14,265. Pays on acceptance. Publishes ms an average of 6 months after acceptance. Byline given. Offers 100% kill fee.

Generally purchases first North American serial rights; also buys all rights, simultaneous rights, second serial (reprint) rights or one-time rights. Submit seasonal/holiday material 4 months in advance. Simultaneous, photocopied, and previously published submissions OK. Query for electronic submissions. Computer printout submissions acceptable; no dot-matrix. Reports in 1 month. Sample copy $2.50 in postage and 9x12 SAE; writer's guidelines for #10 SAE and 44¢. (Canadian funds). U.S. postage cannot be used in Canada.

Nonfiction: Humor (related to family life or husband/wife relations); inspirational (anything that depicts people responding to adverse conditions with courage, hope and love); personal experience (with religious dimensions); and photo feature (particularly in search of photo essays on human/religious themes and on persons whose lives are an inspiration to others). Phone queries OK. Buys 72-88 unsolicited mss/year. Pays expenses of writers on assignment.

Photos: Photos purchased with or without accompanying ms. Pays $35 for 5x7 or larger b&w glossy prints and color photos (which are converted into b&w). Offers additional payment for photos accepted with ms (payment for these photos varies according to their quality). Free photo spec sheet with SASE.

Fiction: Humorous and religious. "Anything true to human nature. No romance, he-man adventure material, science fiction, moralizing or sentimentality." Buys 1 ms/issue. Send complete ms. Length: 700-3,000 words. Pays 7-10¢/word minimum for original material. Free fiction requirement guide with SASE.

Poetry: Avant-garde, free verse, haiku, light verse and traditional. Buys 4-10 poems/issue. Length: 3-30 lines. Pays 75¢-$1/line.

Fillers: Jokes, gags, anecdotes and short humor. Buys 2-10/issue.

Tips: "Writers should ask themselves whether this is the kind of an article, poem, etc. that a busy housewife would pick up and read when she has a few moments of leisure. We are particularly looking for articles on the spirituality of marriage. We will be concentrating more on recent movements and developments in the church to help make people aware of the new church of which they are a part."

PARISH FAMILY DIGEST, Our Sunday Visitor, Inc., 200 Noll Plaza, Huntington IN 46750. (219)356-8400. Editor: George P. Foster. 100% freelance written. Works with small number of new/unpublished writers each year. Bimonthly magazine. "*Parish Family Digest* is geared to the Catholic family and to that family as a unit of the parish." Circ. 150,000. Pays on acceptance. Publishes ms an average of 6 months after acceptance. Byline given. Buys first North American rights. Submit seasonal/holiday material 6 months in advance. Photocopied submissions OK. Computer printout submissions acceptable; prefers letter-quality. Reports in 2 weeks on queries; 3 weeks on mss. Sample copy and writer's guidelines for 9½x6½ SAE and 2 first class stamps.

Nonfiction: General interest, historical, inspirational, interview, nostalgia (if related to overall Parish involvement) and profile. No personal essays or preachy first person "thou shalt's or shalt not's." Send complete ms. Buys 72 unsolicited mss/year. Length: 1,000 words maximum. Pays $5-50.

Photos: State availability of photos with ms. Pays $10 for 3x5 b&w prints. Buys one-time rights. Captions preferred; model releases required.

Fillers: Anecdotes and short humor. Buys 6/issue. Length: 100 words maximum.

Tips: "If an article does not deal with some angle of Catholic family life, the writer is wasting time in sending it to us. We rarely use reprints; we prefer fresh material that will hold up over time, not tied to an event in the news. We will be more oriented to families with kids and the problems such families face in the Church and society, in particular, the struggle to raise good Catholic kids in a secular society. Articles on how to overcome these problems will be welcomed."

PENTECOSTAL EVANGEL, The General Council of the Assemblies of God, 1445 Boonville, Springfield MO 65802. (417)862-2781. FAX: (417)862-8558. Editor: Richard G. Champion. 33% freelance written. Works with a small number of new/unpublished writers each year. Weekly magazine. Emphasizes news of the Assemblies of God for members of the Assemblies and other Pentecostal and charismatic Christians. Circ. 280,000. Pays on acceptance. Publishes ms an average of 4-6 months after acceptance. Byline given. Buys first serial rights, second serial (reprint) rights or one-time rights. Submit seasonal/holiday material 6 months in advance. Computer printout submissions acceptable; prefers letter-quality. Reports in 3 months. Free sample copy and writer's guidelines.

Nonfiction: Informational (articles on homelife that convey Christian teachings); inspirational; and personal experience. Buys 5 mss/issue. Send complete ms. Length: 500-2,000 words. Pays 5¢/word maximum. Sometimes pays the expenses of writers on assignment.

Photos: Photos purchased without accompanying ms. Pays $7.50-15 for 8x10 b&w glossy prints; $10-35 for 35mm or larger color transparencies. Total purchase price for ms includes payment for photos.

Poetry: Religious and inspirational. Buys 1 poem/issue. Submit maximum 6 poems. Pays 20-40¢/line.

Tips: "Break in by writing up a personal experience. We publish first-person articles concerning spiritual experiences; that is, answers to prayer for help in a particular situation, of unusual conversions or healings through faith in Christ. All articles submitted to us should be related to religious life. We are Protestant, evangelical, Pentecostal, and any doctrines or practices portrayed should be in harmony with the official position of our denomination (Assemblies of God)."

THE PENTECOSTAL MESSENGER, Messenger Publishing House, 4901 Pennsylvania, Box 850, Joplin MO 64802. (417)624-7050. Editor: Don Allen. Managing Editor: Peggy Lee Allen. 25% freelance written. Works with small number of new/unpublished writers each year. Monthly (excluding July) magazine covering Pentcostal Christianity. "*The Pentecostal Messenger* is the official organ of the Pentecostal Church of God. Goes to ministers and church members." Circ. 8,000. Pays on publication. Publishes ms an average of 6 months after acceptance. Byline given. Buys second serial (reprint) rights or simultaneous rights. Submit seasonal/holiday material 4 months in advance. Simultaneous, photocopied and previously published submissions OK. Computer printout submissions OK; prefers letter-quality. Reports in 4 weeks on mss. Sample copy for 9x12 SAE and 4 first class stamps; free writer's guidelines.
Nonfiction: Inspirational, personal experience and religious. Special issue includes Sunday School Enlargement (October). Buys 35 mss/year. Send complete ms. Length: 1,800 words. Pays 1½¢/word.
Photos: Send photos with submission. Reviews 2¼x2¼ transparencies and prints. Offers $10-25 per photo. Captions and model releases required. Buys one-time rights.
Tips: "Articles need to be inspirational, informative, written from a positive viewpoint, not extremely controversial."

PRESBYTERIAN RECORD, 50 Wynford Dr., Don Mills, Ontario M3C 1J7 Canada. (416)444-1111. FAX: (416)441-2825. 50% freelance written. Eager to work with new/unpublished writers. Monthly magazine for a church-oriented, family audience. Circ. 71,444. Buys 35 mss/year. Pays on publication. Publishes ms an average of 4 months after acceptance. Buys first serial rights, one-time rights, simultaneous rights. Submit seasonal material 3 months in advance. Computer printout submissions acceptable. Reports on ms accepted for publication in 2 months. Returns rejected material in 3 months. Sample copy and writer's guidelines for 9x12 SAE with $1 Canadian postage or IRCs.
Nonfiction: Material on religious themes. Check a copy of the magazine for style. Also, personal experience, interview, and inspirational material. No material solely or mainly American in context. When possible, black-and-white photos should accompany manuscript; i.e., current events, historical events and biographies. Buys 15-20 unsolicited mss/year. Query. Length: 1,000-2,000 words. Pays $45-55 (Canadian funds). Sometimes pays expenses of writers on assignment.
Photos: Pays $15-20 for b&w glossy photos. Uses positive color transparencies for cover. Pays $50. Captions required.
Tips: "There is a trend away from maudlin, first-person pieces redolent with tragedy and dripping with simplistic pietistic conclusions."

PURPOSE, 616 Walnut Ave., Scottdale PA 15683-1999. (412)887-8500. Editor: James E. Horsch. 95% freelance written. Weekly magazine "for adults, young and old, general audience with interests as varied as there are people. My readership is interested in seeing how Christianity works in difficult situations." Circ. 19,250. Pays on acceptance. Publishes ms an average of 8 months after acceptance. Byline given, including city, state/province. Buys one-time rights. Submit seasonal material 6 months in advance. Photocopied and simultaneous submissions OK. Computer printout submissions acceptable; prefers letter-quality. Submit complete ms. Reports in 6 weeks. Free sample copy and writer's guidelines for 6x9 SAE with 2 first class stamps.
Nonfiction: Inspirational articles from a Christian perspective. "I want stories that go to the core of human problems in family, business, politics, religion, sex and any other areas—and show how the Christian faith resolves them. I want material that's upbeat. *Purpose* is a story paper which conveys truth either through quality fiction or through articles that use the best story techniques. Our magazine accents Christian discipleship. Christianity affects all of life, and we expect our material to demonstrate this. I would like to see story-type articles about individuals, groups and organizations who are intelligently and effectively working at some of the great human problems such as overpopulation, hunger, poverty, international understanding, peace, justice, etc., because of their faith." Buys 175-200 mss/year. Submit complete ms. Length: 1,100 words maximum. Pays 5¢/word maximum.
Photos: Photos purchased with ms. Pays $5-25 for b&w, depending on quality. Must be sharp enough for reproduction; prefers prints in all cases. Can use color prints. Captions desired.
Fiction: Humorous, religious and historical fiction related to discipleship theme. "Produce the story with specificity so that it appears to take place somewhere and with real people. It should not be moralistic."
Poetry: Traditional poetry, blank verse, free verse and light verse. Length: 12 lines maximum. Pays 50¢-$1/line.
Fillers: Anecdotal items from 200-800 words. Pays 4¢/word maximum.
Tips: "We are looking for articles which show the Christian faith working at issues where people hurt; stories need to be told and presented professionally. Good photographs help place material with us."

QUEEN OF ALL HEARTS, Montfort Missionaries, 26 S. Saxon Ave., Bay Shore NY 11706. (516)665-0726. Managing Editor: Roger Charest, S.M.M. 50% freelance written. Bimonthly magazine covering Marian doctrine and devotion. "Subject: Mary, Mother of Jesus, as seen in the sacred scriptures, tradition, history of the church, the early Christian writers, lives of the saints, poetry, art, music, spiritual writers, apparitions, shrines, ecumenism, etc." Circ. approx 6,000. Pays on acceptance. Publishes ms an average of 6 months after acceptance. Byline given. Not copyrighted. Buys second serial (reprint) rights. Submit seasonal/holiday material 6 months in advance. Reports in 6 weeks. Sample copy $2.

Nonfiction: Essays, inspirational, personal experience and religious. Buys 25 ms/year. Send complete ms. Length: 750-2,500 words. Pays $40-60. Sometimes pays writers in contributor copies or other premiums "by mutual agreement. Poetry paid by contributor copies."

Photos: Send photos with submission. Reviews transparencies and prints. Offers variable payment per photo. Buys one-time rights.

Fiction: Religious. Buys 6 mss/year. Send complete ms. Length: 1,500-2,500 words. Pays $40-60.

Poetry: Poetry Editor: Joseph Tusiani. Free verse. Buys approximately 10 poems/year. Submit 2 poems maximum at one time. Pays in contributor copies.

REVIEW FOR RELIGIOUS, 3601 Lindell Blvd., Room 428, St. Louis MO 63108. (314)535-3048. Editor: David L. Fleming, S.J. 100% freelance written. "Each ms is judged on its own merits, without reference to author's publishing history." Bimonthly. For Roman Catholic priests, brothers and sisters. Pays on publication. Publishes ms an average of 9 months after acceptance. Byline given. Buys first North American serial rights and rarely second serial (reprint) rights. Computer printout submissions acceptable. Reports in 8 weeks.

Nonfiction: Articles on ascetical, liturgical and canonical matters only; not for general audience. Length: 2,000-8,000 words. Pays $6/page.

Tips: "The writer must know about religious life in the Catholic Church and be familiar with prayer, vows and problems related to them."

ST. ANTHONY MESSENGER, 1615 Republic St., Cincinnati OH 45210. Editor-in-Chief: Norman Perry. 55% freelance written. "Willing to work with new/unpublished writers if their writing is of a professional caliber." Monthly magazine for a national readership of Catholic families, most of which have children in grade school, high school or college. Circ. 390,000. Pays on acceptance. Publishes ms an average of 9 months after acceptance. Byline given. Buys first North American serial rights. Submit seasonal/holiday material 6 months in advance. Query for electronic submissions. Sample copy and writer's guidelines for 9x12 SASE.

Nonfiction: How-to (on psychological and spiritual growth, problems of parenting/better parenting, marriage problems/marriage enrichment); humor; informational; inspirational; interview; personal experience (if pertinent to our purpose); personal opinion (limited use; writer must have special qualifications for topic); and profile. Buys 35-50 mss/year. Length: 1,500-3,500 words. Pays 14¢/word. Sometimes pays the expenses of writers on assignment.

Fiction: Mainstream and religious. Buys 12 mss/year. Submit complete ms. Length: 2,000-3,500 words. Pays 14¢/word.

Tips: "The freelancer should ask why his or her proposed article would be appropriate for us, rather than for *Redbook* or *Saturday Review.* We treat human problems of all kinds, but from a religious perspective. Get authoritative information (not merely library research); we want interviews with experts. Write in popular style. Word length is an important consideration."

ST. JOSEPH'S MESSENGER & ADVOCATE OF THE BLIND, Sisters of St. Joseph of Peace, St. Joseph's Home, Box 288, Jersey City NJ 07303. Editor-in-Chief: Sister Ursula Maphet. 30% freelance written. Eager to work with new/unpublished writers. Quarterly magazine. Circ. 25,000. Pays on acceptance. Publishes ms an average of 3 months after acceptance. Buys first serial rights and second serial (reprint) rights, but will reassign rights back to author after publication asking only that credit line be included in next publication. Submit seasonal/holiday material 3 months in advance (no Christmas issue). Computer printout submissions OK; prefers letter-quality. Simultaneous and previously published submissions OK. Reports in 3 weeks. Sample copy and writer's guidelines 8½x11 SAE with 45¢ postage.

Nonfiction: Humor, inspirational, nostalgia, personal opinion and personal experience. Buys 24 mss/year. Submit complete ms. Length: 300-1,500 words. Pays $3-15.

Fiction: Romance, suspense, mainstream and religious. Buys 30 mss/year. Submit complete ms. Length: 600-1,600 words. Pays $6-25.

Poetry: Light verse and traditional. Buys 25 poems/year. Submit maximum 10 poems. Length: 50-300 words. Pays $5-20.

Tips: "It's rewarding to know that someone is waiting to see freelancers' efforts rewarded by 'print'. It's annoying, however, to receive poor copy, shallow material or inane submissions. Human interest fiction, touching on current happenings, is what is most needed. We look for social issues — woven into story form. We also seek non-preaching articles that carry a message that is positive."

SCP JOURNAL AND SCP Newsletter, Spiritual Counterfeits Project, Box 4308, Berkeley CA 94704. (415)540-0300. Editor: Robert J. L. Burrows. 5% freelance written. Prefers to work with published/established writers. "The *SCP Journal* and *SCP Newsletter* ares occasional publications that analyze new religious movements and spiritual trends from a Christian perspective. Their targeted audience is the educated lay person." Circ. 16,500. Pays on publication. Publishes ms an average of 6 months after acceptance. Byline given. Simultaneous and previously published submissions OK. Computer printout submissions acceptable. Sample copy for 8½x11 SAE and 4 first class stamps.

Nonfiction: Book excerpts, essays, exposé, interview/profile, opinion, personal experience and religious. Buys 10 mss/year. Query with published clips. Length: 2,500-3,500 words. Pays $20-35/typeset page.

Photos: State availability of photos with submission. Reviews contact sheets and prints. Offers no additional payment for photos accepted with ms. Captions, model releases and identification of subjects required. Buys one-time rights.

Tips: "The area of our publication most open to freelancers is reviews of books relevant to subjects covered by *SCP*. These should not exceed 6 typewritten, double-spaced pages, 1,500 words. Send samples of work that are relevant to the *SCP's* area of interest."

II CHRONICLES MAGAZINE, Box 42, Medford OR 97501. (503)664-3072. Editor: Mack Lloyd Lewis. 30% freelance written. A tabloid on contemporary Christian lifestyles, in Southern Oregon. "*II Chronicles Magazine* is a contemporary monthly Christian lifestyles magazine designed to encourage people in a relationship with Christ. We're most interested in work that ties in with our region." Circ. 5,000. Pays on publication. Publishes ms an average of 3 months after acceptance. Byline given. Buys one-time rights. Submit seasonal/holiday material 3 months in advance. Simultaneous and photocopied submissions OK. Computer printout submissions OK; prefers letter-quality. Reports quarterly on queries. Sample copy and writer's guidelines for 9x12 SAE and 4 first class stamps.

Nonfiction: Lloyd Neske, articles editor. Essays, general interest, historical/nostalgic, inspirational, interview/profile and religious. Buys 8 mss/year. Query with published clips. Length: 1,250-2,500 words. Pays $30-100. Sometimes pays in contributor copies for articles.

Fiction: Buck Ryehead, fiction editor. Adventure, historical, mainstream, religious and suspense. "Does not have to be 'religious' but it should be based upon biblical values." Buys 12 mss/year. Send complete ms. Length: 800-1,200 words. Pays $30.

Fillers: Anecdotes, cartoons facts, gags to be illustrated by cartoonist, newsbreaks and short humor. Buys 12/year. Length: 25-150 words. Pays with $5, byline and copies.

Tips: "Freelancers can best begin by writing to us. Nonfiction topics are usually assigned to those we know. Fiction writers can best begin simply through submitting their work. We're always looking for good Christian fiction. Historical articles on Biblical times with a unique slant are of interest to us. Unique slants in general will always help one's chances. We're known for being different."

SEEK, Standard Publishing, 8121 Hamilton Ave., Cincinnati OH 45231. (513)931-4050, ext. 365. Editor: Eileen H. Wilmoth. 98% freelance written. Prefers to work with published/established writers; works with a small number of new/unpublished writers each year. Sunday school paper. Quarterly, in weekly issues for young and middle-aged adults who attend church and Bible classes. Circ. 45,000. Pays on acceptance. Publishes ms an average of 1 year after acceptance. Byline given. Buys first serial rights and second serial (reprint) rights. Buys 100-150 mss/year. Submit seasonal material 1 year in advance. Computer printout submissions acceptable; prefers letter-quality. Reports in 6 weeks. Sample copy and writer's guidelines for 6x9 SAE and 2 first class stamps.

Nonfiction: "We look for articles that are warm, inspirational, devotional, of personal or human interest; that deal with controversial matters, timely issues of religious, ethical or moral nature, or first-person testimonies, true-to-life happenings, vignettes, emotional situations or problems; communication problems and examples of answered prayers. Article must deliver its point in a convincing manner but not be patronizing or preachy. They must appeal to either men or women, must be alive, vibrant, sparkling and have a title that demands the article be read. We always need stories of families, marriages, problems on campus and life testimonies." No poetry. Buys 100-150 mss/year. Submit complete ms. Length: 400-1,200 words. Pays 3¢/word.

Photos: B&w photos purchased with or without mss. Pays $20 minimum for good 8x10 glossy prints.

Fiction: Religious fiction and religiously slanted historical and humorous fiction. Length: 400-1,200 words. Pays 3¢/word.

Tips: Submit mss which tell of faith in action or victorious Christian living as central theme. "We select manuscripts as far as one year in advance of publication. Complimentary copies are sent to our published writers immediately following printing."

SHARING THE VICTORY, Fellowship of Christian Athletes, 8701 Leeds Rd., Kansas City MO 64129. (816)921-0909. Editor: Skip Stogsdill. Managing Editor: Don Hilkemeir. 60% freelance written. Prefers to work with published/established writers, but works with a growing number of new/unpublished writers each year. A bimonthly magazine. "We seek to encourage and enable athletes and coaches at all levels to take their faith seriously on and off the 'field.' " Circ. 50,000. Pays on publication. Publishes ms an average of 4 months after acceptance. Byline given. Buys first rights. Submit seasonal/holiday material 3 months in advance. Computer printout submissions acceptable; prefers letter-quality. Reports in 1 week on queries; 2 weeks on manuscripts. Sample copy $1 with 9x12 SAE and 3 first class stamps; free writer's guidelines for #10 SASE.

Nonfiction: Humor, inspirational, interview/profile (with "name" athletes and coaches solid in their faith), personal experience, and photo feature. No "sappy articles on 'I became a Christian and now I'm a winner.' " Buys 5-20 mss/year. Query. Length: 500-1,000 words. Pays $100-200 for unsolicited articles, more for the exceptional profile.
Photos: State availability of photos with submission. Reviews contact sheets. Pay depends on quality of photo but usually a minimum $75. Model releases required for "name" individuals. Buys one-time rights.
Columns/Departments: Sports Conscience (deals with a problem issue in athletics today and some possible solutions or alternatives). Buys 4 mss/year. Query. Length: 700-1,200 words. Pays $100 minimum.
Poetry: Free verse. Buys 3 poems/year. Pays $50.
Tips: "Profiles and interviews of particular interest to coed athlete primarily high school and college age. We have redesigned our graphics and editorial content to appeal to youth. The area most open to freelancers is profiles on or interviews with well-known athletes or coaches (male, female, minorities or of offbeat but interscholastic team sports)."

SIGNS OF THE TIMES, Pacific Press Publishing Association, Box 7000, Boise ID 83707. (208)465-2500. FAX: (208)465-2531. Editor: Kenneth J. Holland. Managing Editor: B. Russell Holt. 40% freelance written. Works with a small number of new/unpublished writers each year. Monthly magazine on religion. "We are a Christian publication encouraging the general public to put into practice the principles of the Bible." Circ. 400,000. Pays on acceptance. Publishes ms an average of 5 months after acceptance. Byline given. Offers $100 kill fee. Buys first North American serial rights and simultaneous rights. Submit seasonal/holiday material 8 months in advance. Simultaneous queries and submissions, and photocopied and previously published submissions OK. Computer printout submissions acceptable; prefers letter-quality. Reports in 2 weeks on queries; 1 month on mss. Free sample copy and writer's guidelines.
Nonfiction: General interest (home, marriage, health – interpret current events from a Biblical perspective); how-to (overcome depression, find one's identity, answer loneliness and guilt, face death triumphantly); humor; inspirational (human interest pieces that highlight a Biblical principle); interview/profile; personal experience (overcome problems with God's help); and photo feature. "We want writers with a desire to share the good news of reconciliation with God. Articles should be people-oriented, well-researched and should have a sharp focus and include anecdotes." Buys 150 mss/year. Query with or without published clips, or send complete ms. Length: 500-3,000 words. Pays $100-400. Sometimes pays the expenses of writers on assignment.
Photos: Ed Guthero, photo editor. Send photos with query or ms. Reviews b&w contact sheets; 35mm color transparencies; 5x7 or 8x10 b&w prints. Pays $35-300 for transparencies; $20-50 for prints. Model releases and identification of subjects required (captions helpful). Buys one-time rights.
Tips: "One of the most frequent mistakes made by writers in completing an article assignment for us is trying to cover too much ground. Articles need focus, research and anecdotes. We don't want essays."

SISTERS TODAY, The Liturgical Press, St. John's Abbey, Collegeville MN 56321. Editor-in-Chief: Sister Mary Anthony Wagner, O.S.B. Associate Editor: Sister Andre Marthaler, O.S.B. Review Editor: Sister Stefanie Weisgram, O.S.B. 80% freelance written. Prefers to work with published/established writers; works with a small number of new/unpublished writers each year. Magazine, beginning with January 1990, will be published bimonthly, for women of the Roman Catholic Church, primarily. Circ. 9,000. Pays on publication. Publishes ms 1-2 years after acceptance. Byline given. Buys first rights. Submit seasonal/holiday material 4 months in advance. Computer printout submissions acceptable; no dot-matrix. Reports in 3 months. Sample copy $1.50.
Nonfiction: How-to (pray, live in a religious community, exercise faith, hope, charity etc.); informational; and inspirational. Also articles concerning religious renewal, community life, worship, and the role of sisters in the Church and in the world today. Buys 50-60 unsolicited mss/year. Query. Length: 500-2,500 words. Pays $5/printed page.
Poetry: Free verse, haiku, light verse and traditional. Buys 3 poems/issue. Submit maximum 4 poems. Pays $10.
Tips: "Some of the freelance material evidences the lack of familiarity with *Sisters Today*. We would prefer submitted articles not to exceed eight or nine pages."

SOCIAL JUSTICE REVIEW, 3835 Westminister Place, St. Louis MO 63108. (314)371-1653. Contact: editor. 25% freelance written. Works with a small number of new/unpublished writers each year. Bimonthly. Publishes ms an average of 3 months after acceptance. Not copyrighted; "however special articles within the magazine may be copyrighted, or an occasional special issue has been copyrighted due to author's request." Buys first serial rights. Computer printout submissions acceptable; prefers letter-quality.
Nonfiction: Wants scholarly articles on society's economic, religious, social, intellectual and political problems with the aim of bringing Catholic social thinking to bear upon these problems. Query. Length: 2,500-3,500 words. Pays about 2¢/word.

SONLIGHT/SUN, (formerly *Soloing and Sonlight*), Christian newspaper, 4118 10th Ave., N. Lake Worth FL 33461. (407)439-3509. Editor/Publisher: Dennis Lombard. Managing Editor: Dave Van Way. 50-75% freelance written. Eager to work with new/unpublished writers. Monthly tabloids distributed free to churches and the public, geared to all denominations. Circ. 10,000. Pays on publication. Publishes ms an average of 2 months after acceptance. Byline given. Buys first North American serial rights, one-time rights, second serial (reprint) rights, or simultaneous rights, and makes work-for-hire assignments (locally). Submit seasonal/holiday material 2 months in advance. Simultaneous, photocopied, or previously published submissions OK. Computer printout submissions acceptable; prefers letter-quality. Reports in 2 weeks. Sample copies $1 with 9x12 SAE; writer's guidelines for #10 SASE.

Nonfiction: Books excerpts and reviews; essays; (or "Op-Ed" pieces on Christian issues); general interest (Christian subjects); how-to; humor; inspirational; interview/profile; opinion; personal experience; photo feature; and religious. "All require inter-denominational, non-doctrinal viewpoint." No critical attitudes. Buys 50 mss/year. Send complete ms only. Length: 500-1,200 words. Pays $25-75 for assigned articles; pays $15-35 for unsolicited articles. Sometimes pays expenses of writers on assignment.

Photos: Send photos with submission. Reviews 4x5 b&w glossy prints. Offers $3-5/photo. Captions, model releases and identification of subjects required. Buys one-time rights.

Fiction: Now buying humorous, religious, romance. Must have Christian perspective, but should not be preachy. Send complete ms. Length: 500-1,500 words.

Poetry: Light verse and traditional. Buys 3-5 poems/year. Submit maximum 3 poems. Length: 4-20 lines. Pays $5. Nothing too abstract or overly sentimental.

Tips: "We will be buying much more as our newspapers expand. We re-launched *Sonlight*, a general Christian newspaper for all denominations in 1988. We will be buying twice as much this year—and we encourage new writers. We also have launched another new paper called *The New Sun*, a "kingdom view" community newspaper which buys dozens of articles weekly from syndicates, freelancers, local writers on assignment, etc. Must see to know what to submit. Send additional $1 for *Sun* sample. We would like to receive testimonies, how-to for Christians (singles too) essays, and humor in the Christian life. New writers are welcome. How-to and personal experience articles are most open to freelancers. Testimonial articles should include an informal b&w photo of subject and subject's signed release. We're looking for the light and inspirational side. Send for samples and guidelines."

‡**SPIRIT, Lectionary-based Weekly for Catholic Teens**, Editorial Development Associates, 1884 Randolph Ave., St. Paul MN 55434. (612)690-7005. Editor: Joan Mitchell, CSJ. Managing Editor: Therese Sherlock, CSJ. 50% freelance written. Weekly newsletter for religious education of high schoolers. "We want realistic fiction and nonfiction that raises current ethical and religious questions and conflicts in multi-racial contexts." Estab. 1988. Circ. 13,000. Pays on publication. Publishes ms an average of 6 months after acceptance. Byline given. Buys all rights. Submit seasonal/holiday material 4-6 months in advance. Simultaneous submissions OK. Computer printout submissions OK. Reports in 2 weeks on queries; 6 weeks on mss. Free sample copy and writer's guidelines.

Nonfiction: Interview/profile, personal experience, photo feature (homelessness, illiteracy), religious, Roman Catholic leaders, human interest features, social justice leaders, projects, humanitarians. "No Christian confessional pieces." Buys 12 mss/year. Query. Length: 1,100-1,200 words. Pays $100-135 for assigned articles; $75-135 for unsolicited articles.

Photos: State availability of photos with submission. Reviews contact sheets, transparencies and prints. Offers $15-25 per photo. Identification of subjects required. Buys one-time rights.

Fiction: Fantasy and slice-of-life vignettes. "We want realistic pieces for and about teens—nonpedantic, nonpious." Buys 12 mss/year. Query. Length: 1,100-1,200 words. Pays $100-135.

Tips: "Query to receive call for stories, spec sheet, sample issues."

SPIRITUAL LIFE, 2131 Lincoln Rd. NE, Washington DC 20002. (202)832-6622. Editor: Rev. Steven Payne, O.C.D. 80% freelance written. Prefers to work with published/established writers; works with a small number of new/unpublished writers each year. Quarterly. "Largely Catholic, well-educated, serious readers. A few are nonCatholic or nonChristian." Circ. 17,000. Pays on acceptance. Publishes ms an average of 1 year after acceptance. Buys first North American serial rights. "Brief autobiographical information (present occupation, past occupations, books and articles published, etc.) should accompany article." Computer printout submissions OK; prefers letter-quality. Reports in 1 month. Sample copy and writer's guidelines for SASE (9x6 or larger) with 4 first class stamps.

Nonfiction: Serious articles of contemporary spirituality. High quality articles about our encounter with God in the present day world. Language of articles should be college level. Technical terminology, if used, should be clearly explained. Material should be presented in a positive manner. Sentimental articles or those dealing with specific devotional practices not accepted. Buys inspirational and think pieces. No fiction or poetry. Buys 20 mss/year. Length: 3,000-5,000 words. Pays $50 minimum. "Five contributor's copies are sent to author on publication of article." Book reviews should be sent to Rev. Steven Payne, O.C.D.

‡**STANDARD**, Nazarene International Headquarters, 6401 The Paseo, Kansas City MO 64131. (816)333-7000, ext. 555. Editor: Beth A. Fisher. 95% freelance written. Works with a small number of new/unpublished writers each year. Weekly inspirational paper with Christian reading for adults. Circ. 177,000. Pays on acceptance. Publishes ms an average of 15 months after acceptance. Byline given. Buys one-time rights and second

serial (reprint) rights. Submit seasonal/holiday material 10 months in advance. Computer printout submissions acceptable; prefers letter-quality to dot-matrix. Reports in 6 weeks. Free sample copy; writer's guidelines for SAE with 2 first class stamps.

Nonfiction: How-to (grow spiritually); inspirational; social issues; and personal experience (with an emphasis on spiritual growth). Buys 100 mss/year. Send complete ms. Length: 300-1,500 words. Pays 3½¢/word for first rights; 2¢/word for reprint rights.

Photos: Pays $25-45 for 8x10 b&w prints. Buys one-time rights. Accepts photos with ms.

Fiction: Adventure, religious, romance and suspense—all with a spiritual emphasis. Buys 100 mss/year. Send complete ms. Length: 500-1,500 words. Pays 3½¢/word for first rights; 2¢/word for reprint rights.

Poetry: Free verse, haiku, light verse and traditional. Buys 50 poems/year. Submit maximum 5 poems. Length: 50 lines maximum. Pays 25¢/line.

Fillers: Jokes, anecdotes and short humor. Buys 52/year. Length: 300 words maximum. Pays same as nonfiction and fiction.

Tips: "Articles should express Biblical principles without being preachy. Setting, plot and characterization must be realistic. Fiction articles should be labeled 'Fiction' on the manuscript. True experience articles may be first person, 'as told to,' or third person."

SUNDAY DIGEST, David C. Cook Publishing Co., 850 N. Grove Ave., Elgin IL 60120. Editor: Janette L. Pearson. 75% freelance written. Prefers to work with established writers. Issued weekly to Christian adults in Sunday School. "*Sunday Digest* provides a combination of original articles and reprints, selected to help adult readers better understand the Christian faith, to keep them informed of issues within the Christian community, and to challenge them to a deeper personal commitment to Christ." Pays on acceptance. Publishes ms an average of 1 year after acceptance. Buys first or reprint rights. Computer printout submissions acceptable; no dot-matrix. Reports in 2 months. Sample copy and writer's guidelines for 6½x9½ SAE with 2 first class stamps.

Nonfiction: Needs articles applying the Christian faith to personal and social problems, articles on family life and church relationships, inspirational self-help, personal experience; how-to and interview articles preferred over fiction. Submit a detailed query letter including the article's introduction. Length: 400-1,700 words. Pays $40-180.

Tips: "It is crucial that the writer is committed to quality Christian communication with a crisp, clear writing style. Christian message should be woven in, not tacked on."

SUNDAY SCHOOL COUNSELOR, General Council of the Assemblies of God, 1445 Boonville, Springfield MO 65802. (417)862-2781. Editor: Sylvia Lee. 60% freelance written. Works with small number of new/unpublished writers each year. Monthly magazine on religious education in the local church—the official Sunday school voice of the Assemblies of God channeling programs and help to local, primarily lay, leadership. Circ. 35,000. Pays on acceptance. Publishes ms an average of 9 months after acceptance. Byline given. Offers variable kill fee. Buys first North American serial rights, one-time rights, all rights, simultaneous rights, first serial rights, or second serial (reprint) rights; makes work-for-hire assignments. Submit seasonal/holiday material 7 months in advance. Simultaneous and previously published submissions OK. Computer printout submissions acceptable; prefers letter-quality. Reports in 2 weeks on queries; 1 month on mss. Free sample copy and writer's guidelines for SASE.

Nonfiction: How-to, inspirational, interview/profile, personal experience and photo feature. All related to religious education in the local church. Buys 100 mss/year. Send complete ms. Length: 300-1,800 words. Pays $25-90. Sometimes pays expenses of writers on assignment.

Photos: Send photos with ms. Reviews b&w and color prints. Model releases and identification of subjects required. Buys one-time rights.

TEACHERS INTERACTION, A Magazine Church School Workers Grow By, Concordia Publishing House, 3558 S. Jefferson, St. Louis MO 63118. Mail submissions to LCMS, 1333 S. Kirkwood Rd., St. Louis MO 63122-7295. Editor: Martha Streufert Jander. 20% freelance written. Quarterly magazine (newsletter seven times/year) of practical, inspirational, theological articles for volunteer church school teachers. Material must be true to the doctrines of the Lutheran Church—Missouri Synod. Circ. 20,400. Pays on acceptance. Publishes ms an average of 1 year after acceptance. Byline given. Buys all rights. Submit seasonal/holiday material 7 months in advance. Query for electronic submissions. Computer printout submissions acceptable; prefers letter-quality. Reports in 1 month on queries; 2 months on mss. Sample copy $1; writer's guidelines for 9x12 SAE (with sample copy); for #10 SAE (without sample copy).

Nonfiction: How-to (practical helps/ideas used successfully in own classroom); inspirational (to the church school worker—must be in accordance with LCMS doctrine); and personal experience (of a Sunday school classroom nature—growth). No theological articles. Buys 6 mss/year. Send complete ms. Length: 750-1,500 words. Pays $35.

Fillers: Cartoons. Buys 14/year. *"Teachers Interaction* buys short items – activities and ideas planned and used successfully in a church school classroom." Buys 50/year. Length: 100 words maximum. Pays $10.
Tips: "Practical, or 'it happened to me' experiences articles would have the best chance. Also short items – ideas used in classrooms; seasonal and in conjunction with our Sunday school material; Our Life in Christ. Our format includes all volunteer church school teachers, not just Sunday school teachers."

THE UNITED CHURCH OBSERVER, 85 St. Clair Ave. E., Toronto, Ontario M4T 1M8 Canada. (416)960-8500. Publisher and Editor: Hugh McCullum. Managing Editor: Muriel Duncan. 40% freelance written. Prefers to work with published/established writers. A 60-page monthly newsmagazine for people associated with The United Church of Canada. Deals primarily with events, trends and policies having religious significance. Most coverage is Canadian, but reports on international or world concerns will be considered. Pays on publication. Publishes ms an average of 4 months after acceptance. Byline usually given. Buys first serial rights and occasionally all rights. Computer printout submissions acceptable; no dot-matrix.
Nonfiction: Occasional opinion features only. Extended coverage of major issues usually assigned to known writers. No opinion pieces, poetry. Submissions should be written as news, no more than 1,200 words length, accurate and well-researched. Queries preferred. Rates depend on subject, author and work involved. Pays expenses of writers on assignment "as negotiated."
Photos: Buys photographs with mss. B&w should be 5x7 minimum; color 35mm or larger format. Payment varies.
Tips: "The writer has a better chance of breaking in at our publication with short articles; it also allows us to try more freelancers. Include samples of previous *news* writing with query. Indicate ability and willingness to do research, and to evaluate that research. The most frequent mistakes made by writers in completing an article for us are organizational problems, lack of polished style, short on research, and a lack of inclusive language."

UNITED EVANGELICAL ACTION, Box 28, Wheaton IL 60189. (312)665-0500. Editor: Donald R. Brown. Managing Editor: Brad Davis. 50% freelance written. Prefers to work with published/established writers. Bimonthly magazine. Offers "an objective evangelical viewpoint and interpretive analysis of specific issues of consequence and concern to the American Church and updates readers on ways evangelicals are confronting those issues at the grass roots level." Circ. 10,500. Pays on publication. Publishes ms an average of 2 months after acceptance. Buys first serial rights. Phone queries OK. Query for electronic submissions. Computer printout submissions acceptable; prefers letter-quality. Reports in 1 month. Sample copy for 9x12 SAE with 85¢ postage; writer's guidelines with #10 SASE.
Nonfiction: Issues and trends in the Church and society that affect the ongoing witness and outreach of evangelical Christians. Content should be well thought through, and should provide practical suggestions for dealing with these issues and trends. Buys 8-10 mss/year. "Always send a query letter before sending an unsolicited manuscript." Length: 900-1,000 words. Pays $50-175. Sometimes pays expenses of writers on assignment.
Tips: Editors would really like to see news (action) items that relate to the National Association of Evangelicals. "We are interested in expanding coverage of NAE activities throughout the country. Send query letter about important topics facing evangelicals or news features about local works by evangelicals. Keep writing terse, to the point, and stress practical over theoretical."

UNITED METHODIST REPORTER, Box 660275, Dallas TX 75266-0275. (214)630-6495. Editor/General Manager: Spurgeon M. Dunnam, III. Managing Editor: John A. Lovelace. Weekly newspaper for a United Methodist national readership. Circ. 475,000. Pays on publication. Byline given. Not copyrighted. Free sample copy and writer's guidelines.
Nonfiction: "We accept occasional short features, approximately 500 words. Articles need not be limited to a United Methodist angle but need to have an explicit Protestant angle, preferably with evidence of participation in a local congregation. Write about a distinctly Christian response to human need or how a person's faith relates to a given situation." Send complete ms. Pays 4¢/word.
Photos: Purchased with accompanying ms. "We encourage the submission of good action photos (5x7 or 8x10 b&w glossy prints) of the persons or situations in the article." Pays $10.

‡UNITY MAGAZINE, Unity School of Christianity, Unity Village MO 65065. (816)524-3550. Editor: Philip White. 90% freelance written. Monthly magazine on the metaphysical. Circ. 500,000. Pays on acceptance. Publishes ms an average of 7 months after acceptance. Byline given. Buys first North American serial rights. Submit seasonal/holiday material 6-7 months in advance. Computer printout submissions OK; prefers letter-quality. Reports in 3 weeks on queries; 2 months on mss. Free sample copy and writer's guidelines.
Nonfiction: Inspirational, personal experience, religious. Buys 200 mss/year. Send complete ms. Length: 2,000 words. Pays $15/page.
Photos: State availability of photos with submission. Reviews transparencies and prints. Offers $35-200/photo. Model release and identification of subjects required. Buys one-time rights.
Poetry: "Any type fitting magazine." Buys 100 poems/year. Submit maximum 10 poems. Length: 30 lines maximum. Pays $20 minimum.

THE UPPER ROOM, DAILY DEVOTIONAL GUIDE, The Upper Room, 1908 Grand Ave., Nashville TN 37202. (615)340-7250. FAX: (615)340-7006. World Editor: Janice T. Grana. Managing Editor: Mary Lou Redding. 95% freelance written. Eager to work with new/unpublished writers. Bimonthly magazine "offering a daily inspirational message which includes a Bible reading, text, prayer, 'Thought for the Day,' and suggestion for prayer. Each day's meditation is written by a different person and is usually a personal witness about discovering meaning and power for Christian living through some experience from daily life." Circ. 2.2 million (U.S.); 385,000 outside U.S. Pays on publication. Publishes ms an average of 1 year after acceptance. Byline given. Buys first North American serial rights and translation rights. Submit seasonal/holiday material 14 months in advance. Computer printout submissions acceptable; prefers letter-quality. Reports in 6 weeks on mss. Sample copy and writer's guidelines for SAE and 2 first class stamps.
Nonfiction: Inspirational and personal experience. No poetry, lengthy "spiritual journey" stories. Buys 360 unsolicited mss/year. Send complete ms. Length: 250 words maximum. Pays $12.
Tips: "The best way to break into our magazine is to send a well-written manuscript that looks at the Christian faith in a fresh way. Standard stories and sermon illustrations are immediately rejected. We very much want to find new writers and welcome good material. We are particularly interested in meditations based on Old Testament characters and stories. Good repeat meditations can lead to work on longer assignments for our other publications, which pay more. A writer who can deal concretely with everyday situations, relate them to spiritual truths, and write clear, direct prose should be able to write for *The Upper Room*. We want material that provides for more interaction on the part of the reader — meditation suggestions, journaling suggestions, space to reflect and link personal experience with the meditation for the day."

‡VENTURE AND VISIONS, Lectionary-based weeklies for Catholic youth, Pflaum/Editorial Development Associates, 1884 Randolph Ave., St. Paul MN 55105. (612)690-7010. Editor: Joan Mitchell,CSJ. Managing Editor: Therese Sherlock, CSJ. 40% freelance written. Weekly newsletter on religious education for intermediate and junior high students. "We want realistic fiction and nonfiction that raises current ethical and religious questions and conflicts in multiracial contexts to which intermediate and junior high youth can relate." Circ. 140,000. Pays on publication. Byline given. Publishes ms an average of 6 months after acceptance. Buys all rights. Submit seasonal/holiday material 4-6 months in advance. Simultaneous submissions OK. Computer printout submissions OK; prefers letter-quality. Reports in 2 weeks on queries; 2 months on mss. Free sample copy. Writer's guidelines for #10 SASE.
Nonfiction: Marianne W. Nold. General interest (human interest features), interview/profile, personal experience, photo feature (students in other countries), religious, Roman Catholic leaders, humanitarians and social justice projects. "No Christian confessional pieces." Buys 14 mss/year. Query. Length: 900-1,100 words. Pays $100-125 for assigned articles; $75-125 for unsolicited articles.
Photos: State availability of photos with submission. Reviews contact sheets, transparencies and prints. Offers $15-50 per photo. Identification of subjects required. Buys one-time rights.
Fiction: Fantasy, religious and slice-of-life-vignettes. "No 'Christian'. We want realistic pieces for and about intermediate and junior-high aged students — non-pedantic, non-pious." Buys 30-40 mss/year. Query. Length: 900-1,100 words. Pays $100-125.
Tips: "Query to receive call for stories, spec sheet, sample issues."

VIRTUE, The Christian Magazine for Women, 548 Sisters Pkwy, Box 850, Sisters OR 97759. (503)549-8261. Editor: Becky Durost Fish. Managing Editor: Ruth Nygren Keller. 75% freelance written. Works with small number of new/unpublished writers each year. Bimonthly magazine that "encourages women in their development as individuals and provides practical help for them as they minister to their families, churches and communities." Circ. 130,000. Pays on acceptance. Publishes ms an average of 4 months after acceptance. Byline given. Buys first North American serial rights. Submit seasonal/holiday material 9 months in advance. Photocopied submissions OK. Computer printout submissions OK; prefers letter-quality. Reports in 6 weeks on queries; 2 months on mss. Sample copy $3; writer's guidelines for #10 SASE.
Nonfiction: Book excerpts, how-to, humor, inspirational, interview/profile, opinion, personal experience and religious. Buys 70 mss/year. Query. Length: 600-1,800 words. Pays 10¢/word. Sometimes pays the expenses of writers on assignment.
Photos: State availability of photos with submission.
Columns/Departments: In My Opinion (reader editorial); One Woman's Journal (personal experience); Equipped for Ministry (practical how-to for helping others). Buys 25 mss/year. Query. Length: 1,000-1,500. Pays 10¢/word.
Fiction: Fantasy, humorous and religious. Buys 4-6 mss/year. Send complete ms. Length: 1,500-1,800 words. Pays 10¢/word.
Poetry: Free verse, haiku and traditional. Buys 7-10 poems/year. Submit maximum 3 poems. Length: 3-30 lines. Pays $15-50.

VISTA, Wesleyan Publishing House, Box 50434, Indianapolis IN 46250-0434. Editor: Rebecca Higgins. 80% freelance written. Eager to work with new/unpublished writers — "quality writing a must, however." Weekly publication of The Wesleyan Church for adults. Circ. 60,000. Pays on acceptance. Publishes ms an average of 10 months after acceptance. Byline given. Not copyrighted. Buys first rights, simultaneous rights, second rights and reprint rights. Submit seasonal/holiday material 10 months in advance. Computer printout submissions acceptable; prefers letter-quality. Reports in 2 months. Sample copy for 9x12 SAE with 45¢ postage. Writer's guidelines for #10 SASE.

Nonfiction: Testimonies, how-to's, humor, interviews, opinion pieces from conservative Christian perspective. Length: 500-1,200 words.

Photos: Pays $15-40 for 5x7 or 8x10 b&w glossy print natural-looking close-ups of faces in various emotions, groups of people interacting. Various reader age groups should be considered.

Fiction: Believable, quality articles, no Sunday "soaps." Length: 500-1,200 words. Pays 2-4¢/word.

Tips: "Read the writer's guide carefully before submitting."

VITAL CHRISTIANITY, Warner Press, Inc., 1200 E. 5th St., Anderson IN 46018. (317)644-7721. Editor-in-Chief: Arlo F. Newell. Managing Editor: Richard L. Willowby. 20-25% freelance written. Prefers to work with published/established writers; works with small number of new/unpublished writers each year. Monthly magazine covering Christian living for people attending local Church of God congregations. Circ. 26,000. Pays on acceptance. Byline given. Offers kill fee. Buys one-time rights. Submit seasonal/holiday material 6 months in advance. Query for electronic submissions. Computer printout submissions OK; no dot-matrix. Reports in 6 weeks. Sample copy and writer's guidelines for SASE and $1.

Nonfiction: Humor (with religious point); inspirational (religious—not preachy); interview/profile (of church-related personalities); opinion (religious/theological); and personal experience (related to putting one's faith into practice). Buys 125 mss/year. Query. Length: 1,000 words maximum. Pays $10-100.

Photos: State availability of photos. Pays $50-300 for 5x7 color transparencies; $20-40 for 8x10 b&w prints. Identification of subjects (when related directly to articles) required. Buys one-time rights. Reserves the right to reprint material it has used for advertising and editorial purposes (pays second rights for editorial re-use).

Fiction: Fiction with a religious message. "It should show reality from a Christian point of view."

Tips: "Fillers, personal experience, personality interviews, profiles and good holiday articles are areas of our magazine open to freelancers. Writers should request our guidelines and list of upcoming topics of interest to determine if they have interest or expertise in writing for us. Always send SASE."

WAR CRY, The Official Organ of the Salvation Army, 799 Bloomfield Ave., Verona NJ 07044. Editor: Henry Gariepy. 10% freelance written. Prefers to work with published/established writers. Biweekly magazine for "persons with evangelical Christian background; members and friends of the Salvation Army; the 'man in the street.'" Circ. 450,000. Pays on acceptance. Publishes ms an average of 8 months after acceptance. Buys first serial rights and second serial (reprint) rights. Computer printout submissions OK; no dot-matrix. Reports in 2 months. Sample copy and guidelines for 9x12 SAE and 65¢ postage.

Nonfiction: Inspirational and informational articles with a strong evangelical Christian slant, but not preachy. In addition to general articles, needs articles slanted toward most of the holidays including Easter, Christmas, Mother's Day, Father's Day, etc. Buys 12 mss/year. Length: approximately 700-1,400 words. Pays 10¢/word.

Photos: Pays $25-35 for b&w glossy prints; $150 for color prints.

THE WESLEYAN ADVOCATE, The Wesleyan Publishing House, Box 50434, Indianapolis IN 46250-0434. (317)576-1313. FAX: (317)841-7147. Editor: Dr. Wayne E. Caldwell. 10% freelance written. A biweekly magazine by the Wesleyan Church. Circ. 20,000. Pays on publication. Publishes ms an average of 1 year after acceptance. Byline given. Buys first rights or simultaneous rights. Submit seasonal/holiday material 1 year in advance. Simultaneous submissions OK. Query for electronic submissions. Computer printout submission OK; prefers letter-quality. Reports in 2 weeks. Sample copy for $1; writer's guidelines for #10 SASE.

Nonfiction: Humor, inspirational and religious. Buys 5 mss/year. Send complete ms. Length: 250-650 words. Pays $10-40 for assigned articles; $5-25 for unsolicited articles.

Photos: Send photos with submission. Reviews color transparencies. Buys one-time rights.

Tips: "Write for a guide."

‡WOMAN'S TOUCH, Assemblies of God Women's Ministries Department (GPH), 1445 Boonville, Springfield MO 65802. (417)862-2781. Editor: Sandra Goodwin Clopine. Associate Editor: Aleda Swartzendruber. 75-90% freelance written. Eager to work with new/unpublished writers. A bimonthly inspirational magazine for women. "Articles and contents of the magazine should be compatible with Christian teachings as well as human interests. The audience is women, both homemakers and those who are career-oriented." Circ. 21,000. Pays on acceptance. Byline given. Buys one-time rights. Submit seasonal/holiday material 8 months in advance. Photocopied and previously published submissions OK. Computer printout submissions OK; prefers letter-quality to dot-matrix. Reports in 6 weeks. Sample copy 9½x11 SAE with 85¢ postage; writer's guidelines for #10 SASE.

Nonfiction: General interest, how-to, inspirational, personal experience, religious and travel. Buys 100 mss/year. Send complete ms. Length: 800-1,000 words. Pays $10-35 for unsolicited articles.
Photos: State availability of photos with submission. Reviews negatives, transparencies and 4x6 prints. Offers no additional payment for photos accepted with ms. Identification of subjects required. Buys one-time rights.
Columns/Departments: An Added Touch (special crafts, holiday decorations, family activities); A Personal Touch (articles relating to personal development such as fashion accents, skin care, exercises, etc.). "We've added 'A Lite Touch' for short human interest articles – home and family or career-oriented." Buys 15 mss/year. Query with published clips. Length: 500-1,000 words. Pays $20-35.
Poetry: Free verse, light verse and traditional. Buys 20 poems/year. Submit maximum 6-8 poems. Length: 4-50 lines. Pays $5-20.
Fillers: Facts. Buys 10/year. Length: 50-200. Pays $5-15.

Retirement

Retirement magazines have changed to meet the active lifestyles of their readers and dislike the kinds of stereotypes people have of retirement magazines. More people are retiring in their 50s, while others are starting a business or traveling and pursuing hobbies. These publications give readers specialized information on health and fitness, medical research, finances and other topics of interest, as well as general articles on travel destinations and recreational activities.

During the past year, a number of new "maturity" publications have started publication. Many are regional titles, but a number are national. Many of these publications, including *New Choices* and the nostalgic *Memories*, do not accept freelance submissions. As Madison Avenue takes notice of the buying power of the mature market, experts say more magazines in this category will be supported by advertisers.

GOLDEN YEARS MAGAZINE, Golden Years Senior News, Inc., 233 E. New Haven Ave., Melbourne FL 32902-0537. (407)725-4888. FAX: (407)724-0736. Editor: Carol Brenner Hittner. 50% freelance written. Prefers to work with published/established writers. Bimonthly national magazine covering the needs and interests of our fastest growing generation. Editorial presented in a positive, uplifting, straightforward manner." Circ. 400,000. Pays on publication. Publishes ms an average of 7 months after acceptance. Byline given. Buys first serial rights and first North American serial rights. Submit seasonal/holiday material 1 year in advance. Simultaneous queries and photocopied submissions OK. Computer printout submissions acceptable; no dot-matrix. SASE for return of ms *required* for acceptance. Sample copy for 9x12 SAE and $2; writer's guidelines for #10 SASE.
Nonfiction: Profile (senior celebrities), travel, second careers, hobbies, retirement ideas and real estate. Limited need for poetry and cartoons. Nostalgia articles generally not accepted. Buys 100 mss/year. Query with published clips or send complete ms. Length: 500 words maximum. Pays 70¢/standard one-third-column line.
Photos: "We like to include a lot of photos." Send photos with query or ms. Pays $25 for color transparencies. Captions, model releases, and identification of subjects required. Buys one-time rights. Pays $10 per each b&w photo.
Tips: "Our magazine articles are short and special – that's why we are successful."

HARVEST MAGAZINE, The Reader's Hearth, 2322 Latona Dr. NE, Salem OR 97303. Managing Editor: William Michaelian and Jay Thomas Collins. Bimonthly magazine of writing by those age 50 and older. "Dedicated to preserving the voice of our older generation." Estab. 1988. Circ. 3,000. Pays on publication. Publishes ms an average of 3 months after acceptance. Byline given. Buys one-time rights. Submit seasonal/holiday material 4 months in advance. Photocopied and previously published submissions OK. Computer printout submissions OK. Reports in 5 weeks on queries; 6 weeks on mss. Sample copy $2. Writer's guidelines for #10 SASE.

The double dagger before a listing indicates that the listing is new in this edition. New markets are often the most receptive to freelance submissions.

Nonfiction: Book excerpts, historical/nostalgic, humor, interview/profile, opinion, personal experience. Buys 50 mss/year. Query with or without published clips, or send complete ms. Length: 400-6,000 words. Pays $10-60.

Photos: Send photos with submission. Reviews prints. Offers no additional payment for photos accepted with ms. Model releases and identification of subjects required. Buys one-time rights.

Fiction: Ethnic, historical, humorous, novel excerpts, slice-of-life vignettes. Buys 6 mss/year. Send complete ms. Length: 200-4,000 words. Pays 5-10 copies.

Poetry: Avant-garde, free verse, traditional. Buys 24 poems/year. Submit maximum 12 poems at one time. Length: 100 lines maximum. Pays 5-10 copies.

Fillers: Anecdotes, short humor. Pays 5-10 copies.

Tips: "Interviews and articles on interesting seniors may be written by anyone. Due to financial restrictions, our current policy is to pay for this service only. Above all, we look for honest stories written from the heart."

‡MATURE LIFESTYLES, Keystone Publishing Inc. 9261 130 Ave. N., Largo FL 34643. (813)586-5400. Editor: Stephen N. Ream. 75% freelance written. Monthly tabloid on general interest news and features for mature reader over 50. Estab. 1988. Circ. 40,000. Pays on publication. Publishes ms an average of 2-3 months after acceptance. Byline given. Buys all rights. Submit seasonal/holiday material 2 months in advance. Simultaneous, photocopied and previously published submissions OK. Computer printout submissions OK; prefers letter-quality. Reports in 2 weeks. Sample for 9x12 SAE with 4 first class stamps. Writer's guidelines for #10 SASE.

Nonfiction: Essays, general interest, historical/nostalgic, humor, interview/profile, opinion (does not mean letters to the editor), personal experience, photo feature, travel and health. Buys 12-15 mss/year. Send complete ms. Length: 600-800 words. Pays $15.

Photos: Send photos with submission. Reviews contact sheets and 3x5 prints. Offers $5 per photo. Buys one-time rights.

Columns/Departments: Health (senior citizen), 600-800 words. Buys 12-15 mss/year. Send complete ms. Pays $15.

Fiction: Humorous and slice-of-life vignettes.

Tips: "Don't write down to seniors. Seniors are interested in everything, except possibly child care and rock-n-roll. We need good humor."

MATURE LIVING, A Christian Magazine for Senior Adults, Sunday School Board of the Southern Baptist Convention, 127 9th Ave. N., Nashville TN 37234. (615)251-2274. Assistant Editor: Judy Pregel. 70% freelance written. A monthly leisure reading magazine for senior adults 60 and older. Circ. 340,000. Pays on acceptance. Byline given. Buys all rights and sometimes one-time rights. Submit seasonal/holiday material 18 months in advance. Photocopied submissions OK. Computer printout submissions acceptable; prefers letter-quality. Reports in 8 weeks. Sample copy for 9x12 SAE with 85¢ postage; writer's guidelines for #10 SASE.

Nonfiction: General interest, historical/nostalgic, how-to, humor, inspirational, interview/profile, personal experience, photo feature and travel. No pornography, profanity, occult; liquor, dancing, drugs, gambling; no book reviews. Buys 100 mss/year. Send complete ms. Length: 1,475 words maximum, prefers 950 words. Pays 5¢/word (accepted).

Photos: State availability of photos with submission. Offers $10-15/photo. Pays on publication. Buys one-time rights.

Fiction: Humorous, mainstream and slice-of-life vignettes. No reference to liquor, dancing, drugs, gambling; no pornography, profanity or occult. Buys 12 mss/year. Send complete ms. Length: 900-1,475 words. Pays 5¢/word.

Poetry: Light verse and traditional. Buys 50 poems/year. Submit maximum 5 poems. Length: open. Pays $5-24.

Fillers: Anecdotes, facts and short humor. Buys 15/issue. Length: 50 words maximum. Pays $5.

‡MATURE OUTLOOK, Meredith Corp. 1716 Locust St., Des Moines IA 50336. Editor: Marjorie P. Groves, Ph.D. 80% freelance written. A bimonthly magazine and newsletter on travel, health, nutrition, money and garden for over-50 audience. They may or may *not* be retired. Circ. 870,000. Pays on acceptance. Publishes ms an average 3 months after acceptance. Byline given. Offers 20% kill fee. Buys all rights or makes work-for-hire assignments. Submit seasonal/holiday material 9 months in advance. Query for electronic submissions. Computer printout submissions OK; prefers letter-quality. Reports in 2 weeks. Sample copy $1. Writer's guidelines for #10 SASE.

Nonfiction: How-to, interview/profile, technical and travel. No humor, personal experience or poetry. Buys 50-60 mss/year. Query with published clips. "Definite preference for queries. To date have purchased 1 ms of the hundreds sent." Length: 500-2,000 words. Pays $200-1,000 for assigned articles. Pays telephone expenses of writers on assignment.

Photos: State availability of photos with submission.

Tips: "Please query. Please don't call."

MATURE YEARS, 201 8th Ave., S., Nashville TN 37202. Editor: Donn C. Downall. 30% freelance written. Prefers to work with published/established writers; works with a small number of new/unpublished writers each year. Quarterly magazine for retired persons and those facing retirement; persons seeking help on how to handle problems and privileges of retirement. Pays on acceptance. Publishes ms an average of 14 months after acceptance. Rights purchased vary with author and material; usually buys first North American serial rights. Submit seasonal material 14 months in advance. Query for electronic submissions. Computer printout submissions OK. Reports in 6 weeks. Sample copy for 9x12 SAE and $2; writer's guidelines for #10 SASE.

Nonfiction: "*Mature Years* is different from the secular press in that we like material with a Christian and church orientation. Usually we prefer materials that have a happy, healthy outlook regarding aging. Advocacy (for older adults) articles are at times used; some are freelance submissions. We need articles dealing with many aspects of pre-retirement and retirement living, and short stories and leisure-time hobbies related to specific seasons. Give examples of how older persons, organizations, and institutions are helping others. Writing should be of interest to older adults, with Christian emphasis, though not preachy and moralizing. No poking fun or mushy, sentimental articles. We treat retirement from the religious viewpoint. How-to, humor and travel are also considered." Buys 24 unsolicited mss/year. Submit complete ms (include SASE and Social Security number with submissions). Length: 1,200-1,500 words. Sometimes pays expenses of writers on assignment.

Photos: 8x10 b&w glossy prints, color prints or color transparencies purchased with ms or on assignment.

Fiction: "We buy fiction for adults. Humor is preferred. No children's stories and no stories about depressed situations of older adults." Length: 1,000-1,500 words. Payment varies, usually 4¢/word.

Tips: "We like writing to be meaty, timely, clear and concrete."

‡**MERIDIAN, Canada's Magazine for the 55 plus**, Troika Publishing Inc., Box 13337, Kanata, Ontario K2K 1X5 Canada. (613)592-5623. Editor: Maureen Grenier. 70% freelance written. Bimonthly magazine. "Articles and poems must be of interest to the older reader and show a *positive* view of aging." Circ. 25,000. Pays on publication. Publishes ms an average of 8 months after acceptance. Byline given. Offers 50% kill fee. Buys first North American serial rights, second serial (reprint) rights or first Canadian rights. Submit seasonal/holiday material 6 months in advance. Photocopied submissions and previously published submissions OK. Computer printout submissions OK. Reports in 3 weeks on queries; 2 months on mss. Sample copy for $2 and 8½x11 SAE with 2 first class stamps (Canada). Writer's guidelines for #10 SASE (Canada), or USA with international coupon.

Nonfiction: General interest, historical/nostalgic, humor and personal experience. "We have accepted our quota of health, fitness and travel for 1990." Buys 24 mss/year. Send complete ms. Length: 150-800 words. Pays $50-75 for assigned articles; $10-50 for unsolicited articles.

Photos: Send photos with submission. Reviews prints. Offers $5 minimum per photo. Identification of subjects required. Buys one-time rights.

Fiction: Humorous, romance and slice-of-life vignettes. "No stories about the horrors of entering nursing or retirement homes, or of losing one's independence or memory." Buys 6 mss/year. Length: 300-800 words. Pays $30-50.

Poetry: Free verse, light verse and traditional. Buys 12 poems/year. Submit maximum 5 poems. Length 4-20 lines. Pays $5.

Tips: "Because our magazine is small, we prefer short articles and like to see the complete ms rather than deal with queries. Try to include a photo or two when appropriate. (We return photos after publication.) Usually our main feature article is assigned to one of our regular writers and we do not accept freelance finance articles or recipes. Almost all other material is written by freelancers. Tip: keep it short and stay positive about the aging process."

MODERN MATURITY, American Association of Retired Persons, 3200 E. Carson, Lakewood CA 90712. Editor-in-Chief: Ian Ledgerwood. 50% freelance written. Prefers to work with published/established writers. Bimonthly magazine for readership of persons 50 years of age and over. Circ. 20 million. Pays on acceptance. Publishes ms an average of 4-6 months after acceptance. Byline given. Buys first North American serial rights. Submit seasonal/holiday material 6 months in advance. Query for electronic submissions. Computer printout submissions acceptable; no dot-matrix. Reports in 6-8 weeks. Free sample copy and writer's guidelines.

Nonfiction: Careers, workplace, practical information in living, investments, financial and legal matters, personal relationships, and consumerism. Query first. Length: up to 2,000 words. Pays up to $3,000. Sometimes pays expenses of writers on assignment.

Photos: Photos purchased with or without accompanying ms. Pays $250 and up for color and $150 and up for b&w.

Fiction: Write for guidelines.

Tips: "The most frequent mistake made by writers in completing an article for us is poor follow-through with basic research. The outline is often more interesting than the finished piece. We do not accept unsolicited manuscripts."

PRIME TIMES, Grote Deutsch & Co., Suite 120, 2802 International Ln., Madison WI 53704. Executive Editor: Joan Donovan. 80% freelance written. Prefers to work with published/established writers, but "we will work at times with unpublished writers." Quarterly magazine "for people who are in prime mid-life or at the height of their careers and planning a dynamic retirement lifestyle or second career." Circ. 75,000. Pays on publication. Buys first North American serial rights and second serial (reprint) rights. Publishes ms an average of 6 months after acceptance. Submit seasonal material 6 months in advance. Previously published submissions OK as long as they were not in another national maturity-market magazine. Computer printout submissions acceptable; no dot-matrix. Reports in 2 months. Sample copy available only with 9x12 SAE and 5 first class stamps; *also* $2.50 check or money order made payable to Grote Deutsch & Company; writer's guidelines for #10 SASE.

Nonfiction: Investigative journalism, new research and updates (related to financial planning methods, consumer activism, preventive health and fitness, travel, and careers/dynamic lifestyle after retirement); opinion; profile; travel; popular arts; self-image; personal experience; humor; and photo feature. "No rocking-chair reminiscing." Articles on health and medical issues and research *must* be founded in sound scientific method and must include current, up-to-date data. "Health-related articles are an easy sale, but you must do your homework and be able to document your research. Don't waste your time or ours on tired generalizations about how to take care of the human anatomy. If you've heard it before, so have we. We want to know who is doing new research, what the current findings may be, and what scientists on the cutting edge of new research say the future holds, preferably in the next one to five years. Is anyone doing basic research into the physiology of the aging process? If so, who? And what have they found? What triggers the aging process? Why do some people age faster than others? What are the common denominators? Does genetic coding and recombinant DNA research hold the answers to slowing or halting the aging process? Give us the facts, only the facts, and all of the facts. Allow the scientists and our audience to draw their own conclusions." Buys 30-40 mss/year, about half from new talent. Query with published clips. Length: 1,000-3,000 words. Pays $50-1,000. "Be sure to keep a photocopy—just in case gremlins pinch the original." Sometimes pays the expenses of writers on assignment.

Photos: Payment is based on one-time publication rights; $75 for less than ½ page, $125 for ½ page and $250 for full page. Cover photos, photo spreads, multiple purchases and work done on assignment to be negotiated. Payment is upon publication. Photo release is necessary to prove ownership of copyright. No standard kill fee. "Do not send irreplaceable *anything*."

Fiction: Length: 1,500-3,500 words. Pays $200-750. "If you are not sure your work is of outstanding quality, please do not submit it to us."

Tips: "Query should reflect writing style and skill of the author. Special issues requiring freelance work include publications on adult relationships and developmental transitions such as mid-life and 'empty-nest' passages and couple renewal; mid-life women's issues; health and medical research and updates; second careers; money management; continuing education; consequences of the ongoing longevity revolution; and the creation of new lifestyles for prime-life adults (ages 40-70 primarily) who are well-educated, affluent, and above all, *active*. About 55% of our readers are women. All are active and redefining the middle years with creative energy and imagination. Age-irrelevant writing is a must. The focus of *Prime Times* in 1990 will be on presenting readers with refreshing and newsworthy material for dynamic mid-lifers, people who have a forever-forty mentality."

‡RETIREMENT LIFESTYLES, Club 55, Suite 212, 5438 11th St. NE, Calgary Alberta T2E 7E9 Canada. (403)295-0567. Editor: David Todd. Magazine published 10 times/year on retirement topics. Audience: age 40 plus. Circ. 50,000. Pays on publication. Publishes ms an average of 3 months after acceptance. Byline given. Buys one-time rights. Simultaneous, photocopied and previously published submissions OK. Computer printout submissions OK. Prefers letter-quality. Reports in 2 months. Free sample copy and writer's guidelines.

Nonfiction: General interest, historical/nostalgic, humor, interview/profile, new product, personal experience, photo feature. Buys 10 mss/year. Send complete ms. Length: 500-2,000 words. Pays $50-300.

Photos: State availability of photos with submission. Reviews contact sheets. Captions required. Buys one-time rights.

Fillers: Anecdotes and gags illustrated by cartoonist. Buys 10/year. Pays $5-15.

SENIOR, California Senior Magazine, 3565 S. Higuera St., San Luis Obispo CA 93401. (805)544-8711. Editor: George Brand. Associate Editor: Herb Kamm, R. Judd. 90% freelance written. Monthly magazine covering senior citizens to inform and entertain the "over-50" audience. Circ. 40,000. Pays on publication. Byline given. Publishes ms an average of 1 month after acceptance. Not copyrighted. Buys first rights or second rights. Submit seasonal/holiday material 2 months in advance. Computer printout submissions OK; prefers letter-quality. Reports in 2 weeks. Sample copy for 9x11 SAE and 6 first class stamps; free writer's guidelines.

Nonfiction: Historical/nostalgic, humor, inspirational, personal experience and travel. Special issue features War Years (November); Christmas (December); and Travel (April). Buys 30-75 mss/year. Query. Length: 300-900 words. Pays $1.50/inch. Sometimes pays the expenses of writers on assignment.

Photos: Send photos with submission. Reviews 8x10 prints. Offers $10-25 per photo. Captions and identification of subjects required. Buys one-time rights.

Columns/Departments: Finance (investment); Taxes; Auto; Medicare. Length: 300-900 words. Pays $1.50/inch.

Fillers: Herb Kamm, editor. Anecdotes and facts. Length: 25-30 words. Pays $1.50/inch.

SENIOR EDITION AND USA/COLORADO, SEI Publishing Corporation, Suite 2240, 1660 Lincoln, Denver CO 80264. (303)837-9100. Editor: Allison St. Claire. 15% freelance written. Monthly tabloid. "Colorado newspaper for seniors (with national distribution) emphasizing legislation, opinion and advice columns, local and national news, features and local calendar aimed at over-55 community." Circ. 25,000. Pays on publication. Publishes ms an average of 1-6 months after acceptance. Byline given. Offer 25-50% kill fee for assigned stories only. Buys first North American serial rights and simultaneous rights. Submit seasonal/holiday material 3 months in advance. Reports in 2 weeks on queries; 3 weeks on mss. Sample copy $1; writer's guidelines for SASE.

Nonfiction: Historical/nostalgic, humor, inspirational, opinion, personal experience and travel. Does not want "anything aimed at less than age 55-plus market; anything patronizing or condescending to seniors." Buys 12 mss/year. Query with or without published clips, or send complete ms. Length: 50-1,000 words. Pays $5-100 for assigned articles; $5-50 for unsolicited articles. Sometimes pays expenses of writers on assignment.

Photos: Send photos with submission (or photocopies of available pictures). Offers $3-10 per photo. Identification of subjects required. Buys one-time rights.

Columns/Departments: Senior Overlook (opinions of seniors about anything they feel strongly about: finances, grandkids, love, life, social problems, etc. May be editorial, essay, prose or poetry). Buys 12 mss/year. Send complete ms. Length: 50-1,000 words. Pays $10 maximum.

Fillers: Short humor. Buys 4/year. Length: 300 words maximum. Pays $10 maximum.

Tips: Areas most open to freelancers are "Opinion: have a good, reasonable point backed with personal experience and/or researched data. Diatribes, vague or fuzzy logic or overworked themes not appreciated. Advice: solid information and generic articles accepted. We will not promote any product or business unless it is the only one in existence. Must be applicable to senior lifestyle."

SENIOR LIFE MAGAZINE, The Magazine for Active Adults, Suite 200 "L", 1420 E. Cooley Dr., Colton CA 92324. (714)824-6681. Editor: Bobbi Mason. Monthly magazine of general interest to people 50+. "Readers are 50+, mobile and active. Most live in California full or part time." Circ. 30,000. Pays on publication. Byline given. Buys first rights, second serial (reprint) rights, or simultaneous rights. Submit seasonal/holiday material 4 months in advance. Simultaneous, clear photocopies and previously published submissions OK. Computer printout submissions OK, letter quality preferred. Sample copy $2.25.

Nonfiction: General interest, historical/nostalgic, how-to (crafts, other than needlework), humor, inspirational, interview/profile, personal experience, financial, sports and photo feature. Buys 5 mss/year. Send complete ms. Length: 300-800 words. Pays $50-75 for assigned articles; $10-45 for unsolicited articles.

Photos: State availability of photos with submission. Reviews transparencies and prints. Offers no additional payment for photos accepted with ms "unless negotiated up front." Captions, model releases and identification of subjects required. Buys one-time rights.

Columns/Departments: Special to this issue (open to stories on fashion, financial, nostalgia, or a highlight of a not-famous-but-special-senior) 500-800 words. Send complete ms. Length: 300-700 words. Pays $10-50.

Fiction: Adventure, fantasy, historical, humorous, mainstream, mystery, romance, slice-of-life-vignettes, westerns. Buys 6 mss/year. Send complete ms. Length: 200 words minimum. Pays $10-75.

Tips: "Write tightly: space for us is a problem. Short articles with photo(s) most likely accepted. No travel or food/recipe articles."

SENIOR WORLD OF CALIFORNIA, Californian Publishing Co., Box 1565, 1000 Pioneer Way, El Cajon CA 92022. (619)442-4404. Executive Editor: Laura Impastato. Travel Editor: Jerry Goodrum. Health Editor: Ron Miller. Lifestyle Editor: Sandy Pasqua. 10% freelance written. Prefers to work with published/established writers. Monthly tabloid newspaper for active older adults living in San Diego, Orange, Los Angeles, Santa Barbara, Ventura, Riverside and San Bernardino counties. Circ. 400,000. Pays on publication. Publishes ms an average of 3 months after acceptance. Buys first serial rights. Simultaneous and photocopied submissions OK. Reports in 2 months. Sample copy $2; free writer's guidelines.

Nonfiction: "We are looking for stories on health, stressing wellness and prevention; travel—international, domestic and how-to; profiles of senior celebrities and remarkable seniors; finance and investment tips for seniors; and interesting hobbies." Send query or complete ms. Length: 500-1,000 words. Pays $30-100.

Photos: State availability of photos with submission. Need b&w with model release. Will pay extra for photos. Buys all rights to photos selected to run with a story.

Columns/Departments: Most of our columns are local or staff-written. We will consider a query on a column idea accompanied by a sample column.

Tips: "No pity the poor seniors material. Remember that we are primarily a news publication and that our content and style reflect that. Our readers are active, vital adults 55 years of age and older." No telephone queries.

Romance and Confession

Listed here are publications that need stories of romance ranging from ethnic and adventure to romantic intrigue and confession. Each magazine has a particular slant; some are written for young adults, others to family-oriented women. Some magazines also are interested in general interest nonfiction on related subjects.

AFFAIRE DE COEUR, Keenan Enterprises, Suite B, 1555 Washington Ave., San Leandro CA 94577. (415)357-5665. Editor: Barbara N. Keenan. 56% freelance written. Monthly magazine of book reviews, articles and information on publishing for romance readers and writers. Circ. 15,000. Pays on publication. Publishes ms an average of 6-12 months after acceptance. Byline given. Buys one-time rights. Submit seasonal/holiday material 3 months in advance. Simultaneous, photocopied and previously published submissions OK. Reports in 3-4 months. Sample copy $3; writer's guidelines for #10 SAE and 1 first class stamp.

Nonfiction: Book excerpts, essays, general interest, historical/nostalgic, how-to, interview/profile, personal experience and photo feature. Buys 2 mss/year. Query. Length: 500-2,200 words. Pays $5-15. Sometimes pays writers with contributor copies or other premiums.

Photos: State availability of photos with submission. Review prints. Identification of subjects required. Buys one-time rights.

Columns/Departments: Reviews (book reviews). Query. Length: 125-150 words. Does not pay.

Fiction: Historical, mainstream and romance. Buys 2 mss/year. Query. Length: 1,500-2,200. Pays $15.

Poetry: Light verse. Buys 2 poems/year. Submit 1 poem. Does not pay.

Fillers: Newsbreaks. Buys 2/year. Length: 50-100 words. Does not pay.

Tips: "Please send clean copy. Do not send material without SASE. Do not expect a return for 2-3 months. Type all information. Send some sample of your work."

BLACK CONFESSIONS, Lexington Library, Inc., 355 Lexington Ave., New York NY 10017. (212)949-6850. Editor: Nathasha Brooks. See *Jive*.

BRONZE THRILLS, Lexington Library, Inc., 355 Lexington Ave., New York NY 10017. (212)949-6850. Editor: Nathasha Brooks. See *Intimacy/Black Romance*. "Stories can be a bit more extraordinary than in the other magazines. They have to be romantic just like the other stories in the other magazines."

INTIMACY/BLACK ROMANCE, 355 Lexington Ave., New York NY 10017. (212)949-6850. FAX: (212)986-5926. Editor: Nathasha Brooks. 100% freelance written. Eager to work with new/unpublished writers. A bimonthly magazine covering romance and love. Circ. 100,000. Pays on publication. Publishes ms an average of 6 months after acceptance. Byline given. Buys first and one-time rights. Submit seasonal/holiday material 6 months in advance. Photocopied submissions OK. Computer printout submissions OK. Reports in 2 months on queries; 3-6 months on mss. Sample copy for 9x12 SAE with 5 first class stamps; writer's guidelines for #10 SAE with 3 first class stamps.

Nonfiction: How-to (relating to romance and love); personal experience (confessions); and feature articles on any aspect of love and romance. "I would not like to see any special features that are overly researched." Buys 100 mss/year. Query with published clips, or send complete ms. Length: 3-5 typed pages. Pays $100.

Photos: Send photos with submission. Reviews contact sheets, negatives, transparencies. All photos are now solicited through the art department.

Columns/Departments: Beauty (Black skin, hair, foot and hand care); Fashion (any articles about current fashions that our audience may be interested in will be considered). Buys 50 mss/year. Query with published clips or send complete ms. Length: 3-5 typed pages. Pays $100.

Fiction: Confession and romance. "I would not like to see anything that stereotypes Black people. Stories which are too sexual in content and lack romance are unacceptable." Buys 300 mss/year. *Bronze Thrills* accepts stories which are a bit more out of the ordinary and are more uninhibited in concept than those written for *Jive*, *Black Confession* or *Black Romance*. Send complete ms (12-15 typed pages). Pays $75-100.

Tips: "This is a great market for beginning, unpublished writers. I am a tough editor because I want quality material and would like to encourage serious writers to submit to us on a regular basis. I discourage sloppiness, carelessness and people who give lip service to wanting to be a writer and not doing the work involved. I would like to emphasize to the writers that writing is not easy, and not to think that they will get a break here. Contemporary issues and timely subjects should be the basis of any stories submitted to us."

JIVE, Lexington Library, Inc., 355 Lexington Ave., New York NY 10017. (212)949-6850. Editor: Nathasha Brooks. 100% freelance written. Eager to work with new/unpublished writers. A bimonthly magazine covering romance and love. Circ. 100,000. Pays on publication. Publishes ms an average of 3 months after acceptance. Byline given. Buys first and one-time rights. Submit seasonal/holiday material 6 months in advance. Clear, legible photocopied submissions OK. Computer printout submissions OK; prefers letter-quality. Reports in 2 months on queries; 3-6 months on mss. Sample copy for 9x12 SAE with 5 first class stamps; free writer's guidelines.

Nonfiction: How-to (relating to romance and love); personal experience (confessions); and feature articles on any aspect of love and romance. "I would not like to see any special features that are overly researched." Buys 100 mss/year. Query with published clips, or send complete ms. Length: 3-5 typed pages. Pays $100.

Columns/Departments: Beauty (Black skin, hair, foot and hand care); Fashion (any articles about current fashions that our audience may be interested in will be considered); Health (about topics that deal with issues pertaining to safe sex, birth control, etc.); how-to special features that deal with romance. Buys 50 mss/year. Query with published clips or send complete ms. Length: 3-5 typed pages. Pays $100.

Fiction: Confession and romance. "I would not like to see anything that stereotypes Black people. Stories which are too sexual in content and lack romance are unacceptable. However, all stories must contain one or two love scenes that are romantic, not lewd." All love scenes should not show the sex act, but should allude to it through the use of metaphors and tags. Buys 300 mss/year. Send complete ms (12-15 typed pages). Pays $75-100.

Tips: "We will continue to buy material that is timely and is based on contemporary themes. However, we are leaning toward more of the romantic themes as opposed to the more graphic themes of the past. We reach an audience that is comprised mostly of women who are college students, high school students, housewives, divorcees and older women. The audience is mainly Black and ethnic. Our slant is Black and should reinforce Black pride. Our philosophy is to show our experiences in as positive a light as possible without addressing any of the common stereotypes that are associated with Black men, lovemaking prowess, penile size, etc. Stereotypes of any kind are totally unacceptable. The fiction section which accepts romance stories and confession stories about love and romance are most open to freelancers. Also, our special features section is very open. We would like to see stories that are set outside the U.S.—perhaps they should be set in the Caribbean, Europe, Africa, etc. Women should be shown as being professional, assertive, independent, but should still enjoy being romanced and loved by a man. We'd like to see themes that are reflective of things happening around us in the 80's—crack, AIDS, living together, surrogate mothers, etc. The characters should be young, but not the typical 'country bumpkin girl who was turned out by a big city pimp' type story. Cosmopolitan storylines would be great too. Please, writers who are not Black, research your story to be sure that it depicts Black people in a positive manner. Do not make Black characters a caricature of a white character. This is totally unacceptable."

MODERN ROMANCES, Macfadden Women's Group, Inc., 215 Lexington Ave., New York NY 10016. Editor: Colleen Brennan. 100% freelance written. Monthly magazine for blue-collar, family-oriented women, ages 18-65 years old. Circ. 300,000. Pays the last week of the month of issue. Buys all rights. Byline given. Submit seasonal/holiday material 6 months in advance. Reports in 3 months. Writer's guidelines for #10 SASE.

Nonfiction: General interest, baby and child care, how-to (homemaking subjects), humor, inspirational, and personal experience. Submit complete ms. Length: 200-1,500 words. Pay depends on merit. "Confession stories with reader identification and a strong emotional tone. No third-person material." Buys 14 mss/issue. Submit complete ms. Length: 1,500-8,500 words. Pays 5¢/word.

Poetry: Light, romantic poetry. Length: 24 lines maximum. Pay depends on merit.

SECRETS, Macfadden Holdings, Inc., 215 Lexington Ave., New York NY 10016. (212)340-7500. Editorial Director: Susan Weiner. Editor: Pat Byrdsong. 100% freelance written. Monthly magazine for blue-collar black family women, ages 18-35. *Secrets* is a woman's confession/romance magazine geared toward a black audience. We are particularly interested in seeing true to life stories that address contemporary social issues as well as light romance." Pays on publication. Publishes ms an average of 4 months after acceptance. Buys all rights. Submit seasonal material *at least* 5 months in advance. Reports in 3 months.

Nonfiction and Fiction: Wants true stories of special interest to women: family, marriage and emotional conflict themes, "woman-angle articles," or self-help or inspirational fillers. "No pornographic material; no sadistic or abnormal angles. Stories must be written in the first person." Buys about 150 mss/year. Submit complete ms. Length: 300-1,000 words for features; 2,500-7,500 words for full-length story. Occasional 10,000-worders. Greatest need: 4,500-6,000 words. Pays 3¢/word for story mss.

Columns/Departments: Woman (readers share anecdotes about their lives, loves and families); My Best Friend (photographs of pets and children with article of 50 words or less). Pays $50.

Tips: "Know our market. We are keenly aware of all contemporary lifestyles and activities that involve black women and family—i.e.; current emphasis on child abuse, or renewed interest in the image of marriage, etc."

TRUE CONFESSIONS, Macfadden Holdings, Inc., 215 Lexington Ave., New York NY 10016. (212)340-7500. Editor: H. Marie Atkocius. 90% freelance written. Eager to work with new/unpublished writers. For high-school-educated, blue-collar women, teens through maturity. Monthly magazine. Circ. 250,000. Buys all rights. Byline given on some articles. Pays during the last week of month of issue. Publishes ms an average of 4 months after acceptance. Submit seasonal material 6 months in advance. Reports in 6-8 months. Submit complete ms. Computer printout submissions acceptable; prefers letter-quality. No simultaneous submissions.

Stories, Articles, and Fillers: Timely, exciting, emotional first-person stories on the problems that face today's women. The narrators should be sympathetic, and the situations they find themselves in should be intriguing, yet realistic. Many stories may have a strong romantic interest and a high moral tone; however, personal accounts or "confessions," no matter how controversial the topic, are encouraged and accepted. Careful study of a current issue is suggested. Length: 2,000-6,000 words; 5,000-word stories preferred; also book lengths of 8,000-10,000 words. Pays 5¢/word. Also publishes articles poetry, recipes and mini-stories (1,200 words maximum).

TRUE LOVE, Macfadden Holdings Inc., 215 Lexington Ave., New York NY 10016. (212)340-7500. Editor: Marcia Pomerantz. 100% freelance written. Monthly magazine. For young, blue-collar women, teens through mid-30's. Confession stories based on true happenings, with reader identification and a strong emotional tone. No third-person material; no simultaneous submissions. Circ. 200,000. Pays the last week of the month of the issue. Buys all rights. Submit seasonal material 6 months in advance. Reports within 2 months. Sample copy for 9x12 SAE and $2. Writer's guidelines for #10 SASE.

Nonfiction and Fiction: Confessions, true love stories; problems and solutions; health problems; marital and child-rearing difficulties. Avoid graphic sex. Stories dealing with reality, current problems, everyday events, with emphasis on emotional impact. Buys 14 stories/issue. Submit complete ms. Length: 1,500-8,000 words. Pays 3¢/word. Informational and how-to articles. Byline given. Length: 250-800 words. Pays 5¢/word minimum.

Columns/Departments: "The Life I Live," $100; "How I Know I'm In Love," 700 words or less; $75. Interesting, true-to-life short pieces.

Poetry: Light romantic poetry. Length: 24 lines maximum. Pay depends on merit.

Tips: "The story must appeal to the average blue-collar woman. It must deal with her problems and interests. Characters—especially the narrator—must be sympathetic. Focus is especially on teenagers, young working (or student) women."

TRUE ROMANCE, Macfadden Women's Group, 215 Lexington Ave., New York NY 10016. (212)340-7500. Editor: Jean Sharbel. Monthly magazine. 100% freelance written. Readership primarily young, blue-collar women, teens through mid-30's. Confession stories based on true happenings, with reader identification and strong emotional tone; couple-oriented stories with emphasis on love and romance. No third-person material; no simultaneous submissions! Circ. 225,000. Pays 1 month after publication. Buys all rights. Submit seasonal/holiday material at least 5 months in advance. Reports in 2-3 months.

Fiction and Nonfiction: Confessions, true love stories; problems and solutions; dating and marital and child-rearing difficulties. Realistic stories dealing with current problems, everyday events, with strong emotional appeal. Buys 14 stories/issue. Submit complete ms. Length 1,500-7,500 words. Pays 3¢/word; slightly higher rates for short-shorts. Informational and how-to articles. Byline given. Length: 250-800 words. Pays 5¢/word minimum.

Poetry: Light romantic poetry. Buys 100/year. Length: 24 lines maximum. Pay depends on merit.

Tips: "A timely, well-written story that is told by a sympathetic narrator who sees the central problem through to a satisfying resolution is all important to break into *True Romance*. We are always looking for good love stories."

TRUE STORY, Macfadden Women's Group, 215 Lexington Ave., New York NY 10016. (212)340-7585. Editor: Susan Weiner. 80% freelance written. For young married, blue-collar women, 20-35; high school education; increasingly broad interests; home-oriented, but looking beyond the home for personal fulfillment. Monthly magazine. Circ. 1.7 million. Buys all rights. Byline given "on articles only." Pays 1 month after publication.

Submit seasonal material 4 months in advance; make notation on envelope that it is seasonal material. Reports in 6 months.

Nonfiction: Pays a flat rate for columns or departments, as announced in the magazine. Query for fact articles.

Photos: Lisa Fischer, art director. Query about all possible photo submissions.

Nonfiction: "First-person stories covering all aspects of women's interests: love, marriage, family life, careers, social problems, etc. The best direction a new writer can be given is to carefully study several issues of the magazine; then submit a fresh, exciting, well-written true story. We have no taboos. It's the handling and believability that make the difference between a rejection and an acceptance." Buys about 125 full-length mss/year. Submit only complete mss for stories. Length: 1,500-10,000 words. Pays 5¢/word; $150 minimum.

Rural

Readers may be conservative or liberal, but these publications draw them together with a focus on rural lifestyles. Surprisingly, many readers are from urban centers who dream or plan to build a house in the country.

COUNTRY JOURNAL, Box 8200, Harrisburg PA 17105. FAX: (717)657-9526. Editor: Peter V. Fossel. Managing Editor: Tracy Lynn. 90% freelance written. Works with a small number of new/unpublished writers each year. Bimonthly magazine featuring country living for people who live in rural areas or who are thinking about moving there. Circ. 320,000. Average issue includes 6-8 feature articles and 10 departments. Pays on acceptance. Rates range from 30-50¢/word. Byline given. Buys first North American serial rights. Submit seasonal material 1 year in advance. Photocopied submissions OK. Computer printout submissions acceptable, prefers letter-quality; "dot-matrix submissions are acceptable if double-spaced." Reports in 1 month. Sample copy $3; writer's guidelines for SASE.

Nonfiction: Book excerpts; general interest; opinion (essays); profile (people who are outstanding in terms of country living); how-to; issues affecting rural areas; and photo feature. Query with published clips. Length: 2,000-3,500 words. Pays 30-50¢/word. Pays the expenses of writers on assignment.

Photos: Ed Henry, assistant art director. State availability of photos. Reviews b&w contact sheets, 5x7 and 8x10 b&w glossy prints and 35mm or larger color transparencies. Captions, model release, and identification of subjects required. Buys one-time rights.

Columns/Departments: Listener (brief articles on country topics, how-to's, current events and updates). Buys 5 mss/issue. Query with published clips. Length: 200-400 words. Pays approximately $75.

Poetry: Free verse, light verse and traditional. Buys 1 poem/issue. Pays $50/poem. Include SASE.

Tips: "Be as specific in your query as possible and explain why you are qualified to write the piece (especially for how-to's and controversial subjects). The writer has a better chance of breaking in at our publication with short articles."

FARM & RANCH LIVING, Reiman Publications, 5400 S. 60th St., Greendale WI 53129. (414)423-0100. Editor: Bob Ottum. 80% freelance written. Eager to work with new/unpublished writers. A bimonthly lifestyle magazine aimed at families engaged full time in farming or ranching. "*F&RL* is *not* a 'how-to' magazine – it deals with people rather than products and profits." Circ. 280,000. Pays on acceptance. Publishes ms an average of 1 year after acceptance. Byline given. Offers 25% kill fee. Buys first serial rights and one-time rights. Submit seasonal/holiday material 6 months in advance. Previously published submissions OK. Computer printout submissions acceptable. Reports in 6 weeks. Sample copy $2; writer's guidelines for #10 SASE.

Nonfiction: Interview/profile, photo feature, historical/nostalgic, humor, inspirational and personal experience. No how-to articles or stories about "hobby farmers" (doctors or lawyers with weekend farms), or "hard-times" stories (farmers going broke and selling out). Buys 50 mss/year. Query first with or without published clips; state availability of photos. Length: 1,000-3,000 words. Pays $150-500 for text-and-photos package. Pays expenses of writers on assignment.

Photos: Scenic. Pays $75-200 for 35mm color slides. Buys one-time rights.

Fillers: Clippings, jokes, anecdotes and short humor. Buys 150/year. Length: 50-150 words. Pays $20 minimum.

Tips: "In spite of poor farm economy, most farm families are proud and optimistic, and they especially enjoy stories and features that are upbeat and positive. *F&RL*'s circulation continues to increase, providing an excellent market for freelancers. A freelancer must see *F&RL* to fully appreciate how different it is from other farm publications ordering a sample is strongly advised (not available on newsstands). Query first – we'll give plenty of help and encouragement if story looks promising, and we'll explain why if it doesn't. Photo features (about interesting farm or ranch families); Most Interesting Farmer (or Rancher) I've Ever Met (human interest profile); and Prettiest Place in the Country (tour in text and photos of an attractive farm or ranch) are most open to freelancers. We can make separate arrangements for photography if writer is unable to provide photos."

FARM FAMILY AMERICA, Fieldhagen Publishing, Inc., Suite 121, 333 On Sibley, St. Paul MN 55101. (612)292-1747. Editor: George Ashfield. 75% freelance written. A quarterly magazine published by American Cyanamid and written to the lifestyle, activities and travel interests of American farm families. Circ. 295,000. Pays on acceptance. Publishes ms an average of 2 months after acceptance. Byline given. Offers 25% kill fee. Buys first or second serial (reprint) rights. Submit seasonal/holiday material 6 months in advance. Simultaneous and photocopied submissions OK. Query for electronic submissions. Computer printout submissions OK. Reports in 6 weeks. Writer's guidelines for #10 SASE.
Nonfiction: General interest and travel. Buys 24 mss/year. Query with published clips. Length: 1,000-1,800 words. Pays $300-650. Sometimes pays the expenses of writers on assignment.
Photos: State availability of photos with submission. Reviews 35mm transparencies and prints. Offers $160-700 per photo. Model releases and identification of subjects required. Buys one-time rights.

HARROWSMITH, The Magazine of Country Life, The Creamery, Charlotte VT 05445. (802)425-3961. FAX: (802)425-3307. Editor: Thomas H. Rawls. Bimonthly magazine covering country living, gardening, shelter, food, and environmental issues. "*Harrowsmith* readers are generally college educated country dwellers, looking for good information." Circ. 225,000. Pays 30-45 days after acceptance. Byline given. Offers 25% kill fee. Buys first North American serial rights. Reports in 6 weeks. Sample copy $4; writer's guidelines for #10 SASE.
Nonfiction: Book excerpts, essays, exposé (environmental issues), how-to (gardening/building), humor, interview/profile, opinion. Buys 36 mss/year. Query with published clips. Length: 500-5,000 words. Pays $500-1,500. Pays expenses of writers on assignment.
Photos: State availability of photos with submission. Reviews 35mm transparencies. Offers $100-325/photo. Model releases and identification of subjects required. Buys one-time rights.
Columns/Departments: Sourcebank (ideas, tips, techniques relating to gardening, the environment, food, health), 50-400 words; Gazette (brief news items). Buys 30 mss/year. Query with published clips. Length: 40-400 words. Pays $25-150.
Tips: "While main feature stories are open to freelancers, a good way for us to get to know the writer is through our Screed (essays), Sourcebank (tips and ideas) and Gazette (brief news items) departments. Articles should contain examples, quotations and anecdotes. They should be fairly detailed and factual."

HARROWSMITH MAGAZINE, Camden House Publishing, Ltd., Camden East, Ontario K0K 1J0 Canada. (613)378-6661. Editor: Wayne Grady. 75% freelance written. Published 6 times/year "for those interested in country life, nonchemical gardening, energy, self-sufficiency, small-stock husbandry, owner-builder architecture and alternative styles of life." Circ. 154,000. Pays on acceptance. Publishes ms an average of 4 months after acceptance. Byline given. Buys first North American serial rights. Submit seasonal/holiday material 6 months in advance. Computer printout submissions acceptable; prefers letter-quality. Reports in 6 weeks. Sample copy $5; free writer's guidelines.
Nonfiction: Exposé, how-to, general interest, humor, environmental and profile. "We are always in need of quality gardening articles geared to northern conditions. No articles whose style feigns 'folksiness.' No how-to articles written by people who are not totally familiar with their subject. We feel that in this field simple research does not compensate for lack of long-time personal experience." Buys 10 mss/issue. Query. Length: 500-4,000 words. Pays $150-1,250 but will consider higher rates for major stories.
Photos: State availability of photos with query. Pays $50-250 for 35mm or larger color transparencies. Captions required. Buys one-time rights.
Tips: "We have standards of excellence as high as any publication in the country. However, we are by no means a closed market. Much of our material comes from unknown writers. We welcome and give thorough consideration to all freelance submissions. Our magazine is read by Canadians who live in rural areas or who hope to make the urban to rural transition. They want to know as much about the realities of country life as the dreams. They expect quality writing, not folksy clichés."

THE MOTHER EARTH NEWS, Box 70, Hendersonville NC 28791. (704)693-0211. Editor: Bruce Woods. 40% freelance written. Magazine published 10 times/year. Emphasizes "country living and country skills, for both long-time and would-be ruralites." Circ. 700,000. Pays on acceptance. Byline given. Submit seasonal/holiday material 5 months in advance. Computer printout submissions acceptable; prefer letter-quality. No handwritten mss. Reports within 3 months. Publishes ms an average of 1 year after acceptance. Sample copy $3; writer's guidelines for SASE with 2 first class stamps.
Nonfiction: Terry Krautwurst, submissions editor. How-to, home business, alternative energy systems, home building, home retrofit and home maintenance, energy-efficient structures, seasonal cooking, gardening and crafts. Buys 300-350 mss/year. Query or send complete ms. "A short, to-the-point paragraph is often enough. If it's a subject we don't need at all, we can answer immediately. If it tickles our imagination, we'll ask to take a look at the whole piece. No phone queries, please." Length: 300-3,000 words.

Photos: Purchased with accompanying ms. Send prints or transparencies. Uses 8x10 b&w glossies; any size color transparencies. Include type of film, speed and lighting used. Total purchase price for ms includes payment for photos. Captions and credits required.

Columns/Departments: "Contributions to Mother's Down-Home Country Lore and Barters and Bootstraps are paid by subscription."

Fillers: Short how-to's on any subject normally covered by the magazine. Query. Length: 150-300 words. Pays $7.50-25.

Tips: "Probably the best way to break in is to study our magazine, digest our writer's guidelines, and send us a concise article illustrated with color transparencies that we can't resist. When folks query and we give a go-ahead on speculation, we often offer some suggestions. Failure to follow those suggestions can lose the sale for the author. We want articles that tell what real people are doing to take charge of their own lives. Articles should be well-documented and tightly written treatments of topics we haven't already covered. The critical thing is length, and our payment is by space, not word count." No phone queries.

‡**OKLAHOMA RURAL NEWS**, Oklahoma Association of Electric Co-Op, 23245 N.E. Expressway, Box 11047, Oklahoma City OK 73136. (405)478-1455. Editor: Vernon E. Kouts. 20% freelance written. Monthly tabloid on rural electrification. Circ. 231,000. Pays on publication. Byline given sometimes. Not copyrighted. Buys one-time rights. Submit seasonal/holiday material 4-6 months in advance. Computer printout submissions OK; prefers letter-quality. Free sample copy.

Nonfiction: General interest, historical/nostalgic, humor and interview/profile. Buys 4-6 mss/year. Send complete ms. Length: 1,400 words maximum. Pays 10¢/word. Pays expenses of writers on assignment.

Photos: Send photos with submission. Reviews 35mm transparencies and 5x7 or bigger prints. Offers $10 per photo. Captions and identification of subjects required. Buys one-time rights.

‡**RURAL HERITAGE**, Box 516, Albia IA 52531. (515)932-2947. Editor & Publisher: Allan Young. 98% freelance written. Works with a small number of new/unpublished writers each year. Quarterly magazine covering individuals dedicated to preserving traditional American life. Circ. 10,000. Pays on publication. Publishes ms an average of 1 year after acceptance. Byline given. Buys first North American rights. Submit seasonal/holiday material 1 year in advance. Computer printout submissions acceptable. Reports in 2 months. Sample copy $4.50; writer's guidelines #10 SASE.

Nonfiction: Essays; historical/nostalgic; how-to (all types of crafting and farming); interview/profile (especially people using draft animals); photo feature; and travel (emphasizing our theme, "rural heritage"). No articles on *modern* farming. Buys 100 mss/year. Send complete ms. Length: 500-1,500 words. Pays $15-400.

Photos: Send photos with ms. (B&w 5x7 or larger.) No negatives. Pays $5-40. Captions, model releases and identification of subjects (if applicable or pertinent) required. Buys one-time rights.

Columns/Departments: Self-Sufficiency (modern people preserving traditional American lifestyle), 500-1,500 words; Drafter's Features (draft horses and mules used for farming, horse shows and pulls—their care), 500-2,000 words; and Crafting (new designs and patterns), 500-1,500 words. Buys 75 mss/year. Send complete ms. Pays $15-125.

Poetry: Traditional. Pays $5-25.

Fillers: Anecdotes and short humor. Pays $15-25.

Tips: "Profiles/articles on draft horses and draft horse shows and pulling events are *very* popular with our readers."

Science

These publications are published for laymen interested in technical and scientific developments and discoveries, applied science and technical or scientific hobbies. Publications of interest to the personal computer owner/user are listed in the Personal Computer section. Journals for scientists, engineers, repairmen, etc., are listed in Trade in various sections.

AD ASTRA, (formerly *Space World*), 922 Pennsylvania Ave. SE, Washington DC 20003. (202)543-3991. FAX: (202)546-4189. Editor-in-Chief: Leonard David. Managing Editor: Kate McMains. 80% freelance written. A monthly magazine covering the space program. "We publish non-technical, lively articles about all aspects of international space programs, from shuttle missions to planetary probes to plans for the future." Estab. 1989. Circ. 24,000. Pays on publication. Byline given. Buys first North American serial rights. Simultaneous, photocopied and previously published submissions OK. Query for electronic submissions. Computer printout submissions acceptable. Reports in 6 weeks on queries; 1 month on mss. Sample copy for 9x12 SAE; writer's guidelines for #10 SASE.

Nonfiction: Book excerpts, essays, exposé, general interest, historical/nostalgic, interview/profile, opinion, personal experience, photo feature and technical. No science fiction. Query with published clips. Length: 1,200-3,000 words. Pays $150-300 for features.
Photos: State availability of photos with submission. Reviews 4x5 color transparencies and b&w prints. Negotiable payment. Identification of subjects required. Buys one-time rights.
Columns/Departments: Mission Control (news about space from around the world), 100-300 words; Space Ed (information for educators), 700-750 words; Spaceware (reviews of space or astronomy software), 700-750 words; Reviews (reviews of books or other media); Enterprises (commercial space activities); and Touchdown (opinion pieces). Query with published clips. Pay $75-100.
Fillers: Newsbreaks. Length: 100-500 words. Pays $30-50.

‡ARCHAEOLOGY, Archaeological Institute of America, 15 Park Row, New York NY 10038. (212)732-5154. FAX: (212)732-5707. Editor: Peter A. Young. 5% freelance written. "We generally commission articles from professional archaeologists." Bimonthly magazine on archaeology. "The only magazine of its kind to bring worldwide archaeology to the attention of the general public." Circ. 120,000. Pays on publication. Byline given. Offers kill fee of ⅕ of agreed upon fee. Buys first North American serial rights. Submit seasonal/holiday material 6 months in advance. Simultaneous submissions OK. Free sample copy and writer's guidelines.
Nonfiction: Essays and general interest. Buys 6 mss/year. Length: 1,000-3,000 words. Pays $750 maximum. Sometimes pays expenses of writers on assignment.
Photos: Send photos with submission.

‡BIOLOGY DIGEST, Plexus Publishing Inc., 143 Old Marlton Pike, Medford NJ 08055. (609)654-6500. Editor: Mary S. Hogan. Monthly abstracts journal covering life sciences. Circ. 2,000. Pays "after publication is returned from printer." Byline given. Not copyrighted.
Nonfiction: Thomas H. Hogan, publisher. Essays. "A list of suggested further readings must accompany each article." Buys 9 mss/year. Send complete ms. Length: 18-25 double-spaced ms pages.
Photos: "A minimum of 5 photos and/or finished drawings are required to go along with the feature article. If drawings are used, there should be at least 2 photos. Photos are a must because the feature article is always depicted on the cover of the issue through the use of a photo."
Tips: "Although *Biology Digest* is intended for students at the high school and college levels, the feature articles published are of a serious nature and contain scientifically accurate material—not conjecture or opinion. Articles should be self-contained; i.e. the author should assume no previous knowledge of the subject area, and scientific terms should be defined. However, avoid 'talking down' to the reader—he or she is probably smarter than you think."

THE ELECTRON, CIE Publishing, 4781 E. 355th St., Willoughby OH 44094. (216)946-9065. Managing Editor: Janice Weaver. 80% freelance written. Prefers to work with published/established writers. Bimonthly tabloid on electronics and high technology. Circ. 50,000. Pays on publication. Publishes ms an average of 2 months after acceptance. Byline given. Buys all rights unless negotiated otherwise. Simultaneous queries, and photocopied and previously published submissions OK. Computer printout submissions acceptable; prefers letter-quality. Reports in 1 month or earlier. Free sample copy and writer's guidelines.
Nonfiction: Technical (tutorial and how-to), technology news and feature, photo feature, career/educational. All submissions must be electronics/technology-related. Query with published clips or send complete ms. Pays $35-1,000. Sometimes pays expenses of writers on assignment.
Photos: State availability of photos. Reviews 8x10 and 5x7 b&w prints. Captions and identification of subjects required.
Tips: "We would like to receive educational electronics/technical articles. They must be written in a manner understandable to the beginning-intermediate electronics student. We are also seeking news/feature-type articles covering timely developments in high technology."

FINAL FRONTIER, The Magazine of Space Exploration, Final Frontier Publishing, Box 11519 Washington DC 20008 for editorial submissions. FAX: (202)244-0322. 2400 Foshay Tower, Minneapolis MN 55402. (612)332-3001. Editor: Tony Reichhardt. 95% freelance written. Bimonthly magazine on space exploration. "We are not a technical journal nor a science fiction magazine. We're looking for well told, factual articles about the people, events and exciting possiblities of the world's space programs." Estab. 1988. Circ. 75,000. Pays on acceptance. Byline given. Pays 33% kill fee. Buys first North American serial rights. Submit seasonal/holiday material 6 months in advance. Simultaneous and photocopied submissions OK. Query for electronic submissions. Computer printout submissions OK; prefers letter-quality. Reports in 2 months. Sample copy for $3 and a 9x12 SAE with 6 first class stamps. Writer's guidelines for #10 SASE.
Nonfiction: Book excerpts, essays, expose, general interest, historical/nostalgic, humor, interview/profile, new product, personal experience, photo feature. No technical papers, no science fiction or UFOs. Buys 60 mss/year. Query with published clips. Length: 1,000-3,000 words. Pays 25¢/word (or $500-750). Sometimes pays expenses of writers on assignment.

Photos: State availability of photos with submission. Offers no additional payment for photos accepted with ms "except as agreed ahead of time."

Column/Departments: Boundaries (the cutting edge of exploration); The Private Vector (space businesses); Earthly Pursuits (spinoffs of space technology); Global Currents (international space happenings); Reviews (books, films, videos, computer programs), all 800 words; Notes from Earth (miscellaneous short items), 200-250 words. Buys 120 mss/year. Query with published clips. Pays $50-150.

Tips: "Look for fresh approaches to familiar subjects. Rather than simply suggesting a story on the space shuttle or Mars exploration, we need a tie-in to a specific project or personality. Think behind-the-scenes. 'Notes from Earth' is a grab-bag of short, quick stories—no more than 250 words. Send your ideas!"

MODERN ELECTRONICS, For electronics and computer enthusiasts, CQ Communications, 76 N. Broadway, Hicksville NY 11801. (516)681-2922. FAX: (516)681-2926. 90% freelance written. Monthly magazine covering consumer electronics, personal computers, electronic circuitry, construction projects and technology for readers with a technical affinity. Circ. 70,000. Pays on acceptance. Publishes ms an average of 3 months after acceptance. Byline given. Offers 25% kill fee. Buys first North American serial rights. Submit seasonal/holiday material minimum 4 months in advance. Computer printout submissions acceptable; prefers near letter-quality to coarse dot-matrix. Reports in 1 week on queries; 3 weeks on mss. Sample copy for 9x12 SAE and $2; writer's guidelines for #10 SASE.

Nonfiction: General interest (new technology, product buying guides); how-to (construction projects, applications); new product (reviews); opinion (experiences with electronic and computer products); technical (features and tutorials: circuits, applications); includes stereo, video, communications and computer equipment. "Articles must be technically accurate. Writing should be 'loose,' not textbookish." No long computer programs. Buys 75 mss/year. Query. Length: 500-4,000 words. Pays $80-150/published page. Sometimes pays expenses of writers on assignment.

Photos: Send photos with query or ms. Reviews color transparencies and 5x7 b&w prints. Captions, model releases, and identification of subjects required. Buys variable rights depending on mss.

Tips: "The writer must have technical or applications acumen and well-researched material. Articles should reflect the latest products and technology. Sharp, interesting photos are helpful, as are rough, clean illustrations for re-drawing. Cover 'hot' subjects (avoid old technology). Areas most open to freelancers include feature articles, technical tutorials, and projects to build. Some writers exhibit problems with longer pieces due to limited technical knowledge and/or poor organization. We can accept more short pieces."

OMNI, 1965 Broadway, New York NY 10023-5965. Editor: Patrice Adcroft. 90% freelance written. Prefers to work with published/established writers; works with a small number of new/unpublished writers each year. Monthly magazine of the future covering science fact, fiction, and fantasy for readers of all ages, backgrounds and interests. Circ. 934,000. Average issue includes 2-3 nonfiction feature articles and 1-2 fiction articles; also numerous columns and 2 pictorials. Pays on acceptance. Publishes ms an average of 5 months after acceptance. Offers 25% kill fee. Buys exclusive worldwide and exclusive first English rights and rights for *Omni* anthologies. Submit seasonal material 4-6 months in advance. Photocopied submissions OK. Computer printout submissions acceptable; prefers letter-quality. Reports in 6 weeks. Free writer's guidelines with SASE (request fiction or nonfiction).

Nonfiction: "Articles with a futuristic angle, offering readers information on housing, energy, transportation, medicine and communications. People want to know, want to understand what scientists are doing and how scientific research is affecting their lives and their future. *Omni* publishes articles about science in language that people can understand. We seek very knowledgeable science writers who are ready to work with scientists and futurists to produce articles that can inform, interest and entertain our readers with the opportunity to participate in many ground breaking studies." Send query/proposal. Length: 2,500-3,500 words. Pays $2,500-3,500.

Photos: Frank DeVino, graphic director. State availability of photos. Reviews 35mm slides and 4x5 transparencies. Pays the expenses of writers on assignment.

Columns/Departments: Explorations (unusual travel or locations on Earth); Mind (by and about psychiatrists and psychologists); Earth (environment); Space (technology); Arts (theatre, music, film, technology); Interview (of prominent person); Continuum (newsbreaks); Star Tech (new products); Antimatter and UFO Update (unusual newsbreaks, paranormal); Stars (astronomy); First/Last Word (editorial/humor); Artificial Intelligence (computers); The Body (medical). Query with clips of previously published work. Length: 1,500 words maximum. Pays $900; $150 for Continuum and Antimatter items.

Fiction: Contact Ellen Datlow. Fantasy and science fiction. Buys 2 mss/issue. Send complete ms. Length: 10,000 words maximum. Pays $1,250-2,000.

Tips: "To get an idea of the kinds of fiction we publish, check recent back issues of the magazine."

POPULAR SCIENCE, 2 Park Ave., New York NY 10016. Editor-in-Chief: C.P. Gilmore. 30% freelance written. Prefers to work with published/established writers. Monthly magazine. For the well-educated adult, interested in science, technology, new products. Circ. 1.8 million. Pays on acceptance. Publishes ms an average of 4 months after acceptance. Byline given. Buys all rights. Pays negotiable kill fee. Free guidelines for writers.

Any electronic submission OK. Computer printout submissions acceptable; prefers letter-quality. Submit seasonal material 4 months in advance. Reports in 3 weeks. Query. Writer's guidelines for #10 SASE.

Nonfiction: "*Popular Science* is devoted to exploring (and explaining) to a nontechnical but knowledgeable readership the technical world around us. We cover the physical sciences, engineering and technology, and above all, products. We are largely a 'thing'-oriented publication: things that fly or travel down a turnpike, or go on or under the sea, or cut wood, or reproduce music, or build buildings, or make pictures or mow lawns. We are especially focused on the new, the ingenious and the useful. We are consumer-oriented and are interested in any product that adds to the enjoyment of the home, yard, car, boat, workshop, outdoor recreation. Some of our 'articles' are only a picture and caption long. Some are a page long. Some occupy 4 or more pages. Contributors should be as alert to the possibility of selling us pictures and short features as they are to major articles. Freelancers should study the magazine to see what we want and avoid irrelevant submissions. No biology or life sciences." Buys several hundred mss/year. Pays $200/published page minimum. Uses mostly color and some b&w photos. Pays expenses of writers on assignment.

Tips: "Probably the easiest way to break in here is by covering a news story in science and technology that we haven't heard about yet. We need people to be acting as scouts for us out there and we are willing to give the most leeway on these performances. We are interested in good, sharply focused ideas in all areas we cover. We prefer a vivid, journalistic style of writing, with the writer taking the reader along with him, showing the reader what he saw, through words. Please query first."

TECHNOLOGY REVIEW, The Association of Alumni and Alumnae of the Massachusetts Institute of Technology, W59-200, Massachusetts Institute of Technology, Cambridge MA 02139. FAX: (617)258-7264. Editor-in-Chief: Jonathan K. Schlefer. 30% freelance written. Emphasizes technology and its implications for scientists, engineers, managers and social scientists. Magazine published 8 times/year. Circ. 82,000. Pays on publication. Publishes ms an average of 3-6 months after acceptance. Buys first rights and some exclusive rights. Phone queries OK but much prefer written queries. Submit seasonal/holiday material 6 months in advance. Simultaneous and photocopied submissions OK. Computer printout submissions acceptable. Reports in 6 weeks. Sample copy $2.50; writer's guidelines for #10 SASE. "Please send two copies of all submissions and a self-addressed stamped envelope for return of manuscripts."

Nonfiction: General interest, interview, photo feature and technical. Buys 5-10 mss/year. Query. Length: 1,000-6,000 words. Pays $50-750. Sometimes pays the expenses of writers on assignment.

Columns/Departments: Book Reviews; Trend of Affairs; Technology and Economics; and Prospects (guest column). Also special reports on other appropriate subjects. Query. Length: 750-4,000 words. Pays $50-750.

UFO REVIEW, Global Communications, Box 1994, JAF Station, New York NY 10116. (212)685-4080. Editor: Timothy Beckley. Emphasizes UFOs and space science. 50% freelance written. Published 4 times/year. Tabloid. Circ. 50,000. Pays on publication. Publishes ms an average of 4 months after acceptance. Phone queries OK. Photocopied submissions OK. Reports in 3 weeks. Sample copy $1.25.

Nonfiction: Exposé (on government secrecy about UFOs). "We also want articles detailing on-the-spot field investigations of UFO landings, contact with UFOs, and UFO abductions. No lights-in-the-sky stories." Buys 1-2 mss/issue. Query. Length: 1,200-2,000 words. Pays $25-75.

Photos: Send photos with ms. Pays $5-10 for 8x10 b&w prints. Captions required.

Fillers: Clippings. Pays $2-5.

Tips: "Read the tabloid first. We are aimed at UFO fans who have knowledge of the field. Too many submissions are made about old cases everyone knows about. We don't accept rehash. We get a lot of material unrelated to our subject."

Science Fiction, Fantasy and Horror

Additional science fiction, fantasy and horror markets are in the Literary and "Little" section.

ABORIGINAL SCIENCE FICTION, Absolute Entertainment Inc., Box 2449, Woburn MA 01888. Editor: Charles C. Ryan. 99% freelance written. A bimonthly science fiction magazine. "We publish short, lively and entertaining science fiction short stories and poems, accompanied by full-color art." Circ. 31,000. Pays on publication. Publishes ms an average of 6 months after acceptance. Byline given. Buys first North American seial rights, non-exclusive options on other rights. Photocopied submissions OK. Query for electronic submission. Computer printout submissions OK; prefers letter-quality. Sample copy $3, 9 × 12 SAE and 90¢ postage; writer's guidelines for #10 SASE.

Fiction: Science fiction of all types. "We do not use fantasy, horror, sword and sorcery or 'Twilight Zone' type stories." Buys 36 mss/year. Send complete ms. Length: 2,000-6,000 words. Pays $250.

Poetry: Science and science fiction. Buys 8-12 poems/year.

Tips: "Read science fiction novels and other science fiction magazines. Do not rely on science fiction movies or TV. We are open to new fiction writers who are making a sincere effort."

‡AFTER HOURS, A Magazine of Dark Fantasy & Horror, 21541 Oakbrook, Mission Viejo CA 92692-3044. Editor: William G. Raley. 95% freelance written. Quarterly magazine. "All stories *must* take place after dark! No excessive violence. Keep the blood and slime to a minimum." Estab. 1988. Circ. 6,000. Pays on acceptance. Publishes ms an average of 6 months after acceptance. Byline given. Buys first North American serial rights or second serial (reprint) rights. Photocopied and previously published submissions OK. Query for electronic submissions. Computer printout submissions OK; prefers letter-quality. Reports in 2 months on mss. (2 weeks on stories not accepted). Sample copy $4. Writer's guidelines for #10 SASE.

Fiction: Fantasy (including S&S), horror, humorous (macabre), mystery and suspense. No science fiction, "typical" crime stories (where the only motive is murder, rape, or robbery). Buys 50 mss/year. Send complete ms. Length: 6,000 words maximum. Pays 1¢/word.

Tips: "I'm eager to work with new/unpublished writers. I need action (or at least an atmosphere of dread) on *page one*. Good characterization is important. Don't be afraid to be original—if it's too weird or off-the-wall for other magazines, send it here!"

AMAZING® Stories, TSR, Inc., Box 111, Lake Geneva WI 53147-0111. Editor: Patrick L. Price. 90% freelance written. Bimonthly magazine of science fiction and fantasy short stories. "Audience does not need to be scientifically literate, but the authors must be, where required. *AMAZING* is devoted to the best science fiction and fantasy. There is no formula. We require the writers using scientific concepts be scientifically convincing, and that every story contain believable and interesting characters and some overall point. We accept story manuscripts submitted only by literary agents, by profesional authors whose works have been previously published in the science-fiction and fantasy genres, by members of professional writers' organizations (e.g., Science Fiction Writers of America, Mystery Writers of America, etc.), or by attendees of the major science-fiction/fantasy workshops (e.g., Clarion, Clarion West, Writers of the Future, etc.)." Circ. 13,000. Pays on acceptance. Publishes ms an average of 18 months after acceptance. Byline given. Buys first worldwide serial rights in the English language only; "single, non-exclusive re-use option (with additional pay)." Photocopied submissions OK. Computer printout submissions acceptable; no dot-matrix. Reports in 10 weeks. Sample copy for $2.50; writer's guidelines for #10 SASE.

Nonfiction: Historical (about science fiction history and figures); interview/profile and science articles of interest to science fiction audiences; reviews and essays about major science fiction movies written by big names. No "pop pseudo-science trends: The Unified Field Theory Discovered; How I Spoke to the Flying Saucer People; Interpretations of Past Visits by Sentient Beings, as Read in Glacial Scratches on Granite, etc." Buys 4-8 mss/year. Query with or without published clips. Length: 1,000-5,000 words. Pays 10-12¢/word 3,000-5,000 words. Sometimes pays the expenses of writers on assignment.

Fiction: Contemporary and ethnic fantasy; science fiction. "We are looking for hard or speculative science fiction, space fantasy/opera, and fantasy. Horror fiction is OK if it has a science-fictional or fantastic setting. No 'true' experiences, media-derived fiction featuring *Star Wars* (etc.) characters, stories based on UFO reports or standard occultism." Buys 50-60 mss/year. Send complete ms. Length: 500-25,000 words. "Anything longer, ask." Pays 8¢/word to 6,000 words; 5¢/word for 12,000 or more words.

Poetry: All types are OK. No prose arranged in columns. Buys 10 poems/year. Submit maximum 3 poems. Length: 30 lines maximum; ideal length, 20 lines or less. Pays $1/line.

Tips: "We are particularly interested in shorter fiction: stories of 7,000 or fewer words; we are currently overstocked on novelettes and novellas. We look for larger pieces by established writers, because their names help sell our product. Don't try to especially tailor one for our 'slant.' We want original concepts, good writing, and well-developed characters. Avoid certain obvious clichés: UFO landings in rural areas, video games which become real (or vice-versa), stories based on contemporary newspaper headlines. 'Hard' science fiction, that is, science fiction which is based on a plausible extrapolation from real science, is increasingly rare and very much in demand. We are moving away from heroic, pseudo-medieval European fantasies, and more toward ethnic (Japanese, Arabian, Central American, etc.) and contemporary fantasies. All sorts of hard, speculative or militaristic science fiction desired."

ANALOG SCIENCE FICTION/SCIENCE FACT, 380 Lexington Ave., New York NY 10017. Editor: Dr. Stanley Schmidt. 100% freelance written. Eager to work with new/unpublished writers. For general future-minded audience. Monthly. Buys first North American serial rights and nonexclusive foreign serial rights. Pays on acceptance. Publishes ms an average of 6-10 months after acceptance. Byline given. Computer printout submissions (with dark ink) acceptable; prefers letter-quality or near-letter-quality. Reports in 1 month. Sample copy $2.50 (no SASE needed); writer's guidelines for #10 SASE.

Nonfiction: Illustrated technical articles dealing with subjects of not only current but future interest, i.e., with topics at the present frontiers of research whose likely future developments have implications of wide interest. Buys about 12 mss/year. Query. Length: 5,000 words. Pays 6¢/word.

Fiction: "Basically, we publish science fiction stories. That is, stories in which some aspect of future science or technology is so integral to the plot that, if that aspect were removed, the story would collapse. The science can be physical, sociological or psychological. The technology can be anything from electronic engineering to biogenetic engineering. But the stories must be strong and realistic, with believable people doing believable things—no matter how fantastic the background might be." Buys 60-100 unsolicited mss/year. Send complete ms on short fiction; query about serials. Length: 2,000-80,000 words. Pays 4¢/word for novels; 5-6¢/word for novelettes; 6-8¢/word for shorts under 7,500 words; $450-550 for intermediate lengths.

Tips: "In query give clear indication of central ideas and themes and general nature of story line—and what is distinctive or unusual about it. We have no hard-and-fast editorial guidelines, because science fiction is such a broad field that I don't want to inhibit a new writer's thinking by imposing 'Thou Shalt Not's.' Besides, a really good story can make an editor swallow his preconceived taboos. I want the best work I can get, regardless of who wrote it—and I need new writers. So I work closely with new writers who show definite promise, but of course it's impossible to do this with *every* new writer. No occult or fantasy."

BEYOND . . ., Science Fiction and Fantasy, Other World Books, Box 1124, Fair Lawn NJ 07410-1124. (201)791-6721. Editor: Shirley Winston. Managing Editor: Roberta Rogow. 80% freelance written. Eager to work with new/unpublished writers. A science fiction and fantasy magazine published 4 times a year. "Our audience is mostly science fiction fans." Circ. 300. Pays on publication. Publishes ms an average of 6-9 months after acceptance. Byline given. Buys first North American serial rights. Submit seasonal/holiday material 6 months in advance. Photocopied submissions OK. Query for electronic submissions. Computer printout submissions acceptable; prefers letter-quality. Reports in 3 weeks. Sample copy $4.50 and 9X12 SAE; writer's guidelines for #10 SASE.

Nonfiction: Essays and humor. Buys 3 mss/year. Send complete ms. Length: 500-1,500 words. Pays $1.25-3.75 and 1 copy.

Columns/Departments: Reviews (of books and periodicals in science fiction and fantasy area), 500-1,500 words. Buys 3 mss/year. Send complete ms. Length: 500-1,500 words. Pays $1.25-3.75.

Fiction: Fantasy and science fiction only. "We enjoy using stories with a humorous aspect. No horror stories, excessive violence or explicit sex; nothing degrading to women or showing prejudice based on race, religion, or planet of origin. No predictions of universal destruction; we prefer an outlook on the future in which the human race survives and progresses." Buys 20 mss/year. Send complete ms. Length: 500-8,000 words; prefers 4,000-5,000 words. Pays $1.25-20 and 1 copy.

Poetry: Free verse, haiku, light verse and traditional. "Poetry should be comprehensible by an educated reader literate in English, take its subject matter from science fiction or fantasy, need not rhyme but should fall musically on the ear." No poetry unrelated to science fiction or fantasy. Buys 18 poems/year. Submit maximum 3 poems. Length: 4-65 words. Pays 2¢/line and 1 copy.

Tips: Fiction and poetry are most open to freelancers.

HAUNTS, Nightshade Publications, Box 3342, Providence RI 02906. (401)781-9438. Editor: Joseph K. Cherkes. 98% freelance written. Prefers to work with published/established writers; works with small number of new/unpublished writers each year. "We are a literary quarterly geared to those fans of the 'pulp' magazines of the 30's, 40's and 50's, with tales of horror, the supernatural, and the bizarre. We are trying to reach those in the 18-35 age group." Circ. 1,000. Pays on publication. Publishes ms an average of 8 months after acceptance. Byline given. Buys first North American serial rights. Photocopied submissions OK. Computer printout submissions acceptable; prefers letter-quality. Reports in 3 weeks on queries; 2 months on mss. Sample copy $3.50 and $1.25 postage; writer's guidelines for #10 SASE.

Fiction: Fantasy, horror and suspense. "No fiction involving blow-by-blow dismemberment, explicit sexual scenes or pure adventure." Buys 36 fiction mss/year. Query. Length: 1,500-8,000 words. Pays $5-50.

Poetry: Free verse, light verse and traditional. Buys 4 poems/year. Submit maximum 3 poems. Offers contributor's copies.

Tips: "Market open from June 1 to December 1 inclusive. How the writer handles revisions often is a key to acceptance."

ISAAC ASIMOV'S SCIENCE FICTION MAGAZINE, Davis Publications, Inc., 380 Lexington Ave., New York NY 10017. (212)557-9100. Editor-in-Chief: Gardner Dozois. 98% freelance written. Works with a small number of new/unpublished writers each year. Emphasizes science fiction. 13 times a year magazine. Circ. 100,000. Pays on acceptance. Buys first North American serial rights, nonexclusive foreign serial rights and occasionally reprint rights. "Clear and dark" photocopied submissions OK but no simultaneous submissions. Legible computer printout submissions acceptable; prefers letter-quality. "Don't justify right margins." Reports in 6 weeks. Sample copy for 6½x9½ SAE and $2; writer's guidelines for #10 SASE.

Nonfiction: Science. Query first.
Fiction: Science fiction primarily. Some fantasy and poetry. "It's best to read a great deal of material in the genre to avoid the use of some *very* old ideas." Buys 10 mss/issue. Submit complete ms. Length: 100-20,000 words. Pays 5-8¢/word except for novel serializations at 4¢/word.
Tips: Query letters not wanted, except for nonfiction.

‡**JABBERWOCKY, A Magazine of Imaginative Writing**, Chimera Connections, Inc., 7701 SW 7th Pl., Gainesville FL 32605. (904)332-6586. Editor: Duane Bray/Jeff VanderMeer. Managing Editor: Penelope Miller. 100% freelance written. Semiannual magazine on science fiction/horror/fantasy with a surreal/unreal bent, though not exclusively. Estab. 1988. Circ. 500-1,000. Pays on acceptance. Publishes ms an average of 4-6 months after acceptance. Byline given. Offers $25 kill fee. Buys first North American serial rights or first rights. Photocopied submissions OK. Computer printout submissions OK; prefers letter-quality. Reports in 2 weeks on queries; 1-3 weeks on mss. Sample copy $4.50. Writer's guidelines for #10 SASE.
Nonfiction: Essays and interview/profile. Interviews must at least be partially integrated, not just question-answer. No essays on horror at this time. Buys 4 mss/year. Query with or without published clips, or send complete ms. Length: 1,000-5,000 words. Pays $10-50. Sometimes pays expenses of writers on assignment.
Photos: Send photos with submission. Reviews 5x7 prints. Offers $10 per photo. Identification of subjects required. Buys one-time rights.
Fiction: Experimental, fantasy, horror, humorous if SF/L/F, novel excerpts and science fiction. "No short (1,000 words) short stories with twist at end. No 'formula stories' (i.e., pact w/devil, stories about writers)." Buys 25 mss/year. Send complete ms. Length: 500-5,000 words. Pays $10-50.
Poetry: Avant-garde and free verse. "No overtly religious. No end rhyme (slant rhyme OK). Nothing that tells rather than shows (imagery with substance optimum)." Buys 5-15 poems/year. Submit maximum 10 poems. Length: 3-1,000 lines. Pays $5-30.
Tips: "Always include a cover letter with publication credits, where the listing for *Jabber* was seen, and any amusing/interesting facts about the submitter. Send your best piece. We treat writers royally and expect such treatment in return. We are very selective. The best way to know what we take is to buy a sample copy because our slant is rather different."

‡**NEW BLOOD MAGAZINE**, Suite 3730, 540 W. Foothill Blvd., Glendora CA 91740. Editor: Chris B. Lacher. 90% freelance written. Quarterly magazine that uses fiction considered too strong or bizarre for ordinary periodicals. "*NB* is an outlet for work that is otherwise unpublishable because of content, view, opinion, or other. We reach all readers — horror, fantasy, sci-fi, mystery/suspense, erotic — becuase we do not print generic forms of fiction." Circ. 15,000. Pays mostly half on acceptance, half on publication; sometimes pays up to 3 months after publication. Publishes ms an average of 6 months after acceptance. Byline given. Offers 50% kill fee. All rights revert to author upon publication. Submit seasonal/holiday material 6 months in advance. Photocopied and previously published submissions OK. Computer printout submissions OK; no preference, except clear dark type. Reports in 2 weeks. Sample copy $4. Writer's guidelines for #10 SASE.
Nonfiction: Book excerpts (query), essays, exposé, humor, interview/profile, new product, opinion and photo feature. Buys 4 mss/year. Query or send complete ms. Length: 500-3,000 words. Pays 3¢/word for assigned articles.
Photos: State availability of photos with submission. Reviews contact sheets. Offers no additional payment for photos accepted with ms. Model releases required. Buys one-time rights.
Columns/Departments: Shelf-Life (book reviews), 100-500 words; Prose & Conversation (novel excerpt/opinion), 1,000-5,000 words. Buys 4-8 mss/year. Query or send complete ms. Pays 1-5¢/word.
Fiction: Adventure, erotica, experimental, fantasy, horror/gore, humorous, mainstream, mystery, novel excerpts, science fiction, slice-of-life vignettes and suspense. Open to all subjects, except libelous fiction, fiction that portrays children in pornographic situations. Buys 50-100 mss/year. Send complete ms. Length: 750-5,000 words. Pays 1-5¢/word; higher for special.
Poetry: Avant-garde, free verse, Haiku, light verse, traditional. Buys 50-100 poems/year. Submit maximum 5 poems. Length: 3-25 lines. Pays $5 minimum.
Fillers: Anecdotes, facts, gags to be illustrated by cartoonist, newsbreaks and short humor. Buys 10-25/year. Pays $5 minimum.
Tips: "I support you by answering your submission personally — always, with no exceptions — so I hope you will support me. *NB* was created as an outlet not only for the unpublishable, but also for the beginning or less established author, hence the title. I try not to discourage any contributor — if you're brave enough and dedicated enough to submit your work professionally, I believe you will eventually become successful. Don't get discouraged. I submitted my work for 8 years before I made my first sale, so be persistent."

PANDORA, 2844 Grayson, Ferndale MI 48220. Editors: Meg MacDonald. 95% freelance written. Works with a number of new/unpublished writers each year. Magazine published 4 times/year covering science fiction and fantasy. Circ. 500. Pays on publication. Publishes ms an average of 6-12 months after acceptance. Byline given. Buys first North American serial rights and second serial (reprint) rights; one-time rights on some poems. Photocopied submissions OK. Readable computer printout submissions on white 8½x11 paper acceptable. Reports in 6 weeks. Sample copy $3.50, $5; overseas; subscriptions $15.16 U.S., $20.16 Canada, $25.16 Overseas; writer's guidelines for #10 SASE.

Columns/Departments: "We buy short reviews of science fiction and fantasy books that a reader feels truly exemplify fine writing and will be of interest and use to other writers. Small press titles as well as major press titles are welcome." Buys 2-4 mss/year. Query or send complete ms. Length: under 500 words. Pays $5 and up.

Fiction: Fantasy, science fiction. "No pun stories. Nothing x-rated (no vulgar language or subject matter). No inaccurate science and no horror." Buys 15 mss/year. Send complete ms. Length: 1,000-4,000 words. Pays 1-2¢/word.

Poetry: Ruth Berman, poetry editor. 2809 Drew Ave. S., Minneapolis MN 55417. Buys 9-12 poems/year. Payment starts at $2.50. Length: open. No romance, occult or horror.

Tips: "Send us stories about characters our readers can sympathize with and care about. Then give them convincing, relevant problems they must overcome. Stories about people and their difficulties, victories, and losses are of more interest to us than stories about futuristic gadgets. What impact does the gadget have on society? *That's* what we want to know. Stories must have a point—not just a pun. Happy endings aren't necessary, but we urge authors to leave the reader with a sense that no matter the outcome, something has been accomplished between the first and last pages. Reading our magazine is the best way to determine our needs, and we strongly recommend all contributors read at least one sample. Better yet, subscribe for a while, then start submitting. We like to see whole stories, the shorter the better, and we will make attempts to respond personally with a critique. Foreign contributors, please use two IRCs."

‡**THE SCREAM FACTORY, The Magazine of Horrors, Past, Present, and Future**, Deadline Publications, 145 Tully Rd., San Jose CA 95111. (408)267-1159. Editors: Clifford Brooks, Peter Enfantino and Joe Lopez. 40% freelance written. Quarterly literary magazine about horror in films and literature. Estab. 1988. Circ. 300. Pays on acceptance. Publishes ms an average of 6 months after acceptance. Buys first North American serial rights. Submit seasonal/holiday material 6 months in advance. Photocopied submissions OK. Reports in 2 weeks on queries, 1 month on ms. Sample copy $5; writer's guidelines for #10 SASE.

Nonfiction: Book excerpts, essays, historical/nostalgic, interview/profile, new product and personal experience. Buys 10-15 mss/year. Query. Pays 1/2¢/word.

Photos: Send photos with submission. Reviews prints. Offers no additional payment for photos accepted with ms. Captions required. Buys one-time rights.

Columns/Departments: Book reviews of horror novels/collections; Writer's Writing (what horror authors are currently working on); A Tale of Wyrmwood (fiction saga about haunted town). Query or send complete ms. Pays 1/2¢/word.

Fiction: Horror and dark fantasy. No explicit sexual content. Buys 4-10 mss/year. Send complete ms. Pays 1/2¢/word.

Fillers: Facts, newsbreaks. Pays 1/2¢/word.

Tips: "Looking for reviews of horror fiction, especially the lesser known authors. News on the horror genre, interviews with horror authors and strong opinion pieces."

‡**SERENDIPITY, The Magazine of Everything**, Solarquest Publications, 4295 Silver Lake Rd., Pinson AL 35126. Editor: Joseph Dickerson. 60% freelance written. Bimonthly magazine on science fiction, fantasy, and horror. Circ. 3,000. Pays on publication. Publishes ms an average of 3 months after acceptance. Byline given. Buys first North American serial rights. Submit seasonal/holiday material 6 months in advance. Simultaneous, photocopied and previously published submissions OK. Computer printout submissions OK; prefers letter-quality. Reports in 1 month on queries; 2 months on mss. Sample copy $2. Writer's guidelines for #10 SASE.

Nonfiction: Book excerpts, essays, historical/nostalgic, humor, interview/profile, technical and space exploration. Buys 6 mss/year. Query with or without published clips, or send complete ms. Length: 750-3,000 words. Pays $15-60.

Photos: Send photos with submission. Reviews 4x5 transparencies. Offers $5-15 per photo. Buys one-time rights.

Columns/Departments: Jeff Tatarek. Future Words (SF/F/H book reviews), 600-1,500 words; Critical Hits (role playing games reviews), 600-1,500 words; Trekking (*Star Trek* articles), 600-2,000 words and Thought Balloons (comic book reviews), 600-1,500 words. Buys 25 mss/year. Query with published clips. Pays $15-30.

Fiction: Adventure, condensed novels, experimental, fantasy, historical, horror, humorous, mainstream, mystery, novel excerpts, science fiction and suspense. Buys 40 mss/year. Send complete ms. Length: 750-3,000 words. Pays $15-75.

Poetry: Avant-garde, free verse, haiku, light verse and traditional. Buys 60 poems/year. Submit maximum 4 poems. Length: 3-30 lines. Pays $1-3.

Fillers: Les Crane. Gags to be illustrated by cartoonist, newsbreak and short humor. Buys 10/year. Length: 5-300 words. Pays $1-6.

Tips: "Ask yourself: Would *I* like to read what I'm writing? If the answer is no, then just forget it. If it's yes, then send it in. Have faith in what you have written; and find out beforehand if it's something that I would publish (by buying a sample issue). Be creative; write something original. Or, if your story's plot is an often-used one, write it *with* originality."

STARLOG MAGAZINE, The Science Fiction Universe, Starlog Group, 8th Floor, 475 Park Ave. S., New York NY 10016. (212)689-2830. FAX: (212) 889-7933. Editor: David McDonnell. 85% freelance written. Works with a number of new/unpublished writers each year and is very eager to work with new/unpublished writers. Monthly magazine covering "the science fiction-fantasy-adventure genre: its films, TV, books, art and personalities. We explore the fields of science fiction and fantasy with occasional forays into adventure (i.e., the James Bond and Indiana Jones films). We concentrate on the personalities and behind-the-scenes angles of science fiction/fantasy films with comprehensive interviews with actors, directors, screenwriters, producers, special effects technicians and others. Be aware that '*sc-fi*' is mostly considered a derogatory term by our readers and by us." Pays on publication. Publishes ms an average of 3 months after acceptance. Byline given. All contributors are also credited in masthead. Offers kill fee "only to mss *written* or interviews *done*." Buys first North American serial rights to material with option to reprint (for an additional fee) certain articles in twice annual *Starlog Yearbook*. Buys second serial (reprint) rights to certain other material. Submit seasonal/holiday material 6 months in advance. Simultaneous queries (*if* we are aware they are being made) and photocopied submissions OK. Computer printout submissions acceptable (separate sheets first); prefers letter-quality. Reports in 4 weeks on queries; 6 weeks on mss. "We provide an assignment sheet to *all* writers with deadline and other info, thus authorizing a queried piece." Sample copy and writer's guidelines for $3.95 and 8½x11 SAE with 3 first class stamps. Writer's guidelines for #10 SASE.

Nonfiction: Interview/profile (actors, directors, screenwriters who've made past or current science fiction films, and science fiction novelists); photo features; special effects how-tos (on filmmaking only); retrospectives of famous SF films and TV series; occasional pieces on science fiction fandom, conventions, etc. "We also sometimes cover animation (especially Disney and WB)." No personal opinion think pieces/essays on *Star Wars, Star Trek. No* first person. "We prefer article format as opposed to question-and-answer interviews." Buys 150 or more mss/year. Query first with published clips. "We prefer queries by mail to phone queries. If we've never talked to you before, please *avoid* making first contact with us by phone." Length: 500-3,000 words. Pays $35 (500-word pieces); $50-75 (sidebars); $100-225 (1,000-word and up pieces). Avoids articles on horror films/creators and comic book/comic strip creators and creations.

Photos: State availability of photos. Pays $10-25 for color slide transparencies and 8x10 b&w prints depending on quality. "No separate payment for photos provided by film studios." Captions, model releases, identification of subjects and credit line on photos required. Photo credit given. Buys all rights.

Columns/Departments: Other Voices (essays by well-known, *published*, science fiction writers on their genre work, the writing life or their opinions, immediate need), $200 and up, 2,000 words plus; Fan Network (articles on fandom and its aspects—mostly staff-written); Booklog (book reviews, $10 each, by assignment only); Medialog (news of upcoming science fiction films and TV projects and mini-interviews with those involved, $35); Videolog (videocassette and disk releases of genre interest, staff-written). New comics news department, focusing on science fiction, is being introduced. Buys 24-30 mss/year. Query with published clips. Length: 300-500 words. No kill fee on logs.

Tips: "Absolutely *no fiction*. We expect to emphasize literary science fiction much more in 1990 and will need further interviews with writers and coverage of science fiction/fantasy literature. We especially *need* writers who know a prospective interviewee's literary work. Additionally, we expect to cover classic science fiction/fantasy TV series and films in much more detail especially with interviews with the quest stars from the original *Star Trek* episodes. A writer can best break in to *Starlog* with short news pieces or by getting an unusual interview that we can't get through normal channels or by *out-thinking* us and coming up with something new on a current film or book before we can think of it. We are always looking for *new* angles on *Star Trek: The Next Generation, Star Wars*, the original *Star Trek, Doctor Who, Blake's 7* and seek a small number of features investigating aspects (i.e., cast & crew) of series which remain very popular with many readers: *Starman, Lost in Space, Space 1999, Battlestar Galactica, The Twilight Zone, The Outer Limits*. Know your subject before you try us. Most full-length major assignments go to freelancers with whom we're already dealing. But if we like your clips and ideas, we'll be happy to give *you* a chance. Discovering new freelancers and helping them to break into print is always enjoyable. We love it. We're fans of this material—and a prospective writer must be, too—but we were *also* freelancers. And if your love for science fiction shows through, we would love to *help* you break in as we've done with others in the past."

STARWIND, The Starwind Press, Box 98, Ripley OH 45167. (513)392-4549. Editors: David F. Powell and Susannah C. West. 75% freelance written. Eager to work with new/unpublished writers. A quarterly magazine "for older teenagers and adults who have an interest in science and technology, and who also enjoy reading well-crafted science fiction and fantasy." Circ. 2,500. Pays on publication. Publishes ms an average of 1 year after acceptance. Byline given. Rights vary with author and material; negotiated with author. Usually first serial rights and second serial reprint rights (nonfiction). Photocopied submissions OK. Query for electronic submissions. Computer printout submissions acceptable. Photocopied and dot-matrix submissions OK. "In fact, we encourage disposable submissions; easier for us and easier for the author. Just enclose SASE for our response. We prefer non-simultaneous submissions." Reports in 2-3 months. Sample copy for $3.50 and 9x12 SAE; writer's guidelines for #10 SASE.

Nonfiction: How-to (technological interest, e.g., how to build a robot eye, building your own radio receiver, etc.); interview/profile (of leaders in science and technology fields); and technical ("did you know" articles dealing with development of current technology). "No speculative articles, dealing with topics such as the Abominable Snowman, Bermuda Triangle, etc. At present, most nonfiction is staff-written or reprinted from other sources. We hope to use more freelance written work in the future." Query. Length: 1,000-7,000 words. Pays 1-4¢/word.

Photos: Send photos with accompanying query or ms. Reviews b&w contact sheets and prints. Model releases and identification of subjects required. "If photos are available, we prefer to purchase them as part of the written piece." Buys negotiable rights.

Fiction: Fantasy and science fiction. "No stories whose characters were created by others (e.g. *Lovecraft*, *Star Trek*, *Star Wars* characters, etc.)." Buys 15-20 mss/year. Send complete ms. Length: 2,000-10,000 words. Pays 1-4¢/word. "We prefer previously unpublished fiction." No query necessary.

Tips: "Our need for nonfiction is greater than for fiction at present. Almost all our fiction and nonfiction is unsolicited. We rarely ask for rewrites, because we've found that rewrites are often disappointing; although the writer may have rewritten it to fix problems, he/she frequently changes parts we liked, too."

THRUST – SCIENCE FICTION AND FANTASY REVIEW, Thrust Publications, 8217 Langport Terrace, Gaithersburg MD 20877. (301)948-2514. Editor: D. Douglas Fratz. 20-40% freelance written. Prefers to work with published/established writers; works with small number of new/unpublished writers each year. A quarterly literary review magazine covering science fiction and fantasy literature. "*THRUST – Science Fiction and Fantasy Review* is the highly acclaimed, Hugo-Award-nominated magazine about science fiction and fantasy. Since 1973, *THRUST* has been featuring in-depth interviews with science fiction's best known authors and artists, articles and columns by the field's most outspoken writers, and reviews of current science fiction books. *THRUST* has built its reputation on never failing to take a close look at the most sensitive and controversial issues concerning science fiction and continues to receive the highest praise and most heated comments from professionals and fans in the science fiction field." Circ. 1,800. Pays on publication. Publishes ms an average of 6 months after acceptance. Byline given. Buys first North American serial rights, one-time rights and second serial (reprint) rights. Submit seasonal/holiday material 3-6 months in advance. Simultaneous queries, and simultaneous, photocopied and previously published submissions OK. Query for electronic submissions. Computer printout submissions acceptable; prefers letter-quality. Reports in 2 weeks on queries; 2 months on mss. Sample copy for $2.50.

Nonfiction: Humor, interview/profile, opinion, personal experience and book reviews. Buys 50-100 mss/year. Query or send complete ms. Length: 200-10,000 words. Pays 1-2¢/word.

Photos: "We publish only photos of writers being interviewed." State availability of photos. Pays $2-15 for smaller than 8x10 b&w prints. Buys one-time rights.

Columns/Departments: Uses science fiction and fantasy book reviews and film reviews. Buys 40-100 mss/year. Send complete ms. Length: 100-1,000 words. Pays 1¢/word. (Reviews usually paid in subscriptions, not cash.)

Tips: "Reviews are best way to break into *THRUST*. Must be on current science fiction and fantasy books. The most frequent mistake made by writers in completing articles for us is writing to a novice audience; *THRUST*'s readers are science fiction and fantasy experts."

2 AM MAGAZINE, Box 6754, Rockford IL 61125. Editor: Gretta M. Anderson. 100% freelance written. A quarterly magazine of fiction, poetry, articles and art for readers of fantasy, horror and science fiction. Circ. 1000. Pays on acceptance. Publishes ms an average of 9 months after acceptance. Byline given. Buys first North American serial rights. Submit seasonal/holiday material 1 year inadvance. Photocopied submissions OK. Computer printout submission OK; no dot-matrix. Reports in 1 month on queries; 2-3 months on mss. Sample copy $5.95; writer's guidelines for #10 SAE with 1 first class stamp.

Nonfiction: How-to, interview/profile, opinion. "No essays originally written for high school or college courses." Buys 5 mss/year. Query with or without published clips or send complete ms. Length: 500-2,000 words. Pay ½-1¢/word.

Photos: State availability of photos with submission. Offers no additional payment for photos accepted with ms. Identification of subjects required. Buys one-time rights.

Fiction: Fantasy, horror, mystery, science fiction and suspense. Buys 50 mss/year. Send complete ms. Length: 500-5,000 words. Pays ½-1¢/word.

Poetry: Free verse and traditional. "No haiku/zen or short poems without imagery." Buys 20 poems/year. Submit up to 5 poems at one time. Length: 5-100 lines. Pays $1-5.

Tips: "We are looking for taut, imaginative fiction. Please use proper manuscript format; all manuscripts must include a SASE to be considered. We suggest to Canadian and foreign writers that they send disposable manuscripts with one IRC and a #10 SAE for response, if U.S. postage stamps are unavailable to them."

For information on setting your freelance fees, see How Much Should I Charge? in the Business of Writing section.

Sports

A number of new sports magazines have started publication, each with its area of specialization. In the Juvenile section, *Sports Illustrated* debuted *Sports Illustrated for Kids*. Covered in this section are several new regional titles and a magazine for athletes called *Proathlete*.

For the convenience of writers who specialize in one or two areas of sport and outdoor writing, the publications are subcategorized by the sport or subject matter they emphasize. Publications in related categories (for example, Hunting and Fishing; Archery and Bowhunting) often buy similar material. Writers should read through this entire category to become familiar with the subcategories. Publications on horse breeding and hunting dogs are classified in the Animal category, while horse racing is listed here. Publications dealing with automobile or motorcycle racing can be found in the Automotive and Motorcycle category. Markets interested in articles on exercise and fitness are listed in the Health and Fitness section. Outdoor publications that promote the preservation of nature, placing only secondary emphasis on nature as a setting for sport, are in the Nature, Conservation and Ecology category. Regional magazines are frequently interested in sports material with a local angle. Camping publications are classified in the Travel, Camping and Trailer category.

Archery and Bowhunting

BOW AND ARROW HUNTING, Box HH/34249 Camino Capistrano, Capistrano Beach CA 92624. Editorial Director: Roger Combs. 80% freelance written. Eager to work with new/unpublished writers. Bimonthly magazine for bowhunters. Pays on acceptance. Publishes ms an average of 6 months after acceptance. Buys first serial rights. Byline given. Computer printout submissions acceptable; prefers letter-quality. Reports on submissions in 2 months. Author must have some knowledge of archery terms.
Nonfiction: Articles: bowhunting, techniques used by champs, how to make your own tackle and off-trail hunting tales. Likes a touch of humor in articles. "No dead animals or 'my first hunt.' " Also uses one technical and how-to article per issue. Submit complete ms. Length: 1,500-2,500 words. Pays $150-300.
Photos: Purchased as package with ms; 5x7 minimum. Pays $100 for cover chromes, 35mm or larger.
Tips: "Subject matter is more important than style—that's why we have editors and copy pencils. Good b&w photos are of primary importance. Don't submit color prints. We staff-write our shorter pieces."

‡**BOWBENDER**, Mr. Bill Windsor, 65 McDonald Close; Box 912, Carstairs, Alberta T0M 0N0 Canada. Editor: Kathleen Windsor. 100% freelance written. Quarterly magazine on archery/bowhunting. "All submissions must concern archery in Canada, especially hunting with the bow and arrow." Circ. 33,000. Pays on publication. Publishes ms an average of 6 months after acceptance. Byline given. Buys first North American serial rights. Submit seasonal/holiday material 6-9 months in advance. Photocopied submissions OK. Computer printout submissions OK; prefers letter quality. Reports in 1 week on queries; 3 weeks on mss. Sample copy $2.50 with 9x12 SAE and Canadian $1 postage; U.S. $2 in Canadian stamps or (cash). Writer's guidelines for #10 SAE with 37¢ Canadian stamp or 30¢ American stamp.
Nonfiction: General interest (archery), how-to (hunting tips), humor (archery), new product (archery), opinion (Canadian bowhunting), personal experience (bowhunting) and technical (bowhunting). Spring—guides directory; Summer—archery dealer directory; Fall—big game summary. "No anti-hunting; American hunts." Buys 40 mss/year. Query. Length: 500-2,500 words. "Does not assign articles." Pays $300 maximum for unsolicited articles. Sometimes pays in other premiums (ad swap).
Photos: Send photos with submission. Reviews 35mm transparencies and 3x5 prints. Offers no additional payment for photos accepted with ms. Captions, model releases and identification of subjects preferred, not required. Buys one-time rights.
Columns/Departments: Spotlight On . . . (regular column describing archery personality, club, manufacturer, etc. from Canada), 1,200-1,500 words. Buys 12 mss/year. Send complete ms. Pays $100-150.
Fillers: Anecdotes, facts, gags to be illustrated by cartoonist, newsbreaks and short humor. Pays 10¢/word maximum.
Tips: "Make sure articles(s) is typed. *Please* read the guidelines; that's what they are for. Remember that a quarterly cannot (because of space) accept all manuscripts—this is not a final rejection. Send a cover letter. Guest articles: factual; descriptive but not flowery, add tips for education; enjoy your own story."

BOWHUNTER, The Magazine for the Hunting Archer, Cowles Magazines, 2245 Kohn Rd. Box 8200, Harrisburg PA 17105-8200. (717)540-8192. FAX (717) 657-9526. Editor: M.R. James. Managing Editor: Dave Canfield. 85% freelance written. Bimonthly magazine (with two special issues) on hunting big and small game with bow and arrow. "We are a special interest publication, produced by bowhunters for bowhunters, covering all aspects of the sport. Material included in each issue is designed to entertain and inform readers, making them better bowhunters." Circ. 250,000. Pays on acceptance. Publishes ms an average of 10-12 months after acceptance. Byline given. Kill fee varies. Buys first North American serial rights and one-time rights. Submit seasonal/holiday material 8 months in advance. Photocopied submissions OK (sometimes). Computer printout submissions OK; prefers letter-quality. Reports in 2-4 weeks on queries; 4-5 weeks on mss. Sample copy $2. Free writer's guidelines.

Nonfiction: General interest, how-to, interview/profile, opinion, personal experience and photo feature. "We publish a special 'Big Game' issue each Fall (September) but need all material by mid-March. Our other annual publication, *Whitetail Bowhunter*, is staff written or by assignment only. We don't want articles which graphically deal with an animal's death. And, please, no articles written from the animal's viewpoint." Buys 100 mss/year. Query. Length: 250-2,500 words. Pays $500 maximum for assigned articles; $25-500 for unsolicited articles. Sometimes pays expenses of writers on assignment.

Photos: Send photos with submission. Reviews 35mm and 2¼x2¼ transparencies and 5x7 and 8x10 prints. Offers $35-200 per photo. Captions required. Buys one-time rights.

Columns/Departments: Would You Believe (unusual or offbeat hunting experiences), 250-1,000 words. Buys 6-8 mss/year. Send complete ms. Pays $25-100.

Tips: "A writer must know bowhunting and be willing to share that knowledge. Writers should anticipate *all* questions a reader might ask, then answer them in the article itself or in an appropriate sidebar. Articles should be written with the reader foremost in mind; we won't be impressed by writers seeking to prove how good they are—either as writers or bowhunters. We care about the reader and don't need writers with 'I' trouble. Features are a good bet since most of our material comes from freelancers. The best advice is: Be yourself. Tell your story the same as if sharing the experience around a campfire. Don't try to write like you think a writer writes."

‡BOWHUNTING WORLD (formerly *Archery World*), Ehlert Publishing Group, Suite 101, 319 Barry Ave., S., Wayzata MN 55391. (612)476-2200. Managing Editor: Tim Dehn. 70% freelance written. A magazine published 9 times/year and written for bowhunting and archery enthusiasts who participate in the sport year-round. Circ. 208,000. Pays on publication. Publishes manuscripts an average of 5 months after acceptance. Byline given. Offers 50% kill fee. Buys first rights. Simultaneous submissions OK. Reports in 3 weeks on queries, 4-6 weeks on manuscripts. Sample copy for 9×12 SAE and $2 postage; free writer's and photographers guidelines.

Nonfiction: Hunting adventure and scouting and hunting how-to features, primarily from a first-person point of view. Also interview/profile pieces, historical articles, humor and assigned product reviews. Buys 60 mss/year. Query or send complete ms. Length: 1,500-3,000 words. Pays from less than $200 to more than $400.

Photos: Send photos with submission. Reviews 35mm transparencies and b&w prints. Captions required. Buys one-time rights. Send for separate photo guidelines.

Tips: "Good writing is paramount. Authors should be bowhunters or, in the case of interviews or profiles, familiar enough with the sport to write well about it. Read bowhunting stories in *Bowhunting World*, *Field & Stream*, *Outdoor Life* and *Sports Afield* for an idea of the level of writing required and the types of subjects most often used. Submit polished manuscripts and support them with a variety of good slides or b&w prints."

‡GREAT LAKES BOWHUNTER MAGAZINE, Midwest Manufacturer Marketing Service, Rt. 1 Box 41E, Box 67, Pillager MN 56473-0067. (218)746-3333. Editor: Johnny E. Boatner. 95% freelance written. Magazine publishes seven issues per year on bowhunting. "We are interested in any kind of articles that deal with bowhunting. We pride ourselves as a magazine written by hunter/writers, rather than writer/hunters. We are not interested in articles that just fill pages, we like each paragraph to say something." Circ. 7,000-15,000. Pays on publication. Publishes ms an average of 1 or 2 months after acceptance. Byline sometimes given. Buys first rights. Submit seasonal/holiday material 4 months in advance. Photocopied submissions OK. Computer printout submissions OK; prefers letter-quality. Reports in 1 week on queries; 6 weeks on mss. Free sample copy and writer's guidelines.

Nonfiction: Historical/nostalgic, how-to, humor, interview/profile, new product, personal experience, photo feature, technical, travel; bowhunting and archery related. "No commercials of writers' pet products; articles including bad ethics, gory, target archery." Buys 75 mss/year. Send complete ms. Length: 600-3,500 words. Pays $25 minimum for assigned articles; $25-75 for unsolicited articles. Sometimes pays in contributor copies or other premiums (trade ads for articles). Sometimes pays expenses of writers on assignments.

Photos: Send photos with submission. Reviews transparencies and prints. Offers no additional payment for photos accepted with ms. Captions and identification of subjects required. Buys one-time rights.
Fiction: Adventure (bowhunting related) and historical (bowhunting). Send complete ms. Length: 600-3,500 words. Pays $25-75.
Fillers: Anecdotes, facts, gags to be illustrated by cartoonist, newsbreaks and short humor. Buys 10/year. Length: 100-500 words. Pays $10-25.
Tips: "We do mainly first person accounts as long as it relates to hunting with the bow and arrow, If they have a bowhunting story they want to tell, then type it up and send it in, we probably publish more first time writers than any other bowhunting magazine today. Keep the articles clean,entertaining and informative. We do a few how-tos, but mainly want articles about bowhunting and the great outdoors that relate to bowhunting."

Baseball

‡CALIFORNIA BASEBALL MAGAZINE, California Football Magazine, Inc., Suite 301, 1801 Catalina Ave., Redondo Beach CA 90277. (213)373-3630 or (213)326-5859. 40% freelance written. Bimonthly magazine on baseball. (See *California Football Magazine*).

Basketball

‡CALIFORNIA BASKETBALL MAGAZINE, Suite 300, 1801 S. Catalina Ave., Redondo Beach CA 90277. (See *California Football Magazine*).

Bicycling

BICYCLE GUIDE, Raben Publishing Co., 711 Boylston St., Boston MA 02116. (617)236-1885. FAX (617) 267-1849. Editor: Theodore Costantino. 25% freelance written. "We're equally happy working with established writers and new writers." Magazine published 9 times/year covering "the world of high-performance cycling. We cover racing, touring and mountain biking from an enthusiast's point of view." Circ. 200,000. Pays on publication. Publishes ms an average of 4 months after acceptance. Byline given. Offers kill fee. Buys first North American serial rights. Submit seasonal/holiday material 6 months in advance. Simultaneous submissions OK. Computer printout submissions acceptable; prefers letter-quality. Reports in 3 weeks on queries; 1 month on mss. Sample copy for 8½x11 SAE with 2 first class stamps; writer's guidelines for #10 SASE.
Nonfiction: Humor, interview/profile, new product, opinion, photo feature, technical, and travel (short rides in North America only). Buyers' annual published in April. "We need 'how-to-buy' material by preceding November." No entry-level how-to repairs or projects; long overseas tours; puff pieces on sports medicine; or 'my first ride' articles. Buys 18 mss/year. Query. Length: 900-3,500 words. Pays $200-600. Sometimes pays expenses of writers on assignment.
Photos: Send photos with submissions. Reviews transparencies and 5x8 b&w prints. Offers $50-250/photo. Captions, model releases, and identification of subjects required. Buys one-time rights.
Columns/Departments: What's Hot (new product reviews, personalities, events), 100-200 words; En Route (helpful hints for high performance cycling; on-the-road advice), 100 words; and Guest Column (thoughtful essay of interest to our readers), 900-1,200 words. Buys 30 mss/year. Query. Pays $25-450.
Tips: "Freelancers should be cyclists with a thorough knowledge of the sport. Area most open to freelancers are Training Methods (cover specific routines); Rides (75-100-mile loop rides over challenging terrain in continental U.S.); and Technical Pages (covers leading edge, technical innovations, new materials)."

‡BICYCLING, Rodale Press, Inc., 33 E. Minor St., Emmaus PA 18098. FAX: (215)965-5670. Editor and Publisher: James C. McCullagh. 20-25% freelance written. Prefers to work with published/established writers. Publishes 10 issues/year (7 monthly, 3 bimonthly); 104-250 pages. Circ. 300,000. Pays on acceptance or publication. Publishes ms an average of 6 months after acceptance. Byline given. Buys all rights. Submit seasonal/holiday material 5 months in advance. Query for electronic submissions. Computer printout submissions acceptable; prefers letter-quality to dot-matrix. Writer's guidelines for SASE.
Nonfiction: How-to (on all phases of bicycle touring, bike repair, maintenance, commuting, new products, clothing, riding technique, nutrition for cyclists, conditioning). Fitness is more important than ever. Also travel (bicycling must be central here); photo feature (on cycling events of national significance); and technical

(component review—query). "We are strictly a bicycling magazine. We seek readable, clear, well-informed pieces. We rarely run articles that are pure humor or inspiration but a little of either might flavor even our most technical pieces. No poetry or fiction." Buys 1-2 unsolicited mss/issue. Send complete ms. Length: 1,500 words average. Pays $25-1,200. Sometimes pays expenses of writers on assignment.

Photos: State availability of photos with query letter or send photo material with ms. Pays $15-50 for b&w prints and $35-250 for color transparencies. Captions preferred; model release required.

Fillers: Anecdotes and news items for Paceline section.

Tips: "We're alway seeking interesting accounts of cycling as a lifestlye."

‡**BIKEOHIO**, Peter Wray, Publisher, Box 141287, Columbus OH 43214. (614)262-1447. Editor: Linda Hanlon. 20% freelance written. Monthly tabloid on bicycling in state of Ohio. "All aspects of adult bicycling covering both racing and recreational riding." Estab. 1988. Circ. 25,000. Pays on publication. Byline given. Buys first rights and second serial (reprint) rights. Simultaneous submissions OK. Query for electronic submissions. Computer printout submissions OK; prefers letter-quality. Sample copy and writer's guidelines for 10x13 SAE with 65¢ postage. Writer's guidelines for #10 SASE.

Nonfiction: How-to (athletics), humor (bicycle related), interview/profile (bicycle related), new product (bicycle related), personal experience (bicycle related) and photo feature (bicycle related). Buys 10 mss/year. Query. Length: 500-2,500 words. Pays $25-50. Sometimes pays expenses of writers on assignment.

Photos: Send photos with submission. Reviews contact sheets and 5x7 prints. Offers no additional payment for photos accepted with ms. Identification of subjects required. Buys one-time rights.

Tips: "Consult with editor. Looking for reports of racing/riding events, previews, interviews with personalities. Inclusion of art is very important."

BIKEREPORT, Bikecentennial, Inc., The Bicycle Travel Association, Box 8308, Missoula MT 59807. (406)721-1776. Editor: Daniel D'Ambrosio. 75% freelance written. Works with a small number of new/unpublished writers each year. Bimonthly bicycle touring magazine for Bikecentennial members. Circ. 18,000. Pays on publication. Publishes ms an average of 8 months after acceptance. Byline given. Include short bio with manuscript. Buys first serial rights. Submit seasonal/holiday material 3 months in advance. Simultaneous queries and photocopied submissions OK. Query for electronic submissions. Computer printout submissions acceptable; no dot-matrix. Reports in 2 weeks on queries; 1 month on mss. Sample copy and guidelines for 9x12 SAE with $1 postage.

Nonfiction: Historical/nostalgic (interesting spots along bike trails); how-to (bicycle); humor (touring); interview/profile (bicycle industry people); personal experience ("my favorite tour"); photo feature (bicycle); technical (bicycle); travel ("my favorite tour"). Buys 20-25 mss/year. Query with published clips or send complete ms. Length: 800-2,500 words. Pays 3¢/word and up.

Photos: Bicycle, scenery, portraits. State availability of photos. Model releases and identification of subjects required.

Fiction: Adventure, experimental, historical, humorous. Not interested in anything that doesn't involve bicycles. Query with published clips or send complete ms. Length: 800-2,500 words. Pays 3¢/word and up.

Tips: "We don't get many good essays. Consider that a hint. But we are still always interested in travelogs."

‡**CYCLING USA, The Official Publication of the U.S. Cycling Federation**, 1750 E. Boulder St., Colorado Springs CO 80909. (719)578-4581. Editor: Diane Fritschner. 50% freelance written. Monthly magazine covering reportage and commentary on American bicycle racing, personalities and sports physiology, for USCF licensed cyclists. Circ. 32,000. Pays on publication. Publishes ms an average of 2 months after acceptance. Byline given. Simultaneous queries, and photocopied and previously published submissions OK. Computer printout submissions acceptable; no dot-matrix. Reports in 2 weeks. Sample copy for 10x12 SAE and 60¢ postage.

Nonfiction: How-to (train, prepare for a bike race); interview/profile; opinion; personal experience; photo feature; technical; and race commentary on major cycling events. No comparative product evaluations. Buys 15 mss/year. Query with published clips. Length: 500-2,000 words. Pays 10¢/word.

Photos: State availability of photos. Pays $10-25 for 5x7 b&w prints; $100 for color transparencies used as cover. Captions required. Buys one-time rights.

Columns/Departments: Athlete's Kitchen, Nuts & Bolts, Coaches Column.

Tips: "A background in bicycle racing is important because the sport is somewhat insular, technical and complex. Most major articles are generated inhouse. Race reports are most open to freelancers. Be concise, informative and anecdotal. The most frequent mistake made by writers in completing an article for us is that it is too lengthy; our format is more compatible with shorter (500-800 word) articles than longer features."

‡**SOUTHWEST CYCLING**, Suite 201, 301 W. California, Glendale CA 91203. (818)247-9384. Editor: Rachelle Berlatsky-Kaplan. 80% freelance written. Monthly tabloid on bicycling—commuting, touring, racing, off-road and triathlon. Circ. 60,000. Pays 30 days after publication. Publishes ms an average of 2 months after acceptance. Byline given. Buys first rights. Submit seasonal/holiday material 6 months in advance. Photocopied submissions OK. Query for electronic submissions. Computer printout submissions OK; prefers

letter-quality. Reports in 1 month. Sample copy $2. Free writer's guidelines with SAE.
Nonfiction: How-to, humor, interview/profile, personal experience and travel. Buys 75 or more mss/year. Query with or without published clips, or send complete ms. Length: 400-2,000 words. Pays $40-200. Sometimes pays expenses of writers on assignment.
Photos: State availability of photos with submission. Reviews 5x7 or 8x10 prints. Offers $25-75 per photo. Captions, model releases and identification of subjects required. Buys one-time rights.
Columns/Departments: Sprockets (the funny side of bicycling), 800-1,200 words and Southwest Reoprt (short news items from our region), 250-600 words. Buys 1-12 mss/year. Query with published clips. Pays $25-120.
Tips: "Unsolicited articles that have been published include first-person accounts no one else could have written. Also news items that we are unaware of have a chance of reaching print. Send a query on a cycling personality from our region."

VELONEWS, A Journal of Bicycle Racing, 5595 Arapahoe Ave., Apt. G, Boulder CO 80303. (303)440-0601. Managing Editor: Tim Johnson. 35% freelance written. Monthly tabloid October-March, biweekly April-September covering bicycle racing. Circ. 14,000. Pays on publication. Publishes ms an average of 2 weeks after acceptance. Byline given. Buys one-time rights. Simultaneous queries, and simultaneous, photocopied, and previously published submissions OK. Electronic submissions OK; call first. Computer printout submissions acceptable; prefers letter-quality. Reports in 2 weeks. Sample copy for 9x12 SAE plus $1.05 postage.
Nonfiction: In addition to race coverage, opportunities for freelancers include reviews (book and videos) and health-and-fitness departments. Buys 30 mss/year. Query. Length: 300-2,500 words. Pays up to 10¢/word.
Photos: State availability of photos. Pays $16.50-34.50 for b&w prints. Captions and identification of subjects required. Buys one-time rights.

Boating

BAY & DELTA YACHTSMAN, Recreation Publications, 2019 Clement Ave., Alameda CA 94501. (415)865-7500. Editor: Bill Parks. 45% freelance written. Works with a small number of new/unpublished writers each year. Emphasizes recreational boating for small boat owners and recreational yachtsmen in northern California. Monthly tabloid newspaper. Circ. 22,000. Pays on publication. Publishes ms an average of 6 months after acceptance. Byline given. Buys one-time serial rights. Submit seasonal/holiday material 3 months in advance. Photocopied submissions OK. Query for electronic submissions. Computer printout submissions OK. Reports in 1 month. Free writer's guidelines.
Nonfiction: Historical (nautical history of northern California); how-to (modifications, equipment, supplies, rigging, etc., aboard both power and sailboats); humor (no disaster or boating ineptitude pieces); informational (government legislation as it relates to recreational boating); interview; nostalgia; personal experience ("How I learned about boating from this" type of approach); photo feature (to accompany copy); profile; and travel. Buys 5-10 unsolicited mss/issue. Query. Length: 1,200-2,000 words. Pays $1/column inch.
Photos: Photos purchased with accompanying ms. Pays $5 for b&w glossy or matte finish photos. Total purchase price for ms includes payment for photos. Captions required.
Fiction: Adventure (sea stories, cruises, races pertaining to West Coast and points South/Southwest); fantasy; historical; humorous; and mystery. Buys 4 mss/year. Query. Length: 500-1,750 words. Pays $1/column inch.
Tips: "Think of our market area: the waterways of northern California and how, why, when and where the boatman would use those waters. Writers should be able to comprehend the boating and Bay Area references in our magazine. Think about unusual onboard applications of ideas (power and sail), special cruising tips, etc. We're very interested in local boating interviews—both the famous and unknown. Write for a knowledgeable boating public."

BOAT PENNSYLVANIA, Pennsylvania Fish Commission, Box 1673, Harrisburg PA 17105. (717)657-4520. Editor: Art Michaels. 60-80% freelance written. Quarterly magazine covering motorboating, sailing, canoeing, water skiing, kayaking and rafting in Pennsylvania. Prefers to work with published/established contributors, but works with a few unpublished writers and photographers every year. Pays 6-8 weeks after acceptance. Publishes ms an average of 8 months after acceptance. Byline given. Buys variable rights. Submit seasonal/holiday material 8 months in advance. Computer printout submissions acceptable; prefers letter-quality. Reports in 2 weeks on queries; 2 months on manuscript. Writer's guidelines for #10 SASE.
Nonfiction: How-to, photo feature, technical and historical/nostalgic, all related to water sports in Pennsylvania. No saltwater material. Buys 40 mss/year. Query. Length: 300-3,000 words. Pays $25-300.
Photos: Send photos with submission. Reviews 35mm and larger color transparencies and 8x10 b&w prints. Captions, model releases and identification of subjects required.

CANOE MAGAZINE, Canoe Associates, Box 3146, Kirkland WA 98083. (206)827-6363. FAX: (206)827-5177. Managing Editor: George Thomas. 80-90% freelance written. A bimonthly magazine on canoeing, whitewater kayaking and sea-kayaking. Circ. 55,000. Pays on publication. Publishes ms an average of 2-3 months after acceptance. Byline given. Offers 25% kill fee (rarely needed). Buys all rights. Submit seasonal/holiday material 4 months in advance. Query for electronic submissions. Computer printout submissions acceptable; no dot-matrix. Reports in 1 month. Free sample copy and writer's guidelines for 9x12 SASE.

Nonfiction: Bart Parrott, articles editor. Essays, general interest, historical/nostalgic, how-to, humor, interview/profile, new product, opinion, personal experience, photo feature, technical and travel. Plans a special entry-level guide to canoeing and kayaking. No "trip diaries." Buys 60 mss/year. Query with or without published clips, or send complete ms. Length: 500-2,500 words. Pays $5/column inch. Pays the expenses of writers on assignment.

Photos: State availability of photos with submission or send photos with submission. Reviews contact sheets, negatives, transparencies and prints. "Some activities we cover are canoeing, kayaking, canoe sailing or poling, canoe fishing, camping, backpacking (when compatible with the main activity) and occasionally inflatable boats. We are not interested in groups of people in rafts, photos showing disregard for the environment, gasoline-powered, multi-horsepower engines unless appropriate to the discussion, or unskilled persons taking extraordinary risks." Offers $50-150/photo. Model releases and identification of subjects occasionally required. Buys one-time rights.

Columns/Departments: Bart Parrott, column/department editor. Competition (racing); Continuum (essay); Counter Currents (environmental); Put-In (short interesting articles) – all 1,500 words. Buys 60 mss/year. Pays $5/column inch.

Fiction: Uses very little fiction. Buys 5 mss/year.

Fillers: Anecdotes, facts and newsbreaks. Buys 20/year. Length: 500-1,000 words. Pays $5/column inch.

Tips: "Start with Put-In articles (short featurettes) of approximately 500 words, book reviews, or short, unique equipment reviews. Or give us the best, most exciting article we've ever seen – with great photos. Short Strokes is also a good entry forum focusing on short trips on good waterways accessible to lots of people. Focusing more on technique and how-to articles. Query for specifics."

‡**COASTAL CRUISING.** New World Publishing Group, Inc., Box 157, Beaufort NC 28516. (919)247-4185. Editor: Ted Jones. 75% freelance written. Monthly magazine. A boating and yachting travelogue for North America covering cruising/racing/cruising grounds. Circ. 30,000. Pays on acceptance or publication. Publishes ms an average of 6 months after acceptance. Byline given. Buys one-time rights or second serial (reprint) rights. Submit seasonal/holiday material 6 months in advance. Simultaneous, photocopied and previously published submissions OK. Query for electronic submissions. Computer printout submissions OK; prefers letter-quality. Free sample copy and writer's guidelines.

Nonficton: How-to (technical items dealing with boating – both power and sail), humor, new product (boating items), personal experience, photo feature, technical and travel. "I do not read anything that does not deal with boating and/or travel along our waterways and coastline." Buys 75 mss/year. Send complete ms. Length: 500-3,000 words (6,000 if it is a 2-part series). Pays $100-300. Sometimes pays expenses of writers on assignment.

Photos: Send photos with submission. Reviews transparencies and 3x5 or 5x7 prints. Offers no additional payment for photos accepted with ms (except for certain assignments). Model releases and identification of subjects required. Buys one-time rights.

Columns/Departments: Scuttlebutt (club news, upcoming boating events, boat shows, etc.); Race Reports (racing reports from around N. America. Include photos if possible); and New Products (new product information on boating gear, products, equipment, etc.), all 100-800 words. Buys 25 mss/year. Send complete ms. Pays $25-50.

Fiction: Adventure and humorous. "Nothing that does not deal with boating." Buys 5 ms/year. Send complete ms. Length: 500-3,000 words. Pays $35-50.

Fillers: Gags to be illustrated by cartoonist and short humor. Buys 5/year. Length: 100-500 words. Pays $35-50.

CRUISING WORLD, Cruising World Publications, Inc., 5 John Clarke Rd., Newport RI 02840. (401)847-1588. Editor: Bernadette Brown. 70% freelance written. Eager to work with new/unpublished writers. For all those who cruise under sail. Monthly magazine; 200 pages. Circ. 133,000. Pays on acceptance. Publishes ms an average of 8 months after acceptance. Offers variable kill fee, $50-150. Buys first North American periodical rights or first world periodical rights. Reports in about 2 months. Query for electronic submissions. Computer printout submissions acceptable; prefers letter-quality. Free writer's guidelines.

Nonfiction: Book excerpts, how-to, humor, inspirational, opinion and personal experience. "We are interested in seeing informative articles on the technical and enjoyable aspects of cruising under sail. Also subjects of general interest to seafarers." Buys 135-140 unsolicited mss/year. Submit complete ms. Length: 500-3,500 words. Pays $150-800.

Photos: 5x7 b&w prints and color transparencies purchased with accompanying ms. Captions and identification of subjects required. Buys one-time rights.

Columns/Departments: People & Food (recipes for preparation aboard sailboats); Shoreline (sailing news, vignettes); and Workbench (projects for upgrading your boat). Send complete ms. Length: 150-500 words. Pays $25-150.

Tips: "Cruising stories should be first person narratives. In general, authors must be sailors who read the magazine. Color slides always improve a ms's chances of acceptance. Technical articles should be well-illustrated."

CURRENTS, Voice of the National Organization for River Sports, 314 N. 20th St., Colorado Springs CO 80904. (719)473-2466. Editor: Eric Leaper. Managing Editor: Mary McCurdy. 25% freelance written. Bimonthly magazine covering river running (kayaking, rafting, river canoeing). Circ. 10,000. Pays on publication. Publishes ms an average of 6 months after acceptance. Byline given. Offers 25% kill fee. Buys first North American serial rights, first rights and one-time rights. Submit seasonal/holiday material 2 months in advance. Simultaneous queries, and simultaneous, photocopied and previously published submissions OK. Computer printout submissions acceptable; prefers letter-quality. Reports in 2 weeks on queries; in 1 month on mss. Sample copy for $1 and 9x12 SAE with 3 first class stamps; writer's guidelines for #10 SASE.

Nonfiction: How-to (run rivers and fix equipment); in-depth reporting on river conservation and access issues and problems; humor (related to rivers); interview/profile (any interesting river runner); new product; opinion; personal experience; technical; travel (rivers in other countries). "We tell river runners about river conservation, river access, river equipment, how to do it, when, where, etc." No trip accounts without originality; no stories about "my first river trip." Buys 20 mss/year. Query with or without clips of published work. Length: 500-2,500 words. Pays $12-75.

Photos: State availability of photos. Pays $10-35. Reviews b&w or color prints or slides; b&w preferred. Captions and identification of subjects (if racing) required. Buys one-time rights.

Columns/Departments: Book and film reviews (river-related). Buys 5 mss/year. Query with or without clips of published work or send complete ms. Length: 100-500 words. Pays $5-50.

Fiction: Adventure (river). Buys 2 mss/year. Query. Length: 1,000-2,500 words. Pays $25-75. "Must be well-written, on well-known river and beyond the realm of possibility."

Fillers: Clippings, jokes, gags, anecdotes, short humor, newsbreaks. Buys 5/year. Length: 25-100 words. Pays $5-10.

Tips: "We need more material on river news—proposed dams, wild and scenic river studies, accidents, etc. If you can provide brief (300-500 words) on these subjects, you will have a good chance of being published. Material must be on whitewater rivers. Go to a famous river and investigate it; find out something we don't know—especially about rivers that are *not* in Colorado or adjacent states—we already know about the ones near us."

GREAT LAKES SAILOR, Mid-America's Freshwater Sailing Magazine, Great Lakes Sailor, Inc., Box 951, Akron OH 44309. (216)762-2300. Editor: Drew Shippy. 55% freelance written. A monthly magazine on Great Lakes sailing. Circ. 24,000. Pays on publication. Byline given. Buys first North America serial rights. Submit seasonal material 3 months in advance. Simultaneous submisions OK. Computer printout submissions OK; prefers letter-quality. Free sample copy and writer's guidelines. Reports on queries in 1 month; 6 weeks on mss.

Nonfiction: How-to (major and minor sailboat upgrades), humor (sailing oriented), interview/profile (sailing personality), new product (sailboat oriented), personal experience (sailing oriented), photo feature (sail racing), travel (sailing destination). Buys 60 mss/year. Query. Length: 1,000-3,500 words. Pays $50-500.

Photos: Send photos with submissions. Reviews, transparencies and 4x5 or 8x10 prints. Offers no additional payment for photos accepted with ms. Captions required. Buys one-time rights.

Columns/Departments: Yard & Loft (major sailboat upgrades) 1,500-2,000 words; Sailor's Projects (minor sailboat upgrades—under $250) 250-1,000 words; Boat Handling (sailing techniques) 1,500-2,000 words; News (Great Lakes events/developments of interest) 300-500 words. Buys 36 mss/year. Query. Pays $50-250.

Fillers: Anecdotes, facts, newsbreaks, short humor. Length: 50-500 words. Pays $20-75.

‡HEARTLAND BOATING, Heartland Boating Publications, Route 1, Box 145, Martin TN 38237. (901)587-6971. Editor: Molly Lightfoot Blom. 40% freelance written. Bimonthly magazine on boating. "Magazine is devoted to both power and sail boating enthusiasts throughout middle America. The focus is on the freshwater inland rivers and lakes of the Heartland; primarily the Tennessee, Cumberland, Ohio and Mississippi rivers and the Tennessee-Tombigbee Waterway. No Great Lakes of salt water material wil be considered unless it applies to our area." Estab. 1988. Circ. 9,000. Pays on publication. Publishes ms an average of 3 months after acceptance. Byline given. Buys first North American serial rights and sometimes second serial (reprint) rights. Submit seasonal/holiday material 6 months in advance. Simultaneous submissions OK. Query for electronic submission. Computer printout submissions OK. Reports in 1 month. Sample copy $3; free writer's guidelines.

Nonfiction: General interest, historical/nostalgic, how-to, humor, interview/profile, new product, personal experience, photo feature, technical, travel. Buys 20-30 mss/year. Query with or without published clips, or send complete ms. Length: 800-3,000 words. Pays 5-25¢/word.
Photos: Send photos with query. Reviews contact sheets, transparencies. Buys one-time rights.
Columns/Departments: Buys 10 mss/year. Query. Pays 5-25¢/word.

HOT BOAT, LFP Publishing, Suite 525, 9171 Wilshire Blvd., Beverly Hills CA 90210. (213)858-7866. FAX: (213)275-3857. Editor: Kevin Spaise. 30% freelance written. A monthly magazine on performance boating (16-35 feet), water skiing and water sports in general. "We're looking for concise, technically oriented 'how-to' articles on performance modifications; personality features on interesting boating-oriented personalities, and occasional event coverage." Circ. 88,000. Pays on acceptance. Publishes ms an average of 2 months after acceptance. Byline given. Offers 40% kill fee. Buys first North American serial rights; also reprint rights occasionally. Submit seasonal/holiday material 3 months in advance. Simultaneous, photocopied and previously published submissions OK. Computer printout submissions OK; no dot-matrix. Reports in 3 weeks on queries; 1 month on mss. Sample copy for SAE with $1.35 postage.
Nonfiction: How-to (increase horsepower, perform simple boat related maintenance), humor, interview/profile (racers and manufacturers), new product, personal experience, photo feature, technical. "Absolutely no sailing—we deal strictly in powerboating." Buys 30 mss/year. Query with published clips. Length: 200-3,500 words. Pays $50-300. Sometimes pays expenses of writers on assignment.
Photos: Send photos with submission. Reviews contact sheets, negatives, transparencies, prints. Captions, model releases and identification of subjects required. Buys one-time rights.
Tips: "We're always open to new writers. If you query with published clips and we like your writing, we can keep you on file even if we reject the particular query. It may be more important to simply establish contact. Once we work together there will be much more work to follow."

‡MOTORBOAT, Power & Motoryacht Magazine, 1234 Summer St. 5th Fl., Stamford CT 06950. FAX: (203)327-7039. Editor: Richard Thiel. Managing Editor: Catherine Cusmano. 85% freelance written. Magazine which will be published 3 times first year, 6 second year and 12 third year. "This is a how-to magazine about small powerboats. It concentrates on basic skills, product review and some destination pieces." Estab. 1988. Circ. 160,000. Pays on acceptance. Publishes ms an average of 3 months after acceptance. Byline given. Offers negotiable kill fee. Buys first North American serial rights. Query for electronic submissions. Computer printout submissions OK. Sample copy for 9x12 SAE and $1; writer's guidelines for #10 SASE.
Nonfiction: How-to (fishing boating maintenance repair), new product, photo feature and technical. "No reminiscence, ma and pa cruise, fish stories." Buys 45-50 mss/year. Query with published clips. Length: 1,200-1,600 words. Pays $400 and up. Pays expenses of writers on assignment.
Photos: State availability of photos with submission. Captions and model releases required. Buys one-time rights.

OFFSHORE, Boating Magazine of New England and the Northeast, Offshore Publications, Inc., 220-9 Reservoir St., Needham MA 02194. (617)449-6204. Editor: Herbert Gliick. 80% freelance written. Eager to work with new/unpublished writers. Monthly magazine (oversize) covering boating and the coast from Maine to New Jersey. Circ. 35,000. Pays on acceptance. Publishes ms an average of 2 months after acceptance. Byline given. Offers negotiable kill fee. Buys first North American serial rights. Submit seasonal/holiday material 3 months in advance. Simultaneous queries, and simultaneous, photocopied, and previously published submissions OK. Query for electronic submissions. Computer printout submissions acceptable. Reports in 1 week. Sample copy for 10x12 SAE and $1.50 postage; writer's guidelines for #10 SAE.
Nonfiction: Articles on boats, boating, New York, New Jersey and New England coastal places and people. Coastal history of NJ, NY, CT, RI, MA, NH and ME. Boat-related fiction. Thumbnail and/or outline of topic will elicit immediate response. Buys 125 mss/year. Query with writing sample or send complete ms. Length: 1,000-3,500 words. Pays 10¢/word and up.
Photos: Reviews photocopies of 5x7 b&w prints. Identification of subjects required. Buys one-time rights.
Tips: "Demonstrate familiarity with boats or region and ability to recognize subjects of interest to regional boat owners. Those subjects need not be boats. *Offshore* is serious but does not take itself as seriously as most national boating magazines. The most frequent mistake made by writers in completing an article for us is failing to build on a theme (what is the point of the story?)."

‡PADDLER, 152 Silver Birch Ave., Toronto, Ontario M4B 3L3 Canada. (416)640-5103. Editor: Kathy Fremes. 60% freelance written. Quarterly magazine on canoeing & kayaking. Circ. 23,000. Pays on publication. Byline given. Buys first North American serial rights. Submit seasonal/holiday material 4 months in advance. Simultaneous, photocopied and previously published submissions OK. Computer printout submissions OK.
Nonfiction: Interview/profile, opinion, photo feature and travel. Buys 20 mss/year. Query. Length: 750-3,500 words. Pays $50-150 for assigned articles. Sometimes pays expenses of writers on assignment.
Photos: State availability of photos with submission or send photos with submission. Reviews contact sheets. Offers $10-65 per photo. Identification of subjects required. Buys one-time rights.

RIVER RUNNER MAGAZINE, Rancher Publications, Box 458, Fallbrook CA 92028. (619)723-8155. Editorial office: Box 2073, Durango CO 81302. Editor: Ken Hulick. 90% freelance written. "Interested in working with new/unpublished writers who understand our needs and who submit material professionally." Seven-time-per-year magazine covering whitewater rafting, canoeing and kayaking. "Audience is predominately male, college educated, and approximately 20-45 years old. The editorial slant favors whitewater action. Stories reflect the natural beauty and excitement of running rivers." Circ. 20,000. Pays on publication. Publishes ms an average of 4 months after acceptance. Byline given. Buys first North American serial rights. Submit seasonal/holiday material 6 months in advance. Computer printout submissions acceptable; prefers letter-quality. Reports in 1 month on queries; 2 months on mss. Sample copy $2.50; writer's guidelines for #10 SASE.

Nonfiction: Features on running a specific river (or region), with practical information for other paddlers, that convey a sense of place as well as whitewater action. How-to articles on techniques (mostly for immediate-level readers). Equipment overviews of canoes, kayaks, rafts, paddles, clothing and accessories. Occasional features on sea kayaking, competition whitewater racing, historical/personality profile, conservation and alternative water sports (wave skiing, bathtub racing, etc.). No fiction or poetry. "We focus primarily on the United States, but regularly run features on other North American and international destinations." Buys 40-50 mss/year. Query with or without published clips or send complete ms. Length: 1,500-2,500 words. Pays 7-10¢/word. Sometimes pays the expenses of writers on assignment.

Photos: State availability of photos with query letter or submit with ms. Pays $20-125 for color transparencies; $15-65 for b&w prints. "We need good, sharp photographs that portray the total whitewater experience." Captions required. Buys first North American serial rights.

Columns/Departments: Hotline (news, conservation, trends); snapshots (people, history, competition); strokes (techniques, tips); shorelines (places, mini-features, reviews, outfitters); gear (equipment, products, evaluations). Buys 30-40 mss/year. Query or send complete ms. Length: 500-1,000 words. Pays 5-10¢/word.

Tips: "Submit fresh, original story ideas with strong supporting photographs. The prime need is for original, well-written river feature stories. Stories should be written for the intermediate-level paddler and display an understanding of our editorial needs."

SAILING MAGAZINE, 125 E. Main St., Port Washington WI 53074. (414)284-3494. FAX: (414)284-0067. Editor and Publisher: William F. Schanen, III. Monthly magazine. For readers ages 25-44, majority professionals. About 75% of them own their own sailboat. Circ. 35,000. Pays on publication. Photocopied and simultaneous submissions OK. Reports in 6 weeks. Sample copy for 12x15 SAE and $1 postage; writer's guidelines for #10 SASE.

Nonfiction: Micca Leffingwell Hutchins, editor. "Experiences of sailing, whether cruising, racing or learning. We require no special style. We're devoted exclusively to sailing and sailboat enthusiasts, and particularly interested in articles about the trend toward cruising in the sailing world." Informational, personal experience, profile, historical, travel and book reviews. Buys 24 mss/year. Query or submit complete ms. Length: open. Payment negotiable. Must be accompanied by photos.

Photos: B&w and color photos purchased with or without accompanying ms. Captions required. Pays flat fee for article.

SAILING WORLD, N.Y. Times Magazine Group, 5 John Clarke Rd., Newport RI 02840. FAX: (401)848-5048. Editor: John Burnham. 40% freelance written. Magazine published 12 times/year. Circ. 57,000. Pays on publication. Publishes ms an average of 4 months after acceptance. Buys first North American serial rights. Byline given. Query for electronic submissions. Computer printout submissions acceptable. Sample copy $1.95.

Nonfiction: How-to for racing and performance-oriented sailors, photo feature, profile, regatta reports, and charter. No travelogs. Buys 5-10 unsolicited mss/year. Query. Length: 500-1,500 words. Pays $50 per column of text.

Tips: "Send query with outline and include your experience. The writer may have a better chance of breaking in with short articles and fillers such as regatta news reports from his or her own area."

SANTANA, The So-Cal Sailing Rag, Santana Publications, Inc., #101, 5132 Bolsa, Huntington Beach CA 92649. (714)893-3432. Editor: David Poe. Managing Editor: Kitty James. 50% freelance written. A monthly magazine on sailing. "We publish conversationally written articles of interest to Southern California sailers, including technical, cruising, racing, fiction, etc." Circ. 25,000. Pays on publication. Publishes ms an average of 2 months after acceptance. Byline given. Publication not copyrighted. Buys first North American serial rights or second serial (reprint) rights. Submit seasonal/holiday material 3 months in advance. Photocopied and previously published submissions OK. Computer printout submissions OK. Reports in 1 month. Sample copy for 9x12 SAE with 5 first class stamps.

Nonfiction: Essays, general interest, historical/nostalgic, how-to (technical articles), humor, interview/profile, personal experience. Buys 50 mss/year. Query with or without published clips or send complete ms. Length: 1,000-4,000 words. Pays $50-150.

Photos: State availability of photos with submission. Reviews contact sheets, negatives, transparencies (35mm) and prints (5x7 or 8x10). Offers $10/photo. Captions and identification of subjects required. Buys one-time rights.

Fiction: Adventure, humorous. Send complete ms. Length: 1,000-5,000. Pays $50-150.

Tips: "Reading the publication is best as our style tends towards conversational, frequently irreverent, but we are also interested in technical articles. We are also happy to critique submissions with suggestions on how to break in. Virtually the entire range of topics covered is open to freelance submissions."

SEA, The Magazine of Western Boating for 80 years, Duncan McIntosh Co., Inc., Box 1579, Newport Beach CA 92663. FAX: (714)642-8980. Editor and Publisher: Duncan McIntosh Jr. Executive Editor: Linda Yuskaitis. 70% freelance written. A monthly magazine covering recreational power and sail boating, offshore fishing and coastal news of the West Coast, from Alaska to Hawaii. Also includes separate regional sections on Southern California and the Pacific Northwest. "*Sea* readers are well educated boat owners, knowledgeable about sail and power boating beyond the fundamentals." Circ. 60,000, all regional editions combined. Pays on publication. Publishes ms an average of 4 months after acceptance. Byline given. Negotiable kill fee. Buys first North American serial rights or second serial (reprint) rights. Query for disk submissions. Computer printout submissions OK; prefers letter-quality. Reports in 1 month on queries; 6 weeks on mss. Free writer's guidelines, deadline schedule and sample copy with 9x12 SASE.

Nonfiction: General interest (on boating and coastal topics); how-to (tips on maintaining a boat, engine, and gear); interview/profile (of a prominent boating personality); travel (West Coast cruising or fishing destination); historical/nostalgic. Buys 150 mss/year. Query with or without published clips, or send complete ms. Length: 250 (news items) to 2,500 (features) words. Pays $50 (news items) to $300 (features). Some assignment expenses covered if requested in advance.

Photos: Stories accompanied by photos are preferred. Color transparencies or b&w prints only; no color negatives or prints. Pays $25 (inside b&w) to $200 (color cover) for photos. Identification of photo subjects required. Buys one-time rights.

Columns/Departments: West Coast Focus (boating and fishing news with color photos); Southern California Focus (boating and fishing news from Ventura to San Diego with b&w photos); Northwest Focus (boating and fishing news in Alaska, Washington and Oregon with b&w photos); Nautical Elegance (feature on a spectacular modern or renovated classic yacht); Fish Hooks (sportfishing tips); Mexico Report (short features on boating and fishing destinations in Mexico).

Tips: "*Sea*'s editorial focus is on West Coast boating and sportfishing. We are not interested in stories about the East Coast, Midwest or foreign countries. First-time contributors should include resume or information about themselves that identifies their knowledge of subject. Written queries appreciated. No first-person 'what happened on our first cruise' stories. No poetry, fiction or cartoons."

‡**SEA KAYAKER**, Sea Kayaker, Inc., 1670 Duranleau St., Vancouver, British Columbia V6H 3S4 Canada. (604)263-1471. Editor: John Dowd. Managing Editor: Beatrice Dowd. 50% freelance written. Works with small number of new/unpublished writers each year. A quarterly magazine on the sport of sea kayaking. Circ. 12,000. Pays on publication. Publishes ms. an average of 6 months after acceptance. Byline sometimes given. Offers 20% kill fee. Buys first North American serial rights or second serial (reprint) rights. Submit seasonal/holiday material 6 months in advance. Previously published submissions OK. Computer printout submissions acceptable; prefers letter-quality to dot-matrix. Reports in 2 months. Sample copy $4.60; free writer's guidelines.

Nonfiction: Essays, historical/nostalgic, how-to (on making equipment), humor, inspirational, interview/profile, opinion, personal experience, photo feature, technical and travel. Buys 15 mss/year. Query with or without published clips, or send complete ms. Length: 750-4,000 words. Pays $5-10¢/word (U.S.). Sometimes pays the expenses of writers on assignment.

Photos: Send photos with submission. Reviews contact sheets. Offers $15-35/photo. Captions, model releases, and identification of subjects required. Buys one-time rights.

Columns/Department: History, Safety, Environment, and Humor. Buys 6 mss/year. Length: 750-4,000 words. Pays 5-10¢/word (U.S.).

Fiction: Adventure, experimental, fantasy, historical, horror, humorous, mainstream, mystery, science fiction, slice-of-life vignettes and suspense. Buys 2 mss/year. Send complete ms. Length: 750-4,000 words. Pays 5-10¢/word (U.S.).

Tips: "We consider unsolicited mss that include a SASE, but we give greater priority to brief (several paragraphs) descriptions of proposed articles accompanied by at least two samples—published or unpublished—of your writing. Enclose a statement as to why you're qualified to write the piece and indicate whether photographs or illustrations are available to accompany the piece."

SMALL BOAT JOURNAL, 2100 Powers Ferry Rd., Atlanta GA 30339. (404)955-5656. Editor: Thomas Baker. Managing Editor: Richard Lebovitz. 95% freelance written. Bimonthly magazine covering recreational boating. "*Small Boat Journal* focuses on the practical and enjoyable aspects of owning and using small boats. *Small Boat Journal* covers all types of watercraft under 30 feet in length—powerboats, sailboats, rowing boats, sea kayaks and canoes. Topics include cruising areas and adventures, boat evaluations, and helpful tips for building, upgrading and maintaining, and safely handling small boats." Circ. 61,000. Pays on acceptance. Publishes ms an average of 6 months after acceptance. Byline given. Offers 50% kill fee. Buys first rights. Submit seasonal/holiday material 6 months in advance. Simultaneous (as long as author agrees to give first rights to *SBJ*) and photocopied submissions OK. Query for electronic submissions. Computer printout submissions OK; prefers letter-quality. Reports in 5 weeks on queries; 3 weeks on mss. Sample copy for 8½x11 SAE with 7 first class stamps; writer's guidelines for #10 SASE.

Nonfiction: Book excerpts, essays, historical/nostalgic, how-to (boating, maintenance, restoration and improvements), humor, interview/profile, new product, personal experience, photo feature, technical and travel. Plans special issues on sea kayaking, rowing, electronics, engines, fishing boats and equipment, boatbuilding. Buys 60 mss/year. Query with or without published clips, or send complete ms. Length: 800-3,000 words. Pays $150-600 for assigned articles; pays $75-400 for unsolicited articles. Sometimes pays the expenses of writers on assignment.

Photos: Send photos with submission. Reviews contact sheets, transparencies and prints. Offers $15-200 per photo. Model releases and identification of subjects required. Buys one-time rights.

Columns/Departments: Seamanship (boating safety, piloting and navigation), 1,500 words; Rigs & Rigging (care and improvement of rigging and sails), 1,500 words; Ripples (personal experiences and reflections on boating), 1,000 words; Boatcraft (ideas for improving a boat), 1,500 words; Inside Outboards (care and maintenance of outboard engines), 1,500 words. Buys 40 mss/year. Query with published clips. Length: 900-2,500 words. Pays $50-400.

Tips: "Our best stories provide comprehensive, in-depth information about a particular boating subject. *SBJ*'s readers are experienced and sophisticated boating enthusiasts—most own more than one type of boat—and expect well-researched articles with a practical, how-to slant. Excellent photos are a must, as are stories with engaging tales drawn from the author's experience." Most open to freelancers are "topics related to seamanship, engine maintenance and repair, boat handling, boat building, hull maintenance and repair, restoration and historical subjects related to small boats."

SOUNDINGS, The Nation's Boating Newspaper, Pratt St., Essex CT 06426. (203)767-3200. FAX: (203)767-1048. Editor: Arthur R. Henick. Managing Editor: Milton Moore. Works with a small number of new/unpublished writers each year. National monthly boating newspaper with nine regional editions. Features "news—hard and soft—for the recreational boating public." Circ. 100,000. Pays after "the 10th of the month of publication." Publishes ms an average of 3 months after acceptance. Byline given. Buys one-time rights. Deadline 1st of month before issue. Simultaneous queries and simultaneous and photocopied submissions OK. Query for electronic submissions. Computer printout submissions acceptable; prefers letter-quality. Reports in 2 months on queries; 5 weeks on mss. Sample copy for 8½x11 SAE and 7 first class stamps; free writer's guidelines.

Nonfiction: General interest, historical/nostalgic, interview/profile, opinion and photo feature. Race coverage is also used; supply full names, home towns and the full scores for the top 10 winners in each division. Send complete ms. Length: 250-1,000 words. Pays $2/column inch-$4/column inch. Sometimes pays the expenses of writers on assignment.

Photos: Send photos with ms. Pays $20-25 for 8x10 b&w prints. Identification of subjects required. Buys one-time rights.

TRAILER BOATS MAGAZINE, Poole Publications, Inc., 20700 Belshaw Ave., Carson CA 90746-3510. (213)537-6322. FAX: (213)537-8735. Editor: Chuck Coyne. 30-40% freelance written. Works with a small number of new/unpublished writers each year. Monthly magazine (November/December issue combined). Emphasizes legally trailerable boats and related powerboating activities. Circ. 80,000. Pays on publication. Publishes ms 2-6 months after acceptance. Byline given. Buys all rights. Submit seasonal/holiday material 3 months in advance. Query for electronic submissions. Computer printout submissions acceptable; prefers letter-quality. Reports in 1 month. Sample copy $1.25; writer's guidelines for #10 SASE.

Nonfiction: General interest (trailer boating activities); historical (places, events, boats); how-to (repair boats, installation, etc.); humor (almost any boating-related subject); nostalgia (same as historical); personal experience; photo feature; profile; technical; and travel (boating travel on water or highways). No "How I Spent My Summer Vacation" stories, or stories not even remotely connected to trailerable boats and related activities. Buys 18-30 unsolicited mss/year. Query or send complete ms. Length: 500-3,000 words. Pays up t6o $7/column inch. Pays expenses of writers on assignment.

Photos: Send photos with ms. Pays $10-75 for 8 × 10 b&w prints; $25-350 for color transparencies. Captions required.

Columns/Departments: Boaters Bookshelf (boating book reviews); Over the Transom (funny or strange boating photos); and Patent Pending (an invention with drawings). Buys 2/issue. Query. Length: 100-500 words. Pays 7¢-10¢/word. Mini-Cruise (short enthusiastic approach to a favorite boating spot). Need map and photographs. Length: 500-750 words. Pays $100. Open to suggestions for new columns/departments.

Fiction: Adventure, experimental, historical, humorous and suspense. "We do not use too many fiction stories but we will consider them if they fit the general editorial guidelines." Query or send complete ms. Length: 500-1,500 words. Pays $50 minimum.

Tips: "Query should contain short general outline of the intended material; what kind of photos; how the photos illustrate the piece. Write with authority covering the subject like an expert. Frequent mistakes are not knowing the subject matter or the audience. Use basic information rather than prose, particularly in travel stories. The writer may have a better chance of breaking in at our publication with short articles and fillers if they are typically hard to find articles. We do most major features inhouse."

‡**WATERWAY GUIDE**, Communication Channels, Inc., 6255 Barfield Rd., Atlanta GA 30328. (404)256-9800. FAX: (404)256-3116. Editor: Judith Powers. 90% freelance written. Quarterly magazine on intracoastal waterway travel for recreational boats. "Writer must be knowledgeable about navigation and the areas covered by the Guide." Circ. 45,000. Pays on publication. Publishes ms an average of 3 months after acceptance. Byline given sometimes. Kill fee varies. Buys all rights. Photocopied submissions OK. Computer printout submissions OK; prefers letter-quality. Reports in 2 month on queries; 3 months on mss. Sample copy $23.95 and $3 postage.

Nonfiction: Historical/nostalgic, how-to, photo feature, technical and travel. "No personal boating experiences." Buys 25 mss/year. Query with or without published clips, or send complete ms. Length: 200 words minimum. Pays $50-2,000 for assigned articles. Pays in contributor copies or other premiums for brief articles, information and sidebars.

Photos: Send photos with submission. Reviews 3x5 prints. Offers $50 per photo. Identification of subjects required. Buys one-time rights.

Fillers: Facts. Buys 6/year. Length: 250-1,000 words. Pays $50-150.

Tips: "Must have on-the-water experience and be able to provide new and accurate information on geographic areas covered by Waterway Guide."

WOODENBOAT MAGAZINE, The Magazine for Wooden Boat Owners, Builders, and Designers, WoodenBoat Publications, Inc., Box 78, Brookline ME 04616. (207)359-4651. Editor: Jon Wilson. Managing Editor: Jennifer Elliott. Senior Editor: Mike O'Brien. 50% freelance written. Works with a small number of new/unpublished writers each year. Bimonthly magazine for wooden boat owners, builders, and designers. "We are devoted exclusively to the design, building, care, preservation, and use of wooden boats, both commercial and pleasure, old and new, sail and power. We work to convey quality, integrity, and involvement in the creation and care of these craft, to entertain, to inform, to inspire, and to provide our varied readers with access to individuals who are deeply experienced in the world of wooden boats." Circ. 103,000. Pays on publication. Publishes ms an average of 6-12 months after acceptance. Byline given. Offers variable kill fee. Buys first North American serial rights. Submit seasonal/holiday material 6 months in advance. Simultaneous queries and submissions (with notification) and photocopied and previously published submissions OK. Query for electronic submissions. Computer printout submissions acceptable. Reports in 3 weeks on queries; 4 weeks on mss. Sample copy $4; writer's guidelines for SASE.

Nonfiction: Technical (repair, restoration, maintenance, use, design and building wooden boats). No poetry, fiction. Buys 100 mss/year. Query with published clips. Length: 1,500-5,000 words. Pays $6/column inch. Sometimes pays expenses of writers on assignment.

Photos: Send photos with query. Negatives must be available. Pays $15-75 for b&w; $25-350 for color. Identification of subjects required. Buys one-time rights.

Columns/Departments: On the Waterfront pays for information on wooden boat-related events, projects, boatshop activities, etc. Buys 25/year. "We use the same columnists for each issue." Send complete information. Length: 250-1,000 words. Pays $5-50 for information.

Tips: "We appreciate a detailed, articulate query letter, accompanied by photos, that will give us a clear idea of what the author is proposing. We appreciate samples of previously published work. It is important for a prospective author to become familiar with our magazine first. It is extremely rare for us to make an assignment with a writer with whom we have not worked before. Most work is submitted on speculation. The most common failure is not exploring the subject material in enough depth."

YACHTING, Times-Mirror, 2 Park Ave., New York NY 10016. Publishing Director: Oliver S. Moore III. Managing Editor: Cynthia Taylor. 30% freelance written. "The magazine is written and edited for experienced, knowledgeable yachtsmen." Circ. 150,000. Pays on acceptance. Byline given. Offers 50% kill fee. Buys first rights. Submit seasonal/holiday material 6 months in advance. Computer printout submissions OK; prefers letter-quality. Reports in 2 weeks on queries; 1 month on mss.

Nonfiction: Book excerpts, personal experience, photo feature and travel. No cartoons, fiction, poetry. Query with published clips. Length: 250-2,500 words. Pays $250-1,000 for assigned articles. Pays expenses of writers on assignment.

Photos: Send photos with submission. Reviews 35mm transparencies. Offers no additional payment for photos accepted with ms. Captions, model releases and identification of subjects required.

Columns/Departments: Cruising Yachtsman (stories on cruising; contact Cynthia Taylor, managing editor); Racing Yachtsman (stories about sail or power racing; contact Lisa Gosselin). Buys 30 mss/year. Send complete ms. Length: 750 words maximum. Pays $250-500.

Tips: "We require considerable expertise in our writing because our audience is experienced and knowledgeable. Vivid descriptions of quaint anchorages and quainter natives are fine, but our readers want to know how the yachtsmen got there, too."

Bowling

‡**BOWLERS JOURNAL**, 101 E. Erie St., Chicago IL 60611. (312)266-7171. Editor-in-Chief: Mort Luby. Managing Editor: Jim Dressel. 30% freelance written. Prefers to work with published/established writers; works with a small number of new/unpublished writers each year. Emphasizes bowling. Monthly magazine; 100 pages. Circ. 22,000. Pays on acceptance. Publishes ms an average of 2 months after acceptance. Buys all rights. Submit seasonal/holiday material 3 months in advance of issue date. Photocopied submissions OK. Computer printout submissions acceptable; prefers letter-quality to dot-matrix. Reports in 6 weeks. Sample copy $2.

Nonfiction: General interest (stories on top pros); historical (stories of old-time bowlers or bowling alleys); interview (top pros, men and women); and profile (top pros). "We publish some controversial matter, seek outspoken personalities. We reject material that is too general; that is, not written for high average bowlers and bowling proprietors who already know basics of playing the game and basics of operating a bowling alley." Buys 15-20 unsolicited mss/year. Query, phone queries OK. Length: 1,200-3,500 words. Pays $75-200.

Photos: State availability of photos with query. Pays $5-15 for 8x10 b&w prints; and $15-25 for 35mm or 2¼x2¼ color transparencies. Buys one-time rights.

‡**WOMAN BOWLER**, 5301 S. 76th St., Greendale WI 53129. (414)421-9000. FAX: (414)421-4420. Editor: Karen Sytsma. 3% freelance written. Works with a small number of new/unpublished writers each year. Published eight times a year with combined March/April, May/June, August/September, November/December issues. Circ. 150,000. Emphasizes bowling for women bowlers, ages 18-90. Buys all rights. Pays on acceptance. Publishes ms an average of 3 months after acceptance. Byline given "except on occasion, when freelance article is used as part of a regular magazine department. When this occurs, it is discussed first with the author." Submit seasonal/holiday material 2 months in advance. Photocopied and previously published submissions OK; prefers letter-quality to dot-matrix. Reports in 1 month. Free sample copy and writer's guidelines.

Nonfiction: Interview; profile; and spot news. Buys 25 mss/year. Query. Length: 1,500 words maximum (unless by special assignment). Pays $25-100.

Photos: Purchased with accompanying ms. Query. Pays $25 for b&w glossy prints. Model releases and identification of subjects required.

Football

‡**CALIFORNIA FOOTBALL MAGAZINE**, California Football Magazine, Inc., Suite 301, 1801 S. Catalina Ave., Redondo Beach CA 90277. (213)375-9860, (213)373-3630 or (213)326-5839. Editor: David Raatz. 40% freelance written. Bimonthly magazine. "*California Football, Basketball and Baseball Magazines* cover all levels of activity in the state, high school through pro, as well as Californians who are excelling in other states. Target audience: 14-24 year-old males and females." Circ. 100,000. Pays on publication. Publishes 1½ months after acceptance. Byline given. Buys one-time rights. Simultaneous, photocopied and previously published submissions OK. Computer printout submissions OK; prefers letter-quality. Reports in 3 weeks on queries; 2 weeks on mss. Free sample copy and writer's guidelines.

Nonfiction: How-to (training tips), humor, inspirational, new product (sporting goods) and personal experience (athlete's perspective). "Anything unsuitable for family reading is unacceptable." Buys 12 mss/year. Length: 250-3,000 words. Pays $35-250. Sometimes pays expenses of writers on assignment.

Photos: State availability of photos with submission. Reviews 1½x1 tranparencies and 8x10 prints. Offers $15-150 per photo. Captions, model releases and identification of subjects required. Buys one-time rights.

Columns/Departments: Winning Edge (overcome adversity to gain success), 750-2,000 words; Training Room (performance tips), 750-2,000 words; New Products (sporting goods), 50-500 words; and Extra Points (mini-features with human interest), 50-500 words. Query with published clips. Pays $35-250.

Fillers: Anecdotes, facts, gags to be illustrated by cartoonist, newsbreaks, short humor and statistics. Buys 4/year. Length: 50-750 words. Pays $35-75.

Tips: "Submission of a completed manuscript (with a cover letter) followed up by a phone call and then a personal interview is the best bet (for freelancers). Extra points (or Free Throws for basketball) is the easiest section to get freelanced material published. We look for human/general interest stories, with humor or drama being good attributes. This is the off-the-field part of the magazine."

Gambling

‡THE PLAYER, Nation's Largest Gaming Guide, Player's Intl./ACE Marketing, 2524 Arctic Ave., Atlantic City NJ 08401. (609)344-9000. FAX: (609)345-3469. Editor: Glenn Fine. Managing Editor: Roger Gros. 15% freelance written. Monthly tabloid on gambling. "We cover any issue that would interest the gambler, from casinos to sports betting, to race tracks. Articles should be light, entertaining and give tips on how to win." Estab. 1988. Circ. 210,000. Pays on publication. Byline sometimes given. Buys all rights. Submit seasonal/holiday material 3 months in advance. Computer printout submissions OK; prefers letter-quality. Sample copy $1.50 with 9x12 SAE and 5 first class stamps.

Nonfiction: How-to (win!) and new product (gaming equipment). "No articles dependent on statistics/no travelogues. No first person gambling stories." Query with published clips. Length: 500-1,000 words. Pays $50-250 for assigned articles; $50-100 for unsolicited articles. Sometimes pays expenses of writers on assignment.

Photos: Send photos with submission. Reviews contact sheets and 5x7 prints. Offers $10 per photo. Captions and identification of subjects required. Buys all rights.

Columns/Departments: Table Games (best ways to play, ratings); Slots (new machines, methods, casino policies); Nevada (what's new in state, properties); Tournaments (reports on gaming, tournaments) and Caribbean (gaming in the islands), all 500 words. Buys 2 mss/year. Query with published clips. Pays $50-100.

Fillers: Facts and gags to be illustrated by cartoonist. Buys 10/year. Length: 50-250 words. Pays $25-100.

Tips: "Writer must understand the gambler: why he gambles, what are his motivations. The spread of legalized gaming will be an increasingly important topic in the next year. Write as much to entertain as to inform. We try to give the reader information they will not find elsewhere."

General Interest

‡THE BARK EATER, The Bark Eater, Box 33, North River NY 12856. (518)251-2661. Editor: Jeff Fosdick. 100% freelance written. Quarterly magazine on outdoor life in the Adirondack mountains, specifically hunting, fishing, trapping; also interested in history, profiles on Adirondack people and animal profiles. "Must have knowledge of hunting and fishing techniques and tools." Circ. 10,000. Pays on publication. Publishes ms an average of 4 months after acceptance. Byline given. Negotiable kill fee. Will make work for hire assignments. Submit seasonal/holiday material 6 months in advance. Simultaneous and photocopied submissions OK. Computer printout submissions acceptable; prefers letter-quality. Sample copy with 9 × 12 SAE and $1 in postage.

Nonfiction: Essays, general interest, historical/nostalgic, how-to hunt, fish, etc., humor, interview/profile of outdoorsmen, new product, personal experience, photo feature and travel. "Anything related to Adirondack life." Buys 60 mss/year. Query with or without published clips or send complete ms. Length: 1,000-2,000 words. Pays $50. Prefers to pay in copies, subscription. Pays in contributor copies, or local writers/artists/photographers sometimes want an ad promoting their work. Sometimes pays expenses of writers on assignment.

Photos: Send photos with submission. Reviews contact sheets, 35mm transparencies and 4x5 prints. Identification of subjects required. Buys one-time rights. "We also accept drawings and paintings."

Departments/Columns: Book Review (reviews new and old books related to the Adirondack area and/or outdoor life), 500-1,500 words. Send complete ms. Pays $10-50.

Fiction: Adventure, historical, slice-of-life vignettes and suspense. Don't want to see "anything NOT related to the Adirondacks or mountain life." Buys 12 mss/year. Send complete ms. Length: 1,500-2,000 words.

Poetry: Free verse, light verse and traditional. Does not want to see "anything not related to outdoor life." Buys 10 poems/year. Submit maximum 3 poems. Length: 10-50 lines.

Fillers: Anecdotes, facts and short humor. Length: 250-500 words.

Tips: "We welcome freelancers. Since we are a regional magazine, we must receive submissions directly relating to the area of the Adirondacks. Although our main topics are hunting and fishing, we are very open to other subject matter. Try us."

‡**CHAMPION,** Athlete Information Bureau, Suite 204, 1600 James Naismith Dr. Ottawa, Ontario K1B 5N4 Canada. (613)748-5601. FAX: (613)748-5711. Editor: Brenda Gorman. 100% freelance written. Quarterly magazine on high performance amateur sport in Canada. "Canadian content only—high performance amateur sport. Profiles on Canadian athletes, coaches etc. National programs, Olympic Games, Commonwealth Games, Pan American Games and University Games. Sport medicine. Audience is high performance sport community." Pays on acceptance. Publishes ms an average of 2 months after acceptance. Byline given. Buys all rights. Computer printout submissions OK; prefers letter-quality. Reports in 1 month on queries; 6 weeks on mss. Free sample copy.

Nonfiction: General interest related to elite sport; interview profile and sport analysis interviews. "No profiles on U.S. or European personalities or non-Canadian issues." Query with published clips. Length: 750-2,500 words. Pays $300-1,000 for assigned articles. Sometimes pays expenses of writers on assignment.

Photos: State availability of photos with submission.

Columns/Departments: Book Review, 900 words. Buys 4 mss/year. Query with published clips. Pays $100-150.

Tips: "All our features are written by freelancers. Knowledge of the Canadian sport system is a must."

CITY SPORTS MAGAZINE, Box 3693, San Francisco CA 94119. FAX: (415)495-2913. Editors: Jane McConnell in northern California; Sue Levin in southern California (212 Long Beach Blvd., Long Beach CA 90802); 80% freelance written. Works with a small number of new/unpublished writers each year. Monthly controlled circulation tabloid covering nutrition, health, active travel, family fitness and participant sports (such as running, cycling, tennis, skiing, water sports, etc.). Circ. 203,000. Two editions published monthly—for northern California, southern California and California-wide publication. 50% of editorial features run nationally, and 50% run in, one of the regional editions. Pays on acceptance for features. Publishes ms an average of 2 months after acceptance. Uses assignment contracts. Pays ⅓ kill fee. Buys one-time rights. Simultaneous and previously published submissions OK. Query for electronic submissions. Computer printout submissions OK. Reports in 1 month on queries. Sample copy $3.50.

Nonfiction: Interview/profile of participant athletes; travel; instructional and service pieces on sports and fitness; health and nutrition articles; humor. "We accept very few first-person sports accounts unless they are very unusual (such as first-time expeditions or sports participation in exotic locale) or humorous." Special issues include: Health Clubs (February); Sports Vacations (April); Running (May); Bicycling and Outdoors (June); Watersports (July); Sports Medicine (October); Downhill Skiing (November); Cross-Country Skiing (December). Buys 70 mss/year. Query with clips of published work. Length: 1,000-2,000 words. Pays $250-600 for regionally run features.

Photos: Pays $75-150 for 35mm color; $200-500 for covers; $50-100 for 8x10 b&w glossy prints. Model releases and identification of subjects required.

Tips: "We are including more articles on travel and active ideas for families and people over 50 in addition to our mainstay articles on participant sports. We prefer copy on disk."

‡**HIGH SCHOOL SPORTS,** Suite 2000, 1230 Avenue of the Americas, New York NY 10020. (212)765-3300. Editor: Joe Guise. Assistant Editor: Bob Hill. 80% freelance written. Bimonthly magazine. "We are the only national magazine in America that focuses exclusively on the efforts and achievements of high school athletes. Features are on individuals, teams or issues (steroids, small school basketball)." Circ. 500,000. Pays on acceptance. Publishes ms an average of 2 months after acceptance. Byline given. Offers 25% kill fee. Buys first rights. Simultaneous and previously published submissions OK. Query for electronic submissions. Computer printout submissions OK. Sample copy $2 with 8½x11 SAE and 90¢ in postage. Writer's guidelines for #10 SASE.

Nonfiction: Interview (high school retrospect of high profile sports figure). Buys approximately 35 mss/year. Query with published clips. Length: 1,500-2,000. Pays $400-600. Sometimes pays expenses of writers on assignment.

Photos: State availability of photos with submission. Reviews 35mm transparencies. Most photos are assigned. Buys one-time rights.

Columns/Departments: Dateline: USA (7-page round-up of news in different areas of the country), 250 words; Sports Medicine (nutrition, injuries, etc., single subject, technical); Coach's Clinic (how-to on single subject, i.e., vision training, concentration); Time Out (unusual high school activities). Buys 20 mss/year. Query with published clips. Length 300-750. Pays $75-250.

OUTDOOR CANADA MAGAZINE, Suite 301, 801 York Mills Rd., Don Mills, Ontario M3B 1X7 Canada. (416)443-8888. FAX: (416)443-1869. Editor-in-Chief: Teddi Brown. 70% freelance written. Works with a small number of new/unpublished writers each year. Emphasizes noncompetitive outdoor recreation in Canada *only*. Magazine published 9 times/year. Circ. 141,000. Pays on publication. Publishes ms an average of 6-8 months after acceptance. Buys first rights. Submit seasonal/holiday material 1 year in advance of issue date. Byline given. Originals only. Computer printout submissions acceptable; no dot-matrix. *Enclose SASE or IRCs or material not returned.* Reports in 1 month. Mention *Writer's Market* in request for editorial guidelines.

Nonfiction: Adventures, outdoor issues, fishing, exploring, outdoor destinations in Canada, some how-to. Buys 35-40 mss/year, usually with photos. Length: 1,000-2,500 words. Pays $100 and up.
Photos: Emphasize people in the outdoors. Pays $20-50 for 8x10 b&w glossy prints; $30-150 for 35mm color transparencies; and $300/cover. Captions and model releases required.
News: Short news pieces. Buys 70-80/year. Length: 200-500 words. Pays $6/printed inch.

‡**OUTSIDE**, Mariah Publications Corp., 1165 N. Clark St., Chicago IL 60610. (312)951-0990. Editor: John Rasmus. Managing Editor: Mark Bryant. 90% freelance written. Monthly magazine on outdoor recreation and travel. "*Outside* is a monthly national magazine for active, educated, upscale adults who love the outdoors and are concerned about its preservation." Circ. 325,000. Pays on publication. Publishes ms an average of 3 months after acceptance. Byline given. Offers 25% kill fee. Buys first North American serial rights. Submit seasonal/holiday material 4-5 months in advance. Photocopied submissions OK. Electronic submission OK for solicited materials; not unsolicited. Computer printout submissions OK; no dot-matrix. Reports in 1 month on queries; 6 weeks on mss. Sample copy $4 with 8½x11 SAE and $2.40 postage. Writer's guidelines for SASE.
Nonfiction: Todd Balf, senior editor. Book excerpts, essays, reports on the environment, general interest, historical/nostalgic (profiles of pioneers, expeditions, regions), how-to, humor, inspirational, interview/profile (major figures associated with sports, environment, outdoor products), opinion, personal experience (expeditions; trying out new sports), photo feature (outdoor photography), technical (reviews of equipment; how-to) and travel (adventure, sports-oriented travel). All should pertain to the outdoors: sections on cycling; Bike section; Downhill Skiing; Cross-country Skiing; Adventure Travel. Do not want to see articles about sports that we don't cover (basketball, tennis, golf, etc.). Buys 40 mss/year. Query with published clips and SASE. Length: 1,500-4,000 words. Pays 50¢/word. Pays expenses of writers on assignment.
Photos: Send photos with submission. Reviews transparencies. Offers $180 minimum per photo. Captions and identification of subjects required. Buys one-time rights.
Columns/Departments: Dispatches, contact Laura Honhold, (news, events, short profiles relevant to outdoors), 200-1,000 words; Destinations (places to explore, news, and tips for adventure travelers), 250-400 words; Review, contact Dan Ferrara, (evaluations of products), 200-1,500 words. Buys 180 mss/year. Query with published clips. Length: 200-2,000 words. Pays 50¢/word.
Fiction: Adventure, historical, humorous, western and essays. "Must pertain to our subject matter. Most interested in book excerpts." Buys 4-6 mss/year. Query with published clips. Length: 1,500-4,000 words. Pays 50¢/word.
Tips: "Prospective writers should study the magazine before querying. Look at the magazine for our style, subject matter and standards." The departments are the best areas for freelancers to "break in."

‡**PHILLYSPORT**, Lewis Tower Bldg., 15th and Locust Sts., Philadelphia PA 19102. (215)893-4466. Editor: Tim Whitaker. Managing Editor: Linda Belsky Zamost. 100% freelance written. Monthly magazine on sports in Philadelphia. Circ. 75,000. Pays on acceptance. Publishes ms an average of 2 months after acceptance. Byline given. Offers 20% kill fee. Buys first rights. Submit seasonal/holiday material 4 months in advance. Computer printout submissions OK; prefers letter-quality. Reports in 3 weeks in queries. Free sample copy and writer's guidelines.
Nonfiction: Book excerpts, historical/nostalgic, humor, interview/profile and personal experience. "We're only interested in Philadelphia sports." Buys 40 mss/year. Query with published clips. Length: 2,000-5,000 words. Pays $100-3,000 for assigned articles; $100-700 for unsolicited articles. Pays expenses of writers on assignment.
Photos: State availability of photos with submission.
Columns/Departments: Books and Media. Buys 24 mss/year. Query with published clips. Length: 1,000-1,500 words. Pays $300-1,000.

REFEREE, Referee Enterprises, Inc., Box 161, Franksville WI 53126. (414)632-8855. Editor: Tom Hammill. For well-educated, mostly 26- to 50-year-old male sports officials. 20-25% freelance written. Eager to work with new/unpublished writers; works with a small number of new/unpublished writers each year. Monthly magazine. Circ. 42,000. Pays on acceptance of completed manuscript. Publishes ms an average of 3-6 months after acceptance. Rights purchased varies. Submit seasonal/holiday material 6 months in advance. Photocopied and previously published submissions OK. Computer printout submissions acceptable. Reports in 2 weeks. Sample copy for 10x13 SAE and $1.20 postage; writer's guidelines for #10 SASE.
Nonfiction: How-to, informational, humor, interview, profile, personal experience, photo feature and technical. Buys 54 mss/year. Query. Length: 700-3,000 words. Pays 4-10¢/word. "No general sports articles."
Photos: Purchased with or without accompanying ms or on assignment. Captions preferred. Send contact sheet, prints, negatives or transparencies. Pays $15-25 for each b&w used; $25-40 for each color used; $75-100 for color cover.
Columns/Departments: Arena (bios); Law (legal aspects); Take Care (fitness, medical). Buys 24 mss/year. Query. Length: 200-800 words. Pays 4¢/word up to $75 maximum for Law and Take Care. Arena pays about $15 each, regardless of length.

Fillers: Jokes, gags, anecdotes, puzzles and referee shorts. Query. Length: 50-200 words. Pays 4¢/word in some cases; others offer only author credit lines.
Tips: "Queries with a specific idea appeal most to readers. Generally, we are looking more for feature writers, as we usually do our own shorter/filler-type material. It is helpful to obtain suitable photos to augment a story. Don't send fluff—we need hard-hitting, incisive material tailored just for our audience. Anything smacking of public relations is a no sale. Don't gloss over the material too lightly or fail to go in-depth looking for a quick sale (taking the avenue of least resistance)."

‡**SPORTS HISTORY,** Empire Press, 105 Loudoun St. SW, Leesburg VA 22075. (203)771-9400. Editor: John D. Schulz. 95% freelance written. Bimonthly magazine for "any sports buff, any sport—popular history." Circ. 70,000. Pays on publication. Byline given. Buys first North American serial rights. Submit seasonal/holiday material 1 year in advance. Reports in 6 weeks on queries; 2 months on mss. Sample copy $3.95; writer's guidelines for SASE.
Nonfiction: Historical/nostalgic. Buys 24 feature mss/year. Query. Length: 3,000 words. Pays up to $300.
Photos: State availability of photos with submission. May offer additional payment for photos accepted with ms.
Columns/Departments: Personality (profiles); Great Moments (high drama); Stats (faces behind stats). Buys 18 mss/year. Query. Length: 1,000-2,000 words. Pays up to $150.

SPORTS PARADE, Meridian Publishing Co., Inc., Box 10010, Odgen UT 84409. (801)394-9446. 65% freelance written. Works with a small number of new/unpublished writers each year. A monthly general interest sports magazine distributed by business and professional firms to employees, customers, clients, etc. Readers are predominantly upscale, mainstream, family oriented. Pays on acceptance. Publishes ms an average of 8 months after acceptance. Byline given. Buys first rights, second serial (reprint) rights or nonexclusive reprint rights. Submit seasonal/holiday material 6 months in advance. Simultaneous, photocopied and previously published submissions OK. Computer printout submissions acceptable; prefers letter-quality. Reports in 6 weeks. Sample copy $1 with 9x12 SAE; writer's guidelines for #10 SASE.
Nonfiction: General interest and interview/profile. "General interest articles covering the entire sports spectrum, personality profiles on top flight professional and amateur sports figures. Buys 20 mss/year. Query. Length: 1,100-1,200 words. Pays 15¢/word.
Photos: Send with query or ms. Pays $35 for color transparencies; $50 for cover. Captions and model releases required.
Tips: "I will be purchasing more articles based on personalities—today's stars."

‡**WOMEN'S SPORTS AND FITNESS MAGAZINE,** Women's Sports Publications Inc., 330 W. Canton, Winter Park FL 32790. Editor: Lewis Rothlein. 80% freelance written. Works with a small number of new/unpublished writers each year. Magazine published 10 times yearly; 68-125 pages. Emphasizes women's sports, fitness and health. Circ. 350,000. Pays within 30 days of publication. Publishes ms an average of 3 months after acceptance. Generally buys all rights. Submit seasonal/holiday material 3 months in advance. Computer printout submissions acceptable. Reports in 1 month on queries; 6 weeks on mss. Sample copy $2; writer's guidelines for SASE.
Nonfiction: Profile, service piece, interview, how-to, historical, personal experience, personal opinion, new product and sporting event coverage. "All articles should have the latest information from knowledgeable sources. All must be of national interest." Buys 5 mss/issue. Length: 2,500-3,000 words. Pays $300-800 for features, including expenses.
Photos: State availability of photos. Pays about $25-50 for b&w prints; $50-300 for 35mm color transparencies. Buys one-time rights.
Columns/Departments: Buys 8-10/issue. Query with clips. Length: 850-1,250 words. Pays $150-250.
Fillers: Health, fitness and sporting coverage. Length: about 500 words. Pays $75-150.
Tips: "If the writer doesn't have published clips, best advice for breaking in is to concentrate on columns and fillers (the Living Well and Sporting News departments) first. Query letters should tell why our readers—active women (with an average age in the early thirties) who partake in sports or fitness activities four times a week—would want to read the article. We're especially attracted to articles with a new angle, fresh information, or difficult-to-get information. We go after the latest in health, nutrition and fitness research, or reports about lesser-known women in sports who are on the threshold of greatness. We also present profiles of the best athletes and teams. We want the profiles to give insight into the person as well as the athlete. We have a cadre of writers who we've worked with regularly, we are always looking for new writers."

Golf

GOLF DIGEST, 5520 Park Ave., Trumbull CT 06611. (203)373-7000. Editor: Jerry Tarde. 30% freelance written. Emphasizes golfing. Monthly magazine. Circ. 1.3 million. Pays on acceptance. Publishes ms an average of 6 weeks after acceptance. Buys all rights. Byline given. Submit seasonal/holiday material 4 months in advance. Photocopied submissions OK. Computer printout submissions acceptable; prefers letter-quality. Reports in 6 weeks.

Nonfiction: How-to, informational, historical, humor, inspirational, interview, nostalgia, opinion, profile, travel, new product, personal experience, photo feature and technical; "all on playing and otherwise enjoying the game of golf." Query. Length: 1,000-2,500 words. Pays $150-1,500 depending on length of edited mss.

Photos: Nick DiDio, art director. Purchased without accompanying ms. Pays $75-150 for 5x7 or 8x10 b&w prints; $100-300/35mm color transparency. Model release required.

Poetry: Lois Hains, assistant editor. Light verse. Buys 1-2/issue. Length: 4-8 lines. Pays $25.

Fillers: Lois Hains, assistant editor. Jokes, gags, anecdotes and cutlines for cartoons. Buys 1-2/issue. Length: 2-6 lines. Pays $10-25.

GOLF ILLUSTRATED, Family Media, Inc., 3 Park Ave., New York NY 10016. (212)340-9200. Editor-in-Chief: Al Barkow. Managing Editor: David Earl. 50% freelance written. Eager to work with new/unpublished writers. A monthly magazine covering personalities and developments in the sport of golf. Circ. 400,000. Pays on acceptance or publication. Publishes ms an average of 2 months after acceptance. Offers 10% kill fee. Buys all rights. Submit seasonal/holiday material 6 months in advance. Query for electronic submissions. Computer printout submissions acceptable; no dot-matrix. Reports in 3 weeks on queries; 6 weeks on manuscripts.

Nonfiction: Essays, historical/nostalgic, how-to, humor, interview/profile, opinion, personal experience, photo feature and travel. Buys 70 mss/year. Query with published clips. Length: 750-1,750 words. Pays $500-1,500 for assigned articles; pays $250-1,000 for unsolicited articles. Sometimes pays the expenses of writers on assignment.

Photos: State availability of photos with submission. Reviews contact sheets and transparencies. Offers $50-500/photo. Captions and identification of subjects required. Buys one-time rights.

Columns/Departments: Health and Fitness, Food and Opinion (all related to golf), approximately 750 words. Query with published clips. Pays $500-1,000.

Fillers: Anecdotes, facts, gags to be illustrated by cartoonist and short humor. Buys 30/year. Length: 100-500 words. Pays $25-300.

Tips: "A freelancer can best break in to our publication by following the personalities – the PGA, LPGA and PGA Senior tour pros and the nature of the game in general."

GULF COAST GOLFER, Golfer Magazines, Inc., 9182 Old Katy Rd., Houston TX 77055. (713)464-0308. Editor: Bob Gray, Sr. 30% freelance written. Prefers to work with published/established writers. Monthly magazine covering results of major area competition, data on upcoming tournaments, reports of new and improved golf courses, and how-to tips for active, competitive golfers in Texas Gulf Coast area. Circ. 25,000. Pays on publication. Publishes ms an average of 1 month after acceptance. Byline given. Buys one-time rights. Submit seasonal/holiday material 3 months in advance. Reports in 3 weeks. Sample copy for 10x13 SAE and 4 first class stamps; free writer's guidelines.

Nonfiction: How-to and personal experience golf articles. No routine coverage. Query first. Length: by arrangement. Pays negotiable rates.

Tips: Especially wants articles on how-to subjects about golf in Gulf Coast area, but only on assignment basis.

NORTH TEXAS GOLFER, Golfer Magazines, Inc., 9182 Old Katy Rd., Houston TX 77055. (713)464-0308. Editor: Bob Gray. 30% freelance written. A monthly tabloid covering golf in North Texas. Emphasizes "grass roots coverage of regional golf course activities" and detailed, localized information on tournaments and competition in North Texas. Circ. 25,000. Pays on publication. Byline given. Buys one-time rights. Submit seasonal/holiday material 3 months in advance. Reports in 2 weeks. Sample copy for 9x12 SAE and 4 first class stamps.

Nonfiction: How-to, humor, interview/profile, personal experience and travel. Nothing outside of Texas. Buys 20 mss/year. Query. Length: 500-1,500 words. Pays $50-250 for assigned articles.

Photos: Send photos with submission. Offers no additional payment for photos accepted with ms. Identification of subjects required.

Tips: "We publish mostly how-to, where-to articles. They're about people and events in Texas only. We could use profiles of successful amateur and professional golfers in Texas – but only on a specific assignment basis. Most of the tour players already have been assigned to the staff or to freelancers. Do *not* approach people, schedule interviews, then tell us about it."

SCORE, Canada's Golf Magazine, Canadian Controlled Media Communications, 287 MacPherson Ave., Toronto, Ontario M4V 1A4 Canada. (416)928-2909. FAX: (416)928-1357. Managing Editor: John Gordon. 70% freelance written. Works with a small number of new/unpublished writers each year. Magazine published 7 times/year covering golf. "*Score* magazine provides seasonal coverage of the Canadian golf scene, professional, amateur, senior and junior golf for men and women golfers in Canada, the U.S. and Europe through profiles, history, travel, editorial comment and instruction." Circ. over 150,000. Pays on publication. Publishes ms an average of 1-3 months after acceptance. Byline given. Offers negotiable kill fee. Buys all rights and second serial (reprint) rights. Submit seasonal/holiday material 8 months in advance. Computer printout submissions acceptable; prefers letter-quality. Reports within 1 month. Sample copy for $2 (Canadian), 9x12 SAE and IRCs; writer's guidelines for #10 SAE and IRC.

Nonfiction: Book excerpts (golf); historical/nostalgic (golf and golf characters); interview/profile (prominent golf professionals); photo feature (golf); and travel (golf destinations only). The yearly April/May issue includes tournament results from Canada, the U.S., Europe, Asia, Australia, etc., history, profile, and regular features. "No personal experience, technical, opinion or general-interest material. Most articles are by assignment only." Buys 25-30 mss/year. Query with published clips. Length: 700-3,500 words. Pays $140-800.

Photos: Send photos with query or ms. Pays $50-100 for 35mm color transparencies (positives) or $30 for 8x10 or 5x7 b&w prints. Captions, model release (if necessary), and identification of subjects required. Buys all rights.

Columns/Departments: Profile (historical or current golf personalities or characters); Great Moments ("Great Moments in Canadian Golf" – description of great single moments, usually game triumphs); New Equipment (Canadian availability only); Travel (golf destinations, including "hard" information such as greens fees, hotel accommodations, etc.); Instruction (by special assignment only; usually from teaching golf professionals); The Mental Game (psychology of the game, by special assignment only); and History (golf equipment collections and collectors, development of the game, legendary figures and events). Buys 17-20 mss/year. Query with published clips or send complete ms. Length: 700-1,700 words. Pays $140-400.

Tips: "Only writers with an extensive knowledge of golf and familiarity with the Canadian golf scene should query or submit in-depth work to *Score*. Many of our features are written by professional people who play the game for a living or work in the industry. All areas mentioned under Columns/Departments are open to freelancers. Most of our *major* features are done on assignment only."

Guns

AMERICAN HANDGUNNER, Publishers' Development Corp., Suite 200, 591 Camino de la Reina, San Diego CA 92108. (619)297-5352. FAX: (619)297-5353. Editor: Cameron Hopkins. 90% freelance written. Eager to work with new/unpublished writers. A bimonthly magazine covering handguns, handgun sports and handgun accessories. "Semi-technical publication for handgun enthusiasts of above-average knowledge/understanding of handguns. Writers must have ability to write about technical designs of handguns as well as ability to write intelligently about the legitimate sporting value of handguns." Circ. 150,000. Pays on publication. Publishes ms an average of 5-9 months after acceptance. Byline given. Offers $50 kill fee. Buys first North American serial rights. Submit seasonal/holiday material 7 months in advance. Previously published submissions OK. Computer printout submissions acceptable; prefers letter-quality. Reports in 1 week. Free sample copy and writer's guidelines.

Nonfiction: How-to, interview/profile, new product, photo feature, technical and "iconoclastic think pieces." Special issue is the *American Handgunner Annual*. No handgun competition coverage. Buys 60-70 mss/year. Query. Length: 500-3,000 words. Pays $175-600 for assigned articles; pays $100-400 for unsolicited articles. Sometimes pays the expenses of writers on assignment.

Photos: Send photos with submission. Reviews contact sheets, 35mm and 4x5 transparencies and 5x7 b&w prints. Offers no additional payment for b&w photos accepted with ms; offers $50-250/color photo. Captions and identification of subjects required. Buys first North American serial rights.

Columns/Departments: Combat Shooting (techniques, equipment, accessories for sport of combat shooting – no "blood and guts"), 600-800 words. Buys 40-60 mss/year. Query. Pays $175-200.

Tips: "We are always interested in 'round-up' pieces covering a particular product line or mixed bag of different product lines of the same theme. If vacation/travel takes you to an exotic place, we're interested in, say, 'The Guns of Upper Volta.' We are looking more closely at handgun hunting."

GUN DIGEST, HANDLOADER'S DIGEST, DBI Books, Inc., 4092 Commercial Ave., Northbrook IL 60062. (312)272-6310. Editor-in-Chief: Ken Warner. 50% freelance written. Prefers to work with published/established writers and works with a small number of new/unpublished writers each year. Annual journal covering guns and shooting. Pays on acceptance. Publishes ms an average of 20 months after acceptance. Byline given. Buys all rights. Computer printout submissions acceptable if legible; prefers letter-quality. Reports in 1 month.

Nonfiction: Buys 50 mss/issue. Query. Length: 500-5,000 words. Pays $100-600; includes photos or illustration package from author.

Photos: State availability of photos with query letter. Reviews 8x10 b&w prints. Payment for photos included in payment for ms. Captions required.

Tips: Award of $1,000 to author of best article (juried) in each issue.

GUN WORLD, 34249 Camino Capistrano, Box HH, Capistrano Beach CA 92624. Editorial Director: Jack Lewis. 50% freelance written. For ages that "range from mid-teens to mid-60s; many professional types who are interested in relaxation of hunting and shooting." Monthly. Circ. 136,000. Buys 80-100 unsolicited mss/year. Pays on acceptance. Publishes ms an average of 6 months after acceptance. Buys first rights and sometimes all rights, but rights reassigned on request. Byline given. Submit seasonal material 5 months in advance. Reports in 6 weeks. Computer printout submissions acceptable; prefers letter-quality. Copy of editorial requirements for SASE.

Nonfiction and Photos: General subject matter consists of "well-rounded articles—not by amateurs—on shooting techniques, with anecdotes; hunting stories with tips and knowledge integrated. No poems or fiction. We like broad humor in our articles, so long as it does not reflect upon firearms safety. Most arms magazines are pretty deadly, and we feel shooting can be fun. Too much material aimed at pro-gun people. Most of this is staff-written and most shooters don't have to be told of their rights under the Constitution. We want articles on new developments; off-track inventions, novel military uses of arms; police armament and training techniques; do-it-yourself projects in this field." Buys informational, how-to, personal experience and nostalgia articles. Pays up to $300, sometimes more. Purchases photos with mss and captions required. Wants 5x7 b&w photos. Sometimes pays the expenses of writers on assignment.

Tips: "The most frequent mistake made by writers in completing an article for us is surface writing with no real knowledge of the subject. To break in, offer an anecdote having to do with proposed copy."

GUNS MAGAZINE, 591 Camino de la Reina, San Diego CA 92108. (619)297-5352. Editor: Jerome Lee. 50% freelance written. Eager to work with new/unpublished writers. Monthly magazine for firearms enthusiasts. Circ. 150,000. Pays on publication for first North American rights. Publishes manuscripts 4-6 months after acceptance. Computer printout submissions acceptable; no dot-matrix. Free sample copy and writer's guidelines.

Nonfiction: Test reports on new firearms; round-up articles on firearms types; guns for specific purposes (hunting, target shooting, self-defense); custom gunmakers; history of modern guns. Buys approximately 100 ms/year. Length: 1,000-2,500 words. Pays $100-350.

Photos: Major emphasis on quality photography. Additional payment of $50-200 for color, 2¼x2¼ preferred.

INSIGHTS, NRA News for Young Shooters, National Rifle Association of America, 1600 Rhode Island Ave. NW, Washington DC 20036. (202)828-6290. FAX: (202)223-2691. Editor: Brenda K. Dalessandro. Managing Editor: John Robbins. 55% freelance written. Monthly magazine covers the shooting sports. "*InSights* is educational yet entertaining. It teaches young shooters and hunters proper and safe shooting techniques and gun handling. Readers are 8-20 years old; 88% are boys." Circ. 45,000. Pays on acceptance. Publishes ms an average of 1 month to 1 year after acceptance. Byline given. Buys first North American serial rights and second serial (reprint) rights. Submit seasonal/holiday material 6 months in advance. Photocopied submissions OK. Computer printout submissions OK. Reports in 1 month on queries; 2 months on mss. Free sample copy for 9x12 SAE with 65¢ postage; writer's guidelines for #10 SASE.

Nonfiction: Historical/nostalgic, how-to, humor, interview/profile, personal experience, technical. "We do not accept manuscripts that are anti-guns or anti-hunting. Nor do we buy articles that describe unsafe or unethical shooting practices." Buys 45 mss/year. Query. Length: 800-1,500 words. Pays $150-200 for assigned articles; $80-200 for unsolicited articles.

Photos: Send photos with submission. Reviews contact sheets and 8x10 b&w prints. Offers $10-25 per photo. Captions and identification of subjects required. Buys one-time rights only.

Fiction: Adventure, historical, humorous, western. No unsafe or unethical shooting practices in fiction. Buys 8 mss/year. Query. Length: 800-1,500 words. Pays $80-150.

Tips: "We buy many mss about hunting trips that are unique somehow or teach our young readers about a certain of game. How-to articles like refinishing a gun stock or mounting a scope are purchased as well. Match results or event descriptions for competition shooting are also published; we must receive queries for competition shooting articles."

Horse Racing

HOOF BEATS, United States Trotting Association, 750 Michigan Ave., Columbus OH 43215. (614)224-2291. FAX: (614)228-1385. Editor: Dean A. Hoffman. 35% freelance written. Works with a small number of new/unpublished writers each year. Monthly magazine covering harness racing for the participants of the sport of harness racing. "We cover all aspects of the sport—racing, breeding, selling, etc." Circ. 26,000. Pays on publication. Publishes ms an average of 3 months after acceptance. Byline given. Buys negotiable rights. Submit seasonal/holiday material 3 months in advance. Computer printout submissions acceptable. Reports in 3 weeks. Free sample copy, postpaid.

Nonfiction: General interest, historical/nostalgic, humor, inspirational, interview/profile, new product, personal experience, photo feature. Buys 15-20 mss/year. Query. Length: open. Pays $100-400. Pays the expenses of writers on assignment "with approval."
Photos: State availability of photos. Pays variable rates for 35mm transparencies and prints. Identification of subjects required. Buys one-time rights.
Fiction: Historical, humorous, interesting fiction with a harness racing theme. Buys 2-3 mss/year. Query. Length: open. Pays $100-400.

SPUR, Box 85, Middleburg VA 22117. (703)687-6314. Editor: Kerry Phelps. 80% freelance written. Prefers to work with published/established writers; works with a small number of new/unpublished writers each year. Bimonthly magazine covering thoroughbred horses and the people who are involved in the business and sports of flat racing, steeplechasing and polo. Circ. 10,000. Pays on publication. Publishes ms an average of 3 months after acceptance. Byline given. Buys all rights. Computer printout submissions acceptable; prefers letter-quality. Reports in 1 month on mss and queries. Sample copy $3.50; writer's guidelines for #10 SASE.
Nonfiction: Historical/nostalgic, thoroughbred care, personality profile, farm, special feature, regional, photo essay, steeplechasing and polo. Buys 50 mss/year. Query with clips of published work, "or we will consider complete manuscripts." Length: 300-4,000 words. Payment negotiable. Sometimes pays the expenses of writers on assignment.
Photos: State availability of photos. Reviews color and b&w contact sheets. Captions, model releases and identification of subjects required. Buys all rights "unless otherwise negotiated."
Columns/Departments: Query or send complete ms to Editorial Dept. Length: 100-500 words. Pays $50 and up.
Tips: "Writers must have a knowledge of horses, horse owners, breeding, training, racing, and riding—or the ability to obtain this knowledge from a subject."

Hunting and Fishing

ALABAMA GAME & FISH, Game & Fish Publications, Inc., Suite 110, 2250 Newmarket Parkway, Marietta GA 30067. (404)953-9222. Editor: Jimmy Jacobs. 90% freelance written. Monthly magazine on in-state outdoor topics of interest to an avid hunting and fishing audience. Circ. 25,000. Pays 75 days prior to cover date of issue. Publishes ms an average of 6 months after acceptance. Byline given. Offers negotiable kill fee. Buys first North American serial rights. Submit seasonal/holiday material 10 months in advance. Computer printout submissions OK; no dot-matrix. Editor prefers to hold queries on file until article is assigned or writer informs of prior sale. Reports in 3 months on mss. Sample copy for $2 and 9x12 SAE with 7 first class stamps; writer's guidelines for #10 SASE.
Nonfiction: Send photos with submission. Reviews 2x2 transparencies and 8x10 prints. Offers $25-250 per photo. Captions and identification of subjects required. Buys one-time rights.
Fiction: Gordon Whittington, fiction editor. Humorous (hunting and fishing topics). Buys 12 mss/year. Send complete ms. Length: 2,200-2,500 words. Pays $250-300.
Tips: "We publish hard-core hunting and fishing features for the purpose of informing and entertaining a loyal, state-specific outdoor audience. We do not publish the standard type or outdoor article in quantity. Study our magazine and restrict query ideas to major species in the state."

AMERICAN HUNTER, Suite 1000, 470 Spring Park Pl., Herndon VA 22070. Editor: Tom Fulgham. 90% freelance written. For hunters who are members of the National Rifle Association. Circ. 1.4 million. Buys first North American serial rights. Byline given. Computer printout submissions acceptable; prefers letter-quality. Free sample copy for 9x12 SAE with 85¢ postage; writer's guidelines for #10 SASE.
Nonfiction: Factual material on all phases of hunting. Not interested in material on fishing or camping. Prefers queries. Length: 2,000-3,000 words. Pays $250-450.
Photos: No additional payment made for photos used with mss. Pays $25 for b&w photos purchased without accompanying mss. Pays $50-300 for color.

ARKANSAS SPORTSMAN, Game & Fish Publications, Inc., Box 741, Marietta GA 30061. (404)953-9222. Editor: Bill Hartlage. 90-95% freelance written. Works with a small number of new/unpublished writers each year. Monthly how-to, where-to and when-to hunting and fishing magazine covering Arkansas. Pays 3 months before publication. Byline given. Buys one-time rights. Submit seasonal material 8 months in advance. Simultaneous queries, and simultaneous and photocopied submissions OK. Computer printout submissions acceptable; prefers letter-quality. Reports in 2 months. Sample copy for $2.50 and 10x12 SAE; writer's guidelines for SASE.

Nonfiction: How-to (hunting and fishing *only*); humor (on limited basis); interview/profile (of successful hunter/angler); personal experience (hunting or fishing adventure). No hiking, backpacking or camping. No "my first deer" articles. Buys 60 mss/year. Query with or without published clips. Length: 2,200-2,500 words. Pays $150.
Photos: State availability of photos. Pays $75 for full-page, color leads; $225 for covers; $25 for b&w photos not submitted as part of story package. Captions and identification of subjects required. Buys one-time rights.

BADGER SPORTSMAN, Vercauteren Publishing, Inc., 19 E. Main, Chilton WI 53014. (414)849-4651. Editor: Tom Woodrow. Managing Editor: Gary Vercauteren. 80% freelance written. Monthly tabloid covering Wisconsin outdoors. Circ. 26,260. Pays on publication. Publishes ms an average of 1 month after acceptance. Byline given. Buys one-time rights. Submit seasonal/holiday material 2 months in advance. Previously published submissions OK. Computer printout submissions acceptable. Sample copy for 10x13 SAE with 3 first class stamps; free writer's guidelines.
Nonfiction: General interest; how-to (fishing, hunting, etc., in the Midwest outdoors); humor; interview/ profile; personal experience; technical. Buys 400-500 mss/year. Query. Length: open. Pays 35¢/column inch ($15-40).
Photos: Send photos with accompanying query or ms. Reviews 3x5 or larger b&w and color prints. Pays by column inch. Identification of subjects required.
Tips: "We publish stories about *Wisconsin* fishing, hunting, camping; outdoor cooking; and general animal stories."

BASSIN', Box 185, Bixby OK 74008. (918)366-4441. FAX: (918)366-6250. Editor: Thayne Smith. 90% freelance written. Eager to work with new/unpublished writers. Magazine published 8 times/year covering freshwater fishing with emphasis on black bass. Circ. 265,000. Publishes ms an average of 8 months after acceptance. Pays within 30 days of acceptance. Byline given. Buys first serial rights. Submit seasonal material 8 months in advance. Prefers queries but will examine mss accompanied by SASE. Query for electronic submissions. Computer printout submissions acceptable; no dot-matrix. Reports in 2-3 weeks. Sample copy $2; writer's guidelines for #10 SASE.
Nonfiction: How-to and where-to stories on bass fishing. Prefers completed ms. Length: 1,200-1,500 words. Pays $275-500 on acceptance.
Photos: Send photos with ms. Pays $300 for color cover; $100 for color cover inset. Send b&w prints or color transparencies. Buys one-time rights. Photo payment on publication.
Columns/Departments: Product reviews. Length: 100-700 words. Pays $50-150 on publication. Send complete ms.
Tips: "Reduce the common fishing slang terminology when writing for *Bassin'* (and other outdoor magazines). This slang is usually regional and confuses anglers in other areas of the country. Good strong features will win me over more quickly than short articles or fillers. Absolutely no poetry. We need stories on fishing tackle and techniques to catch largemouth, smallmouth and spotted (Kentucky) bass."

BASSMASTER MAGAZINE, B.A.S.S. Publications, Box 17900, Montgomery AL 36141. (205)272-9530. Editor: Dave Precht. 80% freelance written. Prefers to work with published/established writers. Magazine (10 issues/ year) about largemouth, smallmouth, spotted bass for dedicated beginning and advanced bass fishermen. Circ. 550,000. Pays on acceptance. Publication date of ms after acceptance "varies—seasonal material could take years"; average time is 8 months. Byline given. Buys all rights. Submit seasonal material 6 months in advance. Computer printout submissions OK; letter-quality only, not justified. Reports in 1 month. Sample copy $2; writer's guidelines for #10 SASE.
Nonfiction: Historical; interview (of knowledgable people in the sport); profile (outstanding fishermen); travel (where to go to fish for bass); how-to (catch bass and enjoy the outdoors); new product (reels, rods and bass boats); and conservation related to bass fishing."No 'Me and Joe Go Fishing' type articles." Query. Length: 400-2,100 words. Pays 20¢/word.
Columns/Departments: Short Cast/News & Views (upfront regular feature covering news-related events such as new state bass records, unusual bass fishing happenings, conservation, new products and editorial viewpoints); 250-400 words.
Photos: "We want a mixture of b&w and color photos." Pays $50 minimum for b&w prints. Pays $300-350 for color cover transparencies. Captions required; model releases preferred. Buys all rights.
Fillers: Anecdotes, short humor and newsbreaks. Buys 4-5 mss/issue. Length: 250-500 words. Pays $50-100.
Tips: "Editorial direction continues in the short, more direct how-to article. Compact, easy-to-read information is our objective. Shorter articles with good graphics, such as how-to diagrams, step-by-step instruction, etc., will enhance a writer's articles submitted to *Bassmaster Magazine*. The most frequent mistakes made by writers in completing an article for us are poor grammar, poor writing, poor organization and superficial research."

BC OUTDOORS, SIP Division, Maclean Hunter Ltd., 202-1132 Hamilton St., Vancouver, British Columbia V6B 2S2 Canada. (604)687-1581. FAX: (604)687-1925. Editor: George Will. 80% freelance written. Works with a small number of new/unpublished writers each year. Outdoor recreation magazine published 7 times/

year. *BC Outdoors* covers fishing, camping, hunting, and the environment of outdoor recreation. Circ. 40,000. Pays on acceptance. Publishes ms an average of 3 months after acceptance. Byline given. Offers negotiable kill fee. Buys first North American serial rights. Query for electronic submissions. Computer printout submissions acceptable; prefers letter-quality. Reports in 1 month on queries; 2 months on mss. Sample copy and writer's guidelines for 8x10 SAE with $2 postage.

Nonfiction: How-to (new or innovative articles on outdoor subjects); personal experience (outdoor adventure); and outdoor topics specific to British Columbia. "We would like to receive how-to, where-to features dealing with hunting and fishing in British Columbia and the Yukon." Buys 80-90 mss/year. Query. Length: 1,500-2,000 words. Pays $300-500. Sometimes pays the expenses of writers on assignment.

Photos: State availability of photos with query. Pays $25-75 on publication for 5x7 b&w prints; $35-150 for color contact sheets and 35mm transparencies. Captions and identification of subjects required. Buys one-time rights.

Tips: "More emphasis on saltwater angling and less emphasis on self-propelled activity, like hiking and canoeing will affect the types of freelance material we buy in 1989-90. Subject must be specific to British Columbia. We receive many manuscripts written by people who obviously do not know the magazine or market. The writer has a better chance of breaking in at our publication with short, lesser-paying articles and fillers, because we have a stable of regular writers in constant touch who produce most main features."

CALIFORNIA ANGLER, The Magazine For Fresh and Saltwater Fishing, Outdoor Ventures, Ltd., Suite N, 1921 Carnegie, Santa Ana CA 92705. (714)261-9779. FAX: (714)261-9853. Editor: Jim Matthews. Associate Editor: Rob Breeding. 90% freelance written. A recreational fishing magazine published monthly. Circ. 20,000. Pays during month prior to publication for columns, shorts and photos; 2-3 months before publication for features. Publishes ms 2-12 months after acceptance. Byline given. Buys one-time rights. Submit seasonal/holiday material 6-12 months in advance. Simultaneous and photocopied submissions OK. Computer printout submissions OK. Query for electronic submissions. Reports immediately if possible. Sample copy and writer's guideliens sent on request.

Nonfiction: Heavily how-to and where-to, with emphasis on California and Baja California places and techniques. Most new product, opinion written by staff. Interview/profile pieces would be considered. Annual where-to-go subject themes include: Canada (Jan), Bass (Feb), Eastern Sierra (Apr), Flyfishing (June), Baja (September), New Products (Nov), Alaska (Dec). "We see a lot of just horrible material—some of it from established writers—so we are ripe for a talented young writer who knows what research and reporting are all about." Buys minimum of 60 mss/year. Query first "and I don't care about clips, dazzle me with a three paragraph query." Length: 1,500-2,500 words. Pays $300 average for mss with photos, occasionally more.

Photos: Send photos with submission (not query). Reviews transparencies. Offers no additional payment for photos accepted with ms. Cover photos: pays $25-300.

Columns/Departments: Travel, Tactics, Reviews, Conservation, Flyfishing and Hot Bite. "Our *Hot Bite* column offers a good opportunity to sell a short, where-to-go piece (200 to 500 words) for a quick $100." Length: to 1,500 words. Pays $100 for *Hot Bite*; $200 other columns. Photos required. Buys 50-70 *Hot Bites* per year, 40-50 other columns.

Tips: "Write for our new, entertaining guidelines, ask for the current contributor's newsletter (which goes to our regular writers), and an issue of the magazine. Better yet, subscribe. We try to stay on the leading edge of the latest in fishing techniques, emerging fishing places and conservation. But remember our name is *California Angler*—emphasis on the California. Most of our travel material is written by our regular contributors."

‡**CALIFORNIA GAME & FISH**, Game & Fish Publications, Inc., Box 741, Marietta GA 30061. Editor: Stan Warren. See *Alabama Game & Fish*.

DAKOTA GAME & FISH, Game & Fish Publications, Inc., Box 741, Marietta GA 30061. (404)953-9222. Editor: Jim Schlender. See *Alabama Game & Fish*.

DEER AND DEER HUNTING, The Stump Sitters, Inc., Box 1117, Appleton WI 54912. (414)734-0009. FAX: (414)734-2919. Editors: Al Hofacker and Dr. Rob Wegner. 80% freelance written. Prefers to work with published/established writers. Bimonthly magazine covering deer hunting for individuals who hunt with bow, gun or camera. Circ. 120,000. Pays on publication. Publishes ms an average of 6 months after acceptance. Byline given. Offers $50 kill fee. Buys first North American serial rights and second serial (reprint) rights. Submit seasonal/holiday material 8 months in advance. Computer printout submissions acceptable; prefers letter-quality. Reports in 1 week on queries; 2 weeks on mss. Sample copy for 9x12 SAE with 7 first class stamps; writer's guidelines for #10 SASE.

Nonfiction: Historical/nostalgic; how-to (hunting techniques); opinion; personal experience; photo feature; technical. "Our readers desire factual articles of a technical nature that relate deer behavior and habits to hunting methodology. We focus on deer biology, management principles and practices, habitat requirements, natural history of deer, hunting techniques and hunting ethics." No hunting "Hot Spot" or "local" articles.

Buys 40 mss/year. Query with clips of published work. Length: 1,000-4,000 words. Pays $50-400. Sometimes pays the expenses of writers on assignment.

Photos: State availability of photos. Pays $125 for 35mm color transparencies; $500 for front cover; $40 for 8x10 b&w prints. Captions and identification of subjects required. Buys one-time rights.

Columns/Departments: Deer Browse (unusual observations of deer behavior). Buys 20 mss/year. Length: 200-800 words. Pays $10-50.

Fillers: Clippings, anecdotes, newsbreaks. Buys 20/year. Length: 200-800 words. Pays $10-40.

Tips: "Break in by providing material of a technical nature, backed by scientific research, and written in a style understandable to the average deer hunter. We focus primarily on white-tailed deer."

FIELD & STREAM, 2 Park Ave., New York NY 10016. Editor: Duncan Barnes. 50% freelance written. Eager to work with new/unpublished writers. Monthly. Buys first rights. Byline given. Reports in 6 weeks. Query. Writer's guidelines for 8x10 SAE with 1 first class stamp.

Nonfiction and Photos: "This is a broad-based service magazine for the hunter and fisherman. Editorial content ranges from very basic how-to stories detailing a useful technique or a device that sportsmen can make to articles of penetrating depth about national hunting, fishing, and related activities. Also humor and personal essays, nostalgia and 'mood pieces' on the hunting or fishing experience." Prefers color photos to b&w. Query first with photos. Length: 1,000-2,000 words. Payment varies depending on the quality of work, importance of the article. Pays $750 and up for major features. *Field & Stream* also publishes regional sections with feature articles on hunting and fishing in specific areas of the country. The sections are geographically divided into Northeast, Midwest, Far West, West and South, and appear 12 months a year. Usually buys photos with mss. When purchased separately, pays $450 minimum for color. Buys first rights to photos.

Fillers: Buys "how it's done" fillers of 500-900 words. Must be unusual or helpful subjects. Pays $250 on acceptance. Also buys "Field Guide" pieces, short (750-word maximum) articles on natural phenomena as specifically related to hunting and fishing; and "Myths and Misconceptions," short pieces debunking a commonly held belief about hunting and fishing. Pays $500.

‡THE FISHERMAN, LIF Publishing Corp., 14 Ramsey Rd., Shirley NY 11967-4704. (516)345-5200. FAX: (516)345-5304. Editor: Fred Golofaro. Senior Editor: Pete Barrett. 4 regional editions: *Long Island*, *Metropolitan New York*, Fred Golofaro, editor; *New England*, Tim Coleman, editor; *New Jersey*, Ken Freel, editor; and *Delaware-Maryland-Virginia*, Eric Burnley, editor. 75% freelance written. A weekly magazine covering fishing and boating. Combined circ. 82,000. Pays on publication. Byline given. Offers variable kill fee. Buys all rights. Articles may be run in one or more regional editions by choice of the editors. Submit seasonal/holiday material 2 months in advance. Computer printout submissions acceptable; prefers letter-quality to dot-matrix. Reports in 3 weeks. Free sample copy and writer's guidelines.

Nonfiction: Send submission to editor of regional edition. General interest, historical/nostalgic, how-to, interview/profile, personal experience, photo feature, technical and travel. Special issues include Trout Fishing (April), Bass Fishing (June), Offshore Fishing (July), Surf Fishing (September), Tackle (October) and Electronics (November). "No 'me and Joe' tales. We stress how, where, when, why." Buys approx. 400 mss/year, each edition. Length: 1,500-2,400 words. Pays $100-150 for unsolicited feature articles.

Photos: Send photos with submission; also buys single photos for cover use. Offers no additional payment for photos accepted with ms. Identification of subjects required.

Tips: "Focus on specific how-to and where-to subjects within each region."

FISHING & BOATING ILLUSTRATED, Gallant/Charger Publications, Inc., Box HH, Capistrano Beach CA 92624. (714)493-2101. Editor: Jack Lewis. Managing Editor: Burt Carey. 50% freelance written. A bimonthly magazine covering fishing and boating. "*Fishing & Boating Illustrated* is aimed at recreational fishermen and boaters who enjoy both. Geographic coverage is national, with how-to stories on many fish species." Circ. 50,000. Pays on acceptance. Byline given. Buys one-time rights and makes work-for-hire assignments. Query first. Computer printout submissions acceptable. Reports in 1 month. Sample copy $3.

Nonfiction: How-to (catching specific species of fish, maintaining boats) and technical (on boating projects). Buys 100 mss/year. Query. Length: 250-3,000 words. Pays $25-350.

Photos: Send photos with accompanying query or manuscript. Reviews 35mm transparencies and 8x10 prints. Pays $5-10 for prints, $25-100 for transparencies. Captions, model releases and identification of subjects required.

Tips: "We need queries by late spring for editorial planning. If a manufacturer's product tie-in is possible, so state. Photography must be excellent."

FISHING & HUNTING JOURNAL, The Magazine of the Midwestern Outdoors, North Town Center, #3A, Box 440, Sparta IL 62282. Editor: John Stahlman. 95% freelance written. Works with new writers. Bimonthly magazine on the where-to, how-to and when-to of fishing and hunting in 16 states (North Dakota, South Dakota, Nebraska, Kansas, Oklahoma, Arkansas, Missouri, Iowa, Minnesota, Wisconsin, Illinois, Kentucky, Tennessee, Indiana, Michigan and Ohio). Byline given. Pays on acceptance. Buys one-time rights. Queries preferred. Computer printout submissions acceptable. Reports in 2 months. Sample copy for 9x12 SASE; writer's guidelines for SASE.

Nonfiction: Hunting and fishing in Midwest only. Pays $75-350. Length: 750-2,000 words. Photos with captions accompanying text improves chance of acceptance dramatically.

Tips: "Best place for new writers to break into the magazine is with a 750 word where-to article for Midwestern Adventures section. Tell me about a midwestern technique used to catch or bag a midwestern species in the midwest and you have my attention. Then if it is well-written, interesting and with a unique slant, you made a sale."

FISHING AND HUNTING NEWS, Outdoor Empire Publishing Co., Inc., 511 Eastlake Ave. E., Box 19000, Seattle WA 98109. (206)624-3845. Managing Editor: Vence Malernee. Emphasizes fishing and hunting. Weekly tabloid. Circ. 140,000. Pays on acceptance. Buys all rights. Submit seasonal/holiday material 3 months in advance. Photocopied submissions OK. Computer printout submissions OK.

Nonfiction: Short how-to (fish and hunt successfully, things that make outdoor jaunts more enjoyable/productive); photo feature (successful fishing/hunting in the western U.S.); informational. No first-person personal accounts of the 'me and Joe' variety or dated materials, as we are a weekly news publication." Buys 25 or more mss/year. Query. Length: 100-1,000 words. Pays $25 minimum.

Photos: Purchased with or without accompanying ms. Captions required. Submit prints or transparencies. Pays $15 minimum for b&w glossy prints; $25 minimum for 35mm or 2¼x2¼color transparencies. Looking for top-notch cover material. Transparencies preferred. Happy fishermen, hunters with their fish, game in tasteful setting."

Tips: "Competition in the outdoor publishing industry is very keen, and we are meeting it with increasingly timely and prognosticative articles. Writers should look for the new, the different, and the off-the-beaten track in western hunting, fishing and outdoor activities."

FISHING WORLD, 51 Atlantic Ave., Floral Park NY 11001. FAX: (516)437-6841. Editor: Keith Gardner. 100% freelance written. Bimonthly. Circ. 350,000. Pays on acceptance. Buys first North American serial rights. Pays on acceptance. Publishes ms an average of 6 months after acceptance. Photocopied submissions OK. Reports in 2 weeks. Free sample copy; writer's guidelines for #10 SASE.

Nonfiction: "Feature articles range from 1,000-2,000 words with the shorter preferred. A good selection of color transparencies should accompany each submission. Subject matter can range from a hot fishing site to tackle and techniques, from tips on taking individual species to a story on one lake or an entire region, either freshwater or salt. However, how-to is definitely preferred over where-to, and a strong biological/scientific slant is best of all. Where-to articles, especially if they describe foreign fishing, should be accompanied by sidebars covering how to make reservations and arrange transportation, how to get there, where to stay. Angling methods should be developed in clear detail, with accurate and useful information about tackle and boats. Depending on article length, suitability of photographs and other factors, payment is up to $500 for feature articles accompanied by suitable photography. Color transparencies selected for cover use pay an additional $300. B&w or unillustrated featurettes are also considered. These can be on anything remotely connected with fishing." Query. Length: 1,000 words. Pays up to $250 depending on length and photos. Brief queries accompanied by photos are preferred.

Photos: "Cover shots are purchased separately, rather than selected from those accompanying mss. The editor favors drama rather than serenity in selecting cover shots. Underwater horizontal portraits of fish are purchased (one-time rights) for centerfold use at the rate of $300 per transparency."

Tips: Looking for "quality photography and more West Coast fishing."

FLORIDA GAME & FISH, Game & Fish Publications, Inc., Box 741, Marietta GA 30061. (404)953-9222. Editor: Jimmy Jacobs. See *Alabama Game & Fish.*

FLORIDA SPORTSMAN, Wickstrom Publishers Inc., 5901 S.W. 74 St., Miami FL 33143. (305)661-4222. Editor: Vic Dunaway. Managing Editor: Biff Lampton. 80% freelance written. Eager to work with new/unpublished writers. A monthly magazine covering fishing, boating and related sports—Florida and Caribbean only. Circ. 100,000. Pays on publication. Publishes ms an average of 6 months after acceptance. Byline given. Offers 50% kill fee. Buys first North American serial rights. Submit seasonal/holiday material 6 months in advance. Computer printout submissions acceptable; prefers letter-quality. Reports in 1 week on queries; 1 month on mss. Free sample copy; writer's guidelines for #10 SASE.

Nonfiction: Essays (environment or nature); how-to (fishing, hunting, boating); humor (outdoors angle); personal experience (in fishing, etc.); and technical (boats, tackle, etc., as particularly suitable for Florida specialties). "We use reader service pieces almost entirely—how-to, where-to, etc. One or two environmental pieces per issue as well. Writers *must* be Florida based, or have lengthy experience in Florida outdoors. All articles must have strong Florida emphasis. We do not want to see general how-to-fish-or-boat pieces which might well appear in a national or wide-regional magazine." Buys 120 mss/year. Query with or without published clips, or send complete ms. Length: 2,000-3,000 words. Pays $300-400 for assigned articles; pays $150-300 for unsolicited articles.

Photos: Send photos with submission. Reviews 35mm transparencies and 4x5 and larger prints. Offers no additional payment for photos accepted with ms. Buys one-time rights.
Columns/Departments: Sportsman Scene (news-feature items on outdoors subjects), 100-500 words. Buys 25 mss/year. Send complete ms. Pays $15-100.
Tips: "Feature articles are most open to freelancers; however there is little chance of acceptance unless contributor is an accomplished and avid outdoorsman *and* a competent writer-photographer with considerable experience in Florida."

FLORIDA WILDLIFE, Florida Game & Fresh Water Fish Commission, 620 South Meridian St., Tallahassee FL 32399-1600. (904)488-5563. FAX: (904)488-6988. Editor: Andrea H. Blount. About 40% freelance written. Bimonthly state magazine covering hunting, natural hisotry, fishing and wildlife conservation. "In outdoors sporting articles we seek themes of wholesome recreation. In nature articles we seek accuracy and conservation purpose." Circ. 29,000. Pays on publication. Publishes ms 2 months to 2 years after acceptance. Byline given. Buys first North American serial rights and occasionally second serial (reprint) rights. Submit seasonal/holiday material 6 months in advance. Simultaneous queries, and simultaneous, photocopied, and previously published submissions OK. "Inform us if it is previously published work." Computer printout submissions acceptable if double-spaced. Reports in 6 weeks on queries; variable on mss. Sample copy $1.25; free writer's/photographer's guidelines for SASE.
Nonfiction: General interest (bird watching, hiking, camping, boating); how-to (hunting and fishing); humor (wildlife related; no anthropomorphism); inspirational (conservation oriented); personal experience (wildlife, hunting, fishing, outdoors); photo feature (Florida species: game, nongame, botany); and technical (rarely purchased, but open to experts). "In a nutshell, we buy general interest hunting, fishing and nature stories. No stories that humanize animals, or opinionated stories not based on confirmable facts." Buys 40-50 mss/year. Send slides/manuscript. Length: 500-1,500 words. Generally pays $50/published page; including use of photos.
Photos: State availability of photos with story query. Prefer 35mm color slides of hunting, fishing, and natural science series of Florida wildlife species. Pays $20-50 for inside photos; $100 for front cover photos, $50 for back cover. "We like short, specific captions." Buys one-time rights.
Fiction: "We rarely buy fiction, and then only if it is true to life and directly related to good sportsmanship and conservation. No fairy tales, erotica, profanity, or obscenity." Buys 2-3 mss/year. Send complete mss and label "fiction." Length: 500-1,200 words. Generally pays $50/published page.
Tips: "Read and study recent issues for subject matter, style and examples of our viewpoint, philosophy and treatment. We look for wholesome recreation, ethics, safety, and good outdoor experience more than bagging the game in our stories. Of special need at this time are well-written hunting and fishing in Florida articles."

FLY FISHERMAN, Historical Times, Inc., 2245 Kohn Rd., Box 8200, Harrisburg PA 17105. (717)657-9555. Editor and Publisher: John Randolph. Associate Editors: Jack Russell and Philip Hanyok. 85-90% freelance written. Magazine published 6 times/year on fly fishing. Circ. 140,000. Pays on acceptance. Publishes ms an average 10 months after acceptance. Byline given. Buys first North American serial rights and (selectively) all rights. Submit seasonal/holiday material 1 year in advance. Query for electronic submissions. Computer printout submissions acceptable; prefers letter-quality. Reports in 6 weeks. Sample copy for 9x12 SAE and 4 first class stamps. Writer's guidelines for #10 SASE.
Nonfiction: Book excerpts, how-to, humor, interview/profile, technical and essays on fly fishing, fly tying, shorts and fishing technique shorts and features. Where-to. No other types of fishing, including spin or bait. Buys 75 mss/year. Query before submitting ms. Length: 50-3,000 words. Pays $35-500.
Photos: State availability of photos or send photos with query or ms. Reviews b&w contact sheets and 35mm transparencies. Pays $35-100 for contact sheets; $35-200 for transparencies; $500 for cover photos. Captions, model releases and identification of subjects required. Buys one-time rights.
Columns/Departments: Fly Fisherman's Bookshelf, 500-750 word book reviews ($75 each); reviews of fly fishing video tapes $75, same length. Buys 8 mss/year. Query. Length: 500-1,000 words. Pays $75.
Fiction: Essays on fly fishing, humorous and serious. No articles over 2,500 words. Buys 2 mss/year. Query before submitting ms. Length: 1,200-3,000 words. Pays $125-500.
Fillers: Short humor and newsbreaks. Buys 30/year. Length: 25-1,000 words. Pays $25-250.
Tips: "Our magazine is a tightly focused, technique-intensive special interest magazine. Articles require fly fishing expertise, and writing must be tight and in many instances well researched. The novice fly fisher has little hope of a sale with us, although perhaps 30 percent of our features are entry-level or intermediate-level in nature. Fly-fishing technique pieces that are broadly focused have great appeal. Both features and departments—short features—have the best chance of purchase. Accompany submissions with excellent color slides (35mm), black and white 8x10 prints or line drawing illustrations."

FUR-FISH-GAME, 2878 E. Main, Columbus OH 43209. Editor: Mitch Cox. 65% freelance written. Works with a small number of new/unpublished writers each year. Monthly magazine. For outdoorsmen of all ages who are interested in hunting, fishing, trapping, dogs, camping, conservation and related topics. Circ. 180,000. Pays on acceptance. Publishes ms an average of 7 months after acceptance. Byline given. Buys first serial rights or all rights. Prefers nonsimultaneous submissions. Computer printout submissions acceptable; prefers letter-quality. Reports in 6 weeks. Query. Sample copy for $1 and 8×11 SAE. Writer's guidelines for #10 SASE.

Nonfiction: "We are looking for informative, down-to-earth stories about hunting, fishing, trapping, dogs, camping, boating, conservation and related subjects. Nostalgic articles are also used. Many of our stories are 'how-to' and should appeal to small-town and rural readers who are true outdoorsmen. Some recent articles have told how to train a gun dog, catch big-water catfish, outfit a bowhunter and trap late-season muskrat. We also use personal experience stories and an occasional profile, such as an article about an old-time trapper. 'Where-to' stories are used occasionally if they have broad appeal. Length: 1,500-3,000 words. Pays $75-150 depending upon quality, photo support, and importance to magazine. Short filler stories pay $35-80."

Photos: Send photos with ms. Photos are part of ms package and receive no additional payment. Prefer b&w but color prints or transparencies OK. Prints can be 5x7 or 8x10. Caption information required.

Tips: "We are always looking for quality articles that tell how to hunt or fish for game animals or birds that are popular with everyday outdoorsmen but often overlooked in other publications, such as catfish, bluegill, crappie, squirrel, rabbit, crows, etc. We also use articles on standard seasonal subjects such as deer and pheasant, but like to see a fresh approach or new technique. Trapping articles, especially instructional ones based on personal experience, are useful all year. Articles on gun dogs, ginseng and do-it-yourself projects are also popular with our readers. An assortment of photos and/or sketches greatly enhances any ms, and sidebars, where applicable, can also help."

GEORGIA SPORTSMAN, Game & Fish Publications, Box 741, Marietta GA 30061. (404)953-9222. Editor: Jimmy Jacobs. See *Alabama Game & Fish*.

GULF COAST FISHERMAN, Harold Wells Gulf Coast Fisherman, Inc., 403 W. Main St., Port Lavaca TX 77979. (512)552-8864. Editor: Gary M. Ralston. 95% freelance written. A quarterly magazine covering Gulf Coast saltwater fishing. "All editorial material is designed to expand the knowledge of the Gulf Coast angler and promote saltwater fishing in general. Our audience is composed principally of persons from managerial/professional occupations." Circ 15,000. Pays on publication. Publishes ms an average of 2 months after acceptance. Byline given. Buys first North American serial rights. Submit seasonal/holiday material 2 months in advance. Computer printout submissions acceptable; prefers letter-quality. Submissions of manuscripts on Macintosh 3½ diskette most preferred. Sample copy and writer's guidelines for 9x12 SAE and 5 first class stamps.

Nonfiction: How-to (any aspect relating to saltwater fishing that provides the reader specifics on use of tackle, boats, finding fish, etc.); interview/profile; new product; personal experience; and technical. Buys 25 mss/year. Query with or without published clips, or send complete ms. Length: 900-1,800 words. Pays $90-200.

Photos: State availability of photos with submission. Offers no additional payment for photos accepted with ms. Captions and identification of subjects required. Buys one-time rights.

Tips: "Features are the area of our publication most open to freelancers. Subject matter should concern some aspect of or be in relation to saltwater fishing in coastal bays or offshore."

ILLINOIS GAME & FISH, Game & Fish Publications, Inc., Box 741, Marietta GA 30061. (404)953-9222. Editor: Jim Low. See *Alabama Game & Fish*.

INDIANA GAME & FISH, Game & Fish Publications, Inc., Box 741, Marietta GA 30061. (404)953-9222. Editor: Jim Low. See *Alabama Game & Fish*.

IOWA GAME & FISH, Game & Fish Publications, Inc., Box 741, Marietta GA 30061. (404)953-9222. Editor: Jim Schendler. See *Alabama Game & Fish*.

KANSAS GAME & FISH, Game & Fish Publications, Inc., Box 741, Marietta GA 30061. (404)953-9222. Editor: Steve Lightfoot. See *Alabama Game & Fish*.

KENTUCKY GAME & FISH, Game & Fish Publications, Inc., Box 741, Marietta GA 30061. (404)953-9222. Editor: Bill Hartlage. See *Alabama Game & Fish*.

LOUISIANA GAME & FISH, Game & Fish Publications, Inc., Box 741, Marietta GA 30061. (404)953-9222. Editor: Robert Sloan. See *Alabama Game & Fish*.

THE MAINE SPORTSMAN, Box 365, Augusta ME 04330. Editor: Harry Vanderweide. 100% freelance written. "Eager to work with new/unpublished writers, but because we run over 30 regular columns, it's hard to get into *The Maine Sportsman* as a beginner." Monthly tabloid. Circ. 30,000. Pays "during month of publication." Buys first rights. Publishes ms an average of 3 months after acceptance. Byline given. Computer printout submissions acceptable; prefers letter-quality. Reports in 2-4 weeks.

Nonfiction: "We publish only articles about Maine hunting and fishing activities. Any well-written, researched, knowledgeable article about that subject area is likely to be accepted by us." Exposé, how-to, general interest, interview, nostalgia, personal experience, opinion, profile and technical. Buys 25-40 mss/issue. Submit complete ms. Length: 200-2,000 words. Pays $20-300. Sometimes pays the expenses of writers on assignment.

Photos: "We can have illustrations drawn, but prefer 1-3 b&w photos." Submit photos with accompanying ms. Pays $5-50 for b&w print.

Tips: "It's rewarding finding a writer who has a fresh way of looking at ordinary events. Specific where-to-go about Maine is needed."

‡MARLIN, The International Sportfishing Magazine, Marlin Magazine, a division of EBSCO Industries, Inc., 21 S. Tarragona St., Pensacola FL 32501. (904)434-5571. Editor: Margaret Fifield. 90% freelance written. Bimonthly magazine on big game fishing. "*Marlin* covers the sport of big game fishing (billfish, tuna, sharks, dorado and wahoo). Our readers are sophisticated, affluent and serious about their sport—they expect a high-class, well-written magazine that provides information and practical advice." Circ. 20,000. Pays on acceptance. Publishes ms an average of 3 months after acceptance. Byline given. Offers ⅓ kill fee. Not copyrighted. Buys first North American serial rights. Submit seasonal/holiday material 2-3 months in advance. Photocopied submissions OK. Query for electronic submissions. Computer printout submissions OK; prefers-letter quality. Reports in 2 weeks. Free sample copy and writer's guidelines.

Nonfiction: General interest, how-to (bait-rigging, tackle maintenance, etc.), new product, personal experience, photo feature, technical and travel. "No freshwater fishing stories. No 'me & Joe went fishing' stories, unless top quality writing." Buys 30-50 mss/year. Query with published clips. Length: 800-2,000 words. Pays $250-500.

Photos: State availability of photos with submission. Reviews negatives, transparencies and prints. Offers $25-300 per photo. $300 is for a cover. Buys one-time rights.

Columns/Departments: Newsline (notable catches, conservation news, legislation), 200-300 words; Tournament Reports (reports on winners of big game fishing tournaments), 300-600 words; Blue Water Currents (news features similar to newsline), 300-900 words; and Boats of Interest (reviews of featured fishing boats), 400-500 words. Buys 25 mss/year. Query. Pays $100-250.

Tips: "Tournament reports are a good way to break in at *Marlin*. Make them short but accurate, and provide photos of fishing action (*not* dead fish hanging up at the docks!). We always need how-tos, and news items. Our destination pieces (travel stories) emphasize where and when to fish, but include information on where to stay also. For features: crisp, high action stories—nothing flowery or academic. Photos! Technical/How-to: concise and informational—specific details. Photos. News: Again, concise with good details—watch for legislation affecting big game fishing, outstanding catches, new clubs and organizations, new trends and conservations issues."

MARYLAND-DELAWARE GAME & FISH, Game & Fish Publications, Inc., Box 741, Marietta GA 30061. (404)953-9222. Editor: Ken Freel. See *Alabama Game & Fish*.

MICHIGAN OUT-OF-DOORS, Box 30235, Lansing MI 48909. (517)371-1041. Editor: Kenneth S. Lowe. 50% freelance written. Works with a small number of new/unpublished writers each year. Emphasizes outdoor recreation, especially hunting and fishing, conservation and environmental affairs. Monthly magazine. Circ. 130,000. Pays on acceptance. Publishes ms an average of 6 months after acceptance. Byline given. Buys first North American serial rights. Phone queries OK. Submit seasonal/holiday material 6 months in advance. Computer printout submissions acceptable; prefers letter-quality. Reports in 1 month. Sample copy $1.50; free writer's guidelines.

Nonfiction: Exposé, historical, how-to, informational, interview, nostalgia, personal experience, personal opinion, photo feature and profile. No humor. "Stories *must* have a Michigan slant unless they treat a subject of universal interest to our readers." Buys 8 mss/issue. Send complete ms. Length: 1,000-3,000 words. Pays $75 minimum for feature stories. Pays expenses of writers on assignment.

Photos: Purchased with or without accompanying ms. Pays $15 minimum for any size b&w glossy prints; $60 maximum for color (for cover). Offers no additional payment for photos accepted with accompanying ms. Buys one-time rights. Captions preferred.

Tips: "Top priority is placed on true accounts of personal adventures in the out-of-doors—well-written tales of very unusual incidents encountered while hunting, fishing, camping, hiking, etc. The most rewarding aspect of working with freelancers is realizing we had a part in their development. But it's annoying to respond to queries that never produce a manuscript."

MICHIGAN SPORTSMAN, Game & Fish Publications, Inc., Box 741, Marietta GA 30061. (404)953-9222. Editor: Ken Dunwoody. See *Alabama Game & Fish*.

MID WEST OUTDOORS, Mid West Outdoors, Ltd., 111 Shore Drive, Hinsdale (Burr Ridge) IL 60521. (312)887-7722. FAX: (312)887-1958. Editor: Gene Laulunen. Emphasizes fishing, hunting, camping and boating. Monthly tabloid. 100% freelance written. Circ. 42,811. Pays on publication. Buys simultaneous rights. Byline given. Submit seasonal material 2 months in advance. Simultaneous, photocopied and previously published submissions OK. Reports in 3 weeks. Publishes ms an average of 3 months after acceptance. Sample copy $1; free writer's guidelines with #10 SASE.
Nonfiction: How-to (fishing, hunting, camping in the Midwest) and where-to-go (fishing, hunting, camping within 500 miles of Chicago). "We do not want to see any articles on 'my first fishing, hunting or camping experiences,' 'Cleaning My Tackle Box,' 'Tackle Tune-up,' or 'Catch and Release.' " Buys 1,200 unsolicited mss/year. Send complete ms. Length: 1,000-1,500 words. Pays $15-25.
Photos: Offers no additional payment for photos accompanying ms; uses b&w prints. Buys all rights. Captions required.
Columns/Departments: Fishing, Hunting. Open to suggestions for columns/departments. Send complete ms. Pays $25.
Tips: "Break in with a great unknown fishing hole or new technique within 500 miles of Chicago. Where, how, when and why. Know the type of publication you are sending material to."

MINNESOTA SPORTSMAN, Game & Fish Publications, Inc., Box 741, Marietta GA 30061. (404)953-9222. Editor: Ken Dunwoody. See *Alabama Game & Fish*.

MISSISSIPPI GAME & FISH, Game & Fish Publications, Inc., Box 741, Marietta GA 30061. (404)953-9222. Editor: Robert Sloan. See *Alabama Game & Fish*.

MISSOURI GAME & FISH, Game & Fish Publications, Inc., Box 741, Marietta GA 30061. (404)953-9222. Editor: Bill Hartlage. See *Alabama Game & Fish*.

‡**MUSKY HUNTER MAGAZINE**, Esox Publishing, Inc., 959 W. Mason St., Green Bay WI 54303. (414)496-0334. Editor: Joe Bucher. 90% freelance written. Magazine published 6 times a year (Feb., May, June, July, Sept. and Dec.) on Musky fishing. "Serves the vertical market of Musky fishing enthusiasts. We're interested in advanced how-to articles." Estab. 1989. Circ. 16,000. Pays on publication. Publishes ms an average of 3 months after acceptance. Byline sometimes given. Buys first rights or one-time rights. Submit seasonal/holiday material 4 months in advance. Photocopied submissions OK. Computer printout submissions OK. Reports in 2 weeks. Sample copy for 9x12 SAE with 5 first class stamps. Writer's guidelines for #10 SASE.
Nonfiction: Historical/nostalgic (related only to Musky fishing), how-to (modify lures, boats and tackle for Musky fishing), personal experience (must be Musky fishing experience), technical (fishing equipment) and travel (to lakes and areas for Musky fishing). Buys 50 mss/year. Send complete ms. Length: 1,000-2,000 words. Pays $100-200 for assigned articles; $50-200 for unsolicited articles. Payment of contributor copies or other premiums negotiable.
Photos: Send photos with submission. Reviews 35mm transparencies and 3x5 prints. Offers no additional payment for photos accepted with ms. Identification on subjects required. One-time rights.

NEBRASKA GAME & FISH, Game & Fish Publications, Inc., Box 741, Marietta GA 30061. (404)953-9222. Editor: Jim Schlender. See *Alabama Game & Fish*.

NEW ENGLAND GAME & FISH, Game & Fish Publications, Inc., Box 741, Marietta GA 30061. (404)953-9222. Editor: Mike Toth. See *Alabama Game & Fish*.

NEW JERSEY GAME & FISH, Game & Fish Publications, Inc., Box 741, Marietta GA 30061. (404)953-9222. Editor: Ken Freel. See *Alabama Game & Fish*.

NEW YORK GAME & FISH, Game & Fish Publications, Inc., Box 741, Marietta GA 30061. (404)953-9222. Editor: Mike Toth. See *Alabama Game & Fish*.

‡**NORTH AMERICAN FISHERMAN, Official Publication of North American Fishing Club**, Box 35861, Minneapolis MN 55435. (612)936-0555. Editor: Mark LaBarbera. Managing Editor: Steve Pennaz. 45% freelance written. Bimonthly magazine on fresh- and saltwater fishing across North America. Estab. 1988. Circ. 100,000. Pays on acceptance. Publishes ms an average of 4 months after acceptance. Offers $150 kill fee. Buys first North American serial rights, one-time rights and all rights. Submit seasonal/holiday material 6 months in advance. Computer printout submissions OK. Reports in 3 weeks. Sample copy $3 with 9x12 SAE and 6 first class stamps.
Nonfiction: How-to (species specific information on how-to catch fish), new product (news brief on fishing from various state agencies) and travel (where to information on first class fishing lodges). Buys 35-40 mss/year. Query. Length: 700-2,100. Pays $100-325.

Photos: Send photos with submission. Offers no additional payment for photos accepted with ms. Captions and identification of subjects required. Buys one-time rights.

Fillers: Facts and newsbreaks. Buys 60/year. Length: 50-100. Pays $35-50.

Tips: "We are looking for news briefs on important law changes, new lakes, etc. Areas most open for freelancers are: full-length features, cover photos and news briefs. Know what subject you are writing about. Our audience of avid fresh and saltwater anglers know how to fish and will see through weak or dated fishing information. Must be on cutting edge for material to be considered."

NORTH AMERICAN HUNTER, Official Publication of the North American Hunting Club, North American Hunting Club, Box 35557, Minneapolis MN 55435. (612)941-7654. FAX: (612)944-2687. Publisher: Mark LaBarbera. Editor: Bill Miller. 60% freelance written. A bimonthly magazine for members of the North American Hunting Club covering strictly North American hunting. "The purpose of the NAHC is to enhance the hunting skill and enjoyment of its 215,000 members." Circ. 215,000. Pays on acceptance. Publishes ms an average of 6-10 months after acceptance. Byline given. Buys first North American serial rights, first rights, one-time rights, second serial (reprint) rights or all rights. Submit seasonal/holiday material 1 year in advance. Query for electronic submissions. Computer printout submissions acceptable; prefers letter-quality. Reports in 3 weeks. Sample copy $3; writer's guidelines for #10 SASE.

Nonfiction: Exposé (on hunting issues); how-to (on hunting); humor; interview/profile; new product; opinion; personal experience; photo feature and where-to-hunt. No fiction or "Me and Joe." Buys 18-24 mss/year. Query. Length: 1,000-2,500 words. Pays $200-325 for assigned articles; pays $25-325 for unsolicited articles.

Photos: Send photos with submissions. Reviews transparencies and 5x7 or 8x10 prints. Offers no additional payment for photos accepted with ms. Captions and identification of subjects required. Buys one-time rights.

Tips: "Write stories as if they are from one hunting friend to another."

NORTH AMERICAN WHITETAIL, The Magazine Devoted to the Serious Trophy Deer Hunter, Game & Fish Publications, Inc., Suite 110, 2250 Newmarket Parkway, Marietta GA 30067. (404)953-9222. Editor: Gordon Whittington. 70% freelance written. Magazine, published 8 times/year, about hunting trophy-class white-tailed deer in North America, primarily the U.S. "We provide the serious hunter with highly sophisticated information about trophy-class whitetails and how, when and where to hunt them. We are not a general hunting magazine or a magazine for the very occasional deer hunter." Pays 75 days prior to cover date of issue. Publishes ms an average of 6 months after acceptance. Byline given. Offers negotiable kill fee. Buys first North American serial rights. Submit seasonal/holiday material 10 months in advance. Computer printout submissions OK; no dot-matrix. Reports in 3 months on mss. Editor prefers to keep queries on file, without notification, until the article can be assigned or author informs of prior sale. Sample copy $3 with 9x12 SAE and 7 first class stamps. Writer's guidelines for #10 SASE.

Nonfiction: How-to, interview/profile. Buys 50 mss/year. Query. Length: 1,400-3,000 words. Pays $150-400.

Photos: Send photos with submission. Reviews 2x2 transparencies and 8x10 prints. Offers no additional payment for photos accepted with ms. Captions and identification of subjects required. Buys one-time rights.

Columns/Departments: Trails and Tails (nostalgic, humorous or other entertaining styles of deer-hunting material, fictional or nonfictional), 1,400 words. Buys 8 mss/year. Send complete ms. Pays $150.

Tips: "Our articles are written by persons who are deer hunters first, writers second. Our hard-core hunting audience can see through material produced by non-hunters or those with only marginal deer-hunting expertise. We have a continual need for expert profiles/interviews. Study the magazine to see what type of hunting expert it takes to qualify for our use, and look at how those articles have been directed by the writers. Good photography of the interviewee and his hunting results must accompany such pieces."

NORTH CAROLINA GAME & FISH, Game & Fish Publications, Inc., Box 741, Marietta GA 30061. (404)953-9222. Editor: Aaron Pass. See *Alabama Game & Fish.*

OHIO GAME & FISH, Game & Fish Publications, Inc., Box 741, Marietta GA 30061. (404)953-9222. Editor: Jim Low. See *Alabama Game & Fish.*

OKLAHOMA GAME & FISH, Game & Fish Publications, Box 741, Marietta GA 30061. (404)953-9222. FAX: (404)933-9510. Editor: Jim Schlender. See *Alabama Game & Fish.*

OUTDOOR LIFE, Times Mirror Magazines, Inc., 2 Park Ave., New York NY 10016. (212)779-5000. Editor: Mr. Clare Conley. Executive Editor: Vin T. Sparano. 95% freelance written. A monthly magazine covering hunting and fishing. Circ. 1.5 million. Pays on acceptance. Publishes ms an average of 6-12 months after acceptance. Byline given. Buys first North American serial rights. Submit seasonal/holiday material 6 months in advance. Previously published submissions OK on occasion. Computer printout submissions acceptable; prefers letter-quality. Reports in 1 month on queries; 2 months on mss. Writer's guidelines for SASE.

Nonfiction: Book excerpts; essays; how-to (must cover hunting, fishing or related outdoor activities); humor; interview/profile; new product; personal experience; photo feature; technical; and travel. Special issues include Bass and Freshwater Fishing Annual (March), Deer and Big Game Annual (Aug.), and Hunting Guns Annual (Sept.). No articles that are too general in scope—need to write specifically. Buys 400 mss/ year. Query or send ms—"either way, photos are *very important*." Length: 800-3,000 words. Pays $350-600 for 1,000-word features and regionals; pays $900-1,200 for 2,000-word or longer national features. "We receive and encourage queries over CompuServe."

Photos: Send photos with submission. Reviews 35mm transparencies and 8x10 prints. Offers variable payment. Captions and identification of subjects required. Buys one-time rights. "May offer to buy photos after first use if considered good and have potential to be used with other articles in the future (file photos)." Pay for freelance photos is $100 for ¼ page color to $800 for 2-page spread in color; $1,000 for covers. All photos must be stamped with name and address.

Columns/Departments: This Happened to Me (true-to-life, personal outdoor adventure, harrowing experience), approximately 300 words. Buys 12 mss/year. Pays $50.

Fillers: Newsbreaks and do-it-yourself for hunters and fishermen. Buys unlimited number/year. Length: 1,000 words maximum. Payment varies.

Tips: "It is best for freelancers to break in by writing features for one of the regional sections—East, Midwest, South, West. These are where-to-go oriented and run from 800-1,500 words. Writers must send one-page query with photos."

PENNSYLVANIA ANGLER, Pennsylvania Fish Commission, Box 1673, Harrisburg PA 17105-1673. (717)657-4518. Editor: Art Michaels. 60-80% freelance written. Prefers to work with published/established writers but works with a few unpublished writers every year. A monthly magazine covering fishing and related conservation topics in Pennsylvania. Circ. 55,000. Pays 6-8 weeks after acceptance. Publishes ms an average of 7-9 months after acceptance. Byline given. Rights purchased vary. Submit seasonal/holiday material 8 months in advance. Computer printout submissions acceptable; prefers letter-quality. Reports in 2 weeks on queries; 2 months on mss. Sample copy for 9x12 SAE with 5 first class stamps; writer's guidelines for #10 SASE.

Nonfiction: Historical/nostalgic, how-to, where-to and technical. No saltwater or hunting material. Buys 120 mss/year. Query. Length: 300-3,000 words. Pays $25-300.

Photos: Send photos with submission. Reviews 35mm and larger color transparencies and 8x10 b&w prints. Offers no additional payment for photos accepted with ms. Captions, model releases and identification of subjects required.

Tips: "Our mainstays are how-tos, where-tos, and conservation pieces, but we seek more top-quality fiction, first-person stories, humor, reminiscenses and historical articles. These pieces must a strong, specific Pennsylvania slant."

PENNSYLVANIA GAME & FISH, Game & Fish Publications, Inc., Box 741, Marietta GA 30061. (404)953-9222. Editor: Mike Toth. See *Alabama Game & Fish.*

‡PENNSYLVANIA GAME NEWS, Pennsylvania Game Commission, 2001 Elmerton Ave., Harrisburg PA 17110-9797. (717)787-3745. Editor: Bob Bell. 60% freelance written. Works with a small number of new/ unpublished writers each year. "We have a large inventory; nevertheless, we read everything that comes in." A monthly magazine covering hunting and outdoors in Pennsylvania. Emphasizes sportsmanlike actions of hunters. Circ. 175,000. Pays on acceptance. Publishes ms an average of 8-10 months after acceptance. Byline given. Buys all rights; "we return unused rights after publication." Submit seasonal/holiday material 6 months in advance. Photocopied submissions OK. Computer printout submissions acceptable; prefers letter-quality to dot-matrix. Reports in 3 weeks on queries; 6 weeks on mss. Free sample copy and writer's guidelines.

Nonfiction: General interest and personal hunting experiences. "We consider material on any outdoor subject that can be done in Pennsylvania *except* fishing and boating." Buys 60 mss/year. Query. Length: 2,500 words maximum. Pays $250 maximum.

Photos: Send photos with submission. Offers $5-20/photo. Captions required. Buys all rights.

Fiction: Must deal with hunting or outdoors; no fishing. Buys very few mss/year. Send complete ms.

Tips: "True hunting experiences—'me and Joe' stuff—are best chances for freelancers. Must take place in Pennsylvania."

PENNSYLVANIA SPORTSMAN, Northwoods Publications Inc., Suite 206, 2101 N. Front St., Harrisburg PA 17110. (717)233-4797. Editor: Lou Hoffman. Managing Editor: Sherry Ritchey. 50% freelance written. Magazine appears 8 times a year on regional—state of Pennsylvania hunting, fishing sports. Circ. 57,000. Pays on acceptance. Publishes ms an average of 4 months after acceptance. Byline given. Buys one-time rights. Buys first North American serial rights. Simultaneous submissions OK. Computer printout submissions OK; prefers letter-quality. Reports in 2 weeks on queries; 3 weeks on mss. Sample copy $2. Free writer's guidelines for #10 SASE.

Nonfiction: How-to, new product, personal experience and photo feature. September—Hunting annual; March—Fishing annual. Buys 80 mss/year. Query. Length: 600-1,800 words. Pays $25-125. Sometimes pays the expenses of writers on assignment.

Photos: Send photos with submissions. Reviews negatives (slides). Offers no additional payment for photos accepted with ms. Captions required. Buys one-time rights.

Fiction: Mainstream and slice-of-life vignettes. Buys 10 mss/year. Query. Length: 600-1,500 words. Pays $25-125.

Fillers: Facts and newsbreaks. Buys 10/year. Length: 300-600 words. Pays $20-50.

PETERSEN'S HUNTING, Petersen's Publishing Co., 8490 Sunset Blvd., Los Angeles CA 90069. (213)854-2184. Editor: Craig Boddington. Managing Editor: Jeanne Frissell. 40% freelance written. Works with a small number of new/unpublished writers each year. A monthly magazine covering sport hunting. "We are a 'how-to' magazine devoted to all facets of sport hunting, with the intent to make our readers more knowledgeable, more successful and safer hunters." Circ. 325,000. Pays on acceptance. Publishes ms an average of 9 months after acceptance. Byline given. Offers $50 kill fee. Buys all rights. Submit seasonal/holiday material 9 months in advance. Computer printout submissions acceptable; prefers letter-quality. Reports in 2 weeks. Free sample copy and writer's guidelines.

Nonfiction: General interest; historical/nostalgic; how-to (on hunting techniques); humor; and travel. Special issues include Hunting Annual (August) and the Deer Hunting Annual (September). Buys 50 mss/year. Query. Length: 2,000-3,000 words. Pays $350 minimum.

Photos: Send photos with submission. Reviews 35mm transparencies and 8x10 b&w prints. Offers no additional payment for b&w photos accepted with ms; offers $50-250/color photo. Captions, model releases and identification of subjects required. Buys one-time rights.

‡ROCKY MOUNTAIN GAME & FISH, Game & Fish Publications, Inc., Box 741, Marietta GA 30061. Editor: Stan Warren. See *Alabama Game & Fish*.

‡SAFARI MAGAZINE, The Journal of Big Game Hunting, Safari Club International, 4800 W. Gates Pass Rd., Tucson AZ 85745. (602)620-1220. Editor: William R. Quimby. 90% freelance written. Bimonthly club journal covering international big game hunting and wildlife conservation. Circ. 17,000. Pays on publication. Publishes ms an average of 1 year after acceptance. Byline given. Offers $100 kill fee. Buys all rights. Submit seasonal/holiday material 1 year in advance. Computer printout submissions acceptable; prefers letter-quality to dot-matrix. Reports in 2 weeks on queries; 1 month on mss. Sample copy $3.50; writer's guidelines for SAE.

Nonfiction: Doug Fulton; articles editor. Photo feature (wildlife); and technical (firearms, hunting techniques, etc.). Buys 42 mss/year. Query or send complete ms. Length: 1,500-2,500 words. Pays $200.

Photos: State availability of photos with query or ms, or send photos with query or ms. Payment depends on size in magazine. Pays $35 for b&w; $50-150 color. Captions, model releases and identification of subjects required. Buys one-time rights.

Tips: "Study the magazine. Send manuscripts and photo packages with query. Make it appeal to affluent, knowledgable, world-travelled big game hunters. Features on conservation contributions from big game hunters around the world are most open to freelancers. We have enough stories on first-time African safaris and North American hunting. We need South American, Asian and South Pacific hunting stories, plus stories dealing with hunting and conservation."

SALT WATER SPORTSMAN, 280 Summer St., Boston MA 02210. (617)439-9977. FAX: (617)439-9357. Editor-in-Chief: Barry Gibson. Emphasizes saltwater fishing. 85% freelance written. Works with a small number of new/unpublished writers each year. Monthly magazine. Circ. 150,000. Pays on acceptance. Publishes ms an average of 5 months after acceptance. Byline given. Buys first North American serial rights. Offers 100% kill fee. Submit seasonal material 8 months in advance. Computer printout submissions acceptable; no dot-matrix. Reports in 1 month. Sample copy and writer's guidelines for 8½x11 SAE with $1.41 postage.

Nonfiction: How-to, personal experience, technical and travel (to fishing areas). "Readers want solid how-to, where-to information written in an enjoyable, easy-to-read style. Personal anecdotes help the reader identify with the writer." Prefers new slants and specific information. Query. "It is helpful if the writer states experience in salt water fishing and any previous related articles. We want one, possibly two well-explained ideas per query letter—not merely a listing." Buys 100 unsolicited mss/year. Length: 1,200-1,500 words. Pays $350 and up. Sometimes pays the expenses of writers on assignment.

Photos: Purchased with or without accompanying ms. Captions required. Uses 5x7 or 8x10 b&w prints and color slides. Pays $600 minimum for 35mm, 2¼x2¼ or 8x10 color transparencies for cover. Offers additional payment for photos accepted with accompanying ms.

Columns: Sportsman's Workbench (how to make fishing or fishing-related boating equipment), 100-300 words.

Tips: "There are a lot of knowledgeable fishermen/budding writers out there who could be valuable to us with a little coaching. Many don't think they can write a story for us, but they'd be surprised. We work with writers. Shorter articles that get to the point which are accompanied by good, sharp photos are hard for us to turn down. Having to delete unnecessary wordage—conversation, clichés, etc.—that writers feel is mandatory is annoying. Often they don't devote enough attention to specific fishing information."

SOUTH CAROLINA GAME & FISH, Game & Fish Publications, Inc., Box 741, Marietta GA 30061. (404)953-9222. Editor: Aaron Pass. See *Alabama Game & Fish*.

SOUTH CAROLINA WILDLIFE, Box 167, Rembert Dennis Bldg., Columbia SC 29202. (803)734-3972. Editor: John Davis. Managing Editor: Linda Renshaw. For South Carolinians interested in wildlife and outdoor activities. 75% freelance written. Bimonthly magazine. Circ. 69,000. Byline given. Pays on acceptance. Publishes ms an average of 6 months after acceptance. Buys first rights. Free sample copy. Reports in 6 weeks. Computer printout submissions acceptable "if double-spaced."

Nonfiction and Photos: Articles on outdoor South Carolina with an emphasis on preserving and protecting our natural resources. "Realize that the topic must be of interest to South Carolinians and that we must be able to justify using it in a publication published by the state wildlife department—so if it isn't directly about hunting, fishing, a certain plant or animal, it must be somehow related to the environment and conservation. Readers prefer a broad mix of outdoor related topics (articles that illustrate the beauty of South Carolina's outdoors and those that help the reader get more for his/her time, effort, and money spent in outdoor recreation). These two general areas are the ones we most need. Subjects vary a great deal in topic, area and style, but must all have a common ground in the outdoor resources and heritage of South Carolina. Review back issues and query with a one-page outline citing sources, giving ideas for graphic design, explaining justification and giving an example of the first two paragraphs." Does not need any column material. Generally does not seek photographs. The publisher assumes no responsibility for unsolicited material. Buys 25-30 mss/year. Length: 1,000-3,000 words. Pays an average of $200-400 per article depending upon length and subject matter. Sometimes pays the expenses of writers on assignment.

Tips: "We need more writers in the outdoor field who take pride in the craft of writing and put a real effort toward originality and preciseness in their work. Query on a topic we haven't recently done. The most frequent mistakes made by writers in completing an article are failure to check details and go in-depth on a subject."

SOUTHERN OUTDOORS MAGAZINE, B.A.S.S. Publications, 1 Bell Rd., Montgomery AL 36141. Editor: Larry Teague. Emphasizes Southern outdoor activities, including hunting, fishing, boating, shooting, camping. 90% freelance written. Prefers to work with published/established writers. Published 9 times/year. Circ. 240,000. Pays on acceptance. Publishes ms an average of 6 months after acceptance. Buys all rights. Computer printout submissions acceptable; no dot-matrix. Reports in 1 month. Sample copy for 9x12 SAE, 5 first class stamps, and $2.50.

Nonfiction: Articles should be service-oriented, helping the reader excel in outdoor sports. Emphasis is on techniques and trends. Some "where-to" stories purchased on Southern destinations with strong fishing or hunting theme. Buys 120 mss/year. Length: 2,000 words maximum. Pays 15¢/word. Sometimes pays the expenses of writers on assignment.

Photos: Usually purchased with manuscripts. Pays $50-75 for 35mm color transparencies without ms, and $250-400 for covers.

Fillers: Needs short articles (50-500 words) with newsy slant for Southern Shorts. Emphasis on irony and humor. Also needs humorous or thought-provoking pieces (750-1,200 words) for S.O. Essay feature.

Tips: "It's easiest to break in with short features of 500-1,000 words on 'how-to' fishing and hunting topics. We buy very little first-person. Query first and send sample of your writing if we haven't done business before. Stories most likely to sell: bass fishing, deer hunting, other freshwater fishing, inshore saltwater fishing, bird and small-game hunting, shooting, camping and boating. The most frequent mistakes made by writers in completing an article for us are first-person usage; clarity of articles; applicability of topic to the South; lack of quotes from qualified sources."

SOUTHERN SALTWATER MAGAZINE, B.A.S.S. Communications, 1 Bell Rd., Montgomery AL 36117. (205)272-9530. Editor: Colin Moore. A magazine on coastal fishing in the southern United States (Delaware to Texas) published 8 times/year. Circ. 100,000. Pays on acceptance. Publishes ms an average of 6 months after acceptance. Byline given. Buys all rights. Reports in 2 weeks. Sample copy for $1; include 8½x11 SASE. Free writer's guidelines with SASE.

Nonfiction: Associate Editor: Susan Shehane. General interest, how-to, interview/profile, photo feature, technical, travel. Buys 40 mss/year. Send complete ms. Length: 1,500-2,000 words. Pays 15-20¢/word.
Photos: Send photos with submission. Reviews 35mm transparencies and 5x7 prints. Captions and identification of subjects required. Buys all rights.
Columns/Departments: Salt South (general review applying to southern region); Coast Watch (state-by-state items). Buys 40 mss/year. Send complete ms. Length: 800-1,000 words. Pays 15¢/word.
Fillers: Facts, newsbreaks. Buys 75 mss/year. Length: 250-450 words. Pays 15¢/word.

‡**SPORTING CLASSICS,** Live Oak Press, Highway 521 S., Box 1017, Camden SC 29020. (803)425-1003. Executive Editor: Charles A. Wechsler. 90% freelance written. Prefers to work with published/established writers; works with a small number of new/unpublished writers each year. A bimonthly magazine covering hunting and fishing for well-educated and above-average-income sportsmen. Circ. 30,000. Pays on publication. Publishes ms an average of 3-4 months after acceptance. Byline given. Buys one-time rights. Submit seasonal/holiday·material 6 months in advance. Simultaneous submissions and photocopied submissions OK. Computer printout submissions acceptable. Reports in 3-5 weeks. Free sample copy and writer's guidelines.
Nonfiction: 'Classic" hunting and fishing adventures, historical/nostalgic, humor, personal experience, photo feature, travel. Buys 1 ms/year. Query with or without published clips or send complete ms. Length 2,000-3,000 words. Pays $300-750 for assigned articles; pays $300-500 for unsolicited articles. Sometimes pays expenses of writers on assignment.
Photos: Send photos with submissions and state availability of other photos. Reviews 35mm and larger transparencies. Offers no additional payment for photos accepted with ms. Buys one-time rights.
Columns/Departments: This N That (bits and pieces on hunting, fishing, wildlife and conservation). Length: 50-500 words. Pays $50-150.
Fillers: Anecdotes, facts, newsbreaks and short humor. Buys 6/year. Query. $25-100.
Tips: "We're always looking for well-written features—about hunting and fishing, exotic or unusual places to hunt and fish; about great sportsmen; conservation issues that affect game species; sporting dogs; wildlife painters, carvers and sculptors; firearms; decoys; knives; and collectible fishing tackle. Material must be fact-laden with unique, high-interest experience and insights."

SPORTS AFIELD, 2 Park Ave., New York NY 10016. Editor: Tom Paugh. Executive Editor: Fred Kesting. 20% freelance written. Eager to work with new/unpublished writers. For people of all ages whose interests are centered around the out-of-doors (hunting and fishing) and related subjects. Monthly magazine. Circ. 518,010. Buys first North American serial rights for features, and all rights for *SA Almanac*. Pays on acceptance. Publishes ms an average of 6 months after acceptance. Byline given. "Our magazine is seasonal and material submitted should be in accordance. Fishing in spring and summer; hunting in the fall; camping in summer and fall." Submit seasonal material 6 months in advance. Computer printout submissions acceptable; prefers letter-quality. Reports in 1 month. Query or submit complete ms. Sample copy for $1; writer's guidelines for 1 first class stamp.
Nonfiction and Photos: "Informative where-to and how-to articles and personal experiences with good photos on hunting, fishing, camping, boating and subjects such as conservation, environment and travel related to hunting and fishing. We want first-class writing and reporting." Buys 15-17 unsolicited mss/year. Length: 500-2,500 words. Pays $750 minimum, depending on length and quality. Photos purchased with or without ms. Pays $50 minimum for 8x10 b&w glossy prints. Pays $50 minimum for 35mm or larger transparencies. Sometimes pays the expenses of writers on assignment.
Fiction: Adventure, humor (if related to hunting and fishing).
Fillers: Send to *Almanac* editor. *Almanac* pays $25 and up depending on length, for newsworthy, unusual, how-to and nature items. Payment on publication. Buys all rights.
Tips: "We seldom give assignments to other than staff. Top-quality 35mm slides to illustrate articles a must. Read a recent copy of *Sports Afield* so you know the market you're writing for. Family-oriented features will probably become more important because more and more groups/families are sharing the outdoor experience."

TENNESSEE SPORTSMAN, Game & Fish Publications, Box 741, Marietta GA 30061. (404)953-9222. Editor: Bill Hartlage. See *Alabama Game & Fish*.

TEXAS FISHERMAN, #150, 4550 Post Oak Place Dr., Houston TX 77027. FAX: (713)877-1438. Editor: Todd Woodard. 90% freelance written. Prefers to work with published/established writers; works with a small number of new/unpublished writers each year. Published 9 times a year for freshwater and saltwater fishermen in Texas. Circ. 80,000. Rights purchased vary with author and material. Byline given. Usually buys second serial (reprint) rights. Buys 4-6 mss/month. Pays on acceptance. Publishes ms an average of 3 months after acceptance. Query with hard copy and photos at Houston address, but electronic filing a must after acceptance. Computer printout submissions acceptable; no dot-matrix. Reports in 1 month. Query. Sample copy and writer's guidelines for 9x12 SAE and 9 first class stamps.

Nonfiction and Photos: General how-to, where-to, features on all phases of fishing in Texas. Strong slant on informative pieces. Strong writing. Good saltwater stories (Texas only). Length: 1,200-2,000 words. Pays 10-20¢/word, ($100-400), depending on quality of writing and photos. Mss must include 4-7 good action b&w photos or illustrations. Color slides will be considered for cover or inside use.
Tips: "Query should be a short, but complete description of the story that emphasizes a specific angle. When possible, send black and white and/or color photos with queries. Good art will sell us a story that is mediocre, but even a great story can't replace bad photographs, and better than half submit poor quality photos. How-to, location, or personality profile stories are preferred." Will consider mood or humor Texas-based articles, but rejection rate is higher on those story types.

TEXAS SPORTSMAN, Game & Fish Publications, Inc., Box 741, Marietta GA 30061. (404)953-9222. Editor: Steve Lightfoot. See *Alabama Game & Fish*.

‡TROUT, The Magazine for Trout and Salmon Anglers, Trout Unlimited, Inc., Box 6225, Bend OR 97708. (503)382-2327. Editor: Thomas R. Pero. Associate Editor: James A. Yuskavitch. 90% freelance written. Quarterly magazine on trout and salmon fishing and conservation. Circ. 70,000. Pays on acceptance. Byline given. Offers $100 kill fee. Buys first North American rights. Reports in 1 month on queries; 2 months on mss. Sample $4. Free writer's guidelines.
Nonfiction: Essays, historical/nostalgic, how-to, humor, interview/profile, personal experience, conservation, photo feature and travel. "No fly tying, new product reviews, simplistic where-to-go pieces." Buys 25 mss/year. Query. Send complete ms. Length: 600-6,000. Pays $750 maximum.
Photos: Send photos with submission. Reviews b&w contact sheets and 35mm transparencies. Offers no additional payment for photos accepted with ms. Captions required. Buys one-time rights.
Columns/Departments: The Fishing in Print (reviews of quality fishing books), to 1,500 words. Pays $300 maximum.

TURKEY CALL, Wild Turkey Center, Box 530, Edgefield SC 29824. (803)637-3106. Editor: Gene Smith. 50-60% freelance written. Eager to work with new/unpublished writers and photographers. An educational publication for members of the National Wild Turkey Federation. Bimonthly magazine. Circ. 53,000. Buys one-time rights. Byline given. Pays on acceptance. Publishes ms an average of 6 months after acceptance. Reports in 1 month. No queries necessary. Submit complete package. Wants original ms only. Computer printout submissions acceptable; prefers letter-quality. "Double strike dot-matrix OK." Sample copy $3 with 9x12 SAE. Writer's guidelines for #10 SASE.
Nonfiction and Photos: Feature articles dealing with the hunting and management of the American wild turkey. Must be accurate information and must appeal to national readership of turkey hunters and wildlife management experts. No poetry or first-person accounts of unremarkable hunting trips. May use some fiction that educates or entertains in a special way. Length: up to 3,000 words. Pays $35 for items, $65 for short fillers of 600-700 words, $200-350 for illustrated features. "We want quality photos submitted with features." Art illustrations also acceptable. "We are using more and more inside color illustrations." For b&w, prefer 8x10 glossies, but 5x7s OK. Color transparencies of any size are acceptable. Wants no typical hunter-holding-dead-turkey photos or setups using mounted birds or domestic turkeys. Photos with how-to stories must make the techniques clear (example: how to make a turkey call; how to sculpt or carve a bird in wood). Pays $20 minimum for one-time rights on b&w photos and simple art illustrations; up to $75 for inside color, reproduced any size. Covers: Most are donated. Any purchased are negotiated.
Tips: The writer "should simply keep in mind that the audience is 'expert' on wild turkey management, hunting, life history and restoration/conservation history. He/she *must know the subject*. We are buying more third-person, more fiction, more humor—in an attempt to avoid the 'predictability trap' of a single subject magazine."

VIRGINIA GAME & FISH, Game & Fish Publications, Inc., Box 741, Marietta GA 30061. (404)953-9222. Editor: Aaron Pass. See *Alabama Game & Fish*.

‡WASHINGTON-OREGON GAME & FISH, Game & Fish Publications, Inc., Box 741, Marietta GA 30061. Editor: Stan Warren. See *Alabama Game & Fish*.

WEST VIRGINIA GAME & FISH, Game & Fish Publications, Inc., Box 741, Marietta GA 30061. (404)953-9222. Editor: Ken Freel. See *Alabama Game & Fish*.

WESTERN OUTDOORS, 3197-E Airport Loop, Costa Mesa CA 92626. (714)546-4370. Editor: Jack Brown. 75% freelance written. Works with a small number of new/unpublished writers each year. Emphasizes hunting, fishing, camping, boating for 11 Western states only, Baja California, Canada, Hawaii and Alaska. Publishes 10 issues/year. Circ. 150,000. Pays on acceptance. Publishes ms an average of 6 months after acceptance. Buys first North American serial rights. Query (in writing). Submit seasonal material 4-6 months in advance. Photocopied submissions OK. Computer printout submissions are acceptable if double-spaced;

no dot-matrix. Reports in 4-6 weeks. Sample copy $1.75; writer's guidelines for #10 SASE.

Nonfiction: Where-to (catch more fish, bag more game, improve equipment, etc.); how-to informational; photo feature. "We do not accept fiction, poetry, cartoons." Buys 70 assigned mss/year. Query. Length: 1,000-1,800 words maximum. Pays $300-500.

Photos: Purchased with accompanying ms. Captions required. Uses 8x10 b&w glossy prints; prefers Kodachrome II 35mm slides. Offers no additional payment for photos accepted with accompanying ms. Pays $200-250 for covers.

Tips: "Provide a complete package of photos, map, trip facts and manuscript written according to our news feature format. Excellence of color photo selections make a sale more likely. The most frequent mistake made by writers in completing an article for us is that they don't follow our style. Our guidelines are quite clear."

WESTERN SPORTSMAN, Box 737, Regina, Saskatchewan S4P 3A8 Canada. (306)352-8384. Editor: Rick Bates. 90% freelance written. For fishermen, hunters, campers and others interested in outdoor recreation. "Note that our coverage area is Alberta and Saskatchewan." Bimonthly magazine. Circ. 30,000. Rights purchased vary with author and material. May buy first North American serial rights or second serial (reprint) rights. Byline given. Pays on publication. Publishes ms an average of 2-12 months after acceptance. "We try to include as much information as possible on all subjects in each edition. Therefore, we usually publish fishing articles in our winter issues along with a variety of winter stories. If material is dated, we would like to receive articles 2 months in advance of our publication date." Computer printout submissions OK; no dot-matrix. Reports in 1 month. Sample copy $3.50; free writer's guidelines.

Nonfiction: "It is necessary that all articles can identify with our coverage area of Alberta and Saskatchewan. We are interested in mss from writers who have experienced an interesting fishing, hunting, camping or other outdoor experience. We also publish how-to and other informational pieces as long as they can relate to our coverage area. We are more interested in articles which tell about the average guy living on beans, guiding his own boat, stalking his game and generally doing his own thing in our part of Western Canada than a story describing a well-to-do outdoorsman traveling by motorhome, staying at an expensive lodge with guides doing everything for him except catching the fish, or shooting the big game animal. The articles that are submitted to us need to be prepared in a knowledgeable way and include more information than the actual fish catch or animal or bird kill. Discuss the terrain, the people involved on the trip, the water or weather conditions, the costs, the planning that went into the trip, the equipment and other data closely associated with the particular event in a factual manner. We're always looking for new writers." Buys 120 mss/year. Submit complete ms. Length: 1,500-2,000 words. Pays $100-325. Sometimes pays the expenses of writers on assignment.

Photos: Photos purchased with ms with no additional payment. Also purchased without ms. Pays $20-25/5x7 or 8x10 b&w print; $175-250/35mm or larger transparency for front cover.

WISCONSIN SPORTSMAN, Game & Fish Publications, Inc., Box 741, Marietta GA 30061. Editor: Ken Dunwoody. See *Alabama Game & Fish*.

Martial Arts

BLACK BELT, Rainbow Publications, Inc., 1813 Victory Place, Burbank CA 91504. (818)843-4444. Executive Editor: Jim Coleman. 80-90% freelance written. Works with a small number of new/unpublished writers each year. Emphasizes martial arts for both practitioner and layman. Monthly magazine. Circ. 100,000. Pays on publication. Publishes ms an average of 3-5 months after acceptance. Buys first North American serial rights, retains right to republish. Submit seasonal/holiday material 6 months in advance. Photocopied submissions OK. Computer printout submissions acceptable; prefers letter-quality. Reports in 3 weeks.

Nonfiction: Exposé, how-to, informational, interview, new product, personal experience, profile, technical and travel. Buys 8-9 mss/issue. Query or send complete ms. Length: 1,200 words minimum. Pays $10-20/page of manuscript.

Photos: Very seldom buys photos without accompanying mss. Captions required. Total purchase price for ms includes payment for photos. Model releases required.

Fiction: Historical and modern day. Buys 2-3 mss/year. Query. Pays $100-200.

Tips: "We also publish an annual yearbook and special issues periodically. The yearbook includes our annual 'Black Belt Hall of Fame' inductees."

THE FIGHTER—INTERNATIONAL, The Fighter Magazine Group, Inc., 1017 Highland Ave., Largo FL 33640. (813)584-0054. FAX: (813)584-0592. Editor: John M. Corcoran. Bimonthly magazine covering martial arts. "We cover the entire spectrum of the industry, but are particularly interested in controversial issues that affect the martial arts masses." Circ. 150,000 (English language). Pays on publication. Publishes ms an average of 2-3 months after acceptance. Byline given. Offers $25 kill fee. Buys first rights (worldwide) or second serial (reprint) rights. Simultaneous, photocopied and previously published submissions OK (only if published in mainstream magazines). Computer printout submissions OK; no dot-matrix. Reports in 2 weeks on queries; 3-4 weeks on mss. Sample copy $3.50 with 8x10 SAE and $1.65 postage; free writer's guidelines.

Nonfiction: Expose, historical/nostalgic, humor, inspirational, interview/profile (on assignment only) and photo feature. No how-to/technical articles. Buys 25-30 mss/year. Query. Length: 1,500 words or what the story requires. Pays $200-300 for assigned articles; $150-200 for unsolicited articles.

Photos: State availability of photos with query. Reviews contact sheets, transparencies (3x5) and prints (8x10). Offers no additional payment for photos accepted with ms. Captions and identification of subjects required. Buys one-time rights.

Tips: "We prefer queries instead of completed manuscripts. Submit article ideas of substance and significance. Omit ideas which have been done to death by other martial arts publications. We are the only full color magazine in the genre; therefore, visual impact can increase chances of acceptance."

FIGHTING WOMAN NEWS, Martial Arts, Self-Defense, Combative Sports Quarterly, Box 1459, Grand Central Station, New York NY 10163. (212)228-0900. Editor: Valerie Eads. Mostly freelance written. Prefers to work with published/established writers. Quarterly magazine. Our audience is composed of adult women actually practicing martial arts with an average experience of 4+ years. Since our audience is also 80+% college grads and 40% holders of advanced degrees we are an action magazine with footnotes. Our material is quite different from what is found in newsstand martial arts publications." Circ. 3,500. Pays on publication. "There is a backlog of poetry and fiction—hence a *very* long wait. A solid factual martial arts article would go out 'next issue' with trumpets and pipes." Byline given. Buys one-time rights. Submit seasonal/holiday material 6 months in advance. Simultaneous queries, and simultaneous, photocopied and previously published submissions OK. "For simultaneous and previously published we *must* be told about it." Query for electronic submissions. Readable computer printout submissions acceptable. Reports as soon as possible. Sample copy $3.50; writer's guidelines for #10 SASE.

Nonfiction: Book excerpts, exposé (e.g. discrimination against women in martial arts governing bodies); historical/nostalgic; how-to (martial arts, self-defense techniques); humor; inspirational (e.g., self-defense success stories); interview/profile ("we have assignments waiting for writers in this field"); new product; opinion; personal experience; photo feature; technical; travel. Buys 6 mss/year. Query. Length: 1,000-3,000 words. Pays in copies, barter or $10 maximum. Some expenses negotiated, but we can't pay major costs such as planes or hotels.

Photos: Nancy Green, photo editor. State availability of photos with query or ms. Reviews "technically competent" b&w contact sheets and 8x10 b&w prints. "We negotiate photos and articles as a package. Sometimes expenses are negotiated. Captions and identification of subjects required. The need for releases depends on the situation."

Columns/Departments: Notes & News (short items relevant to our subject matter); Letters (substantive comment regarding previous issues); Sports Reports; and Reviews (of relevant materials in any medium). Query or send complete ms. Length: 100-1,000 words. Pays in copies or negotiates payment.

Fiction: Muskat Buckby, fiction editor. Adventure, fantasy, historical and science fiction. "Any fiction must feature a woman skilled in martial arts." Buys 0-1 ms/year. Query. Length: 1,000-5,000 words. "We will consider serializing longer stories." Pays in copies or negotiates payment.

Poetry: Muskat Buckby, poetry editor. "We'll look at all types. Must appeal to an audience of martial artists." Buys 3-4 poems/year. Length: open. Pays in copies or negotiates payment.

Tips: "First, read the magazine. Our major reason for rejecting articles is total unsuitability for our publication. A prime example of this is the writer who submitted numerous articles on subjects that we very much wanted to cover, but written in a gosh-gee-wow progress-to-the-abos style that was totally inappropriate. The second most common reason for rejections is vagueness; we need the old Who, What, When, Where, Why and How and if your article doesn't have that save yourself the postage. Several articles returned by *FWN* have later shown up in other martial arts magazines and since they pay a lot more, you're better off trying them first unless an audience of literate, adult, female, martial artists is what you're aiming at."

INSIDE KARATE, The Magazine for Today's Total Martial Artist, Unique Publications, 4201 Vanowen Pl., Burbank CA 91505. (818)845-2656. FAX: (818)845-7761. Editor: John Steven Soet. 90% freelance written. Works with a small number of new/unpublished writers each year. Monthly magazine covering the martial arts. Circ. 120,000. Publishes ms an average of 3 months after acceptance. Byline given. Buys first North American serial rights. Computer printout submissions acceptable; prefers letter-quality. Reports in 3 weeks on queries; in 6 weeks on mss. Sample copy $2.50, 9x12 SAE and 5 first class stamps; free writer's guidelines for #10 SASE.

Nonfiction: Book excerpts; exposé (of martial arts); historical/nostalgic; humor; interview/profile (with approval only); opinion; personal experience; photo feature; and technical (with approval only). *Inside Karate* seeks a balance of the following in each issue: tradition, history, glamor, profiles and/or interviews (both by assignment only), technical, philosophical and think pieces. To date, most "how to" pieces have been done inhouse. Buys 70 mss/year. Query. Length: 1,000-2,500 words; prefers 10-12 page mss. Pays $25-125.

Photos: Send photos with ms. Prefers 3x5 bordered b&w. Captions and identification of subjects required. Buys one-time rights.

Tips: "In our publication, writing style and/or expertise is not the determining factor. Beginning writers with martial arts expertise may submit. Trends in magazine publishing that freelance writers should be aware of include the use of less body copy, better (and interesting) photos to be run large with 'story' caps. If the photos are poor and the reader can't grasp the whole story by looking at photos and copy, forget it."

INSIDE KUNG-FU, The Ultimate In Martial Arts Coverage!, Unique Publications, 4201 Vanowen Pl., Burbank CA 91505. (818)845-2656. FAX: (818)845-7761. Editor: Dave Cater. 75% freelance written. Monthly magazine covering martial arts for those with "traditional, modern, athletic and intellectual tastes. The magazine slants toward little-known martial arts, and little-known aspects of established martial arts." Circ. 100,000. Pays on publication. Publishes ms an average of 6 months after acceptance. Byline given. Buys first North American serial rights. Submit seasonal/holiday material 4 months in advance. Simultaneous queries, and simultaneous and photocopied submissions OK. Computer printout submissions acceptable; no dot-matrix. Reports in 3 weeks on queries; 4 weeks on mss. Sample copy $2.50 with 9x12 SAE and 5 first class stamps; free writer's guidelines for #10 SASE.

Nonfiction: Exposé (topics relating to the martial arts); historical/nostalgic; how-to (primarily technical materials); cultural/philosophical; interview/profile; personal experience; photo feature; and technical. "Articles must be technically or historically accurate." No "sports coverage, first-person articles or articles which constitute personal aggrandizement." Buys 120 mss/year. Query or send complete ms. Length: 8-10 pages, typewritten and double-spaced.

Photos: Send photos with accompanying ms. Reviews b&w contact sheets, b&w negatives and 8x10 b&w prints. "Photos are paid for with payment for ms." Captions and model release required.

Fiction: Adventure, historical, humorous, mystery and suspense. "Fiction must be short (1,000-2,000 words) and relate to the martial arts. We buy very few fiction pieces." Buys 2-3 mss/year.

Tips: "The writer may have a better chance of breaking in at our publication with short articles and fillers since smaller pieces allow us to gauge individual ability, but we're flexible—quality writers get published period. The most frequent mistakes made by writers in completing an article for us are ignoring photo requirements and model releases (always number one—and who knows why? All requirements are spelled out in writer's guidelines)."

KARATE/KUNG-FU ILLUSTRATED, Rainbow Publications, Inc., 1813 Victory Place, Burbank CA 91504. (818)843-4444. Publisher: Michael James. Executive Editor: Marian K. Castinado. 80% freelance written. Eager to work with new/unpublished writers. Emphasizes karate and kung fu from the traditional standpoint and training techniques. Bimonthly magazine. Circ. 80,000. Pays on publication. Buys all rights. Photocopied submissions OK. Reports in 1 month. Sample copy for 8½x11 SAE.

Nonfiction: Expose, historical, how-to, informational, interview, new product, opinion, photo feature, technical and travel. Need historical and contemporary kung fu pieces, including styles, how-tos, Chinese philosophy. Buys 6 mss/issue. Query or submit complete ms. Pays $100-200.

Photos: Purchased with accompanying ms. Submit 5x7 b&w prints or color transparencies. Total purchase price for ms includes payment for photos.

Tips: "Style must be concise, authoritative and in third person."

M.A. TRAINING, Rainbow Publications, 1813 Victory Pl., Box 7728, Burbank CA 91510-7728. (818)843-4444. FAX: (818)953-9244. Executive Editor: Ian C. Blair. 75% freelance written. Works with a small number of new/unpublished writers each year. Quarterly magazine about martial arts training. Circ. 60,000. Pays on publication. Publishes ms an average of 3-6 months after acceptance. Buys first North American serial rights. Submit seasonal material 4 months in advance, but best to send query letter first. Simultaneous and photocopied submissions OK. Computer print-out submissions acceptable; prefers letter-quality. Reports in 6 weeks. Writer's guidelines for SASE.

Nonfiction: How-to: want training related features. Buys 30-40 unsolicited mss/year. Send query or complete ms. Length: 1,000-2,000 words. Pays $50-200.

Photos: State availability of photos. Most ms should be accompanied by photos. Reviews 5x7 and 8x10 b&w and color glossy prints. Can reproduce prints from negatives. Will use illustrations. Offers no additional payment for photos accepted with ms. Model releases required. Buys all rights.

Tips: "I'm looking for how-to, nuts-and-bolts training type stories which are martial arts related. I need stories about developing speed, accuracy, power, etc."

Miscellaneous

‡BALLOON LIFE, Balloon Life Magazine, Inc., 3381 Pony Express Dr., Sacramento CA 95834. (916)922-9648. Editor: Tom Hamilton. 75% freelance written. Monthly magazine for sport of hot air ballooning. Circ.

3,500. Pays on publication. Byline given. Offers 50-100% kill fee. Buys first North American serial rights or second serial (reprint) rights. Submit seasonal/holiday material 3-4 months in advance. Previously published submissions OK. Query for electronic submissions. Computer printout submissions OK; prefers letter-quality. Reports in 3 weeks on queries; 2 weeks on mss. Sample copy for 9x12 SAE with $1.45 postage. Writer's guidelines for letter SASE.

Nonfiction: Book excerpts, general interest, how-to (flying hot air balloons, equipment techniques), interview/profile, new product, letters to the editor, technical. Buys 150 mss/year. Query with or without published or send complete ms. Length: 800-5,000 words. Pays $50-75 for assigned articles; $25-50 for unsolicited articles. Sometimes pays expenses of writers on assignment.

Photos: Send photos with submission. Reviews transparencies and prints. Offers $15-50 per photo. Identification of subjects required. Buys one-time rights.

Columns/Departments: Hangar Flying (real life flying experience that others can learn from), 800-1,500 words; Preflight (a news and information column), 100-500 words; Logbook (recent balloon events—events that have taken place in last 3-4 months), 300-500 words. Buys 60 mss/year. Send complete ms. Pays $15-50.

Fiction: Humorous. Buys 3-5 mss/year. Send complete ms. Length: 800-1,500 words. Pays $50.

Tips: "This magazine slants toward the technical side of ballooning. We are interested in articles that help to educate and provide safety information. Also stories and/or individuals with manufacturers, and important individuals in the field of ballooning. The magazine attempts to present articles that show "how-to" (fly, business opportunities, weather, equipment). Both our Feature Stories section and Logbook section are where most mss are purchased."

BALLS AND STRIKES, Amateur Softball Association, 2801 NE 50th St., Oklahoma City OK 73111. (405)424-5266. Editor: Pat Madden. Senior Editor: Bill Plummer III. 20% freelance written. Works with a small number of new/unpublished writers each year. "Only national monthly tabloid covering amateur softball." Circ. 300,000. Pays on publication. Publishes ms an average of 2 months after acceptance. Buys first rights. Byline given. Computer printout submissions acceptable; no dot-matrix. Reports in 3 weeks. Free sample copy.

Nonfiction: General interest, historical/nostalgic, interview/profile and technical. Query. Length: 2-3 pages. Pays $50-65.

Tips: "We generally like shorter features because we try to get many different features in each issue. There is a possibility we will be using more freelance material in the future."

‡FLEX, For Tomorrow's Superstars, Weider Health & Fitness, 21100 Erwin St., Woodland Hills CA 91367. (818)884-6800. 1-800-423-5590. FAX: (818)704-5734. Editor: Bill Reynolds. Managing Editor: Jerry Kindela. 5-10% freelance written. Monthly magazine on bodybuilding (competitive). "Highly specialized. Must be authentic to bodybuilding competitors." Circ. 165,000 in USA, 30,000 in Canada. Pays 30 days after acceptance. Byline usually given. Buys all rights. "Many articles are translated into German, Spanish, Japanese, etc., and reprinted in *Flex* in those countries." Reports in 2 weeks on queries; 3 weeks on mss, "slower if on tour for fall competitions."

Nonfiction: General interest, historical/nostalgic, how-to (training, psychology nutrition), inspirational, technical, travel and major competition reports. "No fiction, poetry, softcore shape-up stories, articles on lesser known competitors." Buys 20-25 mss/year. Query with published clips. Length: "Query. Assigned articles can be up to 15 pages." Pays $150-500 for assigned. Pays reasonable expenses of writers on assignment.

Photos: State availability of photos with submission. Reviews contact sheets and negatives, 35mm or 60mm transparencies and prints. Offers $30-500 per photo. Captions, model releases and identification of subjects required. Buys all rights.

Columns/Departments: Julian Schmidt. Rising Stars (2½ pages stories with photo ,b&w or color, of upcoming athlete); Flexible Cuisine (recipes of the champs, 2½ pages) and Nutrition (various nutrition topics, 2½ pages) Buys 30-35 mss/year. Query with published clips. Pays $150.

Tips: "If someone has expertise in the sport but is deficient in writing mechanics, I'll work with him/her. Authenticity and total mastery of subject are everything. Attend a competition, read the magazines. Look, learn and pick out good rising stars to write about."

HOCKEY ILLUSTRATED, Lexington Library, Inc., 355 Lexington Ave., New York NY 10017. (212)391-1400. FAX: (212)986-5926. Editor: Stephen Ciacciarelli. 90% freelance written. Published 3 times in season. Magazine covering NHL hockey. "Upbeat stories on NHL superstars—aimed at hockey fans, predominantly a younger audience." Pays on acceptance. Publishes ms an average of 1-2 months after acceptance. Byline given. Buys first North American serial rights. Photocopied submissions OK. Computer printout submissions OK; prefers letter-quality. Reports in 2 weeks. Sample copy $1.95 with 9x12 SAE with 3 first class stamps.

Nonfiction: Inspirational and interview/profile. Buys 40-50 mss/year. Query with or without published clips, or send complete ms. Length: 1,500-3,000 words. Pays $75-125 for assigned and unsolicited articles.
Photos: State availability of photos with submission. Reviews transparencies and prints. Offers no additional payment for photos accepted with ms. Identification of subjects required. Buys one-time rights.

INSIDE TEXAS RUNNING, 9514 Bristlebrook Dr., Houston TX 77083. (713)498-3208. Editor: Joanne Schmidt. 50% freelance written. A monthly tabloid covering running, cycling and triathloning. "Our audience is Texas runners and triathletes who may also be into cross training with biking and swimming." Circ. 10,000. Pays on acceptance. Publishes ms an average of 1-2 months after acceptance. Byline given. Buys first rights, one-time rights, second serial (reprint) rights and all rights. Submit seasonal/holiday material 2 months in advance. Previously published submissions OK; no dot-matrix. Reports in 1 month on queries; 6 weeks on mss. Sample copy $1.50; writer's guidelines for #10 SASE.
Nonfiction: Book excerpts, exposé, historical/nostalgic, humor, interview/profile, opinion, photo feature, technical and travel. "We would like to receive controversial and detailed news pieces which cover both sides of an issue; for example, how a race director must deal with city government to put on an event. Problems seen by both sides include cost, traffic congestion, red tape, etc." No personal experience such as "Why I Love to Run," "How I Ran My First Marathon." Buys 18 mss/year. Query with published clips, or send complete ms. Length: 500-2,500 words. Pays $100 maximum for assigned articles; $50 maximum for unsolicited articles. Sometimes pays the expenses of writers on assignments.
Photos: Send photos with submission. Offers $25 maximum/photo. Captions required. Buys one-time rights.
Tips: "General material on running will be replaced in 1990 by specific pieces which cite names, places, costs and references to additional information. Writers should be familiar with the sport and understand race strategies, etc. The basic who, what, where, when and how also applies. The best way to break in to our publication is to submit brief (3 or 4 paragraphs) write-ups on road races to be used in the Results section. We also need more cycling articles for new biking section."

‡INTERNATIONAL GYMNAST, Sundby Sports, Inc., 225 Brooks St., Box G, Oceanside CA 92054. (619)722-0030. Editor: Dwight Normile. 50% freelance written. Monthly magazine on gymnastics. "*IG* is dedicated to serving the gymnastics community with competition reports, personality profiles, training and coaching tips and innovations in the sport." Circ. 25,000. Pays on publication. Publishes ms an average of 3 months after acceptance. Byline given. Buys one-time rights. Submit seasonal/holiday material 3 months in advance. Computer printout submissions OK; prefers letter-quality. Sample copy $3.25. Writer's guidelines for #10 SASE.
Nonfiction: How-to (coaching/training/ business, i.e. running a club), interview/profile, opinion, photo feature (meets or training sites of interest, etc.), competition reports and technical. "Nothing unsuitable for young readers." Buys 25 mss/year. Send complete ms. Length: 500-2,250 words. Pays $15-25. Pays in contributor copies or other premiums when currency exchange is not feasible i.e., foreign residents.
Photos: Send photos with submission. Reviews transparencies and prints. Offers $5-40 per photo published. Identification of subjects required. Buys one-time rights.
Columns/Departments: Innovations (new moves, new approaches, coaching tips); Nutrition (hints for the competitive gymnast); Dance (ways to improve gymnasts through dance, all types); Club Corner (business hints for club owners/new programs, etc.) and Book Reviews (reviews of new books pertaining to gymnastics). Buys 10 mm/year. Send complete ms. Length: 750-1,000. Pays $15-25.
Fiction: Humorous, anything pertaining to gymnastics, nothing inappropriate for young readers. Buys 1-2 ms/year. Send complete ms. Length: 1,500 words maximum. Pays $15-25.
Tips: "To *IG* readers, a lack of knowledge sticks out like a sore thumb. Writers are generally coaches, ex-gymnasts and 'hardcore' enthusiasts. Most open area would generally be competition reports. Be concise, but details are necessary when covering gymnastics. Again, thorough knowledge of the sport is indispensable."

INTERNATIONAL OLYMPIC LIFTER, IOL Publications, 3602 Eagle Rock, Box 65855, Los Angeles CA 90065. (213)257-8762. Editor: Bob Hise. Managing Editor: Herb Glossbrenner. 5% freelance written. Magazine published 6 times per year covering the Olympic sport of weightlifting. Circ. 10,000. Pays on publication. Publishes ms an average of 3 months after acceptance. Byline given. Offers $25 kill fee. Buys one-time rights or negotiable rights. Submit seasonal/holiday material 5 months in advance. Photocopied submissions OK; prefers letter-quality. Reports in 6 weeks. Sample copy $4; writer's guidelines for 9x12 SAE and 5 first class stamps.
Nonfiction: Training articles, contest reports, diet—all related to Olympic weight lifting. Buys 4 mss/year. Query. Length: 250-2,000 words. Pays $25-100.
Photos: Action (competition and training). State availability of photos. Pays $1-5 for 5x7 b&w prints. Identification of subjects required.
Poetry: Dale Rhoades, poetry editor. Light verse, traditional—related to Olympic lifting. Buys 6-10 poems/year. Submit maximum 3 poems. Length: 12-24 lines. Pays $10-20.
Tips: "First—a writer must be acquainted with Olympic-style weight lifting. Since we are an international publication we do not tolerate ethnic, cultural, religious or political inclusions. Articles relating to AWA are readily accepted."

‡**NEW YORK RUNNING NEWS**, New York Road Runners Club, 9 E. 89th St., New York NY 10128. (212)860-2280. FAX: (212)860-9754. Editor: Raleigh Mayer. 75% freelance written. A bimonthly regional sports magazine covering running, racewalking, nutrition and fitness. Material should be of interest to members of the New York Road Runners Club. Circ. 45,000. Pays on publication. Time to publication varies. Byline given. Offers ⅓ kill fee. Buys first North American serial rights. Submit seasonal/holiday material 4 months in advance. Simultaneous submissions and previously published submissions OK. Computer printout submissions acceptable; no dot-matrix. Reports in 1 month. Sample copy for 9x12 SAE with $1.75 postage; writer's guidelines for #10 SASE.
Nonfiction: Running and marathon articles. Special issues include N.Y.C. Marathon (submissions in by August 1). No non-running stories. Buys 25 mss/year. Query. Length: 750-1,750 words. Pays $50-250. Pays documented expenses of writers on assignment.
Photos: Send photos with submission. Reviews 8x10 b&w prints. Offers $35-300/photo. Captions, model releases and identification of subjects required. Buys one-time rights.
Columns/Departments: Essay (running-related topics). Query. Length: 750 words. Pays $50-125.
Fiction: Running stories. Query. Length: 750-1,750 words. Pays $50-150.
Fillers: Anecdotes. Length: 250-500 words. No payment for fillers.
Tips: "Be knowledgeable about the sport of running. Write like a runner."

‡**ON COURT**, Fourhand Inc., Suite 400, 1200 Sheppard Ave. E, Willowdale, Ontario M2K 2S5 Canada. (416)497-1370. Editor: Tom Tebbutt. 5% freelance written. Tabloid published 8 times yearly on tennis and squash. Circ. 40,000. Pays on publication. Publishes ms an average of 2 months after acceptance. Byline given. Buys one-time rights. Submit seasonal/holiday material 2 months in advance. Simultaneous, photocopied and previously published submissions OK. Computer printout submissions OK.
Nonfiction: Length 400-2,000 words. Sometimes pays expenses of writers on assignment.
Photos: State availability of photos with submission.

‡**POLO**, Fleet Street Corp., 656 Quince Orchard Rd., Gaithersburg MD 20878. (301)977-3900. Editor: Ami Shinitzky. Managing Editor: Martha LeGrand. Magazine, published 10 times per year on polo—the sport and lifestyle. "Our readers are an affluent group. Most are well-educated, well-read and highly sophisticated." Circ. 5,000. Pays on acceptance. Publishes ms an average of 2-4 months after acceptance. Kill fee varies. Buys first North American serial rights and makes work-for-hire assignments. Submit seasonal/holiday material 3 months in advance. Simultaneous submissions OK. Computer printout submissions OK; prefers letter-quality. Reports in 1 month on queries; 2 months on mss. Free writer's guidelines.
Nonfiction: Articles Editor: Dale Leatherman. Historical/nostalgic, interview/profile, personal experience, photo feature, technical, travel. Buys 20 mss/year. Query with published clips or send complete ms. Length: 800-3,000 words. Pays $150-400 for assigned articles; $100-300 for unsolicited articles—(Polo Report game coverage somewhat lower). Sometimes pays expenses of writers on assignment.
Photos: State availability of photos with submission or send photos with submission. Reviews contact sheets, transparencies and prints. Offers $20-150 per photo. Captions required. Buys one-time rights.
Columns/Departments: Yesteryears (historical pieces), 500 words; Polo Scene (club and player profiles), 800-1,000 words. Buys 15 mss/year. Query with published clips. Pays $100-300.
Tips: "Query us on a personality or club profile or historic piece or, if you know the game, state availability to cover a tournament. Keep in mind that ours is a sophisticated, well-educated audience."

PRIME TIME SPORTS & FITNESS, GND Prime Time Publishing, Box 6091, Evanston IL 60204. (312)869-6434. Editor: Dennis A. Dorner. Managing Editor: Nicholas J. Schmitz. 80% freelance written. Eager to work with new/unpublished writers. A monthly magazine covering seasonal pro sports and racquet and health club sports and fitness. Circ. 35,000. Pays on publication. Publishes ms an average of 6 months after acceptance. Byline given. Buys all rights; will assign back to author in 85% of cases. Submit seasonal/holiday material 6 months in advance. Simultaneous, photocopied and previously published submissions OK. Computer printout submissions acceptable; prefers letter-quality. Reports in 6 weeks. Sample copy for 9x11 SAE and 7 first class stamps.
Nonfiction: Book excerpts (fitness and health); exposé (in tennis, fitness, racquetball, health clubs, diets); adult (slightly risqué and racy fitness); how-to (expert instructional pieces on any area of coverage); humor (large market for funny pieces on health clubs and fitness); inspirational (on how diet and exercise combine to bring you a better body, self); interview/profile; new product; opinion (only from recognized sources who know what they are talking about); personal experience (definitely—humor); photo feature (on related subjects); technical (on exercise and sport); travel (related to fitness, tennis camps, etc.); news reports (on racquetball, handball, tennis, running events). Special issues: Swimsuit and Resort Issue (March); Baseball Preview (April); Summer Fashion (July); Pro Football Preview (August); Fall Fashion (October); Ski Issue (November); Christmas Gifts and related articles (December). "We love short articles that get to the point. Nationally oriented big events and national championships. No articles on local only tennis and racquetball tournaments without national appeal." Buys 150 mss/year. Length: 2,000 words maximum. Pays $20-150. Sometimes pays the expenses of writers on assignment.

Photos: Randy Lester, photo editor. Send photos with ms. Pays $5-75 for b&w prints. Captions, model releases and identification of subjects required. Buys all rights, "but returns 75% of photos to submitter."

Columns/Departments: Linda Jefferson, column/department editor. New Products; Fitness Newsletter; Handball Newsletter; Racquetball Newsletter; Tennis Newsletter; News & Capsule Summaries; Fashion Spot (photos of new fitness and bathing suits and ski equipment); related subjects. Buys 100 mss/year. Send complete ms. Length: 50-250 words ("more if author has good handle to cover complete columns"). Pays $5-25.

Fiction: Judy Johnson, fiction editor. Erotica (if related to fitness club); fantasy (related to subjects); humorous (definite market); religious ("no God-is-my shepherd, but Body-is-God's-temple OK"); romance (related subjects). "Upbeat stories are needed." Buys 20 mss/year. Send complete ms. Length: 500-2,500 words maximum. Pays $20-150.

Poetry: Free verse, haiku, light verse, traditional on related subjects. Length: up to 150 words. Pays $10-25.

Tips: "Looking for articles charting the 1992 Olympics. Send us articles dealing with court club sports, exercise and nutrition that exemplify an upbeat 'you can do it' attitude. Pro sports previews 3-4 months ahead of their seasons are also needed. Good short fiction or humorous articles can break in. Expert knowledge of any related subject can bring assignments; any area is open. A humorous/knowledgeable columnist in weight lifting, aerobics, running and nutrition is presently needed. We consider everything as a potential article, but are turned off by credits, past work and degrees. We have a constant demand for well-written articles on instruction, health and trends in both. Other articles needed are professional sports training techniques, fad diets, tennis and fitness resorts, photo features with aerobic routines. A frequent mistake made by writers is length — articles are too long. When we assign an article, we want it newsy if it's news and opinion if opinion."

‡**PROATHLETE, Magazine for Professional Athletes**, Freeway Publications, Box 89, Berkeley CA 94701. (415)843-5062. Editor: Jeanne B. Ewing, Ph.D. 80% freelance written. Monthly magazine. "This publication's purpose is to provide information and insights that will help professional athletes cope with the challenges of their unique occupational and social status." Estab. 1988. Circ. 50,000. Pays on acceptance or publication or sometimes on assignment. Publishes ms an average of 3 months after acceptance. Byline given. Buys first rights, all rights and makes work-for-hire assignments. Submit seasonal/holiday material 3-4 months in advance. Simultaneous and photocopied submissions OK. Query for electronic submissions. Computer printout submissions OK; prefers letter-quality. Reports in 3 weeks on queries; 1 month on mss. Writer's guidelines for #10 SASE.

Nonfiction: Book excerpts, essays (opinion or controversy of interest to readers), general interest (hobbies, home, garden), how-to (find a lawyer, cope with the IRS, select. . .), humor, inspirational, interview/profile (celebreties of interest to our readers), new product (computers, cars, clothing), opinion, personal experience, photo feature, technical (computers), travel (hideaways and tips), health and fitness and entertainment/recreation. "Please don't try to recount sports events to our readers; no academic approaches." Buys 70 mss/year. Query with or without published clips or send complete ms. Length: 200-950 words. Pays $5-300. Sometimes pays expenses of writers on assignment.

Photos: Send photos with submission. Reviews transparencies. Offers $10-50 per photo. Model releases and identification of subjects required. Buys all rights.

Columns/Departments: Touchdown (recreation/entertainment/travel); Time-Out (vacations and hideaways); Financial Advisor (problem-solving for athletes); Your Agent & You (problem-solving for athletes); Media Strategy (helping athletes cope with media); Profiles ; Pro-At-Home; Pro-How-To; Pro-Business (opportunities) and On the Edge (personal, mind and body). We use many sidebars. Query with published clips or send complete ms. Length: 500-800 words. Pays $5-150.

Fiction: Adventure, ethnic, historical, humorous, mainstream, novel exerpts, serialized novels, slice-of-life vignettes and suspense. "We may use very little fiction. Must be exceptional. No erotica, confessions, horror, mystery, religious." Send complete ms. Length: 1,000 words maximum.

Poetry: Light verse and traditional. "We rarely use poetry, but we will consider it. (Nothing 'cute' or mysterious, please.)" Pays $5.

Fillers: Newsbreaks and short humor. Buys 100/year. Length: 50-100 words. Pays $5.

Tips: "Address our readership in a friendly, helpful way. Offer something new, crisp, and interesting. Be willing to work with us to get it right. We want quality in writing and concern for our readership. Travel — authentic, first-hand information *with* slides that provide information not accessible from the travel agent are most open to freelancers. Save our readers stress, money; give them pleasure, make their lives easier, tell them something they don't already know. Make it snappy and easy to read, but don't talk down to us."

‡**RUNNING TIMES, The National Calendar Magazine for Runners**, LFP, Inc., Suite 300, 9171 Wilshire Blvd., Beverly Hills CA 90210. (213)858-7100. Editor: Ed Ayres. 70% freelance written. Monthly magazine on running. "*Running Times* readers range from recreational enthusiasts to world-class marathoners; but whether turtles or hounds, they share a conviction that running is an important part of their lives." Circ. 60,000. Pays on publication. Publishes ms an average of 4 months after acceptance. Byline given. Offers 50% kill fee. Buys one-time rights and makes work-for-hire assignments. Submit seasonal/holiday material 4 months in advance. Simultaneous and photocopied submissions OK. Computer printout submissions OK.

Reports in 10 weeks. Sample copy $2.95 with 9x12 SAE and 7 first class stamps; free writer's guidelines.

Nonfiction: Essays, historical/nostalgic, interview/profile, photo feature. "We have no need for rehashed advice, cute humor, slick or glitzy profiles or anything lacking in real depth, humor or authenticity." Query with published or send complete ms. Length: 200-3,000 words. Pays $50-1,000 for assigned articles; $50-500 for unsolicited articles. Sometimes pays expenses of writers on assignment.

Photos: State availability of photos with submission or send photos with submission. Reviews any color transparencies or b&w prints. Captions required. Buys one-time rights.

Fillers: Anecdotes, facts. Buys 50/year. Length: 50-200 words. Pays $15-50.

Tips: "Our greatest needs are for short anecdotes or news pieces on current trends, offbeat occurrences, issues or phenomena of interest to runners; and well-researched expositions on cutting-edge developments in the scientific and medical aspects of distance running. These types of submissions, if well written, have a high probability of acceptance."

SIGNPOST MAGAZINE, Suite 518, 1305 Fourth Ave., Seattle WA 98101. Publisher: Washington Trails Association. Editor: Ann L. Marshall. 10% freelance written. "We will consider working with both previously published and unpublished freelancers." Monthly about hiking, backpacking and similar trail-related activities, mostly from a Pacific Northwest viewpoint. Will consider any rights offered by author. Buys 12 mss/year. Pays on publication. Publishes ms an average of 6 months after acceptance. Free sample copy; writer's guidelines available for SASE. Will consider photocopied submissions. Reports in 6 weeks. Query or submit complete ms. Computer printout submissions acceptable; no dot-matrix. Sample copy and writer's guidelines for SASE.

Nonfiction and Photos: "Most material is donated by subscribers or is staff-written. Payment for purchased material is low, but a good way to break in to print and share your outdoor experiences."

Tips: "We cover only *self-propelled* backcountry sports and won't consider manuscripts about trail bikes, snowmobiles, or power boats. We *are* interested in articles about modified and customized equipment, food and nutrition, and personal experiences in the backcountry (primarily Pacific Northwest, but will consider nation- and world-wide)."

SKYDIVING, Box 1520, DeLand FL 32721. (904)736-9779. Editor: Michael Truffer. 25% freelance written. Works with a small number of new/unpublished writers each year. Monthly tabloid featuring skydiving for sport parachutists, worldwide dealers and equipment manufacturers. Circ. 8,600. Average issue includes 3 feature articles and 3 columns of technical information. Pays on publication. Publishes ms an average of 3 months after acceptance. Byline given. Buys one-time rights. Simultaneous, photocopied and previously published submissions OK, if so indicated. Query for electronic submissions. Computer printout submissions acceptable. Reports in 1 month. Sample copy $2; writer's guidelines with 9x12 SAE and 4 first class stamps.

Nonfiction: "Send us news and information on equipment, techniques, events and outstanding personalities who skydive. We want articles written by people who have a solid knowledge of parachuting." No personal experience or human-interest articles. Query. Length: 500-1,000 words. Pays $25-100. Sometimes pays the expenses of writers on assignment.

Photos: State availability of photos. Reviews 5x7 and larger b&w glossy prints. Offers no additional payment for photos accepted with ms. Captions required.

Fillers: Newsbreaks. Length: 100-200 words. Pays $25 minimum.

Tips: "The most frequent mistake made by writers in completing articles for us is that the writer isn't knowledgeable about the sport of parachuting."

‡SPORT DETROIT MAGAZINE, Suite 150, 32270 Telegraph, Birmingham MI 48010. (313)433-3162. FAX: (313)645-6645. Editor: Dave Aretha and Michael Haines. 60% freelance written. Monthly magazine on pro and college sports in Michigan. It's geared toward Michigan's casual sports fan. *Sport Detroit* is featured-oriented and it focuses heavily on Michigan's pro and college teams. Circ. 50,000. Pays 30 days after publication. Publishes ms an average of 1-2 months after acceptance. Byline given. Offers 30% kill fee. Buys first North American serial rights. Photocopied and previously published submissions OK. Query for electronic submissions. Computer printout submissions OK; prefers letter-quality. Reports in 3 weeks. Free sample copy.

Nonfiction: Exposé, general interest and interview/profile; all sports related. "No opinion, personal experience, nostalgia." Buys 75-100. Query with published clips. Length: 250-3,000 words. Pays $30-250 for assigned articles (possible exceptions); $30-150 for unsolicited articles. Pays writers' expenses on assignment.

Photos: State availability of photos with submission. Reviews contact sheets and transparencies. Offers $25-100 per photo. Captions and identification of subjects required. Buys one-time rights (on-assignment become property of *Sport Detroit*).

Columns/Departments: Short shorts (short, off-beat features on interesting characters or unusual happenings in the world of sports), 200-500 words. Buys 30-50 mss/year. Query with published clips. Pays $30.

Tips: "We're always looking for out-of-state freelancers who can write about Michigan sports celebrities who have fled their state. For example we recently needed an L.A. writer to write about the Dodgers' Kirk Gibson. Interested freelancers should query with published clips of feature stories and/or sports–oriented analytical articles."

‡**TAVERN SPORTS INTERNATIONAL**, National Bowlers Journal Inc., Suite 850 101 E. Erie St., Chicago IL 60611. (312)266-9499. FAX: (312)266-7215. Managing Editor: Jocelyn Hathaway. 50% freelance written. Bimonthly magazine on organized tavern sports and coin-operated games. "*TSI* targets organized tavern sports in league/tournament play and the coin-operated game industry, i.e. pool, darts, shuffleboard and video games. Editorial content reads like a newspaper sports page and includes coverage of major tournaments, legislation affecting the industry, personality profiles and instructional tips." Estab. 1988. Circ. 40,000. Pays on publication. Publishes ms an average of 2-4 months after acceptance. Byline usually given. Offers $25 kill fee. Buys first North American serial rights. Submit seasonal/holiday material 4 months in advance. Simultaneous, photocopied and previously published submissions OK. Computer printout submissions OK; prefers letter-quality. Reports in 2-4 weeks. Sample copy for 9x12 SAE with $1.25 in postage. Free writer's guidelines.
Nonfiction: Book excerpts, general interest, historical/nostalgic, how-to (trick shots extremely difficult shots; pool/billiards/darts), humor, interview/profile, personal experience, photo feature and tournament coverage. Buys 40-50 mss/year. Query with or without published clips or send complete ms. Length: 600-1,500. Pays $50-200.
Photos: Send photos with submission. Reviews contact sheets, negatives, transparencies and prints (color slides preferred). Offers $5-50 per photo. Identification of subjects required. Buys all rights.
Column/Departments: Outtakes (tournament briefs), 100-200 words. Query. Pays $10-20.
Tips: "Extensive knowledge of or possessing a competitive history in tavern-based sports and related areas is most desired, but not required. Letters addressed to the managing editor detailing proposed topic preferred. Enclosing published clips and daytime telephone number helpful."

VOLLEYBALL MONTHLY, Straight Down, Inc., 2308 Broad St., San Luis Obispo CA 93401. (805)541-2294. FAX: (805)541-2438. Editor: Jon Hastings. 25% freelance written. Monthly magazine covering volleyball. "National publication geared to players, coaches and fans of the sport of volleyball." Circ. 60,000. Pays on publication. Publishes ms an average of 2 months after acceptance. Byline given. Buys first rights. Submit seasonal/holiday material 4 months in advance. Computer printout submissions OK. Reports in 2 weeks on queries. Sample copy and writer's guidelines for 9x12 SAE and $2.
Nonfiction: How-to, humor, interview/profile, personal experience, photo feature and travel. No "USC beat UCLA last week" articles. Buys 22 mss/year. Send complete ms. Length: 750-3,000 words. Pays $75-250 for assigned articles; pays $50-200 for unsolicited articles. Sometimes pays the expenses of writers on assignment.
Photos: State availability of photos with submission or send photos with submission. Reviews transparencies and 8x10 prints. Offers $25-100 per photo. Identification of subjects required. Buys one-time rights.
Columns/Departments: Buys 6 mss/year. Send complete ms. Length: 750-2,000 words. Pays $50-250.
Fiction: Buys 1-5 mss/year. Send complete ms. Pays $50-250.

‡**WRESTLING WORLD**, Lexington Library Inc., 355 Lexington Ave., New York NY 10017. (212)949-6850. FAX: (212)986-5926. Editor: Stephen Ciacciarelli. 100% freelance written. Magazine published bimonthly. "Professional wrestling fans are our audience. We run profiles of top wrestlers and managers and articles on current topics of interest on the mat scene." Circ. 100,000. Pays on acceptance. Byline given. Buys first North American serial rights. Photocopied submissions OK. Computer printout submissions OK; prefers letter-quality to dot-matrix. Reports in 2 weeks. Sample copy $3.
Nonfiction: Interview/profile and photo feature. "No general think pieces." Buys 100 mss/year. Query with or without published clips or send complete ms. Length: 1,500-2,500 words. Pays $75-125.
Photos: State availability of photos with submision. Reviews 35 mm transparencies and prints. Offers $25-50/photo package. Pays $50-150 for color transparencies. Identification of subjects required. Buys one-time rights.
Tips: "Anything topical has the best chance of acceptance. Articles on those hard-to-reach wrestlers stand an excellent chance of acceptance."

Skiing and Snow Sports

‡**AMERICAN SKATING WORLD, Independent Publication of the American Ice Skating Community,** Business Communications Inc., 2545-47 Brownsville Rd., Pittsburgh PA 15210. (412)885-7600. FAX: (412)885-7617. Editor: Robert A. Mock. Magazine Editor: Doug Graham. 70% freelance written. Eager to work with new/unpublished writers. Monthly tabloid on figure skating. Circ. 15,000. Pays on publication. Publishes ms an average of 2-3 months after acceptance. Byline given. Buys first North American serial rights

and occasionally second serial rights. Submit seasonal/holiday material 3 months in advance. Computer printout submissions acceptable; prefers letter-quality to dot-matrix. Reports in 6 weeks. Sample copy and writer's guidelines $2.

Nonfiction: Expose; general interest; historical/nostalgic; how-to (technique in figure skating); humor; inspirational; interview/profile; new product; opinion; personal experience; photo feature; technical and travel. Special issues include recreational (July), classic skaters (August), annual fashion issue (September), adult issue (December). No fiction. AP Style Guidelines are the primary style source. Short, snappy paragraphs desired. Buys 200 mss/year. Send complete ms. "Include phone number; response time longer without it." Length: 600-1,000 words. Pays $25-75.

Photos: Send photos with query or ms. Reviews color transparencies and b&w prints. Pays $5 for b&w; $15 for color. Identification of subjects required. Buys all rights for b&w; one-time rights for color.

Columns/Departments: Buys 60 mss/year. Send complete ms. Length: 500-750 words. Pays $25-50.

Fillers: Clippings and anecdotes. No payment for fillers.

Tips: Event coverage is most open to freelancers; confirm with managing editor to ensure event has not been assigned. Questions are welcome, call managing editor EST, 11 a.m. to 3 p.m., Tuesdays, Wednesdays and Thursdays.

SKATING, United States Figure Skating Association, 20 First St., Colorado Springs CO 80906. (303)635-5200. Editor: Dale Mitch. Published 10 times a year except August/September. Circ. 31,000. Official Publication of the USFSA. Pays on publication. Publishes ms an average of 3 months after acceptance. Buys all rights. Byline given.

Nonfiction: Historical; humor; informational; interview; photo feature; historical biographies; profile (background and interests of national-caliber amateur skaters); technical; and competition reports. Buys 4 mss/issue. Query.

Photos: Photos purchased with or without accompanying ms. Pays $15 for 8x10 or 5x7 b&w glossy prints and $35 for color prints or transparencies. Query.

Columns/Departments: Ice Abroad (competition results and report from outside the U.S.); Book Reviews; People; and Music column (what's new and used for music for skating). Buys 4 mss/issue. Query or send complete ms. Length: 500-2,000 words.

Tips: "We want sharp, strong, intelligent writing by experienced persons knowledgeable in the technical and artistic aspects of figure skating with a new outlook on the development of the sport. Knowledge and background in technical aspects of figure skating are essential to the quality of writing expected. We would also like to receive articles on former national and international champions; and personalities and humorous features directly related to figure skating. No professional skater material."

‡SKI GUIDE, Canada's Ski Magazine, Canadian Controlled Media Communications, 287 McPherson Ave. Toronto, Ontario M6V 1A6 Canada. (416)928-2909. Editor: Bob Weeks. Managing Editor: John Gordon. 80% freelance written. Annual magazine on ski equipment and travel. "Readers are looking for details that will assist them in making purchases of equipment or vacation. Price, quality and details are imperative." Pays on acceptance. Publishes ms an average of 2 months after acceptance. Byline given. Offers negotiable kill fee. Buys all rights. Query for electronic submissions. Computer printout submissions OK. Sample copy $2 with SAE and Canadian postage or IRC. Free writer's guidelines.

Nonfiction: Interview/profile (top skiers, ski-industry people), photo feature (travel areas) and travel (ski destinations). "No how I learned to ski," no personal experiences. Buys 5-7 mss/year. Query with published clips. Length: 750-2,000 words. Pays $150-500. Sometimes pays expenses of writers on assignment.

Photos: State availability of photos with submission. Reviews contact sheets. Offers $50-150 per photo. Buys one-time rights.

Columns/Departments: Lift Lines (short, newsy items of interest to skiers), 100 words. Buys 5-10 mss/year. Query. Pays $25-100.

Tips: "We look for unusual travel destinations; something besides the typical Aspen, Whistler, Jackson's Hole. Tell us why this place is different."

SKI MAGAZINE, 2 Park Ave., New York NY 10016. (212)779-5000. Editor: Dick Needham. Managing Editor: Andrea Rosengarten. 15% freelance written. A monthly magazine on snow skiing. "*Ski* is written and edited for recreational skiers. Its content is intended to help them ski better (technique), buy better (equipment and skiwear), and introduce them to new resort experiences and ski adventures." Circ. 430,000. Pays on acceptance. Publishes ms an average of 3 months after acceptance. Byline given. Offers 15% kill fee. Buys first North American serial rights. Submit seasonal/holiday material 8 months in advance. Photocopied submission OK. Computer printout submissions OK; prefers letter-quality. Reports in 1 week on queries; 2 weeks on ms. Sample copy for 8½x11 SAE and 5 first class stamps.

Nonfiction: Essays, historical/nostalgic, how-to, humor, interview/profile and personal experience. Buys 5-10 mss/year. Send complete ms. Length: 1,000-3,500 words. Pays $500-1,000 for assigned articles; pays $300-700 for unsolicited artiicles. Pays the expenses of writers on assignment.

Photos: Send photos with submission. Offers $75-300/photo. Captions, model releases and identification of subjects required. Buys one-time rights.

Columns/Departments: Ski Life (interesting people, events, oddities in skiing), 150-300 words; Discoveries (special products or services available to skiers that are out of the ordinary), 100-200 words; and It Worked for Me (new ideas invented by writer that make his skiing life easier, more convenient, more enjoyable), 50-150 words. Buys 20 mss/year. Send complete ms. Length: 100-300 words. Pays $50-100.

Fillers: Facts and short humor. Buys 10/year. Length: 60-75 words. Pays $50-75.

Tips: "Writers must have an extensive familiarity with the sport and know what concerns, interests and amuses skiers. Ski Life, Discoveries and It Worked for Me are most open to freelancers."

SNOW COUNTRY, New York Times Magazine Group, 5520 Park Ave., Trumbull CT 06611. (203)723-7030. Editor: John Fry. Managing Editor: Bob LaMarche. 50% freelance written. Monthly magazine on sports and leisure activity in North American snow country. "Story ideas should be hooked to a person or people; best market for freelancers are front- and back-of-book pieces which are short—500-700 words." Estab. 1988. Circ. 200,000. Pays on acceptance. Byline given. Offers ⅓ kill fee. Buys first North American serial rights. Query for electronic submission. Computer printout submissions OK. Reports in 2 weeks.

Nonfiction: Historical/nostalgic, humor, interview/profile, personal experience, photo feature. Buys 150 mss/year. Query or query with published clips. Length: 200-1,000 words. Pays $150-750.

Photos: State availability of photos with submission or send photos with submission. Reviews contact sheets, transparencies and prints. Offers $25-600/photo. Model releases and identification of subjects required. Buys one-time rights.

Columns/Departments: Datebook (events, occasions, anniversaries in snow country; also odd, lively, or poignant quotes from people living in snow country or about snow country) 50 words. Send complete ms. Pays $20-40. Snow Country Store is a department of 150-word takes on artist, artisan, craftsperson, inventor, even cook or songwriter living in snow country who has product that can be purchased locally or by mail. This is not standard mail-order column—no souvenirs, household helps, objects conceived by marketing departments. Interesting people, unique or well-executed products. Query first. $100 minimum payment; extra for 2 pictures—one of person, one of product.

Tips: "We are looking for excellent writing, genuine fondness or interest in the subject. Please query and send clips. Magazine began regular publication in September 1988, monthly thereafter, and will be on newsstands. Most libraries will have, eventually. We do not send copies. We are developing writer's guidelines."

‡SNOWMOBILE MAGAZINE, Ehlert Publishing Group, Inc., Suite 101, 319 Barry Ave., Wayzata MN 55391. (612)476-2200. Editor: Dick Hendricks. Managing Editor: Jackie Walcome. 10% freelance written. A seasonal magazine (September, October, December and January) covering recreational snowmobiling. Circ. 500,000. Pays on publication. Byline given. Buys first North American serial rights. Submit seasonal/holiday material 5 months in advance. Computer printout submissions OK. Reports in 1 month. Sample copy $2.50; free writer's guidelines.

Nonfiction: How-to, interview/profile, new product, photo feature and travel. Buys 5-6 mss/year. Query. Length: 300-1,000 words. Pays $150-500. Sometimes pays the expenses of writers on assignment.

Photos: Send photos with submission. Reviews 35mm transparencies and 3x5 prints. Offers no additional payment for photos accepted with ms. Captions and identification of subjects required. Buys one-time rights.

Tips: The areas most open to freelancers include "travel and tour stories (with photos) on snowmobiling and snowmobile resorts and event coverage (races, winter festivals, etc.)."

Soccer

SOCCER AMERICA, Box 23704, Oakland CA 94623. (415)549-1414. Editor-in-Chief: Lynn Berling-Manuel. 10% freelance written. Works with a small number of new/unpublished writers each year. Weekly tabloid for a wide range of soccer enthusiasts. Circ. 20,000. Pays on publication. Publishes ms an average of 2 months after acceptance. Buys all rights. Byline given. Submit seasonal/holiday material 30 days in advance. Query for electronic submissions. Computer printout submissions OK; prefers letter-quality. Reports in 2 months. Sample copy and writer's guidelines $1.

Nonfiction: Expose (why a pro franchise isn't working right, etc.); historical; how-to; informational (news features); inspirational; interview; photo feature; profile; and technical. "No 'Why I Like Soccer' articles in 1,000 words or less. It's been done. We are very much interested in articles for our 'special issues': fitness, travel, and college selection process." Buys 1-2 mss/issue. Query. Length: 200-1,500 words. Pays 50¢/inch minimum.

Photos: Photos purchased with or without accompanying ms or on assignment. Captions required. Pays $12 for 5x7 or larger b&w glossy prints. Query.
Tips: "Freelancers mean the addition of editorial vitality. New approaches and new minds can make a world of difference. But if they haven't familiarized themselves with the publication—total waste of my time and theirs."

Tennis

WORLD TENNIS, Family Media, 3 Park Ave., New York NY 10016. (212)340-9688. Editor: Neil Amdur. Managing Editor: Peter M. Coan. Monthly tennis magazine. "We are a magazine catering to the complete tennis player." Circ. 500,000. Pays on acceptance. Byline given. Offers 25% kill fee. Buys all rights. Submit seasonal/holiday material 3 months in advance. Photocopied submissions OK. Query for electronic submissions. Computer printout submissions OK. Query for electronic submissions. Computer printout submissions OK; no dot-matrix. Reports in 2 weeks on queries; 1 month on manuscripts. Sample copy for 8×11 SAE and 5 first class stamps.
Nonfiction: Book excerpts (tennis, fitness, nutrition), essays, interview/profile, new product, personal experience, photo feature, travel (tennis resorts). No instruction, poetry or fiction. Buys 30-40 mss/year. Query with published clips. Length: 750-3,000 words. Pays $100 and up. Sometimes pays expenses of writers on assignment.
Photos: State availability of photos with submission. Reviews contact sheets. Payment varies. Requires captions and identification of subjects. Buys one-time rights.
Columns/Departments: My Ad (personal opinion on hot tennis topics); 200-1,000 words. Buys 25-30 mss/year. Query with published clips. Pays $100 and up.
Fillers: Anecdotes, facts, people/player news, international tennis news. Buys 10-15/year. Length: 750-1,000 words. Pays $100.

Water Sports

‡**THE DIVER**, Diversified Periodicals, Box 249, Cobalt CT 06414. (203)342-4730. Editor: Bob Taylor. 50% freelance written. Magazine published 10 times/year for divers, coaches and officials. Circ. 1,500. Pays on publication. Byline given. Submit material at least 2 months in advance. Simultaneous queries and simultaneous, photocopied and previously published submissions OK. Reports in 2 weeks on queries; 1 month on mss. Sample copy for 9x12 SAE and 85¢ postage.
Nonfiction: Interview/profile (of divers, coaches, officials); results; tournament coverage; any stories connected with platform and springboard diving; photo features and technical. Buys 35 mss/year. Query. Length: 500-2,500 words. Pays $15-40.
Photos: Pays $5-25 for b&w prints. Captions and identification of subjects required. Buys one-time rights.
Tips: "We're very receptive to new writers."

‡**PACIFIC DIVER**, Western Outdoors Publications, 3197-E Airport Loop Dr., Costa Mesa CA 92626. (714)546-4370. Editor: John Brumm. Send all mss and queries to Editor, *Pacific Diver*, Box 6218, Huntington Beach CA 92615 (714)536-7252. 75% freelance written. Bimonthly magazine on scuba diving. "Aimed at scuba diving in the South Pacific, covering events, destinations and activities from Hawaii to the Pacific Coast to Mexico and beyond. Aimed at all divers interested in Pacific diving." Estab. 1988. Circ. 25,000. Pays on acceptance. Publishes an average of 2 months after acceptance. Byline given. Offers $50 kill fee. Buys first North American serial rights and one-time rights. Submit seasonal/holiday material 3 months in advance. Photocopied submissions OK. Query for electronic submissions. Computer printout submissions OK. Reports in 3 weeks. Sample copy $2. Free writer's guidelines.
Nonfiction: General interest, historical/nostalgic, how-to, humor, interview/profile, new product, opinion, personal experience, photo feature, technical and travel; all must relate to scuba diving in the Pacific. "No poems, fiction." Buys 60 mss/year. Query or send complete ms. Length: 1,500-2,000. Pays $150-350.
Photos: Send photos with submission. Reviews 35mm transparencies. Offers no additional payment for photos accepted with ms. Captions and identification of subjects required. Buys one-time rights.

SKIN DIVER, Petersen Publishing Co., 8490 Sunset Blvd., Los Angeles CA 90069. (213)854-2960. Executive Editor: Bonnie J. Cardone. Managing Editor: Jim Warner. 85% freelance written. Eager to work with new/unpublished writers. Monthly magazine on scuba diving. "*Skin Diver* offers broad coverage of all significant aspects of underwater activity in the areas of foreign and domestic travel, recreation, ocean exploration, scientific research, commercial diving and technological developments." Circ. 224,786. Pays on publication.

Publishes ms an average of 9 months after acceptance. Byline given. Buys one-time rights. Submit seasonal/holiday material 6 months in advance. No simultaneous submissions. Computer printout submissions acceptable. Reports in 3 weeks on queries; 3 months on mss. Sample copy $3; free writer's guidelines.

Nonfiction: How-to (catch game, modify equipment, etc.); interview/profile; personal experience; travel; local diving; adventure and wreck diving). No Caribbean travel; "how I learned to dive." Buys 200 mss/year. Send complete ms. Length: 300-2,000 words; 1,200 preferred. Pays $50/published page.

Photos: Send photos with query or ms. Reviews 35mm transparencies and 8x10 prints. Pays $50/published page. Captions and identification of subjects required. Buys one-time rights.

Fillers: Newsbreaks and cartoons. Length: 300 words. Pays $25 for cartoons; $50/published page.

Tips: "Forget tropical travel articles and write about local diving sites, hobbies, game diving, local and wreck diving."

SURFER, Surfer Publications, 33046 Calle Aviador, San Juan Capistrano CA 92675. (714)496-5922. Editor: Paul Holmes. 20% freelance written. A monthly magazine "aimed at experts and beginners with strong emphasis on action surf photography." Circ. 110,000. Pays on publication. Byline given. Buys all rights. Submit seasonal/holiday material 6 months in advance. Simultaneous and photocopied submissions OK. Query for electronic submissions. Computer printout submissions acceptable; prefers letter-quality. Reports in 1 month on queries; 10 weeks on manuscripts. Sample copy for 8½x11 SAE with $3.50; writer's guidelines for SASE.

Nonfiction: How-to (technique in surfing); humor, inspiratonal, interview/profile, opinion, and personal experience (all surf-related); photo feature (action surf and surf travel); technical (surfboard design); and travel (surf exploration and discovery—photos required). Buys 30-50 mss/year. Query with or without published clips, or send complete ms. Length: 500-2,500 words. Pays 10-15¢/word. Sometimes pays the expenses of writers on assignment.

Photos: Send photos with submission. Reviews 35mm negatives and transparencies. Offers $10-250/photo. Identification of subjects required. Buys one-time and reprint rights.

Columns/Departments: Our Mother Ocean (environmental concerns to surfers), 1,000-1,500 words; Surf Stories (personal experiences of surfing), 1,000-1,500 words; Reviews (surf-related movies, books), 500-1,000 words; and Sections (humorous surf-related items with b&w photos), 100-500 words. Buys 25-50 mss/year. Send complete ms. Pays 10-15¢/word.

Fiction: Surf-related adventure, fantasy, horror, humorous, and science fiction. Buys 10 mss/year. Send complete ms. Length: 750-2,000 words. Pays 10-15¢/word.

Tips: "All sections are open to freelancers but interview/profiles are usually assigned. Stories must be authoritative and oriented to the hard-core surfer."

SWIM MAGAZINE, Sports Publications, Inc., Box 45497, Los Angeles CA 90045. (213)674-2120. Editor: Kim A. Hansen. 50% freelance written. Prefers to work with published/selected writers. Bimonthly magazine. "*Swim Magazine* is for adults interested in swimming for fun, fitness and competition. Readers are fitness-oriented adults from varied social and professional backgrounds who share swimming as part of their lifestyle. Readers' ages are evenly distributed from 25 to 90, so articles must appeal to a broad age group." Circ. 9,390. Pays approximately 1 month after publication. Publishes ms an average of 4 months after acceptance. Byline given. Submit seasonal/holiday material 4 months in advance. Simultaneous queries and photocopied submissions OK. Computer printout submissions OK; no dot-matrix. Reports in 1 month on queries; 3 months on mss. Sample copy for $2.50 prepaid and 9x12 SAE with 11 first class stamps. Free writer's guidelines.

Nonfiction: How-to (training plans and techniques); humor (sophisticated adult-oriented humor); interview/profile (people associated with fitness and competitive swimming); new product (articles describing new products for fitness and competitive training). "Articles need to be informative as well as interesting. In addition to fitness and health articles, we are interested in exploring fascinating topics dealing with swimming for the adult reader. Send complete ms. Length: 1,000-3,500 words. Pays $3/published column inch. "No payment for articles about personal experiences."

Photos: Send photos with ms. Offers no additional payment for photos accepted with ms. Captions, model releases, and identification of subjects required.

Tips: "Our how-to articles and physiology articles best typify *Swim Magazine*'s projected style for fitness and competitive swimmers. *Swim Magazine* will accept medical guideline and diet articles only by M.D.s and Ph.Ds."

UNDERCURRENT, Box 1658, Sausalito CA 94966. Managing Editor: Ben Davison. 20-50% freelance written. Works with a small number of new/unpublished writers each year. Monthly consumer-oriented *scuba diving newsletter*. Circ. 15,000. Pays on publication. Publishes ms an average of 2 months after acceptance. Buys first rights. Pays $50 kill fee. Byline given. Simultaneous (if to other than diving publisher), photocopied and previously published submissions OK. Computer printout submissions OK. Reports in 4-6 weeks. Free sample copy and writer's guidelines; mention *Writer's Market* in request.

Nonfiction: Equipment evaluation, how-to, general interest, new product and travel review. Buys 2 mss/issue. Query with brief outline of story idea and credentials. Will commission. Length: 2,000 words maximum. Pays 10-20¢/word. Sometimes pays the expenses of writers on assignment.

THE WATER SKIER, 799 Overlook Dr., Winter Haven FL 33884. (813)324-4341. Editor: Duke Cullimore. Official publication of the American Water Ski Association. 50% freelance written. Published monthly. Circ. 25,000. Buys North American serial rights. Byline given. Buys limited amount of freelance material. Query. Pays on acceptance. Publishes ms an average of 3 months after acceptance. Reports on submissions within 10 days. Computer printout submissions acceptable "if double-spaced and standard ms requirements are followed"; prefers letter-quality. Sample copy for 9x12 SAE and 4 first class stamps.
Nonfiction and Photos: Occasionally buys exceptionally offbeat, unusual text/photo features on the sport of water skiing. Emphasis on technique, methods, etc.
Tips: "Freelance writers should be aware of specialization of subject matter; need for more expertise in topic; more professional writing ability."

Teen and Young Adult

The publications in this category are for young people ages 13-19. Publications for college students are listed in Career, College and Alumni.

BREAD, Nazarene Publishing House, 6401 The Paseo, Kansas City MO 64131. (816)333-7000. Editor: Karen DeSollar. 20% freelance written. Works with a small number of new/unpublished writers each year. A monthly magazine for Nazarene teens. Circ. 26,000. Pays on acceptance. Publishes ms an average of 8 months after acceptance. Byline given. Buys one-time rights. Submit seasonal/holiday material 10 months in advance. Simultaneous, photocopied, and previously published submissions OK. Computer printout submissions acceptable; no dot-matrix. Reports in 6 weeks on queries; 2 months on mss. Sample copy and writer's guidelines for 9x12 SAE with 2 first class stamps.
Nonfiction: How-to and personal experience, both involving teens and teen problems and how to deal with them. Buys 25 mss/year. Send complete ms. Length: 1,200-1,500 words. Pays 3-3½¢/word.
Fiction: Adventure, humorous and romance, all demonstrating teens living out Christian commitment in real life.

CAMPUS LIFE MAGAZINE, Christianity Today, Inc., 465 Gundersen Dr., Carol Stream IL 60188. Senior Editor: Jim Long. Associate Editors: Chris Lutes and Diane Eble. Assistant Editor: Kris Bearss. 30-40% freelance written. Prefers to work with published/established writers. For a readership of young adults, high school and college age. "Though our readership is largely Christian, *Campus Life* reflects the interests of all young people—music, bicycling, photography, media and sports." Largely staff-written. "*Campus Life* is a Christian magazine that is *not* overtly religious. The indirect style is intended to create a safety zone with our readers and to reflect our philosophy that God is interested in all of life. Therefore, we publish message stories side by side with general interest, humor, etc." Monthly magazine. Circ. 180,000. Pays on acceptance. Publishes ms an average of 3-6 months after acceptance. Buys first serial and one-time rights. Byline given. Submit seasonal/holiday material 6 months in advance. Simultaneous, photocopied and previously published submissions OK. Query for electronic submissions. Computer printout submissions acceptable. Reports in 2 months. Sample copy for 9x12 SAE and $2; writer's guidelines for SASE.
Nonfiction: Personal experiences, photo features, unusual sports, humor, short items—how-to, college or career and travel, etc. *Query only.* Length: 500-3,000 words. Pays $100-300. Sometimes pays the expenses of writers on assignment.
Photos: Pays $50 minimum/8x10 b&w glossy print; $90 minimum/color transparency; $250/cover photo. Buys one-time rights.
Fiction: Stories about problems and experiences kids face. Trite, simplistic religious stories are not acceptable.
Tips: "The best ms for a freelancer to try to sell us would be a well-written first-person story (fiction or nonfiction) focusing on a common struggle young people face in any area of life—intellectual, emotional, social, physical or spiritual. Most manuscripts that miss us fail in quality or style. We are always looking for good humor pieces for high school readers. These could be cartoon spreads, or other creative humorous pieces that would make kids laugh."

CHRISTIAN LIVING FOR SENIOR HIGHS, David C. Cook Publishing Co., 850 N. Grove, Elgin IL 60120. (312)741-2400. Editor: Anne E. Dinnan. 75% freelance written. Prefers to work with published/established writers, and works with a small number of new/unpublished writers each year. Quarterly magazine. "A take-home paper used in senior high Sunday School classes. We encourage Christian teens to write to us." Pays on acceptance. Publishes ms an average of 15 months after acceptance. Buys all rights. Query for electronic submissions. Computer printout submissions acceptable; prefers letter-quality. Reports in 2-3 months. Sample copy and writer's guidelines for SASE.

Nonfiction: How-to (Sunday School youth projects); historical (with religious base); humor (from Christian perspective); inspirational and personality (nonpreachy); personal teen experience (Christian); poetry written by teens and photo feature (Christian subject). "Nothing not compatible with a Christian lifestyle." Submit complete ms. Length: 900-1,200 words. Pays $100; $40 for short pieces.

Fiction: Adventure (with religious theme); historical (with Christian perspective); humorous; and religious. Submit complete ms. Length: 900-1,200 words. Pays $100. "No preachy experiences."

Photos: Gail Russell, photo editor. Photos purchased with or without accompanying ms or on assignment. Send contact sheets, prints or transparencies. Pays $25-40 for 8½x11 b&w photos; $50 minimum for color transparencies. "Photo guidelines available."

Tips: "Our demand for manuscripts should increase, but most of these will probably be assigned rather than bought over-the-transom. Our features are always short. A frequent mistake made by writers in completing articles for us is misunderstanding our market. Writing is often not Christian at all, or it's too 'Christian,' i.e. pedantic, condescending and moralistic."

‡CLASS ACT, Harvard Publishing Co. Ltd., 2-1835 Sargent Ave., Winnipeg, Manitoba Canada R3H 0E2. (204)783-2681. Editor: Guy R. Rochom. 50% freelance written. Monthly tabloid for a teen audience. "Editorial content aimed at enlightening teens on a number of topics concerning their peers." Circ. 15,000. Pays on publication. Byline given. Offers 10% kill fee. Buys first North American serial rights, second or simultaneous rights. Submit seasonal/holiday material 4 months in advance. Simultaneous, photocopied and previously published submissions OK. Query for electronic submissions. Computer printout submissions OK; prefers letter-quality. Reports in 3 months on queries. Sample copy for 9x12 SAE with 1 first class stamp. Free writer's guidelines.

Nonfiction: Book excerpts, expose, general interest, humor, inspirational, interview/profile, new product, personal experience, photo feature, religious, technical, travel, entertainment and education. Buys 30 mss/year. Query with published clips. Length: 250-800 words. Pays 5¢/word.

Photos: Send photos with submission. Reviews contact sheets. Offers $10 per photo. Captions, model releases and identification of subjects required. Buys one-time rights.

Columns/Departments: What's New (new products, merchandise aimed at teens); fashion (new trends); and Education (schools abroad), all 500 words.

Fillers: Facts and newsbreaks. Buys 24/year. Length: 200-300 words. Pays 5¢/word.

EXPLORING MAGAZINE, Boy Scouts of America, 1325 Walnut Hill Ln., Box 152079, Irving TX 75015-2079. (214)580-2365. FAX: (214)580-2502. Executive Editor: Scott Daniels. 85% freelance written. Prefers to work with published/established writers; works with a small number of new/unpublished writers each year. Magazine published 4 times/year—January, March, May, September. Covers the educational teen-age Exploring program of the BSA. Circ. 400,000. Pays on acceptance. Publishes ms an average of 6 months after acceptance. Byline given. Buys one-time and first rights. Submit seasonal/holiday material 6 months in advance. Simultaneous queries OK. Computer printout submissions acceptable; prefers letter-quality. Reports in 2 weeks. Sample copy for 9x12 SAE and 4 first class stamps; writer's guidelines for #10 SASE. Write for guidelines and "What is Exploring?" fact sheet.

Nonfiction: General interest, how-to (achieve outdoor skills, organize trips, meetings, etc.); interview/profile (of outstanding Explorer); travel (backpacking or canoeing with Explorers). Buys 15-20 mss/year. Query with clips. Length: 800-1,800 words. Pays $300-450. Pays expenses of writers on assignment.

Photos: Brian Payne, photo editor. State availability of photos with query letter or ms. Reviews b&w contact sheets and 35mm color transparencies. Captions required. Buys one-time rights.

Tips: "Contact the local Exploring Director in your area (listed in phone book white pages under Boy Scouts of America). Find out if there are some outstanding post activities going on and then query magazine editor in Irving, Texas. Strive for shorter texts, faster starts and stories that lend themselves to dramatic photographs."

FREEWAY, Box 632, Glen Ellyn IL 60138. Editor: Billie Sue Thompson. For "young Christian adults of high school and college age." 80% freelance written. Works with a small number of new/unpublished writers each year; eager to work with new/unpublished writers. Weekly. Circ. 50,000. Prefers first serial rights but buys some reprints. Purchases 100 mss/year. Byline given. Reports on material accepted for publication in 2 months. Publishes ms an average of 1 year after acceptance. Returns rejected material in 2 months. Computer printout submissions acceptable; prefers letter-quality. Free sample copy and writer's guidelines.

Nonfiction: "*FreeWay*'s greatest need is for personal experience stories showing how God has worked in teens' lives. Stories are best written in first-person, 'as told to' author. Incorporate specific details, anecdotes, and dialogue. Show, don't tell, how the subject thought and felt. Weave spiritual conflicts and prayers into entire manuscript; avoid tacked-on sermons and morals. Stories should show how God has helped the person resolve a problem or how God helped save a person from trying circumstances (1,000 words or less). Avoid stories about accident and illness; focus on events and emotions of everyday life. (Examples: How I overcame shyness; confessions of a food addict.) Short-short stories are needed as fillers. We also need self-help or how-to articles with practical Christian advice on daily living, and trend articles addressing secular fads from a Christian perspective. We do not use devotional material, poetry, or fictionalized Bible stories." Pays 4-7¢/word. Sometimes pays the expenses of writers on assignment.

Photos: Whenever possible, provide clear 8x10 or 5x7 b&w photos to accompany mss (or any other available photos). Payment is $5-30.

Fiction: "We use little fiction, unless it is allegory, parables, or humor."

Tips: "Study our 'Tips to Writers' pamphlet and sample copy, then query or send complete ms. In your cover letter, include information about who you are, writing qualifications, and experience working with teens. Include SASE."

GUIDE MAGAZINE, 55 W. Oak Ridge Dr., Hagerstown MD 21740. Editor: Jeannette Johnson. 90% freelance written. Works with a small number of new/unpublished writers each year. A journal for junior youth and early teens. "Its content reflects Christian beliefs and standards. Another characteristic which probably distinguishes it from many other magazines is the fact that all its stories are nonfiction." Weekly magazine. Circ. 50,000. Buys first serial rights, simultaneous rights, and second serial (reprint) rights to material originally published elsewhere. Pays on acceptance. Publishes ms an average of 6-9 months after acceptance. Byline given. Submit seasonal/holiday material 6 months in advance. Query for electronic submissions. Computer printout submissions acceptable; no dot-matrix. Reports in 3 weeks. Free sample copy.

Nonfiction: Wants nonfiction stories of character-building and spiritual value. All stories must be true and include dialogue. Should emphasize the positive aspects of living, obedience to parents, perseverance, kindness, etc. "We use a number of stories dealing with problems common to today's Christian youth, such as peer pressure, parents' divorce, chemical dependency, etc. We can always use 'drama in real life' stories that show God's protection and seasonal stories—Christmas, Thanksgiving, special holidays. We do not use stories of hunting, fishing, trapping or spiritualism." Buys about 300 mss/year. Send complete ms (include word count and Social Security number). Length: up to 1,600 words. Pays 3-4¢/word. Also buys serialized true stories. (Inquire first.) Length: 10 chapters.

Tips: "Typical topics we cover in a yearly cycle include choices (music, clothes, friends, diet); friend-making skills; school problems (cheating, peer pressure, new school); death; finding and keeping a job; sibling relationships; divorce; step-families; runaways/throwaways; drugs; communication; and suicide. Write for our story schedule. We often buy short fillers, and an author who does not fully understand our needs is more likely to sell with a short-short. Our target age is 10-14. Our most successful writers are those who present stories from the viewpoint of a young teen-ager. Stories that sound like an adult's sentiments passing through a young person's lips are *not* what we're looking for. Use believable dialogue."

IN TOUCH, Wesley Press, Box 50434, Indianapolis IN 46250-0434. Editor: Rebecca Higgins. 80% freelance written. Eager to work with new/unpublished writers—"quality writing a must, however." A weekly Christian teen magazine. Circ. 25,000. Pays on acceptance. Publishes ms an average of 6-18 months after acceptance. Byline given. Offers 30% kill fee. Not copyrighted. Buys first rights or second serial (reprint) rights. Submit seasonal/holiday material 10 months in advance. Simultaneous and previously published submissions OK. Computer printout submissions acceptable; prefers letter-quality. Reports in 2 months on manuscripts. Sample copy for 9x12 SAE with 45¢ postage. Writer's guidelines for #10 SASE.

Nonfiction: Book excerpts, essays, how-to, humor, interview/profile, opinion, personal experience, photo feature from Christian perspective. "Our articles are teaching-oriented and contain lots of humor." Also needs true experiences told in fiction style, humorous fiction and allegories. No Sunday "soap." Buys 100 mss/year. Send complete ms. Length: 500-1,000 words. Pays $15-45.

Photos: Send photos with submissions. Pays $15-40/photo. Buys one-time rights.

KEYNOTER, Key Club International, 3636 Woodview Trace, Indianapolis IN 46268. (317)875-8755, ext. 172. Executive Editor: Jack Brockley. 65% freelance written. Works with a small number of new/unpublished writers each year, and is eager to work with new/unpublished writers willing to adjust their writing styles to *Keynoter*'s needs. A youth magazine published monthly Oct.-May (Dec./Jan. combined issue), distributed to members of Key Club International, a high school service organization for young men and women. Circ. 120,000. Pays on acceptance. Publishes ms an average of 5 months after acceptance. Byline given. Buys first North American serial rights. Submit seasonal/holiday material 7 months in advance. Simultaneous queries and submissions (if advised), photocopied and previously published submissions OK. Computer printout

ALWAYS submit unsolicited manuscripts or queries with a self-addressed, stamped envelope (SASE) within your country or International Reply Coupons (IRC) purchased from the post office for other countries.

submissions acceptable; prefers letter-quality. Reports in 1 month. Sample copy for 9x12 SAE and 3 first class stamps; writer's guidelines for #10 SASE.

Nonfiction: Book excerpts (may be included in articles but are not accepted alone); general interest (must be geared for intelligent teen audience); historical/nostalgic (generally not accepted); how-to (if it offers advice on how teens can enhance the quality of lives or communities); humor (accepted very infrequently; if adds to story, OK); interview/profile (rarely purchased, "would have to be on/with an irresistible subject"); new product (only if affects teens); photo feature (if subject is right, might consider); technical (if understandable and interesting to teen audience); travel (sometimes OK, but must apply to club travel schedule); subjects that entertain and inform teens on topics that relate directly to their lives. "We would also like to receive self-help and school-related nonfiction on leadership, community service, and teen issues. Please, no first-person confessions, no articles that are written down to our teen readers." Buys 10-15 mss/year. Query. Length: 1,500-2,500 words. Pays $125-250. Sometimes pays the expenses of writers on assignment.

Photos: State availability of photos. Reviews b&w contact sheets and negatives. Identification of subjects required. Buys one-time rights. Payment for photos included in payment for ms.

Tips: "We want to see articles written with attention to style and detail that will enrich the world of teens. Articles must be thoroughly researched and must draw on interviews with nationally and internationally respected sources. Our readers are 13-18, mature and dedicated to community service. We are very committed to working with good writers, and if we see something we like in a well-written query, we'll try to work it through to publication."

THE MAGAZINE FOR CHRISTIAN YOUTH! The United Methodist Publishing House, 201 Eighth Ave. S., Box 801, Nashville TN 37202. (615)749-6463. FAX: (615)749-6078 or 749-6079. Editor: Christopher B. Hughes. Monthly magazine. Circ. 40,000. Pays on acceptance. Publishes ms an average of 9 months after acceptance. Byline given. Buys one-time and all rights. Submit seasonal/holiday material 1 year in advance. Photocopied and previously published submissions OK. Computer printout submissions OK. Sample copy for 9x12 SAE with $1.25 postage. Writer's guidelines for SASE.

Nonfiction: Book excerpts; general interest; how-to (deal with problems teens have); humor (on issues that touch teens' lives); inspirational; interview/profile (well-known singers, musicians, actors, sports); personal experience; religious and travel (include teen culture of another country). Buys 5-10 mss/year. Queries welcome. Length: 700-2,000 words. Pays $80-110 for assigned articles; 4¢/word for unsolicited articles. Pays expenses of writers on assignment. "Writers should give indication before expenses happen."

Photos: State availability of photos with submission. Reviews transparencies and 8x10 prints. Offers $25-150/photo. Captions and model releases required. Buys one-time rights.

Fiction: Adventure, ethnic, fantasy, historical, humorous, mainstream, mystery, religious, romance, science fiction, suspense and western. No stories where the plot is too trite and predictable—or too preachy. Buys 15 mss/year. Send complete ms. Length: 700-2,000 words. Pays 4¢/word.

Poetry: Free verse, haiku, light verse and traditional. Buys 6-8 poems/year. Submit maximum of 5 poems at one time. Pays $10-100.

Fillers: Gags to be illustrated by cartoonists and short humor. Buys 6-8/year. Length: 10-75 words. Pays $15-80.

Tips: "Stay current with the youth culture so that your writing will reflect an insight into where teenagers are. Be neat, and always proofread and edit your own copy. Use faith language in a natural manner."

PIONEER, Baptist Brotherhood Commission, 1548 Poplar Ave., Memphis TN 38104. (901)272-2461. Editor-in-Chief: Timothy D. Bearden. 5% freelance written. For "boys age 12-14 who are members of a missions organization in Southern Baptist churches." Monthly magazine. Circ. 35,000. Byline given. Pays on acceptance. Publishes ms an average of 6-8 months after acceptance. Buys simultaneous rights. Submit seasonal/holiday material 8 months in advance. Simultaneous submissions OK. Computer printout submissions acceptable; prefers letter-quality. Reports in 1 month. Sample copy and writer's guidelines for 8½x11 SAE with $1.20 postage; writer's guidelines only for #10 SASE.

Nonfiction: How-to (crafts, hobbies); informational (youth, religious especially); inspirational (sports/entertainment personalities); photo feature (sports, teen subjects). No "preachy" articles, fiction or excessive dialogue. Submit complete ms. Length: 500-1,500 words. Pays $20-50.

Photos: Purchased with accompanying ms or on assignment. Captions required. Query. Pays $10 for 8x10 b&w glossy prints.

Tips: "The writer has a better chance of breaking in at our publication with short articles and fillers. Most topics are set years in advance. Regulars and fun articles are current. The most frequent mistake made by writers is sending us preachy articles. They don't read the guide carefully. Aim for the mid-teen instead of younger teen."

PURPLE COW Newspaper for Teens, Suite 320, 3423 Piedmont Rd. NE, Atlanta GA 30305. (404)239-0642. FAX: (404)261-2214. Editor: Todd Daniel. 5% freelance written. Works with a small number of new/unpublished writers each year. A monthly tabloid circulated to Atlanta area high schools. Circ. 59,000. Pays on publication. Buys one-time rights. "Manuscripts are accepted on a 'space-available' basis. If space becomes available, we publish the manuscript under consideration 1-12 months after receiving." Byline given. Submit seasonal/holiday material 2 months in advance. Simultaneous queries, photocopied, and previously published submissions OK. Computer printout submissions acceptable; prefers letter-quality. Sample copy for $1 with 9x12 SAE and 2 first class stamps; writer's guidelines for #10 SASE.

Nonfiction: General interest, how-to, humor and anything of interest to teenagers. Especially looking for college and work/career related stories. No opinion or anything which talks down to teens. No fiction. Buys 7-10 mss/year. Send complete ms. Length: 1,000 words maximum. Pays $10-25.

Cartoons and Photos: Must be humorous, teen-related, up-to-date with good illustrations. Buys 10/year. Send photos with ms. Buys one-time rights. Pays $5.

Tips: "A freelancer can best break in to our publication with articles which help teens. Examples might be how to secure financial aid for college or how to survive your freshman year of college."

SCHOLASTIC SCOPE, Scholastic Magazines, Inc., 730 Broadway, New York NY 10003. Editor: Fran Claro. 5% freelance written. Works with a small number of new/unpublished writers each year. Weekly. 4-6th grade reading level; 15-18 age level. Circ. 800,000. Publishes ms an average of 8 months after acceptance. Buys all rights. Byline given. Computer printout submissions acceptable; no dot-matrix. Reports in 6 weeks. Sample copy for 10x14 SAE with $1.75 postage.

Nonfiction and Photos: Articles with photos about teenagers who have accomplished something against great odds, overcome obstacles, performed heroically, or simply have done something out of the ordinary. Prefers articles about people outside New York area. Length: 400-1,200 words. Pays $125 and up.

Fiction and Drama: Problems of contemporary teenagers (drugs, prejudice, runaways, failure in school, family problems, etc.); relationships between people (interracial, adult-teenage, employer-employee, etc.) in family, job, and school situations. Strive for directness, realism, and action, perhaps carried through dialogue rather than exposition. Try for depth of characterization in at least one character. Avoid too many coincidences and random happenings. Although action stories are wanted, it's not a market for crime fiction. Occasionally uses mysteries and science fiction. Length: 400-1,200 words. Uses plays up to 15,000 words. Pays $150 minimum.

SEVENTEEN, 850 3rd Ave., New York NY 10022. Editor-in-Chief: Midge Turk Richardson. Managing Editor: Mary Anne Baumgold. 80% freelance written. Works with a small number of new/unpublished writers each year. Monthly. Circ. 1.9 million. Buys one-time rights for nonfiction and fiction by adult writers and work by teenagers. Pays 25% kill fee. Pays on acceptance. Publishes ms an average of 6 months after acceptance. Byline given. Computer printout submissions acceptable; prefers letter-quality. Reports in 6 weeks.

Nonfiction: Roberta Anne Myers, articles editor. Articles and features of general interest to young women who are concerned with the development of their own lives and the problems of the world around them; strong emphasis on topicality and helpfulness. Send brief outline and query, including a typical lead paragraph, summing up basic idea of article. Also like to receive articles and features on speculation. Query with tearsheets or copies of published articles. Length: 1,200-2,000 words. Pays $50-150 for articles written by teenagers but more to established adult freelancers. Articles are commissioned after outlines are submitted and approved. Fees for commissioned articles generally range from $650-1,500. Sometimes pays the expenses of writers on assignment.

Photos: Kay Spear Gibson, art director. Photos usually by assignment only.

Fiction: Adrian LeBlanc, fiction editor. Thoughtful, well-written stories on subjects of interest to young women between the ages of 12 and 20. Avoid formula stories—"My sainted Granny," "My crush on Brad," etc.—heavy moralizing, condescension of any sort. Humorous stories and mysteries are welcomed. Best lengths are 1,000-3,000 words. Pays $500-1,000.

Poetry: Contact teen features editor. By teenagers only. Pays $15. Submissions are nonreturnable unless accompanied by SASE.

Tips: "Writers have to ask themselves whether or not they feel they can find the right tone for a *Seventeen* article—a tone which is empathetic yet never patronizing; lively yet not superficial. Not all writers feel comfortable with, understand or like teenagers. If you don't like them, *Seventeen* is the wrong market for you. The best way for beginning teenage writers to crack the *Seventeen* lineup is for them to contribute suggestions and short pieces to the New Voices and Views section, a literary format which lends itself to just about every kind of writing: profiles, essays, exposes, reportage, and book reviews."

STRAIGHT, Standard Publishing Co., 8121 Hamilton Ave., Cincinnati OH 45231. (513)931-4050. Editor: Carla J. Crane. 90% freelance written. "Teens, age 13-19, from Christian backgrounds generally receive this publication in their Sunday School classes or through subscriptions." Weekly (published quarterly) magazine. Pays on acceptance. Publishes ms an average of 1 year after acceptance. Buys first rights, second serial (reprint) rights or simultaneous rights. Byline given. Submit seasonal/holiday material 1 year in advance. Reports in 6 weeks. Computer printout submissions acceptable. Include Social Security number on ms. Free sample copy; writer's guidelines with #10 SASE and 2 first class stamps.

Nonfiction: Religious-oriented topics, teen interest (school, church, family, dating, sports, part-time jobs), humor, inspirational, personal experience. "We want articles that promote Christian values and ideals." No puzzles. Query or submit complete ms. "We're buying more short pieces these days; 12 pages fill up much too quickly." Length: 800-1,500 words.

Fiction: Adventure, humorous, religious and suspense. "All fiction should have some message for the modern Christian teen." Fiction should deal with all subjects in a forthright manner, without being preachy and without talking down to teens. No tasteless manuscripts that promote anything adverse to the Bible's teachings. Submit complete ms. Length: 1,000-1,500 words. Pays 2-3½¢/word; less for reprints.

Photos: May submit photos with ms. Pays $20-25 for 8x10 b&w glossy prints and $100 for color slides. Model releases should be available. Buys one-time rights.

Tips: "Don't be trite. Use unusual settings or problems. Use a lot of illustrations, a good balance of conversation, narration, and action. Style must be clear, fresh—no sermonettes or sickly-sweet fiction. Take a realistic approach to problems. Be willing to submit to editorial policies on doctrine; knowledge of the *Bible* a must. Also, be aware of teens today, and what they do. Language, clothing, and activities included in mss should be contemporary. We are becoming more and more selective about freelance material and the competition seems to be stiffer all the time."

'TEEN MAGAZINE, 8490 Sunset Blvd., Hollywood CA 90069. Editor: Roxanne Camron. 20-30% freelance written. Prefers to work with published/established writers. For teenage girls. Monthly magazine. Circ. 1 million. Publishes ms an average of 6 months after acceptance. Buys all rights. Reports in 4 months. Computer printout submissions acceptable; prefers no dot-matrix. Sample copy and writer's guidelines for 8½x11 SAE and $2.50.

Fiction: Dealing specifically with teenage girls and contemporary teen issues. More fiction on emerging alternatives for young women. Suspense, humorous and romance. "Young love is all right, but teens want to read about it in more relevant settings." Length: 2,500-4,000 words. Pays $100. Sometimes pays the expenses of writers on assignment.

Tips: "No fiction with explicit language, casual references to drugs, alcohol, sex, or smoking; no fiction with too depressing outcome."

TEENAGE, The Magazine for Christian Young People, Thom Schultz Publications, 2890 N. Monroe, Box 481, Loveland CO 80539. Editorial Director: Joani Schultz. 80% freelance written. Prefers to work with published/established writers; works with small number of new/unpublished writers each year. Magazine published 10 times/year. For members of high-school-age Christian youth groups. Circ. 30,000. Pays on acceptance. Publishes ms an average of 4 months after acceptance. Byline given. Buys all rights. Submit seasonal/holiday material 6 months in advance. Computer printout submissions acceptable; prefers letter-quality. Special Easter, Thanksgiving and Christmas issues and college issues. Reports in 1 month. Sample copy and writer's guidelines for $1 and 9x12 SAE with 2 first class stamps.

Nonfiction: Contact: Jolene L. Roehlkepartain. Humor, interview/profile, opinion, personal experience, religion, current fads, trends and teen culture. Length: 500-1,000. Pays $25-100 for articles. Buys 30 mss/year. Query. Length: 500-1,000 words. Pays up to $100. Sometimes pays expenses of writers on assignment.

Photos: State availability of photos with submissions. Reviews contact sheets, transparencies, 35mm slides and 8x10 prints. Offers $25-150 per b&w photo. Model releases required. Buys one-time rights.

TEENS TODAY, Church of the Nazarene, 6401 The Paseo, Kansas City MO 64131. (816)333-7000. Editor: Karen De Sollar. 25% freelance written. Eager to work with new/unpublished writers. For junior and senior high teens, to age 18, attending Church of the Nazarene Sunday School. Weekly magazine. Circ. 55,000. Pays on acceptance. Publishes ms an average of 8 months after acceptance. Byline given. Buys first rights and second rights. Submit seasonal/holiday material 10 months in advance. Simultaneous, photocopied and previously published submissions OK. Computer printout submissions acceptable; no dot-matrix. Reports in 2 months. Sample copy and writer's guidelines for 9x12 SAE with 2 first class stamps.

Photos: Pays $10-30 for 8x10 b&w glossy prints.

Fiction: Adventure (if Christian principles are apparent); humorous; religious; and romance (keep it clean). Buys 1 ms/issue. Send complete ms. Length: 1,200-1,500 words. Pays 3½¢/word, first rights; 3¢/word, second rights.

Poetry: "We accept poetry written by teens—no outside poetry accepted." Buys 50 poems/year.

Tips: "We're looking for quality fiction dealing with teen issues: peers, self, parents, vocation, Christian truths related to life, etc."

TIGER BEAT MAGAZINE, D.S. Magazines, Inc., 1086 Teaneck Road, Teaneck NJ 07666. (201)833-1800. Editors: Tom Arndt and Janice Loprieno. 10% freelance written. For teenage girls ages 11 to 16. Monthly magazine. Circ. 400,000. Pays on publication. Publishes ms an average of 3 months after acceptance. Buys all rights. Buys 50 manuscripts per year. Query for electronic submissions. Computer printout submissions acceptable; no dot-matrix.

Nonfiction: Stories about young entertainers; their lives, what they do, their interests. Also service-type, self-help articles. Quality writing expected, but must be written with the 14-18 age group in mind. "Skill, style, ideas, and exclusivity are important to *Tiger Beat*. If a writer has a fresh, fun idea, or access to something staffers don't have, he or she has a good chance." Length: 100-750 words depending on the topic. Pays $50-100. Send query. Sometimes pays the expenses of writers on assignment. Also seeks good teenage fiction, with an emphasis on entertainment and romance.

Photos: Pays $25 for b&w photos used with mss; captions optional. Pays $50-75 for color used inside; $75 for cover. 35mm transparencies preferred.

Tips: "A freelancer's best bet is to come up with something original and exclusive that the staff couldn't do or get. Writing should be aimed at a 17- or 18-year-old intelligence level. Trends in magazine publishing that freelance writers should be aware of include shorter articles, segmenting of markets, and much less 'I' journalism. The most frequent mistake made by writers in completing an article for us is a patronizing attitude toward teens or an emphasis on historical aspects of subject matter. Don't talk down to young readers; they sense it readily."

TIGER BEAT STAR, D.S. Magazines, Inc., 1086 Teaneck Rd., Teaneck NJ 07666. (201)833-1800. FAX: (201)833-1428. Editor: Louise A. Barile. 25% freelance written. Works with a small number of new/unpublished writers each year. Monthly fan magazine for young teens interested in movie, TV and recording stars. Circ. 400,000. Average issue includes 20 feature interviews and 2 or 3 gossip columns. "We have to take each article and examine its worth individually—who's popular this month, how it is written, etc. But we prefer shorter articles most of the time." Pays upon publication. Publishes ms an average of 1 month after acceptance. Byline given. Buys all rights. Submit seasonal material 10 weeks in advance. Previously published submissions discouraged. Computer printout submissions acceptable; no dot-matrix. Reports in 2 weeks.

Nonfiction: Interview (of movie, TV and recording stars). Buys 1-2 mss/issue. Query with clips of previously published work. "Write a good query indicating your contact with the star. Pieces which explore the personal life of a celebrity, with strong teen appeal, are highly desirable. Also willing to purchase transcripts of celebrity interviews." Length: 200-400 words. Pays $50-200.

Photos: State availability of photos. Pays $25 minimum for 5x7 and 8x10 b&w glossy prints. Pays $75 minimum for 35mm and 2¼ color transparencies. Captions and model releases required. Buys all rights.

Tips: "Be aware of our readership (teenage girls, generally ages 9-17); be 'up' on the current TV, movie and music stars; and be aware of our magazine's unique writing style. We are looking for articles that are clearly and intelligently written, factual and fun. Don't talk down to the reader, simply because they are teenaged. We want to give the readers information they can't find elsewhere. Keep in mind that readers are young."

TQ (TEEN QUEST), The Good News Broadcasting Association, Inc., Box 82808, Lincoln NE 68501. (402)474-4567. Editor-in-Chief: Warren Wiersbe. Managing Editor: Barbara Comito. 50% freelance written. Works with a small number of new/unpublished writers each year. Monthly magazine emphasizing Christian living for Protestant church-oriented teens, ages 12-17. Circ. 80,000. Buys first serial rights or second serial (reprint) rights. Publishes ms an average of 8 months after acceptance. Byline given. Submit seasonal/holiday material 1 year in advance. Previously published submissions OK. Computer printout submissions acceptable; prefers letter-quality. Reports in 2 months. Sample copy and writer's guidelines for 9x12 SAE with 4 first class stamps.

Nonfiction: Interviews with Christian sports personalities and features on teens making unusual achievements or involved in unique pursuits—spiritual emphasis a must. "Articles on issues of particular importance to teens—drugs, pregnancy, school, jobs, recreational activities, etc. Christian element not necessary on morally neutral issues." Buys 1-3 mss/issue. Query or send complete ms. No phone queries. Length: 500-1,800 words. Pays 4-7¢/word for unsolicited mss; 7-10¢ for assigned articles. Sometimes pays expenses of writers on assignment.

Fiction: Needs stories involving problems common to teens (dating, family, alcohol and drugs, peer pressure, school, sex, talking about one's faith to non-believers, standing up for convictions, etc.) in which the resolution (or lack of it) is true to our readers' experiences. "In other words, no happily-ever-after endings, last-page spiritual conversions, or pat answers to complex problems. We are interested in the everyday (though still profound) experiences of teen life. If the story was written just to make a point, or grind the author's favorite axe, we don't want it. Most of our stories feature a protagonist 14-17 years old. The key is the spiritual element—how the protagonist deals with or makes sense of his/her situation in light of Christian spiritual principles and ideals, without being preached to or preaching to another character or to the reader." Buys 30 mss/year. Send complete ms. Length: 800-1,800 words. Pays 4-7¢/word for unsolicited mss; 7-10¢/word for assigned fiction.

Fillers: Short puzzles on Biblical themes. Send complete mss. Pays $3-10.

Tips: "Articles for *TQ* need to be written in an upbeat style attractive to teens. No preaching. Writers must be familiar with the characteristics of today's teenagers in order to write for them."

‡WITH MAGAZINE, Faith and Life Press and Mennonite Publishing House, 722 Main St., Box 347, Newton KS 67114. (316)283-5100. Editor: Susan Janzen. 30% freelance written. Monthly magazine for teenagers. "We approach Christianity from an Anabaptist-Mennonite perspective. Our purpose is to disciple youth within congregations." Circ. 6,500. Pays on acceptance. Byline given. Buys one-time rights. Submit seasonal/holiday material 6 months in advance. Simultaneous, photocopied and previously published submissions OK. Query for electronic submissions. Computer printout submissions OK; prefers letter-quality. Reports in 6 weeks on queries; 3 months on mss. Sample copy $1.25 with 9x12 SAE and 85¢ postage. Writer's guidelines for #10 SASE.

Nonfiction: Humor, personal experience, religious, youth. "No articles which use religion as a utopian response to conflict." Buys 10 mss/year. Send complete ms. Length: 900-1,500 words. Pays $36-60 for assigned articles; $18-60 for unsolicited articles.

Photos: Sometimes pays the expenses of writers on assignment. Send photos with submission. Reviews 8x10 prints. Offers $10-50 per photo. Identification of subjects required. Buys one-time rights.

Fiction: Humorous, religious, youth. Buys 30 mss/year. Send complete ms. Length: 900-1,500 words. Pays $18-60.

Poetry: Avant-garde, free verse, haiku, light verse, traditional. Buys 30-49 poems. Pays $10-50.

Tips: "Introduce yourself briefly in a cover letter, but don't overdo it. Flowery resumes and pages of credits mean less to me than a well-written story. Fiction is most open to freelancers. When writing for teens, avoid being preachy or talking down to them. Use anecdotes with which they can identify and avoid using jargon which is out of date quickly."

YOUNG SALVATIONIST, The Salvation Army, 799 Bloomfield Ave., Verona NJ 07044. (201)239-0606. Editor: Capt. Robert R. Hostetler. 75% freelance written. Works with a small number of new/unpublished writers each year. Monthly Christian magazine for high school teens. "Only material with a definite Christian emphasis or from a Christian perspective will be considered." Circ. 48,000. Pays on acceptance. Publishes ms an average of 10 months after acceptance. Byline given. Buys first North American serial rights, first rights, one-time rights or second serial (reprint) rights. Submit seasonal/holiday material 6 months in advance. Computer printout submissions acceptable; prefers letter-quality. Reports in 2 weeks on queries; 1 month on mss. Sample copy for 8½x11 SAE with 3 first class stamps; writer's guidelines for #10 SASE.

Nonfiction: Inspirational, how-to (Bible study, workshop skills), humor, interview/profile, personal experience, photo feature, religious. "Articles should deal with issues of relevance to teens today; avoid 'preachiness' or moralizing." Buys 40 mss/year. Send complete ms. "State whether your submission is for Young Salvationist or The Young Soldier section." Length: 500-1,200 words. Pays 3-4¢/word for unsolicited mss; 5¢/word for assigned articles.

Columns/Departments: Currents (media-related news and human interest from a Christian perspective, book and record reviews). Buys 10-12 mss/year. Send complete ms. Length: 50-200 words. Pays 3-5¢/word.

Fiction: Adventure, fantasy, humorous, religious, romance, science fiction—all from a Christian perspective. Length: 500-1,200 words. Pays 3-5¢/word.

Tips: "Study magazine, familiarize yourself with the unique 'Salvationist' perspective of *Young Salvationist*; learn a little about the Salvation Army; media, sports, sex and dating are strongest appeal."

YOUTH UPDATE, St. Anthony Messenger Press, 1615 Republic St., Cincinnati OH 45210. (513)241-5615. Editor: Carol Ann Morrow. 90% freelance written. Monthly newsletter of faith life for teenagers. Designed to attract, instruct, guide and challenge Catholics of high school age by applying the Gospel to modern problems/situations. Circ. 38,000. Pays when ready to print. Publishes ms an average of 6 months after acceptance. Byline given. Reports in 8 weeks. Sample copy and writer's guidelines for #10 SASE.

Nonfiction: Inspirational, practical self-help and spiritual. Buys 12 mss/year. Query. Length: 2,200-2,300 words. Pays $350. Sometimes pays expenses of writers on assignment.

Travel, Camping and Trailer

Travel agencies and tour companies constantly remind consumers of the joys of traveling. But it's usually the travel magazines that tell potential travelers about the negative as well as positive aspects of potential destinations. Publications in this category tell tourists and campers the where-tos and how-tos of travel. This category is extremely competitive, demanding quality writing, background information and professional photography. All have their own slants and should be studied carefully before sending submissions. Publications that buy how-to camping and travel material with a conservation angle are listed in the Nature, Conservation and Ecology section.

‡**AAA GOING PLACES, Magazine for Today's Traveler**, AAA Florida/Georgia, 1515 No. Westshore Blvd., Tampa FL 33615. (813)289-5923. Editor: Phyllis Zeno. Managing Editor: Janeen Andrews. 50% freelance written. Bimonthly magazine on auto news, driving trips or tips and travel. Circ. 760,000. Pays on publication. Publishes ms an average of 3-6 months after acceptance. Byline given. Buys one-time rights. Submit seasonal/ holiday material 9 months in advance. Simultaneous submissions OK. Computer printout submissions OK; prefers letter-quality. Reports in 2 months. Sample copy for 8x10 SAE with $1 postage. Free writer's guide-lines.

Nonfiction: Historical/nostalgic, how-to, humor, interview/profile, personal experience, photo feature, travel. Special issues include Cruise Guide and Europe Issue. Buys 15 mss/year. Send complete ms. Length: 500-1,500 words. Pays $15 per printed page.

Photos: State availability of photos with submission. Reviews 2x2 transparencies. Offers no additional payment for photos accepted with ms. Captions required.

Columns/Departments: AAAway We Go (local attractions in Florida or Georgia. Bed, breakfast places in Florida or Georgia). Buys 10 ms/year. Send complete ms. Length: 100-200 words. Pays $5.

Poetry: Light verse. "Not interested unless light travel verse." Buys 4 poems/year. Submit maximum 10 poems.

Fillers: Gags to be illustrated by cartoonist, short humor. Buys 6/year. Pays $15 per page printed.

AAA WORLD, Hawaii/Alaska, AAA Hawaii, 590 Queen St., Honolulu HI 96813. (808)528-2600. Editor: Mark Davisson. 80% freelance written. Prefers to work with published/established writers. Bimonthly magazine of travel, automotive safety and legislative issues. Orientation is toward stories that benefit members in some way. Circ. 30,000. Pays on publication. Publishes ms an average of 6-8 months after acceptance. Byline given. Buys one-time rights. Submit seasonal/holiday material 6 months in advance. Photocopied and previously published submissions OK. Query for electronic submissions. Computer printout submissions acceptable. Reports in 1 week on queries; 4 months on mss. Free sample copy.

Nonfiction: How-to (auto maintenance, safety, etc.); and travel (tips, destinations, bargains). Buys 6 mss/ year. Send complete ms. Length: 1,000 words. Pays $100 maximum. Sometimes pays the expenses of writers on assignment.

Photos: State availability of photos. Reviews b&w contact sheet. Pays $10-25. Captions required. Buys one-time rights.

Tips: "Find an interesting, human interest story that affects AAA Hawaii or Alaska members."

‡**ADVENTURE ROAD**, Condé Nast Publications, 360 Madison Ave., 10th Fl., New York NY 10017. (212)880-2282. Editor: Marilyn Holstein. 100% freelance written. Bimonthly magazine that features domestic, general interest travel articles that stimulate reader to travel. Circ. 1.5 million. Pays on acceptance. Publishes ms an average of 4 months after acceptance. Byline given. Offers 25% kill fee. Buys first North American serial rights. Simultaneous, photocopied and previously published submissions OK. Computer printout submissions OK. Sample for 9x12 SAE. Writer's guidelines for letter SAE.

Nonfiction: Travel. "No 1st person articles." Buys 21 mss/year. Query with published clips. Length: 800-1,800 words. Pays $300-750. Sometimes pays expenses of writers on assignment.

Photos: State availability of photos with submission. (Do not send unsolicited transparencies). Offers $200 minimum per photo. Captions required. Buys one-time rights.

Columns/Departments: Calendar (events listing, domestic), 90 entries; Weekend Wanderer (3-day trips from a major city), 1,000 words; Motor Talk (automotive tips), 800 words and Certicare Adviser (Q&A from readers), 800 words. Buys 30 mss/year. Query with published clips. Pays $300-450.

‡**AFRICAN EXPEDITION GAZETTE,"the safari adventure quarterly"**, Kuca Communications Group, Suite 100, One Penn Plaza, New York NY 10119. (201)436-6063. Editor: Joseph V. Kuca. Managing Editor: Tony S. Caporale. 90% freelance written. Quarterly newspaper on African travel, specifically safari adventure travel. Circ. 5,000. Pays on publication. Publishes ms an average of 3 months after acceptance. Byline given. Offers 20% kill fee. Buys all rights. Submit seasonal/holiday material 3 months in advance. Previously published submissions OK. Computer printout submissions OK; prefers letter-quality. Reports in 3 weeks on queries; 6 weeks on mss. Sample copy for 9x12 SAE with two first class stamps. Writer's guidelines for #10 SAE with two first class stamps.

Nonfiction: Book excerpts, historical/nostalgic, how-to (prepare for a trans-Saharan trek, et cetera), interview/profile, new product, personal experience, photo feature, technical and travel. "We especially do not want safari/adventure articles from armchair travelers. We prefer to receive mss from persons active in the areas they are writing about." Buys 10 mss/year. Query with published clips. Length: 1,000-3,000 words. Pays $50-250. Pays in contributor copies or other premiums "if an unpublished writer presents a good ms, we'll gamble and allow generous voucher copies to get them started." Sometimes pays expenses of writers on assignment.

Photos: Send photos with submission. Reviews contact sheets. Offers no additional payment for photos accepted with ms, but offers $15 minimum per photo for photo essays. Captions, model releases and identification of subjects required. Buys one-time rights.

Columns/Departments: Explorer's Journal (column devoted to reprints and re-examination of historical explorer/adventurer text and personality profiles of contemporary persons involved in African conservation, environmental studies, archeology, etc.), 1,800-3,000 words. Buys 4 mss/year. Query with published clips. Pays $25-100.

‡**AMERICAN WEST, Travel & Life,** American West Management Corp., Suite #30, 7000 E. Tanque Verde Rd., Tucson AZ 85715. (602)886-9959. Editor-in-Chief: Thomas W. Pew, Jr. Managing Editor: Mae Reid-Bills. 60% freelance written. Bimonthly magazine which covers travel and life in the American West, often bringing the past into the present. "We look for relevant subject matter skillfully written to interest our readers who travel or want to travel in the West. On the whole, our readers are above average in education, family income, range of interests, and number of trips taken per year." Circ. 180,000. Pays on acceptance. Byline given. Buys first North American serial rights and anthology rights. Submit seasonal/holiday material 8 months in advance. Reports in 1 month on queries; 2 months on mss. Sample copy $3. Writer's guidelines for #10 SASE.
Nonfiction: General interest, historical/nostalgic, humor, personal experience, photo feature and travel. Buys 40 mss/year. Query with published clips. Length: 1,000-2,500 words. Pays $200-800.
Photos: Send photos with submission. Reviews 35mm or 3x5 transparencies and 5x7 or larger prints. Offers $40-200 per photo according to size reproduced. Model releases required. Buys one-time rights.

‡**AMOCO TRAVELER,** K.L. Publications, Suite 105, 2001 Killebrew Dr., Bloomington MN 55425. 80% free-lance written. A quarterly magazine published for the Amoco Traveler Club. Circ. 65,000. Pays on acceptance by client. Byline given. Buys limited rights in work-for-hire. "This publication is a mix of original and reprinted material." Previously published submissions OK. Submit seasonal/holiday material 8 months in advance. Simultaneous and photocopied submissions OK. Reports in 1 month. Sample copy for 9 × 12 SAE with 3 first class stamps. Writer's guidelines for #10 SASE.
Nonfiction: Focus is on U.S. destinations by car, although occasionally will use a foreign destination. Traveler Roads showcases a North American city or area, its attractions, history and accomodations; Traveler Focus features a romantic, getaway destination for the armchair traveler; Traveler Weekends focuses on an activity-oriented destination. Length: 1,000 words. Pays $350-400.
Columns/Departments: Healthwise (travel-related health tips). Length: 500-600 words. Pays $175.
Photos: Send photos with manuscript. Reviews 35mm transparencies, color only, no b&w. Pay varies.

ASU TRAVEL GUIDE, ASU Travel Guide, Inc., 1325 Columbus Ave., San Francisco CA 94133. (415)441-5200. Editor: Brady Ennis. 20% freelance written. Quarterly guidebook covering international travel features and travel discounts for well-traveled airline employees. Circ. 50,000. Payment terms negotiable. Publishes ms an average of 18 months after acceptance. Byline given. Offers kill fee. Buys first North American serial rights, first and second rights to the same material, and second serial (reprint) rights to material originally published elsewhere. Makes work-for-hire assignments. Submit seasonal/holiday material 6 months in advance. Simultaneous queries and simultaneous, photocopied and previously published submissions OK. Computer printout submissions acceptable; prefers letter-quality. Reports in 1 month. Writer's guidelines for #10 SASE.
Nonfiction: International travel articles "similar to those run in consumer magazines." Not interested in amateur efforts from inexperienced travelers or personal experience articles that don't give useful information to other travelers. Buys 16-20 mss/year. Destination pieces only; no "Tips On Luggage" articles. "We will be accepting fewer manuscripts and relying more on our established group of freelance contributors." Unsolicited mss or queries without SASE will not be acknowledged. No telephone queries. Length: 1,200-1,500 words. Pays $200.
Photos: "Interested in clear, high-contrast photos; we prefer not to receive material without photos." Reviews 5x7 and 8x10 b&w prints. "Payment for photos is included in article price; photos from tourist offices are acceptable."
Tips: "We'll be needing more domestic U.S. destination pieces which combine several cities or areas in a logical manner, e.g., Seattle/Vancouver, Savannah/Atlanta. Query with samples of travel writing and a list of places you've recently visited. We appreciate clean and simple style. Keep verbs in the active tense and involve the reader in what you write. Avoid 'cute' writing, excess punctuation (especially dashes and ellipses), coined words and stale cliches. Any article that starts with the name of a country followed by an exclamation point is immediately rejected. The most frequent mistakes made by writers in completing an article for us are: 1) Lazy writing—using words to describe a place that could describe any destination such as 'there is so much to do in (fill in destination) that whole guidebooks have been written about it'; 2) Including fare and tour package information—our readers make arrangements through their own airline."

AWAY, c/o ALA, 888 Worcester St., Wellesley MA 02181. (617)237-5200. Editor: Gerard J. Gagnon. For "members of the ALA Auto & Travel Club, interested in their autos and in travel. Ages range approximately 20-65. They live primarily in New England." Slanted to seasons. 5-10% freelance written. Quarterly. Circ. 117,000. Buys first serial rights. Pays on acceptance. Publishes ms an average of 3 months after acceptance.

Submit seasonal material 6 months in advance. Reports "as soon as possible." Although a query is not mandatory, it may be advisable for many articles. Computer printout submissions acceptable; no dot-matrix. Sample copy for 9x12 SAE with 2 first class stamps.

Nonfiction: Articles on "travel, tourist attractions, safety, history, etc., preferably with a New England angle. Also, car care tips and related subjects." Would like a "positive feel to all pieces, but not the chamber of commerce approach." Buys general seasonal travel, specific travel articles, and travel-related articles; outdoor activities, for example, gravestone rubbing; historical articles linked to places to visit; and humor with a point. "Would like to see more nonseasonally oriented material. Most material now submitted seems suitable only for our summer issue. Avoid pieces on hunting and about New England's most publicized attractions, such as Old Sturbridge Village and Mystic Seaport." Length: 800-1,500 words, "preferably 1,000-1,200 words." Pays approximately 10¢/word.

Photos: Photos purchased with mss. Captions required. B&w glossy prints. Pays $5-10/b&w photo, payment on publication based upon which photos are used. Not buying color photos at this time.

Tips: "The most frequent mistakes we find in articles submitted to us are spelling, typographical errors and questionable statements of fact, which require additional research by the editorial staff. We are buying very few articles at this time."

BAJA TIMES, Editorial Playas De Rosarito, S.A., Box 5577, Chula Vista CA 92012-5577. (706)612-1244. Editor: John W. Utley. 90% freelance written. Monthly tourist and travel publication on Baja California, Mexico. "Oriented to the Baja California, Mexico aficionada—the tourist and those Americans who are living in Baja California or have their vacation homes there. Articles should be slanted to Baja." Pays on publication. Publishes ms an average of 8 months after acceptance. Byline given. Buys first rights. Submit seasonal/holiday material 4 months in advance. Computer printout submissions OK; prefers letter-quality. Sample copy for 9x12 SAE with 4 first class stamps; free writer's guidelines.

Nonfiction: General interest, historical/nostalgic, humor, personal experience, photo feature, travel. All with Baja California slant. "Nothing that describes any negative aspects of Mexico (bribes, bad police, etc.). We are a positive publication." Query with or without published clips, or submit complete ms. Length: 750-2,100 words. Pays $50-100 for assigned articles; $35-50 for unsolicited articles. Sometimes pays expenses of writers on assignment.

Photos: Send photos with submission. Reviews 5x7 prints. Captions and identification of subjects required. Buys one-time rights.

Tips: "Take a chance—send in that Baja California related article. We guarantee to read them all. Over the years we have turned up some real winners from our writers—many who do not have substantial experience. The entire publication is open. We buy an average of 6 freelance each issue. Virtually any subject is acceptable as long as it has a Baja California slant. Remember Tijuana, Mexico (on the border with San Diego, CA) is the busiest border crossing in the world. We are always interested in material relating to Tijuana, Rosarito, Ensenada, LaPaz."

THE CAMPER TIMES, Royal Productions, Inc., Box 6294, Richmond VA 23230. (804)288-5653. Editor: Alice Posner Supple. 75% freelance written. Prefers to work with published/established writers; works with a small number of new/unpublished writers each year. Published 8 times a year. Winter issue (January, February, March; monthly, April through October). "We supply the camping public with articles and information on outdoor activities related to camping. Our audience is primarily families that own recreational vehicles." Circ. 35,000. Pays on publication. Publishes ms an average of 4-6 months after acceptance. Byline given. Buys one-time rights, second serial (reprint) rights or simultaneous rights. Submit seasonal/holiday material 2 months in advance. Simultaneous, photocopied and previously published submissions OK. Query for electronic submissions. Computer printout submissions acceptable. Reports in 2 months. Sample copy and writer's guidelines for 9x12 SAE with $2.40 postage.

Nonfiction: How-to and travel; information on places to camp and fishing articles. Also "tourist related articles. Places to go, things to see. Does not have to be camping related." Buys 80 mss/year. Query with or without published clips, or send complete ms. Length: 500-2,000 words. Pays $20-65 for unsolicited articles. Sometimes pays the expenses of writers on assignment.

Photos: State availability of photos with submission. Reviews contact sheets and prints. Uses b&w only. Identification of subjects required. Buys one-time rights.

Tips: "Best approach is to call me. All areas of *The Camper Times* are open to freelancers. We will look at all articles and consider for publication. Return of unsolicited mss is not guaranteed; however, every effort is made to return photos."

‡CAMPING & RV MAGAZINE, Camping Voice of Mid-America, Joe Jones Publishing, Box 337, Iola WI 54945. (715)445-5000. FAX: (715)445-4053. Editor: Deb Lengkeek. 75% freelance written. Monthly magazine on camping in the Midwest and Heartland states. "We accept both casual and technical articles dealing with camping, and destination pieces from our coverage area." Circ. 25,000. Pays on publication. Publishes ms an average of 6 months after acceptance. Byline given. Buys first rights, one-time rights or second serial (reprint) rights. Submit seasonal/holiday material 3 months in advance. Previously published submissions OK. Computer printout submissions OK. Free sample copy and writer's guidelines.

Nonfiction: General interest, how-to, personal experience, photo feature, technical, and travel. "No articles of destinations out of our coverage area." Buys 60 mss/year. Send complete ms. Length: 1,000-2,000 words. Pays 3-5¢/word.

Photos: State availability of photos with submission. Reviews prints. Pays $5 per photo. Identification of subjects required. Buys one-time rights.

Columns/Departments: Living on Wheels; Camping Comforts; RV Wife and Care of RV (hints, suggestions, general interest, technical, equipment care), 1,000 words. Buys 50 mss/year. Query. Pays 3-5¢/word.

Fillers: Anecdotes and facts. Buys 12/year. Length: 500-1,000 words. Pays 3-5¢/word.

Tips: "Write from a campground background—be knowledgeable about how and where to camp as well as camping related activities."

‡CAMPING CANADA, CRV Publishing Canada Ltd., Suite 202, 2077 Dundas St. East, Mississauga, Ontario L4X 1M2 Canada. (416)624-8218. FAX: (416)624-6764. Editor: Tim Stover. Managing Editor: Norman Rosen. 65-80% freelance written. "We have an established group of writers but are always willing to work with newcomers." A magazine published 7 times/year, covering camping and RVing. Circ. 100,000. Pays on publication. Publishes ms an average of 2-3 months after acceptance. Byline given. Buys first rights. Computer printout submissions acceptable; no dot-matrix. Reports in 2 months. Free sample copy and writer's guidelines.

Nonfiction: Canadian recreational life, especially as it concerns or interests Canadian RV and camping enthusiasts; historical/nostalgic (sometimes); how-to; new product; personal experience; technical; and travel. Will accept occasional material unrelated to Canada. Buys 25-30 mss/year. "Only mss from solicited writers will be considered." Query first. Length: 1,000-2,500 words. Pays $150-300. Sometimes pays the expenses of writers on assignment.

Photos: Will buy occasional photos. Query first. Mss must be accompanied by photos, unless otherwise agreed upon.

Tips: "Deep, accurate, thorough research and colorful detail are required for all features. Travel pieces should include places to camp (contact information, if available). We would like to receive profiles of celebrity RVers, preferably Canadians, but will look at celebrities known in the U.S. and Canada."

CAMPING TODAY, Official Publication of National Campers & Hikers Association, 126 Hermitage Rd., Butler PA 16001. (412)283-7401. Editors: DeWayne and June Johnston. 50% freelance written. Prefers to work with published/established writers. The monthly official membership publication of the NCHA, "the largest nonprofit camping organization in the United States and Canada. Members are heavily oriented toward RV travel, both weekend and extended vacations. A small segment is interested in hiking and backpacking. Concentration is on activities of members within chapters, conservation, wildlife, etc. The majority of members are retired." Circ. 30,000. Pays on publication. Publishes ms an average of 6 months after acceptance. Byline given. Buys one-time rights. Submit seasonal/holiday material 3 months in advance. Simultaneous, photocopied, and previously published submissions OK. Computer printout submissions acceptable if letter-quality. Reports in 1 month. Sample copy for $1 in stamps or writer's guidelines for #10 SASE.

Nonfiction: Travel (interesting places to visit by RV, camping, hiking); humor (camping or travel related); interview/profile (interesting campers); new product (RVs and related equipment); and technical (RVs). Buys 20-30 mss/year. Send complete ms. Length: 750-1,000 words. Pays $75-150. Sometimes pays the expenses of writers on assignment.

Photos: Send photos with ms. Reviews color transparencies and 5x7 b&w prints. Pays $25 maximum for color transparencies. Color cover every month requires vertical slide. Captions required.

Tips: "Freelance material on RV travel, RV technical subjects and items of general camping and hiking interest throughout the United States and Canada will receive special attention."

CARIBBEAN TRAVEL AND LIFE, Suite 830, 8403 Colesville Rd., Silver Spring MD 20910. (301)588-2300. Editor: Veronica Gould Stoddart. 90% freelance written. Prefers to work with published/established writers. A bimonthly magazine covering travel to the Caribbean, Bahamas and Bermuda. Circ. 75,000. Pays on publication. Publishes ms an average of 3 months after acceptance. Byline given. Offers 25% kill fee. Buys first North American serial rights. Submit seasonal/holiday material 6 months in advance. Photocopied submissions OK. Computer printout submissions OK; prefers letter-quality. Reports in 2 months. Sample copy for 9x12 SAE with 5 first class stamps; writer's guidelines for #10 SASE.

Nonfiction: General interest, how-to, interview/profile, culture, personal experience and travel. No "guidebook rehashing; superficial destination pieces or critical exposes." Buys 30 mss/year. Query with published clips. Length: 2,000-2,500 words. Pays $550.

Photos: Send photos with submission. Reviews 35mm transparencies. Offers $75-400 per photo. Captions and identification of subjects required. Buys one-time rights.

Columns/Departments: Resort Spotlight (in-depth review of luxury resort); Tradewinds (focus on one particular kind of water sport or sailing/cruising); Island Buys (best shopping for luxury goods, crafts, duty-free); Island Spice (best cuisine and/or restaurant reviews with recipes); all 1,000-1,500 words; Caribbeana (short items on great finds in travel, culture, and special attractions), 500 words. Buys 36 mss/year. Query with published clips or send complete ms. Length: 500-1,250 words. Pays $75-200.

Tips: "We are especially looking for stories with a personal touch and lively, entertaining anecdotes, as well as strong insight into people and places being covered. Also prefers stories with focus on people, i.e, colorful personalities, famous people, etc. Writer should demonstrate why he/she is the best person to do that story based on extensive knowledge of the subject, frequent visits to destination, residence in destination, specialty in field."

CRUISE TRAVEL MAGAZINE, World Publishing Co., 990 Grove St., Evanston IL 60201. (312)491-6440. Editor: Robert Meyers. Managing Editor: Charles Doherty. 95% freelance written. A bimonthly magazine on cruise travel. "This is a consumer oriented travel publication covering the world of pleasure cruising on large cruise ships (with some coverage of smaller ships), including ports, travel tips, roundups." Pays on acceptance. Publishes ms an average of 5 months after acceptance. Byline given. Offers ½ kill fee. Buys first North American serial rights, one-time rights, or second serial (reprint) rights. Simultaneous, photocopied and previously published submissions OK. Computer printout submissions OK; prefers letter-quality. Sample copy $3 with 9x12 SAE and 5 first class stamps. Writer's guidelines for #10 SASE.

Nonfiction: General interest, historical/nostalgic, interview/profile, personal experience, photo feature, travel. "No daily cruise 'diary'; My First Cruise; etc." Buys 72 mss/year. Query with or without published clips or send complete ms. Length: 500-2,000 words. Pay $75-350.

Photos: Send photos with submission. Reviews transparencies and prints. "Must be color, 35m preferred (other format OK); color prints second choice." Offers no additional payment for photos accepted with ms "but pay more for well-illustrated ms." Captions and identification of subjects required. Buys one-time rights.

Fillers: Anecdotes, facts. Buys 3 mss/year. Length: 300-700 words. Pays $75-200.

Tips: "Do your homework. Know what we do and what sorts of things we publish. Know the cruise industry—we can't use novices. Good, sharp, bright color photography opens the door fast."

‡DISCOVERY, One Illinois Center, Suite 1700, 111 E. Wacker Dr., Chicago IL 60601. Editor: John Fink. 75% freelance written. Prefers to work with published/established writers, and works with a small number of new/unpublished writers each year. A quarterly travel magazine for Allstate Motor Club members. Circ. 1.6 million. Buys first North American serial rights. Pays on acceptance. Publishes ms an average of 8 months after acceptance. Computer printout submissions acceptable; no dot-matrix. Submit seasonal queries 8-14 months in advance to allow for photo assignment. Reports in 5 weeks. Sample copy for 9x12 SAE and $1 postage; writer's guidelines for #10 SASE.

Nonfiction: "The emphasis is on North America and its people." Emphasizes automotive travel, offering a firsthand look at the people and places, trends and activities that help define the American character. "We're looking for polished magazine articles that are people-oriented and promise insight as well as entertainment—not narratives of peoples' vacations. Destination articles must rely less on the impressions of writers and more on the observations of people who live or work or grew up in the place and have special attachments. We seek ideas for a 'Best of America' department, which is a roundup of particular kinds of places (i.e beaches, national park lodges, space museums) often related to the season." Query. "Submit a thorough proposal suitable for *Discovery*. It must be literate, concise and enthusiastic. Accompany query with relevant published clips and a resume." Buys 12 assigned mss/year. Length: 1,500-2,000 words, plus a 500-word sidebar on other things to see and do. Rates vary, depending on assignment and writer's credentials; usual range is $800-plus. Sometimes pays the expenses of writers on assignment.

Photography: Color transparencies (35mm or larger). Pays day rate. For existing photos, rates depend on use. Photos should work as story; captions required. Send transparencies by registered mail. Buys one-time rights.

Tips: "No personal narratives, mere destination pieces or subjects that are not particularly visual. We have a strong emphasis on photojournalism and our stories reflect this. The most frequent mistakes made by writers in completing an article for us are: not writing to assignment, which results in a weak focus or central theme and poor organization and a lack of development, which diminishes the substance of the story. Word precision frequently is the difference between a dull and an exciting story. Writers will benefit by studying several issues of the publication before sending queries."

ENDLESS VACATION, Endless Vacation Publications, Inc., Box 80260, Indianapolis IN 46280. (317)871-9500. Editor: Helen A. Wernle. Prefers to work with published/established writers. A bimonthly magazine covering travel destinations, activities and issues that enhance the lives of vacationers. Circ. 608,872. Pays on acceptance. Publishes ms an average of 3 months after acceptance. Byline given. Buys first worldwide serial rights. Simultaneous and photocopied submissions OK. Query for electronic submissions. Computer printout submissions acceptable; prefers letter-quality. Reports in 1 month on queries; 3 weeks on manuscripts. Sample copy $5; writer's guidelines for SAE with 1 first class stamp.

Nonfiction: Contact Manuscript Editor. Travel. Buys 24 mss/year (approx). Query with published clips. Length: 1,200-2,200 words. Pays $500-1,200 for assigned articles; pays $250-800 for unsolicited articles. Sometimes pays the expenses of writers on assignment.

Photos: State availability of photos with submissions. Reviews 4x5 transparencies and 35mm slides. Offers $100-500/photo. Model releases and identification of subjects required. Buys one-time rights.

Columns/Departments: Gourmet on the Go (culinary topics of interest to travelers whether they are dining out or cooking in their condominium kitchens; no reviews of individual restaurants). Buys 4 mss/year. Query with published clips. Length: 800-1,200 words. Pays $150-300. Sometimes pays the expenses of writers on assignment.

Tips: "We will continue to focus on travel trends and resort and upscale destinations. Articles must be packed with pertinent facts and applicable how-tos. Information — addresses, phone numbers, dates of events, costs — must be current and accurate. We like to see a variety of stylistic approaches, but in all cases the lead must be strong. A writer should realize that we require first-hand knowledge of the subject and plenty of practical information. For further understanding of *Endless Vacations*' direction, the writer should study the magazine and guidelines for writers."

FAMILY MOTOR COACHING, Official Publication of the Family Motor Coach Association, 8291 Clough Pike, Cincinnati OH 45244-2796. (513)474-3622. Editor: Pamela Wisby Kay. Associate Editor: Robbin Maue. 80% freelance written. "We prefer that writers be experienced RVers." Emphasizes travel by motorhome, motorhome mechanics, maintenance and other technical information. Monthly magazine. Circ. 75,000. Pays on acceptance. Publishes ms an average of 8 months after acceptance. Buys first North American serial rights. Byline given. Submit seasonal/holiday material 4 months in advance. Computer printout submissions acceptable; prefers letter-quality. Reports in 2 months. Sample copy $2.50; writer's guidelines for #10 SASE.

Nonfiction: Motorhome travel and living on the road; travel (various areas of country accessible by motor coach); how-to (modify motor coach features); bus conversions; humor; interview/profile; new product; technical; and nostalgia. Buys 240 mss/issue. Query with published clips . Length: 1,000-2,000 words. Pays $100-500.

Photos: State availability of photos with query. Offers no additional payment for b&w contact sheets, 35mm or 2¼x2¼ color transparencies. Captions and model releases required. Buys one-time rights.

Tips: "The greatest number of contributions that we receive are travel; therefore that area is the most competitive. However, it also represents the easiest way to break in to our publications. Articles should be written for those traveling by self-contained motor home. The destinations must be accessible to RV travelers and any peculiar road conditions should be mentioned."

GREAT EXPEDITIONS, Adventure Travel Magazine, Box 8000-411, Sumas WA 98295; or Box 8000-411, Abbotsford, BC V2S 6H1 Canada. Editor: Craig Henderson. 90% freelance written. Eager to work with new/unpublished writers. Quarterly magazine covering "off-the-beaten-path" destinations, outdoor recreation, cultural discovery, budget travel, and working abroad. Circ. 5,000. Pays on publication. Buys first and second (reprint) rights. Simultaneous queries, and simultaneous, photocopied and previously published submissions OK. Computer printout submissions acceptable. Send SASE for return of article and photos. Reports in 6 weeks. Sample copy $2; free writer's guidelines.

Nonfiction: Articles range from very adventurous (living with an isolated tribe in the Philippines) to mildly adventurous (Spanish language school vacations in Guatemala and Mexico). We also like to see "how-to" pieces for adventurous travelers (i.e., How to Sail Around the World for Free, Swapping Homes with Residents of Other Countries, How to Get in on an Archaeological Dig). Buys 30 mss/year. Pays $50 maximum. Length 1,000-3,000 words.

Photos: B&w photos, color prints or slides should be sent with article. Captions required.

Tips: "It's best to send for a sample copy for a first-hand look at the style of articles we are looking for. If possible, we appreciate practical information for travelers, either in the form of a sidebar or incorporated into the article, detailing how to get there, where to stay, specific costs, where to write for visas or travel information."

GUIDE TO THE FLORIDA KEYS, Humm's, Crain Communications Inc., Box 330712, Miami FL 33133. (305)665-2858. Editor: William A. Humm. 80% freelance written. A quarterly travel guide to the Florida Keys. Circ. 60,000. Pays on publication. Byline given. Buys first rights and second serial (reprint) rights. Submit seasonal/holiday material 6 months in advance. Previously published submissions OK. Computer

For explanation of symbols, see the Key to Symbols and Abbreviations on Page 5. For unfamiliar words, see the Glossary.

printout submissions acceptable. Reports in 2 weeks on queries; 3 weeks on manuscripts. Free sample copy.
Nonfiction: General interest, historical/nostalgic, personal experience and travel, all for the Florida Keys area. Buys 30-40 mss/year. Send complete ms. Length: 500-1,500 words. Pays $5/column inch. Sometimes pays the expenses of writers on assignment.
Photos: State availability of photos with submission. Reviews negatives, 35mm and 2x2¾ transparencies, and 5x7 and 8x10 prints. Offers $40-100/photo. Captions and model releases required. Buys one-time rights.
Columns/Departments: Fishing and Diving (primarily about the Florida Keys), 500-1,500 words. Pays $5/column inch.

‡HIDEAWAYS GUIDE, Hideaways International, 15 Goldsmith St., Littleton MA 01460. Editor: Michael Thiel. Managing Editor: Gail Richard. 10% freelance written. Magazine published 2 times/year—February, August. Also publishes 4 quarterly newsletters. Features travel/leisure and real estate information for upscale, affluent, educated, outdoorsy audience. Deals with unique vacation opportunities: vacation home renting, buying, exchanging, yacht/houseboat charters, adventure vacations, country inns and small resorts. Circ. 12,000. Pays on publication. Publishes ms an average of 4 months after acceptance. Byline given. Buys first North American serial rights, one-time rights and second serial (reprint) rights. Submit seasonal/holiday material 6 months in advance. Previously published submissions OK. Query for electronic submissions. Computer printout submissions OK; no dot-matrix. Reports in 1 month on queries; 2 months on mss. Sample copy $10; writer's guidelines for #10 SASE.
Nonfiction: How-to (with focus on personal experience: vacation home renting, exchanging, buying, selling, yacht and house boat chartering); travel (intimate out-of-the-way spots to visit). Articles on "learning" vacations: scuba, sailing, flying, cooking, shooting, golf, tennis, photography, etc. Buys 5-10 mss/year. Query. Length: 800-1,500 words. Pays $75-150.
Photos: State availability of photos with query letter or ms or send photos with accompanying query or ms. Reviews color transparencies. Pays negotiable fee. Captions and identification of subjects required. Buys one-time rights.
Tips: "The most frequent mistakes made by writers in completing an article for us are that they are too impersonal with no photos and not enough focus or accommodations."

THE ITINERARY MAGAZINE, "The" Magazine for Travelers with Physical Disabilities, Box 1084, Bayonne NJ 07002. (201)858-3400. Editor: Robert S Zywicki. Managing Editor: Elizabeth C. Zywicki. 60-70% freelance written. Works with established and new writers. A bimonthly magazine covering travel for the disabled. Circ. 10,400. Pays on publication. Publishes ms an average of 6 months after acceptance. Buys first North American serial rights, first rights, one-time rights, second serial (reprint) rights, all rights, makes work-for-hire assignments. Submit seasonal/holiday material 6 months in advance. Simultaneous, photocopied and previously published submissions OK. Computer printout submissions acceptable. Reports in 1 month on queries; 2 months on manuscripts. Sample copy for 9x12 SAE with 4 first class stamps; writer's guidelines for #10 SASE.
Nonfiction: How-to, interview/profile, new product, personal experience, photo feature and travel (especially adventure/wilderness/sports related travel for persons with disabilities). Special issues will feature accessible travel articles for Thanksgiving/Christmas time; national parks, regional tourist sites in USA and Canada. No articles that do not deal with travel for the disabled. Buys 24-30 mss/year. Query with or without published clips, or send complete ms. Length: 750-2,000 words. Pays $100-300 for assigned articles; pays $50-150 for unsolicited articles. Sometimes pays the expenses of writers on assignment.
Photos: Send photos with submission. Reviews contact sheets and prints. Offers no additional payment for photos accepted with ms. Captions, model releases and identification of subjects required. Buys one-time rights.
Columns/Departments: Book Reviews (only containing information on travel for the disabled), 300-500 words. Buys 6-10 mss/year. Query. Pays $25-50.
Tips: "Be disabled or a relative, friend or co-worker of the disabled. Be aware of the needs of the disabled in travel-related situations. Describe the venues, sightseeing, lodging, etc. The areas most open to freelancers are travelogues featuring access data for the disabled, how-to features for travelers with disabilities, and reports on hotels, transportation, etc."

JOURNAL OF CHRISTIAN CAMPING, Christian Camping International, Box 646, Wheaton IL 60189. Editor: Daniel Bostrom. 75% freelance written. Prefers to work with published/established writers. Emphasizes the broad scope of organized camping with emphasis on Christian camping. "Leaders of youth camps and adult conferences read our magazine to get practical help in ways to run their camps." Bimonthly magazine. Circ. 6,000. Pays on acceptance. Publishes ms an average of 2 months after acceptance. Buys all rights. Offers 25% kill fee. Byline given. Computer printout submissions acceptable; prefers letter-quality. Reports in 6 weeks. Sample copy for 9x12 SAE and $2.50; writer's guidelines for #10 SASE.
Nonfiction: General interest (trends in organized camping in general and Christian camping in particular); how-to (anything involved with organized camping from motivating staff, to programming, to record keeping, to camper follow-up); inspirational (limited use, but might be interested in practical applications of Scriptural

principles to everyday situations in camping, no preaching); interview (with movers and shakers in camping and Christian camping in particular; submit a list of basic questions first); and opinion (write a letter to the editor). Buys 30-50 mss/year. Query required. Length: 600-2,500 words. Pays 5¢/word.

Photos: Send photos with ms. Pays $10/5x7 b&w contact sheet or print; price negotiable for 35mm color transparencies. Buys all rights. Captions required.

Tips: "The most frequent mistake made by writers is that they have not read the information in the listing and send articles unrelated to our readers."

‡THE MATURE TRAVELER, Travel Bonanzas for 49ers-Plus, GEM Publishing Group, Box 50820, Reno NV 89513. (702)786-7419. Editor: Gene E. Malott. 30% freelance written. Monthly newsletter on senior citizen travel. Circ. 1,800. Pays on acceptance. Publishes an average of 2 months after acceptance. Byline given. Offers 25% kill fee. Buys one-time rights. Submit seasonal/holiday material 3 months in advance. Simultaneous (if we know about it) and previously published submissions OK. Query for electronic submissions. Computer printout submissions OK; prefers letter-quality. Reports in 2 weeks. Sample copy for $1 and #10 SAE with 45¢ postage. Writer's guidelines for SAE with 45¢ postage.

Nonfiction: Travel for seniors. "No general travel and destination pieces not aimed at 49ers +." Query. Length: 200-1,200 words. Pays $20-100.

Photos: State availability of photos with submission. Reviews contact sheets and b&w (only) prints. Captions required. Buys one-time rights.

Fillers: Newsbreaks of interest to senior travelers. Buys 6-10/year. Length: 40-200 words. Pays $5-10.

Tips: "Read the guidelines and write stories to our readers' needs—not the general public."

MEXICO MAGAZINE, Team Mexico, 303 Main St., Box 700, Carbondale CO 81623. (303)963-2330. Editor: Peggy DeVilbiss. Managing Editor: Harlan Feder. 60% freelance written. A quarterly magazine on Mexico travel. "We like information on all aspects of travel to Mexico to enable travelers to travel knowledgeably and confidently for a rewarding Mexico experience." Circ. 20,000 controlled. Pays on publication. Publishes ms an average of 3-6 months after acceptance. Buys first North American serial rights, second serial (reprint) rights, simultaneous rights and makes work-for-hire assignments. Submit seasonal/holiday material 5 months in advance. Simultaneous, photocopied and previously published material OK. Query for electronic submissions. Computer printout submissions OK. Reports in 2 months on queries; 4 months on mss. Free sample copy; writer's guidelines for #10 SASE.

Nonfiction: General interest (on Mexico), how-to (travel tips), humor, interview/profile (Mexican personalities), opinion (sympathetic to Mexico), personal experience, photo feature, travel, Mexico culture and recreation. No "dated travel writing, unverified facts, over-reliance on secondary sources or 'vacation diary.' No articles condescending or disrespectful of Mexico." Buys 40-60 mss/year. Query with published clips (if available), or send complete mss. Length: 400-2,000 words, prefer 1,500 maximum. Pays $50-250.

Photos: State availability of photos with submission. Reviews contact sheets, negatives, transparencies and b&w prints. Offers $50-200/photo. Identification of subjects required. Buys one-time rights.

Fillers: Facts, short humor, personal anecdotes. Length: 35-50 words. Pays $10.

Tips: "Preference is given to material that presents Mexico's uniqueness and culture as differences to be appreciated; material that helps travelers understand, accept and cope with these differences respectfully; material that reflects a genuine concern, caring, acceptance or love of Mexico on the part of the writer. All areas open to freelancers. Experienced Mexico travel writers favored for longer regional features. For City Highlights, Resort Reports, Travel Choices, Specialty Spotlights and departments, we seek fresh perspectives, first-hand knowledge and experience, timely information and affection for Mexico."

‡MÉXICO TODAY!, Travel & Leisure for the Mature Reader, Mexico Today!, Suite 311, 1420 N. St. NW, Washington DC 20005. (202)387-5142. Editor: Michael J. Zamba. 60% freelance written. Quarterly newsletter. "*México Today!* is an English-language publication for the resident Americans and British in Mexico, as well as the frequent traveler. Most readers are retirees enjoying the travel and leisure aspects of Mexico." Pays on publication. Publishes ms an average of 4-6 months after acceptance. Byline given. Buys first rights. Submit seasonal/holiday material 8 months in advance. Simultaneous and photocopied submissions OK. Computer printout submissions OK; prefers letter-quality. Reports in 6 weeks on queries. Sample copy $3. Writer's guidelines for #10 SASE.

Nonfiction: Book excerpt, how-to (i.e. how to buy a home in Mexico), humor, interview/profile, photo feature and travel, all about Mexico. No politics, pollution or controversial issues. Buys 12-15 mss/year. Send complete ms. Length: 500-1,200 words. Pays $50.

Photos: Send photos with submission. Reviews 5x7 or 8x10 prints. Offers $25 per photo. Identification of subjects required. Buys one-time rights.

Columns/Departments: Vecinos (neighbors, personal experiences about living or traveling in Mexico), 500-1,200 words. Buys 4 mss/year. Send complete ms. Pays $25.

Tips: "Be familiar with Mexico and its people. Avoid the beaches, tourist locations and the overwritten topics. Don't be too general. Examine a topic indepth so the reader knows it as well as you. Use quotes and good images."

‡**MEXICO WEST**, Mexico West Travel Club, Inc., Suite 107, 3450 Bonita Rd., Chula Vista CA 92010. (619)585-3033. Editor: Shirley Miller. 50% freelance written. Monthly newsletter on Baja California; Mexico as a travel destination. "Yes, our readers are travelers to Mexico, especially Baja California. They are knowledgeable but are always looking for new places to see." Circ. 3,000. Pays on publication. Publishes an average of 2 months after acceptance. Byline given. Buys first North American serial rights. Submit seasonal/holiday material 3 months in advance. Photocopied and previously published submissions OK. Computer printout submissions OK; prefers letter-quality. Free sample copy. Writer's guidelines for #10 SAE with 2 first class stamps.
Nonfiction: Historical, humor, interview, personal experience and travel. Buys 36-50 mss/year. Send complete ms. Length: 900-1,500 words. Pays $50.
Photos: State availability of photos with submission. Reviews 3x5 prints. Offers no additional payment for photos accepted with ms. Captions required. Buys one-time rights.

MICHIGAN LIVING, AAA Michigan, 17000 Executive Plaza Drive, Dearborn MI 48126. (313)336-1211. Editor: Len Barnes. 50% freelance written. Emphasizes travel and auto use. Monthly magazine. Circ. 1 million. Pays on acceptance. Publishes ms an average of 6 months after acceptance. Buys first North American serial rights. Offers 100% kill fee. Byline given. Submit seasonal/holiday material 3 months in advance. Reports in 6 weeks. Free sample copy and writer's guidelines.
Nonfiction: Travel articles on U.S. and Canadian topics. Buys 50-60 unsolicited mss/year. Send complete ms. Length: 200-1,000 words. Pays $88-315.
Photos: Photos purchased with accompanying ms. Captions required. Pays $367 for cover photos; $50-220 for color transparencies; total purchase price for ms includes payment for b&w photos.
Tips: "In addition to descriptions of things to see and do, articles should contain accurate, current information on costs the traveler would encounter on his trip. Items such as lodging, meal and entertainment expenses should be included, not in the form of a balance sheet but as an integral part of the piece. We want the sounds, sights, tastes, smells of a place or experience so one will feel he has been there and knows if he wants to go back."

THE MIDWEST MOTORIST, AAA Auto Club of Missouri, 12901 North Forty Dr., St. Louis MO 63141. (314)576-7350. Editor: Michael J. Right. Managing Editor: Jean Kennedy. Associate Editor: Bret Berigan. 70% freelance written. Bimonthly magazine on travel and auto-related topics. Primarily focuses on travel throughout the world; prefers stories that tell about sights and give solid travel tips. Circ. 375,000. Pays on acceptance. Publishes ms an average of 8 months after acceptance. Byline given. Not copyrighted. Buys one-time rights, simultaneous rights (rarely), and second serial (reprint) rights. Submit seasonal/holiday material 6-8 months in advance. Simultaneous queries, and simultaneous, photocopied and previously published submissions OK. Query for electronic submissions. Computer printout submissions acceptable as long as they are readable and NOT ALL CAPS; no dot-matrix. Reports in 1 month when query is accompanied by SASE. Sample copy for 9x12 SAE and 4 first class stamps. Writer's guidelines for #10 SASE.
Nonfiction: General interest; historical/nostalgic; how-to; humor (with motoring or travel slant); interview/profile; personal experience; photo feature; technical (auto safety or auto-related); and travel (domestic and international), all travel-related or auto-related. March/April annual European travel issue; November/December annual cruise issue. No religious, philosophical arguments or opinion not supported by facts. Buys 25 mss/year. Query with published clips. Length: 500-2,000 (1,500 preferred) words. Pays $50-200.
Photos: State availability of photos. Prefers color slides and b&w with people, sights, scenery mentioned. Reviews 35mm transparencies and 8x10 prints. Payment included in ms purchase. Captions, model releases and identification of subjects required. Buys one-time rights.
Tips: "Query should be informative and entertaining, written with as much care as the lead of a story. Feature articles on travel destinations and tips are most open to freelancers."

MOTORHOME, TL Enterprises, Inc., 29901 Agoura Rd., Agoura CA 91301. (818)991-4980. FAX: (818)991-8102. Editor: Bob Livingston. Managing Editor: Gail Harrington. 60% freelance written. A monthly magazine covering motorhomes. "*MotorHome* is exclusively for motorhome enthusiasts. We feature road tests on new motorhomes, travel locations, controversy concerning motorhomes, how-to and technical articles relating to motorhomes." Circ. 130,000. Pays on acceptance. Publishes ms an average of 4 months after acceptance. Byline given. Buys first North American serial rights. Submit seasonal/holiday material 8 months in advance. Query for electronic submissions. Computer printout submissions acceptable. Reports in 3 weeks on queries; 2 months on mss. Free sample copy and writer's guidelines.
Nonfiction: General interest; historical/nostalgic; how-to (do it yourself for motorhomes); humor; new product; photo feature; and technical. Buys 80 mss/year. Query with published clips. Length: 1,000-2,000 words. Pays $250-600 for assigned articles; pays $200-500 for unsolicited articles. Sometimes pays expenses of writers and/or photographers on assignment.
Photos: Send photos with submission. Reviews contact sheets and 35mm/120/4x5 transparencies. Offers no additional payment for photos accepted with ms except for use on cover. Captions, model releases and identification of subjects required. Buys first North American serial rights.

Tips: "If a freelancer has an idea for a good article it's best to send a query and include possible photo locations to illustrate the article. We prefer to assign articles and work with the author in developing a piece suitable to our audience. We are in a specialized field with very enthusiastic readers who appreciate articles by authors who actually enjoy motorhomes. The following areas are most open: Travel—places to go with a motorhome, where to stay, what to see etc.; we prefer not to use travel articles where the motorhome is secondary; and How-to—personal projects on author's motorhomes to make travel easier, etc., unique projects, accessories. Also articles on unique personalities, motorhomes, humorous experiences."

NATIONAL GEOGRAPHIC TRAVELER, National Geographic Society, 17th and M Sts. NW, Washington DC 20036. (202)857-7721. Editorial Director: Richard Busch. 90% freelance written. A bimonthly travel magazine. "*Traveler* highlights mostly U.S. and Canadian subjects, but about 30% of its articles cover other foreign destinations—most often Europe, Mexico, and the Caribbean, occasionally the Pacific." Circ. 775,000. Pays on acceptance. Publishes ms an average of 12-15 months after acceptance. Byline given. Offers 50% kill fee. Computer printout submissions OK; prefers letter-quality. Reports in 2 months. Sample copy $4.50; writer's guidelines for #10 SASE.
Nonfiction: Travel. Buys 50 mss/year. Query with published clips. Length: 1,200-3,500 words. Pays $1/word. Pays expenses of writers on assignment.
Photos: Reviews transparencies and prints.

‡NEWSDAY, Melville, Long Island NY 11747. (516)454-2980. Travel Editor: Steve Schatt. Assistant Travel Editor: Barbara Shea. 75% freelance written. For general readership of Sunday Travel Section. Newspaper. Weekly. Circ. 680,000. Buys all rights for New York area only. Buys 175 mss/year. Pays on publication. Will consider photocopied submissions. Simultaneous submissions considered if others are being made outside the New York area. Query for electronic submissions. Computer printout submissions acceptable; prefers letter-quality to dot-matrix. Reports in 1 month.
Nonfiction and Photos: Travel articles with strong focus and theme for Sunday Travel Section, but does not accept pieces based on freebies, junkets, discount or subsidies of any sort. Emphasis on accuracy, honesty, service, and quality writing to convey mood and flavor. Destination pieces must involve visit or experience that a typical traveler can duplicate. Skip diaries, "My First Trip Abroad" pieces or laundry lists of activities; downplay first person. Submit complete ms. Length: 600-1,500 words; prefers 800- to 1,000-word pieces. Pays 12-20¢/word. Photos extra. Also, regional "Weekender" pieces of 700-800 words plus service box, but query Barbara Shea first.
Tips: "We look for professional material with a writer's touch, and it makes no difference who produces it. The test is quality, not experience."

NORTHEAST OUTDOORS, Northeast Outdoors, Inc., Box 2180, Waterbury CT 06722. (203)755-0158. Editor: Camilo Falcon. 80% freelance written. Works with a small number of new/unpublished writers each year, and is eager to work with new/unpublished writers. A monthly tabloid covering family camping in the Northeastern U.S. Circ. 14,000. Pays on publication. Publishes ms an average of 8 months after acceptance. Byline given. Offers 50% kill fee. Buys first rights, one-time rights, second serial (reprint) rights, simultaneous rights, and regional rights. Submit seasonal/holiday material 5 months in advance. Simultaneous, photocopied and previously published submissions OK. Query for electronic submissions. Computer printout submissions acceptable; no dot-matrix. Reports in 1 month. Sample copy for 9x12 SAE with 6 first class stamps; writer's guidelines for #10 SASE.
Nonfiction: Book excerpts; general interest; historical/nostalgic; how-to (on camping); humor; new product (company and RV releases only); personal experience; photo feature; and travel. "No diaries of trips, dog stories, or anything not camping and RV related." Length: 300-1,500 words. Pays $40-80 for articles with b&w photos; pays $30-75 for articles without art.
Photos: Send photos with submission. Reviews contact sheets and 5x7 prints or larger. Captions and identification of subjects required. Buys one-time rights.
Columns/Departments: Mealtime (campground cooking), 300-900 words. Buys 12 mss/year. Query or send complete ms. Length: 750-1,000 words. Pays $30-75.
Fillers: Camping related anecdotes, facts, newsbreaks and short humor. Buys few fillers. Length: 25-200 words. Pays $5-15.
Tips: "We most often need material on campgrounds and attractions in New England. Go camping and travel in the Northeastern states, especially New England. Have a nice trip, and tell us about it. Travel and camping articles, especially first-person reports on private campgrounds and interviews with owners, are the areas of our publication most open to freelancers."

‡ONTARIO MOTOR COACH REVIEW, Naylor Communications Ltd., 6th Fl., 920 Yonge St., Toronto, Ontario M4W 3C7 Canada. (416)961-1028. FAX: (416)924-4408. Editor: J.D. Corcoran. 50% freelance written. Annual magazine on travel and tourist destinations. Circ. 3,000. Pays 30 days from deadline. Byline given. Offers 33⅓% kill fee. Buys first North American serial rights and all rights. Submit seasonal/holiday material 2 months in advance. Simultaneous and photocopied submissions OK. Query for electronic submissions. Computer printout submissions OK; prefers letter-quality. Free sample copy and writer's guidelines.

Nonfiction: General interest, historical, interview/profile, new product, personal experience (related to motor coach travel), photo feature, technical and travel. Buys 5-10 mss/year. Query with published clips. Length: 500-3,000 words. Pays 20-25¢/word. Pays expenses of writers on assignment.

Photos: State availability of photos with submission. Reviews transparencies and prints. Offers $25-200 per photo. Identification of subjects required.

‡PREFERRED TRAVELLER, "The magazine ENCORE members prefer", Encore Marketing International, Inc., 4501 Forbes Blvd., Lanham MD 20706. Editor: Karen M. Jones. 80% freelance written. Bimonthly magazine on travel. "We are a practical guide for members making travel plans – not a travel 'dream' book. We give them useful information, insider tips, advice on getting the most for their travel dollar. We like short, snappy, entertaining pieces that use colorful writing – not long narrative – to familiarize readers with various locales." Publishes ms an average of 3 months after acceptance. Byline given. Offers 50% kill fee. Buys first North American serial rights. Submit seasonal/holiday material 5 months in advance. Computer printout submissions OK; prefers letter-quality. Reports in 2 months on queries. Sample copy for 8x11 SAE with 2 first class stamps. Writer's guidelines for letter #10 SASE.

Nonfiction: Book excerpts, how-to, humor, new product, photo feature and travel, all travel related. Annual ski issue - Nov./Dec.; Annual cruise issue - Sept./Oct. Buys 36-40 mss/year. Query with published clips. Length: 1,500-2,000 words. Pays $500-700 for assigned articles. Pay only phone, mail charges of writers on assignment.

Photos: State availability of photos with submission. Reviews transparencies. Offers $50-500 per photo. Model releases and identification of subjects required.

Columns/Departments: Business Travel Bulletin (brief news items of current interest to frequent business travelers), 700-800 words; Comic Trips (one-page humorous look at some aspect of travel), 500-600 words; CityScope (fast facts, useful guide to specific city for business travelers), 700-800 words; Picture Perfect (tips on taking better travel photos), 400-500 words. Buys 24 mss/year. Query with published clips. Send complete ms with humor only. Pays $300-400.

Tips: "Do not send unassigned manuscripts (except humor). Even unsolicited queries are not encouraged. Best approach is to send list of travel destinations or topics in which the writer specializes – places frequently visited or lived in. Keep editor abreast of travel plans. Topics are determined by staff and assigned to specialists as needed. Please – no phone queries!"

RV WEST MAGAZINE, Outdoor Publications, Inc., Suite 226, 2033 Clement Ave., Alameda CA 94501. (415)769-8338. Editor: Dave Preston. 85% freelance written. Works with a small number of new/unpublished writers each year. A monthly magazine for Western recreational vehicle owners. Circ. 30,000. Pays on publication. Publishes ms an average of 6 months after acceptance. Byline given. Buys one-time rights. Submit seasonal/holiday material 6 months in advance. Simultaneous, photocopied, and previously published submissions OK. Query for electronic submissions. Computer printout submissions acceptable. Reports in several weeks on queries; several months on mss. Free writer's guidelines.

Nonfiction: Historical/nostalgic; how-to (fix your RV); new product; personal experience (particularly travel); technical; and travel (destinations for RVs). No non-RV travel articles. Buys 36 mss/year. Query with or without published clips, or send complete ms. Length: 1,000-3,000 words. Pays $1.50/inch.

Photos: Send photos with submissions. Reviews contact sheets, negatives, transparencies and prints. Offers $5 minimum/photo. Identification of subjects required.

Tips: "RV travel/destination stories are most open to freelancers. Include all information of value to RVers, and reasons why they would want to visit the location (12 Western states)."

TOURS & RESORTS, The World-Wide Vacation Magazine, World Publishing Co., 990 Grove St., Evanston IL 60201-4370. (312)491-6440. Editor/Associate Publisher: Bob Meyers. Managing Editor: Ray Gudas. 90% freelance written. A bimonthly magazine covering world-wide vacation travel features. Circ. 250,000. Pays on acceptance. Byline given. Buys first North American serial rights. Submit seasonal/holiday material 6 months in advance. Previously published submissions acceptable, dependent upon publication – local or regional OK. Computer printout submissions acceptable; prefers letter-quality. Reports in 3 weeks on queries; 6 weeks on mss. Sample copy $2.50 with 9x12 SASE.

Nonfiction: Primarily destination-oriented travel articles, "Anatomy of a Tour" features, and resort/hotel profiles and roundups, but will consider essays, how-to, humor, company profiles, nostalgia, etc. – if travel-related. "It is best to study current contents and query first." Buys 75 mss/year. Average length: 1,500 words. Pays $150-500.

The double dagger before a listing indicates that the listing is new in this edition. New markets are often the most receptive to freelance submissions.

Photos: Top-quality original color slides preferred. Captions required. Buys one-time rights. Prefers photo feature package (ms plus slides), but will purchase slides only to support a work in progress.

Columns/Departments: Travel Views (travel tips; service articles), and World Shopping (shopping guide). Buys 8-12 mss/year. Query or send complete ms. Length: 800-1,500 words. Pays $125-250.

Tips: "Travel features and the Travel Views department are most open to freelancers. Because we are heavily photo-oriented, superb slides are our foremost concern. The most successful approach is to send 2-3 sheets of slides with the query or complete ms. Include a list of other subjects you can provide as a photo feature package."

TRAILS-A-WAY, 120 S. Lafayette, Greenville MI 48838. (616)754-2251. Editor: Martha Higbie. 25% freelance written. Newspaper published 12 times/year on camping in the Midwest (Michigan, Ohio, Western Pennsylvania, Indiana, Illinois, Wisconsin and Minnesota). "Fun and information for campers who own recreational vehicles." Circ. 62,000. Pays on publication. Byline given. Buys first and second rights to the same material, and second (reprint) rights to material originally published elsewhere. Submit seasonal/holiday material 3 months in advance. Simultaneous queries and submissions OK. Computer printout submissions acceptable; no dot-matrix. Reports in 1 month. Sample copy for 10x13 SAE with 4 first class stamps; writer's guidelines for #10 SAE and 2 first class stamps.

Nonfiction: How-to (use, maintain recreational vehicles—5th wheels, travel and camping trailers, pop-up trailers, motorhomes); humor; inspirational; interview/profile; new product (camp products); personal experience; photo feature; technical (on RVs); travel. March/April issue: spring camping; September/October: fall camping. Winter issues feature southern hot spots. "All articles should relate to RV camping in Michigan, Ohio, Indiana, Illinois and Wisconsin—or south in winter. No tenting or backpacking." Buys 40-50 mss/year. Send complete ms. Length: 1,000-1,500 words. Pays $75-125.

Photos: Send photos with ms. Captions required.

TRANSITIONS ABROAD, 18 Hulst Rd., Box 344, Amherst MA 01004. (413)256-0373. Editor/Publisher: Prof. Clayton A. Hubbs. 80-90% freelance written. Eager to work with new/unpublished writers. The resource magazine for low-budget international travel with an educational or work component. Bound magazine. Circ. 13,000. Pays on publication. Buys first rights and second (reprint) rights to material originally published elsewhere. Byline given. Written queries only. Computer printout submissions acceptable; prefers letter-quality. Reports in 2 months. Sample copy $3.50; writer's guidelines and topics schedule for #10 SASE.

Nonfiction: How-to (find courses, inexpensive lodging and travel); interview (information on specific areas and people); personal experience (evaluation of courses, special interest and study tours, economy travel); and travel (what to see and do in specific areas of the world, new learning and travel ideas). Foreign travel only. Few destination ("tourist") pieces. Emphasis on information and on interaction with people in host country. Buys 30 unsolicited mss/issue. Query with credentials. Length: 500-2,000 words. Pays $25-150. Include author's bio with submissions.

Photos: Send photos with ms. Pays $10-25 for 8x10 b&w glossy prints, $125 for covers. No color. Additional payment for photos accompanying ms. Photos increase likelihood of acceptance. Buys one-time rights. Captions and ID on photos required.

Columns/Departments: Study/Travel Program Notes (evaluation of courses or programs); Traveler's Advisory/Resources (new information and ideas for offbeat independent travel); Jobnotes (how to find it and what to expect); and Book Reviews (reviews of single books or groups on one area). Buys 8/issue. Send complete ms. Length: 1,000 words maximum. Pays $20-50.

Fillers: Info Exchange (information, preferably first-hand—having to do with travel, particularly offbeat educational travel and work or study abroad). Buys 10/issue. Length: 1,000 words maximum. Pays $20-50.

Tips: "We like nuts and bolts stuff, practical information, especially on how to work, live and cut costs abroad. Our readers want usable information on planning their own travel itinerary. Be specific: names, addresses, current costs. We are particularly interested in educational travel and study abroad for adults and senior citizens. More and more readers want information not only on work but retirement possibilities. We have a new department on exchange programs, homestays, and study/tours for precollege students. *Educational Travel Directory and Travel Planner* published each year in July provides descriptive listings of resources and information sources on work, study, and independent travel abroad along with study/travel programs abroad for adults."

TRAVEL & LEISURE, American Express Publishing Corp., 1120 Avenue of the Americas, New York NY 10036. (212)382-5600. Editor-in-Chief: Pamela Fiori. Executive Editor: Christopher Hunt. Managing Editor: Maria Shaw. 80% freelance written. Monthly magazine. Circ. 1.1 million. Pays on acceptance. Byline given. Offers 25% kill fee. Buys first world and foreign edition rights. Reports in 3 weeks. Sample copy $3. Free writer's guidelines.

Nonfiction: Travel. Buys 200 mss/year. Query. Length open. Payment varies. Often pays the expenses of writers on assignment.
Photos: Discourages submission of unsolicited transparencies. Payment varies. Captions required. Buys one-time rights.
Tips: "Read the magazine. Regionals and Taking Off section are best places to start."

TRAVEL SMART, Communications House, Inc., Dobbs Ferry NY 10522. (914)693-4208. Editor/Publisher: H.J. Teison. Managing Editor: Deborah Gaines. Covers information on "good-value travel." Monthly newsletter. Pays on publication. Buys all rights. Photocopied submissions OK. Computer printout submissions acceptable. Reports in 6 weeks. Sample copy and writer's guidelines for #10 SAE with 3 first class stamps.
Nonfiction: "Interested primarily in bargains or little-known deals on transportation, lodging, food, unusual destinations that won't break the bank. Also information on trends in industry. No destination stories on major Caribbean islands, London, New York, no travelogs, my vacation, poetry, fillers. No photos or illustrations. Just hard facts. We are not part of 'Rosy fingers of dawn . . .' school. Write for guidelines, then query. Length: 100-1,000 words. Pays "up to $50."
Tips: "When you travel, check out small hotels offering good prices, little known restaurants, and send us brief rundown (with prices, phone numbers, addresses). Information must be current. Include your phone number with submission, because we sometimes make immediate assignments."

TRAVELORE REPORT, Suite #100, 1512 Spruce St., Philadelphia PA 19102. (215)735-3838. Editor: Ted Barkus. For affluent travelers; businessmen, retirees, well-educated readers; interested in specific tips, tours, and bargain opportunities in travel. Monthly newsletter. Buys all rights. Pays on publication. Submit seasonal material 2 months in advance. Computer printout and disk submissions acceptable. Sample copy $2; writer's guidelines for #10 SASE.
Nonfiction: "Brief insights (25-200 words) with facts, prices, names of hotels and restaurants, etc., on offbeat subjects of interest to people going places. What to do, what not to do. Supply information. We will rewrite if acceptable. We're candid—we tell it like it is with no sugar coating. Avoid telling us about places in United States or abroad without specific recommendations (hotel name, costs, rip-offs, why, how long, etc.). No destination pieces which are general with no specific 'story angle' in mind, or generally available through PR departments." Buys 10-20 mss/year. Pays $5-20.
Tips: "Destinations confronted with political disturbances should be avoided. We'll put more emphasis on travel to North American destination and Caribbean, and/or South Pacific, while safety exists. We're adding more topics geared to business-related travel and marketing trends in leisure-time industry."

‡TRIP & TOUR, Allied Publications, 1776 Lake Worth Rd., Lake Worth FL 33460. (407)582-2099. FAX: (407)582-4667. Editor: Richard Champlin. 95% freelance written. Bimonthly magazine. "We focus on travel through agents and tour operators and on destinations." Pays on publication. Publishes ms an average of 6 months after acceptance. Byline given. Buys first North American serial rights, one-time rights, second serial (reprint) rights or simultaneous rights. Submit seasonal/holiday material 6-8 months in advance. Simultaneous, photocopied and previously published submissions OK. Query for electronic submissions. Computer printout submissions OK; prefers letter-quality. Reports in 2 weeks on queries; 6 months on mss. Sample copy $1. Free writer's guidelines.
Nonfiction: Travel (international). Two cruise issues each year: June/July and December/January. "No hiking or camping stories." Buys 6-12 mss/year. Query with or without published clips, or send complete ms. Length: 600-1,500 words. Pays $5-25 for unsolicited articles. Pays in contributor copies or other premiums only at author request.
Photos: State availability of photos with submission. Reviews contact sheets and transparencies. Pays $5 per photo. Captions, model releases and identification of subjects required. Buys one-time rights.

VISTA/USA, Box 161, Convent Station NJ 07961. (201)538-7600. Editor: Kathleen M. Caccavale. Managing Editor: Martha J. Mendez. 90% freelance written. Will consider ms submissions from *unpublished* writers. Quarterly magazine of Exxon Travel Club. "Our publication uses articles on North American areas. We strive to help our readers gain an in-depth understanding of cities, towns and areas as well as other aspects of American culture that affect the character of the nation." Circ. 900,000. Pays on acceptance. Publishes ms an average of 1 year after acceptance. Buys first North American serial rights. Query about seasonal subjects 18 months in advance. Computer printout submissions acceptable; prefers letter-quality. Reports in 6 weeks. Sample copy for a 9x12 or larger SAE with 5 first class stamps; writer's and photographer's guidelines for #10 SASE.
Nonfiction: Geographically oriented articles on North America focused on the character of an area or place; photo essays (recent examples include city lights, Thoreau's Cape Cod, reflections); and some articles dealing with nature, Americana, crafts and collecting. Usually one activity-oriented article per issue. "We buy feature articles on the U.S., Canada, Mexico and the Caribbean that appeal to a national audience and prefer that destination queries have a hook or angle to them that give us a clear, solid argument for covering the average subject 'soon' rather than 'anytime.' " No feature articles that mention driving or follow routes on a map.

Uses 7-15 mss/issue. Query with outline and clips of previously published work. Length: 1,200-2,000 words. Pays $450 minimum for features. Pays the expenses of writers on assignment.

Columns/Departments: "MiniTrips are point to point or loop driving tours of from 50 to 350 miles covering a healthy variety of stops along the way. 'Close Focus' covers openings or changing aspects of major attractions, small or limited attractions not appropriate for a feature article (800-1,000 words). 'American Vignettes' covers anything travel related that also reveals a slice of American life, often with a light or humorous touch, such as asking directions from a cranky New Englander, or the phenomenon of vanity plates. 'Information, Please' provides practical information on travel safety, trends, tips; a service column."

Photos: Contact: photo researcher. Send photos with ms. Pays $100 minimum for color transparencies. Captions preferred. Buys one-time rights.

Tips: "We are looking for readable pieces with good writing that will interest armchair travelers as much as readers who may want to visit the areas you write about. Queries about well-known destinations should have someting new or different to say about them, a specific focus or angle. Articles should have definite themes and should give our readers an insight into the character and flavor of an area or topic. Stories about personal experiences must impart a sense of drama and excitement or have a strong human-interest angle. Stories about areas should communicate a strong sense of what it feels like to be there. Good use of anecdotes and quotes should be included. Study the articles in the magazine to understand how they are organized, how they present their subjects, the range of writing styles, and the specific types of subjects used. Afterwards, query and enclose samples of your best writing. We continue to seek department shorts and inventory articles of a general, nonseasonal nature (1,500 to 1,800 words)."

‡VOYAGER/SUN SCENE, K.L. Publications, Suite 105, 2001 Killebrew Dr., Bloomington MN 55425. Quarterly magazine published for Gulf Motor Club/Sun Travel Club. 80% freelance written. Circ. 114,000. Pays on acceptance by client. Byline given. Considers mostly previously published articles. Submit seasonal/holiday material 6-8 months in advance. Reports in 1 month. Sample copy for 9x12 SAE with 3 first class stamps; writer's guidelines for #10 SASE.

Nonfiction: Travel (U.S. destinations by car and some foreign destinations), general interest, lifestyle, how-to (travel-related), historical/nostalgic. Length: 500-1,500 words. Pays $50-100.

Photos: Send photos with manuscript. Reviews 35mm transparencies, color only. Pay varies.

YACHT VACATIONS MAGAZINE, Box 1657, Palm Harbor FL 34682-1657. (813)785-3101. Editor: Charity Cicardo. 50% freelance written. Prefers to work with published/established writers. *"Yacht Vacations* is a people-oriented yacht charter magazine with a positive approach." Circ. 30,000. Pays on publication. Publishes ms an average of 3 months after acceptance. Buys first North American serial rights. Submit seasonal/holiday material at least 5 months in advance. Simultaneous queries, simultaneous and photocopied submissions OK. Query for electronic submissions. Computer printout submissions acceptable. Reports in 6 weeks. Writer's guidelines for #10 SASE.

Nonfiction: General interest (worldwide, charter boat-oriented travel); historical/nostalgic (charter vacation oriented); how-to (bareboating technique); interview/profile (charter brokers, charter skippers, positive); new product (beach fashion, hair care products, sun screens, etc.); opinion; personal experience (charter boat related, worldwide, positive people-oriented travel); photo feature (charter boat, worldwide, positive, people-oriented travel); travel (charter vacation-oriented); and ancillary topics such as fishing, scuba or underwater photography. Special issues will focus on the Caribbean, diving, and Mediterranean. Buys 30-40 mss/year. Query with published clips. Length: 600-1,500 words. Pays $100 per 600 words. Rarely pays expenses of writers on assignment.

Photos: "We would like to receive quality cover photos reflecting the charter yacht vacation experience, i.e., water, yacht, and people enjoying." State availability of photos or send photos with query or ms. Pays with article for b&w and color negatives, color transparencies (35mm), and b&w and color prints (3x5 or larger), plus buys cover photos. Requires model releases and identification of subjects. Buys one-time rights.

Tips: "We are happy to look at the work of any established freelancer who may have something appropriate to offer within our scope—travel with a charter vacation orientation. We prefer submissions accompanied by good, professional quality photography. The best first step is a request for editorial guidelines, accompanied by a typed letter and work sample."

Women's

Women have an incredible variety of publications available to them these days—about 50 appear on newsstands in an array of specialties. A number of titles in this area have been redesigned during the past year to compete in the crowded marketplace. Many of the fashion magazines also are following the European trend of putting models in casual minimal settings, especially out-of-doors. Magazines that also use material slanted to women's interests can be found in the following categories: Business and Finance; Child Care and Parental Guidance; Contemporary Culture; Food and Drink; Health and Fitness; Hobby and Craft; Home and Garden; Relationships; Religious; Romance and Confession; and Sports.

‡BRIDAL GUIDE, The How-To For I Do, Globe Communications Corp., 441 Lexington Ave., New York NY 10017. (212)949-4040. FAX: (212)286-0072. Editor: Deborah Harding. 80% freelance written. Prefers to work with experienced/published writers. A bimonthly magazine covering wedding planning, fashion, beauty, contemporary relationship articles, honeymoon travel and planning for the first home. Sample copy for 9x12 SAE and $2.40 postage (1st class), or $1.50 postage (3rd class); writer's guidelines for #10 SASE.

Nonfiction: The editors prefer queries rather than actual manuscript submissions. All correspondence accompanied by a SASE will be answered (response is usually within 1 month). Length: 800-1,600 words. Pays $200-600 on acceptance. Buys 120 mss/year. Offers 20% kill fee. Buys first North American serial rights. Sample copy for $3.50.

Photos: Design Director: Jean L. Oberholtzer. Cartoons and photography submissions should be handled through the Art Department.

Columns/Departments: Regular departments include Finance, Sex, Remarriage, and Advice for the Groom.

BRIDAL TRENDS, Meridian Publishing, Inc., Box 10010, Ogden UT 84409. (801)394-9446. 65% freelance written. Monthly magazine with useful articles for today's bride. Circ. 60,000. Pays on acceptance. Publishes ms an average of 10 months after acceptance. Byline given. Buys first rights, second serial (reprint) rights and non-exclusive reprint rights. Simultaneous, photocopied and previously published submissions OK. Reports in 6 weeks. Sample copy for $1 and 9x12 SAE; writer's guidelines for #10 SASE. All requests for sample copies and guidelines should be addressed Attn: Editor.

Nonfiction: "General interest articles about traditional and modern approaches to weddings. Topics include all aspects of ceremony and reception planning; flowers; invitations; catering; wedding apparel and fashion trends for the bride, groom, and other members of the wedding party, etc. Also featured are honeymoon destinations, how to build a relationship and keep romance alive, and adjusting to married life." Buys approximately 15 mss/year. Query. Length: 1,200 words. Pays 15¢/word for first rights plus non-exclusive reprint rights. Payment for second rights is negotiable.

Photos: State availability of photos with query letter. Color transparencies and 5x7 or 8x10 prints are preferred. Pays $35 for inside photo; pays $50 for cover. Captions, model release, and identification of subjects required.

Tips: "We publish articles that detail each aspect of wedding planning: invitations, choosing your flowers, deciding on the style of your wedding, and choosing a photographer and caterer."

BRIDE'S, Conde Nast Bldg., 350 Madison Ave., New York NY 10017. (212)880-8800. Editor-in-Chief: Barbara D. Tober. 40% freelance written. Eager to work with new/unpublished writers. A bimonthly magazine for the first- or second-time bride, her family and friends, the groom and his family and friends. Circ. 410,000. Pays on acceptance. Publishes ms an average of 2 months after acceptance. Buys all rights. Also buys first and second serial rights for book excerpts on marriage, communication, finances. Offers 20% kill fee, depending on circumstances. Buys 40 unsolicited mss/year. Byline given. Reports in 2 months. Computer printout submissions acceptable; no dot-matrix. Address mss to Features Department. Writer's guidelines for #10 SASE.

Nonfiction: "We want warm, personal articles, optimistic in tone, with help offered in a clear, specific way. All issues should be handled within the context of marriage. How-to features on all aspects of marriage: communications, in-laws, careers, money, sex, housing, housework, family planning, marriage after a baby, religion, interfaith marriage, step-parenting, second marriage, reaffirmation of vows; informational articles on the realities of marriage, the changing roles of men and women, the kind of troubles in engagement that are likely to become big issues in marriage; stories from couples or marriage authorities that illustrate marital problems and solutions to men and women; book excerpts on marriage, communication, finances, sex; and how-to features on wedding planning that offer expert advice. Also success stories of marriages of long duration. We use first-person pieces and articles that are well researched, relying on quotes from authorities in the field, and anecdotes and dialogues from real couples. We publish first-person essays on provocative topics unique to marriage." Query or submit complete ms. Article outline preferred. Length: 1,000-3,000 words. Pays $300-800.

Columns/Departments: The Love column accepts reader love poems, for $25 each. The Something New section accepts reader wedding planning and craft ideas; pays $25.

Tips: "Since marriage rates are up and large, traditional weddings are back in style, and since more women work than ever before, do *not* query us on just living together or becoming a stay-at-home wife after marriage. Send us a query or a well-written article that is both easy to read and offers real help for the bride or groom as she/he adjusts to her/his new role. No first-person narratives on wedding and reception planning, home furnishings, cooking, fashion, beauty, travel. We're interested in unusual ideas, experiences, and lifestyles. No 'I used baby pink rose buds' articles."

CHATELAINE, 777 Bay St., Toronto, Ontario M5W 1A7 Canada. Editor-in-Chief: Mildred Istona. 75% freelance written. Prefers to work with published/established writers. Monthly general-interest magazine for Canadian women, from age 20 and up. "*Chatelaine* is read by one woman in three across Canada, a readership that spans almost every age group but is concentrated among those 25 to 45 including homemakers and working women in all walks of life." Circ. over 1 million. Pays on acceptance. Publishes ms an average of 3 months after acceptance. Byline given. Computer printout submissions OK; prefers letter-quality. Reports within 2 weeks. All mss must be accompanied by a SASE (IRCs in lieu of stamps if sent from outside Canada). Sample copy $2 and postage; free writer's guidelines.

Nonfiction: Elizabeth Parr, senior editor, articles. Submit an outline or query first. Full-length major pieces run from 1,500 to 3,000 words. Pays minimum $1,200 for acceptable major article. Buys first North American serial rights in English and French (the latter to cover possible use in *Chatelaine's* sister French-language edition, edited in Montreal for French Canada). "We look for important national Canadian subjects, examining any and all facets of Canadian life, especially as they concern or interest women. Upfront columns include stories about relationships, health, nutrition, fitness and parents and kids. Submit outline first. Pays $350 for about 600 words. Prefers queries for nonfiction subjects on initial contact plus a resume and writing samples. Also seeks full-length personal experience stories with deep emotional impact. Pays $750. Pays expenses of writers on assignment.

Tips: Features on beauty, food, fashion and home decorating are supplied by staff writers and editors, and unsolicited material is not considered.

‡COSMOPOLITAN, The Hearst Corp., 224 W. 57th St., New York NY 10019. Exec. Editor: Roberta Ashley. 90% freelance written. Monthly magazine about 18- to 35-year-old single, married, divorced—all working. Pays on acceptance. Byline given. Offers 10% kill fee. Buys all magazine rights and occasionally negotiates first North American rights. Submit seasonal/holiday material 6 months in advance. Previously published submissions in minor publications OK. Computer printout submissions OK; prefers letter-quality. Reports in 1 week on queries; 3 weeks on mss. Sample copy $2.50. Writer's guidelines for #10 SASE.

Nonfiction: Book excerpts, how-to, humor, opinion, personal experience and anything of interest to young women. Buys 350 mss/year. Query with published clips or send complete ms. Length: 500-3,500 words. Pays expenses of writers on assignment.

Fiction: Betty Kelly. Condensed novels, humorous, novel excerpts, romance and original short stories with romantic plots. Buys 18 mss/year. Query. Length: 750-3,000 words.

Poetry: Free verse and light verse. Buys 30 poems/year. No maximum number. Length: 4-30 lines.

Fillers: Irene Copeland. Facts. Buys 240/year. Length: 300-1,000 words.

COUNTRY WOMAN, Reiman Publications, Box 643, Milwaukee WI 53201. (414)423-0100. Editor: Ann Kaiser. Managing Editor: Kathy Pohl. 75-85% freelance written. Eager to work with new/unpublished writers. Bimonthly magazine on the interests of country women. "*Country Woman* is for contemporary rural women of all ages and backgrounds and from all over the U.S. and Canada. It includes a sampling of the diversity that makes up rural women's lives—love of home, family, farm, ranch, community, hobbies, enduring values, humor, attaining new skills and appreciating present, past and future all within the content of the lifestyle that surrounds country living." Circ. 550,000. Pays on acceptance. Publishes ms an average of 1 year after acceptance. Byline given. Buys first North American serial rights, one-time rights, and second serial (reprint) rights; makes some work-for-hire assignments (very few). Submit seasonal/holiday material 4-5 months in advance. Photocopied and previously published (on occasion) submissions OK. Computer printout submissions acceptable; no dot-matrix. Reports in 1 month on queries; 2 months on mss. Sample copy for $2.50; writer's guidelines for #10 SASE.

Nonfiction: General interest, historical/nostalgic, how-to (crafts, community projects, family relations, self-improvement, decorative, antiquing, etc.); humor; inspirational; interview/profile; personal experience; photo feature; and travel, all pertaining to a rural woman's interest. Articles must be written in a positive, light and entertaining manner. Buys 100 mss/year. Query or send complete ms. Length: 1,000 words maximum.

Photos: Send photos with query or ms. Reviews 35mm or 2¼ transparencies. "We pay for photo/feature packages." Captions, model releases and identification of subjects required. Buys one-time rights.

Columns/Departments: Why Farm Wives Age Fast (humor), I Remember When (nostalgia), Country Decorating, and Shopping Comparison (new product comparisons). Buys 20 mss (maximum)/year. Query or send complete ms. Length: 500-1,000 words. Pays $75-125.

Fiction: Adventure, humorous, mainstream and western. Main character *must* be a country woman. All fiction must have a country setting. Fiction must have a positive, upbeat message. Buys 5 mss (maximum)/year. Query or send complete ms. Length: 750-1,000 words. Pays $90-125.

Poetry: Traditional and light verse. "Poetry must have rhythm and rhyme! It must be country-related. Always looking for seasonal poetry." Buys 40 poems/year. Submit maximum 6 poems. Length: 5-24 lines. Pays $10-40.

Fillers: Jokes, anecdotes, short humor and consumer news (e.g. safety, tips, etc.). Buys 40/year. Length: 40-250 words. Pays $25-40.

Tips: "We have recently broadened our focus to include 'country' women, not just women on farms and ranches. This allows freelancers a wider scope in material. Write as clearly and with as much zest and enthusiasm as possible. We love good quotes, supporting materials (names, places, etc.) and strong leads and closings. Readers relate strongly to where they live and the lifestyle they've chosen. They want to be informed and entertained, and that's just exactly why they subscribe. Readers are busy—not too busy to read—but when they do sit down, they want good writing, reliable information and something that feels like a reward. How-to, humor, personal experience and nostalgia are areas most open to freelancers. Profiles, to a certain degree, are also open. We are always especially receptive to short items—250 words, 400 words and so on. Be accurate and fresh in approach."

ESSENCE, 1500 Broadway, New York NY 10036. Editor-in-Chief: Susan L. Taylor. Editor: Stephanie Stokes Oliver. Executive Editor: Cheryll Y. Greene. Senior Editor: Elsie B. Washington. Edited for Black women. Monthly magazine; 150 pages. Circ. 850,000. Pays on acceptance. Makes assignments on work for hire basis. 3 month lead time. Pays 25% kill fee. Byline given. Submit seasonal/holiday material 6 months in advance. Computer printout submissions acceptable. Reports in 2 months. Sample copy $1.50; free writer's guidelines.

Features: "We're looking for articles that inspire and inform Black women. Our readers are interested and aware; the topics we include in each issue are provacative. Every articles should move the *Essence* woman emotionally and intellectually. We welcome queries form good writers on a wide range of topics; general interest, health and fitness, historical, how-to, humor, self-help, relationships, work, personality interview, personal experience, political issues, business and finances and personal opinion." Buys 200 mss/year. Query only; word length will be given upon assignment. Pays $500 minimum.

Photos: Charles Dixon, III, art director. State availability of photos with query. Pays $100 for b&w page; $300 for color page. Captions and model release required. "We particularly would like to see photographs for our travel section that feature Black travelers."

Columns/Departments: Query department editors: Contemporary Living (home, food, lifestyle, travel, consumer information): Harriette Cole, Contemporary Living, editor; Arts & Entertainment: Martha Southgate; Health & Fitness: Linda Villarosa; Business and Finance: Evette Porter. Query only; word length will be given upon assignment. Pays $100 minimum. "We are interested in buying short poetry to be used as filler material."

Tips: "Please note that *Essence* no longer accepts unsolicited mss for fiction, poetry or nonfiction, except for the Brothers and Speak! pages and our Interiors column. So please only send query letters for nonfiction story ideas."

FAIRFIELD COUNTY WOMAN, FCW, Inc., 15 Bank St., Stamford CT 06901. (203)323-3105. Editor: Joan Honig. 90% freelance written. A women's regional monthly tabloid focusing on careers, education, health, relationships and family life. Circ. 40,000. Pays 60 days after publications. Byline given. Buys first rights. Submit seasonal/holiday material 3 months in advance. Simultaneous, photocopied and previously published submissions OK. Query for electronic submissions. Requires hard copy with submission; computer printout OK, letter-quality preferred. Sample copy for 10x13 SAE with $1.25 postage.

Nonfiction: Book excerpts, essays, general interest, how-to, humor, inspirational and local interview/profile. Buys 125 mss/year. Query with published clips. Length: 800-2,000 words. Pays $35-100 for assigned articles; $25-75 for unsolicited articles. Sometimes pays expenses of writers on assignment.

Photos: State availability of photos with submission. Reviews 5x7 prints. Offers no additional payment with ms. Buys one-time rights.

Columns/Departments: Health, auto, finance and home. Length: 1,200 words. Buys 50 mss/year. Query with published clips. Pays $25-50.

‡FAMILY CIRCLE MAGAZINE, 110 Fifth Ave., New York NY 10011. (212)463-1000. Editor-in-Chief: Jacqueline Leo. 70% freelance written. For women. Published 17 times/year. Usually buys all rights. Offers 20% kill fee. Byline given. Pays on acceptance. "We are a national women's magazine which offers advice, fresh information and entertainment to women. Query should stress the unique aspects of an article and expert sources; we want articles that will help our readers." Reports in 1 month.

Nonfiction: Susan Ungaro, articles editor. Women's interest subjects such as family and personal relationships, children, physical and mental health, nutrition, self-improvement and profiles of ordinary women doing extraordinary things for her community or the nation. Service articles. For travel, interested mainly in local material. "We look for well-written, well-reported stories told in terms of people. We want well-researched

service journalism on all subjects." Query. Length: 1,000-2,500 words. Pays $1/word.
Tips: Query letters should be "concise and to the point." Also, writers should "keep close tabs on *Family Circle* and other women's magazines to avoid submitting recently run subject matter."

GLAMOUR, Conde Nast, 350 Madison Ave., New York NY 10017. (212)880-8800. Editor-in-Chief: Ruth Whitney. 75% freelance written. Works with a small number of new/unpublished writers each year. For college-educated women, 18-35 years old. Monthly. Circ. 2.3 million; 7 million readers. Pays on acceptance. Offers 20% kill fee. Publishes ms an average of 6-12 months after acceptance. Byline given. Computer printout submissions OK "if the material is easy to read"; prefers letter-quality. Reports in 5 weeks. Writer's guidelines for #10 SASE.
Nonfiction: Judy Coyne, articles editor. "Editorial approach is 'how-to' with articles that are relevant in the areas of careers, health, psychology, interpersonal relationships, etc. We look for queries that are fresh and include a contemporary, timely angle. Fashion, beauty, decorating, travel, food and entertainment are all staff-written. We use 1,000-word opinion essays for our Viewpoint section. Pays $500. Our His/Hers column features generally stylish essays on relationships or comments on current mores by male and female writers in alternate months." Pays $1,000 for His/Hers mss. Buys first North American serial rights. Buys 10-12 mss/ issue. Query "with letter that is detailed, well-focused, well-organized, and documented with surveys, statistics and research, personal essays excepted." Short articles and essays (1,500-2,000 words) pay $1,000 and up; longer mss (2,500-3,000 words) pay $1,500 minimum on acceptance. Sometimes pays the expenses of writers on assignment.
Tips: "We're looking for sharply focused ideas by strong writers and constantly raising our standards. We are interested in getting new writers, and we are approachable, mainly because our range of topics is so broad. We've increased our focus on male-female relationships."

GOOD HOUSEKEEPING, Hearst Corp., 959 8th Ave., New York NY 10019. (212)649-2000. Editor-in-Chief: John Mack Carter. Executive Editor: Mina Mulvey. Managing Editor: Mary Fiore. Prefers to work with published/established writers. Monthly. Circ. 5 million. Pays on acceptance. Buys all rights. Pays 25% kill fee. Byline given. Submit seasonal/holiday material 6 months in advance. Computer printout submissions acceptable; no dot-matrix. Reports in 6 weeks. Sample copy $2. Free writer's guidelines with SASE.
Nonfiction: Joan Thursh, articles editor. Medical; informational; investigative stories; inspirational; interview; nostalgia; personal experience; and profile. Buys 4-6 mss/issue. Query. Length: 1,500-2,500 words. Pays $1,500 on acceptance for full articles from new writers. Regional Editor: Shirley Howard. Pays $250-350 for local interest and travel pieces of 2,000 words. Pays the expenses of writers on assignment.
Photos: Herbert Bleiweiss, art director. Photos purchased on assignment mostly. Some short photo features with captions. Pays $100-350 for b&w; $200-400 for color photos. Query. Model releases required.
Columns/Departments: Light Housekeeping & Fillers, edited by Rosemary Leonard. Humorous short-short prose and verse. Jokes, gags, anecdotes. Pays $25-50. The Better Way, edited by Erika Mark. Ideas and in-depth research. Query. Pays $250-500. "Mostly staff written; only outstanding ideas have a chance here."
Fiction: Naome Lewis, fiction editor. Uses romance fiction and condensations of novels that can appear in one issue. Looks for reader identification. "We get 1,500 unsolicited mss/month—includes poetry; a freelancer's odds are overwhelming—but we do look at all submissions." Send complete mss. Length: 1,500 words (short-shorts); novel according to merit of material; average 5,000-word short stories. Pays $1,000 minimum for fiction short-shorts; $1,250 for short stories.
Poetry: Arleen Quarfoot, poetry editor. Light verse and traditional. "Presently overstocked." Poems used as fillers. Pays $5/line for poetry on acceptance.
Tips: "Always send an SASE. We prefer to see a query first. Do not send material on subjects already covered in-house by the Good Housekeeping Institute—these include food, beauty, needlework and crafts."

HOMEWORKING MOTHERS, Mothers' Home Business Network, Box 423, East Meadow NY 11554. (516)997-7394. Editor: Georganne Fiumara. 80% freelance written. Eager to work with new/unpublished writers. Quarterly newsletter "written for mothers who have home businesses or would like to. These mothers want to work at home so that they can spend more time with their children." Circ. 10,000. Pays on publication. Publishes ms an average of 3-6 months after acceptance. Byline given. Buys one-time rights. Submit seasonal/ holiday material 8 months in advance. Simultaneous, photocopied and previously published submissions OK. Computer printout submissions OK. Reports in 1 month on queries; 6 weeks on mss. Sample copy $2 with #10 SAE and 65¢ postage.
Nonfiction: Book excerpts, essays, how-to, humor, inspirational, personal experience and technical—home business information "all relating to working at home or home-based businesses." Special issues feature excerpts and reviews of books and periodicals about working at home (spring) and tax-related articles (winter). No articles about questionable home business opportunities. Buys 16-20 mss/year. Query with published clips, or send complete ms. Length: 300-1,000 words. Payment varies. Sometimes pays writers with contributor copies or in advertising or promoting a writer's business if applicable. "We would like to receive in-depth descriptions of one home business possibility, i.e., bookkeeping, commercial art, etc.—at least 3,000 words to be published in booklet form. (Pays $150 and buys all rights)."

Columns/Departments: It's My Business (mothers describe their businesses, how they got started, and how they handle work and children at the same time); Advice for Homeworking Mothers (business, marketing and tax basics written by professionals); Considering the Possibilities (ideas and descriptions of legitimate home business opportunities); A Look at a Book (excerpts from books describing some aspect of working at home or popular work-at-home professions); and Time Out for Kids (inspirational material to help mothers cope with working at home). Length: Varies, but average is 500 words. Buys 4 mss/year. Send complete ms.

Poetry: Free verse, light verse and traditional. "About being a mother working at home or home business." Submit maximum 5 poems. Pays $5.

Fillers: Facts and newsbreaks "about working at home for 'Take Note' page." Length: 150 words maximum. Pays $10.

Tips: "We prefer that the writer have personal experience with this lifestyle or be an expert in the field when giving general home business information. It's My Business and Time Out for Kids are most open to freelancers. Writers should read *HM* before trying to write for us."

THE JOYFUL WOMAN, For and About Bible-believing Women Who Want God's Best, The Joyful Woman Ministries, Inc., Business Office: Box 90028, Chattanooga TN 37412. (615)698-7318. Editor: Elizabeth Handford, 118 Shannon Lake Circle, Greenville SC 29615. 50% freelance written. Works with small number of new/unpublished writers each year. Bimonthly magazine covering the role of women in home and business. *"The Joyful Woman* hopes to encourage, stimulate, teach, and develop the Christian woman to reach the full potential of her womanhood." Circ. 12,000. Pays on publication. Publishes ms an average of 4 months after acceptance. Byline given. Buys first rights. Submit seasonal/holiday material 4 months in advance. Photocopied submissions OK. Computer printout submissions acceptable; prefers letter-quality. Reports in 3 months. Sample copy for 9x12 SAE with 4 first class stamps; writer's guidelines for #10 SASE.

Nonfiction: Book excerpts, how-to (housekeeping, childrearing, career management, etc.); inspirational; interview/profile (of Christian women); and personal experience. "We publish material on every facet of the human experience, considering not just a woman's spiritual needs, but her emotional, physical, and intellectual needs and her ministry to others." Buys 80-100 mss/year. Send complete ms. Length: 700-2,500 words. Pays about 2¢/word.

Tips: "The philosophy of the woman's liberation movement tends to minimize the unique and important ministries God has in mind for a woman. We believe that being a woman and a Christian ought to be joyful and fulfilling personally and valuable to God, whatever her situation—career woman, wife, mother, daughter."

LADIES' HOME JOURNAL, Meredith Corporation, 100 Park Ave., New York NY 10017. (212)953-7070. Publishing Director and Editor-in-Chief: Myrna Blyth. Executive Editor: Lynn Langway. 50% freelance written. A monthly magazine focusing on issues of concern to women. *"LHJ* reflects the lives of the contemporary mainstream woman and provides the information she needs and wants to live in today's world." Circ. 5.1 million. Pays on acceptance. Publishes ms an average of 3 months after acceptance, but varies according to needs. Byline given. Offers 25% kill fee. Rights bought vary with submission. Submit seasonal/holiday material 6 months in advance. Photocopied submissions OK. Computer printout submissions OK; prefers letter-quality. Reports in 6 weeks. Sample copy $1.75 with SAE and $2.40 postage. Issues older than 2 years: $3.50 plus $2.40 postage. Free writer's guidelines.

Nonfiction: Lynn Langway, executive editor, oversees the entire department and may be queried directly. In addition, submissions may be directed to Linda Peterson, articles editor, and on the following subjects to the editors listed for each: Relationships (senior editor Margery Rosen); medical/health (Nelly Edmondson Gupta); investigative reports or news related features (senior editor Jane Farrell); and celebrities (executive editor Lynn Langway). Travel pieces for Prime Shopper may be sent to Assistant Managing Editor Nina Keilin. Query with published clips. Length: 1,500-3,500 words. Fees vary; average is between $1,000 and $3,500. Pays expenses of writers on assignment.

Photos: State availability of photos with submission. Offers variable payment for photos accepted with ms. Captions, model releases and identification of subjects required. Rights bought vary with submissions.

Columns/Departments: Query the following editors for column ideas. A Woman Today (Pam Guthrie O'Brien, associate editor); Money News (Linda Peterson, articles editor); Parent News (Mary Mohler, managing editor); and Pet News (Nina Keilin).

Fiction: "We consider any short story or novel that is submitted by an agent or publisher that we feel will work for our audience." Buys 12 mss/year. Length: 3,500 words. Fees vary with submission.

LADY'S CIRCLE, Lopez Publications, Inc., 111 East 35th St., New York NY 10016. (212)689-3933. Editor: Mary F. Bemis. 50% freelance written. Bimonthly magazine. "Midwest homemakers. Christian. Middle to low income. A large number of senior citizens read *Lady's Circle.*" Circ. 200,000. Pays on publication. Byline given. Submit seasonal/holiday material 6 months in advance. Photocopied and previously published submissions OK. Reports in 2 months on queries; 3 months on mss. Sample copy for 9x12 SAE with $1.25 postage. Writer's guidelines for #10 SASE.

Nonfiction: Historical/nostalgic, how-to (crafts, cooking, hobbies), humor, inspirational, interview/profile, opinion, personal experience and religious. No travel. Buys 50-75 mss/year. Query. Pays $125 for unsolicited articles. Sometimes pays expenses of writers on assignment.
Photos: State availability of photos with submission. Reviews negatives, transparencies and prints. Offers $10/photo. Model releases and identification of subjects required.
Columns/Departments: Sound Off (pet peeves) 250 words; Readers' Cookbook (readers send in recipes); and Helpful Hints (hints for kitchen, house, etc.) 3-4 lines per hint. Send complete ms. Pays $5-10.
Fiction: Humorous, mainstream, religious, romance, and slice-of-life vignettes. Nothing experimental. No foul language. Buys 3 mss/year. Send complete ms. Pays $125.
Fillers: Contact Adrian B. Lopez. Anecdotes and short humor. Buys 35/year. Length: 100 words. Pays $5-25.
Tips: "Write for guidelines. A good query is always appreciated. Fifty percent of our magazine is open to freelancers."

LEAR'S, Lear's Publishing, 505 Park Ave., New York NY 10022. (212)888-0007. Editor: Myra Appleton. Executive Editor: Audreen Ballard. Articles Editor: Nelson W. Aldrich, Jr. Bimonthly magazine for women. Circ. 375,000. Pays on acceptance. Byline given. Offers ⅓ kill fee. Buys first North American serial rights and second serial reprint rights. Computer printout submissions OK. Reports in 6 weeks. Free writer's guidelines.
Nonfiction: Book excerpts, essays, general interest, interview/profile, opinion, personal experience, travel. Query with published clips. Length: 800-1,200 words. Pays $1 per word. Sometimes pays expenses of writers on assignment.
Columns/Departments: Self-Center, Money & Worth, Features, and Pleasures. Query with published clips. Length: 800-1,000 words. Pays $1 per word.

LUTHERAN WOMAN TODAY, Women of the ELCA/Augsburg Publishing House, 8765 West Higgings Rd., Chicago IL 60631. (380)312-2743. Editor: Nancy Stelling. Managing Editor: Sue Edison-Swift. 25% freelance written. Monthly magazine designed for all women of the Evangelical Lutheran Church in American. Estab. 1988. Circ. 300,000. Pays on acceptance or 2 months post due date. Byline given. Buys first rights and one-time rights. Submit seasonal/holiday material 7 months in advance. Photocopied submissions OK. Computer printout submissions OK. Reports in 2 months on queries; 3 months on mss. Sample copy for 6x9 SAE and $1; writer's guidelines for #10 SAE.
Nonfiction: Book excerpts, historical/nostalgic, humor, inspirational, interview/profile, opinion, personal experience, photo feature religious. Buys 24 mss/year. Send complete ms. Length: 350-1,400 words. Pays $50-250.
Photos: State availability of photos or send photos with submission. Reviews contact sheet and prints. Pays variable rate. Captions and identification of subjects required. Buys one-time rights.
Columns/Departments: Women's Scene, Seasons' Best (essay featuring church year theme); About Women (featuring 3 women of faith); Forum (essay/editorial). Send complete ms. Length: 350-1,000 words. Pays $50-250.
Fiction: Historical humorous, religious, thought-provoking devotions. "All with a women's and Christian focus." Buys 5 mss/year. Send complete ms. Length: 350-1,400 words. Pays $50-250.
Poetry: Free verse, haiku, light verse and traditional. Buys 5 poems/year. Submit maximum 5 poems. Length: 60 lines maximum. Pays $15-50.
Fillers: Anecdotes, newsbreaks, short humor. Buys occasionally. Length: 350 maximum. Pays $15-50.

McCALL'S, 230 Park Ave., New York NY 10169. (212)551-9500. Editor: Elizabeth Sloan. Managing Editor: Lisel Eisenheimer. 90% freelance written. "Study recent issues." Our publication "carefully and conscientiously services the needs of the woman reader—concentrating on matters that directly affect her life and offering information and understanding on subjects of personal importance to her." Monthly. Circ. 5 million. Pays on acceptance. Publishes ms an average of 6 months after acceptance. Offers 20% kill fee. Byline given. Buys first or exclusive North American rights. Computer printout submissions acceptable; no dot-matrix. Reports in 2 months. Writer's guidelines for SASE.
Nonfiction: Lisel Eisenheimer, managing editor. No subject of wide public or personal interest is out of bounds for *McCall's* so long as it is appropriately treated. The editors are seeking meaningful stories of personal experience, fresh slants for self-help and relationship pieces, and well-researched articles and narratives dealing with social problems concerning readers. *McCall's* buys 200-300 articles/year, many in the 1,000- to 1,500-word length. Pays variable rates for nonfiction. Helen Del Monte and Andrea Thompson are editors of nonfiction books, from which *McCall's* frequently publishes excerpts. These are on subjects of interest to women: personal narratives, celebrity biographies and autobiographies, etc. Almost all features on food, household equipment and management, fashion, beauty, building and decorating are staff-written. Query. "All manuscripts must be submitted on speculation, and *McCall's* accepts no responsibility for unsolicited manuscripts." Sometimes pays the expenses of writers on assignment.
Columns/Departments: Child Care (edited by Maureen Smith Williams); short items that may be humorous, helpful, inspiring and reassuring. Pays $100 and up. Vital Signs (edited by Saralie Falvelson-Neustadt); short items on health and medical news. Pay varies.

Fiction: Helen Del Monte, department editor. Not considering unsolicited fiction. "Again the editors would remind writers of the contemporary woman's taste and intelligence. Most of all, fiction can awaken a reader's sense of identity, deepen her understanding of herself and others, refresh her with a laugh at herself, etc. *McCall's* looks for stories which will have meaning for an adult reader of some literary sensitivity. *No* stories that are grim, depressing, fragmentary or concerned with themes of abnormality or violence. *McCall's* principal interest is in short stories; but fiction of all lengths is considered." Length: about 3,000 words average. Length for short-shorts: about 2,000 words. Payment begins at $1,500; $2,000 for full-length stories.

Poetry: Helen Del Monte, poetry editor. Poets with a "very original way of looking at their subjects" are most likely to get her attention. *McCall's* needs poems on love, the family, relationships with friends and relatives, familiar aspects of domestic and suburban life, Americana, and the seasons. Pays $5/line on acceptance for first North American serial rights. Length: no longer than 30 lines.

Tips: "Except for humor, query first. We are interested in holiday-related pieces and personal narratives. We rarely use essays. We don't encourage an idea unless we think we can use it." Preferred length: 750-2,000 words. Address submissions to Margot Gilman unless otherwise specified.

MADEMOISELLE, 350 Madison Ave., New York NY 10017. Michelle Stacey, executive editor, articles. 95% freelance written. Prefers to work with published/established writers. Columns are written by columnists; "sometimes we give new writers a 'chance' on shorter, less complex assignments." Directed to college-educated, unmarried working women 18-34. Circ. 1.1 million. Reports in 1 month. Buys first North American serial rights. Pays on acceptance; rates vary. Publishes ms an average of 1 year after acceptance. Computer printout submissions are acceptable "but only letter-quality, double-spaced; no dot-matrix."

Nonfiction: Particular concentration on articles of interest to the intelligent young woman, including personal relationships, health, careers, trends, and current social problems. Send health queries to Ellen Welty, health editor. Send entertainment queries to Gini Sikes, entertainment editor. Query with published clips. Length: 1,500-3,000 words.

Photos: Kati Korpijaakko, art director. Commissioned work assigned according to needs. Photos of fashion, beauty, travel. Payment ranges from no-charge to an agreed rate of payment per shot, job series or page rate. Buys all rights. Pays on publication for photos.

Fiction: Eileen Schnurr, fiction and books editor. Quality fiction by both established and unknown writers. "We are interested in encouraging and publishing new writers and welcome unsolicited fiction manuscripts. However we are not a market for formula stories, genre fiction, unforgettable character portraits, surprise endings or oblique stream of consciousness sketches. We are looking for well-told stories that speak in fresh and individual voices and help us to understand ourselves and the world we live in. Stories of particular relevance to young women have an especially good chance, but stories need not be by or from the point of view of a woman—we are interested in good fiction on any theme from any point of view." Buys first North American serial rights. Pays $1,500 for short stories (10-25 pages); $1,000 for short shorts (7-10 pages). Allow 3 months for reply. SASE required. In addition to year-round unqualified acceptance of unsolicited fiction manuscripts, *Mademoiselle* conducts a once-a-year fiction contest open to unpublished writers, male and female, 18-30 years old. First prize is $1,000 plus publication in *Mademoiselle*; second prize, $500 with option to publish. Watch magazine for announcement, usually in January or February issues, or send SASE for rules, after Jan 1.

Tips: "We are looking for timely, well-researched manuscripts."

MODERN BRIDE, CBS Magazines, 475 Park Ave., South, New York NY 10016. (212)779-1999. Editor: Cele Lalli. Managing Editor: Mary Ann Cavlin. Pays on acceptance. Offers 25% kill fee. Buys first periodical rights. Previously published submissions OK. Reports in 1 month.

Nonfiction: Book excerpts, general interest, how-to, personal experience. Buys 70 mss/year. Query with published clips. Length: 500-2,000 words. Pays $600-1,200.

Columns/Departments: Risa Weinreb, editor. Travel.

Poetry: Free verse, light verse and traditional. Buys very few. Submit maximum 6 poems.

‡MS. MAGAZINE, Matilda Publications Inc., 1 Times Square, 9th Fl., New York NY 10036. (212)719-9800. Editor: Anne Summers. Managing Editor: Joanne Edgar. Executive Editor: Marcia Ann Gillespie. 75% freelance written. Monthly magazine on women's issues and news. Circ. 550,000. Pays on publication. Byline given. Offers 20% kill fee. Buys all rights. Submit seasonal/holiday material 6 months in advance. Query for electronic submissions. Computer printout submissions OK; prefers letter-quality. Reports in 6 weeks. Sample copy $2.25. Writer's guidelines for #10 SASE.

Nonfiction: Book excerpts, essays, exposé, general interest, historical/nostalgic, how-to, humor, interview/profile, new product, opinion, personal experience, photo feature, travel, women's news and sports. "Has special issue on women's health; special issue on Smart Money. No fiction, poetry." Buys 150 mss/year. Query with published clips. Length: 300-4,000 words. Pays $150-6,000 for assigned articles; $150-1,000 for unsolicited articles. Pays expenses of writers on assignment.

Photos: State availability of photos with submission. Offers $75-300 per photo. Model releases and identification of subjects required. Buys one-time rights.
Columns/Departments: Our Bodies (women's health), 300-1,000 words; Ms. Adventure (travel), 600-1,000 words; Arts & Books (reviews), 300-750 words; and Technology, 600-750 words. Buys 100 mss/year. Query with published clips. Length: 500-1,000 words. Pays $250-1,000.

NA'AMAT WOMAN, Magazine of NA'AMAT USA, the Women's Labor Zionist Organization of America, NA'AMAT USA, 200 Madison Ave., New York NY 10016. (212)725-8010. Editor: Judith A. Sokoloff. 80% freelance written. Magazine published 5 times/year covering Jewish themes and issues; Israel; women's issues; Labor Zionism; and social, political and economic issues. Circ. 30,000. Pays on publication. Byline given. Not copyrighted. Buys first North American serial, one-time and first serial rights; second serial (reprint) rights to book excerpts; and makes work-for-hire assignments. Reports in 1 month on queries, 2 months on mss. Writer's guidelines for SASE.
Nonfiction: Expose; general interest (Jewish); historical/nostalgic; interview/profile; opinion; personal experience; photo feature; travel (Israel); art; and music. "All articles must be of interest to the Jewish community." Buys 35 mss/year. Query with clips of published work or send complete ms. Pays 8¢/word.
Photos: State availability of photos. Pays $10-30 for 4x5 or 5x7 prints. Captions and identification of subjects required. Buys one-time rights.
Columns/Departments: Film and book reviews with Jewish themes. Buys 20-25 mss/year. Query with clips of published work or send complete ms. Pays 8¢/word.
Fiction: Historical/nostalgic, humorous, women-oriented, and novel excerpts. "Good intelligent fiction with Jewish slant. No maudlin nostalgia or trite humor." Buys 3 mss/year. Send complete ms. Length: 1,200-3,000 words. Pays 8¢/word.

‡NEW WOMAN MAGAZINE, Murdoch Magazines, 215 Lexington Ave., New York NY 10016. (212)685-4790. Editor-in-Chief: Gay Bryant. Managing Editor: Karen Walden. 80% freelance written. Prefers to work with published/established writers, and works with a small number of new/unpublished writers each year. A monthly general interest women's magazine for ages 25-45. "We're especially interested in self-help in love and work (career); we also cover food, fashion, beauty, travel, money." Circ. 1.15 million. Pays on acceptance. Publishes ms an average of 6 months after acceptance. Byline given. Offers 20% kill fee. Buys first North American and British serial rights. Submit seasonal/holiday material 8 months in advance. Simultaneous, photocopied and previously published submissions OK. Computer printout submissions acceptable (double space and leave a wide righthand margin); prefers letter-quality. Reports in 2 months. Writer's guidelines for #10 SASE.
Nonfiction: Articles or essays on relationships, psychology, personal experience, travel, health, career advice and money. Does one special section on Money, Careers and/or Health every year. No book or movie reviews, advice columns, fashion, food or beauty material. Buys 75-100 mss/year. Query with published clips or send complete ms. Length: 2,000 words. Pays $500-2,000. Pays the telephone expenses of writers on assignment.
Photos: State availability of photos with submission. Offers no additional payment for photos accepted with ms. Captions, model releases and identification of subjects required. Buys one-time rights.
Fillers: Rosemarie Lennon, fillers editor. Facts, newsbreaks and newspaper clips (for Briefing section). Buys 3/year. Length: 200-500 words. Pays $10-200.
Tips: "The best approach for breaking in to our publication is a personal letter, with clippings of published work, telling us what you're interested in, what you really like to write about, and your perceptions of *New Woman*. It counts a lot when a writer loves the magazine and responds to it on a personal level. Psychology and relationships articles are most open to freelancers. Best tip: *familiarity with the magazine*. We look for originality, solid research, depth, and a friendly, accessible style."

QUARANTE, Magazine for the Woman Who's Arrived, Savoir Inc., Box 2875, Crystal City, Arlington VA 22202. (703)920-3333. Editor: Michele R. Linden. Managing Editor: Linda Wozniak. 90% freelance written. A quarterly magazine with humor, politics, finance, business, fashion, cuisine, health, beauty, travel, media and sociology, "for educated, affluent women over 40. We respect their experience and intelligence." Circ. 50,000. Pays on publication. Byline given. Buys one-time rights. Submit seasonal/holiday material 3 months in advance. Simultaneous, photocopied and previously published submissions OK. Computer printout submissions OK. Sample copy for 8½x11 SAE and $3.
Nonfiction: Book excerpts, humor, inspirational, interview/profile, new product, opinion, personal experience, religious, travel. Publishes an annual bridal guide for Washington DC only. No articles on aging or "homemaker" or "working woman" articles. Buys 4 mss/year. Query with published clips. Length: 250-1,500 words. Pays up to $200.

For information on setting your freelance fees, see How Much Should I Charge? in the Business of Writing section.

Photos: State availability of photos or send photos with submission. Reviews color transparencies (4x5) or prints (4x5). Offers no additional payment for photos accepted with ms. Captions, model releases and identification of subjects required. Buys one-time rights.

Fiction: Adventure, humorous, novel excerpts, suspense. Buys 4 mss/year. Query with published clips. Length: 800-1,500 words. Pays $25-200.

Poetry: Avant-garde, free verse, light verse, traditional. Buys 9 poems/year. Submit maximum of 3 poems. Length: 10-50 lines. Pays $25-50.

Fillers: Anecdotes, facts, short humor. Buys 10-20 mss/year. Length: 20-50 words.

Tips: "Profiles on fascinating, sophisticated women (100-500 words in length) and topics that are rarely covered in women's magazine such as an anthropology project interest us. We will include more finance, health, fashion and beauty."

RADIANCE, The Magazine for Large Women, Box 31703, Oakland CA 94604. (415)482-0680. Editor: Alice Ansfield. 75% freelance written. A quarterly magazine encouraging "self-esteem for large women—the physical, emotional, social, cultural, spiritual aspects." Circ. 30,000. Pays on publication. Publishes ms an average of 3 months after acceptance. Byline given. Offers $15 kill fee. Buys one-time and second serial (reprint) rights. Submit seasonal/holiday material 3 months in advance. Simultaneous, photocopied and previously published submissions OK. Query for electronic submissions. Computer printout submissions OK; no dot-matrix. Reports in 2 weeks. Sample copy $1.50; writer's guidelines for #10 SASE.

Nonfiction: Book excerpts (related to large women), essays, expose, general interest, historical/nostalgic, how-to (on health/well-being/growth/awareness/fashion/movement, etc.), humor, inspirational, interview/profile, new product, opinion, personal experience, photo feature and travel. Future issues will focus on children and weight, interviews with large men, fashion update, emerging spirituality, women and the arts, and women in the media. "No diet successes or articles condemning people for being fat." Query with published clips. Length: 1,000-2,000 words. Pays $35-100. Sometimes pays writers with contributor copies or other premiums—"negotiable with writer and us."

Photos: State availability of photos with submission. Offers $15-50 per photo. Captions and identification of subjects preferred. Buys one-time rights.

Columns/Departments: Up Front and Personal (personal profiles of women in all areas of life); Health and Well-Being (physical/emotional well-being, self care, research); Images (designer interviews, color/style/fashion, features); Inner Journeys (spirituality awareness and growth, methods, interviews); Perspectives (cultural and political aspects of being in a larger body); Heart to Heart (poetry, artwork, inspiring). Buys 60 mss/year. Query with published clips. Length: 1,000-2,000 words. Pays $50-100.

Fiction: Condensed novels, ethnic, fantasy, historical, humorous, mainstream, novel excerpts, romance, science fiction, serialized novels and slice-of-life vignettes relating somehow to large women. Buys 15 mss/year. Query with published clips. Length: 800-1,500 words. Pays $35-100.

Poetry: Nothing "too political and jargony." Buys 15 poems/year. Length: 4-45 lines. Pays $20-50.

Tips: "We need talented, sensitive and openminded writers from across the country. We profile women from all walks of life who are all sizes of large, of all ages and from all ethnic groups and lifestyles. We welcome writers' ideas on successful and interesting large women from their local areas. We're an open, light-hearted magazine that's working to help women feel good about themselves now, whatever their body size. *Radiance* is one of the major forces nationwide working for size acceptance. We want articles to address all areas of vital importance in their lives."

REDBOOK MAGAZINE, 224 W. 57th St., New York NY 10019. (212)649-3450. Editor-in-Chief: Annette Capone. Managing Editor: Jennifer Johnson. 80% freelance written. Monthly magazine. Circ. 3.9 million. Pays on acceptance. Publishes ms an average of 1 year after acceptance. Rights purchased vary with author and material. Computer printout submissions acceptable; prefers letter-quality. Reports in 3 months. Free writer's guidelines for *Redbook* for SASE.

Nonfiction: Karen Larson, executive editor. Jean Maguire, health editor. "*Redbook* addresses young mothers between the ages of 25 and 44. Most of our readers are married with children under 18; more than half of *Redbook*'s readers work outside the home. The articles in *Redbook* entertain, guide and inspire our readers. A significant percentage of the pieces stress 'how-to,' the ways a woman can solve the problems in her everyday life. Writers are advised to read at least the last *six* issues of the magazine (available in most libraries) to get a better understanding of what we're looking for. We prefer to see queries, rather than complete manuscripts. Please enclose a sample or two of your writing as well as a stamped, self-addressed envelope." Length: articles, 2,500-3,000 words; short articles, 1,000-1,500 words. Also interested in submissions for Young Mother's Story. "We are interested in stories for the Young Mother series offering the dramatic retelling of an experience involving you, your husband or child. Possible topics might include: how you have handled a child's health or school problem, or conflicts within the family. For each 1,500-2,000 words accepted for publication as Young Mother's Story, we pay $750. Mss accompanied by a large, stamped, self-addressed envelope, must be signed, and mailed to: Young Mother's Story, c/o *Redbook Magazine*. Young Mother's reports in 4-6 months." Pays the expenses of writers on assignment.

Fiction: Deborah Purcell, fiction editor. "Of the 40,000 unsolicited manuscripts that we receive annually, we buy about 36 or more stories/year. We also find many more stories that, are not necessarily suited to our needs but are good enough to warrant our encouraging the author to send others. *Redbook* looks for stories by and about men and women, realistic and offbeat stories, humorous or poignant stories, stories about families, couples, or people alone, stories with familiar and exotic settings, love stories and work stories, medical and mystery stories. Those elements common to all of them are the high quality of their prose and the distinctiveness of their characters and plots. We also look for stories with emotional resonance. Cool stylistic or intellectually experimental stories are of greater interest, we feel, to readers of literary magazines than readers of a magazine like *Redbook* which tries to offer insights into the hows and whys of day-to-day living; all of our stories reflect some aspect of the experience, the interests, or the dreams of *Redbook*'s readership." We buy short-short stories (9 pages) and short stories (25 pages or fewer). "We do not read unsolicited novels." Manuscripts must be typewritten, double-spaced, and accompanied by SASE. Payment begins at $850 for short shorts; $1,200 for short stories.

Tips: "Shorter, front-of-the-book features are usually easier to develop with first-time contributors. It is very difficult to break into the nonfiction section, although we do buy Young Mother's stories, dramatic personal experience pieces (1,500-2,000 words), from previously unpublished writers. The most frequent mistakes made by writers in completing an article for us are 1) Poor organization. A piece that's poorly organized is confusing, repetitive, difficult to read. I advise authors to do full outlines before they start writing so they can more easily spot structure problems and so they have a surer sense of where their piece is headed. 2) Poor or insufficient research. Most *Redbook* articles require solid research and include: full, well-developed anecdotes from real people (not from people who exist only in the writer's imagination); clear, substantial quotes from established experts in a field; and, when available, additional research such as statistics and other information from reputable studies, surveys, etc."

‡SAVVY, For the Successful Woman, Family Media, 3 Park Ave., New York NY 10016. (212)340-9200. Editor-in-Chief: Annalyn Swan. Managing Editor: Curtis Feldman. 90% freelance written. A monthly magazine. "*Savvy* articles are written for successful women. We try to use as many women as possible for our sources. The age group of our readers falls primarily between 25 and 45 and we address both their home and office lives." Circ. 400,000. Pays 4-6 weeks after due date. Publishes ms an average of 2-5 months after acceptance. Byline given. Offers 15-20% kill fee. Buys first North American serial rights, and reprint rights. Submit seasonal/holiday material 4 months in advance. Photocopied submissions OK. Computer printout submissions acceptable; prefers letter-quality. Reports as soon as possible. Free writer's guidelines with SASE.

Nonfiction: Book excerpts, humor, interview/profile, opinion, personal experience and travel. No limit on mss bought/year. Query with published clips. Length: 800-3,000 words ("depends on its position"). Pays $500 minimum. Pays the expenses of writers on assignment.

Columns/Departments: Savvy Money (how to manage, invest and save money), 900-1,000 words; Health (any topics pertaining to health: illnesses, cures, new findings, etc.), 1,000-1,200 words; and Savvy Manager (how to handle career situations, gain ground at work, change jobs, etc.), 900-1,200 words. Query with published clips. Pays $500 minimum. Travel, 1,000-1,200 words; Dining In/Dining Out, 1,000-1,200 words.

Tips: "The best advice is to read the magazine before querying. We have expanded our Savvy Money and Savvy Manager sections to include several shorter pieces."

SELF, Conde-Nast, 350 Madison Ave., New York NY 10017. (212)880-8834. Executive Editor: Anthea Disney. Managing Editor: Linda Rath. 50% freelance written. "We prefer to work with writers—even relatively new ones—with a degree, training or practical experience in specialized areas, psychology to nutrition." Monthly magazine emphasizing self improvement of emotional and physical well-being for women of all ages. Circ. 1 million. Average issue includes 12-20 feature articles and 4-6 columns. Pays on acceptance. Publishes ms an average of 6 months after acceptance. Byline given. Offers 20% kill fee. Buys first North American serial rights. Submit seasonal material 4 months in advance. Simultaneous and photocopied submissions OK. Computer printout submissions acceptable; prefers letter-quality. Reports in 1 month. Writer's guidelines for SASE.

Nonfiction: Well-researched service articles on self improvement, mind, the psychological angle of daily activities, health, careers, nutrition, fitness, medicine, male/female relationships and money. "We try to translate major developments and complex information in these areas into practical, personalized articles." Buys 6-10 mss/issue. Query with clips of previously published work. Length: 1,000-2,500 words. Pays $800-1,500. "We are always looking for any piece that has a psychological or behavioral side. We rely heavily on freelancers who can take an article on contraceptive research, for example, and add a psychological aspect to it. Everything should relate to the whole person." Pays the expenses of writers on assignment "with prior approval."

Photos: Submit to art director. State availability of photos. Reviews 5x7 b&w glossy prints.

Columns/Departments: Your Health (800-1,200 words on health topics); Your Work (800-1,200 words on career topics); and Your Money (800-1,200 words on finance topics). Buys 4-6 mss/issue. Query. Pays $800-2,000.

Tips: "Original ideas backed up by research, rarely personal experiences and anecdotes, open our doors. We almost never risk blowing a major piece on an untried-by-us writer, especially since these ideas are usually staff-conceived. It's usually better for everyone to start small, where there's more time and leeway for re-writes. The most frequent mistakes made by writers in completing an article for us are swiss-cheese research (holes all over it which the writer missed and has to go back and fill in) and/or not personalizing the information by applying it to the reader, but just reporting it."

TODAY'S CHRISTIAN WOMAN, 465 Gundersen Dr., Carol Stream IL 60188. (312)260-6200. FAX (312) 260-0114. Managing Editor: Rebecca K. Grosenbach. 25% freelance written. Works with a small number of new/unpublished writers each year. A bimonthly magazine for Christian women of all ages, single and married, homemakers and career women. Circ. 215,000. Pays on acceptance. Publishes ms an average of 2 years after acceptance. Byline given. Buys first rights only. Submit seasonal/holiday material 9 months in advance. Computer printout submissions acceptable; prefers letter-quality. Sample copy $3.50; writer's guidelines for #10 SASE.
Nonfiction: How-to, narrative, inspirational and opinion. Query only; no unsolicited mss. "The query should include article summary, purpose and reader value, author's qualifications, suggested length and date to send, availability of photos if applicable." Pays 7-15¢/word.
Tips: "Nature of the articles are: relational, psychological, philosophical or spiritual. All articles should be highly anecdotal, personal in tone, and universal in appeal."

‡TODAY'S IMAGES, Allied Publications, 1776 Lake Worth Rd. Lake Worth FL 33460. (407)582-2099. FAX: (407)582-4667. Editor: Richard Champlin. 95% freelance written. Bimonthly magazine on style/beauty/fashion/self improvement. Pays on publication. Publishes ms an average of 2-3 months after acceptance. Byline given. Buys first North American serial rights, one-time rights or second serial (reprint) rights. Submit seasonal/holiday material 6-8 months in advance. Simultaneous, photocopied and previously published submissions OK. Query for electronic submissions. Computer printout submissions OK; prefers letter-quality. Reports in 2 weeks on queries; 6 weeks on mss. Sample copy $1. Free writer's guidelines with SASE.
Nonfiction: General interest, humor, inspirational, interview/profile, personal experience. Buys 20 mss/year. Query with or without published clips, or send complete ms. Length: 600-1,500 words. Pays $5-25 for unsolicited articles. Pays in contributor copies or other premiums only at writer's request.
Photos: State availability of photos with submission. Reviews contact sheets, transparencies and b&w prints. Offers $5 per photo. Captions, model releases (when necessary) and identification of subjects required. Buys one-time rights.
Columns/Departments: Galleria (news briefs), 50-600 words. Buys 6-12 mss/year. Query or send complete ms.
Fiction: "No love stories." Buys 2-6 mss/year. Send complete ms. Length: 600-1,200 words. Pays $5-25.
Fillers: Anecdotes, gags to be illustrated, newbreaks and short humor. Buys 10/year. Pays $5.

‡TORONTO LIFE FASHION, Key Publishers, 6 Church St., Toronto, Ontario M5E 1M1 Canada. (416)364-3333. Editor: Tim Blanks. Managing Editor: Alicia Perry-Blackwell. 20% freelance written. Magazine published 9 times a year on fashion and style. "Personal style counts for more than the latest trends. That means an individual's taste in movies, books, music, decor, food and travel has become a vehicle of self-expression just as just as valid as her taste in clothing." Pays on acceptance. Publishes ms an average of 2 months after acceptance. Byline given. Offers 50% kill fee. Buys first North American serial rights. Submit seasonal/holiday material 3 months in advance. Computer printout submissions OK. Reports in 2 weeks. Free sample copy.
Nonfiction: General interest, interview/profile, travel, fitness, health, book and film reviews, and manners. "No articles on politics of fashion, opinions of fashion, personal preferences unless they are high profile writers." Buys 50 mss/year. Query with published clips. Length: 200-2,000 words. Pays $250-2,000. Sometimes pays expenses of writers on assignment.
Photos: State availability of photos with submission. Reviews contact sheets. "Payment is negotiated with art director." Identification of subjects required. Buys one-time rights.
Columns/Departments: Barbara Righton. First in Fashion; Books; Theatre; Film; Photography (newsworthy, trendworthy, stylish), 250-1,500 words. Buys 40 mss/year. Query with published clips. Pays $200-800.
Tips: "Non-fashion sections: Health, fitness, film and book reviews, profiles of actors/writers/directors in the news. The writing must be informed, concise, accurate and interesting. Our target market is primarily women 30-45 with varied interests, brains and style."

WOMAN MAGAZINE, Conde Nast, 350 Madison Ave., New York NY 10017. (212)880-2341. Editor: Pat Miller. 80% freelance written. Magazine published 12 times/year covering "every aspect of a woman's life. Offers self-help orientation, guidelines on lifestyles, careers, relationships/sex, finances, health, etc." Circ. 550,000. Pays on acceptance. Byline given. Buys one-time rights. Offers 25% kill fee. Computer printout submissions acceptable; prefers letter-quality. Reports in 6 weeks. Sample copy $1.95; writer's guidelines for #10 SASE.

Nonfiction: Relationships; self-esteem; humor; inspirational (how I solved a specific problem); interview/profile (200-1,000 words with successful or gutsy women); round-ups; and personal experience (how a woman took action and helped herself—emotional punch, but not "trapped housewife" material). "The *Woman* reader is evolving into a smarter, cannier woman who wants to reach her full potential." No articles on "10 ways to pep up your marriage"—looking for unique angle. Short medical and legal updates for Woman to Woman column. Query with published clips or send complete ms. Length: 200-1,500 words. Pays up to $1 per word. Pays phone expenses.

Columns/Departments: Suddenly Single (1,000 words on getting over a breakup and beyond); Moving Up (1,000 words on getting ahead at work); Dieter's Notes (900-1,700 words on diets); More Money (1,000 words on stretching you dollars) and Women in the News (200-500 words on successful/inspiring women).

Tips: "We're for all women—ones in and out of the home. We don't condescend; neither should you."

WOMAN'S DAY, 1515 Broadway, New York NY 10036. (212)719-6250. Articles Editor: Rebecca Greer. 75% or more of articles freelance written. 15 issues/year. Circ. 6 million. Pays negotiable kill fee. Byline given. Pays on acceptance. Computer printout submissions acceptable; no dot-matrix. Reports in 1 month on queries; longer on mss. Submit detailed queries first to Rebecca Greer.

Nonfiction: Uses articles on all subjects of interest to women—marriage, family life, childrearing, education, homemaking, money management, careers, family health, work and leisure activities. Also interested in fresh, dramatic narratives of women's lives and concerns. "These must be lively and fascinating to read." Length: 500-3,500 words, depending on material. Payment varies depending on length, type, writer, and whether it's for regional or national use, but rates are high. Pays the expenses of writers on confirmed assignment. *Woman's Day* has a page called Reflections, a full-page essay running 1,000 words. "We're looking primarily for tough, strong pieces on matters of real concern and relevance to women. We're seeking strong points of view, impassioned opinions, and fresh insights. The topics can be controversial, but they have to be convincing and relevant to readers. We look for significant issues—medical ethics and honesty in marriage—rather than the slight and the trivial."

Fiction: Contact Eileen Jordan, department editor. Uses high quality, genuine human interest, romance and humor, in lengths between 1,500 and 3,000 words. Payment varies. "We pay any writer's established rate, however."

Fillers: Neighbors and Tips to Share columns also pay $50/each for brief practical suggestions on homemaking, childrearing and relationships. Address to the editor of the appropriate section.

Tips: "Our primary need is for ideas with broad appeal that can be featured on the cover. We're buying more short pieces. Writers should consider Quick section which uses factual pieces of 100-500 words." Editor: Mary-Ellen Banashek.

WOMAN'S WORLD, The Woman's Weekly, Heinrich Bauer North American, Inc., 270 Sylvan Ave., Englewod Cliffs NJ 07632. Editor-in-Chief: Dennis Neeld. 95% freelance written. Weekly magazine covering "controversial, dramatic, and human interest women's issues" for women across the nation. Pays on acceptance. Publishes ms an average of 4 months after acceptance. Byline given. Offers kill fee. Buys first North American serial rights. Submit seasonal/holiday material 4 months in advance. Simultaneous queries, and simultaneous, photocopied and previously published submissions OK. Computer printout submissions acceptable; prefers letter-quality. Reports in 6 weeks on queries; 2 months on mss. Sample copy $1 and self-addressed mailing label; writer's guidelines for #10 SASE.

Nonfiction: Well-researched material with "a hard-news edge and topics of national scope." Reports of 1,000 words on vital trends and major issues such as women and alcohol or teen suicide; dramatic, personal women's stories; articles on self-improvement, medicine and health topics; and the economics of home, career and daily life. Features include In Real Life (true stories); Turning Point (in a woman's life); Families (highlighting strength of family or how unusual families deal with problems); True Love (tender, beautiful, touching and unusual love stories). Other regular features are Report (1,500-word investigative news features with national scope, statistics, etc.); Scales of Justice (true stories of 1,000-1,200 words on women and crime "if possible, presented with sympathetic" attitude); Between You and Me (600-word humorous and/or poignant slice-of-life essays); and Relationships (800 words on pop psychology or coping). Queries should be addressed to Gerry Hunt, senior editor. We use no fillers, but all the Between You and Me pieces are chosen from mail. Sometimes pays the expenses of writers on assignment.

Fiction: Jeanne Muchnick, fiction editor. Short story, romance and mainstream of 3,600 words and mini-mysteries of 1,200-2,000 words. "Each of our stories has a light romantic theme with a protagonist no older than forty. Each can be written from either a masculine or feminine point of view. Women characters may be single, married or divorced. Plots must be fast moving with vivid dialogue and action. The problems and dilemmas inherent in them should be contemporary and realistic, handled with warmth and feeling. The stories must have a positive resolution." Not interested in science fiction, fantasy, historical romance or foreign locales. No explicit sex, graphic language or seamy settings. Humor meets with enthusiasm. Specify "short story" on envelope. Always enclose SASE. Reports in 2 months. No phone queries. Pays $1,000 on acceptance for North American serial rights for 6 months. "The mini-mysteries, at a length of 1,600 words, may feature either a 'whodunnit' or 'howdunnit' theme. The mystery may revolve around anything from a theft to a murder. However, we are not interested in sordid or grotesque crimes. Emphasis should be on intricacies of plot rather than gratuitous violence. The story must include a resolution that clearly states the villain is getting his or her come-uppance." Pays $500 on acceptance. Pays approximately 50¢ a published word on acceptance. Buys first North American serial rights. Queries with clips of published work are preferred; accepts complete mss. Specify "mini mystery" on envelope. Enclose SASE. Stories slanted for a particular holiday should be sent at least 6 months in advance. No phone queries.

Photos: State availability of photos. "State photo leads. Photos are assigned to freelance photographers." Buys one-time rights.

Tips: "Come up with good queries. Short queries are best. We have a strong emphasis on well-researched material. Writers must send research with manuscript including book references and phone numbers for double checking. The most frequent mistakes made by writers in completing an article for us are sloppy, incomplete research, not writing to the format, and not studying the magazine carefully enough beforehand."

WOMEN OF OHIO, 4565 N. High St., Columbus OH 43214. (614)263-3080. Executive Editor: Claire Kessler. 100% freelance written. Bimonthly magazine on Ohio women and women in general. "Subject matter is Ohio places and personalities—including, occasionally, women of note from Ohio." Circ. 27,000. Pays on publication. Publishes ms an average of 3 months after acceptance. Byline given. Buys first North American serial rights. Submit seasonal/holiday material 5 months in advance. Query for electronic submissions. Computer printout submissions OK. Reports in 5 weeks. Sample copy for 9x12 SAE with 4 first class stamps. Writer's guidelines for #10 SASE.

Nonfiction: Essays, expose, general interest, historical/nostalgic, how-to, humor (not jokes), interview/profile, new product, personal experience, photo feature, travel. Buys 60-80 mss/year. Query with published clips. *"Women of Ohio* has some issues built around themes and solicits queries on specific topics. However, many articles are chosen from queries sent by writers. Our topics, Ohio women and/or articles of general interest to women is, in itself limiting. Anything unsolicited *must* be accompanied by SASE or will not be returned." Length: 500-1,500 words. Pays $50-150.

Photos: Send photos with submission. Offers no additional payment for photos accepted with ms. Captions, identification of subjects and model releases are required. Buys one-time rights.

Columns/Departments: Books (reviews, not necessarily best-selling books, but on women's topics); Money (sound advice and management); Fashion (what's new, seasonal); Health (mental and physical health, philosophical); Restaurant (not critique, basic facts); Autos (car maintenance as well as general info). Books and Fashion run occasionally. Buys 30 mss/year. Query with published clips. Length: 500-750 words. Pays $50-125.

Tips: "Send letter with published clips outlining familiarity with Ohio subjects and suggesting type of story and subject that writer would like to submit. Features area is where we are most in need of freelance submissions. We're looking for short (under 1,500 word) stories, tightly written, on the subject queries and assigned pursuant to editorial schedule/invitation to query."

WOMEN'S CIRCLE, Box 299, Lynnfield MA 01940-0299. Editor: Marjorie Pearl. 100% freelance written. Bimonthly magazine for women of all ages. Buys all rights. Pays on acceptance. Byline given. Publishes ms an average of 6 months to 1 year after acceptance. Submit seasonal material 8 months in advance. Reports in 3 months. Sample copy $2. Writer's guidelines for #10 SASE.

Nonfiction: Especially interested in stories about successful, home-based female entrepreneurs with b&w photos or color transparencies. Length: 1,000-2,000 words. Also interesting and unusual money-making ideas. Welcomes good quality crafts and how-to directions in any media—crochet, fabric, etc.

‡THE WOMEN'S QUARTERLY, University of California, Irvine Media Board, Women's Resource Center, 1st Fl., Gateway Commons, University of California, Irvine CA 92717. (714)856-6000. Editor: Tiffany Kern. Managing Editor: Julia Smedley. 90% freelance written. Tabloid which is published 3 times/year on feminism/women's issues. "We want to be a forum for women and feminists. We want all women (and men) to read our paper, but we will not 'water down' the feminism." Circ. 10,000. Pays on publication. Publishes ms an average of 4 months after acceptance. Byline given. Offers $5 kill fee. Buys one-time rights. Submit seasonal/holiday material 3 months in advance. Simultaneous, photocopied submissions and previously published submissions OK. Query for electronic submissions. Computer printout submissions OK; prefers letter-quality. Reports in 3 weeks on queries; 2 months on mss.

Nonfiction: Essays, exposé, general interest, historical, interview/profile, opinion, personal experience, photo feature (b&w) and religious. Buys 30 mss/year. Send complete ms. Length: 8,000 words maximum. Pays $4-20. Pays in contributor copies if requested.

Photos: State availability of photos with submission. Reviews contact sheets. Offers $2-5 per photo. Captions required. Buys one-time rights.

Columns/Departments: Book/film reviews (feminist), 100-1,000 words; Art reviews. Open to suggestion on columns. Buys 10 mss/year. Send complete ms. Pays $4-20.

Fiction: "We will accept any fiction that is about women or women's issues." Buys 10 mss/year. Send complete ms. Length: 8,000 words maximum. Pays $4-20.

Poetry: Avant-garde, free verse, haiku, light verse and traditional. Buys 20 poems/year. Submit maximum 5 poems. Length: 100 lines maximum. Pays $4-20.

Tips: "*The Women's Quarterly* is essentially wide open. Our only restrictions are the limitations of time to read manuscripts and space to print them in."

WORKING MOTHER MAGAZINE, WWT Partnership, 230 Park Ave., New York NY 10169. (212)551-9412. Editor: Judsen Culbreth. Executive Editor: Mary McLaughlin. 90% freelance written. Prefers to work with published/established writers; works with a small number of new/unpublished writers each year. For women who balance a career with the concerns of parenting. Monthly magazine. Circ. 600,000. Pays on acceptance. Publishes ms an average of 4 months after acceptance. Byline given. Buys first North American Serial Rights and all rights. Pays 20% kill fee. Submit seasonal/holiday material 6 months in advance. Computer printout submissions acceptable; no dot-matrix. Reports in 1 month. Sample copy $1.95; writer's guidelines for SASE.

Nonfiction: Service, humor, material pertinent to the working mother's predicament. "Don't just go out and find some mother who holds a job and describe how she runs her home, manages her children and feels fulfilled. Find a working mother whose story is inherently dramatic." Query. Buys 9-10 mss/issue. Length: 750-2,000 words. Pays $300-1,200. "We pay more to people who write for us regularly." Pays the expenses of writers on assignment.

Tips: "We are looking for pieces that help the reader. In other words, we don't simply report on a trend without discussing how it specifically affects our readers' lives and how they can handle the effects. Where can they look for help if necessary?"

WORKING WOMAN, WWT Partnership, 342 Madison Ave., New York NY 10173. (212)309-9800. Managing Editor: Lisa Higgins. Editor: Anne Mollegen Smith. 85% freelance written. Works with a small number of new/unpublished writers each year. Monthly magazine for executive, professional and entrepreneurial women. "Readers are ambitious, educated, affluent managers, executives, and business owners. Median age is 34. Material should be sophisticated, witty, not entry-level, and focus on work-related issues." Circ. 950,000. Pays on acceptance. Publishes ms an average of 8 months after acceptance. Byline given. Offers 20% kill fee after attempt at rewrite to make ms acceptable. Buys all rights, first rights for books, and second serial (reprint) rights. Submit seasonal/holiday material 6 months in advance. Computer printout submissions acceptable only if legible; prefers letter-quality. Sample copy for $2.95 and 8½x12 SAE; writer's guidelines for #10 SASE.

Nonfiction: Lisa Higgins, managing editor, or Jacqueline Johnson, book excerpts editor. Book excerpts; how-to (management skills, small business); humor; interview/profile (high level executive or entrepreneur preferred); new product (office products, computer/high tech); opinion (issues of interest to managerial, professional, entrepreneur women); personal experience; technical (in management or small business field); and other (business). No child-related pieces that don't involve work issues; no entry-level topics; no fiction/poetry. Buys roughly 200 mss/year. Query with clips. Length: 250-3,000 words. Pays $400 and up for most articles. Pays the expenses of writers on assignment.

Photos: State availability of photos with ms.

Columns: Management/Enterprise, Basia Hellwig; Manager's Shoptalk, Louise Washer; Lifestyle, Food, Freddi Greenberg; Fitness, Health, Janette Scandura; Business Trends, Michele Morris; Computers, Technology, Anne Russell. Query with clips of published work. Length: 1,200-1,500 words.

Tips: "Be sure to include clips with queries and to make the queries detailed (including writer's expertise in the area, if any). The writer has a better chance of breaking in at our publication with short articles and fillers as we prefer to start new writers out small unless they're very experienced elsewhere. Columns are more open than features. We do not accept phone submissions."

For explanation of symbols, see the Key to Symbols and Abbreviations on Page 5. For unfamiliar words, see the Glossary.

Close-up

Mary McLaughlin
Executive Editor
Working Mother

In May, 1989, *Working Mother* celebrated its tenth anniversary. Executive Editor Mary McLaughlin says changes in the magazine's format have not been great over the past 10 years. More surprising than the lack of changes, she says, is the consistency with which the editors and publishers have viewed their mission. In the test issue of the magazine in May, 1979, a statement of purpose was made. It said: "*Working Mother* is here because working mothers are here. We want to be part of a working mother's support network." Although circulation has more than tripled since then, that philosophy has been a constant throughout the 10 years of the magazine.

Prior to working at *Working Mother*, she worked as an editor on *McCall's*. McLaughlin was also a copywriter for *Harper's Bazaar*, a reporter for the *Buffalo Evening News*, and she has written articles for various magazines.

McLaughlin says they receive about 200 unsolicited submissions a month. "I'm really looking for ideas, not topics. For example, on the subject of childcare, I'm not interested in general ideas to do with childcare such as: 'How to find good childcare for your child.' I'm more interested in ideas like: 'What do you do with a child who doesn't want to go to his day care?' 'How should you interpret a child's crying when you return to pick the child up from day care?' 'How can you resolve a conflict with a childcare giver whom you like very much but can't somehow communicate effectively with?' These are *ideas*, not topics. I look for a writer who says this is what I think the solution is. I need writers whose ideas ring true to the experience of the working mother.

"The most important thing for a writer to do is to write a simple, clear letter so that I can get an idea of how straight her thinking is." McLaughlin says she reads proposals from writers and if she finds an attractive idea, she will give that writer a try, although if it's from someone without clips the piece may be assigned on speculation.

Working Mother began as a "support system for the still small but growing league of mothers who by choice and economic necessity were slowly making their way into the workforce.

"The reason we're still around is that our readers see us as a magazine with whom they have a bond. These women don't have the traditional places to meet other mothers, like outside the school while waiting to pick their kids up or on the playground after school. The magazine serves as a 'back fence' over which they can exchange their problems and concerns," says McLaughlin.

She says the magazine and the readers have changed only in the respect that now it's a given that mothers will go to work. The majority of the population of mothers have a career outside the home. Ten years ago that position had to be defended and justified but today it really no longer does. "I think the job is just as hard now as it was, and in a way, the readers need us more than before because now the assumption is 'oh, everybody does it; it's easy to do.' But the dual role of a working mother remains difficult and at times extremely stressful."

—Deborah Cinnamon

Other Consumer Publications

The following listings are inactive for the 1990 edition because the firms are backlogged with submissions, will not accept unsolicited submissions, are completely staff-written or indicated a need for few freelance submissions in 1990.

Animal Press
American Catfisherman
Conde Nast's Traveler
Consumer Reports
Contemporanea
Electronics Today
Episcopal Church Facts

Inc Magazine
Life
Memories
National Geographic World
New Choices
New York Times Magazine
Rolling Stone

Sports Illustrated
Space and Time
Thinking Families
Time Magazine
Town and Country
U.S. News and World Report
Utne Reader

The following firms did not return a verification to update an existing listing or a questionnaire to begin a new listing by press time.

ACM
Absolute Sound
Accent
Adam
Aero
Alaska Flying Magazine
American Atheist
American Book Collector
American Brewer
American Clay Exchange
American Collectors Journal
American Karate
American Newspaper Carrier
American Politics
Ann Arbor Scene Magazine
Antique Review
Arizona Singles
Army Magazine
Arts Journal
Asia-Pacific Defense Forum
Asymptotical World
ATA Magazine
ATV Sports Magazine
Austin Magazine
Backstretch
Baltimore Jewish Times
Bakersfield Lifestyle
Bank Note Reporter
Basketball Weekly
BC Business
Bestways Magazine
Better Nutrition
Biblical Illustrator
Blade Magazine
Bloomsbury Review
Boston Business Journal
Bowhunter Magazine
Bowling
Buffalo Spree Magazine
Business Atlanta
California Business
Car Craft
Careers
CBIA News
Chevy Outdoors
Chicago Life
Chicago Tribune Travel Section
Child Life
Chronicle Guidance Publications
Cincinnati Magazine

Civil War Times Illustrated
COA Review
Coast & Country Magazine
College Outlook and Career Opportunities
Commentary
Common Boundary
Companion of St. Francis and St. Anthony
Congress Monthly
Connecticut Traveler
CQ: The Radio Amateur's Journal
Critique
Current Health 1 and 2
Dallas Magazine
Diabetes Self-Management
Dinosaur Review
Diver
Diversion Magazine
Ear
Edges
80 Micro
Elle
Equilibrium
Erie & Chautauqua Magazine
Erotic Fiction Quarterly
Eternity Magazine
Exceptional Parent
Expecting
Faces: The Magazine About People
Farming Uncle
Fessenden Review
Flight Reports
Florida Horse
Flyfisher
Fortune
Franklin Mint Almanac
Freedom Magazine
Friends Magazine
Front Page Detective
Gambling Times Magazine
'GBH Magazine
Glass
Glass Studio
Globe
Golfweek
Gourmet
Grapevine's Finger Lakes Magazine
Gray Panther Network

Great Lakes Fisherman
Greyhound Review
Group
Healthplex Magazine
HG
Horoscope Guide
Horror Show
Ideals Magazine
Illinois Times
Indiana Review
In These Times
Inner-View
Inside Detective
Jack and Jill
Jacksonville Today
Journal of the North Shore Jewish Community
Kansas!
Kansas City Magazine
L'apache
Leatherneck
Lighted Pathway
Log Home Guide for Builders & Buyers
Log Homes
Lone Star Horse Report
Loose Change
Los Angeles Reader
MACazine
McCall's Needlework & Crafts Magazine
Magick Theatre
Magical Blend
Magazine of the Midlands
Maine Motorist
Manhattan
Manuscripts
Marriage Partnership
Maryland Magazine
MCS
Men's Fitness
Metropolis
Metropolis, Art and Entertainment News
Milkweek Chronicle/Milkweed Editions
Missouri Life
Mothers Today
Motorboating & Sailing
Mountain Bike Action
Mushing
Mustang Monthly

National Forum: The Phi
   Kappa Phi Journal
National Guard
National Parks
National Racquetball
National Show Horse
Natural History
Near West Gazette
Needlepoint News
Nevada Business Journal
New Alaskan
New England Getaways
New England Senior Citizen/
   Senior American News
New Jersey Business
New Vistas
New York Antique Almanac
Nightmoves
Nine-O-One Network
Northeast Magazine
Northwest
Off Duty
Off-Road's Thunder Trucks
   and Truck Pulls
Ohio Fisherman
Optimist Magazine
Original New England Guide
Our Sunday Visitor Magazine
Pacific Boating Almanac
Pacific Coast Journal
Palm Beach Jewish World
Palm Springs Life
Passion Magazine
PC
PC Clones
PC World
Penthouse
People
Phoenix Metro Magazine
Piloting Careers Magazine
Pittsburgh Magazine
Playgirl
Popular Cars
Popular Ceramics
Popular Lures
Popular Mechanics
Popular Woodworking

Ports O'Call
Powerboat Magazine
Prairie Messenger
Presbyterian Survey
Private Pilot
Professional Pilot
Public Citizen
Pulse!
Quilter's Newsletter Magazine
Radio-Electronics
Rainbow Magazine
Ranch & Coast
Rave
Reform Judaism
Return Receipt Requested
Rider
Right On!
Ripon College Magazine
Road & Track
Rock & Roll Disc
Rod Serling's Twilight Zone
   Magazine
Rosicrucian Digest
Sail
Sample Case
San Antonio Business Journal
Santa Clarita Valley Magazine
Sassy
Saturday Night Magazine
Scuba Times
Seattle's Child
Select Homes Magazine
Senior Voice Newspaper
Short Story Review
Sierra Life Magazine
Sing Heavenly Muse
Singlelife Magazine
Skies America
Skiing
Smithsonian Magazine
Special Interest Autos
Speedhorse Magazine/The
   Racing Report
Splice Magazine
Sport
Sportscan
Springfield! Magazine

Star*Line
Start, the ST Quarterly
Stories
Student Leadership
Success
SunCities Life Magazine
Sunday Morning
Tallahassee Magazine
TDR: The Drama Review
Team
Tennis
Texas Highways Magazine
Today's Living
Today's Parish
Trailer Life
Travel Smart for Business
Tri-State Bass Fisherman
Tucson Lifestyle
Turkey
Turtle Quarterly Magazine
TWA Ambassador
University Man
University of Windsor
Vanity Fair
Veteran
Victor Valley Magazine
Vietnam
Vision
Vision, A Lifestyle Magazine
   for Young Adults
Vista
Vogue
VW & Porsche
Walking Tours of San Juan &
   Restaurant Menu Guide
Western Reserve Magazine
Westways
Wine World
Winning Sweepstakes Letter
Windsor This Month Magazine
Wisconsin Silent Sports
Worcester Magazine
World & I
YM
You Magazine
Zymurgy

The following listings were deleted following the 1990 edition of *Writer's Market* because the company asked to have the listing removed, went out of business, charges a fee to consider manuscripts or has unresolved complaints on file.

A Matter of Crime (ceased publication)
Action (recently sold; new information unavailable at press time)
Albuquerque Senior Scene Magazine (no longer a separate publication; now a section of On the
   Scene)
America Entertains (suspended publication)
Ampersand's Entertainment Guide (suspended publication)
Antaeus (asked to be deleted)
Black Mountain Review (suspended publication)
Chariot (out of business)
City Paper (asked to be deleted)
Coast Magazine (asked to be deleted)
College Woman (suspended publication)
Common Cause Magazine (asked to be deleted; received too many inappropriate submissions)
Common Ground (asked to be deleted)
Destination (suspended publication)
Facet (suspended publication)

Four Seasons Hotels (asked to be deleted)
Funnnies (asked to be deleted)
Golf Magazine (asked to be deleted)
Guide Magazines (pays in copies)
Home (unable to contact)
Internal Arts (does not pay)
Lifeline (suspended publication)
LV/Reno (suspended publication)
Magazine, The (suspended publication)
Meet People (out of business)
Millionaire (suspended publication)
New England Church Life (asked to be deleted; received too many inppropriate submissions)
Orange Coast Magazine (asked to be deleted)
Orben's Current Comedy (sold; see Current Comedy for Speakers)
Patches (suspended publication)
Pico (sold to Portable Computer Review)
Political Woman (suspended publication)
Prelude Magazine (asked to be deleted)
Pulpsmith (suspended publication)
Quarry (asked to be deleted)
San Angelo Magazine (asked to be deleted; uses only local writers)
SHR (no longer publishing under this title)
Single Impact (suspended publication)
Southern Magazine (acquired by Time, Inc.; name change to Southpoint; new information not available at press time)
Southern Style (suspended publication)
Southern Travel (name change to *Travel South*; no updated information available at press time)
Stone Country (asked to be deleted)
Sylvia Porter (bought by *Changing Times*)
Tara's Literary Art Journal (temporarily ceased publication)
Threshold of Fantasy (suspended publication)
Travel-Holiday Magazine (asked to be deleted)
Uncommon Reader (out of business)
US (sold to Straight Arrow; no new information available)
Wholistic Living News (asked to be deleted)
Wide Open Magazine (charges a fee)
Youth Sports (unable to contact)

Trade, Technical and Professional Journals

Often overlooked by beginners, trade publications can be an excellent place to start or augment a writing career. A writer who delivers can build long-term working relationships with the editors of trade publications.

The general term for all publications focusing on a particular occupation or industry is *trade*. Other terms used to describe the different types of trade publications are: business, technical and professional journals. (Trade magazines are also called "books" by editors and publishers.) "Trade magazines are *business* magazines that must help readers do their jobs better," says the editor of an aviation trade magazine. Technical journals contain highly technical articles and columns written by professionals working in a specific industry. Many are written for industrial and science trades and contain articles focusing on new technology or research. Professional journals contain articles from practitioners, but focus on all aspects of an occupation. Physicians, educators and lawyers have their own professional journals.

Study several trade journals in the field to get a feel for trends and popular topics. "Read our magazine and other industry magazines. Give readers something they can walk away with and use the minute they put the magazine down," says an editor of a business magazine. Newspapers are another good source of information. Note changes in tax legislation and government regulations—several industries may be affected. Top market magazine editors at a recent writers' conference told writers to look for material first in their own backyards. Local news can be expanded upon and written for regional, national and special interest magazines.

Although most trade journals have smaller circulations than consumer publications, writing for the trades is similar to writing for consumer magazines in many ways. Trade publication editors, like their consumer counterparts, seek professionally-presented submissions aimed specifically at their readers. An editor of a trade medical magazine says: "Short, snappy, energetic articles that inform with style are what our readers want, written in a way that imparts information without talking down to them *or* going over their heads." Another editor says, "Articles must be adequately researched as readers of trade magazines are intelligent, literate and knowledgeable about their fields and can spot editorial not researched."

Most trade articles are shorter than consumer features and they tend to use more fillers, newsbreaks and short pieces. "Brevity is a blessing in a publication going primarily to busy executives," says one editor. "Writing style should be lively, informal and straightforward, but the subject matter must be as functional and down-to-earth as possible," says another.

A survey conducted by the Association of Business Publishers (ABP) reports that 23% of trade magazines get more than one-half of their copy from freelance writers. The survey reports that editors most often pay freelance writers on acceptance. The ABP also reported that most publishers pay for expenses incurred by writers on assignment.

Another survey, this one by *Publishing News*, states that 15% of editors say they don't attempt to buy specific rights when buying manuscripts from freelancers. Forty percent say they buy all rights or make work-for-hire assignments as opposed to 31% of consumer magazine editors who buy less restrictive rights. The survey also reported that business publications pay better for articles of a given length, usually shorter articles, than their consumer counterparts. Yet you will sometimes be competing with professionals in the field who submit articles for prestige instead of pay. Trade editors are eager to work with new writers, however, and often need writers based in smaller cities to cover conventions and trade shows.

Photos help increase the value of most stories for trade. If you can provide photos, mention that in your query, or even send photocopies. Like consumer magazines, trade publications are becoming more visual. The availability of computer graphics has also increased the need (and desire) for charts, graphs and other explanatory visuals.

Training or experience in a particular field is a definite plus, but not always necessary if you know where to look and who to ask for information. Access to experts is essential for highly technical information. In fact, many trade journal editors will ask for a list of sources in order to verify information. Keep this in mind when querying—provide names of experts you talked with or plan to contact. Professionals will often consider a coauthor arrangement; his expertise, your writing ability. Many professionals are willing interview subjects, eager to talk about trends or important developments in their field.

Query a trade journal as you would a consumer magazine. Most trade editors like to discuss an article idea with a writer first and will sometimes offer names of helpful sources. Some will provide a list of questions they want you to ask an interview subject. It is important to mention any direct experience you may have in the industry in your cover letter. Send a resume and include clips if they show you have some background or related experience in the specific subject area. Don't forget to include a SASE with your unsolicited query or manuscript.

One way to break into the trade field and to increase your income at the same time is to rewrite a consumer story to fit a trade publication. While working on a consumer story, you may also uncover a good trade story lead, such as an interesting new business or a manager with innovative ideas about increasing productivity. Remember to be alert for problem-solving material; readers want to know how they can apply this information to their own situations.

A story for a city magazine, for example, could generate a number of trade articles. A report on the local rise of using HMO dental insurance plans could be rewritten for a dental trade journal or for an insurance trade publication. You'll need to dig deeper into different aspects of your original story, but the effort could mean additional sales.

In a survey conducted by *WM* editors, magazine editors were asked how they dealt with unsolicited manuscripts. Responding to the question were 309 editors. Of these, some editors (about 15%) say they accept no unsolicited manuscripts and will return manuscripts unread (those with SASE). Others, however (about 64%), treat unsolicited manuscripts the same as solicited ones and are eager to work with new writers who are familiar with specific subjects the trade magazine deals with. According to our respondents, 225 trade magazine editors receive 121,425 manuscripts over-the-transom per year, an average of about 540 per editor. Reading and paying close attention to submission guidelines gives the freelance writer a greater chance of placing his well-written and well-researched manuscript.

New magazines begin publishing almost daily. Writers should watch for new start-ups. This information can be found in *Publishers Weekly*, *Folio* and *Advertising Age*, as well as several other publications that stay abreast of the publishing industry. For example, a new magazine for journalists with ethics questions and situations encountered on the job will find a market in Barry Bingham Jr.'s *FineLine* at 600 E. Main St., Louisville KY 40202. Accounts must be from the journalists who were involved in the ethics questions and made the decisions.

This section contains over 550 listings for trade, technical and professional publications; approximately 200 listings are new for 1990.

For information on additional trade publications not listed in *Writer's Market*, see Other Trade Publications at the end of this section.

—— *Advertising, Marketing and PR*

Trade journals for advertising executives, copywriters and marketing and public relations professionals are listed in this category. Those whose main focus are the advertising and marketing of specific products, such as home furnishings, are classified under individual product categories. Journals for sales personnel and general merchandisers can be found in the Selling and Merchandising category.

ADVERTISING AGE, 740 N. Rush, Chicago IL 60611-2590. (312)649-5200. Managing Editor: Valerie Mackie. Special Projects-Director: Robert Goldsborough. Managing Editor/Special Reports; Edward L. Fitch. Executive Editor: Dennis Chase. Deputy Editor: Larry Doherty. New York office: 220 E 42 St., New York NY 10017. (212)210-0100. Editor: Fred Danzig. Currently staff-produced. Includes weekly sections devoted to one topic (i.e. marketing in Southern California, agribusiness/advertising, TV syndication trends). Much of this material is done freelance – on assignment only. Pays kill fee "based on hours spent plus expenses." Byline given "except short articles or contributions to a roundup."

AMERICAN DEMOGRAPHICS, American Demographics, Inc., Box 68, Ithaca NY 14851. (607)273-6343. Editor: Cheryl Russell. Managing Editor: Caroline Arthur. 25% freelance written. Works with a small number of new/unpublished writers each year. For business executives, market researchers, media and communications people, public policymakers. Monthly magazine. Circ. 30,000. Pays on publication. Publishes ms an average of 6 months after acceptance. Buys all rights. Submit seasonal/holiday material 6 months in advance. Query for electronic submissions. Computer printout submissions acceptable. Reports in 1 month on queries; in 2 months on mss. Include self-addressed stamped postcard for return word that ms arrived safely. Sample copy for $5 with 9 × 11 SAE. Writer's guidelines for #10 SASE.
Nonfiction: General interest (on demographic trends, implications of changing demographics, profile of business using demographic data); and how-to (on the use of demographic techniques, psychographics, understand projections, data, apply demography to business and planning). No anecdotal material or humor. Sometimes pays the expenses of writers on assignment.
Tips: "Writer should have clear understanding of specific population trends and their implications for business and planning. The most important thing a freelancer can do is to read the magazine and be familiar with its style and focus."

THE COUNSELOR MAGAZINE, Advertising Specialty Institute, NBS Bldg., 1120 Wheeler Way, Langhorne PA 19047. (215)752-4200. Editor: Daniel B. Cartledge. 25% freelance written. Works with a small number of new/unpublished writers each year. For executives, both distributors and suppliers, in the ad specialty industry. Monthly magazine. Circ. 6,000. Pays on publication. Publishes ms an average of 3 months after acceptance. Buys first rights only. No phone queries. Submit seasonal/holiday material 4 months in advance. Simultaneous, photocopied and previously published submissions OK. Computer printout submissions OK; prefers letter-quality. Reports in 2-3 months. Sample copy of *Imprint* for 9x12 SAE with 3 first class stamps.
Nonfiction: Contact managing editor. How-to (promotional case histories); interview (with executives and government figures); profile (of executives); and articles on specific product categories. "Articles almost always have a specialty advertising slant and quotes from specialty advertising practitioners." Buys 30 mss/year. Length: Open. Query with samples. Pays according to assigned length. Sometimes pays the expenses of writers on assignment.
Photos: State availability of photos. B&w photos only. Prefers contact sheet(s) and 5x7 prints. Offers some additional payment for original only photos accepted with ms. Captions and model releases required. Buys one-time rights.
Tips: "If a writer shows promise, we can help him or her modify his style to suit our publication and provide leads. Writers must be willing to adapt or rewrite their material for a specific audience. If an article is suitable for 5 or 6 other publications, it's probably not suitable for us. The best way to break in is to write for *Imprint*,

a quarterly publication we produce for the clients of ad specialty counselors."

THE FLYING A, Aeroquip Corp., 300 S. East Ave., Jackson MI 49203. (517)787-8121. Editor-in-Chief: Wayne D. Thomas. 10% freelance written. Emphasizes Aeroquip customers and products. Quarterly magazine. Circ. 35,000. Pays on acceptance. Buys first or second rights, depending upon circumstances. Simultaneous submissions OK. Reports in 2 months.
Nonfiction: General interest (feature stories with emphasis on free enterprise, business-related or historical articles with broad appeal, human interest.) "An Aeroquip tie-in in a human interest story is helpful." No jokes, no sample copies; no cartoons, no short fillers. Buys 2-4 mss/year. Query with biographic sketch and clips. Length: Not to exceed five typewritten pages. Pays $100 minimum.
Photos: Accompanying photos are helpful.
Fillers: Human interest. No personal anecdotes, recipes or how-to articles. "Suggest the writer contact editor by letter with proposed story outline."
Tips: "We publish a marketing-oriented magazine, with a section devoted to employee news. Our products are used in a wide variety of markets, including aerospace, automotive, construction equipment and others. Our primary products are hose lines and fittings and plastics for aerospace, automotive and industrial markets."

HIGH-TECH SELLING, For Electronics, Telecommunications, and Other High-Tech Industries, Bureau of Business Practice/Simon & Schuster, 24 Rope Ferry Rd., Waterford CT 06385. (800)243-0876. FAX: (203)434-3341. Editor: Michele S. Rubin. Managing Editor: Wayne Muller. 75% freelance written. Prefers to work with published/established writers, but also is eager to work with new/unpublished writers. A monthly training newsletter covering selling. Pays on acceptance. Publishes ms an average of 3 months after acceptance. Byline not given. Buys all rights. Submit seasonal/holiday material 6 months in advance. Photocopied submissions OK. Computer printout submissions acceptable; prefers letter-quality. Reports in 1 week. Sample copy and writer's guidelines for #10 SASE.
Nonfiction: How-to. Buys 50 mss/year. Query. Length: 1,000-1,500 words. Pays 10-15¢/word.
Tips: "Our entire publication is interview-based with high-tech sales people who sell on the business, not retail, level."

IDEAS, The Monthly Magazine of the International Newspaper Marketing Association, 11600 Sunrise Valley Dr., Reston VA 22091. (703)648-1094. FAX: (703)620-4557. Editor: Mayhugh H. "Skip" Horne III. Art Director: Kent O'Daniel. A monthly magazine of newspaper marketing and promotion ideas. "*IDEAS* highlights successful marketing and promotion ideas for newspapers of all circulation groups. Each month, it includes a feature article examining a pertinent, timely marketing topic of interest to newspaper executives." Pays on publication. Publishes ms an average of 2 months after acceptance. Byline given. Makes work-for-hire assignments. Submit seasonal/holiday material 2 months in advance. Simultaneous, photocopied and previously published submissions OK. Computer printout submissions OK; prefers letter-quality. Sample copy for 9x12 SAE.
Nonfiction: Book excerpts, general interest, how-to, new product and technical. Buys up to 12 mss/year. Send complete ms. Length: 1,200-2,000 words. Pays $250.
Photos: Send photos with submission. Reviews contact sheets, negatives and prints (5x7). Offers no additional payment for photos accepted with ms. Identification of subjects required. Buys one-time rights.
Columns/Departments: Focus (monthly feature article which examines marketing topics of interest to newspaper promotion and marketing executives). Buys up to 12 mss/year. Send complete ms. Length: 1,200-2,000 words. Pays $250 maximum.
Tips: "Writers for *IDEAS* must have a keen knowledge of the newspaper marketing field—previous work in this area or with an ad agency on a newspaper account is definitely a plus. Writers must also be up on current trends in newspaper marketing (i.e., marketing to younger readers, conversions to a.m. publication, competition with broadcast media). The area most open to freelancers is the Focus section of *IDEAS*."

‡IMPRINT, The Magazine of Specialty Advertising Ideas, Advertising Specialty Institute, 1120 Wheeler Way, Langhorne PA 19047. (215)752-4200. Managing Editor: Arn Bernstein. 25% freelance written. Works with a small number of new/unpublished writers each year. Quarterly magazine covering specialty advertising. Circ. 60,000. Pays on publication. Publishes ms an average of 6 months after acceptance. Byline given. Buys one-time rights. Submit seasonal/holiday material 6 months in advance. Simultaneous queries OK. Query for electronic submissions. Computer printout submissions acceptable; prefers letter-quality to dot-matrix. Reports in 3 months. Sample copy for 9x12 SAE with 3 first class stamps.

 The double dagger before a listing indicates that the listing is new in this edition. New markets are often the most receptive to freelance submissions.

Nonfiction: How-to (case histories of specialty advertising campaigns); and features (how ad specialties are distributed in promotions). "Emphasize effective use of specialty advertising. Avoid direct-buy situations. Stress the distributor's role in promotions. No generalized pieces on print, broadcast or outdoor advertising." Buys 10-12 mss/year. Query with published clips. Length: varies. Payment based on assigned length. "We pay authorized phone, postage, etc."

Photos: State availability of 5x7 b&w photos. Pays "some extra for *original* photos *only*." Captions, model release and identification of subjects required.

Tips: "The predominant cause of misdirected articles is the fact that many new writers simply don't understand the medium of specialty advertising, or our target audience—end-users. Writers are urged to investigate the medium a bit before attempting an article or suggesting an idea for one. We can also provide additional leads and suggestions. All articles, however, are specifically geared to specialty advertising (or premium) use."

MORE BUSINESS, 11 Wimbledon Court, Jericho NY 11753. Editor: Trudy Settel. 50% freelance written. "We sell publications material to business for consumer use (incentives, communication, public relations)—look for book ideas and manuscripts." Monthly magazine. Circ. 10,000. Pays on acceptance. Publishes ms an average of 1 month after acceptance. Buys all rights. Computer printout submissions acceptable; no dot-matrix. Reports in 1 month.

Nonfiction: General interest, how-to, vocational techniques, nostalgia, photo feature, profile and travel. Reviews new computer software. Buys 10-20 mss/year. Word length varies with article. Payment negotiable. Query. Pays $4,000-7,000 for book mss.

SALES & MARKETING MANAGEMENT IN CANADA, Sanford Evans Communications Ltd., Suite 103, 3500 Dufferin St., Downsview, Ontario M3K 1N2 Canada. (416)633-2020. FAX: (416)633-5725. Editor: Ernie Spear. Monthly magazine. Circ. 13,000. Pays on publication. Byline given. Buys first North American serial rights. Simultaneous queries and photocopied submissions OK. Reports in 2 weeks.

Nonfiction: How-to (case histories of successful marketing campaigns). "Canadian articles only." Buys 3 mss/year. Query. Length: 800-1,500 words. Pays $200 maximum.

SIGNCRAFT, The Magazine for the Sign Artist and Commercial Sign Shop, SignCraft Publishing Co., Inc., Box 06031, Fort Myers FL 33906. (813)939-4644. Editor: Tom McIltrot. 20% freelance written. Bimonthly magazine of the sign industry. "Like any trade magazine, we need material of direct benefit to our readers. We can't afford space for material of marginal interest." Circ. 20,400. Pays on publication. Publishes ms an average of 9 months after acceptance. Byline given. Offers negotiable kill fee. Buys first North American serial rights or all rights. Photocopied and previously published submissions OK. Computer printout submissions acceptable. Reports in 1 month. Sample copy and writer's guidelines for $2 and 5 first class stamps.

Nonfiction: Interviews and profiles. "All articles should be directly related to quality commercial signage. If you are familiar with the sign trade, we'd like to hear from you." Buys 20 mss/year. Query with or without published clips. Length: 500-2,000 words. Pays up to $150.

‡SIGNS OF THE TIMES, The Industry Journal since 1906, ST Publications, 407 Gilbert Ave., Cincinnati OH 45202. (513)421-2050. FAX: (513)421-5144. Editor: Tod Swormstedt. Managing Editor: Wade Swormstedt. 15-30% freelance written. "We are willing to use more freelancers." Magazine published 13 times/year; special buyer's guide between November and December issue. Circ. 18,000. Pays on publication. Publishes ms an average of 3 months after acceptance. Byline given. Buys variable rights. Simultaneous queries, and simultaneous, photocopied and previously published submissions OK. Computer printout submissions acceptable; no dot-matrix. Reports in 3 months. Free sample copy. Writer's guidelines "flexible."

Nonfiction: Historical/nostalgic (regarding the sign industry); how-to (carved signs, goldleaf, etc.); interview/profile (usually on assignment but interested to hear proposed topics); photo feature (query first); and technical (sign engineering, etc.). Nothing "nonspecific on signs, an example being a photo essay on 'signs I've seen.' We are a trade journal with specific audience interests." Buys 15-20 mss/year. Query with clips. Pays $150-500. Sometimes pays the expenses of writers on assignment.

Photos: Send photos with ms. "Sign industry-related photos only. We sometimes accept photos with funny twists or misspellings."

Fillers: Open to queries; request rates.

Tips: "A background in telecommunications and/or telemarketing is desired; general business management helpful. We want very *specific* ideas for articles; i.e. the *area* of telemarketing or telecommunications such as training with audio/visual materials, research of Fortune 50 companies in the field, today's hybrid PBX, etc. Research of the marketplace, i.e.; number of industry participants, future trends, No. 1 companies in the field, is most open to freelancers."

VM & SD (Visual Merchandising and Store Design), ST Publications, 407 Gilbert Ave., Cincinnati OH 45202. FAX: (513)421-4144. Editor: Ms. P.K. Anderson. 30% freelance written. Emphasizes store design and merchandise presentation. Monthly magazine. Circ. 18,000. Pays on publication. Buys first and second rights to the same material. Simultaneous and previously published submissions OK. Computer printout submissions acceptable. Reports in 1 month. Publishes ms an average of 3 months after acceptance. Sample copy for 8½x11 SAE with $2.70. Writer's guidelines for #10 SAE.

Nonfiction: How-to (display); informational (store design, construction, merchandise presentation); interview (display directors and store owners, industry personalities); profile (new and remodeled stores); new product; photo feature (window display); and technical (store lighting, carpet, wallcoverings, fixtures). No "advertorials" that tout a single company's product or product line. Buys 24 mss year. Query or submit complete ms. Length: 500-3,000 words. Pays $250-500.

Photos: Purchased with accompanying ms or on assignment.

Tips: "Be fashion and design conscious and reflect that in the article. Submit finished manuscripts with photos or slides always. Look for stories on department and specialty store visual merchandisers and store designers (profiles, methods, views on the industry, sales promotions and new store design or remodels). The size of the publication could very well begin to increase in the year ahead. And with a greater page count, we will need to rely on an increasing number of freelancers."

Art, Design and Collectibles

The businesses of art, art administration, architecture, environmental/package design and antiques/collectibles are covered in these listings. Art-related topics for the general public are located in the Consumer Art and Architecture category. Antiques and collectibles magazines for enthusiasts are listed in Consumer Hobby and Craft. (Listings of markets looking for freelance artists to do art work can be found in *Artist's Market* — see Other Books of Interest).

ANTIQUEWEEK, Mayhill Publications Inc., 27 N. Jefferson St., Box 90, Knightstown IN 46148. (317)345-5133. Managing Editor: Tom Hoepf. 60% freelance written. Weekly tabloid on antiques, collectibles and genealogy. *AntiqueWeek* publishes two editions: Mid-Atlantic and Mid-Central. "*AntiqueWeek* has a wide range of readership from dealers and auctioneers to collectors, advanced and novice. Our readers demand accurate information presented in an entertaining style." Circ. 60,000. Pays on publication. Publishes ms an average of 1-2 months after acceptance. Byline given. Buys first and second serial (reprint) rights. Submit seasonal/holiday material 1 month in advance. Simultaneous, photocopied and previously published submissions OK. Computer printout submissions OK; prefers letter-quality. Reports in 1 month. Free sample copy and writer's guidelines.

Nonfiction: Historical/nostalgic, how-to, interview/profile, opinion, personal experience, photo feature, antique show and auction reports, feature articles on particular types of antiques. Buys 400-500 mss/year. Query with or without published clips, or send complete ms. Length: 1,000-2,000 words. Pays $25-125.

Photos: Send photos with submission. Reviews 3½x5 prints. Offers $10-15 per photo. Identification of subjects required. Buys one-time rights.

Columns/Departments: Insights (opinions on buying, selling and collecting antiques), 500-1,000 words; Your Ancestors (advice, information on locating sources for genealogists), 1,500-2,000 words. Buys 150 mss/ year. Query. Length: 500-1,000 words. Pays $15-50.

Tips: "Writers should know their topic thoroughly to write about it. Feature articles must be well-researched and clearly written. An interview and profile article with a knowledgeable collector might be the break for a first-time contributor. As we move toward the year 2000, there is much more interest in 20th-century collectibles. *Antiqueweek* also seeks articles that reflect the current popularity of Victorian-era antiques."

ART BUSINESS NEWS, Myers Publishing Co., 60 Ridgeway Plaza, Stamford CT 06905. (203)356-1745. Editor: Jo Yanow-Schwartz. Managing Editor: Beth Fleckenstein. 25% freelance written. Prefers to work with published/established writers. Monthly tabloid covering news relating to the art and picture framing industry. Circ. 28,000. Pays on publication. Publishes ms an average of 3 months after acceptance. Byline given. Buys first-time rights. Submit seasonal/holiday material 2 months in advance. Photocopied and simultaneous submissions OK. Computer printout submissions acceptable; prefers letter-quality. Reports in 2-3 months. Sample copy for 12x15¾ SAE and $2.40.

Nonfiction: News in art and framing field; interview/marketing profiles (of dealers, publishers in the art industry); new products; articles focusing on small business people — framers, art gallery management, art trends; and how-to (occasional article on "how-to frame" accepted). Buys 8-20 mss/year. Length: 1,000 words maximum. Query first. Pays $75-250. Sometimes pays the expenses of writers on assignment. "Useful if writer can photograph."

ARTS MANAGEMENT, 408 W. 57th St., New York NY 10019. (212)245-3850. Editor: A.H. Reiss. For cultural institutions. Published five times/year. 2% freelance written. Circ. 6,000. Pays on publication. Byline given. Buys all rights. Mostly staff-written; uses very little outside material. Computer printout submissions acceptable; no dot-matrix. Query. Reports in "several weeks." Writer's guidelines for #10 SASE.
Nonfiction: Short articles, 400-900 words, tightly written, expository, explaining how art administrators solved problems in publicity, fund raising and general administration; actual case histories emphasizing the how-to. Also short articles on the economics and sociology of the arts and important trends in the nonprofit cultural field. Must be fact-filled, well-organized and without rhetoric. Payment is 2-4¢/word. No photographs or pictures.

CALLIGRAPHY REVIEW, Box 1511, Norman OK 73070. (405)364-8794. Editor: Karyn L. Gilman. 98% freelance written. Eager to work with new/unpublished writers with calligraphic expertise and language skills. A quarterly magazine on calligraphy and related book arts, both historical and contemporary in nature. Circ. 5,500. Pays on publication. Publishes ms an average of 6 months after acceptance. Byline given. Offers 20% kill fee. Buys first rights. Submit seasonal/holiday material 3-4 months in advance. Photocopied submissions OK. Query for electronic submissons. Computer printout submissions acceptable. Sample copy for 9x12 SAE with 7 first class stamps; free writer's guidelines.
Nonfiction: Interview/profile, new product, opinion and historical. Buys 50 mss/year. Query with or without published clips, or send complete ms. Length: 1,000-2,000 words. Pays $50-200 for assigned articles; pays $25-200 for unsolicited articles. Sometimes pays the expenses of writers on assignment.
Photos: State availability of photos with submission. Reviews contact sheets, negatives, transparencies and prints. Pays agreed upon cost. Captions and identification of subjects required. Buys one-time rights.
Columns/Departments: Book Reviews Viewpoint (critical), 500-1,500 words; Ms. (discussion of manuscripts in collections), 1,000-2,000 words; and Profile (contemporary calligraphic figure), 1,000-2,000 words. Query. Pays $50-200.
Tips: "*Calligraphy Review*'s primary objective is to encourage the exchange of ideas on calligraphy, its past and present as well as trends for the future. Practical and conceptual treatments are welcomed, as are learning and teaching experiences. Third person is preferred, however first person will be considered if appropriate."

THE CRAFTS REPORT, The Newsmonthly of Marketing, Management and Money for Crafts Professionals, The Crafts Report Publishing Co., 3632 Ashworth North, Seattle WA 98103. (206)547-7611. FAX: (206)547-7113. Editor: Michael Scott. 50% freelance written. A monthly tabloid covering business subjects for crafts professionals. Circ. 17,000. Pays on publication. Byline given. Offers $50 kill fee. Buys first rights. Photocopied submissions and sometimes previously published submissions OK. Query for electronic submissions. Computer printout submissions OK. Reports in 2 weeks. Sample copy $2.
Nonfiction: Business articles for crafts professionals. No articles on art or crafts techniques. Buys approximately 70 mss/year. Query with published clips. Length: 800-1,200 words. Pays $100-150.
Photos: State availability of photos with submission or send photos with submission. Reviews 5x7 b&w prints, color prints and color transparencies. Identification of subjects required. Buys one-time rights.

‡THE FRONT STRIKER BULLETIN, The Retskin Report, Box 8101, Alexandria VA 22306-8101. (703)768-1051. Editor: Bill Retskin. 70% freelance written. Quarterly newsletter for matchcover collectors and historical enthusiasts. Circ. 500. Pays on publication. Publishes ms an average of 3 months after acceptance. Byline given. Offers 20% kill fee. Buys first North American serial rights. Submit seasonal/holiday material 6 months in advance. Query for electronic submission. Computer printout submissions OK; prefers letter-quality. Sample copy for 8 1/2x11 SAE with 2 first class stamps; writer's guidelines for #10 SASE.
Nonfiction: General interest, historical/nostalgic, how-to (collecting techniques), humor, personal experience and photo feature; all relating to match industry or ephemera. Buys 2 mss/year. Query with published clips. Length: 200-1,200 words. Pays $25-50 for assigned articles; $10-25 for unsolicited articles.
Photos: State availability of photos with submission. Reviews b&w contact sheets and 5x7 prints. Offers $2-5/photo. Captions and identification of subjects required.
Fiction: Historical (match cover related only). Buys 2 mss/year. Query with published clips. Length: 200-1,200 words. Pays $25-50.
Tips: "We are interested in clean, direct style with the collector audience in mind."

‡GLASS ART, The Magazine for Stained and Decorative Glass, Travin, Inc., Suite 202, 1008 Depot Hill Rd., Broomfield CO 80020. (303)465-4965. FAX: (303)469-5730. Editor: Shawn Waggoner. Publisher: Kevin Borgmann. 40% freelance written. Bimonthly magazine. "*Glass Art* magazine covers the spectrum of the glass art industry. We feature national artists and their work as well as provide information on getting commissions, legal issues, safety issues and business issues." Circ. 7,000. Byline given. Buys first North American serial rights. Submit seasonal/holiday material 2 months in advance. Simultaneous and photocopied submissions OK. Computer printout submissions OK; prefers letter-quality. Reports in 4 weeks. Free sample copy and writer's guidelines.

Nonfiction: How-to (any glass process articles are of interest); personal experience (glass artists with experiences of interest to other artists may submit materials); religious (articles relaying crossover between religion and stained glass) and technical (any technical information pertaining to glass and its use as art media). "*Glass Art* rarely accepts freelance material written by persons who are not professional glass artists, engineers, kilnmakers, etc." Query with published clips. Length: 700-2,000 words. Pays $75-250.

Photos: Send photos with submission. Reviews transparencies and prints. Offers no additional payment for photos accepted with ms. Identification of subjects required. Buys one-time rights.

Column/Departments: Hot Glass, Safety, Good Business and Tips & Tricks (technical).

Tips: "Technical information is always needed. If you are a glass artist who can write, simply call with your ideas. Must be well-versed in glass art processes and techniques."

‡**HOW, Ideas and Techniques in Graphic Design**, 1507 Dana Ave., Cincinnati OH 45207. (513)531-2222. Editor: Laurel Harper. 75% freelance written. Bimonthly magazine; graphic design and illustration trade journal. "*HOW* gives a behind-the-scenes look at how the world's best graphic artists and designers conceive and create their work." Circ. 35,000. Pays on acceptance. Byline given. Buys first North American serial rights. Query for electronic submission. Reports in 1 month. Sample copy for $8.50. Writer's guidelines for #10 SASE.

Nonfiction: Interview/profile and new product. Special issues—Sept/Oct: Business Annual; Nov/Dec: Self-Promotion Annual. No how-to articles for beginning artists or fine-art-oriented articles. Buys 40 mss/year. Query with published clips and samples of subjects work (artwork or design). Length: 1,200-2,500 words. Pays $250-600. Sometimes pays expenses of writers on assignment.

Photos: State availability of artwork with submission. Reviews 35mm or larger transparencies. May reimburse mechanical photo expenses. Captions are required. Buys one-time rights.

Columns/Departments: Marketplace, (focuses on lucrative fields for designers/illustrators); Design Talk, (Q&A interviews with top designers); and Production, (ins, outs and tips on production). Buys 40 mss/year. Query with published clips. Length: 1,000-1,800 words. Pays $150-400.

Tips: "We look for writers who can recognize graphic designers on the cutting-edge of their industry. Writers must have an eye for detail, and be able to relay *HOW*'s step-by-step approach in an interesting, concise manner—without omitting any details. Showing you've done your homework on a subject—and that you can go beyond asking 'those same old questions'—will give you a big advantage."

‡**MANHATTAN ARTS MAGAZINE**, Renee Phillips Associates, Suite 26L, 200 East 72 St., New York NY 10021. (212) 472-1660. Editor: Renee Phillips. Managing Editor: Michael Jason. 100% freelance written. Monthly magazine coving fine art. Audience is comprised of art professionals, artists and emerging collectors. Educational, informative, easy-to-read style, making art more accessible. Highly promotional of new artists. Circ. 50,000. Pays on publication. Publishes ms an average of 1 month after acceptance. Byline given. Makes work for hire assignments. Submit seasonal/holiday material 3 months in advance. Simultaneous and photocopied submissions OK. Sample copy $1 with 9x12 SAE and 85¢ postage.

Nonfiction: Book excerpts (art), essays (art world), general interest (collecting art), inspirational (artists success stories), interview/profile (major art leaders), new product (art supplies), technical (art business). Buys 100 mss/year. Query with published clips. Length: 150-750 words. Pays $25-100. New writers receive byline and promotion, art books. Sometimes pays expenses of writers on assignment.

Photos: Send photos with submission. Offers no additional payment for photos accepted with ms. Captions, model releases and identification of subjects required.

Columns/Departments: Reviews/Previews (art critiques of exhibitions in galleries and museums), 150-250 words; Profiles (features on major art leaders), 400-650 words; The New Collector (collectibles, interviews with dealers, collectors), 150-650 words; Artopia (inspirational features, success stories), 150-650 words; Art Books, Art Services, 150-300 words. Buys 100 mss/year. Query with published clips. Pays $25-100.

Tips: "A knowledge of the current, contemporary art scene is a must. An eye for emerging talent is an asset."

‡**THE MIDATLANTIC ANTIQUES MAGAZINE, Monthly Guide to Antiques, Art, Auctions & Collectibles**, The Henderson Daily Dispatch Company, Inc. Box 908, Henderson NC 27536. (919)492-4001. Editor: Kay Compston. 65% freelance written. Monthly tabloid that covers antiques, art, auctions and collectibles. "The *MidAtlantic* is a monthly trade publication that reaches dealers, collectors, antique shows and auction houses primarily on the east coast, but circulation includes 48 states and Europe." Circ. 12,000. Pays on publication. Byline given. Buys first rights, second serial (reprint) rights or simultaneous rights (noncompeting markets). Submit seasonal/holiday material 3 months in advance. Simultaneous, photocopied and previously published submissions OK. Computer printout submissions OK. Reports in 1 month on queries; 2 months on mss. Free sample copy and writer's guidelines.

Nonfiction: Book excerpts, historical/nostalgic, how-to (choose an antique to collect; how to sell your collection; how to identify market trends), interview/profile, personal experience, photo feature, and technical. Buys 96-120 mss/year. Query. Length: 800-2,000 words. Pays $50-150. Trade for advertising space. Rarely pays expenses of writers on assignment.

Photos: Send photos with submission. Offers no additional payment for photos accepted with ms. Identification of subjects required. Buys one-time rights.

Columns/Departments: Ask An Appraiser, Knock on Wood, Rinker on Collectibles, Lindquist on Antiques and Collecting For Fun (Insights on buying, selling, collecting antiques, art, collectibles, *not* looking for columnists at this time.), 800-2,000 words. Buys 96 mss/year. Query with published clips. Pays $3-50.

Tips: "Please contact by mail first, but may call with specific ideas after initial contact. Looking for writers who have extensive knowledge in specific areas of antiques. Articles should be educational in nature. We are also interested in how-to articles, i.e., how to choose antiques to collect; how to sell your collection and get the most for it; looking for articles that focus on future market trends. We want writers that are active in the antiques business and can predict good investments. (Articles with photographs are given preference.) We are looking for people who are not only knowledgeable, but can write well."

NEAA NEWS, New England Appraisers Association Newsletter, New England Appraisers Assocation, 5 Gill Terrace, Ludlow VT 05149. (802)228-7444. Editor: Linda L. Tucker. 75% freelance written. Works with a small number of new/unpublished writers each year. Monthly newsletter on the appraisals of antiques, art, collectibles, jewelry, coins, stamps and real estate. "The writer should be extremely knowledgeable on the subject, and the article should be written with appraisers in mind with prices quoted for objects, good pictures and descriptions of articles being written about." Circ. 1,300. Pays on publication. Publishes ms an average of 2 months after acceptance. Byline given, with short biography to establish writer's credibility. Buys first rights, second serial (reprint) rights, and simultaneous rights. Submit seasonal/holiday material 2 months in advance. Simultaneous and previously published submissions OK. Computer printout submissions acceptable; prefers letter-quality. Reports in 1 week on queries; 3 weeks on mss. Sample copy for 8½x11 SAE with 45¢ postage; writer's guidelines for #10 SASE.

Nonfiction: Interview/profile, personal experience, technical and travel. "All articles must be geared toward professional appraisers." Query with or without published clips, or send complete ms. Length: 800 words. Pays $50.

Photos: Send photos with submission. Reviews negatives and prints. Offers no additional payment for photos accepted with ms. Identification of subjects required. Buys one-time rights.

Tips: "Interviewing members of the Association for articles, reviewing art books, shows and large auctions are all ways for writers who are not in the field to write articles for us."

NEW ENGLAND ANTIQUES JOURNAL, Turley Publications. 4 Church St., Ware MA 01082. (413)967-3505. FAX: (413)967-6009. Editor: Rufus Foshee. 50% freelance written. A monthly newspaper concentrating on antiques for antique dealers, collectors and the general public. Circ. 20,000. Pays on publication. Byline given. Buys first rights. Computer printout submissions OK; prefers letter-quality, double-spaced copy. Reports in 1 month on queries; 2 months on mss.

Nonfiction: Queries advisable, all manuscripts considered. Fees negotiable. "We want original, in-depth articles on all types of antiques, preferably by experts in their fields." Mss under 1,000 words not desirable, no limit on length. Articles must be accompanied by photos.

Tips: "Read our publication, send inquiries first."

‡PROGRESSIVE ARCHITECTURE, 600 Summer St., Box 1361, Stamford CT 06904. Editor: John M. Dixon. 5-10% freelance written. Prefers to work with published/established writers. Monthly. Pays on acceptance. Publishes ms an average of 4 months after acceptance. Buys all rights for use in architectural press. Query for electronic submissions. Computer printout submissions acceptable.

Nonfiction: "Articles of technical, professional interest devoted to architecture, interior design, and urban design and planning and illustrated by photographs and architectural drawings. We also use technical articles which are prepared by technical authorities and would be beyond the scope of the lay writer. Practically all the material is professional, and most of it is prepared by writers in the field who are approached by the magazine for material." Pays $150-400. Sometimes pays the expenses of writers on assignment.

Photos: Buys one-time reproduction rights to b&w and color photos.

‡TEXAS ARCHITECT, Texas Society of Architects, Suite 1400, 114 W. Seventh, Austin TX 78701. (512)478-7386. Editor: Joel Warren Barna. Managing Editor: Don Tilley. 30% freelance written. Bimonthly trade journal of architecture and architects of Texas. "*Texas Architect* is a highly visually-oriented look at Texas architecture, design and urban planning. Articles cover varied subtopics within architecture. Readers are mostly architects and related building professionals." Circ. 10,000. Pays on publication. Publishes an average of 2 months after acceptance. Byline given. Buys one-time rights, all rights or makes work-for-hire assignments. Submit seasonal/holiday material 4 months in advance. Photocopied submissions OK. Query for electronic submissions. Computer printout submissions OK; prefers letter-quality. Reports in 2 weeks. Free sample copy and writer's guidelines.

Nonfiction: Book excerpts, essays, historical/nostalgic, humor, interview/profile, opinion, photo feature and technical. Buys 15 mss/year. Query with or without published clips, or send complete ms. Length: 100-2,000 words. Pays $50-500 for assigned articles; $25-300 for unsolicited articles.

Photos: Send photos with submission. Reviews contact sheets, 35mm or 4x5 transparencies and 4x5 prints. Offers no additional payment for photos accepted with ms. Identification of subjects required. Buys one-time rights.

Columns: Ray Don Tilley. News (timely reports on architectural issues, projects and people); 100-500 words. Buys 10 mss/year. Query with published clips. Pays $50-100.

Auto and Truck

These publications are geared to automobile, motorcycle and truck dealers; professional truck drivers; service department personnel; or fleet operators. Publications for highway planners and traffic control experts are listed in the Government and Public Service category, Aviation and Space.

In this section are journals for aviation business executives, airport operators and aviation technicians. Publications for professional and private pilots can be found in the Consumer Aviation section.

AUTO GLASS JOURNAL, Grawin Publications, Inc., Suite 101, 303 Harvard E., Box 12099, Seattle WA 98102-0099. (206)322-5120. Editor: Burton Winters. 45% freelance written. Prefers to work with published/established writers. Monthly magazine on auto glass replacement. National publication for the auto glass replacement industry. Includes step-by-step glass replacement procedures for current model cars as well as shop profiles, industry news and trends. Circ. 5,500. Pays on acceptance. Publishes ms an average of 5 months after acceptance. No byline given. Buys all rights. Query for electronic submissions. Computer printout submissions acceptable; prefers letter-quality. Reports in 2 weeks on queries; 1 week on mss. Sample copy for 6x9 SAE and 3 first class stamps. Writer's guidelines for #10 SAE and 1 first class stamp.

Nonfiction: How-to (install all glass in a current model car); and interview/profile. Buys 22-36 mss/year. Query with published clips. Length: 2,000-3,500 words. Pays $75-250, with photos.

Photos: State availability of photos. Reviews b&w contact sheets and negatives. Payment included with ms. Captions required. Buys all rights.

Tips: "Be willing to visit auto glass replacement shops for installation features."

‡**AUTO LAUNDRY NEWS,** Columbia Communications, 370 Lexington Ave., New York NY 10017. (212)532-9290. FAX: (212)779-8345. Publisher/Editor: Ralph Monti. 20% freelance written. Prefers to work with published/established writers, and works with a small number of new/unpublished writers each year. For sophisticated car wash operators. Monthly magazine; 45-100 pages. Circ. 15,000. Pays on publication. Publishes ms an average of 2 months after acceptance. Buys all rights. Submit seasonal/holiday material 2 months in advance. Query for electronic submissions. Computer printout submissions acceptable; no dot-matrix. Reports in 1 month. Sample copy for 9x12 SAE with 70¢ postage. Free writer's guidelines.

Nonfiction: How-to, historical, informational, new product, nostalgia, personal experience, technical, interviews, photo features and profiles. Buys 15 mss/year. Query. Length: 1,000-2,000 words. Pays $75-175. Sometimes pays the expenses of writers on assignment.

Tips: "We would mainly like to receive car wash profiles. Read the magazine; notice its style and come up with something interesting to the industry. Foremost, the writer has to know the industry."

AUTOMOTIVE BOOSTER OF CALIFORNIA, Box 765, LaCanada CA 91011. (213)790-6554. FAX: (818)957-3889. Editor: Don McAnally. 2% freelance written. Prefers to work with published/established writers. For members of Automotive Booster clubs, automotive warehouse distributors, and automotive parts jobbers in California. Monthly. Circ. 3,400. Not copyrighted. Byline given. Pays on publication. Publishes ms an average of 1 month after acceptance. Buys first rights only.

Nonfiction: Will look at short articles and pictures about successes of automotive parts outlets in California. Also can use personnel assignments for automotive parts people in California. Query first. Pays $1.25/column inch (about 2½¢/word).

Photos: Pays $7.50 for b&w photos used with mss.

AUTOMOTIVE EXECUTIVE, Official Publication of National Auto Dealers, NADA Services Corporation. 8400 Westpart Dr., McLean VA 22102. (703)821-7150. FAX: (703)821-7075. Editor-in-Chief: Marc H. Stertz. Managing Editor: Joe Phillips. 80% freelance written. A monthly magazine on the retail new-car and truck business. "We offer a broad view of developments in the nation's $283 billion retail new car and truck market. We seek examples of excellence in sales, service, product, and customer relations." Circ. 24,000. Pays on publication. Publishes ms an average of 2 months after acceptance. Byline given. Kill fee negotiable. Buys all rights. Query for electronic submissions. Computer printout submissions OK; prefers letter-quality. Reports in 1 week on queries; 2 weeks on mss. Free sample copy and writer's guidelines.

Nonfiction: Dealership managament (sales, service, parts, finance, personnel), interview/profile, new product and technical. February—annual convention issue; May—annual dealership design issue; August—annual buyers guide issue; December—annual forecast issue. Buys 50-60 mss/year. Query with published clips. Length: 2,500 words. Pays $200-500 for assigned articles. Pays the expenses of writers on assignment.

Photos: State availability of photos with submission or send photos with submission. Reviews contact sheets. Offers no additional payment for photos accepted with ms. Buys all rights.

Columns/Departments: Column/Department Editor: Joan Mooney. On Track (reports on current auto-industry events /trends and new-car introductions), 100-250 words; pays $50-75. Opinion Page (opinions on current industry controversies/policies) 750-1,000 words; pays $250-300; Showcase (highlights new products related to retail auto market) 750-1,000 words; pays $250-300; Service Department (ideas for efficient servicing of cars/trucks), 750-2,500 words; pays $250-300. Buys 40-50 mss/year. Query with published clips.

Tips: "We're looking for articles dealing with all aspects of retail new car/truck sales/service/customer relations, interviews with manufacturing/import executives, stories on unusual dealers/dealerships and stories from related industry that focus on excellence. We look for current economic and retrail trends in the auto industry and changes in the global economy that may impact dealers (i.e., merging car manufacturers, labor relations, trade, etc.)."

‡THE BATTERY MAN, Independent Battery Manufacturers Association, Inc., 100 Larchwood Dr., Largo FL 34640. (813)586-1409. Editor: Celwyn E. Hopkins. 40% freelance written. Emphasizes SLI battery manufacture, applications and new developments. For battery manufacturers and retailers (garage owners, servicemen, fleet owners, etc.). Monthly magazine. Circ. 5,200. Pays on acceptance. Publishes ms an average of 1 year after acceptance. Buys all rights. Submit seasonal/holiday material 4 months in advance. Simultaneous, photocopied and previously published submissions OK. Computer printout submissions acceptable; no dot-matrix. Reports in 2 months. Send SASE for return of manuscript. Sample copy $3 and 9 × 12 SAE. Writer's guidelines for #10 SASE.

Nonfiction: Technical articles. "Articles about how a company is using batteries as a source of uninterruptable power supply for its computer systems or a hospital using batteries for the same (photos with article are nice) purpose as well as for life support systems, etc." Submit complete ms. Buys 19-24 unsolicited mss/year. Recent article examples: "State-of-the-Art Ventilation Engineering Principles of Laminar Flow and Recirculation in the Battery Industry" (April 1989); "North American SLI Battery Market Review and Forecast" (January 1989). Length: 750-1,200 words. Pays 6¢/word.

Tips: "Most writers are not familiar enough with this industry to be able to furnish a feature article. They try to palm off something that they wrote for a hardware store, or a dry cleaner, by calling everything a 'battery store.' We receive a lot of manuscripts on taxes and tax information (such as U.S. income tax) and mss on business management in general and managing a family-owned business. Since this is an international publication, we try to stay away from such subjects, since U.S. tax info is of no use or interest to overseas readers."

‡BRAKE & FRONT END, 11 S. Forge St., Akron OH 44304. (216)535-6117. Publisher: Jeffrey S. Davis. Editor: Jim Davis. 5% freelance written. Works with a small number of new/unpublished writers each year. For owners of automotive repair shops engaged in brake, suspension, driveline exhaust and steering repair, including: specialty shops, general repair shops, new car and truck dealers, gas stations, mass merchandisers and tire stores. Monthly magazine; 68 pages. Circ. 28,000. Pays on publication. Publishes ms an average of 3-4 months after acceptance. Byline given. Buys first North American serial rights. Computer printout submissions acceptable; prefers letter-quality to dot-matrix. Reports immediately. Sample copy and editorial schedule $3; guidelines for SASE.

Nonfiction: Specialty shops taking on new ideas using new merchandising techniques; growth of business, volume; reasons for growth and success. Expansions and unusual brake shops. Prefers no product-oriented material. Query. Length: about 800-1,500 words. Pays 7-9¢/word. Sometimes pays expenses of writers on assignment.

Photos: Pays $8.50 for b&w glossy prints purchased with mss.

COLLISION, Kruza Kaleidoscopix, Inc., Box 389, Franklin MA 02038. Editor: Jay Kruza. For auto dealers, auto body repairmen and managers, and tow truck operators. Magazine published every 6 weeks. Pays on acceptance. Buys all rights. Submit seasonal/holiday material 4 months in advance. Simultaneous, photocopied and previously published submissions OK. Reports in 3 weeks. Sample copy $3; writer's guidelines and editorial schedule for SASE.

Nonfiction: Expose (on government intervention in private enterprise via rule making; also how any business skims the cream of profitable business but fails to satisfy needs of motorist); and how-to (fix a dent, a frame, repair plastics, run your business better). No general business articles such as how to sell more, do better bookkeeping, etc. Query before submitting interview, personal opinion or technical articles. "Journalism of newsworthy material in local areas pertaining to auto body is of interest." Buys 20 or more articles/year. Length: 100-1,500 words. Pays $25-125.

Photos: "Our readers work with their hands and are more likely to be stopped by photo with story." Send photos with ms. Pays $25/first, $10/each additional for 5x7 b&w prints. Captions preferred. Model release required if not news material.

Columns/Departments: Stars and Their Cars, Personalities in Auto Dealerships, Auto Body Repair Shop Profiles, Association News and Lifestyle (dealing with general human interest hobbies or pastimes). Almost anything automotive that would attract readership interest. "Photos are very important. Stories that we have purchased are: 'Post office commandeered cars to deliver help during 1906 San Francisco Quake'; 'Bob Salter has rescued 3,000 people with his tow truck'; 'Telnack's design of T-Bird and Sable set new trends in style'; 'Snow increases body shop business for Minnesota shop'; 'Race against the clock with funny wheels on frozen lake.' "

‡**HEAVY TRUCK SALESMAN, The Magazine for Truck Sales and Leasing Professionals**, Newport Publications, Suite 214, 1045 Taylor Ave., Baltimore MD 21204. (301)828-1092. Editor-in-Chief: David A. Kolman. 25% freelance written. Bimonthly trade magazine on truck sales and leasing industry/trucking industry. "The editorial purpose is to supply timely business and career related articles for those who sell or lease medium and heavy duty trucks. Articles are intended to further sharpen the reader's selling skills and product knowledge in order to sell and lease more trucks." Circ. 22,000. Pays on publication. Pays $450 minimum. Publishes ms an average of 2 months after acceptance. Byline given. Buys first North American serial rights. Submit seasonal/holiday material 6 months in advance. Query for electronic submissions. Computer printout submissions OK. Reports in 1 month. Free sample copy.

Nonfiction: How-to (selling, truck engineering), interview/profile (industry personnel), new product, technical (product knowledge, truck engineering). Buys 6 mss/year. Query with or without published clips, or send complete ms. Sometimes pay expenses of writers on assignment.

Photos: Send photo with submission. Reviews contact sheets, negatives, transparencies and prints. Offers $75 minimum per photo. Captions are required. Buys one-time rights.

Tips: "Profiles of successful business and salespeople are most open to freelancers. Find interesting or unique subject that would appeal to *HTS* readers."

JOBBER TOPICS, 7300 N. Cicero Ave., Lincolnwood IL 60646. (312)588-7300. FAX: (312)674-7015. Articles Editor: Jack Creighton. 10% freelance written. Prefers to work with published/established writers, works with a small number of new/unpublished writers each year, and is eager to work with new/unpublished writers. "A magazine dedicated to helping its readers—auto parts jobbers and warehouse distributors—succeed in their business via better management and merchandising techniques; and a better knowledge of industry trends, sales activities and local or federal legislation that may influence their business activities." Monthly. Pays on acceptance. No byline given. Buys all rights. Computer printout submissions OK; prefers letter-quality. Sample copy and writer's guidelines for 8½x11 SASE.

Nonfiction: Most editorial material is staff-written. "Articles with unusual or outstanding automotive jobber procedures, with special emphasis on sales, merchandising and machine shop; any phase of automotive parts and equipment sales and distribution. Especially interested in merchandising practices and machine shop operations. Most independent businesses usually have a strong point or two. We like to see a writer zero in on that strong point(s) and submit an outline (or query), advising us of those points and what he/she intends to include in a feature. We will give him, or her, a prompt reply." Length: 2,500 words maximum. Pay based on quality and timeliness of feature. Pays the expenses of writers on assignment.

Photos: 5x7 b&w glossies or 35mm color transparencies purchased with mss.

MODERN TIRE DEALER, 110 N. Miller Rd., Box 5417, Akron OH 44313. (216)867-4401. FAX: (216)867-0019. Editor: Lloyd Stoyer. 15-20% freelance written. Prefers to work with published/established writers, and works with a small number of new/unpublished writers each year. For independent tire dealers. Monthly tabloid, plus 2 special emphasis issue magazines. Published 14 times annually. Buys all rights. Photocopied submissions OK. Computer printout submissions acceptable. Reports in 1 month. Publishes ms an average of 2 months after acceptance. Sample copy $5. Writer's guidelines for #10 SASE.

Nonfiction: "How independent tire dealers sell tires, accessories and allied services such as brakes, wheel alignment, shocks and mufflers. The emphasis is on merchandising and management. We prefer the writer to zero in on some specific area of interest; avoid shotgun approach." Query. Length: 1,500 words. Pays $300 and up. Sometimes pays the expenses of writers on assignment.

Photos: 8x10, 4x5, 5x7 b&w glossy prints purchased with mss.
Tips: "Changes in the competitive situation among tire manufacturers and/or distributors will affect the types of freelance material we buy. We want articles for or about tire dealers, not generic articles adapted for our publication."

‡**MOTOR SERVICE**, Hunter Publishing Co., 950 Lee, Des Plaines IL 60016. Editor: Jim Halloran. 25% freelance written. Monthly magazine for professional auto mechanics and the owners and service managers of repair shops, garages and fleets. Circ. 131,000. Pays on acceptance. Buys all rights. Pays kill fee. Byline given. Computer printout submissions acceptable. Publishes ms an average of 2 months after acceptance. Free sample copy.
Nonfiction: Technical how-to features in language a mechanic can enjoy and understand; management articles to help shop owners and service managers operate a better business; technical theory pieces on how something works; new technology roundups, etc. No "generic business pieces on management tips, increasing sales, employee motivation or do-it-yourself material, etc." Length: 1,500-2,500 words. Pays $75 for departmental material, $200-$500 for feature articles. Buys 10 mss/year, mostly from regular contributing editors. Query first. "Writers must know our market."
Photos: Photos and/or diagrams must accompany technical articles. Uses 5x7 b&w prints or 35mm transparencies. Offers no additional payment for photos accepted with ms. Captions and model releases required. Also buys color transparencies for cover use. Pays $125-200.
Tips: "We're always looking for new faces but finding someone who is technically knowledgeable in our field who can also write is extremely difficult. Good tech writers are hard to find."

O AND A MARKETING NEWS, Box 765, LaCanada CA 91011. (213)790-6554. Editor: Don McAnally. For "service station dealers, garagemen, TBA (tires, batteries, accessories) people, gasoline jobbers and distributors, and oil company marketing management." Bimonthly. 5% freelance written. Circ. 9,500. Not copyrighted. Pays on publication. Buys first rights only. Reports in 1 week.
Nonfiction: "Straight news material; management, service and merchandising applications; emphasis on news about or affecting markets and marketers *within the publication's geographic area of the 11 Western states*. No restrictions on style or slant. We could use straight news of our industry from some Western cities, notably Phoenix, Seattle and Salt Lake City. Query with a letter that gives a capsule treatment of what the story is about." Buys 25 mss/year. Length: maximum 1,000 words. Pays $1.25/column inch (about 2½¢ a word).
Photos: Photos purchased with or without mss; captions required. No cartoons. Pays $7.50.

‡**PRO TRUCKER and OVER THE ROAD**, Ramp Enterprises, 1160-G Grimes Bridge Rd., Roswell GA 30075. (404)587-0311. Editor: Ryan R. Rees. 5-10% freelance written. Monthly magazine on trucking. *"Over the Road* is published the first of each month, *Pro Trucker* the 15th of each month." Circ. 50,000. Pays on acceptance. Publishes ms an average of 2 months after acceptance. Byline given. Buys first rights and second serial (reprint) rights. Submit seasonal/holiday material 3 months in advance. Computer printout submissions OK. Sample copy for 6x9 SAE with $1.25 in postage.
Nonfiction: Humor, interview/profile and technical. Query. Length: 300-3,000 words. Pays $150-500 for assigned articles. Sometimes pays expenses of writers on assignment.
Photos: State availability of photos with submission. Reviews transparencies and 5x7 prints. Offers no additional payment for photos accepted with ms or may pay—depending on subject. Identification of subjects required. Buys all rights.
Columns/Departments: J.R. Morgan. Puzzler (word search & crossword), 1 page. Query. Pays $100-250.

RENEWS, Kona Communications, Inc., Suite 300, 707 Lake Cook Rd., Deerfield IL 60015. (312)498-3180. FAX: (312)498-3197. Editor: Terry Haller. Managing Editor: Denise L. Rondini. 40% freelance written. Works with a small number of new/unpublished writers each year. Magazine published 12 times/year covering automotive engine/parts rebuilding. Emphasizes technology and management issues affecting automotive rebuilders. Circ. 21,000. Pays on publication. Publishes ms an average of 2 months after acceptance. Byline sometimes given. Buys first rights. Photocopied submissions OK. Computer printout submissions acceptable; prefers letter-quality. Reports in 1 month.
Nonfiction: Interview/profile, photo feature and technical. "No articles that are too general to be helpful to our readers." Buys 8 mss/year. Query. Length: 1,000-2,500 words. Pays $75-300. Sometimes pays the expenses of writers on assignment.
Photos: Send photos with submission. Reviews contact sheets, transparencies and prints. Offers no additional payment for photos accepted with ms. Captions, model releases and identification of subjects required. Buys one-time rights.
Tips: "A strong automotive technical background or a special expertise in small business management is helpful. Technical and business management sections are most open to freelancers. Most of our writers are thoroughly experienced in the subject they write on. It is difficult for a 'generalist' to write for our audience."

‡**SOUTHERN MOTOR CARGO**, Wallace Witmer Co., 1509 Madison, Memphis TN 38104. (901)276-5424. Editor: Pearce Hammond. Managing Editor: Randy Duke. 15% freelance written. Monthly trade journal on heavy-duty truck equipment and safety. Circ. 61,000. Pays on acceptance. Publishes ms an average of 2 months after acceptance. Byline sometimes given. Buys all rights. Submit seasonal/holiday material 2 months in advance. Computer printout submissions OK; prefers letter-quality. Free sample copy.
Nonfiction: Interview/profile, new product, technical, trucking industry news and other safety related articles. "We do not want articles about drivers." Buys 10 mss/year. Send complete ms. Length: 500-25,000 woods. Pays 10-15¢/word. Pays expenses of writers on assignment.
Photos: Send photos with submission. Reviews contact sheets and negatives. Pays for film and processing. Captions, model releases and identification of subjects required. Buys all rights.
Columns/Departments: Bettie O. Franklin. Southern Trucking (articles that affect the writer's region. Consists of state news which deals with trucking.) and Industry News (deals with company expansions, closings, etc.). Send complete ms. Length: 300-1,500 words. Pays 10-15¢/word.
Tips: "We have recently begun publishing *regional* sections. We *need* freelancers in the Atlantic, West South Central, and East South Central regions. These writers will report on truck news in their city and surrounding area."

THE SUCCESSFUL DEALER, Kona-Cal, Inc., 707 Lake Cook Rd., Deerfield IL 60015. (312)498-3180. FAX: (312)498-3187. Editor: Terry Haller. Managing Editor: Denise Rondini. 30% freelance written. "We will consider material from both established writers and new ones." Magazine published 6 times/year covering dealership management of medium and heavy duty trucks, construction equipment, forklift trucks, diesel engines and truck trailers. Circ. 19,000. Pays on publication. Byline sometimes given. Buys first serial rights only. Simultaneous queries, and simultaneous and photocopied submissions OK. Computer printout submissions acceptable; prefers letter-quality. Reports in 2 weeks. Publication date "depends on the article; some are contracted for a specific issue, others on an as need basis."
Nonfiction: How-to (solve problems within the dealership); interview/profile (concentrating on business, not personality); new product (exceptional only); opinion (by readers—those in industry); personal experience (of readers); photo feature (of major events); and technical (vehicle componentry). Special issues include: March-April: American Truck Dealer Convention; September-October: Parts and Service. Query. Length: open. Pays $75/page. Sometimes pays the expenses of writers on assignment.
Tips: "Phone first, then follow up with a detailed explanation of the proposed article. Allow two weeks for our response. Articles should be based on real problems/solutions encountered by truck or heavy equipment dealership personnel. We are *not* interested in general management tips."

TOW-AGE, Kruza Kaleidoscopix, Inc., Box 389, Franklin MA 02038. Editor: J. Kruza. For readers who run their own towing service business. 5% freelance written. Prefers to work with published/established writers, and works with a small number of new/unpublished writers each year. Published every 6 weeks. Circ. 18,000. Buys all rights; usually reassigns rights. Buys about 18 mss/year. Pays on acceptance. Publishes ms an average of 1 month after acceptance. Photocopied and simultaneous submissions OK. Reports in 1-4 weeks. Computer printout submissions acceptable. Sample copy $3; writer's guidelines for #10 SASE.
Nonfiction: Articles on business, legal and technical information for the towing industry. "Light reading material; short, with punch." Informational, how-to, personal, interview and profile. Query or submit complete ms. Length: 200-800 words. Pays $50-150. Spot news and successful business operations. Length: 100-800 words. Technical articles. Length: 400-1,000 words. Pays expenses of writers on assignment.
Photos: Buys up to 8x10 b&w photos purchased with or without mss, or on assignment. Pays $25 for first photo; $10 for each additional photo in series. Captions required.

‡**TRUCK WORLD**, Truck World Publications Ltd., Suite 205, 2550 Boundary Rd., Burnaby, British Columbia V5M 3Z3 Canada. FAX: (604)433-4882. Trade journal on the trucking industry. "*Truck World* is designed to reach people directly or indirectly employed in the Canadian trucking industry. Readers are generally assumed to have an understanding of the industry." Pays on publication. Publishes an average of 2 months after acceptance. Byline given. Buys first North American serial rights. Previously published submissions OK. Query for electronic submissions. Computer printout submissions OK; prefers letter quality. Reports in 2 weeks on queries; 1 month on mss. Free sample copy.
Nonfiction: Humor, interview/profile, new product, photo feature and technical. "No personal trucking experiences. Stick to objective reporting on industry issues in Canada and the U.S." Buys 25 mss/year. Query with published clips. Length: 200-2,000 words. Pays $75-800. Pays expenses of writers on assignment.
Photos: State availability of photos with submissions or send photos with submission. Reviews 5x7 color or b&w prints. Offers no additional payment for photos accepted with ms. Captions and identification of subjects required. Buys one-time rights.
Columns/Departments: Finance (general pieces on finance and leasing relating to trucking industry), 500-1,000 words; Maintenance (general tips on trucking maintenance), 50-500 words; and Computers (latest in computer systems for trucking industry), 500-1,000 words. Buys 10 mss/year. Query with published clips. Pays $20-500.

Tips: "Potential contributors should have an awareness of the trucking industry. Do not attempt to write technical articles unless you have substantial knowledge in truck maintenance and operation. We are looking for more contributors from eastern Canada to report on the trucking industry generally. U.S. writers are needed to report on the latest trends in the industry."

WARD'S AUTO WORLD, % 28 W. Adams, Detroit MI 48226. (313)962-4433. FAX: (313)962-4456. Editor-in-Chief: David C. Smith. Editor: Edward K. Miller. 10% freelance written. Prefers to work with published/established writers; works with a small number of new/unpublished writers each year. For top and middle management in all phases of auto industry. Also includes heavy-duty vehicle coverage. Monthly magazine. Circ. 85,000. Pays on publication. Pay varies for kill fee. Byline given. Buys all rights. Phone queries OK. Submit seasonal/holiday material 1 month in advance. Query for electronic submissions. Computer printout submissions acceptable; check first before submitting dot-matrix. Reports in 2 weeks. Publishes ms an average of 1 month after acceptance. Free sample copy and writer's guidelines.
Nonfiction: Expose, general interest, international automotive news, historical, humor, interview, new product, photo feature and technical. Few consumer type articles. No "nostalgia or personal history type stories (like 'My Favorite Car')." Buys 4-8 mss/year. Query. Length: 700-5,000 words. Pays $200-750. Sometimes pays the expenses of writers on assignment.
Photos: "We're heavy on graphics." Submit photo material with query. Pay varies for 8x10 b&w prints or color transparencies. Captions required. Buys one-time rights.
Tips: "Don't send poetry, how-to and 'My Favorite Car' stuff. It doesn't stand a chance. This is a business newsmagazine and operates on a news basis just like any other newsmagazine. We like solid, logical, well-written pieces with *all* holes filled."

Aviation and Space

In this section are journals for aviation business executives, airport operators and aviation technicians. Publications for professional and private pilots can be found in the Consumer Aviation section.

‡AG-PILOT INTERNATIONAL MAGAZINE, Tomelupa, Inc., 405 Main St., Mt Vernon WA 98273. FAX: (206)336-2506. Editor: Tom J. Wood. Executive Editor: Rocky Kemp. Emphasizes agricultural aerial application (crop dusting). "This is intended to be a fun-to-read, technical, as well as humorous, and serious publication for the ag pilot and operator. They are our primary target." 20% freelance written. Monthly magazine; 60 pages. Circ. 12,400. Pays on publication. Publishes ms an average of 3 months after acceptance. Buys all rights. Byline given unless writer requests name held. Computer printout submissions acceptable; prefers letter-quality to dot-matrix. Reports in 2 weeks. Sample copy for 9×12 SAE with $1.80 postage; writer's guidelines for #10 SASE.
Nonfiction: Expose (of EPA, OSHA, FAA or any government function concerned with this industry); general interest; historical; interview (of well-known ag/aviation person); nostalgia; personal opinion; new product; personal experience; and photo feature. "If we receive an article, in any area we have solicited, it is quite possible this person could contribute intermittently. The international input is what we desire. Industry-related material is a must. *No newspaper clippings.*" Send complete ms. Length: 800-1,500 words. Pays $50-200. Sometimes pays the expenses of writers on assignment.
Photos: "We would like one color or b&w (5x7 preferred) with the manuscript, if applicable—it will help increase your chance of publication." Four color. Offers no additional payment for photos accepted with ms. Captions preferred, model release required.
Columns/Departments: International (of prime interest, crop dusting-related); Embryo Birdman (should be written, or appear to be written, by a beginner spray pilot); The Chopper Hopper (by anyone in the helicopter industry); Trouble Shooter (ag aircraft maintenance tips); and Catchin' The Corner (written by a person obviously skilled in the crop dusting field of experience or other interest-capturing material related to the industry). Send complete ms. Length: 800-1,500 words. Pays $25-100.
Poetry: Interested in all agri-aviation related poetry. Buys 1/issue. Submit no more than 2 at one time. Maximum length: one 20 inch x 48 picas maximum. Pays $10-50.
Fillers: Short jokes, short humor and industry-related newsbreaks. Length: 10-100 words. Pays $5-20.
Tips: "Writers should be witty and knowledgeable about the crop dusting aviation world. Material *must* be agricultural/aviation-oriented. *Crop dusting or nothing!*"

‡AIR LINE PILOT, Magazine of Professional Flight Crews, Air Line Pilots Association, 535 Herndon Parkway, Box 1169, Herndon VA 22069. (703)689-4176. Editor: Esperison Martinez, Jr. 10% freelance written. Prefers to work with published/established writers; works with a small number of new/unpublished writers each year. A monthly magazine for airline pilots covering "aviation industry information—economics, avionics, equipment, systems, safety—that affects a pilot's life in professional sense." Also includes information about management/labor relations trends, contract negotiations, etc. Circ. 42,000. Pays on acceptance. Publishes ms an average of 6 months after acceptance. Offers 35% kill fee. Buys first serial rights and makes work-for-hire assignments. Submit seasonal/holiday material 6 months in advance. Query for electronic submissions. Computer printout submissions acceptable. Reports in 2 months. Sample copy $1 with 9x12 SAE; writer's guidelines for #10 SASE.

Nonfiction: Historical/nostalgic, humor, interview/profile, photo feature and technical. "We are backlogged with historical submissions and prefer not to receive unsolicited submissions at this time." Buys 20 mss/year. Query with or without published clips, or send complete ms. Length: 1,000-3,000 words. Pays $100-800 for assigned articles; pays $50-500 for unsolicited articles.

Photos: Send photos with submission. Reviews contact sheets, 35mm transparencies and 8x10 prints. Offers $10-25/photo. Identification of subjects required. Buys one-time rights.

Tips: "For our feature section, we seek aviation industry information that affects the life of a professional airline pilot from a career standpoint. We also seek material that affects his life from a job security and work environment standpoint. Historical material that addresses the heritage of the profession or the advancement of the industry is also sought. Any airline pilot featured in an article must be an Air Line Pilots Association member in good standing."

AIRPORT SERVICES MAGAZINE, Lakewood Publications, 50 S. 9th St., Minneapolis MN 55402. (612)333-0471. Managing Editor: Karl Bremer. 33% freelance written. Emphasizes management of airports and airport-based businesses. Monthly magazine. Circ. 20,000. Pays on acceptance. Publishes ms an average of 3 months after acceptance. Buys one-time rights, exclusive in our industry. Byline given. Phone queries OK. Submit seasonal/holiday material 3 months in advance. Photocopied submissions OK but must be industry-exclusive. Query for electronic submission. Computer printout submissions acceptable; prefers letter-quality. Reports in 1 month. Free sample copy and writer's guidelines.

Nonfiction: How-to (manage an airport or aviation service company; work with local governments, etc.); interview (with a successful operator); and technical (how to manage a maintenance shop, snow removal operations, airport terminal, security operations). "No flying, no airport nostalgia or product puff pieces. We don't want pieces on how one company's product solved everyone's problem (how one airport or aviation business solved its problem with a certain type of product is okay). No descriptions of airport construction projects (down to the square footage in the new restrooms) that don't discuss applications for other airports. Plain 'how-to' story lines, please." Buys 40-50 mss/year, "but at least half are short (750-1,000 words) items for inclusion in one of our monthly departments." Query. Length: 750-3,000 words. Pays $100 for most department articles, $200-300 for features.

Photos: State availability of photos with query. Payment for photos is included in total purchase price. Uses b&w photos, charts and line drawings.

Tips: "Writing style should be lively, informal and straightforward, but the *subject matter* must be as functional and as down-to-earth as possible. Trade magazines are *business* magazines that must help readers do their jobs better. Frequent mistakes are using industry vendors/suppliers rather than users and industry officials as *sources*, especially in endorsing products or approaches, and directing articles to pilots or aviation consumers rather than to our specialized audience of aviation business managers and airport managers."

‡INTERNATIONAL AVIATION MECHANICS JOURNAL, I.A.P., Inc., Box 10,000, Casper WY 82602. (800)443-9250. Editor: Marlon R. Atkins. 60% freelance written. Monthly magazine on all aspects of aviation maintenance. "Looking for good 'how-to' and troubleshooting articles. Anything that will help the mechanic in his/her job. Keep it positive and up-beat." Circ. 36,000. Pays on publication. Byline given. Buys all rights and makes work-for-hire assignments. Submit seasonal/holiday material 6 months in advance. Query for electronic submissions. Computer printout submissions OK; prefers letter-quality. Reports in 2 weeks on queries; 1 month on mss. Free sample copy and writer's guidelines.

Nonfiction: General interest, historical/nostalgic, how-to and technical, (all related to maintenance of aircraft). "No articles on flying—articles 'slamming' government agencies such as FAA or DOT." Buys 40 mss/year. Send complete ms. Length: 2,000-2,500 words. Pays $250 maximum. "Pays in contributors copies for agency or company written material about a company."

Photos: Send photos with submission. Reviews 5x7 prints. Offers no additional payment for photos accepted with ms. Captions required. Buys one-time rights (on historical) and all rights.

Columns/Departments: Maintenance Tip (short "trick-of-the-trade" with illustration or photo.), 100 words. Buys 12 mss/year. Send complete ms. Pays $25 maximum.

Tips: "I am never too busy to talk to a potential writer. The best way for me to find out a little about them is for the writer to call me at our toll-free number. But don't call to talk about the weather—be specific, tell me what your qualifications are and what you have in mind. We're always looking for new, talented writers."

‡**WINGS WEST, The Western Aviation Magazine**, CAVU Communications, Inc., 89 Sherman St. Denver CO 80203. (303)778-7145. Editor: Babette André. 50% freelance written. Bimonthly magazine on aviation and aerospace in the west. Circ. 20,000. Pays on publication. "Writer must bill us." Publishes ms an average of 6 months after acceptance. Byline given. Offers $25 kill fee. Buys all rights. Submit seasonal/holiday material 6 months in advance. Photocopied and previously published submissions OK. Query for electronic submissions. Computer printout submissions OK; prefers letter-quality. Sample copy available. Free writer's guidelines.

Nonfiction: General interest, how-to, humor, new product, opinion, mountain flying, photo feature and travel. (July/August—Airshow issue; Nov./Dec.—Holidays.) Buys 18 mss/year. Query with published clips. Length: 800-1,800 words. Pays $50-150.

Fiction: Interested in new ideas. Query.

Photos: Send photos with submission. Reviews contact sheets, transparencies and prints. Offers $25-50. Captions, model releases and identification of subjects required. Buys all rights.

Columns/Departments: Aero Wayne (personal experiences, seasoned columnist); Medical (aeromedical factors); and Legal (FARS, enforcement), 800 words. Query with published clips. Pays $25-50.

Fillers: Anecdotes, facts, newsbreaks and short humor. Buys 14/year. Length: 50-150 words. Pays $10-15.

Tips: "Read the past 3 issues as well as a dozen other av pubs every month. Imagination is the key. We like to do things other aviation publications don't do. Know the national and regional aviation publication market."

Beverages and Bottling

Manufacturers, distributors and retailers of soft drinks and alcoholic beverages read these publications. Publications for bar and tavern operators and managers of restaurants are classified in the Hotels, Motels, Clubs, Resorts and Restaurants category.

‡**BEVERAGE WORLD**, Keller International Publishing Corp., 150 Great Neck Rd., Great Neck NY 11021. (516)829-9210. Editor: Alan Wolf. Monthly magazine on the beverage industry. Circ. 32,000. Pays on acceptance. Publishes ms an average of 2 months after acceptance. Byline given. Buys all rights. Submit seasonal/holiday material 2 months in advance. Simultaneous submissions OK. Free sample copy and writer's guidelines.

Nonfiction: How-to (increase profit/sales), interview/profile and technical. Buys 15 mss/year. Query with published clips. Length:1,000-2,500 words. Pays $200-600. Sometimes pays expenses of writers on assignment.

Photos: State availability of photos with submission. Reviews contact sheets. Captions required. Buys one-time rights.

Columns/Departments: Buys 5 mss/year. Query with published clips. Length: 750-1,000 words. Pays $150-400.

Tips: "Requires background in beverage production and marketing. Business and/or technical writing experience *a must*."

LA BARRIQUE, Kylix Media Inc.. Suite 414, 5165 Sherbrooke St. W., Montreal H4A 1T6 Canada. (514)481-5892. Editor: Nicole Barette-Ryan. 20% freelance written. A magazine on wine published 7 times/year. "The magazine, *written in French*, covers wines of the world specially written for the province of Québec consumers and restaurant trade. It covers wine books, restaurants, vintage reports and European suppliers." Pays on publication. Publishes ms an average of 2 months after acceptance. Byline given. Buys first North American serial rights. Submit seasonal/holiday material 6 months in advance. Simultaneous submissions OK. Computer printout submissions OK; no dot-matrix. Reports in 6 weeks on queries.

Nonfiction: General interest, how-to, humor, interview/profile, new product, opinion and travel. Knowledge of wines given primary consideration. Length: 500-1,500 words. Pays $25-100 for unsolicited articles.

Photos: Send photos with submission. Reviews transparencies and prints. Offers $25-100 per photo. Identifiction of subjects required. Buys one-time rights.

MID-CONTINENT BOTTLER, 10741 El Monte, Overland Park KS 66207. (913)341-0020. FAX: (913)341-3025. Publisher: Floyd E. Sageser. 5% freelance written. Prefers to work with published/established writers, and works with a small number of new/unpublished writers each year. For "soft drink bottlers in the 20-state Midwestern area." Bimonthly. Not copyrighted. Pays on acceptance. Publishes ms an average of 2 months after acceptance. Buys first rights only. Reports "immediately." Computer printout submissions acceptable.

Sample copy for 8½x12 SAE with $2.50 postage; guidelines for #10 SASE.

Nonfiction: "Items of specific soft drink bottler interest with special emphasis on sales and merchandising techniques. Feature style desired." Buys 2-3 mss/year. Length: 2,000 words. Pays $15-100. Sometimes pays the expenses of writers on assignment.

Photos: Photos purchased with mss.

SOUTHERN BEVERAGE JOURNAL, 13225 S.W. 88th Ave., Miami FL 33176. (305)233-7230. FAX: (305)252-2580. Senior Editor: Jackie Preston. 60% freelance written. Works with a small number of new/unpublished writers each year, and is eager to work with new/unpublished writers. A monthly magazine for the alcohol beverage industry. Readers are personnel of bars, restaurants, package stores, night clubs, lounges and hotels—owners, managers and salespersons. Circ. 30,000. Pays on acceptance. Publishes ms an average of 3-4 months after acceptance. Byline given. Buys first rights. Submit seasonal/holiday material 3 months in advance. Computer printout submissions acceptable; no dot matrix. Query for electronic submissions. Reports in 1 month.

Nonfiction: General interest, historical, personal experience, interview/profile and success stories. No canned material. Buys 3 mss/year. Send complete ms. Length: 1,000-2,500 words. Pays $200 maximum for assigned articles.

Photos: State availability of photos with submission. Reviews 7x8 transparencies and 3x5 prints. Offers $10 maximum/photo. Identification of subjects required. Buys one-time rights.

Tips: "We are interested in legislation having to do with our industry and also views on trends, drinking and different beverages."

TEA & COFFEE TRADE JOURNAL, Lockwood Book Publishing Co., 130 W. 42nd St., New York NY 10036. (212)661-5980. FAX: (212)827-0945. Editor: Jane Phillips McCabe. 50% freelance written. Prefers to work with published/established writers. A monthly magazine covering the international coffee and tea market. "Tea and coffee trends are analyzed; transportation problems, new equipment for plants and packaging are featured." Circ. approximately 5,000. Pays on publication. Publishes ms an average of 2 months after acceptance. Byline given. Makes work-for-hire assignments. Submit seasonal/holiday material 1 month in advance. Simultaneous submissions OK. Computer printout submissions acceptable; no dot-matrix. Free sample copy.

Nonfiction: Exposé, historical/nostalgic, interview/profile, new product, photo feature and technical. Special issue includes the Coffee Market Forecast and Review (January). "No consumer related submissions. I'm only interested in the trade." Buys 60 mss/year. Query. Length: 750-1,500 words. Pays $5.50/published inch.

Photos: State availability of photos with submission. Reviews contact sheets, negatives, transparencies and prints. Pays $5.50/published inch. Captions and identification of subjects required. Buys one-time rights.

Columns/Departments: Specialties (gourmet trends); and Transportation (shipping lines). Buys 36 mss/year. Query. Pays $5/published inch.

VINEYARD & WINERY MANAGEMENT, 103 Third St., Box 231, Watkins Glen NY 14891. (607)535-7133. FAX: (607)535-2998. Editor: J. William Moffett. 80% freelance written. A bimonthly trade journal on the management of winemaking and grape growing. Circ. 4,500. Pays on publication. Byline given. Buys first North American serial rights and occasionally simultaneous rights. Photocopied submissions OK. Query for electronic submissions (preferred). Reports in 3 weeks on queries; 1 month on mss. Free sample copy; writer's guidelines for #10 SAE.

Nonfiction: How-to, interview/profile and technical. Buys 30 mss/year. Query. Length: 300-5,000 words. Pays $20-750 for assigned articles; pays $20-500 for unsolicited articles. Pays some expenses of writers on some assignments.

Photos: State availability of photos with submission. Reviews contact sheets, negatives and transparencies. Identification of subjects required. "Black and white often purchased for $10 each to accompany story material; 35mm and/or 4x5 transparencies for $50 and up; 6 per year of vineyard and/or winery scene related to story. Query."

Fiction: Occasional short, humorous fiction related to vineyard/winery operation.

Tips: "We're looking for long term relationships with authors who know the business and write well."

WINES & VINES, 1800 Lincoln Ave., San Rafael CA 94901. FAX: (415)453-2517. Editor: Philip E. Hiaring. 10-20% freelance written. Works with a small number of new/unpublished writers each year. For everyone concerned with the grape and wine industry including winemakers, wine merchants, growers, suppliers, consumers, etc. Monthly magazine. Circ. 4,500. Buy first North American serial rights or simultaneous rights. Pays on acceptance. Publishes ms an average of 3 months after acceptance. Submit special material (water, January; vineyard, February; Man-of-the-Year, March; Brandy, April; export-import, May; enological, June; statistical, July; merchandising, August; marketing, September; equipment and supplies, November; champagne, December) 3 months in advance. Computer printout submissions OK; no dot-matrix. Reports in 2 weeks. Sample copy for 11×14 SAE with $2.05 postage; free writer's guidelines.

Close-up

J. William Moffett
Publisher/Editor
Vineyard & Winery Management

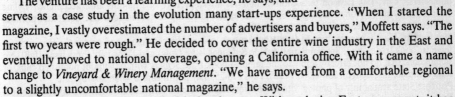

As the owner of a vineyard in the Finger Lakes area of New York, Bill Moffett saw the need for a magazine serving Eastern grape growers. Since he also had a background in publishing, Moffett decided to launch a magazine, *Eastern Grape Grower*, in 1975.

The venture has been a learning experience, he says, and serves as a case study in the evolution many start-ups experience. "When I started the magazine, I vastly overestimated the number of advertisers and buyers," Moffett says. "The first two years were rough." He decided to cover the entire wine industry in the East and eventually moved to national coverage, opening a California office. With it came a name change to *Vineyard & Winery Management*. "We have moved from a comfortable regional to a slightly uncomfortable national magazine," he says.

The magazine has prospered with the changes. Without losing Eastern support, it has gained circulation in all states, Moffett says.

Although he sold his own vineyard in 1978, Moffett continues to learn about the business. "We had to double our knowledge when we went national." The magazine also has to provide information to a diverse set of readers, "from professional grape growers with hundreds of acres of expensive vineyard in their care, to winemakers caring for millions of gallons of wine, to smaller vineyard/winery operators who are highly skilled craftspeople—more like modern Michelangelos in that they have to innovate everything from a vineyard spray schedule to the spring marketing promotions for their wines."

Moffett prefers queries from freelancers. "I like a query first to help me get a feeling for the author's ability to penetrate the story," he says. "We're pretty deep into the subject areas and most freelancers have a tendency to skim over our actual target area. We don't go in for wine appreciation stuff."

He likes articles on both vineyard and winery sides of the operation. There is the "how-to-do-it-better article where an operation is examined in detail at one or more successful practitioners' places of business and its anatomy described for our readers," he says. "We like successful management articles. We like indepth discussions of state-of-the-art technology—winery or vineyard. We also like marketing success stories, label and point-of-sale art design. We like stories that show how to cut costs and make money."

Freelancers, especially those new to a trade, must be willing to work on their knowledge of the industry to write for any trade journal. "The one tip I'd like to pass along to prospective authors is this: Ask the people you interview for your story who they recommend to read your manuscript before you submit it for our review," Moffett says. "Too often freelancers' material comes in under-researched and too shallow for our level of reader knowledge. We recommend this especially when the author is new to the business. Better to debug it before it goes to print than after."

— Glenda Tennant Neff

Nonfiction: Articles of interest to the trade. "These could be on grape growing in unusual areas; new winemaking techniques; wine marketing, retailing, etc." Interview, historical, spot news, merchandising techniques and technical. No stories with a strong consumer orientation as against trade orientation. Author should know the subject matter, i.e., know proper grape growing/winemaking terminology. Buys 3-4 ms/year. Query. Length: 1,000-2,500 words. Pays 5¢/word. Sometimes pays the expenses of writers on assignment.
Photos: Pays $10 for 4x5 or 8x10 b&w photos purchased with mss. Captions required.
Tips: "Ours is a trade magazine for professionals. Therefore, we do not use 'gee-whiz' wine articles."

Book and Bookstore

Publications for book trade professionals from publishers to bookstore operators are found in this section. Journals for professional writers are classified in the Journalism and Writing category.

THE FEMINIST BOOKSTORE NEWS, Box 882554, San Francisco CA 94188. (415)626-1556. Editor: Carol Seajay. Managing Editor: Christine Chia. 10% freelance written. Works with a small number of new/unpublished writers each year. A bimonthly magazine covering feminist books and the women-in-print industry. "*Feminist Bookstore News* covers 'everything of interest' to the feminist bookstores, publishers and periodicals, books of interest to feminist bookstores, and provides an overview of feminist publishing by mainstream publishers." Circ. 450. Pays on publication. Publishes ms an average of 2 months after acceptance. Byline sometimes given. Buys one-time rights. Simultaneous and photocopied submissions OK. Computer printout submissions acceptable; prefers letter-quality. Reports in 3 weeks. Sample copy $5.
Nonfiction: Essays, exposé, how-to (run a bookstore); new product; opinion; and personal experience (in feminist book trade only). Special issues include Sidelines issue (July) and University Press issue (fall). No submissions that do not directly apply to the feminist book trade. Query with or without published clips, or send complete ms. Length: 250-2,000 words. Pays $10-25; may pay in copies when appropriate.
Photos: State availability of photos with submission. Model release and identification of subjects required. Buys one-time rights.
Fillers: Anecdotes, facts, newsbreaks and short humor. Length: 100-400 words. Pays $5-15.
Tips: "Have several years experience in the feminist book industry. We publish very little by anyone else."

THE HORN BOOK MAGAZINE, The Horn Book, Inc., 14 Beacon St., Boston MA 01208. (617)227-1555. Editor: Anita Silvey. 25% freelance written. Prefers to work with published/established writers. Bimonthly magazine covering children's literature for librarians, booksellers, professors, and students of children's literature. Circ. 22,000. Pays on publication. Publishes ms an average of 4 months after acceptance. Byline given. Buys one-time rights. Submit seasonal/holiday material 6 months in advance. Simultaneous queries, and simultaneous and photocopied submissions OK. Computer printout submissions acceptable; no dot-matrix. Reports in 6 weeks on queries; 2 months on mss. Free sample copy; writer's guidelines for SAE with 1 first class stamp.
Nonfiction: Interview/profile (children's book authors and illustrators). Buys 20 mss/year. Query or send complete ms. Length: 1,000-2,800 words. Pays $25-250.
Tips: "Writers have a better chance of breaking in to our publication with a query letter on a specific article they want to write."

PUBLISHERS WEEKLY, 249 W. 17th St., New York NY 10011. (212)463-6758. Editor-in-Chief: John F. Baker. Weekly. Buys first North American serial rights. Pays on publication. Computer printout submissions acceptable; prefers letter-quality. Reports "in several weeks."
Nonfiction: "We rarely use unsolicited manuscripts because of our highly specialized audience and their professional interests, but we can sometimes use news items about publishers, publishing projects, bookstores and other subjects relating to books. We will be paying increasing attention to electronic publishing." No pieces about writers or word processors. Payment negotiable; generally $150/printed page.
Photos: Photos occasionally purchased with and without mss.

ALWAYS submit unsolicited manuscripts or queries with a self-addressed, stamped envelope (SASE) within your country or International Reply Coupons (IRC) purchased from the post office for other countries.

Brick, Glass and Ceramics

These publications are read by manufacturers, dealers and managers of brick, glass and ceramic retail businesses. Other publications related to glass and ceramics are listed in the Consumer Art and Architecture and Consumer Hobby and Craft sections.

AMERICAN GLASS REVIEW, Box 2147, Clifton NJ 07015. (201)779-1600. Editor-in-Chief: Donald Doctorow. 10% freelance written. Monthly magazine. Pays on publication. Byline given. Phone queries OK. Buys all rights. Submit seasonal/holiday material 2 months in advance of issue date. Reports in 2-3 weeks. Free sample copy and writer's guidelines; mention *Writer's Market* in request.
Nonfiction: Glass plant and glass manufacturing articles. Buys 3-4 mss/year. Query. Length: 1,500-3,000 words. Pays $100.
Photos: State availability of photos with query. No additional payment for b&w contact sheets. Captions preferred. Buys one-time rights.

CERAMIC SCOPE, 3632 Ashworth North, Seattle WA 98103. (206)547-7611. FAX: (206)547-7113. Editor: Michael Scott. Bimonthly magazine covering hobby ceramics business. For "ceramic studio owners and teachers operating out of homes as well as storefronts, who have a love for ceramics but meager business education." Also read by distributors, dealers and supervisors of ceramic programs in institutions. Circ. 8,000. Pays on publication. Byline given unless it is a round-up story with any number of sources. Submit seasonal/holiday material 5 months in advance. Computer printout submissions acceptable. Reports in 2 weeks. Sample copy $1.
Nonfiction: "Articles on operating a small business specifically tailored to the ceramic hobby field; photo feature stories with in-depth information about business practices and methods that contribute to successful studio operation." Pays 12½¢/published word.
Photos: State availability of photos or send photos with ms. Pays $5/4x5 or 5x7 glossy b&w print. Captions required.

GLASS MAGAZINE, For the Architectural and Automotive Glass Industries, National Glass Association, Suite 302, 8200 Greensboro Drive, McLean VA 22102. (703)442-4890. FAX: (703)442-0630. Editor: Patricia Mascari. 50% freelance written. Prefers to work with published/established writers; works with a small number of new/unpublished writers each year. A monthly magazine covering the architectural glass industry. Circ. 18,000. Pays on acceptance. Publishes ms an average of 3-6 months after acceptance. Byline given. Offers varying kill fee. Buys first rights only. Computer printout submissions acceptable; prefers letter-quality. Reports in 1 month. Sample copy for $5 and 10x13 SAE with $2.40 postage; free writer's guidelines.
Nonfiction: Interview/profile (of various glass businesses; profiles of industry people or glass business owners); and technical (about glazing processes). Buys 30 mss/year. Query with published clips. Length: 1,500 words minimum. Pays $200-600. Sometimes pays the expenses of writers on assignment.
Photos: State availability of photos. Reviews b&w and color contact sheets. Pays $15-30 for b&w; $25-75 for color. Identification of subjects required. Buys one-time rights.
Tips: "We are a growing magazine and do not have a large enough staff to do all the writing that will be required. We need more freelancers."

Building Interiors

Owners, managers and sales personnel of floor covering, wall covering and remodeling businesses read the journals listed in this category. Interior design and architecture publications may be found in the Consumer Art, Design and Collectibles category. For journals aimed at other construction trades see the Construction and Contracting section.

‡**ALUMI-NEWS**, Work-4 Projects Ltd., Box 400 Victoria Station, Westmount, Québec H3Z 2V8 Canada. (514)489-4941. FAX: (514)489-5505. Publisher: Nachmi Artzy. Exec. Director: Shelley Blidner. 75% freelance written. Home renovation — exterior building products trade journal published 6 times/year. "We are dedicated to the grass roots of the industry. i.e. installers, dealers, contractors. We do not play up to our advertisers nor government." Circ. 18,000. Pays on publication. Byline usually given. Buys all rights. Simultaneous, photocopied and previously published submissions OK. Computer printout submissions OK; prefers letter-quality. Free sample copy.

Nonfiction: Exposé, how-to (pertaining to dealers i.e. profit, production, or management.); new product (exterior building products); technical and survey results (trends or products in our industry). Buys 12-24 mss/year. Query with published clips. Length: 200-2,000 words. Pays 10-20¢/word. Pays in contributor copies or other premiums if mutually suitable. Sometimes pays expenses of writers on assignment.

Photos: State availability of photos with submission. Reviews negatives, transparencies and prints. Pays $300 maximum per photo. Captions and identification of subjects required. Buys all rights.

Columns/Departments: Industry News (company profile: new location, product, personnel), 100-250 words; and Profiles (interviews), 1,000-2,500 words. Query with published clips. Length: 75-300 words. Pays 10-20¢/word.

Fillers: Facts and short humor. Length 5-50 words. Pays 10-20¢/word.

Tips: "Submit articles not found in *every* similar publication. Find a new angle; Canadian content."

FLOOR COVERING BUSINESS, International Thomson Retail Press, 345 Park Ave. S., New York NY 10010. (212)686-7744. FAX: (212)686-0948. Editor: Michael Karol. 15-20% freelance written. Prefers to work with published/established writers. Monthly tabloid featuring profit-making ideas on floor coverings, for the retail community. Circ. 28,000. Pays on acceptance. Publishes ms an average of 3 months after acceptance. Byline given. Buys first rights only. Makes work-for-hire assignments. Computer printout submissions acceptable; prefers letter-quality. "Better to write first. Send resume and cover letter explaining your qualifications and business writing experience." Sample copy for 8½x11 SASE. Writer's guidelines for #10 SASE.

Nonfiction: Interview and features/profiles. Send complete ms. Length: 1,000-10,000 words. Pays $300-500.

Tips: "Polished, professional writing is always a plus. We now have more of a focus on consumer buying habits, the economy, taxes/legislation and products selling at retail — all of course, as they relate to the floor covering specialty retailer."

REMODELING, Hanley-Wood, Inc., Suite 475, 655 15th St. NW, Washington DC 20005. (202)737-0717. FAX: (202)737-2439. Editor: Wendy Jordan. 5% freelance written. A monthly magazine covering residential and light commercial remodeling. "We cover the best new ideas in remodeling design, business, construction and products." Circ. 82,000. Pays on publication. Publishes ms an average of 3 months after acceptance. Byline given. Offers 5¢/word kill fee. Buys first North American serial rights. Photocopied submissions OK. Query for electronic submissions. Computer printout submissions acceptable. Reports in 1 month. Free sample copy and writer's guidelines.

Nonfiction: Interview/profile, new product and technical. Buys 4 mss/year. Query with published clips. Length: 250-1,000 words. Pays 20¢/word. Sometimes pays the expenses of writers on assignment.

Photos: State availability of photos with submission. Reviews slides, 4x5 transparencies, and 8x10 prints. Offers $25-100/photo. Captions, model releases, and identification of subjects required. Buys one-time rights.

Tips: "The areas of our publication most open to freelancers are news and new product news."

WALLS & CEILINGS, 8602 N. 40th St., Tampa FL 33604. (813)989-9300. FAX: (813)980-3982. Managing Editor: Melissa Wells. 10% freelance written. Prefers to work with published/established writers, and works with a small number of new/unpublished writers each year. For contractors involved in lathing and plastering, drywall, acoustics, fireproofing, curtain walls, movable partitions together with manufacturers, dealers, and architects. Monthly magazine. Circ. 15,000. Pays on publication. Publishes ms an average of 4-6 months after acceptance. Buys first North American serial rights. Byline given. Phone queries OK. Submit seasonal/holiday material 3 months in advance. Query for electronic submissions. Computer printout submissions OK. Reports in 3 weeks. Sample copy with 9x12 SAE and $2 postage.

Nonfiction: How-to (drywall and plaster construction and business management); and interview. Buys 12 mss/year. Query. Length: 200-1,500 words. Pays $50-150 maximum. Sometimes pays the expenses of writers on assignment.

Photos: State availability of photos with query. Pays $5 for 8x10 b&w prints. Captions required. Buys one-time rights.

Tips: "We would like to receive wall and ceiling finishing features about unique designs and applications in new buildings (from high-rise to fast food restaurants), fireproofing, and acoustical design with photography (b&w and color)."

_____ *Business Management*

These publications cover trends, general theory and management practices for business owners and top-level business executives. Publications that use similar material but have a less technical slant are listed in the Consumer Business and Finance section. Journals for middle management, including supervisors and office managers, appear in the Management and Supervision section. Those for industrial plant managers are listed under Industrial Operations and under sections for specific industries, such as Machinery and Metal. Publications for office supply store operators are included in the Office Environment and Equipment section.

‡CHIEF EXECUTIVE, 205 Lexington Ave. New York NY 10016. (212)213-3666. FAX: (212)684-2048. Editor: J.P. Donlon. 25% freelance written. Bimonthly magazine for CEO's. Circ. 38,000. Pays on acceptance. Publishes ms an average of 2-3 months after acceptance. Byline given. Offers 10% kill fee. Buys world serial rights. Free writer's guidelines.
Nonfiction: Amenities, personal finance for the CEO, and travel. Buys 18 mss/year. Query. Length: 1,000-1,500 words. Pays $300-2,000 for assigned articles. Pays previously agreed upon expenses of writers on assignment.
Photos: State availability of photos with submission. Reviews 4-color transparencies and slides. Offers $100 maximum per photo. Captions required. Buys one-time rights.
Column/Departments: Editor: Margaret Alison Hart. N.B. (profile of chairman or president of mid- to large-size company), 325-400 words. Query. Pays $300-800.

COMMON SENSE, Upstart Publishing Company, 12 Portland St., Dover NH 03820. (603)749-5071. Editor: David Durgin. 25% freelance written. Prefers to work with published/established writers. A monthly newsletter covering small business and personal finance. Pays on acceptance. Publishes ms an average of 2-4 months after acceptance. $25 kill fee. Buys all rights and makes work-for-hire assignments. Does not accept unsolicited mss. Queries welcome. Computer printout submissions acceptable; prefers letter-quality. Reports in 6 weeks. Sample copy and writer's guidelines for 8½x11 SAE and 2 first class stamps.
Nonfiction: How-to, interview/profile and technical. "We are looking for clear, jargon-free information. We often sell our publications in bulk to banks so must avoid subjects and stances that clearly run counter to their interests." No highly technical or pompous language, or politically contentious articles. Buys 15-20 mss/year. Query with published clips. Length: 3,500 words maximum. Pays 10¢/word for assigned articles.
Columns/Departments: Breakthroughs (technological, medical breakthroughs or innovations, new applications for old materials or products; scientific information of interest to the business community). Query with published clips. Length: 300-600 words. Pays $30-60.

COMMUNICATION BRIEFINGS, Encoders, Inc., 140 S. Broadway, Pitman NJ 08071. (609)589-3503. FAX: (609)582-6572. Executive Editor: Frank Grazian. 15% freelance written. Prefers to work with published/established writers. A monthly newsletter covering business communication and business management. "Most readers are in middle and upper management. They comprise public relations professionals, editors of company publications, marketing and advertising managers, fund raisers, directors of associations and foundations, school and college administrators, human resources professionals, and other middle managers who want to communicate better on the job." Circ. 35,000. Pays on acceptance. Publishes ms an average of 2-3 months after acceptance. Byline given sometimes on Bonus Items and on other items if idea originates with the writer. Buys one-time rights. Submit seasonal/holiday material 2 months in advance. Previously published submissions OK, "but must be rewritten to conform to our style." Computer printout submissions acceptable; prefers letter-quality. Reports in 1 month. Sample copy and writer's guidelines for #10 SAE and 2 first class stamps.
Nonfiction: "Most articles we buy are of the 'how-to' type. They consist of practical ideas, techniques and advice that readers can use to improve business communication and management. Areas covered: writing, speaking, listening, employee communication, human relations, public relations, interpersonal communication, persuasion, conducting meetings, advertising, marketing, fund raising, telephone techniques, teleconferencing, selling, improving publications, handling conflicts, negotiating, etc. Because half of our subscribers are in the nonprofit sector, articles that appeal to both profit and nonprofit organizations are given top priority." *Short Items:* Articles consisting of one or two brief tips that can stand alone. Length: 40-70 words. *Articles:* A collection of tips or ideas that offer a solution to a communication or management problem or that show a better way to communicate or manage. Examples: "How to produce slogans that work," "The wrong way to criticize employees," "Mistakes to avoid when leading a group discussion," and "5 ways to overcome writer's block." Length: 125-150 words. *Bonus Items:* In-depth pieces that probe one area of com-

munication or management and cover it as thoroughly as possible. Examples: "Producing successful special events," "How to evaluate your newsletter," and "How to write to be understood." Length: 1,300 words. Buys 30-50 mss/year. Pays $15-35 for 40- to 150-word pieces; Bonus Items, $200. Pays the expenses of writers on assignment.

Tips: "Our readers are looking for specific and practical ideas and tips that will help them communicate better both within their organizations and with outside publics. Most ideas are rejected because they are too general or too elementary for our audience. Our style is down-to-earth and terse. We pack a lot of useful information into short articles. Our readers are busy executives and managers who want information dispatched quickly and without embroidery. We omit anecdotes, lengthy quotes and long-winded exposition. The writer has a better chance of breaking in at our publication with short articles and fillers since we buy only six major features (bonus items) a year. We require queries on longer items and bonus items. Writers may submit short tips (40-70 words) without querying. The most frequent mistakes made by writers in completing an article for us are failure to master the style of our publication and to understand our readers' needs."

‡**CONVENTION SOUTH,** Covey Communications Corp. 519 Secor Bank Bldg., 550 Greensboro Ave., Tuscaloosa AL 35401. (205)752-8144. Editor: J.Talty O'Connor. 50% freelance written. Trade journal on planning meetings and conventions in the South. Circ. 7,000. Pays on publication. Byline given. Buys first rights or second serial (reprint) rights. Submit seasonal/holiday material 2 months in advance. Simultaneous, photocopied and previously published submissions OK. Query for electronic submissions. Computer printout submissions OK; prefers letter-quality. Reports in 2 months on queries. Free sample copy.

Nonfiction: How-to (relative to meeting planning/travel), photo feature and travel. Buys 20 mss/year. Query. Length: 1,250-3,000 words. Pays $75. Pays in contributor copies or other premiums if arranged in advance. Sometime pays expenses of writers on assignment.

Photos: Send photos with submission. Reviews 5x7 prints. Offers no additional payment for photos accepted with ms. Captions and identification of subjects required. Buys one-time rights.

‡**DIRECTIONS IN CHILDCARE, Trade Journal of the National Childcare Association, Inc.,** National Childcare Association, Inc., Box 48400, Ft. Worth TX 76148. (817)656-0988. Senior Editor: J.L. Balderas. 90% freelance written. Monthly magazine on child care industry. "The thrust of *Directions in Childcare* is to educate our readers to be better business people and to improve the quality of services they offer." Estab. 1988. Circ. 50,000. Pays on publication. Publishes ms an average of 2 months after acceptance. Byline given. Buys first rights, second serial (reprint) rights or simultaneous rights. Submit seasonal/holiday material 4 months in advance. Simultaneous and previously published submissions OK. Query for electronic submissions. Computer printout submissions OK; prefers letter-quality. Reports in 6 weeks. Sample copy $3. Writer's guidelines for #10 SAE with 1 first class stamp.

Nonfiction: Book excerpts, exposé, how-to, humor, interview/profile, new product, opinion, personal experience, technical and regional reports. "No negative articles describing horror stories from child care situations. Solid factual articles with objective approaches will be considered." Buys 80 mss/year. Send complete ms. Length: 1,500-3,000 words. Pays $500-1,000 for assigned articles; $300-800 for unsolicited articles. Sometimes pays expenses of writers on assignment.

Photos: State availability of photos with submission. Reviews 5x8 prints. Offers $5-50 per photo. Model releases and identification of subjects required. Buys one-time rights.

Columns/Departments: Child Development, Food, Crafts and Decorations, Fashion and Beauty, Health, Personnel Problems, Product Review and Safety. Buys 80 mss/year. Send complete ms. Length: 1,500-3,000 words. Pays $300-800.

Fillers: Anecdotes, facts, newsbreaks and short humor. Buys 20 mss/year. Length: 50 words maximum. Pays $10-50.

Tips: "Approach the child care industry as a business, not a hobby, with the most critical consumer need being quality child care. The child care industry is undergoing intensive development and incredible growth. Concise, positive reading that guides and directs readers is the *most* valuable. All areas are open to freelancers. Manuscripts must not look to blame for problems in industry but provide options/solutions. Small business tips and information is extremely useful."

‡**EARLY CHILDHOOD NEWS,** Peter Li, Inc. 2451 E. River Rd., Dayton OH 45420. (513)294-5785. FAX: (513)294-7840. Editor: Janet Coburn. 75% freelance written. Bimonthly trade journal on child care centers. "Our publication is a news and service magazine for owners, directors and administrators of child care centers serving children from age 6 weeks to 2nd grade." Estab. 1988. Circ. 30,000. Pays on publication. Publishes ms an average of 3-4 months after acceptance. Copyright pending. Buys first rights. Submit seasonal/holiday material 5-6 months in advance. Photocopied submissions OK. Query for electronic submissions. Computer printout submissions OK; prefers letter-quality. Sample copy $2 with 9x12 SAE and 50¢ postage.

Nonfiction: How-to (how I solved a problem other center directors may face), interview/profile (profiles of interesting child care centers), personal experience and business aspects of child care centers. "No articles directed at early childhood teachers or lesson plans." Buys 15 mss/year. Query with or without published clips, or send complete ms. Length: 500-1,500 words. Pays $50-150.

Photos: Send photos with submission. Reviews 35mm and 4x5 transparencies and 5x7 prints. Captions, model releases and identification of subjects required. Buys one-time rights.

Fillers: Facts and newsbreaks. Length: 100-250 words. Pays $10-25.

Tips: "Send double-spaced typed mss and pay attention to grammar and punctuation. Enclose SASE for faster reply. No scholarly pieces with footnotes and bibliography. No activities/lesson plans for use with kids. We need short, easy-to-read articles written in popular style that give child care center owners information they can use right away to make their centers better, more effective, more efficient, etc. Feature stories and fillers are most open to freelancers. Be specific and concrete; use examples. Tightly focused topics are better than general 'The Day Care Dilemma' types."

‡**FARM STORE MERCHANDISING**, Miller Publishing, Box 2400, Minneapolis MN 55343. (612)931-0211. Editor: Jan Johnson. 20% freelance written. Eager to work with new/unpublished writers. A monthly magazine for small business owners who sell to farmers. Primary busines lines are bulk and bagged feed, animal health products, grain storage, agricultural chemicals. Pays on publication. Publishes ms an average of 3 months after acceptance. Byline given. Buys one-time rights. Submit seasonal/holiday material 4 months in advance. Simultaneous, photocopied and previously published submissions OK. Computer printout submissions acceptable; prefers letter-quality to dot-matrix. Reports in 1 month. Free sample copy and writer's guidelines.

Nonfiction: How-to (subjects must be business-oriented, credit, taxes, inventory, hiring, firing, etc.); interview/profile (with successful agribusiness dealers or industry leaders); opinion (on controversial industry issues); personal experiences (good or bad ways to run a business); photo features (people-oriented); and technical (how to maintain sprayers, what's the best fertilizer spreader, etc.). Buys 15 mss/year. Query. Length: 500-2,000 words. Pays $100-300 for assigned articles; pays $50-150 for unsolicited articles. Sometimes pays the expenses of writers on assignment.

Photos: State availability of photos with submission. Reviews contact sheets, 2x4 transparencies and 5x7 prints. Offers $10-50 per photo. Identification of subjects required. Buys one-time rights.

Columns/Departments: Shop Talk (short pieces on merchandising, sales, promotion, advertising, business management and marketing). Buys 10 mss/year. Send complete ms. Length: 50-200 words. Pays $10-50.

Tips: "The area of our publication most open to freelancers is features on successful farm store dealers. Submit two to three black and white photos. Keep the article under 2,000 words and don't get bogged down in technical details. Tell what sets their business apart and why it works. General business articles also are needed, especially if they have a rural, small-business slant."

FINANCIAL EXECUTIVE, Financial Executives Institute, 10 Madison Ave., Morriston NJ 07960. Editor: Robert A. Parker. 10% freelance written. A bimonthly magazine for corporate financial management. "*Financial Executive* is published for senior financial executives of major corporations and explores corporate accounting and treasury related issues without being anti-business." Circ. 19,000. Pays following acceptance. Byline given. Buys first North American serial rights. Reports in 1 week on queries; 2 weeks on mss. Sample copy $5; writer's guidelines for #10 SASE.

Nonfiction: Analysis, based on interviews, of accounting, finance, and tax developments of interest to financial executives. Buys 6 mss/year. Query with published clips; no unsolicited mss. Length: 1,500-3,000 words. Pays $500-1,000.

Tips: "Most article ideas come from editors, so the query approach is best. We use business or financial articles that follow a Wall Street Journal approach—a fresh idea, with its significance (to financial executives), quotes, anecdotes and an interpretation or evaluation. Our content will follow developments in market volatility, M&A trend, regulatory changes, tax legislation, Congressional hearings/legislation, re business and financial reporting. Growing interest in international business and impact of technology, such as exchanges. We have very high journalistic standards."

HIGH TECHNOLOGY BUSINESS, Infotechnology Publishing, Inc. 270 Lafayette St., New York NY 10012. (212)431-5511. FAX: (212)431-4209. Editor: Mark Estven. 20% freelance written. A monthly magazine covering businesses in high-tech. "Stories should be aimed at a business person who wants to profit personally or corporately from knowing the latest developments in high-tech and how those developments will help or hurt specific companies or industries financially. Covers broad range of technologies." Circ. 130,000. Publishes ms an average of 3 months after acceptance. Byline given. Buys all rights. Simultaneous submissions OK. Query for electronic submissions. Computer printout submissions OK. Reports in 5 weeks.

Nonfiction: Mel Mandell. Essays and general interest. No articles of a strictly technical nature. Buys 18 mss/year. Query with published clips. Length: 2,500 words. Pays $1,250 plus expenses. State availability of photos with submission. Offers no additional payment for photos accepted with ms.

Columns/Departments: New Developments (high-tech developments of interest to business community), 50-200 words; Personal Technology (new products in high-tech for use by individuals), 50-200 words; Japan Watch (major new technical developments from Far East), 750 words. Buys 18 mss/year. Send complete ms. Length: 50-750 words. Pays $25-400.

Tips: "Read the magazine. Try to think what cutting-edge technologies are important to a CEO or R&D manager. Stories should have business focus rather than dealing with technology abstractly. No how-tos, please, or stories about the troubles you had getting used to your computer."

LOOKING FIT, The Magazine for Health Conscious Tanning & Toning Centers, Virgo Publishing, Inc.. Box C-5400, Scottsdale AZ 85261. (602)483-0014. FAX: (602)483-1247. Managing Editor: Andrew McGavin. Editorial Director: Brent Diamond. 15% freelance written. A monthly magazine on issues related to the indoor tanning and toning industries. "*Looking Fit* is interested in material dealing with any aspect of operating a tanning or toning salon. Preferred style is light whenever subject matter doesn't preclude it. Technical material should be written in a manner interesting and intelligible to the average salon operator." Circ. 28,000. Pays 1 month after publication. Byline given. Buys all rights. Submit seasonal/holiday material 3 months in advance. Simultaneous submissions OK. Query for electronic submissions. Computer printout submissions OK. Reports in 1 month. Sample copy for 10x13 SAE and $2.50.
Nonfiction: How-to (operational—how to choose a location, buy equipment, etc.), humor, new product and technical. Buys 10-20 mss/year. Query with or without published clips, or send complete ms. Length: 1,500-9,000 words. Pays $50-175 for assigned articles. Pays $50-150 for unsolicited articles.
Photos: Send photos with submission. Reviews contact sheets, transparencies (2x4) and prints (2x4). Offers no additional payment for photos accepted with ms. Model releases and identification of subjects required.
Columns/Departments: Clublines (profiles of unusual/successful salons), 750-1,500 words; Profiles (profiles of unusual/successful manufacturers/distributors), 1,000-2,500 words. Buys 5-10 mss/year. Query or send complete ms. Length: 750-2,500 words. Pays $25-75.
Tips: "The best way to break in is to call or write with a good story idea. If it's workable, we'll have the writer do it. Unsolicited manuscripts are welcome, but may not fit into the magazine's goals. We're happy to offer direction or style angles by phone. In general, *Looking Fit* follows AP style. Full-length (1,500-7,500 words) features are what we most often buy. For best results, contact us with story ideas and we can supply the names and numbers of industry contacts."

‡**MANAGEMENT DIGEST**, Allied Publications, 1776 Lake Worth Rd., Lake Worth FL 33460. (407)582-2099. FAX: (407)582-4667. Editor: Richard Champlin. 95% freelance written. Monthly magazine for executives. Pays on publication. Publishes ms an average of 2-3 months after acceptance. Byline given. Buys first North American serial rights, one-time rights, second serial (reprint) rights or simultaneous rights. Submit seasonal/holiday material 6-8 months in advance. Simultaneous, photocopied and previously published submissions OK. Query for electronic submissions. Computer printout submissions OK; prefers letter-quality. Reports in 1-2 weeks on queries; 1-6 months on mss. Sample copy $1. Free writer's guidelines with SASE.
Nonfiction: Essays, how-to, humor, interview/profile, personal experience and photo feature. Buys 50 mss year. Query with or without published clips, or send complete ms. Length: 600-1,500 words. Pays $5-25 for unsolicited articles. Pays writers with contributor copies or other premiums "only at writer's request."
Photos: State availability of photos with submission. Reviews contact sheets and transparencies. Offers $5 per photo. Captions, model releases (when necessary) and identification of subjects required. Buys one-time rights.
Columns/Departments Department Editor. Worldwise (origins of words) and On-The-Books (reviews of business books). Buys 24 mss/year. Query with published clips. Length: 500-600 words. Pays $25 maximum.
Fiction: Humorous and business related. Buys 8-12 mss/year. Send complete ms. Length: 600-1,200 words. Pays $5-25.
Fillers: Anecdotes, gags to be illustrated by cartoonist and short humor. Buys 40- 50/year. Pays $5.

MAY TRENDS, George S. May International Company. 303 S. Northwest Hwy., Park Ridge IL 60068. (312)825-8806. Editor: John E. McArdle. 20% freelance written. Works with a small number of new/unpublished writers each year. For owners and managers of small and medium-sized businesses, hospitals and nursing homes, trade associations, Better Business Bureaus, educational institutions and newspapers. Magazine published without charge 3 times a year. Circulation: 30,000. Buys all rights. Byline given. Buys 10-15 mss/year. Pays on acceptance. Publishes ms an average of 4-6 months after acceptance. Returns rejected material immediately. Query or submit complete ms. Computer printout submissions acceptable; prefers letter-quality. Reports in 2 weeks. Sample copy available on request for 9x12 SAE with 2 first class stamps.
Nonfiction: "We prefer articles dealing with how to solve problems of specific industries (manufacturers, wholesalers, retailers, service businesses, small hospitals and nursing homes) where contact has been made with key executives whose comments regarding their problems may be quoted. We want problem solving articles, *not* success stories that laud an individual company. We like articles that give the business manager concrete suggestions on how to deal with specific problems—i.e., '5 steps to solve . . .,' '6 key questions to ask when . . .,' and '4 tell-tale signs indicating . . . .' " Focus is on marketing, economic and technological trends

Close-up

Ruth Benedict
Publisher/Editor
Magna Publications

As the need for concise, up-to-date business information increases, so do the number of companies publishing professional and trade newsletters. Freelancers interested in writing for these publications may find breaking in tough, says Ruth Benedict, publisher of Magna Publications' Hospitality and Travel Newsletter Group. Benedict adds, however, that the demand is steadily increasing for those freelance writers who have expertise in the management of a particular field.

Magna Publications publishes nine newsletters—six for managers and administrators in higher education and three for managers in the hospitality field. In addition to heading the hospitality newsletters group, Benedict is editor of Magna's only magazine, *In Business*, a Wisconsin business publication focused on the state's capital. Before coming to Magna, she was managing editor of *Country Woman* (formerly *Farm Woman*) magazine for nine years. Her background has made her aware of the differences between writing for magazines and writing for newsletters.

"Trade newsletters require tighter writing than magazines," she says. "Our stock in trade is short, concise information—with our biggies being 400 to 500 words max. That calls for economic writing: Sophistication in the approach—get into the piece right away.

"The appeal and benefit of newsletters have been targeting specialized information, very narrowly focused. A newsletter's claim to fame is expertise, hard-sought and presented, and there's long been a feeling of immediacy and direct relevance tied in with what's published—very much a 'from us directly to you' feeling."

It's important, therefore, to know your subject and your readers, says Benedict. "Newsletters permit more of a 'psst—here's the inside info' approach in writing. That is, if the writer is truly an expert or someone who's checked in with the major industry leaders and can thus write with some authority on this insider info."

The best way to approach any of the company's newsletters or the magazine is to query, says Benedict. She receives five to six queries a month for the newsletters. "We buy about 25 percent of the few queries we get. We will probably buy more freelance for the newsletters, but with great caution, again because of our very specific editorial niches."

Specific, practical information is the key, she says, regardless of the field. But each field has its own particular needs. Writers must research the field to find exactly what information is needed. For example, the needs of Magna's two groups of readers—college administrators and hotel managers—are very different.

"In higher education, it's a matter of an ever-changing perspective. What's appropriate this year? What is our mission about now and how should we operate in terms of that change? With hotel publications, it's a matter of publishing material that helps operate a hotel—sell rooms in a very competitive time, make huge decisions about management, renovation, capital improvements. These are not topics for the generalist writer, but for those who study or have expertise, it's a wide-open field."

—*Robin Gee*

that have an impact on medium- and small-sized businesses, not on the "giants"; automobile dealers coping with existing dull markets; and contractors solving cost-inventory problems. Will consider material on successful business operations and merchandising techniques. Length: 2,000-3,000 words. Pays $150-250.

Tips: Query letter should tell "type of business and problems the article will deal with. We specialize in the problems of small (20-100 employees, $500,000-3,000,000 volume) businesses (manufacturing, wholesale, retail and service), plus medium and small health care facilities. We are now including nationally known writers in each issue—writers like the Vice Chairman of the Federal Reserve Bank, the U.S. Secretary of the Treasury; names like George Bush and Malcolm Baldridge; titles like the Chairman of the Joint Committee on Accreditation of Hospitals; and Canadian Minister of Export. This places extra pressure on freelance writers to submit very good articles. Frequent mistakes: 1) Writing for big business, rather than small, 2) using language that is too academic."

‡THE MEETING MANAGER, Meeting Planners International, Suite 5018, 1950 Stemmons, Dallas TX 75207. (214)746-5222. FAX: (214)746-5248. Editor: Tina Berres Filipski. 50% freelance written. Monthly magazine on meetings/hospitality/travel. Circ. 10,000. Pays on acceptance. Publishes an average of 2 months after acceptance. Byline given. Offers $150 kill fee. Buys first rights. Query for electronic submissions. Computer printout submissions OK; prefers letter-quality. Reports in 4 weeks. Free sample and writer's guidelines.

Nonfiction: How-to, trends, humor, inspirational, interview/profile, opinion and personal experience. Buys 4 mss/year. Query with published clips. Length: 500-2,500 words. Pay "depends on subject."

Photos: State availability of photos with submission. Reviews contact sheets and transparencies. Offers no additional payment for photos accepted with ms. Captions required.

MEETING NEWS, Facts, News, Ideas For Convention, Meeting and Incentive Planners Everywhere, Gralla Publications, 1515 Broadway, New York NY 10036. (212)869-1300. Editorial Director/Co-Publisher: Peter Shure. Editor: Leah Krakinowski. A monthly tabloid covering news, facts, ideas and methods in meeting planning; industry developments, legislation, new labor contracts, business practices and costs for meeting planners. Circ. 74,000. Pays on acceptance. Byline given. Buys all rights. Computer printout submissions acceptable; prefers letter-quality. Reports in 1 month on queries; 2 weeks on mss. Free sample copy.

Nonfiction: Travel; and specifics on how a group improved its meetings or shows, saved money or drew more attendees. "Stress is on business articles—facts and figures." Seven special issues covering specific states as meeting destination—Florida/Colorado/Texas/California/New York and Arizona. No general or philosophical pieces. Buys 25-50 mss/year. Query with published clips. Length: varies. Pays variable rates.

Tips: "Special issues focusing on certain states as meeting sites are most open. Best suggestion—query in writing, with clips, on any area of expertise about these states that would be of interest to people planning meetings there. Example: food/entertainment, specific sports, group activities, etc."

‡NATION'S BUSINESS, Chamber of Commerce of the United States, 1615 H St., NW, Washington DC 20062. (202)463-5650. Editor: Robert Gray. Deputy Editor: Ripley Hotch. 25% freelance written. Monthly magazine of useful information for business people about managing a business. Audience includes owners and managers of businesses of all sizes, but predominantly smaller to medium-sized businesses. Circ. 850,000. Pays on acceptance. Publishes an average of 3 months after acceptance. Byline given. Offers 30% kill fee. Buys all rights. Submit seasonal/holiday material 6 months in advance. Simultaneous queries, and simultaneous and photocopied submissions OK, but only for exclusive use upon acceptance. Query for electronic submissions. Computer printout submissions acceptable; prefers letter-quality to dot-matrix. Reports in 2 months on queries; 3 months on mss. Sample copy for 9x12 SAE and $3; writer's guidelines for #10 SASE.

Nonfiction: How-to (run a business); interview/profile (business success stories; entrepreneurs who successfully implement ideas); and business trends stories. Buys 40 mss/year. Query. Length: 700-2,500 words. Pays $200 minimum. Pays expenses of writers on assignment.

Tips: "Ask for guidelines and read them carefully before making any approach."

‡OUTSIDE BUSINESS, Mariah Publications, a Division of Burke Communication Industries, 1165 N. Clark St., Chicago IL 60610. (312)951-0990. Editor: Andrea Horwich. Associate Editor: Molly Mattaliano. 50% freelance written. Monthly magazine on retailing of outdoor recreational products. "Our readers are retailers of upscale equipment and apparel used for outdoor activities. Writers must be familiar with the business issues involved in retailing, or with the products themselves, or both." Circ. 12,500. Pays on publication. Publishes an average of 3 months after acceptance. Byline given. Buys first rights, second serial (reprint) rights and makes work-for-hire assignments. Query for electronic submissions. Computer printout submissions OK. Reports in 2 months on queries. Sample copy for 9x12 SAE with $1.85 postage.

Nonfiction: Interview/profile, technical (equipment and/or apparel round-ups) and business issues (affecting retailing). "Not responsible for unsolicited manuscripts." Buys 40-48 mss/year. Query. Length: 1,500-3,000 words. Pays $350-700 for assigned articles. Sometimes pays expenses of writers on assignment.

Photos: State availability of photos with submission. Reviews 35mm transparencies. Captions, model releases and identification of subjects required. Buys one-time rights.

Columns/Departments: Management, Advertising/Promotion, Merchandising, and Financial Planning: all written for retail audience and all 1,500 words. Buys 36 mss/year. Query. Pays $300-350.

Tips: "We value knowledge of outdoor equipment and apparel, *and* familiarity with business issues affecting retailers."

RECOGNITION & PROMOTIONS BUSINESS, (formerly *Awards Specialist*), DF Publications, 26 Summit St., Box 1230, Brighton MI 48116. (313)227-2614. FAX: (313)229-8230. Editor: James J. Farrell. Managing Editor: Michael J. Davis. 40% freelance written. Prefers to work with published/established writers, and works with a small number of new/unpublished writers each year. A monthly magazine for the recognition and specialty advertising industry, especially awards. "*RPB* is published for retail business owners and owners involved in the recognition/specialty industry. Our aim is to provide solid, down-to-earth information to help them succeed in business, as well as news and ideas about our industry." Pays on acceptance. Publishes ms an average of 4 months after acceptance. Buys all rights or makes work-for-hire assignments. Submit seasonal/holiday material 6 months in advance. Previously published submissions OK "if we are so informed." Query for electronic submissions. Computer printout submissions OK. Reports in 3 weeks. "Sample copy and writer's guidelines sent to those who send us writing samples or query about an article."

Nonfiction: Historical, how-to, interview/profile, new product, photo feature, technical and business and marketing. "Our readers are becoming more involved in the specialty advertising industry. No vague, general articles which could be aimed at any audience. We prefer to receive a query from writers before reviewing a manuscript. Also, a large number of our freelance articles are given to writers on assignment." Buys 20-30 mss/year. Query with clips ("clips do not have to be published, but should give us an indication of writer's ability"). Length: depends on subject matter. Pays $50-225.

Photos: Send photos with submission. Reviews 8x10 prints. Offers no additional payment for photos accepted with ms, "but we take the photos into consideration when deciding rate of compensation for the assignment." Captions, model releases and identification of subjects required. Buys all rights; "semi-exclusive rights may be purchased, for our industry, depending on subject."

Tips: "The best way to work for *RPB* is to write to us with information about your background and experience (a resume, if possible), and several samples of your writing. We are most interested in receiving business and marketing articles from freelancers. These would provide solid, down-to-earth information for the smaller business owner. For example, recent articles we have included were on tips for writing good business letters; the proper use of titles for awards; legal and practical considerations of setting up a corporation vs. a sole proprietorship. Articles should be written in clear, plain English with examples and anecdotes to add interest to the subject matter."

RECORDS MANAGEMENT QUARTERLY, Association of Records Managers and Administrators, Inc., Box 4580, Silver Spring MD 20904. Editor: Ira A. Penn, CRM, CSP. 10% freelance written. Eager to work with new/unpublished writers. Quarterly magazine covering records and information management. Circ. 10,000. Pays on publication. Publishes ms an average of 6 months after acceptance. Byline given. Buys all rights. Photocopied and simultaneous submissions OK. Computer printout submissions acceptable; prefers letter-quality. Reports in 1 month on mss. Sample copy $14; free writer's guidelines.

Nonfiction: Professional articles covering theory, case studies, surveys, etc. on any aspect of records and information management. Buys 24-32 mss/year. Send complete ms. Length: 1,500 words minimum. Pays $25-125. Pays a "stipend"; no contract.

Photos: Send photos with ms. Does not pay extra for photos. Prefers b&w prints. Captions required.

Tips: "A writer *must* know our magazine. Most work is written by practitioners in the field. We use very little freelance writing, but we have had some and it's been good. A writer must have detailed knowledge of the subject he/she is writing about. Superficiality is not acceptable."

SECURITY DEALER, PTN Security Group, 210 Crossways Park Drive, Woodbury NY 11797. (516)496-8000. Editorial Director: Thomas Kapinos, CPP. Managing Editor: Tami Goldberg. 5% freelance written. A monthly magazine for electronic alarm dealers; burglary and fire installers, with technical, business, sales and marketing information. Circ. 25,000. Pays 3 weeks after publication. Publishes ms an average of 4 months after acceptance. Byline given sometimes. Buys first North American serial rights. Simultaneous and previously published submissions OK. Letter quality computer printout submissions mandatory.

Nonfiction: How-to, interview/profile and technical. No consumer pieces. Query or send complete ms. Length: 1,000-3,000 words. Pays $200 for assigned articles; pays $100-150 for unsolicited articles. Sometimes pays the expenses of writers on assignment.

Photos: State availability of photos with submission. Reviews contact sheets and transparencies. Offers $25 additional payment for photos accepted with ms. Captions and identification of subjects required.
Columns/Departments: Closed Circuit TV, and Access Control (both on application, installation, new products), 500-1,000 words. Buys 25 mss/year. Query. Pays $100-150.
Tips: "The areas of our publication most open to freelancers are technical innovations, trends in the alarm industry and crime patterns as related to the business as well as business finance and management pieces."

‡**SELF-EMPLOYED AMERICA, The News Publication for your Small Business,** National Association for the Self-Employed, Box 612067, Dallas TX 75261. (817)589-2475 or (800)232-NASE. FAX: (817)595-5456. Editor: Karen C. Jones. 90% freelance written. Published 6 times per year for association members. "Keep in mind that the self-employed don't need business news tailored to meet needs of what government considers 'small business'. We reach those with few, if any, employees. Our readers are independent business owners going it alone—and in need of information." Estab. 1988. Circ. 150,000. Pays on acceptance. Byline given. Offers 10% kill fee. Buys first North American serial rights and makes work-for-hire assignments. Submit seasonal/holiday material 6 months in advance. "Please no phone queries." Query for electronic submissions. Computer printout submissions OK; prefers letter-quality. Reports in 2 weeks on queries; 4 weeks on mss. Sample copy for 9x12 with 2 first class stamps. Writer's guidelines for #10 SAE with 1 first class stamp.
Nonfiction: Book excerpts, how-to, interview/profile, new product, personal experience and travel (how to save money on travel or how to combine business and personal travel). "No big business or how to claw your way to the top stuff. Generally my readers are happy as small businesses." Buys 50-60 mss/year. Query with published clips. Length: 150-700 words. Pays $200-350 for assigned articles; $100-250 for unsolicited articles. Sometimes pays expenses of writers on assignment.
Photos: State availability of photos with submission. Reviews 3x5 prints. Offers $25-50 per photo. Captions, model releases and identification required. Buys one-time rights.
Columns/Departments: Tax Tips. Send complete ms. Length: 200-300. Pays $50-100.
Fillers: Anecdotes, facts, newsbreaks and short humor. Buys 50/year. Length: 75-125 words. Pays $25-50.
Tips: "Be considerate—This is a start-up stage; one-person staff desperately seeks capable freelancers who understand my time constraints. Hopefully will increase staff and frequency in one-two years. Keep in mind reader demographics show 150,000 people with nothing in common except desire to be independent."

‡**THE SERVICING DEALER,** The Communications Group, Suite 202, 3703 N. Main St., Rockford IL 61103. (815)633-2680. FAX: (815)633-0923. Editor: Craig Wyatt. 15% freelance written. Trade journal, published 9 times per year, on outdoor power equipment retailing. "Editorial is basic retail management oriented. Readers are servicing dealers of lawn and other outdoor power equipment. They're good mechanics but not-so-good businessmen." Circ. 25,000. Pays on publication. Publishes ms an average of 2 months after acceptance. Byline given. Offers 20% kill fee. Buys one-time rights and exclusive rights within industry. Submit seasonal/holiday material 4 months in advance. Simultaneous, photocopied and previously published submissions OK. Query for electronic submissions. Computer printout submissions OK. Sample copy $1 with 9x12 SAE and 5 first class stamps. Writer's guidelines for #10 SASE.
Nonfiction: How-to (marketing, personnel management and financial management) and technical (dealing with small air-cooled engines and lawn equipment repair). Buys 10 mss/year. Query with published clips. Length: 600-1,200 words. Pays $150-300 for assigned articles; $50-250 for unsolicited articles. Sometimes pays expenses of writers on assignment.
Photos: Send photos with submission. Reviews contact sheets, transparencies and prints. Offers no additional payment for photos accepted with ms. Captions and identification of subjects required.
Columns/Departments: Sales Tips (basic sales methods and suggestions); Out Back (personnel management topics for small business); Greenbacks (financial management) and Ad-Visor (advertising and promotion for small business). Buys 7 mss/year. Query with published clips. Length: 450-675 words. Pays $50-250.
Tips: "Any prior knowledge of the outdoor power equipment industry, retail management topics, small engine repair is a plus. Read our magazine and other industry magazines. Small business management is a plus. Use electronic media to transfer directly into our Mac system. Give readers something they can walk away with and use the minute they put the magazine down."

‡**SIGN BUSINESS,** National Business Media Inc., 1008 Depot Hill Rd., Box 1416, Broomfield CO 80020. (303)469-0424. FAX: (303)469-5730. Editor: Emerson Schwartzkopf. 15-25% freelance written. Trade journal on the sign industry—electric, commercial, architectural. "This is business-to-business writing; we try to produce news you can use, rather than human interest." Circ. 20,500. Pays on publication. Publishes ms an average of 1-2 months after acceptance. Byline given. Buys first North American serial rights. Submit seasonal/holiday material 4 months in advance. Query for electronic submissions. Computer printout submissions OK; prefers letter-quality. Reports in 1 week on queries; 2 weeks on mss. Sample copy $2.50. Free writer's guidelines for #10 SASE.
Nonfiction: How-to (sign-painting techniques, new uses for computer cutters, plotters lettering styles); interview/profile (sign company execs, shop owners with *unusual;* work etc.) and other (news on sign codes, legislation, unusual signs, etc.). "No humor, human interest, generic articles with sign replacing another

industry, no first person writing, no profiles of a sign shop just because someone nice runs the business." Buys 24-30 mss/year. Query with published clips. Length: 500-3,000 words. Pays $125-200.

Photos: Send photos with submission. Reviews 3x5 transparencies and 3x5 prints. Offers $5-10 per photo. Identification of subjects required. Buys one-time rights and/or reprint rights.

Columns/Departments: Vinyl (new uses and trends in pressure-sensitive films) and Airbrush (artists and techniques in commercial airbrush). Buys 6-10 mss/year. Query with published clips. Length: 500-1,500 words. Pays $100-150.

Tips: "Find a sign shop, or sign company, and take some time to learn the business. The sign business is easily a $5 billion-plus industry every year in the United States, and we treat it like a business, not a hobby. If you see a sign that stops you in your tracks, find out who made it, if it's a one-in-10,000 kind of sign, chances are good we'll want to know more. Writing should be factual and avoid polysyllabic words that waste a reader's time. I'll work with writers who may not know the trade, but can write well."

‡**SMALL BUSINESS CHRONICLE**, Suite 3, 426 Pennsylvania Ave., Ft. Washington PA 19034. (215)540-9440. FAX: (215)540-9442. 50% freelance written. Monthly business tabloid "for 20,000 business executives in Bucks and Montgomery counties, PA. Short, general, how-to articles related to all aspects of operating a business." Circ. 20,000. Pays on publication. Byline given. Buys first North American serial rights, first rights, one-time rights, second serial (reprint) rights and simultaneous rights. Simultaneous, photocopied and previously published submissions OK. Query for electronic submissions. Computer printout submissions OK. Reports in 2-4 weeks. Sample copy for 8x11 SAE with 85¢ postage.

Nonfiction: Book excerpts, essays, humor, interview/profile, opinion and personal experience. Buys 36 mss/ year. Send complete ms. Length: 750 words maximum. Pays $5-50.

Photos: Send photos with submission. Reviews 5x7 prints. Offers no additional payment for payment for photos accepted with ms. Captions, model releases and identification of subjects required. Buys one-time rights.

WOMEN IN BUSINESS, The ABWA Co., Inc.. 9100 Ward Parkway, Kansas City MO 64114. (816)361-6621. Editor: Laura Luckert. 30% freelance written. A bimonthly magazine for members of the American Business Women's Association. "We publish articles of interest to the American working woman." Circ. 110,000. Pays on acceptance. Publishes ms an average of 2 months after acceptance. Byline given. Kill fee negotiable. Buys all rights. Submit seasonal/holiday material 4 months in advance. Computer printout submissions OK; prefers letter-quality. Reports in 1 week. Sample copy for 9x12 SAE with 4 first class stamps. Writer's guidelines for #10 SAE with 1 first class stamp.

Nonfiction: "We cannot use success stories about individual businesswomen." Buys 30 mss/year. Query with published clips or send complete ms. Length: 1,000-3,000 words. Pays 15¢/word.

Photos: State availability of photos with submission. Offers no additional payment for photos accepted with ms. Identification of subjects required.

Columns/Departments: Wendy Myers, column/department editor. Working Capital (personal finance for women), 1,500 words; Health Scope (health topics for women); Moving up (advice for the up-and-coming woman manager). Buys 18 mss/year. Query with published clips or send complete ms. Length: 1,000-1,500 words. Pays 15¢/word.

Tips: "It would be very difficult to break into our columns. We have regular contributing freelance writers for those. But we are always on the look out for good feature articles and writers. We are especially interested in writers who provide a fresh, new look to otherwise old topics, such as time management etc."

_____ Church Administration and Ministry

Publications in this section are written for clergy members, church leaders and teachers. Magazines for lay members and the general public are listed in the Consumer Religious section.

CHRISTIAN EDUCATION TODAY: For Teachers, Superintendents and Other Christian Educators, Box 15337, Denver CO 80215. Editor: James E. Burkett, Jr.. Research Editor: Kenneth O. Gangel. 60% freelance written. Works with a small number of new/unpublished writers each year. Quarterly magazine. Pays prior to publication. Publishes ms an average of 6-9 months after acceptance. Byline given. Buys reprint rights with magazines of different circulations. Computer printout submissions acceptable; prefers letter-quality.

Reports in 2 months. Sample copy $1 or 9x12 SAE with 3 first class stamps. Writer's guidelines for #10 SASE.

Nonfiction: Articles which provide information, instruction and/or inspiration to workers at every level of Christian education. May be slanted to the general area or to specific age-group categories such as preschool, elementary, youth or adult. Simultaneous rights acceptable *only* if offered to magazines which do not have overlapping circulation. Length: 1,000-2,000 words. Payment commensurate with length and value of article to total magazine (5-10¢/word).

Tips: "Often a freelance short article is followed up with a suggestion or firm assignment for more work from that writer."

CHRISTIAN LEADERSHIP, Board of Christian Education of the Church of God, Box 2458, Anderson IN 46018-2458. (317)642-0257. Editor: Sherrill D. Hayes. 50% freelance written. Works with a small number of new/unpublished writers each year. A bimonthly magazine covering local Sunday school teaching and administrating, youth work, worship, family life and other local church workers. Circ. 4,000. Pays on publication. Publishes ms an average of 6 months after acceptance. Byline given. Buys first rights and second serial (reprint) rights. Submit seasonal/holiday material 6 months in advance. Simultaneous queries OK. Computer printout submissions acceptable; no dot-matrix. Reports in 4 months. Sample copy and writer's guidelines for 9x12 SAE with 3 first class stamps.

Nonfiction: General interest, how-to, inspirational, personal experience, guidance for carrying out programs for special days, and continuing ministries. No articles that are not specifically related to local church leadership. Buys 20 mss/year. Send complete ms, brief description of present interest in writing for church leaders, background and experience. Length: 300-1,200 words. Pays 2¢/word ($10 minimum).

Photos: Send photos with ms. Pays $15-25 for 5x7 b&w photos.

Tips: "How-to articles related to Sunday school teaching, program development and personal teacher enrichment or growth, with illustrations of personal experience of the authors, are most open to freelancers."

CHURCH EDUCATOR, Creative Resources for Christian Educators, Educational Ministries, Inc., 2861-C Saturn St., Brea CA 92621. (714)961-0622. Editor: Robert G. Davidson. Managing Editor: Linda S. Davidson. 80% freelance written. Works with a small number of new/unpublished writers each year. A monthly magazine covering religious education. Circ. 5,200. Pays on publication. Publishes manuscript an average of 4 months after acceptance. Byline given. Buys first rights, second serial (reprint) rights, or all rights. "We prefer all rights." Submit seasonal/holiday material 4 months in advance. Simultaneous submissions OK. Computer printout submissions acceptable; prefers letter-quality. Reports in 3 months. Sample copy for 9x12 SAE and 3 first class stamps; free writer's guidelines.

Nonfiction: Book reviews; general interest; how-to (crafts for Church school); inspirational; personal experience; and religious. "Our editorial lines are very middle of the road—mainline Protestant. We are not seeking extreme conservative or liberal theology pieces." No testimonials. Buys 100 mss/year. Send complete ms. Length: 100-2,000 words. Pays 2-4¢/word.

Photos: Send photos with submissions. Reviews 5x7 b&w prints. Offers $5-10/photo. Captions required. Buys one-time rights.

Fiction: Mainstream, religious and slice-of-life vignettes. Buys 15 mss/year. Send complete ms. Length: 100-2,000 words. Pays 2-4¢/word.

Fillers: Anecdotes and short humor. Buys 15/year. Length: 100-700 words. Pays 2-4¢/word.

Tips: "Send the complete manuscript with a cover letter which gives a concise summary of the manuscript. We are looking for how-to articles related to Christian education. That would include most any program held in a church. Be straightforward and to the point—not flowery and wordy. We're especially interested in youth programs. Give steps needed to carry out the program: preparation, starting the program, continuing the program, conclusion. List several discussion questions for each program."

‡CHURCH TRAINING, 127 9th Ave. N., Nashville TN 37234. (615)251-2843. Publisher: The Sunday School Board of the Southern Baptist Convention. Editor: Ralph Hodge. 5% freelance written. Works with a small number of new/unpublished writers each year. Monthly. For all workers and leaders in the Church Training program of the Southern Baptist Convention. Circ. 30,000. Pays on acceptance. Publishes ms an average of 18 months after acceptance. Byline given. Buys all rights. Query for electronic submissions. Computer printout submissions acceptable; letter-quality only. Reports in 6 weeks. Free sample copy and writer's guidelines.

Nonfiction: Articles that pertain to leadership training in the church; success stories that pertain to Church Training; association articles; informational, how-to's that pertain to church training using Sunday School Board resources and personal testimonies. Buys 15 unsolicited mss/year. Query with rough outline. Length: 500-1,500 words. Pays 5¢/word. Sometimes pays the expenses of writers on assignment.

Tips: "Write an article that reflects the writer's experience of personal growth through church training or tell how to use BSSB resources to train Christians. Keep in mind the target audience: workers and leaders of Church Training organizations in churches of the Southern Baptist Convention. Often subjects and treatment are too general."

CIRCUIT RIDER, A Journal for United Methodist Ministers, United Methodist Publishing House, Box 801, Nashville TN 37202. (615)749-6137. FAX: (615)749-6079. Editor: Keith I. Pohl. Editorial Director: J. Richard Peck. 60% freelance written. Works with a small number of new/unpublished writers each year. A monthly magazine covering professional concerns of clergy. Circ. 40,000. Pays on acceptance. Publishes ms an average of 1 year after acceptance. Byline given. Buys all rights. Submit seasonal/holiday material 6 months in advance. Photocopied submissions OK. Computer printout submissions acceptable; prefers letter-quality. Reports in 3 weeks. Sample copy for 8½x11 SAE with $1 postage. Writer's guidelines for #10 SASE.

Nonfiction: How-to (improve pastoral calling, preaching, counseling, administration, etc.). No personal experience articles; no interviews. Buys 50 mss/year. Send complete ms. Length: 600-2,000 words. Pays $30-100. Pays the expenses of writers on assignment.

Photos: State availability of photos. Pays $25-50 for 8x10 b&w prints. Model release required. Buys one-time rights.

Tips: "Know the concerns of a United Methodist pastor. Be specific. Think of how you can help pastors."

THE CLERGY JOURNAL, Church Management, Inc., Box 162527, Austin TX 78716. (512)327-8501. Editor: Manfred Holck, Jr. 20% freelance written. Eager to work with new/unpublished writers. Monthly (except June and December) on religion. Readers are Protestant clergy. Circ. 30,000. Pays on publication. Publishes ms an average of 4 months after acceptance. Byline given. Offers 50% kill fee. Buys all rights. Submit seasonal/holiday material 6 months in advance. Photocopied submissions OK. Computer printout submissions acceptable; prefers letter-quality. Reports in 2 weeks on queries; 1 month on mss. Sample copy for $3 and 9x12 SAE with 8 first class stamps.

Nonfiction: How-to (be a more efficient and effective minister/administrator). No devotional, inspirational or sermons. Buys 20 mss/year. Query. Length: 500-1,500 words. Pays $25-40.

LEADERSHIP, A Practical Journal for Church Leaders, Christianity Today, Inc., 465 Gundersen Dr., Carol Stream IL 60188. (312)260-6200. Editor: Marshall Shelley. 75% freelance written. Works with a small number of new/unpublished writers each year. A quarterly magazine covering church leadership. Writers must have a "knowledge of and sympathy for the unique expectations placed on pastors and local church leaders. Each article must support points by illustrating from real life experiences in local churches." Circ. 90,000. Pays on acceptance. Publishes ms an average of 6 months after acceptance. Byline given. Buys first North American serial rights. Submit seasonal/holiday material 6 months in advance. Photocopied and previously published submissions OK. Computer printout submissions OK; prefers letter-quality. Reports in 6 weeks on queries; 2 months on mss. Sample copy $3; free writer's guidelines.

Nonfiction: How-to, humor and personal experience. No "articles from writers who have never read our journal." Buys 50 mss/year. Send complete ms. Length: 100-5,000 words. Pays $30-300. Sometimes pays the expenses of writers on assignment.

Photos: State availability of photos with submission. Offers no additional payment for photos accepted with ms. Identification of subjects required. Buys one-time rights.

Columns/Departments: People in Print (book reviews with interview of author), 1,500 words. James D. Berkley, editor, To Illustrate (short stories or analogies that illustrate a biblical principle), 100 words. Buys 25 mss/year. Send complete ms. Pays $25-100.

MINISTRIES TODAY, Strang Communications Co., 190 N. Westmonte Dr., Altamonte Springs FL 32714. (305)869-5005. Owner: Stephen Strang. Publisher: Tim Gilmore. Editor-in-Chief: Jamie Buckingham. Associate Editor: E.S. Caldwell. 20% freelance written. Bimonthly magazine for pastors and leaders in Evangelical/Pentecostal/Charismatic ministries. Circ. 30,000. Pays on publication. Publishes ms an average of 6 months after acceptance. Byline given. Buys first rights. Photocopied submissions OK. Computer printout submissions acceptable; prefers letter-quality. Reports in 1 month. Sample copy $3, with 9×12 SAE and 2 first class stamps; writer's guidelines for #10 SAE and 1 first class stamp.

Nonfiction: How-to (for pastors), and interview/profile. Buys 20 mss/year. Query or send complete ms to Ed Caldwell, associate editor. Length: 1,700-2,000 words. Pays $50-200. Sometimes pays expenses.

Photos: Eric Jessen, photo editor.

Tips: "We need practical, proven ideas with both negative and positive anecdotes. We have a specialized audience—pastors and leaders of churches. We suggest you study back issues of the magazine before submitting. It is unlikely that persons not fully understanding this audience would be able to provide appropriate manuscripts."

PASTORAL LIFE, Society of St. Paul, Route 224, Canfield OH 44406. Editor: Jeffrey Mickler, SSP. 66% freelance written. Works with a small number of new/unpublished writers each year, and is eager to work with new/unpublished writers. Emphasizes priests and those interested in pastoral ministry. Monthly magazine. Circ. 5,000. Buys first rights only. Byline given. Pays on publication. Publishes ms an average of 6 months after acceptance. Sample copy to writer on request. Query with a outline before submitting ms. "New contributors are expected to include, in addition, a few lines of personal data that indicate academic and professional background." Computer printout submissions acceptable; no dot-matrix. Reports within 1 month. Free sample copy and writer's guidelines.

Nonfiction: *"Pastoral Life* is a professional review, principally designed to focus attention on current problems, needs, issues and all important activities related to all phases of pastoral work and life." Buys 30 unsolicited mss/year. Length: 2,000-3,400 words. Pays 3¢/word minimum.

Tips: "Projected increase in number of pages will warrant expansion of our material needs."

THE PREACHER'S MAGAZINE, Nazarene Publishing House, 6401 The Paseo, Kansas City MO 64131. (816)333-7000. Editor: Randal E. Denny. Assistant Editor: Mark D. Marvin. 15% freelance written. Works with a small number of new/unpublished writers each year. Quarterly magazine of seasonal/miscellaneous articles. "A resource for ministers; Wesleyan-Arminian in theological persuasion." Circ. 17,000. Pays on acceptance. Publishes ms an average of 9 months after acceptance. Byline given. Buys first serial rights, second serial (reprint) rights and simultaneous rights. Submit seasonal/holiday material 9 months in advance. Simultaneous queries and photocopied submissions OK. Computer printout submissions acceptable; prefers letter-quality. Sample copy for 9x12 SAE and 2 first class stamps; writer's guidelines for #10 SASE.

Nonfiction: How-to, humor, inspirational, opinion and personal experience, all relating to aspects of ministry. No articles that present problems without also presenting answers to them; things not relating to pastoral ministry. Buys 48 mss/year. Send complete ms. Length: 700-2,500 words. Pays 3½¢/word.

Photos: Send photos with ms. Reviews 35mm color transparencies and 35mm b&w prints. Pays $25-35. Model release and identification of subjects required. Buys one-time rights.

Columns/Departments: Today's Books for Today's Preacher—book reviews. Buys 24 mss/year. Send complete ms. Length: 300-400 words. Pays $7.50.

Fillers: Anecdotes and short humor. Buys 10/year. Length: 400 words maximum. Pays 3½¢/word.

Tips: "Writers for the *Preacher's Magazine* should have insight into the pastoral ministry, or expertise in a specialized area of ministry. Our magazine is a highly specialized publication aimed at the minister. Our goal is to assist, by both scholarly and practical articles, the modern-day minister in applying Biblical theological truths."

Clothing

APPAREL INDUSTRY MAGAZINE, Shore Publishing, Suite 300-South, 180 Allen Rd., Atlanta GA 30328. Editor: Karen Schaffner. Managing Editor: Gary Fong. 30% freelance written. Monthly magazine for executive management in apparel companies with interests in equipment, fabrics, licensing, distribution, finance, management and training. Circ. 18,700. Pays on publication. Publishes ms an average of 4 months after acceptance. Byline given. Buys first serial rights. Will consider legible photocopied submissions. Query for electronic submissions. Computer printout submissions acceptable. Reports in 1 month. Sample copy $3; writer's guidelines for #10 SASE.

Nonfiction: Articles dealing with equipment, manufacturing techniques, training, finance, licensing, fabrics, quality control, etc., related to the industry. "Use concise, precise language that is easy to read and understand. In other words, because the subjects are often technical, keep the language comprehensible. Material must be precisely related to the apparel industry. We are not a retail or fashion magazine." Informational, interview, profile, successful business operations and technical articles. Buys 30 mss/year. Query. Length: 3,000 words maximum. Pays 20¢/word. Sometimes pays expenses of writers on assignment.

Photos: Pays $5/photo with ms.

Tips: "Frequently articles are too general due to lack of industry-specific knowledge by the writer."

‡SPECIALTY STORE SERVICE, Vanguard Publications, Inc., 6604 W. Saginaw Hwy., Lansing MI 48917. (517)321-0671. FAX: (517)371-1015. Editor: Jill Powell. 70% freelance written. Monthly newsletter for women's specialty clothing stores. "The *SSS Bulletin* is a management newsletter geared specifically toward running a women's specialty store business, and current fashion trends." Circ. 1,400. Pays on acceptance. Publishes ms an average of 3 months after acceptance. Byline given. Buys first North American serial rights and second serial (reprint) rights. Submit seasonal/holiday material 5 months in advance. Simultaneous and photocopied submissions OK. Query for electronic submissions. Computer printout submissions OK. Reports in 2 weeks on queries; 6 weeks on mss. Free sample copy and writer's guidelines.

Nonfiction: General interest (retail trends), how-to (retail sales, inventory management, retail promotion) and interview/profile (A Store Like Yours). No color analysis. Buys 120 mss/year. Query with published clips. Length: 350-3,000 words. Pays $50-375. Pays in contributor copies "only if requested by contributor."

Photos: Send photos with submission. Offers $15-50 per photo. Buys all rights.
Columns/Departments: Retailing Trends (current trends in women's fashion cents how it will affect stores), minimum 1,100 words; Promotional Ideas (new, creative, unique ideas for store promotions), minimum 275 words and A Store Like Yours (review of well-run, nicely designed, etc. specialty shop), minimum 850 words. Buys 50 mss/year. Query with published clips. Send complete ms. Length: 275-3,000 words. Pays $50-375.
Fillers: Facts and newsbreaks. Buys 12/year. Length: 125 words maximum. Pays $10-25.
Tips: "Keep abreast of the fashion industry—read *WWD* (a must), *Vogue*, *Elle*, etc. All areas are open to freelancers. The more specifics given in an article, the better your chances of being published."

‡**T-SHIRT RETAILER AND SCREEN PRINTER**, WFC, Inc., 195 Main St., Metuchen NJ 08840. (201)494-2889. Editor: Bruce Sachenski. Associate Editor: Deborah Miller. 10% freelance written. A monthly magazine for persons in imprinted garment industry and screen printing. Circ. 27,000. Pays on publication. Publishes ms an average of 3 months after acceptance. Byline given. Buys one-time rights. Submit seasonal/holiday material 3 months in advance. Photocopied and previously published submissions OK. Computer printout submissions OK; prefers letter-quality to dot-matrix. Reports in 1 month. Sample copy $5; writer's guidelines for 5x7 SAE with 1 first class stamp.
Nonfiction: How-to, new product, photo feature, technical and business. Buys 6 mss/year. Send complete ms. Length: 1,500-3,500 words. Pays $100-200 for assigned articles.
Photos: Send photos with submission. Reviews contact sheets. Offers no additional payment for photos accepted with ms. Identification of subjects required.
Columns/Departments: Query. Length: 1,000-2,000 words. Pays $50-150.
Tips: "We need general business stories: equipment, advertising, store management, etc."

‡**WESTERN & ENGLISH FASHIONS**, Bell Publishing, 2403 Champa, Denver CO 80205. (303)296-1600. FAX: (303)292-1903. Editor: Larry Bell. Managing Editor: Lee Darrigrand. 90% freelance written. Prefers to work with published/established writers; works with a small number of new/unpublished writers each year. For "Western and English apparel and equipment retailers, manufacturers and distributors. The magazine features retailing practices such as marketing, merchandising, display techniques, buying and selling to help business grow or improve, etc. Every issue carries feature stories on Western/English/square dance apparel stores throughout the U.S." Monthly magazine; 50 pages. Circ. 13,000. Pays on publication. Publishes ms an average of 2 months after acceptance. Not copyrighted. Byline given unless extensive rewriting is required. Phone queries OK. Submit seasonal/holiday material 3 months in advance. Simultaneous (to noncompeting publications), photocopied and previously published submissions OK. Computer printout submissions acceptable; no dot-matrix. No fiction or foreign material. Sample copy and writer's guidelines for 9x11½ SAE with $1.50 postage.
Nonfiction: Current trends in fashion of English riding attire, square dance and western; exposé (of government as related to industry or people in industry); general interest (pertaining to Western lifestyle); interview (with Western/English store owners); new product (of interest to Western/English clothing retailers—send photo); and photo feature. "We will be doing much more fashion-oriented articles and layouts." Buys 20-25 mss/year. Query with outline. Length: 800-3,600 words. Pays $50-150. Sometimes pays the expenses of writers on assignment.
Photos: "We buy photos with manuscripts." State availability of photos. Captions required with "names of people or products and locations." Buys one-time rights.
Tips: "We will be highlighting current fashion trends and continuing to feature retail store operations. We continue to look for material relating to the fashion end of the western and English industry. 'Store stories' are particularly important. Currently we receive *too many* business type articles."

Coin-Operated Machines

AMERICAN COIN-OP, 500 N. Dearborn St., Chicago IL 60610. (312)337-7700. Editor: Ben Russell. 30% freelance written. Monthly magazine for owners of coin-operated laundry and dry cleaning stores. Circ. 19,500. Rights purchased vary with author and material but are exclusive to the field. Pays two weeks prior to publication. Publishes ms an average of 4 months after acceptance. Byline given for frequent contributors. Computer printout submissions acceptable; prefers letter-quality. Reports as soon as possible; usually in 2 weeks. Free sample copy.

Nonfiction: "We emphasize store operation and use features on industry topics: utility use and conservation, maintenance, store management, customer service and advertising. A case study should emphasize how the store operator accomplished whatever he did—in a way that the reader can apply to his own operation. Manuscript should have a no-nonsense, business-like approach." Uses informational, how-to, interview, profile, think pieces and successful business operations articles. Length: 500-3,000 words. Pays 6¢/word minimum.

Photos: Pays $6 minimum for 8x10 b&w glossy photos purchased with mss. (Contact sheets with negatives preferred.)

Fillers: Newsbreaks and clippings. Length: open. Pays $6 minimum.

Tips: "Query about subjects of current interest. Be observant of coin-operated laundries—how they are designed and equipped, how they serve customers and how (if) they advertise and promote their services. Most general articles are turned down because they are not aimed well enough at audience. Most case histories are turned down because of lack of practical purpose (nothing new or worth reporting). A frequent mistake is failure to follow up on an interesting point made by the interviewee—probably due to lack of knowledge about the industry."

‡**PLAY METER MAGAZINE,** Skybird Publishing Co., Inc., Box 24970. New Orleans LA 70184. Publisher: Carol Lally. Editor: Valerie Cognevich. 25% freelance written. "We will work with new writers who are familiar with the amusement industry." Monthly trade magazine, 100 pages, for owners/operators of coin-operated amusement machine companies, e.g., pinball machines, video games, arcade pieces, jukeboxes, etc. Circ. 6,500. Pays on publication. Publishes ms an average of 2 months after acceptance. Byline given. Buys all rights. Submit seasonal/holiday material 2 months in advance. Photocopied and previously published submissions OK. Computer printout submissions acceptable; prefers letter-quality to dot-matrix. Query answered in 2 months. Sample copy $5; free writer's guidelines.

Nonfiction: How-to (get better locations for machines, promote tournaments, evaluate profitability of route, etc.); interview (with industry leaders); new product. "Our readers want to read about how they can make more money from their machines, how they can get better tax breaks, commissions, etc. Also no stories about *playing* pinball or video games. Also, submissions on video-game technology advances; technical pieces on troubleshooting videos, pinballs and novelty machines (all coin-operated); trade-show coverage (query) submissions on the pay-telephone industry. Our readers don't play the games per se; they buy the machines and make money from them." Buys 48 mss/year. Submit complete ms. Length: 250-3,000 words. Pays $30-215. Sometimes pays expenses of writers on assignment.

Photos: "The photography should have news value. We don't want 'stand 'em up-shoot 'em down' group shots." Pays $15 minimum for 5x7 or 8x10 b&w prints. Captions preferred. Buys all rights. Art returned on request.

Tips: "We need feature articles more than small news items or featurettes. Query first. We're interested in writers who either have a few years of reporting/feature-writing experience or who know the coin-operated amusement industry well but are relatively inexperienced writers."

VENDING TIMES, 545 8th. Avenue, New York NY 10018. Editor: Arthur E. Yohalem. Monthly. For operators of vending machines. Circ. 14,700. Pays on publication. Buys all rights. "We will discuss in detail the story requirements with the writer." Sample copy $3.

Nonfiction: Feature articles and news stories about vending operations; practical and important aspects of the business. "We are always willing to pay for good material." Query.

Confectionery and Snack Foods

These publications focus on the bakery, snack and candy industries. Journals for grocers, wholesalers and other food industry personnel are listed under Groceries and Food Products.

CANDY INDUSTRY, Edgell Communications, Inc., 7500 Old Oak Blvd., Cleveland OH 44130. (216)243-8100. FAX: (216)819-2683. Managing Editor: Susan Tiffany-Jones. 5% freelance written. Monthly. Prefers to work with published/established writers. For confectionery manufacturers. Publishes ms an average of 4 months after acceptance. Buys all rights. Computer printout submissions acceptable; prefers letter-quality. Reports in 1 month. Writer's guidelines for #10 SASE.

Nonfiction: "Feature articles of interest to large scale candy manufacturers that deal with activities in the fields of production, packaging (including package design), merchandising; and financial news (sales figures, profits, earnings), advertising campaigns in all media, and promotional methods used to increase the sale or distribution of candy." Length: 1,000-1,250 words. Pays 15¢/word; "special rates on assignments."
Photos: "Good quality glossies with complete and accurate captions, in sizes not smaller than 5x7." Pays $15 b&w; $20 for color.
Fillers: "Short news stories about the trade and anything related to candy and snacks." Pays 5¢/word; $1 for clippings.

PACIFIC BAKERS NEWS, 1809 Sharpe Ave., Walnut Creek CA 94596. (415)932-1256. Publisher: C.W. Soward. 30% freelance written. Eager to work with new/unpublished writers. Monthly business newsletter for commercial bakeries in the western states. Pays on publication. No byline given; uses only one-paragraph news items. Computer printout submissions acceptable.
Nonfiction: Uses bakery business reports and news about bakers. Buys only brief "boiled-down news items about bakers and bakeries operating only in Alaska, Hawaii, Pacific Coast and Rocky Mountain states. We welcome clippings. We need monthly news reports and clippings about the baking industry and the donut business. No pictures, jokes, poetry or cartoons." Length: 10-200 words. Pays 6¢/word for clips and news used.

Construction and Contracting

Builders, architects and contractors learn the latest industry news in these publications. Journals targeted to architects are also included in the Consumer Art, Design and Collectibles category. Those for specialists in the interior aspects of construction are listed under Building Interiors.

ACCESS CONTROL, 6255 Barfield Rd., Atlanta GA 30328. (404)256-9800. FAX: (404)256-3116. Editor/ Associate Publisher: Steven Lasky. 50% freelance written. Prefers to work with published/established writers. Monthly tabloid for retailers and installers of access control equipment. Circ. 21,000. Pays on publication. Publishes ms an average of 2 months after acceptance. Buys all rights. Query for electronic submissions. Computer printout submissions acceptable; no dot-matrix. Reports in 3 months. Free sample copy for 8x10 SASE; writer's guidelines for #10 SASE.
Nonfiction: Case histories, large-scale access control "systems approach" equipment installations. A format for these articles has been established. Query for details. Buys 10-12 unsolicited mss/year. Query. Length: 4,500 words maximum.
Columns/Departments: Also take technical or practical application features for following monthly columns dealing with perimeter security fencing and accessories, gate systems, sensor technology card access systems, and CCTV technology. Length: 2,000 words maximum.
Photos: Pays $10 for 5x7 b&w photos purchased with mss. Captions required.
Tips: "We will place more focus on access control installations."

‡**ATLANTIC CONSTRUCTION**, Naylor Communications Ltd., 6th Fl., 920 Yonge St., Toronto, Ontario M4W 3C7 Canada. (416)961-1028. FAX: (416)924-4408. Editor: J.D. Corcoran. 50% freelance written. Annual trade journal for the construction industry in region of Atlantic Canada. "*Construction Atlantic* focuses on issues of interest to the members of four provincial construction associations. A topical and informed style is sought from all writers supplying material." Circ. 5,000. Pays 30 days "from deadline." Byline given. Offers 33⅓% kill fee. Buys first North American serial rights. Submit seasonal/holiday material 2 months in advance. Simultaneous, photocopied and previously published submissions OK. Query for electronic submissions. Computer printout submissions OK; prefers letter-quality.
Nonfiction: General interest, historical, interview/profile, new product, photo feature and technical. "Our publishing date is normally mid-November each year. Articles or ideas for same should be looked at in summer months and as late as September. No promotional, inspirational or personal fluff." Buys 10 mss/ year. Query with published clips. Length: 500-2,500 words. Pays 20-25¢/word. Pays expenses of writers on assignment.

Photos: State availability of photos with submission or send photos with submission. Reviews transparencies and prints. Offers $25-200 per photo. Identification of subjects required. Buys all rights.
Tips: "Query with examples of work. I always respond to every inquiry even if it's to say we're not interested. Major tip: Research facts and quote experts in particular fields."

AUTOMATED BUILDER, CMN Associates, Inc., Box 120, Carpinteria CA 93013. (805)684-7659. FAX: (805)684-1765. Editor-in-Chief: Don Carlson. 15% freelance written. Monthly magazine specializing in management for industrialized (manufactured) housing and volume home builders. Circ. 25,000. Pays on acceptance. Publishes ms an average of 3 months after acceptance. Buys first North American serial rights. Phone queries OK. Computer printout submissions acceptable; no dot-matrix. Reports in 2 weeks. Free sample copy and writer's guidelines.
Nonfiction: Case history articles on successful home building companies which may be 1) production (big volume) home builders; 2) mobile home manufacturers; 3) modular home manufacturers; 4) prefabricated home manufacturers; 5) house component manufacturers; or 6) special unit (in-plant commercial building) manufacturers. Also uses interviews, photo features and technical articles. "No architect or plan 'dreams'. Housing projects must be built or under construction." Buys 15 mss/year. Query. Length: 500-1,000 words maximum. Pays $300 minimum.
Photos: Purchased with accompanying ms. Query. No additional payment for 4x5, 5x7 or 8x10 b&w glossies or 35mm or larger color transparencies (35mm preferred). Captions required.
Tips: "Stories often are too long, too loose; we prefer 500 to 750 words. We prefer a phone query on feature articles. If accepted on query, usually article will not be rejected later."

‡**BUILDER INSIDER,** Box 191125, Dallas TX 75219-1125. (214)871-2913. Editor: Mike Anderson. 18% freelance written. Works with a small number of new/unpublished writers each year. Covers the entire north Texas building industry for builders, architects, contractors, remodelers and homeowners. Circ. 8,000. Publishes ms an average of 2 months after acceptance. Photocopied submissions OK. Computer printout submissions OK; prefers letter-quality to dot-matrix. Free sample copy.
Nonfiction: "What is current in the building industry" is the approach. Wants "advertising, business builders, new building products, building projects being developed and helpful building hints localized to the Southwest and particularly to north Texas." Submit complete ms. Length: 100-900 words. Pays $30-50.

‡**THE CONCRETE TRADER,** Box 660, Dublin OH 43017-0660. (614)793-9711. FAX: (614)793-8380. Editor John D. Cowan. Managing Editor: Jeri Sizemore. 25% freelance written. Monthly newspaper of business information related to concrete industry. Circ. 9,500. Pays on publication. Byline given. Offers $25 kill fee. Buys all rights. Photocopied and previously published submissions OK. Query for electronic submissions. Computer printout submissions OK; prefers letter-quality. Free sample copy and writer's guidelines.
Nonfiction: General interest, interview/profile, new product and technical. Buys 5-12 mss/year. Query with published clips. Length: 500-1,000 words. Pays $100-200 for assigned articles; $100 maximum for unsolicited articles.
Photos: State availability of photos with submission. Reviews contact sheets. Offers no additional payment for photos accepted with ms. Captions required. Buys all rights.
Fillers: Facts. Buys 10/year. Length: 50-200 words. Pays $10-50.
Tips: "Submit all work to Jeri L. Sizemore."

‡**CONSTRUCTION COMMENT,** Naylor Communications Ltd. 6th Fl., 920 Yonge St., Toronto, Ontario M4W 3C7 Canada. (416)961-1028. FAX: (416)924-4408. Editor: J.D. Corcoran. 50% freelance written. Semiannual magazine on construction industry in Ottawa. "*Construction Comment* reaches all members of the Ottawa Construction Association and most senior management of firms relating to the industry." Circ. 3,000. Pays 30 day from deadline. Byline given. Offers 33⅓% kill fee. Buys first North American serial rights. Submit seasonal/holiday material 2 months in advance. Simultaneous and photocopied submissions OK. Query for electronic submissions. Computer printout submissions OK; prefers letter-quality.
Nonfiction: General interest, historical, interview/profile, new product, photo feature and technical. "We publish a spring/summer issue and a fall/winter issue. Submit correspondingly or inquire two months ahead of these times." Buys 20 mss/year. Query with published clips. Length: 500-2,500 words. Pays 20-25¢/word. Pays expenses of writers on assignment.
Photos: State availability of photos with submission. Send photos with submission. Reviews transparencies and prints. Offers $25-200 per photo. Identification of subjects required. Buys one-time rights.
Tips: "Please send copies of work and a general query. I will respond as promptly as my deadlines allow."

If you have an IBM or IBM-compatible personal computer and would like to know more about Writer's Market on disk, see the bind-in card between pages 904 and 905.

CONSTRUCTION SPECIFIER, 601 Madison St., Alexandria VA 22314. (703)684-0300. FAX: (703)684-0465. Editor: Kimberly C. Young. 50% freelance written. Works with a small number of new/unpublished writers each year. Monthly professional society magazine for architects, engineers, specification writers and project managers. Monthly. Circ. 19,000. Pays on publication. Publishes ms an average of 4 months after acceptance. Deadline: 60 days preceding publication on the 1st of each month. Buys North American serial rights. Computer printout submissions acceptable; prefers letter-quality. "Call or write first." Model release, author copyright transferral requested. Reports in 3 weeks. Sample copy for 8½x11 SAE and 6 first class stamps. Writer's guidelines for #10 SASE.

Nonfiction: Articles on selection and specification of products, materials, practices and methods used in commercial (nonresidential) construction projects, specifications as related to construction design, plus legal and management subjects. Query. Length: 3,000-5,000 words maximum. Pays 15¢/published word (negotiable), plus art. Pays minor expenses of writers on assignment, to an agreed upon limit.

Photos: Photos desirable in consideration for publication; line art, sketches, diagrams, charts and graphs also desired. Full color transparencies may be used. 8x10 glossies, 3¼ slides preferred. Payment negotiable.

Tips: "We are increasing in size and thus will need more good technical articles."

‡**COST CUTS**, The Enterprise Foundation, 500 American City Bldg., Columbia MD 21044. (301)964-1230. Editor Cecilia Cassidy. 25% freelance written. Newsletter published 9 times/year on rehabilitation of low-income housing. "As the construction arm of The Enterprise Foundation, the Rehab Work Group, which publishes *Cost Cuts*, seeks ways to reduce the cost of rehabbing and constructing low-income housing. *Cost Cuts* is distributed nationally to rehab specialists, agencies, and others involved in the production of low-income housing." Circ. 5,000. Pays on publication. Byline given. Buys one-time rights. Submit seasonal/holiday material 3 months in advance. Photocopied and previously published submissions OK. Query for electronic submissions. Computer printout submissions OK; prefers letter-quality. Reports in 1 month. Sample copy for 8½x11 SAE with 2 first class stamps. Writer's guidelines for #10 SAE with 1 first class stamp.

Nonfiction: How-to, interview/profile and technical. "No personal experience of do-it-yourselfers in single-family homes. We want articles that contribute to the low cost and high production of low-income housing." Buys 12-20 mss/year. Query with published clips. Length: 100-1,500 words. Pays $50-200 for assigned articles; $200 maximum for unsolicited articles. Sometimes pays expenses of writers on assignment.

Photos: Send photos with submission. Reviews contact sheets and 3x5 and 5x7 prints. Captions and identification of subjects required. Buys one-time rights.

Fillers: Facts and newsbreaks. Buys 20/year. Length: 100-500 words. Pays $25-50.

Tips: "The Foundations's missions is to develop new systems to help poor people help themselves move out of poverty and dependence—into fit and livable housing and self-sufficiency. Freelancers must be conscious of this context. Articles must include case studies of specific projects where costs have been cut. Charts of cost comparisons to show exactly where cuts were made are most helpful."

DIXIE CONTRACTOR, The Regional Construction Journal of the Southeast, Dixie Contractor, Inc. 209-A Swanton Way, Box 280, Decatur GA 30031. (404)377-2683. Editor: Steve Hudson. 50% freelance written. A bimonthly magazine for contractors, construction professionals, equipment suppliers, developers and builders, local and regional officials, and others involved in heavy or commercial construction in the Southeast (Alabama, Florida, Georgia, South Carolina, most of Tennessee). Circ. 10,000. Pays on publication. Byline given. Buys first North American serial rights. Submit seasonal/holiday material 3 months in advance. Query for electronic submissions. Computer printout submissions OK. Reports in 1 week. Sample copy for 9x12 SAE with 8 first class stamps. Writer's guidelines SAE with 2 first class stamps.

Nonfiction: Project profiles, how-to, interview/profile, photo feature and technical. We cannot use articles on projects outside our coverage area. Buys 30-40 mss/year. Query. Length: 600-1,800. Pays $50/published page.

Photos: Send photos with submission. Reviews transparencies (for cover use only) and b&w prints (5x7 or 8x10). Captions required. Buys first North American serial rights.

Tips: "As construction activiity continues to increase in the Southeastern U.S., our need for well-written articles on certain projects is greater than ever before. If you can supply such articles, *Dixie Contractor* can keep you busy."

FINE HOMEBUILDING, The Taunton Press, Inc., 63 S. Main St., Box 355, Newtown CT 06470. (203)426-8171. Editor: Mark Feirer. Less than 5% freelance written. Bimonthly magazine covering house building, construction, design for builders, architects and serious amateurs. Circ. 230,000. Pays advance, balance on publication. Publishes ms an average of 6-12 months after acceptance. Byline given. Offers negotiable kill fee. Buys first rights and "use in books to be published." Query for electronic submissions. Computer printout submissions acceptable; prefers letter-quality. Reports as soon as possible. Free writer's guidelines.

Nonfiction: Technical (techniques in design or construction process). Query. Length: 2,000-3,000 words. Pays $150-1,200.

Columns/Departments: Tools and Materials (products or techniques that are new or unusual); Great Moments in Building History (humorous, embarrassing, or otherwise noteworthy anecdotes); Reviews (short reviews of books on building or design) and Reports and Comment (essays, short reports on construction and architecture trends and developments). Query. Length: 300-1,000 words. Pays $50-250.

‡**HOME BUILDER,** Work-4 Projects Ltd., Box 400, Victoria Stn. Westmount, Quebec H3Z 2V8 Canada. (514)489-4941. Publisher: Natchmi Artzy. Editor: Rob Bradford. 80% freelance written. Magazine that covers new home construction, published 6 times annually. "*Home Builder Magazine* reports on builders, architects, mortgage, sub-trades, associations and government. We keep the readers' concerns in the forefront, not the advertisers." Estab. 1988. Circ. 12,000. Pays on publication. Publishes ms an average of 4 months after acceptance. Byline sometimes given. Buys all rights. Simultaneous and photocopied submissions OK. Computer printout submissions OK; prefers letter-quality. Reports in 2-3 weeks on queries. Free sample copy.

Nonfiction: Exposé, how-to (builders, administration, production, etc.), interview/profile, new product and technical. Buys 20-30 mss/year. Query with published clips. Length: 100-500 words. Pays 10-20¢/word. Pays in contributor copies or other premiums "if suitable for both parties." Sometimes pays expenses of writers on assignment.

Photos: Send photos with submission. Reviews transparencies and prints. Offers expense-$300 per photo. Captions and identification of subjects required. Buys all rights.

Columns/Departments: Perspective (general news of importance to audience), 100-300 words; and Industry News (specific company information of relevance – not sales pitch), 75-300 words. Buys 20 mss/year. Query with published clips. Pays 10-20¢/word.

Fillers: Facts and gags. Buys 5/year. Length: 5-50 words. Pays 10¢/word-$25.

Tips: "Keep audience in mind. Give them something that will affect them, not something they will forget five minutes after reading it. Keep in mind Canadian content."

INLAND ARCHITECT, The Midwestern Magazine for the Building Arts, Inland Architect Press, 10 West Hubbard St., Box 10394, Chicago IL 60610. (312)321-0583. Editor: Cynthia Davidson-Powers. 80% freelance written. Prefers to work with published/established writers. Bimonthly magazine covering architecture and urban planning. "*Inland Architect* is a critical journal covering architecture and design in the midwest for an audience primarily of architects. *Inland* is open to all points of view, providing they are intelligently expressed and of relevance to architecture." Circ. 7,000. Pays on publication. Publishes ms an average of 2 months after acceptance. Byline given. Offers 60% kill fee. Buys first rights. Computer printout submissions OK; no dot-matrix. Reports in 1 month on queries; 2 months on mss. Sample copy $4 with 9½x12½ SAE. Writer's guidelines for #10 SASE.

Nonfiction: Book excerpts, essays, historical/nostalgic, interview/profile, criticism and photo feature of architecture. Every summer *Inland* focuses on a midwestern city, its architecture and urban design. Call to find out 1990 city. No new products, "how to run your office," or technical pieces. Buys 40 mss/year. Query with or without published clips, or send complete ms. Length: 750-3,500 words. Pays $100-300 for assigned articles; pays $75-250 for unsolicited articles. Sometimes pays the expenses of writers on assignment.

Photos: Send photos with submission. Reviews 4x5 transparencies, slides and 8x10 prints. Offers no additional payment for photos accepted with ms. Identification of subjects required. Buys one-time rights.

Columns/Departments: Books (reviews of new publications on architecture, design and, occasionally, art), 250-1,000 words. Buys 10 mss/year. Query. Length: 250-1,000 words. Pays $25-100.

Tips: "Propose specific articles, e.g., to cover a lecture, to interview a certain architect. Articles must be written for an audience primarily consisting of well-educated architects. If an author feels he has a 'hot' timely idea, a phone call is appreciated."

‡**THE JOURNAL OF LIGHT CONSTRUCTION,** Hanley-Wood Partners, RR2, Box 146, Richmond VT 05477. (802)864-3680. Editor: Steven Bliss. Managing Editor: Kate O'Brien. 50% freelance written. Monthly tabloid on residential and light-commercial construction/remodeling. "Most of our articles offer practical solutions to problems that small contractors face on the job site or in the office. For that reason, most of our authors have practical experience in construction. In fact, the accuracy of the information is more important to us than the quality of the writing." Pays on publication. Publishes ms an average of 4 months after acceptance. Byline given. Negotiable kill fee. Buys first North American serial rights and non-exclusive reprint rights. Query for electronic submissions. Computer printout submissions OK; prefers letter-quality. Sample copy $3. Writer's guidelines for SASE.

Nonfiction: How-to, new product and technical. Buys 40 mss/year. Query. Length: 1,300-2,500 words. Pays $150-400. Sometimes pays expenses of writers on assignment.

Photos: Send photos with submission. Reviews contact sheets, transparencies and prints. Offers no additional payment for photos accepted with ms. Captions required. Buys first first and non-exclusive reprint rights.

Columns/Departments: Miscellaney (news shorts in areas of business, technology, codes, human interest related to home construction), 300-1,000 words. Buys 12 mss/year. Send complete ms. Pays $50-200.

‡**LOUISIANA CONTRACTOR**, Rhodes Publishing Co., Inc., 18271 Old Jefferson Hwy., Baton Rouge LA 70817. (504)292-8980. Editor: Joyce Elson. 10% freelance written. Works with Louisiana freelance writers with knowledge of the construction industry. Monthly comprehensive magazine covering heavy commercial, industrial and highway construction in Louisiana. Circ. 7,750. Pays on publication. Publishes ms an average of 2 months after acceptance. Offers negotiable kill fee. Buys all rights. Computer printout submissions OK; prefers letter-quality to dot-matrix. Reports in 2 weeks on queries; 2½ months on mss. Sample copy $1.50.
Nonfiction: "We are particularly interested in writers who can get clearance into a chemical plant or refinery and detail unusual maintenance jobs. Our feature articles are semitechnical to technical, balanced by a lot of name dropping of subcontractors, suppliers and key job personnel. We want quotes, and we never run a story without lots of photos either taken or procured by the writer. Stories on new methods of construction and unusual projects in the state are always wanted. Nothing from anyone unfamiliar with the construction industry in Louisiana." Buys 8-12 mss/year. Query. Length: 1,000-3,500 words. Pays negotiable rate. Sometimes pays the expenses of writers on assignment.
Photos: State availability of photos. Reviews 5x7 or 8x10 b&w glossy prints. Captions and identification of subjects required. "It is absolutely essential that a writer understand construction terms and practices."

MIDWEST CONTRACTOR, Construction Digest, Inc., 3170 Mercier, Box 419766, Kansas City MO 64141. (816)931-2080. 5% freelance written. Biweekly magazine covering the public works and engineering construction industries in Iowa, Nebraska, Kansas and western and northeastern Missouri. Circ. 8,426. Pays on publication. Byline given depending on nature of article. Computer printout submissions acceptable; prefers letter-quality. Reports in 1 month. Sample copy for 11x15 SAE with 8 first class stamps.
Nonfiction: How-to, photo feature, technical, "nuts and bolts" construction job-site features. "We seek two-to three-page articles on topics of interest to our readership, including marketing trends, tips, and construction job-site stories. Providing concise, accurate and original news stories is another freelance opportunity." Buys 4 mss/year. Query with three published clips. Length: 175 typewritten lines, 35 character count, no maximum. Pays $50/published page.
Tips: "We need writers who can write clearly about our specialized trade area. An engineering/construction background is a plus. The most frequent mistake made by writers is that they do not tailor their article to our specific market—the nonresidential construction market in Nebraska, Iowa, Kansas and Missouri. We are not interested in what happens in New York unless it has a specific impact in the Midwest."

PACIFIC BUILDER & ENGINEER, Vernon Publications Inc.. Suite 200, 3000 Northup Way, Bellevue WA 98004. (206)827-9900. Editor: John M. Watkins. Editorial Director: Michele Dill. 20% freelance written. A biweekly magazine on heavy construction. "We cover non-residential construction in Washington, Oregon, Idaho, Montana and Alaska." Circ. 12,000. Pays on publication. Byline given. Buys first North American serial rights. Submit seasonal material 2 months in advance. Photocopied submissions OK. Computer printout submissions OK; prefers letter-quality. Reports in 3 weeks on queries; 6 weeks on mss.
Nonfiction: How-to (construction), interview/profile and technical (construction). Buys 10 mss/year. Query with published clips. Length: 1,000-2,500 words. Pays $100-200. Does not pay for unsolicited manuscripts. Sometimes pays the expenses of writers on assignment.
Photos: Send photos with submission. Reviews contact sheets, transparencies (35mm) and prints (8x10). Payment is by the page. Buys North American rights.

‡**ROOFER MAGAZINE**, D&H Publications, 10990 Metro Pky. SE, Ft. Myers FL 33912. (813)275-7663. Editor: Shawn Holiday. 10% freelance written. Eager to work with new/unpublished writers, and works with a small number of new/unpublished writers each year. Monthly magazine covering the roofing industry for roofing contractors. Circ. 16,000. Pays on publication. Publishes ms an average of 5 months after acceptance. Byline given. Buys first serial rights and second serial (reprint) rights. Submit seasonal/holiday material 4 months in advance. Computer printout submissions acceptable; no dot-matrix. Reports in 2 weeks on queries; 1 month on mss. Sample copy and writer's guidelines for SAE and $1.50 postage.
Nonfiction: Historical/nostalgic; how-to (solve application problems, overcome trying environmental conditions); interview/profile; and technical. "Write articles directed toward areas of specific interest; don't generalize too much." Buys 7 mss/year. Query. Length: 3,000-7,000 words. Pays $125-250.
Photos: Send photos with accompanying query. Reviews 8x10 b&w prints and standard size transparencies. Identification of subjects required. Buys all rights.
Tips: "We prefer substantial articles (not short articles and fillers). Slant articles toward roofing contractors. Don't embellish too much. Our audience has proven itself to be educated, intelligent and demanding. The submitted freelance article should exemplify those traits. We have little use for generic articles that can appear in any business publication and give little consideration to such material submitted. The tone of articles submitted to us needs to be authoritative but not condescending. Authors of successful freelance articles know the roofing industry."

RSI, Roofing/Siding/Insulation, Edgell Communications, 7500 Old Oak Blvd., Cleveland OH 44130. (216)243-8100. Editor: Michael Russo. 15% freelance written. A monthly magazine about roofing, siding and insulation fields. "Our audience is almost entirely contractors in the roofing, siding and/or insulation fields. The publication's goal is to help them improve their business, with heavy emphasis on application techniques." Circ. 20,000. Pays on publication. Publishes ms an average of 3 months after acceptance. Byline sometimes given. Buys all rights. Computer printout submissions OK; no dot-matrix. Free sample copy.
Nonfiction: How-to (application of RSI products), new product, technical (on roofing, siding and/or insulation) and business articles directed at subcontractors. "No consumer-oriented articles. Our readers sell to consumers and building owners." Buys 6 mss/year. Query. Length: 1,000-3,000 words. Pays $100-800 for assigned articles. Pays $50-400 for unsolicited articles. Sometimes pays the expenses of writers on assignment.
Photos: State availability of photos with submission. Reviews transparencies (2¼x2¼) and prints (5x7). Offers no additional payment for photos accepted with ms. Captions and identification of subjects required.

‡SOUTHWEST CONTRACTOR, Akers-Runbeck Publishing, Suite 490, 3101 Central Ave., Phoenix AZ 85012. (602)230-0598. FAX: (602)230-8704. Editor: Elaine M. Beall. 20% freelance written. Monthly magazine on construction industry/engineering. "Problem-solving case histories of projects in Arizona, New Mexico, Nevada and West Texas emphasizing engineering, equipment, materials and people." Circ. 6,200. Pays on publication. Byline given. Buys first rights and makes work-for-hire assignments. Submit seasonal/holiday material 3 months in advance. Previously published submissions OK. Computer printout submissions OK; prefers letter-quality. Sample $3 with 9x12 SAE and 90¢ postage. Writer's guidelines for #10 SAE with 1 first class stamp.
Nonfiction: Interview/profile and technical. (June — Aggregate/Asphalt; July — Concrete/Ready Mix and December — Mining.) Buys 12 mss/year. Query. Length: 1,000-3,000 words. Pays $4/column inch at 14 picas wide. Sometimes pays expenses of writers on assignment.
Photos: State availability of photos with submission. Reviews 3x5 prints. Offers $10 maximum per photo. Captions and identification of subjects required. Buys one-time rights.
Columns/Departments: People; Around Southwest (general construction activities), Association News (all associations involved with industry), Manufacturer's News, Legal News (construction only).

Dental

DENTAL ECONOMICS, Penwell Publishing Co., Box 3408, Tulsa OK 74101. (918)835-3161. FAX: (918)831-9497. Editor: Dick Hale. 50% freelance written. A monthly dental trade journal. "Our readers are actively practicing dentists who look to us for current practice-building, practice-administrative and personal finance assistance." Circ. 110,000. Pays on acceptance. Publishes ms an average of 3-4 months after acceptance. Byline given. Buys first rights. Submit seasonal/holiday material 6 months in advance. Computer printout submissions OK; prefers letter-quality. Reports in 3 weeks on queries; 1 month on mss. Free sample copy and writer's guidelines.
Nonfiction: General interest, how-to and new product. "No human interest and consumer-related stories." Buys 40 mss/year. Query. Length: 750-3,500 words. Pays $150-500 for assigned articles; pays $75-350 for unsolicited articles. Sometimes pays the expenses of writers on assignment.
Photos: State availability of photos with submission. Reviews contact sheets. Offers no additional payment for photos accepted with ms. Model releases and identification of subjects required. Buys one-time rights.
Columns/Departments: Ron Combs, editor. Tax Q&A (tax tips for dentists), 1,500 words; Capitolgram (late legislative news — dentistry), 750 words; and Econ Report (national economic outlook), 750 words. Buys 36 mss/year. Pays $50-300.
Tips: "How-to articles on specific subjects such as practice-building, newsletters and collections should be relevant to a busy, solo-practice dentist."

DENTIST, Dental Market Network, Stevens Publishing Corp., 225 N. New Rd., Box 7573, Waco TX 76714. (817)776-9000. FAX: (817)776-9018. Editor: Mark S. Hartley. 25% freelance written. Eager to work with new/unpublished writers. A bimonthly trade journal for dentists. Any news or feature story of interest to dentists is considered. Circ. 154,860. Pays 60 days after acceptance. Publishes ms an average of 2 months after acceptance. Byline given. Offers 25% kill fee. Buys first North American serial rights. Submit seasonal/holiday material 1 year in advance. Simultaneous submissions OK. Computer printout submissions OK; prefers letter-quality. Reports in 1 month on queries; 2 months on mss. Sample copy and writer's guidelines for 12½x15 SAE with 7 first class stamps.

Nonfiction: How-to, humor, interview/profile, new product and technical. Buys 20 mss/year. Query with or without published clips, or send complete ms. Length: 30 inches of copy. Pays $50-200 for assigned articles. Sometimes pays the expenses of writers on assignment

Photos: Send photos with submission. Reviews contact sheets. Offers $10-100 per photo. Captions and identification of subjects required. Buys one-time rights.

Tips: "Purchased freelance material reflects a knowledgeable, analytical insight into issues concerning the dental profession. Audience is very intelligent and literate; readers can easily spot editorial that is not adequately researched. The emphasis in 1990 will continue to be on obtaining timely, newsworthy editorial pertinent to dentistry: cosmetic dentistry, infection control, periodontics, patient insurance, and alternative methods of patient payment."

GENERAL DENTISTRY, Academy of General Dentistry. Suite 1200, 211 E. Chicago Ave., Chicago IL 60611. (312)440-4344. FAX: (312)440-4315. Managing Editor: Terrance Stanton. 5% freelance written. A bimonthly magazine about dentistry. "Our focus is continuing eduction in dentistry. Our readers are dentists. Articles should be written at a dentist's level of knowledge." Circ. 45,000. Pays on acceptance. Publishes ms an average of 4 months after acceptance. Offers 50% kill fee. Buys all rights. Simultaneous and photocopied submissions OK. Computer printout submissions OK; prefers letter-quality. Reports in 1 month. Sample copy for 8½x11 SAE with 5 first class stamps; writer's guidelines for #10 SASE.

Nonfiction: Essays, historical/nostalgic, interview/profile, new product and technical. No articles written for dental patients. Buys 10 mss/year. Query with or without published clips, or send complete ms. Pays $125-500 for assigned articles. Pays $125-400 for unsolicited articles. Pays the expenses of writers on assignment.

Photos: State availability of photos with submission. Reviews contact sheets. Offers no additional payment for photos accepted with ms. Captions, model releases and identification of subjects required. All rights for dental market acquired.

Tips: "Understand that our focus is scientific. Any article we buy must be of special interest to the members of our association, which is devoted to fostering continuing education in dentistry. Writers are advised to call or query so that we can assist in developing an idea. Stories that have to do with improvements in clinical practice are the best prospects for our magazine."

PROOFS, The Magazine of Dental Sales and Marketing, Box 3408, Tulsa OK 74101. (918)835-3161. FAX: (918)831-9497. Publisher: Dick Hale. Editor: Mary Elizabeth Good. 10% freelance written. Magazine published 10 times/year; combined issues July/August, November/December. Pays on publication. Byline given. Computer printout submissions acceptable; prefers letter-quality. Reports in 2 weeks. Free sample copy.

Nonfiction: Uses short articles, chiefly on selling to dentists. Must have understanding of dental trade industry and problems of marketing and selling to dentists and dental laboratories. Query. Pays about $75.

Tips: "The most frequent mistakes made by writers are having a lack of familiarity with industry problems and talking down to our audience."

RDH, The National Magazine for Dental Hygiene Professionals, Stevens Publishing Corp., 225 N. New Rd., Waco TX 76714. (817)776-9000. Editor: Laura Albrecht. 65% freelance written. Eager to work with new/unpublished writers. Monthly magazine, covering information relevant to dental hygiene professionals as business-career oriented individuals. "Dental hygienists are highly trained, licensed professionals; most are women. They are concerned with ways to develop rewarding careers, give optimum service to patients and to grow both professionally and personally." Circ. 63,210. Usually pays on publication; sometimes on acceptance. Publishes ms an average of 8 months after acceptance. Byline given. Buys first serial rights. Computer printout submissions acceptable. Reports in 2 weeks on queries; 2 months on mss. Sample copy for 9×11 SAE; writer's guidelines for SASE.

Nonfiction: Essays, general interest, interview/profile, personal experience, photo feature and technical. "We are interested in any topic that offers broad reader appeal, especially in the area of personal growth (communication, managing time, balancing career and personal life). No undocumented clinical or technical articles; how-it-feels-to-be-a-patient articles; product-oriented articles (unless in generic terms); anything cutesy-unprofessional." Length: 1,500-3,000 words. Pays $100-350 for assigned articles; pays $50-200 for unsolicited articles. Sometimes pays expenses of writers on assignment.

Photos: Send photos with submission. Reviews 3x5 prints. Model releases required. Buys one-time rights.

Tips: "Freelancers should have a feel for the concerns of today's business-career woman – and address those interests and concerns with practical, meaningful and even motivational messages. We want to see good-quality manuscripts on both personal growth and lifestyle topics. For clinical and/or technical topics, we prefer the writers be members of the dental profession. New approaches to old problems and dilemmas will always get a close look from our editors. *RDH* is also interested in manuscripts for our feature section. Other than clinical information, dental hygienists are interested in all sorts of topics – finances, personal growth, educational opportunities, business management, staff/employer relations, communication and motivation, office rapport and career options. Other than clinical/technical articles, *RDH* maintains an informal tone. Writing style can easily be accommodated to our format."

_____ *Drugs, Health Care and Medical Products*

THE APOTHECARY, Health Care Marketing Services, #200, 95 First St., Box AP, Los Altos CA 94023. (415)941-3955. FAX: (415)941-2303. Editor: Jerold Karabensh. Publication Director: Janet Goodman. 100% freelance written. Prefers to work with published/established writers. Quarterly magazine. "*The Apothecary* aims to provide practical information to community retail pharmacists." Circ. 60,000. Pays on acceptance. Publishes ms an average of 5 months after acceptance. Byline given. Buys all rights. Submit seasonal material 8 months in advance. Simultaneous queries and photocopied submissions OK. Computer printout submissions acceptable; prefers letter-quality. Reports in 6 weeks on queries; 5 months on mss. Sample copy for 9x12 SAE with 4 first class stamps. Writer's guidelines for #10 SASE.

Nonfiction: How-to (e.g., manage a pharmacy); opinion (of registered pharmacists); and health-related feature stories. "We publish only those general health articles with some practical application for the pharmacist as business person. No general articles not geared to our pharmacy readership; no fiction." Buys 4 mss/year. Query with published clips. Length: 750-3,000 words. Pays $100-300.

Columns/Departments: Commentary (views or issues relevant to the subject of pharmacy or to pharmacists). Send complete ms. Length: 750-1,000 words. "This section is unpaid; we will take submissions with byline."

Tips: "Submit material geared to the *pharmacist* as *business person*. Write according to our policy, i.e., business articles with emphasis on practical information for a community pharmacist. We suggest reading several back issues and following general feature story tone, depth, etc. Stay away from condescending use of language. Though our articles are written in simple style, they must reflect knowledge of the subject and reasonable respect for the readers' professionalism and intelligence."

CANADIAN PHARMACEUTICAL JOURNAL, 1785 Alta Vista Dr., Ottawa, Ontario K1G 3Y6 Canada. (613)523-7877. FAX: (613)523-0445. Editor: Jane Dewar. Clinical Editor: Mary MacDonald-LaPrade. New & Features Editor: Diana Gibbs. 40% freelance written. Works with a small number of new/unpublished writers each year. Monthly journal for pharmacists. Circ. 12,500. Pays after editing. Publishes ms an average of 3 months after acceptance. Buys first serial rights. Computer printout submissions acceptable; no dot-matrix. Reports in 2 months. Free sample copy and writer's guidelines.

Nonfiction: Relevant to Canadian pharmacy. Publishes exposés (pharmacy practice, education and legislation); how-to (pharmacy business operations); historical (pharmacy practice, Canadian legislation, education); and interviews with and profiles on Canadian and international pharmacy figures. Length: 200-400 words (for news notices); 800-1,500 words (for articles). Query. Payment is contingent on value, usually 18¢/word. Sometimes pays expenses of writers on assignment.

Photos: B&w (5x7) glossies purchased with mss. Pays $25 first photo; $5 for each additional photo. Captions and model release required.

Tips: "Query with complete description of proposed article, including topic, sources (in general), length, payment requested, suggested submission date, and whether photographs will be included. It is helpful if the writer has read a *recent* (1989) copy of the journal; we are glad to send one if required. References should be included where appropriate (this is vital where medical and scientific information is included). Send 3 copies of each ms. Author's degree and affiliations (if any) and writing background should be listed."

‡CORPORATE HEALTH, Top Management's Source on Employee Health, 2506 Gross Point Rd., Evanston IL 60201. (312)475-7510. Editor: Lisbeth R. Maxwell. 50-75% freelance written. Bimonthly magazine on employee health and benefits. "Our readers are executives of medium to large companies. They need substantive yet not exhaustively detailed information on all aspects of employee health." Estab. 1988. Circ. 17,000. Pays on publication. Publishes ms an average of 3 months after acceptance. Byline given. Offers negotiable kill fee. Makes work-for-hire assignments. Submit seasonal/holiday material 5 months in advance. Query for electronic submissions. Computer printout submissions OK; prefers letter-quality. Reports in 2 weeks on queries; 2 months on mss. Free sample copy and writer's guidelines.

Nonfiction: General interest and how-to (health/fitness in the business setting). "No promotions for specific products or services; general health/fitness articles with a business slant." Query with published clips if possible, or send complete ms. Length: 2,100-4,200 words. Payment negotiable. Pays expenses of writers on assignment.

Photos: Send photos with submission. Reviews 5x7 prints. Captions, model releases and identification of subjects required. Buys one-time rights.

Columns/Departments: Health Watch (health issues of import to employers and employees); Focus on Fitness (fitness issues of import to employers and employees); and Case Study ("how they did it" approach to one benefits, health, fitness or safety topic—one company's method of dealing with issue). Query with published clips if possible. Send complete ms. Length: 1,400-2,800 words. Payment negotiable.

Tips: "Well researched, balanced pieces with authoritative sources will always be welcomed. Brevity is a blessing in a publication going primarily to busy executives. Short, snappy, energetic articles that inform with style are what our readers want, written in a way that imparts information without talking down to them *or* going over their heads."

‡FAHS REVIEW, (formerly *Federation of America Health Systems Review*), Suite 308, 1405 N. Pierce St., Little Rock AR 72207. (501)661-9555. FAX: (501)663-4903. Editor: John Herrmann. 10% freelance written. Bimonthly trade journal on health care issues and health care politics (federal and state). "*FAHS Review* publishes news and articles concerning the politics of health care, covers legislative activities and broad grassroots stories involving particular hospitals or organizations and their problems/solutions. Goes to health care managers, executives, to all members of the Congress and key administrative people." Circ. 35,000. Pays on acceptance. Byline given. Offers $100 kill fee. Buys first North American serial rights and second serial (reprint) rights. Submit seasonal/holiday material 4-5 months in advance. Simultaneous and photocopied submissions OK. Query for electronic submissions. Computer printout submissions OK; prefers letter-quality. Reports in 1 week on queries; 1 month on mss. Sample copy for 9x12 SAE with $1.25 in postage.

Nonfiction: Essays, interview/profile, opinion and personal experience. "No articles about health care or medical procedures. No new products pieces. No articles about health care organizations and the stock market." Buys 15 mss/year. Query with published clips. Length: 1,500-3,500 words. Pays $150-500. "Articles by health care leaders, members of Congress and staff and legal columns generally not paid." Pays expenses of writers on assignment.

Photos: Send photo with submission. Reviews contact sheets, transparencies and prints. Offers no additional payment for photos accepted with ms. Captions and identification of subjects required. Buys one-time rights and all rights.

Columns/Departments: Shirley Brainard. Health Law Perspectives (analysis of legislative activity; interpretation of laws as they apply to hospitals, etc.), 2,000-3,000 words; Health Care Financing (business issues in health care), 1,500-3,500 words; and Supply Side (health care suppliers news update), 1,500-3,500 words. Buys 6 mss/year. Query with published clips. Pays $100-200.

Tips: "Any specific information on Medicare/Medicaid problems; a good hospital/business story (failure or success story); good contacts with state or federal senators and representatives and/or their staff members for close-ups, profiles. No writing in supply side that sells the supplier or its products but, rather, how it sees current issues from its perspective."

‡PHARMACY TIMES, Romaine Pierson Publishers, 80 Shore Rd., Port Washington NY 11050. (516)883-6350. Publisher/Editor-in-Chief: Raymond A. Gosselin, R.Ph.. Executive Editor: Joseph Cupolo. 15% freelance written. Monthly magazine on the pharmaceutical industry. Circ. 89,076. Pays on publication. Publishes ms an average of 4 months after acceptance. Byline given. Buys one-time rights. Submit seasonal/holiday material 6 months in advance. Query for electronic submissions. Computer printout submissions OK; no dot-matrix. Reports in 3 weeks on queries; 6 weeks on mss. Free sample copy and writer's guidelines.

Nonfiction: Interview/profile, new product, opinion, personal experience, photo feature, technical and travel. Buys 12-15 mss/year. Send complete ms. Length: 800-1,500 words. Pays $250-400 for assigned articles; $100-250 for unsolicited articles. Pays in contributor copies or other premiums "per author request or for reprinted material."

Photos: State availability of photos with submission. Reviews negatives and 3x5 prints. Offers no additional payment for photos accepted with ms. Captions, model releases and identification of subjects required. Buys one-time rights.

Education and Counseling

Professional educators, teachers, coaches and counselors—as well as other people involved in training and education—read the journals classified here. Many journals for educators are nonprofit forums for professional advancement; writers contribute articles in return for a byline and contributor's copies. *Writer's Market* includes only educational journals that pay freelancers for articles. Education-related publications for students are included in the Consumer Career, College and Alumni and Teen and Young Adult sections.

THE AMERICAN SCHOOL BOARD JOURNAL, National School Boards Association, 1680 Duke St., Alexandria VA 22314. (703)838-6722. Editor: Gregg Downey. 10% freelance written. "We have no preference for published/unpublished writers; it's the quality of the article and writing that count." Monthly magazine. Emphasizes public school administration and policymaking for elected members of public boards of education throughout U.S. and Canada, and high-level administrators of same. Circ. 42,000. Pays on acceptance. Publishes ms an average of 3 months after acceptance. Buys all rights. Phone queries OK. Photocopied submissions OK. Computer printout submissions acceptable; prefers letter-quality. Reports in 2 months. Sample copy and guidelines for 8½x11 SAE.
Nonfiction: Publishes how-to articles (solutions to problems of public school operation including political problems). "No material on how public schools are in trouble. We all know that; what we need are *answers*." Buys 20 mss/year. Query. Length: 400-2,000 words. Payment for feature articles varies, "but never less than $100."
Photos: B&w glossies (any size) purchased on assignment. Captions required. Pays $10-50. Model release required.
Tips: "Can you lend a national perspective to a locally observed school program? Do you prefer writing for a general audience or a specific, knowledgeable-on-this-issue audience?"

ARTS & ACTIVITIES, Publishers' Development Corporation, Suite 200, 591 Camino de la Reina, San Diego CA 92108. (619)297-5352. FAX: (619)297-5353. Editor: Dr. Leven C. Leatherbury. Managing Editor: Maryellen Bridge. 95% freelance written. Eager to work with new/unpublished writers. Monthly (except July and August) art education magazine covering art education at levels from preschool through college for educators and therapists engaged in arts and crafts education and training. Circ. 25,433. Pays on publication. Publishes ms an average of 6 months after acceptance. Byline given. Buys first North American rights. Submit seasonal/holiday material 4 months in advance. Photocopied submissions OK. Computer printout submissions acceptable; prefers letter-quality. Reports in 2 months. Sample copy for 9x12 envelope and 8 first class stamps; writer's guidelines for #10 SAE and 1 first class stamp.
Nonfiction: Historical/nostalgic (arts activities history); how-to (classroom art experiences, artists' techniques); interview/profile (of artists); opinion (on arts activities curriculum, ideas on how to do things better); personal experience in the art class room ("this ties in with the how-to, we like it to be *personal*, no recipe style"); and articles on exceptional art programs. Buys 50-80 mss/year. Length: 200-2,000 words. Pays $35-150.
Tips: "Frequently in unsolicited manuscripts, writers obviously have not studied the magazine to see what style of articles we publish. Send for a sample copy to familiarize yourself with our style and needs. The best way to find out if his/her writing style suits our needs is for the author to submit a manuscript on speculation."

CLASSROOM COMPUTER LEARNING, Suite A4, 2169 Francisco Blvd. E., San Rafael CA 94901. FAX: (415)457-4378. Editor-in-Chief: Holly Brady. 50% freelance written. Works with a small number of new/unpublished writers each year. Monthly magazine published during school year emphasizing elementary through high school educational computing topics. Circ. 83,000. Pays on acceptance. Publishes ms an average of 8 months after acceptance. Buys all rights or first serial rights. Submit seasonal/holiday material 6 months in advance. Computer printout submissions acceptable; prefers letter-quality. Reports in 2 months. Writer's guidelines with SAE and 1 first class stamp; sample copy for 8x10 SAE and 6 first class stamps.
Nonfiction: "We publish manuscripts that describe innovative ways of using computers in the classroom as well as articles that discuss controversial issues in computer education." Interviews, brief computer-related activity ideas and longer featurettes describing fully developed and tested classroom ideas. Recent article example: "A Network Primer: How They're Used ... and How They Could be Used" (April, 1988). Buys 50 mss/year. Query. Length: 500 words or less for classroom activities; 1,000-1,500 words for classroom activity featurettes; 1,500-2,500 words for major articles. Pays $25 for activities; $150 for featurettes; varying rates for longer articles. Educational Software Reviews: Assigned through editorial offices. "If interested, send a letter telling us of your areas of interest and expertise as well as the microcomputer(s) you have available to you." Pays $150 per review. Sometimes pays expenses of writers on assignment.
Photos: State availability of photos with query.
Tips: "The talent that goes into writing our shorter hands-on pieces is different from that required for features (e.g., interviews, issues pieces, etc.) Write whatever taps your talent best. A frequent mistake is taking too 'novice' or too 'expert' an approach. You need to know our audience well and to understand how much they know about computers. Also, too many manuscripts lack a definite point of view or focus or opinion. We like pieces with clear, strong, well thought out opinions."

COMPUTERS IN EDUCATION, Moorshead Publications, 1300 Don Mills Rd., North York, Toronto, Ontario M3B 3M8 Canada. (416)445-5600. Editor: Richard Evers. 90% freelance written. Eager to work with new/ unpublished writers. Magazine published 10 times/year. Articles of interest to teachers, computer consultants and administrators working at the kindergarten to post secondary level. Circ. 18,000. Pays on publication. Publishes ms an average of 2 months after acceptance. Byline given. Buys first serial rights, first North American serial rights, one time rights, second serial (reprint) rights, and all rights. Phone queries OK. Photocopied submissions OK. Query for electronic submissions. Computer printout submissions acceptable; prefers letter-quality. Sample copy and writer's guidelines with SASE or IRC.
Nonfiction: Use of computers in education and techniques of teaching using computers; lesson plans, novel applications, anything that is practical for the teacher. Does not want overviews, "Gee Whizzes," and reinventions of the wheel. Length 700-2,000 words. Pays 6-10¢/word. Sometimes pays the expenses of writers on assignment.
Photos: Photos and/or artwork all but mandatory. Pays extra for photos. Captions required.
Tips: "We are looking for practical articles by working teachers. Nothing too general, no overviews, or the same thing that has been said for years."

‡COTTONWOOD MONTHLY, Cottonwood Press, Suite 398, 305 W. Magnolia, Ft. Collins CO 80521. (303)493-1286. Editor: Cheryl Thurston. 25% freelance written. Monthly, Sept.-May newsletter for language arts teachers, grades 5 and up. "The *Cottonwood Monthly* publishes ideas, activities, lessons, games and assignments for language arts teachers to use in the classroom. Our emphasis is upon practical materials that a teacher can photocopy and use tomorrow. We also like to use material with a humorous slant." Circ. 300. Pays on publication. Publishes ms an average of 3 months after acceptance. Byline sometimes given. Buys all rights. Submit seasonal/holiday material 4 months in advance. Simultaneous and photocopied submissions OK. Computer printout submissions OK. Sample copy $1 with SAE and 1 first class stamp.
Nonfiction: How-to (practical ideas on anything that can make a teacher's life easier), humor, (games lessons, activities, assignments for language arts classes grades 5 and up). "Nothing theoretical. We want only practical material teachers can actually *use* in their classrooms." Buys 20 mss/year. Send complete ms. Length: 250-750 words. Pays $20-25 for unsolicited articles.
Columns/Departments: Teacher Tips (practical tips on anything of concern to language arts teachers: discipline, stress management, school programs, motivating students, grading papers, communicating with parents, etc.). Buys 9 mss/year. Send complete ms. Length: 75-200 words. Pays $10.
Tips: "Show us that you know kids, real life kids. If your material will appeal to modern-day students, we are interested and flexible. We don't like to see dry, textbook-like material. We are interested in material that takes a lighter, humorous, even offbeat approach to language arts."

INSTRUCTOR MAGAZINE, Edgell Communications, Inc.. 7500 Old Oak Blvd., Cleveland OH 44130. Editor: Ben Miyares. 30% freelance written. Eager to work with new/unpublished writers, "especially teachers." Monthly magazine. Emphasizes elementary education. Circ. 300,000. Pays on acceptance. Publishes ms an average of 1 year after acceptance. Byline given. Buys all rights. Submit seasonal/holiday material 6 months in advance. Photocopied submissions OK. Query for electronic submissions. Computer printout submissions OK; prefers letter-quality. Reports in 1 month on queries; 2 months on mss. Send a SASE for a free writer's guidelines; mention *Writer's Market* in request.
Nonfiction: How-to articles on elementary classroom practice—practical suggestions as well as project reports, opinion pieces on professional issues, and current first-person stories by teachers about the teaching experience. Buys 100 mss/year. Query. Length: 400-2,000 words. Pays $15-100 for short items; $125-400 for articles and features. Send all queries to Attention: manuscripts editor. No poetry.
Photos: Send photos with submission. Reviews 4x5 transparencies and prints. Offers no additional payment for photos accepted with ms. Model releases and identification of subjects required. Buys all rights.
Columns/Departments: OTS (slice-of-life vignettes); Speakout (controversial points-of-view); Teachers Express (quick teacher tips and ideas); Planner (activities, bulletin boards and crafts). Buys 100 mss/year. Query with SASE. Length: 50-900 words. Pays $30-100.
Fiction: Ethnic, historical, humorous and slice-of-life vignettes. Buys 50 mss/year. Query with SASE. Length: 500-2,500 words. Pays $75-200.
Tips: "The most frequent mistake writers make is writing to a general audience rather than teachers. We'll be looking for writing that considers the increasing ethnic diversity of classrooms and the greater age-range among elementary teachers."

JOURNAL OF CAREER PLANNING & EMPLOYMENT, College Placement Council, Inc., 62 Highland Ave., Bethlehem PA 18017. (215)868-1421. FAX: (215)868-0208. Editor: Patricia Sinnott. 25% freelance written. Published Nov., Jan., March and May. A magazine for career development professionals who counsel and/ or hire college students, graduating students, employees and job-changers. Circ. 4,000. Pays on acceptance. Publishes ms an average of 4 months after acceptance. Byline given. Buys first rights. Photocopied submissions OK. Computer printout submissions acceptable; no dot-matrix. Reports in 1 month on queries; 2 months on mss. Free writer's guidelines for #10 SASE.

Nonfiction: Book excerpts, how-to, humor, interview/profile, opinion, photo feature, new techniques/innovative practices and current issues in the field. No articles that speak directly to job candidates. Buys 7-10 mss/year. Query with published clips, or send complete ms. Length: 2,000-4,000 words. Pays $200-400.

Tips: "A freelancer can best break into our publication by sending query with clips of published work, by writing on topics that aim directly at the journal's audience—professionals in the college career planning, placement and recruitment field—and by using an easy-to-read, narrative style rather than a formal, thesis style. The area of our publication most open to freelancers is nonfiction feature articles only. Make sure that the topic is directly relevant to the career planning and employment of the college educated and that the style is crisp and easy to read."

LEARNING 90, 1111 Bethlehem Pike, Springhouse PA 19477. Editor: Charlene F. Gaynor. 45% freelance written. Published monthly during school year. Emphasizes elementary and junior high school education topics. Circ. 275,000. Pays on acceptance. Buys all rights. Submit seasonal/holiday material 9 months in advance. Photocopied submissions OK. Computer printout submissions acceptable. Reports in 3 months. Sample copy $3; free writer's guidelines.

Nonfiction: "We publish manuscripts that describe innovative, practical teaching strategies or probe controversial and significant issues of interest to kindergarten to 8th grade teachers." How-to (classroom management, specific lessons or units or activities for children—all at the elementary and junior high level, and hints for teaching in all curriculum areas): personal experience (from teachers in elementary and junior high schools); and profile (with teachers who are in unusual or innovative teaching situations). Strong interest in articles that deal with discipline, teaching strategy, motivation and working with parents. Buys 250 mss/year. Query. Length: 1,000-3,500 words. Pays $50-350.

Photos: State availability of photos with query. Model release required. "We are also interested in series of photos that show step-by-step projects or tell a story that will be of interest."

Tips: "We're looking for practical, teacher-tested ideas and strategies as well as first-hand personal accounts of dramatic successes—or failures—with a lesson to be drawn. We're also interested in examples of especially creative classrooms and teachers. Emphasis on professionalism will increase: top teachers telling what they do best and others can also."

LOLLIPOPS, The Magazine for Early Childhood Educators, Good Apple, Inc., 1204 Buchanan, Box 299, Carthage IL 62321. (212)357-3981. Editor: Jerry Aten. 20% freelance written. A magazine published 5 times a year providing easy-to-use, hands-on practical teaching ideas and suggestions for early childhood education. Circ. 17,000. Pays on publication. Months until publication vary. Buys all rights. Submit seasonal/holiday material 6 months in advance. Computer printout submissions acceptable; prefers letter-quality. Sample copy for 8×12 SAE with 3 first class stamps; writer's guidelines for #10 SAE with 2 first class stamps.

Nonfiction: How-to (on creating usable teaching materials). Buys varying number of mss/year. Query with or without published clips, or send complete ms. Length: 200-1,000 words. Pays $25-100 for assigned articles; pays $10-30 for unsolicited articles. Writer has choice of cash or Good Apple products worth twice the contract value.

Photos: State availability of photos with submission. Reviews contact sheets and transparencies. Offers $10 minimum/photo. Model releases and identification of subjects required. Buys all rights.

Columns/Departments: Accepts material dealing with the solving of problems encountered by early childhood education. Buys varying number of mss/year. Query with published clips. Length: varies. Pays $25-100.

Fiction: Adventure and fantasy (for young children). Query with published clips.

Poetry: Light verse. Buys varying number of poems/year.

Tips: "I'm always looking for something that's new and different—something that works for teachers of young children."

‡MEDIA PROFILES: The Health Sciences Edition, Olympic Media Information, 550 1st St., Hoboken NJ 07030. (201)963-1600. Publisher: Walt Carroll. 100% freelance written. For hospital education departments, nursing schools, schools of allied health, paramedical training units, colleges, community colleges, local health organizations. Serial, in magazine format, published every 2 months. Circ. 1,000+. Pays on publication. Publishes ms an average of 6 months after acceptance. Buys all rights. Buys 240 mss/year. Electronic submissions OK on PC DOS only. Computer printout submissions acceptable. "Sample copies and writer's guidelines sent on receipt of resume, background, and mention of audiovisual hardware you have access to. Enclose $5 for writer's guidelines and sample issue. (Refunded with first payment upon publication)." Reports in 1 month. Query.

Nonfiction: "Reviews of all kinds of audiovisual media. We are the only review publication devoted exclusively to evaluation of audiovisual aids for hospital and health training. We have a highly specialized, definite format that must be followed in all cases. Samples should be seen by all means. Our writers should first have a background in health sciences; second, have some experience with audiovisuals; and third, follow our format precisely. Writers with advanced degrees and teaching affiliations with colleges and hospital education departments given preference. We are interested in reviews of media materials for nursing education, in-service education, continuing education, personnel training, patient education, patient care and medical problems. We will assign audiovisual aids to qualified writers and send them these to review for us. Unsolicited mss not welcome." Pays $15/review.

MOMENTUM, National Catholic Educational Association, 1077 30th St. NW, Washington DC 20007. Editor: Patricia Feistritzer. 10% freelance written. Quarterly magazine. For Catholic administrators and teachers, some parents and students, in all levels of education (preschool, elementary, secondary, higher). Circ. 20,000. Pays on publication. Buys first serial rights. Reports in 3 months. Free sample copy.
Nonfiction: Articles concerned with educational philosophy, psychology, methodology, innovative programs, teacher training, research, financial and public relations programs and management systems — all applicable to nonpublic schools. Book reviews on educational/religious topics. Avoid general topics or topics applicable *only* to public education. "We look for a straightforward, journalistic style with emphasis on practical examples, as well as scholarly writing and statistics. All references must be footnoted, fully documented. Emphasis is on professionalism." Buys 28-36 mss/year. Query with outline. Length: 1,500-2,000 words. Pays 2¢/word.
Photos: Pays $25 for b&w glossy photos purchased with mss. Captions required.

NATIONAL BEAUTY SCHOOL JOURNAL, Milady Publishing Corp., 3839 White Plains Rd., Bronx NY 10467. (212)881-3000. Editor: Mary Jane Tenerelli. Associate Editor: Mary Healy. 75% freelance written. Works with a small number of new/unpublished writers each year. A monthly magazine covering cosmetology education. "Articles must address subjects pertinent to cosmetology education (i.e. articles which will assist the instructor in the classroom or the school owner to run his or her business)." Circ. 4,000 schools. Pays on publication. Publishes ms an average of 2 months after acceptance. Byline given. Buys first rights. Submit seasonal/holiday material 3 months in advance. Simultaneous submissions, photocopied submissions, and previously published submissions OK. Computer printout submissions acceptable; prefers letter-quality. Free sample copy with writer's guidelines.
Nonfiction: Book excerpts, essays, historical/nostalgic, how-to (on doing a haircut, teaching a technique) humor, interview/profile, new product, personal experience, photo feature and technical. No articles geared to the salon owner or operator instead of the cosmetology school instructor or owner. Buys 24 mss/year. Query with published clips, or send complete ms. Length: 500-3,000 words. Pays $150 if published.
Photos: Send photos with submissions. Reviews 5x7 b&w prints. Offers no additional payment for photos accepted with ms. Identification of subjects required. Buys first rights; make sure reprint permission is granted.
Columns Departments: Buys 6 mss/year; willing to start new departments. Length: 500-1,000 words. Pays $150.
Fiction: Humorous and slice-of-life vignettes. No fiction relating to anything other than the classroom or the beauty school business. Send complete ms. Length: 500-3,000 words. Pays $150.
Tips: "Talk to school owners and instructors to get a feel for the industry. All areas of our publication are open. Write in clear, simple language."

‡PHI DELTA KAPPAN, Box 789, Bloomington IN 47402-0789. Editor: Pauline B. Gough 2% freelance written. Monthly magazine; 80 pages. For educators — teachers, kindergarten-12 administrators and college professors. All hold BA degrees; one-third hold doctorates. Circ. 150,000. Buys all rights. Pays on publication. Publishes ms an average of 6 months after acceptance. Reports in 2 months. Free sample copy.
Nonfiction: Feature articles on education — emphasizing policy, trends, both sides of issues, controversial developments. Also informational, how-to, personal experience, inspirational, humor, think articles and expose. "Our audience is scholarly but hard-headed." Buys 5 mss/year. Submit complete ms. Length: 500-4,000 words. Pays $250-800. "We pay a fee only occasionally, and then it is usually to an author whom *we* seek out. We do welcome inquiries from freelancers, but it is misleading to suggest that we buy very much from them."
Photos: Pays average photographer's rates for b&w photos purchased with mss, but captions are required. Will purchase photos on assignment. Sizes: 8x10 or 5x7 preferred.

SCHOOL ARTS MAGAZINE, 50 Portland St., Worcester MA 01608. Editor: Kent Anderson. 85% freelance written. Monthly, except June, July and August. Serves arts and craft education profession, kindergarten-12, higher education and museum education programs. Written by and for art teachers. Pays on publication. Publishes ms an average of 3 months "if timely; if less pressing, can be 1 year or more" after acceptance. Buys first serial rights and second serial (reprint) rights. Computer printout submissions acceptable; prefers letter-quality. Reports in 3 months. Sample copy for 8½x11 SAE and $1.50; free writer's guidelines.
Nonfiction: Articles, with photos, on art and craft activities in schools. Should include description and photos of activity in progress as well as examples of finished art work. Query or send complete ms. Length: 600-1,400 words. Pays $20-100.
Tips: "We prefer articles on actual art projects or techniques done by students in actual classroom situations. Philosophical and theoretical aspects of art and art education are usually handled by our contributing editors. Our articles are reviewed and accepted on merit and each is tailored to meet our needs. Keep in mind that art teachers want practical tips, above all. Our readers are visually, not verbally, oriented. Write your article

with the accompanying photographs in hand." The most frequent mistakes made by writers are "bad visual material (photographs, drawings) submitted with articles, or a lack of complete descriptions of art processes; and no rationale behind programs or activities. It takes a close reading of *School Arts* to understand its function and the needs of its readers. Some writers lack the necessary familiarity with art education."

SCHOOL SHOP, Prakken Publications, Inc., Box 8623, Ann Arbor MI 48107 FAX: (313)769-8383. Editor: Alan H. Jones. 100% freelance written. Eager to work with new/unpublished writers. A monthly (except June and July) magazine covering issues, trends and projects of interest to industrial, vocational, technical and technology educators at the secondary and post secondary school levels. Special issue in April deals with varying topics for which mss are solicited. Circ. 45,000. Buys all rights. Pays on publication. Publishes ms an average of 8-12 months after acceptance. Byline given. Prefers authors who have direct connection with the field of industrial and/or technical education. Submit seasonal material 6 months in advance. Simultaneous queries, and simultaneous, photocopied, and previously published submissions OK. Computer printout submissions acceptable; prefers letter-quality. Reports in 6 weeks. Free sample copy and writer's guidelines.

Nonfiction: Uses articles pertinent to the various teaching areas in industrial education (woodwork, electronics, drafting, machine shop, graphic arts, computer training, etc.). "The outlook should be on innovation in educational programs, processes or projects which directly apply to the industrial/technical education area." Buys general interest, how-to, opinion, personal experience, technical and think pieces, interviews, humor, and coverage of new products. Buys 135 unsolicited mss/year. Length: 200-2,000 words. Pays $25-150.

Photos: Send photos with accompanying query or ms. Reviews b&w and color prints. Payment for photos included in payment for ms.

Columns/Departments: Shop Kinks (brief items which describe short-cuts or special procedures relevant to the industrial arts classroom). Buys 30 mss/year. Send complete ms. Length: 20-100 words. Pays $15 minimum.

Tips: "We are most interested in articles written by industrial, vocational and technical educators about their class projects and their ideas about the field. We need more and more technology-related articles."

TEACHING/K-8, The Professional Magazine, Early Years, Inc., 40 Richards Ave., 7th Fl., Norwalk CT 06854. (203)454-1020. Editor: Allen Raymond. 90% freelance written. "We prefer material from classroom teachers." A monthly magazine covering teaching of kindergarten through eighth grades. Pays on publication. Publishes ms an average of 2-7 months after acceptance. Byline given. Buys all rights. Submit seasonal/holiday material 6 months in advance. Computer printout submissions acceptable; prefers letter-quality. Reports in 6 weeks. Sample copy $2 with 9x12 SASE; writer's guidelines for #10 SAE with 1 first class stamp.

Nonfiction: Patricia Broderick, editorial director. Classroom curriculum material. Send complete ms. Length: 1,200-1,500 words. Pays $35 maximum.

Photos: Offers no additional payment for photos accepted with ms. Model releases and identification of subjects required.

Columns/Departments: Patricia Broderick, editorial director. Send complete ms. Length: 1,100 word maximum. Pays $25 maximum.

Tips: "Manuscripts should be specifically oriented to a successful teaching strategy, idea, project or program. Broad overviews of programs or general theory manuscripts are not usually the type of material we select for publication. Because of the definitive learning level we cover (pre-school through grade eight) we try to avoid presenting general groups of unstructured ideas. We prefer classroom tested ideas and techniques."

‡TEACHING TODAY, 6112-102 Ave., Edmonton, Alberta T6A-0N4 Canada. (403)465-2990. Editor: Betty Coderre. Managing Editor: Max Coderre. 90% freelance written. Educational magazine published 5 times per year. Circ. 16,921. Pays on publication. Publishes ms an average of 6-12 months after acceptance. Byline given. Buys first rights, one-time rights or all rights. Simultaneous, photocopied and previously published submissions OK. Query for electronic submissions. Computer printout submissions OK; prefers letter-quality. Free sample and writer's guidelines.

Nonfiction: How-to (related to teaching), humor (related to education), inspirational, interview/profile (publicly visible people's views on education), personal experience (if related to teaching), communication skills and professional development (teacher). Buys 40-50 mss/year. Query with published clips. Length: 150-1,500 words. Pays $20-225 for assigned articles; $15-150 for unsolicited articles. Sometimes pays expenses of writers on assignment.

For explanation of symbols, see the Key to Symbols and Abbreviations on Page 5. For unfamiliar words, see the Glossary.

Photos: Send photos with submission. Reviews 4x5 prints. Offers $25-100 per photo. Model releases and identification of subjects required. Buys one-time rights.

Fillers: Anecdotes and gags to be illustrated by cartoonist. Buys 20/year. Length: 20-100 words. Pays $5-25.

Tips: "A freelancer can best break into our magazine with articles, cartoons, fillers related to education. Articles primarily that will *help* educators personally or professionally."

TODAY'S CATHOLIC TEACHER, 26 Reynolds Ave., Ormond Beach FL 32074. (904)672-9974. Editor-in-Chief: Ruth A. Matheny. 40% freelance written. Works with a small number of new/unpublished writers each year. For administrators, teachers and parents concerned with Catholic schools, both parochial and CCD. Circ. 65,000. Pays after publication. Publishes ms an average of 3 months after acceptance. Byline given. Buys all rights. Phone queries OK. Submit seasonal/holiday material 3 months in advance. Sample copy $3; writer's guidelines for #10 SASE; mention *Writer's Market* in request.

Nonfiction: How-to (based on experience, particularly in Catholic situations, philosophy with practical applications); interview (of practicing educators, educational leaders); personal experience (classroom happenings); and profile (of educational leader). Buys 40-50 mss/year. Submit complete ms. Length: 800-2,000 words. Pays $15-75.

Photos: State availability of photos with ms. Offers no additional payment for 8x10 b&w glossy prints. Buys one-time rights. Captions preferred; model release required.

Tips: "We prefer articles based on the author's own expertise, and/or experience, with a minimum of quotations from other sources. We use many one-page features."

Electronics and Communication

These publications are edited for broadcast and telecommunications technicians and engineers, electrical engineers and electrical contractors. Included are journals for electronic equipment designers and operators who maintain electronic and telecommunication systems. Publications for appliance dealers can be found in Home Furnishings and Household Goods.

BROADCAST TECHNOLOGY, Box 420, Bolton, Ontario L7E 5T3 Canada. (416)857-6076. FAX: (416)857-6045. Editor-in-Chief: Doug Loney. 50% freelance written. Monthly (except August, December) magazine. Emphasizes broadcast engineering. Circ. 9,000. Pays on publication. Byline given. Buys all rights. Phone queries OK.

Nonfiction: Technical articles on developments in broadcast engineering, especially pertaining to Canada. Query. Length: 500-1,500 words. Pays $100-300.

Photos: Purchased with accompanying ms. B&w or color. Captions required.

Tips: "Most of our outside writing is by regular contributors, usually employed full-time in broadcast engineering. The specialized nature of our magazine requires a specialized knowledge on the part of a writer."

‡**BROADCASTER,** Northern Miner Press Ltd., 7 Labatt Ave., Toronto, Ontario M5A 3P2 Canada. (416)363-6111. FAX: (416)861-9564. Editor: Lynda Ashley. Monthly broadcasting trade journal. "Must be Canadian in focus, and relevant to a national audience." Circ. 8,500. Pays on publication. Publishes ms an averate of 2 months after acceptance. Byline given. Offers 10% kill fee. Buys all rights. Submit seasonal/holiday material 3 months in advance. Photocopied submissions OK. Computer printout submissions OK; prefers letter-quality. Reports in 3 weeks on queries; 2 weeks on mss. Free sample copy.

Nonfiction: Interview/profile and new product. Buys 20 mss/year. Query with published clips. Length: 1,000-2,000 words. Pays $200-400 for assigned articles; $200-350 for unsolicited articles. Pays expenses of writers on assignment.

Photos: Send photos with submission. Reviews 8x10 prints. Offers no additional payment for photos accepted with ms. Identification of subjects required. Buys one-time rights.

‡**BUSINESS RADIO,** National Assoc. of Business & Educational Radio, 1501 Duke St., Alexandria VA 22314. (703)739-0300. Editor: Mark C. Huey. Managing Editor: Diane C. Flaherty. 25% freelance written. Magazine is published 10 times/year on two-way radio communications. "Magazine is for land mobile equipment users, dealers, service shop operators, manufacturers, communications technicians, SMR owners and operators. To acquaint members with the diversity of uses to which land mobile radio can be applied. To identify and

discuss new and developing areas of RF technology and their application." Circ. 6,000. Pays on acceptance. Publishes ms an average of 3 months after acceptance. Byline given. Buys first rights. Photocopied and previously published submissions OK. Query for electronic submissions. Computer printout submissions OK; prefers letter-quality. Reports in 1 month. Sample copy for 9x12 SAE with 5 first class stamps. Writer's guidelines for 9x12 SASE.

Nonfiction: General interest, interview/profile, new product, technical, and general — small business or management articles all related to two-way (land mobile) communications. Buys 5 mss/year. Query with or without published clips, or send complete ms. Length: 2,500-4,000 words. Pays $150-300 for unsolicited articles. Manufacturers often write articles for us. Sometimes pays expenses of writers on assignment.

Photos: Send photos with submission. Reviews contact sheets, negatives, transparencies and prints. Offers no additional payment for b&w photos accepted with ms. Offers $200-250 per photo if color used for cover. Captions, model releases and identification of subjects required. Buys one-time rights.

Columns/Departments: Management Notebook (small business, general management), 2,000-3,000 words. Buys 8 mss/year. Query or send complete ms. Pays $50-150.

Tips: "Many people use two-way radios. Any of them could be a potential article."

CABLE MARKETING, The Marketing/Management Magazine for Cable Television Executives, Jobson Publishing, 352 Park Ave. So., New York NY 10010. (212)685-4848. Editor: Ellis Simon. 10% freelance written. Prefers to work with published/established writers. Monthly magazine for cable industry executives dealing with marketing and management topics, new trends and developments and their impact. Circ. 15,000. Pays on publication. Publishes ms an average of 2 months after acceptance. Byline given. Buys first North American serial rights. Photocopied submissions OK. Computer printout submissions acceptable; prefers letter-quality. Reports in 1 month. Free sample copy.

Columns/Departments: Cable Tech (technology, engineering and new products); and Cable Scan (news items and marketing featurettes mostly about cable system activities and developments). Buys 20 mss/year. Query with published clips. Length: 200-3,000 words. Pays $50-500. Pays the expenses of writers on assignment.

Tips: "Learn something about the cable TV business before you try to write about it. Have specific story ideas. Have some field of expertise that you can draw upon (e.g., marketing, management or advertising). Short articles and fillers give us a chance to better assess a writer's real abilities without exposing us to undue risk, expense, aggravation, etc., on a feature. Not interested in reviews of programming. Editorial focus is on the *business* of cable television."

‡CABLE TELEVISION BUSINESS MAGAZINE, Cardiff Publishing Co., #650, 6300 S. Syracuse Way, Englewood CO 80111. (303)220-0600. FAX: (303)773-9716. Editor: Chuck Moozakis. 10% freelance written. Prefers writers with telecommunications background. Semimonthly magazine about cable television for CATV system operators and equipment suppliers. Circ. 12,000. Pays on publication. Publishes ms an average of 1 month after acceptance. Byline given. Makes work-for-hire assignments. Phone queries OK. Query for electronic submissions. Computer printout submissions acceptable. Reports in 2 weeks on queries; 1 month on mss. Free sample copy and writer's guidelines.

Nonfiction: Exposé (of industry corruption and government mismanagement); historical (early days of CATV); interview (of important people in the industry); profiles (of people or companies); how-to (manage or engineer cable systems); new product (description and application); and case history. "We use articles on all aspects of cable television from programming through government regulation to technical pieces. We use both color and b&w photos, charts and graphs. A writer should have some knowledge of cable television, then send a letter with a proposed topic." No first person articles. Buys 5 mss/year. Query. Length: 1,800-3,500 words. Pays $100/page of magazine space. Sometimes pays expenses of writers on assignment.

Photos: State availability of photos. Reviews 35mm color transparencies. Pays $50/page of magazine space for contact sheets. Offers no additional payment for photos accepted with ms. Captions required.

Tips: "The most frequent mistake made by writers in completing an article for us is not being specific enough about what the story topic really means to cable management — i.e., dollars and cents, or operational strategy. Freelancers are only used for major features."

‡CABLECASTER, Northern Miner Press Ltd., 7 Labatt Ave., Toronto, Ontario M5A 3P2 Canada. (416)363-6111. FAX: (416)861-9564. Editor: Lynda Ashley. Monthly magazine on the cable industry. "National magazine for the Canadian cable industry. Focus on management/technical regulatory issues." Estab. 1989. Pays on publication. Offers 10% kill fee. Buys all rights. Submit seasonal/holiday material 3 months in advance. Photocopied submissions OK. Computer printout submissions OK; prefers letter-quality. Reports in 3 weeks on queries; 2 weeks on mss. Free sample copy.

Nonfiction: General interest, interview/profile and new product. Buys 20 mss/year. Query with published clips. Length: 1,000-2,000 words. Pays $300-400 for assigned articles; $200-350 for unsolicited articles. Pays expenses of writers on assignment.

Photos: Send photos with submission. Reviews 8x10 prints.

Tips: "Focus must be on the Canadian cable industry—the people, issues and technology that drive the industry."

‡**HAM RADIO MAGAZINE**, Main St., Greenville NH 03048. (603)878-1441. Editor: T.H. Tenney, Jr. Managing Editor: Terry Northrup. 75% freelance written. Monthly magazine on amateur radio theory and equipment construction. Circ. 36,000. Pays on publication. Publishes ms an average of 6 months after acceptance. Byline given. Buys first rights. Query for electronic submissions. Computer printout submissions OK. Reports in 1 month. Sample copy $5. Writer's guidelines for #10 SASE.

Nonfiction: Contact: Marty Durham, technical editor. How-to and technical. "We have four special issues per year: January: Construction Issue; May: Antenna Issue; July: VHF/UHF Issue; and November: Receiver Issue. No human interest stories (like 'How I Saved the World with my Ham Radio'), contest information, information on awards. We are a technical publication." Send complete ms. Pays $40 per published page. "We have given subscriptions or books from our bookstore authors have requested such a payment instead."

Photos: Send photos with submission. Reviews 5x7 prints. Offers no additional payment for photos accepted with ms. Captions and identification of subjects required. Buys one-time rights.

Columns/Departments: Ham Notes (Quick fixes for problems with equipment, antennas, etc.). Send complete ms.

Tips: "The best way a writer can 'break in' to our publication is to have a working knowledge of amateur radio and a project of interest to other hams. Our Author's Guide offers tips on how to get started writing for our publication. Authors are welcome to submit feature articles or short pieces for our Ham Notes section."

INFORMATION TODAY, Learned Information Inc., 143 Old Marlton Pike, Medford NJ 08055. (609)654-6266. FAX: (609)654-4309. Publisher: Thomas H. Hogan. Editor: Patricia Lane. 30% freelance written. A tabloid for the users and producers of electronic information services, published 11 times per year. Circ. 10,000. Pays on publication. Publishes ms an average of 1 month after acceptance. Byline given. Buys first North American serial rights. Submit seasonal/holiday material 2 months in advance. Computer printout submissions acceptable; prefers letter-quality. Reports in 2 weeks. Free sample copy and writer's guidelines.

Nonfiction: Book reviews; interview/profile and new product; technical (dealing with computerized information services); and articles on library technology, artificial intelligence, database and Videotex services." We also cover software and optical publishing (CD-ROM). More focus on coverage of integrated online library systems." Buys approximately 25 mss/year. Query with published clips or send complete ms on speculation. Length: 500-1,500 words. Pays $80-200.

Photos: State availability of photos with submission.

Tips: "We look for clearly-written, informative articles dealing with the electronic delivery of information. Writing style should not be jargon-laden or heavily technical."

‡**INSTALLATION NEWS, The Technical Journal of Automotive Electronics**, Bobit Publishing, 2512 Artesia Blvd., Redondo Beach CA 90278. (213)376-8788. FAX: (213)376-9043. Editor: Doug Newcomb. 10-20% freelance written. Monthly magazine on aftermarket automotive electronics. "Our readers install and sell market automotive electronics (car audio, car security, cellular telephones, etc.). We are looking for technical, hands-on types of articles that will make their jobs easier." Circ. 17,000. Pays on acceptance. Publishes an average of 1-2 months after acceptance. Byline given. Buys first rights. Simultaneous and photocopied submissions OK. Computer printout submissions OK; prefers letter-quality. Reports in 2 weeks. Free sample copy.

Nonfiction: How-to (technical how-to articles dealing with automotive electronics), photo feature and technical. Length: 1,000-2,000 words. Sometimes pays expenses of writers on assignment.

Photos: State availability of photos with submissions. Reviews contact sheets, negatives, transparencies and 5x7 prints. Offers no additional payment for photos accepted with ms. Identification of subjects required. Buys one-time rights.

Tips: "Freelancers are most often used for writing highly technical or research-heavy stories. The freelancer does not necessarily have to be a technical person, but her or she must be able to relay the information in a concise, clear and interesting form."

MICROWAVES & RF, Ten Holland Dr., Hasbrouck Heights NJ 07604. (201)393-6285. FAX: (201)393-6388. Associate Publisher/Editor: Michael Kachmar. 50% freelance written. Eager to work with new/unpublished writers. Monthly magazine emphasizing radio frequency design. "Qualified recipients are those individuals actively engaged in microwave and RF research, design, development, production and application engineering, engineering management, administration or purchasing departments in organizations and facilities where

For information on setting your freelance fees, see How Much Should I Charge? in the Business of Writing section.

application and use of devices, systems and techniques involve frequencies from HF through visible light." Circ. 65,000. Pays on publication. Publishes ms an average of 6 months after acceptance. Buys all rights. Phone queries OK. Photocopied submissions OK. Query for electronic submissions. Computer printouts acceptable "if legible." Reports in 1 month. Free sample copy and writer's guidelines; mention *Writer's Market* in request.

Nonfiction: "We are interested in material on research and development in microwave and RF technology and economic news that affects the industry." How-to (circuit design), new product, opinion, and technical. Buys 100 mss/year. Query. Pays $100.

OUTSIDE PLANT, Box 183, Cary IL 60013. (312)639-2200. FAX: (312)639-9542. Editor: John S. Saxtan. 50% freelance written. Prefers to work with published/established writers. Trade publication focusing exclusively on the outside plant segment of the telephone industry. Readers are end users and/or specifiers at Bell and independent operating companies, as well as long distance firms whose chief responsibilities are construction, maintenance, planning and fleet management. Readership also includes telephone contracting firms. Published 10 issues in 1989. Circ. 17,000. Buys first rights. Pays on publication. Publishes ms an average of 3 months after acceptance. Computer printout submissions OK; prefers letter-quality. Reports in 1 month. Free sample copy and guidelines for #10 SASE.

Nonfiction: Must deal specifically with outside plant construction, maintenance, planning and fleet vehicle subjects for the telephone industry. "Case history application articles profiling specific telephone projects are best. Also accepts trend features, tutorials, industry research and seminar presentations. Preferably, features should be by-lined by someone at the telephone company profiled." Pays $35-50/published page, including photographs; pays $35 for cover photos.

Departments: OSP Tips & Advice (short nuts-and-bolts items on new or unusual work methods); and OSP Tommorrow (significant trends in outside plant), 300-600 word items. Pays $5-50. Other departments include new products, literature, vehicles and fiber optics.

Tips: Submissions should include author bio demonstrating expertise in the subject area."

PRO SOUND NEWS, International News Magazine for the Professional Sound Production Industry, 2 Park Ave., New York NY 10016. (212)213-3444. Editor: Jeffrey Schwartz. 20% freelance written. Works with a small number of new/unpublished writers each year. Monthly tabloid covering the music recording, concert sound reinforcement, TV and film sound industry. Circ. 18,000. Pays on publication. Publishes ms an average of 1 month after acceptance. Byline given. Buys first serial rights. Simultaneous queries, and photocopied and previously published submissions OK. Query for electronic submissions. Computer printout submissions acceptable. Reports in 2 weeks.

Nonfiction: Query with published clips. Pays $150-300 for assigned articles (approximately 1,000 words). Sometimes pays the expenses of writers on assignment.

‡RADIO WORLD NEWSPAPER, Industrial Marketing Advisory Services, Suite 310, 5827 Columbia Pike, Falls Church VA 22041. (703)998-7600. FAX: (703)998-2966. Editor: Judith Gross. News Editor: Alan Carter. 50% freelance written. Bimonthly newspaper on radio station technology and regulatory news. "Articles should be geared toward radio station engineers, producers, technical people and managers wishing to learn more about technical subjects. The approach should be more how-to than theoretical, although emerging technology may be approached in a more abstract way." Pays on publication. Publishes ms an average of 1-2 months after acceptance. Byline given. Buys first North American serial rights. Submit seasonal/holiday material 2 months in advance. Photocopied submissions OK. Query for electronic submissions. Computer printout submissions OK; prefers letter-quality. Reports in 1-2 months. Free sample copy and writer's guidelines.

Nonfiction: Exposé, historical/nostalgic, how-to (radio equipment maintenance and repair), humor, interview/profile, new product, opinion, personal experience, photo feature and technical. "No general financial, or vogue management concept pieces." Busy 24-40 mss/year. Query. Length: 750-1,250 words. Pays $75-200. Pays in contributor copies or other premiums "if they request it, and for one special feature called Great Idea." Sometimes pays expenses of writers on assignment.

Photos: Send photos with submission. Reviews 3x5 or larger prints. Offers no additional payment for photos accepted with ms. Identification of subjects required. Buys one-time rights.

Columns/Departments: Richard Farrell, Buyers Guide editor. Buyers Guide User Reports (field reports from engineers on specific pieces of radio station equipment). Buys 100 mss/year. Query. Length: 750-1,250 words. Pays $25-125.

Fillers: Newsbreaks and short humor. Buys 6/year. Length: 500-1,000 words. Pays $25-75.

Tips: "I frequently assign articles by phone. Sometimes just a spark of an idea can lead to a story assignment or publication. The best way is to have some radio station experience and try to think of articles other readers would benefit from reading."

SATELLITE RETAILER, Triple D Publishing, Inc., Box 2384, Shelby NC 28151. (704)482-9673. FAX: (704)484-8558. Editor: David B. Melton. 75% freelance written. Monthly magazine covering home satellite TV. "We look for technical, how-to, marketing, sales, new products, product testing, and news for the satellite television dealer." Circ. 12,000. Pays on publication. Byline given. 30% kill fee. Buys all rights. Submit seasonal/holiday material 3 months in advance. Simultaneous and photocopied submissions OK. Query for electronic submissions. Computer printout submissions OK. Free sample copy and writer's guidelines.

Nonfiction: How-to, new product, personal experience, photo feature, technical. Buys 24 mss/year. Query with or without published clips, or send complete ms. Length: 1,800-3,600 words. Pays $150-400. Sometimes pays expenses of writers on assignment.

Photos: Send photos with submission. Reviews contact sheets, transparencies (135 to 4x5). Captions, model releases and identification of subjects required. Buys all rights.

Tips: "Familiarity with electronics and television delivery systems is a definite plus."

‡SHOPTALK, Natl. Assoc. of Business and Educational Radio, 1501 Duke St., Alexandria VA 22314. (703)739-0300. Editor: Mark C. Huey. Managing Editor: Diane C. Flaherty. 25% freelance written. Monthly newsletter about two-way radios. "Newsletter targeted toward dealers, service shop owners and manufacturers of two-way radio. Newsletter supplies info. to help readers manage businesses better." Circ. 1,000. Pays on acceptance. Publishes ms an average of 2 months after acceptance. Byline given. Buys first rights. Submit seasonal/holiday material 2 months in advance. Photocopied and previously published submissions OK. Query for electronic submissions. Computer printout submissions OK; prefers letter-quality. Reports in 1 month. Sample copy for #10 SAE with 2 first class stamps. Writer's guidelines for #10 SAE with 1 first class stamp.

Nonfiction: Book excerpts, essays, how-to, new product and technical, all small business or two-way radio related. Buys 9 mss/year. Query with or without published clips, or send complete ms. Length: 1,500-2,500 words. Pays $50-125 for unsolicited articles.

Photos: Send photos with submission. Reviews contact sheets. Offers no additional payment for photos accepted with ms. Captions, model releases and identification of subjects required. Buys one-time rights.

Tips: "All material should be written clearly and simply. Sidebars are helpful."

‡TECHTALK, Natl. Assoc. of Business and Educational Radio, 1501 Duke St., Alexandria VA 22314. (703)739-0300. Editor: Mark C. Huey. Managing Editor: Diane C. Flaherty. Bimonthly newsletter on two-way radio communications. "Newsletter is for technicians in communications field, especially two-way radio. Material relates to technical changes in the industry, installation procedures, testing and repair methods and self-improvement." Circ. 2,500. Pays on acceptance. Publishes ms an average of 2 months after acceptance. Byline given. Buys first rights. Photocopied and previously published submissions OK. Query for electronic submissions. Computer printout submissions OK; prefers letter-quality. Reports in 1 month. Sample copy for #10 SAE with 2 first class stamps. Writer's guidelines for #10 SAE with 1 first class stamp.

Nonfiction: Book excerpts, essays, how-to, new product and technical, all dealing with communications. Query with or without published clips, or send complete ms. Length: 1,000-2,500 words. Pays $50-125. Pays in contributor copies for "a member of the industry interested in disseminating info."

Photos: Send photos with submission. Reviews contact sheets. Offers no additional payment for photos accepted with ms. Captions, model releases and identification of subjects required.

Tips: "Writer needs a technical background such as tech school training and/or experience in communications, especially land-mobile."

‡TELEVISION BROADCAST, Covering Television Equipment, News Applications and Technology, P.S.N. Publications, Inc., Suite 1820, 2 Park Ave., New York NY 10016. (212)779-1919. Editor: Elliot Luber. 40% freelance written. Monthly tabloid newsmagazine covering television station technology. "We publish a timely, colorful news tabloid targeted toward managers and engineers at television stations and teleproduction facilities in the U.S. The magazine is a balance between news and technology features." Circ. 30,000. Pays on publication. Usually publishes manuscripts the month they are accepted. Byline given. Offers 50% kill fee. Buys all rights. Submit seasonal/holiday material three months in advance. Query for electronic submissions. Computer printout submissions OK. Free sample copy and writer's guidelines.

Nonfiction: Spot news. How-to (on using technology to improve signal quality, profits or community image), interview/profile, personal experience and technical. No articles that appeal mostly to TV viewers. No product reviews. Buys 100 mss per year. Query with published clips and brief résumé. Length: 500-1,500 words. Pays $100-300 for articles. Sometimes pays expenses of writers on assignment.

Photos: Send photos with submission. Reviews contact sheets. Captions, model releases and identification of subjects required.

Columns/Departments: Opinion, Newsmaker (Q&A interview), Engineering Close-up (quarterly special focus section), ENG/News Technology, Teleproduction, Audio for Video, Post Production, Electronic Graphics, Business/Industrial, Transmission, Product Spotlight (technology close-up), Station Breaks (station news), People & Places, New Products. Columns are 800 words; short features for departments up to 1,200 words.

Fillers: 25-100 word news items regarding television stations. Pays up to $30 each.

Tips: "Every city has a leading TV station and a leading video production company. What technological changes are they experiencing in their businesses, and how have they reacted? What have the consequences been?"

‡**VIDEO MANAGER, Management Insights for the Decision Maker**, Montage Publishing, Inc., Suite 314, 25550 Hawthorne Blvd., Torrance CA 90505. (213)373-9993. Editor: Neil Heller. Managing Editor: John Lehrer. 80% freelance written. Monthly magazine of the professional video industry. Circ. 25,000. Pays on publication. Byline given. Offers 50% kill fee. Buys first North American serial rights. Submit seasonal/ holiday material 2 months in advance. Simultaneous, photocopied and previously published submissions OK. Query for electronic submissions. Computer printout submissions OK; prefers letter-quality. Reports in 3 weeks. Free sample copy.
Nonfiction: New product and technical. Buys 75 mss/year. Query with or without published clips, or send complete ms. Length: 1,200-1,500 words. Pays $175-250 for assigned articles. Sometimes pays expenses of writers on assignment.
Photos: Send photos with submission. Reviews transparencies and 5x7 prints. Offers no additional payment for photos accepted with ms. Captions and identification of subjects required. Buys all rights.

‡**VOICE PROCESSING MAGAZINE**, Information Publishing Corp., Suite 100, 3721 Briarpark, Box 42382, Houston TX 77242. (713)974-6637. Editor: Tim Cornitius. Managing Editor: Cheryl Van De Walle. 10% freelance written. Quarterly magazine about the voice processing industry. Estab. 1989. Pays on publication. Publishes ms an average of 2 months after acceptance. Byline given. Offers $100 kill fee. Buys one-time rights. Simultaneous and photocopied submissions OK. Query for electronic submissions. Computer submissions OK. Free sample copy.
Nonfiction: How-to select a voice messaging system, interview/profile, new product and technical. Buys 8-10 mss/year. Query. Length: 2,000-2,400 words. Pays 15¢/word. "Doesn't pay industry insiders for contributions."
Photos: Send photos with submission. Offers no additional payment for photos accepted with ms. Captions required. Buys one-time rights.

———— *Energy and Utilities*

People who supply power to homes, businesses and industry read the publications in this section. This category includes journals covering the electric power, natural gas, petroleum, solar and alternative energy industries.

ALTERNATIVE ENERGY RETAILER, Zackin Publications, Inc., Box 2180, Waterbury CT 06722. (203)755-0158. FAX: (203)755-3480. Editor: Ed Easley. 20% freelance written. Prefers to work with published/established writers. Monthly magazine on selling alternative energy products—chiefly solid fuel burning appliances. "We seek detailed how-to tips for retailers to improve business. Most freelance material purchased is about retailers and how they succeed." Circ. 14,000. Pays on publication. Publishes ms an average of 2 months after acceptance. Buys first North American serial rights. Submit seasonal/holiday material 4 months in advance. Computer printout submissions OK; no dot-matrix. Reports in 2 weeks on queries. Sample copy for 8½x11 SAE with 4 first class stamps; writer's guidelines for #10 SASE.
Nonfiction: How-to (improve retail profits and business know-how); and interview/profile (of successful retailers in this field). No "general business articles not adapted to this industry." Buys 10-20 mss/year. Query. Length: 1,000 words. Pays $200.
Photos: State availability of photos. Pays $25-125 maximum for 5x7 b&w prints. Reviews color slide transparencies. Identification of subject required. Buys one-time rights.
Tips: "We've redesigned into a more sophisticated, visual format. A freelancer can best break in to our publication with features about readers (retailers). Stick to details about what has made this person a success."

ELECTRICAL APPARATUS, The Magazine of the Electrical Aftermarket, Barks Publications, Inc., 400 N. Michigan Ave., Chicago IL 60611-4198. (312)321-9440. Editorial Director: Elsie Dickson. Managing Editor: Kevin N. Jones. Prefers to work with published/established writers. Uses very little freelance material. A monthly magazine for persons working in electrical maintenance, chiefly in industrial plants, who install and service electrical motors, transformers, generators, and related equipment. Circ. 16,000. Pays on acceptance. Publishes ms an average of 2-3 months after acceptance. Byline given. Buys all rights unless other arrangements made. Query for electronic submissions. Computer printout submissions acceptable. Reports in 1 week on queries; 1 month on mss. Sample copy $4.
Nonfiction: Technical. Buys very few mss/year. Query essential, along with letter outlining credentials. Length: 1,500-2,500. Pays $250-500 for assigned articles only. Pays the expenses of writers on assignment by advance arrangement.

Photos: Send photos with submission. "Photos are important to most articles. We prefer 35mm color slides, but sometimes use color or b&w prints." Offers additional payments, depending on quality and number. Captions and identification of subjects required. Buys one-time rights. "If we reuse photos, we pay residual fee."

Columns/Departments: Electrical Manager (items on managing businesses, people), 150-600 words; and Electropix (photo of interest with electrical slant), brief captions. "We are interested in expanding these departments." Pays $50-100.

Tips: "Queries are essential. Technical expertise is absolutely necessary, preferably an E.E. degree, or practical experience. We are also book publishers and some of the material in *EA* is now in book form, bringing the authors royalties."

ELECTRICAL CONTRACTOR, 7315 Wisconsin Ave., Bethesda MD 20814. (301)657-3110. Editor: Larry C. Osius. 10% freelance written. Monthly. For electrical contractors. Circ. 67,000. Publishes ms an average of 3 months after acceptance. Buys first serial rights, second serial (reprint) rights or simultaneous rights. Usually reports in 1 month. Byline given. Free sample copy.

Nonfiction: Installation articles showing informative application of new techniques and products. Slant is product and method contributing to better, faster and more economical construction process. Query. Length: 800-2,500 words. Pays $100/printed page, including photos and illustrative material.

Photos: Photos should be sharp, reproducible glossies, 5x7 and up.

‡NATIONAL UTILITY CONTRACTOR, Suite 606, 1235 Jefferson Davis Hwy., Arlington VA 22202. (703)486-2100. FAX: (703)979-8628. Editor: James B. Gardner. Staff Editor: Jennifer J. Whiteaker. 40% freelance written. Monthly magazine on construction of sewer and water systems (pipe and sewage and water treatment facilities). "Our publication is edited for contractors who construct underground utility systems—primarily sewer and water pipelines and sewage and water treatment plants. Slant: What's new and interesting out on the jobsite." Circ. 12,000. Pays on acceptance. Publishes ms an average of 2 months after acceptance. Byline given. Buys first North American serial rights. Submit seasonal/holiday material 4 months in advance. Query for electronic submissions. Computer printout submissions OK. Reports in 3 weeks on mss. Free sample copy and writer's guidelines.

Nonfiction: How-to, opinion, photo feature, technical and photo job story. Buys 15 mss/year. Query. Length: 1,000-3,000 words. Pays $200-500 for assigned articles; $100-300 for unsolicited articles. Does not return rejected, unsolicited mss. Sometimes pays expenses of writers on assignment.

Photos: Send photos with submission. Reviews contact sheets. Offers $5-25 per photo. Captions and identification of subjects preferred. Buys one-time rights.

Columns/Departments: Safety (articles intended to promote all aspects of safety on the job site), 1,500 words. Buys 10 mss/year. Query. Length: 700-1,500 words. Pays $100-300.

Tips: "Be a photographer and a decent writer. Call the editor, get the names of some members of our association in the writer's local area, and plan to visit the construction sites and write a succinct article about what the contractor is doing on that job site that would interest our other contractor-readers. Most open area is job-site stories. Before writing, contact editor to obtain samples of good stories. Be prepared to supply photographs with informative captions. Other writing opportunities are published in our editorial calendar, which can be requested by phone or in writing."

PUBLIC POWER, 2301 M St. NW, Washington DC 20037. (202)775-8300. Editor/Publisher: Jeanne Wickline LaBella. 20% freelance written. Prefers to work with published/established writers. Bimonthly. Not copyrighted. Pays on acceptance. Publishes ms an average of 3 months after acceptance. Byline given. Query for electronic submissions. Computer printout submissions acceptable. Free sample copy and writer's guidelines.

Nonfiction: Features on municipal and other local publicly-owned electric systems. Payment negotiable. Pays the telephone expenses of writers on assignment.

Photos: Uses b&w glossy and color slides.

UTILITY AND TELEPHONE FLEETS, Practical Communications, Inc., 37 W. Main, Box 183, Cary IL 60013. (312)639-2200. FAX: (312)639-9542. Managing Editor: Alan Richter. 5% freelance written. Bimonthly magazine for fleet managers and maintenance supervisors for electric gas and water utilities; telephone, interconnect and cable TV companies and contractors. "We seek case history/application features covering specific fleet management and maintenance projects/installations. Instructional/tutorial features are also welcome." Circ.18,000. Pays on publication. Publishes ms an average of 1 month after acceptance. Byline given. 20% kill fee. Buys all rights. Submit seasonal/holiday material 2 months in advance. Photocopied submissions OK. Computer printout submissions OK. Reports in 2 weeks. Free sample copy and writer's guidelines.

Nonfiction: How-to (ways for performing fleet maintenance/improving management skills/vehicle tutorials), technical, case history/application features. No advertorials in which specific product or company is promoted. Buys 2-3 ms/year. Query with published clips. Length: 1,000-2,800 words. Pays $50/page.

Photos: Send photos with submission. Reviews contact sheets, negatives, transparencies (3x5) and prints (3x5). Offers no additional payment for photos accepted with ms. Captions required. Buys one-time rights.
Columns/Departments: Vehicle Management and Maintenance Tips (nuts-and-bolts type items dealing with new or unusual methods for fleet management, maintenance and safety). Buys 2 mss/year. Query with published clips. Length: 100-400 words. Pays $10-20.
Tips: "Working for a utility or telephone company and gathering information about a construction, safety or fleet project is the best approach for a freelancer."

Engineering and Technology

Engineers and professionals with various specialties read the publications in this section. Publications for electrical, electronics and telecommunications engineers are classified separately under Electronics and Communication. Magazines for computer professionals are in the Information Systems section.

AMERICAN MACHINIST & Automated Manufacturing, Penton Publishing, Suite 2119, 122 E. 42nd St., New York NY 10168. (212)867-9191. Editor: Joseph Jablonowski. A monthly magazine about durable-goods manufacturing. Circ. 70,000. Pays on acceptance. Publishes ms an average of 4 months after acceptance. Sometimes byline given. Makes work-for-hire assignments. Query for electronic submissions. Computer printout submissions OK. Reports in 2 months on queries; 3 months on mss. Free sample copy.
Nonfiction: Technical. Query with or without published clips, or send complete ms. Length: 1,500-4,000 words. Pays $300-700. Pays the expenses of writers on assignment. Send photos with submission. Offers no additional payment for photos accepted with ms. Buys all rights.
Tips: "Articles that are published are probably 85% engineering details. We're interested in feature articles on technology of manufacturing in the metalworking industries (automaking, aircraft, machinery, etc.). Aim at instructing a 45-year-old degreed mechanical engineer in a new method of making, say, a pump housing."

‡BIONICS, Box 1553, Owosso MI 48867. Editor: Ben Campbell. Managing Editor: Ray Band. 50% freelance written. Quarterly newsletter on bionics. Estab. 1988. Circ. 1,500. Pay on publication. Buys first North American serial rights, first rights, one-time rights, second serial (reprint) rights and simultaneous rights. Submit seasonal/holiday material 3 months in advance. Simultaneous, photocopied and previously published submissions OK. Computer printout submissions OK; prefers letter-quality. Reports in 2 weeks on queries. Sample copy $10. Free writer's guidelines.
Nonfiction: Book excerpts, how-to, interview/profile, new product, opinion, personal experience and technical. Buys 24 mss/year. Query with or without published clips, or send complete ms. Length: 50-5,000 words. Pays 3-5¢/words. Sometimes pays expenses of writers on assignment.
Photos: Send photos with submission. Reviews negatives and 5x8 transparencies. Offers $10-50 per photo. Model releases required. Buys one-time rights.
Columns/Departments: Bionics, Bi-sensors, Bio-Medical and Robotics. Buys 24 mss/year. Send complete ms. Length: 50-1,000 words.
Fiction: Ethnic, experimental and novel excerpts. Buys 12 mss/year. Query. Length: 50-5,000 words.
Fillers: Facts and newsbreaks. Buys 36/year. Length: 50-200 words.
Tips: "Consult with industry experts. Read the latest magazine articles."

‡CANADIAN RESEARCH, Maclean Hunter, Suite 500, 245 Fairview Mall Dr., Wilburdale, Ontario M2J 4T1 Canada. (416)490-0220. Editor: Tom Gale. 60% freelance written. Monthly magazine on hard sciences at PhD level. Circ. 15,000. Pays on acceptance. Publishes ms an average of 3 months after acceptance. Byline given. Offers 50% kill fee. Buys first North American serial rights and one-time rights. Query for electronic submissions. Computer printout submissions OK; prefers letter-quality. Sample copy $3.
Nonfiction: How-to (science techniques), new product, opinion and technical. Buys 50 mss/year. Query. Length: 150-3,000 words. Pays 23¢/word. Sometimes pays expenses of writers on assignment.
Photos: Send photos with submission. Reviews transparencies and prints. Offers $25 per photo. Captions, model releases and identification of subjects required. Buys one-time rights.
Fillers: Facts and newsbreaks. Buys 50/year. Length: 50-200 words. Pays 23¢/word.
Tips: "Be damn good, and *scientifically accurate!*"

‡DESIGN MANAGEMENT, (formerly *Design Graphics World*), Communication Channels, Inc., 6255 Barfield Rd., Atlanta GA 30328. (404)256-9800. FAX: (404)256-3116. Editor: Eric Torrey. 10% freelance written. Works with a small number of new/unpublished writers each year. A monthly magazine covering design graphics in the architecture, engineering and construction community. Circ. 41,500. Pays on publication. Publishes ms an average of 2 months after acceptance. Byline given. 10% kill fee. Buys all rights. Submit seasonal/holiday material 3 months in advance. Computer printout submissions acceptable; no dot-matrix. Reports in 1 month on queries; 2 weeks on mss. Sample copy for 10x13 SAE.
Nonfiction: How-to, interview/profile, new product and technical. "Articles should be knowledgeable, informative and written for professional architects, engineers and designers." No product sales information, brand- or product-specific information features. Buys 8 mss/year. Query with published clips. Length: 500-2,000 words. Pays $50-500 for assigned article. Sometimes pays the expenses of writers on assignment.
Photos: Send photos with submission. Reviews 2x2 transparencies and 5x7 prints. Offers no additional payment for photos accepted with ms. Identification of subjects required. Buys all rights.
Tips: "Writers should be capable of dropping consumer-prose writing styles and adopt more technical language and usage."

GRADUATING ENGINEER, McGraw-Hill, 1221 Avenue of the Americas, New York NY 10020. (212)512-4123. FAX: (212)512-3334. Editor: J. Robert Connor. Managing Editor: Bill D. Miller. 90% freelance written. Prefers to work with published/established writers. Published September-March "to help graduating engineers make the transition from campus to the working world." Circ. 83,000. Pays on acceptance. Publishes ms an average of 2 months after acceptance. Byline given. Buys first North American serial rights. Reports in 3 weeks. Free sample copy and writer's guidelines.
Nonfiction: General interest (on management, human resources); and career entry, interpersonal skills, job markets, careers, career trends. Special issues include Minority, Women and Computer. Buys 100 mss/year. Query. Length: 2,000-3,000 words. Pays $300-700.
Photos: State availability of photos, illustrations or charts. Reviews 35mm color transparencies, 8x10 b&w glossy prints. Captions and model release required.
Tips: "We're generating new types of editorial. We closely monitor economy here and abroad so that our editorial reflects economic, social, and global trends."

HIGH TECHNOLOGY CAREERS, %Writers Connection, Suite 180, 1601 Saratoga-Sunnyvale Rd., Cupertino CA 95014. (408)973-0227. FAX: (408)973-1219. Managing Editor: Meera Lester. 100% freelance written. Monthly tabloid on high technology industries. "Articles must have a high technology tie-in and should be written in a positive and lively manner. The audience includes managers, engineers and other professionals working in the high technology industries." Circ. 348,000. Pays on publication. Publishes ms an average of 3 months after acceptance. Byline given. Offers 25% kill fee. Buys all rights. Query for electronic submissions. Computer printout submissions OK; prefers letter-quality. Reports in 3 weeks. Free sample copy; writer's guidelines for #10 SASE.
Nonfiction: General interest (with high tech tie-in), technical. No career-oriented material, company or personal profiles. Buys 36 mss/year. Query with or without published clips, or send complete ms. Length: 1,500-2,000 words. Pays 17½¢/word. Sometimes pays expenses of writers on assignment.
Photos: State availability of photo with submission.

LASER FOCUS WORLD MAGAZINE, One Technology Park Dr., Box 989, Westford MA 01886. (508)692-0700. FAX: (508)692-0525. Publisher: Dr. Morris Levitt. Editor-in-Chief: Dr. Lewis M. Holmes. Managing Editor: Barbara Murray. Less than 10% freelance written. A monthly magazine for physicists, scientists and engineers involved in the research and development, design, manufacturing and applications of lasers, laser systems and all other segments of electro-optical technologies. Circ. 60,000. Publishes ms an average of 6 months after acceptance. Byline given unless anonymity requested. Retains all rights. Query for electronic submissions. Computer printout submissions acceptable; submission on floppy disk preferred. Free sample copy and writer's guidelines.
Nonfiction: Lasers, laser systems, fiberoptics, optics, imaging and other electro-optical materials, components, instrumentation and systems. "Each article should serve our reader's need by either stimulating ideas, increasing technical competence or improving design capabilities in the following areas: natural light and radiation sources, artificial light and radiation sources, light modulators, optical materials and components, image detectors, energy detectors, information displays, image processing, information storage and processing, subsystem and system testing, support equipment and other related areas." No "flighty prose, material not written for our readership, or irrelevant material." Query first "with a clear statement and outline of why the article would be important to our readers." Pay rate negotiable.
Photos: Send photos with ms. Reviews 8x10 b&w glossies or 4x5 color transparencies. Drawings: Rough drawings acceptable, are finished by staff technical illustrator.
Tips: "The writer has a better chance of breaking in at our publication with short articles since shorter articles are easier to schedule, but must address more carefully our requirements for technical coverage. We use few freelancers that are independent professional writers. Most of our submitted materials come from technical

experts in the areas we cover. The most frequent mistake made by writers in completing articles for us is that the articles are too commercial, i.e. emphasize a given product or technology from one company. Also articles are not the right technical depth, too thin or too scientific."

THE MINORITY ENGINEER, An Equal Opportunity Career Publication for Professional and Graduating Minority Engineers, Equal Opportunity Publications, Inc., 44 Broadway, Greenlawn NY 11740. (516)261-8917. FAX: (516)261-8935. Editor: James Schneider. 60% freelance written. Prefers to work with published/established writers. Magazine published 4 times/year (fall, winter, spring, April/May) covering career guidance for minority engineering students and professional minority engineers. Circ. 16,000. Pays on publication. Publishes ms an average of 3-6 months after acceptance. Byline given. Buys all rights. "Deadline dates: fall, May 1; winter, July 15; spring, October 15; April/May, January 1." Simultaneous, photocopied and previously published submissions OK. Computer printout submissions acceptable; no dot-matrix. Sample copy and writer's guidelines for 9x12 SAE with 5 first class stamps; writer's guidelines for #10 SASE.

Nonfiction: Book excerpts; articles (on job search techniques, role models); general interest (on specific minority engineering concerns); how-to (land a job, keep a job, etc.); interview/profile (minority engineer role models); new product (new career opportunities); opinion (problems of ethnic minorities); personal experience (student and career experiences); and technical (on career fields offering opportunities for minority engineers). "We're interested in articles dealing with career guidance and job opportunities for minority engineers." Query or send complete ms. Length: 1,250-3,000 words. Sometimes pays the expenses of writers on assignment. Pays 10¢/word.

Photos: Prefers 35mm color slides but will accept b&w. Captions and identification of subjects required. Buys all rights. Pays $15. Cartoons accepted. Pays $25.

Tips: "Articles should focus on career guidance, role model and industry prospects for minority engineers. Prefer articles related to careers, not politically or socially sensitive."

‡NSBE JOURNAL, National Society of Black Engineers Official Publication, Journals, Inc., Suite 3, 1240 S. Broad St., New Orleans LA 70125. (504)822-3533. Editor: Bill Bowers. Copy Editor: Sonya Stinson. 50% freelance written. Works with a small number of new/unpublished writers each year. A bimonthly magazine covering engineering, science studies and careers. "The majority of our readers are college students in engineering and other technical fields. Readership also includes professional engineers and academic personnel." Circ. 20,000. Pays on publication. Publishes ms an average of 1 month after acceptance. Byline given. Buys all rights. Photocopied submissions OK. Query for electronic submissions. Computer printout submissions acceptable; no dot-matrix. Reports in 2 weeks. Free sample copy and writer's guidelines.

Nonfiction: Historical/nostalgic, how-to, inspirational, interview/profile, photo feature, technical and travel. No highly technical articles on engineering projects, products, etc. Buys 50 mss/year. Query. Length: 3,500 words maximum. Pays $150-400. Sometimes pays the expenses of writers on assignment.

Photos: Send photos with submission. Reviews contact sheets. Model releases and identification of subjects required.

Columns/Departments: NSBE Updates (trivia, news on outstanding students and professional engineers, statistical information). Buys 15 mss/year. Query. Length: 200 words maximum. Pays $150.

THE WOMAN ENGINEER, An Equal Opportunity Career Publication for Graduating Women and Experienced Professionals, Equal Opportunity Publications, Inc., 44 Broadway, Greenlawn NY 11740. (516)261-8917. Editor: Anne Kelly. 60% freelance written. Works with a small number of new/unpublished writers each year. Magazine published 4 times/year (fall, winter, spring, April/May) covering career guidance for women engineering students and professional women engineers. Circ. 16,000. Pays on publication. Publishes ms 3-12 months after acceptance. Byline given. Buys all rights. Computer printout submissions OK; not dot-matrix. Free sample copy and writer's guidelines.

Nonfiction: "Interested in articles dealing with career guidance and job opportunities for women engineers. Looking for manuscripts showing how to land an engineering position and advance professionally. Wants features on job-search techniques, engineering disciplines offering career opportunities to women, companies with affirmative action and career advancement opportunities for women, problems facing women engineers and how to cope with such problems, in addition to role-model profiles of successful women engineers, especially in government, military and defense-related industries." Query. Length: 1,000-2,500 words. Pays 10¢/word.

Photos: Prefers color slides but will accept b&w. Captions, model release and identification of subjects required. Buys all rights. Pays $15.

Tips: "We will be looking for shorter manuscripts (800-1,000 words) on job-search techniques, and first-person Endpage Essay."

Entertainment and the Arts

The business of the entertainment/amusement industry in arts, film, dance, theater, etc. is covered by these publications. Journals that focus on the people and equipment of various music specialties are listed in the Music section, while art and design business publications can be found in Art, Design and Collectibles. Entertainment publications for the general public can be found in the Consumer Entertainment section.

AMUSEMENT BUSINESS, Billboard Publications, Inc., Box 24970, Nashville TN 37202. (615)321-4267. FAX: (615)327-1575. Managing Editor: Tim O'Brien. 25% freelance written. Works with a small number of new/ unpublished writers each year. Weekly tabloid emphasizing hard news of the amusement, sports business, and mass entertainment industry. Read by top management. Circ. 15,000. Pays on publication. Publishes ms an average of 3 weeks after acceptance. Byline sometimes given; "it depends on the quality of the individual piece." Buys all rights. Submit seasonal/holiday material 3 weeks in advance. Phone queries OK. Computer printout submissions acceptable; no dot-matrix. Sample copy for 11x14 SAE with 5 first class stamps.
Nonfiction: How-to (case history of successful advertising campaigns and promotions); interviews (with leaders in the areas we cover highlighting appropriate problems and issues of today, i.e. insurance, alcohol control, etc.); new product; and technical (how "new" devices, shows or services work at parks, fairs, auditoriums and conventions). Likes lots of financial support data: grosses, profits, operating budgets and per-cap spending. Also needs in-depth looks at advertising and promotional programs of carnivals, circuses, amusement parks, fairs: how these facilities position themselves against other entertainment opportunities in the area. No personality pieces or interviews with stage stars. Buys 500-1,000 mss/year. Query. Length: 400-700 words. Pays $3/published inch. Sometimes pays the expenses of writers on assignment.
Photos: State availability of photos with query. Pays $3-5 for 8x10 b&w glossy prints. Captions and model release required. Buys all rights.
Columns/Departments: Auditorium Arenas; Fairs, Fun Parks; Food Concessions; Merchandise; Promotion; Shows (carnival and circus); Talent; Tourist Attractions; and Management Changes.
Tips: There will be more and more emphasis on financial reporting of areas covered. "Submission must contain the whys and whos, etc. and be strong enough that others in the same field will learn from it and not find it naive. We will be increasing story count while decreasing story length."

BOXOFFICE MAGAZINE, RLD Publishing Corp., Suite 710, 1800 N. Highland Ave., Hollywood CA 90028. (213)465-1186. Editor: Harley W. Lond. 5% freelance written. Monthly business magazine about the motion picture industry for members of the film industry: theater owners, film producers, directors, financiers and allied industries. Circ. 10,000. Pays on publication. Publishes ms an average of 2-4 months after acceptance. Byline given. Buys one-time rights. Submit seasonal material 2 months in advance. Simultaneous, photocopied and previously published submissions OK. Computer printout submissions acceptable. Reports in 2 months. Sample copy for 8½x11 SAE with 6 first class stamps.
Nonfiction: Exposé, interview, profile, new product, photo feature and technical. "We are a general news magazine about the motion picture industry and are looking for stories about trends, developments, problems or opportunities facing the industry. Almost any story will be considered, including corporate profiles, but we don't want gossip or celebrity stuff." Query with clips. Length: 1,500-2,500 words. Pays $100-150.
Photos: State availability of photos. Pays $10 maximum for 8x10 b&w prints. Captions required.
Tips: "Request a sample copy, indicating you read about *Boxoffice* in *Writer's Market*. Write a clear, comprehensive outline of the proposed story and enclose a resume and clip samples. We welcome new writers but don't want to be a classroom. Know how to write. We look for 'investigative' articles."

THE ELECTRIC WEENIE, Box 2715, Quincy MA 02269. (617)749-6900 ext. 248. FAX: (617)749-3691. Publisher: Jerry Ellis. Editor: James J. Donohue. 80% freelance written. Monthly magazine covering "primarily radio, for 'personalities' worldwide (however, mostly English speaking). We mail flyers mainly to radio people, but obviously no one is excepted if he/she wants a monthly supply of first-rate gags, one liners, zappers, etc." Circ. 1,500. Pays on publication. Publishes ms an average of 2 months after acceptance. No byline given. Buys all rights. Computer printout submissions acceptable. Free sample copy and writer's guidelines.
Fillers: Jokes, gags, short humor, one liners, etc. "Short is the bottom line; if it's over two sentences, it's too long." Uses 300/month. Pays $2/gag used – higher price paid for quality material.
Tips: "We like to receive in multiples of 100 if possible; not mandatory, just preferred. And we like a few original 'grossies.' We also publish a tamer version for speakers and toastmasters called '*The Ad-Lib Helper*'."

FESTIVITY!, Profitable Plans for the Party Professional, Festivities Publications, 1205 W. Forsyth St., Jacksonville FL 32204. (904)634-1902. Editorial Director: Debra Paulk. Editor: Ann White. 50% freelance written. Monthly trade journal for the party industry. Estab. 1988. Circ. 10,000. Pays on publication. Publishes ms an average of 3 months after acceptance. Byline given. Buys one-time rights. Submit seasonal/holiday material 8 months in advance. Simultaneous, photocopied and previously published submissions OK. Query for electronic submissions. Computer printout submissions OK. Reports in 3 weeks on queries; 2 weeks on mss. Sample copy for 9x12 SAE with $2 in postage.
Nonfiction: Interview/profile, new product, photo feature, technical. Buys 24 mss/year. Query with or without published clips, or send complete ms. Length: 500-2,000 words. Pays $50-200 for assigned articles.
Photos: Send photos with submission. Reviews 2x2 transparencies and 3x5 prints. Offers no additional payment for photos accepted with ms. Captions, model releases and identification of subjects required. Buys one-time rights.
Columns/Departments: Party Business (ideas on store management, finance), 500-1,000 words; Party Display (in-store display ideas, products), 500-1,000 words. Buys 24 mss/year. Query with published clips. Length: 500-1,000 words. Pays $50-200.
Tips: "Be very specific with how-to tips and programs for building business."

‡**THE HOLLYWOOD REPORTER**, Verdugo Press, 6715 Sunset Blvd., Hollywood CA 90028. (213)464-7411. Publisher: Tichi Wilkerson. Editor: Teri Ritzer. Emphasizes entertainment industry, film, TV and theatre and is interested in everything to do with financial news in these areas. 15% freelance written. Daily entertainment trade publication: 25-100 pages. Circ. 25,000. Publishes ms an average of 1 month after acceptance. Send queries first. Reports in 1 month. Sample copy $1.
Tips: "Short articles and fillers fit our format best. The most frequent mistake made by writers in completing an article for us is that they are not familiar with our publication."

‡**IDEA TODAY**, (formerly *Dance Exercise Today*), The Association for Fitness Professionals, Suite 204, 6190 Cornerstone Court E., San Diego CA 92121. (619)535-8979. Editor: Patricia A. Ryan. Associate Editor: Nancy Lee. 70% freelance written. A trade journal published 10 times/year for the dance-exercise and personal training industry. "All articles must be geared to fitness professionals—aerobics instructors, one-to-one trainers and studio and health club owners—covering topics such as aerobics, nutrition, injury prevention, entrepreneurship in fitness, fitness-oriented research and exercise programs." Circ. 18,000. Pays on acceptance. Publishes ms an average of 4 months after acceptance. Byline given. Buys all rights. Simultaneous and photocopied submissions OK. Computer printout submissions OK. Reports in 6 weeks on queries. Sample copy $4.
Nonfiction: How-to, technical. No general information on fitness; our readers are pros who need detailed information. Buys 10 mss/year. Query. Length: 1,000-3,000 words. Pays $100-300. Photos: State availability of photos with submission. Offers no additional payment for photos with ms. Model releases required. Buys all rights.
Columns/Departments: Exercise Technique (detailed, specific info; must be written by expert), 750-1,500 words; Industry News (short reports on research, programs conferences), 150-300 words; Student Handout (exercise and nutrition info for participants), 750 words; Program Spotlight (detailed explanation of specific exercise program), 1,000-1,500 words. Buys 80 mss/year. Query. Length: 150-1,500 words. Pays $15-150.
Tips: "We don't accept fitness information for the consumer audience on topics such as why exercise is good for you. Industry News (column) is most open to freelancers. We're looking for short reports on fitness-related conferences and conventions, research, innovative exercise programs, trends, news from other countries and reports on aerobics competitions. Writers who have specific knowledge of, or experience working in the fitness industry have an edge."

‡**LOCATION UPDATE**, Suite 612, 6922 Hollywood Blvd., Hollywood CA 90028. (213)461-8887. Editor: Jean Drummond. Bimonthly entertainment industry magazine covering all aspects of filming on location. "*Location Update* communicates the issues, trends, problems, solutions and business matters which affect productions working on location. Features include interviews with industry professionals, controversial issues, regional spotlights, hard-to-find or difficult locations, etc. Audience is producers, directors, production managers, location managers—any person who works on location for film, tv, commercials and videos." Circ. 15,000. Pays on publication. Publishes ms an average of 2 months after acceptance. Byline given. Offers 50% kill fee. Publication is not copyrighted. Buys first north American serial rights. Query for electronic submissions. Computer printout submissions OK. Reports in 3 weeks. Sample copy for 9x12 SAE with 7 first class stamps; free writer's guidelines. Nonfiction: Expose, General interest, historical/nostalgic, interview/profile, new product, opinion, photo feature, technical and features about productions on location. No fluffy or glitzy "Hollywood" slants. Buys 75 mss/year. Query with published clips. Length: 1,000-2,500 words. Pays $50-200 for assigned articles; $50-100 for unsolicited articles. Sometimes pays expenses of writers on assignment.
Photos: State availability of photos with submission. Reviews contact sheets, 35mm, 2¼x2¼ transparencies and 8x10 prints. Offers no additional payment for photos accepted with ms. Identification of subjects required. Buys one-time rights.

Columns/Departments: Commentary (opinion pieces on issues and problems in film industry), 500-750 words; Locations (hard to find or difficult locations and how to use them), 1,000-1,500 words; Supporting Roles (support services used on location, ie, security companies, catering, etc.), 1,000-1,500 words; Newsreel (short news briefs on location-related issues), 250 words. Buys 25-30 mss/year. Query with published clips. Pays $25-100.

Tips: "The best way to break in is to query with story ideas and to be familiar with film, TV, video and commercials. Know the workings of the entertainment industry and the roles of producers, directors and location managers. Articles about locations is the area most open to freelance writers. Everything is a possible location for productions. Every state has a film commission who can help with who is filming where and how to go about using particular locations."

THE LONE STAR COMEDY MONTHLY, Lone Star Publications of Humor, Suite #103, Box 29000, San Antonio TX 78229. Editor: Lauren Barnett. Less than 1% freelance written. Eager to work with new/unpublished writers. Monthly comedy service newsletter for professional humorists – DJs, public speakers, comedians. Includes one-liners and jokes for oral expression. Pays on publication "or before." Publishes ms an average of 4-6 months after acceptance. Byline given if 2 or more jokes are used. Buys all rights, exclusive rights for 6 months from publication date. Submit seasonal/holiday material 1 month in advance. Photocopied submissions OK. Computer printout submissions acceptable; no dot-matrix. Reports in 2-3 months. Inquire for update on prices of sample copies. Writer's guidelines for #10 SASE.

Fillers: Jokes, gags and short humor. Buys 20-60/year. Length: 100 words maximum. "We don't use major features in *The Lone Star Comedy Monthly*." Inquire for update on rates. "Submit several (no more than 20) original gags on one or two subjects only."

Tips: "Writers should inquire for an update on our needs before submitting material."

MIDDLE EASTERN DANCER, Mideastern Connection, Inc., Box 1572, Casselberry FL 32707-1572. (407)788-0301. Editor: Karen Kuzsel. Managing Editor: Tracie Harris. 60% freelance written. Eager to work with new/unpublished writers. A monthly magazine covering Middle Eastern dance and culture (belly dancing). "We provide the most current news and entertainment information available in the world. We focus on the positive, but don't shy away from controversy. All copy and photos must relate to Middle Eastern dance and cultural activities. We do not get into politics." Circ. 2,500. Pays on acceptance. Publishes ms an average of 4 months after acceptance, usually sooner, but it depends on type of article and need for that month. Byline given. Buys first rights, simultaneous rights or second serial (reprint) rights. Submit seasonal/holiday material 3 months in advance. Simultaneous, photocopied and previously published submissions OK, unless printed in another belly dance publication. Computer printout submissions acceptable; prefers letter-quality. Reports in 2 weeks on queries; 3 weeks on mss. Sample copy for 9x12 SAE with 4 first class stamps; writer's guidelines for #10 SAE with 1 first class stamp.

Nonfiction: Essays; general interest; historical/nostalgic; how-to (on costuming, putting on shows, teaching and exercises); humor; inspirational; interview/profile; personal experience; photo features; travel (to the Middle East or related to dancers); and reviews of seminars, movies, clubs, restaurants and museums. Special issues include costuming (March); and anniversary issue (October). No politics. Buys 60 mss/year. Query. Pays $20 for assigned articles; pays $10 for unsolicited articles. May provide free advertising in trade. Sometimes pays the expenses of writers on assignment.

Photos: Send photos with submission. Offers $5 additional payment for each photo accepted with ms. Identification of subjects required. Buys one-time rights.

Columns/Departments: Critic's Corner (reviews of books, videotapes, records, movies, clubs and restaurants, museums and special events); Helpful Hints (tips for finding accessories and making them easier or for less); Putting on the Ritz (describes costume in detail with photo); and Personal Glimpses (autobiographical) and Profiles (biographical – providing insights of benefit to other dancers). Query.

Fiction: Open to fiction dealing with belly dancers as subject.

Poetry: Avant-garde, free verse, light verse and traditional. Buys 5 poems/year. Submit maximum 3 poems. Pays $5 maximum.

Tips: "It's easy to break in if you stick to belly dancing related information and expect little or no money (advertising instead). Although we are the second largest in the world in this field, we're still small."

OPPORTUNITIES FOR ACTORS & MODELS, "A Guide to Working in Cable TV-Radio-Print Advertising," Copy Group, Suite 315, 1900 N. Vine St., Hollywood CA 90068. FAX: (213)465-5161. Editor: Len Miller. 50% freelance written. Works with a small number of new/unpublished writers each year. A monthly newsletter "serving the interests of those people who are (or would like to be) a part of the cable-TV, radio, and print advertising industries." Circ. 10,000. Pays on acceptance. Publishes ms an average of 3 months after acceptance. Byline given. Buys all rights. Simultaneous queries OK. Computer printout submissions OK; prefers letter-quality. Reports in 3 weeks. Free sample copy and writer's guidelines #10 SASE.

Nonfiction: How-to, humor, inspirational, interview/profile, local news, personal experience, photo feature and technical (within cable TV). Coverage should include the model scene, little theatre, drama groups, comedy workshops and other related events and places. "Detailed information about your local cable TV

station should be an important part of your coverage. Get to know the station and its creative personnel."
Buys 120 mss/year. Query. Length: 100-950 words. Pays $50 maximum.
Photos: State availability of photos. Model release and identification of subjects required. Buys one-time or all rights.
Columns/Departments: "We will consider using your material in a column format with your byline." Buys 60 mss/year. Query. Length: 150-450 words. Pays $50 maximum.
Tips: "Good first person experiences, interviews and articles, all related to modeling, acting, little theatre, photography (model shots) and other interesting items are needed."

‡**TOURIST ATTRACTIONS & PARKS MAGAZINE,** Kane Communications, Inc., Suite 210, 7000 Terminal Square, Upper Darby PA 19082. (215)925-9744. FAX: (215)734-2420. Editor: Chuck Tooley. A bimonthly magazine covering mass entertainment and leisure facilities. Emphasizes management articles. Circ. 19,600. Pays on publication. Buys all rights. Computer printout submissions acceptable; prefers letter-quality to dot-matrix. Reports in 3 weeks. Sample copy for 9x12 SAE with $1.50 postage.
Nonfiction: Interview/profile and new product. Buys 10 mss/year. Query. Length: 1,000-2,500 words. Pays $50-250 for assigned articles; sometimes payment arranged individually with publisher. Sometimes pays expenses of writers on assignment.
Photos: State availability of photos with submission. Captions and model releases required.
Tips: "Inquire about covering trade shows for us, such as C.M.A."

UPB MAGAZINE, The Voice of the United Polka Boosters, The United Polka Boosters, Box 681, Glastonbury CT 06033. (203)537-1880. Editor: Irene Kobelski. 50-60% freelance written. Eager to work with new/unpublished writers. A bimonthly magazine of the polka music industry. "Our readers share a common love for polka music and are dedicated to its preservation. They want information-packed pieces to help them understand and perform better in the polka industry." Circ. 1,100. Pays on acceptance. Publishes ms an average of 6 months after acceptance. Byline given. Offers 5% kill fee. Buys first or second serial (reprint) rights. Submit seasonal/holiday material 6 months in advance. Simultaneous, photocopied and previously published submissions OK; prefers letter-quality. Computer printout submissions OK. Reports in 6 weeks. Sample copy for 9x12 SAE with 4 first class stamps; free writer's guidelines for #10 SASE.
Nonfiction: Historical/nostalgic (polka-related), how-to (have published "How to Make a Polka album," "How to Protect Your Songs," "How to Read Music"), humor (polka-related), interview/profile (polka personalities), opinion (on polka issues), technical and the origins and history of well-known polkas. "No submissions that portray polkas as the dictionary definition 'a Bohemian dance in ¾ time.' Articles should be clearly written and easily understandable. Polka music in the U.S.A. is what we want—not old world music." Buys 15 mss/year. Query with or without published clips, or send complete ms. Length: 300-1,500 words. Pays $10-35 for assigned articles; pays $5-30 for unsolicited articles. Sometimes pays the expenses of writers on assignment.
Photos: State availability of photos with submission; photos required for all profiles/interviews. Reviews 8x10 or 5x7 prints, b&w only. Offers $1-3 per photo. Model releases and identification of subjects required. Buys one-time rights.
Columns/Departments: Behind the Scenes (in-depth report of 'how' and 'why' a polka-related or music-related process is followed), to 1,000 words; Personality Profiles (emphasize the subject's contributions to polka music); 500-1,500 words; Origins of Songs (show dates and facts—pack it with research, tie in a contemporary recording if possible), 300-1,500 words. Buys 16 mss/year. Query or send complete ms. Pays $5-35.
Fillers: Anecdotes, facts, newsbreaks, short humor and puzzles, all polka related. Buys 30/year. Length: 150-750 words. Pays $2-20 and contributor copy.
Tips: "We'd love to see some round-up pieces—for example, 'What 10 top bandleaders say about—' or 'Polka fans speak out about—.' Know the polka industry! We need info to help our readers survive in the world of performance and business. Articles should be well researched and should reflect the writer's knowledge of the present polka industry. A list of sources should accompany your ms. Our publication serves both industry professionals (musicians, DJs, composers, arrangers and promoters), and polka fans. Articles should be both informative and entertaining. We are very eager to work with freelance writers on a regular basis. We'd like pieces on recording, performing, promoting, composing, dancing—all types of well-written polka-oriented pieces."

Farm

The successful farm writer focuses on the business side of farming. For technical articles, editors feel writers should have a farm background or agricultural training, but there are opportunities for the general freelancer too. The following farm publications are divided into seven categories, each specializing in a different aspect of farming: agricultural equipment; crops and soil management; dairy farming; livestock; management; miscellaneous and regional.

Agricultural Equipment

CUSTOM APPLICATOR, Little Publications, Suite 540, 6263 Poplar Ave., Memphis TN 38119. (901)767-4020. Editor: Rob Wiley. 50% freelance written. Works with a small number of new/unpublished writers each year. For "firms that sell and custom apply agricultural fertilizer and chemicals." Circ. 16,100. Pays on publication. Publishes ms an average of 2 months after acceptance. Buys all rights. "Query is best. The editor can help you develop the story line regarding our specific needs." Computer printout submissions acceptable; prefers letter-quality. Free sample copy and writer's guidelines.
Nonfiction: "We are looking for articles on custom application firms telling others how to better perform jobs of chemical application, develop new customers, handle credit, etc. Lack of a good idea or usable information will bring a rejection." Length: 1,000-1,200 words "with 3 or 4 b&w glossy prints." Pays 20¢/word.
Photos: Accepts b&w glossy prints. "We will look at color slides for possible cover or inside use."
Tips: "We don't get enough shorter articles, so one that is well-written and informative could catch our eyes. Our readers want pragmatic information to help them run a more efficient business; they can't get that through a story filled with generalities."

Crops and Soil Management

ONION WORLD, Columbia Publishing, 111C S. 7th Ave., Box 1467, Yakima WA 98907. (509)248-2452. Editor: D. Brent Clement. 90% freelance written. A monthly magazine covering "the world of onion production and marketing" for onion growers and shippers. Circ. 5,500. Pays on publication. Publishes ms an average of 1 month after acceptance. Byline given. Not copyrighted. Buys first North American serial rights. Submit seasonal/holiday material 1 month in advance. Simultaneous submissions OK. Computer printout submisions acceptable; prefers letter-quality. Reports in several weeks. Sample copy for 8½x11 SAE with 4 first class stamps.
Nonfiction: General interest, historical/nostalgic and interview/profile. Buys 60 mss/year. Query. Length: 1,200-1,500 words. Pays $75-150 for assigned articles.
Photos: Send photos with submission. Offers no additional payment for photos accepted with ms unless cover shot. Captions and identification of subjects required. Buys all rights.
Tips: "Writers should be familiar with growing and marketing onions. We use a lot of feature stories on growers, shippers and others in the onion trade—what they are doing, their problems, solutions, marketing plans, etc."

SINSEMILLA TIPS, Domestic Marijuana Journal, New Moon Publishing, 215 SW 2nd, Box 2046, Corvallis OR 97339. (503)757-8477. FAX: (503)757-0028. Editor: Don Parker. 50% freelance written. Eager to work with new/unpublished writers. Quarterly magazine tabloid covering the domestic cultivation of marijuana. Circ. 15,000. Pays on publication. Publishes ms an average of 3 months after acceptance. Byline given. "Some writers desire to be anonymous for obvious reasons." Buys first serial rights and second serial (reprint) rights. Submit seasonal/holiday material 2 months in advance. Query for electronic submissions. Computer printout submissions acceptable. Reports in 2 months. Sample copy $6; writer's guidelines for #10 SASE.
Nonfiction: Book excerpts and reviews; expose (on political corruption); general interest; how-to; interview/profile; opinion; personal experience; and technical. Send complete ms. Length: 500-2,000 words. Pays 2½¢/word. Sometimes pays the expenses of writers on assignment.
Photos: Send photos with ms. Pays $10-20 for b&w prints; $20-50 color inside print; $50-75 color cover photo. Captions optional; model release required. Buys all rights.
Tips: "Writers have the best chance of publication if article is *specifically* related to the American marijuana industry."

SOYBEAN DIGEST, Box 41309, 777 Craig Rd., St. Louis MO 63141-1309. (314)432-1600. FAX: (314)567-7642. Editor: Gregg Hillyer. 75% freelance written. Works with a small number of new/unpublished writers each year. Emphasizes soybean production and marketing. Published monthly except semi-monthly in February and March, and bimonthly in June/July and August/September. Circ. 200,000. Pays on acceptance.

Buys all rights. Byline given. Phone queries OK. Submit seasonal material 2 months in advance. Query for electronic submissions. Computer printout submissions OK; prefers letter-quality. Reports in 3 weeks. Sample copy $3; mention *Writer's Market* in request. Free writer's guidelines.

Nonfiction: How-to (soybean production and marketing); and new product (soybean production and marketing). Buys 100 mss/year. Query or submit complete ms. Length: 1,000 words. Pays $50-350. Sometimes pays the expenses of writers on assignment.

Photos: State availability of photos with query. Pays $25-100 for 5x7 or 8x10 b&w prints, $50-275 for 35mm color transparencies, and up to $350 for covers. Captions and/or ms required. Buys all rights.

TOBACCO REPORTER, Suite 300, 3000 Highwoods Blvd., Box 95075, Raleigh NC 27625. Editor: Dayton Matlick. 5% (by those who *know* the industry) freelance written. International business journal for tobacco processors, exporters, importers, manufacturers and distributors of cigars, cigarettes and other tobacco products. Monthly. Buys all rights. Pays on publication. Computer printout submissions acceptable; no dot-matrix. Publishes ms an average of 2 months after acceptance.

Nonfiction: Uses exclusive original material on request only. Pays 10-15¢/word.

Photos: Pays $25 for photos purchased with mss.

Fillers: Wants clippings on new tobacco product brands, smoking and health, and tobacco and tobacco products: job promotions, honors, equipment, etc. Pays $5-10/clipping on use only.

Dairy Farming

BUTTER-FAT, Fraser Valley Milk Producers' Cooperative Association, Box 9100, Vancouver, British Columbia V6B 4G4 Canada. (604)420-6611. Editor: Grace Hahn. Managing Editor: Carol A. Paulson. Eager to work with new/unpublished writers. 50% freelance written. Monthly magazine emphasizing this dairy cooperative's processing and marketing operations for dairy farmers and dairy workers in British Columbia. Circ. 3,500. Pays on acceptance. Publishes ms an average of 4 months after acceptance. Byline given. Buys first rights. Makes work-for-hire assignments. Phone queries preferred. Submit seasonal material 4 months in advance. Simultaneous, photocopied and previously published submissions OK. Computer printout submissions acceptable. Reports in 1 week on queries; in 1 month on mss. Free sample copy.

Nonfiction: Interview (character profile with industry leaders); local nostalgia; opinion (of industry leaders); and profile (of association members and employees).

Photos: Reviews 5x7 b&w negatives and contact sheets and color photos. Offers $10/published photo. Captions required. Buys all rights.

Columns/Departments: "We want articles on the people, products, business of producing, processing and marketing dairy foods in this province." Query first. Buys 3 mss/issue. Length: 500-1,500 words. Pays 7¢/word.

Fillers: Jokes, short humor and quotes. Buys 5 mss/issue. Pays $10.

Tips: "Make an appointment to come by and see us!"

‡DAIRY GOAT JOURNAL, Kane Communications, Inc., Suite 210, 7000 Terminal Sq., Upper Darby PA 19082. (215)734-2420. Editor: Ann Miller. 25% freelance written. Monthly magazine about dairy goats. "We are the bible of dairy goat breeding and accessory products." Circ. 10,000. Pays on publication. Byline given. Buys all rights. Submit seasonal/holiday material 3 months in advance. Computer printout submissions OK; prefers letter-quality. Reports in 2 weeks on queries. Sample copy for 9x12 SAE with first class stamp.

Nonfiction: Book excerpts, essays, historical/nostalgic, how-to, humor, interview/profile, new product, personal experience, photo feature, technical and travel. "We publish a special Buyers Guide and have special goat breed issues." Query for times of publication. Send complete ms. Length: 800-1,500 words. Pays $40 minimum. Pays in contributor copies or other premiums if writer desires. Sometimes pays expenses of writers on assignment.

Photos: Send photos with submission. Captions, model releases and identification of subjects required. Buys all rights.

Columns/Departments: Quiz (Cream-Judging contest), 1 page; Vet (questions and answers), 600-800 words; and Cheese Marketing (how-to), 800-1,500 words. Send complete ms. Pays $40.

Livestock

ANGUS JOURNAL, Angus Publications, Inc., 3201 Frederick Blvd., St. Joseph MO 64501. (816)233-0508. FAX: (816)233-0508, ext. 112. Editor: Jim Cotton. 10% freelance written. Monthly (except June/July, which are combined) magazine. "Must be Angus-related or beef cattle with no other breeds mentioned." Circ. 15,000. Pays on acceptance. Byline given. Buys first North American serial rights, second serial(reprint) rights, simultaneous rights and makes work-for-hire assignments. Submit seasonal/holiday material 3 months in advance. Simultaneous submissions, photocopied submissions and previously published submissions OK. Computer printout submissions OK; prefer letter-quality. Reports in 2 weeks. Samples copy $1.50 wtih 10x13 SAE and 4 first class stamps.

Nonfiction: Historical/nostalgic, how-to, humor, interview/profile and photo feature. Nothing without an angus slant. Buys 6 mss/year. Send complete ms. Length: 1,000-5,000 words. Pays $50-300.

Photos: Send photos with submission. Review contact sheets and transparencies. Offers no additional payment for photos accepted with ms. Identification of subjects required. Buys one-time rights.

Columns/Departments: The Grazier (pasture, fencing, range management). Send complete ms. Length: 500-1,000 words. Pays $25-75.

Fiction: Historical, humorous and rural. Must be short, with an angus slant. Send complete ms. Length: 2,000-4,000 words. Pays $100-300.

Poetry: Light verse and traditional. Nothing without an angus or beef cattle slant. Submit up to 4 poems at one time. Length: 4-20 lines. Pays $10-75.

Tips: Areas most open to freelancers are "farm and ranch profiles – breeder interviews."

BEEF, The Webb Co., 1999 Shepard Rd., St. Paul MN 55116. (612)690-7374. Editor-in-Chief: Paul D. Andre. Managing Editor: Joe Roybal. 5% freelance written. Prefers to work with published/established writers. Monthly magazine for readers who have the same basic interest – making a living feeding cattle or running a cow herd. Circ. 120,000. Pays on acceptance. Publishes ms an average of 4 months after acceptance. Buys all rights. Byline given. Phone queries OK. Submit seasonal material 3 months in advance. Computer printout submissions acceptable. Reports in 2 months. Free sample copy and writer's guidelines.

Nonfiction: How-to and informational articles on doing a better job of producing, feeding cattle, market building, managing, and animal health practices. Material must deal with beef cattle only. Buys 8-10 mss/year. Query. Length: 500-2,000 words. Pays $25-300. Sometimes pays the expenses of writers on assignment.

Photos: B&w glossies (8x10) and color transparencies (35mm or 2¼x2¼) purchased with or without mss. Query or send contact sheet, captions and/or transparencies. Pays $10-50 for b&w; $25-100 for color. Model release required.

Tips: "Be completely knowledgeable about cattle feeding and cowherd operations. Know what makes a story. We want specifics, not a general roundup of an operation. Pick one angle and develop it fully. The most frequent mistake is not following instructions on an angle (or angles) to be developed."

‡BEEF TODAY, Farm Journal, Inc., 230 W. Washington Sq., Philadelphia PA 19105. (215)829-4700. Editor: Bill Miller. 10% freelance written. Monthly magazine on cattlemen and the beef-cattle industry. "The audience is larger-scale cattlemen. We emphasize current industry trends, innovative production practices, finances and other business subjects, but also run humor and profiles." Circ. 200,000. Pays on acceptance. Publishes ms an average of 2 months after acceptance. Byline given. Offers $150 kill fee. Buys first rights. Submit seasonal/holiday material 3 months in advance. Computer printout submissions OK; prefers letter-quality. Reports in 2 weeks. Sample copy for 9x12 SAE with 2 first class stamps; free writer's guidelines.

Nonfiction: How-to (do a better job of running a ranch or feed lot), humor, interview/profile and photo feature. "No articles explaining the cattle industry to the general public." Query with published clips. Length: 500-2,500 words. Pays $300-650 for assigned articles; $150-600 for unsolicited articles. Pays expenses of writers on assignment.

Photos: State availability of photos with submissions or send photos with submissions – preferred. Reviews transparencies. Offers $100-200 per photo. Captions and identification of subjects required. Buys one-time rights.

Tips: "Authors should include details in their queries and mention what sort of expertise they bring to the subject. Most of the unsolicited manuscripts that we've accepted have been on lighter subjects – personality profiles and humor, for instance. But even here, freelance writers should remember that we're a business magazine and that our readers are working cattlemen who already know their business. They (and we) want specifics – numbers, results, problems, etc. – rather than a general introduction. Reports from abroad can be slightly more introductory, though."

THE BRAHMAN JOURNAL, Sagebrush Publishing Co., Inc., Box 220, Eddy TX 76524. (817)859-5451. Editor: Joe Ed Brockett. 10% freelance written. A monthly magazine covering Brahman cattle. Circ. 6,000. Pays on publication. Publishes ms an average of 2 months after acceptance. Byline given. Not copyrighted. Buys first North American serial rights, one-time rights, second serial (reprint) rights and makes work-for-hire assignments. Submit seasonal/holiday material 3 months in advance. Previously published submissions OK. Computer printout submissions OK; no dot-matrix. Reports in 1 month. Sample copy for 8½x11 SAE and 5 first class stamps.

Nonfiction: General interest, historical/nostalgic and interview/profile. Special issues include Herd Bull issue (July) and Texas issue (October). Buys 3-4 mss/year. Query with published clips. Length: 1,200-3,000 words. Pays $100-250 for assigned articles.

Photos: Photos needed for article purchase. Send photos with submission. Reviews 4x5 prints. Offers no additional payment for photos accepted with ms. Captions required. Buys one-time rights.

THE CATTLEMAN MAGAZINE, Texas & Southwestern Cattle Raisers Association, 1301 W. 7th St., Ft. Worth TX 76102. (817)332-7155. Editor: Lionel Chambers. Managing Editor: Don C. King. Monthly Magazine emphasizing beef cattle production and feeding. "Readership consists of commercial cattlemen, purebred seedstock producers, cattle feeders and horsemen in the Southwest." Circ. 19,300. Pays on acceptance. Publishes ms an average of 6 months after acceptance. Byline given. Buys all rights. Computer printout submissions acceptable; prefers letter-quality. Reports in 3 weeks. Sample copy $2; writer's guidelines for #10 SAE and 1 first class stamp.
Nonfiction: Need informative, entertaining feature articles on specific commercial ranch operations, cattle breeding and feeding, range and pasture management, profit tips, and university research on beef industry. "We feature various beef cattle breeds most months." Will take a few historical western-lore pieces. Must be well-documented. No first person narratives or fiction or articles pertaining to areas outside the Southwest or outside beef cattle ranching. Buys 24 mss/year. Query. Length 1,500-2,000 words. Pays $75-300. Sometimes pays the expenses of writers on assignment.
Photos: Photos purchased with or without accompanying ms. State availability of photos with query or ms. Pays $15-25 for 5x7 b&w glossies; $100 for color transparencies used as cover. Total purchase price for ms includes payment for photos. Captions, model release, and identification of subjects required.
Fillers: Cartoons.
Tips: "Submit an article dealing with ranching in the Southwest. Too many writers submit stories out of our general readership area. Economics may force staff writers to produce more articles, leaving little room for unsolicited articles."

‡HOG FARM MANAGEMENT, Miller Publishing Co., Suite 160, 12400 Whitewater Dr., Box 2400, Minneapolis MN 55343. (612)931-2900. Editor: Steve Marbery. 25% freelance written. A monthly trade journal on hog production. "Specialized management-oriented features on hog production: feeding, health, finances." Circ. 45,000. Pays on publication. Publishes ms an average of 2 months after acceptance. Byline given. Offers $25 kill fee. Buys all rights. Submit seasonal/holiday material 3 months in advance. Reports in 2 weeks on queries. Sample copy $1; free writer's guidelines.
Nonfiction: General interest, how-to, interview/profile and new product. No humor or excerpts of any kind. Buys 6-8 mss/year. Query with or without published clips, or send complete ms. Length: 200-1,000 words. Pays $150-350.
Photos: State availability of photos with submission. Reviews contact sheets. Offers $10-40 per photo. Model releases and identification of subjects required. Buys all rights.

POLLED HEREFORD WORLD, 4700 E. 63rd St., Kansas City MO 64130. (816)333-7731. Editor: Ed Bible. 1% freelance written. For "breeders of Polled Hereford cattle—about 80% registered breeders, 5% commercial cattle breeders; remainder are agribusinessmen in related fields." Monthly. Circ. 11,500. Not copyrighted. Buys "no unsolicited mss at present." Pays on publication. Publishes ms an average of 2 months after acceptance. Photocopied submissions OK. Computer printout submissions acceptable; prefers letter-quality. Submit seasonal material "as early as possible: 2 months preferred." Reports in 1 month. Query first for reports of events and activities. Query first or submit complete ms for features. Free sample copy.
Nonfiction: "Features on registered or commercial Polled Hereford breeders. Some on related agricultural subjects (pastures, fences, feeds, buildings, etc.). Mostly technical in nature; some human interest. Our readers make their living with cattle, so write for an informed, mature audience." Buys informational articles, how-to's, personal experience articles, interviews, profiles, historical and think pieces, nostalgia, photo features, coverage of successful business operations, articles on merchandising techniques, and technical articles. Length: "varies with subject and content of feature." Pays about 5¢/word ("usually about 50¢/column inch, but can vary with the value of material").
Photos: Purchased with mss, sometimes purchased without mss, or on assignment; captions required. "Only good quality b&w glossies accepted; any size. Good color prints or transparencies." Pays $2 for b&w, $2-25 for color. Pays $25 for color covers.

‡SHEEP! MAGAZINE, Rt. 1, Box 78, Helenville WI 53137. (414)674-3029. FAX: (414)593-8384. Editor: Dave Thompson. 50% freelance written. Prefers to work with published/established writers, and works with a small number of new/unpublished writers each year. Monthly magazine. "We're looking for clear, concise, useful information for sheep raisers who have a few sheep to a 1,000 ewe flock." Circ. 10,500. Pays on publication. Byline given. Offers $30 kill fee. Buys all rights. Makes work-for-hire assignments. Submit seasonal/holiday material 3 months in advance. Computer printout submissions acceptable; prefers letter-quality to dot-matrix. Free sample copy and writer's guidelines.
Nonfiction: Book excerpts; information (on personalities and/or political, legal or environmental issues affecting the sheep industry); how-to (on innovative lamb and wool marketing and promotion techniques, efficient record-keeping systems or specific aspects of health and husbandry). "Health and husbandry articles

should be written by someone with extensive experience or appropriate credentials (i.e., a veterinarian or animal scientist"); profiles (on experienced sheep producers who detail the economics and management of their operation); features (on small businesses that promote wool products and stories about local and regional sheep producer's groups and their activities); new products (of value to sheep producers; should be written by someone who has used them); and technical (on genetics, health and nutrition). First person narratives. Buys 80 mss/year. Query with published clips or send complete ms. Length: 750-2,500 words. Pays $45-150. Pays the expenses of writers on assignment.

Photos: "Color—vertical compositions of sheep and/or people—for our cover. Use only b&w inside magazine. B&w, 35mm photos or other visuals improve your chances of a sale." Pays $100 maximum for 35mm color transparencies; $20-50 for 5x7 b&w prints. Identification of subjects required. Buys all rights.

Tips: "Send us your best ideas and photos!"

Management

ACRES U.S.A., A Voice for Eco-Agriculture, Acres U.S.A., Box 9547, Kansas City MO 64133. (816)737-0064. FAX: (816)737-3346. Editor: Charles Walters, Jr. Monthly tabloid covering biologically sound farming techniques. Circ. 16,000. Pays on acceptance. Byline sometimes given. Buys first rights. Submit seasonal/holiday material 3 months in advance. Query for electronic submissions. Computer printout submissions acceptable, if double spaced. Reports in 1 month. Sample copy $2.25.

Nonfiction: Exposé (farm-related); how-to; and case reports on farmers who have adopted eco-agriculture (organic). No philosophy on eco-farming or essays. Buys 80 mss/year. Query with published clips. Length: open. Pays 6¢/word.

Photos: State availability of photos with submission. Reviews b&w photos only. Top quality photos only. Pays $6 for b&w contact sheets, negatives and 7x10 prints.

Tips: "We need on-scene reports of farmers who have adopted eco-farming—good case reports. We must have substance in articles and need details on systems developed. Read a few copies of the magazine to learn the language of the subject."

‡AGWAY COOPERATOR, Box 4933, Syracuse NY 13221. (315)477-6231. Editor: Jean Willis. 2% freelance written. For farmers. Published 9 times/year. Pays on acceptance. Publishes ms an average of 6 months after acceptance. Time between acceptance and publication varies considerably. Usually reports in 1 week. Computer printout submissions acceptable; no dot-matrix. Free sample copy.

Nonfiction: Should deal with topics of farm or rural interest in the Northeastern U.S. Length: 1,200 words maximum. Pays $100, usually including photos.

Tips: "We prefer an Agway tie-in, if possible. Fillers don't fit into our format. We do not assign freelance articles."

FARM FUTURES, The Farm Business Magazine, AgriData Resources, 330 E. Kilbourn, Milwaukee WI 53202. (414)283-4411. Editor: Claudia Waterloo. 40% freelance written. Eager to work with new/unpublished writers. Circ. 200,000. Pays on acceptance. Publishes ms an average of 2 months after acceptance. Byline given. Offers negotiable kill fee. Buys first serial rights only. Simultaneous queries, and photocopied and previously published submissions OK; no simultaneous submissions. Query for electronic submissions. Reports in 1 month. Free sample copy and writer's guidelines.

Nonfiction: Practical advice and insights into managing commercial farms, farm marketing how-to's, financial management, use of computers in agriculture, and farmer profiles. Buys 45 mss/year. Query first; do not send unsolicited mss. Length: 250-2,000 words. Pays $35-400. Sometimes pays the expenses of writers on assignment.

Tips: "The writer has a better chance of breaking in at our publication with short articles and fillers since our style is very particular; our stories are written directly to farmers and must be extremely practical. It's a style most writers have to 'grow into.' The most frequent mistakes made by writers in completing an article for us are lack of thoroughness and good examples; language too lofty or convoluted; and lack of precision—inaccuracies. Our magazine is growing—we'll be needing more freelance material."

‡FARM JOURNAL, 230 W. Washington Square, Philadelphia PA 19105. Contact: Editor. "The business magazine of American agriculture" is published 14 times/year with many regional editions. Material bought for one or more editions depending upon where it fits. Buys all rights. Byline given "except when article is too short or too heavily rewritten to justify one." Payment made on acceptance and is the same regardless of editions in which the piece is used.

Nonfiction: Timeliness and seasonableness are very important. Material must be highly practical and should be helpful to as many farmers as possible. Farmers' experiences should apply to one or more of these 8 basic commodities: corn, wheat, milo, soybeans, cotton, dairy, beef and hogs. Technical material must be accurate.

No farm nostalgia. Query to describe a new idea that farmers can use. Length: 500-1,500 words. Pays 10-20¢/word published.

Photos: Much in demand either separately or with short how-to material in picture stories and as illustrations for articles. Warm human-interest-pix for covers—activities on modern farms. For inside use, shots of homemade and handy ideas to get work done easier and faster, farm news photos, and pictures of farm people with interesting sidelines. In b&w, 8x10 glossies are preferred; color submissions should be 2¼x2¼ for the cover, and 35mm for inside use. Pays $50 and up for b&w shot; $75 and up for color.

Tips: "*Farm Journal* now publishes in hundreds of editions reflecting geographic, demographic and economic sectors of the farm market."

‡FARM POND HARVEST, Professional Sportsman's Publishing Company, RR 3, Box 197, Momence IL 60954. (815)472-2686. Editor: Vic Johnson. Managing Editor: Joan Munyon. 75% freelance written; some are reprints from state conservation department magazines. Quarterly magazine for fisheries. "Mainly informational for pond owners—we have many biologists, university libraries and government agencies on our subscription list." Pays on publication. Publishes ms an average of 1-3 months after acceptance. Byline given. Not copyrighted. Buys first rights or second serial (reprint) rights. Submit seasonal/holiday material 2 months in advance. Simultaneous, photocopied, and previously published submissions OK. Free sample copy.

Nonfiction: How-to aquaculture, personal experience, photo feature and technical. Buys 8-10 mss/year. Query with or without published clips, or send complete ms. Length: 1,300-2,500 words. Pays 3¢/word for assigned articles.

Photos: State availability of photos with submission. Reviews negatives 35mm color and 5×7 prints. Offers no additional payment for b&w prints photos accepted with ms. Sometimes pays $5/b&w photo; $10/color photo. Buys one-time rights.

Columns/Departments: What's New (products—news bulletins—magazines—fishery field); Ask Al (answers to questions from readers) and Cutting Bait. Send complete ms.

Tips: Most open to freelancers are "how-to on planning, construction, management, fishing in farm ponds or small lakes. Personal experiences—some light-humorous articles accepted, and seasonal stories, winter, spring, summer or fall."

FARM SHOW MAGAZINE, 20088 Kenwood Trail, Box 1029, Lakeville MN 55044. (612)469-5572. Editor: Mark A. Newhall. 20% freelance written. A bimonthly trade journal covering agriculture. Circ. 150,000. Pays on acceptance. Publishes ms an average of 4 months after acceptance. Byline sometimes given. Buys one-time and second serial (reprint) rights. Previously published submissions OK. Computer printout submissions OK. Reports in 1 week. Free sample copy and writer's guidelines.

Nonfiction: How-to and new product. No general interest, historic or nostalgic articles. Buys 90 mss/year. Send complete ms. Length: 100-2,000 words. Pays $50-300.

Photos: Send photos with submission. Reviews any size color or b&w prints. Offers no additional payment for photos accepted with ms. Captions required. Buys one-time rights.

Tips: "We're looking for first-of-its-kind, inventions of the nuts-and-bolts variety for farmers."

FORD NEW HOLLAND NEWS, 500 Diller Ave., New Holland PA 17557. Editor: Gary Martin. 50% freelance written. Works with a small number of new/unpublished writers each year. Magazine on agriculture; published 8 times/year; designed to entertain and inform farm families. Pays on acceptance. Publishes ms an average of 9 months after acceptance. Byline given. Offers negotiable kill fee. Buys first North American serial rights, one-time rights and second serial (reprint) rights. Submit seasonal/holiday material 6 months in advance. Simultaneous queries and previously published submissions OK. Reports in 1 month. Sample copy and writer's guidelines for 8½x11 SAE and 2 first class stamps.

Nonfiction: "We need strong photo support for short articles up to 1,200 words on farm management and farm human interest." Buys 16-20 mss/year. Query. Length: 1,200 words. Pays $400-600. Sometimes pays the expenses of writers on assignment.

Photos: Send photos with query when possible. Reviews color transparencies. Pays $50-300. Captions, model release and identification of subjects required. Buys one-time rights.

Tips: "We thrive on good article ideas from knowledgeable farm writers. The writer must have an emotional understanding of agriculture and the farm family and must demonstrate in the article an understanding of the unique economics that affect farming in North America. We want to know about the exceptional farm managers, those leading the way in agriculture. We want new efficiencies and technologies presented through the real-life experiences of farmers themselves. Use anecdotes freely. Successful writers keep in touch with the editor as they develop the article."

HIGH PLAINS JOURNAL, "The Farmers Paper," High Plains Publishers, Inc., Box 760, Dodge City KS 67801. (316)227-7171. Editor: Galen Hubbs. 5-10% freelance written. Weekly tabloid with news, features and photos on all phases of farming and livestock production. Circ. 61,000. Pays on publication. Publishes ms an average of 1 month after acceptance. Byline given. Not copyrighted. Buys first serial rights. Submit seasonal/holiday material 1 month in advance. Simultaneous queries and photocopied submissions OK.

Computer printout submissions acceptable; prefers letter-quality. Reports in 3 weeks on queries; 1 month on mss. Sample copy for $1.50.

Nonfiction: General interest (agriculture); how-to; interview/profile (farmers or stockmen within the High Plains area); and photo feature (agricultural). No rewrites of USDA, extension or marketing association releases. Buys 10-20 mss/year. Query with published clips. Length: 10-40 inches. Pays $1/column inch. Sometimes pays the expenses of writers on assignment.

Photos: State availability of photos. Pays $5-10 for 4x5 b&w prints. Captions and complete identification of subjects required. Buys one-time rights.

Tips: "Limit submissions to agriculture. Stories should not have a critical time element. Stories should be informative with correct information. Use quotations and bring out the human aspects of the person featured in profiles. Frequently writers do not have a good understanding of the subject. Stories are too long or are too far from our circulation area to be beneficial."

‡MISSOURI FARM MAGAZINE, Total Concept Small Farming, Gardening, and Rural Living, Missouri Farm Publishing, Rt. 1, Box 237, Clark MO 65243. (314)687-3525. Editor: Ron Macher. 60% freelance written. Bimonthly magazine on small farms. "Magazine for small farmers and small-acreage landowners interested in diversification, direct marketing, alternative crops, minor breeds of livestock, exotics, home-based business, gardening, horses and small stock." Circ. 5,000. Pays on publication. Publishes ms an average of 2 months after acceptance. Byline given. Buys first rights and second serial (reprint) rights to material in our magazine, for use in anthologies. Submit seasonal/holiday material 2 months in advance. Photocopied submissions OK. Computer printout submissions OK. Reports in 2 weeks on queries; 1 month on mss. Sample copy $2. Writer's guidelines for #10 SASE.

Nonfiction: How-to (small farming, gardening, alternative crops/livestock) and interview/profile. "No political opinions, depressing articles." Buys 70 mss/year. Query with or without published clips, or send complete ms. Length: 500-2,500 words. Pays $10-100. Pays in contributor copies or other premiums by individual negotiation.

Photos: Send photos with submission. Reviews contact sheets (b&w only), negatives and 3x5 and larger prints. Offers $4-10 per photo. Captions required. Buys one-time rights and nonexclusive reprint rights (for anthologies).

Columns/Departments: About Books (books about small farming, gardening, rural living, alternative crops, unusual livestock that are useful to small farmers), 500-1,000 words; and Minor Breeds (history, characteristics, use on today's small farm), 500-1,500 words. Buys 15 mss/year. Query or send complete ms. Pays $10-75.

Fillers: Facts, newsbreaks and short humor. Buys 6/year. Length: 50-300 words. Pays $1.50-10.

Tips: "We like upbeat, how-to articles on anything pertaining to the small farm. Also, we need articles on people who are being successful on the small farm through use of diversification, marketing and alternative crops and livestock. Come up with a good idea that we or competing publications haven't done before, and query. Good black and white photos are also a plus. Probably the best area for freelancers is writing interview/profile stories about successful small farmers. We like these articles to include as much concrete, helpful how-to information as possible. Lists of sources for more information (books, associations, etc.) for sidebars are also appreciated. These successful small farmers should be located in Missouri or surrounding states."

THE NATIONAL FUTURE FARMER, 15160, Alexandria VA 22309. (703)360-3600. Editor-in-Chief: Wilson W. Carnes. 20% freelance written. Prefers to work with published/established writers, and is eager to work with new/unpublished writers. Bimonthly magazine for members of the National FFA Organization who are students of agriculture in high school, ranging in age from 14-21 years; major interest in careers in agriculture/agribusiness and other youth interest subjects. Circ. 422,528. Pays on acceptance. Publishes ms an average of 4 months after acceptance. Buys all rights. Byline given. Submit seasonal/holiday material 4 months in advance. Query for electronic submissions. Computer printout submissions acceptable; prefers letter-quality. Usually reports in 1 month. Free sample copy and writer's guidelines.

Nonfiction: How-to for youth (outdoor-type such as camping, hunting, fishing); and informational (getting money for college, farming; and other help for youth). Informational, personal experience and interviews are used only if FFA members or former members are involved. "Science-oriented material is being used more extensively as we broaden people's understanding of agriculture." Buys 15 unsolicited mss/year. Query or send complete ms. Length: 1,000 words maximum. Pays 4-6¢/word. Sometimes pays the expenses of writers on assignment.

Photos: Purchased with mss (5x7 or 8x10 b&w glossies; 35mm or larger color transparencies). Pays $15 for b&w; $30-40 for inside color; $100 for cover.

Tips: "Find an FFA member who has done something truly outstanding that will motivate and inspire others, or provide helpful information for a career in farming, ranching or agribusiness. We've increased emphasis on agriscience and marketing. We're accepting manuscripts now that are tighter and more concise. Get straight to the point."

‡**PROGRESSIVE FARMER**, Southern Progress Corp. Suite 820 Shades Creek Pkwy., Birmingham AL 35209. (205)877-6401. Editorial Director: Tom Curl. Editor: Jack Odle. 3% freelance written. Monthly agriculture trade journal. Country people, farmers, ranchers are our audience. Circ. 865,000. Pays on acceptance. Publishes ms an average of 4 months after acceptance. Byline sometimes given. Buys all rights. Computer printout submissions OK. Reports in 3 weeks. Free sample copy and writer's guidelines.
Nonfiction: How-to (agriculture and country related), humor (farm related) and technical (agriculture). Buys 30-50 mss/year. Query with published clips. Length: 2,000 words maximum. Pays $100 minimum. Sometimes pays expenses of writers on assignment.
Photos: Send photos with submission. Reviews negatives and transparencies. Payment negotiable. Captions and identification of subjects required. Rights depend on assignment.
Columns/Departments: Handy Devices (need photos and short text on the little shop ideas that make farm work easier and rural living more enjoyable). Send complete ms. Length: 20-75 words. Pays $50.
Tips: Query with ideas compatible with basic tone of magazine.

Miscellaneous

FUR TRADE JOURNAL OF CANADA, Titan Publishing Inc., Unit 5, 24 Hayes Ave., Box 1747, Guelph ON N1H 7A1 Canada. (519)763-5058. 40% freelance written. Monthly magazine on fur ranching and trapping. *"Fur Trade Journal* is a publication dedicated to mink, fox and chinchilla husbandry." Circ. 1,500. Pays on publication. Publishes ms an average of 2 months after acceptance. Byline given. Buys first North American serial rights. Simultaneous, photocopied and previously published submissions OK. Computer printout submissions OK; prefers letter-quality. Reports in 6 weeks. Sample copy available for 8x10 SAE with Canadian postage or International Reply Coupon.
Nonfiction: How-to (ranching techniques), interview/profile, new product, technical. Buys 25 mss/year. Query with published clips. Length: 100-3,000 words. Pays up to $100.
Photos: State availability of photos with submission. Reviews 5x7 prints. Offers $5 per photo. Identification of subjects required. Buys one-time rights.
Fillers: Facts, short humor. Length: 10-50 words. Pays $10.
Tips: "Read other publications to become familiar with the trade. The sections most open to freelancers are profiles and interviews and summary of live animal shows."

GLEANINGS IN BEE CULTURE, Box 706, Medina OH 44258. FAX (216)725-5624. Editor: Kim Flottum. 50% freelance written. For beekeepers. Publishes environmentally oriented articles relating to bees or pollination. Monthly. Buys first North American serial rights. Pays on publication, or on acceptance on occasion. Publishes ms an average of 4 months after acceptance. Reports in 15-30 days. Computer printout submissions acceptable; prefers letter-quality. Sample copy for 9x12 SAE and 5 first class stamps; free writer's guidelines.
Nonfiction: Interested in articles giving new ideas on managing bees. Also uses success stories about commercial beekeepers. No "how I began beekeeping" articles. No highly advanced, technical and scientific abstracts or impractical advice. Length: 2,000 words maximum. Pays $30-50/published page—on negotiation.
Photos: Sharp b&w photos (pertaining to honey bees or honey plants) purchased with mss. Can be any size, prints or enlargements, but 4x5 or larger preferred. Pays $5-7/picture.
Tips: "Do an interview story on commercial beekeepers who are cooperative enough to furnish accurate, factual information on their operations. Frequent mistakes made by writers in completing articles are that they are too general in nature and lack management knowledge."

Regional

‡**AGRI-TIMES NORTHWEST**, J/A Publishing Co., 206 S.E. Court, Box 189, Pendleton OR 97801. (503)276-7845. Editor: Virgil Rupp. Managing Editor: Jim Eardley. 50% freelance written. Weekly newspaper on agriculture in western Idaho, eastern Oregon and eastern Washington. "News, features about regional farmers/agribusiness *only*." Circ. 5,200. Pays 15th of month after publication. Publishes ms an average of 1 month after acceptance. Byline given. Buys one-time rights. Submit seasonal/holiday material 1 month in advance. Simultaneous, photocopied and previously published submissions OK. Computer printout submissions OK; prefers letter-quality. Sample 50¢ with 8x10 SAE and 4 first class stamps. Writer's guidelines for #10 SAE with 1 first class stamp.
Nonfiction: How-to (farming and ranching *regional*), humor (regional farming and ranching), interview/profile (regional farmers/ranchers), photo feature (regional agriculture) and technical (regional farming and ranching). Buys 100 mss/year. Query with or without published clips, or send complete ms. Length: 1,000 words maximum. Pays 75¢ per column inch.

Photos: Send photos with submission. Reviews contact sheets, negatives and prints. Offers $5-10 per photo. Captions and identification of subjects required. Buys one-time rights.

Columns/Departments: Agri-Talk (quips, comments of farmers/ranchers). Buys 50 mss/year. Send complete ms. Length: 100 words maximum. Pays 75¢ per column inch.

Tips: "Focus on our regions's agriculture. Be accurate."

CALIFORNIA FARMER, The Business Magazine for Commercial Agriculture, HBJ Farm Publications, 731 Market St., San Francisco CA 94103. (415)495-3340. FAX: (415)777-1958. Editor: Len Richardson. Managing Editor: Ann Senuta. 70% freelance written. Works with a small number of new/unpublished writers each year. Magazine published semimonthly (once a month in July, August, December) covering California agriculture. "We cover all issues of interest to the state's commercial farmers, including production techniques, marketing, politics, and social and economic issues." Circ. 63,000. Pays on acceptance. Publishes ms an average of 1-2 months after acceptance. Byline given. Offers $100 kill fee. Makes work-for-hire assignments. Submit seasonal/holiday material 3 months in advance. Photocopied submissions OK. Query for electronic submissions. Computer printout submissions acceptable, "must be double-spaced"; prefers letter-quality. Reports in 2 months. Sample copy for 8½x11 SASE. Free writer's guidelines for #10 SASE.

Nonfiction: How-to (agricultural, livestock); interview/profile; technical (agricultural; weed and pest control; crop and livestock management; cultural and irrigation practices; financial involvement and marketing of farm products). No "It happened to me"-type stories. Buys 75 mss/year. Query with published clips. Length: 1,500-3,000 words. Pays $200-400 for assigned articles; pays $100-300 for unsolicited articles. Sometimes pays the expenses of writers on assignment.

Photos: Send photos with submission. "We emphasize high-quality color photography. We will give strong preference to well-written, accurate, newsworthy stories that are accompanied by suitable photographs. Reviews 35mm color transparencies and b&w prints (any size). Captions and identification of subjects required. Pays $50-125, depending on published size, per image.

Tips: "We will give preference to writers with a demonstrated knowledge of California agriculture, but we will consider material from and occasionally give assignments to good writers with an ability to research a story, get the facts right and write in a smooth, easy-to-understand style. Stories should be clear, concise, and above all, accurate. We especially welcome pictures of California farmers as illustration."

‡FARMWEEK, Mayhill Publications, Inc. 27 N. Jefferson, Box 90, Knightstown IN 46148. (317)345-5133. FAX: (317)345-5133, ext. 198. Editor: Rod Everhart. 5% freelance written. Agriculture newspaper that covers agriculture in Indiana, Ohio and Kentucky. Circ. 28,000. Pays on publication. Byline given. Buys first rights or second serial (reprint) rights. Submit seasonal/holiday material 1 month in advance. Simultaneous, photocopied and previously published submissions OK. Computer printout submissions OK. Reports in 2 weeks on queries. Free sample copy and writer's guidelines.

Nonfiction: General interest (agriculture), interview/profile (ag leaders), new product, opinion (ag issues) and photo feature (Indiana, Ohio, Kentucky agriculture). "We don't want first person accounts or articles from states outside Indiana, Kentucky, Ohio (unless of general interest to all farmers and agribusiness)." Number of mss/year varies. Query with published clips. Length: 500-1,500 words (2-4 typed pages double spaced). Pays $50 maximum. Sometimes pays expenses of writers on assignment.

Photos: State availability of photos with submission. Reviews contact sheets and 4x5 and 5x7 prints. Offers $5 maximum per photo. Identification of subjects required. Buys one-time rights.

Tips: "We want feature stories about farmers and agribusinessmen in Indiana, Ohio and Kentucky. How do they operate their business? Keys to success, etc.? Best thing to do is call us first with idea, or write. Could also be a story about some pressing issue in agriculture nationally that affects farmers everywhere."

FLORIDA GROWER & RANCHER, F.G.R., Inc., 1331 N. Mills Ave., Orlando FL 32803. (407)894-6522. Editor: Frank Abrahamson. 10% freelance written. A monthly magazine for Florida farmers. Circ. 28,000. Pays on publication. Byline given. Buys one-time rights. Submit seasonal/holiday material 2 months in advance. Query for electronic submissions. Computer printout submissions acceptable; prefers letter-quality. Reports in 2 weeks on queries; 1 month on mss. Free sample copy for 9x12 SAE and free writer's guidelines.

Nonfiction: General interest, historical/nostalgic, how-to, interview/profile, new product, personal experience, photo feature, technical. Articles should coordinate with editorial calendar, determined 1 year in advance. Buys 6 mss/year. Query. Length: 500-1,000 words. Pays $4/printed inch.

Photos: Send photos with submission. Reviews transparencies and prints. Pays $5/b&w print, $50/color cover. Identification of subjects required. Buys one-time rights.

MAINE ORGANIC FARMER & GARDENER, Maine Organic Farmers & Gardeners Association, Box 2176, Augusta ME 04330. (207)622-3118. Editor: Jean English, RR2, Box 595A, Lincolnville ME 04849. 40% freelance written. Prefers to work with published/established writers; works with a small number of new/ unpublished writers each year. Bimonthly magazine covering organic farming and gardening for urban and rural farmers and gardeners and nutrition-oriented, environmentally concerned readers. "*MOF&G* promotes and encourages sustainable agriculture and environmentally sound living. Our primary focus is organic farming, gardening and forestry, but we also deal with local, national and international agriculture, food and environmental issues." Circ. 10,000. Pays on publication. Publishes ms an average of 8 months after acceptance. Byline and bio given. Buys first North American serial rights, one-time rights, first serial rights, or second serial (reprint) rights. Submit seasonal/holiday material 6 months in advance. Simultaneous queries, and simultaneous, photocopied and previously published submissions OK. Computer printout submissions acceptable. Reports in 2 months. Sample copy $2.; free writer's guidelines.

Nonfiction: How-to information can be handled as first person experience, technical/research report, or interview/profile focusing on farmer, gardener, food plant, forests, livestock, weeds, insects, trees, renewable energy, recycling, nutrition, health, non-toxic pest control, organic farm management. We use profiles of New England organic farmers and gardeners and news reports (500-1,000 words) dealing with U.S./international sustainable ag research and development, rural development, recycling projects, environmental problem solutions, organic farms with broad impact, cooperatives, community projects, American farm crisis and issues, food issues. Buys 30 mss/year. Query with published clips or send complete ms. Length: 1,000-3,000 words. Pays $20-100. Sometimes pays expenses of writers on assignment. Humor; book review; poetry.

Photos: State availability of photos with query; send photos or proof sheet with manuscript. Assignment writers can send exposed b&w films, and we process and print. Prefer b&w but can use color slides or negatives in a pinch. Captions, model releases and identification of subjects required. Buys one-time rights.

Tips: "We are a nonprofit organization. Our publication's primary mission is to inform and educate. Our readers want to know how to, but they also want to enjoy the reading and know the source/expert/writer. We don't want impersonal how-to articles that sound like Extension bulletins or textbooks. As consumers' demand for organically grown food increases, we are increasingly interested in issues about certification of organic food, legislation that affects organic growers, and marketing of organic food."

N.D. REC MAGAZINE, N.D. Association of RECs, Box 727, Mandan ND 58554. (701)663-6501. Editor: Karl Karlgaard. 10% freelance written. Prefers to work with published/established writers, and works with a small number of new/unpublished writers each year. Monthly magazine covering rural electric program and rural North Dakota lifestyle. "Our magazine goes to the 70,000 North Dakotans who get their electricity from rural electric cooperatives. We cover rural lifestyle, energy conservation, agriculture, farm family news and other features of importance to this predominantly agrarian state. Of course, we represent the views of our statewide association." Circ. 74,000. Pays on publication; "acceptance for assigned features." Publishes ms average of 6 months after acceptance. Byline given. Buys first North American serial rights. Submit seasonal/holiday material 6 months in advance. Simultaneous queries OK. Computer printout submissions acceptable. Reports in 6 weeks. Sample copy for 9x12 SAE and 6 first class stamps.

Nonfiction: Exposé (subjects of ND interest dealing with rural electric, agriculture, rural lifestyle); historical/nostalgic (ND events or people only); how-to (save energy, weatherize homes, etc.); interview/profile (on great leaders of the rural electric program, agriculture); and opinion (why family farms should be saved, etc.). No fiction that does not relate to our editorial goals. Buys 10-12 mss/year. Length: open. Pays $35-300. Pays expenses of writers on assignment.

Photos: "Good quality photos accompanying ms improve chances for sale."

Fiction: Historical. Buys 2-3 mss/year. Length: 400-1,200 words. Pays $35-150.

Poetry: JoAnn Wimstorfer, family editor. Buys 2-4 poems/year. Submit maximum 8 poems. Pays $5-50.

Tips: "Write about a North Dakotan—one of our members who has done something notable in the ag/energy/rural electric/rural lifestyle areas."

NEW ENGLAND FARM BULLETIN, New England Farm & Home Assn., Box 147, Cohasset MA 02025. Editor-in-Chief: V.A. Lipsett. Managing Editor: M.S. Maire. 5% freelance written. Works with a small number of new/unpublished writers each year. A biweekly newsletter covering New England farming. Circ. 11,000. Pays on publication. Publishes ms an average of 2 months after acceptance. Byline given. Buys first North American serial rights. Submit seasonal/holiday material 6 months in advance. Photocopied submissions OK. Computer printout submissions acceptable. Reports in 1 week. Sample copy and writer's guidelines for #10 SAE and $1.25.

Nonfiction: Essays (farming/agriculture), general interest, historical/nostalgic, how-to, humor, interview/profile (possibly, of New England farm), personal experience, and technical. All articles must be related to New England farming. Buys 6-12 mss/year. Query or send complete ms. Length: 500-1,000 words. Pays 10¢/word.

Tips: "We would probably require the writer to live in New England or to have an unmistakable grasp of what New England is like; must also know farmers." Especially interested in general articles on New England crops/livestocks, specific breeds, crop strains and universal agricultural activity in New England.

‡NEW ENGLAND FARMER, NEF Publishing Co., Box 391, 50 Bay St., St. Johnsbury VT 05819. (802)748-8908. FAX: (802)748-1866. Editors and Publishers: Dan Hurley and Francis Carlet. 40% freelance written. Monthly dairy publication covering New England agriculture for farmers. Circ. 18,000. Pays on publication. Byline given. Buys all rights and makes-work-for-hire assignments. Submit seasonal/holiday material 2 months in advance. Computer printout submissions acceptable. Reports in 3 months. Free sample copy.

Nonfiction: How-to, interview/profile, opinion and technical. No romantic views of farming. "We use on-the-farm interviews with good black and white photos that combine technical information with human interest. No poetics!" Buys 150 mss/year. Send complete ms. Pays $50-100. Sometimes pays the expenses of writers on assignment.

Photos: Send photos with ms. Payment for photos is included in payment for articles. Reviews b&w contact sheets and 8x10 b&w prints.

Tips: "Good, accurate stories needing minimal editing, with art, of interest to commercial farmers in New England are welcome. A frequent mistake made by writers is sending us items that do not meet our needs; generally, they'll send stories that don't have a New England focus."

THE OHIO FARMER, 1350 W. 5th Ave., Columbus OH 43212. (614)486-9637. Editor: Andrew Stevens. 10% freelance written. "We are backlogged with submissions and prefer not to receive unsolicited submissions at this time." For Ohio farmers and their families. Biweekly magazine. Circ. 81,000. Usually buys all rights. Pays on publication. Publishes ms an average of 2 months after acceptance. Will consider photocopied submissions. Reports in 2 weeks. Query for electronic submissions. Sample copy $1; free writer's guidelines.

Nonfiction: Technical and on-the-farm stories. Buys informational, how-to and personal experience. Buys 5 mss/year. Submit complete ms. Length: 600-700 words. Pays $30.

Photos: Photos purchased with ms with no additional payment, or without ms. Pays $5-25 for b&w; $35-100 for color. 4x5 b&w glossies; and transparencies or 8x10 color prints.

Tips: "We are now doing more staff-written stories. We buy very little freelance material."

PENNSYLVANIA FARMER, Harcourt Brace Jovanovich Publications, 704 Lisburn Rd., Camp Hill PA 17011. (717)761-6050. Editor: John Vogel. 20% freelance written. A bimonthly farm business magazine "oriented to providing readers with ideas to help their businesses and personal lives." Circ. 68,000. Pays on publication. Publishes ms an average of 3 months after acceptance. Byline sometimes given. Buys one-time rights. Submit seasonal/holiday material 3 months in advance. Simultaneous submissions OK. Reports in 2 weeks. Writer's guidelines for #10 SASE.

Nonfiction: Humor, inspirational and technical. No stories without a strong tie to modern-day farming. Buys 15 mss/year. Query. Length: 500-1,000 words. Pays $25-100. Sometimes pays the expenses of writers on assignment.

Photos: Send photos with submission. Reviews contact sheets, 35mm transparencies and 5x7 prints. Offers no additional payment for photos accepted with ms. Captions and identification of subjects required. Buys one-time rights.

‡WYOMING RURAL ELECTRIC NEWS, 340 West B St., Casper WY 82601. (307)234-6152. Editor: Gale Eisenhauer. 10% freelance written. Works with a small number of new/unpublished writers each year; eager to work with new/unpublished writers. For audience of rural people, some farmers and ranchers. Monthly magazine; 20 pages. Circ. 58,500. Not copyrighted. Byline given. Pays on publication. Publishes ms an average of 3 months after acceptance. Buys first serial rights. Will consider photocopied and simultaneous submissions. Submit seasonal material 2 months in advance. Computer printout submissions acceptable; prefers letter-quality to dot-matrix. Reports in 1 month. Free sample copy with SAE and 3 first class stamps.

Nonfiction and Fiction: Wants energy-related material, "people" features, historical pieces about Wyoming and the West, and things of interest to Wyoming's rural people. Buys informational, humor, historical, nostalgia and photo mss. Submit complete ms. Buys 12-15 mss/year. Length for nonfiction and fiction: 1,200-1,500 words. Pays $25-50. Buys some experimental, western, humorous and historical fiction. Pays $25-50. Sometimes pays the expenses of writers on assignment.

Photos: Photos purchased with accompanying ms with additional payment, or purchased without ms. Captions required. Pays up to $50 for cover photos. Color only.

Tips: "Study an issue or two of the magazine to become familiar with our focus and the type of freelance material we're using. Submit entire manuscript. Don't submit a regionally set story from some other part of the country and merely change the place names to Wyoming. Photos and illustrations (if appropriate) are always welcomed."

Finance

These magazines deal with banking, investment and financial management. Publications that use similar material but have a less technical slant are listed under the Consumer Business and Finance section.

BANK OPERATIONS REPORT, Warren, Gorham & Lamont, One Penn Plaza, New York NY 10119. (212)971-5000. Managing Editor: Pat Durner. 90% freelance written. Prefers to work with published/established writers, and works with a small number of new/unpublished writers each year. A monthly newsletter covering operations and technology in banking and financial services. Circ. 2,000. Pays on publication. Publishes ms an average of 2 months after acceptance. Buys all rights. Computer printout submissions OK; prefers letter-quality. Free sample copy.
Nonfiction: How-to articles, case histories, "practical oriented for bank operations managers" and technical. Buys 60 mss/year. Query with published clips. Length: 500-1,000 words. Pays $1.50/line. Sometimes pays the expenses of writers on assignment.

BANK PERSONNEL REPORT, Warren, Gorham & Lamont, One Penn Plaza, New York NY 10119. (212)971-5000. Managing Editor: Selvin Gootar. 20% freelance written. Prefers to work with published/established writers, and works with a small number of new/unpublished writers each year. A monthly newsletter covering personnel and human resources, "specifically as they relate to bankers." Circ. 2,000. Pays on publication. Publishes ms an average of 2 months after acceptance. Buys all rights. Computer printout submissions OK; prefers letter-quality. Free sample copy.
Nonfiction: Technical. Query with published clips. Length: 500-1,000 words. Pays $1.20/line. Sometimes pays the expenses of writers on assignment.

BANKING SOFTWARE REVIEW, International Computer Programs, Inc., Suite 200, 9100 Keystone Crossing, Indianapolis IN 46240. (317)844-7461. FAX: (317)574-0571. Editor: Marilyn Gasaway. Quarterly trade magazine covering the computer software industry as it relates to financial institutions. "Editorial slant includes the selection, implementation and use of software in banks and other financial institutions." The audience comprises data processing and end-user management in medium to large financial institutions." Circ. 15,000. Pays on publication. Publishes ms an average of 2 months after acceptance. Byline sometimes given. Buys first or second serial (reprint) rights. Photocopied submissions OK. Query for electronic submissions. Computer printout submissions OK; prefers letter-quality. Reports in 3 weeks on queries; 1 month on mss.
Nonfiction: How-to (successfully install and use software products), interview/profile, new product and technical. No non-software related, non-business software or humorous articles. Buys 8-10 mss/year. Query with published clips. Length: 1,000-2,500 words. Pays $350-600 for assigned articles. Sometimes pays the expenses of writers on assignment. Sometimes pays with contributor copies, "depends on number of copies requested."
Photos: Send photos with submission. Prefers 5x7 prints. Offers no additional payment for photos accepted with ms. Identification of subjects required. Buys all rights.
Columns/Departments: Systems Review (in-depth profile of a specific software product at use in a banking environment; must include comments from 2-3 financial institution users, e.g., the benefits of the product, its use within the institution, etc.). Length: 500-700 words. Pays $50.

‡THE BOTTOM LINE, The News and Information Publication for Canada's Financial Professionals, Bottom Line Publications Inc., 341 Steelcase Rd. W., Markham, Ontario L3R 3W1 Canada. (416)474-9532. FAX: (416)474-9803. Editor: Gundi Jeffrey. 35% freelance written. Monthly tabloid on accounting/ finance/ business. "Reaches 80% of all Canadian accountants. Information should be news/commentary/analysis of issues or issues of interest to or about accountants." Circ. 46,000. Pays on publication. Publishes ms an average of 2 weeks to 4 months after acceptance. Byline given. Buys first rights. Simultaneous submissions OK. Query for electronic submissions. Computer printout submissions OK; prefers letter-quality. Reports in 1-2 weeks. Free sample copy.
Nonfiction: Technical and travel. Buys 12 mss/year. Query. Length: 800-1,200 words. Pays $250-750 for assigned articles.
Photos: State availability of photos with submission. Offers $50 maximum per photo. Buys one-time rights.

CA MAGAZINE, 150 Bloor St., W., Toronto, Ontario M5S 2Y2 Canada. FAX: (416)962-3375. Editor: Nelson Luscombe. 10% freelance written. Works with a small number of new/unpublished writers each year. Monthly magazine for accountants and financial managers. Circ. 60,000. Pays on publication for the article's copyright. Buys all rights. Computer printout submissions acceptable; prefers letter-quality. Publishes ms an average of 4 months after acceptance. Free sample copy and writer's guidelines.
Nonfiction: Accounting, business, finance, management and taxation. Also, subject-related humor pieces and cartoons. "We accept whatever is relevant to our readership, no matter the origin as long as it meets our standards." Length: 3,000-5,000 words. Pays $100 for feature articles, $75 for departments and 10¢/word for acceptable news items. Sometimes pays the expenses of writers on assignment.

‡CONSUMER LENDING REPORT, Warren Gorham & Lamont, 40th Floor, One Penn Plaza, New York NY 10119. (212)971-5000. FAX: (212)971-5025. Editor: Natalie Baumer. 75% freelance written. A monthly trade journal covering all aspects of consumer lending. Circ. 3,000. Pays on publication. No byline given. Computer printout submissions OK; prefers letter-quality to dot-matrix. Free sample copy and writer's guidelines.

Nonfiction: How-to (market, analyze, develop lending products); interview/profile; new product and technical. Query with or without published clips, or send complete ms. Length: 120-150 lines. Pays $1.50/line.

DELUXE, Ideas for the Business of Living, K. L. Publications, Suite 105, 2001 Killebrew Dr., Bloomington MN 55425. (612)854-0155. Editor: George Ashfield. 80% freelance written. A quarterly magazine published by Webb for Deluxe Check Printers, Inc., for employees of financial institutions nationwide. *"Deluxe* is published for new-accounts counselors in banks, savings & loan associations and credit unions. They receive the magazine at work, so we aim to present new, useful and entertaining information that will help them with life at the office, as well as with life at home. New account counselors deal with the public often, both in person and on the phone. They usually serve as the financial institution's main link to customers. Our magazine hopes to help them do their jobs better and reinforce an image of professionalism in themselves." Circ. 100,000. Pays on acceptance by client. Byline given. Offers 25% kill fee. Buys limited rights in work-for-hire arrangement. Submit seasonal/holiday material 8 months in advance. Simultaneous and photocopied submissions OK. Query for electronic submissions. Computer printout submissions OK; prefers letter-quality. Reports in 3 weeks. Sample copy for 8¾x11¾ SAE with 3 first class stamps. Writer's guidelines for #10 SAE with 1 first class stamp.

Nonfiction: General interest, historical/nostalgic and business/career/personal development. No personal articles, essay, opinion, humor, technical finance, first-person, "executive" topics or how to get out of your present job articles. Buys 16 mss/year. Query with published clips and résumé. Length: 600-1,600 words. Pays $300-600. Sometimes pays the expenses of writers on assignment.

Tips: "Writers should learn more about our audience — new accounts counselors at financial institutions — and then gear article ideas specifically to them. Also, they should not be offended if asked to rewrite their stories in order to slant them to the needs/wants of our readers."

EXECUTIVE FINANCIAL WOMAN, Suite 1400, 500 N. Michigan Ave., Chicago IL 60611. (312)661-1700. FAX: (312)661-0769. Editor: Richard G. Kemmer. Managing Editor: Lora Engdahl. 10-30% freelance written. Eager to work with new/unpublished writers. Quarterly magazine for members of the National Association of Bank Women and paid subscribers covering banking, insurance, financial planning, diversified financials, credit unions, thrifts, investment banking and other industry segments. Circ. 25,000. Publishes ms an average of 2 months after acceptance. Byline given. Buys all rights. Submit seasonal material 3 months in advance. Simultaneous queries and photocopied submissions OK. Computer printout submissions acceptable; no dot-matrix. Reports in approximately 1 month. Sample copy $4.

Nonfiction: "We are looking for articles in the general areas of financial services, career advancement, businesswomen's issues and management. Because the financial services industry is in a state of flux at present, articles on how to adapt to and benefit from this fact, both personally and professionally, are particularly apt." Query with resume and clips of published work. Length: 1,000-4,000 words. Pays variable rates.

Photos: "Photos and other graphic material can make an article more attractive to us." Captions and model release required.

Tips: "We're looking for writers who can write effectively about the people who work in the industry and combine that with hard data on how the industry is changing. We're interested in running more Q&As with top executives in the industry, especially women."

‡THE FINANCIAL MANAGER, The Magazine for Financial and Accounting Professionals, Warren, Gorham & Lamont, 40th Fl. One Penn Plaza, New York NY 10119. (212)971-5280. Editor: Joseph P. Burns. 95% freelance written. Bimonthly magazine for accountants and financial executives in business. "Information for CFOs, VPs of Finance, corporate controllers and treasurers on how to manage their companies' finances effectively and efficiently. Estab. 1988. Circ. 30,000. Pays on acceptance. Publishes ms an average of 4 months after acceptance. Byline given. Kill fee varies. Computer printout submissions OK; prefers letter-quality. Reports in 2 months on queries; 4 months on mss. Sample copy for 8½x11 SAE. Free sample copy and writer's guidelines.

Nonfiction: How-to (articles on managing a medium-sized company's finances), professional experience and technical (accounting terms, regulations and procedures). Buys 60 mss/year. Query. Length: 1,500-3,000 words. Pays $100-1,000 for assigned articles; $50-1,000 for unsolicited articles. Pays expenses of writers on assignment.

Columns/Departments: Richard Stockton, senior technical editor; Roslyn Myers, associate editor; Vincent Ryan, assistant editor. Tax Breaks (tax information for medium-sized companies), 1,500-2,000 words. Financial Reporting Update (financial reporting information for medium-sized companies), 1,500-2,000 words; New Products (new accounting software, books, services), 750-1,500 words; The Prudent Manager (issues in insurance, law, compensation, ERISA and ethics); Management Material (winning management tips and strategies); Career Path (maximizing your management potential); Financial Resources (dealing with banks and other capital sources); and Capsule Case (how would you handle this?). Buys 30 mss/year. Query. Length: 1,200-1,500 words. Pays $100-500.

THE FUTURES AND OPTIONS TRADER, DeLong—Western Publishing Co., 13618 Scenic Crest Dr., Yucaipa CA 92399. (714)797-3532. Editor: Charles Kreidl. Managing Editor: Jeanne Johnson. 50% freelance written. Monthly newspaper covering futures and options. Publishes "basic descriptions of trading systems or other commodity futures information which would be useful to traders. No hype or sales-related articles." Circ. 12,000. Pays on acceptance. Publishes ms an average of 1 month after acceptance. Not copyrighted. Buys all rights. Simultaneous and photocopied submissions OK. Query for electronic submissions. Computer printout submissions OK; prefers letter-quality. Free sample copy and writer's guidelines.
Nonfiction: Technical and general trading-related articles. Buys 35 mss/year. Send complete ms. Length: 250-1,000 words. Pays $10-100 for unsolicited articles.
Columns/Departments: Options Trader; Spread Trader (futures and options spread and arbitrage trading); and Index Trader (stock index trading). Buys 35 mss/year. Send complete ms. Length: 250-1,000 words. Pays $10-100.
Tips: "Authors should be active in the markets."

ILLINOIS BANKER, Illinois Bankers Association, Suite 1100, 205 W. Randolph, Chicago IL 60606. (312)984-1500. FAX: (312)782-0485. Vice President, Public Affairs: Martha Rohlfing. Assistant Publisher: Cindy Altman. Assistant Editor: Janet Krause. 10% freelance written. Monthly magazine about banking for top decision makers and executives, bank officers, title and insurance company executives, elected officials and individual subscribers interested in banking products and services. Circ. 3,000. Pays on publication. Publishes ms an average of 4 months after acceptance. Byline given. Buys first serial rights. Phone queries OK. Submit material 6 weeks prior to publication. Simultaneous submissions OK. Computer printout submissions acceptable. Free sample copy, writer's guidelines and editorial calendar.
Nonfiction: Interview (ranking government and banking leaders); personal experience (along the lines of customer relations); and technical (specific areas of banking). "The purpose of the publication is to educate, inform and guide its readers on public policy issues affecting banks, new ideas in management and operations, and banking and business trends in the Midwest. Any clear, fresh approach geared to a specific area of banking, such as agricultural bank management, credit, lending, marketing and trust is what we want." Buys 4-5 unsolicited mss/year. Send complete ms. Length: 825-3,000 words. Pays $50-100.

INDEPENDENT BANKER, Independent Bankers Association of America, Box 267, Sauk Centre MN 56378. (612)352-6546. Editor: Norman Douglas. 15% freelance written. Works with a small number of new/unpublished writers each year. Monthly magazine for the administrators of small, independent banks. Circ. 10,000. Pays on acceptance. Publishes ms an average of 3 months after acceptance. Byline given. Not copyrighted. Buys all rights. Computer printout submissions acceptable; prefers letter-quality. Reports in 1 week. Sample copy and writer's guidelines for 9x12 SAE and $1.25 postage.
Nonfiction: How-to (banking practices and procedures); interview/profile (popular small bankers); technical (bank accounting, automation); and banking trends. "Factual case histories, banker profiles or research pieces of value to bankers in the daily administration of their banks." No material that ridicules banking and finance or puff pieces. Query. Length: 2,000-2,500 words. Pays $300 maximum.
Tips: "In this magazine, the emphasis is on material that will help small banks compete with large banks and large bank holding companies. We look for innovative articles on small bank operations and administration. Resolution of savings and loan industry crisis and third world debt held by U.S. Banks could have impact on editorial content. "

OTC REVIEW, OTC Review, Inc., 37 E. 28th St., Suite 706, New York NY 10016. (212)685-6244. Editor: Robert Flaherty. 50% freelance written. A monthly magazine covering publicly owned companies whose stocks trade in the over-the-counter market. "We are a financial magazine covering the fastest-growing securities market in the world. We study the management of companies traded over-the-counter and act as critics reviewing their performances. We aspire to be 'The Shareholder's Friend.' " Circ. 27,000. Pays on publication. Publishes ms an average of 2 months after acceptance. Byline given. Buys first rights or reprint rights. Sample copy for 8½x11 SAE with 5 first class stamps.
Nonfiction: New product and technical. Buys 30 mss/year. "We must know the writer first as we are careful about whom we publish. A letter of introduction with résumé and clips is the best way to introduce yourself. Financial writing requires specialized knowledge and a feel for people as well, which can be a tough combination to find." Query with published clips. Length: 300-1,500 words. Pays $150-750 for assigned articles. Offers copies or premiums for guest columns by famous money managers who are not writing for cash payments, but to showcase their ideas and approach. Pays expenses of writers on assignment.
Photos: Send photos with submission. Reviews contact sheets, negatives, transparencies and prints. Offers no additional payment for photos accepted with ms. Identification of subjects required.
Columns/Departments: Pays $25-75 for assigned items only.
Tips: "Anyone who enjoys analyzing a business and telling the story of the people who started it, or run it today, is a potential *OTC Review* contributor. But to protect our readers and ourselves, we are careful about who writes for us. Business writing is an exciting area and our stories reflect that. If a writer relies on numbers and percentages to tell his story, rather than the individuals involved, the result will be numbingly dull."

‡**PENSION WORLD**, Communication Channels, Inc., 6255 Barfield Rd. Atlanta GA 30328. (404)256-9800. Editor: Jeffrey S. Atkinson. 10% freelance written. Monthly magazine on pension investment and employee benefits. Circ. 28,146. Pays on pasteup. Publishes ms an average of 1 month after acceptance. Byline given. Offer 10% kill fee. Buys all rights. Submit seasonal/holiday material 4 months in advance. Query for electronic submissions. Computer printout submissions OK; prefers letter-quality. Reports in 2 weeks on queries; 3 weeks on mss. Free sample copy and writer's guidelines.

Nonfiction: General interest, humor, interview/profile, new product and opinion. Buys 18 mss/year. Query with published clips. Length: 1,500-2,500 words. Pays $300-500 for assigned articles. Pays $250-450 for unsolicited articles. Sometimes pays expenses of writers on assignment.

Photos: State availability of photos with submission. Reviews 3¾ transparencies and 5x7 prints. Offers no additional payment for photos accepted with ms. Identification of subjects required. Buys one-time rights.

Tips: "Freelancers should know the major players in the market they are trying to crack, and how those players relate to the market."

RESEARCH MAGAZINE, Ideas for Today's Investors, Research Services, 2201 Third St., San Francisco CA 94107. (415)621-0220. Editor: Anne Evers. 50% freelance written. Monthly business magazine of corporate profiles and subjects of interest to stockbrokers. Circ. 80,000. Pays on publication. Publishes ms an average of 2 months after acceptance. Byline given. Offers 20% kill fee. Buys first North American serial rights or second serial (reprint) rights. Query for electronic submissions. Reports in 1 month. Sample copy for 9x12 SAE with 4 first class stamps; writer's guidelines for #10 SASE.

Nonfiction: How-to (sales tips), interview/profile, new product, financial products. Buys approx. 50 mss/year. Query with published clips. Length: 1,000-3,000 words. Pays 300-900. Sometimes pays expenses of writers on assignment.

Tips: "Only submit articles that fit our editorial policy and are appropriate for our audience. *Only the non-corporate profile section is open to freelancers.* We use local freelancers on a regular basis for coporate profiles."

SAVINGS INSTITUTIONS, U.S. League of Savings Institutions, 111 E. Wacker Dr., Chicago IL 60601. (312)644-3100. FAX: (312)644-9358. Editor: Mary Nowesnick. 5% freelance written. Prefers to work with published/established writers. A monthly business magazine covering management of savings institutions. Circ. 30,000. Pays on acceptance. Publishes ms an average of 3 months after acceptance. Byline given. Buys negotiable rights. Simultaneous queries and photocopied submissions OK. Query for electronic submissions. Computer printout submissions acceptable; prefers letter-quality. Reports in 2 months. Sample copy for SASE.

Nonfiction: How-to (manage or improve operations); new products (application stories at savings institutions); and technical (financial management). No opinion or "puff" pieces. Buys 1-3 mss/year. Query with or without published clips. Length: 3,000-8,000 words. Pays $125/published page. Pays expenses of writers on assignment.

Columns/Departments: Beth Linnen, column/department editor. Operations, Marketing, Personnel, and Secondary Mortgage Market. Buys 10 mss/year. Query with or without published clips. Length: 800-3,000 words. Pays $125/published page.

Tips: "Operations and Marketing departments are most open to freelancers."

SECONDARY MARKETING EXECUTIVE, LDJ Corporation. Box 2151, Waterbury CT 06722. (203)755-0158. FAX: (203)755-3480. Editorial Director: John Florian. 60% freelance written. A monthly tabloid on secondary marketing. "The magazine is read monthly by executives in financial institutions who are involved with secondary marketing. The editorial slant is toward how-to and analysis of trends, rather than spot news." Circ. 34,000. Pays on publication. Publishes ms an average of 1 month after acceptance. Byline given. 30% kill fee. Buys first rights. Submit seasonal/holiday material 4 months in advance. Query for electronic submissions. Computer printout submissions OK; no dot-matrix. Reports in 1 week. Free sample copy and writer's guidelines.

Nonfiction: How-to (how to improve secondary marketing operations and profits) and opinion. Buys 40 mss/year. Query. Length: 800-1,200 words. Pays $200-400.

Photos: State availability of photos with submission. Reviews contact sheets. Offers $25 per photo. Captions, model releases and identification of subjects required. Buys one-time rights.

Fishing

PACIFIC FISHING, Salmon Bay Communications, 1515 NW 51st St., Seattle WA 98107. (206)789-5333. FAX: (206)784-5545. Editor: Bill Marchese. 75% freelance written. Eager to work with new/unpublished writers.

Monthly business magazine for commercial fishermen and others in the West Coast commercial fishing industry. *Pacific Fishing* views the fisherman as a small businessman and covers all aspects of the industry, including harvesting, processing and marketing. Circ. 10,000. Pays on publication. Publishes ms an average of 2 months after acceptance. Byline given. Offers 10-15% kill fee on assigned articles deemed unsuitable. Buys one-time rights. Queries highly recommended. Computer printout submissions acceptable; prefers letter-quality. Reports in 1 month. Free sample copy and writer's guidelines.

Nonfiction: Interview/profile and technical (usually with a business hook or slant). "Articles must be concerned specifically with *commercial* fishing. We view fishermen as small businessmen and professionals who are innovative and success-oriented. To appeal to this reader, *Pacific Fishing* offers four basic features: technical, how-to articles that give fisherman hands-on tips that will make their operation more efficient and profitable; practical, well-researched business articles discussing the dollars and cents of fishing, processing and marketing; profiles of a fisherman, processor or company with emphasis on practical business and technical areas; and in-depth analysis of political, social, fisheries management and resource issues that have a direct bearing on West Coast commercial fishermen." Buys 20 mss/year. Query noting whether photos are available, and enclosing samples of previous work. Length: 1,500-2,500 words. Pays 10-15¢/word. Sometimes pays the expenses of writers on assignment.

Photos: "We need good, high-quality photography, especially color, of West Coast commercial fishing. We prefer 35mm color slides. Our rates are $150 for cover; $50-100 for inside color; $25-50 for b&w and $10 for table of contents."

Tips: "Because of the specialized nature of our audience, the editor strongly recommends that freelance writers query the magazine in writing with a proposal. We enjoy finding a writer who understands our editorial needs and satisfies those needs, a writer willing to work with an editor to make the article just right. Most of our shorter items are staff written. Our freelance budget is such that we get the most benefit by using it for feature material. The most frequent mistakes made by writers are not keeping to specified length and failing to do a complete job on statistics that may be a part of the story."

Florists, Nurseries and Landscaping

Readers of these publications are involved in growing, selling or caring for plants, flowers and trees. Magazines geared to consumers interested in gardening are listed in the Consumer Home and Garden section.

‡**FLORAL & NURSERY TIMES,** XXX Publishing Enterprises Ltd., Box 699, Wilmette IL 60091. (312)256-8777. FAX: (312)256-8791. Editor: Barbara Gilbert. 10% freelance written. A bimonthly trade journal covering wholesale and retail horticulture and floriculture. Circ. 17,500. Pays on publication. Byline given. Buys simultaneous rights. Submit seasonal/holiday material 3 months in advance. Simultaneous and photocopied submissions OK. Reports in 2 weeks. Sample copy for 9x12 SAE and $3; writer's guidelines for #10 SASE.

Nonfiction: General interest and technical. Buys 100 mss/year. Query with or without published clips, or send complete ms. Payment is negotiable.

Photos: State availability of photos with submission. Reviews prints. Offers no additional payment for photos accepted with ms. Captions and identification of subjects required. Buys simultaneous rights.

Columns/Departments: Care & Handling (horticultural products). Query. Payment negotiable.

FLORIST, Florists' Transworld Delivery Association, 29200 Northwestern Hwy., Box 2227, Southfield MI 48037. (313)355-9300. Editor-in-Chief: William P. Golden. Managing Editor: Susan L. Nicholas. 3% freelance written. For retail florists, floriculture growers, wholesalers, researchers and teachers. Monthly magazine. Circ. 28,000. Pays on acceptance. Publishes ms an average of 2 months after acceptance. Buys one-time rights. Pays 10-25% kill fee. Byline given "unless the story needs a substantial rewrite." Phone queries OK. Submit seasonal/holiday material 4 months in advance. Simultaneous, photocopied and previously published submissions OK. Computer printout submissions acceptable; prefers letter-quality. Reports in 1 month.

Nonfiction: How-to (more profitably run a retail flower shop, grow and maintain better quality flowers, etc.); general interest (to floriculture and retail floristry); and technical (on flower and plant growing, breeding, etc.). Buys 5 unsolicited mss/year. Query with published clips. Length: 1,200-3,000 words. Pays 20¢/word.

Photos: "We do not like to run stories without photos." State availability of photos with query. Pays $10-25 for 5x7 b&w photos or color transparencies. Buys one-time rights.
Tips: "Send samples of published work with query. Suggest several ideas in query letter."

‡**FLOWER NEWS,** 549 W. Randolph St., Chicago IL 60606. (312)236-8648. Editor: Lauren C. Oates. For retail, wholesale florists, floral suppliers, supply jobbers and growers. Weekly newspaper; 32 pages. Circ. 17,000. Pays on acceptance. Byline given. Submit seasonal/holiday material at least 2 months in advance. Photocopied and previously published submissions OK. Reports "immediately." Sample copy for 10x13 SAE and $2.40 postage.
Nonfiction: How-to (increase business, set up a new shop, etc.; anything floral related without being an individual shop story); informational (general articles of interest to industry); and technical (grower stories related to industry, but not individual grower stories). Submit complete ms. Length: 3-5 typed pages. Payment varies.
Photos: "We do not buy individual pictures. They may be enclosed with manuscript at regular manuscript rate (b&w only)."

GARDEN SUPPLY RETAILER, Miller Publishing, Box 2400, Minnetonka MN 55343. (612)931-0211. FAX: (612)931-0217. Editor: Kay Melchisedech Olson. 5% freelance written. Prefers to work with published/ established writers but "quality work is more important than experience of the writer." Monthly magazine for lawn and garden retailers. Circ. 40,000. Pays on acceptance in most cases. Publishes ms an average of 3-4 months after acceptance. Buys first serial rights, and occasionally second serial (reprint) rights. Previously published submissions "in different fields" OK as long as not in overlapping fields such as hardware, nursery growers, etc. Computer printout submissions acceptable; prefers letter-quality. Reports in 2 weeks on rejections, acceptance may take longer. Sample copy for 9x12 SAE and $1 postage; writer's guidelines for #10 SAE and 2 first class stamps.
Nonfiction: "We aim to provide retailers with management, merchandising, tax planning and computer information. No technical advice on how to care for lawns, plants and lawn mowers. Articles should be of interest to *retailers* of garden supply products. Stories should tell retailers something about the industry that they don't already know; show them how to make more money by better merchandising or management techniques; address a concern or problem directly affecting retailers or the industry." Buys 10-15 mss/year. Send complete ms or rough draft plus clips of previously published work. Length: 800-1,000 words. Pays $150-200.
Photos: Send photos with ms. Reviews color negatives and transparencies, and 5x7 b&w prints. Captions and identification of subjects required.
Tips: "We will not consider manuscripts offered to 'overlapping' publications such as the hardware industry, nursery growers, etc. Query letters outlining an idea should include at least a partial rough draft; lists of titles are uninteresting. We want business-oriented articles specifically relevant to interests and concerns of retailers of lawn and garden products. We seldom use filler material and would find it a nuisance to deal with freelancers for this. Freelancers submitting articles to our publication will find it increasingly difficult to get acceptance as we will be soliciting stories from industry experts and will not have much budget for general freelance material."

‡**THE GROWING EDGE,** New Moon Publishing Inc., 206 SW Jefferson, Box 1027, Corvallis OR 97339. (503)757-0027. FAX: (503)757-0028. Editor: Don Parker. 60% freelance written. Eager to work with new or unpublished writers. Quarterly magazine signature covering indoor and outdoor high-tech gardening techniques and tips. Circ. 15,000. Pays on publication. Publishes ms an average of 3 months after acceptance. Byline given. Buys first serial rights and reprint rights. Submit seasonal/holiday material at least 6 months in advance. Query for electronic submissions. Sample copy $6.
Nonfiction: Book excerpts and reviews relating to high-tech gardening, general interest, how-to, interview/ profile, personal experience and technical. Query first. Length: 500-2,500 words. Pays 7.5¢/word.
Photos: Pays $50/color cover photos; $10-30/color inside photo; $10-20/b&w inside photos; $50-150/text/ photo package. Pays on publication. Credit line given. Buys first and reprint rights. Simultaneous and previously published submissions OK.
Tips: Looking for information which will give the reader/gardener/farmer the "growing edge" in high-tech gardening and farming on topics such as hydroponics, high intensity grow lights, water conservation, drip irrigation, advanced organic fertilizers, new seed varieties and greenhouse cultivation.

The double dagger before a listing indicates that the listing is new in this edition. New markets are often the most receptive to freelance submissions.

INTERIOR LANDSCAPE INDUSTRY, The Magazine for Designing Minds and Growing Businesses, American Nurseryman Publishing Co., Suite 545, 111 N. Canal St., Chicago IL 60606. (312)782-5505. FAX: (312)454-6158. Editor: Brent C. Marchant. 10% freelance written. Prefers to work with published/established writers. "Willing to work with freelancers as long as they can fulfill the specifics of our requirements." Monthly magazine on business and technical topics for all parties involved in interior plantings, including interior landscapers, growers and allied professionals (landscape architects, architects and interior designers). "We take a professional approach to the material and encourage our writers to emphasize the professionalism of the industry in their writings." Circ. 4,000. Pays on publication. Publishes ms an average of 5 months after acceptance. Byline given. Buys all rights. Submit material 2 months in advance. Query for electronic submissions. Computer printout submissions acceptable; prefers letter-quality. Reports in 3 weeks on queries; 2 weeks on mss. Free sample copy and writer's guidelines.
Nonfiction: How-to (technical and business topics related to the audience); interview/profile (companies working in the industry); personal experience (preferably from those who work or have worked in the industry); photo feature (related to interior projects or plant producers); and technical. No shallow, consumerish-type features. Buys 30 mss/year. Query with published clips. Length: 3-15 ms pages double spaced. Pays $2/ published inch. Sometimes pays expenses of writers on assignment.
Photos: Send photos with query. Reviews b&w contact sheet, negatives, and 5x7 prints; standard size or 4x5 color transparencies. Pays $5-10 for b&w; $15 for color. Identification of subjects required. Buys all rights.
Tips: "Demonstrate knowledge of the field—not just interest in it. Features, especially profiles, are most open to freelancers. We are currently increasing coverage of the design professions, specifically as they relate to interior landscaping."

‡PRO, Helping Lawn Maintenance Firms Operate Profitably, Johnson Hill Press, 1233 Janesville Ave., Ft. Atkinson WI 53538. (414)563-6388. Editor: Rod Dickens. Managing Editor: Julie DeYoung. 25% freelance written. Bimonthly tabloid on lawn maintenance firms. Estab. 1988. Circ. 40,000. Pays on publication. Byline given. Buys all rights. Submit seasonal/holiday material 6 months in advance. Computer printout submissions OK; prefers letter-quality. Reports in 1 month. Free sample copy and writer's guidelines.
Nonfiction: How-to (business management, employee management, marketing, advertising), interview/profile (successful lawn maintenance firms), new product, and technical (equipment selection, use and care). Buys 12 mss/year. Query with or without published clips, or send complete ms. Length: 500-1,400 words. Pays $10-300 for assigned articles; $10-200 for unassigned articles. Sometimes pays writers with contributor copies or other premiums rather than a cash payment. Pays expenses of writers on assignment.
Photos: Send photos with submission. Reviews negatives, transparencies, and prints. Offers no additional payment for photos accepted with ms. Captions and identification of subjects required. Buys all rights.
Columns/Departments: Rx for Downtime (lawncare equipment preventive maintenance); Safety pen (safe equipment operation); In-gear (better procedures for bigger profits, employee productivity); Business management (business management techniques); and Ask the Computerman (business use of computers). Buys 24 mss/year. Query with published clips. Length: 500-1,400 words. Pays $10-100.
Tips: "Have experience in this industry. Query with article idea before writing article. Provide color photos with stories."

‡TURF MAGAZINE, Box 391, 50 Bay St., St. Johnsbury VT 05819. (802)748-8908. FAX: (802)748-1866. Editors and Publishers: Francis Carlet and Dan Hurley. 40% freelance written. "Primarily focused on the professional turf grass applicators and users, e.g.: superintendents of grounds for golf courses, cemeteries, athletic fields, parks, recreation fields, lawn care companies, landscape contractors/architects." Circ. 22,000. Pays on publication. Byline given. Buys all rights or makes work-for-hire assignments. Submit seasonal/ holiday material 2 months in advance. Computer printout submissions acceptable. Reports in 3 months. Free sample copy.
Nonfiction: How to, interview/profile, opinion and technical. We use on-the-job type interviews with good b&w photos that combine technical information with human interest. "No poetics!" Buys 150 mss/year. Send complete ms. Pays $75-150. Sometimes pays the expenses of writers on assignment.
Photos: Send photos with ms. Payment for photos is included in payment for articles. Reviews b&w contact sheets and 8x10 b&w prints.
Tips: "Good, accurate stories needing minimal editing, with art, of interest to commercial applicators from New England down to Maryland, are welcomed."

‡YARD & GARDEN, Helping Readers Sell More Profitably, Johnson Hill Press, 1233 Janesville Ave., Ft. Atkinson WI 53538. (414)563-6388. Editor: Rod Dickens. Managing Editor: Julie DeYoung. 5% freelance written. Monthly tabloid on lawn and garden retailing. "Editorial mission is to help yard and garden retailers become more successful sellers and managers and covers topics such as sales strategies, marketing, new products and improved business practices." Circ. 38,000. Pays on publication. Byline given. Buys all rights. Submit seasonal/holiday material 6 months in advance. Query for electronic submissions. Computer printout submissions OK; prefers letter-quality. Reports in 1 month. Free sample copy and writer's guidelines.

Nonfiction: How-to (merchandising, sales, advertising, business management, computers), interview/profile (successful yard and garden retailers) and new product. Business Management issue in December. Buys 12 mss/year. Query with or without published clips, or send complete ms. Length: 500-1,400 words. Pays $15-300 for assigned articles; $15-200 for unsolicited articles. Pays with contributor copies "if affiliated with an association or agency which is promoted by having the author's byline in the magazine." Pays expenses of writers on assignment.

Photos: Send photos with submission. Reviews negatives, transparencies and prints. Offers no additional payment for photos accepted with ms. Captions and identification of subjects required. Buys all rights.

Columns/Departments: Money (money management for businesses), 800 words; Legal Adviser (legal issues of interest to retailers), 800 words; and Retail Market Clinic (marketing, advertising information for retailers), 800 words. Buys 48 mss/year. Query with published clips. Pays $15-100.

Tips: "Send specific article ideas with previous work samples to the editor. Call the editor to discuss any upcoming article needs. State your willingness to revise, rewrite if needed to fit publication. Be specific to the industry we serve. Ask for a copy of our editorial calendar and suggest articles that match."

_____ Government and Public Service

Listed here are journals for people who provide governmental services at the local, state or federal level or for those who work in franchised utilities. Journals for city managers, politicians, bureaucratic decision makers, civil servants, firefighters, police officers, public administrators, urban transit managers and utilities managers are listed in this section. Those for private citizens interested in government and public affairs are classified in the Consumer Politics and World Affairs category.

THE CALIFORNIA FIREMAN, The Official Publication of the California State Firemen's Association, Suite 1, 2701 K St., Sacramento CA 95816. Editor: Gary Giacomo. 80% freelance written. Monthly fireservice trade journal. Circ. 30,000. Pays on publication. Publishes ms an average of 2 months after acceptance. Byline given. Buys first North American serial rights. Submit seasonal/holiday material 4 months in advance. Simultaneous submissions OK. Computer printout submissions OK; prefers letter-quality. Reports in 1 month. Sample copy for $1.50; writer's guidelines for #10 SASE.

Nonfiction: Expose (circumvention of fire regulations), historical/nostalgic (California slant), how-to (fight specific types of fires), interview/profile (innovative chiefs and/or departments and their programs), new product (fire suppression/fire prevention), opinion (current issues related to the fire service), personal experience (fire or rescue related), photo features (large or dramatic fires in California), technical (fire suppression/fire prevention). Special issue includes: January 1990: firefighter's wages and hours survey. For this issue we will be looking for submissions dealing with wages and benefits of firefighters and privitization. "The CSFA does sponsor a legislative program in Sacramento. All political items are staff written or assigned to experts; therefore, we do not want any political submissions." Buys 24 mss/year. Query with or without published clips, or send complete ms. Length: 400-1,200 words. Pays $55-100 for assigned articles; $35-55 for unsolicited articles. Pays in contributor's copies for opinion pieces and book reviews.

Photos: State availability of photos with submission or send photos with submission. Reviews contact sheets, trasparencies and 5x7 prints. Captions and identification of subjects required. Buys one-time rights. Pays $10-15.

Columns/Departments: Opinion (essay related to an issue facing the modern fire service. Some examples: AIDS and emergency medical services; hazardous materials cleanup and cancer) 400-700 words. Buys 9 mss/year. Send complete ms. Pays in contributor's copies.

Fillers: Anecdotes, facts, newsbreaks. Buys 60 fillers/year. Length: 30-180. Pays $2.

Tips: "Send for writer's guidelines, an editorial calendar and sample issue. Study our editorial calendar and submit appropriate articles as early as possible. We are always interested in articles that are accompanied by compelling fire or firefighting photographs. Articles submittted with quality photographs, graphs or other illustrations will receive special consideration. Fire Breaks is a good area to break in. In Fire Breaks we are looking for fire related newsbreaks, facts and anecdotes from around the U.S. and the world. Bear in mind that we only pay for the first submission, since many Fire Breaks submissions are duplicates. Also, if you're a good photojournalist and you submit photographs with complete information there is a good chance you can develop into a regular contributor. Remember that we have members from all over California—and from urban as well as forestry and rural departments."

‡**CANADIAN DEFENCE QUARTERLY**, Revue Canadienne de Défense, Baxter Publications Inc., 310 Dupont St., Toronto, Ontario M5R 1V9 Canada. (416)968-7252. FAX: (416)968-2377. Editor: John Marteinson. 90% freelance written. Professional bimonthly journal on strategy, defense policy, military technology, history. "A professional journal for officers of the Canadian Forces and for the academic community working in Canadian foreign and defense affairs. Articles should have Canadian or NATO applicability." Pays on publication. Byline given. Offers $150 kill fee. Buys all rights. Simultaneous submissions OK. Reports in 4 weeks. Free sample copy and writer's guidelines.

Nonfiction: Historical, new product, opinion, technical and military strategy. Buys 45 mss/year. Query with or without published clips, or send complete ms. Length: 2,500-4,000 words. Pays $150-300.

Photos: State availability of photos with submission. Offers no additional payment for photos accepted with ms. Buys one-time rights.

Tips: "Submit a well-written manuscript in a relevant field that demonstrates an original approach to the subject matter. Manuscripts *must* be double-spaced, with good margins."

CHIEF OF POLICE MAGAZINE, National Association of Chiefs of Police, 1100 NE 125th St., Miami FL 33161. (305)891-9800. FAX: (305)891-1884. Editor: Gerald S. Arenberg. A bimonthly trade journal for law enforcement commanders (command ranks). Circ. 10,000. Pays on acceptance. Publishes ms an average of 4-6 months after acceptance. Byline given. Full payment kill fee offered. Buys first rights. Submit seasonal/holiday material 6 months in advance. Simultaneous, photocopied and previously published submissions OK. Computer printout submissions OK. Reports in 2 weeks. Sample copy $3, 8½x11 SAE and 5 first class stamps; writer's guidelines for #10 SASE.

Nonfiction: General interest, historical/nostalgic, how-to, humor, inspirational, interview/profile, new product, personal experience, photo feature, religious and technical. "We want stories about interesting police cases and stories on any law enforcement subject or program that is positive in nature. No exposé types. Nothing anti-police." Buys 50 mss/year. Send complete ms. Length: 600-2,000 words. Pays $25-75 for assigned articles; pays $10-50 for unsolicited articles. Sometimes (when pre-requested) pays the expenses of writers on assignment.

Photos: Send photos with submission. Reviews 5x6 prints. Offers $5-75 per photo. Captions required. Buys one-time rights.

Columns/Departments: New Police (police equipment shown and tests), 200-600 words. Buys 6 mss/year. Send complete ms. Pays $5-25.

Fillers: Anecdote and short humor. Buys 100/year. Length: 100-1,600 words. Pays $5-25.

Tips: "Writers need only contact law enforcement officers right in their own areas and we would be delighted. We want to recognize good commanding officers from sergeant and above who are involved with the community. Pictures of the subject or the department are essential and can be snapshots. We are looking for interviews with police chiefs and sheriffs on command level with photos."

FIREHOUSE MAGAZINE, Firehouse Communications, Inc., 33 Irving Pl., New York NY 10003. (212)475-5400. FAX: (212)353-2863. Editor: Dennis Smith. Executive Editor: Janet Kimmerly. 85% freelance written. Works with a small number of new/unpublished writers each year. Monthly magazine covering fire service. "*Firehouse* covers major fires nationwide, controversial issues and trends in the fire service, the latest firefighting equipment and methods of firefighting, historical fires, firefighting history and memorabilia. Fire-related books, firefighters with interesting avocations, fire safety education, hazardous materials incidents and the emergency medical services are also covered." Circ. 110,000. Pays on publication. Byline given. Exclusive submissions only. Query for electronic submissions. Computer printout submissions acceptable; prefers letter-quality. Reports ASAP. Sample copy for 8½x11 SAE with 7 first class stamps; free writer's guidelines.

Nonfiction: Book excerpts (of recent books on fire, EMS and hazardous materials); historical/nostalgic (great fires in history, fire collectibles, the fire service of yesteryear); how-to (fight certain kinds of fires, buy and maintain equipment, run a fire department); interview/profile (of noteworthy fire leader, centers, commissioners); new product (for firefighting, EMS); personal experience (description of dramatic rescue, helping one's own fire department); photo feature (on unusual apparatus, fire collectibles, a spectacular fire); technical (on almost any phase of firefighting, techniques, equipment, training, administration); and trends (controversies in the fire service). No profiles of people or departments that are not unusual or innovative, reports of nonmajor fires, articles not slanted toward firefighters' interests. Buys 100 mss/year. Query with or without published clips, or send complete ms. Length: 500-3,000 words. Pays $50-400 for assigned articles; pays $50-300 for unsolicited articles. Sometimes pays the expenses of writers on assignment.

Photos: Mike Delia, art director. Send photos with query or ms. Pays $15-45 for 8x10 b&w prints; $30-200 for color transparencies and 8x10 color prints. Captions and identification of subjects required.

Columns/Departments: Command Post (for fire service leaders); Training (effective methods); Book Reviews; Fire Safety (how departments teach fire safety to the public); Communicating (PR, dispatching); Arson (efforts to combat it); Doing Things (profile of a firefighter with an interesting avocation, group projects by firefighters). Buys 50 mss/year. Query or send complete ms. Length: 750-1,000 words. Pays $100-300.

Tips: "Read the magazine to get a full understanding of the subject matter, the writing style and the readers before sending a query or manuscript. Send photos with manuscript or indicate sources for photos. Be sure to focus articles on firefighters."

FOREIGN SERVICE JOURNAL, 2101 E St. NW, Washington DC 20037. (202)338-4045. Editor: Ann Luppi. 80% freelance written. For Foreign Service personnel and others interested in foreign affairs and related subjects. Monthly (July/August combined). Pays on publication. Publishes ms an average of 3 months after acceptance. Byline given. Buys first North American serial rights. Computer printout submissions acceptable; prefers letter-quality. Sample copy $2.
Nonfiction: Uses articles on "diplomacy, professional concerns of the State Department and Foreign Service, diplomatic history and articles on Foreign Service experiences. Much of our material is contributed by those working in the profession. Informed outside contributions are welcomed, however." Query. Buys 5-10 unsolicited mss/year. Length: 1,000-4,000 words. Offers honoraria.
Tips: "The most frequent mistakes made by writers in completing an article for us are that the items are not suitable for the magazine, and they don't query."

FOUNDATION NEWS MAGAZINE: Philanthropy and the Nonprofit Sector, Council on Foundations, 1828 L St. NW, Washington DC 20036. (202)466-6512. FAX: (202)785-3926. Editor: Arlie Schardt. Managing Editor: Susan Calhoun. 70% freelance written. Prefers to work with published/established writers. Bimonthly magazine covering the world of philanthropy, nonprofit organizations and their relation to current events. Read by staff and executives of foundations, corporations, hospitals, colleges and universities and various nonprofit organizations. Circ. 20,000. Pays on acceptance. Publishes ms an average of 3 months after acceptance. Byline given. Offers negotiable kill fee. Not copyrighted. Buys all rights. Submit seasonal/holiday material 5 months in advance. Simultaneous queries and previously published submissions OK. Computer printout submissions acceptable; prefers letter-quality. Reports in 6 weeks.
Nonfiction: Book excerpts, exposé, general interest, historical/nostalgic, how-to, interview/profile and photo feature. Submit written query; not telephone calls. Length: 500-3,000 words. Pays $200-2,000. Pays expenses of writers on assignment.
Photos: State availability of photos with submission. Pays negotiable rates for b&w contact sheet and prints. Captions and identification of subjects required. Buys one-time rights; "some rare requests for second use."
Columns/Departments: Buys 12 mss/year. Query. Length: 900-2,000 words. Pays $100-750.
Tips: "We have a great interest in working with writers familiar with the nonprofit sector."

‡GOVERNMENT CONTRACTOR, Federal Buyers Guide, 600 Ward Dr. Santa Barbara CA 93111. (805)683-6181. Editor: Stuart Miller. 60% freelance written. Monthly magazine on government buying. Pays on publication. Publishes ms an average of 3 months after acceptance. Byline sometimes given. Buys all rights. Simultaneous, photocopied and previously published submissions OK. Computer printout submissions OK; prefers letter-quality. Reports in 2 weeks on queries; 1 week on mss.
Nonfiction: Government. Buys 50 mss/year. Query. Length: 200-10,000 words. Pays $50-500 for assigned articles; $50-250 for unsolicited articles. Sometimes pays expenses of writers on assignment.
Photos: State availability of photos with submission. Reviews 3x5 prints. Offers no additional payment for photos accepted with ms. Captions and model releases are required. Buys all rights.

LAW AND ORDER, Hendon Co., 1000 Skokie Blvd., Wilmette IL 60091. (312)256-8555. Editor: Bruce W. Cameron. 90% freelance written. Prefers to work with published/established writers. Monthly magazine covering the administration and operation of law enforcement agencies, directed to police chiefs and supervisors. Circ. 30,000. Pays on publication. Publishes ms an average of 6 months after acceptance. Byline given. Buys first North American serial rights. Submit seasonal/holiday material 3 months in advance. No simultaneous queries. Query for electronic submissions. Computer printout submissions acceptable; no dot-matrix. Reports in 1 month. Sample copy for 9x12 SAE; free writer's guidelines.
Nonfiction: General police interest; how-to (do specific police assignments); new product (how applied in police operation); and technical (specific police operation). Special issues include Buyers Guide (January); Communications (February); Training (March); International (April); Administration (May); Small Departments (June); Police Science (July); Equipment (August); Weapons (September); Mobile Patrol (November); and Community Relations (December). No articles dealing with courts (legal field) or convicted prisoners. No nostalgic, financial, travel or recreational material. Buys 100 mss/year. Length: 2,000-3,000 words. Pays 10¢/word.
Photos: Send photos with ms. Reviews transparencies and prints. Identification of subjects required. Buys all rights.
Tips: "*L&O* is a respected magazine that provides up-to-date information that chiefs can use. Writers must know their subject as it applies to this field. Case histories are well received. We are upgrading quality for editorial—stories *must* show some understanding of the law enforcement field. A frequent mistake is not getting photographs to accompany article."

‡**9-1-1 MAGAZINE**, Official Publications, Inc. 18201 Weston Pl., Tustin CA 92680. (714)544-7776. Editor: Jim Voelkl. 50% freelance written. Quarterly magazine for emergency response personnel. "Our readers are emergency response personnel at all levels and all agencies. We report on trends, health, equipment, safety and we run features." Estab. 1988. Circ. 7,000. Pays on publication. Publishes ms an average of 2 months after acceptance. Byline given. Offers 50% kill fee. Buys one-time rights and second serial (reprint) rights. Submit seasonal/holiday material 3 months in advance. Simultaneous, photocopied and previously published submissions OK. Computer printout submissions OK; prefers letter-quality. Reports in 1 month on queries; 3 months on mss. Sample copy for 9x12 SAE with 5 first class stamps. Writer's guidelines for #10 SASE.
Nonfiction: Humor, new product, photo feature, technical and travel. Buys 10 mss/year. Send complete ms. Length: 200-1,000 words. Pays $20-150 for unsolicited articles.
Photos: Send photos with submission. Reviews contact sheets, transparencies and prints. Offers $5-100 per photo. Captions and identification of subjects required. Buys one-time rights.
Fiction: Experimental, historical and humorous.
Fillers: Gags to be illustrated by cartoonist and short humor. Buys 10/year. Length: 25-100 words. Pays $5-25.
Tips: "We are looking for submissions relating to the emergency response community and their families. Know what your're talking about and use currently accepted terms used by law enforcement, fire prevention, etc."

PLANNING, American Planning Association, 1313 E. 60th St., Chicago IL 60637. (312)955-9100. Editor: Sylvia Lewis. 25% freelance written. Emphasizes urban planning for adult, college-educated readers who are regional and urban planners in city, state or federal agencies or in private business or university faculty or students. Monthly. Circ. 25,000. Pays on publication. Publishes ms an average of 3 months after acceptance. Buys all rights or first rights. Byline given. Photocopied and previously published submissions OK. Computer printout submissions acceptable; prefers letter-quality. Reports in 2 months. Sample copy and writer's guidelines for 9x12 SAE.
Nonfiction: Exposé (on government or business, but on topics related to planning, housing, land use, zoning); general interest (trend stories on cities, land use, government); how-to (successful government or citizen efforts in planning; innovations; concepts that have been applied); and technical (detailed articles on the nitty-gritty of planning, zoning, transportation but no footnotes or mathematical models). Also needs news stories up to 500 words. "It's best to query with a fairly detailed, one-page letter. We'll consider any article that's well written and relevant to our audience. Articles have a better chance if they are timely and related to planning and land use and if they appeal to a national audience. All articles should be written in magazine feature style." Buys 2 features and 1 news story/issue. Length: 500-2,000 words. Pays $50-600. "We pay freelance writers and photographers only, not planners."
Photos: "We prefer that authors supply their own photos, but we sometimes take our own or arrange for them in other ways." State availability of photos. Pays $25 minimum for 8x10 matte or glossy prints and $200 for 4-color cover photos. Caption material required. Buys one-time rights.

POLICE, Hare Publications, 6200 Yarrow Dr., Carlsbad CA 92008. (619)438-2511. Editor: Sean T. Hilferty. 90% freelance written. A monthly magazine covering topics related to law enforcement officials. "Our audience is primarily law enforcement personnel such as patrol officers, detectives and security police." Circ. 45,000. Pays on acceptance. Publishes ms an average of 6 months after acceptance. Buys all rights (returned to author 45 days after publication). Submit theme material 3 months in advance. Computer printout submissions acceptable. Reports in 2 months. Sample copy $2; writer's guidelines for #10 SAE with 2 first class stamps.
Nonfiction: General interest, expose, humor, inspirational, interview/profile, new product, opinion, personal experience and technical. Buys 60 mss/year. Query or send complete ms. Length: 2,000-4,000 words. Pays $200-250 for unsolicited articles.
Photos: Send photos with submission. Reviews color transparencies. Captions required. Buys all rights.
Columns/Departments: The Beat (entertainment section—humor, fiction, first-person drama, professional tips) 1,000 words; pays $75; The Arsenal (weapons, ammunition and equipment used in the line of duty); and Officer Survival (theories, skills and techniques used by offices for street survival). Buys 75 mss/year. Query or send complete ms. Length: 1,500-2,500 words. Pays $75-250
Tips: "You are writing for police officers—people who live a dangerous and stressful life. Study the editorial calendar—yours for the asking—and come up with an idea that fits into a specific issue. We are actively seeking talented writers."

POLICE AND SECURITY NEWS, Days Communications, Inc.. 15 Thatcher Rd., Quakertown PA 18951. (215)538-1240. Editor: James Devery. 40% freelance written. A bimonthly tabloid on public law enforcement and private security. "Our publication is designed to provide educational and entertaining information directed toward management level. Technical information written for the expert in a manner that the non-expert can understand." Circ. 23,590. Pays on publication. Publishes ms an average of 2 months after acceptance. Byline given. Buys first North American serial rights. Submit seasonal/holiday material 2 months in advance. Simultaneous, photocopied and previously published submissions OK. Computer printout submissions OK. Free sample copy and writer's guidelines.

Nonfiction: Al Menear, articles editor. Exposé, historical/nostalgic, how-to, humor, interview/profile, opinion, personal experience, photo feature and technical. Buys 12 mss/year. Query. Length: 200-8,000 words. Pays $50-200. Sometimes pays in trade-out of services.

Photos: State availability of photos with submission. Reviews prints (3x5). Offers $10-100 per photo. Buys one-time rights.

Fillers: Anecdotes, facts, gags to be illustrated by cartoonist, newsbreaks and short humor. Buys 6/year. Length: 200-2,000 words. Pays $50-150.

POLICE TIMES, American Police Academy, 1100 NE 125th St., North Miami FL 33161. (305)891-1700. Editor-In-Chief: Jim Gordon. 80% freelance written. Eager to work with new/unpublished writers. A bimonthly tabloid covering "law enforcement (general topics) for men and women engaged in law enforcement and private security, and citizens who are law and order concerned." Circ. 55,000. Pays on acceptance. Publishes ms an average of 3-6 months after acceptance. Byline given. Offers 50% kill fee. Buys second serial (reprint) rights. Submit seasonal/holiday material 4 months in advance. Simultaneous, photocopied and previously published submissions OK. Computer printout submissions acceptable; prefers letter-quality. Sample copy for 9x12 SAE with 3 first class stamps; writer's guidelines for #10 SASE.

Nonfiction: Book excerpts; essays (on police science); exposé (police corruption); general interest; historical/nostalgic; how-to; humor; interview/profile; new product; personal experience (with police); photo feature; and technical—all police-related. "We produce a special edition on police killed in the line of duty. It is mailed May 15 so copy must arrive six months in advance. Photos required." No anti-police materials. Buys 50 mss/year. Send complete ms. Length: 200-4,000 words. Pays $5-50 for assigned articles; pays $5-25 for unsolicited articles. Sometimes pays the expenses of writers on assignment.

Photos: Send photos with submission. Reviews 5x6 prints. Offers $5-25/photo. Identification of subjects required. Buys all rights.

Columns/Departments: Legal Cases (lawsuits involving police actions); New Products (new items related to police services); and Awards (police heroism acts). Buys variable number of mss/year. Send complete ms. Length: 200-1,000 words. Pays $5-25.

Fillers: Anecdotes, facts, newsbreaks and short humor. Buys 100/year. Length: 50-100 words. Pays $5-10. Fillers are usually humorous stories about police officer and citizen situations. Special stories on police cases, public corruptions, etc. are most open to freelancers.

SUPERINTENDENT'S PROFILE & POCKET EQUIPMENT DIRECTORY, Profile Publications, 220 Central Ave., Box 43, Dunkirk NY 14048. (716)366-4774. Editor: Robert Dyment. 60% freelance written. Prefers to work with published/established writers. Monthly magazine covering "outstanding" town, village, county and city highway superintendents and Department of Public Works Directors throughout New York state only. Circ. 2,500. Publishes ms an average of 4 months after acceptance. Pays within 90 days. Byline given for excellent material. Buys first serial rights. Submit seasonal/holiday material 3 months in advance. Simultaneous queries OK. Computer printout submissions acceptable; no dot-matrix. Reports in 2 weeks on queries; 1 month on mss. Sample copy for 9x12 SAE and 4 first class stamps.

Nonfiction: John Powers, articles editor. Interview/profile (of a highway superintendent or DPW director in NY state who has improved department operations through unique methods or equipment); and technical. Special issues include winter maintenance profiles. No fiction. Buys 20 mss/year. Query. Length: 1,500-2,000 words. Pays $125 for a full-length ms. "Pays more for excellent material. All manuscripts will be edited to fit our format and space limitations." Sometimes pays the expenses of writers on assignment.

Photos: John Powers, photo editor. State availability of photos. Pays $5-10 for b&w contact sheets; reviews 5x7 prints. Captions and identification of subjects required. Buys one-time rights.

Poetry: Buys poetry if it pertains to highway departments. Pays $5-15.

Tips: "We are a widely read and highly respected state-wide magazine, and although we can't pay high rates, we expect quality work. Too many freelance writers are going for the exposé rather than the meat-and-potato type articles that will help readers. We use more major features than fillers. Frequently writers don't read sample copies first. We will be purchasing more material because our page numbers are increasing."

VICTIMOLOGY: An International Journal, 2333 N. Vernon St., Arlington VA 22207. (703)536-1750. Editor-in-Chief: Emilio C. Viano. "We are the only magazine specifically focusing on the victim, on the dynamics of victimization; for social scientists, criminal justice professionals and practitioners, social workers and volunteer and professional groups engaged in prevention of victimization and in offering assistance to victims of rape, spouse abuse, child abuse, incest, abuse of the elderly, natural disasters, etc." Quarterly magazine. Circ. 2,500. Pays on publication. Buys all rights. Byline given. Reports in 2 months. Sample copy $5; free writer's guidelines.

Nonfiction: Exposé, historical, how-to, informational, interview, personal experience, profile, research and technical. Buys 10 mss/issue. Query. Length: 500-5,000 words. Pays $50-150.
Photos: Purchased with accompanying ms. Captions required. Send contact sheet. Pays $15-50 for 5x7 or 8x10 b&w glossy prints.
Poetry: Avant-garde, free verse, light verse and traditional. Length: 30 lines maximum. Pays $10-25.
Tips: "Focus on what is being researched and discovered on the victim, the victim/offender relationship, treatment of the offender, the bystander/witness, preventive measures, and what is being done in the areas of service to the victims of rape, spouse abuse, neglect and occupational and environmental hazards and the elderly."

YOUR VIRGINIA STATE TROOPER MAGAZINE, Box 2189, Springfield VA Editor: Kerian Bunch. 90% freelance written. Biannual magazine covering police topics for troopers, police, libraries, legislators and businesses. Circ. 10,000. Pays on acceptance. Publishes ms an average of 3 months after acceptance. Byline given. Buys first North American serial rights and all rights on assignments. Submit seasonal/holiday material 2 months in advance. Simultaneous and photocopied submissions OK. Computer printout submissions acceptable; prefers letter-quality. Reports in 2 months. Sample copy for 9x12 SAE and $2 postage.
Nonfiction: Book excerpts, exposé (consumer or police-related), general interest, nutrition/health, historical/nostalgic, how-to (energy saving), humor, interview/profile (notable police figures), opinion, personal experience, technical (radar) and recreation. Buys 40-45 mss/year. Query with clips or send complete ms. Length: 2,500 words. Pays $250 maximum/article (10¢/word). Sometimes pays expenses of writers on assignment.
Photos: Send photos with ms. Pays $25 maximum/5x7 b&w glossy print. Captions and model release required. Buys one-time rights.
Fiction: Adventure, humorous, mystery, novel excerpts and suspense. Buys 4 mss/year. Send complete ms. Length: 2,500 words minimum. Pays $250 maximum (10¢/word) on acceptance.
Tips: "The writer may have a better chance of breaking in at our publication with short articles and fillers due to space limitations."

Groceries and Food Products

In this section are publications for grocers, food wholesalers, processors, warehouse owners, caterers, institutional managers and suppliers of grocery store equipment. See the section on Confectionery and Snack Foods for bakery and candy industry magazines.

AUTOMATIC MERCHANDISER, (formerly *American Automatic Merchandiser*), Edgell Communications, 7500 Old Oak Blvd., Cleveland OH 44130. (216)826-2870 or (216)243-8100. FAX: (216)891-2683. Editor: David R. Stone. Managing Editor: Mark L. Dlugoss. 5% freelance written. Prefers to work with published/established writers. A monthly trade journal covering vending machines, contract foodservice and office coffee service. "*AM's* readers are owners and managers of these companies; we profile successful companies and report on market trends." Circ. 12,500. Pays on acceptance. Publishes ms an average of 3 months after acceptance. Byline sometimes given. Buys first North American serial rights, all rights or makes work-for-hire assignments. Submit seasonal/holiday material 4 months in advance. Photocopied submissions OK. Computer printout submissions OK; prefers letter-quality. Reports in 1 month. Free sample copy and writer's guidelines.
Nonfiction: Buys 30 mss/year. Query. Length: 1,000-6,000 words. Pays $150-600. Sometimes pays the expenses of writers on assignment.
Photos: Send photos with submission. Reviews contact sheets, transparencies and prints. Offers $50 maximum per photo. Buys all rights.

CANADIAN GROCER, Maclean-Hunter Ltd., Maclean Hunter Building, 777 Bay St., Toronto, Ontario M5W 1A7 Canada. (416)596-5772. Editor: George H. Condon. 10% freelance written. Prefers to work with published/established writers. Monthly magazine about supermarketing and food retailing for Canadian chain and independent food store managers, owners, buyers, executives, food brokers, food processors and manufacturers. Circ 18,000. Pays on publication. Publishes ms an average of 2 months after acceptance. Byline given. Buys first Canadian rights. Phone queries OK. Submit seasonal material 2 months in advance. Previously published submissions OK. Computer printout submissions acceptable; prefers letter-quality. Reports in 1 month. Sample copy $5.

Nonfiction: Interview (Canadian trendsetters in marketing, finance or food distribution); technical (store operations, equipment and finance); and news features on supermarkets. "Freelancers should be well versed on the supermarket industry. We don't want unsolicited material. Writers with business and/or finance expertise are preferred. Know the retail food industry and be able to write concisely and accurately on subjects relevant to our readers: food store managers, senior corporate executives, etc. A good example of an article would be 'How a Six Store Chain of Supermarkets Improved Profits 2% and Kept Customers Coming.' " Buys 14 mss/year. Query with clips of previously published work. Pays 25¢/word. Sometimes pays the expenses of writers on assignment.

Photos: State availability of photos. Pays $10-25 for prints or slides. Captions preferred. Buys one-time rights.

Tips: "Suitable writers will be familiar with sales per square foot, merchandising mixes and direct product profitability."

‡**CITRUS & VEGETABLE MAGAZINE, and the Florida Farmer**, 1819 N. Franklin St. Tampa FL 33602. (813)223-7628. FAX: (813)223-6878. Editor: Sarah Carey. Monthly magazine on the citrus and vegetable industries. Circ. 10,000. Pays on publication. Publishes ms an average of 1 month after acceptance. Byline given. Kill fee varies. Buys exclusive first rights. Photocopied submissions OK. Computer printout submissions OK; prefers letter-quality. Reports in 2 months on queries. Free sample copy and writer's guidelines.

Nonfiction: Book excerpts (if pertinent to relevant agricultural issues), how-to (grower interest - cultivation practices, etc.), new product (of interest to Florida citrus or vegetable growers), personal experience and photo feature. Buys 50 mss/year. Query with published clips or send complete ms. Length: 3-5 typewritten pages. Pays $4 per column inch.

Photos: Send photos with submission. Reviews 5x7 prints. Offers $10 minimum per photo. Captions and identification of subjects required. Buys first rights.

Columns/Departments: Citrus Summary (news to citrus industry in Florida: market trends, new product lines, anything focusing the competition at home or abroad) and Vegetable Vignettes (new cultivars, anything on trends or developments withing vegetable industry of Florida). Send complete ms. Length: 600 words maximum. Pays $4 per column inch.

Tips: "Show initiative—don't be afraid to call whomever you need to get your information for story together— accurately and with style. Submit ideas and/or completed ms. well in advance. Focus on areas which have not been widely written about elsewhere in the press. Looking for fresh copy. Have something to sell and be convinced of its value. Become familiar with the key issues, key players in the citrus industry in Florida. Have a specific idea in mind. for a news or feature story and try to submit manuscript at least 1 month in advance of publication."

‡**DELI-DAIRY**, Hubsher Publications, Box 373, Cedarhurst NY 11516. (516)295-3680. Editor Stan Hubsher. 100% freelance written. Quarterly magazine for deli/dairy buyers in supermarkets. "Audience is volume deli/ dairy buyers at chain, supermarket level—how they determine showcase purchases, layout of department, all buying functions as well as training etc." Circ. 8,500. Pays on acceptance. No byline. Buys all rights. Submit seasonal/holiday material 2 months in advance. Computer printout submissions OK. Free sample copy and writer's guidelines.

Nonficiton: Buys 4-6 mss/year. Query. Length: 2,000 words. Pays $150 minimum to negotiable maximum. Sometimes pays expenses of writers on assignment.

Photos: Send photos with submission. Offers no additional payment for photos accepted with ms. Captions and identification of subjects required. Buys one-time rights.

FANCY FOOD, The Business Magazine for Specialty Foods, Confections & Wine, Talcott Publishing, Inc., 1414 Merchandise Mart, Chicago IL 60654. (312)670-0800. Editor: Larry Natta. 35-40% freelance written. Works with a small number of new/unpublished writers each year. A trade magazine covering specialty food and confections. Published 12 times a year. Circ. 27,000. Pays on publication. Publishes an average of 3 months after acceptance. Byline sometimes given. Buys all rights. Submit seasonal/holiday material 3 months in advance. Computer printout submissions acceptable; prefers letter-quality. Sample copy $4.

Nonfiction: Interview/profile and new product. Buys 30 mss/year. Query with published clips. Length: 1,500-4,000 words. Pays $100-250 for assigned articles. Expenses must be approved and estimated in advance.

Photos: Send photos with submission. Reviews transparencies and prints. Offers no additional payment other than for film and development for photos accepted with ms. Captions and identification of subjects required. Buys all rights.

Columns/Departments: Across The Nation, Supply Side, Distributor's Inquiries and Buyer's Mart. Buys 20 mss/year. Query with published clips. Length: 2,000-3,000 words. Pays $100-200.

Tips: "We prefer submissions from food writers with practical experience in gourmet retail or prepared food business."

FLORIDA GROCER, Florida Grocer Publications, Inc., Box 430760, South Miami FL 33243. (305)441-1138. Editor: Dennis Kane. 5% freelance written. "*Florida Grocer* is a 16,000 circulation monthly trade newspaper, serving members of the Florida food industry. Our publication is edited for chain and independent food store owners and operators as well as members of allied industries." Circ. 16,000. Pays on acceptance. Byline given. Buys all rights. Submit seasonal/holiday material 6 months in advance. Sample copy for #10 SAE with 6 first class stamps.

Nonfiction: Book excerpts, expose, general interest, humor, features on supermarkets and their owners, new product, new equipment, photo feature and video. Buys variable number of mss/year. Query with or without published clips, or send complete ms. Length: varies. Payment varies. Sometimes pays the expenses of writers on assignment.

Photos: State availability of photos with submission. Terms for payment on photos "included in terms of payment for assignment."

Tips: "We prefer feature articles on new stores (grand openings, etc.), store owners, operators; Florida based food manufacturers, brokers, whole sales, distributors, etc. We also publish a section in Spanish and also welcome the above types of materials in Spanish (Cuban)."

‡**FOOD BUSINESS**, Putman Publishing Corp., 301 E. Erie St., Chicago IL 60611. (312)644-2020. Senior Editor: Bryan Salvage. 33% freelance written. Bimonthly magazine on food business. "Everything is written from a *news* slant." Estab. 1988. Circ. 40,000-45,000. Pays on acceptance. Publishes ms an average of 1 month after acceptance. Byline sometimes given. Offers 100% kill fee. Buys first rights and second serial (reprint) rights. Query for electronic submissions. Computer printout submissions OK; prefers letter-quality. Free writer's guidelines.

Nonfiction: Exposé, interview/profile (people/companies/trends), new product and news. Columns on some aspect of the food industry. Buys 40 mss/year. Send article abstract. Length: 2,000-3,500 words. Averages $500 per feature. Sometimes pays expenses of writers on assignment.

Photos: Send photos with submission—as assigned. Reviews contact sheets transparencies and prints. Offers no additional payment for photos accepted with ms (with exceptions based on assignment). Identification of subjects required. Buys one-time rights and reprint rights.

Columns/Departments: News Editor: Rex Davenport. Packaging (food-related news/trends), New Products (new foods), International (food people/companies) and Finance (performance). Buys 40 mss/year. Query with published clips. Length: 500-1,000 words. Pays average of $250.

FOOD PEOPLE, Olson Publications, Inc., Box 1208, Woodstock GA 30188. (404)928-8994. Editor: Warren B. Causey. 75% freelance written. Prefers to work with published/established writers, and works with a small number of new/unpublished writers each year. Always willing to consider new writers, but they must have a basic command of their craft. Monthly tabloid covering the retail food industry. Circ. 40,000. Pays on publication. Publishes ms an average of 1 month after acceptance. Byline given. Buys all rights. Will reassign subsidiary rights after publication and upon request. Submit seasonal/holiday material 6 weeks in advance. Photocopied submissions acceptable; prefers letter quality. Computer modem submissions encouraged. Reports in 6 weeks. Sample copy for 9x12 SAE with 5 first class stamps; writer's guidelines for #10 SASE.

Nonfiction: Interview/profile (of major food industry figures), photo features of ad campaigns, marketing strategies, important new products and services. "We would like to receive feature articles about people and companies that illustrate trends in the food industry. Articles should be informative, tone is upbeat. Do not send recipes or how-to shop articles; we cover food as a business." Buys 250-300 mss/year. Query or send complete ms. Length: 500-1,500 words. Pays $3/published inch minimum. Pays the expenses of writers on assignment.

Photos: "Photos of people. Photos of displays, or store layouts, etc., that illustrate points made in article are good, too. But stay away from storefront shots." State availability of photos with query or send photos with ms. Pays $10 plus expenses for 5x7 b&w prints; and $25 plus expenses for color transparencies. Captions required. Buys one-time rights.

Columns/Departments: Company news, People, Organizations, New Products, and Morsels . . . a Smorgasbord of Tidbits in the National Stew. Send complete ms. Pays $3/inch.

Tips: "Begin with an area news event—store openings, new promotions. Write that as news, then go further to examine the consequences. We are staffing more conventions, so writers should concentrate on features about people, companies, trends, new products, innovations in the food industry in their geographic areas and apply these to a national scope when possible. Talk with decision makers to get 'hows' and 'whys.' We now are more feature than news oriented. We look for contributors who work well, quickly and always deliver. We are now buying some international material."

‡**FOODSERVICE DIRECTOR**, Bill Communications, 633 Third Ave., New York NY 10017. (212)984-2356. Editor: Walter J. Schruntek. Managing Editor: Karen Weisberg. 20% freelance written. Monthly tabloid on non-commercial foodservice operations for operators of kitchens and dining halls in schools, colleges, hospitals/health care, office and plant cafeterias, military, airline/transportation, correctional institutions. Estab. 1988. Circ. 45,000. Pays on publication. Byline given sometimes. Offers 25% kill fee. Buys all rights. Submit seasonal/holiday material 2-3 months in advance. Simultaneous submissions OK. Computer printout submissions OK. Free sample copy.

Nonfiction: How-to, interview/profile. Buys 60-70 mss/year. Query with published clips. Length: 700-900 words. Pays $250-500. Sometimes pays the expenses of writers on assignment.

Photos: Send photos with submission. Reviews transparencies. Offers no additional payment for photos accepted with ms. Identification of subjects required. Buys all rights.

Columns/Departments: Equipment (case studies of kitchen/serving equipment in use), 700-900 words; Food (specific category studies per publication calendar), 750-900 words. Buys 20-30 mss/year. Query. Length: 400-600 words. Pays $150-250.

‡GOURMET TODAY, Incorporating *Telefood Magazine*, Cummins Publishing Company, Suite 204, 26011 Evergreen Rd., Southfield MI 48076. (313)358-4900. FAX: (313)358-3965. Editor: Andrew J. Cummins. Managing Editor: Eric Nordwall. 65% freelance written. Bimonthly magazine on specialty food retailers, distributors and manufacturers, as well as the food itself. "Our readers are purveyors of gourmet foods and as such are concerned with stories that will help them enhance their business. Our stories are designed to introduce them to new or unusual products and retailing ideas, explore the possibilities of established products or introduce the readers to innovative people who are leaving their mark on the industry." Circ. 20,000. Pays on publication. Byline given. Buys first North American serial rights and first industry rights. Submit seasonal/holiday material 6-8 months in advance. Computer printout submissions OK; prefers letter-quality. Reports in 1 month on queries; 2 months on mss. Sample copy for 9x12 SAE with 5 first class stamps. Writer's guidelines for #10 SASE.

Nonfiction: Exposé, how-to, interview/profile, new product, personal experience, technical and travel. "Our publication is directed specifically toward retailers, distributors and manufacturers of specialty foods. Any stories that do not directly address these groups are of no use to us." Buys 36 mss/year. Query with published clips. Length: 800-1,300 words. Pays $150 for assigned articles; $100-150 for unsolicited articles. Pays phone and auto mileage of writers on assignment.

Photos: State availability of photos with submission. Reviews negatives, at least 4x5 transparencies and at least 4x5 prints. Model releases and identification of subjects required.

Tips: "An understanding of gourmet foods is important, as is a good general knowledge of running a business operation. Clips that demonstrate an ability to make a business-related story informative and readable, as well as a capacity for descriptive narrative, always catch our eye. Good phone skills are important, as many of our assignments require extensive telephone interviews. In query letters, tell us why you want to write about the specialty food industry—and why we should want you to do so. Good query letters can be all the difference. More than anything else, we use freelancers in writing retailer profiles. We ask that stories tell us both about the shop itself—size, years in business, types of products carried, location—as well as something about the owner and his or her approach to business. We also use frelancers for stories on their eating experiences abroad, with particular emphasis on the types of gourmet foods eaten (and where those foods are available domestically). Narrative that is descriptive without being superfluous is important in these pieces."

HEALTH FOODS BUSINESS, Howmark Publishing Corp., 567 Morris Ave., Elizabeth NJ 07208. (201)353-7373. FAX: (201)353-8221. Editor: Gina Geslewitz. 40% freelance written. Eager to work with new/unpublished writers if competent and reliable. For owners and managers of health food stores. Monthly magazine. Circ. 11,000. Pays on publication. Publishes ms an average of 4 months after acceptance. Byline given "if story quality warrants it." Buys first serial rights and first North American serial rights; "also exclusive rights in our trade field." Phone queries OK. "Query us about a good health food store in your area. We use many store profile stories." Simultaneous and photocopied submissions OK if exclusive to their field. Previously published work OK, but please indicate where and when material appeared previously. Computer printout submissions acceptable if double-spaced and in upper and lower case; no dot-matrix. Reports in 1 month. Sample copy $5 plus $2 for postage and handling; writer's guidelines for #10 SASE.

Nonfiction: Exposé (government hassling with health food industry); how-to (unique or successful retail operators); informational (how or why a product works; technical aspects must be clear to laymen); historical (natural food use); interview (must be prominent person in industry or closely related to the health food industry or well-known or prominent person in any arena who has undertaken a natural diet/lifestyle;); and photo feature (any unusual subject related to the retailer's interests). Buys 1-2 mss/issue. Query for interview and photo features. Will consider complete ms in other categories. Length: long enough to tell the whole story without padding. Pays $50 and up for feature stories, $75 and up for store profiles.

Photos: "Most articles must have photos included"; negatives and contact sheet OK. Captions required. No additional payment.

Tips: "A writer may find that submitting a letter with a sample article he/she believes to be closely related to articles read in our publication is the most of expedient way to determine the appropriateness of his/her skills and expertise."

MEAT PLANT MAGAZINE, 9701 Gravois Ave., St. Louis MO 63123. (314)638-4050. FAX: (314)638-3880. Editor: Tony Nolan. 10% freelance written. Prefers to work with published/established writers; works with a small number of new/unpublished writers each year. For meat processors, locker plant operators, freezer provisioners, portion control packers, meat dealers and food service (food plan) operators. Monthly. Pays on publication. Publishes ms an average of 6 months after acceptance. Computer printout submissions acceptable. Reports in 2 weeks.

Nonfiction and Fillers: Buys feature-length articles and shorter subjects pertinent to the field. Length: 1,000-1,500 words for features. Pays 10¢/word. Sometimes pays the expenses of writers on assignment.

Photos: Pays $5 for photos.

‡**MINNESOTA GROCER, Official Publication of the Minnesota Grocers Association,** Minnesota Grocers Council, Inc., 533 St. Clair Ave., St. Paul MN 55102. (612)228-0973. FAX: (612)228-1949. Editor: Randy Schubring. 25% freelance written. Bimonthly magazine on the retail grocery industry in Minnesota. Circ. 4,800. Pays on publication. Publishes ms an average of 1-2 months after acceptance. Byline given. Buys all rights. Submit seasonal/holiday material 3 months in advance. Photocopied and previously published submissions OK. Computer printout submissions OK; prefers letter quality. Reports in 1 month on queries; 2 weeks on mss. Free sample copy and writer's guidelines.

Nonfiction: How-to (better market, display and sell food, and other items in a grocery store. How to find new markets.), interview/profile and new products. Special issues: "We do an economic forecast in Jan/Feb. issue." Buys 6 mss/year. Query with published clips. Length: 300-1,500 words. Pays $100-500 for assigned articles. Sometimes pays expenses of writers on assignment.

Photos: State availability of photos with submission. Reviews contact sheets and 5x7 prints. Captions, model releases and identification of subjects required. Buys all rights.

Columns/Departments: Query with published clips.

Tips: "The best way to be considered for a freelance assignment is first and foremost to have a crisp journalistic writing style on clips. Second it is very helpful to have a knowledge of the issues and trends in the grocery industry. The most open area is the feature stories about issues and trends."

PRODUCE NEWS, 2185 Lemoine Ave., Fort Lee NJ 07024. FAX: (201)592-0809. Editor: Gordon Hochberg. 10-15% freelance written. Works with a small number of new/unpublished writers each year. For commercial growers and shippers, receivers and distributors of fresh fruits and vegetables, including chain store produce buyers and merchandisers. Weekly. Circ. 9,500. Pays on publication. Publishes ms an average of 2 weeks after acceptance. Deadline is Tuesday afternoon before Thursday press day. Computer printout submissions acceptable. Free sample copy and writer's guidelines.

Nonfiction: News stories (about the produce industry). Buys profiles, spot news, coverage of successful business operations and articles on merchandising techniques. Query. Pays minimum of $1/column inch for original material. Sometimes pays the expenses of writers on assignment.

Photos: B&w glossies. Pays $8-10 for each one used.

Tips: "Stories should be trade-oriented, not consumer-oriented. As our circulation grows in the next year, we are interested in stories and news articles from all fresh fruit-growing areas of the country. Looking especially for writers in southern California and lower Rio Grande Valley of Texas."

QUICK FROZEN FOODS INTERNATIONAL, E.W. Williams Publishing Co., 80 8th Ave., New York NY 10011. (212)989-1101. FAX: (212)242-5991. Editor: John M. Saulnier. 20% freelance written. Works with a small number of new/unpublished writers each year. Quarterly magazine covering frozen foods around the world— "every phase of frozen food manufacture, retailing, food service, brokerage, transport, warehousing, merchandising. Especially interested in stories from Europe, Asia and emerging nations." Circ. 13,500. Pays on publication. Publishes ms an average of 3 months after acceptance. Byline given. Offers kill fee; "if satisfactory, we will pay promised amount. If bungled, half." Buys all rights, but will relinquish any rights requested. Submit seasonal/holiday material 6 months in advance. Photocopied submissions OK "if not under submission elsewhere." Computer printout submissions acceptable; prefers letter-quality. Sample copy $5.

Nonfiction: Book excerpts, general interest, historical/nostalgic, interview/profile, new product (from overseas), personal experience, photo feature, technical and travel. No articles peripheral to frozen food industry such as taxes, insurance, government regulation, safety, etc. Buys 20-30 mss/year. Query or send complete ms. Length: 500-4,000 words. Pays 5¢/word or by arrangement. "We will reimburse postage on articles ordered from overseas." Sometimes pays the expenses of writers on assignment.

Photos: "We prefer photos with all articles." State availability of photos or send photos with accompanying ms. Pays $7 for 5x7 b&w prints (contact sheet if many shots). Captions and identification of subject required. Buys all rights. Release on request.

Columns/Departments: News or analysis of frozen foods abroad. Buys 20 columns/year. Query. Length: 500-1,500 words. Pays by arrangement.

Fillers: Newsbreaks. Length: 100-500 words. Pays $5-20.

Tips: "We are primarily interested in feature materials, (1,000-3,000 words with pictures). We plan to devote more space to frozen food company developments in Pacific Rim countries. Stories on frozen food merchandising and retailing in foreign supermarket chains in Europe, Japan and Australia/New Zealand are welcome. National frozen food prouduction profiles are also in demand worldwide. A frequent mistake is submitting general interest material instead of specific industry-related stories."

SEAFOOD LEADER, Waterfront Press Co., 1115 NW 45th St., Seattle WA 98107. (206)789-6506. FAX: (206)548-9346. Editor: Wayne Lee. Associate Editor: Laune Underwood. 20% freelance written. Works with a small number of new/unpublished writers each year. A trade journal on the seafood business published 6 times/year. Circ. 15,000. Pays on publication. Publishes ms an average of 3 months after acceptance. Byline given. Buys first rights and second serial (reprint) rights. Simultaneous, photocopied and previously published submissions OK. Query for electronic submissions. Computer printout submissions OK. Reports in 1 month on queries; 2 months on mss. Sample copy $3 with 8½x11 SAE.

Nonfiction: General seafood interest, marketing/business, historical/nostalgic, interview/profile, opinion and photo feature. Each of *Seafood Leader's* six issues has a slant: international (Feb/March), foodservice (April/May), international aquaculture and retail merchandising (June/July), shrimp and aquaculture (Aug/Sept) and the annual Seafood Buyer's Guide (Dec/Jan). Still, each issue includes stories outside of the particular focus, particularly shorter features and news items. No recreational fishing; no first person articles. Buys 12-15 mss/year. Query with or without published clips, or send complete ms. Length: 1,000-2,500 words. Pay rate is 15-20¢/word published depending upon amount of editing necessary. Sometimes pays the expenses of writers on assignment.

Photos: State availability of photos with submission. Reviews contact sheets and transparencies. Offers $50-100 per photo. Buys one-time rights.

Fillers: Newsbreaks. Buys 10-15/year. Length: 100-250 words. Pays $50-100.

Tips: "*Seafood Leader* is steadily increasing in size and has a growing need for full-length feature stories and special sections. Articles on innovative, unique and aggressive people or companies involved in seafood are needed. Writing should be colorful, tight and fact-filled, always emphasizing the subject's formula for increased seafood sales. Readers should feel as if they have learned something applicable to their business."

SNACK FOOD, Edgell Communicattions, Inc., 131 W. 1st St., Duluth MN 55802. (218)723-9343. Executive Editor: Jerry L. Hess. 15% freelance written. For manufacturers and distributors of snack foods. Monthly magazine. Circ. 10,000. Pays on acceptance. Publishes ms an average of 2 months after acceptance. Buys first serial rights. Occasional byline given. Phone queries OK. Photocopied submissions OK. Computer printout submissions acceptable. Reports in 2 months. Free sample copy and writer's guidelines.

Nonfiction: Informational, interview, new product, nostalgia, photo feature, profile and technical articles. "We use an occasional mini news feature or personality sketch." Length: 300-600 words for mini features; 750-1,200 words for longer features. Pays 12-15¢/word. Sometimes pays the expenses of writers on assignment.

Photos: Purchased with accompanying ms. Captions required. Pays $20 for 5x7 b&w photos. Total purchase price for ms includes payment for photos when used. Buys all rights.

Tips: "Query should contain specific lead and display more than a casual knowledge of our audience. The most frequent mistakes made by writers are not writing to our particular audience, and lack of a grasp of certain technical points on how the industry functions."

‡THE WISCONSIN GROCER, Wisconsin Grocers Association, Suite 203, 802 W. Broadway, Madison WI 53713. (608)222-4515. Editor: Dianne Calgaro. 40% freelance written. Eager to work with new/unpublished writers. Bimonthly magazine covering grocery industry of Wisconsin. Circ. 1,500. Pays on publication. Publishes ms an average of 3 months after acceptance. Byline given. Not copyrighted. Buys first North American serial rights, second serial (reprint) rights or simultaneous rights. Submit seasonal/holiday material 5 months in advance. Simultaneous and previously published submissions OK. Computer printout submissions OK. Reports in 2 weeks on queries; 2 months on mss. Sample copy for 9x12 SAE with 51¢ postage.

Nonfiction: How-to (money management, employee training/relations, store design, promotional ideas); interview/profile (of WGA members and Wisconsin politicans only); opinion; technical (store design or equipment). No articles about grocers or companies not affiliated with the WGA. Buys 6 mss/year. Query. Length: 500-2,000 words. Pays $15 for unsolicited articles. Pays in copies if the writer works for a manufacturer or distributor of goods or services relevant to the grocery industry, or if a political viewpoint is expressed.

Photos: Send photos with submission. Reviews 5x7 prints. Offers no additional payment for photos accepted with ms. Identification of subjects required. Buys one-time rights.

Columns/Departments: Security (anti-shoplifting, vendor thefts, employee theft, burglary); Employee Relations (screening, training, management); Customer Relations (better service, corporate-community relations, buying trends); Money Management (DPP programs, bookkeeping, grocery–specific computer applications); Merchandising (promotional or advertising ideas), all 1,000 words. Buys 6 mss/year. Query. Length: 500-1,500 words. Pays $15.

Fillers: Facts and newsbreaks. Buys 6/year. Length: 50-250 words. Pays $5.

Tips: "How-tos are especially strong with our readers. They want to know how to increase sales and cut costs. Cover new management techniques, promotional ideas, customer services and industry trends."

Hardware

Journals for general and specialized hardware wholesalers and retailers are listed in this section. Journals specializing in hardware for a certain trade, such as plumbing or automotive supplies, are classified with other publications for that trade.

CHAIN SAW AGE, 3435 N.E. Broadway, Portland OR 97232. Editor: Ken Morrison. 1% freelance written. "We will consider any submissions that address pertinent subjects and are well-written." For "mostly chain saw dealers (retailers); small businesses—usually family-owned, typical ages, interests and education." Monthly. Circ. 20,000. Pays on acceptance or publication. Publishes ms an average of 4 months after acceptance. Photocopied submissions OK. Computer printout submissions acceptable. Free sample copy.
Nonfiction: "Must relate to chain saw use, merchandising, adaptation, repair, maintenance, manufacture or display." Buys informational articles, how-to, personal experience, interview, profiles, inspirational, personal opinion, photo feature, coverage of successful business operations, and articles on merchandising techniques. Buys very few mss/year. Query first. Length: 500-1,000 words. Pays $20-50 "5¢/word plus photo fees." Sometimes pays the expenses of writers on assignment.
Photos: Photos purchased with or without mss, or on assignment. For b&w glossies, pay "varies." Captions required.
Tips: "Frequently writers have an inadequate understanding of the subject area."

HARDWARE AGE, Chilton Co., Chilton Way, Radnor PA 19089. (215)964-4275. Editor: Terry Gallagher. Managing Editor: Rick Carter. 2% freelance written. Emphasizes retailing, distribution and merchandising of hardware and building materials. Monthly magazine. Circ. 71,000. Buys first North American serial rights. No guarantee of byline. Simultaneous, photocopied and previously published submissions OK, if exclusive in the field. Reports in 1-2 months. Sample copy for $1; mention *Writer's Market* in request.
Nonfiction: Rick Carter, managing editor. How-to more profitably run a hardware store or a department within a store. "We particularly want stories on local hardware stores and home improvement centers, with photos. Stories should concentrate on one particular aspect of how the retailer in question has been successful." Also wants technical pieces (will consider stories on retail accounting, inventory management and business management by qualified writers). Buys 1-5 unsolicited mss/year. Submit complete ms. Length: 1,500-3,000 words. Pays $75-200.
Photos: "We like store features with b&w photos. Usually use b&w for small freelance features." Send photos with ms. Pays $25 for 4x5 glossy b&w prints. Captions preferred. Buys one-time rights.
Columns/Departments: Retailers' Business Tips; Wholesalers' Business Tips; and Moneysaving Tips. Query or submit complete ms. Length: 1,000-1,250 words. Pays $100-150. Open to suggestions for new columns/departments.

Home Furnishings and Household Goods

Readers rely on these publications to learn more about new products and trends in the home furnishings and appliance trade. Magazines for consumers interested in home furnishings are listed in the Consumer Home and Garden section.

CHINA GLASS & TABLEWARE, Doctorow Communications, Inc., Box 2147, Clifton NJ 07015. (201)779-1600. FAX: (201)779-3242. Editor-in-Chief: Amy Stavis. 60% freelance written. Works with a small number of new/unpublished writers each year. Monthly magazine for buyers, merchandise managers and specialty store owners who deal in tableware, dinnerware, glassware, flatware and other tabletop accessories. Pays on publication. Publishes ms an average of 3-4 months after acceptance. Buys one-time rights. Byline given. Phone queries OK. Submit seasonal/holiday material 3 months in advance. Computer printout submissions acceptable; no dot-matrix. Reports in 3 weeks. Free sample copy for 8½ × 11 SAE and writer's guidelines; mention *Writer's Market* in request.
Nonfiction: General interest (on store successes, reasons for a store's business track record); interview (personalities of store owners, how they cope with industry problems, why they are in tableware); and technical (on the business aspects of retailing china, glassware and flatware). "Bridal registry material always

welcomed." No articles on how-to or gift shops. Buys 2-3 mss/issue. Query. Length: 1,500-3,000 words. Pays $50/page. Sometimes pays the expenses of writers on assignment.

Photos: State availability of photos with query. No additional payment for b&w or color contact sheets. Captions required. Buys first serial rights.

Tips: "Show imagination in the query; have a good angle on a story that makes it unique from the competition's coverage and requires less work on the editor's part for rewriting a snappy beginning."

ENTREE, Fairchild, 7 East 12th St., New York NY 10003. (212)337-3467. Editor: Marie Griffin. 20% freelance written. Monthly business magazine covering housewares, lifestyle and tabletop (i.e.: cookware, small electrical appliances, RTA furniture, etc.) wherever they are sold, including department stores, mass merchants, specialty stores. Circ. 15,000. Average issue includes 5-11 features, 3 columns, special pullout sections, news and 50% advertising. Pays on acceptance. Publishes ms an average of 2½ months after acceptance. Byline given. Kill fee varies. Buys all rights. Written queries OK. Computer printout submissions acceptable; prefers letter-quality. Reports in 6 weeks on queries; 3 weeks on mss. Sample copy $3.

Nonfiction: Corporate profiles (of major retailers and manufacturers); industry news analysis; new product ("hot product categories"); photo feature; and technical (cookware and specialty food in terms retailers can apply to their businesses). No first person, humor, cartoons and unsolicited stories on obscure retailers or general pieces of any kind such as accounting or computer stories. Buys 1-2 mss/issue. Query. Length: 750-1,000 words. Pays $250-600. Sometimes pays the expenses of writers on assignment.

Photos: Art Director. Always looking for illustrations and photographs.

Tips: "We have established a core of regular writers we rely on. We want writers who can thoroughly analyze a market, whether it be cutlery, drip coffee makers, food processors or cookware and who can do in-depth profiles of major retailers. We are especially looking for stories with statistical information. We welcome information on foreign markets."

FLOORING MAGAZINE, 7500 Old Oak Blvd., Cleveland OH 44130. FAX: (216)826-2832. Editor: Dan Alaimo. Send ms or letter and writing sample to: Robert Blumel, managing editor. 10-20% freelance written by assignment only. Prefers to work with published/established writers. Monthly magazine for floor covering retailers, wholesalers, contractors, specifiers and designers. Circ. 24,000. Pays on acceptance. Publishes ms an average of 3 months after acceptance. Byline given. Buys all rights. Computer printout submissions acceptable; prefers letter-quality. Query for electronic submissions. "Send letter with writing sample to be placed in our freelance contact file." Editorial calendar available on request. Send #10 SASE.

Nonfiction: Mostly staff-written. Will not be buying a significant number of manuscripts. However, has frequent need for correspondents skilled in 35mm photography for simple, local assignments. Sometimes pays the expenses of writers on assignment.

‡GIFT & STATIONERY, 1515 Broadway, New York NY 10036. (212)869-1300. Editor: Joyce Washnik. 10% freelance written. Prefers to work with published/established writers. Monthly for "merchants (department store buyers, specialty shop owners) engaged in the resale of giftware, china and glass, stationery and decorative accessories." Monthly. Circ. 37,500. Buys all rights. Byline given "by request only." Pays on publication. Publishes ms an average of 2 months after acceptance. Will consider photocopied submissions. Query for electronic submissions. Computer printout submissions acceptable; prefers letter-quality to dot-matrix.

Nonfiction: "Retail store success stories. Describe a single merchandising gimmick. We are a tabloid format—glossy stock. Descriptions of store interiors are less important than sales performance unless display is outstanding. We're interested in articles on aggressive selling tactics. We cannot use material written for the consumer." Buys coverage of successful business operations and merchandising techniques. Query or submit complete ms. Length: 750 words maximum. Sometimes pays the expenses of writers on assignment.

Photos: Purchased with mss and on assignment; captions required. "Individuals are to be identified." Reviews b&w glossy prints (preferred) and color transparencies.

Tips: "All short items are staff produced. The most frequent mistake made by writers is that they don't know the market. As a trade publication, we require a strong business slant, rather than a consumer angle."

GIFTWARE NEWS, Talcott Corp., 112 Adrossan, Box 5398, Deptford NJ 08096. (609)227-0798. Editor: Anthony DeMasi. 50% freelance written. A monthly magazine covering gifts, collectibles, and tabletops for giftware retailers. Circ. 41,000. Pays on publication. Publishes ms an average of 2 months after acceptance. Byline given. Buys all rights. Submit seasonal/holiday material 4 months in advance. Reports in 2 months on mss. Sample copy $1.50.

Nonfiction: How-to (sell, display) and new product. Buys 50 mss/year. Send complete ms. Length: 1,500-2,500 words. Pays $150-250 for assigned articles; pays $75-100 for unsolicited articles.

Photos: Send photos with submission. Reviews 4x5 transparencies and 5x7 prints. Offers no additional payment for photos accepted with ms. Identification of subjects required.

Columns/Departments: Tabletop, Wedding Market and Display—all for the gift retailer. Buys 36 mss/year. Send complete ms. Length: 1,500-2,500 words. Pays $75-200.

Tips: "We are not looking so much for general journalists but rather experts in particular fields who can also write."

HOME FURNISHINGS REVIEW, The Digest of Profitable Ideas for Busy Decision-Makers,, Box 581207, Dallas TX 75258. (214)741-7632. Editor: Darrell Hofheinz. 10% freelance written. Quarterly magazine for home furnishings retail dealers, manufacturers, their representatives and others in related fields. Circ. 25,000. Pays on acceptance. Publishes ms an average of 2 months after acceptance. Buys first serial rights. Computer printout submissions acceptable; no dot-matrix. Sample copy for 10x13 SAE and $3 postage.
Nonfiction: Presents information pertinent to home furnishings retailers, primarily digested from business magazines, consumer magazines, trade journals, books, newsletters, etc. Always interested in seeing original or previously published information regarding the home-furnishings industry, retail sales, consumer buying-habit research, general business information or economic trends. Emphasis on short, "how-to" articles. Query. Length: 100-350 words, appropriate to subject and slant. Photos desirable. Sometimes pays the expenses of writers on assignment.

HOME LIGHTING & ACCESSORIES, Box 2147, Clifton NJ 07015. (201)779-1600. FAX: (201)779-3242. Editor: Peter Wulff. 5% freelance written. Prefers to work with published/established writers. For lighting stores/departments. Monthly magazine. Circ. 9,000. Pays on publication. Publishes ms an average of 4-6 months after acceptance. Buys all rights. Submit seasonal/holiday material 6 months in advance. Computer printout submissions acceptable; no dot-matrix. Free sample copy.
Nonfiction: Interview (with lighting retailers); personal experience (as a businessperson involved with lighting); profile (of a successful lighting retailer/lamp buyer); and technical (concerning lighting or lighting design). Buys 10 mss/year. Query. Pays $60/published page. Sometimes pays the expenses of writers on assignment.
Photos: State availability of photos with query. Offers no additional payment for 5x7 or 8x10 b&w glossy prints. Pays additional $90 for color transparencies used on cover. Captions required.
Tips: "We don't need fillers—only features."

THE PROFESSIONAL UPHOLSTERER, Official Publication of the National Association of Professional Upholsterers, Communications Today Ltd., 200 S. Main St., High Point NC 27261. (919)889-0113. Associate Editor: Karl Kunkel. Group Editor: Gary Evans. 30% freelance written. A bimonthly magazine on reupholstering and building of custom-made upholstered furniture. "Our publication is geared to professional upholsterers and/or owners of independently owned/operated upholstery shops and custom interior decoration houses. The emphasis is on new products, sales ideas, profiles of upwardly mobile, marketing-oriented businesses. The biggest need is in how-to pieces." Circ. 22,000. Pays on publication. Publishes ms an average of 2 months after acceptance. Buys all rights. Submit seasonal/holiday material 4 months in advance. Photocopied submissions OK. Computer printout submissions OK. Reports in 2 weeks on queries; 3 weeks on mss. Sample copy $4. Writer's guidelines for #10 SASE.
Nonfiction: Historical/nostalgic, how-to (tips, techniques on producing all types of upholstered furniture and antiques, pillows, draperies, upholstered headboards, etc.), humor (topical cartoons), new products and unusual time-saving pieces of equipment), opinion (good or bad experiences of a reupholsterer), personal experience, technical and travel. "No boiler plate sales pieces or motivational pieces in which plumber, carpenter, etc. has been removed and upholsterer inserted. I can usually tell if the writer knows our reading audience." Buys 10 mss/year. Query. Length: 50 words. Pays $25-150 for assigned articles. Pays $25-100 for unsolicited articles. Prefer initial contact prior to receiving articles.
Photos: State availability of photos with submission. Reviews contact sheets. Offers no additional payment for photos accepted with ms. Captions required. Buys all rights.
Columns/Departments: Buys 6 mss/year. Query. Length: 140-200 words. Pays $25-100.
Fillers: Anecdotes, facts and short humor. Buys 2/year. Length: 100 words. Pays $10-25.
Tips: "Learn tips, unusual areas of specialization (not auto-related, prefer furniture—residential, hotel, restaurant, office, related items). Prefers neat writer. Call me or write a query letter, allowing me to focus piece better."

‡**RETAILER AND MARKETING NEWS,** Box 191105, Dallas TX 75219-1105. (214)871-2930. Editor: Michael J. Anderson. Monthly for retail dealers and wholesalers in appliances, TVs, furniture, consumer electronics, records, air conditioning, housewares, hardware, and all related businesses. Circ. 10,000. Photocopied submissions OK. Free sample copy.
Nonfiction: "How a retail dealer can make more profit" is the approach. Wants "sales promotion ideas, advertising, sales tips, business builders and the like, localized to the Southwest and particularly to north Texas." Submit complete ms. Length: 100-900 words. Pays $30.

SEW BUSINESS, 15400 Knoll Trail, Suite 112, Dallas TX 75248. Editor: Keven Todd. National monthly business magazine for retailers of creative sewing, needle arts and related crafts. Circ. 20,000. Pays on publication. Publishes ms 3-4 months after acceptance. Computer printout submissions OK. Reports in 5 weeks on queries; 6-8 weeks on ms. Sample copy and writer's guidelines for 8½x11 SAE with 5 first class stamps.

Nonfiction: Business-oriented articles that concentrate on fabric, needleworkor quilting shop operations — retailing in terms of cash flow, display and marketing. Interviews with retailers and suppliers concerning fashion trends, new products and services. Buys 15 unsolicited mss/year. Query. Length: 750 words. Pays $75 minimum.
Photos: Photos purchased with mss. Typically use b&w, occasionally color. Additional payment possible depending upon the situation.

TILE WORLD, Tradelink Publishing Co.. 485 Kinderkamack Rd., Oradell NJ 07649. (201)599-0136. FAX: (207)599-2378. Editor: Mike Lench. Managing Editor: John Sailer. 25% freelance written. A quarterly magazine on tile. "Our readers are tile users and specifiers; write for that market." Circ. 18,000. Pays on publication. Publishes ms an average of 4 months after acceptance. Byline given. Buys first rights and makes work-for-hire assignments. Submit seasonal/holiday material 6 months in advance. Simultaneous, photocopied and previously published submissions OK. Computer printout submissions OK; prefers letter-quality. Reports in 1 month on queries; 2 months on mss. Sample copy $5. Free writer's guidelines.
Nonfiction: How-to (install tile), interview/profile, new product, photo feature (architectural design) and technical. Buys 10 mss/year. Query with published clips. Length: 600-2,000 words. Pays $80-240.
Photos: Send photos with submission. Reviews transparencies and prints. Captions and identification of subjects required. Buys one-time rights.
Columns/Departments: News; New Products (new types of tiles); New Equipment (for installing tile); 200 words. Send complete ms. Pays $15-40.
Tips: "Reports on architectural designs using tile are most open to freelancers. Architects are very willing to be quoted and provide good photos. Be sure to include in features all players involved with tile distribution and installation."

Hospitals, Nursing and Nursing Homes

In this section are journals for medical and nonmedical nursing home personnel, clinical and hospital staffs and medical laboratory technicians and managers. Journals publishing technical material on medical research and information for physicians in private practice are listed in the Medical category.

AMERICAN JOURNAL OF NURSING, 555 West 57th St., New York NY 10019. (212)582-8820. Editor: Mary B. Mallison, RN. 2% freelance written. Eager to work with new/unpublished writers. Monthly magazine covering nursing and health care. Circ. 330,000. Pays on publication. Publishes ms an average of 6 months after acceptance. Byline given. Simultaneous queries OK. Computer printout submissions acceptable; prefers letter-quality. Reports in 3 weeks on queries, 4 months on mss. Sample copy $3; free writer's guidelines.
Nonfiction: How-to, satire, new product, opinion, personal experience, photo feature and technical. No material other than nursing care and nursing issues. "Nurse authors mostly accepted for publication." Query. Length: 1,000-1,500 words. Payment negotiable. Pays the expenses of writers on assignment.
Photos: Forbes Linkhorn, art editor. Reviews b&w and color transparencies and prints. Model release and identification of subjects required. Buys variable rights.
Columns/Departments: Buys 20 mss/year. Query with or without clips of published work.

‡**CONTEMPORARY LONG-TERM CARE,** Advantage Publishing, Suite 500, 1801 West End Ave., Nashville TN 37203. (615)329-1973. Editor: John Mitchell. 70% freelance written. Monthly magazine on long-term health care (nursing homes, retirement facilities, etc.). "*CLTC* is the leading trade journal for the long-term care industry and is circulated each month to some 34,000 nursing home and retirement facility administrators/owners and others active in the aging network (legislators, investment bankers, insurance companies, equipment and service providers, etc.)." Pays on publication. Publishes ms an average of 2-6 months after acceptance. Byline given. Buys first North American serial rights and second serial (reprint) rights. Submit seasonal/holiday material 3-4 months in advance. Simultaneous submissions OK. Query for electronic submissions. Computer printout submissions OK; no dot-matrix. Reports in 2 weeks on queries; 1 month on mss. Free sample copy and writer's guidelines.
Nonfiction: How-to, interview/profile, new product, opinion, personal experience and technical. "We do not accept any articles *not* related to long-term care specifically." Buys 30-40 mss/year. Send complete ms. Length: 750-2,000 words. Pays $50-300 for assigned articles; $200 maximum for unsolicited articles. Some-

times pays in "free issues, occasionally free reprints." Sometimes pays expenses of writers on assignment.

Photos: State availability of photos with submission. Reviews contact sheets, 2¼x2¼ transparencies and 5x7 prints. Offers no additional payment for photos accepted with ms. Model releases and identification of subjects required. Buys all rights.

Columns/Departments: LTC Financing (*Current* issues in long-term care) and LTC Marketing (impact/benefits to *LTC* providers). Buyers 4-8 mss/year. Query with published clips. Length: 750-1,200 words. Pays $50-200.

Tips: "Knowledge of long-term health care is a *must*, given esoteric nature of the industry and regulatory requirements at federal, state and local levels."

‡**FLORIDA NURSING NEWS,** Landmark Community Newspapers, Inc., Suite 205, 8360 W. Oakland Pk. Blvd., Ft. Lauderdale FL 33351. (305)748-3660. Managing Editor: Steven Ricci. 65% freelance written. Biweekly newspaper on nursing in Florida. "News and feature articles about the nursing profession, especially in Florida." Circ. 90,000. Pays on publication. Publishes ms an average of 1-2 months after acceptance. Byline given. Offers $25-50 kill fee. Buys first rights. Submit seasonal/holiday material 3 months in advance. Reports in 3 weeks on queries; 1-2 months on mss. Sample copy for 5x7 SAE with 2 first class stamps. Free writer's guidelines.

Nonfiction: Interview/profile (nursing), opinion (nursing related), personal experience (nursing stories) and technical (nursing). Buys 50 mss/year. Query with published clips. Length: 750-2,500 words. Pays $75-250. Sometimes pays expenses of writers on assignment.

Photos: Send photos with submission. Reviews 5x7 prints. Offers $10 maximum per photo. Captions, model releases and identification of subjects required. Buys one-time rights.

Columns/Departments: Nurses Forum (articles/opinion on or about nursing/by nurses). Buys 10 mss/year. Query. Length: 750-1,000 words. Pays $50 maximum.

Tips: "Cover what's new and different about nursing in Florida! Send stories about outstanding and different Florida nurses."

HOSPITAL GIFT SHOP MANAGEMENT, Creative Age Publications, 7628 Densmore Ave., Van Nuys CA 91406. (818)782-7232. Editor: Barbara Feiner. 25% freelance written. Works with a small number of new/unpublished writers each year. Monthly magazine covering hospital gift shop management. "*HGSM* presents practical and informative articles and features to assist in expanding the hospital gift shop into a comprehensive center generating large profits." Circ. 15,000. Pays on acceptance. Publishes ms an average of 4 months after acceptance. Byline given. Buys first North American serial rights. Submit seasonal/holiday material 8 months in advance. Computer printout submissions acceptable; dot-matrix OK "if readable and double-spaced." Reports in 1 month. Sample copy and writer's guidelines for $4 postage.

Nonfiction: How-to, interview/profile, photo feature and management-themed articles. "No fiction, no poetry, no first-person 'I was shopping in a gift shop' kinds of pieces." Buys 12-25 mss/year. Length: 750-2,500 words. Pays $10-100. Query first.

Photos: State availability of photos with query. "If you are preparing a gift shop profile, think of providing gift shop photos." Reviews 5x7 color or b&w prints; payment depends on photo quality and number used. Captions, model release and identification of subjects required.

Fillers: Cartoons only. Buys 12/year. Pays $20.

Tips: "A freelancer's best bet is to let us know you're out there. We prefer to work on assignment a lot of the time, and we're very receptive to freelancers—especially those in parts of the country to which we have no access. Call or write; let me know you're available. Visit your nearby hospital gift shop—it's probably larger, more sophisticated than you would imagine. I've noticed that query letters are becoming sloppy and lack direction. I wouldn't mind finding writers who can communicate well, explain story ideas in a one-page letter, spell correctly and wow me with original ideas. Make your query letter stand out. Convince me that your story is going to be exciting. A boring query usually yields a boring story."

HOSPITAL SUPERVISOR'S BULLETIN, Bureau of Business Practice, 24 Rope Ferry Rd., Waterford CT 06386. Editor: Michele Dunaj. 40% freelance written. Works with a small number of new/unpublished writers each year. For non-medical hospital supervisors. Semimonthly newsletter. Circ. 3,300. Pays on acceptance. Publishes ms an average of 5 months after acceptance. Buys all rights. No byline. Submit seasonal/holiday material 6 months in advance. Photocopied submissions OK. Computer printout submissions acceptable; prefers letter-quality. Reports in 1 month. Sample copy and writer's guidelines for SAE with 2 first class stamps.

Nonfiction: Publishes interviews with non-medical hospital department heads. "You should ask supervisors to pinpoint current problems in supervision, tell how they are trying to solve these problems and what results they're getting—backed up by real examples from daily life." Also publishes interviews on people problems and good methods of management. People problems include the areas of training, planning, evaluating, counseling, discipline, motivation, supervising the undereducated, getting along with the medical staff, dealing with change, layoffs, etc. No material on hospital volunteers. "We prefer six- to eight-page typewritten articles. Articles must be interview-based." Pays 12-15¢/word after editing.

Tips: "Often stories lack concrete examples explaining general principles. I want to stress that freelancers interview supervisors (not high-level managers, doctors, or administrators) of non-medical departments. Interviews should focus on supervisory skills or techniques that would be applicable in any hospital department. The article should be conversational in tone: not stiff or academic. Use the second person to address the supervisor/reader."

‡**NURSING90**, Springhouse Corporation, 1111 Bethlehem Pike, Springhouse PA 19477. (215)646-8700. Editor: Maryanne Wagner. Managing Editor: Jane Benner. 100% freelance written. Monthly magazine on the nursing field. "Our articles are written by nurses for nurses; we look for practical advice for the working nurse that reflects the author's experience." Circ. 500,000. Pays on publication. Publishes ms an average of 10-12 months after acceptance. Byline given. Offers 50% kill fee. Buys all rights. Submit seasonal/holiday material 6-8 months in advance. Photocopied submissions OK. Query for electronic submissions. Computer printout submissions OK. Reports in 2 weeks on queries; 3 months on mss. Sample copy for $3 with 9x12 SAE. Free writer's guidelines.

Nonfiction: Book excerpts, exposé, how-to (specifically as applies to nursing field), inspirational, new product, opinion, personal experience and photo feature. No articles from patients' point of view; humor articles, poetry, etc. Buys 100 mss/year. Query. Length: 100 words minimum. Pays $50-400.

Photos: State availability of photos with submission. Offers no additional payment for photos accepted with ms. Model releases required. Buys all rights.

—— Hotels, Motels, Clubs, Resorts and Restaurants

These publications offer trade tips and advice to hotel, club, resort and restaurant managers, owners and operators. Journals for manufacturers and distributors of bar and beverage supplies are listed in the Beverages and Bottling section.

BARTENDER MAGAZINE, Foley Publishing, Box 158, Liberty Corner NJ 07038. (201)766-6006. FAX: (201)766-6607. Publisher: Raymond P. Foley. Editor: Jaclyn M. Wilson. Emphasizes liquor and bartending for bartenders, tavern owners and owners of restaurants with liquor licenses. 100% freelance written. Prefers to work with published/established writers; eager to work with new/unpublished writers. Magazine published 5 times/year. Circ. 140,000. Pays on publication. Publishes ms an average of 3 months after acceptance. Buys first serial rights, first North American serial rights, one-time rights, second serial (reprint) rights, all rights, and simultaneous U.S. rights. Byline given. Phone queries OK. Submit seasonal/holiday material 3 months in advance. Simultaneous, photocopied, and previously published submissions OK. Computer printout submissions acceptable; prefers letter-quality. Reports in 2 months. Sample copies for 9x12 SAE with $2.50 for postage.

Nonfiction: General interest, historical, how-to, humor, interview (with famous bartenders or ex-bartenders); new products, nostalgia, personal experience, unique bars, opinion, new techniques, new drinking trends, photo feature, profile, travel and bar sports or bar magic tricks. Send complete ms. Length: 100-1,000 words. Sometimes pays the expenses of writers on assignment.

Photos: Send photos with ms. Pays $7.50-50 for 8x10 b&w glossy prints; $10-75 for 8x10 color glossy prints. Caption preferred and model release required.

Columns/Departments: Bar of the Month; Bartender of the Month; Drink of the Month; New Drink Ideas; Bar Sports; Quiz; Bar Art; Wine Cellar; Tips from the Top (from prominent figures in the liquor industry); One For The Road (travel); Collectors (bar or liquor-related items); Photo Essays. Query. Length: 200-1,000 words. Pays $50-200.

Fillers: Clippings, jokes, gags, anecdotes, short humor, newsbreaks and anything relating to bartending and the liquor industry. Length: 25-100 words. Pays $5-25.

Tips: "To break in, absolutely make sure that your work will be of interest to all bartenders across the country. Your style of writing should reflect the audience you are addressing. The most frequent mistake made by writers in completing an article for us is using the wrong subject."

ALWAYS submit unsolicited manuscripts or queries with a self-addressed, stamped envelope (SASE) within your country or International Reply Coupons (IRC) purchased from the post office for other countries.

CATERING TODAY, The Professional Guide to Catering Profits, ProTech Publishing, 738 Pearl, Denver CO 80203. (303)861-4040. Editor: Amy Lorton. Managing Editor: Jane Kulbeth. 40% freelance written. Prefers to work with published/established writers. A monthly magazine for the off-premise and on-site catering industry covering food trends, business and management advice and features on successful caterers. Circ. 37,000. Pays on publication. Publishes ms an average of 5-6 months after acceptance. Byline given. Offers 10-30% kill fee. Buys all rights. Submit seasonal/holiday material 3 months in advance. Simultaneous, photocopied and previously published submissions OK. Computer printout submissions acceptable; prefers letter-quality. Reports in 2 weeks on queries; 3 weeks on mss. Sample copy and writer's guidelines for 9x12 SAE with 5 first class stamps.

Nonfiction: How-to (on ice carving, garnishes, cooking techniques, etc); interview/profile, new product and photo feature. "Also valuable to caterers are advice and ideas on marketing, advertising, public relations and promotion." No humor, poetry or fiction. Buys 35-40 mss/year. Query with published clips. Length: 800-2,500. Pays $50/printed word minimum; $150/printed word maximum.

Photos: Send photos with submission. Reviews contact sheets, negatives, 4x5 transparencies, and 5x7 prints. Offers $5-25/photo. Captions required.

Columns/Departments: Book reviews. Buys 25/year. Send complete ms. Length: 500-1,200 words. Pays $75/printed page.

Fillers: Buys 10/year. Length: 50-100 words. Pays $25.

Tips: "Write from a viewpoint that a caterer/business person can understand, appreciate and learn from. Submissions should be neat, accurate and not flowery or wordy. Areas of our publication most open to freelancers are food trends and uses, equipment reviews and feature-length profiles of caterers."

FLORIDA HOTEL & MOTEL JOURNAL, The Official Publication of the Florida Hotel & Motel Association, Accommodations, Inc., Box 1529, Tallahassee FL 32302. (904)224-2888. Editor: Mrs. Jayleen Woods. 10% freelance written. Prefers to work with published/established writers. Monthly magazine for managers in the lodging industry (every licensed hotel, motel and resort in Florida). Circ. 6,800. Pays on publication. Publishes ms an average of 2 months after acceptance. Byline given. Offers $50 kill fee. Buys all rights and makes work-for-hire assignments. Submit seasonal/holiday material 3 months in advance. Photocopied submissions OK. Computer printout submissions acceptable; no dot-matrix. Reports in 1 month. Sample copy for 9x12 SAE and 5 first class stamps; writer's guidelines for #10 SASE.

Nonfiction: General interest (business, finance, taxes); historical/nostalgic (old Florida hotel reminiscences); how-to (improve management, housekeeping procedures, guest services, security and coping with common hotel problems); humor (hotel-related anecdotes); inspirational (succeeding where others have failed); interview/profile (of unusual hotel personalities); new product (industry-related and non brand preferential); photo feature (queries only); technical (emerging patterns of hotel accounting, telephone systems, etc.); travel (transportation and tourism trends only—no scenics or site visits); and property renovations and maintenance techniques. Buys 10-12 mss/year. Query with clips of published work. Length: 750-2,500 words. Pays $75-250 "depending on type of article and amount of research." Sometimes pays the expenses of writers on assignment.

Photos: Send photos with ms. Pays $25-100 for 4x5 color transparencies; $10-15 for 5x7 b&w prints. Captions, model release and identification of subjects required.

Tips: "We prefer feature stories on properties or personalities holding current membership in the Florida Hotel and Motel Association. Membership and/or leadership brochures are available (SASE) on request. We're open to articles showing how hotel management copes with energy systems, repairs, renovations, new guest needs and expectations. The writer may have a better chance of breaking in at our publication with short articles and fillers because the better a writer is at the art of condensation, the better his/her feature articles are likely to be."

‡FLORIDA RESTAURATEUR, Florida Restaurant Association, 2441 Hollywood Blvd., Hollywood FL 33020. (305)921-6300. FAX (305)925-6381. Editor: Hugh P. (Mickey) McLinden. 15% freelance written. Monthly magazine for food service and restaurant owners and managers—"deals with trends, legislation, training, sanitation, new products, spot news." Circ. 17,142. Pays on publication. Publishes ms an average of 2 months after acceptance. Byline given. Offers $100 kill fee. Buys one-time rights. Submit seasonal/holiday material 3 months in advance. Simultaneous submissions OK. Query for electronic submissions. Computer printout submissions OK; prefers letter-quality. Reports in 1 week on queries; 2 weeks on mss. Sample copy for 9x12 SAE and 3 first class stamps.

Nonfiction: How-to, general interest, interview/profile, new product, personal experience and technical. Query. Length: 500-2,000 words. Pays $200-300 for assigned articles; $150-250 for unsolicited articles.

Photos: State availability of photos with submission. Reviews transparencies and 5x7 prints. Offers $50-250 per photo. Model releases and identification of subjects required. Buys one-time rights.

FOOD & SERVICE, Texas Restaurant Association, Box 1429, Austin TX 78767. (512)444-6543 (in Texas, 1-800-252-9360). FAX: (512)444-7811. Editor: Bland Crowder. 50% freelance written. Magazine published 11 times/year providing business solutions to Texas restaurant owners and operators. Circ. 5,000. Written queries required. Reports in 1 month. Byline given. Not copyrighted. Buys first rights. Simultaneous queries, photocopied submissions OK. No previously published submissions. Query for electronic submissions. Sample copy and editorial calendar for 9x12 SAE and 6 first class stamps. Free writer's guidelines. Pays on acceptance; rates vary.

Nonfiction: Features must provide business solutions to problems in the restaurant and food service industries. Topics vary but always have business slant; usually particular to Texas. No restaurant critiques, human interest stories or seasonal copy. Quote members of the Texas Restaurant Association; substantiate with facts and examples. Query. Length: 2,000-2,500 words, features; shorter articles sometimes used; product releases, 300-word maximum. Payment rates vary.

Photos: State availability of photos, but photos usually assigned.

Columns/Departments: Written in-house only.

HOTEL AMENITIES IN CANADA, Titan Publishing Inc., Unit 5, 24 Hayes Ave., Box 1747, Guelph ON N1H 7A1 Canada. (519)763-5058. Editor: Jayne Guild. 30% freelance written. Bimonthly magazine covering the lodging hospitality industry. "*Hotel Amenities in Canada* is a publication dedicated to the promotion of amenities and essential supplies and services in the Canadian hospitality industry." Circ. 3,600. Pays on publication. Publishes ms an average of 2 months after acceptance. Byline given. Buys first North American serial rights. Submit seasonal/holiday material 3 months in advance. Simultaneous and previously published submissions OK. Computer printout submissions OK; prefers letter-quality. Reports in 6 weeks. Sample copy for 8x10 SAE with Canadian postage or International Reply Coupon.

Nonfiction: New product, company feature. "*Hotel Amenities in Canada* is aimed primarily at the lodging hospitality industry so we do not need foodservice articles." Buys 12 mss/year. Query with published clips. Length: 500-1,500 words. Pays up to $100.

Photos: State availability of photos with submission. Reviews 5x7 prints. Offers $5/photo. Identification of subjects required. Buys one-time rights.

Columns/Departments: Products and Services (new products). Length 50-100 words. Pays up to $10.

Tips: "Research the amenities trend in the hospitality industry."

‡**HOTEL AND MOTEL MANAGEMENT,** Edgell Communications Inc. 7500 Old Oak Blvd., Cleveland OH 44130. (216)243-8100. FAX: (216)826-2832. Editor: Michael Deluca. Managing Editor: Robert Nozar. 25% freelance written. Prefers to work with published/established writers. Newsmagazine published every 3 weeks about hotels, motels and resorts in the continental U.S. and Hawaii for general managers, corporate executives, and department heads (such as director of sales; food and beverage; energy; security; front office; housekeeping, etc.) Circ. 45,000. Pays on acceptance. Publishes ms an average of 2 months after acceptance. Byline given. Buys first North American serial rights. No phone queries. Computer printout submissions acceptable; prefers letter-quality. Reports in 3 weeks on queries; do not send mss. Sample copy for 12x16 SAE and $2 postage.

Nonfiction: "A how-to, nuts-and-bolts approach to improving the bottom line through more innovative, efficient management of hotels, motels and resorts in the continental U.S. and Hawaii. Articles consist largely of specific case studies and interviews with authorities on various aspects of the lodging market, including franchising, financing, personnel, security, energy management, telecommunications, food service operations, architecture and interior design, and technological advances. We use freelance coverage of spot news events (strikes, natural disasters, etc.). Query with published clips. "Write a query letter outlining your idea and be specific." Length: 800-1,000 words. Sometimes pays expenses of writers on assignment.

Photos: State availability of photos. Captions preferred. Buys one-time rights.

Tips: "The writer may have a better chance of breaking in at our publication with short articles and fillers because we are a newsmagazine that covers an industry of people who don't have time to read longer articles. We need 'hands on' articles which explain the topic."

‡**HYATT,** Hotel Magazine Network, 1729 H St. NW, Washington DC 20006. Editor: Edwin S. Grosvenor. Bimonthly magazine for guests of hotels, upper and middle management business travelers. Also publishes *Marriott Portfolio.* Pays on publication. Byline given. Buys one-time rights. Submit seasonal/holiday material 3 months in advance. Simultaneous, photocopied and previously published submissions OK. Query for electronic submissions. Computer printout submissions OK; prefers letter-quality. Sample copy for 8½x11 SAE with $2.40 postage for both magazines.

Nonfiction: Book excerpts, general interest, historical/nostalgic, how-to, humor, inspirational, interview/profile, photo feature, travel and business/management advice. Buys 12 mss/year. Query with or without published clips, or send complete ms. Length: 1,500-3,200 words. Pays $200-400. Pays in contributor copies or other premiums under "negotiable" circumstances. Sometimes pays expenses of writers on assignment.

Photos: State availability of photos with submission. Reviews contact sheets, transparencies and prints. Captions, model releases and identification of subjects required. Buys one-time rights.

Columns/Departments: Finance, Lifestyles, Managment, Communication and Travel Advice; all of interest to business people who make $40,000 and over per year. Upper and middle management. Buys 24 mss/year. Query or send complete ms. Length: 1,200-3,000 words. Pays $100-400.

INNKEEPING WORLD, Box 84108, Seattle WA 98124. Editor/Publisher: Charles Nolte. 75% freelance written. Eager to work with new/unpublished writers. Emphasizes the hotel industry worldwide. Published 10 times a year. Circ. 2,000. Pays on acceptance. Publishes ms an average of 4 months after acceptance. Buys all rights. No byline. Submit seasonal/holiday material 1 month in advance. Computer printout submissions acceptable; no dot-matrix. Reports in 1 month. Sample copy and writer's guidelines for 9x12 SAE with 3 first class stamps.

Nonfiction: Managing—interviews with successful hotel managers of large and/or famous hotels/resorts (600-1,200 words); Marketing—interviews with hotel marketing executives on successful promotions/case histories (300-1,000 words); Sales Promotion—innovative programs for increasing business (100-600 words); Bill of Fare—outstanding hotel restaurants, menus and merchandising concepts (300-1,000 words); and Guest Relations—guest service programs, management philosophies relative to guests (200-800 words). Pays $100 minimum or 15¢/word (whichever is greater) for main topics. Other topics—advertising, creative packages, cutting expenses, frequent guest profile, guest comfort, hospitality, ideas, public relations, reports and trends, special guestrooms, staff relations. Length: 50-500 words. Pays 15¢/word. "If a writer asks a hotel for a complimentary room, the article will not be accepted, nor will *Innkeeping World* accept future articles from the writer."

Tips: "We need more in-depth reporting on successful case histories—results-oriented information."

‡LODGING HOSPITALITY MAGAZINE, Penton Publishing, 1100 Superior Ave., Cleveland OH 44114. (216)696-7000. Editor: Edward Watkins. 25% freelance written. Prefers to work with published/established writers. A monthly magazine covering the lodging industry. "Our purpose is to inform lodging management of trends and events which will affect their properties and the way they do business. Audience: owners and managers of hotels, motels, resorts." Circ. 50,000. Pays on acceptance. Publishes ms an average of 2 months after acceptance. Byline given. Buys first rights. Submit seasonal/holiday material 2 months in advance. Computer printout submissions OK; no dot-matrix. Reports in 1 month.

Nonfiction: General interest, how-to, interview/profile and travel. Special issues include technology (January); interior design (April); foodservice (May); investments (June); franchising (July); marketing (September); and state of the industry (December). "We do *not* want personal reviews of hotels visited by writer, or travel pieces. All articles are geared to hotel executives to help them in their business." Buys 25 mss/year. Query. Length: 700-2,000 words. Pays $150-600. Sometimes pays the expenses of writers on assignment.

Photos: State availability of photos with submission. Reviews contact sheets and transparencies. Offers no additional payment for photos accepted with ms. Captions and identification of subjects required. Buys one-time rights.

Columns/Departments: Budget Line, Suite Success, Resort Report, Executive on the Spot, Strategies Marketwatch, Report from Washington, Food for Profit, Technology Update—all one-page reports of 700 words. Buys 25 mss/year. Query. Pays $150-250.

‡MARRIOTT PORTFOLIO, Hotel Magazine Network, 1729 H. St. NW, Washington DC 20006. Editor: Edwin S. Grosvenor. Bimonthly magazine for guests of hotels; upper and middle management business travelers. (see *Hyatt* for guidelines).

‡MOTEL/HOTEL INSIDER, Magna Publications, Inc., 2718 Dryden Dr., Madison WI 53704-3006. (608)249-2455. Editor: Bill Merrick. 10% freelance written. A semimonthly newsletter for executives, managers, management companies and owners in the lodging industry. "The magazine is a high-priced publication that takes seriously its purpose of offering useful, current, provocative lodging management information to its audience. The *Insider* newsletter has no advertising, its articles are brief and targeted. Its checklists, interviews, promotional digests, how-to and perspective pieces are all tightly written to save the reader's valuable time." Publishes ms an average of 2 months after acceptance. Byline given. Offers 25% kill fee. Buys first North American serial rights and (some) second serial rights. Submit seasonal material 4 months in advance. Query for electronic submissions. Reports in 3 weeks. Sample copy $8; writer's guidelines for 6x9 SASE. Query or send complete ms. Length 175-400 words: pays $75-125; 400-650 words: pays $125-200; 650-800 words: Pays $200-300.

Tips: "This newsletter's audience is very knowledgeable about the industry, and tends to be decision makers with profits, better management on its mind. Therefore, we welcome sophisticated hotel management information: articles, interviews or checklists on new technology, energy management, theft prevention, renovation strategy, etc."

PIZZA TODAY, The Professional Guide To Pizza Profits, ProTech Publishing and Communications, Inc., Box 114, Santa Claus IN 47579. (812)937-4464. Editor: Amy Lorton. Managing Editor: Ramona Chun. 30% freelance written. Prefers to work with published/established writers. A monthly magazine for the pizza industry, covering trends, features of successful pizza operators, business and management advice, etc. Circ. 40,000. Pays on publication. Publishes ms an average of 2 months after acceptance. Byline given. Offers 10-30% kill fee. Buys all rights and negotiable rights. Submit seasonal/holiday material 3 months in advance. Simultaneous, photocopied and previously published submissions OK. Query for electronic submissions.

Computer printout submissons acceptable; prefers letter-quality. Reports in 2 weeks on queries; 3 weeks on manuscripts. Sample copy and writer's guidelines for 10x13 SAE with 6 first class stamps.

Nonfiction: Interview/profile, new product, entrepreneurial slants, time management, pizza delivery and employee training. No fillers, fiction, humor or poetry. Buys 40-60 mss/year. Query with published clips. Length: 750-2,500 words. Pays $50-125/page. Sometimes pays the expenses of writers on assignment.

Photos: Send photos with submission. Reviews contact sheets, negatives, 4x5 transparencies, color slides and 5x7 prints. Offers $5-10/photo. Captions required.

Tips: "We would like to receive nutritional information for low-cal, low-salt, low-fat, etc. pizza. Writers must have strong business and foodservice background."

‡RESTAURANT EXCHANGE NEWS, 2 New Hempstead Rd., New City NY 10956. (914)638-1108. FAX: (914)638-2549. Executive Editor: Eric Daum. 10% freelance written. Monthly tabloid for foodservice industry in metro New York. "*Restaurant Exchange News* covers timely news, legislation, trends, serving restaurants, caterers, and the entire food service industry (health care, etc.) plus supporting services in New York, New Jersey, Connecticut and Pennsylvania." Circ. 22,000. Pays on publication. Byline given. Offers negotiable kill fee. Not copyrighted. Buys one-time rights. Submit seasonal/holiday material 2 months in advance. Computer printout submissions OK; prefers letter-quality. Reports in 1 month on queries. Free sample copy and writer's guidelines.

Nonfiction: Book excerpts, how-to, interview/profile (on chefs and restaurateurs), new products, food service association reports and legislative news. "We do not want opinion or personal experience." Query with published clips. Length: 250-2,000 words. Pays $50-250 for assigned articles; $50-175 for unsolicited articles.

Photos: State availability of photos with submission. Reviews negatives and transparencies. Offers no additional payment for photos accepted with ms. Captions and identification of subjects required. Buys one-time rights.

Fillers: Newsbreaks.

‡THE SUCCESSFUL HOTEL MARKETER, The Newsletter of Profit-Building Ideas for the Lodging Industry, Magna Publications, Inc., 2718 Dryden Dr., Madison WI 53704-3006. (608)249-2455. Editor: Sylvia McNair. 15% freelance written. "The magazine is a high-priced, semimonthly publication that takes seriously its mission to offer practical, useful, innovative and transferable marketing strategies and success stories to its lodging industry audience. It has no advertising, its articles are brief and targeted. Its checklists, interviews, promotional digests, how-to and perspective pieces are all tightly written to save the reader's valuable time." Publishes ms an average of 2 months after acceptance. Byline given. Offers 25% kill fee. Buys first North American serial rights and (some) second serial rights. Submit seasonal material 4 months in advance. Query for electronic submissions. Reports in 3 weeks. Sample copy $6. Writer's guidelines for 6x9 SASE. Query or send complete ms. Length 175-400 words: pays $75-125; 400-650 words: pays $125-200; 650-800 words: Pays $200-300.

Tips: "This newsletter's audience is very knowledgeable about the industry, hungry for fresh marketing ideas and at the same time tends to know all the well-publicized promotional strategies in vogue. It is our mission to find the unpublished ones, by building contacts with creative hotel marketers around the country. Therefore, we welcome sophisticated hotel marketing information: articles, interviews or checklists on new promotional packages, dos and don'ts, marketing for new properties and renovations, successful strategies by B&B's, etc."

VACATION INDUSTRY REVIEW, Worldex Corp., Box 431920, South Miami FL 33243. (305)667-0202. FAX: (305)667-5321. Managing Editor: George Leposky. 10% freelance written. Prefers to work with published/ established writers. A quarterly magazine covering leisure lodgings (timeshare resorts, fractionals, condo hotels, and other types of vacation ownership properties). Circ. 10,000. Pays on publication. Publishes ms an average of 3-6 months after acceptance. Byline given. Buys all rights and makes work-for-hire assignments. Submit seasonal/holiday material 6 months advance. Photocopied submissions OK. "Electronic submissions—query for details." Computer printout submissions acceptable; prefers letter-quality. Reports in 1 month. Sample copy $2; writer's guidelines with #10 SASE.

Nonfiction: How-to, interview/profile, new product, opinion, personal experience, technical and travel. No consumer travel or non-vacation real-estate material. Buys 5 mss/year. Query with published clips. Length: 1,000-2,500 words. Pays $75-175. Pays the expenses of writers on assignment, if previously arranged.

Photos: Send photos with submission. Reviews contact sheets, 35mm transparencies, and 5x7 prints. Offers no additional payment for photos accepted with ms. Captions and identification of subjects required. Buys one-time rights.

Tips: "We want articles about the business aspect of the vacation industry: entrepreneurship, project financing, design and construction, sales and marketing, operations, management—in short, anything that will help our readers plan, build, sell and run a quality vacation property that satisfies the owners/guests while earning a profit for the proprietor. Our destination pieces are trade-oriented, reporting the status of tourism and the development of various kinds of leisure lodging facilities in a city, region or country. We're interested in homeowners associations at vacation ownership resorts (not residential condos). You can discuss things to see and do in the context of a resort located near an attraction, but that shouldn't be the main focus or reason for the article."

——— Industrial Operations

Industrial plant managers, executives, distributors and buyers read these journals. Some industrial management journals are also listed under the names of specific industries. Publications for industrial supervisors are listed in Management and Supervision.

APPLIANCE MANUFACTURER, The Magazine for Design for Manufacturing Solutions,, Corcoran Communications, Inc., 6200 Som Center Rd., C-14, Solon OH 44139. (216)349-3060. Editor: Norman C. Remich, Jr. 5% freelance written. A monthly magazine covering design for manufacturing in high-volume automated manufacturing industries. Circ. 35,000. Pays on publication. Publishes ms an average of 3 months after acceptance. Byline given sometimes. Buys all rights. Simultaneous submissions OK. Computer printout submissions acceptable; prefers letter-quality. Reports in 3 weeks. Free sample copy.
Nonfiction: How-to; interview/profile (sometimes); new product; and technical. Buys 12 mss/year. Send complete ms. Length: open. Pays $50/published page. Pays expenses of writers on assignment.
Photos: Captions and identification of subjects required.
Tips: "We are emphasizing the 'design for manufacturing solutions' aspect. It is so important to us, we changed our cover design to feature a more updated look. What the appliance manufacturer wants is solutions to manfacturing problems."

CHEMICAL BUSINESS, Schnell Publishing Company, 80 Broad St., New York NY 1004. FAX: (212)248-4901. Editor: J. Robert Warren. Managing Editor: Alan Serchuk. 60% freelance written. A monthly magazine covering chemicals and related process industries such as plastics, paints, some minerals, essential oils, soaps, detergents. Publishes features on the industry, management, financial (Wall Street), marketing, shipping and storage, labor, engineering, environment, research, international and company profiles. Circ. 40,000. Pays on acceptance. Publishes ms an average of 3 months after acceptance. Byline given. Offers $100 kill fee. Buys all rights. Call before submitting seasonal/holiday material. Photocopied submissions and previously published book excerpts OK. Computer printout submissions acceptable; prefers letter-quality. Free sample copy and writer's guidelines.
Nonfiction: No broad, general industrial submissions on how-to. Buys 60 mss/year. Query. Length: 1,500-2,000 words. Pays $500 for assigned articles. Pays the expenses of writers on assignment.
Photos: Send photos with submission. Reviews contact sheets, negatives and 35mm or 70mm ("almost any size") transparencies. No pay for company photos; offers $10-25/photo taken by writer. Model releases required. Buys all rights.

COMPRESSED AIR, 253 E. Washington Ave., Washington NJ 07882. Editor/Publications Manager: S.M. Parkhill. 75% freelance written. Emphasizes applied technology and industrial management subjects for engineers and managers. Monthly magazine. Circ. 150,000. Buys all rights. Publishes ms an average of 3 months after acceptance. Computer printout submissions acceptable; no dot-matrix. Reports in 6 weeks. Free sample copy, editorial schedule; mention *Writer's Market* in request.
Nonfiction: "Articles must be reviewed by experts in the field." Buys 48 mss/year. Query with published clips. Pays negotiable fee. Sometimes pays expenses of writers on assignment.
Photos: State availability of photos in query. Payment for slides, transparencies and glossy prints is included in total purchase price. Captions required. Buys all rights.
Tips: "We are presently looking for freelancers with a track record in industrial/technology/management writing. Editorial schedule is developed in the summer before the publication year and relies heavily on article ideas from contributors. Resume and samples help. Writers with access to authorities preferred; and prefer interviews over library research. The magazine's name doesn't reflect its contents. We suggest writers request sample copies."

INDUSTRIAL FABRIC PRODUCTS REVIEW, Industrial Fabrics Assoc., Suite 450, 345 Cedar Bldg., St. Paul MN 55101. (612)222-2508. Editor: Sue Hagen. Director of Publications: Roger Barr. 10% freelance written. Monthly magazine covering industrial textiles for company owners, salespersons and researchers in a variety of industrial textile areas. Circ. 9,000. Pays on publication. Publishes ms an average of 2 months after acceptance. Byline given. Buys all rights. Submit seasonal material 4 months in advance. Simultaneous queries, and photocopied and previously published submissions OK. Computer printout submissions acceptable; prefers letter-quality. Reports in 1 month. Sample copy free "after query and phone conversation."

Nonfiction: Technical, marketing and other topics related to any aspect of industrial fabric industry from fiber to finished fabric product. Special issues include new products, industrial products and equipment. No historical or apparel oriented articles. Buys 30 mss/year. Query with phone number. Length: 1,200-3,000 words. Pays $75/published page. Sometimes pays the expenses of writers on assignment.

Photos: State availability of photos. Reviews 8x10 b&w glossy and color prints. Pay is negotiable. Model release and identification of subjects required. Buys one-time rights.

Tips: We encourage freelancers to learn our industry and make regular, solicited contributions to the magazine."

MANUFACTURING SYSTEMS, The Management Magazine of Integrated Manufacturing, Hitchcock Publishing Co., 191 S. Gary Ave., Carol Stream IL 60188. (Split office operation between San Jose and Illinois). (312)665-1000. FAX: (312)462-2225 (staff); (408)272-0403 (editor). Editor: Tom Inglesby. Managing Editor: Mary Emrich. Senior Editor: Barbara Dutton. 10-15% freelance written. A monthly magazine covering computers/information in manufacturing for upper and middle-level management in manufacturing companies. Circ. 115,000. Pays on acceptance. Publishes ms an average of 2 months after acceptance. Byline given. Offers 35% kill fee on assignments. Buys all rights. Simultaneous and photocopied submissions OK. Query for electronic submissions. Computer printout submissions acceptable; prefers letter-quality. Reports in 4-6 weeks. Free sample copy and writer's guidelines.

Nonfiction: Book excerpts, essays, general interest, interview/profile, new product, opinion, technical, case history—applications of system. "Each issue emphasizes some aspect of manufacturing. Editorial schedule available, usually in September, for next year." Buys 6-8 mss/year. Query with or without published clips, or send complete ms. Length: 500-2,500 words. Pays $150-600 for assigned articles; pays $50/published page for unsolicited articles. Sometimes pays limited, pre-authorized expenses of writers on assignment.

Photos: State availability of photos with submission. Reviews contact sheets, negatives, 2x2 and larger transparencies and 5x7 and larger prints. Offers no additional payment for photos accepted with ms. Captions and identification of subjects required. Buys one-time rights.

Columns/Departments: Forum (VIP-to-VIP, bylined by manufacturing executive), 1,000-1,500 words. Buys 1-2 mss/year. Query. Sometimes pays $100-200. "These are *rarely* paid for but we'd consider ghost written pieces bylined by 'name.'"

Fillers: Kimberly Bates Miller, assistant editor. Anecdotes, facts and newsbreaks. Buys 3-6/year. Length: 25-100 words. Pays $10-50.

Tips: "We are moving more toward personal management issues and away from technical articles—how to manage, not what tools are available. Check out success stories of companies winning against overseas competition in international marketplace. New trends in manufacturing include application of artificial intelligence (expert systems); standards for comuter systems, networks, operating systems; computer trends, trade, taxes; movement toward "lights-out" factory (no human workers) in Japan and some U.S. industries; desire to be like Japanese in management style; more computer power in smaller boxes. Features are the most open area. We will be happy to provide market information, reader profile and writer's guidelines on request. We are moving to 'require' submission in electronic form—diskette, MCI-mail, Source Mail. Rekeying ms into our word processing system is more work (and cost)."

OCCUPATIONAL HEALTH & SAFETY MAGAZINE, Stevens Publishing, 225 N. New Road, Box 7573, Waco TX 76714. (817)776-9000. FAX: (817)776-9018. Managing Editor: Margoret Leary. Assistant Managing Editor: Ann R. Hawkins. 10% freelance written. Works with a small number of new/unpublished writers each year. A monthly magazine covering health and safety in the workplace. Circ. 86,000. Pays 2 months after publication. Publishes ms an average of 3 months after acceptance. Byline given. Buys first serial rights and first North American serial rights. FAX queries OK. Computer printout submissions acceptable. Reports in 1 month on queries; 2 months on mss. Free sample copy with writer's guidelines and editorial calendar.

Nonfiction: How-to (for health/safety professionals); interview/profile. Subjects of interest include OSHA and EPA regulations; Department of Labor statistics; carpal tunnel syndrome; asbestos; interviews with health and safety personnel of interest to general readers; drug testing; stress management. No unsubstantiated material; no advertorials; no columns; no first-person articles. Query editors on specific subjects only. Length 2,000-3,000 words. Payment varies. Sometimes pays the expenses of writers on assignment.

Photos: Reviews contact sheets, negatives, 4x5 transparencies and prints—prefer color. Captions, model releases of subjects required. Will request print dupes for photo files. Works with stock agencies.

Tips: "There is an increasing merger between OSHA and EPA regulations regarding employee health and safety in such areas as hazardous waste cleanup and emergency response. Writers can judge whether their expertise will suit our needs by noting the technical quality of material in our magazine and reviewing the editorial calendar. Prefer writers with scientific or medical experience. Expanding on news events such as drug testing or AIDS in the workplace is also a good source of editorial material. Send résumé and clips if looking for an assignment."

PLANT MANAGEMENT & ENGINEERING, Suite 500, 245 Fairview Mall Dr., Willowdale/Ontario, Ontario M2J 4T1 Canada. FAX: (416)490-0220. Editor: Ron Richardson. 10% freelance written. Prefers to work with published/established writers. For Canadian plant managers and engineers. Monthly magazine. Circ. 26,000. Pays on acceptance. Publishes ms an average of 2 months after acceptance. Buys first Canadian rights. Computer printout submissions acceptable; prefers letter-quality. Reports in 3 weeks. Free sample copy.
Nonfiction: How-to, technical and management technique articles. Must have Canadian slant. No generic articles that appear to be rewritten from textbooks. Buys fewer than 20 unsolicited mss/year. Query. Pays 22¢/word minimum. Sometimes pays the expenses of writers on assignment.
Photos: State availability of photos with query. Pays $25-50 for b&w prints; $50-100 for 2¼x2¼ or 35mm color transparencies. Captions required. Buys one-time rights.
Tips: "Increased emphasis on the use of computers and programmable controls in manufacturing will affect the types of freelance material we buy. Read the magazine. Know the Canadian readers' special needs. Case histories and interviews only—no theoretical pieces. We have gone to tabloid-size format, and this means shorter (about 800 word) features."

PURCHASING EXECUTIVE'S BULLETIN, Bureau of Business Practice, 24 Rope Ferry Rd., Waterford CT 06386. (203)442-4365. Editor: Wayne Mueller. Managing Editor: Wayne Muller. For purchasing managers and purchasing agents. Semimonthly newsletter. Circ. 5,500. Pays on acceptance. Buys all rights. Submit seasonal/holiday material 3 months in advance. Reports in 2 weeks. Free sample copy and writer's guidelines.
Nonfiction: How-to (better cope with problems confronting purchasing executives); and direct interviews detailing how purchasing has overcome problems and found better ways of handling departments. No derogatory material about a company; no writer's opinions; no training or minority purchasing articles. "We don't want material that's too elementary (things any purchasing executive already knows)." Buys 2-3 mss/issue. Query. Length: 750-1,000 words.

QUALITY CONTROL SUPERVISOR'S BULLETIN, National Foremen's Institute, 24 Rope Ferry Rd., Waterford CT 06386. (800)243-0876. FAX: (203)434-3341. Editor: Steven J. Finn. 80% freelance written. Biweekly newsletter for quality control supervisors. Pays on acceptance. No byline given. Buys all rights. Computer printout submissions acceptable. Reports in 2 weeks on queries; 1 month on mss. Free sample copy and writer's guidelines.
Nonfiction: Interview and "articles with a strong how-to slant that make use of direct quotes whenever possible." Buys 70 mss/year. Query. Length: 800-1,500 words. Pays 8-15¢/word.
Tips: "Write for our freelancer guidelines and follow them closely. We're looking for steady freelancers we can work with on a regular basis."

WEIGHING & MEASUREMENT, Key Markets Publishing Co., Box 5867, Rockford IL 61125. (815)229-1818. FAX: (815)229-4086. Editor: David M. Mathieu. For users of industrial scales and meters. Bimonthly magazine. Circ. 15,000. Pays on acceptance. Buys all rights. Pays 20% kill fee. Byline given. Reports in 2 weeks. Free sample copy.
Nonfiction: Interview (with presidents of companies); personal opinion (guest editorials on government involvement in business, etc.); profile (about users of weighing and measurement equipment); and technical. Buys 25 mss/year. Query on technical articles; submit complete ms for general interest material. Length: 750-1,500 words. Pays $100-175.

_____ *Information Systems*

These publications give computer professionals more data about their field. Consumer computer publications are listed under Personal Computers.

‡COMPUTER LANGUAGE, Miller Freeman Publications, 500 Howard St., San Francisco CA 94105. (415)397-1881. Editor: J.D. Hildebrand. Managing Editor: Kathy Kincade. 75% freelance written. A monthly trade journal on software. "*Computer Language* editorial contains practical information on programming and design for programmers and software developers." Circ. 60,000. Pays on publication. Publishes ms an average of 6 months after acceptance. Byline given. Buys first or second rights. Query for electronic submissions. Computer printout submissions OK; prefers letter-quality. Reports in 1 month on queries; 2 months on mss. Free writer's guidelines. "Writer's guidelines, editorial calendar and other information may be obtained from the magazine's on-line electronic bulletin board: (415)882-9915.
Nonfiction: Interview/profile, technical. Buys 70 mss/year. Query. Length: 2,500-5,000 words. Pays $200-600.
Columns/Departments: Computer Visions (interview—technical—of leader in software development industry) 2,500 words. Buys 10 mss/year. Query. Pays $250-400.
Tips: Emphasis will be on new techniques: CASE, OS/2, 386, object-oriented programming.

‡DBMS, M&T Publishing, Inc., 501 Galveston Dr., Redwood City CA 94063. (415)366-3600. Editor: Kevin Strehlo. Managing Editor: Steve Wilnet. 60% freelance written. Monthly magazine covering database applications and technology. "Our readers are database developers, consultants, VARs, programmers in MIS/DP departments, and serious users." Estab. 1988. Circ. 55,000 (estimate). Pays on acceptance. Publishes ms 3 months after acceptance. Byline given. Offers 33% kill fee. Buys all rights. Query for electronic submissions. Reports in 6 weeks on queries. Samply copy for 9x12 SAE with 8 first class stamps.
Nonfiction: Technical. Buys 40-50 mss/year. Query with published clips. Length: 750-6,000 words. Pays $800.
Photos: Send photos with submission. Offers no additional payment for photos accepted with ms. Captions, model releases and identification of subjects required. Buys all rights.
Tips: "New writers should submit clear, concise queries of specific article subjects and ideas. *Read the magazine* to get a feel for the kind of articles we publish. This magazine is written for a highly technical computer database developer, consultant and user readership. We need technical features that inform this audience of new trends, software, hardware and techniques, including source code, screen caps, and procedures."

‡DG REVIEW, For Data General and Compatible Users, Data Base Publications, Suite 385, 8310 Capital of Texas Hwy., Austin TX 78731. (512)343-9066. Editor: Wendell Watson. Managing Editor: S. Elizabeth Brown. 50% freelance written. Works with a small number of new/unpublished writers each year. A monthly magazine covering Data General computer systems. "*Data Base Monthly* is the primary independent source of technical and market-specific information for people who use Data General computer systems or sell to the Data General market." Circ. 25,000. Pays on publication. Publishes ms an average of 3 months after acceptance. Byline given. Buys first North American serial rights and second serial (reprint) rights. Submit seasonal/holiday material 3 months in advance. Query for electronic submissions. Computer printout submissions acceptable; prefers letter-quality to dot-matrix. Reports in 1 month. Free sample copy and writer's guidelines.
Nonfiction: How-to, new product (computer-related), and technical all specific to Data General systems. No articles which cannot be related to Data General. Buys 25 mss/year. Query with published clips. Length: 1,000-3,500 words. Pays $100-500 for assigned articles; pays $0-500 for unsolicited articles. Sometimes pays the expenses of writers on assignment.
Photos: State availability of photos with submission. Reviews contact sheets, transparencies and 5x7 prints. Offers $0-25/photo. Captions, model releases, and identification of subjects required. Buys first serial rights.
Columns/Departments: Technical columns (instructive articles on Data General computer hardware and software, including reviews by users), 1,000-2,500 words. Query with published clips. Pays $0-300.
Tips: "Feature articles are the area of our publication most open to freelancers."

DR. DOBB'S JOURNAL, Software Tools for Advanced Programmers, M&T Publishing, Inc., 501 Galveston Dr., Redwood City CA 94063. (415)366-3600. Editor: Jon Erickson. Managing Editor: Monica Berg. 60% freelance written. Eager to work with new/unpublished writers. Monthly magazine on computer programming. Circ. 80,000. Pays on publication. Publishes ms an average of 5 months after acceptance. Byline given. Buys all rights. Photocopied submissions OK. Query for electronic submissions. Computer printout submissions acceptable; prefers letter-quality. Reports in 1 month on queries; 9 weeks on mss. Writer's guidelines for #10 SASE.
Nonfiction: How-to and technical. Buys 70 mss/year. Send complete ms. Word length open. Pays $75-1,000.
Tips: "We are happy to look at outlines or queries to see if an author is suitable. They may also obtain writer's guidelines. We are a 'hot rodding' magazine for experienced programmers. Our articles show how to write faster, yet smaller, code. Almost all articles are programmers talking to programmers."

ID SYSTEMS, The Magazine of Keyless Data Entry, Helmers Publishing, Inc.. 174 Concord St., Peterborough NH 03458. (603)924-9631. FAX: (603)924-7408. Editor: Gisela Rank. Associate Editor: Margaret Ann McCauley. 80% freelance written. A magazine about automatic identification technologies, published 10 times/year. Circ. 48,000. Pays at dummy date of issue. Byline given. Buys all rights. Query for electronic submissions. Computer printout submissions OK. Reports in 2 months on queries; 2 weeks on mss. Free sample copy and writer's guidelines.
Nonfiction: Application stories. "We want articles we have assigned, not spec articles." Buys 50/year. Query with published clips. Length: 1,500-1,800 words. Pays $300. Sometimes pays the expenses of writers on assignment.
Photos: Send photos with submission. Reviews contact sheets, transparencies (35mm) and prints. Offers no additional payment for photos accepted with ms. Identification of subjects required. Rights vary article to article.
Tips: "Send letter, fesumé and clips. If background is appropriate, we will contact writer as needed. We give detailed instructions."

IEEE SOFTWARE, IEEE Computer Society, 10662 Los Vagueros Circle, Los Alamitos CA 90720. (714)821-8380. FAX: (714)821-4010. Managing Editor: Angela Burgess. 2% freelance written. Works with a small number of new/unpublished writers each year. A bimonthly magazine on computer software. Circ. 25,000.

Pays on acceptance. "We buy news reports, not feature articles." Publishes ms an average of 1 month after acceptance. Byline given. Offers 25% kill fee. Buys all rights. Simultaneous and photocopied queries OK. Query for electronic submissions. Computer printout submissions OK; prefers letter-quality. Reports in 3 weeks on queries; 5 weeks on mss. Sample copy for 9x12 SAE with 4 first class stamps; writer's guidelines for #10 SASE.

Nonfiction: Interview/profile and technical. "Our news articles show how the technology is being applied and how it affects people. Examples: costs of new languages, problems in SDI software, copyright law, changes in ways of doing things." Buys 10-12 mss/year. Query with published clips. Length: 300-2,000 words. Pays $100-800 for assigned news reports. Sometimes pays the expenses of writers on assignment.

Photos: State availability of photos with submission. Reviews contact sheets. Offers $25-50 per photo. Captions and identification of subjects required. Buys one-time rights.

Tips: "The approach is to pitch an idea. If the idea is good, there's a good chance (budget allowing) a story will follow. Be concise and direct."

‡INFO GUIDE, Info Media Intl., 140 Cloverdale #207, Dorval, Quebec H9S 3H9 Canada. (514)631-8438. Editor: Loran P. Villiers. Managing Editor: Ray Duquesnes. Annual magazine with 4-6 updates yearly that covers computers, office automation, high tech. Circ. 250,000. Pays on publication. Byline given. Buys one-time rights. Submit seasonal material 6 months in advance. Simultaneous submissions OK. Dot-matrix submissions OK; letter-quality preferred. Reports in 2 months. Free writer's guidelines.

Nonfiction: Essays (business), how-to (computers, OA productivity, etc.), interview/profile (business personalities), new product (high-tech), personal experience (business), photo feature (products, corporate) and technical (computers, OEM) "Don't submit anything not related to how businesses use modern technology to increase productivity and profitability." Buys 20 mss/year. Query with published clips. Pays $2,000-2,400 for assigned articles. Sometimes pays expenses of writers on assignment.

Photos: Send photos with submission. Reviews 7x10 prints. Each case discussed on its own merit. Captions, model releases and identification of subjects required. Buys one-time rights.

Columns/Departments: Perspectives on High Tech (current trends on High Tech for Businesses). Buys 2-4 mss/year. Query with published clips. Pays $400-2,500 "depending on length and interest of features."

Tips: "*Info Guide* consists of an Editorial section and a Directory section. Freelancers are welcome to contribute to the entire Editorial section. Articles must be well documented, up to date and informative."

‡INFORM, The Magazine of Information and Image Management, Association for Information and Image Management, 1100 Wayne Ave., Silver Spring MD 20910. (301)587-8202. FAX: (301)587-2711. Editor: Gregory E. Kaebnick. 30% freelance written. Prefers to work with writers with business/high tech experience. A monthly trade magazine on information and image processing. "Specifically we feature coverage of micrographics, electronic imaging and developments in storage and retrieval technology like optical disk, computer-assisted retrieval." Circ. 10,000. Pays on publication. Publishes ms an average of 3 months after acceptance. Byline given. Offers $50 kill fee. Buys first North American serial and second serial (reprint) rights. Submit seasonal/holiday material 2 months in advance. Simultaneous and photocopied submissions OK. Computer printout submissions OK; prefers letter-quality to dot-matrix. Free sample copy and writer's guidelines.

Nonfiction: Interview/profile, new product, photo feature and technical. Buys 4-12 mss/year. Query. Length: 1,500-4,000 words. Pays $200-500 for assigned articles. Sometimes pays the expenses of writers on assignment.

Photos: State availability of photos with submission. Reviews negatives, 4x5 transparencies and prints. Offers no additional payment for photos accepted with ms. Captions and identification of subjects required. Buys all rights.

Columns/Departments: Trends (developments across industry segments); Technology (innovations of specific technology); Management (costs, strategies of managing information), all 500-1,500 words. Query. Length: 500-1,500 words. Pays $250.

Fillers: Facts and newsbreaks. Length: 150-500 words. Pays $50-250.

Tips: "We would encourage freelancers who have access to our editorial calendar to contact us regarding article ideas, inquiries, etc. We also cover numerous trade shows during the year, and the availability of freelancers to cover these events would be valuable to us. Our feature section is the area where the need for quality freelance coverage of our industry is most desirable. The most likely candidate for acceptance is someone who has a proven background in business writing, and/or someone with demonstrated knowledge of high-tech industries as they relate to information management."

INFORMATION WEEK, CMP Inc., 600 Community Dr., Manhasset NY 11030. (516)365-4600. FAX: (516)562-5474. Editor: Dennis Eskow. Assistant Managing Editor: John McCormick. 20% freelance written. Weekly magazine covering strategic use of information systems and telecom. "Our readers are busy executives who want excellent information or thoughtful opinion on making computers and associated equipment improve the competitiveness of their companies." Circ. 145,000. Pays on publication. Publishes ms an average of 1 month after acceptance. Byline given. Offers 25% kill fee. Buys first North American serial rights and second serial (reprint) rights. Submit seasonal/holiday material 2 months in advance. Previously published submissions rarely OK. Query for electronic submissions. Computer printout submissions OK; prefers letter-

quality to dot-matrix. Reports in 3 weeks on queries; 2 week on mss. Sample copy for 8x11 SAE.
Nonfiction: Book excerpts (information management); exposé (government computing, big vendors); humor (850 word piece reflecting on our information era and its people); and interview/profile (corporate chief information officers). No software reviews, product reviews, no "gee whiz—computers are wonderful" pieces. Buys 20-30 mss/year. Query with or without published clips. Length: 500-3,500 words. Pays $300-1,500. Pays expenses of writers on assignment.
Photos: Send photos with submission. Reviews negatives and transparencies. Pays negotiable rates. Captions, model releases and identification of subjects required. Buys one-time rights.
Columns/Departments: Final Word (a humorous or controversial personal opinion page on high-level computer-oriented business), 850 words; Chiefs (interview, portrait of chief information officer in Fortune 500 Company), 2,000-3,000 words. Buys 100 mss/year. Length: 800-900 words. Pays $100-1,500.
Tips: "We appreciate a *one-paragraph* lead, a headline, a deck and a very brief outline. This evokes the quickest response. Humor is the most difficult thing to create and the one we crave the most. Humor is especially difficult when the subject is management information systems. Good humor is an easy sell with us."

NETWORK WORLD, Network World Publishing, Box 9171, 375 Cochituate Rd., Framingham MA 01701. (508)820-2543. FAX: (508)879-3167. Editor: John Gallant. Features Editor: Steve Moore. 25% freelance written. A weekly tabloid covering data, voice and video communications networks (including news and features on communications management, hardware and software, services, education, technology and industry trends) for senior technical managers at large companies. Circ. 70,000. Pays on acceptance. Byline given. Offers negotiable kill fee. Buys all rights. Submit all material 2 months in advance. Query for electronic submissions. Computer printout submissions acceptable; prefers letter-quality. Reports in 3 weeks. Free sample copy and writer's guidelines.
Nonfiction: Exposé, general interest, how-to (build a strong communications staff, evaluate vendors, choose a value-added network service), humor, interview/profile, opinion and technical. Editorial calendar available. "Our readers are users: avoid vendor-oriented material." Buys 100-150 mss/year. Query with published clips. Length: 500-2,500 words. Pays $600 minimum—negotiable maximum for assigned or unsolicited articles.
Photos: Send photos with submission. Reviews 35mm, 2¼ and 4x5 transparencies and b&w prints (prefers 8x10 but can use 5x7). Captions, model releases and identification of subjects required. Buys one-time rights.
Fiction: Adventure, mainstream, slice-of-life vignettes and suspense. "We want literate, technically correct stories that entertain while illustrating an issue, problem or trend that affects our readership. No obtrusive styles or 'purple prose.'" Buys 4-5 mss/year. Query with published clips. Length: 1,500-2,500 words. Pays $600 minimum—negotiable maximum.
Tips: "We look for accessible treatments of technological, managerial or regulatory trends. It's OK to dig into technical issues as long as the article doesn't read like an engineering document. Feature section is most open to freelancers. Be informative, stimulating, controversial and technically accurate."

RESELLER MANAGEMENT, (formerly *Computer Dealer*), Gordon Publications, Inc., Box 650, Morton Plains NJ 07950-0650. (201)292-5100. Editor: Tom Farre. 50% freelance written. Eager to work with new/unpublished writers if they know the field. Monthly management and technology magazine for computer resellers, including dealers, VARs and systems houses. Circ. 55,000. Pays on publication. Publishes ms an average of 3 months after acceptance. Buys all rights. Query for electronic submissions. Computer printout submissions OK.
Nonfiction: Management and business issues for resellers. "Writers must know microcomputer hardware and software and be familiar with computer *reselling*—our readers are computer-industry professionals in an extremely competitive field." Buys 3-6 mss/issue. Query with published clips. Length: 400-2,000 words. Pays 10-25¢/word. Sometimes pays the expenses of writers on assignment.
Photos: B&w or color.
Columns/Departments: Solicited by editor. "If the writer has an idea, query by mail to the editor, with clips."
Tips: "We've changed our name to *Reseller Management* from *Computer Dealer*—so all articles must have a heavy managerial slant, while still covering the microcomputer industry for resellers."

‡SUNTECHNOLOGY, The Journal for Sun Users, Sun Microsystems, 2550 Garcia Ave, M/S 6-14, Mountain View CA 94043. (415)336-6700. Editor: Mark Hall. Managing Editor: John Barry. 75% freelance written. Quarterly magazine that covers engineering computers. "*SunTechnology* covers the technical and application issues relating to scientific and engineering computers and the UNIX operating system." Buys first rights. Simultaneous submissions, photocopied and previously published submissions OK. Query for electronic submissions. Computer printout submissions OK; prefers letter-quaity. Reports in 2 weeks on queries; 3 weeks on mss. Free sample copy and writer's guidelines.
Nonfiction: How-to (e.g., write a RISC compiler), new product and technical. "Marketing-oriented articles are taboo. Technical audience must be kept in mind." Buys 6-12 mss/year. Query. Length: 2,000-4,000 words. Pays $500-1,000 for assigned articles. Sometimes pays expenses of writers on assignment.

Photos: Send figures, charts and program listings with submission. Offers no additional payment for photos accepted with ms. Captions and identification of subjects required. Buys all rights except advertising.
Columns/Departments: Synergy ("success" story of technical application), 750-1,500 words; and user profile (profile of scientist or engineer using Sun computers), 750-1,500 words. Buys 8 mss/year. Query. Pays $250 maximum.
Fillers: Gags. Buys 4/year. Pays $250.
Tips: "Writers should be technically sophisticated. *SunTechnology* readers are some of the most technically astute people in the world, which is why their companies/universities give them the powerful computers from Sun to work with. User profiles are the best entry into *SunTechnology*. Some of the most interesting scientists and engineers in the world use Sun equipment, (e.g., those monitoring Voyager II; those who found the *Titanic*, etc.). This work makes for exciting reading when handled by a fine writer."

‡**SYSTEM BUILDER, The Manager's Guide for Applications Development,** ICP, Inc., Suite 200, 9100 Keystone Crossing, Indianapolis IN 46240. (317)844-7461. Executive Editor: Sheila Cunningham. Managing Editor: Brenda Pace. 20% freelance written. Bimonthly magazine on software for application development. "Our readers are MIS, project and application development managers at IBM mainframe sites. The articles provide strategies to deal with the problems of selecting and implementing technology." Estab. 1988. Circ. 30,000. Pays on publication. Buys all rights. Simultaneous submissions OK. Query for electronic submissions. Computer printout submissions OK. Reports in 1 month. Free sample copy and writer's guidelines.
Nonfiction: Book excerpts and technical. "No product-oriented articles or news stories." Query with or without published clips, or send complete ms. Length: 1,000-3,500 words. Pays $500-600 for assigned articles; $100-400 for unsolicited articles. Pays writer with contributor copies or other premiums with prior agreement between author and editor. Sometimes pays expenses of writers on assignment.
Photos: Send photos with submission. Reviews prints. Offers no additional payment for photos accepted with ms. Buys first North American serial rights.
Columns/Departments: Design (software design issues); Programming (programming issues); Maintenance (software maintenance issues); and DBMS (DBMS issues). Buys 4 mss/year. Query. Length: 1,000-2,000 words. Pays $100-300.

SYSTEMS INTEGRATION, (formerly *Mini-Micro Systems*), Cahners Publishing Co., 275 Washington St., Newton MA 02158. (617)964-3030. FAX: (617)558-4700. Editor-in-Chief: George Kotelly. 40% freelance written. Monthly magazine covering systems integration and technology for manufacturers and users of computers, peripherals and software. Circ. 110,000. Pays on publication. Byline given. Publishes ms an average of 3 months after acceptance. Buys all rights. Simultaneous queries and photocopied submissions OK. Computer printout submissions acceptable; prefers letter-quality. Reports in 1 month on queries. Free sample copy; writer's guidelines for #10 SASE.
Nonfiction: Articles about new computer technologies and trends, interpretive news. Buys 25-50 mss/year. Query with published clips. Length: 500-2,500 words. Pays $70-100/printed page, including illustrations. Sometimes pays expenses of writers on assignment.
Photos: Send line art, diagrams, photos or color transparencies.
Tips: "Call with a definite idea or focus to your study. Focus on new technology, but also the impact that technology has on systems builders. Will also consider profiles of major systems integration projects."

‡**SYSTEMS/3X WORLD,** Hunter Publishing, 950 Lee St., Des Plaines IL 60016. (312)296-0770. FAX: (312)803-3328. Editor: Anne Hedin. 10% freelance written. Works with a small number of new/unpublished writers each year. Monthly magazine covering applications of IBM minicomputers (S/34/36/38/ and AS/400) in business. Circ. 46,000. Pays on acceptance. Publishes ms an average of 2 months after acceptance. Byline given. Buys all rights. Submit seasonal/holiday material 4 months in advance. Query for electronic submissions. Computer printout submissions acceptable; prefers letter-quality. Reports in 2 weeks on queries. Sample copy for 9x12 SAE and 4 first class stamps; writer's guidelines for #10 SAE.
Nonfiction: How-to (use the computer in business); and technical (organization of a data base or file system). "A writer who submits material to us should be an expert in computer applications. No material on large scale computer equipment." No poetry. Buys 8 mss/year. Query. Length: 3,000-4,000 words. Sometimes pays expenses of writers on assignment.
Tips: "We only buy long features, mostly ones that we commission. Frequent mistakes are not understanding the audience and not having read the magazine (past issues)."

Insurance

COMPASS, Marine Office of America Corporation (MOAC), 180 Maiden Lane, New York NY 10038. (212)440-7735. Editor: Abbe Bates. 100% freelance written. Prefers to work with published/established writers. Semiannual magazine of the Marine Office of America Corporation. Magazine is distributed in the U.S. and overseas to persons in marine insurance (agents, brokers, risk managers), government authorities and employees. Circ. 8,000. Pays half on acceptance, half on publication. Publishes ms an average of 6 months after acceptance. Byline given. Offers $750 kill fee on manuscripts accepted for publication, but subsequently cancelled. Offers $250 kill fee on solicited ms rejected for publication. Not copyrighted. Buys first North American serial rights. Does not accept previously published work, unsolicited mss or works of fiction. Query first. Simultaneous queries OK. Query for electronic submissions. Computer printout submissions acceptable; no dot-matrix. Reports in 1 month on queries. Free sample copy and writer's guidelines.

Nonfiction: General interest, historical/nostalgic and technical. U.S. or overseas locale. "Historical/nostalgia should relate to ships, trains, airplanes, balloons, bridges, sea and land expeditions, marine archeology, seaports and transportation of all types. General interest includes marine and transportation subjects; fishing industry; farming; outdoor occupations; environmental topics such as dams, irrigation projects, water conservations inland waterways; space travel and satellites. Articles must have human interest. Technical articles may cover energy exploration and development—offshore oil and gas drilling, developing new sources of electric power and solar energy; usages of coal, water and wind to generate electric power; special cargo handling such as containerization on land and sea; salvage; shipbuilding; bridge or tunnel construction. Articles must not be overly technical and should have strong reader interest." No book excerpts, first-person, exposes, how-to, or opinion. Buys 8 mss/year. Query with published clips. Length: 1,500-2,000 words. Pays $1,500 maximum. Sometimes pays the expenses of writers on assignment.

Photos: Robert A. Cooney, photo editor. (212)995-8001. State availability of photos. Reviews b&w and color transparencies and prints. Captions and identification of subjects required. Buys one-time rights.

Tips: "We want profiles of individuals connected with marine, energy, and transportation fields who are unusual. Send a brief outline of the story idea to editor mentioning also the availability of photographs in b&w and color. All articles must be thoroughly researched and original. Articles should have human interest through the device of interviews. We only publish full-length articles—no fillers."

‡**FLORIDA UNDERWRITER**, National Underwriter Company, Suite 115, 1345 S. Missouri Ave., Clearwater FL 34616. (813)442-9189. FAX: (813)443-2479. Editor: James E. Seymour. Mangaing Editor: J. Kenneth Duff. 20-40% freelance written. Monthly magazine about insurance. "*Florida Underwriter* covers insurance for Florida insurance professionals: producers, executives, risk managers, employee benefit administrators. We want material about any insurance line, Life & Health or Property & Casualty, but *must* have a Florida tag—Florida authors preferred." Circ. 10,000. Pays on publication. Publishes ms an average of 2-3 months after acceptance. Byline given. Buys all rights. Submit seasonal/holiday material 3 months in advance. Simultaneous, photocopied and previously published submissions OK (notification of other submission, publications required). Query for electronic submissions. Computer printout submissions OK; prefers letter-quality. Reports in 2-3 weeks. Free sample copy and writer's guidelines.

Nonfiction: Essay, exposé, historical/nostalgic, how-to, interview/profile, new product, opinion and technical. "We don't want articles that aren't about insurance for insurance people or those that lack Florida angle. No puff pieces." Buys 6 mss/year. Query with or without published clips, or send complete ms. Length: 500-1,500 words. Pays $50-150 for assigned articles; $25-100 for unsolicited articles. "Industry experts contribute in return for exposure." Sometimes pays expenses of writers on assignment.

Photos: State availability of photos with submission. Send photos with submission. Reviews 5x7 prints. Offers no additional payment for photos accepted with ms. Identification of subjects required.

INSURANCE REVIEW, Insurance Information Institute, 110 William St., New York NY 10038. (212)669-9200. Editor: Olga Badillo-Sciortino. Managing Editor: Kenneth M. Coughlin. 100% freelance written. A monthly magazine covering property and casualty insurance for agents, brokers, insurers, risk managers, educators, lawyers, financial analysts and journalists. Circ. 70,000. Pays on acceptance. Publishes ms an average of 2 months after acceptance. Byline given. Offers 25% kill fee. Buys first North American serial rights; rights returned to author 90 days after publication. "We retain right to reprint." Query for electronic submissions. Reports in 1 month. Free sample copy and writer's guidelines.

Nonfiction: How-to (improve agency business), interview/profile, opinion, industry issues, technical and business articles with insurance information. Buys 75 mss/year. Query with published clips. Length: 750-2,500 words. Pays $350-1,200 for assigned articles. Pays expenses of writers on assignment.

Photos: Send photos with submission. Reviews contact sheets and transparencies. Captions, model releases and identification of subjects required.

Columns/Departments: By Line (analysis of one line of business p/c), Analysis (financial aspects of p/c industry); Technology (innovative uses for agents or insurers); Agency Profitability; Agency Business. Query. Length: 750-1,200 words. Pays $300-500.

Tips: "Become well-versed in issues facing the insurance industry. Identify provocative topics worthy of in-depth treatment. Profile successful agents or brokers."

INSURANCE SOFTWARE REVIEW, International Computer Programs, Inc., Suite 200, 9100 Keystone Crossing, Indianapolis IN 46240. (317)844-7461. FAX: (317)574-0571. Editor: Marilyn Gasaway. 50% freelance written. Bimonthly magazine covering the computer software industry as it relates to insurance companies and large agencies. "Editorial slant includes the selection, implementation and use of software in insurance companies, agencies and brokerages. Audience comprises data processing and end-user management in medium to large insurance concerns." Circ. 20,000. Pays on publication. Publishes ms an average of 2 months after acceptance. Byline sometimes given. Buys first and second serial (reprint) rights. Photocopied submissions OK. Query for electronic submissions. Computer printout submissions OK; prefers letter-quality. Reports in 3 weeks on queries; 1 month on mss. Free sample copy and writer's guidelines.
Nonfiction: How to (successfully install and use software products), interview/profile, new product and technical. No non-software related, non-business software or humorous articles. Buys 8-10 mss/year. Query with published clips. Length: 1,000-2,500 words. Pays $350-600 for assigned articles. Sometimes pays the expenses of writers on assignment.
Photos: Send photos with submission. Prefers 5x7 prints. Offers no additional payment for photos accepted with ms. Identification of subjects required. Buys all rights.
Columns/Departments: Systems Review (in-depth profile of a specific software product at use in an insurance environment; must include comments from 2-3 insurance users [e.g., the benefits of the product, its use within the insurance firm, etc.]). Length: 500-700 words. Pays $50.

‡**THE LEADER,** Fireman's Fund Insurance Co., 777 San Marin Dr., Novato CA 94998. (415)899-2109. FAX: (415)899-2126. Editor: Jim Toland. 50% freelance written. Monthly magazine on insurance. "*The Leader* contains articles and information for Fireman's Fund employees and retirees about the many offices and employees nationwide—emphasizing the business of insurance and the unique people who work for the company." Pays on acceptance. Publishes ms an average of 1 month after acceptance. Byline given. Buys one-time rights. Simultaneous and photocopied submissions OK. Reports in 2 weeks on mss. Free sample copy.
Nonfiction: Interview/profile, new products and employees involved in positive activities in the insurance industry and in the communities where company offices are located. Query with published clips. Length: 200-2,500 words. Pays $50-300.
Photos: Reviews contact sheets and prints. Sometimes buys color slides. Offer $25-100 per photo for b&w, more for color. Buys one-time rights.
Tips: "It helps to work in the insurance business and/or know people at Fireman's Fund. Writers with business reporting experience are usually most successful—though we've published many first time writers. Research the local Fireman's Fund branch office (not sales agents who are independents). Look for newsworthy topics. Strong journalism and reporting skills are greatly appreciated."

‡**PROFESSIONAL AGENT MAGAZINE,** Professional Insurance Agents, 400 N. Washington St., Alexandria VA 22314. (703)836-9340. Editor: John S. Demott. 75% freelance written. Prefers to work with published/established writers, especially those with knowledge of the workings of insurance. Monthly magazine covering insurance/small business for independent insurance agents. Circ. 40,000. Pays on acceptance. Publishes ms an average of 2 months after acceptance. Byline given. Buys exclusive rights in the industry. Query for electronic submissions. Computer printout submissions acceptable; prefers letter-quality to dot-matrix. Reports ASAP. Sample copy for SAE.
Nonfiction: Insurance management for small businesses and self-help. Special issues on life insurance and computer interface. Buys 36 mss/year. Query with published clips or send complete ms. Length: 1,000-3,000 words. Pays $100-800. Sometimes pays the expenses of writers on assignment.
Photos: State availability of photos. Pays $35-200 for 5x7 b&w prints; $50-300 for 35mm color transparencies. Captions, model release, and identification of subjects required. Buys one-time rights.

_____ *International Affairs*

These publications cover global relations, international trade, economic analysis and philosophy for business executives and government officials involved in foreign affairs. Publications for the general public on related subjects appear in Consumer Politics and World Affairs.

DEFENSE & FOREIGN AFFAIRS, International Media Corporation, Suite 307, 110 North Royal Street, Alexandria VA 22314. (703)684-8455. FAX: (703)684-2207. Editor-In-Chief: Gregory R. Copley. A monthly magazine on defense, strategy and international affairs. Circ. 9,000. Pays within 1 month after publication.

Publishes ms an average of 1 month after acceptance. Byline given. Buys all rights. Photocopied submissions OK. Electronic submissions preferred. Computer printout submissions OK; prefers letter-quality. Reports in 1 week.

Nonfiction: Interview/profile, new product, photo feature, technical. Buys 40 mss/year. Query with or without published clips. Length: 1,500-3,000 words. Pays $150-300. Sometimes pays expense of writers on assignment.

Photos: State availability of photos with submission. Reviews negatives, transparencies and prints. Offers no additional payment for photo accepted with ms. Identification of subjects required. Buys one-time rights.

Columns/Departments: Current estimates: country surveys (political forecasts/assessments, etc.). Length: 1,500 words. Pays $150.

FOREIGN AFFAIRS, 58 E. 68th St., New York NY 10021. (212)734-0400. Editor: William G. Hyland. Primarily freelance written. For academics, businessmen (national and international), government, educational and cultural readers especially interested in international affairs of a political nature. Published 5 times/year. Circ. 100,000. Pays on publication. Byline given. Photocopied submissions OK. Query for electronic submissions. Computer printout submissions acceptable; prefers letter-quality. Reports in 2 months.

Nonfiction: "Articles dealing with international affairs; political, educational, cultural, economic, scientific, philosophical and social sciences. Develop an original idea in depth, with a strong thesis usually leading to policy recommendations. Serious analyses by qualified authors on subjects with international appeal." Buys 25 unsolicited mss/year. Submit complete ms, double-spaced. Length: 5,000 words. Pays approximately $750.

Tips: "We like the writer to include his/her qualifications for writing on the topic in question (educational, past publications, relevant positions or honors), and a clear summation of the article: the argument (or area examined), and the writer's policy conclusions."

Jewelry

CANADIAN JEWELLER, 777 Bay St., Toronto, Ontario M5W 1A7 Canada. Editor: Simon Hally. Monthly magazine for members of the jewelry trade, primarily retailers. Circ. 7,500. Pays on acceptance. Buys first North American serial rights.

Nonfiction: Wants "stories on the jewelry industry internationally." Query. Length: 200-2,000 words. Pays $50-750 (Canadian).

Photos: Reviews 5x7 and 8x10 b&w prints and 35mm and 2¼x2¼ color transparencies. "We pay more if usable photos accompany ms. Payment is based on space used in the book including both text and photos."

THE ENGRAVERS JOURNAL, Box 318, 26 Summit St., Brighton MI 48116. (313)229-5725. FAX: (313)229-8320. Co-Publisher and Managing Editor: Michael J. Davis. 15% freelance written. "We are eager to work with published/established writers as well as new/unpublished writers." A bimonthly magazine covering the recognition and identification industry (engraving, marking devices, awards, jewelry, and signage.) "We provide practical information for the education and advancement of our readers, mainly retail business owners." Pays on acceptance. Publishes ms an average of 1 year after acceptance. Byline given "only if writer is recognized authority." Buys all rights (usually). Query with published clips and resume. Photocopied and previously published submissions OK. Query for electronic submissions. Computer printout submissions acceptable; prefers letter-quality. Reports in 2 weeks. Free writer's guidelines; sample copy to "those who send writing samples with inquiry."

Nonfiction: General interest (industry-related); how-to (small business subjects, increase sales, develop new markets, use new sales techniques, etc.); interview/profile; new product; photo feature (a particularly outstanding signage system); and technical. No general overviews of the industry. Buys 12 mss/year. Query with writing samples "published or not," or "send samples and resume to be considered for assignments on speculation." Length: 1,000-5,000 words. Pays $75-250, depending on writer's skill and expertise in handling subject.

Photos: Send photos with query. Reviews 8x10 prints. Pays variable rate. Captions, model release and identifiction of subjects required.

Tips: "Articles should always be down to earth, practical and thoroughly cover the subject with authority. We do not want the 'textbook' writing approach, vagueness, or theory—our readers look to us for sound practical information."

FASHION ACCESSORIES, S.C.M. Publications, Inc., 65 W. Main St., Bergenfield NJ 07621-1696. (201)384-3336. FAX: (201)384-6776. Managing Editor: Samuel Mendelson. Monthly newspaper covering costume or fashion jewelry. "Serves the manufacturers, manufacturers' sales reps., importers and exporters who sell exclusively through the wholesale level in ladies' fashion jewlery, mens' jewelry, gifts and boutiques and related novelties." Circ. 8,000. Pays on acceptance. Byline given. Not copyrighted. Buys first rights. Submit seasonal/holiday material 3 months in advance. Photocopied submissions OK. Computer printout submissions OK; no dot-matrix. Sample copy $2 and 9x12 SAE.

Nonfiction: Essays, general interest, historical/nostalgic, how-to, humor, interview/profile, new product and travel. Buys 20 mss/year. Query with published clips. Length: 1,000-2,000 words. Pays $100-300. Sometimes pays the expenses of writers on assignment.

Photos: Send photos with submission. Reviews 4x5 prints. Offers no additional payment for photos accepted with ms. Identification of subjects required. Buys one-time rights.

Columns/Departments: Fashion Report (interviews and reports of fashion news), 1,000-2,000 words.

Tips: "We are interested in anything that will be of interest to costume jewelry buyers at the wholesale level."

Journalism and Writing

Journalism and writing magazines cover both the business and creative sides of writing. Writing publications offer inspiration and support for professional and beginning writers. Although there are many valuable writing publications that do not pay, we only have space to list those writing publications that pay for articles.

BOOK DEALERS WORLD, American Bookdealers Exchange, Box 2525, La Mesa CA 92041. (619)462-3297. Editorial Director: Al Galasso. Senior Editor: Judy Wiggins. 50% freelance written. Quarterly magazine covering writing, self-publishing and marketing books by mail. Circ. 20,000. Pays on publication. Publishes ms an average of 3 months after acceptance. Byline given. Buys first serial rights and second serial (reprint) rights to material originally published elsewhere. Simultaneous and previously published submissions OK. Computer printout submissions acceptable; no dot-matrix. Reports in 1 month. Sample copy for $2.

Nonfiction: Book excerpts (writing, mail order, direct mail, publishing); how-to (home business by mail, advertising); and interview/profile (of successful self-publishers). Positive articles on self-publishing, new writing angles, marketing, etc. Buys 10 mss/year. Send complete ms. Length: 1,000-1,500 words. Pays $25-50.

Columns/Departments: Print Perspective (about new magazines and newsletters); Small Press Scene (news about small press activities); and Self-Publisher Profile (on successful self-publishers and their marketing strategy). Buys 20 mss/year. Send complete ms. Length: 250-1,000 words. Pays $5-20.

Fillers: Fillers concerning writing, publishing or books. Buys 6/year. Length: 100-250 words. Pays $3-10.

Tips: "Query first. Get a sample copy of the magazine."

BRILLIANT IDEAS FOR PUBLISHERS, Creative Brilliance Associates, 4709 Sherwood Rd., Box 4237, Madison WI 53711. (608)271-6867. Editor: Naomi K. Shapiro. 3% freelance written. A bimonthly magazine covering the newspaper and shopper industry. "We provide business news and ideas to publishers of the daily, weekly, community, surburban newspaper and shopper publishing industry." Circ. 17,000. Pays on publication. Publishes ms an average of 4 months after acceptance. Byline given. Buys all rights. Photocopied submissions OK. Query for electronic submissions. Computer printout submissions OK; no dot-matrix. Reports in 3 weeks. Sample copy for 9x12 SAE with 4 first class stamps.

Nonfiction: *Only submit articles related to the newspaper industry*, i.e., sales, marketing or management. General interest, historical/nostalgic, how-to (tips and hints regarding editorial, production, etc.), humor, interview/profile, new product and opinion. "The writer has to know and understand the industry." Buys 3 mss/year. Query. Length: 200 words maximum. Pays $10-50 for unsolicited articles. May pay writers with contributor copies or other premiums if writer requests.

Photos: State availability of photos with submission. Offers no additional payment for photos accepted with ms. Captions, model releases and identification of subjects required. Buys all rights.

Columns/Departments: "Any books or brochures related to sales, marketing, management, etc. can be submitted for consideration for our BIFP Press department." Buys 3 mss/year. Query. Length: 200 words maximum. Pays $10-50.

For explanation of symbols, see the Key to Symbols and Abbreviations on Page 5. For unfamiliar words, see the Glossary.

Tips: "We are interested in working with any writer or researcher who has good, solid, documented pieces of interest to this specific industry."

BYLINE, Box 130596, Edmond OK 73013. (405)348-3325. Executive Editor/Publisher: Marcia Preston. Managing Editor: Kathryn Fanning. 80-90% freelance written. Eager to work with new/unpublished writers. Monthly magazine for writers and poets. "We stress encouragement of beginning writers." Publishes ms an average of 6 months after acceptance. Byline given. Buys first North American serial rights. Computer printout submissions OK; prefers letter-quality. Reports within 1 month. Sample copy and guidelines for $3.
Nonfiction: How-to, humor, inspirational, personal experience, *all* connected with writing and selling. Read magazine for special departments. Buys approximately 72 mss/year. Prefers queries; will read complete mss. Length: 1,500-2,000 words. Usual rate for features is $50, on acceptance. Needs short humor on writing (400-800 words). Pays $35.
Fiction: General fiction. Writing or literary slant preferred, but not required. Send complete ms: 2,000-3,000 words preferred. Pays $50 on acceptance.
Poetry: Any style, on a writing theme. Preferred length: 4-30 lines. Pays $5 on publication plus free issue.

CANADIAN AUTHOR & BOOKMAN, Canadian Authors Association, Suite 104, 121 Avenue Rd., Toronto, Ontario M5R 2G3 Canada. Contact: Editor. 95% freelance written. Prefers to work with published/established writers. "For writers—all ages, all levels of experience." Quarterly magazine. Circ. 3,000. Pays on publication. Publishes ms an average of 6 months after acceptance. Buys first Canadian rights. Byline given. Written queries only. Computer printout submissions acceptable; prefers letter-quality. Sample copy for $4.50; writer's guidelines for #10 SASE.
Nonfiction: How-to (on writing, selling; the specifics of the different genres—what they are and how to write them); informational (the writing scene—who's who and what's what); interview (on writers, mainly leading ones, but also those with a story that can help others write and sell more often); and opinion. No personal, lightweight writing experiences; no fillers. Query with immediate pinpointing of topic, length (if ms is ready), and writer's background. Length: 1,000-2,500 words. Pays $30/printed page.
Photos: "We're after an interesting-looking magazine, and graphics are a decided help." State availability of photos with query. Offers $5/photo for b&w photos accepted with ms. Buys one-time rights.
Poetry: High quality. "Major poets publish with us—others need to be as good." Buys 60 poems/year. Pays $15.
Tips: "We dislike material that condescends to its reader and articles that advocate an adversarial approach to writer/editor relationships. We agree that there is a time and place for such an approach, but good sense should prevail. If the writer is writing to a Canadian freelance writer, the work will likely fall within our range of interest."

CANADIAN WRITER'S JOURNAL, Gordon M. Smart Publications, Box 6618, Depot 1, Victoria BC V8P 5N7 Canada. (604)477-8807. Editor: Gordon M. Smart. Quarterly digest-size magazine for writers. Circulation 350. 50% freelance written. Will accept well-written articles by inexperienced writers. Pays on publication, an average of 2-4 months after acceptance. Byline given. Computer printout submissions OK. Sample copy for $3 plus $1 postage; writer's guidelines for #10 SAE with $1 postage.
Nonfiction: How-to articles for writers. Buys 30-35 mss/year. Query. Length: 500-1,000 words. Pays up to $15.
Tips: "We prefer short, how-to articles; 1,000 words is our limit and we prefer 700 words. U.S. writers should be advised that U.S. postage cannot be used from Canada and is therefore wasted. Two or more quarters taped to a cardboard piece can be used to buy postage here."

CHRISTIAN WRITERS NEWSLETTER, Box 8220, Knoxville TN 37996-4800. Editor/Publisher: David E. Sumner. Markets Editor: Sandy Brooks. 60% freelance written. A bimonthly newsletter for Christian writers. "The purpose of the newsletter is to provide inspiration, information and education for Christian writers. Articles should teach, educate, help, inspire or motivate the reader in some way." Circ. 400. Pays on acceptance. Computer printout submissions acceptable. Reports in 2 weeks on queries; 1 month on mss. Sample copy for $2; writer's guidelines for #10 SASE.
Nonfiction: Short inspirational and how-to. Length: 500 words maximum. Pays up to $25. Also accepts anecdotes and humor. Pays $5-10. No poetry or fiction.
Tips: "Focus on providing some practical help or inspiration for the *reader*. We don't accept writers' personal experience articles unless they're able to do this."

COLUMBIA JOURNALISM REVIEW, 700 Journalism Bldg., Columbia University, New York NY 10027. (212)280-5595. Managing Editor: Gloria Cooper. "We welcome queries concerning media issues and performance. *CJR* also publishes book reviews. We emphasize in-depth reporting, critical analysis and good writing. All queries are read by editors."

THE COMICS JOURNAL, THE Magazine of News and Criticism, Fantagraphics, Inc., 7563 Lake City Way, Seattle WA 98115. (206)524-1967. Managing Editor: Greg Baisden. 90% freelance written. A monthly magazine covering the comic book industry. "Comic books can appeal intellectually and emotionally to an adult audience, and can express ideas that other media are inherently incapable of." Circ. 11,500. Pays on publication. Publishes ms an average of 2 months after acceptance. Byline given. Buys first rights. Submit seasonal/holiday material 5 months in advance. Photocopied submissions OK. Computer printout submissions acceptable; prefers letter-quality. Reports in 2 weeks. Sample copy $3.50.

Nonfiction: Essays, exposé, historical, interview/profile, opinion and magazine reviews. Buys 120 mss/year. Send complete ms. Length: 500-3,000 words. Pays 1.5¢/word; writers may request trade for merchandise. Pays the expenses of writers on assignment.

Photos: Send photos with submission. Offers additional payment for photos accepted with ms. Identification of subjects required. Buys one-time rights.

Columns/Departments: Opening Shots (brief commentary, often humorous), 1,000 words; Executive Forum; (written by publishers offering, opinions on various subjects), 3,000 words; The Comics Library (graphic review), and Ethics (examining the ethics of the comic-book industry), both 3,000 words. Buys 60 mss/year. Send complete ms. Pays 1.5¢/word.

Tips: "Have an intelligent, sophisticated, critical approach to writing about comic books."

EDITOR & PUBLISHER, 11 W. 19th St., New York NY 10011. Editor: Robert U. Brown. 10% freelance written. Weekly magazine. For newspaper publishers, editors, executives, employees and others in communications, marketing, advertising, etc. Circ. 29,000. Pays on publication. Publishes ms an average of 2 weeks after acceptance. Buys first serial rights. Computer printout submissions acceptable; prefers letter-quality. Sample copy $1.

Nonfiction: John P. Consoli, managing editor. Uses newspaper business articles and news items; also newspaper personality features and printing technology. Query.

Fillers: "Amusing typographical errors found in newspapers." Pays $5.

THE EDITORIAL EYE, Focusing on Publications Standards and Practices, Editorial Experts, Inc., Suite 400, 85 S. Bragg St., Alexandria VA 22312. (703)642-3040. FAX: (703)642-3046. Editor: Ann R. Molpus. 5% freelance written. Prefers to work with published/established writers. Monthly professional newsletter on editorial subjects: writing, editing, proofreading and levels of editing. "Our readers are professional publications people. Use journalistic style." Circ. 3,000. Pays on acceptance. Publishes ms an average of 3 months after acceptance. Byline given. Kill fee determined for each assignment. Buys first North American serial rights. "We retain the right to use articles in our training division and in an anthology of collected articles." Submit seasonal/holiday material 3 months in advance. Computer printout submissions acceptable; prefers letter-quality. Reports in 1 month. Sample copy for 6x9 SAE and 2 first-class stamps; writer's guidelines for #10 SASE.

Nonfiction: Editorial and production problems, issues, standards, practices and techniques; publication management; publishing technology; style, grammar and usage. No word games, vocabulary building, language puzzles, or jeremiads on how the English language is going to blazes. Buys 12 mss/year. Query. Length: 300-1,200. Pays $25-100.

Tips: "We seek mostly lead articles written by people in the publications field about the practice of publications work. Our style is journalistic with a light touch (not cute). We are interested in submissions on the craft of editing, levels of edit, editing by computer, publications management, indexing, lexicography, usages, proofreading. Our back issue list provides a good idea of the kinds of articles we run."

EDITORS' FORUM, Editors' Forum Publishing Company, Box 411806, Kansas City MO 64141. (913)236-9235. Managing Editor: William R. Brinton. 50% freelance written. Prefers to work with published/established and works with a small number of new/unpublished writers each year. A monthly newsletter geared toward communicators, particularly those involved in the editing and publication of newsletters and company publications. Circ. 900. Pays on publication. Publishes ms an average of 4 months after acceptance. Byline given. Offers 25% kill fee. Buys first North American serial rights, second serial (reprint) rights and makes work-for-hire assignments. Photocopied submissions OK. Previously published submissions OK depending on content. Computer printout submissions acceptable; no dot-matrix. Reports in 2 weeks on queries. Sample copy for 9x12 SAE and 45¢ postage. Writer's guidelines for #10 SASE.

Nonfiction: How-to on editing and writing, etc. "With the advent of computer publishing, *EF* is running a regular high tech column on desk top publishing, software, etc. We can use articles on the latest techniques in computer publishing. Not interested in anything that does not have a direct effect on writing and editing newsletters. This is a how-to newsletter." Buys 22 mss/year. Query. Length: 250-1,000 words. Pays $20/page maximum.

Photos: State availability of photos with submission. Reviews contact sheets. Offers $5/photo. Captions, model releases and identification of subjects required. Buys one-time rights.
Tips: "We are necessarily interested in articles pertaining to the newsletter business. That would include articles involving writing skills, layout and makeup, the use of pictures and other graphics to brighten up our reader's publication, and an occasional article on how to put out a good publication inexpensively."

THE FINAL DRAFT, Writer's Refinery, Box 47786, Phoenix AZ 85068-7786. (602)944-5268. Editorial Director: Elizabeth "Libbi" Goodman. Submissions Editor: Marguerite Zody. Senior Editor: Robert Cree. A monthly newsletter on writing published by a volunteer group. "The premise of our publication is to teach and impart useful information to published and aspiring writers. We also provide an opportunity for new writers to get published." Circ. 800. Pays on publication. Publishes mss an average of 2-10 months after acceptance. Byline given. Buys first North American serial rights, second serial (reprint) rights or makes work-for-hire assignments. Submit seasonal/holiday material 6 months in advance. Photocopied and previously published submissions OK. Computer printout submissions OK; prefers letter-quality. Reports in 6 weeks. Sample copy for $1.50; writer's guidelines for #10 SASE.
Nonfiction: Book excerpts, essays, exposé, general interest, historical/nostalgic, how-to, humor, motivational, interview/profile (especially with writers of juvenile fiction), new product, opinion, personal experience, technical and travel. "No interviews with people not associated with the craft of writing. No book reviews of fiction. Will accept reviews on books dealing with the craft/writing." Buys 100 mss/year. Send complete ms. Length: 500-3,000 words. Pays $5-20 for unsolicited articles. Pays in contributor's copies if article is of interest "but needs major rewriting author cannot do." Sometimes pays the expenses of writers on assignment.
Fiction: Adventure, experimental, fantasy, historical, horror, humorous, mystery, romance, science fiction, slice-of-life vignettes, suspense and western. "We are open to most fiction that uses writing or writers as the theme. We do not want to see any fiction not slanted toward writers." Buys 12 mss/year. Send complete ms. Length: 500-1,500 words. Pays $4-15.
Poetry: "Must be of interest to writers. Open to all forms. No religious themes." Buys 12 poems/year. Submit maximum 5 poems. Length: 4-25 lines. Pays $2-5.
Fillers: Anecdotes, facts, gags and short humor. Length: up to 375 words. Pays $2-5.
Tips: "We are anxious to help new writers get started, but that does not mean we accept articles/fiction that are poorly written. Mss should be finely tuned *before* we see them. We are increasing the size of our publication, and are actively looking to purchase a wide variety of articles. The most frequent reason for rejection by our staff is material submitted is not suitable for our publication or the writer has not focused the article. No response to any correspondence if SASE is not included with query or submission. Actively looking for well-written 'writing technique' articles."

FREELANCE WRITER'S REPORT, Cassell Communications Inc., Box 9844, Fort Lauderdale FL 33310. (305)485-0795. Editor: Dana K. Cassell. 15% freelance written. Prefers to work with published/established writers. Monthly newsletter covering writing and marketing advice for established freelance writers. Pays on publication. Publishes ms an average of 6 months after acceptance. Byline given. Buys one-time rights. Submit seasonal/holiday material 2 months in advance. Simultaneous queries, and simultaneous, photocopied and previously published submissions OK. Computer printout submissions OK; no dot-matrix. Reports in 1 month. Sample copy $4. No writer's guidelines; refer to this listing.
Nonfiction: Book excerpts (on writing profession); how-to (market, write, research); interview (of writers or editors); new product (only those pertaining to writers); photojournalism; promotion and administration of a writing business. No humor, fiction or poetry. Buys 36 mss/year. Query or send complete ms. Length: 500 words maximum. Also buys longer material (2,000-2,500 words) for Special Reports; must be timeless and of interest to many writers. Pays 10¢/edited word.
Tips: "Write in terse newsletter style, eliminate flowery adjectives and edit mercilessly. Send something that will help writers increase profits from writing output—must be a proven method. We're targeting to the more established writer, less to the beginner."

‡GUIDELINES NEWSLETTER, Box 608, Pittsburg MO 65724. Editor: Susan Nelene Salaki. 97% freelance written. Quarterly at present "but plan to go bi-monthly soon." *GN* is a magazine where writers and editors communicate. "We are interested in what writers on both sides of the desk have to say about the craft of writing." Estab. 1988. Circ. 700. Pays on publication. Byline given. Rights revert to contributors after publication. Reports in 1 month. Sample copy $4; SASE for writer's guidelines and themes for upcoming issues.
Nonfiction: General interest, historical articles on writers/writing, psychological aspects of being a writer, how-to, interview/profile, personal experience, humor and fillers. "Write to me and present your ideas." Buys 12 mss/year. OK to send in complete mss. Include SASE with all correspondence. Length: 50-1,500 words. Pays $10 maximum.
Photos: State availability of photos with submission. Reviews b/w glossies. Buys one-time rights on exceptional prints for cover on occasion. Prefer nature scene photos for cover. Pays $2-25 per photo. Captions, model releases and identification of subjects required.

Columns/Departments: Survey questions (questions writers want answers to), 200 words. Buys 6-24 mss/year. Send complete ms. Pays $5 maximum.

Fiction: Only short-short fiction with writing/editing as theme. Can be any genre, but must be good. Buys 3-6 mss/year. Send complete mss. Length: 300 words or less. Pays $5.

Poetry: Short poetry, any form, having to do with writing or editing. Submit minimum of 3 poems. Pays $1 maximum. Length: up to 20 lines "unless it is exceptional."

Fillers: Facts about writing or writers, short humor and cartoons,"wide-open to any facts of interest to writers or editors." Pays $1 maximum.

Tips: "If you believe what you have to say about writing or editing has needed to be said for some time now, then I'm interested. If you say it well, I'll buy it. This is a unique publication in that we offer original guidelines for over 200 magazine and book publishers and because of this service, writers and editors are linked in a new and exciting way—as correspondents. Articles that help to bridge the gap which has existed between these two professions have the best chance of being accepted. Publishing background does not matter. Writers should query for theme list. Include a short biography and cover letter with your submissions. Published writers who want to have their credits published with byline must include tearsheets. All contributors receive a copy of the issue in which their work appears."

HOUSEWIFE-WRITER'S FORUM, Drawer 1518, Lafayette CA 94549. (415)932-1143. Editor: Deborah Haeseler. 90% freelance written. Bimonthly newsletter and literary magazine for women writers. "We are a support network and writer's group on paper directed to the unique needs of women who write and juggle home life." Estab. 1988. Circ. 600. Pays on acceptance. Publishes ms an average of 6-12 months after acceptance. Byline given. Buys one-time rights. Submit seasonal/holiday material 6 months in advance. Simultaneous, photocopied and previously published submissions OK. Computer printout submissions OK. Reports in 2 weeks on queries; 1 month on mss. Sample copy $3; writer's guidelines for #10 SASE.

Nonfiction: Book excerpts, essays, historical/nostalgic, how-to, humor, interview/profile, opinion, personal experience. Buys 60-100 mss/year. Query with or without published clips, or send complete ms. Length: 2,000 words maximum, 400-750 words preferred. Pays $1-10.

Columns/Departments: Confessions of Housewife-Writers (essays pertaining to our lives as women, writers, our childhoods, etc.), 25-800 words; Reviews (books, reference texts, products for housewife writers), 50-300 words. Buys 6-20 mss/year. Send complete ms. Length: 25-800 words. Pays $1 maximum.

Fiction: Confession, experimental, fantasy, historica, horror, humorous, mainstream, mystery, novel excerpts, romance, science fiction, slice-of-life vignettes, suspense. No pornography. Buys 6-12 mss/year. Send complete ms. Length: 2,000 words maximum. Pays $1-10.

Poetry: Avant-garde, free verse, haiku, light verse, traditional, humorous. Buys 15-20 poems/year. Submit maximum 10 poems at one time. Pays $1 maximum.

Fillers: Anecdotes, facts, short humor, hints on writing and running a home. Length: 25-300 words. Pays $1 maximum.

Tips: "We consider ourselves a beginner's market for women who want to write for the various major women's markets. Like any woman, I like to laugh and I love a good cry. I also like to be educated. More importantly, I want to know about you as a person. My goal is to help each other become the best writers we can be. Everything is open to freelancers."

MAGAZINE ISSUES, Serving Under 500,000 Circulation Publications, Feredonna Communications, Drawer 9808, Knoxville TN 37940. Editor: Michael Ward. 50% freelance written. Bimonthly magazine covering magazine publishing. Circulated to approximately 13,000 publishers, editors, ad managers, circulation managers, production managers and art directors of magazines. Circ. 13,000. Publishes ms an average of 2 months after acceptance. Byline given. Submit seasonal/holiday material 6 months in advance. Query for electronic submissions. Computer printout submissions OK; prefers letter-quality. Reports in 2 months on queries. Sample copy and writer's guidelines available for 9x12 SASE.

Nonfiction: How-to (write, sell advertising, manage production, manage creative and sales people, etc.); interview/profile (*only* after assignment—must be full of "secrets" of success and how-to detail); personal experiences; new product (no payment); and technical (aspects of magazine publishing). "Features deal with every aspect of publishing, including: creating an effective ad sales team; increasing ad revenue; writing effective direct-mail circulation promotion; improving reproduction quality; planning and implementing ad sales strategies; buying printing; gathering unique information; writing crisp, clear articles with impact; and designing publications with visual impact." No general interest. "Everything must be keyed directly to our typical reader—a 39 year-old publisher/editor producing a trade magazine for 30,000 or more readers." Buys 18-24 mss/year. Query. Length: 900-3,000 words.

Photos: Send photos with ms.

Tips: "Articles must present practical, useful, new information in how-to detail, so readers can do what the articles discuss. Articles that present problems and discuss how they were successfully solved also are welcome. These must carry many specific examples to flesh out general statements. We don't care who you are, just how you write."

‡**NEW WRITER'S MAGAZETTE**, 'The Friend of the Writing Class,' Independent Publishing Co., Box 15126, Sarasota FL 34277. (813)922-7080. Editor: Ned Burke. 95% freelance written. Bimonthly magazine for new writers. *"New Writer's Magazette* believes that *all* writers are *new* writers in that each of us can learn from one another. So, we reach *pro* and non-pro alike." Circ. 2,500. Pays on publication. Byline given. Buys first rights. Submit seasona/holiday material 2 months in advance. Photocopied submission OK. Query for electronic submissions. Computer printout submissions OK; prefers letter-quality. Reports in 2 weeks on queries; 1 month on mss. Sample copy $2. Writer's guidelines for #10 SASE.

Nonfiction: General interest, historical/nostalgic (writers), how-to (for new writers and desktop publishers), humor, interview/profile, opinion, personal experience (with *pro* writer) and photo feature ("Pals with Pens" uses photos/write-ups of writers). "We are planning a special fiction edition for Sept./Oct. – deadline August 15. "We don't want anything *not* for writing or the new writer." Buys 30-60 mss/year. Send complete ms. Length: 300-1,200 words. Pays $10-35 for assigned articles; $5-25 for unsolicited articles. Pays in contributor copies or other premiums for short items, poetry, fillers, etc.

Photos: Send photos with submission. Reviews 5x7 prints. Offers no additional payment for photos accepted with ms. Captions required. Buys one-time rights.

Columns/Departments: Lasting Impressions (a "one-on-one" interview or meeting with a recognized professional writer), 500-1,000 words. Buys 5-10 mss/year. Send complete ms. Length: 300-750 words. Pays $5-15.

Fiction: Experimental, historical, humorous, mainstream and slice-of-life vignettes. "Again, we do *not* want anything that does not have a tie-in with the writing life or writers in general." Buys 2-6 mss/year. "We offer a special fiction contest held each year with cash prizes." Send complete ms. Length: 750-1,500 words. Pays $5-20.

Poetry: Free verse, light verse and traditional. Does not want anything *not* for writers. Buys 10-20 poems/year. Submit maximum 3 poems. Length: 8-20 lines. Pays $5 maximum.

Fillers: Anecdotes, facts, gags to illustrated by cartoonist, newsbreaks and short humor. Buys 5-15/year. Length: 20-100 words. Pays $5 maximum.

Tips: "Any article *with photos* has a good chance, especially an *up close & personal* interview with an established professional writer offering advice, etc. *Desktop Publishing* section is always in need of good, in-depth articles or interesting columns."

OHIO WRITER, Box 79464, Cleveland OH 44107. Co-Editors: Susan and Mary Grimm, Kristin Blumberg and Jeff Erdie. 50% freelance written. Bimonthly newsletter on writing-related activities in Ohio. "We are a service newsletter only interested in articles, interviews, surveys, etc. which illuminate some aspect of writing. Our readers and contributors are mostly Ohioans." Publishes ms an average of 6 months after acceptance. Byline given. Buys one-time rights or second serial (reprint) rights. Submit seasonal/holiday material 5 months in advance. Simultaneous, photocopied and previously published material OK. Computer printout submissions OK. Reports in 3 months. Guidelines free; send $.45 in stamps for sample copy.

Nonfiction: Feature articles (on some aspect of writing), interview/profile (of Ohio authors), personal experience (writing related), book reviews, event reviews. Buys 30 mss/year. Send complete ms. Length: 400-2,000 words. Pays $50 for lead articles; $5-10 for reviews.

Columns/Departments: Alternative Paychecks (how writers make a living writing outside their preferred genre); Focus (a concentrated look at writing activities in one area). Buys 3 mss/year. Query. Length: 1,000-1,200 words. Pays $5-35.

Tips: "Any area is open; however, since we print more reviews than articles, that might be an easier opening. Reviews must be critical but balanced – we do not wish to trash someone's work. If it's that bad, we don't want to review it anyway. With lead articles we are not interested in formulaic how-tos (i.e.; 'The 7 Golden Rules to Good Fiction'), rather, we want a deeper examination of some aspect of writing – although not academic – coming from real experience."

RIGHTING WORDS, The Journal of Language and Editing, Righting Words Corp., Box 6811, F.D.R. Station, New York NY 10150. (718)761-0235. Editor: Jonathan S. Kaufman. 80% freelance written. Eager to work with new/unpublished writers. A bimonthly magazine on language usage, trends and issues. "Our readers include copy editors, book and magazine editors, and journalism and English teachers – people interested in the changing ways of the language and in ways to improve their editing and writing skills." Pays on acceptance. Publishes ms an average of 1 month after acceptance. Byline given. Offers $100 kill fee. Buys first North American serial rights. Query for electronic submissions. Computer printout submissions OK; no dot-matrix. Reports in 1 month. Sample copy $4.50 with 9x12 SAE and 3 first class stamps; writer's guidelines for #10 SASE.

Nonfiction: Buys 30 mss/year. Send complete ms. Length: 3,000 words. Pays $100 minimum for assigned articles; pays $75 minimum for unsolicited articles.

Tips: "Our contributors have included Rudolf Flesch and Willard Espy, but we welcome freelance submissions on editing and language topics that are well-written, contain hard information of value to editors, and that display wit and style. Yes, the editor reads *all* submissions, and often suggests approaches to writers whose material may be good but whose approach is off. No book reviews, please; other than that, all parts of the magazines are open to freelancers."

RISING STAR, 47 Byledge Rd., Manchester NH 03104. (603)623-9796. Editor: Scott E. Green. 50% freelance written. A bimonthly newsletter on science fiction and fantasy markets for writers and artists. Circ. 150. Pays on publication. Publishes ms an average of 3 months after acceptance. Byline given. Not copyrighted. Buys first rights. Simultaneous, photocopied and previously published submissions OK. Reports in 2 weeks on queries. Sample copy $1 with #10 SASE; free writer's guidelines.
Nonfiction: Book excerpts, essays, interview/profile and opinion. Buys 8 mss/year. Query. Length: 500-900 words. Pays $3 minimum.

ST. LOUIS JOURNALISM REVIEW, 8380 Olive Blvd., St. Louis MO 63132. (314)991-1699. FAX: (314)997-1848. Editor/Publisher: Charles L. Klotzer. 50% freelance written. Prefers to work with published/established writers. Works with a small number of new/unpublished writers each year; eager to work with new/unpublished writers. Monthly tabloid newspaper critiquing St. Louis media, print, broadcasting, TV and cable primarily by working journalists and others. Also covers issues not covered adequately by dailies. Occasionally buys articles on national media criticism. Circ. 6,500. Buys all rights. Byline given. Computer printout submissions OK. Sample copy $2.
Nonfiction: "We buy material which analyzes, critically, St. Louis metro area media and, less frequently, national media institutions, personalities or trends." No taboos. Payment depends. Pays the expenses of writers on assignment subject to prior approval.

SCAVENGER'S NEWSLETTER, 519 Ellinwood, Osage City KS 66523. (913)528-3538. Editor: Janet Fox. 25% freelance written. Eager to work with new/unpublished writers. A monthly newsletter covering markets for science fiction/fantasy/horror materials especially with regard to the small press. Circ. 800. Publishes ms an average of 8 months after acceptance. Byline given. Not copyrighted. Places copyright symbol on title page; rights revert to contributor on publication. Buys one-time rights. Simultaneous, photocopied and previously published submissions OK. Computer printout submissions acceptable; prefers letter-quality. Reports in 2 weeks. Sample copy $1.50; writer's guidelines for #10 SASE.
Nonfiction: Essays; general interest; how-to (write, sell, publish sf/fantasy/horror); humor; interview/profile (writers, artists in the field); and opinion. Buys 12-15 mss/year. Send complete ms. Length: 1,000 words maximum. Pays $4 on acceptance.
Poetry: Avant-garde, free verse, haiku and traditional. All related to science fiction/fantasy/horror genres. Buys 36 poems/year. Submit maximum 3 poems. Length: 10 lines maximum. Pays $2 on acceptance.
Tips: "Because this is a small publication, it has occasional overstocks. We're especially looking for sf/fantasy/horror commentary as opposed to writer's how-to's."

SCIENCE FICTION CHRONICLE, Box 2730, Brooklyn NY 11202-0036. (718)643-9011. Editor: Andrew Porter. 3% freelance written. Works with a small number of new/unpublished writers each year. Monthly magazine about science fiction, fantasy and horror publishing for readers, editors, writers, et al., who are interested in keeping up with the latest developments and news. Publication also includes market reports, UK news, letters, reviews, columns. Circ. 5,100. Buys first serial rights. Pays on publication. Publishes ms an average of 2 months after acceptance. Makes work-for-hire assignments. Submit seasonal material 4 months in advance. Computer printout submissions acceptable; prefers letter-quality. Reports in 1 month. Sample copy for 9x12 SAE and 5 first class stamps.
Nonfiction: New product and photo feature. No articles about UFOs, or "news we reported six months ago." Buys 10 unsolicited mss/year. Send complete ms. Length: 200-500 words. Pays 3-5¢/word.
Photos: Send photos with ms. Pays $5-15 for 4x5 and 8x10 b&w prints. Captions preferred. Buys one-time rights.
Tips: "News of publishers, booksellers and software related to sf, fantasy and horror is most needed from freelancers. **No fiction**—This is a news magazine, like *Publishers Weekly* or *Time*. (I still get 10-20 story mss a year, which are returned, unread.)"

‡SE LA VIE WRITER'S JOURNAL, Rio Grande Press, Box 371371, El Paso TX 79937. (915)595-2625. Editor: Rosalie Avara. 70% freelance written. Quarterly magazine on writing and poetry. "*Se La Vie* is a 50 pp. digest-sized journal with contests in poetry, short stories, essays, plays and freelance humor in the way of cartoons, short fillers, all reflecting 'La Vie' or 'Life theme.' Open to new and experienced poets and writers." Circ. 200. Pays on publication. Publishes ms an average of 3 months after acceptance. Byline given. Buys first North American serial rights. Submit seasonal/holiday material 2 months in advance. Photocopied submissions OK. Reports in 2 weeks on queries; 6-8 weeks on mss. Sample copy $3 with 7x10 SAE and 2 first class stamps. Writer's guidelines for #10 SASE.
Nonfiction: Book excerpts (chapbook reviews), essays (contest mostly), general interest (to writers and poets), how-to (write a prize-winning poem), humor (cartoons, jokes, short poems), opinion (Poet's Poll Rhyme vs. free verse, etc.), personal experience (humorous), technical (techniques of writing poetry) and

writing song lyrics. "No religious, political, erotica or porn, historical or war stories." Buys 20 mss/year. Query for current needs. Length: 150-500 words. Pays $3-10 for assigned articles. "Pays in contributor copies if artist may need copies for their portfolio. Authors may want clips or advertising. Guest judges receive free subscription."

Columns/Departments: Poet's Poll (opinion on various forms or subjects dealing with poetry), 500 words; New Markets (for poetry, stories), up to 4 lines; How To (current series on writing prize-winner poems), 500 words and Riter's Remedies (a "Dear Abby" for writers, about 4-5 w/answers), 500 words. Buys 12 mss/year. Query for current needs. Pays $3-10.

Fiction: Adventure, ethnic, humorous, romance, slice-of-life vignettes and suspense. "No religious, political, historical, erotica, science fiction, long narratives, war stories or novel length." Buys 4 mss/year. Query. Length: 400-500 words. Pays $3-10.

Poetry: Free verse, Haiku, light verse and traditional. "No erotica, religious, political, war stories, or cowboy poetry." Buys 80 poems/year. Submit maximum 10 poems (entry fee) contest(s) regular and subscribers only. Length: 3-30 lines. Pays $5-25.

Fillers: Anecdotes, gags to be illustrated by cartoonist, and short humor. Buys 24/year. Length: 50-150 words. Pays $3-5.

Tips: "Send post card or short letter explaining types of material writer has done in past (clips unnecessary). Include SASE for reply. All short humor fillers or cartoons considered, best to query first. Enter one of our many contests in poetry, essays, short, short stories, one-act plays, and sometimes artwork or cover designs. Receive free copy."

‡SMALL PRESS, The Magazine & Book Review of Independent Publishing, Meckler Corporation, 11 Ferry Ln. W., Westport CT 06880. (203)226-6967. FAX: (203)454-5840. Editor: Brenda Mitchell-Powell. Managing Editor: Doreen Beauregard. 90% freelance written. Bimonthly magazine on independent publishers/independent publishing. "The writers and reviewers of *Small Press*, in cooperation with the publishers, editors, booksellers and trade participants, work to create a periodical that affirms and nurtures independent-press publishing and that epitomizes the ideology and strength of our industry." Circ. 5,400. Pays on publication. Publishes ms an average of 2-6 months after acceptance. Byline given. Makes work-for-hire assignments. Submit seasonal/holiday material 3-6 months in advance. "While *Small Press* does, occasionally, reprint articles, we strive to publish only original material; articles of particular relevance to the trade are accepted on other bases with the editor's approval." Query for electronic submissions. Computer printout submissions OK. Reports in 6 weeks on queries; 2 months on mss. Free sample copy and writer's guidelines.

Nonfiction: Essays, general interest to the trade, how-to (practical applications), interview/profile, new product, technical, use of computers, legal/financial strategies, promotion and marketing. "Interested parties should write for an editorial calendar. Such a calendar is available upon request, and there is no charge. Editorial agenda is fixed to a degree, but certain items are subject to change. NO FICTION!! I prefer not to receive blind submissions. Please inquire before mailing. Articles of a strictly personal nature—not genre-oriented—are discouraged. Articles must relate to the independent-press industry." Buys 10-12 mss/year. Query with published clips or send complete ms. Length: 250-4,000 words. Pays $45-65/page. Book reviewers receive only the title sent for review and a copy of the issue in which the review appears. Sometimes pays expenses of writers on assignment.

Photos: Send photos with submission. Offers no additional payment for photos accepted with ms. Captions, model releases and identification of subjects required.

Columns/Departments: "Columns are assigned to contributing editors. Only practical/advice for trade use columns are available to freelance writers at this time." not assigned (practical and advisory columns on technical, legal, financial, promotional strategies [e.g., marketing to independent bookstores, tax advice for publishers, non-traditional marketing techniques, implementation of graphics with computer systems, etc.]), 250-2,000 words. Buys 30-50 mss/year. Query with published clips. Send complete ms. Pays $45-65/page.

Fillers: Facts and newsbreaks. Buys 6/year. Length: 250-1,500 words. Pays $65 maximum.

Tips: "Please familiarize yourself with the independent-press industry. I neither want nor need writers who have neither knowledge nor appreciation of the industry *Small Press* serves. Writing skills are not sufficient qualification. Genre-oriented articles are sought and preferred. Filler articles on a variety of subjects of practical advice to the trade are the most open to freelance writers. I am amenable to submissions of feature articles relating to publishers, inventories, traditional, and desktop-publishing systems, trade events (London Book Fair, Frankfurt, ABA, etc.), publishing trends, regional pieces (with a direct relationship to the independent-press industry), production issues, business-oriented advice, promotion and marketing strategies, interviews with industry participants."

SMALL PRESS REVIEW, Box 100, Paradise CA 95967. Editor: Len Fulton. Monthly for "people interested in small presses and magazines, current trends and data; many libraries." Circ. 3,000. Byline given. "Query if you're unsure." Reports in 2 months. Free sample copy.

Nonfiction: News, short reviews, photos, short articles on small magazines and presses. Uses how-to, personal experience, interview, profile, spot news, historical, think, photo, and coverage of merchandising techniques. Accepts 50-200 mss/year. Length: 100-200 words. Payment is negotiable.

‡**WDS BOOK AUTHOR'S NEWSLETTER,** Writer's Digest School, 1507 Dana Ave., Cincinnati OH 45207. (513)531-2222. Editor: Kirk Polking. Semi-annual newsletter covering writing and marketing information for students of workshops in novel and nonfiction book writing offered by Writer's Digest School. Circ. 3,000. Pays on acceptance. Publishes ms an average of 6 months after acceptance. Byline given. Pays 25% kill fee. Buys first serial rights and second serial (reprint) rights. Simultaneous, photocopied and previously published submissions OK. Query for electronic submissions. Computer printout submissions acceptable; not dot-matrix. Reports in 3 weeks. Free sample copy.
Nonfiction: How-to (write or market novels or nonfiction books); and interviews with published authors or novels and books. Buys six mss/year. "Query by mail, please, not phone." Length: 500-1,000 words. Pays $10-25.

WDS FORUM, Writer's Digest School, 1507 Dana Ave., Cincinnati OH 45207. (513)531-2222. Editor: Kirk Polking. 100% freelance written. Quarterly newsletter covering writing techniques and marketing for students of courses in fiction and nonfiction writing offered by Writer's Digest School. Circ. 13,000. Pays on acceptance. Publishes ms an average of 6 months after acceptance. Byline given. Pays 25% kill fee. Buys first serial rights and second serial (reprint) rights. Submit seasonal/holiday material 4 months in advance. Simultaneous, photocopied, and previously published submissions OK. Query for electronic submissions. Computer printout submissions acceptable; no dot-matrix. Reports in 3 weeks. Free sample copy.
Nonfiction: How-to (write or market short stories, articles, novels, etc.); and interviews (with well-known authors of short stories, novels and books). Buys 12 mss/year. "Query by mail, please, not phone." Length: 500-1,000 words. Pays $10-25.

‡**WEST COAST REVIEW OF BOOKS,** Rapport Publishing Co., Inc., 5265 Fountain Ave., Upper Terrace #6, Los Angeles CA 90029. (213)660-0433. Editor: D. David Dreis. Bimonthly magazine for book consumers. "Provocative articles based on specific subject matter, books and author retrospectives." Circ. 80,000. Pays on publication. Byline given. Offers kill fee. Buys one-time rights and second serial (reprint) rights to published author interviews. Sample copy $2.
Nonfiction: General interest, historical/nostalgic and profile (author retrospectives). "No individual book reviews." Buys 25 mss/year. Query. Length: open.
Tips: "There must be a reason (current interest, news events, etc.) for any article here. Example: 'The Jew-Haters' was about anti-semitism which was written up in six books; all reviewed and analyzed under that umbrella title. Under no circumstances should articles be submitted unless query has been responded to." No phone calls.

THE WRITER, 120 Boylston St., Boston MA 02116. Editor-in-Chief/Publisher: Sylvia K. Burack. 20-25% freelance written. Prefers to buy work of published/established writers. Monthly. Pays on acceptance. Publishes ms an average of 6-8 months after acceptance. Buys first serial rights. Uses some freelance material. Computer printout submissions acceptable; no dot-matrix. Sample copy $2.50.
Nonfiction: Practical articles for writers on how to write for publication, and how and where to market manuscripts in various fields. Will consider all submissions promptly. No assignments. Length: approximately 2,000 words.
Tips: "New types of publications and our continually updated market listings in all fields will determine changes of focus and fact."

WRITER'S DIGEST, 1507 Dana Ave., Cincinnati OH 45207. (513)531-2222. Submissions Editor: Bill Strickland. 90% freelance written. Monthly magazine about writing and publishing. "Our readers write fiction, poetry, nonfiction, plays and all kinds of creative writing. They're interested in improving their writing skills, improving their sales ability, and finding new outlets for their talents." Circ. 225,000. Pays on acceptance. Publishes ms an average of 1 year after acceptance. Buys first North American serial rights for one-time editorial use, microfilm/microfiche use and magazine promotional use. Pays 20% kill fee. Byline given. Submit seasonal/holiday material 8 months in advance. Previously published and photocopied submissions OK. Query for electronic submissions. "We're able to use electronic submissions only for accepted pieces/and will discuss details if we buy your work. We'll accept computer printout submissions, of course—but they *must* be readable. We strongly recommend letter-quality. If you don't want your manuscript returned, indicate that on the first page of the manuscript or in a cover letter." Reports in 2 weeks. Sample copy $2.75; writer's guidelines for #10 SASE.
Nonfiction: "Our mainstay is the how-to article—that is, an article telling how to write and sell more of what you write. For instance, how to write compelling leads and conclusions, how to improve your character descriptions, how to become more efficient and productive. We like plenty of examples, anecdotes and $$$ in our articles—so other writers can actually see what's been done successfully by the author of a particular piece. We like our articles to speak directly to the reader through the use of the first-person voice. Don't submit an article on what five book editors say about writing mysteries. Instead, submit an article on how you cracked the mystery market and how our readers can do the same. But don't limit the article to your experiences; include the opinions of those five editors to give your article increased depth and authority."

General interest (about writing); how-to (writing and marketing techniques that work); humor (short pieces); inspirational; interview and profile (query first); new product; and personal experience (marketing and freelancing experiences). "We can always use articles on fiction and nonfiction technique, and solid articles on poetry or scriptwriting are always welcome. No articles titled 'So You Want to Be a Writer,' and no first-person pieces that ramble without giving a lesson or something readers can learn from in the sharing of the story." Buys 90-100 mss/year. Queries are preferred, but complete mss are OK. Length: 500-3,000 words. Pays 10¢/word minimum. Sometimes pays expenses of writers on assignment.

Photos: Used only with interviews and profiles. State availability of photos or send contact sheet with ms. Pays $25 minimum for 5x7 or larger b&w prints. Captions required.

Columns/Departments: Chronicle (first-person narratives about the writing life; length: 1,200-1,500 words; pays 10¢/word); The Writing Life (length: 50-800 words; pays 10¢/word); Tip Sheet (short, unbylined items that offer solutions to writing- and freelance business-related problems that writers commonly face; pays 10¢/word); and My First Sale (an "occasional" department; a first-person account of how a writer broke into print; length: 1,000 words; pays 10¢/word). "For First Sale items, use a narrative, anecdotal style to tell a tale that is both inspirational and instructional. Before you submit a My First Sale item, make certain that your story contains a solid lesson that will benefit other writers." Buys approximately 200 articles/year for Writing Life section, Tip Sheet and shorter pieces. Send complete ms.

Poetry: Light verse about "the writing life"—joys and frustrations of writing. "We are also considering poetry other than short light verse—but related to writing, publishing, other poets and authors, etc." Buys 2-3/issue. Submit poems in batches of 1-8. Length: 2-20 lines. Pays $10-50/poem.

Fillers: Anecdotes and short humor, primarily for use in The Writing Life column. Uses 4/issue. Length: 50-250 words. Pays 10¢/word.

WRITER'S GUIDELINES, S.O.C.O. Publications, RD 1 Ward Rd., Box 71, Mohawk NY 13407. (315)866-7445. Editor: Carol Ann Vercz. 100% freelance written. A monthly magazine with writing information and general interest features. "We are trying to inform all writers about new techniques, advancements as well as educate, to some degree, the novice to get him started in his career." Circ. 1,000. Pays on publication. Byline sometimes given. Buys one-time rights. Submit seasonal/holiday material 6 months in advance. Simultaneous and previously published submissions OK. Query for electronic submissions. Computer printout submissions OK; no dot-matrix. Reports in 6 weeks on queries. Sample copy $3. Free writer's guidelines.

Nonfiction: General interest, historical/nostalgic, how-to, humor, inspirational, photo feature, technical and travel. Buys 200 mss/year. Query. Length: 500-1,200 words. Pays 2¢/word. Pays 1¢/word for reprints.

Photos: Send photos with submission. Reviews prints (3x5). Pays $3.50 per photo. Identification of subjects required. Buys one-time rights.

Columns/Departments: Conferences. Buys 100 mss/year. Query. Length: 500-1,200 words. Pays 2¢/word.

Fiction: Adventure, historical and humorous.

Poetry: Traditional. Buys 100 poems/year. Submit maximum 6 poems. Length: 6-25 lines. Pays 25¢/line.

Fillers: Anecdotes and facts. Buys 15/year. Pays $1-5.

Tips: "Query first about any article. We're always looking for new ideas for columns."

WRITER'S INFO, Box 1870, Hayden ID 83835. (208)772-6184. Editor: Linda Hutton. 90% freelance written. Eager to work with new/unpublished writers. Monthly newsletter on writing. "We provide helpful tips and advice to writers, both beginners and old pros." Circ. 200. Pays on acceptance. Publishes ms an average of 6 months after acceptance. Byline given. Buys first North American serial rights and second serial (reprint) rights. Submit seasonal/holiday material 9 months in advance. Simultaneous queries, and simultaneous, photocopied and previously published submissions OK. Computer printout submissions acceptable; prefers letter-quality. Reports in 1 month. Sample copy for #10 SAE and 2 first class stamps; writer's guidelines for #10 SASE.

Nonfiction: How-to, humor and personal experience, all related to writing. No interviews or re-hashes of articles published in other writers magazines. Buys 50-75 mss/year. Send complete ms. Length: 300 words. Pays $1-10.

Poetry: Free verse, light verse and traditional. No avant-garde or shaped poetry. Buys 40-50/year. Submit maximum 6 poems. Length: 4-20 lines. Pays $1-10.

Fillers: Jokes, anecdotes and short humor. Buys 3-4/year. Length: 100 words maximum. Pays $1-10.

Tips: "Tell us a system that worked for you to make a sale or inspired you to write. All departments are open to freelancers."

WRITER'S JOURNAL, Minnesota Ink, Inc., Box 9148 N., St. Paul MN 55109. (612)433-3626. Publisher/Managing Editor: Valerie Hockert. Associate Editor: John Hall. 30% freelance written. Monthly. Circ. 10,000. Pays on publication. Publishes ms an average of 2 months after acceptance. Byline given. Buys first North American serial rights. Submit seasonal/holiday material 4 months in advance. Simultaneous queries OK. Query for electronic submissions. Computer printout submissions acceptable; prefers letter-quality. Reports in 1 month on queries; 6 weeks on mss. Sample copy $2; writer's guidelines for #10 SAE and 1 first class stamp.

Nonfiction: How-to (on the business and approach to writing); motivational; interview/profile; opinion. *"Writer's Journal* publishes articles on style, technique, editing methods, copy writing, research, writing of news releases, writing news stories and features, creative writing, grammar reviews, marketing, the business aspects of writing, copyright law and legal advice for writers/editors, independent book publishing, interview techniques, and more." Also articles on the use of computers by writers and a book review section. Buys 30-40 mss/year. Send complete ms. Length: 500-1,500 words. Pays $15-50.

Poetry: Avant-garde, free verse, haiku, light verse and traditional. "The *Inkling* runs one poetry contest each year in the spring: Winner and 2nd place cash prizes and two honorable mentions." Buys 10-15 poems/year. Submit maximum 3 poems. Length: 25 lines maximum. Pays $4-15.

Tips: "Articles must be *well* written and slanted toward the business (or commitment) of writing and/or being a writer. Interviews with established writers should be in-depth, particularly reporting interviewee's philosophy on writing, how (s)he got started, etc. Tape interviews, transcribe, then edit. Monthly 'theme' emphasizes a particular genre or type of writing. Opinion pieces (researched and authoritative) on any of the monthly themes welcomed. (Theme schedule available with guidelines.)"

THE WRITER'S NOOK NEWS, 10957 Chardon Rd., Chardon OH 44024. (216)285-0942. Editor: Eugene Ortiz. 100% freelance written. A quarterly newsletter for professional writers. "We don't print fluff, anecdotes or platitudes. Articles must be specific, terse, pithy and contain information my readers can put to immediate, practical use. Every article should be the kind you want to cut out and tape to your desk somewhere." Circ. 5,000. Pays on acceptance. Publishes ms an average of 5 months after acceptance. Byline given. Publication is not copyrighted. Buys first North American serial rights. Submit seasonal/holiday material 5 months in advance. Photocopied submissions OK. Computer printout submissions OK; no dot-matrix. Reports in 6 weeks. Sample copy $3. Writer's guidelines for 9x12 SAE with 2 first class stamps.

Nonfiction: How-to and interview/profile (how he or she wrote or writes and markets his or her work). "I do not want to see essays, poetry, fiction, ruminations, anecdotes, or anything of no immediate, practical value to my readers." Buys 100 mss/year. Send complete ms with credits and short bio. Length: 100-400 words. Pays $8-32.

Photos: Send photos with submission. Reviews prints (2½x2½). Offers $5 maximum per photo. Identification of subjects required. Buys one-time rights.

Columns/Departments: Bolton's Book Bench (short reviews of books related to writing), 400 words; Conferences & Klatches (listings of conferences and gatherings), 400-1,200 words; Contests & Awards (listings of contests and awards), 400 words; Writer's Rights (latest information on what's happening on Capital Hill), 400 words; Markets (listings of information on markets for writers), 400 words. Buys 20 mss/year. Query with published clips and short bio. Length: 400 words. Pays $3-32.

Fillers: Facts and newsbreaks. Buys 20/year. Length: 20-100 words. Pays $1.60-8.

Tips: "Take the writer's guidelines very seriously. 90% of the best submissions are still about 25% fluff. Cut till it bleeds! Very short cover letter. Word count (400 max) and rights offered (First North American serial) in upper right of page one of ms. Typed SASE (#10 or larger) with proper postage. Short bio with submission. Don't tell me how hard or impossible it is to write anything of worth in only 400 words—others are doing it in each issue of *The Writer's Nook News*. This is not a market for beginners. Particularly looking for genre tips. Tell me how you did it, what it takes, or what you are doing to keep your writing fresh. I need more helpful information for established writers. I also need information on alternative ways of earning money as a writer. Finally, I could use information on songwriting, playwriting and screenwriting. We also sponsor an annual short fiction contest. Details can be found in any current issue of *TWNN*. We also publish a quarterly conference bulletin and a quarterly markets bulletin (both 12 pages, digest-size)."

WRITER'S YEARBOOK, 1507 Dana Ave., Cincinnati OH 45207. Submissions Editor: Bill Strickland. 90% freelance written. Newsstand annual for freelance writers, journalists and teachers of creative writing. "Please note that the *Yearbook* is currently using a 'best of' format. That is, we are reprinting the best of writing about writing published in the last year: articles, fiction, and book excerpts. The *Yearbook* now uses little original material, so do not submit queries or original manuscripts to the *Yearbook*. We will, however, consider already-published material for possible inclusion." Buys reprint rights. Pays 20% kill fee. Byline given. Pays on acceptance. Publishes ms an average of 6 months after acceptance. High-quality photocopied submissions OK. Computer printout submissions acceptable; prefers letter-quality. "If you don't want your manuscript returned, indicate that on the first page of the manuscript or in a cover letter."

Nonfiction: "In reprints, we want articles that reflect the current state of writing in America. Trends, inside information and money-saving and money-making ideas for the freelance writer. We try to touch on the various facets of writing in each issue of the *Yearbook*—from fiction to poetry to playwriting, and any other endeavor a writer can pursue. How-to articles—that is, articles that explain in detail how to do something—are very important to us. For example, you could explain how to establish mood in fiction, how to improve interviewing techniques, how to write for and sell to specialty magazines, or how to construct and market a good poem. We are also interested in the writer's spare time—what she/he does to retreat occasionally from the writing wars; where and how to refuel and replenish the writing spirit. 'How Beats the Heart of a Writer' features interest us, if written warmly, in the first person, by a writer who has had considerable success. We also want interviews or profiles of well-known bestselling authors, always with good pictures. Articles on writing techniques that are effective today are always welcome. We provide how-to features and information to help our readers become more skilled at writing and successful at selling their writing." Buys 10-15 mss (reprints only)/year. Length: 750-4,500 words. Pays 2½¢/word minimum.

Photos: Interviews and profiles must be accompanied by high-quality photos. Reviews b&w photos only, depending on use; pays $20-50/published photo. Captions required.

Law

While all of these publications deal with topics of interest to attorneys, each has a particular slant. Be sure that your subject is geared to a specific market — lawyers in a single region, law students, paralegals, etc. Publications for law enforcement personnel are listed under Government and Public Service.

ABA JOURNAL, American Bar Association, 750 N. Lake Shore Dr., Chicago IL 60611. (312)988-5000. FAX: (312)988-6014. Editor: Larry Bodine. Articles Editor: Robert Yates. 35% freelance written. Prefers to work with published/established writers. Monthly magazine covering law and laywers. "The content of the *Journal* is designed to appeal to the association's diverse membership with emphasis on the general practitioner." Circ. 370,000. Pays on acceptance. Publishes ms an average of 2 months after acceptance. Byline given. "Editor works with writer until article is in acceptable form." Buys all rights. Submit seasonal/holiday material 3 months in advance. Simultaneous queries, and simultaneous and photocopied submissions OK. Query for electronic submissions. Computer printout submissions acceptable; no dot-matrix. Reports in 3 weeks. Free sample copy and writer's guidelines.

Nonfiction: Book excerpts; general interest (legal); how-to (law practice techniques); interview/profile (law firms and prominent individuals); and technical (legal trends). "The emphasis of the *Journal* is on the practical problems faced by lawyers in general practice and how those problems can be overcome. Articles should emphasize the practical rather than the theoretical or esoteric. Writers should avoid the style of law reviews, academic journals or legal briefs and should write in an informal, journalistic style. Short quotations from people and specific examples of your point will improve an article." Special issues have featured women and minorities in the legal profession. Buys 30 mss/year. Query with published clips or send complete ms. Length: 1,000-3,000 words. Pays $300-800. Pays expenses of writers on assignment.

Tips: "Write to us with a specific idea in mind and spell out how the subject would be covered. Full length profiles and feature articles are always needed. We look for practical information. Don't send us theory, philosophy or wistful meanderings. Our readers want to know how to win cases and operate their practices more efficiently. We need more writing horsepower on lifestyle, profile and practice pieces for lawyers. If the New York Times or Wall Street Journal would like your style, so will we."

THE ALTMAN & WEIL REPORT TO LEGAL MANAGEMENT, Altman & Weil Publications, Inc., Box 472, Ardmore PA 19003. (215)649-4646. Editor: Robert I. Weil. 15-20% freelance written. Works with a small number of new/unpublished writers each year. Monthly newsletter covering law office purchases (equipment, insurance services, space, etc.) and technology. Circ. 2,200. Pays on publication. Publishes ms an average of 3-6 months after acceptance. Byline given. Buys all rights; sometimes second serial (reprint) rights. Photocopied and previously published submissions OK. Query for electronic submissions. Computer printout submissions acceptable; no dot-matrix. Reports in 1 month on queries; 6 weeks on mss. Sample copy for #10 SASE.

Nonfiction: How-to (buy, use, repair), interview/profile and new product. Buys 6 mss/year. Query. Submit a sample of previous writing. Length: 500-2,500 words. Pays $125/published page.

Photos: State availability of photos. Reviews b&w prints; payment is included in payment for ms. Captions and model release required. Buys one-time rights.

‡BENCH & BAR OF MINNESOTA, Minnesota State Bar Association, Suite 403, 430 Marquette Ave., Minneapolis MN 55401. (612)333-1183. FAX: (612)333-4927. Editor: Judson Haverkamp. 10% freelance written. A magazine on the law/legal profession published 11 times/year. "Audience is mostly Minnesota lawyers. *Bench & Bar* seeks reportage, analysis, and commentary on developments in the law and the legal profession, especially in Minnesota. Preference to items of practical/human interest to professionals in law." Circ. 12,500. Pays on acceptance. Publishes ms an average of 3 months after acceptence. Byline given. Buys first North American serial rights and makes work-for-hire assignments. Photocopied submissions OK. Computer printout submissions OK; prefers letter-quality. Reports in 2 weeks on queries; 1 month on mss. Sample copy for 9x12 SAE and $1 postage; free writer's guidelines.

Nonfiction: General interest, historical/nostalgic, how-to (how to handle particular types of legal, ethical problems in office management, representation, etc.), humor, interview/profile and technical/legal. "We do not want one-sided opinion pieces or advertorial." Buys 4-5 mss/year. Query with published clips, or send complete ms. Length: 1,500-4,000 words. Pays $250-650. Sometimes pays expenses of writers on assignment.
Photos: State availability of photos with submission. Reviews 5x7 or larger prints. Offers $25-100 per photo upon publication. Model releases and identification of subjects required. Buys one-time rights.

‡**COMPUTER USER'S LEGAL REPORTER,** Computer Law Group, Inc., Box 375, Charlottesville VA 22902. (804)977-6343. FAX: (804)977-8570. Editor: Charles P. Lickson. 20% freelance written. Prefers to work with published/established writers or "experts" in fields addressed. Newsletter published 9 times per year featuring legal issues and considerations facing users of computer and processed data. "The *Computer User's Legal Reporter* is written by a fully qualified legal and technical staff for essentially nonlawyer readers. It features brief summaries on developments in such vital areas as computer contracts, insurance, warranties, crime, proprietary rights and privacy. Each summary is backed by reliable research and sourcework." Circ. 1,000. Pays on publication. Publishes ms an average of 1 month after acceptance. Offers 50% kill fee. Buys first North American serial rights. Simultaneous queries, and simultaneous, photocopied, and previously published submissions OK. Computer printout submissions acceptable; prefers letter-quality to dot-matrix. Reports in 2 weeks. Sample copy for $10 with #10 SAE and 5 first class stamps.
Nonfiction: Book excerpts; expose; how-to (protect ideas, etc.); humor (computer law . . . according to Murphy); interview/profile (legal or computer personality); and technical. No articles not related to computers or high-tech and society. Buys 15 mss/year. Query with published clips. Length: 250-1,000 words. Pays $50; $150 for scenes.
Columns/Departments: Computer Law . . . according to Murphy (humorous "laws" relating to computers, definitions, etc.). The editor buys all rights to Murphyisms which may be included in his book, *Computer Law . . . According to Murphy.* Buys 10 mss/year. Length: 25-75 words. Pays $10-50.
Tips: "Send materials with a note on your own background and qualifications to write what you submit. We invite intelligently presented and well-argued controversy within our field. Our audience is non-lawyers."

‡**THE DOCKET,** Nat'l Assoc. of Legal Secretaries, Suite 550, 2250 E. 73rd St., Tulsa OK 74136. (918)493-3540. Editor: Debora L. Riggs. 20% freelance written. Bimonthly magazine that covers continuing legal education for legal support staff. "*The Docket* is written and edited for legal secretaries, legal assistants and other non-attorney personnel. Feature articles address general trends and emerging issues in the legal field, provide practical information to achieve proficiency in the delivery of legal services, and offer techniques for career growth and fulfillment." Circ. 20,000. Pays on publication. Publishes ms an average of 3-6 months after acceptance. Byline given. Offers 25-35% of original commission fee as kill fee. Buys first North American serial rights. Simultaneous and previously published submissions OK. Computer printout submissions OK; prefers letter-quality. Reports in 2-3 weeks on queries; 3-4 weeks on mss. Free sample copy and writer's guidelines.
Nonfiction: How-to (enhance the delivery of legal services or any aspect thereof), new product (must be a service or equipment used in a legal office), personal experience (legal related) and technical (legal services and equipment). Buys 20-25 mss/year. Query with or without published clips, or send complete ms. Length: 500-3,000 words. Pays $50-250. Sometimes pays expenses of writers on assignment.
Photos: State availability of photos with submission. Reviews contact sheets, negatives, transparencies and prints. Offers no additional payment for photos accepted with ms. Buys one-time rights.

‡**LAWYERS MONTHLY,** Lawyers Weekly Publications, Inc., 30 Court Sq., Boston MA 02108. (617)227-6034. Editor: Carolee Morrison. 50% freelance written. Monthly newspaper feature supplement for law newpapers concerning law, lawyers, law-related events. "We are writing for a highly educated, generally affluent, professional, active national readership, age-range 25-75 — busy men and women who are intimately involved with the subjects we cover and who therefore requir the best in authority, expertise, timeliness, uniqueness and readability. Circ. 85,000. Pays on publication. Publishes ms an average of 2 months after acceptance. Byline given. Buys first rights. Submit seasonal/holiday material 3 months in advance. Photocopied submissions OK. Query for electronic submissions. Computer printout submissions OK; prefers letter-quality. Reports in 4 weeks on queries. Free sample copy.
Nonfiction: National reporting (investigative pieces about important cases or trends), historical/academic (legal history), how-to (concerning law office management and new products), interview/profile (prominent judges and attorneys, or lawyers with serious nonlawyer involvements — professional or hobby) and opinion (columns from experts or prominent individuals on current national legal issues and controversies). Buys 25-50 mss/year. Send complete ms. Length: 1,000-2,500 words. Pays $25-500. Sometimes pays expenses of writers on assignment.

Photos: Send photos or appropriate graphic material with submission. Reviews prints. Payment policy negotiable. Buys one-time rights.

Tips: "Our publication is only open to individuals with an intimate familiarity with the law, either as legal journalists or practitioners of the law. Submissions must be clear, professional, readable, well-researched, timely, crucial, enterprising, original and authoritative."

THE LAWYER'S PC, A Newsletter for Lawyers Using Personal Computers, Shepard's/McGraw-Hill, Inc.; editorial office at Box 1108, Lexington SC 29072. (803)359-9941. Editor: Robert P. Wilkins. Managing Editor: Daniel E. Harmon. 50% freelance written. A biweekly newsletter covering computerized law firms. "Our readers are lawyers who want to be told how a particular microcomputer program or type of program is being applied to a legal office task, such as timekeeping, litigation support, etc." Circ. 4,000. Pays end of the month of publication. Publishes ms an average of 1-2 months after acceptance. Byline given. Buys first North American serial rights and the right to reprint. Submit seasonal/holiday material 5 months in advance. Query for electronic submissions. Computer printout submissions acceptable; prefers letter-quality. Reports in 1 month on queries; 2 months on mss. Sample copy for 9x12 SAE with 3 first class stamps; free writer's guidelines.

Nonfiction: How-to (applications articles on law office computerization) and software reviews written by lawyers who have no compromising interests. No general articles on why lawyers need computers or reviews of products written by public relations representatives or vending consultants. Buys 30-35 mss/year. Query. Length: 500-2,500 words. Pays $25-125. Sometimes pays the expenses of writers on assignment.

Tips: "Most of our writers are lawyers. If you're not a lawyer, you need to at least understand why general business software may not work well in a law firm. If you understand lawyers' specific computer problems, write an article describing how to solve one of those problems, and we'd like to see it."

THE LAWYERS WEEKLY, The Newspaper for the Legal Profession in Canada, Butterworth (Canada) Inc., Suite 201, 423 Queen St. W., Toronto, Ontario M5V 2A5 Canada. (416)598-5211. FAX: (416)598-5659. Editor: D. Michael Fitz-James. 20% freelance written. "We will work with any *talented* writer of whatever experience level." Works with a small number of new/unpublished writers each year. A 48-times-per-year tabloid covering law and legal affairs for a "sophisticated up-market readership of lawyers and accountants." Circ. 37,000. Pays on publication. Publishes ms an average of 1 month after acceptance. Byline given. Offers 50% kill fee. Usually buys all rights. Submit seasonal/holiday material 6 weeks in advance. Simultaneous queries and submissions, and photocopied submissions OK. Query for electronic submissions. Electronic submissions on PC compatible disks, WordStar or WordPerfect. Printout backup a must. Computer printout submissions acceptable. Reports in 1 month. Sample copy $1.50 Canadian funds and 8½x11 SAE.

Nonfiction: Expose; general interest (law); historical/nostalgic; how-to (professional); humor; interview/profile (lawyers and judges); opinion; technical; news; and case comments. "We try to wrap up the week's legal events and issues in a snappy informal package with lots of visual punch. We especially like news stories with photos or illustrations. We are always interested in feature or newsfeature articles involving current legal issues, but contributors should keep in mind our audience is trained in *English/Canadian common law* — not U.S. law. That means most U.S. constitutional or criminal law stories will generally not be accepted. Special Christmas issue. No routine court reporting or fake news stories about commercial products. Buys 200-300 mss/year. Query or send complete ms. Length: 700-1,500 words. Pays $25 minimum, negotiable maximum (have paid up to $350 in the past). Payment in Canadian dollars. Sometimes pays the expenses of writers on assignment.

Photos: State availability of photos with query letter or ms. Reviews b&w contact sheets, negatives, and 5x7 prints. Identification of subjects required. Buys one-time rights.

Columns/Departments: Buys 90-100 mss/year. Send complete ms or Wordstar or WordPerfect disk. Length: 500-1,000 words. Pays negotiable rate.

Fillers: Clippings, jokes, gags, anecdotes, short humor and newsbreaks. Cartoon ideas will be drawn by our artists. Length: 50-200 words. Pays $10 minimum.

Tips: "Freelancers can best break into our publication by submitting news, features, and accounts of unusual or bizarre legal events. A frequent mistake made by writers is forgetting that our audience is intelligent and learned in law. They don't need the word 'plaintiff' explained to them." No unsolicited mss returned without SASE (or IRC to U.S. destinations).

LEGAL ECONOMICS, The Magazine of Law Office Management, A magazine of the section of Economics of Law Practice of the American Bar Association, Box 11418, Columbia SC 29211. Managing Editor/Art Director: Delmar L. Roberts. 10% freelance written. For the practicing lawyer and legal administrator. Magazine published 8 times/year. Circ. 24,168 (BPA). Rights purchased vary with author and material. Usually buys all rights. Byline given. Pays on publication. Publishes ms an average of 8 months after acceptance. Computer printout submissions acceptable. Query. Free writer's guidelines; sample copy $7 (make check payable to American Bar Association). Returns rejected material in 90 days, if requested.

Nonfiction: "We assist the practicing lawyer in operating and managing his or her office by providing relevant articles and departments written in a readable and informative style. Editorial content is intended to aid the lawyer by conveying management methods that will allow him or her to provide legal services to clients in a prompt and efficient manner at reasonable cost. Typical topics of articles include fees and billing; client/lawyer relations; computer hardware/software; mergers; retirement/disability; marketing; compensation of partners and associates; legal data base research; and use of paralegals." No elementary articles on a whole field of technology, such as, "why you need word processing in the law office." Pays $75-300.
Photos: Pays $30-60 for b&w photos purchased with mss; $50-75 for color; $100-125 for cover transparencies.
Tips: "We have a theme for each issue with two to three articles relating to the theme. We also publish thematic issues occasionally in which an entire issue is devoted to a single topic, primarily in the area of new office technology."

‡LOS ANGELES LAWYER, Los Angeles County Bar Association, Box 55020, Los Angeles CA 90055. (213)627-2727, ext. 265. Editor: Susan Pettit. 100% freelance written. Prefers to work with published/established writers. Monthly (except for combined July/August issue) magazine covering legal profession with "journalistic and scholarly articles of interest to the legal profession." Circ. 25,000. Pays on acceptance. Publishes ms an average of 2 months after acceptance. Byline given. Buys first serial rights only. Submit seasonal/holiday material 4 months in advance. Simultaneous queries and photocopied submissions OK. Query for electronic submissions. Computer printout submissions acceptable; prefers letter-quality to dot-matrix. Reports in 1 month on queries; 2 months on mss. Sample copy $1.50; free writer's guidelines.
Nonfiction: How-to (tips for legal practitioners); interview (leading legal figures); opinion (on area of law, lawyer attitudes or group, court decisions, etc.); travel (very occasionally); and consumer-at-law feature articles on topics of interest to lawyers. No first person, nonlegal material. Buys 22 mss/year. Query with published clips. Length: 3,000-4,000 words for feature (cover story); 1,500-2,500 words for consumer article. Pays $500-600 for cover story, $225-300 for consumer article. Sometimes pays the expenses of writers on assignment.
Tips: "Writers should be familiar with the Los Angeles legal community as the magazine has a local focus."

THE PARALEGAL, The Publication for the Paralegal Profession, Paralegal Publishing Corp./National Paralegal Association, Box 406, Solebury PA 18963. (215)297-8333. FAX: (215)297-8358. Editor: William Cameron. 90% freelance written. Works with published/established writers; works with a number of new/unpublished writers each year; eager to work with new/unpublished writers. Bimonthly magazine covering the paralegal profession for practicing paralegals, attorneys, paralegal educators, paralegal associations, law librarians and court personnel. Special and controlled circulation includes law libraries, colleges and schools educating paralegals, law schools, law firms and governmental agencies, etc. Circ. 22,000. Byline given. Buys all or limited rights. Simultaneous queries, and simultaneous, photocopied and previously published submissions OK. Computer printout submissions acceptable; no dot-matrix. Reports in 2 weeks on queries; 1 month on mss. Writer's guidelines and suggested topic sheet for #10 SASE.
Nonfiction: Book excerpts, exposé, general interest, historical/nostalgic, how-to, humor, interview/profile, new product, opinion, personal experience, photo feature, technical and travel. Suggested topics include the paralegal (where do they fit and how do they operate within the law firm in each specialty); the government; the corporation; the trade union; the banking institution; the law library; the legal clinic; the trade or professional association; the educational institution; the court system; the collection agency; the stock brokerage firm; and the insurance company. Articles also wanted on paralegals exploring "Where have they been? Where are they now? Where are they going?" Query or send complete ms. Length: 1,500-3,000 words. Pays variable rates; submissions should state desired fee. Ask amount when submitting ms or other material to be considered. Sometimes pays the expenses of writers on assignment.
Photos: Send photos with query or ms. Captions, model release, and identification of subjects required.
Columns/Departments: Case at Issue (a feature on a current case from a state or federal court which either directly or indirectly affects paralegals and their work with attorneys, the public, private or governmental sector); Humor (cartoons, quips, short humorous stories, anecdotes and one-liners in good taste and germane to the legal profession); and My Position (an actual presentation by a paralegal who wishes to share with others his/her job analysis). Query. Submissions should state desired fee.
Fillers: Clippings, jokes, gags, anecdotes, short humor and newsbreaks.

THE PENNSYLVANIA LAWYER, Pennsylvania Bar Association, 100 South St., Box 186, Harrisburg PA 17108. (717)238-6715. Managing Editor: Donald C. Sarvey. Associate Editor: Marcy Carey Mallory. 25% freelance written. Prefers to work with published/established writers. Magazine published 8 times/year as a service to the legal profession. Circ. 27,000. Pays on acceptance. Publishes ms an average of 3-6 months after acceptance. Byline given. Buys negotiable serial rights; generally first rights, occasionally one-time rights or second serial (reprint) rights. Submit seasonal/holiday material 6 months in advance. Simultaneous submissions are discouraged. Computer printout and disk submissions acceptable; prefers letter-quality. Reports in 4-6 weeks. Free sample copy and writer's guidelines.

Nonfiction: General interest, how-to, humor, interview/profile, new product, and personal experience. All features *must* relate in some way to Pennsylvania lawyers or the practice of law in Pennsylvania. Buys 10-12 mss/year. Query. Length: 600-1,500 words. Pays $75-350. Sometimes pays the expenses of writers on assignment.

STUDENT LAWYER, American Bar Association, 750 N. Lake Shore Dr., Chicago IL 60611. (312)988-6048. Editor: Sarah Hoban. Managing Editor: Miriam R. Krasno. 95% freelance written. Works with a small number of new/unpublished writers each year. Monthly (September-May) magazine. Circ. 40,000. Pays on publication. Buys first serial rights and second serial (reprint) rights. Pays negotiable kill fee. Byline given. Submit seasonal/holiday material 4 months in advance. Photocopied submissions OK. Computer printout submissions acceptable; prefers letter-quality. Reports in 6 weeks. Publishes ms an average of 3 months after acceptance. Sample copy $3; free writer's guidelines.

Nonfiction: Exposé (government, law, education and business); profiles (prominent persons in law-related fields); opinion (on matters of current legal interest); essays (on legal affairs); interviews; and photo features. Recent article examples: "Caught on Death Row" (January 1988) and "The Wrongs of Legal Writing" (October 1987). Buys 5 mss/issue. Query. Length: 3,000-5,000 words. Pays $250-600 for main features. Covers some writer's expenses.

Columns/Departments: Briefly (short stories on unusual and interesting developments in the law); Legal Aids (unusual approaches and programs connected to teaching law students and lawyers); Esq. (brief profiles of people in the law); End Note (short pieces on a variety of topics; can be humorous, educational, outrageous); Pro Se (opinion slot for authors to wax eloquent on legal issues, civil rights conflicts, the state of the union); and Et Al. (column for short features that fit none of the above categories). Buys 4-8 mss/issue. Length: 250-1,000 words. Pays $75-250.

Fiction: "We buy fiction only when it is very good and deals with issues of law in the contemporary world or offers insights into the inner workings of lawyers. No mystery or science fiction accepted."

Tips: "*Student Lawyer* actively seeks good new writers. Legal training definitely not essential; writing talent is. The writer should not think we are a law review; we are a feature magazine with the law (in the broadest sense) as the common denominator. Past articles concerned gay rights, prison reform, the media, pornography, capital punishment, and space law. Find issues of national scope and interest to write about; be aware of subjects the magazine — and other media — have already covered and propose something new. Write clearly and well."

_____ *Leather Goods*

NSRA NEWS, National Shoe Retailers Association, Suite 400, 9861 Broken Land Pkwy., Columbia MD 21046. (301)381-8282. FAX: (301)381-1167. Editor: Cynthia Emmel. 10% freelance written. Bimonthly newsletter covering footwear/accessory industry. Looks for articles that are "informative, educational, but with wit, interest, and creativity. I hate dry, dusty articles." Circ. 4,000-5,000. Byline given. Buys one-time rights. Submit seasonal/holiday material 3 months in advance. Photocopied submissions OK. Computer printout submissions OK; no dot-matrix. Reports in 2 weeks. Free sample copy and writer's guidelines.

Nonfiction: How-to, interview/profile, new product and technical. January and July are shoe show issues. Buys 4 mss/year. Length: 450 words. Pays $125 for assigned articles. Pays up to $175 for "full-fledged research — 1,000 words or more on assigned articles.

Photos: State availability of photos with submission. Offers no additional payment for photos accepted with ms. Buys one-time rights.

Columns/Departments: Query. Pays $50-125.

Tips: "We are a trade magazine/newsletter for the footwear industry. Any information pertaining to our market is helpful: ex. advertising/display/how-tos."

‡**SHOE SERVICE**, SSIA Service Corp., 5024 Campbell Blvd., Baltimore MD 21236. (301)256-8100. FAX: (301)529-4612. Editor: Mitchell Lebovic. 50% freelance written. "We want well-written articles, whether they come from new or established writers." Monthly magazine for business people who own and operate small shoe repair shops. Circ. 17,000. Pays on publication. Publishes ms an average of 3 months after acceptance. Byline given. Buys first serial rights, first North American serial rights, and one-time rights. Submit seasonal/holiday material 3 months in advance. Simultaneous queries, and photocopied and previously published submissions OK. Computer printout submissions acceptable; prefers letter-quality to dot-matrix. Reports in 6 weeks. Sample copy $2 and 9x12 SAE; free writer's guidelines.

Nonfiction: How-to (run a profitable shop); interview/profile (of an outstanding or unusual person on shoe repair); and business articles (particularly about small business practices in a service/retail shop). Buys 12-24 mss/year. Query with published clips or send complete ms. Length: 500-2,000 words. Pays 5¢/word.

Photos: "Quality photos will help sell an article." State availability of photos. Pays $10-30 for 8x10 b&w prints. Uses some color photos, but mostly uses b&w glossies. Captions, model release, and identification of subjects required.

Tips: "Visit some shoe repair shops to get an idea of the kind of person who reads *Shoe Service*. Profiles are the easiest to sell to us if you can find a repairer we think is unusual."

Library Science

Librarians read these journals for advice on promotion and management of libraries, library and book trade issues and information access and transfer. Be aware of current issues such as censorship, declines in funding and government information policies. For journals on the book trade see Book and Bookstore.

AMERICAN LIBRARIES, 50 E. Huron St., Chicago IL 60611. (312)944-6780. Editor: Arthur Plotnik. 5-10% freelance written. Works with a small number of new/unpublished writers each year. Magazine published 11 times/year for librarians. "A highly literate audience. They are for the most part practicing professionals with a down-to-earth interest in people and current trends." Circ. 48,000. Buys first North American serial rights. Publishes ms an average of 4 months after acceptance. Pays negotiable kill fee. Byline given. Will consider photocopied submissions if not being considered elsewhere at time of submission. Computer printout submissions acceptable; prefers letter-quality. Submit seasonal material 6 months in advance. Reports in 10 weeks.

Nonfiction: "Material reflecting the special and current interests of the library profession. Nonlibrarians should browse recent journals in the field, available on request in medium-sized and large libraries everywhere. Topic and/or approach must be fresh, vital or highly entertaining. Library memoirs and stereotyped stories about old maids, overdue books, fines, etc., are unacceptable. Our first concern is with the American Library Association's activities and how they relate to the 46,000 reader/members. Tough for an outsider to write on this topic, but not to supplement it with short, offbeat or significant library stories and features." No fillers. Buys 2-6 freelance mss/year. Pays $15 for news tips used, and $25-300 for briefs and articles.

Photos: "Will look at color transparencies and bright color prints for inside and cover use." Pays $50-200 for photos.

Tips: "You can break in with a sparkling, 300-word report on a true, offbeat library event, use of new technology, or with an exciting color photo and caption. Though stories on public libraries are always of interest, we especially need arresting material on academic and school libraries."

CHURCH MEDIA LIBRARY MAGAZINE, 127 9th Ave. N., Nashville TN 37234. (615)251-2752. Editor: Floyd B. Simpson. Quarterly magazine. For adult leaders in church organizations and people interested in library work (especially church library work). Circ. 16,000. Pays on publication. Buys all rights, first serial rights and second serial (reprint) rights. Byline given. Phone queries OK. Submit seasonal/holiday material 14 months in advance. Previously published submissions OK. Reports in 1 month. Free sample copy and writer's guidelines.

Nonfiction: "We are primarily interested in articles that relate to the development of church libraries in providing media and services to support the total program of a church and in meeting individual needs. We publish how-to accounts of services provided, promotional ideas, exciting things that have happened as a result of implementing an idea or service; human interest stories that are library-related; and media training (teaching and learning with a media mix). Articles should be practical for church library staffs and for teachers and other leaders of the church." Buys 10-15 mss/issue. Query. Pays 5¢/word.

EMERGENCY LIBRARIAN, Dyad Services, Box 46258, Stn. G, Vancouver, British Columbia V6R 4G6 Canada. Editor: Ken Haycock. Publishes 5 issues/year. Circ. 5,500. Pays on publication. Photocopied submissions OK. No multiple submissions. Reports in 6 weeks. Free writer's guidelines.

Nonfiction: Emphasis is on improvement of library service for children and young adults in school and public libraries. Also annotated bibliographies. Buys 3 mss/issue. Query. Length: 1,000-3,500 words. Pays $50.

Columns/Departments: Five regular columnists. Also Book Reviews (of professional materials in education, librarianship). Query. Length: 100-300 words. Payment consists of book reviewed.

THE LIBRARY IMAGINATION PAPER, Carol Bryan Imagines, 1000 Byus Dr., Charleston WV 25311. (304)345-2378. 30% freelance written. Quarterly newspaper covering public relations education for librarians, clip art included in each issue. Circ. 3,000. Pays on publication. Publishes ms an average of 6 months after acceptance.

Byline given. Buys one-time rights. Submit seasonal/holiday material 3 months in advance. Simultaneous, photocopied and previously published submissions OK. Computer printout submissions OK; prefers letter-quality. Reports in 6 weeks on queries; 3 weeks on mss. Sample copy $5; writer's guidelines for SASE.

Nonfiction: How-to (on "all aspects of good library public relations both mental tips and hands-on methods. We need how-to and tips pieces on all aspects of PR, for library subscribers—both school and public libraries. In the past we've featured pieces on taking good photos, promoting an anniversary celebration, working with printers, and producing a slide show.") No articles on "what the library means to me." Buys 4-6 mss/year. Query with or without published clips, or send complete ms. Length: 500-2,200 words. Pays $35.

Photos: Send photos with submission. Reviews 5x7 prints. Offers $5 per photo. Captions required. Buys one-time rights.

Tips: "Someone who has worked in the library field and has first-hand knowledge of library PR needs, methods and processes will do far better with us. Our readers are people who cannot be written down to—but their library training has not always incorporated enough preparation for handling promotion, publicity and the public."

LIBRARY JOURNAL, 249 W. 17th St., New York NY 10011. Editor-in-Chief: John N. Berry III. 60% freelance written by librarians. Eager to work with new/unpublished writers. For librarians (academic, public, special). Magazine published 20 times/year. Circ. 30,000. Buys all rights. Pays on publication. Publishes ms an average of 12-18 months after acceptance. Computer printout submissions OK; prefers letter-quality. "Our response time is slow, but improving."

Nonfiction: *"Library Journal* is a professional magazine for librarians. Freelancers are most often rejected because they are not librarians or they submit one of the following types of article: 'A wonderful, warm, concerned, loving librarian who started me on the road to good reading and success'; 'How I became rich, famous, and successful by using my public library'; 'Libraries are the most wonderful and important institutions in our society, because they have all of the knowledge of mankind—praise them.' We need material of greater sophistication, government information, dealing with issues related to the transfer of information, access to it, or related phenomena. (Current hot are copyright, censorship, the decline in funding for public institutions, the local politics of libraries, trusteeship, U.S. government information policy, etc.)" Professional articles on criticism, censorship, professional concerns, library activities, historical articles, information technology, automation and management, and spot news. Outlook should be from librarian's point of view. Buys 50-65 unsolicited mss/year. Submit complete ms. Length: 1,500-2,000 words. Pays $50-350. Sometimes pays the expenses of writers on assignment.

Photos: Payment for b&w or color glossy photos purchased without accompanying mss is $35. Must be at least 5x7. Captions required.

Tips: "We're increasingly interested in material on library management, public sector fundraising, and information policy."

THE NEW LIBRARY SCENE, Library Binding Institute, 8013 Centre Park Dr., Austin TX 78754. (512)836-4141. FAX: (512)836-4849. 50% freelance written. A bimonthly magazine on library book binding and conservation. Circ. 3,000. Pays on acceptance. Publishes ms an average of 2 months after acceptance. Byline given. Buys first North American serial rights. Computer printout submissions OK; prefers letter-quality. Reports in 1 month on queries. Sample copy for 9x12 SAE and 85¢ postage and writer's guidelines for #10 SASE.

Nonfiction: How-to (libraries, book binding, conservation), interview/profile and technical. Buys 6-10 mss/year. Query. Pays $100.

Photos: State availability of photos with submission. Reviews contact sheets and prints (3x5 or 5x7). Offers no additional payment for photos accepted with ms. Identification of subjects required. Buys one-time rights.

‡WILSON LIBRARY BULLETIN, 950 University Ave., Bronx NY 10452. (212)588-8400. FAX: (212)538-2716. Editor: Mary Jo Godwin. 80% freelance written. Monthly (September-June) for professional librarians and those interested in the book and library worlds. Circ. 30,000. Pays on publication. Publishes ms an average of 2 months after acceptance. Buys first North American serial rights. Sample copies may be seen on request in most libraries. "Manuscript must be original copy, double-spaced; additional photocopy or carbon is appreciated." Computer printout submissions acceptable; prefers letter-quality to dot-matrix. Deadlines are a minimum 2 months before publication. Reports in 3 months. Free sample copy and writer's guidelines.

Nonfiction: Uses articles "of interest to librarians and information professionals throughout the nation and around the world. Style must be lively, readable and sophisticated, with appeal to modern professionals; facts must be thoroughly researched. Subjects range from the political to the comic in the world of media and libraries, with an emphasis on the human as well as the technical aspects of any story. No condescension: no library stereotypes." Buys 30 mss/year. Send complete ms. Length: 2,500-6,000 words. Pays about $100-400, "depending on the substance of article and its importance to readers." Sometimes pays the expenses of writers on assignment.

Tips: "The best way you can break in is with a first-rate black and white or color photo and caption information on a library, library service or librarian who departs completely from all stereotypes and the commonplace. Libraries have changed. You'd better first discover what is now commonplace."

Lumber

‡**CANADIAN FOREST INDUSTRIES WEST**, Southam Communications Ltd., 4285 Canada Way, Burnaby, British Columbia V5G 1H2 Canada. (604)433-6125. Editor: Paul MacDonald. 10% freelance written. Monthly magazine. "*Canadian Forest Industries West* covers all facets of the logging and sawmilling sectors of the forest industry." Circ. 22,000. Pays on acceptance. Byline given. Buys first rights. Previously published submissions OK. Computer printout submissions OK. Reports in 6 weeks on queries; 1 month on mss. Free writer's guidelines.
Nonfiction: Humor, interview/profile, new product and technical. "We do not want fiction." Buys 6 mss/year. Query with published clips. Length: 800-1,500 words. Payment varies. Sometimes pays expenses of writers on assignment.
Photos: State availability of photos with submission. Reviews transparencies. Payment varies. Buys one-time rights.

NORTHERN LOGGER AND TIMBER PROCESSOR, Northeastern Loggers' Association, Box 69, Old Forge NY 13420. (315)369-3078. FAX: (315)369-3736. Editor: Eric A. Johnson. 40% freelance written. Monthly magazine of the forest industry in the northern U.S. (Maine to Minnesota and south to Virginia and Missouri). "We are not a purely technical journal, but are more information oriented." Circ. 13,600. Pays on publication. Publishes ms an average of 3 months after acceptance. Byline given. Buys all rights. Submit seasonal/holiday material 3 months in advance. Photocopied and previously published submissions OK. "Any computer print-out submission that can be easily read is acceptable." Reports in 2 weeks. Free sample copy and writer's guidelines.
Nonfiction: Expose, general interest, historical/nostalgic, how-to, interview/profile, new product and opinion. "We only buy feature articles, and those should contain some technical or historical material relating to the forest products industry." Buys 12-15 mss/year. Query. Length: 500-2,500 words. Pays $50-250.
Photos: Send photos with ms. Pays $35 for 35mm color transparencies; $15 for 5x7 b&w prints. Captions and identification of subjects required.
Tips: "We accept most any subject dealing with this part of the country's forest industry, from historical to logging, firewood, and timber processing."

‡**SILVICULTURE, Journal of the New Forest**, Maclean Hunter Ltd., Maclean Hunter Bldg., 777 Bay St., Toronto, Ontario M5W 1A7 Canada. (416)596-5868. FAX: (416)593-3193. Editor: Scott Olson. 50% freelance written. Bimonthly magazine that covers reforestation and forest management. "*Silviculture* covers proper forest management techniques from a *business* point of view; forestry and environment protection are complementary; proper forest management will ensure trees for tomorrow." Circ. 13,000. Pays on acceptance. Byline given. Offers $50 kill fee. Buys first North American serial rights. Query for electronic submissions. Computer printout submissions OK; prefers letter-quality. Free sample copy and writer's guidelines.
Nonfiction: How-to (plant, brush, slash-burn, scarify), interview/profile and technical. Buys 10 mss/year. Query with published clips, or send complete ms. Length: 800-3,000 words. Pays $150-400 Canadian for assigned articles. Sometimes pays expenses of writers on assignment.
Photos: Send photos with submission. Reviews 5x7 prints. Captions and identification of subjects required. Buys one-time rights.

SOUTHERN LUMBERMAN, Greysmith Publishing, Inc., Suite 116, 128 Holiday Ct., Franklin TN 37064. (615)791-1961. FAX: (615)790-6188. Editor: Nanci P. Gregg. 20-30% freelance written. Works with a small number of new/unpublished writers each year. A monthly trade journal for the lumber industry. Circ. 12,000. Pays on publication. Publishes ms an average of 3 months after acceptance. Byline given. Not copyrighted. Buys all rights. Submit seasonal/holiday material 6 months in advance. Query for electronic submissions. Computer printout submissions OK; prefers letter-quality. Reports in 1 month on queries; 2 months on mss. Sample copy $1 with 9x12 SAE and 5 first class stamps; writer's guidelines for #10 SASE.
Nonfiction: Exposé, historical, interview/profile, new product, technical. Buys 20-30 mss/year. Query with or without published clips, or send complete ms. Length: 500-2,000 words. Pays $150-350 for assigned articles; pays $150-250 for unsolicited articles. Sometimes pays the expenses of writers on assignment.
Photos: Send photos with submission. Reviews transparencies and 4x5 b&w prints. Offers $10-25 per photo. Captions and identification of subjects required.
Tips: "Like most, we appreciate a clearly-worded query listing merits of suggested story—what it will tell our readers they need/want to know. We want quotes, we want opinions to make others discuss the article. Best hint? Find an interesting sawmill operation owner and start asking questions—I bet a story idea develops. We need b&w photos too. Most open is what we call the Sweethart Mill stories. We publish at least one per month, and hope to be printing two or more monthly in the immediate future. Find a sawmill operator and

ask questions—what's he doing bigger, better, different. We're interested in new facilities, better marketing, improved production."

Machinery and Metal

‡**AUTOMATIC MACHINING**, 100 Seneca Ave., Rochester NY 14621. (716)338-1522. Editor: Donald E. Wood. For metalworking technical management. Buys all rights. Byline given. Computer printout submissions acceptable.
Nonfiction: "This is not a market for the average freelancer. A personal knowledge of the trade is essential. Articles deal in depth with specific job operations on automatic screw machines, chucking machines, high production metal turning lathes and cold heading machines. Part prints, tooling layouts always required, plus written agreement of source to publish the material. Without personal background in operation of this type of equipment, freelancers are wasting time. No material researched from library sources." Query. Length: no limit. Pays $20/printed page.
Tips: "In the year ahead there will be more emphasis on plant and people news so less space will be available for conventional articles."

CANADIAN MACHINERY & METALWORKING, 777 Bay St., Toronto, Ontario M5W 1A7 Canada. (416)596-5714. Editor: James Barnes. 10% freelance written. Monthly. Buys first North American rights. Pays on acceptance. Query. Publishes ms an average of 6 weeks after acceptance.
Nonfiction: Technical and semi-technical articles dealing with metalworking operations in Canada and in the U.S., if of particular interest to Canadian readers. Accuracy and service appeal to readers is a must. Pays minimum 30¢ (Canadian)/word.
Photos: Purchased with mss and with captions only. Pays $10 minimum for b&w features.

MODERN MACHINE SHOP, 6600 Clough Pike, Cincinnati OH 45244. Editor: Ken Gettelman. 25% freelance written. Monthly. Pays 1 month following acceptance. Publishes ms an average of 6 months after acceptance. Byline given. Query for electronic submissions. Computer printout submissions acceptable; prefers letter-quality. Reports in 5 days. Writer's guidelines for #10 SASE.
Nonfiction: Uses articles dealing with all phases of metal working, manufacturing and machine shop work, with photos. No general articles. "Ours is an industrial publication, and contributing authors should have a working knowledge of the metalworking industry." Buys 10 unsolicited mss/year. Query. Length: 1,000-3,500 words. Pays current market rate. Sometimes pays the expenses of writers on assignment.
Tips: "The use of articles relating to computers in manufacturing is growing."

Maintenance and Safety

BUILDING SERVICES CONTRACTOR, MacNair Publications Inc., 101 W. 31st St., New York NY 10001. (212)279-4455. Editor: Frank C. Falcetta. 0-5% freelance written. Bimonthly magazine covering building services and maintenance. Circ. 8,000. Pays on publication. Publishes ms an average of 2-4 months after acceptance. Byline sometimes given. Buys one-time rights and second serial (reprint) rights. Simultaneous, photocopied and previously published submissions OK "as long as not published in competitive magazine." Computer printout submissions OK; prefers letter-quality. Reports in 2 weeks. Writer's guidelines for #10 SASE.

Nonfiction: How-to, humor, interview/profile, new product and technical. Buys 1-5 mss/year. Query only. Pays $75 minimum.
Photos: State availability of photos with submission. Reviews contact sheets. Offers no additional payment for photos accepted with ms, but "offers higher payment when photos are used." Buys one-time rights.
Tips: "I'd love to do more with freelance, but market and budget make it tough. I do most of it myself."

CLEANING MANAGEMENT, The Magazine for Today's Building Maintenance Housekeeping Executive, Harris Communications, 15550-D Rockfield Blvd., Irvine CA 92718. (714)770-5008. Editor: R. Daniel Harris Jr. Monthly magazine covering building maintenance/housekeeping operations in large institutions such as hotels, schools, hospitals, etc., as well as commercial and industrial, recreational and religious buildings, stores and markets. For managers with on-staff cleaning operations, contract cleaning service companies, and professional carpet cleaning companies. Circ. 42,000. Pays on publication. Byline given. Offers "full payment, if article has been completed." Buys all rights. Submit seasonal/holiday material 3 months in advance. Simultaneous queries and photocopied submissions OK. Reports in 1 month. Free sample copy and writer's guidelines.
Nonfiction: How-to (custodial operations); interview/profile (of custodial managers); opinion (of custodial managers); personal experience (on-the-job). Special issues include: March—Carpet Care; April and June—Floor Care; May—Exterior Building Maintenance; September—Office Cleaning. Buys 5-6 mss/year. Query. Length: 1,000-2,000 words. Pays $100-300.
Photos: State availability of photos. Pays $5-15 for 8x10 b&w prints; $20-75 for 4x5 color transparencies. Captions, model release, and identification of subjects required.
Tips: "We want writers familiar with our field or who can pick it up quickly."

MAINTENANCE SUPPLIES, MacNair Publishing, 101 West 31st St., New York NY 10001. (212)279-4455. Editor: Dominic Mariana. 20% freelance written. A monthly magazine on maintenance/sanitary supplies and equipment., "Articles should be geared to the distributors of janitorial supplies." Circ. 15,000. Pays on publication. Publishes ms an average of 2 months after acceptance. Byline given. Publication not copyrighted. Buys one-time rights. Submit seasonal/holiday material 2 months in advance. Photocopied and previously published submissions OK. Computer printout submissions OK; letter-quality preferred. Reports in 1 week. Sample copy for 8x11 SAE with 2 first class stamps. Free writer's guidelines for #10 SASE.
Nonfiction: Essays, how-to (sell products to distributors), interview/profile, new product, technical. Buys 15 mss/year. Send complete ms. Length: 1,000-5,000 words. Pays $150-200. Sometimes pays expenses of writers on assignment.
Photos: Send photos with submission. Reviews contact sheets, transparencies and prints. Offers no additional payment for photos accepted with ms. Captions and identification of subjects required. Buys one-time rights.

PEST CONTROL MAGAZINE, 7500 Old Oak Blvd., Cleveland OH 44130. (216)243-8100. Editor: Jerry Mix. For professional pest control operators and sanitation workers. Monthly magazine. Circ. 15,000. Buys all rights. Buys 12 mss/year. Pays on publication. Submit seasonal material 2 months in advance. Reports in 1 month. Query or submit complete ms.
Nonfiction: Business tips, unique control situations, personal experience (stories about 1-man operations and their problems) articles. Must have trade or business orientation. No general information type of articles desired. Buys 3 unsolicited mss/year. Length: 4 double-spaced pages. Pays $150 minimum. Regular columns use material oriented to this profession. Length: 8 double-spaced pages.
Photos: No additional payment for photos used with mss. Pays $50-150 for 8x10 color or transparencies.

‡SAFETY COMPLIANCE LETTER, with OSHA Highlights, Bureau of Business Practice, 24 Rope Ferry Rd., Waterford CT 06386. (203)442-4365. Editor: Margot Loomis. Managing Editor: Wayne Muller. 80% freelance written. Bimonthly newsletter covering occupational safety and health. Publishes interview-based 'how-to' and 'success' stories for personnel in charge of safety and health in manufacturing/industrial environments. Circ. 8,000. Pays on acceptance after editing. Publishes ms an average of 3-6 months after acceptance. No byline given. Offers 50% kill fee. Buys all rights. Submit seasonal/holiday material 4 months in advance. Reports in 1 week on queries; 1 month on mss. Free sample copy and writer's guidelines.
Nonfiction: How-to (implement an occupational safety/health program), changes in OSHA regulations and examples of safety/health programs. No articles that aren't based on an interview. Buys 24 mss/year. Query. Length: 750-1,200 words. Pays 10¢-15¢/word. Sometimes pays the expenses of writers on assignment.

Market conditions are constantly changing! If this is 1991 or later, buy the newest edition of Writer's Market at your favorite bookstore or order directly from Writer's Digest Books.

SERVICE BUSINESS, Published Quarterly for the Self-Employed Professional Cleaner, Suite 345, 1916 Pike Place, Seattle WA 98101. (206)622-4241. Publisher: William R. Griffin. Editor: Martha Ireland. Associate Editor: Jim Saunders. 80% freelance written. Quarterly magazine covering technical and management information relating to cleaning and self-employment. "We cater to those who are self-employed in any facet of the cleaning and maintenance industry who seek to be top professionals in their field. Our readership is small but select. We seek concise, factual articles, realistic but definitely upbeat." Circ. 6,000. Pays 1 month after publication. Publishes ms an average of 3 months after acceptance. Byline given. Buys first serial rights, second serial (reprint) rights, and all rights; makes work-for-hire assignments. Submit seasonal/holiday material 4 months in advance. Simultaneous queries and previously published work (rarely) OK. Computer printout submissions acceptable; prefers letter-quality. Reports in 3 months. Sample copy $3, 9x7½ SAE and 3 first class stamps; writer's guidelines for #10 SASE.

Nonfiction: Exposé (safety/health business practices); how-to (on cleaning, maintenance, small business management); humor (clean jokes, cartoons); interview/profile; new product (must be unusual to rate full article—mostly obtained from manufacturers); opinion; personal experience; and technical. Special issues include "What's New?" (Feb. 10). No "wordy articles written off the top of the head, obviously without research, and needing more editing time than was spent on writing." Buys 40 mss/year. Query with or without published clips. Length: 500-3,000 words. Pays $5-80. ("Pay depends on amount of work, research and polishing put into article much more than on length.") Pays expenses of writers on assignment with prior approval only.

Photos: State availability of photos or send photos with ms. Pays $5-25 for "smallish" b&w prints. Captions, model release, and identification of subjects required. Buys one-time rights and reprint rights. "Magazine size is 8½x7—photos need to be proportionate."

Columns/Departments: "Ten regular columnists now sell four columns per year to us. We are interested in adding a Safety & Health column (related to cleaning and maintenance industry). We are also open to other suggestions—send query." Buys 36 columns/year; department information obtained at no cost. Query with or without published clips. Length: 500-1,500 words. Pays $15-85.

Fillers: Jokes, gags, anecdotes, short humor, newsbreaks and cartoons. Buys 40/year. Length: 3-200 words. Pays $1-20.

Tips: "We are constantly seeking quality freelancers from all parts of the country. A freelancer can best break in to our publication with fairly technical articles on how to do specific cleaning/maintenance jobs; interviews with top professionals covering this and how they manage their business; and personal experience. Our readers demand concise, accurate information. Don't ramble. Write only about what you know and/or have researched. Editors don't have time to rewrite your rough draft. Organize and polish before submitting."

Management and Supervision

This category includes trade journals for middle management business and industrial managers, including supervisors and office managers. Journals for business executives and owners are classified under Business Management. Those for industrial plant managers are listed in Industrial Operations.

DATA TRAINING, Weingarten Publications, Inc. 38 Chauncy St., Boston MA 02111. (617)542-0146. Editor: Douglas W. Roberts. 50% freelance written. A monthly magazine on computer training and training management. "*Data Training* is aimed at people who teach other people how to use computers. We try to help our readers advance in their profession by including information on management and business." Circ. 20,000. Pays on acceptance. Publishes ms an average of 3 months after acceptance. Byline given. Query for electronic submissions. Computer printout submissions OK. Free sample copy; writer's guidelines for #10 SASE.

Nonfiction: How-to, interview/profile, opinion, technical. Buys 24 mss/year. Query with or without published clips or send complete ms. Length: 500-5,000 words. Pays $100-600. Sometimes pays expenses of writers on assignment.

Photos: State availability of photos with submission.

Tips: "Writers should be familiar with computers and/or training. A knowledge of our publication would help. Writers should keep in mind that *Data Training* is a business publication and our readers appreciate clear, concise writing on well-defined topics. We will help writers find sources and shape topics if they have the business background and training familiarity."

EMPLOYEE RELATIONS AND HUMAN RESOURCES BULLETIN, Bureau of Business Practice, 24 Rope Ferry Rd., Waterford CT 06386. Senior Editor: Barbara Kelsey. 75% freelance written. Works with a small number of new/unpublished writers each year. For personnel, human resources and employee relations managers on the executive level. Semimonthly newsletter. Circ. 5,500. Pays on acceptance. Publishes ms an average of 3 months after acceptance. Buys all rights. No byline. Phone queries OK. Submit seasonal/holiday material 6 months in advance. Photocopied submissions OK. Computer printout submissions acceptable; prefers letter-quality. Reports in 1 month. Free sample copy and writer's guidelines.

Nonfiction: Interviews about all types of business and industry such as banks, insurance companies, public utilities, airlines, consulting firms, etc. Interviewee should be a high level company officer — general manager, president, industrial relations manager, etc. Writer must get signed release from person interviewed showing that article has been read and approved by him/her, before submission. Some subjects for interviews might be productivity improvement, communications, compensation, labor relations, safety and health, grievance handling, human relations techniques and problems, etc. No general opinions and/or philosophy of good employee relations or general good motivation/morale material. Buys 3 mss/issue. Query. Length: 1,500-2,000 words. Pays 10-15¢/word after editing. Sometimes pays the expenses of writers on assignment.

HUMAN RESOURCE EXECUTIVE, Axon Group, 1035 Camphill Rd., Ft. Washington PA 19034. (215)540-1180. Editor: David Shadovitz. 15% freelance written. A monthly magazine for human resource professionals/executives. "The magazine serves the information needs of chief human resource executives in companies, government agencies and nonprofit institutions with 500 or more employees." Estab. 1987. Circ. 40,000. Pays on acceptance. Publishes ms an average of 2 months after acceptance. Byline given. Offers 50% kill fee. Buys first rights and second serial (reprint) rights. Query for electronic submissions. Computer printout submissions OK; prefers letter-quality. Reports in 1 month. Sample copy for 13x10 SAE with 2 first class stamps. Writer's guidelines for #10 SAE with 1 first class stamp.

Nonfiction: Book excerpts, interview/profile. Buys 16 mss/year. Query with published clips. Length: 1,700-2,400 words. Pays $200-700. Sometimes pays expenses of writers on assignment.

Photos: State availability of photos with submission. Reviews contact sheets. Offers no additional payment for photos accepted with ms. Identification of subjects required. Buys first and repeat rights.

‡INDUSTRY WEEK, "The industry management magazine," Penton Publishing Inc., 1100 Superior Ave., Cleveland OH 44114. (216)696-7000. Editor: Perry Pascarella. Mangaging Editor: Charles R. Day, Jr. 8-10% freelance written. Industrial management magazine published on the first and third Monday of each month. "*Industry Week* is designed to help its audience — mid- and upper-level managers in industry — manage and lead their organizations better. Every article should address this editorial mission." Circ. 300,200. Pays on acceptance. Publishes ms an average of 2-4 months after acceptance. Byline given. Buys first North American serial rights. Computer printout submissions OK; prefers letter-quality. Free sample copy and writer's guidelines. "An SAE speeds replies."

Nonfiction: Interview/profile. "Any article submitted to *Industry Week* should be consistent with its mission. We suggested authors contacting us before submitting anything." Buys 10-15 mss/year. Query with or without published clips, or send complete ms. Length: 750-2,500 words. Pays $350 minimum. "We pay *routine* expenses; we do *not* pay for travel unless arranged in advance."

Photos: State availability of photos with submission. Send photo with submission. Reviews contact sheets, transparencies and prints. Payment arranged individually. Captions and identification of subjects required. Buys one-time rights.

Tips: "Become familiar with *Industry Week*. We're after articles about managing in industry, period. While we do not use freelancers too often, we do use some. The stories we accept are written with an understanding of our audience, and mission. We prefer multi-source stories that offer lessons for all managers in industry."

MANAGE, 2210 Arbor Blvd., Dayton OH 45439. (513)294-0421. Editor-in-Chief: Douglas E. Shaw. 60% freelance written. Works with a small number of new/unpublished writers each year. Quarterly magazine. For first-line and middle management and scientific/technical managers. Circ. 75,000. Pays on acceptance. Publishes ms an average of 6 months after acceptance. Buys North American magazine rights with reprint privileges; book rights remain with the author. Computer printout submissions OK; prefers letter-quality. Reports in 1 month. Free sample copy for 8½x11 SAE; free writer's guidelines.

Nonfiction: "All material published by *Manage* is in some way management oriented. Most articles concern one or more of the following categories: communications, executive abilities, human relations, job status, leadership, motivation and productivity and professionalism. Articles should be specific and tell the manager how to apply the information to his job immediately. Be sure to include pertinent examples, and back up statements with facts and, where possible, charts and illustrations. *Manage* does not want essays or academic reports, but interesting, well-written and practical articles for and about management." Buys 6 mss/issue. Phone queries OK. Submit complete ms. Length: 600-2,000 words. Pays 5¢/word.

Tips: "Keep current on management subjects; submit timely work."

MANAGEMENT REVIEW, American Management Association, 135 West 50th St., New York NY 10020. (212)903-8393. Managing Editor: Lisa Fried. Monthly magazine covering all aspects of managing in the workplace—private, public, nonprofit. "We have an audience of well-educated, middle- and high-level executives. They are a sophisticated audience looking for pragmatic, *nontheoretical* information and advice on how to run organizations, manage people and operations and compete in domestic and global markets. Strong emphasis on case studies." Pays on acceptance. Publishes ms an average of 4 months after acceptance. Byline given. Offers 50% kill fee. Buys first North American serial rights, second serial (reprint) rights and all rights. Submit seasonal material 4 months in advance. Previously published submissions sometimes OK. Computer printout submissions OK; no dot-matrix. Reports in 3 months due to overflow of queries. Free sample copy and writer's guidelines.

Nonfiction: Book excerpts, essays, general interest (business/trade/economics), how-to (case studies and advice for managers), interview/profile, opinion, personal experience (infrequently), other (management, global business, corporate culture topics). "Write for editorial calendar—monthly themes. No cartoons, academic papers, or short 'humorous' looks at management." Query with published clips and send an explanation of your business expertise or publishing background, or send complete ms. Length: 500-3,000 words. Pays $250-2,000 for assigned articles; pays $250-1,000 for unsolicited articles. Pays in contributor's copies "when no pay is requested—happens often." Sometimes pays the expenses of writers on assignment.

Photos: State availability of photos with submission. Reviews 8x10 prints. Black and white preferred.

Columns/Departments: Management in Practice (case studies of good management—how problems/opportunities were handled); Global Perspective (information/case studies on international business & trade); Perspective (essays on management or business topics-opinion); On-Line (case studies or advice/information on information technology in management); and Decision Makers (profiles of top executives/managers; focus on their management styles). Query with published clips. Length: 1,000-1,500. Pays $250-750.

Tips: "Don't write down to audience—the average *MR* reader has a graduate degree, and/or years of hands-on business and management experience. Need practical, *detailed* information on 'how-to' manage all kinds of situations, operations, and people. *Don't* rehash others' work—the audience has already read Drucker, Tom Peters, *et. al.* We do not want press kits or stories on software packages in general. We do want more stories on international business, managing nonprofit organizations and growing companies and managing technology in the workplace. For Decision Makers, Management in Practice, Global Perspective and Perspective columns, we're always looking for good writers. Same goes for features—but always query first. Phone queries okay, but letters preferred."

MIDWEST PURCHASING MANAGEMENT and PURCHASING MANAGEMENT, Meyer Associates, Inc., 14 7th Ave. N., St. Cloud MN 56301. (612)259-4000. FAX: (612)259-4044. Editor: Murdock Johnson. Managing Editor: Peg Meyer. 40% freelance written. Monthly magazines covering all aspects of purchasing and materials management. "We prefer 'How to Buy' or 'Ten Tips for Buying' format. Articles should feature a class of products (i.e. 'How to Choose Office Equipment) rather than single products ('Ten Tips for Buying a Copier'). Must apply to all levels of buyer—entry level to manager." Circ. 12,500. Pays on publication. Publishes ms an average of 6 months after acceptance. Byline given. Negotiable kill fee. Buys first rights. Photocopied submissions OK. Query for electronic submissions. Computer printout submissions OK; prefers letter-quality. Reports in 1 month. Sample copy for 8½x11 SAE with 3 first class stamps. Free writer's guidelines.

Nonfiction: Interview/profile, personal experience, technical. No general interest or general business articles, with single exception of economics. Buys 6 mss/year. Query with published clips. Length: 1,200-3,000 words. Pays $25-150. Sometimes pays expenses of writers on assignment.

Photos: State availability of photos with submission. Reviews contact sheets, negatives, transparencies and prints. Offers no additional payment for photos accepted with ms. Model releases and identification of subjects required.

Tips: "The best ideas and articles come directly from practitioners in the field. Short interviews, or telephone calls, will yield topic ideas. Go for the unusual, the off-the-beaten-path industry or technique. And send an outline first—let's work together to save time and money. A purchaser or materials manager must be all things to all people. He or she doesn't need more general information. Instead, he or she needs very specific information to help do the job better."

‡NEW MEXICO BUSINESS JOURNAL, Southwest Publications, Inc., Box 1788 Albuquerque NM 87103. (505)243-5581. Editor-in-Chief: George Hackler. Managing Editor: Todd R. Staats. 80% freelance written. A monthly magazine covering the state's business community. Circ. 20,000. Pays on acceptance. Publishes ms an average of 3 months after acceptance. Byline given. Buys first rights. Submit seasonal/holiday material 4 months in advance. Simultaneous and photocopied submissions OK. Computer printout submissions OK; prefers letter-quality. Reports in 3 weeks on queries. Sample copy 9 × 12 SAE with $1.25 (5 first class stamps) guidelines for #10 SAE with a first class stamp.

Nonfiction: How-to interview/profile, trends, technical and general interest (real estate, economic development, finance, mining, construction, etc.). Buys 100+ mss/year. Query with published clips or send complete manuscript. Length: 8-5,000 words. Pays $50-500 for assigned articles. Sometimes pays the expenses of writers on assignment.

Tips: We are interested in well-researched articles of interest to owners and top management of small to medium sized businesses. Include several b&w prints with manuscript if the piece lends itself to illustration. We offer no additional payment for photos accepted with manuscripts. Special emphasis on New Mexico business preferred.

PERSONNEL ADVISORY BULLETIN, Bureau of Business Practice, 24 Rope Ferry Rd., Waterford CT 06386. (203)442-4365, ext. 778. Editor: Jill Whitney. 75% freelance written. Eager to work with new/unpublished writers. Emphasizes all aspects of personnel practices for personnel managers in all types and sizes of companies, both white collar and industrial. Semimonthly newsletter. Pays on acceptance. Publishes ms an average of 5 months after acceptance. Buys all rights. Phone queries OK. Submit seasonal/holiday material 4 months in advance. Computer printout submissions acceptable; prefers letter-quality. Reports in 2 weeks. Free sample copy and writer's guidelines for 10x13 SAE and 2 first class stamps.

Nonfiction: Interviews with personnel managers or human resource professionals on topics of current interest in the personnel field. Avoid articles on hiring and interviewing, discipline or absenteeism/tardiness control. Buys 30 mss/year. Query with brief, specific outline. Length: 1,500-1,800 words.

Tips: "We're looking for concrete, practical material on how to solve problems. We're providing information about trends and developments in the field. We don't want filler copy. It's very easy to break in. Just query by phone or letter and we'll discuss the topic. Send for guidelines first, though, so we can have a coherent conversation."

‡PERSONNEL JOURNAL, The Management Magazine for Personnel Executives, AC Croft, Inc., 245 Fischer Ave., B-2, Costa Mesa CA 92626. (714)751-1883. FAX: (714)751-4106. Editor: Allan Halcrow. Managing Editor: Stephanie Lawrence. 10% freelance written. Monthly magazine that covers everything related to human resources management. "*Personnel Journal* is targeted to senior human resources executives in companies with 500 or more employees. The editorial content is aimed at helping readers define and improve corporate policy on personnel issues, as well as to identify trends and issues in the field and provide case examples of successful personnel programs." Circ. 30,000. Pays on acceptance. Publishes ms an average of 2 months after acceptance. Byline given. Offers kill fee of ½ original fee plus expenses. Buys all rights (can be negotiable). Photocopied submissions OK. Computer printout submissions OK; prefers letter-quality. Reports in 3 weeks on queries; 1 month on mss. Free sample copy and writer's guidelines.

Nonfiction: How-to (explanation of a personnel-related program or system), opinion, informed commentary on some aspect of personnel management), personal experience (case study detailing a personnel program's development and implementation) and technical (how to use computers in the personnel department; analysis of recent legislation or court decisions). "We do not want literature surveys (a round-up of all published thought on a topic, such as performance appraisals). We do not want anything written to or for employees." Buys 6-8 mss/year. Query with published clips. Length: 4,000 word minimum. Pays $700-3,000 for assigned articles; $500-2,000 for unsolicited articles. Pays with contributor copies when articles submitted by practitioners (not writers) and when terms are understood up-front. Pays expenses of writers on assignment.

Photos: State availability of photos with submission. Reviews 35mm transparencies. Offers $50-200 per photo. Model releases are required. Buys one-time rights.

Tips: "The best way to get into *Personnel Journal* is to base material in reality. Too many writers present management theory with no evidence it has been tried or write a how-to that does not include examples. Be specific—*why* was a program developed, *how* (step-by-step) was it implemented. Also, it's best to assume readers have some sophistication—they do not need basic techniques defined; they want *new* ideas."

PRODUCTION SUPERVISOR'S BULLETIN, Bureau of Business Practice, 24 Rope Ferry Rd., Waterford CT 06386. (800)243-0876. FAX: (203)434-3341. Editor: Anna Maria Trusky. Managing Editor: Wayne N. Muller. 75% freelance written. Biweekly newsletter. "The audience is primarily first-line production supervisors. Articles are meant to address a common workplace issue faced by such a supervisor, (absenteeism, low productivity, etc.) and explain how interviewee dealt with the problem." Circ. 5,000. Pays on acceptance. Publishes ms an average of 4 months after acceptance. Byline not given. Buys all rights. Computer printout submissions OK; prefers letter-quality. Reports in 2 weeks on queries; 3 weeks on mss. Free sample copy and writer's guidelines.

Nonfiction: How-to (on managing people, solving workplace problems, improving productivity). No high-level articles aimed at upper management. Buys 60-70 mss/year. Query. Length: 800-1,500 words. Pays 9-15¢/word.

Tips: "Freelancers may call me at (800)243-0876 or (203)434-6799. Or write for further information. Sections of publication most open to freelancers are lead story; inside stories (generally 3 to 4 per issue); and Production Management Clinic (in every other issue). Simply include lots of concrete, how-to steps for dealing effectively with the topic at hand."

SALES MANAGER'S BULLETIN, The Bureau of Business Practice, 24 Rope Ferry Rd., Waterford CT 06386. Editor: Paulette S. Withers. 33% freelance written. Prefers to work with published/established writers. Newsletter published twice a month. For sales managers and salespeople interested in getting into sales management. Pays on acceptance. Publishes ms an average of 3-6 months after acceptance. Written queries only except from regulars. Submit seasonal/holiday material 6 months in advance. Original submissions only. Buys all rights. Computer printout submissions acceptable; prefers letter-quality. Reports in 2 weeks. Sample copy and writer's guidelines only when request is accompanied by SAE with 2 first clas stamps.

Nonfiction: How-to (motivate salespeople, cut costs, create territories, etc.); interview (with working sales managers who use innovative techniques); and technical (marketing stories based on interviews with experts). No articles on territory management, saving fuel in the field, or public speaking skills. Break into this publication by reading the guidelines and sample issue. Follow the directions closely and chances for acceptance go up dramatically. One easy way to start is with an interview article ("Here's what sales executives have to say about . . ."). Query is vital to acceptance: "send a simple postcard explaining briefly the subject matter, the interviewees (if any), slant, length, and date of expected completion, accompanied by a SASE. Do not accept unqueried mss." Length: 800-1,000 words. Pays 10-15¢/word.

Tips: "Freelancers should always request samples and writer's guidelines, accompanied by SASE. Requests without SASE are discarded immediately. Examine the sample, and don't try to improve on our style. Write as we write. Don't 'jump around' from point to point and don't submit articles that are too chatty and with not enough real information. The more time a writer can save the editors, the greater his or her chance of a sale and repeated sales, when queries may not be necessary any longer. We will focus more on selling more product, meeting intense competiton, while spending less money to do it."

SECURITY MANAGEMENT: PROTECTING PROPERTY, PEOPLE & ASSETS, Bureau of Business Practice, 24 Rope Ferry Rd., Waterford CT 06386. Editor: Alex Vaughn. 75% freelance written. Eager to work with new/unpublished writers. Semimonthly newsletter. Emphasizes security for industry. "All material should be slanted toward security directors, primarily industrial, retail and service businesses, but others as well." Circ. 3,000. Pays on acceptance. Buys all rights. Phone queries OK. Photocopied submissions OK. Computer printout submissions acceptable; prefers letter-quality. Reports in 2 weeks. Free sample copy and writer's guidelines.

Nonfiction: Interview (with security professionals only). "Articles should be tight and specific. They should deal with new security techniques or new twists on old ones." Buys 2-5 mss/issue. Query. Length: 750-1,000 words. Pays 15¢/word.

SUPERVISION, 424 N. 3rd St., Burlington IA 52601. Publisher: Michael S. Darnall. Editorial Supervisor: Doris J. Ruschill. Editor: Barbara Boeding. 95% freelance written. Monthly magazine for first-line foremen, supervisors and office managers. Circ. 6,075. Pays on publication. Publishes ms an average of 6 months after acceptance. Buys all rights. Computer printout submissions OK; prefers letter-quality. Reports in 3 weeks. Sample copy and writer's guidelines for 9x12 SAE with 4 first class stamps; mention *Writer's Market* in request.

Nonfiction: How-to (cope with supervisory problems, discipline, absenteeism, safety, productivity, goal setting, etc.); and personal experience (unusual success story of foreman or supervisor). No sexist material written from only a male viewpoint. Include biography and/or byline with ms submissions. Author photos requested. Buys 12 mss/issue. Query. Length: 1,500-1,800 words. Pays 4¢/word.

Tips: "Following AP stylebook would be helpful." Uses no advertising.

‡SUPERVISOR'S BULLETIN, Bureau of Business Practice, 24 Rope Ferry Rd., Waterford CT 06386. (203)442-4365. Editor: Kelly Donlon. 50-75% freelance written. "We work with both new or established writers, and are always looking for fresh talent." Bimonthly newsletter for manufacturing supervisors wishing to improve their managerial skills. Pays on acceptance. Publishes ms on average of 6 weeks after acceptance. No byline given. Buys all rights. Computer printout submissions acceptable; prefers letter-quality to dot-matrix. Reports in 2 weeks on queries, 6 weeks on mss. Free sample copy and writer's guidelines.

Nonfiction: How-to (solve a supervisory problem on the job); and interview (of top-notch supervisors). Sample topics could include: how-to increase productivity, cut costs, achieve better teamwork." No filler or non-interview based copy. Buys 72 mss/year. Query first. "Strongly urge writers to study guidelines and samples." Length: 750-1,000 words. Pays 8-14¢/word.

Tips: "We need interview-based articles that emphasize direct quotes. Each article should include a reference to the interviewee's company (location, size, products, function of the interviewee's department and number of employees under his control). Define a problem and show how the supervisor solved it. Write in a light, conversational style, talking directly to supervisors who can benefit from putting the interviewee's tips into practice. We will focus on more safety issues. More articles will cover how supervisors can ensure safety in the workplace."

TRAINING, The Magazine of Human Resources Development, Lakewood Publications, 50 S. Ninth St., Minneapolis MN 55402. (612)333-0471. Editor: Jack Gordon. Managing Editor: Chris Lee. 10% freelance written. A monthly magazine covering training and employee development in the business world. "Our core readers are managers and professionals who specialize in employee training and development (e.g., corporate training directors, VP-human resource development, etc.). We have a large secondary readership among managers of all sorts who are concerned with improving human performance in their organizations. We take a businesslike approach to training and employee education." Circ. 52,000. Pays on acceptance. Publishes ms an average of 3 months after acceptance. Byline given. Buys first North American serial rights and second serial (reprint) rights. Simultaneous and photocopied submissions OK. Computer printout submissions acceptable; prefers letter-quality. Reports in 2 weeks on queries; 6 weeks on mss. Sample copy for 9x11 SAE with 4 first class stamps. Writer's guidelines for #10 SASE.

Nonfiction: Essay; exposé; how-to (on training, management, sales, productivity improvement, etc.); humor; interview/profile; new product; opinion; photo feature; and technical (use of audiovisual aids, computers, etc.). "No puff, no 'testimonials' or disguised ads in any form, no 'gee-whiz' approaches to the subjects." Buys 10-12 mss/year. Query with or without published clips, or send complete ms. Length: 200-3,000 words. Pays $50-500.

Photos: State availability of photos or send with submission. Reviews contact sheets and prints. Offers no additional payment for photos accepted with ms. Identification of subjects required. Buys one-time rights and reprint rights.

Columns/Departments: Training Today (news briefs, how-to tips, reports on pertinent research, trend analysis, etc.), 200-800 words. Buys 6 mss/year. Query or send complete ms. Pays $50-75.

Tips: "We would like to develop a few freelancers to work with on a regular basis. We almost never give firm assignments to unfamiliar writers, so you have to be willing to hit us with one or two on spec to break in. Short pieces for our Training Today section involve least investment on your part, but also are less likely to convince us to assign you a feature. When studying the magazine, freelancers should look at our staff-written articles for style, approach and tone. Do not concentrate on articles written by people identified as consultants, training directors, etc."

UTILITY SUPERVISION, Bureau of Business Practice, 24 Rope Ferry Rd., Waterford CT 06386. (203)739-0169. Editor: DeLoris Lidestri. 80% freelance written. "We're willing to work with a few new writers if they're willing to follow guidelines carefully." Semimonthly newsletter emphasizing all aspects of utility supervision. Pays on acceptance. Publishes ms an average of 4 months after acceptance. Buys all rights. Phone queries OK. Submit seasonal material 4 months in advance. Computer printout submissions OK; no dot-matrix. Reports in 6 weeks. Free sample copy and writer's guidelines.

Nonfiction: Publishes how-to (interview on a single aspect of supervision with utility manager/supervisor concentrating on how reader/supervisor can improve in that area). Buys 100 mss/year. Query. Length: 360-750 words. Pays 10-15¢/word.

Photos: Purchased with accompanying ms. Pays $10 for head and shoulders photo of person interviewed. Total purchase price for ms includes payment for photo.

Tips: "A writer should call before he or she does anything. I like to spend a few minutes on the phone exchanging information."

‡**WAREHOUSING SUPERVISOR'S BULLETIN**, Bureau of Business Practice, 24 Rope Ferry Rd., Waterford CT 06386. (203)442-4365. FAX: (203)434-3341. Editor: April L. Katz. 75-90% freelance written. "We work with a wide variety of writers, and are always looking for fresh talent." Biweekly newsletter covering traffic, materials handling and distribution for warehouse supervisors "interested in becoming more effective on the job." Pays on acceptance. Publishes ms an average of 3 months after acceptance. No byline given. Buys all rights. Computer printout submissions acceptable. Reports in 2 weeks on queries; 6 weeks on mss. Free sample copy and writer's guidelines.

Nonfiction: How-to (increase efficiency, control or cut costs, cut absenteeism or tardiness, increase productivity, raise morale); and interview (of warehouse supervisors or managers who have solved problems on the job). No descriptions of company programs, noninterview articles, textbook-like descriptions or union references. Buys 50 mss/year. Query. "A resumé and sample of work are helpful." Length: 1,580-2,900 words. Pays 10-15¢/word. Sometimes pays the expenses of writers on assignment.

Tips: "All articles must be interview-based and emphasize how-to information. They should also include a reference to the interviewee's company (location, size, products, function of the interviewee's department and number of employees under his control). Focus articles on one problem, and get the interviewee to pinpoint the best way to solve it. Write in a light, conversational style, talking directly to warehouse supervisors who can benefit from putting the interviewee's tips into practice."

Marine and Maritime Industries

‡**BOATING INDUSTRY**, Communication Channels, Inc., 390 Fifth Ave., 3rd Floor, New York NY 10018. (212)613-9700. Editor-in-Chief/Publisher: Charles A. Jones. Editor: Paul Larsen. 15% freelance written. Prefers to work with published/established writers. Monthly for boating retailers and distributors. Circ. 27,200. Pays on publication. Publishes ms an average of 3 months after acceptance. Byline given. Buys all rights. Best practice is to check with editor first on story ideas for go-ahead. Submit seasonal material 4 months in advance. Reports in 2 months.
Nonfiction: Business-oriented pieces about marine management. Interested in good column material, too. Buys 10-15 mss/year. Query. Length: 1,500-4,000 words. No clippings. Pays 9-15¢/word.
Photos: B&w glossy photos purchased with mss; "also some color."

‡**PROCEEDINGS**, U.S. Naval Institute, Annapolis MD 21402. (301)268-6110. Editor: Fred H. Rainbow. Managing Editor: John G. Miller. 95% freelance written. Eager to work with new/published writers. Monthly magazine covering naval and maritime subjects. Circ. 100,000. Pays on acceptance. Publishes ms an average of 5 months after acceptance. Byline given. Buys all rights. Submit seasonal/holiday material 3 months in advance. Photocopied submissions OK. Computer printout submissions OK; prefers letter-quality. Reports in 2 weeks on queries; 1 month on mss. Free sample copy and writer's guidelines.
Nonfiction: Essays, exposé, general interest, historical/nostalgic, how-to (related to sea service professional subjects), humor, interview/profile, new product, opinion, personal experience, photo feature and technical. "*Proceedings* is an unofficial, open forum for the discussion of naval and maritime topics." Special issues include International Navies (March) and Naval Review (May). Buys 250 mss/year. Query or send complete ms. Length: up to 3,500 words. Pays $50-600. Sometimes pays writers with contributor copies or other premiums "if author desires." Sometimes pays the expenses of writers on assignment.
Photos: Send photos with submission. Reviews contact sheets, negatives, transparencies and prints. Offers $10-100 per photo. Buys one-time rights.
Columns/Departments: Book Reviews, Nobody Asked Me About . . ., and Crossword Puzzles (all with naval or maritime slants), all 500-2,000 words. Buys 90 mss/year. Query. Pays $50-200.
Fiction: Adventure, historical and humorous. Buys 4 mss/year. Query. Length: 500-3,000 words. Pays $50-600.
Fillers: Anecdotes. Buys 50/year. Length: 1,000 words maximum. Pays $25-150.
Tips: "Write about something you know about, either from first-hand experience or based on primary source material. Our letters to the editor column is most open to freelancers."

‡**WORKBOAT**, Box 1348, Mandeville LA 70470. (504)626-0298. FAX: (504)624-4801. Editor: Robert Carpenter. Assoc. Editor: Marilyn Barrett. 60% freelance written. Bimonthly magazine on all working boats: commerical inland and near shore. Target work boat owners, boat captains, operators, service companies and related businesses." Pays on acceptance or publication. Publishes ms an average of 2 months after acceptance. Byline given. Offers negotiable kill fee. Buys first time rights. Query for electronic submissions. Computer printout submissions OK; prefers letter-quality. Sample copy for 9x12 SAE and $1.50; writer's guidelines for #10 SASE.
Nonfiction: General interest, historical/nostalgic, how-to, interview/profile and technical. Query or query with published clips. Sometimes pays expenses of writers on assignment.
Photos: State availability of photos with submission. Reviews contact sheets and transparencies. Pay negotiable. Identification of subjects required. Buys one-time rights.
Tips: "Learn all you can about tugs, barges, supply boats, passenger vessels (excursion & ferry), dredges, fire boats, patrol boats and any vessel doing business on America's inland waterways, harbors and close to shore. Also, familiarity with issues affecting the maritime industry is a plus."

Medical

Through these journals physicians, pharmacists, therapists and mental health professionals learn how other professionals help their patients and manage their medical practices.

Publications for nurses, laboratory technicians and other medical personnel are listed in the Hospitals, Nursing and Nursing Home section. Publications for drug store managers and drug wholesalers and retailers, as well as hospital equipment suppliers, are listed with Drugs, Health Care and Medical Products. Publications for consumers that report trends in the medical field are found in the Consumer Health and Science categories.

AMERICAN MEDICAL NEWS, American Medical Association, 535 N. Dearborn St., Chicago IL 60610. (312)645-5000. Editor: Dick Walt. Executive Editor: Barbara Bolsen. 5-10% freelance written. "Prefers writers already interested in the health care field—not clinical medicine." Weekly tabloid providing nonclinical information for physicians—information on socio-economic, political and other developments in medicine. "*AMN* is a specialized publication circulating to physicians, covering subjects touching upon their profession, practices and personal lives. This is a well-educated, highly sophisticated audience." Circ. 375,000 physicians. Pays on acceptance. Publishes ms an average of 2 months after acceptance. Byline given. Offers variable kill fee. Buys all rights. Rights sometimes returnable on request after publication. Simultaneous queries OK. Computer printout submissions acceptable. Reports in 1 month. Sample copy for 9x12 SAE and 2 first class stamps. Free writer's guidelines.
Nonfiction: Flora Johnson Skelly, assistant executive editor for outside contributions. Interview/profile (occasional); opinion (mainly from physicians); and news and interpretive features. Special issues include "Year in Review" issue published in January. No clinical articles, general-interest articles physicians would see elsewhere, or recycled versions of articles published elsewhere. Buys 200 mss/year. Query. Length: 200-4,000 words. Pays $400-750 for features; $50-100 for opinions and short news items. "We have limited travel budget for freelancers; we pay minimal local expenses."
Tips: "We are trying to create a group of strong feature writers who will be regular contributors."

‡THE BEST REPORT, Exploring the World of Quality, Wilton Communications, Inc., 140 E. 45th St., 36th Fl., New York NY 10017. (212)983-4320. Editor: Bonnie Davidson. Managing Editor: Dan Richards. 20% freelance written. Monthly magazine. "*The Best Report* is an upscale lifestyle magazine distributed by pharmaceutical companies to doctors nationwide. Articles cover an eclectic mix of luxury goods, services and travel destinations. Our only restriction: everything we write about must be top-of-the-line." Circ. 150,000. Pays on acceptance. Publishes ms an average of 3 months after acceptance. No byline, but contributors are listed in masthead under "Contributors to this issue." Offers 25% kill fee. Buys first rights. Submit seasonal/holiday material 4 months in advance. Query for electronic submissions. Computer printout submissions OK; prefers letter-quality. Reports in 1 month. Free sample copy and writer's guidelines.
Nonfiction: General interest (collectibles, sporting and cultural events, shopping, food, restaurants, roundups—i.e. the best places to scuba dive in the world), travel and other (feature on a classic best—i.e. the Jaguar). "We do not want fiction." Buys about 40 mss/year. Query with published clips. Length: 600-1,400 words. Pays 30¢/word for all articles accepted. Sometimes pays phone and other incidentals of writers on assignment.
Photos: Send photos with submission. Reviews color transparencies and prints (b&w preferred). Offers no additional payment for photos accepted with ms. Identification of subjects required.
Columns/Departments: Best Finds (highlights of interesting new gadgets, resorts, restaurants; unusual events), 300-800 words or less. Query with published clips. Pays 30¢/word.
Tips: "In general, articles should be lively, authoritative and concise. Writers should consult with experts whenever possible, and should always include prices, addresses and phone numbers for more information."

CARDIOLOGY WORLD NEWS, Medical Publishing Enterprises, Box 1548, Marco Island FL 33969. (813)394-0400. Editor: John H. Lavin. 75% freelance written. Prefers to work with published/established writers. Monthly magazine covering cardiology and the cardiovascular system. "We need short news articles *for doctors* on any aspect of our field—diagnosis, treatment, risk factors, etc." Pays on acceptance. Publishes ms an average of 2 months after acceptance. Byline given "for special reports and feature-length articles." Offers 20% kill fee. Buys first North American serial rights. Photocopied submissions OK. Query for electronic submissions. Computer printout submissions acceptable. Reports in 1 month. Sample copy $1; free writer's guidelines with #10 SASE.
Nonfiction: New product and technical (clinical). No fiction, fillers, profiles of doctors or poetry. Query with published clips. Length: 250-1,500 words. Pays $50-300; $50/column for news articles. Pays expenses of writers on assignment.
Photos: State availability of photos with query. Pays $50/published photo. Rough captions, model release and identification of subjects required. Buys one-time rights.
Tips: "Submit written news articles of 250-500 words on speculation with basic source material (not interview notes) for fact-checking. We demand clinical or writing expertise for full-length feature. Clinical cardiology conventions/symposia are the best source of news and feature articles."

CINCINNATI MEDICINE, Academy of Medicine, 320 Broadway, Cincinnati OH 45202. (513)421-7010. Managing Editor: Vicki L. Black. 40-50% freelance written. Works with a small number of new/unpublished writers each year. Quarterly membership magazine for the Academy of Medicine of Cincinnati. "We cover socio-economic and political factors that affect the practice of medicine in Cincinnati. For example: How will changes in Medicare policies affect local physicians and what will they mean for the quality of care Cincinnati's elderly patients receive. (Ninety-nine percent of our readers are Cincinnati physicians.)" Circ. 3,500. Pays on acceptance. Publishes ms an average of 3-6 months after acceptance. Byline given. Makes work-for-hire assignments. Simultaneous queries and photocopied submissions OK. Computer printout submissions acceptable; prefers letter-quality. Reports in 6 weeks on queries; 1 month on mss. Sample copy for $3 and 9x12 SAE and 7 first class stamps; writer's guidelines for 4½x9½ SAE with 1 first class stamp.
Nonfiction: Historical/nostalgic (history of, or reminiscences about, medicine in Cincinnati); interview/profile (of nationally known medical figures or medical leaders in Cincinnati); and opinion (opinion pieces on controversial medico-legal and medico-ethical issues). "We do not want: scientific-research articles, stories that are not based on good journalistic skills (no seat-of-the-pants reporting), or why my 'doc' is the greatest guy in the world stories." Buys 10-12 mss/year. Query with published clips or send complete ms. Length: 800-2,500 words. Pays $125-300. Sometimes pays expenses of writers on assignment.
Photos: State availability of photos with query or ms. Captions and identification of subjects required. Buys one-time rights.
Tips: "Send published clips; do some short features that will help you develop some familiarity with our magazine and our audience; and show initiative to tackle the larger stories. First-time writers often don't realize the emphasis we place on solid reporting. We want accurate, well-balanced reporting or analysis. Our job is to *inform* our readers."

CONSULTANT PHARMACIST, American Society of Consultant Pharmacists, Suite 515, 2300 S. Ninth St., Arlington VA 22204. (703)920-8492. FAX: (703)892-2084. Editor: L. Michael Posey. Managing Editor: Joanne Kaldy. 10% freelance written. A bimonthly magazine on consultant pharmacy. "We do not promote drugs or companies but rather ideas and information." Circ. 10,000. Pays on acceptance. Publishes ms an average of 2 months after acceptance. Byline given. Buys first North American serial rights. Photocopied submissions OK. Query for electronic submissions. Computer printout submissions OK; prefers letter-quality. Reports in 2 weeks. Sample copy for 9x12 SAE with 4 first class stamps. Writer's guidelines for #10 SAE with 1 first class stamp.
Nonfiction: How-to (related to consultant pharmacy), interview/profile, technical. Buys 10 mss/year. Query with published clips. Length: 750-2,000 words. Pays $300-1,200. Sometimes pays expenses of writers on assignment.
Photos: Send photos with submission. Offers $100/per photo session. Captions, model releases, identification of subjects required. Buys one-time rights.
Tips: "This journal is devoted to consultant pharmacy, so articles must relate to this field."

COPE MAGAZINE, Oncology News for Professionals, Pulse Publications, Inc., Box 1677, Franklin TN 37065-1677. (615)791-5900. Managing Editor: Jacki Moss. 30% freelance written. Magazine covering oncology published 10 times a year. "All information must directly relate to oncology and be new research, treatment, therapy or conference reports." Circ, 30,000. Pays on publication. Publishes ms an average of 2 months after acceptance. Byline given. Offers $25 kill fee. Buys first North American serial rights. Submit seasonal/holiday material 3 months in advance. Computer printout submissions OK; prefers letter-quality. Reports in 3 weeks on queries; 1 month on mss. Sample copy $3.50 with 10x12 SAE with $1.25 postage. Writer's guidelines for 25¢ postage.
Nonfiction: Book excerpts (oncology), exposé, new products (for oncologists), opinion, research, technical (oncology), treatment and conference coverage. "We will not consider anything that does not have a current oncology angle." Buys 100 mss/year. Query with published clips or send complete ms. Length: 500-1,500 words. Pays $50-250 for assigned articles; $10-200 for unsolicited articles. Sometimes pays expenses of writers on assignment.
Photos: State availability of photos with submission. Reviews contact sheets, transparencies and prints. Offers $10-25 per photo. Captions, model releases and identification of subjects required. Buys one-time rights.
Columns/Departments: Second Opinion, Nutrition, Pain, Conferences, Pharmacology (all on oncology issues) 750-1,200 words. Buys 10 mss/year. Query with published clips. Pays $50-250.
Tips: "Conference coverage of new oncology reports is most open to freelancers. We generally assign conferences to freelancers who either already live there. Writers must have a firm medical writing background. No general health pieces are used. We cannot use any information more than six months old – it must be cutting edge technology and research. Articles must be medically/scientifically accurate and verifiable."

‡DOCTOR'S REVIEW, The Leisure-Time Journal for Physicians, Parkhurst Publishing, Suite 302, 640 St. Paul St. W., Montreal, Quebec H3C 1L9 Canada. (514)397-8833. FAX: (514)397-0228. Editor: David Elkins. Associate Editor: Madeleine Partous. 30% freelance written. Monthly magazine on travel & leisure – upscale for *Canadian* doctors. "We have a wide range of interests and wil cover broad topics, as long as the pieces can be loosely grouped as 'Leisure.' Tone *must* be light, airy, snappy. Avoid history or anything potentially dry. Chatty stuff." Circ. 37,000. Pays on publication. Publishes ms an average of 6 months after acceptance. Byline given. Offers $200 kill fee. Buys one-time rights. Submit seasonal/holiday material 6 months in advance. Simultaneous, photocopied and previously published submissions OK as long as clearly stated where other submissions have been sent. Query for electronic submissions. Computer printout submissions OK; prefers letter-quality. Reports in 1 month on queries; 2 months on mss. Sample copy $4. Free writer's guidelines.

Nonfiction: Book excerpts, general interest, how-to, humor, interview/profile, new product, personal experience, photo feature and travel. "We do not want political, economical, religious, extremist, elitist, racist, sexist articles. Send complete ms. Length: 1,800-2,500 words. Pays $200-300 for assigned articles; $125-300 for unsolicited articles. "We pay less for reprints, more for originals—some flexibility."

Photos: Send photos with submission. Reviews transparencies and 5x7 prints. Offers $25 per photo. Identification of subjects required. Buys one-time rights.

Columns/Departments: Humor (anything funny), 1,000 words. Buys 12 mss/year. Send complete ms. Length: 1,000-1,800 words. Pays $100-200.

Tips: "Since we can't pay much, we welcome reprints, as long as the piece has never been published for Canadian doctors! Being a trade book, it doesn't matter whether the article has been published a few times, even. Keep the audience in mind. We will pay Americans in U.S. funds."

‡**DOCTORS SHOPPER,** Marketing Communications, Inc., 949 E. 99 St., Brooklyn NY 11236. (718)257-8484. FAX: (718)257-8845. Publisher: Ralph Selitzer. 35% freelance written. Quarterly magazine on medical business, travel, finances, lifestyle articles for doctors. Circ. 211,000. Pays on publication. Byline given. 100% freelance written. Buys one-time rights. Submit seasonal/holiday material 6 months in advance. Previously published submissions OK. Reports in 4 weeks. Free sample copy for 9x12 SAE and $3 postage. Writer's guidelines for #10 SASE.

Nonfiction: General interest, new product, photo feature, technical, travel and financial. Buys 8 mss/year. Send complete ms. Length: 250-2,000 words. Pays $500-1,000 for assigned articles; $250-1,000 for unsolicited articles. Sometimes pays expenses of writers on assignment.

Photos: State availability of photos with submission. Reviews contact sheets and 2x2 transparencies. Offers no additional payment for photos accepted with ms. Captions, model releases and identification of subjects required. Buys one-time rights.

Columns/Departments: CME Travel (travel articles for doctors attending continuing education conferences), 500-1,000 words. Buys 4 mss/year. Pays $350-750.

Fillers: Anecdotes, facts, gags to be illustrated by cartoonist, only *medical*. Buys 8/year. Length: 100-500 words. Pays $50-300.

Tips: "Contribute self help articles for physicians on serving patients better, run a more efficient practice, enjoy leisure time, travel, etc. Travel articles, new medical office methods, actual physician case histories are areas most open to freelancers."

EMERGENCY, The Journal of Emergency Services, 6200 Yarrow Drive, Carlsbad CA 92009. (619)438-2511. FAX: (619)931-5809. Editor: Laura M. Gilbert.100% freelance written. Works with a small number of new/unpublished writers each year. A monthly magazine covering pre-hospital emergency care. "Our readership is primarily composed of EMTs, paramedics and other EMS personnel. We prefer a professional, semitechnical approach to pre-hospital subjects." Circ. 25,000. Pays on acceptance. Publishes ms an average of 3 months after acceptance. Byline given. Buys all rights, nonexclusive. Submit seasonal/holiday material 6 months in advance. Photocopied submissions OK. Computer printout submissions acceptable; no dot-matrix. Reports in 2 months. Sample copy $3; writer's guidelines for #10 SASE.

Nonfiction: Semi-technical exposé, how-to (on treating pre-hospital emergency patients), interview/profile, new techniques, opinion and photo feature. "We do not publish cartoons, color *print* photos, term papers, product promotions disguised as articles or overly technical manuscripts." Buys 10 mss/year. Query with published clips. Length 1,500-3,000 words. Pays $100-400.

Photos: Send photos with submission. Reviews color transparencies and b&w prints. Offers no additional payment for photos accepted with ms. Offers $20-30/photo without ms. Captions and identification of subjects required.

Columns/Departments: Open Forum (opinion page for EMS professionals), 500 words. Trauma Primer (pre-hospital care topics, treatment of injuries, etc.), 1,000-2,000 words. Drug Watch (focus on one particular drug a month). Buys 10 mss/year. Query first. Pays $100-250.

Fillers: Facts and newsbreaks. Buys 10/year. Length: no more than 500 words. Pays $0-75.

Tips: "Writing style for features and departments should be knowledgeable and lively with a clear theme or story line to maintain reader interest and enhance comprehension. The biggest problem we encounter is dull, lifeless term-paper-style writing with nothing to perk reader interest. Keep in mind we are not a textbook. Accompanying photos are a plus.We appreciate a short, one paragraph biography on the author."

FAMILY THERAPY NEWS, American Association for Marriage and Family Therapy, #407, 1717 K St. NW, Washington DC 20006. (202)429-1825. Editor: William C. Nichols. Managing Editor: Kimberly A. Tilley. 10% freelance written. Newspaper for professional organization covering family therapy, family policy, mental health and behavior sciences. *FT News* is a professional newspaper serving marital and family therapists. Writers should be able to reach both doctoral level and graduate student readers. Circ. 16,000. Pays on acceptance. Publishes ms an average of 3 months after acceptance. Byline given. Buys first North American serial rights. Submit seasonal/holiday material 6 months in advance. Query for electronic submissions. Computer printout submissions OK; prefers letter-quality. Reports in 2 weeks. Free sample copy; writer's guidelines for 9x12 SAE with 65¢ postage.

Nonfiction: Only want materials pertaining to the field of family therapy, family policy, family research, mental health and behavioral science for professionals. Query with or without published clips, or send complete ms. Length: 300-1,800 words. Pays $25-200.

Photos: State availability of photos with submission. Reviews 8x10 prints. Payment negotiable. Identification of subjects required. Buys one-time rights.

Columns/Departments: Family Therapy Forum (wide variety of topics and slants on family therapy, education, training, practice, service delivery, the therapists, family therapists in various countries, opinion), to 1,800 words; In Focus (interview with outstanding therapists, other leaders), to 1,500 words. Send complete ms. Length: 600-1,800. Pays $25-100.

Fillers: Facts. Length: 100-300 words. Pays $10-25.

Tips: "The annual conference is a major source of good material for writers, such as those of the American Family Therapy Association. Query editor. Also, we are in need of short, well-written features on current developments in the field. Materials could be developed into columns as well for Family Therapy Forum in some instances, but straight news-based features are the best bet."

FITNESS MANAGEMENT, The Magazine for Professionals in Adult Physical Fitness, Leisure Publications, Inc., Suite 213, 215 S. Highway 101, Box 1198, Solana Beach CA 92075. (619)481-4155. Editor: Edward H. Pitts. 50% freelance written. Bimonthly magazine covering commercial, corporate and community fitness centers. "Readers are owners, managers and program directors of physical fitness facilities. *FM* helps them run their enterprises safely, efficiently and profitably. Ethical and professional positions in health, nutrition, sports medicine, management, etc., are consistent with those of established national bodies." Circ. 21,000. Pays on publication. Publishes ms an average of 5 months after acceptance. Byline given. Pays 50% kill fee. Buys all rights. Submit seasonal/holiday material 6 months in advance. Query for electronic submissions. Computer printout submissions OK; prefers letter-quality. Reports in 1 month on queries; 2 months on mss. Writer's guidelines for #10 SASE. Sample copy for $5.

Nonfiction: Book excerpts (prepublication), how-to (manage fitness center and program), new product (no pay), photo feature (facilities/programs), technical and other (news of fitness research and major happenings in fitness industry). No exercise instructions or general ideas without examples of fitness businesses that have used them successfully. Buys 30 mss/year. Query. Length: 750-2,000 words. Pays $60-300 for assigned articles; pays up to $160 for unsolicited articles. Pays expenses of writers on assignment.

Photos: Send photos with submission. Reviews contact sheets, 2x2 and 4x5 transparencies and 5x7 prints. Offers $10 per photo. Captions and model releases required.

Tips: "We seek writers who are expert in a business or science field related to the fitness-service industry or who are experienced in the industry. Be current with the state of the art/science in business and fitness and communicate it in human terms (avoid intimidating academic language; tell the story of how this was learned and/or cite examples of quotes of people who have applied the knowledge successfully)."

GERIATRIC CONSULTANT, Medical Publishing Enterprises, Box 1548, Marco Island FL 33969. (813)394-0400. Editor: John H. Lavin. 70% freelance written. Prefers to work with published/established writers. Bimonthly magazine for physicians covering medical care of the elderly. "We're a clinical magazine directed to doctors and physician assistants. All articles must *help* these health professionals to help their elderly patients. We're too tough a market for nonmedical beginners." Circ. 97,500. Pays on acceptance. Publishes ms an average of 3 months after acceptance. Byline given. Offers 20% kill fee. Buys first North American serial rights. Simultaneous queries OK. Query for electronic submissions. Computer printout submissions acceptable. Reports in 1 month. Sample copy for $1; free writer's guidelines with #10 SASE.

Nonfiction: How-to (diagnosis and treatment of health problems of the elderly) and technical/clinical. No fiction or articles directed to a lay audience. Buys 20 mss/year. Query. Length: 750-3,000 words. Pays $100-300. Pays expenses of writers on assignment.

Photos: State availability of photos. (Photos are not required.) Model release and identification of subjects required. Buys one-time rights.

Tips: "Many medical meetings are now held in the field of geriatric care. These offer potential sources and subjects for us."

GROUP PRACTICE JOURNAL, American Group Practice Association, 1422 Duke St., Alexandria VA 22314-3430. (703)838-0033. FAX: (703)548-1890. Editor: Charles Honaker. 30% freelance written. Bimonthly magazine on medical group practices. Circ. 46,000. Pays on publication. Publishes ms an average of 6 months after acceptance. Byline given. Buys first North American serial rights. Query for electronic submissions. Computer printout submissions OK; prefers letter-quality. Free sample copy for 11x14 SAE and writer's guidelines with #10 SASE.
Nonfiction: How-to, opinion, photo feature, technical, travel, socio-economic aspects of medical group practices. Buys 10 mss/year. Send complete ms. Length: 1,000-3,000 words. Pays $500-1,000.
Photos: State availability of photos with submissions. Reviews contact sheets, negatives, transparencies, prints. Captions, model releases and identification of subjects required. Buy all rights.
Columns/Departments: Taxes (tax tips); Marketing (medical marketing tips); Legal Forum (law-legislation analysis). Query. Length: 500-1,000 words. Pays $300-500.
Tips: "Call the editor and chat. Discuss story ideas, news needs. Visit a medical group practice and learn what the doctors, CEOs read and want to read."

HEALTHCARE PROFESSIONAL PUBLISHING, Division of TM Marketing, Inc., 105 Main Street, Hackensack NJ 06701. (201)342-6511. Managing Editor: Michael Kaufman. 35% freelance written. "Produces single-sponsored publications. Work is made on assignment only. An ability to work with specialized scientific material and condense it into tightly written news stories for physicians is important." Pays on acceptance. Publishes ms an average of 1-2 months after acceptance. Byline sometimes given. Makes work-for-hire assignments.

THE JOURNAL, Addiction Research Foundation of Ontario, 33 Russell St., Toronto, Ontario M5S 2S1 Canada. (416)964-9235. Editor: Anne MacLennan. Managing Editor: Elda Hauschildt. 50% freelance written. Prefers to work with published/established writers. Monthly tabloid covering addictions and related fields around the world. "*The Journal* alerts professionals in the addictions and related fields or disciplines to news events, issues, opinions and developments of potential interest and/or significance to them in their work, and provides them an informed context in which to judge developments in their own specialty/geographical areas." Circ. 10,000. Pays on publication. Publishes ms an average of 3 months after acceptance. Byline given. Kill fee negotiable. Not copyrighted. Buys first serial rights and second serial (reprint) rights. Computer printout submissions acceptable. Reports in 2 months on queries; 3 months on mss. Sample copy and writer's guidelines 9x12 SAE.
Nonfiction: Only. Query with published clips or send complete ms. Length: 1,000 words maximum. Pays 21¢/word minimum. Sometimes pays the expenses of writers on assignment.
Photos: Elda Hauschildt, managing editor. State availability of photos. Pays $25 and up for 5x7 or 8x10 b&w prints. Captions, model release, and identification of subjects required. Buys one-time rights.
Columns/Departments: Under contract.
Tips: "A freelancer can best break in to our publication with six years reporting experience, preferably with medical/science writing background. We rarely use untried writers."

THE MAYO ALUMNUS, Mayo Clinic, 200 SW 1st St., Rochester MN 55905. (507)284-4077. Editor: Teresa Opheim. 10% freelance written. "We usually use our own staff for writing, and only occasionally use freelancers." For physicians, scientists and medical educators who trained at the Mayo Clinic. Quarterly magazine. Circ. 12,000. Pays on acceptance. Publishes ms an average of 3 months after acceptance. Buys all rights. Computer printout submissions acceptable; prefers letter-quality. Free sample copy; mention *Writer's Market* in request. Writer's guidelines available on request.
Nonfiction: "We're interested in seeing interviews with members of the Mayo Alumni Association — stories about Mayo-trained doctors/educators/scientists/researchers who are interesting people doing interesting things in medicine, surgery or hobbies of interest, etc." Query with clips of published work. Length: 1,500-3,000 words. Payment negotiable. Sometimes pays the expenses of writers on assignment.
Photos: "We need art and must make arrangements if not provided with the story." State availability of photos with query. Captions preferred. Buys all rights.
Tips: "I keep a file of freelance writers, and when I need an alumnus covered in a certain area of the country, I contact a freelancer from that area. Those who suit my needs are the writers in the right place at the right time or those who have a story about an interesting alumnus."

MD MAGAZINE, MD Publications, 3 E. 54th St., New York NY 10022. (212)355-5432. Editor: Sharon AvRutick. Managing Editor: Judith Weinblatt. 90% freelance written. Monthly magazine on culture/travel; a general interest magazine for physicians, covering all aspects of human experience. "Our readers are practicing physicians. *MD's* role is to broaden their horizons, enlighten and entertain them." Circ. 130,000. Pays on acceptance. Publishes ms an average of 6 months after acceptance. Byline given. Offers 33⅓% kill fee. Buys one-time rights. Submit seasonal/holiday material 6 months in advance. Photocopied and previously published submissions OK. Computer printout submissions acceptable; prefers letter-quality. Reports in 1 month. Sample copy for 9x12 SAE, 10 first class stamps and $2; writer's guidelines for #10 SASE.

Nonfiction: Book excerpts, culture, essays (by doctors), opinion (by doctors), personal experience, general interest, historical/nostalgic, photo feature and travel. Buys 100 mss/year. Query with published clips. Length: 1,000-2,500 words. Pays $200-700. Rarely pays expenses of writers on assignment.

Photos: Send photos with ms. Reviews b&w and color transparencies (35mm or larger) and 8x10 prints and b&w contact sheets. Payment varies. Captions required.

Columns/Departments: Doctor After Hours (profile); Word Play (on language); Travel (short, focused, unique) and Artists Worth Watching (up-and-coming visual artist). Buys 25 mss/year. Query with published clips. Length: 1,200-1,500 words. Pays $350.

Tips: "It is fresh ideas and writing that make things and people come alive. Think about what cultural subject would capture a busy doctor's attention and keep it."

THE MEDICAL BUSINESS JOURNAL, Medical Business Publishing Corp., 3461 Rt. 22 E., Somerville NJ 08876. (201)231-9695. Editor: Satish Tyagi. 25% freelance written. "Our authors generally have health care industry credentials." Publishes ms an average of 1-2 months after acceptance. Byline given. Electronic submissions preferred; computer printout submissions OK.

Nonfiction: Query with published clips, or send complete ms. Length: 1,800 words. Pays for articles accepted.

Tips: "We would like to receive profiles of health care business segments and interesting small companies written for a highly sophisticated business audience. Articles should be oriented toward strategic planning executives and exhibit an understanding of the links between operating companies and the financial markets."

‡MEDICAL MEETINGS, The International Guide for Healthcare Meetings Planners, The Laux Co., Inc., 63 Great Rd., Maynard MA 01754. FAX: (508)897-6824. Editor: Betsy Bair Cassidy. 60% freelance written. A bimonthly trade journal covering the medical meetings market. Circ. 13,500. Pays on publication. Publishes ms an average of 2 months after acceptance. Byline given. Offers negotiable kill fee. Makes work-for-hire assignments. Computer printout submissions OK; prefers letter-quality. Reports in 1 month. Sample copy for 9x12 SAE with $1.65 postage; writer's guidelines for #10 SASE.

Nonfiction: How-to, trends, interview/profile and travel. Buys 30 mss/year. Length: 1,000-2,500 words. Pays $150-700 for assigned articles; no unsolicited manuscripts accepted.

Photos: State availability of photos with submission. Reviews 5x7 transparencies and 5x7 prints. Captions required. Buys one-time rights.

Tips: "Request our editorial calender and follow up with specific destination or feature articles you would like to write. Knowledge of meetings industry is very helpful."

THE NEW PHYSICIAN, 1890 Preston White Dr., Reston VA 22091. Editor: Richard Camer. 30% freelance written. For medical students, interns and residents. Published 9 times/year. Circ. 40,000. Buys first serial rights. Pays on publication. Publishes features an average of 2 months after acceptance. Will consider simultaneous submissions. Computer printout submissions acceptable; prefers letter-quality. Reports in 2 months or less. Sample copy for 10x13 SAE with 5 first class stamps; writer's guidelines for SASE.

Nonfiction: Articles on social, political, economic issues in medicine/medical education. "We want skeptical, accurate, professional contributors to do well-researched, comprehensive, incisive reports and offer new perspectives on health care problems. Not interested in highly technical or clinical material. Humorous articles and cartoons welcome." Buys about 12 features/year plus 6 departments. Query or send complete ms. Length: 500-3,500 words. Pays $75-650 with higher fees for selected pieces. Pays expenses of writers on assignment.

Tips: "We need more practically oriented articles for physicians-in-training—how-tos for young doctors starting out. They must be authoritative, and from objective sources, not a consultant trying to sell his services. Our magazine demands sophistication on the issues we cover. We are a professional magazine for readers with a progressive view on health care issues and a particular interest in improving the health care system. We are not however, *Medical Economics*. Freelancers should be willing to look deeply into the issues in question and not be satisfied with a cursory review of those issues."

‡THE NEW YORK DOCTOR, Metro Publications, affiliate of Milstein Enterprises, 11 E. 36th St., New York NY 10016. (212)779-0101. Biweekly news and city magazine for physicians in the five boroughs, Long Island and Westchester. "Our magazine covers AIDS; nursing shortages, malpractice and legislative issues affecting New York-area doctors. Circ. 31,000. Pays on acceptance. Byline given. Offers 35% kill fee. Buys first North American serial rights; also second rights if work has not appeared in another New York metropolitan-area publication or in another publication for physicians. Photocopied submissions OK. Query for electronic submissions. Letter-quality computer printout submissions OK. Reports in 1 month on mss. Sample copy for 8x10 SAE with 3 first class stamps.

Nonfiction: "We do not want anything too clinical or technical. Buys 35-60 mss/year. Query with published clips. Length: 250-1,500 words. Pays $150-750 for assigned articles. Pays expenses of writers on assignment.
Photos: State availability of photos with submission. Reviews contact sheets, negatives and prints. Payment varies. Captions and identification of subjects required.
Columns/Departments: Inside-talk (hospitals, government, pharmaceutical companies), Medicare, The Environment/Medical Waste Management, After Hours (New York area physicians' hobbies, life-styles), Recruitment (trends at hospitals, managed-care companies, pharmaceutical companies), Malpractice, Office Labs, Op-Ed (by health-care experts), Research (human-interest behind the effort), As Written (exquisitely detailed portraits of New York doctors by literary writers). Query June Zimmerman for departments (senior editor), Michelle Eldredge for As Written (associate editor), Glenn Deutsch for news (editor in chief).

‡THE PHYSICIAN AND SPORTSMEDICINE, McGraw-Hill, 4530 W. 77th St., Edina MN 55435. (612)835-3222. Features Editor: Debra Giel Adams. Managing Editor: Robin Bodishbaugh. Executive Editor: Frances Munnings. 30% freelance written. Prefers to work with published/established writers. Monthly magazine covering medical aspects of sports and exercise. "We look in our feature articles for subjects of practical interest to our physician audience." Circ. 130,000. Pays on acceptance. Publishes ms an average of 2 months after acceptance. Byline given. Buys one-time rights. Submit seasonal/holiday material 6 months in advance. Computer printout submissions OK; no dot-matrix. Reports in 1 month. Sample copy for $4; writer's guidelines for #10 SASE.
Nonfiction: Interview (persons active in this field); and technical (new developments in sports medicine). Query. Length: 250-2,500 words. Pays $150-900.
Photos: Marty Duda, photo editor. State availability of photos. Buys one-time rights.

PHYSICIAN'S MANAGEMENT, Edgell Communications Health Care Publications, 7500 Old Oak Blvd., Cleveland OH 44130. (216)243-8100. Editor: Bob Feigenbaum. Prefers to work with published/established writers. Monthly magazine emphasizes finances, investments, malpractice, socioeconomic issues, estate and retirement planning, small office administration, practice management, leisure time, computers, travel, automobiles, and taxes for primary care physicians in private practice. Circ. 110,000. Pays on acceptance. Publishes ms an average of 6 months after acceptance. Buys first serial rights only. Submit seasonal or holiday material 5 months in advance. Query for electronic submissions. Computer printout submissions acceptable; prefers letter-quality. Reports in 1 month. Sample copy $3.50. Writer's guidelines for #10 SASE.
Nonfiction: *"Physician's Management* is a practice management/economic publication, not a clinical one." Publishes how-to articles (limited to medical practice management); informational (when relevant to audience); and personal experience articles (if written by a physician). No fiction, clinical material or satire that portrays MD in an unfavorable light; or soap opera, "real-life" articles. Length: 2,000-2,500 words. Query with SASE. Pays $125/3-column printed page. Use of charts, tables, graphs, sidebars and photos strongly encouraged. Sometimes pays expenses of writers on assignment.
Tips: "Talk to doctors first about their practices, financial interests, and day-to-day nonclinical problems and then query us. Also, the ability to write a concise, well-structured and well-researched magazine article is essential. Freelancers who think like patients fail with us. Those who can think like MDs are successful. Our magazine is growing significantly. The opportunities for good writers will, therefore, increase greatly."

‡PHYSICIANS' TRAVEL & MEETING GUIDE, Cahners Publishing Company, 249 W. 17th St., New York NY 10011. (212)463-6405. Editor: Bea Riemschneider. Managing Editor: Susann Tepperberg. 70% freelance written. Monthly magazine that covers continuing medical education and travel. *Physicians' Travel & Meeting Guide* supplies continuing medical education events listings, education features and extensive travel coverage of international and national destinations. Circ. 250,000. Pays on acceptance. Byline given. Buys first North American serial rights. Submit seasonal material 4-6 months in advance. Computer printout submissions OK; prefers letter-quality. Reports in 3 months.
Nonfiction: Photo feature and travel. Buys 25-30 mss/year. Query with published clips. Length: 450-3,000 words. Pays $100-1,000 for assigned articles.
Photos: State availability of photos with submission. Send photos with submission. Reviews 35mm or 4x5 transparencies. Captions and identification of subjects required. Buys one-time rights.

PODIATRY MANAGEMENT, Box 50, Island Station NY 10044. (212)355-5216. Publisher: Scott C. Borowsky. Editor: Barry Block, D.P.M. Managing Editor: M.J. Goldberg. Business magazine published 8 times/year for practicing podiatrists. "Aims to help the doctor of podiatric medicine to build a bigger, more successful practice, to conserve and invest his money, to keep him posted on the economic, legal and sociological changes that affect him." Circ. 11,000. Pays on publication. Byline given. Buys first North American serial rights and second serial (reprint) rights. Submit seasonal/holiday material 4 months in advance. Simultaneous queries, and simultaneous, photocopied and previously published submissions OK. Reports in 2 weeks. Sample copy $2 with 9x12 SAE; free writer's guidelines for #10 SASE.

Nonfiction: General interest (taxes, investments, estate planning, recreation, hobbies); how-to (establish and collect fees, practice management, organize office routines, supervise office assistants, handle patient relations); interview/profile about interesting or well-known podiatrists; and personal experience. "These subjects are the mainstay of the magazine, but offbeat articles and humor are always welcome." Buys 25 mss/year. Query. Length: 1,000-2,500 words. Pays $150-350.

Photos: State availability of photos. Pays $15 for b&w contact sheet. Buys one-time rights.

PRIVATE PRACTICE, Box 12489, Oklahoma City OK 73157. Executive Editor: Brian Sherman. 60% freelance written. Eager to work with new/unpublished writers. For "medical doctors in private practice." Monthly. Buys first North American serial rights. "If an article is assigned, it is paid for in full, used or killed." Byline given "except if it was completely rewritten or a considerable amount of additional material is added to the article." Pays on publication. Publishes ms an average of 6 months after acceptance. Query. "Computer printout submissions acceptable; prefers letter-quality. Free sample copy and writer's guidelines.

Nonfiction: "Articles that indicate importance of maintaining freedom of medical practice or which detail outside interferences in the practice of medicine, including research, hospital operation, drug manufacture, etc. Straight reporting style. No clichés, no scare words, no flowery phrases to cover up poor reporting. Stories must be actual, factual, precise and correct. Copy should be lively and easy to read." No general short humor, poetry or short stories. "Please, no first person humor or other type of personal experiences with your doctor—i.e., my account of when my doctor told me I needed my first operation, etc." Buys 50-60 unsolicited mss/year. Length: up to 2,500 words. Pays "usual minimum $150."

Photos: Photos purchased with mss only. B&w glossies, 8x10. Payment "depends on quality, relevancy of material, etc."

Tips: "The article we are most likely to buy will be a straight report on some situation where the freedom to practice medicine has been enhanced, or where it has been intruded on to the detriment of good health."

‡**SENIOR PATIENT**, McGraw-Hill, 4530 W. 77th St., Edina MN 55435. (612)835-3222. Managing Editor: Cindy Christian Rogers. Features and Currents Editor: Kathleen Kimball-Baker. Special Reports Editor: Terry Monahan. Bimonthly magazine covering the health care needs of the elderly. "As the American population ages, doctors need more information to help them better care for the psychosocial—as well as the medical—needs of the elderly." 20-50% freelance written. Estab. 1989. Circ. 135,000. Pays on acceptance. Publishes ms an average of 4 months after acceptance. Byline given. (Sometimes byline shared with physician.) Buys limited rights. Send seasonal/holiday material 6 months in advance. Query for electronic submissions. Computer printout submissions OK. Reports in 6 weeks. Sample copy for $5; writer's guidelines for #10 SASE.

Nonfiction: Articles include journalistic features (Special Reports) on political, economic and social issues of interest to physicians who treat older adults; "not-exactly-medical" features (Features) that share one doctor's experiences about managing senior patients; and short news stories (Currents) with up-to-date information on Medicare policies, ethical concerns and recent studies that have immediate applicability to our readers' practices. Query. Length: 100-2,500 words. Pays $50-1,000.

Photos: Tina Adamek, photo editor. State availability of photos. Buys one-time rights.

‡**SPORTCARE & FITNESS, Preventing and Rehabilitating Athletic and Exercise Injury**, Sportcare & Fitness, Inc., 2400 W. 4th St., Wilmington DE 19805. (302)984-2600. Editor: Ali Kalamchi, M.D. Managing Editor: Linda Jones. 5% freelance written. Bimonthly magazine about sportsmedicine. "*Sportcare & Fitness* is read by sportcare professionals who are directly involved with the training and care of athletes (athletic trainers, coaches, sport PTs, nutritionists, psychologists). *Sportcare & Fitness* is an educational tool providing innovative, immediately useful material, not research or case reports." Estab. 1988. Circ. 35,000. Pays on publication. Publishes an average of 6 months after acceptance. Byline given. Offers $100 kill fee. Buys all rights. Submit seasonal material 6 months in advance. Simultaneous submissions OK. Query for electronic submissions. Computer printout submissions OK; prefers letter-quality. Free sample copy and writer's guidelines.

Nonfiction: How-to (medical exercise, coaching procedures) and technical (medical, clinical). "We do not want human interest, big name sports profiles, or laymen's fitness tips." Buys 3 mss/year. Query with published clips. Length: 900-1,500 words. Pays 20¢/word. Sometimes pays expenses of writers on assignment.

Photos: State availability of photos with submission. Reviews transparencies. Offers $50-200 per photo. Captions, model releases and identification of subjects required. Buys one-time rights.

Columns/Departments: Sports Nutrition (nutritional recommendations for *elite athletes*), 1,000 words; Equipment Connection (reviews of trends, design changes etc. [no manufac. comparisons]), 1,000 words; Training & Conditioning (T&C programs applicable to all sports from an accomplished trainer), 1,000 words and Exercise & Fitness (updates, strategies for sportcare professionals), 1,000 words. Buys 2 mss/year. Query with published clips. Length: 900-1,500 words. Pays 20¢/word.

Fillers: Facts, newsbreaks. Length: 100-300 words. Pays 20¢/word.
Tips: "Columns listed are most open to freelance. Most important: remember that we are a trade publication written for professional sportcare—but *not* physicians. Medical/technical material must be well explained, but not oversimplified."

STRATEGIC HEALTH CARE MARKETING, Health Care Communications, 211 Midland Ave., Box 594, Rye NY 10580. (914)967-6741. Editor: Michele von Dambrowski. 20% freelance written. Prefers to work with published/established writers. "Will only work with unpublished writer on a 'stringer' basis initially." A monthly newsletter covering health care services marketing in a wide range of settings including hospitals and medical group practices, home health services and urgent care centers. Emphasizing strategies and techniques employed within the health care field and relevant applications from other service industries. Pays on publication. Publishes ms an average of 2 months after acceptance. Byline given. Offers 25% kill fee. Buys first North American serial rights. Computer printout submissions acceptable; no dot-matrix. Reports in 1 month. Sample copy for 9x12 SAE and 3 first class stamps; guidelines sent with sample copy only.
Nonfiction: How-to, interview/profile, new product and technical. Buys 15 mss/year. Query with published clips. No unsolicited mss accepted. Length: 700-2,000 words. Pays $75-350. Sometimes pays the expenses of writers on assignment with prior authorization.
Photos: State availability of photos with submissions. (Photos, unless necessary for subject explanation, are rarely used.) Reviews contact sheets. Offers $10-30/photo. Captions and model releases required. Buys one-time rights.
Tips: "Writers with prior experience on business beat for newspaper or newsletter will do well. This is not a consumer publication—the writer with knowledge of both health care and marketing will excel. Interviews or profiles are most open to freelancers. Absolutely no unsolicited manuscripts; any received will be returned or discarded unread."

Music

Publications for musicians and for the recording industry are listed in this section. Other professional performing arts publications are classified under Entertainment and the Arts. Magazines featuring music industry news for the general public are listed in the Consumer Entertainment and Music sections. (Markets for songwriters can be found in *Songwriter's Market*—see Other Books of Interest).

‡**THE CHURCH MUSICIAN,** 127 9th Ave. N., Nashville TN 37234. (615)251-2961. Editor: William Anderson. 30% freelance written. Works with a small number of new/unpublished writers each year; eager to work with new/unpublished writers. Southern Baptist publication for Southern Baptist church music leaders. Monthly. Circ. 20,000. Buys all rights. Pays on acceptance. Publishes ms an average of 1 year after acceptance. No query required. Reports in 2 months. Free sample copy.
Nonfiction: Leadership and how-to features, success stories and articles on Protestant church music. "We reject material when the subject of an article doesn't meet our needs. And they are often poorly written, or contain too many 'glittering generalities' or lack creativity." Length: maximum 1,300 words. Pays up to 5¢/word.
Photos: Purchased with mss; related to mss content only. "We use only b&w glossy prints."
Fiction: Inspiration, guidance, motivation and morality with Protestant church music slant. Length: to 1,300 words. Pays up to 5¢/word.
Poetry: Church music slant, inspirational. Length: 8-24 lines. Pays $5-15.
Fillers: Short humor. Church music slant. No clippings. Pays $5-15.
Tips: "I'd advise a beginning writer to write about his or her experience with some aspect of church music; the social, musical and spiritual benefits from singing in a choir; a success story about their instrumental group; a testimonial about how they were enlisted in a choir—especially if they were not inclined to be enlisted at first. A writer might speak to hymn singers—what turns them on and what doesn't. Some might include how music has helped them to talk about Jesus as well as sing about Him. We would prefer most of these experiences be related to the church, of course, although we include many articles by freelance writers whose affiliation is other than Baptist. A writer might relate his experience with a choir of blind or deaf members. Some people receive benefits from working with unusual children—retarded, or culturally deprived, emotionally unstable, and so forth."

THE INSTRUMENTALIST, Instrumentalist Publishing Company, 200 Northfield Rd., Northfield IL 60093. (312)446-5000. Editor: Elaine Guregian. Approximately 95% freelance written. Works with a small number of new/unpublished writers each year. A monthly magazine covering instrumental music education for school band and orchestra directors, as well as performers and students. Circ. 22,000. Pays on publication. Publishes ms an average of 6-9 months after acceptance. Byline given. Buys all rights. Submit seasonal/holiday material 4 months in advance. Photocopied submissions OK. Computer printout submissions acceptable; prefers letter-quality. Reports in 1 month. Sample copy for 9x12 SAE and $2.50; free writer's guidelines.

Nonfiction: Book excerpts (rarely); essays (on occasion); general interest (on occasion, music); historical/ nostalgic (music); how-to (teach, repair instruments); humor (on occasion); interview/profile (performers, conductors, composers); opinion; personal experience; photo feature; and travel. Buys 100 mss/year. Send complete ms. Length: 750-1,750 words. Pays $30-45/published page.

Photos: State availability of photos with submission. Reviews slides and 5x7 prints. Payment varies. Captions and identification of subjects required. Buys variable rights.

Columns/Departments: Challenge (opinions on issues facing music educators), 500-750 words; Personal Perspective (advice and ideas from experienced educators and performers), 500-750 words; Idea Exchange ('how-tos' from educators), 250-500 words. Send complete ms. Length: 250-500 words. Pays $30-45.

Fillers: Anecdotes and short humor. Buys 5/year. Length: 250 words maximum. Pays $25-45.

Tips: "Know the music education field, specifically band and orchestra. Interviews with performers should focus on the person's contribution to education and opinions about it. We are interested in interviews and features that focus on ideas rather than on personalities."

INTERNATIONAL BLUEGRASS, International Bluegrass Music Association, 326 St. Elizabeth St., Owensboro KY 42301. (502)684-9025. Editor: Art Menius. 30% freelance written. Bimonthly newsletter covering bluegrass music industry. "We are the business publication for the bluegrass music industry. IBMA believes that our music has growth potential. We are interested in hard news and features concerning how to reach that potential and how to conduct business more effectively." Circ. 3,000. Pays on publication. Publishes ms an average of 2 months after acceptance. Byline given. Not copyrighted. Buys one-time rights. Submit seasonal/ holiday material 4 months in advance. Simultaneous, photocopied and previously published submissions OK. Query for electronic submissions. Computer printout submissions OK. Reports in 1 month on queries; 6 weeks on mss. Sample copy for 6x9 SAE and 2 first class stamps.

Nonfiction: Book excerpts, essays, how-to (conduct business effectively within bluegrass music), new product and opinion. No interview/profiles of performers (rare exceptions) or fans. Buys 6 mss/year. Query with or without published clips, or send complete ms. Length: 300-1,200 words. Pays $25 maximum for assigned articles. Pays in contributor's copies unless payment in cash agreed at assignment.

Photos: Send photos with submission. Reviews 5x8 prints. Offers no additional payment for photos accepted with ms. Captions and identification of subjects required. Buys one-time rights.

Columns/Departments: At the Microphone (opinion about the bluegrass music industry). Buys 6 mss/year. Send complete ms. Length: 300-1,200 words. Pays $0-25.

Fillers: Anecdotes, facts, newsbreaks and short humor. Buys 2/year. Length: 60-200 words.

Tips: "The easiest break-in is to submit an article about an organizational member of IBMA—such as a bluegrass association, instrument manufacturer or dealer, or performing venue. We're interested in a slant strongly toward the business end of bluegrass music. At the Microphone is the most open to freelancers. We're especially looking for material dealing with audience development and how to book bluegrass bands outside of the existing market."

OPERA NEWS, 1865 Broadway, New York NY 10023. Editor: Patrick J. Smith. 75% freelance written. Monthly magazine (May-November); biweekly (December-April). For all people interested in opera; the opera professional as well as the opera audience. Circ. 120,000. Pays on publication. Publishes ms an average of 3 months after acceptance. Buys first serial rights only. Pays negotiable kill fee. Byline given. Computer printout submissions acceptable; prefers letter-quality. Sample copy $2.50.

Nonfiction: Most articles are commissioned in advance. Monthly issues feature articles on various aspects of opera; in biweekly issues articles relate to the weekly broadcasts from the Metropolitan Opera. Emphasis is on high quality writing and an intellectual interest to the opera-oriented public. Informational, personal experience, interview, profile, historical, think pieces, personal opinion and opera reviews. Query; no telephone inquiries. Length: 2,500 words maximum. Pays 13¢/word for features; 11¢/word for reviews. Rarely pays the expenses of writers on assignment.

Photos: Pays minimum of $25 for photos purchased on assignment. Captions required.

‡RECORDING ENGINEER/PRODUCER, The Applications Magazine for Audio Professionals, Intertec Publishing, Suite C, 8330 Allison Ave., La Mesa CA 92041. (619)464-5577. FAX: (619)464-2643. Editor: Michael Fay. Managing Editor: Tom Cook. 85% freelance written. Monthly magazine that covers professional audio: engineers, producers, studios, concert sound. "We use applications articles on professional audio hardware use, function, technology. We look for material that will help audio professionals do their jobs better or easier." Circ. 20,094. Pays on acceptance. Publishes ms an average of 2-3 months after acceptance. Offers 50% kill fee. Buys all rights. Submit seasonal/holiday material 3 months in advance. Query for electronic submissions. Computer printout submissions OK. Reports in 2 weeks. Sample copy for 8x11 SAE with 6 first class stamps. Writer's guidelines for 8x11 SAE with 3 first class stamps.

Nonfiction: Interview/profile (audio engineers), new product (technical reports), opinion (does not mean letters to the editor) (guest editorials relative to professional audio) and technical (pro audio applications). "We do not want musician, artist or act profiles. This is not a music mag. No fanzine type articles." Buys 40-60 mss/year. Query. Length: 1,000-4,000 words. Pays $200-500 for assigned articles; $500 maximum for unsolicited articles. Sometimes pays expenses of writers on assignment.

Photos: Send photos with submission. Reviews 35mm transparencies and 4x5 prints. Offers no additional payment for photos accepted with ms. Captions and identification of subjects required. Buys all rights.

Columns/Departments: Buys 24 mss/year.

Tips: "Most of our articles are written by experts or specialists in the pro audio field. Other manuscripts come from equipment manufacturers. This is a very specialized market. If the writer is familiar with the publication already, and the level of experience and technological understanding required to write to the pro audio market, then all feature article subjects are open. We work from an editorial calendar for about half our features. Query re. calendar."

Office Environment and Equipment

GEYER'S OFFICE DEALER, 51 Madison Ave., New York NY 10010. (212)689-4411. Editor: Robert D. Rauch. 20% freelance written. For independent office equipment and stationery dealers, and special purchasers for store departments handling stationery and office equipment. Monthly. Buys all rights. Byline given. Pays on publication. Publishes ms an average of 3 months after acceptance. Computer printout submissions acceptable; prefers letter-quality. Reports "immediately."

Nonfiction: Articles on dealer efforts in merchandising and sales promotion; programs of stationery and office equipment dealers. Problem-solving articles related to retailers of office supplies, social stationery items, office furniture and equipment and office machines. Must feature specific stores. Query. Length: 300-1,000 words. Pays $175 minimum but quality of article is real determinant.

Photos: B&w glossies are purchased with accompanying ms with no additional payment.

MODERN OFFICE TECHNOLOGY, Penton Publishing, 1100 Superior Ave., Cleveland OH 44114. (216)696-7000. Editorial Director: John Dykeman. Editor: Lura K. Romei. Production Manager: Vickie Friess. 5-10% freelance written. A monthly magazine covering office automation for corporate management and corporate personnel, financial management, administrative and operating management, systems and information management, managers and supervisors of support personnel, and purchasing. Circ. 160,000. Pays on publication. Publishes ms an average of 6 months after acceptance. Byline given. Buys first and one-time rights. Photocopied submissions OK. Query for electronic submissions. Computer printout submissions acceptable. Reports in 1 month. Sample copy and writer's guidelines for 8½x11 SAE and 2 first class stamps.

Nonfiction: New product, opinion and technical. Query with or without published clips, or send complete ms. Length: open. Pays $250-500 for assigned articles; pays $250-400 for unsolicited articles. Pays expenses of writers on assignment.

Photos: Send photos with submission. Reviews contact sheets, 4x5 transparencies and prints. Additional payment for photos accepted with ms: consult editorial director. Captions and identification of subjects required. Buys one-time rights.

Columns/Departments: Reader's Soapbox (opinions on office-related subjects), 750 words. Buys 3 mss/year. Send complete ms. Pays $75-150.

Tips: "Submitted material should alway present topics, ideas, on issues that are clearly and concisely defined. Material should describe problems and solution. Writer should describe benefits to reader in tangible results whenever possible."

Paint

AMERICAN PAINT & COATINGS JOURNAL, American Paint Journal Co., 2911 Washington Ave., St. Louis MO 63103. (314)534-0301. FAX: (314)534-4458. Editor: Chuck Reitter. 10% freelance written. Weekly maga-

zine. For the coatings industry (paint, varnish, lacquer, etc.); manufacturers of coatings, suppliers to coatings industry, educational institutions, salesmen. Circ. 7,300. Pays on publication. Pays kill fee "depending on the work done." Buys all rights. Simultaneous and photocopied submissions OK. Computer printout submissions acceptable. Reports in 3 weeks. Free sample copy and writer's guidelines.

Nonfiction: Informational, historical, interview, new product, technical articles and coatings industry news. Buys 2 mss/issue. Query before sending long articles; submit complete ms for short pieces. Length: 75-1,200 words. Pays $5-100. Sometimes pays expenses of writers on assignment.

Photos: B&w (5x7) glossies purchased with or without mss or on assignment. Query. Pays $3-10.

Paper

PAPERBOARD PACKAGING, 111 E. Wacker Dr., 16th Floor, Chicago IL 60601. (312)938-2345. Editor: Mark Arzoumanian. 10% freelance written. Works with a small number of new/unpublished writers each year. Monthly. For "executives, managers, supervisors, and technical personnel who operate corrugated box manufacturing, folding carton converting and rigid box companies and plants." Circ. 15,000. Pays on publication. Publishes ms an average of 2 months after acceptance. Buys all rights. Photocopied submissions OK. Submit seasonal material 3 months in advance. Computer printout submissions acceptable; no dot-matrix. Sample copy on request.

Nonfiction: "Application articles, installation stories, etc. Contact the editor first to establish the approach desired for the article. Especially interested in box plant stories that have a human interest angle or history that makes company stand out." Buys semi-technical articles. Query. Length: open. Pays "$100/printed page (about 1,000 words to a page), including photos." Sometimes pays the expenses of writers on assignment.

Tips: "Writing style is not as much a concern to me as individual's knowledge of my industry (paperboard converting) and objective in writing article in first place. Nature of publication (trade) automatically means limited use of freelancers."

PULP & PAPER CANADA, Southam Information and Communications Group Inc., Suite 410, 3300 Côte Vertu, St. Laurent Quebec H4R 2B7 Canada. (514)339-1399. FAX: (514)339-1396. Editor: Peter N. Williamson. Managing Editor: Graeme Rodden. 5% freelance written. Prefers to work with published/established writers. Monthly magazine. Circ. 9,309. Pays on acceptance. Publishes ms "as soon as possible" after acceptance. Byline given. Offers kill fee according to prior agreement. Buys first North American serial rights. Computer printout submissions acceptable; prefers letter-quality. Reports in 2 weeks on queries; 3 weeks on mss. Free sample copy and writer's guidelines.

Nonfiction: How-to (related to processes and procedures in the industry); interview/profile (of Canadian leaders in pulp and paper industry); and technical (relevant to modern pulp and/or paper industry). No fillers, short industry news items, or product news items. Buys 10 mss/year. Query first with published clips or send complete ms. Articles with photographs (b&w glossy) or other good quality illustrations will get priority review. Length: 1,500-2,000 words (with photos). Pays $150 (Canadian funds)/published page, including photos, graphics, charts, etc. Sometimes pays the expenses of writers on assignment.

Tips: "Any return postage must be in either Canadian stamps or International Reply Coupons *only*."

Pets

Listed here are publications for professionals in the pet industry—pet product wholesalers, manufacturers, suppliers, and retailers, and owners of pet specialty stores, grooming businesses, aquarium retailers and those interested in the pet fish industry. The Veterinary section lists journals for animal health professionals. Publications for pet owners are listed in the Consumer Animal section.

‡**GROOM & BOARD, Incorporating "Groomers Gazette Kennelnews,"** H.H. Backer Associates Inc., Suite 504, 207S. Wabash Ave., Chicago IL 60604. (312)663-4040. Editor: Karen Long MacLeod. 10% freelance written. Magazine about grooming and boarding pets published 9 times/year. *"Groom & Board* is the

only national trade publication for professional pet groomers and boarding kennel operators. It provides news, technical articles and features to help them operate their businesses more successfully." Circ. 16,000. Pays on acceptance. Publishes ms an average of 6 months after acceptance. Byline given. Buys first North American serial rights, first rights, one-time rights, second serial (reprint) rights, all rights or exclusive to industry. Submit seasonal/holiday material 6 months in advance. Photocopied and previously published submissions OK (rarely). Query for electronic submissions. Computer printout submissions OK; prefers letter-quality. Reports in 2 months on queries; 1 month on mss. Sample copy $2.50. Writer's guidelines for #10 SASE.

Nonfiction: How-to (groom specific breeds of pets, run business, etc.), interview/profile (successful grooming and/or kennel operations) and technical. "We do not want consumer-oriented articles or stories about a single animal (animal heroes, grief, etc.)." Buys 3-6 mss/year. Query with or without published clips, or send complete ms. Length: 1,000-3,000 words. Pays $90 minimum for assigned articles; $65-200 for unsolicited articles. Sometimes pays expenses of writers on assignment.

Photos: Send photos with submission. Reviews contact sheets, transparencies and prints. Offers $5 per photo. Captions and identification of subjects required. Buys variable rights.

PET AGE, The Largest Circulation Pet Industry Trade Publication, H.H. Backer Associates, Inc., 207 S. Wabash Ave., Chicago IL 60604. (312)663-4040. Editor: Karen Long MacLeod. 10-20% freelance written. Prefers to work with published/established writers. Monthly magazine about the pet industry for pet retailers and industry. Circ. 17,000. Pays on acceptance. Publishes ms an average of 3-6 months after acceptance. Byline given. Buys first serial rights, first rights, all rights, or exclusive industry rights. Submit seasonal/holiday material 6 months in advance. Query for electronic submissions. Computer printout submissions acceptable; prefers letter-quality. Reports in 1 month. Sample copy for $2.50 and 9x12 SASE; writer's guidelines for #10 SASE.

Nonfiction: Book excerpts, profile (of a successful, well-run pet retail operation); how-to; interview; photo feature; and technical—all trade-related. Query first with published clips. Buys 6-12 mss/year. "Query as to the name and location of a pet operation you wish to profile and why it would make a good feature. No general retailing articles or consumer-oriented pet articles." Length: 1,000-3,000 words. Pays $75-200 for assigned articles; $50-150 for unsolicited articles. Sometimes pays the expenses of writers on assignment.

Photos: Reviews 5x7 b&w glossy prints. Captions and identification of subjects required. Offers $5 (negotiable) for photos. Buys one-time rights or all rights.

Tips: "Our readers already know about general animal care and business practices. This is a business publication for busy people, and must be very informative in easy-to-read, concise style. The type of article we purchase most frequently is the pet shop profile, a story about an interesting/successful pet shop. We need queries on these (we get references on the individual shop from our sources in the industry). We supply typical questions to writers when we answer their queries."

PET BUSINESS, 10850 SW 57th Ave., Miami FL 33156. (305)667-4402. Editor: Amy Jordan Smith. 20% freelance written. Eager to work with new/unpublished writers. "Our monthly news magazine reaches retailers, distributors and manufacturers of companion animals and pet products. Groomers, veterinarians and serious hobbyists are also represented." Circ. 15,000. Pays on publication. Publishes ms an average of 2 months after acceptance. Byline sometimes given. Buys first rights. Submit seasonal/holiday material 3 months in advance. Computer printout submissions OK; no dot-matrix. Sample copy $3. Writer's guidelines for SASE.

Nonfiction: "Articles must be newsworthy and pertain to animals routinely sold in pet stores (dogs, cats, fish, birds, reptiles and small animals). Research, legislative and animal behavior reports are of interest. All data must be attributed. No fluff!" Buys 40 mss/year. Send complete ms. "No queries—the news gets old quickly." Length: 50-800 words. Pays $5 per column inch.

Photos: Send photos (slides or prints) with submission. Offers $10-20 per photo. Buys one-time rights.

Tips: "We are open to national and international news written in standard news format. Buys cartoons; pays $10 each on publication."

THE PET DEALER, Howmark Publishing Corp., 567 Morris Ave., Elizabeth NJ 07208. (201)353-7373. FAX: (201)353-8221. Editor: Donna Eastman. 40% freelance written. Prefers to work with published/established writers; works with a small number of new/unpublished writers each year; and eager to work with new/published writers. "We want writers who are good reporters and clear communicators." Monthly magazine. Emphasizes merchandising, marketing and management for owners and managers of pet specialty stores, departments, and pet groomers and their suppliers. Circ. 16,000. Pays on publication. Publication "may be many months between acceptance of a manuscript and publication." Byline given. Phone queries OK. Submit seasonal/holiday material 3 months in advance. Computer printout submissions acceptable; no dot-matrix. Reports in 1 month. Sample copy and writer's guidelines for 8x10 SAE and $5.

Nonfiction: How-to (store operations, administration, merchandising, marketing, management, promotion and purchasing). Consumer pet articles—lost pets, best pets, humane themes—*not* welcome. Emphasis is on *trade* merchandising and marketing of pets and supplies. Buys 8 unsolicited mss/year. Length: 800-1,500 words. Pays $100.

Photos: Submit photo material with ms. No additional payment for 5x7 b&w glossy prints. "Six photos with captions required." Buys one-time rights. Will give photo credit for photogrpahy students.

Tips: "We're interested in store profiles outside the New York, New Jersey, Connecticut and Pennsylvania metro areas. Photos are of key importance. Articles focus on new techniques in merchandising or promotion. Want to see more articles from retailers and veternarians.Submit query letter first, with writing background summarized; include samples. We seek one-to-one, interview-type features on retail pet store merchandising. Indicate the availability of the proposed article, your willingness to submit on exclusive or first-in-field basis, and whether you are patient enough to await payment on publication."

Photography Trade

Journals for professional photographers are listed in this section. Magazines for the general public interested in photography techniques are in the Consumer Photography section. (For listings of markets for freelance photography use *Photographer's Market*—see Other Books of Interest.)

AMERICAN CINEMATOGRAPHER, A.S.C. Holding Corp., Box 2230, Hollywood CA 90078. (213)876-5080. FAX: (213)876-4973. Editor: George Turner. 50% freelance written. Monthly magazine. An international journal of film and video production techniques "addressed to creative, managerial, and technical people in all aspects of production. Its function is to disseminate practical information about the creative use of film and video equipment, and it strives to maintain a balance between technical sophistication and accessibility." Circ. 31,000. Pays on publication. Publishes ms an average of 3 months after acceptance. Buys all rights. Phone queries OK. Simultaneous and photocopied submissions OK. Query for electronic submission. Computer printout submissions OK. Sample copy for 9x12 SAE with $1 postage; writer's guidelines for #10 SASE.

Nonfiction: Jean Turner, associate editor. Descriptions of new equipment and techniques or accounts of specific productions involving unique problems or techniques; historical articles detailing the production of a classic film, the work of a pioneer or legendary cinematographer or the development of a significant technique or type of equipment. Also discussions of the aesthetic principles involved in production techniques. Recent article example: "Chances Are—Bridges the Generation Gap" (April 1989). Length 2,000-2,500 words. Pays according to position and worth. Negotiable. Sometimes pays the expenses of writers on assignment.

Photos: B&w and color purchased with mss. No additional payment.

Tips: "No unsolicited articles. Call first. Doesn't matter whether you are published or new. Queries must describe writer's qualifications and include writing samples. We expect expansion of videography."

PHOTO MARKETING, Photo Marketing Assocation Intl., 3000 Picture Place, Jackson MI 49201. (517)788-8100. Managing Editor: Margaret Hooks. 2% freelance written. A monthly magazine for photo industry retailers, finishers and suppliers. "Articles must be specific to the photo industry and cannot be authored by anyone who writes for other magazines in the photo industry. We provide management information on a variety of topics as well as profiles of successful photo businesses and analyses of current issues in the industry." Circ. 22,000. Pays on acceptance. Publishes ms an average of 2 months after acceptance. Byline given. Buys one-time rights and exclusive photo magazine rights. Simultaneous and photocopied submissions OK. Computer printout submissions OK. Reports in 2 weeks. Free sample copy and writer's guidelines.

Nonfiction: Interview/profile (anonymous consumer shops for equipment); personal experience (interviews with photo retailers); technical (photofinishing lab equipment); new technology (still electronic video). Buys 5 mss/year. Send complete ms. Length: 1,000-2,300 words. Pays $150-350.

Photos: State availability of photos with submission. Reviews negatives, 5x7 transparencies and prints. Offers $25-35 per photo. Buys one-time rights.

Columns/Departments: Anonymous Consumer (anonymous shopper shops for equipment at photo stores) 1,800 words. Buys 5 mss/year. Query with published clips. Length: 1,800 words. Pays up to $200.

Tips: "All main sections use freelance material: business tips, promotion ideas, employee concerns, advertising, coop, marketing. But they must be geared to and have direct quotes from members of the association."

THE PHOTO REVIEW, 301 Hill Ave., Langhorne PA 19047. (215)757-8921. Editor: Stephen Perloff. 50% freelance written. A quarterly magazine on photography with reviews, interviews and articles on art photography. Circ. 900. Pays on publication. Publishes ms an average of 3 months after acceptance. Byline given. Buys one-time rights. Simultaneous, photocopied and previously published submissions OK. Computer printout submissions OK. Reports in 3 weeks on queries; 2 months on mss. Sample copy for 8½x11 SAE with 6 first class stamps. Writer's guidelines for #10 SASE.

Nonfiction: Essays, historical/nostalgic, interview/profile and opinion. No how-to articles. Buys 10-15 mss/year. Query. Pays $25-200.

Photos: Send photos with submission. Reviews 8x10 prints. Offers no additional payment for photos accepted with ms. Captions and identification of subjects required. Buys one-time rights.

PHOTOLETTER, PhotoSource International, Pine Lake Farm, Osceola WI 54020. (715)248-3800. Fax: (715)248-7394. Editor: Don Wittman. Managing Editor: H.T. White. 10% freelance written. A monthly newsletter on marketing photographs. "The *Photoletter* pairs photobuyers with photographers' collections." Circ. 780. Pays on acceptance. Publishes ms an average of 6 months after acceptance. Byline given. Buys one-time rights and simultaneous rights. Submit seasonal/holiday material 3 months in advance. Simultaneous, photocopied, and previously published submissions OK. Query for electronic submissions. Computer printout submissions acceptable. Reports in 2 weeks on queries. Sample copy $3; writer's guidelines for #10 SASE.

Nonfiction: How-to market photos and personal experience in marketing photos. "Our readers expect advice in how-to articles." No submissions that do not deal with selling photos. Buys 6 mss/year. Query. Length: 300-850 words. Pays $50-100 for unsolicited articles.

Columns/Departments: Jeri Engh, columns department editor. "We would welcome column ideas." Length: 350 words. Pays $45-75.

Fillers: Facts. Buys 20/year. Length: 30-50 words. Pays $10.

Tips: "Columns are most open to freelancers. Bring an *expertise* on marketing photos or some other aspect of aid to small business persons."

PROFESSIONAL PHOTOGRAPHER, The Business Magazine of Professional Photography, Professional Photographers of America, Inc., 1090 Executive Way, Des Plaines IL 60018. (312)299-8161. Editor: Alfred DeBat. 80% freelance written. Monthly magazine of professional portrait, wedding, commercial, corporate and industrial photography. Describes the technical and business sides of professional photography—successful photo techniques, money-making business tips, legal considerations, selling to new markets, and descriptions of tough assignments and how completed. Circ. 32,000. Publishes ms an average of 6-9 months after acceptance. Byline given. Buys one-time rights. Submit seasonal/holiday material 6 months in advance. Simultaneous queries, and photocopied and previously published submissions OK. Computer printout submissions acceptable; prefers letter-quality. Reports in 2 months. Sample copy $3.25; free writer's guidelines.

Nonfiction: How-to. Professional photographic techniques: How I solved this difficult assignment, How I increased my photo sales, How to buy a studio . . . run a photo business etc. Special issues include February: Portrait Photography; April: Wedding Photography; May: Commercial Photography; and August: Industrial Photography. Buys 8-10 ms/issue. Query. Length: 1,000-3,000 words. "We seldom pay, as most writers are PP of A members and want recognition for their professional skills, publicity, etc."

Photos: State availability of photos. Reviews color transparencies and 8x10 unmounted prints. Captions and model release required. Buys one-time rights.

PTN, (formerly *Photographic Video Trade News*), PTN Publishing Corp, 210 Crossways Park Dr., Woodbury NY 11797. (516)496-8000. FAX: (516)496-8013. Editor: Bill Schiffner. 20-25% freelance written. A semimonthly magazine about the photographic/video and photofinishing industries. Circ. 15,000. Pays on publication. Publishes ms an average of 2 months after acceptance. Byline given. Buys first North American serial rights. Submit seasonal/holiday material 3 months in advance. Simultaneous, photocopied and previously published submissions OK. Reports in 2 weeks on queries; 3 weeks on mss. Free sample copy and writer's guidelines.

Nonfiction: Interview/profile, technical. Buys 50 mss/year. Send complete ms. Length: 750-1,500 words. Pays $75-300. Sometimes pays expenses of writers on assignment.

Photos: Send photos with submission. Reviews 5x7 prints. Offers no additional payment for photos accepted with ms. Captions and identification of subjects required. Buys one-time rights.

Tips: "Know the photo and video and photofinishing industries."

‡THE RANGEFINDER, 1312 Lincoln Blvd., Santa Monica CA 90406. (213)451-8506. FAX: (213)395-9058. Editor: Arthur C. Stern. Associate Editor: Carolyn Ryan. Monthly magazine; 80 pages. Emphasizes professional photography. Circ. 55,000. Pays on publication. Publishes ms an average of 3 months after acceptance. Byline given. Buys first North American serial rights. Phone queries OK. Submit seasonal material 4 months in advance. Computer printout submissions acceptable; prefers letter-quality to dot-matrix. Reports in 6 weeks. Sample copy $2.50; writer's guidelines for SASE.

Nonfiction: How-to (solve a photographic problem; such as new techniques in lighting, new poses or setups); profile; and technical. "Articles should contain practical, solid information. Issues should be covered in depth. Look thoroughly into the topic." No opinion or biographical articles. Buys 5-7 mss/issue. Query with outline. Length: 800-1,200 words. Pays $60/published page.

Photos: State availability of photos with query. Captions preferred; model release required. Buys one-time rights.
Tips: "Exhibit knowledge of photography. Introduce yourself with a well-written letter and a great story idea."

STUDIO PHOTOGRAPHY, PTN Publishing Corp., 210 Crossways Park Dr., Woodbury NY 11797. (516)496-8000. Editor: G. Faye Guercio. 85% freelance written. Prefers to work with published/established writers or experienced photographers with writing skills. Monthly magazine. Circ. 65,000. Pays on publication. Publishes ms an average of 6 months after acceptance. Not copyrighted. Buys first serial rights only. Submit seasonal/holiday material 5 months in advance. Computer printout submissions acceptable; prefers letter-quality. Reports in 6 weeks. Sample copy for 9½x12½ SAE and 5 first class stamps.
Nonfiction: Interview, personal experience, photo feature, communication-oriented, technical, travel and business-oriented articles. Buys 5-6 mss/issue. Length: 1,000-3,000 words. Pays about $75/page.
Photos: State availability of photos with query. Photos and article in one package.
Tips: "We look for professional quality writing coupled with top-notch photographs. Submit photos with all articles. No original transparencies, only fine quality duplicates. Only people with definite ideas and a sense of who they are need apply for publication. Read the magazine and become familiar with it before submitting work. Write for editorial schedule and writer/photographer's guidelines."

Plumbing, Heating, Air Conditioning and Refrigeration

DISTRIBUTOR, The Voice of Wholesaling, Technical Reporting Corp., 651 Washington St., #300, Chicago IL 60606-2180. (312)537-6460. Editorial Director: Steve Read. Managing Editor: James Butschli. 30% freelance written. Prefers to work with published/established writers. Monthly magazine for heating, ventilating, air conditioning and refrigeration wholesalers. Editorial material shows "executive wholesalers how they can run better businesses and cope with personal and business problems." Circ. 10,000. Pays on publication. Publishes ms an average of 1 month after acceptance. Byline sometimes given. Buys one-time rights. Submit seasonal/holiday material 3 months in advance. "We want material exclusive to the field (industry)." Photocopied submissions OK. Query for information on electronic submissions. Computer printout submissions acceptable; prefers letter-quality. Reports in 1 month. Sample copy $4.
Nonfiction: How-to (run a better business, cope with problems); and interview/profile (the wholesalers). No flippant or general approaches. Buys 12 mss/year. Query with or without published clips or send complete ms. Length: 1,000-2,000 words. Pays $100-200 (10¢/word). Sometimes pays the expenses of writers on assignment.
Photos: State availability of photos or send photos with query or ms. Pays $5 minimum. Captions and identification of subjects required.
Tips: "Know the industry—come up with a different angle on an industry subject (one we haven't dealt with in a long time). Wholesale ideas and top-quality business management articles are most open to freelancers."

DOMESTIC ENGINEERING MAGAZINE, Delta Communications, Inc., 385 N. York Rd., Elmhurst IL 60126. FAX: (312)530-3670. Executive Editor: Stephen J. Shafer. 15% freelance written. Prefers to work with published/established writers. Monthly magazine emphasizing plumbing, heating, air conditioning and piping for specialty contractors. Gives information on management, marketing and merchandising. Circ. 48,000. Pays on acceptance. Publishes ms an average of 6 months after acceptance. Buys all rights. Simultaneous, photocopied and previously published submissions OK. Computer printout submissions acceptable; prefers letter-quality. Reports in 1 month. Sample copy for 9x12 SAE.
Nonfiction: How-to (some technical in industry areas). Exposé, interview, profile, personal experience, photo feature and technical articles are written on assignment only and should be about management, marketing and merchandising for plumbing and mechanical contracting businessmen. Buys 12 mss/year. Query. Pays $25 minimum. Sometimes pays the expenses of writers on assignment.
Photos: State availability of photos. Pays $10 minimum for b&w prints (reviews contact sheets) and color transparencies.

EXPORT, 386 Park Ave. S., New York NY 10016. FAX: (212)779-7475. Editor: Jack Dobson. For importers and distributors in 183 countries who handle hardware, air conditioning and refrigeration equipment and related consumer hardlines. Bimonthly magazine in English and Spanish editions. Circ. 38,000. Buys first rights and second (reprint) rights to material originally published elsewhere. Byline given. Buys about 10 mss/year. Pays on acceptance. Publishes ms an average of 5 months after acceptance. Reports in 1 month. Query. Free sample copy and writer's guidelines.

Nonfiction: News stories of products and merchandising of air conditioning and refrigeration equipment, hardware and related consumer hardlines. Informational, how-to, interview, profile and successful business operations. Length: 1,000-3,000 words. Pays $400 maximum.

Tips: "One of the best ways to break in here is with a story originating outside the U.S. or Canada. Our major interest is in new products and new developments—but they must be available and valuable to overseas buyers. We also like company profile stories. Departments and news stories are staff-written."

FLORIDA FORUM, FRSA, Drawer 4850, Winter Park FL 32793. (305)671-3772. Editor: Glenda Arango-Meekins. 10% freelance written. Eager to work with new/unpublished writers. Monthly magazine covering the roofing, sheet metal and air conditioning industries. Circ. 8,500. Pays on publication. Publishes ms an average of 2 months after acceptance. Byline given. Buys one-time rights. Submit seasonal/holiday material 2 months in advance. Simultaneous queries, and simultaneous, photocopied, and previously published submissions OK. Query for electronic submissions. Computer printout submissions acceptable; prefers letter-quality. Reports in 2 weeks. Sample copy and writer's guidelines for #10 SASE.

Nonfiction: Interview/profile, new product, changes in roofing and sheet metal industries, and technical. Buys 25 mss/year. Send complete ms. Length: open. Pays variable rates.

Photos: Send photos with ms. Pays variable rates for b&w prints.

Columns/Departments: Buys 12/year. Send complete ms. Length: open. Pays variable rates.

HEARTH & HOME, (formerly *Wood'N Energy*), Gilford Publishing Inc., Box 2008, Laconia NH 03247. (603)528-4285. Editor: Jason Perry. 10% freelance written. Works with a small number of new/unpublished writers each year. Monthly magazine covering wood, coal and solar heating (residential). "*Hearth & Home* is mailed to retailers, distributors and manufacturers of wood, coal and solar heating equipment in the U.S. and Canada. A majority of our readers are small businessmen who need help in running their businesses and want to learn secrets to prospering in a field that has seen better days when oil embargoes were daily happenings." Circ. 32,000. Pays on publication. Publishes ms an average of 2 months after acceptance. Byline given. Buys one-time rights and all rights. Submit seasonal/holiday material 4 months in advance. Simultaneous queries OK. Query for electronic submissions. Computer printout submissions OK; prefers letter-quality. Reports in 2 weeks. Sample copy $2.50.

Nonfiction: Interview/profile (of stove dealers, manufacturers, others); photo feature (of energy stores); and technical (nuts and bolts of stove design and operation). Special issue includes Buyers Guide/Retailers Handbook (annual issue with retail marketing articles), "how to run your business," accounting. "The best times of year for freelancers are in our fall issue (our largest) and also in February and March." No "how wonderful renewable energy is" and experiences with stoves. "This is a *trade* book." Buys 25 mss/year. Query with or without published clips or send complete ms. Pays $25-300. Sometimes pays expenses of writers on assignment.

Photos: State availability of photos or send photos with query or ms. Pays $35 minimum for b&w contact sheets; $125 maximum for color contact sheets. Identification of subjects required. Buys one-time rights.

Columns/Departments: Reports (energy news; potpourri of current incentives, happenings); Regulations (safety and standard news); and Retailers Corner (tips on running a retail shop). "We are also looking for freelancers who could serve in our 'network' around the country. If there's a law passed regulating wood-stove emissions in their town, for example, they could send us a clip and/or rewrite the story. These pay $50 or so, depending on the clip. Contact editor on an individual basis (over the phone is OK) for a green light." Query with or without published clips. Length: 150-500 words. Pays $35-150.

Tips: "Short, hot articles on retailers (500 words and photographs) are desperately needed. We're looking for serious business articles. Freelancers who know the ins and outs of running a business have an excellent shot at being published."

HEATING, PLUMBING, AIR CONDITIONING, 1450 Don Mills Rd., Don Mills, Ontario M3B 2X7 Canada. (416)445-6641. FAX: (416)442-2077. Editor: Ronald H. Shuker. 20% freelance written. Monthly. For mechanical contractors; plumbers; warm air and hydronic heating, refrigeration, ventilation, air conditioning and insulation contractors; wholesalers; architects; consulting and mechanical engineers who are in key management or specifying positions in the plumbing, heating, air conditioning and refrigeration industries in Canada. Circ. 14,500. Pays on publication. Publishes ms an average of 3 months after acceptance. Computer printout submissions acceptable; prefers letter-quality to dot-matrix. Reports in 2 months. For a prompt reply, "enclose a sheet on which is typed a statement either approving or rejecting the suggested article which can either be checked off, or a quick answer written in and signed and returned." Free sample copy.

Nonfiction: News, technical, business management and "how-to" articles that will inform, educate, motivate and help readers to be more efficient and profitable who design, manufacture, install, sell, service, maintain or supply all mechanical components and systems in residential, commercial, institutional and industrial installations across Canada. Length: 1,000-1,500 words. Pays 20¢/word. Sometimes pays expenses of writers on assignment.

Photos: Photos purchased with ms. Prefers 4x5 or 5x7 glossies.

Tips: "Topics must relate directly to the day-to-day activities of *HPAC* readers in Canada. Must be detailed, with specific examples, quotes from specific people or authorities—show depth. We specifically want material from other parts of Canada besides southern Ontario. Not really interested in material from U.S. unless specifically related to Canadian readers' concerns. We primarily want articles that show *HPAC* readers how they can increase their sales and business step-by-step based on specific examples of what others have done."

SNIPS MAGAZINE, 407 Mannheim Rd., Bellwood IL 60104. (312)544-3870. Editor: Nick Carter. 2% freelance written. Monthly. For sheet metal, warm air heating, ventilating, air conditioning and roofing contractors. Publishes ms an average of 3 months after acceptance. Buys all rights. "Write for detailed list of requirements before submitting any work."

Nonfiction: Material should deal with information about contractors who do sheet metal, warm air heating, air conditioning, ventilation and roofing work; also about successful advertising campaigns conducted by these contractors and the results. Length: "prefers stories to run less than 1,000 words unless on special assignment." Pays 5¢ each for first 500 words, 2¢ each for additional word.

Photos: Pays $2 each for small snapshot pictures, $4 each for usable 8x10 pictures.

Printing

‡CANADIAN PRINTER & PUBLISHER, Maclean Hunter Ltd., 777 Bay St., Toronto, Ontario M5W 1A7 Canada. (416)596-5000. Editor: Jack Homer. Executive Editor: Wm. B. Forbes. 30% freelance written. Monthly magazine for printing and the allied industries. "*Canadian Printer & Publisher* wants technical matter on graphic arts, printing, binding, typesetting, packaging, specialty production and trends in technology. Circ. 11,000. Pays on acceptance. Publishes ms an average of 1-3 months after acceptance. Byline given. Buys first North American serial rights and second serial (reprint) rights. Simultaneous submissions OK. Reports in 2 weeks on queries; 3 weeks on mss. Free sample copy.

Nonfiction: Technical. "We do not want U.S. plant articles—this is a Canadian magazine. No profiles." Buys 30-40 mss/year. Query or send complete ms. Length: 400-1,600 words. Pays $50-350 Canadian. Pays expenses of writers on assignment "on prior arrangement."

Photos: Send photos with submission. Reviews 4x5 prints. Offers $10-30 per photo. Captions and identification of subjects required. Buys one-time rights.

‡COPY MAGAZINE, The Journal of New Imaging Technologies, Copy Magazine, Inc. 800 W. Huron St., Chicago IL 60622 (312)226-5600. FAX: (312)226-4640. Managing Editor: Dan Witte. 25% freelance written. Monthly magazine that covers toner-on-paper and other non-impact printing. "*Copy Magazine* seeks to present a technical understanding of the new imaging technologies and the businesses that use them." Circ. 20,000. Pays on publication. Byline given. Offers 50% kill fee. Buys all rights. Simultaneous and photocopied submissions OK. Query for electronic submissions. Computer printout submissions OK; prefers letter-quality. Reports in 1 month on queries. Sample copy $3 with 9x12 SAE and 65¢ postage. Writer's guidelines for #10 SASE.

Nonfiction: Book excerpts (DTP, copying), how-to (DTP, copying), interview/profile (industry suppliers), new product (relevant to trade), opinion, personal experience (in industry), photo feature (on DTP) and technical. "We do not want general business stuff (taxes, employee morale, etc.)" Buys 8-10 mss/year. Query. Length: 100-100,000 words. Pays $100-300 for assigned articles; $100-250 for unsolicited articles. Pays in contributor copies or other premiums "if they request such."

Photos: State availability of photos with submission. Reviews contact sheets. Offers no additional payment for photos accepted with ms. Captions, model releases and identification of subjects required. Buys all rights.

Columns/Departments: Fast Copy (minutiae, trivial news). Buys 40-50 mss/year. Query. Length: 100-1,000 words. Pays $25-75.

HIGH VOLUME PRINTING, Innes Publishing Co., Box 368, Northbrook IL 60062. (312)564-5940. Editor: Rod Piechowski. 20% freelance written. Eager to work with new/unpublished writers. Bimonthly magazine for book, magazine printers, large commercial printing plants with 20 or more employees. Aimed at telling the reader what he needs to know to print more efficiently and more profitably. Circ. 30,000. Pays on publication. Publishes ms an average of 9 months after acceptance. Byline given. Buys first and second serial rights. Simultaneous queries OK. Query for electronic submissions. Computer printout submissions acceptable. Reports in 2 weeks. Writer's guidelines, sample articles provided.

Nonfiction: How-to (printing production techniques); new product (printing, auxiliary equipment, plant equipment); photo feature (case histories featuring unique equipment); technical (printing product research and development); shipping; and publishing distribution methods. No product puff. Buys 12 mss/year. Query. Length: 700-3,000 words. Pays $50-300. Sometimes pays the expenses of writers on assignment.

Photos: Send photos with ms. Pays $25-150 for any size color transparencies and prints. Captions, model release, and identification of subjects required.

Tips: "Feature articles covering actual installations and industry trends are most open to freelancers. Be familiar with the industry, spend time in the field, and attend industry meetings and trade shows where equipment is displayed. We would also like to receive clips and shorts about printing mergers."

‡PRINT & GRAPHICS, Box 9525, Arlington VA 22209. (703)525-4800. FAX: (703)525-4805. Editor: Geoff Lindsay. 20% freelance written. Eager to work with new/unpublished writers. Monthly tabloid of the commercial printing industry for owners and executives of graphic arts firms. Circ. 18,000. Pays on acceptance. Publishes ms an average of 1 month after acceptance. Byline given. Buys one-time rights. Simultaneous queries, and simultaneous, photocopied and previously published submissions OK. Electronic submissions OK via standard protocols, but requires hard copy also. Computer printout submissions acceptable; prefers letter-quality to dot-matrix. Reports in 1 week. Sample copy for $1.50.

Nonfiction: Book excerpts, historical/nostalgic, how-to, interview/profile, new product, opinion, personal experience, photo feature and technical. "All articles should relate to graphic arts management or production." Buys 20 mss/year. Query with published clips. Length: 750-2,000 words. Pays $50-150.

Photos: State availability of photos. Pays $25-75 for 5x7 b&w prints. Captions and identification of subjects required.

PRINTING VIEWS, For the Midwest Printer, Midwest Publishing, 8328 N. Lincoln, Skokie IL 60077. (312)539-8540. FAX: (312)674-0081. Editor: Ed Schwenn. 10% freelance written. Prefers to work with published/established writers. Monthly magazine about printing and graphic arts for Midwest commercial printers, typographers, platemakers, engravers and other trade people. Circ. 15,000. Average issue includes 2-3 features. Pays on publication. Publishes ms an average of 2 months after acceptance. Byline given. Buys one-time rights. Phone queries OK. Reports in 2 weeks. Sample copy $2.

Nonfiction: Interview (possibly with graphic arts personnel); new product (in graphic arts in a Midwest plant); management/sales success in Midwest printing plant; and technical (printing equipment). Buys 6 feature mss/year. Query with clips of previously published work. "We will entertain query letters; no unsolicited manuscripts." Length: 2-9 typed pages. Pays $250 and up for assigned mss only.

Photos: State availability of photos. Reviews b&w contact sheets. Offers additional payment for photos accepted with ms. Captions preferred. Buys one-time rights.

QUICK PRINTING, The Information Source for Commercial Copyshops and Printshops, Coast Publishing, 1680 SW Bayshore Blvd., Port St. Lucie FL 34984. (407)879-6666. Publisher: Cyndi Schulman. Editor: Bob Hall. 50% freelance written. A monthly magazine covering the quick printing industry. "Our articles tell quick printers how they can be more profitable. We want figures to illustrate points made." Circ. 50,000. Pays on acceptance. Publishes ms an average of 4 months after acceptance. Byline given. Buys first North American serial rights, all rights. Submit seasonal/holiday material 6 months in advance. Photocopied submissions OK, if identified as such. Rarely uses previously published submissions. Query for electronic submissions. Computer printout submissions acceptable; prefers letter-quality. Reports in 1 month. Sample copy for $3 and 9x12 SAE with 7 first class stamps; writer's guidelines for #10 SAE with 1 first class stamp.

Nonfiction: How-to (on marketing products better or accomplishing more with equipment); new product; opinion (on the quick printing industry); personal experience (from which others can learn); technical (on printing). No generic business articles, or articles on larger printing applications. Buys 75 mss/year. Send complete ms. Length: 1,500-3,000 words. Pays $100 and up.

Photos: State availability of photos with submission. Reviews transparencies and prints. Offers no payment for photos. Captions and identification of subjects required.

Columns/Departments: Viewpoint/Counterpoint (opinion on the industry); QP Profile (shop profiles with a marketing slant); Management (how to handle employees and/or business strategies); and Marketing Impressions, all 500-1,500 words. Buys 10 mss/year. Send complete ms. Pays $75.

Tips: "The use of electronic publishing systems by quick printers is of increasing interest. Show a knowledge of the industry. Try visiting your local quick printer for an afternoon to get to know about us. When your articles make a point, back it up with examples, statistics, and dollar figures. We need good material in all areas, but avoid the shop profile. Technical articles are most needed, but they must be accurate. No puff pieces for a certain industry supplier."

‡**SCREEN PRINTING,** 407 Gilbert Ave., Cincinnati OH 45202. (513)421-2050. FAX: (513)421-5144. Editor: Susan Venell. 30% freelance written. Works with a small number of new/unpublished writers each year. Monthly magazine; 175 pages. For the screen printing industry, including screen printers (commercial, industrial and captive shops), suppliers and manufacturers, and ad agencies and allied professions. Circ. 15,000. Pays on publication. Publishes ms an average of 3-4 months after acceptance. Byline given. Buys all rights. Computer printout submissions acceptable; prefers letter-quality to dot-matrix. Reporting time varies. Free sample copy and writer's guidelines.

Nonfiction: "Since the screen printing industry covers a broad range of applications and overlaps other fields in the graphic arts, it's necessary that articles be of a significant contribution, preferably to a specific area of screen printing. Subject matter is fairly open, with preference given to articles on administration or technology; trends and developments. We try to give a good sampling of technical business and management articles; articles about unique operations. We also publish special features and issues on important subjects, such as material shortages, new markets and new technology breakthroughs. While most of our material is nitty-gritty, we appreciate a writer who can take an essentially dull subject and encourage the reader to read on through concise, factual, 'flairful' and creative, expressive writing. Interviews are published after consultation with and guidance from the editor." Interested in stories on unique approaches by some shops. No general, promotional treatment of individual companies. Buys 6-10 unsolicited mss/year. Query. Unsolicited mss not returned. Length: 1,500-3,500 words. Pays minimum of $150 for major features. Sometimes pays the expenses of writers on assignment.

Photos: Cover photos negotiable; b&w or color. Published material becomes the property of the magazine.

Tips: "If the author has a working knowledge of screen printing, assignments are more readily available. General management articles are rarely used."

Real Estate

AREA DEVELOPMENT MAGAZINE, 525 Northern Blvd., Great Neck NY 11021. (516)829-8990. Editor-in-Chief: Tom Bergeron. 40% freelance written. Prefers to work with published/established writers. Emphasizes corporate facility planning and site selection for industrial chief executives worldwide. Monthly magazine. Circ. 33,000. Pays when edited. Publishes ms an average of 2 months after acceptance. Buys first rights only. Byline given. Photocopied submissions OK. Computer printout submissions acceptable; prefers letter-quality. Reports in 1-3 weeks. Free sample copy. Writer's guidelines for #10 SASE.

Nonfiction: How-to (case histories of companies; experiences in site selection and all other aspects of corporate facility planning); historical (if it deals with corporate facility planning); interview (corporate executives and industrial developers); and related areas of site selection and facility planning such as taxes, labor, government, energy, architecture and finance. Buys 8-10 mss/yr. Query. Pays $30-40/ms page; rates for illustrations depend on quality and printed size. Sometimes pays the expenses of writers on assignment.

Photos: State availability of photos with query. Prefer 8x10 or 5x7 b&w glossy prints. Captions preferred.

Tips: "Articles must be accurate, objective (no puffery) and useful to our industrial executive readers. Avoid any discussion of the merits or disadvantages of any particular areas or communities. Writers should realize we serve an intelligent and busy readership—they should avoid 'cute' allegories and get right to the point."

BUSINESS FACILITIES, Bus Fac Publishing Co., 121 Monmouth St., Box 2060, Red Bank NJ 07701. (201)842-7433. FAX: (201)758-6634. Editor: Eric Peterson. Managing Editor: James Picerno. 20% freelance written. Prefers to work with published/established writers. A monthly magazine covering economic development and commercial and industrial real estate. "Our audience consists of corporate site selectors and real estate people; our editorial coverage is aimed at providing news and trends on the plant location and corporate expansion field." Circ. 32,000. Pays on publication. Publishes ms an average of 3 months after acceptance. Byline given. Buys all rights. Photocopied and previously published submissions OK. Computer printout submissions acceptable; prefers letter-quality. Reports in 2 weeks. Free sample copy and writer's guidelines.

Nonfiction: General interest, how-to, interview/profile and personal experience. No news shorts and no clippings; feature material only. Buys 12-15 mss/year. Query. Length: 1,000-3,000 words. Pays $200-1,000 for assigned articles, pays $200-600 for unsolicited articles. Sometimes pays the expenses of writers on assignment.

Photos: State availability of photos with submission. Reviews contact sheets, negatives, transparencies and 8x10 prints. Payment negotiable. Captions and identification of subjects required. Buys one-time rights.

Tips: "First, remember that our reader is a corporate executive responsible for his company's expansion and/or relocation decisions and our writers have to get inside that person's head in order to provide him with something that's helpful in his decision-making process. And second, the biggest turnoff is a telephone query.

We're too busy to accept them and must require that all queries be put in writing. Submit major feature articles only; all news departments, fillers, etc., are staff prepared. A writer should be aware that our style is not necessarily dry and business-like. We tend to be more upbeat and a writer should look for that aspect of our approach. We are currently overstocked, however, and for the near future will be accepting fewer pieces."

FINANCIAL FREEDOM REPORT, 1831 Fort Union Blvd., Salt Lake City UT 84121. (801)943-1280. FAX: (801)942-7489. Chairman of the Board: Mark O. Haroldsen. Managing Editor: Carolyn Tice. 25% freelance written. Eager to work with new/unpublished writers. For "professional and nonprofessional investors and would-be investors in real estate—real estate brokers, insurance companies, investment planners, truck drivers, housewives, doctors, architects, contractors, etc. The magazine's content is presently expanding to interest and inform the readers about other ways to put their money to work for them." Monthly magazine. Circ. 50,000. Pays on publication. Publishes ms an average of 3 months after acceptance. Buys all rights. Phone queries OK. Simultaneous submissions OK. Query for electronic submissions. Computer printout submissions acceptable; prefers letter-quality. Reports in 2 weeks. Sample copy $3; free writer's guidelines.
Nonfiction: How-to (find real estate bargains, finance property, use of leverage, managing property, developing market trends, goal setting, motivational); and interviews (success stories of those who have relied on own initiative and determination in real estate market or related fields). Buys 25 unsolicited mss/year. Query with clips of published work or submit complete ms. Length: 1,500-3,000 words. "If the topic warranted a two- or three-parter, we would consider it." Pays 5-10¢/word. Sometimes pays the expenses of writers on assignment.
Photos: Send photos with ms. Uses 8x10 b&w or color matte prints. Makes additional payment for photos accepted with ms. Captions required.
Tips: "We would like to find several specialized writers in our field of real estate investments. A writer would need to have had some hands-on experience in the real estate field."

JOURNAL OF PROPERTY MANAGEMENT, Institute of Real Estate Management, Box 109025, Chicago IL 60610-9025. (312)661-1930. FAX: (312)661-0217. 15% freelance written. Bimonthly magazine covering real estate management and development. "The *Journal* has a feature/information slant designed to educate readers in the application of new techniques and to keep them abreast of current industry trends." Circ. 17,500. Pays on acceptance. Publishes ms an average of 3 months after acceptance. Byline given. Buys all rights. Simultaneous submissions OK. Query for electronic submissions. Computer printout submissions OK; no dot-matrix. Reports in 6 weeks on queries; 3 weeks on mss. Free sample copy and writer's guidelines.
Nonfiction: How-to, interview, technical (building systems/computers), demographic shifts in business employment and buying patterns, oversupply of real estate. "No non-real estate subjects personality or company, humor." Buys 8-12 mss/year. Query with published clips. Length: 1,500-4,000 words. Pays $100-750 for assigned articles; pays $50-750 for unsolicited articles. Pays in contributor's copies "if so agreed." Sometimes pays the expenses of writers on assignment.
Photos: State availability of photos with submission. Reviews contact sheets. Offers no additonal payment for photos accepted with ms. Model releases and identification of subjects required. Buys one-time rights.
Columns/Departments: Bridget Gorman, editor. Insurance Insights, Tax Corner, Investment Corner and Legal Corner. Buys 6-8 mss/year. Query. Length: 750-1,500 words. Pays $50-350.

‡REAL ESTATE COMPUTING, Real Estate Software Company, Inc., Suite D, 10622 Montwood Dr., El Paso TX 79935. (915)598-2435. Editor: Kevin L. Chestnut. Managing Editor: C. Bryant Crawford. 25% freelance written. Bimonthly tabloid on computers and computerization of/for real estate professionals. Circ. 85,000. Pays on publication. Publishes ms an average of 2 months after acceptance. Byline given. Offers 25% kill fee. Buys first rights, one-time rights, or second serial (reprint) rights. Submit seasonal/holiday material 3 months in advance. Photocopied submissions and previously published submissions OK. Query for electronic submissions. Computer printout submissions OK; prefers letter-quality. Reports in 3 weeks on queries. Free sample copy and writer's guidelines.
Nonfiction: Book excerpts, how-to (computerize, increase production with computers), interview/profile (real estate pros, computer experts, opinion (on real estate computerization trends, needs, state of), photo feature, technical and real estate sales and management success secrets. "No articles on competing companies or products or articles which do not involve both computers and real estate. We don't want articles that involve Apple or other non-IBM-compatible computers." Query. Length: 500-1,500 words. Pays $50-150 for assigned articles; $25-100 for unsolicited articles. Sometimes pays expenses of writers on assignment.
Photos: State availability of photos with submission. Reviews contact sheets and prints. Offers $10-35 per photo. Model releases and identification of subjects required. Buys one-time rights.
Fillers: Facts, gags to be illustrated by cartoonist, newsbreaks and short humor. Buys 10/year. Length: 50-500 words. Pays $10-50.
Tips: "Although originally produced to keep in touch with users of our software products, the strong response from non-users has let us to greatly expand our editorial aim. We now mail to every real estate broker in the USA. Our readers are not technical wizards; they're busy real estate professionals and residential property managers. They look to us for plain-English solutions to their everyday computerization problems. Our

publication is colorful and illustrated with graphs, charts and 'button-by-button examples'. We like interviews with agents who've successfully implemented computers into their offices. We expect facts to be researched and well documented."

Resources and Waste Reduction

‡**GROUND WATER AGE**, National Trade Publications, 13 Century HIll Dr., Latham NY 12110. (518)783-1281. Editor: Alan M. Petrillo. 30% freelance written. Monthly magazine that covers water well drilling and pump installation. "We want good, solid writing, accurate facts and up-to-date information on technical subjects." Circ. 27,000. Pays on acceptance. Publishes ms an average of 3-4 months after acceptance. Byline given. Buys first North American serial rights. Submit seasonal/holiday material 6 months in advance. Simultaneous and previously published submissions OK. Query for electronic submissions. Computer printout submissions OK; prefers letter-quality. Reports in 2 weeks on queries; 1 month on mss. Sample copy for 9x12 SAE with 5 first class stamps.
Nonfiction: Historical/nostalgic, interview/profile, new product, photo feature and technical. Buys 12-20 mss/year. Query with published clips. Length: 750-3,000 words. Pays $50-350 for assigned articles; $50-250 for unsolicited articles. "Trades articles for advertising, on occasion and when desirable." Sometimes pays expenses of writers on assignment.
Photos: State availability of photos with submission. Reviews contact sheets, negatives, transparencies and prints. Offers no additional payment for photos accepted with ms. Identification of subjects required. Buys one-time rights.
Columns/Departments: Strategic Marketing (info on how to best market the services of well drillers and pump installers), 500-600 words; and Inside Business (tips for improving business productivity, etc.), 500-600 words. Buys 12 mss/year. Query with published clips. Length: 500-600 words. Pays $50-150.

THE PUMPER, COLE Publishing Inc., Drawer 220, Three Lakes WI 54562. (715)546-3347. Production Manager: Ken Lowther. 50% freelance written. Eager to work with new/unpublished writers. A monthly tabloid covering the liquid waste hauling industry (portable toilet renters, septic tank pumpers, industrial waste haulers, chemical waste haulers, oil field haulers, and hazardous waste haulers). "Our publication is read by companies that handle liquid waste and manufacturers of equipment." Circ. 15,000. Pays on publication. Publishes ms an average of 1 month after acceptance. Byline given. Buys first serial rights. Submit seasonal/holiday material 3 months in advance. Simultaneous queries, and simultaneous, photocopied, and previously published submissions OK. Query for electronic submissions. Computer printout submissions acceptable; no dot-matrix. Reports in 1 month. Free sample copy and writer's guidelines.
Nonfiction: Exposé (government regulations, industry problems, trends, public attitudes, etc.); general interest (state association meetings, conventions, etc.); how-to (related to industry, e.g., how to incorporate septage or municipal waste into farm fields, how to process waste, etc.); humor (related to industry, especially septic tank pumpers or portable toilet renters); interview/profile (including descriptions of business statistics, type of equipment, etc.); new product; personal experience; photo feature; and technical (especially reports on research projects related to disposal). "We are looking for quality articles that will be of interest to our readers; length is not important. We publish trade journals. We need articles that deal with the trade. Studies on land application of sanitary waste are of great interest." Query or send complete ms. Pays 7½¢/word.
Photos: Send photos with query or ms. Pays $15 for b&w and color prints that are used. No negatives. "We need good contrast." Captions "suggested" and model release required. Buys one-time rights.
Tips: "Material must pertain to liquid waste-related industries listed above. We hope to expand the editorial content of our monthly publications. We also have publications for sewer and drain cleaners with the same format as *The Pumper*; however, *The Cleaner* has a circulation of 18,000. We are looking for the same type of articles and pay is the same."

RESOURCE RECYCLING, North America's Recycling Journal, Resource Recycling, Inc., Box 10540, Portland OR 97210. (503)227-1319. FAX: (503)227-3864. Editor: Jerry Powell. 25% freelance written. Eager to work with·new/unpublished writers. A trade journal published 12 times/year, covering recycling of paper, plastics, metals and glass. Circ. 6,000. Pays on publication. Publishes ms an average of 3-9 months after acceptance. Byline given. Buys first rights. Simultaneous, photocopied and previously published submissions OK. Query for electronic submissions. Computer printout submissions OK; prefers letter-quality. Reports in

1 month on queries. Sample copy and writer's guidelines for 9x12 SAE with 5 first clas stamps. "No nontechnical or opinion pieces." Buys 15-20 mss/year. Query with published clips. Length: 1,200-1,800 words. Pays $100-250. Pays with contributor copies "if writers are more interested in professional recognition than financial compensation." Sometimes pays the expenses of writers on assignment.

Photos: State availability of photos with submission. Reviews contact sheets, negatives and prints. Offers $5-50. Identification of subjects required. Buys one-time rights.

Tips: "Overviews of one recycling aspect in one state (e.g., oil recycling in Alabama) will receive attention. We will increase coverage of plastics recycling."

Selling and Merchandising

Sales personnel and merchandisers interested in how to sell and market products successfully consult these journals. Publications in nearly every category of Trade also buy sales-related material if it is slanted to the product or industry with which they deal.

THE AMERICAN SALESMAN, 424 N. 3rd St., Burlington IA 52601. Publisher: Michael S. Darnall. Editorial Supervisor: Doris J. Ruschill. Editor: Barbara Boeding. 95% freelance written. Prefers to work with published/established writers; works with a small number of new/unpublished writers each year. Monthly magazine for distribution through company sales representatives. Circ. 1,855. Pays on publication. Publishes ms an average of 4 months after acceptance. Buys all rights. Computer printout submissions OK; no dot-matrix. Sample copy and writer's guidelines for 9½x6½ SAE and 2 first class stamps; mention *Writer's Market* in request.

Nonfiction: Sales seminars, customer service and follow-up, closing sales, sales presentations, handling objections, competition, telephone usage and correspondence, managing territory and new innovative sales concepts. No sexist material, illustration written from a salesperson's viewpoint. No ms dealing with supervisory problems. Query. Length: 900-1,200 words. Pays 3¢/word. Uses no advertising. Follow AP Stylebook. Include biography and/or byline with ms submissions. Author photos used.

‡ANSOM, Army/Navy Store & Outdoor Merchandiser, Howmark Publishing, 567 Morris Ave. Elizabeth NJ 07208. (201)353-7373. Editor: Timothy Herbrick. Managing Editor: Mitch Harrison. 35% freelance written. Monthly tabloid that covers apparel, hunting, camping, surplus markets. "A business journal for independent retailers of surplus, apparel, camping, hunting, work and outdoor merchandise." Circ. 11,299. Pays on publication. Publishes ms an average of 2 months after acceptance. Byline given. Buys one-time rights. Submit seasonal/holiday material 6 months in advance. Photocopied submissions OK. Reports in 2 weeks on queries. Sample copy for 10 SAE with $2.40 postage.

Nonfiction: For special issues, *ANSOM* needs material on store management in November, Christmas in June, and back to school in April. "We do not want first person, non-business related material." Buys 10 mss/year. Send complete ms. Length: 500-3,000 words. Pays $50-125.

Photos: Send photos with submission. Reviews 5x10 prints. Offers no additional payment for photos accepted with ms. Identification of subjects required. Buys one-time rights.

Columns/Departments: Camping Corner (camping market updates—products and sales), 700 words; and Business Insights (anything related to retailing), 700 words. Buys 6 mss/year. Query. Length: 500-1,000 words. Pays $50-75.

ART MATERIAL TRADE NEWS, The Journal of All Art, Craft, Engineering and Drafting Supplies, Communication Channels Inc., 6255 Barfield Rd., Atlanta GA 30328. (404)256-9800. Editor: Tom C. Cooper. 15% freelance written. Works with a small number of new/unpublished writers each year. Monthly magazine on art materials. "Our editorial thrust is to bring art materials retailers, distributors and manufacturers information they can use in their everyday operations." Circ. 12,000. Pays on publication. Publishes ms an average of 3 months after acceptance. "All assigned manuscripts are published." Buys first serial rights. Submit seasonal/holiday material 3 months in advance. Photocopied submissions OK. Computer printout submissions acceptable; prefers letter-quality to dot-matrix. Reports in 6 weeks. Sample copy for 9x12 SAE and $1 postage; writer's guidelines for #10 SAE and 1 first class stamp.

Nonfiction: How-to (sell, retail/wholesale employee management, advertising programs); interview/profile (within industry); and technical (commercial art drafting/engineering). "We encourage a strong narrative style where possible. We publish an editorial 'theme' calendar at the beginning of each year." Buys 15-30 mss/year. Query with published clips. Length: 1,000-3,000 words (prefers 2,000 words). Pays $75-300.

Photos: State availability of photos. Pays $10 maximum for b&w contact sheets. Identification of subjects required.
Columns/Departments: Creative Corner (crafts) and Print & Framing. Buys 12-15 mss/year. Query with published clips. Length: 1,000-2,000 words. Pays $75-200.
Tips: "We are very interested in developing a cadre of writers who know the art materials industry well. We would like to receive articles that show knowledge of the specifics of the art materials industry. We reject many general business articles that are not useful to our readers because they fail to take into account the nature of the industry. A current, solid background in any one of these areas helps—commercial art, retail selling, wholesale selling, business finance, employee management, interviewing or advertising. We're refocusing on articles that will help art material storeowners run their business better (less focus on manufacturers). More news-you-can-use articles."

BALLOONS TODAY MAGAZINE, The Original Balloon Magazine of New-Fashioned Ideas, Festivities Publications, 1205 W. Forsyth St., Jacksonville, FL 32204. (904)634-1902. Editor: Debra Paulk. 10% freelance written. Monthly international trade journal for professional party decorators, and for gift delivery businesses. Circ. 12,000. Pays on pubilcation. Publishes ms an average of 3 months after acceptance. Byline given. Buys one-time rights. Submit seasonal/holiday material 6 months in advance. Query for electronic submissions. Computer printout submissions OK. Reports in 3 weeks on queries; 2 weeks on mss. Sample copy for 9x12 SAE with $2 in postage.
Nonfiction: Interview/profile, photo feature, technical, craft. Buys 24 mss/year. Query with or without published clips, or send complete ms. Length: 500-1,500 words. Pays $100-300 assigned articles; $50-200 for unsolicited articles. Sometimes pays expenses of writers on assignment.
Photos: Send photos with submission. Reviews 2x2 transparencies and 3x5 prints. Pays $25 per photo accepted with manuscript (designs, arrangements, decorations only—no payment for new products). Captions, model releases and identification of subjects required. Buys one-time rights.
Columns/Departments: Great Ideas (craft projects using balloons, large scale decorations), 200-500 words. Send full manuscript with photos. Pays $25 per photo, $20-50.
Tips: "Show unusual, lavish, and outstanding examples of balloon sculpture, design and decorating. Offer specific how-to information. Be positive and motivational in style."

BEAUTY AGE, Tramedia, Inc., Suite B, 113 West 85th St., New York NY 10024. (212)580-2756. Editor: Paul M. Cohen. 25% freelance written. A bimonthly magazine about cosmetics, fragrances and cosmetic accessories for retail buyers, merchandisers and corporate personnel. Circ. 26,000. Pays on publication. Byline given. Offers 100% kill fee. Buys first and second serial (reprint) rights. Submit seasonal/holiday material 3 months in advance. Computer printout submissions OK. Sample copy for 9x12 SAE with $2 postage.
Nonfiction: Interview/profile, new product. Buys 30 mss/year. Query. Length: 1,000-1,500 words. Pays $200-400 for assigned articles. Sometimes pays expenses of writers on assignment.
Photos: Send photos with submission. Reviews negatives, transparencies and prints. Offers no additional payment for photos accepted with ms. Captions, model releases and identification of subjects required. Buys all rights.

‡CANADIAN COMPUTER DEALER NEWS, Plesman Publication Ltd., Suite 110, 255 Consumers Rd., Willowdale, Ontario M2J 5B1 Canada. (416)497-9562. Editor: Gord Campbell. Managing Editor: Cathy Hilborn. 10% freelance written. Biweekly newspaper about computers, for retailers. Circ. 7,600. Pays on publication. Publishes ms an average of 1 month after acceptance. Byline given. Offers negotiable kill fee. Buys first North American serial rights. Submit seasonal/holiday material 2 months in advance. Query for electronic submissions. Computer printout submissions OK; prefers letter-quality. Free sample copy and writer's guidelines.
Nonfiction: Exposé, how-to (market computers effectively, establish advertising budgets or choose a P.R. firm), interview/profile, new product, personal experience (applications) and other. Buys 250 mss/year. Query with or without published clips, or send complete ms. Length: 600-1,000 words. Pays $200-400 for assigned articles. Negotiable payment for unsolicited articles. Sometimes pays expenses of writers on assignment.
Photos: Send photos with submission. Reviews 3x5 b&w prints. Identification of subjects required.
Columns/Departments: Dealer Report (profile of Canadian computer dealer), 800 words; Distribution (profile of Canadian computer distributor), 800 words; Var Tracks (profile of a Canadian VAR *or* of vendors VAR program), 800 words and Vendor Update (profile of a Canadian computer vendor), 800 words. Buys 50 mss/year. Query with published clips. Pays $200-400.
Tips: "If freelancer is familiar with the computer industry, they might call to discuss story ideas. They would then be asked to send a more detailed outline. Managing editor might suggest contacts, sources, if necessary."

‡CANADIAN COMPUTER RESELLER, Maclean Hunter, 777 Bay St., Maclean Hunter Bldg., 5th Fl., Toronto, Ontario M5W1A7 Canada. (416)596-5994. FAX: (416)593-3166. Editor: Tracy Peverett. 50% freelance written. Magazine that covers computer industry, specifically distribution (dealers, retailers of computers), which is published 10 times yearly. "The magazine goes to companies who sell computers rather than those who buy and use them."Circ. 8,500. Pays on acceptance. Publishes ms an average of 2 months after acceptance. Byline given. Buys first Canadian serial rights. Submit seasonal/holiday material 2 months in advance. Simultaneous submissions and photocopied submissions OK. Computer printout submissions OK; prefers letter-quality. Free sample copy and writer's guidelines.

Nonfiction: Essays, exposé, general interest, technical, merchandising, marketing, and selling (specifically of technology). "We do not want fiction." Buys 30 mss/year. Query with or without published clips, or send complete ms. Length: 900-1,500 words. Pays $300-500. Sometimes pays expenses of writers on assignment.

Photos: State availability of photos with submission. Reviews contact sheets and prints. Identification of subjects required.

CASUAL LIVING, Columbia Communications, 370 Lexington Ave., New York NY 10164. (212)532-9290. FAX: (212)779-8345. Publisher/Editor: Ralph Monti. A monthly magazine covering outdoor furniture for outdoor furniture specialists, including retailers, mass merchandisers and department store buyers. Circ. 11,000. Pays on publication. Buys first North American serial rights. Submit seasonal/holiday material 2 months in advance. Computer printout submissions acceptable. Reports in 1 month. Sample copy for 9x12 SAE with 45¢ postage.

Nonfiction: Interview/profile (case histories of retailers in the industry); new product; opinion; and technical. Buys 7-8 mss/year. Query with clips, then follow up with phone call. Length: 1,000 words average. Pays $200-400.

Photos: State availability of photos with query letter or ms. "Photos are essential with all articles." Reviews b&w contact sheet. Pays $75-100 for b&w prints. Buys all rights.

Tips: "Know the industry, trades and fashions, and what makes a successful retailer."

‡DEALER COMMUNICATOR, Fichera Publications, 777 S. State Road 7, Margate FL 33068. (305)971-4360. FAX: (305)971-4362. Editor: Steve Spence. Publisher: Mike Fichera. 20% freelance written. Works with a small number of new/unpublished writers each year. A monthly magazine covering personnel and news developments for the graphic arts industry. Circ. 13,000. Pays on publication. Publishes ms an average of 1 month after acceptance. Byline given. Not copyrighted. Buys one-time rights. Simultaneous and photocopied submissions OK. Computer printout submissions OK; prefers letter-quality to dot-matrix. Reports in 1 week on queries.

Nonfiction: Interview/profile. Buys a varying number of mss/year. Query with published clips. Length: 500-1,500 words. Pays 3-7¢/word. Pays the expenses of writers on assignment.

Photos: State availability of photos with submissions. Offers $5-10/photo. Captions required.

Fillers: Facts and newsbreaks. Buys a varying number/year. Length: 10-50 words. Pays $1-1.50.

Tips: "We cover a national market. Find out what local printing/graphic arts dealers are doing and what is news in the area."

‡EDUCATIONAL DEALER, Fahy-Williams Publishing, Inc. 171 Reed St., Box 1080, Geneva NY 14456. (315)789-0458. Editor: J. Kenn Fahy. 3% freelance written. A publication that covers the educational supply industry, published 5 times per year—January, March, May, August and October. "Slant should be toward educational Supply *dealers, not* teachers or educators, as most commonly happens." Circ. 12,500. Pays on publication. Byline given. Buys one-time rights. Simultaneous, photocopied and previously published submissions OK. Computer printout submissions OK. Reports in 3 weeks on queries; 1 month on mss. Sample copies $3.

Nonfiction: New product and technical. Buys 3 mss/year. Query. Length: 1,500 words minimum. Pays $50 minimum.

Photos: Send photos with submission. Reviews contact sheets. Offers no additional payment for photos accepted with ms. Identification of subjects required. Buys one-time rights.

Tips: "Our special features section is most open to freelancers. Become familiar with the educational supply industry, which is growing quickly. While the industry is a large one in terms of dollars spent on school supply products, it's a 'small' one in terms of its players and what they're doing. Everyone knows everyone else; they belong to the same organizations: NSSEA and EDSA."

FAIR TIMES, Independent Dealers Association, Box 455, Arnold MO 63010. (314)464-2616. Editor: Georgia Goodridge. 20-90% freelance written. A monthly tabloid covering fairs, celebrations and indoor expositions for vendors who travel North America working these various events. Byline given. Buys first rights. Submit seasonal/holiday material 3 months in advance. Photocopied and previously published submissions OK. Free sample copy and writer's guidelines.

Nonfiction: How-to, interview/profile and new product. Special issues include an annual fair directory and semi-annual flea market directory. No submissions unrelated to selling at events. Query. Length: 400-750 words. Pays $2.50/column inch; may offer premiums instead of cash. Sometimes pays the expenses of writers on assignment.

Photos: Send photos with submission. Reviews contact sheets. Offers $5/photo. Captions required. Buys one-time rights.
Columns/Departments: 3 columns monthly (must deal with vending at events in North America). Query with published clips. Length: 400-750 words. Pays $3/column inch.

FOOD & DRUG PACKAGING, 7500 Old Oak Blvd., Cleveland OH 44130. FAX: (216)891-2735 or 2683. Editor: Sophia Dilberakis. 5% freelance written. Prefers to work with published/established writers. For packaging decision makers in food, drug and cosmetic firms. Monthly. Circ. 77,000. Rights purchased vary with author and material. Pays on acceptance. Publishes ms an average of 2-4 months after acceptance. Query for electronic submissions. Computer printout submissions OK; prefers letter-quality.
Nonfiction and Photos: "Looking for news stories about local and state (not federal) packaging legislation, and its impact on the marketplace. Newspaper style." Query only. Length: 1,000-2,500 words; usually 500-700. Payments vary; usually 5¢/word.
Photos: Photos purchased with mss. 5x7 glossies preferred. Pays $5. Sometimes pays the expenses of writers on assignment.
Tips: "Get details on local packaging legislation's impact on marketplace/sales/consumer/retailer reaction; etc. Keep an eye open to *new* packages. Query when you think you've got one. New packages move into test markets every day, so if you don't see anything new this week, try again next week. Buy it; describe it briefly in a query."

INCENTIVE, Bill Communications, 633 3rd Ave., New York NY 10017. (212)986-4800. FAX: (212)867-4395. Editor: Bruce Bolger. Managing Editor: Mary A. Riordan. Monthly magazine covering sales promotion and employee motivation: managing and marketing through motivation. Circ. 41,000. Pays on acceptance. Publishes ms an average of 3 months after acceptance. Byline sometimes given. Buys all rights. Query for electronic submissions. Computer printout submissions OK; no dot-matrix. Reports in 1 month on queries; 2 months on mss. Sample copy for 9x12 SAE; writer's guidelines for #10 SAE.
Nonfiction: General interest (motivation, demographics), how-to (types of sales promotion, buying product categories, using destinations), interview/profile (sales promotion executives); corporate case studies; and travel (incentive-oriented). Buys up to 48 mss/year. Query with 2 published clips. Length: 500-2,000 words. Pays $100-700 for assigned articles; pays $0-100 for unsolicited articles. Sometimes pays the expenses of writers on assignment.
Photos: Send photos with submission. Reviews contact sheets and transparencies. Offers no additional payment for photos accepted with ms. Identification of subjects required.
Tips: "Read the publication, then query."

OPPORTUNITY MAGAZINE, 6 N. Michigan Ave., Chicago IL 60602. Managing Editor: Jack Weissman. 33% freelance written. Eager to work with new/unpublished writers. Monthly magazine "for anyone who is interested in making money, full or spare time, in selling or in an independent business program." Circ. 190,000. Pays on publication. Buys all rights. Byline given. Submit seasonal/holiday material 6 months in advance. Free sample copy; writer's guidelines for #10 SASE.
Nonfiction: "We use articles dealing with sales techniques, sales psychology or general self-improvement topics." How-to, inspirational and interview (with successful salespeople selling products offered by direct selling firms, especially concerning firms which recruit salespeople through *Opportunity Magazine*). Articles on self-improvement should deal with specifics rather than generalities. Would like to have more articles that deal with overcoming fear, building self-confidence, increasing personal effectiveness and other psychological subjects. Submit complete ms. Buys 35-50 unsolicited mss/year. Length: 250-900 words. Pays $20-35.
Photos: State availability of photos with ms. Offers no additional payment for 8x10 b&w glossy prints. Captions and model release required. Buys all rights.
Tips: "Many articles are too academic for our audience. We look for a free-and-easy style in simple language which is packed with useful information, drama and inspiration. Check the magazine before writing. We can't use general articles. The only articles we buy deal with material that is specifically directed to readers who are opportunity seekers—articles dealing with direct sales programs or successful ventures that others can emulate. Try to relate the article to the actual work in which the reader is engaged. Look for fresh approaches. Too many people write on the same or similar topics."

PROFESSIONAL SELLING, 24 Rope Ferry Rd., Waterford CT 06386. (203)442-4365. Editor: Paulette S. Withers. 33% freelance written. Prefers to work with published/established writers, and works with a small number of new/unpublished writers each year. Bimonthly newsletter in two sections for sales professionals covering industrial or wholesale sales. "*Professional Selling* provides field sales personnel with both the basics and current information that can help them better perform the sales function." Pays on acceptance. Publishes ms an average of 4-6 months after acceptance. No byline given. Buys all rights. Submit seasonal/holiday material 4 months in advance. Computer printout submissions acceptable; no dot-matrix. Reports in 2 weeks. Sample copy and writer's guidelines for #10 SAE and 2 first class stamps.

Nonfiction: How-to (successful sales techniques); and interview/profile (interview-based articles). "We buy only interview-based material." Buys 12-15 mss/year. No unsolicited manuscripts; written queries only. Length: 800-1,000 words.

Tips: "*Professional Selling* has recently expanded to 8 pages, with a 4-page clinic devoted to a single topic of major importance to sales professionals. Only the lead article for each section is open to freelancers. That must be based on an interview with an actual sales professional. Freelancers may occasionally interview sales managers, but the slant must be toward field sales, *not* management."

SOUND MANAGEMENT, Radio Advertising Bureau, 304 Park Ave. S., New York NY 10010. (212)254-4800. FAX: (212)254-8908. Editor-in-Chief: Daniel Flamberg. Executive Editor: Andrew Giangola. 15% freelance written. A monthly magazine covering radio sales and marketing. "We write practical business and how-to stories for the owners and managers of radio stations on topics geared toward increasing ad sales and training salespeople." Circ. 10,000. Pays on publication. Publishes ms an average of 4 months after acceptance. Byline given. Buys one-time rights, exclusive rights for the field or makes work-for-hire assignments. Submit seasonal/holiday material 3 months in advance. Previously published submissions OK. Sample copy for 9x12 SAE with 54¢ postage; writer's guidelines for #10 SASE.

Nonfiction: Essays, how-to, interview/profile and personal experience. No articles on disc jockeys or radio programming. Buys 5-10 mss/year. Query with published clips. Length: 400-750 words. Pays $350-650 for assigned articles; pays $50-150 for unsolicited articles. May pay contributor copies for republished items.

Photos: State availability of photos with submission. Reviews contact sheets, negatives and transparencies. Captions, model releases, and identification of subjects required. Buys one-time rights.

Tips: "Our cover story is most open to freelancers, but proven experience in writing about media advertising and marketing is necessary, with strong interviewing and critical writing skills."

‡SOUVENIR MAGAZINE, Talcott Publishing, 1414 Merchandise Mart, Chicago IL 60654. (312)670-0800. FAX: (312)670-0830. Editor: Janet Wilmoth. 40% freelance written. Bimonthly magazine that covers souvenir/gift centers in specialty areas. "*Souvenir* serves souvenir/gift centers in transient areas: airports, hotels, museums, hospital gift shops, university/college bookstores, theme parks and gift stores in tourist areas. Our readers are the owners/buyers for these stores and this *must* be kept in mind." Circ. 20,000. Pays on publication. Publishes ms an average of 2 months after acceptance. Byline sometimes given. Offers 25% kill fee. Buys first rights. Submit seasonal/holiday material 6 months in advance. Computer printout submissions OK; prefers letter-quality. Reports in 2 weeks on queries; 1 month on mss. Sample copy for 9x12 SAE with 4 first class stamps. Free writer's guidelines.

Nonfiction: Interview/profile (retailers/unusual gift shops). "No advertisements clothed as features." Buys 12-15 mss/year. Query. Length: 750-2,000 words. Pays $100-300 for assigned articles; $100-200 for unsolicited articles. Sometimes pays expenses of writers on assignment.

Photos: State availability of photos with submission. Reviews contact sheets and transparencies. Offers no additional payment for photos accepted with ms. Captions required. Buys one-time rights.

Columns/Departments: Retailer Profile (retailers of specialty stores—listed on cover or masthead), 1,200 words. Buys 4 mss/year. Query. Length: 750-1,200 words. Pays $150-200.

Tips: "Story ideas abound—in every area of USA. Newspaper background would help with trade magazine writing. Feature stories are most practical. I use a map and try to run stories from a 'balance' of USA—not just coastal areas of big cities. Find an unusual gift shop or one that has become a *success* story—and tell me how, why and what my readers might learn."

Sport Trade

Retailers and wholesalers of sports equipment and operators of recreation programs read these journals. Magazines about general and specific sports are classified in the Consumer Sports section.

AMERICAN BICYCLIST, Suite 305, 80 8th Ave., New York NY 10011. (212)206-7230. FAX: (212)633-0079. Editor: Konstantin Doren. 40% freelance written. Prefers to work with published/established writers. Monthly magazine for bicycle sales and service shops. Circ. 11,200. Pays on publication. Publishes ms an average of 4 months after acceptance. Only staff-written articles are bylined, except under special circumstances. Buys all rights. Computer printout submissions acceptable; no dot-matrix.

Nonfiction: Typical story describes (very specifically) unique traffic-builder or merchandising ideas used with success by an actual dealer. Articles may also deal exclusively with moped sales and service operation within conventional bicycle shops. Emphasis on showing other dealers how they can follow similar pattern and increase their business. Articles may also be based entirely on repair shop operation, depicting efficient and profitable service systems and methods. Buys 12 mss/year. Query. Length: 1,000-2,800 words. Pays 9¢/word, plus bonus for outstanding manuscript. Pays expenses of writers on assignment.

Photos: Reviews relevant b&w photos illustrating principal points in article purchased with ms; 5x7 minimum. Pays $8/photo. Captions required. Buys all rights.

Tips: "A frequent mistake made by writers is writing as if we are a book read by consumers instead of professionals in the bicycle industry."

AMERICAN FITNESS, The Official Publication of the Aerobics and Fitness Association of America, Suite 310, 15250 Ventura Blvd., Sherman Oaks CA 91403. (818)905-0040. FAX: (818)990-5468. Editor: Peg Jordan, R.N. Managing Editor: Rhonda Wilson. 80% freelance written. Eager to work with new/unpublished writers. Bimonthly magazine covering exercise and fitness, health and nutrition. "We need timely, in-depth informative articles on health, fitness, aerobic exercise, sports nutrition, sports medicine and physiology." Circ. 20,000. Pays on publication. Publishes ms an average of 6 months after acceptance. Byline given. Buys first North American serial rights and simultaneous rights (in some cases). Submit seasonal/holiday material 4 months in advance. Simultaneous queries and simultaneous, photocopied and previously published submissions OK. Query for electronic submissions. Computer printout submissions acceptable; prefers letter-quality to dot-matrix. Reports in 2 weeks. Sample copy for $1 or SAE with 6 first class stamps; writer's guidelines for SAE.

Nonfiction: Book excerpts (fitness book reviews); exposé (on nutritional gimmickry); historical/nostalgic (history of various athletic events); humor (personal fitness profiles); inspirational (sports leader's motivational pieces); interview/profile (fitness figures); new product (plus equipment review); opinion (on clubs); personal experience (successful fitness story); photo feature (on exercise, fitness, new sport); and travel (spas that cater to fitness industry). No articles on unsound nutritional practices, popular trends or unsafe exercise gimmicks. Buys 18-25 mss/year. Query. Length: 800-2,500 words. Pays $65-120. Sometimes pays expenses of writers on assignment.

Photos: Sports, action, fitness, aerobic competitions and exercise classes. Pays $30-60 for 8x10 b&w prints; $35 for color transparencies. Captions, model release, and identification of subjects required. Buys one-time rights; other rights purchased depend on use of photo.

Columns/Departments: Fitness Industry News, shorts on health and fitness, and profiles on successful fitness figures. Buys 50 mss/year. Query with published clips or send complete ms. Length: 50-150 words. Pays 1¢/word.

Poetry: Buys 2 poems/year. Submit maximum 1 poem. Length: 20-80 lines. Pays $20.

Fillers: Cartoons, clippings, jokes, short humor and newsbreaks. Buys 12/year. Length: 75-200 words. Pays $20.

Tips: "Cover an athletic event, get a unique angle, provide accurate and interesting findings, and write in a lively, intelligent manner. We are looking for new health and fitness reporters and writers. *A&F* is a good place to get started. I have generally been disappointed with short articles and fillers submissions due to their lack of force. Cover a topic with depth."

AMERICAN HOCKEY MAGAZINE, Amateur Hockey Association of the United States, 2997 Broadmoor Valley Rd., Colorado Springs CO 80906. (719)576-4990. FAX: (719)576-4975. Contact: Publisher. Managing Editor: Mike Schroeder. 80% freelance written. Monthly magazine covering hockey in general (with amateur/youth hockey emphasis) for teams, coaches and referees of the Amateur Hockey Association of the U.S., ice facilities in the U.S. and Canada, buyers, schools, colleges, pro teams, and park and recreation departments. Circ. 35,000. Pays on publication. Publishes ms an average of 1 month after acceptance. Byline given. Buys first serial rights; makes work-for-hire assignments. Phone queries OK. Submit seasonal/holiday material 4 months in advance. Photocopied and previously published submissions OK. Reports in 1 month. Sample copy for 9x12 SAE; writer's guidelines for #10 SASE.

Nonfiction: General interest, profile, new product and technical. Query. Length: 500-3,000 words. Pays $50 minimum.

Photos: Reviews 5x7 b&w glossy prints and color slides. Offers no additional payment for photos accepted with ms. Captions preferred. Buys one-time rights.

Columns/Departments: Rebound Shots (editorial); Americans in the Pros (U.S. players in the NHL); College Notes; Rinks and Arenas (arena news); Equipment/Sports Medicine; Referees Crease; Coaches Playbook; For the Record; and Features (miscellaneous). Query.

BICYCLE BUSINESS JOURNAL, Box 1570, 1904 Wenneca, Fort Worth TX 76101. FAX: (817)332-1619. Editor: Rix Quinn. Works with a small number of new/unpublished writers each year. 10% freelance written. Monthly. Circ. 10,000. Pays on acceptance. Publishes ms an average of 3 months after acceptance. Buys all rights. Computer printout submissions acceptable. Sample copy for 7x10 SAE and 2 first class stamps.

Nonfiction: Stories about dealers who service what they sell, emphasizing progressive, successful sales ideas in the face of rising costs and increased competition. Length: 3 double-spaced pages maximum. Sometimes pays the expenses of writers on assignment.

Photos: B&w or color glossy photo a must; vertical photo preferred. Query.

FISHING TACKLE RETAILER, B.A.S.S. Publications, 1 Bell Rd., Montgomery AL 36141. (205)272-9530. Editor: Dave Ellison. 90% freelance written. Prefers to work with published/established writers. Magazine published 10 times/year, "designed to promote the economic health of retail sellers of freshwater and saltwater angling equipment." Circ. 22,000. Byline usually given. Publishes ms an average of 1 year after acceptance. Buys all rights. Submit seasonal/holiday material 6 months in advance. Query for electronic submissions. Computer printout submissions acceptable; prefers letter-quality. Reports in 6 weeks. Sample copy $2; writer's guidelines for #10 SASE.
Nonfiction: How-to (merchandising and management techniques); technical (how readers can specifically benefit from individual technological advances); and success stories (how certain fishing tackle retailers have successfully overcome business difficulties and their advice to their fellow retailers). Articles must directly relate to the financial interests of the magazine's audience. Buys 100 mss/year. Query with published clips. Length: 50-3,000 words. Pays $10-600. Sometimes pays expenses of writers on assignment.
Photos: State availability of photos. Payment included with ms.
Tips: "Long stories are usually assigned to writers with whom we have an established relationship. The writer has a better chance of breaking in at our publication with short, lesser-paying articles and fillers."

GOLF COURSE MANAGEMENT, Golf Course Superintendents Association of America, 1617 St. Andrews Dr., Lawrence KS 66046. (913)841-2240. FAX: (913)841-2407. Editor: Clay Loyd. 30% freelance written. Eager to work with new/unpublished writers. Monthly magazine covering golf course and turf management. Circ. 22,000. Byline given. Buys all rights. Submit seasonal/holiday material 6 months in advance. Publishes ms an average of 3 months after acceptance. Simultaneous queries and submissions OK. Computer printout submissions acceptable; prefers letter-quality. Reports in 2 weeks on queries; 1 month on mss. Free sample copy; writer's guidelines for #10 SASE.
Nonfiction: Book excerpts, historical/nostalgic, interview/profile, personal experience and technical. "All areas that relate to the golf course superintendent—whether features or scholarly pieces related to turf/grass management. We prefer all submissions to be written *simply.*" Special issues include January "conference issue"—features on convention cities used each year. Buys 50 mss/year. Query with clips of published work. Length: 1,500-3,000 words. Pays $100-300 or more. Sometimes pays the expenses of writers on assignment.
Photos: Send photos with ms. Pays $50-250 for color, slides or transparencies preferred. Captions, model release and identification of subjects required. Buys one-time rights.
Tips: "Call communications department (913)841-2240, offer idea, follow with outline and writing samples. Response from us is immediate."

GOLF SHOP OPERATIONS, 5520 Park Ave., Trumbull CT 06611. (203)373-7232. Editor: David Gould. 20% freelance written. Works with a small number of new/unpublished writers each year. Magazine published 8 times/year for golf professionals and shop operators at public and private courses, resorts, driving ranges and golf specialty stores. Circ. 13,200. Pays on publication. Publishes ms an average of 2 months after acceptance. Byline given. Submit seasonal material (for Christmas and other holiday sales, or profiles of successful professionals with how-to angle emphasized) 4 months in advance. Photocopied submissions OK. Computer printout submissions acceptable; prefers letter-quality. Reports in 1 month. Sample copy free.
Nonfiction: "We emphasize improving the golf retailer's knowledge of his profession. Articles should describe how pros are buying, promoting, merchandising and displaying wares in their shops that might be of practical value. Must be aimed only at the retailer." How-to, profile, successful business operation and merchandising techniques. Buys 6-8 mss/year. Phone queries preferred. Pays $500 maximum for assigned articles. Sometimes pays expenses of writers on assignment.
Columns/Departments: Shop Talk (interesting happenings in the golf market), 250 words; Roaming Range (new and different in the driving range business), 500 words. Buys 4 mss/year. Send complete ms. Pays $50-150.

POOL & SPA NEWS, Leisure Publications, 3923 W. 6th St., Los Angeles CA 90020. (213)385-3926. FAX: (213)383-1152. Editor-in-Chief: J. Field. 25-40% freelance written. Semimonthly magazine emphasizing news of the swimming pool and spa industry for pool builders, pool retail stores and pool service firms. Circ. 15,000. Pays on publication. Publishes ms an average of 1-2 months after acceptance. Buys all rights. Photocopied submissions OK. Query for electronic submissions. Computer printout submissions acceptable; no dot-matrix. Reports in 2 weeks. Sample copy for 9x12 SAE and $2.50 postage; writer's guidelines for #10 SASE.
Nonfiction: Interview, new product, profile and technical. Phone queries OK. Length: 500-2,000 words. Pays 10-12¢/word. Pays expenses of writers on assignment.
Photos: Pays $10 per b&w photo used.

‡PRORODEO SPORTS NEWS, Professional Rodeo Cowboys Association, 101 Pro Rodeo Dr., Colorado Springs CO 80919, (719)593-8840. Editor: Timothy C. Bergsten. Very little freelance printed. Biweekly tabloid that covers PRCA Rodeo. "The *Prorodeo Sports News* is the official publication of the PRCA. It covers PRCA rodeo and all parts thereof, including PRCA cowboys, stock contractors, contract members and general rodeo-related news about the PRCA membership and PRCA sponsors. We do not print material about any non-sanctioned rodeo event, or other rodeo associations." Circ. 28,000. Pays on publication. Publishes ms 1 month after acceptance. Byline given. Submit seasonal/holiday material 2 months in advance. Sample copy for 8x10 SAE and $1 postage; free writer's guidelines.

Nonfiction: Interview/profile and photo feature. Buys 5 mss/year. Query. Length: 1,500 words maximum. Pays $50-100. Sometimes pays expenses of writers on assignment.

Photos: Send photos with submission. Reviews negatives and 5x7 and 8x10 prints. Offers $10-50 per photo. Identification of subjects required.

Tips: "Feature stories written about PRCA cowboys will always be considered for publication. Along with feature stories on PRCA members, I foresee the *Prorodeo Sports News* printing more articles about rodeo sponsorship and creative rodeo promotions. Like all professional sports, PRCA rodeo is a business. The *Prorodeo Sports News* will reflect the business aspect of professional rodeo, as well as cover the people who make it all happen."

SKI BUSINESS, 537 Post Rd., Darien CT 06820. Managing Editor: Frank Hammel. 70% freelance written. Works with a small number of new/unpublished writers each year. Tabloid magazine published 11 times/year. For ski retailers, both alpine and cross-country. Circ. 18,000. Byline given, except on "press releases and round-up articles containing passages from articles submitted by several writers." Pays within 1 month of publication. Buys first rights plus reprint rights for promotional use and republication in special editions. Submit seasonal material 6 weeks in advance. Query for electronic submissions. Computer printout submissions acceptable; no dot-matrix. Reports in 1 month. Publishes ms an average of 2 months after acceptance. Free sample copy available to qualified writers; writer's guidelines for #10 SAE and 35¢ postage.

Nonfiction: Will consider ski shop profiles; mss about unique and successful merchandising ideas and equipment rental operations. "All material should be slanted toward usefulness to the ski shop operator. Always interested in in-depth interviews with successful retailers." Uses round-ups of preseason sales and Christmas buying trends across the country from September to December. Would like to see reports on what retailers in major markets are doing. Buys about 100 mss/year. Query first. Pays $50-250. Pays expenses of writers on assignment.

Photos: Photos purchased with accompanying mss. Buys b&w glossies and slides. Pays minimum of $35/photo.

Tips: "We are most interested in retailer profiles of successful ski shop operators, with plenty of advice and examples for our readers. We anticipate a shift in editorial direction to more closely meet the needs of retailers, which will require more retailer-oriented pieces."

‡SPORT STYLE, Fairchild Publication, 7 E. 12th St., New York NY 10003. (212)741-5971. Editor: Mark Sullivan. Managing Editor: Dusty Kidd. 10% freelance written. Biweekly tabloid that covers all sports. "Submit material on product technology, business and marketing trends that are helpful for sports *retailers* in selling and running their stores." Circ. 30,000. Pays on acceptance. Publishes ms an average of 1 month after acceptance. Byline given. Buys all rights. Submit seasonal/holiday material 1 month in advance. Query for electronic submissions. Computer printout submissions OK. Free sample copy and writer's guidelines.

Nonfiction: Interview/profile, new product, photo feature, technical and marketing information. Buys 20 mss/year. Query with published clips. Length: 300-1,500 words. Pays $100-500. Sometimes pays expenses of writers on assignment.

Photos: State availability of photos with submission. Reviews contact sheets and negatives. Offers negotiable payment. Identification of subjects required. Buys one-time rights.

Columns/Departments: Sidelines (sports events—unusual first-time marketing oriented), up to 300 words; and Sport Seen (photo essay on trends). Buys 20 mss/year. Query with published clips. Length: 100-500 words. Pays $50-150.

THE SPORTING GOODS DEALER, 1212 N. Lindbergh Blvd., St. Louis MO 63132. (314)997-7111. FAX: (314)993-7726. President/Chief Executive Officer: Richard Waters. Editor: Steve Fechter. 20% freelance written. Prefers to work with published/established writers. For members of the sporting goods trade: retailers, manufacturers, wholesalers and representatives. Monthly magazine. Circ. 27,000. Buys second serial (reprint) rights. Buys about 15 mss/year. Pays on publication. Computer printout submissions acceptable; no dot-matrix. Publishes ms an average of 3 months after acceptance. Query. Sample copy $4 (refunded with first ms).

Nonfiction: "Articles about specific sporting goods retail stores, their promotions, display techniques, sales ideas, merchandising, timely news of key personnel; expansions, new stores, deaths—all in the sporting goods trade. Specific details on how individual successful sporting goods stores operate. What specific retail sporting goods stores are doing that is new and different. We would also be interested in features dealing with stores doing an outstanding job in retailing of exercise equipment, athletic footwear, athletic apparel, baseball, fishing, golf, tennis, camping, firearms/hunting and allied lines of equipment. Query on these." Successful business operations and merchandising techniques. Does not want to see announcements of doings and engagements. Length: open. Rates negotiated by assignment. Also looking for material for the following columns: Terse Tales of the Trade (store news); Selling Slants (store promotions); and Open for Business (new retail sporting goods stores or sporting goods departments). All material must relate to specific sporting goods stores by name, city and state; general information is not accepted.

Photos: Pays minimum of $3.50 for sharp clear b&w photos; size not important. These are purchased with or without mss. Captions optional, but identification requested.

Fillers: Clippings. These must relate directly to the sporting goods industry. Pays 2¢/published word.

Tips: "The writer has to put himself or herself in our readers' position and ask: Does my style and/or expertise help retailers run their business better?"

SWIMMING POOL/SPA AGE, Communication Channels, Inc., 6255 Barfield Rd., Atlanta GA 30328. (404)256-9800. Editor: Terri Simmons. 30% freelance written. Works with a small number of new/unpublished writers each year. Monthly tabloid emphasizing pool, spa and hot tub industry. Circ. 17,500. Pays on publication. Publishes ms an average of 3 months after acceptance. Buys all rights. Submit seasonal/holiday material 3 months in advance. Query for electronic submissions.

Nonfiction: How-to (installation techniques, service and repairs, tips, etc.); interview (with people and groups within the industry); photo feature (pool/spa/tub construction or special use); technical (should be prepared with expert within the industry); industry news; and market research reports. Also, comparison articles exploring the same type of products produced by numerous manufacturers. Buys 1-3 unsolicited mss/year. Mss must be double-spaced on *white* paper. Query. Length: 250-2,500 words. Pays 10¢/word. Sometimes pays the expenses of writers on assignment.

Photos: Purchased with accompanying ms or on assignment. Query or send contact sheet. Will accept 35mm transparencies of good quality. Captions required.

Tips: "If a writer can produce easily understood technical articles containing unbiased, hard facts, we are definitely interested. We will be concentrating on technical and how-to articles because that's what our readers want."

TENNIS BUYER'S GUIDE, New York Times Magazine Group, 5520 Park Ave., Trumbull CT 06611. (203)373-7232. FAX: (203)373-7170. Editor: Robert Carney. Managing Editor: Sandra Dolbow. 5% freelance written. A bimonthly tabloid on the tennis industry. "We publish for the tennis retailer. We favor a business angle, providing information that will make our readers better tennis professionals and better business people." Circ. 11,000. Pays on publication. Publishes ms an average of 3 months after acceptance. Byline given. Offers 15% kill fee. Buys one-time rights. Submit seasonal/holiday material 6 months in advance. Simultaneous and photocopied submissions OK. Computer printout submissions OK; no dot-matrix. Reports in 6 weeks on queries; 1 month on mss. Free sample copy and writer's guidelines.

Nonfiction: How-to, humor, interview/profile, new product, photo feature, technical and travel. No professional tennis tour articles. Buys 8 mss/year. Send complete ms. Length: 500-2,000 words. Pays $75-300 for assigned articles. Pays $50-300 for unsolicited articles. Sometimes pays the expenses of writers on assignment.

Photos: Reviews transparencies and prints (35mm). Captions, model releases and identification of subjects required. Buys one-time rights.

Columns/Departments: Court Report (interesting happenings in the tennis market). Buys 4 mss/year. Send complete ms. Length: 250-500 words. Pays $50-150.

Tips: "Express an interest and knowledge in tennis or a business management field and an understanding of retail business."

‡WATERSPORTS BUSINESS, International Trade Magazine for Watersports Industry, Sports Ink Magazines, Inc., 2 South Park Place, Box 159, Fair Haven VT 05743. (802)265-8153. Editor: Mark Gabriel. Managing Editor: Robert Gray. 5% freelance written. Monthly magazine about watersports industry. "We are a trade magazine covering a number of watersports markets, including water skis, sailboard, personal watercraft, paddlecraft. inflatables, etc. Our audience consists of retailers, suppliers and sales reps in these markets." Estab. 1989. Circ. 19,000. Pays on publication. Publishes ms an average of 2 months after acceptance. Byline given. Buys first North American serial rights. Submit seasonal/holiday material 2 months in advance. Simultaneous, photocopied and previously published submissions OK. Computer printout submissions OK. Reports in 2 months. Sample copy $2 with SAE and 3 first class stamps; free writer's guidelines.

Nonfiction: How-to (retailing techniques), interview/profile (retailer profiles) and travel. Buys 6 mss/year. Query with published clips. Length: 250-750 words. Pays $50-150. Also trades ad space for article.

Photos: Send photos with submission. Reviews 5x7 prints. Offers no additional payment for photos accepted with ms. Buys one-time rights.

Tips: "The best way to break in is to approach us with a proposal to interview up to six retailers in a given region and to write a general piece on these shops, with photos."

WOODALL'S CAMPGROUND MANAGEMENT, Woodall Publishing Co., Suite 100, 100 Corporate North, Bannockburn IL 60015-1253. (312)295-7799. Editor: Mike Byrnes. 66% freelance written. Works with a small number of new/unpublished writers each year. A monthly tabloid covering campground management and operation for managers of private and public campgrounds throughout the U.S. Circ. 16,000. Pays after publication. Publishes ms an average of 4 months after acceptance. Byline given. Buys all rights. Will reassign rights to author upon written request. Submit seasonal/holiday material 4 months in advance. Simultaneous queries OK. Computer printout submissions acceptable; prefers letter-quality. Reports in 1 month on queries; 2 months on mss. Free sample copy and writer's guidelines.

Nonfiction: How-to, interview/profile and technical. "Our articles tell our readers how to maintain their resources, manage personnel and guests, market, develop new campground areas and activities, and interrelate with the major tourism organizations within their areas. 'Improvement' and 'profit' are the two key words." Buys 24 mss/year. Query. Length: 500 words minimum. Pays $50-200. Sometimes pays expenses of writers on assignment.

Photos: Send contact sheets and negatives. "We pay for each photo used."

Tips: "Contact us and give us an idea of your ability to travel and your travel range. We sometimes have assignments in certain areas. The best type of story to break in with is a case history type approach about how a campground improved its maintenance, physical plant or profitability."

Stone and Quarry Products

‡DIMENSIONAL STONE, Dimensional Stone Institute, Inc., Suite 400, 20335 Ventura Blvd., Woodland Hills CA 91364. (818)704-5555. FAX: (818)704-6500. Editor: Jerry Fisher. 25% freelance written. A bimonthly magazine covering dimensional stone use for managers of producers, importers, contractors, fabricators and specifiers of dimensional stone. Circ. 14,986. Pays on publication. Publishes ms an average of 2 months after acceptance. Byline given. Buys first rights or second serial (reprint) rights. Photocopied submissions and previously published submissions OK. Computer printout submissions acceptable; prefers letter-quality. Sample copy for 9x12 SAE and $2.54 postage; writer's guidelines for #10 SAE.

Nonfiction: Interview/profile and technical, only on users of dimensional stone. Buys 6-7 mss/year. Send complete ms. Length: 1,000-3,000 words. Pays $100 maximum. Sometimes pays the expenses of writers on assignment.

Photos: Send photos with submission. Reviews any size prints. Offers no additional payment for photos accepted with ms. Identification of subjects required.

Tips: "Articles on outstanding uses of dimensional stone are most open to freelancers."

STONE REVIEW, National Stone Association, 1415 Elliot Place NW, Washington DC 20007. (202)342-1100. Editor: Frank Atlee. Bimonthly magazine covering quarrying and supplying of crushed stone. "Designed to be a communications forum for the crushed stone industry. Publishes information on industry technology, trends, developments and concerns. Audience are quarry operations/management, and manufacturers of equipment, suppliers of services to the industry." Circ. 3,000. Pays on publication. Publishes ms an average of 3 months after acceptance. Byline given. Negotiable kill fee. Buys one-time rights. Simultaneous, photocopied and previously published submissions OK. Computer printout submissions OK; prefers letter-quality. Reports in 1 month. Sample copy sent upon request.

Nonfiction: Technical. Query with or without published clips, or send complete ms. Length: 1,000-2,500 words. "Note: We have no budget for freelance material, but I'm willing to get monetary payment OK for right material."

Photos: State availability of photos with query, then send photos with submission. Reviews contact sheets, negatives, transparencies and prints. Offers no additional payment for photos accepted with ms. Identification of subjects required. Buys one-time rights.

Tips: "At this point, most features are written by contributors in the industry, but I'd like to open it up. Articles on unique equipment, applications, etc. are good, as are those reporting on trends (e.g., there is a strong push on now for automation of operations). Also interested in stories on family-run operations involving three or more generations."

STONE WORLD, Tradelink Publishing Company. 485 Kinderkamack Rd., Oradell NJ 07649-1502. (201) 599-0136. FAX: (201)599-2378. Editor: Mike Lench. Managing Editor: John Sailer. A monthly magazine on natural building stone for producers and users of granite, marble, limestone, slate, sandstone, onyx and other natural stone products. Circ. 18,000. Pays on publication. Publishes ms an average of 2 months after acceptance. Byline given. Buys first rights or second serial (reprint) rights. Submit seasonal/holiday material 4 months in advance. Photocopied and previously published submissions OK. Computer printout submissions OK; prefers letter-quality. Reports in 2 weeks on queries; 1 month on mss. Free sample copy.

Nonfiction: How-to (fabricate and/or install natural building stone), interview/profile, photo feature, technical, architectural design, artistic stone uses, statistics, factory profile, equipment profile and trade show review. Buys 5 mss/year. Query with or without published clips, or send complete ms. Length: 600-3,000 words. Pays $75-150. Pays the expenses of writers on assignment.
Photos: State availability of photos with submission. Reviews transparencies and prints. Offers no additional payment for photos accepted with ms. Captions and identification of subjects required. Buys one-time rights.
Columns/Departments: News (pertaining to stone or design community); New Literature (brochures, catalogs, books, videos, etc. about stone); New Products (stone products); New Equipment (equipment and machinery for working with stone); Calendar (dates and locations of events in stone and design communities). Query or send complete ms. Length: 300-600 words. Pays $25-50.
Tips: "Articles about architectural stone design accompanied by professional photographs and quotes from designing firms are often published, as are articles about new techniques of quarrying and/or fabricating natural building stone."

Toy, Novelty and Hobby

Publications focusing on the toy and hobby industry are listed in this section. For magazines for hobbyists see the Consumer Hobby and Craft section.

‡**MINIATURES DEALER MAGAZINE**, 21027 Crossroads Circle, Waukesha WI 53186. Editor: Geraldine Willems. 50% freelance written. Eager to work with new/unpublished writers. For "retailers in the dollhouse/miniatures trade. Our readers are generally independent, small store owners who don't have time to read anything that does not pertain specifically to their own problems." Monthly magazine; 40 pages. Circ. 1,300. Pays on publication. Publishes ms an average of 3 months after acceptance. Buys all rights. Byline given. Phone queries OK. Submit seasonal/holiday material 4 months in advance. Photocopied, previously published and simultaneous submissions (if submitted to publications in different fields) OK. Computer printout submissions acceptable; prefers letter-quality. Reports in 1 month. Sample copy $1.50; writer's guidelines for SASE.
Nonfiction: How-to (unique articles — e.g., how to finish a dollhouse exterior — are acceptable if they introduce new techniques or ideas; show the retailer how learning this technique will help sell dollhouses); profiles of miniatures shops; and business information pertaining to small store retailers. Buys 2-4 mss/issue. Query or send complete ms. "In query, writer should give clear description of intended article, when he could have it to me plus indication that he has studied the field, and is not making a 'blind' query. Availability of b&w photos should be noted." Pay negotiable.
Photos: "Photos must tie in directly with articles." State availability of photos. Pays $7 for each photo used. Prefers 5x7 b&w glossy prints (reviews contact sheets). Captions and model release preferred.
Tips: "We are interested in articles on full-line miniatures stores. The best way for a freelancer to break in is to study several issues of our magazine, then try to visit a miniatures shop and submit an *M&D* Visits . . . article. This is a regular feature that can be written by a sharp freelancer who takes the time to study and follow the formula this feature uses. Also, basic business articles for retailers — inventory control, how to handle bad checks, etc., that are written with miniatures dealers in mind, are always needed. *M&D* is extremely interested in good business articles."

PLAYTHINGS, Geyer-McAllister, 51 Madison Ave., New York NY 10010. (212)689-4411. FAX: (212)683-7929. Editor: Frank Reysen, Jr. Senior Editor: Eugene Gilligan. 20-30% freelance written. A monthly merchandising magazine covering toys and hobbies aimed mainly at mass market toy retailers. Circ. 15,000. Pays on acceptance. Publishes ms an average of 3 months after acceptance. Byline sometimes given. Buys one-time rights. Submit seasonal/holiday material 3 months in advance. Simultaneous and photocopied submissions OK. Reports in 2 weeks. Free sample copy and writer's guidelines.
Nonfiction: Interview/profile, photo feature and retail profiles of toy and hobby stores and chains. Annual directory, May. Buys 10 mss/year. Query. Length: 900-2,500 words. Pays $100-350. Sometimes pays the expenses of writers on assignment.
Photos: Send photos with submission. Captions and identification of subjects required. Buys one-time rights.
Columns/Departments: Buys 5 mss/year. Query. Pays $50-100.

SOUVENIRS & NOVELTIES MAGAZINE, Kane Communications, Inc., Suite 210, 7000 Terminal Square, Upper Darby PA 19082. President: Scott Borowsky. Editor: Chuck Tooley. A magazine published 7 times/year for resort and gift industry. Circ. 21,000. Pays on publication. Byline given. Buys all rights. Computer printout submissions acceptable; prefers letter-quality. Reports in 3 weeks. Sample copy for 6x9 SAE with 5 first class stamps.

Nonfiction: Interview/profile and new product. Buys 6 mss/year. Query. Length: 700-1,500 words. Pays $25-175 for assigned articles. Sometimes pays the expenses of writers on assignment.

Photos: State availability of photos with submission. Captions, model releases and identification of subjects required.

THE STAMP WHOLESALER, Box 706, Albany OR 97321. Executive Editor: Dane S. Claussen. 80% freelance written. Newspaper published 28 times/year for philatelic businessmen; many are part-time and/or retired from other work. Circ. 6,000. Pays on publication. Byline given. Buys all rights. Computer printout submissions acceptable; prefers letter-quality. Reports in 10 weeks. Free sample copy and writer's guidelines.

Nonfiction: How-to information on how to deal more profitably in postage stamps for collections. Emphasis on merchandising techniques and how to make money. Does not want to see any so-called "humor" items from nonprofessionals. Buys 60 ms/year. Submit complete ms. Length: 1,000-1,500 words. Pays $35 and up/article.

Tips: "Send queries on business stories. Send manuscript on stamp dealer stories. We need stories to help dealers make and save money."

Transportation

These publications are for professional movers and people involved in transportation of goods. For magazines focusing on trucking see also Auto and Truck.

AMERICAN MOVER, American Movers Conference, 2200 Mill Rd., Alexandria VA 22314. (703)838-1938. FAX: (703)838-1925. Editor: Ann S. Dinerman. 10% freelance written. Works with a small number of new/unpublished writers each year. A monthly trade journal on the moving and storage industry for moving company executives. Circ. 2,200. Pays on publication. Publishes ms an average of 3 months after acceptance. Byline given. Offers $100 kill fee. Buys first North American serial rights. Submit seasonal/holiday material 3 months in advance. Query for electronic submissions. Computer printout submissions OK; prefers letter-quality. Reports in 3 weeks on queries. Free sample copy and writer's guidelines.

Nonfiction: How-to, interview/profile, new product, personal experience, photo feature, technical and small business articles. "No fiction or articles geared toward consumers." Buys 6 mss/year. Query with published clips. Length: 1,000-5,000 words. Pays $100-200 for assigned articles. Pays contributor copies at writer's request.

Photos: Send photos with submission. Reviews 5x7 prints. Offers no additional payment for photos accepted with ms. Captions required. Buys one-time rights.

Tips: "We have an editorial calendar available that lists topics we'll be covering. Articles on small business are helpful. Feature articles are most open to freelancers. Articles must slant toward moving company presidents on business-related issues. Timely topics are safety, deregulation, drug testing, computers, insurance, tax reform and marketing."

BUS WORLD, Magazine of Buses and Bus Systems, Stauss Publications, Box 39, Woodland Hills CA 91365. (818)710-0208. Editor: Ed Stauss. 75% freelance written. Quarterly trade journal covering the transit and intercity bus industries. Extensive photographic coverage." Circ. 6,000. Pays on publication. Publishes ms an average of 4 months after acceptance. Byline given. Buys first North American serial rights. Computer printout and disk submissions acceptable; prefers letter-quality. Reports in 3 weeks. Sample copy with writer's guidelines $1.

Nonfiction: Primary coverage is North America. No tourist or travelog viewpoints. Buys 8-12 mss/year. Query. Length: 500-2,000 words. Pays $30-100.

Photos: "We buy photos with manuscripts under one payment." Reviews 35mm color transparencies and 8x10 b&w prints. Captions required. Buys one-time rights.

Fillers: Cartoons. Buys 4-6/year. Pays $10.

Tips: "Be employed in or have a good understanding of the bus industry. Be enthusiastic about buses—their history and future—as well as current events. Acceptable material will be held until used and will not be returned unless requested by sender. Unacceptable and excess material will be returned only if accompanied by suitable SASE."

‡**THE CANADIAN SHIPPER,** Naylor Communications Ltd., 920 Yonge St., 6th Fl., Toronto, Ontario M4W 3C7 Canada. (416)961-1028. FAX: (416)924-4408. Editor: J.D. Corcoran. 50% freelance written. Bimonthly magazine that covers transportation/shipping, focusing on analytical and concisely organized journalism on

transportation issues. Circ. 5,000. Pays 30 days after receipt. Byline given. Offers 33⅓% kill fee. Buys all rights. Simultaneous, photocopied and previously published submissions OK. Query for electronic submissions. Computer printout submissions OK; prefers letter-quality. Reports in 3 weeks. Free sample copy and writer's guidelines.

Nonfiction: Historical, interview/profile, photo feature and technical. Buys 25 mss/year. Query with published clips. Length: 500-3,000 words. Pays 20-30¢/word. Sometimes pays expenses of writers on assignment.

Photos: State availability of photos with submission. Offers $25-250 per photo. Identification of subjects required. Buys all rights.

INBOUND LOGISTICS, Thomas Publishing Co., 1 Penn Plaza, 26th Fl., New York NY 10019. (212)290-7336. FAX: (212)290-7362. Senior Editor: Douglas J. Bowen. 20% freelance written. Prefers to work with published/established writers. Monthly magazine covering the transportation industry. "*Inbound Logistics* is distributed to people who buy, specify, or recommend inbound freight transportation services and equipment. The editorial matter provides basic explanations of inbound freight transportation, directory listings, how-to technical information, trends and developments affecting inbound freight movements, and expository, case history feature stories." Circ. 43,000. Pays on publication. Publishes ms an average of 3 months after acceptance. Byline given. Buys all rights. Simultaneous queries, and simultaneous and photocopied submissions OK. Computer printout submissions acceptable; no dot-matrix. Reports in 2 weeks. Sample copy and writer's guidelines for 8½11 SAE ad 5 first class stamps.

Nonfiction: How-to (basic help for purchasing agents and traffic managers) and interview/profile (purchasing and transportation professionals). Buys 15 mss/year. Query with published clips. Length: 750-1,000 words. Pays $300-1,200. Pays expenses of writers on assignment.

Photos: Michael Ritter, photo editor. State availability of photos with query. Pays $100-500 for b&w contact sheets, negatives, transparencies and prints; $250-500 for color contact sheets, negative transparencies and prints. Captions and identification of subjects required.

Columns/Departments: Viewpoint (discusses current opinions on transportation topics). Query with published clips.

Tips: "Have a sound knowledge of the transportation industry; educational how-to articles get our attention."

‡LIFTING & TRANSPORTATION INTERNATIONAL, B&B Publishing, Inc., Box 2575, Washington DC 20013. (703)641-9898. FAX: (703)573-7273. Editor: Graham Brent. Managing Editor: Jane Pratt. 35% freelance written. Monthly magazine that covers cranes, heavy trucks and trailers. "LTI covers all the significant events in the crane and rigging and specialized transportation industries. LTI reports on buying trends and market developments as they happen and adds an extra dimension to its reporting of international stories with its bilingual treatment of selected features." Circ. 21,000. Pays on acceptance. Publishes ms an average of 2 months after acceptance. Byline given. Buys one-time rights, simultaneous rights and makes work-for-hire assignments. Submit seasonal/holiday material 2 months in advance. Simultaneous, photocopied and previously published submissions OK. Query for electronic submissions. Computer printout submissions OK; prefers letter-quality. Reports in 2 weeks. Sample copy for 9x11 SAE. Sample copy $7.

Nonfiction: Book excerpts, how-to, (maintenance), interview/profile, new product, opinion, personal experience, photo feature and technical. Buys 30 mss/year. Query with published clips. Pays $200/1,000 words. Pays in contributor copies or other premiums "as contributor wishes." Sometimes pays expenses of writers on assignment.

Photos: Send photos with submission. Reviews slides and larger transparencies and 5x7 or larger prints. Offers $10 per photo. Captions, model releases and identification of subjects required. Buys one-time rights.

THE PRIVATE CARRIER, Private Carrier Conference, Inc.. Suite 720, 1320 Braddock Place, Alexandria VA 22314. (703)683-1300. FAX: (703)683-1217. Editor: Don Tepper. 30% freelance written. A monthly magazine on freight transportation. "*The Private Carrier* is the national publication for private fleet managers. Its goal is to help them manage their private fleets and their other transportation activities as efficiently and cost-effectively as possible." Circ. 35,000. Pays on publication. Publishes ms an average of 2 months after acceptance. Byline given. Offers $100 maximum kill fee. "We buy first rights and retain right for reprint. However, after publication, writer may use/sell article as he/she sees fit." Submit seasonal/holiday material 3 months in advance. Photocopied submissions OK. Computer printout submissions OK; prefers letter-quality. Reports in 1 week on queries; 2 weeks on mss. Sample copy for 9x12 SAE and $1.05 postage.

Nonfiction: Exposé, interview/profile, opinion and photo feature. Buys 10 mss/year. Query. Length: 1,000-3,000 words. Pays $100-250. Sometimes pays the expenses of writers on assignment.

Photos: Send photos with submission. Reviews transparencies (35mm) and prints (5x7 or 8x10). Offers no additional payment for photos accepted with ms. When necessary model releases and identification of subjects required. Buys one-time rights.

Columns/Departments: Computer Briefs (computer software for transportation); On The Road (humorous true items dealing with transportation); Picture This (humorous photos dealing with transportation). Send complete ms. Length: 100-300 words. Pays $10-50.

Tips: "Tailor articles to our readers. Writing style is less important than clean, well-written copy. We love good photos or articles that lend themselves to good illustrations. We like the slightly off-beat, unconventional or novel way to look at subjects. Articles for whatever department that profile how a private fleet solved a problem (i.e., computers, drivers, maintenance, etc.). The structure is: 1) company identifies a problem, 2) evaluates options, 3) selects a solution, and 4) evaluates its choice."

‡**SHIPPING DIGEST, The National Shipping Weekly of Export Transportation,** Geyer McAllister Publications Inc., 51 Madison Ave., New York NY 10010. (212)689-4411. Editor: Maria Reines. 20% freelance written. Weekly magazine that covers ocean, surface, air transportation, ports, intermodal or EDI. "Read by executives responsible for exporting U.S. goods to foreign markets. Emphasis is on services offered by ocean, surface and air carriers, their development and trends; port developments; trade agreements; government regulation; electronic data interchange." Pays on publication. Publishes ms an average of 1 month after acceptance. Byline given. Offers $150 kill fee. Buys first rights. Computer printout submissions OK; prefers letter-quality. Reports in 1 week. Free sample copy and writers guidelines.
Nonfiction: Interview/profile. Buys 25 mss/year. Query. Length: 800-1,500 words. Pays $125-300. Sometimes pays expenses of writers on assignment.
Photos: State availability of photos with submission. Reviews contact sheets and 5x7 prints. Offers no payment for photos accepted with ms. Identification of subjects required. Buys one-time rights.

‡**TRUCKS MAGAZINE, Dedicated to the People Behind the Wheel,** 20 Waterside Plaza, New York NY 10010-2615. (212)691-8215. FAX: (212)691-1191. Editor: John Stevens. Publisher: Chris Krieg. 25% freelance written. Magazine covering long haul, heavy-duty trucking. "Trucks magazine is dedicated to the health, safety, image and profitability of long haul, heavy-duty truck drivers and their families." Circ. 100,000. Pays within 30 days of publication. Publishes ms an average of 6-10 months after acceptance. Byline given. Buys first rights. Submit seasonal/holiday material 10 months in advance. Reports in 1 week on queries; sample copy for 9x12 SAE with $1.50 postage.
Nonfiction: Exposé, general interest, how-to, inspirational, new product, personal experience and photo feature. Buys 10 mss/year. Send complete ms. Length: 1,500 words maximum. Pays $50/published page.
Photos: Send photos with submission. Reviews transparencies and prints. Offers no additional payment for photos accepted with ms. Captions, model releases and identification of subjects required. Buys one-time rights.

Travel

Travel professionals read these publications to keep up with trends, tours and changes in transportation. Magazines about vacations and travel for the general public are listed in the Consumer Travel section.

ABC STAR SERVICE, ABC International, 131 Clarendon St., Boston MA 02116. (617)262-5000. Contact: Managing Editor. "Eager to work with new/unpublished writers as well as those working from a home base abroad, planning trips that would allow time for hotel reporting, or living in major ports for cruise ships." Worldwide guide to accommodations and cruises founded in 1960 (as *Sloan Travel Agency Reports*) and sold to travel agencies on subscription basis. Pays 15 days prior to publication. Publishes ms an average of 3 months after acceptance. Buys all rights. Query for electronic submissions. Computer printout submissions OK; prefers letter-quality. Query. Query should include details on writer's experience in travel and writing, clips, specific forthcoming travel plans, and how much time would be available for hotel or ship inspections. Buys 5,000 reports/year. Pays $18 and up/report used (higher for ships). Sponsored trips are acceptable. "Higher rates of payment and of guaranteed acceptance of set number of reports will be made after correspondent's ability and reliability have been established." Writer's guidelines and list of available assignments for #10 SASE.
Nonfiction: Objective, critical evaluations of hotels and cruise ships suitable for international travelers, based on personal inspections. Freelance correspondents ordinarily are assigned to update an entire state or country. "Assignment involves on-site inspections of all hotels we review; revising and updating published reports; and reviewing new properties. Qualities needed are thoroughness, precision, perseverance and keen judgment. Solid research skills and powers of observation are crucial. Travel and travel writing experience are highly desirable. Reviews should be colorful, clear, and documented with hotel's brochure, rate sheet, etc. We accept no hotel advertising or payment for listings, so reviews should dispense praise and criticism where deserved."
Tips: "We may require sample hotel or cruise reports on facilities near freelancer's hometown before giving the first assignment. No byline because of sensitive nature of reviews."

‡**ASTA AGENCY MANAGEMENT, Official Publication of the American Society of Travel Agents**, American Society of Travel Agents, 666 Fifth Ave., New York NY 10103. (212)765-5454. Editor: Patrick D. O. Arton. 75% freelance written. Monthly magazine on the travel industry. "The magazine covers the business side of the travel industry and the management of travel agencies. Readers are primarily travel agency owner/managers." Pays on acceptance. Publishes an average of 2-4 months after acceptance. Byline given. Offers 25% kill fee. Buys first North American serial rights. Simultaneous and photocopied submissions OK. Reports in 2 weeks. Free sample copy and writer's guidelines.
Nonfiction: How-to (run a travel agency), interview/profile, new product and travel industry. "We don't want the 'sun, sand & sea' descriptive travel articles." Buys 100 mss/year. Query or send complete ms. Length: 600-1,500 words. Pays $150-400. Pays expenses of writers on assignment.
Photos: State availability of photos with submission. Offers $25 minimum-negotiable maximum per photo. Captions, model releases and identification of subjects required. Buys one-time rights.
Tips: "Freelancers should preferably have an in-depth knowledge of the travel industry or the industry segment being written about. Articles covering the business of the travel industry are what we need most."

‡**BUS RIDE**, Friendship Publications, Inc., Box 1472, Spokane WA 99210. (509)328-9181. FAX: (509)325-5396. Editor: William A. Luke. Magazine published 8 times/year covering bus transportation. Circ. 12,500. Byline given. Not copyrighted. Sample copy $3; free writer's guidelines.
Nonfiction: How-to (on bus maintenance, operations, marketing); new product; and technical. Only bus transportation material is acceptable. Query. Length: 500-1,500 words. No payment from publication; "writer may receive payment from company or organization featured."
Photos: State availability of photos. Reviews b&w 8x10 prints. Captions required.
Fillers: Newsbreaks. Length: 50-100 words.
Tips: "A freelancer can contact bus companies, transit authorities, suppliers and products for the bus industry to write articles which would be accepted by our publication."

‡**BUS TOURS MAGAZINE, The Magazine of Bus Tours and Long Distance Charters**, National Bus Trader, Inc., 9698 W. Judson Rd., Polo IL 61064. (815)946-2341. Editor: Larry Plachno. Editorial Assistant: Ginger Riehle. 80% freelance written. Eager to work with new/unpublished writers. Bimonthly magazine for bus companies and tour brokers who design or sell bus tours. Circ. 9,306. Pays as arranged. Publishes ms an average of 6 months after acceptance. Byline given. Not copyrighted. Buys rights as arranged. Submit seasonal/holiday material 9 months in advance. Simultaneous queries OK. Computer printout submissions acceptable; no dot-matrix. Reports in 1 month. Free sample copy and writer's guidelines.
Nonfiction: Historical/nostalgic, how-to, humor, interview/profile, new product, professional, personal experience and travel; all on bus tours. Buys 10 mss/year. Query. Length: open. Pays negotiable fee.
Photos: State availability of photos. Reviews 35mm transparencies and 6x9 or 8x10 prints. Caption, model release and identification of subjects required.
Columns/Departments: Bus Tour Marketing; and Buses and the Law. Buys 15-20 mss/year. Query. Length: 1-1½ pages.
Tips: "Most of our feature articles are written by freelancers under contract from local convention and tourism bureaus. Specifications sent on request. Writers should query local bureaus regarding their interest. Writer need not have extensive background and knowledge of bus tours."

‡**NATIONAL BUS TRADER, The Magazine of Bus Equipment for the United States and Canada**, 9698 W. Judson Rd., Polo IL 61064. (815)946-2341. Editor: Larry Plachno. 25% freelance written. Eager to work with new/unpublished writers. Monthly magazine for manufacturers, dealers and owners of buses and motor coaches. Circ. 7,354. Pays on either acceptance or publication. Publishes ms an average of 3 months after acceptance. Byline given. Not copyrighted. Buys rights "as required by writer." Simultaneous queries, and simultaneous, photocopied and previously published submissions OK. Computer printout submissions acceptable; no dot-matrix. Reports in 1 month. Free sample copy.
Nonfiction: Historical/nostalgic (on old buses); how-to (maintenance repair); new products; photo feature; and technical (aspects of mechanical operation of buses). "We are finding that more and more firms and agencies are hiring freelancers to write articles to our specifications. We are more likely to run them if someone else pays." No material that does *not* pertain to bus tours or bus equipment. Buys 3-5 unsolicited mss/year. Query. Length: varies. Pays variable rate. Sometimes pays the expenses of writers on assignment.
Photos: State availability of photos. Reviews 5x7 or 8x10 prints and 35mm transparencies. Captions, model release and identification of subjects required.
Columns/Departments: Bus maintenance; Buses and the Law; Regulations; and Bus of the Month. Buys 20-30 mss/year. Query. Length: 1-1½ pages. Pays variable rate.
Tips: "We are a very technical publication. Writers should submit qualifications showing extensive background in bus vehicles. We're very interested in well-researched articles on older bus models and manufacturers, or current converted coaches. We would like to receive history of individual bus models prior to 1953 and history of GMC 'new look' models. Write or phone editors with article concept or outline for comments and approval."

RV BUSINESS, TL Enterprises, Inc., 29901 Agoura Rd., Agoura CA 91301. (818)991-4980. Executive Editor: Katherine Sharma. 60% freelance written. Prefers to work with published/established writers. Semi-monthly magazine covering the recreational vehicle and allied industries for people in the RV industry—dealers, manufacturers, suppliers, campground management, and finance experts. Circ. 25,000. Pays on acceptance. Publishes ms an average of 2 months after acceptance. Byline given. Offers 50% kill fee. Buys first North American serial rights. Submit seasonal/holiday material 6 months in advance. Photocopied submissions OK. Query for electronic submissions. Computer printout submissions acceptable; prefers letter-quality. Reports in 3 weeks on queries; 6 weeks on mss. Sample copy for 9x12 SAE and 3 first class stamps; writer's guidelines for #10 SAE and 1 first class stamp.

Nonfiction: Technical, financial, legal or marketing issues; how-to (deal with any specific aspect of the RV business); interview/profile (persons or companies involved with the industry—legislative, finance, dealerships, manufacturing, supplier); specifics and verification of statistics required—must be factual; and technical (photos required, 4-color preferred). General business articles may be considered. Buys 75 mss/year. Query with published clips. Send complete ms—"but only read on speculation." Length: 1,000-1,500 words. Pays variable rate up to $500. Sometimes pays expenses of writers on assignment.

Photos: State availability of photos with query or send photos with ms. Reviews 35mm transparencies and 8x10 b&w prints. Captions, model release, and identification of subjects required. Buys one-time or all rights; unused photos returned.

Columns/Departments: Guest editorial; News (50-500 words maximum, b&w photos appreciated); and RV People (color photos/4-color transparencies; this section lends itself to fun, upbeat copy). Buys 100-120 mss/year. Query or send complete ms. Pays $10-200 "depending on where used and importance."

Tips: "Query. Phone OK; letter preferable. Send one or several ideas and a few lines letting us know how you plan to treat it/them. We are always looking for good authors knowledgable in the RV industry or related industries. Change of editorial focus requires more articles that are brief, factual, hard hitting, business oriented and in-depth. Will work with promising writers, published or unpublished."

TRAVELAGE MIDAMERICA, Official Airlines Guide, Inc., A Dun & Bradstreet Co., Suite 601, 320 N. Michigan, Chicago IL 60601. (312)346-4952. Editor/Publisher: Martin Deutsch. Managing Editor: Karen Goodwin. 15% freelance written. Weekly magazine "for travel agents in the 13 midAmerica states and in Ontario and Manitoba." Circ. 20,000. Pays on publication. Publishes ms an average of 2 months after acceptance. Buys one-time rights and second serial (reprint) rights. Submit seasonal/holiday material 3 months in advance. Simultaneous, photocopied, and previously published submissions OK. Computer printout submissions acceptable ("but not pleased with"); prefers letter-quality. Query first. Reports in 2 months. Free sample copy and writer's guidelines with SASE.

Nonfiction: "News on destinations, hotels, operators, rates and other developments in the travel business." Also runs human interest features on retail travel agents in the readership area. No stories that don't contain prices; no queries that don't give detailed story lines. No general destination stories, especially ones on "do-it-yourself" travel. Buys 20 mss/year. Query. Length: 400-1,500 words. Pays $2/column inch.

Photos: State availability of photos with query. Pays $2/column inch for glossy b&w prints.

Tips: "Our major need is for freelance human interest stories with a marketing angle on travel agents in our readership area. Buying freelance destination stories is a much lower priority."

TRAVELAGE WEST, Official Airline Guides, Inc., 100 Grant Ave., San Francisco CA 94108. Executive Editor: Donald C. Langley. 5% freelance written. Prefers to work with published/established writers. Weekly magazine for travel agency sales counselors in the western U.S. and Canada. Circ. 35,000. Pays on publication. Publishes ms an average of 1 month after acceptance. Byline given. Buys all rights. Offers kill fee. Submit seasonal/holiday material 2 months in advance. Query for electronic submissions. Computer printout submissions acceptable; prefers letter-quality. Reports in 1 month. Free writer's guidelines.

Nonfiction: Travel. "No promotional approach or any hint of do-it-yourself travel. Emphasis is on news, not description. No static descriptions of places, particularly resort hotels." Buys 40 mss/year. Query. Length: 1,000 words maximum. Pays $2/column inch.

Tips: "Query should be a straightforward description of the proposed story, including (1) an indication of the news angle, no matter how tenuous, and (2) a recognition by the author that we run a trade magazine for travel agents, not a consumer book. I am particularly turned off by letters that try to get me all worked up about the 'beauty' or excitement of some place. Authors planning to travel might discuss with us a proposed angle before they go; otherwise their chances of gathering the right information are slim."

ALWAYS submit unsolicited manuscripts or queries with a self-addressed, stamped envelope (SASE) within your country or International Reply Coupons (IRC) purchased from the post office for other countries.

Veterinary

Journals for veterinarians and pet health professionals are located in this section. For publications targeted to pet shop and grooming business managers and the pet supply industry see the Pets section. For magazines for pet owners see the Consumer Animal section.

‡NEW METHODS, The Journal of Animal Health Technology, Box 22605, San Francisco CA 94122-0605. (415)664-3469. Managing Editor: Ronald S. Lippert. *"New Methods* is an educational and informational newsletter about animal health technology." Circ. 5,600. Pays on publication. Byline given. Buys simultaneous rights. Submit seasonal/holiday material 2 months in advance. Simultaneous and photocopied submissions OK. Computer printout submissions OK; prefers letter-quality. Reports in 2 weeks. Sample copy for #10 SAE and 2 first class stamps; writer's guidelines for #10 SASE.

Nonfiction: How-to (technical), new product and technical. Buys 1 ms/year. Query. Pays in contributor copies or other premiums. Sometimes pays expenses of writers on assignment.

Photos: State availability of photos with submission. Reviews contact sheets. Offers variable payment. Captions, model releases and identification of subjects required. Buys one-time rights.

Columns/Departments: Buys 12 mss/year. Query. Length: variable. Payment variable.

Poetry: We do not want unrelated subject matter, very long or abstract poetry. Buys 2 poems/year. Submit maximum 1 poem. Length: variable. Payment variable.

Fillers: Facts and newsbreaks. Buys 12/year.

Tips: "Contact *New Methods* in writing with a SASE before writing or submitting any finished material; ideas first."

VETERINARY ECONOMICS MAGAZINE, 9073 Lenexa Dr., Lenexa KS 66215. (913)492-4300. Editor: Becky Turner. 75% freelance written. Prefers to work with published/established writers but will work with several new/unpublished writers each year. Monthly business magazine for all practicing veterinarians in the U.S. Buys exclusive rights in the field. Pays on publication. Publishes ms 3-6 months after acceptance. Computer printout submissions acceptable. Free sample copy and writer's guidelines.

Nonfiction: Publishes non-clinical case studies on business and management techniques that will strengthen a veterinarian's private practice. Also interested in articles on financial problems, investments, insurance and similar subjects of particular interest to professionals. "We look for carefully researched articles that are specifically directed to our field." Pays negotiable rates. Pays expenses of writers on assignment.

Tips: "Our stories will focus more on nuts-and-bolts practice management techniques prescribed by experts in the practice management field. Stories must be useful and appeal to a broad section of our readers."

VETERINARY PRACTICE MANAGEMENT, Whittle Communications, 505 Market St., Knoxville TN 37902. (615)595-5211. Senior Editor: Margaret Morrow Leske. 80% freelance written. Prefers to work with published/established business writers. Triannual magazine—"a business guide for small animal practitioners." Circ. 33,000. Pays on acceptance. Publishes ms an average of 3-4 months after acceptance. Byline given. Offers kill fee. Buys first serial rights. Simultaneous queries OK. Query for electronic submissions. Computer printout submissions acceptable; prefers letter-quality. Writer's guidelines and free sample copy to experienced business writers.

Nonfiction: How-to, and successful business (practice) management techniques supported by veterinary anecdotes and expert advice. No "how to milk more dollars out of your clients" articles. Buys 18 mss/year. Query with published clips; no unsolicited manuscripts. Pays $600-2,000 (average $1,200). Pays expenses of writers on assignment.

Columns/Departments: On the Job; In School; and In the Know departments. "Most department items are written in-house, but we will consider ideas. We are actively seeking new writers who can provide snappy as well as informative writing in our columns and features." Query with published clips. Pays up to $400.

Other Trade Journals

The following firms did not return a verification to update an existing listing or a questionnaire to begin a new listing by press time.

AB Bookman's Weekly
Activewear Business
American Banker
American Fire Journal

American Firearms Industry
American Trucker Magazine
Appliance Service News
Applied Radiology
Arms & Outdoor Digest

Art Direction
ATI
Auto Trim News
Automotive Booster of
   California

Barrister
Barter Communique
Beverage Retailer Weekly
Bobbin
Boxboard Containers
BPME Image
Broadcast Management/Engineering
Business Software
Cable Communications Magazine
California Pharmacist
Canadian Aquaculture
Canadian Auto Review
Canadian Jeweller
Canadian Premiums & Incentives
Candy Wholesaler
CGA Magazine
Chain Store Age
Church Administration
Clavier
Cleaning Management
Coal People Magazine
Computer Reseller
Concrete Construction Magazine
Construction Supervision & Safety Letter
Contractors Market Center
Corporate Finance
Corporate Fitness
CPI Purchasing
Cross-Canada Writers' Magazine
Curriculum Review
Dairyman
Diamond Registry Bulletin
Draperies & Window Coverings
Electronic Servicing & Technology
Equipment Management
Executive Communications
FBO
Federal Credit Union
Flowers &
Futures Magazine
Glass Digest
Gold prospector
Grassroots Fundraising Journal

Happi
Hospital Risk ManagementlHP Design & Automation
Industrial Chemist
Info Franchise Newsletter
In-plant Printer and Electronic Publisher
In-plant Reproductions & Electronic Publishing
Insulation Outlook
Iowa Rec News
Jet Cargo News
Journal of Defense & Diplomacy
Journal of Systems Management
Leisure Wheels Magazine
Lightwave
Llamas Magazine
Machine Design
Management Accounting
Mart
Mass High Tech
Mechanical Engineering
Media & Methods
Medical Economics
Micro Cornucopia
Mini-Storage Messenger
Multi-Housing News
Music & Sound Output
National Defense
National Fisherman
National Law Journal
NATPE Programmer
National Petroleum News
Newman Report
NSGA Sports Retailer
Nursing Homes
Nursingworld Journal
OA Magazine
On Page
On Radio
Overdrive
Perinatal Press
Pet/Supplies/Marketing
Philatelic Journalist
Photo Lab Management
Photovideo
Pipeline & Underground Utilities Construction
Preaching

Private Label
Professional Furniture Merchant Magazine
Progress
Purchasing World
Refrigerated Transporter
Response!
Retailer News
Restaurant Hospitality
Restaurant Management
Risk & Benefits Management
Rock Products
Roseburg Woodsman
Safety & Health
Sailboard News
Sales Motivation
School Library Journal
Selling Direct
Shopping Center World
Shopping Centers Today
Skylines
Southwest Real Estate News
Sports Marketing News
Successful Farming
Sunshine Service News
Surgical Rounds
Team Sports Business
Technical Photography
Telecommunications Equipment Retailer
Textile World
Today's Furniture Designer
Top Shelf Magazine
Tradeshow
Transaction/Society
Truckers/USA
United Caprine News
Unix world
Vehicle Leasing Today
Verdict Magazine
Video Business
Visual Communications Canada
Watch and Clock Review
Waterbed Magazine
Western Publisher
Wisconsin Restaurateur
Woodheat
Writer's Haven Journal
Yarn Market News

The following listings were deleted following the 1989 edition of *Writer's Market* because the company asked to have the listing removed, went out of business or is no longer accepting freelance submissions.

Advertising Techniques (suspended publication)
Ag Review (suspended publication)
American Screenwriter (suspended publication)
Association & Society Manager (unable to contact)
Cincinnati Bell Magazine (suspended publication)
Dvorak Developments (suspended publication)
Electronic Education (only accepting submissions from school administrators)

Farm Supplier (merged with Farm Store Merchandising)
Fish Boat (suspended publication)
Glass News (suspended publication)
Hardware Merchandiser (suspended publication)
Information Marketing (suspended publication)
Productivity Improvement Bulletin (suspended publication)
Raytheon Magazine (suspended publication)

Real Estate Information Network (unable to contact)
Rx Home Care (recently sold; no updated information available at press time)
Teacher Update (asked to be deleted)
Western Roofing/Insulation/Siding (asked to be deleted)
Western Washington Writers' Market Report (suspended publication)
Writers Gazette (suspended publication)

Scriptwriting

by Michael Singh

The video revolution has been changing the scriptwriter's world. Video rental stores are bursting with films old and new and the cable market is saturated and will no longer pay high prices for films anymore. The vacuum has been filled and demand for new material is not as high as it was.

Adventuresome film producers are not as welcome by video distributors, who have become reluctant to pay for films that are not mainstream. Says Los Angeles screenwriter Jeff Scheftel of video stores, "They no longer line their shelves with a variety of independent or off-beat titles. They just buy 50 copies of 'Indiana Jones.' " Alive Pictures is just one of many highly respected and decorated independent film concerns that has competed successfully with Hollywood but had to end its distribution business recently because video franchises were not willing to pay the previous high prices for its films.

It is a rare accomplishment for a writer to walk into a studio executive's office with an idea and leave with a five-or six-figure development deal. The industry trend of demanding completed scripts has a positive side: it places writers nationwide on more equal footing.

For business/education films, the video trend also is beneficial since more establishments nationwide see the advantage of producing what are now relatively inexpensive films. The market encompasses business, law and education fields, the industrial/military complex, churches, advertising and even the business side of entertainment.

Analyzing actual scripts is the best way to become familiar with the particular genre you choose. Most scriptwriting forms, except plays, share the traits of minimal dialogue, strong emphasis on visuals and action and a dramatic structure.

Selling scripts requires research and perseverence. Industrial film producers pay about half the Hollywood Writers Guild minimum per page of scripts, but in turn usually provide a steadier source of income once the initial contact and successful first assignment have been accomplished. Each market requires a different approach. Read the specific section introductions and be sure to follow individual submission instructions detailed in the listings.

For information on additional scriptwriting markets not in *Writer's Market*, see Other Scriptwriting Markets at the end of this section.

Business and Educational Writing

Business and educational films comprise a substantially larger market than their more

Michael Singh has written the introductions of the Business and Educational Writing, Playwriting and Screenwriting sections of this edition of Writer's Market. He has taught screenwriting and film production for the USC-Universal Studios program and has also written children's fiction and nonfiction for Holt, Rinehart & Winston. He currently is an ad copywriter for the Twentieth Century Fox and directs documentary and evidentiary films for law firms.

famous Hollywood cousins. Writers willing to research technical subjects or already able to write on them will find corporations, school and universities, the armed forces, hospitals, manufacturers and even law firms all requiring their brand of service.

The company is the producer, and, as in Hollywood, it calls the shots in terms of scope, content, style and tone. The film's main purpose is usually recruitment, training, advertising and dissemination of data—more long-term goals than box office profits. Since these films are shown to a nonpaying and often captive audience, any zest or entertainment value they display will probably be due to the writer's ingenuity and ability to make dry material lively.

In doing research on a topic or a target corporation, capitalize on your own experiences. If you are familiar with the workings of a law firm, a factory or a branch of the armed forces, your knowledge will put you ahead of those who must spend the sponsors' and their own time and money researching, interviewing and perhaps even traveling.

Whether your knowledge is from experience or through research, a personal computer outfitted with a telephone modem can greatly enhance your ability to produce an informative piece. Information available through your computer is bountiful, instantly accessible, and despite high telephone charges, often more cost-effective than travel.

More than expertise, it is perseverence and work experience that will help you persuade a large corporation to add you to their writers' pool. If called on, a process that may take months, you will probably be asked to submit a bid or budget for a completed script. This will include your travel expenses or computer modem expenses, if any. Experience at this point can help you defray research costs and present a lower, more competitive budget. Often, assignments are awarded to the lowest bidder. Fees of $50 to $150 per page are normal. (The Hollywood Writers Guild minimum for full-length screenplays works out to about $250 per page.)

Many organizations stagger payments: the first for a treatment or story; second for a rough draft; third for a polish. Each typically must be approved by various members of the organization.

A good script minimizes jargon and details and exploits the advantage of film over print media by concentrating on visuals, potentially dramatic moments and narrative conflict within the material. Information and data are best conveyed in print since the viewer will not or cannot rewind the film as easily as flipping the pages of a manual. A good script effectively conveys feelings of, say, a hospital emergency procedure, or a manufacturer's new product or a law firm's attractiveness to a potential law school recruit.

Avoid showing the narrator on camera as that information is redundant. Keep in mind that extensive on-screen dialogue also may result in wooden performance unless the producer has decided that it is appropriate, and affordable, to hire professional actors. Writers will find that a host of still photographs, and even recorded bites in specialized and general libraries, are available and can be incorporated into your script.

The conventional appearance or format for business and educational filmscripts is not as standard as one for a motion picture scripts, so it is best to obtain copies or actual scripts from your target client. The look of the page is crucial.

A square ☐ to the left of a listing denotes firms interested in cable TV scripts.

‡**A.V. MEDIA CRAFTSMAN, INC.**, Suite 600, 110 E. 23rd St., New York NY 10010. (212)228-6644. FAX: (212)979-0544. President: Carolyn Clark. Produces audio visual training material for corporations and educational material for publishers. Works with New York area writers only. Contracts scripts for 10-15 projects per year. Query with samples and resume. Call later. Samples and resumes filed by area of expertise.
Needs: "Most of our projects are 10-15 minute training scripts with related study materials for corporations and educational publishers. We create multi-screen presentations for conferences as well." Produces slide shows, sound filmstrips, videos, multiscreen shows, multimedia kits, overhead transparencies, tapes and cassettes. Pays $350-500 per project.
Tips: "Accept changes, do accurate research, and enjoy the subject matter. Send resume and cover letter. State special areas of interest (ie., economics, science, fashion, health, etc.)."

ABS & ASSOCIATES, Box 5127, Evanston IL 60204. (312)982-1414. President: Alan Soell. "We produce material for all levels of corporate, medical, cable, and educational institutions for the purposes of training and development, marketing and meeting presentations. We also are developing programming for the broadcast areas. 75% freelance written. We work with a core of three to five freelance writers from development to final drafts." All scripts published are unagented submissions. Buys all rights. Previously produced material OK. Computer printout submissions acceptable. Reports in 2 weeks on queries. Catalog for 8x10 SAE and 6 first class stamps.

Needs: Videotape, 16mm films, silent and sound filmstrips, multimedia kits, overhead transparencies, realia, slides, tapes and cassettes, and television shows/series. Currently interested in "sports instructional series that could be produced for the consumer market on tennis, gymnastics, bowling, golf, aerobics, health and fitness, cross-country skiing and cycling. Also home improvement programs for the novice—for around the house—in a series format. These two areas should be 30 minutes and be timeless in approach for long shelf life." Sports audience, age 25-45; home improvement, 25-65. "Cable TV needs include the two groups of programming detailed here. We are also looking for documentary work on current issues, nuclear power, solar power, urban development, senior citizens—but with a new approach." Query or submit synopsis/outline and resume. Pays by contractual agreement.

Tips: "I am looking for innovative approaches to old problems that just don't go away. The approach should be simple and direct so there is immediate audience identification with the presentation. I also like to see a sense of humor used. Trends in the audiovisual field include interactive video with tape and video disk—for training purposes."

ADMASTER, INC., 95 Madison Ave., New York NY 10016. (212)679-1134. Director: Andrew Corn. Produces sales and training material. Purchases 50-75 scripts/year. Works with 5-10 writers/year. Buys all rights. No previously published material. Reports in 1 month.

Needs: Charts, filmstrips (sound), multimedia kits, slides, tapes and cassettes. "We need material for multimedia industrial and financial meetings." Submit synopsis/outline, complete script or résumé. Makes outright purchase of $250-500.

Tips: "We want local writers only."

AMERICAN MEDIA INC., 1454 30th St., West Des Moines IA 50265. (515)224-0919. Contact: Art Bauer. Produces material for the business and industry training market (management, motivation, sales). Buys 10 scripts/year. Buys all rights. Previously produced material OK. Reports in 3 weeks. Catalog for 8½x11 SAE with 5 first class stamps.

Needs: Produces 16mm films and 1-inch videotapes. Submit synopsis/outline or completed script. Payment varies depending on script and quality.

Tips: "Do your homework, don't rush, think a project thru, ask and find out what your client needs. Not just what you think. Work long and hard."

‡ANIMATION ARTS ASSOCIATES, INC., 1100 E. Hector St., Conshohocken PA 19428. (215)825-8530. Contact Rozaida Keely or Harry E. Ziegler, Jr. For government, industry, engineers, doctors, scientists, dentists, general public, military. 100% freelance written. Buys average 12 scripts/year.

Needs: Produces 3½-minute 8mm and 16mm film loops; 16mm and 35mm films (ranging from 5-40 minutes); 2¼x2¼ or 4x5 slides; complete film and video productions; and teaching machine programs for training, sales, industry and public relations. Also produces software—motion picture scripts for training sales promotion and recruitment films. Send resume of credits for motion picture and filmstrip productions and software. "The writer should have scriptwriting credits for training, sales, promotion and public relations." Payment dependent on client's budget.

Tips: "Send us a resume listing writing and directing credits for films and sound/slide programs."

ARNOLD AND ASSOCIATES PRODUCTIONS, INC., 2159 Powell St., San Francisco CA 94133. (415)989-3490. President: John Arnold. Executive Producers: James W. Morris and Peter Dutton. Produces material for the general public (entertainment/motion pictures) and for corporate clients (employees/customers/consumers). Buys 10-15 scripts/year. Works with 3 writers/year. Buys all rights. Previously produced material OK. Reports in 1 month.

Needs: Films (35mm) and videotape. Looking for "upscale image and marketing programs. Dramatic writing for "name narrators and post scored original music; and motion picture. $5-6 million dollar budget. Dramatic or horror." Query with samples or submit completed script. Makes outright purchase of $1,000.

Tips: Looking for "upscale writers that understand corporate image production, and motion picture writer(s) that understands story and dialogue."

A/V CONCEPTS CORP., 30 Montauk Blvd., Oakdale NY 11769. (516)567-7227. Contact: P. Solimene or K. Brennan. Produces material for elementary-high school students, either on grade level or in remedial situations. 100% freelance written. Works with a small number of new/unpublished writers each year. Buys 25 scripts/year from unpublished/unproduced writers. Employs filmstrip, book and personal computer media.

Computer printout submissions acceptable. Reports on outline in 1 month; on final scripts in 6 weeks. Buys all rights.
Needs: Interested in original educational computer (disk-based) software programs for Apple +, 48k. Main concentration in language arts, mathematics and reading. "Manuscripts must be written using our lists of vocabulary words and meet our reading ability formula requirements. Specific guidelines are devised for each level. Length of manuscript and subjects will vary according to grade level for which material is prepared. Basically, we want material that will motivate people to read." Pays $300 and up.
Tips: "Writers must be highly creative and highly disciplined. We are interested in high interest-low readability materials."

‡**BARR FILMS**, 12801 Schabarum Ave., Irwindale CA 91706. (818)338-7878. FAX: (818)814-2672. Vice President, Product Development: George Holland. Produces material for schools, health agencies, libraries, colleges, business and government." Buys 10-20 scripts/year. Buys all rights. Reports in 1 month. Free catalog.
Needs: Films (16mm). Looking for "short, 10-25-minute films on any educational or training subject." Submit synopsis/outline. Makes outright purchase of $1,000-3,000.

SAMUEL R. BLATE ASSOCIATES, 10331 Watkins Mill Dr., Gaithersburg MD 20879-2935. (301)840-2248. President: Samuel R. Blate. Produces audiovisual and educational material for business, education, institutions, state and federal governments. "We work with two to six *local* writers per year on a per project basis—it varies as to business conditions and demand." Buys first rights when possible. Query for electronic submissions. Computer printout submissions acceptable; prefers letter-quality. Reports in 1 week on queries; 2 weeks on submissions. SASE for return.
Needs: Filmstrips (silent and sound), multimedia kits, slides, tapes and cassettes. Query with samples. SASE for return. Payment "depends on type of contract with principal client." Pays expenses of writers on assignment.
Tips: "Writers must have a strong track record of technical and aesthetic excellence. Clarity is not next to divinity—it is above it."

CABSCOTT BROADCAST PRODUCTION, INC., #1 Broadcast Center, Blackwood NJ 08012. (609)228-3600. FAX: (609)227-9624. Contact: Larry Scott. Produces industrial and broadcast material. 10% freelance written. Works with a small number of new/unpublished writers each year. Buys 10-12 scripts/year. Buys all rights. No previously produced material. Query for electronic submissions. Computer printout submissions acceptable; prefers letter-quality. Reports in 1 month.
Needs: Tapes and cassettes and video. Query with samples. Makes outright purchase. Sometimes pays expenses of writers on assignment.

‡**LEE CAPLIN PRODUCTIONS**, 8274 Grand View Trail, Los Angeles CA 90046. (213)650-1882. Vice President Development: Sonia Mintz. Produces feature films for theatrical audience and TV audience. Buys 2 scripts/year, works with 10 writers/year. Buys all rights. Reports on submissions in 2 months.
Needs: Films (35mm) and videotapes. Feature scripts 100-120 pp. Submit completed script. Pays on a deal by deal basis/some WGA, some not.
Tips: "Don't send derivitive standard material. Emphasis on unique plot and characters, realistic dialogue. *Discourage* period pieces, over-the-top comedy, graphic sex/violence. *Encourage* action, action/comedy, horror, thriller, thriller/comedy."

CLEARVUE, INC., 6465 N. Avondale, Chicago IL 60631. (312)775-9433. President: W.O. McDermed. Produces material for educational market—grades kindergarten-12. 90% freelance written. Prefers to work with published/established writers; works with a small number of new/unpublished writers each year. Buys 20-50 scripts/year from previously unpublished/unproduced writers. Buys all rights. Previously produced material OK. Query for electronic submissions. Computer printout submissions acceptable; prefers letter-quality. Reports in 2 weeks on queries; 3 weeks on submissions. Free catalog.
Needs: Videos, filmstrips (sound), multimedia kits, and slides. "Our filmstrips are 35 to 100 frames—8 to 30 minutes for all curriculum areas." Query. Makes outright purchase, $100-5,000. Sometimes pays the expenses of writers on assignment.
Tips: "Our interests are in filmstrips and video for the elementary and high school markets on all subjects."

Market conditions are constantly changing! If this is 1991 or later, buy the newest edition of Writer's Market at your favorite bookstore or order directly from Writer's Digest Books.

COMPASS FILMS, 921 Jackson Dr., Cleveland WI 53015. Executive Producer: Robert Whittaker. Produces material for educational, industrial and general adult audiences. Specializes in Marine films, stop motion and special effects with a budget . . . and national and worldwide filming in difficult locations. 60% freelance written. Works with 3 writers/year. Buys 2-4 scripts/year. 100% of scripts are unagented submissions. Buys all rights. Query with samples or submit resume. Computer printout submissions acceptable. Reports in 6 weeks. Buys all rights.

Needs: Scripts for 5- to 30-minute business films, and general documentaries. "We would like to review writers to develop existing film treatments and ideas with strong dialogue." Also needs ghost writers, editors and researchers. Produces 16mm and 35mm films and video tape products. Payment negotiable, depending on experience. Pays expenses of writers on assignment.

Tips: Writer/photographers receive higher consideration "because we could also use them as still photographers on location and they could double-up as rewrite men . . . and ladies. Experience in videotape editing supervision an asset. We are producing more high 'fashion-tech' industrial video."

CONTINENTAL FILM PRODUCTIONS CORPORATION, Box 5126, 4220 Amnicola Hwy., Chattanooga TN 37406. (615)622-1193. Executive Vice President: James L. Webster. Produces "AV and video presentations for businesses and non profit organizations for sales, training, public relations, documentation, motivation, etc." Works with many writers annually. Buys all rights. No previously produced material. Unsolicited submissions not returned. Reports in 1 week.

Needs: "We do need new writers of various types. Please contact us by mail with samples and resume. Samples will be returned postpaid." Produces slides, filmstrips, motion pictures, multi-image presentations, and videos. Query with samples and resume. Outright purchase: $250 minimum.

Tips: Looks for writers whose work shows " technical understanding, humor, common sense, practicality, simplicity, creativity, etc. Important for writers to adapt script to available production budget." Suggests writers "increase use of humor in training films." Also seeking scripts on "human behavior in industry" and on "why elementary and high school students should continue their educations."

NICHOLAS DANCY PRODUCTIONS, INC., 333 W. 39th St., New York NY 10018. (212)564-9140. President: Nicholas Dancy. Produces media material for corporate communications, the health care field, general audiences, employees, members of professional groups, members of associations and special customer groups. 60% freelance written. Prefers to work with published/established writers. Buys 5-10 scripts/year; works with 5-10 writers/year. None of scripts are unagented submissions. Buys all rights. Query for electronic submissions. Computer printout submissions acceptable; prefers letter-quality. Reports in 1 month.

Needs: "We use scripts for videotapes or films from 5 minutes to 1 hour for corporate communications, sales, orientation, training, corporate image, medical and documentary." Format: videotape, occasionally 16mm films. Query with résumé. "No unsolicited material. Our field is too specialized." Pays by outright purchase of $800-5,000. Pays expenses of writers on assignment.

Tips: "Writers should have a knowledge of business and industry and professions, an ability to work with clients and communicators, a fresh narrative style, creative use of dialogue, good skills in accomplishing research, and a professional approach to production. New concept trends are important in business. We're looking for new areas. The cautious loosening of FDA processes will create an even sharper need for skilled and talented scriptwriters in the medical field."

EDUCATIONAL IMAGES LTD., Box 3456, Elmira NY 14905. (607)732-1090. Executive Director: Dr. Charles R. Belinky. Produces material (sound filmstrips, multimedia kits and slide sets) for schools, kindergarten through college and graduate school, public libraries, parks, nature centers, etc. Also produces science-related software material. Buys 50 scripts/year. Buys all AV rights. Computer printout submissions OK. Free catalog.

Needs: Slide sets and filmstrips on science, natural history, anthropology and social studies. "We are looking primarily for complete AV programs; we will consider slide collections to add to our files. This requires high quality, factual text and pictures." Query with a meaningful sample of proposed program. Pays $150 minimum.

Tips: The writer/photographer is given high consideration. "Once we express interest, follow up. Potential contributors lose many sales to us by not following up on initial query. Don't waste our time and yours if you can't deliver. The market seems to be shifting to greater popularity of video and computer software formats."

‡EDUCATIONAL INSIGHTS, 19560 S. Rancho Way, Dominguez Hills CA 90220. (213)637-2131. FAX: (213)605-5048. VP/Director of Development: Dennis J. Graham. Produces material for elementary schools and retail "home-learning" markets. Works with 10 writers/year. Buys all rights. Previously produced material OK. Reports in 2 weeks. Catalog for 9x12 SAE with 47¢ postage.

Needs: Charts, models, multimedia kits, study prints, tapes and cassettes, and teaching machine programs. Query with samples. Pays varied royalties or makes outright purchase.

Tips: "Keep up-to-date information on educational trends in mind. Study the market before starting to work. We receive 20 manuscripts per week—all reviewed and returned, if rejected."

EDUCATIONAL VIDEO NETWORK, 1401 19th St., Huntsville TX 77340. (409)295-5767. President: Dr. Kenneth L. Russell. Produces material for junior high, senior high, college and university audiences. Buys "perhaps 20 scripts/year." Buys all rights or pays royalty on gross retail and wholesale. Previously produced material OK. Reports in 1 week on queries; in 1 month on submissions. Free catalog.
Needs: "Filmstrips and video for educational purposes." Produces filmstrips with sound and video. "Photographs on 2x2 slides must have good saturation of color." Query. Royalty varies.
Tips: Looks for writers with the "ability to write and illustrate for educational purposes. Schools are asking for more curriculum oriented live-action video. Recent trends include more emphasis on video; less emphasis on filmstrips."

EMC CORP, 300 York Ave., St. Paul MN 55101. Editor: Eileen Slater. Produces material for children and teenagers in the primary grades through high school. "We sell strictly to schools and public libraries." Software submissions accepted. 100% freelance written by published/produced writers. All scripts produced are unagented submissions. Buys 2-3 scripts/year. Buys world rights. Query for electronic submissions. Computer printout submissions acceptable; prefers letter-quality. Catalog for 9x12 SASE.
Needs: Career education, consumer education and vocational education (as related to language arts especially). "No standard requirements, due to the nature of educational materials publishing." No religious topics. Query with resume and one or more samples of previously produced work. No unsolicited manuscripts accepted. Payment varies.

‡FIRE PREVENTION THROUGH FILMS, INC., Box 11, Newton Highlands MA 02161. (617)965-4444. Manager: Julian Olansky. Produces material for audiences involved with fire prevention and general safety: grades kindergarten through 12, colleges and universities, laboratories, industry and home safety. 50% freelance written. Works with a small number of new/unpublished writers each year. Purchases 1-3 scripts/year. "We work with several local scriptwriters on a yearly basis." Buys all rights. No previously produced material. Computer printout submissions acceptable; prefers letter-quality to dot-matrix. Reports in 3 weeks. Free catalog.
Needs: Films (16mm). "We will need scripts for films dealing with general safety in an office setting (20 minutes). Will consider any script dealing with fire prevention and/or general safety (20-minute film or less). Query with or without samples. Makes outright purchase.

FIRST RING, 15303 Ventura Blvd., #800, Sherman Oaks CA 91403-3155. Assistant Editor: Phil Potters. Estab. 1987. "Audio material only. Humorous telephone answering machine messages. Intended for use by all persons who utilize telephone answering machines." Buys 100 scripts/year. Buys all rights. No previously produced material. Reports in 1 week on queries; 4 months on submissions.
Needs: Write for guidelines. Scripts must not exceed 20 seconds in their finished production; however there is no minimum duration. Produces tapes and cassettes. Query. Outright purchase of $100 upon acceptance.
Tips: Looking for writers with "the ability to write hilarious scripts as set forth in guidelines. All submissions are considered even from writers whose prior work was not accepted."

FLIPTRACK LEARNING SYSTEMS, Division of Mosaic Media, Inc., Suite 200, 999 Main St., Glen Ellyn IL 60137. (312)790-1117. Publisher: F. Lee McFadden. Contact: Patricia Menges. Produces training courses for microcomputers and business software. Works with a small number of new/unpublished writers each year. 35% freelance written. Buys 3-5 courses/year; 1-2 from unpublished/unproduced writers. All courses published are unagented submissions. Works with 3-5 writers/year. Buys all rights. Query for electronic submissions. Computer printout submissions OK. Reports in 3 weeks. Free product literature; sample copy for 9x12 SAE.
Needs: Training courses on how to use personal computers/software, video or audio geared to the adult student in a business setting and usually to the novice user; a few courses at advanced levels. Primarily audio, also some reference manuals, video, and feature articles on personal computers. Query with resume and samples if available. Pays negotiable royalty or makes outright purchase.
Tips: "We prefer to work with Chicago-area writers with strong teaching/training backgrounds and experience with microcomputers. Writers from other regions are also welcome. We also need feature/journalism writers with strong microcomputer interest and experience."

PAUL FRENCH & PARTNERS, INC., 503 Gabbettville Rd., LaGrange GA 30240. (404)882-5581. Contact: Gene Ballard. 20% freelance written. Buys all rights. Computer printout submissions acceptable. Reports in 2 weeks.
Needs: Wants to see multi-screen scripts (all employee-attitude related) and/or multi-screen AV sales meeting scripts or resumes. Produces silent and sound filmstrips, videotapes, cassettes and slides. Query or submit resume. Pays in outright purchase of $500-5,000. Payment is in accordance with Writers Guild standards.

‡GESSLER PUBLISHING CO., INC., Gessler Educational Software, 55 W. 13th St., New York NY 10011. (212)627-0099. FAX: (212)627-5948. President: Seth C. Levin. Produces material for students learning ESL and foreign languages. 50% freelance written. Eager to work with new/unpublished writers. Buys about 60-

75 scripts/year. 100% of scripts are unagented submissions. Prefers to buy all rights, but will work on royalty basis. Do not send disk submission without documentation. Query for electronic submissions. Computer printout submissions acceptable; prefers letter-quality to dot-matrix. Reports in 3 weeks on queries; 2 months on submissions.

Needs: Video and filmstrips "to create an interest in learning a foreign language and its usefulness in career objectives; also culturally insightful video/filmstrips on French, German, Italian and Spanish speaking countries." Produces sound filmstrips, multimedia kits, overhead transparencies, games, realia, tapes and cassettes, computer software. Also produces scripts for videos. Submit synopsis/outline or software with complete documentation, introduction, objectives. Makes outright purchase and pays royalties.

Tips: "Be organized in your presentation; be creative but keep in mind that your audience is primarily junior/senior high school teachers. We will be looking for new filmstrips, videotapes, software and videodisks which can be used in foreign language and ESL classes. Also, more of a concentration on hypercard and interactive video projects."

‡**GOODWIN, KNAB & COMPANY,** 1415 N. Dayton St., Chicago IL 60622-2603. (312)337-2010. Creative Director: Michael Knab. "Most of our work is marketing and corporate image communications." Produces about 200 scripts/year. Buys variable rights. Query for electronic submission. Computer printout submissions acceptable. Reports in 2 weeks.

Needs: 16 and 35mm films, multimedia kits and all forms of print, including advertising. Query with samples. Pays in royalty or outright purchase.

Tips: "We look for advertising writing in our Print Department and we look for strongly conceptual writing in our AV Department."

‡**BRAD HAGERT,** Box 18642, Irvine CA 92713. (714)261-7266. Produces material for corporate executives. Buys 10 scripts/year. Buys all rights. No previously produced material. SASE. Reports in 1 month.

Needs: Films, videotapes, multimedia kits, slides, tapes and cassettes. Query with samples. Makes outright purchase.

HAYES SCHOOL PUBLISHING CO., INC., 321 Pennwood Ave., Wilkinsburg PA 15221. (412)371-2373. FAX: (800)543-8771. President: Clair N. Hayes, III. Produces material for school teachers, principals, elementary through high school. Also produces charts, workbooks, teacher's handbooks, posters, bulletin board material, and reproducible blackline masters (grades kindergarten through 12). 25% freelance written. Prefers to work with published/established writers; works with a small number of new/unpublished writers each year. Buys 5-10 scripts/year from unpublished/unproduced writers. 100% of scripts produced are unagented submissions. Buys all rights. Query for electronic submissions. Computer printout submissions acceptable; prefers letter-quality. Catalog for 3 first class stamps; writer's guidelines for #10 SAE and 2 first class stamps.

Needs: Educational material only. Particularly interested in educational material for elementary school level. Query. Pays $25 minimum.

IMAGE INNOVATIONS, INC., Suite 201, 29 Clyde Rd., Somerset NJ 08873. President: Mark A. Else. Produces material for business, education and general audiences. 50% freelance written. "Credentials and reputation means much—published or unpublished." Buys 15-20 scripts/year from previously unpublished/unproduced writers. All scripts produced are unagented submissions. Computer printout submissions acceptable; prefers letter-quality. Reports in 2 weeks. Buys all rights.

Needs: Subject topics include education, sales, public relations and technical. Produces sound/slide, multi-image programs, and hi-image 1" and ¾" Betacam video and tapes and cassettes. Query with samples. Pays in outright purchase of $800-5,000. Sometimes pays the expenses of writers on assignment.

IMPERIAL INTERNATIONAL LEARNING CORP., 329 E. Court St., Kankakee IL 60901. (815)933-7735. Editor: Patsy Gunnels. Material intended for kindergarten through grade 12 audience. 60% freelance written. Prefers to work with published/established writers; works with a small number of new/unpublished writers each year. Buys 2-4 scripts/year from unpublished/unproduced writers. Buys all rights. No previously produced material. Query for electronic submissions. Computer printout submissions acceptable. Reports in 2 weeks on queries; 1 month on submissions. Free catalog.

Needs: "Supplemental learning materials of various lengths in the areas of reading, math, social studies and science with emphasis on using the microcomputer." Produces microcomputer programs. Query with samples or submit complete script and resume. Pays negotiable rates.

Tips: "We are interested in software and interactive videodisks that meet curricular needs in the math, science, language arts, social studies and special education classroom."

☐**INTERNATIONAL MEDIA SERVICES INC.,** 718 Sherman Ave., Plainfield NJ 07060. (201)756-4060. President/General Manager: Stuart Allen. Produces varied material depending on assignment or production in house; includes corporate, public relations, sales, radio/TV, CATV, teleconferencing/CCTV, etc. 60-75% freelance written. 90% of scripts produced are unagented submissions. "We normally issue assignments to writers in the freelance market who specialize in appropriate fields of interest." Buys all rights. No previously produced material. Computer printout submissions acceptable. Reporting time varies depending on job requirements and specifications.

Needs: Charts, dioramas, 8/16mm film loops, 16/35mm films, silent and sound filmstrips, kinescopes, multimedia kits, overhead transparencies, phonograph records, slides, tapes and cassettes, television shows/series and videotape presentations. "We routinely hire writers from a freelance resource file." Cable TV needs include educational and entertainment marketplaces. Query with or without samples, or submit synopsis/outline and resume. "All work must be copyrighted and be original unpublished works." Pays in accordance with Writers Guild standards, negotiated contract or flat rate.

Tips: "We are not responsible for unsolicited material and recommend not submitting complete manuscripts for review without prior arrangement."

JACOBY/STORM PRODUCTIONS INC., 22 Crescent Road, Westport CT 06880. (203)227-2220. Contact: Doris Storm. Produces material for business people, students of all ages, professionals (e.g. medical). Works with 4-6 writers annually. Buys all rights. No previously produced material. Reports in 2 weeks.

Needs: "Short dramatic films on business subjects, educational filmstrips on varied subjects, sales and corporate image films." Produces 16mm films, filmstrips (sound), slides, tapes and cassettes, videotapes and videodisks. Query. Makes outright purchase (depends on project).

Tips: "Prefers local people. Look for experience, creativity, dependability, attention to detail, enthusiasm for project, ability to interface with client. Wants more film/video, fewer filmstrips, more emphasis on creative approaches to material."

PAUL S. KARR PRODUCTIONS, 2949 W. Indian School Rd., Box 11711, Phoenix AZ 85017. (602)266-4198. Utah Division: 1024 N. 250 E., Box 1254, Orem UT 84057. (801)226-8209. Produces films and videos for industry, business, education, TV spots and entertainment. *Do not submit material unless requested.* Works on co-production ventures that have been funded.

Needs: Produces 16mm films and videos. Query. Payment varies.

Tips: "One of the best ways for a writer to become a screenwriter is to come up with a client that requires a film or video. He can take the project to a production company, such as we are, assume the position of an associate producer, work with an experienced professional producer in putting the production into being, and in that way learn about video and filmmaking and chalk up some meaningful credits, and share in the profits. Direct consumer TV spots (that is, 800-number sales spots) have become a big business in the Phoenix market the last few years. Our company is set up to handle all facets of this area of television marketing."

KIMBO EDUCATIONAL-UNITED SOUND ARTS, INC., 10-16 N. 3rd Ave., Box 477, Long Branch NJ 07740. (201)229-4949. Contact: James Kimble or Amy Laufer. Produces materials for the educational market (early childhood, special education, music, physical education, dance, and preschool children 6 months and up). 50% freelance written. Buys approximately 12-15 scripts/year; works with approximately 12-15 writers/year. Buys 5 scripts/year from unpublished/unproduced writers. Most scripts are unagented submissions. Buys all rights or first rights. Previously produced material OK "in some instances." Reports in 1 month. Free catalog.

Needs: "For the next two years we will be concentrating on general early childhood songs and movement oriented products, new albums in the fitness field and more. Each will be an album/cassette with accompanying teacher's manual and, if warranted, manipulatives." Phonograph records and cassettes, "all with accompanying manual or teaching guides." Query with samples and synopsis/outline or completed script. Pays 5-7% royalty on lowest wholesale selling price, and by outright purchase. Both negotiable.

Tips: "We look for creativity first. Having material that is educationally sound is also important. Being organized is certainly helpful. Fitness is growing rapidly in popularity and will always be a necessary thing. Children will always need to be taught the basic fine and gross motor skills. Capturing interest while reaching these goals is the key."

‡DAVID LANCASTER PRODUCTIONS, 3356 Bennett, Los Angeles CA 90068. (213)874-1415. President: David Lancaster. Buys approximately 5 scripts/year. Buys all rights. Reports in 1 month on queries.

Needs: Feature films (35 mm). Submit completed script. Pays in accordance with Writers Guild standards.

Tips: "Submit clean format per industry—no less than 90 pages, no more than 125."

‡MARSHFILM ENTERPRISES, INC., Box 8082, Shawnee Mission KS 66208. (816)523-1059. President: Joan K. Marsh. Produces software and filmstrips for elementary and junior/senior high school students. 100% freelance written. Works with a small number of new/unpublished writers each year. Buys 8-16 scripts/year. All scripts produced are unagented submissions. Buys all rights. Computer printout submissions acceptable; prefers letter-quality to dot-matrix.

Needs: 50-frame; 15-minute scripts for sound filmstrips. Query only. Pays by outright purchase of $250-500/script.

Tips: "We are seeking generic, curriculum-oriented educational scripts suitable for interactive video disk development."

‡MOTIVATION MEDIA, INC., 1245 Milwaukee Ave., Glenview IL 60025. (312)297-4740. FAX: (312)297-6829. Executive Producer: Frank Stedronsky. Produces customized material for salespeople, customers, corporate/industrial employees and distributors. 90% freelance written. Buys 100 scripts/year from unpublished/unproduced writers. Prefers to work with published/established writers. All scripts produced are unagented submissions. Buys all rights. Computer printout submissions acceptable. Reports in 1 month.
Needs: Material for all audiovisual media—particularly marketing-oriented (sales training, sales promotional, sales motivational) material. Produces sound filmstrips, 16mm films, multimedia sales meeting programs, videotapes, cassettes and slide sets. Software should be AV oriented. Query with samples. Pays $150-5,000. Pays the expenses of writers on assignment.

‡HENRY NASON PRODUCTIONS, INC., 1900 Superfine Lane, Wilmington DE 19802. President: Henry Nason. Producers of video presentations for corporate clients. 90% freelance written. Buys all rights.
Needs: Usually 10- to 15-minute scripts on wide variety of corporate subjects, such as sales, marketing, employee benefits, finance, health and safety, pharmaceuticals, etc. "The style should be clear and relaxed, well-researched and organized. Welcome video scripts submissions or inquiries from writers in the Philadelphia to Baltimore area." Pays an average of $3,000 plus expenses.

NYSTROM, 3333 N. Elston Ave., Chicago IL 60618. (312)463-1144. Editorial Director: Darrell A. Coppock. Produces material for school audiences (kindergarten through 12th grade). Computer printout and disk submissions OK. Free catalog.
Needs: Educational material on social studies, earth and life sciences, career education, reading, language arts and mathematics. Produces charts, sound filmstrips, models, multimedia kits, overhead transparencies and realia. Required credentials depend on topics and subject matter and approach desired. Query. Pays according to circumstances.

OMNI COMMUNICATIONS, Suite 207, 101 E. Carmel Drive, Carmel IN 46032. (317)844-6664. Vice President: Dr. Sandra M. Long. Produces commercial, training, educational and documentary material. Buys all rights. No previously produced material.
Needs: "Educational, documentary, commercial, training, motivational." Produces slides, shows and multi-image videotapes. Query. Makes outright purchase.
Tips: "Must have experience as writer and have examples of work. Examples need to include print copy and finished copy of videotape if possible. A résumé with educational background, general work experience and experience as a writer must be included. Especially interested in documentary-style writing. Writers' payment varies, depending on amount of research needed, complexity of project, length of production and other factors."

OUR SUNDAY VISITOR, INC., Religious Education Dept., 200 Noll Plaza, Huntington IN 46750. (219)356-8400. Produces print and video material for students (pre-K through 12th grade), adult religious education groups and teacher trainees. "We are very concerned that the materials we produce meet the needs of today's church." Free catalog.
Needs: "Proposals for projects should be no more than 2 pages in length, in outline form. Programs should display up-to-date audiovisual techniques and cohesiveness. Broadly speaking, material should deal with religious education, including liturgy and daily Christian living, as well as structured catechesis. It must not conflict with sound Catholic doctrine and should reflect modern trends in education." Produces educational books, charts and videos. "Work-for-hire and royalty arrangements possible."

PHOTO COMMUNICATION SERVICES, INC., 6410 Knapp NE, Ada MI 49301. (616)676-1499 or (616)676-2429. President: Michael Jackson. Produces commercial, industrial, sales, training material etc. 95% freelance written. No scripts from unpublished/unproduced writers. 95% of scripts produced are unagented submissions. Buys all rights and first serial rights. Query for electronic submissions. Computer printout submissions acceptable. Reports in 1 month. SASE if you wish to have material returned.
Needs: Multimedia kits, slides, tapes and cassettes, and video presentations. Primarily interested in 35mm multimedia, 1-24 projectors and video. Query with samples or submit completed script and résumé. Pays in outright purchase or by agreement.

PREMIER VIDEO FILM & RECORDING CORP., 3033 Locust, St. Louis MO 63103. (314)531-3555. Secretary/Treasurer: Grace Dalzell. Produces material for the corporate community, religious organizations, political arms, and hospital and educational groups. 100% freelance written. Prefers to work with published/established writers. Buys 50-100 scripts/year. All scripts are unagented submissions. Buys all rights; "very occasionally the writer retains rights." Previously produced material OK; "depends upon original purposes and markets." Computer printout submissions acceptable; prefers letter-quality. Reports "within a month or as soon as possible."

Needs: "Our work is all custom produced with the needs being known only as required." 35mm film loops, super 8mm and 35mm films, silent and sound filmstrips, multimedia kits, overhead transparencies, phonograph records, slides, and tapes and cassettes. Produces TV, training and educational scripts for video. Submit complete script and resume. Pays in accordance with Writers Guild standards or by outright purchase of $100 or "any appropriate sum." Sometimes pays the expenses of writers on assignment.

Tips: "Always place without fail *occupational pursuit*, name, address and phone number in upper right hand corner of resume. We're looking for writers with creativity, good background and a presentable image."

RHYTHMS PRODUCTIONS, Box 34485, Los Angeles CA 90034. President: Ruth White. Produces children's educational cassettes/books. Buys all rights. Previously published material OK "if it is suitable for our market and is not now currently on the market. We also look for tapes that have been produced and are ready for publication." Reports on mss in 3 weeks. Catalog for 8½x11 SAE and 3 first class stamps.

Needs: Phonograph records and tapes and cassettes. "Looking for children's stories with musical treatments if possible. Must have educational content or values." Query with samples. Payment is negotiable.

‡SANFORD/PILLSBURY PRODUCTION, Suite 216, 1640 S. Sepulveda, Los Angeles CA 90025. (213)479-8200. Development Executives: Jacqueline Stansbury and Patty Clark. Reports in 1 month on queries.

Needs: Films (35 mm). Query. Writers without agents must sign a release form. Pays in accordance with Writer's Guild standards.

PETER SCHLEGER COMPANY, 135 W. 58th St., New York NY 10019. (212)765-7129. President: Peter R. Schleger. Produces material "primarily for employee populations in corporations and non-profit organizations." Buys all rights, "most work is paid for for a one-time use, and that piece may have no life beyond one project." Previously produced material OK. Reports in 1 month. "Typical programs are customized workshops or specific individual programs from subjects such as listening and presentation skills to medical benefits communication. No program is longer than 10 minutes. If they need to be, they become shorter modules."

Needs: Produces sound filmstrips, video and printed manuals and leader's guides. Send completed script and resume. Makes outright purchase; payment "depends on script length."

Tips: "We are looking to receive and keep on file a resume and short, completed script sample of a program not longer than 10 minutes. The shorter the better to get a sense of writing style and the ability to structure a piece. We would also like to know the fees the writer expects for his/her work. Either per-diem, by project budget or by finished script page. We want communicators with a training background or who have written training programs, modules and the like. We want to know of people who have written print material, as well. We do not want to see scripts that have been written and are looking for a producer/director. We will look at queries for possible workshops or new approaches for training, but these must be submitted as longshots only; it is not our primary business."

☐SEVEN OAKS FOUNDATION, 9145 Sligo Creek Pkwy., Silver Spring MD 20901. (301)587-0030. FAX: (301)587-8649. Production Manager: M. Marlow. 80% freelance written. Produces material for pastoral counselors on marriage and family counseling techniques; medical and psychiatric programs for hospital in-service and patient outreach training and preventive medicine programs on staying well and happy for a variety of age groups; and special interest educational training programs. Buys 20-30 scripts from 10-20 writers/year. 55% of scripts are unagented submissions. Will consider new writers with prior credits in other media but does give writers on successful projects repeat business. Buys all rights or first rights; rights purchased negotiable. Computer printout submissions acceptable; prefers letter-quality. Reports in 6 months.

Needs: Health care, leisure time, positive thinking, "enjoy a fuller life after 50" audio and video subjects. Also interested in safety, "how-to" self improvement subjects for kids, teenagers, young marrieds, and handicapped as well as general entertainment for K-6 grades. Writers should know film and TV formats. Programs are released under Seven Oaks Foundation, Seven Oaks Productions or Maritime Media depending on subjects and distribution markets. Presently expanding in home video market place. Query only first: will keep on file. Will not return unsolicited material. Payment negotiable according to project.

Tips: "Looking for budget features for cable TV set in either US or other countries—unique travel oriented scripts, maritime-related stories and educational subjects for consumer cassette market."

SPENCER PRODUCTIONS, INC., 234 5th Ave., New York NY 10001. (212)697-5895. General Manager: Bruce Spencer. Executive Producer: Alan Abel. Produces material for high school students, college students and adults. Occasionally uses freelance writers with considerable talent.

Needs: 16mm films, prerecorded tapes and cassettes. Satirical material only. Query. Pay is negotiable.

‡SPOTTSWOOD STUDIOS, 2524 Old Shell Rd., Box 7061, Mobile AL 36607. (205)478-9387. Co-owner: M.W. Spottswood. "We normally work for sponsors (but not always) who seek public attention." Buys 1-2 scripts/year. Buys all rights. Computer printout submissions acceptable. Reports in 2 weeks.

Needs: Business, religious and general. Produces 16mm films and 8mm loops, sound filmstrips, videotape and slide sets. Query with resume and samples. Pays by outright purchase.

Tips: "As documentary producers of video/films, we will be getting deeper into *historic* material."

TALCO PRODUCTIONS, 279 E. 44th St., New York NY 10017. (212)697-4015. President: Alan Lawrence. Vice President: Marty Holberton. Produces variety of material for motion picture theatres, TV, radio, business, trade associations, non-profit organizations, etc. Audiences range from young children to senior citizens. 20-40% freelance written. Buys scripts from published/produced writers only. All scripts produced are un-agented submissions. Buys all rights. No previously published material. Computer printout submissions acceptable; prefers letter-quality. Reports in 3 weeks on queries.

Needs: Films (16-35mm), filmstrips (sound), phonograph records, slides, radio tapes and cassettes and videotape. "We maintain a file of writers and call on those with experience in the same general category as the project in production. We do not accept unsolicited manuscripts. We prefer to receive a writer's resume listing credits. If his/her background merits, we will be in touch when a project seems right." Makes outright purchase/project and in accordance with Writer's Guild standards (when appropriate). Sometimes pays the expenses of writers on assignment.

Tips: "In the next year, we will have a greater concentration in TV productions. Production budgets will be tighter. Productions will be of shorter length to save money."

‡**TEL-AIR INTERESTS, INC.**, 1755 N.E. 149th St., Miami FL 33181. (305)944-3268. President: Grant H. Gravitt. Produces material for groups and theatrical and TV audiences. Buys all rights. Submit resume.

Needs: Documentary films on education, travel and sports. Produces films and videotape. Pays by outright purchase.

TRANSLIGHT MEDIA ASSOCIATES, 931 W. Liberty, Wheaton IL 60187. (312)690-7780. Producer: John Lorimer. Produces material for business people and religious organizations. Buys 4-8 scripts/year. Buys all rights. No previously produced material. "We like to keep samples as part of file for reference. If writer wants something back they should obtain permission to send it first." Reports as project arises in writer's skill area.

Needs: "We produce primarily slide/tape, multi-image and video programs. Our needs are generally for short (5-10 minute) creative scripts for sales, fund raising, business meeting, or corporate image applications. No commercial or TV shows." Query with samples. Outright purchase $250-3,000.

Tips: "We look for creative concepts, and ability to communicate clearly and concisely. We also look for writers that recognize that often in an audiovisual script the visuals are more important than the words— writers that write a visual concept, not just copy. We prefer to work with local writers (Chicago market). Initial query should include 2 or 3 short scripts or excerpts that show range and style. No phone queries please."

TRANSTAR PRODUCTIONS, INC., Suite C, 9520 E. Jewell Ave. Denver CO 80231. (303)695-4207. Producer/Director: Doug Hanes. Produces primarily industrial material. 10% freelance written. Buys 1-2 scripts/year from unpublished/unproduced writers. 100% of scripts are unagented submissions. Buys all rights. No previously produced material. Computer printout submissions acceptable; prefers letter-quality. Reporting time varies.

Needs: 16mm films, slides, tapes and cassettes, and videotape presentations. Also produces scripts for industrial sales and training. Submit resume. Pays negotiable rate.

TRI VIDEO TELEPRODUCTION—Lake Tahoe, Box 8822, Incline Village NV 89450-8822. (702)323-6868. California seasonal address: Suite 7, 751 Rancheros Dr., San Marcos CA 92069. Production Manager: Beth Davidson. Produces material primarily for corporate targets (their sales, marketing and training clients). Works with 3-4 writers each year developing contracted material. Could work with more, and could produce more programs if the right material were available. Buys all rights or negotiable rights. No previously produced material. Does not return material unless requested.

Needs: "Will have a need for writing contract projects; would consider other projects which are either sold to a client and need a producer, or which the writer wishes to sell and have produced. In all cases, corporate sales, marketing and training materials. Perhaps some mass audience (how-to) video programs." Produces videtapes only. Query. Makes outright purchase in accordance with Writers Guild standards.

Tips: "We are strong on production skill; weak on sales, so if your idea needs to be sold to an end user before it is produced, we may not be the right avenue. However, give us a try. We might be able to put the right people together." Looks for "creativity, of course, but solid understanding of the buying market. We don't go in for highly symbolic and abstract materials."

TROLL ASSOCIATES, 100 Corporate Dr., Mahwah NJ 07430. (201)529-4000. Contact: M. Schecter. Produces material for elementary and high school students. Buys approximately 200 scripts/year. Buys all rights. Reports in 3 weeks. Free catalog.

Needs: Produces multimedia kits, tapes and cassettes, and (mainly) books. Query or submit outline/synopsis. Pays royalty or by outright purchase.

UNIVERSITY OF WISCONSIN STOUT TELEPRODUCTION CENTER, 800 S. Broadway, Menomonie WI 54751. (715)232-2624. Center Director: Rosemary Jacobson. Produces instructional TV programs for primary, secondary, post secondary and specialized audiences. 10% freelance written. All scripts produced are unagented submissions. "We produce ITV programs for national, regional and state distribution to classrooms around the U.S. and Canada." Buys all rights. Computer printout submissions acceptable; prefers letter-quality.
Needs: "Our clients fund programs in a 'series' format which tend to be 8-12 programs each." Produces with one-inch and BETACAM broadcast quality. "We have a need for writers in Wisconsin and Minnesota whom we can call on to write single or multi-program/series in instructional television." Query with resume and samples of TV scripts. Sometimes pays the expenses of writers on assignment.
Tips: "Freelance writers should be aware of the hardware advances in broadcast and nonbroadcast. There are new avenues for writers to pursue in adult learning, computer-assisted programming and interactive programming. Our focus is moving from K-12 to post-secondary and adult education."

VISUAL HORIZONS, 180 Metro Park, Rochester NY 14623. (716)424-5300. FAX: (716)424-5313. President: Stanley Feingold. Produces material for general audiences. Buys 5 programs/year. Reports in 5 months. Free catalog.
Needs: Business, medical and general subjects. Produces silent and sound filmstrips, multimedia kits, slide sets and videotapes. Query with samples. Payment negotiable.

WMC COMPANY, 5 Independence Way, Princeton NJ 08540. (609)520-8500. President: Karl Faller. Produces various sales and marketing presentations for Fortune 500 corporate clients. 100% freelance written. Buys 30-40 scripts/year from previously produced writers only. All scripts produced are unagented submissions. Buys all rights. No previously published material. Query for electronic submissions. Computer printout submissions acceptable. Reports in 3 weeks.
Needs: "WMC produces sales and marketing tools in a variety of media. We need freelance writers who can assimilate technical or business-oriented subject matter (e.g., telecommunications services, automotive, financial). They must be able to present this material in a clear, entertaining presentation that *sells* the product." Query with samples. Pays $400-7,000/job. Sometimes pays expenses of writers on assignment.
Tips: "Freelance writers should be aware of interactive video disk, tape trend. It's the coming wave in training and P.O.P. sales."

ZM SQUARED, Box C-30, Cinnaminson NJ 08077. (609)786-0612. Contact: Pete Zakroff. "We produce AVs for a wide range of clients including education, business, industry and labor organizations." Buys 10 scripts/year; works with 4-5 writers/year. Buys all rights. No previously produced material. Query for electronic submissions. Computer printout submissions acceptable. Reports in 2 weeks on queries; 1 month on submissions.
Needs: Silent filmstrips, kinescopes, multimedia kits, overhead transparencies, slides, tapes and cassettes, and videotape presentations. Query with or without samples. Pays 3-10% royalty or by outright purchase, $150-750.

Playwriting

Both established playwrights and newcomers are finding theaters throughout the country open to new and diverse works for the stage. More than any other group of writers in the U.S., playwrights remain prolific and continue to inspire and be rewarded by audiences who value their work.

The playwright's words are honored more than those of any other writer and are universally protected from change without permission. Since most budgets are far smaller than those for films, the target audience need not be as large. Playwrights also enjoy far more freedom of choice of topics, degree of frankness and subtlety, and range of style than other scriptwriters.

On the other hand, budgetary considerations influence the choice of plays. Aspiring playwrights who stay within a reasonable range for size of cast, complexity of costumes and scene changes and number and type of special effects will have a better chance of having their plays performed.

While the video revolution has made it possible for anyone to be a scriptwriter, director and/or actor, live theater remains the most popular venue for the dramatic arts. Community theaters abound, and most organizations from the Scouts to local church groups devote time to producing plays.

Playwriting is not as lucrative as screenplay writing, yet there are few experiences as rewarding for a writer as watching his characters come to life on stage. Screenwriters exercise little if any influence at all over the fashion in which their work is interpreted, while a playwright's ability and desire to direct the talent and mold the production to his vision is rarely questioned.

Although some successfully produced plays are adapted to the screen, that transition remains rare. Theaters that pay playwrights have varied policies. Some pay royalties, others give outright sums and still others negotiate a combination. For the most part, playwrights tend to be challenged more by the desire to entertain and enlighten a live audience than by the desire to clear a profit.

For more playwriting opportunities, see also the listings in the Contests and Awards section.

‡A.D. PLAYERS, 2710 W. Alabama, Houston TX 77098. (713)526-2721. Artistic Director: Jeannette Clift George. Produces 4-6 plays/year. "These are professional productions that are performed either in our mainstage season or on tour. On tour the performance-arenas vary. The full-length road show productions are performed in civic auditoriums, theaters, opera houses. The one-act and revue shows are performed in various settings; churches. Our audiences are primarily family-oriented, a majority come from a church affiliation." Query and synopsis or submit complete ms. Reports in 6 weeks. Pays per performance.
Needs: "We produce one-act and full length plays, any style. As a professional Christian repertory company, we produce shows that express a Christian world view, i.e. God's reality in everyday life. This can range from Biblical to contemporary to anything in between. We produce two children's shows a season and do a lot of touring performances for high school age groups. We are looking for plays that have no more than 14 characters. We have the limitation of a proscenium stage with no fly space."
Tips: "Because of our specific signature as a Christian repertory company, plays that have nothing to do with God or man's search for spiritual significance in his world, would be of interest to us."

ACADEMY THEATRE, Box 77070, Atlanta GA 30357. (404)873-2518. Artistic Director: Frank Wittow. Literary Manager: Linda Anderson. Produces 7-9 plays/year; 389 seat Phoebe Theatre (modified thrust stage); 250 seat Phoenix Theatre and 80 seat Genesis Theatre with flexible stages. Genesis Series consists of three minimal productions of plays from local playwrights. Theatre for Youth seeks plays that can be staged and toured for grades 3-8 and high school. Only local playwrights are considered. Playwrights from other regions can send plays for new play production, but world premiere plays are preferred. Query and/or send synopsis and short sample of dialogue. Reports in 6 months. Rights vary according to type of production.
Needs: Full-length, one-act, plays for young audiences. Special interests: non-traditional plays with elements of poetic language and surrealism; plays that deal with important issues in unique ways. Cast: 8 maximum. Simple sets.
Tips: "The Academy Theatre looks for new plays that show writers have found their own unique voice and are not imitating current theatrical trends. We get excited by writers who have a facility with language along with the ability to disturb, amuse and interest an audience in theatrical, dramatic ways. We look for unusual works that show promise of a playwright who has something important to say and says it in an imaginative way."

ACTORS THEATRE OF LOUISVILLE, 316 West Main St., Louisville KY 40202. (502)584-1265. Producing Director: Jon Jory. Produces approximately 30 new plays of varying lengths/year. Professional productions are performed for subscription audience from diverse backgrounds. Agented submissions only for full-length plays. Reports in 6-9 months on submissions. No dot-matrix computer printout submissions. Buys production (in Louisville only) rights. Offers variable royalty.
Needs: "No children's shows or musicals. We produce both full-lengths and short one-acts."

AMAS REPERTORY THEATRE, INC., 1 E. 104th St., New York NY 10029. (212)369-8000. Artistic Director: Rosetta LeNoire. Produces 3 plays/year. 1 or 2 scripts produced are unagented submissions. "AMAS is a professional, off-off-Broadway showcase theater. We produce three showcase productions of original musicals each season; these are presented for a sophisticated New York theater audience. A number have gone on to commercial productions, the best known of which is *Bubbling Brown Sugar*. We also present two children's theater productions and one summer tour." Query with synopsis or submit complete script with cassette tape of score or of partial score and SASE. Computer printout submissions acceptable; prefers letter-quality. Reports in 2 months. "Be prepared to wait at least two years or more between acceptance and production. Our standard contract calls for a small percentage of gross and royalties to AMAS, should the work be commercially produced within a specified period."

Needs: "*Musicals only*; in addition, all works will be performed by multi-racial casts. Musical biographies are especially welcome. Cast size should be under 13 if possible, including doubling. Because of the physical space, set requirements should be relatively simple."

Tips: "AMAS is dedicated to bringing all people—regardless of race, creed, color or religion—together through the performing arts. In writing for AMAS, an author should keep this overall goal in mind."

THE AMERICAN LINE, #5C, 810 W. 18 3rd St., New York NY 10033. (212)740-9277. Artistic Director: Richard Hoehler. Produces 3 plays/year. Query with synopsis. Reports in 3 months. Rights and payment negotiable.

Needs: "Contemporary straight plays (one-act or full lengths) that make a point about American people of all races and ethnic backgrounds. Works which address issues and human conflicts relevant to the day."

THE AMERICAN PLAYWRIGHTS' THEATRE, 1742 Church St. NW, Washington DC 20036. (202)232-4527. Contact: Literary Manager. Produces 5 musicals and straight plays and 7-10 readings/year. 15% of scripts produced are unagented submissions. "Plays are produced in professional productions in the 125-seat American Playwrights' Theatre in the Dupont Circle area of the city for a subscription audience as well as large single-ticket buying followers." Works with varying number of writers annually. Will not accept unsolicited mss, only synopsis plus 10 pages of finished script, "typed to form, suitably bound." All musicals must be accompanied by cassette tape recording of songs in proper order. Reports in 6-9 months on synopsis; 9-12 months on scripts. "Rights purchased and financial arrangements are individually negotiated." SASE, acknowledgement postcard. No rights requested on readings. Pays 6% royalty against a $300/week minimum.

Needs: "All styles, traditional to experimental, straight plays to musicals and music-dramas, revues and cabaret shows, and full-lengths only. No one-act plays, verse plays, puppet plays or film scripts. Staging: performance space adaptable.

Tips: "We prefer a strong plot line, be the play realistic, expressionistic or non-realistic, with an emphasis on vital, lively, visceral energy in writing. We look at a wide range of styles from the old-fashioned 'well-made play' to more avant-garde structures. We are a theater of content with a humanist perspective focusing on the personal and public issues of our time. Black dramatists sponsor festival featuring 4 staged readings in the fall followed by a fully staged production in the spring of the previous year's outstanding work from the staged reading."

‡AMERICAN STAGE COMPANY, 211 3rd St. So., St. Petersburg FL 33731. (813)823-1600. Artistic Director: Victoria Holloway. Produces 5 plays/year. Plays performed on "our mainstage, in the park (Shakespeare) or on tour in schools." Submit query and synopsis. Reports in 4 months. Payment varies.

Needs: New American plays for small cast. No musicals.

‡AMERICAN STAGE FESTIVAL, Box 225, Milford NH 03055. Artistic Director: Richard Rose. "The ASF is a central New England professional theater (professional equity company) with a 3 month summer season (June-August)" for audience of all ages, interests, education and sophistication levels. Query with synopsis. Produces musicals (20%) and nonmusicals (80%). 5 are mainstage and 10 are children's productions; 40% are originals. Royalty option and subsequent amount of gross: optional. Reports in 3 months.

Needs: "The Festival can do comedies, musicals and dramas. However, the most frequent problems are bolder language and action than a general mixed audience will accept. Prefer not to produce plays with strictly urban themes. We have a 40-foot proscenium stage with 30-foot wings, but no fly system. Festival plays are chosen to present scale and opportunities for scenic and costume projects far beyond the 'summer theater' type of play." Length: Mainstage: 2-3 acts; children's productions: 50 minutes.

Recent Productions: *Woody Guthrie's American Song* Adapted by Peter Slazer and *Starmites* Music & Lyric by Barry Keating, Book by Stuart Ross & Barry Keating.

Tips: Writers could improve submissions with "dramatic action, complexity, subplot and a unique statement. Try to get a staged reading of the script before submitting the play to us. Our audiences prefer plays that deal with human problems presented in a conventional manner."

ANGEL'S TOUCH PRODUCTIONS, 7962 Hollywood Way, Sun Valley CA 91352. (818)768-6369. Director of Development: Phil Nemy. Professional Broadway productions for all audiences. Send script, query and synopsis. Reports in 6 months. Rights negotiated between production company and author. Payment negotiated.
Needs: All types, all genres, only full-length plays and screenplays—no one-acts or pieces involving homosexuality.
Tips: "Keep in mind the costs involved in mounting a Broadway or regional theater production and try to write accordingly."

ARAN PRESS, 1320 S. 3rd St., Louisville KY 40208. (502)636-0115. Publishes a varying number of professional theater, community theater, college and university theater, dinner theater and summer stock plays. Query. Reports in 3 weeks. Acquires stage production rights. Pays 10% royalty on book; or 50% of standard royalty (i.e. half of $35 or $50 per performance).
Needs: "Anything the writer deems suitable for one or more of our five targeted markets. Inquire first." No children's plays.

ARENA STAGE, 6th and Maine Ave. SW, Washington DC 20024. (202)554-9066. Artistic Director: Zelda Fichandler. Produces 8-11 plays/year. Works with 1-4 unpublished/unproduced writers annually in "Play Lab," a play development project. Stages professional productions in Washington for intelligent, educated, sophisticated audiences using resident Equity company. Virtually none of the scripts produced are unagented submissions. Prefers query and synopsis plus the first 10 pages of dialogue, or agented submissions. Reports in 4 months. "We obtain an option to produce for one year or other term; percentage of future earnings." Pays 5% royalty. Computer printout submissions acceptable "as long as they are easily readable; no dot-matrix."
Needs: Produces classical, contemporary European and American plays; new plays, translations and adaptations without restrictions. No sitcoms, blank verse, pseudo-Shakespearean tragedies, movies-of-the-week or soap operas.
Tips: "We can consider large casts, though big plays are expensive and must justify that expense artistically. Be theatrical. Plays with relevance to the human situation—which cover a multitude of dramatic approaches—are welcome here."

THE ARKANSAS ARTS CENTER CHILDREN'S THEATRE, Box 2137, MacArthur Park, Little Rock AR 72203. (501)372-4000. Artistic Director: Bradley Anderson. Produces 5-6 mainstage plays, 3 tours/year. Mainstage season plays performed at The Arkansas Arts Center for Little Rock and surrounding area; tour season by professional actors throughout Arkansas and surrounding states. Mainstage productions perform to family audiences in public performances; weekday performances for local schools in grades kindergarten through senior high school. Tour audiences generally the same. Accepts unsolicited scripts. Submit complete script. Computer printout submissions acceptable; prefers letter-quality to dot-matrix. Reports in several months. Buys negotiable rights. Pays $250-1,500 or negotiable commission.
Needs: Original adaptations of classic and contemporary works. Also original scripts. "This theater is defined as a children's theater; this can inspire certain assumptions about the nature of the work. We would be pleased if submissions did not presume to condescend to a particular audience. We are not interested in 'cute' scripts. Submissions should simply strive to be good theater literature."
Recent Title: *Dracula*.
Tips: "We would welcome scripts open to imaginative production and interpretation. Also, scripts which are mindful that this children's theater casts adults as adults and children as children. Scripts which are not afraid of contemporary issues are welcome."

‡ARROW ROCK LYCEUM, Main St., Arrow Rock MO 65320. (816)837-3311. Artistic Director: Michael Bollinger. Produces 8 plays/year. "Lyceum has two main projects: a 29-year-old summer season, performing seven plays in repertory in the historic village of Arrow Rock and a Holiday Production, based in a much larger house in Columbia, MO. The Lyceum is a regional theater, and employs professional actors." Query and synopsis throughout year or submit complete ms with synopsis and résumé for contest subs. Also sponsors the National Playwrights Contest. "Lyceum and original artistic staff to get future credit, and Lyceum to retain 5% of author's gross commissions for first 5 years only. Lyceum either commissions w/separate deals, or simply pays a flat fee to National Playwrights Contest winners, which also receive world premiere."
Needs: The repertory season includes seven diverse plays, including musicals, classic, comedy, drama, wild card. Generally each season will feature one world premiere, contest winner or a commissioned work. "I would suggest plays with casts not exceeding 12, and one set, or rather open space with various locales."
Tips: "Who knows—if it works, anything can go! However, keeping budgets in mind, etc., works that have a bit of flexibility are best—could be produced with all 20 characters, or could be produced with 6 actors doubling supporting roles. Also, keep in mind set. Generally two or three realistic sets in one play could hinder original chances; one set or open staging could help. I do feel it is important for professional theaters to be 'theatrical creators' as well as mere 'consumers'!"

ART CRAFT PUBLISHING CO., 232 Dows Bldg., Cedar Rapids IA 52406. (319)364-6311. Publisher: C. McMullen. Publishes plays for the junior and senior high school market. Query with synopsis or send complete ms. Reports in 2 months. Acquires amateur rights only. Makes outright purchase for $250-1,500 or pays royalty.
Needs: One- and three-acts—preferably comedies or mystery comedies. Currently needs plays with a larger number of characters for production within churches and schools. Prefers one-set plays. No "material with the normal 'taboos'—controversial material."

‡ARTREACH TOURING THEATRE, 3074 Madison Rd., Cincinnati OH 45209. (513)871-2300. Director: Kathryn Schultz Miller. Produces 4 plays/year to be performed in area schools and community organizations. "We are a professional company. Our audience is primarily young people in schools and their families." Submit complete ms. Reports in 6 weeks. Buys exclusive right to produce for 9 months. Pays $4/show (approximately 150 performances).
Needs: Plays for children and adolescents. Serious, intelligent plays about contemporary life or history/legend. "Limited sets and props. Can use scripts with only 2 men and 2 women; 45 minutes long. Should be appropriate for touring." No clichéd approaches, camp or musicals.
Tips: "We look for opportunities to create innovative stage effects using few props, and we like scripts with good acting opportunities."

ASOLO STATE THEATRE, Postal Drawer E, Sarasota FL 34234. (813)355-7115. Resident Director: John Gulley. Produces 7 plays/year. 20% freelance written. 100% of scripts produced are unagented submissions. A LORT theater with an intimate performing space. "We play to rather traditional middle-class audiences." Works with 2-4 unpublished/unproduced writers annually. "We do not accept unsolicited scripts. Writers must send us a letter and synopsis with self-addressed stamped postcard." Computer printout submissions acceptable; no dot-matrix. Reports in 8 months. Negotiates rights and payment.
Needs: Play must be *full length*. "We do not restrict ourselves to any particular genre or style—generally we do a good mix of classical and modern works."
Tips: "We have no special approach—we just want well written plays with clear, dramatic throughlines. Don't worry about trends on the stage. Write honestly and write for the stage, not for a publication. We will be entering a new complex next year and be upgrading to a higher LORT status. In addition, we are undertaking to produce more new plays."

‡AT THE FOOT OF THE MOUNTAIN THEATER, 2000 S. 5th St., Minneapolis MN 55454. (612)375-9487. Executive Director: Nayo Barbara Malcolm Watkins. "Put yourself on our newsletter mailing list and watch for when scripts are called for (approximately bi-annually)." No unsolicited scripts are accepted. Submit complete script. Reports in 6 months. Pay $25-30/performance. Submissions returned with SASE.
Needs: All genres: full-length plays, one acts, and musicals by women. Encourages experimental plays. Plays that reflect women's perspectives on the world as it is: multi-cultural, multi-racial, multi-generational, global, personal and political.
Tips: "The theater prefers small casts and simple sets."

AVILA COLLEGE, DEPARTMENT OF HUMANITIES, 11901 Wornall Rd., Kansas City MO 64145. (816)942-8400, Ext. 289. Chairman: Dr. Daniel Paul Larson. Produces 6-8 plays/year. Possibility of 1-2 scripts produced by unagented submission. Performs collegiate amateur productions (4 main stage, 2-4 studio productions) for Kansas City audiences. Query with synopsis. Computer printout submissions acceptable; prefers letter-quality. Reports in 3 months. Buys rights arranged with author. Pay rate arranged with author.
Needs: All genres with wholesome ideas and language—musicals, comedies, dramas. Length 1-2 hours. Small to medium casts (2-8 characters), few props, simple staging.
Tips: Example of play just done: *Towards The Morning*, by John Fenn. Story: "Mentally confused bag lady and 17-year-old egocentric boy discover they need each other; she regains mental stability; he grows up a bit and becomes more responsible. Trends in the American stage freelance writers should be aware of include (1) point-of-view one step beyond theater of the absurd—theater that makes light of self-pity; and (2) need for witty, energetic social satire done without smut in the style of *Kid Purple*, by Don Wollner."

‡BAKER'S PLAY PUBLISHING CO., 100 Chauncy St., Boston MA 02111. Editor: John B. Welch. 80% freelance written. Plays performed by amateur groups, high schools, children's theater, churches and community theater groups. "We are the largest publisher of chancel drama in the world." 90% of scripts are unagented submissions. Works with 2-3 unpublished/unproduced writers annually. Submit complete script. Submit complete cassette of music with musical submissions. Computer printout submissions acceptable. Publishes 18-25 straight plays and musicals; all originals. Pay varies; outright purchase price to split in production fees. Reports in 4 months.
Needs: "We are finding strong support in our new division—plays for young adults featuring contemporary issue-oriented dramatic pieces for high school production."

MARY BALDWIN COLLEGE THEATRE, Mary Baldwin College, Staunton VA 24401. (703)887-7192. Artistic Director: Dr. Virginia R. Francisco. Produces 5 plays/year. 10% freelance written. 0-1% of scripts are unagented. Works with 0-1 unpublished/unproduced writer annually. An undergraduate women's college theater with an audience of students, faculty, staff and local community (adult, conservative). Query with synopsis. Query for electronic submissions. Computer printout submissions acceptable; prefers letter-quality. Reports in 6 months. Buys performance rights only. Pays $10-50/performance.
Needs: Full-length and short comedies, tragedies, musical plays, particularly for young women actresses, dealing with women's issues both contemporary and historical. Experimental/studio theater not suitable for heavy sets. Cast should emphasize women. No heavy sex; minimal explicit language.
Tips: "A perfect play for us has several roles for young women, few male roles, minimal production demands, a concentration on issues relevant to contemporary society, and elegant writing and structure."

BEREA COLLEGE THEATRE, Box 591, Berea KY 40404. (606)986-9341, ext. 6357. Produces 4 full-length and 10 one-act plays/year. "Amateur performances; college audience with community persons in audience also." Send query and synopsis or submit complete ms. Reports in 3 weeks. Obtains negotiable rights. Pays $35-50/performance.
Needs: Medium cast plays (10-20 persons); no musicals.
Tips: "Single-page business letter with synopsis will be good to start with."

‡**BERKSHIRE PUBLIC THEATRE**, 30 Union St., Box 860, Pittsfield MA 01202. (413)445-4631. Artistic Director: Frank Bessell. Produces 10 plays/year. Year-round regional theater. Professional, non-Equity. Query and synopsis or submit complete ms. Reports in 3 months. Various payment arrangements.

‡**BOARSHEAD THEATER**, 425 S. Grand Ave., Lansing MI 48933. (517)484-7800. Artistic Director: John Peakes. Produces 7-9 plays/year. Mainstage AEA company; also Youth Theater—touring to schools by our Intern company. Query, synopsis, cast list (with descriptions), 5-10 pages of representative dialogue, SASE postcard. "Reports on query and synopsis , etc. in 1 week. Full manuscripts (when requested by us) in 4-8 months." Pays royalty.
Needs: Thrust stage. Cast usually 8 or less; ocassionally up to 12-14. Prefer staging which depends on theatricality rather than multiple sets.

‡**BOSTON POST ROAD STAGE COMPANY**, Box 1719, Fairfield CT 06430. (203)255-1719. Artistic Director: Douglas Moser. Produces 6 plays/year. "Small professional (Equity) theater playing to audiences in Fairfield County. Audiences are adult, seniors and interested students." Submit complete ms. Reports in 2 months. Right to produce a 4 week run of the play with an option for several months following conclusion of run to explore further production possibilities. Pays 4-5% royalty.
Needs: Off-Broadway in Connecticut. Emphasis on originality of script. We will take risks if the play is good. We produce a wide range of plays, comedy, drama, musical (small). Budgetary considerations, three quarter round and no flies are our limitations. Maximum eight characters, we prefer less however. We are eligible for grants to develop new plays if something were to strike us which was more expensive than our budget would allow.
Tips: "We're tired of NYC apartment tirades and moot-point 'true' biographies. No obviously large cast or panoramic history plays. The dramatic structure of a play must stimulate an audience. Foul language acceptable only when inherent to the dramatic situation; no headline plays that cannot transcend the ordinary details of everyday life. Even a 'slice-of-life' play must inform us about life, not just illustrate it. Energy, guts, vision and the ability to pull it all together. Those are the well written, stimulating playwrights and plays which will get the most of our attention."

‡**CALIFORNIA THEATER CENTER**, Box 2007, Sunnyvale CA 94087. (408)245-2978. Artistic Director: Gayle Cornelison. Produces 12 plays/year. Plays are for young audiences in both our home theater and for tour. Query and synopsis. Reports in 3 months. We negotiate a set fee.
Needs: All plays must be suitable for young audiences, must be under one hour in length. Cast sizes vary, 6 or less. Sets must be able to tour easily.
Tips: "No plays with heavy music requirements."

‡**THE CHANGING SCENE THEATER**, 1527½ Champa St., Denver CO 80202. Director: Alfred Brooks. Year-round productions in theater space. Cast may be made up of both professional and amateur actors. For public audience; age varies, but mostly youthful and interested in taking a chance on new and/or experimental works. No limit to subject matter or story themes. Emphasis is on the innovative. "Also, we require that the playwright be present for at least one performance of his work, if not for the entire rehearsal period. We have a small stage area, but are able to convert to round, semi-round or environmental. Prefer to do plays with limited sets and props." one-act, two-act and three-act. Produces 8-10 nonmusicals a year; all are originals. 90% freelance written. 65% of scripts produced are unagented submissions. Works with 3-4 unpublished/unproduced writers annually. "We do not pay royalties or sign contracts with playwrights. We function

on a performance-share basis of payment. Our theater seats 76; the first 50 seats go to the theater; the balance is divided among the participants in the production. The performance-share process is based on the entire production run and not determined by individual performances. We do not copyright our plays." Send complete script. Reporting time varies; usually several months.

Recent Title: *The Malignancy of Henrietta Lacks*, by August Baker.

Tips: "We are experimental: open to young artists who want to test their talents and open to experienced artists who want to test new ideas/explore new techniques. Dare to write 'strange and wonderful' well-thought-out scripts. We want upbeat ones. Consider that we have a small performance area when submitting."

‡CHARLOTTE REPERTORY THEATRE, 110 E. 7th St., Charlotte NC 28202. (704)375-4796. Artistic Director: Mark Woods. Produces approximately 10 plays/year. Submit complete ms. Reports in 3 months. Payment depends on "what use is made of script."
Needs: Any but children's, musicals or one-act plays.

CIRCLE REPERTORY CO., 161 Avenue of the Americas, New York NY 10013. (212)691-3210. Associate Artistic Director: Rod Marriott. Produces 5 mainstage plays, 5 Projects in Progress/year. Accepts unsolicited mss for full-length plays only; "we no longer produce one-acts."

CIRCUIT PLAYHOUSE/PLAYHOUSE ON THE SQUARE, 51 S. Cooper, Memphis TN 38104. (901)725-0776. Artistic Director: Jackie Nichols. Produces 2 plays/year. 100% freelance written. Professional plays performed for the Memphis/Mid-South area. Member of the Theatre Communications Group. 100% of scripts are unagented submissions. Works with 1 unpublished/unproduced writer annually. A play contest is held each fall. Submit complete ms. Computer printout submissions acceptable. Reports in 3 months. Buys "percentage of royalty rights for 2 years." Pays $500-1,000 in outright purchase.
Needs: All types; limited to single or unit sets. Cast of 20 or fewer.
Tips: "Each play is read by three readers through the extended length of time a script is kept. Preference is given to scripts for the southeastern region of the U.S."

CITY THEATRE COMPANY, B39 CL, University of Pittsburgh, Pittsburgh PA 15260. Literary Manager: Lynne Conner. Produces 4 full productions and 6 readings/year. "We are a small professional theater, operating under an Equity contract, and committed to twentieth-century American plays. Our seasons are innovative and challenging, both artistically and socially. We perform in a 117-seat thrust stage, playing usually 6 times a week, each production running 5 weeks or more. We have a committed audience following." Query and synopsis or submit through agent. Obtains no rights. Pays 5-6% royalty.
Needs: "No limits on style or subject, but we are most interested in theatrical plays that have something to say about the way we live. No light comedies or TV-issue dramas." Normal cast limit is 8. Plays must be appropriate for small space without flies.
Tips: "American playwrights only. We run a staged reading series of 6 plays a year, choosing work that we wish to consider for full production."

I.E. CLARK, INC., Saint John's Rd., Box 246, Schulenburg TX 78956. (409)743-3232. Publishes 15 plays/year for educational theater, children's theater, religious theater, regional professional theater and amateur community theater. 20% freelance written. 3-4 scripts published/year are unagented submissions. Works with 2-3 unpublished writers annually. Submit complete script. Computer printout submissions acceptable; prefers letter-quality. Reports in 6 months. Buys all available rights; "we serve as an agency as well as a publisher." Pays standard book and performance royalty, "the amount and percentages dependent upon type and marketability of play." Catalog for $1.50; writer's guidelines for #10 SAE with 1 first class postage stamp.
Needs: "We are interested in plays of all types—short or long. Audio tapes of music or videotapes of a performance are requested with submissions of musicals. We prefer that a play has been produced (directed by someone other than the author); photos and reviews of the production are helpful. No limitations in cast, props, staging, etc.; however, the simpler the staging, the larger the market. Plays with more than one set are difficult to sell. So are plays with only one or two characters. We insist on literary quality. We like plays that give new interpretations and understanding of human nature. Correct spelling, punctuation and grammar (befitting the characters, of course) impress our editors."
Tips: "Entertainment value and a sense of moral responsibility seem to be returning as essential qualities of a good play script. The era of glorifying the negative elements of society seems to be fading rapidly. Literary quality, entertainment value and good craftsmanship rank in that order as the characteristics of a good script in our opinion. 'Literary quality' means that the play must—in beautiful, distinctive, and un-trite language—say something; preferably something new and important concerning man's relations with his fellow man; and these 'lessons in living' must be presented in an intelligent, believable and creative manner. Plays for children's theater are tending more toward realism and childhood problems rather than fantasy or dramatization of fairy tales."

‡**THE CLEVELAND PLAY HOUSE**, 8500 Euclid Ave., Cleveland OH 44106. (216)795-7010. Artistic Director: Josephine Abady. Produces 12 plays/year. Resident LORT theater. Audience: subscribers and single ticket buyers; three different theaters with different audience needs/requirements: 160-experimental, 499 & 615-mainstage subscription theaters. Agented submissions only. Reports in 4-6 months. Negotiated rights. Pay negotiable.
Needs: Full length; emphasis on American realism; all styles and topics given full consideration, however. Musicals also welcome.
Tips: "No translations of foreign works. No previously produced works which got national attention."

‡**COLONY STUDIO THEATRE**, 1944 Riverside Dr., Los Angeles CA 90039. Managing Director: Barbara Beckley. Produces 5 plays/year. Professional 99-seat theater, (year round) for general audiences. SASE for submission guidelines. Reports in 2 weeks on queries; on scripts: in 6 months. Negotiated rights. Pays $25-35 per performance.
Needs: "Produce *full length* (at least 90 minutes) of all genres, topics and styles, but *no musicals*. We cast from a company of resident, professional actors. Extreme casting types could be a problem."
Tips: "Trends are *created* by the skillful writer. An accepted, professional format (like 'Samuel French's Format Guidelines') to the appearance of a script, helps in the reading process."

COMPANY ONE, 94 Allyn St., Hartford CT 06103. (203)278-6347. Literary Manager: Sherry Stidolph. Produces 6-8 plays/year. "One-act plays submitted to Company One, if selected, will be performed at the Hartford Arts Center as part of our Lunchtime Theater series. Our audience members are generally downtown employees looking for an entertaining break in their workday. This, however, does not preclude the presentation of thought-provoking material." Submit complete ms with SASE.
Needs: "Best suited to the Lunchtime format is the 40 minute, 2 or 3 character, single or multi-purpose set piece. Although a good play can find its way around limitations, Company One tries to keep its casts small (four or less), its sets and props simple, and special effects to a minimum. Each play receives about 12 performances.
Tips: "Company One also welcomes new translations, adaptations from other sources and pieces incorporating music or dance. This year we are initiating a radio play project and seek original radio scripts as well."

CONTEMPORARY DRAMA SERVICE, Meriwether Publishing Ltd., Box 7710, Colorado Springs CO 80933. (303)594-4422. FAX: (719)594-9916. Editor-in-Chief: Arthur Zapel. Publishes 50-60 plays/year. "We publish for the secondary school market and colleges. We also publish for mainline liturgical churches—drama activities for church holidays, youth activities and fundraising entertainments. These may be plays or drama-related books." Query with synopsis or submit complete ms. Reports in 5 weeks. Obtains either amateur or all rights. Pays 10% royalty or outright negotiated purchase.
Needs: "Most of the plays we publish are one-acts, 15 to 45 minutes in length. We occasionally publish full-length three-act plays. We prefer comedies in the longer plays. Musical plays must have name appeal either by prestige author, prestige title adaptation or performance on Broadway or TV. Comedy sketches, monologues and 2-character plays are welcomed. We prefer simple staging appropriate to high school, college or church performance. We like playwrights who see the world positively and with a sense of humor. Offbeat themes and treatments are accepted if the playwright can sustain a light touch and not take himself (herself) too seriously. In documentary or religious plays we look for good research and authenticity. We will probably be publishing more textbooks on the theatrical arty rather than trade books."

‡**CREATIVE PRODUCTIONS, INC.**, 2 Beaver Pl., Aberdeen NJ 07747. (201)566-6985. Artistic Director: Walter L. Born. Produce 4 musicals/year. Amateur, year-around productions. "We use plays/musicals with folks with disabilities and the older performers in addition to 'normal' performers, for the broad spectrum of viewers." Submit query and synopsis. Reports in 2 weeks. Buys rights to perform play for specified number of performances. Pays $75-150 per performance.
Needs: Plays/musicals about people with disabilities where they are actually used as performers; unusual subjects out of ordinary human experiences plus music. Limitations: Cast: maximum 12, sets can't "fly," facilities are schools, no mammoth sets and multiple scene changes.
Tips: No blue material; pornographic; obscene language. Submit info on any performances plus pix of set and actors in costume. Demo tape (musicals); list of references on users of their material to confirm bio info.

‡**CROSSROADS THEATRE COMPANY**, 320 Memorial Parkway, New Brunswick NJ 08901. (201)249-5581. Producing Artistic Director: Rick Khan. Produces 5 plays/year. Regional theater that stages Equity professional productions. Query with synopsis. Computer printout submissions acceptable. Reports in 6 months. Returns rights to percentage of future productions. Pays royalty.
Needs: "We need plays that offer honest, imaginative and insightful examinations of the African American experience. Black (African-American, African and Caribbean) and interracial plays are preferred." Productions should be suited to a 150-seat theater.
Tips: "We look for issue-oriented, experimental scripts that reflect the complexity of the human experience."

DALTON LITTLE THEATRE NEW PLAY PROJECT, Box 841, Dalton GA 30722. (404)226-6618. Contact: Project Coordinator. Amateur productions each year. Submit complete ms. Reports in 3 months. Obtains first performance rights. Pays $400.
Needs: "Any full-length play or musical is accepted." Writers should keep in mind small stage/playing area. No less-than-full-length or previously produced plays.

‡FREDERIC DEFEIS, 296 Rt. 109, E. Farmingdale NY 11735. (516)293-0674. Produces 20 plays/year. Professional summer theater for general audiences. Submit complete ms. Reports in 3-12 months. Pays royalty.
Needs: All types. Cast 4-10 or 12.
Tips: "Know your subject! Write dialogue that is natural, believable and is really representative of the character who is speaking."

DELAWARE THEATRE COMPANY, Box 516, Wilmington DE 19899. (302)594-1104. Artistic Director: Cleveland Morris. Produces 5 plays/year. 10% freelance written. "Plays are performed as part of a five-play subscription season in a 300-seat auditorium. Professional actors, directors and designers are engaged. The season is intended for a general audience." 10% of scripts are unagented submissions. Works with 1 unpublished/unproduced writer every two years. Query with synopsis. Computer printout submissions acceptable; prefers letter-quality. Reports in 6 months. Buys variable rights. Pays 5% (variable) royalty.
Needs: "We present comedies, dramas, tragedies and musicals. All works must be full length and fit in with a season composed of standards and classics. All works have a strong literary element. Plays showing a flair for language and a strong involvement with the interests of classical humanism are of greatest interest. Single-set, small-cast works are likeliest for consideration." Recent trend towards "more economical productions."

‡DENVER CENTER THEATRE COMPANY, 1050 13th St., Denver CO 80204. (303)893-4200. Artistic Director: Donovan Marley. Produces 8 plays/year. "Denver Center Theater Company produces an annual New Plays Festival, entitled Prima Facie. 8-10 new scripts are rehearsed and presented in staged readings. From this festival, 4 are selected for full production in the following DCTC Theatre season." Submit complete ms. Reports in 4-6 weeks. Prima Facie submittals must be previously unproduced. DCTC negotiates for production rights on scripts selected for full presentation but does not hold rights on Prima Facie scripts. Royalty to be negotiated.
Needs: Full-length unproduced scripts. We do not accept one-acts, adaptations, children's plays, or musicals at this time.
Tips: "DCTC is a regional theater, producing new plays as a part of a subscription series that also includes classics. We tend to be interested in plays that explore issues larger than personal growth and comic moments."

‡DISCOVERY '90, Paul Mellon Arts Center, Wallingford CT 06492. (203)269-1113. Artistic Director: Terrence Ortwein. Produces 3-5 plays/year. "Choate Rosemary Hall in Wallingford, Connecticut, will host its sixth summer theater program committed to the discovery and development of new scripts written specifically for secondary school production. Students with an interest in theater from around the country will join directors and writers-in-residence in order to rehearse and perform new works in July. Playwrights will have the opportunity to hear, see and rewrite their scripts during three-week residencies. Public workshop performances will provide audience reactions to the works-in-progress and will enable the playwrights to further develop their scripts for future productions." Submit complete ms. Reports in 3 months. Playwrights selected must agree to be in residence at Choate Rosemary Hall from July 9-August 9. Room, board, and a stipend of $700 will be given each playwright selected. The workshop productions, script-in-hand so that the playwright will have every opportunity to rewrite during every step of his *discovery*, will be the responsibility of Choate Rosemary Hall.
Tips: The content should appeal strongly and directly to teenagers. Although all the characters don't have to be teenagers, the actors will be. In most high schools, more girls than boys participate in drama. Most high schools have limited technical resources and limited budgets. Although we will look at full-length scripts, the real need and interest is in the one-act and hour-length play. This program is established to help playwrights develop scripts, not to produce already finished scripts. *Only unproduced scripts may be submitted.*

THE DRAMATIC PUBLISHING CO., 311 Washington St., Woodstock IL 60098. (815)338-7170. FAX: (815)338-8981. Publishes about 30 new shows a year. 60% freelance written. 40% of scripts published are unagented submissions. "Current growth market is in plays and musicals for children, plays and small-cast musicals for stock and community theater." Also has a large market for plays and musicals for schools and other amateur theater groups. Works with 2-6 unpublished/unproduced writers annually. Reports in 2-6 months. Buys stock and amateur theatrical rights. Pays by usual royalty contract, 10 free scripts and 40% discount on script purchases.
Tips: "Avoid stereotype roles and situations. Submit cassette tapes with musicals whenever possible. Always include SASE if script is to be returned. Only one intermission (if any) in a show running up to two hours."

ELDRIDGE PUBLISHING CO., Box 216, Franklin OH 45005. (513)746-653l. Publishes 15-20 plays/year. For elementary, junior high, senior high, church and community audience. Query with synopsis (acceptable) or submit complete ms (preferred). Please send cassette tapes with any operettas. Reports in 2 months. Buys all rights. Pays 35% royalty (three-act royalties approximately $50/$35, one-act royalty rates usually $10/$10); outright purchase from $100-300 or occasionally offers 10% of copy sale receipts. Writer's guidelines for #10 SASE.
Needs: "We are always on the lookout for Xmas plays (religious for our church market or secular for the public school market). Also lighthearted one-acts and three-acts. We do like some serious, high caliber plays reflective of today's sophisticated students. Also operettas for jr/sr high school and more limited elementary (third grade and above) market. We prefer larger casts for our three-acts and operettas. Staging should be in keeping with school budgets and expertise. We are *not* interested in plays that are highly sexually suggestive or use abusive language."
Tips: "Submissions are welcomed at any time but during our fall season, response will definitely take 2 months. Authors are paid royalties twice a year. They receive complimentary copies of their published plays, the annual catalog and 50% discount if buying additional copies."

‡**EMPIRE STATE INSTITUTE FOR THE PERFORMING ARTS**, Empire State Plaza, Albany NY 12223. (518)443-5222. Artistic Director: Patricia B. Snyder. Produces 4-5 plays/year. Professional regional productions for adult and family audiences. Query with synopsis. Reports in 3 months. Pay varies.

THE EMPTY SPACE, 95 S. Jackson St., Seattle WA 98104. (206)587-3737. Artistic Director: M. Burke Walker. Produces 6 plays/year. 100% freelance written. Professional plays for subscriber base and single ticket Seattle audience. 1 script/year is unagented submission. Works with 5-6 unpublished/unproduced writers annually. Query with synopsis before sending script. Computer printout submissions OK; prefers letter-quality. Response in 3 months. LOA theater.
Needs: "Other things besides linear, narrative realism, but we are interested in that as well. No restriction on subject matter. Generally we opt for broader, more farcical comedies and harder-edged, uncompromising dramas. We like to go places we've never been before."

‡**THE ENSEMBLE STUDIO THEATRE**, 549 W. 52nd St., New York NY 10019. (212)247-4982. Artistic Director: Curt Dempster. Literary Manager: Sari Bodi. Produces 15-20 plays/year for off-off Broadway theater. 100-seat house, 60-seat workshop space. Submit complete ms. Reports in 3 months. Standard production contract: mini contract with AEA or letter of agreement. Pays $80-1,000.
Needs: Full-lengths and one-acts with strong dramatic actions and situations. No musicals, verse-dramas or elaborate costume dramas.
Tips: Submit work September through April.

RICHARD FICARELLI, Financial East Building, Suite 404, 2801 E. Oakland Park Blvd., Ft. Lauderdale FL 33306. Produces 1-2 plays/year. Plays are Equity productions performed in NY, Broadway and off-Broadway theaters. Regional possibilities. Submit query and synopsis. Reports in 6 weeks. Acquires DGA (standard) rights. Pays standard royalty.
Needs: Situation comedies *only*. Prefers cast of fewer than 14. No dramas.
Tips: "Stronger possibilities for regional and dinner theater productions as well as Broadway and off-Broadway."

THE FIREHOUSE THEATRE, 514 S. 11th St., Omaha NE 68102. (402)346-6009. Artistic Director: Dick Mueller. Produces 7 plays/year. Has produced 4 unagented submissions in 14 years. Computer printout submissions acceptable; prefers letter-quality.
Needs: "We produce at the Firehouse Dinner Theater in Omaha. Our interest in new scripts is the hope of finding material that can be proven here at our theater and then go on from here to find its audience." Submit complete ms. Reporting times vary; depends on work load. Buys negotiable rights. Pays $100/week or negotiable rates.
Tips: "We are a small theater. Certainly size and cost are a consideration. Quality is also a consideration. We can't use heavy drama in this theater. We might, however, consider a production if it were a good script and use another theater."

FLORIDA STUDIO THEATRE, 1241 N. Palm Ave., Sarasota FL 34236. (813)366-9017. New plays director: Jack Fournier. Produces 4 established scripts and 3 new plays/year. "FST is a professional not-for-profit theater." Plays are produced in 165-seat theater for a subscription audience (primarily). FST operates under a small professional theater contract of Actor's Equity. Submit query and synopsis. Reports in 2 months on queries; 7 months on mss. Pays $200 for workshop production of new script.
Needs: Contemporary plays ("courageous and innovative"). Prefers casts of no more than 8, and single sets.

‡**THE FREELANCE PRESS**, Box 548, Dover MA 02030. (508)785-1260 or 0068. Artistic Director: Priscilla B. Dewey. Publishes 4 plays/year. Children/young adults. Query and synopsis. Reports in 2 months. Pays 2-3% royalty. Pays $25 or 10% of the price of each script and score.
Needs: "Publish original musical theater for young people, dealing with issues of importance to them, also adapt 'classics' into musicals for 8-16 year old age groups to perform." Large cast; flexible, simple staging and props.

SAMUEL FRENCH, INC., 45 W. 25th St., New York NY 10010. Editor: Lawrence Harbison. 100% freelance written. "We publish about 80-90 new titles a year. We are the world's largest publisher of plays. 10-20% are unagented submissions. In addition to publishing plays, we occasionally act as agents in the placement of plays for professional production—eventually in New York. Pays on royalty basis. Submit complete ms (bound). "Always type your play in the standard, accepted stageplay manuscript format used by all professional playwrights in the U.S. If in doubt, send $3 to the attention of Lawrence Harbison for a copy of 'Guidelines.' We require a minimum of two months to report."
Needs: "We are willing at all times to read the work of freelancers. Our markets prefer simple-to-stage, light, happy romantic comedies or mysteries. If your work does not fall into this category, we would be reading it for consideration for agency representation. No 25-page 'full-length' plays; no children's plays to be performed *by* children; no puppet plays; no adaptations of public domain children's stories; no verse plays; no large-cast historical (costume) plays; no seasonal and/or religious plays; no television, film or radio scripts; no translations of foreign plays."

GASLAMP QUARTER THEATRE COMPANY, 547 4th Ave., San Diego CA 92101. (619)232-9608. Company Manager: Jean Hauser. Produces 8 plays/year. A professional, not-for-profit theater. Query with synopsis. Variable contract, usually a weekly amount, "scale depends on author."
Needs: "We like a drawing room touch, also have a penchant for Pinter." Maximum cast: 10. No more than 4 sets. Small cast musicals accepted also.
Tips: "Small cast (under 8), not too many scenery changes, not too current (meaning not trendy), some lasting comment about the human condition."

THE WILL GEER THEATRICUM BOTANICUM, Box 1222, Topanga CA 90290. (213)455-2322. Artistic Director: Ellen Geer. Produces 3 plays/year. Professional summer theater. Query with synopsis. Reports in 6 months. Obtains negotiable rights. Pays royalty.
Needs: Seeks full-length plays appropriate for repertory company in large outdoor arena: musical, political, humanistic. "Not over 10 in cast—we do *not* have a large technical budget."

‡**GEORGE STREET PLAYHOUSE**, 9 Livingston Ave., New Brunswick NJ 08901. (201)846-2895. Producing Director: Gregory Hurst. Produces 8 plays/year. Professional regional theater (LORT D). Submit complete ms, submit through agent or send synopsis with cast list, dialogue sample and letter of inquiry. Reports in 3 months.
Needs: Full-length dramas, comedies and musicals that present a fresh perspective on our society and embrace theatricity. Prefers cast size under 10.
Tips: "We present a series of 6 staged readings each year and a playwright's project. We also select at least one new play and one new musical for production each season."

GEORGETOWN PRODUCTIONS, 7 Park Ave., New York NY 10016. Producers: Gerald van de Vorst and David Singer. Produces 1-2 plays/year for a general audience. Works with 2-3 unpublished/unproduced writers annually. Dramatist Guild membership required. Submit complete ms only. Standard Dramatists Guild contract.
Needs: Prefers plays with small casts and not demanding more than one set. Interested in new unconventional scripts dealing with contemporary issues, comedies, mysteries, musicals or dramas. No first drafts, outlines, one-act plays.
Tips: "The current trend is toward light entertainment, as opposed to meaningful or serious plays."

‡**GEVA THEATRE**, 75 Woodbury Blvd., Rochester NY 14607. (716)232-1366. Produces 2 mainstage plays plus annual production of "A Christmas Carol." LORT B Theatre (537 seats) for a subscription audience/single ticket market. Query and synopsis. "I cannot guarantee a reading because of large volume for a single person office, I do not take unsolicited scripts." Reports in 2 months. Pays royalty.
Needs: "In each season we produced one new, previously unproduced work. These have tended to be dramas and the more hard-hitting, adventuresome works of the season. We have a play development series (six works) best defined as contemporary dramas and comedies." Cast size tends to be limited to 10-12. Main limitation is fly space.
Tips: "Would like to see contemporary work that speaks to our lives and that broadens out beyond 'kitchen' drama and the need for individuals to find self-fulfillment."

‡**EMMY GIFFORD CHILDREN'S THEATER**, 3504 Center St., Omaha NE 68105. (402)345-4849. Artistic Director: James Larson. Produces 6 plays/year. "Our target audience is children, preschool – jr. high and their parents." Query with synopsis with SASE. Reports in 9 months. Royalty negotiable.
Needs: "Plays must be geared to children and parents (PG rating). Titles recognized by the general public have a stronger chance of being produced. Cast limit: 25 (8-10 adults). No adult scripts."
Tips: "Previously produced plays may be accepted only after a letter of inquiry (familiar titles only!)."

‡**GLOUCESTER STAGE CO.**, 267 E. Main St., Gloucester MA 01930. (508)281-4099. Artistic Director: Israel Horovitz. Produces 12 plays/year in "The Gorton Theatre, a flexible space (approx. 99 seats), in professional Equity productions. The audience comes from Boston and the North Shore, with a large percentage of working-class people (Gloucester is a fishing town)." Submit complete ms w/SASP for acknowledgment of receipt. Reports in 6-8 weeks. Pay negotiated individually (1-5% royalty). Favored nations contract – $100/wk.
Needs: All lengths (including one-acts) will be considered. Any genre. Very theatrical plays that make ingenious use of stage convention seem to work best. Topics of interest to New Englanders are especially welcome. No fly space – no traps. Theatre is flexible "black box."
Tips: "Small cast plays (1-6 characters) more likely to be accepted."

‡**GUTHRIE THEATER**, 725 Vineland Pl., Minneapolis MN 55403. (612)347-1100. Artistic Director: Garland Wright. Produces 8 plays/year. At the Guthrie Theater, a professional Lort A Theater; season lasts from May through March. Query and synopsis or submit complete ms (agents). Reports in 3 months. Royalty varies; Advance against performance royalties.
Needs: "We produce full-length plays of consequence in an innovative style on important contemporary issues."
Tips: No One-Acts or Historical Costume Dramas.

‡**HARTFORD STAGE COMPANY**, 50 Church St., Hartford CT 06103. (203)525-5601. Artistic Director: Mark Lamos. Produces 6 plays/year. Professional regional theater with subscriber base. Query with synopsis. Reports in 8 months. Buys only one time production rights. Pays royalty.
Needs: Full-length plays, translations, adaptations. Limitations are figured on a per-season, rather than per-script basis.
Tips: No one-acts, work for children.

HEUER PUBLISHING CO., 233 Dows Bldg., Box 248, Cedar Rapids IA 52406. (319)364-6311. Publishes plays for junior and senior high school and church groups. Query with synopsis or submit complete ms. Reports in 2 months. Purchases amateur rights only. Pays royalty or cash.
Needs: "One- and three-act plays suitable for school production. Preferably comedy or mystery comedy. All material should be of the capabilities of high school actors. We prefer material with one set." No "special day material, material with controversial subject matter."

HONOLULU THEATRE FOR YOUTH, Box 3257, Honolulu HI 96801. (808)521-3487. Artistic Director: John Kauffman. Produces 6 plays/year. 50% freelance written. Plays are professional productions in Hawaii, primarily for youth audiences (youth aged 2 to 20). 80% of scripts are unagented submissions. Works with 2 unpublished/unproduced writers annually. Computer printout submissions acceptable; prefers letter-quality. Reports in 3 months. Buys negotiable rights.
Needs: Contemporary subjects of concern/interest to young people; adaptations of literary classics; fantasy including space, fairy tales, myth and legend. "HTY wants well-written plays, 60-90 minutes in length, that have something worthwhile to say and that will stretch the talents of professional adult actors." Cast not exceeding 8; *no* technical extravaganzas; *no* full-orchestra musicals; simple sets and props, costumes can be elaborate. No plays to be enacted by children or camp versions of popular fairytales. Query with synopsis. Pays $1,000-2,500.
Tips: "Young people are intelligent and perceptive; if anything, more so than lots of adults, and if they are to become fans and eventual supporters of good theater, they must see good theater while they are young. Trends on the American stage that freelance writers should be aware of include a growing awareness that we are living in a world community. We must learn to share and understand other people and other cultures."

HUDSON GUILD THEATRE, 414 West 26th St., New York NY 10001. (212)760-9836. Literary Manager: Steven Ramay. Produces 5 mainstage plays annually, and conducts readings/workshops. "The plays are performed at the Hudson Guild Theatre. Our audiences (largely subscription) are from the greater New York City area, including parts of New Jersey, Connecticut and all Manhattan boroughs." Submit complete ms; prefers synopsis in addition to ms. Reports in 2 months. All rights agreements are worked out individually in production contract negotiations. Pays flat $1,000 fee for mainstage productions.

Needs: "Our interests are varied and international in scope. Socially and politically aware plays are preferred. We usually limit our casts to no more than 8, although exceptions can be made depending on the project."
Tips: "Don't submit your complete works. Submitting one play at a time usually insures a more thoughtful consideration of your material."

WILLIAM E. HUNT, 801 West End Ave., New York NY 10025. Interested in reading scripts for stock production, off-Broadway and even Broadway production. "Small cast, youth-oriented, meaningful, technically adventuresome; serious, funny, far-out. Must be about people first, ideas second. No political or social tracts." No one-act, anti-Black, anti-Semitic or anti-gay plays. "I do not want 1920, 1930 or 1940 plays disguised as modern by 'modern' language. I do not want plays with 24 characters, plays with 150 costumes, plays about symbols instead of people. I do not want plays which are really movie or television scripts." Works with 2-3 unpublished/unproduced writers annually. Pays royalties on production. Off-Broadway, 5%; on Broadway, 5%, 7½% and 10%, based on gross. No royalty paid if play is selected for a showcase production. Reports in "a few weeks." Must have SASE or script will not be returned.
Tips: "Production costs and weekly running costs in the legitimate theater are so high today that no play (or it is the very rare play) with more than six characters and more than one set, by a novice playwright, is likely to be produced unless that playwright will either put up or raise the money him or herself for the production."

‡**INDIANA REPERTORY THEATRE**, 140 W. Washington, Indianapolis IN 46204. (317)635-5277. Artistic Director: Tom Haas. Produces 10 full-length, 9 90-minute cabarets/year. Plays are professional productions, LORT B and C contracts, in 2 theaters. Mainstage seats 600, Cabaret seats 150. Subscription audience composed of cross section of Indianapolis community. Query with synopsis. Reports in 3 months. Retains rights for first- or second-class production with 60 days after production closes; retains percent on subsequent productions elsewhere. Pays 5% royalty; $500-1,000 nonrefundable advance over royalties.
Needs: "On our Mainstage we produce exclusively classics, with a heavy emphasis on American work, adaptations of classic work or new translations of classic work. Upperstage is currently closed. Cabaret produces exclusively small cast (5 or less) satirical musicals. Prefer under 10 casts, staging which can be adapted—that is, not rigidly realistic; prefer one set or unit set which can be adapted. We tend to be attracted to plays that display an acute interest in using language vigorously. We are interested in epic proportion and in plays that speak very directly to concerns of 1980s. No TV scripts, movie scripts, plays which depend on excessive profanity or explicit sexual behavior or one-acts."

INVISIBLE THEATRE, 1400 N. 1st Ave., Tucson AZ 85719. (602)882-9721. Artistic Director: Susan Claassen. Literary Manager: Deborah Dickey. Produces 5-7 plays/year. 10% freelance written. Semiprofessional regional theater for liberal, college-educated audiences. Plays performed in 78-seat non-Equity theater with small production budget. Works with 1-5 unpublished/unproduced writers annually. Query with synopsis. Computer printout submissions acceptable; prefers letter-quality. Reports in 6 months. Buys non-professional rights. Pays 10% royalty.
Needs: "Two-act plays, generally contemporary, some historical, comedies, drama, small musicals, wide range of topics. Limited to plays with small casts of 10 or less, strong female roles, simple sets, minimal props." No large musicals, complex set designs, casts larger than 10.
Tips: "Trends in the American stage that will affect the types of scripts we accept include social issues—social conscience—i.e. South Africa, coming to terms with elderly parents, overcoming effects of disease, family relationships, things that the average person can relate to and think about. Challenges we can all relate to, common experiences, because people enjoy people. Our audiences include some older, somewhat conservative, members (although *not* rigid or dogmatic) as well as younger, more liberal groups. We try to have broad appeal—mixing experimental with comedy and drama throughout the year."

JEWEL BOX THEATRE, 3700 North Walker, Oklahoma City OK 73118. (405)521-1786. Artistic Director: Charles Tweed. Produces 6 plays/year. Amateur productions. Intended for 2,800 season subscribers and general public. Submit complete ms. Reports in 3 months. "We would like to have first production rights and 'premiere' the play at Jewel Box Theatre." Pays $500 contest prize.
Needs: "Write theater for entry form during September-October. We produce dramas, comedies and musicals. Usually we have two-act plays, but one and three acts are acceptable. Plays usually run two hours. Our theater is in-the-round, so we adapt plays accordingly. We have not used multi-media projections. We do not use excessive profanity. We will dilute dialogue if necessary."

‡**JEWISH REPERTORY THEATRE**, 344 E 14th St., New York NY 10003., (212)674-7200. Artistic Director: Ran Avni. Produces 5 plays, 15 readings/year. New York City professional off B'way production. Submit complete ms. Reports in 4 weeks. 1st production/option to move to B'way or off B'way. Pays royalty.
Needs: Full length only. Straight plays & musicals. Must have some connection to Jewish life, characters, history. Maximum 10 characters. Limited technical facilities.
Tips: No biblical plays.

KUMU KAHUA, 1770 East-West Rd., Honolulu HI 96822. (808)948-7677. Executive Director: Dennis Carroll. Produces 4 productions, 4 public readings/year. "Plays performed at various theaters for community audiences. Actors are not paid. It's a nonprofit company." Submit complete ms. Royalty is $25 per performance; usually 10 performances of each production.
Needs: "Plays must have some interest for local audiences, preferably by being set in Hawaii or dealing with some aspect of the Hawaiian experience. Prefer small cast, with simple staging demands. We don't like 'commercial' plays structured and designed for BO success of a Broadway sort. No trivial commercial farces, whodunits, plays like made-for-TV movies or sitcoms."
Tips: "We need some time to evaluate, and may want to hold the script awhile. We're not trendy."

LAMB'S PLAYERS THEATRE, 500 Plaza Blvd., Box 26, National City CA 92050. (619)474-3385. Artistic Director: Robert Smyth. Produces 7 plays/year. 15% freelance written. A professional non-Equity resident company with a year-round production schedule. Audience is varied; high percentage of family and church interest. Works with 1-2 unpublished/unproduced writers annually. Submit synopsis. Computer printout submissions acceptable. Reports in 4 months. Buys first production rights, touring option. Pays $500-5,000.
Needs: "We produce a wide variety of material which, while not necessarily 'religious' in nature, often reflects a broad-based Christian perspective." Prefers smaller cast (2-10); adaptable staging (arena stage). "We are not interested in material that is 'preachy,' or material intended to shock or titillate with sex, violence or language."
Tips: "Trends freelance writers should be aware of include productions which offer hope without being clichéd or sentimental; productions needing small cast and imaginative yet inexpensive sets; and an interest in presentational style pieces – acknowledgment of and/or interaction with the audience."

‡THE LAMB'S THEATRE COMPANY, 130 W. 44th St., New York NY 10036. (212)997-0210. Artistic Director: Carolyn Rossi Copeland. Produces 3 plays/year. Off-Broadway, and then they are frequently produced around the country once they are published. We do a lot of material that is suitable for families, as well as "adult" shows. Performances are in 90-seat black box theater or 360-seat proscenium mainstage. Query and synopsis; address queries to the Literary Manager. Reports in 6 months. "We have a standard contract that is in accordance with accepted Dramatist's Guild policies." Payment is flat option fee leading to royalty arrangement upon recoupment.
Needs: Musicals, comedies, serious dramas that leave audiences with an affirmation of hope. We are not a nihilistic theater. Casts of over eight are problematic, though sometimes possible. Shows with complex technical effects are discouraged.
Tips: "We do not produce one-acts. We do not produce works with nudity, explicit sex, or obscene language. Writers should be mindful of the need to reach wider audiences, and make the theater as common a need for everyday people as television seems to be. They should avoid the avant-garde habit of despising the audience, and to return to the age old theatrical traditions of delighting them with magic that can only occur on the living stage."

LILLENAS PUBLISHING CO., Box 419527, Kansas City MO 64141. (816)931-1900. Editor: Paul M. Miller. "We publish on two levels: (1) Program Builders – seasonal and topical collections of recitations, sketches, dialogues and short plays. (2) Drama Resources. These assume more than one format: (a) full length scripts, (b) shorter plays and sketches all by one author, (c) collection of short plays and sketches by various authors. All program and play resources are produced with local church and Christian school in mind. Therefore there are taboos." Queries are encouraged, but synopses and complete manuscripts are read. Computer printout submissions are acceptable, if highly readable. "First rights are purchased for Program Builder manuscripts. For our line of Drama Resources, we purchase all print rights, but this is negotiable." Writer's guidelines for #10 SASE.
Needs: 98% of Program Builder materials are freelance written. Manuscripts selected for these publications are outright purchases; verse is 25 cents per line, prose (play scripts) are $5 per double-spaced page. Lillenas Drama Resources is a line of play scripts that are, for the most part, written by professionals with experience in production as well as writing. However, while we do read unsolicited manuscripts, more than half of what we publish is written by experienced authors whom we have already published. Drama Resources (whether full-length scripts, one-acts, or sketches) are paid on a 10% royalty. There are no advances.
Tips: "All plays need to be presented in standard play script format. We welcome a summary statement of each play. Purpose statements are always desirable. Approximate playing time, cast and prop lists, etc. are important to include. We are interested in fully scripted traditional plays, reader's theater scripts, choral speaking pieces. Contemporary settings generally have it over Biblical settings. Christmas and Easter scripts must have a bit of a twist. Secular approaches to these seasons (Santas, Easter bunnies, and so on), are not considered. We sell our product in 10,000 Christian bookstores. We are probably in the forefront as a publisher of religious drama resources."

LOS ANGELES THEATRE CENTER, 514 S. Spring St., Los Angeles CA 90013. (213)627-6500. Literary Managers:Peter Sagal and Stephen Weeks. Produces 15-20 plays/year. 90% freelance written. A professional theater for a multicultural metropolitan audience. 10% of scripts are unagented submissions. Works with 7-10 unproduced writers annually. Query with synopsis plus 10 pages of script. *No unsolicited ms.* Reports in 8 months. Buys first production rights, options to extend and move, subsidiaries. Pays 4-7% royalty. Computer printout submissions acceptable; no dot-matrix.

Needs: Plays with social or political awareness preferred. 10 actors maximum. No "television scripts or movies pretending to be theater."

Tips: "The most important and exciting new work in the theater is non-naturalistic. It takes risks with its subject matter and form and, therefore, it is dramatic writing that cannot be easily transferred to another form, i.e., television or film."

‡MAD RIVER THEATER WORKS, Box 248, W. Liberty OH 43357. (513)465-6751. Artistic Director: Jeffrey Hooper. Produces 3 plays/year. "Mad River is a professional company. We present over 150 performances each year at colleges, universities and in small towns, for a broad, multigenerational audience. Our intended audience is primarily rural." Query and synopsis. Reports in 1 month. Buys exclusive production rights for a limited time. Pays negotiable royalty.

Needs: "We primarily produce works that deal with rural themes and/or issues. A small cast is most likely to be accepted. As a touring company, simple technical requirements are also a factor."

Tips: "We reach out to many different kinds of people, particularly audiences in rural areas without other access to professional theater. We seek to challenge, as well as entertain, and present works which can speak to conservative individuals as well as seasoned theatergoers."

MAGNUS THEATRE COMPANY, 137 N. May St., Thunder Bay, Ontario P7C 3N8 Canada. (807)623-5818. Artistic Director: Michael McLaughlin. Produces 6 plays/year. Professional stock theater produced in 197-seat facility, and performed for a demographically diverse general audience.

Needs: "Fairly general in genres, but with a particular emphasis on new plays, must be full-length. Smaller (i.e., up to seven) casts are viewed favorably; some technical limitations. Always, budget limitations. Also produces one-act theater-in-education scripts for all age ranges, with emphasis on socially and curriculum-relevant material."

Tips: "Thunder Bay is a very earthy, working city, and we try to reflect that sensibility in our choice of plays. Beyond that, however, Magnus has gained a national reputation for its commitment to the development and production of new plays, including, where possible, workshops. Scripts should be accessible to Canadian audiences in theme; should be produceable within realistic budget limitations."

MANHATTAN PUNCH LINE, 3rd Floor, 410 W. 42nd St., New York NY 10036. (212)239-0827. Artistic Director: Steve Kaplan. Produces 6-7 plays/year. Professional off-off Broadway theater company. Submit complete ms. Reports in 3 months. Pays $325-500.

Needs: "Manhattan Punch Line is devoted to producing comedies of all types. We are a developmental theater interested in producing serious plays with a comedic point of view."

Tips: "The most important and successful playwrights (Durang, Wasserstein, Innaurato) are all writing comedies. Don't worry about being funny, just try to be honest. Large-cast plays are back in."

MANHATTAN THEATRE CLUB, 453 W. 16th Ave., New York NY 10011. Literary Manager: Tom Szentgyorgyi. Produces 9 plays/year. All freelance written. A two-theater performing arts complex classified as off-Broadway, using professional actors. Computer printout submissions acceptable; no dot-matrix. No unsolicited scripts. Query with synopsis. Reports in 6 months. Payment is negotiable.

Needs: "We present a wide range of new work, from this country and abroad, to a subscription audience. We want plays about contemporary problems and people. Comedies are welcome. No verse plays, historical dramas or large musicals. Very heavy set shows or multiple detailed sets are out. We present shows with casts not more than 15. No skits, but any other length is fine."

‡MERRIMACK REPERTORY THEATRE, Box 228, Lowell MA 01853. (508)454-6324. Dramaturg/Literary Manager: David Kent. Produces 6 plays/year. Professional LORT D. Agented submissions only. Also sponsors Merrimack Repertory Theatre First Annual Playwriting Contest. Reports in 3-6 months.

Needs: All styles & genres. No avant-garde. "We are a small 300 seat theater—with a modest budget. Plays should appeal to working class/Catholic/and urban-immigrant populations."

MIAMI BEACH COMMUNITY THEATRE, 2231 Prairie Ave., Miami Beach FL 33139. (305)532-4515. Artistic Director: Jay W. Jensen. Produces 5 plays/year. "Amateur productions performed during the year for the Miami Beach community." Send query and synopsis or submit complete ms. Reports in 3 weeks. Pays $35-75/performance (if published work); does not pay for unpublished plays.

Needs: "All types. Interested in Spanish themes—Latin American plots, etc. Interested in new plays dealing with AIDS and short plays dealing wth AIDS that could be used in junior highs and senior highs for motivation—about 30 minutes long. Avoid sex."

MILL, MOUNTAIN THEATRE, Market Square Center in Square, Roanoke VA 24011. (703)342-5730. Artistic Director: Jere Lee Hodgin. Produces 7 established plays, 10 new one-acts and 2 new full-length plays/year. "Some of the professional productions will be on the main stage and some in our alternative theater B." Submit complete ms. Reports in 8 months. Payment negotiable on individual play. Writer's guidelines for #10 SAE with 1 first class stamp; do not include loose stamps or money.
Needs: "We are interested in plays with racially mixed cast, but not to the exclusion of others. We are constantly seeking one-act plays for 'Centerpieces', our Lunch Time Program of Script-in-Hand Productions. Playing time should be between 25-35 minutes. Cast limit is 15 for plays and 24 for musicals."
Tips: "Subject matter and character variations are open, but gratuitous language and acts are not acceptable. A play based on large amounts of topical reference or humor has a very short life. Be sure you have written a play and not a film script. Roanoke is a fairly conservative community—good taste is always in order."

MISE EN SCENE THEATRE, 11305 Magnolia Blvd., North Hollywood CA 91601. (818)763-3101. Artistic Director: Herb Rodgers. Produces 6-16 plays/year at two theaters. For Los Angeles audiences, casting directors, agents and producers. Equity waiver; 99-seat house. Submit complete ms. Reports in 2 months. Payment negotiable.
Needs: "Only original, unproduced, full-lengths and one-acts. Any genre, topic, style." Stage has 28-foot opening, 21-foot depth.
Tips: "No previously produced plays. Our objective is to give playwrights the opportunity to work in production with the directors and actors, to better prepare the play for professional productions. Our plays are reviewed by the *Los Angeles Times*, *Variety*, *Hollywood Reporter* and other local papers. Productions are videotaped."

‡**MISSOURI REPERTORY THEATRE,** 4949 Cherry St., Kansas City MO 64110. (816)276-2727. Artistic Director: George Keathley. Produces 7 plays/year. Regional professional theater for artistically conservative audience. Query and synopsis. Reports in 2 months. Buys standard Dramatists Guild contract.
Needs: Well-known contemporary American, a few classics, almost zero "originals".
Tips: "No offensive language or weak narrative line."

NATIONAL ARTS CENTRE-ENGLISH THEATRE, Box 1534, Station B, Ottawa, Ontario K1P 5W1 Canada. (613)996-5051. Theater Producer: Andis Celms. Produces and/or presents 12 plays/year. 0-5% freelance written. Works with 1-2 unpublished/unproduced writers annually. All scripts produced are agented submissions. Professional productions performed in the theater and studio of the National Arts Centre (also, workshop productions in a rehearsal space). Audience ranges from young/middle-aged professionals (especially civil servants) to students. Computer printout submissions acceptable; prefers letter-quality.
Tips: "Our 'mainstage' audience likes a solid, well-written play with an intelligible story line and no coarse language. Our 'workshop' audience likes to be challenged, both in language and structure, but not abused. We are interested in the smaller cast, 'human interest' style of theater and film. For example, last season we produced *Children of a Lesser God*. Our audience likes the combination of having heard of the play and being moved by the emotions."

‡**NATIONAL JEWISH THEATER,** 5050 W. Church, Skokie IL 60077. (312)675-2200. Artistic Director: Sheldon Patinkin. Produces 4 plays/year. Submit complete ms. Reports in 1 month. Buys first Chicago—Midwestern production rights.

NECESSARY ANGEL THEATRE, #400, 553 Queen St. W., Toronto, Ontario M5V 2B6 Canada (416)365-0533. Dramaturg: D. D. Kugler. Produces 2 plays/year. Plays are Equity productions in various Toronto theaters and performance spaces for an urban audience between 20-55 years of age. Submit complete ms. Please include SASE (international postal coupon if USA). Reports in 6 months. Obtains various rights "based on the manuscript (original, translation, adaptation) and the playwright (company member, etc.)." Pays 10% royalty.
Needs: "We are open to new theatrical ideas, environmental pieces, unusual acting styles and large casts. The usual financial constraints exist, but they have never eliminated a work to which we felt a strong commitment." No "TV-influenced sit-coms and melodramas."
Tips: "All submissions are considered for long-term script/playwright development, including one-day readings and one-week workshops, leading to company productions. Playwrights should be aware of our interdisciplinary approach to performance (music, dance and visual arts which support the text)."

THE NEW CONSERVATORY CHILDREN'S THEATRE COMPANY AND SCHOOL, Zephyr Theater Complex, 25 Van Ness, Lower Level, San Francisco CA 94102. (415)861-4814. Artistic Director: Ed Decker. Produces 4-5 plays/year. "The New Conservatory is a children's theater school (ages four to nineteen) which operates year-round. Each year we produce several plays, for which the older students (usually eleven and up, but younger depending on the readiness of the child) audition. These are presented to the general public at the

Zephyr Theatre Complex San Francisco (50-350 seats). Our audience is approximately age 10 to adult." Send query and synopsis. Reports in 1 month. Pays 5% royalty.

Needs: "We emphasize works in which children play *children*, and prefer relevant and controversial subjects, although we also do musicals. We have a commitment to new plays. Examples of our shows are: Mary Gail's *Nobody Home* (world premiere; about latchkey kids); Brian Kral's *Special Class* (about disabled kids), and *The Inner Circle*, by Patricia Loughrey (commissioned scripts about AIDS prevention for kids). As we are a non-profit group on limited budget, we tend not to have elaborate staging; however, our staff is inventive — includes choreographer and composer. Write innovative theater that explores topics of concern/interest to young people, that takes risks. We concentrate more on ensemble than individual roles, too. We do *not* want to see fairytales or trite rehashings of things children have seen/heard since the age of two. See theater as education, rather than 'children are cute'."

Tips: "It is important for young people and their families to explore and confront issues relevant to growing up in the '80s. Theatre is a marvelous teaching tool that can educate while it entertains."

‡NEW MEXICO REPERTORY THEATRE, Box 789, Albuquerque NM 87103-0789. (505)243-4577. Artistic Director: Andrew Shea. Produces 6 plays/year. Query and synopsis, "no unsolicited mss please." Reports in 1 month. Pays royalty.

Needs: "We produce classic, modern & contemporary plays of all kinds. We are interested especially in plays about the American West & the Hispanic experience in the US."

NEW PLAYS INCORPORATED, Box 371, Bethel CT 06801. (203)792-4342. Publisher: Patricia Whitton. Publishes an average of 4 plays/year. Publishes plays for producers of plays for young audiences and teachers in college courses on child drama. Query with synopsis. Reports in 2 months. Agent for amateur and semi-professional productions, exclusive agency for script sales. Pays 50% royalty on productions; 10% on script sales. Free catalog.

Needs: Plays for young audiences with something innovative in form and content. Length: usually 45-90 minutes. "Should be suitable for performance by adults for young audiences." No skits, assembly programs, improvisations or unproduced manuscripts.

‡NEW PLAYWRIGHTS' PROGRAM, THE UNIVERSITY OF ALABAMA, Box 870239, Tuscaloosa AL 35487-0239. (205)348-9032. Produces at least 1 new play/year. University Theatre, The University of Alabama. Submit complete ms. Reports in 1-3 months.

NEW TUNERS THEATRE, 1225 W. Belmont Ave., Chicago IL 60657. (312)929-7367. Artistic Director: Byron Schaffer, Jr. Produces 3-4 new musicals/year. 66% freelance written. "Nearly all" scripts produced are unagented submissions. Plays performed in a small off-Loop theater seating 148 for a general theater audience, urban/suburban mix. Submit complete ms and cassette tape of the score, if available. Reports in 6 months. Buys exclusive right of production within 80-mile radius. "Submit first, we'll negotiate later." Pays 5-10% of gross. "Authors are given a stipend to cover a residency of at least two weeks." Computer printout submissions acceptable; prefers letter-quality.

Needs: "We're interested in traditional forms of musical theater as well as more innovative styles. We have less interest in operetta and operatic works, but we'd look at anything. At this time, we have no interest in nonmusical plays unless to consider them for possible adaptation — please send query letter first. Our production capabilities are limited by the lack of space, but we're very creative and authors should submit anyway. The smaller the cast, the better. We are especially interested in scripts using a younger (35 and under) ensemble of actors. We mostly look for authors who are interested in developing their script through workshops, rehearsals and production. No interest in children's theater. No casts over 15. No one-man shows."

Tips: "Freelance writers should be aware that musical theater can be more serious. The work of Sondheim and others who follow demonstrates clearly that musical comedy can be ambitious and can treat mature themes in a relevant way. Probably 90 percent of what we receive would fall into the category of 'fluff.' We have nothing against fluff. We've had some great successes producing it and hope to continue to offer some pastiche and farce to our audience; however, we would like to see the musical theater articulating something about the world around us, rather than merely diverting an audience's attention from that world."

NEW WORLD THEATER, INC., Suite 212, 7600 Red Rd., South Miami FL 33143. (305)663-0208. Executive Director: Kenneth A. Cotthoff. Produces 5 plays/year. "We are a professional (AEA — LOA) resident theater performing in Miami Beach. Our season begins in the Fall with the winners of our annual National New Play Competition, which is followed with a season of contemporary off-Broadway format plays. Audience upwardly mobile, average age approximately 40-ish." Submit complete ms — "must be typed, bound with address on fly sheet." Reports in 3 months for play competition; 1 month otherwise. "We maintain a six month exclusive limited option on any play produced." Pays $500 for competition or season. Writer's guidelines available for #10 envelope and 25¢ postage.

Needs: Contemporary comedies or dramas. Off-Broadway budgets and sensibilities; also interested in young authors and Florida themes. "Currently limiting to cast of four for competition and season. Prefer one main set and no extraordinary budget-breaking items."

Tips: "Prefers contemporary format, standard length, one intermission, intelligent, thought provoking (even if comedy). No high budget, children's plays or musicals (small ones OK). This may change as budget expands."

NEW YORK SHAKESPEARE FESTIVAL/PUBLIC THEATER, 425 Lafayette St., New York NY 10003. (212)598-7100. Producer: Joseph Papp. Plays and Musical Development Director: Gail Merrifield. Co Director: Tom Ross. Interested in plays, musicals, operas, translations, adaptations. No restriction as to style, form, subject matter. Produces 6-10 new works year-round at Public Theater complex housing 5 theaters (100-300 seat capacity): Newman, Anspacher, Shiva, LuEsther Hall, Martinson. Also Delacorte 2100-seat ampitheater, Broadway; film and television. Unsolicited and unagented submissions accepted. Computer printout manuscripts and electronic submissions via VHS OK with hard copy. Send music cassette with musical work. All scripts: include cast of characters with age and brief description; musical works: submit cassette with at least 3 songs. Standard options and production agreements. Reports in 2 months.

‡NEW YORK THEATRE WORKSHOP, 220 W. 42 St., 18th Fl., New York NY 10036. (212)302-7737. Artistic Director: James C. Nicola. Produces 6 full productions; approximately 50 readings per annum. Plays are performed Off-Broadway, Equity mini-contract theater; Audience: New York theatergoing audience and theater professionals. Query and synopsis or submit complete ms. Reports in 3-5 months. Option to produce commercially; percentage of box office gross of subsidiary rights from commercial productions within a specified time limit from our original production; percentage of author's net subsidiary rights within specified time limit from our original production. Pays fee because of limited run: $1,500.
Needs: Full-length plays, one-acts, translations/adaptations, music-theater pieces; proposals for performance projects. Large issues, socially relevant issues, innovative form and language, minority issues. Plays utilizing over eight actors usually require outside funding.
Tips: No overtly commercial, traditional Broadway-type "musicals."

JACKIE NICHOLS, 51 S. Cooper, Memphis TN 38104. Artistic Director: Jackie Nichols. Produces 16 plays/year. Professional productions. Submit complete ms. Reports in 5 months. Pays $500.
Needs: All types. "Small cast, single or unit set."
Tips: "Playwrights from the South will be given preference. South is defined as the following states: Alabama, Florida, Georgia, Kentucky, Louisiana, Mississippi, Missouri, North Carolina, South Carolina, Tennessee, Texas, Virginia and West Virginia. This means we will read all shows and when final decisions are made, if every other aspect of the plays are equal we will choose a Southern author."

NINE O'CLOCK PLAYERS, 1367 N. St. Andrews Pl, Los Angeles CA 90028. (213)469-1973. Artistic Director: Fluff McLean. Produces 2 plays/year. "Plays produced at Assistance League Playhouse by resident amateur and semi-professional company. All plays are musical adaptations of classical children's literature. Plays must be appropriate for children ages 4-12." Query and synopsis. Reports in 1 month. Pays negotiable royalty or per performance.
Needs: "Plays must have at least 15 characters and be 1 hour 15 minutes long. Productions are done on a proscenium stage in classical theater style. All plays must have humor, music and good moral values. No audience participation improvisational plays."

‡NO EMPTY SPACE THEATRE, 568 Metropolitan Ave., Staten Island NY 10301-3431. Artistic Director: James E. Stayoch. Produces 1 play/year. Performed locally on S.I., usually Equity Showcase, intended for NYC audience. Submit complete ms. Reports in 1 month. Buys 1 time production rights. Award - $500. Also sponsors contest. Write for more information.

‡THE NORTH CAROLINA BLACK REPERTORY COMPANY, Box 2793, Winston-Salem NC 27012. (919)723-7907. Artistic Director: Larry Leon Hamlin. Produces 4-6 plays/year. Plays produced primarily in North Carolina, New York City, and possible touring throughout the South. Submit complete ms. Reports in 5 months. Obtains negotiable rights. Negotiable payment.
Needs: "Full-length plays and musicals: mostly African-American with special interest in historical or contemporary *statement* genre. A cast of 10 would be a comfortable limit; we discourage multiple sets."
Tips: "The best time to submit manuscript is between September and February."

‡NORTHLIGHT THEATRE, 2300 Green Bay Rd., Evanston IL 60201. (312)869-7732. Artistic Director: Russell Vandenbroucke. Produces 5 plays/year. Plays receive full, professional productions (6-8 week run), with Equity casts. All plays are produced at the Northlight facility, which is a 300 seat proscenium house. Query and synopsis (for non-agented writers) or agented submissions. Reports in 2 months. Buys production rights. Pays royalty.
Needs: Ambitious works of a heightened theatricality; works which concern themselves with sociopolitical or cultural issues; works which transcend circumstantial specificity. Seldom work with casts larger than 12-15.

ODYSSEY THEATRE ENSEMBLE, 12111 Ohio Ave., Los Angeles CA 90025. (213)826-1626. Literary Manager: Jan Lewis. Produces 12 plays/year. Plays performed in a 3-theater facility. "All three theaters are Equity 99-seat theater plan; Odyssey 1 and 2 each have 99 seats, while Odyssey 3 has 72-90 seats. We have a subscription audience of 2,000 who subscribe to a six-play main season and a 3-4 play lab season, and are offered a discount on our remaining non-subscription plays. Remaining seats are sold to the general public." Query with synopsis, cast breakdown and 8-10 pages of sample dialogue. Scripts must be securely bound. Reports in 1 month on queries; 6 months on scripts. Buys negotiable rights. Pays 5-7% royalty or $25-35/performance. "We will *not* return scripts without SASE."
Needs: Full-length plays only with "either an innovative form or extremely provocative subject matter. We desire more theatrical pieces that explore possibilities of the live theater experience. We are seeking full-length musicals. We are not reading one-act plays or light situation comedies. We are seeking Hispanic material for our resident Hispanic Unit"

OLDCASTLE THEATRE COMPANY, Box 1555, Bennington VT 05201. (802)447-0564. Artistic Director: Eric Peterson. Produces 7 plays/year. Plays are performed in a small (104 seat) theater on a former estate now used by Southern Vermont College, by a professional Equity theater company (in a season from April through October) for general audiences, including residents of a three-state area and tourists during the vacation season. Submit complete ms. Pays "by negotiation with the playwright. A not-for-profit theater company."
Needs: Produces classics, musicals, comedy, drama, most frequently American works. Usual performance time is 2 hours. "With a small stage, we limit to small cast."

EUGENE O'NEILL THEATER CENTER'S NATIONAL PLAYWRIGHTS CONFERENCE/NEW DRAMA FOR TELEVISION PROJECT, Suite 901, 234 W. 44th St., New York NY 10036. (212)382-2790. Artistic Director: Lloyd Richards. Administrator: Peggy Vernieu. Develops staged readings of 10-12 stage plays, 2-3 teleplays/year for a general audience. "We accept unsolicited mss with no prejudice toward either represented or unrepresented writers. Our theater is located in Waterford, Connecticut and we operate under an Equity LORT Contract. We have 3 theaters: Barn-250 seats, Amphitheater-300 seats, Instant Theater-150. Send #10 SASE in the fall for submission guidelines. Complete bound, unproduced, original plays are eligible (no adaptations). Decision by late April. Pays stipend plus room, board and transportation. Computer printout submissions acceptable. We accept script submissions from Sept. 15-Dec. 1 of each year. Conference takes place during four weeks in July each summer."
Needs: "We use modular sets for all plays, minimal lighting, minimal props and no costumes. We do script-in-hand readings with professional actors and directors. Our focus is on new play/playwright development."

THE OPEN EYE: NEW STAGINGS, 270 W. 89th St., New York NY 10024. (212)769-4143. Artistic Director: Amie Brockway. Produces 3-4 full-length plays/year plus a series of readings and workshop productions of one-acts. "The Open Eye is a professional, Equity LOA, 104-seat, off-off Broadway theater. Our audiences include a broad spectrum of ages and backgrounds." Submit complete ms in clean, bound copy with SASE for its return. Reports in 6 months. Playwright fee for mainstage: $500.
Needs: "New Stagings is particularly interested in one-act and full-length plays that take full advantage of the live performance situation. We tend not to do totally realistic plays. We especially like plays that appeal to young people and adults alike."

OREGON SHAKESPEARE FESTIVAL ASSOCIATION, Box 158, Ashland OR 97520. (503)482-2111. Literary Manager: Cynthia White. Produces 16 plays/year. "The Angus Bowmer Theater has a thrust stage and seats 600. The Black Swan is an experimental space and seats 150; The Elizabethan Outdoor Theatre seats 1,200 (we do almost exclusively Shakespearean productions there—mid-June through September). OSFA also produces a separate five-play season at the Portland Center for The Performing Arts in a 725 seat proscenium theater. Producing director of OSFA Portland Center Stage: Dennis Bigelow. Query and synopsis plus 10 pages of dialogue from unsolicited sources/also resume. Complete scripts from agents only. Reports in 9 months. Negotiates individually for rights with the playwright's agent. "Most plays run within our 10 month season for 6-10 months, so royalties are paid accordingly."
Needs: "A broad range of classic and contemporary scripts. One or two fairly new scripts per season. Also a play readings series which focuses on new work. Plays must fit into our 10-month rotating repertory season. Black Swan shows usually limited to 6 actors." No one-acts or musicals.
Tips: "Send your work through an agent if possible. Send the best examples of your work rather than all of it. Don't become impatient or discouraged if it takes 6 months or more for a response. Don't expect detailed critiques with rejections. As always, I want to see plays with heart and soul, intelligence, humor and wit. I

The double dagger before a listing indicates that the listing is new in this edition. New markets are often the most receptive to freelance submissions.

also think theater is a place for the *word*. So, the word first, then spectacle and high-tech effects."

‡THE ORGANIC THEATER COMPANY, 3319 N. Clark St., Chicago IL 60657. (312)327-2427. Literary Manager: Lawrence Santoro. "We're a developmental theater and do only previously unproduced work." Number of productions per year varies. Professional (AEA) productions. Send query, synopsis and sample first. Reports in 2-3 months. Rights bought vary: Some scripts require Chicago-area rights only. Pays negotiable percentage of receipts.
Needs: Vary. Social commentary, day-to-day comedy/drama, science fiction OK. Artistic director, Richard Fire, wants to see plays in which the writer is "passionately involved."
Tips: "Write something which is meaningful to you, about wich you have a passionate interest, and we'll like it better than one you wrote because you thought you couild sell it."

‡PAJ PUBLICATIONS, #318 325 Spring St., New York NY 10013. (212)243-3885. Publishers/Editors: Bonnie Marranca and Gautam Dasgupta. Publishes 3-15 plays/year. Publishes for theater, academia, library and audiences. Query and synopsis. Reports in 4 months. Buys publication rights only. Pays royalty or outright purchase.
Needs: International drama, primarily; for *Performing Arts Journal*: produces plays of highest calibre only; experimental work, avant garde and traditional.

‡THE PASSAGE THEATRE COMPANY, 221 E. State St., Trenton NJ 08608. Artistic Director: Veronica Brady. Produces 4 plays/year. "Passage is a professional theater company. Most of our work is performed at the Mill Hill Playhouse, which is in Trenton NJ. Our work is intended for all audiences, culturally and artistically." Query and synopsis or submit complete ms. Reports in 3-4 weeks. Pays royalty.
Needs: "We are committed to producing only new American plays. 1-3 act plays (this is general, based on previous experience) dealing with social, cultural and artistic issues. We also do workshops and readings of plays. We work actively with the writers in developing their work."

‡PCPA THEATERFEST, Box 1700, Santa Monica CA 93456. (805)928-7731. Artistic Director: Jack Shouse. Produces 14 plays/year. "We have year-round theater: the Marian Theatre seats 500, the Interim Theatre seats 160; the Festival Theatre m Solvang is open-air, seats 750 and is for summer only. Our audience is broad spectrum." Accept only query and synopsis with sample pages. No unsolicited scripts. Reports within 6 months. Rights negotiaged with each playwright on an individual basis. Pay negotiable.
Needs: All genres. All topics. All styles. All lengths. "We have 2 distinct play series in winter—one for large scale producitons, the other for smaller scale, more contemporary/experimental. We also do a variety of outreach projects for schools and community groups. All plays must deal with aspects of the human condition.
Tips: "No formulaic writing or television-style writing. Works *should be theatrical*, using the elements which make theater a distinctive art form. Works should *say* something moving, interesting, thought-provoking and entertaining about the human condition. We want fresh voices. Originality, not repetition is key here. We are looking for top-quality plays with fresh insights/approaches. Musicals should have top-quality music, lyrics and book."

‡PENNSYLVANIA STAGE COMPANY, 837 Linden St., Allentown PA 18101. (215)437-6110. Artistic Director: Peter Wrenn-Meleck. Produces 7 plays and musicals/year. "We are a LORT D theater and our season runs from October through June. The large majority of our audience comes from the Lehigh Valley. Our audience consists largely of adults. We also offer special student and senior citizen matinees." Query and synopsis; also would like a character breakdown and SASE or postcard. Reports in 3 months for scripts; 2 weeks for synopsis. Payment negotiable.
Needs: "The PSC produces full-length plays and musicals which are innovative and imaginative and that broaden our understanding of ourselves and society. Looking for wide range of styles and topics." Prefers 12 characters or fewer (will consider up to 18) for musicals; 8 or fewer for plays.
Tips: "Works presented at the Stage Company have a passion for being presented now, should be entertaining and meaningful to our local community, and perpetuate our theatrical and literary heritage. We do not want to limit our options in achieving this artistic mission. No one-acts and material that contains grossly offensive language. We appreciate also receiving a sample of dialogue with the synopsis. We have a staged reading program where a director, actors and the playwright work together during an intensive 3-day rehearsal period. A discussion with the audience follows the staged reading."

PEOPLE'S LIGHT & THEATRE COMPANY, 39 Conestoga Rd., Malvern PA 19355. (215)647-1900. Producing Director: Danny S. Fruchter. Produces 5 full-length plays/year; no more than 1 new play/year. "LORT D Actors' Equity plays are produced in Malvern 30 miles outside Philadelphia in 350-seat main stage and 150-seat second stage. Our audience is mainly suburban, some from Philadelphia." Query with synopsis and cast list. Computer printout submissions acceptable; prefers letter-quality. Reports in 10 months. Buys "rights to production in our theater, sometimes for local touring." Pays 2-5% royalty.

Needs: "We will produce anything that interests us." Prefers single set, maximum cast of 12 (for full length), fewer for one act. No musicals, mysteries, domestic comedies.
Tips: "Writers should be aware of trend away from naturalistic family drama and trend toward smaller cast size."

‡**PERSEVERANCE THEATRE**, 914 3rd St., Douglas AK 99801. (907)364-2421. Artistic Director: Molly Smith. Produces 5 mainstage, 2-3 second stage plays/year. Professional productions, Southeast Alaska. Primarily Juneau audiences; occasional tours to other places. Submit query and synopsis, no unsolicited mss. Reports in 6 months. Pays $25-50 per performance.
Tips: "We are producing very few original pieces from writers outside of Alaska. Because of that, we are reading few new plays."

‡**PHILADELPHIA FESTIVAL THEATRE FOR NEW PLAYS**, 3900 Chestnut St., Philadelphia PA 19104. (215)222-5000. Artistic Director: Dr. Carol Rocamora. Produces 6 plays/year. Professional productions (LORT D contract), subscriber series. Submit complete ms. Reports in 6 months.
Needs: A wide variety of new works without previous professional production.

PIER ONE THEATRE, Box 894, Homer AK 99603. (907)235-7333. Artistic Director: Lance Petersen. Produces 5-8 plays/year. "Plays to various audiences for various plays—e.g. children's, senior citizens, adult, family, etc. Plays are produced on Kemai Peninsula." Submit complete ms. Reports in 2 months. Pays $25-125/performance.
Needs: "No restrictions—willing to read *all* genres." No stock reviews, hillbilly or sit-coms.
Tips: "There are slightly increased opportunities for new works. Don't start your play with a telephone conversation. New plays ought to be risky business; they ought to be something the playwright feels is terribly important."

PIONEER DRAMA SERVICE, Box 22555, Denver CO 80222. (303)759-4297. Publisher: Shubert Fendrich. 10% freelance written. Plays are performed by high school, junior high and adult groups, colleges, churches and recreation programs for audiences of all ages. "We are one of the largest full-service play publishers in the country in that we handle straight plays, musicals, children's theater and melodrama." Publishes 10 plays/year; 40% musicals and 60% straight plays. Query only; no unsolicited manuscripts. Computer printout submissions acceptable; prefers letter-quality. Buys all rights. Outright purchase only with a few exceptions for major musicals. Reports in 2 months.
Needs: "We use the standard two-act format, two-act musicals, religious drama, comedies, mysteries, drama, melodrama and plays for children's theater (plays to be done by adult actors for children)." Length: two-act musicals and two-act comedies up to 90 minutes; and children's theater of 1 hour. Prefer many female roles, one simple set. Currently overstocked on one-act plays.

PLAYERS PRESS, INC., Box 1132, Studio City CA 91604. Senior Editor: Robert W. Gordon. "We deal in all areas and handle works for film and television as well as theater. But all works must be in stage play format for publication." Also produces scripts for video, and material for cable television. 80% freelance written. 10-12 scripts/year are unagented submissions. Works with 1-10 unpublished/unproduced writers annually. Submit complete ms. "Must have SASE or play will not be returned, and two #10 SASEs for update and correspondence. All submissions must have been produced and should include a flyer and/or program with dates of performance." Reports in 3 months. Buys negotiable rights. "We prefer all area rights." Pays variable royalty "according to area; approximately 10-75% of gross receipts." Also pays in outright purchase of $100-25,000 or $5-5,000/performance.
Needs: "We prefer comedies, musicals and children's theater, but are open to all genres. We will rework the ms after acceptance. We are interested in the quality, not the format."
Tips: "Send only material requested. Do not telephone."

PLAYS, The Drama Magazine for Young People, 120 Boylston St., Boston MA 02116. Editor: Sylvia K. Burack. Publishes approximately 75 one-act plays and dramatic program material each school year to be performed by junior and senior high, middle grades, lower grades. Mss should follow the general style of *Plays*. Stage directions should not be typed in capital letters or underlined. No incorrect grammar or dialect. Desired lengths for mss are: junior and senior high—18-20 double-spaced ms pages (25 to 30 minutes playing time). Middle grades—10 to 15 pages (15 to 20 minutes playing time). Lower grades—6 to 10 pages (8 to 15 minutes playing time). Pays "good rates on acceptance." Query first for adaptations. Reports in 2-3 weeks. Sample copy $3.50; send SASE for mss specification sheet.
Needs: "Can use comedies, farces, melodramas, skits, mysteries and dramas, plays for holidays and other special occasions, such as Book Week; adaptations of classic stories and fables; historical plays; plays about black history and heroes; puppet plays; folk and fairy tales; creative dramatics; and plays for conservation, ecology or human rights programs."

THE PLAYWRIGHTS CENTER, 2301 Franklin Ave. E., Minneapolis MN 55406. (612)332-7481. Director of Public Relations: Lisa Stevens. "Midwest Playlabs is a 2-week developmental workshop for new plays. The program is held in Minneapolis and is open by script competition. It is an intensive two-week workshop focusing on the development of a script and the playwright. 4-6 new plays are given rehearsed public readings at the site of the workshop." Announcements of playwrights by end of April. Playwrights receive honoraria, travel expenses, room and board.

Needs: "We are interested in playwrights with talent, ambitions for a sustained career in theater and scripts which could benefit from an intensive developmental process involving professional dramaturgs, directors and actors. US citizens, only: no musicals or children's plays. Participants must attend all or part of conference depending on the length of their workshop. Full lengths only. No previously produced materials. Submit complete ms. Submission deadline: March 1, 1990.

Tips: "We do not buy scripts or produce them. We are a service organization that provides programs for developmental work on scripts for members. Pre-conference: May 18-21, 1990; conference: July 29-August 12, 1990."

‡PLAYWRIGHTS HORIZONS, 416 W. 42nd St., New York NY 10036. (212)564-1235. Artistic Director: André Bishop. Literary Manager: Tim Sanford. Produces 4-8 plays/year. Non-profit, Off-Broadway professional productions. Subscription audiences of approximately 5,000. 2 stages: One seating about 174; and a Studio Theatre seating about 74. Query and synopsis (we do accept and review synopses, if so desired) or submit complete ms (include SASE, cover letter; résumé optional). Reports in 1-3 months. Rights vary. Some rights retained. Fee and royalty vary.

Needs: Original, full-length plays by American authors only. Also musicals. "Our largest theater is 170 seats with limited fly and wing space. Huge casts and elaborate sets are not possible. No overly familiar styles: naturalism, topical satires, adaptations, TV writing.

Tips: "We like professional, literate plays with strong, original voices. Also, we like unconventional but accessible plays: verbal, intelligent & stylish. Writers should include bios and production histories."

‡PLAYWRIGHTS OF PHILADELPHIA/PHILADELPHIA DRAMA GUILD, Robert Morris Bldg., 100 North 17th St., Philadelphia PA 19103. (215)563-7530. POP Director: Charles Conwell. Producing Director: Greg Poggi. Produces readings for 4 staged readings/year. Professional readings for adults in Philadelphia. Submit complete ms. SASE required. Reports Feb. 1 or June 1. "Plays are read in January and May." Buys 6 month option. Pays $100 reading and $1,000 production.

Needs: Anything but children's plays, musical, video scripts, movie scripts, adaptations, and one-acts (less than an hour).

‡PLAYWRIGHTS PREVIEW PRODUCTIONS, #304, 1160 5th Ave., New York NY 10029. Artistic Director: Frances Hill. Produces 4-6 plays/year. Professional productions Off or Off Off Broadway, 1 production Kennedy Center—throughout the year. General audience. Submit complete ms. Reports in 1-2 months. If produced, option for six months. Pays royalty.

Needs: Both one-act and full-length; generally one set or styled playing dual. Cast of 3-7. Good imaginative, creative writing. Cast limited to 3-7.

Tips: "We tend to reject 'living-room' plays. We look for imaginative settings. Be creative and interesting with intellectual content."

‡PLAYWRIGHTS THEATRE OF NEW JERSEY, 33 Green Village Rd., Madison NJ 07940. (201)514-1787. Artistic Director: Buzz McLaughlin. Produces 3 productions/6 staged readings/6 sit-down readings/year. "We operate under a small professional theater contract with Actors' Equity Association for all productions and readings." Submit complete ms. Short bio and prod. history required. Reports in 2 months. "For productions and staged readings we ask the playwright to sign an agreement which gives us exclusive rights to the play for the production period and for 30 days following. After the 30 days we give the rights back with no strings attached, except for productions, we ask that our developmental work be acknowledged in any other professional productions." Pays $100 for productions and staged readings.

Needs: Any style or length; full-length, one-acts, musicals.

Tips: "No plays that simply reflect the world's chaos. We are interested in developing plays that illuminate the human spirit. We're looking for plays which are in their early stages of development."

PRIMARY STAGES COMPANY, INC., 584 Ninth Ave., New York NY 10036. (212)333-7471. Artistic Director: Casey Childs. Produces 4 plays, 4 workshops, over 100 readings/year. All of the plays are produced professionally off-Broadway at the 45th Street Theatre, 354 West 45th St. Query and synopsis. Reports in 3 months. "If Primary Stages produces the play, we ask for the right to move it for up to six months after the closing performance." Writers paid "same as the actors."

Needs: "We are looking for highly theatrical works that were written exclusively with the stage in mind. We do not want TV scripts or strictly realistic plays."

Tips: No "living room plays, disease-of-the-week plays, back-porch plays, father/son work-it-all-out-plays, etc."

THE QUARTZ THEATRE, Box 465, Ashland OR 97520. (503)482-8119. Artistic Director: Dr. Robert Spira. Produces 5 plays/year. "Semi-professional mini-theater. General audience." Send 3 page dialogue and personal bio. Reports in 2 weeks. Pays 5% royalty after expenses.
Needs: "Any length, any subject, with or without music. We seek playwrights with a flair for language and theatrical imagination."
Tips: "We look at anything. We do not do second productions unless substantial rewriting is involved. Our theatre is a steppingstone to further production. Our playwrights are usually well-read in comparative religion, philosophy, psychology, and have a comprehensive grasp of human problems. We seek the 'self-indulgent' playwright who pleases him/herself first of all."

‡RADIO REPERTORY COMPANY, INC., Box 23179, Cincinnati OH 45223. Artistic Director: Jon C. Hughes. Produces 6 plays/year. Public radio. Submit complete ms. Reports in 3 months. Buys first rights. Payment depends on non-profit funding: 1989 authors' honorarium $400.
Needs: Genres: drama/mystery/science fiction. Length: 24-27 minutes (about 20 pages). No more than 10 characters.
Tips: "The ms must be in the appropriate format. Request free copy of guidelines and format before submitting ms. Enclose SASE."

‡THE ROAD COMPANY, Box 5278 EKS, Johnson City TN 37603. (615)926-7726. Artistic Director: Robert H. Leonard. Produces 3 plays/year. "Our professional productions are intended for a general adult audience." Query and synopsis. Reports in 4 months. Pays royalty. "When we do new plays we generally try to have the playwright in residence during rehearsal for 3-4 weeks for about $1,000 plus room and board."
Needs: We like plays that experiment with form, that challenge, inform and entertain. We are a small ensemble based company. We look for smaller cast shows 4-6."
Tips: "We are always looking for 2 character (male/female) plays. We are interested in plays set in the south. We are most interested in new work that deals with new forms. We write our own plays using improvisational techniques which we then tour throughout the Southeast. When funding permits, we include one of our own new plays in our home season."

‡SEATTLE GROUP THEATRE CO., 3940 Brooklyn Ave. NE, Seattle WA 98105. (206)545-4969. Artistic Director: Ruben Sierra. Produces 6 mainstage and Multicultural Playwright's Festival (2 workshops and 4-6 readings). Ethnic Theatre (200 seats) plus Glenn Hughes Playhouse (213 seats) small professional Theatre Contract AEA. Intended for general public. 2,500 subscribers. No unsolicited scripts; synopsis, dialogue sample, resumé and letter of inquiry. Reports in 6 weeks on queries; 9 months on script submissions. Buys licensing for production. Payment negotiated royalties (per performance minimum or % of total box).
Needs: Full length, translations, adaptations. Serious plays with social/cultural issues; satires or comedies with bite. Plays must be suitable for multi-ethnic casts. Cast limit of 10 prefer unit set or simple sets.
Tips: "No non-solicited topics. No fluff."

‡SECOND STAGE, Box 1807, Ansonia Station, New York NY 10023. (212)685-5873. Artistic Directors: Robyn Goodman and Carole Rothman. Produces 4 plays/year. Professional productions. Off-Broadway. Query and synopsis. Reports in 2 months. Standard Off-Broadway contract. Pays royalty.
Needs: No one-acts.

‡SHAW FESTIVAL, Box 774, Niagara-on-the-Lake, Ontario L0S 1J0 Canada. Artistic Director: Christopher Newton. Produces 10 plays/year. 4% freelance written. "Professional summer festival operating three theaters (Festival: 845 seats, Court House: 370 seats and Royal George: 250 seats). We also host some music and some winter rentals. Mandate is based on the works of G.B. Shaw and his contemporaries." No scripts are unagented submissions. Works with 2 unpublished/unproduced writers annually. Submit complete ms. Computer printout submissions acceptable; no dot-matrix. Reports in 6 months. "We prefer to hold rights for Canada and northeastern U.S., also potential to tour." Pays 5-6% royalty. SASE or SAE and IRCs.
Needs: "We operate an acting ensemble of up to 75 actors, this includes 14 actor/singers and have sophisticated production facilities. We run a winter season in Toronto for the production of new works. During the summer season (April-October) the Academy of the Shaw Festival organizes several workshops of new plays."

THE SHAZZAM PRODUCTION COMPANY, 418 Pier Ave., Santa Monica CA 90405. Artistic Director: Edward Blackoff. Produces 2 plays/year. Equity-waiver productions for adult audience. Query with complete ms and synopsis. Reports in 6 weeks. Obtains negotiable rights. Pays $15-25/performance.
Needs: "Full-length plays dealing with important contemporary social and political human issues. Limit of 2 sets and requiring no more than 12 actors. No musicals or drawing-room farces."

SOUTH COAST REPERTORY, Box 2197, Costa Mesa CA 92628. (714)957-2602. Dramaturg: Jerry Patch. Literary Manager: John Glore. Produces 6 plays/year on mainstage, 5 on second stage. A professional non-profit theater; a member of LORT and TCG. "We operate in our own facility which houses a 507-seat mainstage theater and a 161-seat second stage theater. We have a combined subscription audience of 24,000." Submit query and synopsis; manuscripts considered if submitted by agent. Reports in 4 months. Acquires negotiable rights. Pays negotiable royalty.

Needs: "We produce mostly full-lengths but will consider one-acts. Our only-iron-clad restriction is that a play be well written. We prefer plays that address contemporary concerns and are dramaturgically innovative. A play whose cast is larger than 15-20 will need to be extremely compelling and its cast size must be justifiable."

Tips: "We don't look for a writer to write for us – he or she should write for him or herself. We look for honesty and a fresh voice. We're not likely to be interested in writers who are mindful of *any* trends. Originality and craftsmanship are the most important qualities we look for."

SOUTHEAST PLAYWRIGHTS PROJECT, Box 14252, Atlanta GA 30324. (404)242-5906. Executive Director: Gayle Austin. Produces approximately 30 readings/workshops/year and provides career development services, including ongoing Writers' Lab, newsletter and workshops. This is the Atlanta New Play Project restructured to have playwrights as members. Write (includng SASE) for general membership applications. After joining, members may submit full-length script to be considered for Associate or Full membership.

Needs: General membership open to any playwright who lives, or has lived in the Southeast. Associate member must have had public reading of one full-length or two one-act plays. Full Member must have had at least one full production of a full-length play or be Associate Member.

Tips: "We aim at becoming a regional type of New Dramatists organization. Selection committee is looking for a distinctive voice, imaginative use of the stage, not just TV movies or sitcoms in play form."

SOUTHERN APPALACHIAN REPERTORY THEATRE (SART), Mars Hill College, Box 53, Mars Hill NC 28754. (704)689-1384. Managing Director: James W. Thomas. Produces 5-6 plays/year. "Since 1975 the Southern Appalachian Repertory Theatre has produced 625 performances of 71 plays and played to over 90,000 patrons in the 152-seat Owen Theatre on the Mars Hill College campus. The theater's goals are quality, adventurous programming and integrity, both in artistic form and in the treatment of various aspects of the human condition. SART is a professional summer theater company whose audiences range from students to senior citizens." Send query with synopsis. Reports in 2 months. Pays flat fee of $500.

Needs: "Since 1975, one of SART's goals has been to produce at least one original play each summer season. To date, 23 original scripts have been produced. Plays by southern Appalachian playwrights or about southern Appalachia are preferred, but by no means exclusively. New scripts, synopses of letters of inquiry welcomed."

STAGE ONE: The Louisville Children's Theatre, 425 W. Market St., Louisville KY 40202. (502)589-5946. Producing Director: Moses Goldberg. Produces 6-7 plays/year. 20% freelance written. 15-20% of scripts produced are unagented submissions (excluding work of playwright-in-residence). Plays performed by an Equity company for young audiences aged 4-18; usually does different plays for different age groups within that range. Submit complete ms. Computer printout submissions acceptable. Reports in 4 months. Pays negotiable royalty or $25-50/performance.

Needs: "Good plays for young audiences of all types: adventure, fantasy, realism, serious problem plays about growing up or family entertainment." Cast: ideally, 10 or less. "Honest, visual potentiality, worthwhile story and characters are necessary. An awareness of children and their schooling is a plus." No "campy material or anything condescending to children. No musicals unless they are fairly limited in orchestration."

CHARLES STILWILL, Managing Director, Community Playhouse, Box 433, Waterloo IA-50704. (319)235-0367. Plays performed by Waterloo Community Playhouse with a volunteer cast. Produces 9-10 plays (7 adult, 4 children's); 1-3 musicals and 11 nonmusicals/year; 1-4 originals. 17% freelance written. Most scripts produced are unagented submissions. Works with 1-4 unpublished/unproduced writers annually. "We are one of few community theaters with a commitment to new scripts. We do at least one and have done as many as four a year. We have 4,300 season members." Average attendance at main stage shows is 3,000; at studio shows 1,600. "We try to fit the play to the theater. We do a wide variety of plays. Our public isn't going to accept nudity, too much sex, too much strong language. We don't have enough Black actors to do all-Black shows." Theatre has done plays with as few as two characters, and as many as 98. "On the main stage, we usually pay between $300 and $500. In our studio, we usually pay between $50 and $500. We also produce children's theater. Send complete script. Computer printout submissions acceptable, "Please, no loose pages." "Reports negatively within 1 year, but acceptance takes longer because we try to fit a wanted script into the balanced season. We sometimes hold a script longer than a year if we like it but cannot immediately find the right slot for it. Next year we will be doing the world premier of *Veranda Promise* and this year we did *Anna's Brooklyn Promise*, which we've had since 1983."

Needs: "We are looking for good adaptations of name children's shows and very good shows that don't necessarily have a name. We produce children's theater with both adult and child actors. We also do a small (2-6 actors) cast show that tours the elementary schools in the spring. This can only be about 35-45 minutes long."

‡STOP-GAP, 523 N. Grand, Santa Ana CA 92701. (714)648-0135. Artistic Director: Don Laffoon. Produces 3 plays/year. Professional productions for general audiences. Query and synopsis. Reports in 4 months. Buys no rights except directorial syle. Payment for production only. Standard royalty, rates negotiable.
Needs: Full-length plays dealing with topical social issues: substance abuse, AIDS, aging, physical abuse, disabilities, etc. Casts should be small.
Tips: "Plays too individualized to have broader meaning are discouraged. On the other hand we certainly recognize that plays concern individuals and not institutions. Non-traditional forms in staging, casting, and linear development are very acceptable and often exciting. Anything goes, though, doesn't. Grab us with the story and the characters and we'll follow you in offbeat directions. Keep stage directions clean and clear. Don't pile too much information and detail on the reader or viewer."

‡STOREFRONT THEATRE, 615 NW Couch, Portland OR 97209. (503)224-9598. Artistic Director: Gary O'Brien. Produces 6-8 plays/year. "Productions are professional/semi-professional; we have a 158-seat theater and a 310-seat theater, a subscription audience of around 3,000." Query and synopsis. Reports in 2 months. Pays 6-8% royalty.
Needs: "No Broadway comedies or TV sitcom-type material, non-mainstream, offbeat, occasional small musicals. Interested in plays that have something to say, but not didactic, heavy."

‡STREET PLAYERS THEATRE, Box 2687, Norman OK 73070. (405)364-0207. Artistic Director: Thomas C. Lategola. Produces 6 play/year. Professional productions performed for midwestern university community. One Children's theater piece is toured throughout the region. Submit complete ms. Reports in 6 months. Limited production rights.
Needs: Produces previously unproduced work, with preference given to Oklahoma and Southwest regional writers. Full-length plays preferred; all styles and topics considered. Small cast (5-6), single set preferred. Storefront-type theater, which holds up to 99 people. Fall Festival Contest pays $250, no guarantee of production; deadline: June 30 each year. New Plays Series and Children's 50-minute piece: Negotiated average: $250.

TEJAS ART PRESS, 207 Terrell Rd., San Antonio TX 78209. Editor: Robert Willson. Publishes poetry, plays, or "illustrated books" relating to the American Indian experience, by American Indians only. Submit complete ms. Reports in 2 months. Pays royalty.

THEATER ARTISTS OF MARIN, Box 473, San Rafael CA 94915. (415)454-2380. Artistic Director: Charles Brousse. Produces 5-6 plays/year. Professional non-equity productions for a general adult audience. Submit complete ms. Reports in 3 months. Pays outright $250.
Needs: "All types of scripts: comedy, drama, farce. Prefers contemporary setting, with some relevance to current issues in American society. Will also consider 'small musicals,' reviews or plays with music." No children's shows, domestic sitcoms, one-man shows or commercial thrillers.

‡THEATRE CALGARY, 220 9th Ave. SE, Calgary, Alberta T2G 5C4 Canada. (403)294-7440. Artistic Director: Martin Kinch. Produces 6-8 plays/year. Professional productions. Reports in 3 months. Buys production rights usually, "but it can vary with specific contracts." Payments and commissions negotiated under individual contracts.
Needs: "Theater Calgary is a major Canadian Regional Theater."
Tips: "Theatre Calgary still accepts unsolicited scripts, but does not have a significant script development program at the present time. We cannot guarantee a quick return time, and we will not return scripts without pre-paid envelopes."

‡THEATRE DE LA JEUNE LUNE, Box 25170, Minneapolis MN 55458. (612)332-3968. Artistic Directors: Barbra Berlovitz Desbois, Vincent Garcieux, Robert Rosen, Dominique Serrand. Produces 4 plays/year. Professional non-profit company producing September-May for general audience. Query and synopsis. Reports in 2 months. Pays royalty or per performance.
Needs: "All subject matter considered, although plays with universal themes are desired; plays that concern people of today. We are constantly looking for plays with large casts. Generally *not* interested in plays with 1-4 characters. No psychological drama or plays that are written alone in a room without the input of outside vitality and life."
Tips: "We are an acting company that takes plays and makes them ours; this could mean cutting a script or not heeding a writer's stage directions. We are committed to the performance in front of the audience as the goal of all the contributing factors; therefore, the actors' voice is extremely important."

‡THEATER LUDICRUM, INC., Suite 83, 64 Charlesgate E., Boston MA 02215. (617)424-6831. Contact: Director. Produces 2-3 plays/year. Plays are performed in a small, non-equity theater in Boston. "Our audience includes minority groups (people of color, gays, women)." Submit complete ms. Reports in 2 weeks. Rights revert to author after production. Pays $15-30/performance.

Needs: "As a small theater with a small budget, we look for scripts with minimal sets, costumes, props and expense in general. We are interested in scripts that emphasize the word and acting."

‡**THEATRE ON THE MOVE**, Box 462, Islington, Ontario M9A 4X4 Canada. (416)622-1423. Artistic Director: Anne Hines. Produces 5 plays/year for families and young audiences—elementary and high schools and special venues (museums, etc.). Uses professional, adult, union actors. Submit query and synopsis or complete ms. Reports in 2 months. Acquires exclusive rights to Ontario, usually for a minimum of 1 year. Pays royalty, or commission for works-in-progress.
Needs: Musicals or dramas for small casts (limit 4 actors) which deal with current topics of interest to children and families. Uncomplicated, 'tourable' sets.
Tips: "Our shows have to educate the audience about some aspect of modern life, as well as entertain. The trend is away from fairy tales, etc."

THEATREWORKS, University of Colorado, Box 7150, Colorado Springs CO 80933. (719)593-3232. Producing Director: Whit Andrews. Produces 4 full-length plays/year and two new one-acts. "New full-length plays produced on an irregular basis. Casts are semi-professional and plays are produced at the university." Submit query and synopsis. No unsolicited manuscripts. One-act plays are accepted as Playwrights' Forum competition entries—submit complete ms. Deadline: December 15; winners announced February 15. Two one-act competition winners receive full production, cash awards and travel allowances. Acquires exclusive regional option for duration of production. Full rights revert to author upon closing. Pays $300-1,200.
Needs: Full-lengths and one-acts—no restrictions on subject. "Cast size should not exceed 20; stage area is small with limited wing and fly space. Theatreworks is interested in the exploration of new and inventive theatrical work. Points are scored by imaginative use of visual image. Static verbosity and staid conventionalism not encouraged." No formulaic melodrama or children's plays.
Tips: "Too often, new plays seem far too derivative of television and film writing. We think theater is a medium which an author must specifically attack. The standard three-act form would appear to be on the way out. Economy, brevity and incisiveness are favorably received."

THEATREWORKS/USA, 890 Broadway, New York NY 10003. (212)677-5959. Artistic Director: Jay Hamick. Literary Manager: Barbara Pasternack. Produces 3 new musical plays/season. Produces professional musicals that primarily tour but also play (TYA contract) at an off-Broadway theater for a young audience. Submit query and synopsis or sample song. Reports in 6 months. Buys all rights. Pays 6% royalty; offers $1,500 advance against future royalties for new, commissioned plays.
Needs: Musicals and plays with music. Historical/biographical themes (ages 9-15), classic literature, fairy tales, and issue-oriented themes suitable for young people ages 9-15. Five person cast, minimal lighting. "We like well-crafted shows with good dramatic structure—a protagonist who wants something specific, an antagonist, a problem to be solved—character development, tension, climax, etc. No Saturday Afternoon Special-type shows, shows with nothing to say or 'kiddie' theater shows."
Tips: "Writing for kids is just like writing for adults—only better (clearer, cleaner). Kids will not sit still for unnecessary exposition and overblown prose. Long monologues, soliloquies and 'I Am' songs and ballads should be avoided. Television, movies and video make the world of entertainment highly competitive. We've noticed lately how well popular children's titles, contemporary and in public domain, sell. We are very interested in acquiring adaptations of this type of material."

TRINITY SQUARE ENSEMBLE, Box 1798, Evanston IL 60204. (312)328-0330. Artistic Director: Karen L. Erickson. Produces 4-6 plays/year. "Professional non-equity company, member of League of Chicago Theatres, ensemble company of artists. We look for scripts adapted from classics suited to our ensemble as well as new works. Writers are encouraged to research our company. We produce new children's pieces—must blend stories with school curriculum." Send query and synopsis. "We do not want full ms submissions. If we request, then we'll return." Reports in 6 months. Obtains negotiated percentage of rights, ususally 10%.
Needs: Cast: prefer no more than 10. Set: preferably simple.
Tips: "Our ensemble is 70% women/30% men. Keep this in mind as you develop scripts. No male-dominated, fluffy comedies. Get to know us—write for our performers. Looks for strength in female characters."

‡**UNICORN THEATRE**, 3820 Main St., Kansas City MO 64111. (816)531-PLAY. Artistic Director: Cynthia Levin. Produces 8 plays/year. "We are a professional Equity Theatre. Typically, we produce contemporary plays." Query and synopsis or submit complete ms. Buys 5% subsidiary rights to Unicorn's Playwright Project. Pays $1,000 cash prize plus mainstage professional production.
Needs: Contemporary, unpublished, professionally unproduced, maximum 10 characters, firmly bound scripts, legible scripts, no dot-matrix. Include: manuscript, cover letter w/*brief* bio, SASE, 1 pg. synopsis w/ character description. Maximum 10 characters. No musicals, one-acts, or historical plays.

‡**UNIVERSITY OF MINNESOTA, DULUTH THEATRE**, 10 University Dr., Duluth MN 55812. (218)726-8562. Artistic Director: Richard Durst. Produces 13 plays/year. Plays are performed at the University Theatre, American College Theatre Festival and the Minnesota Repertory Theatre (summer). Submit query and

synopsis only. Reports in 3 weeks. Acquires performance rights. Pays $35-100/performance.

Needs: All genres. Prefers younger casting requirements and single set or unit setting shows. No previously produced work or one-act plays.

Tips: "We are a very active undergraduate theater program that is very interested in producing new work. We annually produce a new play for the American College Theatre Festival in which there are several major playwriting awards."

‡MIRIAM COLON VALLE, 141 W. 94th St., New York NY 10036. (212)354-1293. Produces 4 plays/year. Three plays performed bi-lingually, January to July. One play performed in the street parks and playgrounds of the five boroughs of New York City. Submit complete ms. Reports in 6 months. Fee to be negotiated.

Needs: Plays about the Latino experience in English and Spanish. Serious or comedies. Any style—prefer plays with psychological or social substance. Cast limitations: No more than eight. No wing or fly space. No childrens plays. Avoid TV drama & sitcoms.

VIGILANTE PLAYERS, INC., MSU Media and Theatre Arts. Bozeman MT 59717. (406)994-5884. Artistic Director: John M. Hosking. Produces 3-4 plays/year. Plays by professional touring company that does productions by or about people and themes of the Northwest. "Past productions were concerned with homeless people, agriculture, literature by Northwest writers, one-company towns and spouse abuse in rural areas." Submit complete ms. Reports in 6 months. Pays $10-50/performance.

Needs: Produces full-length plays and some one-acts. "Staging suitable for a small touring company and cast limited to four actors (two men, two women). Double casting actors for more play characters is also an option."

Tips: "No musicals requiring orchestras and a chorus line. Although we prefer a script of some thematic substance, the company is very adept at comedy and would prefer the topic to include humor."

WALNUT STREET THEATRE, 9th and Walnut Streets, Philadelphia PA 19107. (215)574-3550. Executive Director: Bernard Havard. Produces 5 mainstage and 5 studio plays/year. "Our plays are performed in our own space. WST has 3 theaters—a proscenium (mainstage), audience capacity: 1,052; 2 studios, audience capacity: 79-99. We have a subscription audience, the third largest in the nation." Query with synopsis and 10 pages. Reports in 5 months. Rights negotiated per project. Pays royalty (negotiated per project) or outright purchase.

Needs: "Full-length dramas and comedies, musicals, translations, adaptations and revues. The studio plays must be small cast, simple sets."

Tips: "We will consider anything. Bear in mind that on the mainstage we look for plays with mass appeal, Broadway-style. The studio spaces are our Off-Broadway. No children's plays. Our mainstage audience goes for work that is entertaining and light. Our studio season is when we look for plays that have bite, are more provocative."

WASHINGTON STATE UNIVERSITY THEATRE, Theatre Arts and Drama, Pullman WA 99164-2432. (509)335-3239. Contact: General Manager. Produces 10 plays/year. Plays performed in university environment. Submit query and synopsis. Do not send full script. Royalties paid in accordance with standard rates.

WEST COAST ENSEMBLE, Box 38728, Los Angeles CA 90038. (213)871-1052. Artistic Director: Les Hanson. Produces 6 plays/year. Plays will be performed in one of our two theaters in Hollywood in an Equity-waiver situation. Submit complete ms. Reports in 5 months. Obtains the exclusive rights in southern California to present the play for the period specified. All ownership and rights remain with the playwright. Pays $25-45/performance.

Needs: Prefers a cast of 6-12.

Tips: "Submit the manuscript in acceptable dramatic script format."

THE WESTERN STAGE, 156 Homestead Ave., Salinas CA 93901. Dramaturg: Joyce Lower. The Steinbeck Playwriting Competition.

Needs: Submissions: Subject matter in the spirit of John Steinbeck. Works must be full length, unproduced (workshops, readings excepted) and original. No musicals, one-acts, adaptations, translations. Bound, typed works only on good quality 8½ × 11 inch paper. Please include a cast list with a short description of each character and a synopsis of the plot. Also include a list of all workshops and readings of the play to date. Enclose a 9 × 12 SASE for ms. Only one submission per playwright. Submissions accepted Oct. 1-Dec. 31 only. Response by April 15. All finalists will receive a staged reading at the internationally acclaimed Steinbeck Festival and royalties for the reading of the play. One play will be chosen from the readings to receive a full scale production, the playwright will receive a $1000 cash award (amount tentative), royalties for the production, residency, and publication, if possible. Current staff, students and contractors of The Western Stage are not eligible.

THE ANN WHITE THEATRE, 5266 Gate Lake Rd., Fort Lauderdale FL 33319. (305)772-4371. Artistic Director: Ann White. Produces 6 plays/year. "Alternative theater, professional productions for mature audiences. Plays performed in various settings: libraries, theaters, colleges and universities, hotels and dinner theaters." Conducts annual playwrights' competition and festival. Send mss August through November 15 for productions in spring. SASE for guidelines. Winning playwright receives $500.
Tips: "We are always interested in plays that focus on contemporary issues."

‡WILLIAMSTOWN THEATRE FESTIVAL, 341 W 38th St., 10th Fl., New York NY 10018. (212)967-8170. Artistic Director: Nikos Psacharopoulos. Publishes 10-12 plays/year. Professional productions of classics, contemporary classics and new works performed in Williamstown, Massachusetts - home of the Williamstown Theatre Festival. Season dates: June 22 - Aug. 26. Query and synopsis. Also, full scripts from agents, or we solicit scripts from playwrights and producers directly. Reports in 2-3 months. Pays royalty.
Needs: Most interested in new works with manageable cast size (up to 10 or 12) minimal production requirements and of "important" subject matter . . . very interested in serious works with social and political import. We avoid musicals (logistical limitations) and one-acts, unless there is a companion piece.
Tips: "Make sure script is readable—often copy quality and typos make scripts difficult to read!"

WOOLLY MAMMOTH THEATRE COMPANY, 1401 Church St. NW, Washington DC 20005. (202)393-3939. Artistic Director: Howard Shalwitz. Literary Manager: Martin Blank. Produces 5 plays/year. 50% freelance written. Produces professional productions for the general public in Washington, DC. 2-3 scripts/year are unagented submissions. Works with 1-2 unpublished/unproduced writers annually. Accepts unsolicited scripts; reports in 6 weeks on scripts; very interesting scripts take much longer. Buys first- and second- class production rights. Pays 5% royalty.
Needs: "We look only for plays that are highly unusual in some way. Apart from an innovative approach, there is no formula. One-acts are not used." Cast limit of 8.

WORCESTER FOOTHILLS THEATRE COMPANY, 074 Worcester Center, Worcester MA 01608. (508)754-3314. Artistic Director: Marc P. Smith. Literary Manager: Greg DeJarnett. Produces 7 plays/year. Full time professional theater, general audience. Query and synopsis. Reports in 3 weeks. Pays royalty.
Needs: "Produce plays for general audience. No gratuitous violence, sex or language. Prefer cast under 10 and single set. 30' proscenium with apron but no fly space."

YWAM/ACADEMY OF PERFORMING ARTS, Box 1324, Cambridge, Ontario N1R 7G6 Canada. Artistic Director: Stuart Scadron-Wattles. Produces 3 plays/year. Semi-professional productions for a general audience. Send query and synopsis. Reports in 6 months. Pays $50-100/performance.
Needs: "One-act or full-length; comedy or drama; musical or straight; written from a biblical world view." No cast above 10; prefers unit staging.
Tips: Looks for "non-religious writing from a biblical world view for an audience which loves the theater. Avoid current trends toward shorter scenes. Playwrights should be aware that they are writing for the stage—not television."

Screenwriting

"Is it a good movie?" a caller recently asked an advertising executive at one of Hollywood's major studios.

"Yes, it already grossed $60 million," he answered, then laughed at his unabashed admission that show business remains first a business, and then, perhaps, an art.

To a writer, this fundamental business premise means writing stories that are highly accessible to the general public. Banks loan studios cash to produce films that the studios believe will most likely return the huge investment. The studios in turn put up their assets as collateral. Audience numbers, meaning public acceptance, remain a financial necessity.

For this reason, scripts with universal appeal stand a better chance to make it beyond the first line of professional readers that all studios (and most agents) employ in their quest for a fresh new twist to proven plots and themes.

The studios' desire for less subtle and more easily accessible material can cause writers to lament the material that ends up on screen. In reality, the best story offers something for everyone but also is unique and it usually comes from personal or autobiographical sources. If your story touches on the basic themes of love, honor, courage, revenge or pathos, it can be a comedy, drama, adventure or romance, and it will naturally elicit the sort of empathy in studio readers that it would with any filmgoer. "Moonstruck" is a good example. If you have lived it and felt it, that experience is probably a good one to dramatize.

Despite fads and trends, certain patterns have remained a constant in American films. Comedy remains king. "Down" endings may be big in Japan, or on the European festival circuit, but such stories rarely find backers in Hollywood.

Because widespread public acceptance is such a high priority, studio executives who are willing to place black, Hispanic or Oriental actors in romantic heroes' roles remain rare. This phenomenon is hardly unique: in India, for example, which produces far more films than Hollywood, the chance for a white male to land a leading role is equally slim.

It is also rare in Hollywood to come across non-narrative films, or stories in which a distinctly Jewish person is portrayed as a villain or those in which a distinctly Arab or German person is portrayed a hero. On the other hand, there are no rules in Hollywood, and many young and more iconoclastic filmmakers such as Spike ("Do the Right Thing") Lee have succeeded in bucking these trends and encourage others to follow their lead.

Thematic conventions of Hollywood screenplays are not nearly as strong as the aesthetic and technical ones. A good screenplay is a page turner. Scene divisions are outlined, but instructions to actors are avoided since they are the director's and actors' prerogative. Each page represents about one minute of screen time and takes about 20 second to read. Scenes can range from one sentence (usually a segue scene) to several pages. As in any drama, each has a specific purpose, offers specific expectations and resolves the conflict in an unexpected or surprising manner. Most screenplays contain between 40 and 60 scenes, but no reader is going to count yours, especially if engrossed in your story and your characters.

A screenplay's goal is not to be a blueprint for a good movie as much as it is to entertain the reader enough to champion it up the corporate ladder of a studio's story department. The story that hurtles along is the one that endures longest through that gauntlet.

The look of the page is critical. Obtain actual screenplays to study, not published "after-the-fact" transcripts of completed films, since the latters' formats are different. *Five Screenplays by Preston Sturgess* is a good example of actual screenplays (edited with an introduction by Brian Henderson, University of California press, $18.95). So is *The Best American Screenplays*, a collection of 12 classic and modern screenplays (edited by Sam Thomas, Crown Books, $24.95).

Watching films while following their original screenplays will illustrate how a good writer achieves maximum effect with the fewest words and develops a character's inner conflict without actually describing it to the reader as a novelist would. Flashbacks are considered awkward; "inner monologue" narration (although used expertly in many of Woody Allen's films) is unconventional. Screenplays that are not between 90 and 130 pages/minutes discourage studio readers. Exhibitors are reluctant to book films that are too short – audiences presumably won't pay to see a one-hour film – or too long – meaning fewer screenings per day.

Development deals were once relatively common. The fabled Hollywood "pitch," a writer's sales speech during which he enacts his story for the producer, has become a rare occasion. With a development deal, a writer is paid in steps for his idea, then his story, then outline, then his first section of first draft, the second section, etc. Today only 10% of all development projects are made into films, and only about half of those return their investments.

Treatments are also not as eagerly sought, since a desirable treatment requires offering the writer a development deal. It is more economical for studios to read and purchase completed scripts. This now-common practice benefits non-Southern California writers because it frees them from the obligation to be on call to "take a meeting" in Hollywood to discuss the latest draft.

Although writers are individually in a more difficult position than last year, they are in general at least perceived as a more important link in the industry. Last year's Writers Guild strike brought the motion picture and television industries to a complete standstill. The consensus remains that both sides lost more than they won in this battle over rights, residuals and overseas percentages. What remains unchanged is that scripts are as crucial and good writers as necessary to the process as ever.

☐**BACHNER PRODUCTIONS, INC.**, 360 First Ave., #5D, New York NY 10010. (212)673-2946. President: Annette Bachner. Produces material for television, home video cassettes, cable TV. Buys 4 scripts/year. Buys all rights. No previously produced material. Does not return unsolicited submissions. "Do not want unsolicited material." Reports on queries in 1 month; on solicited submissions in 2 months.
Needs: 35mm and 16mm films, realia, tapes and cassettes. Natural history subjects only. Query. Pays by outright purchase in accordance with Writer's Guild standards.
Tips: Looks for writers with "experience in visual media."

BLAZING PRODUCTIONS, INC., Suite 125, 4712 Avenue N, Brooklyn NY 11234. Producer: David Krinsky. Produces material for "major and minor theatrical distribution of quality low budget 35mm films." Buys 1-3 scripts/year. Buys all rights. No previously produced material. Reports in 2 weeks on queries; 1 month on mss.
Needs: Films (35mm). "I need well-written, original, low budget movie screenplays in the comedy, drama, actions and thriller genres *only*." Submit synopsis/outline. "Send synopsis of film and I'll contact if I wish to see script. Send SASE." Payment "depends—sometimes percentage, sometimes outright, sometimes both."
Tips: "*Follow instructions.* Do *not* send a script or treatment unless *requested. Only* send a *one*-page synopsis of screenplay and query letter. Writers should be flexible and open to suggestion regarding changes/improvements in their material. Intelligent scripts with teenage characters are an easier sell. No exploitation comedy or slashers. Don't expect instant sales. Once I approve a script, my investors have to approve. Be patient. Send standard script format."

‡**ANTHONY CARDOZA ENTERPRISES**, Box 4163, North Hollywood CA 91607. (818)985-5550. President: Anthony Cardoza. Produces material for "theater, TV and home." Buys one screenplay/year. Buys all rights. No previously produced material. Reports in 1 month.
Needs: Feature films. Submit completed script. Outright purchase.

CAREY-IT-OFF PRODUCTIONS, Suite 4, 14316 Riverside Dr., Sherman Oaks CA 91423. (818)789-0954. President: Kathi Carey. Audience is general moviegoers. Works with 5-6 writers/year. Buys all rights. No previously produced material. Reports in 6 weeks on queries; 3 months on mss.
Needs: 35mm films. Wants feature films—strong male and female lead, action/adventure or suspense/thriller or police/action dramas. Query with synopsis. Makes outright purchase in accordance with Writer's Guild standards.
Tips: "Keep in mind that feature films/film packages need stars in the lead roles, and these roles should be written with a star's ego in mind."

‡**CHERRY ST. FILMS**, c/o Columbia, Columbia Plaza West, Room 12, Burbank CA 91505. (818)954-4671. Director of Development: Karen J. Moy. Buys 5-10 scripts/year. Buys all rights. Reports in 1 month on queries; 2 months on submissions.
Needs: Films (35-70mm). "We are only interested in reading full-length feature screenplays (approximately 120 pages in length) of most genres, except for westerns and high budgeted sci-fi." Submit query "which indicates the genre of the piece and a one-liner about the story. If we are interested in reading it, we will send author a release form to fill out before we can take a look at it." Pays in accordance with Writers Guild standards and options other films.
Tips: "Writers should write on what they know and/or feel strongly about. Please do not call us; we'd rather hear from interested parties via letters."

THE CHICAGO BOARD OF RABBIS BROADCASTING COMMISSION, 1 South Franklin St., Chicago IL 60606. (312)444-2896. Director of Broadcasting: Mindy Soble. "Television scripts are requested for *The Magic Door*, a children's program produced in conjunction with CBS's WBBM-TV 2 in Chicago." 26 scripts are purchased per television season. Buys all rights. Reports in 1 month. Writers guidelines for #10 SASE.
Needs: "*Magic Door* is a weekly series of 26 shows that contain Jewish content and have universal appeal. The program takes place backstage in a theatre where a company of actors brings stories to life for a puppet-child, Mazel. (Mazel is a large hand puppet who is worked by a member of the company, Wendy). The company consists of approximately 30 actors and actresses. Most of the programs utilize 3 or 4 of the above, including Wendy." Submit synopsis/outline, resume or a completed script with the right to reject. Outright purchase of $125.

Tips: "A Judaic background is helpful, yet not critical. Writing for children is key. We prefer to use Chicago writers, as script rewrites are paramount."

‡☐ **CHRISTIAN BROADCASTING NETWORK**, Virginia Beach VA 23463. (804)424-7777. Head Writer, Producers Group: David Wimbish. Produces material for a general mass audience as well as Christian audiences. "We are looking for family-oriented material. Query first and ask for a release form before submitting a short (two-or-three pages) synopsis of your script. Letter-quality please." Reports in 2 months.
Tips: "We are interested in well-written scripts which can attract a family audience. Please, no dramatic retellings of the Second Coming or the Apocalypse. We've seen dozens upon dozens of these!"

CINE/DESIGN FILMS, INC., 255 Washington St., Denver CO 80203. (303)777-4222. Producer/Director: Jon Husband. Produces educational material for general, sales-training and theatrical audiences. 75% freelance written. 90% of scripts produced are unagented submissions. "Original, solid ideas are encouraged." Computer printout submissions acceptable. Rights purchased vary.
Needs: "Motion picture outlines in the theatrical and documentary areas. We are seeking theatrical scripts in the low-budget area that are possible to produce for under $1,000,000. We seek flexibility and personalities who can work well with our clients." Produces 16mm and 35mm films. Send an 8-10 page outline before submitting ms or script. Pays $100-200/screen minute on 16mm productions. Theatrical scripts negotiable.
Tips: "Understand the marketing needs of film production today. Materials will not be returned."

CORMAN PRODUCTIONS, 6729 Dume Dr., Box 371, Malibu CA 90265. (213)457-7524. Producer: Dick Corman. Material for feature films and television needed. Buys 10-12 scripts or stories in treatment format per year. Buys all rights. No previously produced material.
Needs: Wants true stories, any genre, short stories. Query with synopsis. Material is optioned for studios and networks.
Tips: "We are looking for unusual, different stories which haven't reached the news wire services. High concept will continue to be the front runner in the business. Happy, fun-oriented stories will also begin surfacing."

‡**DIVIDED ARTISTS**, 5439 Red Oak Dr., Los Angeles CA 90068. (213)461-1961. Producer: Mitchell Kledambly. Purchases about 5 scripts/year. Buys all rights. Reports in 2 weeks on queries; 2 months on submissions.
Needs: Films (70mm). Submit complete ms. Pays in accordance with Writers Guild standards.

‡**ENTERTAINMENT PRODUCTIONS, INC.**, 2210 Wilshire Blvd. #744, Santa Monica CA 90403. (213)456-3143. Producer: Edward Coe. Estab. 1972. Produces material for theatrical and television (worldwide) clients. Buys all rights. No previously produced material. Reports in 1 month (only if SASE is enclosed for return).
Needs: Films (35mm) and videotapes. Entertainment only material needed. Query with synopsis. Pays outright purchase. Price negotiated on a project-by-project basis.
Tips: "Learn your trade. Be flexible."

FELINE PRODUCTIONS, 1125 Veronica Springs Rd., Santa Barbara CA 93105. Executive Producer: Deby DeWeese. Produces material for educational institutions, non-profit agencies and home video markets. Number of scripts purchased "varies year to year—rarely more than 10/year." Rights vary. Previously produced material OK. Reports in 3 months.
Needs: "Low-budget 30- and 60-minute scripts in dual slide or video format. Fiction or non-fiction. Alternative media scripts encouraged. Particularly interested in feminist slant. Also looking for gay and/or lesbian-oriented themes. Prefer single-camera approach. Query.
Tips: "All material must be feminist. No military themes. Delete violence and sexism. Our audience is radical, educated, politically savvy—qualities you need to produce the scripts we buy. Actively seeking lesbian theatre scripts that can be produced on video. No film scripts—video only."

☐**LEE MAGID PRODUCTIONS**, Box 532, Malibu CA 90265. (213)463-5998. President: Lee Magid. Produces material for all markets, teenage-adult; commercial—even musicals. 90% freelance written. 70% of scripts produced are unagented submissions. Works with "many" unpublished/unproduced writers. Buys all rights or will negotiate. No previously produced material. Does not return unsolicited material. Query for electronic submissions. Reports in 6 weeks.
Needs: Films, sound filmstrips, phonograph records, television shows/series, videotape presentations. Currently interested in film material, either for video (television) or theatrical. "We deal with cable networks, producers, live-stage productions, etc." Works with musicals for cable TV. Prefers musical forms for video comedy. Submit synopsis/outline and resume. Pays in royalty, in outright purchase, in accordance with Writer's Guild standards, or depending on author.
Tips: "We're interested in comedy material. Forget drug-related scripts."

‡MAGNUSFILMS, 225 Santa Monica Blvd., 5th Floor, Santa Monica CA 90401. (213)458-3323. Manager, Development: Gayle Reavlin. Approximately 20 projects—including books—optioned/year. Reports in 1 month.
Needs: Films (35mm). Submit complete script and resume. Pays in accordance with Writers Guild standards.

‡MERIWETHER PUBLISHING LTD. (**Contemporary Drama Service**), 885 Elkton Dr., Colorado Springs CO 80907. Editor: Arthur Zapel. "We publish how-to materials in book, video and game formats. We are interested in materials for high school and college level students only. Our contemporary drama division publishes 60-70 plays/year." 95% freelance written. Eager to work with new/unpublished writers. Buys 40-60 scripts/year from unpublished/unproduced writers. 95% of scripts are unagented submissions. Computer printout submissions acceptable if readable. Reports in 4 weeks on queries; 6 weeks on full-length submissions. Query should include synopsis/outline, resume of credits, sample of style and SASE. Catalog available for $1 postage. Offers 10% royalty or outright purchase.
Needs: Book mss on theatrical arts subjects. Christian activity book mss also accepted. We will consider elementary level religious materials and plays. Query. Pays royalty; buys some mss outright.
Tips: "We publish a wide variety of speech contest materials for high school students. We are publishing more reader's theatre scripts and musicals based on classic literature or popular TV shows, provided the writer includes letter of clearance from the copyright owner."

THE MERRYWOOD STUDIO, (formerly Da Silva Associates), 137 E. 38th St., New York NY 10016-2650. Creative Director: Raul da Silva. 40% freelance written. Produces animated motion pictures for entertainment audiences. No children's material sought or produced.
Needs: Proprietary material only. Human potential themes woven into highly entertaining drama, high adventure, comedy. This is a new market for animation with only precedent in the illustrated novels published in France and Japan. Cannot handle unsolicited mail/scripts and will not return mail. Open to credit sheets, concepts and synopses only. Profit sharing depending upon value of concept and writer's following. Will pay at least Writer's Guild levels or better, plus expenses.
Tips: "This is not a market for beginning writers. Established, professional work with highly unusual and original themes is sought. If you love writing, it will show and we will recognize it and reward it in every way you can imagine. We are not a 'factory' and work on a very high level of excellence."

PACE FILMS, INC., 411 E. 53rd St., New York NY 10022. (212)755-5486. President: R. Vanderbes. Produces material for a general theatrical audience. Buys all rights. Reports in 2 months.
Needs: Theatrical motion pictures. Produces and distributes 35mm motion pictures for theatrical and videocassettes. Query with synopsis/outline and writing background/credits. Completed scripts should be submitted together with an outline. Pays in accordance with Writer's Guild standards.

□ TOM PARKER MOTION PICTURES, 18653 Ventura Blvd., Tarzana CA 91356. (818)342-9115. President: Tom Parker. Produces and distributes feature length motion pictures worldwide (Member AFMA) for theatrical, home video, pay and free TV. Works with 5-10 scripts per year. Previously produced and distributed "Wackiest Wagon Train in the West," (Rated G); "S S Girls," (Rated R); and "Initiation" (Rated R). Will acknowledge receipt of material and report within 90 days. "Follow the instructions herein and do not phone for info or to inquire about your script."
Needs: Completed scripts *only* for low budget (under $500,000) "R" or "PG" rated action/thriller, action/adventure, comedy, adult romance (R), sex comedy (R), family action/adventure to be filmed in 35mm film for the theatrical and home video market (do not send TV movie scripts, series, teleplays, stage plays). *Very limited dialogue.* Scripts should be action oriented and fully described. Screen stories or scripts OK, but no camera angles please. No heavy drama, documentaries, social commentaries, dope stories, weird or horror. Violence or sex OK, but must be well motivated with strong story line. Submit synopsis and description of characters with finished scripts. Outright purchase: $5,000-25,000. Will consider participation, co-production.
Tips: "Absolutely will not return scripts or report on rejected scripts unless accompanied by SASE."

□ TELEVISION PRODUCTION SERVICES CORP., Box 1233, Edison NJ 08818. (201)287-3626. Executive Director/Producer: R.S. Burks. Produces video music materials for major market distributor networks, etc. Buys 50-100 scripts/year. Buys all rights. Computer printout submissions OK; prefers letter-quality. Reports in 2 weeks.

□   ***Open box preceding a listing indicates a cable TV market.***

Needs: "We do video music for record companies, MTV, HBO, etc. We use treatments of story ideas from the groups' management. We also do commercials for over-the-air broadcast and cable. We are now doing internal in-house video for display on disco or internally distributed channels." Submit synopsis/outline or completed script, and resume; include SASE for response.

Tips: Looks for rewrite flexibility and availability. "We have the capability of transmission electronically over the phone modem to our printer or directly onto disk for storage."

THEME SONG: A Musical and Literary Production House, 396 Watchogue Rd., Staten Island NY 10314. (718)698-4178. Director: Lawrence Nicastro. Produces material for theater (stage/screen); radio; television (entertainment/educational documentary). Buys 50 scripts/year. Buys first rights. Previously published material OK, if a revision is sought. Reports in 1 month.

Needs: Phonograph records, tapes and cassettes and ¾" video tape. Query. "I'll answer each query individually. We enjoy newsworthy subjects and investigative/collaborative themes." Pays negotiable royalty.

Tips: "I am interested in political lyrics/songs/parodies, religious hymns, satirical sketches, epic poetry, and concrete criticism of American life, with prescriptive institutional changes necessary to improve our condition; also, international themes or cooperative themes. I am a member of The Dramatists Guild and The Songwriters Guild."

‡**VICTOR & GRAIS PRODUCTIONS,** 450 N. Roxbury #202, Beverly Hills CA 90210. (213)281-4150. Contact: Joel Castleberg. Produces material for feature films. Buys 10-12 screenplays/year. Buys all rights. No previously produced material. Reports in 1 month on queries.

Needs: Films (35mm). Looking for 90-minute feature screenplays. Submit synopsis/outline, completed script or resume. Pays in accordance with Writer's Guild standards.

Other Scriptwriting Markets

The following firms did not return a verification to update an existing listing or a questionnaire to begin a new listing by press time.

Actors Theatre of Tulsa
African Caribbean Poetry Theater
Alley Theatre
An Claidheamh Soluis/Celtic Arts Center
Arztco Pictures, Inc.
Barter Theatre
Berkeley Jewish Theatre
Bristol Riverside Theatre
Casa Manana Musicals Inc.
Center Stage
Chambra Organization
Clavis Theatre One Act Festival
Comark
Comprenetics, Inc.
Compro Productions
Condyne/The Oceana Group
Cricket Theatre
Dinner Playhouse Inc.

Dobama Theatre
Dorset Theatre Festival
Dramatika
East West Players
Effective Communication Arts, Inc.
Florida Production Center
GI-Step Audio/Visual
Goldsholl Design & Film, Inc.
Griffin Media Design
Ironbound Theatre Inc.
William V. Levine Associates, Inc.
Little Sister Pictures Inc.
McCarter Theatre Co.
Magic Theatre Inc.
Mediacom Development Corp.
Monad Trainer's Aide
New American Theater
New Rose Theatre
Nickelodeon MTV Networks

Inc.
Old Globe Theatre
Pasetta Productions
Paulist Productions
Bill Rase Productions, Inc.
Save the Children
Scott Resources Inc.
Screenscope, Inc.
Frank Silvera Writer's Workshop
Snowmass Repertory Theatre
Soho Repertory Theatre
Spectrum Theatre
E.J. Stewart Inc.
Valley Studios
Vancouver Playhouse
Virginia Stage Company
Westbeth Theatre Center, Inc.
Wichita State University Theatre

The following listings were deleted following the 1989 edition of *Writer's Market* because they went out of business, asked to be deleted or could not be contacted.

Alaska Repertory Theatre (out of business)
Alexi Productions Ltd. (closed U.S. office)
Arts Club Theatre (accepting only Canadian manuscripts)
CP Films Inc. (ceased production)

EFC, Inc. (asked to be deleted)
Heaping Teaspoon Animation (unable to handle volume of submissions)
Dennis Hommel Associates Inc. (asked to be deleted)
Julian Theatre (unable to contact)

Oracle Press (no longer publishes plays)
Philadelphia Theatre Co. (unable to contact)
Story Source (unable to contact)
Video Wonderland (out of business)

During the past year, syndicates have launched columns with topics ranging from living with disabilities to the political views of former U.S. Attorney General Edwin Meese. In a move toward recognition of social problems, 100 cartoonists also banded together to publicize the plight of America's homeless with their cartoons.

Syndication remains a competitive and challenging field for writers. A Creators Syndicate editor said the syndicate received 7,000 submissions last year and accepted four.

Producing a lively, appealing column on a regular basis requires a certain set of skills and most editors want proof of your ability to produce consistently good work. A good place to start is your local newspaper. Many small papers welcome columnists and freelancers, especially if you are willing to start at little or no pay. If you can publish regularly at this level, you have a better chance of building your portfolio and being considered for syndication. Some newspapers do readership surveys and a favorable response to your column also is a definite plus when you approach a syndicate.

Make it a practice to study popular syndicated columns and their structure. Most columns are short—from 500 to 750 words—so columnists learn how to make every word count. Don't make the mistake of imitating a well-known columnist or of submitting a column on a topic already covered by one of the syndicate's columnists.

The more unique your column idea, the greater chance you have at syndication. It's important, however, not to narrow your topic down too much. Remember, you want to be able to generate ideas on the topic for a long time.

Editors look for writers with unique viewpoints on lifestyles or politics, but they also seek how-to columns and one-shot features on a variety of subjects. One-shot features tend to be longer than columns and can be tied to a news peg or event. Other one-shot items include puzzles, cartoons and graphics. Syndicates which accept these features have included that information in their listings.

When you submit material, most syndicate editors prefer a query letter and about six sample columns with a self-addressed, stamped envelope. If you have a particular field of expertise, be sure to mention this in your letter. For highly specialized or technical matter, you also should provide some credentials to show you are qualified to handle the topic.

Most syndicated writers advise you to submit to several syndicates at the same time to speed up the process. Unlike most magazines, you also can resubmit material to syndicates—perhaps with newly-published material included. Continue to work on your writing while you submit to syndicates; it can keep you from becoming preoccupied with the often lengthy process involved. Keep in mind that even very successful columnists and cartoonists have faced rejection. Mike Peters, editorial cartoonist of the *Dayton Daily News*, told a group in New York he sent out submissions for seven years before his work was picked up for syndication.

Syndicates act as agents or brokers for the material they sell. The syndicate promotes and markets the work, usually as part of a package, and keeps a record of sales. Writers usually receive 40-60% of gross receipts. Syndicates may pay a small salary or flat fee for one-shot items.

Syndicates usually acquire all rights to accepted material, but a few offer writers and artists the option of retaining ownership. When selling all rights, writers give up all ownership to the work. This has been one reason some writers choose to self-syndicate their work. Others choose self-syndication with hopes of attracting a major syndicate. Some self-syndicate after leaving a major syndicate and a few others do it because they like retaining control and 100% of their earnings.

If you choose self-syndication, remember that you must assume the duties of business management, marketing and sales. Payment for your columns will be negotiated on a case-by-case basis. Some small newspapers may offer only $10 per column, while larger papers may pay $50-100. You also should look for non-newspaper outlets like specialty magazines. The number of outlets is limited only by your marketing budget and sales ability. You also may need up-to-date equipment to compete successfully. Today, most columnists find they must be able to deliver their columns to newspapers and magazines electronically.

If your self-syndicated column will be used by a non-copyrighted publication, you must copyright your own material. For information about copyright procedures, see Copyrighting Your Writing in the Business of Writing section.

For information on column writing and syndication you may find these publications helpful: *Editor and Publisher Syndicate Directory* (11 W. 19th St., New York NY 10011) and *How to Make Money in Newspaper Syndication*, by Susan Lane (Newspaper Syndication Specialists, Suite 326, Box 19654, Irvine CA 92720).

For information on syndicates not listed in *Writer's Market*, see Other Syndicates at the end of this section.

ADVENTURE FEATURE SYNDICATE, 329 Harvery Dr., Glendale CA 91206. (818)247-1721. Editor: Orpha Harryman Barry. Reports in 1 month. Buys all rights, first North American serial rights and second serial (reprint) rights. Free cartoonist's guidelines.
Needs: Fiction (spies) and fillers (adventure/travel), action/adventure comic strips and graphic novels. Submit complete ms.

AMERICA INTERNATIONAL SYNDICATE, 3801 Oakland St., St. Joseph MO 64506. (816)271-5250. FAX: (816)271-5290. Executive Director: Gerald A. Bennett. Associate Director (London Office): Paul Eisler. 100% freelance written by cartoonists on contract. Works with 6 previously unpublished cartoonists/year. "We sell to newspapers, trade magazines, puzzle books and comic books." Reports in 6 weeks. Buys all rights.
Needs: Short fictional crime story "You Are The Detective" for magazines, books and comics; also comic strips of adventure, western or family type. Children's features and games also needed. Scientific or unusual features with art and written text needed. Send 6-8 samples with SASE. Pays 50% of gross sales. Currently syndication features: "Alphonso," "Silent Sam," "Tex Benson," "Double Trouble," "Buccaneers," "A.J. Sowell," "Figment," "Nath' n Tyler," "Small Potatoes" and "Dad's Place" (comic strips). Panel Features are "Staccy," "Girls," "Our Family," "Funny Bones," "The Edge" and "Sports Laffs."
Tips: "Keep the art simple and uncluttered as possible: Know your subject and strive for humor."

AMERICAN NEWSPAPER SYNDICATE, 9 Woodrush Dr., Irvine CA 92714. (714)559-8047. Executive Editor: Susan Smith. 50% regular columns by writers under contract; 50% freelance articles and series by writers on a one-time basis. Plan to syndicate up to 7 new U.S. and Canadian columnists this year. Plan to buy 20 one-time articles/series per year. Syndicates to U.S. and Canadian medium-to-large general interest and special interest newspapers. Works with previously unpublished and published writers. Pays 50% of net sales, salary on some contracted columns. Buys first North American serial rights. Computer printout submissions acceptable. Reports in 3 weeks. Writer's guidelines for SASE.
Needs: Newspaper columns and one-time articles/series on travel, entertainment, how-to, human interest, business, personal finance, lifestyle, health, legal issues. "Practical, money-saving information on everyday needs such as medicine, insurance, automobiles, education, home decoration and repairs, and travel is always in great demand by newspapers." Will not return material without SASE. Columns should be 700 words in length; one-time articles should be 1,500 words.
Tips: "We seek fresh, innovative material that may be overlooked by the other syndicates. Because we know the newspaper syndication market, we feel we can find a place for the previously-unpublished writer if the material is well-executed. Be sure to research your idea thoroughly. Good, solid writing is a must. This is a very tough business to penetrate—but the rewards can be great for those who are successful."

ARKIN MAGAZINE SYNDICATE, 761 NE 180th St., North Miami Beach FL 33162. Editor: Joseph Arkin. 20% freelance written by writers on contract; 70% freelance written by writers on a one-time basis. "We regularly purchase articles from several freelancers for syndication in trade and professional magazines." Previously published submissions OK, "if all rights haven't been sold." Computer printout submissions acceptable; no dot-matrix. Reports in 3 weeks. Buys all North American magazine and newspaper rights.

Needs: Magazine articles (nonfiction, 750-2,200 words), directly relating to business problems common to several (not just one) different types of businesses); and photos (purchased with written material). "We are in dire need of the 'how-to' business article." Will not consider article series. Submit complete ms; "SASE required with all submissions." Pays 3-10/word; $5-10 for photos; "actually, line drawings are preferred instead of photos." Pays on acceptance.

Tips: "Study a representative group of trade magazines to learn style, needs and other facets of the field."

ARTHUR'S INTERNATIONAL, Box 10599, Honolulu HI 96816. (808)922-9443. Editor: Marvin C. Arthur. Syndicates to newspapers and magazines. Computer printout submissions acceptable; prefers letter-quality. Reports in 1 week. "SASE must be enclosed." Buys all rights.

Needs: Fillers, magazine columns, magazine features, newspaper columns, newspaper features and news items. "We specialize in timely nonfiction and historical stories, and columns, preferably the unusual. We utilize humor. Travel stories utilized in 'World Traveler.'" Buys one-shot features and article series. "Since the majority of what we utilize is column or short story length, it is better to submit the article so as to expedite consideration and reply. Do not send any lengthy manuscripts." Pays 50% of net sales, salary on some contracted work and flat rate on commissioned work. Currently syndicates Marv, by Marvin C. Arthur (informative, humorous, commentary); Humoresque, by Don Alexander (humorous); and World Spotlight, by Don Kampel (commentary).

Tips: "We do not use cartoons but we are open for fine illustrators."

BUDDY BASCH FEATURE SYNDICATE, 771 West End Ave., New York NY 10025. (212)666-2300. Editor/Publisher: Buddy Basch. 10% written by writers on contract; 2% freelance written by writers on a one-time basis. Buys 10 features/year; works with 3-4 previously unpublished writers annually. Syndicates to print media: newspapers, magazines, house organs, etc. Computer printout submissions acceptable; no dot-matrix. Reports in 2 weeks. Buys first North American serial rights.

Needs: Magazine features, newspaper features, and one-shot ideas that are really different. "Try to make them unusual, unique, real 'stoppers,' not the usual stuff." Will consider one-shots and article series on travel, entertainment, human interest—"the latter, a wide umbrella that makes people stop and read the piece. Different, unusual and unique are the key words, not what the *writer* thinks is, but has been done nine million times before." Query. Pays 20-50% commission. Additional payment for photos $10-50. Currently syndicates It Takes a Woman, by Frances Scott (woman's feature), Travel Whirl, Scramble Steps and others.

Tips: "Never mind what your mother, fiancé or friend thinks is good. If it has been done before and is old hat, it has no chance. Do a little research and see if there are a dozen other similar items in the press—and don't just try a very close 'switch' on them. You don't fool anyone with this. There are fewer and fewer newspapers, with more and more people vying for the available space. But there's *always* room for a really good, different feature or story. Trouble is few writers (amateurs especially) know a good piece, I'm sorry to say."

BLACK CONSCIENCE SYNDICATION INC., 21 Bedford St., Wyandanch NY 11798. (516)491-7774. President: Clyde Davis. 65% of material freelance written. Buys 1,000 features annually. Uses material for magazines, newspapers, radio and television. Computer printout submissions OK; no dot-matrix. Reports in 2 weeks. Buys all rights. Writer's guidelines for SASE.

Needs: Magazine columns, magazine features, newspaper columns, newpaper features and news items. Buys single features and article series. Query only. Pays 50% commission.

Tips: "The purpose of Black Conscience Syndication Inc., is to serve God and provide writers who produce material vital to the well-being of the black community an avenue to have their copy published in black newspapers and trade publications throughout the world. We are interested in all material that is informative and enlightening: book reviews, interviews, feature articles, cartoons, poetry and travel information. Black Conscience Syndication submits material to 700 publications world-wide three-fourths of those publications are black."

BUSINESS FEATURES SYNDICATE, Box 9844, Ft. Lauderdale FL 33310. (305)485-0795. Editor: Dana K. Cassell. 100% freelance written. Buys about 100 features/columns a year. Syndicates to trade journal magazines, business newspapers and tabloids. Computer printout submissions acceptable; no dot-matrix. Buys exclusive rights while being circulated. Writer's guidelines for #10 SAE and 1 first class stamp. Reports in 1 month.

Needs: Buys single features and article series on generic business, how-to, marketing, merchandising, security, management and personnel. Length: 1,000-2,500 words. Complete ms preferred. Pays 50% commission. Currently syndicates Retail Market Clinic.

Tips: "We need nonfiction material aimed at the independent retailer or small service business owner. Material must be written for and of value to more than one field, for example: jewelers, drug store owners and sporting goods dealers. We aim at retail trade journals; our material is more how-to business oriented than that bought by other syndicates."

CONTINENTAL FEATURES/CONTINENTAL NEWS SERVICE, Suite 265, 341 W. Broadway, San Diego CA 92101. (619)492-8696. Editor: Gary P. Salamone. 100% written by writers on contract; 30% freelance written by writer's on a one-time basis. "Writers who offer the kind and quality of writing we seek stand an equal chance regardless of experience." Syndicates to the print media. Reports in 1 month. Writer's guidelines for #10 SASE.

Needs: Magazine features, newspaper features, "Feature material should fit the equivalent of one-quarter to one-half standard newspaper page, and Continental News considers an ultra-liberal or ultra-conservative slant inappropriate." Query. Pays 85% author's percentage. Currently syndicates News and Comment by Charles Hampton Savage (general news commentary/analysis); Continental Viewpoint, by Staff (political and social commentary); Portfolio, by William F. Pike (cartoon/caricature art); FreedomWatch, by Glen Church; The Happy Wanderer by Ann Hattes; and Middle East Cable, by Mike Maggio.

Tips: "Continental News seeks country profiles/background articles that pertain to foreign countries. Writers who possess such specific knowledge/personal experience stand an excellent chance of acceptance, provided they can focus the political, economic and social issues. We welcome them to submit their proposals. We forsee the possibility of diversifying our feature package by representing writers and feature creators on more one-shot projects."

CONTINUUM BROADCASTING NETWORK/CONTINUUM NEWS FEATURES, INC., Suite 1670, 208 East 51 St., New York NY 10022. (212)713-5165 and (415)541-5032 (San Francisco). Executive Editor: Donald J. Fass. Associate Editor: Stephen Vaughn. Broadcast Feature Producer: Deanna Baron. 60% freelance written. 45% written by writers on contract; 5% freelance written by writers on a one-time basis. Buys 300 features/interviews/year. Works with 25-30 previously unpublished writers annually. Syndicates to newspapers and radio. Computer printout submissions acceptable; no dot-matrix. Buys all rights. Writer's guidelines for business size SAE and 2 first-class stamps. Reports in 5 weeks.

Needs: Newspaper columns (all kinds of weekly regular features for newspapers); radio broadcast material (90-second and 2½-minute regular daily radio features: lifestyle, comedy, music and interview—scripts as well as taped features); 30-minute and 60-minute specials. One-shot features for radio only-for 30- and 60-minute specials; scripts and completed productions. Query with 1 or 2 clips of published work only and 1 page summary on proposed articles. Demo tape and/or full script for broadcast; not necessary to query on tapes, but return postage must be provided. Pays 25-50% commission or $25-175, depending on length. Offers no additional payment for photos accompanying ms. Currently syndicates The World of Melvin Belli, Getting It Together (weekly youth-oriented music and lifestyle column); Keeping Fit (daily series); Rockweek and Backstage (weekly entertainment series); On Bleecker Street (weekly music/interview series).

Tips: "We seek a unique or contemporary concept with broad appeal that can be sustained indefinitely and for which the writer already has at least some backlog. Unique health, fitness, lifestyle, music, entertainment and trivia material will be emphasized, with a decrease in pop psychology, child psychology, history, seniors and parenting material."

COPLEY NEWS SERVICE, Box 190, San Diego CA 92112. (619)293-1818. Editorial Director: Nanette Wiser. Buys 85% of work from contracted stringers; 15% from freelancers on a one-time basis. Offers 200 features/week. Sells to magazines, newspapers, radio. Computer printout submissions OK; no dot-matrix. Reports in 1-2 months. Buys all rights or second serial (reprint) rights (sometimes).

Needs: Fillers, magazine columns, magazine features, newspaper columns and newspaper features. Subjects include interior design, outdoor recreation, fashion, antiques, real estate, pets and gardening. Buys one-shot and articles series. Query with clips of published work. Pays $50-100 flat rate or $400 salary/month.

‡CREATIVE SYNDICATION SERVICES, Box 40, Eureka MO 63025. (314)938-9116. FAX (314)343-0966. Editor: Debra Holly. 10% written by writers on contract; 50% freelance written by writers on a one-time basis. Syndicates to magazines, newspapers and radio. Query for electronic submissions. Computer printout submissions OK. Reports in 1 month. Buys all rights. Currently syndicates The Weekend Workshop, by Ed Baldwin; and Woodcrafting, by Ed Baldwin (woodworking).

CREATORS SYNDICATE, INC., 1554 S. Sepulveda Blvd. Los Angeles CA 90025. (213)477-2776. Estab. 1987. Syndicates to newspapers. Computer printout submissions OK. Reports in 2 months. Buys negotiable rights. Reports in 2 months. Writer's guidelines for SASE.

Needs: Newspaper columns and features. Query with clips of published work or submit complete ms. Author's percentage: 50%. Currently syndicates Ann Landers (advice) B.C. (comic strip) and Herblock (editorial cartoon).

Tips: "Syndication is very competitive. Writing regularly for your local newspaper is a good start."

For information on setting your freelance fees, see How Much Should I Charge? in the Business of Writing section.

THE CRICKET LETTER, INC., Box 527, Ardmore PA 19003. (215)789-2480. Editor: J.D. Krickett. 10% written by writers on contract; 10% freelance written by writers on a one-time basis. Works with 2-3 previously unpublished writers annually. Syndicates to trade magazines and newspapers. Computer printout submissions acceptable; prefers letter-quality. Reports in 3 weeks. Buys all rights.

Needs: Magazine columns, magazine features, newspaper columns, newspaper features and news items— all tax and financial-oriented (700-1,500 words); newspaper columns, features and news items directed to small business. Query with clips of published work. Pays $50-500. Currently syndicates Hobby/Business, by Mark E. Battersby (tax and financial); Farm Taxes, by various authors; and Small Business Taxes, by Mark E. Battersby.

CROWN SYNDICATE, INC., Box 99126, Seattle WA 98199. President: L.M. Boyd. Buys countless trivia items and cartoon and panel gag lines. Syndicates to newspapers, radio. Reports in 1 month. Buys first North American serial rights. Free writer's guidelines.

Needs: Filler material used weekly, items for trivia column, gaglines for specialty comic strip (format guidelines sent on request). Pays $1-5/item, depending on how it's used, i.e., trivia or filler service or comic strip. Offers no additional payment for photos accompanying ms. Currently syndicates puzzle panels and comic strips.

EDITORIAL CONSULTANT SERVICE, Box 524, West Hempstead NY 11552. Editorial Director: Arthur A. Ingoglia. 40% written by writers on contract; 25% freelance written by writers on a one-time basis. "We work with 75 writers in the U.S. and Canada." Previously published writers only. Adds about 5 new columnists/ year. Syndicates material to an average of 60 newspapers, magazines, automotive trade and consumer publications, and radio stations with circulation of 50,000-575,000. Computer printout submissions acceptable; letter-quality submissions preferred. Buys all rights. Writer's guidelines for #10 SASE. Reports in 3 weeks.

Needs: Magazine and newspaper columns and features, news items and radio broadcast material. Prefers carefully documented material with automotive slant. Also considers automotive trade features. Will consider article series. No horoscope, child care, lovelorn or pet care. Query. Author's percentage varies; usually averages 50%. Additional payment for 8x10 b&w and color photos accepted with ms. Submit 2-3 columns. Currently syndicates Let's Talk About Your Car, by R. Hite.

Tips: "Emphasis is placed on articles and columns with an automotive slant. We prefer consumer-oriented features, i.e., how to save money on your car, what every woman should know about her car, how to get more miles per gallon, etc."

EDITORS PRESS SERVICE, INC., 330 West 42nd St., New York NY 10036. (212)563-2252. FAX (212)563-2517. Editor: Hilda Marbán 2% written by writers on contract. "Editors Press primarily acts as the foreign sales representative for various U.S. based newspaper syndicates. We represent for sale outside the continental United States and Canada only the material they produce. The little in-house we have is Spanish." Syndicates to foreign language newspapers and magazine outside the United States. Reports in 2 weeks. Free writer's guidelines.

Needs: We handle only material that has already been syndicted by the syndicates we represent. Query only.

Tips: "We recommend that a writer contact the established syndicates who operate within the United States before getting in touch with us. Syndicates are merging, and so there is less of a market in newspaper syndication than there was twenty years ago. Also, the newspapers have a limited budget and amount of space for syndicated features. A new author would be wise to take this into account, and when developing a feature, should try to work toward developing something that has a distinctive appeal which will give it an edge over the competition."

‡FEATURE ENTERPRISES, Box 55625, Birmingham AL 35255. (205)939-3303. Editor: Maury M. Breecher. 10% written by writers on contract; 90% freelance written by writers on a one-time basis. Syndicates 100 mss/year. Works with 10-20 previously unpublished writers/year. Syndicates to magazines and newspapers. Query for electronic submissions. Reports in 1 month. Buys first North American serial rights and second serial (reprint) rights. Writer's guidelines for $1.

Needs: Currently syndicates On Health, by Maury Brechder (medicine/health); and Kinship Korner, by Kimberly Amber (family relationships). Payment on 50/50 standard syndicate split.

Tips: "More intense push on popular psychology and medical breakthroughs."

FICTION NETWORK, Box 5651, San Francisco CA 94101. (415)391-6610. Editor: Jay Schaefer. 100% freelance written by writers on a one-time basis. Syndicates fiction to newspapers and regional magazines. Buys 100 features/year. Works with 25 previously unpublished writers annually. Computer printout submissions acceptable; letter-quality only. Reports in 3 months. Buys first serial rights. Sample catalog of syndicated stories for $5; writer's guidelines SAE with 1 first class stamp.

Needs: All types of fiction (particularly holiday) under 2,000 words. "We specialize in quality literature." Submit complete ms; do not send summaries or ideas. "Send one manuscript at a time; do not send second until you receive a response to the first." Pays 50% commission. Syndicates short fiction only; authors include

Alice Adams, Ann Beattie, Max Apple, Andre Dubus, Bobbie Ann Mason, Joyce Carol Oates and others.
Tips: "We seek and encourage previously unpublished authors. Keep stories short, fast-paced and interesting. We need short-short stories under 1,000 words."

FOTOPRESS, INDEPENDENT NEWS SERVICE INTERNATIONAL, Box 1268, Station Q, Toronto, Ontario M4T 2P4 Canada. 50% written by writers on contract; 25% freelance written by writers on a one-time basis. Works with 30% previously unpublished writers. Syndicates to domestic and international magazines, newspapers, radio, TV stations and motion picture industry. Computer printout submissions acceptable; prefers letter-quality. Reports in 6 weeks. Buys variable rights. Writer's guidelines for $3 in IRCs.
Needs: Fillers, magazine columns, magazine features, newspaper columns, newspaper features, news items, radio broadcast material, documentary, travel and art. Buys one-shot and article series for international politics, scientists, celebrities and religious leaders. Query or submit complete ms. Pays 50-75% author's percentage. Offers $5-150 for accompanying ms.
Tips: "We need all subjects from 500-3,000 words. Photos are purchased with or without features. All writers are regarded respectfully—their success is our success."

(GABRIEL) GRAPHICS NEWS BUREAU, Box 38, Madison Square Station, New York NY 10010. (212)254-8863. Editor: J. G. Bumberg. 25% freelance written by writers on contract; 50% freelance written by writers on one-time basis. Syndicates to weeklies (selected) and small dailies. Computer printout submissions OK; prefers letter-quality. Reports in 1 month. Buys all rights for clients, packages. Writer's guidelines for SASE.
Needs: Fillers, magazine features, newspaper columns and features and news items for PR clients custom packages. Pays 15% from client. Also has consulting services in communicaltions/graphics/management.

GENERAL NEWS SYNDICATE, 147 W. 42nd St., New York NY 10036. (212)221-0043. 25% written by writers on contract; 12% freelance written by writers on a one-time basis. Works with 12 writers/year; average of 5 previously unpublished writers annually. Syndicates to an average of 12 newspaper and radio outlets averaging 20 million circulation; buys theatre and show business people columns (mostly New York theatre pieces). Computer printout submissions acceptable; prefers letter-quality. Reports on accepted material in 3 weeks. Buys one-time rights. Writer's guidelines for #10 SASE.
Needs: Entertainment-related material.
Tips: Looking for "shorter copy (250-500 words)."

DAVE GOODWIN & ASSOCIATES, Drawer 54-6661, Surfside FL 33154. FAX (305)531-5490. Editor: Dave Goodwin. 70% written by writers on contract; 10% freelance written by writers on a one-time basis. Buys about 25 features a year from freelancers. Works with 2 previously unpublished writers annually. Rights purchased vary with author and material. May buy first rights or second serial (reprint) rights or simultaneous rights. Will handle copyrighted material. Query for electronic submissions. Computer printout submissions acceptable; prefers letter-quality. Query or submit complete ms. Reports in 3 weeks.
Nonfiction: "Money-saving information for consumers: how to save on home expenses; auto, medical, drug, insurance, boat, business items, etc." Buys article series on brief, practical, down-to-earth items for consumer use or knowledge. Rarely buys single features. Currently handling Insurance for Consumers. Length: 300-5,000 words. Pays 50% on publication. Submit 2-3 columns.

HERITAGE FEATURES SYNDICATE, 214 Massachusetts Ave. NE, Washington DC 20002. (202)543-0440. Managing Editor: Andy Seamans. 99% written by writers on contract; 1% freelance written by writers on one-time basis. Buys 3 columns/year. Works with 2-3 previously unpublished writers annually. Syndicates to over 150 newspapers with circulations ranging from 2,000 to 630,000. Works with previously published writers. Computer printout submissions acceptable; prefers letter-quality. Buys first North American serial rights. Reports in 3 weeks.
Needs: Newspaper columns (practically all material is done by regular columnists). One-shot features. "We purchase 750-800 word columns on political, economic and related subjects." Query. "SASE a must." Pays $50 maximum. Currently syndicates 10 columnists, including A Minority View, by Walter E. Williams; Fed Up, by Don Feder; and The Answer Man, by Andy Seamans.
Tips: "We may be going to op-ed page material exclusively."

‡HISPANIC LINK NEWS SERVICE, 1420 N St. NW, Washington DC 20005. (202)234-0280. Editor/Publisher: Charles A. Ericksen. 50% freelance written by writers on contract; 50% freelance written by writers on a one-time basis. Buys 156 columns and features/year. Works with 50 writers/year; 5 previously unpublished writers. Syndicates to 200 newspapers and magazines with circulations ranging from 5,000 to 300,000. Computer printout submissions acceptable; prefers letter-quality. Reports in 2 weeks. Buys second serial (reprint) or negotiable rights. Free writer's guidelines.
Needs: Magazine columns, magazine features, newspaper columns, newspaper features. One-shot features and article series. "We prefer 650-700 word op/ed or features geared to a general national audience, but focus on issue or subject of particular interest to Hispanic Americans. Some longer pieces accepted occasion-

ally." Query or submit complete ms. Pays $25-150. Currently syndicates Hispanic Link, by various authors (opinion and/or feature columns).

Tips: "This year we would especially like to get topical material and vignettes relating to Hispanic presence and progress in the United States. Provide insights on Hispanic experience geared to a general audience. Eighty-five to 90 percent of the columns we accept are authored by Hispanics; the Link presents Hispanic viewpoints, and showcases Hispanic writing talent to its 200 subscribing newspapers and magazines. Copy should be submitted in English. We syndicate in English and Spanish."

HOLLYWOOD INSIDE SYNDICATE, Box 49957, Los Angeles CA 90049. (714)678-6237. Editor: John Austin. 10% written by writers on contract; 40% freelance written by writers on a one-time basis. Purchases entertainment-oriented mss for syndication to newspapers in San Francisco, Philadelphia, Detroit, Montreal, London, Sydney, Manila, South Africa, etc. Works with 2-3 previously unpublished writers annually. Previously published submissions OK, if published in the U.S. and Canada only. Computer printout submissions acceptable; prefers letter-quality. Reports in 6 weeks. Negotiates for first rights or second serial (reprint) rights.

Needs: News items (column items concerning entertainment—motion picture—personalities and jet setters for syndicated column; 750-800 words). Also considers series of 1,500-word articles; "suggest descriptive query first. We are also looking for off-beat travel pieces (with pictures) but not on areas covered extensively in the Sunday supplements. We can always use pieces on 'freighter' travel. Not luxury cruise liners but lower cost cruises. We also syndicate nonfiction book subjects—sex, travel, etc., to overseas markets. No fiction. Must have b&w photo with submissions if possible." Also require 1,500 word celebrity profiles on internationally recognized celebrities." Query or submit complete ms. Pay negotiable. Currently syndicates Books of the Week column.

Tips: "Study the entertainment pages of Sunday (and daily) newspapers to see the type of specialized material we deal in. Perhaps we are different from other syndicates, but we deal with celebrities. No 'I' journalism such as 'when I spoke to Cloris Leachman.' Many freelancers submit material from the 'dinner theatre' and summer stock circuit of 'gossip type' items from what they have observed about the 'stars' or featured players in these productions—how they act off stage, who they romance, etc. We use this material."

‡HYDE PARK MEDIA, Chicago Metro News Services, Suite 2, 1314 Howard St., Chicago IL 60626. (312)274-3337. Editor: Anthony DeBartolo. 10% freelance written by writers on a one-time basis. Syndicates to Chicago area newspapers and magazines. Query for electronic submissions. Computer printout submissions acceptable; prefers letter-quality. Reports in 2 weeks. Buys first and second serial rights.

Needs: Unusual, off-beat magazine features (1,500-3,000 words) and newspaper features with a local hook (750-1,500 words). Buys single (one-shot) features only. Send complete manuscript and SASE. No phone queries. Pays 50% commission on sale.

Tips: "Please read 'Needs' graph before sending material. Why waste anyone's time?"

INTERNATIONAL PHOTO NEWS, Box 2405, West Palm Beach FL 33402. (305)793-3424. Editor: Elliott Kravetz. 10% written by freelance writers under contract. Buys 52 features/year. Works with 25 previously unpublished writers/year. Syndicates to newspapers. Query for electronic submissions. Computer printout submissions OK. Reports in 1 week. Buys second serial (reprint) rights. Writer's guidelines for SASE.

Needs: Magazine columns and features (celebrity), newspaper columns and features (political or celebrity), news items (political). Buys one-shot features. Query with clips of published work. Pays 50% author's percentage. Pays $5 for photos accepted with ms. Currently syndicates Celebrity Interview, by Jay and Elliott Kravetz.

Tips: "Go after celebrities who are on the cover on major magazines."

INTERPRESS OF LONDON AND NEW YORK, 400 Madison Ave., New York NY 10017. (212)832-2839. Editor: Jeffrey Blyth. 50% freelance written by writers on contract; 50% freelance written by writers on a one-time basis. Works with 3-6 previously unpublished writers annually. Buys British and European rights mostly, but can handle world rights. Will consider photocopied submissions. Previously published submissions OK "for overseas." Computer printout submissions acceptable; prefers letter-quality. Pays on publication or agreement of sale. Reports immediately or as soon as practicable.

Needs: "Unusual nonfiction stories and photos for British and European press. Picture stories, for example, on such 'Americana' as a five-year-old evangelist; the 800-pound 'con-man'; the nude-male calendar; tallest girl in the world; interviews with pop celebrities such as Yoko Ono, Michael Jackson, Bill Cosby, Tom Selleck, Cher, Priscilla Presley, Cheryl Tiegs, Eddie Murphy, Liza Minelli, also news of stars on such shows as 'Dynasty'/'Dallas'; cult subjects such as voodoo, college fads, anything amusing or offbeat. Extracts from books such as Earl Wilson's *Show Business Laid Bare*, inside-Hollywood type series ('Secrets of the Stuntmen'). Real life adventure dramas ('Three Months in an Open Boat,' 'The Air Crash Cannibals of the Andes'). No length limits—short or long, but not too long. Query or submit complete ms. Payment varies; depending on whether material is original, or world rights. Pays top rates, up to several thousand dollars, for exclusive material."

Photos: Purchased with or without features. Captions required. Standard size prints. Pay $50-100, but no limit on exclusive material.

Tips: "Be alert to the unusual story in your area—the sort that interests the American tabloids (and also the European press)."

‡JEWISH TELEGRAPHIC AGENCY, 330 7th Ave., New York NY 10001-5010. (212)643-1890. Editor: Mark Joffe. Managing Editor: Elli Wohlgelernter. 40% written by writers on contract; 40% freelance written by writers on a one-time basis. Buys 40 features/year. Syndicates to newspapers. Query for electronic submissions. Computer printout submissions OK. Submissions with SASE will not be returned. Reports in 2 months. Buys second serial (reprint) rights.
Needs: Fillers, magazine features, newspaper features and news items. "Anything of Jewish interest, 500-1,000 words. Can be first-person or op-ed; news stories should be balanced." Buys one-shot features and article series. Submit complete ms. Pays $25-50-75 flat rate. Currently syndicates American News Report, by Ben Gallob; and Commentary, by Rabbi Marc Tanenbaum.
Tips: "Simply put, good writing will get published. Anything of Jewish interest, nationally or worldwide, will be considered. I'm looking for good stories on whatever trends are happening in Jewish life."

JSA PUBLICATIONS, Box 37175, Oak Park MI 48237. (313)546-9123. Editor: Joseph S. Ajlouny. 20% of writing bought from freelancers under contract; 20% from freelancers writing on one-time basis. "We purchase 20-40 illustrations per year. We use charts and graphs as well as contemporary/entertainment-oriented columnists." Syndicates to magazines and weekly newspapers. Query for electronic submissions. Computer printout submissions OK; prefers letter-quality. Reports in 1 month. Buys all rights. Writer's guidelines for SASE.
Needs: Fiction (short, contemporary), fillers (illustrations especially), magazine columns, magazine features, comic strips and panels. Buys single features and article series. Query with clips of published work. Pays flat rate of $60-500. Pays $100-300 for photos accepted with ms. Currently syndicates Party Ranks, by Joe Stuart and Mike Pascale (comic strip). Travel features and nonfiction articles for trade publications also needed; query first.

KING FEATURES SYNDICATE, INC., 235 E. 45th St., New York NY 10017. (212)455-4000. Editorial Director: Dennis R. Allen. Syndicates material to newspapers. Submit brief cover letter with samples of column or comic proposal. Reports in 1 month by letter.
Needs: Newspaper features, comics, political cartoons and columns. Pays revenue commission percentage. Special single-article opportunity is King Features Select, a weekly one-shot service. Buys world rights to celebrity profiles, off-beat lifestyle and consumer pieces. Query with SASE to Sue Jarzyk for Select one-shot articles.
Tips: "Be brief, thoughtful and offer some evidence that the feature proposal is viable. Read newspapers to find out what already is out there. Don't try to buck established columns which newspapers would be reluctant to replace with new and untried material. We're always looking for new ideas. Please send *copies* of your work to us. Do not send original material. All submissions *must* have SASE."

LOS ANGELES TIMES SYNDICATE, Times Mirror Square, Los Angeles CA 90053. Vice President/Editor: Don Michel. Special Articles Editor: Dan O'Toole. Syndicates to U.S. and worldwide markets. Usually buys first North American serial rights and world rights, but rights purchased can vary. Submit seasonal material six weeks in advance. Material ranges from 800-2,000 words.
Needs: Reviews continuing columns and comic strips for U.S. and foreign markets. Send columns and comic strips to Don Michel. Also reviews single articles, series, magazine reprints, and book serials. Send these submissions to Dan O'Toole. Send complete mss. Pays 50% commission. Currently syndicates Art Buchwald, Dr. Henry Kissinger, Dr. Jeane Kirkpatrick, William Pfaff, Paul Conrad and Lee Iacocca.
Tips: "We're dealing with fewer undiscovered writers but still do review material."

MINORITY FEATURES SYNDICATE, Box 421, Farrell PA 16146. (412)342-5300. Editor: Merry Frable. Reports in 5 weeks. 60% written by freelance writers on contract; 40% freelance written by writers on a one-time basis. Works with 500 previously unpublished writers annually. Buys first North American serial rights. Computer printout submissions acceptable; no dot-matrix. Reports in 5 weeks. Writer's guidelines for #10 SAE with 2 first class stamps.
Needs: Fillers, magazine features, newspaper features. Also needs comic book writers for Bill Murray Productions. Query with published clips. Pays open commission. Pays $25 minimum for photos. Currently syndicates Sonny Boy, Those Browns and The Candyman, by Bill Murray (newspaper features).
Tips: "We are getting in the comic book market. Writers should write for guidelines. Also looking for family-style humor."

NATIONAL NEWS BUREAU, 1318 Chancellor St., Philadelphia PA 19107. (215)546-8088. Editor: Harry Jay Katz. "We work with more than 200 writers and buy over 1,000 stories per year." Syndicates to more than 500 publications. Reports in 2 weeks. Buys all rights. Writer's guidelines for 9x12 SAE and 3 first class stamps.
Needs: Newspaper features; "we do many reviews and celebrity interviews. Only original, assigned material." One-shot features and article series; film reviews, etc. Query with clips. Pays $5-200 flat rate. Offers $5-200 additional payment for photos accompanying ms.

NEW YORK TIMES SYNDICATION SALES CORP., 130 Fifth Ave., New York NY 10011. (212)645-3000. Senior Vice President/Editorial Director: Paula Reichler. Syndicates numerous one-shot articles. Buys first serial rights, first North American serial rights, one-time rights, second serial (reprint) rights, or all rights. Computer printout submissions acceptable; no dot-matrix.

Needs: Wants magazine and newspaper features; magazine and newspaper columns. "On syndicated articles, payment to author is varied. We only consider articles that have been previously published. Send tearsheets of articles published." Submit approximately 4 samples of articles, 12 samples of columns. Photos are welcome with articles.

Tips: "Topics should cover universal markets and either be by a well-known writer or have an off-beat quality. Quizzes are welcomed if well researched."

‡NEWS USA INC., 1199 National Press Bldg., Washington DC 20045. (202)682-2400. Editor: Dennis Williams. 50% written by writers on contract; 50% freelance written by writers on a one-time basis. Buys 75 mss/month. Works with 50 previously unpublished writers/year. Syndicates to U.S. newspapers. Query for electronic submissions. Computer printout submissions OK. Submissions with SASE will not be returned. "Takes staff time." Reports in 1 week. Buys all rights.

Needs: Fillers, newspaper columns, newspaper features, news items, editorial cartoons and graphics. Buys one-shot features and article series. Health, seniors and consumer. "We consider all features, documents etc." Query with clips of published work or submit complete ms. Pays $100/item flat rate. Pays $100 for photos. Currently syndicates Consumer Watch, by Esther Peterson (consumer); Your Medicines, by Todd Dankmyer (health) and Bank Notes, by Virginia Stafford (money).

NEWSPAPER ENTERPRISE ASSOCIATION, INC., 200 Park Ave., New York NY 10166. (212)557-5870/(212)692-3700. Editorial Director: David Hendin. Director, International Newspaper Operations: Sidney Goldberg. Executive Editor: D.L. Drake. Director of Comics: Sarah Gillespie. 100% written by writers on contract. "We provide a comprehensive package of features to mostly small- and medium-sized newspapers." Computer printout submission acceptable; prefers letter-quality to dot-matrix. Reports in 6 weeks. Buys all rights.

Needs: "Any column we purchase must fill a need in our feature lineup and must have appeal for a wide variety of people in all parts of the country. We are most interested in lively writing. We are also interested in features that are not merely copies of other features already on the market. The writer must know his or her subject. Any writer who has a feature that meets all of those requirements should send a few copies of the feature to us, along with his or her plans for the column and some background material on the writer." Current columnists include Bob Walters, Bob Wagman, Chuck Stone, Dr. Peter Gott, Tom Tiede, Ben Wattenberg and William Rusher. Current comics include Born Loser, Frank & Ernest, Eek & Meek, Kit 'n' Carlyle, Bugs Bunny, Berry's World, Arlo and Janis, and Snafu.

Tips: "We get enormous numbers of proposals for first person columns—slice of life material with lots of anecdotes. While many of these columns are big successes in local newspapers, it's been our experience that they are extremely difficult to sell nationally. Most papers seem to prefer to buy this sort of column from a talented local writer."

NORTH AMERICA SYNDICATE, (formerly News America Syndicate), 235 E. 45th St., New York NY 10017. See King Features Syndicate.

‡PACHECO AUTOMOTIVE NEWS SERVICE, Box 6691, Concord CA 94524. (415)228-7821. Editor: Bob Hagin. 100% written by writers on contract. Buys 1 feature/month. Syndicates to 45 U.S. and Canadian daily papers.

Nonfiction: Newspaper features—auto-related only. Currently syndicates Auto Feature, Collectible Car, Road Test, Motor Sports.

ROYAL FEATURES, Box 58174, Houston TX 77258. (713)280-0777. Executive Director: Fay W. Henry. 80% written by writers on contract; 10% freelance written by writers on one-time basis. Syndicates to magazines and newspapers. Computer printout submissions OK; no dot-matrix. Reports in 2 months. Buys all rights or first North American serial rights.

Needs: Magazine and newspaper columns and features. Buys one-shot features and article series. Query with or without published clips. Send SASE with unsolicited queries or materials. Pays authors percentage, 40-60%.

SAN FRANCISCO STYLE INTERNATIONAL, 20 San Antonio Place, San Francisco CA 94133. (415)788-6589. Editor: Christina Tom. 50% of material is bought from freelancers under contract; 10% from freelancers writing on one-time basis. Works regularly with 6-10 writers. Syndicates to newspapers, magazines and radio. Query for electronic submissions. Computer printout submissions OK; prefers letter-quality. Reports in 6 weeks. Buys all rights. Writer's guidelines for $1.

NEW! WRITER'S MARKET ON DISK!

Now you can let your PC — instead of your fingers — do the walking through the pages of 1990 Writer's Market *to find markets that are just right for you!*

1990 WRITER'S MARKET® INFOBASE

Now you can use your IBM-compatible personal computer and 1990 Writer's Market Infobase to quickly and easily search for writing markets by word count, category, pay rates, terms ... the possibilities are phenomenal!

Here's how Writer's Market Infobase can help you sell more of what you write:

Q.What does the Writer's Market Infobase package include?

A.You'll get a set of disks — one set with all the current *1990 Writer's Market* listing information and one set (called "Previews") that provides text retrieval, search, and sort capabilities.   You'll also receive a complete, easy-to-understand user's manual, an on-screen tutorial, and a quick reference card to acquaint you with the program.

Q.What can I use Writer's Market Infobase for?

A.This package offers a sophisticated search program that lets you find anything in the database, retrieve it, and pull together related information. For instance, you can search for "baseball" and get all the *Writer's Market* listings in which the word "baseball" appears. Better than that is the ability of the software to search for specific phrases, word lengths, and payment

(over)

Don't miss this chance to spend more time writing and less time searching. Use the coupon below to order your package today, or for more information, call 1-800-289-0963!

- -

To order, drop this postpaid card in the mail.

☐ **Yes!** I want the new 1990 Writer's Market® Infobase! Please send me:

Writer's Market Infobase/Previews @ $120 per package*

____ (#01001) 5¼" 360 K
____ (#01002) 5¼" 1.2 MB
____ (#01003) 3½" 720 K
____ (#01004) 3½" 1.4 MB

Writer's Market Infobase/Views @ $502.50 per package**

____ (#01005) 5¼" 360 K
____ (#01006) 5¼" 1.2 MB
____ (#01007) 3½" 720 K
____ (#01008) 3½" 1.4 MB

____ (#10108) 1990 Writer's Market @ $26.95***

___Payment enclosed (Slip this card and your payment into an envelope)
___Please charge my: ___Visa ___MasterCard

Account #_____ Exp. Date_____

Signature_____

Name_____

Address_____

City_____

State_____Zip_____

* $115.00 plus $5.00 postage & handling
** $495.00 plus $7.50 postage & handling
*** $23.95 plus $3.00 postage & handling
Ohio residents add 5½% sales tax

Writer's Digest Books

1507 Dana Avenue
Cincinnati, OH 45207

5444

ranges. You also can conduct multiple searches at one time. For instance, say you want all the magazines about baseball that are located in California and offer additional payment for photos. Or all the baseball magazines located in California that buy one-time or first North American serial rights. Or all the baseball magazines in California except those that are in San Diego. You can do all this, as well as print out selected text on your computer printer.

Q.How computer literate do I need to be in order to use this package?

A.If you are comfortable with any word processing program, you'll be able to load Writer's Market Infobase and do the on-screen tutorial in about 20 minutes. Once you've familiarized yourself with the system, it's as easy to access as your favorite word processing program.

Q.How much is 1990 Writer's Market Infobase, and will I really get my money out of it?

A.1990 Writer's Market Infobase (with the Previews software), is $115.00, and, like your personal computer, will pay for itself again and again by saving you valuable time that you can use to write, instead of search. It also makes your freelancing more efficient. With one search, you can find markets you may not have noticed otherwise and make more sales. Also, the Previews software is only a one-time charge. In the future, all you'll buy each year is an updated Writer's Market disk.

If you use *Writer's Market* daily, or even weekly, you might want to consider the "upgraded" version of Writer's Market Infobase. It's called "Views" and gives you the ability to update and add your own information to the database (like adding new markets featured in the monthly *Writer's Digest* magazine, or making changes when a market's address or contact name changes); to create "views" or files of information that you'll use often (such as grouping together listings you refer to frequently); and to integrate word processing — use your own word processing package with the Views package. The cost for this version is $495.00 — which is the cost of the Views package alone — so you're actually getting the Writer's Market Infobase FREE!

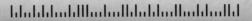

WOULD YOU USE THE SAME CALENDAR YEAR AFTER YEAR?

Of course not! If you scheduled your appointments using last year's calendar, you'd risk missing important meetings and deadlines, so you keep up-to-date with a new calendar each year. Just like your calendar, *Writer's Market®* changes every year, too. Many of the editors move or get promoted, rates of pay increase, and even editorial needs change from the previous year. You can't afford to use an out-of-date book to plan your marketing efforts!

So save yourself the frustration of getting manuscripts returned in the mail, stamped MOVED: ADDRESS UNKNOWN. And of NOT submitting your work to new listings because you don't know they exist. **Make sure you have the most current writing and marketing information by ordering** *1991 Writer's Market* **today.** All you have to do is complete the attached post card and return it with your payment or charge card information. Order now, and there's one thing that won't change from your *1990 Writer's Market*—the price! That's right, we'll send you the 1991 edition for just $23.95. *1991 Writer's Market* will be published and ready for shipment in September 1990.

Let an old acquaintance be forgot, and toast the new edition of *Writer's Market*. Order today!

(See other side for more new market books to help you get published)

- -

GREAT NEWS FOR WRITERS!

3 NEW Market Books to Help You Get Published!

1990 Novel & Short Story Writer's Market (Formerly Fiction Writer's Market)
Edited by Robin Gee
Now in paperback, with all the facts and information you need to get your short stories and novels published. Includes 1,900 detailed listings of commercial books and magazine publishers, small presses, and little/literary magazines, PLUS advice on/listings of agents who handle fiction.
672 pages/$18.95, paperback (available February, 1990)

1990 Children's Writer's & Illustrator's Market
Edited by Connie Eidenier
Now in its second year, this annual is even bigger and better with the addition of market listings for audiovisual aids, songs, coloring books, comic books, and puzzles. Again includes markets for writing by children. Includes a "Business of Writing & Illustrating" article, subject and age-level indexes, and many other features to help you sell in this lucrative market.
256 pages/$15.95, paperback (available February, 1990)

1990 Humor & Cartoon Markets
Edited by Bob Staake
This first edition is filled with 600 listings of magazine, newsletter, greeting card, and comic book publishers, plus articles on the "Business of Freelancing." You'll find out where and how to sell your gags, cartoons, and funny articles, stories, and songs, and then find yourself laughing all the way to the bank!
256 pages/$15.95, paperback (available February, 1990)

Use coupon on other side to order your copies today!

Needs: Magazine columns and features, newspaper columns and features, fiction, cartoons, puzzles, games and juvenile activities. Purchases one-shot features and articles series. Submit complete ms. Pays author's percentage of 50%; books: 15% for US and Canada, 20% foreign sales commission. 50% additional payment for photos.

SINGER MEDIA CORPORATION, 3164 Tyler Ave., Anaheim CA 92801. (714)527-5650. Editors: Kurt Singer and Donna Hollingshead. 25% written by writers on contract; 25% freelance written by writers on a one-time basis. Syndicates to magazines, newspapers, cassettes and book publishers. Computer printout submissions acceptable; prefers letter-quality. Reports in 3 weeks. Rights negotiable, world rights preferred. Writer's guidelines for #10 SAE and $1.
Needs: Short stories, crosswords, puzzles, quizzes, interviews, entertainment and psychology features, cartoons, books for serialization and foreign reprints. Syndicates one-shot features and article series on celebrities. Query with clips of published work or submit complete ms. Pays 50% author's percentage. Currently syndicates Solve a Crime, by B. Gordon (mystery puzzle) and Hollywood Gossip, by N. Carr (entertainment).
Tips: "Good interviews with celebrities, men/women relations, business and real estate features have a good chance with us. Aim at world distribution and therefore have a universal approach."

‡THE SOUTHAM SYNDICATE, 20 Yorks Mills Rd., Toronto, Ontario M2P 2C2 Canada. (416)222-8000. Editor: Jeffrey McBain. 70% written by writers on contract; 5% freelance written by writers on a one-time basis. Buys 40 features/year. Works with 3-4 previously unpublished writers/year. Syndicates to newspapers. Query for electronic submissions. Computer printout submissions OK. Reports in 2 months. Buys Canadian rights.
Needs: Fillers (400-500 words), newspaper columns (700-800 words, self help) and newpaper features (1,000 words). Buys one-shot features and article series. Query with clips of published work. Pays 50% author's percentage. Currently syndicates Claire Hoy, Bill Fox, William Johnson and Ben Wicks.

THE SPELMAN SYNDICATE, INC., 26941 Pebblestone, Southfield MI 48034. (313)355-3686. Editor: Philip Spelman. Syndicates to newspapers and TV. Computer printout submissions OK. Reports in 1 month. Buys all rights.
Needs: Newspaper columns. Query only. Pays 50% author's percentage. Currently syndicates Easy Tax Tips.
Tips: "Get a column started in a small newspaper, develop a following and expand on your own until you become attractive to a syndicate."

SPORTS FEATURES SYNDICATE/WORLD FEATURES SYNDICATE, 1005 Mulberry, Marlton NJ 08053. (609)983-7688. Editor: Ronald A. Sataloff. 1-5% written by freelancers under contract; 1-5% freelance written by writers on one-time basis. Nearly all material is syndicated to daily newspapers and the Associated Press's supplemental sports wire. Computer printout submissions OK; no dot-matrix. Reports in 1 month. Buys all rights.
Needs: Currently syndicates Sports Lists, by staff; No Kidding?, by Karl Van Asselt; Mr. Music, by Jerry Osborne.
Tips: "No surprise—space is at a premium and one wishing to sell a column is at a disadvantage unless he is an expert in a chosen field and can relate that area of expertise in layman's language. Concentrate on features that take little space and that are helpful to the reader as well as interesting. *USA Today* has revolutionized newspapering in the sense that it is no longer a sin to be brief. That trend is here for a long time, and a writer should be aware of it. Papers are also moving toward more reader-oriented features, and those with an ability to make difficult subjects easy reading have an advantage."

TEENAGE CORNER, INC., 70-540 Gardenia Ct., Rancho Mirage CA 92270. President: David J. Lavin. Buys 122 items/year for use in newspapers. Submit complete ms. Reports in 1 week. Material is not copyrighted.
Needs: 500-word newspaper features. Pays $25.

TRIBUNE MEDIA SERVICES, 64 E Concord St., Orlando FL 32801. (407)839-5600. President: Robert S. Reed. Editor: Michael Argirion. Syndicates to newspapers. Reports in 1 month. Buys all rights, first North American serial rights or second serial (reprint) rights.
Needs: Newspaper columns, comic strips. Query with published clips. Currently syndicates the columns of Mike Royko, Bob Greene, Liz Smith, Andy Rooney and Marilyn Beck; and cartoons of Jeff MacNelly and Mike Peters.

‡UNITED CARTOONIST SYNDICATE, Box 7081, Corpus Christi TX 78415. (512)855-2480. Comic Editor: Pedro R. Moreno. 10% freelance written by writers on a one-time basis. Works with 24 cartoonists annually. Syndicates to newspapers, newsletters, magazines, books or book publishers, and licensing companies. Reports in 1 week on submissions. Simultaneous submissions OK. Guidelines $10. Also publishes the newsletter "Cartoonist's Progressive Report."

Needs: Newspaper features (comic panel and comic strips in a family entertainment slant). Purchases single (one-shot) features and article series. Will consider metaphysical, UFOs, and human- and animal-interest stories or articles. Query with published clips or 6-12 samples of unpublished artwork (reduced) or articles. Include SASE for their return. Pays author 40%. Additional payment for photos: $10-25. Currently syndicates Brother Simon and Lucus, by Pedro R. Moreno.
Tips: "We do not accept any material that deals with sex, or put-down material against anything or anybody."

UNITED MEDIA, 200 Park Ave., New York NY 10166. (212)692-3700. 100% written by writers on contract. Syndicates to newspapers. Computer printout submission acceptable; prefers letter-quality. Reports in 6 weeks. Writer's guidelines for #10 SAE and 1 first class stamp.
Needs: Newspaper columns and newspaper features. Query with photocopied clips of published work. "Authors under contract have negotiable terms." Currently syndicates Miss Manners, by Judith Martin (etiquette); Dr. Gott, by Peter Gott, M.D. (medical) and Supermarket Shopper, by Martin Sloane (coupon clipping advice), Jack Anderson and Dale van Atta (investigative reporting).
Tips: "We include tips in our guidelines. We buy very few of the hundreds of submissions we see monthly. We are looking for the different feature as opposed to new slants on established columns."

WASHINGTON POST WRITERS GROUP, 1150 15th St. NW, Washington DC 20071. (202)334-6375. Editor/General Manager: William B. Dickinson. Currently syndicates 31 features (columns and cartoons). A news syndicate which provides features for newspapers nationwide. Query for electronic submissions. Computer printout submissions OK. Responds in 1 week. Buys all rights. Free writer's guidelines.
Needs: Newspaper column (editorial, lifestyle, humor), and newspaper features (comic strips, political cartoons). Query with clips of published work. Pays combination of salary and percentage. Currently syndicates George F. Will columns (editorial); Ellen Goodman column (editorial).
Tips: "At this time, The Washington Post Writers Group will review editorial page and lifestyle page columns, as well as political cartoons and comic strips. Will not consider games, puzzles, or similar features. Send sample columns to the attention of William Dickinson, general manager. Send sample cartoons or comic strips (photocopies—no original artwork, please) to the attention of Al Leeds, sales manager. Enclose a SASE for the return and response."

WHITEGATE FEATURES SYNDICATE, 71 Faunce Dr., Providence RI 02906. (401)274-2149. Editor: Ed Isaac. Estab. 1988. Buys 100% of material from freelance writers. Syndicates to newspapers; planning to begin selling to magazines and radio. Query for electronic submissions. Reports in 3 months. Buys all rights.
Needs: Fiction for Sunday newspaper magazines; magazine columns and features, newspaper columns and features, cartoon strips. Buys one-shots and article series. Query with clips of published work. For cartoon strips, submit samples. Pays 50% author's percentage on columns. Additional payment for photos accepted with ms. Currently syndicates Indoor Gardening, by Jane Adler; Looking Great, by Gloria Lintermans and Strong Style, by Hope Strong; On Marriage and Divorce, by Dr. Melmyn Berke.
Tips: "Please aim for a topic that is fresh. Newspapers seem to want short text pieces, 400-800 words."

WORDS BY WIRE, Suite #24, 1500 Massachusetts Ave., Washington DC 20009. Editors: Kathleen Currie, Sara Lowen. 5% freelance written by writers on contract; 95% freelance written by writers on once-time basis. Buys about 200 articles/year; works with 150 writers. Works with 25-50 previously unpublished writers/year. Query for electronic submissions. Computer printout submissions OK; no dot-matrix. Reports in 2 months. Buys newspaper syndication rights. Writer's guidelines for SASE.
Needs: Magazine features, newspaper features and op-ed columns. Buys one-shot features. Query with clips of published work or submit complete ms. Pays author's percentage 50%. Currently syndicates Political Commentary by Mark Shields; Essays, by André Codrescu.
Tips: "We are looking for original offbeat features on breaking trends for such sections as Arts, Entertainment, Food, Style, Travel Commentaries and stories. No first-person, sports or business."

Other Syndicates

The following firms did not return a verification to update an existing listing by press time.

AP Newsfeatures	News Flash International Inc.	United Feature Syndicate (see
Chronicle Features	Syndicated News Service	United Media)
First Draft	Syndicated Writers & Artists	Universal Press Syndicate
Interstate News Service	Inc.	

The following listings were deleted after the 1989 *Writer's Market* because the firm asked to be deleted, does not need freelance submissions or could not be contacted.

Didato Associates (asked to be deleted)	Mercury Syndications (unable to contact)	Walnut Press (no longer accepting freelance submissions)

Greeting Card Publishers

Industry leaders predict Americans will spend an estimated $3.9 billion buying 7.1 billion greeting cards this year, including 2.3 billion Christmas cards, says Patti Brickman, director of communications for the Greeting Card Association. It is estimated that more than one third will come from freelance material but the market remains highly competitive and successful freelancers know they must keep up with rapid changes in both taste and style.

"We encourage greeting card freelancers to study the market *throughly*. Look at cards currently on the market for appropriate tone, style, theme, length, etc.," says Elizabeth Gordon, humor editor for Paramount Cards, Inc.

Keeping aware requires careful study of the market. A visit to your local card shop is a good first step. Take a look at the card racks, talk to the clerk and watch to see who buys what. Some card companies will provide a market list or catalog of their card lines for a self-addressed, stamped envelope or a small fee. Industry magazines such as *Greetings* also help to keep you informed of changes and happenings within the field.

Although you may spot several new growth areas or trends each year, some factors remain constant and are important to keep in mind. For example, women buy an estimated 90% of all greeting cards. The market is geared to women between ages 17 and 35. This fact has added to the need for cards women can send to other women, Gordon says.

The three basic card categories—traditional, studio (or contemporary) and alternative—have remained the same for a number of years. Note, however, these categories are loosely defined and do change focus from year to year. Traditional cards, after a slight lull in popularity in the early 1980s, are once again in demand.

Alternative cards continue to increase in popularity. This category includes cards with offbeat messages or that celebrate nontraditional events such as a salary raise, a divorce or new job. Many smaller card companies have built their businesses on alternative card lines. Sparked by the success of these firms, larger firms are developing their own lines of nontraditional cards.

"Think funny" may be the best advice this year, because the majority of editors say they cannot get enough humorous cards—especially ones that say something funny in a new or unique way.

Illustration has always been an important component of greeting cards, but in recent years editors say they've been looking for an even closer relationship between artwork and copy. It is important to think visually—to think of the card as an entire product—even if you are not artistically talented. Although most editors do not want to see artwork unless it is professional, they do appreciate suggestions from writers who have visualized a card as a whole unit. If your verse depends on an illustration to make its point or if you have an idea for a unique card shape or foldout, include a dummy card with your writing samples.

Payment for greeting card verse varies, but most firms pay on a per card or per idea basis, while a handful pay small royalties. Some firms will pay for card ideas and, if you are gifted artistically, complete cards are welcome. Payment is made for each separate component of the card. Some card companies prefer to test a card first and will pay a small fee for a test card idea.

Greeting card companies will also buy ideas for gift products and may plan to use card material for a number of subsequent items. Licensing—the sale of rights to a particular character for a variety of products from mugs to T-shirts—is a growing part of the greetings industry. Because of this, however, note that most card companies buy all rights. Many companies also require writers to provide a release form, guaranteeing the material submitted is original and has not been sold elsewhere. Before signing a release form or a contract to sell all rights, be sure you understand the terms.

Submission requirements may vary slightly from company to company, so send a SASE for writer's guidelines if they are available. To submit conventional card material, type or neatly print your verses or ideas on 8½x11, 4x6 or 3x5 slips of paper or index cards. The usual submission includes from 5 to 15 cards and an accompanying cover letter. Be sure to include your name and address on the back of each card as well as on the cover letter. For studio cards, or cards with pop-outs or attachments also send a mechanical dummy card. For more help on card submissions see the samples in *The Writer's Digest Guide to Manuscript Formats* (Writer's Digest Books).

A word about recordkeeping—since you will be sending out many samples, Larry Sandman, author of *A Guide to Greeting Card Writing* (also Writer's Digest Books), suggests labeling each sample with a three-letter code. Establish a master card for each verse or idea and record where and when each was sent and whether it was rejected or purchased. One way to code the cards is to give each one a code with the first letter of each of the first three words of your verse. Keep all cards sent to one company in a batch and give each batch a number. Write this number on the back of your return SASE to help you match up your verses if they are returned.

AMBERLEY GREETING CARD CO., 11510 Goldcoast Dr., Cincinnati OH 45249. (513)489-2775. Editor: Ned Stern. 90% freelance written. Bought 250 freelance ideas/samples last year; receives an estimated 25,000 submissions annually. Reports in 1 month. Material copyrighted. Buys all rights. Pays on acceptance. Writer's guidelines for #10 SAE and 1 first class stamp. Market list is regularly revised.
Needs: Humorous, informal and studio. No seasonal material or poetry. Prefers unrhymed verses/ideas. Humorous cards sell best. Pays $40/card idea.
Tips: "Amberley publishes specialty lines and humorous studio greeting cards. We accept freelance ideas, including risque and nonrisque. Also looking for more women-oriented cards. Make it short and to the point. Nontraditional ideas are selling well. Include SASE (with correct postage) for return of rejects."

AMERICAN GREETINGS, 10500 American Rd., Cleveland OH 44144. (216)252-7300. Contact: Director-Creative Recruitment. No unsolicited material. "We like to receive a letter of inquiry describing education or experience, or a resume first. We will then screen those applicants and request samples from those that interest us."

‡ARGUS COMMUNICATIONS, 1 DLM Park, Allen TX 75002. (214)248-6300. Editor: Jane R. Bennett. 70% freelance written. Bought 300 freelance ideas last year; receives an estimated 20,000 submissions annually. Interested in everyday material for cards, posters and postcards all year. Submit seasonal/holiday material 1 year in advance: Christmas and Valentine only. Reports in 2 months. Buys all rights. Pays on acceptance. Submission guidelines available for #10 SASE.
Needs: Humorous, informal, sensivity and unique "lifestyle" concepts. No rhymed verse or poetry. Prefers humorous sentiments/ideas. Pays $50-125.
Other Product Lines: Greeting cards, postcards and posters.
Tips: "Greeting cards are a personalized, 'me-to-you' form of communication that express a wish for the recipient, a greeting, or an expression of endearment. Concentrate on warm humor that supports the relationship. Writers should focus on humorous birthday and friendship material. Target audience is women ages 18-45."

BLUE MOUNTAIN ARTS, INC., Dept. WM, Box 1007, Boulder CO 80306. Contact: Editorial Staff. Buys 50-75 items/year. Reports in 3-5 months. Buys all rights. Pays on publication.
Needs: "Primarily need sensitive and sensible writings about love, friendships, families, philosophies, etc.—written with originality and universal appeal." Also poems and writings for specific holidays (Christmas, Valentine's Day, etc.), and special occasions, such as birthdays, get well, and sympathy. Seasonal writings should be submitted at least 4 months prior to the actual holiday. Pays $200/card or poem.
Other Product Lines: Calendars, gift books and greeting books. Payment varies.
Tips: "Get a feel for the Blue Mountain Arts line prior to submitting material. Our needs differ from other card publishers; we do not use rhymed verse, preferring instead a more honest, person-to-person style. Have a specific person or personal experience in mind as you write. We use unrhymed, sensitive poetry and prose

on the deep significance and meaning of life and relationships. A very limited amount of freelance material is selected each year, either for publication on a notecard or in a gift anthology, and the selection prospects are highly competitive. But new material is always welcome and each manuscript is given serious consideration."

BRILLIANT ENTERPRISES, 117 W. Valerio St., Santa Barbara CA 93101. Contact: Editorial Dept. Buys all rights. Submit words and art in black on 3½x3⅓ horizontal, thin white paper in batches of no more than 15. Reports "usually in 2 weeks." Catalog and sample set for $2.
Needs: Postcards. Messages should be "of a highly original nature, emphasizing subtlety, simplicity, insight, wit, profundity, beauty and felicity of expression. Accompanying art should be in the nature of oblique commentary or decoration rather than direct illustration. Messages should be of universal appeal, capable of being appreciated by all types of people and of being easily translated into other languages. Since our line of cards is highly unconventional, it is essential that freelancers study it before submitting." No "topical references, subjects limited to American culture or puns." Limit of 17 words/card. Pays $50 for "complete ready-to-print word and picture design."

‡THE CALLIGRAPHY COLLECTION, 2604 NW 7th Place, Gainesville FL 32606. (904)378-0748. Editor: Katy Fischer. Submit seasonal/holiday material 6 months in advance. Reports in 2 months. Buys all rights. Pays on publication.
Needs: "Ours is a line of framed prints of watercolors with calligraphy." Conventional, humorous, informal, inspirational, sensitivity, soft line and studio. Prefers unrhymed verse, but will consider rhymed. Submit 3 ideas/batch. Pays $50-100/framed print idea.
Other Product Lines: Gift books, greeting books and plaques.
Tips: Sayings for friendship are difficult to get. Bestsellers are humorous, sentimental, inspirational and conventional cards—such as wedding announcements, thank you, all occasions, and birthday plaques. "Our audience is women 20 to 50 years of age. Write something they would like to give or receive as a lasting gift."

COLORTYPE, 1640 Market St., Corona CA 91720. (714)734-7410. Editor: Mike Gribble. 100% freelance writen. Buys 75 freelance ideas/samples per year; receives 200 annually. Submit seasonal/holiday material 9 months in advance. Reports in 3 weeks. Buys all rights. Pays on acceptance. Writer's guidelines/market list for 6x9 SASE.
Needs: Humorous, assemble-it-yourself cards or other novelty cards. Prefers to receive 6 or more card ideas/batch. Pays $100-150/card idea. Royalty "open for discussion."
Tips: "Prefer humorous. Photos of humorous subjects are difficult to get."

‡COMSTOCK CARDS, Suite 18, 600 S. Rock, Reno NV 89502. FAX: (702)333-9406. Owner: Patti P.Wolf. Art Director: David Delacroix. Estab. 1986. "Just starting to purchase freelance material." 25% freelance written. Buys 20 freelance ideas/samples per year; receives 50 submissions annually. Submit seasonal/holiday material 1 year in advance. Reports in 5 weeks. Buys all rights. Pays on acceptance. Free writer's guidelines/market list. Market list issued one time only.
Needs: Humorous, informal, invitations and "puns, put-downs, put-ons, outrageous humor aimed at a sophisticated, adult female audience. No conventional, soft line or sensitivity hearts and flowers, etc." Prefers to receive 25 cards/batch. Pays $50-75/card idea.
Other Product Lines: Notepads.
Tips: "Always keep holiday occasions in mind and personal me-to-you expressions that relate to today's occurrences. Ideas must be simple and concisely delivered. A combination of strong image and strong gag line make a successful greeting card. Consumers relate to themes of work, sex and friendship combined with current social, political and economic issues."

CONTENOVA GIFTS, Box 69130, Postal Station K, Vancouver, British Columbia V5K 4W4 Canada. (604)253-4444. Editor: Jeff Sinclair. 100% freelance written. Bought over 100 freelance ideas last year; receives an estimated 15,000 submissions annually. Submit ideas on 3x5 cards or small mock-ups in batches of 10-15. Buys world rights. Pays on acceptance. Current needs list for SAE and IRC.
Needs: Humorous and studio. Both risqué and nonrisqué. "Short gags with good punch work best." Birthday, belated birthday, get well, anniversary, thank you, congratulations, miss you, new job, etc. Seasonal ideas needed for Christmas and Valentine's Day. Pays $50.
Tips: "Not interested in play-on-words themes. We're leaning toward more 'cute risqué' and no longer using drinking themes. Put together your best ideas and submit them. One great idea sent is much better than 20 poor ideas filling an envelope. We are always searching for new writers who can produce quality work. You need not be previously published. Our audience is 18-65—the full spectrum of studio card readers. We do *not* use poetry."

CREATE-A-CRAFT, Box 330008, Fort Worth TX 76163-0008. (817)292-1855. Editor: Mitchell Lee. 5% freelance written. Buys 2 freelance ideas/samples per year; receives 300 submissions annually. Submit seasonal/holiday material 1 year in advance. Submissions not returned even if accompanied by SASE—"not enough staff to take time to package up returns." Buys all rights. Sample greeting cards are available for $2.50 and a #10 SASE.

Needs: Announcements, conventional, humorous, juvenile and studio. "Payment depends upon the assignment, amount of work involved, and production costs involved in project."

Tips: No unsolicited material. "Send letter of inquiry describing education, experience, or resume with one sample first. We will screen applicants and request samples from those who interest us."

EARTH CARE PAPER INC., Box 3335, Madison WI 53704. (608)256-5522. Editor: Carol Magee. Submit seasonal/holiday material 1 year in advance. Prefers to keep on file rather than return by SASE. Reports in 2 months. Buys card rights. Pays on acceptance. Free writer's guidelines.

Needs: Humorous, informal, sensitivity, soft line. Prefers unrhymed verse, but will consider rhymed. Pays $25/minimum.

Tips: "Our company features cards printed on recycled paper. We are interested in humor relating to nature, environmental protection or social issues. Submit illustration ideas with verse."

‡ELDERCARDS, INC., Box 202, Piermont NY 10968. (914)359-7137. Editor: Steve Epstein and Lenore Berkowitz. 10% of material is freelance written. Receives 20 submissions annually. Submit seasonal/holiday material 3 months in advance. Reports in 1 month. Pays royalties.

Needs: Announcements, conventional, humorous, informal, invitations, sensitivity and studio. Prefers unrhymed verse. Submit 24 ideas/batch. Pays $10-200.

Other Product Lines: Calendars ($10-200), post cards ($10-200) and posters ($10-200).

Tips: "Market is contemporary, upbeat, humorous, for 20-50 years old. Writers should be mindful of babies and the baby boom and President George Bush likes."

FREEDOM GREETING CARD CO., Box 715, Bristol PA 19007. (215)945-3300. Editor: J. Levitt. 90% freelance written. Submit seasonal/holiday material 1 year in advance. Reports in 2 weeks. Pays on acceptance. Free writer's guidelines/market list. Market list available to writer on mailing list basis.

Needs: Announcements, conventional, humorous, inspirational, invitations, juvenile and sensitivity. Payment varies.

Tips: "General and friendly cards sell best for Freedom."

GALLANT GREETINGS, 2654 W. Medill, Chicago IL 60647. Editorial Coordinator: Pamela Hendee. 90% of material bought is freelance written. Bought 500 freelance ideas/samples last year. Reports in 1 month. Buys world greeting card rights. Pays 60-90 days after acceptance. Writer's guidelines for SASE.

Needs: Announcements, conventional, humorous, informal, inspirational, invitations, juvenile, studio. Submit 20 cards in one batch.

Tips: "Greeting cards should and do move with the times, and sometimes writers don't. Keep aware of what is going on around you."

HALLMARK CARDS, INC., Box 419580, 2501 McGee, Mail Drop 276, Kansas City MO 64141. Contact: Carol King with letter of inquiry only; no sample. Reports in 2 months. Request guidelines if not on current Hallmark freelance roster; include SASE.

Needs: Humorous, studio cards, and conversational prose.

Tips: "Purchasing writing for everyday and seasonal greeting cards. Because Hallmark has an experienced and prolific writing staff, freelance writers must show a high degree of skill and originality to interest editors who are used to reading the very best."

‡INDUSTRIAL WHIMSY CO., Box 1330, Cedar Ridge CA 95924. (916)272-5062. Editor: J. Thom. Helsom. 75% of material is freelance written. Buys 50 plus freelance ideas/samples per year; receives 500 plus submissions annually. Reports in 2 months. Buys all rights. Pays on acceptance. Writer's guidelines for #10 SAE with one first class stamp. Market list available to writer on mailing list basis.

Needs: Humorous, informal, Grafitti-style sayings—intellectual or otherwise—unrhymed. Prefers unrhymed verse. Submit 1-10 card ideas/batch.

Other Product Line: Bumper stickers ($10-50), calendars ($10-50), plaques ($10-50), post cards ($10-50) and posters ($10-50).

For explanation of symbols, see the Key to Symbols and Abbreviations on Page 5. For unfamiliar words, see the Glossary.

Close-up

Ann Asel-Wagner
Writer/Editor
Hallmark Cards

"I just find it easy and entertaining and fun to think like a kid," says Hallmark writer/editor Ann Asel-Wagner. A veteran writer and editor with the company, Asel-Wagner started with the company after college and most recently moved to Hallmark Juvenile Properties after editing product lines for 13 years and working on the creative writing staff for three years.

"I entered the creative field after taking our writer/editor test," she says. "I edited various product lines, focusing on kids' products—books, cards and specialty items—before joining our Creative Writing Staff. After three years there, I took my experience with kids' products to Hallmark Juvenile Properties. It's not a bad deal to make a living pretending you're not a grown-up!"

During her tenure at Hallmark, she's seen a number of changes in the styles of greeting cards. "Cards are much more interesting," she says. "The best card used to ramble on and say very little of substance. Today we make more cards for more specific reasons. The standards for new writing are higher. A new card has to be well written, original and say something significant."

The majority of card buyers are still women from 25 to 40, but cards have changed to reflect other market segments and changing lifestyles. "We often think in terms of particular needs and lifestyles these days—coping, support, problems in relationships—over age ranges," Asel-Wagner says. "People are more communicative than they used to be—or at least they feel the need to be. There are more reasons for people to be separated from friends and family than ever before. Family life is more complicated with divorce and remarriage mixing families in so many ways. And finally—this is my own little theory—I think people simply know more people than they used to in today's mobile society."

Freelancers should keep these changes in mind when submitting material, Asel-Wagner says. "They often neglect the issue of 'sendability,' " she says. "The stated or implied 'me-to-you' message that turns a piece of writing into something many people will send as a greeting card is very important."

Asel-Wagner's experience has given her an appreciation for both writing and editing greeting cards. "I enjoy the pure creativity of writing, but I love working with copy as an editor too," she says.

Staying creative is not a problem. "I usually find that it's not too difficult to think of new ideas," she says. "You really just have to have a wealth of relationships, activities, memories, feelings, a sense of humor—in other words, it helps to lead a very full life. Since I love people, and since relationships are so varied and multi-faceted, there is always something new to say."

—Glenda Tennant Neff

‡**INNOVISIONS, INC.**, 445 W. Erie St., #B3, Chicago IL 60610. (312)642-4871. Editor: Jay Blumenfeld. 100% of material freelance written. Buys 50 freelance ideas/samples per year; receives 400 submissions annually. Submit seasonal/holiday material 1 year in advance. Reports in 3 weeks. Buys all rights. Pays within 30 days of publication. Market list issued one time only.

Needs: Humorous. Prefers unrhymed verse. Submit any amount/batch.

Tips: Looks for "off-the-wall humor and novelty cards (small 'joke' items that are the punch line)."

‡**KALAN, INC.**, 97 S. Union Ave., Lansdowne PA 19050. (215)623-1900. Contact: Editor. 90% freelance written. Buys 125 freelance ideas/samples per year; receives 1,000 annually. Submit seasonal/holiday material 10 months in advance. Reports in 1 month. Buys all rights. Pays on acceptance. Writer's guidelines for #10 SAE with 1 first class stamp. Submit ideas on 3x5 cards or small mock-ups. If artwork is necessary for the understanding of the gag, it may be described briefly for our art department.

Needs: Risque and knock-'em-dead funny messages for birthday, friendship, seasonal, etc. "We seek clever and suggestive material. For our new 5x7 full-color line, we need copy for the following: modern friendship, birthday, fun love, thinking of you, coping with men, work, life, etc. Our studio cards are gags geared toward a specific occasion. The x-rated line uses humorous gags with the artwork usually completing the gag. The x-rated line is beyond risqué—very daring! We prefer humorous prose for all lines, but will consider serious verse." Payment schedule on guidelines. "Put 'Attn: Editor' on submission envelope."

Other Product Lines: Bumper stickers, buttons, key rings, etc. Payment for new product ideas is negotiable.

Tips: "Send for guidelines and samples before submitting. Write for a specific occasion: birthday, celebrating love, good-bye, Christmas, etc. Once you've decided on an occasion, write with a specific person in mind—your best friend, mother, coworker, etc. This tends to produce specific, funny copy able to be sent to many different types of people. The editor is waiting to be impressed by your neatness and creativity."

‡**LANDMARK GENERAL CORP.**, 51 Digital Dr., Novato CA 94948, (415)883-1600. FAX (415)883-6725. Editor: Thomas Biela. 90% of material is freelance written. Buys 90 freelance ideas/samples per year; receives 500 submissions annually. Submit seasonal/holiday material 6 months in advance. Reports in 3 months. Pays on publication.

Needs: Humorous and soft line. Submit as few as 15-20 ideas/batch.

Other Product Lines: Calendars. "Payment in this area is discussed upon review of concept. There is no minimum or maximum. Royalties or flat fee may be involved."

Tips: "Our primary line is of the strictly humorous nature. Our audience is 95% women, ages 18 to 65. The greeting card industry has opened up to a wide range of acceptable areas. No longer does the message have to be sweet and syrupy. Copy lines depicting 'slam' and 'risqué' are no longer regarded as 'alternative.' "

MAINE LINE CO., Box 947, Rockland ME 04841. (207)594-9418. Editor: Perri Ardman. 95% freelance written. Buys 200-400 freelance ideas/samples per year. Receives approximately 2,500 submissions/year. Submit photocopies (1 idea per page) or index cards. Please send SASE for return of samples. Reports in 2 months. Material copyrighted. Buys greeting card rights. Pays on acceptance. Writer's guidelines for #10 SAE and 2 first class stamps. Market list is regularly revised.

Needs: "We use non-humorous, as well as humorous material. We are expanding into 'sensitive language,' and 'inspirational' greeting cards and 'light, cute' greeting cards. Still, we do not want clichés or corny sap. Messages, whether 'light' or 'sensitive', must be real and reflect attitudes and feelings of real people in today's world. Unrhymed material is preferred."

Other Product Lines: Wacky, outrageous humor needed for buttons, mugs, key chains, magnets, tee-shirts, plaques and other novelty items. "We prefer copy that stands on its own humor rather than relies on four-letter words or grossly suggestive material. Material that is *mildly* suggestive is OK. 'Inspirational' material for the above items also requested."

Tips: "Please send for our guidelines. Copy should speak to universal truths that most people will recognize. Writers need not submit any visuals with copy but may suggest visuals. Lack of drawing ability does not decrease chances of having your work accepted; however, we also seek people who can both write and illustrate. Writers who are also illustrators or graphic artists are invited to send samples or tearsheets. Be sure to send an SASE with appropriate postage for return of your material if you want to get it back."

MERLYN GRAPHICS, Box 9087, Canoga Park CA 91309. (818)349-2775. Editor: Bettie Galling. Estab. 1987. 50% of material bought is freelance written. Bought 50 freelance ideas last year; receives 2,000 submissions annually. Submit seasonal/holiday material 1 year in advance. Reports in 1 month. Buys all rights. Pays on publication. Writer's guidelines for #10 SASE.

Needs: "Humorous everyday cards: birthday, friendship, get well, miss you. The only holiday/occasion cards we are currently publishing are Christmas and Valentine's. We want *very* funny, clever, witty, slightly twisted, belly-busting lines that lend themselves to a very strong visual. We do not want sentimental, 'hearts & flowers,' or cute traditional material. Neither do we want vulgar or 'x-rated' material. Go for clever 'double entendre' and unpredictable punch lines."

Tips: "Please send for and really study our guidelines. Suggested visuals are OK but not required. Only once have we used a writer's suggested visual. However, you must think visually! Remember that you are not writing for 'stand-up comedy.' You should also ask yourself if the card is 'sendable.' Who would you send it to and why? Always remember that most cards (93%) are purchased by women! Our cards are 100% photographic, and almost exclusively photographed in a studio setting. They are 5x7, with the photo on the front and the punchline on the inside, with little or no set-up on the front. Stay away from outlandish 'flying dinosaurs' type concepts. We are not currently accepting outside photography or artwork. Submit your material on index cards, or individual sheets of paper. Do not group more than one idea/line to a card/sheet. Your name, address and phone number should be on the back of each submission. Always send the correct size SASE with the correct amount of postage for the return of your material; however, we do not guarantee the return of your submissions, so please keep copies. We publish two or three times annually in groups of 36 designs. As a result, when we find material we want to use we may hold it for as long as six months before publishing it. You may write or submit material as often as you wish, but please, no phone calls or certified mail. We provide samples of the finished cards at no charge to the writers, and we give a writer's credit line on the back of the card."

‡MIRAGE IMAGES INC., Box #6, Elk CA 95432. Editor: Caroline Selden. 100% of material is freelance written. Buys 2 ideas/samples per year; receives 10 submissions annually. Submit seasonal/holiday material 6 months in advance. Reports in 2 months. Buys all rights. Pays on acceptance "when artist and producer are in *total* agreement."
Needs: Humorous and juvenile.
Other Product Lines: Gift boxes.

‡NOBLEWORKS, 52 Gansevoort St., New York NY 10014. (800)346-6253. Editor: Christopher Noble. 75% freelance written. Buys about 100 submissions/year; received about 1,000 last year. Submit seasonal/holiday material 1 year in advance for Christmas; 8-9 months for other holidays. Reports in 3 weeks. Buys greeting card rights only. Pays initial fee no later than publication and a royalty up to a specified amount. Guidelines for SASE. Market list is regularly updated.
Needs: Humorous. Prefers to receive 12-24 card ideas/batch.
Tips: "Through many years of trial and error, we have found that very humorous, silly, irreverent and outrageously humorous cards are what we sell. Our cards are aimed at a sophisticated urban market with humor that is unexpected and off-center (though not sleazy and sexual). Our humor is modern, on the edge and takes risks! A card must be instantly understandable. Though an idea may be clever, it will never fly if the reader must complete the thought in order to get at the gist of the joke. Satire, political and social is very popular if applied correctly."

OATMEAL STUDIOS, Box 138W3, Rochester VT 05767. (802)767-3171. Editor: David Stewart. 85% freelance written. Buys 200-300 greeting card lines/year. Pays on acceptance. Reports in 6 weeks. Current market list for self-addressed, #10 SAE and 1 first class stamp.
Needs: Birthday, friendship, anniversary, get well cards, etc. Also Christmas, Chanukah, Mother's Day, Father's Day, Easter, Valentine's Day, etc. Will review concepts. Humorous material (clever and *very* funny) year-round. "Humor, conversational in tone and format, sells best for us." Prefers unrhymed contemporary humor. Current pay schedule available with guidelines.
Other Product Lines: Notepads.
Tips: "The greeting card market has become more competitive with a greater need for creative and original ideas. We are looking for writers who can communicate situations, thoughts, and relationships in a funny way and apply them to a birthday, get well, etc., greeting and we are willing to work with them in targeting our style. We will be looking for material that says something funny about life in a new way. We tend to see a lot of the same ideas over and over. It's harder to find something different and fresh. Reading card racks is a good way for a writer to stay one step ahead."

‡OCCASIONS SOUTHWEST GREETINGS, 2665 N. Indian Ridge Dr., Tucson AZ 85715. (602)721-1378. Editor: Tim Harrington. 75% of material is freelance written. Buys 75 freelance ideas/samples per year; receives 150 submissions annually. Submit seasonal/holiday material 1 year in advance. Reports in 3 weeks. Buys all rights. Pays on publication. Free writer's guidelines/market list. Market list is regularly revised.
Needs: Conventional, humorous, informal, inspirational (non-religious) and sensitive Southwest themes. Prefers unrhymed verse. Submit 1 or more card ideas/batch.

OUTREACH PUBLICATIONS, Box 1010, Siloam Springs AR 72761. (501)524-9381. Editor: Joan Aycock. Submit seasonal/holiday material 1 year in advance. Reports in 2 months. Pays on acceptance. Guidelines for #10 SAE with 1 first class stamp.
Needs: Announcements, invitations, juvenile get well and birthday, all major seasonal and special days, all major everyday cards—birthday, anniversary, get well, friendship, etc. Material must be usable for the Christian market.

Tips: "Study our line, Day Spring Greeting Cards, before submitting. We are looking for sentiments with relational, inspirational messages that minister love and encouragement to the receiver." Accepting unrhynmed and rhymed verse.

‡**PAPER MOON GRAPHICS, INC.**, Box 34672, Los Angeles CA 90266. (213)202-4800. FAX (213)559-5897. Editors: Robert Fitch/Fred Zax. 80% of material is freelance written. Buys 200 freelance ideas/samples per year. Submit seasonal/holiday material 1 year in advance. Reports in 8 months. Buys all rights. Pays on acceptance. Free writer's guidelines.
Needs: Humorous, informal, invitations, sensitivity and studio. Prefers unrhymed verse. Submit 30 ideas/ batch.
Tips: "Funny, friendly, conversational dialogue – no poems, no age insults." Audience is female generally age 20-35.

PAPERPOTAMUS PAPER PRODUCTS INC., Box 966, Point Roberts WA 98281 or Box 35008, Station E, Vancouver, British Columbia VGM 4G1 Canada. (604)874-3520. FAX: (604)874-3420. Editor: George Jackson. Buys 100% freelance written material. Buys 75-125 freelance ideas/samples annually; receives 500-600 submissions/year. Reports in 1 month. Buys all rights. Gives credit to writer on back of cards. Prefers typed copy on 3×5 cards and/or mock-ups with SASE. Catalog available for 9×12 SASE or send $1. "Looking to develop lines of cards as well as individual ideas. Send only everyday and Christmas ideas. Pays $55 per accepted idea. Will pay flat fee or royalty for continuous line of cards. Prefers concept for card to come with copy. Submit 10-20 ideas/batch."
Needs: Off-the-wall, wacko, slightly twisted, unpredictable humor. Prefers unrhymed verse.

‡**PARAMOUNT CARDS INC.**, Box 6546, Providence RI 02940-6546. Editorial Director: Mark Acey. Over 10% of material is freelance written. Buys 300 greeting card ideas/samples per year. Submit seasonal/material at least 6 months in advance. Reports in 1 month. Buys all rights. Pays on acceptance. Writer's guidelines for SASE.
Needs: All types of conventional verses. Fresh, inventive humorous verses, especially general birthday cards. Submit in batches of 10-15.

‡**PAWPRINTS**, Box 446, Jaffrey NH 03452. Editor: Marcy Tripp. 10% freelance written. Bought 70 freelance ideas/samples last year; receives an estimated 1,000 submissions annually. Submit seasonal/holiday material 1 year in advance. Reports in 1 month. Buys reproduction rights. Pays on acceptance.
Needs: Conventional, humorous, sensitivity and soft line. "Witty, humorous, anthropomorphic animal cards aimed at a bright, fun-loving audience sell best for us. Card ideas with the right mix of word-play, humor and appropriateness to an occasion – like a birthday – are difficult to get." Prefers unrhymed verses/ideas. Pays $50-100.
Tips: "Keep it fun, clean and witty. The trend is back to romance – away from the off-color."

PLUM GRAPHICS INC., Box 136 Prince Station, New York NY 10012. (212)966-2573. Editor: Yvette Cohen. Buys 100% of material from freelancers; purchased 21 samples in past year. Does not return samples accompanied by SASE. Reports in 3-4 months. Buys greeting card and stationery rights. Pays on publication. Free guidelines sheet. "Sent out about twice a year in conjunction with the development of new cards."
Needs: Humorous. "We don't want general submissions. We want them to relate to our next line." Prefers unrhymed verse. Greeting cards pay $20-40, depending on series and strength of line. Pays $50 for very good lines.
Tips: "Sell to all ages. Humor is always appreciated. Wants short to-the-point lines."

RED FARM STUDIO, Box 347, 334 Pleasant St., Pawtucket RI 02862. (401)728-9300. Art Director: Mary M. Hood. Buys 50 ideas/samples per year. Reports in 2 weeks. Buys all rights. Pays on acceptance. Market list for #10 SAE with 1 first class stamp.
Needs: Conventional, inspirational, sensitivity and soft line cards. "We cannot use risqué or insult humor." Submit no more than 10 ideas/samples per batch. Pays $3 per line of copy.
Tips: "Write verses that are direct and honest. Flowery sentiments are not in fashion right now. It is important to show caring and sensitivity, however. Our audience is middle to upper middle class adults of all ages."

‡**RENAISSANCE GREETING CARDS**, Box 126, Springvale ME 04083. (207)324-4153. Editor: Ronnie Sellers. 5% of material freelance written. Bought 20-50 freelance ideas/samples last year; receives 1,000-1,500 submissions annually. Submit seasonal/holiday material at least 9 months in advance. Reports in 2 months, longer on seasonal submissions. Pays on acceptance or publication, "probably acceptance with writers." Market list for #10 SAE with 1 first class stamp. Market list regularly revised.
Needs: "Most interested in humorous submissions. Always interested in receiving inspirational, but not heavily religious cards." Sensitivity cards are also important. "We publish 'upbeat,' positive and sincere greetings that enhance relationships. No off-color material or 'put-down' material." Usually pays flat fee of

$25-50 (per accepted written submission), more if provided with illustrations or graphics.
Other Product Lines: Calendars, gift books, greeting books, postcards, posters and puzzles. Payment negotiable.
Tips: "Address the specific occasions for which greeting cards are sent (birthday, get well, friendship, etc.). Be original but be sincere. Be clever but stay upbeat and positive. We are a contemporary card company. Our customers expect written context that is more 'original' than that normally associated with the traditional publishers. Write material that will appeal to younger, 'baby boom' audience. We are interested in expanding our humor lines—no slang or off-color. We prefer occasion-oriented but are open to other ideas."

ROCKSHOTS, INC., 632 Broadway, New York NY 10012. (212)420-1400. Editor: Bob Vesce. "We buy 75 greeting card verse (or gag) lines annually." Submit seasonal/holiday material 1 year in advance. Reports in 2 months. Buys rights for greeting-card use. Writer's guidelines for SAE and 1 first class stamp.
Needs: Humorous ("should be off-the-wall, as outrageous as possible, preferably for sophisticated buyer"); soft line; combination of sexy and humorous come-on type greeting ("sentimental is not our style"); and insult cards ("looking for cute insults"). No sentimental or conventional material. "Card gag can adopt a sentimental style, then take an ironic twist and end on an off-beat note." Submit no more than 10 card ideas/samples per batch. Send to attention: Submissions. Pays $50 per gagline. Prefers gag lines on 8x11 paper with name, address, and phone and social security numbers in right corner, or individually on 3x5 cards.
Tips: "Think of a concept that would normally be too outrageous to use, give it a cute and clever wording to make it drop-dead funny and you will have commercialized a non-commercial message. It's always good to mix sex and humor. Our emphasis is definitely on the erotic. Hard-core eroticism is difficult for the general public to handle on greeting cards. The trend is toward 'light' sexy humor, even cute sexy humor. 'Cute' has always sold cards, and it's a good word to think of even with the most sophisticated, crazy ideas. 80% of our audience is female. Remember that your gag line will be illustrated by a photographer. So try to think visually. If no visual is needed, the gag line *can* stand alone, but we generally prefer some visual representation. It is a very good idea to preview our cards at your local store if this is possible to give you a feeling of our style."

‡SAM CARDS, 249-11 37th Ave., Little Neck NY 11363. (718)279-2766. Editor: Susan A. M. Solotoff. 10% of material is freelance written. Buys 20 freelance ideas/samples per year. Submit seasonal/holiday material 6 months to 1 year in advance. Reports in 3 months. Buys all rights. Pays on acceptance. Free writer's guidelines/market list. Market list issued one time only.
Needs: Humorous, inspirational and sensitivity (enlightenment oriented). Unrhymed verse only.
Other Product Lines: Gift books and greeting books.
Tips: Looking for "humorous, simple, short, punchy or biting. Anything that creates a strong reaction!"

MARCEL SCHURMAN CO., INC., 2500 North Watney Way, Fairfield CA 94533. Editor: Susan Perry. 25% freelance written. Buys 50 freelance ideas/samples per year; receives 500 submissions per year. Reports in 1 month. Pays on acceptance. Writer's guidelines for #10 SAE with 1 first class stamp.
Needs: Conventional, light humor, informal, invitations, juvenile, sensitivity, soft religious and inspirational; seasonal and everyday categories. Prefers unrhymed verse, but on juvenile cards rhyme is OK. Submit 5-20 cards in one batch.
Tips: "Historically, our nostalgic and art museum cards sell best. However, we are moving towards more contemporary cards. Target market: upscale, professional, well-educated; average age 40; more female."

‡SCOTT CARDS INC., Box 906, Newbury Park CA 91319. Editor: Larry Templeman. 95% of material is freelance written. Buys 75 freelance ideas/samples per year. Not printing seasonal/holiday cards at present. Reports in 3 months. Pays on acceptance. Writer's guidelines/market list for SAE and 2 first class stamps.
Needs: Conventional, humorous and sensitivity. Submit 10-20 ideas/batch.
Tips: "New ways to say 'I love you' always sell if they aren't corny or too obvious. Humor helps, especially if there is a twist. We are looking for non-traditional sentiments that are sensitive, timely and sophisticated. Our cards have a distinct flavor, so before submitting your work, write for our guidelines and sample brochure."

SILVER VISIONS, Box 49, Newton Highlands MA 02161. (617)244-9504. Editor: B. Kaufman. Submit seasonal/holiday material 9 months to 1 year in advance. Reports in 2 months. Pays on publication. Guidelines are available for SAE.
Needs: Humorous, humorous Jewish, contemporary occasion for photography line. Send 10-16 card ideas/batch.

‡SNAFU DESIGNS, Box 16643, St. Paul MN 55116. (612)290-0943. Editor: Scott F. Austin. Reports in 6 weeks. Buys all rights. Pays on acceptance. "Before we send you our guidelines, please send us something that is representative of your sense of humor (include a SASE). We will send you our guidelines if we feel your humor is consistent with ours."

Needs: Humorous, informal, birthday, love and friendship, thank you, anniversary, congratulations, get well and new baby. Prefers unrhymed verse. Submit no more than 10 ideas per batch. Pays $55/idea.

Other Product Lines: Post cards.

Tips: "We're a small card company, and we plan to continue emphasizing quality over quantity. Humor is what we are interested in (but not the cutesy type). Our audience is intelligent. With our cards, a strong yet simple image is very important, and the inside copy should tie in with a clever twist. Try to think visually, and use a conversational tone."

‡SUNRISE PUBLICATIONS, INC., Box 2699, Bloomington IN 47402. (812)336-9900. Contact: Editorial Coordinator. 75% freelance written. Bought 200 freelance ideas/samples last year; receives an estimated 2,000 submissions annually. Reports in 2 months. Acquires greeting card rights only. Pays on acceptance. Free writer's guidelines. Market list is regularly revised.

Needs: Conventional, humorous, informal. No "off-color humor or lengthy poetry." Prefers unrhymed verses/ideas. "We like short one- or two-line captions, sincere or clever. Our customers prefer this to lengthy rhymed verse. Submit ideas for birthday, get well, friendship, wedding, baby congrats, sympathy, thinking of you, anniversary, belated birthday, thank yous, fun and love." Payment varies.

Tips: "Think always of the sending situation and both the person buying the card and its intended recipient. Most card purchasers are aged between 18 and 45 years, and are female."

VAGABOND CREATIONS, INC., 2560 Lance Dr., Dayton OH 45409. (513)298-1124. Editor: George F. Stanley, Jr. 30% freelance written. Buys 30-40 ideas annually. Submit seasonal/holiday material 6 months in advance. Reports in 1 week. Buys all rights. Ideas sometimes copyrighted. Pays on acceptance. Writer's guidelines for #10 SAE. Market list issued one time only.

Needs: Cute, humorous greeting cards (illustrations and copy) often with animated animals or objects in people-situations with short, subtle tie-in message on inside page only. No poetry. Pays $10-25/card idea.

WARNER PRESS, INC., Box 2499, Anderson IN 46018. (317)644-7721. Product Editor: Cindy M. Grant. 70% freelance written. Buys $3,000-4,000 worth of freelance material/year. Scheduled reading times: everyday verses (Feb.-March); Christmas verses (May-June). Reports in 5 weeks. Buys all rights. Pays on acceptance. Writer's guidelines for #10 SAE with 1 first class stamp. Market list is regularly revised.

Needs: Conventional, informal, inspirational, juvenile, sensitivity and verses of all types with contemporary Christian message and focus. No off-color humor. "Cards with a definite Christian perspective that is subtly stressed, but not preachy, sell best for us." Uses both rhymed and unrhymed verses/ideas "but we're beginning to move away from 'sing-song' rhyme, toward contemporary prose." Pays $15-35 per card idea.

Other Product Lines: Pays $60-150 for calendars; $15-30 for plaques; $15-50 for posters; $20-50 for short meditations; negotiates payment for coloring books.

Tips: "Try to avoid use of 'I' or 'we' on card verses. A majority of what we purchase is for box assortments. An estimated 75% of purchases are Christian in focus; 25% good conventional verses. Religious card ideas that are not preachy are difficult to find. The market is moving away from the longer verses in a variety of card types, though there is still a market for good inspirational verses. Our best sellers are short poems or sensitivity verses that are unique, meaningful and appropriate for many people. We do not purchase verses written specifically to one person (such as relative or very close friend) but rather for boxed assortments. Please request guidelines before submitting."

‡WESTERN GREETING, INC., Box 81056, Las Vegas NV 89180. Editor: Barbara Jean Sullivan. 100% of material is freelance written. Buys 15 freelance ideas/samples per year. Reports in 1 month. Buys all rights. Pays on acceptance. Writer's guidelines/market list for #10 SAE with one first class stamp.

Needs: Humorous, sensitivity, soft line, Western and Indian themes. Prefers unrhymed verse. Submit 10-20 ideas/batch.

Tips: "The Western cards include the cowboy, mountain man, Indian, cowgirl, western stilllife and landscape. Our cards are reproduced from Western and Southwest art. Target audiences are people who love the West, the outdoors and history of the West."

‡WILDWOOD DESIGN GROUP, Box 3140, McLean VA 22103. (703)642-5394. Editor: Brian Smolens. 5% of material is freelance written. Reports in 1 month. Buys all rights. Pays on publication. Writer's guidelines/market list for 8½x11 SAE with 3 first class stamps. Must submit samples with request for guidelines.

Needs: Humorous only. "We supply pictures—caption must be written to match." Submit 10 ideas/batch.

Other Product Lines: Post cards ($5-20) and posters ($10-50).

CAROL WILSON FINE ARTS, INC., Box 17394, Portland OR 97217. Editor: Gary Spector. 90% freelance written. Buys 100 freelance ideas/samples per year; receives thousands annually. Submit seasonal/holiday material 1 year in advance. Reports in 6 weeks. Buys negotiable rights. Whether payment is made on acceptance or publication varies, with type of agreement. Writer's guidelines/market list for #10 SAE and 1 first class stamp.

Needs: Humorous and unrhymed. Pays $40-80 per card idea. "Royalties could be considered for a body of work."

Other Product Lines: Postcards.

Tips: "We are looking for laugh-out-loud, unusual and clever ideas for greeting cards. All occasions are needed but most of all birthday cards are needed. It's OK to be outrageous or risque. Cards should be 'personal'—ask yourself—is this a card that someone would buy for a specific person?"

‡WIZWORKS, Box 240, Masonville CO 80541-0240. Editor: Tom Cannon. Estab. 1988. 90% of material is freelance written. Submit seasonal/holiday material 6 months in advance. Reports in 6 weeks. Writer's guidelines/market list for $1. Market list available to writer on mailing list basis.

Needs: Conventional, humorous, informal, inspirational, juvenile, sensitivity, soft line, studio, all types non-occasion and holidays, favor orientation to specific market segments rather than generalized. No preference for rhymed or unrhymed; however, no more than 4 lines in rhymed. Submit 10 ideas/batch. Pays royalty on sales.

Tips: "We sell to all types of extremely segmented audiences. We want verse ideas which are specific to age, gender, lifestyle, etc. Our cards are intended to be printed on the retail site by a computer controlled high resolution color printer. Consumers will preview cards on a color CRT before printing. This allows cards to be extremely specific."

Other Greeting Card Publishers

The following firms asked to be deleted or did not return a verification to update an existing listing or a questionnaire to begin a new listing by press time.

Carolyn Bean Publishing Ltd.
Creative Directions (unable to contact)
Current Inc. (asked to be deleted)

Fravessi-Lamont Inc.
Grand Slam Greetings, Inc.
Life Greetings
Life Lines
Manhattan Greeting Card Co.

Mark I, Inc.
Pacific Paper Greetings Inc.
Roserich Designs Ltd.
Son Mark, Inc.
Stabur Press Inc.

Services & Opportunities

Author's Agents

Many writers — especially beginning writers — think they must have an agent to sell their work. An author looks for an agent because he needs someone who understands the publishing business; he needs an agent to negotiate contracts and subsidiary rights; and he needs an agent to help get his manuscript or outline read by an editor. In general, agents are a combination of sales representatives and business managers. They are specialists who keep in touch with editors needs; they know where to sell marketable manuscripts and how to negotiate contracts; they help collect payments from publishers and keep accurate records of earnings.

The fact is, though, not everyone needs an agent and not all authors prefer having an agent. Some writers are perfectly capable of handling the placement of their manuscripts and enjoy being involved in all stages of selling and negotiating. They do their own deal-making with editors, hire an attorney to review the legal terms of the contract and keep the 15% for themselves.

Book publishing today

There are writers who have no interest, time or talent for the business side of writing and feel their agents are invaluable. Admittedly, in the area of book-length fiction the need for an agent has become increasingly important. It is estimated that 90% of everything commercially published is handled by agents. The book publishing industry has been transformed over the last 10 years by mergers and consolidation. Although *Writer's Market* has over 700 listings in the Book Publishers section, there are now about six mega-publishers backed by major corporations. According to the industry newsletter *BP Report*, the top six publishing houses get 60% of all adult-book revenues, up from 50% in 1983.

The "big" book is part of this trend. Editors of large publishing houses are shying away from mid-list books (those that sell fewer than 20,000 copies). *Time* (June 12, 1989) reports the general-interest segment of a $15 billion book publishing industry is on a binge. The advances negotiated for potential best-selling authors have risen to six figures.

Like any other business, a publishing company that fails to make a profit will not survive. Few publishers can afford to hire a staff of editors or freelance readers to go through hundreds of unsolicited manuscripts; they receive simply too many unpublishable manuscripts for each one that is publishable. More and more publishers look to agents to do the screening for them. This has led to an increasing importance of agents in the marketplace.

The greater demand for agented submissions has resulted in an increase in the number of literary agencies. Now more agencies are opening throughout the U.S., dispensing with the notion that long-distance selling could never be successful.

Picking an agent

The good news for new writers is that the independent publishers are willing to take a chance on a new, but good writer and a small agent is willing to take on a mid-list title in hopes of developing the author into a best-selling one. As far as what an agent can and will do, each agency is different in the services it offers, the clients it prefers, its contacts in the industry and the style in which it conducts business. Before contacting an agent, the writer should determine why he wants or needs an agent and then match his requirements with the agent provides those services. Read the listings carefully, pay close attention to the areas that an agent indicates he handles and look at the Author's Agents Subject Index at the back of the book to find the category that matches your writing subject.

Although some agents say in their listing they will handle articles, short stories and filler material, they generally only handle these manuscripts for authors they already have under contract for books because of the low commissions they generate and the time and money involved in marketing them. Consult the consumer and trade listings for these markets. Agents are generally not necessary for submitting articles, columns, short fiction or filler material.

Ask yourself the following questions when evaluating your need for an agent:

- Do you have the skills necessary to handle the tasks of an agent?
- Can you take care of marketing your book and analyzing your contract?
- Can you afford to pay an agent 10-20% of your royalties?
- Would you like working through a middleman on all aspects of your book's future?
- Will you have more time to write if you have an agent?
- Are you interested in approaching markets that won't accept unagented submissions?

No matter how much you want or need an agent, you'll be wasting time and money if your writing isn't ready for an agent. Try to be objective about whether or not you have truly polished your work and studied the marketplace for your kind of writing. You should talk to other writers who have agents and read all you can find about working with an agent. Local writers' groups often share information about agents with whom they have established a relationship. Make every effort to obtain some published credits and always correspond with an agent in a professional manner.

How do I contact an agent?

Most agents will not look at unsolicited manuscripts and some will consider queries only if you've been recommended by a client or editor. But the majority will look at a query and possibly an outline and sample chapters from an unknown writer. The importance of reading the listings carefully and submitting queries, outlines or manuscripts in the manner preferred cannot be overlooked. In a poll conducted by *Writer's Market*, agents responded to the question, "What is the volume of unsolicited manuscripts you receive and what are your procedures for handling them?" The average number of unsolicited manuscripts received in a year was 2,030. Over 50% ask writers to send SASE with all correspondence and 46% say they accept no unsolicited manuscripts and discard those without SASE. Only 23% of the agents said they handle unsolicited submissions the same as solicited ones.

If an agent asks to see more of your work, don't assume you now have an agent. Just as you need to find out more about the agent, the agent has to know more about you and your writing. Give an agent time to read your work. Don't expect an immediate response to your query or manuscript. If you receive no response or a negative one, don't be discouraged. Continue to contact other agents. It may take several tries before an agent asks to see more of your writing.

How a literary agent works

In an interview with *Publishers Weekly* (November 1988), agent Jean Naggar says, "I am the author's business partner. And as a partner, and working as I do with a writer, I really try, even from the beginning, to take the long view, to look at every deal in the context of the author's overall career, rather than just as a deal for which I am a broker." In general, an agent's tasks can be divided into those done before a sale, during a sale and after a sale.

Before the sale, an agent evaluates your manuscript and sometimes makes suggestions about revisions. If the agent wants to represent you, you'll usually receive a contract or letter of agreement specifying the agent's commission, fees and the terms of the agreement. When that's signed, the agent talks to editors and sends your manuscript out. The agent repeats this sequence until the manuscript sells, you withdraw it or your agreement expires. Agents are getting more involved in the overall publishing of a manuscript by acting as packagers. See the Book Packagers and Producers section introduction for more information.

The agent negotiates your book contract for you, offering certain rights to the publisher and usually reserving other rights for future sale. The agent tries to get additional rights, like book jacket approval, galley approval, etc. Opportunities in commercial, cable and public television, as well as feature films, are increasing for an author's work and need a degree of expertise to negotiate. Your agent can explain the contract to you and make recommendations, but the final decision is always yours.

Understanding commissions and fees

Agents usually charge between 10-20% commission on manuscripts they place with publishers or producers. The commission is subtracted from the author's advance and royalty payments from the publisher. A commission arrangement means the writer doesn't pay the agent a commission until the manuscript has been sold. A commission paid to an agent is comparable to the commission a Realtor is paid for selling a house.

Charges to a writer for things like photocopying manuscripts, telephone calls, cables, telexes, postage and messenger service have become, for the most part, standard practice. Some agents also charge fees for marketing, critiques and consultant services. Remember that payment of a reading or criticism fee almost never guarantees that the agency will represent you. Payment of a fee may or may not give the kind of constructive criticism you need. As approximately 85% of all literary agencies now charge some kind of fee, there is no way to generalize about fee-charging agencies. If you decide to pay a fee, be sure you know *exactly* what you will receive in return. Several firms that charge fees regard them as one-time payments; if the writer becomes a client, no more fees will be charged for future manuscripts. Some agencies will reimburse the writer for the original fee when the manuscript is sold.

Judging an agent

After you have made the decision to contact an agent, you must decide what your expectations are for an agent. To make a knowledgeable decision, you need information and that means asking questions.

Although the answers to many of these questions appear in an agency's listing, it is a good idea to ask them again. Policies change and reporting times, commission amounts and fees may vary.
- How soon do you report on queries? On manuscripts?
- Do you charge a reading or criticism fee? If yes, how much? What kind of feedback will I receive? What is the ratio of the agency's income from fees compared to income from marketing books? If the manuscript is accepted, will my fee be returned? Credited against my marketing expenses? Or is it a nonreturnable charge to cover reading/criticism fees?
- Do you charge any other fees?
- How many clients do you represent?
- Will you provide me with a list of recent sales, titles published or clients?
- May I contact any of your clients for referrals?

- Who will work with me and what kind of feedback can I expect—regular status reports, rejection letters, etc.?
- Who will negotiate my contracts?
- Which subsidiary rights do you market directly? Which are marketed through sub-agents? Which are handled by the publisher?
- Do you offer any special services—tax/legal consultation (for attorneys), manuscript typing, book promotion or lecture tour coordination, etc.? Which costs extra? Which are covered by commission?
- Do you offer editorial support? How much?
- Do you offer a written agreement? If yes, how long does it run? What kind of projects are covered? Will (or must) all of my writing be represented? What will your commission be on domestic, foreign and other rights? Which expenses am I responsible for? Are they deducted from earnings, billed directly or paid by initial deposit? How can the agreement be terminated? After it terminates, what happens to work already sold, current submissions, etc.?

If the agency doesn't offer a contract or written agreement of any kind, you should write a letter of your own that summarizes your understanding on all these issues. Ask the agent to return a signed copy to you. A few agents prefer verbal agreements. No matter how personal a relationship you have with an agent, it's still a business matter. If the agent refuses to sign a simple letter of understanding, you may want to reconsider your choice of agencies.

Additional resources

The search for an agent can be a frustrating and time-consuming task, especially if you don't know what you're looking for. You can learn more about agents by studying several books on the subject. Read *Literary Agents: How to Get and Work with the Right One for You*, by Michael Larsen (Writer's Digest Books) and *Literary Agents: A Writer's Guide*, by Debby Mayer (Poet's & Writer's, Inc., 201 W. 54th St., New York NY 10019). *Literary Agents of North America* (Author Aid/Research Associates International, 340 E. 52nd St., New York NY 10022) is a directory of agents indexed by name, geography, subjects and specialities, size and affiliates. Your library may have a copy of *Literary Market Place*, which includes names and addresses of agents.

Remember that agents are not required to have any special training or accreditation. Some are members of a number of professional organizations or writers' groups, depending on their special interests. Each of the following organizations has a code of ethics or standard practices.

- ASJA—American Society of Journalists and Authors, Suite 1907, 1501 Broadway, New York NY 10036. Service organization providing exchange of ideas, market information. Regular meetings, annual writer's conference, professional referral service and annual membership directory. (For regional ASJA information see *Literary Market Place*).
- DGA—Directors Guild of America.
- ILAA—Independent Literary Agents Association, Inc., Suite 1205, 432 Park Ave., S., New York NY 10016. Founded in 1977, ILAA is a nationwide association of fulltime literary agents. An informative brochure, list of members and copy of the association's code of ethics are sent on request to writers who enclose #10 SAE with two first class stamps. ILAA does not provide information on specialties of individual members.
- RWA—Romance Writers of America, Suite 208, 5206 FM 1960 West, Houston TX 77069. (713)440-6885. Promotes recognition of the romance genre writing as a serious book form. Conducts workshops, regional and national conferences and awards for members.
- SAR—Society of Author's Representatives, Inc., 10 S. Portland Ave., Brooklyn NY 11217. (212)353-3709. Founded in 1928, SAR is a voluntary association of New York agents. A brochure and membership list are available for SASE. Members are identified as special-

izing in literary or dramatic material.

● WGA—Writers Guild of America. Agents and producers in the TV, radio and motion picture industry can become members or signatories of WGA by signing the guild's basic agreement which outlines minimum standards for treatment of writers. For a list of agents who have signed the WGA agreement, send a money order for $1.25 (except New York state residents, $1.33) to one of the WGA offices. If you live east of the Mississippi River, write to WGA East, 555 W. 57th St., New York NY 10019; west of the Mississippi, write WGA West, 8955 Beverly Blvd., Los Angeles CA 90048.

Like *Writer's Market*, these agencies will not make recommendations of agents but will provide information to help you in your search.

For information on author's agents not listed in *Writer's Market*, see Other Author's Agents at the end of this section.

‡A.M.C. LITERARY AGENCY, 234 Fifth Ave., New York NY 10001. (212)529-1803. President: Alexandra Chalusiak. Estab. 1987. Represents 6 clients. 98% of clients are new/unpublished writer. Specializes in nonfiction and fiction.
Will Handle: Nonfiction books, novels, movie scripts, TV scripts. Currently handles 60% nonfiction books; 30% novels; 10% TV scripts. Will read—at no charge—unsolicited queries and outlines. Does not read unsolicited mss. Reports in 2 weeks.
Terms: Agent receives 15% commission on domestic sales; 15% on dramatic sales; and 25% on foreign sales.
Fees: Writers must provide 3 copies of manuscript.
Recent Sales: No information given.

DOMINICK ABEL LITERARY AGENCY, INC., Suite 12C, 498 West End Ave., New York NY 10024. (212)877-0710. President: Dominick Abel. Estab. 1975. Member of ILAA.
Will Handle: Will read—at no charge—unsolicited queries and outlines. Reports in 2 weeks on queries. "Enclose SASE."
Terms: Agent receives 10% commission on domestic sales; 15% on dramatic sales; and 20% on foreign sales. Charges for overseas postage, phone and cable expenses.
Recent Sales: *Smoke and Mirrors*, by Barbara Michaels (Simon & Schuster); *Blood Shot*, by Sara Paretsky (Delacorte); *In the Blink of an Eye*, by Alan Doelp (Prentice Hall).

ACTON AND DYSTEL, INC., (formerly Edward J. Acton, Inc.), 928 Broadway, New York NY 10010. (212)473-1700. Contact: Edward Novak and Stephen Schacht. Estab. 1975. Member of ILAA. Represents 150 clients. Works with a small number of new/unpublished authors. Specializes in politics, celebrities, sports, business and commercial fiction.
Will Handle: Nonfiction books and novels. Currently handles 60% nonfiction; 40% novels. Will read—at no charge—unsolicited queries and outlines. No unsolicited manuscripts. Reports in 1 month on queries.
Terms: Agent receives 15% commission on domestic sales; 15% on dramatic sales; and 19% on foreign sales. Charges for photocopy expenses. 100% of income derived from commission on ms sales.
Recent Sales: *Funny, You Don't Look Like a Grandmother*, by Lois Wyse (Crown); and *Palace Coup*, by Michael Moss (Doubleday).

LEE ALLAN AGENCY, Box 18617, Milwaukee WI 53218. (414)357-7708. Agent: Lee A. Matthias. Estab. 1983. Member of WGA, Horror Writers of America, Inc. and Wisconsin Screenwriter's Forum. Represents 50 clients. 80% of clients are new/unpublished writers. "A writer must have a minimum of one (in our judgment) salable work. Credentials are preferred, but we are open to new writers." Specializes in "screenplays for mass film audience, low to medium budget preferred, but of high quality, not exploitation; and novels of high adventure, genre fiction such as mystery and science fiction—no romance, nonfiction, textbooks, or poetry."
Will Handle: Novels (male adventure, mystery, science fiction, literary) and movie scripts (low to medium budget, mass appeal material). Currently handles 50% novels; 50% movie scripts. Will read—at no charge—unsolicited queries and outlines. Does not read unsolicited mss. Must be queried first. Reports in 2 weeks on queries; 6 weeks on mss.
Terms: Agent receives 10% commission on domestic sales; 10% on dramatic sales; and 20% on foreign sales; occasionally higher. Foreign rights handled by Mildred Hird. Charges for photocopying, binding, occasional shipping/postage costs.
Recent Sales: *Valley of the Shadow* (Presidio Press); *Sea Lion* (New American Library); and *Shadowdale* and *Tantras* (TSR, Inc.).

MARCIA AMSTERDAM AGENCY, Suite 9A, 41 W. 82nd St., New York NY 10024. (212)873-4945. Contact: Marcia Amsterdam. Estab. 1969. Member of WGA. 20% of clients are new/unpublished writers. Eager to work with new/unpublished writers. Specializes in fiction, nonfiction, young adult, TV and movies.
Will Handle: Nonfiction books, novels, juvenile books (young adult), and movie and TV scripts. Will read — at no charge — unsolicited queries, synopsis and outlines. Reports in 2 weeks on queries; 1 month on mss. "SASE essential."
Terms: Agent receives 15% commission on domestic sales; 10% on dramatic sales; and 15% on foreign sales.
Fees: Charges for telegraph, cable, phone, and legal fees (when client agrees to them).
Recent Sales: *Ash Ock*, by Christopher Hinz (St. Martin's); *Silvercat*, by Kristopher Franklin (Bantam); and *Face the Dragon*, by Joyce Sweeney (Delacorte).

BART ANDREWS & ASSOCIATES, 1321 N. Stanley Ave., Los Angeles CA 90046. (213)851-8158. Contact: Bart Andrews. Estab. 1982. Member ILAA. Represents 50 clients. 10% of clients are new/unpublished writers. Works with small number of new/unpublished writers. Specializes in nonfiction only. "Seventy-five percent of books I represent are in the show business genre — biographies, autobiographies, books about TV, etc."
Will Handle: Nonfiction books. Handles 100% nonfiction books. Will read — at no charge — unsolicited queries and outlines. Reports in 3 weeks on queries.
Terms: Agent receives 15% commission on domestic sales; 10% on dramatic sales; and 25% on foreign sales.
Fees: "New clients are charged $150 marketing fee to offset out-of-pocket costs, i.e. phone, postage, etc." Charges writers for postage, photocopying, long distance phone calls. 95% of income derived from commission on manuscript sales; 5% of income derived from fees.
Recent Sales: *Once Before I Go*, by Wayne Newton with Dick Maurice (William Morrow); *Ringmaster!*, by Kristopher Antekeier (E.P. Dutton); *Film Flubs*, by Bill Givens (Citadel Press).

‡JOSEPH ANTHONY AGENCY, 8 Locust Ct. Rd. 20, Mays Landing NJ 08330. (609)625-7608. President: Joseph Anthony. Estab. 1964. Member of WGA. Represents 10 clients. 90% of clients are new/unpublished writers. Eager to work with new/unpublished writers. "Specializes in general fiction and nonfiction. Always interested in screenplays."
Will Handle: Magazine fiction, nonfiction books, novels, juvenile books (6-12 years), movie scripts, stage plays and TV scripts. Currently handles 5% magazine articles; 10% magazine fiction; 13% nonfiction books; 60% novels; 2% textbooks; 5% juvenile books; 5% movie scripts; 2% stage plays and 3% syndicated material. Will read — at no charge — unsolicited queries and outlines. Reports in 2 weeks on queries; 1 month on mss.
Terms: Agent receives 15% commission on domestic sales; 15% on dramatic sales; and 20% on foreign sales.
Fees: Charges $75 up to 100,000 words; $125 over 100,000 words for reading fee.
Recent Sales: No information given.

APPLESEEDS MANAGEMENT, Suite 302, 200 E. 30th St., San Bernardino CA 92404. (714)882-1667. Executive Manager: S. James Foiles. Estab. 1988. Signatory to Writers Guild of America-Association of Agents Basic Agreement; licensed by the state of California. Represents 25 clients. 40% of our clients are new/unpublished writers.
Will Handle: Specializes in action, mystery and science fiction novels; also in materials that could be adapted from novel to screen; also in screenplays; also in TV scripts for existing serials; and also in nonfiction including crime stories, biography, and educational materials dealing with self-improvement, self-esteem, abuse of controlled substances, etc. 25% nonfiction books; 40% novels; 20% movie scripts; 15% TV scripts. Reports in 2 weeks on queries; 2 months on manuscripts.
Terms: Agent receives 10-15% commission on domestic sales; 10-15% on dramatic sales; and 20% on foreign sales. 100% of income derived from sales of writer's work.

‡THE ARTISTS GROUP, 1930 Century Parkway West, Suite 403, Los Angeles CA 90067. (213)552-1100. President: Arnold Soloway. Estab. 1975. Member of Association of Talent Agents. Represents 30 clients. 10% of clients are new/unpublished writers. Works with a small number of new/unpublished authors. Specializes in episodic television and motion pictures.
Will Handle: Nonfiction books, novels, movie scripts, stage plays, TV scripts and syndicated material. Currently handles 5% nonfiction books; 5% novels; 40% movie scripts; 35% TV scripts; 10% syndicated material and 5% plays. Does not read unsolicited manuscripts.
Terms: Agent receives 10%. "We do not charge office expenses — but writers are responsible for photocopying their materials i.e. all scripts and manuscripts must be furnished by the writers themselves."
Recent Sales: No information given.

AUTHOR AID ASSOCIATES, 340 E. 52nd St., New York NY 10022. (212)758-4213; 697-2419. Editorial Director: Arthur Orrmont. Estab. 1967. Represents 150 clients. 10% of clients are new/unpublished writers. Works with a small number of new/unpublished authors. Publishers of *Literary Agents of North America*.

Will Handle: Magazine fiction, nonfiction books, novels, juvenile books, movie scripts, stage plays, TV scripts and poetry collections. Currently handles 5% magazine fiction; 35% nonfiction books; 38% novels; 5% juvenile books (ages 5-8; 9-11; and 12 and up); 5% movie scripts; 2% stage plays; 5% poetry and 5% other. Will read—at no charge—unsolicited queries and outlines. "Queries answered by return mail." Reports within 1 month on mss.

Terms: Agent receives 10-15% commission on domestic sales; 15% on dramatic sales; and 20% on foreign sales.

Fees: Charges a reading fee "only to new authors, refundable from commission on sale." Charges for cable, photocopy and messenger express. Offers a consultation service through which writers not represented can get advice on a contract. 15% of income derived from reading fees; 85% of income from sales of writer's work.

Recent Sales: *The Judgment Day Archives*, by Igor Yefimov (Mercury House Publishing); *Dialogue*, by Lewis Turco (Writer's Digest).

‡MALAGA BALDI LITERARY AGENCY, INC., Box 591, Radio City Station, New York NY 10101. (212)222-1221. President: Malaga Baldi. Estab. 1986. Represents 42 clients. 60% of clients are new/unpublished writers. Eager to work with talented writers, published or unpublished. Specializes in first fiction, literary fiction, a variety of nonfiction work.

Will Handle: Literary novels (non genre); nonfiction books and proposals and magazine articles and fiction (with the promise of a larger work forthcoming). Currently handles 15% magazine articles; 35% nonfiction books and 50% novels. Will read—at no charge—unsolicited queries, outlines and manuscripts. Requires SASE. Reports in 6 weeks on queries; 2 months on manuscripts. "Suggest to authors that they contact other agents, if no response within 2 months."

Terms: Agent receives 15% commission on domestic sales; 15% on dramatic sales; and 10-20% on foreign sales.

Fees: Charges writers for messenger, overseas mail costs, photocopying costs, cable/telegram/overseas phone calls *to* author, when necessary, lawyer's fees if agreed to prior to signing agent/author agreement.

Recent Sales: *Crossing the River*, by Fenton Johnson (Birch Lane Press/Lyle Stuart/Carol Management); *Water Boys*, by Eric Gabriel (Mercury House); and *The Bed*, by Aleecia Beldegreen (Stewart, Tabori and Chang).

MAXIMILIAN BECKER, 115 E. 82nd St., New York NY 10028. (212)988-3887. President: Maximilian Becker. Associate: Aleta Daley. Estab. 1950. Works with a small number of new/unpublished authors.

Will Handle: Nonfiction books, novels and stage plays. Will read—at no charge—unsolicited queries, outlines and mss, but may charge a criticism fee or service charge for work performed after the initial reading if requested. Reports in 2 weeks on queries; 3 weeks on mss.

Terms: Agent receives 15% commission on domestic sales; 20% on foreign sales.

Fees: Charges a criticism fee "if detailed criticism is requested. Writers receive a detailed criticism with suggestions—five to ten pages. No criticism is given if manuscript is hopeless."

Recent Sales: *Goering*, by David Irving (William Morrow); *Enigma*, by David Kahn (Houghton Mifflin); and *Cecile*, by Jamine Boissard (Little, Brown).

‡MEREDITH BERNSTEIN, 2112 Broadway, Suite 503 A, New York NY 10023. (212)799-1007. FAX: (212)799-1145 (must notify us you are faxing). President: Meredith Bernstein. Estab. 1981. Member of ILAA. Represents about 100 clients. 10% of our clients are new/unpublished writers. Eager to work with new/unpublished writers. Specializes in fiction and nonfiction; contemporary novels, mysteries, child care, business and money, romances, sagas, fashion and beauty, humor, visual books and psychology.

Will Handle: Nonfiction books, novels, juvenile books and movie scripts. Currently handles 45% nonfiction books; 45% novels; 5% juvenile books; and 5% miscellaneous. Will read unsolicited queries, outlines and mss. Reports in 1 week on queries; 3 weeks on mss.

Terms: Agent receives 15% commission on domestic sales and 20% on foreign sales.

Fees: Charges a reading fee. 5% of income derived from reading fees.

Recent Sales: *Anne Frank Remembered*, by Miep Gies and Alison Gold (Simon and Schuster); *Good Behavior*, by Robyn Spizman, Steven and Maryann Garber (Villard Books); and *Dead Crazy*, by Nancy Picard (Scribners).

THE BLAKE GROUP LITERARY AGENCY, Suite 600, One Turtle Creek Village, Dallas TX 75219. (214)520-8562. Director/Agent: Ms. Lee B. Halff. Estab. 1979. Member of Texas Publishers Association (TPA) and Texas Booksellers Association (TBA). Represents 40 clients. Prefers to work with published/established authors; works with a small number of new/unpublished authors.

Will Handle: Fiction and nonfiction books, novels, textbooks, juvenile books, movie scripts, TV scripts and poetry collections. Currently handles 11% fiction; 30% nonfiction books; 40% novels; 2% textbooks; 9% juvenile books; 2% movie scripts; 1% TV scripts; 2% poetry; and 3% science fiction. "Will read at no charge

query letter and two sample chapters. Charges criticism fee; $100 for 3-page critique. Reports within 3 months. Pre-stamped return mailer must accompany submissions."
Terms: Agent receives 10% commission on domestic sales; 15% on dramatic sales; and 20% on foreign sales. Sometimes offers a consultation service through which writers not represented can get advice on a contract; charges $50/hour. Income derived from commission on ms sales and critique fees.
Recent Sales: *Captured Corregidor: Diary of an American P.O.W. in WWII*, by John M. Wright, Jr. (McFarland & Co); *Modern Language for Musicians*, by Julie Yarbrough (Pendragon Press); and *Weight Loss for Super Wellness*, by Ted L. Edwards Jr., M.D. (life enhancement).

REID BOATES LITERARY AGENCY, 44 Mountain Ridge Dr., Wayne NJ 07470. (201)628-7523. Contact: Reid Boates. Represents 45 clients. 20% of clients are new/unpublished writers. "To be represented writers must have a writing background, though not necessarily in books." Specializes in biography and nonfiction; topical documentary, autobiography; wellness and general how-to, business (investigative); fiction: good, clear writing; strong story and character.
Will Handle: Nonfiction books, novels. Currently handles 90% nonfiction books; 10% novels. Will read—at no charge—unsolicited queries and outlines. Does not read unsolicited mss. Reports in 2 weeks.
Terms: Agent receives 15% commission on domestic sales; 15% on dramatic sales; 10% on foreign sales, "plus 10% for the foreign co-agent."
Fees: Charges for photocopying over $50.
Recent Sales: *United on the American Night*, by Kevin Coyne (Random House); and *Mankind's First Family*, by Donald Johansen and Kevin O'Farrell (Villard).

THE BOOK PEDDLERS, 18326 Minnetonka Blvd., Deephaven MN 55391. (612)475-3527. Owner/Agent: Vicki Lansky. Estab. 1984. Member of ILAA. "Also provides, on occasion, book packaging services and does publish a few titles." Represents 26 clients. 80% of clients are new/unpublished writers. Prefers to work with published/established authors. "Small agency because owner is also an author and columnist."
Will Handle: Nonfiction books and syndicated material. Currently handles 100% nonfiction books. Will read—at no charge—unsolicited queries and outlines. Does not read unsolicited mss. Reports in 2 weeks on queries. "We take on very few new clients."
Terms: Agent receives 15% commission on domestic sales; and 20% on foreign sales.
Fees: Does not charge reading fee "at this time (May 1989). We do charge, however, a fee of $5 per submission. If we cannot sell your material after submitting it to 10 publishers (or any number mutually agreed upon), we will submit a bill which is payable upon receipt. This is a fee that we feel accurately represents our time, postage, phone calls, typing and copying expense." 90% of agency income derived from commission on ms sales.
Recent Sales: *My Writing Book*, by Joyce Baumgartner (Scholastic); *Jewish-American Baby Name Book*, by Smadar Sidi (Harper and Row); and *Buying, Raising and Showing Your Pedigree Dog*, by Jeannie Burt (Wynwood).

BOOKSTOP LITERARY AGENCY, 67 Meadow View Rd., Orinda CA 94563. (415)254-2664. Owner: Kendra Marcus. Estab. 1984. Represents 60 clients. 20% of clients are new/unpublished writers. Specializes in juvenile and young adult fiction and nonfiction.
Will Handle: Only juvenile books (ages 6 months to 16 years). Will read submissions at no charge, but may charge a criticism fee or service charge for work performed after the initial reading. Reports in 6 weeks on mss. Please do not send queries except with nonfiction. Send ms complete.
Terms: Agent receives 15% commission on domestic sales; 20% on dramatic sales; and 20% on foreign sales.
Fees: Charges criticism fee "if the author has asked for a detailed critique." .001% of income derived from criticism fees. Charges $200 for 300-page double-spaced book manuscript. "Agent provides critiques of three or four pages (general) with line by line where necessary." Charges for postage, phone and copying. Sometimes offers consultation service through which writers can get advice on a contract. "We work out the fee." 95% of income derived from commission on mss sales; 5% of income derived from fees.
Recent Sales: *Bronco Dogs*, by Cohen/Shepherd (Dutton), *City, San Francisco*, by Climo (Macmillan); and *Jenny*, by Wilson/Johnson (Macmillan).

GEORGES BORCHARDT INC., 136 E. 57th St., New York NY 10022. (212)753-5785. FAX: (212)838-6518. President: Georges Borchardt. Estab. 1967. Member of SAR. Represents 200 clients. 1-2% of our clients are new/unpublished writers. "We do not consider new clients unless highly recommended by someone we trust." Prefers to work with published/established authors; also works with a small number of new/unpublished authors. Specializes in fiction, biography and general nonfiction of unusual interest.
Will Handle: Nonfiction books and novels. Does not read unsolicited mss.
Terms: Agent receives 10% commission on domestic sales; 10% on dramatic sales; and 20% on foreign sales (15% on British).
Fees: Charges for photocopy expenses.
Recent Sales: *If The River Was Whiskey*, by T. Coraghessan Boyle (Viking Press); *Among School Children*, by Tracy Kidder (Houghton Mifflin); and *Jazz Cleopatra*, by Phyllis Rose (Doubleday).

THE BRADLEY-GOLDSTEIN AGENCY, Suite 6E, 7 Lexington Ave., New York NY 10010. President: Paul Bradley. Director: Martha Goldstein. Estab. 1985. Represents 50 clients. 25% of clients have been new/unpublished writers. Will consider taking on a small number of new/unpublished authors. Specializes in "quality" nonfiction: biographies, politics, science, social science, business, current affairs, and the arts. "No fiction queries, please (in 1990)."
Will Handle: Nonfiction books. Currently handles 90% nonfiction books; 10% novels. Will read—at no charge—unsolicited query letters and outlines only. Do not send mss. Reports in 2 months on queries.
Terms: Agent receives 15% commission on domestic sales; and 25% on foreign sales.
Fees: Charges for postage, photocopying, and telephone expenses. 90% of income is derived from commission on ms sales; 10% on consultations.
Recent Sales: *Mixed Feelings*, by Cynthia Ehrlich (E.P. Dutton); *The Book of Crabs and Lobsters*, by Christopher Reaske (Lyons & Burford); *Bomber One: Story of The B-1 Bomber*, by James L.H. Peck (Paragon House).

‡BRANDT & BRANDT LITERARY AGENTS, INC., 1501 Broadway, New York NY 10036. (212)840-5760. Estab. 1914. Member of SAR. Represents 250 clients. Works with a small number of new/unpublished authors.
Will Handle: Nonfiction books and novels. "We read and answer letters from writers about their work only."
Terms: Agent receives 10% commission on domestic sales; 10% on dramatic sales; and 20% on foreign sales.
Recent Sales: No information given.

‡RUTH HAGY BROD LITERARY AGENCY, 15 Park Ave., New York NY 10016. (212)683-3232. FAX: (212)269-0313. President: A.T. Brod. Estab. 1975. Represents 10 clients. 10% of clients are new/unpublished authors. Prefers to work with published/established authors. Specializes in trade books.
Will Handle: Nonfiction books. Currently handles 95% nonfiction books and 5% novels. Will read submissions at no charge, but may charge a criticism fee or service charge for work performed after the initial reading. Reports in 5 weeks on queries; 2 months on mss.
Terms: Agent receives 15% commission on domestic sales and 20% on foreign sales.
Fees: Charges a reading fee; waives reading fee when representing writer. 5% of income derived from reading fees. Charges a criticism fee. 5% of income derived from criticism fees.
Recent Sales: No information given.

NED BROWN INC., Box 1044, Malibu CA 90265. (213)456-8068. President: Ned Brown. Estab. 1963. Writer must be previously published or have a recommendation from other client or publisher. Prefers to work with published/established authors.
Will Handle: Magazine fiction, nonfiction books, novels, movie scripts, stage plays and TV scripts. Does not read unsolicited mss.
Terms: Agent receives 15% commission on domestic sales; 15% on dramatic sales; and 20% on foreign sales.
Fees: Charges writers for "extraordinary expenses."
Recent Sales: No information given.

ANDREA BROWN, LITERARY AGENCY, 301 West 53rd St., New York NY 10019. (212)581-7068. Owner: Andrea Brown. Estab. 1981. Member of ILAA. Number of clients: confidential. 50% of our clients are new/unpublished writers. Specializes in children's books—all ages.
Will Handle: Juvenile books (preschool, ages 6-9 and 8-12). Currently handles 5% adult nonfiction books; 95% juvenile books. "Young adult is dead, so I'm mostly looking for middle-group books." Will read—at no charge—unsolicited queries and outlines. Reports in 2 weeks on queries; 3 months on manuscripts.
Terms: Agent receives 15% commission on domestic sales; 20% on foreign sales.
Recent Sales: *How to Find a Ghost*, by James Deem (Houghton Mifflin); *Harry Newberry and The Raiders of the Red Drink*, by Mel Gilden (Holt); and *Nothing To Fear*, by Jackie French Koller (HBJ).

PEMA BROWNE LTD., 185 E. 85th St., New York NY 10028. (212)369-1925. Treasurer: Perry J. Browne. Estab. 1966. Member of WGA. Represents 35 clients. 25% of clients are new/unpublished writers. "We review only new projects and require that writers have not sent manuscript to publishers or other agents." Specializes in men's adventure, thrillers, mainstream, historical, regencies and contemporary romances; young adult; children's; reference; how-to and other types of nonfiction.
Will Handle: Nonfiction books, novels, juvenile books. Currently handles 25% nonfiction books; 25% novels; 10% juvenile books; and 40% mass-market.
Terms: Agent receives 15% commission on domestic sales; 10% on dramatic sales; and 15% on foreign sales.
Fees: "In some cases, a reading fee."
Recent Sales: *Travelling Salesman*, by Ron Dee (Dell); *Across the Creek*, by Marga Smith (Arcade/Little Brown); and *Sussex Summer*, by Luci Le Moore (Harlequin).

THE MARSHALL CAMERON AGENCY, Rt. 1, Box 125, Lawtey FL 32058. (904)964-7013. Contact: Margo Prescott. California: Box 922101, Sylmar, CA 91341. (818)365-3400. Contact: Wendy Zhorne. Represents 30 clients. "Prefer writers with credits but we are always open to new talent." Specializes in screenplays and

MFT's; published novels (no vanity) with screenplay potential; writers and producers with 50% project financing in place.

Will Handle: Novels and nonfiction.

Terms: Agent receives 15% commission on domestic and dramatic sales; 20% on foreign sales.

Fees: Charges $50 reading/evaluation (offers recommendation)/250 pages (novels, nonfiction); $45 for screenplays. Comprehensive critique is provided at writer's request. Will read queries and synopses at no charge. "We are a 'full service' agency, providing 'hands-on' editing, revising, script doctoring, as well as researchers, ghostwriters and typing, for both clients and nonclients. We also provide pre-production services to film producers."

Recent Sales: Confidential.

RUTH CANTOR, LITERARY AGENT, Rm. 1133, 156 5th Ave., New York NY 10010. (212)243-3246. Contact: Ruth Cantor. Estab. 1952. Represents 40 clients. Writer must have "a good, sound track record in the publishing field ... A skimpy one will sometimes get you a reading if I'm convinced that talent might be lurking in the bulrushes." Prefers to work with published/established authors; works with a small number of new/unpublished authors. Specializes in "any good trade book, fiction of quality, good, competent mysteries with new elements, juvenile books above the age of 8, up through young adult (12-16)."

Will Handle: Nonfiction books, novels and juvenile books. Will read—at no charge—unsolicited queries and outlines. Reports in 1 month on queries; 2 months on mss.

Terms: Agent receives 10% commission on domestic sales; 10% on dramatic sales; and 10% on foreign sales.

Recent Sales: *The Rod of Sybil* (Harcourt); *The Players* (Warner); and *Lady Divine*, by Barbara Sherrod (Warner).

MARTHA CASSELMAN, LITERARY AGENT, Box 342, Callstoga CA 94515-0342. (707)942-4341. Estab. 1978. Member ILAA. 25% of clients are new/unpublished writers. Works with small number of new/unpublished writers. Specializes in food books, general nonfiction, fiction, occasional humor, small number of children's books.

Will Handle: Nonfiction books; novels, juvenile books. Will read—at no charge—unsolicited queries and outlines. Does not read unsolicited mss. Reports in 1 month. "Cannot return long distance query phone calls."

Terms: Agent receives 15% commission on domestic sales.

Fees: Charges for copying, overnight mail or travel made at author's request.

Recent Sales: Confidential.

‡THE CATALOG™ LITERARY AGENCY, Box 2964, Vancouver WA 98668. (206)694-8531. Contact: Douglas Storey. Estab. 1986. Represents 23 clients. 50% of clients are new/unpublished writers. Eager to work with new/unpublished writers. Specializes in nonfiction, mainstream fiction, technical, textbooks and juvenile manuscripts.

Will Handle: Popular, professional and textbooks in all subjects (but especially in business, health, money, science and women's interests), how-to and self-help. Will read—at no charge—unsolicited queries, outlines and manuscripts. Reports in 3 weeks on queries. Does not return material unless accompanied by SASE.

Terms: Agent receives 15% commission on domestic sales; 20% on dramatic sales; and 20% on foreign sales.

Fees: Charges a criticism fee "if the writer requests a written evaluation of the submitted manuscript." 2% of income derived from criticism fees. Charges $150/300 pages. Critique is four to six pages and includes overall evaluation with specific examples, marketing advice included—if ms is marketable. Critiques provided by Douglas Storey. Except for recently published authors, charges an upfront handling fee that covers photocopying, postage and telephone expense. 80% of income derived from sales of writers' work; 20% of income derived from criticism services.

Recent Sales: *In the Mouth of the Dragon*, (Avery Publishing Group) and *Did God Make Them Black*, (Winston-Derek Publishers).

‡JAMES CHARLTON ASSOCIATES, 680 Washington St., New York NY 10014. (212)691-4951. FAX: (212)691-4952. Contact: Lisa Friedman. Estab. 1981. Represents 20 clients. 50% of clients are new/unpublished writers. To be represented, writer must "have published more than one article or be authority in his/her field." Specializes in self-help, working, finance and sports.

Will Handle: Nonfiction books. Currently handles 99% nonfiction books and 1% novels. Will read—at no charge—unsolicited queries and outlines. Reports in 2 weeks on queries.

Terms: Agent receives 15% commission on domestic sales and 20% on foreign sales.

Fees: Charges writers for photocopies and postage if it exceeds $50.

Recent Sales: *Cook School of Umbria*, by Soviero (Macmillan); *Personal Finance Series*, 10 books (Houghton-Mifflin); and *Shield of the Republic*, by Isenberg (St. Martin's).

TERRY CHIZ AGENCY, Suite E, 5761 Whitnall Hwy., North Hollywood CA 91601. (818)506-0994. President: Terry Chiz. Vice President: Shan Sia. Estab. 1984. Represents 18 clients. 20% of clients are new/unpublished writers. Prefers to work with published/established authors; works with a small number of new/unpublished authors. Specializes in film and TV.
Will Handle: Novels, movie scripts and TV scripts. No romance or historical. Currently handles 20% novels; 40% movie scripts; and 40% TV scripts. Will read — at no charge — unsolicited queries and outlines. Reports in 2 weeks. Will not respond without SASE.
Terms: Agent receives 10% commission.
Recent Sales: "Film deals pending on several properties that are in book and script — not for public information."

‡**CONNIE CLAUSEN ASSOCIATES**, 250 E. 87th St., New York NY 10128. (212)427-6135. Contact: Connie Clausen (nonfiction); Susan Lipson (fiction). Estab. 1976. Member ASJA. Represents approximately 90 clients. Prefers to work with published authors who have prior magazine and/or book credits; works with a small number of new authors. Considers recommendations from clients and publishers. Specializes in trade nonfiction of all kinds: self-help, how-to, health, beauty, biographies, true crime and cookbooks, and mainstream and literary fiction for adults and children.
Will Handle: Nonfiction books, novels and juvenile books (ages 4-12). No magazine articles, romance or sci-fi novels, screenplays or humor books. Will sell movie rights for books we handle. Currently handles 75% nonfiction; 23% novels; and 2% juvenile. Does not read unsolicited mss. Reports in 6 weeks on full manuscripts, 1 month on proposals.
Terms: Agent receives 15% commission on domestic sales and dramatic sales; and 20% on foreign sales.
Fees: Charges for photocopying and shipping. No reading fees.
Recent Sales: *Happier Ever After*, by Dr. Sonya Friedman (Little, Brown); *The Don Juan Dilemma*, by Jane Carpineto, MSW, (Morrow); *Jackson Pollock*, by Steven Naifeh and Gregory White Smith (Clarkson-Potter).

DIANE CLEAVER INC., 55 5th St., New York NY 10003. (212)206-5600. Estab. 1982. Member ILAA. Specializes in general trade fiction/nonfiction.
Will Handle: Nonfiction books, novels. Will read — at no charge — unsolicited queries and outlines. Does not read unsolicited mss. Reports in 3 weeks on queries; 5 weeks on mss.
Terms: Agent receives 15% commission on domestic sales; 15% on dramatic sales and 19% on foreign sales.
Fees: Charges for photocopying. 100% of income derived from mss sales.
Recent Sales: Confidential.

RUTH COHEN, INC., Box 7626, Menlo Park CA 94025. (415)854-2054. President: Ruth Cohen. Estab. 1982. Member of ILAA. Represents 45-60 clients. 30% of clients are new/unpublished writers. Writers must have a book that is well written. Prefers to work with published/established authors; eager to work with new/unpublished writers. Specializes in juvenile fiction, young adult fiction and nonfiction and adult genre books — mystery, western, historical romance, horror and thrillers. No poetry or screenplays.
Will Handle: Fiction and nonfiction books for adults, juvenile books (for ages 3-14) adult and young adult books, and genre novels — mystery, western, mainstream romance, regency romances and historical romance. Currently handles 20% nonfiction books; 30% novels; and 50% juvenile books. Will read — at no charge — unsolicited queries with 10 opening pages of manuscripts, outlines and partial mss with SASE. "No complete manuscripts unless requested." Reports in 3 weeks on queries; 1 month on mss. "No multiple agency submissions." Must include SASE with all mss on queries.
Terms: Agent receives 15% commission on domestic sales; 15% on dramatic sales; and 20% on foreign sales.
Fees: Charges writers only for photocopying and foreign postage.
Recent Sales: *Wormholes*, by Lensey Namioka (Harper YA); *Dearly Beloved*, by Mary Jo Pritney (NAL); and *Irish Piper*, by Jim Latimer (Scribners).

HY COHEN LITERARY AGENCY, LTD., Suite 1400, 111 W. 57th St., New York NY 10019. (212)757-5237. Mail queries and manuscripts to Box 743, Upper Montclair NJ 07043. President: Hy Cohen. Estab. 1975. Represents 20 clients. 50% of our clients are new/unpublished writers.
Will Handle: Nonfiction books and novels. Currently handles 50% nonfiction books and 50% novels. Will read — at no charge — unsolicited queries, outlines and mss, accompanied by SASE. Reports in 2 weeks on queries; 1 month on mss.
Terms: Agent receives 10% commission on domestic sales; 10% on dramatic sales; and 20% on foreign sales.
Fees: Charges for "unusual" postage and phone expenses. 100% of income derived from commission on ms sales.
Recent Sales: *Common Sense ESP*, by Robert Ferguson (St. Martin's); *How Long Can You Love A Lemon*, by Daniel Hayes (Godine); and *South Texas*, by Ann Gabriel (Ballantine).

COLLIER ASSOCIATES, 2000 Flat Run Rd., Seaman OH 45679. (513)764-1234. Manager: Oscar Collier. Associate: Carol Cartaino. Estab. 1976. Member of SAR and ILAA. Represents 80 clients. Rarely works with new/unpublished authors. Specializes in fiction trade books (war, crime and historical novels) and nonfiction trade books on business and finance, biographies, math for general audience, politics, exposes, nature and outdoors and history.
Terms: Agent receives 15% commission on domestic sales; 15% on dramatic sales; and 20% on foreign sales.
Fees: Charges for books ordered from publishers for rights submissions, Express Mail and copying expenses.
Recent Sales: *The Economic Time Bomb*, by Harry Browne (St. Martin's Press); *Sizzle*, by Barbara Brett (Zebra); and *How Do I Clean the Moosehead?*, by Don Aslett (NAL).

FRANCES COLLIN LITERARY AGENCY, 110 West 40th St., New York NY 10018. (212)840-8664. Contact: Frances Collin. Estab. 1948. Member of SAR. Represents 90 clients. Almost always works only with published/established authors; works with a very small number of new/unpublished authors. Has a "broad general trade list."
Will Handle: Nonfiction books and novels. Currently handles 50% nonfiction books; 50% fiction books. Will read—at no charge—unsolicited queries. Reports in 1 week on queries.
Terms: Agent receives 15% commission on domestic sales; 20% on dramatic sales; and 25% on foreign sales.
Fees: Charges for overseas postage, photocopy and registered mail expenses and copyright registration fees.
Recent Sales: Confidential.

CONNOR LITERARY AGENCY, 640 W. 153rd St., New York NY 10031. (212)491-5233. Owner: Marlene Connor. Estab. 1985. Represents 28 clients. 25% of clients are new/unpublished writers. "Seeking books with strong promotion possibilities; published writers with good track records; new writers with solid credentials."
Will Handle: Nonfiction: parenting, illustrated books, self-help, beauty, fitness, relationships, how-to, cookbooks, true crime. Fiction: mysteries, horror, espionage, suspense, mainstream.Will read—at no charge—unsolicited queries and outlines. Reports in 2 months on queries. "Material will not be returned without SASE."
Terms: Agent receives 15% commission on domestic sales; and 25% on foreign sales.
Fees: Reading fees $40 for proposals with sample chapter; $65 and up for full ms. Charges for photocopy, postage, telephone and messenger expenses, and special materials for presentation. 2% of income derived from fees; 98% of income derived from commission on ms sales.
Recent Sales: *Venus Unbound: Actualizing the Power of Being Female*, by Dina von Zweck and Jaye Smith (Fireside); *Hotwire*, by Randy Russell (Bantam); *Shattered Lullabies*, by Morton Reed (Zebra).

ROBERT CORNFIELD LITERARY AGENCY, 145 West 79th St., Apt. 16C, New York NY 10024. (212)874-2465. Associate Director: Jeffrey Essmann. Estab. 1980. Member ILAA. Represents 70 clients. 50% of client's are new/unpublished writers. Specializes in fiction, food, music, film, literary criticism and art.
Will Handle: Magazine articles, magazine fiction, nonfiction books and novels. Currently handles 20% magazine articles; 60% nonfiction books and 20% novels. Will read—at no cost—unsolicited queries, outlines and manuscripts. Reports in 2 weeks on queries; 1 month on mss.
Terms: Agent receives 15% commission on domestic sales; 15% on dramatic sales; and 20% on foreign sales.
Fees: Charges for foreign postage and ms photocopying.
Recent Sales: *Encyclopedia of Bad Taste*, by Jane and Michael Stern (Harper & Row); *Music of Bob Dylan*, by Tim Riley (Knopf/Vintage); *Animal Politics*, by Vicki Hearne (Weidenfeld & Nicolson).

‡CREATIVE CONCEPTS LITERARY AGENCY, Suite V, 509 67th Ave. N., Myrtle Beach SC 29577. Director: Michele Glance Serwach. Estab. 1987. Represent 15 clients. 80% of clients are new/unpublished writers. "We welcome new/unpublished writers—the only requirement is that you have an outline or manuscript ready to submit." Eager to work with new/unpublished writers. Specializes in how-to books, self-help books, cookbooks, general interest novels, romance novels and poetry.
Will Handle: Magazine articles, nonfiction books, novels, juvenile books, movie scripts, TV scripts, syndicated material, poetry. Currently handles 5% magazine articles; 50% nonfiction books; 20% novels; 5% juvenile books; 5% movie scripts; 5% TV scripts; 5% syndicated material; 5% poetry. Will read—at no charge—unsolicited queries and outlines. Reports in 3 weeks on queries; 5 weeks on mss.
Terms: Agent receives 12% commission on domestic sales; 12% on dramatic sales; and 12% on foreign sales.
Recent Sales: Confidential.

RICHARD CURTIS ASSOCIATES, INC., Suite 1, 164 E. 64th St., New York NY 10021. (212)371-9481. President: Richard Curtis. Contact: Elizabeth Waxse, Rob Cohen, Rich Henshaw, associates. Estab. 1969. Member of ILAA. Represents 100 clients. 5% of clients are new/unpublished writers. Writer must have some published work and either a finished novel or proposed nonfiction book. Prefers to work with published/established authors; works with a small number of new/unpublished authors. Specializes in commercial fiction of all genres, mainstream fiction and nonfiction. Especially interested in health, science, how-to, New Age, psychology, biography, social history, women's issues, relationships, business, true crime.

Will Handle: Nonfiction books, novels, movie scripts and juvenile books. Currently handles 1% magazine articles; 1% magazine fiction; 25% nonfiction books; 70% novels; 3% juvenile books. Will read—at no charge—unsolicited queries and outlines. Reports in 2 weeks on queries; 1 month on mss.

Terms: Agent receives 10% commission on domestic fiction, 15% nonfiction sales; 15% on dramatic sales; and 20% on foreign sales.

Fees: Occasionally charges a reading fee; less than 1% of income derived from reading fee. Charges for photocopying, messengers, purchase of books for subsidiary exploitations, cable, air mail and express mail. Offers a consultation service through which writers not represented can get advice on a contract; charges $200/hour.

Recent Sales: *Masquerade*, by Janet Dailey (Little, Brown); *Phases of Gravity*, by Dan Simmons (Bantam); and *Queen of Angels*, by Greg Bear (Warner).

‡ELAINE DAVIE LITERARY AGENCY, Village Gate Square, 274 North Goodman St., Rochester NY 14607. (716)442-8030. President: Elaine Davie. Estab. 1986. Represents 40 clients. 30% of clients are new/unpublished writers. Works with a small number of new/unpublished authors. Specializes in adult fiction and nonfiction, particularly books by and for women and genre/fiction (romances, historicals, mysteries, horror, westerns, etc.). "We pride ourselves on prompt and personal responses." Please query first with letter and synopsis or brief description of manuscript.

Will Handle: Nonfiction books, novels, juvenile books (no children's books or poetry). Handles 30% nonfiction; 60% novels; 10% juvenile books. Will read—at no charge—unsolicited queries and outlines. Reports in 2 weeks on queries. "If our agency does not respond within 1 month to your request to become a client, you may submit requests elsewhere."

Terms: Agent receives 15% commission on domestic sales; 20% on dramatic sales; and 20% on foreign sales.

Recent Sales: *City of Glan*, by Paul Bagdon (Ballantine), *Perfect Morning*, by Marcia Evanick (Bantam); and *Captive Heart*, by Roberta Stalberg (Dell).

‡DOROTHY DEERING, LITERARY AGENCY, 251 Jason Dr., Nicholasville KY 40356. (606)887-2881. Literary Agent: Dorothy Deering. Estab. 1989. Represents 7 clients. 75% of clients are new/unpublished writers. "We are a new agency and are anxious to work with new, unpublished authors as well as published authors." Specializes in fiction i.e., science fiction, mystery, romance, juvenile novels as well as short stories and articles.

Will Handle: Magazine articles, magazine fiction, nonfiction books, novels, juvenile books, movie scripts, stage plays and TV scripts. Currently handles 10% magazine articles; 10% magazine fiction; 20% nonfiction books; 50% novels; and 10% juvenile books. Will read—at no charge—unsolicited queries and outlines. Reports in 2 weeks on queries; 3-6 weeks on manuscripts.

Terms: Agent receives 12% commission on domestic sales; 15% on dramatic sales; and 15% on foreign sales.

Fees: Charges a reading fee; provides free critiques. Charges $100 for book manuscript-charges for postage, copying, phone calls. 5% of income derived from reading fees. Provides 3-5 page critique from agent.

Recent Sales: *The Sleepers*, *The Unseen* and *The Secret of the Temple*.

ANITA DIAMANT, THE WRITER'S WORKSHOP, INC., #1508, 310 Madison Ave., New York NY 10017. (212)687-1122. President: Anita Diamant. Estab. 1917. Member of SAR. Represents 100 clients. 30% of clients are new/unpublished writers. Prefers to work with published/established authors; works with a small number of new/unpublished authors. Specializes in general and commercial fiction (hard and soft cover) such as historical romances, general romances, horror and science fiction; and nonfiction such as health, politics and biography.

Will Handle: Magazine articles, nonfiction books and novels. Currently handles 40% nonfiction books; 40% novels; 10% young adult books; and 10% other. Will read—at no charge—unsolicited queries. Reports in 1 month on queries.

Terms: Agent receives 15% commission for up to $20,000 advance on domestic sales—10% thereafter; 15% on dramatic sales; and 15-20% on foreign sales.

Fees: Charges for photocopy, messenger, special mailing and telephone expenses.

Recent Sales: *Gates of Paradise*, by V.C. Andrews (Poseidon); *New McGarr*, by Bartholemew Gill (Morrow); and *Crazy English*, by Richard Lederer (Pocket).

SANDRA DIJKSTRA LITERARY AGENCY, Suite 515C, 1237 Camino Del Mar, Del Mar CA 92014. (619)755-3115. FAX: (619)792-1494. Contact: Sandra Dijkstra. Estab. 1981. Member of ILAA. Represents 50 clients. 60% of clients are new/unpublished writers. "We, of course, prefer to take on established authors, but are happy to represent any writer of brilliance or special ability. Most of our sales have been nonfiction, but we are building a quality fiction list."

Will Handle: Nonfiction books (author must have expertise in the field) and novels. "We are expanding our fiction client list through our new associate agent, Katherine Goodwin, to include category and commercial fiction as well as contemporary/literary novels. We are interested in thriller-suspense fiction of all kinds, horror, science fiction/fantasy and historical romance by writers with distinctive voices and mainstream potential." Currently handles 75% nonfiction books; 25% novels. Will read—at no charge—unsolicited queries and outlines accompanied by SASE. Reports in 3 weeks on queries.

Terms: Receives 15% commission on domestic sales; 20% on British sales (10% to British agent); and 30% on translation (20% to foreign agent who represents world rights).

Fees: Charges a $175 yearly expense fee to cover phone, postage, photocopy costs incurred in marketing ms of authors under contract.

Recent Sales: *The Joy Luck Club*, by Amy Tan (Putnam's); *White Rabbit: A Doctor's Story of Her Addiction and Recovery*, by Martha Morrison, M.D. (Crown); and *If I'm So Wonderful Why Am I Still Single?*, by Susan Page (Viking).

THE JONATHAN DOLGER AGENCY, Suite 9B, 49 E. 96th St., New York NY 10128. (212)427-1853. President: Jonathan Dolger. Estab. 1980. Represents 70 clients. 25% of clients are new/unpublished writers. Writer must have been previously published if submitting fiction. Prefers to work with published/established authors; works with a small number of new/unpublished writers. Specializes in adult trade fiction and nonfiction, and illustrated books.

Will Handle: Nonfiction books, novels and illustrated books. Will read—at no charge—unsolicited queries and outlines with SASE included.

Terms: Agent receives 15% commission on domestic sales; 10% on dramatic sales; and 25-30% on foreign sales.

Fees: Charges for "standard expenses."

Recent Sales: Confidential.

‡DYKEMAN ASSOCIATES, INC., 4115 Rawlins, Dallas TX 75219. (214)528-2991. FAX (214)528-0241. President: Alice Dykeman. Estab. 1973. Represents 15 clients. Prefers to work with published/established authors.

Will Handle: Nonfiction books, novels, movie scripts. Currently handles 30% nonfiction books; 10% novels; 40% movie scripts; 20% TV scripts. Will read submissions at no charge, but may charge a criticism fee or service charge for work performed after the initial reading.

Terms: Agent receives 15% commission.

Fees: Charges writers for out-of-pocket expenses, photocopies, faxes, long distance phone charges.

Recent Sales: "Several in the works, cannot release titles yet."

EDUCATIONAL DESIGN SERVICES, INC., Box 253, Wantagh NY 11793. (718)539-4107/(516)221-0995. Vice President: Edwin Selzer. President: Bertram Linder. Estab. 1979. Represents 18 clients. 90% of clients are new/unpublished writers. Eager to work with new/unpublished writers in the educational field. Specializes in educational materials aimed at the kindergarten through 12th grade market; primarily textual materials.

Will Handle: Nonfiction books and textbooks. Currently handles 100% textbooks. Reports in 1 month. "You must send SASE."

Terms: Agent receives 15% commission on domestic sales and 25% on foreign sales.

Fees: Charges for phone, postage and delivery expenses, and retyping "if necessary"; charges $50/hour.

Recent Sales: *Money* (Schoolhouse Press); *Nueva Historia de Los Estados Unidos* (Minerva Books); and *Comprehensive Social Studies* (Barrons Education Series).

‡VICKI EISENBERG LITERARY AGENCY, 4514 Travis, Dallas TX 75205. (214)521-8430. FAX: (214)521-8454. President: Vicki Eisenberg. Literary Agent: Ann Whitley. Estab. 1984. Represents 20 clients. Prefers to work with published/established authors; works with a small number of new/unpublished authors. Specializes in adult novels and nonfiction books, especially humor, social and political commentary, mysteries, true crime; magazine articles and fiction for authors who also write books.

Will Handle: Nonfiction books, novels, stage plays and syndicated material. Currently handles 5% magazine articles; 42% nonfiction books; 18% novels; 8% movie scripts; 3% radio scripts; 8% stage plays; 11% TV scripts and 5% syndicated material. Will read—at no charge—unsolicited queries and outlines. Does not read unsolicited manuscripts. Reports in 3 weeks on queries.

Terms: Agent receives 15% commission on domestic sales; 15% on dramatic sales; and 20% on foreign sales.

Fees: Charges writers for photocopies of manuscripts, overnight mail and messenger expenses.

Recent Sales: *White Like Me: Joe Bob Returns to the Drive-in*, by Joe Bob Briggs (Delacorte); *The Death Shift*, by Peter Elkind (Viking); and *How to Improve Your Cat*, by William J. Helmer (Tor Books).

PETER ELEK ASSOCIATES, Box 223, Canal St. Station, New York NY 10013. (212)431-9368. FAX: (212)966-5768. Associate: Carol Diehl. Assistant: Liza Lagunoff. Estab. 1979. Also provides book packaging services. Represents 25 clients. 10% of our clients are new/unpublished writers. "An applicant must be, or is clearly intending to be, self-supporting through their writing." Prefers to work with published/established authors; works with a small number of new/unpublished authors. Specializes in illustrated nonfiction, current affairs, self-help (not pop-psych), contemporary biography/autobiography, food, popular culture (all for adults); and preschool and juvenile illustrated fiction, nonfiction and novelties; and contemporary adventure for adults.

Will Handle: Nonfiction books, novels and juvenile books. No category fiction. Currently handles 75% non-fiction books and 25% juvenile books. Will read—at no charge—unsolicited queries and outlines. Reports in 2 weeks on queries.

Terms: Agent receives 15% commission on domestic sales; 20% on dramatic sales; and 20% on foreign sales.

Fees: Charges for manuscript retyping, "if required." 5% of income derived from fees; 30% of income derived from commission on ms sales ("65% derived from sale of finished packaged books").

Recent Sales: *Vegetarian Celebrations* (Little, Brown); *The Spirit of Columbus* (Simon and Schuster); *The Great Rosy Radish* (Joy Street).

ETHAN ELLENBERG, LITERARY AGENT, #5-C, 548 Broadway, New York NY 10012. (212)431-4554. FAX: (212)941-4652. President: Ethan Ellenberg. Estab. 1984. Represents 40 clients. 30% of clients are new/unpublished writers. Eager to work with new/unpublished writers. Specializes in quality fiction and nonfiction, first novels, thriller, glitz, spy, military, history, biography, science fiction.

Will Handle: Nonfiction books, novels, juvenile books. Currently handles 25% nonfiction books; 70% novels; 5% juvenile books. Will read—at no charge—unsolicited queries, outlines and mss. Must include SASE. Reports in 3 weeks on queries; 6 weeks on mss. Prefers outline and first 3 chapters.

Terms: Agent receives 15% commission on domestic sales; 15% on dramatic sales; and 20% on foreign sales.

Fees: Charges for cost of photocopies up to 10 mss for sale, finished copies for submission to foreign markets and Hollywood.

Recent Sales: *Danang Diary*, by Tom Yarborough (St. Martin's); *Brack +1*, by Johnney Quarles (Berkley); and *Royal Chaos +1*, by Dan McGirt (NAL).

THE ERIKSON LITERARY AGENCY, 223 Via Sevilla, Santa Barbara CA 93109. (805)564-8782. Agent: George Erikson. Estab. 1987. Represents 32 clients. 70% of clients are new/unpublished writers. Eager to work with new/unpublished writers.

Will Handle: Nonfiction books, novels and movie scripts. Currently handles 60% nonfiction books; 30% novels and 10% movie scripts. Reports in 1 month on queries; 2 months on mss. Writer's guidelines available for #10 SAE with 2 first class stamps.

Terms: Receives 15% commission on domestic sales; 15% on dramatic sales and 20% on foreign sales.

Fees: Charges reading fee of $100 for full ms; $75 for screenplay. Reading fee will be deducted from agency's earned commissions. 10% of income derived from reading fees. Writer receives one-page evaluation with marketing advice. Charges for photocopying, mailing and telephone are charged against advances. 90% of income derived from sales of writer's work; 10% of income derived from criticism services.

Recent Sales: *Elvis, My Brother*, by Billy Stanley (St. Martin's); *Imagine That*, by Ken Cohen (Capra Press); *The Don Juan Papers*, by Richard de Mille (Goodyear Publishing).

EVANS AND ASSOCIATES, 14330 Caves Rd., Novelty OH 44072. (216)338-3264. Agent/Owner: Clyde Evans. Estab. 1987. "This agency will represent any author whose work, based on agency review, is of such quality that it is deemed sellable." Eager to work with new/unpublished writers.

Will Handle: Various types of material. Will read—at no charge—unsolicited queries, outlines and mss. Reports in 3 weeks on queries; 2 months on mss.

Terms: Agent receives 15% commission on domestic sales; 10% on dramatic sales; and 20% total on foreign sales—10% to foreign agent.

Fees: Charges for photocopying over 75 pages, legal advice beyond normal agency services, messenger.

Recent Sales: No information given.

JOHN FARQUHARSON LTD., Suite 1007, 250 W. 57th St., New York NY 10107. (212)245-1993. Director: Jane Gelfman. Agent: Deborah Schneider. Estab. 1919 (London); 1980 (New York). Member of SAR and ILAA. Represents 125 clients. 5% of clients are new/unpublished writers. Prefers to work with published/established authors; works with a small number of new/unpublished authors. Specializes in general trade fiction and nonfiction. No poetry, short stories or screenplays.

Will Handle: Fiction and nonfiction; handles magazine articles and magazine fiction only for authors already represented. Currently handles 49% nonfiction books; 49% novels; and 2% juvenile books. Will read—at no charge—unsolicited queries and outlines. Reports in 3 weeks on queries. SASE necessary.

Terms: Agent receives 10% commission on domestic sales; 10% on dramatic sales; and 20% on foreign sales.

Fees: Charges for messengers, photocopying and overseas calls.

Recent Sales: *Letourneau's Used Auto Parts*, by Carolyn Chute (Ticknor & Fields); and *A Great Deliverance*, by Elizabeth George (Bantam).

FARWESTERN CONSULTANTS, INC., Box 47786, Phoenix AZ 85068-7786. (602)861-3546. President: Elizabeth "Libbi" Goodman. Estab. 1987. Represents 38 clients. "50% of our clients are new/unpublished writers. We have a strong background in literature, editing; and cover the NY and regional markets. We devote whatever time is needed to help a writer develop his full potential. We believe a dynamic relationship between author and agent is necessary for success." Eager to work with new/unpublished writers if they are ready.

"We also work with a number of established authors. We specialize in popular fiction (western, mystery, contemporary/historical romance, espionage, medical thriller, horror, occult and action/adventure), women's fiction and ethnic fiction/nonfiction."

Will Handle: Most book-length nonfiction, contemporary fiction, literary novels, short story collections by established authors. Represents screenplays only for established clients. Does not handle magazine articles, short stories, poetry, juvenile or young adult fiction.

Terms: Receives 15% commission on domestic sales; 15% on dramatic sales; and 20% on foreign sales. Currently handles 70% novels; 25% nonfiction; and 5% screenplays. Prefers query letters, but will read—at no charge—unsolicited queries consisting of a cover letter, outline or synopsis, and first 10 pages of manuscript. No response, to any correspondence, unless SASE is included with submission. Reports in 2 weeks on queries; 3 months from date of receipt for solicited mss and partials. "No complete manuscripts unless requested. We do not charge a reading fee, therefore, we do not read any requested material that is a multiple submission."

Fees: Charges writers for photocopying and unusual expenses agreed upon in advance.

Recent Sales: *Slate Creed Series*, by Zachary Harte (Berkley Publishing); *Rumor Has It*, by Sandra Lee (Harlequin); short story collection, by Clyde James Aragon (Golden West).

FLORENCE FEILER LITERARY AGENCY, 1524 Sunset Plaza Dr., Los Angeles CA 90069. (659)652-6920/652-0945. Associate: Audrey Rugh. Estab. 1967. Represents 40 clients. No unpublished writers. "Quality is the criterion." Specializes in fiction, nonfiction, essays and screen; very little TV and no short stories.

Will Handle: Textbooks (for special clients), juvenile books, movie scripts. Will read—at no charge—queries and outlines only. Reports in 2 weeks on queries; 10 weeks on mss. "We will not accept simultaneous queries to other agents."

Terms: Agent receives 10% commission on domestic sales; 10% on dramatic sales; and 20% on foreign sales.

Recent Sales: *Babette's Feast* (best foreign film); *The Dreamers & Echoes* (Dinesen-Orson Wells).

MARJE FIELDS/RITA SCOTT, 165 W. 46th, New York NY 10036. (212)764-5740. Literary Manager: Ray Powers. Member ILAA. Represents 50 clients. 50% of clients are new/unpublished writers. Prefers to work with published/established writers, works with a small number of new/unpublished authors. Specializes in novels, nonfiction and plays.

Will Handle: Nonfiction books, novels (including young adult) and stage plays. Currently handles 25% nonfiction books; 75% novels. Reports in 1 week on queries.

Terms: Agent receives 15% commission on domestic sales; 15% on dramatic sales; and 20% on foreign sales.

Recent Sales: *Exit Wounds*, by John Westermann (Soho Press); *Death of a Blue Movie Star*, by Jeff Deaver (Bantam); *Live Free or Die*, by Ernest Hebert (Viking).

FRIEDA FISHBEIN LTD., 2556 Hubbard St., Brooklyn NY 11235. (212)247-4398. President: Janice Fishbein. Estab. 1925. Represents 30 clients. 50% of clients are new/unpublished writers. "We agree to represent a writer solely on the basis of a *complete* work." Eager to work with new/unpublished writers. Specializes in historical romance, historical adventure, male adventure, mysteries, thrillers and family sagas. Books on the environment, how-to, plays and screenplays.

Will Handle: Nonfiction books, novels, young adult, movie scripts, stage plays and TV scripts. No poetry or magazine articles. Currently handles 20% nonfiction books; 30% novels; 5% textbooks; 10% juvenile books; 10% movie scripts; 15% stage plays; and 10% TV scripts. Will read—at no charge—unsolicited queries and brief outlines. Reports in 2 weeks on queries; 1 month on mss.

Terms: Agent receives 10% commission on domestic sales; 10% on dramatic sales; and 20% on foreign sales.

Fees: Charges reading fee; $75/TV script, screenplay or play; $60/50,000 words for manuscripts, $1 for each 1,000 additional words. Only *complete* mss are reviewed. Fee will be returned if representing writer. "Our readers are freelance workers who also serve as editors at magazines and/or publishers. Our reports are always longer for larger manuscripts. The usual reader's report varies between three to five pages, and may or may not include a line-to-line critique, but it always includes an overall evaluation." 20% of income derived from fees; 80% of income derived from commission on ms sales. Payment of a criticism fee does not ensure that agency will represent a writer.

Recent Sales: *Dr. Death*, by Herbert L. Fisher (Berkley Publishing Co.); "Double Cross," by Gary Bohlke (play); and *The Frenchwoman*, by Jeanne Mockin (St. Martin's Press).

JOYCE A. FLAHERTY, LITERARY AGENT, 816 Lynda Court, St. Louis MO 63122. (314)966-3057. Agent: Joyce A. Flaherty. Estab. 1980. Member Romance Writers of America and Mystery Writers of America. Represents 63 clients. 25% of clients are new/unpublished writers. "Most new clients come through referral by clients and/or editors." Works with small number of new/unpublished authors. Specializes in mainstream women's fiction, general fiction, genre fiction such as horror, historical, romance, family sagas, thrillers, mysteries, contemporary romance, mainstream historicals. General nonfiction, including biographies, cookbooks, true crime, health/science, self-help, how-to and techni-military.

Will Handle: Nonfiction books, novels. Currently handles 40% nonfiction books; 60% novels. Will read—at no charge—unsolicited queries and outlines. "No response without SASE." Reports in 6 weeks on queries.
Terms: Agent receives 10-15% commission on domestic sales—10% published authors; 15% first book sale for unpublished authors, 10% on subsequent sales; 15% all sales for juvenile authors.
Fees: Charges reading fee "at my discretion for unpublished authors." 1% of income derived from reading fees. Charges $100-150 for 300-page, typed, double-spaced ms. 99% of income derived from commission on mss sales; 1% derived from reading fees.
Recent Sales: *The World of International Modeling*, by Eve Matheson (Holt); *Defcon-One*, by Joe Weber (Presidio); and *Gentle Pardon*, by Gloria Skinner (Warner).

FLAMING STAR LITERARY ENTERPRISES, 320 Riverside Dr., New York NY 10025-9998. (212)222-0083. President: Joseph B. Vallely. Estab. 1985. Represents 50 clients. 50% of clients are new/unpublished writers. Eager to work with new/unpublished writers. Specializes in adult commercial and literary fiction and nonfiction.
Will Handle: Nonfiction books and novels. Currently handles 50% nonfiction books and 50% novels. Will read submissions at no charge. Reports in 1 week on queries; 2 weeks on mss. "No phone calls."
Terms: Agent receives 15% commission on domestic sales; 15% on dramatic sales; and 20% on foreign sales. (All rates are for unpublished authors. Commissions are 5% lower for previously published authors.)
Recent Sales: Confidential.

‡FLANNERY, WHITE & STONE, Suite 110, 180 Cook, Denver CO 80206. (303)399-2264. Literary Agent: Barbara Schoichet. Estab. 1987. Member of International Women's Writer's Guild and Society of Children's Literature. Represents 25 clients. 90% of clients are new/unpublished writer. Specializes in literary fiction, nonfiction business books and children's picture books with exceptional illustrations.
Will Handle: Nonfiction books, novels, juvenile books, movie scripts. Currently represents 19% nonfiction; 60% novels; 20% juvenile books; 1% movie scripts. Will read submissions at no charge, but may charge a criticism fee or service charge for work performed after the initial reading. Reports in 2 weeks on queries; 6 weeks on mss.
Terms: Agent receives 15% commission on domestic sales; 15% on dramatic sales; and 20% on foreign sales.
Fees: Usually we don't charge unless a writer wants a written evaluation of his/her work. Charges $1/page of mss for reading/evaluation. Critiques are 3-5 pages of both line-by-line and overall evaluation. Marketing advice is included and the critiques are done by professional editors and/or published authors. 25% of income derived from criticism fees. Charges writers for photocopying unless the author provides copies.
Recent Sales: *I Get on the Bus*, by Reginald McKnight (Little, Brown); *The Powwow Highway*, by David Seals (NAL); *Drain that Swamp*, by John Brown (Amacom).

THE FOLEY AGENCY, 34 E. 38th St., New York NY 10016. (212)686-6930. Partners: Joan and Joseph Foley. Estab. 1956. Represents 30 clients. Works with a small number of new/unpublished authors (1% of new material received).
Will Handle: Nonfiction books and novels. Currently handles 50% nonfiction books and 50% novels. Will read—at no charge—unsolicited queries and outlines if SASE is enclosed. Reports in 2 weeks on queries. Do not submit manuscripts unless requested.
Terms: Agent receives 10% commission on domestic sales; 10-20% on dramatic sales; and 10-20% on foreign sales.
Fees: Charges for occasional messenger fee and special phone expenses.
Recent Sales: "Deals with all major publishers."

ROBERT A. FREEDMAN DRAMATIC AGENCY, INC., Suite 2310, 1501 Broadway, New York NY 10036. (212)840-5760. President: Robert A. Freedman. Vice President: Selma Luttinger. Member of SAR. Prefers to work with established authors; works with a very small number of new/unpublished authors. Specializes in plays, motion picture and television scripts.
Will Handle: Movie scripts, stage plays and TV scripts. Does not read unsolicited mss. Usually reports in 2 weeks on queries; 6 weeks on mss.
Terms: Agent receives 10% on dramatic sales; "and, as is customary, 20% on amateur rights."
Fees: Charges for photocopying.
Recent Sales: "We will tell any author directly information on our sales that are relevant to his/her specific script."

SAMUEL FRENCH, INC., 45 W. 25th St., New York NY 10010. (212)206-8990. Editor: William Talbot. Assistant Editor: Lawrence Harbison. Estab. 1830. Member of SAR. Represents "hundreds" of clients. Prefers to work with published/established authors; works with a small number of new/unpublished authors. Specializes in plays.

Will Handle: Stage plays. Currently handles 100% stage plays. Will read – at no charge – unsolicited queries and mss. Replies "immediately" on queries; decision in 2-8 months regarding publication. "Enclose SASE."
Terms: Agent receives usually 10% professional production royalties; and 20% amateur production royalties.
Recent Sales: *Shirley Valentiné*, by Willie Russell.

‡**CANDICE FUHRMAN LITERARY AGENCY**, Box F, Forest Knolls CA 94933. (415)488-0161. President: Candice Fuhrman. Estab. 1987. Represents 25 clients. 90% of clients are new/unpublished writers. Eager to work with new/unpublished writers. Specializes in self-help and how-to nonfiction; adult commercial fiction. No genre or children's books.
Will Handle: Nonfiction and adult fiction novels. Handles 90% nonfiction books; 10% novels. Will read – at no charge – unsolicited queries, outlines and manuscripts. Reports in 2 weeks on queries; 1 months on mss.
Terms: Agent receives 15% commission on domestic sales; 20% on dramatic sales; and 20% on foreign sales.
Fees: Charges for postage and telephone expenses.
Recent Sales: *Co-Dependent's Recovery Plan*, by Brian Des Roches (Dell); *Romantic Dreaming*, by Patricia Maybruck (Pocket Books); and *Reclaiming the Heart*, by Mary Beth McClure (Warner Books).

JAY GARON-BROOKE ASSOCIATES INC., 17th Floor, 415 Central Park West, New York NY 10025. (212)866-3654. President: Jay Garon. Estab. 1952. Member of ILAA and Author's Guild Inc. Represents 100 clients. 15% of clients are new/unpublished writers. Prefers to work with published/established authors; works with small number of new/unpublished writers.
Will Handle: Nonfiction books, novels, juvenile books (young adult), movie scripts and stage plays. Currently handles 25% nonfiction books; 70% novels; 2% juvenile books; 1% movie scripts; 1% stage plays and 1% TV scripts. Does not read unsolicited material. Submit query letters with bio and SASE. Reports in 1 month.
Terms: Agent receives 15% commission on domestic sales; 10-15% on dramatic sales; and 30% on foreign sales.
Recent Sales: *Port of Missing Men*, by Mary Ann T. Smith (Wm. Morrow); *Glimpse of Stocking*, by Elizabeth Gage (Simon & Schuster and Pocket Books); *Redeye*, by Richard Aellen (Donald Fine, Inc. and Bantam Books).

MAX GARTENBERG, LITERARY AGENT, 15 W. 44th St., New York NY 10036. (212)860-8451. Contact: Max Gartenberg. Estab. 1954. Represents 30 clients. 10% of clients are new/unpublished writers. "The writer must convince me of his or her professional skills, whether through published or unpublished materials he/ she has produced." Prefers to work with published/established authors; works with a small number of new/ unpublished authors. Specializes in nonfiction and fiction trade books.
Will Handle: Nonfiction books and novels. Currently handles 75% nonfiction books and 25% novels. Will read – at no charge – unsolicited queries and outlines. Reports in 1 week on queries. "SASE required."
Terms: Agent receives 10% commission on domestic sales; 10% on dramatic sales; and 15% on foreign sales.
Recent Sales: *Greetings from Wisdom, Montana*, by Ruth Rudner (Fulcrum); *Encyclopedia of North American Sports History*, by Ralph Hickok (Facts on File); and *Penguins, Puffins and Auks*, by Art Wolfe and William Ashworth (Crown Publishers).

GELLES-COLE LITERARY ENTERPRISES, Woodstock Towers, Suite 801, 320 E. 42nd St., New York NY 10017. (212)573-9857. President: Sandi Gelles-Cole. Estab. 1983. Represents 50 clients. 25% of clients are new/unpublished writers. "We concentrate on published and unpublished, but we try to avoid writers who seem stuck in mid-list." Specializes in commercial fiction and nonfiction.
Will Handle: Nonfiction books and novels. "We're looking for more nonfiction – fiction has to be complete to submit – publishers buying fewer unfinished novels." Currently handles 50% nonfiction books; 50% novels. Does not read unsolicited mss. Reports in 3 weeks.
Terms: Agent receives 15% commission on domestic sales; 15% on dramatic sales; and 20% on foreign sales.
Fees: Charges reading fee of $75 for proposal; $100, ms under 250 pages; $150, ms over 250 pages. "Our reading fee is for evaluation. Writer receives total evaluation, what is right, what is wrong, is book 'playing' to market, general advice on how to fix." Charges writers for overseas calls, overnight mail, messenger. 5% of income derived from fees charged to writers. 50% of income derived from sales of writer's work; 45% of income derived from editorial service.
Recent Sales: *So Close to the Flame*, by Dee Pace (Crown); and *Wolfman*, by Art Bourgeau (Don Fine, Inc.).

‡**GLADDEN & ASSOCIATES**, Box 12001, Portland OR 97212. (503)287-9015. Principal: Carolan Gladden. Represents 10 clients. 70% of clients are new/unpublished writers. Eager to work with new/unpublished writers. Specializes in mainstream, action-adventure, science fiction, and thriller fiction – self-help, how-to, and celebrity bio nonfiction. "No romance, mystery, western, children's, poetry or short fiction. Also handle movie scripts."
Will Handle: Nonfiction books, novels and movie scripts. Currently handles 25% nonfiction books; 74% novels and 1% movie scripts. Will read – at no charge – unsolicited queries. SASE required. Reports in 3 weeks on queries.

Terms: Agent receives 15% commission on domestic sales; 20% on dramatic sales; and 20% on foreign sales.
Fees: We charge $100 for a marketability evaluation. It is refunded when ms is placed with publisher. 25% of income derived from criticism fees. The marketability evaluation is comprised of general observations, ideas toward marketability and specific items needing attention. It runs 6-10 pages. Also offers other authors' services.
Recent Sales: Confidential.

GOODMAN ASSOCIATES, LITERARY AGENTS, 500 West End Ave., New York NY 10024. Contact: Arnold or Elise Goodman. Estab. 1976. Member of ILAA. Represents 100-125 clients. 10% of clients are new/unpublished writers. Specializes in general adult trade fiction and nonfiction. No short stories, articles, poetry, computer books, science fiction, plays, screenplays or textbooks.
Will Handle: Will read—at no charge—unsolicited queries and outlines. "Include SASE for response."
Terms: Agent receives 15% commission on domestic sales; 15% on dramatic sales; and 20% on foreign sales.
Fees: Charges for photocopying, long-distance phone, messenger, telex and book purchases for subsidiary rights submissions.
Recent Sales: No information given.

IRENE GOODMAN LITERARY AGENCY, 521 5th Ave., 17th Floor, New York NY 10017. (212)688-4286. Contact: Irene Goodman, president. Estab. 1978. Member of ILAA. Represents 100 clients. 20% of clients are new/unpublished writers. Works with a small number of new/unpublished authors. Specializes in women's fiction (mass market, category, and historical romance), popular nonfiction, reference and mysteries.
Will Handle: Novels and nonfiction books. Currently handles 20% nonfiction books; 80% novels. Will read—at no charge—unsolicited queries. Reports in 3 weeks. "No reply without SASE."
Terms: Agent receives 15% commission on domestic sales and 20% on foreign sales. 100% of income from commission on ms sales.
Recent Sales: *Free Flows the River* (TOR) and *Jenny's Dream* (Pocket).

‡CHARLOTTE GORDON AGENCY, 235 E. 22nd St., New York NY 10010. (212)679-5363. Contact: Charlotte Gordon. Estab. 1986. Represents 16 clients. 30% of clients are new/unpublished writers. "I'll work with writers whose work is interesting to me." Specializes in "books (not magazine material, except for my writers, and then only in special situations). My taste is eclectic."
Will Handle: Nonfiction books, novels and juvenile books (all ages). Currently handles 30% nonfiction books; 30% novels; 10% textbooks and 30% juvenile. Will read—at no charge—unsolicited queries and outlines. Does not read unsolicited manuscripts. Reports in 2 weeks on queries.
Terms: Agent receives 15% commission on domestic sales; 10% on dramatic sales; and 10% on foreign sales.
Fees: Charges writers for photocopying manuscripts.
Recent Sales: No information given.

GRAHAM AGENCY, 311 W. 43rd St., New York NY 10036. (212)489-7730. Owner: Earl Graham. Estab. 1971. Member of SAR. Represents 35 clients. 35% of clients are new/unpublished writers. Willing to work with new/unpublished writers. Specializes in full-length stage plays and musicals.
Will Handle: Stage plays and musicals. Will read—at no charge—unsolicited queries and outlines, "and plays and musicals which we agree to consider on the basis of the letters of inquiry." Reports in 6 weeks on queries.
Terms: Agent receives 10% commission on domestic sales; 10% on dramatic sales; and 10% on foreign sales.
Recent Sales: No information given.

‡HAROLD R. GREENE, INC., Suite 309, 8455 Beverly Blvd., Los Angeles CA 90048. (213)852-4959. President: Harold Greene. Estab. 1985. Member of WGA and DGA. Represents 12 clients, primarily screenwriters. Specializes in screenplay writing and novels that are adaptable to films or TV movies.
Will Handle: Novels and movie scripts. Currently handles 5% novels and 95% movie scripts. Does not read unsolicited mss.
Terms: Agent receives 10% commission on domestic sales; 10% on dramatic sales; and 10% on foreign sales.
Recent Sales: *The Long Walk,* by George La Fountaine (Putnam); *Lifter,* by Crawford Kilian (Berkeley); and *Forever And a Day,* by Pamela Wallace (Silhouette).

‡ROSE HASS, AGENT, 2020 Ave. V, Apt. 5-C, Brooklyn NY 11229. (718)646-1418 (evenings); (212)529-8900 (days). FAX: (212)529-7399. Contact: Rose Hass. Estab. 1987. Represents 3 clients. To be represented, writer must have published at least three magazine articles. Specializes in selling juvenile fiction and nonfiction, adult fiction and nonfiction, art books (illustrated), some literary criticism.
Will Handle: Nonfiction books, novels and juvenile books (ages 5-12). Currently handles 50% nonfiction books; 25% novels and 25% juvenile books. Will read—at no charge—unsolicited queries and outlines. Does not read unsolicited manuscripts. Reports in 1 month on queries.

Terms: Agent receives 15% commission on domestic sales; 15% on dramatic sales; and 15% on foreign sales.
Fees: "If ms is sent to more than four publishers, writer pays postage."
Recent Sales: *The Toscanini Musicians Knew*, by B.H. Haggin (DaCapo); *Conversations with Toscanini*, by B.H. Haggin (DaCapo) and *The Poem Itself*, by B.H. Haggin (Simon & Schuster).

‡JOHN HAWKINS & ASSOCIATES, INC., Suite 1600, 71 W. 23rd St., New York NY 10010. (212)807-7040. FAX: (212)807-9555. Agents: John Hawkins, William Reiss and Sharon Friedman. Estab. 1893 (Originally Paul R. Reynolds Agency). Member of SAR. Eager to work with new/unpublished writers. Specializes in fiction, nonfiction, children's, young adult, women's fiction and nonfiction, history.
Will Handle: Nonfiction books, novels and juvenile books. Currently handles 40% nonfiction books; 50% novels and 10% juvenile books. Will read—at no charge—unsolicited queries and outlines. Reports in 3 weeks on queries.
Terms: Agent receives 10% commission on domestic sales and 20% on foreign sales.
Recent Sales: No information given.

HEACOCK LITERARY AGENCY, INC., Suite 14, 1523 6th St., Santa Monica CA 90401. (213)393-6227. President: Jim Heacock. Vice President: Rosalie Heacock. Estab. 1978. Member of ILAA and the Association of Talent Agents (writers only). Represents 60 clients. 35% of clients are new/unpublished writers. Works with a small number of new/unpublished authors. Specializes in nonfiction on a wide variety of subjects—health, nutrition, diet, exercise, sports, psychology, crafts, women's studies, business expertise, pregnancy and parenting, alternative health concepts, starting a business and celebrity biographies.
Will Handle: Nonfiction books; novels (by authors who have been previously published by major houses); movie scripts (prefer Writer's Guild members); and TV scripts (prefer Writer's Guild members). Currently handles 85% nonfiction books; 5% novels; 5% movie scripts and 5% TV scripts. "We want to see health oriented works by professionals with credentials and something original to say. Selected New Age subjects are a growing market at all levels of publishing. Celebrity biographies will continue to sell well if they cover contemporary personalities." Will read—at no charge—unsolicited queries and outlines. Reports in 1 month on queries if SASE is included.
Terms: Agent receives 15% commission on domestic sales; 10% on dramatic sales; 25% on foreign sales (if a foreign agent is used. If we sell direct to a foreign publisher, the commission is 15%).
Fees: Charges writers for postage, phone and photocopying.
Recent Sales: *Making Miracles*, by Arnold Fox, M.D. and Barry Fox (Rodale Press); *Retin-A And Other Youth Miracles*, by Joseph Bark, M.D. (Prima/St. Martinns Press); *Little Piggies*, by Don and Audrey Wood (Harcourt Brace Jovanovich).

THE JEFF HERMAN AGENCY, INC., 166 Lexington Ave., New York NY 10016. (212)725-4660. FAX: (212)779-9713. President: Jeffrey H. Herman. Estab. 1985. Member ILAA. Represents 50 clients. 50% of clients are new/previously unpublished writers. To be represented writer must have marketable proposal or manuscript and appropriate credentials. Eager to work with new/unpublished writers. Specializes in general nonfiction and fiction.
Will Handle: Nonfiction books, novels, textbooks. Currently handles 80% nonfiction; 10% textbooks; 10% general fiction. Will read—at no charge—unsolicited queries. Reports in 2 weeks on queries; 6 weeks on mss.
Terms: Agent receives 10-15% commission on domestic sales; 15% on foreign sales.
Fees: Charges for proposal/ms photocopying, overseas calls and cables.
Recent Sales: *The People's Religion, American Faith In The '90s*, by George Gallup and Jim Castelli (Macmillan); *Kids Who Don't Grow Up*, by Cindy Graves and Larry Stockman (contemporary); and *Have I Got a Match For You, Secrets of an International Matchmaker*, by Helena Amram (Random House).

SUSAN HERNER RIGHTS AGENCY, Suite 1403, 110 W. 40 St., New York NY 10018. (212)221-7515. Contact: Susan Herner or Sue Yuen. Estab. 1987. Represents 50 clients. 25% of clients are new/unpublished writers. Eager to work with new/unpublished writers. Trade expertise in fiction (literary and genre), romance, science fiction, nonfiction, juvenile and children's books.
Will Handle: Nonfiction books and novels. Currently handles 40% nonfiction books; 50% novels; 10% juvenile books (pre-school to age 7). Will read—at no charge—unsolicited queries, outlines and mss. Reports in 1 month on queries; 6 weeks on mss.
Terms: Agent receives 15% commission on domestic sales; 20% on dramatic sales; and 20% on foreign sales.
Fees: Charges for extraordinary postage and handling, photocopying. "Agency has two divisions: one represents writers on a commission-only basis; the other represents the rights for small publishers and packagers who do not have in-house subsidiary rights representation. Percentage of income derived from each division is currently 50-50."
Recent Sales: *Dreamfields*, by Libby Sydes (Dell); *Divination Handbook*, by B.A. Crawford (NAL); *Guide to America's Haunted Houses*, by Bingham & Riccio (Pocket); and *Bad Voltage*, by Jonathan Littell (NAL).

FREDERICK HILL ASSOCIATES, 1842 Union St., San Francisco CA 94123. (415)921-2910. FAX: (415)921-2802. Contact: Bonnie Nadell. Estab. 1979. Represents 100 clients. 50% of clients are new/unpublished writers. Specializes in general nonfiction, fiction and young adult fiction.
Will Handle: Nonfiction books and novels.
Terms: Agent receives 15% commission on domestic sales; 15% on dramatic sales; and 20% on foreign sales.
Fees: Charges for overseas airmail (books, proofs only), overseas Telex, cable, domestic Telex. 100% of income derived from commission on ms sales.
Recent Sales: No information given.

ALICE HILTON LITERARY AGENCY, 13131 Welby Way, North Hollywood CA 91606. (818)982-2546. Estab. 1986. Affiliated with Ann Waugh Agency (WGA). Eager to work with new/unpublished writers. Specializes in movie and TV scripts—"Interested in any quality material, although agent's personal taste runs in the genre of 'Cheers,' 'L.A. Law,' 'American Playhouse,' 'Masterpiece Theatre' and Woody Allen vintage humor."
Will Handle: Movie and TV scripts and booklength mss.
Terms: Agent receives 10% commission.
Fees: Charges for phone, postage and photocopy expenses. Charges evaluation fee of $2/1,000 words. Will read movie and TV scripts at no charge if invited. Brochure available. Preliminary phone call appreciated.
Recent Sales: Soap opera comedy, by Kris Meijer to VOO Television (Amsterdam); *Counterparts*, by Kurt Fischel (New Saga) and *The Cradled and the Called*, by Roger Sargeant (New Saga).

SCOTT HUDSON TALENT REPRESENTATION, 2B, 215 East 76th St., New York NY 10021. (212)570-9645. President: Scott Hudson. Estab. 1983. Member of WGA. Represents 30 clients. Prefers to work with published/established authors; works with a small number of new/unpublished authors. Specializes in selling for the entertainment field: screenwriters, television writers, playwrights and some book writers.
Will Handle: Movie scripts, stage plays and TV scripts. Currently handles 30% movie scripts; 30% stage plays; and 40% TV scripts. Will read—at no charge—unsolicited queries and outlines with a synopsis and resume. We "only respond if we are interested."
Terms: Agent receives 10% commission on domestic sales; 10% on dramatic sales; and 15% on foreign sales.

INTERNATIONAL LITERATURE AND ARTS AGENCY, 50 E. 10th St., New York NY 10003. (212)475-1999. Director: Bonnie R. Crown. Estab. 1977. Represents 10 clients. 10% of clients are new/unpublished writers. Works with a small number of new/unpublished authors; eager to work with new/unpublished writers in area of specialization, and established translators from Asian languages. Specializes in translations of literary works from Asian languages, arts- and literature-related works, and "American writers who have been influenced by some aspect of an Asian culture, for example, a novel set in Japan or India, or nonfiction works about Asia."
Will Handle: Novels, stage plays (related to Asia or Asian American experience), and poetry (translations of Asian classics). Currently handles 50% nonfiction books; 25% novels; and 25% classics from Asian languages. Will read—at no charge—unsolicited queries and brief outlines. Reports in 1 week on queries; 2 weeks on mss. "For details of policy, send query with SASE."
Terms: Agent receives 15% commission on domestic sales; and 20% on foreign sales.
Fees: "We do not do critiques, as such, but do give the writer a brief evaluation of marketing potential based on my reading. There is a processing fee of $25-45. May charge for phone and photocopy expenses." ½% of income derived from fees; 99½% of income is derived from commission on ms sales.
Recent Sales: *New Translation of the I Ching*, by Richard John Lynn (Shambhala).

INTERNATIONAL PUBLISHER ASSOCIATES, INC., 746 West Shore, Sparta NJ 07871. Executive Vice President: Joe DeRogatis. Estab. 1982. Represents 30 clients. 80% of clients are new/unpublished writers. Eager to work with new/unpublished writers. Specializes in all types of nonfiction. Writer's guidelines for #10 SASE.
Will Handle: Nonfiction books and novels. Currently handles 80% nonfiction books and 20% fiction. Will read—at no charge—unsolicited queries and outlines. Reports in 3 weeks on queries.
Terms: Agent receives 15% commission on domestic sales; and 20% on foreign sales. 100% of income derived from commission on ms sales.
Recent Sales: *Guerilla Tactics for Women Over Forty*, by Anne Cardoza and Mavis Sutton (Mills and Sanderson); *Under the Clock*, by George Carpozi, Jr. and William Balsam; *Success on the Line*, by Martin Novich (American Management Association).

J&R LITERARY AGENCY, 28 East 11 St., New York NY 10003. (212)677-4248. Owner: Jean Rosenthal. Represents published writers only. Specializes in nonfiction.
Will Handle: Nonfiction books, novels, textbooks, juvenile books. "The lower dollar will cause my focus to switch from European co-productions to some extent, and I shall look for material from U.S. authors and publishers who would like a subsidiary rights agent." Does not read unsolicited mss. Reports in 1 month on queries.

Terms: Agent receives 15% commission on domestic sales; 25% on foreign sales.

Fees: Charges for mailing and telephone. 50% of income derived from commission on ms sales.

Recent Sales: A six volume series of paperback travel books entitled *Off The Beaten Track Italy, France, Switzerland, Spain, Austria, Germany* (Harper and Row); a five-volume *Encyclopedia of Mammals*, by Bernhard Grzimek (McGraw Hill); *The Vineyards of France*, by Don Philpott (Globe Pequot).

SHARON JARVIS AND CO., INC., 260 Willard Ave., Staten Island NY 10314. (718)720-2120. President: Sharon Jarvis. Estab. 1985 (previously known as Jarvis, Braff Ltd. Established 1979). Member of ILAA. Represents 70 clients. 20% of clients are new/unpublished writers. Prefers to work with published/established authors; works with a small number of new/unpublished authors. Considers types of genre fiction, commercial fiction and nonfiction.

Will Handle: Nonfiction books and novels. Currently handles 20% nonfiction books; 80% novels. Does not read unsolicited mss. Reports in 1 month on queries.

Terms: Agent receives 15% commission on domestic sales; extra 10% on dramatic sales (splits commission with dramatic agent); and extra 10% on foreign sales. ("We have sub-agents in ten different foreign markets.") "SASE must be included."

Fees: Charges reading fee; $50 per manuscript ("fee goes to outside reader; recommended material then read by agency at no extra charge"). Critique is an analysis "aimed toward agency evaluation of author's talent and marketability." Charges for photocopying. 100% of income derived from commission on ms sales.

Recent Sales: *Ultrafit*, by Joe Davis, M.D.; *Magic Words*, by Thorarinn Gunnarsson; and *Birds of Paradise*, by Elizabeth Lane.

ASHER D. JASON ENTERPRISES, INC., Suite 3B, 111 Barrow St., New York NY 10014. (212)929-2179. President: Asher D. Jason. Estab. 1983. Represents 25 clients. 15% of clients are new/unpublished writers. "Writers must be either published or have a salable nonfiction idea or an excellent finished fiction ms." Prefers to work with published/established authors; works with a small number of new/unpublished authors. Specializes in fiction, nonfiction, romance, espionage, horror/suspense and mystery.

Will Handle: Nonfiction books and novels. Currently handles 15% magazine articles; 70% nonfiction books; and 15% novels. Will read—at no charge—unsolicited queries and outlines. Reports in 1 week on queries; 3 weeks on mss.

Terms: Agent receives 15% commission on domestic sales; 15% on dramatic sales; and 20% on foreign sales.

Fees: Charges for photocopy and foreign postage expenses.

Recent Sales: *New Classic Beauty* (Villard); *Good Sound* (Morrow/Quill); and *Mapping of Manhattan* (Abbeville).

JCA LITERARY AGENCY, Suite 4A, 242 West 27th St., New York NY 10001. (212)807-0888. Agents: Jane Cushman, Jeff Gerecke, Tom Cushman. Estab. 1978. Member SAR. Represents 100 clients. 10% of clients are new/unpublished writers. Specializes in general fiction and nonfiction.

Will Handle: Nonfiction books and novels; no science fiction or juvenile. "We would be interested in adding *high-quality* commercial novelists to our client list." Currently handles 65% nonfiction books; 35% novels. Will read—at no charge—unsolicited queries and outlines. Reports in 1 month on queries; 2 months on mss.

Terms: Agent receives 10% commission on domestic sales; 10% on dramatic sales; 20% on foriegn sales.

Fees: Charges for bound galleys and finished books used in subsidiary rights submissions; manuscripts copied for submissions to publishers.

Recent Sales: *From Cradle to Grave*, by Joyce Egginton (Morrow, true crime); *Widows*, by William Corson, Joseph Trento, Susan Trento (Crown, nonfiction espionage); and *The Geography of Desire*, by Robert Boswell (Knopf, literary novel).

JET LITERARY ASSOCIATES, INC., 124 E. 84th St., New York NY 10028. (212)879-2578. President: James Trupin. Estab. 1976. Represents 85 clients. 5% of clients are new/unpublished writers. Writer must have published articles or books. Prefers to work with published/established authors. Specializes in nonfiction.

Will Handle: Nonfiction books and novels. Currently handles 50% nonfiction books and 50% novels. Does not read unsolicited mss. Reports in 2 weeks on queries; 1 month on mss.

Terms: Agent receives 15% commission on domestic sales; 15% on dramatic sales; and 25% on foreign sales.

Fees: Charges for phone and postage expenses. 100% of income derived from commission on ms sales.

Recent Sales: *When Do Fish Sleep*, by David Feldman (Harper & Row); *Age Wave*, by Dr. Ken Dyctwald (J.P. Tarcher); *Making It,* by Oliver Lange (E.P. Dutton).

LARRY KALTMAN LITERARY AGENCY, 1301 S. Scott St., Arlington VA 22204. (703)920-3771. Director: Larry Kaltman. Estab. 1984. Represents 11 clients. 75% of clients are new/unpublished writers. Works with a small number of new/unpublished authors. Specializes in novels, novellas (mainstream). Sponsors the Washington Prize For Fiction (see contests and awards section).

Will Handle: Nonfiction books, novels. Currently handles 25% nonfiction books; 75% novels. Reports in 2 weeks.

Terms: Agent receives 15% commission on domestic sales; 15% on dramatic sales; 15% on foreign sales.

Fees: Charges reading fee for all unsolicited mss. Criticism fee automatically included in reading fee. Charges $150/300-page, typed double-spaced book ms. "I don't distinguish between reading fees and criticism fees. Manuscript author receives an approximately 1,000-word letter commenting on writing style, organization and marketability. I write all the critiques." Charges for postage. 80% of income derived from commission on ms sales; 20% derived from fees charged to writers.

Recent Sales: *Rastus on Capitol Hill*, by Samuel Edison (Hunter House).

ALEX KAMAROFF ASSOCIATES, Suite 303 East, 200 Park Ave., Pan Am Bldg., New York NY 10166. (212)557-5557. President: Alex Kamaroff. Associate: Paul Katz. Estab. 1985. Represents 77 clients. 25% of clients are new/unpublished writers. Specializes in men's adventure, science fiction, mysteries, horror, category and historical romances, contemporary women's fiction.

Will Handle: Novels. Currently handles 5% nonfiction books; 95% novels. Will read—at no charge—unsolicited queries and outlines; no reply without SASE. Reports in 1 week on queries; 3 weeks on mss.

Fees: Charges $85 reading fee ("includes feedback") refundable upon sale of ms.

Terms: Agent receives 10% commission on domestic sales; 10% on dramatic sales; and 20% on foreign sales.

Recent Sales: Four-book deal by Diana Morgan (Berkley); *Louis Rukeyser Business Almanac*, by Louis Rukeyser and John Cooney (Simon & Schuster).

‡J. KELLOCK & ASSOCIATES CO. LTD., 11017 - 80 Avenue, Edmonton Alberta T6G 0R2 Canada. (403)433-0274. President: Joanne Kellock. Estab. 1981. Represents 60 clients. 40% of clients are new/unpublished writers. Specializes in pre-school, juvenile, young adult fiction; literature and all genre fiction; nonfiction trade material.

Will Handle: Nonfiction books, novels, juvenile books, movie scripts. Currently handles 45% novels; 5% movie scripts; 50% nonfiction. Will read—at no charge—unsolicited queries and outlines. Reports in 2 weeks on queries.

Terms: Agent receives 15% English language rights; 15% commission on domestic sales; 15% on dramatic sales; and 20% on foreign sales.

Fees: Charges a criticism fee if author has no previous publication in book form. 25% of income derived from criticism fee. Charges $248/300 pages (Canadian funds). Critique is two to three single spaced pages with overall evaluation and line-by-line in terms of grammar, spelling and punctuation by agent or one of two qualified readers. Charges writers a handling charge; postage for submission to publisher, necessary long distance calls at negotiation of contract with publisher.

Recent Sales: *History of the Cowboy*, by Andy Russell (McClelland & Stewart); *Teach Me to Pick My Nose*, by Martyn Godfrey (Avon); *A Promise to the Sun*, by Tololwa Marti Mollel (Little, Brown & Co).

NATASHA KERN LITERARY AGENCY, Box 2908, Portland OR 97208-2908. Contact: Natasha Kern. Estab. 1986. Represents 55 clients. 35% of clients are new/unpublished writers. Eager to work with new/unpublished writers. Specializes in business, health, New Age, self-help (on all topics—by authorities only), how-to and cookbooks. Represents mainstream and genre fiction, including romances, historicals, thrillers and westerns. For children's books, specialize in middle grade and YA fiction.

Will Handle: Nonfiction books, novels and juvenile books. Currently handles 45% nonfiction books; 45% novels; 10% juvenile books. Will read—at no charge—unsolicited queries. Reports in 2 weeks on queries; 6 weeks on mss.

Terms: Agent receives 15% commission on domestic sales; 15% on dramatic sales; and 20% on foreign sales.

Fees: Charges $35 reading fee for unpublished writers which is credited on sales; no marketing charges except overseas mail and calls and Express Mail. 90% of income derived from sales of writer's work; 5% from speaking and workshops; 5% from reading fees.

Recent Sales: *Words That Heal*, by Douglas Block (Bantam); *Grab the Brass Ring*, by Ann Hinds (Crown); *It's Just a Stage*, by Laura Sonnenmark (Scholastic).

DANIEL P. KING, LITERARY AGENT, 5125 N. Cumberland Blvd., Whitefish Bay WI 53217. (414)964-2903. FAX: (414)964-6860. President: Daniel P. King. Estab. 1974. Member of Crime Writer's Association. Represents 125 clients. 25% of clients are new/unpublished writers. Eager to work with new/unpublished writers. Specializes in crime and mystery, science fiction, mainstream fiction, short stories, and books in English for foreign sales. Representative offices in Japan, England and Spain.

Will Handle: Magazine articles (crime, foreign affairs, economics); magazine fiction (mystery, romance); nonfiction books (crime, politics); novels (mystery, science fiction, romance, mainstream); movie scripts (from California office); TV scripts (from California office); syndicate material (general, politics, economics). Currently handles 5% magazine articles; 10% magazine fiction; 30% nonfiction books; 50% novels; 2% movie scripts; 2% TV scripts; 1% syndicated material. Will read—at no charge—unsolicited queries and outlines. Does not read unsolicited ms. Reports in 1 week.

Terms: Agent receives 10% commission on domestic sales; 10% on dramatic sales; and 20% on foreign sales.
Fees: "Reading and evaluation fees range from $90-175 depending upon the length and complexity of the manuscript submitted. For this fee, we will provide a critique of the work which will address the author's writing skill level, analysis of story line and suggestions for rewriting. Rereadings of revised manuscripts are done without further charge, and telephone consultation is available to assist the author in revisions. Writers having published at least 1 trade book within the last year are exempt from any fees."
Recent Sales: Confidential — available to writers on request.

‡**KIRCHOFF/WOHLBERG**, Suite 525, 866 United Nations Plaza, New York NY 10017. (212)644-2020. FAX: (212)223-4387. Author's Representative: Liza Pulitzer; John Whitman. Estab. 1930s. Member of A.A.P. Represents 20 clients. 50% of clients are new/unpublished writers. Works with a small number of new/unpublished authors. Specializes in picture book manuscripts for children; nonfiction for children of all ages; and fiction for ages 8 through teens.
Will Handle: Juvenile books. Currently handles 100% juvenile books. Will read — at no charge — unsolicited queries and outlines. (*must* include SASE return envelope for response). Reports in 1 month on queries.
Terms: Agent receives 15% commission on domestic sales.
Recent Sales: *Planting a Rainbow*, by Lois Ehlert (Harcourt Brace Jovanovich); *The Silver Whistle*, by Ann Tompert (Macmillan) and *Baby Walk*, by Anne Miranda (Dutton).

HARVEY KLINGER, INC., 301 W. 53rd St., New York NY 10019. (212)581-7068. President: Harvey Klinger. Estab. 1977. Represents 100 clients. 25% of our clients are new/unpublished writers. "We seek writers demonstrating great talent, fresh writing and a willingness to listen to editorial criticism and learn." Works with a small number of new/unpublished authors. Specializes in mainstream fiction, (not category romance or mysteries, etc.), nonfiction in the medical, social sciences, autobiography and biography areas.
Will Handle: Nonfiction books and novels. Currently handles 60% nonfiction books and 40% novels. Will read — at no charge — unsolicited queries and outlines. Reports in 2 weeks on queries.
Terms: Agent receives 15% commission on domestic sales; 15% on dramatic sales; and 25% on foreign sales.
Fees: Charges for photocopying expenses. 100% of income derived from commission on ms sales.
Recent Sales: *Green City In The Sun*, by Barbara Wood (Random); *The Proprietor's Daughter*, by Lewis Orde (Little, Brown); and *How to Make Love All The Time*, by Barbara DeAngelis (Rawson).

PAUL KOHNER, INC., 9169 Sunset Blvd., Los Angeles CA 90069. (213)550-1060. FAX: (213)276-1083. Agent: Gary Salt. Estab. 1938. Represents 100 clients. Writer must have sold material in the market or category in which they are seeking representation. Prefers to work with published/established authors. Specializes in film and TV scripts and related material, and dramatic rights for published or soon-to-be published books — both fiction and nonfiction. No plays, poetry or short stories. "We handle dramatic and performing rights only."
Will Handle: Magazine articles and nonfiction books (if they have film or TV potential); novels (only previously published or with publication deals set); movie scripts; and TV scripts. Currently handles 5% magazine articles; 12½% nonfiction books; 12½% novels; 40% movie scripts; and 30% TV scripts. Only queries accompanied by SASE will be answered. *Absolutely no unsolicited material.* Reports in 1 week on queries.
Terms: Agent receives 10% commission on dramatic sales.
Fees: Charges for photocopy and binding expenses.
Recent Sales: *The Flight of The Intruder* (Naval Institute Press); *Men Who Hate Women and The Women Who Love Them* (Bantam); *Trust Me On This* (Mysterious Press). All recent sales refer to film/TV rights.

BARBARA S. KOUTS, (Affiliated with Philip G. Spitzer Literary Agency), 788 9th Ave., New York NY 10019. (212)265-6003. Literary Agent: Barbara S. Kouts. Estab. 1980. Member of ILAA. Represents 50 clients. 50% of clients are new/unpublished writers. Specializes in fiction, nonfiction and children's books.
Will Handle: Nonfiction books, novels and juvenile books. Currently handles 40% nonfiction books; 40% novels; and 20% juvenile books. Will read — at no charge — unsolicited queries and outlines. Reports in 3 weeks on queries; 2 months on mss.
Terms: Agent receives 10% commission on domestic sales; and 20% on foreign sales.
Fees: Charges writers for photocopy expenses.
Recent Sales: *Short and Shivery*, by Robert San Souci (Doubleday); *Bed and Breakfast, North America*, by Hal Gieseking (Simon & Schuster); *Beethoven's Cat*, by Elisabeth McHugh (Atheneum).
Terms: Agent receives 10% commission on domestic sales, dramatic sales and foreign sales. Charges a reading fee. 10% of income derived from reading fees. Writer receives "a total breakdown of scripts — chances of sale, demands for re-write, etc." 10% of income derived from fees charged to writer; 90% from commission on ms sales.
Recent Sales: No information given.

‡**LUCY KROLL AGENCY**, 390 W. End Ave., New York NY 10024. (212)877-0627. Agent: Barbara Hogenson. Member of SAR and WGA East and West. Represents 60 clients. 5% of clients are new/unpublished writers. "Recommendations are useful, but good writing is the most important qualification for representation." Specializes in nonfiction, screenplays and plays.

Will Handle: Nonfiction books, novels, movie scripts and stage plays. Currently handles 60% nonfiction books; 5% novels; 15% movie scripts and 20% stage plays. Will read—at no charge—unsolicited queries and outlines "provided SASE is sent." Does not read unsolicited manuscripts. Reports in 1 month.
Terms: Agent receives 10% commission on domestic sales; 10% on dramatic sales; and 10% on foreign sales.
Recent Sales: No information given.

PETER LAMPACK AGENCY, INC., 2015, 551 5th Ave., New York NY 10017. (212)687-9106. FAX: (212)687-9109. President: Peter Lampack. Estab. 1977. Represents 90 clients. 10% of clients are new/unpublished writers. Majority of clients are published/established authors; works with a small number of new/unpublished authors. Specializes in "commercial fiction, particularly contemporary relationships, male-oriented action/adventure, mysteries, horror and historical romance; literary fiction; and upscale, serious nonfiction or general interest nonfiction only from a recognized expert in a given field."
Will Handle: Nonfiction books, novels, movie scripts and TV scripts ("but not for espiodic TV series—must lend itself to movie-of-the-week or mini-series format.") Currently handles 15% nonfiction books; 75% novels; 5% movie scripts; 5% TV scripts. Will read—at no charge—unsolicited queries, outlines and mss. Reports in 2 weeks on queries; 6 weeks on mss.
Terms: Agent receives 15% commission on domestic sales; 15% on dramatic sales; and 20% on foreign sales.
Fees: Charges for photocopy expenses "although we prefer writers supply copies of their work. Writers are required to supply or bear the cost of copies of books for overseas sales."
Recent Sales: *Rightfully Mine*, by Doris Mortman (Bantam); *Murder On Martha's Vineyard*, by David Osborn (Lynx Books); *The Wolf's Hour*, by Robert McCammon (Pocket Books).

MICHAEL LARSEN/ELIZABETH POMADA LITERARY AGENTS, 1029 Jones St., San Francisco CA 94109. (415)673-0939. Contact: Mike Larsen or Elizabeth Pomada. Member of ILAA. Represents 100 clients. 50-55% of clients are new/unpublished writers. Eager to work with new/unpublished writers. "We have very catholic tastes and do not specialize. We handle literary, commercial, and genre fiction, and the full range of nonfiction books."
Will Handle: Adult nonfiction books and novels. Currently handles 75% nonfiction books and 25% novels. Will read—at no charge—unsolicited queries, the first 30 pages and synopsis of completed novels, and nonfiction book proposals. Reports in 8 weeks on queries. "Always include SASE. Send SASE for brochure."
Terms: Agent receives 15% commission on domestic sales; 15% on dramatic sales; and 20% on foreign sales.
Fees: May charge writer for printing, postage for multiple submissions, foreign mail, foreign phone calls, galleys, books, and legal fees. Offers a separate consultation service; charges $100/hour. 100% of income derived from commission on ms sales.
Recent Sales: *Beyond Compulsive Living*, by Carla Perez (Fireside Books); *Polar City Blues*, by Katharine Kerr (Foundation), and *Chantal*, by Yvone Lenard (Delacorte).

‡THE LAZEAR AGENCY, INCORPORATED, Suite 416, 430 First Ave. N, Minneapolis MN 55401. Contact: Kathy Erickson. Estab. 1984. Represents 240 clients. 30% of clients are new/unpublished writers. Works with a small number of new/unpublished authors. "A full-service entertainment agency."
Will Handle: Nonfiction books, novels, textbooks, juvenile books, movie scripts, radio scripts, stage plays, TV scripts and syndicated material. Currently handles 2% magazine articles; 2% magazine fiction; 35% nonfiction books; 35% novels; 2% textbooks; 5% juvenile books; 5% movie scripts; 2% radio scripts; 2% stage plays; 5% TV scripts. Will read—at no charge—unsolicited queries, outlines and manuscripts. Reports in 2 months.
Terms: Agent receives 15% commission on domestic sales; 15% on dramatic sales; and 20% on foreign sales.
Fees: Charges writers for photocopy, messenger, foreign shipping, overnight mail.

L. HARRY LEE LITERARY AGENCY, Box 203, Rocky Point NY 11778. (516)744-1188. President: L. Harry Lee. Agents: Ralph Schiano (science fiction); Katie Polk (mystery); Vito Brenna (mainstream); Lisa Judd (historical/adventure); Colin James (mainstream/horror); Mary Lee Gaylor (West Coast representative). Estab. 1979. Member of WGA. Represents 160 clients. 35% of clients are new/unpublished writers. "Mainly interested in screenwriters." Specializes in movies, TV (episodic, movies-of-the-week and sit-coms) and contemporary novels.
Will Handle: Novels, movie scripts, stage plays, and TV scripts (movies, mini-series, MOW's, episodic, and sit-coms). Currently handles 12% novels; 65% movie scripts; 3% stage plays; 20% TV scripts. Will read—at no charge—unsolicited queries and outlines; does not read material submitted without SASE. Does not consider unsolicited complete mss. No dot-matrix. Reports in 2 weeks on queries; 6 weeks on mss.
Terms: Agent receives 15% commission on domestic sales; 15% on dramatic sales; and 20% on foreign sales.
Fees: Charges a marketing fee. Charges for photocopies, line editing, proofing, typing and postage expenses. 10% of income derived from marketing fees; 90% of income derived from commission on ms sales.
Recent Sales: *Curtains for Sure, Snake-Check, Marrakesh.*

‡LEE SHORE AGENCY, 1687 Washington Rd., Pittsburgh PA 15228. (412)831-1299. Owner: Cynthia Semelsberger. Estab. 1988. Member of ILAA. Represents 12 clients. 50% of clients are new/unpublished writers. "We have no set criteria; we are on the look out for good, consistent writers. We love new talent." Eager to work with new/unpublished writers. Specializes in nonfiction, mainstream fiction and poetry.
Will Handle: Nonfiction books, novels, textbooks, juvenile books and poetry. Currently handles 30% nonfiction books; 50% novels and 20% poetry. Will read submissions at no charge, but may charge a criticism fee or service charge for work performed after the initial reading. Reports in 1 week on queries; 2 weeks on mss.
Terms: Agent receives 15% commission on domestic sales; 15% on dramatic sales; and 20% on foreign sales.
Fees: Charges a reading fee for proposal and first 3 chapters. 10% of income derived from reading fees. Charges nothing/300 pages if the manuscript is requested once the proposal and chapters have been reviewed. Charges a criticism fee if we are solicited by a client to do so. 30% of income derived from criticism fees. Charges $300/300 pages. "Writer receives general overview (½-1 page); comments on technical problems, storyline, characters, focus, marketability (2-3 pages); evaluation checkoff sheet (1 page); light editing throughout manuscript; manuscript reviewed first by agent—then at least one editor; many times client is contacted via phone, and copy of editing symbols is included."
Recent Sales: *Walk Yourself Healthy,* by Dick Harding (Diabetes Center; George Cleveland Publishing).

‡ELLEN LEVINE LITERARY AGENCY, INC., Suite 1205, 432 Park Ave. So., New York NY 10016. (212)889-0620. Contact: Diana Finch. Estab. 1980. Member of SAR and ILAA. Represents 100 clients. 10% of clients are new/unpublished writers.
Will Handle: Nonfiction books and novels. Currently handles 40% nonfiction books; 55% novels; and 5% juvenile books. Will read—at no charge—unsolicited queries and outlines. Does not read unsolicited manuscripts. Reports in 1 week on queries.
Terms: Agent receives 10% commission on domestic sales; 10% on dramatic sales; and 20% on foreign sales.
Fees: Charges writer for photocopying mss for submissions, overseas calls, cables and postage incurred in representation of foreign rights, cost of books bought to submit for foreign rights and other subsidiary rights. 100% of income derived from commission on ms sales.
Recent Sales: "We do not release this information except by individual request from prospective clients."

LIGHTHOUSE LITERARY AGENCY, Box 2105, 1112 Solana Ave., Winter Park FL 32790. (407)647-2385. Director: Sandra Kangas. Estab. 1988. Represents 36 clients. 30% of clients are new/unpublished writers. "We are interested in working with any new or established writer whose goal is to advance his/her writing career. Some prior success is a plus, but not a requirement." Specializes in nonfiction, novels, TV and movie scripts, treatments, juveniles, young adult novels.
Will Handle: Short story collections, nonfiction books, novels, textbooks, juvenile books, movie scripts, TV scripts, poetry. Currently handles 32% nonfiction books; 30% novels; 22% juvenile books; 2% poetry, 14% scripts. Reports in 2 weeks on queries; 2 months on manuscripts.
Terms: Agent receives 15% commission on domestic sales; 10-15% on dramatic sales; and 20% on foreign sales.
Fees: "We read for acceptance or rejection at no charge. If we feel a rewrite might make a marketable work, we offer to write a critique. We suggest new writers use it." Charges $300/300 pages. The author is mailed a written critique of one or more typewritten single-spaced pages. Emphasis is on clarity, plot, characterization, viewpoint, marketability and style. Lighthouse hires published readers to help with this service." 90% of income derived from sales of writers' work; 10% of income derived from criticism service.
Recent Sales: *The Draper Solution,* by Galen C. Dukes and *Tooting Your Own Horn,* by Dennis C. Hill.

WENDY LIPKIND AGENCY, Suite 3E, 165 E. 66th St., New York NY 10021. (212)935-1406. President: Wendy Lipkind. Estab. 1977. Member of ILAA. Represents 50 clients. 20% of clients are new/unpublished writers. Works with a small number of new/unpublished authors. Specializes in nonfiction (social history, adventure, biography, science, sports, history) and fiction ("good story telling. I do not specialize in genre mass-market fiction").
Will Handle: Nonfiction books and novels. Currently handles 80% nonfiction books and 20% novels. Will read—at no charge—unsolicited queries and outlines. Reports in 2 weeks on queries.
Terms: Agent receives 10-15% commission on domestic sales; 10-15% on dramatic sales; and 20% on foreign sales.
Fees: Charges $100 one-time handling fee if sells work. Charges for phone, foreign postage, photocopy, cables and messenger expenses.
Recent Sales: *Travelling Through Historic France* (Doubleday); *Buying Out America* (Crown); *Murderous Remedy* (Crime Club).

LITERARY/BUSINESS ASSOCIATES, Box 2415, Hollywood CA 90078. (213)465-2630. President: Shelley Gross. Estab. 1979. Member ILAA. Represents 5 clients. 80% of clients are new/unpublished writers. Specializes in nontechnical nonfiction, especially New Age, health and fitness, popular business, psychology, spirituality, philosophy.

Will Handle: Nonfiction books and novels. Curently handles 60% nonfiction; 40% novels. Will read—at no charge—unsolicited queries and outlines. Reports in 1 week on queries; 6 weeks on mss.

Terms: Agent receives 15% commission on domestic sales; 20% on foreign sales.

Fees: Charges criticism fee to new and unpublished writers. 50% is refundable after sale is made. 40% of income derived from criticism fees. Charges $75/300-page, typed double-spaced book ms. "Writer receives approximately 2 single-spaced typewritten pages of detailed editorial and marketing evaluation including advice for ms improvement. Some penciled comments on pages themselves. Also included is typed guidesheet for either fiction or nonfiction mss. Writers pay marketing fee which is nonrefundable." Offers full editorial consultation service, which includes professional book editing and consultations on book contracts, etc. Charges $35-45 per hour. 40-60% of income derived from commission on ms sales; 35-40% from fees charged to writers.

Recent Sales: *The Top Ten*, by Theroux Gilbert (Simon & Schuster).

PETER LIVINGSTON ASSOCIATES, INC., Suite 304, 120 Carlton St., Toronto, Ontario M5A 4K2 Canada. (416)928-1010. FAX: (416)924-3393. Estab. 1984. Member of ILAA. Represents 150 clients. Works with a small number of new/unpublished authors. Specializes in nonfiction sociological and political books, fiction both literary and commercial, some TV and film, biographies.

Will Handle: Currently handles 60% nonfiction books; 30% novels; 4% movie scripts; and 6% TV scripts. Will read—at no charge—unsolicited queries and outlines. Does not read unsolicited mss. Reports in 3 weeks.

Terms: Agent receives 15% commission on domestic sales; and 20% on foreign sales.

Fees: Charges a reading fee of $40 for outline and 5-6 sample chapters. Reading fee waived if represents writer. Charges writers for photocopying, long distance, faxes, legal fees (if necessary) courier charges.

Recent Sales: *Intelligence Running Wild*, by Dr. Edward Rodvoll (Harper & Row); *The CrossKiller*, by Marcel Montecino (Arbor House) and *The Potato Baron*, by John Thorndike (Villard Books).

NANCY LOVE AGENCY, 250 E. 65th St., New York NY 10021. (212)980-3499. Contact: Nancy Love. Estab. 1984. Member of ILAA. Represents 50 clients. 40% of clients are new/unpublished writers. Prefers to work with published writers. Specializes in adult fiction and nonfiction with the exception of romance novels.

Will Handle: Nonfiction books and novels. Curently handles 75% nonfiction books; 25% novels. Will read—at no charge—unsolicited queries, outlines and mss. Reports in 1 month on queries; 6 weeks on mss. "Length of exclusivity negotiated on a per case basis."

Terms: Agent receives 15% commission on domestic sales; 15% TV and movie sales; 20% on foreign sales.

Recent Sales: *Everybody Says Freedom*, by Pete Seeger and Bob Reiser (W.W. Norton); *Famous For 15 Minutes*, by Ultraviolet (Harcourt Brace Jovanovich); and *Bloomingdale's Tabletop Sourcebook*, by Elizabeth Knight (Doubleday).

MARGARET MCBRIDE LITERARY AGENCY, Box 8730, LaJolla CA 92038. (619)459-0559. Contact: Winifred Golden. Estab. 1980. Member of ILAA. Represents 25 clients. 10-20% of clients are new/unpublished writers. Specializes in historical biographies, literary fiction, mainstream fiction and nonfiction.

Will Handle: Nonfiction books, novels, movie scripts and syndicated material. Will read—at no charge—unsolicited queries and outlines. Does not read unsolicited mss. Reports in 6 weeks on queries. "We are looking for two more novelists to complete our client list."

Terms: Agent receives 15% commission on domestic sales; 10% on dramatic sales; and 25% on foreign sales. Charges writers for Telex and Federal Express made at author's request. 100% of income derived from commission on ms sales.

Recent Sales: *Barbarian to Bureaucrats*, by Lawrence M. Miller (Clarkson Potter); *The Memoirs of Senator John G. Tower* (Little, Brown); and *Men and Women*, by Jonathon Kraner and Diane Dunaway (Pocket).

‡DONALD MACCAMPBELL INC., 12 E. 41st St., New York NY 10017. (212)683-5580. Editor: Maureen Moran. Estab. 1940. Represents 50 clients. "The agency does not handle unpublished writers." Specializes in women's book-length fiction in all categories.

Will Handle: Novels. Currently handles 100% novels. Does not read unsolicited mss. Reports in 1 week on queries.

Terms: Agent receives 10% commission on domestic sales; and 20% on foreign sales.

Recent Sales: *Love & Smoke*, by Jennifer Blake (Ballantine); *Special Assistant*, by Emilie McGee (Silhouette); *Tycoon's Daughter*, by Lynn Drennan (Doubleday).

RICHARD P. MCDONOUGH, LITERARY AGENT, Box 1950, Boston MA 02130. (617)522-6388. Estab. 1986. Represents 20 clients. 80% of clients are new/unpublished writers. Works with unpublished and published writers "whose work I think has merit and requires a committed advocate." Specializes in nonfiction for general contract and fiction.

Will Handle: Nonfiction books, novels and syndicated material. Currently handles 80% nonfiction books; 10% novels; and 10% juvenile. Will read—at no charge—unsolicited queries, outlines and mss if accompanied by SASE. Reports in 2 weeks on queries; 5 weeks on mss.

Terms: Agent receives 15% commission on domestic sales; 15% on dramatic sales; 15% on foreign sales.

Fees: Charges for photocopying, phone beyond 300 miles; postage for sold work only.

Recent Sales: *Guide to Museums in N.Y. City*, by R. Garrett (Chelsea Green); *Mystic Lakes*, by D. Musello (Donald Fine); and *Saying Goodbye*, by M.R. Montgomery (Knopf).

‡JANET WILKENS MANUS LITERARY AGENCY INC., Suite 906, 370 Lexington Ave., New York NY 10017. (212)685-9558. President: Janet Wilkens Manus. Estab. 1981. Member of ILAA. Represents 40 clients. 20% of our clients are new/unpublished writers. Prefers to work with published/established authors; works with a small number of new/unpublished writers. Specializes in general adult trade fiction and nonfiction.

Will Handle: Nonfiction books (trade oriented); novels (adult and young adult); and juvenile books. Currently handles 5% magazine articles; 5% magazine fiction; 40% nonfiction books; 45% novels; and 5% juvenile books. Will read—at no charge—unsolicited queries and outlines. Reports in 2 weeks on queries; 5 weeks on manuscripts.

Terms: Agent receives 15% commission on domestic sales; 15% on dramatic sales; and 20% on foreign sales. Charges for photocopying, messenger, overseas phone, and postage expenses.

Recent Sales: *The New Mother's Body*, by Paula Siegel (Bantam); *Reading Your Future in the Cards*, by Louise Woods (Pocket); and *A Gift for the King*, by Christopher Manson (Holt).

‡MARCH TENTH, INC., 4 Myrtle St., Haworth NJ 07641. (201)387-6551. FAX: (201)387-6552. President: Sandra Choron. Estab. 1981. Represents 40 clients. 5% of clients are new/unpublished writers. "Writers must have professional expertise in the field in which they are writing." Prefers to work with published/established writers.

Will Handle: Nonfiction books. Currently handles 100% nonfiction books. Does not read unsolicited mss. Reports in 1 month.

Terms: Agent receives 15% commission on domestic sales; 20% on dramatic sales; and 20% on foreign sales.

Fees: Charges writers for postage, photocopy and overseas phone expenses. 10% of income is derived from fees; 90% of income derived from commission of ms sales.

Recent Sales: *Trash Trio*, by John Waters (three screenplays); The Heart of Rock & Soul, by Dave Marsh; *How to Avoid Bad Credit*, by Pearl Polto.

DENISE MARCIL LITERARY AGENCY, INC., 685 West End Ave., 9C, New York NY 10025. (212)932-3110. President: Denise Marcil. Estab. 1977. Member of ILAA. Represents 80 clients. Works with a small number of new/unpublished authors. Specializes in "solid, informative nonfiction including such areas as money, business, health, child care, parenting, self-help and how-to's and commercial fiction, especially women's fiction; also mysteries, psychological suspense and horror."

Will Handle: Nonfiction books and novels. Currently handles 40% nonfiction books and 60% novels. Will read—at no charge—unsolicited queries and outlines when submitted with an SASE mailer. Reports in 2 weeks on queries; 3 months on mss.

Terms: Agent receives 15% commission on domestic sales; 15% on dramatic sales; and 22% on foreign sales.

Fees: Charges a reading fee: $45/first 3 chapters and outline. Less than .1% of income derived from reading fees. Charges for disbursements, postage, copying and messenger service. 99.9% of income derived from commission on ms sales. Always send SASE.

Recent Sales: *Parent's Guide to Raising Sexually Healthy Children*, by Lynn Leight (Rawson Assoc.); *Blood and Sable*, by Carol J. Kane (McGraw-Hill); and *Corsican Woman*, by Madge Swindells (Warner).

BETTY MARKS, Suite 9F, 176 E. 77th St., New York NY 10021. (212)535-8388. Contact: Betty Marks. Estab. 1969. Member of ILAA. Represents 35 clients. Prefers to work with published/established authors; works with a small number of new/unpublished authors. Specializes in journalists' nonfiction.

Will Handle: Nonfiction books, cookbooks and novels. Will read—at no charge—unsolicited queries and outlines. Reports in 1 week on queries; 6 weeks on mss.

Terms: Agent receives 15% commission on domestic sales; and 10% on foreign sales (plus 10% to foreign agent).

Fees: Charges a reading fee for unpublished writers; fee will be waived if representing writer. Charges criticism fee. "Writers receive two-page letter covering storyline, plot, characters, dialogue, language, etc." Written by agent. Charges for "extraordinary" postage, phone and messenger expenses. 95% of income derived from commission on ms sales. Payment of criticism fee does not ensure that agency will represent a writer.

Recent Sales: *Mad Dreams, Saving Graces*, by Michael Kaufman (Random House); *Druglord*, by Terrence Poppa (Pharos Books); and *100 Views of the Adirondacks*, by Nathan Farb (Rizzoli).

ELAINE MARKSON LITERARY AGENCY, 44 Greenwich Ave., New York NY 10011. Estab. 1972. Member of ILAA. Represents 200 clients. 10% of clients are new/unpublished writers. Specializes in literary fiction, commercial fiction and trade nonfiction.
Will Handle: Nonfiction books and novels. Currently handles 30% nonfiction books; 40% novels; 20% juvenile books; 5% movie scripts. Will read—at no charge—unsolicited queries and outlines. Reports in 2 weeks on queries.
Terms: Agent receives 15% commission on domestic sales; 10% on dramatic sales; and 20% on foreign sales.
Fees: Charges for postage, photocopying, special long distance telephone. 100% of income derived from commission on ms sales.
Recent Sales: No information given.

‡THE EVAN MARSHALL AGENCY, 228 Watchung Ave., Upper Montclair NJ 07043. (201)744-1661. FAX: (201)744-6312. President: Evan Marshall. Estab. 1987. Member of ILAA and Romance Writers of America. Represents 75 clients. 10% of clients are new/unpublished writers. To be represented, a writer must demonstrate talent as well as knowledge of the market for which he or she is writing. Specializes in adult fiction and nonfiction.
Will Handle: Nonfiction books, novels, movie scripts and TV scripts. Currently handles 45% nonfiction; 45% novels; 5% movie scripts and 5% TV scripts. Does not read unsolicited manuscripts. Reports in 2 weeks on queries.
Terms: Agent receives 15% commission on domestic sales; 20% on dramatic sales; and 20% on foreign sales.
Recent Sales: Confidential.

THE MARTELL AGENCY, 555 5th Ave., New York NY 10017. (212)692-9770. Contact: Alice Fried Martell, Esq. Estab. 1985. Represents approximately 80 clients. Works with published/established writers. Specializes in "very diversified material. Must be commercial. We do not handle science fiction; otherwise, we're equally receptive to fiction and nonfiction."
Will Handle: Nonfiction books and novels. Currently handles approximately 65% nonfiction books and 35% novels. Will read—at no charge—unsolicited queries, outlines and mss. Send query first.
Terms: Agent receives 15% commission on domestic sales; 20% on foreign sales.
Fees: Charges for messenger, photocopying, overseas postage and telephone, galleys and books ordered for ancillary rights sales.
Recent Sales: *Oil and Honor*, by Thomas Petzinger, Jr. (Putnam); *Tempting Fate*, by Laurie Alberts (Houghton Mifflin); and *The Red Truck*, by Rudy Wilson (Knopf).

SCOTT MEREDITH, INC., 845 3rd Ave., New York NY 10022. (212)245-5500. FAX: (212)755-2972. Vice President and Editorial Director: Jack Scovil. Estab. 1946. Represents 2,000 clients. 10% of clients are new/unpublished writers. "We'll represent on a straight commission basis writers who've sold one or more recent books to major publishers, or several (three or four) magazine pieces to major magazines, or a screenplay or teleplay to a major producer. We're a very large agency (staff of 51) and handle all types of material except individual cartoons or drawings, though we will handle collections of these as well."
Will Handle: Magazine articles, magazine fiction, nonfiction books, novels, textbooks, juvenile books, movie scripts, radio scripts, stage plays, TV scripts, syndicated material and poetry. Currently handles 5% magazine articles; 5% magazine fiction; 23% nonfiction books; 23% novels; 5% textbooks; 10% juvenile books; 5% movie scripts; 2% radio scripts; 2% stage plays; 5% TV scripts; 5% syndicated material; and 5% poetry. Will read—at no charge—unsolicited queries, outlines, and manuscripts "if from a writer with track record as described previously; charges a fee if no sales." Reports in 2 weeks.
Terms: Agent receives 10% commission on domestic sales; 10% on dramatic sales; and 20% on foreign sales.
Fees: Charges "a single fee which covers multiple readers, revision assistance or critique as needed. When a script is returned as irreparably unsalable, the accompanying letter of explanation will usually run two single-spaced pages minimum on short stories or articles, or from 4 to 10 single-spaced pages on book-length manuscripts, teleplays, or screenplays. All reports are done by agents on full-time staff. No marketing advice is included, since, if it's salable, we'll market and sell it ourselves." 10% of income derived from fees; 90% of income derived from commission on ms sales.
Recent Sales: *Murder at the Kennedy Center*, by Margaret Truman (Random House); *Rendezvous with Rama II*, by Arthur C. Clarke (Bantam Books); *Stand Up!*, by Roseanne Barr (Harper & Row).

MEWS BOOKS LTD.—Sidney B. Kramer, 20 Bluewater Hill, Westport CT 06880. (203)227-1836. FAX: (203)226-6928. Secretary: Fran Pollak. Estab. 1972. Represents 35 clients. Prefers to work with published/established authors; works with small number of new/unpublished authors "producing professional work. No editing services." Specializes in juvenile (pre-school through young adult), cookery, adult nonfiction and fiction, technical and medical.
Will Handle: Nonfiction books, novels, juvenile books, character merchandising and video use of illustrated published books. Currently handles 20% nonfiction; 20% novels; 50% juvenile books and 10% miscellaneous. Will read—at no charge—unsolicited queries and outlines with character description and a few pages of writing sample.

Terms: Agent receives 10% commission on domestic sales for published authors; 15% for unpublished; total 20% on foreign. $500 minimum commission if book is published.

Fees: Charges writers for photocopy and postage expenses and other direct costs. Principle agent is an attorney and former publisher. Offers consultation service through which writers can get advice on a contract or on publishing problems.

Recent Sales: No information given.

‡DAVID H. MORGAN LITERARY AGENCY, INC., Box 40566, Portland OR 97240. (503)221-1643. President: David H. Morgan. Estab. 1988. Represents 25 clients. 30% of clients are new/unpublished writers. Eager to work with new/unpublished writers. Specializes in fiction, nonfiction: adult and juvenile.

Will Handle: Nonfiction books, novels, juvenile books. Currently handles 40% nonfiction books; 40% novels; and 20% juvenile books. Will read—at no charge—unsolicited queries and outlines. Does not read unsolicited manuscripts. Send SASE for free brochure describing agency and submission policies. Reports in 1-1½ weeks on queries.

Terms: Agent receives 15% commission on domestic sales; 15% on dramatic sales; and 20% on foreign sales.

Fees: Charges a criticism fee for new/unpublished writers. "All submissions by unpublished writers are reviewed by our acquisitions department which is a fee-based division that evaluates all works by new writers. If a new/unpublished writer's submission is accepted as is by the agency—or with minor revisions—the fee is returned." 20% of income derived from criticism fees. Charges $55-160/300 pages. For $55 fee: 2-3 page evaluation of specific narrative (fiction) or expository (nonfiction) weaknesses of work; for $160 fee: in-depth line-by-line manuscript critique of first 60 pages (15,000 words). Clients pay charges for overseas mail and overnight mail (i.e., unusual or extraordinary mailing costs).

Recent Sales: *A Field of Innocence*, by Jack Estes (Headline Books); *How to Stop Your Husband's Snoring*, by Derek Lipman, M.D. (Rodale Press); and *Prophecies and Predictions*, by Moira Timms (Ballantine).

MULTIMEDIA PRODUCT DEVELOPMENT, INC., Suite 724, 410 S. Michigan Ave., Chicago IL 60605. (312)922-3063. FAX (312)922-1905. President: Jane Jordan Browne. Estab. 1971. Member of ILAA. Represents 100 clients. 10% of clients are new/unpublished writers. Works with a small number of new/unpublished authors. "We are generalists, taking on nonfiction and fiction that we believe will be on target for the market."

Will Handle: Nonfiction books ("new idea" books, how-to, science and biography) and novels (mainstream and genre). Currently handles 68% nonfiction books; 30% novels; and 2% juvenile books. Will read—at no charge—unsolicited queries and outlines. Reports in 3 weeks on queries. "We review manuscripts only if we solicit submission and only as 'exclusives.'"

Terms: Agent receives 15% commission on domestic sales; 15% on dramatic sales; and 20% on foreign sales.

Fees: Charges for photocopying, overseas telegrams and telephone calls, and overseas postage expenses.

Recent Sales: *Time Off From Good Behavior*, by Susan Sussman (Pocket); *Chanel*, by Axel Madsen (Henry Holt); *The Name of the Demon*, by Jackie Hyman (William Morrow).

JEAN V. NAGGAR LITERARY AGENCY, 216 East 75th St., New York NY 10021. (212)794-1082. President: Jean Naggar. Estab. 1978. Member of ILAA and SAR. Represents 80 clients. "If a writer is submitting a first novel, this must be completed and in final draft form before writing to query the agency." Prefers to work with published/established authors; works with small number of new/unpublished authors. Specializes in mainstream fiction and nonfiction—no category romances, no occult.

Will Handle: Nonfiction books, novels and juvenile books. Handles magazine articles and magazine fiction from authors who also write fiction/nonfiction books. Will read—at no charge—unsolicited queries and outlines. Reports in 2 weeks on queries.

Terms: Agent receives 15% commission on domestic sales; 15% on dramatic sales; and 20% on foreign sales.

Fees: Charges writers for photocopying, long distance telephone, cables and overseas postage expenses.

Recent Sales: *A Vision of Light*, by Judith Merkle Riley (Delacorte/Dell); *A Gift Upon the Shore*, by M.K. Wren (Ballantine); and *Tables*, by John Lucas (Little, Brown).

RUTH NATHAN LITERARY AGENCY, 242 West 27th St., New York NY 10001. (212)807-6292. President: Ruth Nathan. Estab. 1987. Member of ILAA. Represents 10 clients. 50% of clients are new/unpublished writers. Works with small number of new/unpublished writers and specialized writers of biography, art history and art. Specializes in nonfiction.

Will Handle: Nonfiction books. Currently handles 80% nonfiction books; 20% novels. Does not read unsolicited mss. Reports in 1 month on queries.

Terms: Agent receives 15% commission on domestic sales; 10% on foreign sales.

Fees: Charges for long distance phone calls, copying of ms, FAX, and Telex, extra galleys. 100% of income derived from commission on ms sales.

Recent Sales: *We Deliver*, by Joan Lisante; *Verve* (anthology); and *Texas Collects*, by Paul Nathan.

CHARLES NEIGHBORS, INC., Suite 3607A, 7600 Blanco Rd., San Antonio TX 78216. (512)342-5324. Owner: Charles Neighbors. Manager: Margaret Neighbors. Estab. 1966. Represents 60 clients. 10% of clients are new/unpublished writers. Works with a small number of new/unpublished authors.
Will Handle: Nonfiction books, novels and movie scripts. Currently handles 30% nonfiction books; 60% novels; and 10% movie scripts. Will read—at no charge—unsolicited queries and outlines. Reports in 1 month on queries; 2 months on mss.
Terms: Agent receives 15% commission on domestic sales; 15% on dramatic sales; and 20% on foreign sales.
Fees: Charges for photocopying and foreign postage expenses.
Recent Sales: *Best Sellers*, by Robert Laurance (Prentice Hall); *The Tree House*, by Victor Mullen (Zebra).

NEW AGE WORLD SERVICES, 62091 Valley View Circle, Joshua Tree CA 92252. (619)366-2833. Owner: Victoria Vandertuin. Estab. 1957. Member of Academy of Science Fiction, Fantasy and Horror Films. Represents 12 clients. 100% of clients are new/unpublished writers. Eager to work with new/unpublished writers. Specializes in all New Age fields: occult, astrology, metaphysical, yoga, U.F.O., ancient continents, para sciences, mystical, magical, health, beauty, political, and all New Age categories in fiction and nonfiction. Writer's guidelines for #10 SAE with four first class stamps.
Will Handle: Magazine articles, magazine fiction, nonfiction books, novels and poetry. Currently handles 10% magazine articles; 10% magazine fiction; 40% nonfiction books; 30% novels and 10% poetry. Will read—at no charge— unsolicited queries, outlines and mss; will read submissions at no charge, but may charge a criticism fee or service charge for work performed after the initial reading. Reports in 6 weeks.
Terms: Receives 15% commission on domestic sales; and 20% on foreign sales.
Fees: Charges reading fee of $95 for 300-page, typed, double-spaced ms; reading fee waived if representing writer. Charges criticism fee of $110 for 300-page, typed, double-space ms; 10% of income derived from criticism fees. "I personally read all manuscripts for critique or evaluation, which is typed, double-spaced with about four or more pages, depending on the manuscript and the service for the manuscript the author requests. If requested, marketing advice is included. We charge a representation fee if we represent the author's manuscript." Charges writer for editorial readings, compiling of query letter and synopsis, printing of same, compiling lists and mailings.
Recent Sales: No information given.

‡NEW ENGLAND PUBLISHING ASSOCIATES, INC., Box 5, Chester CT 06412. New York: (718)788-6641 or Connecticut: (203)345-4976. President: Elizabeth Frost Knappman. Estab. 1983. Represents 45-50 clients. 25% of clients are new/unpublished writers. Specializes in serious nonfiction. "We would like to see mss reflecting long-term research."
Will Handle: Nonfiction books. Currently handles 100% nonfiction books. Will read—at no charge—unsolicited queries and outlines. Phone queries are OK. Reports in 1 month on queries. Simultaneous queries OK.
Terms: Agent receives 15% on domestic sales; and 10% on dramatic and foreign sales (plus 10% to co-agent). 100% of income derived from commission on ms sales.
Recent Sales: *Body Mike*, by Tom Reaner and Joe Cantolupo (Villard); *Lillian Hellman*, by Carl Rollyson (St. Martin's); and *How to Get Your Lover Back*, by Dr. Blase Harris (Dell).

NEW WRITERS LITERARY PROJECT, LTD., Suite 177, 2809 Bird Ave., Coconut Grove FL 33133. (305)443-2158. FAX: (305)443-6756. President: Robert S. Catz. Estab. 1987. Member of ILAA. Represents 10 clients. 90% of clients are new/unpublished writers. Specializes in fiction and nonfiction, motion picture and television screenplays.
Will Handle: Magazine articles, magazine fiction, nonfiction books, novels, movie scripts, stage plays, TV scripts. Handles 5% magazine articles; 80% nonfiction books; 5% movie scripts; and 10% TV scripts. Will read—at no charge—unsolicited queries, outlines and mss. Reports in 3 weeks on queries; 5 weeks on mss. "Please indicate if submission is simultaneous!"
Terms: Agent receives 15% commission on domestic sales; 15% on dramatic sales; and 20% on foreign sales.
Fees: Charges writers for mail, telephone and photocopying expenses. Charge is individually negotiated per project. 95% of income derived from commission on ms sales; 5% from fees.
Recent Sales: *Power and Greed: A History of Teamster Corruption*, by Friedman and Schwarz (Watts); *Two Nightmares and a Dream*, by Rimmer and Morris (William Morrow).

For information on author's agents' areas of interest, see the nonfiction and fiction sections in the Author's Agents Subject Index.

THE BETSY NOLAN LITERARY AGENCY, Suite 9 West, 50 W. 29th St., New York NY 10001. (212)779-0700. FAX: (212)689-0376. President: Betsy Nolan. Agents: Donald Lehr and Carla Glasser. Estab. 1980. Represents 26 clients. 50% of clients are new/unpublished writers. Works with a small number of new/unpublished authors.
Will Handle: Nonfiction books and novels. Currently handles 60% nonfiction books and 40% novels. Will read—at no charge—unsolicited queries and outlines. Reports in 2 weeks on queries; 1 month on mss.
Terms: Agent receives 15% commission on domestic sales; and 20% on foreign sales.
Recent Sales: No information given.

THE NORMA-LEWIS AGENCY, 521 5th Ave., New York NY 10175. (212)751-4955. Contact: Norma Liebert. Estab. 1980. 50% of clients are new/unpublished writers. Prefers to work with published/established authors; eager to work with new/unpublished writers. Specializes in young adult and children's books.
Will Handle: Novels, textbooks, juvenile books (pre-school through high school), movie scripts, radio scripts, stage plays and TV scripts. Currently handles 10% nonfiction books; 10% novels; 10% textbooks; 50% juvenile books; 5% movie scripts; 5% radio scripts; 5% stage plays; and 5% TV scripts. Will read—at no charge—unsolicited queries and outlines. Reports in 2 weeks on queries.
Terms: Agent receives 15% commission on domestic sales; 15% on dramatic sales; and 20% on foreign sales.
Recent Sales: No information given.
of income derived from commission on ms sales.
Recent Sales: *Making the Words Stand Still*, by Don Lyman (Houghton Mifflin); *Working It Out*, by Judi Sprankle (Walker and Co.); *Putting Work In Its Place*, by Henry Ebel and Judi Sprankle (Walker and Co.).

NUGENT AND ASSOCIATES, INC., 170 10th Street North, Naples FL 33940. (813)262-3683. President: Ray E. Nugent. Estab. 1976. Represents 41 clients. 50% of clients are new/unpublished writers. Eager to work with new/unpublished writers. Specializes in adult fiction and nonfiction—screenplays.
Will Handle: Nonfiction books, novels, movie scripts, stage plays and TV scripts. Currently handles 25% nonfiction books; 55% novels; 5% juvenile books (preschool through grade 5); 5% movie scripts; 3% stage plays; 5% TV scripts; and 2% poetry. Will read—at no charge—unsolicited queries, outlines and mss. Reports in 1 month on queries; 2 months on submissions.
Terms: Receives 15% commission on domestic sales; 15% on dramatic sales; and 20% on foreign sales.
Fees: First book authors are charged $100 to cover ms typing, copies, long distance calls, etc.; balance refundable. Less than 1% of income derived from fees. Charges writers for long distance phone calls, copies, ms typing, any other extraordinary expenses directly associated with the author's specific material.
Recent Sales: *Hirohito*, by Leonard Mosley (Stein and Day); *Osteoporosis*, by Bruce/McIlwain (John Wiley); *50+*, by Bruce/McIlwain (John Wiley).

FIFI OSCARD ASSOCIATES, 19 W. 44th St., New York NY 10036. (212)764-1100. Contact: Ivy Fischer Stone, Literary Department. Estab. 1956. Member of SAR and WGA. Represents 108 clients. 5% of clients are new/unpublished writers. "Writer must have published articles or books in major markets or have screen credits if movie scripts, etc." Works with a small number of new/unpublished authors. Specializes in literary novels, commercial novels, mysteries and nonfiction, especially celebrity biographies and autobiographies.
Will Handle: Nonfiction books, novels, movie scripts and stage plays. Currently handles 40% nonfiction books; 40% novels; 5% movie scripts; 5% stage plays; and 10% TV scripts. Will read—at no charge—unsolicited queries and outlines. Reports in 1 week on queries if SASE enclosed.
Terms: Agent receives 15% commission on domestic sales; 10% on dramatic sales; and 20% on foreign sales.
Fees: Charges for photocopy expenses.
Recent Sales: *Kaffir Boy in America*, by Mark Mathabane (Scribner's); *TekWar*, by William Shatner (Putnam's); and *Beastly Tales, The 1989 Mystery Writers of America Anthology* (Wynwood Press).

THE OTTE COMPANY, 9 Goden St., Belmont MA 02178. (617)484-8505. Contact: Jane H. Otte or L. David Otte. Estab. 1973. Represents 25 clients. 33% of clients are new/unpublished writers. Works with a small number of new/unpublished authors. Specializes in quality adult trade books.
Will Handle: Nonfiction books and novels. Currently handles 40% nonfiction books; and 60% novels. Will consider unsolicited query letters. Reports in 1 week on queries; 1 month on mss.
Terms: Agent receives 15% commission on domestic sales; 7½% on dramatic sales; and 10% on foreign sales plus 10% to foreign agent.
Fees: Charges for photocopy, overseas phone and postage expenses. 100% of income derived from commission on ms sales.
Recent Sales: *Jack and Susan in 1933*, by Michael McDowell (Ballantine); *Abbott and Avery*, by Robert Shaw (Viking Penguin); and *Candles Burning*, by Michael McDowell (Berkley).

‡THE PANETTIERI AGENCY, 142 Marcella Rd., Hampton VA 23666. President: Eugenia A. Panettieri. Estab. 1988. Member of Romance Writers of America. Represents 36 clients. 70% of clients are new/unpublished writers. Prefers to work with published/established authors; eager to work with new/unpublished writers.

Specializes in romance and women's fiction, young adult, historical, nonfiction (how-to and self-help), mystery, suspense and horror.
Will Handle: Magazine articles, magazine fiction, nonfiction books, novels and juvenile books. Currently handles 20% nonfiction books; 70% novels; and 10% juvenile books. Will read—at no charge—unsolicited queries, outlines and manuscripts. Reports in 1 week on queries; 2 weeks on mss.
Terms: Agent receives 10% commission on domestic sales; 20% on foreign sales.
Recent Sales: *The Devil's Web*, by Kathy Cawthon and Pat Pulling (Prescott Press); *Place for the Heart*, by Catherine Leigh (Harlequin); *The Valiant Heart*, by Anita Gordon (Berkely Publishing Group).

JOHN K. PAYNE LITERARY AGENCY, INC., Box 1003, New York NY 10276. (212)475-6447. President: John K. Payne. Estab. 1923 (as Lenniger Literary Agency). Represents 30 clients. 20% of clients are new/unpublished writers. Prefers writers who have one or two books published. Specializes in popular women's fiction, historical romance, biography, sagas.
Will Handle: Nonfiction books, novels, and juvenile books (young adult fiction, nonfiction). Currently publishes 20% nonfiction books and 80% novels. Charges reading/criticism fee to unpublished writers—$1/page; $100 minimum. Writer receives 3-5 single-spaced pages for partial scripts, 5 and up for entire scripts.
Terms: Agent receives 10% commission on domestic sales; 10% on dramatic sales; and 20% on foreign sales.
Fees: Charges for express mail expenses and photocopies. 5% of income derived from fees charged to writers; 95% of income derived from commission on ms sales.
Recent Sales: *But That Was Yesterday*, by Kathleen Eagle (Silhouette); *Ragtown Scim*, by Elmer Kelton (Doubleday); *Sons of Texas*, by Tom Early (Berkley).

PEGASUS INTERNATIONAL, INC., Box 5470, Winter Park FL 32793-5470. (407)831-1008. Director: Gene Lovitz. Assistant Director/Client Contact: Carole Morling. Estab. 1987. Represents 300 clients. 85% of clients are new/unpublished writers. Eager to work with new/unpublished writers. Specializes in how-to, self-help, technical, business, health, political; mainstream novels, regency, contemporary and historical romance, horror, experimental, sci-fi, mystery.
Will Handle: Nonfiction books, novels, textbooks, juvenile books, movie scripts, TV scripts and video. Currently handles 25% nonfiction books; 45% novels; 5% cookbooks; 5% juvenile books (middle school-high school); 20% film/TV scripts. Will read—at no charge—unsolicited queries and outlines accompanied by SASE. Does not read unsolicited manuscripts. Reports in 2 weeks.
Terms: Agent receives 10% commission on domestic sales; 10% on dramatic sales; 15% on foreign sales.
Fees: Charges reading fee. "We return fee when and if a publishing contract is obtained. No charge for postage or phone expenses." 25% of income derived from reading fees. Charges $200 for up to a 400-page, typed, double-spaced ms. Lower fees for pamphlets, chapbooks, etc. "We charge one fee only. We term it an 'evaluation' fee which is both a reading fee as well as a criticism fee. The length of our critiques depends upon how much is needed. Usually 1½ pages to 10 pages. Some are longer. We do both line-by-line when needed while concentrating on the overall work. Marketing is always a part of the critique. Discuss ways to improve and make the manuscript marketable." 75% of income is derived from commission on mss sales; 25% derived from fees.
Recent Sales: *Dead Season*, by J. Bradley Owen (Leisure Books); *Pasaquina*, by Erin O'Shaughnessy (Saybrook); *John Wayne Gacy: Man or Monster*, by Harlan Mendenhall (Rhino Film Works, Ltd.).

‡**PENMARIN BOOKS**, Suite 8, 16 Mary St., San Rafael CA 94901. (415)457-7746. FAX: (415)454-0426. President: Hal Lockwood. Estab. 1987. Represents 8 clients. 80% of clients are new/unpublished writers. "No previous publication is necessary. We do expect authoritative credentials in terms of history, politics, science and the like." Works with a small number of new/unpublished authors. Specializes in general trade nonfiction and illustrated books.
Will Handle: Nonfiction books. Currently handles 100% nonfiction books. Will read—at no charge—unsolicited queries and outlines. Will read submissions at no charge, but may charge a criticism fee or service charge for work performed after the initial reading. Reports in 2 weeks on queries; 1 months on mss.
Terms: Agent receives 10% commission on domestic sales; 10% on dramatic sales; and 10% on foreign sales.
Fees: "We normally do not provide extensive criticism as part of our reading but, for a fee, will prepare guidance for editorial development." Charges $200/300 pages. "Our editorial director writes critiques. These may be two to ten pages long. They usually include an overall evaluation and then analysis and recommendations about specific sections, organization, or style."
Recent Sales: *Teenage Drug Abuses*, by R. Gaetano (Union Hospital Foundation); *Bank of America Guide to Making the Most of Your Money*, by R. Darden Chambliss, Jr. (Dow Jones-Irwin); and *The Picture Fixer: A Problem-Solving Guide to Taking Great Photos with a Point-and-Shoot Camera* (Amphoto).

PERKINS' LITERARY AGENCY, Box 48, Childs MD 21916. (301)398-2647. Agent/Owner: Esther R. Perkins. Estab. 1979. Represents 35 clients; 75% of clients are new/unpublished authors. Will be adding a few clients, professional or newcomers, in the next year. Specializes in historicals, mysteries, men's adventure, horror, regencies, a few historical/romance.

Will Handle: Novels. Currently handles 100% novels. Does not read unsolicited material. Reports in 1 week. **Terms:** Agent receives 15% commission on domestic sales; 20% on dramatic sales; 20% on foreign sales. **Fees:** Charges a reading fee "if writer has not had a book published by a major house in the past two years. Fee refunded if sale made within one year." 5% of income derived from reading fees. Charges $75 for 300-page, typed, double-spaced book ms. "I provide an overall critique of the ms—could be long or short, but not line-by-line. Marketing advice for clients only. I am the only reader." 95% of income is derived from commission on ms sales; 5% from fees. **Recent Sales:** *Sweet Treason*, by Patricia Gaffney (Leisure); *Sweet Texas Nights*, by Vivian Vaughan (Zebra); and *An Improper Companion*, by Karla Hocker (Zebra).

‡JAMES PETER ASSOCIATES, INC., Box 772, Tenafly NJ 07670. (201)568-0760. FAX: (201)568-2959. President: Bert Holtje. Estab. 1970. Member of ILAA. Represents 49 clients. "We are especially interested in writers whose backgrounds include psychology, medicine, history, business and politics. Prior publication is important, but not critical." Prefers to work with published/established authors. Specializes in nonfiction only. Psychology, health and related subjects, history, politics,how-to, popular culture, and business—all for general readers. **Will Handle:** Nonfiction books. Currently handles 100% nonfiction books. Will read—at no charge—unsolicited queries and outlines. Does not read unsolicited manuscripts. Reports in 1 month on queries. **Terms:** Agent receives 15% commission on domestic sales; 20% on foreign sales. **Fees:** Charges writers for duplicating proposals. **Recent Sales:** *Between You and Your Doctor*, by David Stutz, M.D. and Bernard Feder (Consumer Reports Books); *Exotic Diseases of the Mind*, by Richard Noll (Berkley); and *Your Rights on the Job*, by Steven Mitchell Sack, J.D. (Facts on File).

ALISON PICARD, LITERARY AGENT, Box 2000, Cotuit MA 02635. (508)888-3741. Contact: Alison Picard. Estab. 1985. Represents 40 clients. 30% of clients are new/unpublished writers. "I prefer writers who have been published (at least in magazines) but am willing to consider exceptional new writers." Works with a small number of new/unpublished authors. Specializes in nonfiction. Also handle literary and category fiction, contemporary and historical romances, juvenile/YA books, short stories and articles if suitable for major national magazine. **Will Handle:** Magazine articles, magazine fiction, nonfiction books, novels, juvenile books. Currently handles 5% magazine articles; 5% magazine fiction; 30% nonfiction books; 40% novels; and 20% juvenile books. Will read—at no charge—unsolicited queries, outlines and manuscripts. Reports in 1 week on queries; 1 month on manuscripts. "Authors *must* send written query first before submitting material." **Terms:** Agent receives 15% commission on domestic sales; 15% on dramatic sales; and 15% on foreign sales. **Fees:** Charges for copying of ms. 100% of income derived from sales of writers' work. **Recent Sales:** *From: The President*, by Bruce Oudes (Harper & Row); *Annabelle Anderson*, by Patricia Beaver (Four Winds Press/Macmillan); and *Secrets for Young Scientists*, by Ray Staszako (Doubleday).

ARTHUR PINE ASSOCIATES, INC., 1780 Broadway, New York NY 10019. (212)265-7330. Contact: Agent. Estab. 1967..Represents 100 clients. 20% of clients are new/unpublished writers. Works with a small number of new/unpublished authors. **Will Handle:** Nonfiction books and novels. Currently handles 75% nonfiction books and 25% novels. Does not read unsolicited mss. Reports in 2 weeks on queries. **Terms:** Agent receives 15% commission on domestic sales; 15% on dramatic sales; and 15% on foreign sales. **Fees:** Charges a reading fee. .1% of income derived from reading fees. Gives 1-3 pages of criticism. Charges for photocopy expenses. 99.9% of income derived from sales of writers' work. **Recent Sales:** *Take My Life Please*, by Henny Youngman (Beech Tree/Morrow); *Saturday Night USA*, by Susan Orlean (Simon & Schuster); and *Your Erroneous Zones*, by Dr. Wayne W. Dyer.

‡JULIE POPKIN/NANCY COOKE, 15340 Albright St., #204, Pacific Palisades CA 90272 (Popkin). (213)459-2834; 236 E. Davie St., Raleigh NC 27601 (Cooke). (919)834-1456. Estab. 1989. Member of ILAA. Represents 6 clients. 33% of clients are new/unpublished writers. Specializes in selling book-length mss including fiction—all genres—and nonfiction. **Will Handle:** Nonfiction books and novels. Currently handles 50% nonfiction books and 50% novels. Will read submissions at no charge, but may charge a criticism fee or service charge for work performed after the initial reading. Reports in 1 months on queries; 2 months on mss. **Terms:** Agent receives 10% commission on domestic sales; 10% on dramatic sales; and 20% on foreign sales. **Fees:** Charges writers for photocopying, extraordinary mailing fees. **Recent Sales:** *Moments of Light*, by Fred Chappell (New South).

SIDNEY E. PORCELAIN, Box 1229, Milford PA 18337. (717)296-6420. Manager: Sidney Porcelain. Estab. 1952. Represents 20 clients. 50% of clients are new/unpublished writers. Prefers to work with published/established authors; works with a small number of new/unpublished authors. Specializes in fiction (novels, mysteries, and suspense) and nonfiction (celebrity and exposé).

Will Handle: Magazine articles, magazine fiction, nonfiction books, novels and juvenile books. Currently handles 2% magazine articles; 5% magazine fiction; 5% nonfiction books; 50% novels; 5% juvenile books; 2% movie scripts; 1% TV scripts; and 30% "comments for new writers." Will read—at no charge—unsolicited queries, outlines and mss. Reports in 2 weeks on queries; 3 weeks on mss.

Terms: Agent receives 10% commission on domestic sales; 10% on dramatic sales; and 10% on foreign sales. 50% of income derived from commission on ms sales.

Recent Sales: No information given.

JULIAN PORTMAN & ASSOCIATES, Suite 283, 7337 Lincoln Ave., Chicago IL 60646. (312)509-6421. Branch office: Suite 964, 8033 Sunset Blvd., Hollywood CA 90046. (213)281-7391. Senior partner: Julian Portman. Estab. 1969. Represents 35 clients. 25% of our clients are new/unpublished writers. "Our interest is a good writer, storyteller and plot creator, whether they be a new writer or one who has had a book previously published. Our interest is to find stories that would sell for books and could be turned into potential TV/ motion pictures." Works with a small number of new/unpublished authors.

Will Handle: Nonfiction books, novels, movie scripts, TV scripts. Currently handles 30% nonfiction books, 35% novels, 20% movie scripts; 15% TV scripts. Will read—at no charge—unsolicited queries and outlines. Reports in 3 weeks on queries; 7 weeks on mss.

Terms: Agent receives 15-25% commission on domestic sales; 15% on dramatic sales and 25% on foreign sales.

Fees: Charges a reading and criticism fee for new writers; reading fee will be waived if represents the writer. 3% of income derived from reading fees. Charges $150-200/300-page, typed double-spaced book ms. Writer receives an "overall evaluation of 2-3 pages depending on the quality of the ms. Uses both published authors and journalists on a flat fee arrangement to evaluate mss." Charges a handling fee. 1% of income derived from handling fees. 15% of total income derived from fees. Payment of a criticism fee does not ensure that agency will represent a writer.

Recent Sales: *Escape From Terror*, by Julian John Portman, Carol Ryzak and Walter Eckes (Pocket Books); *Sebastian Longfellow Mysteries*, by Robert Hill and Julian John Portman (St. Martin's); *The Senator From Illinois*, by Julian John Portman and Lori Simon.

AARON M. PRIEST LITERARY AGENCY, Suite 3902, 122 E. 42nd St., New York NY 10168. (212)818-0344. Contact: Aaron Priest, Molly Friedrich and Robert Colgan.

Will Handle: Fiction and nonfiction books. Currently handles 50% nonfiction books and 50% fiction. Will read submissions at no charge. Reports in 1 month on mss.

Terms: Agent receives 15% commission on domestic sales.

Fees: Charges for photocopy and foreign postage expenses.

Recent Sales: *The Man Who Heard Too Much*, by Bill Granger; *I Want to Grow Up, I Want to Grow Hair, I Want to Go to Boise*, by Erma Bombeck; and *Edge of Eden*, by Nicholas Proffitt.

‡D. RADLEY-REGAN & ASSOCIATES, Box 243, Jamestown NC 27282. (919)454-5040. President and Editor: D. Radley-Regan. Estab. 1987. Eager to work with new/unpublished writers. Specializes in fiction, nonfiction, mystery, thriller.

Will Handle: Nonfiction books, novels, movie scripts and TV scripts. Currently handles 10% nonfiction books; 40% novels; 25% movie scripts; 25% TV scripts. Will read submissions at no charge, but may charge a criticism fee or service charge for work performed after the initial reading. Reports in 2 weeks on queries; 10 weeks on mss.

Terms: Agent receives 15% commission on domestic sales; 15% on dramatic sales; and 15% on foreign sales.

Fees: Charges reading for full mss. Writer receives overall evaluation, marketing advice and agency service. 10% of income derived from commission on mss sales. Payment of criticism fee does not ensure that writer will be represented.

Recent Sales: *Wentworth Place*, and *Return to Wentworth Place*, by D. Radley-Regan.

RAINES & RAINES, 71 Park Ave., New York NY 10016. (212)684-5160. Contact: Joan Raines, Theron Raines. Estab. 1961. Represents 110 clients. 3% of clients are new/unpublished writers. Prefers to work with published/established writers; works with small number of new/unpublished writers.

Will Handle: Nonfiction books, novels. Does not read unsolicited mss. Reports on queries in 2 weeks; 3 weeks on mss.

Terms: Agent receives 15% commission on domestic sales; 15% on dramatic sales; and 20% on foreign sales (½ for foreign agent).

Fees: Charges writers for overseas calls, copying and copies of books.

Recent Sales: *Thalassa*, by James Dickey (Houghton Mifflin); *Freud's Vienna and Other Essays*, by Bruno Betthlheim (Knopf); and *The Shawl*, by Cynthia Ozick (Knopf).

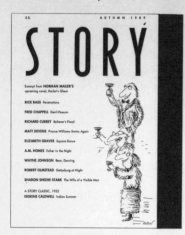

ONE OF THE MOST TALKED-ABOUT REVIVALS IN MAGAZINE PUBLISHING.....

STORY

The first issues of STORY were cranked out on an old mimeograph machine in 1931 by two American newspaper correspondents in Vienna. Editors Whit Burnett and his wife Martha Foley had no money—just a vision to create a forum for outstanding short stories, regardless of their commercial appeal. The magazine was an instant literary success, and was hailed "the most distinguished short story magazine in the world."

Now STORY returns with the same commitment to publishing the best new fiction written today. It will also provide a workshop for new material from today's more established writers, as well as feature at least one piece reprinted from an original issue of STORY. Printed on heavy premium paper, each issue is meant to be read and cherished for years to come. (Those first mimeographed copies of STORY are collectors' items today!)

Share in the rebirth of a literary legend. Become a Charter Subscriber to STORY today!

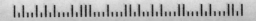

Writer's® DIGEST

Writer's®
DIGEST

THE WORLD'S LEADING MAGAZINE FOR WRITERS

How would you like to get:

- up-to-the-minute reports on new markets for your writing
- professional advice from editors and writers about what to write and how to write it to maximize your opportunities for getting published
- in-depth interviews with leading authors who reveal their secrets of success
- expert opinion about writing and selling fiction, nonfiction, poetry and scripts
- ...all at a $13.00 discount?

(See other side for details.)

HELEN REES LITERARY AGENCY, 308 Commonwealth Ave., Boston MA 02116. (617)262-2401. Contact: Catherine Mahar. Estab. 1982. Member of ILAA. Represents 55 clients. 25% of our clients are new/unpublished writers. Writer must have been published or be an authority on a subject. Prefers to work with published/established authors; works with a small number of new/unpublished authors. Specializes in nonfiction—biographies, health and business.
Will Handle: Nonfiction books and novels. Currently handles 90% nonfiction books and 10% novels. Will read—at no charge—unsolicited queries and outlines. Reports in 2 weeks on queries; 3 weeks on mss.
Terms: Agent receives 15% commission on domestic sales and 20% on foreign sales.
Fees: Occasionally charges a reading fee "for clients who are unpublished and want that service. I don't solicit this." Reading fee will be waived if representing the writer. Charges criticism fee of $250; writer receives criticism of characters, dialogue, plot, style and suggestions for reworking areas of weakness.
Recent Sales: *Price Waterhouse Guide to the New Tax Law* (Bantam); *Senator Barry Goldwater's Autobiography* (Doubleday); and *Minding the Body, Mending the Mind* (Addison Wesley).

RHODES LITERARY AGENCY INC., 140 West End Ave., New York NY 10023. (212)580-1300. President: Joan Lewis. Estab. 1971. Member of ILAA.
Will Handle: Nonfiction books, novels (a limited number), and juvenile books. Will read—at no charge—unsolicited queries and outlines. Include SASE. Reports in 2 weeks on queries.
Terms: Agent receives 10% commission on domestic sales; and 20% on foreign sales.
Recent Sales: No information given.

JOHN R. RIINA LITERARY AGENCY, 5905 Meadowood Rd., Baltimore MD 21212. (301)433-2305. Contact: John R. Riina. Estab. 1977. Works with "authors with credentials to write on their subject." Specializes in college textbooks, professional books and serious nonfiction.
Will Handle: Textbooks. Currently handles 30% nonfiction books and 70% textbooks. Does not read unsolicited mss. Reports in 3 weeks.
Terms: Agent receives 10% commission on domestic sales; 10% on dramatic sales; 15% on foreign sales.
Fees: Charges "exceptional long distance telephone and express of manuscripts." 90% of income is derived from commission on manuscript sales; 10% from fees.
Recent Sales: "Not available for listing."

THE ROBBINS OFFICE, INC., 12th Floor, 866 Second Ave., New York NY 10017. (212)223-0720. Contact: Kathy P. Robbins. Represents 140 clients. Writers must be published or come to us by referral. Specializes in selling mainstream nonfiction, commercial and literary fiction.
Will Handle: Nonfiction books and novels. Currently handles 75% nonfiction books and 25% novels. Will handle magazine articles for book writers under contract. Does not read unsolicited mss. Reports in 2 weeks on queries.
Terms: Agent receives 15% commission on domestic sales; 10-15% on dramatic sales; and 15% on foreign sales.
Fees: Bills back specific expenses incurred in doing business for a client.
Recent Sales: *1959*, by Thulani Davis (Weidenfeld & Nicolson); untitled on Moscow, by David Remnick (Farrar, Straus & Giroux); and *Article 35*, by Michael Grant (Bantam).

RICHARD H. ROFFMAN ASSOCIATES, Suite 6A, 697 West End Ave., New York NY 10025. (212)749-3647/ 3648. President: Richard H. Roffman. Estab. 1967. 70% of clients are new/unpublished writers. Prefers to work with published/established writers. Specializes in "nonfiction primarily, but other types, too."
Will Handle: Nonfiction books. Currently handles 10% magazine articles; 5% magazine fiction; 5% textbooks; 5% juvenile books; 5% radio scripts; 5% movie scripts; 5% TV scripts; 5% syndicated material; 5% poetry; and 50% other. Does not read unsolicited mss. Reports in 2 weeks. "SASE if written answer requested, please."
Terms: Agent receives 10% commission on domestic sales; 10% on dramatic sales; and 10% on foreign sales.
Fees: "We do not read material (for a fee) actually, only on special occasions. We prefer to refer to other people specializing in that." 10% of income derived from reading fees. "We suggest a moderate montly retainer." Charges for mailings, phone calls, photocopying and messenger service. Offers consultation service through which writers can get advice on a contract. "I am also an attorney at law."
Recent Sales: No information given.

STEPHANIE ROGERS AND ASSOCIATES, 3855 Lankershim Blvd.—#218, N. Hollywood CA 91604. (818)509-1010. Owner: Stephanie Rogers. Estab. 1981. Represents 22 clients. 20% of clients are new/unpublished writers. Prefers that the writer has been produced (motion pictures or TV), his/her properties optioned or has references. Prefers to work with published/established authors. Specializes in screenplays—dramas (contemporary), action/adventure, romantic comedies and supsense/thrillers for motion pictures and TV.

Will Handle: Novels (only wishes to see those that have been published and can translate to screen) and movie and TV scripts (must be professional in presentation and not over 125 pages). Currently handles 10% novels; 50% movie scripts and 40% TV scripts. Does not read unsolicited mss.
Terms: Agent receives 10% commission on domestic sales; 10% on dramatic sales; and 20% on foreign sales.
Fees: Charges for phone, photocopying and messenger expenses.
Recent Sales: *Shoot to Kill*, for Touchstone Pictures; *Steel Dawn*, for Vestron; and *South of Picasso*, for Tri-Star.

JANE ROTROSEN AGENCY, 318 East 51st St., New York NY 10022. (212)593-4330. Estab. 1974. Member of ILAA. Represents 100 clients. 70% of clients were new/unpublished writers. Works with published and unpublished writers. Specializes in general trade fiction and nonfiction.
Will Handle: Nonfiction books, novels and juvenile books. Currently handles 30% nonfiction books and 70% novels. Will read—at no charge—unsolicited queries and short outlines. Reports in 2 weeks.
Terms: Receives 15% commission on domestic sales; 15% on dramatic sales; and 20% on foreign sales.
Fees: Charges writers for photocopies, long-distance/transoceanic telephone, telegraph, Telex, messenger service and foreign postage.
Recent Sales: "Our client list remains confidential."

THE SAGALYN AGENCY, 1717 N St., NW, Washington DC 20036. (202)835-0320. FAX: (202)835-0323. Agents: Raphael Sagalyn or Lisa DiMona. Estab. 1980. Member ILAA. Represents 75 clients. 10% of clients are new/unpublished writers. Specializes in journalism, biography, history, business, autobiography, popular science and medicine, and psychology.
Will Handle: Adult trade nonfiction books and novels. Currently handles 98% nonfiction books and 2% novels. Will read—at no charge—unsolicited queries and outlines when accompanied by SASE. Reports in 2 weeks.
Terms: Agent receives 15% to $100,000; 10% thereafter.
Fees: Charges for faxes, overnight mail, photocopy, international calls, etc.
Recent Sales: *Innumeracy*, by John Allen Paulos (Farrar, Straus); *Landslide: The Unmaking of the President 1984-1988*, by Jane Meyer and Doyle McManus (Houghton Mifflin); and *Food Pharmacy*, by Jean Carper (Bantam).

‡SANDUM & ASSOCIATES, 114 E. 84th St., New York NY 10028. (212)737-2011. President: Howard E. Sandum. Estab. 1987. Represents 25 clients. 20% of clients are new/unpublished writers. Specializes in general nonfiction—all categories of adult books; commerical and literary fiction.
Will Handle: Nonfiction books and novels. Currently handles 60% nonfiction books and 40% novels. Will read—at no charge—unsolicited queries and outlines. "Do not send full ms unless requested. Include SASE." Reports in 1 week on queries.
Terms: Agent receives 15% commission. Agent fee adjustable on dramatic and foreign sales.
Fees: Charges writers for copying, air express, long distance telephone.
Recent Sales: Nonfiction books in psychology (daydreaming); family values; 20th century American history.

SBC ENTERPRISES, INC., 11 Mabro Dr., Denville NJ 07834-9607. (201)366-3622. Agents: Alec Bernard, Eugenia Cohen. Estab. 1979. 50% of clients are new/unpublished writers. Specializes in trade fiction, nonfiction and screenplays.
Will Handle: Nonfiction books, novels, textbooks, movie scripts, TV scripts. Currently handles 25% nonfiction books; 25% novels; 10% textbooks; 20% movie scripts; 20% TV scripts. Will read—at no charge—unsolicited queries and outlines "provided SASE included." Does not read unsolicited manuscripts. Reports in 2 weeks on queries.
Terms: Agent receives 15% commission on domestic sales for first-time writers up to $10,000, 10% thereafter—all others 10%; 15% on dramatic rights sales; 20% on foreign sales.
Recent Sales: No information given.

JACK SCAGNETTI LITERARY AGENCY, Suite 210, 5330 Lankershim Blvd., N. Hollywood CA 91601. (818)762-3871. Owner: Jack Scagnetti. Estab. 1974. Member of WGA. Represents 50 clients. 10% of clients are new/unpublished writers. Prefers to work with published/established authors.
Will Handle: Nonfiction books, novels, movie scripts and TV scripts. Currently handles 20% nonfiction books; 10% novels; 40% movie scripts; and 30% TV scripts. Will read—at no charge—unsolicited queries and outlines. Reports in 2 weeks on queries; 1 month on mss.
Terms: Agent receives 10% commission on domestic sales; 10% on dramatic sales; and 15% on foreign sales.
Fees: Charges for postage on multiple submissions.
Recent Sales: *Superstition Gold* (Dorchester Publishing); *How to Win at Car Buying*, by Steve Ross (Stackpole Books).

‡**JOHN SCHAFFNER ASSOCIATES, INC.**, 4th Fl., 264 5th Ave., New York NY 10001. (212)689-6888. Contact: Timothy Schaffner or Patrick Delahunt. Estab. 1948. Member of SAR and ILAA. Represents 50-60 clients. 15% of clients are new/unpublished writers. Works with a small number of new/unpublished authors. Specializes in speculative fiction, science fiction, fantasy, celebrity bios, popular self-help, and general nonfiction and fiction.
Will Handle: Nonfiction books and novels. Currently handles 5% magazine fiction; 30% nonfiction books; 60% novels; and 5% juvenile books. Query first. $10 handling fee for regular submissions. Reports in 2 weeks on queries; 6 weeks on mss. "If our agency does not respond within 6 weeks to your request to become a client, you may submit requests elsewhere."
Terms: Agent receives 15% commission on domestic sales; 15% on dramatic sales; and 20% on foreign sales. Charges writers for "extra services," photocopy expenses, overseas courier, etc. 100% of income derived from commission on ms sales.
Recent Sales: *How to Be Funny*, by Steve Allen (McGraw-Hill); *Menken and Sara: A Life In Letters*, edited by Marion Elizabeth Rodgers (McGraw-Hill); and *Trip-Master Monkey: His Fake Book*, by Maxine Hong Kingston (Knopf).

‡**SCHLESSINGER-VAN DYCK AGENCY**, 2814 PSFS Bldg., 12 S. 12th St., Philadelphia PA 19107. (215)627-4665. FAX: (215)627-0448. Partners: Blanche Schlessinger and Barrie Van Dyck. Estab. 1987. Represents 40 clients. 30% of clients are new/unpublished writers. Specializes in mainstream fiction, nonfiction, how-to, mysteries, children's.
Will Handle: Nonfiction books, novels, juvenile books. Handles 55% nonfiction books; 35% novels; 10% juvenile books. Will read—at no charge—unsolicited queries and outlines. Reports in 2 weeks on queries; 1 month on mss.
Terms: Agent receives 15% commission on domestic sales; 15% on dramatic sales; and 20% on foreign sales.
Fees: Charges writers for copying, UPS, long-distance phone.
Recent Sales: *Indecent Proposal* (Donald I. Fine); *Living with Angina* (Harper & Row); *Getting Strong In All The Hurting Places* (Rawson Associates/Macmillan).

‡**THE SUSAN SCHULMAN LITERARY AGENCY, INC.**, 454 W. 44th St., New York NY 10036. (212)713-1633/4/5. FAX: (212)315-4782. President: Susan Schulman. Estab. 1978. Member of SAR and ILAA. 10-15% of clients are new/unpublished writers. Prefers to work with published/established authors; works with a small number of new/unpublished authors.
Will Handle: Nonfiction books, novels, plays, movie scripts, treatments for television movies of the week, and dramatic and comedy series. Currently handles 50% nonfiction books; 10% novels; 10% movie scripts; 5% stage plays; and 20% TV scripts. Will read—at no charge—unsolicited queries and outlines. Reports in 2 weeks on queries; 6 weeks on mss as long as SASE enclosed.
Terms: Agent receives 15% commission on domestic sales; 10-20% on dramatic sales; and 7½-10% on foreign sales (plus 7½-10% to co-agent).
Fees: Charges a $50 reading fee if detailed analysis requested; fee will be waived if repesenting the writer. Less than 1% of income derived from reading fees. Charges for foreign mail, special messenger or delivery services.
Recent Sales: *When Parents Love Too Much*, by Meyerson and Ashner (William Morrow); *The Devil in London*, by Christopher Fowler (Ballantine); *Hardball: A Mystery*, by Barbara D'Amato (Scribner's).

LAURENS R. SCHWARTZ, ESQUIRE, Suite 15D, 5 E. 22nd St., New York NY 10010-5315. (212)228-2614. Contact: Laurens R. Schwartz. Estab. 1984. Specializes in nonfiction books—"primary specialty is high-tech; others includes medicine, social topics, music, art, biography; videocassette, CD-ROM—will place or package."
Will Handle: Nonfiction books, videocassettes, computer programs, CD-ROM. Currently handles 65% nonfiction books; 15% computer or videocassette-related; 20% art and advertising. "Do not like receiving mass mailings sent to all agents. Be selective—do your homework. Do not send *everything* you have ever written. Choose *one* work and promote that. *Always* include an SASE. *Never* send your only copy. *Always* include a background sheet on yourself and a *one*-page synopsis of the work (too many summaries end up being as long as the work)." No longer handle screenplays except as tied in to a book, or unless we solicit the screenwriter directly. Does not read unsolicited mss. Reports in 1 month.
Terms: Agent receives 10% commission on domestic sales; 15% on foreign sales.
Fees: "To keep my rates low, I require that a writer provide as many copies of material as I need. All other costs are absorbed by me. I am an entertainment law lawyer. I provide simple negotiations as part of commission. Complex packaging or development of ancillaries necessitates an hourly charge (my then current fee)."

‡**ARTHUR P. SCHWARTZ, LITERARY AGENT**, % Corey Business Services, Box 9132, Christchurch 2, New Zealand. (03)664-717 or (03)385-647. New York office: 435 Riverside Dr. New York NY 10025. (212)864-3182. Literary Agent: Arthur P. Schwartz. Estab. 1975. Member of ILAA. Represents 70 clients. 20% of

clients are new/unpublished writers. Prefers to work with published/established authors; works with a small number of new/unpublished authors.
Will Handle: Nonfiction books and novels. Currently handles 50% nonfiction books and 50% novels. Reports in 1 month on queries.
Terms: Agent receives 12½% commission on domestic sales; 12½% on dramatic sales and 12½% on foreign sales.
Recent Sales: *Power Speech* by, Roy Alexander (AMAcom); *Angel's Wing*, by Jill Dubois (Ballantine) and *Einstein's Dream*, by Dr. Barry Parker (Plenum).

‡**SCRIBE AGENCY**, Box 580393, Houston TX 77258-0393. (713)333-1094. Literary Agent: Marta White or Carl Sinclair. Estab. 1988. Member of Writers Guild of America. Represents 9 clients. 60% of clients are new/unpublished writers. Specializes in book-length literary fiction for adults; film and television rights; motion picture and TV scripts.
Will Handle: Novels, movie scripts, TV scripts. Currently handles 40% novels; 40% movie scripts; and 20% TV scripts. Will read—at no charge—unsolicited queries, outlines and manuscripts. Reports in 3 weeks.
Terms: Agent receives 10% commission on domestic sales; 15-20% on foreign sales.
Recent Sales: "Currently negotiating movie rights for a screenplay and a book contract."

‡**SEBASTIAN AGENCY**, Box 1369, San Carlos CA 94070. (415)598-0310. FAX: (415)637-9615. Owner/Agent: Laurie Harper. Estab. 1985. Represents 35 clients. "If previously unpublished, the book must be completed. If previously published but outside of current book's category—book must be complete. If published within same area or category as present book—may contact with proposal and outline plus 3 sample chapters." Works with a small number of new/unpublished authors. Particulary interested in nonfiction: psychology, health, self-help, women's issues, business; fiction: mainstream, adventure, suspense, historical or literary.
Will Handle: Nonfiction books and novels. Currently handles 70% nonfiction books and 30% novels. Will read—at no charge—unsolicited queries, outlines and sample chapters. "No submissions during February or September." Reports in 3 weeks on queries; 1 month on sample material.
Terms: Agent receives 15% commission on domestic sales; 20% on dramatic sales and 20% on foreign sales.
Fees: "There will be a $100, nonrefundable fee, one time upon contracting with this agency—for previously *unpublished* authors. This is to cover extra costs of marketing a new author." Charges writers for postage after 15 submissions; cable fees; copies of manuscript for submissions.
Recent Sales: *The Urge to Splurge*, by Carolyn Wessen (St. Martin's Press); *The Monogamy Myth*, by Peggy Vaughan (Newmarket Press), *God Was An Atheist Sailor*, by Burgess Cogill (W.W. Norton).

‡**SHAPIRO-LICHTMAN TALENT AGENCY**, 8827 Beverly Blvd., Los Angeles CA 90048. (213)859-8877. FAX: (213)859-7153. Contact: Martin Shapiro. Estab. 1969. Writer must have appropriate academic background and recommendations. Prefers to work with published/established authors.
Will Handle: Movie scripts and TV scripts. Currently handles 90% movie and TV scripts. Does not read unsolicited mss. Reports in 2 weeks on queries.
Terms: Agent receives 10% commission on domestic sales; 10% on dramatic sales; and 20% on foreign sales.
Recent Sales: No information given.

SHORR STILLE AND ASSOCIATES, Suite 6, 800 S. Robertson Blvd., Los Angeles CA 90035. (213)659-6160. Member of WGA. Writer must have an entertainment industry referral. Works with a small number of new/unpublished authors. Specializes in screenplays, teleplays, high concept action-adventure and romantic comedy.
Will Handle: Movie scripts and TV scripts. Currently handles 50% movie scripts and 50% TV scripts. Will read—at no charge—unsolicited queries. Reports in 1 month on queries; 6 weeks on mss.
Terms: Agent receives 10% commission on domestic sales.
Fees: Charges for photocopy expenses.
Recent Sales: No information given.

BOBBE SIEGEL, LITERARY AGENCY, 41 W. 83rd St., New York NY 10024. (212)877-4985. Estab. 1975. Represents 60 clients. 40% of clients are new/unpublished writers. "The writer must have a good project, have the credentials to be able to write on the subject and must deliver it in proper fashion. In fiction it all depends on whether I like what I read and if I feel I can sell it." Prefers to work with published/established authors. "Prefer track records, but am eager to work with talent." Specializes in literary fiction, detective and suspense fiction, historicals, how-to, health, woman's subjects, fitness, beauty, feminist sports, biographies and crafts.
Will Handle: Nonfiction books and novels. Currently handles 65% nonfiction books and 35% novels. Does not read unsolicited mss. Reports in 2 weeks on queries; 2 months on mss.
Terms: Agent receives 15% commission on domestic sales; 10% on dramatic sales; and 10% on foreign sales.
Fees: "If writer wishes critique, will refer to a freelance editor. Charges for photocopying, telephone, overseas mail, express mail expenses. 70% of income derived from commission on ms sales; 30% comes from foreign representation."

Recent Sales: *Other Peoples' Trades*, by Primo Levi (Summit); *A Light From Within*, by Dalene Berry (Dutton); *The Yeast Control Diet*, by Gail Burton (NAL).

‡**SIERRA LITERARY AGENCY**, 468-165 Bass Hill Rd., Janesville CA 96114. (916)253-3250. Owner: Mary Barr. Estab. 1988. Eager to work with new/unpublished writers. Specializes in contemporary women's novels, mainstream fiction and nonfiction, self-help, self-esteem books.
Will Handle: Magazine articles, magazine fiction, nonfiction books and novels. Will read—at no charge—unsolicited queries, outlines and manuscripts. Reports in 2 weeks on queries; 6 weeks on mss.
Terms: Agent receives 10% commission on domestic sales; 15% on dramatic sales; and 20% on foreign sales.
Fees: Charge writers for copying, phone and overseas postage.
Recent Sales: "We are a new agency."

EVELYN SINGER LITERARY AGENCY, Box 594, White Plains NY 10602. Agent: Evelyn Singer. Estab. 1951. Represents 50 clients. To be represented, writer must have $20,000 in past sales of freelance works. Prefers to work with published/established authors. Specializes in fiction and nonfiction books, adult and juvenile (picture books only if writer is also the artist).
Will Handle: Nonfiction books (bylined by authority or celebrity); novels (no romances, or pseudo-science, violence or sex); and juvenile books. Currently handles 25% nonfiction books; 25% novels; and 50% juvenile books. Does not read unsolicited mss.
Terms: Agent receives 15% commission on domestic sales; 20% on dramatic sales; and 20% on foreign sales.
Fees: Charges for phone and expenses authorized by the author. 100% of income derived from commission on ms sales.
Recent Sales: *Secret Kills*, by William Beechcroft (Dodd, Mead); *Volcanoes*, by Mary Elting (Simon and Schuster); and *How Things Work*, by Mike and Marcia Folsom (Macmillan).

SINGER MEDIA CORPORATION, INC., 3164 Tyler Ave., Anaheim CA 92801. (714)527-5650. Associate Editor: Donna Hollinghead. Estab. 1940. 10% of clients are new/unpublished writers. Prefers to work with published/established authors; works with a small number of new/unpublished authors. Specializes in contemporary romances, nonfiction and biographies.
Will Handle: Magazine articles and syndicated material (submit tearsheets); nonfiction books (query); and romance novels. Currently handles 5% nonfiction books; 20% novels; 75% syndicated material. Will read—at no charge—unsolicited queries and outlines; but may charge a criticism fee or service charge for work performed after the initial reading. Reports in 2 weeks on queries; 6 weeks on mss.
Terms: Agent receives 15% commission on domestic sales and 20% on foreign sales.
Fees: Charges a reading fee to unpublished writers which will be credited on sales; 5% of income derived from reading fees. Criticism included in reading fee. "A general overall critique averages 3-6 pages. It does not cover spelling or grammar, but the construction of the material. A general marketing critique is also included." 95% of income derived from sales of writers' work; 5% of income derived from criticism services. "Payment of a criticism fee does not ensure that agency will represent a writer. The author may not be satisfied with our reply, or may need help in making the manuscript marketable."
Recent Sales: "Dozens of magazines, W.H. Allen; Mondadori, Pocketbooks Inc."

MICHAEL SNELL LITERARY AGENCY, Bridge and Castle Rd., Truro MA 02666. (508)349-3718. President: Michael Snell. Estab. 1980. Represents 150 clients. 25% of our clients are new/unpublished writers. Eager to work with new/unpublished writers. Specializes in business books (from professional/reference to popular trade how-to); college textbooks (in all subjects, but especially business, science and psychology); and how-to and self-help (on all topics, from diet and exercise to sex and personal finance). All types of computer books: professional and reference, college textbooks, general interest. Increased emphasis on popular and professional science books and science textbooks in all disciplines.
Will Handle: Nonfiction books and textbooks. Currently handles 80% nonfiction books; 10% novels; and 10% textbooks. Will read—at no charge—unsolicited queries and outlines. Reports in 3 weeks on queries. "Will not return rejected material unless accompanied by SASE."
Terms: Agent receives 15% commission on domestic sales; 15% on dramatic sales; and 15% on foreign sales.
Fees: "When a project interests us, we provide a two- to three-page critique and sample editing, a brochure on *How to Write a Book Proposal* and a model book proposal at no charge." Charges collaboration, ghostwriting and developmental editing fee "as an increased percentage of manuscript sale—no cash fee."
Recent Sales: *How to Write for Children*, by Catherine Wooley (NAL); *The Total Lotus Handbook*, by Steve Bennett (Simon & Schuster); *Europe 1992*, by Michael Silva (Wiley).

SOUTHERN WRITERS, Suite 1020, 635 Gravier St., New Orleans LA 70130. (504)525-6390. FAX: (504)524-7349. Agent: Pamela G. Ahearn. Estab. 1979. Member Romance Writers of America. Represents 30 clients; 33% of clients are new/unpublished writers. Works with small number of new/unpublished writers. Specializes in fiction or nonfiction with a Southern flavor or background; romances—both contemporary and historical.

Will Handle: Nonfiction books (no autobiographies), novels. Currently handles 30% nonfiction books and 70% novels. Accepts submissions for young adults 12 and up. Will read—at no charge—unsolicited queries and outlines. Reports in 2 weeks on queries; 1 month on mss.

Terms: Agent receives 12-15% commission on domestic sales; 20% on dramatic sales; 20% on foreign sales.

Fees: Charges reading fee "to unpublished authors and to authors writing in areas other than that of previous publication." 40% of income derived from reading fees; charges $175/300-page, typed, double-spaced book ms. "Criticism fee is charged to unpublished authors who request *only* criticism and not representation." 5% of income derived from criticism fees; charges $300/300-page, typed, double-spaced book ms. Writers receive a letter, usually 3-4 pages long, single-spaced. Includes evaluation of manuscript's writing quality, marketability, and more specific discussion of problems within book (plot, characterization, tone, author's credentials for writing such book, etc.). Specific examples are cited wherever possible. Letter is written by Pamela G. Ahearn. Charges for postage. 55% of income derived from commission on manuscript sales. Payment of fees does not ensure representation.

Recent Sales: *Where The Towers Pierce the Sky*, by Marie Goodwin (Macmillan); *The Heart's Haven*, by Jillian Stadler (Pocket); *I Loved the 30's*, by Mary Lou Widmer (Pelican).

F. JOSEPH SPIELER LITERARY AGENCY, 410 W. 24th St., New York NY 10011. (212)757-4439. Contact: Joseph Spieler. Estab. 1983. Represents 53 clients. 7.25% of clients are new/unpublished writers. Specializes in "fiction and nonfiction." No genre books.

Will Handle: Nonfiction books, novels, textbooks, juvenile (all ages) and poetry. Will read—at no charge—unsolicited queries and outlines. Does not read unsolicited mss. Reports in 1 week.

Terms: Agent receives 15% commission on domestic sales; 15% on dramatic sales; and 20% on foreign sales.

Fees: Charges for bulk and international mail, photocopies, toll and international phone calls and Telexes, etc. 99% of income derived from commission on ms sales.

Recent Sales: *The Age of Miracles*, by Catherine MacCoun (Atlantic Monthly Press); and *I'll Be Home Before Midnight*, by Tony Wolf (Vintage/Random House); *Baseball Lives*, by Mike Bryan (Pantheon).

PHILIP G. SPITZER LITERARY AGENCY, 788 9th Ave., New York NY 10019. (212)265-6003. Member of SAR. Represents 50 clients. 10% of clients are new/unpublished writers. Prefers to work with published/established authors; works with a small number of new/unpublished authors. Specializes in general nonfiction (politics, current events, sports, biography) and fiction, including mystery/suspense.

Will Handle: Nonfiction books, novels and movie scripts. Currently handles 45% nonfiction books; 45% novels; and 10% movie scripts. Will read—at no charge—unsolicited queries and outlines. Reports in 2 weeks on queries; 5 weeks on mss. "If our agency does not respond within 1 month to your request to become a client, you may submit requests elsewhere."

Terms: Agent receives 10% commission on domestic sales; 10% on dramatic sales; and 20% on foreign sales.

Fees: Charges for photocopying expenses. 100% of income derived from commission on ms sales.

Recent Sales: *Black Cherry Blues*, by James Lee Burke (Little, Brown); *King of the Hustlers*, by Eugene Izzi (Bantam); *The Hotel*, by Sonny Kleinfield (Simon & Schuster).

LYLE STEELE & COMPANY, Suite 7, 511 E. 73rd St., New York NY 10021. (202)288-2981. President: Lyle Steele. Estab. 1984. Represents 40 clients. To be represented writers "ideally should have published at least one work." Works with small number of new/unpublished writers. Specializes in continuing paperback series and nonfiction.

Will Handle: Nonfiction books, series and novels. Currently handles 50% nonfiction books; 50% novels. Will read—at no charge—unsolicited queries, outlines and manuscripts. Reports in 2 weeks on queries; 1 month on mss.

Terms: Agent receives 15% commission on domestic sales; 15% on dramatic sales; and 15% on foreign sales. 100% of income derived from commission on ms sales.

Recent Sales: *Cracking the Over 50 Job Market*, by J. Robert Connor (NAL); *Aunt Celia*, by Jane Gillespie (St. Martin's Press).

MICHAEL STEINBERG, Box 274, Glencoe IL 60022. (312)835-8881. Literary Agent/Attorney: Michael Steinberg. Estab. 1980. Represents 15 clients. 40% of clients are new/unpublished writers. "Not currently accepting new writers except by referral from editors or current authors." Specializes in business and general nonfiction, science fiction and mystery.

Will Handle: Nonfiction books and novels. Currently handles 70% nonfiction books and 30% novels. Does not read unsolicited mss.

Terms: Agent receives 15% commission on domestic sales and 20% on foreign sales.

Fees: Charges a reading fee when accepting new material; 4% of income derived from reading fees. Charges writers for postage and phone expenses. Offers a consultation service through which writers not represented can get advice on a contract; charges $75/hour, with a minimum of $125. 95% of income derived from commission on ms sales.

Recent Sales: *New Prosperity*, by Jake Bernstein (NYIF); *Long Wave Trading*, by Jake Bernstein (Probus); *The Black Star Murders* and *The Mother Murders*, by Dale Gilbert (St. Martin's).

STEPPING STONE LITERARY AGENCY, 59 West 71st St., New York NY 10023. (212)362-9277. President: Sarah Jane Freymann. Estab. 1974. Member of ILAA. Represents 60 clients. 15% are new/unpublished writers. Although I prefer to work with established authors. I am always interested and excited about finding new talent. In fiction, it's simply a question of can the author really write and do I feel I can sell the work. With nonfiction, I look for authors who have achieved some recognition, have some experience, or are authorities in their field. I do not specialize; I like my list to be eclectic." Particularly interested in mainstream and commercial fiction, contemporary women's fiction, quality mystery/suspense, metaphysical fiction. In nonfiction, women's issues, biography, health, psychology, self-help, spiritual and science/New Age, design and lifestyle books.
Will Handle: Nonfiction and novels. Currently handles 70% nonfiction books and 30% novels. Will read — at no charge — unsolicited queries and outlines. Reports in 2 weeks on queries; 6 weeks on mss.
Terms: Agent receives 15% commission on domestic sales; 10% on dramatic sales; and 20% on foreign sales. Charges for photocopying, messenger and out-of-the-ordinary postage and phone expenses. Offers a consultation service through which writers not represented can get advice on a contact; charges a negotiable fee. Will also critique a ms we're not representing for a negotiable fee. 99% of income derived from commission.
Recent Sales: *Design for a Livable Planet: The Whole Earth Ecology Handbook*, by Jon Naar (Harper & Row); *The Texas Trilogy*, by Leigh Briston (Warner); *Trylon and Perisphere*, by Barbara Cohen, Steven Heller and Seymour Chwast (Harry N. Abrams).

GLORIA STERN AGENCY, 1230 Park Ave., New York NY 10128. (212)289-7698. Agent: Gloria Stern. Estab. 1976. Member of ILAA. Represents 30 clients. 2% of our clients are new/unpublished writers. Prefers to work with published/established authors; works with a small number on new/unpublished authors.
Will Handle: Nonfiction books (no how-to; must have expertise on subject); and novels ("serious mainstream," mysteries, accepts very little fiction). Currently handles 90% nonfiction books and 10% novels. Will read — at no charge — unsolicited queries and outlines (no unsolicited ms). Reports in 1 week on queries; 2 months on manuscripts.
Terms: Agent receives 10-15% commission on domestic sales; and 20% shared with foreign coagent.
Fees: Charges for photocopy expenses. Charges a criticism fee "if the writer requests it and I think that it could be publishable with help. Criticism includes appraisal of style, development of characters and action. Sometimes suggests cutting or building scene. No guarantee that I can represent finished work." Offers a consultation service ("as a courtesy to some authors") through which writers not represented can get advice on a contract; charges $125. .5% of income derived from fee charged to writers; 99.5% of income derived from commission of manuscript sales.
Recent Sales: *How to Learn Math*, by Sheila Tobias (The College Board); *A Taste of Astrology*, by Lucy Ash (Knopf); and *Parent Power*, by Sherry Ferguson and Lawrence Mazin (Clarkson Potter).

CHARLES M. STERN ASSOCIATES, 319 Coronet, Box 790742, San Antonio TX 78279-0742. (512)349-6141. Owners: Charles M. Stern and Mildred R. Stern. Estab. 1978. 75% of clients are new/unpublished writers. Prefers to work with published/established authors; eager to work with new/unpublished writers. Specializes in historical romances, category romances, how-to, mystery and adventure.
Will Handle: Nonfiction books and novels. Currently handles 50% nonfiction books and 50% novels. Does not read unsolicited mss. Only markets completed mss. Reports in approximately 6 weeks on queries. Writer must supply all copies of ms.
Terms: Agent receives 15% commission on domestic sales; and 20% on foreign sales.
Recent Sales: No information given.

GLORIA STERN, Suite 3, 12535 Chandler Blvd., North Hollywood CA 91607. (818)508-6296. Contact: Gloria Stern. Estab. 1984. Represents 18 clients. 65% of clients are new/unpublished writers. Writer must query with project description or be recommended by qualified reader. Prefers to work with published/established authors; works with a number of new/unpublished authors. Specializes in novels and scripts, some theatrical material, dramas or comedy.
Will Handle: Novels, movie scripts and TV scripts (movie of the week). Currently handles 30% novels; and 70% movie and TV scripts. Will read submissions at charge and may charge a criticism fee or service charge for on-going consultation and editing. Reports in 3 weeks on queries; 6 weeks on mss.
Terms: Agent receives 10-15% commission on domestic sales; 10-15% on dramatic sales; and 18% on foreign sales.
Fees: Occasionally waives fee if representing the writer. Charges criticism fee; $35/hour (may vary). "Initial report averages four or five pages with point-by-point recommendation. I will work with the writers I represent to point of acceptance." Charges for postage, photocopy and long distance phone expenses. Percentage of

income derived from commission on ms sales varies with sales. Payment of criticism fee usually ensures that agency will represent writer.
Recent Sales: *Able Team*, by Dick Stivers (Gold Eagle).

GUNTHER STUHLMANN, AUTHOR'S REPRESENTATIVE, Box 276, Becket MA 01223. (413)623-5170. Associate: Barbara Ward. Estab. 1954. Prefers to work with published/established authors. Specializes in high quality literary material, fiction and nonfiction.
Will Handle: Nonfiction books, novels, young adult, movie and TV rights on established properties (no original screenplays). Will read—at no charge—unsolicited queries and outlines. Reports in 2 weeks on queries. "Include SASE for reply."
Terms: Receives 10% commission on domestic sales; 15% on British sales; 20% on translation.
Recent Sales: *Prisoner's Dilemma*, by Richard Powers (Beech Tree/Morrow); *Henry & June*, by Anais Nin (Harcourt Brace Jovanovich); and *A Literate Passion*, by Henry Miller and Anais Nin (Harcourt Brace Jovanovich).

THE TANTLEFF OFFICE, Suite 4F, 360 W. 20th St., New York NY 10011. (212)627-2105. President: Jack Tantleff. Estab. 1986. Member WGA. Represents 30 clients. 20% of clients are new/unpublished writers. Specializes in television, theatre and film.
Will Handle: Movie scripts, stage plays, TV scripts. Currently handles 15% movie scripts; 50% stage plays; 35% TV scripts. Will read—at no charge—unsolicited queries and outlines.
Terms: Agent receives 10% commission on domestic sales; 10% on dramatic sales; and 10% on foreign sales.
Fees: "Charges for unusual expenses agreed upon in advance."
Recent Sales: No information given.

PATRICIA TEAL LITERARY AGENCY, 2036 Vista del Rosa, Fullerton CA 92631. (714)738-8333. Owner: Patricia Teal. Estab. 1978. Member of ILAA, RWA and WGA. Represents 40 clients. 20% of clients are new/unpublished writers. "Writer must have honed his skills by virtue of educational background, writing classes, previous publications. Any of these *may* qualify him to query." Works with a small number of new/unpublished authors. Limited to category fiction such as mysteries, romances (contemporary and historical), westerns, men's adventure, horror, etc. Also handles nonfiction, limited to self-help and how-to.
Will Handle: Nonfiction books (self-help and how-to) and novels (category only). Currently handles 20% nonfiction books and 80% category novels. Will read—at no charge—unsolicited queries and outlines. No response if not accompanied by SASE. Reports in 3 weeks on queries.
Terms: 15% commission for new, unpublished writers; and 10% for published. Agent receives 10-15% commission on domestic sales; 20% on dramatic sales; and 20% on foreign sales.
Fees: Charges for phone, postage and photocopy expenses. 5% of total income derived from fees charged to writers; 95% of income derived from commission on ms sales.
Recent Sales: *Rose*, by Jill Marie Landis (The Berkley Publishing Group); *The Masseuse*, by B.L. Wilson (Pocket Books); and *Bonds of Blood*, by June Triglia (NAL).

‡PHYLLIS TORNETTA AGENCY, Box 423, Croton-on-Hudson NY 10521. (914)737-3464. President: Phyllis Tornetta. Estab. 1979. Represents 22 clients. 35% of clients are new/unpublished writers. Specializes in romance, contemporary, mystery.
Will Handle: Novels and juvenile. Currently handles 90% novels and 10% juvenile. Will read—at no charge—unsolicited queries and outlines. Does not read unsolicited mss. Reports in 1 month.
Terms: Agent receives 15% commission on domestic sales and 20% on foreign sales.
Fees: Charges a reading fee "for full manuscripts." Charges $75/300 pages.
Recent Sales: *Intimate Strangers*, by S. Hoover (Harlequin); *Accused* (Silhouette) and *Ride Eagle* (Worldwide).

A TOTAL ACTING EXPERIENCE, Suite 100, Dept. 77B, 14621 Titus St., Panorama City CA 91402. Agent: Dan A. Bellacicco. Estab. 1984. Member of WGA. Represents 24 clients. 70% of clients are new/unpublished writers. Will accept new and established writers. Specializes in romance, science fiction, mysteries, humor, how-to and self-help books, and video/audio tapes on all topics.
Will Handle: Movie scripts, radio scripts, stage plays, TV scripts, nonfiction books, novels, juvenile books, syndicated material, lyricists and composers. (No heavy violence, drugs or sex.) Currently handles 2% magazine articles; 2% magazine fiction; 5% nonfiction books; 5% novels; 2% juvenile books; 50% movie scripts; 2% radio scripts; 5% stage plays; 19% TV scripts; and 8% from lyricists/composers. Will read—at no charge—unsolicited queries, outlines and mss. Reports in 3 months. "Submit only first 10 pages of your ms; include a one-page synopsis of story, resume and letter of introduction with SASE. No exceptions please. No phone calls, please. No heavy violence, sex or drugs."
Terms: Agent receives 10% commission on domestic sales; 10% on dramatic sales; and 10% on foreign sales. 100% of income derived from commission on ms sales.
Recent Sales: "Confidential."

2M COMMUNICATIONS LTD., Suite 601, 121 West 27th St., New York NY 10001. President: Madeleine Morel. Estab. 1982. Member ABPA- American Book Producers Association. Represents 30 clients. 25% of clients are new writers. Specializes in nonfiction, humor, biographies, lifestyle, pop psychology, health, nutrition, how-to, New Age, cookbooks.
Will Handle: Currently handles 100% nonfiction books. Will read—at no charge—unsolicited queries and outlines. Does not read unsolicited mss. Reports in 2 weeks on queries.
Terms: Agent receives 15% commission on domestic sales and 25% on foreign sales.
Fees: Charges for photocopying, mailing and messengers.
Recent Sales: *Diet For a Poisoned Planet*, by David Steinman (Crown); *Future Stuff*, by M. Abrams and H. Bernstein (Viking).

SUSAN P. URSTADT, INC., Suite 708, 271 Madison Ave., New York NY 10016. (212)744-6605. President: Susan P. Urstadt. Estab. 1975. Member of ILAA. Represents 50-60 clients. 5% of clients are new/unpublished writers. Specializes in literary and commercial fiction, decorative arts and antiques, architecture, literary, gardening, armchair cookbooks, biography, performing arts, current affairs, lifestyle and current living trends.
Will Handle: Nonfiction books and novels. "We look for serious books of quality with fresh ideas and approaches to current situations and trends." Currently handles 65% nonfiction books; 25% novels; and 10% juvenile books. No unsolicited queries or mss.
Terms: Agent receives 15% commission on domestic sales; 15% on dramatic sales; and 20% on foreign sales.
Fees: Charges for phone, photocopying, foreign postage and Express Mail expenses.
Recent Sales: *Equinox: A Gardener's Autumn*, by Allen Lacy (Atlantic Monthly Press); *Democracy*, by Patrick Watson and B. Barber (Little Brown); and *Irish Cooking*, by Myrtle Allen (Stewart, Tabori and Chang).

VAN DER LEUN AND ASSOCIATES, 464 Mill Hill Dr., Southport CT 06490. (203)259-4897. President: Patricia Van Der Leun. Estab. 1985. Represents 20 clients; 50% of clients are new/unpublished writers. Works with small number of new/unpublished authors. Specializes in science, art, illustrated books, fiction.
Will Handle: Nonfiction books and novels. Currently handles 50% nonfiction books; 50% novels. Will read—at no charge—unsolicited queries and outlines "if accompanied by SASE." Reports in 2 weeks on queries; 1 month on mss.
Terms: Agent receives 15% commission on domestic sales; 15% on dramatic sales; and 15% on foreign sales.
Fees: Charges for photocopying.
Recent Sales: *Everything I Really Need To Know I Learned in Kindergarten*, by Robert Fulghum (Villard Books); *Cosmogenesis*, by David Layzer (Oxford University Press); and *Deep Time: The Journey of a Single Sub-Atomic Particle From The Moment of Creation to the Death of the Universe—And Beyond*, by David Darling (Delacorte Press).

RALPH VICINANZA LTD., Suite 1205, 432 Park Ave. South, New York NY 10016. (212)725-5133. Assistant: Christopher Lotts. Estab. 1978. Represents agents, authors and publishers. Works with a small number of new/unpublished authors. Specializes in science fiction, fantasy and thrillers.
Will Handle: Nonfiction books and novels. Currently handles 10% nonfiction books and 90% novels.
Terms: Agent receives 10% commission on domestic sales and 20% on foreign sales.
Fees: Charges for photocopy expenses and special mailings. 100% of income derived from commission on ms sales.
Recent Sales: *At Winter's End*, by Robert Silverberg (Warner); *Love and Sleep*, by John Crowley (Bantam); and *Funland*, by Richard Laymon (New American Library).

‡VICTORIA MANAGEMENT CO., Suite 2R, 23 W. 87th St., New York NY 10024. (212)873-0972. President: Frank Weimann. Estab. 1985. Represents 22 clients. Eager to work with new/unpublished writers. Specializes in films, TV scripts, nonfiction, self-help and biography.
Will Handle: Nonfiction books, novels, movie scripts and syndicated material. Currently handles 60% nonfiction books; 10% novels; and 30% movie scripts. Will read—at no charge—unsolicited queries, outlines and mss. Reports in 2 weeks on queries; 1 month on mss.
Terms: Agent receives 10% commission on domestic sales; 10% on dramatic sales; and 20% on foreign sales.
Recent Sales: *It's Not What You Eat . . . It's What's Eating You*, by Dr. Janet Greeson (Pocket Books).

CARLSON WADE, Room K-4, 49 Bokee Ct., Brooklyn NY 11223. (718)743-6983. President: Carlson Wade. Estab. 1949. Represents 40 clients. 50% of clients are new/unpublished writers. Eager to work with new/unpublished writers. Will consider all types of fiction and nonfiction.
Will Handle: Magazine articles, magazine fiction, nonfiction books and novels. Currently handles 10% magazine articles; 10% magazine fiction; 40% nonfiction books; and 40% novels. Will read submissions at no charge, but may charge a criticism fee or service charge for work performed after the initial reading. Reports in 2 weeks.

Terms: Agent receives 10% commission on domestic sales; 10% on dramatic sales; and 10% on foreign sales.
Fees: Charges handling fee: $1/1,000 words on short ms; $50/book. 20% of income derived from reading and handling fees. Charges a criticism fee if ms requires extensive work. 10% of income derived from criticism fees. "Short manuscript receives 5 pages of critique, book receives 15 (single space, page-by-page critique)." 20% of income derived from reading and handling fees; 80% of income derived from commission on ms sales. Payment of a criticism fee does not ensure that agency will represent a writer. "If a writer revises a manuscript properly, then we take it on. Futher help is available at no cost."
Recent Sales: *Eat Away Illness* (Prentice Hall) and *Nutritional Therapy* (Prentice Hall).

BESS WALLACE LITERARY AGENCY, 1502 N. Mitchell, Payson AZ 85541. (602)474-2983 and (602)486-2389. Owner: Bess Wallace. Estab. 1977. Represents 32 clients. 80% of clients are new/unpublished writers. Eager to work with new/unpublished writers. Specializes in nonfiction.
Will Handle: Nonfiction books and novels. Will read—at no charge—unsolicited queries and outlines. Reports in 3 weeks.
Terms: Agent receives 15% commission on domestic sales; 10% on dramatic sales; and 10% on foreign sales.
Fees: Charges for editing and retyping. 80% of income derived from commission on ms sales; 20% from fees. "Ghostwriters available."
Recent Sales: *Child Abuse, Neglect and Molestation, Terrorism,* and *Our Social Service Agencies,* by M.J. Philippus and Bess Wallace (P.P.I. Publishers); *Language in Tears,* by Robert Thompson (CAP Publishers); and *Children of Alcoholics,* by Bess Wallace and M.J. Philippus, PhD. (P.P.I. Publishers).

THE GERRY B. WALLERSTEIN AGENCY, Suite 12, 2315 Powell Ave., Erie PA 16506. (814)833-5511. President/Owner: Gerry B. Wallerstein. Estab. 1984. Member Author's Guild, Society of Professional Journalists. Represents 40 clients. 23% of clients are new/unpublished writers. "I read/critique works by writers who have sold regularly to major periodicals, or have had a prior book published, or sold a script, on the basis of no reading fee. Works by new writers are read/critiqued on the basis of a reading fee, according to length of ms. I will represent writers of either category. All potential clients should request a brochure." Specializes in both fiction and nonfiction books, articles, short stories, no poetry or song/lyrics, scripts or juvenile material.
Will Handle: Magazine articles and magazine fiction (clients only); nonfiction books; novels. Currently handles 22% magazine articles; 6% magazine fiction; 37% nonfiction books; 35% novels. Will read—at no charge—unsolicited queries and short outlines. Reports in 1 week on queries.
Terms: Agent receives 15% commission on domestic sales; 15% on dramatic sales; and 20% on foreign sales.
Fees: Charges reading fee "for writers who have not sold their work regularly to major periodicals, or have not had a prior book published or a script sold to a producer." Reading fee waived if writer represented. 50% of income derived from reading fees. Charges $300 for 300-page typed, double-spaced book ms. "Criticism included in reading fee. Our reading/critique averages 1-2 pages for short material and book proposals; 2-4 pages for book-length manuscripts. I indicate any problem areas, suggest possible ways to solve the problems, and provide marketing advice. Revised ms read at no additional fee. All reading is done by Gerry B. Wallerstein." Charges for manuscript typing or copying, copyright fees, attorney's fees (if required, and approved by author), travel fees (if required and approved by author) and a monthly fee of $20 for postage/telephone expenses. 50% of income derived from commission on ms sales. Payment of a reading fee does not ensure that the agency will represent a writer.
Recent Sales: *Caring For Your Own,* by Darla J. Neidrick, R.N. (John Wiley & Sons, Inc.); *Cars Detroit Never Built,* by Edward Janicki (Main Street Press); *American Dreaming,* by Donald Cobbs (Holloway House).

JOHN A. WARE LITERARY AGENCY, 392 Central Park West, New York NY 10025. (212)866-4733. Contact: John Ware. Estab. 1978. Represents 60 clients. 40% of clients are new/unpublished writers. Writers must have appropriate credentials for authorship of proposal (nonfiction) or manuscript (fiction); no publishing track record required. "Open to good writing and interesting ideas, by 'new' or 'veteran' writers." Specializes in biography; memoirs; investigative journalism; history; health and psychology (academic credentials required); serious and accessible non-category fiction; thrillers and mysteries; current issues and affairs; sports; oral history; Americana and folklore.
Will Handle: Nonfiction books and novels. Currently handles 75% nonfiction books and 25% novels. Will read unsolicited queries and outlines; does not read unsolicited mss. Reports in 2 weeks on queries.
Terms: Agent receives 10% commission on domestic sales; 10% on dramatic sales; and 20% on foreign sales. Charges for messengering, photocopying and extraordinary expenses.
Recent Sales: *Cycles of Rock and Water: At The Pacific Edge,* by Kenneth Brown (Harper and Row); *Fires In The Sky: A Novel of the Trojan War,* by Phillip Parotti (Ticknor & Fields); *South Pass: A Memoir Along The Oregon Trail,* by Laton McCartney (Doubleday).

JAMES WARREN LITERARY AGENCY, 13131 Welby Way, North Hollywood CA 91606. (818)982-5423. Agent: James Warren. Editors: Ellen Reed, Bob Carlson. Estab. 1969. Represents 60 clients. 60% of clients are new/unpublished writers. "We are willing to work with select unpublished writers." Specializes in fiction, history, textbooks, professional books, craft books, how-to books, self-improvement books, health books and diet books.

Will Handle: Juvenile books, historical romance novels, movie scripts (especially drama and humor), and TV scripts (drama, humor, documentary). Currently handles 40% nonfiction books; 20% novels; 10% textbooks; 5% juvenile books; 10% movie scripts; and 15% TV scripts and teleplays. Will read—at no charge—unsolicited queries and outlines. Does not read unsolicited mss. Reports in 1 week on queries; 1 month on mss.

Terms: Receives 10% commission on first domestic sales; 20% on foreign sales.

Fees: Charges reading fee of $2 per thousand words. 20% of income derived from reading fees; refunds reading fee if material sells. 20% of total income derived from fees charged to writers; 80% of income derived from commission on ms sales. Payment of fees does not ensure that agency will represent writer.

Recent Sales: *The Woman Inge*, by Audrey R. Langer (New Saga) and *Ashes Under Uricon*, by Audrey R. Langer (New Saga).

WATERSIDE PRODUCTIONS, INC., Suite 2, 832 Camino del Mar, Del Mar CA 92014. (619)481-8335. (Additional office in New York City (1 Union Square West, #209, New York NY 10003). Estab. 1982. Represents 200 clients. 20% of clients are new/unpublished writers. To be represented "fiction authors must be published in major magazines; nonfiction authors must be recognized experts in their field; computer authors must have superb technical skills." Works with small number of new/unpublished writers. Specializes in computer books and books about new technology; fiction and general nonfiction of exceptional quality. Writer's guidelines for #10 SAE and 2 first class stamps.

Will Handle: Nonfiction books; novels; textbooks. Currently handles 90% nonfiction books; 4% novels; 4% textbooks. Will read—at no charge—unsolicited queries and outlines. Does not read unsolicited mss. Reports in 1 month on queries.

Terms: Agent receives 15% commission on domestic sales; 20% on dramatic sales; and 25% on foreign sales.

Fees: Charges reading fee for "first time novelists or personal nonfiction." Negotiable income derived from reading fees. Charges $300/300-page, typed, double-spaced book ms. 99.9% of income derived from commission on ms sales; .1% derived from fees.

Recent Sales: *Peter Norton's Insider's Guides*, by Peter Norton (Bantam); *Never Be Tired Again!*, by Gardner and Beatty (Rawson/MacMillan); and *Alfred H. Barr Jr.: Missionary for the Modern*, by Alice Goldfarb (Marquis Contemporary).

SANDRA WATT & ASSOCIATES, Suite 4053, 8033 Sunset Blvd., Los Angeles CA 90046. (213)653-2339. FAX: (213)653-3320. President: Sandra Watt. Estab. 1976. Member of ILAA and WGA West. Represents 100 clients. Eager to work with new/unpublished writers. Specializes in literary and category fiction, popular nonfiction, metaphysical works, and gay/lesbian fiction and nonfiction. Works extensively with television and film.

Will Handle: Nonfiction books, novels, movie scripts and TV scripts. Will read—at no charge—unsolicited queries and outlines. Reports in 1 week on queries. No unsolicited mss.

Terms: Agent receives 15% commission on domestic sales; 10% on dramatic sales; and 25% on foreign sales.

Fees: Charges marketing fee for new writers to cover expenses generated in promotion of their project alone.

Recent Sales: *Hungry Women*, by B. Laramie Dunaway (Warner); *Lemons . . . & Lemonade*, by Portia Toples (NAL); AND *Families*, by David Watmough (the first in an anticipated nine-book series with Knights Press).

‡CHERRY WEINER LITERARY AGENCY, 28 Kipling Way, Manalapan NJ 07726. (201)446-2096. President: Cherry Weiner. Estab. 1980. Represents 50 clients. 20% of clients are new/unpublished writers. To be represented, writer should be recommended by people agency knows. Prefers to work with published/established authors; works with a small number of new/unpublished authors. Specializes in fiction—all genres; some nonfiction, depending on topic.

Will Handle Nonfiction books and novels. Does not read unsolicited manuscripts.

Terms: Agent receives 15% commission on domestic sales; 15% on dramatic sales; and 15% on foreign sales.

Fees: Charges writers for special mailings—overseas phone calls, etc.

Recent Sales: No information given.

RHODA WEYR AGENCY, 216 Vance St., Chapel Hill NC 27514. (919)942-0770. President: Rhoda A. Weyr. Estab. 1983. Member of SAR and ILAA. Prefers to work with published/established authors; works with a small number of new/unpublished authors. Specializes in general nonfiction and fiction of high quality.

For information on author's agents' areas of interest, see the nonfiction and fiction sections in the Author's Agents Subject Index.

Will Handle: Nonfiction books and novels. Will read — at no charge — unsolicited queries, outlines and sample chapters sent with SASE.
Terms: Agent receives 10% commission on domestic sales; 10-15% on dramatic sales; and 20% on foreign sales.
Recent Sales: Confidential.

WIESER & WIESER, INC., 118 E. 25th St., New York NY 10010. (212)260-0860. President: Olga B. Wieser. Estab. 1976. Represents 60 clients. 10% of clients are new/unpublished writers. Prefers to work with published/established authors; works with a small number of new/unpublished authors. Specializes in literary and mainstream fiction, serious and popular historical fiction, mass market regencies, general nonfiction, business, finance, aviation, sports, photography, Americana, cookbooks, travel books and popular medicine.
Will Handle: Nonfiction books and novels. Currently handles 50% nonfiction books and 50% novels. Will read — at no charge — unsolicited queries and outlines. Reports in 1 week on queries accompanied by SASE.
Terms: Agent receives 15% commission on domestic sales; 15% on dramatic sales; and 20% on foreign sales.
Fees: Charges for photocopy, cable and overnight postage expenses.
Recent Sales: *Day of the Cheetah*, by Dale Brown (Donald I. Fine, Inc.); *Recovering Together*, by Carol Cox Smith (Hazelden and Harper & Row trade edition); and *Born of the Sun*, by Joan Wolf (NAL hardcover).

WINGRA WOODS PRESS/Agenting Division, Suite 3, 33 Witherspoon St., Princeton NJ 08542. (609)683-1218. Agent: Anne Matthews. Estab. 1985. Member of American Booksellers Association and American Book Producers Association. Represents 12 clients. 70% of clients are new/unpublished writers. "Books must be completed, and designed for a distinct market niche." Works with small number of new/unpublished authors. Specializes in nonfiction, children's, Americana and travel.
Will Handle: Currently handles 60% nonfiction books and 40% juvenile books.
Terms: Receives 15% commission on domestic sales; 15% on dramatic sales; and 15% on foreign sales.
Recent Sales: *A Rose for Abby*, by Donna Guthrie (Abingdon); and *The Gone With the Wind Handbook*, by Pauline Bartel (Taylor); *What Sign Is Your Pet?*, by Donald Wolf, DVM (Taylor).

RUTH WRESCHNER, AUTHORS' REPRESENTATIVE, 10 W. 74th St., New York NY 10023. (212)877-2605. Agent: Ruth Wreschner. Estab. 1981. Represents 40 clients. 70% of clients are new/unpublished writers. "In fiction, if a client is not published yet, I prefer writers who have written for magazines; in nonfiction, a person well-qualified in his field is acceptable." Prefers to work with published/established authors; works with new/unpublished authors. "I will always pay attention to a writer referred by another client." Specializes in popular medicine, health, how-to books and fiction (no pornography, screenplays or dramatic plays).
Will Handle: Adult and young adult fiction; nonfiction; textbooks; magazine articles (only if appropriate for commercial magazines). Currently handles 5% magazine articles; 80% nonfiction books; 10% novels; 5% textbooks; and 5% juvenile books. Will read — at no charge — unsolicited queries and outlines. Reports in 2 weeks on queries.
Terms: Agent receives 15% commission on domestic sales and 20% on foreign sales.
Fees: Charges for photocopying expenses. "Once a book is placed, I will retain some money from the second advance to cover airmail postage of books, long distance calls, etc. on foreign sales." 100% of income derived from commission on ms sales. "I may consider charging for reviewing contracts in future. In that case I will charge $50/hour plus long distance calls, if any."
Recent Sales: *Our Choice of Gods*, by Richard Parrish (Birch Lane Press); *The Beloved Prison*, by Lucy Freeman (St. Martin's Press); and *Richer Than You Dreamed, Poorer Than You Think*, by Steven Sisgold and Kathryn Maxwell (Clarkson N. Potter).

ANN WRIGHT REPRESENTATIVES, INC., 136 E. 56th St., 2C, New York NY 10022. (212)832-0110. Head of Literary Department: Dan Wright. Estab. 1963. Member of WGA. Represents 34 clients. 25% of clients are new/unpublished writers. "Writers must be skilled or have superior material for screenplays, stories or novels that can eventually become motion pictures or television properties." Prefers to work with published/established authors; works with a small number of new/unpublished authors. "Eager to work with any author with material that we can effectively market in the motion picture business worldwide." Specializes in themes that make good motion picture projects.
Will Handle: Novels, movie scripts, stage plays and TV scripts. Currently handles 10% novels; 75% movie scripts; and 15% TV scripts. Will read — at no charge — unsolicited queries and outlines; does not read unsolicited mss. Reports in 3 weeks on queries; 2 months on mss.
Terms: Agent receives 10% commission on domestic sales; 10% on dramatic sales; 10% on foreign sales; 20% on packaging. Will critique only works of signed clients.
Fees: Charges for photocopying expenses.
Recent Sales: No information given.

WRITER'S CONSULTING GROUP, Box 492, Burbank CA 91503. (818)841-9294. Director: Jim Barmeier. Estab. 1983. Represents 10 clients. 50% of clients new/unpublished writers. "We prefer to work with established writers unless the author has an unusual true story."

Will Handle: Magazine articles (if written about a true story for which the author has the rights); nonfiction books (celebrity books, true crime accounts, unusual true stories); novels; movie scripts. Currently handles 40% nonfiction books; 20% novels; and 40% movie scripts. Will read—at no charge—unsolicited queries and outlines. Include SASE. Reports in 1 month on queries; 3 months on mss.

Terms: "We will explain our terms to clients when they wish to sign. We receive a 10% commission on domestic sales. Additionally, we offer ghostwriting and editorial services, as well as book publicity services for authors." 100% of income derived from commission on ms sales.

Recent Sales: "We have helped writers sell everything from episodes for children's TV shows ("Smurfs") to move-of-the-week options (including the Craig Smith espionage story)."

WRITERS HOUSE, INC., 21 W. 26 St., New York NY 10010. (212)685-2400. President: Albert Zuckerman. Estab. 1974. Member of ILAA. Represents 120 clients. 20% of clients are new/unpublished writers. Specializes in fiction of all types, adult fiction, juvenile novels, and nonfiction books on business, parenting, lifestyles, science, sci-fi and fantasy, and rock and pop culture.

Will Handle: Nonfiction books, novels and juvenile books. Currently handles 30% nonfiction books; 40% novels; and 30% juvenile books. Will read—at no charge—unsolicited queries and outlines. Reports in 2 weeks on queries.

Terms: Agent receives 15% commission on sale of adult books, 10% on juvenile and young adult domestic sales; 15% on dramatic sales; and 20% on foreign sales.

Fees: Charges for overseas postage, Telex, messenger, phone and photocopy expenses. 95% of income derived from commission on ms sales; 5% from scouting for foreign publishers.

Recent Sales: *Pillars of the Earth*, by Ken Follett (Morrow); *Sweet Valley Summer*, by Francine Pascal (Bantam); and *A Brief History of Time*, by Stephen Hawking (Bantam).

WRITERS' PRODUCTIONS, Box 630, Westport CT 06881. (203)227-8199. Agent: David L. Meth. Estab. 1981. Eager to work with new/unpublished writers. Specializes in "fiction of literary quality, unique, intriguing nonfiction and photo-essay books. We are especially interested in works of Asian American writers about the Asian American experience, and are specializing in works about the Orient. No historical romances, science fiction, mysteries, westerns, how-to, health, cookbooks, occult, philosophy, etc ."

Will Handle: Nonfiction books and novels. Currently handles 15% nonfiction books and 85% novels. Will read—at no charge—unsolicited queries, outlines and mss. "We want complete manuscripts. Too many people call themselves authors and send 25-30-page samples of uncompleted works, making such submissions premature and a waste of time." Reports in 2 weeks on queries; 1 month on mss. "All correspondence must have a SASE for any response and return of manuscript, due to the large volume of submissions we receive. No phone calls please."

Terms: Agent receives 15% commission on domestic sales; 20% on dramatic sales; and 20% on foreign sales. 100% of income derived from commission on ms sales.

Recent Sales: *The Silver Stallion*, by Ahn Junghyo (Soho); *Children of the Paper Crane*, by Masamoto Nasu (M.E. Sharpe); and *Jinsei Annai: Letters To the Advice Column of the* Yomiuri Shimbun *(Japan)*, by Prof. John McKinstry (M.E. Sharpe).

WRITERS' REPRESENTATIVES, INC., 25 W. 19th St., New York NY 10011-4202. (212)620-9009. Contact: Glen Hartley or Lynn Chu. Estab. 1985. Represents 35 clients.

Will Handle: Nonfiction books and novels. Journalism handled for our established clients by special arrangement only. Currently handles 66% nonfiction; 33% fiction. Nonfiction submissions should include book proposal, detailed table of contents and sample chapters. For fiction submissions, send sample chapters, not synopses. All submissions should include author bio, publication list, and if available, clips. SASE required. All retained rights (serial, audiovisual, world territories, translation, etc.) handled in-house or through sub-agents.

Terms: Agent receives 15% commission on domestic sales; 20% if sub-agent retained for ancillary rights sales. Charges for out-of-pocket expenses, such as photocopying, long-distance phone calls, etc.

Recent Sales: *The Perfect Murder*, by David Lehman (Free Press); *The Dead Girl*, by Melanie Thernstrom (Pocket); *Fugitive Spring*, by Deborah Digges (Knopf).

SUSAN ZECKENDORF ASSOCIATES, Suite 11B, 171 W. 57th St., New York NY 10019. (212)245-2928. President: Susan Zeckendorf. Estab. 1979. Member of ILAA. Represents 45 clients. 60% of clients are new writers. Specializes in fiction of all kinds—literary, historical, and commercial women's, mainstream thrillers and mysteries; science, music, self-help and parenting books.

Will Handle: Nonfiction books (by a qualified expert) and novels. Currently handles 40% nonfiction books and 60% novels. Will read—at no charge—unsolicited queries. Reports in 2 weeks on queries; 1 month on mss.

Terms: Agent receives 15% commission on domestic sales; 15% on dramatic (movie or TV) sales; and 20% on foreign sales.

Fees: Charges for phone, photocopy and foreign postage expenses.

Recent Sales: *Temptations*, by Una-Mary Parker (NAL); *Vanderbilt Style*, by Jerry Patterson (Harry Abrams); and *Jeremiah Martin*, by Robert Fowler (St. Martin's).

TOM ZELASKY LITERARY AGENCY, 3138 Parkridge Crescent, Chamblee GA 30341. (404)458-0391. Agent: Tom Zelasky. Estab. 1984. Represents 5 clients. 90% of clients are new/unpublished writers. Prefers to work with published/established authors. Specializes in mainstream fiction or nonfiction, categorical romance, historical romance, historical fiction, westerns, action/detective mysteries, suspense, science fiction.

Will Handle: Nonfiction books, novels, juvenile books, movie scripts, stage plays and TV scripts. Will read—at no charge—unsolicited queries and outlines. "SASE is compulsory; otherwise, manuscript will be in storage and destroyed after 2 years." Reports in 3 weeks on queries; 3 months on mss.

Terms: Agent receives 10-15% commission on domestic sales; 10-15% on dramatic sales; and 15-25% on foreign sales.

Fees: Charges a reading fee; will waive fee if representing the writer. "A critique of one to three pages is mailed to writer when manuscript is rejected. I do my own reading and critique. It is usually a one- to three-page item, single space, citing craft skills, marketability and overall evaluation." Charges writers for phone calls to writers and publishers and postage.

Recent Sales: No information given.

‡GEORGE ZIEGLER LITERARY AGENCY, 160 East 97th St., New York NY 10029. (212)348-3637. Proprietor: George Ziegler. Estab. 1977. Represents 30 clients. 30% of clients are new/unpublished writers. Specializes in "nonfiction of strong human interest, or unique consumer books. Genre fiction if it is fresh and original; mainstream fiction if it is both well written and commercial."

Will Handle: Nonfiction books. Currently handles 90% nonfiction books; 10% novels. Will read—at no charge—unsolicited queries and outlines. Does not read unsolicited manuscripts. Reports in 2 weeks on queries; 2 months on mss.

Terms: Receives 15% of commission on domestic sales; and 20% on foreign sales or dramatic sales if a subagent is used.

Recent Sales: *Women On War* (anthology), edited by Daniela Gioseffi (Touchstone Books); *Kimura*, by Robert Davis (Walker Books); *Confessions of a Mail-Order Bride*, by Wanwadee Larsen (New Horizon Press).

Other Author's Agents

The following listings were deleted from the 1990 edition because the firms are backlogged with submissions, asked to be deleted or were unable to be contacted.

Linda Allen Agency (taking on few new clients)
David Cutler & Associates (asked to be deleted)
D.J. Enterprises (not accepting submissions)

Dorese Agency Ltd. (unable to contact)
Joseph Elder Agency (asked to be deleted)
Janus Literary Agency (not seeking new clients)

Literary Marketing Consultants (not accepting submissions)
Ann Waugh Agency (out of business)

The following firms did not return a verification to update an existing listing or a questionnaire to begin a new listing by press time.

Carole Abel Literary Agency
James Allen, Literary Agent
Adrian Anbry Literary Agency, Inc.
Harry Bloom
Boston Literary Agency
Curtis Brown Ltd.
Jane Butler, Art and Literary Agent
Canadian Speakers' and Writers' Service Ltd.
Maria Carvainis Agency Inc.
Columbia Literary Associates Inc.
Bill Cooper Assoc. Inc.

Joan Daves
Athos Demetriou
Diamond Literary Agency
Lucianne S. Goldberg Literary Agents Inc.
John Hochmann Books
Janklow & Nesbit
Kidde, Hoyt and Picard Literary Agency
Law Offices of Robert L. Fenton, P.C.
Lowenstein Associates, Inc.
Gerard McCauley Agency
Peter Miller Agency Inc.
Susan Ann Protter Literary

Agent
Publishing Enterprises/Literary Agency
Mitchell Rose Literary Agency
Schumaker Artists Talent Agency
Ellen Lively Steele and Associates
H.N. Swanson Inc.
Kathe Telingator
Wecksler-Incomco
Writers' Associates Literary Agency
Writers Workshop Inc.
Writers' World Forum

Contests and Awards

Contests and awards offer writers the opportunity to have their work judged for quality alone, once entry requirements are met. Writers' works are compared to the work of other writers, whose submissions are subject to identical conditions. Aside from the monetary reward many contests offer, there is the satisfaction of having your work recognized for excellence by established writers and other professionals in the field. Writers often receive the added benefit of having their work published or produced after the contest is over.

Some competitions focus on form, such as a short story or poetry contest, while others reward writers who handle a particular subject well. This year, for example, there are contests listed for best bowling writing, best writing about dogs and for best children's book on a Jewish theme. In addition to contests for poetry, short stories and journalism, we've included listings of competitions for plays, novels, film and radio scripts and even for book jacket blurbs.

Some contests are free, while others charge entry fees. Not all contests are open to everyone—some are for published authors, others for beginning writers or students. Eligibility may be based on the writer's age, geographic location or whether the work has been previously published. It's important to read contest rules carefully to avoid submitting to contests for which you do not qualify.

If rules are unclear or you are unsure how a particular contest defines terms, send the director a self-addressed, stamped envelope along with a brief letter asking for clarification. It's best to ask a specific question—contest directors have little time to answer lengthy letters.

A number of contests require someone to nominate the work for consideration. If nomination by a publisher is required, just ask—most publishers welcome the opportunity to promote a work in this way. Make the publisher aware of the contest in plenty of time before the deadline.

In addition to contests and awards, we also list grants, scholarship and fellowship programs. Additional information on funding for writers can be found in most large public libraries. See the *Annual Register of Grant Support* (National Register Publishing Co., Inc., 3004 Glenview Road, Wilmette IL 60091); *Foundation Grants to Individuals* (Foundation Center, 79 Fifth Ave., New York NY 10003) and *Grants and Awards Available to American Writers* (PEN American Center, 568 Broadway, New York NY 10012).These books are available in most large public libraries.

For more listings of contests and awards for fiction writers see *Novel & Short Story Writer's Market* or for poets see *Poet's Market* (both by Writer's Digest Books). A good source of contests for journalists is the annual Journalism Awards Issue of *Editor and Publisher* magazine, published in the last week of December.

The contests in this section are listed by title, address, contact person, type of competition and deadline. Deadlines that state a range—for example, July to September—will only accept entries within that period. If a contest sounds interesting, send a self-addressed, stamped envelope to the contact person for information, rules and details about prizes. Don't enter any contest without first seeking this information.

AAAS PRIZE FOR BEHAVIORAL SCIENCE RESEARCH, American Association for the Advancement of Science, Office of Science and Technology Education, 11th Floor, 1333 H. St. NW, Washington DC 20005. Anthropology/psychology/social sciences/sociology. Deadline: July 1.

HERBERT BAXTER ADAMS PRIZE, Committee Chairman, American Historical Association, 400 A St. SE, Washington DC 20003. European history (first book). Deadline: June 15.

‡JANE ADDAMS PEACE ASSOCIATION CHILDREN'S BOOK AWARD, Jane Addams Peace Association and Women's International League for Peace and Freedom, 777 United Nations Plaza, New York NY 10017. (212)682-8830. Award Director: Jean Gore. Send books to Jean Gore: 980 Lincoln Pl., Boulder CO 80302. Previously published book that promotes peace, social justice, and the equality of the sexes and races. Deadline: April 1.

ADRIATIC AWARD, International Society of Dramatists, Box 1310, Miami FL 33153. (305)674-1831. Award Director: A. Delaplaine. Full-length play either unproduced professionally, *or* with one professional production (using Equity actors). Deadline: Nov. 1. Query.

‡AIM MAGAZINE SHORT STORY CONTEST, Box 20554, Chicago IL 60620. (312)874-6184. Publisher: Ruth Apilado. Unpublished short stories (4,000 words maximum) "promoting brotherhood among people and cultures." Deadline: Aug. 15.

ALBERTA NEW FICTION COMPETITION, Alberta Culture, Film and Literary Arts, 12th Fl., CN Tower, Edmonton, Alberta T5J 0K5 Canada. (403)427-2554. Accept manuscripts 60-100,000 words (250 pages) in one of three categories: (1) novel; (2) short stories; (30 novella/short stories combination. Open only to Alberta resident authors. Deadline: Dec. 31.

AMELIA STUDENT AWARD, *Amelia Magazine*, 329 E St., Bakersfield CA 93304. (805)323-4064. Editor: Frederick A. Raborg, Jr. Previously unpublished poems, essays and short stories by high school students. Deadline: May 15.

AMERICAN-SCANDINAVIAN FOUNDATION/TRANSLATION PRIZE, American-Scandinavian Foundation, 127 E. 73rd St., New York NY 10021. (212)879-9779. Contact: Publishing Division. Contemporary Scandinavian fiction and poetry translations. Deadline: June 1.

AMERICAN SOCIETY OF JOURNALISTS & AUTHORS EXCELLENCE AWARDS, Room 1907, 1501 Broadway, New York NY 10036. (212)997-0947. Executive Director: Alexandra Cantor. Author, article and magazine awards. Nominations accepted after January 1 for May 31 deadline each year.

‡AMERICAN SPEECH-LANGUAGE-HEARING ASSOCIATION (ASHA), NATIONAL MEDIA AWARD, 10801 Rockville Pike, Rockville MD 20852. (301)897-5700. Speech-language pathology and audiology (radio, TV, newspaper, magazine). Deadline: June 30.

AMWA MEDICAL BOOK AWARDS COMPETITION, American Medical Writers Association, 9650 Rockville Pike, Bethesda MD 20814. (301)493-0003. Contact: Book Awards Committee. Previously published and must have appeared in print previous year. Contest is to honor the best medical book published in the previous year in each of three categories: Books for Physicians, Books for Allied Health Professionals and Trade Books. Deadline April 1. Charges $10 fee.

AMY WRITING AWARDS, The Amy Foundation, Box 16091, Lansing MI 48901. (517)323-3181. President: James Russell. Articles communicating Biblical truth previously published in the secular media. Deadline: Jan. 31.

ANNUAL INTERNATIONAL NARRATIVE CONTEST, Poets and Patrons, Inc., 10053 Avenue L., Chicago IL 60617. Director: Veronica Robertson. Unpublished poetry. Deadline: Sept. 1.

ANNUAL INTERNATIONAL SHAKESPEAREAN SONNET CONTEST, Poets Club of Chicago. 2930 Franklin, Highland IN 46322. Chairman: June Shipley. "Classic" Shakespearean sonnet form. Deadline; Sept. 1. Request rules after March 1.

ANNUAL JOURNALISM AWARDS COMPETITION, Big Brothers/Big Sisters of America, 230 North 13th St., Philadelphia PA 19107. (215)567-7000. Director of Publications: George L. Beiswinger. Previously published stories "communicating the difficulties experienced by children from one-parent homes and how such problems are handled." Cash prizes and plaques to winning writers; plaques to the writer's publications. Deadline: March 15.

THE ANNUAL NISSAN FOCUS AWARDS, Nissan Motor Corporation and Eastman Kodak Company, 10 E. 34th St., 6th Floor, New York NY 10016. (212)779-0404. Executive Director: Sam Katz. Narrative filmmaking; documentary; animation/experimental; screenwriting; sound achievement; film editing; cinematography, Women in Film Foundation Award, Renee Valente Producers Award. Charges $15 fee. Open to student filmmakers only enrolled in a U.S. college, university, art institute or film school. Deadline: Varies annually—late spring.

ANNUAL NJ POETRY CONTEST, NJIT Alumni Association, NJ Institute of Technology, Newark NJ 07102. (201)596-3441. Contest/Award Director: Dr. Herman A. Estrin. Poetry by elementary, junior high, secondary and college students who are New Jersey residents.

ANNUAL NORTH AMERICAN ESSAY CONTEST, *The Humanist* magazine, 7 Harwood Dr., Box 146, Amherst NY 14226. (716)839-5080. Contest/Award Director: Lloyd Morain. Unpublished essay by writers age 29 or younger. Deadline: Oct. 15.

ARIZONA AUTHORS' ASSOCIATION ANNUAL NATIONAL LITERARY CONTEST, Arizona Authors' Association, Suite 117WM, 3509 E. Shea Blvd., Phoenix AZ 85028-3339. (602)996-9706. Contact: Velma Cooper. Previously unpublished poetry, short stories, essays. Deadline: July 29. Charges $4 for poetry; $6 for short stories and essays.

ARTIST'S FELLOWSHIP AWARD, New York Foundation for the Arts, Suite 600, 5 Beekman St., New York NY 10038. (212)233-3900. Contact: Penny Stegenga. New York State resident artists' career awards to be used at the artist's discretion to support their work. Deadlines begin in late summer.

ARTS RECOGNITION AND TALENT SEARCH, National Foundation for Advancement in the Arts, 3915 Biscayne Blvd., Miami FL 33137. (305)573-0490. Vice President, Programs: Dr. William Banchs. For achievements in dance, music, theater, visual arts and writing. Students fill in and return the application, available at every public and private high school around the nation. Deadline: May 16-Oct. 1. Charges $25 registration fee.

‡ASPIRATIONS ©, 727 Dodge Ave., Evanston IL 60202. Director: Gail Plunkett. Short fiction, nonfiction and essays by unpublished writers. Fee. Deadline: twice a year.

VINCENT ASTOR MEMORIAL LEADERSHIP ESSAY CONTEST, U.S. Naval Institute, Preble Hall, U.S. Naval Academy, Annapolis MD 21402. (301)268-6110. Award Director: James A. Barber, Jr. Essays on the topic of leadership (junior officers and officer trainees). Deadline: March 1.

THE ATHENAEUM OF PHILADELPHIA LITERARY AWARD, The Athenaeum of Philadelphia, 219 S. 6th St., Philadelphia PA 19106. (215)925-2688. Award Director: Nathaniel Burt. Nominated book by a Philadelphia resident. Deadline: Dec. 31.

‡AUTHORS/WRITERS ANNUAL SHORT STORY CONTEST, Authors/Writers Network, c/o Alumni House, Montclair State College, Upper Montclair NJ 07043. (201)754-4829 or (201)893-4141. Award Director: Kitt Chisholm. Unpublished children's picture book; older children's stories; pre-adult stories and adult stories. Deadline: mid-July. Entries limited to New Jersey residents and community college. Charges $5 entry fee.

AVON FLARE YOUNG ADULT NOVEL COMPETITION, Avon Books, 105 Madison Ave., New York NY 10016. Editor: Gwen Montgomery. Unpublished novel written by an author 13-18 years old. Deadline: Jan. 1-Aug. 31. Contest held every other year.

‡AWARD FOR LITERARY TRANSLATION, American Translators Association, 109 Croton Ave., Ossining NY 10562. (914)941-1500. Contact: Chair, Honors & Awards. Previously published book translated from German to English. In even years, Lewis Galentière Prize awarded for translations other than German to English. Deadline: March 15.

EMILY CLARK BALCH AWARD, *Virginia Quarterly Review*, 1 West Range, Charlottesville VA 22903. (804)924-3124. Editor: Staige D. Blackford. Best short story/poetry accepted and published by the *Virginia Quarterly Review* during a calendar year. No deadline.

‡BANTA AWARD, Wisconsin Library Association/Banta Foundation of the George Banta Company, Inc., 1922 University Ave., Madison WI 53705. (608)231-1513. Executive Director: Faith B. Miracle, WLA. Book by a Wisconsin author published during the previous year. Deadline: December 31.

THE MARGARET BARTLE PLAYWRITING AWARD, Community Children's Theatre of Kansas City, 8021 E. 129th Terrace, Grandview MO 64030. (816)761-5775. Award Director: E. Blanche Sellens. Unpublished play for elementary school audiences. Deadline: Jan. 28.

THE ELIZABETH BARTLETT AWARD, 2875 Cowley Way-1302, San Diego CA 92110. (619)276-6199. Contest/Award Director: Elizabeth Bartlett. For best unpublished 12-tone poem.

GEORGE LOUIS BEER PRIZE, Committee Chairman, American Historical Assoc., 400 A St. SE, Washington DC 20003. European international history since 1895 (scholarly work). Deadline: June 15.

BEST OF BLURBS CONTEST, Writer's Refinery, Box 47786, Phoenix AZ 85068-7786. Contest Director: Libbi Goodman. "To foster the joy of writing a concise statement of the plot of a novel, write back cover or jacket flap copy for a hypothetical novel." Deadline: Sept. 30. Write "Best of Blurbs/WM" on SASE for rules.

BEST OF *HOUSEWIFE-WRITER'S FORUM*: THE CONTESTED WILLS TO WRITE, *Housewife-Writer's Forum*, Drawer 1518, Lafayette CA 94549. (415)932-1143. Contest Director: Deborah Haeseler.Unpublished prose and poetry categories. Deadline: Dec. 15. Charges $3 fee for subscribers and $4 for nonsubscribers for prose; $1.50 fee for subscribers and $2 for nonsubscribers for poetry.

ALBERT J. BEVERIDGE AWARD, Committee Chairman, American Historical Association, 400 A St. SE, Washington DC 20003. American history of U.S., Canada and Latin American (book). Deadline: June 15.

THE BEVERLY HILLS THEATRE GUILD-JULIE HARRIS PLAYWRIGHT AWARD COMPETITION, 2815 N. Beachwood Drive, Los Angeles CA 90068. (213)465-2703. Playwright Award Coordinator: Marcella Meharg. Original full-length plays, unpublished, unproduced and not currently under option. Application required, available upon request with SASE. Deadline: Nov. 1.

‡**BIENNIAL PROMISING PLAYWRIGHT AWARD**, The Colonial Players, Inc. Theater in the Round, 108 E. St., Annapolis MD 21401. (301)268-7373. Contact: Doris S. Cummins. Contest is offered every two years for an outstanding unpublished script by a promising playwright. Deadline Dec. 31. Charges $5 per entry.

BITTERROOT MAGAZINE POETRY CONTEST, *Bitterroot*, Spring Glen NY 12483. Editor-in-Chief: Menke Katz. For information and guidelines include SASE. Sponsors William Kushner Annual Awards and Heershe Dovid-Badonneh Awards for unpublished poetry. Deadline: Dec. 31.

IRMA SIMONTON BLACK AWARD, Bank Street College of Education, 610 W. 112th St., New York NY 10025. (212)222-6700. Award Director: William H. Hooks. Previously published children's book, for excellence of both text and illustration. Deadline: Jan. 15.

HOWARD W. BLAKESLEE AWARDS, American Heart Association, 7320 Greenville Ave., Dallas TX 75231. (214)706-1340. Award Director: Howard L. Lewis. Previously published or broadcast reports on cardiovascular diseases. Deadline: Feb. 1.

‡**NELTJE BLANCHAN MEMORIAL AWARD**, Wyoming Council on the Arts, 2320 Capitol Ave., Cheyenne WY 82002. (307)777-7742. Literature Consultant: Jean Hanson. "This award is given to honor the most promising work by a previously published or unpublished writer who takes inspiration from nature." June 15. May call WCA offices for guidelines, (307)777-7742; guidelines are also printed in Wyoming Council on the Arts Literature Newsletter, a monthly free publication. Applicants must have been Wyoming residents for one year prior to entry deadline, and may not be full-time students or tenured faculty.

‡**BMI UNIVERSITY MUSICAL SHOW COMPETITION**, Broadcast Music Inc., 320 W. 57 St., New York NY 10019. (212)586-2000. Contact: Norma Grossman. To encourage the creation of musical shows by unpublished student composers and lyricists; and the nurturing of new talent by their representative organizations. Deadline June 30. Applicants must be enrolled in accredited private, public, parochial colleges, universities or conservatories and must not have reached their 26th birthday by Dec. 31.

BODY STORY CONTEST, *American Health* Magazine, 80 5th Ave., New York NY 10011. (212)242-2460. Contact: Erica Franklin. 2,000-word fiction or nonfiction story. Deadline: September 1.

BOSTON GLOBE-HORN BOOK AWARDS, *The Boston Globe*, Boston MA 02107. Children's Book Editor: Stephanie Loer. Fiction, nonfiction and illustrated book. Deadline: May 1.

BOWLING WRITING COMPETITION, American Bowling Congress, Public Relations, 5301 S. 76th St., Greendale WI 53129. Director: Dave DeLorenzo, Public Relations Manager. Feature, editorial and news. Deadline: December.

‡**BRODY ARTS FUND FELLOWSHIP**, California Community Foundaiton, Suite 1660, 3580 Wilshire Blvd., Los Angeles CA 90010. (213)413-4042. "The Brody Arts Fund is designed to serve the needs of emerging, artists and arts organizaitons, especially those rooted in the diverse, multicultural communities of Los Angeles. The fellowship program rotates annually between 3 main subsections of the arts. Literary artists will be considered in 1990 (for 1991 awards) and 1993."

ARLEIGH BURKE ESSAY CONTEST, U.S. Naval Institute, Preble Hall, U.S. Naval Academy, Annapolis MD 21402. (301)268-6110. Award Director: James A. Barber, Jr. Essay that advances professional, literary or scientific knowledge of the naval and maritime services. Deadline: Dec. 1.

BUSH ARTIST FELLOWSHIPS, The Bush Foundation, E-900 First Natl. Bank Bldg., St. Paul MN 55101. (612)227-0891. Contact: Sally F. Dixon. Award for Minnesota, South and North Dakota residents "to buy 6-18 months of time for the applicant to do his/her own work." Up to 15 fellowships annually. Deadline: Oct. 31.

BYLINE MAGAZINE Contests, Box 130596, Edmond OK 73013. (405)348-3325. Publisher: Marcia Preston. Unpublished short stories, poems and other categories. Awards on monthly basis. Deadline on annual award, which is for subscribers only, Dec. 1. Charges fee of $5 for short story; $2 for poems.

CALIFORNIA WRITERS' CLUB CONFERENCE CONTEST, 2214 Derby St., Berkeley CA 94705. (415)841-1217. Unpublished adult fiction, adult nonfiction, juvenile fiction or nonfiction, poetry and scripts. "Ourconference is biennial, next being in 1991." Deadline: varies in spring. Charges fee.

‡**CALIFORNIA YOUNG PLAYWRIGHTS PROJECT**, Gaslamp Quarter Theatre Company, 547 Fourth Ave., San Diego CA 92101. (619)232-9608. Contact: Deborah Salzer. Contest is to encourage young writers to create for the stage and to develop audiences for live theatre. Every writer receives an individualized script critique; selected scripts receive professional productions. Deadline varies from May to June. Request for poster is sufficient. California residents under 19 years of age.

‡**CANADIAN AUTHOR & BOOKMAN STUDENT CREATIVE WRITING AWARDS**, Canadian Authors Association, 121 Ave. Rd., Toronto, Ontario M5R 2G3 Canada. (416)926-8084. Contact: Editor of Canadian Author & Bookman. Contest is to encourage creative writing of unpublished fiction, nonfiction and poetry at the secondary school level. Deadline: Mid-February. Must purchase fall or winter issue of CA&B and use tearsheet entry form. Teacher must nominate (and may only nominate one student). Must be secondary school student and nominated by his/her instructor.

CANADIAN BOOKSELLERS ASSOCIATION AUTHOR OF THE YEAR AWARD, 301 Donlands Ave., Toronto, Ontario M4J 3R8 Canada. Contact: Board of Directors of the Association. Canadian author for body of work over many years. No applications may be made by authors.

CANADIAN FICTION MAGAZINE, Contributor's Prize. Box 946, Station F, Toronto Ontario M4Y 2N9 Canada. Contact: Editor-in-Chief. Best story of year in French or English; Canadian citizens only. Deadline: Sept. 15.

MELVILLE CANE AWARD, Poetry Society of America, 15 Gramercy Park S., New York NY 10003. (212)254-9268. Contact: Award Director. Published book of poems or prose work on a poet or poetry submitted by the publisher. Deadline: Dec. 31.

THE THOMAS H. CARTER MEMORIAL AWARD FOR LITERARY CRITICISM, *Shenandoah*, Box 722 Lexington VA 24450. (703)463-8765. Editor: Dabney Stuart. Unpublished quality essays and/or literary criticism.

‡**CATHOLIC PRESS ASSOCIATION JOURNALISM AWARDS**, Catholic Press Association, 119 N. Park Ave., Rockville Centre NY 11570. (516)766-3400. Contact: Owen McGovern. To recognize quality work of journalists published between January and December of previous year who work for a Catholic publication. There are numerous categories for newspapers and magazines. Deadline: Mid-February. Charges $30 fee. Only journalists who are published in Catholic publications are eligible.

‡**CCLM EDITOR'S GRANT AWARDS**, Coordinating Council of Literary Magazines, 666 Broadway, New York NY 10012. (212)614-6551. Contact: Beth O'Rourke. Awards for editors of noncommercial literary magazines in CCLM. Deadline: April 30.

‡**CCLM SEED GRANTS**, Coordinating Council of Literary Magazines, 666 Broadway, New York NY 10012. (212)614-6551. Contact: Beth O'Rourke. For literary magazines that have published fewer than 3 issues. Deadline: March 1.

RUSSELL L. CECIL ARTHRITIS WRITING AWARDS, Arthritis Foundation, 1314 Spring St. NW, Atlanta GA 30309. (404)872-7100. Contact: Public Relations Department. Medical and features (news stories, articles and radio/TV scripts) published or broadcast during the previous calendar year. Deadline: Feb. 15.

CELEBRATION OF ONE-ACTS, West Coast Ensemble, Box 38728, Los Angeles CA 90038. Artistic Director: Les Hanson. Unpublished (in Southern California) one-act plays. Deadline: Oct. 15. "Up to 3 submissions allowed for each playwright." Casts should be no more than 6 and plays no longer than 40 minutes.

PAULETTE CHANDLER AWARD, Council for Wisconsin Writers, Box 55322, Madison WI 53705. (608)233-0531. "For a Wisconsin poet or short story writer based on need and ability." Deadline: Jan. 15. Poets in even years (1990); short story writers in odd years (1991). Applications do not open until November.

‡**CHICANO LITERARY CONTEST**, Dept of Spanish and Portuguese, University of California, Irvine, Irvine CA 92717. (714)856-5702. Contact: Richard Barrutia. "To promote the dissemination of unpublished Chicano literature, and to encourage its development. We accept entries in 3 divisions: short story, poetry and theater." Deadline: January. "Interested parties may call or write for entry procedures. The contest is open to all residents of the U.S. who are Chicano or who identify strongly with the Chicano movement."

CHILDREN'S SCIENCE BOOK AWARDS, New York Academy of Sciences, 2 E. 63rd St., New York NY 10021. (212)838-0230. Public Relations Director: Ann E. Collins. General or trade science books for children under 17 years. Deadline: June 30.

THE CHRISTOPHER AWARD, The Christophers, 12 E. 48th St., New York NY 10017. (212)759-4050. Award Director: Peggy Flanagan. Outstanding books published during the calendar year that "affirm the highest values of the human spirit."

‡**CINTAS FELLOWSHIP**, Inst. of International Education, 809 United Nations Pl., New York NY 10017-3580. (212)984-5564. Contact: Rebecca A. Sayles. "Cintas Fellowships are intended to acknowledge demonstrated creative accomplishment and to encourage the professional development of talented, previously published or unpublished creative artists in the fields of architecture, visual arts, music composition and literature." Deadline: March 1. Eligibility is limited to professionals living outside Cuba, who are of Cuban citizenship or direct lineage and who have completed their academic and technical training. Fellowships are not awarded more than twice to the same person. The fellowships are not awarded toward the furtherance of academic study, research on writing, nor to performing artists."

GERTRUDE B. CLAYTOR MEMORIAL AWARD, Poetry Society of America, 15 Gramercy Park S., New York NY 10003. (212)254-9628. Contact: Award Director. Poem in any form on the American scene or character. Deadline: Dec. 31. Members only.

‡**CLEVELAND STATE UNIVERSITY POETRY CENTER PRIZE**, Cleveland State University Poetry Center, Cleveland State University, Cleveland OH 44115. (216)687-3986. Director of the CSU Poetry Center: Alberta T. Turner. To identify, reward and publish the best unpublished book-length poetry manuscript submitted. Deadline: Postmarked on or before March 1. Charges $10 fee. "Submission implies willingness to sign contract for publication of the manuscript if manuscript wins." Send SASE for guidelines and entry form.

COLLEGIATE POETRY CONTEST, *The Lyric,* 307 Dunton Dr. SW, Blacksburg VA 24060. Editor: Leslie Mellichamp. Unpublished poems (36 lines or less) by fulltime undergraduates in U.S. or Canadian colleges. Deadline: June 1.

ALBERT B. COREY PRIZE IN CANADIAN-AMERICAN RELATIONS, Office of the Executive Director, American Historical Association, 400 A St. SE, Washington DC 20003. History, Canadian-U.S. relations or history of both countries (book). Deadline: Varies. Award offered every two years.

COUNCIL FOR WISCONSIN WRITERS, INC. ANNUAL AWARDS COMPETITION, Box 55322, Madison WI 58705. (608)233-0531. Contact: Awards committee. Book-length fiction, short fiction, book-length and short nonfiction, poetry, play, juvenile books, children's picture books and outdoor writing by Wisconsin residents published preceding year. Deadline: Jan. 15. Applications do not open until November.

CREATIVE ARTS CONTEST, Women's National Auxiliary Convention, Free Will Baptists, Box 1088, Nashville TN 37202. Contact: Lorene Miley. Unpublished articles, plays, poetry, programs and art from Auxiliary members. Deadline: March 1.

CREATIVITY FELLOWSHIP, Northwood Institute Alden B. Dow Creativity Center, Midland MI 48640-2398. (517)832-4478. Award Director: Carol B. Coppage. Ten-week summer residency for individuals in any field who wish to pursue a new and different creative idea that has the potential of impact in that field. Deadline: Dec. 31.

GUSTAV DAVIDSON MEMORIAL AWARD, Poetry Society of America, 15 Gramercy Park S., New York NY 10003. (212)254-9628. Contact: Award Director. Sonnet or sequence in traditional forms. Deadline: Dec. 31. Members only.

MARY CAROLYN DAVIES MEMORIAL AWARD, Poetry Society of America, 15 Gramercy Park S., New York NY 10003. (212)254-9628. Contact: Award Director. Unpublished poem suitable for setting to music. Deadline: December 31. Members only.

‡DAYTON PLAYHOUSE NATIONAL PLAYWRITING COMPETITION, The Dayton Playhouse, 1301 E. Siebenthaler Ave., Dayton OH 45414. (513)277-0144. Managing Director: Jim Payne. "To encourage and support new unpublished playwrights." Deadline Nov. 30.

DEEP SOUTH WRITERS CONTEST, Deep South Writers Conference, Box 44691, University of Southwestern Louisiana, Lafayette LA 70504. (318)231-6908. Contact: Contest Clerk. Unpublished works of short fiction, nonfiction, novels, poetry, drama and French literature. Deadline: July 15. Charges $25 fee for novels; $5 for other submissions.

DELACORTE PRESS PRIZE FOR A FIRST YOUNG ADULT NOVEL, Delacorte Press, 666 5th Ave., New York NY 10103. (212)765-6500. Contest Director: Lisa Oldenburg. Previously unpublished contemporary young adult fiction. Deadline: Dec. 31.

BILLEE MURRAY DENNY POETRY CONTEST, Lincoln College, 300 Keokuk St., Lincoln IL 62656. (217)732-3155. Contest/Award Director: Valecia Crisafulli. Unpublished poetry. Deadline: May 31. Charges $2 fee per poem (limit 3).

MARIE-LOUISE D'ESTERNAUX STUDENT POETRY CONTEST, The Brooklyn Poetry Circle, 61 Pierrepont St., Brooklyn NY 11201. Contest Chairman: Gabrielle Lederer. Poetry by students between 16 and 21 years of age. Deadline: April 15. For rules of contest send SASE.

ALICE FAY DI CASTAGNOLA AWARD, Poetry Society of America, 15 Gramercy Park S., New York NY 10003. (212)254-9628. Contact: Award Director. Manuscript in progress: poetry, prose (on poetry) or verse-drama. Deadline: Dec. 31. Members only.

EMILY DICKINSON AWARD, Poetry Society of America, 15 Gramercy Park S., New York NY 10003. (212)254-9628. Contact: Award Director. Poem inspired by Emily Dickinson. Deadline: Dec. 31. Members only.

‡GORDON W. DILLON/RICHARD C. PETERSON MEMORIAL ESSAY PRIZE, American Orchid Society, Inc., 6000 S. Olive Ave., West Palm Beach FL 33405. (407)585-8666. Contact: Dr. Alec M. Pridgeon. "To honor the memory of two outstanding former editors of the *American Orchid Society Bulletin*. Annual themes of the essay competitions are announced by the Editor of the *A.O.S. Bulletin* in the May issue. Themes in past years have included Orchid Culture, Orchids in Nature and Orchids in Use. The contest is open to all individuals with the exception of A.O.S. employees and their immediate families."

DISCOVERY/THE NATION, The Poetry Center of the 92nd Street YM-YWHA, 1395 Lexington Ave., New York NY 10128. (212)415-5760. Poetry (unpublished in book form). Deadline: February 2. Write or call for competition guidelines.

‡THE DOBIE-PAISANO FELLOWSHIP, Texas Institute of Letters, Office of Graduate Studies, Ths University of Texas at Austin, Austin TX 78712. (512)471-7213. Contact: Dr. Audrey N. Slate. "The competition offers 2 fellowships per year to creative writers—can be fiction,poetry, playwriting or nonfiction. Provides writers with opportunity to work without distraction for six months at the ranch-retreat of the late Texas writer and folklorist, J. Frank Dobie. The ranch is 256 acres and house is furnished." Deadline: Jan. 23. Charges $5 fee. Must be native Texan, living in Texas at time of application, or focus of work is on Texas and Southwest.

‡THE GERALDINE R. DODGE FOUNDATION NEW AMERICAN PLAY AWARD, Geraldine R. Dodge Foundation, % Playwrights Theatre of New Jersey, 33 Green Village Rd., Madison NJ 07940. (201)514-1194. Contact: Buzz McLaughlin. Offered every two years. "To find unpublished quality new American plays and help the playwrights develop the scripts." Offered every other year. Next contest will be in 1990-91.

DOG WRITER'S ASSOCIATION OF AMERICA ANNUAL WRITING CONTEST, 1828 Shady Lane, Louisville KY 40205. Contest Director: Susan Jeffries. Previously published writing about dogs—their rearing, training, care and all aspects of companionship. For material published from Oct. 1 1988, through Sept. 30, 1989. Deadline Oct. 1, 1989. Charges $10 fee.

‡**FRANK NELSON DOUBLEDAY MEMORIAL AWARD**, Wyoming Council on the Arts, 2320 Capitol Ave., Cheyenne WY 82002. (307)777-7742. Literature Consultant: Jean Hanson. "This award is given to honor the most promising work by a woman writer." May call WCA offices for guidelines, (307)777-7742; guidelines are also printed in Wyoming Council on the Arts Literature Newsletter, a monthly free publication. Applicants must have been Wyoming residents for one year prior to entry deadline, must be women writers, not full-time students or tenured faculty.

‡**DRURY COLLEGE ONE-ACT PLAY CONTEST**, Drury College, 900 N. Benton Ave., Springfield MO 65802. (417)865-8731. Contact: Sandy Asher. Contest is offered every two years. Plays must be unpublished and professionally unproduced. One play per playwright. Deadline: Dec. 10. Send SASE for complete guidelines.

DUBUQUE FINE ARTS PLAYERS, 569 S. Grandview Ave., Dubuque IA 52001. (319)582-5558. Contact: Sally T. Ryan. Produces 3 one acts, plays/year. Obtains first productions rights. Winning plays produced in September. Deadline: Jan. 31. Charges $5 fee.

JOHN H. DUNNING PRIZE IN AMERICAN HISTORY, Committee Chairman, American Historical Association, 400 A St. SE, Washington DC 20003. Annual award for U.S. history monograph/book. Deadline: June 15.

EATON LITERARY ASSOCIATES LITERARY AWARDS PROGRAM, Box 49795, Sarasota FL 34230-6795. (813)355-4561. Editorial Director: Lana Bruce. Previously unpublished short stories and book-length manuscripts. Deadline: March 31 (short story); Aug. 31 (book length).

EDITORS' BOOK AWARD, Pushcart Press, Box 380, Wainscott NY 11975. (516)324-9300. Unpublished books. Deadline: Aug. 30. "All manuscripts must be nominated by an editor in a publishing house."

‡**EMERGING PLAYWRIGHT AWARD**, Playwrights Preview Productions, 1160 5th Ave. #304, New York NY 10029. (212)289-2168. Contact: Thais Fitzsimmons. Submissions required to be unpublished. Awards are announced in the Spring. Submissions accepted year-round.

THE RALPH WALDO EMERSON AWARD, Phi Beta Kappa (The Phi Beta Kappa Society), 1811 Q St. NW, Washington DC 20009. (202)265-3808. Contact: Administrator, Phi Beta Kappa Book Awards. Studies of the intellectual and cultural condition of man published in the U.S. during the 12-month period preceding the entry deadline, and submitted by the publisher. Deadline: April 30.

‡**LAWRENCE S. EPSTEIN PLAYWRITING AWARD**, 280 Park Ave. S., New York NY 10010. (212)979-0865. Contact: Lawrence Epstein. Unpublished submissions. Deadline: October. Published in Dramatist's Guild and other newsletters.

‡**DAVID W. AND BEATRICE C. EVANS BIOGRAPHY AWARD**, Mountain West Center for Regional Studies Utah Sate University, University Hill, Logan UT 84322-0735. (801)750-3630. Contact: F. Ross Peterson. Submissions to be published or unpublished. To encourage the writing of biography about people who have played a role in Mormon Country. (Not the religion, the country i.e., Intermountain West with parts of Southwestern Canada and North Western Mexico.) Deadline: March. Publishers may nominate book. Criteria for consideration: Work must be a biography or autobiography on "Mormon Country"; must be submitted for consideration for publication year's award; (i.e. for 1989--January 1989-March 1990); new editions or reprints are not eligible; manuscripts are accepted. Send 5 copies of the biography to the Mountain West Center for Regional Studies, Utah State University.

JOHN K. FAIRBANK PRIZE IN EAST ASIAN HISTORY, Committee Chairman, American Historical Association, 400 A St. SE, Washington DC 20003. Book on East Asian history. Deadline: June 15.

NORMA FARBER FIRST BOOK AWARD, Poetry Society of America, 15 Gramercy Park S., New York NY 10003. (212)254-9628. Contact: Award Director. Book of original poetry. Deadline: Dec. 31. Charges $5 entry fee for non-members. Publishers only.

VIRGINIA FAULKNER AWARD FOR EXCELLENCE IN WRITING, *Prairie Schooner*, 201 Andrews, University of Nebraska, Lincoln NE 68588-0334. (402)472-3191. Editor: Hilda Raz. All genres eligible for consideration. The winning piece must have bee npublished in *Prairie Schooner* during that calendar year.

FAW LITERARY AWARD, Friends of American Writers, 506 Rose, Des Plaines IL 60016. (312)827-8339. Contact: Vivian Mortensen. Previously published books. Author must be a resident (or previously been a resident for approximately 5 years) of Arkansas, Illinois, Indiana, Iowa, Kansas, Michigan, Minnesota, Missouri, North Dakota, Nebraska, Ohio, South Dakota, or Wisconsin; or the locale of the book must be in the region above. Author shall not have published more than 3 books under his own and/or pen name. Deadline: Jan. 1-Dec. 15.

‡*FELICITY* AWARDS, Star Rt. Box 21AA, Artemas PA 17211. (814)458-3102. Contact: Kay Weems. "Monthly award to help previously published or unpublished poets & writers become published by winning contests or through contributions with cash awards to winners and publication in our newsletter. We work with the beginning writers and poets." Deadline: 30th each month. Charges an entry fee.

FESTIVAL OF NEW WORKS, Department of Theater, University of Cincinnati Mail Location 003, Cincinnati OH 45221. (513)556-5803. Artistic Director: Michael Hankins. Unpublished full-length and one-act plays or musicals. Deadline Sept. 30. Scripts should be typed and bound. Musicals must include tapes of songs.

FICTION WRITERS CONTEST, *Mademoiselle Magazine*, 350 Madison Ave., New York NY 10017. Contest Director: Eileen Schnurr. Short stories by unpublished writers aged 18-30. Deadline: March 15.

‡**FIEJ GOLDEN PEN OF FREEDOM**, International Federation of Newspaper Publishers, 25 rue d'Astorg, Paris France 75008. (011)47 42 85 00. FAX: 47 42 49 48. To recognize the outstanding actions of an individual, group or institution in favor of freedom of the press. Nominations are made by FIEJ member associations and other free press organizations invited to do so by the FIEJ Secretariat.

FLORIDA INDIVIDUAL ARTIST FELLOWSHIPS, Florida Department of State, Bureau of Grants Services, Division of Cultural Affairs, The Capitol, Tallahassee FL 32399-0250. (904)487-2980. Director: Peyton Fearington. Fellowship for Florida writers only. Deadline: mid-February.

‡**FMCT'S BIENNIAL PLAYWRIGHTS COMPETITION (MID-WEST)**, Fargo-Moorhead Community Theatre, Box 644, Fargo ND 58107. (701)235-1901. Contact: Krystine Cramer. Contest offered every two years (next contest will be held 1990-91). Submissions required to be unpublished. Deadline: Dec. 1. Midwestern playwrights only.

FOLIO, Dept. of Literature, American University, Washington DC 20016. Fiction, poetry, essays, interviews and b&w artwork. Published twice a year. Manuscripts read Aug.-April.

CONSUELO FORD AWARD, Poetry Society of America, 15 Gramercy Park S., New York NY 10003. (212)254-9628. Contact: Award Director. Unpublished lyric. Deadline: Dec. 31. Members only.

‡**THE 49th PARALLEL POETRY CONTEST**, The Signpost Press Inc., 1007 Queen St., Bellingham WA 98226. (206)734-9781. Contest Director: Knute Skinner. Unpublished poetry. Submission period: Sept. 15-Dec. 1.

FOSTER CITY ANNUAL WRITERS CONTEST, Foster City Committee for the Arts, 650 Shell Blvd., Foster City CA 94404. Chairman: Ted Lance. Unpublished fiction, poetry, humor and childrens' stories. Deadline: April 1-Aug. 31. Before submitting, send SASE for contest rules.

‡**FOURTH ESTATE AWARD**, American Legion National Headquarters, 700 N. Pennsylvania, Indianapolis IN 46204. (317)635-8411. Contact: National Public Relations. Previously published or broadcast piece on an issue of national concern. Deadline: Jan. 31.

GEORGE FREEDLEY MEMORIAL AWARD, Theatre Library Association, 111 Amsterdam Ave., New York NY 10023. (212)870-1670. Award Committee Chair: James Poteat, Museum of Broadcasting, Research Services, 810 7th Ave., New York NY 10019. (212)977-2210. Published books related to performance in theatre. Deadline: Feb. 1.

‡**FULBRIGHT SCHOLAR PROGRAM**, Council for International Exchange of Scholars, 3400 International Dr. NW, Washington DC 20008-3097. (202)686-7866. Academic & University Liaison: Carlota Baca. "Approximately 1,000 awards are offered annually in virtually all academic disciplines for university lecturing or research in over 100 countries. The opportunity for multicountry research also exists in many areas. Grant duration ranges from 3 months to an academic year." Deadlines are: June 15 – Australasia, India, Latin America and Sept. 15 – Africa, Asia, Western Europe, East Europe/USSR and the Middle East. Eligibility criteria include U.S. citizenship at the time of application; M.F.A., Ph.D or equivalent professional qualifications; for lecturing awards, university teaching experience.

‡**LEWIS GALANTIÈRE PRIZE FOR LITERARY TRANSLATION**, American Translators Association, 109 Croton Ave., Ossining NY 10562. (914)941-1500. Contact: Chair, Honors & Awards Committee. Award offered in even years recognizing the outstanding translation of a previously published work from languages other than German published in the United States." Deadline: March 15.

GALLAUDET JOURNALISM AWARD, Gallaudet University, Public Relations Office, 800 Florida Ave., N.E., Washington DC 20002. (202)651-5505. Contact: Barbara H. Dennis. Previously published "accurate, substantive, and insightful articles which provide the general public with a broad awareness and understanding of the achievements of deaf people, research in the field of deafness and the continuing documentation of deaf expression. Work of reporters and writers employed by U.S. wire services, newspapers or magazines of general circulation may be submitted for consideration. Newsletters or publication written specifically for the deaf community are *not* eligible for this award." Deadline: March 31.

JOHN GASSNER MEMORIAL PLAYWRITING AWARD, The New England Theatre Conference. 50 Exchange St., Waltham MA 02154. (617)893-3120. Unpublished one-act and full-length plays. Deadline: April 15. Charges $5 fee; free for members of New England Theatre Conference.

THE CHRISTIAN GAUSS AWARD, Phi Beta Kappa (The Phi Beta Kappa Society), 1811 Q St. NW, Washington DC 20009. (202)265-3808. Contact; Administrator, Phi Beta Kappa Book Awards. Works of literary criticism or scholarship published in the U.S. during the 12-month period preceding the entry deadline, and submitted by the publisher. Deadline: April 30.

‡**GENERAL ELECTRIC FOUNDATION AWARDS FOR YOUNGER WRITERS**, Coordinating Council of Literary Magazines, 666 Broadway, New York NY 10012. (212)614-6551. Contact: Beth O'Rourke. Previously published poetry, fiction or literary essays in literary magazines. Deadline: April 30.

‡**GERMAN PRIZE FOR LITERARY TRANSLATION**, American Translators Association, 190 Croton Ave., Ossining NY 10562. (914)941-1500. Contact: Chair, Honors & Awards Committee. Prize offered every two years. Submissions must be previously published and appeared in print between January, two years previous and March 15, current year in odd-numbered calendar. "Recognizes outstanding translations of a literary work from German published in the United States." Deadline March 15.

‡**JOHN GLASSCO TRANSLATION PRIZE**, Literary Translators' Association of Canada, Suite 510, 1030 rue Cherrier, Montreal, Quebec H2L 1H9 Canada. (514)482-6508. Contact: Mrs. Jane Brierley. Submissions are required to be previously published between Jan. 1 and Dec. 31 of previous year. The aim of the contest is to gain recognition for new literary translators and make the public aware of the contribution of literary translation. Deadline Feb. 15. Anyone may nominate the work, provided the application form is filled out and returned to the Glassco Prize Committee, with three copies of the published translation and one copy of the original. The translator must be a Canadian resident. The entry must be booklength, the body of the book done by a single translator (or a team working indivisibly). This must be the translator's first published booklength literary translation. The book must have been published in Canada during the previous year. Target languages must be French or English.

‡**GOLDEN GATE ACTORS ENSEMBLE PLAYWRIGHT'S CONTEST**, American Theatre Ventures, Inc., 580 Constanzo St., Stanford CA 94305. (415)326-0336. Contact: David Arrow, John Goodman. Playwrighting contest held to seek out and develop scripts from previously published or unpublished (cannot be produced previously in an Equity contract) American writers. Its goal is to encourage and stimulate the writing of new and original plays." Contest and dates will vary. Charges $20 fee.

GOLDEN KITE AWARDS, Society of Children's Book Writers (SCBW), Box 296 Mar Vista Station, Los Angeles CA 90066. (818)347-2849. Coordinator: Sue Alexander. Calendar year published children's fiction, nonfiction and picture illustration books by a SCBW member. Deadline: Dec. 15.

GOLF WRITER'S CONTEST, Golf Course Superintendents Association of America, 1617 St. Andrews Dr., Lawrence KS 66046. Public Relations Manager: Bob Still. Previously published work pertaining to golf superintendents. Deadline: Jan. 10. Must be a member of GWAA.

THE JEANNE CHARPIOT GOODHEART PRIZE FOR FICTION, *Shenandoah*, Box 722, Lexington VA 24450. (703)463-8765. Editor: Dabney Stuart. Unpublished short stories.

GOODMAN AWARD, Thorntree Press, 547 Hawthorn Lane, Winnetka IL 60093. (312)446-8099. Contact: Eloise Bradley Fink or John Dickson. Imagery is important. Submit 10 photocopied pages and $4 readers' fee. Mss not returned. Deadline: Jan. 1-Feb. 14.

GOVERNOR GENERAL'S LITERARY AWARDS, Canada Council, Box 1047, Ottawa, Ontario K1P 5V8 Canada. (613)237-3400. Contact: Gwen Hoover. Translation award for the best translations of Canadia works; one for a translation from English into French and one for a translation from French into English. Also offers annual children's literature award for best English-language and French-language work in text and illustration. Awards to honor published *Canadian* writers and illustrators of children's books.

GRANTS TO INDIVIDUAL ARTISTS , Maryland State Arts Council, 15 W. Mulberry St., Baltimore MD 21201. (301)333-8232. Grants Officer: Charles Camp. Grants to Maryland residents for completed works (fellowships) or works-in-progress. Deadline: Early Fall.

THE GREAT AMERICAN TENNIS WRITING AWARDS, Tennis Week/Smith Corona, 124 East 40th St., New York NY 10016. (212)808-4750. Publisher: Eugene L. Scott. Category 1: unpublished manuscript by an aspiring journalist with no previous national byline. Category 2: unpublished manuscript by a non-tennis journalist. Category 3: unpublished manuscript by a tennis journalist. Categories 4-6: published articles and one award to a book. Deadline: Nov. 18.

‡GREAT LAKES COLLEGES ASSOCIATION NEW WRITERS AWARD, The Great Lakes Colleges Association, % English Dept, Albion College, Albion MI 49224. (517)629-5511, ext. 271. Director: Paul Loukides. Entries must have appeared between February and subsequent January of year submitted. The GLCA New Writer's Award is given each year to the best *first* book of poetry and fiction submitted by publishers. "To encourage writers of previously published poetry and fiction whose publishers consider their work especially meritorious and to bring those writers together with the students and faculty of the twelve sponsoring colleges of the GLCA to their mutual benefit." Deadline: Feb. 28/29. "Publishers must nominate the works to be considered and may do so by sending *four copies* of the nominated work together with a statement assuring the contest director that the nominated author will accept the prize under the terms stipulated in the official contest announcement.

‡SARAH JOSEPHA HALE AWARD, Trustees of the Richards Library, 58 N. Main, Newport NH 03773. (603)863-3430. The award is to a New England author for the full body of his/her work. Open only to New England authors.

ERNEST HEMINGWAY FOUNDATION AWARD, P.E.N. American Center, 568 Broadway, New York NY 10012. First-published novel or short story collection by American author. Deadline: Dec. 31.

CECIL HEMLEY MEMORIAL AWARD, Poetry Society of America, 15 Gramercy Park S., New York NY 10003. (212)254-9628. Contact: Award Director. Unpublished lyric poem on a philosophical theme. Deadline: Dec. 31. Members only.

HIGHLIGHTS FOR CHILDREN FICTION CONTEST, *Highlights for Children*, 803 Church St., Honesdale PA 18431. Editor: Kent L. Brown, Jr. Category for 1990 is humor. Stories should not exceed 900 words and be appropriate for children ages 2-12. Entries for contest may also be considered for regular purchase. Deadline: Jan. 1-Feb. 28.

SIDNEY HILLMAN PRIZE AWARD, Sidney Hillman Foundation, Inc., 15 Union Square, New York NY 10003. (212)242-0700. Executive Director: Joyce D. Miller. Social/economic themes related to ideals of Sidney Hillman (daily or periodical journalism, nonfiction, radio and TV). Deadline: Jan. 15.

HOOVER ANNUAL JOURNALISM AWARDS, Herbert Hoover Presidential Library Assn., Box 696, West Branch IA 52358. Contact: Tom Walsh. Previously published newspaper and magazine journalism that contributes to public awareness and appreciation of the lives of Herbert and Lou Henry Hoover or is based on research at the Herbert Hoover Presidential Library in West Branch, Iowa. Deadline: Jan. 31.

DARRELL BOB HOUSTON PRIZE, 1931 Second Ave., Seattle WA 98101. (206)441-6239. Journalism published within the previous year in Washington State which shows "some soul, some color, some grace, robustness, mirth and generosity," to honor the memory of writer Darrell Bob Houston. Deadline: contact for exact date, usually in May.

THE ROY W. HOWARD AWARDS, The Scripps Howard Foundation, Box 5380, Cincinnati OH 45201. (513)977-3036. Public service reporting for newspapers.

IDAHO WRITER IN RESIDENCE, Idaho Commission on the Arts, 304 W. State, Boise ID 83720. (208)334-2119. Program Coordinator: Jim Owen. Previously published works by Idaho writers; award offered every two years. Deadline: June 30.

INDEPENDENT SCHOLARS, LOWELL, MARRARO, SHAUGHNESSY AND MILDENBERGER AWARDS, MLA, 10 Astor Place, New York NY 10003. (212)614-6314. Contact: Adrienne M. Ward. Mildenberger Prize: research publication on teaching foreign languages and literatures. Shaughnessy Prize: research publication on teaching English. Lowell Prize: previously published literary, linguistic study or critical edition or biography. Marraro Prize: scholarly book or essay on Italian literature. Independent Scholars: published research in modern languages and literature. Lowell and Marraro awards only open to MLA members in good standing.

INDIVIDUAL ARTISTS FELLOWSHIP, Ohio Arts Council, 727 E. Main St., Columbus OH 43205-1796 (614)466-2613. Contact: Susan Dickson. Nonfiction, fiction, criticism, poetry and plays. (Ohio resident, nonstudent). Deadline: Jan. 15.

‡INNER CITY CULTURAL CENTER'S NATIONAL SHORT PLAY COMPETITION, Inner City Cultural Center, 1308 S. New Hampshire Ave., Los Angeles CA 90006. (213)387-1161. Contact: C. Bernard Jackson. Offered annually. Submissions to be unpublished. Deadline: August. Charges $25. "All entries are presented live before an audience. All writers must have a sponsor capable of assisting the writer in preparing the work for live presentation."

‡INTERNATIONAL FILM & FILM LITERATURE AWARDS, International Film & Film Literature Society, Box 12193, La Jolla CA 92037. Previously published or unpublished. To encourage excellence in films and the literature of film production, pre-production and post-production. Deadline Dec. 20. Entries postmarked after Dec. 20 automatically entered into next competition.

INTERNATIONAL LITERARY CONTEST, Writer's Refinery/WM, Box 47786, Phoenix AZ 85068-7786. Contest Director: Libbi Goodman. Unpublished fiction, poetry and essays. Deadline: Nov. 31. Send SASE for guidelines.

‡INTERNATIONAL READING ASSOCIATION CHILDREN'S BOOK AWARD, International Reading Association, Box 8139, 800 Barksdale Rd., Newark DE 19714-8139. (302)731-1600. Director: IRA Children's Book Award Subcommittee. The IRA Children's Book Awards will be given for a first or second book, either fiction or nonfiction, by an author who shows unusual promise in the children's book field. Two categories: younger readers, ages 4-10; older readers, ages 10-16+. Deadline: Dec 1.

INTERNATIONAL READING ASSOCIATION PRINT MEDIA AWARD, International Reading Association, Box 8139, 800 Barksdale Rd., Newark DE 19714-8139. (302)731-1600. FAX: (302)731-1057. Contact: Patricia Du Bois. Reports by professional journalists from newspapers, magazines and wire services on reading programs. Deadline: Jan. 15.

‡IOWA SHORT FICTION AWARD/JOHN SIMMONS SHORT FICTION AWARD, University of Iowa Press, Dept. of English, University of Iowa, Iowa City IA 52242. Submissions to be unpublished. Deadline: Sept. 1 to Oct. 30. "Any writer who has not previously published a volume of prose fiction is eligible to enter the competition for these prizes. Revised mss which have been previously entered may be resubmitted. Writers who have published a volume of poetry are elible. Stories previously published in periodicals are eligible."

JOSEPH HENRY JACKSON/JAMES D. PHELAN LITERARY AWARDS, The San Francisco Foundation, Suite 910, 685 Market St., San Francisco CA 94105. (415)543-0223. Awards Coordinator: Katherine Brody. Jackson Award: unpublished, work-in-progress—fiction (novel or short story), nonfiction or poetry by author age 20-35, with 3-year consecutive residency in N. California or Nevada prior to submission. Phelan: unpublished, work-in-progress fiction, nonfiction, short story, poetry or drama by California-born author age 20-35. Deadline: Jan. 15.

‡1990 JAPAN-U.S. FRIENDSHIP COMMISSION PRIZE FOR THE TRANSLATION OF JAPANESE LITERATURE, Donald Keene Center of Japanese Culture, 407 Kent Hall, Columbia University, New York NY 10027. (212)854-5036/5027. Book-length works of any period or genre of Japanese literature by a not widely recognized American translator. Deadline: Dec. 1.

‡JCC THEATRE OF CLEVELAND PLAYWRITING COMPETITION, Jewish Community Center, 3505 Mayfield Rd., Cleveland Heights OH 44118. (216)382-4000, ext. 275. Contact: Elaine Rembrandt. All entries must be original works, not previously produced, suitable for a full-length presentation; directly concerned with the Jewish experience.

ANSON JONES AWARD, % Texas Medical Association, 1801 N. Lamar Blvd., Austin TX 78701. (512)477-6704. Health (Texas newspaper, magazine—trade, commercial, association, chamber or company—radio and TV). Deadline: Jan. 15.

‡**THE CHESTER H. JONES NATIONAL POETRY COMPETITION**, Box 498, Chardon OH 44024. An annual competition for persons in the U.S., Canada and U.S. citizens living abroad. Winning poems plus others, called "commendations," are published in a chapbook available for $3.50 from the foundation. Deadline: March 31. Charges $1/poem, no more than 10 entries, no more than 32 lines each; must be unpublished.

‡**MARGO JONES PLAYWRITING COMPETITION**, Texas Woman's University, Department of Music & Drama, Box 23865, Denton TX 76204. (817)898-2500. Contest Contact: Mary Lou. Contest offered every two years for unpublished plays. "Playwrights are encouraged to submit plays which are for and about women. By no means should this be taken to mean that men should not appear in the cast, or the male playwrights are excluded from the competition itself." Deadline Feb. 1.

‡**JUVENILE BOOK AWARDS**, Friends of American Writers, 15237 Redwood, Libertyville IL 60048. (312)362-3782. Contest is offered annually. Submissions are required to be published in the previous year. Author must be a native or current resident (5 years) of the following states: AR, IL, IN, IA, KS, MI, MN, MO, NE, ND, OH, SD or WI.

THE JANET HEIDINGER KAFKA PRIZE, English Department, Susan B. Anthony Center, 538 Lattimore Hall, University of Rochester, Rochester NY 14627. (716)275-8318. Attenton: Bonnie G. Smith. Book-length fiction (novel, short story or experimental writing) by U.S. woman citizen submitted by publishers.

ROBERT F. KENNEDY BOOK AWARD, 1031 31st St. NW, Washington DC 20007. (202)333-1880. Executive Director: Caroline Croft. Book which reflects "concern for the poor and the powerless, justice, the conviction that society must assure all young people a fair chance and faith that a free democracy can act to remedy disparities of power and opportunity." Deadline: Jan. 8. Charges $20 entry fee.

ROBERT F. KENNEDY JOURNALISM AWARDS, 1031 31st St. NW, Washington DC 20007. (202)333-1880. Executive Director: Linda Semans. Previously published entries on problems of the disadvantaged. Deadline: Jan. 31.

‡**GEORGE R. KERNODLE ONE-ACT PLAYWRITING COMPETITION**, University of Arkansas, Department of Drama, 406 Kimpel Hall, Fayetteville AR 72701. (501)575-2953. Contact: Dr. Donald Seay. Submissions to be unpublished. Deadline: June 1. Charges $3 fee. Open to entry to all playwrights residing in the United States and Canada.

‡**LEE KORF PLAYWRITING AWARDS**, The Original Theatre Works, Cerritos College, 11110 E. Alondra, Norwalk CA 90650. (213)924-2100. Contact: Nancy J. Payne Award for previously published or unpublished plays. Deadline Jan. 1. "Full length plays only, no special criteria."

RUTH LAKE MEMORIAL AWARD, Poetry Society of America, 15 Gramercy Park S., New York NY 10003. (212)254-9628. Contact: Award Director. Unpublished poem of retrospection. Deadline: Dec. 31. Charges $5 fee.

LAMONT POETRY SELECTION, Academy of American Poets, 177 E. 87th St., New York NY 10128. (212)427-5665. Contest/Award Director: Alex Thorburn. Second book of unpublished poems by an American citizen, submitted by publisher in manuscript form.

THE HAROLD MORTON LANDON TRANSLATION PRIZE, The Academy of American Poets, 177 E. 87th St., New York NY 10128. (212)427-5665. Award Director: Alex Thorburn. Previously published translation of poetry (book) from any language into English by an American translator. Deadline: end of calendar year.

THE PETER I.B. LAVAN YOUNGER POETS AWARD, The Academy of American Poets, 177 East 87th St., New York NY 10128. (212)427-5665. American poets under 40 who have published at least one full-length collection of poetry. Recipients are selected by the Academy's Chancellors. No applications.

LAWRENCE FOUNDATION AWARD, *Prairie Schooner*, 201 Andrews, University of Nebraska, Lincoln NE 68588-0334. (402)472-3191. Editor: Hilda Raz. Short story published in *Prairie Schooner*. Winner announced in the spring issue of the following year.

STEPHEN LEACOCK MEMORIAL AWARD FOR HUMOUR, Stephen Leacock Associates, Box 854, Orillia Ontario L3V 6K8 Canada. (705)325-6546. Contest Director: Jean Dickson. Previously published book of humor by a Canadian author. Include 10 books each entry and a black & white photo with bio. Deadline: Dec. 31. Charges $25 fee.

‡LEAGUE OF CANADIAN POETS AWARDS, National Poetry Contest, F.R. Scott Translation Award, Gerald Lampert Memorial Award, and Pat Lowther Memorial Award. 24 Ryerson Ave., Toronto, Ontario M5T 2P3 Canada. (416)363-5047. Submissions to be previously published (awards) in the preceding year or previously unpublished (poetry contest). To promote new Canadian poetry/poets and also to recognize exceptional work in each category. Awards Deadline: Jan. 30. Contest Deadline: Dec. 1. Enquiries from publishers welcome. Charges $5 per poem fee for contest *only*. Open to Canadians living here and abroad. The candidate must be a Canadian citizen or landed immigrant, although publisher need not be Canadian.

ELIAS LIEBERMAN STUDENT POETRY AWARD, Poetry Society of America, 15 Gramercy Park S., New York NY 10003. (212)254-9628. Contact: Award Director. Unpublished poem by student (grades 9-12). Deadline: Dec. 31. Charges $5 fee.

LIGHT AND LIFE WRITING CONTEST, *Light and Life* Magazine, 901 College Ave., Winona Lake IN 46590. (219)267-7656. Editor: Bob Haslam. Write for guidelines after November. Deadline: April 15. New categories each year.

THE RUTH LILLY POETRY PRIZE, The Modern Poetry Association and The American Council for the Arts, 60 W. Walton St., Chicago IL 60610. (312)413-2210. Contact: Joseph Parisi. Annual prize to poet "whose accomplishments in the field of poetry warrant extraordinary recognition." No applicants or nominations are accepted. Deadline: varies.

LINCOLN MEMORIAL ONE-ACT PLAYWRITING CONTEST, International Society of Dramatists, Box 1310, Miami FL 33153. (305)674-1831. Award Director: A. Delaplaine. Unpublished one-act plays, any type, any style. Awards and reading, and possible future production. Deadline: Jan. 15.

LINDEN LANE MAGAZINE ENGLISH-LANGUAGE POETRY CONTEST, Linden Lane Magazine & Press, Inc., Box 2384, Princeton NJ 08543-2384. (609)921-2833. Editor: Belkis Cuza Male. Unpublished Spanish and English poetry, short story and essay prizes. Deadline: May 15. Charges $12 fee.

JOSEPH W. LIPPINCOTT AWARD, Donated by Joseph W. Lippincott, Jr., Administered by American Library Association, 50 E. Huron, Chicago IL 60611. (312)944-6780. For distinguished service to the profession of librarianship, including notable published professional writing.

LOCKERT LIBRARY OF POETRY IN TRANSLATION, Princeton University Press, 41 William St., Princeton NJ 08540. (609)452-4900. Poetry Editor: Robert E. Brown. Book-length poetry translation of a single poet.

‡LOFT CREATIVE NONFICTION RESIDENCY PROGRAM. The Loft, 2301 E. Franklin Ave., Minneapolis MN 55406. (612)341-0431. Program Director: Lois Vossen. Opportunity to work in month-long seminar with resident writer and cash award to six creative nonfiction writers. "Must live close enough to Minneapolis to participate fully." Deadline: April.

LOFT-MCKNIGHT WRITERS AWARD, The Loft, 2301 E. Franklin Ave., Minneapolis MN 55406. (612)341-0431. Program Director: Lois Vossen. Eight awards and two awards of distinction for Minnesota writers of poetry and creative prose. Deadline: November.

LOFT-MENTOR SERIES, The Loft, 2301 Franklin Ave., Minneapolis MN 55406. (612)341-0431. Program Director: Lois Vossen. Opportunity to work with five nationally known writers and cash award available to eight winning poets and fiction writers. "Must live close enough to Minneapolis to participate fully in the series." Deadline: May.

‡LOUISIANA LITERARY AWARD, Louisana Literary Assoc., Box 3058, Baton Rouge LA 70821. (504)342-4928. Contact: Literary Award Committee. Submissions to be previously published. "Must be related to Louisiana. Write for details."

LOUISIANA LITERATURE PRIZE FOR POETRY, Box 792, Southeastern Louisiana University, Hammond LA 70402. Contest Director: Dr. Tim Gautreaux. Unpublished poetry. Deadline: Feb. 15. Write for rules.

‡MCDONALD'S LITERARY ACHIEVEMENT AWARDS, McDonald's & The Negro Ensemble Company, Box 778, Times Square Station, New York NY 10108. (312)443-8739. Burrell Public Relations: Phyllis D. Banks. Offered annually. Submissions to be previously published or unpublished. Writing on the black experience in America. Categories consist of poetry (up to 15 pages, 5 poems) Fiction (up to 50 pages of long work or two short works) Playwriting (at least 20 pages). Deadline: June 1. Must be 18 or older. Due to volume of entries, materials will not be returned.

MCLEMORE PRIZE, Mississippi Historical Society, Box 571, Jackson MS 39205. (601)359-1424. Contact: Secretary/Treasurer. Scholarly book on a topic in Mississippi history/biography published in the year of competition. Deadline: Jan. 1.

HOWARD R. MARRARO PRIZE IN ITALIAN HISTORY, Office of the Executive Director, American Historical Association, 400 A St. SE, Washington DC 20003. Work on any epoch of Italian history, Italian cultural history or Italian-American relations. Deadline: June 15.

THE LENORE MARSHALL/NATION PRIZE FOR POETRY, The New Hope Foundation and *The Nation* Magazine, 72 5th Ave., New York NY 10011. (212)242-8400. Administrator: Peter Meyer. Book of poems published in the United States during the previous year and nominated by the publisher. Deadline: June 1. Books must be submitted *directly* to judges.

‡WALTER RUMSEY MARVIN GRANT, Ohioana Library Association, Room 1105 State Departments Bldg., 65 S. Front St., Columbus OH 43215. (614)466-3831. Director: Linda Hengst. Award given every 2 years, (even years). Applicant must have been born in Ohio or have lived in Ohio for 5 years or more. Deadline Jan. 31.

JOHN MASEFIELD MEMORIAL AWARD, Poetry Society of America, 15 Gramercy Park S., New York NY 10003. (212)254-9628. Contact: Award Director. Unpublished narrative poem in English. No translations. Deadline: Dec. 31. Charges $5 fee.

HAROLD MASON REFERENCE BOOK AWARD, Association of Jewish Libraries, Library, YIVO Institute for Jewish Research, 1048 Fifth Ave., New York NY 10028. (212)535-6700. Conctact: Zachary Baker. Outstanding reference book published during the previous year in the field of Jewish studies.

THE MAYFLOWER SOCIETY CUP COMPETITION, North Carolina Literary and Historical Association, 109 E. Jones St., Raleigh NC 27611. (919)733-7305. Contact: Award Director. Previously published nonfiction by a North Carolina resident. Deadline: July 15.

LUCILLE MEDWICK MEMORIAL AWARD, Poetry Society of America, 15 Gramercy Park S., New York NY 10003. (212)254-9628. Contact: Award Director. Original poem on a humanitarian theme. Deadline: Dec. 31. Members only.

THE EDWARD J. MEEMAN AWARDS, The Scripps Howard Foundation, Box 5380, Cincinnati OH 45201. (513)977-3036. Environmental reporting for newspapers.

MELCHER BOOK AWARD, Unitarian Universalist Association, 25 Beacon St., Boston MA 02108. Staff Liaison: Lenore Fogel. Previously published book on religious liberalism. Deadline: Dec. 31.

MENCKEN AWARDS, Free Press Association, Box 15548, Columbus OH 43215. FPA Executive Director: Michael Grossberg. Defense of human rights and individual liberties; news story or investigative report, feature story, editorial or op-ed column, editorial cartoon; and book published or broadcast during previous year. Entry *must* have been published. *Must* send SASE for entry form, rules. Deadline: April 1. Late fee deadline: May 1 (for work published previous year).

‡THE MERRIMACK REPERTORY THEATRE FIRST ANNUAL PLAYWRITING CONTEST, Merrimack Repertory Theatre, Box 228, Lovell MA 01853. (508)454-6324. Contact: David Kent. Accepts original full length, unpublished and unproduced scripts from residents of Massachusetts, Connecticut, Rhode Island, Maine, Vermont and New Hampshire. Deadline March 15, winners announced in June.

‡MIDSOUTH, Circuit Playhouse/Playhouse on the Square, 51 S. Cooper, Memphis TN 38104. (901)725-0776. Contact: Jackie Nichols. Deadline: April 1.

MILL MOUNTAIN THEATRE NEW PLAY COMPETITION, Mill Mountain Theatre, Center in the Square, One Market Sq., Roanoke VA 24011. (703)342-5730. Literary Manager: Jo Weinstein. Previously unpublished and unproduced plays for up to 10 cast members. Deadline: Jan. 1.

MISSISSIPPI VALLEY POETRY CONTEST, Box 3188, Rock Island IL 61204. (309)788-8041. Director: Sue. Unpublished poetry: adult general, student division, Mississippi Valley, senior citizen, religious, rhyming, humor, haiku, historical, ethnic and jazz. Deadline: Sept. 15. Charges $3 to enter contest. Up to 5 poems may be submitted without line limitation.

‡**MIXED BLOOD VERSUS AMERICA**, Mixed Blood Theatre Company, 1501 S. 4th St., Minneapolis MN 55454. (612)338-0984. For a copy of contest guidelines contact: David B. Kunz by letter with SASE. "Mixed Blood Versus America" encourages and seeks out the emerging playwright. Please note that Mixed Blood is not necessarily looking for scripts that have multi-racial casts, it is interested primarily in good scripts that will be cast with the best actors available." Open to all playwrights who have had at least one of their works produced or workshopped (either professionally or educationally). Only unpublished unproduced plays are eligible for contest. Subject matter and length are open. Limit two submissions per playwright. No translations or adaptations.

FELIX MORLEY MEMORIAL PRIZES, Institute for Humane Studies, George Mason University, 4400 University Dr., Fairfax VA 22030. (703)323-1055. Contact: Marty Zupan or Jane Cocking. Awards for "young writers dedicated to individual liberty." Deadline: June 15.

FRANK LUTHER MOTT-KAPPA TAU ALPHA RESEARCH AWARD IN JOURNALISM, 107 Sondra Ave., Columbia MO 65202. (314)443-3521. Executive Director, Central Office: William H. Taft. Research in journalism (book). Deadline: Jan. 15.

MULTICULTURAL PLAYWRIGHTS' FESTIVAL, The Seattle Group Theatre Company, 3940 Brooklyn Ave. NE, Seattle WA 98105. (206)545-4969. Director: Tim Bond. One-act and full-length plays by Black, Native American, Hispanic and Asian playwrights. Honorarium, airfare and housing for 2 playwrights plus workshop productions. 4-6 playwrights receive readings. Deadline: Sept. 15.

‡**NATIONAL ARCHIVES ONE-ACT PLAYWRITING COMPETITION**, National Archives and Records Administration, Education Branch, NEE-E, Washington DC 20408. Contact: Cynthia A. Hightower. To educate playwrights about the vast resources within the records of the National Archives. Script must be unpublished and based on Bill of Rights, 14th and/or 15th amendment issues such as freedom of speech, religion, press, due process, voting rights. Scripts must be based on records held by the National Archives in Washington, DC and/or its regional archives, and/or any of the presidential libraries. Deadline Jan. 15. Open to all except the employees of the National Archives and Records Administration, its field branches and the presidential libraries.

‡**NATIONAL AWARDS FOR EDUCATION REPORTING**, Education Writers Association, 1001 Connecticut Ave. NW, Washington DC 20036. (202)429-9680. Submissions to be previously published, previous year. There are 17 categories; write for more information. Deadline, mid-January. Charges $30 for first entry, $20 for each additional.

NATIONAL BOOK AWARDS, Studio 1002D, 155 Bank St., New York NY 10014. (212)206-0024. Executive Director: Barbara Prete. Fiction and general nonfiction books by American authors. "Publishers must enter the books." Deadline: varies. Charges $100 fee.

‡**NATIONAL ENDOWMENT FOR THE ARTS: ARTS ADMINISTRATION FELLOWS PROGRAM/FELLOWSHIP**, National Endowment for the Arts, 1100 Pennsylvania Ave., NW, Washington DC 20506. (202)682-5786. Contact: Anya Nykyforiak. Offered three times each year: Spring, Summer and Fall. "The Arts Administration Fellowships are for arts managers and administrators in the non-profit literary publishing field or writers' centers. Fellows come to the NEA for a 13-week residency to acquire an overview of this Federal agency's operations. Deadline: Jan./April/July. Guidelines may be requested by letter or telephone.

‡**NATIONAL JEWISH BOOK AWARD—AUTOBIOGRAPHY/MEMOIR**, Sandra Brand and Arik Weintraub Award, 15 E. 26th St., New York NY 10010. (212)532-4949. Director: Paula G. Gottlieb. Given to an author of an autobiography or a memoir of the life of a Jewish person.

NATIONAL JEWISH BOOK AWARD—CHILDREN'S LITERATURE, Shapolsky Family Award, Jewish Book Council, 15 E. 26th St., New York NY 10010. (212)532-4949. Director: Paula G. Gottlieb. Children's book on Jewish theme. Deadline: Nov. 25.

NATIONAL JEWISH BOOK AWARD—CHILDREN'S PICTURE BOOK, Marcia and Louis Posner Award, Jewish Book Council, 15 E. 26th St., New York NY 10010. (212)532-4949. Director: Paula G. Gottlieb. Author and illustrator of a children's book on a Jewish theme. Deadline: Nov. 25.

‡**NATIONAL JEWISH BOOK AWARD—CONTEMPORARY JEWISH LIFE**, Muriel and Phil Berman Award, 15 E. 26th St., New York NY 10010. (212)532-4949. Contact: Paula G. Gottlieb. Nonfiction work dealing with the sociology of modern Jewish life.

NATIONAL JEWISH BOOK AWARD—FICTION, William and Janice Epstein Award, 15 E. 26th St., New York NY 10010. (212)532-4949. Director: Paula G. Gottlieb. Jewish fiction (novel or short story collection). Deadline: Nov. 25.

NATIONAL JEWISH BOOK AWARD—HOLOCAUST, Leon Jolson Award, Jewish Book Council, 15 E. 26th St., New York NY 10010. (212)532-4949. Contact: Paula G. Gottlieb. Nonfiction book concerning the Holocaust. Deadline: Nov. 25.

NATIONAL JEWISH BOOK AWARD—ISRAEL, Morris J. and Betty Kaplun Memorial Award, Jewish Book Council, 15 E. 26th St., New York NY 10010. (212)532-4949. Director: Paula G. Gottlieb. Nonfiction work about the State of Israel. Deadline: Nov. 25.

NATIONAL JEWISH BOOK AWARD—JEWISH HISTORY, Gerrard and Ella Berman Award, Jewish Book Council, 15 E. 26th St., New York NY 10010. (212)532-4949. Director: Paula G. Gottlieb. Book of Jewish history. Deadline: Nov. 25.

NATIONAL JEWISH BOOK AWARD—JEWISH THOUGHT, Jewish Book Council, 15 E. 26th St., New York NY 10010. (212)532-4949. Director: Paula G. Gottlieb. Book dealing with some aspect of Jewish thought, past or present. Deadline: Nov. 25.

NATIONAL JEWISH BOOK AWARD—SCHOLARSHIP, Sarah H. and Julius Kushner Memorial Award, Jewish Book Council, 15 E. 26th St., New York NY 10010. (212)532-4949. Director: Paula G. Gottlieb. Book which makes an original contribution to Jewish learning. Deadline: Nov. 25.

NATIONAL JEWISH BOOK AWARD—VISUAL ARTS, Leon L. Gildesgame Award, Jewish Book Council, 15 E. 26th St., New York NY 10010. (212)532-4949. Director: Paula G. Gottlieb. Book about Jewish art. Deadline: Nov. 25.

NATIONAL ONE-ACT PLAY CONTEST, Actors Theatre of Louisville, 316 W. Main St., Louisville KY 40202. (502)584-1265. Literary Manager: Michael Bigelow Dixon. Previously unproduced (professionally) one-act plays (60 pages or less). "Entries must *not* have had an Equity or Equity-waiver production." Deadline: April 15.

‡NATIONAL ONE-ACT PLAYWRITING COMPETITION, Little Theatre of Alexandria, 600 Wolfe St., Alexandria VA 22314. (703)683-0778. To encourage original writing for theatre. Criteria: submissions must be original, unpublished, unproduced one-act stage plays. Deadline: March 31. Send SASE for guidelines.

‡NATIONAL PLAYWRIGHTS' COMPETITION, Unicorn Theatre, 3820 Main St., Kansas City MO 64111. (816)531-PLAY. Contact: Jan Kohl. To present unpublished, original scripts and new playwrights to the Kansas City area. Only full-length plays are eligible with a maximum of 10 actors. No musicals, one-acts or historical plays. Limit 2 submissions, entered separately. Deadline: March 1.

‡NATIONAL PLAYWRIGHTS COMPETITION ON THEMES OF RURAL AMERICA, Arrow Rock Lyceum Theatre, Main St., Arrow Rock MO 65320. Contact: Michael Bollinger. Offered every two years to unpublished full length plays dealing with the smalltown/rural American experience. Submit between March and November.

NATIONAL SOCIETY OF NEWSPAPER COLUMNISTS, Box 8318, Newark CA 94537. Public Relations: Pat Kite. Annual contest. Quarterly newsletter. Humor and general interest columns and "About Town" columns in small and large weekly and/or daily newspapers. Deadline: varies, between Jan. 31 and March 1. Charges $10 fee.

THE NEBRASKA REVIEW AWARDS IN FICTION AND POETRY, *The Nebraska Review*, ASH 215, University of Nebraska-Omaha, Omaha NE 68182-0324. (402)554-2771. Contact: Arthur Homer (poetry) and Richard Duggin (fiction). Previously unpublished fiction and a poem or group of poems. Deadline: Nov. 30.

‡NELSON ALGREN AWARDS, The Chicago Tribune. 435 N. Michigan, Chicago IL 60611. (312)222-3232. Contest/Award Coordinator: Nadia Cowen. Unpublished short fiction between 2,500-10,000 words by an American writer. Deadline: Oct. 1-Feb. 1.

NEUSTADT INTERNATIONAL PRIZE FOR LITERATURE, 110 Monnet Hall, Norman OK 73019. (405)325-4531. Director: Dr. Ivar Ivask. Previously published fiction, poetry and drama. Nominations are made only by members of the jury, which changes every two years.

NEW DAY POETRY/SHORT STORY CONTEST, New Day Publications, Route 4, Box 10, Eupora MS 39744. (601)258-2935. Director: Brenda Davis. Award offered 10 times per year; contest for poets and authors. Deadline: various. Charges $3 per poem, $5 per short story. Guidelines available for SASE.

NEW LETTERS LITERARY AWARDS, University of Missouri-Kansas City, Kansas City MO 64110. Awards Coordinator: Glenda McCrary. Unpublished fiction, poetry and essays. Deadline: May 15. Charges $10 fee.

‡NEW PLAY COMPETITION, Theatre Memphis, 630 Perkins Extended, Memphis TN 38117-4799. (901)682-8323. Co-Chairman: Martha Graber, Iris Dichtel. Competition offered every three year for unpublished scripts. Deadline: Oct. 1. Contest is staged every three years, so deadlines vary slightly. Generally in early fall. No musicals.

NEW PLAYWRIGHTS COMPETITION AND FESTIVAL, The Ann White Theatre, 5266 Gate Lake Road, Ft. Lauderdale FL 33319. (305)722-4371. Director: Ann White. Unpublished full-length play scripts. Award: $500, production by the Ann White Theatre. Deadline Nov. 15.

NEW WRITERS AWARDS, Great Lakes Colleges Association, c/o English Department, Albion College, Albion MI 49224. (517)629-5511. Director: Paul Loukides. Published poetry or fiction (first book) 4 copies submitted by publisher to arrive no later than Feb. 28.

‡JOHN NEWBERY MEDAL, Association for Library Service to Children/American Library Association, 50 E. Huron St., Chicago IL 60611. (312)944-6780. Award Director: Susan Roman. For children's literature published in the previous year.

NHS BOOK PRIZE, National Historical Society, 2245 Kohn Rd., Box 8200, Harrisburg PA 17105. (717)657-9555. Editor in Chief: William C. Davis. NHS Book Prize first book published by author. Deadline: July 31.

‡DON AND GEE NICHOLL FELLOWSHIPS IN SCREENWRITING, Academy of Motion Picture Arts & Sciences, 8949 Wilshire Blvd., Beverly Hills CA 90211. (213)278-8990. Director: Richard Miller. Unpublished or produced screenplays. Deadline: June 1. Charges $25 fee.

‡CHARLES H. AND N. MILDRED NILON EXCELLENCE IN MINORITY FICTION AWARD, University of Colorado at Boulder and the Fiction Collective, University of Colorado Campus, Box 226, Boulder CO 80309. Contact: Donald Laing. Unpublished book-length fiction.

NIMROD, ARTS AND HUMANITIES COUNCIL OF TULSA PRIZES, 2210 South Main, Tulsa OK 74114. (918)584-3333. Editor: Francine Ringold. Unpublished fiction (Katherine Anne Porter prize) and poetry (Pablo Neruda Prize). Deadline: April 15. Fee $10, for which you receive an issue of *Nimrod*. (Writers entering both fiction and poetry contest need only pay once.) Send SASE for complete guidelines.

‡O. HENRY FESTIVAL SHORT STORY CONTEST, O. Henry Festival, Inc., Box 29484, Greensboro NC 27429. Contact: Susan B. DeVaney. Contest offered every other year to encourage unpublished writing of literary quality short fiction. No children's stories. Deadline date is variable depending on the festival date. Charges $7 per story. SASE requested on all correspondence.

‡ELI M. OBOLER MEMORIAL AWARD, American Library Association's Intellectual Freedom Round Table, 50 E. Huron St., Chicago IL 60611. (312)944-6780. Chairman: Intellectual Freedom Round Table. Award offered every two years to previously unpublished author or authors of an article (including a review article), a series of thematically connected articles, a book, or a manual published on the local, state or national level, in English or in English translation. It need *not* have appeared in the "library press," nor have been written by a librarian. The works to be considered must have as their central concern one or more issues, events, questions or controversies in the area of intellectual freedom, including matters of ethical, political, or social concern related to intellectual freedom. The work for which the award is granted must have been published within the *two-year* period ending the December prior to the ALA Annual Conference at which it is granted. Deadline: Dec. 15. For 1990 award, send to: Sue Kamm, P.O. Box 26467, Los Angeles, CA 90026. Chair, Eli M. Oboler Committee.

For explanation of symbols, see the Key to Symbols and Abbreviations on Page 5. For unfamiliar words, see the Glossary.

THE FLANNERY O'CONNOR AWARD FOR SHORT FICTION, The University of Georgia Press, Terrell Hall, Athens GA 30602. (404)542-2830. Senes Editor: Charles East. Submission period: June-July 31. Charges $10 fee.

SCOTT O'DELL AWARD FOR HISTORICAL FICTION, 1100 E. 57th St., Chicago IL 60637. (312)702-8293. Director: Zena Sutherland. Previously published historical fiction book for children set in the Americas. Entries must have appeared in print between Jan. 1 and Dec. 31 of previous year. Deadline: Dec. 31.

‡OFF-OFF-BROADWAY ORIGINAL SHORT PLAY FESTIVAL, Double Image Theatre, 445 W. 59th St., New York NY 10019. (212)245-2489. Contact: William Talbot. Previously unpublished submissions. "The festival was developed in 1976 to bolster those theatre companies and schools who offer workshops, programs and instruction in playwriting. It proposes to encourage them by offering them and their playwrights the opportunity of having their plays seen by new audiences and critics, and of having them reviewed for publication." Deadline: March/April. "No individual writer may enter on his own initiative. Entries must come from theatre companies, professional schools or colleges which foster playwriting by conducting classes, workshops or similar programs of assistance to playwrights."

‡OGLEBAY INSTITUTE/TOWNGATE THEATRE PLAYWRITING, Oglebay Institute, Oglebay Park, Wheeling WV 26003. (304)242-4200. Contact: Debbie Hynes. Deadline: Jan. 1. All full-length *non*-musical plays that have never been professionally produced or published are eligible.

OHIOANA BOOK AWARD, Ohioana Library Association, Room 1105, Ohio Departments Bldg., 65 S. Front St., Columbus OH 43215. (614)466-3831. Award Director: Linda Hengst. Books published within the past 12 months by Ohioans or about Ohio and Ohioans. Submit two copies of book on publication.

‡OMMATION PRESS BOOK CONTEST, 5548 N. Sawyer, Chicago IL 60625. (312)539-5745. Contact: Effie Mihopoulos. Previously unpublished chapbook manuscripts. Deadline: Dec. 30.

THE C.F. ORVIS WRITING CONTEST, The Orvis Company, Inc., Manchester VT 05254. (802)362-3622. Contest/Award Director: Doug Truax. Outdoor writing about upland bird hunting and fly fishing (magazine and newspaper). Deadline: Feb. 1.

‡OVERSEAS PRESS CLUB OF AMERICA, Suite 2116, 310 Madison Ave., New York NY 10017. (212)983-4655. Contact: Morton Frank. Annual awards for newspaper, magazine, wire service, syndicate, cartoon, book & photographic reporting and/or interpretation from abroad – published or broadcast in the US during the previous calendar year. Deadline: Jan. 30. Charges $40 fee.

‡PANHANDLER POETRY CHAPBOOK COMPETITION, *The Panhandler Magazine*, English Dept. University of West Florida, Pensacola FL 32514. (904)474-2923. Editor: Michael Yots. Individual poems may have been published. To honor excellence in the writing of short collections of poetry. Two winning manuscripts are published each year. Deadline: Jan. 15. Charges $7 (includes copy of winning chapbooks).

FRANCIS PARKMAN PRIZE, Society of American Historians, 610 Fayerweather Hall, Columbia University, New York NY 10027. Contact: Professor Kenneth T. Jackson. Colonial or national U.S. history book. Deadline: Jan. 15.

‡PEN CENTER USA WEST AWARDS, PEN Center USA West, 1100 Glendon Ave., Los Angeles CA 90024. (213)824-2041. Directors: Marjorie Marks & Marilee Zdenek. Award offered for previously published work in a calendar year.
Deadline: Feb. 1. Open to writers living west of the Mississippi River whose books have been published in the calendar year.

PEN/JERARD FUND, PEN American Center, 568 Broadway, New York NY 10012. (212)334-1660. Contact: John Morrone. Estab. 1986. Grant for American woman writer of nonfiction for a booklength work in progress. Deadline: Feb. 15.

PEN MEDAL FOR TRANSLATION, PEN American Center, 568 Broadway, New York NY 10012. (212)334-1660. Translators nominated by the PEN Translation Committee. Given every 3 years.

PEN PUBLISHER CITATION, PEN American Center, 568 Broadway, New York NY 10012. (212)334-1660. "Awarded every two years to a publisher who has throughout his career, given distinctive and continuous service." Nominated by the PEN Executive Board.

PEN/ROGER KLEIN AWARD FOR EDITING, PEN American Center, 568 Broadway, New York NY 10012. (212)334-1660. "Given every two years to an editor of trade books who has an outstanding record of recognizing talents." Nominated by authors, agents, publishers and editors. Deadline: Oct. 1.

‡PEN SYNDICATED FICTION PROJECT, Box 15650, Washington DC 20003. (202)543-6322. Director: Caroline Marshall. Syndicates unpublished short fiction (2,500 words maximum) to newspapers and produces radio show. Receives submissions January 1-31 annually. Send SASE for guidelines, further info.

PEN TRANSLATION PRIZE, PEN American Center, 568 Broadway, New York NY 10012. Contact: Chairman, Translation Committee. One award to a literary book-length translation into English. (No technical, scientific or reference.) Deadline: Dec. 31.

PEN WRITING AWARDS FOR PRISONERS, PEN American Center, 568 Broadway, New York NY 10012. (212)334-1660. "Awarded to the authors of the best poetry, plays, short fiction and nonfiction received from prison writers in the U.S." Deadline: Sept. 1.

PERKINS PLAYWRITING CONTEST, International Society of Dramatists, Box 1310, Miami FL 33153. (305)756-8313. Award Director: A. Delaplaine. Unproduced full-length plays, any genre, any style. Awards plus staged reading and possible future production. Travel and expenses. Deadline: Dec. 6.

‡PHI BETA KAPPA BOOK AWARDS, The Phi Beta Kappa Society, 1811 Q St. NW, Washington DC 20009. (202)265-3808. Contact: Mary Mladinov. "Annual award to recognize and honor outstanding scholarly books published in the United States in the fields of the humanities, the social sciences, and the natural sciences and mathematics." Deadline: April 30. "Authors may request information, however it is requested that books be submitted by the publisher." Entries must be the works of authors who are U.S. citizens or residents.

‡PLAYWRIGHTS' CENTER JEROME PLAYWRIGHT—IN-RESIDENCE FELLOWSHIP, The Playwrights' Center, 2301 Franklin Ave. E, Minneapolis MN 55406. (612)332-7481. To provide emerging playwrights with funds and services to aid them in the development of their craft. Deadline: Feb. 1. Open to playwrights only—may not have had more than 2 fully staged productions of their works by professional theaters. Must spend fellowship year in MN at Playwrights' Center. US Citizens only.

‡PLAYWRIGHTS' CENTER MCKNIGHT FELLOWSHIP, The Playwrights' Center, 2301 Franklin Ave. E, Minneapolis MN 55406. (612)332-7481. Recognition of playwrights whose work has made a significant impact on the contemporary theater. Deadline: Dec. 1. Open to playwrights only. Must have had a minimum of two fully staged productions by professional theaters. Must spend 2 months at Playwrights' Center. US citizens only.

‡THE PLAYWRIGHTS' CENTER MIDWEST PLAYERS, The Playwrights' Center, 2301 Franklin Ave. E, Minneapolis MN 55406.(612)332-7481. Assists in the development of unproduced or unpublished new plays. Deadline: March 1. Playwrights only; must be associated with Midwest or member of Playwrights' Center; no one acts, musicals or childrens plays; and must be available for entire pre-conference and conference.

‡PLAYWRIGHTS' FORUM AWARDS, Theatreworks/Colorado, Box 7150, Colorado Springs CO 80933-7150. (719)593-3232. Producing Director: Whit Andrews. Submissions to be unpublished. To recognize excellence in playwriting in the one-act form. Deadline: Dec. 15.

PLAYWRIGHT'S-IN-RESIDENCE GRANTS, c/o HPRL, INTAR Hispanic-American Theater, Box 788, New York NY 10108. (212)695-6134. Residency grant for Hispanic-American playwrights. Deadline: June 30.

‡EDGAR ALLAN POE AWARD, Mystery Writers of America, Inc. 236 W. 27th St. #600, New York NY 10001. (212)255-7005. Previously published entries must be copyrighted in the year they are submitted. Deadline: Dec. 1. Entries for the book categories are usually submitted by the publisher but may be submitted by the author or his agent.

POETRY ARTS PROJECT CONTEST, United Resource Press, Suite 388, 4521 Campus Drive, Irvine CA 92715. Director: Charlene B. Brown. Poetry with social commentary. Prizes awarded in US Savings Bonds. Deadline: April 15. Send SASE for entry form. Must sign release. Charges $3 per poem jury fee.

POETRY MAGAZINE POETRY AWARDS, 60 W. Walton St., Chicago IL 60610. (312)280-4870. Contest/Award Director: Joseph Parisi, Editor. All poems published in *Poetry* are automatically considered for prizes.

‡POETS AND PATRONS, INC. INTERNATIONAL NARRATIVE CONTEST, 10053 Avenue L, Chicago IL 60617. Chairman: Veronica Robertson. Deadline: Sept. 1.

‡**POETS CLUB OF CHICAGO INTERNATIONAL SHAKESPEAREAN CONTEST**, 2930 Franklin St., Highland IN 46332. Chairman: June Shipley. Deadline: Sept. 1.

RENATO POGGIOLI TRANSLATION AWARD, PEN American Center, 568 Broadway, New York NY 10012. (212)334-1660. "Given to encourage a beginning and promising translator who is working on a first book length translation from Italian into English." Deadline: Feb. 1.

PRAIRIE SCHOONER STROUSSE AWARD, *Prairie Schooner*, 201 Andrews, University of Nebraska, Lincoln NE 68588-0334. (402)472-3191. Editor: Hilda Raz. Poem or group of poems previously published in *Prairie Schooner*. Annual award given for the best poem or group of poems in that year's volume.

PRESENT TENSE/JOEL H. CAVIOR LITERARY AWARDS, *Present Tense Magazine*, 165 East 56th St., New York NY 10022. Director: Murray Polner. Published books of fiction, history, religious thought, current affairs, juvenile and autobiography with Jewish themes, nominated by publisher. Deadline: Nov. 30.

PROMETHEUS AWARD/HALL OF FAME, Libertarian Futurist Society, 89 Gebhardt Road, Penfield NY 14526. (716)288-6137. Contact: Victoria Varga. Prometheus Award: pro-freedom, anti-authoritarian novel published during previous year. Hall of Fame: one classic libertarian novel at least five years old. Deadline: March 1.

PULITZER PRIZES, The Pulitzer Prize Board, 702 Journalism, Columbia University, New York NY 10027. Contact: Robert C. Christopher, Secretary. Awards for journalism in U.S. newspapers (published daily or weekly), and in literature, drama and music by Americans. Deadline: Feb. 1 (journalism); March 14 (music); March 1 (drama) and Nov. 1 (letters).

PULP PRESS INTERNATIONAL 3-DAY NOVEL WRITING CONTEST, Pulp Press Book Publishers Ltd., 100-1062 Homer St., Vancouver, British Columbia V6B 2W9 Canada. (604)687-4233. Contact: Brian Lam. Best novel written in three days; specifically, over the Labor Day weekend. Entrants return finished novels to Pulp Press for judging. Deadline: Friday before Labor Day weekend. Charges $5 fee.

‡**PURE-BRED DOGS MAGAZINE AWARD.** See listing in Consumer Animal section.

‡**PURGATORY THEATRE ANNUAL NATIONAL PLAYWRITING COMPETITION**, Purgatory Resort, Box 666, Durango CO 81302. (303)247-9000. Contact: Anthony Haigh. Submissions to be unpublished. Deadline: March 24. Plays should full-length (2 hours), suitable for summer theatre production. One play submission limit.

ERNIE PYLE AWARD, Scripps Howard Foundation, Box 5380, Cincinnati OH 45201. (513)977-3036. Human-interest reporting for newspaper men and women.

QRL POETRY SERIES, *Quarterly Review of Literature*, 26 Haslet Ave., Princeton NJ 08540. (609)921-6976. Contact: Renée Weiss. A book of miscellaneous poems, a single long poem, a poetic play, a book of translation. May and October *only*. "They must be received in those 2 months." Charges $20 subscription to the series. Send SASE for complete information.

SIR WALTER RALEIGH AWARD, North Carolina Literary and Historical Association, 109 E. Jones St., Raleigh NC 27611. (919)733-7305. Previously published fiction by a North Carolina resident. Deadline: July 15.

READER RITER POLL, *Affaire de Coeur*, 1555 Washington Ave., San Leandro CA 94577. (415)357-5665. Director: Barbara N. Keenan. Awards for previously published material in five categories appearing in magazine. Deadline: March 15.

REDBOOK'S SHORT STORY CONTEST, *Redbook Magazine*, 224 W. 57th St., New York NY 10019. Fiction Editor: Deborah Purcell. Short stories by writers who have not previously published fiction in a major publication. Contest rules appear in the March issue of *Redbook* annually or send SASE, attn: Contest Guidelines. Deadline: May 31.

REUBEN AWARD, National Cartoonists Society, 9 Ebony Ct., Brooklyn NY 11229. (718)743-6510. "Outstanding Cartoonist of the Year" chosen from National Cartoonists Society membership.

RHODE ISLAND STATE COUNCIL ON THE ARTS FELLOWSHIP, Suite 103, 95 Cedar St., Providence RI 02903. (401)277-3880. Award Director: Edward Holgate. Poetry, fiction or play, must be a resident of Rhode Island and cannot be a student in a degree – or certificate – granting program of study. Deadline: April 1.

Close-up

Deborah Purcell
Fiction Editor
Redbook Short Story Contest

Redbook has launched several well-known writers nationally, including John Irving, Mary Gordon and Tim O'Brien, and it regularly runs excerpts from novels by authors such as Barbara Taylor Bradford, Judith Krantz and Dominick Dunne. But the magazine also is interested in less widely known writers from whom the next John Irving may appear, says Fiction Editor Deborah Purcell. With that idea in mind, the magazine conducts an annual short story contest, attracting up to 8,000 entries each year.

The *Redbook* Short Story Contest began as the *Redbook* Young Writer's Contest in 1977. It was started because editors noted "over the years we were publishing relatively few stories by people in their late teens and early twenties." It seemed to be harder for the younger writers to compete, so the Young Writer's Contest began to offer them encouragement and the chance for recognition, according to former contest editor Mimi Jones.

The contest now is open to anyone 18 years of age or older who has not been published in a commercial magazine with a circulation of 25,000 or more. Stories must be no longer than 5,000 words and contestants are limited to one entry. The prizes are publication and $2,000 for first; $1,000 and $500 for second and third prizes. *Redbook* reserves the right to purchase rights to publish any of the contest entries for six months after the contest. Contest rules, along with the first place winner, are published each March in the magazine.

Purcell says the stories are first read by "a small, select group of freelance readers, who generally pass along several hundred stories to our contest editor.

"The contest editor then chooses up to 50 semifinalists, which are then evaluated by the fiction department. The fiction editor then turns over the department's selections for first, second and third prize to the editor-in-chief. The editor-in-chief reserves the right to make the final decision."

With 8,000 stories, Purcell says readers see a variety of writing styles, levels and topics. "If there is a trend, it is that submissions reflect contemporary issues and concerns. In recent years, the subjects of semifinalist stories have included wife and child abuse, AIDS, poverty, parental aging and illness," she says. "Which is not to say that all submissions are bleak—we do see a great deal of humor, as well."

At a time when fewer women's magazines consider and publish fiction on a regular basis, *Redbook* remains committed to including fiction in the magazine each month. "*Redbook* began as a short story magazine in 1903 and only many years later evolved into a women's service magazine," Purcell notes. "Perhaps *Redbook*'s fiction weathered the transition and continues to rate exceptionally because of its diversity, quality and its meaningful treatment of issues without sacrificing entertainment value."

— Glenda Tennant Neff

RHYME TIME CREATIVE WRITING COMPETITION, *Rhyme Time/Story Time*, Box 1870, Hayden ID 83835. (208)772-6184. Award Director: Linda Hutton. Rhymed poetry, fiction and essays. Deadline: first and fifteenth of each month.

THE HAROLD U. RIBALOW PRIZE, *Hadassah Magazine*, 50 W. 58th St., New York NY 10019. Executive Editor: Alan M.Tigay. English-language book of fiction on a Jewish theme. Deadline: Feb/March.

MARY ROBERTS RINEHART FUND, English Department, George Mason University, 4400 University Dr., Fairfax VA 22030. (703)323-2220. Contact: Roger Lathbury. Grants by nomination to unpublished creative writers for fiction, poetry, drama, biography, autobiography or history with a strong narrative quality. Grants are given in fiction and poetry in even years, and nonfiction and drama in odd years. Deadline: Nov. 30.

ROANOKE-CHOWAN AWARD FOR POETRY, North Carolina Literary and Historical Association, 109 E. Jones St., Raleigh NC 27611. (919)733-7305. Previously published poetry by a resident of North Carolina. Deadline: July 15.

FOREST A. ROBERTS PLAYWRITING AWARD, Shiras Institute, Forest A. Roberts Theatre, Northern Michigan University, Marquette MI 49855-5364. (906)227-2553. Award Director: Dr. James A. Panowski. Unpublished, unproduced plays. Scripts must be *received* on or before Nov. 17.

‡ROBERTS WRITING AWARDS, H.G. Roberts Foundation, Inc., Box 1868, Pittsburg KS 66762. (316)231-2998. Contact: Stephen Meats. Competitions in unpublished: poetry, short fiction, informal essays. No limitations on subject matter or form. Deadline: Sept. 1. Charges $5 for 1-5 poems; additional poems $1 each. Short fiction, essays, $5 each. Open to English language works by writers with a U.S. social security number. SASE for guidelines and entry form.

NICHOLAS ROERICH POETRY PRIZE, Story Line Press, 403 Continental St., Santa Cruz CA 95062. (408)426-5539. Contact: Robert McDowell. First full-length book of poetry. Any writer who has not published a full-length collection of poetry (48 pages or more) in English is eligible to apply. Deadline: Oct. 15. Charges $10 fee.

ROLLING STONE COLLEGE JOURNALISM COMPETITION, Rolling Stone/Smith Corona, Suite 2208, 745 5th Ave., New York NY 10151. (212)758-3800. Contact: David M. Rheins. Entertainment reporting, essays, criticism and general reporting among college writers. Deadline: June 1. Must have been published before April 1.

THE LOIS AND RICHARD ROSENTHAL NEW PLAY PRIZE, Cincinnati Playhouse in the Park. Box 6537, Cincinnati OH 45206. (513)421-5440. Unpublished plays. "Scripts must not have received a full-scale professional production." Deadline: Oct. 15-Jan. 15.

THE CARL SANDBURG LITERARY ARTS AWARDS, The Friends of the Chicago Public Library, 78 E. Washington St., Chicago IL 60602. (312)269-2922. Chicago writers of fiction, nonfiction, poetry and children's literature.

‡SCHOLASTIC WRITING AWARDS, Scholastic Inc., 730 Broadway, New York NY 10003. (212)505-3000. Fiction, nonfiction, poetry and drama (grades 7-12). Write for complete information. Cash prizes, equipment prizes and scholarships. Deadline: August-December.

THE CHARLES M. SCHULZ AWARD,The Scripps Howard Foundation, Box 5380, Cincinnati OH 45201. (513)977-3035. For college cartoonists.

SCIENCE IN SOCIETY JOURNALISM AWARDS, National Association of Science Writers, Box 294, Greenlawn NY 11740. Contact: Diane McGurgan. Newspaper, magazine and broadcast science writing. Deadline: July 1 for work published June 1-May 31 of previous year.

CHARLES E. SCRIPPS AWARD,The Scripps Howard Foundation, Box 5380, Cincinnati OH 45201. (513)977-3036. Combatting illiteracy. For newspapers, television and radio stations.

THE EDWARD WILLIS SCRIPPS AWARD, The Scripps Howard Foundation, Box 5380, Cincinnati OH 45201. (513)977-3036. Service to the First Amendment for newspapers.

SENIOR AWARD, International Society of Dramatists, Box 1310, Miami FL 33153. Award Director: A. Delaplaine. Previously unpublished scripts (any media or length) written by college students. Award plus staged reading and possible future production. Deadline: May 1.

‡*SEVENTEEN MAGAZINE*/DELL FICTION CONTEST, 850 Third Ave., New York NY 10022. Previously unpublished short stories from writers 13-20 years old. Deadline: Jan. 31.

SFWA NEBULA AWARDS, Science Fiction Writers of America, Inc., Box 4236, West Columbia SC 29171. Science fiction or fantasy in the categories of novel, novella, novelette and short story recommended by members.

MINA P. SHAUGHNESSY PRIZE, Modern Language Association, 10 Astor Place, New York NY 10003. Contact: Adrienne Ward, Administrative Assistant. Outstanding research publication in the field of teaching English language and literature; book or article published in the year previous to the award year. Nomination deadline: May 1.

SHELLEY MEMORIAL AWARD, Poetry Society of America, 15 Gramercy Park S., New York NY 10003. (212)254-9628. Contact: Award Director. Deadline: Dec. 31. By nomination only to a living American poet.

‡THE SHORT STORY AWARD, *Follow Me Gentlemen Magazine* & British Airways. 2nd Fl, 2-4 Bellevue St. Surry Hills NWS 2001 Australia. (2)2125344. FAX: (2)2126037. Contact: Jane Nicholls. To find high quality unpublished short stories, less than 5,000 words in length. One prize for winner and if the quality is of a high enough standard, 10 or more stories will be collected into a book. Noentry form. One story only per entrant.

SHORT STORY WRITERS COMPETITION, Hemingway Days Festival, Box 4045, Key West FL 33041. (305)294-4440. Director: Michael Whalton. Unpublished short stories. Deadline: early July. Contact the Hemingway Days Festival for specific date each year. Charges $10 fee.

‡SIENA COLLEGE PLAYWRIGHTS' COMPETITION, Siena College Theatre Program, Department of Fine Arts, Loudonville NY 12211. (518)783-2381. Director of Theatre: Mark A. Heckler. Contest offered every two years to recognize unpublished and unproduced works of playwrights, professional and amateur. Winning playwright required to participate in six-week residency on college campus to prepare play for production. Deadline: Feb. 1 - June 30. Even numbered years. Next deadlines occur in 1990.

SIERRA REPERTORY THEATRE, Box 3030, Sonora CA 95370. (209)532-3120. Producer: Dennis C. Jones. Full-length plays. Deadline: May 15.

SILVER GAVEL AWARDS, American Bar Association, 750 N. Lake Shore Dr., Chicago IL 60611. (312)988-6137. Contact: Marilyn Giblin. Previously published, performed or broadcast works that promote "public understanding of the American system of law and justice." Deadline: Feb. 1.

JOHN SIMMONS SHORT FICTION AWARD and IOWA SHORT FICTION AWARDS, Department of English, University of Iowa. English-Philosophy Building, Iowa City IA 52242. Previously published or unpublished fiction. Two awards and publiclations. Deadline: Aug. 1-Sept. 30.

‡CHARLIE MAY SIMON AWARD, Arkansas State Dept. of Education, University of Central Arkansas, Conway AR 72032. (501)450-3177. Co-Chairs: Dr. Jody Charter and Dr. Selvin Royal. Award for books published three years previous to award year that allows Arkansas children in grades 4-6 to vote for their favorite book from a list selected by a committee designated by Elementary Council, Arkansas DOE Books for committee's reading selected in June each year. Nominations are collected in the spring from schools or other interested parties.

BERNICE SLOTE AWARD, *Prairie Schooner*, 201 Andrews, University of Nebraska, Lincoln NE 68588-0334. (402)472-3191. Editor: Hilda Raz. Work by a beginning writers previously published in *Prairie Schooner*. Annual award given for best work by a beginning writer from that year's volume.

SMALL PRESS PUBLISHER OF THE YEAR, Quality Books Inc., 918 Sherwood Dr., Lake Bluff IL 60044-2204. (312)295-2010. Contact: Tom Drewes. "Each year a publisher is named that publishes titles we stock and has demonstrated ability to produce a timely and topical title, suitable for libraries, and supports their distributor." Title must have been selected for stocking by Quality Books Inc. QBI is the principal nationwide distributor of small press titles to libraries.

‡R. GAINES SMITH MEMORIAL WRITING CONTEST, What's Happening (Alternative Weekly Newspaper), 449 Howard, Eugene OR 97404. (503)689-9074. Contact: Anne Kern. Contest for unpublished work. Deadline: Nov. 10. Charges $10 entry fee. For writers who are Oregon residents.

C.L. SONNICHSEN BOOK AWARD, Texas Western Press of the University of Texas at El Paso, El Paso TX 79968-0633. (915)747-5688. Press Director: Dale L. Walker. Previously unpublished nonfiction manuscript dealing with the history, literature or cultures of the Southwest. Deadline: March 1.

‡SOUTHERN PLAYWRITING COMPETITION, Festival of Southern Theatre, Dept. of Theatre Arts Univ. of Mississippi, University MS 38677. (601)232-5816. Contact: Scott McCoy. Competiton for unpublished and unproduced original full-length scripts for the theatre by a Southern writer or with a markedly Southern theme. Deadline: Dec. 1.

THE SOUTHERN REVIEW/LOUISIANA STATE UNIVERSITY SHORT FICTION AWARD, Louisiana State University, 43 Allen Hall, Baton Rouge LA 70803. (504)388-5108. Selection Committee Chairman: Veronica Makowsky. Previously published first collection of short stories by an American published in the U.S. Deadline: Jan. 31. A publisher or an author may submit an entry by mailing two copies of the collection to the *Southern Review* Short Story Award.

‡SOVEREIGN AWARD OUTSTANDING NEWSPAPER STORY, OUTSTANDING FEATURE STORY, The Jockey Club of Canada, Box 156, Rexdale, Ontario M9W 5L2 Canada. (416)675-7756. Contact: Nigel P.H. Wallace. To recognize outstanding achievement in the area of Canadian thoroughbred racing of work published in the previous year. Newspaper Story: Appeared in a newspaper by a racing columnist on Canadian Racing subject matter. Outstanding Feature Story: Appeared in a magazine book or newspaper, written as feature story on Canadian Racing subject matter. Deadline: Oct. 31. There is no nominating process other than the writer submitting no more than two entries per category. Special Criteria: Must be published between Nov. 1 and Oct. 31 and be of Canadian racing content.

BRYANT SPANN MEMORIAL PRIZE, History Dept., Indiana State University, Terre Haute IN 47809. Social criticism in the tradition of Eugene V. Debs. Deadline: April 30. SASE required.

‡SPECIAL LIBRARIES ASSOCIATION PUBLIC RELATIONS AWARD, Special Libraries Association, 1700 18th St., NW, Washington DC 20009. (202)234-4700. Director, Communications: David Malinak. SLA's Public Relations Award is presented to the writer published the previous year who develops an outstanding feature story on the special libraries profession, which appears in a general circulation publication (i.e., not a library magazine or journal). Deadline: Dec. 31. The article must appear in a general-circulation magazine or newspaper during the calendar year. (Library journal magazine articles or submissions from librarians are not eligible).

SPUR AWARDS (WESTERN WRITERS OF AMERICA, INC.), WWA, 1753 Victoria, Sheridan WY 82801. (307)672-2079. Director: Barbara Ketcham. Ten categories of western: novel, historical novel, nonfiction book, juvenile nonfiction, juvenile fiction, nonfiction article, fiction short story, best TV script, movie screenplay, cover art. Also, Medicine Pipe Bearer's Award for best first novel. Deadline: Dec. 31. Submissions must be published in the calendar year they are submitted.

‡THE STAND MAGAZINE SHORT STORY COMPETITION, *Stand Magazine* and the Harrogate International Festival, 19 Haldane Terrace, Newcastle upon Tyne U.K. NE2 3AN. (091)-2812614. Contact: Editors of *Stand Magazine*. "This competition is an open international contest for unpublished writing in the English language intended to foster a wider interest in the short story as a literary form and to promote and encourage excellent writing in it." Deadline: March 31. Please note that intending entrants enquiring from outside the U.K. should send International Reply Coupons, not stamps from their own countries. In lieu of an entry fee we ask for a minimum donation of £3 or $6 U.S. per story entered. Editorial inquiries should be made with SAE to: Professor Jack Kingsbury, Box 1161, Florence AL 35631-1161.

STANLEY DRAMA AWARD, Wagner College, Staten Island NY 10301. (212)390-3256. Unpublished and nonprofessionally produced full-length plays, musicals or related one-acts by American playwrights. Submissions must be accompanied by completed application and written recommendation by theatre professional or drama teacher. Deadline: Sept. 1.

THE AGNES LYNCH STARRETT POETRY PRIZE, University of Pittsburgh Press, 127 N. Bellefield Ave., Pittsburgh PA 15260. (412)624-4110. First book of poetry for poets who have not had a full-length book published. Deadline: March and April only. Write for complete guidelines for manuscript submission.

THE WALKER STONE AWARDS, The Scripps Howard Foundation, Box 5380, Cincinnati OH 45201. (513)977-3036. Editorial writing for newspaper men and women.

‡STUDENT GRANT-IN-AID, American Translators Association, 109 Croton Ave., Ossining NY 10562. (914)941-1500. Contact: Chair, Honors & Awards Committee. Support is granted for a promising project to an unpublished student enrolled in a translation program at a U.S. college or university. Deadline: Feb. 28.

Open to any student enrolled in a translation program at a U.S. college or university. Must be sponsored by a faculty member.

SYDNEY TAYLOR BOOK AWARDS, % National Federation for Jewish Culture, 330 7th Ave., 21st Floor, New York NY 10001. (201)744-3836. Director: Aileen Grossberg. Previously published children's books, submitted by publisher. Deadline: Jan. 10.

MARVIN TAYLOR PLAYWRITING AWARD, Sierra Repertory Theatre, Box 3030, Sonora CA 95370. (209)532-3120. Producing Director: Dennis C. Jones. Full-length plays. Deadline: May 15.

THE TEN BEST "CENSORED" STORIES OF 1989, Project Censored—Sonoma State University, Rohnert Park CA 94928. (707)664-2149. Award Director: Carl Jensen, Ph.D. Current published, nonfiction stories of national social significance that have been overlooked or under-reported by the news media. Deadline: March 1990.

TEXAS BLUEBONNET AWARD, Texas Association of School Libraries and Children's Round Table, Suite 603, 3355 Bee Cave Rd., Austin TX 78746. (512)328-1518. Contact: Patricia Smith. Published books for children recommended by librarians, teachers and students.

THE THEATRE LIBRARY ASSOCIATION AWARD, 111 Amsterdam Ave., New York NY 10023. Awards Committee Chair: James Poteat, Museum of Broadcasting, Research Services, 810 7th Ave., New York NY 10019. (212)977-2210. Book published in the United States in the field of recorded performance, including motion pictures and television. Deadline: Feb. 1.

TOWSON STATE UNIVERSITY PRIZE FOR LITERATURE, College of Liberal Arts, Towson State University, Towson MD 21204. (301)321-2128. Award Director: Dean Annette Chappell. Book or book-length manuscript that has been accepted for publication, written by a Maryland author of no more than 40 years of age. Deadline: May 15.

THE TRANSLATION CENTER AWARDS, The Translation Center, 412 Dodge, Columbia University, New York NY 10027. (212)854-2305. Executive Director: Diane G.H. Cook. Awards are grants to a translator for an outstanding translation of a substantial part of a book length literary work.

HARRY S. TRUMAN BOOK PRIZE, Harry S. Truman Library Institute, Independence MO 64050. Secretary of the Institute: Dr. Benedict K. Zobrist. Previously published book written between January 1, 1988, and December 31, 1989, dealing primarily with the history of the United States between April 12, 1945 and January 20, 1953, or with the public career of Harry S. Truman. Deadline: Jan. 20.

UCROSS FOUNDATION RESIDENCY, Ucross Rt., Box 19, Ucross WY 82835. (307)737-2291. Contact: Ron Wray. Four concurrent positions open for artists-in-residence in various disciplines extending from 2 weeks-4 months. No charge for room, board or studio space. Deadline: March 1 for August-December program; Oct. 1 for January-May program.

UFO RESEARCH AWARD, Fund for UFO Research, Box 277, Mt. Rainier MD 20712. (703)684-6032. Contact: Executive Committee, Fund for UFO Research. Unscheduled cash awards for published works on UFO phenomena research or public education.

UNDERGRADUATE PAPER COMPETITION IN CRYPTOLOGY, *Cryptologia*, Rose-Hulman Institute of Technology, Terre Haute IN 47803. Contact: Editor. Unpublished papers on cryptology. Deadline: Jan. 1.

DANIEL VAROUJAN AWARD, New England Poetry Club, Erika Mumford Award and Norma Farber Prize, 2 Farrar St., Cambridge MA 02138. Unpublished poems in duplicate. Deadline: June 30. Charges $2 per poem; no charge for New England Poetry Club members.

‡VERBATIM ESSAY COMPETITION, Verbatim, *The Language Quarterly*, 4 Laurel Heights, Old Lyme CT 06371. (203)434-2104. Award Director: Laurence Urdang. Unpublished articles on any topic pertaining to language, not exceeding 2,000 words. Deadline: varies. Send SASE for current information.

CELIA B. WAGNER AWARD, Poetry Society of America, 15 Gramercy Park St. S., New York NY 10003. (212)254-9628. Contact: Award Director. Unpublished poem. "Poem worthy of the tradition of the art in any style." Deadline: Dec. 31. Charges $5 fee.

EDWARD LEWIS WALLANT BOOK AWARD, Mrs. Irving Waltman, 3 Brighton Rd., West Hartford CT 06117. Published fiction with significance for the American Jew (novel or short stories) by an American writer. Book must have been published during current year. Deadline: Dec. 31.

‡**THEODORE WARD PRIZE FOR PLAYWRITING,** Columbia College Theater/Music Center, 72 E 11th St., Chicago IL 60605. Contact: Chuck Smith. To uncover and identify new unpublished African American plays that are promising and produceable." Deadline: July 1. All rights for music or biographies must be secured prior to submission. All entrants must be of African American descent and residing within the US. Only one completed script per playwright will be accepted.

‡**WAREHOUSE THEATRE ONE-ACT COMPETITION,** Warehouse Theatre Company, Stephens College, Columbia MO 65215. (314)876-7194. Contact: Elizabeth Pendergrass-Rainey. Offered annually. Submissions to be unpublished. Deadline: Nov. 4. Varies according to school year. Charges $7.50.

‡**WASHINGTON PRIZE FOR FICTION,** Larry Kaltman Literary Agency, 1301 S. Scott St., Arlington VA 22204. (703)920-3771. Contact: Larry Kaltman. Fiction, previously unpublished, of at least 75,000 words. Deadline: Nov. 30. Charges $25 fee.

ARNOLD WEISSBERGER PLAYWRITING AWARD, New Dramatists, 424 West 44th St., New York NY 10036. (212)757-6960. Contest/Award Director: Kirk Aanes. Unpublished plays; no musicals or children's plays. Deadline: Feb. 1.

WEST COAST ENSEMBLE FULL PLAY COMPETITION, CELEBRATION OF ONE-ACTS, West Coast Ensemble, Box 38728, Los Angeles CA 90038. Artistic Director: Les Hanson. Unpublished (in Southern California) plays. No musicals or children's plays for full-play competition. No restrictions on subject matter for one-acts. Deadline: Oct. 15; Nov.1 for one-act play.

WESTERN STATES BOOK AWARDS, Western States Arts Federation, 236 Montezuma, Santa Fe NM 87501. (505)988-1166. Director of Special Projects: Cheryl Alters Jamison. Unpublished fiction, poetry or creative nonfiction, that has been accepted for publication in the award year, by a press in a Western States Arts Federation member state. Deadline: spring of the year preceding the award year. Open to authors in Alaska, Arizona, California, Colorado, Hawaii, Idaho, Montana, Nevada, New Mexico, Oregon, Utah, Washington, and Wyoming. Manuscript duplication and return postage fee of $10.

‡**WHITING WRITERS' AWARDS,** Mrs. Giles Whiting Foundation, Rm. 3500, 30 Rockefeller Plaza, New York NY 10112. Director: Gerald Freund. Direct applications and informal nominations are not accepted by the Foundation.

‡**WHITNEY-CARNEGIE AWARD,** American Library Association Publishing Services, 40 E. Huron, Chicago IL 60611. (312)944-6780. Contact: Edgar S. McLarin. Submissions to be unpublished. "The grants are awarded to individuals for the preparation of bibliographic aids for research. The aids must be aimed at a scholarly audience but have a general applicability. Products prepared under this project must be offered to ALA Publishing Services for first consideration." Deadline: Feb. 28.

WICHITA STATE UNIVERSITY PLAYWRITING CONTEST, Wichita State University Theatre, WSU, Box 31, Wichita KS 67208. (316)689-3185. Contest Director: Professor Bela Kiralyfalvi. Two or three short, unpublished, unproduced plays or full-length plays by graduate or undergraduate U.S. college students. Deadline: Feb. 15.

LAURA INGALLS WILDER AWARD, Association for Library Service to Children/American Library Association, 50 E. Huron St., Chicago IL 60611. (312)944-6780. Contact: Award Director. Awarded every three years to an author or illustrator whose books, published in the United States,have over a period of years made a substantial and lasting contribution to literature for children.

BELL I. WILEY PRIZE, National Historical Society, 2245 Kohn Rd., Box 8200, Harrisburg PA 17105. (717)657-9555. Civil War and Reconstruction nonfiction (book). Biennial award. Deadline: July 31.

WILLIAM CARLOS WILLIAMS AWARD, Poetry Society of America, 15 Gramercy Park S., New York NY 10003. (212)254-9628. Contact: Award Director. Deadline: Dec. 31. Small press, nonprofit, or university press book of poetry submitted by publisher.

‡**H.W. WILSON LIBRARY PERIODICAL AWARD,** donated by H.W. Wilson Company, administered by the American Library Association, 50 E. Huron, Chicago IL 60611. (312)944-6780. Periodical published by a local, state or regional library, library group, or association in U.S. or Canada.

J. J. WINSHIP BOOK AWARD, *The Boston Globe*, 135 Morissey Blvd., Boston MA 02107. (617)929-2649. New England-related book. Deadline: June 30.

‡WISCONSIN ARTS BOARD FELLOWSHIP PROGRAM, 131 W. Wilson St., #301, Madison WI 53702. (608)266-0190. Contact: Grants Coordinator. Literary fellowship for Wisconsin writers in the categories of poetry, drama, fiction and essay/criticism. Deadline: Sept. 15.

WITTER BYNNER FOUNDATION FOR POETRY, INC. GRANTS, Box 2188, Santa Fe NM 87504. (505)988-3251. Executive Director: Steven D. Schwartz. Grants for poetry and poetry-related projects. Deadline: Feb. 1.

‡WOODBINE HOUSE AWARD, #512, 10400 Connecticut Ave., Kensington MD 20895. (301)949-3590. Editor: Susan Stokes. Unpublished nonfiction. Deadline: Sept. 1.

WORLD FANTASY AWARDS, Box 4236, W. Columbia SC 29171. Contest/Award Director: Peter Dennis Pautz. Previously published work recommended by previous convention attendees in several categories, including life achievement, novel, novella, short story, anthology, collection, artist, special award-pro and special award non-pro. Deadline: July 1. Works are recommended by attendees of previous two years' conventions.

‡WORLD HUNGER MEDIA AWARDS, World Hunger Year, #1402, 261 W. 35th St., New York NY 10001. (212)629-8850. Director: Bill Ayres. Critical issues of domestic and world hunger (newspaper, periodical, TV, radio, photojournalism, books). Deadline: Jan. 31.

WRITER'S BIENNIAL, Missouri Arts Council. Suite 105, 111 N. 7th St., St. Louis MO 63101. (314)444-6845. Contest/Award Director: Teresa Goettsch Wingert. Unpublished prose essays and poetry by Missouri writers. "All entrants must have lived in Missouri for two years at the time of the entry and cannot be a student in a degree-granting program." Send a SASE for complete competition guidelines. Deadline: August.

‡*WRITERS DIGEST* WRITING COMPETITION, *Writer's Digest Magazine*, 1507 Dana Ave., Cincinnati OH 45207. (513)531-2222. Contest Director: Bill Strickland. Submissions to be unpublished. Deadline: May 31.

WRITERS GUILD OF AMERICA WEST AWARDS, Writers Guild of America West, 8955 Beverly Blvd., Los Angeles CA 90048. Scripts (screen, TV and radio). Members only. Deadline: September.

WRITERS' JOURNAL ANNUAL FICTION CONTEST, Minnesota Ink, Inc. Box 9148 N, St. Paul MN 55109. (612)433-3626. Contact: Valerie Hockert. Previously unpublished fiction. Deadline: March 15. Charges $5 per entry.

WRITERS' JOURNAL SEMI-ANNUAL POETRY CONTEST, Minnesota Ink, Inc., Box 9148 N, St. Paul MN 55109. (612)433-3626. Contact: Esther M. Leiper. Previously unpublished poetry. Deadline: Nov. 30 & April 15. Charges fee: $2 first poem; $1 each thereafter.

‡WRITERS OF THE FUTURE CONTEST, L. Ron Hubbard, Box 1630, Los Angeles CA 90078. (213)466-3310. Award Director: Fred Harris of Author Services, Inc. Unpublished science fiction and fantasy.

‡WYOMING COUNCIL ON THE ARTS LITERARY FELLOWHIPS, Wyoming Council on the Arts, 2320 Capitol Ave. Cheyenne WY 82002. (307)777-7742. Literature Consultant: Jean Hanson. Fellowships to honor the most outstanding previously published or unpublished new work of Wyoming writers (all creative writing, fiction, non-fiction, drama, poetry). Aug. 15 for 89-90. Has changed according to WCA schedule. Writers may call WCA offices; guidelines are also printed in WCA Literature Newsletter, a free monthly publication. Applicants must have been Wyoming residents for one year prior to entry deadline; and may not be full-time students.

‡XANADU: A LITERARY JOURNAL'S ANNUAL POETRY CONTEST, The Long Island Poetry Collective, Box 773, Huntington NY 11743. Contact: Editors. Submissions to be unpublished. Deadline: Sept. 1. Charges $3 for up to 10 poems. Manuscripts will not be returned. Send SASE for list of winners.

PETER ZENGER AWARD, Brooklyn Writers' Network, 2509 Avenue K, Brooklyn NY 11210. (718)377-4945. Contact: Ruth Schwartz. Previously published work by author/journalist "who best furthers the cause of freedom of the press." Deadline: May 31.

‡ANNA ZOINEO MEMORIAL THEATRE FOR YOUTH PLAYWRITING AWARD, U of NH Youth Drama Program /TRY, Paul Creative Arts, Durbam NH 03824. (603)862-2150. Contact: Carol Lucha-Burns/Susan Golden. To bring quality unpublished plays & musicals (45 minutes-1 hour in length) to young audiences. Deadline: September. Production is planned—usually Sept. 1.

Other Contests

The following contest sponsors did not return a verification to update an existing listing by press time.

AAAS-Westinghouse Science Journalism Awards
Alberta Non-fiction Award
American Association of University Women Award
Annual Fiction and Poetry Contest (Rambunctious Press)
Association for Education in Journalism Awards
Baltic American Freedom League Article Award
Black Warrior Review Literary Awards
Boston Globe Literary Press Competition
Brittingham Prize in Poetry
Arnold and Dorothy Burger Playwriting Competition
Commonwealth of Pennsylvania Council on the Arts Literature Fellowships
Connecticut Writers League, Inc., Annual Writing Awards
Bernard F. Conners Prize for Poetry
Creative Artists Grant
De La Torre Bueno Prize
David James Ellis Memorial Award
Fellowships for Translators/ Creative Writers

Festival of Firsts
Firman Houghton Award
Don Freeman Memorial Grant-in-Aid
French-American Foundation Translation Prize
Golden Heart/Golden Medallion
Governor General's Literary Award: Children's Literature
Guideposts Magazine Youth Writing Contest
Drue Heinz Literature Prize
Honolulu Magazine Fiction Contest
Illinois State University Fine Arts Playwriting Award
Jamestown Prize
Juniper Prize
Kansas Quarterly/Kansas Arts Commission Awards, Seaton Awards
Aga Khan Prize for Fiction
Marc A. Klein Playwriting Award for Students
D.H. Lawrence Fellowship
John H. McGinnis Memorial Award
Kenneth W. Midenberger Prize
Morse Poetry Prize
MS Public Education Awards Contest

National Play Award
National Psychology Awards for Excellence in the Media
Allen Nevins Prize
New World Theater New Play Competition
New York State Historical Association Manuscript Award
Newcomen Awards in Business History
NMMA Directors Award
Alicia Patterson Foundation Fellowship Program for Journalists
Prix Alvine-Belisle
Science Award
Science-Writing Award in Physics and Astronomy
Senior Fellowships for Literature
Society for Technical Communication Technical Publications
Elizabeth Matchett Stover Memorial Award
Sydney Taylor Manuscript Contest of AJL
Towngate Theatre Playwriting Contest
John Train Humor Prize
Virginia Prize for Literature
Work-in-Progress Grant

The following listings were deleted after the 1989 edition because the sponsor discontinued the contest, asked for the listing to be deleted, or was unable to be contacted for information.

Ruby Lloyd Apsey Playwriting Award (inactive for year)
Charlotte Repertory Theatre New Script Competition (discontinued)
FS Drama Award (inactive for year)
Giralt Publishers (asked to be deleted)

Governor General's Literary Award: Translation (asked to be deleted)
National Awards Program (unable to contact)
New Play Festival (asked to be deleted)
Oktoberfest Short Fiction Competition (discontinued)

PEN/Nelson Algren Fiction Award (discontinued)
Princeton Series of Contemporary Poets (not accepting unsolicited submissions)
Sydney Taylor Children's Book Awards (unable to contact)
Texas Literary Awards (unable to contact)

Glossary

Key to symbols and abbreviations is on page 5.

Advance. A sum of money that a publisher pays a writer prior to the publication of a book. The advance is paid against the royalty money that will be earned by the book.

Advertorial. Advertising presented in such a way as to resemble editorial material. Information may be the same as that contained in an editorial feature, but it is paid for or supplied by an advertiser and the word "advertisement" appears at the top of the page.

All rights. See Rights and the Writer in the Business of Writing article.

Anthology. A collection of selected writings by various authors or works by one author.

Assignment. Editor asks a writer to do a specific article for a certain price to be paid upon completion.

Auction. Publishers sometimes bid for the acquisition of a book manuscript that has excellent sales prospects. The bids are for the amount of the author's advance, guaranteed dollar amounts, advertising and promotional expenses, royalty percentage, etc.

B&W. Abbreviation for black and white photographs.

Backlist. A publisher's list of its books that were not published during the current season, but which are still in print.

Belles lettres. A term used to describe fine or literary writing—writing more to entertain than to inform or instruct.

Bimonthly. Every two months. See also *semimonthly*. (Note: Some publications indicated bimonthly when they are published twice a month.)

Bionote. A sentence or brief paragraph about the writer. Also called a "bio," it can appear at the bottom of the first or last page of a writer's article or short story or on a contributor's page.

Biweekly. Every two weeks.

Boilerplate. A standardized contract. When an editor says "our standard contract," he means the boilerplate with no changes. Writers should be aware that most authors and/or agents make many changes on the boilerplate.

Book auction. Selling the rights (i.e. paperback, movie, etc.) of a book to the highest bidder. A publisher or agent may initiate the auction.

Book packager. Draws all elements of a book together, from the initial concept to writing and marketing strategies, then sells the book package to a book publisher and/or movie producer. Also known as book producer or book developer.

Business size envelope. Also known as a #10 envelope, it is the standard size used in sending business correspondence.

Byline. Name of the author appearing with the published piece.

Caption. Originally a title or headline over a picture, but now a description of the subject matter of a photograph; includes names of people where appropriate. Also called cutline.

Category fiction. A term used to include labels attached to types of fiction. See also *genre*.

Chapbook. A small booklet, usually paperback, of poetry, ballads or tales.

Clean copy. Free of errors, cross-outs, wrinkles or smudges.

Clippings. News items of possible interest to trade magazine editors.

Clips. Samples, usually from newspapers or magazines, of your *published* work.

Coffee table book. An oversize book, heavily illustrated, suitable for display on a coffee table.

Column inch. All the type contained in one inch of a typeset column.

Commercial novels. Novels designed to appeal to a broad audience. These are often broken down into categories such as western, mystery and romance. See also *genre*.

Commissioned work. See *assignment*.

Compatible. The condition which allows one type of computer/word processor to share information or communicate with another type of machine.

Concept. A statement that summarizes a screenplay or teleplay—before the outline or treatment is written.

Contributor's copies. Copies of the issues of magazines sent to the author in which the his/her work appears.

Co-publishing. An arrangement in which author and publisher share the publication costs and profits of a book. See also *subsidy publisher*.

Copyediting. Editing a manuscript for grammar, punctuation and printing style, not subject content.

Copyright. A means to protect an author's work. See Copyrighting Your Writing in the Business of Writing article.)

Cover letter. A brief letter, accompanying a complete manuscript, especially useful if responding to an editor's request for a manuscript. A cover letter may also accompany a book proposal. (A cover letter is *not* a query letter; see Approaching Markets in the Business of Writing article.

Cutline. See *caption*.

Derivative works. A work that has been translated, adapted, abridged, condensed, annotated or otherwise produced by altering a previously created work. Before producing a derivative work, it is necessary to secure the written permission of the author or copyright owner of the original piece.

Desktop publishing. A publishing system designed for a personal computer. The system is capable of typesetting, some illustration, layout, design and printing—so that the final piece can be distributed and/or sold.

Disk. A round, flat magnetic plate on which computer data may be stored.

Docudrama. A fictional film rendition of recent newsmaking events and people.

Dot-matrix. Printed type where characters are composed of a matrix or pattern of tiny dots.

El-hi. Elementary to high school.

Epigram. A short, witty sometimes paradoxical saying.

Erotica. Usually fiction that is sexually-oriented, although it could be art on the same theme.

ESL. Abbreviation for English as a second language.

Fair use. A provision of the copyright law that says short passages from copyrighted material may be used without infringing on the owner's rights.

Fanzine. A noncommercial, small circulation magazine dealing with fantasy or science fiction literature and art.

FAX. A communication system used to transmit documents over telephone lines.

Feature. An article giving the reader information of human interest rather than news. Also used by magazines to indicate a lead article or distinctive department.

Filler. A short item used by an editor to "fill" out a newspaper column or magazine page. It could be a timeless news item, a joke, an anecdote, some light verse or short humor, puzzle, etc.

First chapter novel. A book for children that is roughly the size of an adult novel's first chapter.

First North American serial rights. See Rights and the Writer in the Business of Writing article.

Formula story. Familiar theme treated in a predictable plot structure—such as boy meets girl, boy loses girl, boy gets girl.

Galleys. The first typeset version of a manuscript that has not yet been divided into pages.

Genre. Refers either to a general classification of writing, such as the novel or the poem, or to the categories within those classifications. (Also called category fiction.)

Ghostwriter. A writer who puts into literary form an article, speech, story or book based on another person's ideas or knowledge.

Glossy. A black and white photograph with a shiny surface as opposed to one with a non-shiny matte finish.

Gothic novel. A fiction category or genre in which the central character is usually a beautiful young girl, the setting an old mansion or castle, and there is a handsome hero and a real menace, either natural or supernatural.

Graphic novel. A term to describe an adaptation of a novel in graphic form, long comic strip or heavily illustrated story, of 40 pages or more, produced in paperback form.

Hard copy. The printed copy of a computer's output.

Hardware. All the mechanically-integrated components of a computer that are not software. Circuit boards, transistors and the machines that are the actual computer are the hardware.

Honorarium. Token payment—small amount of money, or a byline and copies of the publication.

Illustrations. May be photographs, old engravings, artwork. Usually paid for separately from the manuscript. See also *package sale*.

Imprint. Name applied to a publisher's specific line or lines of books (e.g., Delacorte Press is an imprint of Dell Publishing).

Interactive fiction. Works of fiction in book or computer software format in which the reader determines the path the story will take. The reader chooses from several alternatives at the end of a "chapter," and thus determines the structure of the story.

Invasion of privacy. Writing about persons (even though truthfully) without their consent.

Kill fee. Fee for a complete article that was assigned but which was subsequently cancelled.

Letter-quality submission. Computer printout that looks like a typewritten manuscript.

Libel. A false accusation or any published statement or presentation that tends to expose another to public contempt, ridicule, etc. Defenses are truth; fair comment on a matter of public interest; and privileged communication—such as a client's communication to a lawyer.

Little magazine. Publications of limited circulation, usually on literary or political subject matter.

LORT. An acronym for League of Resident Theatres. Letters from A to D follow LORT and designate the size of the theater.

Mainstream fiction. Fiction that transcends popular novel categories such as mystery, romance and science fiction. Using conventional methods, this kind of fiction tells stories about people and their conflicts with greater depth than the more narrowly focused genre novels.

Mass market. Nonspecialized books of wide appeal directed toward an extremely large audience.

Microcomputer. A small computer system capable of performing various specific tasks with data it receives. Personal computers are microcomputers.

Midlist. Those titles on a publisher's list that are not expected to be big sellers, but are expected to have limited sales.

Model release. A paper signed by the subject of a photograph (or the subject's guardian, if a juvenile) giving the photographer permission to use the photograph, editorially or for advertising purposes or for some specific purpose as stated.

Modem. A small electrical box that plugs into the serial card of a computer, used to transmit data from one computer to another, usually via telephone lines.

Monograph. Thoroughly detailed and documented scholarly study concerning a singular subject.

MOW. Movie of the week.

Multiple submissions. Sending more than one poem, gag or greeting card idea at the same time. This term is often used synonymously with simultaneous submission.

Mystery Writers of America. Room 600, 236 W. 27 St., New York NY 10001. (212)255-7005. Open to professional writers in mystery and other fields and to students and fans of mystery.

National Writers Union. 13 Astor Place, New York NY 10003. (212)254-0279. Organization for better treatment of freelance writers by publishers. Also negotiates union contracts with publishers, grievance procedures, health insurance and conferences.

Net receipts. A royalty payment based on the amount of money a book publisher receives on the sale of a book after booksellers' discounts, special sales discounts and returned copies.

New age. A generic term for works linked by a common interest in metaphysical, spiritual, holistic and other alternative approaches to living. It embraces astrology, psychic phenomena, spiritual healing, UFOs, mysticism — anything that deals with reality beyond everyday material perception.

Newsbreak. A brief, late-breaking news story added to the front page of a newspaper at press time or a magazine news item of importance to readers.

NLQ. Near letter-quality print required by some editors for computer printout submissions.

Novelette. A short novel, or a long short story; 7,000 to 15,000 words approximately. Also known as a novella.

Novelization. A novel created from the script of a popular movie, usually called movie "tie-ins" and published in paperback.

Offprint. Copies of an author's article taken "out of issue" before a magazine is bound and given to the author in lieu of monetary payment. An offprint could be used by the writer as a published writing sample.

On spec. An editors expresses an interest in a proposed article idea and agrees to consider the finished piece for publication "on speculation." The editor is under no obligation to buy the finished manuscript.

One-time rights. See Rights and the Writer in the Business of Writing article.

Outline. A summary of a book's contents in five to 15 double-spaced pages; often in the form of chapter headings with a descriptive sentence or two under each one to show the scope of the book. A screenplay's or teleplay's outline is a scene-by-scene narrative description of the story (10-15 pages for a ½-hour teleplay; 15-25 pages for a 1-hour teleplay; 25-40 pages for a 90-minute teleplay; 40-60 pages for a 2-hour feature film or teleplay).

Over-the-transom. Unsolicited material submitted by a freelance writer.

Package sale. The editor buys manuscript and photos as a "package" and pays for them with one check.

Page rate. Some magazines pay for material at a fixed rate per published page, rather than per word.

Payment on acceptance. The editor sends you a check for your article, story or poem as soon as he reads it and decides to publish it.

Payment on publication. The editor doesn't send you a check for your material until it is published.

Pen name. The use of a name other than your legal name on articles, stories or books when you wish to remain anonymous. Simply notify your post office and bank that you are using the name so that you'll receive mail and/or checks in that name. Also called a pseudonym.

Photo feature. Feature in which the emphasis is on the photographs rather than on accompanying written material.

Photocopied submissions. Submitting *photocopies* of an original manuscript is acceptable to some editors instead of the author sending the original manuscript. Do not assume that an editor who accepts photocopies will also accept multiple or simultaneous submissions.

Plagiarism. Passing off as one's own the expression of ideas and words of another writer.

Potboiler. Refers to writing projects a freelance writer does to "keep the pot boiling" while working on major articles — quick projects to bring in money with little time or effort. These may be fillers such as anecdotes or how-to tips, but could be short articles or stories.

Proofreading. Close reading and correction of a manuscript's typographical errors.

Pseudonym. See *pen name*.

Public domain. Material which was either never copyrighted or whose copyright term has run out.

Publication not copyrighted. Publication of an author's work in such a periodical places it in the public domain and it cannot subsequently be copyrighted. See Copyrighting Your Writing in the Business of Writing article.

Query. A letter to an editor aimed to get his/her interest in an article you purpose to write.

Rebus. Stories, quips, puzzles, etc., in juvenile magazines that convey words or syllables with pictures, objects or symbols whose names resemble the sounds of intended words.

Realia. Activities that relate classroom study to real life.

Release. A statement that your idea is original, has never been sold to anyone else and that you are selling the negotiated rights to the idea upon payment.

Remainders. Copies of a book that are slow to sell and can be purchased from the publisher at a reduced price. Depending on the author's book contract, a reduced royalty or no royalty is paid on remainder books.

Reporting time. The time it takes for an editor to report to the author on his/her query or manuscript.

Reprint rights. See Rights and the Writer in the Business of Writing article.

Round-up article. Comments from, or interviews with, a number of celebrities or experts on a single theme.

Royalties, standard hardcover book. 10% of the retail price on the first 5,000 copies sold; 12½% on the next 5,000; 15% thereafter.

Royalties, standard mass paperback book. 4 to 8% of the retail price on the first 150,000 copies sold.

Royalties, trade paperback book. No less than 6% of list price on the first 20,000 copies; 7½% thereafter.

Science Fiction Writers of America, SFWA. Box 4236, West Columbia SC 29171. An organization of professional writers, editors, agents, artists and others in the science fiction and fantasy field.

Screenplay. Script for a film intended to be shown in theaters.

Self-publishing. In this arrangement, the author keeps all income derived from the book, but he pays for its manufacturing, production and marketing.

Semimonthly. Twice a month.

Semiweekly. Twice a week.

Serial. Published periodically, such as a newspaper or magazine.

Sidebar. A feature presented as a companion to a straight news report (or main magazine article) giving sidelights on human-interest aspects or sometimes elucidating just one aspect of the story.

Simultaneous submissions. Sending the same article, story or poem to several publishers at the same time. Some publishers refuse to consider such submissions. No simultaneous submissions should be made without stating the fact in your letter.

Slant. The approach or style of a story or article that will appeal to readers of a specific magazine.

Slides. Usually called transparencies by editors looking for color photographs.

Slush pile. The stack of unsolicited manuscripts received by an editor or book publisher.

Software. Programs and related documentation for use with a particular computer system.

Speculation. See "On Spec."

Style. The way something is written—for example, short, punchy sentences or flowing narrative.

Subsidiary rights. All those rights, other than book publishing rights included in a book contract—such as paperback, book club, movie rights, etc.

Subsidy publisher. A book publisher who charges the author for the cost to typeset and print his book, the jacket, etc. as opposed to a royalty publisher who pays the author.

Syndication rights. See Rights and the Writer in the Business of Writing article.

Synopsis. A brief summary of a story, novel or play. As part of a book proposal, it is a comprehensive summary condensed in a page or page and a half, single-spaced. See also *outline*.

Tabloid. Newspaper format publication on about half the size of the regular newspaper page, such as the *National Enquirer*.

Tagline. A caption for a photo or a comment added to a filler.

Tearsheet. Page from a magazine or newspaper containing your printed story, article, poem or ad.

Trade. Either a hardcover or paperback book; subject matter frequently concerns a special interest. Books are directed toward the layperson rather than the professional.

Transparencies. Positive color slides; not color prints.

Treatment. Synopsis of a television or film script (40-60 pages for a 2-hour feature film or teleplay).

Unsolicited manuscript. A story, article, or book that an editor did not specifically ask to see.

User friendly. Easy to handle and use. Refers to computer hardware and software designed with the user in mind.

Vanity publisher See *subsidy publisher*.

Word processor. A computer that produces typewritten copy via automated typing, text-editing and storage and transmission capabilities.

Work-for-hire. See Copyrighting Your Writing in the Business of Writing article.

YA. Young adult books.

For hundreds of additional definitions and other information of importance to writers, see the *Writer's Encyclopedia* (Writer's Digest Books).

Book Publishers Subject Index

Nonfiction

This index will help you find publishers that consider books on specific subjects—the subjects you choose to write about. Remember that a publisher may be listed here under a general subject category like Art and Architecture, while the company publishes *only* art history or how-to books. Be sure to consult each company's detailed individual listing, its book catalog and several of its books before you send your query or manuscript.

Agriculture/Horticulture. Between the Lines Inc.; Countrywoman's Press, The; Gordon and Breach; Gower Publishing Co.; Interstate Publishers, Inc. The; Lyons & Burford, Publishers, Inc.; Michigan State University Press; S.C.E.-Editions L'Etincelle; Science Tech Publishers, Inc.; Scojtia Publishing Co., Inc.; Stipes Publishing Co.; Stormline Press; Texas A&M University Press; University of Minnesota Press; Woodbridge Press.

Americana. American Studies Press, Inc.; Ancestry Incorporated; Arbor House; Atheneum Children's Books; Bantam Books; Bear Flag Books; Blair, Publisher, John F.; Bragdon Publishers, Inc., Allen D.; Branden Publishing Co., Inc..; Camden House, Inc.; Carol Publishing; Caxton Printers, Ltd., The; Cherokee Publishing Company; Christopher Publishing House, The; Clarion Books; Clark Co., Arthur H.; Countrywoman's Press, The; Creative Publishing Co.; Crown Publishers, Inc.; Devin-Adair Publishers, Inc.; Down East Books; Eakin Publications, Inc.; Eriksson, Publisher, Paul S.; Faber & Faber, Inc.; Four Winds Press; Gaslight Publications; Glenbridge Publishing Ltd.; Godine, Publisher, David R.; Hancock House Publishers Ltd.; Harper & Row Publishers, Inc.; Heyday Books; Holmes & Meier Publishers, Inc.; International Publishers Co., Inc.; International Resources; Interurban Press/Trans Anglo Books; Lexikos; Library Research Associates, Inc.; Lyons & Burford, Publishers, Inc.; McFarland & Company, Inc., Publishers; Madison Books; Main Street Press, The; Media Productions and Marketing, Inc.; Middle Atlantic Press; Miller Books; Monitor Book Co.; Mosaic Press Miniature Books; Mott Media, Inc., Publishers; Mountain Press Publishing Company; Mustang Publishing Co.; New England Press, Inc., The; Oregon Historical Society Press; Outbooks; Overlook Press; Pacific Books, Publishers; Paragon House Publishers; Pelican Publishing Company; Peter Pauper Press, Inc.; Pickering Press, The; Pomegranate Press, Ltd.; Potomac-Pacific Press; Purdue University Press; Renaissance House Publishers; Schiffer Publishing Ltd.; Scribner's Sons, Charles; Second Chance Press/Permanent Press; Seven Locks Press, Inc.; Shoe Tree Press; Sierra Club Books; Silver Burdett Press; Smith, Publisher, Gibbs; Stemmer House Publishers, Inc.; Sterling Publishing; Stevens, Inc., Gareth; Stormline Press; Tapley, Publisher, Inc., Lance; Texas Christian University Press; Transaction Books; University of Arizona Press; University of Illinois Press; University of Minnesota Press; University of Oklahoma Press; University of Pennsylvania Press; University Press of Kentucky; University Press of Mississippi; University Press of Virginia; Utah State University Press; Vesta Publications, Ltd.; Washington State University Press; Westernlore Press; Wilderness Adventure Books; Windriver Publishing Company; Winston-Derek Publishers, Inc.; Woodbine House; Workman Publishing Company, Inc.

Animals. Alpine Publications Inc.; Atheneum Children's Books; Barron's Educational Series, Inc.; Bear Flag Books; Bergh Publishing, Inc.; Canadian Plains Research Center; Carol Publishing; Carolina Biological Supply Co.; Carolrhoda Books, Inc.; Crown Publishers, Inc.; Denlingers Publishers, Ltd.; Dillon Press, Inc.; Dutton Children's Books; Eriksson, Publisher, Paul S.; Faber & Faber, Inc.; Flora And Fauna Publications; Four Winds Press; Greenhaven Press, Inc.; Harper & Row Publishers, Inc.; Homestead Publishing; International Resources; Kesend Publishing, Ltd., Michael; Lyons & Burford, Publishers, Inc.; Miller Books; Mosaic Press Miniature Books; Outbooks; Pineapple Press, Inc.; Pippin Press; Plexus Publishing, Inc.; Random House, Inc./Alfred A. Knopf, Inc. Juvenile Books; Rocky Top Publications; S.C.E.-Editions L'Etincelle; S.O.C.O. Publications; Shoe Tree Press; Southfarm Press; Stemmer House Publishers, Inc.; Stormline Press;

ARE YOU SERIOUS?

About learning to write better? Getting published? Getting paid for what you write?

If you're dedicated to your writing, **Writer's Digest School** can put you on the fast track to writing success.

Study With A Professional

When you enroll in a **Writer's Digest School** course, you get more than writing textbooks and assignments. You get a one-on-one relationship with a professional writer who is currently writing *and selling* the kind of material you're interested in. Your training as a writer is built around this personal guidance from an experienced pro who knows what it takes to succeed in the competitive literary marketplace.

Four Courses Available

Writer's Digest School offers four courses: Writing to Sell Nonfiction (Articles), Writing to Sell Fiction (Short Stories), Elements of Effective Writing, and a Novel-Writing Workshop. Each course is described in more detail on the reverse side.

We've Been Teaching Creative People Since 1920

Writer's Digest School was founded over 60 years ago by the same people who publish **Writer's Digest,** the world's leading magazine for writers, and **Writer's Market,** the indispensable annual reference directory for writers. When you enroll in a **Writer's Digest School** course, you get the quality and expertise that are the hallmarks of the **Writer's Digest** name.

If you're serious about your writing, you owe it to yourself to check out **Writer's Digest School.** Mail the coupon below today for *free* information!

Yes, I'm Serious!

I want to learn to write and sell from the professionals at **Writer's Digest School.** Send me free information about the course I've checked below:

☐ Writing to Sell Nonfiction (Articles)

☐ Writing to Sell Fiction (Short Stories)

☐ Novel-Writing Workshop

☐ Elements of Effective Writing

NAME

ADDRESS

CITY STATE ZIP

(   )

Area Code   Phone Number

Mail this card today! No postage needed   WM00

Writer's Digest School has been teaching people like you to write for more than 60 years.

Writer's Digest School

1507 Dana Avenue
Cincinnati, Ohio 45207

Four **Writer's Digest School** courses to help you write better and sell more:

- **Writing to Sell Nonfiction.** Master the fundamentals of writing/selling nonfiction articles: finding article ideas, conducting interviews, writing effective query letters and attention-getting leads, targeting your articles to the right publication, and other important elements of a salable article. Course includes writing assignments and one complete article manuscript (and its revision). Your instructor will critique each assignment and help you adapt your article to a particular magazine.

- **Writing to Sell Fiction.** Learn the basics of writing/selling short stories: plotting, characterization, dialogue, theme, conflict, and other elements of a marketable short story. Course includes writing assignments and one complete short story (and its revision). Your instructor will critique each assignment and give you suggestions for selling your story.

- **Novel-Writing Workshop.** A professional novelist helps you iron out your plot, develop your main characters, write the background for your novel, and complete the opening scene and a summary of your novel's complete story. You'll even identify potential publishers, write a query letter, and get practical advice on the submission process.

- **Elements of Effective Writing.** Refresher course covers the basics of grammar, punctuation and elements of composition. You review the nine parts of speech and their correct usage, and learn to write clearly and effectively. Course includes 12 lessons with a grammar exercise and editing or writing assignment in each lesson.

Mail this card today for **free** information!

NO POSTAGE
NECESSARY
IF MAILED
IN THE
UNITED STATES

BUSINESS REPLY MAIL

FIRST CLASS   PERMIT NO. 17   CINCINNATI, OHIO

POSTAGE WILL BE PAID BY ADDRESSEE

WRITER'S DIGEST SCHOOL
1507 Dana Ave.
Cincinnati OH 45207-9965

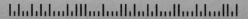

Tab Book, Inc.; Tapley, Publisher, Inc., Lance; Wilderness Adventure Books; Williamson Publishing Co.

Anthropology/Archaelogy. Bantam Books; Bear Flag Books; Blue Dolphin Publishing, Inc.; Gordon and Breach; Horizon Publishers & Distributors; Howell Press, Inc.; International Resources; Kent State University Press; Milkweed Editions; Noyes Data Corp.; Pennsylvania Historical and Museum Commission; Princeton University Press; Routledge, Chapman & Hall, Inc.; Rutgers University Press; Scojtia Publishing Co., Inc.; Stanford University Press; Stevens, Inc., Gareth; Tapley, Publisher, Inc., Lance; Thomas, Publisher, Charles C.; University of Alabama Press; University of Arizona Press; University of Iowa Press; University of Michigan Press; University of Nevada Press; University of Pennsylvania Press; University of Tennessee Press, The; University of Texas Press; University of Utah Press; University Press of Kentucky; Westernlore Press; Wilderness Adventure Books.

Art/Architecture. ABC-CLIO, Inc.; Apollo Books; Arbor House; Atheneum Children's Books; Barron's Educational Series, Inc.; Branden Publishing Co., Inc..; Caratzas, Publisher, Aristide D.; Carol Publishing; Carolrhoda Books, Inc.; Chelsea Green; Cheribe Publishing Co.; Christopher Publishing House, The; Consultant Press, The; Coteau Books; Crown Publishers, Inc.; Davenport, Publishers, May; Davis Publications, Inc.; Dunburn Press Ltd.; Eriksson, Publisher, Paul S.; Fairleigh Dickinson University Press; Family Album, The; Fitzhenry & Whiteside, Ltd.; Fleet Press Corp.; Forman Publishing; Godine, Publisher, David R.; Gordon and Breach; Gower Publishing Co.; Guernica Editions; Harper & Row Publishers, Inc.; Holmes & Meier Publishers, Inc.; Homestead Publishing; Howell Press, Inc.; Hudson Hill Press, Inc.; International Resources; Intervarsity Press; Iowa State University Press; Kent State University Press; Lang Publishing, Peter; Library Research Associates, Inc.; Loyola University Press; Lyons & Burford, Publishers, Inc.; McFarland & Company, Inc., Publishers; McGraw Hill Ryerson; Main Street Press, The; Mazda Publishers; Meriwether Publishing Ltd.; Milkweed Editions; Morrow and Co., William; Mosaic Press Miniature Books; Museum of Northern Arizona Press; National Book Company; National Gallery of Canada; Nichols Publishing; Nimbus Publishing Limited; North Light; Noyes Data Corp.; Ohio State University Press; Oregon Historical Society Press; Outbooks; PBC International, Inc.; Pennsylvania Historical and Museum Commission; Pickering Press, The; Pomegranate Press, Ltd.; Potter, Inc., Clarkson N.; Prakken Publications, Inc.; Prentice Hall Canada, Inc. ; Prentice Hall Press; Preservation Press, The; Princeton Architectural Press; Princeton University Press; Professional Publications, Inc.; Q.E.D. Press Of Ann Arbor, Inc.; Real Comet Press, The; Rosen Publishing Group, The; Rutgers University Press; Sasquatch Books; Schiffer Publishing Ltd.; Scojtia Publishing Co., Inc.; Shapolsky Publishers; Shoe Tree Press; Simon & Schuster; Smith, Publisher, Gibbs; ST Publications, Inc.; Starrhill Press; Stemmer House Publishers, Inc.; Sterling Publishing; Stevens, Inc., Gareth; Stormline Press; Sunstone Press; Tab Book, Inc.; Tapley, Publisher, Inc., Lance; Texas Monthly Press Inc.; Tuttle Publishing Company, Inc., Charles E.; Umi Research Press; University of Alberta Press, The; University of California Press; University of Massachusetts Press; University of Michigan Press; University of Minnesota Press; University of Missouri Press; University of Tennessee Press, The; University of Texas Press; University Press of America, Inc.; Vesta Publications, Ltd.; Walch, Publisher, J. Weston; Washington State University Press; Westgate Press; Whitney Library of Design; Whitson Publishing Co., The; Workman Publishing Company, Inc.; Zoland Books, Inc.

Astrology/Psychic/New Age. ACS Publications, Inc.; America West Publishers; Aquarian Press Ltd., The; Cassandra Press; Delta Books; Garber Communications, Inc.; Humanics Publishing Group; Melior Publications; Newcastle Publishing Co., Inc.; Prentice Hall Press; Theosophical Publishing House, The; Westgate Press; Whitford Press; Wingbow Press.

Audiocassette. Abingdon Press; Accelerated Development Inc.; Asher-Gallant Press; Boston Mills Press, The; Chatham Press; CompCare Publishers; Consultant Press, The; Craftsman Book Company; Devin-Adair Publishers, Inc.; Global Business and Trade Communications; Gower Publishing Co.; Human Kinetics Publishers, Inc.; Humanics Publishing Group; Interstate Publishers, Inc. The; Ishiyaku Euroamerica, Inc.; Kar-Ben Copies Inc.; Liguori Publications; Longman Financial Services Publishing; Metamorphous Press; Muir Publications, John; National Association of Social Workers; National Textbook Co.; Peterson's; Potentials Development for Health & Aging Services; Price Stern Sloan, Inc.; Professional Publications, Inc.; Rainbow Books; Rodale Press; Saint Anthony Messenger Press; Saint Bede's Publications; Sasquatch Books; Scojtia Publishing Co., Inc.; Shapolsky Publishers; Shore Associates, Michael; Stemmer House Publishers, Inc.; Tabor Publishing; Trillium Press; Troubador Press; Utah State University Press; Walch, Publisher, J. Weston; Willow Creek Press; Wilshire Book Co.; Winston-Derek Publishers, Inc.

Autobiographies. Arbor House; Daniel and Company, Publishers, John; Poseidon Press; Potter, Inc., Clarkson N.; Soho Press, Inc.

Bibliographies. Avon Books; Borgo Press, The; Chosen Books Publishing Co.; Family Album, The; Garland Publishing, Inc.; Klein Publications, B.; Princeton University Press; Reymont Associates; Scarecrow Press, Inc.; Second Chance Press/Permanent Press; University Press of Virginia; Whitson Publishing Co., The.

Biography. Advocacy Press; Aegina Press, Inc.; American Atheist Press; American Studies Press, Inc.; Apollo Books; Atheneum Children's Books; Avon Books; Baker Book House Company;

Ballantine/Epiphany Books; Bantam Books; Bart Books; Bear Flag Books; Bergh Publishing, Inc.; Binford & Mort Publishing; Blair, Publisher, John F.; Blue Dolphin Publishing, Inc.; Borgo Press, The; Bosco Publications, Don; Branden Publishing Co., Inc..; Breakwater Books; Canadian Plains Research Center; Carol Publishing; Carolrhoda Books, Inc.; Carroll & Graf Publishers, Inc.; Catholic University of America Press; Chelsea Green; Cherokee Publishing Company; Chockstone Press, Inc.; Christopher Publishing House, The; Citadel Press; Clarion Books; Clark Co., Arthur H.; Contemporary Books, Inc.; Creative Arts Book Company; Creative Publishing Co.; Crown Publishers, Inc.; Cuff Publications Limited, Harry; Daniel and Company, Publishers, John; Dante University Of America Press, Inc.; Delta Books; Dillon Press, Inc.; Dunburn Press Ltd.; E.P. Dutton; Eakin Publications, Inc.; Ediciones Universal; Enslow Publishers; Eriksson, Publisher, Paul S.; Faber & Faber, Inc.; Family Album, The; Fell Publishers, Inc., Frederick; Fine, Inc., Donald I.; Fitzhenry & Whiteside, Ltd.; Fleet Press Corp.; Fulcrum, Inc.; Gallaudet University Press; Gardner Press, Inc.; Gaslight Publications; Global Business and Trade Communications; Godine, Publisher, David R.; Gordon and Breach; Gospel Publishing House; Great Northwest Publishing and Distributing Company, Inc.; Greenhaven Press, Inc.; Guernica Editions; Hancock House Publishers Ltd.; Harbinger House, Inc.; Harper & Row Publishers, Inc.; Harper & Row, San Francisco; Harvest House Publishers; Here's Life Publishers, Inc.; Hippocrene Books Inc.; Holmes & Meier Publishers, Inc.; Homestead Publishing; Horizon Publishers & Distributors; Houghton Mifflin Co.; Huntington House, Inc.; ILR Press; International Publishers Co., Inc.; International Resources; Iowa State University Press; Java Publishing Company; Kent State University Press; Kesend Publishing, Ltd., Michael; Lang Publishing, Peter; Library Research Associates, Inc.; Little, Brown and Co., Inc.; Liturgical Publications, Inc.; Longwood Academic; Loyola University Press; McGraw Hill Ryerson; Madison Books; Madison Books; Media Forum International, Ltd.; Media Productions and Marketing, Inc.; Melior Publications; Mercer University Press; Metamorphous Press; Monitor Book Co.; Moonfall Publishing, Inc.; Morrow and Co., William; Mosaic Press Miniature Books; Mother Courage Press; Motorbooks International Publishers & Wholesalers, Inc.; Mott Media, Inc., Publishers; Naval Institute Press; New England Press, Inc., The; New Leaf Press, Inc.; New Victoria Publishers; Nimbus Publishing Limited; Noble Press, Incorporated, The; Northland; Ohio State University Press; Old Army Press, The; Oregon Historical Society Press; Oregon State University Press; Outbooks; Pacific Press Publishing Association; Paragon House Publishers; Pelican Publishing Company; Pineapple Press, Inc.; Pippin Press; Plexus Publishing, Inc.; Pocket Books; Pomegranate Press, Ltd.; Poseidon Press; Potomac-Pacific Press; Potter, Inc., Clarkson N.; Prairie Publishing Company, The; Prima Publishing and Communications; Princeton Book Company, Publishers; Princeton University Press; Purdue University Press; Quill; Random House, Inc./Alfred A. Knopf, Inc. Juvenile Books; Roundtable Publishing, Inc.; Routledge, Chapman & Hall, Inc.; Rutledge Hill Press; S.C.E.-Editions L'Etincelle; S.O.C.O. Publications; St. Martin's Press; St. Paul Books and Media; San Francisco Press, Inc.; Sandlapper Publishing, Inc.; Schirmer Books; Science Tech Publishers, Inc.; Scojtia Publishing Co., Inc.; Scribner's Sons, Charles; Second Chance Press/Permanent Press; Seven Locks Press, Inc.; Simon & Schuster; Smith, Publisher, Gibbs; Soho Press, Inc.; Stemmer House Publishers, Inc.; Stevens, Inc., Gareth; Stormline Press; Tapley, Publisher, Inc., Lance; Texas Monthly Press Inc.; Times Books; Transaction Books; University of Alabama Press; University of Alberta Press, The; University of Illinois Press; University of Massachusetts Press; University of Nevada Press; University of Pennsylvania Press; University Press of Kansas; University Press of Kentucky; University Press of Mississippi; Unlimited Publishing Co.; Utah State University Press; Vehicule Press; Vesta Publications, Ltd.; Walker and Co.; Washington State University Press; Westernlore Press; Wilderness Adventure Books; Windriver Publishing Company; Winston-Derek Publishers, Inc.; Woodbine House; Woodsong Graphics, Inc.; Zebra Books; Zoland Books, Inc.

Booklets. P.P.I. Publishing.

Business/Economics. Abbott, Langer & Associates; Adams, Inc., Bob; Allen Publishing Co.; American Hospital Publishing, Inc.; Arbor House; Asher-Gallant Press; Atheneum Children's Books; Avon Books; Bantam Books; Barron's Educational Series, Inc.; Benjamin Company, Inc., The; Betterway Publications, Inc.; Between the Lines Inc.; BNA Books; Brethren Press; Brick House Publishing Co.; Canadian Plains Research Center; Carol Publishing; Cassell Publications; Cheribe Publishing Co.; Chilton Book Co.; Christopher Publishing House, The; Cleaning Consultant Services, Inc.; Commerce Clearing House, Inc.; Communications Press; Compact Books; Consultant Press, The; Contemporary Books, Inc.; Davenport, Publishers, May; Devin-Adair Publishers, Inc.; Devonshire Publishing Co.; Eakin Publications, Inc.; Enslow Publishers; Enterprise Publishing Co., Inc.; Eriksson, Publisher, Paul S.; Facts On File, Inc.; Fairchild Books & Visuals; Fairleigh Dickinson University Press; Federal Buyers Guide, Inc.; Fell Publishers, Inc., Frederick; Financial Sourcebooks; Fitzhenry & Whiteside, Ltd.; Forman Publishing; Fraser Institute, The; Free Press, The; Glenbridge Publishing Ltd.; Global Business and Trade Communications; Gollehon Press Inc.; Gordon and Breach; Gower Publishing Co.; Greenhaven Press, Inc.; Harbor House Publishers; Harper & Row Publishers, Inc.; Health Administration Press; Holmes & Meier Publishers, Inc.; Humanics Publishing Group; ILR Press; Industrial Press, Inc.; Intercultural Press, Inc.; International Foundation Of Employee Benefit Plans; International Publishers Co., Inc.; International Resources; International Self-Counsel Press, Ltd.; Iowa State University Press; Klein Publications, B.; Knowledge Industry Publications, Inc.; Krieger Publishing Co., Inc., Robert E.; Lang Publishing, Peter; Liberty House; Library Research Associates, Inc.; Lomond Publications, Inc.; Longman Financial Services Publishing; Loompanics Unlimited; McFarland & Company, Inc., Publishers; McGraw Hill Ryerson; Madison Books; Mazda Publishers; Meadowbrook Press; Metamorphous Press; MGI Management Institute, Inc., The; Michigan State University Press; Morgan-Rand Publications Inc.; Mosaic Press Miniature Books; Muir Publications, John; National Book Company; National Textbook Co.; NavPress; Nichols Publishing; Oryx Press; Overlook Press; Pelican Publishing Company; Pilot Books; Poseidon Press; Potomac-Pacific Press; Prentice Hall Canada, Inc. ; Prentice Hall Canada, Inc.; Prentice Hall Canada, Inc.; Prentice Hall Press; Prima Publishing and Communications; Probus Publishing Co.; Professional Publications, Inc.; Purdue University Press; R&E Publishers; Reymont Associates; Ronin Publishing; Ross Books; Roundtable Publishing, Inc.; Routledge, Chapman & Hall, Inc.; Roxbury Publishing Co.; Russell Sage Foundation; S.C.E.-Editions L'Etincelle; S.O.C.O. Publications; Scojtia Publishing Co., Inc.; Seven Locks Press, Inc.; Sterling Publishing; Stipes Publishing Co.; Studio Press; Tab Book, Inc.; Texas Monthly Press Inc.; Times Books; Transaction Books; Trend Book Division; Tuttle Publishing Company, Inc., Charles E.; Twin Peaks Press; Union Square Press; University Associates, Inc.; University of Illinois Press; University of Michigan Press; University of Minnesota Press; University of Pennsylvania Press; University of Texas Press; University Press of America, Inc.; Unlimited Publishing Co.; Wadsworth Publishing Company; Walch, Publisher, J. Weston; Walker and Co.; Washington State University Press; Wiley & Sons, Inc., John; Williamson Publishing Co.; Windsor Books; Wordware Publishing, Inc.

Child Guidance/Parenting. African American Images; ALA Books; Augsburg Books; Baker Book House Company; Bantam Books; Barron's Educational Series, Inc.; Bart Books; Blue Bird Publishing; Bookmakers Guild, Inc.; Cambridge Career Products; Carol Publishing; Center for Applied Linguistics; Child Welfare League Of America; College Board, The; CompCare Publishers; Delta Books; Fisher Books; Gallaudet University Press; Gardner Press, Inc.; Harbinger House, Inc.; Hensley, Inc., Virgil W.; Horizon Publishers & Distributors; Lion Publishing Corporation; Meadowbrook Press; Middle Atlantic Press; NavPress; Parenting Press; R&E Publishers; Spence Publishing; Tabor Publishing; Tapley, Publisher, Inc., Lance; Thomas, Publisher, Charles C.; University of Minnesota Press; Victor Books; Walker and Co.; Westport Publishers, Inc.; Williamson Publishing Co.

Coffee Table Book. Apollo Books; Bantam Books; Bentley, Inc., Robert; Breakwater Books; Canadian Plains Research Center; Caxton Printers, Ltd., The; Chockstone Press, Inc.; Dunburn Press Ltd.; E.P. Dutton; Fell Publishers, Inc., Frederick; Fiddlehead Poetry Books & Goose Lane Editions; Gallaudet University Press; Harbor House Publishers; Homestead Publishing; Howell Press, Inc.; Imagine, Inc.; Lexikos; Library Research Associates, Inc.; Melior Publications; Middle Atlantic Press; Moonfall Publishing, Inc.; Multnomah Press; Museum of Northern Arizona Press; Nimbus Publishing Limited; Pelican Publishing Company; Pennsylvania Historical and Museum Commission; Pomegranate Press, Ltd.; Princeton Book Company, Publishers; Rutledge Hill Press; S.O.C.O. Publications; Schiffer Publishing Ltd.; Tapley, Publisher, Inc., Lance; Texas Monthly Press Inc.; Union Square Press; Westport Publishers, Inc.; Willow Creek Press; Wolgemuth & Hyatt, Publishers; Workman Publishing Company, Inc.; Zoland Books, Inc.

Communications. Communications Press; Tab Book, Inc.; Union Square Press; Univelt, Inc.; Wadsworth Publishing Company.

Community/Public Affairs. Jalmar Press, Inc.; Taylor Publishing Company; University Associates, Inc.; University of Alabama Press.

Computers/Electronics. ALA Books; Arcsoft Publishers; Bantam Books; Branden Publishing Co., Inc..; Breakwater Books; Career Publishing, Inc.; Carol Publishing; Carolina Biological Supply Co.; Center for Applied Linguistics; Cheribe Publishing Co.; Compute! Books; Computer Science Press, Inc.; Digital Press; Dustbooks; Entelek; Financial Sourcebooks; Gifted Education Press; Gordon and Breach; Grapevine Publications, Inc.; Industrial Press, Inc.; MGI Management Institute, Inc., The; New York Zoetrope, Inc.; Nichols Publishing; Prentice Hall Canada, Inc.; Princeton University Press; Q.E.D. Information Sciences, Inc.; Que Corporation; R&E Publishers; Ross Books; S.C.E.-Editions L'Etincelle; San Francisco Press, Inc.; Sybex, Inc.; Tab Book, Inc.; Teachers College Press; Union Square Press; University of Pennsylvania Press; VGM Career Horizons; Walch, Publisher, J. Weston; Wordware Publishing, Inc.

Consumer Affairs. International Foundation Of Employee Benefit Plans; Pharos Books; Woodsong Graphics, Inc.

Cooking/Foods/Nutrition. Applezaba Press; Arbor House; Atheneum Children's Books; Bantam Books; Barron's Educational Series, Inc.; Bart Books; Benjamin Company, Inc., The; Bergh Publishing, Inc.; Better Homes and Gardens Books; Betterway Publications, Inc.; Blue Dolphin Publishing, Inc.; Bragdon Publishers, Inc., Allen D.; Breakwater Books; Breakwater Books; Briarcliff Press Publishers; Bristol Publishing Enterprises, Inc.; Cambridge Career Products; Carol Publishing; Cassandra Press; Christopher Publishing House, The; Compact Books; Contemporary Books, Inc.; Countryman Press, Inc., The; Countrywoman's Press, The; Crossing Press, The; Crown Publishers, Inc.; Down East Books; E.P. Dutton; Eakin Publications, Inc.; Eriksson, Publisher, Paul S.; Evans and Co., Inc., M.; Facts On File, Inc.; Fell Publishers, Inc., Frederick; Fine, Inc., Donald I.; Fisher Books; Five Star Publications; Forman Publishing; Godine, Publisher, David R.; Golden West Publishers; Hancock House Publishers Ltd.; Harbor House Publishers; Harper & Row Publishers, Inc.; Harvard Common Press, The; Hawkes Publishing, Inc.; Horizon Publishers & Distributors; Jonathan David Publishers; Leisure Press; Little, Brown and Co., Inc.; Lyons & Burford, Publishers, Inc.; McGraw Hill Ryerson; Mazda Publishers; Meadowbrook Press; Media Forum International, Ltd.; Middle Atlantic Press; Miller Books; Morrow and Co., William; Mosaic Press Miniature Books; Nimbus Publishing Limited; Outbooks; Pacific Press Publishing Association; Peachtree Publishers, Ltd.; Pelican Publishing Company; Pennsylvania Historical and Museum Commission; Peter Pauper Press, Inc.; Pocket Books; Potter, Inc., Clarkson N.; Prairie Publishing Company, The; Prentice Hall Canada, Inc. ; Prentice Hall Press; Prima Publishing and Communications; Quill; R&E Publishers; Rodale Press; Rutledge Hill Press; S.C.E.-Editions L'Etincelle; S.O.C.O. Publications; Sasquatch Books; Scojtia Publishing Co., Inc.; Shapolsky Publishers; Shoe Tree Press; Spence Publishing; Stemmer House Publishers, Inc.; Sterling Publishing; Stevens, Inc., Gareth; Stoeger Publishing Company; Stormline Press; Tapley, Publisher, Inc., Lance; Taylor Publishing Company; Texas Monthly Press Inc.; Times Books; Tuttle Publishing Company, Inc., Charles E.; Twin Peaks Press; Unlimited Publishing Co.; Vesta Publications, Ltd.; Westport Publishers, Inc.; Williamson Publishing Co.; Wine Appreciation Guild, Ltd.; Woodbridge Press; Woodsong Graphics, Inc.; Workman Publishing Company, Inc.

Counseling/Career Guidance. Accelerated Development Inc.; Adams, Inc., Bob; Career Publishing, Inc.; Fairchild Books & Visuals; Milady Publishing Company; National Association of Social Workers; National Textbook Co.; Octameron Associates; Peterson's; Pilot Books; Potomac-Pacific Press; Rutgers University Press; Scojtia Publishing Co., Inc.; Teachers College Press; VGM Career Horizons; Wiley & Sons, Inc., John; Williamson Publishing Co.

Crafts. Barron's Educational Series, Inc.; Better Homes and Gardens Books; Briarcliff Press Publishers; Chilton Book Co.; Coles Publishing Co., Ltd.; Davis Publications, Inc.; Down East Books; Naturegraph Publishers, Inc.

Education(al). ABC-CLIO, Inc.; Accelerated Development Inc.; Advocacy Press; African American Images; ALA Books; American Catholic Press; Barron's Educational Series, Inc.; Benjamin Company, Inc., The; Between the Lines Inc.; Blue Bird Publishing; Bookmakers Guild, Inc.; Bosco Publications, Don; Breakwater Books; Cambridge Career Products; Canadian Plains Research Center; Center for Applied Linguistics; Coles Publishing Co., Ltd.; College Board, The; Colorado Associated University Press; Dante University Of America Press, Inc.; Denison & Co., Inc., T.S.; Dillon Press, Inc.; Duquesne University Press; EES Publications; Education Associates; Entelek; ETC Publications; Fairleigh Dickinson University Press; Fearon Education; Gallaudet University Press; Gardner Press, Inc.; Gifted Education Press; Global Business and Trade Communications; Gordon and Breach; Gospel Publishing House; Holmes & Meier Publishers, Inc.; Horizon Publishers & Distributors; Humanics Publishing Group; Incentive Publications, Inc.; Instructor Books; Intercultural Press, Inc.; Interstate Publishers, Inc. The; Ishiyaku Euroamerica, Inc.; Jalmar Press, Inc.; Kent State University Press; Knopf, Inc., Alfred A.; Lang Publishing, Peter; Liguori Publications; Longwood Academic; Metamorphous Press; Morehouse Publishing Co.; National Book Company; Naturegraph Publishers, Inc.; Nichols Publishing; Noble Press, Incorporated, The; Ohio State University Press; Oise Press; Peterson's; Pilot Books; Porter Sargent Publishers, Inc.; Prakken Publications, Inc.; Prentice Hall Canada, Inc.; Prentice Hall Canada, Inc.; Preservation Press, The; Princeton Book Company, Publishers; Que Corporation; R&E Publishers; Routledge, Chapman & Hall, Inc.; Russell Sage Foundation; San Francisco Press, Inc.; Speech Bin, Inc., The; Standard Publishing; Tabor Publishing; Teachers College Press; Thomas, Publisher, Charles C.; Trillium Press; University Associates, Inc.; University Press of America, Inc.; Walch, Publisher, J. Weston; Whitaker House; Williamson Publishing Co.

Entertainment/Games. Borgo Press, The; Broadway Press; Citadel Press; Delta Books; Dembner Books; Drama Book Publishers; Faber & Faber, Inc.; Fairleigh Dickinson University Press; Focal Press; Holloway House Publishing Co.; Intergalactic Publishing Co.; McFarland & Company, Inc., Publishers; New York Zoetrope, Inc.; Quill; Speech Bin, Inc., The; Standard Publishing; Sterling Publishing.

Ethnic. Aegina Press, Inc.; African American Images; Between the Lines Inc.; Carol Publishing; Coteau Books; Fairleigh Dickinson University Press; Four Winds Press; Gardner Press, Inc.; Gordon and Breach; Holmes & Meier Publishers, Inc.; Indiana University Press; International Publishers Co., Inc.; Kar-Ben Copies Inc.; Luramedia; Media Forum International, Ltd.; Muir Publications, John; Noble Press, Incorporated, The; Oregon Historical Society Press; R&E Publishers; Stormline Press; University of Massachusetts Press; University of Oklahoma Press; University of Tennessee Press, The; University of Texas Press; University Press of America, Inc.; University Press of Mississippi; University Press of Virginia.

Fashion/Beauty. Acropolis Books, Ltd.; Fairchild Books & Visuals.

Feminism. Crossing Press, The; Firebrand Books; New Victoria Publishers.

Film/Cinema/Stage. Focal Press; French, Inc., Samuel; Imagine, Inc.; Indiana University Press; Knowledge Industry Publications, Inc.; Leonard Publishing Corp.; McFarland & Company, Inc., Publishers; Madison Books; Main Street Press, The; Media Forum International, Ltd.; Meriwether Publishing Ltd.; Players Press, Inc.; Prentice Hall Press; Roundtable Publishing, Inc.; Rutgers University Press; Schirmer Books; Southfarm Press; Starrhill Press; Tab Book, Inc.; Teachers College Press; Umi Research Press; University of Michigan Press; University of Texas Press; University Press of America, Inc.; Vestal Press, Ltd., The; VGM Career Horizons; Windriver Publishing Company.

Gardening. Apollo Books; Better Homes and Gardens Books; Briarcliff Press Publishers; Countrywoman's Press, The; Fisher Books; Godine, Publisher, David R.; Horizon Publishers & Distributors; Lyons & Burford, Publishers, Inc.; McGraw Hill Ryerson; Main Street Press, The; Naturegraph Publishers, Inc.; Prentice Hall Press; Sasquatch Books; Scojtia Publishing Co., Inc.; Stackpole Books; Stormline Press; Timber Press, Inc.; Williamson Publishing Co.; Woodbridge Press.

Gay/Lesbian. Alyson Publications, Inc.; Bantam Books; Between the Lines Inc.; Carol Publishing; Cleis Press; Crossing Press, The; Firebrand Books; Gardner Press, Inc.; University of Minnesota Press.

General Nonfiction. Aegina Press, Inc.; American Atheist Press; American Psychiatric Press, Inc., The; Avon Flare Books; Davis Publishing, Steve; Dimension Books, Inc.; Evans and Co., Inc., M.; Fleet Press Corp.; Fulcrum, Inc.; Indiana University Press; Jonathan David Publishers; Kent State University Press; Lang Publishing, Peter; Leisure Books; Media Productions and Marketing, Inc.; Mercury House Inc.; Mills & Sanderson, Publishers; Morrow and Co., William; Norton Co., Inc., W.W.; Ohio State University Press; Ohio University Press; Peachtree Publishers, Ltd.; Pocket Books; Potentials Development for Health & Aging Services; Renaissance House Publishers; St. Anthony Messenger Press; St. Martin's Press; Shaw Publishers, Harold; Time-Life Books Inc.; University of Calgary Press, The; University of Wisconsin Press; Wiley & Sons, Inc., John; Writer's Digest Books; Yankee Books.

Government/Politics. ABC-CLIO, Inc.; American Atheist Press; Arbor House; Avon Books; Bantam Books; Bergh Publishing, Inc.; Between the Lines Inc.; Carol Publishing; Christopher Publishing House, The; Cleis Press; Communications Press; Crown Publishers, Inc.; Cuff Publications Limited, Harry; Devin-Adair Publishers, Inc.; Ediciones Universal; Eriksson, Publisher, Paul S.; Federal Buyers Guide, Inc.; Federal Personnel Management Institute, Inc.; Financial Sourcebooks; Fraser Institute, The; Glenbridge Publishing Ltd.; Gower Publishing Co.; Greenhaven Press, Inc.; Guernica Editions; Harper & Row Publishers, Inc.; Health Administration Press; Holmes & Meier Publishers, Inc.; Humanities Press International, Inc.; Huntington House, Inc.; Indiana University Press; Intercultural Press, Inc.; International Publishers Co., Inc.; Lang Publishing, Peter; Library Research Associates, Inc.; Life Cycle Books; Lomond Publications, Inc.; Loompanics Unlimited; McGraw Hill Ryerson; Madison Books; Mazda Publishers; Media Productions and Marketing, Inc.; Michigan State University Press; Milkweed Editions; Moonfall Publishing, Inc.; Mott Media, Inc., Publishers; National Book Company; Noble Press, Incorporated, The; Northern Illinois University Press; Oregon Historical Society Press; Paragon House Publishers; Pelican Publishing Company; Pennsylvania Historical and Museum Commission; Plenum Publishing; Poseidon Press; Potomac-Pacific Press; Prentice Hall Canada, Inc.; Prima Publishing and Communications; Princeton University Press; R&E Publishers; Regnery/Gateway, Inc.; Riverdale Company, Inc., Publishers, The; Roundtable Publishing, Inc.; Russell Sage Foundation; S.C.E.-Editions L'Etincelle; St. Martin's Press; San Francisco Press, Inc.; Sasquatch Books; Scojtia Publishing Co., Inc.; Second Chance Press/Permanent Press; Seven Locks Press, Inc.; Shapolsky Publishers; Stanford University Press; Tapley, Publisher, Inc., Lance; Teachers College Press; Texas Monthly Press Inc.; Transaction Books; Transnational Publishers, Inc.; Trend Book Division; Tuttle Publishing Company, Inc., Charles E.; University of Alabama Press; University of Alberta Press, The; University of Illinois Press; University Press of Kansas; University Press of Kentucky; University Press of Mississippi; Utah State University Press; Vehicule Press; Vesta Publications, Ltd.; Walch, Publisher, J. Weston; Washington State University Press.

Hi-lo/ESL. Cambridge Career Products; Fearon Education; Miller Books; National Textbook Co.; New Readers Press; Prolingua Associates; Rosen Publishing Group, The; University of Michigan Press.

Health/Medicine. Accelerated Development Inc.; Acropolis Books, Ltd.; ACS Publications, Inc.; Aegina Press, Inc.; America West Publishers; American Hospital Publishing, Inc.; Arbor House; Atheneum Children's Books; Avon Books; Ballantine/Epiphany Books; Bantam Books; Bart Books; Benjamin Company, Inc., The; Betterway Publications, Inc.; Between the Lines Inc.; Blue Dolphin Publishing, Inc.; Bookmakers Guild, Inc.; Branden Publishing Co., Inc..; Brethren Press; Briarcliff Press Publishers; Cambridge Career Products; Camden House, Inc.; Carol Publishing; Carolina Biological Supply Co.; Cassandra Press; Catholic Health Association of the United States, The; Cheribe Publishing Co.; Cherokee Publishing Company; Christopher Publishing House, The; Cleaning Consultant Services, Inc.; Compact Books; CompCare Publishers; Contemporary Books, Inc.; Crossing Press, The; Crown Publishers, Inc.; Dembner Books; Devin-Adair Publishers, Inc.; EES Publications; Elysium Growth Press; Enslow Publishers; Eriksson, Publisher, Paul S.; Evans and Co., Inc., M.; Facts On File, Inc.; Fell Publishers, Inc., Frederick; Fisher Books; Fitzhenry & Whiteside, Ltd.; Forman Publishing; Gallaudet University Press; Gardner Press, Inc.; Gordon and Breach; Government Institutes, Inc.; Harbinger House, Inc.; Harper & Row Publishers, Inc.; Hawkes Publishing, Inc.; Hazelden Educational Materials; Health Administration Press; Horizon Publishers & Distributors; Houghton Mifflin Co.; Human Kinetics Publishers, Inc.; Hunter House, Inc., Publishers; Information Resources Press; International Foundation Of Employee Benefit Plans; Iowa State University Press; Ishiyaku Euroamerica, Inc.; Kesend Publishing, Ltd., Michael;

Krieger Publishing Co., Inc., Robert E.; Leisure Press; Life Cycle Books; Lion Publishing Corporation; Longwood Academic; Luramedia; McFarland & Company, Inc., Publishers; M Graw Hill Ryerson; Marathon International Publishing Company, Inc.; Medmaster, Inc.; Metamorphous Press; Middle Atlantic Press; Mills & Sanderson, Publishers; Mosaic Press Miniature Books; Mother Courage Press; Muir Publications, John; National Association of Social Workers; National Book Company; Naturegraph Publishers, Inc.; New Idea Press, Inc.; Newcastle Publishing Co., Inc.; Oryx Press; Pacific Press Publishing Association; Pelican Publishing Company; Perspectives Press; Potomac-Pacific Press; Prentice Hall Canada, Inc. ; Prima Publishing and Communications; Princeton Book Company, Publishers; R&E Publishers; Rocky Top Publications; Rodale Press; Rosen Publishing Group, The; Roundtable Publishing, Inc.; S.C.E.-Editions L'Etincelle; Science Tech Publishers, Inc.; Scojtia Publishing Co., Inc.; Scribner's Sons, Charles; Shoe Tree Press; Sierra Club Books; Speech Bin, Inc., The; Spence Publishing; Sterling Publishing; Tab Book, Inc.; Theosophical Publishing House, The; Thomas, Publisher, Charles C.; Times Books; Transaction Books; Twin Peaks Press; Ultralight Publications, Inc.; University of Minnesota Press; University of Pennsylvania Press; University of Texas Press; University Press of Virginia; VGM Career Horizons; Walch, Publisher, J. Weston; Walker and Co.; Weiser, Inc., Samuel; Whitaker House; Williamson Publishing Co.; Wilshire Book Co.; Winston-Derek Publishers, Inc.; Woodbine House; Woodbridge Press; Workman Publishing Company, Inc.

History. ABC-CLIO, Inc.; African American Images; American Atheist Press; American Studies Press, Inc.; Ancestry Incorporated; Appalachian Mountain Club Books; Arbor House; Atheneum Children's Books; Atlantic Monthly Press; Aviation Book Co.; Avon Books; Aztex Corp.; Bear Flag Books; Binford & Mort Publishing; Blair, Publisher, John F.; Borgo Press, The; Boston Mills Press, The; Branden Publishing Co., Inc..; Breakwater Books; Brethren Press; Canadian Plains Research Center; Caratzas, Publisher, Aristide D.; Carol Publishing; Carolrhoda Books, Inc.; Carroll & Graf Publishers, Inc.; Catholic University of America Press; Chatham Press; Cherokee Publishing Company; Christopher Publishing House, The; Citadel Press; Clark Co., Arthur H.; Coteau Books; Countryman Press, Inc., The; Creative Publishing Co.; Crossway Books; Crown Publishers, Inc.; Cuff Publications Limited, Harry; Dembner Books; Devin-Adair Publishers, Inc.; Devonshire Publishing Co.; Dillon Press, Inc.; Down East Books; Dunburn Press Ltd.; Eerdmans Publishing Co., William B.; Eriksson, Publisher, Paul S.; Facts On File, Inc.; Fairleigh Dickinson University Press; Family Album, The; Fiddlehead Poetry Books & Goose Lane Editions; Fine, Inc., Donald I.; Fitzhenry & Whiteside, Ltd.; Fleet Press Corp.; Fulcrum, Inc.; Gallaudet University Press; Gaslight Publications; Glenbridge Publishing Ltd.; Godine, Publisher, David R.; Golden West Publishers; Gospel Publishing House; Greenhaven Press, Inc.; Guernica Editions; Hancock House Publishers Ltd.; Harbinger House, Inc.; Harper & Row Publishers, Inc.; Hawkes Publishing, Inc.; Heart Of The Lakes Publishing; Heritage Books, Inc.; Heyday Books; Hippocrene Books Inc.; Holmes & Meier Publishers, Inc.; Homestead Publishing; Horizon Publishers & Distributors; Houghton Mifflin Co.; Howell Press, Inc.; Humanities Press International, Inc.; ILR Press; Indiana University Press; International Publishers Co., Inc.; International Resources; Interurban Press/ Trans Anglo Books; Intervarsity Press; Iowa State University Press; Kent State University Press; Kesend Publishing, Ltd., Michael; Kinseeker Publications; Krieger Publishing Co., Inc., Robert E.; Lang Publishing, Peter; Lexikos; Library Research Associates, Inc.; Library Research Associates, Inc.; Life Cycle Books; Little, Brown and Co., Inc.; Longwood Academic; Loyola University Press; McGraw Hill Ryerson; Madison Books; Madison Books; Mazda Publishers; Media Productions and Marketing, Inc.; Melior Publications; Michigan State University Press; Middle Atlantic Press; Milkweed Editions; Miller Books; Morehouse Publishing Co.; Morrow and Co., William; Mosaic Press Miniature Books; Motorbooks International Publishers & Wholesalers, Inc.; National Book Company; Naval Institute Press; New England Press, Inc., The; New Victoria Publishers; Nimbus Publishing Limited; Noble Press, Incorporated, The; Northern Illinois University Press; Noyes Data Corp.; Oddo Publishing, Inc.; Ohio State University Press; Ohio University Press; Old Army Press, The; Oregon Historical Society Press; Oregon State University Press; Outbooks; Overlook Press; Paragon House Publishers; Paragon House Publishers; Peachtree Publishers, Ltd.; Penkevill Publishing Company, The; Pennsylvania Historical and Museum Commission; Pickering Press, The; Pineapple Press, Inc.; Poseidon Press; Potomac-Pacific Press; Prentice Hall Canada, Inc.; Preservation Press, The; Princeton University Press; Purdue University Press; Quill; R&E Publishers; Renaissance House Publishers; Riverdale Company, Inc., Publishers, The; Russell Sage Foundation; Rutgers University Press; S.C.E.-Editions L'Etincelle; S.O.C.O. Publications; St. Bede's Publications; St. Martin's Press; San Francisco Press, Inc.; Sandlapper Publishing, Inc.; Sasquatch Books; Schiffer Publishing Ltd.; Scojtia Publishing Co., Inc.; Second Chance Press/ Permanent Press; Seven Locks Press, Inc.; Shapolsky Publishers; Shaw Publishers, Harold; Shoe Tree Press; Sierra Club Books; Silver Burdett Press; Simon & Schuster; Smith, Publisher, Gibbs; Southfarm Press; Stanford University Press; Stemmer House Publishers, Inc.; Stevens, Inc., Gareth; Stormline Press; Sunstone Press; Tapley, Publisher, Inc., Lance; Teachers College Press; Texas A&M University Press; Texas Monthly Press Inc.; Texas Western Press; Three Continents Press; Timber Press, Inc.; Times Books; Transaction Books; Transportation Trails; Trend Book Division; Tuttle Publishing Company, Inc., Charles E.; Tyndale House Publishers, Inc.; Umi Research Press; University of Alabama Press; University of Alberta Press, The; University of Illinois Press; University of Iowa Press; University of Massachusetts Press; University of Michigan Press; University of

Missouri Press; University of Nevada Press; University of Oklahoma Press; University of Pennsylvania Press; University of Tennessee Press, The; University of Texas Press; University of Utah Press; University Press of America, Inc.; University Press of Kansas; University Press of Kentucky; University Press of Mississippi; University Press of Virginia; Vehicule Press; Vesta Publications, Ltd.; Vestal Press, Ltd., The; Walch, Publisher, J. Weston; Walker and Co.; Washington State University Pess; Westernlore Press; Wilderness Adventure Books; Windriver Publishing Company; Woodbine House; Workman Publishing Company, Inc.

Hobby. Ancestry Incorporated; Arcsoft Publishers; Atheneum Children's Books; Benjamin Company, Inc., The; Betterway Publications, Inc.; Bragdon Publishers, Inc., Allen D.; Carstens Publications, Inc.; Coles Publishing Co., Ltd.; Compact Books; Crown Publishers, Inc.; Devonshire Publishing Co.; Doll Reader; Dunburn Press Ltd.; Enslow Publishers; Eriksson, Publisher, Paul S.; Facts On File, Inc.; Fell Publishers, Inc., Frederick; Gollehon Press Inc.; Hawkes Publishing, Inc.; Horizon Publishers & Distributors; International Resources; Interurban Press/Trans Anglo Books; Interweave Press; Java Publishing Company; Kalmbach Publishing Co.; Kesend Publishing, Ltd., Michael; Klein Publications, B.; Main Street Press, The; Meriwether Publishing Ltd.; Mosaic Press Miniature Books; Mustang Publishing Co.; Pomegranate Press, Ltd.; Prentice Hall Press; Rocky Top Publications; S.C.E.-Editions L'Etincelle; S.O.C.O. Publications; Schiffer Publishing Ltd.; Scribner's Sons, Charles; Shoe Tree Press; Stackpole Books; Standard Publishing; Sterling Publishing; Sunstone Press; Symmes Systems; Tab Book, Inc.; Travel Keys; Ultralight Publications, Inc.; Union Square Press; Unlimited Publishing Co.; Vestal Press, Ltd., The; Williamson Publishing Co.; Wilshire Book Co.; Woodbine House; Woodsong Graphics, Inc.; Workman Publishing Company, Inc.

How-to. AASH Press; Abbott, Langer & Associates; ABC-CLIO, Inc.; Accent Books; Acropolis Books, Ltd.; Aegina Press, Inc.; Allen Publishing Co.; Alpine Publications Inc.; Ancestry Incorporated; Andrews and McMeel; Appalachian Mountain Club Books; Arbor House; Arman Publishing, Inc., M.; Asher-Gallant Press; Atheneum Children's Books; Avon Books; Aztex Corp.; Ballantine/Epiphany Books; Bantam Books; Bart Books; Benjamin Company, Inc., The; Bentley, Inc., Robert; Better Homes and Gardens Books; Betterway Publications, Inc.; Blue Bird Publishing; Blue Dolphin Publishing, Inc.; Bragdon Publishers, Inc., Allen D.; Briarcliff Press Publishers; Brick House Publishing Co.; Cambridge Career Products; Carol Publishing; Cassandra Press; Cassell Publications; Cheribe Publishing Co.; Chilton Book Co.; Chockstone Press, Inc.; Chosen Books Publishing Co.; Christopher Publishing House, The; Cleaning Consultant Services, Inc.; Coles Publishing Co., Ltd.; College Board, The; Compact Books; Contemporary Books, Inc.; Cornell Maritime Press, Inc.; Countryman Press, Inc., The; Countrywoman's Press, The; Craftsman Book Company; Crossing Press, The; Crown Publishers, Inc.; Dembner Books; Denlingers Publishers, Ltd.; Devin-Adair Publishers, Inc.; EES Publications; E.P. Dutton; Education Associates; Enslow Publishers; Eriksson, Publisher, Paul S.; Federal Buyers Guide, Inc.; Fell Publishers, Inc., Frederick; Fisher Books; Five Star Publications; Flores Publications, J.; Focal Press; Forman Publishing; Gifted Education Press; Global Business and Trade Communications; Gollehon Press Inc.; Grapevine Publications, Inc.; Graphic Arts Technical Foundation; Great Northwest Publishing and Distributing Company, Inc.; Greene Press, The Stephen/Pelham Books; Hamilton Institute, Alexander; Hancock House Publishers Ltd.; Harper & Row Publishers, Inc.; Harper & Row, San Francisco; Harvard Common Press, The; Harvest House Publishers; Hawkes Publishing, Inc.; Here's Life Publishers, Inc.; Heritage Books, Inc.; Heyday Books; Hippocrene Books Inc.; Holloway House Publishing Co.; Horizon Publishers & Distributors; Human Kinetics Publishers, Inc.; Hunter House, Inc., Publishers; Imagine, Inc.; Intercultural Press, Inc.; International Resources; International Self-Counsel Press, Ltd.; International Wealth Success; Interweave Press; Java Publishing Company; Kalmbach Publishing Co.; Kesend Publishing, Ltd., Michael; Klein Publications, B.; Leisure Press; Library Research Associates, Inc.; Linch Publishing, Inc.; Little, Brown and Co., Inc.; Liturgical Publications, Inc.; Longman Financial Services Publishing; Loompanics Unlimited; Lyons & Burford, Publishers, Inc.; M Graw Hill Ryerson; Meadowbrook Press; Media Productions and Marketing, Inc.; Meriwether Publishing Ltd.; Metamorphous Press; MGI Management Institute, Inc., The; Middle Atlantic Press; Milady Publishing Company; Miller Books; Modern Books and Crafts, Inc.; Moonfall Publishing, Inc.; Morrow and Co., William; Mother Courage Press; Motorbooks International Publishers & Wholesalers, Inc.; Mott Media, Inc., Publishers; Mountaineers Books, The; Muir Publications, John; Mustang Publishing Co.; Naturegraph Publishers, Inc.; New England Press, Inc., The; Newcastle Publishing Co., Inc.; Nimbus Publishing Limited; Noble Press, Incorporated, The; North Light; Overlook Press; Pacific Press Publishing Association; Paladin Press; Pelican Publishing Company; Pennsylvania Historical and Museum Commission; Perspectives Press; Pickering Press, The; Pineapple Press, Inc.; Pomegranate Press, Ltd.; Potomac-Pacific Press; Potter, Inc., Clarkson N.; Prima Publishing and Communications; Princeton Book Company, Publishers; Probus Publishing Co.; Q.E.D. Press Of Ann Arbor, Inc.; Que Corporation; R&E Publishers; Resource Publications, Inc.; Reymont Associates; Rocky Top Publications; Rodale Press; Ronin Publishing; Ross Books; Roundtable Publishing, Inc.; S.C.E.-Editions L'Etincelle; S.O.C.O. Publications; Schiffer Publishing Ltd.; Schirmer Books; Scojtia Publishing Co., Inc.; Shore Associates, Michael; Sierra Club Books; Speech Bin, Inc., The; Spence Publishing; ST Publications, Inc.; Standard Publishing; Sterling Publishing; Stoeger Publishing Company; Sunstone Press; Tab Book, Inc.; Tapley, Publisher, Inc., Lance; Thomas Publications; Travel Keys;

Tuttle Publishing Company, Inc., Charles E.; Twin Peaks Press; Ultralight Publications, Inc.; Union Square Press; University of Alberta Press, The; Unlimited Publishing Co.; Weiser, Inc., Samuel; Western Marine Enterprises, Inc.; Whitaker House; Whitford Press; Wilderness Adventure Books; Wilderness Press; Wiley & Sons, Inc., John; Williamson Publishing Co.; Willow Creek Press; Wilshire Book Co.; Windsor Books; Wine Appreciation Guild, Ltd.; Wolgemuth & Hyatt, Publishers; Woodsong Graphics, Inc.; Workman Publishing Company, Inc.; Zebra Books.

Humanities. Asian Humanities Press; Duquesne University Press; Free Press, The; Garland Publishing, Inc.; Indiana University Press; Plenum Publishing; Riverdale Company, Inc., Publishers, The; Roxbury Publishing Co.; Southern Illinois University Press; Stanford University Press; Umi Research Press; Whitson Publishing Co., The.

Humor. Aegina Press, Inc.; American Atheist Press; American Studies Press, Inc.; Andrews and McMeel; Atheneum Children's Books; Baker Book House Company; Bale Books; Ballantine/Epiphany Books; Bantam Books; Bart Books; Blue Dolphin Publishing, Inc.; Breakwater Books; C S.S. Publishing Co.; Carol Publishing; CCC Publications; Citadel Press; Clarion Books; Cliffs Notes, Inc.; Compact Books; Contemporary Books, Inc.; Corkscrew Press; Coteau Books; Countryman Press, Inc., The; Crown Publishers, Inc.; Cuff Publications Limited, Harry; Daniel and Company, Publishers, John; Davenport Publishers, May; E.P. Dutton; Ediciones Universal; Eriksson, Publisher, Paul S.; Faber & Faber, Inc.; Fell Publishers, Inc., Frederick; Fine, Inc., Donald I.; Gollehon Press Inc.; Guernica Editions; Harper & Row Publishers, Inc.; Horizon Publishers & Distributors; Java Publishing Company; Jonathan David Publishers; Media Forum International, Ltd.; Meriwether Publishing Ltd.; Middle Atlantic Press; Mosaic Press Miniature Books; Mustang Publishing Co.; Nimbus Publishing Limited; Once Upon a Planet, Inc.; Paladin Press; Peachtree Publishers, Ltd.; Pelican Publishing Company; Peter Pauper Press, Inc.; Pharos Books; Pomegranate Press, Ltd.; Potomac-Pacific Press; Pocket Books; Potter, Inc., Clarkson N.; Price Stern Sloan, Inc.; R&E Publishers; Random House, Inc./Alfred A. Knopf, Inc. Juvenile Books; Ronin Publishing; Rutledge Hill Press; S.O.C.O. Publications; Sandlapper Publishing, Inc.; Scojtia Publishing Co., Inc.; Scribner's Sons, Charles; Sterling Publishing; Stoeger Publishing Company; Stormline Press; Tapley, Publisher, Inc., Lance; Taylor Publishing Company; Texas Monthly Press Inc.; Tuttle Publishing Company, Inc., Charles E.; Unlimited Publishing Co.; Willow Creek Press; Woodsong Graphics, Inc.; Workman Publishing Company, Inc.; Zebra Books.

Illustrated Book. American References Inc.; American Studies Press, Inc.; Atheneum Children's Books; Bantam Books; Bear and Co., Inc.; Bear Flag Books; Bergh Publishing, Inc.; Betterway Publications, Inc.; Boston Mills Press, The; Branden Publishing Co., Inc..; Breakwater Books; Canadian Plains Research Center; Carol Publishing; Chockstone Press, Inc.; Cleaning Consultant Services, Inc.; Coteau Books; Davis Publications, Inc.; Dial Books For Young Readers; E.P. Dutton; Elysium Growth Press; Five Star Publications; Flores Publications, J.; Gallaudet University Press; Godine, Publisher, David R.; Graphic Arts Center Publishing Co.; Greenhaven Press, Inc.; Harbor House Publishers; Harvest House Publishers; Homestead Publishing; Horizon Publishers & Distributors; Howell Press, Inc.; Imagine, Inc.; International Resources; Kesend Publishing, Ltd., Michael; Lexikos; Lodestar Books; Main Street Press, The; Meadowbrook Press; Melior Publications; Metamorphous Press; Middle Atlantic Press; Milkweed Editions; Mosaic Press Miniature Books; Multnomah Press; New England Press, Inc., The; Nimbus Publishing Limited; Noble Press, Incorporated, The; Once Upon a Planet, Inc.; Parenting Press; Pelican Publishing Company; Pennsylvania Historical and Museum Commission; Philomel Books; Pickering Press, The; Prentice Hall Press; Princeton Architectural Press; R&E Publishers; Random House, Inc./Alfred A. Knopf, Inc. Juvenile Books; Sandlapper Publishing, Inc.; Schiffer Publishing Ltd.; Scojtia Publishing Co., Inc.; Speech Bin, Inc., The; Spence Publishing; Stemmer House Publishers, Inc.; Stormline Press; Tapley, Publisher, Inc., Lance; Texas Monthly Press Inc.; Tuttle Publishing Company, Inc., Charles E.; UAHC Press; Union Square Press; University of Minnesota Press; University Press of Virginia; Unlimited Publishing Co.; Westgate Press; Wilderness Adventure Books; Williamson Publishing Co.; Willow Creek Press; Woodsong Graphics, Inc.; Workman Publishing Company, Inc.; Bragdon Publishers, Inc., Allen D.

Juvenile Books. Abingdon Press; Advocacy Press; African American Images; Atheneum Children's Books; Augsburg Books; Baker Book House Company; Bantam Books; Barron's Educational Series, Inc.; Behrman House Inc.; Bergh Publishing, Inc.; Betterway Publications, Inc.; Blue Bird Publishing; Blue Dolphin Publishing, Inc.; Bookmakers Guild, Inc.; Bosco Publications, Don; Branden Publishing Co., Inc..; Cambridge Career Products; Carolrhoda Books, Inc.; Clarion Books; Coteau Books; Crown Publishers, Inc.; Davenport, Publishers, May; Denison & Co., Inc., T.S.; Dial Books For Young Readers; Dillon Press, Inc.; Dunburn Press Ltd.; Dutton Children's Books; Eakin Publications, Inc.; Education Associates; Enslow Publishers; Fawcett Juniper; Fitzhenry & Whiteside, Ltd.; Five Star Publications; Fleet Press Corp.; Four Winds Press; Gallaudet University Press; Godine, Publisher, David R.; Greenhaven Press, Inc.; Guernica Editions; Harbinger House, Inc.; Harcourt Brace Jovanovich; Harper Junior Books Group, West Coast; Harvest House Publishers; Hazelden Educational Materials; Herald Press; Homestead Publishing; Horizon Publishers & Distributors; Houghton Mifflin Co.; Huntington House, Inc.; Incentive Publications, Inc.; Kar-Ben Copies Inc.; Lodestar Books; McElderry Books, Margaret K.; MacMillan Publishing Co.; Mazda Publishers; Meadowbrook Press; Metamorphous Press; Middle Atlantic Press; Morehouse Publishing Co.; Morrow Junior Books; Mott Media, Inc., Publishers; Multnomah Press;

NavPress; New Idea Press, Inc.; Nimbus Publishing Limited; Noble Press, Incorporated, The; Oddo Publishing, Inc.; P.P.I. Publishing; Pacific Press Publishing Association; Parenting Press; Pelican Publishing Company; Perspectives Press; Philomel Books; Platt & Munk Publishers; Players Press, Inc.; Potter, Inc., Clarkson N.; Price Stern Sloan, Inc.; Random House, Inc./Alfred A. Knopf, Inc. Juvenile Books; Review and Herald Publishing Association; St. Paul Books and Media; Sandlapper Publishing, Inc.; Scojtia Publishing Co., Inc.; Shaw Publishers, Harold; Shoe Tree Press; Sierra Club Books; Silver Burdett Press; Speech Bin, Inc., The; Standard Publishing; Stemmer House Publishers, Inc.; Sterling Publishing; Stevens, Inc., Gareth; Stormline Press; Tapley, Publisher, Inc., Lance; Texas A&M University Press; Texas Christian University Press; Troubador Press; UAHC Press; Victor Books; Woodbine House; Woodsong Graphics, Inc.; Workman Publishing Company, Inc.

Labor/Management. Abbott, Langer & Associates; Acropolis Books, Ltd.; ALA Books; Asher-Gallant Press; BNA Books; Catholic Health Association of the United States, The; Communications Press; Drama Book Publishers; Enterprise Publishing Co., Inc.; Fairchild Books & Visuals; Federal Personnel Management Institute, Inc.; Hamilton Institute, Alexander; ILR Press; International Publishers Co., Inc.; Lomond Publications, Inc.; MGI Management Institute, Inc., The; Teachers College Press; University Associates, Inc.

Language and Literature. Asian Humanities Press; Baker Book House Company; Bantam Books; Barron's Educational Series, Inc.; Breakwater Books; Camden House, Inc.; Caratzas, Publisher, Aristide D.; Cassell Publications; Catholic University of America Press; Center for Applied Linguistics; Clarion Books; Coles Publishing Co., Ltd.; College Board, The; Coteau Books; Creative Arts Book Company; Crossing Press, The; Daniel and Company, Publishers, John; Dante University Of America Press, Inc.; Dunburn Press Ltd.; Facts On File, Inc.; Family Album, The; Fiddlehead Poetry Books & Goose Lane Editions; Gallaudet University Press; Gaslight Publications; Godine, Publisher, David R.; Humanities Press International, Inc.; Indiana University Press; Intervarsity Press; Kent State University Press; Lang Publishing, Peter; Longwood Academic; McFarland & Company, Inc., Publishers; Michigan State University Press; Milkweed Editions; Modern Language Association of America; National Textbook Co.; Ohio State University Press; Ohio University Press; Oregon State University Press; Penkevill Publishing Company, The; Pippin Press; Potter, Inc., Clarkson N.; Prentice Hall Canada, Inc.; Princeton University Press; Prolingua Associates; Purdue University Press; Regnery/Gateway, Inc.; Sasquatch Books; Scojtia Publishing Co., Inc.; Stanford University Press; Tapley, Publisher, Lance; Thomas, Publisher, Charles C.; Three Continents Press; Tuttle Publishing Company, Inc., Charles E.; University of Alabama Press; University of California Press; University of Illinois Press; University of Iowa Press; University of Michigan Press; University of Oklahoma Press; University of Texas Press; University Press of America, Inc.; University Press of Mississippi; Utah State University Press; Vehicule Press; Wake Forest University Press; Walch, Publisher, J. Weston; Wiley & Sons, Inc., John; York Press Ltd.; Zoland Books, Inc.

Law. Anderson Publishing Co.; Banks-Baldwin Law Publishing Co.; BNA Books; Commerce Clearing House, Inc.; Copyright Information Services; EES Publications; Enterprise Publishing Co., Inc.; Government Institutes, Inc.; Hamilton Institute, Alexander; International Self-Counsel Press, Ltd.; Linch Publishing, Inc.; Monitor Book Co.; Ohio State University Press; Rutgers University Press; Transaction Books; Transnational Publishers, Inc.; Trend Book Division; University of Michigan Press; University of Pennsylvania Press.

Literary Criticism. Barron's Educational Series, Inc.; Borgo Press, The; Dunburn Press Ltd.; ECS Press; Fairleigh Dickinson University Press; Firebrand Books; Graywolf Press; Holmes & Meier Publishers, Inc.; Lang Publishing, Peter; Longwood Academic; Mysterious Press, The; Northern Illinois University Press; Q.E.D. Press Of Ann Arbor, Inc.; Routledge, Chapman & Hall, Inc.; Texas Christian University Press; Three Continents Press; Umi Research Press; University of Alabama Press; University of Massachusetts Press; University of Missouri Press; University of Pennsylvania Press; University of Tennessee Press, The; University Press of Mississippi; University Press of Virginia; York Press Ltd.

Marine Subjects. Binford & Mort Publishing; Cornell Maritime Press, Inc.; Fiddlehead Poetry Books & Goose Lane Editions; Flores Publications, J.; Harbor House Publishers; International Marine Publishing Co.; Tab Book, Inc.; Transportation Trails; Western Marine Enterprises, Inc.

Military/War. ABC-CLIO, Inc.; Avon Books; Bantam Books; Beau Lac Publishers; Crown Publishers, Inc.; Eakin Publications, Inc.; Fine, Inc., Donald I.; Flores Publications, J.; Global Business and Trade Communications; Gower Publishing Co.; Howell Press, Inc.; McFarland & Co., Inc; Modern Books and Crafts, Inc.; Old Army Press, The; Oregon Historical Society Press; Outbooks; Paladin Press; Prentice Hall Press; Princeton University Press; Schiffer Publishing Ltd.; Scojtia Publishing Co., Inc.; Southfarm Press; Stackpole Books; Sterling Publishing; Texas A&M University Press; University Press of Kansas; Weiser, Inc., Samuel.

Money/Finance. Allen Publishing Co.; Bale Books; Bantam Books; Better Homes and Gardens Books; Briarcliff Press Publishers; Brick House Publishing Co.; Cambridge Career Products; Carol Publishing; Catholic Health Association of the United States, The; Contemporary Books, Inc.; Davenport, Publishers, May; Enterprise Publishing Co., Inc.; Financial Sourcebooks; Global Business and Trade Communications; Gollehon Press Inc.; Hancock House Publishers Ltd.; Hensley, Inc., Virgil W.; Horizon Publishers & Distributors; Intergalactic Publishing Co.; International

Resources; International Wealth Success; Liberty House; Longman Financial Services Publishing; McGraw Hill Ryerson; NavPress; Nichols Publishing; Pilot Books; Probus Publishing Co.; R&E Publishers; Scojtia Publishing Co., Inc.; Tuttle Publishing Company, Inc., Charles E.; ULI, The Urban Land Institute; United Resource Press; Wilshire Book Co.; Windsor Books

Music and Dance. American Catholic Press; Atheneum Children's Books; Bantam Books; Bergh Publishing, Inc.; Betterway Publications, Inc.; Branden Publishing Co., Inc..; Carol Publishing; Carolrhoda Books, Inc.; Creative Arts Book Company; Dance Horizons; Davenport, Publishers, May; Delta Books; Dembner Books; Devin-Adair Publishers, Inc.; Drama Book Publishers; Eriksson, Publisher, Paul S.; Faber & Faber, Inc.; Facts On File, Inc.; Fairleigh Dickinson University Press; Glenbridge Publishing Ltd.; Godine, Publisher, David R.; Gordon and Breach; Guernica Editions; Harper & Row Publishers, Inc.; Holmes & Meier Publishers, Inc.; Horizon Publishers & Distributors; Krieger Publishing Co., Inc., Robert E.; Lang Publishing, Peter; Leonard Publishing Corp.; Longwood Academic; McFarland & Company, Inc., Publishers; Meriwether Publishing Ltd.; Mosaic Press Miniature Books; National Book Company; Pelican Publishing Company; Pippin Press; Platt & Munk Publishers; Pomegranate Press, Ltd.; Prima Publishing and Communications; Princeton Book Company, Publishers; Princeton University Press; Q.E.D. Press Of Ann Arbor, Inc.; Quill; R&E Publishers; Real Comet Press, The; Resource Publications, Inc.; Rosen Publishing Group, The; San Francisco Press, Inc.; Scarecrow Press, Inc.; Schirmer Books; Scojtia Publishing Co., Inc.; Shoe Tree Press; Stipes Publishing Co.; Tab Book, Inc.; Timber Press, Inc.; Transaction Books; University of Illinois Press; University of Michigan Press; University of Minnesota Press; University Press of America, Inc.; Vestal Press, Ltd., The; Wadsworth Publishing Company; Walch, Publisher, J. Weston; Walker and Co.; Writer's Digest Books.

Nature Environment. Appalachian Mountain Club Books; Atheneum Children's Books; Backcountry Publications; Bear Flag Books; Binford & Mort Publishing; BNA Books; Bookmakers Guild, Inc.; Breakwater Books; Canadian Plains Research Center; Carol Publishing; Carolina Biological Supply Co.; Carolrhoda Books, Inc.; Chelsea Green; Clarion Books; Colorado Associated University Press; Countryman Press, Inc., The; Countrywoman's Press, The; Crown Publishers, Inc.; Daniel and Company, Publishers, John; Devin-Adair Publishers, Inc.; Devonshire Publishing Co.; Down East Books; Dustbooks; Dutton Children's Books; Eakin Publications, Inc.; Elysium Growth Press; Eriksson, Publisher, Paul S.; Facts On File, Inc.; Flora And Fauna Publications; Forman Publishing; Four Winds Press; Fulcrum, Inc.; Godine, Publisher, David R.; Gordon and Breach; Government Institutes, Inc.; Greene Press, The Stephen/Pelham Books; Greenhaven Press, Inc.; Hancock House Publishers Ltd.; Harbinger House, Inc.; Harper & Row Publishers, Inc.; Heyday Books; Homestead Publishing; Horizon Publishers & Distributors; Houghton Mifflin Co.; International Resources; Kesend Publishing, Ltd., Michael; Lexikos; Lyons & Burford, Publishers, Inc.; Milkweed Editions; Mosaic Press Miniature Books; Mountain Press Publishing Company; Muir Publications, John; Museum of Northern Arizona Press; New England Press, Inc., The; Noble Press, Incorporated, The; Northland Publishing Co., Inc.; Oregon Historical Society Press; Outbooks; Overlook Press; Pacific Press Publishing Association; Pennsylvania Historical and Museum Commission; Pineapple Press, Inc.; Pippin Press; Plexus Publishing, Inc.; Potter, Inc., Clarkson N.; Prentice Hall Press; Princeton University Press; R&E Publishers; Random House, Inc./ Alfred A. Knopf, Inc. Juvenile Books; Review and Herald Publishing Association; Rocky Top Publications; S.C.E.-Editions L'Etincelle; S.O.C.O. Publications; Sasquatch Books; Scojtia Publishing Co., Inc.; Scribner's Sons, Charles; Seven Locks Press, Inc.; Shoe Tree Press; Sierra Club Books; Silver Burdett Press; Stemmer House Publishers, Inc.; Stevens, Inc., Gareth; Symmes Systems; Tapley, Publisher, Inc., Lance; Texas A&M University Press; Texas Monthly Press Inc.; Thomas, Publisher, Charles C.; Timber Press, Inc.; University of Alberta Press, The; University of Arizona Press; University of California Press; University of Minnesota Press; University of Texas Press; University Press of Mississippi; Unlimited Publishing Co.; Walker and Co.; Washington State University Press; Wilderness Adventure Books; Williamson Publishing Co.; Willow Creek Press; Woodbridge Press; Workman Publishing Company, Inc.; Zoland Books, Inc.

Philosophy. American Atheist Press; Aquarian Press Ltd., The; Asian Humanities Press; Atheneum Children's Books; Atlantic Monthly Press; Baker Book House Company; Bantam Books; Brethren Press; Carol Publishing; Cassandra Press; Catholic University of America Press; Christopher Publishing House, The; Daniel and Company, Publishers, John; Ediciones Universal; Eerdmans Publishing Co., William B.; Elysium Growth Press; Enslow Publishers; Eriksson, Publisher, Paul S.; Facts On File, Inc.; Fairleigh Dickinson University Press; Fairleigh Dickinson University Press; Fell Publishers, Inc., Frederick; Gifted Education Press; Glenbridge Publishing Ltd.; Gordon and Breach; Gower Publishing Co.; Greenhaven Press, Inc.; Guernica Editions; Harper & Row Publishers, Inc.; Harper & Row, San Francisco; Humanities Press International, Inc.; Indiana University Press; Intercultural Press, Inc.; International Publishers Co., Inc.; Intervarsity Press; Krieger Publishing Co., Inc., Robert E.; Lang Publishing, Peter; Library Research Associates, Inc.; Longwood Academic; Loompanics Unlimited; Mercer University Press; Michigan State University Press; Miller Books; Noble Press, Incorporated, The; Ohio State University Press; Ohio University Press; Paragon House Publishers; Paulist Press; Princeton University Press; Purdue University Press; Q.E.D. Press Of Ann Arbor, Inc.; R&E Publishers; Renaissance House Publishers; Rocky Top Publications; Routledge, Chapman & Hall, Inc.; Roxbury Publishing Co.; St. Bede's Publications; Scojtia Publishing Co., Inc.; Second Chance Press/Permanent Press; Shapolsky Publishers;

Sierra Club Books; Simon & Schuster; Tabor Publishing; Teachers College Press; Theosophical Publishing House, The; Thomas, Publisher, Charles C.; Transaction Books; Tuttle Publishing Company, Inc., Charles E.; University of Alabama Press; University of Alberta Press, The; University of Arizona Press; University of Massachusetts Press; University of Minnesota Press; University of Utah Press; University Press of America, Inc.; University Press of Kansas; Vesta Publications, Ltd.; Wadsworth Publishing Company; Washington State University Press; Weiser, Inc., Samuel; Wingbow Press; Winston-Derek Publishers, Inc.; Wizards Bookshelf; Woodsong Graphics, Inc.

Photography. Atheneum Children's Books; Bear Flag Books; Branden Publishing Co., Inc..; Breakwater Books; Carstens Publications, Inc.; Clarion Books; Consultant Press, The; Coteau Books; Crown Publishers, Inc.; Cuff Publications Limited, Harry; Elysium Growth Press; Eriksson, Publisher, Paul S.; Fiddlehead Poetry Books & Goose Lane Editions; Focal Press; Godine, Publisher, David R.; Gordon and Breach; Homestead Publishing; Howell Press, Inc.; Hudson Hill Press, Inc.; International Resources; Milkweed Editions; Miller Books; Moonfall Publishing, Inc.; Motorbooks International Publishers & Wholesalers, Inc.; Oregon Historical Society Press; PBC International, Inc.; Pennsylvania Historical and Museum Commission; Pomegranate Press, Ltd.; Potter, Inc., Clarkson N.; Prentice Hall Press; Purdue University Press; Real Comet Press, The; S.O.C.O. Publications; Sasquatch Books; Scojtia Publishing Co., Inc.; Scribner's Sons, Charles; Shapolsky Publishers; Sierra Club Books; Sterling Publishing; Stormline Press; Studio Press; Symmes Systems; Tab Book, Inc.; Tapley, Publisher, Inc., Lance; Texas Monthly Press Inc.; University of Minnesota Press; University of Texas Press; Wake Forest University Press; Workman Publishing Company, Inc.; Writer's Digest Books; Zoland Books, Inc.

Psychology. African American Images; American Psychiatric Press, Inc., The; American Studies Press, Inc.; Aquarian Press Ltd., The; Arbor House; Atheneum Children's Books; Baker Book House Company; Ballantine/Epiphany Books; Bantam Books; Bart Books; Bergh Publishing, Inc.; Betterway Publications, Inc.; Blue Dolphin Publishing, Inc.; Bookmakers Guild, Inc.; Brethren Press; Carol Publishing; Carroll & Graf Publishers, Inc.; Cassandra Press; Cheribe Publishing Co.; Christopher Publishing House, The; Citadel Press; Compact Books; CompCare Publishers; Contemporary Books, Inc.; Crown Publishers, Inc.; Devonshire Publishing Co.; Dimension Books, Inc.; Ediciones Universal; Education Associates; Eerdmans Publishing Co., William B.; Elysium Growth Press; Enslow Publishers; Eriksson, Publisher, Paul S.; Facts On File, Inc.; Fairleigh Dickinson University Press; Fell Publishers, Inc., Frederick; Fisher Books; Gallaudet University Press; Gardner Press, Inc.; Gifted Education Press; Glenbridge Publishing Ltd.; Gordon and Breach; Greene Press, The Stephen/Pelham Books; Guernica Editions; Harbinger House, Inc.; Harper & Row Publishers, Inc.; Harper & Row, San Francisco; Hawkes Publishing, Inc.; Horizon Publishers & Distributors; Houghton Mifflin Co.; Humanics Publishing Group; Hunter House, Inc., Publishers; Intercultural Press, Inc.; International Self-Counsel Press, Ltd.; Intervarsity Press; Ishiyaku Euroamerica, Inc.; Krieger Publishing Co., Inc., Robert E.; Lang Publishing, Peter; Libra Publishers, Inc.; Luramedia; Metamorphous Press; Moonfall Publishing, Inc.; Mother Courage Press; NavPress; New Idea Press, Inc.; Newcastle Publishing Co., Inc.; Penkevill Publishing Company, The; Perspectives Press; Pickering Press, The; Plenum Publishing; Poseidon Press; Potomac-Pacific Press; Prentice Hall Press; Prima Publishing and Communications; Quill; R&E Publishers; Riverdale Company, Inc., Publishers, The; Ronin Publishing; Roundtable Publishing, Inc.; Routledge, Chapman & Hall, Inc.; Roxbury Publishing Co.; Russell Sage Foundation; S.C.E.-Editions L'Etincelle; St. Paul Books and Media; Scojtia Publishing Co., Inc.; Shaw Publishers, Harold; Tabor Publishing; Theosophical Publishing House, The; Thomas, Publisher, Charles C.; Transaction Books; Tyndale House Publishers, Inc.; University of Minnesota Press; University Press of America, Inc.; Victor Books; Walch, Publisher, J. Weston; Walker and Co.; Washington State University Press; Weiser, Inc., Samuel; Westport Publishers, Inc.; Williamson Publishing Co.; Wilshire Book Co.; Wingbow Perss; Woodbridge Press; Woodsong Graphics, Inc.

Real Estate. Contemporary Books, Inc.; Government Institutes, Inc.; Liberty House; Linch Publishing, Inc.; ULI, The Urban Land Institute.

Recreation. Appalachian Mountain Club Books; Arbor House; Atheneum Children's Books; Backcountry Publications; Bear Flag Books; Binford & Mort Publishing; Breakwater Books; Cambridge Career Products; Carol Publishing; Chatham Press; Chockstone Press, Inc.; Compact Books; Countryman Press, Inc., The; Countrywoman's Press, The; Crown Publishers, Inc.; Down East Books; Elysium Growth Press; Enslow Publishers; Eriksson, Publisher, Paul S.; Facts On File, Inc.; Falcon Press Publishing Co.; Fell Publishers, Inc., Frederick; Gardner Press, Inc.; Golden West Publishers; Gollehon Press Inc.; Greene Press, The Stephen/Pelham Books; Guernica Editions; Hancock House Publishers Ltd.; Heyday Books; Hippocrene Books Inc.; Horizon Publishers & Distributors; Java Publishing Company; Kalmbach Publishing Co.; Krieger Publishing Co., Inc., Robert E.; Mc Farland & Company, Inc., Publishers; McGraw Hill Ryerson; Meriwether Publishing Ltd.; Mountain Press Publishing Company; Mountaineers Books, The; Muir Publications, John; Mustang Publishing Co.; Outbooks; Overlook Press; Peachtree Publishers, Ltd.; Pelican Publishing Company; Princeton Book Company, Publishers; Random House, Inc./Alfred A. Knopf, Inc. Juvenile Books; Riverdale Company, Inc., Publishers, The; Sasquatch Books; Scojtia Publishing Co., Inc.; Scribner's Sons, Charles; Shoe Tree Press; Sierra Club Books; Sterling Publishing; Stipes Publishing Co.; Tapley, Publisher, Inc., Lance; Texas Monthly Press Inc.; Thomas, Publisher, Charles C.;

Twin Peaks Press; Westport Publishers, Inc.; Wilderness Press; Wilshire Book Co.; Workman Publishing Company, Inc.

Reference. AASH Press; Abbott, Langer & Associates; ABC-CLIO, Inc.; Accelerated Development Inc.; Acropolis Books, Ltd.; Adams, Inc., Bob; ALA Books; American Atheist Press; American Hospital Publishing, Inc.; American Psychiatric Press, Inc., The; American References Inc.; Ancestry Incorporated; Andrews and McMeel; Apollo Books; Appalachian Mountain Club Books; Arman Publishing, Inc., M.; Asher-Gallant Press; Asian Humanities Press; Backcountry Publications; Baker Book House Company; Banks-Baldwin Law Publishing Co.; Bart Books; Bear Flag Books; Behrman House Inc.; Bethany House Publishers; Betterway Publications, Inc.; Binford & Mort Publishing; Blue Bird Publishing; BNA Books; Bookmakers Guild, Inc.; Borgo Press, The; Branden Publishing Co., Inc..; Breakwater Books; Brick House Publishing Co.; Broadway Press; Camden House, Inc.; Caratzas, Publisher, Aristide D.; Cassell Publications; Cheribe Publishing Co.; Chockstone Press, Inc.; Christopher Publishing House, The; Clark Co., Arthur H.; Cleaning Consultant Services, Inc.; College Board, The; Communications Press; Compact Books; Compute! Books; Computer Science Press, Inc.; Contemporary Books, Inc.; Coteau Books; Crown Publishers, Inc.; Cuff Publications Limited, Harry; Dante University Of America Press, Inc.; Davis Publishing, Steve; Dembner Books; Devonshire Publishing Co.; Drama Book Publishers; EES Publications; ECS Press; Ediciones Universal; Eerdmans Publishing Co., William B.; Enslow Publishers; Evans and Co., Inc., M.; Facts On File, Inc.; Fairleigh Dickinson University Press; Fiddlehead Poetry Books & Goose Lane Editions; Financial Sourcebooks; Five Star Publications; Flora And Fauna Publications; Focal Press; Gallaudet University Press; Gardner Press, Inc.; Garland Publishing, Inc.; Gaslight Publications; Genealogical Publishing Co., Inc.; Glenbridge Publishing Ltd.; Gordon and Breach; Government Institutes, Inc.; Gower Publishing Co.; Graphic Arts Technical Foundation; Greenhaven Press, Inc.; Guernica Editions; Harper & Row Publishers, Inc.; Harper & Row, San Francisco; Harvard Common Press, The; Harvest House Publishers; Health Administration Press; Here's Life Publishers, Inc.; Heritage Books, Inc.; Heyday Books; Hippocrene Books Inc.; Holmes & Meier Publishers, Inc.; Homestead Publishing; Human Kinetics Publishers, Inc.; Hunter Publishing, Inc.; ILR Press; Imagine, Inc.; Indiana University Press; Industrial Press, Inc.; Information Resources Press; Intercultural Press, Inc.; International Foundation Of Employee Benefit Plans; International Publishers Co., Inc.; International Resources; International Self-Counsel Press, Ltd.; Ishiyaku Euroamerica, Inc.; Jonathan David Publishers; Kinseeker Publications; Klein Publications, B.; Krieger Publishing Co., Inc., Robert E.; Lang Publishing, Peter; Leisure Press; Libraries Unlimited; Library Research Associates, Inc.; Liturgical Publications, Inc.; Longman Financial Services Publishing; Longwood Academic; Loompanics Unlimited; McFarland & Company, Inc., Publishers; McGraw Hill Ryerson; Madison Books; Mazda Publishers; Meadowbrook Press; Media Forum International, Ltd.; Mercer University Press; Meriwether Publishing Ltd.; Metamorphous Press; Michigan State University Press; Milady Publishing Company; Modern Language Association of America; Monitor Book Co.; Morgan-Rand Publications Inc.; Muir Publications, John; Museum of Northern Arizona Press; Mysterious Press, The; National Book Company; New York Zoetrope, Inc.; Nichols Publishing; Noble Press, Incorporated, The; Old Army Press, The; Oregon Historical Society Press; Oryx Press; Our Sunday Visitor, Inc.; Outbooks; Overlook Press; Pacific Books, Publishers; Paragon House Publishers; Penkevill Publishing Company, The; Pennsylvania Historical and Museum Commission; Pharos Books; Pineapple Press, Inc.; Plexus Publishing, Inc.; Pocket Books; Porter Sargent Publishers, Inc.; Princeton Book Company, Publishers; Princeton University Press; Professional Publications, Inc.; Prolingua Associates; Que Corporation; R&E Publishers; Rainbow Books; Rocky Top Publications; Rodale Press; Rosen Publishing Group, The; Routledge, Chapman & Hall, Inc.; Rutledge Hill Press; S.C.E.-Editions L'Etincelle; St. Martin's Press; Sandlapper Publishing, Inc.; Scarecrow Press, Inc.; Schiffer Publishing Ltd.; Schirmer Books; Science Tech Publishers, Inc.; Scojtia Publishing Co., Inc.; Seven Locks Press, Inc.; Shaw Publishers, Harold; Speech Bin, Inc., The; ST Publications, Inc.; Standard Publishing; Starrhill Press; Sterling Publishing; Stevens, Inc., Gareth; Storie/McOwen Publishers, Inc.; Tapley, Publisher, Inc., Lance; Texas Monthly Press Inc.; Thomas Publications; Transaction Books; Transnational Publishers, Inc.; Trend Book Division; Tuttle Publishing Company, Inc., Charles E.; Twin Peaks Press; Ultralight Publications, Inc.; Union Square Press; United Resource Press; University of Alberta Press, The; University of Illinois Press; University of Michigan Press; University of Minnesota Press; University Press of Kentucky; Unlimited Publishing Co.; Utah State University Press; Vesta Publications, Ltd.; Victor Books; Walker and Co.; Westport Publishers, Inc.; Whitford Press; Whitson Publishing Co., The; Wiley & Sons, Inc., John; Wingbow Perss; Woodbine House; Woodsong Graphics, Inc.; York Press Ltd.

Regional. Aegina Press, Inc.; Appalachian Mountain Club Books; Bear Flag Books; Binford & Mort Publishing; Blair, Publisher, John F.; Borealis Press, Ltd.; Boston Mills Press, The; Breakwater Books; Carol Publishing; Caxton Printers, Ltd., The; Chatham Press; Cherokee Publishing Company; Colorado Associated University Press; Coteau Books; Countryman Press, Inc., The; Creative Arts Book Company; Creative Publishing Co.; Cuff Publications Limited, Harry; Dillon Press, Inc.; Down East Books; Dunburn Press Ltd.; Eakin Publications, Inc.; ECS Press; Eerdmans Publishing Co., William B.; Faber & Faber, Inc.; Family Album, The; Fiddlehead Poetry Books & Goose Lane Editions; Fitzhenry & Whiteside, Ltd.; Gallaudet University Press; Godine, Publisher, David R.; Golden West Books; Golden West Publishers; Great Northwest Publishing and Distributing

Company, Inc.; Greene Press, The Stephen/Pelham Books; Guernica Editions; Hancock House Publishers Ltd.; Harbor House Publishers; Heart Of The Lakes Publishing; Heritage Books, Inc.; Heyday Books; Howell Press, Inc.; Indiana University Press; Interurban Press/Trans Anglo Books; Kent State University Press; Lexikos; McGraw Hill Ryerson; Melior Publications; Mercer University Press; Middle Atlantic Press; Milkweed Editions; Mountain Press Publishing Company; Museum of Northern Arizona Press; National Gallery of Canada; Nimbus Publishing Limited; Northern Illinois University Press; Ohio University Press; Oregon Historical Society Press; Outbooks; Pacific Books, Publishers; Pacific Press Publishing Association; Pennsylvania Historical and Museum Commission; Pickering Press, The; Prentice Hall Canada, Inc. ; Purdue University Press; R&E Publishers; Renaissance House Publishers; Sandlapper Publishing, Inc.; Sasquatch Books; Schiffer Publishing Ltd.; Stormline Press; Sunstone Press; Syracuse University Press; Tapley, Publisher, Inc., Lance; Texas A&M University Press; Texas Christian University Press; Texas Monthly Press Inc.; Texas Western Press; Timber Press, Inc.; Trend Book Division; Tuttle Publishing Company, Inc., Charles E.; University of Alberta Press, The; University of Arizona Press; University of Michigan Press; University of Minnesota Press; University of Missouri Press; University of Nevada Press; University of Tennessee Press, The; University of Texas Press; University Press of Kansas; University Press of Mississippi; Utah State University Press; Vehicule Press; Vestal Press, Ltd., The; Washington State University Press; Westernlore Press; Westport Publishers, Inc.; Wilderness Adventure Books; Wordware Publishing, Inc.; Yankee Books; Zoland Books, Inc.

Religion. Abingdon Press; Accent Books; Aglow Publications; Alban Institue, Inc., The; American Atheist Press; American Catholic Press; Aquarian Press Ltd., The; Asian Humanities Press; Atheneum Children's Books; Augsburg Books; Baker Book House Company; Ballantine/Epiphany Books; Bantam Books; Beacon Hill Press of Kansas City; Bear and Co., Inc.; Bethany House Publishers; Blue Dolphin Publishing, Inc.; Bookcraft, Inc.; Bosco Publications, Don; Brethren Press; Broadman Press; C.S.S. Publishing Co.; Caratzas, Publisher, Aristide D.; Cassandra Press; Catholic University of America Press; Chosen Books Publishing Co.; Christopher Publishing House, The; Christopher Publishing House, The; College Press Publishing Co.; Compact Books; Crossway Books; Devonshire Publishing Co.; Dimension Books, Inc.; Eerdmans Publishing Co., William B.; Facts On File, Inc.; Fell Publishers, Inc., Frederick; Fleet Press Corp.; Franciscan Herald Press; Fraser Institute, The; Gardner Press, Inc.; Gospel Publishing House; Gower Publishing Co.; Greenhaven Press, Inc.; Guernica Editions; Harper & Row, San Francisco; Harper & Row Publishers, Inc.; Harvest House Publishers; Hendrickson Publishers Inc.; Hensley, Inc., Virgil W.; Herald Press; Here's Life Publishers, Inc.; Horizon Publishers & Distributors; Howell Press, Inc.; Human Kinetics Publishers, Inc.; Indiana University Press; Intervarsity Press; Jalmar Press, Inc.; Krieger Publishing Co., Inc., Robert E.; Lang Publishing, Peter; Life Cycle Books; Liguori Publications; Lion Publishing Corporation; Liturgical Publications, Inc.; Living Flame Press; Longwood Academic; Loyola University Press; McFarland & Company, Inc., Publishers; Meriwether Publishing Ltd.; Michigan State University Press; Moonfall Publishing, Inc.; Morehouse Publishing Co.; Morrow and Co., William; Mott Media, Inc., Publishers; Multnomah Press; NavPress; New Leaf Press, Inc.; Newcastle Publishing Co., Inc.; Noble Press, Incorporated, The; Our Sunday Visitor, Inc.; Pacific Press Publishing Association; Paragon House Publishers; Paulist Press; Pelican Publishing Company; Pennsylvania Historical and Museum Commission; Peter Pauper Press, Inc.; Pickwick Publications; Princeton University Press; Purdue University Press; Religious Education Press; Resource Publications, Inc.; Revell, Fleming H. Co.; Review and Herald Publishing Association; S.C.E.-Editions L'Etincelle; St. Anthony Messenger Press; St. Bede's Publications; St. Paul Books and Media; St. Vladimir's Seminary Press; Scojtia Publishing Co., Inc.; Servant Publications; Seven Locks Press, Inc.; Shapolsky Publishers; Standard Publishing; Tabor Publishing; Tapley, Publisher, Inc., Lance; Theosophical Publishing House, The; Thomas, Publisher, Charles C.; Tuttle Publishing Company, Inc., Charles E.; Tyndale House Publishers, Inc.; UAHC Press; University of Alabama Press; University of Tennessee Press, The; University Press of America, Inc.; Vesta Publications, Ltd.; Victor Books; Wadsworth Publishing Company; Weiser, Inc., Samuel; Whitaker House; Wingbow Perss; Winston-Derek Publishers, Inc.; Wolgemuth & Hyatt, Publishers; Workman Publishing Company, Inc.; Zondervan Corp., The.

Scholarly. Humanities Press International, Inc.; Lomond Publications, Inc.; Longwood Academic; McFarland & Company, Inc., Publishers; Mazda Publishers; Mercer University Press; Michigan State University Press; Mott Media, Inc., Publishers; Nelson-Hall; Ohio University Press; Oise Press; Oregon State University Press; Pacific Books, Publishers; Penkevill Publishing Company, The; Pickwick Publications; Princeton University Press; Purdue University Press; Religious Education Press; Riverdale Company, Inc., Publishers, The; Rutgers University Press; St. Vladimir's Seminary Press; Schirmer Books; Southern Illinois University Press; Stanford University Press; Texas Christian University Press; Texas Western Press; Three Continents Press; Transaction Books; Transnational Publishers, Inc.; Umi Research Press; University of Alabama Press; University of Alberta Press, The; University of Arizona Press; University of Calgary Press, The; University of California Press; University of Illinois Press; University of Missouri Press; University of Pennsylvania Press; University of Tennessee Press, The; University of Texas Press; University of Utah Press; University of Wisconsin Press; University Press of America, Inc.; University Press of Kansas; University Press of Kentucky; University Press of Mississippi; Utah State University Press; Washington State University Press; Westernlore Press; Whitson Publishing Co., The; Whitson Publishing Co., The; York Press Ltd.

Science/Technology. American Astronautical Society; American Institute of Physics; Arcsoft Publishers; Baen Publishing Enterprises; Bantam Books; Bear and Co., Inc.; Carol Publishing; Carolina Biological Supply Co.; College Board, The; Crown Publishers, Inc.; Dillon Press, Inc.; Dutton Children's Books; Enslow Publishers; Focal Press; Gallaudet University Press; Gordon and Breach; Grapevine Publications, Inc.; Harper & Row Publishers, Inc.; Houghton Mifflin Co.; Industrial Press, Inc.; Interstate Publishers, Inc. The; Iowa State University Press; Krieger Publishing Co., Inc., Robert E.; Little, Brown and Co., Inc.; Lomond Publications, Inc.; Longwood Academic; Lyons & Burford, Publishers, Inc.; Metamorphous Press; Mountain Press Publishing Company; Museum of Northern Arizona Press; National Book Company; Naturegraph Publishers, Inc.; Noyes Data Corp.; Oddo Publishing, Inc.; Outbooks; Platt & Munk Publishers; Plenum Publishing; Prentice Hall Canada, Inc.; Prentice Hall Canada, Inc.; Princeton University Press; Quill; R&E Publishers; Random House, Inc./Alfred A. Knopf, Inc. Juvenile Books; Rocky Top Publications; Ross Books; Routledge, Chapman & Hall, Inc.; Rutgers University Press; St. Martin's Press; Scojtia Publishing Co., Inc.; Scribner's Sons, Charles; Sierra Club Books; Silver Burdett Press; Simon & Schuster; Stackpole Books; Stanford University Press; Theosophical Publishing House, The; Thomas, Publisher, Charles C.; Times Books; Transaction Books; Union Square Press; Univelt, Inc.; University of Arizona Press; University of Michigan Press; University of Pennsylvania Press; University of Texas Press; Walker and Co.; Woodbine House.

Self-Help. AASH Press; Accent Books; Acropolis Books, Ltd.; Advocacy Press; African American Images; Aglow Publications; Allen Publishing Co.; Arbor House; Atheneum Children's Books; Augsburg Books; Avon Books; Baker Book House Company; Ballantine/Epiphany Books; Bantam Books; Bart Books; Benjamin Company, Inc., The; Betterway Publications, Inc.; Blue Dolphin Publishing, Inc.; C.S.S. Publishing Co.; Cambridge Career Products; Carol Publishing; Carolina Biological Supply Co.; Cassandra Press; CCC Publications; Cheribe Publishing Co.; Chosen Books Publishing Co.; Christopher Publishing House, The; Cleaning Consultant Services, Inc.; Cliffs Notes, Inc.; Coles Publishing Co., Ltd.; College Board, The; Compact Books; CompCare Publishers; Contemporary Books, Inc.; Crown Publishers, Inc.; Daniel and Company, Publishers, John; E. P. Dutton; Elysium Growth Press; Enslow Publishers; Enterprise Publishing Co., Inc.; Eriksson, Publisher, Paul S.; Fell Publishers, Inc., Frederick; Fine, Inc., Donald I.; Fisher Books; Flores Publications, J.; Forman Publishing; Fulcrum, Inc.; Gallaudet University Press; Gardner Press, Inc.; Global Business and Trade Communications; Gollehon Press Inc.; Gospel Publishing House; Grapevine Publications, Inc.; Greene Press, The Stephen/Pelham Books; Hancock House Publishers Ltd.; Harbinger House, Inc.; Harper & Row Publishers, Inc.; Harper & Row, San Francisco; Harvard Common Press, The; Harvest House Publishers; Hawkes Publishing, Inc.; Hazelden Educational Materials; Herald Press; Here's Life Publishers, Inc.; Hippocrene Books Inc.; Horizon Publishers & Distributors; Human Kinetics Publishers, Inc.; Humanics Publishing Group; Hunter House, Inc., Publishers; Huntington House, Inc.; Intercultural Press, Inc.; International Resources; International Self-Counsel Press, Ltd.; International Wealth Success; Java Publishing Company; Kesend Publishing, Ltd., Michael; Klein Publications, B.; Liguori Publications; Liturgical Publications, Inc.; Living Flame Press; Loompanics Unlimited; Luramedia; McGraw Hill Ryerson; Media Productions and Marketing, Inc.; Meriwether Publishing Ltd.; Metamorphous Press; Middle Atlantic Press; Miller Books; Mills & Sanderson, Publishers; Modern Books and Crafts, Inc.; Moonfall Publishing, Inc.; Mother Courage Press; Mott Media, Inc., Publishers; Multnomah Press; Mustang Publishing Co.; New Idea Press, Inc.; New Leaf Press, Inc.; Newcastle Publishing Co., Inc.; Noble Press, Incorporated, The; Pacific Press Publishing Association; Parenting Press; Paulist Press; Pelican Publishing Company; Perspectives Press; Pickering Press, The; Pomegranate Press, Ltd.; Poseidon Press; Potomac-Pacific Press; Potter, Inc., Clarkson N.; Prentice Hall Press; Price Stern Sloan, Inc.; Prima Publishing and Communications; Princeton Book Company, Publishers; R&E Publishers; Rainbow Books; Rocky Top Publications; Rodale Press; Rosen Publishing Group, The; Roundtable Publishing, Inc.; S.C.E.-Editions L'Etincelle; S.O.C.O. Publications; St. Martin's Press; St. Paul Books and Media; Scojtia Publishing Co., Inc.; Shaw Publishers, Harold; Shore Associates, Michael; Spence Publishing; Spinsters/Aunt Lute Books; Sterling Publishing; Symmes Systems; Tapley, Publisher, Inc., Lance; Taylor Publishing Company; Theosophical Publishing House, The; Thomas, Publisher, Charles C.; Trillium Press; Twin Peaks Press; Ultralight Publications, Inc.; United Resource Press; Unlimited Publishing Co.; Victor Books; Walker and Co.; Weiser, Inc., Samuel; Whitford Press; Wiley & Sons, Inc., John; Williamson Publishing Co.; Wilshire Book Co.; Wingbow Perss; Wolgemuth & Hyatt, Publishers; Woodbine House; Woodbridge Press; Woodsong Graphics, Inc.; Workman Publishing Company, Inc.

Social Sciences. African American Images; Borgo Press, The; Brethren Press; C Q Press; Canadian Plains Research Center; Caratzas, Publisher, Aristide D.; Catholic University of America Press; Chelsea Green; Duquesne University Press; Eerdmans Publishing Co., William B.; Enslow Publishers; Fleet Press Corp.; Free Press, The; Garland Publishing, Inc.; Greene Press, The Stephen/Pelham Books; Harbinger House, Inc.; Indiana University Press; International Publishers Co., Inc.; Madison Books; Mazda Publishers; Prentice Hall Canada, Inc.; Riverdale Company, Inc., Publishers, The; Routledge, Chapman & Hall, Inc.; Roxbury Publishing Co.; Stanford University

Press; Teachers College Press; University of California Press; Wadsworth Publishing Company; Walch, Publisher, J. Weston; Whitson Publishing Co., The.

Sociology. Atheneum Children's Books; Baker Book House Company; Ballantine/Epiphany Books; Bantam Books; Betterway Publications, Inc.; Branden Publishing Co., Inc..; Breakwater Books; Brethren Press; Canadian Plains Research Center; Child Welfare League Of America; Christopher Publishing House, The; Cleis Press; Compact Books; Cuff Publications Limited, Harry; Dembner Books; Devonshire Publishing Co.; Ediciones Universal; Eerdmans Publishing Co., William B.; Elysium Growth Press; Eriksson, Publisher, Paul S.; Faber & Faber, Inc.; Fairleigh Dickinson University Press; Fell Publishers, Inc., Frederick; Fraser Institute, The; Gallaudet University Press; Gardner Press, Inc.; Glenbridge Publishing Ltd.; Gordon and Breach; Gower Publishing Co.; Greenhaven Press, Inc.; Harbinger House, Inc.; Harper & Row Publishers, Inc.; Harrow And Heston; Health Administration Press; Holmes & Meier Publishers, Inc.; Humanics Publishing Group; Humanities Press International, Inc.; ILR Press; Intercultural Press, Inc.; Intervarsity Press; Krieger Publishing Co., Inc., Robert E.; Lang Publishing, Peter; Libra Publishers, Inc.; Life Cycle Books; Lomond Publications, Inc.; McFarland & Company, Inc., Publishers; Madison Books; Mazda Publishers; Mercer University Press; Metamorphous Press; Moonfall Publishing, Inc.; Mother Courage Press; New Idea Press, Inc.; Noble Press, Incorporated, The; Ohio State University Press; Penkevill Publishing Company, The; Perspectives Press; Plenum Publishing; Potomac-Pacific Press; Princeton Book Company, Publishers; Princeton University Press; Purdue University Press; R&E Publishers; Riverdale Company, Inc., Publishers, The; Roxbury Publishing Co.; Russell Sage Foundation; Rutgers University Press; S.C.E.-Editions L'Etincelle; Seven Locks Press, Inc.; Stanford University Press; Stevens, Inc., Gareth; Teachers College Press; Thomas Publications; Thomas, Publisher, Charles C.; Transaction Books; Twin Peaks Press; University of Alabama Press; University of Alberta Press, The; University of Illinois Press; University of Massachusetts Press; University of Missouri Press; University Press of America, Inc.; University Press of Kansas; University Press of Kentucky; Unlimited Publishing Co.; Vehicule Press; Walch, Publisher, J. Weston; Washington State University Press; Woodbine House; Arbor House; Atheneum Children's Books.

Software. Accelerated Development Inc.; Anderson Publishing Co.; Arcsoft Publishers; Barron's Educational Series, Inc.; Branden Publishing Co., Inc..; Breakwater Books; Career Publishing, Inc.; Cheribe Publishing Co.; Compute! Books; Computer Science Press, Inc.; Devin-Adair Publishers, Inc.; Digital Press; Dustbooks; Family Album, The; Grapevine Publications, Inc.; Michigan State University Press; Milady Publishing Company; National Book Company; National Textbook Co.; New York Zoetrope, Inc.; Pacific Press Publishing Association; Que Corporation; R&E Publishers; Sybex, Inc.; Tab Book, Inc.; Trillium Press; Wordware Publishing, Inc.

Sports. Avon Books; Backcountry Publications; Bantam Books; Bart Books; Benjamin Company, Inc., The; Bergh Publishing, Inc.; Briarcliff Press Publishers; Cambridge Career Products; Carol Publishing; Chockstone Press, Inc.; Contemporary Books, Inc.; Crown Publishers, Inc.; Dembner Books; Devin-Adair Publishers, Inc.; Eakin Publications, Inc.; Enslow Publishers; Eriksson, Publisher, Paul S.; Facts On File, Inc.; Fine, Inc., Donald I.; Fisher Books; Gallaudet University Press; Gardner Press, Inc.; Greene Press, The Stephen/Pelham Books; Hancock House Publishers Ltd.; Harper & Row Publishers, Inc.; Howell Press, Inc.; Human Kinetics Publishers, Inc.; Java Publishing Company; Jonathan David Publishers; Kesend Publishing, Ltd., Michael; Krieger Publishing Co., Inc., Robert E.; Leisure Press; Little, Brown and Co., Inc.; Lyons & Burford, Publishers, Inc.; McFarland & Company, Inc., Publishers; McGraw Hill Ryerson; Milkweed Editions; Mosaic Press Miniature Books; Motorbooks International Publishers & Wholesalers, Inc.; Mountaineers Books, The; Muir Publications, John; Mustang Publishing Co.; Ohara Publications, Inc.; Overlook Press; Pennsylvania Historical and Museum Commission; Prentice Hall Canada, Inc. ; Prentice Hall Press; Princeton Book Company, Publishers; Random House, Inc./Alfred A. Knopf, Inc. Juvenile Books; Rodale Press; S.C.E.-Editions L'Etincelle; S.O.C.O. Publications; Sasquatch Books; Scribner's Sons, Charles; Shapolsky Publishers; Shoe Tree Press; Sierra Club Books; Stackpole Books; Sterling Publishing; Stoeger Publishing Company; Tapley, Publisher, Inc., Lance; Taylor Publishing Company; Texas Monthly Press Inc.; Thomas, Publisher, Charles C.; Times Books; Tuttle Publishing Company, Inc., Charles E.; Twin Peaks Press; University of Illinois Press; Wilderness Adventure Books; Willow Creek Press; Workman Publishing Company, Inc.

Technical. Abbott, Langer & Associates; ALA Books; American Astonautical Society; American Hospital Publishing, Inc.; American Psychiatric Press, Inc., The; Arcsoft Publishers; Arman Publishing, Inc., M.; Aviation Book Co.; Bentley, Inc., Robert; Branden Publishing Co., Inc..; Brick House Publishing Co.; Broadway Press; Camden House, Inc.; Canadian Plains Research Center; Caratzas, Publisher, Aristide D.; Carolina Biological Supply Co.; Cheribe Publishing Co.; Chilton Book Co.; Cleaning Consultant Services, Inc.; Coles Publishing Co., Ltd.; Commerce Clearing House, Inc.; Communications Press; Computer Science Press, Inc.; Cornell Maritime Press, Inc.; Craftsman Book Company; Cuff Publications Limited, Harry; Denlingers Publishers, Ltd.; Devonshire Publishing Co.; Digital Press; Dustbooks; EES Publications; Enslow Publishers; Federal Buyers Guide, Inc.; Federal Personnel Management Institute, Inc.; Fell Publishers, Inc., Frederick; Financial Sourcebooks; Flora And Fauna Publications; Focal Press; Gallaudet University Press; Gordon and Breach; Government Institutes, Inc.; Gower Publishing Co.; Grapevine Publications, Inc.; Graphic Arts Technical Foundation; Human Kinetics Publishers, Inc.; ILR Press; Industrial

Press, Inc.; Information Resources Press; International Foundation Of Employee Benefit Plans; Interweave Press; Iowa State University Press; Krieger Publishing Co., Inc., Robert E.; Leisure Press; Library Research Associates, Inc.; Lomond Publications, Inc.; McFarland & Company, Inc., Publishers; Medmaster, Inc.; Metamorphous Press; MGI Management Institute, Inc., The; Michigan State University Press; Morgan-Rand Publications Inc.; Mountain Press Publishing Company; Museum of Northern Arizona Press; National Book Company; New York Zoetrope, Inc.; Nichols Publishing; Pacific Books, Publishers; Pennsylvania Historical and Museum Commission; Princeton University Press; Probus Publishing Co.; Professional Publications, Inc.; Q.E.D. Information Sciences, Inc.; Que Corporation; R&E Publishers; Religious Education Press; Riverdale Company, Inc., Publishers, The; Rocky Top Publications; S.O.C.O. Publications; San Francisco Press, Inc.; Science Tech Publishers, Inc.; Scojtia Publishing Co., Inc.; ST Publications, Inc.; Sterling Publishing; Stipes Publishing Co.; Sybex, Inc.; Tab Book, Inc.; Texas Western Press; Thomas, Publisher, Charles C.; Transaction Books; ULI, The Urban Land Institute; Ultralight Publications, Inc.; Union Square Press; Univelt, Inc.; University of Alberta Press, The; University of Minnesota Press; Unlimited Publishing Co.; Vestal Press, Ltd., The; Willow Creek Press; Windsor Books; Wordware Publishing, Inc.

Textbook. Overlook Press; AASH Press; Abingdon Press; Accelerated Development Inc.; American Hospital Publishing, Inc.; American Psychiatric Press, Inc., The; Arman Publishing, Inc., M.; Asian Humanities Press; Baker Book House Company; Barron's Educational Series, Inc.; Behrman House Inc.; Bosco Publications, Don; Branden Publishing Co., Inc.; Breakwater Books; C Q Press; Canadian Plains Research Center; Caratzas, Publisher, Aristide D.; Career Publishing, Inc.; Catholic Health Association of the United States, The; Cheribe Publishing Co.; Christopher Publishing House, The; Cleaning Consultant Services, Inc.; Cliffs Notes, Inc.; College Press Publishing Co.; Commerce Clearing House, Inc.; Communications Press; Computer Science Press, Inc.; Cuff Publications Limited, Harry; Devonshire Publishing Co.; Drama Book Publishers; EES Publications; Education Associates; Eerdmans Publishing Co., William B.; Elysium Growth Press; ETC Publications; Fairchild Books & Visuals; Fell Publishers, Inc., Frederick; Financial Sourcebooks; Fitzhenry & Whiteside, Ltd.; Flora And Fauna Publications; Focal Press; Free Press, The; Gallaudet University Press; Gardner Press, Inc.; Glenbridge Publishing Ltd.; Global Business and Trade Communications; Gordon and Breach; Gower Publishing Co.; Grapevine Publications, Inc.; Graphic Arts Technical Foundation; Greenhaven Press, Inc.; Guernica Editions; Hardy—Publisher, Max; Harrow And Heston; Harvest House Publishers; Hazelden Educational Materials; Health Administration Press; Holmes & Meier Publishers, Inc.; Horizon Publishers & Distributors; Human Kinetics Publishers, Inc.; ILR Press; Information Resources Press; Intercultural Press, Inc.; International Foundation Of Employee Benefit Plans; International Publishers Co., Inc.; International Resources; Interstate Publishers, Inc. The; Intervarsity Press; Iowa State University Press; Ishiyaku Euroamerica, Inc.; Krieger Publishing Co., Inc., Robert E.; Libraries Unlimited; Liturgical Publications, Inc.; Longman Financial Services Publishing; Longwood Academic; Loyola University Press; Mazda Publishers; Media Productions and Marketing, Inc.; Mercer University Press; Metamorphous Press; Michigan State University Press; Milady Publishing Company; Miller Books; Mott Media, Inc., Publishers; National Association of Social Workers; National Book Company; National Textbook Co.; Nelson-Hall; New York Zoetrope, Inc.; Oise Press; Pacific Press Publishing Association; Penkevill Publishing Company, The; Pomegranate Press, Ltd.; Porter Sargent Publishers, Inc.; Prentice Hall Canada, Inc.; Prentice Hall Canada, Inc.; Princeton Architectural Press; Princeton Book Company, Publishers; Professional Publications, Inc.; Prolingua Associates; Purdue University Press; Que Corporation; R&E Publishers; Religious Education Press; Rosen Publishing Group, The; Routledge, Chapman & Hall, Inc.; Roxbury Publishing Co.; S.O.C.O. Publications; St. Bede's Publications; St. Martin's Press; San Francisco Press, Inc.; Sandlapper Publishing, Inc.; Schiffer Publishing Ltd.; Schirmer Books; Science Tech Publishers, Inc.; Scojtia Publishing Co., Inc.; Seven Locks Press, Inc.; ST Publications, Inc.; Standard Publishing; Stanford University Press; Stipes Publishing Co.; Tabor Publishing; Thomas Publications; Thomas, Publisher, Charles C.; Transaction Books; Transnational Publishers, Inc.; Trend Book Division; Trillium Press; UAHC Press; University of Alberta Press, The; University of Michigan Press; University of Minnesota Press; University Press of America; Utah State University Press; VGM Career Horizons; Wadsworth Publishing Company; York Press Ltd.

Translation. Alyson Publications, Inc.; Arcsoft Publishers; Asian Humanities Press; Aztex Corp.; Barron's Educational Series, Inc.; Bosco Publications, Don; Briarcliff Press Publishers; Camden House, Inc.; Chatham Press; Citadel Press; Clarion Books; Cleis Press; Dante University Of America Press, Inc.; Davis Publications, Inc.; Devin-Adair Publishers, Inc.; Dimension Books, Inc.; Drama Book Publishers; Ediciones Universal; Enslow Publishers; ETC Publications; Free Press, The; Gallaudet University Press; Gardner Press, Inc.; Garland Publishing, Inc.; Godine, Publisher, David R.; Guernica Editions; Harbinger House, Inc.; Indiana University Press; Longwood Academic; Mazda Publishers; Mercury House Inc.; Motorbooks International Publishers & Wholesalers, Inc.; National Gallery of Canada; Northern Illinois University Press; Pacific Books, Publishers; Paulist Press; Pickwick Publications; Porter Sargent Publishers, Inc.; Potter, Inc., Clarkson N.; Princeton University Press; Ross Books; S.C.E.-Editions L'Etincelle; Scojtia Publishing Co., Inc.; Sybex, Inc.; Tab Book, Inc.; Theosophical Publishing House, The; Three Continents Press; Timber Press, Inc.; University of Alabama Press; University of Massachusetts Press; University of Texas

Press; University of Utah Press; Vesta Publications, Ltd.; Wake Forest University Press; Wizards Bookshelf; Zoland Books, Inc.

Transportation. Arman Publishing, Inc., M.; Aviation Book Co.; Aztex Corp.; Boston Mills Press, The; Carstens Publications, Inc.; Golden West Books; Howell Press, Inc.; Hungness Publishing, Carl; Interurban Press/Trans Anglo Books; Iowa State University Press; Transportation Trails; Ultralight Publications, Inc.

Travel. Aegina Press, Inc.; Appalachian Mountain Club Books; Atheneum Children's Books; Bantam Books; Barron's Educational Series, Inc.; Bear Flag Books; Bergh Publishing, Inc.; Binford & Mort Publishing; Briarcliff Press Publishers; Caratzas, Publisher, Aristide D.; Carol Publishing; Chelsea Green; Christopher Publishing House, The; Countryman Press, Inc., The; Daniel and Company, Publishers, John; Devin-Adair Publishers, Inc.; Eerdmans Publishing Co., William B.; Elysium Growth Press; Eriksson, Publisher, Paul S.; Falcon Press Publishing Co.; Gallaudet University Press; Godine, Publisher, David R.; Golden West Publishers; Gollehon Press Inc.; Harper & Row Publishers, Inc.; Harvard Common Press, The; Heyday Books; Hippocrene Books Inc.; Homestead Publishing; Howell Press, Inc.; Hunter Publishing, Inc.; Intercultural Press, Inc.; International Resources; Interurban Press/Trans Anglo Books; Kesend Publishing, Ltd., Michael; Library Research Associates, Inc.; Loompanics Unlimited; Lyons & Burford, Publishers, Inc.; Meadowbrook Press; Middle Atlantic Press; Mills & Sanderson, Publishers; Mosaic Press Miniature Books; Mountain Press Publishing Company; Mountaineers Books, The; Muir Publications, John; Mustang Publishing Co.; Nimbus Publishing Limited; Outbooks; Passport Press; Peachtree Publishers, Ltd.; Pelican Publishing Company; Pennsylvania Historical and Museum Commission; Peterson's; Pomegranate Press, Ltd.; Prentice Hall Canada, Inc. ; Prentice Hall Press; R&E Publishers; Riverdale Company, Inc., Publishers, The; S.C.E.-Editions L'Etincelle; S.O.C.O. Publications; Sasquatch Books; Scojtia Publishing Co., Inc.; Shapolsky Publishers; Shoe Tree Press; Sierra Club Books; Soho Press, Inc.; Storie/McOwen Publishers, Inc.; Taylor Publishing Company; Texas Monthly Press Inc.; Transportation Trails; Travel Keys; Trend Book Division; Tuttle Publishing Company, Inc., Charles E.; Twin Peaks Press; Umbrella Books; University of Minnesota Press; Unlimited Publishing Co.; Wilderness Adventure Books; Wiley & Sons, Inc., John; Williamson Publishing Co.; Wine Appreciation Guild, Ltd.; Woodbine House; Workman Publishing Company, Inc.; Zoland Books, Inc.

Women's Issues/Studies. ABC-CLIO, Inc.; Advocacy Press; Asian Humanities Press; Baker Book House Company; Between the Lines Inc.; Carol Publishing; Cheribe Publishing Co.; Cleis Press; Contemporary Books, Inc.; Coteau Books; Eakin Publications, Inc.; Fairleigh Dickinson University Press; Gardner Press, Inc.; Harbinger House, Inc.; Hensley, Inc., Virgil W.; Holmes & Meier Publishers, Inc.; Horizon Publishers & Distributors; Indiana University Press; International Publishers Co., Inc.; International Resources; Longwood Academic; Luramedia; McFarland & Company, Inc., Publishers; Milkweed Editions; Multnomah Press; NavPress; Noble Press, Incorporated, The; Princeton Book Company, Publishers; Princeton University Press; R&E Publishers; Routledge, Chapman & Hall, Inc.; Russell Sage Foundation; Rutgers University Press; Scarecrow Press, Inc.; Scojtia Publishing Co., Inc.; Spinsters/Aunt Lute Books; Times Books; Transnational Publishers, Inc.; Umi Research Press; University of Massachusetts Press; University of Michigan Press; University of Minnesota Press; University of Tennessee Press, The; University Press of Virginia; Victor Books; Whitaker House; Wingbow Perss; Zoland Books, Inc.

World Affairs. ABC-CLIO, Inc.; Atlantic Monthly Press; Carroll & Graf Publishers, Inc.; Davis Publishing, Steve; Dillon Press, Inc.; Family Album, The; Fraser Institute, The.

Young Adult. ABC-CLIO, Inc.; Atheneum Children's Books; Augsburg Books; Bale Books; Barron's Educational Series, Inc.; Cliffs Notes, Inc.; College Board, The; Davenport, Publishers, May; Dial Books For Young Readers; Dillon Press, Inc.; Education Associates; Enslow Publishers; Falcon Press Publishing Co.; Fitzhenry & Whiteside, Ltd.; Houghton Mifflin Co.; Hunter House, Inc., Publishers; Lodestar Books; McElderry Books, Margaret K.; Philomel Books; Pineapple Press, Inc.; Rosen Publishing Group, The; Silver Burdett Press.

Fiction

This subject index for fiction will help you pinpoint fiction markets without having to scan all the book publishers' listings. As with the nonfiction markets, read the complete individual listings for each publisher for advice on what types of fiction the company buys. For more detailed advice and additional fiction markets that offer a royalty or copies as payment, consult *Novel and Short Story Writer's Market* (Writer's Digest Books).

Adventure. Advocacy Press; Aegina Press, Inc.; Arbor House; Atheneum Children's Books; Avalon Books; Avon Books; Avon Flare Books; Bantam Books; Bart Books; Bergh Publishing, Inc.; Branden Publishing Co., Inc..; Breakwater Books; Camelot Books; Carol Publishing; Chockstone Press, Inc.; Clarion Books; Daniel and Company, Publishers, John; Davenport, Publishers, May; Dial

Books For Young Readers; Dutton Children's Books; Fine, Inc., Donald I.; Gallaudet University Press; Gospel Publishing House; Harper & Row Publishers, Inc.; Horizon Publishers & Distributors; Kar-Ben Copies Inc.; Knights Press; Laura Books, Inc.; Library Research Associates, Inc.; Lodestar Books; Middle Atlantic Press; Miller Books; Moonfall Publishing, Inc.; Mother Courage Press; Mountaineers Books, The; NavPress; New Victoria Publishers; Overlook Press; Pippin Press; Players Press, Inc.; Quality Publications; Random House, Inc./Alfred A. Knopf, Inc. Juvenile Books; Scojtia Publishing Co., Inc.; Second Chance Press/Permanent Press; Shoe Tree Press; Soho Press, Inc.; Stemmer House Publishers, Inc.; Stevens, Inc., Gareth; Tapley, Publisher, Inc., Lance; Unlimited Publishing Co.; Walker and Co.; Wilderness Adventure Books; Woodsong Graphics, Inc.; Worldwide Library; Zebra Books.

Confession. Carol Publishing; Moonfall Publishing, Inc.; Players Press, Inc.; Second Chance Press/Permanent Press; Zebra Books.

Erotica. Bergh Publishing, Inc.; Carroll & Graf Publishers, Inc.; Devonshire Publishing Co.; Greenleaf Classics, Inc.; Knights Press; New Victoria Publishers; Quality Publications; Tapley, Publisher, Inc., Lance

Ethnic. African American Images; Atheneum Children's Books; Avon Flare Books; Branden Publishing Co., Inc..; Breakwater Books; Coteau Books; Cuff Publications Limited, Harry; Daniel and Company, Publishers, John; Davenport, Publishers, May; Faber & Faber, Inc.; Fiction Collective; Gallaudet University Press; Graywolf Press; Guernica Editions; Hermes House Press; Holloway House Publishing Co.; Kar-Ben Copies Inc.; Knights Press; Overlook Press; Players Press, Inc.; Scojtia Publishing Co., Inc.; Second Chance Press/Permanent Press; Soho Press, Inc.; Stemmer House Publishers, Inc.; Texas Monthly Press Inc.; University of Illinois Press; University of Minnesota Press.

Experimental. Aegina Press, Inc.; Atheneum Children's Books; Avon Flare Books; Breakwater Books; Daniel and Company, Publishers, John; Devonshire Publishing Co.; Faber & Faber, Inc.; Fiction Collective; Fiddlehead Poetry Books & Goose Lane Editions; Garber Communications, Inc.; Hermes House Press; Horizon Publishers & Distributors; Knights Press; Players Press, Inc.; Porcépic Books; Scojtia Publishing Co., Inc.; Second Chance Press/Permanent Press; Speech Bin, Inc., The; University of Minnesota Press; Unlimited Publishing Co.; Woodsong Graphics, Inc.; York Press Ltd.

Fantasy. Aegina Press, Inc.; Arbor House; Atheneum Children's Books; Avon Books; Baen Publishing Enterprises; Bantam Books; Bergh Publishing, Inc.; Bookmakers Guild, Inc.; Breakwater Books; Camelot Books; Carol Publishing; Coteau Books; Crossway Books; Daniel and Company, Publishers, John; Davenport, Publishers, May; Daw Books, Inc.; Del Rey Books; Dial Books For Young Readers; Dutton Children's Books; Fine, Inc., Donald I.; Gallaudet University Press; Gospel Publishing House; Green Tiger Press Inc.; Harper & Row Publishers, Inc.; Horizon Publishers & Distributors; Imagine, Inc.; Intervarsity Press; Iron Crown Enterprises; Kar-Ben Copies Inc.; Knights Press; Laura Books, Inc.; Lion Publishing Corporation; Lodestar Books; Moonfall Publishing, Inc.; Mother Courage Press; New Victoria Publishers; Overlook Press; Pippin Press; Players Press, Inc.; Random House, Inc./Alfred A. Knopf, Inc. Juvenile Books; Scojtia Publishing Co., Inc.; Second Chance Press/Permanent Press; Tor Books; TSR, Inc.; Woodsong Graphics, Inc.

Feminist. Advocacy Press; Bantam Books; Bergh Publishing, Inc.; Blue Dolphin Publishing, Inc.; Breakwater Books; Coteau Books; Firebrand Books; Graywolf Press; Hermes House Press; Soho Press, Inc.; Stevens, Inc., Gareth; University of Minnesota Press.

Gay/Lesbian. Alyson Publications, Inc.; Bantam Books; Carol Publishing; Cleis Press; Firebrand Books; Knights Press; Mother Courage Press; Naiad Press, Inc., The; University of Minnesota Press.

Gothic. Atheneum Children's Books; Harper & Row Publishers, Inc.; Knights Press; Laura Books, Inc.; Woodsong Graphics, Inc.

Historical. Advocacy Press; Aegina Press, Inc.; Atheneum Children's Books; Avalon Books; Avon Books; Bantam Books; Bart Books; Bradbury Press; Branden Publishing Co., Inc..; Breakwater Books; Brethren Press; Carolrhoda Books, Inc.; College Press Publishing Co.; Cuff Publications Limited, Harry; Daniel and Company, Publishers, John; Devonshire Publishing Co.; Dial Books For Young Readers; Fine, Inc., Donald I.; Gallaudet University Press; Gospel Publishing House; Guernica Editions; Harlequin Books; Harper & Row Publishers, Inc.; Heart Of The Lakes Publishing; Hermes House Press; Houghton Mifflin Co.; Kar-Ben Copies Inc.; Knights Press; Leisure Books; Library Research Associates, Inc.; Lion Publishing Corporation; Lodestar Books; Melior Publications; Middle Atlantic Press; Miller Books; Mother Courage Press; New England Press, Inc., The; New Victoria Publishers; Overlook Press; Pelican Publishing Company; Pineapple Press, Inc.; Pippin Press; Players Press, Inc.; Pocket Books; Poseidon Press; Quality Publications; Random House, Inc./Alfred A. Knopf, Inc. Juvenile Books; Scojtia Publishing Co., Inc.; Second Chance Press/Permanent Press; Shoe Tree Press; Soho Press, Inc.; Stemmer House Publishers, Inc.; University of Minnesota Press; Unlimited Publishing Co.; Wilderness Adventure Books; Willow Creek Press; Winston-Derek Publishers, Inc.; Woodsong Graphics, Inc.; Zebra Books.

Horror. Aegina Press, Inc.; Atheneum Children's Books; Bantam Books; Bart Books; Carol Publishing; Devonshire Publishing Co.; Fine, Inc., Donald I.; Leisure Books; Middle Atlantic Press; Players Press, Inc.; Random House, Inc./Alfred A. Knopf, Inc. Juvenile Books; Tor Books; TSR, Inc.; Zebra Books.

Humor. Aegina Press, Inc.; Atheneum Children's Books; Avon Flare Books; Bart Books; Blue Dolphin Publishing, Inc.; Breakwater Books; Camelot Books; Carol Publishing; Clarion Books; Corkscrew Press; Coteau Books; Cuff Publications Limited, Harry; Daniel and Company, Publishers, John; Fine, Inc., Donald I.; Five Star Publications; Gallaudet University Press; Gospel Publishing House; Intervarsity Press; Knights Press; Lodestar Books; Miller Books; New Victoria Publishers; Once Upon a Planet, Inc.; Pelican Publishing Company; Pippin Press; Players Press, Inc.; Random House, Inc./Alfred A. Knopf, Inc. Juvenile Books; Scojtia Publishing Co., Inc.; Second Chance Press/Permanent Press; Shoe Tree Press; Stevens, Inc., Gareth; Tapley, Publisher, Inc., Lance; Unlimited Publishing Co.; Willow Creek Press.

Juvenile. Aegina Press, Inc.; African American Images; Atheneum Children's Books; Bantam Books; Bookmakers Guild, Inc.; Bradbury Press; Breakwater Books; Camelot Books; Carolrhoda Books, Inc.; Coteau Books; Crossway Books; Down East Books; Dutton Children's Books; Eakin; Faber & Faber; Farrar, Straus and Giroux, Inc.; Fawcett Juniper; Four Winds Press; Gallaudet University Press; Gospel Publishing House; Green Tiger Press Inc.; Harcourt Brace Jovanovich; Harper Junior Books Group, West Coast; Horizon Publishers & Distributors; Houghton Mifflin Co.; Lion Publishing Corporation; Macmillan Publishing Co.; Middle Atlantic Press; Morrow Junior Books; Multnomah Press; NavPress; New Idea Press, Inc.; Pelican Publishing Company; Philomel Books; Pippin Press; Platt & Munk Publishers; Random House, Knopf; St. Paul Books and Media; Scojtia Publishing Co., Inc.; Stevens, Inc., Gareth; Thistledown Press; Trillium Press; Victor Books; Walker and Co.; Winston-Derek Publishers, Inc.

Literary. Aegina Press, Inc.; Applezaba Press; Bantam Books; Bergh Publishing, Inc.; Blue Dolphin Publishing, Inc.; Bookmakers Guild, Inc.; Breakwater Books; Carol Publishing; Coteau Books; Fine, Inc., Donald I.; Gallaudet University Press; Harper & Row Publishers, Inc.; Houghton Mifflin Co.; Little, Brown and Co., Inc.; Longwood Academic; Peachtree Publishers, Ltd.; Pineapple Press, Inc.; Poseidon Press; Q.E.D. Press Of Ann Arbor, Inc.; Scojtia Publishing Co., Inc.; Soho Press, Inc.; Stormline Press; Thistledown Press; Three Continents Press; University of Minnesota Press; Zoland Books, Inc.

Mainstream/Contemporary. Aegina Press, Inc.; Atheneum Children's Books; Avalon Books; Avon Flare Books; Bantam Books; Bart Books; Bergh Publishing, Inc.; Blair, Publisher, John F.; Bradbury Press; Branden Publishing Co., Inc..; Breakwater Books; Camelot Books; Carroll & Graf Publishers, Inc.; Chelsea Green; Child Welfare League Of America; Citadel Press; Clarion Books; Coteau Books; Crossway Books; Cuff Publications Limited, Harry; Daniel and Company, Publishers, John; Delacorte Press; E.P. Dutton; Ediciones Universal; Eriksson, Publisher, Paul S.; Faber & Faber, Inc.; Fawcett Juniper; Fiddlehead Poetry Books & Goose Lane Editions; Fine, Inc., Donald I.; Gallaudet University Press; Graywolf Press; Harbinger House, Inc.; Hardy—Publisher, Max; Harlequin Books; Hermes House Press; Houghton Mifflin Co.; International Marine Publishing Co.; International Publishers Co., Inc.; Intervarsity Press; Little, Brown and Co., Inc.; Lodestar Books; Middle Atlantic Press; Morrow and Co., William; New American Library; Norton Co., Inc., W.W.; Overlook Press; Peachtree Publishers, Ltd.; Pelican Publishing Company; Perspectives Press; Pineapple Press, Inc.; Players Press, Inc.; Porcépic Books; Quality Publications; St. Luke's Press; St. Martin's Press; Scojtia Publishing Co., Inc.; Second Chance Press/Permanent Press; Shoe Tree Press; Simon & Schuster; Soho Press, Inc.; Stemmer House Publishers, Inc.; Texas Monthly Press Inc.; TSR, Inc.; University of Illinois Press; University of Iowa Press; University of Nevada Press; University Press of Mississippi; Woodsong Graphics, Inc.; Word Beat Press.

Military/War. Laura Books, Inc.; Mother Courage Press.

Mystery. Aegina Press, Inc.; Atheneum Children's Books; Avon Books; Avon Flare Books; Bantam Books; Bart Books; Bergh Publishing, Inc.; Breakwater Books; Camden House, Inc.; Camelot Books; Carol Publishing; Carroll & Graf Publishers, Inc.; Clarion Books; Cliffhanger Press; Countryman Press, Inc., The; Daniel and Company, Publishers, John; Dembner Books; Dial Books For Young Readers; Doubleday & Co., Inc.; Fine, Inc., Donald I.; Gallaudet University Press; Gospel Publishing House; Guernica Editions; Harper & Row Publishers, Inc.; Horizon Publishers & Distributors; Knights Press; Laura Books, Inc.; Library Research Associates, Inc.; Lodestar Books; Miller Books; Moonfall Publishing, Inc.; Mother Courage Press; Mysterious Press, The; Overlook Press; Pippin Press; Players Press, Inc.; Pocket Books; Random House, Inc./Alfred A. Knopf, Inc. Juvenile Books; Scholastic, Inc.; Scojtia Publishing Co., Inc.; Second Chance Press/Permanent Press; Soho Press, Inc.; Stevens, Inc., Gareth; TSR, Inc.; Unlimited Publishing Co.; Walker and Co.; Windriver Publishing Company; Woodsong Graphics, Inc.; Worldwide Library.

Occult. Bart Books; Bergh Publishing, Inc.; Blue Dolphin Publishing, Inc.; Cassandra Press; Laura Books, Inc.; Middle Atlantic Press; Moonfall Publishing, Inc.; Tor Books.

Picture Books. Advocacy Press; Bradbury Press; Breakwater Books; Coteau Books; Dutton Children's Books; Five Star Publications; Four Winds Press; Gallaudet University Press; Harbinger House, Inc.; Harcourt Brace Jovanovich; Horizon Publishers & Distributors; Lodestar Books; Moonfall Publishing; New Idea Press, Inc.; Philomel Books; Pippin Press; Platt & Munk Publishers; Random House, Inc./Alfred A. Knopf, Inc. Juvenile Books; Stevens, Inc., Gareth; Tapley, Publisher, Inc., Lance.

Plays. Breakwater Books; Coteau Books; Drama Book Publishers; French, Inc., Samuel; Gallaudet University Press; Meriwether Publishing Ltd.; Playwrights Canada; Scojtia Publishing Co., Inc.; University of Minnesota Press; University of Missouri Press; Zoland Books, Inc.

Poetry. American Studies Press, Inc.; Applezaba Press; Atheneum Children's Books; Branden Publishing Co., Inc.; Camden House, Inc.; Chatham Press; Christopher Publishing House, The; Cleveland State University Poetry Center; Daniel and Company, Publishers, John; Dante University Of America Press, Inc.; Fiddlehead Poetry Books & Goose Lane Editions; Firebrand Books; Guernica Editions; Harper Junior Books Group, West Coast; International Publishers Co., Inc.; Mazda Publishers; Morrow and Co., William; Overlook Press; Paragon House Publishers; Sheep Meadow Press, The; Sparrow Press; Sunstone Press; Thistledown Press; Three Continents Press; Tuttle Publishing Company, Inc., Charles E.; University of California Press; University of Iowa Press; University of Massachusetts Press; University of Missouri Press; University of Utah Press; Vehicle Press; Vesta Publications, Ltd.; Wake Forest University Press; Wilderness Adventure Books; Winston-Derek Publishers, Inc.

Regional. Eakin Publications, Inc.; Blair, Publisher, John F.; Borealis Press, Ltd.; Cuff Publications Limited, Harry; Faber & Faber, Inc.; Heart Of The Lakes Publishing; Philomel Books; Porcépic Books; Sunstone Press; Texas Christian University Press; Texas Monthly Press Inc.; Thistledown Press; University of Utah Press.

Religious. Accent Books; Ballantine/Epiphany; Bethany House Publishers; Branden Publishing Co., Inc.; Brethren Press; Broadman Press; Cassandra Press; Devonshire Publishing Co.; Gospel Publishing House; Herald Press; Intervarsity Press; Kar-Ben Copies Inc.; Moonfall Publishing, Inc.; NavPress; Players Press, Inc.; Revell, Fleming H. Co.; St. Paul Books and Media; Standard Publishing; Tyndale House Publishers, Inc.; UAHC Press; Victor Books; Winston-Derek Publishers, Inc.; Wolgemuth & Hyatt, Publishers.

Romance. Arbor House; Atheneum Children's Books; Avalon Books; Avon Books; Avon Flare Books; Bantam Books; Breakwater Books; Dial Books For Young Readers; Doubleday & Co., Inc.; Evans and Co., Inc., M.; Harlequin Books; Knights Press; Leisure Books; Moonfall Publishing, Inc.; Mother Courage Press; Players Press, Inc.; Pocket Books; Scholastic, Inc.; Scojtia Publishing Co., Inc.; Silhouette Books; Walker and Co.; Woodsong Graphics, Inc.; Zebra Books.

Science Fiction. Aegina Press, Inc.; Arbor House; Atheneum Children's Books; Avon Books; Baen Publishing Enterprises; Bantam Books; Carol Publishing; Cheribe Publishing Co.; Crossway Books; Daw Books, Inc.; Del Rey Books; Devonshire Publishing Co.; Fine, Inc., Donald I.; Gallaudet University Press; Harper & Row Publishers, Inc.; Hermes House Press; Horizon Publishers & Distributors; Imagine, Inc.; Intervarsity Press; Iron Crown Enterprises; Knights Press; Laura Books, Inc.; Lodestar Books; Middle Atlantic Press; Moonfall Publishing, Inc.; Mother Courage Press; New Victoria Publishers; Overlook Press; Players Press, Inc.; Pocket Books; Porcépic Books; Random House, Inc./Alfred A. Knopf, Inc. Juvenile Books; Scojtia Publishing Co., Inc.; TSR, Inc.; Woodsong Graphics, Inc.

Short Story Collection. Aegina Press, Inc.; Applezaba Press; Bookmakers Guild, Inc.; Breakwater Books; Coteau Books; Dutton Children's Books; Faber & Faber, Inc.; Fiction Collective; International Publishers Co., Inc.; Muir Publications, John; Pippin Press; Platt & Munk; San Francisco Press; Science Tech Publishers; Scojtia Publishing Co., Inc.; University of Missouri Press; Word Beat Press; Zoland Books, Inc.

Spiritual. Graywolf Press.

Sports. Willow Creek Press.

Suspense. Arbor House; Atheneum Children's Books; Avon Books; Avon Flare Books; Bantam Books; Bart Books; Bergh Publishing, Inc.; Breakwater Books; Carroll & Graf Publishers, Inc.; Clarion Books; Cliffhanger Press; Dembner Books; Dial Books For Young Readers; Doubleday & Co., Inc.; Fine, Inc., Donald I.; Gallaudet University Press; Harper & Row Publishers, Inc.; Horizon Publishers & Distributors; Knights Press; Library Research Associates, Inc.; Lodestar Books; Middle Atlantic Press; Moonfall Publishing, Inc.; Mysterious Press, The; Overlook Press; Pippin Press; Players Press, Inc.; Pocket Books; Random House, Inc./Alfred A. Knopf, Inc. Juvenile Books; Scojtia Publishing Co., Inc.; Second Chance Press/Permanent Press; Soho Press, Inc.; Tor Books; Walker and Co.; Winston-Derek Publishers, Inc.; Woodsong Graphics, Inc.; Zebra Books.

Western. Atheneum Children's Books; Avalon Books; Avon Books; Bantam Books; Evans and Co., Inc., M.; Fine, Inc., Donald I.; Harper & Row Publishers, Inc.; Horizon Publishers & Distributors; Knights Press; Laura Books, Inc.; Lodestar Books; Middle Atlantic Press; Miller Books; New Victoria Publishers; Players Press, Inc.; Pocket Books; Quality Publications; Scojtia Publishing Co., Inc.; Walker and Co.; Woodsong Graphics, Inc.

Young Adult. Advocacy Press; Breakwater Books; Dutton Children's Books; Fawcett Juniper; Horizon Publishers & Distributors; Pelican Publishing Company; Aegina Press, Inc.; African American Images; Bantam Books; Bergh Publishing, Inc.; Crossway Books; Farrar, Straus and Giroux, Inc.; Fearon Education; Four Winds Press; Gallaudet University Press; Gospel Publishing House; Green Tiger Press Inc.; Harcourt Brace Jovanovich; Harper Junior Books Group, West Coast; Herald Press; Houghton Mifflin Co.; Lodestar Books; Lodestar Books; McElderry Books, Margaret K.; Middle Atlantic Press; NavPress; Random House, Inc./Alfred A. Knopf, Inc. Juvenile Books; Saint Paul Books and Media; Scholastic, Inc.; Science Tech Publishers, Inc.; Scojtia Publishing Co., Inc.; Texas Christian University Press; Wilderness Adventure Books.

Author's Agents Subject Index

This index will help you find agents who consider book manuscripts, articles and scripts on the subjects you write about. Nonfiction categories are listed before fiction categories in the index. Be sure to consult each agent's individual listing for submission information before sending a query or manuscript.

Nonfiction

Americana. Ware Literary Agency, John A.; Wieser & Wieser, Inc.; Wingra Woods Press.

Anthropology. Watt & Associates, Sandra.

Art/Architecture. Bradley-Goldstein Agency, The; Cornfield Literary Agency, Robert; Hass, Agent, Rose; Nathan Literary Agency, Ruth; Schwartz, Esquire, Laurens R.; Urstadt, Inc., Susan P.; Van Der Leun and Associates.

Astrology/Psychic/New Age. Literary/Business Associates; New Age World Services; Stepping Stone Literary Agency; 2-M Communications Ltd.

Audiocassettes. Creative Concepts Literary Agency; Feiler Literary Agency, Florence; Herman Agency, Inc., The Jeff.

Autobiographies. Andrews & Associates, Bart; Boates Literary Agency, Reid; Elek Associates, Peter; Klinger, Inc., Harvey; Oscard Associates, Fifi; Sagalyn Agency, The.

Biography. Andrews & Associates, Bart; Appleseeds Management; Boates Literary Agency, Reid; Borchardt Inc., Georges; Bradley-Goldstein Agency, The; Clausen Associates, Connie; Collier Associates; Diamant, The Writer's Workshop, Inc., Anita; Elek Associates, Peter; Ellenberg, Literary Agent, Ethan; Flaherty, Literary Agent, Joyce A.; Gladden & Associates; Heacock Literary Agency, Inc.; Klinger, Inc., Harvey; Lipkind Agency, Wendy; Livingston Associates, Inc., Peter ; MacBride Literary Agency, Margaret; Multimedia Product Development, Inc.; Nathan Literary Agency, Ruth; Oscard Associates, Fifi; Payne Literary Agency, The John K.; Porcelain, Sidney E.; Rees Literary Agency, Helen; Sagalyn Agency, The; Schaffner Associates, Inc., John; Schwartz, Esquire, Laurens R.; Siegel, Literary Agency, Bobbe; Singer Media Corporation, Inc.; Spitzer Literary Agency, Philip G.; Stepping Stone Literary Agency; 2-M Communications Ltd.; Urstadt, Inc., Susan P.; Victoria Management Co.; Ware Literary Agency, John A.

Business/Economics. Acton and Dystel, Inc.; Bernstein, Meredith; Boates Literary Agency, Reid; Bradley-Goldstein Agency, The; Collier Associates; Heacock Literary Agency, Inc.; King, Literary Agent, Daniel P.; Literary/Business Associates; Pegasus International, Inc.; Peter Associates, Inc., James; Rees Literary Agency, Helen; Sagalyn Agency, The; Sebastian Agency; Snell Literary Agency, Michael; Steinberg, Michael; Wieser & Wieser, Inc.; Writers House, Inc.

Child Guidance/Parenting. Bernstein, Meredith; Connor Literary Agency; Heacock Literary Agency, Inc.; Writers House, Inc.; Zeckendorf Associates, Susan.

Computers/Electronics. Snell Literary Agency, Michael; Waterside Productions, Inc.

Cooking/Foods/Nutrition. Casselman, Literary Agent, Martha; Clausen Associates, Connie; Connor Literary Agency; Cornfield Literary Agency, Robert; Creative Concepts Literary Agency; Elek Associates, Peter; Kern Literary Agency, Natasha; Mews Books Ltd.; 2-M Communications Ltd.; Urstadt, Inc., Susan P.; Warren Literary Agency, James; Wieser & Wieser, Inc.

Crafts. Siegel, Literary Agency, Bobbe; Warren Literary Agency, James.

Entertainment/Games. Andrews & Associates, Bart.

Ethnic. Farwestern Consultants, Inc.; Writers' Production.

Fashion/Beauty. Bernstein, Meredith; Clausen Associates, Connie; Connor Literary Agency; Siegel, Literary Agency, Bobbe.

Film/Cinema/Stage. Cornfield Literary Agency, Robert.

Gardening. Urstadt, Inc., Susan P.

Gay/Lesbian. Watt & Associates, Sandra.

General Nonfiction. Rees Literary Agency, Helen; A. M.C. Literary Agency; Acton and Dystel, Inc.; Amsterdam Agency, Marcia; Andrews & Associates, Bart; Anthony Agency, Joseph; Artists Group, The; Author Aid Associates; Baldi Literary Agency, Inc., Malaga; Becker, Maximilian; Bernstein, Meredith; Blake Group Literary Agency, The; Boates Literary Agency, Reid; Book Peddlers, The; Borchardt Inc., Georges; Brandt & Brandt Literary Agents, Inc.; Brod Literary Agency, Ruth Hagy; Brown Inc., Ned; Brown, Literary Agency, Andrea; Browne Ltd., Pema; Cameron Agency, The Marshall; Cantor, Literary Agent, Ruth; Casselman, Literary Agent, Martha; Cleaver Inc., Diane; Cohen, Inc., Ruth; Cohen Literary Agency, Ltd., Hy; Collin Literary Agency, Frances; Davie Literary Agency, Elaine; Deering, Literary Agency, Dorothy; Dijkstra Literary Agency, Sandra; Dolger Agency, The Jonathan; Dykeman Associates, Inc.; Eisenberg Literary Agency, Vicki; Erikson Literary Agency, The; Evans and Associates; Farquharson Ltd., John; Farwestern Consultants, Inc.; Fields/Rita Scott, Marje; Fishbein Ltd., Frieda; Flaming Star Literary Enterprises; Flannery, White & Stone; Foley Agency, The; Garon-Brook Associates, Inc., Jay; Gartenberg, Literary Agent, Max; Gelles-Cole Literary Enterprises; Goodman Associates, Literary Agents; Gordon Agency, Charlotte; Herman Agency, Inc., The Jeff; Herner Rights Agency, Susan; Hill Associates, Frederick; International Publisher Associates, Inc.; J&R Literary Agency; Jarvis and Co., Inc., Sharon; Jason Enterprises, Inc., Asher D.; JCA Literary Agency; Jet Literary Associates, Inc.; Kaltman Literary Agency, Larry; Kamaroff Associates, Alex; Kellock & Associates Co. Ltd., J.; Kern Literary Agency, Natasha; Kohner, Inc., Paul; Kouts, Barbara S.; Kroll Agency, Lucy; Lampack Agency, Inc., Peter; Larsen/Elizabeth Pomada Literary Agents, Michael; Lazear Agency, Inc., The; Lee Shore Agency; Levine Literary Agency, Inc., Ellen ; Lighthouse Literary Agency; Love Agency, Nancy; MacBride Literary Agency, Margaret; MacDonough, Literary Agent, Richard P.; Marshall Agency, The Evan; Martell Agency, The; Meredith, Inc., Scott; Morgan Literary Agency, Inc., David H.; Naggar Literary Agency, Jean V.; Neighbors, Inc., Charles; New England Publishing Associates, Inc.; New Writers Literary Project, Ltd.; Nolan Literary Agency, The Betsy; Nugent and Associates, Inc.; Otte Company, The; Pine Associates, Inc., Arthur ; Popkin, Julie/Nancy Cooke; Portman & Associates, Julian; Priest Literary Agency, Aaron M.; Radley-Regan & Associates, D.; Raines & Raines; Rhodes Literary Agency Inc.; Riina Literary Agency, John, R.; Robbins Office, Inc., The; Rotrosen Agency, Jane; Sandum & Associates; SBC Enterprises, Inc.; Scagnetti Literary Agency, Jack; Schulman Literary Agency, Inc., The Susan; Schwartz, Literary Agent, Arthur P.; Singer Literary Agency, Evelyn; Steele & Company, Lyle; Steinberg, Michael; Stern Agency, Gloria; Stuhlmann, Author's Representative, Gunther; Vicinanza Ltd., Ralph; Wade, Carlson; Wallace Literary Agency, Bess; Wallerstein Agency, The Gerry B.; Weiner Literary Agency, Cherry; Weyr Agency, Rhoda; Wingra Woods Press; Writer's Representatives, Inc.; Ziegler Literary Agency, George; Zelasky Literary Agency, Tom.

Government/Politics. Acton and Dystel, Inc.; Bradley-Goldstein Agency, The; Collier Associates; Diamant, The Writer's Workshop, Inc., Anita; Eisenberg Literary Agency, Vicki; King, Literary Agent, Daniel P.; Livingston Associates, Inc., Peter ; Pegasus International, Inc.; Penmarin Books; Peter Associates, Inc., James; Spitzer Literary Agency, Philip G.; Casselman, Literary Agent, Martha; Hawkins & Associates, Inc., John.

Health/Medicine. Clausen Associates, Connie; Diamant, The Writer's Workshop, Inc., Anita; Flaherty, Literary Agent, Joyce A.; Heacock Literary Agency, Inc.; Kern Literary Agency, Natasha; Klinger, Inc., Harvey; Literary/Business Associates; Mews Books Ltd.; New Age World Services; Pegasus International, Inc.; Peter Associates, Inc., James; Sagalyn Agency, The; Schwartz, Esquire, Laurens R.; Sebastian Agency; Siegel, Literary Agency, Bobbe; Stepping Stone Literary Agency; 2-M Communications Ltd.; Ware Literary Agency, John A.; Warren Literary Agency, James; Wieser & Wieser, Inc.; Wreschner, Authors' Representative, Ruth.

History. Collier Associates; Ellenberg, Literary Agent, Ethan; Fishbein Ltd., Frieda; Lipkind Agency, Wendy; Nathan Literary Agency, Ruth; Penmarin Books; Peter Associates, Inc., James; Sagalyn Agency, The; Ware Literary Agency, John A.; Warren Literary Agency, James.

How-to. Boates Literary Agency, Reid; Browne Ltd., Pema; Catalog Literary Agency, The; Clausen Associates, Connie; Connor Literary Agency; Creative Concepts Literary Agency; Flaherty, Literary Agent, Joyce A.; Fuhrman Literary Agency, Candice; Gladden & Associates; Kern Literary Agency, Natasha; Multimedia Product Development, Inc.; Panettieri Agency, The; Pegasus International, Inc.; Peter Associates, Inc., James; Schlessinger-Van Dyck Agency; Siegel, Literary Agency, Bobbe; Snell Literary Agency, Michael; Stern Associates, Charles M.; Teal Literary Agency, Patricia; 2-M Communications Ltd.; Warren Literary Agency, James; Wreschner, Authors' Representative, Ruth.

Humor. Bernstein, Meredith; Eisenberg Literary Agency, Vicki; 2-M Communications Ltd.

Illustrated Book. Connor Literary Agency; Dolger Agency, The Jonathan; Penmarin Books; Van Der Leun and Associates.

Juvenile Books. Amsterdam Agency, Marcia; Author Aid Associates; Bernstein, Meredith; Bookstop Literary Agency; Brown, Literary Agency, Andrea; Browne Ltd., Pema; Cantor, Literary Agent, Ruth; Cohen, Inc., Ruth; Elek Associates, Peter; Ellenberg, Literary Agent, Ethan; Feiler Literary Agency, Florence; Flannery, White & Stone; Hass, Agent, Rose; Herner Rights Agency, Susan; Kirchoff/Wohlberg; Kouts, Barbara S.; Mews Books Ltd.; Morgan Literary Agency, Inc.,

David H.; Naggar Literary Agency, Jean V.; Norma-Lewis Agency, The; Nugent and Associates, Inc.; Pegasus International, Inc.; Roffman Associates, Richard H.

Law. Appleseeds Management; Clausen Associates, Connie; Eisenberg, Vicki; Flaherty, Literary Agent, Joyce A.; King, Literary Agent, Daniel P.; New Age World Services; Writer's Consulting Group.

Literary Criticism. Cornfield Literary Agency, Robert.

Magazine articles. Baldi Literary Agency, Inc., Malaga; Creative Concepts Literary Agency; Curtis Associates Inc., Richard; Deering, Literary Agency, Dorothy; Diamant, The Writer's Workshop, Inc., Anita; Eisenberg Literary Agency, Vicki; Farquharson Ltd., John; Jason Enterprises, Inc., Asher D.; King, Literary Agent, Daniel P.; Kohner, Inc., Paul; Meredith, Inc., Scott; Naggar Literary Agency, Jean V.; New Writers Literary Project, Ltd.; Picard, Literary Agent, Alison; Robbins Office, Inc., The; Roffman Associates, Richard H.; Sierra Literary Agency; Singer Media Corporation, Inc.; Total Acting Experience, A; Wade, Carlson; Wallerstein Agency, The Gerry B.; Wreschner, Authors' Representative, Ruth; Writer's Consulting Group.

Military/War. Collier Associates; Writers House, Inc.; Flaherty, Literary Agent, Joyce A.

Money/Finance. Charlton Associates, James; Wieser & Wieser, Inc.

Music and Dance. Cornfield Literary Agency, Robert; Schwartz, Esquire, Laurens R.; Zeckendorf Associates, Susan.

Nature/Environment. Casselman, Literary Agent, Martha; Collier Associates.

Philosophy. Literary/Business Associates.

Photography. Creative Concepts Literary Agency; International Literature and Arts Agency; Lee Shore Agency; Lighthouse Literary Agency; Meredith, Inc., Scott; New Age World Services; Roffman Associates, Richard H.; Spieler Literary Agency, F. Joseph; Wieser & Wieser, Inc.

Psychology. Bernstein, Meredith; Literary/Business Associates; Peter Associates, Inc., James; Sagalyn Agency, The; Sebastian Agency; Snell Literary Agency, Michael; Stepping Stone Literary Agency; 2-M Communications Ltd.; Ware Literary Agency, John A.

Reference. Browne Ltd., Pema; Goodman Literary Agency, Irene; Snell Literary Agency, Michael.

Regional. Southern Writers.

Religion. Literary/Business Associates; Stepping Stone Literary Agency.

Scholarly. Heacock Literary Agency, Inc.; New England Publishing Associates, Inc.

Science/Technology. Bradley-Goldstein Agency, The; Catalog Literary Agency, The; Lipkind Agency, Wendy; Multimedia Product Development, Inc.; Penmarin Books; Sagalyn Agency, The; Snell Literary Agency, Michael; Van Der Leun and Associates; Waterside Productions, Inc.; Writers House, Inc.; Zeckendorf Associates, Susan.

Self-Help. Appleseeds Management; Catalog Literary Agency, The; Charlton Associates, James; Clausen Associates, Connie; Connor Literary Agency; Creative Concepts Literary Agency; Elek Associates, Peter; Flaherty, Literary Agent, Joyce A.; Fuhrman Literary Agency, Candice; Gladden & Associates; Kern Literary Agency, Natasha; Panettieri Agency, The; Pegasus International, Inc.; Schaffner Associates, Inc., John; Sebastian Agency; Sierra Literary Agency; Snell Literary Agency, Michael; Stepping Stone Literary Agency; Teal Literary Agency, Patricia; Victoria Management Co.; Warren Literary Agency, James; Zeckendorf Associates, Susan.

Social Sciences. Bradley-Goldstein Agency, The; Klinger, Inc., Harvey; Schwartz, Esquire, Laurens R.

Sports. Acton and Dystel, Inc.; Charlton Associates, James; Heacock Literary Agency, Inc.; Lipkind Agency, Wendy; Siegel, Literary Agency, Bobbe; Spitzer Literary Agency, Philip G.; Ware Literary Agency, John A.; Wieser & Wieser, Inc.

Syndicated material. Anthony Agency, Joseph; Artists Group, The; Book Peddlers, The; Creative Concepts Literary Agency; Eisenberg Literary Agency, Vicki; Kellock & Associates Co. Ltd., J.; King, Literary Agent, Daniel P.; Lazear Agency, Inc., The; McBride Literary Agency, Margaret; McDonough, Literary Agent, Richard P.; Meredith, Inc., Scott; Roffman Associates, Richard H.; Singer Media Corporation, Inc.; Total Acting Experience, A; Victoria Management Co.

Technical. Mews Books Ltd.; Pegasus International, Inc.; Schwartz, Esquire, Laurens R.

Textbook. Anthony Agency, Joseph; Catalog Literary Agency, The; Educational Design Services, Inc.; Feiler Literary Agency, Florence; Fishbein Ltd., Frieda; Herman Agency, Inc., The Jeff; J&R Literary Agency; Lazear Agency, Inc., The; Lee Shore Agency; Lighthouse Literary Agency; Meredith, Inc., Scott; Norma-Lewis Agency, The; Pegasus International, Inc.; Riina Literary Agency, John, R.; Roffman Associates, Richard H.; SBC Enterprises, Inc.; Snell Literary Agency, Michael; Spieler Literary Agency, F. Joseph; Warren Literary Agency, James; Waterside Productions, Inc.; Wreschner, Authors' Representative, Ruth.

Translation. International Literature and Arts Agency.

Travel. Wieser & Wieser, Inc.; Wingra Woods Press.

Women's Issues/Studies. Heacock Literary Agency, Inc.; Sebastian Agency; Siegel, Literary Agency, Bobbe; Stepping Stone Literary Agency.

World Affairs. Anthony Agency, Joseph; Norma-Lewis Agency, The.

Young Adult. Bookstop Literary Agency.

Fiction

Adventure. Allan Agency, Lee; Browne Ltd., Pema; Connor Literary Agency; Elek Associates, Peter; Ellenberg, Literary Agent, Ethan; Farwestern Consultants, Inc.; Fishbein Ltd., Frieda; Flaherty, Literary Agent, Joyce A.; Gladden & Associates; Jason Enterprises, Inc., Asher D.; Kamaroff Associates, Alex; Lampack Agency, Inc., Peter; Lee, Literary Agency, L. Harry; Perkins' Literary Agency; Sebastian Agency; Stern Associates, Charles M.; Teal Literary Agency, Patricia; Zelasky Literary Agency, Tom.

Ethnic. Farwestern Consultants, Inc.

Experimental. Pegasus International, Inc.

Fantasy. Schaffner Associates, Inc., John; Vicinanza Ltd., Ralph.

Gay/Lesbian. Watt & Associates, Sandra.

Historical. Collier Associates; Flaherty, Literary Agent, Joyce A.; Panettieri Agency, The; Sebastian Agency; Siegel, Literary Agency, Bobbe; Wieser & Wieser, Inc.; Zeckendorf Associates, Susan; Zelasky Literary Agency, Tom.

Horror. Cohen, Inc., Ruth; Connor Literary Agency; Davie Literary Agency, Elaine; Diamant, The Writer's Workshop, Inc., Anita; Farwestern Consultants, Inc.; Flaherty, Literary Agent, Joyce A.; Jason Enterprises, Inc., Asher D.; Kamaroff Associates, Alex; Lampack Agency, Inc., Peter; Lee, Literary Agency, L. Harry; Panettieri Agency, The; Pegasus International, Inc.; Perkins' Literary Agency; Teal Literary Agency, Patricia.

Juvenile. Anthony Agency, Joseph; Bernstein, Meredith; Blake Group Literary Agency, The; Bookstop Literary Agency; Brown, Literary Agency, Andrea; Browne Ltd., Pema; Cantor, Literary Agent, Ruth; Casselman, Literary Agent, Martha; Catalog Literary Agency, The; Cohen, Inc., Ruth; Curtis Associates, Inc., Richard; Davie Literary Agency, Elaine; Deering, Literary Agency, Dorothy; Elek Associates, Peter; Ellenberg, Literary Agent, Ethan; Farquharson Ltd., John; Feiler Literary Agency, Florence; Gordon Agency, Charlotte; Hass, Agent, Rose; Hawkins & Associates, Inc., John; Herner Rights Agency, Susan; J&R Literary Agency; Kellock & Associates Co. Ltd., J.; Kern Literary Agency, Natasha; Kirchoff/Wohlberg; Kouts, Barbara S.; Lazear Agency, Inc., The; Lee Shore Agency; Levine Literary Agency, Inc., Ellen; Lighthouse Literary Agency; McDonough, Literary Agent, Richard P.; Meredith, Inc., Scott; Mews Books Ltd.; Morgan Literary Agency, Inc., David H.; Naggar Literary Agency, Jean V.; Norma-Lewis Agency, The; Nugent and Associates, Inc.; Pegasus International, Inc.; Picard, Literary Agent, Alison; Rhodes Literary Agency Inc.; Rotrosen Agency, Jane; Scagnetti Literary Agency, Jack; Schlessinger-Van Dyck Agency; Singer Literary Agency, Evelyn; Spieler Literary Agency, F. Joseph; Tornetta Agency, Phyllis; Total Acting Experience, A; Warren Literary Agency, James; Wingra Woods Press; Wreschner, Authors' Representative, Ruth; Writers House, Inc.; Creative Concepts Literary Agency.

Literary. Allan Agency, Lee; Clausen Associates, Connie; Flaming Star Literary Enterprises; Flannery, White & Stone; Herner Rights Agency, Susan; Lampack Agency, Inc., Peter; Livingston Associates, Inc., Peter; McBride Literary Agency, Margaret; Oscard Associates, Fifi; Picard, Literary Agent, Alison; Robbins Office, Inc., The; Scribe Agency; Sebastian Agency; Siegel, Literary Agency, Bobbe; Stuhlmann, Author's Representative, Gunther; Urstadt, Inc., Susan P.; Watt & Associates, Sandra; Wieser & Wieser, Inc.; Zeckendorf Associates, Susan.

Magazine fiction. Anthony Agency, Joseph; Author Aid Associates; Baldi Literary Agency, Inc., Malaga; Brown Inc., Ned; Deering, Literary Agency, Dorothy; Eisenberg Literary Agency, Vicki; Farquharson Ltd., John; King, Literary Agent, Daniel P.; Lazear Agency, Inc., The; Meredith, Inc., Scott; Naggar Literary Agency, Jean V.; New Age World Services; New Writers Literary Project, Ltd.; Picard, Literary Agent, Alison; Roffman Associates, Richard H.; Sierra Literary Agency; Total Acting Experience, A; Wade, Carlson; Wallerstein Agency, The Gerry B.

Mainstream/Contemporary. Acton and Dystel, Inc.; Browne Ltd., Pema; Cantor, Literary Agent, Ruth; Clausen Associates, Connie; Connor Literary Agency; Flaherty, Literary Agent, Joyce A.; Gladden & Associates; Goodman Associates, Literary Agents; Herman Agency, Inc., The Jeff; Hill Associates, Frederick; Kaltman Literary Agency, Larry; Kern Literary Agency, Natasha; King, Literary Agent, Daniel P.; Klinger, Inc., Harvey; Lee, Literary Agency, L. Harry; McBride Literary Agency, Margaret; Multimedia Product Development, Inc.; Naggar Literary Agency, Jean V.; Schlessinger-Van Dyck Agency; Sebastian Agency; Stepping Stone Literary Agency; Stern Associates, Gloria; Tornetta Agency, Phyllis; Wieser & Wieser, Inc.

Military/War. Ellenberg, Literary Agent, Ethan

Movie scripts. A. M.C. Literary Agency; Allan Agency, Lee; Amsterdam Agency, Marcia; Anthony Agency, Joseph; Appleseeds Management; Artists Group, The; Author Aid Associates; Bernstein, Meredith; Brown Inc., Ned; Blake Group Literary Agency, The; Catalog Literary Agency, The; Chiz Agency, Terry; Creative·Concepts Literary Agency; Deering, Literary Agency, Dorothy; Dykeman Associates, Inc.; Eisenberg Literary Agency, Vicki; Erikson Literary Agency, The; Feiler Literary Agency, Florence; Fishbein Ltd., Frieda; Flannery, White & Stone; Freedman Dramatic Agency, Inc., Robert A.; Garon-Brook Associates, Inc., Jay; Gladden & Associates; Greene, Inc., Harold R.; Heacock Literary Agency, Inc.; Hilton Literary Agency, Alice; Hudson Talent Representation, Scott; Kellock & Associates Co. Ltd., J.; King, Literary Agent, Daniel P.; Kohner, Inc.,

Paul; Kroll Agency, Lucy; Lampack Agency, Inc., Peter; Lazear Agency, Inc., The; Lee, Literary Agency, L. Harry; Lighthouse Literary Agency; Livingston Associates, Inc., Peter; McBride Literary Agency, Margaret; Marshall Agency, The Evan; Meredith, Inc., Scott; Neighbors, Inc., Charles; New Writers Literary Project, Ltd.; Norma-Lewis Agency, The; Nugent and Associates, Inc.; Oscard Associates, Fifi; Pegasus International, Inc.; Porcelain, Sidney E.; Portman & Associates, Julian; Radley-Regan & Associates, D.; Roffman Associates, Richard H.; Rogers and Associates, Stephanie; SBC Enterprises, Inc.; Scagnetti Literary Agency, Jack; Schulman Literary Agency, Inc., The Susan; Scribe Agency; Shapiro-Lichtman Talent Agency; Shorr Stille and Associates; Spitzer Literary Agency, Philip G.; Stern, Gloria; Stuhlmann, Author's Representative, Gunther; Tantleff Office, The; Total Acting Experience, A; Victoria Management Co.; Warren Literary Agency, James; Watt & Associates, Sandra; Wright Representatives, Inc., Ann; Writer's Consulting Group; Zelasky Literary Agency, Tom

Mystery. Allan Agency, Lee; Appleseeds Management; Bernstein, Meredith; Cantor, Literary Agent, Ruth; Cohen, Inc., Ruth; Connor Literary Agency; Davie Literary Agency, Elaine; Deering, Literary Agency, Dorothy; Eisenberg Literary Agency, Vicki; Farwestern Consultants, Inc.; Fishbein Ltd., Frieda; Flaherty, Literary Agent, Joyce A.; Goodman Literary Agency, Irene; Jason Enterprises, Inc., Asher D.; Kamaroff Associates, Alex; King, Literary Agent, Daniel P.; Lampack Agency, Inc., Peter; Lee, Literary Agency, L. Harry; Oscard Associates, Fifi; Panettieri Agency, The; Pegasus International, Inc.; Perkins' Literary Agency; Porcelain, Sidney E.; Radley-Regan & Associates, D.; Schlessinger-Van Dyck Agency; Spitzer Literary Agency, Philip G.; Steinberg, Michael; Stepping Stone Literary Agency; Stern Agency, Gloria; Stern Associates, Charles M.; Teal Literary Agency, Patricia; Tornetta Agency, Phyllis; Ware Literary Agency, John A.; Zeckendorf Associates, Susan.

Novels. A. M.C. Literary Agency; Abel Literary Agency, Inc., Dominick ; Acton and Dystel, Inc.; Allan Agency, Lee; Amsterdam Agency, Marcia; Artists Group, The; Author Aid Associates; Baldi Literary Agency, Inc., Malaga; Becker, Maximilian; Bernstein, Meredith; Blake Group Literary Agency, The; Boates Literary Agency, Reid; Borchardt Inc., Georges; Bradley-Goldstein Agency, The; Brandt & Brandt Literary Agents, Inc.; Brown Inc., Ned; Browne Ltd., Pema; Cameron Agency, The Marshall; Cantor, Literary Agent, Ruth; Catalog Literary Agency, The; Chiz Agency, Terry; Cleaver Inc., Diane; Cohen Literary Agency, Ltd., Hy; Collin Literary Agency, Frances; Cornfield Literary Agency, Robert; Creative Concepts Literary Agency; Curtis Associates, Inc., Richard; Davie Literary Agency, Elaine; Diamant, The Writer's Workshop, Inc., Anita; Dijkstra Literary Agency, Sandra; Dolger Agency, The Jonathan; Dykeman Associates, Inc.; Eisenberg Literary Agency, Vicki; Ellenberg, Literary Agent, Ethan; Erikson Literary Agency, The; Evans and Associates; Farquharson Ltd., John; Fields/Rita Scott, Marje; Fishbein Ltd., Frieda; Flaming Star Literary Enterprises; Foley Agency, The; Fuhrman Literary Agency, Candice; Garon-Brook Associates, Inc., Jay; Gartenberg, Literary Agent, Max; Gelles-Cole Literary Enterprises; Gordon Agency, Charlotte; Greene, Inc., Harold R.; Hass, Agent, Rose; Heacock Literary Agency, Inc.; Herman Agency, Inc., The Jeff; International Literature and Arts Agency; International Publisher Associates, Inc.; J&R Literary Agency; Jarvis and Co., Inc., Sharon; JCA Literary Agency; Jet Literary Associates, Inc.; Kaltman Literary Agency, Larry; Kellock & Associates Co. Ltd., J.; Kern Literary Agency, Natasha; Klinger, Inc., Harvey; Kohner, Inc., Paul; Kouts, Barbara S.; Kroll Agency, Lucy; Lampack Agency, Inc., Peter; Larsen/Elizabeth Pomada Literary Agents, Michael; Lazear Agency, Inc., The; Lee, Literary Agency, L. Harry; Lee Shore Agency; Levine Literary Agency, Inc., Ellen; Lighthouse Literary Agency; Lipkind Agency, Wendy; Literary/Business Associates; Love Agency, Nancy; MacCampbell Inc., Donald; McDonough, Literary Agent, Richard P.; Marshall Agency, The Evan; Martell Agency, The; Meredith, Inc., Scott; Morgan Literary Agency, Inc., David H.; Multimedia Product Development, Inc.; Nathan Literary Agency, Ruth; Neighbors, Inc., Charles; New Age World Services; Nolan Literary Agency, The Betsy; Nugent and Associates, Inc.; Oscard Associates, Fifi; Otte Company, The; Payne Literary Agency, The John K.; Pegasus International, Inc.; Pine Associates, Inc., Arthur ; Popkin, Julie/Nancy Cooke; Porcelain, Sidney E.; Portman & Associates, Julian; Priest Literary Agency, Aaron M.; Raines & Raines; Rees Literary Agency, Helen; Rhodes Literary Agency Inc.; Robbins Office, Inc., The; Rotrosen Agency, Jane; Sandum & Associates; SBC Enterprises, Inc.; Scagnetti Literary Agency, Jack; Schulman Literary Agency, Inc., The Susan; Schwartz, Literary Agent, Arthur P.; Sierra Literary Agency; Snell Literary Agency, Michael; Steele & Company, Lyle; Stern, Gloria; Van Der Leun and Associates; Wade, Carlson; Wallace Literary Agency, Bess; Wallerstein Agency, The Gerry B.; Waterside Productions, Inc.; Weiner Literary Agency, Cherry; Weyr Agency, Rhoda; Wreschner, Authors' Representative, Ruth; Wright Representatives, Inc., Ann; Writer's Consulting Group; Writers' Representatives, Inc.; Ziegler Literary Agency, George.

Occult. Farwestern Consultants, Inc.; New Age World Services; Stepping Stone Literary Agency.

Picture Books. Flannery, White & Stone; Kirchoff/Wohlberg; Lighthouse Literary Agency; Singer Literary Agency, Evelyn.

Plays. Anthony Agency, Joseph; Artists Group, The; Author Aid Associates; Becker, Maximilian; Brown Inc., Ned; Deering, Literary Agency, Dorothy; Eisenberg Literary Agency, Vicki; Fields/Rita Scott, Marje; Fishbein Ltd., Frieda; Freedman Dramatic Agency, Inc., Robert A.; French, Inc., Samuel; Garon-Brook Associates, Inc., Jay; Graham Agency; Hudson Talent Representation, Scott; International Literature and Arts Agency ; Kroll Agency, Lucy; Lazear Agency, Inc., The;

Lee, Literary Agency, L. Harry; Meredith, Inc., Scott; New Writers Literary Project, Ltd.; Norma-Lewis Agency, The; Nugent and Associates, Inc.; Oscard Associates, Fifi; Schulman Literary Agency, Inc., The Susan; Tantleff Office, The; Total Acting Experience, A; Wright Representatives, Inc., Ann; Zelasky Literary Agency, Tom.

Poetry. Author Aid Associates.

Romance. Bernstein, Meredith; Cohen, Inc., Ruth; Creative Concepts Literary Agency; Davie Literary Agency, Elaine; Deering, Literary Agency, Dorothy; Diamant, The Writer's Workshop, Inc., Anita; Farwestern Consultants, Inc.; Fishbein Ltd., Frieda; Flaherty, Literary Agent, Joyce A.; Goodman Literary Agency, Irene; Herner Rights Agency, Susan; Jason Enterprises, Inc., Asher D.; Kamaroff Associates, Alex; Kern Literary Agency, Natasha; King, Literary Agent, Daniel P.; Lampack Agency, Inc., Peter; Panettieri Agency, The; Payne Literary Agency, The John K.; Pegasus International, Inc.; Perkins' Litarary Agency; Picard, Literary Agent, Alison; Singer Media Corporation, Inc.; Southern Writers; Stern Associates, Charles M.; Teal Literary Agency, Patricia; Tornetta Agency, Phyllis; Victoria Management Co.; Warren Literary Agency, James; Zelasky Literary Agency, Tom; Browne Ltd., Pema.

Science Fiction. Allan Agency, Lee; Appleseeds Management; Deering, Literary Agency, Dorothy; Diamant, The Writer's Workshop, Inc., Anita; Ellenberg, Literary Agent, Ethan; Gladden & Associates; Herner Rights Agency, Susan; Kamaroff Associates, Alex; King, Literary Agent, Daniel P.; Lee, Literary Agency, L. Harry; Pegasus International, Inc.; Schaffner Associates, Inc., John; Steinberg, Michael; Vicinanza Ltd., Ralph; Writers House, Inc.; Zelasky Literary Agency, Tom.

Short Story Collection. Farwestern Consultants, Inc.; King, Literary Agent, Daniel P.; Lighthouse Literary Agency.

Suspense. Connor Literary Agency; Jason Enterprises, Inc., Asher D.; Kern Literary Agency, Natasha; Panettieri Agency, The; Porcelain, Sidney E.; Radley-Regan & Associates, D.; Sebastian Agency; Siegel, Literary Agency, Bobbe; Spitzer Literary Agency, Philip G.; Stepping Stone Literary Agency; Vicinanza Ltd., Ralph; Ware Literary Agency, John A.; Zeckendorf Associates, Susan; Zelasky Literary Agency, Tom.

TV scripts. A. M.C. Literary Agency; Amsterdam Agency, Marcia; Anthony Agency, Joseph; Appleseeds Management; Artists Group, The; Author Aid Associates; Blake Group Literary Agency, The; Brown Inc., Ned; Literary Agency, The; Chiz Agency, Terry; Creative Concepts Literary Agency; Deering, Literary Agency, Dorothy; Dykeman Associates, Inc.; Eisenberg Literary Agency, Vicki; Fishbein Ltd., Frieda; Freedman Dramatic Agency, Inc., Robert A.; Garon-Brook Associates, Inc., Jay; Heacock Literary Agency, Inc.; Hilton Literary Agency, Alice; Hudson Talent Representation, Scott; King, Literary Agent, Daniel P.; Kohner, Inc., Paul; Lampack Agency, Inc., Peter; Lazear Agency, Inc., The; Lee, Literary Agency, L. Harry; Lighthouse Literary Agency; Livingston Associates, Inc., Peter; Marshall Agency, The Evan; Meredith, Inc., Scott; New Writers Literary Project, Ltd.; Norma-Lewis Agency, The; Nugent and Associates, Inc.; Oscard Associates, Fifi; Pegasus International, Inc.; Porcelain, Sidney E.; Portman & Associates, Julian; Radley-Regan & Associates, D.; Roffman Associates, Richard H.; Rogers and Associates, Stephanie; SBC Enterprises, Inc.; Scagnetti Literary Agency, Jack; Schulman Literary Agency, Inc., The Susan; Scribe Agency; Shapiro-Lichtman Talent Agency; Shorr Stille and Associates; Stern, Gloria; Stuhlmann, Author's Representative, Gunther; Tantleff Office, The; Total Acting Experience, A; Victoria Management Co.; Warren Literary Agency, James; Watt & Associates, Sandra; Wright Representatives, Inc., Ann; Zelasky Literary Agency, Tom.

Western. Cohen, Inc., Ruth; Davie Literary Agency, Elaine; Farwestern Consultants, Inc.; Kern Literary Agency, Natasha; Teal Literary Agency, Patricia; Zelasky Literary Agency, Tom.

Young Adult. Browne Ltd., Pema; Amsterdam Agency, Marcia; Bookstop Literary Agency; Cantor, Literary Agent, Ruth; Cohen, Inc., Ruth; Diamant, The Writer's Workshop, Inc., Anita; Fields/ Rita Scott, Marje; Fishbein Ltd., Frieda; Garon-Brook Associates, Inc., Jay; Hill Associates, Frederick; Kellock & Associates Co. Ltd., J.; Kern Literary Agency, Natasha; Lighthouse Literary Agency; Norma-Lewis Agency, The; Panettieri Agency, The; Payne Literary Agency, The John K.; Picard, Literary Agent, Alison; Stuhlmann, Author's Representative, Gunther.

General Index

If the specific market you are looking for is not listed in the following General Index, check the "Other" section at the end of each major section of the book: Book Publishers and Packagers, pg. 229; Consumer Publications, pg. 668; Trade Journals, pg. 850; Scriptwriting, pg. 895; Greeting Card Publishers, pg. 917; Syndicates, pg. 906; Agents, pg. 966; Contests, pg. 995.

A

A.D. Players 864
A.M.C. Literary Agency 922
A.N.A.L.O.G. Computing 455
A.V. Media Craftsman, Inc. 853
AAA Going Places 638
AAA World 639
AAAS Prize for Behavioral Science Research 968
AASLH Press 50
ABA Journal 795
Abbott, Langer & Associates 51
ABC Star Service 847
ABC-CLIO, Inc. 51
Abel Literary Agency, Inc., Dominick 922
Abingdon Press 51
Aboard 391
Aboriginal Science Fiction 576
Above The Bridge Magazine 500
ABS & Associates 854
Academy Theatre 864
Accelerated Development Inc. 51
Accent Books 52
Accent on Living 340
Access Control 707
Acres U.S.A. 739
Acropolis Books, Ltd. 52
ACS Publications, Inc. 52
Acton and Dystel, Inc. 922
Acton, Inc., Edward J. (see Acton and Dystel 922)
Actors Theatre of Louisville 864
Ad Astra 573
Adams, Inc., Bob 52
Adams Prize, Herbert Baxter 968
Addams Peace Association Children's Book Award, Jane 968
Adirondack Life 508
Admaster, Inc. 854
Adriatic Award 968
Adventure Feature Syndicate 897
Adventure Road 639
Advertising Age 673
Advocacy Press 52
Aegina Press, Inc. 53
Aero Art 263
Affaire de Coeur 568
Africa Report 467
African American Images 53
African Expedition Gazette 639
African-American Heritage 317
After Hours 577
AG-Pilot International Magazine 685
Aglow 534
Aglow Publications 53

Agri-Times Northwest 742
Agway Cooperator 739
Ahsahta Press 221
Aim 277
Aim Magazine 317
Aim Magazine Short Story Contest 968
Aimplus (see Mature Health 344)
Air Alaska 264
Air & Space/Smithsonian Magazine 264
Air Destinations 391
Air Line Pilot 264
Air Line Pilot 685
Airport Services Magazine 686
ALA Books 54
Alabama Game & Fish 603
Alabama Heritage 478
Alaska 479
Alaska Outdoors Magazine 479
Alaska Quarterly Review 409
Alban Institute, Inc., The 54
Alberta New Fiction Competition 968
Alcalde 278
All of Nature 447
Allan Agency, Lee 922
Allen Publishing Co. 54
Aloha 493
Alpine Publications Inc. 54
Alternative Energy Retailer 726
Altman & Weil Report to Legal Management, The 795
Alumi-News 692
Alyson Publications, Inc. 54
AMAS Repertory Theatre, Inc. 864
Amadeus Publishing Company 221
Amazine Heroes 295
Amazing Computing 456
Amazing® Stories 577
Amberley Greeting Card Co. 908
Amelia Magazine 409
Amelia Student Award 968
America International Syndicate 897
America West Airlines Magazine 391
America West Publishers 55
American Art Journal, The 241
American Astronautical Society 55
American Atheist Press 55
American Automatic Merchandiser (see Automatic Merchandiser 758)
American Baby Magazine 287
American Bicyclist 838
American Catholic Press 56
American Cinematographer 825

American Citizen Italian Press, The 317
American Coin-Op 705
American Dane 318
American Demographics 673
American Farriers Journal 232
American Fitness 839
American Forests 448
American Glass Review 691
American Greetings 908
American Handgunner 601
American Health Magazine 340
American Heritage 350
American History Illustrated 350
American Hockey Magazine 839
American Hospital Publishing, Inc. 56
American Hunter 603
American Indian Art Magazine 242
American Institute of Physics 56
American Jewish World 318
American Journal of Nursing 767
American Legion Magazine, The 329
American Libraries 800
American Line, The 865
American Machinist 728
American Media Inc. 854
American Medical News 812
American Motorcyclist 255
American Mover 845
American Newspaper Syndicate 897
American Paint and Coatings Journal 822
American Photographer 465
American Playwrights' Theatre, The 865
American Psychiatric Press, Inc., The 56
American References Inc. 57
American Salesman, The 834
American Scandinavian Foundation/Translation Prize 968
American School Board Journal, The 716
American Showcase, Inc. 221
American Skating World 626
American Society of Journalists & Authors Excellence Awards 968
American Songwriter 439
American Speech-Language-Hearing Association (ASHA), National Media Award 968
American Squaredance 308
American Stage Company 865
American Stage Festival 865
American Studies Press, Inc. 57
American Survival Guide 433

American Voice, The 410
American Way 392
American West 640
American Woman Road Rider 256
Americas 474
America's Civil War 351
Amicus Journal, The 448
Amigaworld 456
Amoco Traveler 640
Amsterdam Agency, Marcia 923
Amusement Business 731
AMWA Medical Book Awards Competition 968
Amy Writing Awards 968
Analog Science Fiction/Science Fact 577
Ancestry Incorporated 57
Ancestry Newsletter 351
Anderson McLean, Inc. 221
Anderson Publishing Co. 57
Andrews & Associates, Bart 923
Andrews and McMeel 57
Angel's Touch Productions 866
Anglo-American Spotlight 329
Anglofile 308
Angus Journal 736
Animal Kingdom 232
Animal World 232
Animals 233
Animation Arts Associates, Inc. 854
Ann Arbor Observer 500
Annals of Saint Anne De Beaupre, The 534
Annual International Narrative Contest 968
Annual International Shakespearean Sonnet Contest 968
Annual Journalism Awards Competition 968
Annual Nissan Focus Awards, The 969
Annual NJ Poetry Contest 969
Annual North American Essay Contest 969
Ansom 834
Anthony Agency, Joseph 923
Antic Magazine 456
Antioch Review 410
Antique Trader Weekly, The 357
Antiques & Auction News 357
Antiqueweek 676
Apollo Books 57
Apothecary, The 714
Appalachian Mountain Club Books 58
Appalachian Trailways News 448
Apparel Industry Magazine 704
Apple IIGS Buyers Guide, The 457
Appleseeds Management 923
Applezaba Press 58
Appliance Manufacturer 774
Aquarian Press Ltd., The 58
Aquarium Fish Magazine 233
Arabian Horse Times 233
Aran Press 866
Ararat 318
Arbor House 58
Archaeology 574
Archery World (see Bowhunting World 584)
ARCsoft Publishers 58
Area Development Magazine 831
Arena Stage 866
Arete 468
Argus Communications 908
Arizona Authors' Association An-

nual National Literary Contest 969
Arizona Business Gazette 270
Arizona Highways 479
Arizona Living Magazine 480
Arizona Trend 270
Arkansas Arts Center Children's Theatre, The 866
Arkansas Business 270
Arkansas Sportsman 603
Arkansas Times 480
Arkin Magazine Syndicate 897
Arman Publishing, Inc., M. 59
Armed Forces Journal International 433
Arnold and Associates Productions, Inc. 854
Arrow Rock Lyceum 866
Art Business News 676
Art Craft Publishing Co. 867
Art Material Trade News 834
Art Times 242
Arthritis Today 305
Arthur's International 898
Artilleryman, The 351
Artist's Fellowship Award 969
Artists Group, The 923
Artist's Magazine, The 242
Artreach Touring Theatre 867
Arts & Activities 716
Arts Indiana 495
Arts Management 677
Arts Recognition and Talent Search 969
ASU Travel Guide 640
Asher-Gallant Press 59
Asian Humanities Press 59
Asolo State Theatre 867
Aspirations 969
Associate Reformed Presbyterian, The 534
Association Executive 246
Asta Agency Management 848
Astor Memorial Leadership Essay Contest, Vincent 969
Astro Signs 253
At the Foot of the Mountain Theater 867
Atari Explorer 457
Athenaeum of Philadelphia Literary Award, The 969
Atheneum Children's Books 60
Atlanta Singles Magazine 528
Atlantic City Magazine 505
Atlantic Construction 707
Atlantic Monthly Press 60
Atlantic Monthly, The 329
Atlantic Salmon Journal, The 448
Audubon 450
Augsburg Books 60
Author Aid Associates 923
Authors' Unlimited 212
Authors/Writers Annual Short Story Contest 969
Auto Book Press 221
Auto Glass Journal 680
Auto Laundry News 680
Automated Builder 708
Automatic Machining 803
Automatic Merchandiser 758
Automotive Booster of California 680
Automotive Executive 681
A/V Concepts Corp. 854
Avalon Books 61
Aviation Book Co. 61

Avila College, Department of Humanities 867
Avon Books 61
Avon Flare Books 61
Avon Flare Young Adult Novel Competition 969
Award for Literary Translation 969
Award Specialist (see Recognition & Promotions Business 699)
Away 640
Axios 534
Aztex Corp. 61

B

Baby Talk Magazine 287
Bachner Productions, Inc. 892
Back Pain Magazine (see Back to Health 340)
Back to Health Magazine 340
Backcountry Publications 61
Bad Haircut 410
Badger Sportsman 604
Baen Publishing Enterprises 62
Baja Times 641
Baker Book House Company 62
Baker's Play Publishing Co. 867
Balch Award, Emily Clark 969
Baldi Literary Agency, Inc., Malaga 924
Baldwin College Theatre, Mary 868
Bale Books 62
Ballantine/Epiphany Books 62
Balloon Life 620
Balloons Today Magazine 835
Balls and Strikes 621
Banjo Newsletter 439
Bank Operations Report 746
Bank Personnel Report 746
Banking Software Review 746
Banks-Baldwin Law Publishing Co. 63
Banta Award 969
Bantam Books 63
Baptist Leader 535
Bark Eater, The 596
Barr Films 855
Barron's 266
Barron's Educational Series, Inc. 63
Bart Books 63
Bartender Magazine 769
Bartle Playwriting Award, The Margaret 970
Bartlett Award, The Elizabeth 970
Basch Feature Syndicate, Buddy 898
Bascom Communications 225
Baseball Cards 357
Bassin' 604
Bassmaster Magazine 604
Battery Man, The 681
Bay & Delta Yachtsman 587
Bay Area Parent 287
Bay Windows 528
BC Outdoors 604
Beacon Hill Press of Kansas City 64
Beacon Magazine 513
Bear and Co., Inc. 64
Bear Flag Books 64
Beau Lac Publishers 64
Beauty Age 835
Beauty Digest 341
Becker, Maximilian 924
Beckett Baseball Card Monthly 357
Beef 737
Beef Today 737
Beer Prize, George Louis 970

Behrman House Inc. 64
Believers by the Bay 535
Bench and Bar of Minnesota 795
Bend of the River® Magazine 513
Benjamin Company, Inc., The 65
Bentley, Inc., Robert 65
Berea College Theatre 868
Bergh Publishing, Inc. 65
Berkshire Public Theatre 868
Berkshire Traveller Press 221
Bernstein, Meredith 924
Best of Blurbs Contest 970
Best of Housewife-Writer's Forum:
    The Contested Wills to Write
    970
Best Report, The 812
Bethany House Publishers 65
Better Business 266
Better Health 341
Better Homes and Gardens 377
Better Homes and Gardens Books
    66
Better Life for You, A 329
Betterway Publications, Inc. 66
Between the Lines Inc. 66
Beverage World 687
Beveridge Award, Albert J. 970
Beverly Hills Theatre Guild-Julie
    Harris Playwright Award Com-
    petition, The 970
Beyond . . . 578
Bicycle Business Journal 839
Bicycle Guide 585
Bicycling 585
Biennial Promising Playwright
    Award 970
BikeOhio 586
Bikereport 586
Binford & Mort Publishing 67
Biology Digest 574
Bionics 728
Bird Talk 234
Bird Watcher's Digest 450
Birder's World 234
Bitterroot Magazine Poetry Contest
    970
Black Award, Irma Simonton 970
Black Belt 618
Black Collegian, The 278
Black Confessions 568
Black Conscience Syndication Inc.
    898
Black Warrior Review 411
Blair, Publisher, John F. 67
Blake Group Literary Agency, The
    924
Blakeslee Awards, Howard W. 970
Blanchan Memorial Award, Neltje
    970
Blate Associates, Samuel R. 855
Blazing Productions, Inc. 892
Blue Bird Publishing 67
Blue Dolphin Publishing, Inc. 67
Blue Mountain Arts, Inc. 908
Bluegrass Unlimited 439
Blueridge Country 474
BMI University Musical Show Com-
    petition 970
BMX Plus Magazine 256
BNA Books 68
BNH Magazine 271
Boarshead Theater 868
Boat Pennsylvania 587
Boates Literary Agency, Reid 925
Boating Industry 811
Body, Mind & Spirit 253
Body Story Contest 970

Bomb 300
Bon Appetit 324
Book Creations, Inc. 225
Book Dealers World 784
Book Forum 411
Book Peddlers, The 925
Bookcraft, Inc. 68
Bookmakers Guild, Inc. 68
Bookstop Literary Agency 925
Bookworks, Inc. 225
Borchardt Inc., Georges 925
Borealis Press, Ltd. 69
Borgo Press, The 69
Bosco Publications, Don 69
Boston Globe Magazine 498
Boston Globe-Horn Book Awards
    970
Boston Magazine 498
Boston Mills Press, The 69
Boston Post Road Stage Company
    868
Boston Review 300
Bostonia 499
Bottom Line, The 746
Boulder County Business Report
    271
Bow and Arrow Hunting 583
Bowbender 583
Bowhunter 584
Bowhunting World 584
Bowlers Journal 595
Bowling Writing Competition 971
Boxoffice Magazine 731
Boys Life 394
Bradbury Press 70
Bradley-Goldstein Agency, The 926
Bragdon Publishers, Inc., Allen D.
    70
Brahman Journal, The 737
Brake & Front End 681
Branden Publishing Co., Inc.. 70
Brandt & Brandt Literary Agents,
    Inc. 926
Braniff Magazine 392
Bread 631
Breakers Guide '90 278
Breakwater Books 70
Brethren Press 71
Briarcliff Press Publishers 71
Brick House Publishing Co. 71
Bridal Guide 653
Bridal Trends 653
Bride's 653
Brilliant Enterprises 909
Brilliant Ideas for Publishers 784
Bristol Publishing Enterprises, Inc.
    72
British Car 256
Broadcast Technology 721
Broadcaster 721
Broadman Press 72
Broadway Press 72
Brod Literary Agency, Ruth Hagy
    926
Brody Arts Fund Fellowship 971
Bronze Thrills 568
Brown Inc., Ned 926
Brown, Literary Agency, Andrea
    926
Browne Ltd., Pema 926
Brunswick Publishing Company 212
B-Side 440
Builder Insider 708
Building Services Contractor 803
Burke Essay Contest, Arleigh 971
Bus Ride 848
Bus Tours Magazine 848

Bus World 845
Bush Artist Fellowships 971
Business Age 266
Business Facilities 831
Business Features Syndicate 898
Business Month 266
Business Radio 721
Business Today 297
Business View 271
Butter-Fat 736
Byline 785
Byline Magazine Contests 971
Byte Magazine 457

C

C.L.A.S.S. Magazine 468
C.S.S. Publishing Co. 72
CA Magazine 746
Cable Marketing 722
Cable Television Business Maga-
    zine 722
Cablecaster 722
Cabscott Broadcast Production, Inc.
    855
California Angler 605
California Baseball Magazine 585
California Basketball Magazine 585
California Farmer 743
California Fireman, The 753
California Football Magazine 595
California Game & Fish 605
California Highway Patrolman 246
California Journal 468
California Magazine 480
California Theater Center 868
California Writers' Club Confer-
    ence Contest 971
California Young Playwrights Proj-
    ect 971
Calligraphy Collection, The 909
Calligraphy Review 677
Calyx 411
Cambridge Career Products 73
Camden House, Inc. 73
Camelot Books 73
Cameron Agency, The Marshall 926
Camper Times, The 641
Camping & RV Magazine 641
Camping Canada 642
Camping Today 642
Campus Life Magazine 631
Canadian Author & Bookman 785
Canadian Author & Bookman Stu-
    dent Creative Writing Awards
    971
Canadian Booksellers Association
    Author of the Year Award 971
Canadian Computer Dealer News
    835
Canadian Computer Reseller 835
Canadian Defence Quarterly 754
Canadian Dimension 300
Canadian Fiction Magazine 411
Canadian Fiction Magazine 971
Canadian Forest Industries West
    802
Canadian Geographic 524
Canadian Grocer 758
Canadian Jeweller 783
Canadian Literature 412
Canadian Machinery & Metalwork-
    ing 803
Canadian Pharmaceutical Journal
    714
Canadian Plains Research Center
    73

Canadian Printer & Publisher 829
Canadian Research 728
Canadian Shipper, The 845
Canadian West 351
Canadian Workshop 377
Canadian Writer's Journal 785
Candy Industry 706
Cane Award, Melville 971
Canoe Magazine 588
Cantor, Literary Agent, Ruth 927
Cape Cod Compass 499
Cape Cod Life 499
Capital Magazine 508
Caplin Productions, Lee 855
Capper's 330
Car Audio and Electronics 257
Car and Driver 257
Car Collector/Car Classics 257
Caratzas, Publisher, Aristide D. 74
Cardiology World News 812
Cardoza Enterprises, Anthony 892
Career Focus 279
Career Publishing, Inc. 74
Career Vision 279
Careers and the Handicapped 305
Carey-It-Off Productions 892
Caribbean Travel and Life 642
Carlton Press, Inc. 212
Carnegie Mellon Magazine 279
Carol Publishing 74
Carolina Biological Supply Co. 75
Carolina Quarterly 412
Carolrhoda Books, Inc. 75
Carpenter Publishing House 225
Carroll & Graf Publishers, Inc. 75
Carrozzeria 258
Carstens Publications, Inc. 75
Carter Memorial Award for Liter-
ary Criticism, The Thomas 971
Cartoon World 296
Cascades East 516
Cassandra Press 75
Cassell Publications 76
Casselman, Literary Agent, Martha
927
Casual Living 836
Cat Fancy 234
Catalog Literary Agency, The 927
Catering Today 770
Catholic Answer,The 535
Catholic Digest 535
Catholic Forester 246
Catholic Health Association of the
United States, The 76
Catholic Life 536
Catholic Near East Magazine 536
Catholic Press Association Journal-
ism Awards 971
Catholic University of America
Press 76
Cats Magazine 235
Cattleman Magazine, The 738
Cavalier 428
Caxton Printers, Ltd., The 76
CCC Publications 77
CCLM Editor's Grant Awards 971
CCLM Seed Grants 972
Cecil Arthritis Writing Awards,
Russell L. 972
Celebration of One-Acts 972
Center for Applied Linguistics 77
Central Coast Parent 289
Century City Magazine 481
Ceramic Scope 691
Chain Saw Age 764
Champion 597
Chandler Award, Paulette 972

Changing Men 528
Changing Scene Theater, The 868
Changing Times 298
Chariton Review, The 412
Charlotte Magazine 512
Charlotte Repertory Theatre 869
Charlton Associates, James 927
Chatelaine 654
Chatham Press 77
Chattanooga Life & Leisure 518
Chelsea Green 77
Chemical Business 774
Cheribe Publishing Co. 77
Cherokee Publishing Company 78
Cherry St. Films 892
Chesapeake Bay Magazine 498
Chess Life 327
Chic Magazine 428
Chicago Board of Rabbis Broad-
casting Commission, The 892
Chicago History 352
Chicago Magazine 494
Chicago Studies 536
Chicano Literary Contest 972
Chickadee Magazine 395
Chief Executive 693
Chief of Police Magazine 754
Child 289
Child and Family 289
Child Welfare League Of America
78
Children's Digest 395
Children's Playmate 395
Children's Science Book Awards
972
Chilton Book Co. 78
China Glass & Tableware 764
Chiz Agency, Terry 928
Chockstone Press, Inc. 78
Chocolatier 324
Chosen Books Publishing Co. 78
Christian Broadcasting Network
893
Christian Education Today 701
Christian Home & School 536
Christian Leadership 701
Christian Living for Senior Highs
631
Christian Outlook 537
Christian Science Monitor, The 330
Christian Single 537
Christian Social Action 537
Christian Writers Newsletter 785
Christianity & Crisis 537
Christianity Today 538
Christmas 538
Christopher Award, The 972
Christopher Publishing House, The
79
Chronicle of the Horse, The 235
Chrysalis 538
Church & State 539
Church Educator 702
Church Herald, The 539
Church Media Library Magazine
800
Church Musician, The 820
Church Training 702
Cincinnati Medicine 813
Cineaste 308
Cine/Design Films, Inc. 893
Cinefantastique Magazine 308
Cintas Fellowshiop 972
Circle K Magazine 280
Circle Repertory Co. 869
Circuit Playhouse/Playhouse on the
Square 869

Circuit Rider 703
Citadel Press 79
Citrus & Vegetable Magazine 759
City Guide 508
City Limits 509
City Sports Magazine 597
City Theatre Company 869
Clarion Books 79
Clarity Press 221
Clark Co., Arthur H. 79
Clark, Inc., I.E. 869
Class Act 632
Classic Auto Restorer 258
Classroom Computer Learning 716
Clausen Associates, Connie 928
Claytor Memorial Award, Gertrude
B. 972
Cleaning Consultant Services, Inc.
80
Cleaning Management 804
Clearvue, Inc. 855
Cleaver Inc., Diane 928
Cleis Press 80
Clergy Journal, The 703
Cleveland Play House, The 870
Cleveland State University Poetry
Center 80
Cleveland State University Poetry
Center Prize 972
Cliffhanger Press 81
Cliffs Notes, Inc. 81
Closing the Gap, Inc. 457
Club Costa Magazine 247
Clubhouse 396
Coastal Cruising 588
Cobblestone 396
Cohen, Inc., Ruth 928
Cohen Literary Agency, Ltd., Hy
928
Coin Enthusiast's Journal, The 358
Coins 358
Coles Publishing Co., Ltd. 81
Collector Editions Quarterly 358
Collectors News & the Antique Re-
porter 359
College Board, The 81
College Monthly 280
College Press Publishing Co. 81
College Preview 280
Collegiate Career Woman 281
Collegiate Poetry Contest 972
Collier Associates 929
Collin Literary Agency, Frances 929
Collision 681
Colony Theatre Studio 870
Colorado Associated University
Press 82
Colorado Homes and Lifestyles 378
Colortype 909
Columbia 539
Columbia Journalism Review 785
Columbus Bride & Groom Maga-
zine 529
Columbus Monthly 514
Comedy Writers Association News-
letter 247
Comico The Comic Company 296
Comics Journal, The 786
Comics Scene 296
Comments 539
Commerce Clearing House, Inc. 82
Commerce Magazine 298
Commodore Magazine 458
Common Sense 693
Commonweal 468
Communication Briefings 693
Communications Press 82

Compact Books 82
Company One 870
Compass 780
Compass Films 856
CompCare Publishers 82
Compressed Air 774
Compute! Books 83
Computer Gaming World 327
Computer Language 458
Computer Language 776
Computer Science Press, Inc. 83
Computer Shopper 458
Computer User's Legal Reporter 796
Computers in Education 717
Compute!'s PC Magazine 459
Computing Now! 459
Computoredge 459
Comstock Cards 909
Conceive Magazine 341
Concrete Trader, The 708
Confident Living 540
Confrontation 412
Connor Literary Agency 929
Conscience 540
Construction Comment 708
Construction Specifier 709
Consultant Pharmacist 813
Consultant Press, The 83
Consumer Action News 298
Consumer Lending Report 746
Consumers Digest Magazine 298
Contemporary Books, Inc. 83
Contemporary Drama Service 870
Contemporary Long-Term Care 767
Contenova Gifts 909
Continental Features/Continental News Service 899
Continental Film Productions Corporation 856
Continuum Broadcasting Network/Continuum News Features, Inc. 899
Convention South 694
Cooking Light 324
Cook's 325
Cope Magazine 813
Coping 341
Copley News Service 899
Copy Magazine 829
Copyright Information Services 84
Coral Springs Monthly 488
Corbin House 221
Corey Prize in Canadian-American Relations, Albert B. 972
Corkscrew Press 84
Corman Productions 893
Cornell Maritime Press, Inc. 84
Cornerstone 540
Cornfield Literary Agency, Robert 929
Corporate Health 714
Corvette Fever 258
Cosmopolitan 654
Cost Cuts 709
Coteau Books 84
Cottonwood Monthly 717
Council for Wisconsin Writers, Inc. Annual Awards Competition 972
Counselor Magazine, The 673
Country Journal 571
Country Roads Quarterly 474
Country Woman 654
Countryman Press, Inc., The 84
Countrywoman's Press, The 85
Covenant Campanion, The 541

CQ Press 72
Craddock Publishing 221
Crafts 'n Things 359
Crafts Report, The 677
Craftsman Book Company 85
Crains Detroit Business 272
Create-a-Craft 909
Creative Arts Book Company 85
Creative Arts Contest 972
Creative Concepts Literary Agency 929
Creative Productions, Inc. 870
Creative Publishing Co. 85
Creative Syndication Services 899
Creativity Fellowship 973
Creators Syndicate, Inc. 899
Cricket 396
Cricket Letter, Inc., The 900
Crossing Press, The 85
Crossroads Theatre Company 870
Crossway Books 86
Crown Publishers, Inc. 86
Crown Syndicate, Inc. 900
Cruise Travel Magazine 643
Cruising World 588
Crusader Magazine 397
Cuff Publications Limited, Harry 86
Current Comedy for Speakers 388
Currents 589
Curtis Associates, Inc., Richard 929
Custom Applicator 735
Cycle World 258
Cycling USA 586
Czeschin's Mutual Fund Outlook & Recommendations 266

D

"D" Magazine 518
Daily Meditation 541
Daily Word 541
Dairy Goat Journal 736
Dakota Game & Fish 605
Dakota Outdoors 517
Dallas Life Magazine 518
Dalton Little Theatre New Play Project 871
Dance Connection 309
Dance Exercise Today (see Idea Today 732)
Dance Horizons 86
Dance Magazine 309
Dancscene—the Magazine of Ballroom Dance 309
Dancy Productions, Inc., Nicholas 856
D&B Reports 267
Daniel and Company, Publishers, John 86
Dante University Of America Press, Inc. 87
Darkroom and Creative Techniques 465
Darkroom Photography Magazine 466
Data Training 805
Davenport, Publishers, May 87
Davidson Memorial Award, Gustav 973
Davie Literary Agency, Elaine 930
Davies Memorial Award, Mary Carolyn 973
Davis Publications, Inc. 87
Davis Publishing, Steve 87
Daw Books, Inc. 88
Dayton Playhouse National Playwriting Competition 973

DBMS 777
De Young Press 212
Dealer Communicator 836
Decision 541
Decorative Artist's Workbook 359
Deep South Writers Contest 973
Deer and Deer Hunting 605
Deering, Literary Agency, Dorothy 930
DeFeis, Frederic 871
Defense and Foreign Affairs 782
Del Rey Books 88
Delacorte Press 88
Delacorte Press Prize for a First Young Adult Novel 973
Delaware Theatre Company 871
Deli-Dairy 759
Delta Books 88
Deluxe 747
Dembner Books 88
Denison & Co., Inc., T.S. 89
Denlingers Publishers, Ltd. 89
Denny Poetry Contest, Billee Murray 973
Dental Economics 712
Dentist 712
Denton Today Magazine 519
Denver Center Theatre Company 871
Denver Quarterly, The 413
Design Graphics World (see Design Management 729)
Design Management 729
D'esternaux Student Poetry Contest, Marie-Louise 973
Details 301
Detective Cases 304
Detective Dragnet 304
Detective Files 304
Detroit Free Press Magazine, The 501
Detroit Monthly 501
Devin-Adair Publishers, Inc. 89
Devonshire Publishing Co. 89
DG Review 777
Di Castagnola Award, Alice Fay 973
Dial Books For Young Readers 90
Dialogue 305
Diamant, The Writer's Workshop, Inc., Anita 930
Diamond Press 221
Dickinson Award, Emily 973
Digital Press 90
Dijkstra Literary Agency, Sandra 930
Dillon Press, Inc. 90
Dillon/Richard C. Peterson Memorial Essay Prize, Gordon W. 973
Dimension Books, Inc. 91
Dimensional Stone 843
Dimi Press 221
Directions 281
Directions in Childcare 694
Dirt Bike 259
Disciple, The 542
Discipleship Journal 542
Discoveries 397
Discovery 643
Discovery '90 871
Discovery/The Nation 973
Distributor, 827
Diver, The 629
Divided Artists 893
Dixie Contractor 709
Dobie-Paisano Fellowship, The 973
Docket, The 796
Doctor's Review 813

Doctors Shopper 814
Dodge Foundation New American Play Award, The Geraldine R. 973
Dog Fancy 235
Dog Writer's Association of America Annual Writing Contest 974
Dolger Agency, The Jonathan 931
Doll Reader 91
Dolls 360
Dolphin Log, The 397
Domestic Engineering Magazine 827
Doubleday & Co., Inc. 91
Doubleday Memorial Award, Frank Nelson 974
Down East Books 91
Dr. Dobb's Journal 777
Dragon® 327
Drama Book Publishers 91
Dramatic Publishing Co., The 871
Dramatics Magazine 309
Drummer 529
Drury College One-Act Play Contest 974
Dry Canyon Press 221
Dubuque Fine Arts Players 974
Dundurn Press Ltd. 92
Dungeon Master 529
Dunning Prize in American History, John H. 974
Duquesne University Press 92
Dustbooks 92
Dutton Children's Books 92
Dykeman Associates, Inc. 931

E

E.P. Dutton 92
Eakin Publications, Inc. 93
Early American Life 360
Early Childhood News 694
Earth Care Paper Inc. 910
Earth Star Publications 221
East West 342
Eastview Editions 212
Eaton Literary Associates Literary Awards Program 974
Ebony Magazine 318
Eclipse Comics 297
Economic Facts 299
ECW Press 93
Ediciones Universal 93
Editor and Publisher 786
Editorial Consultant Service 900
Editorial Eye, The 786
Editors' Book Award 974
Editors' Forum 786
Editors Press Service, Inc. 900
Education Associates 93
Educational Dealer 836
Educational Design Services, Inc. 931
Educational Images Ltd. 856
Educational Insights 856
Educational Video Network 857
Eerdmans Publishing Co., William B. 94
EES* Publications 92
Eisenberg Literary Agency, Vicki 931
El Palacio 352
El Paso Magazine 519
ElderCards, Inc. 910
Eldridge Publishing Co. 871
Eldritch Tales 413

Electric Company Magazine (see Kid City™ 400)
Electric Weenie, The 731
Electrical Apparatus 726
Electrical Contractor 727
Electron, The 574
Electronic Composition and Imaging 459
Electronics Experimenters Handbook 360
Elek Associates, Peter 931
Elks Magazine, The 247
Ellenberg, Literary Agent, Ethan 932
Elysium Growth Press 94
EMC Corp 857
Emergency 814
Emergency Librarian 800
Emerging Playwright Award 974
Emerson Award, The Ralph Waldo 974
Emmy Magazine 310
Empire State Institute for the Performing Arts 872
Employee Relations and Human Resources Bulletin 806
Empty Space, The 872
Endless Vacation 643
Engravers Journal, The 783
Ensemble Studio Theatre, The 872
Enslow Publishers 94
Entelek 94
Enterprise Publishing Co., Inc. 95
Entertainment Productions, Inc. 893
Entree 765
Entrepreneur Magazine 299
Environment 451
Environmental Action 451
Episcopalian, The 542
Epoch 413
Epstein Playwriting Award, Lawrence S. 974
Equal Opportunity 281
Equine Images 243
Equinews 236
Equinox: the Magazine of Canadian Discovery 330
Erikson Literary Agency, The 932
Eriksson, Publisher, Paul S. 95
Esquire 428
Essence 655
ETC Publications 95
Etc Magazine 282
Europe 470
Evangel 543
Evangelical Beacon, The 543
Evangelizing Today's Child 543
Evans and Associates 932
Evans and Co., Inc., M. 95
Evans Biography Award, David W. and Beatrice C. 974
Event 413
Executive Female 267
Executive Financial Woman 747
Exhibit 243
Exploring Magazine 632
Expressions 388

F

Faber & Faber, Inc. 96
Facts On File, Inc. 96
FAHS Review 715
Fair Times 836
Fairbank Prize in East Asian History, John K. 974

Fairchild Books & Visuals 96
Fairfield County Woman 655
Fairleigh Dickinson University Press 96
Fairway Press 212
Falcon Press Publishing Co. 97
Family Album, The 97
Family Circle Magazine 655
Family Fiction Digest 414
Family Magazine 433
Family Motor Coaching 644
Family, The 544
Family Therapy News 815
Fancy Food 759
Fangoria 310
Farber First Book Award, Norma 974
Farm & Ranch Living 571
Farm Family America 572
Farm Futures 739
Farm Journal 739
Farm Pond Harvest 740
Farm Show Magazine 740
Farm Store Merchandising 695
Farmweek 743
Farquharson Ltd., John 932
Farrar, Straus and Giroux, Inc. 97
Farwestern Consultants, Inc. 932
Fashion Accessories 783
Fate 253
Fathers 290
Faulkner Award for Excellence in Writing, Virginia 974
FAW Literary Award 975
Fawcett Juniper 97
FDA Consumer 299
Fearon Education 97
Feature Enterprises 900
Fedco Reporter 248
Federal Buyers Guide, Inc. 97
Federal Personnel Management Institute, Inc. 98
Feiler Literary Agency, Florence 933
Felicity Awards 975
Feline Productions 893
Fell Publishers, Inc., Frederick 98
Feminist Bookstore News, The 690
Festival of New Works 975
Festivity! 732
Fiberarts 361
Ficarelli, Richard 872
Fiction Collective 98
Fiction Network 900
Fiction Network Magazine 414
Fiction Writers Contest 975
Fiddlehead Poetry Books & Goose Lane Editions 98
Fiddlehead, The 414
FIEJ Golden Pen of Freedom 975
Field & Stream 606
Fields/Rita Scott, Marje 933
Fighter International, The 618
Fighting Woman News 619
Film Quarterly 311
Filmclips 311
Final Draft, The 787
Final Frontier 574
Financial Executive 695
Financial Freedom Report 832
Financial Manager, The 747
Financial Sourcebooks 99
Fine Gardening 378
Fine Homebuilding 709
Fine, Inc., Donald I. 99
Fine Woodworking 361
Finescale Modeler 361

Fire Prevention Through Films, Inc. 857
Firebrand Books 99
Firehouse Magazine 754
Firehouse Theatre, The 872
First Hand 529
First Opportunity 282
First Ring 857
Fishbein Ltd., Frieda 933
Fisher Books 99
Fisherman, The 606
Fishing & Boating Illustrated 606
Fishing & Hunting Journal 606
Fishing and Hunting News 607
Fishing Tackle Retailer 840
Fishing World 607
Fithian Press 212
Fitness Management 815
Fitzhenry & Whiteside, Ltd. 100
Five Star Publications 100
Flaherty, Literary Agent, Joyce A. 933
Flaming Star Literary Enterprises 934
Flannery, White & Stone 934
Fleet Press Corp. 100
Flex 621
Fling 428
Fliptrack Learning Systems 857
Floor Covering Business 692
Flooring Magazine 765
Flora And Fauna Publications 100
Floral & Nursery Times 750
Flores Publications, J. 100
Florida Forum 828
Florida Game & Fish 607
Florida Grocer 759
Florida Grower & Rancher 743
Florida Home and Garden 378
Florida Hotel & Motel Journal 770
Florida Individual Artist Fellowships 975
Florida Leader 282
Florida Nursing News 768
Florida Restaurateur 770
Florida Sportsman 607
Florida Studio Theatre 872
Florida Trend 272
Florida Underwriter 781
Florida Wildlife 608
Florist 750
Flower and Garden Magazine 378
Flower News 751
Fly Fisherman 608
Flying A, The 674
FMCT's Biennial Playwrights Competition (Mid-West) 975
Focal Press 101
Foley Agency, The 934
Folio 975
Folio Weekly 488
Follow Me 301
Follow Me Gentleman 301
Food & Wine 325
Food and Drug Packaging 837
Food and Service 770
Food Business 760
Food People 760
Foodservice Director 760
Forbes 267
Ford Award, Consuelo 975
Ford New Holland News 740
Ford Times 331
Fordham Magazine 282
Foreign Affairs 783
Foreign Service Journal 755
Forest Notes 505

Forests & People 451
Forman Publishing 101
49th Parallel Poetry Contest, The 975
Forum 429
Foster City Annual Writers Contest 975
Fotopress, Independent News Service 901
Foundation News 755
Four Wheel and Off-Road 259
Four Wheeler Magazine 259
Four Winds Press 101
Fourth Estate Award 975
FQ 530
Franciscan Herald Press 101
Fraser Institute, The 101
Free Press, The 102
Free Spirit Publishing Inc. 221
Freedley Memorial Award, George 975
Freedman Dramatic Agency, Inc., Robert A. 934
Freedom Greeting Card Co. 910
Freelance Press, The 872
Freelance Writer's Report 787
Freeman, The 470
Freeway 632
French & Partners, Inc., Paul 857
French, Inc., Samuel 102
French, Inc., Samuel 873
French, Inc., Samuel 934
Frequent Flyer 265
Frets Magazine 440
Friedman Publishing Group, Michael 225
Friend, The 398
Friendly Exchange 331
Front Row Experience 221
Front Striker Bulletin, The 677
Frost Associates, Helena 226
Fuhrman Literary Agency, Candice 935
Fulbright Scholar Program 975
Fulcrum, Inc. 102
Fundamentalist Journal 544
Funny Business 388
Fur Trade Journal of Canada 742
Fur-Fish-Game 608
Futures and Options Trader, The 748
Futurific Magazine 331

G

(Gabriel) Graphics News Bureau 901
Galantière Prize for Literary Translation, Lewis 976
Gallant Greetings 910
Gallaudet Journalism Award 976
Gallaudet University Press 102
Gallery Magazine 429
Games Junior and Games 328
Gamut, The 414
Garber Communications, Inc. 103
Garden Design 379
Garden Magazine 379
Garden Supply Retailer 751
Gardner Press, Inc. 103
Garland Publishing, Inc. 103
Garon-Brooke Associates, Inc., Jay 935
Gartenberg, Literary Agent, Max 935
Gaslamp Quarter Theatre Company 873

Gaslight Publications 103
Gassner Memorial Playwriting Award, John 976
Gauss Award, The Christian 976
Geer Theatricum Botanicum, The Will 873
Gelles-Cole Literary Enterprises 935
Gem 429
Gem Show News 362
Gem, The 544
Genealogical Computing 460
Genealogical Publishing Co., Inc. 103
General Dentistry 713
General Electric Foundation Awards for Younger Writers 976
General News Syndicate 901
Gent 429
Gentlemens Quarterly 430
George Street Playhouse 873
Georgetown Productions 873
Georgia Journal 492
Georgia Sportsman 609
Georgia Straight 525
Geriatric Consultant 815
German Prize for Literary Translation 976
Gessler Publishing Co., Inc. 857
GeVa Theatre 873
Geyers Office Dealer 822
Ghost Town Quarterly 353
Giant Crosswords 328
Gifford Children's Theater, Emmy 874
Gift and Stationery 765
Gifted Children Monthly 290
Gifted Education Press 104
Giftware News 765
Gig Magazine 440
Giniger Company, Inc., The K S 226
Gladden & Associates 935
Glamour 656
Glass Art 677
Glass Magazine 691
Glassco Translation Prize, John 976
Gleanings in Bee Culture 742
Glenbridge Publishing Ltd. 104
Global Business and Trade Communications 104
Gloucester Stage Co. 874
Godine, Publisher, David R. 104
Golden Gate Actors Ensemble Playwright's Contest 976
Golden Kite Awards 976
Golden Quill Press 212
Golden West Books 105
Golden West Publishers 105
Golden Years Magazine 563
Golf Course Management 840
Golf Digest 599
Golf Illustrated 600
Golf Shop Operations 840
Golf Writer's Contest 976
Gollehon Press Inc. 105
Good Housekeeping 656
Good News 544
Good Old Days 353
Good Reading 332
Goodheart Prize for Fiction, The Jeanne Charpiot 976
Goodman Associates, Literary Agents 936
Goodman Award 976
Goodman Literary Agency, Irene 936

Goodwin & Associates, Dave 901
Goodwin, Knab & Company 858
Gordon Agency, Charlotte 936
Gordon and Breach 105
Gospel Publishing House 105
Gospel Truth, The 545
Gourmet Today 761
Government Contractor 755
Government Institutes, Inc. 106
Governor General's Literary
  Awards 977
Gower Publishing Co. 106
Graduating Engineer 729
Graham Agency 936
Grand Rapids Magazine 501
Grants to Individual Artists 977
Grapevine Publications, Inc. 106
Graphic Arts Center Publishing Co.
  106
Graphic Arts Technical Foundation
  106
Graywolf Press 107
Great American Tennis Writing
  Awards, The 977
Great Expeditions 644
Great Lakes Bowhunter Magazine
  584
Great Lakes Colleges Association
  New Writers Award 977
Great Lakes Sailor 589
Great Northwest Publishing and
  Distributing Company, Inc. 107
Great Ocean Publishers 222
Greater Phoenix Jewish News 319
Greater Portland Magazine 497
Greater Winnipeg Business 272
Green Tiger Press Inc. 107
Green Timber Publications 222
Greene, Inc., Harold R. 936
Greene Press, The Stephen/Pelham
  Books 107
Greenhaven Press, Inc. 107
Greenleaf Classics, Inc. 108
Groom and Board 823
Ground Water Age 833
Group Practice Journal 816
Group's Junior High Ministry Mag-
  azine 545
Growing Edge, The 751
Growing Parent 290
Gryphon House, Inc. 222
Guernica Editions 108
Guide Magazine 633
Guide, The 530
Guide to the Florida Keys 644
Guidelines Newsletter 787
Guideposts Magazine 546
Guitar Player Magazine 441
Gulf Coast 488
Gulf Coast Fisherman 609
Gulf Coast Golfer 600
Gun Digest and Handloader's Di-
  gest 601
Gun World 602
Guns Magazine 602
Guthrie Theater 874

H

Hadassah Magazine 319
Hagert, Brad 858
Hale Award, Sarah Josepha 977
Hallmark Cards, Inc. 910
Ham Radio Magazine 723
Hamilton Institute, Alexander 108
Hancock House Publishers Ltd. 108
Handmade Accents 243

Hands-On Electronics (see Popular
  Electronics 368)
Handwoven 362
Harbinger House, Inc. 109
Harbor House Publishers 109
Harcourt Brace Jovanovich 109
Hardware Age 764
Hardy—Publisher, Max 109
Harlequin Books 109
Harper & Row Publishers, Inc. 110
Harper & Row, San Francisco 110
Harper Junior Books Group, West
  Coast 110
Harpers Magazine 332
Harrow And Heston 110
Harrowsmith 572
Harrowsmith Magazine 572
Hartford Monthly 486
Hartford Stage Company 874
Hartford Woman 486
Harvard Common Press, The 111
Harvest House Publishers 111
Harvest Magazine 563
Hass, Agent, Rose 936
Haunts 578
Hawaii High Tech Journal 272
Hawkes Publishing, Inc. 111
Hawkins & Associates, Inc., John
  937
Hayes School Publishing Co., Inc.
  858
Hazelden Educational Materials
  111
Heacock Literary Agency, Inc. 937
Headquarters Detective 304
Health Administration Press 114
Health Express 342
Health Foods Business 761
Health Magazine 342
Healthcare Professional Publishing
  816
Heart Of The Lakes Publishing 114
Hearth and Home 828
Heartland Boating 589
Heating, Plumbing, Air Condition-
  ing 828
Heavy Truck Salesman Magazine
  682
Heddle Magazine 362
Helix Press 222
Helm Publishing 222
Hemingway Foundation Award, Er-
  nest 977
Hemley Memorial Award, Cecil 977
Hendrickson Publishers, Inc. 114
Hensley, Inc., Virgil W. 114
Herald Press 114
Herb Companion, The 379
Herb Quarterly, 380
Here's Life Publishers, Inc. 115
Heritage Books, Inc. 115
Heritage Features Syndicate 901
Heritage Florida Jewish News 319
Herman Agency, Inc., The Jeff 937
Hermes House Press 115
Herner Rights Agency, Susan 937
Heuer Publishing Co. 874
Heyday Books 115
Hibiscus Magazine 415
Hicall 546
Hideaways Guide 645
High Adventure 398
High Country News 451
High Plains Journal 740
High School Sports 597
High Society 430
High Technology Business 695

High Technology Careers 729
High Times 301
High Volume Printing 829
Highlander, The 320
Highlights 525
Highlights for Children 398
Highlights for Children Fiction
  Contest 977
High-Tech Selling 674
Hill Associates, Frederick 938
Hillman Prize Award, Sidney 977
Hilton Literary Agency, Alice 938
Hippocrates 343
Hippocrene Books Inc. 116
Hispanic Link News Service 901
Hitchcock's Mystery Magazine, Al-
  fred 447
HOW 678
Hockey Illustrated 621
Hog Farm Management 738
Holloway House Publishing Co. 116
Hollywood Inside Syndicate 902
Hollywood Reporter, The 732
Holmes & Meier Publishers, Inc.
  116
Home and Studio Recording 441
Home Builder 710
Home Business News 267
Home Education Magazine 291
Home Furnishings Review 766
Home Life 291
Home Lighting & Accessories 766
Home Magazine 380
Home Mechanix 362
Home Office Computing 460
Home Shop Machinist, The 363
Homeowner 380
Homestead Publishing 116
Homeworking Mothers 656
Honolulu 493
Honolulu Theatre for Youth 874
Hoof Beats 602
Hoover Annual Journalism Awards
  977
Horizon Publishers & Distributors
  116
Horn Book Magazine, The 690
Horse Digest, The 236
Horse Illustrated 237
Horse World USA 237
Horseman Magazine 237
Horsemen's Yankee Pedlar News-
  paper 238
Horseplay 238
Horses All 238
Horses West 238
Horticulture 380
Hospital Gift Shop Management
  768
Hospital Supervisor's Bulletin 768
Hot Boat 590
Hotel Amenities in Canada 771
Hotel and Motel Management 771
Houghton Mifflin Co. 117
Houghton Mifflin Co., (Children's
  Trade) 117
House Beautiful 381
Housewife-Writer's Forum 788
Houston Magazine 519
Houston Metropolitan Magazine
  519
Houston Prize, Darrell Bob 977
Howard Awards, The Roy W. 977
Howell Press, Inc. 117
Hudson Guild Theatre 874
Hudson Hills Press, Inc. 117
Hudson Review, The 415

Hudson Talent Representation, Scott 938
Human Kinetics Publishers, Inc. 118
Human Resource Executive 806
Humanics Publishing Group 118
Humanities Press International, Inc. 118
Humpty Dumpty's Magazine 399
Hungness Publishing, Carl 118
Hunt, William E. 875
Hunter House, Inc., Publishers 118
Hunter Publishing, Inc. 119
Huntington House, Inc. 119
Hyatt 771
Hyde Park Media 902

I

ID Systems 777
Idaho Writer in Residence 977
Idea Today 732
Ideas 674
IEEE Software 777
ILR Press 119
Illinois Banker 748
Illinois Entertainer 441
Illinois Game & Fish 609
Illinois Magazine 494
Image Innovations, Inc. 858
Imagine, Inc. 119
Imperial International Learning Corp. 858
Imprint 674
In Touch 633
In Touch for Men 531
Inbound Logistics 846
Incentive 837
Incentive Publications, Inc. 120
Incider 460
Income Opportunities 299
Independent Banker 748
Independent Living 306
Independent Scholars, Lowell, Marraro, Shaughnessy and Mildenberger Awards 978
Indiana Business 273
Indiana Game & Fish 609
Indiana Repertory Theatre 875
Indiana University Press 120
Indianapolis Monthly 496
Indianhead Star 523
Individual Artists Fellowship 978
Industrial Fabric Products Review 774
Industrial Press, Inc. 120
Industrial Whimsy Co. 910
Industry Week 806
Infantry 434
Info Guide 778
Inform 778
Information Resources Press 120
Information Today 723
Information Week 778
Inland 475
Inland Architect 710
Inner City Cultural Center's National Short Play Competition 978
Innkeeping World 772
InnoVisions, Inc. 912
Inside 320
Inside Chicago 494
Inside Karate 619
Inside Kung-Fu 620
Inside Texas Running 622
Insights 602
Installation News 723

Institute for Policy Studies 222
Instructor Books 121
Instructor Magazine 717
Instrumentalist, The 820
Insurance Review 781
Insurance Software Review 782
Intercultural Press, Inc. 121
Intergalactic Publishing Co. 121
Interior Landscape Industry 751
Interlit 546
International Aviation Mechanics Journal 686
International Bluegrass 821
International Film & Film Literature Awards 978
International Foundation Of Employee Benefit Plans 121
International Gymnast 622
International Horse's Mouth, The 239
International Literary Contest 978
International Literature and Arts Agency 938
International Living 475
International Marine Publishing Co. 122
International Media Services Inc. 858
International Medical Advances Now! 343
International Musician 442
International Olympic Lifter 622
International Photo News 902
International Publisher Associates, Inc. 938
International Publishers Co., Inc. 122
International Reading Association Children's Book Award 978
International Reading Association Print Media Award 978
International Resources 122
International Self-Counsel Press, Ltd. 122
International Wealth Success 123
International Wildlife 452
International Woodworking 363
Interpress of London and New York 902
Interstate Publishers, Inc. 123
Interurban Press/Trans Anglo Books 123
Intervarsity Press 123
Interweave Press 124
Intimacy/Black Romance 568
Invisible Theatre 875
Iowa Game & Fish 609
Iowa Review, The 415
Iowa Short Fiction Award/John Simmons Short Fiction Award 978
Iowa State University Press 124
Irish & American Review 320
Iron Crown Enterprises 124
Isaac Asimov's Science Fiction Magazine 578
Ishiyaku Euroamerica, Inc. 125
Island Grower, The 381
Island Life 489
Islands 475
Islesboro Island News 497
Italian Times, The 320
Itinerary Magazine, The 645

J

Jabberwocky 579
Jackson Town & Country Magazine 501
Jackson/James D. Phelan Literary Awards, Joseph Henry 978
Jacksonville Magazine 489
Jacoby/Storm Productions Inc. 859
Jalmar Press, Inc. 125
Jam To-Day 415
Jamenair Ltd. 222
J&R Literary Agency 938
Japanophile 415
Japan-U.S. Friendship Commission Prize For the Translation of Japanese Literature, 1990 978
Jarvis and Co., Inc., Sharon 939
Jason Enterprises, Inc., Asher D. 939
Java Publishing Company 125
JCA Literary Agency 939
JCC Theatre of Cleveland Playwriting Competition 978
Jet Literary Associates, Inc. 939
Jewel 363
Jewel Box Theatre 875
Jewish Monthly, The 321
Jewish News 321
Jewish Repertory Theatre 875
Jewish Telegraphic Agency 903
Jewish Weekly News, The 547
Jive 569
Jobber Topics 682
Jonathan David Publishers 125
Jones 21st Century, Inc. 222
Jones Award, Anson 978
Jones National Poetry Competition, The Chester H. 979
Jones Playwriting Competition, Margo 979
Journal of Career Planning & Employment 717
Journal of Christian Camping 645
Journal of Graphoanalysis 472
Journal of Light Construction, The 710
Journal of Property Management 832
Journal, The 816
Journey 283
Joyful Woman, The 657
JSA Publications 903
Juggler's World 364
Junior Scholastic 399
Junior Trails 400
Juvenile Book Awards 979

K

Kafka Prize, The Janet Heidinger 979
Kalan, Inc. 912
Kaleidoscope 306
Kalmbach Publishing Co. 125
Kaltman Literary Agency, Larry 939
Kamaroff Associates, Alex 940
Kansas Game & Fish 609
Karate/Kung-Fu Illustrated 620
Kar-Ben Copies Inc. 126
Karr Productions, Paul S. 859
Kashrus Magazine 325
Keepin' Track of Vettes 260
Kellock & Associates Co. Ltd., J. 940
Kennedy Book Award, Robert F. 979

Kennedy Journalism Awards, Robert F. 979
Kent State University Press 126
Kentucky Game & Fish 609
Kentucky Happy Hunting Ground 496
Kentucky Living 496
Kern Literary Agency, Natasha 940
Kernodle One-Act Playwriting Competition, George R. 979
Kesend Publishing, Ltd., Michael 126
Key to Victoria/Essential Victoria 525
Keyboard Magazine 442
Keynoter 633
Kid City™ 400
Kimbo Educational-United Sound Arts, Inc. 859
King Features Syndicate, Inc. 903
King, Literary Agent, Daniel P. 940
Kinseeker Publications 127
Kirchoff/Wohlberg 941
Kitplanes 364
Kiwanis 248
Klein Publications, B. 127
Klinger, Inc., Harvey 941
Knights Press 127
Knopf, Inc., Alfred A. 127
Knowledge 332
Knowledge Industry Publications, Inc. 127
Knucklehead Press 388
Kohner, Inc., Paul 941
Korf Playwriting Awards, Lee 979
Kouts, Barbara S. 941
Krieger Publishing Co., Inc., Robert E. 127
Kroll Agency, Lucy 941
Kumu Kahua 875

L

L.A. Parent 291
L.A. Style 481
L.A. West 481
La Barrique 687
La Red/The Net 321
Ladies' Home Journal 657
Lady's Circle 657
Lake Memorial Award, Ruth 979
Lake Superior Magazine 502
Lamb's Players Theatre 876
Lamb's Theatre Company, The 876
Lamont Poetry Selection 979
Lampack Agency, Inc., Peter 942
Lancaster Productions, David 859
Landmark General Corp. 912
Landon Translation Prize, The Harold Morton 979
Lang Publishing, Peter 128
Larsen/Elizabeth Pomada Literary Agents, Michael 942
Laser Focus World Magazine 729
Laser Publishing Systems, Inc. 212
Latest Jokes 389
Laura Books, Inc. 128
Lavan Younger Poets Award, The Peter I.B. 979
Law and Order 755
Lawrence Foundation Award 979
Lawyers Monthly 796
Lawyer's PC, The 797
Lawyers Weekly, The 797
Lazear Agency, Inc., The 942
Leacock Memorial Award for Humour, Stephen 979

Leader, The 782
Leadership 703
League of Canadian Poets Awards 980
Learning 90 718
Lear's 658
Leather Craftsman, The 364
Lector 321
Lee, Literary Agency, L. Harry 942
Lee Shore Agency 943
Lefthander Magazine 333
Legacy Magazine 364
Legal Economics 797
Leisure Books 128
Leisure Ontario 333
Leisure Press 128
Leonard Publishing Corp., Hal 128
Let's Live Magazine 343
Letters Magazine 416
Levine Literary Agency, Inc., Ellen 943
Lexikos 129
Liberty House 129
Libra Publishers, Inc. 129
Libraries Unlimited 129
Library Imagination Paper, The 800
Library Journal 801
Library Research Associates, Inc. 129
Lieberman Student Poetry Award, Elias 980
Life Cycle Books 130
Life in the Times 434
Lifting and Transportation International 846
Light and Life 547
Light and Life Writing Contest 980
Lighthouse 416
Lighthouse Literary Agency 943
Liguori Publications 130
Liguorian 547
Lillenas Publishing Co. 876
Lily Poetry Prize, The Ruth 980
Linch Publishing, Inc. 130
Lincoln Memorial One-Act Playwriting Contest 980
Linden Lane Magazine English-Language Poetry Contest 980
Link-Up 460
Linn's Stamp News 365
Lintel 222
Lion Publishing Corporation 131
Lion, The 248
Lipkind Agency, Wendy 943
Lippincott Award, Joseph W. 980
Listen Again Music Newsletter, The 442
Listen Magazine 343
Literary Magazine Review 416
Literary Sketches 416
Literary/Business Associates 943
Little, Brown and Co., Inc. 131
Liturgical Publications, Inc. 131
Live 547
Live Steam 365
Living Flame Press 131
Living With Children 291
Living With Preschoolers 292
Living With Teenagers 548
Livingston Associates, Inc., Peter 944
Location Update 732
Lockert Library of Poetry in Translation 980
Lodestar Books 131
Lodging Hospitality Magazine 772

Loft Creative Nonfiction Residency Program 980
Loft-McKnight Writers Award 980
Loft-Mentor Series 980
Log Home Living 381
Lollipops 718
Lomond Publications, Inc. 133
Lone Star Comedy Monthly, The 733
Lone Star Humor 389
Long Island Monthly 509
Longevity 344
Longman Financial Services Publishing 133
Longwood Academic 133
Looking Fit 696
Lookout, The 548
Loompanics Unlimited 133
Los Angeles Lawyer 798
Los Angeles Magazine 482
Los Angeles Theatre Centre 876
Los Angeles Times Book Review 417
Los Angeles Times Magazine 482
Los Angeles Times Syndicate 903
Lost Treasure 365
Lottery! 365
Louisiana Contractor 711
Louisiana Game & Fish 609
Louisiana Literary Award 980
Louisiana Literature Prize for Poetry 980
Love Agency, Nancy 944
Loyola University Press 134
Lucas-Evans Books 226
Luramedia 134
Lutheran Forum 548
Lutheran Journal, The 549
Lutheran Woman Today 658
Lyons & Burford, Publishers, Inc. 134

M

M.A. Training 620
McBride Literary Agency, Margaret 944
MacBusiness Journal 461
McCall's 658
MacCampbell Inc., Donald 944
McDonald Press (see Shoe Tree 177)
McDonald's Literary Achievement Awards 980
McDonough, Literary Agent, Richard P. 944
McElderry Books, Margaret K. 134
McFarland & Company, Inc., Publishers 135
McGraw Hill Ryerson 135
Macintosh Buyer's Guide, The
McLemore Prize 981
Maclean's 333
MacMillan Publishing Co. 135
Mad Magazine 389
Mad River Theater Works 877
Mademoiselle 659
Madison Books 135
Madison Magazine 524
Magazine for Christian Youth!, The 634
Magazine Issues 788
Magid Productions, Lee 893
Magna 430
Magnus Theatre Company 877
Magnusfilms 894
Main Street Press, The 135

Maine Line Co. 912
Maine Organic Farmer & Gardener 743
Maine Sportsman, The 609
Mainline Modeler 366
Mainstream 306
Maintenance Supplies 804
Malahat Review, The 417
Manage 806
Management Digest 696
Management Review 807
Manhattan Arts Magazine 678
Manhattan, Inc. 273
Manhattan Punch Line 877
Manhattan Theatre Club 877
Manscape 2 531
Manufacturing Systems 775
Manus Literary Agency Inc., Janet Wilkens 945
Marathon International Publishing Company, Inc. 136
March Tenth, Inc. 945
Marcil Literary Agency, Denise 945
Marian Helpers Bulletin 549
Marine Corps Gazette 434
Marks, Betty 945
Markson Literary Agency, Elaine 946
Marlin 610
Marraro Prize in Italian History, Howard R. 981
Marriage & Family 549
Marriott Portfolio 772
Marshall Agency, The Evan 946
Marshall/Nation Prize for Poetry, The Lenore 981
Marshfilm Enterprises, Inc. 859
Martell Agency, The 946
Marvel Comics 297
Marvin Grant, Walter Rumsey 981
Maryland-Delaware Game & Fish 610
Masefield Memorial Award, John 981
Mason Reference Book Award, Harold 981
Massachusetts Review, The 417
Massage Magazine 344
Mature Health 344
Mature Lifestyles 564
Mature Living 564
Mature Outlook 564
Mature Traveler, The 646
Mature Years 565
Maverick Publications 222
Maverick Publications 226
Maxwell MacMillan (see MacMillan Publishing Co. 135)
May Trends 696
Mayberry Gazette, The 311
Mayflower Society Cup Competition 981
Mayo Alumnus, The 816
Mazda Publishers 136
MD Magazine 816
Meadowbrook Press 136
Meat Plant Magazine 761
Media Forum International, Ltd. 136
Media History Digest 353
Media Productions and Marketing, Inc. 137
Media Profiles 718
Medical Business Journal, The 817
Medical Meetings 817
Medmaster, Inc. 137

Medwick Memorial Award, Lucille 981
Meeman Awards, The Edward J. 981
Meeting Manager, The 698
Meeting News 698
Melcher Book Award 981
Melior Publications 137
Memphis 518
Memphis Business Journal 274
Mencken Awards 981
Mennonite Brethren Herald 549
Men's Health 344
Mercer University Press 137
Mercury House Inc. 137
Meredith, Inc., Scott 946
Meridian 565
Meriwether Publishing Ltd. 138
Meriwether Publishing Ltd. 894
Merlyn Graphics 912
Merrimack Repertory Theatre 877
Merrimack Repertory Theatre First Annual Playwriting Contest, The 981
Merrywood Studio, The 894
Messenger of the Sacred Heart, The 549
Metamorphous Press 138
Metro 482
Metro Singles Lifestyles 531
Metro Toronto Business Journal 274
Metropolitan Home 381
Mews Books Ltd. 946
Mexico Magazine 646
México Today! 646
Mexico West 647
Meyerbooks, Publisher 222
MGI Management Institute, Inc., The 138
Miami Beach Community Theatre 877
Michigan Living 647
Michigan Natural Resources Magazine 452
Michigan Out-of-Doors 610
Michigan Quarterly Review 417
Michigan Sportsman 610
Michigan State University Press 138
Michigan Woman, The 502
Microage Quarterly 461
Micropendium 461
Microwaves & RF 723
Mid West Outdoors 611
MidAtlantic Antiques Magazine, The 678
Mid-America Review 417
Mid-Continent Bottler 687
Middle Atlantic Press 139
Middle Eastern Dancer 733
Midsouth 981
Midstream 322
Midway Magazine 392
Midwest Contractor 711
Midwest Motorist, The 647
Midwest Poetry Review 418
Midwest Purchasing Management and Purchasing Management 807
Milady Publishing Company 139
Military Engineer, The 435
Military History 353
Military Images 354
Military Lifestyle 435
Military Living R&R Report 435
Military Review 435
Milkweed Editions 139

Mill, Mountain Theatre 877
Mill Mountain Theatre New Play Competition 981
Miller Books 139
Mills & Sanderson, Publishers 140
Miniature Collector 366
Miniatures Dealer Magazine 844
Miniatures Showcase 366
Ministries Today 703
Minnesota Grocer 762
Minnesota Ink, Inc. 418
Minnesota Sportsman 611
Minority Engineer, The 730
Minority Features Syndicate 903
Miraculous Medal, The 550
Mirage Images Inc. 913
Mirror, The 525
Mise En Scene Theatre 878
Mississippi Business Journal 274
Mississippi Game & Fish 611
Mississippi Rag, The 442
Mississippi State University Alumnus 283
Mississippi Valley Poetry Contest 981
Missouri Farm Magazine 741
Missouri Game & Fish 611
Missouri Repertory Theatre 878
Misty Hill Press 222
Mixed Blood Versus America 982
Model Railroader 366
Modern Books and Crafts, Inc. 140
Modern Bride 659
Modern Drummer 443
Modern Electronics 575
Modern Language Association of America 140
Modern Liturgy 550
Modern Machine Shop 803
Modern Maturity 565
Modern Office Technology 822
Modern Romances 569
Modern Secretary 267
Modern Short Stories 418
Modern Tire Dealer 682
Modern Woodmen, The 249
Mom Guess What Newspaper 532
Momentum 719
Money Maker 268
Money World 268
Monitor Book Co., Inc. 140
Monitoring Times 367
Monroe 502
Montana Magazine 504
Monterey Life Magazine 482
Moody Monthly 550
Moonfall Publishing, Inc. 140
Moose Magazine 249
More Business 675
Morehouse Publishing Co. 140
Morgan Literary Agency, Inc., David H. 947
Morgan-Rand Publications Inc. 141
Morley Memorial Prizes, Felix 982
Morrow and Co., William 141
Morrow Junior Books 141
Mosaic Press Miniature Books 141
Motel/Hotel Insider 772
Mother Courage Press 141
Mother Earth News, The 572
Mother Jones Magazine 470
Motivation Media, Inc. 860
Motor Service 683
Motor Trend 260
Motorboat 590
Motorbooks International Publishers & Wholesalers, Inc. 142

Motorhome 647
Mott Media, Inc., Publishers 142
Mott-Kappa Tau Alpha Research Award in Journalism, Frank Luther 982
Mount Ida Press 226
Mountain Press Publishing Company 142
Mountain States Collector 367
Mountain, The 418
Mountaineers Books, The 142
Movie Collector's World 312
Movieline Magazine 312
Mpls. St. Paul Magazine 503
Ms. Magazine 659
MTL Magazine, English 302
Muir Publications, John 143
Multicultural Playwrights' Festival 982
Multimedia Product Development, Inc. 947
Multnomah Press 143
Muscle Mag International 345
Muses Mill 419
Museum & Arts/Washington 244
Museum of Northern Arizona Press 143
Music Express 443
Music Magazine 443
Musical America/Opus 443
Musky Hunter Magazine 611
Mustang Publishing Co. 143
My Daily Visitor 550
Mysterious Press, The 144

N

N.Y. Habitat Magazine 382
Na'Amat Woman 660
Naggar Literary Agency, Jean V. 947
Naiad Press, Inc., The 144
Nanny Times 292
Nason Productions, Inc., Henry 860
Nathan Literary Agency, Ruth 947
Nation, The 470
National Archives One-Act Playwriting Competition 982
National Arts Centre-English Theatre 878
National Association of Social Workers 144
National Awards for Education Reporting 982
National Beauty School Journal 719
National Book Awards 982
National Book Company 144
National Bus Trader 848
National Christian Reporter 550
National Doll World 367
National Endowment for the Arts: Arts Administration Fellows Program/Fellowship 982
National Examiner 334
National Future Farmer, The 741
National Gallery of Canada 145
National Gardening 382
National Geographic Magazine 334
National Geographic Traveler 648
National Jewish Book Award—Autobiography/Memoir 982
National Jewish Book Award—Children's Literature 982
National Jewish Book Award—Children's Picture Book 982
National Jewish Book Award—Contemporary Jewish Life 982

National Jewish Book Award—Fiction 983
National Jewish Book Award—Holocaust 983
National Jewish Book Award—Israel 983
National Jewish Book Award—Jewish History 983
National Jewish Book Award—Jewish Thought 983
National Jewish Book Award—Scholarship 983
National Jewish Book Award—Visual Arts 983
National Jewish Theater 878
National Lampoon 390
National News Bureau 903
National One-Act Play Contest 983
National One-Act Playwriting Competition 983
National Playwrights' Competition 983
National Playwrights Competition on Themes of Rural America 983
National Publishing Company 222
National Society of Newspaper Columnists 983
National Textbook Co. 145
National Utility Contractor 727
National Wildlife 452
Nation's Business 698
Native Peoples Magazine 322
Natural Food & Farming 326
Nature Friend Magazine 400
Naturegraph Publishers, Inc. 145
Naval Institute Press 145
NavPress 146
N.D. REC Magazine 744
NEAA News 679
Nebraska Game & Fish 611
Nebraska Review Awards in Fiction and Poetry, The 983
Nebraska Review, The 419
Necessary Angel Theatre 878
Neighborhood Works, The 249
Neighbors, Inc., Charles 948
Nelson Algren Awards 983
Nelson-Hall Publishers 146
Network 292
Network World 779
Neustadt International Prize for Literature 983
Nevada Magazine 504
Nevadan, The 504
New Age Journal 254
New Age World Services 948
New American Library 146
New Blood Magazine 579
New Body 345
New Business Opportunities 268
New Conservatory Children's Theatre Company and School, The 878
New Day Poetry/Short Story Contest 984
New England Antiques Journal 679
New England Farm Bulletin 744
New England Farmer 744
New England Game & Fish 611
New England Press, Inc., The 146
New England Publishing Associates, Inc. 948
New England Review/Bread Loaf Quarterly 419
New Era, The 551
New Hampshire Alumnus, The 284

New Hampshire Profiles 505
New Home 382
New Idea Press, Inc. 146
New Jersey Game & Fish 611
New Jersey Living 506
New Jersey Monthly 506
New Jersey Reporter 506
New Leaf Press, Inc. 147
New Letters Literary Awards 984
New Library Scene, The 801
New Methods 850
New Mexico Business Journal 807
New Mexico Magazine 507
New Mexico Repertory Theatre 879
New Physician, The 817
New Play Competition 984
New Plays Incorporated 879
New Playwrights Competition and Festival 984
New Playwrights' Program, The University of Alabama 879
New Readers Press 147
New Realities 254
New Tuners Theatre 879
New Victoria Publishers 147
New Ways 307
New Woman Magazine 660
New World Outlook 551
New World Theater, Inc. 879
New Writers Awards 984
New Writers Literary Project, Ltd. 948
New Writer's Magazine 789
New York Alive 509
New York Daily News 509
New York Doctor, The 817
New York Game & Fish 611
New York Habitat 510
New York Magazine 510
New York Running News 623
New York Shakespeare Festival/Public Theater 880
New York Theatre Workshop 880
New York Times Syndication Sales Corp. 904
New York Zoetrope, Inc. 147
New Yorker, The 334
New York's Nightlife and Long Island's Nightlife 510
Newbery Medal, John 984
Newcastle Publishing Co., Inc. 148
News USA Inc. 904
Newsday 511
Newsday 648
Newservice 473
Newspaper Enterprise Association, Inc. 904
Newsweek 471
NHS Book Prize 984
Nibble 462
Nicholl Fellowships in Screenwriting, Don and Gee 984
Nichols, Jackie 880
Nichols Publishing 148
Nilon Excellence in Minority Fiction Award, Charles H. and N. Mildred 984
Nimbus Publishing Limited 148
Nimrod, Arts and Humanities Council of Tulsa Prizes 984
Nine O'Clock Players 880
9-1-1 Magazine 756
Nissan Discovery 260
No Empty Space Theatre 880
Noahs Ark 401
Noble Press, Incorporated, The 148
Nobleworks 913

Nolan Literary Agency, The Betsy 949
Norma-Lewis Agency, The 949
North America Syndicate 904
North American Fisherman 611
North American Hunter 612
North American Review, The 420
North American Voice of Fatima 551
North American Whitetail 612
North Carolina Black Repertory Company, The 880
North Carolina Game & Fish 612
North Dakota Rec 513
North Georgia Journal 492
North Light 149
North Shore 495
North Texas Golfer 600
Northcoast View 483
Northeast Outdoors 648
Northern Illinois University Press 149
Northern Logger and Timber Processor 802
Northern Virginian Magazine 521
Northland Publishing Co., Inc. 149
Northlight Theatre 880
Northwest Living! 476
Northwest Magazine 476
Norton Co., Inc., W.W. 149
Notre Dame Magazine 284
Nova Scotia Business Journal 247
Novascope 522
Now And Then 477
Noyes Data Corp. 149
NSBE Journal 730
NSRA News 799
Nugent and Associates, Inc. 949
Nugget 430
Numismatist, The 367
Nursing 90 769
Nystrom 860

O

O and A Marketing News 683
O. Henry Festival Short Story Contest 984
Oak Tree Publications 222
Oatmeal Studios 913
Oblates Magazine 552
Oboler Memorial Award, Eli M. 984
O'Connor Award for Short Fiction, The Flannery 985
Occasions Southwest Greetings 913
Occupational Health & Safety Magazine 775
Ocean Realm 452
Oceans 453
Oceanus 453
Octameron Associates 150
O'Dell Award for Historical Fiction, Scott 985
Oddo Publishing, Inc. 150
Odyssey 401
Odyssey Theatre Ensemble 881
Off-Off-Broadway Original Short Play Festival 985
Offshore 590
Offshore Financial Report 268
Oglebay Institute Towngate Theatre Playwriting 985
OH! Idaho 493
Ohara Publications, Inc. 150
Ohio Business 274
Ohio Farmer, The 745
Ohio Game & Fish 612

Ohio Magazine 514
Ohio Psychology Publishing Co. 222
Ohio Review, The 420
Ohio State University Press 150
Ohio University Press 150
Ohio Writer 789
Ohioana Book Award 985
Oise Press 150
Oklahoma Game & Fish 612
Oklahoma Home & Lifestyle 515
Oklahoma Rural News 573
Oklahoma Today 515
Old Army Press, The 151
Old Cars Weekly 367
Old Mill News 354
Old Oregon 284
Old West 354
Oldcastle Theatre Company 881
Ommation Press Book Contest 985
Omni 575
Omni Communications 860
O'Neill Theater Center's National Playwrights Conference, Eugene/New Drama for Television Project 881
On Court 623
On Track 260
On the Line 401
On the Scene Magazine 532
On Video 312
Once Upon a Planet, Inc. 151
One Shot 444
1,001 Home Ideas 382
Onion, The 390
Onion World 735
Ontario Motor Coach Review 648
Ontario Out of Doors 525
Open Eye: New Stagings, The 881
Open Wheel Magazine 261
Opera Canada 444
Opera Companion, The 313
Opera News 821
Opportunities for Actors & Models 733
Opportunity Magazine 837
Options 431
Oregon Business 275
Oregon Historical Society Press 151
Oregon Shakespeare Festival Association 881
Oregon State University Press 151
Organic Theater Company, The 882
Original Art Report, The 244
Orlando Magazine 275
Ort Reporter 552
Orvis Writing Contest, The C.F. 985
Oryx Press 151
Oscard Associates, Fifi 949
Ostomy Quarterly 345
OTC Review 748
Other Side, The 552
Ottawa Magazine 526
Otte Company, The 949
Ottenheimer Publishers, Inc. 227
Our Family 552
Our Sunday Visitor, Inc. 152
Our Sunday Visitor, Inc. 860
Our Town 511
Out West 334
Outbooks 152
Outdoor America 453
Outdoor Canada Magazine 597
Outdoor Life 612
Outdoor Photographer 466
Outreach Publications 913
Outside 598
Outside Business 698

Outside Plant 724
Ovation 444
Overlook Press, The 152
Overseas! 436
Overseas Press Club of America 985
Owl Magazine 402

P

P.I. Magazine 304
P.P.I. Publishing 152
P.U.N., The 390
Pace Films, Inc. 894
Pacheco Automotive News Service 904
Pacific Bakers News 707
Pacific Books, Publishers 153
Pacific Builder & Engineer 711
Pacific Discovery 454
Pacific Diver 629
Pacific Fishing 749
Pacific Press Publishing Association 153
Paddler 590
Paint Horse Journal 239
PAJ Publications 882
Paladin Press 153
Palm Beach County Magazine 489
Palm Beach Life 489
Pandora 579
Panettieri Agency, The 949
Panhandler Poetry Chapbook Competition, The 985
Paper Collectors Marketplace 368
Paper Moon Graphics, Inc. 914
Paperboard Packaging 823
Paperpotamus Paper Products Inc. 914
Parade 334
Paragon House Publishers 153
Paralegal, The 798
Parameters: U.S. Army War College Quarterly 436
Paramount Cards Inc. 914
Parenting Magazine 293
Parenting Press 154
Parents and Teenagers 293
Parents Magazine 293
Paris Review, The 420
Parish Family Digest 553
Parker Motion Pictures, Tom 894
Parkman Prize, Francis 985
Partisan Review 420
Partners in Publishing 222
Passage Theatre Company, The 882
Passages North 420
Passport Press 154
Pastoral Life 703
Pathfinder Publications 222
Paulist Press 154
Pawprints 914
Payne Literary Agency, The John K. 950
PBC International, Inc. 154
PCPA Theaterfest 882
PC Computing 462
PCM 462
Peachtree Publishers, Ltd. 154
Peacock Books 222
Pediatrics For Parents 294
Pegasus International, Inc. 950
Pelican Publishing Company 155
PEN Center USA West Awards 985
Pen Dragon Publishing, Co. 223
PEN/Jerard Fund 985
PEN/Medal for Translation 985
PEN/Publisher Citation 985

PEN Roger Klein Award for Editing 986
PEN Syndicated Fiction Project 986
PEN Translation Prize 986
PEN Writing Awards for Prisoners 986
Peninsula Magazine 483
Penkevill Publishing Company, The 155
Penmarin Books 950
Pennsylvania 516
Pennsylvania Angler 613
Pennsylvania Farmer 745
Pennsylvania Game & Fish 613
Pennsylvania Game News 613
Pennsylvania Heritage 516
Pennsylvania Historical and Museum Commission 156
Pennsylvania Lawyer, The 798
Pennsylvania Review 421
Pennsylvania Sportsman 613
Pennsylvania Stage Company 882
Pennywhistle Press 402
Pension World 749
Pentecostal Evangel 553
Pentecostal Messenger, The 554
People in Action 335
People's Light & Theatre Company 882
Perfection Form, The 223
Performing Arts in Canada 313
Periodical 436
Perkins' Litarary Agency 950
Perkins Playwriting Contest 986
Perseverance Theatre 883
Persimmon Hill 354
Personal Computing Magazine 462
Personnel Advisory Bulletin 808
Personnel Journal 808
Perspective 249
Perspectives Press 156
Pest Control Magazine 804
Pet Age 824
Pet Business 824
Pet Dealer, The 824
Peter Associates, Inc., James 951
Peter Pauper Press, Inc. 156
Petersen's Hunting 614
Petersen's Photographic Magazine 466
Peterson's 156
Pets Magazine 239
Pharmacy Times 715
Pharos Books 157
Phi Beta Kappa Book Awards 986
Phi Delta Kappan 719
Philadelphia Festival Theatre for New Plays 883
Philadelphia Magazine 517
Phillysport 598
Philomel Books 157
Phoenix Home and Garden 383
Photo Communication Services, Inc. 860
Photo Marketing 825
Photo Review, The 825
Photographic Video Trade News (see PTN 826)
Photoletter 826
Physician and Sportsmedicine, The 818
Physicians Management 818
Physicians' Travel and Meeting Guide 818
Picard, Literary Agent, Alison 951
Pickering Press, The 157
Pickwick Publications 157

Pier One Theatre 883
Pig Iron Magazine 421
Pilot Books 158
Pine Associates, Inc., Arthur 951
Pineapple Press, Inc. 158
Pioneer 634
Pioneer Drama Service 883
Pipe Smoker & Tobacciana Trader 368
Pippin Press 158
Pizza Today 772
Plain Dealer Magazine 514
Planning 756
Plant Management & Engineering 776
Plate World 268
Platt & Munk Publishers 158
Play Meter Magazine 706
Playbill 313
Playboy 431
Player, The 596
Players Press, Inc. 159
Players Press, Inc. 883
Plays 883
Playthings 844
Playwrights Canada 159
Playwrights' Center, The 884
Playwrights' Center Jerome Playwright—In-Residence Fellowship 986
Playwrights' Center McKnight Fellowship 986
Playwrights' Center Midwest Players, The 986
Playwrights' Forum Awards 986
Playwrights Horizons 884
Playwrights of Philadelphia/Philadelphia Drama Guild 884
Playwrights Preview Productions 884
Playwrights Theatre of New Jersey 884
Playwright's-In-Residence Grants 986
Plenty 302
Plenum Publishing 159
Plexus Publishing, Inc. 159
Ploughshares 421
Plum Graphics Inc. 914
Pocket Books 160
Pockets 402
Podiatry Management 818
Poe Award, Edgar Allan 986
Poetry 421
Poetry Arts Project Contest 986
Poetry Magazine Poetry Awards 986
Poets and Patrons, Inc. International Narrative Contest 986
Poets Club of Chicago International Shakespearean Contest 987
Poggioli Translation Award, Renato 987
Police 756
Police and Security News 756
Police Times 757
Polish American Journal 322
Pollard Press, V. 223
Polled Hereford World 738
Polo 623
Pomegranate Press, Ltd. 160
Pool & Spa News 840
Popkin, Julie/Nancy Cooke 951
Popular Electronics 368
Popular Electronics Hobbyists Handbook 369
Popular Photography 466
Popular Science 575

Porcelain, Sidney E. 951
Porcépic Books 160
Portable 100 463
Porter Sargent Publishers, Inc. 160
Portman & Associates, Julian 952
Poseidon Press 160
Positive Approach, A 307
Postcard Collector 369
Potentials Development for Health & Aging Services 161
Potomac-Pacific Press 161
Potter, Inc., Clarkson N. 161
Practical Homeowner 383
Practical Knowledge 473
Pragmatist, The 471
Prairie Journal, The 421
Prairie Publishing Company, The 161
Prairie Schooner Strousse Award 987
Prakken Publications, Inc. 161
Preacher's Magazine, The 704
Preferred Traveller 649
Preiss Visual Publications, Inc., Byron 227
Premier Video Film & Recording Corp. 860
Premiere 313
Prentice-Hall Canada, Inc. 162
Prentice-Hall Canada, Inc., (College Division) 162
Prentice-Hall Canada, Inc., (Secondary School Division) 162
Prentice-Hall Press 162
Presbyterian Record 554
Present Tense 323
Present Tense/Joel H. Cavior Literary Awards 987
Preservation News 355
Preservation Press, The 162
Press of MacDonald & Reinecke, The 223
Price Stern Sloan, Inc. 163
Priest Literary Agency, Aaron M. 952
Prima Publishing and Communications 163
Primary Stages Company, Inc. 884
Prime Time Sports & Fitness 623
Prime Times 566
Princeton Alumni Weekly 284
Princeton Architectural Press 163
Princeton Book Company, Publishers 163
Princeton University Press 164
Print & Graphics 830
Printing Views 830
Prism International 422
Private Carrier, The 846
Private Practice 819
Pro 752
Pro Sound News 724
Pro Trucker and Over the Road 683
ProAthlete 624
Probus Publishing Co. 164
Proceedings 811
Produce News 762
Produciton Supervisors Bulletin 808
Professional Agent Magazine 782
Professional Photographer 826
Professional Publications, Inc. 164
Professional Quilter, The 369
Professional Selling 837
Professional Upholsterer, The 766
Progressive Architecture 679
Progressive Farmer 742
Progressive, The 471

Prolingua Associates 164
Prometheus Award/Hall of Fame 987
Proofs 713
Prorodeo Sports News 840
Prost! 326
Psychology Today 473
PTN 826
Public Power 727
Publish! 463
Publishers Weekly 690
Puckerbrush Press 223
Pulitzer Prizes 987
Pulp and Paper Canada 823
Pulp Press International 3-Day Novel Writing Contest 987
Pumper, The 833
Purchasing Executive's Bulletin 776
Purdue Alumnus, The 285
Purdue University Press 165
Pure-Bred Dogs American Kennel Gazette 240
Pure-Bred Dogs Magazine Award 987
Purgatory Theatre Annual National Playwriting Competition 987
Purple Cow 634
Purpose 554
Purrrrr! the Newsletter for Cat Lovers 240
Pyle Award, Ernie 987

Q

Q.E.D. Information Sciences, Inc. 165
Q.E.D. Press Of Ann Arbor, Inc. 165
QRL Poetry Series 987
Quality Control Supervisor's Bulletin 776
Quality Living 302
Quality Publications 165
Quarante 660
Quarter Horse Journal, The 240
Quartz Theatre, The 885
Que Corporation 166
Que Pasa 323
Queen Of All Hearts 554
Queen's Mystery Magazine, Ellery 447
Queen's Quarterly 422
Quick Frozen Foods International 762
Quick Printing 830
Quill 166
Quilt World 369
Quilting Today Magazine 370
Quinlan Press 227

R

R-A-D-A-R 404
Radiance 661
Radio Repertory Company, Inc. 885
Radio World Newspaper 724
Radio-Electronics 370
Radley-Regan & Associates, D. 952
Railroad Model Craftsman 370
Rainbow Books 166
Rainbow City Express 254
Raines & Raines 952
Raleigh Award, Sir Walter 987
R&E Publishers 166
Randall Publisher, Peter 212
Random House, Inc. 166
Random House, Inc./Alfred

A.Knopf, Inc. Juvenile Books 167
R&R Entertainment Digest 437
Rangefinder, The 826
Ranger Rick 404
RDH 713
Read Me 335
Reader Riter Poll 987
Reader's Digest 335
Readers Review 336
Real Comet Press, The 167
Real Estate Computing 832
Real People 336
Reason Magazine 471
Recognition & Promotions Business 699
Recording Engineer/Producer 821
Records Management Quarterly 699
Recreation News 250
Red Farm Studio 914
Redbook Magazine 661
Redbook's Short Story Contest 987
Rees Literary Agency, Helen 953
Referee 598
Regardies: The Magazine of Washington Business 275
Regnery/Gateway, Inc. 167
Religious Education Press 167
Relix Magazine 444
Remodeling 692
Renaissance Greeting Cards 914
Renaissance House Publishers 168
Renews 683
Report on Business Magazine 269
Report on the Americas 471
Research Magazine 749
Reseller Management 779
Resolution Business Press 223
Resource Publications, Inc. 168
Resource Recycling 833
Restaurant Exchange News 773
Retailer and Marketing News 766
Retired Officer Magazine, The 437
Retirement Lifestyles 566
Reuben Award 987
Revell, Fleming H. Co. 168
Review 250
Review and Herald Publishing Association 169
Review for Religious 555
Reymont Associates 169
Rhode Island Monthly 517
Rhode Island State Council on the Arts Fellowship 987
Rhodes Literary Agency Inc. 953
Rhyme Time Creative Writing Competition 989
Rhythms Productions 861
Ribalow Prize, The Harold U. 989
Right Here 336
Righting Words 789
Riina Literary Agency, John 953
Rinehart Fund, Mary Roberts 989
Ripon Forum 472
Rising Star 790
River Runner Magazine 591
Rivercross Publishing, Inc. 212
Riverdale Company, Inc., Publishers, The 169
Road Company, The 885
Road King Magazine 261
Roanoke-Chowan Award for Poetry 989
Robbins Office, Inc., The 953
Roberts Playwriting Award, Forest A. 989

Roberts Writing Awards 989
Rochester Business Magazine 511
Rock 445
Rock Hall Reporter 445
Rockshots, Inc. 915
Rocky Mountain Game & Fish 614
Rocky Top Publications 169
Rod & Custom 261
Rodale Press 169
Roerich Poetry Prize, Nicholas 989
Roffman Associates, Richard H. 953
Rogers and Associates, Stephanie 953
Rolling Stone College Journalism Competition 989
Ronin Publishing 170
Roofer Magazine 711
Room of One's Own 422
Rosen Publishing Group, The 170
Rosenthal New Play Prize, The Lois and Richard 989
Ross Books 170
Rotarian, The 251
Rotrosen Agency, Jane 954
Roundtable Publishing, Inc. 170
Routledge, Chapman & Hall, Inc. 171
Roxbury Publishing Co. 171
Royal Features 904
RSI 712
Running Times 624
Rural Heritage 573
Rural Kentuckian (see Kentucky Living 496)
Ruralite 477
Russell Sage, Inc. 171
Rutgers University Press 171
Rutledge Hill Press 171
RV West Magazine 649
Rv Business 849

S

S.C.E.-Editions L'Etincelle 172
S.O.C.O. Publications 172
Sacramento Business Journal 275
Sacramento Magazine 483
Safari Magazine 614
Safety Compliance Letter 804
Sagalyn Agency, The 954
Sagebrush Journal 371
Sailing Magazine 591
Sailing World 591
St. Anthony Messenger 555
St. Anthony Messenger Press 172
St. Bede's Publications 172
St. Joseph's Messenger & Advocate of the Blind 555
St. Louis Journalism Review 790
St. Luke's Press 173
St. Martin's Press 173
St. Paul Books and Media 173
St. Vladimir's Seminary Press 173
Sales & Marketing Management in Canada 675
Sales Manager's Bulletin 809
Salt Water Sportsman 614
Sam Cards 915
Sams and Co., Inc., Howard W. 212
San Diego Home/Garden 383
San Diego Magazine 484
San Francisco Bay Guardian 484
San Francisco Focus 484
San Francisco Press, Inc. 174
San Francisco Style International 904

San Gabriel Valley Magazine, The 484
Sandburg Literary Arts Awards, The Carl 989
Sandlapper Publishing, Inc. 174
Sandpaper, The 507
Sandpiper Press 223
Sandum & Associates 954
Sanford/Pillsbury Production 861
Santana 591
Sasquatch Books 174
Satellite Retailer 724
Savings Institutions 749
Savvy 662
SBC Enterprises, Inc. 954
SCP Journal and SCP Newsletter 555
Scagnetti Literary Agency, Jack 954
Scarecrow Press, Inc. 174
Scavenger's Newsletter 790
Schaffner Associates, Inc., John 955
Schiffer Publishing Ltd. 175
Schirmer Books 175
Schleger Company, Peter 861
Schlessinger-Van Dyck Agency 955
Schneider Performance Series 262
Scholastic, Inc. 175
Scholastic Scope 635
Scholastic Writing Awards 989
School Arts Magazine 719
School Mates 328
School Shop 720
Schuettge & Carleton 227
Schulman Literary Agency, Inc., The Susan 955
Schulz Award, The Charles M. 989
Schurman Co., Inc., Marcel 915
Schwartz, Esquire, Laurens R. 955
Schwartz, Literary Agent, Arthur P. 955
Science Fiction Chronicle 790
Science in Society Journalism Awards 989
Science Tech Publishers, Inc. 175
Scojtia Publishing Co., Inc. 175
Score 600
Scorecard 285
Scott Cards Inc. 915
Scott Stamp Monthly 371
Scouting 251
Scream Factory, The 580
Screen Printing 831
Screw 432
Scribe Agency 956
Scribner's Sons, Charles 176
Scripps Award, Charles E. 989
Scripps Award, The Edward Willis 989
Se Le Vie Writer's Journal 790
Sea 592
Sea Frontiers 454
Sea Kayaker 592
Sea Power 437
Seafood Leader 763
Seattle Business 276
Seattle Group Theatre Co. 885
Sebastian Agency 956
Second Chance Press/Permanent Press 176
II Chronicles Magazine 556
Second Stage 885
Secondary Marketing Executive 749
Secrets 569
Security Dealer 699
Security Management: Protecting Property, People & Assets 809
Seek 556

Selected Reading 336
Self 662
Self-Employed America 700
Senior 566
Senior Award 989
Senior Edition and USA/Colorado 567
Senior Life Magazine 567
Senior Patient 819
Senior World of California 567
Sensible Sound, The 445
Serendipity 580
Servant Publications 176
Service Business 805
Servicing Dealer, The 700
Sesame Street Magazine 294
Seven Locks Press, Inc. 177
Seven Oaks Foundation 861
Seventeen 635
Seventeen Magazine/Dell Fiction Contest 990
Sew Business 766
Sew News 371
Sewanee Review 422
SFWA Nebula Awards 990
Shape 346
Shapiro-Lichtman Talent Agency 956
Shapolsky Publishers 177
Shareware Magazine 463
Sharing the Victory 556
Shaughnessy Prize, Mina P. 990
Shaw Festival 885
Shaw Publishers, Harold 177
Shazzam Production Company, The 885
Sheep! Magazine 738
Sheep Meadow Press, The 177
Shelley Memorial Award 990
Shipmate 285
Shipping Digest 847
Shoe Service 799
Shoe Tree Press 177
Shofar Magazine 404
Shooting Star Review 423
Shoptalk 725
Shore Associates, Michael 178
Shorr Stille and Associates 956
Short Story Award, The 990
Short Story Writers Competition 990
Shuttle Spindle & Dyepot 371
Siegel, Literary Agency, Bobbe 956
Siena College Playwrights' Competition 990
Sierra 454
Sierra Club Books 178
Sierra Literary Agency 957
Sierra Repertory Theatre 990
Sign Business 700
Signcraft 675
Signpost Books 223
Signpost Magazine 625
Signs of the Times 557
Signs of the Times 675
Silhouette Books 178
Silver Burdett Press 179
Silver Gavel Awards 990
Silver Visions 915
Simmons Short Fiction Award and Iowa Short Fiction Awards, John 990
Simon & Schuster 179
Simon Award, Charlie May 990
Singer Literary Agency, Evelyn 957
Singer Media Corporation 905
Singer Media Corporation, Inc. 957

Single Parent, The 294
Sinsemilla Tips 735
Sisters Today 557
Siviculture 802
Skating 627
Ski Business 841
Ski Guide 627
Ski Magazine 627
Skin Diver 629
Sky 393
Skydiving 625
Slote Award, Bernice 990
Small Boat Journal 592
Small Business Chronicle 701
Small Press 791
Small Press Publisher of the Year 990
Small Press Review 791
Smith Memorial Writing Contest, R. Gaines 990
Smith, Publisher, Gibbs 179
SNAFU Designs 915
Snack Food 763
Snell Literary Agency, Michael 957
Snips Magazine 829
Snow Country 628
Snowmobile Magazine 628
Snowy Egret 455
Soap Opera Update 314
Soccer America 628
Social Justice Review 557
Soho Press, Inc. 179
Soldier of Fortune 438
Song Hits 445
Sonlight/Sun 557
Sonnichsen Book Award, C.L. 991
Sons of Norway Viking, The 251
Sound Management 838
Sound View Press 223
Soundings 593
Soundtrack 446
South Carolina Game & Fish 615
South Carolina Wildlife 615
South Coast Repertory 885
South Florida 490
South Florida Poetry Review, The 423
Southam Syndicate, The 905
Southeast Playwrights Project 886
Southern Appalachian Repertory Theatre (SART) 886
Southern Beverage Journal 688
Southern Exposure 512
Southern Homes 384
Southern Illinois University Press 180
Southern Jewish Weekly, The 323
Southern Lumberman 802
Southern Motor Cargo 684
Southern Outdoors Magazine 615
Southern Playwriting Competition 991
Southern Prestigious Homes & Interiors 384
Southern Review, The 423
Southern Review/Louisiana State University Short Fiction Award, The 991
Southern Saltwater Magazine 615
Southern Sensations 477
Southern Tier Images 511
Southern Writers 957
Southfarm Press 180
Southwest Contractor 712
Southwest Cycling 586
Southwest Profile 507
Southwest Review 424

Souvenir Magazine 838
Souvenirs and Novelties Magazine 844
Sovereign Award, Outstanding Newspaper Story, Outstanding Feature Story 991
Soybean Digest 735
Space World (see Ad Astra 573)
Spann Memorial Prize, Bryant 991
Sparrow Press 180
Special Libraries Association Public Relations Award 991
Special Reports 337
Specialty Store Service 704
Spectrum 424
Speech Bin, Inc., The 180
Spelman Syndicate, Inc., The 905
Spence Publishing 180
Spencer Productions, Inc. 861
Spieler Literary Agency, F. Joseph 958
Spin-Off 372
Spinsters/Aunt Lute Books 181
Spirit 393
Spirit 558
Spiritual Life 558
Spitzer Literary Agency, Philip G. 958
Splash 302
Sport Detroit Magazine 625
Sport Style 841
Sportcare & Fitness 819
Sporting Classics 616
Sporting Goods Dealer, The 841
Sports Afield 616
Sports Collectors Digest 372
Sports Features Syndicate/World Features Syndicate 905
Sports History 599
Sports Illustrated for Kids 404
Sports Parade 599
Spottswood Studios 861
Sproutletter, The 384
Spur 603
Spur Awards (Western Writers of America, Inc.) 991
Spy 303
Square One Publishers 223
St. Louis Magazine 503
ST Publications, Inc. 181
Stackpole Books 181
Stage One 886
Stand Magazine Short Story Competition, The 991
Standard 558
Standard Publishing 181
Stanford University Press 182
Stanley Drama Award 991
Star, The 337
Starlog Magazine 581
Starrett Poetry Prize, The Agnes Lynch 991
Starrhill Press 182
Startling Detective 304
Starwind 581
State, The 512
Steele & Company, Lyle 958
Steinberg, Michael 958
Stemmer House Publishers, Inc. 182
Stepping Stone Literary Agency 959
Stereo Review 446
Sterling Publishing 183
Stern Agency, Gloria 959
Stern Associates, Charles M. 959
Stern, Gloria 959
Stevens, Inc., Gareth 183
Still Point Press 223

Stilwill, Charles 886
Stipes Publishing Co. 183
St-Log 463
Stock Car Racing Magazine 262
Stoeger Publishing Company 183
Stone Awards, The Walker 991
Stone Review 843
Stone Soup 405
Stone Wall Press, Inc. 223
Stone World 843
Stop-Gap 887
Storefront Theatre 887
Storie/McOwen Publishers, Inc. 183
Stormline Press 184
Story 424
Story Friends 405
Storyboard 372
Straight 635
Strategic Health Care Marketing 820
Street Players Theatre 887
Student Grant-in-Aid 991
Student Lawyer 799
Student, The 285
Studio Photography 827
Studio Press 184
Stuhlmann, Author's Representative, Gunther 960
STV Guide 314
Style 495
Successful Dealer, The 684
Successful Hotel Marketer, The 773
Sun, The 425
Sunday 495
Sunday Advocate Magazine 497
Sunday Digest 559
Sunday Journal Magazine 478
Sunday Magazine 485
Sunday School Counselor 559
Sunrise Publications, Inc. 916
Sunshine Artists USA 373
Sunshine Magazine 337
Sunshine: The Magazine of South Florida 490
Sunstone Press 184
Suntechnology 779
Supercuts Style 303
Superintendent's Profile & Pocket Equipment Directory 757
Supervision 809
Supervisor's Bulletin 809
Surfer 630
Swank 432
Swim Magazine 630
Swimming Pool/Spa Age 842
Sybex, Inc. 184
Symmes Systems 185
Syracuse University Press 185
System Builder 780
Systems Integration 780
Systems/3X World 780

T

Tab Books, Inc. 185
Tabor Publishing 185
Talco Productions 862
Tampa Bay Magazine 490
Tampa Review 425
Tantleff Office, The 960
Tapley, Publisher, Inc., Lance 186
Tattoo Advocate Journal 303
Tavern Sports International 626
Taylor Book Awards, Sydney 992
Taylor Playwriting Award, Marvin 992
Taylor Publishing Company 186

Tea & Coffee Trade Journal 688
Teachers College Press 186
Teachers Interaction 559
Teaching K-8 720
Teaching Today 720
Teal Literary Agency, Patricia 960
Technical Analysis of Stocks & Commodities 269
Technology Review 576
TechTalk 725
Teddy Bear Review 373
'Teen Magazine 636
Teenage 636
Teenage Corner, Inc. 905
Teens Today 636
Tejas Art Press 887
Tel-Air Interests, Inc. 862
Television Broadcast 725
Television Production Services Corp. 894
Ten Best "Censored" Stories of 1989, The 992
Tennessee Sportsman 616
Tennis Buyer's Guide 842
Texas A&M University Press 186
Texas Architect 679
Texas Bluebonnet Award 992
Texas Christian University Press 186
Texas Fisherman 616
Texas Gardener 386
Texas Hi-Tech Review 464
Texas Monthly Press, Inc. 187
Texas Sportsman 617
Texas Western Press 187
T.F.H. Publications, Inc. 228
TGNW Press 223
The Roanoker 522
The Seattle Weekly 522
The United Church Observer 560
The Virginian 522
Theater Artists of Marin 887
Theatre Calgary 887
Theatre De La Jeune Lune 887
Theatre Library Association Award, The 992
Theatre Ludicrum, Inc. 887
Theatre on the Move 888
Theatreworks 888
Theatreworks/USA 888
Thedamu 244
Theme Song 895
Theosophical Publishing House, The 187
Thistledown Press 187
Thomas Publications 188
Thomas, Publisher, Charles C. 188
3 & 4 Wheel Action 262
Three Continents Press 188
Threepenny Review, The 425
3-2-1 Contact 405
Thrust—Science Fiction and Fantasy Review 582
TI Computing 464
Tiger Beat Magazine 636
Tiger Beat Star 637
Tile World 767
Timber Press, Inc. 188
Time-Life Books Inc. 189
Timeline 355
Times Books 189
Toastmaster, The 251
Tobacco Reporter 736
Today's Catholic Teacher 721
Today's Christian Woman 663
Today's Images 663
Toledo Magazine 515

Tor Books 189
Tornetta Agency, Phyllis 960
Toronto Life 526
Toronto Life Fashion 663
Torso 532
Total Acting Experience, A 960
Total Health 346
Touch 406
Tourist Attractions & Parks Magazine 734
Tours & Resorts 649
Tow-Age 684
Towers Club, USA Newsletter 299
Towson State University Prize for Literature 992
TQ (Teen Quest) 637
Traces of Indiana and Midwestern History 355
Tradition 446
Traditional Quiltworks 373
Trailer Boats Magazine 593
Trails-A-Way 650
Training 809
Transaction Books 189
Transformation Times 255
Transitions Abroad 650
Translation Center Awards, The 992
Translight Media Associates 862
Transnational Publishers, Inc. 189
Transportation Trails 190
Transtar Productions, Inc. 862
Travel & Leisure 650
Travel Keys 190
Travel Smart 651
Travelage Midamerica 849
Travelage West 849
Travelore Report 651
Treasure 373
Treasure Chest 374
Treasure Search 374
Trend Book Division 190
Tri Video Teleproduction 862
Tribune Media Services 905
Trillium Press 190
Trinity Square Ensemble 888
Trip & Tour 651
Triquarterly 425
Tristate Magazine 515
Troll Associates 862
Tropic Magazine 490
Tropical Fish Hobbyist 241
Troubador Press 190
Trout 617
Truck World 684
Trucks Magazine 847
True Confessions 570
True Love 570
True Police Cases 304
True Romance 570
True Story 570
True West 356
Truman Prize, Harry S. 992
Trumpeter, The 374
T-Shirt Retailer and Screen Printer 705
TSR, Inc. 191
Turf Magazine 752
Turkey Call 617
Turn-On Letters 432
Turtle Magazine for Preschool Kids 406
Tuttle Publishing Company, Inc., Charles E. 191
TV Entertainment 314
TV Guide 315
TV Week Magazine 315

Twentyone® Magazine 386
Twin Peaks Press 191
Twins 294
2 AM Magazine 582
2-M Communications Ltd. 961
Tyndale House Publishers, Inc. 191

U

UAHC Press 191
Ucross Foundation Residency 992
UFO Research Award 992
UFO Review 576
Ukrainian Weekly, The 323
ULI, The Urban Land Institute 192
Ultralight Publications, Inc. 192
Umbrella Books 192
Umi Research Press 192
Uncensored Letters 432
Undercurrent 630
Undergraduate Paper Competition in Cryptology 992
Unicorn Theatre 888
Union Square Press 192
United Cartoonist Syndicate 905
United Evangelical Action 560
United Media 906
United Methodist Reporter 560
United Resource Press 193
Unity Magazine 560
Univelt, Inc. 193
University Associates, Inc. 193
University of Alabama Press 193
University of Alberta Press, The 193
University of Arizona Press 194
University of Calgary Press, The 194
University of California Press 194
University of Illinois Press 194
University of Iowa Press 195
University of Massachusetts Press 195
University of Michigan Press 195
University of Minnesota, Duluth Theatre 888
University of Minnesota Press 195
University of Missouri Press 196
University of Nevada Press 196
University of Oklahoma Press 196
University of Pennsylvania Press 196
University of Tennessee Press, The 197
University of Texas Press 197
University of Toronto Quarterly 425
University of Utah Press 197
University of Wisconsin Press 197
University of Wisconsin Stout Teleproduction Center 863
University Press of America, Inc. 197
University Press of Kansas 198
University Press of Kentucky 198
University Press of Mississippi 198
University Press of Virginia 198
Unlimited Publishing Co. 199
Unspeakable Visions of the Individual Inc., The 426
UPB Magazine 734
Upper Room, The 560
Upstate Magazine 512
Urstadt, Inc., Susan P. 961
U.S. Art 245
USA Weekend 339
USAir Magazine 393
Utah Holiday Magazine 520
Utah State University Press 199
Utility and Telephone Fleets 727

Utility Supervision 810

V

Vacation Industry Review 773
Vagabond Creations, Inc. 916
Vail Magazine 486
Valle, Miriam Colon 889
Valley Magazine 485
Van Der Leun and Associates 961
Vantage Press 212
Varoujan Award, Daniel 992
Vegetarian Journal 346
Vegetarian Times 347
Vehicule Press 199
VeloNews 587
Vending Times 706
Ventura County & Coast Reporter 485
Venture 406
Venture and Visions 561
Verbatim Essay Competition 992
Vermont Business Magazine 276
Vermont Life Magazine 520
Vermont Magazine 521
Vermont Vanguard Press 521
Vesta Publications, Ltd. 199
Vestal Press, Ltd., The 200
Veterinary Economics Magazine 850
Veterinary Practice Management 850
Vette Magazine 262
VFW Magazine 252
VGM Career Horizons 200
Vibrant Life 347
Vicinanza Ltd., Ralph 961
Victimology 757
Victor & Grais Productions 895
Victor Books 200
Victoria Management Co. 961
Victoria's Business Report 276
Victory Press 223
Video 315
Video Choice Magazine 315
Video Magazine 315
Video Manager 726
Video Marketplace Magazine 316
Videomaker™ 375
Videomania 316
Vigilante Players, Inc. 889
Vineyard & Winery Management 688
Virginia Cavalcade 356
Virginia Game & Fish 617
Virginia Quarterly Review, The 426
Virtue 561
Visions 286
Vista 561
Vista/USA 651
Visual Horizons 863
Vital Christianity 562
VM & SD 675
Voice Processing Magazine 726
Volkswagen's World 263
Volleyball Monthly 626
Vortex Communications 223
Voyager/Sun Scene 652

W

Wade, Carlson 961
Wadsworth Publishing Company 200
Wagner Award, Celia B. 992
Wake Forest University Press 201
Walch, Publisher, J. Weston 201

Walker and Co. 201
Walkways 347
Wallace Literary Agency, Bess 962
Wallant Book Award, Edward Lewis 993
Wallerstein Agency, The Gerry B. 962
Walls & Ceilings 692
Walnut Street Theatre 889
Wang in the News 464
War Cry 562
Ward Prize for Playwriting, Theodore 993
Ward's Auto World 685
Ware Literary Agency, John A. 962
Warehouse Theatre One-Act Competition 993
Warehousing Supervisor's Bulletin 810
Warner Press, Inc. 916
Warren Literary Agency, James 962
Washington 523
Washington Blade 532
Washington Jewish Singles Newsletter 533
Washington Monthly 472
Washington Post, The 487
Washington Post Magazine, The 487
Washington Post Writers Group 906
Washington Prize for Fiction 993
Washington State University Press 201
Washington State University Theatre 889
Washingtonian Magazine, The 487
Washington-Oregon Game & Fish 617
Water Skier, The 631
Waterfront Books 223
Waterfront News 492
Waterside Productions, Inc. 963
Watersports Business 842
Waterway Guide 594
Watt & Associates, Sandra 963
WDS Book Author's Newsletter 792
WDS Forum 792
Webster Review 426
Wee Wisdom 407
Weekend Gardener, The 386
Weekly News, The 533
Weighing & Measurement 776
Weight Watchers Magazine 348
Weiner Literary Agency, Cherry 963
Weiser, Inc., Samuel 202
Weissberger Playwriting Award, Arnold 993
Welcome Enterprises, Inc. 228
Wesleyan Advocate, The 562
West 485
West Coast Ensemble 889
West Coast Ensemble Full Play Competition 993
West Coast Review 426
West Coast Review of Books 792
West Texas Sun, The 520
West Virginia Game & Fish 617
Westart 245
Western & English Fashions 705
Western & Eastern Treasures 375
Western Canada Outdoors 526
Western Flyer 265
Western Greeting, Inc. 916
Western Horseman, The 241
Western Humanities Review 426
Western Investor 276

Western Marine Enterprises, Inc. 202
Western New York Magazine 277
Western Outdoors 617
Western People 527
Western Photo Traveler 467
Western Producer, The 527
Western Sportsman 618
Western Stage, The 889
Western States Book Awards 993
Western Tanager Press 223
Westernlore Press 202
Westgate Press 202
Westport Publishers, Inc. 203
Weyr Agency, Rhoda 963
What Makes People Successful 339
What's New Magazine 500
Whitaker House 203
White Theatre, The Ann 890
Whitegate Features Syndicate 906
Whitford Press 203
Whiting Writers' Awards 993
Whitney Library of Design 203
Whitney-Carnegie Award 993
Whitston Publishing Co., The 204
Whole Life 348
Wichita State University Playwriting Contest 993
Wieser & Wieser, Inc. 228
Wieser & Wieser, Inc. 964
Wild West 356
Wilder Award, Laura Ingalls 993
Wilderness Adventure Books 204
Wilderness Press 204
Wildlife Photography 467
Wildwood Design Group 916
Wiley & Sons, Inc., John 204
Wiley Prize, Bell I. 993
Williams Award, William Carlos 993
Williamson Publishing Co. 205
Williamstown Theatre Festival 890
Willow Creek Press 205
Wilshire Book Co. 205
Wilson Fine Arts, Inc., Carol 916
Wilson Library Bulletin 801
Wilson Library Periodical Award, H.W. 993
Windriver Publishing Company 205
Windsor Books 206
Wine Appreciation Guild, Ltd. 206
Wine Spectator, The 326
Wine Tidings 326
Wines & Vines 688
Wingbow Perss 206
Wingra Woods Press 228
Wingra Woods Press (Agenting Division) 964
Wings West 687
Winship Book Award, J.J. 994
Winston-Derek Publishers, Inc. 206
Wisconsin 524
Wisconsin Arts Board Fellowship Program 994
Wisconsin Grocer, The 763
Wisconsin Sportsman 618
Wisconsin Trails 524
With Magazine 637
Witter Bynner Foundation for Poetry, Inc. Grants 994
Wizards Bookshelf 208
Wizworks 917
WMC Company 863
Wolgemuth & Hyatt, Publishers 208
Woman Bowler 595
Woman Engineer, The 730
Woman Magazine 663
Woman's Day 664

Woman's Enterprise 269
Woman's Touch 562
Woman's World 664
Women Artists News 245
Women in Business 701
Women of Ohio 665
Women's Circle 665
Women's Circle Counted Cross-Stitch 375
Women's Household Crochet 376
Women's Quarterly, The 665
Women's Sports and Fitness Magazine 599
Wonder Time 407
Wood 'N Energy (see Hearth & Home 828)
Woodall's Campground Management 842
Woodbine House 208
Woodbine House Award 994
Woodbridge Press 209
Woodenboat Magazine 594
Woodmen of the World Magazine 252
Woodsong Graphics, Inc. 209
Woolly Mammoth Theatre Company 890
Worcester Foothills Theatre Company 890
Word Beat Press 209
Wordperfect, The Magazine 465
Words by Wire 906
Wordware Publishing, Inc. 209
Workbasket, The 376
Workbench 376
Workboat 811
Working Mother Magazine 666
Working Woman 666
Workman Publishing Company, Inc. 210
World Coin News 376
World Fantasy Awards 994
World Hunger Media Awards 994
World of Business Kids, The 407
World Policy Journal 472
World Tennis 629
World Trade 270
World War II 438
Worlds Fair 339
Worldwide Library 210
WPI Journal 286
Wreschner, Authors' Representative, Ruth 964
Wrestling World 626
Wright Representatives, Inc., Ann 964
Writer, The 792
Writer's Biennial 994
Writer's Consulting Group 964
Writer's Digest 792
Writer's Digest Books 210
Writer's Digest Writing Competition 994
Writer's Guidelines 793
Writers Guild of America West Awards 994
Writers House, Inc. 965
Writer's Info 793
Writer's Journal 793
Writers' Journal Annual Fiction Contest 994
Writers' Journal Semi-Annual Poetry Contest 994
Writer's Nook News, The 794
Writers of the Future Contest 994
Writers' Productions 965
Writers' Representatives, Inc. 965

Writer's Yearbook 794
Wyoming Council on the Arts Literary Fellowships 994
Wyoming Rural Electric News 745

X

Xanadu: A Literary Journal's Annual Poetry Contest 994

Y

Yacht Vacations Magazine 652
Yachting 594
Yale Review, The 427
Yankee 478
Yankee Books 210
Yankee Homes 387
Yard & Garden 752
Yellow Silk 427
Yesteryear 377
Yoga Journal, The 348
York Magazine 527
York Press Ltd. 210
Young American 408
Young Salvationist 638
Young Soldier, The 408
Your Health & Fitness 350
Your Health 349
Your Health (Florida) 349
Your Home 387
Your Virginia State Trooper Magazine 758
Youth Update 638
YWAM/Academy of Performing Arts 890

Z

Zebra Books 211
Zeckendorf Associates, Susan 965
Zelasky Literary Agency, Tom 966
Zenger Peter Award 994
Ziegler Literary Agency, George 966
ZM Squared 863
Zoineo Memorial Theatre for Youth Playwriting Award, Anna 995
Zoland Books, Inc. 211
Zondervan Corp. The 211
Zyzzyva 427

Other Books of Interest

Annual Market Books
  Artist's Market, edited by Susan Conner $19.95
  Children's Writer's & Illustrator's Market, edited by Connie Eidenier (paper) $14.95
  Novel & Short Story Writer's Market, edited by Laurie Henry (paper) $17.95
  Photographer's Market, edited by Sam Marshall $19.95
  Poet's Market, by Judson Jerome $18.95
  Songwriter's Market, edited by Mark Garvey $18.95

General Writing Books
  Annable's Treasury of Literary Teasers, by H.D. Annable (paper) $10.95
  Beginning Writer's Answer Book, edited by Kirk Polking (paper) $12.95
  Beyond Style: Mastering the Finer Points of Writing, by Gary Provost $15.95
  Discovering the Writer Within, by Bruce Ballenger & Barry Lane $16.95
  Getting the Words Right: How to Revise, Edit and Rewrite, by Theodore A. Rees Cheney $15.95
  A Handbook of Problem Words & Phrases, by Morton S. Freeman $16.95
  How to Increase Your Word Power, by the editors of Reader's Digest $19.95
  How to Write a Book Proposal, by Michael Larsen $10.95
  Just Open a Vein, edited by William Brohaugh $15.95
  Knowing Where to Look: The Ultimate Guide to Research, by Lois Horowitz (paper) $15.95
  Make Every Word Count, by Gary Provost (paper) $9.95
  On Being a Writer, edited by Bill Strickland $19.95
  Pinckert's Practical Grammar, by Robert C. Pinckert $14.95
  The Story Behind the Word, by Morton S. Freeman (paper) $9.95
  12 Keys to Writing Books that Sell, by Kathleen Krull (paper) $12.95
  The 29 Most Common Writing Mistakes & How to Avoid Them, by Judy Delton $9.95
  Word Processing Secrets for Writers, by Michael A. Banks & Ansen Dibell (paper) $14.95
  Writer's Block & How to Use It, by Victoria Nelson $14.95
  The Writer's Digest Guide to Manuscript Formats, by Buchman & Groves $16.95
  Writer's Encyclopedia, edited by Kirk Polking (paper) $16.95

Nonfiction Writing
  Basic Magazine Writing, by Barbara Kevles $16.95
  How to Sell Every Magazine Article You Write, by Lisa Collier Cool (paper) $11.95
  The Writer's Digest Handbook of Magazine Article Writing, edited by Jean M. Fredette $15.95
  Writing Creative Nonfiction, by Theodore A. Rees Cheney $15.95
  Writing Nonfiction that Sells, by Samm Sinclair Baker $14.95

Fiction Writing
  The Art & Craft of Novel Writing, by Oakley Hall $16.95
  Best Stories from New Writers, edited by Linda Sanders $16.95
  Characters & Viewpoint, by Orson Scott Card $13.95
  Creating Short Fiction, by Damon Knight (paper) $9.95
  Dare to Be a Great Writer: 329 Keys to Powerful Fiction, by Leonard Bishop $15.95
  Dialogue, by Lewis Turco $12.95
  Fiction is Folks: How to Create Unforgettable Characters, by Robert Newton Peck (paper) $8.95
  Handbook of Short Story Writing: Vol. I, by Dickson and Smythe (paper) $9.95
  Handbook of Short Story Writing: Vol. II, edited by Jean M. Fredette $15.95
  One Great Way to Write Short Stories, by Ben Nyberg $14.95
  Plot, by Ansen Dibell $13.95
  Revision, by Kit Reed $13.95
  Spider Spin Me a Web: Lawrence Block on Writing Fiction, by Lawrence Block $16.95
  Storycrafting, by Paul Darcy Boles (paper) $10.95
  Writing the Novel: From Plot to Print, by Lawrence Block (paper) $9.95

Special Interest Writing Books
  The Children's Picture Book: How to Write It, How to Sell It, by Ellen E.M. Roberts (paper) $16.95
  Comedy Writing Secrets, by Melvin Helitzer $18.95
  The Complete Book of Scriptwriting, by J. Michael Straczynski (paper) $11.95

The Craft of Lyric Writing, by Sheila Davis $18.95
Editing Your Newsletter, by Mark Beach (paper) $18.50
Families Writing, by Peter Stillman $15.95
Guide to Greeting Card Writing, edited by Larry Sandman (paper) $9.95
How to Write a Play, by Raymond Hull (paper) $12.95
How to Write Action/Adventure Novels, by Michael Newton $13.95
How to Write & Sell A Column, by Raskin & Males $10.95
How to Write and Sell Your Personal Experiences, by Lois Duncan (paper) $10.95
How to Write Mysteries, by Shannon OCork $13.95
How to Write Romances, by Phyllis Taylor Pianka $13.95
How to Write Tales of Horror, Fantasy & Science Fiction, edited by J.N. Williamson $15.95
How to Write the Story of Your Life, by Frank P. Thomas (paper) $11.95
How to Write Western Novels, by Matt Braun $13.95
Mystery Writer's Handbook, by The Mystery Writers of America (paper) $10.95
The Poet's Handbook, by Judson Jerome (paper) $10.95
Successful Lyric Writing (workbook), by Sheila Davis (paper) $16.95
Successful Scriptwriting, by Jurgen Wolff & Kerry Cox $18.95
Travel Writer's Handbook, by Louise Zobel (paper) $11.95
TV Scriptwriter's Handbook, by Alfred Brenner (paper) $10.95
Writing for Children & Teenagers, 3rd Edition, by Lee Wyndham & Arnold Madison (paper) $12.95
Writing Short Stories for Young People, by George Edward Stanley $15.95
Writing the Modern Mystery, by Barbara Norville $15.95
Writing to Inspire, edited by William Gentz (paper) $14.95

The Writing Business
A Beginner's Guide to Getting Published, edited by Kirk Polking $11.95
The Complete Guide to Self-Publishing, by Tom & Marilyn Ross (paper) $16.95
How to Sell & Re-Sell Your Writing, by Duane Newcomb $11.95
How to Write with a Collaborator, by Hal Bennett with Michael Larsen $11.95
Is There a Speech Inside You?, by Don Aslett (paper) $9.95
Literary Agents: How to Get & Work with the Right One for You, by Michael Larsen $9.95
Professional Etiquette for Writers, by William Brohaugh $9.95
Time Management for Writers, by Ted Schwarz $10.95
The Writer's Friendly Legal Guide, edited by Kirk Polking $16.95
A Writer's Guide to Contract Negotiations, by Richard Balkin (paper) $11.95

To order directly from the publisher, include $3.00 postage and handling for 1 book and 50¢ for each additional book. Allow 30 days for delivery.

Writer's Digest Books
1507 Dana Avenue, Cincinnati, Ohio 45207
Credit card orders call TOLL-FREE
1-800-289-0963
Prices subject to change without notice.

Write to this same address for information on *Writer's Digest* magazine, Writer's Digest Book Club, Writer's Digest School, and Writer's Digest Criticism Service.